FRANZ SCHUBERT – THE COMPLETE SONGS

FRANZ SCHUBERT
THE COMPLETE SONGS
VOLUME ONE
A–I

GRAHAM JOHNSON

translations of the song texts by Richard Wigmore

YALE UNIVERSITY PRESS
NEW HAVEN AND LONDON

The publisher acknowledges the generous sponsorship of the Guildhall School of Music & Drama, London, without which the publication of this work would not have been possible.

Deepest gratitude also to the Marilyn Horne Foundation, a U.S. nonprofit organization devoted exclusively to the art of song, for its support and encouragement of this publication.

For information about this and other Yale University Press publications, please contact:

U.S. office: sales.press@yale.edu   www.yalebooks.com
Europe Office: sales@yaleup.co.uk   www.yalebooks.co.uk

Set in Minion by Toppan Best-set Premedia Limited
Printed in Great Britain by TJ International Ltd, Padstow, Cornwall

Library of Congress Control Number 2013931540

ISBN 978-0-300-11267-2

A catalogue record for this book is available from the British Library.

Published with assistance from the Annie Burr Lewis Fund.

Frontispiece and drawing on p. 958   Schubert by Martha Griebler, 2001

10 9 8 7 6 5 4 3 2 1

This book is dedicated, in loving memory, to four great Schubertians:

accompanist, singer, song scholar, recording producer –

GERALD MOORE (1899–1987)

PETER PEARS (1910–1986)

ERIC SAMS (1926–2004)

EDWARD PERRY (1931–2003)

and to

BRANDON VELARDE

whose strength and companionship have made it possible to complete the task

And Paradise till we are there
Is in these measured lengths of air.

from *The History of Music* by Peter Porter (1929–2010)

FOREWORD AND ACKNOWLEDGEMENTS

This book, covering a large part of Schubert's musical output, the complete vocal works with piano, has taken very many years to come to fruition. The composer played a role in my life over half a century ago: a ten-year old in Bulawayo, I unsuccessfully partnered an equally young violinist in the D major Sonatina D384. Our lack of ensemble drove the violin teacher, the late Richard Thorn, to a state of despair. For years afterwards his name was linked in my mind with the difficulty of the composer's music and the insuperable challenges of accompanying. Like the boy pricked by the rose in *Heidenröslein* D257, I realized that certain things in life must be learned from scratch.

Most young pianists, whatever their future specialism, are taught to play like would-be soloists, except for the lucky ones who grow up in musical households where chamber music is a regular luxury. My Rhodesian upbringing was short of 'luxe' and 'volupté' but I calmly practised Schubert's Impromptus and *Moments musicaux* on my own, of course. What was missing in my Schubert performances seemed beyond both explanation and repair – I felt it and so did my piano teacher, Nora Hutchinson. As far as I was concerned, Schubert was less satisfying than Mozart and Beethoven, a bit of both, and yet neither. When I grew up I would understand him better, or so I was told. In the meantime this composer, like the birds and bees, was an adult mystery and a special case; one could hear this in the irritating way the grown-ups referred to him as if his very name were surrounded by a halo.

The teaching of the piano was a thriving part of the curriculum at the Rhodesian Academy of Music in Bulawayo – but classical singing and vocal literature, something encountered far more rarely in colonial Africa, never came into my ken. The first Schubert lied I ever heard was a song without words. The Rhodesia Broadcasting Corporation allocated an hour every week to a classical music request programme called *Let's Be Serious*. I remember being beguiled by the programme's theme-tune, a piano piece which was never identified. The music, hauntingly played, stirred me in a way that puzzled me; at that stage I would never have been able to identify the composer. It was only some years after I came to the UK that I realized I had been listening to an arrangement of Schubert's *An die Musik* D547 played by Gerald Moore in his own solo arrangement. On looking back it is as if Schubert and one of his great interpreters were calling for my attention, tapping gently on the windowpane, without my being able to recognize either of them, much less guess how huge their importance would be later in my life.

As an eighteen-year-old student at the Royal Academy of Music (R.A.M.) in London I gave an adolescent performance of the Piano Sonata in B flat major D960. The first Schubert song I was asked to play seemed at first much easier than the sonata, but by the time the singer arrived it proved tricky in a different way. I played all the right notes but something remained stubbornly wrong. The poet's faith in the breezes of vernal renewal was sadly misplaced. Poor old Uhland (not that I knew who *he* was at the time) and poor Schubert! My leaden *Frühlingsglaube* D686 – in the booming transposition for bass – postponed the arrival of spring until further notice.

And then, after three years or so, there were signs of seasonal change. By the age of twenty-two I had become an accompanist in bud, ready to unfurl at the first sign of inspirational warmth, and it was Schubert who provided it – the halo around his name was beginning to shed some light. I embarked on *Die schöne Müllerin* D795 with a fellow student, the tenor David Rendall, first at the R. A. M., and then at the Purcell Room in London as a replacement for an indisposed Anthony Rolfe Johnson, a singer who was later to become a regular colleague and musical partner. A year or so earlier I had heard Peter Pears and Benjamin Britten in an unforgettable, indeed life-changing, *Winterreise* D911 at the Maltings, Snape. At that age, and with such music-making as a marker and inspiration, one learns fast. It was as if a thousand pieces of jigsaw had suddenly fallen into place to make a picture that was both new and already familiar. I had always loved languages and history, and as a student-composer of vocal music it was my favourite task to select poetry and scheme and dream of how I might set it to music. I had also been playing for some time at the R. A. M. for singing lessons given by Flora Nielsen – she had been a pupil of that great Schubert singer Elena Gerhardt and a famous mezzo-soprano of her time. With Flora's encouragement I began to blossom; at last there were reasonable grounds for optimism. I was invited to play for Peter Pears's first masterclasses at the Maltings (before the building of the Britten–Pears School). To accompany that great artist as he demonstrated the singing of Schubert's lieder to awestruck students remains the most precious of memories although I did not emerge unscathed (who ever did at Aldeburgh where criticism from Pears and Britten was a rite of passage?). Peter was unquestionably the most magical singer I have ever known, a veritable Prospero. His presence on the dedicatee page of this book is scant acknowledgement of a massive debt of gratitude. Thanks to him the German lied began to play a major part in my life, with Schubert in the forefront.

I started buying music and gramophone records, even though I was unable to afford them on my student subventions. Alongside the LPs, my collecting at the time included a large number of 78 r.p.m. records (still available reasonably cheaply at the time in speciality shops in London) and I spent many hours listening to every interpretation I could find of the songs I was beginning to know in detail. More or less at the same time (and with disastrous effects on my finances) my passion for collecting expanded into printed music – anything I could lay my hands on for voice and piano. This was a process that continued for many years and became more selective (and expensive) as time went on. It was a proud day when I acquired all seven volumes of the Peters Edition of Schubert's lieder in red cloth bindings (after nearly forty years I can confirm that these have proved a more durable investment than the pale green paperback editions). For a short while I proudly thought myself to be in possession of the entire œuvre. Imagine my disappointment when I began to listen to the two recently issued, massive, pale-blue, and dark-blue, boxed sets of Schubert Lieder on Deutsche Grammophon (twenty-nine LPs with Dietrich Fischer-Dieskau and Gerald Moore) and discovered that there were a large number of songs missing from the Peters collection. These were apparently only to be found in the *Gesamtausgabe* of Breitkopf & Härtel – the famous edition of Eusebius Mandyczewski published in 1895 that was out of print and out of my reach. It is true that a few of the reference libraries had these volumes on their shelves, but I longed to have the music readily to hand on my piano. A friend alerted me to the fact that Constable's, the publishing firm in London, was offering, for a few days only, remaindered copies of the Dover hardback reprint of these volumes at a cost of £3.75 each. Even in those days this was a bargain. The ten folio volumes of Mandyczewski were encompassed by five of the Dover reissues, printed in a slightly smaller format, and these became the foundation on which I gradually built a more detailed knowledge of Schubert's songs. The first thing I noticed was that Fischer-Dieskau and Moore had left out many of them from their DGG survey, including all the lieder for women. In those days, 150 years after the composer's death, there was no such thing as a recording of The Complete Schubert.

In the meantime more of the composer's music was coming into my ken and under my fingers. My first broadcast for the BBC at the age of twenty-five included the *Fantasie* for violin and piano D934 with its intricate second-movement variations on the song *Sei mir gegrüsst* D741. This work's relationship to the above-mentioned Sonatina, in terms of pianistic difficulty at least, is that of a hammerhead shark to a trout (both of which swim through different Schubert songs). My teacher at the time, the late Geoffrey Parsons, roared with laughter when he discovered that I had signed the contract for this debut broadcast, blissfully unaware of the challenges in store for me. These turned out to include the violinist's being in the throes of a nervous breakdown (not simply as a result of my playing). At least the fee of £18 came in handy to pay for the Dover reprints of the old *Gesamtausgabe*.

I came to realize that it was the initiate's duty to be an activist (not that I was capable of putting this feeling into words at the time). Faced with a repertoire of this range and excitement, waiting by the 'phone for work was simply not enterprising enough. With the foundation of The Songmakers' Almanac in 1976 I took on the role of pianist and programme planner whereby recitals were presented around a theme and shared between a number of singers. The founder members were my contemporaries Felicity Lott, Ann Murray, Anthony Rolfe Johnson and Richard Jackson, with Dietrich Fischer-Dieskau becoming the group's first patron. For the next twenty years or so Songmakers' concerts, a mixture of vocal music and the spoken word, were given in London with an array of singers, instrumentalists and actors. Many of the programmes included Schubert, of course. In 1975 I had become close friends with the most famous of all accompanists, Gerald Moore, and his wonderful wife Enid. Over the next decade I spent many a day at their home, Beechwood Cottage in the Chilterns, talking about, and listening to, music and regaled by a vast treasury of inimitable anecdotes. With Gerald's encouragement, and in his heartening company, I began to feel at last like a member of his profession, albeit a junior one. In due course I gratefully inherited his music library, including the 'Mandyczewski' – the Schubert edition used by the great accompanist during his recordings with Fischer-Dieskau, filled with his markings and annotations. From Gerald, another mentor–dedicatee of this book, I also received firm support concerning my newfangled ideas about presenting recitals; he too became a patron of the group and his eightieth birthday was celebrated by a Songmakers' Almanac concert in 1979.

The name of the group was inspired by the literary annuals or yearbooks issued between the 1780s and about 1850 where so many composers found texts to set to music, and which often included fold-out supplements of printed lieder. As I discovered much later, the small, compact volumes where Schubert found some of his texts included the *Musenalmanach* of Tieck (1802), the *Poetisches Taschenbuch* of Schlegel (1806), three issues of the Viennese *Selam* (1813–15), *Beckers Taschenbücher* from 1799, 1805, 1808 (as well as 1821, to which the composer was a musical contributor) and *Urania* 1821 and 1823 – this latter was the source of the first twelve *Winterreise* texts. Schubert's first printed song, *Erlafsee* D586 had appeared in an Austrian almanac in 1817. So much for almanacs. As for the other part of my ensemble's name, songmakers (or makers of songs) were not only composers, but also poets and performers; the celebration of all these creative personalities, both past and present, and their connection with the German lied, French mélodie, Spanish cançion, Russian romance, English song and so on, lay within our performing remit. We celebrated, as a good almanac should, important birthdays – Shakespeare's for example and those of Beethoven and Brahms – as well as devoting evenings to Johann Michael Vogl, Peter Pears, Hugues Cuenod and many others. On 31 January 1977 we presented the first of our Birthday Schubertiads in honour of the composer; it is a tradition that survives to this day at the Wigmore Hall with many different artists contributing to the festivities.

In 1978 I accompanied Dame Janet Baker in a Schubert group at the Maltings, the hallowed ground of my *Winterreise* epiphany with Pears and Britten. A recording of this concert later appeared on a CBS compilation. I made my first gramophone recording of Schubert for Hyperion at the age of thirty (again *Die schöne Müllerin*, this time with the tenor Martyn Hill). This was an

LP for which I also wrote the sleeve notes (as such annotations were known at the time). By then I had written programme notes for recitals, which is how many writers on music begin; the progression to the back of a record cover seemed perfectly logical. Nevertheless, there comes a time when every performing artist who aspires to write must learn a hard lesson: excitable after-dinner discussions with friends, verbal eloquence fuelled by glasses of wine, inside knowledge of the music thanks to hours of practice – all this counts for nothing until one is able to sit down and marshal one's thoughts into English prose, that most intractable and slippery of mediums.

I learned this the hard way from the great musicologist Eric Sams who had written the indispensable *The Songs of Hugo Wolf* in 1962. With youthful audacity Felicity Lott and I had asked him to sit in on a rehearsal of songs by this composer. This was in the early 1970s. I soon realized that Eric knew just as much about Schubert (and Schumann, and Brahms, and Shakespeare come to that). He was a Whitehall civil servant in the great British tradition of amateur musicologists (like Frank Walker and those venerable Schubertians Maurice Brown and John Reed) who were more intensely professional and perspicacious than an aula of European professors. Before long I began to send Eric carbon copies of my programme notes, and he returned them, annotated in pencil. These donnish marginalia, faint underlinings and question marks were never designed to discourage or humiliate the fledgling writer. Eric never wrote, or even rewrote, anything for me, but his comments were sufficiently challenging to prompt me to try again and again. He could be a formidable academic opponent of those who crossed his path, but he was above all a supremely gracious and generous man who loved young musicians in whom he saw a spark of talent. He effectively conducted a correspondence course with me on the subject of song and the English language. With each consignment (by the time I was an earning pianist) I gratefully enclosed a cheque; Eric regarded these payments as quixotic, and unnecessary gestures, but for such revelations one must pay; although what Eric taught me was beyond price. Indeed, it was he who fostered in me a love of German literature and the feeling that I had the right to make my own investigations. I stumped up for the first costly issues in the Lieder series of the *Neue Schubert-Ausgabe* in the late 1970s and took delivery of the last of the fourteen volumes some thirty-five years later, providentially only a few months before this book went to press. The majority of information at the cutting edge of Schubertian research is now written in German. Poring through the commentaries of Walther Dürr, doyen of living Schubertians, as well as the supplementary volumes in the *Kritische Bericht* (where we find the most detailed examinations ever undertaken of the songs' autographs) was another labour of love as well as a self-imposed study-course. I was gradually able to do without my dictionary and, instead, read, rehearse, converse and teach in Schubert's language (although I have never broached the Viennese dialect). In the last fifteen years or so I have built up a large poetry library: it became my passion to own the very editions used by Schubert and his song-composing successors so that I could see the poems as they first appeared to the musicians' roving eye, and visit, in effect, the birthplace of each song on the printed page. This gave me the chance not only to study these texts at first hand, but to read around them in each volume while trying to understand the context and depth of each composer's response. In this book, most poems (in terms of versification and punctuation) appear as Schubert, one of the best-read of all musicians, first saw them.

* * * * * *

The story of my relationship to Ted Perry (another of this book's dedicatees) and to Hyperion records is described in detail in an appendix to this book. In 1984 he invited me to plan a double album for Hyperion, a Songmakers' Almanac *Schubertiad*, a small series of thematic Schubert lieder programmes, one on each of the four vinyl sides. Partly as a result of the success of these LPs I was permitted to frame my Schubert explorations in far more ambitious terms. At thirty-seven I began to record the complete songs on CD for Hyperion (all my Schubert recordings have been for this label, apart from a disc on Virgin made with a close friend in New York, the tenor Robert White, and my recordings of the cycles with that extraordinary patron of music and medicine Sir Ralph Kohn, and with the hugely talented Christopher Maltman on Wigmore Hall's own label). What I lacked in experience and knowledge (at that stage I could not read German fluently) I made up for with enthusiasm; I was also very lucky that the late eighties were prosperous times for the recording industry, and Ted felt able to take on a project of this magnitude. A number of critics felt that it would never be completed, but at the age of fifty I brought the series to its conclusion, a little later than planned. The intervening thirteen years had slipped by remarkably quickly and were devoted to a journey which I was privileged to make in the company of some of the greatest singers in the world.

Each of the thirty-seven discs of that series had a booklet of commentaries, the size and detail of which grew as the project showed signs of reaching the finishing line. After the series had come to an end, I was urged to republish these Hyperion notes but this was impossible, mainly because so much had altered. Had these commentaries been republished all together they would have presented a line-up of articles in different styles and of strangely different lengths, and in the years that I was busy in the recording studio Schubert scholarship had advanced and count-less other writers had contributed to the debate with an almost perplexing number of books and articles in both German and English.

In preparing this book, the assimilation of a huge amount of new material and the sifting and arrangement of factual information has been a formidable task – quite apart from the rewriting of countless articles that no longer seemed satisfactory. These three volumes were built on the foundations of the Hyperion notes, but record-collectors able to compare the original booklets with the present work will find that many a shaky construction has been razed and rebuilt, and edifices that were only meant to be temporary at the time have been strengthened or removed. A great deal of largely biographical writing and information from the original booklets had to be swept away (the Calendar at the end of the third volume of this book places the songs in a time frame) and new information has been added that is specific to the songs. In the eleven years of this transformative process I came to terms with Schubert as never before. It is absolutely true that one learns on the job, and the more one studies Schubert the more one realizes how little we know about a great deal of his music, and also about him.

Here I will allow myself an observation that perhaps belongs more properly in a Schubert biography: love for the music has a way of extending its parameters to incorporate a delusion of love of the composer himself, as if he were somehow still alive and in need of champions. There are other great creators who engender in their followers a similar loyalty, normally artists where there is a lack of background information – as in the case of Shakespeare, for example, or Jane Austen – which allows fans to slip into fantasy. Deutsch's *Documentary Biography*, the amateur Schubertian's equivalent to Luther's Bible, has long permitted ordinary people to put their own gloss on the bare facts of Schubertian events, so far as they are known. In the absence of definitive evidence to the contrary, many Schubert lovers fondly imagine the composer to have been someone rather like themselves. This is an indication of the feelings of intimacy and trust engendered between this music and its millions of listeners. Few would dream of being close to Beethoven or Mozart, but Schubert seems cosier – he can tempt the music lover to relate to him as if he were a friendly doppelgänger. This fantasy figure is surely what is meant when people, somewhat possessively, refer to '*My* Schubert' – the great singing teacher Vera Rosza once dismissed a performance by an errant pupil as '*not my Schubert!*'. Christians are convinced the composer was religious, while agnostics regard him approvingly as an enemy of the church. Extroverts imagine the fun the composer must have had with a life of sociable Schubertiads and party games at Atzenbrugg; introverts think of the number of times he failed to turn up to gatherings when invited and how selective he was regarding his friends. Those who are *bon viveurs* want him to have been a merry drinker; those who are abstemious will make the argument that he could not possibly have achieved all he did while suffering from hangovers. How would the non-smokers among us have managed in the company of a man who is said to have smoked a great deal? How would we have reacted if Schubert told us – as Elizabeth McKay believes possible – that he was quite partial to a pipe of opium from time to time? Those who are politically active might wish to see the composer as a brave opponent of Metternich's oppressive regime; and those who are bored by politics will simply see a musician attempting to survive in a tricky environment. The ups and downs of the composer's moods and productivity may have been ascribable to nothing more sinister than an 'artistic temperament', but Elizabeth McKay, having traced evidence of manic-depressive tendencies in members of Schubert's family, suggests that the composer was a lifelong sufferer from cyclothymia, a mild form of manic-depression where the symptoms are 'dark moods manifested by apathy, lethargy, pessimism, self-deprecation and irritability' as well as 'uninhibited people-seeking' and 'a pattern of irresponsibility in personal affairs'. There will be some Schubertians who will take this to be a revelatory personal diagnosis of their own problems; many will dismiss such theories as unlikely. Still others will see in the composer's behaviour a range of self-esteem issues that might require treatment today by a psychoanalyst rather than a medically trained psychiatrist. If McKay uses this putative diagnosis to explain prodigal spending of money and indulgence in unrestrained sexual activity there will be those who will know from first-hand experience that there are differing grounds for such behaviour. It is almost as if we can all decide whom we want 'our' Schubert to be. And all of this because the documents we have at our disposal are silent on many issues, the kind of personal details that would have been monitored by Metternich's secret police if the Schubertians had been foolish enough to allow details of their most private thoughts and activities to be written down and later read by us.

If the evidence that Schubert suffered from syphilis were not incontrovertible we could be certain that some writers would have gone to every length (as was the case with Schumann's illness) to prove that he had not suffered from a disease that seems so horribly unworthy of him and of his music. It is, however, possible to believe that, apart from this single tragic aberration when Schubert apparently visited a prostitute, it was only a series of cruel circumstances (lack of money and social status, crowned by his early death) that denied him the marriage and children that would have brought him later happiness. The Biedermeier culture, of which the composer became something of a personification, was based on a romanticized normality that has been a cornerstone of the Schubert legend for at least 150 years. It is only in the last twenty-five years or so that there has been any public expression of doubt concerning the composer's heterosexuality. This is perhaps the most emotive issue of all. This subject has divided Schubert scholarship for the last two decades and continues to do so, although no longer, perhaps, with the ferocity of the 1990s. Maynard Solomon's article[1] of 1989 quickly became a cause célèbre: interpreting Bauernfeld's observations on Schubert's need for 'the peacocks of Benvenuto Cellini' as applying to young men, Solomon made an argument for the composer's homosexuality. This provoked a considerable backlash, not least in the German-speaking world, particularly because aspects of Solomon's case were based on tenuous assumptions. In the absence of incontrovertible evidence to the contrary the status quo of Schubert's heterosexuality has been maintained with some difficulty (his affection for Therese Grob and Karoline Esterházy is undeniable) although the Viennese scholar Ilija Dürhammer has offered stronger circumstantial evidence for the 'prosecution' (if thus it may be termed, ironically) than the evidence mustered by Solomon.[2] A

---

[1] 'The Peacocks of Benvenuto Cellini' in *19th Century Music*, XII/3, 1989.
[2] Ilje Dürhammer, *Schuberts literarische Heimat*, 1999 and *Geheime Botschaften, Homoerotische Subkulturen im Schubert-Kreis*, 2006.

hung jury might have brought in a fence-sitting verdict of 'bisexual', but in a court of law the composer would have been declared 'Not Guilty' for want of absolute proof to the contrary, notwithstanding some of the company he kept. The words of Philip Brett, however, writing as an avowedly gay musicologist, remain a warning against what might be termed *Lilac Time* complacency:

> *Schubert took on anti-religious, pro-Classical, anti-authoritarian, and pro-sensualist attitudes of the kind that homosexuals have often tended to espouse. Others have done the same, but not with the special edge produced by the constant negation of their feelings by all institutions of society – the courts, the police, the armed forces, all religious sects and all medical authorities (until recently), the educational system, the family. He found a refuge in music and art, suffered profound depressions, and had problems expressing anger, all tell-tale signs of a social sense of exclusion in the modern period in Western countries . . . And it has to be admitted by everyone, I should hope, that it is no more or less a projection, and therefore no more or less reductive or vulgar or essentialist, than an exclusively heterosexual Schubert (why is it that some straight people are so ready to import the category of heterosexuality back into history uncritically while insisting on agonizing historical and epistemological difficulties the moment they sniff homoeroticism in any form?)*[3]

This debate exposed the raw nerve in how Schubert is regarded by those who care deeply for him, as if he were somehow a personal friend whose reputation was at stake. A number of musicologists (and no doubt thousands of music lovers) clearly felt that their own image of the composer, 'their Schubert', had been unacceptably hijacked and appropriated – as if it were inconceivable that music of such depth, sanity and universality might have been composed by someone who was not as 'normal' as they felt themselves to be. The vehemence of the reaction against the very idea that the composer *might* have been gay (he would have been mystified by modern usage of the word) has been a disturbing aspect of a controversy where there have been exaggerations and ad hominem attacks from both sides. The composer has been enlisted in a cultural war of anachronistic labels and sexual identities that would have been entirely foreign to his way of thinking.

In the meantime, Schubert himself, in personal terms at least, is a continuing enigma on this and many other issues. He has kept all of us at arm's length regarding many aspects of his life and it is difficult to say whether this is by accident or design. It is indeed fortunate that I have not attempted a Schubert biography because I feel I know less and less about him as the years go by. Far from believing that I have something in common with the composer, it seems to me that he was so *unlike* the rest of us that all bets are off concerning anything and everything else about him. All commentators can do, when pressed to give an opinion on any number of under-documented issues, is to guess, speculate or admit that this is what we are doing and hope that our intuitions may lead to a measure of disinterested accuracy and understanding. As the French-Canadian philosopher Raymond Joly pointed out, ongoing investigations into the story of Schubert's life, and speculations about it, are more or less inevitable – unless we are to believe that his music was a lucky accident, the fruit of somnambulism, or simply a munificent gift from the heavens:

> *I do not really care for Schubert nor for any other dead person; I am well aware that the 'love' my fellow fans and myself feel for him is just a game we play for our benefit in our fantasy and in conversing with one another. In his own individual fashion he was thwarted and distorted, like every one of us. That was the material he built upon, more courageously than most of us and*

[3] 'Piano Four Hands. Schubert and the Performance of Gay Male Desire' in *19th Century Music*, XXI, 1997, p. 169.

with a genius we do not possess. His music contains an unfathomable amount of knowledge about the glory and misery of being a living creature with a soul, and Schubert obtained that knowledge in the only way possible. Panting and groping he mined this gold at the deepest and darkest levels where few are strong enough to go: the music lover cannot enjoy this treasure as if it were nature-given. It transcends the individual who extracted it, but it is a human product and must be understood in relation to the shape and misshape of the mind that produced it.[4]

* * * * * *

If this book is not a biography of Schubert's life, it is perhaps a biography of his songs. If music is a mirror of the mind that produced it, the 'shape and misshape' of Schubert's longer works (whether songs, sonatas or symphonies) has long been a matter for discussion and criticism. 'Heavenly length', as Robert Schumann described it, has its less flattering corollary in the popular image of Schubert as an amiable but wandering minstrel, a rambler who is scarcely aware of where he is going. (Those who accuse the composer of being a windbag conveniently forget his innumerable tiny songs, page-long creations where, as Maurice Brown puts it, 'with the most modest means he can encompass greatness in a score of bars'.[5]) Between *Adelwold und Emma* D211 (twenty-nine pages in the *Neue Schubert-Ausgabe*) and *Wandrers Nachtlied* D224 (a page long) there is a single month of 1815, yet several worlds of difference. Apart from comparing this composer's Protean gifts to those of Shakespeare, and claiming that he 'contains multitudes', like the self-contradictory Whitman, how can we begin to encapsulate the achievement of Schubert's lieder? Short songs, long songs, simple songs, complicated songs, songs merry and glum, and every shade in between; like Autolycus in *The Winter's Tale*, 'he hath songs for man, or woman, of all sizes; no milliner can so fit his customers with gloves'.

A tidy summation of Schubert's achievement as a lieder composer is scarcely possible because every song, born of a different poem, is a law unto itself. Even after accounting for the various categories and genres – strophic songs, modified strophic songs, through-composed songs, ballads, and endless subtle variations thereof – there is scarcely an example of one work being just like another. This composer was incapable of doing anything by rote and even when writing out copies of songs for friends he could scarcely resist tiny improvements and adaptations as he went along (it is a sad irony that one of the most fastidious and scrupulous of composers, a reviser to his fingertips, should have acquired a reputation for being lackadaisical and careless).

Schubert was a fervent admirer and emulator of Haydn, Mozart, Beethoven and Gluck (strong traces of these Viennese (or adopted Viennese) masters are to be found in his work) but the formation of his lieder style owes more to the Berlin school – Johann Friedrich Reichardt and Carl Friedrich Zelter – and to the Swabian, Johann Rudolf Zumsteeg (qqv under Composers), whose ten books of *Balladen und kleine Lieder* Schubert knew well and took as his models. In a sense his life's work was a glorious elaboration of the principles laid down in Zumsteeg's songs: the setting of a wide range of poetry to music in an attempt to enhance and deepen the text, in ballad or strophic form (or variations on those structures). Recitative and lyrical effusion were combined in whichever way seemed appropriate to the poem in hand with on-the-spot musical illustrations of ideas and events, sometimes merely in passing, playing a crucial part. (I am reminded of Pierre Bernac's response when asked why he had become a singer: 'It gave me the chance to recite the poems I loved with heightened intensity.' Both Zumsteeg and Schubert would have understood this answer.)

Of course Schubert soon overtook the older composer in terms of harmony, the ingenuity of accompaniments and the potency of dramatic narrative – all astounding achievements in one

---

[4] Letter to the author, June 2007.
[5] 'Schubert, Franz' in the *New Grove Dictionary of Music and Musicians*, 1980, Vol. 16, p. 776.

so young. Zumsteeg's decorous ditties were swept aside (albeit respectfully) in favour of memorable tunes from an apprentice who was already an innate master with a gift for melody that had been honed by years of composition exercises (mostly settings of Metastasio and Schiller) supervised by Antonio Salieri. While scarcely aware of his crucial role in the history of German song, the old maestro helped the teenage Schubert to add the immediate sensuality of an Italianate vocal line to the dramatic and intellectually stimulating possibilities of the German lied, a combination of north and south that was to topple Berlin's ascendancy as the song capital of the world. This duality – perhaps only possible in Vienna, a city both grounded in German-speaking traditions and far enough south to be full of Italians – came into powerful focus on that momentous day in October 1814 when Goethe's *Gretchen am Spinnrade* was set to music.

Schubert was one of the most melodically gifted composers of all time – the supple and dramatic *bel canto* of Gretchen's vocal line is one of this song's principal glories – but it is the piano writing – the dynamo driving the song forward – that announces a new mastery and fresh momentum. Schubert himself shines through his accompaniments. The majority of these played to his own strengths as a pianist – a warm singing tone, a variety of touch, a command of colour and a presence that animates, encourages, reflects and controls the song's progress, both musically and emotionally. The movement of Gretchen's spinning wheel puts Schubert on the map not only as a composer but also as a composer–accompanist whose genius enabled him to give each and every song a separate pianistic *raison d'être*. The flexibility and endless inventiveness of this piano writing enabled the lied to rival – and even overtake – opera in terms of dramatic expressivity, with an ever-quickening stride. This ranged from the becalmed semibreves of *Meeres Stille* D216 to the ominous stalking minims of *Der Tod und das Mädchen* D531, from the Harper's crazed and wandering crotchets in *An die Türen will ich schleichen* D478/3 to the ambulatory quavers of *Das Lied im Grünen* D917; from the frenetic horseriding triplets of *Erlkönig* D328 to the cheekily playful semiquavers for roving hands of *Versunken* D715, the watery sextuplets of *Wohin?* D795/2 and the equally watery burbling demisemiquavers of *Liebesbotschaft* D957/1.

Schubert's detailed and complicated progress as a song composer is unfolded chronologically in the Calendar at the end of the third volume of this book, but a bird's-eye picture by way of a preview shows a pattern of long-term relationships with the greatest poets, combined with shorter flings with lesser figures (concentrated and intense over a period of months) and the occasional equivalent of a one-night stand. The first famous poet with whom the fourteen-year-old Schubert had an ongoing relationship (via Zumsteeg, and only on paper of course) was Friedrich Schiller. This was followed by Friedrich von Matthisson, a key figure of 1814, and, like a flash of lightning, Johann Wolfgang von Goethe in the autumn of that year and then into 1815 and beyond – 1816, 1817, 1821, 1822 and 1826 are all Goethe years. Ludwig Hölty was a passion from 1816, as were Klopstock, Uz, Jacobi and several others. Up to now we have mentioned no one whom Schubert knew personally, but the here and now of providing music for poems by his Viennese contemporaries was always important to him and strongly associated with his concept of loyalty and friendship. The year 1817 was one of great settings of Schubert's mentor Johann Mayrhofer (one of several important Mayrhofer years, ending in 1824); settings of his friends Bruchmann, Schelchta and Schober were composed side by side with those of older distinguished Viennese luminaries such as Karoline Pichler, Ladislaus Pyrker and Matthäus von Collin. Throughout Schubert's life his search for new literature continued unabated: in 1818 Aloys Schreiber and translations of Petrarch; in 1819 Friedrich von Schlegel and Novalis; in 1823 Friedrich Rückert and Wilhelm Müller of *Die schöne Müllerin*; in 1825 Karl Lappe, Ernst Schulze and Sir Walter Scott; in 1826 the precocious Austrian poet Johann Gabriel Seidl; in 1827 a return to Müller for *Winterreise* and in 1828 Karl von Leitner (another Austrian), Ludwig Rellstab and Heinrich Heine. All of these poets are accorded separate articles in this book.

This list, in which there are only a few of the more important names, is an indication of Schubert's astonishing range of reading as well as his delight in surrendering to the surprise of unexpected poetic encounters as a source of renewal and inspiration. There is much evidence to support the theory that every poet summoned from him a subtly different musical response, one could almost say style, as if each writer's DNA were imprinted separately on the songs via his poems. Schubert also possessed to a greater degree than any other composer the gift of responding to words by translating a verbal image into a telling musical equivalent, the tonal analogue which Eric Sams so assiduously identified. Thus the imagined whirr of a spinning wheel became a piano figuration that could also be taken to reflect the confused emotions of a young girl desperately in love. Deryck Cooke's *The Language of Music* (1959) posited a communal musical language shared by composers of western music for the expression of emotions, and John A. Sloboda's *The Musical Mind* (1985) argued that the musically literate acquire the ability to read this 'language of music'. The opening motif of *Gretchen am Spinnrade* seems obvious once we have heard it, but like all such obvious things it needed to be discovered by someone of rare imagination, and to be heard by someone with a certain amount of musical understanding. Schubert did not invent word to music relationships of course, they are as old as music itself (they abound in Bach and Handel and a work like Haydn's *Die Schöpfung* which was highly influential on the young Schubert in exactly this sphere). But surrounded by the powerful poetry of a new literary age, Schubert was in the right place at the right time to create tonal analogues with an unprecedented fluency and naturalness born of his command of harmony and melody. In his songs connections and allusions, cross references between words and music, abound with joyous fecundity as Schubert translates the language of poetry into a poem of its own reconstituted in music. All this is not merely the setting of words to music; this is perhaps what Josef von Spaun meant when he wrote that every one of Schubert's songs is 'in reality *a poem on the poem* he set to music' (my italics). And yes, it is true that sometimes the composer's joy in accomplishing these transformations takes precedence over the organizational nature of constructing a musical shape for its own sake. In any case, a song that follows the shape of a poem is far less susceptible to conventional analysis than an instrumental movement constructed to make sense, first and foremost, as a musical argument.

Almost all the great song composers have possessed this word to music gift in large measure and they sometimes pay the price for it and are accused of a facileness of response or a lack of formal control (like Britten, for example, whose word-setting genius in several languages was once witheringly classified as musical 'journalism'). Once Schubert had selected a text (and this clearly involved an evaluation of its suitability as a whole, and the laying down of something of a ground plan) an essential part of his musical fulfilment was going on a journey with it, whatever its length, and responding to its mood while marking the serendipitous events along the way, almost in the spirit of an improvised challenge. This was nearer Robert Schumann's way of working than Hugo Wolf's rigorous quest for great literature in his texts, or Brahms's often melancholic search for poetry that matched and chimed with his own emotions. But all three composers were masters, in their different ways, of the tonal analogue and all three responded to words and verbal ideas with the example of earlier masters not far from their minds. It was their good fortune, as well as ours, that Schubert's wounds and hang-ups (whatever they were) allowed and encouraged him to work ceaselessly, rather than to turn his face to the wall as others might have done. He was a man whose musical gifts were matched by sensitivity and emotional maturity (read the little-known evaluation of his friend Anton Ottenwalt). Without these human qualities Schubert could not have fulfilled his destiny.

It is not the role of this book to demonstrate how Schubert, by dint of hard work and discipline, successfully emulated the example of his forebears in the Viennese classical tradition in terms of his piano sonatas, symphonies or chamber music. Although he contributed to the ongoing evolution of these forms he was unjustly accused of limitation and failure in the composition of larger works. After years of being undervalued for his instrumental music Schubert is now held to be a very great composer, and not 'just' a fine song composer. But the fact that he cared a great deal about the musical coherence of his larger, more formal works means that he perhaps allowed some of his songs to grow wild in the garden of his unbridled imagination. The words 'sonata' and 'symphony' were spoken in Beethoven's shadow (not to mention Mozart's), but song belonged to Schubert, *pace* his need to bow in the direction of other composers, beginning with Zumsteeg. Whatever had been accomplished before him in Berlin and Stuttgart, however beautiful the songs of Mozart and Beethoven, it was he who carried the torch of a form that he had reinvented in his image. Many of his boldest experiments in this field have the confidence of the pioneer and leader who is unabashed by tradition and who refuses to be intimidated by the tracks of earlier explorers.

Schubert's use of harmony was highly individual although seldom trail-blazing. We recognize his musical fingerprints with delight and it is true that they seem to belong to him alone except that, bar some astonishing exceptions, his employment of harmony is largely imaginative reinvention of existing possibilities. One may compare his musical speech to a delightful dialect that derives from an already familiar language as spoken, and variously enriched, by Haydn, Mozart, Gluck and Beethoven. His use of parallel major and minor modes, for example, derives from Mozart's use of this expressive device, but Schubert makes it his own. Take the simple little Matthisson setting *Lebenslied* D508 where the phrase 'Wechslen auf Erden wie Dämmrung und Nacht' ('Alternate on earth between dusk and night') moves to and fro between major and minor keys. This seems supremely apposite because these words crown a stanza where there has been an ongoing pairing of opposite images – arriving/departing, seeking/shunning and so on. In the much more famous *Der Neugierige* from *Die schöne Müllerin* (D795/6) the sudden change from the radiance of B major to the desperation of B minor reflects the miller boy's fear that his confidant, the brook, will fail to reply to the question 'does she love me?' His tense expectations are underlined by a bar's rest as he waits in vain for the reply of a brook unwilling to cooperate as his harbinger of love. Vulnerability expressed in harmonic terms is something of a Schubertian speciality and this use of silence is also a Schubertian thumbprint. In *Lachen und Weinen* D777 the silence following the poem's questions signifies a bemused shrug, but in *Auf der Donau* D553 two beats' rest represent centuries of ancient warfare and tyranny lost in a chasm of time.

Schubert uses harmony to effect countless surprises. The major key is evocative of the innocent beauty of the vanished past in *Winterreise*, but it is employed to gruesome effect at the climax of *Gruppe aus dem Tartarus* D583 with the prospect of an eternity of punishment in hell, and a stentorian outburst of 'Ewigkeit'. He sometimes conveys stark reality, desperation and bitterness by these paradoxical means. The close proximity of this C major outburst and F sharp minor elsewhere in that same Schiller setting, the interval of a tritone – as far apart as one can get in the Western system of keys – shows how bold the composer's harmonic choices can be when he feels the text requires it. Less extreme shifts, moving from one key to the other, sometimes in full-scale modulation, more often in temporary harmonic dalliance, lie at the heart of Schubertian magic. It is these shifts that make Schubert sound like no one else – for example, as he moves to keys located at the interval of a third away from wherever he happens to be at the time. When the beauty of springtime is mentioned in *Wehmut* D772 the chord of A major (the dominant of the tonic) furnishes the internal C sharp whereby the harmony will be led to flower in a sumptuous F sharp major chord (a third away from A major) indicative of an amplitude of beauty ('Schönheit Fülle'). In *Der Musensohn* D764 mediant modulations provide a magic carpet between the G major escapades of the son of the Muses and the more private regions of his feelings as described in B major. The chords of G major and B major have only one note in common but the composer uses this note, B, as his pivot of enchantment. The same juxtaposition of tonalities occurs (in reverse) in *Nacht und Träume* D827 where we are led from the B major of the opening to a deeper realm of the subconscious in G major at the heart of that song. In *Ganymed* D544 in A flat major the central episode (where the poet languishes on the breast of nature – 'Ach, an deinem Busen / Lieg' ich, schmachte') is in the key of C flat major, a minor third away from A flat; C flat major is also the relative major of the tonic minor key of A flat minor. In *Auf dem Wasser zu singen* D774 the shifts between the tonic A flat major and its minor manifestation are as essential to the song's power as the episodes in C flat major. These are a few of many, many examples. An entire essay might also be written about Schubert's fondness for augmented sixth chords termed Italian, French or German sixths – the latter enharmonically identical to a dominant seventh – and his use of them in both conventional (typically resolving on to the dominant) and in less conventional ways. They often serve as a means of changing harmonic direction speedily, as well as dramatizing certain 'hinge moments' in the songs: in the piano interlude between the two verses of *Ihr Bild* (*Schwanengesang* D957/9) a marvellously voiced augmented sixth chord resolves very unconventionally to a tonic B flat minor chord – all the mystery and imponderable horror of this lyric is encapsulated in this eerie juxtaposition. Another Schubertian hallmark is his use of the Neapolitan keys and chords – which is to say the flattened supertonic (second degree of the scale) thus D flat in the context of C major. When the crow's circling flight in the piano introduction to *Die Krähe* (*Winterreise* D911/15) sidles briefly into D flat in the third and fourth bars, before returning to the C minor home key, we hear it as an ill omen – the Neapolitan exerts an irrepressible downward force towards the tonic and yet is very far from it. From that same cycle we also recall the chilling 'side-step' from tonic E minor to D sharp minor in *Auf dem Flusse* D911/7 at the words 'Wie still bist du geworden'. Such semitone manoeuvres, especially by descent, would not become anything resembling standard practice in nineteenth-century music until the Wagnerian tonal revolution twenty years and more after Schubert's death.

That Schubert also genuinely respected the old traditions was part of his nature – he was no iconoclast. He continued to learn as he went along, and the rigorous self-improvement that ensured his mastery in all musical spheres – even arguably in opera, had he only had better librettists – was mirrored in subtle changes and ongoing experiments in the form of his lieder. Indeed it is this constant innovation, quite apart from the changing poets, that makes it impossible to generalize about the shape of Schubert's lieder, much less their content. Here are some signposts along his creative pathway.

In his early opera-influenced songs he delighted in differentiating between recitative and aria; later he much preferred to blur the distinctions so that the two melded together in a unified structure so that it is difficult to tell where recitative or arioso ends and aria begins, and that is exactly how the composer wanted it. This was all part of his quest for unity, and the avoidance of bittiness: many longer songs and ballads were revised and rewritten the better to achieve a sense of their hanging together as single pieces.

The composer's sensitivity to poets from the eighteenth century (like Hölty and Jacobi, Salis-Seewis and Uz) sharpened his interest in the old-fashioned formalities of strophic song that had also been important to Zumsteeg. The hard work he put into this genre, in 1816 in particular, bore fruit in 1823 when he composed *Die schöne Müllerin*, the apotheosis of the strophic song, although some songs in this work were cunningly adapted to give the illusion of sonata form – exposition, development and recapitulation – in lieder terms.

In 1818 Schubert composed a long Mayrhofer poem in six parts, *Einsamkeit* D620, which seems to have been poet and composer's calculated riposte to Beethoven's *An die ferne Geliebte* of 1816 – an unexpected shock that Schubert received from the Titan whom he revered from afar, and whose activity as a song composer had long been reassuringly dormant. This important song, still undervalued, shows Schubert's concern to defend his own patch from Beethovenian incursion, but it also initiates a search to transcend the lied genre, as Beethoven had done, and produce a longer, more meaningful work. From this time on Schubert pondered how best to turn his mastery of song, an essentially miniature form, into the production of something larger and more significant.

His experience of preparing his own songs for publication (from 1821) awakened a feeling for creating songs in groups, the whole opus number sometimes designed (*ex post facto* in terms of the individual songs' composition) to be more than the sum of its parts. Some of the opus numbers with thematic links or carefully related tonalities show the composer's planning hand as a prelude to the composition of his real cycles.

It is possible that he had envisaged a small group of settings (all written on the same day) from the almanac *Selam* in 1815, as Walther Dürr believes, and there is a more controversial theory that he put together a Berlin-style *Liederspiel* in the same year to the poems of Kosegarten. In 1819 Schubert seems to have flirted with the idea of a cycle based on Friedrich Schlegel's *Abendröte* poems. In 1823 the Schober song-rondo, *Viola* D786, stood side by side with *Die schöne Müllerin* as an experiment in creating larger song-structures; a little earlier songs like *Suleika I* D720 and *Der Zwerg* D771 showed the composer flexing his muscles with a kind of symphonic song framed within a through-composed pianistic moto perpetuo. In 1825 he set seven poems from Walter Scott's *The Lady of the Lake* (five solo songs and two vocal ensembles) which seemed designed, in lieder terms, to counter the craze produced by Rossini's opera, *La Donna del lago*, based on the same Scott poem. Also in 1825 he set to music two solo scenes from the play *Lacrimas* (*Delphine* and *Florio*, D857/1–2) where, in Till Gerrit Waidelich's view, he seems to be experimenting with a newly invented genre halfway between lied and piano-accompanied operatic aria.

And so we come to *Winterreise* of 1827, the focus in our own time of so much intense interest in Schubert's lieder, and the successful culmination of his search for cycle. He certainly believed that in writing this work he had taken a step forward and composed his best songs – true to Schubertian form, the cycle, shattering in its uncanny conjunction of sophistication and simplicity, is unlike anything else he wrote. But then the same may be said of the lieder of the composer's final year, 1828, when he encountered, within a few months, poems by Rellstab reputedly passed on to him from Beethoven's deathbed, as well as a commissioned cycle of rather unsuitable popular songs – *Vier Refrain-lieder* – and the brave and astonishing new world of texts by Heinrich Heine. By this time, a year after Beethoven's death, ceaseless work, ongoing experience, and stringent self-criticism had left him, in Spaun's words, 'unexcelled, even unapproached'. And so, in the view of many, he has remained.

There is no shortcut to getting to know Schubert's songs and it is perhaps best to tackle the task slowly, over a number of years. One must be prepared to be surprised again and again, not only by their sheer quantity but also by their range and depth. In 1987 my assigned task to record them all contained an element of ambitious 'completism', but many years later I had learned to agree with Johannes Brahms (the most critical of composers when it came to adumbrating the technical lapses of others) when he said to his pupil Gustav Jenner in 1887, 'Es gibt kein Schubert Lied aus dem man nicht etwas lernen kann' – 'There is no song of Schubert from which one cannot learn something'.

The great art historian, Ernst Gombrich (1909–2001), born in Vienna, who knew so much about works of transcendental beauty in all fields, once said of Schubert's lieder, 'There is very little that quite reaches this kind of refinement'.[6] This is a somewhat laconic evaluation but it

---

[6] *Daily Telegraph*, Gombrich obituary, 6 February 2001.

cannot be bettered as a pithy appraisal. Gombrich, connoisseur of art and music, implies that the 'very little' that *does* reach and match Schubert's 'kind of refinement' includes the greatest works of art known to man, but he is too elegant and clever a commentator to list rival master-pieces. It is not a question of comparisons. To gain an insight into the refinement of which he speaks we must embark on an arduous auditory journey and listen to each song on its own terms (Gombrich chose for one of his Desert Island Discs the supremely appropriate *Der Einsame* D800 – 'The Solitary One'). It is my fervent hope that this book will make the task somewhat easier. I began my Schubert odyssey more than forty years ago, but I still find the lieder so incommensurable en masse that I am relieved that I have to accompany them one at a time - and that this, indeed, is all I am capable of. *'There is very little that quite reaches this kind of refinement.'* For me there is very little in my life and work that quite reaches this kind of happiness.

* * * * * *

This book has been so long in the preparation that it is inevitable that many of the people to whom I owe a debt of gratitude are no longer with us, including four of the five dedicatees, each of them a dear friend and mentor – Peter Pears, Gerald Moore, Eric Sams and Ted Perry. There were many others to whom I was less close but who played a pivotal role long before I began this book. Benjamin Britten as a Schubert pianist was an indispensable guiding spirit, alongside the English Schubertian John Reed who wrote the first alphabetical guide to these songs, the indefatigable Belgian scholar Reinhard Van Hoorickx who generously provided me with all his work on the fragments, and the accompanist Geoffrey Parsons who was a kind teacher at a time when my feverish and newly acquired enthusiasm for Schubert's songs required experienced counsel. Were I also to name the departed singing colleagues whose art has broadened my Schubertian conceptions the list would include the late Arleen Auger, Anthony Rolfe Johnson, Philip Langridge, Lucia Popp and the inimitable Dame Margaret Price. It is impossible not to mention the late Dietrich Fischer-Dieskau, ubiquitous in every Schubertian's progress through life (though I never actually accompanied him), and I also have very strong memories of working on Schubert songs as an accompanist in my twenties with that extraordinary married couple Elizabeth Schwarzkopf and Walter Legge – hardly a comfortable experience, but riveting in a way that made other cosier encounters seem pallid. My gratitude also to them.

Among the great living Schubert scholars I express my thanks for help and advice on several occasions to Walther Dürr (Tübingen; chief editor of the *Neue Schubert-Ausgabe*), Ernst Hilmar (formerly of Vienna), Elizabeth McKay (Oxford), Lorraine Byrne Bodley (National University of Ireland, Maynooth) and Till Gerrit Waidelich (Vienna). Robert Holl, great baritone and Schubert expert and collector *sans pareil*, has been an inspirational colleague for many years. For the redoubtable example of the boundless industry of Susan Youens (University of Notre Dame, Indiana), as well as her faithful and enlightening friendship, I am ever grateful. I am indebted to her for permission to reproduce items from her collection of Schubert first editions. I am also grateful to Matthias Griebler for permission to use the illustrations of Martha Griebler (1948–2006), an artist of genius with an uncanny ability to bring Schubert and his circle to life. My good friend Richard Stokes in London has been the usual tower of strength as colleague, adviser and reader. How many books about song in several languages, some his own, some by his friends, have benefitted from his great-hearted enthusiasm! I am indebted to Leo Black for his unfailingly helpful, and sometimes trenchant, comments – he has taken many hours to read through the manuscript and permitted me to learn from his lifetime of experience at the BBC working on Schubert's music, and with almost every singer of importance. My exemplary colleague Richard Wigmore had published his collection of Schubert translations in 1988; his willingness greatly to expand his brief to include the part-songs and to add new strophes to existing translations has resulted in an entirely new, and much revised, edition of that work which now appears, I am proud to say, within the covers of this book. Uri Liebrecht, master translator in his own right, has also read the book from cover to cover and, with the eagle eye of someone whose mother-tongue is German but whose English is no less splendid, he has spotted mistakes and infelicities in the text that many others have missed. In the publishing of this book I am indebted for the financial and moral support of that remarkable warrior on behalf of song, Marilyn Horne, and the Marilyn Horne Foundation in New York City. I am grateful too for the interest in the project shown on several fronts by my American colleagues Susan Gaustad, Thomas Hampson (wearing his scholar's hat and quite apart from his participation in the Hyperion series as a performer), Irwin Gage (in Zurich), Rosemary Hyler (in Cincinnati), Phillip Moll (in Berlin), Rodney Punt (in Los Angeles) and Robert White (in New York City) – singers and pianists all. To these fellow Schubertians I express my gratitude. I also want to make special mention of my beloved friend, the actress Jill Balcon (1925–2009), one of whose many gifts was to have been an assiduous listener. Her wholehearted attention to the Schubert lieder set a kind of listening standard to which few non-professional musicians can aspire; we performers rarely encounter that level of engagement with our work. I should also not forget to express gratitude to Lucy Hayward for her strong belief that I should be entrusted with the recording of Schubert's complete songs, the project that led eventually to this book.

Among the many communications I received as a result of the Hyperion discs and their commentaries, by far the most extraordinary and helpful were those of Professor Raymond Joly from Montreal. The detail and the learning of his communications over the years (copious commentaries that he referred to, jokingly, as Joly's *Marginalia*) played a large part in the development of my own thoughts on the composer, and thus of this work. Visiting Montreal in 2010 it was an unforgettable privilege to meet Raymond face to face for the first and last time, and to experience, only a few weeks before he died, his gallantry in the face of mortal illness.

In the preparation of the book I am grateful for the collaboration of Dr Natasha Loges in the early stages, and I pay tribute to the unstinting work and efficiency of my youthful research assistant Dr Katy Hamilton in the seven years before I reached the finishing line. I am indebted to Katy for permitting my book to occupy her attentions at many levels, including proof-reading, at the same time as her researches on Brahms, surely only the initial stages of what will be a distinguished musicological career. The efficiency and cooperation of Chris Hinkins in the creation of the song incipits has been beyond praise. The continuing and generous support of Ted Perry's son Simon, managing director of Hyperion Records, has played a large part in enabling this book to be completed. While Ted Perry himself was executive producer of the Hyperion series, I owe special gratitude to Mark Brown and, before him, Martin Compton for the crucial role they played as recording producers for the Hyperion series; likewise to the recording engineers Antony Howell and Julian Millard. The enthusiastic contribution of the photographer Malcolm Crowthers is also gratefully recognized. All these co-workers became seasoned Schubertians over the years. The invaluable and solicitous kindness of my first piano teacher, Nora Hutchinson, and of her husband Ronald Smith, has relieved me of onerous family duties in South Africa, and enabled me to finish this book with fewer interruptions than I feared. Peter Bloor, my valiant manager at Askonas-Holt, as well as the superb Annette Allen, and our overall commander-in-chief Robert Rattray, have played their part in allowing a performing artist the supreme eccentricity of writing a book that requires time off from playing. The enthusiastic invitation to prepare this book for publication by Yale University Press came from John Ryden in New Haven. The director of the Press's London office, Robert Baldock (whom I have known since our shared Rhodesian childhood) has been a model of patience and wisdom, and the editing skills of Candida Brazil at Yale, and of the indefatigable Charlotte Chapman, have contributed enormously to the invigorating, if somewhat stressful, completion of the task. None of us perhaps realized how much work was involved in preparing and proofing such a detailed encyclopaedia, especially when written by a travelling accompanist rather than a team of full-time scholars. At the Guildhall School of Music and Drama where I am Professor of Accompaniment I am grateful for the enthusiasm of the principal, Dr Barry Ife in supporting my research (my work at the Guildhall stands at the centre of my activities as a a scholar and teacher) and for the imaginative co-operation of my tireless colleagues in the piano department, Ronan O'Hora and Pamela Lidiard. Over many years my teaching work with the Young Songmakers project has included a great deal of Schubert and I must salute my close and dear friends Mike and Judy Hildesley as the tireless Young Songmakers organizers; on the night of 31 January 1997 (the bi-centenary of the composer's birth) they hosted a Schubertiad with appropriate food and wine that remains, for events of that kind, unsurpassed in the memory of all those who were there. It was after this occasion that I resolved to write this book. I continue to teach Schubert privately from time to time; the pupil of whom I am most proud is Claus Moser, formerly Chairman of the Royal Opera House – Lord Moser at ninety is a devotee of *Die schöne Müllerin* and he plays the accompaniments beautifully – his love for the music, and his curiosity about every detail, is a delightful reminder that Schubert is ageless. John Gilhooly, director of Wigmore Hall, has played a remarkably supportive role in the year that has led up to the book's publication – I have an ongoing and unashamed devotion to this great auditorium, and its remarkable team, where I believe Schubert songs sound best of all. As I write this I feel slightly pulled in another direction by my gratitude to Gerd Nachbauer, manager of the Hohenems *Schubertiade* and the Angelika-Kauffmannsaal in Schwarzenberg, a centre for Schubert performances unique in a different way – little can compete with the view over the mountains that is visible from the stage.

Of course, all my appearances at Wigmore Hall, Schwarzenberg, in Vienna's Muzikverein and Konzerthaus, and elsewhere throughout the world have been in the company of my colleagues. No accompanist is an island, and his or her achievements can only be measured in performances fronted by singers. It is perhaps because of our utter reliance on singers (and their reliance on us) that accompanists can be very touchy about not getting their due as far as the public is concerned. How very many times have we been completely ignored by those in the audience who come backstage to congratulate the singers, and how often have we found this indifference almost insulting – as if we have been weighed in the balance and our balance found wanting! This is, of course, to imagine each member of the public a terrifically informed connoisseur. I have come to realize that the truth is somewhat different. I am now convinced that no insult is intended (not usually anyway). If a substantial swathe of the listening public declines to comment on the pianist's contribution to the evening it is often a matter of what used to be called aural training: for the untrained ear, belonging to however enthusiastic a vocal fancier, the top line (in this case the sound of the voice) dominates the texture to the point of obliteration of pianistic niceties – they simply have not heard what we pianists have been doing and informed evaluation is duly impossible. At an orchestral concert these same listeners would experience a block of musical sound rather than an assemblage of differentiated orchestral textures where each instrument comes to the fore and shines in turn. It is not every audience-member who rushes backstage after a symphony to congratulate, say, the first horn – although some do, and rightly so.

It is little wonder therefore that the accompanist sometimes seems invisible; it is the singer who carries the tune and phonates the text – it is these things that the average ear picks up first, and we serve the voice which, or rather the person who, assumes these awesome responsibilities. It follows, therefore, that the skills of an accompanist are formed, tempered, honed and in every way refined by the singers with whom he or she works. My greatest debt is to the many hundreds of my contemporaries, singers some a lot (or only somewhat) older than me, a great many younger – my vocal partners are getting younger all the time – who have performed Schubert by my side over the last forty years. To my very many living colleagues, some world famous, some destined to be great, some unknown (sometimes far finer Schubertians than the celebrity singers) I owe a large debt of gratitude. It is they who have enabled me to experience the glories of this composer at first hand while gradually becoming more adept at being in their company – or, to put it another way, accompanying them.

Partnership is indeed one of life's greatest challenges and one of its greatest rewards. For the ongoing companionship for the last eighteen years of my partner Brandon Velarde I can only express my humble gratitude; it was Brandon who encouraged me to take up, and complete, a task that in the beginning seemed simply too large to contemplate – the conversion of disc notes in a variety of lengths and styles into a serious book. I did not think I could do it, but he was certain that I should try and, even in the wake of serious illness in 2009, urged me to stick to the task. It has taken rather a long time, but it has been done with love, and on account of love.

Graham Johnson
London, March 2013

HOW TO USE THIS BOOK

There are three kinds of article in this work – song commentaries, poets' biographies and general subject articles – all arranged within a single alphabetical sequence. The song titles are here treated alphabetically, without reference to their German definite articles – Der, Die and Das (occasionally found in their genitive or dative forms – Des, Der and Dem). *Der Einsame* D800, for example, is listed under 'E' rather than 'D', *Dem Unendlichen* under 'U', *Der zürnenden Diana* under 'Z'. This will be familiar to users of the Peters Edition where the song index at the back of volumes 1 and 7 of Schubert's lieder is similarly arranged. In general, readers will find it easy to find their way around the alphabetical format; an exception to this may be with song titles, such as *Der König in Thule*, which include a vowel with an umlaut. The ö with its umlaut is a German contraction of oe; this is also true of ä (ae), and ü (ue). It follows that the song *Kolmas Klage* should be placed alphabetically *after Der König (Koenig) in Thule* although many English-speakers will probably initially search for it *before* that song, as if ö were simply an o.

The song titles used here are those established by the *Neue Schubert-Ausgabe* (*NSA*), sometimes fairly recently. For example, the famous song known as *Litanei* since it was posthumously published in 1831 is listed here as *Am Tage Aller Seelen* D343, the title that Schubert himself gave it. The publisher's title for the Schulze setting *Tiefes Leid* is replaced by Schubert's own title, *Im Jänner, 1817* D876. In several instances songs that Schubert had simply entitled 'Lied' were given other titles by posthumous publishers (such as *Ins stille Land* D403 and *Die Mutter Erde* D880). Once again following the *Neue Schubert-Ausgabe*, these songs, and several others, are listed here under their authentic title 'Lied' with a differentiating sub-title; these are all supplemented by the necessary cross-references. A new generation of Schubert-lovers will gradually adopt these changes as modern performing editions are used more frequently by singers and pianists, and Schubert's original titles are increasingly printed in concert programmes.

There are several groups of Schubert songs where it made a great deal more sense, certainly in terms of writing commentaries, to present them together in extended articles. This naturally applies to song cycles such as *Die schöne Müllerin* D795, *Winterreise* D911 and *Schwanengesang* D957 (the latter not separated out, as is sometimes the case, into its potentially separate Rellstab, Heine and Seidl constituents). The following song-sets, some twenty-seven songs and ensembles, are also treated in this manner, alphabeticized under the title of their publication, thus under D, G, S, V and Z respectively: *Drei Gesänge für Bass-Stimme und Klavier* Op. 83 D902 (three songs); *Gesänge aus Wilhelm Meister* Op. 62, D877 (three solo songs and one duet); *Gesänge des Harfners* Op. 12 D478 (three songs); *Sieben Gesänge aus Walter Scott's Das Fräulein vom See* Op. 52 D837 (five solo songs, one male voice ensemble and one female voice ensemble); *Vier Canzonen* D588 (four songs); *Vier Refrain-Lieder* Op. 95 D866 (four songs); *Zwei Scenen aus Lacrimas* D857 (two songs). The celebrated *Ave Maria*, for example, is the sixth song in the extended article devoted to the Scott cycle (alphabetically listed here under *Sieben Gesänge*) but there is a cross reference under 'Ave Maria' and also one for 'Ellens Gesänge I–III'; Ellens Gesang I, II and III are the songs' correct titles (sometimes referred to as Ellens erster, zweiter and dritter Gesang) and are separately listed as such within the *Sieben Gesänge* article. The two Schütz settings *Delphine* and *Florio* D857 clearly belong together in terms of plot and background. They are both discussed here under their published title, *Zwei Szenen aus dem Schauspiel Lacrimas*, but they are also separately cross-referenced under 'D' and 'F'. Song arrangements from Schubert's orchestrally accompanied dramatic works appear in articles listed under *Alfonso und Estrella* D732, *Claudine von Villa Bella* D239, *Rosamunde, Fürstin von Zypern* D797 and *Die Verschworenen* D787; once again, all the individual song and ensemble titles are cross-referenced.

The Song Commentaries

The essays on the songs and part-songs constitute by far the largest part of this work. Each of these is preceded by a heading that contains musicological information in abbreviated form: the **Title** in German with its English translation; the surname of the **Poet**; the **Opus number** (if the song was published under the composer's supervision); and the **Deutsch number** assigned to the work by Otto Erich Deutsch in his catalogue of all Schubert's works (1951, revised 1978). Since this monumental work was first published, new research has established many possible variants to Deutsch's chronology. However, with a few exceptions, the numbering has remained immutable and is almost certain to do so in the future. The **H number** is discussed below and at the end of the third volume of this book in the *Schubert Calendar*. The **Date** of composition is given here, where known. The **Tonality** of the song discussed in the commentary is also printed. When a song ends in a different key from the one in which it has begun, this is noted (for example, 'G minor – E minor' for the *Ballade* D134).

If more than one version of the same music exists, as is frequently the case (a different *setting* of the same words is another matter)[1] these are listed with information concerning dates (again, where known), tonality, tempo indication and length.

The principal (and often only) version discussed in the commentary is the subject of the musical **Incipit** which is a reduced outline of a song's accompaniment and vocal line in the manner of a thematic catalogue. These incipits show each song's **Key and Time signatures**, as well as its **Tempo marking** (for translations of these from the German see TEMPO AND EXPRESSION MARKINGS). At the end of each incipit, in brackets, the length of the song is indicated by its number of bars.

Wherever possible the **German Poem** is printed in the versification, and with the punctuation, in which Schubert first encountered it; we can be reasonably certain of the composer's literary sources in a majority of cases, and the look of a poem on the printed page influences song composers more than is generally realized. Changes that Schubert made to the text (apart from punctuation and verbal repetition) are incorporated into the poem as printed here (it is sometimes difficult to tell the difference between the composer's deliberate choices and errors made in haste) and the poet's original wording (where there are any significant differences) is detailed in footnotes. The parallel **English Translations** by Richard Wigmore represent what is, in effect, a revised and enlarged edition of his *Schubert. The Complete Song Texts* (1988).

In the case of longer song texts, **numbered strophes** facilitate discussion of the music within the song commentaries. These numbers are placed in brackets. Only strophe numbers printed without brackets are original to the text source and poets seldom included these in printings of their works.

As indicated above, Schubert often chose to edit a poem for his own purposes. This sometimes entailed leaving out strophes, and even individual lines, from the poet's original. These **strophe omissions** are shown within the printing of the poem in both round and square

---

[1] Different settings of a song text receive separate entries in this book, differentiated by the numbers (I), (II) and (III) as in such songs as *Der Jüngling am Bache (I)* D30, *Der Jüngling am Bache (II)* D192 and *Der Jüngling am Bache (III)* D638.

brackets. Thus [(. . .)] indicates that Schubert decided to leave out a strophe in his setting of a poem; [(. . . 2 . . .)] indicates two strophes, and so on.

In the printing of this book there are also cuts made to a number of long poems which were set strophically by Schubert and which are all but impossible for any singer to perform in their entirety. These **editorial omissions** are represented by numbers in square brackets – for example, a strophe left out in the printing and translation of the original poem is indicated by [. . .], and three strophes by [. . . 3 . . .].

If Schubert set a German translation of an **English poem** (Colley Cibber, Abraham Cowley, Shakespeare, Walter Scott), the original is printed below the German text (which also has its parallel, and literal, translation into English).

Before the beginning of the commentary the poet's full name and dates are given (plus pseudonym if there is one). The date when the poem was written is also given, if known. This is followed by a sentence which places the song discussed in the context of other Schubert settings of the same poet. Following the poems and translation of *Gretchen am Spinnrade*, for example, the following is printed: '*This is the first of Schubert's seventy-five Goethe solo settings (1814–26)*'. The reader is then referred to Goethe's biographical article, and to the full list of Schubert's Goethe settings that is printed there. It is clear that this numbering can only be accurate up to a point: in the case of the Goethe settings, for example, there are a number of contested dates for songs; a change to any one of these (as indeed happened regarding D296 as recently as 2011) could result in a different sequence with a knock-on effect to the whole chronology. A phrase like 'the twenty-ninth of Goethe's solo songs' (in reference to *Erlkönig*) is thus not meant to be definitive, but merely a rough guide. In the case of other poets, particularly those who contributed a smaller list of Schubert settings, it is possible to be more accurate.

At the heart of each song article is a Commentary concerning the history, compositional structure and musical effect of the work in question. These essays often include cross-references to other relevant articles within the book.

Following the commentary a great deal of information is presented in tabular form:

Autograph: This details the libraries and institutions in which the surviving Schubert song autographs may be found and consulted (see also AUTOGRAPHS, ALBUMS AND COLLECTIONS). Information about autographs (which are sometimes in private hands and are sold on to libraries or bequeathed to institutions) can only ever be as up-to-date as the latest auction catalogues, but there is far less fluidity in the location of manuscripts owned by state institutions. If the article covers a song with several variant versions, details are given for all known sources. It is also noted whether extant autographs are first drafts or fair copies.

First Edition: Here are given details of the first publicly available edition of the song, whether as part of an opus number in the composer's lifetime (see OPUS NUMBERS), as an item in Diabelli's fifty instalments of posthumous songs, the so-called *Nachlass* (see NACHLASS), or as further posthumous publications over some 160 years (see POSTHUMOUS SONGS). Many a song, or lesser-known version of a song, has made its first appearance in print as an item in collected editions of the composer's works, right up to the present time. Each song is here given a 'Publication' or 'P' number, which indicates its position within the chronology of published Schubert songs. The reader can more or less follow the history and sequence of these 'P' numbers, over 800 of them, by consulting consecutively the three substantial articles mentioned in brackets above.

Dedicatee: A name is only included here if the dedication was offered by Schubert himself – this clearly applies only to songs published in the composer's lifetime (see DEDICATEES).

Publication reviews: Reviews listed here are all readily available as part of documentary collections published by O. E. Deutsch (in English) and T. G. Waidelich & E. Hilmar (in German). References to these sources are given alongside each listed review.

First known performance: Although many of the songs were first sung and played privately and informally in the houses of Schubert's friends, the information detailed here refers to the first performances in public or private venues, and only where known from documentary sources. Performance information is usually only included if the event occurred during Schubert's lifetime or shortly thereafter.

Performance reviews: These are included from the same sources, and along the same reference principles, as publication reviews.

Subsequent editions: This section details the location of the song in up to four major collected editions of Schubert's lieder. These are:

Peters Edition: the seven volumes of solo lieder, based almost exclusively on the printed opus numbers and the Diabelli *Nachlass*. The most famous Schubert song volumes of Peters Edition were edited by Max Friedlaender and issued in this revised form between 1884 and 1887.

AGA (Alte Gesamtausgabe): the first Schubert collected edition, published by Breitkopf & Härtel from 1894 to 1897 where the songs are arranged chronologically (numbers 1 to 603) according to the information available at the time. The solo Lieder series (Series XX) edited by Eusebius Mandyczewski was published in ten folio volumes, but reference is also made to the various part-song series for different vocal combinations (XVI, XVII, XVIII and XIX).

NSA (Neue Schubert-Ausgabe) sometimes referred to elsewhere as NGA (Neue Gesamtasugabe): the new Schubert collected edition published by Bärenreiter issued its first lieder volume in 1968. The solo Lieder series (Series IV, edited by Walther Dürr) is published in fourteen volumes; Volume 9, which completed the series, appeared in 2012 with an imprint of 2011. This is not exactly a chronological survey in the sense of Mandyczewski's work: the first five volumes follow the sequence of the opus numbers published in Schubert's lifetime, and shortly after his death when he arguably had some say in their publication: Opp. 1–108. In volumes 6–14, those works not published in Schubert's lifetime appear not exactly chronologically (in terms of the latest scholarship) but in the order of Deutsch's catalogue (which attempted a chronological order in the early 1950s which is no longer valid in certain respects). The logic of giving priority to the opus number publications, and removing them from their ordinary Deutsch catalogue chronology, is as follows: Schubert almost always made changes to older works when he prepared them for publication so it is impossible to consign them exactly to their earlier composition dates – the last stage of their composition could be said to have occurred shortly before their publication, sometimes years after their initial composition. For this reason all earlier Schubert songs published by the composer between 1821 and 1828 are problematic in terms of their chronology (Mandyczewski chose to date every song from its inception, and that too is the principal of the 'H' numbers in this book).

Reference is also made to the part-song series of the NSA (Series III, editor Dietrich Berke) of which several volumes have not yet appeared.

Bärenreiter: a performer's lieder edition based on the work of the NSA but in larger format, begun in 2005. Six of the projected eleven volumes had appeared by 2012.

Peters and Bärenreiter references simply provide the volume and page number (if available) of the song in question. AGA references include the series number (in Roman numerals), the number of the song within that series (thus a kind of Mandyczewskian 'H' number) and then the volume and page number for easy reference. The NSA Series IV references include the volume number (volumes 1–5 and 14 are published in two parts, thus (a) and (b), volumes 6–13 are single volumes) followed by the relevant page number.

Bibliography: Here are provided short citations for very selective sources relevant to the song in question. Fuller bibliographic details are to be found at the back of the third volume. This field does not attempt to be a comprehensive list of works and articles that cover the song in question – rather a combination of references that the English-speaking reader will find accessible and helpful, together with authors who have been specifically consulted in the writing of the article.

Further settings and arrangements: Whilst far from complete, this field includes information on further settings, of the same song text by other notable composers, as well as arrangements, orchestrations and transcriptions of the Schubert song in question (*see* ORCHESTRATIONS and TRANSCRIPTIONS).

Discography: A book about notable performances of Schubert songs on disc would be a mighty tome of its own and details of favourite performances (in any case highly subjective) have had to be largely avoided here for reasons of space alone. Details of location and timing are given for the historically essential performances of Dietrich Fischer-Dieskau, readily available on CD, as well as two versions of the Hyperion Schubert Edition, the first issued singer-by-singer between 1987 and 2001 (there are some sixty singers in the series all told), and the second – the chronological re-mastering of 2005. An exception has been made for the Schubert recordings of Peter Pears and Benjamin Britten whose recorded work is also referenced here because it was a major source of inspiration for the author of this book. The information on these recorded performances is provided in the following format:

Title;   volume (if applicable);   disc number or side of LP;   track or band number
For example:
Fischer-Dieskau II 5^{15} = Fischer-Dieskau's *Schubert Lieder*: Volume II, Disc 5, Track 15
Pears–Britten 1^4 = *Schubert Songs*, Decca LP, 1975 Side 1, Track 4

Hyperion I refers to the collection of thirty-seven CDs as originally issued; Hyperion II to the reissue of discs (also thirty-seven in number) with the songs in chronological order. Artist details and disc and track numbers are provided in each case.

At the end of each discography two further song titles are given, one marked ← and the other marked →. These are chronology indicators – the first arrow (←) is the previous song in the Hyperion chronological sequence (the previous H number), the second arrow (→) the following song and H number. H numbers are not an infallible guide to the chronological order in which Schubert composed his songs, but they provide an adequate if necessarily speculative guide. This book, printed alphabetically, was clearly not designed to be read cover to cover, but those readers who may wish to peruse these commentaries in something of a chronological sequence may move from song to song within this work using these arrow indicators. These arrowed titles will also make consecutive song commentaries easier to find for those listening at the same time to the chronological version of the Hyperion Schubert edition.

Poets' Biographies

This book features articles on all known Schubert poets, including recent discoveries such as the almost unknown Ernestine von Krosigk and the celebrated August Varnhagen von Ense whose role as a Schubert poet has been unknown for some 180 years. In considering a song in any depth, the reader is advised to consult the relevant poet's entry for a chronological list of settings, and for biographical information, further reading and the relative importance of the writer to the composer. Each poet article contains:

The Poetic Sources: a detailed list and descriptions of the printed editions (marked S1, S2 and so on) that Schubert used, probably used or might have used, including, where relevant, later editions with textual variants.

The Songs: a chronological list of all of Schubert's settings of texts by the poet in question, with precise page references to the location of each poem within the poetic sources.

A biographical portrait of the poet in question, with occasional bibliographical information where appropriate.

General Subject Articles

These essays vary greatly in their content and format. They cover the following topics: ACCOMPANIMENT; ANTIQUITY; AUTOGRAPHS, ALBUMS and COLLECTIONS; CHRONOLOGY; COMPOSERS; DEDICATEES; *FAUST*; FRIENDS AND FAMILY; GREAT BRITAIN AND BRITISH LITERATURE; GUITAR; HARFNERLIEDER – AN OVERVIEW; INITIALS AND SIGNATURES; ITALY AND ITALIAN LITERATURE; MIGNON LIEDER – AN OVERVIEW; NACHLASS; OPUS NUMBERS; ORCHESTRATIONS; ORNAMENTATION; PART-SONGS; PEDALLING; PIANISTS; PIANOS; POSTHUMOUS SONGS; RELIGION AND RELIGIOUS MUSIC; RUBATO; SINGERS; SCHOLARS; STROPHIC SONGS; TEMPO MARKINGS; TONALITY; TRANSCRIPTIONS; *WEST-ÖSTLICHE DIVAN*; *WILHELM MEISTERS LEHRJAHRE*. Many song commentaries and poet articles include cross-references to these more broadly conceived essays, which provide essential information for scholars, practitioners and students alike. On the subject of singers, and their evaluation historically and artistically, for reasons of professional friendship and sometimes tact, I have declined to comment on those artists with whom I have had the privilege to record the songs of Schubert. The roles of accompanist and critic are, after all, hardly compatible. Accordingly, those living artists who took part in the Hyperion Schubert Edition (many of them still very much active in their careers) are simply listed at the end of the SINGERS article.

A Schubert Song Calendar

This section of the book, printed at the end of the third volume as a kind of index, provides a short biographical introduction to Schubert in the form of a calendar of each year of his life and work from his birth in 1797 to his death in 1828. It is key to this book in chronological, rather than alphabetical, terms. To each relevant year is attached a list of the composer's song output, as well as a selective list of his achievements in other musical areas.

The usefulness of the H numbers goes beyond their link with the Hyperion Edition in terms of orientation. Armed with this number to be found at the head of each commentary within this book (after the Deutsch catalogue number), the reader or listener will be able to refer back to the Schubert Song Calendar at the end of Volume 3 and quickly place any title (otherwise adrift in the alphabetical sequence of an encyclopaedia) in the context of the composer's life, and of his song output as a whole.[2]

Because H numbers have only been attached to songs that were recorded for the Hyperion Edition there are a handful of items listed in the Schubert calendar which did not appear as recordings on the Hyperion discs, but which are nevertheless discussed in commentaries within this book. These are interpolated with brackets [ ] into the calendar sequence and are not assigned an H number. On the other hand, choral items without piano accompaniment, items that are arrangements of arias from the Schubert operas and are not strictly speaking songs at all, readings of Müller texts by Dietrich Fischer-Dieskau – items such as these *are* to be found on the Hyperion recordings and are thus allocated H numbers, or rather **H numbers plus**, as in H425+ for example, the unaccompanied choral setting of *Nur wer die Sehnsucht kennt* D656. This is because these items, as interesting as they may be for background purposes, do not form part of the overall tally of piano-accompanied songs and part-songs at the heart of this book. The allocation of a '+' number ensures that H numbers proper are allocated only to songs that are eligible to be counted as part of this sequence, and that the final tally of H numbers, uninflated by different types of music, will accurately reflect the size of Schubert's output in the realm of piano-accompanied vocal music.

---

[2] The compositional sequence suggested by these 'H' numbers does not pretend to be a definitive solution to the vexed problem of the ordering of Schubert's songs (*see* CHRONOLOGY). In the Schubert Calendar comparative reference is sometimes made to the chronological list suggested by Dr Walther Dürr, editor of the NSA in communication with the author.

Der ABEND

(Matthisson) **D108** [H41]
D minor   July 1814

The evening

(34 bars)

Purpur malt die Tannenhügel
Nach der Sonne Scheideblick,
Lieblich strahlt des Baches Spiegel
Hespers Fackelglanz zurück.

The pine-covered hills are painted with purple
After the sun's parting glance;
The brook's mirror reflects
The lovely gleaming torch of Hesperus.

Wie in Totenhallen düster
Wird's im Pappelweidenhain,
Unter leisem Blattgeflüster
Schlummern alle Vögel ein.

In the poplar grove
It grows dark, as in the vaults for the dead.
Beneath softly whispering leaves
All the birds fall asleep.

Nur dein Abendlied, o Grille!
Tönt noch aus betautem Grün,
Durch der Dämmrung Zauberhülle
Süsse Trauermelodien.

Only your evening song, O cricket,
Echoes from the dewy grass,
Wafting sweet, mournful melodies
Through the enchanted cloak of dusk.

Tönst du einst im Abendhauche,
Grillchen, auf mein frühes Grab,
Aus der Freundschaft Rosenstrauche,
Deinen Klaggesang herab:

Cricket, if one day
You sound your lament in the evening breeze
Over my early grave,
From the rosebush planted by friends,

Wird noch stets mein Geist dir lauschen,[1]
Horchend wie er jetzt dir lauscht,
Durch des Hügels Blumen rauschen,
Wie dies Sommerlüftchen rauscht!

My spirit will always listen to you
As it listens to you now,
And murmur through the flowers on the hillside
As this summer breeze murmurs.

[1] Matthisson writes 'Wird *mein Geist noch stets* dir lauschen'.

FRIEDRICH VON MATTHISSON (1761–1831); poem written in 1780

This is the twelfth of Schubert's twenty-nine Matthisson solo settings (1812–17). See the poet's biography for a chronological list of all the Matthisson settings.

This modified strophic song is less original in musical terms than some of the other Matthisson settings, but it demonstrates Schubert's care for *bel canto* – a respect for the human voice and its possibilities as instilled by Salieri. This was the phase of Schubert's life when he was learning how to appeal not only to his listeners, but to his foot soldiers, the grateful singers of the future. The opening phrase that pivots around A and B flat in the middle of the stave reminds us initially of the opening of *Schäfers Klagelied* D121, and then of the miracle of the vocal line of *Gretchen am Spinnrade* composed a few months later, also in D minor. Here we have a vocal line without the tension and drama of *Gretchen* but with a pleasing and sensual shape that immediately suggests a singer's composer.

The prelude is simple, even perfunctory: three D minor chords pick out a fragment of melody (D-F-D) in the pianist's right hand. The melody, a gentle *siciliana* in dotted rhythm, is appealing without being instantly memorable. The song is in binary form: the first section is entirely strophic, and we hear the same fourteen bars three times in all. The first verse remains the best from the point of view of prosody, but the others show a certain amount of forward thinking on the composer's part. For example, in b. 8 the word 'Lieblich' sounds charming enough as a descending arpeggio, but in the second verse this music is even more appropriate for the falling phrase containing the word 'unter'.

The poem's fourth strophe, addressed to the cricket ('Grillchen'), is set as a recitative. In German poetry the song of this insect is often associated, as here, with the dead. It is much later in Schubert's output that we find a cheerier address to the companionable cricket on the hearth in *Der Einsame* D800 (1825). With the final words of this verse ('Klaggesang herab') the vocal line reverts to melody in dotted rhythm. The last verse is set to music that is identical to that of the first three. The postlude ends with the same chords with which the song began.

There was a craftsmanslike side to Schubert that sought to master the more ordinary, everyday (and rather Germanic) characteristics of strophic song – this self-censorship is something we hear again and again between 1814 and 1816 in Schubert's bid to take his place beside Reichardt and Zumsteeg in the roll call of significant lieder composers. When he is in this mood, Schubert's achievements can seem rather unspectacular on one level; on another they are eloquent testimony to his serious interest in releasing the power of the poem by writing music of minimal fuss. This continuing practice in 'cutting back' in order to be more expressive was to bear its choicest fruit many years later in the strophic songs of *Die schöne Müllerin*.

Autograph:	Missing or lost
First edition:	Published as part of the AGA in 1894 (P543)
Subsequent editions:	Not in Peters; AGA XX 22: Vol. 1/161; NSA IV: Vol. 7/31; Bärenreiter: Vol. 5/131 (high voice) 5/125 (medium low voice)
Discography and timing:	Fischer-Dieskau I 2⁴ 1'46 (omitting verses 2–3)
	Hyperion I 33²¹
	Hyperion II 3¹³ 3'02 Philip Langridge

← *Lied der Liebe* D109   *An Emma* D113 →

Der ABEND

The evening

(KOSEGARTEN) **D221** [H125]
B major   15 July 1815

Der Abend blüht,
Temora glüht
Im Glanz der tiefgesunknen Sonne.
  Es küsst die See
  Die Sinkende,
Von Ehrfurcht schaudernd und von Wonne.

  Ein grauer Duft
  Durchwebt die Luft,
Umschleiert Daura's güldne Auen.
  Es rauscht umher
  Das düstre Meer,
Und rings herrscht ahndungsreiches Grauen.[1]

[. . . 3 . . .]

  O trautes Land,
  O hehrer Strand,
Sei stolz auf deiner Blumen Blume.
  Das heil'ge Meer
  Und rings umher
Die Inseln huld'gen deinem Ruhme. — —

  Nacht hüllt den Strand,
  Temora schwand.
Verlodert sind des Spätrots Gluten.
  Das Weltmeer grollt,
  Und glutrot rollt
Der Vollmond aus den düstern Fluten.

The evening blossoms,
Temora glows
In the light of the setting sun.
  As it sinks
  It kisses the sea,
Trembling in awe and ecstasy.

  A grey haze
  Pervades the air,
Veiling Daura's golden meadows.
  Round about
  The sombre ocean roars,
And a terrible foreboding hangs over all.

[. . . 3 . . .]

  Beloved land
  Noble shore,
Be proud of your fairest flower,
  The sacred sea
  And the surrounding islands
Pay homage to your glory.

  Night shrouds the shore;
  Temora has vanished;
The sunset's last glow has faded.
  The ocean roars,
  And gleaming red,
The full moon rolls from the dark waves.

LUDWIG THEOBUL KOSEGARTEN (1758–1818)

This is the eighth of Schubert's twenty-one Kosegarten solo settings (1815–17). See the poet's biography for a chronological list of all the Kosegarten settings, as well as a discussion of Morten Solvik's Kosegarten Liederkreis and this song's place within it.

Kosegarten played a role in the formative years of Caspar David Friedrich, and this scene is worthy of something painted by the poet's protégé – a magical evening landscape, a coastal scene at

---

[1] Kosegarten writes '*ahnungsreiches* Grauen'.

twilight. Kosegarten was something of an authority on the British poets, and he pays homage to Ossian (the adopted nom de plume of James Macpherson qv) in using the name 'Temora' in the poem's first line; this was the home of the Irish kings as described in Ossian's *The Death of Cuchullin* and the title of Macpherson's second book of Ossianic 'translations' (1763), said by Macpherson to refer to *Tigh-Mòr-rìgh* – 'the house of a great king' and later modernized into 'Tara', the palace of the king of Ireland. 'Daura' in the second strophe is the name of a beautiful but luckless maiden in Ossian's *The Songs of Selma*, kidnapped by Erath and left to die on a rock.

The word 'Temora' lingered strongly in the memory of Schubert's schoolfriend Johann Leopold Ebner (1797–1870); it appears as a song title in a list of Schubert's lieder made by Ebner many years after the composer's death. This suggests that *Der Abend* had enjoyed some favour among Schubert's friends soon after it was composed. Part of the impression the song made on its listeners seems to have been its connection with the contemporary craze for Ossianic poetry.

In the 1788 and 1824 editions of Kosegarten's works, the name 'Temora' does not appear but instead the real place name 'Arkona'. Arkona was local to the poet who lived and worked on the Baltic island of Rügen. Karl Lappe, another significant Schubert poet and pupil of Kosegarten, also lived on Rügen; indeed, this scene, inspired by the island's spectacular sunsets, may be compared to Lappe's *Im Abendrot* D799 and Kosegarten's own *An die untergehende Sonne* D457. John Reed wrongly assumed that the composer had substituted the name 'Temora' for 'Arkona', but the word 'Temora' *is* to be found in the 1802 Leipzig edition of Kosegarten's poems, a

Title page of Kosegarten's *Poesieen*, depicting Cape Arkona ('Temora') in Rügen.

substantial revision of the famous 1798 edition. This publication was undoubtedly the one that came into Schubert's hands. The many departures from Kosegarten's originals that are noted in Schochow 1974 are less to do with Schubert's being cavalier with the texts than with his having used a different edition of the poems. Kosegarten himself had altered his original 'Arkona' to encompass a fashionable Ossianic reference ('Temora') in 1802; the posthumous edition of the *Dichtungen* in 1824 reverted to the poet's original thoughts.

John Reed points out that B major is Schubert's tonality of transcendence (as exemplified by the much later Collin setting *Nacht und Träume* D827). This is fitting for a thumbnail sketch of a fairy kingdom ruled by heroes and eulogized by bards. The descending vocal line for 'der tiefgesunknen Sonne' shows the composer's natural ability to match verbal imagery with appropriate music. As is often the case with Schubert songs on a single page, the overall majesty of the music is created from simple harmonic progressions: the solemn alternation of tonic and dominant in the opening conveys elemental grandeur, as does the 'echo' effect where the vocal line imitates what the piano has proposed in the previous bar. Schubert must have been pleased with the tune; the melody at the opening is found note for note (although in a different key and rhythm, and without the piano interjections) in the Claudius setting *Abendlied* D499 from November 1816.

Der Abend is undated but it shares an autograph sheet (back and front) with another Kosegarten setting, *Geist der Liebe* D233 and the two songs were composed on the same day – 15 July. On 20 July 1815 Schubert set the adjacent poem in the Kosegarten volume, a pendant to *Der Abend* in the same metre, as a terzett for two sopranos and bass (D236). The title of this setting is *Das Abendrot* (qv).

There are seven strophes in Kosegarten's poem – these are all printed in the AGA. Given here are 1, 2, 6 and 7. Three strophes seem sufficient in performance.

Autograph:	Osterreichisches Nationalbibliothek, Vienna
First edition:	Published as Op. post. 118 no. 2 by Joseph Czerny, Vienna in 1829 (P223)
Subsequent editions:	Peters: Vol. 4/146; AGA XX 95: Vol. 2/178; NSA IV: Vol. 8/112
Bibliography:	Clerk 1870, Vol. 2, p. 535
Arrangements:	Arr. Tilman Hoppstock (b. 1961) for guitar accompaniment, in *Franz Schubert: 110 Lieder* (2009)
Discography and timing:	Fischer-Dieskau I 4[12] 2'20
	Hyperion I 22[5]
	Hyperion II 8[8] 2'39 Catherine Wyn-Rogers

← *Geist der Liebe* D233   *Tischlied* D234 →

ABEND   Evening
(TIECK) **D645** [H414]
(Fragment) G minor – A♭ major   early 1819?

Wie ist es denn, dass trüb und schwer so   al-les kommt, vor-ü - ber zieht,

(119 bars)

Wie ist es denn, dass trüb und schwer	How is it that, come what may,
So alles kommt, vorüberzieht,	Everything grim and difficult passes,
Und wechselnd, quälend, immer leer,	And tormented, restless, always empty,
Das arme Herz in sich verglüht?	My poor heart is burning itself out?
Kaum gekommen	No sooner have I come,
Soll ich scheiden,	Than I must leave;
Kaum entglommen	And quench once more,
Löschen wieder	The glimmer
Alle Freuden,	Of new joys,
Und der Leiden	As the dark cloud
Dunkle Wolke senkt sich nieder.	Of pain descends.
Aus den Lichtern in die Nacht,	Away from the lights into the darkness,
Aus den Augen, die mir tagen,	Away from those eyes that shine for me,
Die mein ganzes Herz durchlacht,	Filling my whole heart with laughter,
Bin ich wieder allen Plagen,	I am plunged into all the torments
Dem dürren Leben	And a barren life
Zurückgegeben.	Once more.
[(. . . 6 lines . . .)]	[(. . . 6 lines . . .)]
O als ich dich noch nicht gesehn,	O, before I had seen you,
Da durfte Sehnsucht bei mir sein,	I could live with longing,
Ein Hoffnungswind in meinen Wünschen wehn,	The wind of hope fanned my desires,
Die Zukunft war ein heller Schein:	And the future was a glowing vision.
Jetzt muss ich vom Erinnern kaufen,	Now I must wrest from my memory
Was ich kaum zerstreut empfand;	That which I had enjoyed with scarce a thought.
Wieder durch die wüsten Haufen,	Once more among the uncouth crowd
Wieder durch ein unbewohntes Land,	Once more through deserted country
Soll ich irre, klagend, schweifen,	I must roam and grieve;
Und des Glückes goldne Streifen	The golden strands of happiness
Auch die letzten, ach, abgewandt.[1]	Stripped from me, even to the last.
Noch fühl' ich deine Hand,	Still I can feel your hand,
Noch wie im Traume die Küsse,	Still, as in a dream, your kisses,
Noch folgen mir die holden Blicke,	Your sweet eyes still follow me,
Und die Empfindung, dass ich alles misse,	And the *feeling that all is lost*
Bleibt bei mir zurücke.[2]	*Remains with me.*
[(. . . 14 lines in 2 strophes . . .)]	[(. . . 14 lines in 2 strophes . . .)]

JOHANN LUDWIG TIECK (1773–1853)

This is Schubert's only setting of a Tieck text. See the poet's biography.

This fragment shares the autograph of the remarkable Friedrich von Schlegel setting, *Die Gebüsche*. Schubert's only attempt at setting Ludwig Tieck is thus linked to his interest in the

---

[1] The addition of 'ach' is Schubert's.
[2] The manuscript of D645 breaks off here at 'Empfindung' in mid-word.

poetry of the early German romantics, above all Schlegel and Novalis. As at various times of his life, Schubert was searching for something new in his art, and transcendental poetry of this kind seemed to be the key to a greater depth of musical expression; this is bound up with the composer's own search for a philosophy outside the boundaries of conventional religion. The longing to scale the lofty peaks of romanticism, and the ambition to invent hitherto unheard-of musical and poetic combinations, was to be more or less extinguished with the first signs of illness in 1822–3. It was after this that Schubert pulled in his horns and concentrated on setting less ambitious texts with an ever-deepening musical response.

Tieck had attempted to establish himself in Vienna in 1808 but Schubert never knew him personally. The poet would nevertheless have been a familiar name to anyone who was an avid reader, and some years later his poetry was to feature in the 'Lesegesellschaft', the reading circle associated with Franz von Schober, where important works of literature were read aloud and discussed. Schubert found the poem for *Abend* in the *Musenalmanach für das Jahr 1802* edited by August Schlegel and Tieck himself. Also in this small-format volume was Friedrich Schlegel's cycle *Abendröte* (qv) from which Schubert was to set eleven songs over an extended period. At this stage of his life he was concerned with finding a scheme to intensify the power of his songs in performance – as were these poets who published their work in sets. He was later to publish disparate songs grouped in opus numbers where the juxtapositions could sometimes be of significance, but what is clear is that long before *Die schöne Müllerin*, Schubert hoped to give the lied form a greater weight by grouping single items into something grander than the sum of their parts. Certainly, the publication in 1816 of Beethoven's *An die ferne Geliebte*, officially the first song cycle in musical history, must have been a further spur to these ambitions.

Dietrich Berke avers that the song *Abend* – or rather the sketch for the song – was a preliminary attempt by Schubert to test the waters for a Tieck cycle. In the 1802 almanac, *Abend* is printed as the third of a group of poems entitled *Der Besuch* – 'The Visit'. The other titles are *Morgen*, *Mittag* and *Nacht*, something that brings to mind Philipp Otto Runge's sequence of paintings, *Die Zeiten*. (The idea of a day in the life of a relationship was to be set to music some sixty years later by Fauré in his *Poème d'un jour*.) The tense expectancy of the first two poems is counterbalanced by the desperate disappointment of *Abend* which, in turn, is replaced by *Nacht* where the lover finds his consolation in the starlit heavens as he feels at one with the cosmos. It is worth noting that, in common with Schubert's great song cycles, the protagonist of this story does not get the girl but finds a way out of his depression by moving further into nature's embrace.

Berke believes that the composer deliberately started with the most difficult poems in order to see whether a whole Tieck cycle was viable. Clearly it was not, and so this remains one of those Schubertian ideas that never saw the light of day – yet he made a serious attempt to compose this song, and the fragment is more 'complete' than many. It consists of 119 bars of the vocal line (the sketch was abandoned at the point where fourteen lines of the poem remained). In addition, fragments of the piano part are also provided, although only in terms of snatches of right-hand melody (there is no indication of harmony). Only the first five words of the poem (written out as 'Wie ist es denn, dass') were penned into the score, but these, together with the title, were enough to identify the poem and its author.

If only we could know what sort of accompaniment the composer had already planned when he wrote down this song in skeleton form. The difficult task of reconstructing one for this work was undertaken by the late Reinhard Van Hoorickx. He admitted defeat, however, but the song was unexpectedly rescued for the Hyperion series by the producer Mark Brown who provided a new version of his own. Of course, the challenge of writing music in Schubert's style has defeated every pasticheur, as well as people attempting to complete the fragments, but in these circumstances unpretentious simplicity wins the day over complex, and inevitably inappropriate, sophistication. The single purpose of any completion is to enable Schubert lovers to hear whatever original Schubert there is (in this case the entire vocal line) with a hint of what it might have sounded like in finished form.

The opening section is in G minor and in ⅜. There is no tempo indication. The piano introduction is an exact pre-echo of the vocal line, one of the few pieces of piano writing that was provided for this song by Schubert himself. At 'gekommen' (the poem's fifth line) the music changes into the tonic major, and shifts into ⅔. This section lasts sixteen bars before a return to ⅜, this time in C major ('Aus den Lichtern in die Nacht'). It is only at 'O als ich dich noch nicht gesehn' (Schubert cuts a strophe of Tieck's poem along the way) that the music once again changes key (to E flat major, this time with a ⅜ time signature) which holds sway for the rest of the fragment, despite a number of rather remote chromatic excursions. In the Hyperion recording some twenty extra bars of vocal line were added to this arrangement to bring the poet to the end of his sentence. The manuscript breaks off at b. 119 after the words 'Und die Emp[findung]'.

In many other fragments we can imagine what Schubert would have made of the piece had he added one of his extraordinary accompaniments; the elaboration of a single pianistic motif has a way of making sense of everything else. But the vocal line here changes direction so many times that it is difficult to think of the piano being able to give anything other than relatively simple support. It is as if we are watching Schubert try first one thing, and then another, in order to invest Tieck's work with a musical voice. By the end of the fragment we sense that the composer has lost interest in the struggle to combine the poet's art with his own.

Autograph:	Sketch in private possession (USA)
First edition:	Vocal line published by Dietrich Berke in *Schubert-Kongress 1978* and subsequently in the NSA in 1996; accompaniment realized by Mark Brown for the Hyperion recording in 1998 (P811)
Subsequent editions:	Not in Peters; Not in AGA; NSA IV: Vol. 12/207
Bibliography:	Berke 1979, pp. 305–20
	Dürr, Introduction to NSA IV Volume 12, p. XXVIII
Discography and timing:	Fischer-Dieskau —
	Hyperion I 34^{12}
	Hyperion II 21^{8} 5'32 Martyn Hill

← *Widerschein* D639   *Die Berge* D634 →

ABENDBILDER

(SILBERT) **D650** [H419]

A minor – A major   February 1819

Nocturne

(137 bars)

Still beginnt's im Hain zu tauen;
Ruhig webt der Dämm'rung Grauen
   Durch die Glut
   Sanfter Flut,
Durch das Grün umbüschter Auen,
So die trunk'nen Blicke schauen.

Sieh! der Raben Nachtgefieder
Rauscht auf ferne Eichen nieder. —
   Balsamduft
   Haucht die Luft;
Philomelens Zauberlieder
Hallet zart die Echo wieder.

Horch! des Abendglöckleins Töne
Mahnen ernst der Erde Söhne,
   Dass ihr Herz
   Himmelwärts,
Sinnend ob der Heimat Schöne,
Sich des Erdentands entwöhne.

Durch der hohen Wolken Riegel
Funkeln tausend Himmelssiegel,
   Lunas Bild
   Streuet mild
In der Fluten klarem Spiegel
Schimmernd Gold auf Flur und Hügel.

Von des Vollmonds Wiederscheine
Blitzet das bemooste kleine
   Kirchendach.
   Aber ach!
Ringsum decken Leichensteine[1]
Der Entschlummerten Gebein.[2]

Ruht, o Traute! von den Wehen,
Bis beim grossen Auferstehen
   Aus der Nacht
   Gottes Macht
Einst uns ruft, in seiner Höhen
Ew'ge Wonnen einzugehen.

Softly, dew begins to fall in the grove;
Gently the grey dusk
   Weaves through the red glow
   Of the calm waters,
And through the green meadows, fringed with bushes,
That distort before the eye.

See, the ravens' nocturnal flight
Descends with a swish on distant oaks;
   The air breathes
   A balmy fragrance.
Echo tenderly repeats
Philomel's magic songs.

Hark! The vesper-bell
Solemnly urges the sons of earth
   To forego all earthly dross
   And turn their hearts
Towards heaven,
Reflecting upon that fair dwelling-place.

A thousand celestial stars
Sparkle through chinks in the barrier of high clouds;
   The moon
   Shines gently
In the clear mirror of the waters,
Tingeing hill and meadow with gold.

The mossy roof of the little church
Gleams in the reflection
   Of the full moon.
   But all around
Tombstones cover
The bones of the departed.

Rest, beloved ones, from your cares,
Until, at the Great Resurrection,
   God in His might
   Calls us from the night
To eternal bliss
On high.

JOHANN PETRUS SILBERT (1772–1844)

This is the first of Schubert's two Silbert solo settings (1819). See the poet's biography for a chronological list of the Silbert settings.

The first impression made by those oscillating triplets is of a reworking of *Der Lindenbaum* from *Winterreise*, although *Abendbilder* pre-dates that cycle by some seven years. The undulating sixths

[1] Silbert writes 'Ringsum decken *kühle Steine*'.
[2] Schubert here takes the final syllable away from Silbert's 'Gebeine', thus (inadvertently?) removing the poet's rhyme.

of the opening *Vorspiel* are uncannily descriptive of the gentle movement of an evening breeze wafting through the branches of trees. This sliding figuration (found elsewhere in Schubert's songs, notably in the final section of the Novalis *Nachthymne* D687) goes back to Mozart's *Abendempfindung* which, significantly, is also concerned with intimations of mortality at eventide.

A less immediately audible link is with Beethoven's *An die ferne Geliebte* (1816) and Schubert's longest Mayrhofer setting *Einsamkeit* D620, composed in 1818 at Zseliz. Responding to the Beethovenian challenge, the composer clearly wished to write groups of songs that added up to more than the sum of their parts. He had not yet discovered the separate-song narrative format for his two Müller cycles, *Die schöne Müllerin* and *Winterreise*. Before this he experimented from time to time with episodic lieder that give the impression of a suite of songs joined together without a break in the manner of *An die ferne Geliebte*. The extended song-cantata *Einsamkeit* was closest to the Beethovenian model, but a number of other songs show that Schubert was searching for a new kind of lied, quite separate from the earlier ballade form. An example of a richly episodic song that verges on being a mini-cycle is *An den Mond in einer Herbstnacht* D614 which also dates from 1818.

Abendbilder, fulfilling the promise of its title, is a work in various separate scenes linked together by an accompaniment built upon a single unifying motif. The poem is helpfully episodic for such musical treatment: an introductory strophe about nightfall is followed by the flight of ravens, the sound of the vesper-bell, the sparkling of stars. And then the climactic pay-off of tombstones and lofty thoughts of the Great Resurrection.

There is no doubt that Silbert's heart was in this poem, but there is no reason to suppose that Schubert was attracted to the words because of their religious message. Indeed it is at the end of the song, as the poet's thoughts turn to the triumph of promised immortality, where the music is at its least convincing. Although the composer was interested in lofty metaphysical themes at the time (his settings of Novalis are evidence of this), his own philosophical (and thus musical) quests lay outside conventional Roman Catholic doctrine and the Redemptorist enthusiasms of Silbert. Schubert had become friendly with the rather devout Esterházy family at whose Zseliz residence he spent the summer of 1818 as a music tutor. It is possible that the religious poems of Silbert, like the Marian poems of Schreiber, appealed to the countesses Esterházy, mother and daughters. It is not impossible that Schubert had been asked by his new patrons to set certain poems, or that he simply did so to please them – and some time after his summer sojourn in their employ.

From the very beginning, the idea of an echo (which is established by the poem only in the second strophe) is marked by relatively short vocal phrases followed by piano interludes; in many of these the left hand crosses to the treble reaches of the keyboard (first at bb. 6–7, directly after the verb 'tauen'). The drooping third that is a feature of this crossing of hands is a dotted minim diminishing to a quaver, as delicate as dew forming on a leaf and then falling. The writing for the voice is rather florid, with a number of awkward triplets (at the second 'trunk'nen Blicke schauen' in the first verse for example bb. 20–22). This type of Italianate vocal writing is found quite often in the Schubert songs of this period when the world of grand opera was much on the composer's mind.

The second strophe begins with the ominous ideas of ravens, and ends with a nightingale. After 'Sieh! der Raben Nachtgefieder' (bb. 24–6) the composer cannot resist a tiny musical comment by way of a shudder of apprehension – a falling fifth (already heard in the treble in the first verse after 'Grauen') that now plunges the same interval in the bass. (There is a similar bass-clef frisson, a momentary shadow unnoticed by the casual listener, ushering in the *minore* section of *Der Lindenbaum* D911/5 – at b. 28 – some eight years later.) Now follows a brooding bass-clef commentary (bb. 29–30) like an interjection of a bank of cellos, after 'Rauscht auf ferne Eichen nieder'. The word 'Balsam', as in the Novalis *Nachthymne* D687 where it also occurs, is connected to sensual triplets, as if an unguent were being lovingly applied to the musical texture; here it is part of the compound noun 'Balsamduft' that is rendered into an airy phrase arching upwards before falling gracefully. It is at this point that the Peters Edition (following in the footsteps of the *Nachlass*) lets us down badly; and we must consult the AGA or NSA. What should be b. 33 – a murmuring melodic interlude sets up the song of the nightingale – is missing in Peters (no doubt an oversight of the Diabelli publishing team in 1831 who simply left it out by mistake) and the result is a rather peculiar and unsatisfying harmonic shift between G minor and F major. Philomel's song occasions more hand-crossings, and Schubert thoroughly enjoys the chance to use the upper reaches of the keyboard (after the first 'die Echo wieder') to approximate the high tessitura of birdsong. Word repetitions ('Hallet, hallet zart die Echo wieder') give rise to long phrases of melismas and mini flourishes in duplets and triplets, imitating the showy song of the nightingale, a bird that features in many a Schubert song title but which also makes a number of guest appearances with only a fly-on role, notably in *Ganymed* D544. During this strophe the music moves from A minor into F sharp major.

The tolling of bells (from b. 47) is one of this composer's specialities (cf. *Das Zügenglöcklein* D871). An inverted pedal on F sharp (the triplets are now transferred to the bass line) paints the vesper-bells not, as one might expect, as harbingers of peace and joy but with a hint of angst (the music has now moved into B minor). Here the worshippers are frightened souls, driven by the rather menacing urgings of the bells to renounce earthly dross in favour of future heavenly rewards. The poet may have been certain of these, but this section of the song, with its lack of a solidly grounded bass, shows Schubert rather to have been a doubting Thomas. The composer's opinion of organized religion was not high; he observes these village believers from afar as they scurry to church, without being of their number. One is reminded of the mixture of pity and contempt the singer feels for the cosy bourgeois values of the town dwellers in *Im Dorfe* from *Winterreise*. The ascending phrase on 'Dass ihr Herz / Himmelwärts, / Sinnend' (bb. 54–6) and the descent on 'ob der Heimat Schöne' (bb. 57–60) is a perfect little musical metaphor for mankind's brief struggle to ascend the ladder of life followed by his inevitable descent into the grave: hatch, match and dispatch. The music is restless and, if not exactly doom-laden, has an air of unease.

For the third strophe the change from F sharp major into D major is to move from the oppressive atmosphere of an incense-laden church into the clear air of a starry evening. Here, in communion with Nature, lies the composer's strongest emotional connection with contemplation of the Infinite. The triplets have returned to the right hand of the accompaniment and, in tune with the celestial theme of the words, are in a higher and brighter tessitura than anything that has gone before. At 'Lunas Bild / Streuet <u>mild</u>' (bb. 69–71) there is a beautiful shift to the open fields of C major but, as soon as the hills and meadows are tinged with gold, the music moves into a brighter E major (b. 77). An extended *Zwischenspiel* leads into the next verse, and as the music returns to A minor the effect is of a grand recapitulation, as if the song had something of a sonata movement about it. When writing songs that may be called (very broadly speaking) modified strophic lieder, Schubert often recapitulates the music of the opening in order to achieve a sense of grandeur and inevitability; in this we can hear the experienced composer of instrumental music.

In this manner, 'Von des Vollmonds Wiederscheine' (bb. 82–4) is set to the music of the song's opening, and once again the left-hand echo effect as it crosses into the upper reaches of the keyboard is perfectly suitable for the idea of reflection which, after all, could be thought of as a visual echo. At the words 'Aber ach!' (bb. 92–3) the music is steered in another direction, as if this sensual pleasure at the sights of nature has to come to an end and given way to thoughts of mortality. There is a new note of majesty sounded in bass minims for 'Der Entschlummerten Gebein' (bb. 97–101), and we shall hear similar portentous organ pedal notes at the forte repeat of 'Bis beim grossen Auferstehen' in the last verse. The triplets gently rise and cradle the beautiful, and entirely characteristic, change from A minor to A major at 'Ruht, o Traute! von den Wehen' (from b. 116). There is a note of tenderness here (as always with this particular key change) but this is soon swamped by a rather forced grandeur. 'Auferstehen' (Resurrection, bb. 120–21) is ornamented with a turn, an old-fashioned device. It suggests that Resurrection is a rather old-fashioned idea, or one associated with priestly rhetoric or found in eighteenth-century literary works like Klopstock's *Messias*. But the intimacies of the song form are not suitable for a full-scale depiction of the key moment of Christian doctrine – the words 'Great Resurrection' and 'eternal bliss' suggest a symphonic-sized canvas.

If the more ordinary aspects of evening life earlier in the song have suited Schubert's genius for evocation and delight, this ending has a slightly wooden quality to it. On the last page there are two gigantically long phrases with scarcely room for the singer to draw breath, followed by the quasi-orchestral postlude (with implied right-hand brass and left-hand timpani bb. 132–3 and 134–5) that attempts to set the seal on something large and universal.

Abendbilder is seldom heard on the recital platform. It is full of wonderful illustrative ideas and moments of genuine Schubertian magic, and the incessant triplets give the music a sense of unity and inevitability. Nevertheless, the *pomposo* visionary aspect of the music is ill suited to the rest of the song that is in the more intimate vein of Schubert's pantheistic Nature music (cf. the Schlegel settings from 1819), and it takes a performance of emormous skill and conviction to make of this song-portmanteau a convincing whole.

Autograph:	Wienbibliothek im Rathaus, Vienna
First edition:	Published as Book 9 no. 3 of the *Nachlass* by Diabelli, Vienna in 1831 (P261)
Subsequent editions:	Peters: Vol. 3/134; AGA XX 352: Vol. 6/7; NSA IV: Vol. 12/70
Bibliography:	Black 2003, p. 66
	Capell 1928, pp. 158–9
	Einstein 1951, p. 189
	Fischer-Dieskau 1977, p. 119
Discography and timing:	Fischer-Dieskau II 2[14] 5'13
	Hyperion I 29[1]
	Hyperion II 21[14] 5'11 Marjana Lipovšek

← *Schäfers Klagelied* D121 (second version)   *Himmelsfunken* D651 →

ABENDLIED   Evening song
(STOLBERG) **D276** [H163]
A major   28 August 1815

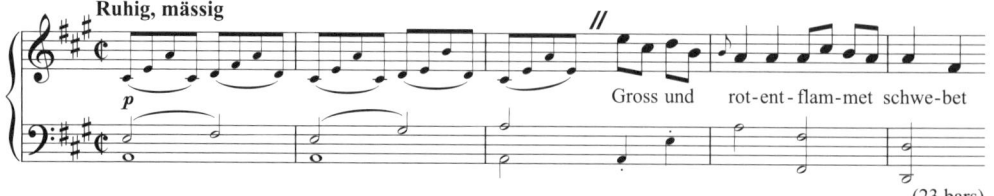

(23 bars)

Gross und rotentflammet schwebet
Noch die Sonn' am Himmelsrand,
Und auf blauen Wogen bebet
Noch ihr Abglanz bis zum Strand;
Aus dem Buchenwalde hebet
Sich der Mond, und winket Ruh'
Seiner Schwester Erde zu.

In geschwollnen Wolken ballet
Dunkler sich die rote Glut,
Zarter Farbenwechsel wallet
Auf der Roggenblüte Flut;
Zwischen schwanken Halmen schallet
Reger Wachteln heller Schlag,
Und der Hirte pfeift ihm nach.

[...]

Ihre Ringeltauben girren
Noch die Täuber sanft in Ruh',
Düstre Fledermäuse schwirren
Nun dem glatten Teiche zu,
Und der Käfer Scharen irren,
Und der Uhu, nun erwacht,
Ziehet heulend auf die Wacht.

[...3...]

Wenn die Nachtigallen flöten,
Hebe dich, mein Geist, empor!
Bei des jungen Tags Erröten
Neig' o Vater, mir dein Ohr!
Von der Erd' und ihren Nöten
Steig, o Geist! Wie Duft der Au,
Send' uns, Vater, deinen Tau!

The sun hovers, massive and flaming red,
On the sky's edge,
And upon the blue waves
Its reflection glistens, touching the shore.
From the beechwood the moon rises,
Heralding peace
To her sister earth.

On the swollen clouds
The red glow darkens;
Delicately changing colours
Play on the sea of burgeoning rye;
Among the slender blades of grass
The lively quails' bright call echoes,
Answered by the shepherd's pipe.

[...]

The pigeons coo their ring-doves
Gently to sleep;
Sombre bats whirr
Against the glassy pond.
The swarming beetles rove,
And the eagle-owl, now awake,
Hoots as it mounts its watch.

[...3...]

When the nightingales warble
Soar aloft, my spirit!
At the first flush of day
Hearken to me, O Father!
Rise, O spirit, above the earth and its cares.
As the meadows spread their fragrance,
Father, bestow on us your dew!

FRIEDRICH LEOPOLD, GRAF ZU STOLBERG-STOLBERG (1750–1819); poem written in 1793

This is the second of Schubert's nine Stolberg settings (1815–23). See the poet's biography for a chronological list of all the Stolberg settings.

Neither the poem or music for *Abendlied* plumb anything like the spiritual depths and winged heights of that great Stolberg setting *Auf dem Wasser zu singen*, but the song is a real little charmer. Its tonality is one that John Reed says 'unlocks the essential Schubert'. Partly because of this the introduction brings to mind the piano figurations of another A major amble through nature's marvels, *Das Lied im Grünen* D917. The tune is delightful and not without ingenuity in mirroring the words: note the rising of the moon from the beechwood ('Aus dem Buchen-walde') as the vocal line floats into the stratosphere – a challenge for the singer this. Staccato left-hand crotchets seem particularly appropriate in the third verse where the sound of cooing doves and pigeons is evoked (cf. another song from 1815, *Die Mainacht* D194).

John Reed finds the piano music at the end rather weak; but its charm surely lies in the surprising extension of what one expects to be a conventional four-bar postlude – a tiny chromatic fall leads into a melting cadence on the *fifth* bar. It is interesting to note that much of the piano writing is in four distinct parts and looks like a short score for a string quartet.

There are eight strophes in Stolberg's poem – these are all printed in the AGA and helpfully laid out under the music in the NSA. Given here are 1, 2, 4 and 8, as recorded in the Hyperion Edition.

Autograph:	British Library, London
First edition:	Published as part of the AGA in 1895 (P578)
Subsequent editions:	Not in Peters; AGA XX 133: Vol. 3/62; NSA IV: Vol. 9/23
Bibliography:	Reed 1985, p. 489
Discography and timing:	Fischer-Dieskau I 5¹⁶　1'35　(first two strophes only)
	Hyperion I 19¹⁵
	Hyperion II 9²⁴　　3'09　Felicity Lott

← *Totenkranz für ein Kind* D275　　　　*Punschlied (Vier Elemente, innig gesellt)* D277 →

ABENDLIED　　　　　　　　Evening song
(ANONYMOUS) **D382** [H227]
F major　24 February 1816

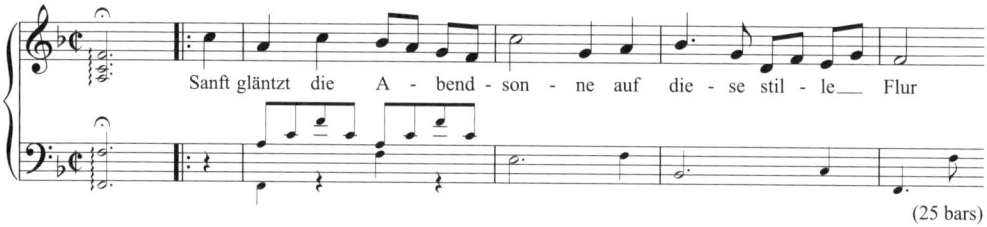

Sanft glänzt die A-bend-son-ne auf die-se stil-le— Flur

(25 bars)

Sanft glänzt die Abendsonne	The evening sun shines gently
Auf diese stille Flur	On these silent meadows,
Und strahlet Ruh' und Wonne	Shedding peace and joy
Auf jede Kreatur.	Over every creature.
Sie zeichnet Licht und Schatten	It traces light and shadow
Auf die beblümte Au,	Upon the flower-decked pastures,
Und auf den grünen Matten	And on the verdant fields
Blitzt der kristallne Tau.	The crystal dew sparkles.
[...2...]	[...2...]
Dir, der die Abendröte	To you, who spread the red glow of evening
Am Himmel ausgespannt	Over the heavens
Und süsses Nachtgeflöte	And brought the sweet song of the night
Auf diese Flur gesandt,	To these meadows,
Dir sei dies Herz geweihet,	To you I dedicate this heart
Das reiner Dank durchglüht,	Glowing with pure gratitude;

Es schlage noch erfreuet,   May it still beat joyfully
Wenn einst das Leben flieht.   When life ceases.

ANONYMOUS/UNKNOWN

*This is the ninth of Schubert's nineteen solo settings of an anonymous poet. See Anonymous/
Unknown for a chronological list of all the songs for which the poets are unknown.*

This is an unpretentious little setting with hymn-like qualities. With the name of *Abendlied* we
think immediately of that most famous of evening hymns, Mozart's song *Abendempfindung* in F
major. This *Abendlied* is in the same key, and the accompaniment rolls and glides in similar
fashion; in the fourth bar after the word 'Flur' one finds a succession of sixths that goes back to
Mozart. As he plays this piece the pianist will also feel a distant premonition of the piano figurations that animate *Das Lied im Grünen* D917, particularly under the words 'Und auf den grünen
Matten'. It seems likely that the unknown poets of this song and of *Morgenlied* D581 are the same.

Despite its melodious and charming qualities, and the seamless fluency of the accompaniment, the song remains rather earthbound. Both the other songs of the same title, the Stolberg
Abendlied D276, and the setting of the famous Claudius *Abendlied* D499, are more distinguished.
However, many lesser composers in Schubert's time made their lifelong reputations with songs
that come nowhere near this in quality. There are six strophes in the poem (two of the poet's
strophes make one of the composer's verses) – these are all printed in the AGA and NSA. Given
here are 1 and 2, and 5 and 6, as recorded in the Hyperion Edition. Wigmore 1988 also translates
verses 3 and 4.

Autograph: Frederick R. Koch Foundation, on loan to Beineke Rare Book and
                             Manuscript Collection, New Haven
First edition: Published as part of the AGA in 1895 (P622)
Subsequent editions: Not in Peters; AGA XX 190: Vol. 4/30; NSA IV: Vol. 10/44
Discography and timing: Fischer-Dieskau I 6[15]   2'47
                             Hyperion I 23[7]
                             Hyperion II 12[22]   1'40   Christoph Prégardien

$\leftarrow$ *Morgenlied D381*   *Laura am Klavier D388* $\rightarrow$

ABENDLIED
(CLAUDIUS) **D499** [H316]   Evening song
B♭ major   November 1816

Ruhig

Der Mond ist auf - ge - gan - gen, die gold - nen Stern - lein pran - gen

pp   (16 bars)

Der Mond ist aufgegangen,   The moon is up,
Die goldnen Sternlein prangen   The golden stars shine
   Am Himmel hell und klar;   Bright and clear in the heavens.

Der Wald steht schwarz und schweiget,	The woods lie dark and silent,
Und aus den Wiesen steiget	And from the meadows, uncannily,
Der weisse Nebel wunderbar.	The white mist rises.

Wie ist die Welt so stille,	How still the world is,
Und in der Dämmrung Hülle	And in dusk's mantle
So traulich und so hold!	How intimate and tender,
Als eine stille Kammer,	Like a peaceful room
Wo ihr des Tages Jammer	Where you may sleep and forget
Verschlafen und vergessen sollt.	The day's cares.

Seht ihr den Mond dort stehen? —	Do you see the moon there?
Er ist nur halb zu sehen,	It is only half visible
Und ist doch rund und schön!	And yet it is so round and fair.
So sind wohl manche Sachen,	Thus it is with many things:
Die wir getrost belachen,	We thoughtlessly mock them
Weil unsre Augen sie nicht sehn.	Because we cannot see them.

Wir stolze Menschenkinder	We proud sons of men
Sind eitel arme Sünder,	Are but poor sinners,
Und wissen gar nicht viel;	And know very little;
Wir spinnen Luftgespinste,	We spin airy fantasies
Und suchen viele Künste,	And seek to master many arts,
Und kommen weiter von dem Ziel.	Yet move further from our goal.

Gott, lass d e i n Heil uns schauen[1]	God, may we behold *Thy* grace,
Auf nichts Vergänglichs trauen	Mistrust all that is transitory,
Nicht Eitelkeit uns freun!	And delight not in vanity.
Lass uns einfältig werden,	May we attain simplicity,
Und vor dir hier auf Erden	And before Thee here on earth
Wie Kinder fromm und fröhlich sein!	Live as children, pious and cheerful.

[. . . 2 . . .]   [. . . 2 . . .]

MATTHIAS CLAUDIUS (1740–1815); poem published in 1779

This is the seventh of Schubert's thirteen Claudius solo settings (1816–17). See the poet's biography for a chronological list of all the Claudius settings.

'Placid and mild' is how Capell describes this song. So it may be, but it contains hidden depths. Despite its simplicity, or perhaps because of it, the music seems to go to the heart of the Claudius poem with a religious feeling that eschews the epic or grandiose. With its gently rocking semi-quaver accompaniment the song glimmers and lours in the evening light, but there is an essential safety and goodness about this music far from the ghostly eeriness of some of the other Schubert song-nocturnes. As in many poems by Claudius, an extremely happy family man, we can hear the security of home and hearth, and an untroubled belief in the goodness of the world. There

---

[1] Claudius writes 'Gott, lass *u n s* und d e i n Heil'. Schubert's alteration allows the line to scan within the parameters of his strophic song.

Illustration for *Abendlied* from *Deutsche Lieder in Volkes Herz und Mund*, 1864.

was much that was domestic and trusting about Schubert too, which is perhaps one of the reasons why, despite the modesty of most of the Claudius settings, this poetry fits our composer's personality like a glove.

The tune starts with the exploration of an arpeggio, frequently the first reconnaissance expedition sent out by Schubert when he is deciding how to conquer a lyric. There is something familiar about the tune for the words 'Der Mond ist aufgegangen'; it is modelled (whether consciously or not is impossible to say) on a figure given to the clarinets and bassoons in the *Larghetto* movement of Beethoven's Second Symphony (b. 32 onwards in that work). The accompanying figurations are discreet except for occasional flashes of temperament – the staccato left hand that comments on the words 'hell and klar' (b. 6), and the hidden tune in the right hand postlude (bb. 13–16), also underpinned by staccato quavers in the bass. The sound of a bassoon in a wind ensemble is so vividly suggested here that perhaps Schubert did have Beethoven's orchestration in mind. Appropriately for the deep, dark woods described in the fourth and fifth lines of the poem, there is a mysterious little legato counter-melody in the pianist's left hand (bb. 7–12). The separation of the rather high vocal line from the low-lying murmuring accompaniment, and the cupola of a night sky that separates the singing and playing protagonists, brings another, rather more profound, nocturne to mind, *Nacht und Träume* D827.

This lyric was praised by Herder as an ideal model of German folksong of its kind. It was set by a number of composers including J.A.P. Schulz, whose simple but beautiful song (to be found in Erk's *Liederschatz*) is still well known in Germany, and was composed in the manner of a chorale. The fame of this setting may be hard for modern-day ears to fathom but at one time it was considered 'arguably the most popular poem and song in the German language' (Rowland 2000). Schubert almost certainly knew it, and must have deliberately attempted to find a different way of setting these famous words. He may also have known the poem through the setting for unaccompanied male quartet (1801) by his admired Michael Haydn (*see* COMPOSERS).

Autograph:	Missing or lost
First edition:	Published as Vol. 7 no. 13 in Friedlaender's edition by Peters, Leipzig in 1885 (P484)
Subsequent editions:	Peters: Vol. 7/13; AGA XX 278: Vol. 4/240; NSA IV: Vol. 11/30
Bibliography:	Black 2003, p. 14
	Capell 1928, p. 120
Further settings and arrangements:	Johann Abraham Peter Schulz (1747–1800) *Abendlied* (c. 1790)
	Johann Friedrich Reichardt (1752–1814) *Abendlied* (1779) and choral setting (1791)

Othmar Schoeck (1886–1957) in *Wandsbecker Liederbuch* Op. 32 no. 10 (1937)
Arr. Tilman Hoppstock (b. 1961) for guitar accompaniment, in *Franz Schubert: 110 Lieder* (2009)

Discography and timing: Fischer-Dieskau I 8[23] 2'26
Hyperion I 18[9]
Hyperion II 16[20] 2'45 Peter Schreier

← *Wiegenlied* D498   *Am Grabe Anselmos* D504 →

ABENDLIED *see* SCHLAFLIED D527

ABENDLIED DER FÜRSTIN   The princess's evening song
(MAYRHOFER) **D495** [H312]
F major   November 1816?

(52 bars)

Der Abend rötet nun das Tal,	The evening tinges the valley with red;
Mild schimmert Hesperus.	Hesperus gleams softly.
Die Buchen stehen still zumal,	The beech trees stand silent,
Und leiser rauscht der Fluss.	And the river murmurs more softly.
Die Wolken segeln goldbesäumt	The clouds, fringed with gold,
Am klaren Firmament;	Sail across the clear sky;
Das Herz, es schwelgt, das Herz, es träumt,	The heart swells, the heart dreams,
Von Erdenqual getrennt.	Free from earthly sorrow.
Am grünen Hügel hingestreckt,[1]	The huntsman, stretched out on the green hillside,
Schläft wohl der Jäger ein —[2]	Falls sound asleep –
Doch plötzlich ihn der Donner weckt,	But then he is suddenly woken by thunder
Und Blitze zischen drein.	And the hiss of lightning.
Wo bist du, heilig Abendrot,	Where are you, sacred evening glow,
Wo, sanfter Hesperus?	Where are you, gentle Hesperus?
So wandelt denn in Schmerz und Not[3]	Thus every pleasure
Sich jeglicher Genuss.[4]	Turns to grief and distress.

[1] Mayrhofer writes '*Auf* grünen Hügel hingestreckt'. For an explanation of the background to these alternative Mayrhofer readings see Editorial Note at the beginning of Johann MAYRHOFER.
[2] Mayrhofer writes 'Schläft *sanft* der Jäger ein'.
[3] Mayrhofer writes '*Es* wandelt *sich* in Schmerz und Not'. The addition of 'denn' when 'sich' is transferred to the next line seems to be Schubert's alteration.
[4] Mayrhofer writes '*Ein* jeglicher Genuss'.

Johann Mayrhofer (1787–1836)

This is the twelfth of Schubert's forty-seven Mayrhofer solo settings (1814–24). See the poet's biography for a chronological list of all the Mayrhofer settings.

This song is in a favourite key for evening songs; and pastoral lullabies in 𝄴 abound. From these points of view this Mayrhofer setting is typical of its genre. We are not told who the princess is, but the poem is obviously steeped in deep Romantic mystery; is she a Mélisande figure, or perhaps a member of the unhappy family that furnished *Der Zwerg* D771 with a royal victim? The tune is pretty enough, and the modulations are typically Schubertian. The passage of the clouds in the second verse induces semiquavers in the accompaniment (from b. 9), and there are unusual touches here like the melisma on the word 'schwelgt' (b. 14). This second verse is awkward for the singer from the point of view of phrasing and breathing.

The aspect of the song most criticized by Reed is the handling of the sudden storm that occurs in the middle of the poem's third verse. This unleashes a Beethovenian streak in the composer, and a near-quote from the *Allegro* section of the first movement of Beethoven's 'Pathétique' Sonata Op. 13. This piano writing, much of it in right-hand octaves, is also reminiscent of the very early fragment *Der Geistertanz* D15. The combination of vocal recitative with pianistic fireworks is quite exciting, but after such a violent upheaval Schubert finds it difficult to re-unify the song. Everything changes, sings the princess – in effect, *tout passe, tout casse*. And yet the composer simply returns to the original melody and accompaniment for the work's closing strophes. How differently Schubert was to handle recoveries from storms in his later music! In *Im Frühling* D882, and in the slow movements of the late A major Piano Sonata D959 and of the String Quintet D956, these peaceful recapitulations are marvellously tinged with a ghost of the preceding outburst so that we *hear* that nothing can be the same again. (Leo Black calls this 'the invaded reprise'.) In *Abendlied der Fürstin* the composer has not yet learned how to convey this subtle transfiguration.

This is in itself a good reason to place this music in 1816. In his studies regarding the dating of manuscript paper (1978), Robert Winter suggests the much later date of 1824. And yet, on stylistic grounds, as Walther Dürr points out, this seems unlikely – the separate marking of a section as 'Recit.' is untypical of the later Schubert. Dürr also cites the composer's musical handwriting as evidence of the earlier date. This and other mysteries remain. Why does the princess wax philosophical just because the thunderstorm has disturbed a huntsman's sleep, and why is this song *her* song? And why, for example, did Schubert decide to make his princess a mezzo-soprano, and place the tessitura of the piece in a much lower range than is usual in his songs specifically for female voices? Other lieder from this period seem destined for the bright, high soprano voice of Therese Grob, the girl Schubert was said to have been in love with at the time. If *Abendlied der Fürstin* does indeed date from November 1816, the composer would have been living with his friend Franz von Schober when he wrote it; the song may have been conceived for a particular voice – a friend (perhaps of regal bearing, for the Schobers prided themselves on their connections) of his host's family.

Autograph:	Staatsbibliothek Preussischer Kulturbesitz, Berlin
First edition:	Published as No. 6 of *Sechs bisher ungedrückte Lieder* by Wilhelm Müller, Berlin in 1868 (P418)
Subsequent editions:	Not in Peters; AGA XX 271: Vol. 4/227; NSA IV: Vol. 11/24
Bibliography:	Black 2003, p. 123
	Winter 1978, p. 500
	Reed 1985, p. 4

Discography and timing: Fischer-Dieskau   —
                          Hyperion I 8[14]
                          Hyperion II 16[15]   2'24   Sarah Walker

←— *Der Geistertanz* D494   *Bei dem Grabe meines Vaters* D496 —→

ABENDLIED FÜR DIE ENTFERNTE   Evening song for the distant beloved
(A. VON SCHLEGEL) OP. 88 NO. 1, **D856** [H575]
F major   September 1825

(176 bars)

Hinaus mein Blick! hinaus ins Tal!	Gaze out, eyes, gaze out to the valley!
Da wohnt noch Lebensfülle;	There abundant life still dwells.
Da labe dich im Mondenstrahl	Refresh yourself there in the moonlight,
Und an der heil'gen Stille.	And in the sacred peace.
Da horch nun ungestört, mein Herz,	Listen, heart, now undisturbed,
Da horch den leisen Klängen,	Listen to the soft sounds
Die, wie von fern, zu Wonn' und Schmerz	That press upon you, as from afar,
Sich dir entgegen drängen.	For joy and for sorrow.
Sie drängen sich so wunderbar,	They teem in so wondrously,
Sie regen all mein Sehnen.	They arouse all my longing.
O sag' mir, Ahnung, bist du wahr?[1]	This intimation, is it real?
Bist du ein eitles Wähnen?	Or is it a vain illusion?
Wird einst mein Aug' in heller Lust,	Will my eyes one day smile in pure pleasure,
Wie jetzt in Tränen, lächeln?	As they do now in tears?
Wird einst die oft empörte Brust	Will blessed peace one day
Mir sel'ge Ruh umfächeln?	Caress my heart, so often incensed?
[(. . .)]	[(. . .)]
Wenn Ahnung und Erinnerung	When presentiment and memory
Vor unserm Blick sich gatten,	Are joined before our eyes,
Dann mildert sich zur Dämmerung	Then at twilight
Der Seele tiefster Schatten.	The soul's deepest shadow turns to gentle half-light.
Ach, dürften wir mit Träumen nicht	Ah, if we could not
Die Wirklichkeit verweben,	Interweave reality with dreams,
Wie arm an Farbe, Glanz und Licht	How poor you would be, human life,
Wärst du, o Menschenleben![2]	In colour, lustre and light!

[1] Schlegel writes '*Ahndung*' – also in Verse 4, line 1.
[2] Schlegel writes 'Wärst *dann du* Menschenleben'.

So hoffet treulich und beharrt	Thus the heart remains constant, hoping faithfully
Das Herz bis hin zum Grabe;	Unto the grave;
Mit Lieb' umfasst's die Gegenwart,	With love it embraces the present,
Und dünkt sich reich an Habe.	And deems itself rich in possessions.
Die Habe, die es selbst sich schafft,	The possessions which it creates itself
Mag ihm kein Schicksal rauben:	No fate can snatch from it.
Es lebt und webt in Wärm' und Kraft,	It lives and works in warmth and strength,
Durch Zuversicht und Glauben.	Through trust and faith.
Und wär in Nacht und Nebeldampf	And if all around lies dead
Auch Alles rings erstorben,	In night and mist,
Dies Herz hat längst für jeden Kampf	This heart has long ago won
Sich einen Schild erworben.	A shield for every battle.
Mit hohem Trotz im Ungemach	In adversity it endures its fate
Trägt es, was ihm beschieden.	With lofty defiance.
So schlummr' ich ein, so werd' ich wach,	And so I fall asleep, so I awake,
In Lust nicht, doch in Frieden.	If not in joy, yet in peace.

AUGUST WILHELM VON SCHLEGEL (1767–1845); poem written in 1807

This is the ninth of Schubert's ten August von Schlegel solo settings (1816–25). See the poet's biography for a chronological list of all the August von Schlegel settings.

Richard Capell refers in his commentary on this long and significant song to 'the tiresome Schlegel', but then it has always been an Anglo-Saxon tendency to make light of the German predilection for solemn introspection, as if omniscient dilettantism (in the name of common sense) could better manage life's mysteries by ignoring them. The ruminative expansiveness offends Capell's sense of proportion, particularly as we hear the tune many times, and, in contrast to a number of Schubert's strophic songs, its tripartite form makes it impossible to leave out any of the verses. (Schubert leaves out the third verse of Schlegel's poem, but that is another matter.) If a poem for a Schubert lied is not by someone as important as Goethe, it is all too easy for English speakers to underestimate it. 'There is nothing in his evening meditation to interest us', writes Capell of Schlegel's poem.

It is clear, however, that it interested Schubert a great deal; indeed it might be one of the handful of songs in his output that have an autobiographical significance. Capell should also have been aware that any Schubert song composed after 1823 – the year of the onset of the composer's illness – is to be taken seriously. The composer suspected that the time left to him was limited and therefore precious, and it is almost impossible to find an example of anything written after this date that can be written off as experimental dalliance. Like the Schober setting *Trost im Liede* D546 in the same key and pulse, it is a personal credo, a meditation on how hope enables us to live without love and come to terms with loneliness. The Distant Beloved to whom the poem is addressed could well be an imaginary figure, perhaps even the chaste virgin or Muse who features in the Novalis-inspired dream (*Mein Traum*) that Schubert noted down in self-revealing fashion in July 1822. The fourth verse of Schlegel's poem makes clear the power of dreams and fantasy as a means not only of making life bearable, but of enriching the artistic imagination. The music moves here into the minor (a change of key signature at b. 75) but the song as a whole seems permanently poised between major and minor; the pastoral gait conveys a feeling of total acceptance of what life has to offer along the way. If there is no overt joy here, neither is there sadness and disappointment. If by 1825 Schubert, with all his considerable troubles and frustrations, had achieved the strength and equanimity of the poem's final lines, 'so werd' ich wach, / In Lust nicht, doch in Frieden', we have only to wonder at the struggles that led him to this resignation without bitterness, this inner peace.

The mention of bells heard in the distance in the first verse clearly delighted the composer, and some of the piano music in the interludes is inspired by this imagery. But the musical mood as a whole takes its cue from the opening lines of the fourth verse (Schlegel's fifth), for the tonality and rhythm are as steadfast and constant as the heart and its pulse. A digression into another key, a mood of 'yes, but on the other hand . . .', would have been inappropriate for this single-minded evening hymn. There is a beautiful harmonic sequence in each verse (bb. 19–23 in the first verse, always in the fifth line of each of Schlegel's strophes) that recalls the melody associated with those vulnerable questions in *Morgengruss* in *Die schöne Müllerin*: 'Verdriesst dich denn mein Gruss so schwer? / Verstört dich denn mein Blick so sehr?'

Schlegel's final verse is reminiscent of the sentiment of Bach's 'Ich bin in mir vergnügt' with overtones of Stoic-Epicurean wisdom that go back to the writings of Horace. The closing words of the song, 'In Lust nicht . . . doch in Frieden' are a superb summing-up of the composer's own day-to-day existence at this stage of his life and of his ability to handle pain and disappointment sufficiently well for his work to continue unabated. Performers are directed to the NSA for phrase-markings that are omitted from other editions.

Autograph:	Missing or lost
First edition:	Published as Op. 88 no. 1 by Thaddäus Weigl, Vienna in 1827 (P137)
Subsequent editions:	Peters: Vol. 3/52; AGA XX 482: Vol. 8/138; NSA IV: Vol. 4a/94; Bärenreiter: Vol. 3/64
Bibliography:	Capell 1928, p. 218
Discography and timing:	Fischer-Dieskau II 7[12] 5'34
	Hyperion I 6[8]
	Hyperion II 30[12] 8'23 Anthony Rolfe Johnson

← *Wiedersehn* D855   *Zwei Lieder aus 'Lacrimas' (Delphine)* D857/1 →

ABENDRÖTE

(*see also* ABENDRÖTE, DIE BERGE, DER FLUSS, DIE GEBÜSCHE, DER KNABE, DAS MÄDCHEN, DIE ROSE, DER SCHMETTERLING, DIE STERNE, DIE VÖGEL, DER WANDERER)

Schubert's eleven songs taken from Friedrich von Schlegel's cycle of poems entitled *Abendröte* are a tantalizing example of what Richard Kramer has called a 'failure of cycle', but there are others. Elsewhere in this book I suggest the idea of creating a new cycle (called *Auf den wilden Wegen*) made up of ten poems from Ernst Schulze's *Poetisches Tagebuch*, although we can only dream of what a real cycle of Schulze songs might have been if Schubert had put his mind to realizing the concept. The same also applies to this group of Schlegel songs where it is well-nigh impossible to force them into a satisfying whole. The fact that Schubert permitted some of the songs to appear as part of three different publications in later years shows that even if he had once conceived the idea of a Schlegel cycle he had given it up by 1826.

Schlegel's cycle, two groups of eleven poems each, written between 1800 and 1801, first appeared in the famous *Musenalmanach für das Jahr 1802* issued in Tübingen by August von Schlegel and Ludwig Tieck (pp. 133–57) where the headings and layout do not make clear whether the poet actually had a cycle in mind. By 1809 and the publication of Friedrich Schlegel's

Gedichte, the sequence is headed *A b e n d r ö t h e* and divided into two parts ('Erster Theil' pp. 12–22 and 'Zweiter Theil' pp. 23–34). This is replicated (in much smaller print) in the edition of Schlegel's *Gedichte* published by Bauer of Vienna (pp. 16–38) in 1816. The first poem in the sequence ('Tiefer sinket schon die Sonne') is without title and is simply marked 'Erster Theil' ('Part One'). On his manuscript of the March 1823 setting of this poem (D690, in A major) Schubert copied Schlegel's heading exactly: 'Abendröthe – erster Theil'. This is one argument for the theory that the composer intended this song, the last to be composed from the set, to stand at the head of a grand cycle. In any case, this is how a single lied came to be known under the poet's collective title of *Abendröte*.

After this introductory *Abendröte*, the sequence of poems, each having a title of its own, proceeds thus in Schlegel's published order:

Die Berge D634	G major; undated, composed March 1820? Published as Op. 57 no. 2 in April 1826
Die Vögel D691	A major; composed March 1820
Der Knabe D692	A major; composed March 1820
Der Fluss D693	B major; composed March 1820
Der Hirt	Not set by Schubert
Die Rose D745	Two versions: F major and G major; composed March 1820? possibly later in 1822. Published as a supplement to the *Wiener Zeitschrift (Modenzeitung)* in May 1822, and as a single song in 1827 without opus number
Der Schmetterling D633	F major; composed March 1820? Published as Op. 57 no. 1 in April 1826
Die Sonne	Not set by Schubert
Die Lüfte	Not set by Schubert
Der Dichter	Not set by Schubert

Thus ends the first part of Schlegel's poetic cycle which has taken place at twilight where the mountains, the birds, the river, the rose, the butterfly, the sun and the winds have all described their feelings and spoken to us in their own words. Schlegel has also permitted human beings, a boy and a shepherd, to be part of the natural tapestry where, in the words of the introductory poem (Schubert's *Abendröte* D690) 'the whole world becomes a single choir singing many a song with one voice'. And all these are speaking to the poet, the elect interpreter of these sounds, who has divined their meaning. Thus the poet's own poem (Der Dichter) serves as something of an epilogue to Part I; this reflection of the poet on nature's voices is a sonnet both here, and at the end of Part II.

The second part of the cycle takes place after night has fallen. There is another reflective poem beginning 'Als die Sonne nun versunken', again without title and not set by Schubert, and once again 'Der Dichter' supplies the epilogue. The sequence unfolds as follows:

Der Wanderer D649	D major; composed February 1819. Published as Op. 65 no. 1 in November 1826, together with two Mayrhofer settings, *Lied eines Schiffers an die Dioskuren* D360, and *Heliopolis I* D753
Der Mond	Not set by Schubert
Zwei Nachtigallen	Not set by Schubert
Das Mädchen D652	A major; composed February 1819
Der Wasserfall	Not set by Schubert
Die Blumen	Not set by Schubert

Der Sänger	Not set by Schubert
Die Sterne D684	E flat major; composed 1820
Die Gebüsche D646	G major; composed January 1819
Der Dichter	Not set by Schubert

From this it is possible to see that Schubert had found the poems by the beginning of 1819, and composed three songs from Part II of Schlegel's cycle. About a year later he moved back to Part I for certainly three (and probably six) from that set, as well as returning to Part II to compose *Die Sterne*. At the same time, he tackled *Der Schiffer* D694, a poem by Schlegel outside the *Abendröte* cycle. And three years later, in 1823, Schubert returned to work on the very first poem in the cycle, *Abendröte*. It is just possible that he had decided at this late stage to try to make a cycle of the songs he had already composed, and so at last set the lyric that gives the unifying tone to Schlegel's group of poems; this was after all the year of *Die schöne Müllerin* D795 when he was taking stock of his achievements and thinking in terms of cycles (the ballad *Viola* D786, also written in that year, represents another attempt to make a larger structure from what might have been seen as a succession of smaller songs).

It seems more likely, however, that the Schlegel settings represent 'a passive flirtation with some form of cyclic arrangement that yet refuses to emerge' (Kramer 1994). Also interesting is the point made by Berke that Schubert found the poems set in 1819 in the *Musen-Almanach für das Jahr 1802*, and that the 1820 settings were taken from one of the later collections of Schlegel's poems – the 1809 Berlin edition or the Vienna edition of 1816. This is not the same as the composer's experience with *Winterreise* (which he first encountered in the almanac *Urania* in a version with only twelve poems) in that, despite small differences between the two versions, *Abendröte* was printed complete in each publication (in the *Musen-Almanach* it is not yet divided into two parts), and the composer was aware of the scope of its cyclic nature from the start. He simply seems to have enjoyed setting these poems singly or in small batches, although Schlegel's conception is arguably best realized in cyclic terms when the various 'characters' in the set are to be found 'singing many a song with one voice'. This last phrase is Schlegel's fervent expression of Romantic pantheism, but to a musician it could also be seen as a pithy demand for a song cycle.

This 'one voice' is a problem for us in a way that it might not have been for Schubert. We know that Vogl sang Ellen's song *Ave Maria* to a rapturous reception in 1825, so it seems likely that male singers of the time would not have been embarrassed to perform *Das Mädchen* or *Die Rose* in public. Present-day singers have more inhibitions in this direction, and Fischer-Dieskau performs neither song in his recorded survey of Schubert. From today's perspective it seems more likely that the Schlegel songs could all be sung by a female singer – she could get away with *Der Knabe* as a *Hosenrolle*, and *Der Wanderer* poses no problem in a musical climate accustomed to the female *Winterreise*. But what type of female singer? Here we must consider the question of voice types, and vocal *Fach*. Could Schubert really have envisaged the same voice singing *Die Rose*, poised so high in the stave, and *Die Sterne* where the tessitura is completely different, not to mention the low notes at the end of *Abendröte*? Whoever sings *Die Sterne* in its original key of E flat will find it difficult, if not impossible, to sing the next song in Schlegel's sequence, *Die Gebüsche*, in its original key of G. The 'failure of cycle' seems to me to be Schubert's failure to have a single singer in mind, or even a single singing type, when conceiving these songs in their original keys. A song like *Die Berge* for example is suited to a bright young tenor, others to a light soprano, and yet others to a high baritone. Only by subjecting Schlegel's descriptive diversity to the practical considerations that would have enabled these poems to find vocal and cyclic unity in the person of a single singer could Schubert have made *Abendröte* into a cycle as we now understand it. Admittedly, by transposing down the higher songs it is possible for a mezzo with 'gravitas' to encompass the cycle as a whole, both in terms of singability and textual suitability (more or less), but it still seems unlikely that Schubert ever thought about this as a possibility. The performer is faced here with a similar problem in Berlioz's *Les Nuits d'été*, another so-called cycle in which different songs suit different sexes and voice types: every performance in which all songs are sung by the same singer is something of a musical compromise.

Nevertheless, modern-day performers who appreciate Schlegel's poetry (and Schubert's music), and who sense an elusive yet demonstrable unity behind the poems and music, have the right to salvage something of a cycle from these songs. The question is how. One solution is to share the *Abendröte* set between two singers, or perhaps even more. Although the best-known shared cycles come after Schubert's time (Schumann's *Myrthen* and Hugo Wolf's *Italienisches Liederbuch*), Schubert was to publish sets of songs that called for at least two singers – the *Gesänge aus* Wilhelm Meister D877, for example, where both Mignon and the Harper participate, albeit unequally. In the Op. 52 *Lady of the Lake* songs we have a larger cast: the famous *Ellens Gesänge* D837, D838 and D839 are interspersed with songs for men's chorus, female chorus, tenor (*Normans Gesang* D846) and baritone (*Lied des gefangenen Jägers* D843). Thus we have a type of operatic casting within a lieder framework. It would be possible for *Abendröte* to be performed by a number of singers, a small operatic cast with a lieder agenda, but perhaps it would make best sense, particularly in a teaching situation, if each song were performed by a different singer keeping their own character, with the pianist as common denominator. The sense of unity in diversity might be enhanced by readings of the unset material whereby the character of the poet himself ('Der Dichter') could provide the thread that binds the work together. One could even envisage an adventurous college (or collage) perform-ance of these songs given as a *Liederspiel*, rather like the one performed by Wilhelm Müller and his friends in Berlin around the subject of *Die schöne Müllerin*.

One practical difficulty, even when the songs are shared, is the unprepossessing sequence of major tonalities (A – G – A – A – B – F – F) when grouped in Schlegel's order. A prime consid-eration for concert performance should be, as far as possible, a comfortable and interesting juxtaposition of tonalities, speeds and moods. In the recording for the Hyperion Schubert Edition Schlegel's ordering was retained as far as possible, but *Die Vögel* and *Der Knabe* were separated because they are in the same key and mood. It may be argued that Schubert intended their enchainment, as did Schlegel, but putting the two merriest items together ensures a long sequence of slow songs elsewhere. Here the soprano sings *Das Mädchen* and *Die Rose*, as well as *Der Fluss*, the silvery colour of which (in the quintessentially Schubertian key of B major) seems particularly threatened by downward transposition. It is unlikely that a definitive order will be found to suit every voice type and every team of singers, but it is nevertheless desirable that the song *Abendröte* should begin the set, and that *Die Gebüsche* should end it.

ABENDRÖTE
(F. VON SCHLEGEL) **D690** [H512]
A major March 1823, perhaps as early as 1820

Evening glow

Tie - fer sin - ket schon_ die Son - ne,

(57 bars)

Tiefer sinket schon die Sonne,	The sun sinks deeper,
Und es atmet alles Ruhe,	All things breathe peace;
Tages Arbeit ist vollendet,	The day's work is finished
Und die Kinder scherzen munter.	And the children play merrily.
Grüner glänzt die grüne Erde,	The green earth shines greener
Eh' die Sonne ganz versunken.	Before the sun goes down.
Milden Balsam hauchen leise	The flowers softly breathe
In die Lüfte nun die Blumen,	Into the air sweet balm
Der die Seele zart berühret,	That tenderly caresses the soul
Wenn die Sinne selig trunken.	While the senses are drunk with rapture.
Kleine Vögel, ferne Menschen,	Small birds, people in the distance,
Berge, himmelan geschwungen,	Mountains soaring heavenwards,
Und der grosse Silberstrom,	And the great silver river
Der im Tale schlank gewunden;	That winds its slender course through the valley:
Alles scheint dem Dichter redend,	All seem to speak to the poet,
Denn er hat den Sinn gefunden;	For he has divined their meaning;
Und das All ein einzig Chor,	And the whole world becomes a single choir,
Manches Lied aus einem Munde.	Singing many a song with one voice.

FRIEDRICH VON SCHLEGEL (1772–1829); poem written in 1800/1801

This is the fifteenth of Schubert's sixteen Friedrich von Schlegel solo settings (1818–25). See the poet's biography for a chronological list of all the Friedrich von Schlegel settings. See also the article about the cycle of which this song is part – Abendröte.

This poem, and its last two lines in particular, are typical of the pantheism long dear to the European Romantic poets and which had been foreshadowed by Pope in his *Essay on Man* (1732):

> All are but parts of one stupendous whole,
> Whose body, Nature is, and God the soul;

Wordsworth in *Lines composed a few miles above Tintern Abbey . . . 1798* wrote of

> . . . a sense sublime
> Of something far more deeply interfused,
> . . .
> A motion and a spirit that impels
> All thinking things, all objects of all thought,
> And rolls through all things.

No English composer of the time even dreamed of setting such lines to music, and when Schubert tackles this Schlegel poem the result is unusual to say the least. Under the fingers of the pianist this accompaniment feels different to any other Schubert song. This is chiefly because the left-hand trills associated with sunset (cf. the opening of *Freiwilliges Versinken* D700) are awkwardly placed (often in the fourth finger of the left hand) and ubiquitous; indeed this is one of only a handful of Schubert songs where an embellishment in the piano writing becomes an important expressive feature in its own right (cf. also *Hippolits Lied* D890 and *Pause* D795/12).

The independence of each strand of the accompaniment (which is what makes those left-hand trills difficult) suggests the layout of a string quartet. The song is cast as a slow dance in compound time, and the ornamentation in both the vocal line (e.g. at 'scherzen munter' b. 15) and the piano part recalls the grandeur of early eighteenth-century music. There is also, in the left-hand line, a suggestion of passacaglia or ground bass, an impression strengthened by the recurring sound of the trills on the third quaver of each bar. As in many a set of variations in the old style, the internal note values quicken as the song progresses: crotchets prevail in the accompaniment for the first twenty bars of the song, semiquavers for the next seventeen and demisemiquavers for the last eighteen. The basic tempo, however, remains that of a stately procession, a measured moto perpetuo of the kind that this composer often uses when describing the stars on their courses and other ineffable workings of God and Nature.

The poem is equally grand in that it describes the regally repetitive rhythm and melody of life pulsating imperceptibly behind the activities of all creation, something hidden from the insensitive and uninitiated. The use of a quasi-contrapuntal texture seems to fit this concept. In line with Schlegel's poetic concepts, only the true and poetic musician is able to pick out and hear inner melodies, at the same time as enjoying the beauty of the combined strands: only the informed ear can appreciate both the particular and the general at the same time.

The first appearance of the singer, like a solo instrument adding its sound to the texture of a Bach cantata, reinforces our feeling that in this song the human voice is one among many, although *primus inter pares*. 'Tages Arbeit ist vollendet' (bb. 11–12) inspires a duet with imaginary cellos, and the next line, about children at play, with flutes. There is a distinct (and rather old-fashioned) feeling of a middle section in the relative minor at 'Milden Balsam hauchen leise / In die Lüfte nun die Blumen' (from b. 21). These six bars, the first three of which are lightened in colour and made more delicate by the fact that both the pianist's hands are in the treble clef, return to the tonic key; 'Der die Seele zart berühret, / Wenn die Sinne selig trunken' repeats this process, relative minor back to tonic. The birds are then delicately placed in the treble clef (b. 32), with a shift to the intimacy of the subdominant. All this while the trills in the piano have illustrated different things as the song progresses: at the beginning, the slow turning of the globe towards night as it shudders on its axis; at 'Und die Kinder scherzen' (where the trills transfer for the first time to the treble clef) the high sound of children's laughter; rustling breezes are evoked at 'Milden Balsam hauchen leise', and (particularly enchantingly) birdsong at 'Kleine Vögel'. Leo Black has pointed out that traces of the song's vocal line (the sequential leaps in fifths for 'Kleine Vögel' and 'ferne Menschen') are also to be found in the contemporary opera *Fierabras* D796 – in the chorus for female voices in Act 1 No. 4d, where Emma sings the words 'Ich reich' für sie'. Returning to the Schlegel song, the mountains of 'Berge, himmelan geschwungen' inspire a reappearance of the ominous bass trills first heard in *Auf der Donau* D553 (from b. 36). That poem contains the words 'Alte Burgen ragen / Himmelan', a related image about castles soaring heavenwards.

These rumblings introduce the song's final section beginning 'Und der grosse Silberstrom' where the rippling watery demisemiquavers of *Liebesbotschaft* from *Schwanengesang* D957/1 are prophesied. These, in combination with more trills in the left hand, herald a true peroration, a drawing together of all the images. When the singer reaches 'Und das All ein einzig Chor' (bb. 48–9), with its matching drops of sevenths in the vocal line, it is as if he has fathomed the meaning of life, and is transfigured by the revelation. The trills here betoken shivers of delight, the vibrating music of the spheres, or perhaps the glowing of the molten fires at the globe's centre. At 'aus einem Munde' (bb. 54–5) the singer plunges into the depths as if to commune with the earth gods, speaking his last tones in the tessitura of Wagner's Erda or Tippett's Sosostris. If Schubert's music sometimes reminds us of Britten's in its textural clarity, these final pages awash with shimmering figuration and heady abandon bring to mind the Tippett of *The Midsummer Marriage* and *The Heart's Assurance*. The music's refusal to reach the tonic until the end of the penultimate bar adds to a state of rapturous suspense, miraculous even by Schubert's exalted standards. There is nothing quite like this greatly undervalued song anywhere else in the repertoire. What a magnificent beginning it might have been to an 1823 Schlegel cycle.

Autograph:	Stiftelsen Musikkulturens främjande, Stockholm (fair copy)
First edition:	Published as Book 7 no. 3 of the *Nachlass* by Diabelli, Vienna in October 1830 (P252)
Subsequent editions:	Peters: Vol. 5/7; AGA XX 376: Vol. 6/94; NSA IV: Vol. 12/151
Bibliography:	Berke 1979, pp. 305–15
	Black 1998, pp. 24–5
	Black 2003, pp. 191–4
	Capell 1928, pp. 165–6
	Fischer-Dieskau 1977, p. 124
Discography and timing:	Fischer-Dieskau II 3[18] 3'18
	Hyperion I 27[8]
	Hyperion II 26[19] 4'06 Matthias Goerne

← *Der zürnende Barde* D785   *Viola* D786 →

Das ABENDROT   Sunset   Trio
(KOSEGARTEN) **D236** [H127]
A major   20 July 1815

(7 bars)

Der Abend blüht!	The evening blooms,
Der Westen glüht!	The west glows!
Wo bist du holdes Licht entglommen?	Fair light, whence your radiance?
Aus welchem Stern herabgekommen?	From which star have you fallen?
[. . .]	[. . .]
Wie sieht so hehr	How sublime
Das düstre Meer!	The dark sea looks!
Die Welle tanzt des Glanzes trunken,	The waves dance, drunk in the iridescence,
Und sprüht lusttaumelnd Feuerfunken.	Spraying sparks of fire with giddy delight.
[. . . 2 . . .]	[. . . 2 . . .]
Viel schöner blüht,	The pale rose's cheeks
Viel wärmer glüht	Bloom much fairer,
Die blasse Rose ihrer Wangen,	Glow far warmer,
Und weckt inbrünstiges Verlangen.	Arousing fervent longing.
[. . . 2 . . .]	[. . . 2 . . .]

Bewunderung	Veneration
Und Huldigung	And homage
Heischt nur das Schön, das ewig lebet,	Are due to eternal beauty alone,
Weil Huld und Heiligkeit es hebet.	For beauty enhances grace and holiness.

LUDWIG THEOBUL KOSEGARTEN (1758–1818)

*See the poet's biography for a chronological list of all the Kosegarten settings, as well as a
discussion of Morten Solvik's Kosegarten Liederkreis and this song's place within it.*

This vocal trio is unusual in that it is marked '1st Voice, 2nd Voice and 3rd Voice' rather than
specifying male or female voices as was the composer's usual custom. Although it is likely that
Schubert had three male voices in mind for this little piece, the mixed clefs of the vocal lines
(two treble and one bass) suggest the possibility of mixing male and female voices in
performance.

The evening mood is effectively peaceful and, as in a number of other Kosegarten settings
on a nocturnal theme, there is a certain quiet majesty about the piece. (For evidence of this one
need go no further than *Der Abend* D221, a solo setting of words in a similar metre that immediately precede these in Kosegarten's *Poesien*, and which Schubert set to music five days earlier.)
There is little in the music in harmonic terms that would not have passed for Haydn's work – a
chromatic progression at the end of the verse under 'abgekommen' strikes us as more modern,
perhaps. The accompaniment is no more than a short score of the vocal parts, suggesting, as
for some Schubert ensembles, a possibility that the piece is supposed to be *a capella* and that
the accompaniment was written only for rehearsal purposes. The final loud A major chord at
the end of each strophe is very much part of the musical effect, however; it seems that the presence of the piano has at least some useful role.

There are nine strophes in this poem – these are all printed in the NSA, Series III. Given
here are 1, 3, 6 and 9 as recorded for the Hyperion Edition.

Autograph:	Österreichische Nationalbibliothek, Vienna
First edition:	Published as part of the AGA in 1892 (P524)
Subsequent editions:	AGA XIX 6: p. 57; NSA III: Vol. 2/44
Discography and timing:	Hyperion I 22[11] 1'43 Lorna Anderson, Catherine
	Hyperion II 8[10] Denley & Michael George

← *Tischlied D234*   *Abends unter der Linde D235* →

Das ABENDROT   Sunset
(SCHREIBER) **D627** [H405]
E major   November 1818

Du hei - lig, glü - hend A - bend- rot!

(83 bars)

Du heilig, glühend Abendrot!	Sacred, glowing sunset.
Der Himmel will in Glanz zerrinnen,	The sky melts into radiance.
So scheiden Märtyrer von hinnen,	Thus do martyrs depart this life,
Holdlächelnd in dem Liebestod.	Serenely smiling as they die for their love.
Des Aufgangs Berge still und grau,	At dawn the mountains are grey and silent,
Am Grab des Tags die hellen Gluten,	The flames glow brightly at the day's grave;
Der Schwan auf purpurroten Fluten,	The swan glides on crimson waters
Und jeder Halm im Silbertau!	And every blade is bathed in silver dew.
O Sonne, Gottesstrahl, du bist	O sun, light of God, you are
Nie herrlicher, als im Entfliehn.	Never more glorious than when you go down!
Du willst uns gern hinüberziehn,	You would gladly draw us with you
Wo deines Glanzes Urquell ist.	To the source of your radiance.

ALOYS SCHREIBER (1761–1841)

This is the last of Schubert's four Schreiber solo settings (1818). See the poet's biography for a chronological list of all the Schreiber settings.

This magisterial work was composed at the end of Schubert's first stay at Zseliz as music teacher to the two daughters of Count Johann Karl Esterházy. The song was written for the count himself, an amateur bass who would have needed every ounce of whatever vocal and musical ability he possessed to sing it.

One fears that Esterházy was not nearly as talented as he might have imagined himself to be for Schubert wrote from Zseliz: 'Not a soul here has any true feeling for Art except (if I am not mistaken) the Countess now and then.' Nevertheless, the count was the boss, and he must have boasted a low E among his accomplishments for the composer to have made such a feature of it. For him Schubert wrote out a transposition of the famous *Der Wanderer* D489, from the original key of E major into D major. It makes us wonder whether the Schiller setting *Der Kampf* D594, despite its being a rather racy text, had also been intended for the same singer some time before the composer's first visit to Hungary (written as an audition work, perhaps).

The Zseliz branch of the Esterházy family seems to have favoured sacred themes in home music-making (exemplified by *Gebet* D815, the Fouqué poem set by Schubert as a quartet during his second visit in 1824). Schubert's Schreiber settings are all from 1818, and although the first, the beautiful *An den Mond in einer Herbstnacht* D614, dates from April (before he went to Zseliz) it seems too good to be true that he hit on an author by chance whose religious outlook chimed with that of the Esterházys. Schubert was employed as a teacher at the count's Vienna establishment before he went to Hungary, and it is from here that he might have borrowed the recently published Schreiber poems.

The ceremonial tone of the opening offers spread E major chords, as if played on the harp of a great minstrel. One is reminded of the majestic introduction to the Kosegarten setting *Der Abend* D221 that shows how well the composer identified with the onset of evening as an ancient and mysterious rite. The bass voice here ensures that echoes of Sarastro and *Die Zauberflöte* are never far away. The four-bar introduction sets the tone in ideal fashion. The entry of the voice signals an aria that roams generously across the stave (the song is notated in the bass clef) in the manner of an old-fashioned *bel canto* showpiece. The music is cleverly assembled from the elements of singing exercises – scales and arpeggios – and the gently rocking piano writing nurses the voice along. If the first performer of this song did not have an infallible sense of rhythm this is exactly the sort of elastic figuration that could expand and contract in the hands of an accommodating and skilled accompanist.

The aria contains more Wagnerian pre-echoes than one might imagine, particularly the spacious and solemn setting of the word 'Liebestod' (bb. 19–20). This anachronistic appearance reminds us how much Wagner's music, while aspiring to be the music of the future, owes to this sort of *scène*. Indeed, if one were searching for the names of composers who might have written the more ordinary passages of *Das Abendrot*, one would think of such names as Marschner and Meyerbeer. The propensity for the lowest vocal range brings Loewe to mind.

The central section of the song (the second strophe) is in C sharp minor (from b. 25) and in the manner of Schubert's *Der Wanderer* D489 (Schmidt von Lübeck). The setting of 'still und grau' (a high C sharp descending to G sharp, a twelfth below bb. 27–8) has a built-in element of vocal showing-off. The gliding-swan imagery of the strophe's third line inspires the composer in a more intense way: at 'Der Schwan auf purpurroten Fluten' the vocal line descends the stave supported by a downy bed of soft semiquavers, while the glinting dew ('Und jeder Halm im Silbertau') is depicted by syncopations, droplets pricked out between the hands (bb. 32–6) also in semiquavers. The repeat of these words inspires music even more picturesque (bb. 37–47). The vocal line remains dignified and spacious, containing just the right amount of regal poise for the progress of the noble swan. Underneath this music that glides and dips horizontally, the rippling-water effect of the spiralling arpeggios, beginning in the treble register and traversing two octaves, is as languidly luxurious as Ravel's accompaniment for *Le Cygne* (*Histoires naturelles*), a song that describes a very similar nature picture. In both pieces the piano writing, leisurely and intricate at the same time, suggests symmetrically patterned circles as the stately galleons of beak and feather cleave the water's surface. There is nothing quite like this in all Schubert, and *Das Abendrot* deserves attention for these ten bars alone (bb. 37–47).

The song's final section, marked 'Feurig, doch nicht zu geschwind', seems composed to an old-fashioned cantata formula, although there is nothing as vulgar (or difficult) as a *cabaletta* on offer. We realize that the voice for which this song is written is unable to move in dazzling fashion – fast coloratura was obviously not possible for the count. Instead, the poem's final strophe is variously repeated to make an extended grand hymn framed by *pomposo* chords and flourishes, and where the harmonies remain more or less within the orbit of I–IV and V, the better to suggest something fundamental – the sunset as a work of nature. The phrase 'als im Entfliehn' is followed by a gentle, even wistful bar (b. 52), a solitary rising phrase prophetic of that extraordinary postlude to Schubert's magisterial sunset song, *Freiwilliges Versinken* D700 (1820). In both cases the downward direction of the vocal line is mirrored by an ascending echo in the piano, as if all things are balanced in nature – the setting of the sun with the rising of the moon.

The last two lines of the strophe, when heard for the fourth and last time, provide the text for an extraordinary twelve-bar coda. Capell finds that the musical interest dwindles at this point, but that is perhaps because he was not a pianist who might have enjoyed the sheer physical sensation of playing it. The bass line switches between tonic and dominant, as if shifting on a giant axis, but this is not so unusual. It is the right-hand writing that is unique amongst Schubert songs: an upper pedal framed by a sumptuous bank of ninths and tenths (from b. 73). It is a pity if one has to cheat and play these chords with the help of the left hand, but the composer probably did. This music creates an impression of immense space and grandeur. The depth of the voice and the pulsating light suggested by the piano (particularly in this unusual chord distribution) are irresistibly complementary. This 'Glanz' is interpreted by Schubert as starlight, the Creator's radiance, so in these solemnly throbbing chords we hear the prototype of such great songs as *Die Sterne* D939 and, above all, *Nachthelle* D892.

Einstein finds in this song 'varying degrees of lyricism, utterly exquisite, yet not superficial'. John Reed on the other hand points out 'a lack of any great depth of subjective feeling'. One sees both points of view because the piece is a strange hybrid: half set piece and commission and half inspired by original thought. Some of the most wonderful things about it, the details that Schubert provided for himself as a shy and patient accompanist, probably went over the head of its first singer, and have gone more or less unnoticed ever since. Walther Dürr avers that the composer would have published this song had he not considered it to be the property of Count Esterházy.

Autograph:	Library of Congress, Washington (fair copy)
First edition:	Published as Op. post. 173 no. 6 by C. A. Spina, Vienna in 1867 (P412)
First known performance:	21 April 1827, Schubertiad, Josef von Spaun's house, Vienna; soloist: Luigi Lablache?
Subsequent editions:	Peters: Vol. 6/123; AGA XX 344: Vol. 5/220; NSA IV: Vol. 12/43
Bibliography:	Capell 1928, p. 145
	Einstein 1951, pp. 184–5
	Fischer-Dieskau 1977, p. 112
Discography and timing:	Fischer-Dieskau II 2[7] 4'24
	Hyperion I 34[11]
	Hyperion II 20[19] 5'15 Neil Davies

← *Blondel zu Marien* D626   *Lob der Tränen* D711 →

ABENDS UNTER DER LINDE (I)   Evening beneath the linden tree
(Kosegarten) **D235** [H128]
F major   24 July 1815

(24 bars)

Woher, o namenloses Sehnen,	Whence this nameless longing
Das den beklemmten Busen presst?	That oppresses my troubled heart?
Woher, ihr bittersüssen Tränen,	Whence these bittersweet tears
Die ihr das Auge dämmernd nässt?	That veil my eyes in moisture?
O Abendrot, o Mondenblitz,	O evening glow, o glittering moon,
Flimmt blasser um den Lindensitz.	Cast a paler light beneath the linden tree.
Es säuselt in dem Laub der Linde;	The leaves of the linden tree rustle,
Es flüstert im Akazienstrauch.	The acacia whispers.
Mir schmeichelt süss, mir schmeichelt linde	Sweetly, gently, I am caressed
Des grauen Abends lauer Hauch.	By the warm evening breeze.
Es spricht um mich wie Geistergruss;	All around it is as if spirits greet me,
Es geht mich an, wie Engelkuss.	And I am touched by an angel's kiss.

Es glänzt, es glänzt im Nachtgefilde.
Der Linde grauer Scheitel bebt—
Verklärte himmlische Gebilde,
Seid ihr es, die ihr mich umschwebt?
Ich fühle eures Atems Kuss,
O Julie! o Emilius!

The nocturnal fields gleam;
The grey locks of the linden tree quiver.
Transfigured celestial forms,
Is it you who hover around me?
I feel the kiss of your breath,
O Julie, O Emilius!

Bleibt, Sel'ge, bleibt in eurem Eden!
Des Lebens Hauch bläst schwer und schwül
Durch stumme leichenvolle Öden.
Elysium ist mild und kühl.
Elysium ist wonnevoll—
Fahrt wohl, ihr Trauten! fahret wohl!

Stay, blessed ones, stay in your Eden!
The breath of life blows heavy and sultry
Through these silent, corpse-laden wastes.
Elysium is serene and cool.
Elysium is blissful.
Farewell, friends! Farewell!

LUDWIG THEOBUL KOSEGARTEN (1758–1818)

This is the ninth of Schubert's twenty-one Kosegarten solo settings (1815–17). See the poet's biography for a chronological list of all the Kosegarten settings.

This is a 'Kindertotenlied' that was written long before Rückert's poems of that name. Kosegarten's children, Johanna Luise Juliana ('Julie') 1794–1797 and Karl Johann Emil ('Emilius') 1796–1797, died when very young. Julie is movingly remembered in the poet's *An Juliens Grabe*; another poem, *An meine Tochter Allwina Louise* gives thanks for the survival of his eldest daughter (pictured in the frontispiece of Volume II of the 1802 edition of poems) while bemoaning the loss of Emil. The two lost children are mentioned at the end of the third strophe of *Abends unter der Linde*. The grieving father sits under the linden tree remembering the son and daughter who used to sit with him there. Schubert responds with a tenderness that shows that he is no stranger to death in the family.

This song has been completely ignored; like so many of its strophic sisters it looks unexceptional on the printed page. It is the type of *bel canto* lied that many singers dread because its musical contours allow no place to hide any deficiency of technique. The work is chiselled out of Mozartian marble, cool to the touch perhaps, but concealing an inner warmth all the more moving because of the simplicity of the conception. John Reed considers this song, and its twin setting, 'unable to carry the weight of emotion suggested by the text'. In amateur performance this might be true, but a fine professional singer can make much of it. A persuasive legato line allows the song to bear its sorrow with dignity. The change of harmonic direction at 'O Abendroth . . . o Mondenblitz' (even more convincing at the confidential 'Es spricht um mich . . . wie Geistergruss' in Verse 2) reveals the stirring of deep emotion; the wafting melismatic setting of the final words of each verse ('Lindensitz' and 'Engelkuss') is enchanting if sung well enough. The second half of the song is accompanied by gently palpitating quavers that urge the vocal line through its twists and turns. The postlude is a delicate evocation of restless melancholy. Unlike some of the most famous of Schubert's songs, *Abends unter der Linde (I)* is not singer-proof, but this is all the more reason for it to be taken up by an artist of patrician abilities.

Autograph: Statsbibliothek Preussicher Kulturbesitz, Berlin
First edition: Published as part of the AGA in 1895 (P568)
Subsequent editions: Not in Peters; AGA XX 100: Vol. 2/204; NSA IV: Vol. 8/131

Discography and timing: Fischer-Dieskau I 4[17]   1'56   (First two strophes only)
                          Hyperion I 6[5]
                          Hyperion II 8[11]   2'41   Anthony Rolfe Johnson

← *Das Abendrot D236*   *Abends unter der Linde (II) D237* →

ABENDS UNTER DER LINDE (II)   Evening beneath the linden tree
(KOSEGARTEN) **D237** [H129]

The song exists in two versions, both of which are discussed below:
(1) 25 July 1815; (2) Date unknown

(1)   'Langsam'   F major   **C**   [21 bars]

(2)   F major

(21 bars)

See previous entry for poem and translation

LUDWIG THEOBUL KOSEGARTEN (1758–1818)

This is the tenth of Schubert's twenty-one Kosegarten solo settings (1815–17). See the poet's biography for a chronological list of all the Kosegarten settings, as well as a discussion of Morten Solvik's Kosegarten Liederkreis and this song's place within it.

Abends unter der Linde (I) was composed on 24 July 1815. Something about the prosodic and emotional challenges of this text of bereavement haunted the composer overnight, and he returned to it the next day. The first setting of the song was written in triple time, the following day's version in duple – a textbook example of how a poem like this can be set in a different metre, with the resulting subtle changes of word emphasis. In some respects the first setting is to be preferred – it is not always true that Schubert's second attempts eclipse the freshness and beauty of his initial response – although we have to admit that in neither song are the two children's names at the end of Verse 3 comfortably adaptable to the music. Both settings require a mastery of breath control, even if the tempo marking is modified by the *alla breve* two-in-the-bar of the time signature.

  The poem is a sad one but Schubert manages to suggest that in the humble acceptance of mortality there is also a corresponding ecstasy. Particularly in the closing bars of the second setting (and in the piano postlude) we can hear Pastor Kosegarten's quiet confidence in the afterlife.

  The first version of this second setting of Kosegarten's words (published for the first time in NSA Vol. 8, 2009) is further evidence of the composer's scrupulous attempts to do his best by a lyric of this kind. It is very similar to the second; apart from its time signature (common time, rather than *alla breve*), there are differences in the vocal line at b. 4 (no triplet) and at bb. 15–16 where a different vocal line is contained within the stave (the highest note is an F rather than the more emotionally expansive higher note of G in the second version). The postlude's final chord in the second version (with an A, rather than an F, at the top) better suggests the poet's ongoing hopes of Elysium for his children.

Autograph:	Österreichische Nationalbibliothek, Vienna (first version)
	In unknown private hands (since 2004; second version)
Publication:	First published as part of the NSA in 2009 (P852; first version)
	Published as No. 10 of *Neueste Folge nachgelassener Lieder und Gesänge* by J. P. Gotthard, Vienna in 1872 (P436; second version)
Subsequent editions:	Not in Peters; AGA XX 101: Vol. 2/206 (second version); NSA IV: Vol. 8/134 (first version) & 138 (second version)
Discography and timing:	Fischer-Dieskau —
	Hyperion I 6[6]
	Hyperion II 8[12] 4'37 Anthony Rolfe Johnson

← *Abends unter der Linde (I) D235*   *Die Mondnacht D238* →

ABENDSTÄNDCHEN AN LINA   Evening serenade to Lina
(BAUMBERG) **D265** [H152]
B♭ major   23 August 1815

(20 bars)

Sei sanft, wie ihre Seele,	Be as gentle as her soul,
Und heiter, wie ihr Blick,	And as serene as her gaze,
O Abend! und vermähle	O evening, and reward
Mit seltner Treu das Glück.	Such rare constancy with happiness!
Wenn alles schläft, und trübe	When all sleep,
Die stille Lampe scheint,	The silent lamp burns dimly;
Und hoffnungslose Liebe	Only hopeless love
Oft helle Tränen weint:	Often sheds its shining tears.
Will ich, lass mir's gelingen!	If only I may succeed in my desire
Zu ihrem Fenster gehn,	To go to her window,
Ein Lied von Liebe singen;	Sing a song of love,
Und schmachtend nach ihr sehn.	And gaze soulfully at her!
Vielleicht, dass Klagetöne	Perhaps the sorrowful tones
Von meinem Saitenspiel	Of my strings
Mehr wirken auf die Schöne,	Will touch the fair maiden more deeply,
Mehr reizen ihr Gefühl;	And stir her feelings.

Vielleicht, dass meine Saiten	Perhaps my strings
Und meine Phantasie'n	And my improvisations
Ein Herz zur Liebe leiten,	Will awaken love in a heart
Das unempfindlich schien.	That seemed unfeeling.
Wenn sie, im sanften Schlummer	When happily aroused from gentle slumber
Durch Lieder gern gestört,	By my songs,
Halbträumend meinen Kummer	She hears, half dreaming,
Und meine Leiden hört;	My grief and suffering.
Dann bang, und immer bänger,	Then she will rise from her bed,
Von ihrem Lager steigt,	Ever more anxious,
Und was er litt, ihr Sänger,	Realizing
Sich selber überzeugt:	How her minstrel has suffered.
Dann leucht' aus deiner Höhe	Then beloved moon, shine down
Herab, geliebter Mond!	From on high,
Dass ich die Tränen sehe,	That I may see her tears
Die meinen Schmerz belohnt.	Reward my pain.

GABRIELE VON BAUMBERG (1775–1839)

This is the sixth of Schubert's seven Baumberg solo settings (1809–10 and 1815). See the poet's biography for a chronological list of all the Baumberg settings.

The Austrian poetess Gabriele von Baumberg was a significant Schubertian literary flirtation from the month of August 1815. In that month alone the composer wrote no fewer than five Baumberg settings, of which this is the fourth. Five years earlier she also had the signal honour of inspiring the thirteen-year-old Schubert to write what was almost certainly his first-ever song – *Lebenstraum* D1A which survives only as a fragment. Baumberg was one of Schubert's few female poets, certainly his first, and the only woman whose work he set in 1815 (Karoline Pichler was to follow in 1816). When he could not know his poetic collaborators personally, the composer seems to have given each of them a character or personality in his mind that became very much a part of the music that he wrote for their texts. Here he seems to treat Baumberg, or at least her work, with gallantry.

The piano preludes to this *Abendständchen* and to another Baumberg setting, the ornate *Der Morgenkuss* D264, share a florid eighteenth-century manner; elegant cascades of notes are like so many ruffles on a dress from the age of Maria Theresa. The style is both feminine and reminiscent of the keyboard writing of Haydn, a composer who loved to charm the ladies. (Both Reed and Einstein mention Haydn in connection with this song.) Baumberg was an extremely passionate and emancipated woman for her time (this passion leaps out of her verse) and Schubert's understanding of this fact seems reflected in the perilousness of an exceptionally demanding tessitura – the vocal line reaches high B flat in its fourth bar. This is as exciting as it is impractical. But then the Baumberg songs are never dull: all are brimful of melody and their passion is usually counterbalanced by an almost magisterial sense of poise (*An die Sonne* D270, despite its simplicity, is one of the grandest hymns to the sun ever written).

The careful ear can also perceive deliciously imaginative touches in the accompaniments. Note for example the exquisite little canonic interchange between left and right hand in the introduction to *Abendständchen*; in his mind's eye Schubert sees the singer communing with Lina, she on the balcony of the treble stave, he at the street level of the bass clef, separated by only one bar, if not by an iron grille. This identification with the song's protagonist is quite natural: what gifted musician at the age of eighteen would not fantasize about his outpourings having the power to move the object of his affections to tears?

The idea of a serenade is thus set up from the beginning, and the gentle floridity of the piano writing seems exactly right for the 'Phantasie'n' – the improvisations mentioned in the fifth verse. References to a lute here are a further excuse for the music's old-fashioned manner; we have a wonderful evocation of the courtly formalities of an earlier age, a stylization rather like that of Fauré's *Mandoline* three-quarters of a century later. In the performance recorded with Ian Bostridge for the Hyperion Schubert Edition the introduction reappears as its postlude. Although this is not specified by the composer, it is common practice in eighteenth-century song; in any case it seems a pity to have only one chance to hear Schubert's inspired *Vorspiel*.

In the AGA there is a misprint: in the fourth bar of the vocal line under the word 'Blick' (in the first verse) a B flat is printed instead of a C.

There are eight strophes in this poem, a translation from the French according to the poet's subtitle. These are all printed in the AGA and NSA. For the Hyperion Edition Bostridge sang verses 1, 2, 4 and 5. The poem is a good one (it shows how manipulative even the most soulful of men can be when it comes to wooing, and Baumberg was an expert on manipulative men) but in performance three strophes, or four at the most, seem sufficient.

Autograph:	Library of Congress, Washington
First edition:	Published as part of the AGA in 1895 (P573)
Subsequent editions:	Not in Peters; AGA XX 125: Vol. 3/52; NSA IV: Vol. 9/9
Bibliography:	Youens 1996, pp. 43–5
Discography and timing:	Fischer-Dieskau I 5[16] 1'35
	Hyperion I 20[27]
	Hyperion II 9[13] 2'54 Ian Bostridge

←— *Der Morgenkuss D264*   *Morgenlied D266* —→

ABENDSTERN   Evening star
(MAYRHOFER) **D806** [H546]
A minor   March 1824

(33 bars)

Was weilst du einsam an dem Himmel,	Why do you linger all alone in the sky,
O schöner Stern? und bist so mild;	Fair star? For you are so gentle;
Warum entfernt das funkelnde Gewimmel	Why does the host of sparkling brothers
Der Brüder sich von deinem Bild?	Shun your sight?
'Ich bin der Liebe treuer Stern,	'I am the faithful star of love;
'Sie halten sich von Liebe fern.'	'They keep far away from love.'

So solltest du zu ihnen gehen,	If you are love,
Bist du der Liebe, zaudre nicht!	You should go to them without delay!
Wer möchte denn dir widerstehen?	For who could resist you,
Du süsses eigensinnig Licht.	Sweet, wayward light?
'Ich säe, schaue keinen Keim,	'I sow, but I see no shoot,
'Und bleibe trauernd still daheim.'	'And remain here, silent and mournful.'

Johann Mayrhofer (1787–1836)

This is the forty-fifth of Schubert's forty-seven Mayrhofer solo settings (1814–24). See the poet's biography for a chronological list of all the Mayrhofer settings.

In March 1824, between the composition of the String Quartets in A minor D804 and D minor ('Death and the Maiden') D810, Schubert bid the poetry of Mayrhofer farewell with five settings (four solo songs and a quartet for male voices), all works of great beauty and importance. The poet had been an important part of Schubert's artistic life since 1814, although it is said that the composer had been estranged from Mayrhofer for two years or so despite the fact that in 1823 he had dedicated his three Op. 6 songs to the poet – hardly the action of an unforgiving enemy. It is often said that this 1824 Mayrhofer renaissance was occasioned by the private publication of the poet's *Gedichte* in 1824, but the songs were composed in March 1824 and the book appeared only in October when the poet sent a copy to Goethe. (Schubert's name had been conspicuously absent from the subscribers' list for this edition of Mayrhofer's poems – but the composer was away in Hungary when that list would have been prepared.)

Abendstern is the second of this new group of songs. Almost all of Schubert's A minor/A major music owes a varying debt of gratitude to the allegretto movement of Beethoven's Seventh Symphony, and the mournful *Abendstern*, an emotionally imposing miniature, is no exception. The rhythm of the Beethoven, however, is dactylic. Here the insistent rhythm is in triple time; the song is propelled ineluctably forward by three quavers, an upbeat figuration that precedes a dotted crotchet at the beginning of each adjacent bar. This quintessentially Schubertian rhythmic dynamo invites comparison with an important later song, *Fülle der Liebe* D854, as well as earlier masterpieces like *Suleika I* D720 and *Der Zwerg* D771, the latter another A minor work, featuring the warped loneliness of a rejected outsider, a murderer and, like Mayrhofer, a suicidal figure, simultaneously depressed and enraged by his unloveability.

Those who love Schubert's A minor String Quartet will not fail to notice that the same haunting ambivalence between major and minor tonalities (in the work's first movement) marks it out as a spiritual, as well as chronological, companion to *Abendstern*. The quartet seems to be music that might offer compassion to the rejected poet. Another A minor work that comes to mind (with the same time signature, but lacking this song's resigned humility) is the Platen setting *Du liebst mich nicht* D756. Like that song, *Abendstern* reflects the poet's loneliness, depression and sense of isolation, and probably for some of the same reasons. The sole star at eventide is of course Venus, solitary in the heavens and here representative of a loveless world. It is well known that Platen was homosexual, and the poem of *Abendstern* might be thought to show Mayrhofer in a similarly self-revealing – not to mention self-punishing – mood. 'I sow no seed', he says, but this could be as much a confession of a life without sexual fulfilment as an indication of sexual difference. He is in any case a loner and someone perpetually excluded from the happiness available to others. If there is a glimmer of A major hope in this poem it is all the more poignant for its fugitive inaccessibility. The warmth of the major key is 'grasped for an instant' (Capell) 'and at the next it slips from love's chilled fingers'. The wonder of the song is that so little is written on the page, yet so much seems to happen in the music.

In a rare example of a tempo indication to modify the mood of an otherwise more or less strophic song, Schubert marks the second verse 'Etwas schneller'. This is less of a sudden gear change than an imperceptible ratcheting up of tension, born of the heightened intensity in the dialogue between the suffering star and the compassionate, involved singer who is here cast as a figure radiating affectionate optimism. This is music by a composer who has already survived the greatest challenge to his mental equilibrium. He has passed through the worst of the depression occasioned by dangerous illness at the same time as the refining fire of *Die schöne Müllerin*. The fact that *Abendstern* is also something of a pre-echo of the devastating emotional landscape of *Der Leiermann* reminds us that Schubert is moving towards another masterpiece of *multum in parvo*, the song cycle *Winterreise*.

Autograph:	Gesellschaft der Musikfreunde, Vienna
First edition:	Published as Book 22 no. 4 of the *Nachlass* by Diabelli, Vienna in 1833 (P302)
Subsequent editions:	Peters: Vol. 5/133; AGA XX 459: Vol. 8/18; NSA IV: Vol. 13/138
Bibliography:	Black 2003, p. 93
	Capell 1928, p. 205
	Fischer-Dieskau 1977, pp. 193–4
	Porter 1961, p. 67
	Youens 1996, pp. 218–21
Arrangements:	arr. Tilman Hoppstock (b. 1961) for guitar accompaniment, in *Franz Schubert: 110 Lieder* (2009)
Discography and timing:	Fischer-Dieskau II 6[14] 2'06
	Pears-Britten 1[6] 2'10
	Hyperion I 6[4]
	Hyperion II 29[1] 2'45 Anthony Rolfe Johnson

← *Des Baches Wiegenlied* D795/20   *Der Sieg* D805 →

Die ABGEBLÜHTE LINDE   The faded linden tree
(SZÉCHÉNYI) OP. 7 NO. 1, **D514** [H331]
A minor – C major   1817?

(99 bars)

Wirst du halten, was du schwurst,	Will you abide by what you pledged to me
Wenn mir die Zeit die Locken bleicht?	When time has made my hair white?
Wie du über Berge fuhrst,	Since you went away over the mountains
Eilt das Wiedersehn nicht leicht.	Reunions are not easy.
Änd'rung ist das Kind der Zeit,	Change is the child of time
Womit Trennung uns bedroht,	With which parting threatens us;

Und was die Zukunft beut,	And what the future offers us
Ist ein blässer's Lebensrot.	Is a paler gleam of life.

Sieh, die Linde blühet noch,	See, the linden tree is still blooming
Als du heute von ihr gehst:	As you leave here today;
Wirst sie wieder finden, doch	You will find it again
Ihre Blüten stiehlt der West.	Though the west wind steals its blossoms.

Einsam steht sie dann, vorbei	Then it will stand alone, people will
Geht man kalt, bemerkt sie kaum.	Pass by, indifferent, scarcely noticing it.
Nur der Gärtner bleibt ihr treu,	Only the gardener will remain true,
Denn er liebt in ihr den Baum.	Since he loves the tree for itself.

LUDWIG VON SZÉCHÉNYI (1781–1855)

This is the first of Schubert's two Széchényi solo settings (1817?). See the poet's biography for a chronological list of the Széchényi settings.

The accompaniment for this song sounds like an operatic orchestration. The opening bar suggests strings, and the next bar, the answering phrase of this *recitativo stromentato*, is a reply from the woodwind. The voice part is marked 'Recit.' at the outset, something that Schubert was less inclined to write in songs as he got older, preferring to integrate recitative and aria without a sense of formal division. After the words 'Wenn mir die Zeit die Locken bleicht' (bb. 9–10) there is a ravishing falling sequence of phrases in the accompaniment (written out like a short score of an orchestral interlude) where each bar seems to represent a different age of man, sharps sinking to naturals and then to flats. The music responds to the idea of fading (the key-word 'bleicht'); in these sequences we can hear colour being drained from the poet's hair and youthful vitality from his body. This portrayal of receding energy serves as an introduction to 'Wie du über Berge fuhrst', music to accompany the beloved friend – or spouse – as he or she goes over the mountains, and we lose sight of them with each harmonic step. The recitative has begun in A minor and wends its way, via a beautifully ornamented cadence full of sighs and longing, towards G major. This is the dominant of the key of the extended section that follows.

There is a great deal about this C major effusion (including the same opening notes of the vocal line) that recalls another aria in the same key, *Liebe schwärmt auf allen Wegen* D239/6, an orchestrated aria from *Claudine von Villa Bella* (qv), a Schubert *Singspiel* with a Goethe text. In both cases the vocal line is interrupted by an echoing orchestral interlude; in *Die abgeblühte Linde* the piano writing suggests cello solos as miniature interjections (bb. 21 and 24). It is interesting too that the theme of both works is 'Treue' or constancy, perhaps the reason the composer has chosen C major, a tonality unsullied by chromatic adulteration. No matter where the piece wanders, it returns to this key. Mention of the future on 'Und was die Zukunft beut' in the second verse takes us into the exotic reaches of B flat minor (b. 26) as if we are being led into uncertainty, not to mention temptation. But the linden tree at the beginning of the third verse ('Sieh, die Linde blühet noch', b. 31) returns us to the security of C major. Unusual phrase lengths are a feature here (4 bars + 3 bars in the opening cantilena) as well as quasi-operatic melismas and in one instance a trill on 'die' – a strange word to have inspired such exuberance (b. 31); even the vocal line seems to have been envisaged in instrumental terms at this point, irrespective of the text.

The sequence of modulations at 'doch / Ihre Blüten stiehlt der West' (bb. 40–43) suggests cunning and trickery as if Time were stealing a march on its ageing victims. The descending bass-line chromatics of 'Einsam steht sie dann' droop and wither most effectively as the accompaniment, with the right hand's group of quavers off the beat, suggests a mood that is *molto patetico* and again operatic. This is very similar to a passage from *Atys* D585 (bb. 47–66) composed in the same year. Mention of the true and trusty gardener (the second line of the fourth verse) prompts one of Schubert's magical transformations from A minor into A major (b. 59), another change that echoes *Atys* (at bb. 17, 94 and 110 of that song). From b. 68 the music is marked 'Etwas geschwinder' – an unusual marking for Schubert in mid-song, and comparable to the 'Un poco accelerando' to be found in *Ganymed* D544, also from 1817. The two remaining lines of text provide all that is necessary for a further seven lines of music. Repetition of this kind is highly unusual in Schubert's lieder; it is as if the composer is treating the poem as a libretto. The singer has his or her work cut out to make these rapturously repetitive phrases sound convincing. Various tricks of the trade (including extending the word 'Nur' as it is sung over shifting harmonies that triumphantly return us to C major once and for all) reinforce the feeling that this song's place in the canon stands somewhere between lied and aria.

The piece closes undramatically in a mood of quiet rapture, murmuring its delight in love and constancy. The way that the piano line entwines with the voice part at bb. 86–93 is again reminiscent of *Ganymed* (at bb. 95–9 for example). The poem enshrines a touching thought about the enduring nature of love and friendship that must have appealed to the composer. The only poem for a solo song he himself penned, and then set to music (*Abschied (Lebe wohl! Du lieber Freund!)* D578 from the summer of 1817), is also about a leave-taking between friends. It seems possible that the departure of his beloved Franz von Schober from Vienna in the summer of that year occasioned this setting – and that would affirm the song's suggested date of 1817.

John Reed has not been the only scholar to doubt whether this song and its Op. 7 sibling, *Der Flug der Zeit* D515, were composed in this year. Reed preferred to think that both these songs were written in 1821 (the year of the song's publication) and offers arguments about when and how the composer might have first encountered Széchényi who was an important member of the Musikverein – someone whom Schubert had to win over in double-quick time in order to obtain his own membership of that organization in 1821. Nevertheless, there is something about these two works that seems stubbornly linked to the other songs of 1817 mentioned above. The operatic nature of *Die abgeblühte Linde* might well suggest that the mature composer of 1821 was pandering to the operatic tastes of the work's dedicatee (none other than the noble poet), but it is equally likely that the twenty-year-old Schubert, a musical gardener taken with the Italian style, was interested in how he could cross-breed the aria with the lied. It is perfectly possible that these songs, composed in 1817, jumped the queue for publication in 1821 in order to help win Széchéyni's support, but the dating of the song remains an open question.

Autograph:	Missing or lost
First edition:	Published as Op. 7 no. 1 by Cappi & Diabelli, Vienna in November 1821 (P18)
Dedicatee:	Graf Ludwig Széchényi von Sarvári-Felsö-Vidék
First known performance:	6 March 1823, *Abend-Unterhaltung* of the Gesellschaft der Musikfreunde, Vienna. Soloist: Franz Ruess (see Waidelich/ Hilmar Dokumente I No. 195 for full concert programme)
Publication reviews:	*Allgemeine musikalische Zeitung* (Vienna), No. 6 (19 January 1822), col. 43ff. [Waidelich/Hilmar Dokumente I No.142; Deutsch Doc. Biog. No. 270]
	F. von Hentl 'Blick auf Schubert's Lieder', *Wiener Zeitschrift für Kunst, Literatur, Theater und Mode* No. 36 (23 March 1822), p. 289f. [Waidelich/Hilmar Dokumente I No. 146; Deutsch Doc. Biog. No. 278]

Subsequent editions:	Peters: Vol. 4/7; AGA XX 300: Vol. 5/29; NSA IV: Vol. 1/59;
	Bärenreiter: Vol. 1/48
Bibliography:	Black 1998, p. 23
	Porter 1961, p. 25
Discography and timing:	Fischer-Dieskau I 9[17] 3'48
	Hyperion I 21[8]
	Hyperion II 17[9] 3'30 Edith Mathis

← *Nur wer die Liebe kennt (Impromptu)* D₂513a   *Der Flug der Zeit* D515 →

ABSCHIED *see* SCHWANENGESANG D957/7

ABSCHIED
(SCHUBERT) **D578** [H380]
B minor   24 August 1817

Farewell to a friend

(18 bars)

Lebe wohl! Du lieber Freund!	Farewell, dear friend!
Ziehe hin in fernes Land,	Go forth to a distant land;
Nimm der Freundschaft trautes Band—	Take this cherished bond of friendship
Und bewahr's in treuer Hand!	And keep it faithfully.
Lebe wohl! Du lieber Freund!	Farewell, dear friend!
Lebe wohl! Du lieber Freund!	Farewell, dear friend!
Hör' in diesem Trauersang	Hear in this mournful song
Meines Herzens innern Drang,	The yearning of my inmost heart,
Tönt er doch so dumpf und bang.	Muffled and anxious.
Lebe wohl! Du lieber Freund!	Farewell, dear friend!
Lebe wohl! Du lieber Freund!	Farewell, dear friend!
Scheiden heisst das bitt're Wort,	Parting is a bitter word;
Weh, es ruft Dich von uns fort	Alas, it calls you from us
Hin an den Bestimmungsort.	To the place decreed for you.
Lebe wohl! Du lieber Freund!	Farewell, dear friend!
Lebe wohl! Du lieber Freund!	Farewell, dear friend!
Wenn dies Lied Dein Herz ergreift,	If this song should stir your heart,
Freundes Schatten näher schweift,	My friendly spirit shall hover close by,
Meiner Seele Saiten streift.	Touching the strings of my soul.
Lebe wohl! Du lieber Freund!	Farewell, dear friend!

Franz Schubert (1797–1828); poem written on, or shortly before, 24 August 1817

This is the only occasion when Franz Schubert set his own words to music for a solo song with piano. (cf. Beitrag zür fünfzigjährigen Jubelfeier des Herrn von Salieri D407)

The song is a touching farewell to the composer's friend Franz von Schober who was leaving Vienna for a while. To explain its background Diabelli chose to issue the song as *Abschied (Lebe wohl! Du lieber Freund!)*, a spurious (if accurate) title that survived in the Peters Edition. The music is heartfelt but simple, as if Schubert was embarrassed (or at least thought it inappropriate) to lavish ornate invention on his own literary efforts. *Pièce d'occasion* it certainly is and was probably penned, words and music almost simultaneously, in a few minutes, and written into his friend's album. The Schober family were Schubert's Viennese hosts at this time; the composer had lived in their apartment for the past eight months. Axel, the elder brother of the family, a first lieutenant in the Austrian Tenth Hussars (and a talented painter of flowers) was due to return on military leave from France, and Schubert had to move back to his parents' home to make enough room for him in the Schober household. Tragically Axel von Schober died before he reached Vienna. He was already ailing when his younger brother Franz (Schubert's friend and poet) left the city to fetch him.

The Schober family's concern over Axel's health must have been well known to Schubert; perhaps they already feared the worst. Was this song meant to comfort and show concern for Schober on his sad and ominous journey? The third verse could apply equally well to the prospect of Schober's sad parting from his brother, and the 'Bestimmungsort' (the decreed place) may refer to the town where Axel lay ill, as well as the grave that parts all friends and brothers. Schubert was devoted to his own brothers; if this song was written as a result of the Schober family crisis, the composer's tactful empathy is as good a reason as any for his having written it.

The doubling of the vocal line by the piano in much of this song seems to show solidarity along the lines of 'Whither thou goest, I will go'. The modulation into the relative major on 'lieber Freund' is as tender as an embrace. John Reed finds pre-echoes of *Vor meiner Wiege* D927 here (it is in the same key of B minor); that song explores the relationship of mother and child, and the tonality is one that the composer often chose when depicting intimate emotional ties (*Grablied für die Mutter* D616 is another example). We sense that Schubert probably considered himself an honorary member of the Schober family; he had certainly been treated as such.

Abschied mirrors Schober's *An die Musik* D547 in terms of its chronology, its key (the D major of *An die Musik* is the relative major of *Abschied*'s B minor) and simply because music and friendship were sacred to Schubert, both containing mingled happiness and sadness in relationships both major and minor. The enigmatic figure of Franz von Schober hovers behind both pieces (*see* poet's biography). After Schubert's death he remained tantalizingly silent (at least on paper) about his friendship with the composer, although – or perhaps because – he was closer to Schubert than any other member of the circle. The enduring strength of this friendship remains one of the unsolved Schubertian mysteries. They were from such different backgrounds, and had such contrasting temperaments, yet the composer remained steadfastly loyal to Schober even when the poet-dilettante's behaviour seemed to have been undeserving of such steadfast devotion. The music with Schoberian connections, usually settings of his poems, always strikes a note that suggests intimacy and special affection. The relationship between this song and *Irrlicht* D911/9 in the same key is discussed in the *Winterreise* commentary.

Autograph:	Conservatoire collection, Bibliothèque Nationale, Paris
First edition:	Published as Book 29 no. 4 of the *Nachlass* by Diabelli, Vienna in 1838 (P323)

Subsequent editions:	Peters: Vol. 5/169; AGA XX 586: Vol. 10/80; NSA IV: Vol. 11/160
Arrangements:	arr. Tilman Hoppstock (b. 1961) for guitar accompaniment, in *Franz Schubert: 110 Lieder* (2009)
Discography and timing:	Fischer-Dieskau II 1[11] 1'48
	Hyperion I 21[16]
	Hyperion II 19[14] 3'30 Edith Mathis

← *Die Entzückung an Laura* D577   *Der Knabe in der Wiege (Wiegenlied)* D579 →

ABSCHIED, NACH EINER WALLFAHRTSARIE

(Mayrhofer) **D475** [H300]
G major   September 1816

Farewell, based on a pilgrim's song

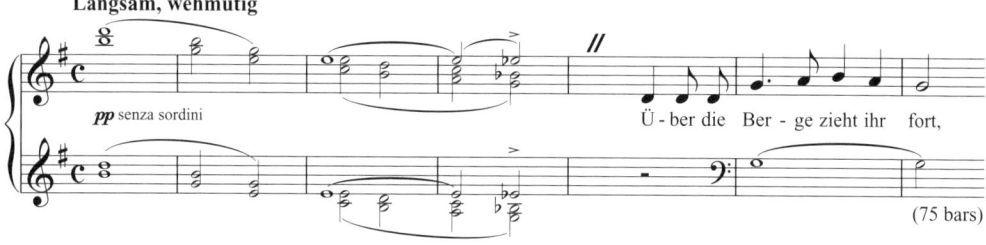

(75 bars)

Über die Berge	You journey
Zieht ihr fort,	Over the mountains
Kommt an manchen	And come upon
Grünen Ort;	Many a green spot;
Muss zurücke	I must return
Ganz allein;	All alone,
Lebet wohl!	Farewell,
Es muss so sein.	It must be so.
Scheiden,	Parting,
Meiden,	Leaving
Was man liebt,	That which we love,
Ach wie wird	Ah, how it grieves
Das Herz betrübt!	The heart.
O Seenspiegel,[1]	Glassy lakes,
Wald und Hügel –	Woods and hills
Schwinden all;	All vanish;
Hör' verschwimmen	I hear the echo
Eurer Stimmen	Of your voices

---

[1] The reversal of Mayrhofer's lines 'Wald und Hügel' and 'O Seenspiegel' is probably Schubert's idea, as are the exclamations 'Ach' (line 12) and 'O' (line 13), as well as the phrase 'Lebt wohl! / Klingt klagevoll' at the end of the setting. For an explanation of the background to these alternative Mayrhofer readings see Editorial Note at the beginning of Johann Mayrhofer.

Wiederhall.	Fade away.
Lebt wohl!	'Farewell'
Klingt klagevoll,	Sounds the lament.
Ach wie wird	Ah, how it grieves
Das Herz betrübt.	The heart.
Scheiden,[2]	Parting,
Meiden,	Leaving
Was man liebt;	That which we love;
Lebt wohl!	'Farewell!'
Klingt klagevoll!	Sounds the lament.

JOHANN MAYRHOFER (1787–1836)

This is the fifth of Schubert's forty-seven Mayrhofer solo settings (1814–24). See the poet's biography for a chronological list of all the Mayrhofer settings.

The pilgrim's aria on which the song is said to be based has never been traced. In the *Gedichte* of 1824 (p. 15) Mayrhofer's poem is entitled *Lunz*, a village in Lower Austria, 30 kilometres from Mariazell. The poet had travelled there on a walking tour in 1816. His companion on that holiday was Hermann Watteroth (see the Deutsch iconographical volume p. 223), the good-looking son of Mayrhofer's university professor Heinrich Watteroth who had been the dedicatee of Schubert's cantata (now lost to posterity) entitled *Prometheus* D451. With this connection in mind John Reed suggests that this *Abschied* may be linked with both poet's and composer's friendship with the Watteroth family. Can it be that the song is based on a melody ('Die Nymphen herbei und Najaden') from this lost *Prometheus* composed in June 1816? Snatches of melody from this otherwise non-existent work were noted down from memory by Leopold von Sonnleithner who heard its only performance. The Sonnleithner quote that matches the melodic contours of the opening vocal line of *Abschied* can be found on p. 444 of the English edition of Deutsch's *Schubert, Memoirs by his Friends* (1958). Because the rise and fall of this kind of horn motif is a common one, Walther Dürr believes this may simply be a coincidence.

Whatever Schubert's inspiration, we can hear the echoing resonances of phrases sung across the mountains by the travellers, and the hauntingly mournful effect of alphorn harmonies merging one into the other in the reverberant mountain acoustic. This is astonishing, bearing in mind that by 1816, as far as we know, Schubert had neither travelled far from Vienna, nor heard any regional music of this kind. (By the time he composed *Der Hirt auf dem Felsen* in 1828 he had journeyed in the mountains of Upper Austria with the singer Vogl.) The wide-open spaces evoked by the song make the listener think of a later musical romanticism. The song's *Vorspiel* is reminiscent of the rainbow of descending chords that open the slow movement of Brahms's F minor Piano Sonata; others have heard an even more modern colour in this song, with its surprising chain of semibreve and minim chords in its introduction and postlude: the whole piece is a bittersweet amalgam of affection and despair that puts one in mind of the mood of some of Mahler's *Des Knaben Wunderhorn* songs.

---

[2] Mayrhofer's final five lines are 'Scheiden, / Meiden, / Was man liebt; / O wie wird / Das Herz betrübt.' Schubert thus dispenses with the poet's rhyme at the end of the setting.

The poet's thoughts of inevitable parting and decay have something in common with a later Schubert song, Collin's *Wehmut* D772. Using the simplest strophic means Schubert elevates Mayrhofer's straightforward text into a universal hymn; the music seems to speak not only of a physical journey, but also of man's final leave-taking into new spiritual realms. Fischer-Dieskau has pointed out the similarity of the introduction to the prisoners' 'schnell schwindest du uns wieder' from Beethoven's *Fidelio*, which is also a kind of farewell. As always Schubert is a Janus, looking backwards to his revered models while anticipating new developments. He was not of the generation to be interested in folksong, but this is as near as he gets to that branch of music that emerged as worthy of study and emulation only later in the nineteenth century.

Autograph:	Missing or lost
First edition:	Published as a solo piano arrangement by Kratochwill, Vienna in 1876; and with vocal line as Vol. 7 no. 7 in Friedlaender's edition by Peters, Leipzig in 1885 (P473)
Subsequent editions:	Peters: Vol. 7/18; AGA XX 251: Vol. 4/176; NSA IV: Vol. 11/2
Bibliography:	Dürr, Introduction to NSA IV Volume 11, p. XVIII
	Fischer-Dieskau 1977, pp. 76–7
Discography and timing:	Fischer-Dieskau I 8³ 5'24
	Hyperion I 3¹⁴
	Hyperion II 16¹ 5'35 Ann Murray

← *Liedesend* D473   *Rückweg* D476 →

ABSCHIED VON DER ERDE *see* LEB' WOHL, DU SCHÖNE ERDE D829

ABSCHIED VON DER HARFE   Farewell to the harp
(SALIS-SEEWIS) **D406** [H241]

This song exists in two versions, the first of which is discussed below:
(1) March 1816; (2) April 1816

(1)   E minor

(2)   'Etwas langsam'   E minor   **C**   [14 bars]

(14 bars)

Noch einmal tön', o Harfe,	Sound once more, o harp;
Die nur Gefühle tönt!	You express only emotion!
Verhalle zart und leise	Softly, tenderly,
Noch jene Schwanenweise,	Let that swansong fade away
Die auf der Flut des Lebens	Which in the flood of life
Uns mit der Not versöhnt!	Reconciles us to our misery!
Im Morgenschein des Lebens	In the dawn of life
Erklangst du rein und hell!	You resounded, pure and bright!
Wer kann den Klang verwahren?	Who can preserve that sound?
Durch Forschen und Erfahren	With our searchings, our experience,
Verhallet' und versiegte	The pure source of your song
Des Liedes reiner Quell.	Fades and runs dry.
In spätern Jugendjahren	In later youth
Hallt es schon zart und bang,	It sounds tender and anxious,
Wie Finkenschlag im Märze;	Like the finch's song in March;
Mit des Entknospens Schmerze	With the pain of budding growth
Erbeben Herz und Saiten	The heart and the strings quiver,
Voll Liebe und Gesang.	Filled with love and song.
Am Sommertag des Lebens	In the summertime of life
Verstummt das Saitenspiel!	The strings fall silent.
Aus sehnsuchtsvoller Seele	From a yearning soul
Lockt's noch, wie Philomele,	They still call, like the nightingale,
Schon seltner, aber rührend,	More rarely now, yet touching us,
Nut Schwermut und Gefühl.	All melancholy and tenderness.
O schlag' im dunkeln Busen	O sound in the dark heart
Der ernsten Abendzeit!	Of solemn eventide!
Will um das öde Leben	When the darkness of fate would spin its web
Des Schicksals Nacht sich weben,	Around life's barrenness,
Dann schlag' und wecke Sehnsucht	Then sound forth, and awaken longing
Nach der Unsterblichkeit!	For immortality!

JOHANN GAUDENZ VON SALIS-SEEWIS (1762–1834); poem written in 1800/1806

This is the ninth of Schubert's thirteen Salis-Seewis solo settings (1816–?21). See the poet's biography for a chronological list of all the Salis-Seewis settings.

This song, one of ten Salis-Seewis settings composed in 1816, is printed in two separate versions in the NSA. They vary in small melodic and rhythmic details. The first of these is marked 'Etwas geschwind'; the second (which shares a manuscript with *Der Herbstabend* D405) is marked 'Etwas langsam'. The first marking is more realistic in terms of the long-breathed vocal lines that are truly impossible to perform in a slow tempo. Yet another version is printed in AGA (this is not an autograph but a copy from the Witteczek collection, thus not included in the NSA) where the marking is 'Etwas bewegt' – perhaps the best musical advice of all.

The minstrel and his harp are a rich theme in Schubert. The Ossian songs were published with a vignette that showed the old Celtic minstrel with a harp. The werewolf is killed by a harp, no less, in *Der Liedler* D209. The angry bard of *Der zürnende Barde* D785 asks who dares to destroy his instrument. We meet the harp in its ancient Greek form in the Anacreontic *An die Leier* D737, and the old minstrel who goes with his harp into the wood to sing his swansong in *Nachtstück* D672 is surely given some of Schubert's greatest music. We meet the zither as the minstrel's accompanying instrument in *Des Sängers Habe* D832 and of course the lute is to be found not only in *An die Laute* D905 but also in *Die schöne Müllerin* D795. We assume that the troubadours in *Der Sänger* D149 and *Die drei Sänger* D329 also played the harp. The most famous of the harp songs are naturally those to Goethe texts from *Wilhelm Meister* D478.

This is one of the earliest examples of Schubert giving the piano a harp-like accompaniment. Flowing semiquavers are underpinned by minims with curious grace-note upbeats that go some way to simulate the sound of the plucked lower strings of the harp. The tune is gently melancholic and somewhat reminiscent of Mozart's *Das Lied der Trennung* K519. The descending bass line at 'Verhalle zart und leise' (bb. 5–7) exactly mirrors in harmonic terms the idea of a tune fading away; the lift of anguish under 'Schwanenweise' (E – E sharp – F sharp in the bass, bb. 9–10) suddenly takes the music into realms of the unknown – exactly where the poem is straying. This is a curiously austere song, difficult to sing, but with a haunting quality.

The poem has five strophes, all printed in the AGA. Only verses 1, 2 and 5 were recorded for the Hyperion Edition, but Salis has proposed an 'ages of man' scenario and the whole poem makes far better sense if read as a whole. Nevertheless, for recital and performing purposes it must be admitted that five strophes seem too many.

Autographs:	In private hands since 1982 (first version)
	Wienbibliothek im Rathaus, Vienna (second version)
Publication:	First published as part of the NSA in 2002 (P833; first version)
	First published by C. A. Spina in 1860 although no copies of this publication have survived. The song next appeared as Vol. 7 no. 34 in Friedlaender's edition by Peters, Leipzig in 1887 (P395; second version)
Subsequent editions:	Peters: Vol. 7/83; AGA XX 208: Vol. 4/80; NSA IV: Vol. 10/120 & 122
Arrangements:	Arr. Tilman Hoppstock (b. 1961) for guitar accompaniment, in *Franz Schubert: 110 Lieder* (2009)
Discography and timing:	Fischer-Dieskau I 6^{29} 1'48
	Hyperion I 23^5
	Hyperion II 13^{15} 2'01 Christoph Prégardien

← *Lied (Ins stille Land)* D403   *Die Herbstnacht ('Die Wehmut')* D404 →

ACCOMPANIMENT AND ACCOMPANYING

Schubert's lieder exemplify the finest piano writing for vocal compositions in all music. In the later nineteenth century, Hugo Wolf and Johannes Brahms wrote accompaniments that on occasion called for greater range and virtuosity; in the early twentieth century lieder by Richard Strauss and Hans Pfitzner sometimes required increased physical strength and more robust instruments than the ones on which Schubert played. But the accompaniments of all these works, and many others, were a logical outcome of Schubert's wonderfully inspired contributions to the art of song with piano.

It is one of the purposes of this book to point out the myriad felicities of Schubert's song accompaniments. Only by encountering the broadest cross section of these can the listener or reader be aware of the extent of the composer's invention in the creation of tonal analogues for verbal ideas, his endlessly imaginative response to words and situations, his mastery of mood-setting and his astonishing resourcefulness in conjuring magic within the minimalist confines of two staves of piano music. From that moment in October 1814 when Schubert decided to imitate the sound of Gretchen's spinning wheel with a whirring, pianistic clatter, the lied was altered for ever. He had already written admirably effective and imaginative accompaniments (as this book points out) but it was with *Gretchen am Spinnrade* D118 that the public, and eventually the musicologists, sat up and took notice. This piano writing was both mechanical and emotional – the unifying moto perpetuo of a spinning wheel running out of control and, with it, a young girl's life. Schubert called for the full-blooded resources of the female voice (the song is extremely demanding for a soprano) but his accompaniment also asks a great deal of the pianist. The sheer confidence and maturity of this piano writing remains as breathtaking as on the day it was conceived. The boldness of the accompaniment played a crucial part in matching Goethe's peerless text in both general terms and in detail, and it marked the beginning of a new era in musical history.

Schubert tended to sketch his vocal lines in conjunction with the bass, before writing out the accompaniments in full. He was under no illusion that a song's success and *raison d'être* were to do with the melody allied to the words, supported by the strength of a bass line. But once these building blocks were in place he lavished infinite care on piano writing that would enhance, illustrate, enliven and sometimes even transfigure his initial melodic inspiration.

Among professional accompanists Schubert's piano writing is regarded as particularly challenging. This is not often a question of technical complexity (Schubert's scores are not difficult to decipher, his harmonies not outlandish by modern standards and many of the accompaniments are relatively easy to sight-read), but often pianists feel exposed in terms of style and interpretation – there is nowhere to hide in a Schubert song. A well-known solo pianist who had been persuaded to accompany a singer once confided to me that he found the undemanding accompaniment to *Heidenröslein* 'terrifying' because there was so little to do. Many of those able to dash off a Rachmaninoff song accompaniment with great brio feel inhibited when it comes to Schubert. (For a description of my own comical difficulties with this music as a young pianist the reader is referred to the Foreword.)

A pianist must always be familiar with the poetic text before they can accompany a song with any confidence. They must be truly aware of every detail of the third stave, both musical and verbal, and a pianist with little understanding of German is at a distinct disadvantage. For English-speaking pianists this is a lifelong challenge. The serious student accompanist has to set his cap at the language with the same dedication that a non-German or Austrian Schubert singer must muster in order to be taken seriously in the sphere. Language is one reason why the singer's line on the top stave is often held at a wary distance by those less experienced accompanists whose musical world has been hitherto bordered by their left and right hands. A pianist has to be able to sing *with* the singer, and by this I mean more than simply play the instrument in a singing manner.

Singers who accompany themselves (countless jazz artists for example) never experience any ensemble difficulties – the human brain is thankfully constructed so that word and tone, when executed by the same person, are always faultlessly together. It follows – and this is one of the great secrets of the profession – that a pianist must fool his or her brain into believing that it is himself or herself who is singing the text. This is achieved by mentally singing every word with the singer (albeit silently and without mouth movements, and yes, even if not every word of the German is understood). In a similar way, when one stands next to someone in church who is more confident with a hymn tune, one gratefully follows them while managing to sing in unison.

Using this ploy, a pianist must think him- or herself *inside* the vocal stave (not merely observing it from a distance), breathing with the singer as if their own life depended on it, and thus anticipating those moments when their colleague's shortness of breath necessitates a slight increase in tempo, as well as those times when a breath successfully taken by the singer allows a more generous use of time-placement or rubato. This is on-the-spot decision-making and the most painstaking rehearsals cannot pre-arrange these moments of give and take that make live music-making such a joy. The pianist must also get used to placing his or her accompanying chords on a singer's vowels, rather than on the initial consonants of words. Pianists who work mainly with instrumentalists often criticize singers for being rhythmically lax, for dragging or being late on the first beat of the bar. Of course singers can sometimes be all these things, but a diagnosis of such ensemble difficulties often reveals that an inexperienced accompanist fails to take into account the fact that a protracted consonant at the beginning of a word will delay the following vowel (and thus the accompanying chord) by a microsecond – and what a crucial microsecond this is! There is a world of difference between a pianist who pushes and hectors the vocal line as if it were written for a violin, making the singer feel rushed without understanding why, and one who allows each word of text to flower in its proper time and place. It takes a good deal of experience to realize that in a song the exactitude of a bar line is relatively meaningless.

When a pianist's brain is firmly superimposed on the singer's line the fingers will automatically bring their playing into perfect, and infinitely flexible, ensemble with even the most wilful and unpredictable of partners. From this perspective any elongation or emphasis of consonants, any sudden variation in tempo or inflexion, will be instantly navigable. The aim is to be in perfect tandem with the singer rather than to run after them, half a second too late. It is a paradox that an accompanist's skill in supposedly 'following' a singer has nothing to do with 'following' in the usual sense, rather is it a kind of shadowing where the vocalist must be allowed to lead, but not imperiously so, and not invariably either. The flexibility of music-making enjoyed by a fine duo should be that of a marriage with both partners guiding each other through thick and thin. Sometimes one person must take the lead, sometimes the other.

This necessary incorporation of the singer's line, both music and words, into the pianist's head (and from there to the heart) applies to all accompaniments by all composers. In Schubert such techniques are rendered especially necessary by the naturalness and honesty of the music – there is no place to hide and every ensemble blemish and clumsiness is heard with merciless clarity. Indeed the transparency of Schubert's writing necessitates scrupulous care for texture, and this in turn demands from the pianist a great command of colour and touch, as well as an impeccable and subtly creative sense of rhythm. All fine accompanists have a sound of their own, very much like singers. Of course these are harder to identify than the distinctive timbres of singing voices, but there are a few seasoned radio listeners who can identify accompanists simply from the tone-quality coming from the piano. Selection of colour and texture, a very personal thing for every pianist, is also strongly affected by the use of the sustaining pedal. Gerald Moore told me that the older he got, the less he used the pedal in Schubert, and I now agree with him that the Schubert accompanist must develop the ability to play a beautiful, singing legato line without the help of the pedal. In Nikolaus Harnoncourt's conducting of the Schubert symphonies it is as if he were taking the metaphorical pedal away from the orchestral sound, revealing the composer's instrumental writing in its unvarnished colours – the antithesis of the interpretations of Karajan, for example. Gerald Moore had no guide like Harnoncourt, but as early as the 1950s he instinctively felt that if the real sound of Schubert was to be made under his fingers, it needed to be created and articulated at the keyboard rather than moderated by a wash of 'helpful' pedal, a softening of contours that achieves an easy warmth of tone at the expense of the composer's specific demands regarding articulation and phrasing, as well as his staccato and mezzo-staccato markings.

Many accompanists continue to employ the pedal almost indiscriminately in Schubert, but Charles Rosen in *The Romantic Generation* reminds us that its use as a default setting developed from about 1830 – two years after Schubert's death.[1] This one consideration makes a composer such as Schumann entirely different from Schubert in terms of pianism. There is surely more excuse to use the pedal in a Schubert work for solo piano than in a song where the singer contributes a seamless vocal legato that the pedal was invented to imitate in the first place. For the latter the accompanist needs to provide a more articulated, somewhat drier, often translucent texture by way of contrast. Of course the pedal remains an essential adjunct in Schubert song accompaniments in terms of colour and the creation of special moments of atmosphere and magic; nevertheless, the almost unthinking operation of the right foot practised by some pianists in every piece they play now sounds inauthentic to me in the Schubert repertoire. The daily practice of Bach preludes and fugues with all the necessary finger legato and melodic connectedness, as well as the clear voicing of contrapuntal entries, played with minimal pedal, is the best possible preparation for Schubert's song accompaniments. In this way the sound of the fortepiano of Schubert's time has inevitably played a part in how today's accompanist should address his works on a modern Steinway.

Mention of this large black instrument that almost exclusively dominates the concert platform raises questions of balance between voice and piano. When Gerald Moore was accused by Hermann Prey's wife of being too loud he replied soothingly that he always appeared to be over-loud for every wife's husband and every mother's son. A singer's voice is not easily swamped by piano sound, but the clarity of the singer's words can all too easily be impaired by insensitive playing. A more sparing use of pedal can often be helpful in rectifying this problem. In other respects balance – exactly how much piano sound seems appropriate in relation to the voice – is a matter of taste, and this in turn is governed by the musical zeitgeist. An indulgent mother would clearly prefer her son's singing voice to be trammelled with as little sonic competition as possible. From the 1980s the Wigmore Hall boasted a set of six black wooden blocks kept backstage; these were exquisitely graded from tiny to rather less tiny and were regularly employed in recitals to open the piano lid to various chink-like apertures. They were smaller alternatives to the smaller of the instrument's two sticks – the one that opens the piano lid to the modest height of nine inches or so. In recent years these blocks have more or less vanished from use: it is extremely rare to see anything less than the smaller stick at a recital, and increasingly often one hears the piano 'on the big stick', in other words fully open. This represents a change of fashion among the younger generation of singers who are less controlling, and less flustered, in this respect than their older counterparts.

Whether or not the big stick is a good idea depends on the player and his or her control of the instrument. Not every accompanist is equipped technically to handle this amount of sound in relation to the voice, and playing the piano in this way in a song recital is to possess a kind of advanced driving licence. But with a certain mastery of touch, it is possible to play more quietly with the larger stick than the smaller because quiet sounds from a fully open piano travel more directly into the hall (particularly in a venue with a fine acoustic like Wigmore Hall) than quiet sounds played on a half-closed instrument where care has to be taken that that the sound does not disappear altogether. I started playing regularly in recital with full stick in the 1980s because Isaac Stern, a famous stickler for balance, told my famous singer at a rehearsal in Finland that I should be permitted to do so. In those days Dame Margaret Price needed convincing, but in time she came to relish the full-toned support of the open instrument. The experience of recording many Schubert discs, always with full stick for technical reasons, contributed to my ease with the open lid. The worst motive for opening the piano to the full stick is a political one: a defiant gesture of pianistic equality with the singer.

[1] Charles Rosen, *The Romantic Generation* (1996), pp. 21–4.

A certain rancour has often been a factor in the relationship between singer and pianist. It has become fashionable, especially in the United States, to drop the word 'accompanist' in favour of 'collaborative pianist' (a phrase that unwittingly conjures connotations of the accompanist cooperating with the enemy – the occupying soloist perhaps!) The use of the new term over the last decades has not resulted in improved fees or working conditions, but perhaps it assuages hurt pride. A more meaningful step would have been to persuade all-powerful North American promoters that accompanists should receive separate contracts for their services rather than appearing on the singer's balance sheet as a deductible expense (in the USA singers' fees include their pianists; in Europe accompanists are usually contracted as individual artists in their own right). Mere terminology will never address problems such as these. The trouble is that if we qualify the simple word 'pianist' with the adjective 'collaborative' we cannot help but imply a sub-category of 'solo' or 'real' pianist; at the same time the impression is given that pianism is all there is to accompanying, whereas it is only one factor in a career that is a state of mind, a way of life and a calling. 'Collaborative pianist' fails, for example, to encompass the convivial and emotionally supportive aspects of the accompanist's métier. Gerald Moore never referred to himself as anything other than an accompanist, wearing his badge in a famously unashamed way.[1] Rather than shun the word because it might seem to indicate diminished status, it would make better sense to redefine it with a renewed pride for younger generations. The accompanist should celebrate, rather than apologize for, a state of mind and commitment that leads to a specialized and highly skilled life's work that is unlike any other career in music.

It is true that a pianist who plays large-scale works with instrumentalists would not today expect to be called an accompanist. It used to be the case, forty or fifty years ago, that every pianistic partner was referred to as such, whatever the work being played. In modern times those who specialize in playing sonatas, trios or other chamber music would properly be known as chamber-music pianists. It is common enough for aspiring accompanists to play both instrumental and vocal music in the earlier stages of a career, but by the time a player has achieved a significant reputation, he or she has almost always come to specialize in one or the other field. This is largely a question of temperament and inclination rather than a barometer of pianistic skill.

In some respects the chamber-music pianist faces more immediate technical challenges – it would be pointless to deny that Schubert's fiendishly difficult *Fantasie* for violin and piano is more taxing to the fingers than the piano writing of, say, *Die schöne Müllerin*. Even in Schubert's time, the pianists Karl Maria von Bocklet (1801–1881) or Josef Gahy (1793–1864) were assigned difficult chamber-music pieces such as the *Fantasie*, as well as solos, while the composer himself preferred to accompany the songs. (Schubert's friend Johann Baptist Jenger (1793–1856), however, a man of exceptional culture and humanity, became known in the Schubert circle as a fine accompanist.) It would be incorrect to imagine Schubert hoping that Bocklet and Gahy would play his songs (and feeling somehow too shy to ask) and it would be equally wrong to suppose that either of these players would have had the skill or experience to provide what was required in an essentially brand new medium of Schubert's own invention – if he was not the actual inventor of the lied, he was most certainly the pioneer of this kind of accompaniment.

Schubert played these piano parts not only because it was fun to do so, not only because he was technically able to cope with the pianistic demands, but because he, among all his contemporaries, was most able to encompass the music's literary and emotional challenges. As for the technical side of being a good accompanist, when a composer plays his own songs he will

---

[1] The book of musical tips and memoirs that made Gerald Moore's name as a writer was entitled *The Unashamed Accompanist* (1943); a third edition was printed in 1983 with a foreword by Geoffrey Parsons and an afterword by Graham Johnson.

doubtless inwardly sing the voice part as he plays (as advocated above) because it was he who invented the vocal line. Schubert united poetry and music to an extent undreamed of by his predecessors; he was fascinated by each of his chosen poets and he understood (as the settings make clear) the literary background. As part of his explorations of every volume of verse Schubert read around his texts – and this is something that pianists of today can also do to the advantage of their performances. The modern accompanist's challenge – no easy task – is to enter the mindset of the person who first played those accompaniments and to acquire a measure of the spark of inspiration and understanding that had given birth to the music in the first place. It is surely no coincidence that almost all the great song composers (Brahms, Wolf, Strauss, Fauré, Debussy, Poulenc, Britten) were said to have played their own accompaniments better than anyone else, and each of these composers had strong working relationships, and often close friendships, with the singers of their choice.

Schubert was the person who knew exactly what to do at the keyboard to get the best possible performance from his somewhat difficult-to-handle colleague, the baritone Johann Michael Vogl (*see* FRIENDS AND FAMILY, and SINGERS). Able to gauge the moods of the touchy retired opera star, Schubert in 1825 defines my ideal of a serious accompanist: someone with whom the singer will give a better performance than he might otherwise have done with a less skilled or experienced player. It was as much thanks to Schubert's pianism as to his compositions that Vogl's lieder-singing career (the first of its kind) took off in that wonderful tour of Upper Austria in the summer and early autumn of that year. The composer wrote to his brother Ferdinand from Gmunden on 12 September 1825: 'The manner in which Vogl sings and the way I accompany him, as though we were one at such a moment, is something quite new and unheard-of for these people.' The true accompanist is able to transmit his or her overall musical experience into playing that makes an audible difference along the way – cradling, inspiring, nudging, suggesting. It is this symbiotic bond that is almost never achieved in opportunistic pairings of singers and celebrity solo pianists – dextrous felicities in preludes and postludes can never replace the seasoned accompanist's capacity to pass on long-accumulated thoughts and understanding to a singer, and often without superfluous words or formal coaching.

What Schubert did was truly to accompany his chosen singers, not merely collaborate with them. Indeed, there is something of the goodness, kindness and companionableness of Schubert himself in the very word 'accompanist'. For me that word 'accompany' implies something of an ongoing personal investment; it is to make music without servility, but also without thin-skinned jostling for equal billing and equal pay. To accompany is to be in for the long haul. Schubert was a good companion on the concert platform, and not above humouring the vanity of those he played for. He listened, persuaded, taught, cajoled, encouraged, explained, advocated, unfolded the story, set up the atmosphere; he moved the music forward when appropriate, pulled it back when appropriate, transposed when necessary, accommodated the breathing. Above all, he clearly provided that ingredient of magic that can only materialize once everything else is safely in place. Schubert's skills in working with singers went far beyond how he executed the piano part per se. If it is impossible to calculate a conductor's charisma, effectiveness and humanity by referring only to his stick technique, it is also impossible to judge an accompanist on the way he plays the piano, *pur sang*.

Dame Janet Baker used to say that in a recital there could only be one captain of the ship, and that had to be the singer. Wise accompanists have to accept this – but on that floating dinghy, *The Recital*, so different from the luxury liner, *Opera*, the pianist must stand in for the rest of the crew: stage director, literary consultant or dramaturg, costume and lighting designer, backstage technician, prompt, pit orchestra and provider of 'props'. It was Schubert himself who first played all these roles, and it gradually became a requirement that his accompanists should show the same inexhaustible versatility.

In terms of money and appreciation there is indeed unfairness in the way many accompanists are treated. Would-be activists, usually young players who arrive on the scene and resolve to change it, may see in this situation an opportunity to take up the cudgels. It seems unkind gently to explain that teachers, nurses, carers, social workers are similarly taken for granted, and that among those professions will be found a similar proportion of great artists, gifted professionals, dutiful drones and hapless incompetents. The idea of an accompanists' guild has occurred to many people over the years, but apart from a unionized minimum wage (and such unions already exist for the truly exploited) there is no way adequately to legislate the relationship between singer and pianist. Indeed the very idea runs counter to the trust that should exist between musical colleagues when music-making is at its best. My own experience of playing Schubert's accompaniments is such that at the moment of performance nothing seems more important than ensuring that the joy of entering into the composer's world becomes something one might be allowed to experience again and again. To play the piano with the voice, for the voice, because of the voice, to help and enhance the singer using the singing voices of the piano keys – this is enough of a challenge for any one life, and it can be a happy destiny and an ongoing delight for the lucky few. On the other hand, if great music and the camaraderie of such team-work are not rewarding enough to compensate for the real risk of being underpaid, overlooked and frequently written off as a second-class musical citizen, it would be best to change career direction. That so many artists stay the course, come what may, has a great deal to do with Schubert's example and his own unflinching devotion to song throughout the vicissitudes of his life and career. There may be no one today who is his kind of composer, but there are very many who already are his kind of accompanist.

See also PEDALLING, PIANISTS, PIANOS, RUBATO, SINGERS, STROPHIC SONGS.

ADELAIDE   Adelaide
(MATTHISSON) **D95** [H33]
A♭ major   1814

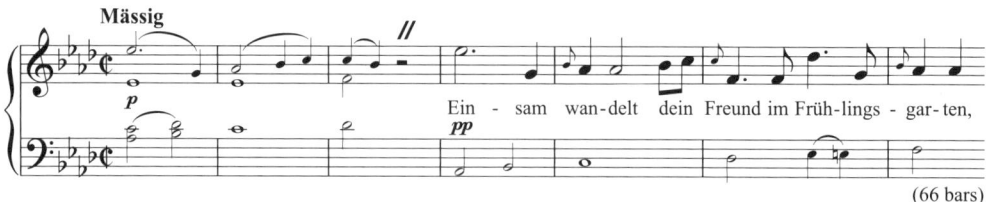

(66 bars)

Einsam wandelt dein Freund im Frühlingsgarten,	In solitude your lover walks in the spring garden
Mild vom lieblichen Zauberlicht umflossen,	Gently bathed in the lovely magic light
Das durch wankende Blütenzweige zittert,	That shimmers through the swaying branches in blossom,
Adelaide!	Adelaide!
In der spiegelnden Flut, im Schnee der Alpen,	In the mirroring waters, in the Alpine snows
In des sinkenden Tages Goldgewölke,[1]	In the golden clouds of the dying day,

[1] Matthisson writes 'Goldge*wölken*'.

Im Gefilde der Sterne strahlt dein Bildnis, Adelaide!	In the meadows of stars your image shines, Adelaide!
Abendlüftchen im zarten Laube flüstern, Silberglöckchen des Mais im Grase säuseln, Wellen rauschen und Nachtigallen flöten: Adelaide!	Evening breezes whisper in the tender leaves Silver bells of May rustle in the grass, Waves plash and nightingales sing: Adelaide!

Einst, o Wunder! entblüht auf meinem Grabe,
 	
Eine Blume der Asche meines Herzens;
Deutlich schimmert auf jedem
   Purpurblättchen:
Adelaide!
	One day, miraculously, a flower from the ashes of
	   my heart
	Shall bloom upon my grave;
	On every tiny purple leaf shall glimmer clearly:
	
	Adelaide!

FRIEDRICH VON MATTHISSON (1761–1831); poem written in 1788

This is the fourth of Schubert's twenty-nine Matthisson solo settings (1812–17). See the poet's biography for a chronological list of all the Matthisson settings.

Mathissson wrote this poem, first printed in Voss's *Musenalmanach* of 1790, inspired by an amateur performance in Switzerland of Voltaire's *Adélaïde de Guesclin* (1734). It is said that the poet was enamoured at the time with a maid of honour of Princess Louise of Dessau, Annette von Glafey (1778–1858). The poet had apparently chosen a woman's name for his poem that incorporated the word 'Adel' or noble. She and Matthisson had encountered each other in the service of their aristocratic patron when the poet was employed as Princess Louise's reader. Despite the difference in their ages the couple were said to have enjoyed an idyllic romance, but Annette's father forbad a relationship with an untitled suitor and she entered the Abbey of Mogiskau near Dessau where she eventually became Abbess. Many years later, at a concert to consecrate the opening of the new organ there (with Prince George of Dessau as the guest of honour), a tenor from the Dresden opera sang Beethoven's *Adelaide* as an encore and the old nun, at first shocked to hear again this poem that had been written for her decades earlier, stood up serenely and was moved to a smile of proud, triumphant joy. Another version of events, and perhaps more accurate, was that Annette's passion for Matthisson was scarcely reciprocated and that she retired into the religious order because she was disappointed by his coolness towards her, despite his earlier dedication to her of a number of his poems.

   Whether the anecdote is true or not, it illustrates the power of Beethoven's music on the listener. Schubert's setting of *Adelaide* has always been eclipsed by the older composer's Op. 46 – a substantial and vocally demanding composition loved throughout the world, and especially valued by tenors and their audiences (it was a Jussi Björling favourite), even those who otherwise have little interest in lieder. Matthisson himself, to whom Beethoven's setting was dedicated, praised the song lavishly at the expense of other settings (the poem was also set by such composers as Pilz and Righini) although there was ambiguity in the poet's endorsement when he said that Beethoven had placed the text deeply in the shade.

   Beethoven's miniature cantata in the Italian manner was published in the year Schubert was born, but it is not certain whether Schubert knew the work as early as 1814; in 1817 he told Josef Hüttenbrenner that he was reluctant to set the poem 'because he would have to write it exactly as Beethoven did'. By 1821, advertisements (almost certainly written with Schubert's collaboration) for the newly published *Gretchen am Spinnrade* Op. 2 proudly claimed that it was as 'original and inimitable' as Beethoven's *Adelaide* and Mozart's *An Chloe* and *Abendemp-findung*. Despite his declared admiration for the Beethoven setting, Schubert at seventeen heard different, more intimate things in the music of Matthisson's words. His song has the flexibility and scale of a personal statement; it is meant to be sung in the home, out of earshot of prince or countess. For Schubert, Adelaide is a real person, a young and graceful girl whom he might have known (or shyly wished to know), whose comely shape is not entirely hidden by eighteenth-century court dress. Einstein avers that the dividing line between classicism and romanticism lies between the two settings. The Beethoven work, for all the ardour of its opening 'Andante', loses something of its spontaneity in the repetitive formula of its 'Allegro con moto'; this echoes the classical grandeur of the opera seria of Mozart's time. But Mozart, on a completely different scale, nevertheless makes an appearance in Schubert's setting: the accompanimental figure of the first and last verses with its seven-note *gruppetto* ascending and then turning in on itself (as in bars 8 and 9) derives from his immortal song *Abendempfindung* which, like *Adelaide*, envisages love outlasting the ashes of the grave.

The new thing about this song, as far as Schubert is concerned, is the happy ability to illustrate depictions of the various workings of nature without interrupting the flow of melody, or compromising the essentially straightforward musical conception. The triplets of the accompaniment's middle section may derive from Beethoven's setting, but the vocal line is set in an entirely different manner. From the very first word 'Einsam' the music beneath shows we are no longer in Beethoven's company. Schubert's dotted minim for the first vowel, leading to a rueful descent of the stave, says more about the solitary state of the poet at the beginning of his plaint than Beethoven's happily ascending crotchets. While Beethoven digs deep into the line for the word 'lieblichen', Schubert lets his setting of the word tumble delightedly from the heights of the stave. These are only two examples among many that show that, here, Schubert was better attuned to the psychological significance of word setting.

In Verse 2 the accompaniment mirrors the 'spiegelnden Flut' in the bar following the words, while the voice part continues with another idea – a subtle canonic variant of illustrative music: one can see (and hear) the setting sun in two banks of descending round semibreves (bb. 24–5). The voice then launches itself into the starry meadows by means of a beautiful and unexpected modulation into G flat. The singer is given a high tessitura here, but not without poetic reason. In Verse 3 (still in G flat) we have breezes, bells, waves and nightingales. The murmuring triplets and the minims ringing out in the pianist's little finger are pressed into service to depict them all. This is the first instance of a song that unites evening and bells in Schubert's output, and the pianistic style of a much later song like *Abendbilder* D650 is already established here. Adelaide's name is sung twice at the end of the verse. In Beethoven's setting the poem's final verse is the cue for an extended allegro movement, but Schubert's last verse is a modest recapitulation of the music of the first. In the final bars, we hear 'Adelaide' three times (marked 'immer leiser und langsamer'); the dying fall of both vocal and bass lines brings the song to a hushed conclusion of murmured quietus.

Autograph:	Missing or lost
First edition:	Published as Book 42 no. 5 of the *Nachlass* by Diabelli, Vienna in 1848 (P363)
Subsequent editions:	Peters: Vol. 6/35; AGA XX 25: Vol. 1/69; NSA IV: Vol. 7/3; Bärenreiter: Vol. 5/102 (high voice) Vol. 5/96 (medium low voice)
Bibliography:	Capell 1928, pp. 32 & 83
	Einstein 1951, pp. 69–70
	Fischer-Dieskau 1977, pp. 29–30
	Reid 2007, pp. 34–7
Further setting:	Ludwig van Beethoven (1770–1827) *Adelaide* Op. 46 (1794–5)

Discography and timing: Fischer-Dieskau I 2[7] 2'36
Hyperion I 12[11]
Hyperion II 3[5] 2'58 Adrian Thompson

← *Don Gayseros III* D93/3 *Trost. An Elisa* D97 →

ADELWOLD UND EMMA Adelwold and Emma

(BERTRAND) **D211** [H105]
F major – B major (5–14 June 1815)

(608 bars)

[(. . . 2 . . .)] [(. . . 2 . . .)]

(1) Hoch und ehern schier von Dauer, A knight's castle, ancient and lofty,
Ragt ein Ritterschloss empor,— Towered up boldly;
Bären lagen an dem Tor Bears lay at the gate,
Beuteschnaubend auf der Lauer;— Snorting, awaiting their prey.
Türme zingelten die Mauer Turrets arose from the walls
Gleich den Riesen—bange Schauer Like giants; eerily the wind
Wehten brausend, wie ein Meer, Gusted from the fir-tops
Von den Tannenwipfeln her. Like the roaring sea.

(2) Aber finstrer Kummer nagte But black care
Mutverzehrend um und an Constantly gnawed away
Hier am wackern deutschen Mann, At the spirit of the valiant German knight
Dem kein Feind zu trotzen wagte;— Whom no foe dared defy.
Oft noch, eh der Morgen tagte, Often, before the morning dawned,
Fuhr er auf vom Traum, und fragte— He would awaken from his dream and ask
Jetzt mit Seufzer—jetzt mit Schrei: Now sighing, now crying out
Wo sein teurer Letzter sei? 'Where is my beloved youngest boy?'

(3) 'Vater! rufe nicht dem Lieben;'— 'Father, do not call to the dear boy,'
Flüstert einstens Emma drein— Emma now whispers,
'Sieh, er schläft im Kämmerlein 'See, he is asleep in his little room,
Sanft and stolz—was kann ihn trüben?' Gentle and proud – what can trouble him?'
'Ich nicht rufen?—sind nicht Sieben 'You ask me not to call? Have not seven
Meiner Söhn' im Kampf geblieben? — Of my sons died in battle?
Weint' ich nicht schon fünfzehn Jahr Have I not for fifteen years
Um das Weib, das euch gebar?' Mourned the woman who bore you?'

(4) Emma hört's—und schmiegt mit Beben Emma listens, and nestles,
Weinend sich an seine Brust.[1] Trembling and weeping, against his breast.

[1] Bertrand writes 'Weinend sich um seine *Knie*'.

'Vater!—sieh dein Kind!—ach früh
War dein Beifall mein Bestreben!' . . .[2]
Wie, wenn, Trosteswort zu geben,
Boten Gottes niederschweben—
Führt der Holden Red' und Blick
Neue Kraft in ihn zurück.

'Father, behold your child! Ah, since I was young
I have sought to win your approval'
And, as when God's messengers
Gently descend to bring words of comfort,
So the fair maiden's words and look
Give him new strength.

(5) Heiter presst er sie ans Herze:[3]
'O vergib, dass ich vergass,
Welchen Schatz ich noch besass,
Übermannt von meinem Schmerze! . . .
Aber—sprachst du nicht im Scherze—
Wohl dann! bei dem Schein der Kerze
Wandle mit mir einen Gang
Stracks den düstern Weg entlang.' . . .

Cheered, he presses her to his heart:
'O forgive me, that I,
Overwhelmed by grief, forgot
What treasure I still possessed!
But you did not speak in jest.
And now, by candlelight
Walk with me straightway
Along the dark path.'

(6) Zitternd folgte sie—bald gelangen
Sie zur Halle, graus und tief,
Wo die Schar der Väter schlief;—
Rings im Kreis' an Silberspangen
Um ein achtes hergehangen,
Leuchteten mit bleichem, bangen
Grabesschimmer fort und fort
Sieben Lämplein diesem Ort.

Trembling, she followed him; soon they reached
The deep and terrible vault
Where their forefathers slept:
Arranged in a circle, seven lamps
Hanging on silver brackets around the eighth
Illuminated this place constantly
With pale, troubled,
Sepulchral gleam.

(7) Unter'n Lämplein war's von Steinen . . .
Traun! erzählen kann ich's nicht . . .
War's so traurig zugericht,
War's so ladend ach!—zum Weinen . . .
'Bei den heiligen Gebeinen
Welchen diese Lampen scheinen'—
Ruft' er laut—'beschwör' ich dich
Traute Tochter, höre mich.

Beneath the lamps were stones . . .
Forsooth! I cannot relate it!
It was so mournful in appearance.
Such an invitation to weeping.
'By the holy remains
For which these lamps shine,'
He cries loudly, 'I entreat you
To hear me, beloved daughter.

(8) 'Mein Geschlecht seit grauen Zeiten
War—wie Rittersmännern ziemt—
Keck, gestreng' und fast berühmt;—
In des Grabes Dunkelheit[4]
Sank die Reih' von Biederleuten—
Sanken die, so mich erfreuten,—

Bis einst der Posaune Hall
Sie wird wecken allzumal.

'Since the misty past, men of my lineage
Have been bold, stern and renowned,
As befits knights;
Honourable men,
Whom I cherished,
Have one by one descended into the grave's
        darkness.
Until the day when the sound of the trumpet
Shall awaken them all.

(9) 'Nie vergassen deine Brüder
Dieser grossen Ahnen Wert;

'Your brothers never forgot
The merit of these great forebears.

[2] Bertrand writes '*sein* Bestreben'.
[3] Bertrand writes '*heisser* presst er sie ans Herze'.
[4] Bertrand writes 'Dunkel*heiten*'.

Reich und Kaiser schütz' ihr Schwert
Wie ein deckendes Gefieder;—
[(. . . 1 line . . .)]
Gib sie, Töchter, gib sie wieder
Mir im wackern Bräutigam,
Dir erkiest aus Heldenstamm! . . .

Their swords, like protective plumage,
Revered the emperor and his realm;
[(. . . 1 line . . .)]
My daughter, restore them to me
In the form of a valiant bridegroom
Chosen from a race of heroes.

(10)   'Aber Fluch!' . . . Und mit dem Worte—
Gleich als schreckt' ihn Nacht und
         Graus—
Zog er plötzlich sie hinaus
Aus dem schauervollen Orte;—
Emma wankte durch die Pforte:
'Ende nicht die Schreckensworte!—
Denk' an Himmel und Gericht!—
O verwirf, verwirf mich nicht!'

         'But a curse . . . !' And with these words,
As if stricken by darkness and horror,

He suddenly dragged her
Out of the fearful place . . .
Emma staggered through the gate:
'Do not finish your terrible words!
Think of heaven, of the Last Judgment!
Do not, ah do not reject me!'

(11)   Bleich, wie sie, mit bangem Zagen
Lehnt des Ritters Knappe hier;—
Wie dem Sünder wirds ihm schier,
Den die Schrecken Gottes schlagen,—
Kaum zu atmen tät er wagen,
Kaum die Kerze vorzutragen,
Hatte, matt und fieberhaft,
Seine Rechte noch die Kraft.

         As pale as the maiden, fearful and apprehensive,
The knight's squire lurks here;
He feels almost as a sinner
Struck by the terrors of God.
He hardly dares breathe;
His right hand, weak and feverish,
Scarcely has the strength
To carry the candle.

(12)   Adelwolden bracht als Waise[5]
Mitleidsvoll auf seinem Ross
Einst der Ritter nach dem Schloss
Heim von einer fernen Reise—
Pflegte sein mit Trank und Speise
Tät ihn hegen in dem Kreise
Seiner Kinder—oft und viel
War er tummelnd ihr Gespiel.

         Adelwold . . . the knight once took pity on him
As an orphan, and brought him on his horse
From distant parts
Home to his castle
He tended him with food and drink,
And raised him among
His own children—long and often
Did they romp about together.

(13)   Aber Emma . . . seine ganze
Zarte Seele webt' um sie . . .
War es frühe Sympathie?. . .
Froh umwand sie seine Lanze
Im Turnier mit einem Kranze—
Schwebte leichter dann im Tanze
Mit dem Ritter keck und treu,
Als das Lüftchen schwebt im Mai . . .

         But Emma . . . his whole tender soul
Wove around her;
Was it the first sign of love?
In the tournament she gaily
Crowned his lance with a wreath
And then she would dance
With the bold and true cavalier
More blithely than the wafting May breeze.

(14)   Rosig auf zum Jüngling blühte
Bald der Niedre von Geschlecht;—
Edler lohnte nie ein Knecht

         Soon the boy of lowly birth
Blossomed into a fine young man
Never did a vassal reward more nobly

[5] Bertrand writes 'Adelwold . . . Ihn bracht' als Waise'.

Seines Pflegens Vatergüte;—
Aber heiss und heisser glühte—
Was zu dämpfen er sich mühte,—
Fester knüpft' ihn fester ach!
An das Fräulein jeder Tag;—

The paternal kindness of his guardian.
But the feelings he sought to quell
Glowed more and more warmly
Each day, alas they bound him more
To the maiden.

(15)   Fest und fester sie an ihren

Süssen, trauten Adelwold . . .
'Was sind Wappen, Land, und Gold—

Sollt' ich Arme dich verlieren?
Was die Flitter, so mich zieren?
Was Bankete bei Turnieren?
Wappen, Land, Geschmuck, und Gold
Lohnt ein Traum von Adelwold!'

And she, too, became more and more closely
     bound
To her dear, sweet Adelwold.
'What do I care for a coat of arms, for land
     and gold
If I, poor maiden, should lose you?
What do I care for the finery that adorns me
For banquets at tournaments?
One dream of Adelwold is worth
A coat of arms land, jewels and gold!'

(16)   So das Fräulein—wenn der Schleier
Grauer Nächte sie umfing.
[(. . . 6 lines . . .)]

So mused the maiden, when the veil
Of dark nights enveloped her.
[(. . . 6 lines . . .)]

(17)   Doch mit eins—als Emma heute
Spät noch betet, weint und wacht,
Steht, gehüllt in Pilgertracht,
Adelwold an ihrer Seite:
'Zürne nicht, Gebenedeite!—
Denn mich treibt's, mich treibt's
     ins Weite;—
Fraülein, dich befehl ich Gott—
Dein im Leben und im Tod!

But this night as Emma stays awake,
Praying and weeping,
Adelwold all of a sudden appears
At her side dressed as a pilgrim.
'Do not be angry, blessed one,
For I am driven far from here!

Sweet maiden, God be with you!
I am yours in life and in death!

(18)   'Leiten soll mich dieser Stecken
Hin in Zions heil'ges Land—
Wo vielleicht ein Häuflein Sand
Bald den Armen wird bedecken . . .
Meine Seele muss erschrecken—
Durch Verrat sich zu beflecken
An dem Mann, der, mild und gross
Her mich trug in seinem Schoss.

'This staff shall lead me
Into the Holy Land of Zion,
Where, perhaps, a mound of sand
Will soon cover this poor man . . .
My soul recoils at the thought
Of being stained with the betrayal
Of the man who, in his kindness and greatness,
Took me to his bosom.

(19)   'Selig träumt' ich einst als Knabe,
Engel—ach vergib es mir —
Denn ein Bettler bin ich schier, —
Nur dies Herz ist meine Habe.'
'Jüngling—ach an diesem Stabe
Führst du treulos mich zum Grabe,—
Du würgest—Gott verzeih es dir!⁶
Die dich liebte für und für!'

'As a boy I once dreamed blissfully.
My angel – o forgive me,
For I am almost a beggar;
This heart is my only possession.'
'Sweet youth with this staff
You would faithlessly lead me to the grave
You would kill her – God forgive you –
Who would love you for ever!'

⁶ The 'Du' at the beginning of this line is Schubert's addition.

(20)   Und schon wankte der Entzückte—
        Als des Fräuleins keuscher Arm—
        Ach, so weiss, so weich und warm!
        Sanft ihn hin zum Busen drückte . . .
        Aber fürchterlicher blickte—

        Was ihm schier ihr Kuss entrückte —[7]
        Und vom Herzen, das ihm schlug,
        Riss ihn schnell des Vaters Fluch.

And already the enraptured youth wavered
As the maiden's chaste arm,
So white, so soft, so warm,
Pressed him gently to her breast . . .
But what her kiss had almost driven from
    his mind
Glared at him more terribly
And swiftly her father's curse
Tore him from the heart that beat for him.

(21)   [(. . . 3 lines . . .)]
        'Lindre, Vater, meine Wunde! . . .
        Keinen Laut aus deinem Munde!
        Keine Zähr' in dieser Stunde!
        Keine Sonne, die mir blickt!
        Keine Nacht, die mich erquickt!'

[(. . . 3 lines . . .)]
'Father, ease my pain –
There is no sound from your lips,
No tears at this hour,
No sun to gaze upon me,
No night to refresh me!'

(22)   Gold, Gestein und Seide nimmer—
        Schwört sie—fort zu legen an,
        Keine Zofe darf ihr nahn,
        Und kein Knappe—jetzt und nimmer;
        Oft bei trautem Mondesschimmer
        Wallt sie barfuss über Trümmer,

        Wild verwachsen, steil und rauh,
        Noch zur hochgelobten Frau.

She swears that henceforth
She will never don gold, jewels or silk;
Neither maid nor squire
May approach her, now and for ever more;
Often, by the moonlight she loved,
She goes, barefoot, on a pilgrimage, through
    ruins
That are wild and overgrown, steep and bleak,
To the revered Lady.

(23)   Ritter! ach schon weht vom Grabe[8]
        Deiner Emma Totenluft!
        Schon umschwärmt der Väter Gruft
        Ahnend Käuzlein, Eul' und Rabe . . .

        Weh dir! weh! an seinem Stabe
        Folgt sie willig ihm zum Grabe—
        Hin, wo mehr denn Helm und Schild
        Liebe, Treu' und Tugend gilt . . .

Knight! Ah, already the wind of death
Blows from your Emma's grave.
Already screech owls and ravens
Flock around your forefathers' tombs, sensing
    death;
Unhappy man! With his staff
She follows him gladly to the grave,
Where, more than helmet and shield,
Love, constancy and virtue are prized.

(24)   Selbst dem Ritter tät sich senken
        Tief und tiefer jetzt das Haupt;—
        Kaum dass er der Mähr noch glaubt:

        Seufzen tät er jetzt—jetzt denken,
        Was den Jüngling konnte kränken?—
        Ob ein Spiel von Neid und Ranken?—
        Ob?. . . Wie ein Gespenst der Nacht
        Schreckt' ihn—was er jetzt gedacht . . .

Even the knight now bowed his head
Lower and lower;
He hardly believed any longer in the frightening
    old tale,
He sighed, and wondered
What could be troubling the youth—
Was it envy and intrigue,
Was it . . . ? As from a nocturnal phantom
He recoils in horror from the thought that now
    struck him.

---

[7] Bertrand writes 'Was ihr Kuss ihm schier entrückte'.
[8] In Schubert's setting he reverses the order of Bertrand's strophes here marked 23 and 24 – thus 24, 23 in the poem as printed in *Beckers Taschenbuch*, 1799.

(25)   [(. . . 4 lines . . .)]]   [(. . . 4 lines . . .)]
       Hergeführt auf schwülen Winden,   Borne on the sultry winds,
       Muss ein Strahl die Burg entzünden,—   A flash of lightning must have set fire to the
                                                     castle.

       [(. . . 2 lines . . .)]   [(. . . 2 lines . . .)]

(26)   Tosend gleich den Wogen wallen   Roaring like the waves
       Rings die Gluten—krachend dräun   The flames rage all around pillars and arches
       Säul und Wölbung, Balk' und Stein,   Crossbeams and stones threaten straight away
       Stracks in Trümmer zu zerfallen;—   To crash down in ruins.
       Angstruf und Verzweiflung schallen   Cries of terror and despair echo
       Grausend durch die weiten Hallen:—   Horribly through the vast halls:
       Stürmend drängt und atemlos   Breathless, servant and squire
       Knecht und Junker aus dem Schloss.   Rush out of the castle.

(27)   'Richter! ach verschone!'[9]   'Lord my Judge! Ah, spare me!'
       Ruft der Greis mit starrem Blick—   Calls the old man, staring fixedly –
       'Gott!—mein Kind!—es bleibt zurück!—   'Lord! My child—she remains within!—
       Rettet—dass euch Gott einst lohne!—   Save her, may God reward you!
       Gold und Silber, Land und Frohne,   Gold and silver, land and farm,
       Jede Burg, die ich bewohne,   Every castle I possess—
       Ihrem Retter zum Gewinn—   All these shall be her rescuer's reward.
       Selbst dies Leben geb' ich hin für sie.'[10] I would even sacrifice my life for her.'

(28)   Gleiten ab von tauben Ohren   His distressed cries
       Tät des Hochbedrängten Schrei . . .   Fall on deaf ears;
       Aber plötzlich stürzt herbei,   But suddenly he appears—
       Der ihr Treue zugeschworen,—   The man who has vowed to be faithful to her.
       Stürzt nach den entflammten Toren,—   He rushes to the flaming gates,
       Gibt mit Freuden sich verloren . . .   And would gladly lose his life;
       Jeder staunend, fern und nah,   All are astonished, near and far,
       Wahnt' ein Blendwerk—was er sah.   Believing what they see to be an illusion.

(29)   Glut an Glut!—und jedes Streben   Flame upon flame! All efforts
       Schien vergebens! . . . endlich fasst[11] Seem in vain! Then, at last,
       Er die teure, süsse Last,   He holds his dear, sweet burden,
       Kalt, und sonder Spur von Leben;—   Cold and without trace of life;
       Doch beginnt ein leises Beben   But then, with a slight trembling,
       Herz und Busen jetzt zu heben,—   Her heart and breast begin to rise,
       Und durch Flamme, Dampf und Graus   And through flames, smoke and terror
       Tragt er glücklich sie hinaus.   He carries her safely out.

(30)   Purpur kehrt auf ihre Wangen—   Crimson returned to her cheeks
       Wo der Traute sie geküsst . . .   Where her beloved has kissed her . . .
       'Jungling!—sage, wer du bist—   'Sweet youth! Tell me in my distress
       Ich beschwöre dich—der Bangen:—   Who you are, I entreat you;

[9] Bertrand writes 'Richter! *Richter!* ach verschone!'.
[10] The words 'für sie' are Schubert's own clarifying addition to this line, in defiance of metre.
[11] Bertrand writes '*schier* vergebens'.

[(... 1 line ...)]
Hält ein Engel mich umfangen,[12]
Der auf seinem Erdenflug
Meines Lieben Bildnis trug?' ...

[(... 1 line ...)]
Am I embraced by an angel
Who, on his flight to earth,
Has assumed the form of my love?'

(31) Starr zusammenschrickt der Blöde,—
Denn der Ritter noch am Tor
Lauscht mit hingewandtem Ohr
Jedem Laut der süssen Rede ...
[(... 4 lines ...)]

The bashful youth is paralysed with fear,
For at the gate the knight
Listens with attentive ears
To every word of her sweet speech.
[(... 4 lines ...)]

(32) Doch den Zweifler tät ermannen

Bald des Ritters Gruss und Kuss,
Dem im süssesten Genuss

Hell der Wonne Zähren rannen:
'Du es?—du?—sag' an, von wannen?
Was dich konnt' von mir verbannen?[13]
Was dich—nimmer lohn' ich's dir!—
Emma wiedergab und mir?'

But the doubting youth's courage was quickly restored
By the knight's welcoming kiss;
Down the old man's cheeks streamed shining tears
Of joy and sweetest pleasure.
'Is it you? Tell me whence you have come.
What could have driven you away from me?
What has restored you to Emma and to me?
For this I can never reward you.'

(33) 'Deines Fluchs mich zu entlasten—
War es Pflicht, dass ich entwich[14]
Eilig, wild und fürchterlich[15]
Trieb's mich sonder Ruh und Rasten;—
Dort im Kloster, wo sie prassten,
Labten Tränen mich und Fasten—
Bis der frommen Pilger Schar
Voll zum Zug versammelt war.

'It was my duty to escape,
In order to release myself from your curse.
In fear I was driven onwards,
Swiftly, harshly and without respite.
In the monastery, where they feasted.
Tears and fasting consoled me
Until the band of devout pilgrims
Was assembled for the journey.

(34) Doch mit unsichtbaren Ketten
Zog mich plötzlich Gottes Hand
Jetzt zurück von Land zu Land
Her zur Burg;— [(... 4 words ...)]
Mein Teuerstes zu retten,—
Nimm sie, Ritter!—nimm und sprich
Das Urteil über mich.' ...[16]

But, with invisible chains
God's hand suddenly drew me
Back through one land after another
To this castle, [(... 4 words ...)]
To rescue my beloved!
Take her now, noble knight, and pronounce
Judgment on me.'

(35) Emma harrt, in düstres Schweigen,
Wie in Mitternacht gehüllt;—
Starrer denn ein Marmorbild,
Harren furchterfüllte Zeugen;
Denn es zweifelten die Feigen,

Emma waits, shrouded in a silence
As dark as midnight
More rigid than marble statues
The fearful onlookers wait.
For the fainthearted among them doubted

---

[12] Bertrand writes '*Jetzt* ein Engel mich umfangen'.
[13] Bertrand writes 'Was dich *tät* von mir verbannen?'.
[14] Bertrand writes 'Wer verdient ihn mehr als ich'. Schubert's changes make Adelwold sound less cocksure and self-righteous.
[15] The original reads '*Ging* ich ... wild und fürchterlich'.
[16] Bertrand writes '*Nun* das Urteil'.

	Ob den Ritterstolz zu beugen	That a noble heart alone,
	Je vermöcht' ein hoher Mut	Without wealth or ancestral glory
	Sonder Ahnenglanz und Gut.	Could ever bend the knight's pride.
(36)	'Dein ist Emma! . . . ewig dein!—	'Emma is yours, yours for ever! Thus heaven
	längst entscheiden[17]	
	Tät der Himmel,—rein wie Gold	Has long since decreed; you are deemed to be
	Bist du funden, Adelwold,—	As pure as gold, Adelwold,
	Gross in Edelmut und Leiden;—	And great in magnanimity and suffering;
	Nimm!—ich gebe sie mit Freuden!—	Take her! With joy I give her to you;
	Nimm!—der Himmel tät entscheiden;	Take her! Heaven has decreed it!
	Nannte selbst im Donnerlaut	In a peal of thunder, before angels,
	Sie vor Engeln deine Braut.	Heaven itself named her as your bride.
(37)	'Nimm sie hin mit Vatersegen!—	'Take her with a father's blessing!
	Ihn wird neben meine Schuld—	He who shall come one day to judge me
	Ach mit Langmut und Geduld!	Will by that blessing on the scales
	Der einst kommt, Gericht zu hegen,	Alongside my guilt—
	Auf die Prüfungswage legen—	May he show patience and forbearance!—
	Mir verzeihn um euretwegen,	And forgive me for what I have done to you;
	Der, von eitlem Stolz befleckt	For, sullied by vain pride,
	Beid' euch schier ins Grab gestreckt.'	I all but drove you both to the grave.'
(38)	Fest umschlungen jetzt von ihnen,	Warmly embraced by the pair,
	Blickt der Greis zum Himmel auf:	The old man now looks up to heaven:
	'Fröhlich endet sich mein Lauf!' . . .	'Thus my days end joyfully!'
	Spuren der Verklärung schienen	Transfigured happiness shone
	Aus des Hochentzückten Mienen—	From the youth's enraptured features,
	Und auf dampfenden Ruinen	And amid the smoking ruins
	Fügt' er schweigend ihre Hand	He silently took her hand
	In das langersehnte Band.	To seal the long-desired bond.

FRIEDRICH ANTON BERTRAND (1787–1830?); poem written in March 1798

This is the second of Schubert's two Bertrand solo settings (1815). See the poet's biography for a chronological list of the Bertrand settings.

In accompanying Dietrich Fischer-Dieskau on his Schubert lieder LP survey of the 1970s, Gerald Moore used as his working copies the ten large, brown and gold volumes of the AGA, the Schubert edition of the 1890s edited by Eusebius Mandyczewski. Moore's heavy tomes are full of pen and pencil markings (fascinating for later generations of accompanists) that betoken hard work at countless recording sessions. But Moore's copy of the twenty-seven pages of this ballad (in Volume 2 of that edition) is as free of spot and stain as Thomas Moore's 'virgin page' and as Emma herself. There could be no more eloquent evidence of the opprobrium heaped on this work (to call it a song is not to do justice to its length) than Fischer-Dieskau's decision entirely to ignore it. Despite the nineteenth-century enthusiasm for the work by Schindler and Kreissle (see NSA Vol. 8/XXIII–XXIV), the jury of more recent commentators had already implied a

---

[17] The words 'ewig dein!' are Schubert's own addition.

damning verdict by focusing on its tiresome length, a tradition continued by Reed, and by Fischer-Dieskau himself in his Schubert book. And of course there are other reasons for this prejudice. Firstly the clumsiness of the text would inevitably tire the patience of, or perhaps worse, amuse, German-speakers (the nearest contender for the longest song, *Der Taucher* D77, at least has an immortal text by Schiller). Schubert lavished ten days of his life on this piece in a year frantically busy with compositions; there is internal evidence in the autograph (as Walther Dürr points out in the NSA – where there is a facsimile of a revised page of the autograph, 8/XXXV) that the composer took this long over it because he had made extensive alterations to the work as he went along, discarding his crossings-out. To have finished this long ballad to his entire satisfaction was clearly important to him.

Maurice Brown and John Reed talk about the 'silent film' music of this piece, an interesting observation in that the silent film stands almost halfway between Schubert's time and ours, and is one of the last vestiges of the sort of melodrama that was so dear to Dickens for example and which dominated the nineteenth century. In Peter Ackroyd's words in his biography of that writer: 'What seems to us now stale, faded, sentimental and grotesque, then hit audiences with a fresh blast of life and truth. For of course every new "realism" eventually seems pale and thin, as "reality" itself changes its form.' In improvising music of this kind, the early film pianists were providing musical illustration in a tradition that in a way stretched back to Schubert, and which he would have understood.

Those who can find nothing special in the appearance on paper of this very long song might have already learned that a great deal of Schubert from this period looks uninteresting on the printed page. Emma's plaint of heartbreak (from b. 384), or the final music of reconciliation (from b. 591) may both be strophic passages, but Emma's music is fit for a languishing Mozartian heroine, and the closing hymn would not be out of place at the end of a passion play – clean-cut and unfussy in a style that reflects a very German idea of simplicity and chivalric goodness.

The first thing to note is that Schubert elected not to set the first two verses of Bertrand's poem – a sentimentalized, romantic variation on the minstrel's prologue invoking the spirit of that great balladeer Stolberg in front of the curtain. Wilhelm Müller, a vastly superior poet, wrote a humorous prologue (and epilogue) to *Die schöne Müllerin*, but Schubert also ignored these apologia and chose to plunge directly into the water music of the millstream and the miller's song of roving. The Heine-esque smile of irony was never Schubert's forte: he takes us to the heart of a story by empathizing with all his characters.

Verses 1–5: In the opening of this piece the poet uses a trick of the present-day cinema – plunging us into the middle of the story at a suitably arresting point (Verses 1–11), leaving the beginning of the narrative, or at least its background (Verses 12–15) to a flashback in the middle. The soap-opera aspect of Wagner's tetralogy (with its story recapitulations in case you missed the first episodes) also comes to mind. Another film trick, from Schubert this time, is the lack of overture, or in film terms opening titles (these seem to come much later); there is a peremptory chord of F major and music begins with a bleak and stark picture, the piano doubling the voice part. Triplets come into the music with the mention of water and wind (b. 13), but this castle, and the life within it, is unadorned, all is primeval German austerity. In this uncompromising male environment the feminine touch emerges with the voice of Emma whose pliant imploring music is reminiscent of the princess in *Der Taucher* D77, pleading with her tyrant father, the king. She is clearly the sole surviving child of this anguished, widowed knight. Life is as obtuse and unexplained in this kingdom as in the Allemonde of *Pelléas et Mélisande*. The knight has been dreaming of the youngest of his dead sons, and calling out for him in his sleep; the word 'Kämmerlein' refers to the burial chamber we encounter later in the poem. Emma's heartfelt lines, 'Father, since I was young I have sought to win your approval', set to ascending chromatic harmonies ('Mit wachsender Bewegung' from b. 53) are probably the ones that struck a chord with the composer. The knight's apology to his daughter is a mixture of recitative and almost unhinged intensity (a modulation into G flat major marked 'Mit steigender, schneller Bewegung' at b. 67, and a change into triple time) which does not bode well. According to Schubert's autograph the knight presses Emma to his heart 'cheerfully' ('heiter' as printed in the AGA), rather than Bertrand's 'more passionately' ('heisser'). The NSA (which usually stands by autograph readings) opts to correct the word to 'heisser' because the agitated patriarch is clearly anything other than happy at this point in the ballad.

Verses 6–7: The main characters established, we are now led into the bowels of the castle with music of labyrinthine meandering (from b. 89 the key changes from A flat minor to F sharp minor) and sinister syncopation ('Mässig, gehend'). In this music, and above all in the rising and falling F sharp minor phrases, there is an astonishing premonition of the second half of *Auf der Donau* (Mayrhofer, D553), another song that features old castles and warriors of yore. The seven lamps, one each to represent the knight's dead sons in the family mausoleum, are briefly described (the eighth reserved for the father himself), but the narrator suddenly finds himself unable to continue the morbid account, and recitative breaks into a ²⁄₄ aria (from b. 83).

Verses 8–9: Here the knight has a set-piece solo, tracing the noble lineage of his family in a proud B flat major polonaise ('Mit Würde' from b. 132), the dotted rhythm accompaniment holding the music back, like a proud warhorse reined in and pawing the ground. The last trump sounds in the pianist's left hand ('Posaune' is mentioned in b. 144), similar to its appearance in *Dem Unendlichen* D291 a few months later. The knight makes his cruel and unrealistic request that Emma marry a real hero, and begins to curse the interloper – any interloper, but including Adelwold of course – whose love for Emma will stand in the way of this plan.

Verses 10–11: At b. 162 panic-stricken ²⁄₄ music returns ('Eilig'); as in Verses 6–7 this has legato left-hand cellos, with pulsating wind-instrument quavers tongued on the offbeat. This music, in its dizzy chromatic sweep and breathless femininity, is uncannily prophetic of the flight of the tormented Viola in Verses 12–13 of the flower ballad of that name, D786. The figure of the unhappy Adelwold is introduced at the end of the verse to enable us to concentrate on his background, in effect a cinematic close-up, and the real beginning of the story, from the next verse.

Verses 12–16: In the manner of a straightforward Loewe ballad, events concerning Adelwold's history over a number of years are quickly covered (E flat major 'Mässig, erzählend' from b. 204). In this narrative style there is a suggestion of horn music, with quavers in a trusty ⁶⁄₈. (This Little Knight Music is appropriate enough for a Ritter in-the-bud.) As soon as Emma comes into the picture (Verse 13 from b. 218), the music blossoms into triplets and the vocal line lifts a semitone (at 'Aber Emma') as if her purity inspires a gaze heavenward. The weaving flourish on 'webt' (b. 211) is appropriate for this turn of events. Narration concerning the blossoming of a May-time romance between the pair inspires a vocal line of tendrils of high-flowering *fioriture*, tricky for any singer. We return to masculine duplets for Verse 14 and more of Adelwold's feelings, a quite deliberate decision to paint him in a steadfast manner. When he is described even thinking of Emma, however, the triplets (like a heart set a-flutter) and the flowing *bel canto* manner, return. In the middle of Verse 15, Emma's music breaks into recitative, brushing aside the prospect of money and finery (with a rather banal money-counting ascending chromatic line for 'Wappen, Land, Geschmuck, und Gold' bb. 259–60) in favour of the most beautiful thought of her lover, and a rapt cadence on the words 'Traum von Adelwold' (to rhyme with

'Gold' of course, bb. 265–6). The two lines of Verse 16 (Schubert cuts 6 lines of Bertrand here) return to the palpitation figure in the piano, this time with a 'Langsam' tempo, the pianist's hands still alternating on the keyboard as they depict feminine desperation (bb. 267–2). Emma's father-respecting suffering is reminiscent of that of Florence Dombey or Little Dorrit, a study for the delicate dejection of Minna in *Lieb Minna* D222 written a fortnight later. We can almost hear in this music the petite build of the heroine as she might have been depicted by 'Phiz'.

Verses 17–20: Enter Adelwold himself (G major, 'Etwas geschwind, mit Ausdruck', from b. 278) and the first of the set pieces in this ballad with the simplicity of a crusader's hymn, a genre to which Schubert was partial throughout his career, though rarely in ¾ as here. The controlled nobility of his aria breaks down under emotional stress, and we begin to glimpse some of the themes that perhaps attracted the composer to this poem – the desire to avoid doing his father dishonour at the same time as the need to leave home on a crusade of self-discovery. After one line of Verse 19 ('Geschwind'), Adelwold is interrupted by a single note on the piano (a high A, b. 307), as if the resonances of his precious childhood memories ('Selig träumt' ich einst als Knabe' in D major) have made time stand still, momentarily staunching the flow of his aria. Emma's hysterically climbing sequences (from b. 325, still 'geschwind' and now accompanied by scrambling pianistic triplets) respond to his decision to leave her. A moment of wild and unwise passion built around rising chromatic patterns in panting quavers and triplets (the symbolic mixing and merging of the two types of note value that have thus far characterized hero and heroine) is as near to sexual intercourse as we come in the entire story. Indeed, this passage is as 'full frontal' as we can find anywhere in the Schubert canon. Adelwold tears himself away only with the help of a rattling piano interlude (bb. 372–8). Schubert then builds in a further interlude, a bridge passage of portentous crotchets that denotes the passing of time, ushering in a cinematic close-up of Emma at prayer, this time imploring her heavenly father. (That there is some confusion as to *which* father she may be addressing is a further sign of Bertrand's ineptitude.) A short aria in A minor with plagal overtones ('Etwas langsam', from b. 373), with tolling left-hand octaves (five bars of an E pedal) sounds the knell of all her hopes. 'Keinen Laut aus deinem Munde' (bb. 375–6) – as if Emma somehow has been expecting God to speak directly to her – is Schubert's clumsy replacement-line for Bertrand's equally inept 'Keinen Laut aus Trösters Munde'. At least the poet's version casts God as the great bringer of consolation rather than a speaking presence.

Verses 22–4: This leads into a beautiful set-piece aria (from b. 394), prophetic of the plaint of the miller boy ('O Bächlein meiner Liebe' from *Der Neugierige* in *Die schöne Müllerin*). The music at the heart of this long ballad (marked 'Trauernd') is partly homage to the spirit of Mozart in the chromatic mood of his later piano music (the Rondo in A minor K511 comes to mind). There has been so much toing and froing that it is a relief at last to have what is, in effect, a strophic lament. Schubert here transposes the order of Bertrand's verses to keep the story of Emma's fading-away within one musical section. This also means that the end of Verse 24 makes a better transition into the music of pre-Wagnerian 'Götterdämmerung'.

Verses 25–9: This music ('Im Takte, schnell', from b. 426) is a little orgy of stirring of semiquaver oscillation and chromaticism. The knight's castle is hit by lightning (jagged descending triplets in bb. 426–7) – an event that even Bertrand seems to find humorous in lines that Schubert chooses not to set. But this is, after all, part of a grand melodramatic tradition. If harmonic coherence seems to give way in this section, it is appropriate that it should do so in the general panic, along with the pillars, arches and crossbeams of the castle. The extra words 'für sie' at the end of Verse 27 are the composer's addition, here showing less sensitivity to rhyme and metre than he was later to develop. Schubert equates the concept of pleas falling on deaf ears (Verse 28) with four solid bars of unchanging B flat rumblings (bb. 463–7), as if to be insensitive to modulation is to be as good as deaf. Adelwold the saviour appears with fanfares in manly quaver octaves; the change from F major to D flat (on 'endlich fasst / Er die teure, süsse Last', from b. 483) mirrors the suspense of his unlikely success in rescuing Emma. Her return to consciousness hinges on the enharmonic change between A flat in a seventh chord on B flat (b. 485), and G sharp in E major (b. 486 at 'Doch beginnt ein leises Beben') and the change from the unmeasured oscillations ('Taktlos') in the piano to the measured semiquavers of heartbeat and pulse ('Im Takte').

Verses 30–35: There has been such a lot of rattling $\frac{4}{4}$ that it is now a happy inspiration to introduce a sensuous $\frac{6}{8}$ passage (B flat major, 'Etwas langsam', from b. 498) with changes in harmonic colour, to depict the return of colour to the heroine's cheeks. This is a wonderful way to contrast external catastrophe with the internal reawakening of the body. Emma's rapt recitative (she seems to have been blissfully asleep, rather than asphyxiated by smoke) is perilously attenuated (encompassing a high B flat, b. 508). After the old knight has recognized Adelwold there is a measured and regal aria in E minor ('Mässig' Verse 33, b. 531), but it is a sign of Adelwold's new stature that it is he who now sings this authoritative music, while the father figure is reduced to the vagaries of recitative. At the beginning of Verse 35 a hushed modulation ('Recit. Schnell declamiert' b. 559) shows Emma's fear, and her suspense in waiting for her father's judgement.

Verses 36–8: Forgiveness is the outcome of course. There are some who would regard the ending of this ballad, three strophic verses from 'Dein ist Emma', as anticlimactic. But the music, in B major ('Mässig, mit Gefühl') is at once courtly and full of generosity. This positively Mozartian trait owes much to the countess's intervention and forgiving in the finale of the last act of *Le nozze di Figaro*. Something of the sacred sensuousness of *Idomeneo* also comes to mind. The impression of strength and tradition, both musical and personal, is absolutely intentional. It makes one realize again that the strophic solution in Schubert's case is no soft option. He is proud to have discovered a tune good enough to fit a number of strophes, and a tune worthy of repetition. Above all he is proud of the character of the ancient patriarch who has proved capable of transformation. Not only has the father figure forgiven Adelwold and Emma, but Schubert himself seems to have forgiven the former curmudgeon. The potential villain of the piece is now transformed, Scrooge-like, into a figure of wisdom and dignified joy. There could be no better indication of Schubert's hopes that the transfiguring power of his music could likewise change his own father, who doubted his musical future, into a loving supporter of his future career.

   This piece still awaits its first great interpreter on the concert platform, someone with story-telling virtuosity who is able to assume different characters and suggest different voices. A cleverly staged (or filmed) semi-staged performance with four voices (Narrator, Knight, Adelwold and Emma – thus three tenors and a soprano) would not be entirely against the spirit in which Schubert envisaged his drama-in-the-home.

Autograph:	Wienbibliothek im Rathaus, Vienna	
First edition:	Published as part of the AGA in 1895 (P566)	
Subsequent editions:	Not in Peters; AGA XX 79: Vol. 2/132; NSA IV: Vol. 8/70	
Discography and timing:	Fischer-Dieskau	—
	Hyperion I 10[10–13]	
	Hyperion II 7[1–4]	27'55 Martyn Hill

← *Die Liebe (Freudvoll und Leidvoll)* D210   *Die Nonne* D208 →

Illustration from W. G. Becker's *Taschenbuch zum geselligen Vergnügen*, 1799.

ADIEU! *see* DUBIOUS, MISATTRIBUTED AND LOST SONGS

Die ADVOKATEN

(ENGELHARDT) OP. 74, **D37** [H15]
G major   (25–7 December 1812)

The Advocates   Trio, TTB

adapted from the music of Anton Fischer

(200 bars)

1. Advocat:
Mein Herr, ich komm' mich anzufragen,
Ob denn der Herr Sempronius
Schon die Expensen abgetragen,
Die er an mich bezahlen muss.

1st Lawyer:
Sir, I've come to enquire
Whether Mr Sempronius
Has settled the costs
Which he must pay me.

2. Advocat:
Noch hab' ich nichts von ihm bekommen,
Doch kommt er heute selbst zu mir,
Da soll er uns nicht mehr entkommen,
Ich bitt', erwarten Sie ihn hier.

2nd Lawyer:
As yet I've had nothing from him,
But this very day he's coming to see me;
He'll not evade us any longer.
I pray you, wait for him here.

1. Advocat:
Die Expensen zu saldieren
Ist der Parteien erste Pflicht.

1st Lawyer:
To settle costs
Is the party's first obligation.

2. Advocat:
Sonst geht es neu an's prozessiren,
Und das behagt den meisten nicht.

2nd Lawyer:
Otherwise it will go back to court,
And most people don't like that.

Beide Advocaten:
O Justitia praestantissima,
Die, wenn sie manchem bitter ist,
Doch der Doktoren nie vergisst.

Both:
O Justitia praestantissima,
Who, if she is harsh to many,
Yet never forgets her initiates.

2. Advocat:
Jetzt trinken wir ein Gläschen Wein,
Doch still, man klopft,
Wer ist's? Herein!

2nd Lawyer:
Let's drink a glass of wine now.
But hush, someone's knocking . . .
Who is it? Come in!

Sempronius:
Ich bin der Herr Sempronius,
Komm grad' vom Land herein,
Die Reise machte ich zu Fuss,
Ich muss wohl sparsam sein,

Sempronius:
I'm Mr Sempronius,
Just arrived from the country;
I made the journey on foot.
I've got to be thrifty, you see,

Denn ich hab's leider auch probiert,
Und hab ein Weilchen prozessiert.

Beide Advocaten:
Mein Herr, wir supplizieren,
Die Noten zu saldieren.

Sempronius:
Ei, ei, Geduld, ich weiss es wohl,
Dass ich die Zech' bezahlen soll.
Nur eine Auskunft möcht' ich gern
Von ihnen, meine Herrn.

Beide Advocaten:
Sehr wohl, sehr wohl,
Doch dies Colloquium
Heisst bei uns ein Consilium
Und kommt ins Expensarium.

Sempronius:
Der Zucker und Kaffee,
Die Lämmer und das Reh,
Schmalz, Butter, Mehl und Eier,
Rosoglio und Tokayer,
Und was ich sonst darneben
Ins Haus hab' hergegeben,
Das rechnet man doch auch mit ein?

Beide Advocaten:
Nein, nein, nein, nein,
Das ist ein Honorarium,
G'hört nicht ins Expensarium,
Davon spricht uns der Richter frei,
Motiva, sind bei der Kanzlei.

Sempronius:
Ei, ei, ei, ei.

Beide Advocaten:
Wir lassen keinen Groschen fahren,
Der Himmel wolle uns bewahren,
Denn uns're Müh' ist nicht gering,
Fiat Justitia.

Sempronius:
Ei, ei, ei, ei
Kling, kling, kling, kling.

Alle:
O Justitia praestantissima,
Kling, kling, kling, kling

For unfortunately I have tried
To take legal action.

Both Lawyers:
Sir, we beg you
To pay our fees.

Sempronius:
All right, have patience; I know well
That now I have to foot the bill.
I'd just like to know one thing,
Gentlemen.

Both Lawyers:
Very well, very well,
But this coloquium
Is a consilium for us
And goes into the expensarium.

Sempronius:
Sugar and coffee,
Lambs and deer,
Fat, butter, flour and eggs,
Rosolio, and Tokay
And everything else
I've stocked up with at home
Should be counted in too.

Both Lawyers:
No, no, no, no,
That's an honorarium,
And doesn't belong with the expensarium,
The judge absolves us from that.
In Chancery there must be cause.

Sempronius:
Ei, ei, ei, ei.

Both Lawyers:
We let no farthing go –
May Heaven preserve us –
For we take no little trouble;
Fiat Justitia.

Sempronius:
Ei, ei, ei, ei
Clink, clink, clink, clink.

All:
O Justitia praestantissima,
Clink, clink, clink, clink

Welche schöne Harmonie,	What sweet harmony,
Kling, kling, kling, kling,	Clink, clink, clink, clink,
Welche schöne Harmonie,	What sweet harmony,
Allgemein verzaubert sie.	Bewitching everyone.
Von ihrem Reiz bleibt niemand frei,	From its charm none remains free.
Motiva sind bei der Kanzlei,	In Chancery there must be cause,
Kling, kling, kling, kling.	Clink, clink, clink clink.

KARL AUGUST ENGELHARDT (1768–1834)

During the Christmas holiday of 1812 Schubert busied himself with a piece whose merry good humour has won more admirers than its musical merits perhaps deserve; everybody tends to remember a piece of music that evokes the sound of money. The history of the work and its publication is rather complicated, and confusion has piled on confusion as more information has emerged over the years. Reinhard Van Hoorickx finally clarified the situation in an article in the *Revue Belge de Musicologie* (*see* Hoorickx 1976[2]).

Die Advokaten was originally composed by Anton Fischer (1782–1808, *see* COMPOSERS). It was published in 1804 by an obscure Viennese publisher, and disappeared utterly from circulation. Until fairly recently no one had seen the Fischer publication or knew its date. It was impossible to say whose work had come first (it was even postulated for a time that Fischer had stolen it from the schoolboy composer). There was disagreement as to whether the original work had been misattributed to Schubert, or whether it was indeed a complete reworking in the same way that Zumsteeg's ballads had been thoroughly 'Schubertized'. A copy of the Fischer trio has emerged in recent years and it is clear that Schubert's version is very different. Fischer's accompaniment is rewritten, the tempo indications are changed and the vocal line is completely reshaped. In 1827 Schubert revised his original reworking of *Die Advokaten*, and it was published in the version performed on the Hyperion recording. For some time there was considerable surprise that at the height of his powers Schubert should have bothered to publish a work manifestly inferior to the other songs of the late 1820s, and not entirely his own into the bargain. The fact is that the trio was popular and had been regularly performed in the Schubert circle for some fourteen years; it was published, it seems, by popular demand, although Maurice Brown believed that such a decision would not have come from the composer himself. In 1827 Schubert was encouraged to compose and prepare for publication another comic trio in G major (this time including a soprano) – the enchanting *Der Hochzeitsbraten* D930 with a text by Franz von Schober.

The comically self-important music says little of substance, but this could be taken as a witty match of musical means to poetic content, and a comment on the emptiness of legal jargon and the vacuous self-importance of the legal profession. Almost all the music pivots around G major, and is in *Singspiel* style. The piece is divided into three main numbers – a duet for the two lawyers, a trio that begins with the entry of their rustic client Sempronius and a concluding trio. These legal quacks are related to the notaries and lawyers of Mozart's operas (Curzio and Despina in disguise) and they bustle with busybody pomposity. One is reminded that the fashion for domestic trios with piano accompaniment began with the deliberate inanities of Mozart's comic trio, *Das Bandel* K441.

Autographs:	University Library of Lund, Sweden; Wienbibliothek im Rathaus, Vienna (first 30 bars)
First edition:	Published as Op. 74 by Diabelli, Vienna in May 1827 (P122)
Subsequent editions:	AGA XIX 1: p. 2; NSA III: Vol. 3

Bibliography: Brown 1966, pp. 244–7 (Brown discusses Franz Lachner's possible role in handing the manuscript to the publisher.)

Discography and timing:

Deutsche Grammophon *Schubert Terzette*	6'41	Peter Schreier, Horst Laubenthal & Dietrich Fischer-Dieskau
Hyperion I 12[4] Hyperion II 2[11]	7'22	John Mark Ainsley, Richard Jackson & Adrian Thompson

← *Serbate, o Dei custodi* D35/3   *Ombre amene, amiche piante (La Serenata)* D990f →

AESCHYLUS (525 BC–456 BC)

THE POETIC SOURCE
Vier Tragödien des Aeschylos übersetzt von Friedrich Leopold Grafen zu Stolberg, Hamburg, bei Friedrich Perthes, 1802

THE SONG
June 1816   *Fragment aus dem Aeschylus* D450 (translation by Mayrhofer, qv)

Franz von Hartmann's diary informs us that the illustrations to Aeschylus by Flaxman (*see* overleaf) were admired by Schober, Schwind and Bauernfeld on 19 December 1826, and that the Greek poet's *Prometheus Bound* was presented at Schober's reading circle on 2 February 1828.

Awarded the title 'Father of Tragedy' by the Greeks, Aeschylus was the first of the three great playwrights of Athens. Born in 525 BC, he was a soldier at the battles of Marathon and Salamis; his play *The Persians* thus recounts recent history of which he had been a part, rather than mythological legend. Of Aeschylus' ninety plays only seven have survived. *Seven against Thebes* cited the Amphiaraus legend that was used by Theodor Körner in a ballad set by Schubert (*Amphiaraos* D166). The *Oresteia* (458 BC) is probably his greatest work and the only extant trilogy of plays from a time when dramatic works were often theme-connected in groups of three. It recounts the events from the return of Agamemnon from Troy to the trial of Orestes. The first play, *Agamemnon*, tells of the old king's murder, *Choephori* or *The Libation Bearers* describes the vengeance of Orestes, and the last of the plays, *The Eumenides* or *The Well Wishers* (a euphemism for the Furies) describes Orestes' trial. Aeschylus effected certain important

reforms, staging his plays with enhanced realism, and it is recorded that the first entrance of the chorus of Furies (a group of twelve actors) in *The Eumenides* struck terror into the public of the time. After many centuries in obscurity, Aeschylus was rediscovered by the Romantics: Napoleon was enthralled by his work, as was Victor Hugo.

The song text for Schubert's *Fragment aus dem Aeschylus* D450 is Mayrhofer's reworking of Friedrich von Stolberg's translation from *The Eumenides* (*Vier Tragödien von Aeschylos*, Hamburg, bei Friedrich Perthes, 1802 pp. 268–9); it is significant that Mayrhofer never printed this paraphrase in his own poetic works – whole lines and phrases (such as Stolberg's 'Wenn an zerschmettertem Maste / Das Wetter die Segel ergreift') are lifted from the older poet's translation. Schubert's song was composed four years before Shelley established the influence of Aeschylus in mainstream English poetry with his epic poem *Prometheus Bound*.

The Furies pursue Orestes, engraving after John Flaxman from *Vier Tragödien von Aeschylos*, translated by Stolberg, 1802.

AL PAR DEL RUSCELLETTO (CANTATE FÜR IRENE KIESEWETTER)
(ANONYMOUS) **D936** [H656]
C major   26 December 1827

Cantata in celebration of the recovery from illness of Irene Kiesewetter

Quartet TTBB & choir (SATB) with piano duet accompaniment

Al par del ruscelletto chiaro
La tua vita scorra, Irene,
Compagne sian le grazie amene,
E l'amistà, virtù e fè.

Like a clear little stream,
Irene, may your life flow,
May your companions be the charming graces,
Friendship, Virtue and Fidelity.

Il suo rigor, le tue pene	May miserly fate
Serbi a noi soli'l fato avaro	Treat us alone harshly,
E sia per noi ancor più amaro	And be even more cruel to us,
Ond' esser prodigo conte.	So that it may be more bountiful with you.
Irene, dea della pace,	Irene, goddess of peace,
Conserva in lei tranquillo il cor	Preserve peace in her heart.
Del suo filial amor	May the torches of filial love
La face per lunga età,	Burn for a long time,
Risplenda ancor per lunga età.	And still longer.
Eviva dunque la bella Irene,	May beautiful Irene,
La delizia del nostro amor.	The delight of our love.

ANONYMOUS/UNKNOWN

Like the quartet for mixed voices, *Der Tanz* D826, this *pièce d'occasion* with piano-duet accompaniment is linked to the slightly enigmatic figure of Irene Kiesewetter (1811–72). She was the daughter of Raphael Georg Kiesewetter von Wiesenbrunn (1773–1850), the distinguished civil servant, musicologist and sometime singer (he had a bass voice). He had taken part in various performances of Schubert's music including the quartet *Geist der Liebe* D747 in 1823, and he was renowned for his collection of ancient choral music from the fifteenth to eighteenth centuries, chiefly in Italian. Italian singers (including the famous Luigi Lablache) were regular visitors to the Kiesewetter home (the virtuoso pianist Karl von Bocklet once improvised there on a theme given him by Lablache). Kiesewetter sometimes took it upon himself to organize entire concerts of music by composers such as Palestrina. In 1832 he published a history of music that was translated into English (with the title of *History of Modern Music in Western Europe*) and published in London in 1848.

The adolescent Irene, adored by her father, was a talented pianist. In a letter to Marie Pachler of 29 January 1828, Johann Baptist Jenger named Irene as 'one of the foremost pianists in Vienna', despite the fact that she was not yet seventeen years old. She was a piano-duettist partner with Jenger for Schubert's *Divertissement à la hongroise*, and an accompanist for that fine singer, Karl von Schönstein. She was thus obviously known to Schubert as a gifted young musician, and she appears to have admired him enormously too – her name is to be found on the subscribers' list for *Schwanengesang*.

It seems that Irene had been very unwell, but had recovered (Jenger's letter to Marie Pachler tells us as much). Schubert had already written *Der Tanz* for her (although the date of that piece is uncertain) and now he was persuaded to write this piece of music – possibly to celebrate her return to health – for very unusual forces – male quartet, mixed chorus and piano duet.

The anonymous text is in Italian. The music was clearly meant to be a surprise for Irene; thus she would have played no part in its performance, and it is almost certain that the piano duettists would have been Schubert himself and Jenger who was on close terms with the family. The modest vocal quartet that begins the piece (two tenors and two basses) might have included artists such as Tietze, Barth, Josef Götz and Lablache. The water imagery of the poem is nicely depicted by the flowing accompaniment that supports a mellifluous vocal cantilena for the four voices. Irene would have been delighted.

The quartet section arrives at a *pomposo* cadence on the dominant. One would think that the piece would soon come to an end but suddenly, with the words 'Eviva dunque la bella Irene', we hear the exciting sound of a four-part male chorus, no less. This must have astonished Irene, from whom the singers were no doubt initially hidden from view, perhaps waiting outside in the spacious Kiesewetter music room, before bursting in at the appropriate moment. And as if this was not enough, these forces are suddenly joined after ten bars by a chorus of sopranos and altos, turning the music into a veritable blazing finale à la Rossini.

The piece could not have been effectively performed without arranging for the whole of Domenico Barbaia's Italian company, or certainly the chorus, from the Kärntnertortheater to serenade Irene in this enchanting way (which further explains the need for an Italian text, rather than a German poem such as was used for the more modest *Der Tanz*). One can discern the extravagant hand of Lablache in a typically Italian celebratory plan, and also Schubert's practical side in providing music that is not difficult to read – thus easily learned – and yet highly effective in performance. The way that the music grows from a small stream into a mighty river is a real *coup de théâtre*, something planned as a one-off event requiring not a little preparation and subterfuge.

Irene lived until 1872. No one could have known, least of all the composer himself, that when this piece was performed on 26 December 1827, Franz Schubert had already celebrated his last Christmas.

Autograph:	Wienbibliothek im Rathaus, Vienna
First edition:	Published as part of the AGA in 1892 (P518)
First known performance:	26 December 1827 at Irene Kiesewetter's home, Salzgries (in the Hanswurstisschenhaus), 184 Vienna
Subsequent editions:	AGA XVII 15: p. 231; NSA III: Vol. 2a/177
Discography and timing:	Tom Raskin, Ashley Catling, Paul
	Hyperion I 36[17] 2'58 Robinson, Charles Gibbs & Holst
	Hyperion II 35[9] Singers, with Graham Johnson & Eugene Asti (piano)

$\longleftarrow$ *Der Kreuzzug* D932   *Der Winterabend* D938 $\longrightarrow$

ALBUMBLATT *see* DUBIOUS, MISATTRIBUTED AND LOST SONGS

ALFONSO UND ESTRELLA
(SCHOBER) **D732**
Late 1821–2

Schubert himself made piano arrangements of two arias from his grand opera of 1821. *See also* DUBIOUS, MISATTRIBUTED AND LOST SONGS for a note on *Die Wolkenbraut* D683, supposedly a solo song with a Schober text, but in fact Froila's Act II aria from *Alfonso und Estrella*.

I DOCH IM GETÜMMEL DER SCHLACHT   But in the tumult of battle
D732/8 [NOT IN HYPERION]
E♭ minor

(93 bars)

Doch im Getümmel der Schlacht,	But in the tumult of battle
Umrungen von Greuel und Blut,	Encircled by horror and blood,
Gab mir nicht Ehre und Macht,	I had neither honour nor power
Zu siegen den blitzenden Mut.	To defeat the foe's flashing mettle.
Nur deine süsse Gestalt,	Only your sweet image,
Die mir im Kampfe erschien,	Which appeared to me in the fray,
Zog mich mit Himmelsgewalt	Drove me with the force of heaven
Durch die drohenden Feinde dahin.	Through the threatening enemy.
Nur dein lächelnder Blick	Only your smiling glance
Gab mir die Stärke, den Sieg,	Gave me strength and victory,
Nur dein liebender Blick	Only your loving gaze
Gibt mir Belohnung und Glück.	Rewards me with happiness.

FRANZ VON SCHOBER (1796–1882); libretto written in 1821

This is the sixth of Schubert's fourteen Schober solo settings (1815–27). See the poet's biography for a chronological list of all the Schober settings.

Schubert arranged the piano score of this aria from *Alfonso und Estrella* (Act 1 No. 8) where it is preceded by a recitative exchange between the general Adolfo and the princess Estrella, daughter of King Mauregato. Adolfo, an unsympathetic character and bully, is enamoured of Estrella and this aria apprises her of the fact. She will soon fall in love with Alfonso, son of the unjustly exiled King of Leon, Froila (her father's enemy in fact), and is unable to return Adolfo's affection – to his fury. It is an effective set piece for heroic baritone – not overly subtle but bracing enough to find a legitimate place, with the help of a good pianist, within a recital framework where a vigorous interlude is required between two slower lieder of greater profundity. It is strange that the first four bars of the vocal line bear an uncanny resemblance to *Auf dem Flusse* from *Winterreise*, the common theme being obsession, through thick and thin, whether on ice or in battle. It is a pity that the character is not more sympathetic. The metronome marking of ♩ = 160 in the orchestral score must have been a slip of the pen on the part of Schubert's factotum of the time, Josef Hüttenbrenner. The correct tempo is ♩ = 106.

Autograph:	Staatsbibliothek Preussicher Kulturbesitz, Berlin
First edition:	Published in this form as 'Tief im Getümmel der Schlacht' in Vol. 42 of the series *Auserlesene Sammlung von Gesängen für eine Bass-Stimme* by Diabelli, Vienna in *c.* 1833 and subsequently as part of the NSA in 1988
Subsequent editions:	Not in Peters; Not in AGA; NSA IV: Vol. 14b/254
Discography and timing:	Fischer-Dieskau —
	Hyperion I —
	Hyperion II

II WENN ICH DICH, HOLDE, SEHE   When I see you, beloved

D732/13 [not in Hyperion]
C major

(46 bars)

Wenn ich dich, Holde, sehe,	When I see you, beloved,
So glaub' ich keinem Schmerz,	I can imagine no pain;
Schon deine blosse Nähe	Knowing that you are nearby
Beseligt dieses Herz.	Is enough to bring joy to my heart.
Die Leiden sind zerronnen,	The sorrows that once plagued my breast
Die sonst die Brust gequält,	Have melted away.
Es leuchten tausend Sonnen	A thousand suns light up
Der Lustentbrannten Welt;	A world inflamed with pleasure,
Und neue Kräfte blitzen	And new powers flare
Ins trunkne Herz hinein,	Into my intoxicated heart.
Ja, ich will dich beschützen,	Yes, I will protect you,
Ich will dein Diener sein.	I will be your knight.

FRANZ VON SCHOBER (1796–1882); libretto written in 1821

This is the seventh of Schubert's fourteen Schober solo settings (1815–27). See the poet's biography for a chronological list of all the Schober settings.

This is one of the arias that Alfonso sings to Estrella in Schubert's opera (Act 2 No. 13). Kreissle von Hellborn, the nineteenth-century biographer who pays most attention to the operas, dismisses this aria as 'commonplace' because it comes hard on the heels of a beautiful G minor duet ('Von Fels und Wald umrungen', no. 12). The music is certainly better than that, particularly if sung well by a high and agile tenor voice. The gently unwinding melismas suggest a character struck by love and beauty to the point of bemused intoxication, and the piano accompaniment from the composer's own hand adds an authentic and graceful touch. The difference between Schubert's arrangement of the accompaniment and the one newly arranged for the publication of the whole vocal score of *Alfonso und Estrella* in 1996 is revealing; the modern version by Catherine and David McShane is more faithful to the full score and its instrumental strands, but Schubert was prepared to abandon many such details in favour of an unfussy, playable piano part. This so-called *Cavatine* was published by Diabelli (and thus also the Peters Edition) in the transposed key of B flat major. If indeed this was first issued in a collection by Diabelli of bass-voice songs and arias, as stated in the NSA, the publisher must have had many dissatisfied customers – even in this lower tonality the music is far too high for any bass voice. In fact the Peters transposition remains a sensible adaption for any but the highest and most accomplished tenors. In the key of B flat it would suit a singer capable of a good performance of, say, *Der Neugierige* from *Die schöne Müllerin*. With its accompaniment of genuine Schubertian provenance, such an aria could find a place within any mixed group of lieder on the recital platform.

Autograph:	Staatsbibliothek Preussicher Kulturbesitz, Berlin
First edition:	Published in this form as 'Cavatine' in Vol. 43 of the series *Auserlesene Sammlung von Gesängen für eine Bass-Stimme* by Diabelli, Vienna, *c.* 1833 and as part of the NSA in 1988
Subsequent editions:	Peters: Vol. 6/132; Not in AGA; NSA IV: Vol. 14b/261
Discography and timing:	Fischer-Dieskau —
	Hyperion I —
	Hyperion II

ALINDE   Alinda
(ROCHLITZ) OP. 81 NO. 1, **D904** [H609]
A major   January 1827

(120 bars)

Die Sonne sinkt in's tiefe Meer,	The sun sinks into the deep ocean,
Da wollte sie kommen.	She was due to come.
Geruhig trabt der Schnitter einher,	Calmly the reaper walks by.
Mir ist's beklommen.	My heart is heavy.
'Hast, Schnitter, mein Liebchen nicht gesehn?	'Reaper, have you not seen my love?
Alinde, Alinde!' —	Alinda! Alinda!'
'Zu Weib und Kindern muss ich gehn,	'I must go to my wife and children,
Kann nicht nach andern Dirnen sehn;	I cannot look for other girls.
Sie warten mein unter der Linde.' —	They are waiting for me beneath the linden tree.'
Der Mond betritt die Himmelsbahn,	The moon enters its heavenly course,
Noch will sie nicht kommen.	She still does not come.
Dort legt der Fischer das Fahrzeug an,	There a fisherman lands his boat.
Mir ist's beklommen.	My heart is heavy.
'Hast, Fischer, mein Liebchen nicht gesehn?	'Fisherman, have you not seen my love?
Alinde, Alinde!' —	Alinda! Alinda!'
'Muss suchen, wie mir die Reusen stehn,	'I must see how my crab nets are,
Hab' nimmer Zeit nach Jungfern zu gehn,	I never have time to chase after girls;
Schau, welch einen Fang ich finde!'	Look what a catch I have!'
Die lichten Sterne ziehn herauf,	The bright stars appear,
Noch will sie nicht kommen.	She still does not come.
Dort eilt der Jäger in rüstigem Lauf,	The huntsman rushes swiftly past.
Mir ist's beklommen.	My heart is heavy.
'Hast, Jäger, mein Liebchen nicht gesehn?	'Huntsman, have you not seen my love?
Alinde, Alinde!' —	Alinda! Alinda!'

'Muss nach dem bräunlichen Rehbock gehn,   'I must go after the brown roebuck,
Hab' nimmer Lust nach Mädeln zu sehn,   I never care to look for girls;
Dort schleicht er im Abendwinde.' —   There he goes in the evening breeze!'

In schwarzer Nacht steht hier der Hain;   The grove lies here in blackest night,
Noch will sie nicht kommen.   She still does not come.
Von allen Lebend'gen irr ich allein,[1]   I am the only living soul around,
Bang und beklommen.   Anxious and troubled.
'Dir, Echo, darf ich mein Leid gestehn: 'To you, Echo, I confess my sorrow:
    Alinde'—Alinde,   Alinda!' Alinda!
Liess Echo leise herüberwehn;   Came the soft echo;
Da sah' ich sie mir zur Seite stehn: Then I saw her at my side.
'Du suchtest so treu: nun finde!' —   'You searched so faithfully. Now you find me.'

JOHANN FRIEDRICH ROCHLITZ (1769–1842); poem written in 1804

This is the third of Schubert's four Rochlitz solo settings (1812–27). See the poet's biography for a chronological list of all the Rochlitz settings.

There were very few occasions when Schubert succumbed to outside pressure regarding the selection of texts, but this seems to have been one of them. Rochlitz was a powerful figure, one of the foremost musical journalists of the time. As founder of the *Allgemeine musikalische Zeitung* in Leipzig his good opinion was of great importance to a young composer. On more than one occasion his paper's critiques of publications of Schubert's music had been favorable, certainly more so than some of the other German (as opposed to Viennese) reviews. The publisher Tobias Haslinger, a friend of Beethoven and a man sophisticated in the way of musical politics, obviously believed that it would be no bad thing for Schubert to choose poems by Rochlitz for musical composition. The resulting songs (the texts taken from Rochlitz's six-volume *Auswahl des Besten aus Friedrich Rochlitz' sämmtlichen Schriften*, 1822) were duly dedicated to the poet and hurried into print scarcely before the ink was dry. The gap between the dating of the manuscript, January 1827, and its publication (May of the same year), represents a quick turnaround in terms of publishing. The wording on the title page is significant: 'Dedicated by the publisher to the creator of these poems . . . in highly esteemed friendship'. In November 1827 Rochlitz, while thanking the composer in a letter for the three settings, seemed greedy for an even closer connection. He proposed that Schubert set a poem of his entitled *Der erste Ton*, having the temerity to take the composer through the musical process step by step in his letter, more or less instructing him line by line as to how the piece should be composed. Schubert's reply was predictably cool, and nothing came of the project.

Alinde is a song that is as interesting as it is famous; at this late stage of his career everything that Schubert touched could turn to gold. The poem, which is wooden and bereft of any genuine emotion, seems to have been selected, *faute de mieux*, because of the musical possibilities inherent in the echo effect in the last verse. The composer is meanwhile content to provide us with a textbook example of the modified strophic song. It is this that makes it such a challenge to the singer's memory in live performance: from verse to verse there is much that is the same, and much that is subtly different. The rhythm of the barcarolle gently insinuates itself from the beginning; as the first line of the poem makes clear this is water music as well as a nocturne.

[1] Rochlitz writes 'Von all*em* Lebend'gen irr ich allein'.

We will rediscover exactly this veiled erotic mood in the Heine setting *Das Fischermädchen*, another § barcarolle. The accompanist plays a six-bar (or four if the opening two bars of strumming A major chords are discounted) ritornello by way of *Vorspiel*. This music serves as an interlude between the verses on three occasions, and as a coda; each of these pianistic appearances is unmodified – although very little else in the song remains unchanged.

The different characterizations of reaper, fisherman and huntsman are a challenge for an imaginative singer. The vocal line is built employing the simplest harmonic means. Schubert can always conjure up a tune from nowhere. Two phrases of interlocking downward arpeggios ('Die Sonne sinkt . . . in's tiefe Meer') are answered by an echo from the dominant back to the tonic ('Da wollte sie kommen'). This latter phrase is marked 'leise' (softly); the following phrase ('Geruhig trabt der Schnitter einher') is marked 'stärker' (louder). It is clear that the composer considers the whole song an exercise in echo technique, with contrasting loud and soft phrases. (We will find these contrasting indications – 'leise' and 'stark' – written above the stave in another song from the same year – *Rast* from the infinitely more profound *Winterreise*.) The music moves from the tonic into the subdominant minor as the singer interrogates various men as to whether they have seen his beloved. This D minor section remains musically unaltered throughout the song. Crushed grace notes in the pianist's left hand suggest the masculine urgency of the singer's quest. The cry of 'Alinde' is first harmonized in B minor moving to F sharp major. The dismissive reply of the reaper offers scant comfort to the concerned enquirer; the return to A major is as leisurely as it is inevitable. A bargain seems to be have been struck in this song: we hear many bars of very simple harmonic progressions in exchange for striking harmonic unpredictability in the middle of each strophe.

The second verse is a conversation with the fisherman. Time has moved on since the first verse: there the sun was sinking, here the moon is already in the sky. The cry to Alinda is now subtly modified to exclude B minor harmony in favour of F sharp major. Why? There seems to be no reason other than Schubert's whim of the moment – as well as his determination to avoid harmonizing the girl's name in F sharp minor. In the third verse the conversation is with a hunter; one may ask what brings this figure to the seaside, but a poet like Rochlitz revels in all the poetic clichés without compunction. The rising of the stars occasions a lift in Schubert's vocal line (at 'Sterne ziehn herauf') rather than the familiar descent of the singer's arpeggio. This is a reversal of what has been established in the previous strophes and typical of Schubert's quixotic (and inspired) approach to setting this poem. The cries of 'Alinde' return to the pattern of the first verse, but the music for the hunter's reply is modified; this is in a lower vocal register, hinting at a slyer (and perhaps more sexually suggestive) response to the singer's questions.

At the final verse it is the dead of night. Rochlitz may have intended a pun with the use of the imagery of the dark grove – the word 'Hain' recalls 'Freund Hain', a nickname for death. There are no more workers on the beach or in the forest. For the first time we hear the name Alinde three times – the first two exclamations are marked 'stark', the third 'leise', a classic echo effect. Here is a chance for a good singer to provide a moment of enchantment with the second 'Alinde' in ravishing *mezza voce*. The actual arrival of the girl on the scene is the singer's final reward, although it seems both perfunctory and unbelievable in terms of the poem. The last line of the text ('Du suchtest so treu, nun finde') is repeated (unlike the clinching lines of the previous verses) as if Echo were still playing a part in the proceedings. Rochlitz seems to have been rather pleased with 'Nun finde' as a rhyme for the girl's name.

Autograph: Wienbibliothek im Rathaus, Vienna
First edition: Published as Op. 81 no. 1 by Tobias Haslinger, Vienna in 1827
                     (P128)

Dedicatee:	Friedrich Rochlitz (dedicated by Haslinger)
Publication reviews:	*Münchener allegemeine Musik-Zeitung*, No. 1 (6 October 1827), col. 8 [Waidelich/Hilmar Dokumente I No. 530; Deutsch Doc. Biog. No. 955]
	Allgemeine musikalische Zeitung (Leipzig), No. 4 (23 January 1828), col. 49ff. [Waidelich/Hilmar Dokumente I No. 569; Deutsch Doc. Biog. No. 1014]
	Berliner allgemeine musikalische Zeitung, No. 20 (14 May 1828), p. 157f. [Waidelich/Hilmar Dokumente II No. 613a]
	Allgemeiner Musikalischer Anzeiger (Vienna), No. 22 (16 May 1829), p. 77 [Waidelich/Hilmar Dokumente I No. 727]
Subsequent editions:	Peters: Vol. 2/154; AGA XX 287: Vol. 4/257; NSA IV: Vol. 4a/18; Bärenreiter: Vol. 3/14
Bibliography:	Capell 1928, p. 128
	Fischer-Dieskau 1977, p. 247
Discography and timing:	Fischer-Dieskau I 9[5] 3'41
	Hyperion I 6[14]
	Hyperion II 32[16] 4'44 Anthony Rolfe Johnson

← *Zur gute Nacht* D903   *An die Laute* D905 →

ALLES UM LIEBE   All for love
(KOSEGARTEN) **D241** [H132]
E major   27 July 1815

Was ist es, das die Seele füllt?
Ach, Liebe füllt sie, Liebe!
Sie füllt nicht Gold noch Goldes Werth;
Nicht, was die schnöde Welt begehrt,
Sie füllt nur Liebe, Liebe!

Was ist es, das die Sehnsucht stillt?
Ach, Liebe stillt sie, Liebe!
Sie stillt nicht Titel, Stand noch Rang,
Und nicht des Ruhmes Schellenklang;
Sie stillt nur Liebe, Liebe!

[. . . 5 . . .]

What is it that fills the soul?
Ah, it is love!
Not gold, nor the worth of gold,
Nor the desires of this base world.
Love alone fills the soul!

What is it that stills our longing?
Ah, it is love.
Not titles, status or rank,
Nor sounding fame.
Love alone stills our longing!

[. . . 5 . . .]

Und wär' ich in der Sklaverei,	If I were in slavery
In freundeloser Wildniss,	In some cheerless wilderness,
Und wäre Dein, nur Dein gewiss,	Yet were only sure of your constancy,
So wäre Sklaverei mir süss,	Slavery would be sweet to me,
Und Paradies die Wildniss.	And the wilderness paradise!
Und hüllte Todesfinsternis	And if the darkness of death
Dich, meines Lebens Sonne,	Shrouded you, sun of my life,
Und stürb' ich nur von Ihr gemeint,	And if I died cherished,
Von Ihr geklagt, von Ihr beweint,	Mourned and lamented by you alone,
So stürb' ich wohl mit Wonne.	Then I would die in bliss.
Viel besser ist's, jung, kräftig, kühn	It is far better to die in the arms of love,
Im Arm der Liebe sterben,	Young, vigorous and bold,
Als ungeliebt und liebelos	Than to grow old and decline,
In dumpfer Freuden mattem Schoss	Unloved and loveless,
Veralten und verderben.	In the lap of weary, faded joys.

LUDWIG THEOBUL KOSEGARTEN (1758–1818)

This is the thirteenth of Schubert's twenty-one Kosegarten solo settings (1815–17). See the poet's biography for a chronological list of all the Kosegarten settings, as well as a discussion of Morten Solvik's Kosegarten Liederkreis and this song's place within it.

This is one of several Kosegarten settings in E major (the others are D229, D230, D233 and D240); it seems that Schubert paired this tonality with the poet's emotional world, searching how best to combine the fervour and simplicity of an older literary style with a new musical vocabulary. Zumsteeg's setting (1800) is in the key of A major and is composed in common time, as opposed to Schubert's ⅜. In Zumsteeg's song, barlines fall on 'Sie füllt nicht <u>Gold</u>, noch Goldes <u>Werth</u>' as opposed to Schubert's 'Sie <u>füllt</u> nicht Gold, noch <u>Gold</u>es Werth'. Whether the poem's metre best suits triple or duple time may be debated, but Zumsteeg's rather four-square and earthbound setting fails to achieve the floating rapture of Schubert's. Textual differences between the two songs (Zumsteeg's 'die öde Welt', Schubert's 'die schnöde Welt') suggest that Book 1 of the older master's *Kleine Balladen und Lieder* was not to hand as Schubert composed. One has a very different impression about *Nachtgesang* D314 composed three months later.

The introduction shows the composer astride two stylistic worlds. The chromaticism of the opening two bars heralds romanticism (indeed these bars remind us of the opening of the much later song *Geheimes* D719) while the courtly ornamented cadence of the two following bars re-establishes a classical manner (although these have a hidden romantic effect, the trill symbolizing the heart a-flutter at the very thought of love). The poem asks a question ('What is it that fills the soul?') which is answered in a phrase that suggests inspired revelation ('Ah, it is love!'). In Schubert's setting the music treats this question as more or less rhetorical. The change of harmony on 'Liebe' is enough to introduce a new colour; instead of dissecting the workings of love in a stiff alternation between hackneyed question and answer, the singer is carried away by the music. The delicacy of the setting is reinforced by a number of tiny but effective touches: the mezzo staccato chords throughout which seem to tread softly so as not to disturb the lover's dreams; the beautiful suspension that provides a note of yearning on the second 'Liebe' in each verse; the pompous little arpeggio which is good for the pedantic 'Goldes Werth' in the first verse, but even better to depict the vain emptiness of 'Titel, Stand noch Rang' in the second.

The 'scoring' of the charming six-bar postlude (strings, plus oboe and bassoon perhaps) reinforces the impression that this little lied would sound well as an aria for Claudine in the opera *Claudine von Villa Bella* (cf. *Liebe schwärmt auf allen Wegen* D239/6) begun on 26 June 1815, the day before *Alles um Liebe* was written.

There are ten strophes in this poem – these are all printed in the AGA. Given here are 1, 2 and 8, 9 and 10. The Hyperion Edition selected 1, 2 and 8 for the recording. Three strophes seem sufficient in performance, but the last two verses of the poem are also included here because they show Kosegarten at his most passionate.

Autograph:	Österreichische Nationalbibliothek, Vienna
First edition:	Published as part of the AGA in 1894 (P571)
Subsequent editions:	Not in Peters; AGA XX 104: Vol. 2/212; NSA IV: Vol. 8
Discography and timing:	Fischer-Dieskau I 4²⁰ 1'48
	Hyperion I 20⁹
	Hyperion II 8¹⁵ 3'05 Patricia Rozario
Further setting:	Johann Rudolf Zumsteeg (1760–1802) *Alles um Liebe* (*Kleine Balladen und Lieder*, Book 1) (1800)

← *Huldigung* D240   *Winterlied* D242a →

Die ALLMACHT (I)   Omnipotence
(Pyrker) Op. 79 no. 2, **D852** [H572]
C major   August 1825

(94 bars)

'Gross ist Jehova, der Herr! denn Himmel
   und Erde verkünden
Seine Macht! — Du hörst sie im brausenden
   Sturm, in des Waldstroms
Lautaufrauschendem Ruf, in des grünenden
   Waldes Gesäusel;[1]
Siehst sie in wogender Saaten Gold,
   in lieblicher Blumen
Glühendem Schmelz, im Glanz des
   sternenbesäeten Himmels!
Furchtbar tönt sie im Donnergeroll, und
   flammt in des Blitzes
Schnellhinzuckendem Flug; doch kündet
   das pochende Herz dir

Great is Jehovah, the Lord! For heaven and earth
   proclaim
His might. You hear it in the roaring storm,
   in the loud, surging cry
Of the forest stream; you hear it in the rustling
   of the greenwood,
You see it in the golden, waving corn,
   in the glowing lustre
Of the lovely flowers, in the sparkling, star-
   strewn heavens;
It echoes terrifyingly in the rolling thunder, and
   flames in the lightning's
Swiftly flickering flight; but your beating heart
   will reveal

[1] Schubert repeats 'Du hörst sie' before 'in des grünenden Waldes Gesäusel'.

Fühlbarer noch Jehova's Macht,   Still more palpably the power of Jehovah,
  des ewigen Gottes,[2]   the eternal God,
Blickst du flehend empor und hoffst auf   If you gaze up in prayer and hope for grace
  Huld und Erbarmen.'[3]   and Mercy.

JOHANN LADISLAUS PYRKER (1772–1847); poem completed before 1821

This is the second of Schubert's two Pyrker solo settings (1825). See the poet's biography for a
chronological list of the Pyrker settings.

The long summer holiday that Schubert took with the singer Vogl in 1825 had a profound effect upon him. The shortness of his life denied him the opportunity to visit such countries as Italy, and even Germany (his forays outside Austria consisted solely of two working summers on Count Esterházy's Hungarian estate at Zseliz). Thus it is no surprise that the composer responded fervently to the spectacular scenery of Upper Austria.

Kreissle von Hellborn tells us that the song was composed in Bad Gastein. *Die Allmacht* reflects a discovery of a new and grander scale in nature, and the 'Great' C major Symphony D944 was conceived at the same time. The similarities of tone and mood between that mighty work and this song in the same key have played some part in finally dating the symphony to the summer of 1825, long a matter of scholastic contention. The composer was at last feeling well and confident again after two years of illness, and his journey through the region was not only the first lieder tour ever undertaken by two artists (Schubert accompanied Vogl along the way in various concerts), but something of a royal progress. It was clear that Schubert's reputation had gone before him, and music lovers of Upper Austria capitulated to the spell of his compositions.

One of the many distinguished people whom Schubert encountered at this time was his old acquaintance Ladislaus Pyrker (he was far too elevated in the state hierarchy to be counted a friend). Schubert had first met Pyrker in 1820 at the home of Matthäus von Collin. A formidable grandee of the church, Pyrker had been patriarch (and ruler) of Venice since 1819 and thus was, needless to say, one of the most hated men in the Austrian-occupied Veneto. In 1821 he had been the dedicatee (at his own request) of Schubert's Op. 4 songs, including the famous *Der Wanderer* D489. As part owner of the Bad Gastein resort he played the summer role of squire, or its Austrian equivalent, and Vogl and Schubert were welcomed there under his aegis. Pyrker, a man with an enormous ego, might have proposed that some of his own writings should be set to music. Perhaps Schubert, prompted by Vogl, was diplomatic enough to request the privilege.

The composer's letters home were expansive and lyrically descriptive; after two years of illness it seems he was fired by rekindled energy. In a way *Die Allmacht* occupies a similar place in the composer's output to the Mörike setting *Der Genesene an die Hoffnung* in Wolf's: both are paeans of praise to the Creator, or the muse – hymns of thanks for the creative power that each composer felt brimming up after a period of depression and setback. To voice this gratitude Schubert asks for something that is not often required in his lieder: a large and sumptuous voice – a voice to cry the message of these rolling hexameters to the heavens. (For the literary background to this poem, including its Old Testament origins, *see* the poet's biography.)

The piano's introduction, in tonality and turn of harmony, is prophetic of the introductory pages of the String Quintet D956. As with the symphony, the musical worlds of 1825 and 1828 somehow join hands, as if the fields of the future were visible from the dizzy mountain heights. The song's accompaniment has a density and grandeur that is not often found in the lied. The

[2] Pyrker writes 'des *unendlichen* Gottes'.
[3] Pyrker writes 'und hoffst *der Erbarmungen Fülle*'.

singer (usually a soprano) must be able to ride the torrent of piano sound with ease; the surprisingly wide-ranging vocal line soars heavenward. The pulsating triplets, these massive chords tending to be Schubert's response to any appearance of mountain imagery (as Leo Black has pointed out) resound almost ceaselessly through the song. The influence of Beethoven is discernible here.

The effect is monumental and dramatic, but the threat of bombast is defused at various crucial quieter moments, notably at the sudden change of mood at bb. 28–9 ('Du hörst sie in des grünenden Waldes Gesäusel'), a passage marked 'piano' that continues for some eight bars. There is a non-recurring middle section ('Furchtbar tönt sie im Donnergeroll' b. 53) where the piano's left hand is unleashed from its triplets to thrilling effect with a succession of whirlwind thunderings. Contemplative music returns at bb. 58–9, and again at bb. 69–80, where the initially implacable triplets serve to illustrate the humble entreaties of mankind. Rhythmic unity and harmonic diversity seek to bind man and nature, all things weak and powerful, all things great and small. In creating a song of considerable majesty Schubert has refused to sacrifice *Innigkeit*. The song's challenge to the singer, and one that is seldom satisfactorily met, is the incorporation of both qualities – a smaller voice can easily sound over-parted, a bigger voice thrilling but insensitive.

The repetition of the first lines of the poem at the end of the song (marked 'Mit Kraft' – with strength) is a magnificent culmination. The arresting progression from C major to the subdominant, F major, thence to G flat major (the flattened supertonic of the subdominant), followed by a glorious vocal and harmonic stretch that carries us into D minor (a high A in the vocal line) and thence back to C major via a 6-4 cadence provides a mighty peroration. After another appearance of the music that opens the String Quintet the song ends, against expectations, in the hushed awe of a piano dynamic.

A good performance of *Die Allmacht* would probably have been beyond the amateur singers of Schubert's acquaintance; he must have had in his ears the heroic voices of some of the great opera artists he had heard – Anna Milder Hauptmann, perhaps, who was capable of taking on Gluck's Iphigenia and Beethoven's Leonora. Nevertheless, the singer who was available to sing his songs, particularly on that Austrian holiday in 1825, was Johann Michael Vogl, a baritone. Another version of the song, printed in Volume 3b of the NSA (and described as the first version of the song in the Deutsch catalogue), is in the lower key of A major; it was clearly intended for Vogl and much else is changed besides the tonality. Walther Dürr has pointed out un-Schubertian details about this arrangement (for instance the piano writing in bb. 18–19), suggesting that Vogl himself might have reworked the song, ironing out difficulties in the original that were uncongenial to him. This adapted version (or 'Veränderung') is no fewer than seven bars longer: the singer has been given – or given himself – breathing space and recovery time between difficult phrases, something that he asked of Schubert in *Erlkönig*. On that occasion the composer obliged, and the adaption passed into immortality; in this instance we are far less sure about the validity of the alterations. Although it is something of a curiosity, this version remains a possibility for the singer of today who feels overstretched by Schubert's original demands, and who might benefit from its concessions [*see* ORNAMENTATION].

Autograph:	Missing or lost
First edition:	Published as Op. 79 no. 2 by Tobias Haslinger, Vienna in May 1827 (P124)
Dedicatee:	Johann Ladislaus Pyrker von Felsö-Eör
Publication reviews:	*Allgemeiner musikalische Zeitung* (Leipzig), No. 4 (23 January 1828), col. 49f. [Waidelich/Hilmar Dokumente I No. 569; Deutsch Doc. Biog. No. 1014]
	Allgemeine Musik-Zeitung (Offenbach), No. 26 (29 March 1828),

col. 208 [Waidelich/Hilmar Dokumente I No. 607; Deutsch Doc. Biog. No. 1070a]

Allgemeiner musikalische Anzeiger (Vienna), No. 12 (21 March 1829), p. 46 [Waidelich/Hilmar Dokumente I No. 711]

First known performance: 26 March 1828 at the Musikverein, Vienna as part of the Schubert 'Privatkonzert'. Soloist: Johann Michael Vogl (see Waidelich/Hilmar Dokumente I No. 603 for full concert programme)

Performance reviews: *Allgemeine musikalische Zeitung* (Leipzig), No. 19 (7 May 1828), col. 307f. [Waidelich/Hilmar Dokumente I No. 613; Deutsch Doc. Biog. No. 1067]

Abend-Zeitung (Dresden), No. 141 (12 June 1828), p. 564 [Waidelich/Hilmar Dokumente I No. 620]

Allgemeine musikalische Zeitung (Berlin), No. 27 (2 July 1828), p. 215 [Waidelich/Hilmar Dokumente I No. 624; Deutsch Doc. Biog. No. 1069]

Subsequent editions: Peters: Vol. 2/150; AGA XX 479: Vol. 8/128; NSA IV: Vol. 3a/158 & Vol. 3b/255 ('Veränderung'); Bärenreiter: Vol. 2/178

Bibliography: Black 2003, pp. 123–5 (The connection between this song and the A flat major Mass D678 is discussed.)

Capell 1928, pp. 213–14

Dürr, Introduction to NSA IV Volume 3, pp. XXVI–XXVIII

Fischer-Dieskau 1977, pp. 216–18

Youens 2002, pp. 190–201

Arrangements: Arr. Franz Liszt (1811–83) for tenor, male chorus and orchestra (1871) [*see* ORCHESTRATIONS]

Arr. Max Spicker (1858–1912) for choir and orchestra (1903) [*see* ORCHESTRATIONS]

Discography and timing: Fischer-Dieskau II 7⁹   4'27

Hyperion I 5⁹

Hyperion II 30⁹   4'54   Elizabeth Connell

← *Das Heimweh* D851   *Fülle der Liebe* D854 →

Die ALLMACHT (II)   Omnipotence   Chorus

(PYRKER) **D875A** [H584]
(Fragment) C major   January 1826

Gross ist Je-ho-va der Herr!

(122 bars)

See previous entry for poem and translation

JOHANN LADISLAUS PYRKER (1772–1847); poem completed before 1821

This piece of music, more or less unknown and seldom performed, comes as a surprise even to the avid Schubertian. The mighty solo song which is a setting of the same text is a mainstay of the repertoire for bigger voices (*Die Allmacht* D852); indeed, it is such an accepted masterpiece that one wonders why Schubert wished to return to the poem five months later to make a second, albeit very different, version. The work has something of a chequered history. It was first mentioned in 1865 (and wrongly classified as a male quartet) in the work list compiled by Schubert's first biographer, Kreissle von Hellborn. For a brief time the manuscript was in the possession of the Viennese conductor Johann Herbeck, and then it was lost. It surfaced in 1952 in a private library in Slovakia and has since been placed in the Bratislava City Library. The version recorded for the Hyperion Schubert Edition – a reconstruction and completion of the work by the late Reinhard Van Hoorickx and Dietrich Knothe, conductor of the Berliner Singakademie – was given its first performance in 1978.

The autograph consists of a full score only until b. 34 (the sixth line of the poem as printed above). Thereafter, the vocal line is complete until b. 119 (and the composer has filled in the text only until b. 99). There is a page missing in the middle of the work (a fact not noted in the Deutsch catalogue which is also inaccurate elsewhere in its description of the fragment). There are five further passages filled in; these relate to crucial interludes for the piano where Schubert has noted his exact thoughts. The whole autograph is a fine example of the composer's working method when in a hurry to complete a work for a specific occasion. (We note something similar in the fragment *Gesang der Geister* D705.) It is clear that the composer could have produced a full score from these sketches with minimum time and effort. In fact, in his own mind, he no doubt regarded the work as complete.

The celebratory key is the same as that of the poem's solo setting. The relationship to the closing fugal section of *Mirjams Siegesgesang* D942 is no accident. Both compositions describe the mighty workings of the Lord, and both derive from passages in the Old Testament where music takes on a visionary and exalted role. In this choice of tonality suitable for trumpets and fanfares, Schubert owes a great deal to the example of earlier composers, such as Handel, and the whole piece deliberately adopts the 'old' or 'learned' style, *pomposo* and effectively written for the choral forces. The 'surging cry of the forest stream' brings forth piano writing that leaps upwards with digit-twisting vigour, but it is not until b. 32, and the first mention of the 'grünenden Waldes Gesäusel', that we hear something incontrovertibly Schubertian – rustling piano writing of the greatest delicacy that sets off a similar weaving between the voice parts. This provides a wonderful contrast to the opening music of hammered conviction. The reconstructed piano writing by Van Hoorickx for the later thunder-and-lightning imagery is less effective because it seldom strays from dutifully doubling the (genuine) vocal line. The gently throbbing 'pochende Herz' section takes its cue from the earlier lilting passagework, and the recapitulation is self-evident. The greater part of the vocal line of the closing fugato is the composer's own work. He would probably have provided more daring and independent piano writing for this passage, but in his absence it was perhaps a wise decision made by the editors to opt for simple effectiveness. The final bars are perhaps the least convincing of the completion.

Although this choral version of *Die Allmacht* is not the composer's greatest work for chorus and piano, it is a worthy study for *Mirjams Siegesgesang* and a welcome reminder of Schubert's command of the choral style.

Autograph:	Státny Archiv, Bratislava, Slovakia
First edition:	Completed by Reinhard Van Hoorickx and Dietrich Knothe in 1978 (privately published) and subsequently published (as an incomplete fragment or sketch) in the NSA in 2006 (P845)

Subsequent editions: Not in AGA; NSA III: Vol. 2b/350
Discography and timing: Hyperion I 31[1]
                           Hyperion II 31[7]   6'42   Holst Singers (dir. Stephen Layton)

← *Mondenschein* D874   *Mignon und der Harfner ('Nur wer die
                                         Sehnsucht kennt')* D877/1 →

Der ALPENJÄGER   The Alpine huntsman
(MAYRHOFER) OP. 13 NO. 3, **D524** [H337]

The song exists in three versions, the third of which is discussed below:
(1) January 1817; (2) Zseliz, summer 1818?; (3) appeared December 1822

(1) 'Froh und frei'   E major   §   [76 bars]

(2) 'Lebhaft'   D major   §   [Vocal line in bass clef, 78 bars]

(3) F major

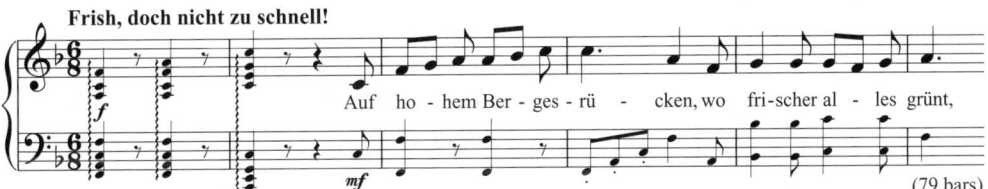

Auf hohem Bergesrücken,   High on the mountain ridge
Wo frischer Alles grünt,   Where everything is greener and fresher,
In's Land hinabzublicken,   The huntsman delights
Das nebelleicht zerrinnt—   In gazing down at the landscape
Erfreut den Alpenjäger.   Veiled in mist.
Je steiler und je schräger   The more steeply the paths
Die Pfade sich verwinden,   Wind upwards,
Je mehr Gefahr aus Schlünden,   The more dangerous the precipices,
So freier schlägt die Brust.   The more freely his heart beats

Er ist der fernen Lieben,   And he thinks more blissfully
Die ihm daheim geblieben,   Of his distant beloved
Sich seliger bewusst.   Who remains at home.

Und ist er nun am Ziele: And when he reaches his goal
So drängt sich in der Stille   A sweet image fills his mind
Ein süsses Bild ihm vor;[1]   In the stillness;
Der Sonne goldne Strahlen,   The sun's golden beams
Sie weben und sie malen,   Weave and paint a portrait of her
Die er im Tal erkor.   Whom he has chosen in the valley.

---

[1] Mayrhofer writes 'Ein süsses *Bildnis* vor'. For an explanation of the background to these alternative Mayrhofer readings
see Editorial Note at the beginning of Johann MAYRHOFER.

JOHANN MAYRHOFER (1787–1836)

This is the sixteenth of Schubert's forty-seven Mayrhofer solo settings (1814–24). See the poet's biography for a chronological list of all the Mayrhofer settings.

This huntsman is not to be confused with the more serious song of the same title to a Schiller text, D588. It is a jolly piece, dated January 1817, with which Schubert began an important year of song composition. This type of genre poem had long been popular and was employed by the greatest poets. Pastoral excursions (as in the Goethe songs *Schäfers Klagelied* D121 and *Jägers Abendlied* D368) evoke an eighteenth-century nostalgia for freedom from the rigours of city life; rustic characters of different occupations and trades are assigned lyrics that can be touching and wise, a practice that goes back to Shakespeare. This poem describes a huntsman, rather than allowing the huntsman to speak for himself (as in Goethe's best work in this manner). Perhaps this is why Capell, in his book of 1928, was not convinced by the song: for him the Alpine huntsman is 'the merry Swiss peasant of German chromolithography'. The song, together with chromolithography itself (the illusion of early colour photography), now strikes us as a picturesque souvenir of a happier and more innocent age. Among the thousands of hearty ditties and quasi-folksongs composed around similar themes by long-forgotten composers, it is Schubert's music that endures.

If Capell finds the song ridiculous, he admits that 'no one else would have done so irresponsible a thing half as well'. From the muggy depths of the Viennese hothouse such an open-air life must have seemed attractive to the poet, for a moment or two at least. Certainly we feel that Mayrhofer's projected alpine world is straightforward and *manly* (like Hemingway perhaps a sign of a guilty inner struggle – the ultra-masculine poem *Der Schiffer* D536 is another example of this). The subtext goes something like this: 'rather than the perils facing me in my own life, give me perilous mountain precipices any day; give me the security of an emotional relationship of picture-book normality and sweetness; give me, in short, an uncomplicated life'. The repeated entreaty 'Give me', though not actually part of this poem, occurs in a long Mayrhofer song that Schubert was to compose in 1818 – *Einsamkeit* D620; there the poet plaintively constructs an extended shopping list of the type of solitary, contemplative existence that he would like to have, far from the life of the big city.

Der Alpenjäger is prophetic of the exile of the poet Johann Senn, intimate of the Schubert circle who was unfortunate enough to be singled out and punished for his political views. In 1820 Senn was ordered back to his native Tyrol where one of his few freedoms was to contemplate life from as many mountain ridges as he pleased. It was as if he were bound to a rock like the unfortunate Prometheus. This punishment which removed him from his circle of friends, and the artistic interchange that nourishes all writers, effectively extinguished Senn's creative abilities. When Mayrhofer wrote this poem, Senn's cruel exile lay in the future; but in 1817 it is clear that the huntsman's life embodies the poet's fantasies of physical and mental freedom – impossible dreams for the free thinker who worked as a censor for the police state.

The opening chords are strummed in carefree manner and Schubert chooses a rhythm suitable for a bracing Arcadia. The unusual tempo marking seems influenced by thoughts of mountain air; this is counterbalanced with the moderating 'doch nicht zu schnell' as if to remind us that this is no elfin song – a strapping body and muscular thighs are contained within these lederhosen. The opening aria is simple in a manner that only Schubert can carry off. He can deliberately restrict harmonic variety without impoverishing his character; rather the reverse. The music is largely grounded in tonics and dominants, and it is no doubt this 'oom pah pah' aspect of the music to which Capell objected; but in-built banality seems entirely suitable for the painting of a man whose eyes traverse vast vistas but whose imagination is limited; we salute his solidity of spirit rather than the power of his brain. The contour of the vocal line moving up and down the stave, and occasionally plunging the octave, suggests the physical movements of a sure-footed climber, and these intervals also tell us that he can yodel into the next valley when necessary. The accompaniment employs the thirds and sixths typical of horn music, and an echo is built into the music: after 'In's Land hinabzublicken' (bb. 7–8) the descending F major arpeggio on that last word is mirrored a beat later by the piano, and the rollicking sixths (which begin after 'Das nebelleicht zerrinnt') bounce back and forth between the piano's middle and high registers as if horn fanfares were reflected back to us at different pitches. The same integrated echo effect in different registers can be heard in another Mayrhofer song written in the same month – *Schlaflied* D527.

The middle section in F minor is marked 'Ein wenig langsamer' in Peters, though not elsewhere. Friedlaender may have taken it upon himself to add this to the score – a very rare intervention on his part if so – because the 'Wie oben' marking at b. 56 (changed to 'Tempo I' in Peters) seems to imply a *minore* middle section at a slower tempo. If the joy of the huntsman in his work is simple, so is his unhappiness; indeed it is almost childlike in its sense of desolation. At 'Er ist der fernen Lieben, / Die ihm daheim geblieben / Sich seliger bewusst' (from b. 27) everything in this music is lovesick with plaintive echoes between voice and piano that border on petulance. It is here, if anywhere, that we can detect an affectionate chuckle on the composer's part. Despite all his bravery and bluster, when it comes to love the huntsman is a big baby. At b. 35, before 'Und ist er nun am Ziele', throbbing triplets are introduced into the piano; the left hand takes up the drooping motif that has already been heard in the treble register; this takes on the character of a mournful horn obbligato resonating through the mountainous terrain. The huntsman seems to be trying to communicate with his faraway love in the time-honoured fashion of alphorn messaging.

It is then that we hear the most authentic Schubertian touch: at 'So drängt sich in der Stille' (b. 39) voice and accompaniment rise to a D flat underpinned by a diminished seventh chord; at 'Ein *süsses* Bild' this changes enharmonically to a C sharp as part of an A^7 chord leading to a modulation into D major. This change summons a vision of sweetness and femininity before our eyes and ears, and the singer is transformed by the radiance. It is as if a healing beam of love has suddenly enabled this rustic soul to communicate in a poetic manner. He recalls choosing his girlfriend in the valley, and Schubert conjures memories of a gathering, a village dance perhaps, where they might have met. The waltz music for the three lines of poetry beginning 'Der Sonne goldne Strahlen' (from b. 44) is simple enough – the harmonies are tonic, dominant and subdominant – but the higher tessitura requires something new of the singer. The song as a whole is conceived for a healthy baritone, but here a high F sharp (on 'im Tal er*kor*' b. 50) has to be sung in a head voice with delicacy and tact. This successfully achieved is like seeing a rugged mountaineer execute a faultless balletic pirouette.

Poets and artists can exist in a world of dreams and fantasy (indeed Mayrhofer finishes his poem with the vision of feminine love, without the reprise that the composer deemed necessary) but real men have to work, and Schubert knows this. The first verse of the poem is exactly recapitulated to make a satisfying whole in conventional ternary form. Having glimpsed another, more vulnerable side of the man's character we are happy to hear his hunting refrain once again. It is perhaps significant that when the song was published in 1822, long after it was written, Schubert dedicated it to his trusty old friend Josef von Spaun, who would have enjoyed this uncomplicated music.

The song exists in three versions of different keys. The first is in E major – the key of the natural horn, as in *Auf dem Strom* – and the second, even lower, in D major. The latter bass-clef version was made for Count Esterházy (an amateur bass) during Schubert's long stay in Zseliz during 1818. When he came to publish the song the composer chose to make a third version in

F major, the one recorded in the Hyperion Edition. This seems to have been influenced by market considerations relating to vocal range and amateur accessibility. The other keys are lugubrious and too low for the majority of male singers. And whereas it is unlikely that many basses will be able to float a delicate high E, one has at least half a hope of finding a baritone with a soft high F sharp. As in the case of this mountaineer, dreams sometimes become reality.

Autograph:	Missing or lost in World War I; photocopy of second version in Staatsbibliothek Preussischer Kulturbesitz, Berlin
Publication:	First published as part of the AGA in 1895 (P668; first version)
	First published as part of the NSA in 1970 (P752; second version)
	First published as Op. 13 no. 3 by Cappi & Diabelli, Vienna in 1822 (P33; third version)
Dedicatee:	Josef von Spaun
Subsequent editions:	Peters: Vol. 2/35; AGA XX 295a & b: Vol. 5/12; NSA IV: Vol. 1a/104 & Vol. 1b/233 (E major) & 266 (D major); Bärenreiter: Vol. 1/83
Bibliography:	Capell 1928, p. 139
Discography and timing:	Fischer-Dieskau I 9[12] 2'05 (Second version)
	Hyperion I 34[1]
	Hyperion II 17[15] 2'14 Christopher Maltman

← *Trost* D523   *Wie Ulfru fischt* D525 →

Der ALPENJÄGER   The Alpine huntsman
(SCHILLER) OP. 37 NO. 2, **D588** [H389]

The song exists in two versions, the second of which is discussed below:
(1) October 1817; (2) appeared in February 1825

(1) 'Mässig'   E flat major – D major $\frac{2}{4}$ [68 bars]

(2) C major – A major

(93 bars)

(1)	Willst du nicht das Lämmlein hüten?	Will you not tend the lamb,
	Lämmlein ist so fromm und sanft,	So meek and mild?
	Nährt sich von des Grases Blüten,	It feeds on flowers in the grass,
	Spielend an des Baches Ranft.	Gambolling beside the brook,
	'Mutter, Mutter, lass mich gehen,	'Mother, let me go
	Jagen nach des Berges Höhen!'	hunting on the high mountains.'
(2)	Willst du nicht die Herde locken	Will you not call the herd
	Mit des Hornes munterm Klang?	With the merry sound of your horn?

Lieblich tönt der Schall der Glocken
In des Waldes Lustgesang.
'Mutter, Mutter, lass mich gehen,
Schweifen auf den wilden Höhen!'

The bells mingle sweetly
With the joyful song of the forest.
'Mother, let me go
and roam the wild heights.'

(3) Willst du nicht der Blümlein warten,
Die im Beete freundlich stehn?
Draussen ladet dich kein Garten,
Wild ist's auf den wilden Höhn!
'Lass die Blümlein, lass sie blühen!
Mutter, Mutter, lass mich ziehen!'

Will you not tend the flowers
That grow so charmingly in their beds?
Out there no garden invites you;
It is harsh on those mountains.
'Let the flowers bloom;
Mother, let me go!'

(4) Und der Knabe ging zu jagen,
Und es treibt und reisst ihn fort,
Rastlos fort mit blindem Wagen
An des Berges finstern Ort;
Vor ihm her mit Windesschnelle
Flieht die zitternde Gazelle.

And the boy went hunting,
Driven relentlessly onwards,
With blind daring,
To the bleak parts of the mountain.
Before him, swift as the wind,
Flees the trembling gazelle.

(5) Auf der Felsen nackte Rippen
Klettert sie mich leichtem Schwung,
Durch den Riss gespaltener Klippen[1]
Trägt sie der gewagte Sprung;
Aber hinter ihr verwogen
Folgt er mit dem Todesbogen.

On the bare rock face
She bounds effortlessly;
Bravely she leaps
Across chasms in the rocks;
But he pursues her boldly
With his deadly bow.

(6) Jetzo auf den schroffen Zinken
Hängt sie, auf dem höchsten Grat,
Wo die Felsen jäh versinken
Und verschwunden ist der Pfad—
Unter sich die steile Höhe,
Hinter sich des Feindes Nähe.

Now she clings to the jagged spur
On the top of the ridge,
Where the cliff falls sheer,
And the path vanishes.
Beneath her is the steep drop,
Behind her is the approaching enemy.

(7) Mit des Jammers stummen Blicken
Fleht sie zu dem harten Mann,
Fleht umsonst, denn loszudrücken
Legt er schon den Bogen an.
Plötzlich aus der Felsenspalte
Tritt der Geist, der Bergesalte.

Gazing in mute distress
She implores the pitiless man;
But in vain, for already he draws his bow
And prepares to shoot.
Suddenly, from a rocky cleft,
The spirit of the mountain steps forth.

(8) Und mit seinen Götterhänden
Schützt er das gequälte Tier.
'Musst du Tod und Jammer senden',
Ruft er, 'bis herauf zu mir?
Raum für alle hat die Erde—
Was verfolgst du meine Herde?'

With his godlike hands
He protects the tormented beast.
'Must you even bring death and woe,'
He cries, 'Up here to me?
The earth has room for all;
Why do you persecute my herd?'

[1] Schiller writes 'Durch den Riss *geborst'ner* Klippen'.

FRIEDRICH VON SCHILLER (1759–1805); poem completed 5 July 1804

This is the thirty-fourth of Schubert's forty-four Schiller solo settings (1811–24). See the poet's biography for a chronological list of all the Schiller settings.

The gracious four-bar piano introduction is Haydnesque – indeed it is prophetic of the grave and reflective beauties of the eighteenth-century-influenced 'Adagio' from Schubert's C minor Piano Sonata D958. (This *Vorspiel* does not exist in the song's first version, and it represents constructive second thoughts on Schubert's part.) There are two bars that announce the music of the mother's entreaties followed by two bars to prophesy the hunting-horn music which symbolizes her tearaway son. This encapsulates the conflict between the matriarch's old-fashioned values (her music is tenderly staid in its ornamented vocal line and simple harmonies) and the wild, destructive youth who can only think of hunting. In the beginning it is the voice of the mother we hear – gentle, pleading and affectionate. The marking is 'Mässig' and the gait seems light hearted and femininely persuasive. The reply of the son is a brusque change of style where civilized values are crushed by brute force: his music is marked 'Geschwind' (the upbeat to b. 15) and in the rather hotheaded insistence on repeated notes and chords it has a Beethovenian cast. One is also reminded of passages in the Brahms folksong settings; in these, as well as in a number of the lieder by the same composer, there are frequent conversations between mothers and headstrong children – in the case of Brahms, daughters rather than sons.

The music is made up of sections, completely strophic until the final dénouement. Once again the mother attempts to persuade her son to find useful employment – perhaps he would like to listen to the music of the cow horn (rather than the hunting horn) in the life of a shepherd? This suggestion meets with the same petulant musical response, as does a third verse where the mother suggests that he take up gardening (this verse is omitted by Janet Baker in the Hyperion recording). After each of the boy's replies there is a six-bar piano postlude plus a bar of silence (bb. 20–26). At the end of this passage the piano harmonies attempt to break out of their A minor prison via an anguished diminished seventh on A flat (b. 24); this falls back with a whimper on to a snatched G^7 chord, and then the glowering silence.

At the end of the third verse we hear this ungracious interlude for the last time before the boy does indeed suddenly break free from his mother's control and go out on the rampage. This section of the song (from the upbeat to b. 49) is marked 'Geschwind', and is the rollicking music of the chase. The key signature switches to four flats and the tessitura of the piano writing is deep and gruff. The light-footed gazelle leaps in terror; the springing staccato accompaniment sprints from A flat major via various tonal paths to a momentary impasse in G flat major (bb. 55–6). The music teeters in this tonality for a bar or so and then continues to spring over cliff and ridge in pursuit of the frightened gazelle. Oafish semiquavers clamber after their prey, their offbeat accents fuelled by testosterone. The wide variety of terrain covered is symbolized by the chromatic explorations of the piano writing and by the nature of the strophic structure – bb. 48 to 64 are repeated three times. This is a pursuit that goes on and on, and around in circles. The obsessive nature of blood sport is ruthlessly depicted. Janet Baker also omits the poem's sixth verse in her recorded performance for Hyperion; it is not essential to the narrative but its inclusion adds to a mounting claustrophobia as the animal is ruthlessly pursued.

For the seventh verse the hunting music we have already heard three times begins for a fourth time. The frightened animal is about to die, the boy's bow and arrow poised to kill it. When we arrive at the (by now) familiar plateau of G flat major, however, the music abruptly breaks off (b. 72). The marking suddenly changes here to 'Langsam', and the tonality rises a semitone; portentous G major chords resound in dotted rhythm. The following five bars of accompanied recitative (bb. 73–7) depict the emergence of the *deus ex machina*. The entry of the mountain

Two illustrations for the final verse of *Der Alpenjäger*,
1853 and 1863.

spirit is illustrated in the tread of separate quaver chords (b. 75) followed by a powerful modulation into E major, although the new key signature for the supernatural being's aria is actually A
major. Schubert cleverly reserves the shift into that key until the end of the song – something
that focuses tonal attention on the spirit's final, unanswerable question. It may be hard to accept
this fairy-tale ending but it gives the singer a marvellous chance to inhabit another character.
A broad legato line restores equilibrium and gravity to the scene and to the song as a whole.
The music here is strong in reproof, but still tender. After characterizing mother and son as
opposites, it is Schubert-Sarastro himself who emerges to defend the weak. He is neither
conservative nor rebellious, but timelessly wise.

At the end of this we feel the hunter might have learned a valuable lesson, rather like
Wagner's 'pure fool' Parsifal who kills a swan and is reproved and instructed by Gurnemanz.
Schiller envisages a mystical metamorphosis and Schubert illustrates it; in this context the two
solemn bars of the postlude (V–I in the key of A) are somehow sufficiently potent to suggest
a Damascene experience for the hunter, the very transformation of his character into someone
responsible and settled. Capell and others have dubbed this song an out-and-out failure, but
on the grounds of its humanity alone it is remarkable, certainly in terms of Schiller's text. It
is a singular voice that will be suited equally to all the challenges of the music – too low at
the end for most tenors or sopranos, it could be sung by an accomplished baritone (as it was
by Fischer-Dieskau). However, the voice of a high mezzo best suits the credibility of the mother's voice for the opening section. Schubert clearly returned to the song's autograph from
October 1817 and revised it for publication at the beginning of 1825; part of this process was
to rethink the high-lying tessitura and transpose the song down a minor third – from E flat
major to C major. The mother's music had been almost ridiculously high, and the boy's replies
(with high B flats) equally impractical. In this first version the final 'Langsam' section (b. 48)
is a third *lower* than the key arrived at when the animal is about to die (thus a shift from A
minor to F major). The abrupt change in the second version from G flat major up to G major

(between bb. 72 and 73) is much more striking. It is possible to speculate that the tenor Tietze sang the song in a higher key for its first performance, but by the time it was taken up by Vogl (accompanied by Schubert) for the great concert tour of 1825, the song had settled down in the lower key that is now considered definitive. It became a special favourite of Georg Nissen (the second husband of Konstanze Mozart) who heard the travelling pair perform this music in Salzburg in September of that year.

While researching *Wilhelm Tell* Schiller found this story of Swiss origin in Carl Victor von Bonstetten's *Briefe über ein Schweizerisches Hirtenland* (1781). Like Goethe, he delighted in making poems out of real incidents or, as in this case, local legends. Those who know Schiller's *Wilhelm Tell* (1804) will recognize in this poem, written the same year, the theme of the mother (Tell's wife) moderating the effects of violent masculinity on the behaviour of her son.

Autographs:	Fitzwilliam Museum, Cambridge (bb. 1–34; first version); Wienbibliothek im Rathaus, Vienna (bb. 35–68; second version)
Publication:	First published as part of the AGA *Revisionsbericht* in 1897 (P728; first version)
	First published as Op. 37 no. 2 by Cappi & Co., Vienna in February 1825 (P78; second version)
Dedicatee:	Ludwig Ferdinand Schnorr von Carolsfeld
First known performance:	10 April 1825, Concert given by Johann Rüttinger, Zum roten Igel, Vienna. Soloist: Ludwig Tietze (see Waidelich/Hilmar Dokumente I No. 325 & II No. 324a for full concert programme and details)
Performance reviews:	*Wiener allgemeine Theaterzeitung* No. 51 (28 April 1825), p. 211 [Waidelich/Hilmar Dokumente I No. 329; Deutsch Doc. Biog. No. 545]
Subsequent editions:	Peters: Vol. 4/28; AGA XX 332: Vol. 5/168; NSA IV: Vol. 2a/138 & Vol. 2b/236 (E♭ major); Bärenreiter: Vol. 2/33
Bibliography:	Capell 1928, pp. 131–2
Further settings:	Johann Friedrich Reichardt (1752–1814) *Der Alpenjäger* (1809)
Discography and timing:	Fischer-Dieskau II 1[17] 5'19
	Hyperion I 1[17]
	Hyperion II 19[23] 4'53 Janet Baker

←— *An den Frühling* D587   *Lied eines Kindes* D596 —→

ALS ICH SIE ERRÖTEN SAH   When I saw her blush
(EHRLICH) **D153** [H66]
G major   10 February 1815

(79 bars)

All' mein Wirken, all' mein Leben,	All that I do, all that I am
Strebt nach dir, Verehrte, hin!	Is for you, my adored one!
Alle meine Sinne weben	All my senses weave
Mir dein Bild, o Zauberin!	An image of you, enchantress!
Du entflammest meinen Busen	You kindle within my heart
Zu der Leier Harmonie,	The sweet sounds of the lyre;
Du begeisterst mehr als Musen,	You inspire me more than the Muses,
Und entzückest mehr als sie.— —	And, more than they, delight me!
Ach, dein blaues Auge strahlet	Your blue eyes shine tenderly
Durch den Sturm der Seele mild,	Through the tempest of the soul,
Und dein süsses Lächeln mahlet	And your sweet smile paints
Rosig mir der Zukunft Bild.	A rosy image of the future.
Herrlich schmückt des Himmels Gränzen	Though the horizon is adorned
Zwar Aurora's Purpurlicht,[1]	By Aurora's crimson glow,
Aber lieblicheres Glänzen	A still fairer radiance
Überdeckt dein Angesicht,	Suffuses your countenance
Wenn mit wonnetrunknen Blicken	When, with ecstatic glances,
Ach! und unaussprechlich schön,	My delighted eyes
Meine Augen voll Entzücken	See the ineffable beauty
Purpurn dich erröten sehn.	Of your crimson blush.

BERNHARD AMBROS EHRLICH (?1765–1827); poem completed before 1791

This is Schubert's only setting of an Ehrlich text. See the poet's biography.

This remarkable song presents a number of problems in performance. Fischer-Dieskau has written that he sees it as a counterpart to *Gretchen am Spinnrade*, and he has sung it accordingly with almost vehement passion. The sextuplets in G major may put listeners in mind of *Wohin?* from *Die schöne Müllerin*. The agitation of *Am Feierabend* D795/5 from the same cycle also comes to mind, particularly since the lines 'All' mein Wirken, all' mein Leben' correspond to the miller boy's efforts to do anything he can to attract the attention of his beloved.

However, in *Als ich sie erröten sah* 'the sweet sounds of the lyre' support a song that is just as much arioso as aria, and the emotions of rapture do not aspire to the driven activity of *Gretchen am Spinnrade* or the Müller songs. The music is ardent at the same time as being tentative, and as shy as a blush. Because the song is a difficult one with long breaths it is all too easy to sing it in a hectoring manner absolutely inappropriate to the seemingly inexperienced lover who encounters so much unworldly rapture due to the glowing hue of a young lady's cheek. The clue to the song's performance is in the marking, 'Mit Liebes-Affekt', that stands at the top of the manuscript. The composer is here using a baroque term that derives from the *Affekten-lehre*, or 'The Doctrine of the Affections', a concept understood by older composers and performers such as Reichardt and Zumsteeg. Music was considered to be oration in sound, and the singer was encouraged to use his own taste to vary his performance in terms of tone, rhythm, contrast of emphasis, all in the pursuit of clear and interesting verbal delivery.

Als ich sie erröten sah is just such a song of the old school; it even looks like Reichardt's music on the printed page. The singer is told to play the part of a young man tenderly in love. In

[1] Ehrlich writes 'Zwar *Aurorens* Purpurlicht'.

practical terms this calls for a flexibility of rhythm where the meaningful and loving declamation of the words is more important than the piano's semiquaver underlay which is utterly different – supportive rather than organically integrated – from that of *Gretchen am Spinnrade*. The nearest counterpart to this Ehrlich setting is not one of the celebrated Schubert songs but another unknown one from 1815, *An die Apfelbäume, wo ich Julien erblickte* D197 which is also in compound time with a long *bel canto* line unfolding over undulating semiquaver sextuplets. There are similar difficulties in the long phrases with scarcely a space to breathe, as well as the feeling that the metre of the poem is perhaps not best suited to the musical solution chosen for it. John Reed writes that the song has a 'wonderful spontaneity and plasticity' but it takes the intervention of the performers (and above all considerable skill on the part of the long-breathed singer) to avoid turning the piece into the merry scherzo that it appears to be at first glance.

Autograph:	Missing or lost
First edition:	Published as Book 39 no. 1 of the *Nachlass* by Diabelli, Vienna in 1845 (P354)
Subsequent editions:	Peters: Vol. 6/18; AGA XX 41: Vol. 2/15; NSA IV: Vol. 7/135; Bärenreiter: Vol. 6/84
Bibliography:	Capell 1928, p. 89
	Einstein 1951, p. 108
	Fischer-Dieskau 1977, p. 54
Discography and timing:	Fischer-Dieskau I 2[19] 2'23
	Hyperion I 20[4]
	Hyperion II 5[5] 2'35 Ian Bostridge

← *Minona* D152   *Das Bild* D155 →

ALTE LIEBE ROSTET NIE   Old love never dies
(MAYRHOFER) **D477** [H302]
B major   September 1816

(16 bars)

Alte Liebe rostet nie,[1]	Old love never dies,
Hört ich oft die Mutter sagen;	I often heard my mother say –
Alte Liebe rostet nie,	Old love never dies;
Muss ich nun erfahrend klagen.	With experience I must now sadly agree.
Wie die Luft umgibt sie mich,	She envelops me like the air,
Die ich einst die Meine nannte,[2]	She whom I once called my own,

[1] Mayrhofer writes 'Alte Liebe rostet *nicht*', also in line 3. For an explanation of the background to these alternative Mayrhofer readings see Editorial Note at the beginning of Johann MAYRHOFER.
[2] Mayrhofer writes 'Die ich einst *mein eigen* nannte'.

Die ich liebte ritterlich,[3]
Die mich in die Ferne sandte.[4]

Whom I loved chivalrously,
Who sent me into the wide world.

Seit die Holde ich verlor,
Hab' ich Meer und Land gesehen,–
Vor der schönsten Frauen Flor[5]
Durft ich unerschüttert stehen.

Since I lost my beloved
I have travelled on sea and land –
Before the fairest flower of womanhood
I could only stand unmoved.

Denn aus mir ihr Bildnis trat,[6]
Zürnend, wie zum Kampf mit ihnen;
Mit dem Zauber, den sie hat,
Musste sie das Spiel gewinnen.

For her image arose from within me,
Angrily, as if in opposition to them;
With the magic she possesses
She had to win the contest.

Da der Garten, dort das Haus,
Wo wir oft so traulich kos'ten![7]
Seh' ich recht? sie schwebt heraus—
Wird die alte Liebe rosten?

There is the garden, there the house
Where we once caressed so lovingly!
Am I seeing things? She glides out towards me –
Will old love never die?

JOHANN MAYRHOFER (1787–1836)

This is the seventh of Schubert's forty-seven Mayrhofer solo settings (1814–24). See the poet's biography for a chronological list of all the Mayrhofer settings.

This entirely enchanting song is of a deceptive simplicity. The lover's restless quest is mirrored by a tonal scheme that reaches the tonic only at the end of each verse. How masterful it is that even the first chord is on the first inversion of B major; this sows a seed of emotional doubt which is only banished in the affirmative postlude. The choice of this key is significant for a love song of faithfulness until death. *Der Neugierige* from *Die schöne Müllerin*, with its 'O Bächlein meiner Liebe' is also in B major, and 'Ich frage keine Blume', the enquiry that precedes that famous cavatina, is similarly accompanied by quaver chords that alternate jauntily between the hands.

In this song the maxim 'Old love never dies' is repeated like a spell or a litany. The touching harmonic sequences which end each verse of Schubert's celebrated *Am Tage aller Seelen (Litanei)* D343 are used here. The quotation from a great song honouring the dead seems to imply that the object of the singer's affections is also dead. The melodic shape for the words 'Alte Liebe rostet nie' ('nicht' in the posthumously printed version of the poem which appeared in 1843 with the title 'Alte Liebe') is Mozart's favourite motto theme that finds its apotheosis in the finale of the 'Jupiter' Symphony in the motto C-D-F-E. The musical effect of this song has a Mozartian magic, and it is in itself a kind of *Tombeau de Mozart*.

In a passage from his diary (earlier in 1816) Schubert had written, 'The magic notes of Mozart's music still haunt me . . . Mozart, immortal Mozart, how endlessly many comforting

---

[3] Mayrhofer writes '*Der* ich *lebte* ritterlich'.
[4] Mayrhofer writes 'Die mich in die *Weite* sandte'.
[5] Mayrhofer writes 'Vor *den* schönsten *Frauenflor*'.
[6] The poem's fourth strophe in the *Gedichte* (1843) is different enough to be quoted in full:
   'Denn *ihr Bild trat vor den Geist*,
   Zürnend, *halb und halb voll Milde*,—
   Und was irgend Zauber heisst,
   Wich beschämt dem lieben Bilde'.
[7] The first two lines of the fifth strophe read (*Gedichte*, 1843):
   '*Hier* der Garten, dort das Haus
   Wo wir *einst* so traulich kos'ten!'

perceptions of a better life have you brought to our souls.' Schubert's old love for Mozart was never to tarnish, much less die. After the failure of his courtship of Therese Grob it is perhaps his way of saying that only in music can he hope to find faithful companionship.

   This song is one of the few Mayrhofer poems set by Schubert that appears to describe a straight-forward romantic feeling between a man and a woman. A closer reading of the poem, however, results in puzzlement and speculation. The poet confesses himself unmoved ('unerschüttert') by womanhood since the loss of this 'alte Liebe' that sent him out into the world. The poet's mother is mentioned in the first stanza. Is she perhaps the old love with whom no one else can ever hope to compete? Her posthumous opposition to other relationships (Verse 4) seems to fit such an hypothesis. Does the final stanza represent a nostalgic visit by the poet to his place of birth? Was the first and only abiding love affair with a woman that Mayrhofer was ever to experience with the spirit who comes to greet him? And one cannot forget that Schubert himself had lost his own mother when still only a young teenager, and that no woman in his own life (certainly in official terms) was destined to replace that oldest and truest of loves.

Autograph:	Österreichische Nationalbibliothek, Vienna
First edition:	Published as part of the AGA in 1895 (P651)
Subsequent editions:	Not in Peters; AGA XX 253: Vol. 4/180; NSA IV: Vol. 11/6
Bibliography:	Youens 1996, pp. 162–3
Discography and timing:	Fischer-Dieskau I 8⁵ 1'33 (Strophes 1, 3 & 4 only)
	Hyperion I 4¹¹
	Hyperion II 16³ 2'56 Philip Langridge

← *Rückweg* D476   *Lied eines Schiffers an die Dioskuren* D360 →

ALTSCHOTTISCHE BALLADE *see* EINE ALTSCHOTTISCHE BALLADE D923

AM BACH IM FRÜHLINGE   By the brook in the spring
(Schober) **D361** [H320]

The song exists in two versions, both of which are discussed below:
(1) 1816; (2) 1816 or 1819?

(1)   D♭ major – C♯ minor

(52 bars)

(2)   'Mässig'   D major   **C**   [51 bars]

Du brachst sie nun die kalte Rinde,	You have now broken your cold crust
Und rieselst froh und frei dahin;	and you ripple merrily and freely forth.
Die Lüfte wehen wieder linde,	The breezes blow gently again,
Und Moos und Gras wird neu und grün.[1]	and moss and grass grow new and green.
Allein, mit traurigem Gemüte[2]	Alone and in a mournful mood
Tret' ich wie sonst zu deiner Flut,	I walk by your waters as of old.
Der Erde allgemeine Blüte	The blossoming of the earth
Kommt meinem Herzen nicht zu gut.	does my soul no good.
Hier treiben immer gleiche Winde,	Here the same old winds are gusting,
Kein Hoffen kommt in meinen Sinn.—	and no hope enters my mind,
Als dass ich hier ein Blümchen finde,	even when I find a little flower here:
Blau, wie sie der Erinnrung blühn.	blue, like the flowers blooming in my memories.

FRANZ VON SCHOBER (1796–1882)

This is the second of Schubert's fourteen Schober solo settings (1815–27). See the poet's biography for a chronological list of all the Schober settings.

This song cast as a *bel canto* aria stems from the purest Schubertian inspiration, as natural and inevitable as the flowing of water and the blossoming of wild flowers beside the brook. This is all the more remarkable because the dilettante Schober's verses lack the originality and deep feeling of his contemporary Mayrhofer's (cf. *Am Strome* D539, related to this song both in terms of its water imagery and in its use of the *da capo* aria form). The poet has adopted the idea of the 'blue flower' from *Heinrich von Ofterdingen* (1802) by Novalis. This 'hohe, lichtblaue Blume', seen in a dream, becomes the symbol of all Heinrich's longing. It also became something of a cliché in the hands of Novalis admirers of the younger generation, like Schober.

This song is so well known in the key of D flat major that it comes as some surprise to discover another version in D major printed in the NSA and marked 'Mässig'. This lacks the single bar of rippling arpeggio introduction, and there is no way of being sure which version came first. The composer's posthumous publishers (above all Diabelli) were perfectly capable of altering details of a Schubert manuscript before publication, and of providing non-authentic piano introductions. Walther Dürr points out, however, that it is unlikely that a song written in the unusual key of D flat would have been changed into the much more common D major. From a musical point of view it is easy to believe that Schubert conceived this 'blue' song for the bass voice (it was a favourite of Hans Hotter). Transposed upwards from D flat the sounds are brighter, but in the lower key the bass tessitura plays a large part in tugging at the heartstrings. A voice singing in this range, whether male or female, has the quality of autumn in springtime, as if chastened by experience and suffering. A high vocal line tends to energize a song, but here the mood is one of introspection and contemplation.

How different is that minor-key song of a river in winter, *Auf dem Flusse* from *Winterreise* where the stream's icy covering has not yet yielded to spring sunshine. In *Am Bach im Frühlinge* the brook flows in the relaxed triplet accompaniment until, a few bars before the phrase 'Der Erde allgemeine Blüte', there is a modulation from D flat into E major. The music becomes livelier and the accompaniment, evoking gently lapping water, cradles the flowering tendrils of the vocal line. The effect is all tender concern, as if a floral poultice were being applied to the lover's

[1] Schober writes '*frisch* und grün'.
[2] Schober writes '*Doch ich* – mit traurigem Gemüte'.

wounds, sadly to no avail. In this passage (bb. 14–15) both the AGA and NSA (unlike Peters) are clear that the piano's accompanying figure in the right hand consists of triplets without the intrusion of a spare semiquaver sounding after them; this semiquaver should sound *with* the third triplet. (This problem is discussed in the commentary for *Leb' wohl, du schöne Erde (Abschied von der Erde)* D829.)

The first section of the song ends mournfully in C sharp minor with a touching three-bar piano interlude (bb. 19–21, which also serves as a postlude). An eight-bar passage marked 'Recit.' follows. The first four of these bars allow the singer to express desperation and pessimism in a forte dynamic, the accompaniment's sturdy chords, marked *colla voce*, leading us back into the key of E major (bb. 22–5 'Hier treiben immer gleiche Winde, / Kein Hoffen kommt in meinen Sinn'). And then the pianissimo miracle at the heart of the song. After a rolled E minor chord in first inversion (b. 25, before 'Als dass ich hier ein Blümchen finde') the voice tells us of something that has hitherto remained elusive. Gently arpeggiated chords ripple as if the pianist's fingers were searching through the undergrowth to find this solitary blue flower; as they do so the music pivots around the chord of B minor in its first inversion (bb. 27–9). We are temporarily lost in watery contemplation, and far away from home; time stands still. A repeat of the words 'Blau, wie sie der Erinnrung blühn' allows the composer to execute one of his masterful tonal exits. When we arrive at the final 'blühn' (b. 31) the voice descends to a G sharp, the lowest note in the song, and it is as if the precious flower has been located at last. Just at that point this note changes its form in the piano writing and is written as A flat. This sets up the return of the key signature of D flat major; no sooner has the elusive flower been found than it slips, by harmonic sleight of hand, from the poet's grasp. Schubert here invents a single bar of piano music to evoke a musical sigh (b. 31); it is so eloquent that he repeats it. This tiny interlude comes to rest on a simple chord of A flat major.

A door has opened onto a changed world. We are now ready for a repeat of the D flat major section of the song, a *da capo* in classical style in which the concluding 'fine' marking comes after the repeat of the first section. It is the performers' task to demonstrate that in a song like this there is no such thing as mere repetition. In the slow movements of the late piano sonatas, or of the String Quintet, the disquiet of the middle section lingers and is written into the recapitulation; here only a change of vocal colour can suggest deepened awareness.

The song remained a favourite of the Schubert circle, on musical grounds certainly, but also because Schober was its author. Wilhelmine von Witteczek invited both composer and poet to a gathering on 15 February 1827 in which she playfully refers in a letter to Vogl as 'Die Nachtigall aus der Alleegasse' (the nightingale of the Alleegasse – the singer's address). She refers to his 'piping' of 'all old crusts' ('aller kalten Rinden') – surely a reference to the first line of this song.

Although it is usually accepted that *Am Bach im Frühlinge* was composed in 1816 this date rests entirely on a copy in the Witteczek-Spaun collection. The blue flower in this song is a reason to suppose that it might have been written in 1819 when the Schubertians were studying Novalis. The song certainly has something in common with other triplet-accompanied songs from this period such as *Der Fluss* D693.

The AGA and Peters published the song as *Am Bach im Frühling*. In Schober the title is simply *Am Bache*, the first of six *Frühlingslieder*. The title *Am Bach im Frühlinge*, restored by NSA in 2002, is to be found in the composer's autograph.

Autograph:	Österreichische Nationalbibliothek, Vienna (second version)
Publication:	First published as Op. post. 109 no. 1 by Diabelli, Vienna in 1829 (P232; first version)
	First published as part of the NSA in 2002 (P826; second version)
Subsequent editions:	Peters: Vol. 4/120; AGA XIX 272: Vol. 4/230; NSA IV: Vol. 10/16 & 18

Bibliography: Capell 1928, p. 126
                               Dürr, Introduction to NSA IV Volume 10 p. XIX
Discography and timing: Fischer-Dieskau I 8[19]   3'32
                               Hyperion I 2[7]
                               Hyperion II 16[24]   4'15   Stephen Varcoe

← *Zufriedenheit* D501   *Herbstlied* D502 →

AM ERLAFSEE *see* ERLAFSEE D586

AM ERSTEN MAIMORGEN   On the first May morning
(CLAUDIUS) **D344** [H215]
G major   *c.* 1816

(46 bars)

Heute will ich fröhlich, fröhlich sein,   Today I shall be merry, merry;
  Keine Weis' und keine Sitte hören;   I shall hear no wisdom and no moralizing
Will mich wälzen, und für Freude schrein,   Shall run about and shout for joy;
  Und der König soll mir das nicht wehren;   And even the king will not stop me.

Denn er kommt mit seiner Freuden Schaar   For today he comes with his retinue of joys
  Heute aus der Morgenröte Hallen,   From the halls of dawn,
Einen Blumenkranz um Brust und Haar   Garlands around his head and breast,
  Und auf seiner Schulter Nachtigallen;   And nightingales on his shoulder.

[. . .]   [. . .]

MATTHIAS CLAUDIUS (1740–1815); poem written in May 1774

This is the first of Schubert's thirteen Claudius solo settings (1816–17). See the poet's biography for a chronological list of all the Claudius settings.

The album of seventeen songs that Schubert put together for Therese Grob in November 1816 contains three items that were found only in that source. The first of these is a *Klage* of doubtful authenticity (formerly D512 but exiled in the second edition of Deutsch to the appendix) and the others are the Hölty setting *Mailied* D503 and *Am ersten Maimorgen* which appears on its last page. These songs are delightful without being very demanding, either vocally or pianistically. They had to wait for private publication by Reinhard Van Hoorickx, but this song has been available in the NSA since 2002.

    Am ersten Maimorgen, with its tune in ascending thirds and its piquant ten-bar postlude, has a charming nursery-rhyme simplicity. This puts us in mind of the Hölty setting *Die frühe Liebe*

D430. In common with Hölty, the North German poet Claudius has an earthy love of the simple joys of life, and this was Schubert's introduction to him. Claudius was soon to lead the composer into darker and more profound utterances (*Bei dem Grabe meines Vaters* D496 for example). Nevertheless, the merry side of Claudius we hear in this song is just as much a part of the personality of *Der Wandsbecker Bote* ('The Wandsbek Messenger', the paper edited by the poet, and also his nickname) as the celebrated *Der Tod und das Mädchen* D531. *Am ersten Maimorgen* is the poem's subtitle, the main heading here is *Der Frühling*.

   In the Grob songbook only the first verse appears; in such cases it is clear that the composer did not always think through all the strophic ramifications in terms of word underlay and emphasis. In the Hyperion Edition the first two verses are sung. All three are given in the NSA.

Autograph:	In private possession in Switzerland (part of the Therese Grob album)
First edition:	Published by Reinhard Van Hoorickx in a private edition and subsequently as part of the NSA in 2002 (P824)
Subsequent editions:	Not in Peters; Not in AGA; NSA IV: Vol. 10/8
Further settings:	Johann Friedrich Reichardt (1752–1814) *Der Frühling (Oden und Lieder)* (1779); *Der Frühling (Lieder geselliger Freude)* (1796) Othmar Schoeck (1886–1957) *Der Frühling* from *Wandsbecker Liederbuch* Op. 52. no. 6 (1937) Hermann Reutter (1900–1985) *Der Frühling* Op. 60 no. 3 (1947)
Discography and timing:	Fischer-Dieskau — Hyperion I 23^{25} Hyperion II 12^{10} 1'30 Christoph Prégardien

← *An mein Klavier* D342   *Klage (Trauer umfliesst mein Leben)* D372 →

AM FEIERABEND *see Die SCHÖNE MÜLLERIN* D795/5

AM FENSTER   At the window
(SEIDL) OP. 105 NO. 3, **D878** [H596]
F major   March 1826

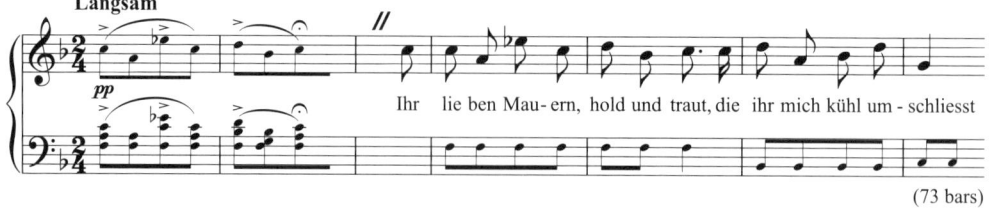

(73 bars)

Ihr lieben Mauern, hold und traut,[1]   Dear, familiar walls,
   Die ihr mich kühl umschliesst,   You enclose me within your coolness,
Und silberglänzend niederschaut,[2]   And gaze down with silvery sheen
   Wenn droben Vollmond ist: When the full moon shines above.

[1] Seidl writes 'Ihr lieben Mauern, *sanft* und traut'.
[2] Seidl writes 'silber*glänzig*'.

Ihr saht mich einst so traurig da,	Once you saw me here so sad,
Mein Haupt auf schlaffer Hand,—	Head buried in weary hands,
Als ich in mir allein mich sah,	Looking only within myself,
Und Keiner mich verstand.	Understood by no one.
Jetzt brach ein ander Licht heran:	Now a new light has dawned,
Die Trauerzeit ist um:	The time of sadness is past,
Und Manche ziehn mit mir die Bahn	And many join me on my path
Durch's Lebensheiligtum.	Through this sacred life.
Sie raubt der Zufall ewig nie	Chance will never steal them
Aus meinem treuen Sinn:	From my faithful heart;
In tiefster Seele trag' ich sie,—	I carry them deep in my soul,
Da reicht kein Zufall hin.	Where fate cannot penetrate.
Du Mauer wähnst mich trüb', wie einst,	Wall, you imagine I am as gloomy as I once was:
Das ist die stille Freud';	That is my silent joy.
Wenn du vom Mondlicht widerscheinst,	When you reflect the moonlight
Wird mir die Brust so weit.	My heart swells.
An jedem Fenster wähn' ich dann	Then I imagine I see at every window
Ein Freundeshaupt, gesenkt,	A friendly face, lowered,
Das auch so schaut zum Himmel an,[3]	That then gazes heavenwards,
Das auch so meiner denkt!	Thinking of me too.

JOHANN GABRIEL SEIDL (1804–1875)

This is the fourth of Schubert's twelve Seidl solo settings (1826–8). See the poet's biography for a chronological list of all the Seidl settings.

This song is a gem, but it remains the orphan of the Seidl settings, seldom performed and seemingly not highly prized, even by Schubertians. Whether this is because of its 'air of understatement' (Reed) or because it is 'a little unusual' (Capell) is difficult to say. The latter critic sums up the background to the poem thus: 'The poet addresses the walls of his old home.' From this alone it seems that Capell, along with the other commentators, has not quite understood the work's scenario, a difficulty also faced by interpreters.

It takes a little detective work on the poem to piece together what is happening. The walls surrounding the poet are cool (Verse 1) which suggests that they are also thick, and perhaps very old. This is no ordinary domestic dwelling. Schubert tells us as much by a dense accompaniment – solid walls of quavers with chords that look like evenly placed bricks. The third line of the poem reveals that the walls are high enough to tower above the narrator, and that they are made of a stone which reflects the moonlight. The scale of this puts one in mind of a castle rather than a private home. Is this a prison of some kind, perhaps? The music implies that the walls contain the poet as much as they shelter him. The song is in F major but we are not allowed to experience the full span of the octave in that key; the top note of the opening phrase is an E flat that flattens and imprisons the scale, as it were. The music which starts in F major is thus deflected into the subdominant. This modal twist to the harmony inevitably suggests early music and religious contemplation.

It is surely clear by now that Seidl has imagined his protagonist as an inmate of a monastery, as is the case in the Leitner setting *Der Kreuzzug* D932. Once this is understood the rest of the

---

[3] Seidl writes '*Und* auch so schaut zum Himmel an'.

poem makes sense. The narrator had arrived at the cloister some years before in a state of profound spiritual crisis (Verse 2). Converted by a 'new light', he has found peace in 'this sacred life' and above all in the fellowship of his religious community (Verse 4). He has embraced the contemplative life where silent joy ('stille Freud', Verse 5) in something as natural and beautiful as the moonlight has replaced his silent anguish. The walls of the monastery have born witness to his development and growth. The final verse is perhaps deliberately ambiguous. Does he refer to the cell windows of his fellow monks who are his companions in prayer, or is he perhaps thinking of his family and friends far away who, in turn, are thinking of him and also offering up their prayers?

Although not conventionally religious himself, Schubert had experienced happy music-making in the monasteries of St Florian and Kremsmünster in the previous year (July 1825) during his holiday with the singer Johann Michael Vogl. Many people led a happy and productive life there in a safe community of contemplation and prayer. There were moments when he also wished to withdraw from the world and concentrate on the inner life that for him meant undisturbed composition.

There are many marvellous touches in the music. After 'Wenn droben Vollmond ist' there is a piano interlude of rare beauty (bb. 15–17) with chords spaced in such a manner as to suggest the transparency of moonlight. The simple change at the beginning of Verse 2 between F major and F minor – the happy present and unhappy past – is beautifully engineered, and this leads naturally into a middle section in D flat (from b. 27) in which the poet describes how he first saw the light. It is no coincidence that these bars at the start of Verse 3 ('Jetzt brach ein ander Licht heran') recall the vocal writing for *Der blinde Knabe* D833 – a German translation of Cibber's lines beginning 'O say! what is that thing call'd Light' There is a bell-like sonority in many of the accompaniment's chords throughout the piece, but the triumphant peal at 'Lebens-heiligtum' is a splendour of lieder campanology (bb. 37–9), with large bells sounding the longer quavers and smaller ones within the chord tinkling in semiquavers.

Verse 4 begins in A flat (from b. 39), and a new sense of agitation creeps into the vocal line; one realizes that this work is related to *Die junge Nonne* D828, both in its subject matter and in its fervour. The triumphant inner feeling that nothing now can take away the poet's faith is remarkably caught by the progression of a line of E flats ('In tiefster Seele' bb. 43–5) which suddenly lifts on to E naturals; the opaqueness of A flat major is thereby replaced and banished by the blazing conviction of A major. The piano interlude with chords syncopated between the hands again suggests the triumphant ringing of bells (bb. 47–9). The quieter musings of Verse 5 are marked 'Leise' in brackets above the vocal line (b. 57); they lead us ingeniously back into a key signature with a single flat, the F major of the opening. This final verse is a gentle recapitulation of the opening music, this time with a vocal line that is ornamented here and there. These flourishes were perhaps included for Vogl who found vocal ornamentation hard to resist, and who would have relished the presentational opportunities of heroic renunciation in this noble music.

The very last line is repeated with flowing semiquavers supported by airy chords high in the treble – the soul, in imagination at least, is free to fly into the heavens, surrounded by love and cherished at last. It is notable that this F major peroration has something in common with that of *Totengräbers Heimwehe* D842 in the same key. The three other Schubert songs mentioned in this commentary are all settings of texts by Craigher von Jachelutta. This song seems a bridge between the composer's Craigher and Seidl styles – the former more self-consciously grand and 'tragic', the latter more intimate and domestic. These are both poets who write about healing and reconciliation, not always without sentimentality. Yet even with poetry of moderate accomplishment these themes inspired Schubert to some of his finest music. With greater poetry such seemingly simple musical means are employed to plumb ever greater depths. One can easily hear this song with its quasi-hymn tune as a forerunner of a song from *Winterreise* – *Das*

Wirtshaus – also in F major with the flattened seventh playing a leading role, and where the singer longs in vain to enter cloistered and secure confines, in that case a grave rather than a monastery. Performers are advised to consult the NSA for phrasing and articulation markings omitted from other editions.

Autograph:	Library of Congress, Washington (first draft)
First edition:	Published as Op. 105 no. 3 by Josef Czerny, Vienna in November 1828 (P176)
Publication reviews:	*Allgemeiner Musikalischer Anzeiger* (Vienna), No. 5 (31 January 1829), p. 19f. [Waidelich/Hilmar Dokumente I No. 688]
Subsequent editions:	Peters: Vol. 3/77; AGA XX 492: Vol. 8/176; NSA IV: Vol. 5/92; Bärenreiter: Vol. 4/12
Bibliography:	Capell 1928, p. 223
	Fischer-Dieskau 1977, pp. 237–8
Discography and timing:	Fischer-Dieskau II 8[1] 3'22
	Hyperion I 15[14]
	Hyperion II 32[2] 4'41 Margaret Price

← *Im Freien* D880   *Sehnsucht* D879 →

AM FLUSSE (I)   By the river
(GOETHE) **D160** [H68]
D minor   27 February 1815

(30 bars)

Verfliesset, vielgeliebte Lieder,	Flow away, beloved songs,
Zum Meere der Vergessenheit!	Into the sea of oblivion.
Kein Knabe sing' entzückt euch wieder,	No enraptured youth, no maiden in the springtime of life
Kein Mädchen in der Blütenzeit.	Will you ever sing again.
Ihr sanget nur von meiner Lieben;	You told only of my beloved,
Nun spricht sie meiner Treue Hohn.	Now she pours scorn on my constancy.
Ihr wart ins Wasser eingeschrieben;	You were inscribed upon the water;
So fliesst denn auch mit ihm davon.	Then with the water flow away.

JOHANN WOLFGANG VON GOETHE (1749–1832); poem written summer 1768/9

This is the eighth of Schubert's seventy-five Goethe solo settings (1814–26). See the poet's biography for a chronological list of all the Goethe settings.

'There are few notes', writes Capell of this song, 'but they are exquisitely disposed.' Certainly this is one of the young Schubert's more potent miniatures. We only know that the composer was not entirely happy with it as a setting of Goethe's text because he returned to it seven years later in a major key setting of completely different mood (D766). Einstein asserts that in this earlier version the river is conspicuous by its absence (it is true that the later version flows in more obvious fashion) but no one seems to have noticed this song's similarity to its near namesake *Auf dem Flusse* from *Winterreise*, also in D minor when sung by baritones. In that song the singer's emotions are numbed by grief, and the river, which has happily rippled in sunnier days, shares the narrator's fate, benumbed by its own covering of ice. The staccato opening chords of *Auf dem Flusse* are reminiscent of the dry accompanying notes in alternating hands in *Am Flusse*. We encounter a similarly powerful concision, and a bitter outburst of grief that is quickly reined back to quiet desperation. Another parallel with the *Winterreise* song is the verbal imagery of Goethe's seventh line ('Ihr wart ins Wasser eingeschrieben') which, as Sterling Lambert points out, is a reminder that 'writing on water might well be a metaphor for the act of engraving on ice'. On the surface of his frozen river the winter traveller will engrave with a sharp stone the name of his beloved, the day and the hour. It is clear that Wilhelm Müller knew his Goethe.

When Schubert chooses the key of D minor he often has something to say about the attempts of mankind to surmount its problems by willpower. The marking of 'Wehmütig' makes no secret of the intensity of the musical mood. The singer commands the river to take his songs away into oblivion, but (unlike in the second setting) it seems unwilling to do so, preferring to burble out the narrator's grief before moving on. The river, *pace* Einstein, is there throughout (particularly after the words 'Ihr sanget', b. 14), but in less 'watery' guise than usual.

Fischer-Dieskau finds the song reminiscent of *Gretchen am Spinnrade* from the previous year; it is certainly in the same key, has a similar Italianate turn of phrase in the vocal line and a similar middle section modulation into the relative major at the moment where songs of past love are evoked. (In Gretchen's song the crucial modulation occurs as she recounts the attractive physical attributes of the manipulative Faust.) The climax at 'meiner Treue Hohn' (bb. 16–17) with the pause on the cadence also recalls Gretchen's 'Und ach, sein Kuss!' with a similarly anguished high G as the climactic note.

This early poem is one of the few song texts that refers to Goethe's infatuation with Kätchen ('Annette') Schönkopf in Leipzig – an episode recounted in *Dichtung und Wahrheit* where she appears as Ännchen. The poet's original title was *An meine Lieder* published in the 1799 Schiller *Musenalmanach* and signed with the pseudonym Justus Amman.

Autograph:	Staatsbibliothek Preussischer Kulturbesitz, Berlin (first draft)
First edition:	Published as part of the AGA in 1895 (P552)
Subsequent editions:	Not in Peters; AGA XX 47: Vol. 2/58; NSA IV: Vol. 13/60
Bibliography:	Capell 1928, p. 100
	Einstein 1951, p. 109
	Fischer-Dieskau 1977, p. 53
	Lambert 2009, pp. 60–68
Further settings and arrangements:	Johann Friedrich Reichardt (1752–1814) *Am Flusse* (1809)
	Václav Tomášek (1774–1850) *Am Flusse* (1815)
	arr. Tilman Hoppstock (b. 1961) for guitar accompaniment, in *Franz Schubert: 110 Lieder* (2009)
Discography and timing:	Fischer-Dieskau I 3³ 1'20
	Hyperion I 10³
	Hyperion II 5⁷ 1'52 Martyn Hill

← *Das Bild* D155   *An Mignon* D161 (first version) →

AM FLUSSE (II)

By the river

(GOETHE) **D766** [H502]
D major   December 1822

See previous entry for poem and translation

JOHANN WOLFGANG VON GOETHE (1749–1832); poem written summer 1768/9

This is the sixty-ninth of Schubert's seventy-five Goethe solo settings (1814–26). See the poet's biography for a chronological list of all the Goethe settings.

The first setting of *Am Flusse* D160 (1815) is in the minor key and portrays the jilted lover's reaction to loss of love and faith in music of anguished sensitivity. Some years later Schubert returned to the poem. Though his second setting is seemingly laconic it is more subtly in tune with the text's deeper implications. All the love songs that used to be superimposed on the watery map have flowed away leaving a blueprint of eternity; all signs of strong emotion have been erased. Here is Schubert the master distiller with a light touch: he allows water to bubble gently, without stirring the pot. Very little happens within the confines of the song's thirty-three bars; the river is encountered, addressed and left in peace to continue its unceasing roundelay. The dotted-rhythm figure in the left hand suggests some eternal beat, an open-fifth drone played on nature's age-old hurdy-gurdy. This motif propels the music forward without any sense of panic or loss of equilibrium.

The poet's beloved songs have flowed into the sea of oblivion. Schubert responds to this idea with music pared down to the bare essentials, and with the minimum of modulation. There is no change from a broad horizon of D major for the first nine bars of music – apart, that is, from the semiquaver G sharp that decorates the left-hand motif. The beloved girl pours scorn on the singer's constancy; in the 1815 version the narrator minds a great deal about this – that song is marked 'Wehmütig' – 'sadly'. In the later setting the poet has *become* the river and he is beyond caring about human affairs. Such things are water under the bridge, unimportant in the broader scheme of things. Theodor Werner, in his 1948 essay on the two *Am Flusse* settings, suggests that Schubert's later version represents Goethe's emotion 'recollected in tranquillity', and that the composer has now entered more fully into the poet's mind.

It is notable that the opening of the vocal line uses the same descending arpeggio phrase (without the upbeat) as that for 'Dort ist ihr Grab' from the song *Ihr Grab* D736 (also 1822). There is a link between the ideas behind the two texts: in *Am Flusse*, having accepted that his love is figuratively dead and buried, the singer harmonizes himself into nature's major key, and his variation is only one possibility in an endless passacaglia.

When he set *Am Flusse* the second time Schubert was only months away from composing *Die schöne Müllerin*, including the marvellously hypnotic water music which ends that cycle, *Des Baches Wiegenlied* – a lullaby for the brook which is both profoundly moving and completely impersonal. This setting of *Am Flusse* is something of a study for that song and its mood of lucidity and unforced naturalness – a tragedy reflected in the major key. Schubert was on the brink of finding a musical language for Wilhelm Müller's poetry that would bestow a musical significance on quasi-folk poetry. This was destined to provide a new intensity that would surpass the heart-on-sleeve of *Sturm und Drang*.

Autograph:	Staatsbibliothek Preussischer Kulturbesitz, Berlin (first draft)
First edition:	Published as No. 3 of *Neueste Folge nachgelassener Lieder und Gesänge* by J. P. Gotthard, Vienna in 1872 (P429)
Subsequent editions:	Not in Peters; AGA XX 418: Vol. 6/56; NSA IV: Vol. 13/62
Bibliography:	Brown 1958, p. 203
	Byrne 2003, pp. 150–54 (both versions)
	Capell 1928, pp. 54 & 181
	Fischer-Dieskau 1977, pp. 167–8
	Lambert 2009, pp. 68–75
Arrangements:	Arr. Tilman Hoppstock (b. 1961) for guitar accompaniment, in *Franz Schubert: 110 Lieder* (2009)
Discography and timing:	Fischer-Dieskau II 5[16] 1'14
	Hyperion I 2[8] 1'30 Stephen Varcoe
	Hyperion I 28[19] 1'15 Maarten Koningsberger
	Hyperion II 26[7] 1'30 Stephen Varcoe

← *Der Musensohn* D764   *Willkommen und Abschied* D767 →

AM GRABE ANSELMOS   By Anselmo's grave
(CLAUDIUS) OP. 6 NO. 3, **D504** [H317]

The song exists in two versions, the first of which is discussed below:
(1) 4 November 1816; (2) End of 1816?

(1)   E♭ minor

(2)   'Sehr langsam'   E♭ minor   3/4   [46 bars]

Dass ich dich verloren habe,	That I have lost you,
Dass du nicht mehr bist,	That you are no more,
Ach! dass hier in diesem Grabe	That my Anselmo lies
Mein Anselmo ist,	Here in this grave:
Das ist mein Schmerz! Das ist mein Schmerz!!!	That is my sorrow! That is my sorrow!!!
Seht, wie liebten wir uns beide,[1]	See, how much we loved each other,
Und so lang ich bin, kommt Freude	And as long as I live joy
Niemals wieder in mein Herz.	Will never return to my heart.

[1] Claudius writes 'Seht, *wir* liebten *uns, wir* beide'.

MATTHIAS CLAUDIUS (1740–1815); poem written late 1772/early 1773

*This is the ninth of Schubert's thirteen Claudius solo settings (1816–17). See the poet's biography
for a chronological list of all the Claudius settings.*

This is one of two graveside songs of Claudius from 1816; the other is *Bei dem Grabe meines
Vaters* D496. Schubert might have thought of them as related as both are in E flat; according to
John Reed this tonality betokens awe and devotion (whether major or minor). These songs
illustrate the love for family that transcends romantic fascination. The first of them describes
Claudius's visit to the grave of his father, but the title of *Am Grabe Anselmos* does not, in itself,
help us with the poem's background. Capell writes: 'A certain sweetness in the music and a
slenderness depict an adolescent mourner whose life is probably not in peril, however sharp the
momentary pain.' In actual fact Claudius and his remarkable wife Rebecca are the bereaved
parents, and it is their first child Matthias (nicknamed 'Anselmo') who has died on the day of
his birth, 30 September 1772. The slender vulnerability which Capell rightly hears in the music
depicts the victim, not the bereaved.

The composer was himself all too familiar with infant mortality in his own family. Because
death in childhood was such a familiar occurrence the tone of the poem, and thus also the
music, depicts resignation rather than surprise and shock. But the dark cloud of a sudden loss
and the pity of a wasted life are beautifully conveyed in the music, a perfect fit for the poem's
restrained, but very deep, emotion. Some time later Claudius wrote a poem entitled *Anselmuccio*
in which he dreams of having another son whom he imagines will be a healthy blue-eyed blond
lad. In writing its closing lines Claudius (who was destined to be father of many children in an
exceptionally happy family life) refers back to the opening line of *Am Grabe Anselmos*:

Nur eines fehlt dir, lieber Knabe!	There's only one thing wrong with you, dear boy,
Eins nur: dass ich dich noch nicht habe.	Just one, and that is, I don't yet have you.

The song, written in the tripartite form of a Mozart aria, is shyly modest in scale, although it
has a gravity which is reinforced by the ceremonial pace in E flat minor. This key feels rather
disconcerting under the fingers of the pianist who has played many Schubert lieder, and is aware
of its rarity. Conversely, the mezzo staccato quavers between the hands in bb. 9 and 35 are
uncannily familiar: the journey to Anselmo's graveside seems signposted, at a distance of eleven
years, by *Der Wegweiser* from *Winterreise*.

If the composer had been initially unaware of the text's biographical background, someone
versed in the lives of older poets – Mayrhofer, for example – might have provided the necessary
information. The very first word 'Dass' is set on an accented suspension that resolves to the
tonic chord only on the second beat of the bar; this is a perfect illustration of all the tension
and pain that is covered by that single word. The child's name is set as 'Anselmo' with a decoration of four semiquavers on the word's last syllable (bb. 10–11), affectionate as a father's caress
– a musical equivalent of the poet's emphasis on the name in the German manner by means of
spacing it when printed. In the accompaniment, mezzo staccato quavers, or quavers played
between the hands and separated by rests, add to the youthful vulnerability. The repeat of the
words 'Das ist mein Schmerz' is the poet's, and Schubert adds a further 'mein Schmerz' of his
own between the two phrases in deference to the three exclamation marks employed by Claudius
at this point. The setting of 'Seht, wie liebten wir uns beide' in the relative major could not
possibly pertain to romantic love, utterly innocent as it is, and so gentle (bb. 19–20). The repeat
of the words (bb. 21–3) occasions a leap upwards like a stifled sob; darker harmonies underscore
the sudden twinge of pain. Under the words 'Und so lang ich bin', the formerly unadorned

quavers of the piano part break down into a figure familiar as a mourning motif: three sighing semiquavers in the right hand set off by quavers in the left. The world of Mozart's lieder is evoked here (as in, for example, *Das Lied der Trennung* K519). Mozart himself was twenty-three when Anselmo died; Schubert has an almost infallible sense of time travel when he sets his eighteenth-century poets.

The song's third section is an exact repeat of the first (as befits its classical form) but the three-bar postlude adds something new and touchingly eloquent: staccato notes in the left hand and a melting tune in the right are played as gently as those same hands might attend to a sick child, stroking a feverish brow in heartbreaking vigil. We hear some consolation in the concluding chord where the arrival into E flat major in b. 45 is decorated with searching quavers before returning to the same chord in b. 46.

The second version of the song (perhaps a version for Vogl?) published in the NSA is marked 'Sehr Langsam'. This was included in the album of songs prepared for Therese Grob in November 1816. It differs in small details from the published version. The vocal line is ornamented in the manner of an old-fashioned aria and the dynamic markings are different.

Schubert's friend Leopold Kupelwieser made a drawing inspired by this song – a young man, old enough nevertheless to be the father of a child, sitting reflectively by a grave.

At Anselmo's Grave, ink drawing (1821) by Leopold Kupelwieser.

Autograph:	Rychenberg-Stiftung, Winterthur (first version; first draft)
	In private possession (second version; part of the Therese Grob album)
Publication:	First published as Op. 6 no. 3 by Cappi & Diabelli, Vienna in 1821 (P17; first version)
	First published as part of the NSA in 1970 (P750; second version)
Dedicatee:	Johann Michael Vogl
Publication reviews:	*Allgemeine musikalische Zeitung* (Vienna), No. 6 (19 January 1822), col. 43ff. [Waidelich/Hilmar Dokumente I No. 142]
	F. von Hentl 'Blick auf Schubert's Lieder', *Wiener Zeitschrift für Kunst, Literatur, Theater und Mode* No. 36 (23 March 1822), p. 289f. [Waidelich/Hilmar Dokumente I No. 146; Deutsch Doc. Biog. No. 278]

First known performance:	9 November 1821, *Abend-Unterhaltung* of the Gesellschaft der Musikfreunde, Vienna. Soloist: Georg Krebner, accompanied by Schubert (see Waidelich/Hilmar Dokumente I No. 128 for full concert programme)
Subsequent editions:	Peters: Vol. 2/14; AGA XX 275: Vol. 4/236; NSA IV: Vol. 1a/56 & Vol. 1b/216; Bärenreiter: Vol. 1/46
Bibliography:	Capell 1928, p. 120
Discography and timing:	Fischer-Dieskau I 8²² 3'11
	Hyperion I 17¹⁷ 3'08 Lucia Popp
	Hyperion II 16²¹

← *Abendlied* D499   *Phidile* D500 →

AM MEER *see SCHWANENGESANG* D957/12

AM SEE
(MAYRHOFER) **D124** [H55]

By the lake

The song exists in two versions, the second of which is discussed below:
(1) December 1814; (2) 7 December 1814

(1)   'Langsam'   G minor   §   [22 bars]

(2)   G minor

(107 bars)

(1)   Sitz' ich im Gras am glatten See,
       Beschleicht die Seele süsses Weh;
       Wie Äolsharfen klingt mich an[1]
       Ein unnennbarer Zauberwahn.

When I sit in the grass by the smooth lake,
Sweet sorrow steals through my soul;
As if by Aeolian harps, I am moved
By nameless magical sounds.

(2)   Das Schilfrohr neiget seufzend sich,
       Die Uferblumen grüssen mich,
       Der Vogel klagt, die Lüfte weh'n,—
       Vor Schmerzeslust möcht' ich vergeh'n!

The bulrushes bow, sighing;
The flowers on the bank greet me;
A bird laments, breezes blow.
I would die of sweet grief!

(3)   Wie mir das Leben kräftig quillt,
       Und sich in raschen Strömen spielt,
       Wie's bald in trüben Massen gärt,
       Und bald zum Spiegel sich verklärt![2]

How vigorously life flows around me,
Playing in rapid currents,
Now fermenting in a dark mass,
And now as bright as a mirror.

[1] Mayrhofer writes '*Mit Äolsharfen*'. For an explanation of the background to these alternative Mayrhofer readings see Editorial Note at the beginning of Johann MAYRHOFER.
[2] Mayrhofer writes 'Und *nun* zum Spiegel'.

(4)   Bewusstsein meiner tiefsten Kraft,[3]   An awareness of my deepest powers
      Ein Wonnemeer in mir erschafft: Creates waves of joy within me.
      Ich stürze kühn in seine Flut,[4]   I plunge boldly into the waters
      Und ringe um das höchste Gut.   And strive for the highest good.

(5)   O Leben, bist so himmlisch schön   O life, you are so celestially beautiful,
      In deinen Tiefen, in deinen Höh'n![5]   In your depths and your peaks!
      Dein freundlich Licht soll ich nicht sehn, If I don't see your fair light;
      Den finstern Pfad des Orkus gehn?[6]   I shall follow the black course to Hades.

(6)   Doch bist du mir das Höchste nicht,[7]   Yet you are not my highest ideal,
      Drum opfr' ich freudig dich der Pflicht;   And I joyfully sacrifice you to duty.
      Ein Strahlenbild schwebt mir voran,   A radiant image draws me onwards;
      Und mutig wag' ich's Leben d'ran!   For it I will bravely risk my life.

(7)   Das Strahlenbild ist oft betränt,   This radiant image is often bathed in tears,
      Wenn es durch meinen Busen brennt,[8]   As it burns through my breast.
      Die Tränen weg vom Wangenrot—   Away with such tears on my youthful cheeks,
      Und dann in tausendfachen Tod!   And let me die a thousandfold death!

(8)   Du warst so menschlich, warst so hold,[9]   You were so humane, so gracious,
      O grosser deutscher Leopold!   So great a German, Leopold;
      Die Menschheit fühlte dich so ganz,[10]   Mankind felt your goodness to the full,
      Und reichte dir den Opferkranz.   And handed you the sacrificial wreath.

(9)   Und hehr geschmückt sprangst du hinab,   Nobly adorned, you leapt down,
      Für Menschen in das Wellengrab.[11]   For men's sake, to death in the waves.
      Vor Dir erbleicht, o Fürstensohn,[12]   Son of princes,
      Thermopylae und Marathon!   Thermopylae and Marathon pale before you.

(10) Das Schilfrohr neiget seufzend sich,   The bulrushes bow, sighing;
      Die Uferblumen grüssen mich,   The flowers on the bank greet me;
      Der Vogel klagt, die Lüfte wehn—   A bird sings, breezes blow.
      Vor Schmerzeslust möcht' ich vergehn!   I would die of sweet grief.

---

[3] Mayrhofer writes 'Bewusstsein meiner *innern* Kraft'.
[4] Mayrhofer writes 'Ich stürze *mich* in seine Flut'.
[5] The second 'in' in this line is Schubert's addition.
[6] Mayrhofer writes 'Den *düstern Gang zum* Orkus gehn'.
[7] The sixth verse as printed in Mayrhofer's *Gedichte* (1824) needs to be quoted in full:
    '*Auch* du bist mir das Höchste nicht:
    Ich opfre heiter dich der Pflicht.
    Ein Strahlenbild schwebt mir voran,
    Und mutig wag' ich *Alles* d'ran.'
[8] Mayrhofer writes '*Wie* es durch meinen Busen brennt'.
[9] Mayrhofer writes 'Du warst so menschlich *und* so hold'.
[10] Mayrhofer writes '*Und gut*, o deutscher Leopold! / Die Menschheit *füllte* Dich, so ganz'.
[11] Mayrhofer writes '*Ein Retter* in das Wellengrab'.
[12] Mayrhofer writes '*Vor Dir erblichen*, Fürstensohn!'.

Johann Mayrhofer (1787–1836)

This is the first of Schubert's forty-seven Mayrhofer solo settings (1814–24). See the poet's biography for a chronological list of all the Mayrhofer settings.

The poem is a sort of retrospective *pièce d'occasion*, a meditation on the fact that Duke Leopold of Brunswick (Braunschweig-Lüneberg), a nephew of Friedrich the Great, died in the drifting ice floes of the river Oder on 27 April 1785 while attempting to save some of his subjects from drowning in a flood. Goethe and Herder also composed elegies to this man whose bravery embodied *noblesse oblige*. In his *Herzog Leopold von Braunschweig*, Goethe imagines the duke slumbering in the depths until awakened to further acts of bravery:

Dich ergriff mit Gewalt der alter Herrscher des Flusses,	The ancient lord of the river seized you by force,
Hält dich und teilet mit dir ewig sein strömendes Reich,	He holds you and eternally shares with you his streaming realm,
Ruhig schlummerst du nun beim stilleren Rauschen der Urne,	You now slumber peacefully as the urn murmurs softly,
Bis dich stürmende Flut wieder zu Taten erweckt.	Until the seething torrent awakens you to further deeds.
Hilfreich werde dem Volke! So wie du ein Sterblicher wolltest,	Aid the people, as you wished to do when mortal,
Und vollend als ein Gott, was dir als Menschen misslang.	And as a god complete what you failed to accomplish as a man.

There was also a rather more openly emotional piece, beloved of reciters in public, by Karl Friedrich Wilhelm Herrosee (1764–1821) entitled *Dem edlen Tode Herzog Leopolds von Braunschweig*, that begins, 'Weep everyone, weep those worthy enough through tears to bring news of the death of the best of princes.' In one of Schubert's school textbooks, the first volume of *Sammlung Deutscher Beyspiele zur Bildung des Styls*, there is a long and laudatory chapter on Duke Leopold. It is likely that the young composer recognized and identified this hero as soon as he read Mayrhofer's poem which came his way via Josef von Spaun. Schubert's setting of it was the foundation of the friendship between poet and composer.

The incident took place two years before Mayrhofer's birth; one can only suppose that the poet admired the man of action (which he himself was not) and was moved by this story of self-sacrifice so different from the behaviour of the feckless aristocracy. There is some justification for patriotic pride in such a German hero, particularly in 1814 when the young Schubert was stirred by the political events that had led up to the defeat of Napoleon by an alliance in which Germany and Austria fought on the same side. When surrounded by sensual aspects of nature (and in this case sensual fantasies concerning gallant young men from the past, whether Duke Leopold or the heroes of Thermopylae), Mayrhofer's happiness is typically modified by self-censoring sadness – thus the use of the hybrid emotion of the strange word 'Schmerzelsust'.

Verses 1–2: The twenty bars which contain these two verses of text (marked 'Nicht zu langsam') are charming and unproblematic in a Mozartian manner. A week before composing *Am See* Schubert had set Goethe's *Schäfers Klagelied* D121 which starts and finishes with a similarly rueful, but not so chromatic, *siciliana*. The time signature, and the lilt of two upbeat semiquavers, also suggest a later lakeside Mayrhofer setting – *Erlafsee* D586. Both poems rhyme 'See' with 'Weh' in the opening lines.

Verses 3–4: An impassioned vocal recitative alternates with piano interludes in turbulent triplets marked 'Geschwind'. The poet swims in the lake for fun but is reminded of someone who found himself in the water for more noble reasons. The currents of the water are a metaphor for the ups and downs of life (cf. *Der Strom* D565). The piano figurations after 'in raschen Strömen spielt' (bb. 23–5) are reflected two bars later in sparkling mirror image (bb. 27–30). The poet dives into the deep end from a high B flat on b. 38 (such high notes are not common in Schubert's lieder, though this song has other such challenges in Verse 7).

Verse 5: At b. 46 the key signature changes to F major, and the tempo marking is 'Mässig'. It is as if the intrepid swimmer has survived the maelstrom and surfaced in a still lagoon, chastened by the experience. Accordingly the poem, and the music, take a somewhat classical turn; in this miniature aria Gluck's shade is evoked, as is often the case when Schubert sets material that refers to the underworld.

Verses 6–7: These verses inspire a novel, though not entirely successful, experiment in unmeasured ('taktlos') recitative; voice and piano come momentarily adrift. There follows frenzied activity where the singer throws himself at the high notes. (The voice is marked 'Sehr schnell' at 'Die Tränen weg vom Wangenrot' (bb. 66–8), then 'mit voller Kraft'.) The piano interlude which follows 'tausendfachen Tod' is also marked 'sehr schnell'. Bars 70–75 bristle with portentous chords in jarringly dotted rhythm.

Verse 8: Prince Leopold's venerable name explains all this introspection and browbeating. At b. 76 the key signature changes to B flat major, the time signature to ¾ ('Mässig'). Schubert dons court dress for a minuet in honour of an eighteenth-century prince (cf. the final section, also in B flat major, old-fashioned, courtly and patriotic, of *Auf der Riesenkoppe* D611).

Verses 9–10: The reference to Greek history introduces us to an aspect of Mayrhofer we will get to know well in later songs. The assertion that the prince's bravery has eclipsed the legends of Thermopylae and Marathon might have been expected of a court poet in Prince Leopold's employ, but Mayrhofer's admiration stems from something quite different to the hyperbole of a paid employee. Here the poet, like the English classicist A. E. Housman, is safely able to distance himself from his admiration of young men and their athletic achievements (and appearance) by the fact that they are all long dead.

A modified recapitulation in the musical manner of Verse 2 ('Tempo primo', b. 83) closes the song in elegiac mood.

The composition of *Am See* was a turning point in Schubert's life; Mayrhofer, in his recollections of Schubert written a few months after the composer's death, remembered their first encounter: 'My connection with Franz Schubert began when a friend from my youth handed him for composition my poem 'Am See'. Hand in hand with this friend, Schubert, in 1814, entered the room we were to occupy jointly five years later'. The friend who introduced composer and poet was Josef von Spaun who had also introduced Schubert to the poet Körner. Perhaps it was also Spaun who drew Schubert's attention to the six Goethe poems (*Gretchen am Spinnrade* among them) which he set between 19 October and 12 December 1814. Within this line-up of famous poetry *Am See*, composed on 7 December, is concealed like a cuckoo in the nest, the work of a more or less unknown local poet. But with it Schubert announces his intention to set modern poetry from far and near, and *Am See* initiated a friendship that was of the greatest artistic and personal importance to the young composer.

The first version of the song is a fragment, crossed out by Schubert; it breaks off after twenty-two bars, shortly after the first vocal recitative. It is more or less this version that Friedlaender published in Volume VII of the Peters Edition, an all-too-convenient means of saving the song's melodious opening page and jettisoning the long ballad that follows. This is an example of Friedlaender allowing his enthusiasm for practical performance (he was after all a singer) to get the better of his musicological duties. He compounded his offence by inviting Max Kalbeck, Brahms's biographer, to add another two verses to the first two of Mayrhofer's poem. Kalbeck clearly found it rather amusing to emulate Mayrhofer's pessimistic style, although one can detect a hint of tongue-in-cheek parody ('Kommt die Nacht mit leisem Schritt / Und nimmt uns Alle, Alle mit').

Autograph:	Wienbibliothek im Rathaus, Vienna (bb. 1–57)
Publication:	Published as Vol. 7 no. 19 in Friedlaender's edition by Peters, Leipzig in 1885 (first 30 bars only); first published in its entirety as part of the AGA in 1894 (P549)
Subsequent editions:	Peters: Vol. 7/42 (first version adapted); AGA XX 36: Vol. 1/210; NSA IV: Vol. 7/65 (second version) & 194 (cancelled first version); Bärenreiter: Vol. 6/10
Bibliography:	Dürr, Introduction to NSA IV Volume 7, pp. XIV–XV Kohlhäufl 1999, p. 180
Arrangements:	Arr. Tilman Hoppstock (b. 1961) for guitar accompaniment, in *Franz Schubert: 110 Lieder* (2009)
Discography and timing:	Fischer-Dieskau I 2[17] 4'18
	Hyperion I 4[10]
	Hyperion II 4[11] 5'03 Philip Langridge

← *Sehnsucht* D123

Szene aus 'Faust' D126 →

AM SEE
By the lake

(Bruchmann) **D746** [H504]
E♭ major   1822–3

(36 bars)

In des Sees Wogenspiele
Fallen durch den Sonnenschein
Sterne, ach, gar viele, viele,
Flammend leuchtend stets hinein.
Wenn der Mensch zum See geworden,
In der Seele Wogenspiele
Fallen aus des Himmels Pforten
Sterne, ach, gar viele, viele.

Into the lake's play of waves,
Through the sunlight,
Stars, O so many stars,
Fall ceaselessly, flaming, gleaming.
When man has become a lake,
Stars, O so many stars,
Will fall from the gates of heaven
Into the play of waves within his soul.

Franz von Bruchmann (1798–1867)

This is the third of Schubert's five Bruchmann solo settings (1822–3). See the poet's biography for a chronological list of all the Bruchmann settings.

There is something about a barcarolle rhythm that suggested the movement of the stars in their courses to Schubert's musical imagination. This song and such settings as *Die Sterne* (Fellinger) D176 and *Die Sternennächte* (Mayrhofer) D670 are barcarolles for heavenly bodies floating in the lagoon of an upside-down world; all employ the same time signature, although each of them has a very different character. Apart from those songs where the stars are made to dance and sparkle cheekily in $\frac{2}{4}$ time (*Die Sterne* D939 of Leitner, and *Auf dem See*, Goethe, D543), the composer seems to have imagined the stars swimming in the heavens like so many tiny islands in an ocean of sky. The combination of stars and water occurs in *Der liebliche Stern* D861, also a song of upside-down reflection, but nowhere is the conjunction of water and celestial light more sensuous than in Bruchmann's *Am See*.

The simultaneous presence of starlight and sunlight is unlikely except at very special moments of dawn and twilight, and the image of man 'becoming like a lake' is fittingly high flown for someone who had attended Schelling's philosophy lectures in Erlangen at the end of 1821. (This surely plays a part in the dating of the song, *see below*.) The text seems to derive its inspiration partly from the Schlegel of *Abendröthe* and partly from Goethe. Schubert was clearly attracted more by the musical opportunities offered in the impressionistic combination of water and light than by the poem's metaphysics. Goethe's *Auf dem See* has similar ingredients, and it is hardly surprising that the composer chose the same key of E flat major and a similar accompanying figure for Bruchmann's lakeside scene. Kreissle's (disputed) date for the Bruchmann song is March 1817, the same month Schubert made a copy for Josef Hüttenbrenner of the Goethe piece which had obviously become a favourite with the circle. In the world of the Schubertiads ideas bounced off each other; one good song might lead to another (just as *Der Tod und das Mädchen* D531 was followed by Josef von Spaun's *Der Jüngling und der Tod* D545). Reed avers that 1817 seems a likely date for *Am See* on stylistic grounds alone. But in 1817 Bruchmann and Schubert had not yet met; most scholars, including those of the NSA, believe that *Am See* was composed in 1822–3, along with the other Bruchmann settings.

As in the Goethe setting, the introduction depicts an oar cleaving the water; the phrasing and the crescendi to the middle point of the bar suggest that the pianist is rowing, albeit in somewhat languid fashion. Perhaps the poem's narrator is lying alone in the bottom of the boat looking up at the stars; on the other hand the purpose of this water-borne journey could well be sensual dalliance *à deux*, without any need for haste or agitation. The image of a soul's openness and receptivity has erotic undertones, and Schubert responds to these. The singer is more stretched than the pianist in the performance of this song: one of Schubert's most daunting challenges from the point of view of breathing. For bar after bar there is scarcely a chink in the vocal line; the singer must take time to oxygenate in one of various places, none of them ideal for the text. These demanding phrases suggest the wondering (and wan--dering) gaze of poet and singer as the vocal line sweeps the heavens taking in all the beauties in its path.

Once the composer has used up all the words of this short poem he repeats the first and the seventh lines in a type of rapturous accompanied cadenza of cascading melody. The outburst of gratitude on the penultimate 'ach, gar viele' (bb. 29–30) encompasses a G, the highest note in the piece, a phrase that seems to overflow with emotion. This section cleverly stays away from the tonic so that we feel ourselves floating unanchored in an expansive wash of luxuriously sybaritic harmony. The coda is no less extraordinary; there are two more separate 'viele' phrases as if the sheer number of stars has defeated the singer's powers of description. A final scale passage (bb. 33–4), as hauntingly beautiful as it is technically treacherous, blossoms out of the final 'Sterne'; the first vowel of the word is held for an entire bar (b. 33) before taking off on its melismatic journey to completion. (This is not a song with which a nervous singer should begin a recital.) And then 'viele' twice more. The sense of space created by this music is remarkable. These final dying falls, sighing appoggiature of rapture, seem to echo far down the wide avenues of a watery universe. It is an indication of the emotions this music can generate that Schubert's closing 'viele', repeated as if in a starry vacuum, puts us in mind of 'Ewig', fervently repeated at the end of Mahler's *Das Lied von der Erde*.

Autograph:	Österreichische Nationalbibliothek, Vienna
First edition:	Published as Book 9 no. 2 of the *Nachlass* by Diabelli, Vienna in 1831 (P260)
Subsequent editions:	Peters: Vol. 5/29; AGA XX 422: Vol. 7/74; NSA IV: Vol. 13/31
Bibliography:	Capell 1928, pp. 47 & 176
	Dürr, Introduction to NSA IV Volume 13, pp. XVI–XVIII
	Fischer-Dieskau 1977, p. 159
	Youens 2007[2], pp. 159–65
Discography and timing:	Fischer-Dieskau II 5[20] 1'51
	Hyperion I 19[9]
	Hyperion II 26[10] 1'50 Felicity Lott

← *Willkommen und Abschied* D767   *Im Haine* D738 →

AM STROME
By the river

(MAYRHOFER) OP. 8 NO. 4, **D539** [H353]
B major   March 1817

(44 bars)

Ist mir's doch, als sei mein Leben	It seems to me that my life
An den schönen Strom gebunden,	Is bound to the fair river;
Hab' ich Frohes nicht an seinem Ufer,[1]	Have I not known joy
Und Betrübtes hier empfunden?	And sorrow on its banks?
Ja, du gleichest meiner Seele;	Yes, you are like my soul;
Manchmal grün und glatt gestaltet,	Sometimes green and unruffled,
Und zu Zeiten—herrschen Stürme—[2]	And sometimes lashed by storms,
Schäumend, unruhvoll, gefaltet!	Foaming, agitated, furrowed.

[1] The words 'an seinem' are Schubert's ametrical interpolation. Mayrhofer writes '*am Ufer*'. For an explanation of the background to these alternative Mayrhofer readings see Editorial Note at the beginning of Johann MAYRHOFER.
[2] Mayrhofer writes 'herrschen *Winde*'. Schubert ignores the implied parenthesis in his setting.

Fliessest zu dem fernen Meere,[3]	You flow to the distant sea,
Darfst allda nicht heimisch werden.	And cannot find your home there.
Mich drängt's auch in mildre Lande—	I, too, yearn for a more welcoming land;
Finde nicht das Glück auf Erden.	I can find no happiness on earth.

JOHANN MAYRHOFER (1787–1836)

This is the twentieth of Schubert's forty-seven Mayrhofer solo settings (1814–24). See the poet's biography for a chronological list of all the Mayrhofer settings.

The shape of this music is similar to that of *Am Bach im Frühlinge*, an aria with triplet accompaniment – water music – which is recapitulated in a *da capo* after a contrasting middle section. A similar if not identical musical architecture is also apparent in the most famous brook song of all, *Der Neugierige* D795/6 from *Die schöne Müllerin*. In that immortal lied, the aria beginning 'O Bächlein meiner Liebe' moves into a questioning recitative and the song concludes with a return of the cantilena, a restating of the spellbinding theme. Like that famous lied, the key of *Am Strome* is B major – one of several reasons why the Mayrhofer setting seems, in retrospect, to have been something of a preparation for other songs in this tonality: first the ornately Italianate Schlegel setting *Der Fluss* D693, and then *Der Neugierige*. Nevertheless, the popularity of *Am Strome* in its own right is not in question. It was published in Schubert's lifetime and has been sung ever since. This is is due entirely to the beauty of the song's ingratiating vocal line, a marvel of *bel canto* that would have made any Italian composer green with envy. The text incorporates the message of *Der Wanderer* D489 while expressing the poet's alienation in a less portentous and self-pitying manner.

In *Am Strome*, as in *Der Neugierige*, man confesses his feelings to nature in the most confidential and intimate terms. The river becomes a metaphor for the poet's soul. By way of contrast the declamatory and disruptive middle section (marked 'Geschwind', from b. 14) is a marvellous example of Schubertian arioso (it is too melodic to be written off as simple recitative). The impetuous setting of the words 'unruhvoll, gefaltet' (bb. 23–5) is particularly impressive as the voice plunges to the bottom of the stave, the word 'gefaltet' set as a shudder. Calm returns. The simple little piano interlude following this outburst is a remarkable example of Schubert pouring oil on troubled waters – two little phrases in F sharp major (bb. 26–7, and bb. 28–9), one gently capping the other. These five bars effect the transition to the *da capo* in the simplest manner; we await a repeat of the B major cantilena with pleasure.

It is notable that the pessimism of Mayrhofer's words has not inclined Schubert to the minor key; instead he used the 'pathetic' major, beloved of *bel canto* composers like Donizetti and Bellini. The song sounds gentle and easy on the ear; in fact it is a huge challenge to any of its interpreters. The pianist is to some extent let off lightly, but the singer who places *Am Strome* on his or her programme has a formidable task in every way – the seamless, controlled line that is required is the hardest kind of vocal challenge imaginable.

Autograph: Wienbibliothek im Rathaus, Vienna
First edition: Published as Op. 8 no. 4 by Cappi & Diabelli, Vienna in May
                             1822 (P24)

---

[3] Mayrhofer writes 'Fliessest *fort zum* fernen Meere'.

Dedicatee: Johann Karl Grafen Esterházy von Galántha
Subsequent editions: Peters: Vol 2/25; AGA XX 306: Vol. 5/54; NSA IV: Vol. 1/82;
                              Bärenreiter: Vol. 1/66
Bibliography: Capell 1928, p. 138
Discography and timing: Fischer-Dieskau I 9²²   2'20
                              Hyperion I 4¹²
                              Hyperion II 18⁴   2'25   Philip Langridge

← *Der Schiffer* D352   *Antigone und Oedip* D542 →

AM TAGE ALLER SEELEN   Litany for the Feast of All Souls
(Litanei)
(Jacobi) **D343** [H293]

The song exists in two versions, the first of which is discussed below:
(1) August 1816; (2) November 1816?

(1)   E♭ major

(2)   'Langsam, mit Andacht'   E♭ major   **C**   [12 bars]

Ruhn in Frieden alle Seelen,   May all souls rest in peace;
Die vollbracht ein banges Quälen,   Those whose fearful torment is past;
Die vollendet süssen Traum,   Those whose sweet dreams are over;
Lebenssatt, geboren kaum,   Those sated with life, those barely born,
Aus der Welt hinüber schieden: Who have left this world:
Alle Seelen ruhn in Frieden!   May all souls rest in peace!

[. . .]   [. . .]

Liebevoller Mädchen Seelen,   The souls of girls in love,
Deren Tränen nicht zu zählen,   Whose tears are without number,
Die ein falscher Freund verliess,   Who, abandoned by a faithless lover,
Und die blinde Welt verstiess: Rejected by the blind world:
Alle, die von hinnen schieden,   May all who have departed hence,
Alle Seelen ruhn in Frieden!   May all souls rest in peace!

[. . . 2 . . .]   [. . . 2 . . .]

Und die nie der Sonne lachten,   And those who never smiled at the sun,
Unterm Mond auf Dornen wachten,   Who lay awake beneath the moon on beds of thorns,

Gott, im reinen Himmelslicht,	So that they might one day see God face to face
Einst zu sehn von Angesicht:	In the pure light of heaven:
Alle, die von hinnen schieden,	May all who have departed hence,
Alle Seelen ruhn in Frieden!	May all souls rest in peace!

[. . . 3 . . .]   [. . . 3 . . .]

JOHANN GEORG JACOBI (1740–1814); poem written between 1775 and 1788

This is the first of Schubert's seven Jacobi solo settings (1816). See the poet's biography for a chronological list of all the Jacobi settings.

When one hears this immortal song in the context of other lieder from the same year it is remarkable how familiar its style already sounds: a rippling accompaniment of deceptive simplicity unfurls beneath a melody that must be sung in the purest and most ineffable legato. One of the tasks that the composer seems to have set himself in 1816 was the creation of melody pure and simple; he had already spent a great deal of time on the recitative and arioso of German dramatic balladry. A work like this could not be more of a contrast; its success proves that, by the middle of the year, Schubert's determination to incorporate the fluidity of *bel canto* into his vocal music had paid off handsomely. The song was composed a few months after the Salieri jubilee celebrations in June 1816 after which it is said that Schubert ceased to work with the Italian master, but perhaps the young composer kept in touch with his teacher and showed him something of his latest work. The old boy would have been beside himself with delight. This song has something for everybody of whatever education, whether a German-speaker moved by profound word-setting, or an Italian who could not have wished for a more memorable or moving tune composed with optimum effect for the voice. As Fischer-Dieskau has written: 'The singer who can execute the long spun-out vocal line with a perfect legato and, at the same time, interpret each phrase meaningfully, probably knows everything that there is to know about singing *piano*.' The patent depth and sincerity of this music unites the musical connoisseur and neophyte; both head and heart judge it to be a masterpiece.

It is easier to salute Schubert's skill than to analyse how he conjures such emotion on a single sheet of paper. As usual the answer lies in the poetry, for the composer has taken the shape of the music from Jacobi. The poet's six-line strophe becomes the carefully plotted ground plan: the music for the first line of poetry and the last (including the piano postlude) are the two elegiac pillars between which the musical edifice is built. Within these noble demarcations, lines 2 to 5 of each verse allow for a pang of anguish or longing (the music moves into the relative minor at b. 3, with the mood more troubled by chromatic harmony). After these perigrinations the cleverly prepared return to E flat major via a cadence in the dominant (b. 7) is an absolving blessing and reassurance. Throughout most of the song the piano is gently supportive, the resonance of the bass line a source of unobtrusive strength but the concluding three solo bars are in that special class occupied by only the greatest of Schubert's postludes. This valedictory commentary, in part made up of new musical ideas, seems to amplify the meaning of the song beyond what the poem itself is capable of saying. This gently stirring piano writing requires both passion and humility from the accompanist; rising sequences match the heavenward gaze of the suppliant who searches for, and finds, musical consolation which lies beyond the power of words.

There are nine verses in the original poem, but most performers find that the song makes greatest impact with the performance of only three. These three verses (as printed above) are included in the first version published in the NSA based on the song's first edition. There is some doubt as to whether the single-bar introduction for the piano is genuine Schubert, but it is effective and time-honoured; it is, after all, perfectly possible that this version was based on a lost autograph. The second version from the Therese Grob songbook, probably from November 1816 (first published in Volume 10 of the NSA, 2002), is without a piano prelude. The vocal line and piano writing are slightly more ornamented (left-hand octaves occur in different places), and only one verse of the poem was written in by Schubert.

Autograph:	Missing or lost (first version)
	In private possession in Switzerland (second version – part of the Therese Grob album)
Publication:	First published as Book 10 no. 5 of the *Nachlass* by Diabelli, Vienna in 1831 (P266; first version)
	First published as part of the NSA in 2002 (P823; second version)
Subsequent editions:	Peters: Vol. 2/212; AGA XX 342: Vol. 5/216; NSA IV: Vol. 10/4 & 6
Bibliography:	Capell 1928, pp. 117–18
	Fischer-Dieskau 1977, pp. 75–6
Arrangements:	Arr. Franz Liszt (1811–1886) for solo piano, no. 1 of *Franz Schuberts Geistliche Lieder* (1840) [*see* TRANSCRIPTIONS]
	Arr. Leopold Godowsky (1870–1938) for solo piano as 'Litany' (1927, 2nd revised edition 1937) [*see* TRANSCRIPTIONS]
	Arr. Max Reger (1873–1916) for voice and orchestra (1913–14) [*see* ORCHESTRATIONS]
Discography and timing:	Fischer-Dieskau II 2^5 3'49 (Strophes 1 & 3 only)
	Hyperion I 17^{15}
	Hyperion II 15^{20} 4'44 Lucia Popp

← *Die Perle* D466   *An den Mond* D468 →

AMALIA
(SCHILLER) **D195** [H97]
A major – A minor   19 May 1815

Amalia

(74 bars)

Schön wie Engel voll Walhallas Wonne,	Fair as angels filled with the bliss of Valhalla.
Schön vor allen Jünglingen war er,	He was fair above all other youths;
Himmlisch mild sein Blick, wie Maien-Sonne,	His gaze had the gentleness of heaven, like the May sun
Rückgestrahlt vom blauen Spiegel-Meer.	Reflected in the blue mirror of the sea.

[. . .]¹   [. . .]

Seine Küsse – paradiesisch Fühlen!   His kisses were the touch of paradise!
  Wie zwei Flammen sich ergreifen, wie   As two flames engulf each other,
Harfentöne in einander spielen   As the sounds of the harp mingle
  Zu der himmelvollen Harmonie—   In celestial harmony.

Stürzen, flogen, schmolzen Geist in   So our spirits rushed, flew and fused together;
  Geist zusammen,
  Lippen, Wangen brannten, zitterten,   Lips and cheeks burned, trembled,
Seele rann in Seele – Erd' und Himmel   Soul melted into soul, earth and heaven
  schwammen
  Wie zerronnen um die Liebenden!   Swam, as though dissolved, around the lovers!

Er ist hin – vergebens, ach vergebens   He is gone – in vain, ah in vain
  Stöhnet ihm der bange Seufzer nach!   My anxious sighs echo after him!
Er ist hin, und alle Lust des Lebens   He is gone, and all life's joy
  Rinnet hin in ein verlor'nes Ach!²   Ebbs away in one forlorn cry!

FRIEDRICH VON SCHILLER (1759–1805); poem written 1777/80

This is the twelfth of Schubert's forty-four Schiller solo settings (1811–24). See the poet's biography for a chronological list of all the Schiller settings.

Amalia von Edelreich is the heroine of Schiller's drama *Die Räuber*; she is the orphaned niece of the aged Graf von Moor to whom she sings this song at the opening of the play's third act, in the garden and accompanying herself on a lute. She has been brought up as a sister to the two Moor brothers, Karl and Franz, and is in love with Karl, who has been banished.

    Amalia's song in the play is a slightly different version of the words from the one set by Schubert. Such was the fame of the play that the composer could well have read it in Volume 1 of the 1810 edition of Schiller's works issued by Anton Doll in Vienna   the same *Ausgabe* in which he found the poem in a somewhat altered guise (Volume 10: *Gedichte*). Some of the texts for Schubert's most dramatic songs were taken from plays; a number of these are still to be heard regularly in the German-speaking theatre. From this point of view *Amalia* is the Schiller counterpart to Goethe's *Gretchen am Spinnrade*, though infinitely less known; legions of actresses have spoken the words of Gretchen on stage without the benefit of Schubert's music, and countless leading ladies have sung Amalia's song to much less sophisticated music by other composers. (The difference between the two poems is that Schiller stipulates music in his play as part of the action, Goethe does not.)

    The subject of Amalia's lyric is the disgraced Karl Moor who has been cheated of his inheritance by his renegade brother, and who has become the leader of a band of robbers. Despite the blandishments and threats of the villainous Franz, Amalia remains steadfastly devoted to Karl's memory – at this stage she believes him to be dead.

    We hear this stoic determination in the opening lines of her song. Amalia's description of Karl's heroic beauty is something of a mystical incantation. The word 'Walhalla' can be traced

¹ There is a further strophe here that appears in the poem as it is printed in *Die Räuber*, Act III Scene 1 (Anton Doll, Wien, 1810).
² Schiller writes '*Wimmert* hin in ein verlor'nes Ach!'.

back to Klopstock's interest in the Hermann legend (*see Hermann und Thusnelda* D322), and this has introduced a tone of ancient minstrelsy into the musical response of a composer who was already becoming attuned to the poetry of Ossian. In this first section the singer is still very much in control of her emotions; the image of a mirror-like sea inspires unruffled music. The vocal line is high and pure; *Strophe aus 'Die Götter Griechenlands'* D677 also comes to mind in this tonality and tessitura. Like that song, this Schiller setting refers to something beautiful that has been irretrievably lost.

The marking changes to 'Recit.'; the key changes from A major to A minor (b. 19). (Reichardt's 1809 strophic setting of this text is also in A major.) The memory of Karl's kiss awakens desire in Amalia, just as the memory of Faust's kiss suddenly brought Gretchen's spinning wheel to a halt. The difference is that Gretchen realizes, even subliminally, that the relationship with Faust is frightening and dangerous. Amalia's memories of Karl are associated with the deepest, truest emotion on both sides. This melting of one soul into another is described in terms of leaping flames and vibrating strings; Schubert rises to the challenge with a tremolando shimmer and snatched chords as if plucked by a harp-playing seer in a moment of ecstatic distraction.

At 'Lippen, Wangen brannten' (again one is reminded of Gretchen's physical description of Faust) Amalia's thoughts race forward. The marking is 'Sehr schnell' – very fast; the panting piano part (chords alternating between the hands) shifts to a new chord in every bar. This restlessness while recalling a powerfully erotic relationship prophesies the intensity of Berlioz's Marguerite. Vistas broaden and the music becomes smoother at 'Erd' und Himmel schwammen' (from b. 37). In order to set up the powerful final strophe of the song Schubert gives the listener, and singer, a moment of respite and Amalia's vision gradually subsides. As we hear the quaver rhythm of the accompaniment melt into crotchet triplets (from b. 45), she appears to let her dream go, bringing her painful longing under control in the interlude's gentle diminuendo. The left-hand melody in the piano's cello register (bb. 45–5) is particularly eloquent.

If we have imagined that Amalia has accepted her fate quietly, the stark grandeur of the final strophe corrects that impression. This is the composer's especial surprise. The song roars to a close with music ('Langsam, traurig') worthy of a Gluck heroine *in extremis*. In a peroration in the grand style of another Schiller setting, *Der Pilgrim* D794, Amalia sings her heart out as if she were an Arianna or a Dido. Schubertians could not fail to note that this A minor tonality is also associated with Mignon in Schubert's last solo setting of Goethe's text (D877/4). Amalia's desolation equals Mignon's (her plight is also tragic and irreversible) but is unique in its expression. The change to C sharp minor (b. 63) for the 'Er ist hin, und alle Lust des Lebens' of the poem's penultimate line, accompanied by hammered dotted minims in the piano, is both chilling and powerful. When we hear the anguish with which Schubert sets Amalia's closing words – 'ein verlor'nes Ach!', bb. 68–70 – a later Schiller setting, *Gruppe aus dem Tartarus* D583 comes to mind (at the typically Schillerian expression 'Qualerpresstes Ach!' in bb. 19–20 of that song).

In Schubert's diary for 14 June 1816 (Deutsch Documentary Biography No. 86) he mentions having given performances of both *Rastlose Liebe* (Goethe) D138 and *Amalia* at a musical gathering – we assume he was both singer and pianist: 'Unanimous applause for the former, less for the latter. Although I myself think that my *Rastlose Liebe* is better than *Amalia*, I cannot deny that Goethe's musical poet's genius contributed much to the success.' Be that as it may, one can scarcely envisage a song of the size and intensity of *Amalia* being effectively performed by a nineteen-year-old amateur male singer, even if that singer were the composer himself.

| Autograph: | Stadtarchiv, Hannover (fair copy) |
| First edition: | Published as Op. post. 173 no. 1 by C. A. Spina, Vienna in 1867 (P407) |

Subsequent editions: Peters: Vol. 6/106; AGA XX 71: Vol. 2/113; NSA IV: Vol. 8/46
Bibliography: Deutsch 1946, p. 60
                           Deutsch 1964, pp. 42–3
Discography and timing: Fischer-Dieskau   —
                           Hyperion I 1[6]
                           Hyperion II 6[17]   3'18   Janet Baker

← *Rastlose Liebe* D138   *An die Nachtigall* D196 →

AMMENLIED

(Lubi) **D122** [H53]
G minor   December 1814

The nurse's song

Am hohen, hohen Turm,   Around the high tower
Da weht ein kalter Sturm: A cold gale blows.
Geduld! die Glöcklein läuten,   Patience! The bells ring;
Die Sonne blinkt von weiten.   The sun gleams from afar.
Am hohen, hohen Turm,   Around the high tower
Da weht ein kalter Sturm.   A cold gale blows.

Im tiefen, tiefen Tal,   In the deep valley
Da rauscht ein Wasserfall: A waterfall rushes.
Geduld! ein bisschen weiter,   Patience! A little further on
Da rinnt das Bächlein heiter.   The brooklet flows merrily.
Im tiefen, tiefen Tal,   In the deep valley
Da rauscht ein Wasserfall.   A waterfall rushes.

Am kahlen, kahlen Baum,   In the bare tree
Deckt sich ein Täubchen kaum,   A dove scarcely finds shelter.
Geduld! bald blühn die Auen,   Patience! Soon the meadows will bloom,
Dann wird's sein Nestchen bauen.   And then it will build its nest.
Am kahlen, kahlen Baum,   In the bare tree
Deckt sich ein Täubchen kaum.   A dove scarcely finds shelter.

Dich friert, mein Töchterlein!   You are frozen, my little daughter!
Kein Freund sagt: komm herein!   No friend asks you to come in!

Lass unser Stündchen schlagen,
Dann werden's Englein sagen.
Das beste Stübchen gibt
Gott jenem, den er liebt.

Let our hour come.
Then angels will invite you in.
God gives his best room
To those he loves.

MICHAEL LUBI (1757–1808)

This is Schubert's only setting of a Lubi text. See the poet's biography.

This is one of the last songs written in 1814, and one of the strangest. It closes the first volume of the Mandyczewski *Gesamtausgabe*, a single page of such simplicity that it seems an enigmatic and downbeat end to a collection that contains much that is astonishing and new. In accordance with the tradition of eighteenth-century strophic song the vocal line is doubled by the piano. Schubert's autograph is lost, and the first printing of the song only includes the first verse. Further verses were added from the author's *Gedichte*, published in Graz in 1804. One wonders why Schubert was attracted to this poem in the first place.

At first glance we would seem to be entering the world of the Viennese *Singspiel* and its style, like watered-down Mozart. But there is a sadder theme behind this music written for a simple working woman. (Is the child the nurse's own, or simply a waif in her care?) Reed talks of the song's playful tenderness, but there is something less than playful about this scenario. Certainly there is a merry little bell-ringing motif at the repeat of 'Am hohen, hohen Turm', but this is surely only whistling down the wind. *Ammenlied* is a winter song, written in winter. There is a faith in spring, a belief that singing about spring will make it come more quickly, and that things will soon change. But the frozen little daughter of the last strophe is not expected to survive the harshness of the season. She can only look forward to death, and the welcome of the angels. The nurse's cries of 'Patience' put us in mind of Mahler's haunting song *Das irdische Leben* where a mother exhorts her starving child to wait for food.

Schubert was no stranger to the death of children, including his younger siblings. Other songs reinforce the notion that *Ammenlied* incorporates a tragic story. In musical terms it is most closely related to another G minor song, *Lied* D373 (1816?) with a text by Fouqué; in this case the theme is parental distress over the loss of a child and grief is depicted through folksong simplicity in $\frac{2}{4}$ time. The repeated quavers pointing towards death in this song will find their apotheosis (once again in G minor) in *Der Wegweiser* from *Winterreise* where the winter traveller's best hope for the future is the peace of the grave. With this in mind it is possible to hear the bells of the first strophe as a peal rung for the dead – a hint here of the passing bell, the so-called *Zügenglöcklein* immortalized in Schubert's song of that name with a text by Seidl, D871.

These signposts to the future may seem fanciful. But Schubert's song output seems more of a piece the longer one studies it; after all it encompasses only fifteen or so years of productivity. Rather than shedding his past he builds bigger and grander edifices on what has always been part of his musical language and understanding. In this way, his early experiments are incorporated, elaborated and refined rather than thrown away. Out of the tiniest song acorns grow the mightiest oaks of lieder.

Autograph:	Missing or lost
First edition:	Published as No. 12 of *Neueste Folge nachgelassener Lieder und Gesänge* by J. P. Gotthard, Vienna in 1872 (P438) where the poet is wrongly named as Marianne Lubi
Subsequent editions:	Not in Peters; AGA XX 38: Vol. 1/224; NSA IV: Vol. 7/59; Bärenreiter: Vol. 6/5

Discography and timing: Fischer-Dieskau   —
                          Hyperion I 33[24]
                          Hyperion II 4[9]   1'56   Catherine Wyn-Rogers

← *Trost in Tränen* D120   *Sehnsucht* D123 →

AMPHIARAOS   Amphiaraus
(Körner) **D166** [H74]
G minor   1 March 1815

(1)   Vor Thebens siebenfach gähnenden   Outside Thebes' seven gaping gates
           Toren
       Lag im furchtbaren Brüderstreit   Lay, in grim fraternal strife,
       Das Heer der Fürsten zum Schlagen   The princes' armies, ready for battle,
           bereit,
       Im heiligen Eide zum Morde   And pledged to murder in sacred oath.
           verschworen.
       Und mit des Panzers blendendem Licht   Clad in dazzling armour,
       Gerüstet, als gält' es, die Welt zu   As if intent on conquering the world,
           bekriegen,
       Träumen sie jauchzend von Kämpfen   They dream joyfully of battle and victory.
           und Siegen,
       Nur Amphiaraos, der Herrliche, nicht. All but the noble Amphiaraus.

(2)   Denn er liest in dem ewigen Kreise   For in the eternal course of stars he reads
           der Sterne,
       Wen die kommenden Stunden feindlich   Whom the coming hours threaten with
           bedrohn.   a hostile fate.
       Des Sonnenlenkers gewaltiger Sohn   The mighty offspring of the sun's master
       Sieht klar in der Zukunft nebelnde Ferne. Sees clearly into the mists of the distant future.
       Er kennt des Schicksals verderblichen He understands destiny's pernicious bond;
           Bund,
       Er weiss, wie die Würfel, die eisernen, He knows how the iron dice fall;
           fallen,
       Er sieht die Möira mit blutigen Krallen; He beholds Fate with her bloody claws;
       Doch die Helden verschmähen den   Yet the heroes scorn his sacred words.
           heil'gen Mund.

(3)   Er sah des Mordes gewaltsame Taten,
Er wusste, was ihm die Parze spann.
So ging er zum Kampf, ein verlorner
    Mann,
Von dem eignen Weibe schmählich
    verraten.
Er war sich der himmlischen Flamme
    bewusst,
Die heiss die kräftige Seele durchglühte,
Der Stolze nannte sich Apolloide,

Es schlug ihm ein göttliches Herz in
    der Brust.

He saw monstrous deeds of murder;
He knew what Fate was spinning for him.
Thus he went to battle, a man doomed,

Shamefully betrayed by his own wife.

He was aware of the heavenly flame

Which burned fiercely through his great soul;
The proud man called himself the son of
    Apollo;
A godlike heart beat in his breast.

(4)   'Wie? – ich, zu dem die Götter geredet,
Den der Wahrheit heilige Düfte umwehn,[1]
Ich soll in gemeiner Schlacht vergehn,
Von Periklymenos' Hand getötet?
Verderben will ich durch eigene Macht,
Und staunend vernehm' es die
    kommende Stunde,
Aus künftiger Sänger geheiligtem Munde,
Wie ich kühn mich gestürzt in die
    ewige Nacht.'

'What? I, whom the gods have addressed,
Bathed in the holy scent of truth,
Am to perish in mean battle,
Slain by Periclymenos' hand?
I wish to die by the power of my own hand.
Future ages will hear, amazed,

From the sacred lips of minstrels
How I plunged boldly into eternal night.'

(5)   Und als der blutige Kampf begonnen,
Und die Ebne vom Mordgeschrei
    widerhallt,
So ruft er verzweifelnd: 'Es naht
    mit Gewalt,
Was mir die untrügliche Parze
    gesponnen.
Doch wogt in der Brust mir ein
    göttliches Blut,
Drum will ich auch wert des
    Erzeugers verderben.'
Und wandte die Rosse auf Leben
    und Sterben,
Und jagt zu des Stromes
    hochbrausender Flut.

And when the bloody fight commenced,
And the plain echoed with murderous cries,

He called in despair: 'What unerring Fate has
    spun for me
Now approaches with mighty force.

But divine blood flows in my breast,

Thus will my death be worthy of my
    progenitor.'
And he turned his horses, for life or for
    death,
And sped to the river's surging flood.

(6)   Wild schnauben die Rosse, laut rasselt
    der Wagen,[2]
Das Stampfen der Hufe zermalmet
    die Bahn.
Und schneller und schneller noch ras't
    es heran,
Als gält' es, die flüchtige Zeit zu erjagen.

The stallions snort fiercely, the chariot rattles
    loudly,
Stamping hooves pound the track.

Faster and faster they approach,

As if striving to catch fleeting Time itself.

---

[1] Körner writes 'Den der *Weisheit* heilige Düfte umwehn'.
[2] Körner writes 'Wild schnauben die *Hengste*'.

Wie wenn er die Leuchte des Himmels geraubt,	As if he had stolen the torch of heaven
Kommt er in Wirbeln der Windsbraut geflogen;	He rushes onwards in a seething whirlwind.
Erschrocken heben die Götter der Wogen	Horrified, the gods of the waves
Aus schäumenden Fluten das schilfichte Haupt.	Raise their reed-covered heads from the foaming floods.

(7)	Und plötzlich, als wenn der Himmel erglüh'te,[3]	But suddenly, as if the heavens were ablaze,
	Stürzt ein Blitz aus der heitern Luft,	A thunderbolt falls from the clear air,
	Und die Erde zerreisst sich zur furchtbaren Kluft;	The earth is ripped open, a terrifying chasm appears.
	Da rief laut jauchzend der Apollonide:	Then, in jubilation, the son of Apollo cried aloud:
	'Dank dir, Gewaltiger, fest steht mir der Bund.	'I thank you, mighty one! My covenant stands firm.
	Dein Blitz ist mir der Unsterblichkeit Siegel,	Your thunderbolt is my seal of immortality.
	Ich folge dir, Zeus!' – und er fasste die Zügel,	I follow you, Zeus!' And he seized the reins
	Und jagte die Rosse hinab in den Schlund.	And spurred his horses down into the abyss.

THEODOR KÖRNER (1791–1813)

This is the fourth of Schubert's sixteen Körner solo settings (1815–18). See the poet's biography for a chronological list of all the Körner settings. See also entry for Aeschylus.

In Greek legend Amphiaraus was a renowned warrior under the special protection of Zeus and Apollo. He married Eriphyle, sister of Adrastus, and one of the marriage stipulations was that if the two brothers-in-law disagreed on any issue, Eriphyle's arbitration was binding. Adrastus (the subject of a Schubert opera to a Mayrhofer text begun in 1814, *Adrast* D137) wanted to make war on Thebes, but Amphiaraus, gifted with a seer's powers, knew that this would be disastrous. Bribed by a gold and diamond necklace, Eriphyle declared herself in favour of the expedition. Bound by his promise, Amphiaraus was forced to take part in a war that he knew would lead to his death. He made his young sons swear to avenge him against Eriphyle, and departed as part of the catastrophic expedition that was the subject of a play by Aeschylus – *Seven against Thebes*. The predicament of Amphiaraus is summed up in lines 608–10 of that work:

a modest, brave, upright and pious man,
a powerful seer allied against his judgement
with blaspheming, boastful men . . .

The war was long, but in combat at the city's Homoloian gate (each of the seven champions attempted to storm one of Thebes' seven gates) Amphiaraus was finally put to flight by the

---

[3] Körner writes '*Doch* plötzlich'.

Theban hero Periclymenus who chased him to the banks of the Ismenus. Amphiaraus would have been slain had Zeus not sent a thunderbolt that made a cleft in the ground into which horse, chariot and driver disappeared. This spot was said to have been something of a tourist attraction as late as the second century AD.

Verse 1: 'Etwas langsam, mit Kraft'. The introduction in common time consists of a powerful rising sequence of chords in dotted rhythm, with a strong tolling bell sounding a solitary octave on the second half of the bar. This musical gesture seems to insist: 'What must be, must be!' Bars 9 to 12 of the slow movement of the Piano Sonata in B flat major D960 use this rhythmic pattern to more sophisticated effect – in that masterpiece from Schubert's final year, the 'bell' in the piano's upper regions is haunting rather than strident. An opening burst of narrative recitative is followed by a recapitulation of this impressive overture. The fighting men's joyful dreams of battle and victory are voiced in deliberately repetitive and banal manner; in contrast, the state of mind of Amphiaraus, who alone knows that their cause is doomed, is emphasized by the superb musical setting of his name (bb. 22–3). It stands alone, without accompaniment except for three chords in dotted rhythm under the longest vowel.

Verses 2–3: Throughout this work Schubert seems to be thinking in longer paragraphs, harmonically speaking, than in some of his earlier ballads. He adopts the form of a march in which to construct a stirring sequence of chords that skilfully suggests the mind-searchings of a man of deep and subtle perceptions; Amphiaraus is clearly different from the members of the herd who think and act only in terms of tonic and dominant harmony. The repetitive hammer blows in the accompaniment under 'Er kennt des Schicksals verderblichen Bund' (from b. 40) represent the immutable fall of iron dice. A change of key into B minor at 'Doch die Helden verschmähen den heil'gen Mund' (at b. 43) describes the hero's misgivings. The dotted march motif returns on 'So ging er zum Kampf' (from b. 56), this time as strangely out of sorts with the harmony of the vocal line as Amphiaraus is with his allies. Another change of key and pace (A major, 'Feurig', b. 63) prompts a movement with scales and arpeggios that throw off sparks of no great originality in order to depict 'the heavenly flame'.

Verse 4: 'Mit steigender Bewegung', from b. 76. This is an effective *recitativo stromentato* built on a falling sequence of harmonies that mirrors the hero's disbelief and depression. At 'Verderben will ich durch eigene Macht' (from b. 86) this black mood is courageously negated by bold vocal arpeggios in D major accompanied by sixteen resolute and insistent D major chords in dotted rhythm.

Verses 5–6: 'Geschwind', from b. 94. This section opens with nine bars of solo warfare for piano, one of Schubert's more effective interludes – different from the battle music of the Kenner *Ballade* D134 but comparable to the depiction of the seething waters of the abyss in *Der Taucher* D77. A different diminished seventh chord is sabre-rattled every two bars, thus suggesting strenuous fighting in first one Theban arena of war, then another. (Those commentators who disparagingly compare passages such as these with silent film music are at least correct in hearing that Schubert, in his ballads, imagines action in terms of what would a century later be praised as ingenious cinematic editing.) The third to the sixth lines of Verse 5 are arioso; this passage forms a bridge between the battle music and the galloping triplets that doubles the vocal line, at 'Und wandte die Rosse auf Leben und Sterben'.

Whipped up to a 'Geschwinder' marking, logically enough at the words 'Und schneller und schneller', the music works itself into a veritable lather of steaming horseflesh and flooding river. The conventional way of playing tremolo passages, octaves together, is inverted to make a long sequence of strident harmonic clashes at the ninth (beginning at 'Erschrocken heben die Götter . . . das schilfichte Haupt', from b. 137). These are technically allowable passing notes that

Illustration of *Amphiaroas* from Laube's edition of Körner's *Sämmtliche Werke* (1882).

resolve, but their unashamed dissonance must have delighted the young composer no end. It is notable that he reserves this grisly effect for the reaction of the gods and their horror at the disaster unfolding below.

Verse 7: The closing dénouement is something of a let-down in musical terms. The thunder of Zeus (at 'Und plöztlich, als wenn der Himmel erglüh'te') is written in the wrong part of the piano for it to sound effectively mighty; the lightning looks good in the score, however (bb. 146–7), descending from the top of the treble stave to the bottom, falling from on high with jagged edges. The tearing open of the earth is effected with abruptly rippled arpeggios, but is again something of an anticlimax in sonic terms. The final address to the deity (from b. 153), suddenly calm and spacious, fails to convince, and an abrupt return of the galloping motif pushes our hero quite unceremoniously over the precipice. One has to admire the composer for the audacity with which he peremptorily drops Amphiaraus in it – and the singer too if he is not careful; the lowest note in the piece (a minim G below middle C, b. 173) opens up at the end of the phrase without any warning. In bb. 159–74 Schubert was possibly attempting to mirror in musical terms the telescopic and laconic verbal endings that are to be found in many a Schiller-inspired narrative ballad.

Theodor Körner's background as a student of law and history gave him a good working knowledge of the classics, although his poems do not often venture into the world of the Greeks and Romans – the only others in this vein (not set by Schubert) are a dialogue between Brutus and Portia, and a hymn to Phoebus. The tale of Amphiaraus seems to tell us something about the poets' own determination to do his patriotic duty and fight no matter what his misgivings and forebodings.

According to the autograph, Schubert composed *Amphiaraos* 'in 5 hours', almost certainly in a rush of emotion that was a mixture of patriotism and affectionate personal gratitude for the memory of Körner, the poet who had encouraged him with kindly words in his fight to be a composer and who had himself died in battle. It is certainly an impressive achievement to have written a work like this within a few hours, but it also explains the uneven nature, sometimes wonderful, sometimes disappointing, of the piece as a whole.

Autograph:	Wienbibliothek im Rathaus, Vienna (first draft)
First edition:	Published as part of the AGA in 1895 (P556)
Subsequent editions:	Not in Peters; AGA XX 52: Vol. 2/68; NSA IV: Vol. 8/7; Bärenreiter: Vol. 6/107
Bibliography:	Capell 1928, p. 91
	Youens 1996, pp. 122–7
Discography and timing:	Fischer-Dieskau I 3[7] 6'04
	Hyperion I 14[2]
	Hyperion II 5[14] 6'12 Thomas Hampson

← *Sängers Morgenlied* D165   *Nun lasst uns den Leib begraben* D168 →

AN CHLOEN   To Chloe
(Uz) **D363** [H209]
(Fragment) G major   June? 1816

Die Munterkeit ist meinen Wangen,   Sprach' ent-gan-gen;   Der Mund will kaum ein Lä-cheln

(23 bars)

In the text printed below, the words and parts of words in italics are those for which Schubert's original music is lost.

Die Munterkeit ist meinen Wangen,
*Den Augen Glut und Sprach' ent*gangen;
Der Mund will kaum ein Lächeln wagen;
Kaum will der welke Leib sich tragen,
Der Blumen am Mittage gleicht,
Wann Flora lechzt und Zephyr weicht.

[...]

Ich seh' auf sie mit bangem Sehnen,
*Und kann den Blick nicht wegge*wöhnen:
Die Anmuth, die im Auge wachet,
Und um die jungen Wangen lachet,
Zieht meinen weggewichnen Blick
Mit güldnen Banden stets zurück.

Mein Blut strömt mit geschwindern Güssen;
Ich brenn', ich zittre, sie zu küssen;
Ich suche sie mit wilden Blicken,
Und Ungeduld will mich ersticken,
Indem ich immer sehnsuchtsvoll
Sie sehn und nicht umarmen soll.

My cheeks have lost their brightness,
My eyes their sparkle;
My lips hardly dare smile;
Like flowers at midday
When Flora thirsts and Zephyr dies,
My wilting body can scarcely support itself.

[...]

I look upon her with anxious longing,
And cannot turn my gaze away.
The grace that wakes in her eyes
And laughs around her young cheeks
Always draws back my averted gaze
With golden fetters.

My blood flows faster;
I burn, I tremble to kiss her;
I seek her out with desperate looks,
Choked with impatience,
For, in my longing I can always see her
But never embrace her.

JOHANN PETER UZ (1720–1796); poem written between 1742–44

This is the second of Schubert's five Uz solo settings (1816). See the poet's biography for a chronological list of all the Uz settings.

Most of the Schubert fragments represent projects abandoned by the composer – for various reasons. The challenge is usually to think of what he might have written had he had the time, interest or energy. Unusually, *An Chloen* was once a complete song and our task is to guess what Schubert *did* write. The manuscript was mutilated, probably by an autograph hunter who cut out part of the vocal line of *Die Nacht* D358, another Uz setting which was written on the back.

This thoughtless vandalism was not directed specifically against *An Chloen*, perhaps, but it left only bars 7 to 23 of the song intact. By chance the bass line of bars 1 to 6 is legible, and Reinhard Van Hoorickx reconstructed the song using material from the unusually long piano postlude to fashion a replacement vocal line where necessary. The poem is one of four with the same title in Book One of Uz's *Lyrische Gedichte*.

The melody has a gently loping gait and, as in that other Uz setting, *Die Liebesgötter* D446, the music is framed by pastoral artificiality. This does not exclude feeling – the tender little chromatic inflections are most affecting – but it is difficult to become deeply involved with this shepherd's plaint. He talks of Flora and Zephyr at the same time as heartbreak, and we somehow know that the gods will arrange for him to recover and revive. So it proves. The left-hand quavers at the beginning were staccato (we can see this much on the autograph). This surely means that the composer's original music was not too lovelorn, and that the tempo was not meant to be lugubrious.

Autograph:	University Library of Lund, Sweden (fragment)
First edition:	Fragment first published in *The Music Review* in 1954 and subsequently completed privately by Reinhard Van Hoorickx. First formally published as part of the NSA in 2002 (P841)
Subsequent editions:	Not in Peters; Not in AGA; NSA IV: Vol. 10/244
Bibliography:	Brown 1954, pp. 93–102
Discography and timing:	Fischer-Dieskau —
	Hyperion I 23[19]
	Hyperion II 12[4] 2'39 Christoph Prégardien

← *Klage um Ali Bey* D140   *Die Nacht* D358 →

AN CHLOEN   To Chloe
(Jacobi) **D462** [H288]
A♭ major   August 1816

(12 bars)

Bei der Liebe reinsten Flammen,	With the purest flames of love
Glänzt das arme Hütten-Dach:	The humble cottage roof shines.
Liebchen! ewig nun beisammen!	Sweetheart, now we are together eternally,
Liebchen! träumend oder wach![1]	Sweetheart, dreaming or awake!

[1] Jacobi writes 'Liebchen! *schlafend* oder wach!'

Süsses, zärtliches Umfangen,	Sweet, tender embrace
Wenn der Tag am Himmel graut:	when day dawns;
Heimlich klopfendes Verlangen,	secret, tremulous longing
Wenn der Abend niedertaut!	when the dew of evening falls.

[. . . 2 . . .]   [. . . 2 . . .]

Und wir teilen alle Freuden,	And we shall share all our joys,
Sonn' und Mond und Sternen-Glanz;	Sun, moon and starlight;
Allen Segen, alles Leiden,	Each blessing, each sorrow,
Arbeit und Gebet und Tanz.	Work, and prayer, and dancing.

So, bei reiner Liebe Flammen,	Thus, with the flames of pure love
Endet sich der schöne Lauf;	Shall the fair course end.
Ruhig schweben wir zusammen,	Peacefully we shall float together,
Liebchen! Liebchen! Himmel auf.	Sweetheart, toward heaven.

JOHANN GEORG JACOBI (1740–1814); poem written between 1775 and 1782

This is the second of Schubert's seven Jacobi solo settings (1816). See the poet's biography for a chronological list of all the Jacobi settings.

In between the famous *Am Tage aller Seelen* D343 and the epic *Lied des Orpheus* D474, both impressive Jacobi songs, lie five little settings of the same poet: *An Chloen* D462, *Hochzeit-Lied* D463, *In der Mitternacht* D464, *Trauer der Liebe* D465 and *Die Perle* D466. They were all composed within the same few days in August 1816, and they comprise if not a miniature Jacobi cycle in their own right, then at least something of a set. The repetitive key sequence of the six songs – A flat; E flat; E flat; A flat; A flat; F major – seems to discourage live performance as a group, although a reordering of the songs (placing *In der Mitternacht* fourth rather than third in the sequence) is a possibility. (Another performing sequence, excluding *Die Perle*, is discussed in the commentary for *Trauer der Liebe*.) We know that in April 1816 Schubert and his friend Spaun had written to Goethe, unsuccessfully trying to interest him in a project that would have included eight books of songs arranged according to the poets. Encouraged by his friends, Schubert already had a feeling for gathering together garlands of songs united by a poetic style, if not yet by a discernible theme.

The shy and elegant musical language of these five Jacobi songs is homogenous and undoubtedly looks back to Mozart. At the end of each verse of *An Chloen*, interludes with left-hand Alberti bass figurations clearly evoke the classical style. In considering this pleasant yet unremarkable little song one remembers one of the most famous Jacobi settings (the prize itself must surely go to Schubert's *Am Tage aller Seelen*, traditionally known as *Litanei*). This was Mozart's *An Chloe* K524 (1787), a setting of a different poem written presumably for the same girl, and a song surely well known to Schubert. The younger composer's music for his different Chloe text is less memorable, but charming nevertheless; it hides more opportunities for vocal and pianistic expression than may at first be thought.

Autograph:	Missing or lost
First edition:	Published as part of the AGA in 1895 (P646)
Subsequent editions:	Not in Peters; AGA XX 244: Vol. 4/149; NSA IV: Vol. 10/200

Discography and timing: Fischer-Dieskau I 7³⁰   1'09
                      Hyperion I 8⁹
                      Hyperion II 15¹⁵   1'41   Sarah Walker

← *Pflicht und Liebe* D467   *Hochzeit-Lied* D463 →

AN CIDLI *see* FURCHT DER GELIEBTEN D285

AN DEM JUNGEN MORGENHIMMEL *see* DON GAYSEROS D93/3

AN DEN FRÜHLING (I)   To the spring
(SCHILLER) **D283** [H169]
F major   6 September 1815

(24 bars)

Willkommen schöner Jüngling!	Welcome, fair youth,
Du Wonne der Natur!	Nature's delight!
Mit deinem Blumenkörbchen	Welcome to the meadows
Willkommen auf der Flur!	With your basket of flowers!
Ei, ei! Da bist du wieder!	Ah, you are here again,
Und bist so lieb und schön!	So dear and lovely!
Und freun wir uns so herzlich,	We feel such joy
Entgegen dir zu gehn.	As we come to meet you.
Denkst auch noch an mein Mädchen?	Do you still think of my sweetheart?
Ei lieber, denke doch!	Ah, dear friend, think of her!
Dort liebte mich das Mädchen	There my girl loved me,
Und's Mädchen liebt mich noch!	And she loves me still!
Für's Mädchen manches Blümchen	I asked you for many flowers
Erbat ich mir von dir—	For my sweetheart
Ich komm' und bitte wieder,	I come and ask you once more,
Und du?—du gibst es mir?	And you? You give them to me?
Willkommen, schöner Jüngling!¹	Welcome, fair youth,
Du Wonne der Natur!	Nature's delight!
Mit deinem Blumenkörbchen	Welcome to the meadows
Willkommen auf der Flur.	With your basket of flowers!

¹On Schubert's exclusion of this strophe in D283, and its inclusion in D587, see commentary.

Illustration from *Album für Deutschlands Töchter*, 1863.

FRIEDRICH VON SCHILLER (1759–1805); poem written in 1782

This is the eighteenth of Schubert's forty-four Schiller solo settings (1811–24). See the poet's biography for a chronological list of all the Schiller settings.

This is the first of Schubert's three settings of the same poem. The second setting, with completely different music, possibly dates from as late as 1823 (D587) but was long thought to have been composed first. D283 was thus initially classified as Schubert's second attempt, perhaps because it had been published first – which was usually the case with the seemingly definitive version of any setting. Confusion was compounded by yet a third setting of the words from circa 1816 which comes chronologically between the two piano-accompanied songs – this is the unaccompanied male voice quartet (D338) that adds a number of 'La La La's to Schiller's poem.

To attempt to analyse this beautiful little violet of a song is to put nature herself under a microscope. There is nothing much to it, and yet only a Schubert could have created the spring-like freshness of a melody that seems invented on the spot. The accompaniment in triplets gently supports the voice until the five-bar postlude where the piano writing is in slightly cheekier mood. The music is radiant, suffused with the uplifting spirit of spring as Mozart might have understood it. Indeed, it is reminiscent of *Sehnsucht nach dem Frühlinge* K596 (1791), a song from Mozart's last year and the inspiration for the last movement of the Piano Concerto K595. The piano concerto is in B flat of course, but Mozart's song and Schubert's share the same key of F, and the same time signature of ⁶⁄₈.

There are five strophes in Schiller's poem – the last an exact repeat of the first. Because each of Schubert's musical verses requires two strophes of poetry he leaves out the fifth strophe in this setting and ends the song with the fourth. In his second setting (*see* below) he incorporates the fifth strophe and repeats the second of Schiller's strophes to complete a third musical verse.

Autograph: University Library of Lund, Sweden
First edition: Published as Op. post. 172 no. 5 by C. A. Spina, Vienna in 1865 (P405)
Subsequent editions: Peters: Vol. 6/103; AGA XX 136: Vol. 3/68; NSA IV: Vol. 11/194
Discography and timing: Fischer-Dieskau —
Hyperion I 7[16]
Hyperion II 10[4]   1'32   Elly Ameling

← *Cronnan* D282   *Lied (Es ist so angenehm)* D284 →

AN DEN FRÜHLING (II)   To the spring
(SCHILLER) **D587** (earlier D245) [H388]

The song exists in two versions, the first of which is discussed below:
(1) October 1817; (2) 1819? 1823?

(1)   A major

(2)   'Etwas geschwind'   B♭ major   §   [27 bars]

See previous entry for poem and translation

FRIEDRICH VON SCHILLER (1759–1805); poem written in 1782

This is the thirty-third of Schubert's forty-four Schiller solo settings (1811–24). See the poet's biography for a chronological list of all the Schiller settings.

Spring is here personified as a handsome, virile youth; Schiller has charmingly cast this vernal visitor as a potential rival for his girl's affections, an exquisitely considerate fellow-suitor, moreover, who keeps handing the poet flowers with which to woo his fair lady. 'A mere trifle' Capell calls this song, but there is nothing insipid or half-hearted about it. On the contrary, the one criticism that may be levelled against the first setting D283 – that it ignores the priapic side of spring in favour of a gentle sweetness – is here rectified. In comparison with that gently perfumed creation, this song is a romp. The opening bars of the accompaniment, a charming variation of a *Ländler* with just the right air of earthy village music-making, immediately betoken rustic flirtatiousness. We are reminded what a very distinguished (and still underestimated) composer of dance music Schubert was. The piano writing calls for different kinds of staccato articulation (the accompaniment for D283 had all been encompassed in a suave legato) and observation of these markings adds to the musical energy.

Schubert adapts Schiller's original five-stanza shape by grouping the strophes in pairs and repeating the second verse of the poem to make up three complete musical verses. The vocal line is flexible and animated by a touch of decorative coloratura. This adds a real sparkle to the music and the song is irresistible in the hands of the right interpreters. The A major version is almost identical to the B flat version (where the vocal line is decorated here and there with mordents). The NSA prints the versions in reverse order to the AGA. Walther Dürr in the NSA admits the difficulty of accurate dating, but the B flat version, on grounds of the manuscript paper used, could only have been written in October 1819 at the earliest. On the basis of the paper and the handwriting, Ernst Hilmar has argued for the even later date of 1823 for the B flat which would make it a work contemporary with *Die schöne Müllerin*.

Autograph:	In private possession; photocopy in Österreichische Nationalbibliothek, Vienna (first version)
	Wienbibliothek im Rathaus (second version)
Publication:	First published as Vol. 7 no. 15 in Friedlaender's edition by Peters, Leipzig in 1885 (P486; first version)
	First published as part of the AGA in 1895 (P572; second version)
Subsequent editions:	Peters: Vol. 7/34; AGA XX 107a Vol. 3/6 (B♭ major) & 107b Vol. 3/8 (A major); NSA IV: Vol. 11/196 (A major) & 198 (B♭ major)
Bibliography:	Dürr, Introduction to NSA IV Volume 11, p. XXVIII
	Hilmar 1991, p. 47
	Hoorickx 1974, pp. 83–4
Discography and timing:	Fischer-Dieskau I 4²² 1'47
	Hyperion I 1¹⁶
	Hyperion II 19²² 2'19 Janet Baker

← *Erlafsee* D586   *Der Alpenjäger* D588 →

AN DEN MOND (I)   To the moon
(GOETHE) **D259** [H145]
E♭ major   19 August 1815

(20 bars)

Füllest wieder Busch und Tal	Once more you silently fill wood and vale
Still mit Nebelglanz,	with your hazy gleam
Lösest endlich auch einmal	and at last
Meine Seele ganz;	set my soul quite free.

Breitest über mein Gefild
Lindernd deinen Blick,
Wie des Freundes Auge, mild
Über mein Geschick.

Jeden Nachklang fühlt mein Herz
Froh- und trüber Zeit,
Wandle zwischen Freud' und Schmerz
In der Einsamkeit.

Fliesse, fliesse, lieber Fluss,
Nimmer werd' ich froh;
So verrauschte Scherz und Kuss,
Und die Treue so.

[. . . 3 . . .]

Selig wer sich vor der Welt
Ohne Hass verschliesst,
Einen Freund am Busen hält
Und mit dem geniesst,

Was, von Menschen nicht gewusst
Oder nicht bedacht,
Durch das Labyrinth der Brust
Wandelt in der Nacht.

You cast your soothing gaze
Over my fields,
With a friend's gentle eye
You watch over my fate.

My heart feels every echo
Of times both glad and gloomy.
I hover between joy and sorrow
In my solitude.

Flow on, beloved river!
I shall never be happy;
Thus have laughter and kisses rippled away.
And with them constancy.

[. . . 3 . . .]

Happy is he who, without hatred,
Shuts himself off from the world,
Holds one friend to his heart,
And with him enjoys

That which, unknown to
And undreamt of by men,
Wanders by night
Through the labyrinth of the heart.

JOHANN WOLFGANG VON GOETHE (1749–1832); poem written in July 1777, second version published in 1789

This is the twenty-sixth of Schubert's seventy-five Goethe solo settings (1814–26). See the poet's biography for a chronological list of all the Goethe settings.

This poem is rightly considered a masterpiece of Goethe's Weimar years. In January 1778 the poet had been shocked by the death of Christiane Lassburg, who was found drowned in the Ilm. He refers to this tragedy – the death of 'poor Christel' – in a letter to Charlotte von Stein that enclosed the poem's (rather different) first version – six strophes rather than nine. Whether or not this incident actually provided any inspiration for the poem is open to question. Goethe's composer friend Johann Philipp Kayser had published his *An den Mond* (1777) with a text by H. L. Wagner – perhaps this played a part in encouraging Goethe to write this text. Ten years later, after Goethe's sudden escape to Italy, an unannounced absence she regarded as a personal betrayal, Charlotte sent him a parody of these verses 'Nach meiner Manier' (In My Manner) as an indication of how much she had suffered. Shortly after his return Goethe revised this lyric and included part of Charlotte's reworking of the poem – the substance of the final version's third stanza about the 'Froh- und trüber Zeit' is actually hers. Dietrich Fischer-Dieskau's autobiography *Nachklang* takes its title and inspiration from this very strophe.

By the time the seventeen-year-old Schubert set the text, he was already a Goethe veteran, as is evident from the serious tone he achieves in music that may appear rather light-hearted on the page. Zelter, as well as Reichardt, had already attempted to set this poem. Challier's lieder

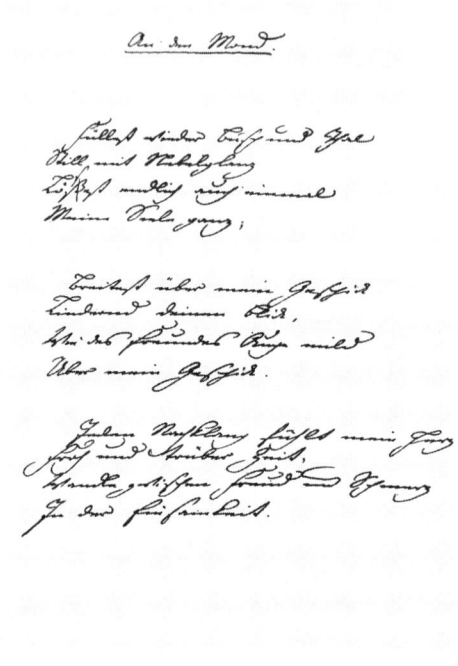

Goethe's autograph of *An den Mond*

catalogue lists thirty-two other settings before 1885, and one must not forget Hans Pfitzner's magnificently over-the-top setting of 1906. Capell outlined the main problem, as he saw it, facing Schubert: 'To catch the various shades of the poet's feelings, in which exalted serenity exists side by side with wild regret, was a hopeless task.'

Well, not quite hopeless. Given that a strophic song has certain limitations (and often these are the limitations of imagination and subtlety on the part of the performing artists), this song is capable of encompassing many moods: rapture, regret, resignation and the rueful smile in the major key that can suggest deep emotion. Schubert does not make clear how many strophes he has in mind for this version in performance. Because each verse of music encompasses two strophes of poetry, a maximum of eight of the poem's nine verses can be sung. The Peters Edition prints only three musical verses (strophes 1 + 2, 3 + 4 and 8 + 9). This is the version recorded for the Hyperion Edition as reflected in the text printed above, a version where text and music seem comfortably reconciled. As well as omitting Verse 5 ('Ich besass es doch einmal') this also removes any mention of the stream's overflowing in Verses 6 and 7 – imagery of turbulence and desperation for which the music is little suited. The AGA, however, prints Verse 5 in brackets; this implies a recommendation for a performance of four musical verses in all, including Verses 6 and 7. This must be the performer's decision. The NSA (Vol. 9/114) unusually offers alternative endings to the song – either strophes 8 and 9 (leaving out 7) or 7 and 8 (leaving out 9). The complete poem is printed below in the commentary for the second setting of *An den Mond* D296.

The profundity and richness of the expansive second setting of this song might encourage people to overlook this first, which would be a pity. The undulating little tune has a simplicity and an inevitability that can be praised for its restraint or damned for its dullness, depending on the tuning and sympathy of the ear. Once heard, it stays in the listener's subconscious. To select only a single passage, the setting of 'Breitest über mein Gefild / Lindernd deinen Blick' is surpassingly beautiful, rich in nostalgia and the profound human understanding born of sad experience. The way that the following melodic sequences echo this phrase, gently winding down the stave to the verse's conclusion, is a small miracle. Above all, in the hands of the right performers this setting need not be 'jaunty' (which is the fault Reed finds with it).

The four-bar postlude is among the most haunting in any of the Schubert single-page songs; on the other hand the four-bar prelude, as printed in Volume 6 of the Peters Edition, is completely spurious – an editorial addition for the song's posthumous publication. (One has only to compare the perfection of the authentic introduction for *An den Mond* D193.) In recital the banality of this introduction could all but ruin any performance.

Autograph: Dated autograph missing or lost; fair copy made for Goethe in
                                  Conservatoire collection, Bibliothèque Nationale, Paris

(4)	Fliesse, fliesse, lieber Fluss, Nimmer werd ich froh, So verrauschte Scherz und Kuss, Und die Treue so.	Flow on, beloved river! I shall never be happy; Thus have laughter and kisses rippled away. And with them constancy.
(5)	Ich besass es doch einmal, Was so köstlich ist! Dass man doch zu einer Qual Nimmer es vergisst.	Yet once I possessed A thing so precious! What torment Never to be able to forget it!
(6)	Rausche, Fluss, das Tal entlang, Ohne Rast und Ruh, Rausche, flüstre meinem Sang Melodien zu!	Murmur on, river, through the valley, Without cease, Murmur on, whispering melodies, To my song,
(7)	Wenn du in der Winternacht Wütend überschwillst, Oder um die Frühlingspracht Junger Knospen quillst.	When on winter nights You angrily overflow, Or when you bathe the springtime splendour Of the young buds.
(8)	Selig, wer sich vor der Welt Ohne Hass verschliesst, Einen Freund am Busen hält Und mit dem geniesst.	Happy he who, without hatred, Shuts himself off from the world, Holds one friend to his heart, And with him enjoys.
(9)	Was, von Menschen nicht gewusst Oder nicht bedacht, Durch das Labyrinth der Brust Wandelt in der Nacht.	That which, unknown to And undreamt of by men, Wanders by night Through the labyrinth of the heart.

JOHANN WOLFGANG VON GOETHE (1749–1832); poem written in July 1777,
second version published in 1789

*This is the thirty-fifth of Schubert's seventy-five Goethe solo settings (1814–26). See the poet's
biography for a chronological list of all the Goethe settings.*

Although the first version of *An den Mond* D259 (1815) is enchantingly melodic, Schubert felt
the need, some five years later, to create something more complex to mirror the shifting moods
of the poem and to incorporate the dramatic episode of the overflowing stream (little suited to
a strophic song) with music especially composed for it. The result is still far from perfect in
terms of expressing the subtleties of Goethe's complex poem (see Reed) but it is a musical
masterpiece. This second version is undated, but paper studies revealed that it was more likely
to date from 1819 than 1815 as earlier judged by Mandyczewski for the AGA. The NSA (2011)
unequivocally dates the song after February 1820; this is based on both paper studies and
Schubert's manner of writing natural signs in this period. Beethoven made a fragmentary sketch
of a setting for this text as late as 1826.

The piano's gentle four-bar introduction warns us that Schubert sees this address to the moon
as something deeply heartfelt, yet ineffably, exquisitely polite. There is no hand-wringing here,
no *Sturm und Drang*. A certain distance is preserved from overtly expressive emotion, reflected

Illustration from Düntzer's edition of *Goethe's Werke* (1882).

in the pianissimo dynamic which increases the power of the poet's entreaty. The *Vorspiel* of the minuet is gestural; quaver rests punctuate a succession of courtly bows – to the public perhaps, to Charlotte von Stein the poem's earthly dedicatee or to the moon itself. The composer imagines Goethe preparing to speak the text in the intimate yet reverential tone with which he addressed Charlotte in the 1770s. These opening bars might also be heard as sighs of romantic longing, but at the same time the formality of the music's phrasing incorporates pre-revolutionary obeisances. (We are reminded of the stately tread of the moon in *An den Mond in einer Herbstnacht* D614, a song from two years earlier.) Despite the use of the familiar 'du' form, Goethe's request to the moon ('Füllest wieder Busch und Tal') is presented in terms of a courtier offering a monarch a petition. Here Schubert holds in his hands the classical and Romantic languages of music, both harnessed to his ineffable purposes. Classicism has the upper hand in terms of rhythm, romanticism in terms of melody and harmony. It is a musical paradox that this plea in the form of a courtly dance, with the dying falls and phrasing of a previous century, is one of the greatest songs of the Romantic era.

Verses 1–4: When the singer enters (bb. 5–6) we find ourselves in heaven. These phrases poised high in the voice are suffused with the silvery glow of moonlight. The composer is usually given to strong bass lines that support and buoy up the vocal line, but here he changes his own rules: the voice part seems unanchored in terms of harmony and floats free, aspiring upwards, seldom settling into the tonic. This is melancholy music, yet sweetly tender. The piano's right hand doubles the vocal line; normally this deadens vocal colour, but here it seems that the poet below is spiritually connected with the moon above as the pianist shadows the singer's line. Schubert uses two strophes of Goethe's poem to make a single music strophe. In the third of the poet's verses Goethe's scanning of the past ('Froh- und trüber Zeit') is overwhelmingly poignant, and the music, strophic so far yet still appropriate to Goethe's changing words, matches this eloquence. The song's grave and dignified moto perpetuo is further justified by the imagery of 'Wandle zwischen Freud' und Schmerz'.

Verses 5–7: Verse 5 ('Ich besass es doch einmal') is another repeat of the music we have already heard. This kind of strophic song grows in stature with each repetition of the refrain, particularly when the music is as beautiful as this. There follows a new development. The poet has already mentioned the stream in Verse 4 but in Verse 6 he returns to address its changing moods. *Die schöne Müllerin* is the high-water mark of Schubert's mastery of musical imagery for brook and stream, but by 1819 he was already a master of the genre. This river, the Ilm, flows through

Weimar; it nourishes and delights as well as being a symbol for tragedy and destruction. In this setting the wide-ranging movement of the stream is reflected in exquisite modulations into ever flatter keys. Rippling semiquavers disrupt the poise of the courtly minuet. The music moves from G flat major to C flat major (b. 34). The harmonization of the passage beginning 'Rausche, flüstre meinem Sang' is extraordinarily daring; the overflowing of the stream reaches the distant shores of D flat minor (b. 40). The most turbulent moment of the poem is also the most self-revealing. Schubert's music strips Goethe of his court dress and wig; the musical manners of the eighteenth century have been overturned, the opening of the floodgates of the *nouvelle régime* has swept away the old proprieties. Schubert, shy as always, yet implacable, reveals himself as an instrument of musical revolution.

Verses 8–9: The overflowing stream has temporarily encouraged the unveiling of the raw emotions that destroy decorum, but Schubert allows the music to recover its former balance, as he almost always does after a musical storm. We return to the music of the earlier strophes, and thanks to this reconciliation the poet is once again in confessional mood. Only a true friend, Goethe says, can understand his mingled emotions. The last stanza of the song depicts this longed-for intimacy in a miraculous way. As a final test Schubert asks the singer to depart from accustomed paths. The moon continues to shine in the piano part while the vocal line buries its head in the lap of the music, delving deep beneath the surface. This change is inspired by the marvellous phrase 'Durch das Labyrinth der Brust'. There is an ineffable distance between lunar serenity (in the aerial accompaniment) and the dark labyrinthine torments of the heart (in an unusually low vocal tessitura, bb. 56–7). This is the 'change of gaze . . . from the natural world to that of the psyche' discussed by Nicholas Marston who compares this passage to one in Beethoven's *An die ferne Geliebte*. No sooner is the singer required to find these dark colours than he or she is commanded to return unflustered to the *mezza voce* heights. There is a single crotchet rest between the low A flat beneath the stave and the E flat floated a twelfth higher. This sudden contrast is the final surprise in a masterpiece full of quiet but subversive innovations.

Autograph:	Staatsbibliothek Preussischer Kulturbesitz, Berlin
First edition:	Published as No. 3 of *Sechs bisher ungedrückte Lieder* by Wilhelm Müller, Berlin in 1868 (P415)
Subsequent editions:	Peters: Vol. 7/50; AGA XX 176: Vol. 3/195; NSA IV: Vol. 9/115
Bibliography:	Black 2003, pp. 146–7
	Capell 1928, pp. 102–3
	Einstein 1951, p. 108
	Fischer-Dieskau 1977, pp. 52–3
	Marston 1998, p. 126
	Winter 1978, p. 500
Further settings:	(*see* previous entry for D259)
Discography and timing:	Fischer-Dieskau I 6[6] 4'58
	Hyperion I 1[12]
	Hyperion II 12[8] 4'19 Janet Baker

← *Hoffnung* D295   *An mein Klavier* D342 →

AN DEN MOND (FRAGMENT WITHOUT TEXT) *see* DUBIOUS, MISATTRIBUTED AND LOST SONGS

AN DEN MOND
(HÖLTY) OP. 57 NO. 3, **D193** [H94]

To the moon

The song exists in two versions, the second of which is discussed below:
(1) 17 May 1815; (2) appeared April 1826

(1)   'Langsam, wehmütig'   F minor   12/8   [34 bars]

(2)   F minor

(37 bars)

Geuss, lieber Mond, geuss deine Silberflimmer	Beloved moon, shed your silver radiance
Durch dieses Buchengrün,	Through these green beeches,
Wo Phantasien und Traumgestalten immer	Where fancies and dreamlike images
Vor mir vorüber fliehn.	Forever flit before me.
Enthülle dich, dass ich die Stätte finde,	Unveil yourself, that I may find the spot
Wo oft mein Mädchen sass,	Where my beloved sat,
Und oft, im Wehn des Buchbaums und der Linde,	Where often, in the swaying branches of the linden,
Der goldnen Stadt vergass.	She forgot the gilded town.
Enthülle dich, dass ich des Strauchs mich freue,	Unveil yourself, that I may delight in the whispering bushes
Der Kühlung ihr gerauscht,	That cooled her,
Und einen Kranz auf jeden Anger streue,	And lay a wreath on every meadow
Wo sie den Bach belauscht.	Where she listened to the brook.
Dann, lieber Mond, dann nimm den Schleier wieder,	Then, beloved moon, take your veil once more,
Und traur um deinen Freund,	And mourn for your friend.
Und weine durch den Wolkenflor hernieder,	Weep down through the hazy clouds,
Wie dein Verlassner weint!	As I, forsaken, weep!

LUDWIG CHRISTOPH HÖLTY (1748–1776); poem written in 1772. Adapted for publication in
1804 by JOHANN HEINRICH VOSS (1751–1826)

*This is the second of Schubert's twenty-three Hölty solo settings (1813–16). See the poet's
biography for a chronological list of all the Hölty settings.*

This is a justly celebrated song. It is famous not only for its melody, but also for its introduction
and accompaniment. The setting universally perfomed is actually the song's second version. Only

the NSA prints the first version ('Langsam, wehmütig') which is dated 17 May 1815. This is almost certainly the copy that Schubert used to prepare the song (with touches of revision) for its publication in 1826. He probably added the *Vorspiel* at that very time and for that purpose. Because the song has an introduction only in the printed version we must suppose that the composer had improvised various introductions for informal performances. Deep in the bass clef the left hand nudges the inexorable melodic line from the tonic to the submediant and back, a mirror image of lunar drift in the night sky. From the beginning the song is aglow with the 'Silberflimmer' demanded by the poet. The undulating triplets of the accompaniment remind us of Beethoven's 'Moonlight' Sonata, although it is unlikely that this represents a conscious homage on Schubert's part (the song is not composed in C sharp minor). Another prophetic similarity of style is that of *bel canto* opera. This song shares its time signature and triplet accompaniment with Bellini's great hymn to the moon, 'Casta Diva' from *Norma*, written sixteen years later. (Both pieces of music are in F – the aria in the major, Schubert's song in the minor.)

The vocal melody is enchanting; like so much of Schubert's introspective music it is tinged with that sad ruefulness that retains a sense of dignity and refuses to topple into moribund self-pity. Memories of past happy times mingle with present loneliness. All is solitary contemplation and containment. A chain of remarkable modulations serves to illustrate the distant realms of 'Phantasien und Traumgestalten' (bb. 7–9). This magical excursion into the world of the supernatural is prolonged over three spacious bars that seem to float above the daily concerns of mankind. A return to the tonic ushers in a hushed two-bar interlude (bb. 11–12).

The middle section changes the mood entirely. This music, marked 'Etwas geschwind', shifts to A flat major without any warning. This is music in the mood of a Mozartian arietta. The poet pleads with the moon to unveil herself, to divest herself of the surrounding dark clouds, in order that he might see those places bathed in moonlight where he once sat with his beloved. The moon is a feminine personality in Italian ('Casta Diva') and French (Fauré's *Diane*, *Séléné*). In German, however, it is a masculine noun. Hölty's pleas of 'Enthülle dich' have no erotic subtext (compare the different use of unveiling and the word 'Schleier' when Actaeon sees Diana bathing in *Der zürnenden Diana* D707). Performers sometimes try to flirt with the moon by singing this passage in too coy a manner, but Schubert sees Hölty's words as an exchange between longsuffering friends, twinned spirits, rather than lovers. The narrator is intimate enough with the moon to refer to himself, when addressing his lunar counterpart, as 'dein Verlassner' – your poor old abandoned friend.

This middle section remains straightforward, firmly anchored in the present. Lightly played staccato quavers add touches of glinting light to the leaves of the beech and lime trees, an illumination that has failed to materialize when the moon moves under cover of a mournful legato. A hearty pair of accompanying hands can make this passage sound rather too jaunty for the good of the whole. The first two strophes of the poem may well be regarded as a plea for a change of weather on a cloudy night – whether this actually happens is scarcely important. From a musical point of view this episode in the relative major sets up a magical return to the atmospheric music of the opening (marked 'Wie oben' b. 28). This ternary form is used in a number of Schubert songs, including *Erlafsee* D586, and sometimes in slow movements of piano pieces and chamber music. We greet the return of a dreamy or nostalgic theme all the more delightedly when the intervening music has taken us temporarily into the here and now. The flattened harmonies, first conceived for 'Phantasien', give rise to a remarkably eloquent melisma (bb. 31–2) on the word 'weine' (weep).

Autograph:	Wienbibliothek im Rathaus, Vienna (first draft without piano prelude) (first version); missing or lost (second version)

Publication:	First published as part of the NSA in 1982 (P779; first version)
	First published as Op. 57 no. 3 by Thaddäus Weigl, Vienna in April 1826 (P96; second version)
Publication reviews:	*Allgemeiner musikalischer Anzeiger* (Frankfurt), No. 33 (10 February 1827), p. 317f. [Waidelich/Hilmar Dokumente I No. 452; Deutsch Doc. Biog. No. 798]
Subsequent editions:	Peters: Vol. 2/116; AGA XX 69: Vol. 2/110; NSA IV: Vol. 3a/81 (second version) & Vol. 3b/175 (first version); Bärenreiter: Vol. 2/115
Bibliography:	Capell 1928, p. 92
	Fischer-Dieskau 1977, pp. 58–9
Discography and timing:	Fischer-Dieskau I 3[19] 2'55
	Hyperion I 7[7]
	Hyperion II 6[14] 2'57 Elly Ameling

←— *Der Jüngling am Bache (II)* D192   *Die Mainacht* D194 —→

AN DEN MOND   To the moon
(Hölty) **D468** [H294]
A major   7 August 1816

Was schau - est du so hell und klar durch die - se Ap - fel - bäu - me,

(18 bars)

Was schauest du so hell und klar	Why do you gaze down, so bright and clear,
Durch diese Apfelbäume,	Through these apple trees,
Wo einst dein Freund so selig war	Where once your friend was so happy,
Und träumte süsse Träume?	Dreaming sweet dreams?
Verhülle deinen Silberglanz,	Veil your silvery radiance,
Und schimmre, wie du schimmerst,	And glimmer as you do
Wenn du den frühen Totenkranz	When you shine upon the funeral wreath
Der jungen Braut beflimmerst!	Of the young bride.
Du blickst umsonst so hell und klar	In vain you gaze down, so bright and clear,
In diese Laube nieder;	Into this arbour.
Nie findest du das frohe Paar	Never again will you find the happy pair
In ihrem Schatten wieder!	Beneath its shade!
Ein schwarzes, feindliches Geschick	Dark, hostile fate
Entriss mir meine Schöne!	Tore my beloved from me.
Kein Seufzer zaubert sie zurück,	No sighs, no tears of longing
Und keine Sehnsuchtsträne!	Can conjure her back.

O wandelt sie hinfort einmal	If one day she should come
An meiner Ruhestelle,	To my resting place,
Dann mache flugs mit trübem Strahl	Then, swiftly, with your sombre light
Des Grabes Blumen helle!	Make bright the flowers on my grave.
Sie setze weinend sich aufs Grab,	May she sit weeping on my grave
Wo Rosen niederhangen,	Where roses droop,
Und pflücke sich ein Blümchen ab,	And pluck a flower,
Und drück' es an die Wangen.	And press it to her cheek.

LUDWIG CHRISTOPH HÖLTY (1748–1776); poem written in 1775. Adapted for publication in 1804 by JOHANN HEINRICH VOSS (1751–1826)

This is the twenty-second of Schubert's twenty-three Hölty solo settings (1813–16). See the poet's biography for a chronological list of all the Hölty settings.

This charming little setting looks to the past and shows Schubert's debt to the heartfelt simplicities of the Berlin school and the songs of such composers as Reichardt, Schulz and Zelter. It was judged harshly by Capell who preferred the more celebrated Hölty setting of the same name (D193). It is perhaps unfair to compare one song with another when they happen simply to share a title and poet rather than a poem, but in some ways they are mirror images of each other. The earlier Hölty song, 'Geuss, lieber Mond', begins in the muted tones of a minor key; the light is soft and veiled with 'fancies and dreamlike images'. At 'Enthülle dich' ('unveil yourself') the music moves into the relative major and everything can be seen with greater clarity before a return to the minor key of the opening.

In 'Was schauest du so hell' (D486) the opposite happens. The A major tonality of the opening and the high-lying vocal line are wonderfully 'hell und klar' – 'bright and clear'. This is music of radiant elegance. The poem's fifth line signals a change of key signature and the three sharps are naturalized (b. 9). The command to the moon is 'veil your silvery radiance' and the music accordingly shifts into A minor – the pivot between major and minor in this tonality is always a special Schubertian moment. The heavenly body has hitherto been characterized by an accompaniment of great simplicity, chastely hugging the ethereal vocal line, but human predicaments of the second section call for a more overtly emotional accompanying figure in semiquavers. Luckily for the composer, who has planned a strophic song, the fifth lines of each of the two remaining verses also contain grounds to justify a change from major to minor (sudden bereavement, weeping on a grave). The result is music that avoids fragmentation, achieving the seamless logic of an integrated whole.

There are also contrasting meteorological conditions in the two Hölty moon songs: the famous F minor setting is probably sung on an overcast summer night; the mood is sultry and languid and the poet sings of a girl who sought the cooling shade. The air surrounding the A major song is crisper and cooler; the light comes through the apple trees which are obviously not at their leafiest. This is probably a song for an autumn evening. The classical poise of another A major work, *An den Mond in einer Herbstnacht* D614, comes to mind. The piano writing in the tonic key ritornello of that work has an etiolated lightness of touch that is also found in the A major sections of this *An den Mond*.

Hölty was fond of the image of the bride's funeral wreath. We find it again ('Die Todtenkränze Manches verstorbenen Mädchens') in his *Auftrag*, set by Peter Cornelius (Op. 5 no. 6, 1861).

Autograph:	Wienbibliothek im Rathaus, Vienna (first draft)
First edition:	Published as part of the AGA in 1895 (P645)
Subsequent editions:	Not in Peters; AGA XX 243: Vol. 4/148; NSA IV: Vol. 10/212

First edition:	Published as Book 47 no. 5 of the *Nachlass* by Diabelli, Vienna in 1850 (P379)
Subsequent editions:	Peters: Vol. 6/57; AGA XX 116: Vol. 3/40; NSA IV: Vol. 9/113
Bibliography:	Byrne 2003, pp. 113–18
Further settings and arrangements:	Johann Friedrich Reichardt (1752–1814) *An den Mond* (1794)
	Carl Friedrich Zelter (1758–1832) *An den Mond* (1811)
	Václav Jan Tomášek (1774–1850) *An den Mond* Op. 56/4 (1815)
	Hans Pfitzner (1869–1949) *An den Mond* Op. 18 (1906)
	Arr. Max Reger (1873–1916) for voice and orchestra (1913–14) [*see* ORCHESTRATIONS]
	Arr. Tilman Hoppstock (b. 1961) for guitar accompaniment, in *Franz Schubert: 110 Lieder* (2009)
Discography and timing:	Fischer-Dieskau I 5⁵ 3'16
	Hyperion I 8¹
	Hyperion II 9⁶ 3'30 Sarah Walker

← *Bundeslied* D258

Wonne der Wehmut D260 →

AN DEN MOND (II)

To the moon

(GOETHE) **D296** [H213][1]

A♭ major   After February 1820

(60 bars)

(1) Füllest wieder Busch und Tal
Still mit Nebelglanz,
Lösest endlich auch einmal
Meine Seele ganz;

Once more you silently fill wood and vale
With your hazy gleam,
And at last
Set my soul quite free.

(2) Breitest über mein Gefild
Lindernd deinen Blick,
Wie des Freundes Auge mild
Über mein Geschick.

You cast your soothing gaze
Over my fields;
With a friend's gentle eye
You watch over my fate.

(3) Jeden Nachklang fühlt mein Herz
Froh- und trüber Zeit,
Wandle zwischen Freud' und Schmerz
In der Einsamkeit.

My heart feels every echo
Of times both glad and gloomy.
I hover between joy and sorrow
In my solitude.

[1] The 2011 re-dating of this song obviously affects its place in the chronology. Had this information been published in 2003, both this song and *Hoffnung* D295 would have been placed between H450 and H470.

Bibliography: Capell 1928, p. 117
Discography and timing: Fischer-Dieskau I 7²⁹   2'06
                           Hyperion I 17¹⁴
                           Hyperion II 15²¹   2'49   Lucia Popp
← *Am Tage Aller Seelen (Litanei)* D343   *Lied des Orpheus (als er in
                                                     die Hölle ging)* D474 →

AN DEN MOND IN EINER HERBSTNACHT

To the moon on an autumn night

(SCHREIBER) **D614** [H397]
A major   April 1818

(139 bars)

Freundlich ist dein Antlitz,
Sohn des Himmels!
Leis sind deine Tritte
Durch des Äthers Wüste
Holder Nachtgefährte!

Dein Schimmer ist sanft und erquickend,
Wie das Wort des Trostes
Von des Freundes Lippe,
Wenn ein schrecklicher Geier
An der Seele nagt.

Manche Träne siehst du,
Siehst so manches Lächeln,
Hörst der Liebe trauliches Geflüster,
Leuchtest ihr auf stillem Pfade;
Hoffnung schwebt auf deinem Strahle,
Herab zum stillen Dulder,
Der verlassen geht auf bedorntem Weg.

Du siehst auch meine Freunde,
Zerstreut in fernen Landen;
Du giessest deinen Schimmer
Auf die frohen Hügel,
Wo ich oft als Knabe hüpfte,[1]

Your face is kind,
Son of heaven.
Softly you move
Through the airy waste,
Fair companion of the night!

Your shimmering light is gentle and refreshing,
Like a word of comfort
From the lips of a friend
When a terrifying vulture
Gnaws at the soul.

You see many a tear,
And many a smile;
You hear lovers' intimate whispers
And you shine for them on their quiet way;
On your beams hope streams down
To the silent sufferer,
Wandering all alone on the thorny path.

You see my friends, too,
Scattered in distant lands:
You shed your light
Upon the happy hills
Where I often played as a boy,

[1] Schubert adds the word 'oft' to Schreiber's line.

Wo oft bei deinem Lächeln	And where, as you smiled down,
Ein unbekanntes Sehnen	An unknown longing
Mein junges Herz ergriff.	Often seized my youthful heart.
Du blickst auch auf die Stätte,	You gaze also upon the place
Wo meine Lieben ruhn,[2]	Where my loved ones rest,
Wo der Tau fällt auf ihr Grab,	Where the dew falls on their graves
Und die Gräser drüber wehn[3]	And the grass above them
In dem Abendhauche.	Blows in the evening breeze.
Doch dein Schimmer	But your light does not penetrate
Dringt nicht in die dunkle Kammer,	The dark chamber
Wo sie ruhen von des Lebens Müh'n,[4]	Where they rest from life's toil,
Wo auch ich bald ruhen werde!	And where I, too, shall soon rest.
Du wirst geh'n und wiederkehren,	You will go and return again;
Du wirst seh'n noch manches Lächeln,[5]	you will see many more smiles.
Dann werd' ich nicht mehr lächeln	Then I shall smile
Dann werd' ich nicht mehr weinen,	and weep no more;
Mein wird man nicht mehr gedenken[6]	I will no longer be remembered
Auf dieser schönen Erde.	On this fair earth.

ALOIS SCHREIBER (1761–1841)

This is the first of Schubert's four Schreiber solo settings (1818). See the poet's biography for a chronological list of all the Schreiber settings.

Einstein has pointed out that this song is half Italian and half German: the aria form (with recitative) is combined with scrupulous word-painting worthy of the lied at its best. The moon is personified as 'son of the heavens' and seems to have acquired human attributes in Schubert's mind. The third line of the poem and the noun 'Tritte' (steps) give us the clue to the haunting ritornello that binds this magnificent hybrid song-rondo together. Although it may be impossible for the moon to 'tread' or 'tramp' in any readable English translation, it is lunar footsteps that we hear in the detached quavers of the pianist's left hand. The right-hand melody traced above this tidal dance is the epitome of ageless elegance with a touch of the antique, perhaps; an imitative retinue flows behind the main theme at a respectful distance, echoes of gentle beams resounding through the stratosphere. The moon seems swathed in veils of contrapuntal mist. At the end of the ritornello, and in preparation for the entry of the voice, the beams are gathered together for a courtly bow in perfect cadence. The tune itself is reminiscent of 'Caro mio ben', attributed to both Tommaseo and Giuseppe Giordani, the same melody that Schumann was to quote so memorably at the end of his Op. 37 Rückert setting *Der Himmel hat eine Träne geweint*. Perhaps Schubert knew this popular *canzonetta*, possibly via Salieri, and that this was a conscious musical quotation in affectionate tribute to the moon, dearest of companions.

The entry of the voice echoes the melody of the ritornello. The stepping motif remains a pronounced feature in the use of the solitary left hand to accompany the vocal line (bb. 5–6).

---

[2] Schreiber writes 'ruh*en*'.
[3] Schreiber writes 'weh*en*'.
[4] Schreiber writes 'von des Lebens *Mühe*'.
[5] Schubert replaces Schreiber's 'Und' at the beginning of this line with another 'Du wirst'.
[6] Schreiber writes 'Mein wird man *dann* nicht mehr gedenken'.

Enharmonic modulations do not cause a change of direction, only a slight bending of the light around astral corners. Another statement of the ritornello and the second verse begins in the same way as the first (b. 30). If we have been led to believe that this is a well-behaved strophic song our mistake will soon be evident. The moon is all-seeing and all-encompassing; his aerial view reveals every shade of light and emotion. The ominous accompaniment under the words 'Wenn ein schrecklicher Geier . . . nagt' (b. 36) changes the music's course. For the third verse (b. 40) flowing triplets and kaleidoscopic modulations reflect first the tears and then the laughter of mankind. The delighted whispering of lovers is uncannily caught in an accompaniment suddenly spiced with playful accidentals (bb. 44–7). Equally suddenly we are with the silent sufferer on his thorny path (b. 53).

This is followed by a marvellous little interlude (bb. 56–61) as if scored for muted brass, which at once melts into the rueful love music of the fourth verse. Triplets rustle in the middle of the texture; the little finger of the pianist's right hand picks out two notes that alternate for five bars (bb. 61–5). Does this repetitive motif illustrate yearning, the constancy of friendship, or both? There are pre-echoes here of *Abendbilder* D650 (1819), another song which gathers varying images into its portmanteau form. Memories of boyhood suddenly make the music gambol with touches of vocal coloratura and pianistic staccato (bb. 69–72). The exit from this mood is achieved by an unaccompanied bar on the words 'Ein unbekanntes': a line of C sharps followed by a semitone lift into 'Sehnen' accompanied by solemn chords and we are transported to a fervent world of longing for we know not what.

The fifth verse (from b. 78) is quite simply a miracle. Hardly ever has Schubert asked the pianist to do so little; the right-hand stave is as empty as the ethereal void. It is as if everything has been cleared away to enable the questing lover to address his sidereal friend, face turned upward, cap (and the barest of chords) in hand. When the right hand joins in again it is merely to add a gesture of the simplest supplication. It is a measure of Schubert's genius that his accentuation of 'auf' in b. 79, and of the same unimportant word in b. 83, breaks all the rules of prosody without disturbing the music's power. This passage (bb. 83–6), where a tiny figuration pivots between two As an octave apart, is prophetic of the piano introduction for the heartbreaking 'Langsam' section of *Frühlingstraum* (b. 27) in *Winterreise*. (If we imagine the singer of that song lying down we must imagine his gaze moving upwards if not to the heavens, as here, at least to the flower pattern etched in ice on the window panes.) The following interlude (bb. 88–93) would hardly be out of place in a work by Mahler. The first real recitative now comes and it is marked as such – 'Recit'. Up till now there have been no tempo changes. The opening 'Mässig' has encompassed myriad internal variations of mood. No doubt this was a source of pride to a composer always in search of musical unity; in this song he illustrates many different verbal images without having to alter the music's overall tempo. The moon, mirror of mankind's hopes, also veers between fragility and strength at this time of year. 'I watch thy gliding, while with watery light / Thy weak eye glimmers through a fleecy veil' writes Coleridge in *To the Autumnal Moon*; the poet then sees Luna emerge with 'radiant might' from the 'wind-rent cloud' as it 'Sails, like a meteor kindling in its flight'.

This changeability is also echoed in Schubert's setting of Schreiber. The realization that death will separate mortals from moonlight temporarily throws the scene into Stygian darkness. There is drama here, but the words 'Wo auch ich bald ruhen werde' (bb. 98–101) do not rage or rant; this moment of doubt, the humble acceptance of human frailty, leads to the ritornello in full sail as the moon briefly emerges from behind the clouds for a final consolatory appearance. 'You must go your way, and I mine', Schreiber says to the heavenly body, and the music adds a smile of resignation without the slightest suggestion of self-pity. An awareness of the beauty of our own planetary home, of our luck simply to be alive, brings music of fervent humility. We are now earthed and the moon's motif has melted away. The phrase 'Auf dieser schönen Erde' is repeated no fewer than four times, the last murmured and ornamented in the lower register of the voice. The effect is almost unbearably beautiful. This long contemplation has brought, if not peace of mind, gratitude for life itself. The rise and fall of the simple five-bar postlude is deeply touching. This music reminds us of the opening of the Andante of the A minor Piano Sonata D784. For Leo Black the steady tread of this song prophesies Bruckner, and he points out that Brahms had intended to orchestrate it. On his copy of the song Brahms wrote the words 'instrumentirt: Flöte Oboe' – 'flute' at the opening and 'oboe' at b. 16.

Mandyczewski in the AGA *Revisionsbericht* unfairly criticizes Schubert for distorting the poetic idea by leaving out one of the poet's verses. An extra strophe does indeed occur in the 1812 edition of Schreiber's works but is not to be found in the 1817 *Poetische Werke*, nor the Viennese edition (Bauer, 1817) which was almost certainly Schubert's source.

Autograph:	Library of Congress, Washington (first draft)
First edition:	Published as Book 18 no. 2 of the *Nachlass* by Diabelli, Vienna in 1832 (P290)
Subsequent editions:	Peters: Vol. 5/88; AGA XX 337: Vol. 5/188; NSA IV: Vol. 12/6
Bibliography:	Black 2003, pp. 62–3, 76 & 84 (mention of connections between this song and *Lazarus* D689 as well as the 'Gloria' and 'Domine Deus Agnus Dei' of the Mass in A flat D678)
	Capell 1928, p. 144
	Einstein 1951, pp. 165–6
	Fischer-Dieskau 1977, pp. 112–13
Discography and timing:	Fischer-Dieskau II 1[21] 7'47
	Hyperion I 8[7]
	Hyperion II 20[6] 7'47 Sarah Walker

← *Auf der Riesenkoppe* D611   *Evangelium Johannis* D607 →

AN DEN SCHLAF   To sleep
(Anonymous) **D447** [H276]
A major   June 1816

(12 bars)

Komm, und senke die umflorten Schwingen,	Come, and lay your gossamer wings,
Süsser Schlummer, auf den müden Blick!	Sweet slumber, upon my weary eyes.
Segner! Freund! in deinen Armen dringen	Benefactor! Friend! In your arms
Trost und Balsam auf's verlorne Glück.	Comfort and balm come to my lost happiness.

ANONYMOUS/UNKNOWN, though long attributed to JOHANN PETER UZ (1720–1796)

This is the eleventh of Schubert's nineteen solo settings of an anonymous poet. See Anonymous/
Unknown for a chronological list of all the songs for which the poets are unknown.

This is only a single page of music yet it contains miraculous things in the modest, almost undemonstrative way that typifies many of the shy glories of the 1816 songs. At the beginning one may think that Haydn has had a hand in its composition (and in a sense, as one of Schubert's revered forbears, he has) but by the third line of the poem we hear the canzonet move over for the lied, as the nineteenth century supplants the eighteenth. The words 'Süsser Schlummer' are exquisitely harmonized with a bass line of three falling semitones (b. 3). This indicates a momentary slipping away from consciousness – not quite enough for the prayer for sleep to be answered immediately. The words 'Segner! Freund!' initiate a throbbing semiquaver accompaniment, and a Romantic sweep of emotion breaks the old-fashioned confines of the chorale. The three-bar postlude is a beautiful little two-part invention, rich in harmonic implications despite its spareness; its chromatic unwindings are a perfect illustration of gradual relaxation. Richard Capell called this song 'a modest relation of *Wanderers Nachtlied I*'. This assessment may seem generous, but it is just.

Autograph:	Missing or lost
First edition:	Published as part of the AGA in 1895 (P643)
Subsequent editions:	Not in Peters; AGA XX 232: Vol. 4/120; NSA IV: Vol. 10/175
Bibliography:	Capell 1928, p. 115
Discography and timing:	Fischer-Dieskau I 7[20] 1'07
	Hyperion I 18[3]
	Hyperion II 15[3] 2'07 Peter Schreier

← *Gott im Frühlinge* D448   *Der gute Hirt* D449 →

AN DEN TOD   To death
(SCHUBART) **D518** [H329]
B major   1816 or 1817

(25 bars)

Tod, du Schrecken der Natur;	Death, terror of nature,
Immer rieselt deine Uhr;	Your hour-glass trickles ceaselessly;
Die geschwung'ne Sense blinkt,—	The swinging scythe flashes,
Gras, und Halm und Blume sinkt.	Grass, stalk and flower fall.

Mähe nicht ohn' Unterschied,	Do not mow down indiscriminately
Dieses Blümchen, das erst blüht;	This little flower just bloomed,
Dieses Röschen, erst halbrot,—	This rose half-opened;
Sei barmherzig, lieber Tod!	Be merciful, dear death!
[. . . 11 . . .]	[. . . 11 . . .]
'Tod, wann kommst du, meine Lust?	'Death, when will you come, my joy,
Ziehst den Dolch aus meiner Brust?	To draw the dagger from my breast,
Streifst die Fesseln von der Hand?—	And slip the fetters from my hands?
Ach, wann deckst du mich mit Sand?'	Ah, when will you cover me with sand?'
[. . .]	[. . .]
Komm, o Tod, wenn's dir gefällt,[1]	Come, death, if it pleases you,
Hol Gefangne aus der Welt:[2]	Take the prisoners from this world,
Komm, vollende meine Not;	Come end my distress;
Sei barmherzig, lieber Tod!	Be merciful, dear death!

CHRISTIAN FRIEDRICH SCHUBART (1739–1791); poem written between 1777–84

This is probably the last of Schubert's four Schubart solo settings (1816–17). See the poet's biography for a chronological list of all the Schubart settings.

This song is tiny and gigantic at the same time; it packs quite a punch. Its masculine thrust is underlined by the fact that it was written in the bass clef (this was changed to the treble clef for the song's appearance in the *Nachlass*, and in Edition Peters). Its tonality of B major is usually reserved for matters of great emotional import, often connected with the ineluctable movement of water. Perhaps Schubert has imagined the movement of the Styx. Here as in *Der Neugierige* from *Die schöne Müllerin* (D795/6) urgent petitions are presented to forces of nature, in the first as a plea, in the second question. In each case the only answer that the singer can expect is deathly silence.

Triplets that pulsate unceasingly in the accompaniment propel forward this impassioned (even imperious) request to spare the newly bloomed rose. In a wildly roving sequence of keys, the composer-barrister makes use of every harmonic argument and angle at his disposal; as Capell says, 'the appellant . . . taking to one failing foothold after another'. There is rage and pain in this face-to-face confrontation, but with this particular interlocutor, both judge and jury, there is nothing to lose in staking all in a plea for mercy. Only at the end of the song (b. 19) does the dynamic soften to piano. There is a conciliatory, and purely rhetorical, appeal to 'dear death', a tone of voice that might be used in a summing-up for the defence. But the case is already lost; on this extraordinary 'Fahrt zum Hades', execution is imminent, and the last hope is that it will at least be humane.

Schubart's original poem has sixteen strophes and the composer uses two stanzas of poetry to make one verse of music. The poet asks death to spare the rose; followed by pleas on behalf of the German hero (Verse 5), the poet (Verse 6), the young bride (Verse 7), the virtuous (Verse 8), the sinner (Verse 9), the prince (Verse 10), the rich (Verse 11), even the gifted young pianist (Verse 4), a category to which Schubert himself, author of *An mein Klavier* D342, once belonged.

---

[1] Schubart writes '*Drum*, o Tod'.
[2] Schubart writes '*Nimm* Gefangne aus der Welt'.

Also autobiographically, he begs death to release the long-term prisoner from his suffering. Schubert wrote out two further verses of the poem – the fourteenth and sixteenth as printed above. These appear as part of the song in both the AGA and the NSA but not in Peters.

It is thought that mention of the well-known poet's unjust imprisonment and suffering would have displeased the Austrian censor. Schubart had been incarcerated in Hohenasperg for ten years (1777–87) for libelling the Duke of Württemberg. Similar restrictions on verbal and literary freedoms held sway in Metternich's Vienna. The possibly offending verses were the twelfth and thirteenth:

Aber musst du töten, Tod,	But you must kill, death!
Ach so tu's, wo dir die Not	Ah, then do so when distress
Aus zerfress'nem Auge winkt	Beckons you from haggard eyes
Und in Staub des Kerkers sinkt.	And crumples in prison's dust.
Wo mit jedem Morgen – Tod!	When with each morning – death!
Wo mit jedem Abend – Tod!	When with each evening – death!
Tod! um Mitternacht erschallt,	Death! At midnight it resounds,
Dass die Schauerzelle hallt.	Making the gruesome cell echo.

Walther Dürr has argued that it is probably for this reason that the song was printed in 1824 with only one musical strophe (the poet's first and second). Modern-day performers have no reason not to revert to what were possibly the composer's original intentions; in any case the song is more effective if this music is heard at least twice. When Brigitte Fassbaender recorded the song for the Hyperion Edition in 1990 she was facing imminent bereavement of her own and could not bear to sing the song more than once through.

Autograph:	Missing or lost
First edition:	Published as a supplement to the *Wiener Allgemeine Musikalische Zeitung* by the Lithographisches Institut, Vienna in June 1824; subsequently issued separately by the Institut in July 1824 (P287)
Publication reviews:	*Allgemeine musikalische Zeitung* (Vienna), No. 104 (29 December 1824), p. 413 [Waidelich/Hilmar Dokumente I No. 299]
Subsequent editions:	Peters: Vol. 5/84; AGA XX 326: Vol. 5/130; NSA IV: Vol. 5a/154; Bärenreiter: Vol. 4/54
Bibliography:	Brown 1958, p. 45
	Capell 1928, p. 35
	Dürr 1983
	Fischer-Dieskau 1977, pp. 107–8
	Porter 1961, pp. 110–11
Discography and timing:	Fischer-Dieskau II 1[10] 2'38
	Hyperion I 11[5]
	Hyperion II 17[7] 1'15 Brigitte Fassbaender

← *Vedi quanto adoro (Didone abbandonata)* D510a   *Nur wer die Liebe kennt (Impromptu)* D₂513a →

AN DIE APFELBÄUME, WO ICH JULIEN ERBLICKTE

To the apple trees where I caught sight of Julia

(HÖLTY) **D197** [H99]
A major   22 May 1815

(28 bars)

Ein heilig Säuseln und ein Gesangeston	Let solemn murmuring and the sound of singing
Durchzittre deine Wipfel, o Schattengang.	Vibrate through the treetops above you, O shaded walk.
Wo bang und wild der ersten Liebe	Where, fearful and impassioned, the blissful frenzy
Selige Taumel mein Herz berauschten.	Of first love sealed my heart.
Die Abendsonne bebte wie lichtes Gold	The evening sun shimmered like brilliant gold
Durch Purpurblüten, bebte wie lichtes Gold	Through purple blossoms; shimmered like brilliant gold
Um ihres Busens Silberschleier;	Around the silver veil on her breast.
Und ich zerfloss in Entzückungsschauer.	And I dissolved in a shudder of ecstasy.
Nach langer Trennung küsse mit Engelkuss	After long separation let a faithful youth
Ein treuer Jungling hier das geliebte Weib,	Kiss with an angel's kiss his beloved wife,
Und schwör' in diesem Blütendunkel	And in the darkness of this blossom
Ewige Treue der Auserkornen.	Pledge eternal constancy to his chosen one.
Ein Blümchen sprosse, wann wir gestorben sind,	May a flower bloom, when we are dead,
Aus jedem Rasen, welchen ihr Fuss berührt,	From every square of turf touched by her foot
Und trag' auf jedem seiner Blätter	And may each of its leaves
Meines verherrlichten Mädchens Namen.	Bear the name of my exalted love.

LUDWIG CHRISTOPH HÖLTY (1748–1776); poem written in 1774. Adapted for publication in 1804 by JOHANN HEINRICH VOSS (1751–1826)

This is the fifth of Schubert's twenty-three Hölty solo settings (1813–16). See the poet's biography for a chronological list of all the Hölty settings.

A sampling of the Schubert songs written in May 1815 is a good indication of the young composer's range of musical and literary sympathies, and his mercurial way of working. In this month there are settings of poems by Matthisson and Schiller (including the imposing *Amalia*

D195) and a *Singspiel* with a text by Theodor Körner entitled *Der vierjährige Posten* D190. But one of his most exciting May discoveries was a poet who would provide him with the texts for a number of exquisite, and still underestimated, songs. He had set one poem by Ludwig Hölty as early as 1813: *Totengräberlied* D44, a Shakespearean graveyard scene with a touch of comedy. On 17 May the first (and probably best known) of the new wave of Hölty settings, *An den Mond* D193, was composed. Five days later Schubert set three more poems: *An die Nachtigall* D196, *An die Apfelbäume, wo ich Julien erblickte* D197 and *Seufzer* D198.

An die Apfelbäume is a tour de force in the use of the alcaic, a Greek poetic stanza of four lines. 'Ein heilig Säuseln und ein Gesangeston', the poet's opening phrase, might almost define piano-accompanied song. Accordingly the composer places the 'Gesangeston' above an accompaniment that murmurs like the rustling of trees in a sacred Delphic grove. Hölty's carefully planned metre is mirrored in music that creates an appropriate spaciousness. This in turn creates a lofty emotional perspective that unites visions of the past, present and future. On a more mundane level, the vocal line seems endless, never giving pause for breath, explaining, perhaps, why so few singers have taken up this song.

The music's challenges are exacerbated by the tempo Schubert chooses for this rapt arioso; time seems to stand still. Given fine singing, this can be rewarding for the listener; but the pianist must know how to move discreetly forward in order to help make sense of Hölty's long sentences (and avoid asphyxiation). The third verse shifts into the tonic minor with a fervent recitative, music for a sacred vow. The last verse is a recapitulation of the first. The vocal melody is no longer accompanied by the rustling semiquavers of the opening, but by imposing triplets. The romance of the present has turned into the legend of the future, and the beloved's name appears on the petal of every flower – an image later appropriated by Matthisson for his *Adelaide*. After 'Meines verherrlichten Mädchens Namen' six mezzo staccato quavers in the piano's miniature postlude seem to whisper (twice) the tri-syllabic name found nowhere in the sung text – Julia, or Julien in its old-fashioned accusative form. There is something in this song of the throbbing ecstasy of another arboreal love song (plane trees rather than apple) – the second setting of the Matthisson setting *Stimme der Liebe* D418.

Autograph:	Missing or lost since 1872 (bb. 1–15)
	Conservatoire collection, Bibliothèque Nationale, Paris (bb. 16 to the end)
First edition:	Published as Book 50 no. 1 of the *Nachlass* by Diabelli, Vienna in 1850 (P389)
Subsequent editions:	Peters: Vol. 6/76; AGA XX 73: Vol. 2/117; NSA IV: Vol. 8/51
Bibliography:	Bell 1964, p. 25
Discography and timing:	Fischer-Dieskau I 3^{22} 2'47
	Hyperion I 10^6
	Hyperion II 6^{19} 3'04 Martyn Hill

← *An die Nachtigall* D196   *Seufzer* D198 →

AN DIE DIOSKUREN *see* LIED EINES SCHIFFERS AN DIE DIOSKUREN D360

AN DIE ENTFERNTE

(GOETHE) **D765** [H500]

G major   December 1822

To the distant beloved

(45 bars)

So hab' ich wirklich dich verloren?	Have I really lost you?
Bist du, o Schöne, mir entflohn?	Have you fled from me, dearest love?
Noch klingt in den gewohnten Ohren	Every word, every tone
Ein jedes Wort, ein jeder Ton.	Still sounds in my well-accustomed ears.
So wie des Wandrers Blick am Morgen	As in the morning the traveller's gaze
Vergebens in die Lüfte dringt,	Searches the heavens in vain
Wenn, in dem blauen Raum verborgen,	When, concealed in the blue firmament,
Hoch über ihm die Lerche singt:	The lark sings high above him:
So dringet ängstlich hin und wieder	So my gaze searches anxiously back and forth
Durch Feld und Busch und Wald mein Blick;	Through field, thicket and woodland;
Dich rufen alle meine Lieder:[1]	All my songs call out to you:
'O komm, Geliebte, mir zurück!'	'Come back to me, beloved!'

JOHANN WOLFGANG VON GOETHE (1749–1832); poem written *c.* 1778? or 1788

This is the sixty-eighth of Schubert's seventy-five Goethe solo settings (1814–26). See the poet's biography for a chronological list of all the Goethe settings.

Other composers had already been drawn to this poem but this small masterpiece, full of wonderful subtleties, caps all the other settings. This is an ABA structure that subtly subverts that form, a song of classical poise which is also the epitome of Romantic longing. Since 1814 the composer, despite his considerable gifts for dramatic narration, had attempted to preserve the important quality of *Innigkeit*, essential to the German lied, in a new and more flexible form. Here we find the choicest fruits of his labour: music that remains true to German aesthetic ideals, yet that is modernized and freed from the traditions of chorale, ballad and strophic repetition.

Schubert had passed through a phase of writing much longer songs, settings of Novalis and Friedrich von Schlegel, and the effusions of his friends Bruchmann and Schober had claimed his attention. By 1822 the return to Goethe via the *West-östlicher Divan* settings inspired a new clarity and lucidity – a genuinely modern fusion of the classical and Romantic. Melody is invented on the spot, and with such naturalness, that we are scarcely aware whether the singer speaks to us or sings. There is a distinct possibility that the Goethe songs of December 1822 were composed

[1] Schubert adds a second 'alle' to Goethe's line.

under the shadow of very recent syphilis diagnosis. The loss of a beloved here, together with a certain sense of shocked disbelief, may be compared to the loss of inner peace and all hope for the future that the composer experienced throughout 1823 and well into 1824.

The falling figure in the *Vorspiel* seems to ask a question, 'Is it true?' An intrusive dissonance in the left hand (b. 2), a momentary twinge of pain before its resolution, leads us to expect an ominous response. The falling figure is repeated; this time it leads to twinned diminished sevenths (b. 3), directing the gaze of the enquirer, and the singer, heavenward. Imitating the piano's introduction, but capping it in terms of intensity, the falling phrase of the vocal line begins unaccompanied on a high G. Fischer-Dieskau writes that this setting 'was to determine the style of musical declamation for a century'. The prosody is refined; the accentuation of 'wirklich' (b. 4) immediately conjures a believable sense of loss. The ghost of Gluck's *Orpheus and Eurydice* appears before us ('J'ai perdu mon Eurydice'), both in terms of Goethe's words and Schubert's musical response.

The poem's first verse encompasses shifts from the home key of G major to G minor (as a rueful mirror of 'mir entflohn' bb. 6–7), B flat and then to F major for the end of the verse. The music for Goethe's second strophe (marked 'Etwas langsamer', from b. 14) is frozen in F minor until the song of the larks takes us into A flat major (bb. 21–2). Taking his cue from Goethe's punctuation at the end of the second verse (a colon rather than a full stop after 'singt'), Schubert annexes half of Verse 3 as part of a tormented bridge passage (marked 'Geschwinder') that begins at 'So dringet ängstlich hin'. This takes us back to F minor, and then C major (b. 26), so that the recapitulation of the first musical idea in G major occurs only in the third line of the poem's last verse.

Repetitions of the few remaining words (note the seemingly improvised power of 'alle, *alle meine Lieder*') build up into a substantial third section – an eloquent plea. Before the closing cadence in the vocal line, there is an unaccompanied bar for the voice ('O komm, Geliebte' for the last time, bb. 37–8) in which Schubert audaciously pays tribute to the tradition of operatic cadenza in the middle of a lied of the highest seriousness. The postlude (from b. 41) repeats the prelude; the singer's entreaties have fallen on deaf ears (that jarring E flat impinges again in the piano) and the final two bars of postlude bring the story to a resigned and crestfallen close.

It is possible that Goethe wrote this poem for Charlotte von Stein as a peace offering on his return to Weimar from Italy in 1788. If so, it was unsuccessful and the friendship between the poet and his former muse never reverted to its former importance. It would not be long before Goethe embarked on his relationship with Christiane Vulpius, the woman whom he was eventually to marry.

Autograph:	Staatsbibliothek Preussischer Kulturbesitz, Berlin (first draft)
First edition:	Published as No. 4 of *Sechs bisher ungedrückte Lieder* by Wilhelm Müller, Berlin in 1868 (P416)
Subsequent editions:	Peters: Vol. 7/541; AGA XX 417: Vol. 7/54; NSA IV: Vol. 13/57
Bibliography:	Capell 1928, p. 181
	Einstein 1951, p. 254
	Fischer-Dieskau 1977, pp. 161–2
Further settings and arrangements:	Johann Friedrich Reichardt (1752–1814) *An die Entfernte* (1809)
	Carl Friedrich Zelter (1758–1832) *An die Entfernte* (1807)
	Vacláv Tomášek (1774–1850) *An die Entfernte* (1815)
	Benedict Randhartinger (1802–93) *An die Entfernte*
	arr. Tilman Hoppstock (b. 1961) for guitar accompaniment, in *Franz Schubert: 110 Lieder* (2009)

Discography and timing: Fischer-Dieskau II 5[15]   3'04
                          Pears-Britten 1[4]   3'16
                          Hyperion I 18[10]   2'58   Peter Schreier
                          Hyperion I 28[20]   3'11   Maarten Koningsberger
                          Hyperion II 26[5]   2'58   Peter Schreier

← *Schicksalslenker, blicke nieder* D763   *Der Musensohn* D764 →

AN DIE FREUDE   Ode to joy
(SCHILLER) **D189** [H91]
E major   May 1815

(32 bars)

Freude, schöner Götterfunken,
   Tochter aus Elysium,
Wir betreten feuertrunken,
   Himmlische, dein Heiligtum.
Deine Zauber binden wieder,
   Was die Mode streng geteilt,
Alle Menschen werden Brüder,
   Wo dein sanfter Flügel weilt.

C h o r :
Seid umschlungen, Millionen!
   Diesen Kuss der ganzen Welt!
   Brüder—überm Sternenzelt
Muss ein guter Vater wohnen.

Wem der grosse Wurf gelungen,
   Eines Freundes Freund zu sein;
Wer ein holdes Weib errungen,
   Mische seinen Jubel ein!
Ja—wer auch nur e i n e Seele
   S e i n nennt auf dem Erdenrund!
Und wer's nie gekonnt, der stehle
   Weinend sich aus diesem Bund!

C h o r :
Was den grossen Ring bewohnet,
   Huldige der Sympathie!
   Zu den Sternen leitet sie,
Wo der U n b e k a n n t e thronet.

Joy, fair divine spark,
   Daughter of Elysium,
We enter your sanctuary,
   Heavenly one, drunk with ardour.
Your magic will reunite
   What custom has harshly severed.
All men become brothers
   Where your gentle wings hover.

Chorus:
Be embraced, ye millions!
   This kiss is for the whole world!
   Brothers above the starry vaults
A good father must dwell.

He who has had the good fortune,
   To give and receive friendship,
He who has found a loving wife,
   Let him add his jubliant voice!
Yes – whoever on this earth
   Calls but *one* living soul his *own*!
And let him who cannot do so
   Creep away, weeping, from this brotherhood!

Chorus:
Let all who inhabit this great globe
   Pay homage to sympathy!
   It leads to the stars,
Where the *unknown being* is enthroned.

Freude trinken alle Wesen
  An den Brüsten der Natur,
Alle Guten, alle Bösen
  Folgen ihrer Rosenspur.
Küsse gab sie uns und Reben,
  Einen Freund, geprüft im Tod,
Wollust ward dem Wurm gegeben,
  Und der Cherub steht vor Gott.

C h o r:
Ihr stürzt nieder, Millionen?
  Ahndest du den Schöpfer, Welt?
  Such Ihn überm Sternenzelt!
  Über Sternen muss er wohnen.

[. . . 5 verses & 5 choruses . . .]

All creatures drink joy
  From nature's breasts;
All men, good and evil,
  Follow her rosy trail.
She gave us kisses, and the vine,
  And a friend, tried in death.
Lust was granted to the worm
  And the Cherub stands before God.

Chorus:
Ye millions, do you bow down?
  World, do you sense your Creator?
  Seek Him beyond the starry vaults!
He must dwell above the stars.

[. . . 5 verses & 5 choruses . . .]

FRIEDRICH VON SCHILLER (1759–1805); poem written in summer 1785

This is the sixth of Schubert's forty-four Schiller solo settings (1811–24). See the poet's biography for a chronological list of all the Schiller settings.

After Schiller's short contract as resident playwright in Mannheim expired in 1784 he had to rely on friends for his next move. It was to be a turning point in his career. Four unknown admirers from Leipzig invited him to come to their city. Chief among them was Christian Gottfried Körner (father of the poet, Theodor) who helped to support Schiller during his two-year sojourn in Saxony. The poet had never felt so happy and at ease; *An die Freude* is a jubilant reflection of his new-found confidence, and first appeared in the almanac *Thalia* in 1786.

It is a *trompe l'oreille*, as it were, of musical chronology that by the time Beethoven came to set this celebrated *Ode to Joy* as part of the finale of his Ninth Symphony (1824) the much younger Schubert had all but finished his own explorations of Schiller's work, including a setting of the same words at least seven years earlier. It is true that Beethoven had toyed with the idea of setting the words from as early as 1793; we know this from a letter written that year to Schiller's wife by one Bartholomäus Fischer of Bonn with which was enclosed a copy of Beethoven's song *Feuerfarb'* (the text not by Schiller), predicting the composer's future fame. Beethoven had evidently told Fischer that he intended to set *An die Freude* to music, paying due attention to each strophe. Before 1822, however, Schiller had hardly featured in Beethoven's musical life except for three occasions (in 1813, 1815 and 1817) when he turned to the poet's work for epigrammatic verses suitable for canons and album-leaf inscriptions for friends and colleagues (including Ludwig Spohr).

No doubt one of the reasons why Beethoven delighted in providing the definitive setting of these words was that since its publication the poem had stood as an insuperable challenge to composers, not least himself. The *Leipziger Allgemeine musikalische Zeitung* of April 1818 pours scorn on all the musicians who had attempted to set the text to music strophically and states that only a through-composed solution would be acceptable.

Beethoven would have been delighted to prove the critics wrong. A simple, singable tune can capture the mood of a lyric such as this better than a fussy line by line response to the poet's various images. The words are populist and they cry out for a populist musical response. Both Schubert and Beethoven understood this, and the younger composer was instinctively on Beethoven's wavelength in a quest for a rugged and noble simplicity. Beethoven even provided a theme where, for most of the melody, the tune moves in single steps, easy for 'Everyman' both to sing and remember. Of course, it was Beethoven's masterstroke to place his tune in a complicated and highly wrought context where grandeur and simplicity could complement each other to their mutual advantage. A parallel may be Britten's decision in *War Requiem* to set poems of Wilfred Owen (impossible to set, surely, as songs for voice and piano) within the context of the Latin mass.

John Reed conjectures that Schubert's tune was perhaps influenced by the final movement of Beethoven's *Fantasie* Op. 80 for piano, chorus and orchestra, a work in which the younger composer might have taken part as a member of the chorus. It is also possible that he was inspired by the example of Zumsteeg whose *An die Freude* appears in his sixth volume of *Kleine Balladen und Lieder* (1803), although when comparing the two settings side by side it is the older composer's that is the more ornate and fussy in terms of melismatic vocal line and pianistic interjection. Schubert's accompaniment is full of orchestral simulation: the gentle beat of the timpani energizes the opening bars, the brass blazes forth at 'Wir betreten feuertrunken', the six-bar postlude suggests singing *divisi* strings. The gear-change into $\frac{3}{4}$ is highly effective for the chorus 'Seid umschlungen, Millionen!' We must remind ourselves again that this music was composed years before Beethoven's, and yet manages to prophesy some of its shining conviction. On the other hand, the tessitura in E major is far too high for a unison choral setting, and the breadth of the lyric is uncontainable by single voice with piano. Although a 'big tune' is required, Schubert's does not bear endless repetition; in the Hyperion Schubert Edition only two (1 and 3) of the eight strophes printed in the AGA were recorded. Strophes 1, 2 and 3 are printed above. It is hard to imagine any concert performance where more would be appropriate. Although the AGA printed this work in its solo song series and it also appears in a Peters lieder volume, the NSA has reserved its appearance for the series devoted to choral music.

Autograph:	Missing or lost
First edition:	Published as Op. post. 111 no. 1 by Josef Czerny, Vienna in 1829 (P197)
Subsequent editions:	Peters: Vol. 4/126; AGA XX 66: Vol. 2/102; NSA III: Vol. 3
Bibliography:	Fischer-Dieskau 1977, pp. 194–5
Further Settings:	Johann Rudolf Zumsteeg (1760–1802) *An die Freude* (1803)
	Benedict Randhartinger (1802–93) *An die Freude* (duet)
Discography and timing:	Fischer-Dieskau I 3[17] 3'18
	Hyperion I 16[6]
	Hyperion II 6[10] 1'56 Thomas Allen

⟵ *Naturgenuss* D188   *Gott, höre meine Stimme* D190/5 ⟶

AN DIE FREUNDE   To his friends
(MAYRHOFER) **D654** [H423]
A minor – A major   March 1819

Im Wald, im Wald, da grabt mich ein,

(76 bars)

Im Wald, im Wald da grabt mich ein,	Bury me in the forest,
Ganz stille, ohne Kreuz und Stein:	Silently, without cross or stone
Denn was ihr türmet, überschneit	For whatever you raise up
Und überrindet Winterszeit.	Winter storms will encrust with snow.
Und wann die Erde sich verjüngt	And when the earth grows young again,
Und Blumen meinem Hügel bringt,[1]	Bringing flowers to my grave,
Das freut euch Guten, freuet euch![2]	Rejoice, good friends, rejoice;
Dies alles ist dem Toten gleich.[3]	All this is nothing to the dead.
Doch nein—denn eure Liebe spannt	But no, for your love extends
Die Äste in das Geisterland:	Its branches into the land of spirits,
Und die euch führt zu meinem Grab,	And as it leads you to my grave,
Zieht mich gewaltiger herab.	It draws me more forcefully downwards.

JOHANN MAYRHOFER (1787–1836)

This is the thirty-second of Schubert's forty-seven Mayrhofer solo settings (1814–24). See the poet's biography for a chronological list of all the Mayrhofer settings.

This was the first Mayrhofer poem to be set after Schubert moved into the poet's lodgings in the Wipplingerstrasse in 1819, although he had already composed some thirty Mayrhofer songs. *An die Freunde* appears in the 1824 *Gedichte* but the composer must have set the poem from a manuscript source. Not for the first time the words of Mayrhofer seem prophetic of the sentiments of the great English poet Thomas Hardy. In *Regret not me* (from *Satires of Circumstance*, 1914) Hardy asks that his friends waste no time in mourning him, and that they get on with the happiness of their own lives. Mayrhofer's command from the grave is 'Rejoice, good friends, rejoice' – both winter storms and springtime flowers are meaningless to the dead. It is pointless, Mayrhofer says, to raise up a stone in his memory because it will be obscured by winter snows (and eventually by the ravages of time – cf. the poem for *Auf der Donau* D553). And in a bitter final line, a Heine-like sudden thrust of the verbal rapier, he warns his friends that visits to his graveside would simply make him appear more dead to them than before; their presence would only serve to drive him more forcefully downwards ('gewaltiger herab') into the nether regions of darkness and obscurity. This aversion to posthumous affection represents a self-loathing that has a far more bitter edge to it than even Hardy's bleak view of the parameters of human existence.

But this song is a rare instance of Schubert wilfully misconstruing the poet's intentions. Far from responding in musical terms to the bleak finality of the text's last line, Schubert's reading seems to imagine a mystical contact between the living and the dead, an exchange of metaphysical energy whereby the poet's friends will be lifted to the land of the spirits by their admiration for him, and Mayrhofer in turn will be drawn back to earthly realms by their affection and devotion. This is neither a statement of belief in a Christian afterlife nor a spiritualist fantasy. The composer seems more influenced by the transcendental poems of Novalis (impossible to define in conventional religious terms) who felt himself in close communion with his beloved

---

[1] Mayrhofer writes 'Sie Veilchen meinem Hügel bringt'. For an explanation of the background to these alternative Mayrhofer readings see Editorial Note at the beginning of Johann MAYRHOFER.
[2] Mayrhofer writes 'Gute' rather than 'Guten'.
[3] Mayrhofer writes '*Ist alles doch* dem Toten gleich'.

Sophie von Kühn after her death (see the biography of this poet). It is no coincidence that Schubert was setting Novalis at exactly this time.

There is a later Mayrhofer song of this year, the wonderful *Nachtstück* D672, where an aged minstrel (an Ossianic figure) prepares for his death without any sense of self-pity or foreboding. He simply feels it is the right time to die. He strides into the depths of the forest and, self-accompanied on his harp, he strikes up a rousing hymn to night. In b. 11 of that song the time signature changes from **C** to *alla breve*, and the hero of the song turns his back on life and goes with his harp into the forest ('So nimmt der Alte seine Harfe') from which he will never return. Such a purposeful left-hand march suggesting a determined stride is also the governing mood of *An die Freunde*, where the manuscript is without tempo marking; Schubert frequently revised time signatures when he prepared songs for publication – this one remained unpublished in his lifetime. There is also no tempo marking on the autograph. Contemporary copies have 'Langsam' while the 'Mässig' of the first edition is clearly an addition of Diabelli's. An *alla breve* tempo seems indicated, despite the **C** of the manuscript.

The whole of the opening section is accompanied by the left hand alone, first in single quavers (not marked staccato, but having that effect due to the intervening rests) and then in octaves. This accompaniment introduces the determined pronouncements of a seer, and it is clear that Schubert regarded Mayrhofer as such. The mood is determinedly anti-sentimental, mirroring the poet's brusque message of 'no fuss'; dying is something natural, and the march-like music is grim without being mournful. One is reminded of another A major song from more or less the same period – *An den Mond in einer Herbstnacht* D614 where at bb. 78–82 the moon shines down on the burial places of loved ones, and the accompaniment, also, is for left hand alone. Single-handed writing of this kind tends to be a Schubertian metaphor for single-minded deci-siveness, but here it also seems to depict the loneliness of the grave, and the withering of hopes that once flowered with abundant musical life. The sheer economy of the writing denotes someone who has long divested himself of earthly vanities.

The magical change from A minor to A major (from b. 18), a Schubertian trademark, is here lavished on Mayrhofer's description of his imagined resting place in springtime. The ray of regenerative light and warmth at 'Und wann die Erde sich verjüngt' (b. 19) is typical of this famous tonal transformation. Instead of the solitary and pitiless left hand the accompaniment blossoms in filled-out harmony and burgeoning counterpoint. An A major cantilena flowers above the dry bass; a thread of oboe-like sound (almost in the manner of a Bach cantata) entwines with string-like writing that seems layered in parts. The vocal line gradually grows from tendril to sturdier branch, already indicative of a network of friendship that will take root and flourish as surely as flowers cover the grave. The almost baroque pacing of the music, suggesting a ground bass without being one, momentarily ceases at b. 33 where the phrase 'Dies alles ist dem Toten gleich' summons an element of portentous canonic imitation between voice and piano. This is music to close the door on any conventional hope of immortality.

The tiny interlude between bb. 37 and 40 that follows this bleak statement is exactly analagous to a passage in *Heliopolis I* D753 (also at a change between major and minor at bb. 21–3 of that song) that similarly makes the piano tread water in harmonic limbo, as if the poet were expecting imminent revelation but is momentarily lost while contemplating the best way forward. This deliberation gives rise to something hushed and wonderful in both songs (they are in any case related in subject matter). In *An die Freunde* the passage beginning 'Doch nein' (from b. 40) is where Schubert intervenes and unashamedly diverts the song's closing moments away from the original intentions of Mayrhofer's poem. The poet's hardness of heart is softened, the chink of light almost visible in the change of harmony on 'nein' in b. 41, invalidating the gloomy prog-nostications with which the poem ends.

From here until the end of the song the voice is in a challenging tessitura; there are a few exposed top notes, but more demanding is the high-lying passage-work that requires a piano dynamic (it was for this reason that the entire song was transposed down a major third by Diabelli). The setting of the words 'spannt / Die Äste' encompasses a semibreve tied to a dotted crotchet poised high on the stave. This passage is remarkable for its suggestion of branches (of sound, by analogy) extending into the land of the spirits. The remainder of the music (from b. 59 more or less anchored on an A pedal) depicts the poet quietly exultant, confident in a kind of afterlife where the artist lives on in the memory of his friends. The distance between the height of the voice and the depth of the piano writing driven ever downwards (as if *this* were the composer's response to 'gewaltiger herab') becomes a musical metaphor for the uncharted realms between heaven and earth. And the very fact that we are discussing this poem (and perhaps listening to Schubert's setting of it) is as fine a vindication of this aim as the composer might ever have wished. The music is fervent here, a triumphant chorale against all the odds; the conclusion to *Trockne Blumen* from *Die schöne Müllerin* D795/18 springs to mind, another song where dry beginnings lead to defiantly unexpected flowerings.

Too inhibited and rigid to accept the love of the living in physical terms, the poet even attempts to deflect affection from those who have outlived him. Schubert chooses to ignore this pessimism and, in doing so, bestows on Mayrhofer a posthumous compensation for a life of unfulfilled yearning. He begins by offering the poet respect, even reverence, but by the end of the song he delivers in musical terms the very things that Mayrhofer insists are of no avail and that he does not merit: solace, flowers, a shift from minor to major – love of a kind.

The choice of key for the unsatisfactory first edition of *An die Freunde* has no doubt contributed to the song's neglect – Schubert's A minor was transposed down to a comfortable if muted F minor (also in the Peters Edition), indubitably easier to sing but lacking the fervid radiance of the original. This is a song that should attract the attention of a fine tenor with a flexible top. Even singers with lower voices who are content to use Peters should consult the NSA to rectify important details – the change between single notes and octaves in the opening bars, the ornamentation of the vocal line in b. 7, the correct bass notes in bb. 57 and 63, and so on. The manuscript of the poem was possibly addressed by Mayrhofer to Josef Kenner (qv), a schoolfriend of Schubert and an aspiring poet, which could account for an incorrect attribution of the text to Kenner in early copies of the song.

Autograph:	Gesellschaft der Musikfreunde, Vienna (first draft)
First edition:	Published as Volume 40 no. 3 of the *Nachlass* by Diabelli, Vienna *c.* 1842 (P350)
Subsequent editions:	Peters: Vol. 6/28 (F minor); AGA XX 356: Vol. 6/20; NSA IV: Vol. 12/87
Bibliography:	Capell 1928, p. 160
	Einstein 1951, p. 189
	Porter 1961, pp. 82–3
	Youens 1996, p. 170
Discography and timing:	Fischer-Dieskau II 2[16] 3'35
	Hyperion I 3[2] 4'01 Ann Murray
	Hyperion II 21[18]

← *Bertas Lied in der Nacht* D653   *Der Jüngling am Bache* D638 →

AN DIE GELIEBTE

(STOLL) **D303** [H183]

G major   15 October 1815

To the beloved

(27 bars)

O dass ich dir vom stillen Auge	Oh that from your silent eyes,
In seinem liebevollen Schein,	In their loving radiance
Die Tränen von der Wange sauge,	I might drink the tears from your cheek
Eh' sie die Erde trinket ein!	Before the earth absorbs them!
Wohl hält sie zögernd auf der Wange,	They remain hesitantly on your cheek,
Und will sich heiss der Treue weihn;	Dedicating themselves warmly to constancy
Nun ich sie so im Kuss empfange,	Now, as I receive them in my kiss,
Nun sind auch deine Schmerzen mein.	Your sorrows, too, are mine.

JOSEF LUDWIG STOLL (1778–1815)

This is the second of Schubert's two Stoll solo settings (1815). See the poet's biography for a chronological list of the Stoll settings See also the article for Selam.

This is one of eight songs composed on 15 October 1815. The others were *Labetrank der Liebe* (Stoll) D302, *Wiegenlied* (Körner) D304, *Mein Gruss an den Mai* (Kumpf) D305, *Skolie* (Deinhard-Deinhardstein) D306, *Die Sternenwelten* (Fellinger) D307, *Die Macht der Liebe* (Kalchberg) D308 and *Das gestörte Glück* (Körner) D309. The composer took all these poems from a single literary source, the third issue of the almanac *Selam* edited by Castelli and published in Vienna in 1814. (He was also to find a number of texts in the 1813 and 1815 issues of the same almanac; *see Selam cycle*) John Reed points out that 15 October was the name-day of Schubert's beloved of the time, Therese Grob. If he was inspired to a large creative outburst in her honour there is little doubt that it is she who is '*die Geliebte*'. On the other hand, the link with the name-day may simply be a coincidence: none of these songs was included in the Therese Grob songbook of the following year.

Nevertheless it seems certain that the young composer was in romantic mood. Like the same unfortunate poet's *Labetrank der Liebe* D302 (and on entirely another, higher, level of intensity Heine's *Am Meer* D957/12) this is about intimate exchange, the mingling of tears as a symbol of one human soul and body melting into another. Such wishful thinking on Schubert's part produces music of considerable intensity.

The melodic line that opens this song reappears note for note (including the surprising F natural in the second bar) in the Claudius setting *An die Nachtigall* D497 (1816). *An die Geliebte* does not achieve the perfect balance of classical and Romantic elements of that famous song, but it is a worthy companion of the other Stoll setting, *Labetrank der Liebe*, which is recommendation enough. All is translucent texture with a succession of gently falling sequences and exquisite suspensions – in short, a perfect page in its modest genre.

Beethoven set this text twice. Both songs are in D major and both in $\frac{2}{4}$, the second version a considerable improvement on the first. In this instance it is clear that Schubert was not in the slightest influenced by his great contemporary.

Autograph: Österreichische Nationalbibliothek, Vienna
First edition: Published as Vol. 7 no. 49 in Friedlaender's edition by Peters,
                              Leipzig in 1887 (P509)
Subsequent editions: Peters: Vol. 7/108; AGA XX 151: Vol. 3/116; NSA IV: Vol. 9/134
Further settings and   Ludwig van Beethoven (1770–1827) *An die Geliebte* (two
arrangements: versions) WoO 140 (1811–14)
                              arr. Tilman Hoppstock (b. 1961) for guitar accompaniment, in
                              Franz Schubert: 110 Lieder (2009)
Discography and timing: Fischer-Dieskau I 5²⁸   1'30
                              Hyperion I 10¹⁸
                              Hyperion II 10¹⁹   2'19   Martyn Hill

← *Labetrank der Liebe* D302   *Wiegenlied* D304 →

AN DIE HARMONIE   To harmony
(Salis-Seewis) **D394** [H239]
A major   March 1816

(27 bars)

Schöpferin beseelter Töne!	Creator of inspired music!
Nachklang dem Olymp enthällt!	Echo, sounding from Olympus!
Holde, körperlose Schöne,	Gracious, disembodied beauty,
Sanfte, geistige Gewalt,	Gentle spiritual power
Die das Herz der Erdensöhne	Who boldly uplifts and tenderly envelops
Kühn erhebt und mild umwallt!	The hearts of mortals;
Die in inn'rer Stürme Drange	Who with soothing magic
Labt mit stillender Magie,	Quells the tempests within us,
Komm mit deinem Sühngesange,	Come with your comforting music,
Himmelstochter, Harmonie!	Harmony, daughter of heaven.
Seufzer, die das Herz erstickte,	For sighs, suppressed by the heart
Das, misskannt, sich endlich schloss –	That, misunderstood, at length became closed;
Tränen, die das Aug' zerdrückte,	For tears, forced back by eyes
Das einst viel' umsonst vergoss,	That had once wept so much in vain,
Dankt dir wieder der Entzückte	I thank you again, enraptured,
Den dein Labequell umfloss.	Lapped by your healing stream.
Der Empfindung zarte Blume,	The tender flower of feeling

Die manch frost'ger Blick versengt,	Blighted by many a frozen look,
Blüht erquickt im Heiligtume	Blossoms, refreshed in the shrine
Einer Brust, die du getränkt.	Of a heart nurtured by you.
[. . . 7 . . .]	[. . . 7 . . .]
Tön' in leisen Sterbe-Chören	In soft funereal strains
Durch des Todes Nacht uns vor!	Sing to us in the night of death.
Bei des äussern Sinns Zerstören	As our external senses are destroyed,
Weile in des Geistes Ohr!	Linger in the spirit's ear.
Die der Erde nicht gehören,	Raise aloft with your swansong
Heb' mit Schwanensang empor!	Those who belong no more on earth.
Löse sanft des Lebens Bande,	Gently loosen life's bonds;
Mildre Kampf und Agonie,	Ease the struggle of our death throes,
Und empfang' im Seelenlande	And receive us in the land of bliss,
Uns, o Seraph, Harmonie!	Seraphic harmony!

JOHANN GAUDENZ VON SALIS-SEEWIS (1762–1834); poem written 1800/6

This is the sixth of Schubert's thirteen Salis-Seewis solo settings (1816–?21). See the poet's biography for a chronological list of all the Salis-Seewis settings.

This is Schubert in public mood (as in *An die Freude*) where the true Schubertian perhaps likes to find him least. Nevertheless *An die Harmonie* is an interesting song. At first hearing the opening seems old-fashioned and formal. (There is no tempo marking in NSA; the AGA version is marked 'Mässig'.) The voice is made to trumpet the opening words in a singularly uninventive A major arpeggio. We soon realize that Schubert's tune deliberately explores the tonic chord as an appropriate salute to harmony itself; for once, melody is not the priority. At 'Die das Herz der Erdensöhne' the music moves into A minor, as if the natural state of wretched mankind is to be in the minor key. As soon as the comforting power of harmony is mentioned, the music softens into C major with an ingratiating piano interlude (bb. 12–13). The chromatic progress back to A major via the words 'Labt mit stillender Magie' has a touch of magic, and 'Himmelstochter' launches its descent from the first of two high As in the piece. This heady tessitura, and the sudden flowering of Mozartian coloratura in b. 19, seems to preclude this music from unison choral performance. Elsewhere the sturdiness of the chordal accompaniment suggests a formal occasion and many voices. From the vocal point of view the song is tiring; ten strophes of it, as printed in the NSA, would test the endurance of audience and performer alike – and this despite the fact that one of the contemporary copies has no fewer than nine of the strophes written out. Printed here are 1, 2 and 10.

Autograph:	Missing or lost
First edition:	Published as part of the AGA in 1895 (P627)
Subsequent editions:	Not in Peters; AGA XX 199: Vol. 4/62; NSA IV: Vol. 10/66
Discography and timing:	Fischer-Dieskau I 6[22] 2'59
	Hyperion I 18[7]
	Hyperion II 13[13] 3'34 Peter Schreier

←— *Die Einsiedelei* D393   *Lied (Ins stille Land)* D403 —→

AN DIE LAUTE
(Rochlitz) Op. 81 no. 2, **D905** [H610]
D major   January 1827

To the lute

(25 bars)

Leiser, leiser, kleine Laute,	Play more softly, little lute,
Flüstre, was ich dir vertraute,	Whisper what I secretly told you
Dort zu jenem Fenster hin!	To that window there!
Wie die Wellen sanfter Lüfte,	Like the ripple of gentle breezes,
Mondenglanz und Blumendüfte,	Like moonlight and the scent of flowers,
Send' es der Gebieterin!	Convey your secret to my mistress.
Neidisch sind des Nachbars Söhne,	The neighbour's sons are envious,
Und im Fenster jener Schöne	And at the fair lady's window
Flimmert noch ein einsam Licht.	A solitary lamp flickers.
Drum noch leiser, kleine Laute:	So play still more softly, little lute:
Dich vernehme die Vertraute,	That my beloved may hear you,
Nachbarn aber—Nachbarn nicht!	But the neighbours – no, not the neighbours!

JOHANN FRIEDRICH ROCHLITZ (1769–1842); poem written in 1803

This is the last of Schubert's four Rochlitz solo settings (1812–27). See the poet's biography for a chronological list of all the Rochlitz settings.

'A flower of a song, a daisy', says Capell, and so it is. This little serenade (with a tempo swift enough to denote the excitement and suspense of a lover) owes much to Don Giovanni's *Deh! vieni alla finestra* – and Rochlitz the music critic would have known every note of Mozart's opera. Here the lute serves as an instrument of seduction in lieu of the mandolin. The four-bar introduction leads us to the pluckings of the serenader simulated in the piano writing by delicately arpeggiated chords. The harmony is pivoted between tonic and dominant; far from being dull this suggests hovering, waiting for an exciting outcome.

It is a miracle that so much is depicted with so little musical activity: excitement and trepidation (note how the vocal line climbs to a *mezza voce* F sharp, then retreats to the middle of the stave), the flickering of the lamp in the window, the way that the moonlight and scent of flowers insinuate themselves into the picture like a lover slipping through a door left discreetly ajar. At bb. 13–14 ('Wie die Wellen sanfter Lüfte') there is a delicious evocation of a rustling breeze, a sensuous *frisson* achieved through clever use of the most simple harmony – Schubert was so confident that his first draft was used as a fair copy for the printer. Intrigue of a delightful kind is everywhere in this song, not least in the point-scoring glee at the expense of the jealous neighbours. The implication is that the singer must be playing the lute himself, but he addresses it as if it has a life and will of its own. This is not unlike an otherwise very different song, the Bruchmann setting *An die Leier* D737, a translation of Anacreon. Perhaps Rochlitz had also read his ancient Greek poetry before producing this Biedermeier trifle. It has become so much more than that in Schubert's hands.

Autograph:	Wienbibliothek im Rathaus, Vienna (first draft)
First edition:	Published as Op. 81 no. 2 by Tobias Haslinger, Vienna in 1827 (P129)
Dedicatee:	Friedrich Rochlitz (dedicated by Haslinger)
Publication reviews:	*Münchener allgemeine Musik-Zeitung* No. 1 (6 October 1827), col. 8 [Waidelich/Hilmar Dokumente I No. 530; Deutsch Doc. Biog. No. 955]
	Allgemeine musikalische Zeitung (Leipzig), No. 4 (23 January 1828), col. 49f. [Waidelich/Hilmar Dokumente I No. 569; Deutsch Doc. Biog. No. 1014]
	Berliner allgemeine musikalische Zeitung No. 20 (14 May 1828), p. 157f. [Waidelich/Hilmar Dokumente II No. 613a]
	Allgemeiner musikalischer Anzeiger (Vienna), No. 20 (16 May 1829), p. 77 [Waidelich/Hilmar Dokumente I No. 727]
Subsequent editions:	Peters: Vol. 4/62; AGA XX 288: Vol. 4/262; NSA IV: Vol. 4/24; Bärenreiter: Vol. 3/18
Bibliography:	Capell 1928, p. 128
	Fischer-Dieskau 1977, p. 247
Discography and timing:	Fischer-Dieskau I 9[6] 1'33
	Hyperion I 6[15]
	Hyperion II 32[17] 1'35 Anthony Rolfe Johnson

← *Alinde* D904   *Der Vater mit dem Kind* D906 →

AN DIE LEIER   To my lyre
(BRUCHMANN) OP. 56 NO. 2, **D737** [H506]
C minor – E♭ major   Winter 1822/3?

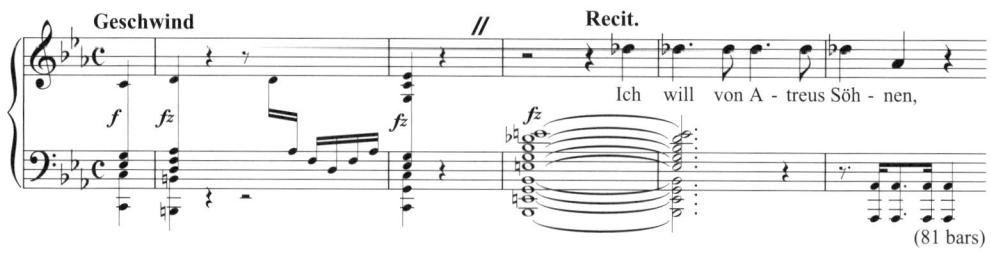

(81 bars)

Ich will von Atreus' Söhnen,	I would sing of Atreus' sons,
Von Kadmus will ich singen!	Of Cadmus,
Doch meine Saiten tönen	But my strings bring forth
Nur Liebe im Erklingen.	Only sounds of love.
Ich tauschte um die Saiten,	I have changed the strings,
Die Leier möcht' ich tauschen!	I should like to change the lyre!
Alcidens Siegesschreiten	Alcides' victorious march
Sollt' ihrer Macht entrauschen!	Should ring out from its might!
Doch auch die Saiten tönen	But these strings, too,
Nur Liebe im Erklingen!	Bring forth only sounds of love!
So lebt denn wohl, Heroen,	Farewell, then, heroes!

Denn meine Saiten tönen,
Statt Heldensang zu drohen,
Nur Liebe im Erklingen.

For my strings,
Instead of threatening with heroic songs,
Bring forth only sounds of love.

FRANZ VON BRUCHMANN (1798–1867), AFTER ANACREON

This is the first of Schubert's five Bruchmann solo settings (1822–3). See the poet's biography for a chronological list of all the Bruchmann settings. See also the entry for Anacreon.

This is Franz von Bruchmann's unpublished translation of a Greek lyric supposedly by Anacreon (fl. sixth century BC), heavily reliant on the translation of the ancient poet by Johann Friedrich Degen, printed in *Anakreons Lieder* (1782). The rather too facile consecutive references to the three most famous Greek epics – the Trojan wars (Atreus), the Theban wars (Cadmus) and the story of Hercules (Alcides) – hardly inspire confidence in the text's contemporary authenticity. An English version of the same poem with the title *This poet sings the Trojan Wars*, or *Anacreon's Defeat*, was set by Purcell in 1686–7. (The English composer treats his subject playfully, as if the notion of a lyre that will not do its owner's bidding suggests the instrument of love getting embarrassingly out of control.)

The popularity of the anacreontic style (where a touch of philosophy counterbalances wine-induced ribaldry) goes back to a celebrated sixteenth-century French translation. This was in turn copied by eighteenth-century German writers: Gleim and Uz, and even Goethe in a certain mood, wrote anacreontic odes. Mörike's *Anakreon und die sogenannten Anakreontischen Lieder* (where another translation of the lyric set by Schubert is entitled simply *Die Leier*) was published in 1864. Leconte de Lisle's *Odes Anacréontiques* were published in 1855 and were set to music by Fauré and Roussel among others. The Italian singing translation of this poem, *Alla cetra*, probably by Nicolaus Craigher de Jachelutta and printed beneath the German text in the song's first edition, is reprinted in the NSA and in Schochow 1974, Vol. 1 p. 46. Italian translations were also printed for the other songs in Op. 56 (*Willkommen und Abschied* and *Im Haine*) and were probably designed to broaden the international appeal of Schubert's songs but there is no evidence that it increased the sales of the music. The original ancient Greek text is reprinted in Schochow 1974, Vol. 1 p. 47.

An die Leier stands on the threshold of the world of *Die schöne Müllerin* and the coming to terms with mortality that was in store for Schubert with the diagnosis of his illness in late 1822 or early 1823. This is among the last songs he wrote that incorporated a classical theme. Once he entered the world of Wilhelm Müller's poetry it is as if he put aside an enthusiasm for the sounding brass and tinkling cymbals of antiquity, marvellous though these evocations are. As the singer attempts to sing of warlike heroes in the opening bars the hollow pomposity of the music is deliberate; we are soon given to understand that only love matters, and when love is the subject we seldom hear Schubert respond in flippant manner. This song is surely a study for *Der Neugierige* D795/6 in *Die schöne Müllerin*: the miller's brook, like the lyre, has a will of its own and fails to respond to the singer's bidding. In both songs the alternation between recitative and aria is similar, including the pregnant silences that usher in love songs both cast in the form of Italian *arie*.

The key of the opening recitative is C minor, usually portentous in Schubert. The song begins with what can seem like frightening intensity; indeed performers must remind themselves not to be unduly fierce in a song that is charming and gentle for the most part. The opening is marked 'Geschwind'. By way of opening fanfare the player of the lyre tries out chords and a couple of sequences of intimidating semiquavers before finding a diminished seventh chord that he strums resoundingly seven times (bb. 3–4), bellicose vacuity turned into music. Atreus was father to Agamemnon and Menelaus, so it seems we are about to hear a tale of the Trojan war, or perhaps a tale about Cadmus, founder of Boethian Thebes. The vocal line is marked 'Recit.' and starts on a succession of strident D flats, underpinned by repeated chords that lead us into

D flat major. From b. 8 the bass line begins to slip like the unwinding of tuning pegs; D flat slides to C flat supporting a right-hand seventh chord on F. From there a tiny loosening takes us to a B flat bass and the dominant seventh chord that will lead us to the key of E flat major. The dense piano writing gradually dissolves into the tentative stutterings of the right hand alone, as if the instrument is autonomous, though not yet certain of what to play – the step by step transformation of a raving Mr Hyde back into a reasonable Dr Jekyll.

The following E flat aria at b. 15 (marked 'Etwas langsamer') is lovingly accompanied in *bel canto* triplets, legato and peacefully tuneful. Generations of singers have made life difficult for themselves by adopting a lachrymose and over-slow tempo for this smiling aria; Anacreon's discomfort at his inability to wage war is just a pose. The opening rant has been merely an excuse to lead us to the radiant heart of this music. Schubert's marking asks that the pace should be only 'rather' slower than the original 'Geschwind', but still fast enough to make this aria flow in two, rather than four, beats to the bar (although it is not actually marked *alla breve*).

The conceit is that the lyre has a will of its own, and all the singer can do is follow its amorous dictates. This is a metaphor, of course, for the urgings of the poet's libido for which he assures us he is not to blame. For the purposes of poetic symmetry (and decency) the narrator must attempt to resist this rebellion. A bar's rest (b. 27) allows the strings to be changed and the pegs to be turned tighter. The singer strums again and, altering his tessitura, works himself up into a higher pitch of warlike intensity. This Herculean task prompts talk of Alcides, another name for Hercules himself. By a rather more circuitous and adventurous harmonic route (as if new strings must resound in different tonalities) the lyre finds its way back to the same chords that set up its entry into the E flat of the love aria (marked 'Langsamer' at b. 46). The singer admits himself defeated and, by now enamoured of his own love music, he bids farewell to the 'threatening' songs (in b. 64 'drohen' is accompanied by a mock ominous bass trill) and to the heroes who have once held him so much in thrall. The darts of love are as potentially wounding in their way as the spears of battle. The postlude has a note of yearning although the Victorian sentimentality that can creep into this music when played too slowly is to be avoided. As in the *rispetti* of Wolf's *Italienisches Liederbuch*, a dramatic situation has been fabricated as a pretext for a gallant compliment. The song should be delightful rather than over-imposing, beguiling rather than forbidding.

Autograph:	Missing or lost
First edition:	Published as Op. 56 no. 2 by A. W. Pennauer, Vienna in July 1826 (P103)
Dedicatee:	Karl Pinterics
Publication reviews:	*Allgemeiner musikalischer Anzeiger* (Frankfurt), No. 2 (8 July 1826), p. 10f. [Waidelich/Hilmar Dokumente I No. 395; Deutsch Doc. Biog. No. 672]
Subsequent editions:	Peters: Vol. 2/10; AGA XX 414: Vol. 7/42; NSA IV: Vol. 3/68; Bärenreiter: Vol. 2/104
Bibliography:	Capell 1928, p. 175
	Einstein 1951, p. 254
	Fischer-Dieskau 1977, pp. 186–7
Discography and timing:	Fischer-Dieskau II 5[12] 3'45
	Hyperion I 14[17]
	Hyperion II 26[12] 4'03 Thomas Hampson

← *Im Haine* D738   *Der Zwerg* D711 →

AN DIE MUSIK
To music
(Schober) Op. 88 no. 4, **D547** [H361]

The song exists in two versions, the second of which is discussed below:
(1) March 1817; (2) appeared December 1827

(1)   'Etwas bewegt'   D major   ₵   [23 bars]

(2)   D major

Du holde Kunst, in wieviel grauen Stunden,	Beloved art, in how many a bleak hour,
Wo mich des Lebens wilder Kreis umstrickt,	When I am enmeshed in life's tumultuous round,
Hast du mein Herz zu warmer Lieb entzunden,[1]	Have you kindled my heart to the warmth of love,
Hast mich in eine bessre Welt entrückt.	And borne me away to a better world!
Oft hat ein Seufzer, deiner Harf entflossen,	Often a sigh, escaping from your harp,
Ein süsser, heiliger Akkord von dir	A sweet, celestial chord
Den Himmel bessrer Zeiten mir erschlossen,[2]	Has revealed to me a heaven of happier times.
Du holde Kunst, ich danke dir dafür.	Beloved art, for this I thank you!

Franz von Schober (1796–1882)

This is the fourth of Schubert's fourteen Schober solo settings (1815–27). See the poet's biography for a chronological list of all the Schober settings.

This has become Schubert's theme song – and few would argue against its use as such. Einstein suggests that another Schober setting, *Trost im Liede* D546, comes closer to defining the composer's attitude to his song-writing art, but there is no denying that Schubert has worked a miracle here and engineered a triumph of pure feeling using relatively modest musical means. The poem (which bears a striking resemblance to a stanza in Ernst Schulze's *Die bezauberte Rose* beginning 'Du holde Kunst, melodisch süsser Klagen') is not great poetry, however familiar and beloved its words have become. There is a handwritten copy of the lyric in Schober's hand in the Wienbibliothek im Rathaus, but it never appeared in any of the poet's printed collections. The resemblance to Schulze noted above is probably purely coincidental as *Die bezauberte Rose* was not printed until 1818.

The setting is entirely conventional (it is even strophic) save for its greatness. Sincerity and heartfelt devotion seem to emanate from every note, as well as a quiet exaltation that enables us to glimpse for a moment the transfigured state in which Schubert is said to have written his music. Finding this mood makes it one of the most daunting of songs for performers. The music has the force of the still, small voice that can hush the world.

[1] In a later hand-written version of the poem Schober writes 'zu *neuer* Lieb entzunden'.
[2] In the same version as above, 'Den Himmel *neuer Hoffnung* mir erschlossen'.

The song is a dialogue between the voice and the pianist's left hand, the quasi-cello bass line of the music. The right hand is the true accompanist in this heavenly conversation; its throbbing quavers mediate between the duettists in a way that is crucial to the mood of the song although the listener may only be subliminally aware of their pulsations. Except in the postlude to each verse these chords have no special thematic significance; the piano needs to repeat notes in order to sustain a harmonic background, and the accompanist has to find a means of allowing these chords to 'happen' without appearing to strike each one individually – something which would break the music into a succession of pedantic downbeats. Underneath this gliding stream of harmony, the left hand sings its heart out, warming the voice into action. The setting of 'Du holde Kunst', with a touching downward leap of a sixth between the second and the third words, suggests obeisance and reverence.

Reference to the bleak hours and the tumult of life are voiced in the lower part of the stave, earthbound and tricky in tessitura for many sopranos and tenors. After 'wilder Kreis umstrickt' an eloquent little falling chromatic motif in the left hand (b. 10) is a prelude that ushers in the lifting of the spirits (and the vocal line) into higher regions. At this point a generous and eloquent four-bar phrase takes wing ('Hast du mein Herz zu warmer Lieb entzunden' bb. 11–14), this time without the dallying on long low notes that has characterized earlier phrases. It is as if the whole song has caught fire and is aglow with the warmth of music itself. The next phrase ('Hast mich in eine bessre Welt entrückt' bb. 14–17) directs its glance heavenward; there is scarcely a phrase in all Schubert more descriptive of longing and aspiration as the inexorably rising bass line shoulders the melody aloft. This phrase ends in the relative minor as if to show us that there is no pleasure without its cost in pain, a paradox, sweetly bitter and bittersweet, that lies at the heart of so much of Schubert's music. The repeat of these words returns us to

First edition of Op. 88 where *An die Musik* occupies a surprisingly modest place.

earth in two succeeding downward leaps, each of a sixth, and as the voice comes to the end of its line we find ourselves back in the D major of the home key. The shape of this vocal line is a musical metaphor to demonstrate that heaven has been brought down to these earthly realms; our dreary planet has been transfigured by Music's beauty.

The piano's interlude (it also serves as the song's postlude, bb. 19–23) mirrors this descent in a succession of chord sequences built around apoggiaturas that lean and sigh, tugging on the sleeve and pulling the heartstrings. A simple excursion into the subdominant (b. 20) subtly emphasizes that this hymn of praise is also a type of prayer. The second strophe introduces the idea of the harp that was probably the inspiration behind the piano's gentle right-hand strumming in the first place. As in all Schubert's great strophic songs, the vocal line fits both verses like a glove; the interval of a sixth that has bowed down to Music on 'holde Kunst' is also descriptive of the sigh of 'ein Seufzer'. The closing words of thanks ('Du holde Kunst, ich danke dir dafür') can be unbearably moving. This song was the last encore sung by the great soprano Lotte Lehmann at her farewell recital at New York's Town Hall in 1951. After a lifetime of service to music she was too choked by tears to sing the final words, and the accompanist finished the song for her. Schubert was also attempting to give voice to the inexpressible. To write music *about* music is the hardest thing of all; in the wordless gratitude of the postlude this most literary of composers retreats into that realm of art where words simply cannot carry the depth of his feeling. 'Such a song', writes Richard Capell, 'wins for the author a tenderness that is more than admiration from the coming and going generations.'

This was actually not always the case and, in the eyes of some literary Germans, the Schober text lets the song down, as can been seen from an entry in Rainer Maria Rilke's *Briefe und Tagebücher aus der Frühzeit*. Carl Hauptmann (best known to recitalists as the poet of *Nacht* in Berg's *Sieben frühe Lieder*) was an indefatigble music enthusiast and loved to arrange impromptu lieder performances for his colleagues. On 10 September 1900, Rilke wrote in his diary: 'Dr Hauptmann had a song with a ghastly text sung to him again and again, an invocation to Art, the bearer of solace, which the soprano, it must be said, sang very well and simply. The words began "O sweet Art, in many a bleak hour. . . etc." '

The song made much more of an impression on the Irish playwright Samuel Beckett, an avid Schubertian who copied both the words and melodic line into his *Whoroscope* notebook in the 1930s. The closing lines of the short story *Walking Out* are 'They sit up to all hours playing the gramophone. *An die Musik* is a great favourite of them both, he finds in her big eyes better worlds than this.'

The NSA prints a first version of the song in Volume 4b. It is this which is dated March 1817. The tempo marking of this slightly plainer version with some different bass notes and fewer dynamic markings is 'Etwas bewegt'. Schubert's first thought might be taken as a warning to certain singers to avoid the slow and sluggish sentimentality that often passes for his published 'Mässig' marking, and one suspects that the 1900 performance for Rilke mentioned above was simply too slow and thus sentimental. In fact there were five autograph versions of the song: the second was the fair copy made for its publication by Weigl in 1827, and a further three were written in private autograph albums.

Autographs:	First draft lost, two surviving fair copies: Conservatoire collection, Bibliothèque Nationale, Paris (first version) and British Library, London (Stefan Zweig Collection) (second version)
Publication:	First published as part of the AGA in 1895 (P672; first version) First published as Op. 88 no. 4 by Thaddäus Weigl, Vienna in 1827 (P140; second version)
Subsequent editions:	Peters: Vol. 1/236 & Vol. 2/166; AGA XX: 314a & b Vol. 5/86 & 87; NSA IV: Vol. 4a/108 & Vol. 4b/240; Bärenreiter: Vol. 3/76

Bibliography:	Capell 1928, pp. 141–2
	Dürhammer 1999, p. 128
	Einstein 1951, p. 143
	Fischer-Dieskau 1977, pp. 83–4
Arrangements:	Arr. Max Reger (1873–1916) for voice and orchestra (1913–14)
	[*see* ORCHESTRATIONS]
	Arr. Gerald Moore (1899–1987) *An die Musik*, for solo piano
	Arr. Tilman Hoppstock (b. 1961) for guitar accompaniment
	(2 arrangements), in *Franz Schubert: 110 Lieder* (2009)
Discography and timing:	Fischer-Dieskau II 1[1] 2'38
	Hyperion I 21[11]
	Hyperion II 18[12] 2'41 Edith Mathis

← *Trost im Liede* D546   *Pax vobiscum* D551 →

AN DIE NACHTIGALL   To the nightingale
(HÖLTY) **D196** [H98]
F♯ minor   22 May 1815

Unruhig, klagend. Im Zeitmasse wachsend bis zur Haltung

Geuss nicht so laut der lieb-ent-flamm-ten Lie-der ton-reich-en Schall

(17 bars)

Geuss nicht so laut der liebentflammten Lieder	Do not pour out so loudly the sonorous strains
Tonreichen Schall	Of passionate love songs
Vom Blütenast des Apfelbaums hernieder,	From the blossom-covered boughs of the apple tree,
O Nachtigall!	O nightingale!
Du tönest mir mit deiner süssen Kehle	The singing from your sweet throat
Die Liebe wach;	Awakens love in me;
Denn schon durchbebt die Tiefen meiner Seele	For already your melting sighs
Dein schmelzend Ach.	Pierce the depths of my soul.
Dann flieht der Schlaf von neuem dieses Lager,	Then sleep once more shuns this bed,
Ich starre dann,	And I stare,
Mit nassem Blick und totenbleich und hager,	Moist-eyed, drawn and deathly pale,
Den Himmel an.	At the heavens.
Fleuch, Nachtigall, in grüne Finsternisse,	Fly away, nightingale, to the green darkness
Ins Haingesträuch,	Of the grove's thickets,
Und spend' im Nest der treuen Gattin Küsse;	And in your nest bestow kisses on your faithful spouse.
Entfleuch, entfleuch!	Fly away!

LUDWIG CHRISTOPH HÖLTY (1748–1776); poem written in 1772. Adapted for publication in 1804 by JOHANN HEINRICH VOSS (1751–1826)

This is the fourth of Schubert's twenty-three Hölty solo settings (1813–16). See the poet's biography for a chronological list of all the Hölty settings.

Brahms's settings of the Hölty poems *An die Nachtigall* and *Die Mainacht* have entirely eclipsed Schubert's songs to the same texts. It is easy to understand the popularity of the Brahms works, rich in sentiment and Romantic nostalgia, but the two composers were aiming to achieve different things. Schubert had chosen to set the poems strophically and Brahms (who knew his Schubert very well) offered a deliberately different through-composed solution. Brahms's *An die Nachtigall* is meditative and lyrical, Schubert's much more urgent, on the wing and a-flutter; as if it is a matter of life and death that the nightingale's painfully evocative song should be silenced. Indeed, the words of the second strophe (the narrator is 'totenbleich') suggest that Schubert might have imagined this as a deathbed scene.

The song boasts one of Schubert's longest directions to his performers: 'Restless, plaintive. Accelerating (growing) in tempo until the fermata' – this 'Haltung' (literally the holding of the note by the singer) is the pause marked on the second beat of b. 7, just before the change of tempo. These first seven bars of music feature a wide-ranging, one might almost say hysterical, vocal line, an outburst of melody with the peremptory flexibility of recitative. The poem's metre, and the overflowing of one line into the other, has encouraged this approach. The piano writing restricts itself at first to arpeggiated chords. At the upbeat to b. 8 ('Du tönest mir mit deiner süssen Kehle') there is a change of gear and the direction 'Mässig' appears as if in mid-stream. The music takes on a more lilting rhythm, though it is notable that the first twelve bars of the song do not contain a single rest in either voice or piano part – the singer must breathe with stealth and good management. At 'Denn schon durchbebt' this temporary poise breaks down and the piano writing suddenly bristles with the tremor of demisemiquavers. These in turn lead to the accompaniment's two final bars where cascading triplets imitate the virtuosity of the nightingale. As the song is strophic, all these features are repeated in the second verse.

In the first half of each verse the harmonies seem almost arbitrary, and thus appropriately distracted: the strummed arpeggios, not to mention the extraordinary piano mini-cadenza at the end of each verse, give an improvised, quasi-Hungarian feel to the music; the sound of the cimbalom is somehow evoked. (One is irresistibly reminded of the savage outbursts, in F sharp minor – also the tonality of this song – in the slow movement of the A major Piano Sonata D959.) Schubert would have known that this warbling rush of notes (under 'Dein schmelzend Ach' and again at 'Entfleuch, entfleuch!') bore no resemblance to the actual song of the nightingale; these melodic pirouettes surely reflect the listener's highly strung emotional reaction to the sound of the bird's singing.

Autograph:	Missing or lost
First edition:	Published as Op. post. 172 no. 3 by C. A. Spina, Vienna in 1865 (P403)
Subsequent editions:	Peters: Vol. 4/100; AGA XX 72: Vol. 2/116; NSA IV: Vol. 8/50
Bibliography:	Einstein 1951, p. 360
	Gülke 1991, pp. 75–6
Further settings:	Johannes Brahms (1833–1897) *An die Nachtigall* Op. 46 no. 4 (1868)

Discography and timing: Fischer-Dieskau I 3²¹   1'51
                          Hyperion I 7⁸
                          Hyperion II 6¹⁸   1'41   Elly Ameling

← *Amalia* D195   *An die Apfelbäume, wo ich Julien erblickte* D201 →

AN DIE NACHTIGALL   To the nightingale
(CLAUDIUS) **D497** [H314]
G major   November 1816

(41 bars)

Er liegt und schläft an meinem Herzen,	He lies sleeping upon my heart;
Mein guter Schutzgeist sang ihn ein;	My tutelary spirit sang him to sleep.
Und ich kann fröhlich sein und scherzen,	And I can be merry and jest,
Kann jeder Blum' und jedes Blatts mich freun.	Delight in every flower and leaf.
Nachtigall, ach! Nachtigall, ach!¹	Nightingale, ah, nightingale,
Sing mir den Amor nicht wach!	Do not awaken my love with your singing!

MATTHIAS CLAUDIUS (1740–1815); poem published in 1771

This is the sixth of Schubert's thirteen Claudius solo settings (1816–17). See the poet's biography for a chronological list of all the Claudius settings.

This is one of the finest songs of 1816: brevity, classical poise and restraint are suffused with achingly beautiful intimations of the Romantic era. The song opens in unconventional fashion in the subdominant, C major. This had already been tried by Schubert a year before in the Stoll setting *An die Geliebte* D303; indeed Schubert liked the opening of that song so much that here he unashamedly borrows from himself, something that was far from his usual practice. It is as if the singer cannot bear to wake the sleeper and has shyly shifted into a backwater tonality, away from the brightness of the tonic key, in order to soothe his dreams. The idea of shaping the vocal line in a sensuously descending sequence perhaps derives from Reichardt's lovely little setting, but the harmonic *trompe l'oreille* is utterly Schubertian.

    The poem is to be found in the first volume of the complete works of Claudius, or the 'Wandsbecker Bote' as he was known. In the 1775 edition, this poem, printed on p. 56, follows *Phidile*, a love song also set by Schubert. Some interpreters see in this song a mother's lullaby but the fact that Claudius had recently become engaged to Rebecca Behn suggests a love song. The opening music is all innocence and a moment of calm. Vivacity enters the music just before the song of the nightingale itself (and the words 'Und ich kann fröhlich sein und scherzen') but

¹ Hölty writes: 'Nachtigall, Nachtigall, ach'. The addition of the first 'Ach' is Schubert's.

the jauntiness of the little birdsong piano interlude (from b. 22) should be tempered by the accompanist – the nightingale is a small bird. In the combination of repose and youthfulness another ⅜ song comes to mind – Friedrich Schlegel's setting *Das Mädchen*.

The sudden change to G minor at b. 30, and a succession of Ds repeated in the vocal line (bb. 30–4) from 'Nachtigall, ach!', is heart-stopping despite (or perhaps because of) the tried and trusted alternation of tonic and dominant harmonies. At this point in the Reichardt setting there is a change from ⅜ to ⅝ and there are two contrasting four-bar phrases for the repeated words 'Nachtigall, Nachtigall, ach! / Sing mir den Amor nicht wach'. The first of these is marked 'Beklommen', the second 'Mit zurückgehaltener Sehnsucht'. The 'apprehension' and 'contained longing' required by Reichardt as interpretative effects are to be heard in the tremulous beauty of Schubert's music, altogether on another plane. But now comes the extraordinary effect of a poised high G harmonized on E flat major for the word 'Amor' (bb. 35–6), and when this melts into the second inversion of G major at the bar line of b. 36 (while the singer holds her high note) we have a quintessential Schubertian moment. The vocal line then makes its gracious descent to the tonic in root position on the word 'wach'. The four-bar postlude (a repetition of a two-bar phrase) combines the piping of the birdsong with the blissful contentment of the singer.

Autograph:	Missing or lost
First edition:	Published as Op. 98 no. 1 by Diabelli, Vienna in July 1829 (P228)
Subsequent editions:	Peters: Vol. 1/252 & Vol. 4/96; AGA XX 276: Vol. 4/238; NSA IV: Vol. 5/74; Bärenreiter: Vol. 3/204
Bibliography:	Einstein 1951, p. 161
Further setting and arrangements:	Johann Friedrich Reichardt (1750–1814) *An die Nachtigall* (1779) Arr. Tilman Hoppstock (b. 1961) for guitar accompaniment, in *Franz Schubert: 110 Lieder* (2009)
Discography and timing:	Fischer-Dieskau — Hyperion I 17[18] Hyperion II 16[18] 1'35 Lucia Popp

← *Klage um Ali Bey* D₂496a   *Wiegenlied* D498 →

AN DIE NATUR   To Nature
(STOLBERG) **D372** [H217]

The song exists in two versions, the first of which is discussed below:
(1) 15 January 1816; (2) November 1816?

(1)   F major

(2)   'Mässig'   A major   ⅝   [12 bars]

Mässig

Süs - se, hei - li - ge____ Na - tur,   lass mich gehn auf dei - ner__ Spur,

p

(12 bars)

Süsse, heilige Natur,	Sweet, holy nature,
Lass mich geh'n auf deiner Spur,	Let me walk upon your pathway,
Leite mich an deiner Hand,	Lead me by the hand,
Wie ein Kind am Gängelband!	Like a child on the reins!
Wenn ich dann ermüdet bin,	Then, when I am weary,
Sink' ich dir am Busen hin,	I shall sink down on your breast,
Atme süsse Himmelslust	And breathe the sweet joys of heaven
Hangend an der Mutterbrust.	Suckling at your maternal breast.
Ach! wie wohl ist mir bei dir!	Ah, how happy I am to be with you!
Will dich lieben für und für;	I shall love you for ever;
Lass mich geh'n auf deiner Spur,	Let me walk upon your pathway,
Süsse, heilige Natur!	Sweet, holy nature!

FRIEDRICH LEOPOLD, GRAF ZU STOLBERG-STOLBERG (1750–1819); poem written in 1775

This is the third of Schubert's nine Stolberg solo settings (1815–23). See the poet's biography for a chronological list of all the Stolberg settings.

Like so many other shy and unassuming creations by Schubert this song lingers in the ear and heart although we are perfectly aware that much greater songs await us on the turn of a page. The composer's radical and reforming instincts (as in *Gretchen am Spinnrade* among many other songs) were balanced by a conservatism that acknowledged the past, and paid more than lip service to the German tradition of word-setting as admired (and required) by Goethe's generation. An inspiration for this discipline came from a composer like J. A. P. Schulz (1747–1800) whose own setting of these words (*Lieder im Volkston*, Teil 1 Nr. 1) may well have been Schubert's source for Stolberg's text. Reichardt's setting appears as the second of his *Oden und Lieder von Klopstock, Stolberg, Claudius und Hölty* (Berlin, 1779). On the other hand the poem also appears in the Viennese school textbook of literary style, *Sammlung Deutscher Beyspiele zur Bildung des Styls*, 1808, which Schubert almost certainly knew as both student and teacher.

This is music of sweet and gentle restraint; in this poem where nature leads a stumbling child by the hand, the song's meek docility seems utterly appropriate. The Schubert biographer, Kreissle von Hellborn, tells us that this was the first song by Schubert known to Therese Grob, the composer's probable sweetheart. However, the dates do not fit this theory: Schubert had known the Grob family too long for a song composed in 1816 to have been the first Therese knew. Either *An die Natur* was composed much earlier, or (and this is more likely) this was one of the manuscripts that came to hand in the making of the Therese Grob songbook – another matter altogether. A second version of *An die Natur* (printed in the NSA) occurs in this anthology from November 1816. Therese was a high soprano, so the key of A major, a third higher than the original F major, was presumably used to suit her voice.

Autograph:	Wienbibliothek im Rathaus, Vienna (first version); in private possession in Switzerland (second version; part of the Therese Grob album)
Publication:	First published as part of the AGA in 1895 (P618; first version)
	First published as part of the NSA in 2002 (P827; second version)

Subsequent editions:	Not in Peters; AGA XX 183: Vol. 4/2; NSA IV: Vol. 10/22 & 23
Bibliography:	Kreissle von Hellborn 1865, Vol. 1, p. 35
Further settings:	Carl Loewe (1796–1869) *An die Natur* (printed without accompaniment, later added by F. H. Schneider, in *Gesang-Lehre*, 1826)
Discography and timing:	Fischer-Dieskau I 6^{12} 1'55
	Hyperion I 5^3
	Hyperion II 12^{12} 2'38 Elizabeth Connell

← *Klage (Trauer umfliesst mein Leben) D371*   *Lied (Mutter geht durch ihre Kammern) D373* →

AN DIE SONNE
(BAUMBERG) **D270** [H156]
E♭ major   25 August 1815?

To the sun

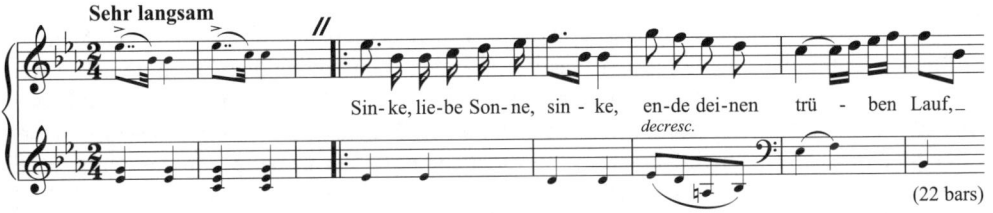

(22 bars)

Sinke, liebe Sonne, sinke!	Sink, dearest sun, sink!
Ende deinen trüben Lauf,	End your dusky course,
Und an deine Stelle winke	And in your place quickly bid
Bald den Mond herauf.	The moon rise.
Herrlicher und schöner dringe	But tomorrow come forth
Aber Morgen dann herfür,	More glorious and more beautiful,
Liebe Sonn'! und mit dir bringe	Dearest sun! And with you
Meinen Lieben mir.	Bring my love.

GABRIELE VON BAUMBERG (1775–1839)

This is the last of Schubert's seven Baumberg solo settings (1809–1810 and 1815). See the poet's biography for a chronological list of all the Baumberg settings.

This miniature displays a marvellous combination of intimacy and grandeur. The natural glory of the sunset is placed in the context of a poem by one of Austria's most gifted woman writers. The date of composition (given in the Witteczek-Spaun catalogue in the absence of an extant autograph) is 25 August 1815, but Reed points out that *An die Sonne* of Tiedge (D272, *see* below) was definitely composed on that day, and there might be room for confusion between two songs with the same title. Nevertheless, as the three Baumberg settings D263–5 were composed in August 1815 the date given for this song is unlikely to be dramatically incorrect.

The original title is 'Als ich einen Freund des nächsten Morgen auf dem Lande zum Besuche erwartete' – 'As I waited in the country for a visit of a friend on the following morning'. On finding the poem in the 1800 edition of Baumberg's *Sämmtliche Gedichte*, Schubert clearly decided on an abbreviation. There may have been a touch of self-censorship here because these words, taken together with the full title and a little reading between the lines, reflect a greater freedom of behaviour for women in the Enlightenment Austria of Josef II than was acceptable during the greater propriety of the Biedermeier years. The passionate poetess has met a handsome man at a formal evening gathering and planned a tryst for the following day. She can scarcely wait for night to come so that the next day will bring his visit. This explains the contained passion of both poem and music – this song is a nature portrait with a definite background. The assignation must take place by day. This might indicate the clandestine circumstances of adultery (the poetess was not yet married, but her prospective lover may have been).

Although the E flat major of this music suggests Mozart's Sarastro, *An die Sonne* has a Beethovenian concision and economy. There is not a single note more than is necessary and there is very little word painting as such. Out of these simple means something lofty and sublime has been fashioned, each phrase seemingly chiselled from sun-warmed marble. Schubert admired Beethoven's nocturnal song *Abendlied unterm gestirnten Himmel* well enough to transpose it in his own hand, and the opening of the *Arietta*, the last movement of Beethoven's C minor Sonata Opus 111, is brought to mind by the falling fourth in dotted rhythm that opens this song.

It is dangerous, however, to make assumptions such as these about the Beethoven/Schubert chronology; although one composer was twenty-seven years older than the other, they were working at the same time. This Schubert song composed in 1815 could not possibly have been influenced by Beethoven's *Abendlied* from 1820, or the Sonata of 1821. Nevertheless, Schubert often prefigures certain characteristics of the older composer's last period – not the contrapuntal complexities and experiments with form, perhaps, but those moments of hymnic simplicity to be found in the slow movements of the late Beethoven piano sonatas, cello sonatas and string quartets, as well as certain of the 'Diabelli' Variations. The power of *An die Sonne*, a single page of music, seems disproportionate to its length and its printed appearance – it has an astonishing maturity and depth of utterance for an eighteen-year-old composer. The drop of a fourth in the key of E flat is exactly how the opening vocal phrase of the Kosegarten setting *An die untergehende Sonne* D457 begins. Again and again one finds that Schubert has a real 'vocabulary' of tonal images: when wishing to compose a hymn to the sun, and without conscious self-quotation, he will respond more than once with an E flat dropping to a B flat (there is a third instance of this in the Tiedge setting *An die Sonne* D272).

Autograph:	Missing or lost
First edition:	Published as Op. post. 118 no. 5 by Josef Czerny, Vienna in 1829 (P226)
Subsequent editions:	Peters: Vol. 4/150; AGA XX 127: Vol. 3/56; NSA IV: Vol. 9/14
Bibliography:	Youens 1996, pp. 41–3
Discography and timing:	Fischer-Dieskau —
	Hyperion I 15[6]
	Hyperion II 9[17] 2'48 Margaret Price

← *Bergknappenlied* D268   *Der Weiberfreund* D271 →

AN DIE SONNE
(TIEDGE) **D272** [H158]
E♭ major   25 August 1815

To the sun

(18 bars)

Königliche Morgensonne,	Regal morning sun,
Sei gegrüsst in deiner Wonne,	I greet you in your rapture;
Hoch gegrüsst in deiner Pracht!	I welcome you in your splendour!
Golden fliesst schon um die Hügel	Already your golden raiment
Dein Gewand; und das Geflügel	Drapes the hills,
Eines jeden Waldes wacht.	And in every forest birds awaken.
Alles fühlet deinen Segen;	Your blessing is felt by all;
Fluren singen dir entgegen,	The meadows sing to greet you;
Alles wird Zusammenklang:	All becomes harmonious.
Und du hörest gern die Chöre	And as you hear with delight the chorus
Froher Wälder, o so höre,	Of the happy forests, so too
Hör' auch meinen Lobgesang.	Hear my song of praise.
[. . . 3 . . .]	[. . . 3 . . .]

CHRISTOPH AUGUST TIEDGE (1752–1841); poem completed before 1795

This is Schubert's only setting of a Tiedge text. See the poet's biography.

Schubert seems to have thought of the rising and setting sun in this key. Both the Baumberg hymns to the sun, *Cora an die Sonne* D263 and *An die Sonne* D270, are in the same tonality, as is Schubert's hymn to the setting sun, *An die untergehende Sonne* (Kosegarten) D457. The majestic workings of nature (and this applies to a great deal of his water music) seems to have been linked in the composer's mind with a trinity of flats. For Schubert, as for Mozart, this key signature denotes awe and an almost religious sense of reverence. The brass-like chords of this song's introduction are reminiscent of the opening of *Die Zauberflöte*. Although poetry of this kind is very much part of the eighteenth-century tradition of extolling the beauties of nature as the workings of God (Tiedge, poet of the famous *Urania*, was very devout), it is just as likely that Schubert was influenced by Ossian's evocations of a majestically pagan world. The Egyptians worshiped the sun as did many ancient cults. This may account for the grandeur that we can detect in this music – so different from the more self-consciously humble settings that reflect Christian pieties.

An die untergehende Sonne D457 is pervaded by downward movement in the melodic line and accompaniment, appropriate to the sinking sun. *An die Sonne*, on the other hand, has a sense of upward momentum. It is very much written for the soprano voice – the stratospheric flight of 'Sei gegrüsst' (accompanied by ceremonial horn fanfares, b. 6) in the poem's second line is capped by 'Hoch gegrüsst' in the third (b. 8). The most interesting passage, however, is the setting of the lines beginning 'Golden fliesst schon um die Hügel' (from b. 10). In the accompaniment an ingeniously built ascent from bass to treble clef mirrors and supports the gradual rising of the sun in the voice (bb. 10–14). This royal progress between the words 'die Hügel' and 'Geflügel' spans almost an octave – A up to A flat – in a ten-note scale that includes a number of semitone intervals. After this high point the melody subsides and bows, giving way to human wonder at all this natural beauty. The postlude, a rising sequence of tonic chords decorated with accented passing notes (bb. 16–18), echoes this phrase in miniature. The final cadence after the ascent is once again in a lower tessitura, a symbol of earthbound awe.

There are five strophes in Tiedge's poem; only the first of these is printed in the AGA – possibly because the poet remained unidentified by Mandyczewski. All five are printed in the NSA. Given here are 1 and 2, which seem sufficient in performance. In the source of the poem, Becker's *Taschenbuch zum geselligen Vergnügen* (1795), there is mention of a setting of this lyric by the Dresden composer Franz Seydelmann (1748–1806).

Autograph:	In private possession
First edition:	Published as No. 9 of *Neueste Folge nachgelassener Lieder und Gesänge* by J. P. Gotthard, Vienna in 1872 (where the poem is wrongly attributed to Baumberg) (P435)
Subsequent editions:	Not in Peters; AGA XX 129: Vol. 3/58; NSA IV: Vol. 9/17
Discography and timing:	Fischer-Dieskau I 5[13] 1'50
	Hyperion I 22[7]
	Hyperion II 9[19] 2'01 Lorna Anderson

⟵ *Der Weiberfreund* D271   *Das Leben ist ein Traum* D269 ⟶

AN DIE SONNE
(Uz) **D439** [H269]
F major   June 1816

                           To the sun   Quartet, SATB

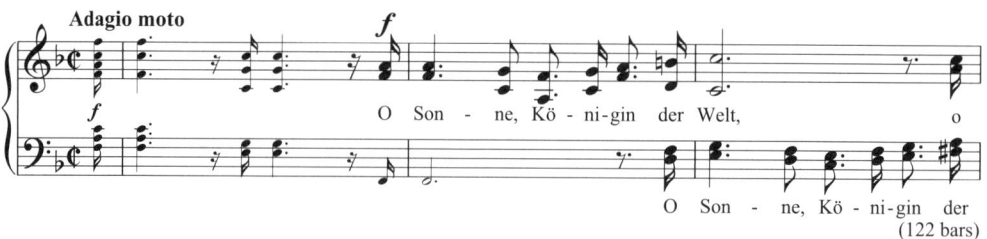

(122 bars)

O Sonne, Königin der Welt,	O sun, queen of the world,
Die unser dunkles Leben erhellt	Who lights our dark lives –
O Sonne, Königin der Welt,	O sun, queen of the world,
Die unser dunkles Rund erhellt,	Who lights our dark round
In lichter Majestät;	In shining majesty;
Erhab'nes Wunder einer Hand,	Sublime marvel of a hand
Die jene Himmel ausgespannt	Which spread out the distant heavens
Und Sterne hingesät!	And strewed the stars within them!

Noch heute seh' ich deinen Glanz,	Today I can still see your radiance;
Mir lacht in ihrem Blumenkranz	In its garlands of flowers
Noch heute die Natur.	Nature still smiles upon me today.
Der Vögel buntgefiedert Heer	Tomorrow the bright-feathered hosts of birds
Singt morgen mir vielleicht nicht mehr	May never again sing to me
Im Wald und auf der Flur.	In the woods and the meadows.
Ich fühle, dass ich sterblich bin,	I feel that I am mortal;
Mein Leben welkt wie Gras dahin,	My life withers away like grass,
Wie ein verschmachtend Laub.	Like languishing leaves.
Wer weiss, wie unerwartet bald	Who knows how unexpectedly, how soon
Des Höchsten Wort an mich erschallt:	The voice of the Almighty will ring out to me:
Komm wieder in den Staub!	'Return to the dust!'
[. . .]	[. . .]

JOHANN PETER UZ (1720–1796); poem written 1763–7

By comparison to the unaccompanied quartet for men's voices (TTBB), the quartet for soprano, alto, tenor and bass is a rarer Schubertian species. From early in his career Schubert had composed for this line-up religious music with orchestra, but piano-accompanied quartets for mixed voices were another matter. In Metternich's Vienna, women did not mix freely in male company, especially in public meeting places and inns. It is therefore no surprise that an evening of quartet-singing in Schubert's time was largely a male affair, a bachelors' night out. This camaraderie remained a strong tradition in Vienna and elsewhere, and had nothing to do with family entertainment and music-making in the drawing room that would follow with the vocal quartets of Schumann and Brahms where Schubertian melody is combined with the domestic plush of later nineteenth-century life.

Schubert, of course, knew nothing of those composers, but Haydn's little-known quartets for SATB and piano must have impressed him. Composed in 1799, these are among Haydn's later creations: profound, humorous, philosophical, even self-deprecating (as in *Der Greis*, where he paints himself, tongue-in-cheek, old and weak, but still witty enough to have the music engraved on his calling-card). Schubert could not have failed to be delighted by this combination of musical grandeur and personal intimacy. Haydn, master of quartets of every kind, took the form as an ideal vehicle for the statements of his last years, whether philosophical in a light-hearted way, or God-fearing (texts from poets like Lessing, Gleim and Gellert, all taken from a single anthology, Ramler's *Lyrische Bluhmenlese* [*sic*] of 1774 – how different from Schubert's far wider pattern of reading). It is perhaps because of Haydn that Schubert's SATB quartets are largely works with metaphysical overtones. This is certainly the case with *An die Sonne*, where the deliberately baroque musical style matches the eighteenth-century text of Haydn's contemporary, the devout Johann Peter Uz, a poet who enjoyed a considerable vogue in Vienna at the beginning of the nineteenth century (if the number of fine Austrian editions of his *Gedichte* is any indication).

Haydn's influence figures here in another important way. He had been astounded by performances of Handel's oratorios in England and had returned to Vienna with the inspiration to write an oratorio of his own – that great work of his late years, *Die Schöpfung* (*The Creation*). This, in turn, was a seminal work for Schubert; its influence (especially concerning musical motifs to do with moon, stars and so on) can be detected in the illustrative details of a large number of the younger composer's vocal works, including *An die Sonne*. This quartet, and others like it, owes a great deal to Haydn's example.

The opening solemn invocation to the sun is introduced by the double-dotted rhythms that are taken up by the singers paired, according to sex, antiphonally. In contrast, at 'erhellt, / In lichter Majestät' bb. 7–10 (where the music modulates into C major, the tonality Haydn used to signify the creation of light), soprano and tenor sing together, followed imitatively by alto and bass. This is typical of the fluidity of this music; ingenious part-writing varies the texture as imposing block harmonies alternate with linear counterpoint. At the end of the first verse, and at the close, the piano writing pulsates in syncopated quavers between the hands at 'Und Sterne hingesät' (bb. 17–24) – an early attempt to depict the electrical energy of the stars in the heavens. (We have to wait until 1827, and the accompaniment to the Leitner setting *Die Sterne*, to hear a more developed version of this idea twinkling in dactylic rhythm.)

The words of the second verse are heard twice, the first time in conventional *pomposo* style in dotted rhythms, relieved by a delightful little piano interjection in triplets after 'Im Wald' as if the composer has imagined the distant sound of hunting horns in the forest (bb. 36–7 and bb. 39–40). When we hear 'Noch heute seh' ich deinen Glanz' for the second time, Schubert allows himself the more personal, conversational tone implied by the word 'ich'. In gently layered solo lines the individual characteristics of the voices are able to shine briefly; all here is simple, sweet goodness in the manner of Haydn. The rise of a semitone in the bass line at the final 'Der Vögel buntgefiedert Heer' (from F to G flat, bb. 49–51) introduces a note of wonder, as if the singer were watching nature with curiosity and awe. This passage sets up a modulation into G flat major – that favourite region of the flattened supertonic.

It is in the poem's third verse, and in tonal regions far away from the home key, that we find the most exceptional music of the piece, and certainly the most Schubertian. There is a reminder here that this composer was of the budding Romantic movement, and a contemporary of neither Haydn nor Uz. From b. 60 the vocal line, marked 'pianissimo', has the four singers breathing as one: 'Ich fühle, ich fühle, dass ich sterblich bin'. This is far removed from threat of hellfire and dry-as-dust renunciation. Instead we hear something nearer to the music for a sensually swooning Ganymede, floating heavenwards as he asks 'Wohin, wohin?' The piano writing in flowing quavers is similar to that which accompanies the shepherd boy's ascent to Olympus. As well as *Ganymed* D544, the mood of this music prophesies the Novalis setting *Nachthymne* D687 where, also, the prospect of death is addressed in ecstatic, rather than fearful, terms.

At 'Wer weiss, wie unerwartet bald' (from b. 90) the return of dotted rhythms implies the majesty of the Last Judgement. The sudden hymnic simplicity of 'Komm wieder in den Staub!' is typical of Schubert's response to music of the grave (the stentorian and frightening unaccompanied men's chorus *Grab und Mond* D893 of 1826 comes to mind). The third strophe is now repeated. 'Ich fühle, ich fühle, dass ich sterblich bin' returns (from b. 78) with the same melody, but this time in D flat major and with a simplified accompaniment. The words 'welkt wie Gras dahin' are heard as a solo for the bass (bb. 85–7). The dotted rhythms of 'Wer weiss, wie unerwartet bald' are set to music a semitone lower than before – this tonal juggling is to ensure that 'Komm wieder in den Staub!' comes to a close in C major. In turn, we are assured of a strong return to the F major of the opening at b. 99. The work closes with a twenty-four-bar repeat of the opening pages, thus framing the quartet with two identical musical pillars, as if the sun were solemnly greeted at both dawn and dusk. The inventive music that lies between these two poles has been substantial enough to make this reprise inevitable and satisfying.

Autograph: Wienbibliothek im Rathaus, Vienna (first draft)
First edition: Published as No. 6 of *Neueste Folge nachgelassener mehrstimmiger Gesänge* by J. P. Gotthard, Vienna in 1872 (P425)
Subsequent editions: AGA XVII 12: p. 218; NSA III: Vol. 2/47

Discography and timing:

	Deutsche Grammophon *Schubert Quartette*	6'26	Elly Ameling, Janet Baker, Peter Schreier & Dietrich Fischer-Dieskau
	Hyperion I 32[12] Hyperion II 14[24]	6'11	Patricia Rozario, Catherine Wyn-Rogers, Jamie MacDougall & Michael George

← *Beitrag zur fünfzigjährigsten Jubelfeier des Herrn von Salieri, erstem K.K. Hofkapellmeister in Wien* D407   *Das grosse Halleluja* D442 →

AN DIE TÜREN WILL ICH SCHLEICHEN *see GESÄNGE DES HARFNERS AUS 'WILHELM MEISTER'* D478/3

AN DIE UNTERGEHENDE SONNE   To the setting sun

(KOSEGARTEN) OP. 44, **D457** [H285]
E♭ major   July 1816–May 1817

(44 bars)

Sonne, du sinkst!	Sun, you are sinking!
Sonne, du sinkst!	Sun, you are sinking!
Sink' in Frieden, o Sonne!	Sink in peace, o sun!
Still und ruhig ist deines Scheidens Gang,	Calm and tranquil is your parting,
Rührend und feierlich deines Scheidens Schweigen.	Touching and solemn that parting's silence.
Wehmut lächelt dein freundliches Auge;	Sadness smiles from your kindly eyes;
Tränen entträufeln den goldenen Wimpern;	Tears fall from your golden lashes;
Segnungen strömst du der duftenden Erde.	You pour blessings upon the fragrant earth.
Immer tiefer,	Ever deeper,
Immer leiser,	Ever softer,
Immer ernster, feierlicher	Ever more grave and solemn,
Sinkest du den Äther hinab![1]	You sink in the heavens.
Sonne, du sinkst!	Sun, you are sinking!
Sonne, du sinkst!	Sun, you are sinking!
Sink in Frieden, o Sonne!	Sink in peace, o sun!

[1] Kosegarten incorrectly prints '*Sinkst* du *die Lüfte nach!*', but Schubert was astute enough to consult the list of printing errors ('Druck- und Schreibfehler') at the beginning of the volume and substitute the correct words.

Es segnen die Völker,	The people bless you,
Es säuseln die Lüfte,	The breezes whisper;
Es räuchern die dampfenden Wiesen dir nach;	Mist drifts towards you from the hazy meadows;
Winde durchrieseln dein lockiges Haar;	The winds blow through your curly hair,
Wogen kühlen die brennende Wange;	The waves cool your burning cheeks;
Weit auf tut sich dein Wasserbett –	Your watery bed opens wide.
Ruh' in Frieden!	Rest in peace,
Ruh' in Wonne!²	Rest in joy!
Die Nachtigall flötet dir Schlummergesang.	The nightingale is singing you lullabies.

Sonne, du sinkst,	Sun, you are sinking.
Sonne, du sinkst,	Sun, you are sinking.
Sink in Frieden, o Sonne!	Sink in peace, o sun!

[(. . . 30 lines, plus 3-line closing refrain . . .)]   [(. . . 30 lines, plus 3-line closing refrain . . .)]

LUDWIG THEOBUL KOSEGARTEN (1758–1818); poem written in 1787

This is the last of Schubert's twenty-one Kosegarten solo settings (1815–17). See the poet's biography for a chronological list of all the Kosegarten settings.

This song of sunset has been damned with faint praise by the commentators. Fischer-Dieskau in 1976 echoes, almost word for word, Richard Capell's lukewarm evaluation of 1928 and John Reed calls it a 'fascinating hybrid'. No one seems to give the song credit for its special grandeur softened, at the end of the day, with gratitude for the goodness and beauty of the world. The haunting Schubertian smile that is a familiar accompaniment to the philosophic acceptance of the inevitable (and what is more inevitable than the daily setting of the sun?) seems to pervade this song: it is bathed in the warm glow of a vocal line that, for all its demands, breathes an air of fulfilment and repose.

The first twenty-one bars of *An die untergehende Sonne* were sketched in 1816; the song was not completed until almost a year later and it is the last of the Kosegarten settings. It is also arguably the finest – the only through-composed setting of this poet. It is obvious that Schubert was fascinated by the rondo form suggested by the look of the printed poem on the page: three lines of invocation (the musical refrain in E flat); a longer passage (nine lines of the poem providing an arioso in A flat in slow ⅜ time); a repeat of the refrain; another passage of a completely different character (another nine lines), a much quicker arioso, also in A flat but modulating via C flat to B major for the song of the nightingales; and back to E flat for the closing invocation – thus ABACA. The composer sets only the first half of Kosegarten's poem, avoiding a pile-up of difficult imagery and repetitive invocations towards the end of the text.

The piano introduction sinks inexorably in stages for five stately bars; each cadence genu-flects in a mood of dignified withdrawal and retreat. It is true that we touch on the chord of E flat in root position in the second bar, but from the very first chord (a first inversion which shows us the sun lowering on the horizon in mid-descent) we are pulled ever downwards towards the moment when the voice enters on the tonic chord of E flat itself (b. 6). This all seems as inevitable as the turning of the world. The vocal refrain ('Sonne, du sinkst!'), modelled

---

² Kosegarten writes '*Schlummr*' in Wonne!'

in the main on the melody of the introduction, unfolds in magisterial fashion. We are quite happy to hear it three times in the course of the work; indeed, such repetition takes on a quasi religious significance, as if something as weighty as the setting of the sun needs to be celebrated by solemn ceremonial. The singer must provide a long-breathed and gleaming vocal line. This is not a song for a thin or unglamorous voice; in order to do it justice the singer must be comfortable playing the role of prophet or seer.

The intervening episodes are also difficult to bring off; the first of these marked 'Ruhig' ('Still und ruhig ist deines Scheidens Gang', from b. 16) is in statuesque triple time (⅜) which, despite the change of metre, retains the poise and gravity of the introduction. The main characteristic of this section in the key of A flat major is that we hear almost all of the phrases twice, suggesting the solemnity of spell or incantation. A small piano postlude has imitative phrases between the hands (again grouped as a pair) as if scored for small wind band (bb. 56–64). After a repeat of the main refrain (from b. 65), the second of the two longer ariosi marked 'Etwas bewegter' ('Es segnen die Völker', from b. 74) is faster and lighter in texture, and serves as an admirable contrast as the heart lifts with the beauties of twilight. This is music of gentle rejoicing; the fleet and palpitating accompaniment captures the playful winds and soothing water cooling the heat of Helios' completed journey. The key signature of this section changes three times. A ten-bar section in five sharps from b. 88 ('Die Nachtigall flötet dir Schlummergesang'), contains the germ of the first *Suleika* song (composed four years later), which is the apotheosis of Schubert's music of the rustling breeze in this tonality. Then the refrain returns for the last time at b. 98; an E flat major chord follows a fermata in B major (b. 97) without preparation or embarrassment. Schubert assumes our ears will cope with the enharmonic change where the third of the old key becomes the new tonic.

Nevertheless, there is something deliberately archaic about this music. In settings of poets such as Klopstock and Hölty, Schubert seems fully aware that he is dealing with old-fashioned literature. The same applies to the Kosegarten settings for, although the poet was younger than Goethe in years and a live wire in his private life, he was perhaps too provincial to be an innovative spirit, and his work looked back to the eighteenth century. To the extent that Schubert's songs often include a musical portrait of their poets as the composer perceives them, this one has about it a learned classical poise as well as a grandeur that owes much to Gluck's example.

Autographs:	Wienbibliothek im Rathaus, Vienna (sketch to bb. 1–17); in private possession, London (complete first draft)
First edition:	Published as Op. 44 by Diabelli, Vienna in January 1827 (P113)
Subsequent editions:	Peters: Vol. 4/45; AGA XX 237: Vol. 4/134; NSA IV: Vol. 3/2; Bärenreiter Vol. 2/70
Bibliography:	Capell 1928, p. 117
	Fischer-Dieskau 1977, p. 74
Discography and timing:	Fischer-Dieskau I 7²⁵ 6'08
	Hyperion I 15¹
	Hyperion II 15¹² 6'37 Margaret Price

← *Das Heimweh* D456   *Aus 'Diego Manazares': Ilmerine* D458 →

AN EINE QUELLE
(CLAUDIUS) **D530** [H345]
A major   February 1817

To a spring

Du klei - ne, grün-um-wachs-ne Quel - le,   an   der   ich Daph-ne jüngst ge - sehn,

(33 bars)

Du kleine grünumwachsne Quelle,	Little spring, mantled in green,
An der ich Daphne jüngst gesehn!	Where lately I saw Daphne!
Dein Wasser war so still und helle![1]	Your water was so still and clear,
Und Daphne's Bild darin so schön![2]	And Daphne's reflection so fair!
O wenn sie sich noch 'mal am Ufer sehen lässt,	O, if she should appear once more on your banks,
So halte du ihr schönes Bild doch fest;	Hold her fair image fast.
Ich schleiche heimlich dann mit nassen Augen hin,	Then I will steal up furtively, with moist eyes,
Dem Bild meine Not zu klagen;[3]	To bewail my distress to her image;
Denn, wenn ich bei ihr selber bin,	For, when I am with her,
Dann, ach! dann kann ich ihr nichts sagen.[4]	Ah, then I cannot say a word to her.

MATTHIAS CLAUDIUS (1740–1815); poem written in 1760

This is the tenth of Schubert's thirteen Claudius solo settings (1816–17). See the poet's biography for a chronological list of all the Claudius settings.

Daphne am Bach D411 from 1816 is written in a classical style – and so, in part at least, is *An eine Quelle*, one of Claudius's earliest poems where another Daphne is the heroine. It is as if Schubert has only to hear a name such as Chloë, Thyrsis, Doris or Daphne for him to take up his pen in eighteenth-century manner. Of course there is often an arch artificiality about this type of poem (although Claudius, as ever, is remarkably fresh and direct) which needs to be framed by music of a formal and old-fashioned kind.

Schubert's achievement in this music is to alternate moments of Mozartian elegance with moments of real Romantic sensibility. For example the first three lines of the poem are set with courtly dotted rhythm and a euphonious success of parallel sixths, but the words 'Und Daphne's Bild darin' plunge us into a watery world of Romantic longing (bb. 6–8): repetition of the words (bb. 8–10) makes a heartfelt sequence, the accompaniment's answering triplets demonstrating that a musical echo is an ideal analogue for the nymph's reflection. The setting of 'so schön' (bb. 10–11) is masterly: Schubert takes the two words out of their metrical place in the line and turns them into a spontaneous exclamation. 'O wenn sie sich noch 'mal am Ufer sehen lässt' (from b. 13) returns us to the jaunty and good-humoured world of the dotted rhythms of Beethoven's Minuet in G WoO10 no. 2. Eric Sams saw in this phrase the prototype of the timid violinist's tune in No. XI of Hugo Wolf's *Italienisches Liederbuch*. On the other hand, the furtive rising chromaticism of 'Ich schleiche heimlich' (bb. 18–20) that suggests the excitement of ungallant

---

[1] In an earlier version of the poem Claudius writes 'Dein Wasser war so still! *so* helle!'
[2] Claudius writes 'Und D a p h n e' s Bild, so schön'. The word 'darin' is Schubert's addition.
[3] For metrical reasons Claudius writes 'Bilde'.
[4] Claudius writes 'Denn, ach! denn' (a north German variant).

voyeurism (for it is not only the face of the bathing Daphne that the river will reflect) could be found in very few songs of the *galant* age. We then return to the music of an earlier convention; when the narrator is face to face with Daphne he can only speak in the stilted language of formality. Thus purity and refinement stand side by side with passion and lust, just as the male protagonist veers between idealism and earthiness.

The introduction (published in the first edition and thus also in Peters) is not authentic. Diabelli took it directly from the postlude which makes it considerably less offensive than some other changes and inventions proposed by him or members of his firm. It was common practice for songs without a printed introduction to have one improvised by the accompanist, almost certainly including Schubert himself. It is possible that the composer might have used the postlude in this manner, or perhaps improvised another which, like the music invented for the pleasure (and dancing) of his friends, vanished into thin air. In this case the music for the final four bars (bb. 30–33) is so appropriate for the narrator struck dumb ('Dann, ach! dann kann ich ihr nichts sagen') that it seems a pity for us to hear it before its relevant place (which is only at the end of the song's narrative).

Autograph:	Bibliotheca Bodmeriana, Cologny, Geneva
First edition:	Published as Op. post. 109 no. 3 by Diabelli, Vienna in 1829 (P234)
Subsequent editions:	Peters: Vol. 4/124; AGA XX 273: Vol. 4/232; NSA IV: Vol. 11/86
Bibliography:	Fischer-Dieskau 1977, p. 87
Further settings:	Johann Reichardt (1752–1814) *An eine Quelle* (1779)
Discography and timing:	Fischer-Dieskau I 8²⁰ 1'47
	Hyperion I 21¹⁰
	Hyperion II 17²³ 2'00 Edith Mathis

← *La pastorella al prato* D513   *Das Lied vom Reifen* D532 →

AN ELISA *see* TROST. AN ELISA D97

AN EMMA   To Emma
(SCHILLER) OP. 58 NO. 2, **D113** [H42]

The song exists in three versions, the third of which is discussed below:
(1) 17 September 1814; (2) Autumn 1814; (3) appeared April 1826

(1) 'Andante'   F major $\frac{2}{4}$ [58 bars]

(2) 'Etwas langsam'   F major $\frac{6}{8}$ [59 bars]

(3) F major

(62 bars)

Weit in nebelgrauer Ferne	Far in the grey, misty distance
Liegt mir das vergang'ne Glück.	Lies my past happiness.
Nur an Einem schönen Sterne	My eyes still linger lovingly
Weilt mit Liebe noch der Blick,	On one fair star alone.
Aber wie des Sternes Pracht	But, like the star's splendour,
Ist es nur ein Schein der Nacht.	It is merely an illusion of the night.
Deckte dir der lange Schlummer,	If the prolonged slumber
Dir der Tod die Augen zu,	Of death closed your eyes
Dich besässe doch mein Kummer,	My sorrow would still possess you;
Meinem Herzen lebtest du.	You live in my heart.
Aber ach! du lebst im Licht,	But, alas, you live in the light,
Meiner Liebe lebst du nicht.	Yet you do not live for my love.
Kann der Liebe süss Verlangen,	Emma, can love's sweet longing
Emma, kann's vergänglich sein?	Pass away?
Was dahin ist und vergangen,	That which is over and past, Emma,
Emma, kann's die Liebe sein?	Can that be love?
Ihrer Flamme Himmelsglut	Does the celestial ardour of its flame
Stirbt sie, wie ein irdisch Gut?	Perish like worldly goods?

FRIEDRICH VON SCHILLER (1759–1805); poem written in 1797

This is the seventh of Schubert's forty-four Schiller solo settings (1811–24). See the poet's biography for a chronological list of all the Schiller settings.

There is no clue in Schiller's life as to who Emma was, or under what circumstances this beautiful elegy for lost love was written. It could well be imagined as a monologue from a play where the mere resonance of a woman's name ('Laura' is another example) creates a gently perfumed atmosphere of innocence and sorrow. The poem dates from the time of Schiller's most intense collaboration with Goethe in the field of poem and ballad and was published in the *Musenalmanach* in 1798. It inspired one of Schubert's most original and successful Schiller settings. In its use of free-flowing recitative and arioso it is comparable to the remarkable first version of the Schiller *Thekla: Eine Geisterstimme* D73 and *Trost. An Elisa* D97, a Matthisson setting from earlier in the same year, which also makes a speciality of ardent rhetorical questions.

    All three versions of this song are published one after the other in the AGA, which would seem to suggest that they were dashed off within a few days of each other, if not on the same day. But it is also possible that Schubert prepared the second version only when it was needed for publication in a supplement to a periodical in 1821, and that he altered this again when the song was published as part of Op. 56 (later changed to Op. 58) in 1826. These three versions of *An Emma* (or *Emma* as the first edition and Peters Edition have it) differ only in tiny details that could scarcely be differentiated by the general listener. They do, however, give the scholar a glimpse into the Schubert workshop and show how much thought the composer gave, as he grew older, to achieving ever more transparent simplicity with texts that he loved and respected.

    All three versions are in F major. The first is in ⁴/₂ and is accompanied almost throughout by flowing triplets. The cadence at the repeat of the words 'Ist es nur ein Schein der Nacht' is in the dominant of the relative minor. In the second version the time changes to ⁶/₈, the triplet movement is broken from time to time by other note values, and words quoted above now lead us into the much darker regions of the relative minor itself. The final version (Op. 58 no. 2) reverts to $\frac{2}{4}$ with an increased use of dotted notes in the vocal line that gives it more of an improvisational feeling and a greater independence from the piano part. There are a number of beautiful details: the interplay of voice and piano in contrary motion, suggesting starlight and its mirror reflection at 'Aber wie des Sternes Pracht' (bb. 13–15); the Italianate vocal line (accompanied by triplets in *bel canto* manner) of 'Deckte dir der lange Schlummer' (bb. 20–23) and the lovely sequence following it (bb. 24–7). The interplay between continuing melody and fragmented recitative makes the music seem spontaneously invented on the spot. After many harmonic peregrinations the song ends in the tonic key, but somehow contrives to leave the poet's final question hanging poignantly in the air.

The revisions, whatever their dates, were largely an exercise in working towards finding the clearest means of notating arioso with enough shape to differentiate it from recitative, and with enough implied freedom to loosen the rhythmic straitjacket of conventional aria. Johann Michael Vogl made a bizarre arrangement of *An Emma* (with a throbbing triplet accompaniment) which shows scant understanding of Schubert's aims; this is discussed in ORNAMENTATION.

Autograph:	Wienbibliothek im Rathaus, Vienna (cancelled version of bb. 1–9 only)
Publication:	First published as part of the AGA in 1894 (P546; first version)
	First published as a supplement to the *Wiener Zeitschrift für Kunst, Literatur, Theater und Mode* in June 1821 (second version), and subsequently as part of the NSA in 1982 (P780)
	First published as Op. 56 (later changed to Op. 58) no. 2 by Thaddäus Weigl, Vienna in April 1826 (P98)
Publication reviews:	*Allgemeiner musikalischer Anzeiger* (Frankfurt), No. 33 (10 February 1827), p. 317f. [Waidelich/Hilmar Dokumente I No. 452; Deutsch Doc. Biog. No. 798]
Subsequent editions:	Peters: Vol. 2/118; AGA XX 26a, b & 9c: Vol. 1/172, 174 & 176 (first, second and third versions); NSA IV: Vol. 3a/90 (third version), Vol. 3b/184 (first version) & 186 (second version); Vol. 3b/250 (Vogl's ornamented version); Bärenreiter: Vol. 2/122
Further settings and arrangements:	Benedict Randhartinger (1802–93) *An Emma*
	Arr. Tilman Hoppstock (b. 1961) for guitar accompaniment, in *Franz Schubert: 110 Lieder* (2009)
Discography and timing:	Fischer-Dieskau I 2[8] 2'26
	Hyperion I 16[7]
	Hyperion II 3[14] 2'19 Thomas Allen

← *Der Abend* D108   *Romanze* D114 →

AN GOTT *see* DUBIOUS, MISATTRIBUTED AND LOST SONGS

AN HERRN JOSEF VON SPAUN, ASSESSOR IN LINZ *see* HERRN JOSEF VON SPAUN, ASSESSOR IN LINZ D749

AN LAURA. ALS SIE KLOPSTOCKS AUFERSTEHUNGSLIED SANG

To Laura, when singing Klopstock's 'Ode to the Resurrection'

(MATTHISSON) **D115** [H46]
E major   2–7 October 1814

(94 bars)

Herzen, die gen Himmel sich erheben,	Hearts raised towards heaven,
Tränen, die dem Auge still entbeben,	Tears silently quivering from the eyes,
Seufzer, die den Lippen leis' entfliehn,	Sighs softly escaping from the lips,
Wangen, die mit Andachtsglut sich malen,	Cheeks coloured with the fire of devotion,
Trunkne Blicke, die Entzückung strahlen,	Enraptured looks, radiant in bliss:
Danken dir, o Heilverkünderin!	All thank you, harbinger of salvation!
Laura! Laura! horchend diesen Tönen,	Laura! Listening to these strains
Müssen Engelseelen sich verschönen,	The souls of angels must grow more beautiful,
Heilige den Himmel offen sehn,	Saints behold the open gates of heaven,
Schwermutsvolle Zweifler sanfter klagen,	Melancholy doubters lament more softly
Kalte Frevler an die Brust sich schlagen,	Heartless sinners beat their breasts
Und wie Seraph Abbadona flehn!	And pray like the seraph Abbadona.
Mit den Tönen des Triumphgesanges	With the strains of the triumphant song
Trank ich Vorgefühl des Überganges	I drank a foretaste of that passage
Von der Grabnacht zum Verklärungsglanz!	From the night of the grave to a transfigured radiance!
Als vernähm' ich Engelmelodieen,	It was as if I heard angels singing;
Wähnt' ich dir, o Erde zu entfliehen,	I imagined I had escaped from you, earth,
Sah schon unter mir der Sterne Tanz!	And already saw the stars dance below me.
Schon umatmete mich des Himmelsmilde,[1]	I was embraced by Heaven's gentleness
Schon begrüsst' ich jauchzend die Gefilde,	With joy I greeted the Elysian fields
Wo des Lebens Strom durch Palmen fleusst!	Where the river of life flows through palm trees;
Glänzend von der nähern Gottheit Strahle	Glowing in the light of the Godhead close by,
Wandelte durch Paradiesestale	My blissful, quivering spirit
Wonnesschauernd mein entschwebter Geist!	Floated through the vales of Paradise.

[1] The word 'des' in this line is Schubert's own metrically disruptive addition. This entire verse signifies the use of the 1802 (or earlier) edition of the poet's *Gedichte* rather than the 1811 edition the composer used for some of his subsequent Matthisson settings. In this later edition Matthisson changed the word 'Himmelsmilde' to 'Himmelslüfte' necessitating a different rhyme ('Totengrüfte') in the second line.

FRIEDRICH VON MATTHISSON (1761–1831); poem written in 1783

This is the fifteenth of Schubert's twenty-nine Matthisson solo settings (1812–17). See the poet's biography for a chronological list of all the Matthisson settings.

Therese Grob, the girl with whom it is said the young Schubert was in love, was the soprano soloist at the first performance of his Mass in F D105. This took place at the local parish church of Liechtenthal, only a few minutes away on foot from Schubert's home in the Säulengasse. The exquisite music of this work (a substantial, not to say astonishing, achievement for a lad not yet seventeen) can thus be heard against a personal background: the soprano is placed on a special musical pedestal in the magical opening *Kyrie*, and her entry crowns the *Benedictus*. The composer's feelings on hearing someone with whom he was in love singing his own music can be gleaned from this Matthisson setting by substituting the name 'Therese' for 'Laura' in the title, and Schubert's Mass for Carl Friedrich Graun's *Auferstehungslied* (1758, text by Klopstock), supposedly sung by the poet's beloved.

This Schubertian devotional style, where the movement of minims and crotchets on the page suggests the hymnal, had been pioneered in *Die Betende* D102 (another Matthisson setting about Laura). The difference is that *An Laura* takes place in a grander public setting. The pace is stately yet passionate – tremendous emotional energy is suppressed and hushed, as seems appropriate in a church. It is unclear whether we are meant to hear Laura herself singing (Capell thought so, and wrote that in his view the piece was never far from Elisabeth's prayer in Wagner's *Tannhäuser*), but it is surely the enraptured poet who sings an ecstatic commentary within himself. The form of the work is most unusual. The music of Verses 2, 3 and 4 is more or less the same apart from relatively small details of declamation carefully altered by Schubert where appropriate for the prosody. This music forms the main body of the work. The first verse, which normally sets the tone of a strophic song, acts as a curtain-raiser and introduction, and ends with a mighty cadence ('Danken dir, o Heilverkünderin' bb. 19–22).

The opening shot of the film (if we imagine it thus presented) is of the whole church resounding with music – something like the opening of *Die Meistersinger* as Walther gazes at Eva. We expect this music to be repeated in strophic manner, but instead there is a close-up of Laura herself, and the music changes style: the organ is re-registered in dulcet tones and public utterance yields to the privacy of dreams and musings of sublimated sexual ardour. The 'Etwas geschwinder' here (b. 26) was added to the manuscript in a hand other than Schubert's, but it is a useful marking in practical terms. Even with this more flowing tempo after the imposing opening, time seems to stand still in music of intimacy and gentleness, a mood that is remarkably sustained for three verses. How different is Schubert's next scene set in a church, the demonic *Szene aus 'Faust'* D126, composed only a few months later. In some ways the undefiled Laura allows Schubert a dry run for the bedevilled Gretchen, the creation of a greater poet.

Autograph:	Wienbibliothek im Rathaus, Vienna (first draft)
First edition:	Published as Book 31 no. 3 of the *Nachlass* by Diabelli, Vienna in 1840 (P334)
Subsequent editions:	Peters: Vol. 5/173; AGA XX 28: Vol. 1/183; NSA IV: Vol. 7/48; Bärenreiter: Vol. 5/148 (high voice), 142 (medium/low voice)
Bibliography:	Capell 1928, p. 83
	Fischer-Dieskau 1977, p. 30

Discography and timing: Fischer-Dieskau I 2[10]   3'10   (strophes 1, 3 & 4 only)
                          Hyperion I 12[17]
                          Hyperion II 4[2]   5'42   Adrian Thompson

← *Die Betende* D102   *Der Geistertanz* D116 →

AN MEIN HERZ   To my heart
(SCHULZE) **D860** [H578]
A minor   December 1825

(119 bars)

O Herz, sei endlich stille!	O heart, be silent at last!
Was schlägst du so unruhvoll?	Why do you beat so restlessly?
Es ist ja des Himmels Wille,	For it is Heaven's will
Dass ich sie lassen soll.	That I should leave her.
Und gab auch dein junges Leben	Even though your youthful life
Dir nichts als Wahn und Pein;	Gave you nothing but delusion and pain,
Hat's ihr nur Freude gegeben,	As long as it gave her joy
So mag's verloren sein!	Then no matter if it was lost to you.
Und wenn sie auch nie dein Lieben	And though she never understood
Und nic dein' Liebe verstand,	Your loving or your love
So bist du doch treu geblieben,	You nevertheless remained faithful,
Und Gott hat's droben erkannt.	And God above saw it.
Wir wollen es mutig ertragen,	Let us bravely endure
So lang nur die Träne noch rinnt,	As long as tears still flow,
Und träumen von schöneren Tagen,	And dream of fairer days
Die lange vorüber sind.	Long since past.
Und siehst du die Blüten erscheinen,	When you see the blossoms appearing,
Und singen die Vögel umher,	When the birds sing all around,
So magst du wohl heimlich weinen,	Then you may weep in secret,
Doch klagen sollst du nicht mehr.	But you should complain no more.
Gehn doch die ewigen Sterne	For the eternal stars above
Dort oben mit goldenem Licht	Move with a golden light,
Und lächeln so freundlich von ferne,	Smiling kindly from afar
Und denken doch unser nicht.	And yet with no thought for us.

ERNST SCHULZE (1789–1817); poem written 23 January 1816

This is the third of Schubert's ten Schulze solo settings (1825–6). See the poet's biography for a chronological list of all the Schulze settings. An outline of a suggested performing version for a Schulze cycle is listed under 'Auf den wilden Wegen'.

The poem's full title in Schulze's *Poetisches Tagebuch* is 'On 23 January, 1816. To my heart.' *An mein Herz* was written in the depths of winter, but the only reference to the seasons is the blooming of spring flowers in the fifth verse. *Über Wildemann* D884 was written in spring and yet its theme is endless winter. It seems that the poet prefers to be wherever he is not in terms of time and place as well as season. Such was Schulze's mental state that what purports to be a 'Verse Diary' is more than capable of disregarding (or 'rising above') the harsh conditions of reality. (For the background to this story and his passion for Adelheid Tychsen, see the biography of the poet.)

This is one of the undoubted musical masterpieces of the Schulze songs, and we hear the poet's blinkered obsession at every turn. The song's tonality is very special for Schubert; it is often reserved for those who live on the emotional edge. Thus the crazed old harper from Goethe's *Wilhelm Meister* sings to us in this key, as does Mignon, his daughter by an incestuous union. The castrated *Atys* D585 of Greek mythology is given voice in A minor, as is August von Platen in the bitter plaint of unreciprocated homosexual love, *Du liebst mich nicht* D756. Johann Mayrhofer is delineated in the same key in his all neurotic vulnerability in *Abendstern* D806, as is the woefully obsessed Hippolytus (*Hippolits Lied* D890). Even more closely connected, by similarities of both tonality and motive, is *Der Zwerg* D771, the tale of a dwarf who kills his queen (and presumably employer) for being unfaithful to him.

The introduction, distantly related to that of *Drang in die Ferne* D770, yet again in A minor, seems to take off in an effort to escape, to fly free of the bars in an ascending melodic curve. At the top of pulsating chords, C naturals (bb. 1–2) rise to C sharps and Ds (bb. 3–4) and we briefly tarry in the second inversion of the subdominant. The forces at hand are then recouped and redirected for an assault on the dominant itself (we expect to move there after bb. 7–8) but at the very last moment sidestep back into the first inversion of the home key. As in *Der Zwerg*, the left hand plays in the rhythm of Beethoven's 'Fate' motif from the Fifth Symphony, here an anacrusis of three semiquavers plus a strong beat crotchet. This rhythm is seldom absent throughout the song, and as a result the work has the momentum of a symphonic movement.

The first line of the poem tells us that the accompaniment's rhythm signifies the beating of the heart. With 'O Herz, sei endlich stille' the poet begs it to be silent, which is to ask not only for relief from palpitations but for release from life itself. However, the request is dismissed out of hand, and the pulses continue to pound. On 'Es ist ja des Himmels Wille' (at bb. 15–16) we move into A major – a tonality suitable for the heavens or, more precisely, cloud-cuckoo-land; the parting of the lovers is nothing to do with God's will, it is his beloved Adelheid's, as Schulze will admit in the third verse. This change of key reflects exactly the sickly-sweet air of sanctimonious masochism inherent in these lines. The third and fourth lines of the strophe are repeated, plus a further repeat of 'Dass ich sie lassen soll' (bb. 23–5). This creation of what is in effect an asymmetrical seven-line strophe is exactly what happens in the first and last verses of *Über Wildemann* D884, but here the pattern pertains to every verse; as strophe succeeds strophe, these repetitions of the final lines seem more and more like an uncontrollable nervous tic, a symptom of illness.

In the second verse we hear the same implied promises of release from A minor, but again they are broken. We are allowed a brief walk down a path that had already been paced by the vocal line of *Lebensmut* D883: on the repeat of 'Hat's ihr nur Freude gegeben' (bb. 35–7) the optimism of the relative major prompts a bold and hearty downward C major arpeggio (the joy he gave to her) which is then contrasted with the muddy chromaticism of what *she* has inflicted on *him* ('So mag's verloren sein', bb. 37–40). Verse 3 is similar to Verse 2 but it slips into the major again for another invocation to God to be the poet's witness; the Deity here inhabits the A major region of impossible dreams. The piano interlude that follows (bb. 58–65) is almost exactly the same as the introduction, and Verse 4 is a repeat of Verse 1. The form reveals itself to be as subtle as that of that other Schulze masterpiece *Im Frühling* D882, this time a rondo as well as a modified strophic song. The inevitable A major excursion in Verse 4 alights on words more touching ('träumen von schöneren Tagen', bb. 73–5) and less manipulative than in previous strophes.

As if to acknowledge a more sincere use of poetic metaphor the composer changes the key signature officially to his beloved A major for Verses 5 and 6. We find ourselves in the open air where Schulze acknowledges the beauties of the real world ('die Blüten', b. 82 and 'die Vögel', b. 84) for the first time, albeit seen through Adelheid's eyes. Because of its high-lying tessitura, the vehement and unhinged final repeat of 'klagen sollst du nicht mehr' seems to be spat out (bb. 93–6). This glimpse of rage is all the more powerful for the fleeting nature of its appearance. One realizes all the anger the poet feels against Adelheid is redirected against himself.

The final verse is a much modified repeat of Verse 5 and we leave Schulze gazing up at the stars, his attention drawn from the tumultuous workings of his own racked body and ruined mind to the impervious workings of nature. Among these celestial messengers there is one, 'der liebliche Stern', which, like so much else in his unhappy short life, he was never to find. The last few bars of the postlude suggest some sort of solution or sign of healing, as if the composer has it in his power to allow a tortured spirit to reach his consoling star after all. The immortality and fame that Schulze so desired were to be his only as part of the shining constellation of Schubert's poets. The composer sometimes adds his own comment to the postlude of a song in the manner of a signature or seal. Schulze had been dead only eight years; the final cadence of *An mein Herz* is plagal, in gentle benison (bb. 118–19), as if to whisper 'rest in peace'.

A word of warning to performers: Schubert's moderating '*Etwas* geschwind' is to be taken just as seriously as the 'sehr unruhig'. A beating heart rather than a seizure is suggested here. Misunderstanding of these markings has led to at least one recorded performance of breath-taking speed, and equally breathtaking stylistic and linguistic aberration.

Autograph:	First draft in private possession, USA
First edition:	Published as Book 13 no. 1 of the *Nachlass* by Diabelli, Vienna in 1832 (P276)
First known performance:	7 February 1833, Musikverein, Vienna. Soloist: Ludwig Tietze
Subsequent editions:	Peters: Vol. 5/73; AGA XX 485: Vol. 8/154; NSA IV: Vol. 13/186
Bibliography:	Capell 1928, p. 216
	Fischer-Dieskau 1977, p. 223
	Youens 1996, pp. 272–8
Discography and timing:	Fischer-Dieskau II 7[14] 3'24
	Hyperion I 18[22]
	Hyperion II 31[1] 3'29 Peter Schreier

⟵ *Zwei Scenen aus Lacrimas (Lied des Florio)* D857/2   *Der liebliche Stern* D861 ⟶

AN MEIN KLAVIER
(SCHUBART) **D342** [H214]
A major   *c.* 1816

To my piano

Etwas geschwind

Sanf - tes Kla- vier,   sanf - tes Kla- vier,   wel - che Ent-zü - ckun-gen schaf-fest du mir,

(17 bars)

Sanftes Klavier,
Welche Entzückungen schaffest du mir,[1]
Sanftes Klavier!
Wenn sich die Schönen
Tändelnd verwöhnen,
Weih' ich mich dir,
Liebes Klavier!

Bin ich allein,
Hauch' ich dir meine Empfindungen ein,
Himmlisch und rein.
Unschuld im Spiele,
Tugendgefühle,
Sprechen aus dir,
Trautes Klavier!

[(. . .)]

Sing' ich dazu,
Goldener Flügel, welch' himmlische Ruh'
Lispelst mir du!
Tränen der Freude
Netzen die Saite;
Silberner Klang
Trägt den Gesang.

[(. . .)]

Sanftes Klavier!
Welche Entzückungen schaffest du mir![2]
Goldnes Klavier!
Wenn mich im Leben
Sorgen umschweben;
Töne du mir,
Trautes Klavier!

Gentle piano,
What delights you bring me,
Gentle piano!
While the spoilt beauties
Dally,
I devote myself to you,
Dear piano!

When I am alone
I whisper my feelings to you,
Pure and celestial.
As I play, innocence
And virtuous sentiments
Speak from you,
Beloved piano!

[(. . .)]

When I sing with you,
Golden keyboard, what heavenly peace
You whisper to me!
Tears of joy
Fall upon the strings.
Silvery tone
Supports the song.

[(. . .)]

Gentle piano,
What delights you awaken within me,
Golden piano!
When in this life
Cares beset me,
Sing to me,
Beloved piano!

[1] Schubart writes the less smooth '*schaffst* du *in* mir'.
[2] As in note 1.

CHRISTIAN FRIEDRICH SCHUBART (1739–1791); poem written in 1781

This is the first of Schubert's four Schubart solo settings (1816–17). See the poet's biography for a chronological list of all the Schubart settings.

This song was probably composed at the end of 1816 or beginning of 1817. It is an unofficial companion piece to the Schiller setting *Laura am Klavier* D388 in which the poet marvels at Laura's exquisite playing. The original title of Schubart's poem is *Serafina an ihr Klavier*, and Serafina's performing skills are much more modest. Her greater depth of feeling, however, is uncontestable, and the composer has fashioned one of his most exquisite miniatures from these lines. Schubert leaves out the third and fifth verses of the poem; in cutting Verse 3 he avoids any reference to the instrument's 'Tanzende Docken' – 'dancing jacks' with their echoes of Shakespeare's Sonnet 128 – which describe the workings of a harpsichord of the poet's time (rather than the fortepiano of the composer's). Verse 5, alone of the six strophes, injects a moral and religious note into the song which is little to Schubert's taste.

Odes and elegies addressed by the poets to their pianos or piano-playing friends became almost a nineteenth-century commonplace. (One thinks of Mörike's *Auf einem Klavierspieler*, or other poems he wrote to Wilhelm Hartlaub.) Schubart wrote another *An mein Klavier* on hearing of the death of his young friend Minette whose music-making he remembered with affection. Schubert's *An mein Klavier* has always enjoyed a popularity because audiences value the supposed autobiographical link between the song and the composer's own piano; in fact it is unlikely that Schubert was thinking of any particular instrument when he wrote it (*see* PIANOS). It has even been suggested that the opening words, 'Sanftes Klavier', describe the soft and gentle sound of that most intimate of instruments, the clavichord. In any case Schubert seems to be aware that the poem is something of a period piece. This is music of matchless simplicity with an accompaniment contained within a clavichord-like keyboard compass. The tonality, as John Reed states, 'unlocks the essential Schubert'. The use of the composer's favourite dactylic rhythm confers a special magic. The repetition of this 'long-short-short' motif (the crotchet and two quavers of 'Sanftes Kla–' poised on a single note before the phrase falls a tone on the syllable '–vier') is worthy of a celestial dance. The way in which the left-hand accompaniment in open fifths echoes this rhythm is another modest delight, as is the piano writing throughout, not least the enchanting rising sequences of the four-bar interludes and postlude (bb. 14–17 and bb. 31–4).

There are three other Schubert settings of Schubart, including the famous *Die Forelle*. Although these poems little reflect the poet's revolutionary political leanings, members of the Schubert circle would have been aware of Schubart's unjust treatment at the hands of Karl Eugen, Duke of Württemberg (who was also the young Schiller's tormentor). Schubart languished in prison for ten years for supposed sedition and all the left-leaning young men of the Schubert circle would have regarded him as a historical martyr and something of a hero. More significant with regard to this song, however, is Schubart's importance as a musician; he was only a modest composer but he was one of the earliest and most important of the music theorists and aestheticians (*see* TONALITY).

Autograph:	Missing or lost
First edition:	Published as a solo piano arrangement by Kratochwill, Vienna in 1876; and with vocal line as Vol. 7 no. 9 in Friedlaender's edition by Peters, Leipzig in 1885 (P474)
Subsequent editions:	Peters: Vol. 7/23; AGA XX 238: Vol. 4/138; NSA IV: Vol. 10/2

Bibliography:	Capell 1928, pp. 118–19
	Fischer-Dieskau 1977, p. 108
	Smeed 1985, pp. 228–40
Arrangement:	Arr. Tilman Hoppstock (b. 1961) for guitar accompaniment, in *Franz Schubert: 110 Lieder* (2009)
Discography and timing:	Fischer-Dieskau I 7²⁶ 3'25
	Hyperion I 17²⁴
	Hyperion II 12⁹ 4'44 Lucia Popp

← *An den Mond* D296   *Am ersten Maimorgen* D344 →

AN MIGNON   To Mignon
(Goethe) Op. 19 no. 2, **D161** [H69 & H71a]

The song exists in two versions, both of which are discussed below:
(1) 27 February 1815; (2) after April 1816

(1) 'Klagend, mässig'   G♯ minor §   [19 bars]

(2) G minor

(19 bars)

Über Tal und Fluss getragen	Borne over valley and river
Ziehet rein der Sonne Wagen.	The sun's chariot moves on inexorably.
Ach! sie regt in ihrem Lauf,	Ah, in its course it stirs
So wie deine, meine Schmerzen,	Your sorrows and mine,
Tief im Herzen,	Deep in our hearts,
Immer morgens wieder auf.	Anew each morning.
Kaum will mir die Nacht noch frommen,	The night brings me scant comfort,
Denn die Träume selber kommen	For then my dreams themselves appear
Nun in trauriger Gestalt,	In mournful guise,
Und ich fühle dieser Schmerzen,	And in my heart
Still im Herzen,	I feel the secret, silent power
Heimlich bildende Gewalt.	Of these sorrows grow.
Schon seit manchen schönen Jahren	For many a long year
Seh' ich unten Schiffe fahren;	I have watched the ships sail below.
Jedes kommt an seinen Ort;	Each one reaches its destination;
Aber ach! die steten Schmerzen,	But alas the sorrows
Fest im Herzen	That forever cling to my heart
Schwimmen nicht im Strome fort.	Do not flow away in the current.

Schön in Kleidern muss ich kommen,	I must come in fine clothes;
Aus dem Schrank sind sie genommen,	They are taken from the closet
Weil es heute Festtag ist;	Because today is a holiday.
Niemand ahnet, dass von Schmerzen	No one guesses
Herz im Herzen	That in my heart of hearts
Grimmig mir zerrissen ist.	I am racked by savage pain.
Heimlich muss ich immer weinen,	Always I must weep in secret,
Aber freundlich kann ich scheinen	Yet I can appear happy,
Und sogar gesund und rot;	Even glowing and healthy.
Wären tödlich diese Schmerzen	If these sorrows could be fatal
Meinem Herzen,	To my heart
Ach! schon lange wär' ich tot.	Ah, I would have died long ago.

JOHANN WOLFGANG VON GOETHE (1749–1832); poem probably written in 1797

This is the ninth of Schubert's seventy-five Goethe solo settings (1814–26). See the poet's biography for a chronological list of all the Goethe settings.

The song exists in two different versions. The second, published as part of Op. 19 is in G minor, the first in G sharp minor – one of only two songs that Schubert was ever to compose in that key. In both cases he actually published them in more user-friendly tonalities – perhaps at the advice of the publishers who wanted to spare their prospective customers tricky accidentals: this one a semitone lower and *Du liebst mich nicht* (Platen) D756 a semitone higher in A minor.

The marking for this earlier version is 'Klagend, mässig' ('Plaintively, in a moderate tempo'), as opposed to the 'Etwas geschwind' of the published version. Schubert had sent the G sharp minor version to Goethe in 1816 as part of a lieder album – a consignment aimed, unsuccessfully, at arousing the great man's interest. Schubert composed this song a full eight months before he embarked on *Mignon (Kennst du das Land?)* D321, the first of his many settings from Goethe's *Wilhelm Meisters Lehrjahre* that include the character of Mignon.

There are various explanations of the poem. The Goethe scholar Eduard von der Hellen in a commentary published in 1902 identifies its inspiration as Magdalena Riggi, a beautiful Milanese girl whom Goethe met on his Italian journey. She envied the poet his freedom, and spoke of watching the ships (as in this poem's third verse) coming and going in Rome's harbour. In this reading *An Mignon* is a woman's lament sung by a real-life Mignon whom Goethe imagines sharing the emotional predicament of his fictional character. If this is the case, a woman should sing *An Mignon* (in the Hyperion Schubert Edition the first version is sung by a soprano, the second by a tenor). Mention of fine clothes on a feast day in the fourth strophe initially seems more feminine than masculine, as does the reference to the narrator being 'gesund und rot' in the fifth.

On the other hand Goethe dressed in ceremonial costume for special occasions at the Weimar court, something he may have regarded as part of the constricting range of his duties before he escaped on his journey to Italy. Nicholas Boyle in his *Goethe* (2000) avers that it is the poet himself, in a period of depression and self doubt who, in this poem, addresses his earlier muse, none other than the 'erotic and ambiguous' fictional Mignon, a symbol of more productive times. She had been created in 1782–3 as part of the little-known and incomplete *Wilhelm Meisters theatralische Sendung*, but as far as the public was concerned she first appeared in 1795–6 in *Wilhelm Meisters Lehrjahre*, a completely overhauled version of the *Sendung*. Schubert was denied Boyle's knowledge of Goethe, but he had well-developed instincts regarding the poet:

Schubert's autograph of *An Mignon* (in G sharp minor) from the album prepared for Goethe, June 1816.

in the musical aspects of the song, for all the ambiguity of its text and background, we sense that he envisaged a male singer.

This is partly because the melody of the first five bars is almost note for note that of *Am Feierabend* from *Die schöne Müllerin* ('Hätt' ich tausend Arme zu rühren') – an unequivocally male song composed eight years later. Both the Müllerin song and *An Mignon* are powered by restless semiquaver accompaniments and secretly nurture unbearably strong passions far from the public gaze. This is probably why the composer responded with a similar melodic shape, if not the same key, in the song from his great cycle. Indeed performers of *Am Feierabend*, a song that is very often sung and played too fast, can learn from *An Mignon* and its marking of 'Klagend mässig', not a bad indication for someone in the miller boy's exhausting predicament as he works himself into the ground to stand out from the other apprentices. In neither of these songs is the unhappy protagonist able to work as fruitfully as he would wish – his hands are metaphorically tied. A clue to the interpretation of both is surely to be found in the 'trauriger Gestalt' of Goethe's words where a dull ache of inadequacy permeates the music rather than a single searing flash of emotion. The mordants in the piano interludes (bb. 16 and 17, 33 and 34) sound flippant in a *Bewegung* sung too fast.

Like Schubert's strophic Goethe song *Die Spinnerin* D247, where a girl's tragic story unfolds in the context of the drudgery of her everyday work, the repetitiveness of the strophic form is here ideal to depict the misery as something recurring. The music, like the poet's feelings, seems to go round in circles, trapped in an emotional maze. The low-lying bass line is strong and thus rather masculine, even brusque; the vocal part tugs against it in eloquent fashion, and the excursion into the Neapolitan key of A flat at bb. 11 and 28 (more like an interrupted cadence perhaps) wrenches the emotions to a higher pitch. Despite a performer's best efforts, the song remains something of an enigma.

Autographs:	Staatsbibliothek Preussischer Kulturbesitz, Berlin (both the G sharp minor first version and the fair copy made for Goethe); another fair copy (the second version in G minor) in the Fitzwilliam Museum, Cambridge
Publication:	First published as part of the AGA in 1894 (P553; first version)
	First published as Op. 19 no. 2 by Diabelli, Vienna in 1825 (P81; second version)
Dedicatee:	Second version dedicated to Johann Wolfgang von Goethe
Subsequent editions:	Peters: Vol. 2/49 (second version); AGA XX 48 a & b: Vol. 2/59 & 60; NSA IV: Vol. 1a/129 (second version) & Vol. 1b/249 (first version); Bärenreiter: Vol. 1/102
Bibliography:	Capell 1928, p. 100
Arrangements:	Arr. Leopold Godowsky for solo piano as 'To Mignon' (1927, 2nd revised edition 1937) [see TRANSCRIPTIONS]
Discography and timing:	Fischer-Dieskau I 3[4] 2'07
	Hyperion I 24[2] 1'36 Christine Schäfer
	Hyperion I 10[4] 3'15 Martyn Hill
	Hyperion II 5[8] 3'15 Christine Schäfer
	Hyperion II 5[11] 3'15 Martyn Hill

← *Am Flusse* D160   *Nähe des Geliebten* D162 →

← *Sängers Morgenlied* D163   *Liebesrausch* D164 →

AN ROSA I   To Rosa
(KOSEGARTEN) **D315** [H194]

The song exists in two versions, the second of which is discussed below:
(1) 19 October 1815; (2) 19 October 1815

(1)   A♭ major   'Mässig' $\frac{3}{4}$ 17 bars

(2)   A♭ major

(17 bars)

Warum bist du nicht hier, meine Geliebteste,	When you are not here, my darling, that your arms
Dass mich gürte dein Arm, dass mich dein Händedruck	May enfold me; that you may press my hand
Labe, dass du mich pressest	To comfort me; that you may clasp me
An dein schlagendes Schwesterherz.	To your beating sisterly heart.
[. . . 2 . . .]	[. . . 2 . . .]

Matte labet der Quell, Müde der Abendstern,	The stream revives the faint, the evening star the weary,
Irre Wandrer der Mond, Kranke das Morgenrot;	The moon revives the lost traveller, the sunrise the sick,
Mich erlabet, Geliebte,	But I, my beloved, am best revived
Dein Umfangen am kräftigsten.	By your embrace.
Warum bist du nicht hier, meine Vertrauteste,	Why are you not here, my beloved,
Dass dich gürte mein Arm, dass ich dir süssen Gruss	That my arm may embrace you, that I may whisper
Lispl' und feurig dich drücke	A sweet greeting and press you ardently
An mein schlagendes Bruderherz.	To my beating fraternal heart?
[. . .]	[. . .]

LUDWIG THEOBUL KOSEGARTEN (1758–1818); poem written in 1787

This is the sixteenth of Schubert's twenty-one Kosegarten solo settings (1815–17). See the poet's biography for a chronological list of all the Kosegarten settings, as well as a discussion of Morten Solvik's Kosegarten Liederkreis and this song's place within it.

This is one of no fewer than eight songs that Schubert wrote on this eventful day, 19 October 1815. Of these, only one, *Hektors Abschied* D312 (Schiller), was not a setting of Kosegarten. Perhaps the story of Hector and Andromache put the composer in the mood for tackling the verse forms of the ancients. The two *An Rosa* poems have a most complicated metre – Asclepiadic, much favoured by Horace though unheard-of in English poetry, and consisting of spondee, two or three coriambs and one iamb (- -/ -UU-/- UU -/ UU-). This does not bend easily to musical treatment, but Schubert's setting works surprisingly well, apart from moments where unimportant words are stressed on the strong first beat of the bar ('Warum <u>bist</u> du nicht hier' at the opening for example, or the 'ste' at the end of the word 'Geliebteste' that awkwardly begins b. 4). On the other hand 'dass mich mein <u>Hände</u>druck / <u>Labe</u>' is more than acceptable; the bar stresses here even add to the sense of longing, like gentle squeezes of the hand. Whether the references to 'Schwesterzherz' and 'Bruderherz' signify a tender platonic relationship, or more literally refer to the sister of Kosegarten's wife, is a moot point.

The tonality, according to Reed, is expressive of 'secret happiness and private joy, and with a secure and reciprocated love'. This astute observation links the Rosa songs with other romantic and intimate lieder written in the same period and in the same key; one is reminded of certain Klopstock settings like *An Sie* D288 as well as *Das Rosenband* D280 written a few months earlier. Without achieving the fluency and memorability of that masterpiece (probably because of the intractable metre) the composer has recaptured something of the same tender sweetness. After an accompaniment that doubles the vocal line almost throughout, the four-bar postlude is particularly affecting: heartbeats depict the 'schlagendes Schwesterherz' in semi-staccato quavers, first in the right hand and then empathetically echoed in the left, the whole making a tender little colloquy in two parts that melt together for the final cadence.

Kosegarten wrote four poems entitled *An Rosa*. The first is tremendously long, as is the fourth, and Schubert did not attempt to set these. It was the second and third much shorter poems that were selected for music. There are five strophes in this Kosegarten poem – printed here are 1, 3 and 4.

| Autographs: | Library of Congress, Washington (first version); in private possession, USA (second version) |

First edition:	Published as part of the AGA in 1895 (P600)
Subsequent editions:	Not in Peters; AGA XX 162: Vol. 3/145; NSA IV: Vol. 9/152 (first version) & 153 (second version)
Bibliography:	Reed 1985, p. 492
Discography and timing:	Fischer-Dieskau I 5[36] 1'25
	Hyperion I 22[13]
	Hyperion II 11[6] 1'24 Jamie MacDougall

← *Nachtgesang* D314   *An Rosa II* D316 →

AN ROSA II   To Rosa
(KOSEGARTEN) **D316** [H195]

The song exists in two versions, the second of which is discussed below:
(1) 19 October 1815; (2) 1816 (?)

(1)   'Langsam'   F minor   ¢   [14 bars]

(2)   F minor

(15 bars)

Rosa, denkst du an mich? Innig gedenk'
  ich dein.
Durch den grünlichen Wald schimmert
  das Abendrot,
    Und die Wipfel der Tannen
      Regt das Säuseln des Ewigen.

Rosa, wärest du hier, säh' ich ins Abendrot
Deine Wangen getaucht, säh' ich vom
  Abendhauch
    Deine Locken geringelt—
      Edle Seele, mir wäre wohl!

[. . . 4 . . .]

Rosa, do you think of me? I think tenderly
  of you.
The evening light glimmers through the green
  forest
    And the pine-tops are stirred
      By the whisper of eternity.

Rosa, if you were here I should see your cheeks
Bathed in the evening glow,

    And your locks ruffled in the evening breeze.
      Dearest soul, how happy I should be!

[. . . 4 . . .]

LUDWIG THEOBUL KOSEGARTEN (1758–1818); poem written in 1787

This is the seventeenth of Schubert's twenty-one Kosegarten solo settings (1815–17). See the poet's biography for a chronological list of all the Kosegarten settings, as well as a discussion of Morten Solvik's Kosegarten Liederkreis and this song's place within it.

Schubert made two versions of this second Rosa song. The first was sketched on the same heroically busy October day (the first anniversary of the composition of *Gretchen am Spinnrade* – and there is some excuse for believing that Schubert was aware of the date's significance). The second version is a reworking of the barring of the first, with small (but crucial) changes of melody and harmony (bb. 7 to 11). These alterations show how far the composer went in the process of refining his initial ideas when the text interested him, as it clearly did. In this case we should assume that the second version represents the composer's final thoughts; it is a real little masterpiece, full of Schubertian tenderness, but never performed in recital – something that is our loss (its absence from the Peters Edition is one reason for this, of course).

The opening, extremely simple in its appearance on the page, offers a masterful interpretation of the words. At the question 'Rosa, do you think of me?' the accompaniment, a solitary line in the pianist's right hand, doubles the voice (b. 1). This is followed by 'I think tenderly of you'; underneath this the left hand joins the conversation in quasi-canon (b. 2) as if summoned by the poet's strength of imagination to take part, the masculine bass cleaving to the feminine treble. This unanimity of thought, a vivid musical depiction of the communing of lovers, puts us in mind of the canonic writing in the introduction to the Brahms song *Wir wandelten* op. 96 no. 2. As the drift of the poem opens outwards from the two lovers to the panorama of nature and from thence to thoughts of eternity, the accompaniment fills out and changes from two-part to four-part, and even six-part, harmony. The whole is conceived in a single sweep without any pauses in the music – quite an achievement when dealing with this type of metre.

We climb high with the voice (bb. 7–9) to reach the tops of the pines ('die Wipfel der Tannen') and then descend again in a long arc (bb. 9–11). The cadence at the first 'Säuseln des <u>Ewigen</u>' (b. 10), which takes us from the second inversion of the tonic chord to the relative minor, is wonderfully appropriate for the mysterious whisperings of eternity, as is the descent of the voice into the depths of its range (a low A flat in b. 13) for the repeat of those words. The postlude takes this deeper tessitura as its starting point with a pair of gentle murmurs – not quite shudders, but the stirring of something deep. It is as if these concluding bars speak for Kosegarten himself: moved by the beauties of his surroundings, he feels that his love for Rosa is part of the vast plan of the universe. In his way the music remains in the present, if conditional, tense.

There are six strophes in Kosegarten's poem – these are all printed in the AGA. Given here are 1 and 2. Only in Verse 6 with mention of Rosa's 'Urne' is it clear the poet sings of someone who has died – a deliberately last-minute revelation. (Kosegarten's fourth poem in the series, not set to music, is an impassioned lament.) A fine and touching performance of this song may be given without introducing this turn of events.

Autograph:	Library of Congress, Washington (first version); in private possession, USA (second version)
Publication:	Both versions published as part of the AGA in 1895 (P601 & P602)
Subsequent editions:	Not in Peters; AGA XX 163a & b: Vol. 3/146 & 147; NSA IV: Vol. 9/155 (first version) & 157 (second version)
Discography and timing:	Fischer-Dieskau I 5[37] 1'45
	Hyperion I 22[14]
	Hyperion II 11[7] 2'02 Jamie MacDougall

← *An Rosa I* D315   *Idens Schwanenlied* D317 →

AN SCHWAGER KRONOS   To coachman Kronos

(GOETHE) OP. 19 NO. 1, **D369** [H222]
D minor – D major   1816

(140 bars)

Spute dich, Kronos!	Make haste, Chronos!
Fort den rasselnden Trott!	Break into a rattling trot!
Bergab gleitet der Weg;	The way runs downhill;
Ekles Schwindeln zögert	I feel a sickening giddiness
Mir vor die Stirne dein Zaudern.	At your dallying.
Frisch, holpert es gleich,	Quick, away, never mind the bumping,
Über Stock und Steine den Trott	Over sticks and stones, trot
Rasch ins Leben hinein!	Briskly into life!
Nun schon wieder	Now once again
Den eratmenden Schritt	Breathless, at walking pace,
Mühsam berghinauf![1]	Struggling uphill;
Auf denn, nicht träge denn	Up then, don't be sluggish,
Strebend und hoffend hinan!	Onwards, striving and hoping.
Weit, hoch, herrlich	Wide, lofty and glorious
Rings den Blick ins Leben hinein[2]	Is the view around into life
Vom Gebirg' zum Gebirg'	From mountain range to mountain range
Schwebet der ewige Geist,	The eternal spirit glides,
Ewigen Lebens ahndevoll.	Bringing promise of eternal life.
Seitwärts des Überdachs Schatten	A shady roof
Zieht dich an	Draws you aside
Und ein Frischung verheissender Blick	And the gaze of a girl
Auf der Schwelle des Mädchens da,	On the step, promising refreshment.
Labe dich – Mir auch, Mädchen,	Refresh yourself! For me too, girl,
Diesen schäumenden Trank,	That foaming draught,
Diesen frischen Gesundheitsblick!	That fresh, healthy look.
Ab denn, rascher hinab!	Down then, down faster!
Sieh, die Sonne sinkt!	Look, the sun is sinking!
Eh' sie sinkt, eh' mich Greisen	Before it sinks, before the mist
Ergreift im Moore Nebelduft,	Seizes me, an old man, on the moor,
Entzahnte Kiefern schnattern	Toothless jaws chattering,
Und das schlotternde Gebein:	Limbs shaking,

[1] Schubert repeats 'Nun schon wieder' at the beginning of this line.
[2] Schubert takes Goethe's nominative from the strophe's first line, and places it into the accusative in the second. The poet writes: 'Weit, hoch, herrlich *der* Blick / Rings ins Leben hinein'.

Trunknen vom letzten Strahl	Snatch me, drunk with its last ray,
Reiss mich, ein Feuermeer	A sea of fire
Mir im schäumenden Aug',	Foaming in my eyes,
Mich geblendeten Taumelnden	Blinded, reeling
In der Hölle nächtliches Tor.	Through hell's nocturnal gate.
Töne, Schwager, in's Horn,	Coachman, sound your horn,
Rassle den schallenden Trab,	Rattle noisily on at a trot.
Dass der Orkus vernehme: wir kommen,	Let Orcus know we're coming.
Dass gleich an der Tür[3]	So that the innkeeper is at the door
Der Wirt uns freundlich empfange.	To give us a kind welcome.

JOHANN WOLFGANG VON GOETHE (1749–1832); poem written 10 October 1774

This is the fortieth of Schubert's seventy-five Goethe solo settings (1814–26). See the poet's biography for a chronological list of all the Goethe settings.

Goethe wrote this poem in a coach on his way back to Frankfurt from Darmstadt. He had recently accompanied Klopstock (qv), then in his mid-fifties, on part of his journey from Karlsruhe to Mannheim, and had been disappointed with the discourse of his famous fellow traveller who seemed to have lost the fire of his youthful creativity. As Lorraine Byrne puts it, 'The poem represents a youthful rebellion against the stagnation Goethe had recognized in Klopstock and the staleness he feared in old age.' The poet later expressed to Charlotte von Stein (letter of 19 May 1778) the wish to die in full command of his faculties rather than be allowed 'to crawl miserably to the final destination'.

Nicholas Boyle in his magisterial *Goethe: The Poet and the Age* (1991–2000) describes *An Schwager Kronos* as 'an exuberant, semi-articulate free-verse hymn'. Boyle continues: 'The poem likens [Goethe's] life to a coach journey, in rhythms now labouring and clotted for the time of difficulty, now smooth and sovereign as it reaches the heights, now rattling rapidly down to a conclusion: let the end be quick and ecstatic, this young Achilles exclaims, a fiery consummation that compels the applause of a pagan underworld.' The poet casts Father Time as a coachman or 'Schwager' (literally brother-in-law, a term that derives from the time when all mail-coach drivers were familiarly addressed thus). This mythical figure, a personification of Father Time himself, is in charge of all our destinies, and inclined to run away with them unless one persuades, or commands, him to take another route.

What an exciting moment for Schubert it must have been to confront the poem for the first time! It is often a sign that a Goethe poem has 'taken' with the composer – like an inoculation – when the result is a feverish moto perpetuo: *Gretchen am Spinnrade* D118, *Rastlose Liebe* D138, *Erlkönig* D328, *Versunken* D715, *Der Musensohn* D764, *Willkommen und Abschied* D767 and *Suleika* D720 are driven by a rhythmic energy that seizes the listener by the scruff of the neck and compels him or her to follow where the composer leads. The agent of this excitement is the accompaniment whose task it is to whip the voice into action, although the pianist must not adopt a speed that is so fast that all the gritty details of the song fail to tell. Schubert uses a relentless staccato accompaniment that connects with every inch of the stony ground, both to paint the 'rasselnden Trott' of the horse and carriage and to lend motivic unity to a challenging text that at first glance might seem to defy musical control and run amok down the page.

---

[3] Goethe writes 'Dass gleich an der *Türe*'.

No other composer succeeded in setting this sprawling poem, despite the obvious musical temptation of the last verse. To bring it to heel Schubert, with devilish cunning, opts for a structure that has the *hint* of the strophic song about it. It is as if he feels the need to point out that although man's span on earth moves in phases, to make musical sense it also has to have certain grandly recurring themes and gathering points. Thus it is that bb. 5–12 (beginning 'Spute dich, Kronos!') have a similar melodic shape to bb. 21–8 ('Frisch, holpert es gleich') as well as bb. 87–100 ('Ab denn, rascher hinab!'). This gives the impression, however mistakenly, that the work is in an ABA form. It is a remarkable part of Schubert's achievement that he gives this song a memorable tune without us being aware that he is creating melody, and that the various episodes hang together seemingly inevitably – to say effortlessly would be to belie the splendid sense of struggle in much of this music (and the way he handles the 'Seitwärts' strophe has its detractors for not being tranquil enough).

Thus the topography of life is built into the song's shape. The first verse starts off on level but difficult terrain, the piano picking its way through sticks and stones with octaves in the left hand shadowed by the right. The direction ('Not too fast') gives a sense of rattling grandeur to the vehicle that sways through life. There is a most subtle variety in the accompaniment: sometimes there are six thrusting quavers per bar in both hands, sometimes the moto perpetuo function is given to either the left or right while the less occupied hand punctuates the texture with jabbed quavers or more sustained dotted crotchets.

At the beginning of the second verse ('Nun schon wieder / Den eratmenden Schritt', b. 29) the rhythm of the accompaniment changes: for a half-dozen bars there is one less quaver on the second beat, with an emphatic sforzando in the middle of the bar. This is as if the heart has skipped a beat, a wonderful tonal analogue for breathlessness and exhaustion under pressure. The climb up life's hill (from 'Auf denn, nicht träge denn', b. 37) is one of the song's glories. The exuberance of youthful determination and willpower is reflected in surging left-hand arpeggios in octaves which lift the post-chaise out of the mud and shoulder it ever upwards. We move from E flat via B major (the beginning of the third verse at 'Weit, hoch, herrlich' b. 41) to E minor, C major, F minor, F sharp minor and thence into A major: all in all a complete tonal definition of what it is to be on an ascending trajectory in life. A condensed history of a young man getting to the top is writ in these progressions. Romantic dalliance is at its best when one is young and successful. Having reached the plateau of A major (b. 56), a short interlude moves the music into D major at the fourth verse ('Seitwärts des Überdachs Schatten' b. 59).

At the top of the hill there is suddenly the leisure to take care of smaller yet highly necessary details; the poet's gaze moves from high goals to lower ones, and wrenching harmonies give way to wenching ones. Suddenly everything is flirtatious and even tender (those rattling staccato quavers have changed their spots if not their dots). The little chromatic left-hand motif (b. 58) just before 'Seitwärts des Überdachs Schatten' plays the coquette and ignites the gleam in the suitor's eye. From b. 66 exchanged glances at 'Und ein Frischung verheissender Blick', underpinned by a frisson of low As in the pianist's left hand, add to a sense of sexual conspiracy.

At the fifth verse ('Ab denn, rascher hinab!' b. 87), with its implied recapitulation (which in turn implies a sudden confrontation of one's mortality around an unexpected corner), it is time to be off. The first encounter is with ascending mist, wonderfully illustrated by a succession of rising chords, thick and opaque in both hands, yet another new texture in this astonishingly varied, and at the same time astonishingly unified, accompaniment. At the beginning of the sixth verse ('Trunknen vom letzten Strahl' b. 101) the piano plainly illustrates that life is now downhill all the way. Perilously precipitous arpeggios, changing the harmony in each bar and threatening the safety of singer and pianist alike, hurtle down the keyboard like rockslides in a narrow mountain pass while the voice hangs on for dear life. But all in vain; the movement of

Schwager Kronos oil painting by Moritz von Schwind, 1827.

the full-handed left-hand harmonies moves inexorably downward by semitones, dragging the vocal line with it. At 'Und das schlotternde Gebein', Richard Stokes observes, Goethe's syntax falls apart, a chaotic construction that is 'ungrammatical, impossible . . . but wonderful'. At rock bottom there is a succession of pounding As (bb. 111–12) that lead to A major chords (the dominant of the home key of D minor) and the composer is ready for his *coup de grâce.*

Goethe commands Kronos to sound his horn, and Schubert triumphantly provides something that poetry can only obliquely imply. A stentorian post-horn motif (a crotchet and two semiquavers) hammered out in an exultant D major by the pianist introduces one of the most powerful pages in all lieder. The gates of hell (Orcus is another name for Hades) hold no terrors for this wild and reckless traveller – he has tasted life in all its glory and even this last experience is one which he will savour and embrace. The imperious fanfare of the coachman, now a virtuoso on his instrument, alternates with the quavers that have rattled throughout the song, but they do so here with a new and imposing grandeur. The postlude is terrific in every sense; it ends with D major chords repeated in the piano's tenor register, only a tone higher than those unforgettable pulsating right-hand thirds that open Beethoven's 'Waldstein' Sonata. (It is not unlikely that Goethe and Beethoven were coupled in Schubert's mind as titans of German culture.) On a page like this, thanks to the composer's ability to capture the poet's tone of voice, the young Goethe himself materializes before our ears – a man for all time who has bent Time to his will, a man to change the world, a man to defy convention, a sinner and bon viveur (and all the better for that) but, above all, a leader and a very great artist. Nine years after the song was composed, the dedication to Goethe (for which the sage of Weimar must have given his permission, in accordance with Austrian law) is proof that he was still a young composer's hero.

Autograph:	Missing or lost
First edition:	Published as Op. 19 no. 1 by Diabelli, Vienna in 1825 (P80)
Dedicatee:	Johann Wolfgang von Goethe
First known performance:	11 Janaury 1827, Gesellschaft der Musizfreunde, Vienna. Soloist: Johann Karl Schoberlechner (see Waidelich/Hilmar Dokumente I No. 440 for full concert programme)
Subsequent editions:	Peters: Vol. 2/44; AGA XX 263: Vol. 4/204; NSA IV: Vol. 1/21; Bärenreiter: Vol. 1/96
Bibliography:	Bell 1964, pp. 34–7
	Byrne 2003, pp. 95–100
	Capell 1928, pp. 123–5
	Einstein 1951, p. 142
	Fischer-Dieskau 1977, pp. 63–4
	Gülke 1991, pp. 117–23
Arrangements:	arr. Johannes Brahms (1833–1897) for voice and orchestra (1862) [see ORCHESTRATIONS]
Discography and timing:	Fischer-Dieskau I 8[11] 2'52
	Hyperion I 24[21]
	Hyperion II 12[17] 2'58 Simon Keenlyside

← *Jägers Abendlied* D368   *Der Tod Oscars* D375 →

AN SIE   To her
(KLOPSTOCK) **D288** [H174]
A♭ major   14 September 1815

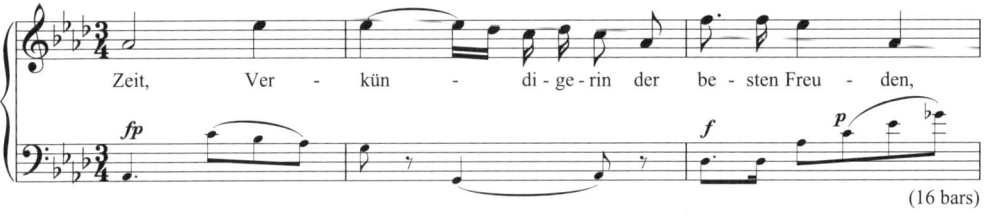

(16 bars)

Zeit, Verkündigerin der besten Freuden,
Nahe selige Zeit, dich in der Ferne
Auszuforschen, vergoss ich
Trübender Tränen zu viel!

   Und doch kommst du! O dich, ja Engel senden,
Engel senden dich mir, die Menschen waren,
Gleich mir liebten, nun lieben
Wie ein Unsterbicher liebt.

Time, herald of the greatest joys,
Approach, blissful Time,
I have shed too many sorrowful tears
Seeking you in the far distance.

   Yet you draw near, sent by angels,

Sent to me by angels who were once human,
Who loved like me, and now love
As immortals do.

Auf den Flügeln der Ruh, in Morgenlüften,	On wings of peace in the morning breezes,
Hell vom Taue des Tages, der höher lächelt,	Bright with the dew of the day that smiles more sublimely
Mit dem ewigen Frühling,	You descend from heaven
Kommst du den Himmel herab.	With the eternal spring.
Denn sie fühlet sich ganz, und giesst Entzückung	For she feels that she is whole,
In dem Herzen empor die volle Seele,	And her overflowing soul exudes rapture within her heart
Wenn sie, dass sie geliebt wird,	When, drunk with love,
Trunken von Liebe, sichs denkt!	She deems herself loved.

FRIEDRICH GOTTLOB KLOPSTOCK (1724–1803); poem written in summer 1752

This is the fifth of Schubert's thirteen Klopstock solo settings (1815–16). See the poet's biography for a chronological list of all the Klopstock settings.

Schubert's discovery of Klopstock in September 1815 unleashed a small flood of creativity. The first song he set to a text by this poet was the masterpiece *Das Rosenband* D280; within a month he had composed music in a number of different styles to match the poet's own different voices. We thus not only have tender love songs (like *An Sie*) but also a jaunty patriotic song (*Vaterlandslied* D287), an imitation of the mysteries of Ossian (*Selma und Selmar* D286), a grandiose religious epic (*Dem Unendlichen* D291) and an imposing ballad about Germany in Roman times (*Hermann und Thusnelda* D322). In all these Schubert uses his gift for melody and his enriched harmonic vocabulary to pay homage to a great poet who may seem passé to today's readers and listeners but who for Schubert's generation was more celebrated than any other German writer (and, in general terms, much more famous than Bach).

An Sie is attractive and dignified. It feeds a more modern harmonic palate (particularly in the second half of the song) at the same time as preserving some of the eighteenth-century conventions. For example, the doubling of voice and piano at 'dich in der Ferne / Auszuforschen' ('seeking you in the far distance', bb. 5–7) is old-fashioned practice but appropriate because of the searching nature of the words; at the same time, the vocal line rises in semitones, a more modern effect than would have been used by Gluck, the composer who had hitherto been most closely associated with Klopstock's poems. The setting of the second word, 'Verkündigerin' (a held note on the second syllable followed by a flurry of semiquavers), is as florid as a courtly bow; it is no doubt seemly to address heraldic Time in so gallant a manner. The poem was written in the fervent hope that the banns of marriage would soon be formally read concerning the union of the poet with his 'Cidli', whose readiness for connubial bliss is confirmed in the fourth verse. 'Time, it is time!' says Klopstock; until now Time has obstinately refused to materialize, but now she ('Zeit' is feminine in German) has finally arrived, sent by compassionate angels who have once known what it is to love in a mortal way. The only possible response is to greet the visitor with a welcome ode. The very title of the poem, 'To Her', might apply equally to Time and Cidli herself.

The device of a held note that culminates in a flourish is repeated for the adjective 'Trübender' (bb. 9–10), suitably describing the flow of sorrowful tears. In short, everything that at first hearing might be eighteenth-century musical mannerism is justified by a Romantic response to the text. The longest note in the vocal line is on the repeat of 'Tränen zu viel' (bb. 12–13).

Underneath this the piano changes chords to moving effect, and the postlude proves itself the jewel of the piece, a little solo that combines the stately poise of classicism with a more modern chromatic poignancy, exemplified by the run of semiquaver triplets in the piano writing of the penultimate bar. Perhaps Schubert knew Reichardt's two-page setting of this poem – ornate by that composer's standards.

Strophes 1 and 4 were sung for the Hyperion Edition (mainly because they are an easier fit for the music in terms of prosody than 2 and 3) but to make complete sense the poem must be read as a whole.

Autograph:	Staatsbibliothek Preussischer Besitz, Berlin
First edition:	Published as part of the AGA in 1895 (P585)
Subsequent editions:	Not in Peters; AGA XX 142: Vol. 3/78; NSA IV: Vol. 9/66
Bibliography:	Fischer-Dieskau 1977, p. 46
Further settings:	Johann Friedrich Reichardt (1752–1814) *An Cidli* (1789)
	Richard Strauss (1864–1949) *An Sie* Op. 43 no. 1 (1899)
Discography and timing:	Fischer-Dieskau I 5²¹ 2'35
	Hyperion I 22³
	Hyperion II 10⁹ 1'48 Jamie MacDougall

← *Vaterlandslied* D287   *Die Sommernacht* D289 →

AN SILVIA *see* GESANG (AN SILVIA) D891

ANACREON (Fl. 520 BC)

THE POETIC SOURCE
Unknown

THE SONG
1822   *An die Leier* D737 (translation by Bruchmann, qv)

The most famous of the Greek lyricists was a native of the island of Teos in Asia Minor. His reputation has always been that of a voluptuary – the poet of wine and love. He spent his youth in Thrace, going on to Samos under the patronage of Polycrates in whose praise he wrote many songs, and whose explosive temper was said to have been softened by the poet's music. Anacreon was a young man at this time which belies his legendary image as an older, grey-haired poet. After the death of Polycrates he was invited to live in Athens by Hipparchus, poetry-loving son of the tyrant Peisistratus, who sent a galley to fetch him (*c.* 525 BC). In Athens he befriended other poets summoned to serve this court, such as the celebrated Simonides, and he became known for his love songs to the beautiful youths of Athens, chief among them Critias, son of Dropides.

There are genuine fragments of Anacreon's poetry that are not at all like the Odes that have come down to us and are now dismissed as being partially, or wholly, spurious.

Anacreon died aged eighty-five – legend has it he choked on a grapestone *c.* 478 BC;

Anacreon, a Roman marble copy of the bronze original
by Phidias, *c.* 450 BC.

the Athenians set up his statue in the Acropolis; the location of his grave eternally awaits discovery as Goethe suggests in his poem, *Anakreons Grab*, memorably set by Hugo Wolf in 1888. Schubert set Franz von Bruchmann's translation of a poem attributed to Anacreon. The same lyric has been translated by many others, including the poet Mörike: 'Ich will des Atreus Söhne, / Ich will den Kadmos singen; / Doch meiner Laute Saiten, / Sie tönen nur von Liebe.' The similarities between this and Bruchmann's version (which could not possibly have been known to Mörike) suggest that Mörike's source of translation (*Anakreons Lieder* by Johann Friedrich Degen) was also the crib on which Bruchmann relied. An inspection of Degen (Anspach, 1782) confirms this: it begins with exactly the same line as Bruchmann's version: 'Ich will von Atreus Söhnen'. It continues: 'Ich will von Kadmus singen, / Doch meiner Laute Saiten / Ertönen nur von Liebe.'

ANDENKEN   Remembrance
(Matthisson) **D99** [H35]

The song exists in two versions, the second of which is discussed below:
(1) April 1814; (2) November 1816?

(1) 'Allegretto'   F major $\frac{2}{4}$ 72 bars

(2) F major

(72 bars)

Ich denke dein,	I think of you
Wenn durch den Hain	When through the grove
Der Nachtigallen	The nightingales'
Akkorde schallen!	Harmonious song echoes!
Wann denkst du mein?[1]	When do you think of me?

[1] Matthisson writes '*Wenn* denkst du mein' (Gedichte, 1811).

Ich denke dein	I think of you
Im Dämmerschein	In the twilight
Der Abendhelle	Of evening
Am Schattenquelle!	At the shady spring!
Wo denkst du mein?	Where do you think of me?
Ich denke dein	I think of you
Mit süsser Pein,	With sweet pain,
Mit bangem Sehnen	With anxious longing,
Und heissen Tränen!	And burning tears!
Wie denkst du mein?	How do you think of me?
O denke mein,	Oh, think of me
Bis zum Verein	Until we meet
Auf besserm Sterne!	In a better world!
In jeder Ferne	However distant you are,
Denk' ich nur dein!	I shall think only of you!

FRIEDRICH VON MATTHISSON (1761–1831); poem written in 1792/3

This is the seventh of Schubert's twenty-nine Matthisson solo settings (1812–17). See the poet's biography for a chronological list of all the Matthisson settings.

Matthisson's poem was published in an almanac in 1802, and Beethoven's famous setting of 1808 (WoO 136) may well have been known to the younger composer. The opening four bars of Schubert's piano introduction might have been scored for wind ensemble: these chords seem suited to flutes and clarinets. The manner of Mozartian wind ensemble extends to the easy, entertaining nature of the whole song. *Andenken* is about melody, pure and simple. Unlike *Adelaide* D95 it does not attempt nature illustrations – the song of the nightingale does not get so much as a trill, and the sweet pain of love and tears of longing stray nowhere near the minor key. Instead an infectious melody repeats to rippling semiquaver accompaniment. (In the second verse this changes to quavers that bounce and glint with a sforzato on the first beat of the bar in an attempt to mirror the evening brightness.)

The cadences on the dominant seventh at the end of each verse ('Wann denkst du mein?') are suitably yearning and an ingenious means of linking the verses. In the last strophe the journey to a better world ('Auf besserm Sterne') occasions a slight change of harmonic direction and a decoration of the vocal line on the word 'Sterne' is like a tiny explosion of stars in the heavens. The word 'Ferne' (bb. 50–51 and bb. 56–7) also encourages the idea of distance with the leap of a sixth. The repetition of 'nur dein' on a falling third (bb. 61–2, 63–4 and yet again at bb. 65–6) denotes the sweet obsession of constancy. This touch owes much to Beethoven's treatment of the poem in 1809, although Schubert avoids that composer's insertion of a rhetorical 'ja' into the penultimate cadence.

A song like Stolberg's *Daphne am Bach* D411 from 1816 has the same overall feeling as *Andenken*, but Schubert had by then refined his motivic language so that a flowing accompaniment in semiquavers almost always denotes water music. Even without water imagery the open-hearted simplicity of *Andenken* is engaging; it is perhaps the first song in which we can detect the germ of the masterful blend of sophistication and naivety later to be found in *Die schöne Müllerin*. It is also one of the songs in the album made for Therese Grob in November 1816.

There are two versions of this song, the second of which was written out in the Therese Grob song album from November 1816, although it is dated there '1814'. Unlike many other songs that appear in the Grob album, this later autograph is the only one to have survived. The earlier version of *Andenken* has come down to us only in a copy. In the NSA the few differences between the two versions are notated in *ossia* passages printed above the stave.

As a supplement to its edition of 27 September 1825, the *Wiener Zeitschrift für Kunst, Literatur, Theater und Mode* published a setting of *Andenken* by Antonio Salieri. Unfortunately the song, clearly from the *Nachlass* of the recently deceased Hofkapellmeister, is not dated. Its courtly style and use of the soprano clef are of no help in this regard, but merely an indication that Salieri was caught in the stylistic time warp of his earlier musical successes. His resistance to German poetry was well known. It would have been fascinating if he had decided to set this text himself as a result of Schubert bringing him the 1814 setting discussed above. The Salieri song is recorded as part of the Hyperion Edition's *Songs by Schubert's Friends and Contemporaries*.

Autograph:	Missing or lost (first version); in private possession in Switzerland (second version; Therese Grob songbook)
Publication:	Published as part of the AGA in 1894 (P538; first version)
	Published as part of the NSA in 1968 (both versions)
Subsequent editions:	Not in Peters: AGA XX 16: Vol. 1/144; NSA IV: Vol. 7/11;
	Bärenreiter: Vol. 5/110 (high voice), 104 (medium/low voice)
Bibliography:	Capell 1928, p. 83
Further settings:	Johann Rudolf Zumsteeg (1760–1802) *Andenken* (1801)
	Ludwig van Beethoven (1770–1827) *Andenken* WoO136 (1809)
	Carl Maria von Weber (1786–1826) *Andenken* Op. 66 No. 3 (1806)
	Hugo Wolf (1860–1903) *Andenken* (1877)
Discography and timing:	Fischer-Dieskau I 1[10] 1'42
	Hyperion I 12[13]
	Hyperion II 3[7] 1'42 Adrian Thompson

← *Trost. An Elisa* D97   *Erinnerung (Todtenopfer)* D101 →

ANONYMOUS/UNKNOWN

There are nineteen solo songs by Schubert with texts by anonymous, or unknown, authors. Such is the lively nature of Schubert scholarship that it is likely that the authorship of some of these texts may well be identified in due course. The songs are listed chronologically:

Autumn 1813	*Auf den Sieg der Deutschen* D81
20 October–4 November 1813	*Zur Namensfeier des Herrn Andreas Siller* D83
11 February 1815	*Das Bild* D155
25 August 1815	*Lilla an die Morgenröte* D273
25 August 1815	*Tischlerlied* D274
12 October 1815	*Lambertine* D301 (formerly attributed to Johann Ludwig Stoll)
January(?) 1816	*Klage (Trauer umfliesst mein Leben)* D292/371
24 February 1816	*Morgenlied* D381
24 February 1816	*Abendlied* D382

May 1816	*Der Leidende* D432
June 1816	*An den Schlaf* D447
November 1816	*Wiegenlied* D498
January 1817	*Trost* D523
February 1817	*Lied (Brüder, schrecklich brennt die Träne)* D535
Autumn 1817?	*Der Strom* D565 (sometimes attributed to Albert Stadler)
November 1817	*Lied eines Kindes* D596
June 1818	*Grablied für die Mutter* D616
September 1818	*Blondel zu Marien* D626 (formerly attributed to Franz Grillparzer)
1827	*Il modo di prender moglie* D902/3

In addition there are a number of part-songs with anonymous authors. Eight of these, as listed chronologically below, have commentaries in this book:

Verschwunden sind die Schmerzen D88 (unaccompanied trio, TTB)
Trinklied (Auf! Jeder sei nun froh und sorgenfrei!) D267 (Chorus, TTBB with piano)
Bergknappenlied D268 (Chorus, TTBB with piano)
Trinklied (Funkelnd im Becher) D356 (Solo tenor and chorus, TTBB with piano, fragment)
Linde Lüfte wehen D725 (Duet, fragment with piano)
Schicksalslenker, blicke nieder (Des Tages Weihe) D763 (Quartet, SATB with piano)
Lied eines Kriegers D822 (Solo bass with unison chorus with piano)
Al par del ruscelletto (Cantate für Irene Kiesewetter) D936 (Quartet, TTBB and Chorus SATB
   with piano duet)

ANTIGONE UND OEDIP   Antigone and Oedipus   Duet
(MAYRHOFER) OP. 6 NO. 2, **D542** [H354]
C major   March 1817

(84 bars)

Antigone:	*Antigone:*
Ihr hohen Himmlischen erhöret	Ye gods on high,
Der Tochter herzentströmtes Flehen:[1]	Hear a daughter's heartfelt entreaty;
Lasst einen kühlen Hauch des Trostes	Let the cool breath of comfort
In des Vaters grosse Seele wehn.[2]	Waft into my father's great soul.

[1] Mayrhofer writes '*Flehn*'. For an explanation of the background to these alternative Mayrhofer readings see Editorial Note at the beginning of Johann MAYRHOFER.
[2] Mayrhofer writes 'In Oedip's grosse Seele wehn'. This alteration to the metre of the poem by Schubert was singled out for criticism by Kanne (qv under COMPOSERS) in his otherwise admiring review in the *Wiener Allgemeine Musikalische Zeitung*, 19 January 1822.

Genüget, euren Zorn zu sühnen,	This young life is sufficient to assuage
Dies' junge Leben—nehmt es hin;	Your anger – take it,
Und euer Rachestrahl vernichte[3]	And let your avenging blow
Die tiefbetrübte Dulderin.	Destroy this deeply distressed sufferer.
Demütig falte ich die Hände—	Humbly I clasp my hands;
Das Firmament bleibt glatt und rein,	The firmament remains serene and clear
Und stille ist's, nur laue Lüfte	And all is calm; now only mild breezes
Durchschauern noch den alten Hain.	Quiver through the ancient grove.
Was seufzt und stöhnt der bleiche Vater?	Why does my pallid father sigh and moan?
Ich ahn's—ein furchtbares Gesicht	I can guess – a terrible vision
Verscheucht von ihm den leichten Schlummer;	Drives away his light sleep;
Er springt vom Rasen auf—er spricht:	He starts up from the grass and speaks:

O e d i p :	*Oedipus:*
Ich träume einen schweren Traum.[4]	I dream a troubled dream.
Schwang nicht den Zepter diese Rechte?	Did not this right hand wield the sceptre?
Doch Hoheit lös'ten starke Mächte	But powerful forces reduced your majesty,
Dir auf, o Greis, in nicht'gen Schaum.	Old man, to mere foam.
Trank ich in schönen Tagen nicht	In happy days, in the halls of my great fathers
In meiner grossen Väter Halle,	Amid the songs of heroes and the peal of horns,
Beim Heldensang und Hörnerschalle,	Did I not drink
O Helios, dein golden Licht,	Your golden light, O Helios,
Das ich nun nimmer schauen kann?	Which now I can never see again?
Zerstörung ruft von allen Seiten:	Destruction calls from all sides:
'Zum Tode sollst du dich bereiten;	'You are to prepare for death;
Dein irdisch Werk ist abgetan.'	Your earthly task is done.'

JOHANN MAYRHOFER (1787–1836)

Antigone und Oedip is a musical dialogue between two characters who never sing simultaneously (a performance for a single singer taking both male and female roles would thus be a possibility). This duet is accordingly listed here as the twenty-third of Schubert's forty-seven Mayrhofer solo settings (1814–24) rather than as an ensemble. See the poet's biography for a chronological list of all the Mayrhofer settings.

The tragedy of Oedipus is one of the most famous in Greek mythology. Sophocles wrote two plays about the king's life and death; *Antigone* is a sequel concerning his ill-fated daughter. The first part of the legend is recounted in *Oedipus Tyrannus*: by unknowingly slaying his father Laius and marrying his mother Jocasta, Oedipus brings down the wrath of the gods upon Thebes. Jocasta hangs herself at the end of this play, and Oedipus blinds himself with her brooch. Deposed from the Theban throne, Oedipus is banished into exile with his daughter Antigone. They wander until they arrive at Colonos in Attica where they fall under the protection of Theseus.

---

[3] Mayrhofer writes 'Und *eurer Rache Strahl* vernichte'.
[4] Mayrhofer writes '*Ich träumte*'; Schubert's 'träume' changes past tense to present.

Oedipus at Colonos dates from 401 BC and was not performed until after Sophocles' death. It opens with the blinded and banished Oedipus' arrival in Colonos, brought by his daughter Antigone to a grove sacred to the Eumenides. Mayrhofer's text reworks this corner of the story, not so much as a duet but as a two-part monologue; Antigone's prayer to the gods is followed by the old king's awakening and voicing his presentiments of death. It is impossible not to imagine the imposing figure of the retired opera singer, and the song's dedicatee, Johann Michael Vogl, relishing the opportunity given him by this magisterial music. This piece is almost always performed as a duet in the present-day concert hall, but it is likely that Vogl took the chance to play the role of Antigone as well as Oedipus, perhaps in the falsetto tones that made his contemporary detractors think of him as 'foppish'. Male singers of the nineteenth century were less inhibited than their present-day counterparts about performing women's songs, and Vogl was also an exponent of Walter Scott's *Ave Maria* (sung by the character of Ellen Douglas in Scott's *Lady of the Lake*).

Antigone und Oedip achieves a different and more subtle dramatic effect than Schiller's *Hektors Abschied* D312, composed two years earlier. It belongs together with the great Mayrhofer setting *Memnon* D541. The song was possibly a planned attempt on the part of poet and composer to woo Vogl, a fan of ancient Greek literature and adept at the language, to the Schubertian cause; in musical terms it panders to the singer's conservative tastes and takes into account his experience as a singer of Gluck's classical roles: the song has the classical virtues of Doric architecture and is free of extraneous detail. The NSA publishes a version that includes Vogl's ornamentation. This is something that Schubert tolerated rather than admired; his older and more distinguished colleague's fussy embellishments add nothing significant to the composer's initial more simple inspiration and were not incorporated in the publication of 1821 (*see* ORNAMENTATION). In Josef Hüttenbrenner's copy of the song Antigone's music is written in the treble clef, that of Oedipus in the bass, but it seems that Vogl regarded both roles as grist to his mill, whether or not Schubert intended the song to be performed as a duet.

Antigone's grandiose and touching opening aria is a type of pagan *Ave Maria* (in that it is similarly concerned with a father's plight). The rippling accompaniment serves to illustrate the flowing nature of the 'herzentströmtes' entreaty, as well as the movement of the long-wished-for cool breath of comfort. Pulsating semiquavers replace undulating arpeggios in the second section (b. 8) with mention of the 'avenging blow' of the gods. The third (b. 14) moves demurely into E minor with a temporary interruption of the pianist's semiquaver *Bewegung*. Perhaps the most beautiful passage in the work begins with the mystery of 'Und stille ist's' – bb. 17–18 – where a peaceful and spacious vocal line floats over a figuration that evokes rustling breezes in a holy place, the composer's sensuous swathes of harmony painting a pagan, rather than Christian, ambience. Antigone's recitative after this, although punctuated by an alert sequence of two-bar piano interludes (marked 'Etwas geschwinder', upbeat to b. 23), employs the unusual and piquant interval of C natural to D sharp for 'seufzt und stöhnt', combining fear and daughterly concern in equal measure.

A sudden marking of 'Schnell' and the twitching of dotted rhythms in the piano allow the daughter to introduce her father to the public ('er spricht . . .') rather in the manner of Victorian melodrama. Yet this Oedipus is a noble creation; we can hear his blindness through Schubert's deliberate use of harmony with a limited field of vision. Fanfares proclaim his former status as king (bb. 42–4), harmony in thirds and sixths (introduced in the piano's interlude at b. 52) evokes the hunting horn, and the rhythm in triplets paints hearty carousings. This is followed by an old-fashioned drinking song (bb. 55–69) as the king recalls the healing beverage of sunlight, never to be tasted by him again. In the last four bars of this aria the simplicity of this good life in sunny C major yields to a heartbreaking change of harmonic circumstance; at 'Das ich nun nimmer schauen kann' the progress from G to E flat major is a short journey for the voice, but it conjures considerable musical pathos.

The portentous last verse softens to include an unmistakable echo of the rhythm and mood of death's utterance in *Der Tod und das Mädchen* D531 written a month earlier: the fateful words Oedipus hears in his imagination are as awe-inspiring and are set to similarly valedictory music in the grand manner.

Autograph:	Conservatoire collection, Bibliothèque Nationale, Paris (first draft)
First edition:	Published as Op. 6 no. 2 by Cappi & Diabelli, Vienna in August 1821 (P16)
Dedicatee:	Johann Michael Vogl
Publication reviews:	*Allgemeine musikalische Zeitung* (Vienna), No. 6 (19 January 1822), col. 43f. [Waidelich/Hilmar Dokumente I No. 142; Deutsch Doc. Biog. No. 270] F. von Hentl 'Blick auf Schubert's Lieder', *Wiener Zeitschrift für Kunst, Literatur, Theater und Mode* No. 36 (23 March 1822), p. 289f. [Waidelich/Hilmar Dokumente I No. 146; Deutsch Doc. Biog. No. 278]
Subsequent editions:	Peters: Vol. 4/3; AGA XX 309: Vol. 5/62; NSA IV: Vol. 1a/50 & Vol. 1b/284 (ornamented version); Bärenreiter: Vol. 1/41
Bibliography:	Capell 1928, pp. 136–7 Fischer-Dieskau 1977, p. 96 Kohlhäufl 1999, p. 165
Discography and timing:	Fischer-Dieskau —

Deutsche Grammophon *Schubert Duette*	5'23	Janet Baker & Dietrich Fischer-Dieskau
Hyperion I 14[11] Hyperion II 18[5]	5'43	Marie McLaughlin & Thomas Hampson

<table>
<tr><td>← Am Strome D539</td><td>Orest D548 →</td></tr>
</table>

❧❧❧❧❧❧

Songs of ANTIQUITY

Perhaps the most significant and fertile theme in Schubert's songs before 1823 is classical antiquity, the result of the prevailing importance of Latin and Greek in European education from the sixteenth century, a tradition that was as much in place for Schubert and his contemporaries as it had been for all his earlier poets. Schubert's principal textbook at school was entitled *Institutio ad Eloquentiam*: the imprint of my copy of this famous educational standby is 'Vindobonae' (the locative case of Vindobona or Vienna), 1808. Classical mythology played an important role in the writing of three of the composer's most important poets, Schiller, Goethe and Mayrhofer, and it is scarcely surprising that there are no fewer than thirty-three Schubert songs, great masterpieces among them, based on classical history, mythology or literature.

With the possible exception of the comical *Dithyrambe*, all these settings were composed before Schubert's illness and the watershed year of 1823. As Walther Dürr points out (NSA Series IV: Volume 11 pp. XVI–XVII), the songs of Schubert's 'Antikenlieder' may be divided into two categories: those with directly classical themes (including two Viennese translations from Aeschylus and Anacreon) and those where the poets have adopted a classical background or setting, or superimposed a classical guise on a more modern theme (the texts may feature classical characters, for example, without having a direct connection with mythology). In the list below songs in this second category – those with a less direct connection to classical literature – are indented. For programme-making purposes any of these songs (with the exception of the longer ballads perhaps – works long enough to stand alone in recital) would fit comfortably within a group of songs arranged around a classical theme.

March 1815	*Amphiaraos* (Körner) D166
August 1815	*Die Bürgschaft* (Schiller) D246
October 1815	*Hektors Abschied* (Schiller) D312
1815–16	*Klage der Ceres* (Schiller) D323
1816	*Lied eines Schiffers an die Dioskuren* (Mayrhofer) D360
1816	*An Schwager Kronos* (Goethe) D369
March 1816	*Die vier Weltalter* (Schiller) D391
March 1816	*Gruppe aus dem Tartarus* I (Schiller) D396
June 1816	*Die Liebesgötter* (Uz) D446
June 1816	*Fragment aus dem Aeschylus* (Mayrhofer) D450
September 1816	*Lied des Orpheus (als er in die Hölle ging)* (Jacobi) D474
December 1816	*Leiden der Trennung* (Collin after Metastasio) D509
January 1817	*Fahrt zum Hades* (Mayrhofer) D526
March 1817	*Philoktet* (Mayrhofer) D540
March 1817	*Memnon* (Mayrhofer) D541
March 1817	*Antigone und Oedip* (Mayrhofer) D542
March 1817	*Ganymed* (Goethe) D544
March 1817	*Orest* (Mayrhofer) D548
April 1817	*Uraniens Flucht* (Mayrhofer) D554
July 1817	*Iphigenia* (Mayrhofer) D573
September 1817	*Gruppe aus dem Tartarus* II (Schiller) D583
September 1817	*Elysium* (Schiller) D584
September 1817	*Atys* (Mayrhofer) D585
November 1818	*Sonnet* ('Apollo, lebet noch') (A. von Schlegel after Petrarch) D628
October 1819	*Prometheus* (Goethe) D674
November 1819	*Strophe aus 'Die Götter Griechenlands'* (Schiller) D677
September 1820	*Der entsühnte Orest* (Mayrhofer) D699
December 1820	*Der zürnenden Diana* (Mayrhofer) D707
March 1821	*Grenzen der Menschheit* (Goethe) D716
1822 or 1823	*An die Leier* (Bruchmann after Anacreon) D737
April 1822	*Heliopolis* I (Mayrhofer) D753
April 1822	*Heliopolis* II (Mayrhofer) D754
1826?	*Dithyrambe* (Schiller) D801

ARIA DELL'ANGELO' *see* QUELL' INNOCENTE FIGLIO D17

ARIA DI ABRAMO *see* ENTRA L'UOMO ALLOR CHE NASCE D33

ARIETTE DER CLAUDINE & ARIETTE DER LUCINDE *see* *CLAUDINE VON VILLA BELLA* D239/1 & 2

Die ART, EIN WEIB ZU NEHMEN *see* *DREI GESÄNGE FÜR BASS-STIMME MIT KLAVIER* D902/3 (IL MODO DI PRENDER MOGLIE)

Der ATLAS *see* *SCHWANENGESANG* D957/8

ATYS   Attis
(Mayrhofer) **D585** [H385]
A minor   September 1817

(116 bars)

Der Knabe seufzt über's grüne Meer,
Vom fernenden Ufer kam er her,[1]
Er wünscht sich mächtige Schwingen:
Die sollten ihn ins heimische Land,[2]
Woran ihn ewige Sehnsucht mahnt,
Im rauschenden Fluge bringen.

'O Heimweh! unergründlicher Schmerz,
Was folterst du das junge Herz;
Kann Liebe dich nicht verdrängen?
So willst du die Frucht, die herrlich reift,[3]
Die Gold und flüssiger Purpur streift,
Mit tödlichem Feuer versengen?

'Ich liebe, ich rase—ich hab' sie gesehn,[4]
Die Lüfte durchschnitt sie im Sturmeswehn
Auf Löwen gezogenem Wagen,
Ich musste flehn: o nimm mich mit!
Mein Leben ist düster und abgeblüht;
Wirst du meine Bitte versagen?

'Sie schaute mit gütigem Lächeln zurück;[5]
Nach Thracien zog uns das Löwengespann,[6]
Da dien' ich als Priester, ihr eigen.
Den Rasenden kränzt ein seliges Glück:
Der Aufgewachte schaudert zurück—
Kein Gott will sich hülfreich erzeigen.

'Dort, hinter den Bergen im scheidenden Strahl[7]
Des Abends, entschlummert mein väterlich Tal;

With a sigh the youth gazes over the green sea;
He came from a distant shore,
And longs for mighty wings
That would take him in intoxicating flight
To the homeland
For which he yearns eternally.

'O longing for home, unfathomable pain,
Why do you torment the young heart?
Can love not drive you out?
Will you then scorch with your deadly fire
The fruit that ripens gloriously,
Kissed by gold and liquid purple?

'I live, I rage, I have seen her;
Like a whirlwind she swept through the air
In a chariot drawn by lions.
I had to entreat: Take me with you!
My life is bleak and barren.
Will you deny my plea?

'She looked back with a kindly smile;
The lions bore us off to Thrace
Where I serve as her priest.
The madman is filled with blissful happiness;
But when he awakes he recoils in fear:
There is no god to lend his aid.

'There beyond the mountain, in the dying rays
Of evening, my native valley begins to slumber.

[1] Mayrhofer writes 'Am dämmernden Ufer kam er her'. For an explanation of the background to these alternative Mayrhofer readings see Editorial Note at the beginning of Johann Mayrhofer.
[2] Mayrhofer writes 'Die sollten ihn zum heimischen Land'.
[3] Mayrhofer writes 'Du willst die Frucht'.
[4] Mayrhofer writes 'Ich liebe und rase'.
[5] Mayrhofer writes 'Sie schaute mit gütigem Lächeln mich an' (this is also given in AGA and Peters editions of the song). Schubert, perhaps unwittingly, destroys Mayrhofer's rhyme here, and singers may prefer to preserve it.
[6] Mayrhofer writes 'Nach Thracien trug uns das Löwengespann'.
[7] Mayrhofer writes 'Dort hinter Gebirgen, im scheidenden Strahl'.

O wär' ich jenseits der Wellen!'	O that I might cross the waters!'
Seufzet der Knabe. Doch Cymbelgetön[8]	Thus sighs the youth. But the clash of cymbals
Verkündet die Göttin; er stürzt von Höh'n[9]	Proclaims the goddess; he plunges from the heights
In Gründe und waldige Stellen.[10]	Into the woods deep below.

JOHANN MAYRHOFER (1787–1836)

This is the twenty-ninth of Schubert's forty-seven Mayrhofer solo settings (1814–24). See the poet's biography for a chronological list of all the Mayrhofer settings.

There are actually two characters named Atys in the works of Schubert: the first is the son of Krösus, a tenor role, in the opera fragment *Adrast* D137 begun in 1814 to a Mayrhofer text. Schubert's second Atys is another Mayrhofer creation. This legend of a Phrygian youth, whose cult was linked to the worship of the fertility goddess Cybele, is one of the strangest of the Greek myths. Grandson of the river-god Sangarios, Attis was famed for his beauty, but was unable to respond to the advances of Cybele, who desired him. Most versions have it that Attis was in love with the wood nymph Sagaritis; in a jealous rage Cybele killed her, and Attis, mad with grief, castrated himself. Thomas Moore, in his translation of Anacreon's Ode XII (published in 1804), tells us that 'Atys, wild with love, / Roams the mount and haunted grove; / Cybele's name he howls around / The gloomy blast returns the sound!' Attis died at the foot of a pine tree where his blood made violets grow. In certain versions of the legend he is changed into a pine. His cult became more important during the Roman epoch, reaching its height during the reign of Claudius, and practised in the east of the empire. Devotees of Cybele worshipped Attis almost on a par with the goddess, and the priests of Cybele castrated themselves and feigned madness as part of their rites.

We do not know how and where Mayrhofer came upon this story. Various contemporary books in German deal with classical mythology, one of the most important of which is *Götterlehre oder mythologische Dichtungen der Alten* (1791) written by the Goethe enthusiast Karl Philipp Moritz. Here the story of Attis is discussed directly after that of *Ganymed* (where Goethe's poem is quoted in full). We read there that 'Atys' (Mayrhofer, like Thomas Moore, also spells it thus) left his home country and hastened, voluntarily, to the Phrygian woods in order to dedicate himself to the service of Cybele. For violating a vow of chastity he was punished by madness and self-inflicted castration ('Entmannung'). Moritz tells his readers that 'in a beautiful poem from the ancient world', Attis, temporarily having regained his sanity, dreams of returning to his homeland over the sea. The goddess appears with her lion-borne chariot and the youth becomes mad again. He serves Cybele for the rest of his days 'in weibischer Weichlichkeit' – a phrase describing effeminate unmanliness that makes Moritz's distaste for such a condition quite clear.

The poem mentioned by Moritz is by Catullus (*Carmina* LXIII). Perhaps Mayrhofer read this in a German translation (for example, J. X. Mayr 1786, Leipzig and Vienna) or even in the original Latin. Indeed all of Mayrhofer's work inspired by mythology seems to owe something to Catullus', practice of re-dramatizing a myth from a new and imaginative angle. It is unlikely, for example, that Mayrhofer would have written the poem for *Lied eines Schiffers an die Dioskuren* D360 without knowing the Catullus poem (*Carmina* IV) concerning the worship of Castor and Pollux. In Catullus, as in Mayrhofer, Attis' love for Sagaritis plays no part in the scenario; instead

[8] Mayrhofer writes '*So* seufzet der Knabe'.
[9] Mayrhofer writes 'Er stürzt von *den* Höh'n'.
[10] Mayrhofer writes '*Zu Gründen* und waldige*n* Stellen'.

the Roman poet concentrates on Attis' enslavement to the cult of Cybele, and a brief moment when the youth desires to escape from its thrall. Catullus (famously bisexual) tells the story from the viewpoint of a man trapped in the body of a 'notha mulier' – an ersatz woman, a being neither male nor female. 'Ego mulier, ego adolescens, ego ephebus, ego puer' Catullus has Attis say – 'a woman I, a young man, an ephebe, a child'. Relieved of his madness for a short while, he longs to return to his homeland where, he claims, he was once the flower of the gymnasium – 'ego gymnasi fui flos' – and admired by all. Now he is condemned to live a life of shame, 'life-long a female slave' as Catullus puts it in Guy Lee's translation. 'Now what I have done appals me; I am sorry for it now', says Attis when awakened to his plight, but any chance of reversing the situation evaporates when the furious goddess unleashes her lion, Ferox, to ensure that he returns to a state of madness and a life in her service.

Like Catullus, Mayrhofer ignores why and when the youth was castrated. What seems important to the Austrian poet is that Attis was the effeminate archetype, unmanned not by his own choosing but as a result of the intervention of the unreasonable gods. (The legend is part of that body of classical references studied by European intellectuals since the Renaissance who looked to Greek history and mythology to explain, or justify, their own same-sex preferences.) The first two strophes of Mayrhofer's poem concentrate on the youth's unassuaged longing to return to the safety and normality of his homeland. This is followed by a flashback that recounts how he begged to enter the goddess's service in the first place. Mayrhofer's third verse describes Attis' life as 'bleak and barren', no doubt because the youth was unable to reconcile his outer physical being with his spiritual centre, a theme also explored in *Memnon* D541, another Schubert-Mayrhofer collaboration. Attis had allowed the goddess to spirit him away to a life of decadent and orgiastic celebration (writing in 1928 Capell refers euphemistically to 'a peculiar priest-hood'). Having lived as 'a Maenad, half me, a male unmanned' (Catallus' words, not Mayrhofer's) Attis realizes, when granted a short period of lucidity, that he yearns for the love and acceptance of his family. On hearing the cymbals of the returning Cybele, rather than submit to a return of the madness of his former life he throws himself from the top of Dindymus, the mountain of the goddess. With the words 'er stürzt von Höh'n', Mayrhofer departs from all the classical sources and conceives a way of ending the boy's life that matches the manner of his own suicide in 1836.

It is little wonder that this is one of Schubert's most elusive songs. The older commentators on the whole find nothing very exceptional about it: Reed states that 'there is little attempt at dramatic immediacy' and Capell finds the music 'mild' and the composer 'untouched'. He notes the absence of 'something exotic . . . some corybantic display' (the Corybantes, who attended Cybele herself, were wild, half-demonic beings, given to orgiastic rituals). But Capell should have understood that the bittersweetness of the human dilemma facing the benighted Attis was what really interested the composer; it was one of the Schubert songs most loved by Peter Pears and Benjamin Britten.

In *Gretchen im Zwinger* D564, the composer had responded to Gretchen as an outcast with empathy, and Attis is similarly treated with an understanding that shows extraordinary emotional maturity. This subject is honoured with music in the key of A minor, with changes into A major – a ravishing tonal ambiguity which here is haunting enough to suggest something as exotic (*pace* Capell) as ambiguity of gender. This is a change of key that the composer reserves for music by which he is deeply touched (cf. the A minor/A major plea for a return to the values of antiquity in *Strophe aus 'Die Götter Griechenlands'* D677). The introduction begins in unison between the hands (Reed notes a similarity to the opening of the *Arpeggione* Sonata; Walther Dürr – in NSA Volume 11 – comments on the resemblance of the piano's *Vorspiel* to the opening of *Die Einsiedelei* D337, a quietly mournful setting of Salis-Seewis for unaccompanied male quartet – Attis is something of a hermit after all).

The rocking 𝄴 rhythm is the gentle background for music of unsettled 'Sehnsucht'. In b. 2 a chromatic decoration is introduced (a motif encompassing the rise of a sharpened Lydian fourth, D sharp in the key of A minor, to E, a semitone higher) which later punctuates the vocal line in obsessive manner. Here, surely, is Capell's required exotic touch, haunting rather than strident. The melodic line strains to go somewhere, to develop, but never manages to do so; thus the tune for 'über's grüne Meer' (bb. 6–7) is the same as for 'Ufer kam er her' (bb. 9–10) by which point we might have expected the melody to have modulated. We slip into the major key at the end of the strophe (at 'Im rauschenden Fluge bringen' bb. 18–20), a change that in this case denotes the feverish hopes of the deluded. We already realize that Attis' request to return home will never be granted.

The melody for the poem's second strophe is based on that of the first. Attis speaks for the first time ('O Heimweh! unergründlicher Schmerz'). This verse remains in the minor tonality. Once again the music seems to be a metaphor for something incomplete. The rippling semiquaver note accompaniment suggests the harp-like arpeggiations of an ancient lyre, and there is water imagery here too. Attis longs for the unattainable, as does the miller boy beside the brook in *Am Feierabend* in *Die schöne Müllerin*. These two pieces of music have much in common, including the tonality, time signature, accompaniment and changes to the major key at the moment when the unattainable is mentioned and made to blossom in the vocal line (this happens at the only moment in that cycle where the lovesick words 'die schöne Müllerin' are given voice). In this verse the metaphor of the wonderfully ripening fruit refers to Attis' beauty and his reputation, previously honoured and praised, hence the mention of gold and purple, colours of honour and nobility – all now ruined by a wound that will never heal.

The middle section of the song is quasi-recitative, an arioso marked 'Geschwind'. Here Schubert seems to have remembered the Gluckian studies of his youth, and with some justification – the appearance of a *deus* (or *dea*) *ex machina* in Verse 2 is worthy of an opera by that composer. The words 'Ich liebe, ich rase—ich hab' sie gesehn' are set to a bracing and wide-ranging vocal line supported by chords punched out at the piano on the second and fourth beats of the bar. Here madness owes its depiction to the manner of the *Iphigenia* operas, and it must have seemed to Schubert that this was appropriate to a Grecian subject; he had learned to identify antiquity closely with Gluck's style. At 'Ich musste flehn' Attis begins to recount his encounter with Cybele. The chromatic wandering of this section paints disorientation, that of a supernatural experience. The accompaniment shepherds the vocal line through a maze of harmonic changes – from C major to D flat major, and thence to C flat major, and a thicket of flats as far removed from the relatively accidental-free regions of A minor as it is possible to imagine. The pleading eloquence of 'Wirst du meine Bitte versagen?' (bb. 53–4) is repeated a semitone higher, anguish voiced in an almost feminine register. The description of the goddess's reaction (marked 'Etwas langsamer') at the words 'Sie schaute mit gütigem Lächeln zurück' is as sweet and unreal as a dream in slow motion. The music here has the silken seductiveness of the Erlking's promises of a happy existence; a major-key simplicity marries charm and gentleness with a sense of something ominous. A short recitative (which, it is true, might have been more dramatic in order to win the admiration of the song's detractors), returns us to the present ('Der Aufgewachte schaudert zurück') and Attis' terrified waking state; the words 'Kein Gott will sich hülfreich erzeigen' are passive, helpless and frozen to the spot. A short interlude prepares the path back to the A minor of the home key.

And so for the last verse of Mayrhofer's poem we hear again the plaintive music of the opening; common time yields to the return of a wafting 𝄴. The change from A minor to A major works its accustomed magic; this time it is at the words 'ich *jen*seits der Wellen' where the raised third of the scale lifts the music into the major key, and with it all of Attis' hopes for a return to a better life. How well this composer understood what it is to dream of what cannot be! The tragedy of Mayrhofer's closing lines (the boy's precipitous suicide) could have been expanded to make something remarkably dramatic, but Schubert prefers a swift recitative for the beleaguered spirit who longs to end a life of shame and pain.

The last words of the poem, 'waldige Stellen', are followed by an E major chord as if in secco recitative. This is an upbeat to an A minor postlude, an aria without voice. The singer is no more; the vocal line suddenly struck dumb is a metaphor for castration, and an accompaniment without a soloist signals the death of the protagonist. The piano is an ersatz singer, standing in for the real thing as much as Attis has been 'notha mulier'. Thus we find ourselves in a state of musical limbo that is unique in Schubert's lieder. This feeling is intensified by the fact that for eight bars, underneath this singerless aria, we are not allowed to hear any chord in root position. That this is almost the longest postlude in all the Schubert songs (eleven bars) suggests how special the song was in the composer's estimation. The first four bars comprise the repeat of a two-bar phrase, the metaphor of unsuccessful lift-off continued, a tentative scale that rises twice, in the treble stave – as if trying to do something that has failed at the first attempt. There is a bass pedal on E for this entire passage (bb. 106–13), and the music is built on various elaborations of E major as the dominant of A minor. The ear longs, like Attis, to go home, for a return to the tonic. Instead, with almost painful rapture, the music blossoms into A major with rippling chord patterns in the right hand, fuller than any we have heard so far. But still the bass is a second inversion (or 6-4 in harmonic terms), and the effect of this passage (again a two-bar cell that is repeated) is gently sensual, infinitely sad as only Schubert's major-key music can be, and offering neither bliss nor resolution.

Only in the last three bars of the postlude does the piano return to the tonic (A minor) with music that derives from the introduction. The left hand's descent is eloquent testimony to Attis' fall in every sense. For the first time in the song the rippling accompanying semiquavers are to be found in the depths of the bass clef; this tessitura reminds us of that wonderful bar of left-hand music at the very end of *Der Müller und der Bach* D795/19 from *Die schöne Müllerin*, also deep in the bass clef, that signals the suicide of the miller boy as he slips beneath the water.

Autograph:	Wienbibliothek im Rathaus, Vienna (fair copy)
First edition:	Published as Book 22 no. 2 of the *Nachlass* by Diabelli, Vienna in 1833 (P300)
Subsequent editions:	Peters: Vol. 5/124; AGA XX 330: Vol. 5/159; NSA IV: Vol. 11/187
Bibliography:	Capell 1928, p. 137
	Porter 1961, p. 128
Discography and timing:	Fischer-Dieskau II 1[15] 4'32
	Pears-Britten 2[5] 4'31
	Hyperion I 34[6]
	Hyperion II 19[19] 4'21 Thomas Hampson

← *Gruppe aus dem Tartarus* D583   *Elysium* D584 →

AUF DEM FLUSSE *see WINTERREISE* D911/7

AUF DEM SEE   On the lake
(GOETHE) OP. 92 NO. 2, **D543** [H356]

The song exists in two versions, the second of which is discussed below:
(1) March 1817; (2) appeared July 1828

(1) 'Mässig, ruhig'   E major   §   [80 bars]

(2) E♭ major

(1) Und frische Nahrung, neues Blut   And I suck fresh nourishment and new blood
     Saug' ich aus freier Welt;   From the wide world;
     Wie ist Natur so hold und gut,   How gracious and kindly is Nature
     Die mich am Busen hält!   Who holds me to her breast!

(2) Die Welle wieget unsern Kahn   The waves rock our boat
     Im Rudertakt hinauf,   To the rhythm of the oars,
     Und Berge, wolkig himmelan,   And soaring, cloud-capped mountains
     Begegnen unserm Lauf.   Meet us in our course.

(3) Aug', mein Aug', was sinkst du nieder?   My eyes, why are you cast down?
     Goldne Träume, kommt ihr wieder?   Golden dreams, will you return?
     Weg, du Traum! so Gold du bist;   Begone, dream, golden as you are;
     Hier auch Lieb' und Leben ist.   There is love here, and life too.

(4) Auf der Welle blinken   On the waves are twinkling
     Tausend schwebende Sterne,   A thousand floating stars;
     Weiche Nebel trinken   Soft mists drink up
     Rings die türmende Ferne;   The looming distances;

(5) Morgenwind umflügelt   The morning breeze wings around
     Die beschattete Bucht,   The shaded bay,
     Und im See bespiegelt   And in the lake
     Sich die reifende Frucht.   The ripening fruit is mirrored.

JOHANN WOLFGANG VON GOETHE (1749–1832); poem written in June 1775

*This is the forty-eighth of Schubert's seventy-five Goethe solo settings (1814–26). See the poet's
biography for a chronological list of all the Goethe settings.*

Goethe, in his mid-twenties, was on holiday with Graf Haugwitz and the von Stolberg brothers
in Switzerland when he wrote the poem. Lake Zurich is the locale, and the 'golden dreams' of
the third verse refer to Lili Schönemann, Goethe's betrothed in his home town of Frankfurt. A

month after the poet's return from Switzerland he abandoned Lili; the writing of this poem seems to have been part of his mental process of freeing himself, with considerable regret and anguish, from her influence and his promise to marry her. Instead he decided to accept the invitation of the Duke of Weimar to live and work in that principality, one of the most important turning points of his life.

There are some musical similarities (the E flat tonality for instance) between this *Auf dem See* and *Am See* (Bruchmann) D746, but the moods of the two songs are as different as waking and dreaming. The setting of the Bruchmann is a languid and sensuous barcarolle but in Goethe's *Auf dem See* the very first notes of the piano introduction delineate energy and determination of a different order: two accented downbeats in each bar proclaim vigorous rowing and manly exercise in the fresh air – *mens sana in corpore sano* (cf. *Der Schiffer* D536, another song in E flat about a strong man and his destiny). When Goethe is in this mood his powers of observation are heightened; he sees things that he would miss if he allowed himself to wallow in past regrets or dreams of the future. The poet possessed the analytical eye of a scientist; compare how earthy and *real* his verses sound when compared to those of many of his predecessors. On the other hand, no one could ever accuse him of cold intellectuality. Goethe's greatness lay in the balance he achieved between serene Apollo and disruptive Dionysus, and the same may be said of Schubert.

The poem is something of an allegory of a round-trip journey through life – morning, afternoon, night and the following morning. Goethe set it out in three strophes – two octaves on either side of a quatrain. For the purposes of this commentary the verses have been numbered to correspond to Schubert's five-part musical treatment of the poem. The vocal line of the first verse (morning) is a marvel and the epitome of outdoor music; we hear great breaths of fresh air taken in to sustain the tenacious arpeggios that sweep up and down across the stave as they follow the poet's confident and grateful gaze. For Lorraine Byrne, Goethe 'depicts nature as a continuum that unites and underpins the universe. He personifies her as a mother and portrays himself as a child enclosed in nature's womb, sucking nourishment and new blood.' The second verse (afternoon in the time-allegory) brings a slight change of weather in the accompaniment (from b. 19). This is triggered by the words 'Die Welle wieget unsern Kahn', prophetic of 'auf den wiegenden Wellen' in *Auf dem Wasser zu singen* D774. The interplay between the left-hand quavers and the syncopated right-hand figure produces a pulsation of semiquavers as the winds rise and the waters of the lake become choppy. This motif is cleverly adapted to reflect the grandeur of the cloud-capped mountains (from b. 24). A short piano interlude leads us away from natural wonders. The composer inserts an eloquent full bar's rest here (b. 34) before we enter into Goethe's silent thoughts in the third verse.

On 'Aug', mein Aug', was sinkst du nieder?' we find ourselves in the relative minor with pairs of left-hand quavers simulating the pounding heartbeats that accompany the involuntary return of sweet and painful memories. The mind weaves golden dreams (the night-phase of the poem in allegorical terms) in the dominant key of B flat (from b. 38) and a canon between vocal line and piano depicts this perfectly: strands of wistful melody, separated by the distance of a bar, stretch out to each other and overlap at the edges. With the words 'Weg, du Traum! so Gold du bist' (bb. 43–4) these musings are quickly banished; voice and piano, reined in from their separate wanderings, return to their common purpose – the celebration of the here and now. The phrase 'Hier auch Lieb' und Leben ist' is heard twice – harmonized for the first time to end in G minor as if to suggest just a shadow of regret (b. 46) and the second time, with greater conviction, making up its mind in B flat major (b. 48). This repetition, and the slight hesitation of resolve it implies, is a superb example of a composer adding an extra layer of meaning to words that appear only once in the poem.

We are now led back to the opening key of E flat and the final section with its change of time signature is a buoyant miracle – nature opens up to the gaze of the poet who is finally free of care. It is a moto perpetuo of refreshed hope, the magic of dawn and a welcome to the early morning hours when the last stars are still visible in the sky and reflected on the dancing waters. A distant relative this of a much later song – the sublime music for dancing stars (also in $\frac{2}{4}$) of *Die Sterne* (Leitner) D939. It is worth noting that there is no new tempo marking here and that many singers make something too fast of this section: quaver = quaver is the possible relationship between the tempi of the $\frac{6}{8}$ and $\frac{2}{4}$ parts of the song, though dotted crotchet = crotchet is a more poised solution. There is certainly no *più mosso*. At b. 58 the interplay of the voice and the alto line of the accompaniment in thirds at 'Morgenwind umflügelt' is music fit for a mischievous putto puffing wind into a ship's sails from the heights of a baroque ceiling. This, Goethe's final verse, is set only once. Schubert returns to the penultimate strophe for his peroration – waves and stars have seldom had such a wealth of loving musical detail lavished upon them. The last 'Welle' (b. 79) rises and breaks on the higher shores of the stave, and the final word 'Sterne' is set as a long note followed by a figuration, a four-note phrase in the manner of a turn, almost the flourish of a signature. (Maurice Brown pointed out that in many of the songs the composer uses a 'little *fioriture* to illustrate his poet's reference to natural objects'; as Schubert comes to the end of his song and takes his leave of the stars, he seems to imprint them with an affectionate coloratura caress.) The simple six-bar postlude is suffused with satisfaction and gratitude. It is interesting to compare this song with Carl Loewe's not inconsiderable (but very different) setting of 1836 with its juxtapostion of phrases in $\frac{6}{8}$ and $\frac{2}{4}$ and its repeat of the poem's first strophe at the end of the song.

Both the AGA and the NSA publish an earlier version of this song in E major; the music is rather less developed (there is a shorter prelude and no postlude) and the vocal line is less gracefully pointed. This tonality brings to mind a song by Johannes Brahms: *Auf dem See* Op. 59 no. 2 (Simrock), also a contemplative poem, which has something in common with Schubert's song in the breezy mood of its opening, and an accompaniment that rows and bobs through the water in a similar manner.

Autograph:	Missing or lost (first and second versions)
Publication:	First published as part of the AGA in 1895 (P670) (first version)
	First published as Op. 87 no. 2 (later corrected to Op. 92 no. 2)
	by M. J. Leidesdorf, Vienna in July 1828 (P163)
Dedicatee:	Josephine von Franck
Publication reviews:	*Münchener Musikzeitung* No. 14 (3 January 1829), col. 209ff.
	[Waidelich/Hilmar Dokumente I No. 680]
Subsequent editions:	Peters: Vol. 2/172; AGA XX 310a & b: Vol. 5/66 (first version) &
	70 (second version); NSA IV: Vol. 5a/9 (second version) & Vol.
	5b/188 (first version); Bärenreiter: Vol. 3/150
Bibliography:	Byrne 2003, pp. 69–74
	Capell 1928, p. 132
	Fischer-Dieskau 1977, p. 89
Further Settings:	Johann Friedrich Reichardt (1752–1814) *Auf dem See* (1794)
	Václav Tomášek (1774–1850) *Auf dem See* Op. 57/3 (1815)
	Carl Loewe (1796–1869) *Auf dem See* Op. 80 (1836)
	Fanny Mendelssohn (1805–1847) *Auf dem See* (1841)
	Hugo Wolf (1860–1903) *Auf dem See* (1875)
	Nikolay Medtner (1880–1951) *Na ozere* Op. 3/3 (1905)

Discography and timing: Fischer-Dieskau I 9[25]   3'19
                           Hyperion I 19[16]
                                                      3'34   Felicity Lott
                           Hyperion II 18[7]

← *Orest* D548   *Ganymed* D544 →

AUF DEM STROM   On the river
(RELLSTAB) **D943** [H660]
E major   March 1828

(210 bars)

Nimm die letzten Abschiedsküsse,	Take these last farewell kisses,
Und die wehenden, die Grüsse,	And the wafted greetings
Die ich noch ans Ufer sende,	That I send to the shore,
Eh' Dein Fuss sich scheidend wende!	Before your foot turns to leave
Schon wird von des Stromes Wogen	Already the boat is pulled away
Rasch der Nachen fortgezogen,	By the waves' rapid current;
Doch den tränendunklen Blick	But longing forever draws back
Zieht die Sehnsucht stets zurück!	My gaze, clouded with tears.
Und so trägt mich denn die Welle	And so the waves bear me away
Fort mit unerflehter Schnelle.	With relentless speed.
Ach, schon ist die Flur verschwunden,	Ah, already the meadows where, overjoyed,
Wo ich selig S i e gefunden!	I found *her*, have disappeared.
Ewig hin, ihr Wonnetage!	Days of bliss, you are gone for ever!
Hoffnungsleer verhallt die Klage	Hopelessly my lament echoes
Um das schöne Heimatland,	Round the fair homeland
Wo ich i h r e Liebe fand.	Where I found *her* love.
Sieh, wie flieht der Strand vorüber,	See how the shore flies past,
Und wie drängt es mich hinüber,	And how mysterious ties
Zieht mit unnennbaren Banden,	Draw me across
An der Hütte dort zu landen,	To a land by yonder cottage,
In der Laube dort zu weilen;	To linger in yonder arbour.
Doch des Stromes Wellen eilen	But the river's waves rush onwards,
Weiter ohne Rast und Ruh,	Without respite,
Führen mich dem Weltmeer zu!	Bearing me on towards the ocean.
Ach, vor jener dunklen Wüste,	Ah, how I tremble with dread
Fern von jeder heitern Küste,	At that dark wilderness,
Wo kein Eiland zu erschauen,	Far from every cheerful shore,
O, wie fasst mich zitternd Grauen!	Where no island can be seen!

Wehmutstränen sanft zu bringen,	No song can reach me from the shore
Kann kein Lied vom Ufer dringen;	To bring forth tears of gentle sadness;
Nur der Sturm weht kalt daher	Only the tempest blows cold
Durch das grau gehob'ne Meer!	Across the grey, angry sea.
Kann des Auges sehnend Schweifen	If my wistful, roaming eyes
Keine Ufer mehr ergreifen,	Can no longer descry the shore,
Nun so schau' ich zu den Sternen	I shall look up to the stars
Auf in jenen heil'gen Fernen!	There in the sacred distance.
Ach, bei i h r e m milden Scheine	Ah! By *their* gentle radiance
Nannt' ich s i e zuerst die Meine;	I first called *her* mine;
Dort vielleicht, o tröstend Glück!	There, perhaps, O consoling fate,
Dort begegn' ich i h r e m Blick.	There I shall meet *her* gaze.

LUDWIG RELLSTAB (1799–1860); poem written before 1825

This is the second of Schubert's ten Rellstab solo settings (1828). See the poet's biography for a chronological list of all the Rellstab settings.

This beautiful and unique piece of music is dominated by thoughts of Beethoven: in writing it Schubert was both paying homage to the memory of his great musical forbear and establishing his right to be considered Beethoven's natural, and worthy, successor. This view of the song's significance is a fairly recent one; Capell judged its sentiment as being 'really only formal'. But a later generation of commentators (chiefly Rufus Hallmark and Christopher Gibbs) has seen in this formality Schubert's conscious attempt to mirror the manner, and honour the spirit, of the older master. *Auf dem Strom* contains a quotation from the 'Eroica' Symphony, a work that Beethoven composed (according to the title page of the first edition) 'per festigiare il Souvenire di un grand'Uomo'. It is apt that in writing *Auf dem Strom* Schubert was, in turn, also paying tribute to the memory of a great man.

It is fairly certain that Schubert did not begin work on this *pièce d'occasion* until after he had decided to hold his first (and only) public concert. This took place, hardly by chance, on the first anniversary of Beethoven's death – 26 March 1828. Rellstab had almost certainly hoped that Beethoven himself would set his text to music. But Schubert saw in an instant how this poem was ideally suited to commemorate the great composer: the narrator who makes his farewell is someone cut off from human contact, unable to hear songs from the distant shore (as if he were deaf). The course of the love affair hinted at in the poem seems as inconclusive as Beethoven's already legendary amatory life was said to have been. This in turn fits in with Beethoven's most famous work for voice and piano, the cycle *An die ferne Geliebte* Op. 98. The significance of this unknown woman in the Rellstab poem is emphasized by the poet's use of italics ('s i e' or 'i h r e') to emphasize her heightened status as someone long dreamed-of and sought. And the sight of the stars 'in the sacred distance' at the end of the poem calls for musical sublimity in the manner of a Beethoven song that Schubert once copied out, the starlit *Abendlied unterm gestirnten Himmel* WoO150. Rellstab's poem is pretentious and over-dramatic but it takes on a completely different resonance if one imagines Beethoven himself singing as he sets sail from life's shore. It is as if Schubert has relinquished the subjectivity of the poem's 'ich' in honour of the older composer's posthumous voice. He could not have known that his own leave-taking was only some eight months away.

Schubert probably thought that his honouring Beethoven in this way might be considered presumptuous; it is little wonder that he never spoke of it. But it would have been enough for him to know that he was paying tribute to the great master in his own way. This is typical of Schubert's attitude to musical homage throughout his life: musical sleuths have uncovered various references to Mozart, Gluck and other composers in Schubert's work, but these entered the fabric of the music without comment from the composer himself. Thus *Auf dem Strom* stands or falls as a piece by Schubert, not as the Beethovenian stylization which, at least in part, it is.

Of course there are a number of important and typical elements that are quintessentially Schubertian, the chief of which is the movement of water, in this case a current of varying strengths and intensities. The liquid triplets propel the departing barque as it makes its way downstream, carrying the narrator with it. We are reminded of the *alla breve* movement of Schubert's Mayrhofer setting *Fahrt zum Hades* D526 where the journey is one of death and anguished farewell. Once the moto perpetuo triplets are set in motion (both underpinned by longer and resonant bass notes) the musical current carries each piece to its final destination. The relentless nature of the journey is reflected by Rellstab's 'Schon wird von des Stromes Wogen / Rasch der Nachen fortgezogen' (Verse 1) and 'mit unerflehter Schnelle' (Verse 2). These words, descriptive of speed, are an indication that the piece should move forward at two in a bar and not at the sluggish crawl of some performances. Also in the second strophe there is the key passage 'Hoffnungsleer verhallt die Klage / Um das schöne Heimatland / Wo ich i h r e Liebe fand' that must have reminded Schubert instantly of that theme of separated lovers, and the link with *An die ferne Geliebte*.

The presence of the horn player on the list of artists for the concert was no doubt partly to do with Schubert's need to have both novelty and celebrity on the bill in order to sell tickets. The distinguished Josef Lewy made himself available, probably as a return favour for Schubert's contribution to *his* benefit concert at the Kärntnertortheater on 22 April 1827, for which the *Nachtgesang im Walde* D913 (for male voice quartet accompanied by four horns) was composed. This had included the participation of Josef Lewy's brother Eduard, also a horn player. But there were artistic reasons for building the horn into the programme. Firstly the sound of the instrument had long been held to be symbolic of heroism and strength of purpose (as in the archetypal aspect of the brave hunter) as well as of heroic death (compare Schubert's use of horn motifs in *Die liebe Farbe* D795/16 from *Die schöne Müllerin*). Secondly the older composer, a hero in his own right, was a noted writer for the horn, both in symphonic and chamber music. We may also wonder whether Schubert had had access to Beethoven's complete Handel edition by this time and noticed – particularly in the operas – how that composer was a master of writing arias with horn obbligato. There is an alternative version for obbligato cello – first performed in 1829 – which was published alongside the horn version but whether this had Schubert's blessing or was simply the publisher's idea is not known. For a discussion as to whether Schubert wrote for a natural or valve horn see NSA Volume 14a p. 27 Note 71. That it was for the latter is now thought likely.

Auf dem Strom is a companion piece to *Der Hirt auf dem Felsen* D965 which was composed later in the same year (perhaps Schubert would have gone on to write a whole series of songs for voice and obbligato instruments) but these are different works both in mood and intention. The cantata for voice and clarinet composed for the famous soprano Anna Milder-Hauptmann was written more or less as a result of a commission (without fee) from a great singer; it is a celebration of vocal virtuosity and picturesque effect. *Auf dem Strom* is no less difficult to sing; it was first performed by the tenor Ludwig Tietze who was well known for his ability in a high tessitura; this type of writing mirrors Beethoven's own merciless challenges to the singing voice. But *Auf dem Strom* does not *sound* like a virtuoso piece because its purpose was too serious for mere display. In this work Schubert was wrestling with his own demons – one may almost say exorcizing the ghost of Beethoven with music to accompany that great soul's crossing from one side to the other.

The accompaniment in the seventeen-bar introduction is framed in simple triplets all the better to support the horn's *bel canto* aria at the opening of this piece which immediately sets a mood that is elegiac – noble and distant, as if other-worldly. This begins with a simple fragment of melody, incorporating a jump of a sixth (bb. 2–4) that is then capped by a sequence which includes a leap of a seventh (bb. 4–6); a third sequence, higher still, is supported by a sudden change from the E major of the home key to a 6–4 of G sharp minor (at b. 7) brought about by the downward slip of a semitone in the bass from E to D sharp. In this way the Schubertian magic begins to take hold. The harmony supporting this D sharp changes from a second inversion of G sharp minor to the dominant of that key, a bar of D sharp major (b. 9) as the horn hovers on a semibreve A sharp; this slips down, in melting fashion, to a semibreve A natural (b. 10), supported by piano triplets on a B major chord that leads us back to E major. In this tiny and tender excursion the mood for the pain of parting, and of strangely unfulfilled longing, has been established. After this, the piano's journeys (in the introduction at least) are less adventurous, although there is a superbly placed but fleeting move to the subdominant (second half of b. 14) – a momentary shift, but one that contributes hugely to the mood of resigned pathos. Ascending semiquavers and a trill in the horn part at b. 13 show that Schubert was not unaware of the player's desire to shine.

Rellstab's poem consists of five eight-line strophes, and each of these is separated from its neighbours by an interlude for horn and piano. The opening vocal line announces a melody, one of two that will be the main threads binding together the various parts of the work. It is a tune of which Beethoven himself might have been proud – gallant and a bit old-fashioned, built partly on a simple tonic-key arpeggio, and yet instantly memorable. This melody uses the first two lines of the poem; the next two lines (ending with 'wende!') are set to almost the identical melody, changing direction only at the cadence where the music veers into the dominant (b. 28). It is notable that the voice and horn, with the breathing space of a suggestion of canonic imitation, are immediately entwined in masterful fashion – one is seldom aware of any balance problems between them in performances of this work. As soon as the boat pulls away from its moorings (at 'Schon wird von des Stromes Wogen' b. 28) the key changes to E minor and the triplets become more restless; the insistent left-hand B naturals followed by split-octave Bs in the right hand suggest the pull of a strong current. At 'Doch den tränendunklen Blick' (b. 34) it seems as if the music is headed for G major but an attempt at a cadence in this key is thwarted at the word 'zurück' where the sudden intrusion of a left-hand D sharp (b. 37) leads us back to the E major of the home key – a superb musical analogue for the pull of the narrator's longing to return from whence he came.

There follows a ten-bar interlude (bb. 41–51) that re-uses the material of the opening. This time Schubert steers the music, with a deft hand on the tiller, into C sharp minor. Now we can no longer doubt that the composer sees in these words a metaphor for death. Rufus Hallmark first pointed out in 1976 that the melody beginning with the words 'Und so trägt mich denn die Welle' (b. 51) is taken, almost note for note, from the *Marcia funebre* of the 'Eroica' Symphony. The tenor sounds an octave lower than written so that the tessitura is the same as the violins' announcement of the theme at the opening of that movement. When the work is performed in E flat major – as it is sometimes to spare the singer – the pitches are also exactly the same as Beethoven's. At the repeat of the words 'Wo ich selig S i e gefunden' (bb. 61–4) the music moves momentarily into C sharp major, a fine example of Schubert's use of major-key tonality to limn the nostalgia of vanished happiness (this type of change is a regular feature of *Winterreise* D911).

In the middle of the work there is an eleven-bar interlude, an interchange of fragments of melody between horn and piano. This begins in C sharp minor (b. 79) but shifts back into E major (bb. 88–9) in order to set up a return of the melody heard in Strophe 1. Strophe 3 is not an exact repetition of the first (Schubert is too subtle a word-setter for that at this stage of his career) but it is very similar. In the first strophe at the word 'zurück' (bb. 36–7) a modulation into G major had been thwarted, but second time around, at the words 'Führen mich dem Weltmeer zu' (bb. 113–14) it is allowed to happen. This opening up of the harmonic landscape suggests larger ocean vistas, as well as triumphant release. For the first time the vocal line is marked 'fortissimo'. This reckless confidence quickly cedes to doubt during the six-bar interlude (bb. 115–20) as the music feels its way, with typically Schubertian ingenuity, into C sharp minor.

The fourth verse is the dramatic centre of the piece, an outburst of feeling accompanied by unceasing triplets. Once again the theme is that of the 'Eroica' *Marcia funebre*, but this is now a water-borne catafalque moving swiftly to its last resting place. The words refer to dread and the dark wilderness, as well as a storm at sea, and it is no surprise that this section of the piece is the most reminiscent of *Fahrt zum Hades*. If the general shape and direction of the music are the same as that for Strophe 2, there are many changes of detail. For example, the expressive instrumental interlude which had been placed between lines 2 and 3 of that verse is now excised in the interests of turning the screw of drama more tightly; and the setting of 'O, wie fasst mich zitternd Grauen!' (bb. 129–31) is tailor-made for those words alone. The horn doubles the bass line (the piano's left hand) and plunges to the lowest tessitura yet in this piece (usually more noted for its heights than its depths). The voice sings the text to the same line an octave higher and, as Leo Black notes, the effect of this 'voice doubling bass' is spine-chilling.

We hear the Beethoven 'Eroica' theme for the fourth time, set to the words 'Wehmutstränen sanft zu bringen, / Kann kein Lied vom Ufer dringen', bb. 135–8. At 'Durch das grau gehob'ne Meer!' (bb. 142–5) this sepulchral horn writing in the depths returns. Despite the differences of detail dictated by new verbal imagery, the music for Strophes 1, 3 and 5, and that for strophes 2 and 4 is, broadly speaking, the same in terms of shape and design. We have noticed this inter-leaving binary structure before – in a long song such as *Schiffers Scheidelied* D910 for example, a work incidentally not unrelated in subject matter to *Auf dem Strom*.

The interlude between Strophes 4 and 5 is eleven bars long (bb. 149–59), and in essence is the music heard right at the beginning of the work. Its purpose here is to calm the triplet-dominated turbulence as the narrator's fear yields to acceptance and a philosophical view of his spiritual metamorphosis. Now on the open sea, he has lost sight of land and looks up to the stars for consolation. Thus might Schubert have imagined Beethoven contemplating his own immortality after the ravages of his unhappy life, as if about to be elevated to the heavenly constellations as one of the gods of music. The music for Strophe 5 is a repeat of that for Strophe 1 (and closer to it than Strophe 3 had been). As in Strophe 1, with the word 'zurück', the modulation into G major we might have expected at 'Dort begegn' ich i h r e m Blick' (bb. 178–9) is prevented at the last minute by the intrusion of a D sharp under 'Blick', a wrench that wonderfully suggests the frisson of the narrator locking glances with his past.

We then find ourselves back in the home reaches of E major for one of Schubert's loveliest codas. He recycles the last four lines of the final strophe and for its second appearance he changes Rellstab's 'Ach, bei i h r e m milden Scheine' to 'Bei der Sterne mildem Scheine'. Here we encounter new musical material of the greatest simplicity and also nobility (from b. 186). It is this passage about starlight that is reminiscent of the Beethoven song *Abendlied unterm gestirnten Himmel*. There is a lovely little counter-melody in the piano under 'Bei der Sterne mildem Scheine' (from b. 187) the which is taken up in canon by the horn as the voice continues with 'vielleicht, o tröstend Glück!' The musical effect of this is enchanting, as if one were seeing banks of stars twinkling in their serried ranks far into the distance. The piano writing is seraphic, as if having undergone a journey through purgatory it finds itself transfigured 'on the other side'. But Schubert does not allow himself to lose the chance of an exciting ending – in fact he has it both ways: with its penultimate 'begegn' ich i h r e m Blick' the voice remains extremely passionate (and loud) to the end of the phrase with the requirement of a ringing high B (something to satisfy the *amour propre* of the tenor Tietze). After this high point, however, the murmurings of horn and piano suggest gentle strolls in Elysium and we are reminded that *Elysium* D584 begins in the same key. Water is no longer the element in which we are moving. All the material is new – meandering triplet scales, partially chromatic, with left hand answering right, and softly reverberant horn notes switching between F sharp and G sharp (bb. 201–3) in a delicious contemplative glow. The idea of encountering the gaze of a loved one produces four lingering last bars that depict a meeting between loving souls in a region where speech is no longer necessary. Schubert fosters this other-worldly atmosphere by making the horn descend right down to a bottom E for its four last sonorous notes, at the same time leaving the piano chords in first inversion and thus without a bass. We feel suspended in time and place. In this peroration Schubert has envisaged a transformation from earthly to heavenly state. The unknown 'ferne Geliebte' – the distant beloved – and her impatient (and also immortal) lover are united thanks to Schubert's intervention. Both composers knew that such love was unlikely to be encountered this side of the grave.

Autograph:	Houghton Library, Harvard University, Cambridge, MA
First edition:	Published as Op. post. 119 by M. J. Leidesdorf, Vienna in October 1829 (P235)
First known performance:	26 March 1828 at the Musikverein, Vienna as part of the Schubert 'Privatkonzert'. Soloist: Ludwig Tietze, with horn player Josef Rudolf Lewy (see Waidelich/Hilmar Dokumente I No. 603 for full concert programme)
Performance reviews:	*Allgemeine Musikalische Zeitung* (Leipzig), No. 19 (7 May 1828), col. 307f. [Waidelich/Hilmar Dokumente I No. 613; Deutsch Doc. Biog. No. 1067]
	Abend-Zeitung (Dresden), No. 141 (12 June 1828), p. 564 [Waidelich/Hilmar Dokumente I No. 620]
	Allgemeine Musikalische Zeitung (Berlin), No. 27 (2 July 1828), p. 215 [Waidelich/Hilmar Dokumente I No. 624; Deutsch Doc. Biog. No. 1069]
Subsequent editions:	Peters: Vol. 3/100 (horn part incorporated into piano part; C major); AGA XX 569: Vol. 10/2; NSA IV: Vol. 14b/196
Bibliography:	Black 2000, p. 89
	Capell 1928, p. 247
	Einstein 1951, pp. 346–7
	Fischer-Dieskau 1977, p. 274
	Gibbs 2000, pp. 157–9
	Hallmark 1982, pp. 25–46
Arrangements:	Arr. Herman Scherchen (1891–1966) as *Auf dem Strom für Sopran, Horn und kleines Orchester* [see ORCHESTRATIONS]
Discography and timing:	Fischer-Dieskau —
	Hyperion I 37[1]
	Hyperion II 35[13] 9'18 Michael Schade & David Pyatt (horn)

← *Der Tanz* D826   *Mirjams Siegesgesang* D942 →

AUF DEM WASSER ZU SINGEN   To be sung on the water
(STOLBERG) OP. 72, **D774** [H519]
A♭ minor   1823

Mässig geschwind

pp

Mit - ten im Schim-mer der   spie - geln - den - Wel - len

(35 bars)

Mitten im Schimmer der spiegelnden Wellen	Amid the shimmer of the mirroring waves
Gleitet, wie Schwäne, der wankende Kahn;	The rocking boat glides, swan-like
Ach, auf der Freude sanft schimmernden Wellen	On gently shimmering waves of joy.
Gleitet die Seele dahin wie der Kahn;	The soul, too, glides like a boat.
Denn von dem Himmel herab auf die Wellen	For from the sky the setting sun
Tanzet das Abendrot rund um den Kahn.	Dances upon the waves around the boat.

Über den Wipfeln des westlichen Haines | Above the treetops of the western grove
Winket uns freundlich der rötliche Schein; | The red glow beckons kindly to us;
Unter den Zweigen des östlichen Haines | Beneath the branches of the eastern grove
Säuselt der Kalmus im rötlichen Schein; | The reeds whisper in the red glow.
Freude des Himmels und Ruhe des Haines | The soul breathes the joy of heaven,
Atmet die Seel' im errötenden Schein. | The peace of the grove, in the reddening glow.

Ach, es entschwindet mit tauigem Flügel | Alas, with dewy wings
Mir auf den wiegenden Wellen die Zeit. | Time vanishes from me on the rocking waves.
Morgen entschwinde mit schimmerndem Flügel | Tomorrow let time again vanish with shimmering wings,
Wieder wie gestern und heute die Zeit, | As it did yesterday and today,
Bis ich auf höherem strahlenden Flügel | Until, on higher, more radiant wings,
Selber entschwinde der wechselnden Zeit. | I myself vanish from the flux of time.

FRIEDRICH LEOPOLD, GRAF ZU STOLBERG-STOLBERG (1750–1819); poem written in 1782

This is the last of Schubert's nine Stolberg solo settings (1815–23). See the poet's biography for a chronological list of all the Stolberg settings.

This is a strophic song but we neither notice nor complain that we hear the same music three times, so beguiling are its many felicities of vocal line and accompaniment. It is a barcarolle with vocal obbligato, a fascinating synthesis of piano piece and lied. It shares its tonality with the fourth Impromptu of Op. 90, D899 which has its own variation on the idea of a gentle descent of semiquavers, wafting between minor and major, with a left-hand obbligato voice singing like a Lorelei amid the pianistic waves. In order to avoid a frozen shoulder and wrenched wrist the accompanist must adopt a seemingly complicated pianistic ruse; as the third finger leaves the pivotal C flat it is replaced, in a split second, by the fourth. This happens throughout as the fingers sidle, crab-like, down the keyboard, a sleight of hand that must be imperceptible.

Professionals in a passage like this are on automatic pilot but for the unpractised accompanist it is like attempting to hold water in a clenched fist.

In a liquid performance where no rigid pattern of bar lines is imposed, the tidal-flow effect is exactly what Schubert intended: music to paint the gentle lapping of waves, the reeds rustling on the shore and, in the final verse, the audible passing of time. The vocal line starts beneath the waterline but rises to hug the piano *fioriture*, note for note, in cascading thirds. The greatest duos create this entwining effect with a hint of mysteriously synchronized rubato, the rest manage to stay together somehow or other. The last line of each verse is repeated; on the long held note the singer, like an intrepid surfer, braves a minor tidal wave to emerge into the sunlight of the major key. I first played this song when accompanying master classes given by Sir Peter Pears at Snape in the early 1970s. When the great tenor was in his sixties he was still capable of demonstrating for his students: it was unforgettable how he made the long-held E flat on the darkened 'a' vowel of 'Tanzet' (b. 26, and the same colour on 'Atmet' in Verse 2) imperceptibly brighten, like the flowering of hope, as the piano music shifted beneath him from A flat minor to A flat major at b. 27. Every singer should be as aware as this of the vocal line's underlying harmony, and a few singers, like Pears, can give the impression of being able to modulate with the piano while singing a single held note.

This harmonic metamorphosis is of course a musical metaphor for the liberation of the soul from its shackles. There was hardly ever a sadder and wiser 'Ach' than the one, fleet dotted quaver though it may be, that signals the beginning of this song's third and final verse. Here, more than ever, the pianist's right hand, in the ecstatic interlude, appears to stretch heavenward, certainly far further than a mere octave, in order to touch the note, an E flat, occupying the highest space on the stave. The song's metaphysical message is not often sufficiently pondered by audiences, diverted as they understandably are by its immediately appealing melody and

First edition of *Auf dem Wasser zu singen*, Op. 72 (1827).

shape. The composer's involvement with the poem's message is nonetheless complete; it was written for Stolberg's beloved wife Agnes (as are many of his best poems), the woman whom Goethe referred to as 'Engel-Grazioso'. At the time of her death Agnes was aged twenty-seven, as was the composer when he wrote this song. It is one of that handful of strophic compositions where the significance of the whole is built into the musical repetitions: human beings are the ephemeral passengers aboard this barge of time, endlessly rocked by the womb-like waters of life. The song seems always to have been resonating somewhere, and the composer has plucked it out of the air before releasing it once more into infinity. In putting it down on paper he has added to it the indefinable ache of sorrow without self-pity that is his special watermark. In the surge of these wonderful piano interludes there is a strange, almost defiant joy that seems to celebrate the beauty of being alive in the here and now while remaining painfully aware of the brevity of life. *Auf dem Wasser zu singen* is contemporary with Schubert's health crisis, as well as the composition of *Die schöne Müllerin*.

Autograph:	Missing or lost
First edition:	Published as a supplement to the *Wiener Zeitschrift für Kunst, Literatur, Theater und Mode* in December 1823 and subsequently as Op. 72 by Diabelli, Vienna in March 1827 (P119)
Subsequent editions:	Peters: Vol. 1/216; AGA XX 428: Vol. 7/106; NSA IV: Vol. 3a/142; Bärenreiter: Vol. 2/164
Bibliography:	Capell 1928, p. 73
	Fischer-Dieskau 1977, pp. 188–9
	Youens 2008, pp. 19–42
Further settings and arrangements:	Arr. Franz Liszt (1811–86) for solo piano as no. 2 of *Lieder von Schubert* (1837–8) [*see* TRANSCRIPTIONS]
	Thomas Adès (b. 1971) *Arcadiana* for String Quartet (inspiration of 3rd movement)
Discography and timing:	Fischer-Dieskau II 6[4] 3'24
	Pears-Britten 1[2] 3'34
	Hyperion I 11[4] 3'21 Brigitte Fassbaender
	Hyperion I 19[14] 3'28 Felicity Lott
	Hyperion II 27[7] 3'28 Felicity Lott

← *Der Pilgrim* D794   *Dass sie hier gewesen* D775 →

AUF DEN SIEG DER DEUTSCHEN

(ANONYMOUS) **D81** [not in Hyperion]

F major   October 1813

On the victory
of the Germans

Voice, 2 violins
& cello

(28 bars)

Verschwunden sind die Schmerzen,	Suffering is over,
Weil aus beklemmten Herzen	For no sighs echo
Kein Seufzer widerhallt.	From oppressed hearts.
Drum jubelt hoch, ihr Deutsche,	Rejoice, then, Germans,
Denn die verruchte Peitsche	For the accursed whip
Hat endlich ausgeknallt.	Has finally cracked its last.
Seht Frankreichs Kreaturen,	Behold the creatures of France!
Sie machten Deutschlands Fluren	They turned Germany's fields
Zum blutigen Altar!	Into a bloody altar.
Die gierige Hyäne	For more than twenty years
Frass Hermanns edle Söhne	The greedy hyena
Durch mehr als zwanzig Jahr.	Devoured Germany's noble sons.
Es wurden Millionen	Millions were terrified
Vom Donner der Kanonen	And made wretched
Zum Jammer aufgeschreckt,	By the thunder of the canons.
Es lag auf Städt' und Flecken	Upon towns and villages
Verwüstung, Todesschrecken,	Lay devastation, and the horror of death,
Vom Satan ausgeheckt.	Plotted by Satan.
[. . .]	[. . .]
Die Menschheit zu erretten	The band of brothers was formed
Von ihren Sklavenketten,	To rescue mankind
Entstand das Bruderband,	From its chains of slavery.
Franz, Wilhelm, Alexander	Franz, Wilhelm, Alexander
Wetteifern mit einander	Vie with each other
Zum wohl furs Vaterland	To do good for the fatherland.
[. . . 2 . . .]	[. . . 2 . . .]
Der Kampf ist nun entschieden,	The struggle is now decided.
Bald, bald erscheint der Frieden	Soon peace will come,
In himmlischer Gestalt.	In heavenly guise.
Drum jubelt hoch, ihr Deutsche,	Rejoice, then, Germans,
Denn die verruchte Peitsche	For the accursed whip
Hat einmal ausgeknallt.	Has finally cracked its last.

ANONYMOUS/UNKNOWN

*This is the first of Schubert's nineteen solo settings of an anonymous poet. See Anonymous/
Unknown for a chronological list of all the songs for which the poets are unknown.*

This merry little string-accompanied victory song in lilting compound time was composed by
Schubert in the autumn of 1813 as an overjoyed reaction to the victory of the Allies (the above-
named Franz of Austria, Wilhelm of Prussia and Alexander of Russia) at the battle of Leipzig
between 16 and 19 October 1813. The work was written almost exactly a year before *Gretchen
am Spinnrade* D118 saw the light of day. It is probable that the composer himself was the singer

and that he was accompanied by his brothers and father on Violin I, Violin II and Violoncello. At that time there was no piano in the Schubert household. The first violin part is the only one that shows any need for virtuosity as it scampers around the stave in gleeful high spirits and Schubert himself may have taken this on instead of the vocal line. The cello part is almost comically easy and was perhaps conceived for the composer's brother Ignaz. The poem gives an accurate idea of the resentment against the French that had long simmered among the good-natured Viennese. The first verse of the poem was set as an unaccompanied trio (*see Verschwunden sind die Schmerzen* D88). The authorship of the anonymous poem has sometimes been ascribed to Schubert, but the mastery of rhyme and metre here and the rough and ready popular vein is simply not the sixteen-year-old composer's style. The poem shows a sophisticated if cynical grasp of history and is typical of the works to be found in the press of the period. Of the eight strophes printed in AGA and NSA we print above 1, 2, 3, 5 and 8.

Autograph:	University Library of Lund, Sweden
First edition:	Published as part of the AGA in 1895 (P706)
Subsequent editions:	AGA XX 583: Vol. 10/72; NSA IV: Vol. 14b/188
Discography and timing:	Fischer-Dieskau —
	Hyperion I —
	Hyperion II

AUF DEN TOD EINER NACHTIGALL (I)   On the death of a nightingale
(HÖLTY) **D201** [H101]
(Fragment) F♯ minor   25 May 1815

(11 bars)

See following entry for poem and translation

LUDWIG CHRISTOPH HÖLTY (1748–76); poem written in 1771. Adapted for publication in
1804 by JOHANN HEINRICH VOSS (1751–1826)

*This is the seventh of Schubert's twenty-three Hölty solo settings (1813–16). See the poet's
biography for a chronological list of all the Hölty settings.*

On 24 May 1815 the composer's love affair with Hölty's texts was suddenly interrupted by the first day's work on the Third Symphony D200, a piece that he finished in the middle of July. But the very day after Schubert had begun this large task he returned to this song, one of a number of fragments and pieces not completed for one reason or another, which are part of his output. In some instances there is not enough material to amplify such sketches into credible performing versions. There are a number of cases, however (and this song is one), where the music is so nearly complete, and where the composer's intentions for finishing the work are so clear, that it seems unforgivable to relegate it to the role of musicological curiosity. Completion by a modern hand seems the lesser of two evils.

The manuscript of this song has disappeared, but Schubert's brother Ferdinand made a copy of it; we owe to Reinhard Van Hoorickx its publication in 1970 in the *Revue Belge de Musicologie*. The composer's original vocal line peters out only in the penultimate bar of the melody and so only three (rather uncontroversial) notes are supplied for the singer. The original piano part stops three bars earlier, after the word 'wenn' in the phrase 'Wenn ich am Bach' (at the end of b. 8). Van Hoorickx provided a prelude and five bars of accompaniment (not printed in the NSA of course). The key is F sharp minor (the gently elegiac slow movement of Mozart's A major Piano Concerto, K488, comes to mind) and the beautiful melody is underpinned by the composer's favourite dactylic rhythm. F sharp is a tonality that Schubert often associates with death and the gentle or ghostly shadows and echoes of remembrance (cf. *Schwestergruss* D762 or *Totengräber-Weise* D869). The second version of this song, D399 (1816) is entirely different and arguably less distinguished.

Autograph:	Missing or lost
First edition:	Completed and published by Reinhard Van Hoorickx in *Revue Belge de Musicologie* in 1970 and then in Volume 10 of NSA in 2002 (P843)
Subsequent editions:	Not in Peters; Not in AGA; NSA IV: Vol. 10/264
Discography and timing:	Fischer-Dieskau —
	Hyperion I 10[8]
	Hyperion II 6[21] 2'41 Martyn Hill

← *Seufzer D198*   *Liebeständelei D206* →

AUF DEN TOD EINER NACHTIGALL (II)   On the death of a nightingale
(HÖLTY) **D399** [H264]
A major   13 May 1816

Traurig. Sehr langsam

Sie ist da - hin, die Mai - en - lie - der tön - te,

(38 bars)

Sie ist dahin, die Maienlieder tönte,
  Die Sängerin,
Die durch ihr Lied den ganzen Hain
    verschönte,
  Sie ist dahin!
Sie, deren Ton mir in die Seele hallte,
  Wenn ich am Bach,

She is no more, the songstress
  Who warbled May songs,
Who adorned the whole grove with her singing.

  She is no more!
She whose notes echoed in my soul,
  When I lay among flowers

Der durch Gebüsch im Abendgolde wallte,	By the brook that flowed through the undergrowth
Auf Blumen lag!	In the golden light of evening.

Sie gurgelte, tief aus der vollen Kehle,	From the depths of her full throat
Den Silberschlag:	She poured forth her silver notes;
Der Widerhall in seiner Felsenhöhle	The echo answered softly
Schlug leis' ihn nach.	In the rocky caves.
Die ländlichen Gesäng' und Feldschalmeien	Rustic melodies and pipers' tunes
Erklangen drein;	Mingled with her song,
Es tanzeten die Jungfrau'n ihre Reihen	As maidens danced
Im Abendschein.	In the glow of evening.

[. . .]   [. . .]

Sie horchten dir, bis dumpf die Abendglocke	They listened until the village angelus
Des Dorfes klang,	Tolled dully,
Und Hesperus, gleich einer goldnen Flocke,	And the evening star emerged from the clouds
Aus Wolken drang;	Like a golden snowflake;
Und gingen dann im Wehn der Maienkühle	Then they went to their cottage
Der Hütte zu,	In the cool May breeze,
Mit einer Brust voll zärtlicher Gefühle,	Their hearts full of tender feeling
Voll süsser Ruh.	And sweet peace.

LUDWIG CHRISTOPH HÖLTY (1748–1776); poem written in 1771. Adapted for publication in 1804 by JOHANN HEINRICH VOSS (1751–1826)

This is the fourteenth of Schubert's twenty-three Hölty solo settings (1813–16). See the poet's biography for a chronological list of all the Hölty settings.

The first version of this song (D201) was composed in May 1815. The poem is typical of the thoughtful Hölty texts that appealed to the composer in that year. This lyric must have haunted Schubert, not only because of its beauty but because he felt that he had failed in the setting of it. He left D201 incomplete and its official status as a fragment (in fact there is not a great deal missing) has denied a touching little song a place in the canon. When he came to set the text again he opted for the same gentle movement (two in a bar with flowing triplet accompaniment) that he had used for a number of other 1816 songs such as *Lied* (*Ins stille Land*) D403 and *Winterlied* D401. *Auf den Tod einer Nachtigall* also shares a key with these two songs, the same mournful tonality that the composer was to use for the laments of the bitter and crazed harper from Goethe's *Wilhelm Meister*. (*Auf den Tod einer Nachtigall* was written on the same double sheet of paper – and on probably the same day – as *Winterlied*, *Frühlingslied* D398, and *Die Knabenzeit* D400, all of these Hölty settings.)

The song has a seamless vocal line with only one quaver rest in thirty-six bars; this holds together the syntax of the poem's phrases while never giving the singer pause for breath. The rhythm of the vocal line is deliberately drab. There are, however, glimmers of consolation, and the modulation into the C major of happier days at 'durch ihr Lied den ganzen Hain verschönte' (bb. 11–15) is noteworthy, as is the dotted quaver and semiquaver melisma at the end of the same phrase – the only moment when there is a touch of rhythmic liveliness in a grove of unadorned crotchets and listless quavers. The mood of the whole of Schubert's little song is

somewhat bleak. Whether it is an improvement on the first setting in F sharp minor is debatable, although a singer at ease in the seemingly improvised spontaneity of Schubert's arioso style
can make an eloquent case for this song. For some inexplicable reason, probably the speed of
copying, in this second version Schubert makes the fifth line of the poem's first verse end with
'hallten' instead of 'hallte' (thus disturbing the rhyme with 'wallte' in the next line). This must
have been an oversight.

Autograph:	Library of Congress, Washington
First edition:	Published as part of the AGA in 1895 (P636)
Subsequent editions:	Not in Peters; AGA XX 218: Vol. 4/98; NSA IV: Vol. 10/90
Bibliography:	Einstein 1951, p. 135
	Fischer-Dieskau 1977, p. 59
Discography and timing:	Fischer-Dieskau I 7[8] 1'30
	Hyperion I 18[5]
	Hyperion II 14[16] 3'33 Peter Schreier

← *Frühlingslied* D398   *Die Knabenzeit* D400 →

AUF DEN WILDEN WEGEN
See also ERNST SCHULZE

In the Hyperion Schubert Edition this group of Schulze settings is sung by Peter Schreier, with
the provisional title above ('On the Wild Paths'), a phrase taken from the song *Auf der Bruck*.
    The order of this putative 'cycle' created for this recording is as follows:

Auf der Bruck D853 [G or A flat major]
Um Mitternacht D862 [B flat major]
O Quell, was strömst du rasch und wild D874 [G major]
Der liebliche Stern D861 [G major]
Im Jänner 1817 (Tiefes Leid) D876 [E minor]
Im Walde D834 [B flat minor]
Im Frühling D882 [G major]
Lebensmut D883 [B flat major]
Über Wildemann D884 [D minor]
An mein Herz D860 [A minor]

The sequence in which Schubert wrote the songs cannot be ascertained; it is possible that D882,
D883 and D884 form an intentional sequence. However the order in which the poems appear
in their poetic source is not best suited for performance: *Im Jänner 1817 (Tiefes Leid)* as a
concluding song is not effective and neither is the juxtaposition of the similarly paced *Auf der
Bruck* and *An mein Herz*. A chronological approach may succeed, however, with the interpolation of readings of poems from Schulze's *Poetisches Tagebuch* that Schubert chose not to set. The
tonalities of the songs (two in B flat and two in G) also raise problems with repetitive key juxtapositions. The tonal relationships in the above order have been arranged so that the 'cycle' (or
rather group of songs) may be performed with, or without, the fragment *O Quell, was strömst
du rasch und wild*.

As *Über Wildemann* was in all likelihood Schubert's last Schulze song, performers may prefer to end the group with this, placing *An mein Herz* after *Im Jänner 1817 (Tiefes Leid)*. A number of the Schulze songs can be performed by female singers in recital, although *Auf der Bruck, Im Walde, Lebensmut* and *Über Wildemann* seem suited exclusively to tenors and baritones. A shared performance of the complete Schulze songs between two singers would be as pointless as it would be in *Winterriese*, defeating the object of indicating the poet's single-minded devotion to the tormented memory of a failed romantic attachment.

AUF DER BRUCK (Auf der Brücke) At Bruck [overlooking Göttingen] (On
(SCHULZE) OP. 93 NO. 2, **D853** [H560]   the bridge)

The song exists in two versions, the second of which is discussed below:
(1) March or August 1825; (2) September 1827?

(1) 'Geschwind'   G major   **C**   [148 bars]

(2) A♭ major

Frisch trabe sonder Ruh und Rast, mein gutes Ross,

Frisch trabe sonder Ruh und Rast,	Trot briskly on, my good horse,
Mein gutes Ross, durch Nacht und Regen!	Without pause for rest, through night and rain!
Was scheust du dich vor Busch und Ast	Why do you shy at bush and branch
Und strauchelst auf den wilden Wegen?	And stumble on the wild paths?
Dehnt auch der Wald sich tief und dicht,	Though the forest stretches deep and dense
Doch muss er endlich sich erschliessen,	It must at last open up,
Und freundlich wird ein fernes Licht	And a distant light will greet us warmly
Uns aus dem dunkeln Tale grüssen.	From the dark valley.
Wohl könnt' ich über Berg und Tal[1]	I could cheerfully speed over mountain and valley
Auf deinem schlanken Rücken fliegen	On your lithe back,
Und mich am bunten Spiel der Welt,	And enjoy the world's varied delights,
An holden Bildern mich vergnügen.	Its fair sights.
Manch Auge lacht mir traulich zu	Many an eye smiles at me affectionately,
Und beut mir Frieden, Lieb' und Freude.	Offering peace, love and joy.
Und dennoch eil' ich ohne Ruh	And yet, restlessly, I hasten
Zurück, zurück zu meinem Leide.	Back to my sorrow.
Denn schon drei Tage war ich fern	For three days now I have been far
Von ihr, die ewig mich gebunden,	From her to whom I am eternally bound;
Drei Tage waren Sonn' und Stern	For three days sun and stars,
Und Erd' und Himmel mir verschwunden.	Earth and heaven, have vanished for me.

[1] Schulze writes 'Berg und *Feld*'.

Von Lust und Leiden, die mein Herz	Of the joy and sorrow which, when I was with her,
Bei ihr bald heilten, bald zerrissen,	Now healed, now tore my heart,
Fühlt' ich drei Tage nur den Schmerz,	I have for three days felt only the pain.
Und ach! die Freude musst' ich missen!	Alas, the joy I have had to forgo!
Weit sehn wir über Land und See[2]	We watch the bird fly far away over land and sea
Zur wärmern Flur den Vogel fliegen;	To warmer pastures.
Wie sollte denn die Liebe je	How, then, should love ever
In ihrem Pfade sich betrügen?	Be deceived in its course?
Drum trabe mutig durch die Nacht!	So trot bravely on through the night!
Und schwinden auch die dunkeln Bahnen,	Though the dark tracks may vanish,
Der Sehnsucht helles Auge wacht,	The bright eye of longing is awake,
Und sicher führt mich süsses Ahnen.	And sweet presentiment guides me safely onwards.

ERNST SCHULZE (1789–1817); poem written 25 July 1814

This is the second of Schubert's ten Schulze solo settings (1825–6). See the poet's biography for a chronological list of all the Schulze settings. An outline of a suggested performing version for a Schulze cycle is listed under 'Auf den wilden Wegen'.

Schulze penned this poem on 25 July 1814 at a lookout point on a hilltop above Göttingen known as 'die Bruck'. There has been a great deal of confusion about the song's title because the first edition, issued in Graz, was entitled *Auf der Brücke*. The addition of an umlaut and an extra 'e' changes the locale from a specific place in Germany to 'on the bridge'. It is still not clear whether this was something Schubert intended (perhaps not wishing his song to be tied down to a pinpoint on the map of Prussia) or if it was the Styrian publisher Kienreich's idea, or a mistake. Given that Schubert altered some of the other Schulze titles, presumably wishing to universalize their significance beyond specific dates and places, it is possible that he approved of a change that was easy to effect, and perhaps rendered the text easier to understand than the original. It also places the protagonist in a place that is both metaphorical and physical; it does not take long to cross a bridge on horseback at full gallop – 'quite a long bridge given the time it takes to perform the song', as Leo Black crisply observes. Nevertheless, at a stretch this bridge might also signify a dividing line between the opposing banks of disappointment and fulfilment, past and future. It could lead either to happiness or to dark and uncharted regions of the spirit.

The question of the title remains open; Reed prints 'Brücke' but the NSA opts for 'Bruck'. (The latter title has been known to many generations using both the AGA and the Peters Edition, and it is true to the poet.) Die Bruck was the final stop on a three-day journey through the Eichsfeld which the poet made that summer. Two days earlier he had written a poem in Bodungen near Nordheim. These two places lie some distance apart and the poet may have conceived the second poem as he galloped through the wild country terrain. The strong iambic rhythm suggests Schulze's determination (strong downbeats thundering through the undergrowth) to reach Göttingen where his beloved lives. For the background to this extraordinary relationship *see* the poet's entry; the story of his obsession with Adelheid Tychsen comes as a surprise to many enthusiasts. Schubert chose not to incorporate this song into any kind of cycle; as a result, generations of singers, not over-concerned with the implications of the Schulze settings as a whole, have taken its musical energy at face value (without burrowing too deeply into the desperation beneath the surface) and performed this song with relish and a gung-ho optimism.

[2] Schubert has reordered the strophe and changed Schulze's original: lines 5–8 as printed above were originally 1–4; lines 1–4 as printed above were 5–8.

This is surely because *Auf der Bruck* is one of the most famous warhorses in the Schubert canon and amateur performers have always felt greatly exhilarated simply getting through it. Gerald Moore used to say that the repeated quaver chords in the pianist's right hand (nearly 150 bars of them) were more tiring to play than the notorious triplets of *Erlkönig*. *Auf der Bruck* is only superficially related to this equestrian masterpiece, as well as to the other famous Schubertian horse-ride, *Willkommen und Abschied* D767. In that song Goethe was speeding on horseback to see Friederike Brion in the Alsatian town of Sesenheim; Schulze had no real hope of being similarly well received by Adelheid Tychsen. In a moment of frankness at the end of the second verse he confesses that he is returning not to joy but to sorrow – 'Zurück, zu meinem Leide' (bb. 61–5). With his almost infallible instinct for empathizing with the deeper resonances of poetry, Schubert understands that the journey of this 'gutes Ross' and its rider is a fruitless quest for peace but that the narrator is trying to keep his spirits up nevertheless. The music is composed accordingly in a circle rather than a straight line: in *Auf der Bruck* there is little sense of starting at one point and actually getting anywhere. (Compare the night ride in *Erlkönig* and how the music moves us forward with it in time and place towards the final catastrophe.) Here the singer seems trapped in a musical web like the Flying Dutchman.

Schulze's journey takes place in the mind, and Schubert fixes it in a repetitive strophic form that matches the obsessive nature of the words. No matter what route the rider tries, he finds himself back at the piano ritornello which is followed by a vocal line on a rising A flat arpeggio (first heard in bb. 10–12) that appears to try to fight its way out of a straitjacket. In this modified strophic form, each one of the four verses begins with the same music for the first four lines of poetry; there is a minor-key adaptation of this music in Verse 3 (bb. 78–9), prompted by imagery of the eclipse of sun and stars. Various excursions lead us hither and thither but we always return to more or less the same place and the grim, forced jollity of the ritornello. Despite the legendary difficulty of the piano's right-hand repetitions, it is the left that holds the reins of power: in a quasi-canon of staccato crotchets at the half bar it echoes the vocal line obsessively, seeming to nudge, stalk, drive the singer forward with jagged spurs. The left hand is the song's driving force, not only in the octaves that thunder out the interludes between verses, but in the subtle way in which it undermines the superficial optimism of the top line; as such one could think of it as the voice of the poet's unconscious. It is seldom in Schubert's songs that you will find a bass line as deep as at 'Dehnt auch der Wald sich tief und dicht' (Verse 1, bb. 21–6), word painting of a high, or here, low, order. At 'Manch Auge lacht mir traulich zu / Und beut mir Frieden' (Verse 2) the bass G flat which clouds the A flat tonality leads the singer on, as if inviting him into the forbidden territory of another key, before erupting into a rumble of warning (bb. 52–7). Schulze's propensity for womanizing leads us to speculate whether the friendly eyes he mentions smile with a professional twinkle. (We know the bitter outcome of what was said to be Schubert's acceptance of such an offer two years earlier, and the heavy price he paid.)

The music seems to waver here, half pulled into D flat; but the obsession for Adelheid, the girl in Göttingen, is stronger, and we turn our gaze once more to the enforced purity of the tonic. Tiny word-setting felicities abound; thus the implicitly violent implication of 'bald zerrissen' (bb. 87–8) is followed by a bar's interlude where the accompaniment is torn from one tessitura to another, and with it the voice. The piano writing for the last line of this verse ('Und ach! die Freude musst' ich missen') pushes its way through a thicket of flats and double flats and this, combined with the high-lying vocal line, powerfully suggests the cry for help of a lost soul. The stormy interlude between verses 3 and 4 (bb. 96–103) is different from the others in that it struggles to take new directions, but, governed by a fixation stronger than its longing for freedom, it returns to the home key for the final verse. For this, Schubert reverses the order of Schulze's last two quatrains, presumably because he relishes the chance to play with the imagery of 'Der Sehnsucht helles Auge wacht' in extended and repetitive musical peroration and also because he did not wish to end the song with the question of 'Wie sollte denn die Liebe je / In ihrem Pfade sich betrügen?' The line 'Und sicher führt mich süsses Ahnen' gives a more upbeat ending, at least on a temporary basis; the word 'Ahnen' providing a beautiful vowel for two elongated vocal cadences (bb. 126–7, and bb. 135–6). The optimistic note struck here, coming after such recent confessions of despair, strikes a false note, but poet and singer are allowed to persist in their belief that all will work out for the best. The composer and pianist know better. The postlude proves we are in the same old place of self-delusion; like Alice in Wonderland we have to run in order to stay in the same place. Ominous staccati falling in sequences deep in the bass seem to take a grim glee in sounding the knell of Schulze's hopes. The horse whose name might be Obsession never comes to a halt at this elusive destination. Two final chords, in tempo, show us that we have merely lost sight of him as he slips over the horizon.

The NSA publishes a 'first version' of the song in G major. It is likely that this was the original key and that Schubert revised the tonality to A flat major – suitable for tenor – when he wrote out the fair copy for the publisher Kienreich in 1827. The G major version in the NSA also contains a certain amount of ornamentation (printed as ossias) that probably goes back to the singer Vogl. The G major version in the middle voice volume of the Peters Edition is simply a transposition of the A flat version.

Autograph:	In private possession (second version)
Publication:	First published as Op. 93 no. 2 by Diabelli, Vienna in 1835 (P308; first version)
	First published as Op. 90 no. 2 by J. A. Kienreich, Graz in May 1828; subsequently corrected to Op. 93 no. 2 in publication of first version (P157; second version)
Subsequent editions:	Peters: Vol. 2/176; AGA XX 477: Vol. 8/106; NSA IV: Vol. 5a/28 & Vol. 5b/214; Bärenreiter: Vol. 3/165
Bibliography:	Black 2003, pp. 117 & 145
	Capell 1928, pp. 215–16
	Einstein 1951, p. 304
	Youens 1996, pp. 267–72
Discography and timing:	Fischer-Dieskau II 7[7] 3'32
	Hyperion I 18[13]
	Hyperion II 29[15] 4'44 Peter Schreier

←— *Des Sängers Habe* D832   *Im Walde* D834 —→

AUF DER DONAU   On the Danube
(MAYRHOFER) OP. 21 NO. 1, **D553** [H365]
E♭ major – F♯ minor   April 1817

(66 bars)

Auf der Wellen Spiegel	Upon the waves' mirror
Schwimmt der Kahn.	Floats our boat;
Alte Burgen ragen	Old castles tower up
Himmelan;	Toward heaven,
Tannenwälder rauschen	Pine forests rustle
Geistergleich—	Ghost-like,
Und das Herz im Busen	And the hearts
Wird uns weich.	In our bosoms melt.
Denn der Menschen Werke	For man's work
Sinken all';	Fails ever:
Wo ist Turm, wo Pforte,[1]	Where is tower, where gate,
Wo der Wall,	Where wall,
Wo sie selbst, die Starken?	Where are they, these strong men?
Erzgeschirmt,	Clad in armour,
Die in Krieg und Jagden	They stormed forth
Hingestürmt.	In war and in hunt.
Trauriges Gestrüppe	Sad undergrowth
Wuchert fort,	Proliferates,
Während frommer Sage	While the strength
Kraft verdorrt.	Of pious words fades:
Und im kleinen Kahne	And in the small boat,
Wird uns bang—	We become timid:
Wellen droh'n, wie Zeiten,	Waves, like Time,
Untergang.	Threaten impending doom.

JOHANN MAYRHOFER (1787–1836)

This is the twenty-fifth of Schubert's forty-seven Mayrhofer solo settings (1814–24). See the poet's biography for a chronological list of all the Mayrhofer settings.

In recent years this has become one of the most frequently performed of all Schubert songs for lower voice. Like the other two songs published as part of Op. 21 (*Der Schiffer* D536 and *Wie Ulfru fischt* D525), it is printed in the bass clef and designated as a bass song by the composer on the title page of the first edition. Basses and baritones are usually pleased to perform a Schubert song in its original key. (*Auf der Donau* is the first in a collection of bass voice songs, twenty-seven items in all, printed by Bärenreiter as Volume 17 of the edition of the NSA issued for singers' use.)

Mayrhofer is here typically pessimistic; this is surely not the mood in which most people would find themselves on a Danube excursion. The song is portentous from the very beginning; there is no lilt of pleasurable barcarolle about the movement of these semiquavers, and the easy rippling that spreads from left-hand octaves on the first beat of each bar is deceptively calm. This opening section is twelve bars long (the first two lines of the poem) and immediately establishes the depth of the river; mirrored in this is the height of castles that tower over the water. At the mention of a pine forest full of ghostly echoes (b. 13) the right hand rustles in

---

[1] Mayrhofer writes 'Wo ist Turm *und* Pforte'. For an explanation of the background to these alternative Mayrhofer readings see Editorial Note at the beginning of Johann MAYRHOFER.

mysterious oscillation, and the water music is transferred to the depths of the bass clef. The hairpin dynamics of these grumbling semiquavers emphasize the poet's disquiet and foreboding. By now we are in the remote key of C flat major; the phrase about the poet's heart melting in his breast is hardly a description of delight or pleasure, but a shudder that is the result of something déjà vu. Other members of the party onboard may be enjoying the scenery, but Mayrhofer, the disaffected imperial censor, foretells disaster for contemporary times by drawing a lesson from history.

The second strophe draws historical pictures that put us in mind of some of Schumann's Eichendorff *Liederkreis* songs (Op. 39), *Auf einer Burg* in particular, and also his Heine setting *Berg' und Burgen* (Op. 24 no. 7) – that poet's Rhine counterpart of Mayrhofer's unsettling journey on the Danube. The power of the castle-building strong men from the twelfth century, as well as their decline and fall, is announced by left-hand trills, the submerged echoes of glories long past. As in the song *Der Schäfer und der Reiter* D517, written in the same month, Schubert uses such trills partly as historical stylization; for him they signify medieval minstrelsy striking up in hollow praise of warriors of yore. At 'die Starken' (bb. 28–9) the key signature switches from three flats to three sharps, from E flat major to F sharp minor; there have been so many extra accidentals that the burden of all those flats forces a sea (or river) change, a tonal crumbling that reflects the demise of both architecture and hope – we feel ourselves drawn into a far more pessimistic mindset.

The singer asks what has become of that armour-clad race of Titans and their once-besieged strongholds? It is a terrible warning to the oligarchs of the present that the visible and ruined traces of that gruesome time now seem perfectly harmless, even picturesque, to the river tourists. A year after this song was composed the English poet Shelley observed that the tyrranical Egyptian, Ozymandias, had once been as terrifying as his statue's inscription ('Look on my works, ye Mighty, and despair!') and yet three thousand years later his effigy lay as rubble, his name an empty threat. *Sic transit gloria.* Having lived through the enlightened reign of Josef II, Mayrhofer felt himself betrayed and endangered by the regime under which he was now forced to exist, but he knew Metternich's power, in the broader scheme of things, was only temporary. Schubert matches and extends the poet's vehement rhetoric by adding (bb. 35–6) the exclamation 'wo'? (where?) on a high C sharp, fortissimo, and again, 'wo'?', an octave lower at the beginning of the next bar – amplifying the text in order to immortalize the very tone of voice and expression of the poet. We know this because Mayrhofer also appears in the verses of Eduard von Bauernfeld's *Ein Buch von uns Wienern*, published in 1858. Bauernfeld describes how Mayrhofer, normally taciturn, holds the company spellbound; 'foaming with clenched fists', he foretells the fall of all tyrants in a corruscating display of emotion. The ghost of that kind of inflamed outburst lingers like a dark shadow in the central section of this song.

Rage subsides, and a complete bar's rest clears the air. We return to the accompanying semiquavers of the opening, though still in F sharp minor. The images and sights of this Danube journey all refer to decay and death. The end of the song is utterly desolate. The voice plunges like a sun setting on man's puny works and destiny. The chordal alternations of the postlude are a minor-key version of that to *Nacht und Träume* D827; here they signify bad dreams and waking nightmares. Mayrhofer often used the stick of classical antiquity with which to beat his contemporaries, but here he sets his parable in the dawn of Austrian history. Bauernfeld described the poet wildly addressing his friends, transfigured by his belief in the triumph of truth and light. This poem, however, finds the unhappy censor on a darker day. The little people are sucked into the vortex and destroyed before their puny lives can make a difference. On this sightseeing excursion even the waves on the Danube seem to threaten destruction. Admirers of the modern German cinema will remember that Oliver Hirschbiegel's film describing the last days of the Third Reich in Hitler's bunker had the title *Untergang*, the same emotive word with which

Mayrhofer ends his poem, the final syllable chillingly set by Schubert on a hollow F sharp, among the lowest notes in all his songs.

It is significant that when *Auf der Donau* was published (together with two others on water themes) as his Op. 21, Schubert dedicated the set to the poet. This was in 1823, the period of the composer's illness when he and Mayrhofer were said to be estranged. (It is possible that because of this personal rift, Schubert's name was absent from the subscription list for the privately printed Mayrhofer *Gedichte* of 1824 – although the composer was a lifelong borrower, rather than buyer, of books.) It is possible that the dedication of this handsome opus was meant as Schubert's peace offering to his old friend.

The castle of Greifenstein, illustration from *Vesta* (1835).

The almanac *Vesta*, published in Vienna in 1835, has an unsigned article about Schloss Greifenstein on the banks of the Danube, in those days some five hours' journey from the capital city. A strophe from Mayrhofer's poem heads this essay. It is possible that Greifenstein and its locale was the poet's inspiration for *Auf der Donau*. The article states that Leopold the Virtuous, Duke of Austria, imprisoned Richard the Lionheart here and that English visitors, knowing Scott's *Ivanhoe*, would take away splinters of wood from the prison where they believed the Plantagenet king had been incarcerated. *Vesta's* contributor is here almost certainly confusing Greifenstein with nearby Dürnstein.

Autograph:	Missing or lost
First edition:	Published as Op. 21 no. 1 by Sauer & Leidesdorf, Vienna in 1823 (P41)

Dedicatee:	Johann Mayrhofer
Publication reviews:	*Allgemeine Musikalische Zeitung* (Leipzig), No. 26 (24 June 1824), col. 425–8 [Waidelich/Hilmar Dokumente I No. 282; Deutsch Doc. Biog. No. 479]
Subsequent editions:	Peters: Vol. 4/24; AGA XX 317: Vol. 5/92; NSA IV: Vol. 1/148; Bärenreiter: Vol. 1/118
Bibliography:	Black 2003, p. 59
	Capell 1928, pp. 60 & 138–9
	Fischer-Dieskau 1977, p. 97
	Newbould 1997, p. 147
	Porter 1961, pp. 129–30
	Youens 1996, pp. 187–94
Discography and timing:	Fischer-Dieskau II 1[4] 2'53
	Hyperion I 2[10]
	Hyperion II 18[16] 3'04 Stephen Varcoe

← *Der Schäfer und der Reiter D517*   *Uraniens Flucht D554* →

AUF DER RIESENKOPPE   On the giant peak

(KÖRNER) **D611** [H396]

D minor – B♭ major   March 1818

(103 bars)

Hoch auf dem Gipfel	High on the summit
Deiner Gebirge	Of your mountains
Steh' ich und staun' ich,	I stand and marvel
Glühend begeistert,	With glowing fervour,
Heilige Koppe,	Sacred peak,
Himmelsanstürmerin!	You that storm the heavens.
Weit in die Ferne	My joyful,
Schweifen die trunknen,	Rapturous gaze
Freudigen Blicke,	Scans the far distance.
Überall Leben,	Everywhere there is life,
Üppiges Streben,	Luxuriant growth,
Überall Sonnenschein.	Everywhere sunshine.
Blühende Fluren,	Meadows in bloom,
Schimmernde Städte,	Sparkling towns,
Dreier Könige	The happy realms
Glückliche Länder	Of three kings:
Schau' ich begeistert,	There I behold with ardour,

Schau' ich mit hoher,	And sublime,
Inniger Lust.	Inward joy.
Auch meines Vaterlands	I behold, too, the borders
Grenze erblick' ich,	Of my homeland,
Wo mich das Leben	Where life bade me
Freundlich begrüsste,	A friendly welcome.
Wo mich der Liebe	Where the sacred longing
Heilige Sehnsucht	Of love
Glühend ergriff.	First glowed within me.
Sei mir gesegnet	Beloved homeland,
Hier in der Ferne,	I bless you
Liebliche Heimat!	From afar.
Sei mir gesegnet,	I bless you,
Land meiner Träume!	Land of my dreams!
Kreis meiner Lieben,	I greet you,
Sei mir gegrüsst!	My loved ones!

THEODOR KÖRNER (1791–1813); poem written in 1809

This is the last of Schubert's sixteen Körner solo settings (1815–18). See the poet's biography for a chronological list of all the Körner settings.

Snezka or 'Schneekoppe' (1,260 metres above sea level) is the highest peak of the Riesengebirge, a ridge of mountains on the present-day Czech-Polish border (37 km long and 25 km wide) often painted by Caspar David Friedrich. One of the most atmospheric of these paintings is *Vor Sonnenaufgang in den Bergen Schlesiens* (reproduced in colour in Volume 2 p. 632 of *Nadler's Literaturgeschichte*, 1938, an indication of the political importance of this area to a Germany under Hitler obsessed with *Lebensraum*). When the athletic young poet Körner tells us that he has climbed the 'Riesenkoppe' he probably means the Schneekoppe, neatly incorporating the name of mountain and mountain-chain in a single word. This was between 22 and 29 July 1809 and here was landscape to inspire poetry – 'it rains sonnets', as the poet wrote to his parents. From these heights he would have been able to see his Saxon homeland as well as Prussian Silesia and Austrian Bohemia where both Schubert's parents were born (Körner never knew about Schubert's ancestry of course, unless the composer had occasion to mention it to him in Vienna). Neither Neudorf (the birthplace of the composer's father, today Vysoká in the Czech Republic), nor Zuckmantel (his mother's birthplace, today Zlaté Hory, also in the Czech Republic) were exactly in the region of the Riesengebirge, but both Franz Theodor Schubert and Elisabeth Schubert, née Vietz, grew up in the shadow of the mountains, he near the Altvatergebirge, she near the Bischofskoppe. Silesians who lived at the crossroads of everybody else's borders were famously patriotic and homesick; it is inconceivable that the young composer had not heard his parents talking about the mountains and scenery associated with their childhood.

The question arises as to why Schubert decided to set this poem when he did; it had been three years since his Körner phase when he set no fewer than thirteen of the poet's texts. The answer is perhaps that it took a new local edition of Körner's works to bring the poet to the composer's attention once again, possibly the paperback edition by Bauer of Vienna in 1817. There the poem appears as the sixth of a set entitled *Erinnerungen aus Schlesien* (Memories from Silesia). The composer had idolized Körner, and these poems, and *Auf der Riesenkoppe* in particular, must

Illustration from Laube's edition of Körner's *Sämmtliche Werke* (1882).

have seemed to unite the poet's past with Schubert's own family history.

The introduction in octaves (like a loud orchestral tutti) strides up the last few steps to the mountain's highest vantage point; we reach the first inversion of the tonic chord in D minor in the forte dynamic (b. 2) followed by a right-hand chord marked piano within the pedalled resonance of the forte, and before the entry of the voice. This sounds like muted strings shimmering in the rarefied atmosphere. The NSA's decision to transfer the piano marking to the beginning of the voice part (b. 3, where the chord in the accompaniment is tied!) seems a misunderstanding of a specialized pianistic effect, but all performers have to beware the harbouring of a preference for the editions which first introduced them to the music they love. There follows a recitative of three bars. The words 'Steh' ich und staun' ich' occasion a repetition of the opening tutti (bb. 5–8), this time a tone lower, a change that suggests knock-down astonishment. The recitative continues, sung with open arms and heart, a mixture of excitement and awe.

For the second verse the key signature changes to D major (b. 16). The broad sweep of this melody is a bird's-eye view over a vast terrain; a benign and noble tune ('Weit in die Ferne') glides over an airy cushion of murmuring quavers in the alto line. As in many descriptions of landscapes, it is impossible to believe that the narrator is rooted to one spot; it is as if he were a camera attached to invisible cranes, hoists or whatever else may support an imagination that fearlessly wings its way into the ether. A change into F major for the piano interlude (bb. 28–31) allows the enraptured narrator, like an eagle who has found a different current of air, to view new vistas from on high. The music for 'Blühende Fluren' (from b. 32) hovers and shimmers; the accompaniment glints with the sparkle of distant lights, an effect that Schubert usually reserves for the depiction of starlight. The three kingdoms seen by the poet are like the 'coloured counties' viewed from Bredon Hill by A. E. Housman's Shropshire Lad. The fourth verse returns for a moment to recitative (bb. 46–8); the poet sings of his fatherland, Saxony, and of the first time he fell in love. What better means could there be of chronicling this new amatory experience than the change of direction in the harmony, a modulation into A major, for 'Wo mich der Liebe / Heilige Sehnsucht / Glühend ergriff'?

At b. 71 the tempo changes to 'Etwas langsam' and the key shifts from A major to B flat major, an unashamed lift of a semitone. Schubert sustains this paean to the homeland in contrast to the trumpet calls and fanfares used by other composers for whom patriotism is more about violence than love. This final section is an *alla breve* hymn – calm and clear-sighted; even the look of the minims on the page implies a lofty, rarefied atmosphere. The fatherland is an empty concept without the cherished friends and family ('Kreis meiner Lieben' bb. 91–2) who live there. The temporary shift into G flat major for this passage has the effect of reining in the boundaries of this enormous vista to encompass only the dimensions of home and hearth, as if the poet's devotion to his family were one kind of patriotism contained within another. There is a classical simplicity and nobility in this closing section about old-fashioned virtues that irresitibly evoke the music, and the spirit, of Josef Haydn who provided Austria with a national anthem. It is notoriously difficult to write nationalistic music that is acceptable to those who are just listeners, rather than inflamed compatriots; even Hugo Wolf fell into tedium and bombast in his *Heimweh* – a scene from another mountain top with a poem by Eichendorff, also a native of Silesia. In his radiant setting Schubert manages to avoid falling into that trap.

Autograph:	Stiftelsen Musikkulturens främjande, Stockholm
First edition:	Published as Book 49 no. 1 of the *Nachlass* by Diabelli, Vienna in *c.* 1850 (P387)
Subsequent editions:	Peters: Vol. 6/68; AGA XX 336: Vol. 5/184; NSA IV: Vol. 12/2
Bibliography:	Black 2003, pp. 120–21
	Fischer-Dieskau 1977, p. 26
	Steblin 1999, p. 243 (for an alternative view of the song's genesis)
	Youens 1996, pp. 144–9
Discography and timing:	Fischer-Dieskau II 1[20] 4'47
	Hyperion I 4[9]
	Hyperion II 20[5] 4'17 Philip Langridge

← *Die Geselligkeit (Lebenslust)* D609   *An den Mond in einer Herbstnacht* D614 →

AUF EINEN KIRCHHOF   On a churchyard
(Schlechta) **D151** [H64]
A major   2 February 1815

(82 bars)

(1) Sei gegrüsst, geweihte Stille,	I greet you, holy stillness
Die mir sanfte Trauer weckt,	Which awakens within me gentle sorrow,
Wo Natur die bunte Hölle	Where kindly nature drapes
Freundlich über Gräber deckt.	Her bright mantle over graves.
(2) Leicht von Wolkenduft getragen	Lightly borne by hazy clouds
Senkt die Sonne ihren Lauf,	The sun sinks in its course.
Aus der finstern Erde schlagen	From the dark earth
Glühend rote Flammen auf!	Glowing red flames leap up!

(3)	Ach, auch ihr, erstarrte Brüder,	Ah, you too, lifeless brothers,
	Habet sinkend ihn vollbracht;	Have sunk down to fulfil your course;
	Sankt ihr auch so herrlich nieder	Did you too, sink so gloriously
	In des Grabes Schauernacht?	Into the dread night of the grave?
(4)	Schlummert sanft, ihr kalten Herzen,	Slumber softly, cold hearts,
	In der düstern langen Ruh',	In your long, sombre peace;
	Eure Wunden, eure Schmerzen	Your wounds, your pain,
	Decket mild die Erde zu!	Are gently covered by the earth!
(5)	Neu zerstören, neu erschaffen	To destroy and to create anew
	Treibt das Rad der Weltenuhr,	The wheel of the world's clock drives on;
	Kräfte, die am Fels erschlaffen,	Forces that languish in the rock
	Blühen wieder auf der Flur!	Blossom again in the meadows.
(6)	Und auch du, geliebte Hülle,	And you too, beloved mortal frame,
	Sinkest zuckend einst hinab,	Will one day sink down, quivering,
	Und erblühst in schönster Fülle	And blossom anew in glorious fullness,
	Neu, ein Blümchen auf dem Grab.	As a flower on the grave.
(7)	Wankst, ein Flämmchen durch die Grüfte,	You will waver, as a flame through the graves.
	Irrest flimmernd durch den Moor,	You will flicker, lost across this moor
	Schwingst, ein Strahl, dich in die Lüfte,	As a shaft of light, you will pierce the air,
	Klingest hell, ein Ton, empor.	As a resonant tone, you will soar upwards.
(8)	Aber du, das in mir lebet,	But you, who live within me,
	Wirst auch du des Wurmes Raub?	Will you, too, fall prey to the worm?
	Was entzückend mich erhebet,	You who exalt and delight me,
	Bist auch du nur eitel Staub?	Are you, too, but vain dust?
(9)	Nein! was ich im Innern fühle,	No! What I feel deep inside me,
	Was entzückend mich erhebt,	That exalts and delights me
	Ist der Gottheit reine Hülle,	Is the pure spirit of the Godhead,
	Ist ihr Hauch, der in mir lebt.	Is His breath, which lives within me.

FRANZ XAVER VON SCHLECHTA (1796–1875)

This is the first of Schubert's six Schlechta solo settings (1815–26). See the poet's biography for a chronological list of all the Schlechta settings.

This song has been denigrated by commentators because it is something of a ragbag, containing samples of all the song techniques Schubert was using in 1815. As a mixture of recitative, aria and arioso it is more audacious than the first Mayrhofer setting, *Am See* D124 from two months earlier. Franz von Schlechta was not as interesting a poet as Mayrhofer and the graveside philosophy of *Auf einen Kirchhof* is clearly the work of a younger man who has not yet questioned the precepts of his strict religious schooling. Schlechta's fiery avowal of faith is among the first poems to be set by Schubert from those of the circle of his contemporaries, although not the first to deal with death and mortality.

   After a spread chord the song opens with a gentle hymn-like melody, a rising scale of four notes prophetic of the opening of the 1816 Uz setting *Die Nacht* D358. The tunefulness of this first verse changes effortlessly and naturally to a new mood for the second, when clouds and sunset (with a downward arpeggio to denote the sinking sun, b. 10) are depicted within the rhythmic haze of recitative. The third verse (from b. 15) changes time signature to § ('Mässig') and quickly reverts to recitative. At the fourth strophe (from b. 21) there is a change of key signature (E major with a marking of 'Langsam' in §), signalling a Mozartian melody with grave 'Magic Flute' formality. This leads to yet more recitative (back to common time, sextuplets briefly illustrate the turning of the big wheel of the world's clock at b. 31) ending with a beautiful cadence on the words 'Blühen wieder auf der Flur' (bb. 33–4 with an added pianistic echo).

The sixth and seventh verses (a section marked 'Mässig geschwind', §, from b. 36) build up to the kind of expansive climax that would have crowned many a ballad by Reichardt; the slightly wayward feeling of these modulations and arpeggios that range across the keyboard is ideal for the image of souls flickering like will-o'-the-wisps across the moor. Shafts of light pierce the mists as the harmonies pass through an arpeggiated thicket of deceptive sharps to the clarity of C major. After 'ein Ton, empor' the representation of soaring tone with a somewhat lame rising arpeggio figure is a device from an earlier age, a last vestige of undigested Zumsteeg; it does not prepare us for the daring of the piece's final recitative (Verse 8). In this music the worm burrows its way purposefully from C to B major, and then writhes up to C sharp major (b. 60).

The fear engendered by this twisting journey is suddenly countermanded with speed and tenacity by the impassioned rebuttal of the god-fearing faithful (marked 'Schnell', from b. 61). The questioning doubt of 'nur eitel Staub', and the context of C sharp major in which it was expressed, are now grandly negated by E naturals in A major arpeggios which are rooted on octaves deep on the keyboard. The pianist's tolling left hand, now a pedal point on A, supports a vocal line that is excitedly vehement. This is prophetic of the peroration of *Hektors Abschied* D312 (also marked 'Schnell' and written eight months later) in which the Trojan Hector proclaims that his love for Andromache is immortal and impervious to Lethe. The finales to both *Hektors Abschied* and *Auf einen Kirchhof* are defiant assertions of belief against all the odds, music of reckless bravery rather than quiet conviction.

The first edition of Schlechta's *Dichtungen*, containing a revised and shortened version of the poem in six strophes, was published in 1824 by which time we may detect the more religiously rigorous influence of Schlechta's friend Franz von Bruchmann and of the deeply Catholic Friedrich von Schlegel.

Autograph:	Wienbibliothek im Rathaus, Vienna (first draft)
First edition:	Published as Book 49 no. 2 of the *Nachlass* by Diabelli, Vienna in *c.* 1850 (P388)
Subsequent editions:	Peters: Vol. 6/69; AGA XX 39: Vol. 2/1; NSA IV: Vol. 7/119; Bärenreiter: Vol. 6/69
Bibliography:	Capell 1928, p. 89
	Fischer-Dieskau 1977, p. 74
Discography and timing:	Fischer-Dieskau I 2[18] 4'00
	Hyperion I 10[2]
	Hyperion II 5[3] 4'38 Martyn Hill

← *Trinklied* D148   *Minona, oder die Kunde der Dogge* D152 →

AUFENTHALT *see SCHWANENGESANG* D957/5

AUFLÖSUNG   Dissolution
(Mayrhofer) **D807** [H548]
G major   March 1824

Verbirg dich, Sonne,   Hide yourself, sun,
Denn die Gluten der Wonne   For the fires of rapture
Versengen mein Gebein;   Burn through my whole being.
Verstummet, Töne,   Be silent, sounds;
Frühlings Schöne   Spring beauty,
Flüchte dich, und lass mich allein!   Flee, and let me be alone!

Quillen doch aus allen Falten   Yet from every recess of my soul
Meiner Seele liebliche Gewalten;   Gentle powers well up
Die mich umschlingen,   And envelop me
Himmlisch singen—   With celestial song.
Geh' unter, Welt, und störe   Dissolve, world, and never more
Nimmer die süssen ätherischen Chöre.   Disturb the sweet ethereal choirs.

JOHANN MAYRHOFER (1787–1836)

This is the forty-sixth of Schubert's forty-seven Mayrhofer solo settings (1814–24). See the poet's biography for a chronological list of all the Mayrhofer settings.

In Book III, chapter 12 of *Wilhelm Meisters Lehrjahre* Goethe uses the word 'Auflösung' as a simple synonym for death. Yet it has many other resonances even if, ultimately, death is Mayrhofer's meaning too. In the *Brockhaus Konversations-Lexicon* for 1820, the leading German encyclopaedia of Schubert's epoch, the first of two entries for the word 'Auflösung' is to do with chemistry, the second with music. The chemical definition, although modern, seems only a step away from the age of magic: 'The process by which two dissimilar substances bind together so that the original substance is separated and a new substance, different to the other two, is formed through new bonds.' The musical definition concerns the resolution of dissonance as well as the naturalization of accidentals. The simmering energy of this music, a bubbling cauldron of harmonic activity, seems nearer to something in the alchemist's laboratory; it certainly suggests that something life-changing is taking place in the crucible of the poet's suffering, not to mention the composer's, in what we know to have been a particularly desperate month in his life. A poem that Schubert had written in May 1823 ends with the words: 'Take my life, my flesh my blood, / Plunge it all in Lethe's flood, / To a purer stronger state / Deign me, Great One, to translate' – in itself a plea that his body, racked by illness, should undergo an 'Auflösung' of a radical kind. The only song remotely like this in the Schubert canon is the Novalis setting, *Nachthymne* D687, another text with a longing for death as a new, transformed life. To hear either of these works for the first time is a moment of discovery for all Schubertians – music that forces us to redefine what we expect from a composer whom we imagine we have fully comprehended.

The piano writing for the opening of *Auflösung* sweeps upwards from the lower reaches of the keyboard, a rhythmic cell made up of a rising arpeggio for the first two beats of the bar; on the third beat there is a shudder of oscillating thirds with a clipped staccato quaver on the fourth. This motif is repeated, ranging through various keys of course, nearly fifty times in the song; only three of its seventy-four bars contain descending accompanimental figurations, and fifteen or so hover transfixed in the same place on the stave. This is music of orchestral scale and inspiration, but it is piano music above all. Thickets of semiquavers harness the energy of every available finger and are at the heart of the song's force field. In composing this music Schubert was offering us a musical demonstration of 'Auflösung' as he understood it, and as defined in Brockhaus. The harmonic writing in this song does indeed offer us 'resolution from dissonance', or 'the necessary stepwise progression of a dissonance into a conforming interval'. Again and again the many sharps and flats of this piece's chromatic harmonies are resolved into naturals – as in the *Vorspiel* where a descending figuration in bb. 3–4 based on diminished seventh harmony finds itself 'aufgelöst' – naturalized and dissolved into waves of G major arpeggios that sweep from one end of the keyboard to the other. Throughout the song excursions into chromatic highways and byways are resolved as the music slips and sinks from its temporary position in and among the black keys to find its release and resolution in an open sea of whites. In a curious way this resolution following chromatic conflict is part of a physical sensation for the pianist; in returning to G major there is a sense of solution as well as resolution, as if the change from one musical state to another were the answer to a problem, a signposted exit. And this is, indeed, a musical analogue for Mayrhofer's triumphant search for an altered state of being.

After six bars of piano introduction the whirring dynamo of the accompaniment is set to generate the birth of an extraordinary vocal line. The voice essays an utterance of cosmic grandeur. The poet-sorcerer emerges as a German Prospero, more powerful than the forces of nature that threaten to engulf him. Unafraid to renounce life entirely, he will choose his moment and manner of going. The major key used in this song is a reflection of the joy, or rather triumph, felt by someone in control of his or her destiny. The depressive (and eventually suicidal) Mayrhofer knew, as A. E. Housman did, the destructive power of a single, self-wielded knife:

I need but stick it in my heart
   And down will come the sky,
And earth's foundations will depart
   And all you folk will die.

Ananchronistic musical comparisons with Wagner come to mind in terms of grandness of scale and audacity, but in the absence of that composer's example we can ascribe the power of this music to the implacable classical rigour of Gluck. In this song Schubert gives musical shape to the poet's self-destructive egocentricity as if Mayrhofer were a great classical figure like Orestes. (In its companion piece, *Abendstern* D806, he gives musical voice to Mayrhofer's insecurity and humility.) *Auflösung* in full swing seems enormous, but in actual fact it is also contained and introspective. Performers who have attempted to place it at the end of the group to generate applause have discovered that it is too disturbing as a piece of music to be a claptrap. Schubert registers the poet's command ('Geh' unter, Welt!') as an intense inward wail, a longing for death that he had probably heard verbalized in real life by his highly strung friend. The sweet ethereal choirs are the sirens of self-delusion that accompany self-immolation. The climactic high A in b. 59 is placed at a deliberately awkward point for the singer, already winded by riding relentless waves of vocal arpeggios with scarcely a pause for breath. The effect looks ecstatic on paper, but in reality this climax can only offer the ecstasy of self-destruction, the enjoyment of power felt by those whose greatest weapon is their own expendability. The poet's pleas (or in this case, imperious demands) for release are a negation of life itself. After this, the rhetoric subsides to a dark, muttering undertone and then the rumbling infinity of silence. One can never forget that this song was composed in the very month that Schubert, his health broken by syphilis, wrote a letter to Kupelwieser in Rome that is his most depressed utterance: '. . . each night on retiring to bed, I hope I may not wake again, and each morning recalls yesterday's grief' (Deutsch 1946, p. 338).

Auflösung is by far the biggest of the four songs written in March 1824 that mark both a return and farewell to the poetry of Mayrhofer after a two-year silence. We shall never know exactly what caused this coldness between old friends; Schubert was otherwise remarkably faithful to members of his circle. The two men had shared a room in the Wipplingerstrasse for eighteen months between 1818 and 1820; it must have seemed to the young composer a very haven of cultivation compared to the aridity of the schoolhouse that was his parental home. Mayrhofer, ten years older than Schubert, was far from being well-to-do, but he had no need to share his space for reasons of impecunity alone. This is a scenario which could encompass anything from Mayrhofer as mentor *in loco parentis* to that of an older man taking advantage of an inexperienced teenager. Josef von Spaun, whose judgement is always to be taken seriously, later warmly attested to the veracity of the former view. Whatever the relationship between Schubert and the poet, Mayrhofer's tastes in literature and philosophy were a force for the good and changed the course of the composer's life.

Fritz Lehner, in his film entitled *Mit meinen heissen Tränen*, conjectures that the composer had gone through a phase of intimacy with Mayrhofer as a younger man but had grown impatient with the importunity of his advances. Those who have read Mayrhofer's poetry (not only the texts set to music) are aware of an integrity and self-control that make the theory of the poet as persistent seducer extremely unlikely. In the new phase of Schubert's life, after the experiences of 1823, the slate was wiped clean of old quarrels and misunderstandings. The fires of *Auflösung*, where the composer temporarily empathizes with the poet's bleak world view, seem to consume and cleanse the petty personal concerns of the past – yet another aspect and definition of the word 'resolution'. The chemical binding together of two dissimilar substances is the brief and explosive reaction between poet and composer, linking them in art and separating them in life. This song, and its aftermath, finds them hurtling, in different directions, towards new and uncharted realms.

The ideal tempo seems to be somewhere in the region of ♩ = 120. The tempo that Pears and Britten adopt for their recording (♩ = 132) has great dramatic fervour, but a febrile atmosphere is created at the expense of the more imposing grandeur required by the composer's cautionary marking, 'Nicht zu geschwind'.

Autograph:	Stiftung des Deutschen Chorwesens, Feuchtwangen, Germany (fair copy)
First edition:	Published as Book 34 no. 1 of the *Nachlass* by Diabelli, Vienna in 1842 (P339)
Subsequent editions:	Peters: Vol. 5/196; AGA XX 460: Vol. 8/20; NSA IV: Vol. 13/140
Bibliography:	Black 2003, pp. 68 & 111 (where he conjectures that 'one relaxation in the Schubert circle was to pass round a hookah loaded with opium and enjoy the supposedly harmless illumination the drugs provided. See also footnote on p. 112 concerning the opinions of Peter Hacks on the drug-taking of the Romantic poets.)

Capell 1928, pp. 204–5
Einstein 1951, p. 303
Fischer-Dieskau 1977, p. 192
Kohlhäufl 1999, p. 300
Youens 1996, pp. 221–7

Discography and timing: Fischer-Dieskau II 6[15]   2'42
Pears-Britten 2[6]   2'07
Hyperion I 11[11]
Hyperion II 29[3]   2'28   Brigitte Fassbaender

← *Der Sieg* D805   *Gondelfahrer* D808 →

AUGENBLICKE IN ELYSIUM *see* DUBIOUS, MISATTRIBUTED AND LOST SONGS

AUGENLIED   Song of the eyes
(MAYRHOFER) **D297** [H340]

The song exists in two versions, the first of which is discussed below:
(1) Early 1817?; (2) Early 1817?

(1)   F major

(104 bars)

(2) 'Mässig'   F major   ¾   [104 bars]

Süsse Augen, klare Bronnen!	Sweet eyes, limpid fountains,
Meine Qual und Seligkeit	My torment and my bliss
Ist fürwahr aus euch gewonnen,[1]	Truly arise from you,
Und mein Dichten euch geweiht.	And my songs I dedicate to you.
Wo ich weile,	Where I linger,
Wie ich eile,	When I hasten,
Liebend strahlet ihr mich an;	You smile upon me, radiant with love;
Ihr erleuchtet,	You illuminate my path,
Ihr befeuchtet,	And moisten it
Mir mit Tränen meine Bahn.	With your tears.

---

[1] Mayrhofer writes 'geronnen'. For an explanation of the background to these alternative Mayrhofer readings see Editorial Note at the beginning of Johann MAYRHOFER.

Treue Sterne, schwindet nimmer,	Faithful stars, never vanish;
Leitet mich zum Acheron!	Lead me to Acheron!
Und mit eurem letzten Schimmer	And with your last glimmer
Sei mein Leben auch entflohn.	May my life, too, fade away.

JOHANN MAYRHOFER (1787–1836)

This is the fourteenth of Schubert's forty-seven Mayrhofer solo settings (1814–24). See the poet's biography for a chronological list of all the Mayrhofer settings.

It was Schubert's friends Josef von Spaun and Franz von Schober who together, eventually, engineered the first encounter between the composer and the famous opera singer Johann Michael Vogl in the spring of 1817. According to Spaun's memoirs the celebrated baritone was little interested and 'took up the nearest sheet of music, containing Mayrhofer's poem *Augenlied*, a pretty, tuneful, but not very significant song. Vogl hummed rather than sang, and then said coldly "Nicht übel!"' (not bad). In time, of course, the singer was to be come a devoted admirer of Schubert's art.

Spaun may have judged the song 'not very significant' (the Schubert enthusiast will understand what he meant) but, by the standards of Schubert's songwriting contemporaries, *Augenlied* is a little jewel – old-fashioned in a Mozartian manner, an undemanding song-baptism for someone inexperienced in 'modern' music. The rippling quaver accompaniment graciously supports a vocal line with just the kind of courtly charm that the singer, something of a composer himself, would have thought appropriate to the text. It is notable too that the range of the song is ideally suited to Vogl's baritone voice, and that the touch of ornamentation at cadences would have been very much to his taste. The classical reference to 'Acheron', river of hell (Mayrhofer could never resist a classical allusion), would have flattered Vogl's reputation as a serious scholar of the classics. Doubtless none of this would have been lost on Schubert's friends who helped him set up the meeting; one can imagine Schober rearranging the pile of music on the piano, leaving *Augenlied* at the top as bait for the big fish.

At the beginning of the music for the poem's third strophe (b. 42) there is a change of tempo ('Geschwinder'). This starlit little dance has something of the mood and movement of the 'Tausend schwebende Sterne' section of Goethe's *Auf dem See* D543. The style is all naïve simplicity; the only ominous touch is the mention of Acheron that occasions a modulation into D minor (bb. 48–9), the key of Don Giovanni's condemnation to the same region, but a very minor event in comparison. Neverthless, the phrase must have appealed to Schubert – we hear it three times in all. The poet's last verse is thus spun out to give more musical substance to the final section. The vocal line becomes less and less demonstrative. At the end of the song we hear a repetition of the phrase 'Sei mein Leben auch entflohn' (from b. 88). The music for this passage dematerializes with great musical charm; the singer's rocking lullaby in quavers yields to minims and crotchets, a fading away as if there were no motivation whatever to live outside the beloved's gaze. The postlude (from b. 100) includes an echo of the voice's closing bars ('auch entflohn'), a touch of Mozartian jauntiness in dotted rhythm that reaffirms an impression of eighteenth-century pastiche.

There are two versions of this song, one in the AGA recorded for the Hyperion Edition, the other, Diabelli's, printed in Peters and marked 'Mässig'. The rather clumsy piano introduction and ornamented accompaniment of the latter suggests a revising hand, and not necessarily Schubert's. The composer affixed his signature to a copy of this second version, but then the good-natured fellow also allowed Vogl to ornament his vocal lines without really approving of them. Perhaps Vogl thought that this song needed his hand to improve it.

Autograph:	Missing or lost
Publication:	First published as part of the AGA in 1895 (P608; first version)
	First published as Book 50 no. 3 of the *Nachlass* by Diabelli,
	Vienna in 1850 (P391; second version)
Subsequent editions:	Peters: Vol. 6/80 (second version); AGA XX 171: Vol. 3/168 (first
	version); NSA IV: Vol. 9/118 (first version), 121 (second version) &
	221 (ornamented version, possibly Vogl's belonging to Anton Schindler)
Discography and timing:	Fischer-Dieskau I 6^3 2'22
	Hyperion I 3^3
	Hyperion II 17^{18} 3'09 Ann Murray

← *Fahrt zum Hades* D526   *Sehnsucht* D516 →

AUS 'DIEGO MANAZARES' (*recte* Manzanares*): ILMERINE (*recte* Almerine)
(Krosigk) **D458** [H286]
F minor – A♭ major   30 July 1816

From 'Diego Manazares': Ilmerine

(23 bars)

Wo irr'st Du durch eisame Schatten der Nacht?

Wo bist Du mein Leben, mein Glück?
Schon sind die Gestirne der Nacht
Aus tauenden Wolken erwacht,
Und ach, der Geliebte kehrt noch nicht zurück!

Why are you wandering through the lonely
   ravines of the night?
Where are you, my life, my happiness?
Already the night stars
Have awoken from their dewy darkness,
And, alas, my beloved has not yet returned.

ERNESTINE VON KROSIGK (1767–1843); poem written in 1804

This is Schubert's only setting of a Krosigk text. See the poet's biography.

This interesting little serenade – and there is nothing else quite like it in all Schubert – has been completely ignored by singers and the commentators. Apart from the *Don Gayseros* cycle D93 (1814), an early set of three songs that tell the tale of Donna Clara's doomed love for a Moorish prince, this is Schubert's only attempt at a Spanish style in his Lieder. The music for *Don Gayseros* is notoriously simple, to the extent that Schubert's authorship has been doubted, but *Aus 'Diego Manazares'* (as far as it goes – it lasts less than a minute) is unquestionably the genuine article. The song's first nine bars even sound convincingly Iberian: offbeat accents in the right hand suggest impulsive southern emotions; left-hand chords, sparking off simulated guitar configurations, accompany the vocal line. As soon as 'Ilmerine' mentions starlight the music moves into throbbing triplets (b. 10) and away from the more fiery regions of F minor; by the time we reach the song's postlude the music has settled into A flat major.

From the earliest days of Schubert scholarship until very recently the author of this text was thought to be Franz von Schlechta, Schubert's contemporary and schoolfriend. The composer himself placed no poet's name on his manuscript. Johann Wolf, the archivist of the publishing firm of Spina, added the name 'Schlechta' to the autograph in 1855; this was only one of many (often accurate) annotations he made to the Schubert songs regarding the dating and authorship of the texts. This information was taken up by Kreissle von Hellborn, Schubert's first biographer, who identified the poet of *Aus Diego Manazares* [*sic*] as 'Freih. v. Schlechta'. Otto Erich Deutsch followed suit in his catalogue, and Walther Dürr in Volume 10 of the NSA (2002) places Schlechta's name unequivocally as the poet, despite the fact that this lyric never appeared in print in any of that poet's writings. (This attribution was subsequently corrected in the *Kritischer Bericht* for Volume 10 (2009).) The poet's six contributions to the Schubert song canon (qv Schlechta) are distributed rather evenly between 1815 and 1826. It was long thought that this was part of a larger literary effort – a play, John Reed suggested, or even an opera libretto.

In fact the author is not Schlechta at all, and with the name Ernestine von Krosigk a new Schubert poet enters the canon. In 2007 I acquired a copy of an obscure almanac – *Egeria, Taschenbuch für das Jahr 1805*, edited by Karl Müchler (poet of several Weber songs) and published in Berlin ('bei Johann Friedrich Unger'). The second item in this book is *Diego Manzanares*, 'translated from the Spanish' (no source given) by Ernestine von Krosigk, 'geboren Krüger'. This story in prose, devoted to the heroic deeds of the noble knight Don Diego Manzanares, runs from p. 47 to p. 82 of the almanac. The great-hearted Manzanares allows Zamet, a captured Moorish soldier of some valour, to return to his beloved, Almerine, daughter of the brave Omar. The spelling of her name is different to the 'Ilmerine' of Schubert's manuscript, but the song she sings as she waits to be reunited with Zamet is identical to the five-line poem set by the composer. There are two further strophes, neither of which fits the music, although with some adjustment (removing the first beats of the vocal line in bb. 15 and 18 – sung to the word 'kehrt' in the first verse – and adding a quaver to the end of each of those two bars) the third strophe of the poem could be made to do so:

Was flüsterst Du quälende Ahnung mir denn;	Why are you whispering distressing words of foreboding?
Ach, dass ich sein Herz wohl verlor?	Ah, have I perhaps lost his heart?
Er könnte vergessen den Bund,	Could he have forgotten the vow
Den oft mir so zärtlich sein Mund	That his lips have often sworn to me so tenderly
In seligen Stunden der Liebe beschwor?	In blissful hours of love?

Aus 'Diego Manzanares' was first issued by J. P. Gotthard, Vienna, 1872, as part of a forty-song collection of hitherto unpublished lieder printed in honour of Schubert's seventy-fifth birthday. It is curious that in this edition the name 'Manzanares' is spelled as we find it in Krosigk when Schubert's autograph, and all subsequent catalogue listings, have 'Manazares'. This is probably because someone working at the publisher knew about the river that runs through Madrid and features in the paintings of Goya, and took an educated guess regarding Diego's true origin. The knowledgeable Johann Peter Gotthard, or one of his employees, might even have known Adolf Jensen's charming setting from Geibel's *Spanisches Liederbuch*, *Am Ufer des Flusses Manzanares*, Op. 21 no. 6, published in 1860. Schubert's misspelling of Manzanares, and that of Almerine, means that he is very unlikely to have had sight of the original source. He clearly worked from a second-hand copy of the poem (and this may indeed have come from Schlechta) where the details of provenance had been hastily, and incorrectly, taken down.

Schubert seems to have conceived this aria in orchestrated terms. John Reed imagines the song's opening figure to be accompanied by 'plucked strings and woodwind'. The postlude could do with an oboe to take over the top line in the final two bars above the throbbing strings. It is a pity that the song is not longer; this might have allowed the composer more time to establish its national character. This tiny flash of light and heat from the imagined south is too brief, too anonymous, to find a place on any but the most unusual of recital programmes, hence my suggestion above that another of Krosigk's verses could be incorporated into performance. This music is a far cry from the convincing Spanish stylizations of Schumann and Wolf who explored the possibilities of pastiche and evocation much more thoroughly. Indeed, by the time this song first appeared in print, Schumann's Spanish-inspired songs and vocal ensembles were already an established part of the repertoire.

Autograph:	Conservatoire collection, Bibliothèque Nationale, Paris
First edition:	Published as No. 25 of *Neueste Folge nachgelassener Lieder und Gesänge* by J. P. Gotthard, Vienna in 1872 (P451)
Subsequent editions:	Not in Peters; AGA XX 242: Vol. 4/146; NSA IV: Vol. 10/198
Bibliography:	Dürr, Introduction to NSA IV Volume 10, pp. XXXI–XXXII
Discography and timing:	Fischer-Dieskau —
	Hyperion I 17^{12}
	Hyperion II 15^{13} 0'58 Lucia Popp

⟵ *An die untergehende Sonne* D457　　　　　　　　　　　　*Pflicht und Liebe* D467 ⟶

AUS HELIOPOLIS *see* HELIOPOLIS I D753 & HELIOPOLIS II D754

AUTOGRAPHS, ALBUMS AND COLLECTIONS

To enter into the study of Schubert's autographs and contemporary copies is to approach the forensic side of Schubert scholarship, and a fascinating and time-consuming process it proves to be.

For the purposes of this book I have attempted to alert the reader to the whereabouts of each of Schubert's song autographs. Many are missing or lost – although any of these might re-emerge at any time. Some are in private possession (another fluid situation as major auctions very occasionally offer significant Schubertian items for sale) but most are in the safe keeping of libraries around the world. As more of these institutions gradually place their holdings online it will be possible for the student or music lover to examine Schubert's autographs at first hand. The main repository of the Schubert song autographs is the former Stadt- und Landesbibliothek in Vienna, now renamed the Wienbibliothek im Rathaus. This library has joined forces with the Österreichische Nationalbibliothek, also in Vienna, to place all its manuscripts online. These are now freely available to users of the Internet who can avail themselves of the opportunity of leafing through these national treasures one by one. The address of this remarkable site where over three hundred Schubert autographs may be viewed instantaneously is www.schubert-online.at.

This still leaves the many autographs in the Gesellschaft der Musikfreunde still to be consulted in person in Vienna, although with the rapid advances of technology this is bound to change to the advantage of the armchair traveller. Outside Vienna the main Schubert song holdings are in Berlin (at the Staatsbibliothek Preussischer Kulturbesitz), at the Bibliothèque Nationale in Paris (comprising the Malherbe collection of manuscripts that was bequeathed to the Paris Conservatoire), the British Library (including items from the Stefan Zweig collection) and the

Pierpont Morgan music library in New York. Other manuscripts emerge in less likely places – a relatively large collection of important material can be found in the University Library of Lund in Sweden, and there are items scattered throughout distinguished libraries in the USA (Harvard, Rochester, Stanford, Yale). Britain can boast the odd treasure in the Bodleian, Oxford or the Fitzwilliam, Cambridge, with an autograph even to be found in the Scottish Record Office in Edinburgh.

COLLECTORS

That all these libraries have such distinguished holdings is the result of careful acquisitions and fortunate bequests over many decades. In the beginning there were powerful collectors whose private Schubertian holdings passed, in due course, into the possession of national institutions. A few people come to mind whose collections were historically important. The first is **Nikolaus von Dumba** (1830–1900), an amateur singer and music lover who was the hugely influential heir to an industrial fortune in Vienna, and who spent his life doing good works on behalf of his native city. He was an out and out Schubertian, a moving spirit in the erection of the composer's statue in the Stadt-park and in the transferral of his remains to a special site in the city cemetery – the grove of honour for musicians in the Zentralfriedhof was purportedly Dumba's idea – as well as in the generous funding of the Breitkopf & Härtel

Nikolaus von Dumba, lithograph by Ignaz Eigner.

Gesamtausgabe in a manner that enabled Eusebius Mandyczewski to do his work unhindered by financial considerations. After the death of the composer's brother Ferdinand in 1859, Dumba bought up Schubert's manuscripts to prevent them from being distributed willy-nilly among hundreds of collectors. He also bought manuscripts from the composer's two nephews, Eduard Schneider and Karl Schubert. In the end he had the biggest collection in private hands, some two hundred items, and these were passed over in part to the City Library, in part (auto-graphs of the symphonies) to the Musikverein. The performer in modern-day Vienna who emerges from the side of the Musikverein building at the stage door will probably return to the Ringstrasse via the Dumba-Strasse, to the left-hand side of the Hotel Imperial.

Other collectors could not hope to possess manuscripts on the scale of the millionaire Dumba. One can list here only a few of the people who collected Schubert manuscripts. The musicologist **Max Kalbeck** (*see* SCHOLARS), Brahms's biographer, was a collector, as was **Johannes Brahms** (1833–1897) himself, and **Robert Schumann** (1810–1856) before him; Schumann owned the third version of *Erlkönig*, the *Grand Duo* for piano duet and the manuscript describing Schubert's dream known as *Mein Traum*. **Max Friedlaender** (*see* SCHOLARS) was also an almost obsessive collector of song manuscripts and Schubertiana although, unlike Dumba, he was not able to ensure his collection's entry into the public domain and most of it was sold by auction in 1930. Other significant names are the Beethoven scholar **Alexander Thayer** (1817–1897) who was a friend of Sir George Grove. In Paris it was the archivist of the Opéra, **Charles-Théodore Malherbe** who was responsible for ensuring that the city was a rich repository of Schubert manuscripts.

In the twentieth century the distinguished collectors include **Louis Koch** in connection with the Floersheim Collection, **Otto Taussig** whose collection is preserved in the Swedish University town of Lund; **Hans Moldenhauer** and the **Wittgenstein Family** whose collections were passed over to the Library of Congress, and the writer and novelist **Stefan Zweig** who substantially enriched the Schubert holdings of the British Library. The collection of **Rudolf Kallir** passed into the possession of the national and city libraries in Vienna.

The only private collection of Schubert manuscripts in modern times that could rival that of Dumba belonged to the wealthy and influential **Hans Peter Wertisch** (1939–1996) in Vienna. His collection of sixty Schubert autographs was the biggest in private hands since Dumba. Wertisch was a strong ally of the Schubertian activities and enthusiasms of Ernst Hilmar and IFSI (*see* SCHOLARS) and, possibly, his early death deprived the city of a Schubert-Stiftung and a number of other initiatives. Wertisch's collection of song manuscripts is now mainly in the possession of the Österreichische Nationalbibliothek.

Not all collectors are interested in autographs: for example, the great Dutch-born Haydn scholar **Anthony van Hoboken** (1887–1983) collected early and rare first editions of Schubert's music as well as exquisite iconographical material. His collection has also now passed over to the Österreichische Nationalbibliothek. Another collection of early printed editions, invaluable to the editors of the *Neue Schubert-Ausgabe*, was assembled by Deutsch's friend and colleague **Ignaz Weinmann** (1896–1976); it is now the property of the Wienbibliothek im Rathaus.

AUTOGRAPH LIEDER ALBUMS

In the collection of the Staatsbibliothek Preussischer Kulturbesitz, Berlin:

THE FIRST ALBUM FOR GOETHE
This is the collection of especially written-out fair copies of Goethe songs that was put together for the poet and sent to him in April 1816 with a covering letter from Josef von Spaun. The receipt of this gift was never acknowledged. After a few months it was sent back to Vienna and Schubert used it as a source of fair copies for the publisher when the works were finally printed in 1821–2. The volume was in Ferdinand Schubert's possession until 1844 when he sold it to a German collector.

Jägers Abendlied D368 [p. 1]; *Der König in Thule* D367 [pp. 2–3]; *Meeres Stille* D216 [pp. 3–4]; *Schäfers Klagelied* D121 [pp. 5–8]; *Die Spinnerin* D247 [p. 9]; *Heidenröslein* D257 [p. 10]; *Wonne der Wehmut* D260 [p. 11]; *Wandrers Nachtlied* I D224 [p. 12]; *Erster Verlust* D226 [pp. 13–14]; *Der Fischer* D225 [pp. 14–15]; *An Mignon* D161 [p. 16]; *Geistes-Gruss* D142 [with a half-page foldout stuck on to the manuscript, p. 17]; *Nähe des Geliebten* D162 [pp. 18–19]; *Gretchen am Spinnrade* D118 [p. 20, at least three pages missing]; *Rastlose Liebe* D138 [pp. 21–4]; *Erlkönig* D328 [pp. 25–31].

THE SECOND ALBUM FOR GOETHE
Anticipating a favourable response from Goethe as a result of Spaun's letter and the dispatch of the first album, Schubert prepared a second album for him that was never sent. The album was broken up and autograph copies of the songs have been preserved in various libraries and collections.

Sehnsucht (Mignon) D123 [pp. 1–5]; *Wer kauft Liebesgötter* D261 [p. 6]; *Trost in Tränen* D120 [pp. 7–8]; *Der Gott und die Bajadere* D254 [p. 9]; *Nachtgesang* D119 [p. 10]; *Sehnsucht* [Mignon]

D310 [pp. 11–13]; *Mignon (Kennst du das Land?)* D321 [pp. 14–16]; *Bundeslied* D258 [pp. 17–18]; *Tischlied* D234 [p. 19]; *An den Mond* D259 [p. 21]; *Der Rattenfänger* D256 [pp. 22–3]; *Der Sänger* D149 [pp. 24–32].

In private possession in Switzerland (the Wilhelm family, Bottmingen bei Basel):

THE THERESE GROB ALBUM

From 1908 when this collection – a bound-together album of songs written on paper of varying size and quality – came to light it was assumed that it had been written out by Schubert for Therese Grob (1798–1875), the composer's first love. It was suspected that the album was put together for Therese in November 1816 – 16 November was her eighteenth birthday. It is agreed that by this time the relationship, such as it was, was almost certainly over, but Schubert stayed in contact with the gifted young amateur singer who married in 1820 and went on to have a family. Then in a long article in *Schubert durch die Brille* (January 2002) Rita Steblin (*see* SCHOLARS) re-examined the whole basis of research on the Grob family. Based on handwriting analysis Steblin came to the conclusion that the album had first belonged not to Therese, but to her brother, Heinrich Grob (b. 1800), a gifted cellist and pianist for whom Schubert wrote the Adagio e Rondo concertante D487. Having established this fact, Steblin argued for the original premise that the gift was meant as a sign of Schubert's suppressed love for Therese, and that in giving it to Heinrich he had meant it to end up in Therese's possession. Three of the songs in the album (marked with an asterisk below) are to be found nowhere else. The second item, *Klage* (formerly D512), is not in Schubert's hand and is now judged to be of doubtful authenticity.

Edone, Klopstock D445; **Klage*, Anon; *An die Natur*, Stolberg [transposed into A major] D372; *Pflügerlied*, Salis-Seewis D392; *Klage* [or *Der Leidende*], Anon D432; *Gott im Frühlinge*, Uz D448; *Lied von Salis* [Ins stille Land], Salis-Seewis D403; *Der Herbstabend*, Salis-Seewis D405; *Am Grabe Anselmos*, Claudius D504; *Andenken*, Matthisson D99; *Am Tage aller Seelen* [Litanei], Jacobi D343; *Lied aus der Ferne*, Matthisson D107; *Zufriedenheit* [second setting], Claudius D501; *Klage* [or *Klage an den Mond*], Hölty D436; **Mailied*, Hölty D503; *Trauer der Liebe*, Jacobi D465; **Am ersten Maimorgen*, Claudius D344.

AUTOGRAPH vs. COPY

In the age before photocopies the only way singers could obtain the music of a song they had heard, perhaps at a party, was to arrange for a copy to be made, or to borrow the original in order to make a copy for themselves. Professional copyists of course abounded in every sphere, not only the musical, but it was an expensive service. If we imagine the sheer industry of Schubert as he put the vast corpus of his creative work on paper (in itself an unfathomable task, even if it were a question of someone else copying down all the notes he had composed afresh) we also have to spare a thought for the unsung heroes of the times in terms of sheer hand-cramping activity, the singers and music lovers who made copies of Schubert's works and lovingly preserved them in collections of their own. This alone is an indication of the powerful charm exerted by Schubert's music on his contemporaries. Without these collections and albums we should undoubtedly have lost many a Schubert song for ever.

SONG ALBUMS AND COLLECTIONS OF IMPORTANT HANDWRITTEN COPIES

The music referred to below is all by Schubert, but not in his own hand.

In the collection of the University Library of Lund, Sweden:
(a)   There are three albums of songs (dated 1815, 1816 and 1817, nearly eighty songs in all) copied and collected by Schubert's friend **Albert Stadler** (qv).
(b)   A less close friend of Schubert's was **Leopold Ebner**. His copies are also in the Lund library, as are those of **Pauline Kner** dating from 1825 when Schubert visited Linz.
(c)   A volume of Schubert songs belonging to Beethoven's factotum (and Schubert's acquaintance) **Anton Schindler** and containing some twenty-five items.

In private possession (Dr Christoph Cornaro, Vienna):
This is the lieder collection of the Spaun-Cornaro family, stemming from the collection of Schubert's devoted friend Josef von Spaun who left fifteen bound volumes of songs to his relatives. Of these, Volumes 1, 3, 5, 7, 8, 10, 11 and 13–15 contain printed copies of the songs, often signed by Schubert himself. Volume 12 has disappeared but Volumes 2, 6 and 9 are made up of handwritten copies that probably date from between 1821 and 1825 – 148 pages of music in all and some forty-one items.

In the collection of the Sächsische Landesbibliothek, Dresden:
A lieder collection belonging to the poet **Franz von Schober** (qv), one of Schubert's closest friends. This includes settings of his own poems *Vergissmeinnicht* D792 and *Jägers Liebeslied* D909 as well as Mayrhofer's *Uraniens Flucht* D554 and *Einsamkeit*, D620. The other songs are Leitner's *Der Kreuzzug* D932 and Goethe's *Gretchen am Spinnrade* D118.

In the collection of the Wienbibliothek im Rathaus, Vienna:
(a)   A Liederalbum, the fifth volume that was once part of a larger collection belonging to **Franziska Tremier**, a young singer who fell in love with Schubert's music at the beginning of 1828. She became an enthusiastic collector of his songs and copied some of the music out for herself. Mixed in with this collection of Schubert songs there are also items by Mozart (including his famous Masonic cantata *Die ihr des unermesslichen Weltalls Schöpfer ehrt* K619) and the Beethoven song *Abendlied unterm gestirnten Himmel* WoO150 transposed up into F major.
(b)   There is another album of songs in this library but the owner is not known apart from a heading stating that the collection stems 'from Schubert's circle'. It is therefore referred to by its catalogue number: MHS24307. It consists of twenty songs, most of them scrupulously dated.

In the Library of the Wiener Schubertbund:
These albums are the work of one **Johann Peterstein** who became enraptured with Schubert's songs and met the composer at the end of 1826. He copied some of the songs from Schubert's manuscripts and some from printed copies (as a student he could not have afforded to buy the songs for himself). There are fifty-two volumes of songs in the collection that were copied between 1822 and 1832. Schubert's works are occasionally interspersed with Peterstein's own compositions or those of one Franz Ripper who set many of the same texts as Schubert.

In the Library of the Stift Kremsmünster:
Pater Georg Benedikt was a friend of the family of the singer Johann Michael Vogl. He probably met Schubert when the composer first visited Steyr with Vogl in 1819. The concerts that Schubert and Vogl gave together in Kremsmünster were legendary, and it is possible that Benedikt was enthused by the music early on. The collection once included the autograph of the Platen setting *Du liebst mich nicht* D756. Some of the collection is written in Benedikt's own hand, other songs by the copyists of the library. There are twenty-six Schubert songs in all.

Another collection made by a Benedictine cleric is in the Library of Stift Seitenstetten in Lower Austria. This was **Father Leopold Puschl** who assiduously collected the printed copies of Schubert songs corresponding with all the Viennese publishers in order to buy them. He dated these songs on receipt which has proved extremely valuable in establishing publication dates that are otherwise doubtful. There are also a number of handwritten copies in Puschl's collection.

In the Library of the Gesellschaft der Musikfreunde, Vienna:

(a) The Witteczek–Spaun Collection:
The most important of all Schubert collections is the one made over three decades by **Josef Wilhelm Witteczek** (1787–1859). He was the dedicatee in 1827 of Schubert's Op. 80 songs and for forty years he gave regular Schubertiads in his home. Baron Schönstein, to whom Schubert had dedicated *Die schöne Müllerin*, often sang there. Witteczek set about making a complete and systematic collection of the Schubert songs (though among the 350 works in the collection there are also twelve important pieces of chamber music). He started by obtaining all the vocal music that had appeared in print and later set about having copies made (by Herr Weiser, a professional copyist) of songs that were still in manuscript. The scope of the collection widened to include pictures of Schubert, letters and critical articles from all over the world. He absorbed Carl Pinterics's collection of autographs into his own in 1831 and, at his death in 1859, left the entire assemblage to his old friend Josef von Spaun who, in

Josef Witteczek, oil painting by J. P. Krafft.

turn, bequeathed it to the Musikverein as agreed. There are eighty-eight volumes which are ordered into nineteen different categories with indices. The lieder are contained in Volumes 23–40 of the collection, as well as 63–70 and 79–80; the contents are listed in detail in the NSA Series VIII, Volume 8 pp. 78–111. Since the earliest days of serious Schubert scholarship the presence of the Witteczek–Spaun collection has been indispensable; our knowledge of certain works depends primarily on its contents, but mostly it is a back-up resource in offering either alternative readings or confirming editorial decisions that would otherwise have depended on slim and solitary evidence. The collection was a major boon to Eusebius Mandyczewski in the preparation of the lieder volumes for the AGA.

(b) The 'Schubert Cupboard' of Ferdinand Schubert:
Schubert died in the home of his brother Ferdinand. Up until then he had been living with the Schober family in the inner city where he had left behind a quantity of his music. After the composer's death Schober kept back only one of the manuscripts, a setting of his own poem *Jägers Liebeslied*. The remainder were sent back to Ferdinand Schubert who sold some items to various publishers or collectors (the *Liederalbum for Goethe* discussed above was sold to a

Prussian collector in 1844) and kept the rest in a box or cupboard. Ferdinand was usually careful to make copies of manuscripts that had left his possession. This collection has been split up between the Musikverein and the Wienbibliothek im Rathaus. It is a motley gathering of music of all kinds including Ferdinand's own music and arrangements of his brother's songs for orchestra and chorus (*Die junge Nonne* D828 for example). Many of these copies are in Ferdinand's own hand.

In private possession in Graz there is a substantial folder of songs (a Schubert-Mappe) that belonged to **Josef Hüttenbrenner**, Schubert's factotum and business secretary in the years 1822–3. This includes some items in Hüttenbrenner's own hand (*Memnon* for example, written out a tone higher than the original) and others made by a professional copyist. There are thirty-nine items in all, including copies of choral works, piano works and even a *Singspiel*. Hüttenbrenner had been closely connected with the composer at a time when many works were being published on commission for the first time.

THE EDITORS' TASK

Even with all these rich resources at their disposal (and sometimes because of the sheer variety of choice) it is clear that the amount of research that needed to be undertaken by the editors of the *Neue Schubert-Ausgabe* was immense – the work was completed in 2011, forty-three years after the first issue in the lieder series. There are different kinds of autographs: the 'Arbeitsmanuskript' is a first draft of the song; the 'Reinschrift' is a fair copy, made at the end of the composition process for performance, or possibly also for a publisher to set the notes in print. In the former the fascinating process of work in progress may be observed, in the latter we are presumably given the composer's final thoughts.

It is never as simple as that of course, and in each case there has to be a weighing up of likelihoods and possibilities before a text can be established that may be thought to represent Schubert's definitive intentions – in as far as these can be discovered. If only it were possible to restrict these editorial decisions to cases where one is working with Schubert's own handwriting. Sometimes the only available copy of a song that the editors have to hand is the first edition, and this may be one of the corrupt editions issued some time after Schubert's death. Even an autograph will not answer all the editor's questions. This may be clearly dated, or it may simply have a day and a month, without mentioning a year. It may also have a year without a month, or no date at all. In these cases paper studies come to the fore, including the analysis of watermarks, although these, also, cannot always be relied upon: music paper can be traced back to a manufacturer and dated, but there is no cast-iron guarantee that it was used immediately, nor, indeed, any indication of how long the paper was kept. This applies also to works that were hastily written down on the nearest piece of available paper – perhaps on the back of extant, older works. In many other instances the autograph has disappeared altogether and the scholars have to rely on a contemporary copy ('Abschrift').

This means that some copies of Schubert's songs are almost as valuable to posterity, in practical terms, as the autographs themselves. It is always difficult to work out whether the variations of detail between different copies go back to Schubert himself – copying a song is rather like a game of Chinese whispers. In any case the choice of options available to a performer when all these variants are taken into account can be confusingly wide, and someone has to take decisions on behalf of those who are not equipped to adjudicate the finer points for themselves.

The reader who wishes to make his or her own decision, or who wishes to follow the train of thought of both Mandyczewski or Dürr, is referred to the bulky *Revisionsbericht* volume of the AGA and the *Quellen und Lesarten* sections at the back of each of the NSA volumes, as well as Walther Dürr's painstaking and separately published volumes of *Kritischer Bericht* (one for each issued volume of the NSA series IV). These contain detailed information regarding Schubert's autographs and copies (with their sometimes conflicting information) and the way in which the editors have come to their conclusions regarding a final reading of the composer's intentions. Particularly fascinating are the quasi-genealogical diagrams provided by Dürr where each autograph or copy of a song is assigned a letter and where he suggests how one version has derived from, or has been dependent on, another.

AVE MARIA *see SIEBEN GESÄNGE AUS WALTER SCOTT'S FRÄULEIN VOM SEE* D839/6 (ELLENS GESANG III)

A student, perhaps Schubert, in the uniform of the Imperial Konvikt, *c.* 1811. From a watercolour by Leo Diet.

B

BACCHUS, FEISTER FÜRST DES WEINS *see* TRINKLIED D888

Des BACHES WIEGENLIED *see Die SCHÖNE MÜLLERIN* D795/20

BALLADE   Ballade
(KENNER) **D134** [H57]
G minor – E minor   Late 1814/early 1815

(136 bars)

(1) Ein Fräulein schaut vom hohen Turm
    Das weite Meer so bang;
    Zum trauerschweren Zitherschlag
    Hallt düster ihr Gesang:
    'Mich halten Schloss und Riegel fest,
    Mein Retter weilt so lang.'

From the high tower a maiden
Looks anxiously down over the vast sea.
To the heavy, mournful chords of her zither
Her gloomy song resounds:
'Lock and bolt keep me captive here,
My saviour tarries so long.'

(2) Sei wohl getrost, du edle Maid!
    Schau, hinterm Kreidenstein
    Treibt in der Buchtung Dunkelheit
    Ein Kriegesboot herein:
    Der Aarenbusch, der Rosenschild,
    Das ist der Retter dein!
    Schon ruft des Hunen Horn zum Streit,
    Hinab zum Muschelrain.

Take comfort, noble maid!
Look, beyond the chalk cliff
A warship approaches
In the darkness of the bay;
With eagle plumes, and rose-decked shield;
Behold your saviour!
Already the giant's horn
Calls to battle on the shell-covered shore.

(3) 'Willkommen, schmucker Knabe, mir!
    Bist du zur Stelle kummen?
    Gar bald vom schwarzen Schilde dir
    Hau' ich die goldnen Blumen.
    Die achtzehn Blumen blutbetaut,
    Les' deine königliche Braut
    Auf aus dem Sand der Wogen,
    Nur flink die Wehr gezogen!'

'Welcome, fair youth,
Have you reached your destination?
Soon I shall cut the golden flowers
From your black shield.
Let the eighteen flowers, stained with blood,
Be gathered by your royal bride
From the sand washed by the waves,
Quickly, draw your sword!'

(4) Zum Turm auf schallt das Schwertgeklirr!	The rattling of swords echoes up to the tower!
Wie harrt die Braut so bang!	How anxiously the bride waits!
Der Kampf dröhnt laut durchs Waldrevier,	The clamour of battle resounded
So heftig und so lang!	Long and fiercely!
Und endlich, endlich däucht es ihr,	Then at length, it seems to her,
Erstirbt der Hiebe Klang.	The clash of weapons ceases.
(5) Es kracht das Schloss, die Tür klafft auf,	The lock is burst, the door opens,
Die Ihren sieht sie wieder;	She sees her people once more;
Sie eilt im atemlosen Lauf	In breathless haste she runs down
Zum Muschelplane nieder.	To the shell-covered shore.
Da liegt der Peiniger zerschellt,	There lies her tormentor's mangled body.
Doch weh! dicht neben nieder,	But alas! Close beside him
Ach! decken's blutbespritzte Feld	Her saviour's pale limbs
Des Retters blasse Glieder.	Cover the blood-bespattered field.
(6) Still sammelt sie die Rosen auf	Silently she gathers the roses
In ihren keuschen Schoss	In her chaste lap,
Und bettet ihren Lieben drauf,	And on them she lays her beloved.
Ein Tränchen stiehlt sich los.	A tear falls,
Und taut die breiten Wunden an,	Bathing his gaping wounds
Und sagt: ich hab das getan!	And signifying: 'I have done the deed.'
(7) Da frass es einem Schandgesell	But an evil accomplice in her abduction
Des Raubes im Gemüt,	Was tortured by the thought
Dass die, die seinen Herrn verdarb,	That she who destroyed his master
Frei nach der Heimat zieht.	Would return home freed.
Vom Busch, wo er verkrochen lag	From the bush where he lay hidden
In wilder Todeslust,	In frenzied blood lust,
Pfeift schnell sein Bolzen durch die Luft,	His arrow whistled rapidly through the air
In ihre keusche Brust.	Into her chaste heart.
(8) Da ward ihr wohl im Brautgemach,	She was happy in her bridal chamber,
Im Kiesgrund, still und klein;	Deep among the pebbles, small and silent;
Sie senkten sie dem Lieben nach,	They lowered her to join her beloved
Dort unter einem Stein,	Beneath a stone
Den ihr von Disteln überweht,	That, overgrown with thistles,
Noch nächst des Turmes Trümmern seht.	You can still see beside the ruined tower.

JOSEPH KENNER (1794–1868); poem written in June 1814

This is the first of Schubert's three Kenner solo settings (1815). See the poet's biography for a chronological list of all the Kenner settings.

This is a companion piece both to Kenner's other ballad *Der Liedler* D209 and to the Matthisson extravaganza, *Romanze* D114, the work on which Kenner seems to have modelled his own story. The Matthisson poem begins 'Ein Fräulein klagt' im finstern Turm, / Am Seegestad' erbaut'; a quick glance at the first line of Kenner's *Ballade* confirms its earnestly plagiaristic provenance. The young Schubert was of course very familiar with this habit of copying a master (Zumsteeg,

Reichardt) in order to improve his own art; perhaps he had advised his friend Kenner to do the same and take Matthisson as his model.

Verse 1: 'Mässig geschwind' § (bb. 1–18). In the beginning it seems that Schubert is quoting from himself on the basis that he is at least as good a model as Zumsteeg. The G minor tonality of *Romanze* is recycled, as is the lilting § of that song's opening. It seems that any mention of an imprisoned maiden in far-off lands must bow in the direction of Mozart's *Die Entführung aus dem Serail* and the character of Pedrillo whose *Romanze* ('In Mohrenland gefangen war / Ein Mädchen hübsch und fein') is of course in §. The maiden's G minor plaint is accompanied by zither (so the poet tells us) rather than Pedrillo's mandolin. Schubert seems to attempt to portray the zither in the arpeggiated piano writing for bb. 10 and 11. The music moves to F major, the dominant of the relative major.

Verse 2: 'Mässig geschwind' ¢ (bb. 19–50). An extraordinary passage of twenty-eight bars is built entirely on three chords in the key of B flat, piano-orchestrated as if for natural horn. Schubert writes the words 'in the distance' for the pianist, and as the rescuing forces get nearer and louder, the narrator, like some benevolent *deus ex machina*, assures the maiden that all will be well. Schubert so expertly builds the excitement (in the manner of Rossini's slowly unwinding crescendos) that the enormous cadence back to F major at the moment when her 'saviour' is announced, seems to solve all problems. He jumps ashore ready for action, as the brusque shift to hammered octaves in D major (bb. 46–9) tells us.

Verse 3: 'Mässig' ¢ (bb. 51–70). This is a formal courtly aria that is reminiscent in mood and key of the opening of *Der Sänger* D149, and also of passages in the longest of the composer's ballads *Adelwold und Emma* D211 (both songs of 1815) – Schubert in courtly vein with music suitable for old-fashioned knights and their ladies.

Verse 4: This decorous courtesy is suddenly interrupted (b. 71) by the pandemonium of battle music of a weirdly jazzy effect, only comparable to the $\frac{12}{32}$ variation in the *Arietta* of the last of Beethoven's piano sonatas, Op. 111, where dotted rhythms suddenly seem to make Vienna swing in crazed anachronism. It would be convenient to claim that Schubert was influenced by Beethoven here, but the sonata was only to be written seven years later. When the waiting heroine is mentioned the music becomes demure and switches back to languishing recitative (b. 76); the techniques of film music come to mind where interiors and outdoor scenes are contrasted and juxtaposed. But then the scene quickly shifts back to the set-piece battle. The noise dies down in ingenious manner as the pianist's fingers limp crab-like to the safety of the bottom of the keyboard (bb. 93–5).

Verse 5: A rather conventional recitative frees the girl from her captivity (bb. 96–101). In a swirl of skirts a coruscating interlude in triplets propels her to the seashore (bb. 101–4). There she finds her captor dead (hurrah!) but alas, her saviour is also slain, his pale limbs spread on the bloody battlefield, although we are spared the grisly details of the exact manner of their dispersal.

Verse 6: 'Sehr langsam, traurig' E minor ¢. A lesser composer, and even a younger, less experienced Schubert, would have turned this verse into tear-drenched recitative, but the music for these words is the most exceptional of the piece, and grandly stoic. Images of a pale body covered with blood, and of a chaste maid, free of sin, summon up in Schubert an altar picture and a miniature Pietà. This is passion music (bb. 112–17) for a secular Christ and Virgin. For six memorable bars the left hand tolls out its spacious notes of mourning, while thirds and sixths, in a manner suggestive of the solemn counterpoint of a former age, weave an old-fashioned elegy that recalls the church music of C. P. E. Bach perhaps, or even that of Graun, as sung by Matthisson's beloved Laura (cf. *An Laura* D115).

Verse 7: We are woken from this requiem by poetry so utterly ludicrous, and attempting to cover so much ground and explanation at such a pace that poor Schubert has little option but to hurry it away in unconvincing recitative. The flight of the treacherous arrow (bb. 123–5) is accompanied by chords moving in contrary motion, rising in semitones in the right hand, falling in semitones in the left. The arrow finds its target at the crest of this progression (on 'ihre keusche Brust', b. 124) and an interlude of descending chords paints the heroine's body sinking to the ground.

Verse 8: There is then a recapitulation of the Passion music of Verse 6, without a trace of the melodrama and grotesque effect that mars the earlier *Romanze*. It is almost as if Schubert, despite himself, has fallen in love with the nameless girl of this unlikely story. All in all, and allowing for the contemporary passion for such balladry, this is far from a ridiculous piece; its treatment is a strong indication of future talent, genius waiting in the wings.

Autograph:	Missing or lost
First edition:	Published as Op. post. 126 Josef Czerny, Vienna in 1830 (P238)
Publication reviews:	*Allgemeiner Musikalischer Anzeiger* (Vienna), No. 7 (13 February 1830), p. 27 [Waidelich/Hilmar Dokumente I No. 765]
	Iris im Gebiete der Tonkunst (Berlin), No. 6 (7 May 1830) [Waidelich/Hilmar Dokumente II No. 775c]
Subsequent editions:	Peters: Vol. 4/152; AGA XX 99: Vol. 2/198; NSA IV: Vol. 7/77; Bärenreiter: Vol. 6/35
Discography and timing:	Fischer-Dieskau I 4[16] 6'33
	Hyperion I 12[21]
	Hyperion II 4[13] 7'12 Adrian Thompson

← *Szene aus 'Faust'* D126   *Der Mondabend* D141 →

EDUARD VON BAUERNFELD (1802–1890)

THE POETIC SOURCES

S1   *William Shakspeare's [sic] Saemmtliche Dramatische Werke* übersetzt im Metrum des Originals. XXXVI Bändchen. Wien, Druck und Verlag von J. P. Sollinger, 1825.
Antonius und Cleopatra von Ferdinand von Mayerhofer, 11te Neue Übersetzung.
Titel und Vignetten, Lithographirt bei Jos. Trentsensky in Wien

S2   *William Shakspeare's Saemmtliche Dramatische Werke* übersetzt im Metrum des Originals. II Bändchen. Wien, Druck und Verlag von J. P. Sollinger, 1825.
Die beiden Edelleute von Verona, von Bauernfeld, Titel und Vignetten, Lithographirt bei Jos. Trentsensky in Wien

S3   *William Shakspeare's sämmtliche dramatische Werke* Übersetzt im Metrum des Originals in einem Bande nebst Supplement, enthaltend Shakspeare's Leben, nebst Anmerkungen und Kritischen Erläuterungen zu seinen Werken Wien, Zu haben bei Rudolph Sammer, Bachhändler, 1826

This is a handsome one-volume edition of Shakespeare's works in large octavo format, very much bigger than the small paperbacks of the individual plays, issued without vignettes and by a different publisher in a completely reset text. It is not impossible that the Schober family acquired this volume in 1826 and that it was Schubert's source.

S4   *Gedichte*, Brockhaus, Leipzig, 1852

THE SONGS

July 1826   *Trinklied* (translation – together with F. Mayerhofer – of Shakespeare, qv) D888
             [S1: Act II Scene 7, p. 47] [S3: p. 864]

             Gesang (An Silvia) (translation of Shakespeare, qv) D891 [S2: Act IV Scene 2,
             p. 53] [S3: p. 32]

January 1827 *Der Vater mit dem Kind* D906 [S4: p. 25]
              Das Todtenhemdchen D864 (music lost) [S4: p. 98]

Eduard von Bauernfeld.

Bauernfeld was a native of Vienna, born there on 13 January 1802. He first met Schubert in January 1822 at the home of the theology professor Vincentius Weintridt, but their friendship was by no means immediate; their eventual collaboration was part of that special flowering of a new generation of Schubertian enthusiasts, a feature of the last three years of the composer's life. Bauernfeld was an inveterate diarist; so we find the first reference to the composer some time before even this first meeting took place. He was present at a performance of Schubert's opera *Die Zauberharfe* on 19 August 1820; on 21 April 1821, he noted the

excellence of *Die Nachtigall* D724 (Unger), a quartet for male voices. His reaction on hearing this music was, 'I must get to know this man!'

A much more intimate friendship between the two men dates from 1825 when the painter Moritz von Schwind, a schoolfriend of Bauernfeld (they had both attended the Schottengymnasium in Vienna), was instrumental in bringing him closer to the composer. At this point Schubert seems to have taken note of the poet's talent, and considered him as a possible librettist for an opera. Bauernfeld's parody on the Schubert circle (written for the New Year's Eve celebrations of 1825–6: see Deutsch 1946, p. 486) would have made the composer aware of this young man's wit and verbal acuity. In May 1826 Bauernfeld began work on the libretto for Schubert entitled *Der Graf von Gleichen* and finished it in eight days. (This was the opera that the composer was working on during the last weeks of his life.) It was also in 1826 that Bauernfeld entered the civil service in order to earn his daily crust; he left it in 1848.

Bauernfeld was at one of the two concerts (attended by Schubert) given by the violinist Paganini in the summer of 1828, and he was also present when Schubert and Franz Lachner (another of the composer's protégés) played the recently composed *Fantasia in F minor* for piano duet. The poet wrote a great deal about

Die beiden Edelleute von Verona by Shakespeare
(Vienna, 1825).

this period of his life in later years. His memoirs, including the poetical *Ein Buch von uns Wienern* (1858, published under the pseudonym 'Rustiocampus') and the *Poetisches Tagebuch* (1887, a diary from 1820 to 1886 in verse form) are a richly informative source on various figures in the Schubert circle, notably Mayrhofer. Bauernfeld was the translator of the German version of Shakespeare's 'Who is Sylvia?' which Schubert set to music in 1826 (*Gesang (An Silvia)* D891). This appeared in *Die beiden Edelleute von Verona* (The Two Gentlemen of Verona), the second of the forty-three slim volumes (booklets in fact) of *Wlm. Shakspeare's saemtliche dramatische Werke* published by Sollinger soon before the song's composition (although officially designated in 1825), and illustrated with title-page vignettes by John Thurston (1774–1822) that are usually

attributed to Moritz von Schwind. (The covers of the booklets, with the Shakespeare bust, were indeed designed by Schwind – for these illustrations, *see* SHAKESPEARE.) With the assistance of his friend Ferdinand Mayerhofer von Grünbühel (1798–1869) Bauernfeld translated *Antony and Cleopatra* but was gallant enough to allow Mayerhofer – not to be confused with the more famous Mayrhofer – to take credit for all the work on the booklet's title page. (Mayerhofer did translate *Love's Labours Lost* on his own.) Other Shakespeare plays translated for the series by Bauernfeld were *The Comedy of Errors*, *King Henry VIII*, *Troilus and Cressida*, *The Rape of Lucrece* ('Tarquin und Lucretia') and *The Passionate Pilgrim* ('Der leidenschaftliche Pilger'). With another friend, Joseph Fick, Bauernfeld translated *Coriolanus*.

Apart from this collaboration on Shakespeare, *Der Vater mit dem Kind* D906 is the only surviving setting that Schubert made of the poetry of his younger friend who became, in due course, an important literary figure in Vienna. The text of this poem was published first in 1852 in the *Gedichte*, so Schubert must have used an autograph copy of the poem from Bauernfeld himself. This volume also contains a poem entitled *Das Todtenhemdchen*, a song that Schubert is said to have composed to a Bauernfeld text in 1826. Curiously enough the *Gedichte* fail to mention Schubert's name in connection with the extant *Der Vater mit dem Kind*, but do so with the second of these poems. The music for *Das Todtenhemdchen* (The Shroud) has not survived (if it ever existed) although the song was assigned the catalogue number D864. There is a Randhartinger setting of that poem; one cannot help but wonder whether someone involved in printing Bauernfeld's *Gedichte* nearly a quarter of a century after Schubert's death confused the two composers' names.

Capell's description of Bauernfeld seems only partly convincing because it undervalues his eventual importance in literary Vienna: '. . . a lively, scatterbrained youth, one imagines – a Murgeresque bohemian, who later wrote successful light comedies in the French

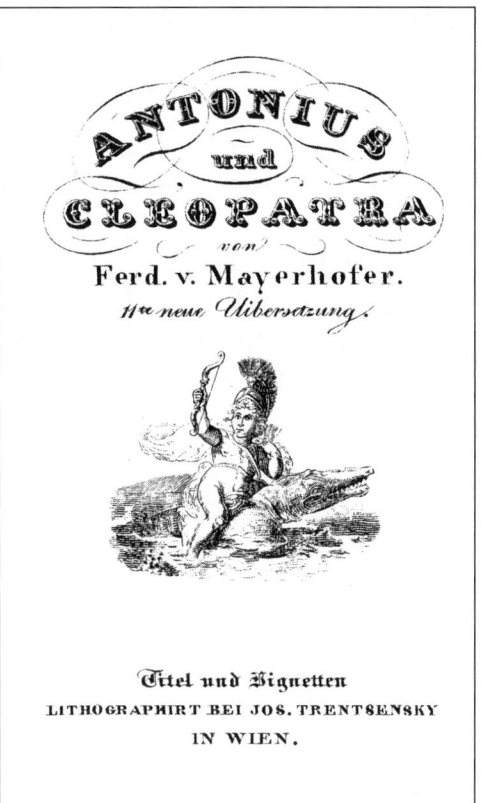

Antonius und Cleopatra by Shakespeare (Vienna, 1825).

vein . . . He could talk, joke, play the piano, and drink . . . Bauernfeld gave us a doubtfully accurate picture of the three [Schubert, Schwind and Bauernfeld himself] sharing one another's lodgings, clothes, and purses – which often meant Schubert's purse – of unflagging activities and spirits, of talk and of merry-makings to all hours of the night.' Such famous Viennese hostelries as 'Zum grünen Anker', 'Schloss Eisenstadt' and Café Bogner were the scenes of such jollifications. At one time the poet was a fellow official with Josef von Spaun at the Lottery Office. He left this work to devote himself to full-time writing. It seems that Schubert was close enough to this young poet to have shared with him his hopes, frustrations and dreams. Bauernfeld was not afraid to visit

Schubert in the last days of his life, when the composer was living in his brother Ferdinand's lodgings (unlike Schober who, it seemed, feared that Schubert might have been infectious); in fact, the poet saw the composer and spoke to him only two days before his death. In 1829 Bauernfeld published an important two-part biographical article about Schubert in the *Wiener Zeitschrift* ('Modenzeitung'). He died in Vienna on 9 August 1890, by then a well-established Viennese celebrity and a famous man of the theatre – if not as famous as Grillparzer. By 1889 the Burgtheater had presented forty-three plays by Bauernfeld in over a thousand performances. His later plays were much admired by Hugo von Hofmannsthal, Richard Strauss's celebrated librettist.

GABRIELE VON BAUMBERG (1775–1839)

THE POETIC SOURCES

S1   *Sämmtliche Gedichte* Gabrielens von Baumberg, Wien Gedruckt bey Joh. Thom. Edl. V. Trattnern, K. K. Hofbuchdrucker und Buchhändler, 1800

Haydn (Joseph) 'Doktor der Musik' is one of the four hundred listed subscribers to this handsome volume.

S2   Gabriele Batsányi, geb. Baumberg *Gedichte* mit einer Abhandlung über die Dichtkunst von F. W. M. [Friedrich Wilhelm Meyer] Gedruckt bey J.V. Degen, 1805

This is a severely edited and shortened edition of the 1805 *Gedichte*. Apart from *Lebenstraum*, the poems for only two Schubert settings of 1815 appear in S2 (D264 and D265) but with different titles.

THE SONGS

Before 1810   *Lebenstraum* (first setting) or *Gesang in c* D1A [S1: where the title is *Ein Jugendtraum* pp. 1–5] [S2: where the title is *Lebenstraum* pp. 3–15]
Lebenstraum (second setting) D39 [S1: pp. 1–5]

August 1815   *Lob des Tokayers* D248 [S1: p. 245]

22 August 1815   *Cora an die Sonne* D263 [S1: p. 240]
Der Morgenkuss D264 [S1: p. 17] [S2: as *Schwärmerey – nach einem Ball*, p. 34]

23 August 1815   *Abendständchen an Lina* D265 [S1: p. 243 with the subtitle *Nach dem Französichen*] [S2: where the title is *An Lina* pp. 26–8]

25 August 1815   *An die Sonne* D270 [S1: p. 18, as *Als ich einen Freund des nächsten Morgens auf dem Lande zum Besuche erwartete*]

Gabriele von Baumberg.

Gabriele von Baumberg was Schubert's first poet. Somehow or other a copy of her *Gedichte* came into the teenager's hands. For his very first settings of her poetry in 1810 (D1A and D39), it is likely the composer had the second edition (1805) at his disposal. Some years later he clearly found a more complete version of the poems (the 1800 edition) for his 1815 songs – only two of these texts appear in the 1805 edition.

Baumberg was born into a well-to-do Viennese family on 24 March 1775. Her father worked at court during the most liberal of epochs in Austria – the period of the reforms of the Emperor Josef II. She displayed literary talent at an early age and several of her poems were published in Viennese almanacs. She was a friend of another Schubert poet, Caroline Pichler (née Greiner), seven years her senior, and she addressed poems to another two of Schubert's collaborators: Gottlieb von Leon and Josef Franz von Ratschky (qqv). Baumberg had a free and uninhibited attitude to love, not unusual in an age of powerful and liberated female figures like Madame de Stäel. At the turn of the century it seemed unlikely that this 'Sappho of Vienna', as she was known, would choose to marry. She met her future husband, the Hungarian poet János Batsányi (1763–1845) just before the much-heralded publication of her *Gedichte* (1800); she was twenty-five, he thirty-six. She was a strong and motivated woman, and during an ardent courtship Batsányi swore that his mission in life would be to promote her genius and her poetry. The reality was very different. Batsányi was obsessed only by his own work as a poet and by his fiery political views. In 1805 he translated Napoleon's exhortation to the Hungarians to revolt against their Habsburg rulers and was punished with imprisonment and banishment.

The rest of Baumberg's life is a sorry tale of decline: exile in Linz, and then penury in Vienna. She died completely forgotten as a poetess; her own epoch, the age of Mozart, had been swept away by revolution, war and the resulting oppression of the Metternich regime in a Biedermeier age less friendly to women of her kind. As beautiful as some of the Schubert settings are (Einstein praises his response to the poet 'as delicately balanced as a pair of jewellers' scales') the Mozart song *Als Luise die Briefe ihres ungetreuen Liebhabers verbrannte* K520 is perhaps Baumberg's finest and best-known musical memorial. She died in Linz on 24 July 1839.

Bibliography: Youens 1996, pp. 1–50

Die BEFREIER EUROPAS IN PARIS   The liberators of Europe in Paris
(Mikan) **D104** [H38]

The song exists in three versions, the third of which is discussed below:
(1) May 1814; (2) May 1814; (3) 16 May 1814

(1) 'Andante moderato'   G major $\frac{2}{4}$ [Vocal line in bass clef, 29 bars]

(2) 'Andante moderato'   G major $\frac{2}{4}$ [Vocal line in bass clef, 29 bars]

(3) 'Andante'   G major

(29 bars)

Sie sind in Paris!
Die Helden! E u r o p a' s B e f r e i e r !
Der V a t e r v o n Ö s t r e i c h, der
    H e r r s c h e r der R e u s s e n,
Der W i e d e r e r w e c k e r der tapferen
    P r e u s s e n.
Das Glück Ihrer Völker – es war ihnen teuer.
Sie sind in Paris!
Nun ist uns der Friede gewiss!

They are in Paris!
The heroes! *Europe's liberators!*
The father of Austria, the ruler of the Russians,

He who aroused once more the brave Prussians.

The happiness of their nations was dear to them.
They are in Paris!
Now we are assured of peace!

JOHANN CHRISTIAN MIKAN (1769–1844); poem written in 1814

This is Schubert's only setting of a Mikan text. See the poet's biography.

There are only two Schubert works that directly show the composer's engagement with political events, and this little ditty is one of them. (The other is *Auf den Sieg der Deutschen* – 'On the victory of the Germans' – D81, written in the autumn of 1813 for voice with string trio accompaniment.) The poem captures the relief of most contemporary Europeans that the Napoleonic nightmare was over – or seemed to be. The allied armies (the Austrians under Franz I, the Russians, as well as the Prussians) had entered Paris on 15 April 1814, and Napoleon, forced to abdicate, was exiled to Elba. As in all the best horror stories, however, the fiend made a return: just when everyone imagined that all the danger was over, Napoleon escaped from his island prison. His ultimate defeat followed at Waterloo in June 1815.

Schubert casts his song in popular style for baritone and piano (the vocal line is in the bass clef). The *pomposo* fanfares and decorations of the piano part and the military dotted rhythms are similarly hackneyed. The repeats of the words 'sie sind in Paris' in a forte dynamic (bb. 16–17) are followed by quiet echoes of the same phrase in the accompaniment (b. 18). This could be put down as the work of an hour at most, had there not been three versions of this song written out on the same folded sheet of music paper (these three versions are all printed in the NSA). Judging by the clearly impassioned crossings-out on the autograph, this rather simple little project seems to have given the composer quite some trouble, and he seems not to have been satisfied by any of the results. The third version is the only one with a postlude. John Reed claims that this is Schubert's dance of joy over Napoleon's downfall. This thesis is undermined by the pastoral nature of this music with its piano markings, and the expressive syncopations that seem to tug at the heartstrings. Everyone was sick and tired of war in Europe; most people had lost friends or family (Schubert's admired Theodor Körner had died in battle) and everyone longed for peace. In this respect this tiny song has a distinct parallel with one Gabriel Fauré composed (against his better judgement) to an undistinguished text that had won a readers' prize in *Le Figaro* in 1918. The poem by the amateur Georgette Debladis, *C'est la paix*, revels in French victory against the Germans (the exact opposite of the events of 1814), and she was apparently mortified by the conciliatory tone adopted by the composer for her triumphalist words. Like Fauré in this instance, Schubert detected sadness in happiness; perhaps he was present at the Redoutensaal on the night of 13 April 1814 when the actress Sophie Schröder declaimed this poem alongside others by Schiller and Körner, and perhaps his three compositional efforts, one after the other, represented his struggle to capture what might have been both the exultation and grateful relief in Schröder's intepretation, more subtle than a barn-storming rant. In any case, Schubert is unexpectedly able to turn a jingoistic poem into a little work of art with a pianissimo ending that seems to express a longing for a return to less violent times. In this respect his wish was eventually granted. After the unexpected blip of Napoleon's 'hundred days' in 1815, there was indeed peace, and for many years, although the cost as far as civil liberties were concerned was high for Austrians: the young composer in 1814 could scarcely have known that in the post-Napoleonic world, a return to the values of the Enlightenment would be out of the question.

Autograph:	Wienbibliothek im Rathaus, Vienna (containing versions one, two and three)
Publication:	First published as part of the NSA in 1968 (P738 & P739; versions one and two)
	First published as part of the AGA in 1895 (P708; third version)
Subsequent editions:	Not in Peters; AGA XX 584: Vol. 10/76 (third version); NSA IV: Vol. 7/24 (third version), 182 (first version) & 184 (second version); Bärenreiter: Vol. 5/122 (high voice), 116 (medium/low voice)

Discography and timing: Fischer-Dieskau   —

Hyperion I 33[20]

Hyperion II 3[10]   2'32   Maarten Koningsberger

← *Geisternähe* D100   *Lied aus der Ferne* D107 →

BEGLEITUNG FÜR KLAVIER *see* DUBIOUS, MISATTRIBUTED AND LOST SONGS

BEGRÄBNISLIED *see* NUN LASST UNS DEN LEIB BEGRABEN D168

BEI ANSELMOS GRABE *see* AM GRABE ANSELMOS D504

BEI DEM GRABE MEINES VATERS   At my father's grave

(Claudius) **D496** [H313]

E♭ major   November 1816

(17 bars)

Friede sei um diesen Grabstein her!	Peace be to this tombstone,
Sanfter Friede Gottes! Ach, sie haben	The tender peace of God.
Einen guten Mann begraben,	Ah, they have buried a good man,
Und mir war er mehr.	And to me he was still more.

Träufte mir von Segen, dieser Mann,   He showered blessings upon me
  Wie ein Stern aus bessern Welten![1]   Like a star from a better world,
Und ich kann's ihm nicht vergelten,   And I can never repay
  Was er mir getan.   What he did for me.

Er entschlief; sie gruben ihn hier ein.   He fell asleep, they buried him here.
  Leiser, süsser Trost von Gott,[2]   May God's sweet, gentle comfort
Und ein Ahnden von dem ew'gen Leben   And a presentiment of eternal life
  Düft' um sein Gebein!   Embalm his mortal remains,

Bis ihn J e s u s C h r i s t u s, gross und hehr!   Until *Jesus Christ*, great and glorious,
  Freundlich wird erwecken – ach sie haben   Lovingly wakens him.
Ihn begraben,[3]   Ah, they have buried him,
  Und mir war er mehr.   And to me he was still more.

Matthias Claudius (1740–1815); poem written in 1773 on the death of the poet's father

This is the fourth of Schubert's thirteen Claudius solo settings (1816–17). See the poet's biography for a chronological list of all the Claudius settings.

[1] The original Claudius reads 'wie ein *milder* Stern . . .'.
[2] The original Claudius reads 'Leiser, süsser Trost, von Gott *gegeben*'.
[3] The original Claudius reads '*Einen guten Mann* begraben'.

The two Claudius songs about bereavement from 1816 (the other is *Am Grabe Anselmos* D504) are somewhat similar: they are both in E flat, and they are both composed in a classical style that seems to place the mourner, and thus the listener, at one remove from a real sense of loss. In *Am Grabe Anselmos* D504 (the music is in the minor key) the poet writes of the death of his child; there the *durchkomponiert* construction of the music is an advantage. *Bei dem Grabe meines Vaters*, however, is strophic and in the major key; the stage hardly seems set for tragedy (admittedly the composer was capable of such sorcery in *Winterreise*). It is not as if Schubert's music lacks invention, indeed the aria-like setting is elaborate almost to a fault; but profound empathy as we understand it in Schubert's songs (and not just those of his maturity) seems to be curiously absent. Reed detects the influence of Beethoven who sometimes wrote his lieder in a similarly formal arioso style. Here and there melodic wafts of *Die Zauberflöte* seem discernible, and some of the the the piano figurations recall Mozart; there is also perhaps even a touch of Gluck and Orpheus' lament for Eurydice.

These are all honourable models. The song is accomplished and unfailingly elegant, despite certain problems of stress in the declamation (where tune takes precedence over prosody) which add to a feeling that this music is ever so slightly stilted. Especially fine is the phrase 'Und ich kann's ihm nicht vergelten' (bb. 9–11) where voice and piano dovetail in courtly imitation at the distance of the bar. There is a similar sense of imitation between the hands at the postlude (bb. 16–17) that seems conceived for string quartet, and which suddenly strikes a more warmly romantic note. Perhaps this exercise in the old-fashioned style was the result of Schubert imagining the type of music that people of his father's generation might have wished to hear at their gravesides.

We know from his diary that in 1816 the composer was thinking back to the death of his own mother. Schubert senior however was in good health, and Schubert seems not to have reacted to this text with a great deal of subjective emotion. At this point in 1816 father and son were hardly seeing eye to eye with regard to Franz's future. *Bei dem Grabe meines Vaters* has all the traces of being written to express condolences for someone else's loss – perhaps a friend's father had died. It is also interesting to compare this music with the wild personal involvement (adolescent rebellion perhaps) of the Schiller *Leichenfantasie* D7 where a father buries a son, or the restrained, yet moving, *Grablied für die Mütter* D616 from 1818.

We are not certain which edition of Claudius poems Schubert used, although it is fairly certain that he had known this particular text from his early teens; it appears in a textbook

Vignette for *Bei dem Grabe meines Vaters* in Claudius's *Asmus Omnia* (1775).

anthology in common use in the Viennese schools, *Sammlung Deutscher Beispiele zur Bildung des Styls*, 1812. It is very possible that he saw the illustration to the poem (reproduced opposite) printed in many German editions which is of a deliberately artificial classical severity. Was this perhaps his inspiration to find a musical style to match the words?

Autograph:	Missing or lost
First edition:	Published as Vol. 7 no. 12 in Friedlaender's edition by Peters, Leipzig in 1885 (P483)
Subsequent editions:	Peters: Vol. 7/28; AGA XX 274: Vol. 4/234; NSA IV: Vol. 11/28
Discography and timing:	Fischer-Dieskau I 8[21] 3'09
	Hyperion I 23[26]
	Hyperion II 16[16] 3'13 Christoph Prégardien

← *Abendlied der Fürstin* D495   *Klage um Ali Bey* D₂496a →

BEI DIR ALLEIN! *see VIER REFRAIN-LIEDER* D866/2

BEIM WINDE   When the wind blows
(MAYRHOFER) **D669** [H432]
G minor – G major   October 1819

(125 bars)

Es träumen die Wolken,	They dream – the clouds,
Die Sterne, der Mond,	Stars, moon,
Die Bäume, die Vögel,	Trees, birds,
Die Blumen, der Strom,	Flowers and stream;
Sie wiegen	Lulled,
Und schmiegen	They nestle
Sich tiefer zurück,	More deeply down
Zur ruhigen Stätte,[1]	O peaceful places,
Zum tauigen Bette,	Dewy beds
Zum heimlichen Glück.	And secret happiness.
Doch Blättergesäusel	But rustling leaves
Und Wellengekräusel	And rippling waves
Verkünden Erwachen:	Herald the awakening;
Denn ewig geschwinde,	For winds,
Unruhige Winde,	Eternally swift and restless,
Sie stöhnen, sie fachen.	Moan and stir.

[1] Schubert reverses lines 8 and 9 of the Mayrhofer poem: in the original these read 'Zum tauigen Bette / Zur ruhigen Stätte'.

Erst schmeichelnde Regung,	First coaxing,
Dann wilde Bewegung;	Then wildly agitated;
Und dehnende Räume.	Dreams are engulfed
Verschlingen die Träume.	By the expanding spaces.
Im Busen, im reinen,	Guard your dreams
Bewahre die deinen;	In your pure heart;
Es ströme dein Blut,	Let your blood course,
Vor rasenden Stürmen	That you may wisely protect
Besonnen zu schirmen	The sacred glow
Die heilige Glut.	From raging storms.

[Schubert repeats the poem's first ten lines to bring the song to a close]

Johann Mayrhofer (1787–1836)

This is the thirty-third of Schubert's forty-seven Mayrhofer solo settings (1814–24). See the poet's biography for a chronological list of all the Mayrhofer settings.

During Schubert's absence in Zseliz (Hungary) in the summer of 1824 the composer's brother Ferdinand loaned the manuscript of this song (with nine others) to the painter Ludwig Mohn. Walther Dürr sees in Schubert's lack of concern for the return of the Mayrhofer settings a sign that the composer himself did not value them. It is more likely that he doubted that this batch of unusual songs would ever find a publisher. In any case, by this time the composer's Mayrhofer phase was over – he had already composed his last setting by the poet. From Schubert's vantage point in 1824, a song composed in 1819 like *Beim Winde*, fruit of a very special friendship at its most intense, might have seemed to come from another world.

The four-bar introduction is followed by the beginning of a vocal line accompanied by watery semiquavers. We are reminded of another much more famous Schubert song in the same key: *Der Müller und der Bach* from *Die schöne Müllerin*. Admittedly the then unwritten masterpiece is in triple time, and this is in duple, but there is nevertheless a powerful similarity between them. Schubert's juxtaposition of major and minor keys stands at the heart of both. In *Beim Winde* the moon and stars are introduced to us in G minor; this mood yields meltingly to a change of key signature, and G major, as soon as the composer shifts his gaze from the skies to the trees rooted in his beloved Earth, and then birds, flowers, and . . . the stream. This is, more than anything else, water music. 'Der Strom' concludes this list of nature's dreamers (surely influenced by Friedrich Schlegel's *Abendröthe* poems) with a strong modulation into D major. It is the stream's gentle ebb and flow that governs the *Bewegung* of *Beim Winde*, and this is what reminds us so much of passages in *Die schöne Müllerin*. At 'Sie wiegen Und schmiegen' (bb. 17–18) we hear a pre-echo of the familiar melody and harmony of 'ein Sternlein, ein neues' from *Der Müller und der Bach* (bb. 32–4 of that song) where the stream cradles the stars' reflection. The imagery of two songs written four years apart thus converges: dreaming, lulling, nestling deep down. In 1823 the drowned miller boy will be offered peace of this kind protected from pain in the millstream's depths.

Tiny contrasts and inflections abound, sometimes implying the same thing looked at in two different ways: at the end of the first section 'heimlichen Glück' is heard twice – the happiness coloured first in diminished seventh secrecy on an E flat (b. 35), and then for an instant on an E natural (b. 37), a fleeting moment when the secret is confessed. Thus ends the song's first section that will be recapitulated in a *da capo*.

It is the second section (beginning at 'Doch Blättergesäusel') that gives the song its name. The sudden storm of another famous Müller song comes to mind – the cold winds that blow the hat off the traveller's head in *Der Lindenbaum* from *Winterreise* and the winds that will blow away like cherished dreams in *Beim Winde*. The piano writing in cascading semiquaver triplets is filled with dangerous accidentals leading the music restlessly from D major to B flat major/ minor (from b. 51). The contrast between major and minor here underlines the difference between 'schmeichelnde Regung' and the more threatening 'wilde Bewegung'. B flat changes enharmonically to an A sharp and at b. 59 we find ourselves wrenched into B minor. At 'dehnende Räume' it is as if we are suspended in a void; Schubert achieves this feeling of limbo by the simple means of allowing the harmony (elsewhere changing with almost every quaver) to remain fixed on an E minor chord for three whole bars; the vocal line is obsessively pegged on the sharpened sixth with no fewer than thirteen C sharps (bb. 60–64) before an ascent to the F sharp of 'Träume'. This extraordinary interruption to the mood of what had seemed a tranquil song is prophetic of the storms that interrupt and transform some of Schubert's instrumental slow movements. This section ends poised on the piano's F sharp chord – the dominant of the B minor tonality that we have already traversed.

The key signature changes, however, to B *major*. What follows is the glory at the heart of the piece: a fervent hymn, twenty-two bars long, of such solemn tenderness and simplicity that we can tell that both composer and poet regard 'die deinen', their own dreams and ideals, as being of paramount importance for their spiritual survival. There is a heart-stopping excursion into A major (b. 73) – the words repeat as if to say 'cherish your dreams *even deeper* in your heart'. The coursing of blood ('Es ströme dein Blut'), and the raging of storms, is quasi-recitative with piano doubling voice. This bridge passage ends on an A sharp that will be reborn as a B flat on the other side of the double bar (a change of key signature to B flat major at b. 82).

With this poignant flattening of the tonality the protecting veil is drawn ever closer, but somehow we are made to realize that the poet's struggle is doomed: we are only men, not gods; we, and our hopes and dreams, are at the mercy of fate. As if to accept this fact the composer now returns to a repeat of the first section; we hear the G minor/major musings from a different perspective the second time around. This is reminiscent of the shape of another Mayrhofer song on a watery theme – *Erlafsee* D586. On paper, Mayrhofer's last words, 'Die heilige Glut', are potentially defiant, even triumphant, but we may be sure that the music's tenderness and wistfulness do not stem from the composer alone, but accurately reflect his mentor's complex personality. It is as if we have been privileged to hear Mayrhofer reading his own verse.

Autograph:	Staatsbibliothek Preussischer Besitz, Berlin
First edition:	Published as a supplement to *Wiener Zeitschrift für Kunst, Literatur, Theater und Mode* in June 1829 and subsequently as Book 22 no. 3 of the *Nachlass* by Diabelli, Vienna in 1833 (P301)
Subsequent editions:	Peters: Vol. 5/129; AGA XX 365: Vol. 6/54; NSA IV: Vol. 12/106
Bibliography:	Capell 1928, p. 161
	Dürr, Introduction to NSA IV Vol. 12, p. XXII
Discography and timing:	Fischer-Dieskau II 3[8] 3'52
	Hyperion I 19[13]
	Hyperion II 22[7] 5'16 Felicity Lott

← *Cantate zum Geburtstag des Sängers Michael Vogl* D666   *Die Sternennächte* D670 →

BEITRAG ZUR FÜNFZIGJÄHRIGSTEN JUBELFEIER DES HERRN VON SALIERI, ERSTEM K.K. HOFKAPELLMEISTER IN WIEN

Contribution to the fiftieth anniversary of Herr von Salieri's appointment as imperial and court Kapellmeister in Vienna

(SCHUBERT?) **D407** [H268 & H268A–C]
Written for 16 June 1816

(a) Terzett, TBB with piano   Bᵇ major

(27 bars)

(b) Quartet, TTBB unaccompanied   'Adagio molto'   Bᵇ major   𝄵   [44 bars]

(c) Aria for tenor and piano   G major

(46 bars)

(d) Three-part canon, TBB unaccompanied   G major

(12 | 8 bars)

Gütigster, Bester!
Weisester, Grösster!
So lang ich Tränen habe
Und an der Kunst mich labe
Sei beides Dir geweiht,
Der beides mir verleiht.

So Güt' als Weisheit strömen mild,
Von Dir, o Gottes Ebenbild,
Engel bist du mir auf Erden
Gern möcht' ich Dir dankbar werden.

Unser aller Grosspapa,
Bleibe noch recht lange da!

Kindest and best of all!
Wisest and greatest of all!
As long as I have tears
And refresh my spirit with art,
Both shall be dedicated to you,
Who bestowed both on me.

Both goodness and wisdom flow benignly
From you, God's image;
You are my angel here on earth;
I long to show my gratitude.

Grandfather to us all,
Stay with us a lot longer!

Franz Schubert? (1797–1828)

In the absence of evidence to the contrary we must assume that the above texts were written by Schubert himself.

Sunday 16 June 1816 was an important day in the annals of Viennese music, and Schubert recounted the festivities in his diary:

> Herr Salieri celebrated his jubilee yesterday, having been fifty years in Vienna, and nearly as long in the service of the Emperor; he was awarded a gold medal by His Majesty and invited many of his pupils of both sexes. The works written for the occasion by his composition students were performed according to the order in which they came under his tuition, from youngest to oldest. The event was framed by a chorus and an oratorio, both by Salieri, entitled Jesus al Limbo. The oratorio is in a genuinely Gluckian manner. The entertainment was interesting for everybody.

Considering the astonishing musical maturity of the composer in 1816, the nineteen-year-old Schubert's prose is that of a well-mannered schoolboy – slightly stilted, as if he is overawed by the grandeur of a formal occasion and the attendant pomp and ceremony of the Imperial court. (We find exactly the same tone in the diaries and letters of the young Benjamin Britten whose music-making far outstripped his literary expression.) It is clear that the young composer already had divided loyalties as far as Salieri and Beethoven were concerned. Beethoven was obviously Salieri's bugbear; the well-ordered and disciplined studio of the old Italian composer was seen (especially by Salieri himself) to foster the old-fashioned virtues of music where Gluck was the paradigm. Salieri believed that his own music, unlike Beethoven's, was made to lift the listener up to God, rather than to incite him to laughter or goad him to madness with 'howlings' and 'Harlequinades'. Schubert himself used these words in his diary in oblique criticism of Beethoven, but we sense that he was not convinced of their truth; on a day devoted to honouring his old teacher he was allowing himself to repeat *idées reçues*. It is the last time that we find him toeing the party line of the old guard in this manner.

Schubert was always torn in his loyalties between the old and the new, a struggle that was to characterize his artistic life. His music, poised between classical and Romantic, takes inspiration, Janus-like, from each, and remains impossible to typecast to this day. This occasion seems to mark the end of Schubert's studentship. Schubert had been flying free of Salieri's influence for quite some time. His ceremonial music written for the occasion is a postlude rather than an overture.

The pupils' gathering took place at Salieri's home. The honoured host sat at the piano with fourteen female pupils arranged in a semicircle on his right; they included Betty Vio and Karoline Unger who were both to become well-known singers – and they were both to sing Schubert's music some years later (*see* SINGERS). Rochlitz's description of Salieri adds to the picture: 'A delicate, attractive little man with fiery eyes, dark skin, always clean and always attractive, with a lively temperament, quick to lose his temper but easily reconciled.' On his left, also in a semicircle, sat twelve male pupils including Anselm Hüttenbrenner and Schubert himself. Josef Weigl, a famous Viennese opera composer more than thirty years older than Schubert, was also included in this line-up. All the composition pupils, past and present, brought a dedicatory work with them, and Moscheles and Hummel, unable to be in Vienna for the occasion, had sent vocal compositions. It must have been a lengthy evening and Schubert's work appeared about a third of the way through.

There is some disagreement, however, about what was actually performed. There are four Schubert pieces associated with this event and three of these were presented to Salieri – certainly the little tenor aria, 'So Güt' als Weisheit strömen mild' D407/2, and the unaccompanied canon 'Unser aller Grosspapa' D407/3. The first and second editions of the Deutsch catalogue disagree on which version of 'Gütigster, Bester! Weisester, Grösster!' was performed. Deutsch 1 (1951) favours the vocal trio with piano (D407/1, second version), even giving it a separate, and later, number, D441. But Deutsch 2 (1978) finds that it is the unaccompanied version for four male voices (D407/1, first version) that appeared in the dedicatory manuscript.

The piano-accompanied vocal trio is thus probably the earlier setting. The introductory bar for piano instigates a mood of Handelian grandeur in oratorio style; the words 'most good', 'best' and 'wisest' cap each other in rising sequence as the double-dotted chords in the piano stride through the stave in *pomposo* fashion. After the concerted opening, the three singers present themselves one by one: with an accompaniment of pulsating semiquavers the bass has a four-bar solo; he is then joined, in the manner of a canon, by the second tenor. When the first tenor joins with the same melody, making a full three-part vocal texture, the accompaniment blossoms into demisemiquavers. The music gathers momentum with a repeat of the opening words and a return to an accompaniment in double-dotted rhythm in a lofty, if rather conventional, style. The high tone of the opening words seems to promise a more substantial work, but Schubert, already a consummate professional, has his eye on the clock and realizes that he needs to keep the piece short.

Why this piano-accompanied trio was not eventually presented at Salieri's party is uncertain. It seems that, in the end, the composer decided to write an unaccompanied vocal quartet instead. Perhaps there was an extra singer who needed to be included in the proceedings, or perhaps Schubert himself took part as the fourth singer rather than as the pianist.

The remaining two items in the triptych of vocal compositions are less musically ambitious. The little tenor aria 'So Güt' als Weisheit strömen mild' (D407/2) is typical of a number of the 1816 songs: sweet and gentle and in the manner of Mozart. The key is an affectionate G major with a middle section where the opening words are set again, this time in B major. The lie of these harmonies, particularly the seventh chord under 'strömen mild' is prophetic of better-known music – the 'O Bächlein meiner Liebe' section of *Der Neugierige* from *Die schöne Müllerin*. The idea of something streaming forth as a source of instruction – whether Salieri's wisdom, or the millstream (in that case, also an oracle) – invokes a similar response in Schubert's mind, and in the special key of B major. Also familiar is the shift into the subdominant for the mention of heavenly things. At 'Engel bist du mir auf Erden' (admittedly not the greatest line ever penned by an amateur poet) the music slips seraphically into C major.

The final little unaccompanied *Canon a tre*, 'Unser aller Grosspapa' (D407/3), might have given the old man the greatest pleasure of all. The Anglo-Saxon might find it embarrassing to address a teacher as 'Grandpa', but it seems to be more a part of the paternalistic German teaching tradition; the famous baritone Gerhard Hüsch, for example, was regularly addressed as 'Papi' by his devoted pupils well into the 1970s.

Autographs:	Wienbibliothek im Rathaus, Vienna (first draft of (c)); Conservatoire collection, Bibliothèque Nationale, Paris (fair copy of three sections)
First edition:	Published as part of the AGA, in 1891/2 (P514)
First known performance:	16 June 1816, Salieri's home, Spiegelgasse (corner of Seilergasse), 1088 Vienna
Subsequent editions:	Not in Peters; AGA XVI 44: p. 211 & XIX 5, p. 53; NSA III: Vol. 3

Discography and timing: Fischer-Dieskau —
Deutsche
Grammophon   2'44
Schubert Terzette

Peter Schreier, Horst Laubenthal &
Dietrich Fischer-Dieskau (trio only)

(a) Daniel Norman, Philip Langridge &
Maarten Koningsberger

Hyperion I 32[4–7]
Hyperion II 14[20–23]   8'03

(b) Toby Spence, Daniel Norman,
Christopher Maltman & Neal Davies
(c) Toby Spence
(d) Toby Spence, Daniel Norman,
Christopher Maltman & Neal Davies

← *Die Erwartung* D159

An die Sonne D439 →

Die BERGE   The mountains
(F. von Schlegel) Op. 57 no. 2, **D634** [H415]
G major   *c.* 1819–March 1820?

(72 bars)

Sieht uns der Blick gehoben,	When we gaze upwards,
So glaubt das Herz die Schwere zu besiegen,	Our hearts believe they can overcome gravity;
Zu den Himmlischen oben	They desire to fly up
Will es dringen und fliegen.	And reach the gods above.
Der Mensch emporgeschwungen,	Soaring aloft, man imagines
Glaubt schon, er sei durch die Wolken gedrungen.	He has already passed through the clouds.
Bald muss er staunend merken,	Soon he must realize with astonishment
Wie ewig fest wir auf uns selbst begründet;	That we are for ever rooted firmly in ourselves;
Dann strebt in sichern Werken,	Then, with concentrated effort,
Sein ganzes Tun, verbündet,	He strives to create lasting achievements,
Vom Grunde nie zu wanken,	Endeavouring never to stray from his roots,
Und baut wie Felsen den Bau der Gedanken.	And builds, as of rock, an edifice of thoughts.
Und dann in neuen Freuden	And then, with new joy,
Sieht er die kühnen Klippen spottend hangen;	He sees the bold cliffs hang in mockery;
Vergessend aller Leiden,	Forgetting all his sorrows,
Fühlt er einzig Verlangen,	He feels only the craving
An dem Abgrund zu scherzen,	To dally on the edge of the abyss,
Denn hoher Mut schwillt ihm in hohem Herzen.	For noble courage swells in his noble heart.

FRIEDRICH VON SCHLEGEL (1772–1829); poem written in 1800/1801

This is the eighth of Schubert's sixteen Friedrich von Schlegel solo settings (1818–25). See the poet's biography for a chronological list of all the Friedrich von Schlegel settings. See also the article about the cycle of which this song is part – Abendröte.

This song, together with *Der Schmetterling*, was (surely erroneously) included by Mandyczewski among the 1815 songs in the AGA, just after *Erlkönig*. Deutsch believed that *Die Berge* must be contemporary with the other *Abendröte* settings (1819–20), and Richard Kramer has pointed out that the sophisticated use of the subdominant is not a characteristic of the 1815 songs. The song's simplicity might be explained by the fact that this is Schubert in outdoor mode, the writing as clean and crisp as mountain air. Nevertheless, the composer's economy goes hand in hand with great sophistication.

The introduction is both bracing and embracing; it endeavours to paint a whole range of mountains in a single sweeping gesture, and it succeeds not only in aural terms, but also visually – on the page we can see a succession of peaks, and a definite summit (bb. 1–3). The left hand is safely anchored in G major but there is a real sense of danger in the ascent in octaves of the right: when we reach a D in the middle of the first bar we descend a third that is in turn a springboard for the highest note, a jump of a sixth that seems Olympian. Once we have reached the highest point we can look down at the view; the piano line descends in a decrescendo to revisit some of the notes used as footholds on the way up. The whole phrase is caught in a nimbus of pedal that gives a sense of open spaces, as if sound were resonating through a valley. The effect is of great effort counterbalanced by a moment of repose, the exhalation of breath after concentration and exertion. And all of this in what is effectively a G major arpeggio!

The singer's first phrase echoes this introduction ('Sieht uns der Blick gehoben'). Mention of gravity in the next line ('die Schwere') prompts a vocal line weighed down and pulled back by the piano, each note doggedly doubled. At 'zu besiegen' the voice breaks free from this and forces the melody into the subdominant (C major) where the mountains, according themselves human qualities, now move around as if no longer rooted to the spot. The left-hand accompaniment has horn-call harmonies beneath an inverted pedal (bb. 11–13), a swirling movement beneath the right hand's constricting blanket of clouds. Man is similarly ambitious; the wise mountains know that his aspirations to be god-like are highly dubious, and this is reflected in the rueful dotted crotchets of 'Glaubt schon, er sei . . .' (bb. 17–18). The extent of human hubris is illustrated by an extraordinary vocal line – a C major arpeggio that ascends the stave and traverses a twelfth in a matter of seconds ('sei durch die Wolken gedrungen' bb. 19–20). This forceful determination triggers the piano into similar action, a dovetailing outburst that returns us to the tonic. We have met these left-hand ascending octaves before in another § song, *An Schwager Kronos* D369 (bb. 41–7, at 'Weit, hoch, herrlich / Rings den Blick ins Leben hinein'), a passage fit for Icarus that describes an ambitious ascent through life. The right-hand scales (bb. 22 and 24) recall the brilliant energy of Weber's piano writing as well as a similar passage in *Die Wetterfahne* from *Winterreise*. In that song the winter traveller comments bitterly on the worldly priorities of the girl's parents who now have a rich bride for a daughter: the vocal and piano writing at both appearances of the words 'reiche Braut' (bb. 32–3 and 42–3) are passages that scale the heights of social climbing and monetary greed.

The middle section (beginning b. 26) takes its cue from the word 'begründet' – 'grounded' or 'rooted' – and this brings the piano once again to double the voice note for note, weighing it down as if it were a hot-air balloon in danger of flying off to dangerous heights. The middle section of the part-song *Widerspruch* D865 comes to mind where the mountains remind mankind of its impotence in comparison to Nature. At 'Dann strebt in sichern Werken, Sein ganzes Tun' (b. 32) the accompaniment blossoms into triplets. This is certainly the most harmonically adventurous passage of the song, and its chromatic restlessness seems linked to the middle section of *Der Fluss* D693, another reason to suppose that *Die Berge* was indeed written at the same time. The activity of man is now shown to be less foolhardy, more connected to hard work in a lower, less giddy part of the stave and thus nearer his roots.

At 'Und baut wie Felsen den Bau der Gedanken' (b. 38) the piano doubles the voice once again, but this time not to contain its boundaries but to widen them. Man has found his vocation as a sculptor of thoughts, and in the interlude after 'den Bau der Gedanken' we hear the philosophical hammer-blows of thesis and antithesis. This is one of those Schubertian middle sections that changes the colour of the recapitulation. When this comes, we have exactly the same music for the second verse – perhaps a weakness of the song – but the new words seem to fit the music very well. Man has learned the lesson that the mountains have known since time immemorial, and this knowledge brings an energy and death-defying daring of its own.

Autograph:	Missing or lost
First edition:	Published as Op. 57 no. 2 by Thaddäus Weigl, Vienna in 1826 (P95)
Publication reviews:	*Allgemeiner musikalischer Anzeiger* (Frankfurt), No. 33 (10 February 1827), p. 317f. [Waidelich/Hilmar Dokumente I No. 452; Deutsch Doc. Biog. No. 798]
Subsequent editions:	Peters: Vol. 4/51; AGA XX 180: Vol. 3/227; NSA IV: Vol. 3a/78; Bärenreiter: Vol. 2/112
Discography and timing:	Fischer-Dieskau I 6¹⁰ 2'03
	Hyperion I 27⁹
	Hyperion II 21⁹ 2'07 Matthias Goerne

← *Abend* D645   *Die Gëbusche* D646 →

BERGKNAPPENLIED
(ANONYMOUS) **D268** [H155]
D minor   25 August 1815

Miners' song   Quartet, TTBB

(17 bars)

Hinab, ihr Brüder, in den Schacht!
Hinab mit frohem Mut!
Es ist ein Gott, der für uns wacht,
Ein Vater gross und gut!

Down into the shaft, brothers,
Down with good cheer.
There is a God who watches over us,
A Father great and good!

A German miner of the period.

ANONYMOUS/UNKNOWN

The music looks and sounds so like a battle march that the text can all too easily be misread, as if men were going into battle ('in die Schlacht') rather than down into the shaft ('in den Schacht'). A single 'l' can make all the difference between hell above ground or below it. The composer makes the miners face the dangers of the depths with a combination of military spirit and religious faith that was absolutely typical of the war songs of the period.

The plunging phrase on 'Es ist ein Gott', first for the basses and later for the tenors, is some indication that the composer understood the terror and danger experienced by the miners, and why they had to call on God to protect them. Nevertheless, we have to admit that the various gravediggers in Schubert's solo songs burrow deeper under the music's surface. This is unexceptional music, but it is unlike anything else in the composer's output which otherwise avoided contact with the stressful occupations that would come to typify the Industrial Revolution. It would certainly have resonated more convincingly in the Welsh valleys than at a Viennese Schubertiad. This quartet shared a manuscript with a song written on the same day, *Der Weiberfreund* D271; which by chance was a setting of a British author, Abraham Cowley, in German translation.

Autograph:	Wienbibliothek im Rathaus, Vienna (fair copy)
First edition:	Published as No. 4 of *Neueste Folge nachgelassener, mehrstimmiger Gesänge mit und ohne Begleitung von Franz Schubert* by J. P. Gotthard, Vienna in 1872 (P512)
Subsequent editions:	AGA XVI 18: p. 133; NSA III: Vol. 3
Discography and timing:	Fischer-Dieskau —

Hyperion I 20[18]
Hyperion II 9[16]   1'22   John Mark Ainsley, Jamie MacDougall, Simon Keenlyside & Michael George

← *Trinklied* D267   *An die Sonne* D270 →

JOSEF KARL BERNARD (1781–1850)

THE POETIC SOURCE
S1   *Selam, Ein Almanach für Freunde des Mannigfaltigen* Herausgegeben von I. F. Castelli Dritter Jahrgang, 1814 im Verlage bey Anton Strauss

THE SONG
April 1815   *Vergebliche Liebe* D177 [S1: p. 199]

Bernard, born in Horatz in Bohemia in 1781, was well known in Vienna as a critic and journalist. He was the librettist for Spohr's opera on the Faust story (composed in 1813, and differing significantly from Goethe's version), and of *Libussa*, the opera by Conradin Kreutzer, a forerunner of Smetana's opera, part of which Schubert heard (he walked out after the first act at the first performance on 4 December 1822). This libretto had originally been meant for Beethoven with whom Bernard was also on friendly terms. He was editor of numerous specialist journals dealing with the arts, such as *Thalia, Zeitschrift für dramatische Kunst* and *Friedenblätter*. As far as we know, Schubert only set one poem by Bernard. The 1822 edition of the Viennese almanac *Aglaja* (p. 68) has a poem by Bernard entitled *Am ersten May* (*sic*) with the 'Musik von Schubert' in brackets underneath. There is no such known song by Franz Schubert, but this may refer to another composer with the same name – Franz Schubert of Dresden (*see* Composers), for example. Bernard died in Vienna on 31 March 1850.

BERTAS LIED IN DER NACHT
(Grillparzer) **D653** [H422]
E♭ minor – F♯ major   February 1819

Bertha's nocturnal song

Sehr langsam

pp

Nacht um-hüllt mit we-hen-dem Flü-gel

pp

(27 bars)

Nacht umhüllt	With fluttering wings,
Mit wehendem Flügel	Night envelops
Täler und Hügel,[1]	Valley and hill,
Ladend zur Ruh'.	Bidding them rest.
Und dem Schlummer,	And to Sleep,
Dem lieblichen Kinde,	That sweet child,
Leise und linde	She whispers
Flüstert sie zu:	Softly and gently:
'Weisst du ein Auge,	'If you know of an eye
Wachend im Kummer,	That stays awake, grieving,
Lieblicher Schlummer,	Sweet Sleep,
Drücke mir's zu!'	Close it for me!'
Fühlst du sein Nahen?	Do you feel him draw near?
Ahnest du Ruh?	Do you have a presentiment of peace?
Alles deckt der Schlummer,[2]	Sleep makes all things well;
Schlummre auch du.	Then sleep also.

[1] In the musical repeat of this strophe (bb. 5–8) the composer adds 'umhüllet' to the beginning of line 3, thus: 'Umhüllet die Täler und Hugel / Ladend zur Ruh'.
[2] In Schubert's musical setting these lines become 'Alles deckt Schlummer / Alles, *alles*, *be*deckt *der* Schlummer / Schlummre, *so* schlummre auch du'.

FRANZ GRILLPARZER (1791–1872); poem written in February 1817

This is Schubert's only Grillparzer solo setting. See the poet's biography.

The NSA has updated this title to the modern orthography of *Bertas Lied in der Nacht*, but Schubert in his autograph writes it as Bertha, unchanged from the Grillparzer play, and identical to the modern English way of spelling this name, rather than the German. Berta is a leading character in *Die Ahnfrau* (The Ancestress), Grillparzer's fourth play, although it was the first to be published and bring him fame. This tragedy in five acts received its first performance at the Hofburg Theatre on the night of Schubert's twentieth birthday, 31 January 1817. The poet wrote the role of Berta for the actress Sophie Schröder who, in a casting twist worthy of modern cinema, also played the eponymous anti-heroine, the Ahnfrau herself, the ghost of the ancestress of the Borotin family. In 1812 Grillparzer, foreshadowing Schubert in 1818 and 1824, had accepted summer employment from a nobleman as a tutor for his children. His employees, Graf Seilern and family, had a castle in Moravia and, inspired by the beautiful landscape, the poet was fortunate to have had the time to work on a new play. Schloss Ullersdorf nearby had once belonged to a family named Jarotin; from local legends and stories about ghosts surrounding this castle Grillparzer spun a story in which the ancestress of the Borotins (having been murdered while engaged in an act of adultery) has cursed her descendants. Her spirit can only achieve peace when there are no more family survivors, and she finds quietus at the end of the drama only through the destruction of Berta and Jaromir Borotin, a brother and sister unwittingly in love with each other. Both these characters die in the course of the story (Bertha commits suicide and Jaromir perishes in the dreadful embrace of the spectre at the final curtain). The play's trochaic metre suggests the influence of Spanish theatre but the overwrought nature of Greek-inspired tragedy also comes to mind, and Grillparzer's drama later struck Sigmund Freud as a modern parallel for the Sophoclean version of Oedipus.

This highly dramatic spectacle was considered excessively shocking at the time and excited fierce critical debate. A song for Berta is required in the first act of the play (p. 11 of the first edition published by Wallishausser in 1817) when she sings a harp-accompanied song to her father, Count Borotin – a lullaby that sends him to sleep as the clock strikes eight. The printed lyric is much longer here than the one set by Schubert, a substantial poem (beginning 'Schlummre ruhig, guter Vater! / Dass doch all die süssen Blumen, / Die du streust auf meinen Pfad, / Dir zum Kranze werden möchten / Auf dein sorgenschweres Haupt.') and more in keeping with the storm that howls outside after the end of the song.

The play was not always meant to be as dramatic or as gruesome (or indeed as long) as the finished product. The original version of *Die Ahnfrau*, the 'Urfassung', was written in 1816, rediscovered only in the 1950s, and given its first performance in Lucerne in 1964. This revealed that Grillparzer's original intention had been a play that was simpler, more direct, less overladen with the angst of 'Schicksal' tragedy, than the work that received its first performance in 1817. The intendant of the Hofburg, Joseph Schreyvogel, had been responsible for pressing the playwright into a change of direction and had persuaded him to cut the play in some parts and greatly to increase it in others; the overall length was expanded from the original four acts to five, and the aim was to create something in the spirit of Schiller's *Die Räuber*, or perhaps in the style of Adolf Müllner's play *Die Schuld* that had been the runaway success of 1816. The work certainly became something else entirely from what Grillparzer had first envisaged. It seems likely that the anodyne but elegant lyric set to music by Schubert had survived from even before this lost 1816 version, a type of 'Ur-Ur-Fassung' of Berta's night song that later appeared as a separate poem in the Viennese periodical *Janus* in 1818; it was here that Schubert almost certainly found it. At this time he did not know Grillparzer personally. Although it is possible that he had seen *Die Ahnfrau*, he would have heard a different text entirely sung at the performance, and it is more than possible (if the name of Berta rang no particular bells) that he was unaware of the poem's link to the play. Grillparzer's name is not on the song's autograph, and early copies ascribe the poem to Kenner; by the time the song was published in the *Nachlass* in 1842 it was possible to establish definitively the link with the now famous playwright. All this is at odds with Ernst Hilmar's contention (Hilmar 1988, p. 97) that Grillparzer actually asked Schubert to set the text for future performances of the play. If this were the case, the lyric here would represent Grillparzer's second thoughts, rather than his first, as also implied in the NSA. Against this theory is the fact that the second printed edition of *Die Ahnfrau* (1819), where we might have expected to find an updated version of the lyric, contains the same longer poem (p. 13) as we find in the first edition mentioned above – and so does the earliest known version from 1816 (Bergland Verlag, Wien, 1959), and all the subsequent editions through the nineteenth century until the present time. The only other possibility is that Schubert's much shorter text was a one-off replacement for the actress replacing Sophie Schröder whose inadequate singing voice made the longer text impossible to perform.

Schubert's choice of opening key is a wonderfully atmospheric E flat minor, although Diabelli inexcusably changed this to D minor for the song's first printing (also in the Peters Edition), no doubt for the ease of sight-reading pianists, but also to render the song accessible for a mezzo soprano in the more demanding passages where a very soft F sharp on the top line of the stave is much more of a challenge than an F natural in the lower tonality. After a two-bar *Vorspiel* where the mysterious pianissimo murmurings of the hands are placed an octave apart in the bass clef, the song gets underway with those ominous doublings of voice and piano that are a sign that the composer is intent on an atmosphere-spinning mood. The subject is night, dreams and a world of whispering spirits and imaginings. It seems obvious to say that no Schubert song is like any other, but Berta's song has a feeling all its own. There is something about the awkwardness of the vocal intervals (between C flat and D natural at 'mit wehendem Flügel' in b. 3, and between G flat and A natural in b. 4) that sets it apart: the brooding chromaticism (like that of *Lied (Des lebens Tag ist schwer)* D788) suggests an Erda-like aura that is Wagnerian *avant la lettre*, at least in these opening eight bars. The low tessitura of the voice and the slightly obsessive quality of the introspection (cf. *Gesang der Norna* D831) intimate that Schubert is in his supernatural or warning mode, and this suggests he might have understood something about the play's overall storyline. John Reed points out a similarity between the 'sinuous unison line' at the beginning of the song and the A minor Piano Sonata D845, as well as Andante con moto of the 'Great' C major Symphony.

At b. 8 we have arrived at a consolatory cadence in G flat major ('ladend zur Ruh'), and at b. 9 there is a change of key signature into F sharp major. This metamorphosis whereby D flats become C sharps is thus a purely enharmonic one. The effect is radiant, however, like something light and golden emerging from a musical fabric of the deepest and richest purple. There seems little argument that F sharp major in this case brings a translucent quality to the song that simply staying in the key of G flat major would not have accomplished. After a bar of C sharps syncopated between the hands, the entry of the voice for 'Und der Schlummer' seraphically banishes all distress: the piano's thatched roof of repeated C sharps continues to be woven aloft in the treble stave while an inverse pedal, holding within its frame a wonderful viola-like tune in the tenor register, entwines sinuously around the vocal line in a descant of caressing sixths and tenths. The accompaniment of the second half of the song could be played by a string quartet with little or no rearrangement, the three-part texture of the accompaniment opening out into four parts in b. 15. There is certainly no trace of the lute as mentioned in the stage directions. Time and place are suspended in the magic of the night, just as in that ghostly song *Schwestergruss* D762 (1822) where the central section of the song – the warning message of Bruchmann's dead sister to the poet's errant soul – is also in F sharp major, and where there is a similar sense of heightened concord between the vocal line and the piano writing, an unearthly harmony to be heard (in Schubert's imagination at least) only in, or coming from, the heavenly regions. Bearing in mind the consistency of the composer's musical responses to verbal imagery over many years, this again seems to suggest (in contradiction to the other evidence) that Schubert was aware that these Grillparzer words came from a play where the supernatural takes on a pivotal part in the story. The whisperings of sleep that are placed in inverted commas from 'Weisst du ein Auge, / Wachend im Kummer' (b. 13) should be sung as if they are coming from another world. In order to achieve this effect, the same singer who has had to begin the song with an excursion deep in the treble stave, is now required to sing pianissimo in the ethereal regions of sleep and dreams, a tessitura that is not very comfortable for most ordinary mezzo sopranos. It may be said that an extraordinary song like this requires, and deserves, an extraordinary singer.

From b. 19 there is the most unusual marking of 'langsamer werdend', a wonderful winding-down effect that suggests that Berta's song for her father is gradually having an effect and making the old man go to sleep. This is a unique marking in the Schubert songs as the composer is content for once to leave the pacing of the long ritardando entirely in the performers' hands. Perhaps the poet would have minded that the metre of the last line was changed by the composer's insertion of an extra 'so schlummre', but it seems more than likely that Grillparzer remained unaware of the song until after Schubert's death. Even the distinction of the orphan poem having been given a wonderful setting by the increasingly famous composer was insufficient to reinstate the lyric in Grillparzer's first edition of *Gedichte*, published as late as 1872 in the year of the poet's death, the same year the first statue of Schubert in Vienna was erected in the Stadtpark. The poem is to be found again (perhaps the sole survivor of the play in an otherwise unknown seminal version, or perhaps genuine second thoughts), in the centenary edition of the poet's works that was published by Cotta in 1891 – but even here Schubert's name is not mentioned.

Autograph:	Gesellschaft der Musikfreunde, Vienna (first draft)
First edition:	Published as Book 40 no. 2 of the *Nachlass* by Diabelli, Vienna in *c.* 1842 (P349)
Subsequent editions:	Peters: Vol. 6/26 (D minor); AGA XX 355: Vol. 6/18; NSA IV: Vol. 12/84
Bibliography:	Capell 1928, pp. 167–8
	Einstein 1951, p. 189
	Fischer-Dieskau 1977, pp. 117–18
Discography and timing:	Fischer-Dieskau —
	Hyperion I 8[17]
	Hyperion II 21[17] 4'57 Sarah Walker

← *Das Mädchen* D652   *An die Freunde* D654 →

FRIEDRICH ANTON FRANZ BERTRAND (1757–*c.* 1829)

THE POETIC SOURCES
S1 *Taschenbuch zum geselligen Vergnügen*, Achtzehnter Jahrgang, 1808, Herausgegeben von W. G. Becker, Leipzig in der Niemannschen Buchhandlung

S2   *Taschenbuch zum geselligen Vergnügen*, von W. G. Becker, 1799 Leipzig bei Voss und Compagnie

S3   *Gedichte und Prosaische Aufsäzze von F. A. F. Bertrand*, Zerbst, 1813

THE SONGS

8 February 1815   *Minona* D152 [S1: pp. 228–30]

5–14 June 1815   *Adelwold und Emma* D211 [S2: pp. 251–64] [S3: pp. 8–25]

Bertrand, a German poet of French descent, was born in Könnern, near Halle an der Saale, on 13 May 1757 (other sources give the date as 17 July 1751). His forbears came from Dauphiné in the French Alps. He is such an obscure figure that Reed mistook him for a member of the Schubert circle, like Kenner (it is doubtful whether the poet ever visited Vienna). He studied in Halle, and worked first in Könnern and then in Köthen. His *Gedichte und Prosaische Aufsätze* appeared at Zerbst near Magdeburg in 1813; these contain versions of the two poems that Schubert set which are radically different from those used by the composer. Bertrand made frequent contributions to almanacs and contributed the libretto to Benda's opera *Pyramus und Thisbe* (1787). He wrote on historical and philosophical subjects, including an essay on suicide. From the rather questionable quality of his writing in these two ballads it seems amazing that Bertrand's work was accepted for periodicals of national renown, and that he achieved greater status than that of a local literary celebrity in his own provincial corner of Germany. Although Schubert changed many words in Bertrand's printed texts it is difficult to imagine what source other than Becker's almanacs from various years (publications that he seemed to have at his disposal for a number of his other settings) could have been available to the composer. In fact, there is another long Bertrand poem entitled *Adelheid von Hohenwall*, a crusader's tale, that was printed in Becker's *Taschenbuch* for 1810; having set the texts from the 1799 and 1808 issues of the same series, it is perhaps just as well that the young composer seems not to have encountered a third Bertrand text. The poet's exact date of death is not known – he died, probably in Dessau, some time after 1829.

Bibliography: Bodendorff 1996, p. 107

Die BETENDE   The maiden at prayer
(MATTHISSON) **D102** [H45]
B major   Autumn 1814

(63 bars)

Laura betet! Engelharfen hallen
  Frieden Gottes in ihr krankes Herz,
Und, wie Abels Opferdüfte, wallen
  Ihre Seufzer himmelwärts.

Laura is praying! Angels' harps sound
  Filling her sick heart with God's peace,
And, like the scents of Abel's sacrifice,
  Her sighs waft heavenwards.

Wie sie kniet, in Andacht hingegossen,	Kneeling, lost in prayer, she is
Schön, wie Raphael die Unschuld malt;	As lovely as Innocence painted by Raphael;
Vom Verklärungsglanze schon umflossen,	Already bathed in that transfigured radiance
Der um Himmelswohner strahlt.	Which shines around those who dwell in heaven.
O sie fühlt, im leisen, linden Wehen,	In the soft, gentle breeze she feels
Froh des Hocherhabnen Gegenwart,	With joy the presence of the Almighty;
Sieht im Geiste schon die Palmenhöhen,	Already she sees in her mind the palm-clad heights
Wo der Lichtkranz ihrer harrt!	Where the crown of light awaits her.
So von Andacht, so von Gottvertrauen	Her angelically pure breast swells
Ihre engelreine Brust geschwellt,	With devotion, with trust in God;
Betend diese Heilige zu schauen,	To behold this saintly maiden at prayer
Ist ein Blick in jene Welt.	Is to look into the world beyond.

FRIEDRICH VON MATTHISSON (1761–1831); poem written in 1778

This is the tenth of Schubert's twenty-nine Matthisson solo settings (1812–17). See the poet's biography for a chronological list of all the Matthisson settings.

This is Schubert's first excursion into B major in his songs, his tonality of sacred, intimate love, the key in which Zuleika will confide her love of Hatem to the East Wind (D720), and the apprentice-miller (in *Der Neugierige*) his love for the beautiful miller girl. The lines 'Vom Verklärungsglanze schon umflossen' – the idea of being bathed in transfiguring radiance – seem significant in a choice of tonality that the composer was later to use in the depiction of a kind of amorous fluidity. B major is also the key of the last of the Mignon songs (D877/3) in which the dying waif seems transfigured by an understanding of the deeper mysteries of life. In *Die Betende*, a strophic song that pre-dates *Gretchen am Spinnrade*, the confessional tone is reserved for where it is most appropriate – a church. Laura is praying, and with a thinly disguised voyeurism the poet watches her, turning his passion into a type of religious ecstasy. This is a forerunner of the exquisite mixture of devotion and blasphemy we find in Heine's poem *Im Rhein, im schönen Strome* that Schumann adopted for his *Dichterliebe*. The remote and exotic tonality limns the girl's sensual beauty rendered infinitely inaccessible by the conventions of society and religion. The musical style seems also to be transfigured: a Protestant chorale keeps its sober dignity in the outer voices, but writhes and falls chromatically in its inner parts – like a plainly covered hymn book that is secretly interleaved with miniatures in the sensuous Italian colours of Raphael. The Abel referred to here is, of course, the biblical character, Cain's brother, and not the Austrian portrait painter Josef Abel (1764–1818) whom Schubert admired and who some believe painted the composer's portrait in 1816.

   When Matthisson mentions the name 'Laura', Klopstock is never far away, and a whiff of a poet from an earlier, more devout, generation makes Schubert partially adopt the musical style of Klopstock's contemporary, C. P. E. Bach, whose settings of Gellert had defined piano-accompanied religious song thirty years before. Schubert is famous for his ability to take us outdoors and into the country (the open-air style is often invoked by the Matthisson poems); but here he shows his uncanny ability to set a song indoors, and light it with the muted, but rich, colours of light pouring through stained glass.

   The popular misconception that Schubert forgot his songs as soon as he had written them is belied by the fact that in the autumn of 1828 he used the opening bars of *Die Betende* in the sketches for his last work, the unfinished opera *Der Graf von Gleichen* D981 (No. 10c, Suleika's aria).

Autograph:	Complete autograph missing or lost; Wienbibliothek im Rathaus, Vienna holds a sketch of the vocal line
First edition:	Published as Book 31 no. 1 of the *Nachlass* by Diabelli, Vienna in 1840 (P332)
Subsequent editions:	Peters: Vol. 5/171; AGA XX 20: Vol. 1/156; NSA IV: Vol. 7/21; Bärenreiter: Vol. 5/119 (high voice), 113 (medium/low voice)
Further settings:	Carl Friedrich Zelter (1758–1832) *Die Betende* (1794) Ferdinand Ries (1784–1838) *Die Betende* Op. 96 no. 4 (1811)
Discography and timing:	Fischer-Dieskau I 2² 3'15 (Strophes 1, 2 and 4 only) Hyperion I 12¹⁶ Hyperion II 4¹ 4'16 Adrian Thompson

←— *Erinnerungen* D98   *An Laura, als sie Klopstocks Auferstehungslied sang* D115 —→

The BIBLE

Schubert set a number of songs taken from biblical themes. These range from D5 to D953 in terms of his solo songs and choral music, including three psalm settings. By far the most important of his 'biblical' works is the substantial 'Szenisches Oratorium' *Lazarus oder: die Feier der Auferstehung* D689 to the text of Hermann Niemeyer (1754–1828). Also on the resurrection theme is the tiny *Chor der Engel* D440 (for SATB) from Goethe's *Faust*. There are many songs in the Schubert canon with religious references that have only a tangential connection with the Bible (the world-famous *Ellens dritter Gesang* – Ave Maria – among them). Whereas a number of Brahms's biblically inspired songs are direct settings of Luther's translation of the Bible, Schubert's songs on biblical themes are either poetic re-workings of famous biblical stories, or translations of the Psalms of David.

Many of the settings of Klopstock, Fouqué, Kleist, Novalis (qqv) and so on, are of a spiritual or religious nature without being directly linked to the Bible. In 1831, as Volume 10 of Diabelli's *Nachlass* series, a book of eight *Geistliche Lieder* was published with poems by Klopstock, Schreiber, Schlegel, Jacobi, Schober, Körner and Silbert (qqv and *see* NACHLASS). Though these poets had a good working knowledge of the Bible, the texts themselves are not, strictly speaking, biblical (*see also* RELIGION AND RELIGIOUS MUSIC).

THE SONGS

30 March 1811	*Hagars Klage* D5 (Clemens Schücking) [derived from Chapters 16 and 21 of *Genesis*, Old Testament]
September–October 1812	*Entra l'uomo allor che nasce* D33 (Pietro Metastasio) [from *Isacco*, inspired by the story of Abraham and Isaac in Chapter 22: 1–24 of *Genesis*, Old Testament]
	There are six different settings in this group of exercises for Salieri: a solo song, a duet for soprano and alto, and terzet (SAT) and three different SATB quartets.
9 March 1815	*Jesus Christus, unser Heiland, der den Tod überwand* ('Osterlied'), D168A (Klopstock) [inspired by the New Testament Resurrection story]

June 1816	*Der gute Hirt* D449 (Johann Peter Uz) [a paraphrase of Psalm 23, Old Testament]
1818	*Evangelium Johannes* D607 (anonymous prose translation of Chapter 6:55–8 of *Gospel according to St John*, New Testament). This is not a Luther translation as is claimed in D₂ According to Reinhard Van Hoorickx, the complete text, including the introductory sentence, is found in the Gospel pericope for the Mass for the Feast of Corpus Christi
June 1819	*Der 13. Psalm* D663 (translation by Moses Mendelssohn, qv of Psalm 13, Old Testament)
December 1820	*Der 23. Psalm* D706 Quartet (SSAA) (translation by Moses Mendelssohn, qv of Psalm 23, Old Testament)
29 August 1823	*Der 8. Psalm* for voice and piano by Maximilian Stadler, arranged by Schubert (translation by Moses Mendelssohn, qv of Psalm 8, Old Testament)
August 1825	*Die Allmacht I* D852 (Pyrker) [Pyrker's text inspired by the story of the prophet Elisha from the book of *Kings* in the Old Testament]
January 1826	*Die Allmacht II* D875A (Pyrker) [*see* above]
March 1828	*Mirjams Siegesgesang* D942 (Grillparzer) [inspired by Chapter 15:19–21 of the book of *Exodus*, Old Testament]
July 1828	*Der 92. Psalm* for baritone solo, SATB Quartet and Chorus (in Hebrew, taken from lines 1–9 of Psalm 92, Old Testament)

Das BILD   The image
(ANONYMOUS) **D155** [H67]
F major   11 February 1815

(20 bars)

Ein Mädchen ist's, das früh und spät   Day and night I see a maiden
Mir vor der Seele schwebet,   In my mind's eye;

Ein Mädchen, wie es steht und geht,	A maiden who stands and moves,
Aus Himmelsreiz gewebet.	Woven from heaven's charms.
Ich seh's, wenn in mein Fenster mild	I see her when, through my window,
Der junge Morgen blinket,	The new morning shines gently;
Ich seh's, wenn lieblich wie das Bild	I see her when the evening star, as sweet as her image,
Der Abendstern mir winket.	Beckons to me.
Mir folgt's, ein treuer Weggenoss',	She follows me, a faithful companion,
Zur Ruh' und in's Getümmel;	Through calm and turmoil;
Ich fänd' es in der Erde Schoss,	I would find her in the depths of the earth,
Ich fänd' es selbst im Himmel.	Or even in the sky.
Es schwebt vor mir in Feld und Wald,	She hovers before me in the fields and the woods;
Prangt über'm Blumenbeete,	She appears radiantly above the flower beds,
Und glänzt in Seraphims Gestalt	And shines, in the form of a seraph,
Am Altar, wo ich bete.	At the altar where I pray.
Allein das Bild, das spät und früh	But this image, which day and night
Mir vor der Seele schwebet,	Hovers before my mind's eye,
Ist's nur Geschöpf der Phantasie,	Is it only a figment of my imagination,
Aus Luft und Traum gewebet?	Woven from air and dreams?
O nein, so warm auch Liebe mir	Oh no, fondly though my love
Das Engelbildniss malet,	Paints this angelic vision,
Ist's doch nur Schatten von der Zier,	The vision is but a shadow of the beauty
Die an dem Mädchen strahlet.	Which irradiates the maiden.

Anonymous/Unknown

This is the third of Schubert's nineteen solo settings of an anonymous poet. See Anonymous/Unknown for a chronological list of all the songs for which the poets are unknown.

Fischer-Dieskau has no hesitation in linking this simple and heartfelt song with Schubert's first love for Therese Grob. It is not, however, one of the works that was collected in the Grob songbook of November 1816. The absence of much specific physical description of the beloved in the poem tallies with the traditional idea of the almost spiritual nature of the relationship between the composer and the young church singer. This was built on admiration of her deeper personal qualities (according to something reportedly said about her by Schubert himself) rather than her beauty. It is also possible that the image is meant to be a heavenly one (of a guardian angel perhaps). The music is probably too flirtatious for this to be the case, but it remains poised in an ambiguous realm between sacred and profane.

In this gently rocking pastoral rhythm each musical verse is made up of two strophes of poetry. The bar of arpeggios by way of introduction printed in the Peters Edition is spurious. The tune is ingratiating in a Mozartian manner with a number of tiny word-setting felicities; the word 'schwebet' (b. 4) is set to a pair of dotted crotchets, the second of these a fourth higher than the first, an effect that sets the vocal line deliciously afloat. At 'Ich seh's, wenn in mein Fenster mild' (b. 9) the sparkling of the new dawn is painted by a jaunty waltz – or *Ländler* – as the left hand vamps in piquant staccati. The music is mostly one note per syllable, but the passage at 'Der Abendstern mir winket' (bb. 12–16) is suddenly expansive. 'Stern' gleams for two beats high in the stave and in unaccompanied splendour. 'Mir winket' is similarly extended, this time over a coquettishly modulating accompaniment that brings us back to the tonic key. The distance between the evening star and its earthbound admirer is evident here, but this passage is much less successful with different words in the later verses. The short postlude, all in the treble clef, is particularly charming; it culminates in a meltingly feminine cadence that redirects our gaze heavenward with a tiny upward scale in sixths, a happy inspiration, even by Schubert's exalted standards. As Fischer-Dieskau writes, this miniature 'outdoes many a sentimental song, or passionate operatic declamation'.

Autograph:	Missing or lost
First edition:	Published as Op. post. 165 no. 3 by C. A. Spina, Vienna in 1862 (P398)
Subsequent editions:	Peters: Vol. 6/90; AGA XX 42: Vol. 2/19; NSA IV: Vol. 7/140; Bärenreiter: Vol. 6/88
Discography and timing:	Fischer-Dieskau I 2[20] 2'36
	Hyperion I 22[15]
	Hyperion II 5[6] 2'26 Jamie MacDougall

← *Als ich sie erröten sah* D153   *Am Flusse* D160 →

BLANKA   Blanka
(F. VON SCHLEGEL) **D631** [H410]
A minor   December 1818

(20 bars)

Wenn mich einsam Lüfte fächeln,	When, in my solitude, breezes fan me,
Muss ich lächeln,	I must smile,
Wie ich kindisch tändelnd kose	As, like a child, I playfully
Mit der Rose.	Fondle the rose.
Wären nicht die neuen Schmerzen,	If it were not for this new suffering,
Möcht ich scherzen;	I should jest.
Könnt' ich, was ich ahnde, sagen,	If I could say what I sense,
Würd' ich klagen,	I should complain,
Und auch bange hoffend fragen:	And ask with anxious hope
Was verkünden meine Lose?	What my fate offers me.
Tändl' ich gleich mit Scherz und Rose,	Even if I jest, and dally with roses,
Muss ich lächelnd dennoch klagen.	Still I must complain as I smile.

FRIEDRICH VON SCHLEGEL (1772–1829); poem written in 1800/1801

This is the first of Schubert's sixteen Friedrich von Schlegel solo settings (1818–25). See the poet's biography for a chronological list of all the Friedrich von Schlegel settings.

Blanka and *Vom Mitleiden Mariä* D632 are the earliest Schubert settings of Friedrich von Schlegel. Both poems appear in the Berlin anthology, *Poetisches Taschenbuch* for 1806. This must have been Schubert's source as the title *Blanka* was not retained in the complete *Gedichte* (1809), and this poem, together with *Vom Mitleiden Mariä*, appears nowhere else. *Blanka* was reprinted under the title *Das Mädchen* in Schlegel's *Gedichte*, the last of nine 'Ansichten' or 'Views', a subdivision of a larger poetic cycle of thirty-one poems entitled *Stimmen der Liebe* ('Voices of Love'). The song is thus not a part of the *Abendröte* cycle, although the poem bears some resemblance to *Das Mädchen* D652; indeed in some early editions it is referred to as *Das Mädchen I*. Both of these exquisite confessions are poised between major- and minor-key feelings – the 'Lachen und Weinen' dichotomy that Schubert loves so much. The alternation between A major and A minor in *Das Mädchen*, and between A minor and A major in *Blanka*, is the purest of Schubert. Raymond Joly, however, found the switching of tonalities almost disorientating – as if the listener were being shunted to and fro, and rather too often, from light-heartedness to misgiving.

Both girls confess an inability to voice their feelings. Blanka's diffidence is reflected by an alternation of long phrases ('Wenn mich einsam Lüfte fächeln', bb. 1–2) with short ones ('Muss ich lächeln', bb. 3–4). In this poem's metre thoughts seem to trail away in mid-air, something that emphasizes the idea of the girl's vulnerability and is reinforced by the poem's printed appearance. Schubert aids this impression most beautifully with two-part writing: sighing figurations in the accompaniment of paired right-hand quavers as if played on a viola, gently phrased away after the impulse of the left-hand dotted crotchet on an imaginary cello. This evanescent music suggests the wilting of roses on the stem. During the pauses between the vocal phrases the piano takes over with an echo-like effect that underlines Blanka's pensiveness. The touches of A major refresh the drooping flower like restorative drops of water – an intimation of hope and of joy-to-come. The girl is on the threshold of life's romantic experiences, and she longs to walk into the gardens of delight. One senses here her trepidation, as well as the concentration needed to play a game of 'He loves me; he loves me not' as in Goethes *Faust*. In this respect, and particularly in terms of their shared tonality, the song is linked to the much longer and more elaborate *Delphine* D857/1.

The second four lines of the poem are set to exactly the same music as the first (a repeat of bb. 6–8). At b. 9 ('Und auch bange hoffend fragen') the texture of the accompaniment changes imperceptibly and becomes richer – three-part writing that suggests a string trio. The vocal line soars upwards as Blanka's feelings blossom; it is as if she has suddenly found her own voice. The triplet accompaniment in compound time supporting a plaintive vocal line in A minor brings to mind the celebrated *Lied der Mignon* D877/4. Blanka is not a tragic figure but, like Mignon, she is faced with a longing that seems larger than her fragile frame. The contained eloquence of the three-bar postlude (including the grace notes in the accompaniment at exactly this pitch in the last bar) suggests that Mozart's Rondo in A minor K511 was familiar music under Schubert's fingers.

Autograph:	In private possession, Vienna
First edition:	Published as Vol. 7 no. 20 in Friedlaender's edition by Peters, Leipzig in 1885 (P471)
Subsequent editions:	Peters: Vol. 7/44; AGA XX 348: Vol. 5/236; NSA IV: Vol. 12/62
Bibliography:	Capell 1928, p. 145
	Einstein 1951, p. 186
	Fischer-Dieskau 1977, p. 124
Discography and timing:	Fischer-Dieskau —
	Hyperion I 9[8] 2'02 Arleen Auger

Hyperion II 27¹⁹   2'12   Christine Schäfer
Hyperion II 21⁴   2'02   Arleen Auger

← *Sonett III D630*   *Vom Mitleiden Mariä D632* →

Der BLINDE KNABE   The blind boy
(CIBBER) OP. 101 NO. 2, **D833** [H562]

This song exists in two versions, the second of which is discussed below:
(1) April 1825; (2) appeared September 1827

(1) 'Langsam'   B♭ major   **C**   [44 bars]

(2) B♭ major

A literal translation of the German is given here. Cibber's original poem is printed below in italics.

O sagt, ihr Lieben, mir einmal,	Now tell me, dear friends,
Welch Ding ist's, Licht genannt?	What is this thing called Light?
Was sind des Sehens Freuden all,	What are all these joys of seeing
Die niemals ich gekannt?	That I have never known?
Die Sonne, die so hell ihr seht,	The sun that you see so bright
Mir Armen scheint sie nie;	Never shines for me, poor boy;
Ihr sagt, sie auf und nieder geht,	You tell me it rises and sets,
Ich weiss nicht wann, noch wie.	Yet I know not when nor how.
Ich mach mir selbst so Tag wie Nacht,	I myself make my day and night
Dieweil ich schlaf und spiel,	Whilst I sleep or play;
Mein inn'res Leben schön mir lacht,	My inner life smiles brightly,
Ich hab' der Freuden viel.	And many are my joys.
Zwar kenn' ich nicht, was euch erfreut,	Though I do not know what gladdens you
Doch drückt mich keine Schuld,	No guilt weighs me down.
Drum freu' ich mich in meinem Leid	Therefore I rejoice in my sorrow
Und trag es mit Geduld.	And bear it patiently.
Ich bin so glücklich, bin so reich	I am so happy and so rich
Mit dem, was Gott mir gab,	With that which God gave me.
Bin wie ein König froh, obgleich	I am as joyful as a king,
Ein armer, blinder Knab'.	Though but a poor, blind boy.

O say! what is that thing call'd light,
Which I must ne'er enjoy;
What are the blessings of the sight,
O tell your poor blind boy!

You talk of wondrous things you see,
You say the sun shines bright;
I feel him warm, but how can he
Or make it day or night?

My day or night myself I make
When e'er I sleep or play;
And could I ever keep awake
With me 'twere always day.

With heavy sighs I often hear
You mourn my hapless woe;
But sure with patience I can bear
A loss I ne'er can know.

Then let not what I cannot have
My cheer of mind destroy:
Whilst thus I sing, I am a king,
Although a poor blind boy.

COLLEY CIBBER (1671–1757), translated by
JACOB NICOLAUS CRAIGHER DE JACHELUTTA (1797–1855)

This is Schubert's only setting of a Cibber text and the second of his three Craigher solo settings
(1825). See Cibber's biography for further information about the poet, and Craigher's biography
for a chronological list of all the Craigher settings.

An early edition of *Der blinde Knabe* (Vienna, *c.* 1830).

'For the sighted complacently to put smooth words into the mouth of the blind, and make a comfortable song of unimagined disaster is a sentimentality and an impertinence.' Thus Richard Capell castigates Schubert's age which was more susceptible to pathos, and more moved by melodrama than our own politically correct century. When this song was performed by Vogl accompanied by the composer it drew tears from the great pianist Johann Nepomuk Hummel who proceeded to improvise on it to great effect. As a child of his time Hummel responded unashamedly to this scenario combining childhood and tragedy, just as the Victorian reader wept at the death of Dickens's Little Nell. The tragedy of blindness had even been broached in an otherwise comical Viennese *Singspiel* composed in 1811 – Adalbert Gyrowetz's *Der Augenarzt* – with which Schubert was clearly familiar as a young man and which included a leading role for Johann Michael Vogl as the regimental doctor. There is a duet in that work for two blind children which influenced Schubert's duet for the two children of Theages in his operatic fragment *Die Bürgschaft* D435 (no. 8 of that work).

Our heart goes out to Hummel for having been one of the very few real musical celebrities of Schubert's day to be receptive to the composer's magic. Those tears were also doubtless occasioned by Vogl's impersonation of the blind boy that was probably completely over the top by the performing standards of our own day (an indication of this can be found in the singer's ornamented version of the song in Volume 5b of the NSA, *see* ORNAMENTATION). Cibber's words (along the lines of 'what you've never had, you never miss') were in questionable taste, yet Schubert's music seems to be centred on the same inner radiance and bravery against the odds that make the celebrated *Frühlingsglaube* D686 such a powerful song. In that work the singer is almost transcendentally convinced that spring will come and that everything will change for the better. For many a listener, the singer's confidence in this improvement of circumstance is merely heart-breaking self-delusion. The distance between optimism and reality is hidden within the setting, voiced by the accompaniment, but we are touched by the bravery of a rare spirit who must almost certainly face further disappointment. This is surely a musical encapsulation of the composer's own refusal to become cynical in the face of tragedy.

For us to appreciate fully the haunting sadness of *Frühlingsglaube*, the song must be performed with radiant conviction. In the same way, the blind boy's pride, strength and independence are what emerge from Schubert's setting, rather than any lament for his handicap. It is left to the listener to be moved by the gulf between the composer's feelings of compassion for the blind boy, and the youngster's own unaccountable lack of self-pity.

The prelude of the opening bars seems to grope for the light. The four-note arpeggio figure is repeated and laid out in such a way that even the rhythm is uncertain; the ear can easily be tricked into believing that the first semiquavers form a weak upbeat rather than a strong downbeat – an effect of deliberate disorientation, a tonal analogue for blindness via the workings of the ear. After two beats we hear the other feature of the introduction that pervades the whole song – two quavers played 'mezzo staccato' in the bass. This rectifies the rhythmical *trompe l'oreille* of the first two beats as it pulls their wayward ramblings into line; these hollow knocking sounds also suggest the tapping of the blind boy's stick which helps him to get his bearings.

The vocal line begins somewhat tentatively, the tune punctuated by rests as if the singer is searching for words – in fact he is searching for the definition of a word. When he names this concept, known to him only by the name 'Licht', we leap out of the dark from the F of 'ist's' (b. 4) to the E flat above, supported by the moderating uncertainty of dominant seventh harmony (b. 5). The elusive word 'light' glows with a halo of mystery like a distant and unknown star. Throughout the song, when the tapping is absent, the voice clings to the tenor line in the pianist's left hand at the interval of a tenth (in performances with a soprano that is, a third when sung by a tenor). This physical contact with another surface suggests that the boy is carefully feeling his way through the music, as if guided by a hand rail.

For the second verse we modulate into the dominant (from b. 10); the sun's music consists of a vocal line of deliberately monotonous Cs (for the boy, the sun neither rises nor sets). For a moment the stoic mezzo-staccato quavers in the left hand that propel the music forward seem prophetic of *Der Wegweiser* in *Winterreise*. In the third verse on the phrase 'Tag wie Nacht' (b. 18) the traditional musical analogues for light and darkness are reversed, with 'Nacht' sung on a note both higher and longer than that for day. The wafting, gently melismatic thirds at bb. 19 and 23 have been sung elsewhere in Schubert's output – in the middle section of *Der Jüngling auf dem Hügel* D702 where the subject matter is another boy (emotionally rather than physically handicapped) and in the same key of B flat as the aria of King Mauregato (*Alfonso und Estrella* D732/32) who dreams in vain of hearing joyful songs resound through his gloomy palace. All three characters describe visions of happiness which their various conditions render unattainable. At 'ich weiss nicht wann, noch wie' (Verse 2, b. 14), and at the similar passage at 'und trag es mit Geduld' (Verse 4, b. 29), the descending sequence, decorated with shrinking appoggiaturas, somehow suggests that the singer is small of stature or frail, perhaps even that he has a limp.

It is the music of the fifth verse, however, which lifts the song on to a different plane. The double-dotted rhythms of 'so glücklich' and 'so reich' (bb. 30–31, and again at bb. 36–7) show a glimmer of defiance, the pride of someone who is king of his own world. The final echo in the major key of 'Ein armer, blinder Knab' (bb. 40–41) is of such tenderness and compassion that it seems the composer himself has taken over from the protagonist who, in any case, does not understand how 'poor' he is. It is as if Schubert had quietly slipped into the picture to give the boy his own affectionate embrace.

Craigher intended to make the song singable in both English and German. It is true that the original poem can be sung to this music, but with a loss of its effectiveness (e.g. the mention of 'light' comes at the wrong point for Schubert's music in the English version). Another translation of Cibber's poem was printed in *Lieder für Blinden und von Blinden*, Wien, 1827, a book Schubert probably knew as it was the possible source of his 1828 Kuffner setting, *Glaube, Hoffnung und Liebe* D955. This translation by Johann Graf Mailáth (qv) (headed 'from the English') is coupled with the name of the composer Simon Sechter (the teacher whom Schubert consulted for lessons in counterpoint in the last year of his life) who spent a good deal of his life working with the institute for the blind in Vienna. There is no music printed in this anthology.

Autographs:	Wienbibliothek im Rathaus, Vienna (first version, first draft); Pierpont Morgan Library, New York (second version, fair copy)
Publication:	First published as part of the AGA in 1895 (P694; first version) First published as a supplement to the *Wiener Zeitschrift* in September 1827, and subsequently as Op. 101 no. 2 by H. A. Probst, Vienna in 1828. A variant of this version was published as the song's third edition in Diabelli's *Philomele* in 1829; the ornamentation perhaps goes back to Johann Michael Vogl (P180; second version)
First known performance:	8 January 1829, *Abend-Unterhaltung* of the Gesellschaft der Musikfreunde, Musikverein, Vienna. Soloist: Ludwig Tietze (see Waidelich/Hilmar Dokumente I No. 682 for full concert programme)
Subsequent editions:	Peters: Vol. 2/196; AGA XX 468a & b: Vol. 8/54 (first version) & 58 (second version); NSA IV: Vol. 5a/162 (first version), 166 (second version) & Vol. 5b/252 (second version variant); Bärenreiter: Vol. 4/58

Bibliography: Black 2003, p. 115
                           Capell 1928, p. 207
                           Fischer-Dieskau 1977, p. 244
Further settings: William Hurlstone (1876–1906) *The Blind Boy* (1906)
Discography and timing: Fischer-Dieskau II 7[2]   2'41
                           Hyperion I 15[16]
                           Hyperion II 29[17]   3'47   Margaret Price

←— *Im Walde* D834   *Totengräbers Heimwehe* D842 —→

BLONDEL ZU MARIEN   Blondel to Mary
(ANONYMOUS) **D626** [H404]

There are two versions of this song, both of which are discussed below:
(1)   E♭ minor – E♭ major   September 1818

(2)   C♯ minor – D♭ major   1812

In düstrer Nacht,   In the dark night,
Wenn Gram mein fühlend Herz umziehet,   When grief envelops my tender heart,
Des Glückes Sonne mir entfliehet,   When the sun of happiness
Und ihre Pracht: And its splendour escape me,
Da leuchtet fern   A fair star
In feurig wonniglichem Glanze,   Shines in the distance
Wie in der Liebe Strahlenkranze,   With a fiery, joyous lustre,
Ein holder Stern.   Like a jewel in the radiant crown of love.

Und ewig rein   Amid joy and sorrow
Lebt unter Wonne, unter Schmerzen,   Its reflection
Im treuen liebevollen Herzen   Remains for ever pure
Sein Wiederschein.   Within my faithful, loving heart.
So hold und mild   Thus your magic image,
Wird unter tröstenden Gestalten   Fair and gentle,
Auch in der Ferne mich umwalten   Will stay by me and comfort me
Dein Zauberbild.   Though I am far away.

ANONYMOUS/UNKNOWN

This is the eighteenth of Schubert's nineteen solo settings of an anonymous poet.
See Anonymous/Unknown for a chronological list of all the songs for which the poets
are unknown.

Schubert composed this song during his first stay in Zseliz, Hungary, as a tutor to the daughters of Count Esterházy. Of all the lieder from this period this must surely be the most elaborately ornate and suggestive of *bel canto* operatic style. Grétry's *Richard Cœur de Lion* (or *Richard Löwenherz* as it was known in translation) was highly popular in Vienna. Blondel de Nesle, the king's minstrel whose song is heard by the imprisoned monarch from outside the castle walls, is a major character in that opera. There were no fewer than forty-five performances of this work at the Theater an der Wien between 1810 and 1822. There are various Blondel serenades in Grétry's opera, but not one of them bears a similarity to this text, and none of them is addressed to the character of Marie – whether this is the minstrel's beloved, or the Virgin Mary, is also not clear. Given the song's place in the Schubert canon, the latter seems more likely. In any case, Blondel's single-minded devotion to England's King Richard I was famous to the exclusion perhaps of his attachment to any female paramour.

Leo Black has made the observation that the closing five lines of this text are reminiscent of Matthisson's *Geisternähe*, but the poem has been long ascribed to Grillparzer. One of the versions of *Blondel zu Marien* (albeit the one for which we are lacking an autograph) shares the same unusual E flat minor tonality as that poet's *Bertas Lied in der Nacht* D653, and Schubert might have had a poem from Grillparzer in autograph form – if this is so it has not survived in that author's published works. A number of other songs of the period have a Marian connection, including Schlegel's *Vom Mitleiden Mariä* D632 and *Das Marienbild* D623 with a text by Aloys Schreiber (who has also been suggested as a possible author). This aspect of the Catholic faith seems to have been dear to the Esterházy family and the young countesses. One could conjecture that Schubert was drawn into the same enthusiasm despite his religious doubts (vehemently expressed in a letter from Zseliz to his brother Ignaz) or that he simply chose a text of this kind (from an unknown volume in the Esterházy library) to please his employers and hosts. A specific request from a member of the family to set these words is also possible. The manuscript of the song stayed in the possession of the Esterházys for many years, although one wonders who might have sung it; everything about this song suggests a light tenor. The tenor Karl von Schönstein was introduced to Schubert in Zseliz in 1818 and he must be a strong contender. As for the Esterházy family, the count was a bass, and the tessitura is far too high to have suited Karoline Esterházy's alto (her mother, the countess, was also an alto). This leaves the other sister, the sixteen-year-old Marie Esterházy, as a possible interpreter; she was a soprano and rather a good one. If Schubert intended the song for her, the poem's title would have seemed particularly apposite. With the recent discovery of an autograph in C sharp minor (*see* below), a much more accessible key, this seems even more of a possibility than before.

The five-bar introduction suggests the grand manner of a fully orchestrated operatic prelude. In bb. 3–4 the flute plays its part in setting the scene with a sequence of upward arpeggios. The portrait of night with which the song starts looks ahead to the heavy triplets and weary vocal line of the opening of *Der Unglückliche* D713. The sunset of happiness is painted by a long and ominous descending bass line under 'Des Glückes Sonne mir entfliehet' (bb. 8–9). Mention of a fair star shining afar makes for a change into the tonic major (b. 11) where the song remains. Mention of a 'fiery, joyous lustre' (b. 12) sparks off an extravagant response in the cascading vocal line. These ornamental passages, clearly authentic Schubert, are somewhat in the style of the vocal embellishments by his singer, Johann Michael Vogl. Once again one imagines a scenario where a song was written to show off the vocal accomplishments of a young Esterházy countess with music written in the newly fashionable Italian *bel canto* style.

The second verse is a modified reworking of the first, but this time in the major key. It seems natural that 'Dein Zauberbild' in the closing bars should prompt further magical melismas. According to copyists' written marginalia it seems almost certain that one of Schubert's autographs, now lost, must have been in E flat minor – the key that is printed definitively in NSA. This tonality, as well as its time signature of $\frac{12}{8}$, had already appeared in a work written during this summer at Zseliz: in the extended Mayrhofer setting *Einsamkeit* D620, a piano-accompanied song cantata, or cycle of sorts, we find a cantilena (beginning 'Ihn bewegt der Sehnsucht Schmerz' bb. 243–56) that is a musical relation of Blondel's hymn.

In the Sotheby's catalogue of 9 June 2010, an autograph of *Blondels zu Marien* re-emerged for sale after a gap of seventy-five years (it was last offered at Sotheby's in 1935, but no Schubert scholar seems to have paid any attention to it at the time). This beautifully penned copy (the handwriting is that of Schubert in 1818) is in the key of C sharp minor, with small differences in the vocal line and piano writing from the version hitherto taken to be definitive. The postlude contains slightly different chromatic inflections. This clearly ranks as another version of the song, although whether first or second is impossible to tell. It might be that the copyists made a mistake concerning Schubert's original key of E flat minor, and that this newly discovered autograph is the original version. It is much more likely, however, to be a written-out transposition made by Schubert for a member of the Esterházy family – it has the appearance of a presentation copy. In the higher key of E flat minor the song seems rather more beautiful, certainly more unusual, but it is significantly harder to sing.

Autograph:	In private possession (second version)
Publication:	Published as Book 34 no. 2 of the *Nachlass* by Diabelli, Vienna in 1842 (P340)
Subsequent editions:	Peters: Vol. 5/200; AGA XX 343: Vol. 5/218; NSA IV: Vol 12/40
Bibliography:	Capell 1928, pp. 146–7
	Einstein 1951, p. 184
Discography and timing:	Fischer-Dieskau II 2[6] 3'35
	Hyperion I 21[23] 2'57 Edith Mathis
	Hyperion I 29[15] 3'18 Marjana Lipovšek
	Hyperion II 20[18] 3'18 Edith Mathis

⟵ *Das Marienbild* D623   *Lob der Tränen* D711 ⟶

Die BLUME UND DER QUELL *see* O QUELL, WAS STRÖMST DU RASCH UND WILD D874

Der BLUMEN SCHMERZ   The flowers' anguish
(MAILÁTH) **D731** [H476]
E minor   September 1821

(99 bars)

Wie tönt es mir so schaurig[1]	With what dread do I hear
Des Lenzes erstes Wehn,	The first breezes of spring;
Wie dünkt es mir so traurig,	How sad it is to me
Dass Blumen auferstehn.	That flowers rise up again.
In ihrer Mutter Armen	They lay so quietly
Da ruhten sie so still,	In their mother's arms,
Nun müssen, ach, die Armen	And now the poor things
Hervor ins Weltgewühl.	Must come out into the teeming world.
Die zarten Kinder heben	The delicate children shyly
Die Häupter scheu empor:	Raise their heads:
'Wer rufet uns ins Leben	'Who summons us into life
Aus stiller Nacht hervor?'	From the peaceful night?'
Der Lenz mit Zauberworten,	Spring, with magic words,
Mit Hauchen süsser Lust,	Breathing sweet delight,
Lockt aus den dunkeln Pforten	Lures them through the dark portals
Sie von der Mutter Brust.	From their mother's breast.
In bräutlich heller Feier	In a lustrous bridal ceremony
Erscheint der Blumen Pracht,	The flowers appear in their glory;
Doch fern schon ist der Freier,	But the groom is already far away,
Wild glüht der Sonne Macht.	And the mighty sun glows harshly.
Nun künden ihre Düfte,	Now their fragrance reveals
Dass sie voll Sehnsucht sind;	That they are full of longing;
Was labend würzt die Lüfte,	The refreshing scent that spices the air
Es ist der Schmerzen Kind.	Is the child of sorrow.
Die Kelche sinken nieder,	The chalices droop,
Sie schauen Erdenwärts:	Gazing earthwards:
'O Mutter, nimm uns wieder,	'O mother, receive us again,
Das Leben gibt nur Schmerz.'	For life gives only pain.'
Die welken Blätter fallen,	The withered leaves fall;
Mild deckt der Schnee sie zu –	The snow gently covers them.
Ach Gott! So gehts mit allen,	O God, so it is with all;
Im Grabe nur ist Ruh.	Only in the grave is there peace.

JOHANN, COUNT MAILÁTH (1768–1855)

This is Schubert's only setting of a Mailáth text. See the poet's biography.

The first thing that the seasoned Schubertian will hear in the introduction is a little sighing motif (bb. 1 and 3) that recalls the Goethe setting *Geheimes* D719, composed six months earlier. The words in that Goethe setting talk of the lover's flirtatious eyes, beguiling and cheeky. The

---

[1] Schubert replaces the poet's 'Wie ist er mir' with 'Wie tönt es mir'.

idea of flowers emerging from the ground to cast their first vulnerable glance into the outside world has inspired the composer to similar musical imagery – a falling figure of two notes, pointedly phrased. Schubert was later to use the same key in the apotheosis of his songs of withered, wilting and dried flowers – *Trockne Blumen* from *Die schöne Müllerin* D795/18.

The sentimentality of the lyrics is 'sickly sweet' for Einstein and 'hard to bear' for Fischer-Dieskau, yet Schubert's music somehow redeems these failings; he has found a means of making us believe in the poet's self-pitying death wish, even if it is disguised in a flower allegory with a strong whiff of Victorian sentiment. The song has something in common with Schubert's *Viola* D786, as well as the *Abendröte* settings (qv) where Schlegel employs the pathetic fallacy to greater effect than Mailáth. In these songs Schubert creates vocal lines of similarly naïve simplicity, as well as rhythmical patterns that reflect the unspoiled childlike simplicity of nature. In *Der Blumen Schmerz* the repeated notes of 'tönt es mir so' at the voice's entrance (b. 5) are typical of this, as is the music for the very similar third and fourth strophes, both in the key of C major, with an accompaniment that inhabits the etiolated treble-clef spheres of *Nachtviolen* D752 (bb. 25–30 and again at bb. 35–40).

The fifth and sixth verses ('In bräutlich heller Feier' bb. 46–56, and 'Nun künden ihre Düfte' bb. 56–6) form an A major variant of the two opening strophes in E minor. The first two lines of the seventh verse ('Die Kelche sinken nieder' bb. 70–72) are set in a semi-melodic way, a quasi-recitative that leads into the flowers' final plea. The ten-bar passage (beginning 'O Mutter, nimm uns wieder') is marked 'Etwas bewegter' in the AGA and NSA, but not in the Peters Edition where the text runs out at this point, and is followed by an eight-bar postlude. This truncated version of *Der Blumen Schmerz* was taken from a manuscript possibly prepared and abridged by the singer Vogl for an early performance. The more authentic version has music for one more verse (marked Tempo I – 'Die welken Blätter fallen') which contains perhaps the most individual ideas of the piece: muted right hand chords in the bass clef are underpinned by tiny funeral march drumbeats on a pedal E. (It is this music that is more or less co-opted for the postlude of what one may term the 'corrupt' version in the Peters Edition.) The song ends in the pathetic major (bb. 96–9) whereby death is a welcome balm; this play between major and minor recalls *Der Müller und der Bach* – another song from *Die schöne Müllerin*.

Autograph:	In private possessision, Basel (part of album for Alois Fuchs)
First edition:	Published as a supplement to *Wiener Zeitschrift für Kunst, Literatur, Theater und Mode* in December 1821 and subsequently as Op. post. 173 no. 4 by C. A. Spina, Vienna in 1867 (P410)
First known performance:	18 April 1822 in a concert organized by Ignaz Sonnleithner, Gesellschaft der Musikfreunde, Vienna. Soloist: Josef Barth (see Waidelich/Hilmar Dokumente I No. 150 for full concert programme)
Subsequent editions:	Peters: Vol. 6/116; AGA XX 399: Vol. 6/210; NSA IV: Vol. 5a/138; Bärenreiter: Vol. 4/50
Bibliography:	Capell 1928, p. 170
	Einstein 1951, p. 252
Discography and timing:	Fischer-Dieskau II 4[15] 3'48
	Hyperion I 19[4]
	Hyperion II 25[2] 4'04 Felicity Lott

←*Johanna Sebus* D728   *Die Rose* D745→

BLUMENBALLADE *see* VERGISSMEINNICHT D792 *and* VIOLA D786

Der BLUMENBRIEF	The message of flowers

(SCHREIBER) **D622** [H402]
D major   August 1818

(28 bars)

Euch Blümlein will ich senden
Zur schönen Jungfrau dort,
Fleht sie, mein Leid zu enden
Mit einem guten Wort.

Du, Rose kannst ihr sagen,
Wie ich in Lieb' erglüh',
Wie ich um sie muss klagen
Und weinen spät und früh.

[(. . .)]

Du Myrte, flüstre leise
Ihr meine Hoffnung zu,
Sag': 'Auf des Lebens Reise
Glänzt ihm kein Stern als du.'

Du Ringelblume, deute
Ihr der Verzweiflung Schmerz,
Sag' ihr: 'des Grabes Beute
Wird ohne dich sein Herz.'

Flowers, I will send you
To that fair lady;
Implore her to end my suffering
With one kind word.

You, rose, can tell her
How I burn with love,
And how I pine for her,
Weeping night and day.

[(. . .)]

You, myrtle, softly whisper
My hopes to her;
Tell her: 'On life's journey
You are the only star that shines for him.'

You, marigold, reveal to her
The pain of despair;
Tell her: 'Without you
His heart will fall prey to the grave.'

ALOYS SCHREIBER (1761–1841)

This is the second of Schubert's four Schreiber solo settings (1818). See the poet's biography for a chronological list of all the Schreiber settings.

This enchanting little song was written in Zseliz in Hungary where Schubert spent the summer of 1818 as music master to the two young Esterházy countesses. Schubert had set the Schreiber poem *An den Mond in einer Herbstnacht* D614 in April 1818. Perhaps the composer, already working as a teacher to the girls, had borrowed a copy of Schreiber's recently published *Poetische Werke* (1817) from the library of the Esterházys in Vienna, kept it and taken it with him to Zseliz in July. It is also possible that Schreiber's works came recommended for musical setting by his employers; this poet, with his devout view of life, was bound to be a favourite with that particular family. *Der Blumenbrief*, with its emphasis on the language of flowers (*see* Die BLUMENSPRACHE D519), would also have pleased the romantic adolescent sensibilities of the composer's two charges, particularly the thirteen-year-old Karoline, the younger of the two, who studied both piano and voice. She was later said to be the woman Schubert most loved.

The four-bar introduction seems to be caught between two possibilities: 'She loves me; she loves me not.' The fate of the singer is balanced within a pair of phrases, the second answering the first. This anticipates the opening of *Der Neugierige* from *Die schöne Müllerin*, a song where the miller boy briefly considers whether he should consult the flowers about his chances in love before deciding against it ('Ich frage keine Blume'). Like that masterpiece, *Der Blumenbrief* is in ⅔ with a similar summery charm and an Italianate cantilena that would have been high even for the talented singer Karl von Schönstein. Schubert met this artist in Zseliz in 1818 and it is possible that the song owes its existence to the burgeoning of their friendship. It is also possible that the tessitura was designed to suit the soprano of the Zseliz household, Marie Esterházy.

The miller boy decides that the brook is his best advocate; the singer of *Der Blumenbrief* allows the symbolic meaning of flowers to declare his love. Schubert must have thought this the appropriate language, unaffected and gently chromatic, in which to address nature. The little four-bar interlude (bb. 12–15, the plucking of staccato quavers, as if blooms were being solicitously picked and arranged) is particularly delightful. At mention of rose, myrtle and marigold the music is paragraphed for each flower as the singer addresses them separately, and one by one, on his stroll through the garden. He is planning the composition of a bouquet that will reveal his feelings to his beloved in a code she will understand. Something about the tentative nature of the vocal line oscillating between adjacent semitones (F sharp and E sharp) in bb. 4 and 8 suggests the discretion and secrecy that makes this kind of subterfuge necessary in their relationship. Perhaps that is why the vocal line of another song about secret love (*Heimliches Lieben* D922 in B flat major) is brought to mind.

Singers who have used the Peters Edition have also come to know *Der Blumenbrief* in B flat major. When the publisher Diabelli issued the song in the *Nachlass* it was clearly his decision that the much higher D major was too demanding a tonality for the amateur singers who made up the majority of his market. In fact the tessitura of the original key still seems impossibly high for even the finest artists; Diabelli's decision has helped to keep the song in recital circulation.

Autograph:	Wienbibliothek im Rathaus, Vienna (first draft)
First edition:	Published as Book 21 no. 1 of the *Nachlass* by Diabelli, Vienna in 1833 (P297)
Subsequent editions:	Peters: Vol. 2/225; AGA XX 340: Vol. 5/213; NSA IV: Vol. 12/36
Bibliography:	Capell 1928, p. 145
Discography and timing:	Fischer-Dieskau II 2[3] 2'08
	Hyperion I 21[22]
	Hyperion II 20[16] 2'04 Edith Mathis

⟵ *Einsamkeit* D620   *Das Marienbild* D623 ⟶

BLUMENLIED
(Hölty) **D431** [H258]   Flower song
E major   May 1816

(22 bars)

Es ist ein halbes Himmelreich,	It is almost heaven
Wenn, Paradiesesblumen gleich,	When, like blooms of paradise,
Aus Klee die Blumen dringen;	The flowers spring up from the clover
Und wenn die Vögel silberhell	And when with silvery voice
Im Garten hier, und dort am Quell,	The birds sing on blossoming boughs
Auf Blütenbäumen singen.	Here in the garden, and yonder by the stream.
Doch holder blüht ein edles Weib,	But lovelier still blooms a noble lady,
Von Seele gut und schön von Leib,	Sweet of soul and fair of form,
In frischer Jugendblüte.	In the freshness of youth.
Wir lassen alle Blumen stehn,	We leave all the flowers be
Das liebe Weibchen anzusehn,	To gaze at that beloved lady
Und freun uns ihrer Güte.	And to delight in her goodness.

LUDWIG CHRISTOPH HÖLTY (1748–1776); poem written in January 1773. Adapted for publication in 1804 by JOHANN HEINRICH VOSS (1751–1826)

This is the nineteenth of Schubert's twenty-three Hölty solo settings (1813–16). See the poet's biography for a chronological list of all the Hölty settings.

This charming Hölty setting is closely related to another song in the same key by the same poet, and composed just before it – *Die frühe Liebe* D430. It also bears comparison with the celebrated *Seligkeit* D433, written in the same month and also in E major. It is as if the composer is searching to establish a special tonality and mood for this poet's lyrics. There is no doubt that during this Maytime Schubert linked innocence and joy with this key and with Hölty. This is in marked contrast to the composer's explorations of a more reflective side of the poet's work in 1815. Other examples of this festival of song-setting in E major are *Erntelied* D434 and *Minnelied* D429.

It is impossible to resist the musical energy and genial high spirits of this music which is never raucous in mood but nevertheless suggests the earthiness of country life. Mention of birds singing 'silberhell' (b. 8) brings forth delicately ringing semiquaver repetitions in the right-hand piano writing, first on F sharps, and later on higher and more silvery Bs (b. 13). The accompaniment here is sufficiently decorative to describe a garden, and liquid enough to describe a stream. Leo Black has pointed out how similar the opening of this song is to the watery trout, *Die Forelle* D550, and how both songs are somehow related to the princess's opening spinning chorus in the opera *Fierabras* D796: 'all three passages touch on freshness and innocence, those of a girl seen by the poet as like a flower, a trout in a stream, and a dreamer princess unaware of the way of the world'. The fermata on the word 'Quell' with its dominant seventh harmony prophesies a famous moment ('Nicht minder freundlich schwimmt im Quell') in the Schulze song

Im Frühling D882. The introduction of a beautiful lady into the picture in the second verse is inevitable in a flower lyric of this type. The music has a springtime jauntiness and the young man's attentions, constrained by the courtly love tradition if the poem is read on its own, take on a rather cheeky immediacy thanks to Schubert's music. The four-bar postlude, as simple as it is ingenious, brings yet another little-known page of Schubert to a close, a flawless miracle within its own modestly defined terms. The lyric is an imitation of, and homage to, a poem entitled *Sô die bluomen ûz dem grase dringent* by Walther von der Vogelweide (1170–1230). This is less clear in J. H. Voss's adaption of the text (as set by Schubert) than in Hölty's original poem, reprinted in Schochow 1974, Vol. 1 pp. 188–9.

Autograph:	Österreichische Nationalbibliothek, Vienna
First edition:	Published as Vol. 7 no. 46 in Friedlaender's edition by Peters, Leipzig in 1887 (P507)
Subsequent editions:	Peters: Vol. 7/100; AGA XX 233: Vol. 4/105; NSA IV: Vol. 10/158
Bibliography:	Black 1998, p. 22
Discography and timing:	Fischer-Dieskau I 7[13] 1'24
	Hyperion I 18[4]
	Hyperion II 14[9] 1'26 Peter Schreier

←—*Die frühe Liebe* D430   *Der Leidende (Klage)* D432—→

Die BLUMENSPRACHE   The language of flowers
(Platner/Plattner?) **D519** [H371]
B♭ major   October 1817?

(117 bars)

Es deuten die Blumen der Herzens Gefühle,	Flowers reveal the feelings of the heart;
Sie sprechen manch heimliches Wort;	They speak many a secret word;
Sie neigen sich traulich am schwankenden Stiele,	They incline confidingly on their swaying stems
Als zöge die Liebe sie fort.	As though drawn by love.
Sie bergen verschämt sich im deckenden Laube,	They hide shyly amid concealing foliage,
Als hätte verraten der Wunsch sie dem Raube.	As though desire had betrayed them to seduction.
Sie deuten im leise bezaubernden Bilde	They reveal, in a delicate, enchanting image,
Der Frauen, der Mädchen Sinn;[1]	The nature of women and maidens;
Sie deuten das Schöne, die Anmut, die Milde,	They signify beauty, grace, gentleness;

[1] In the original poem 'Der Frauen, der *Mägdelein* Sinn'.

Sie deuten des Lebens Gewinn:	They embody life's rewards:
Es hat mit der Knospe, so heimlich verschlungen,	In the bud, so secretly concealed,
Der Jüngling die Perle der Hoffnung gefunden.[2]	The youth has found the pearl of hope.
Sie weben der Sehnsucht, des Harmes Gedanken Aus Farben ins duftige Kleid.	They weave thoughts of yearning and sorrow Into their fragrant dress with coloured strands
Nichts frommen der Trennung gehässige Schranken,	The hateful barriers of separation are of no importance;
Die Blumen verkünden das Leid.	Flowers proclaim our suffering.
Was laut nicht der Mund, der bewachte, darf sagen,	What guarded lips may not speak aloud
Das waget die Huld sich in Blumen zu klagen.	Kindness will dare to lament through flowers.
[(. . .)]	[(. . .)]

EDUARD PLATNER? (1786–1860) OR ANTON PLATTNER? (1787–1855);
poem written before 1805

This is Schubert's only setting of a poet named Platner. Even this name can only be inferred from the 'Pl.' printed in the source of the poem, an almanac from 1805. It is possible that this refers to either Eduard Platner or Anton Plattner, or to someone else altogether. See the article 'Platner' for a discussion of this point.

The language of flowers goes back to Roman times when poets were crowned with laurel. The Elizabethans were versed in its mysteries – Ophelia in *Hamlet* says, 'And there is pansies, that's for thoughts.' The oriental language of flowers was brought back from Constantinople to England by Lady Mary Wortley Montagu in the early eighteenth century, and from this developed a European language of flowers that reached its height in England during the Victorian era. The combination of the love of nature (women were continually encouraged to draw and paint flowers) and sexual repression encouraged the creation of a roundabout means of conveying passionate feelings via carefully chosen garlands and posies.

The practice was probably too artificial and high-flown for most of Schubert's circle; it is extremely doubtful whether he was interested in the Byzantine rules governing the language of flowers. But the composer wrote two songs – *Die Blumensprache* and *Der Blumenbrief* – which refer to this fashionable craze among young courting couples. Both songs are connected with his summer stay in Zseliz in 1818 with the Esterházy family. We know that *Der Blumenbrief* D622 (Schreiber) was written there; the composer's musical charges, the countesses Marie aged sixteen, and Karoline aged thirteen (the latter said to have been loved by Schubert when she was older), were certainly of the age and background to be interested in this etiquette of safe romantic wooing. There was also a fair copy of *Die Blumensprache* in the possession of Karoline Esterházy that makes it a distinct possibility that this song was written for her in 1818. Schubert could have taken it with him to Hungary (the date of October 1817 that Deutsch and Reed ascribe to this song would suggest this) but it is possible that the text was chosen in deference

---

[2] In the original poem 'Der Jüngling die Perle Hoffnung *errungen*' ('*won* the pearl of hope').

to the young countess's teenage preoccupations, and was composed on the spot for her in Zseliz.

The music is that of 'an exquisite Valentine' (Capell), according to Fischer-Dieskau 'whimsically typically Viennese'. The song certainly has the air of the salon about it – this is ingratiating drawing-room music with the perfumed charm (and the same tonality) of *Heimliches Lieben* D922. *Die Blumensprache*, however, is a much faster song; it has the rapidity of *Frühlingssehnsucht* from *Schwanengesang* D957/3; it is this impulsive *Bewegung* that banishes the cloying sentimentality that can all too easily bedevil a work of this kind. The poem's three verses (Schubert ignores the fourth) suggested the straightforward ABA structure. Each six-line strophe is divided into three phrases for the voice: in each of the 'A' sections there are two phrases of seven bars (B flat major to F major, B flat major to G minor), and one of fourteen (F^7 back to B flat major, where there is no pause for breath). The singer must gasp as and when he or she can. The 'B' section begins in D minor and returns to the dominant of the home key by a circuitous garden route. The blossoms are firmly planted within this ground plan, and they sway, gently cosseted by the summer breeze depicted by the accompaniment. The voice dances in almost constant dactylic rhythm; this gives the ardent vocal line an attractive urgency.

Autograph:	Sibley Music Library, University of Rochester, New York (fair copy)
First edition:	Published as Op. post. 173 no. 5 by C. A. Spina, Vienna in 1867 (P411)
Subsequent editions:	Peters: Vol. 6/120; AGA XX 299: Vol. 5/25; NSA IV: Vol. 11/65
Bibliography:	Capell 1928, p. 143
Discography and timing:	Fischer-Dieskau I 9[16] 1'54
	Hyperion I 19[5]
	Hyperion II 19[5] 2'13 Felicity Lott

←*Nach einem Gewitter* D561   *Fischerlied* D562→

JOHANN FRIEDRICH LUDWIG BOBRIK (1781–1844)

THE POETIC SOURCE
S1   *Dichtungen für Kunstredner* ed. Deinhardstein, Geistingerschen Buchhandlung, Wien und Triest, 1815

THE SONG
23 December 1815   *Die drei Sänger* D329, fragment [S1: pp. 130–32]

The poet was born in Marienburg, Prussia, on 13 October 1781 and was educated there. In the year of Schubert's birth he began his legal studies at the University of Königsberg and had a distinguished career as a criminal lawyer. He translated Ossian (*Comala*, 1801) and was an expert translator of Greek and Latin, as well as English. Bobrik long outlived the composer he never knew; his tragedy was that Schubert never completed the fragment begun at the end of 1815. (A complete song might have given the poet the small corner of immortality that eluded him.) Bobrik's *Gedichte* were published by the prestigious Leipzig house of Brockhaus in 1851. He died in Königsberg (now Kaliningrad in Russia) on 22 January 1844 (1848 in other sources).

Die BÖSE FARBE *see Die SCHÖNE MÜLLERIN* D795/17

BOOTGESANG *see SIEBEN GESÄNGE AUS WALTER SCOTT'S FRÄULEIN VOM SEE* D835/3

FRANZ SERAPH RITTER VON BRUCHMANN (1798–1867)

There is no printed source for any of the Bruchmann texts. Schubert must have worked from manuscript copies of the poems.

THE SONGS

Winter 1822/3?   *An die Leier* (translation of Anacreon, qv) D737

1822–3   *Im Haine* D738
                  Am See D746

November 1822   *Schwestergruss* D762

February 1823   *Der zürnende Barde* D785

Franz von Bruchmann by Kupelwieser, 1821.

Bruchmann was born in Vienna on 5 April 1798 into a well-to-do family; his father, originally from Cologne, was director of the Austrian National Bank and was ennobled in 1818. Concerts and readings took place in the family home in the Singerstrasse (895, formerly 951), and later in the Weihburggasse. Figures like Friedrich von Schlegel were visitors to the Bruchmann home; it is possible that Schubert met Schlegel there. The family also rented 'Mutwille' in the summers of 1819–23; this was a sumptuous garden house on the estate of Fürst Karl von Paar in Wien-Hütteldorf. Schubert and Schober visited Mutwille to make music, and perhaps stayed there for a longer period in 1823. There is an attractive sketch of the house by Leopold Kupelwieser.

Bruchmann, exceptionally handsome as a young man, had been introduced into the Schubert circle by Josef Streinsberg, a school-fellow of the composer. As the closest friend of the allegedly seditious poet Johann Senn (qv), Bruchmann was rounded up by the police for questioning (in March 1820) together with Schubert, Streinsberg and Senn himself. At this point Bruchmann was a fourth-year law student and unafraid of inveighing against the police, an incident that led to Senn being charged with sedition, imprisoned and then exiled to the Tyrol. Bruchmann's friendship with Senn, and the literary exchanges between the two men, suggest a relationship of unusual intensity. In 1821 Bruchmann left Austria secretly to study philosophy with Friedrich

Schelling in Erlangen. At the time such travel was forbidden (the Austrian authorities feared the revolutionary ideas taught in foreign universities). While in Erlangen, or possibly shortly before in Vienna, Bruchmann made the acquaintance of August von Platen (qv) who was only two years older. Platen was notoriously susceptible to attractive young men, and was probably drawn to Bruchmann for more than intellectual reasons. It seems that Bruchmann stayed in Erlangen for only two weeks before coming home, possibly summoned by his father. Deutsch informs us that the police had heard about his expedition and that Bruchmann senior feared that his son's prospects in the Austrian civil service had been damaged. Bruchmann almost certainly brought copies of Platen's poems back with him from Erlangen and perhaps gave them to Schubert at Platen's behest; this resulted in the composition of *Die Liebe hat gelogen* D751 and *Du liebst mich nicht* D756. Bruchmann's broad literary interests must have been a stimulating influence on the composer. Schubert composed *Schwestergruss* D762 (November 1822) in memory of the poet's sister Sybilla von Bruchmann who had died in 1820. The songs *Sei mir gegrüsst* D741, *Frühlingsglaube* D686 and *Hänflings Liebeswerbung* D552, gathered together as Schubert's Op. 20, were dedicated to Bruchmann's mother, Justina von Bruchmann.

There were regular Schubertiads at one or other of the Bruchmann homes, with Franz von Schober (qv) playing a key part in the literary proceedings. During the time that Schober had absented himself in Breslau, Bruchmann discovered that his erstwhile friend had become secretly engaged to his sister Justina; his rage and implacable opposition to this union led to a substantial rift in the Schubert circle with Schubert taking Schober's side. Schubert had already noted (in a letter of 30 November 1823) that 'Bruchmann . . . seems to bend to the formalities of the world, and by that alone he loses his halo, which in my opinion was due to his determined disregard of all worldly affairs.' It is significant that Schubert wrote this a few months after the poet's seemingly Damascene reconversion to Catholicism in August 1823. Once Bruchmann had been anti-Catholic, free-thinking and pantheistic: he had written, 'God is none other than lightness, gravity, metal, earth and electricity.' Thus, like Schubert and many of his other friends, he believed in *Gott in der Natur* – 'God in Nature'. Everything now changed. His youthful years yielded to ultra-conservative beliefs and in due course he displayed many of the attributes of a bigoted prelate. Bruchmann's change of direction (seemingly fuelled by a certain amount of guilt and self-loathing) struck his contemporaries as surprising and extreme. He seems to have regarded his earlier life, his Schubertian years, as being riddled with sin. By the age of thirty-five he was married – a short and unhappy union. After the death of his wife he became a Roman Catholic priest in the Redemptorist order and founded a new community at Gars in Bavaria. He broke off contact with all the friends of his early years, and even came to renounce as immoral poets like Goethe. There were few people who knew more about the Schubertians in their great days but, like Schober in later life, Bruchmann always declined to answer questions about his friendship with the composer. His poems were never published. He lives on thanks only to the five settings of his works by Schubert, contemporary drawings by Kupelwieser and photographs of himself in church regalia in older age. Bruchmann died in Gars am Inn, Bavaria, on 23 May 1867.

Bibliography: Dürhammer 1999, pp. 98 & 203

BRÜDER, SCHRECKLICH BRENNT DIE TRÄNE *see* LIED D535

GOTTFRIED AUGUST BÜRGER (1747–1794)

THE POETIC SOURCES
S1   *Gottfried August Bürgers sämmtliche Werke*, Anton Doll, Wien, 1812
[In this edition the *Gedichte* are Volumes 7 and 8 of the collected works]

S2   *Gottfried August Bürgers Gedichte, Bey B. Ph. Bauer*, Wien, 1815

THE SONG
December 1817   *Das Dörfchen* D598 (earlier D641) [S1: *Gedichte*, Erster Theil pp. 45–9]
                           [S2: Volume 1 pp. 36–41]

G. A. Bürger.

A talented writer of narrative ballads and lyrics, Bürger was born in Molmerswende, near Halberstadt on 31 December 1747. He studied in Halle, was a distinguished teacher and became professor at Göttingen where he befriended both Hölty and Stolberg and was a member of the so-called *Göttingen Hainbund*. His career was ruined by personal scandals, particularly in connection with his third marriage – to the writer Elise Hahn. These, and Schiller's scathing review of Bürger's *Ged-ichte*, were said to have contributed to the poet's early death. Schubert was very free in his selection of lines from Bürger's *Das Dörfchen*, a reworking of a French idyll entitled *Le Hameau* ('Rien n'est si beau / Que mon hameau') by Pierre Joseph Bernard (1710–1775). There are 137 lines in the original, of which the composer selected only fifty (he simply leaves out lines 51–119, as well as lines 126–37): the first unaccompanied version of this quartet for men's voices, also D598, is somewhat longer. *Das Dörfchen* is the only lyric by this poet set to music by Schubert, although other composers (Beethoven, Cornelius and particularly Pfitzner) have found much that is interesting in Bürger's work. Both Liszt and Duparc were drawn to his long narrative poem *Lenore* (the poet became a household name when this ballad was published in the *Göttingen Almanach* of 1774). Bürger died in Göttingen on 8 June 1794.

For a discussion of Bürger's unhappy marriage with his third wife, Elise Hahn, and her unlikely connection with *Das Dörfchen*, see the commentary for that song.

Die BÜRGSCHAFT   The hostage
(SCHILLER) **D246** [H134]

G minor – G major   August 1815

(455 bars)

(1)	Zu Dionys, dem Tyrannen, schlich	Moros, his dagger concealed in his cloak,
	Möros, den Dolch im Gewande;	Stealthily approached the tyrant Dionysos.
	Ihn schlugen die Häscher in Bande.	The henchmen clapped him in irons.
	'Was wolltest du mit dem Dolche,	'What did you intend with your dagger? Speak!'
	sprich!'	
	Entgegnet ihm finster der Wüterich	The evil tyrant asked menacingly.
	'Die Stadt vom Tyrannen befreien!'	'To free this city from the tyrant.'
	'Das sollst du am Kreuze bereuen.'	'You shall rue this on the cross.'
(2)	'Ich bin', spricht jener, 'zu sterben	'I am' he said, 'ready to die.
	bereit,	
	Und bitte nicht um mein Leben,	And do not beg for my life
	Doch willst du Gnade mir geben,	But if you will show me clemency
	Ich flehe dich um drei Tage Zeit,	I ask from you three days' grace
	Bis ich die Schwester dem Gatten	Until I have given my sister in marriage.
	gefreit;	
	Ich lasse den Freund dir als Bürgen—	As surety I will leave you my friend—
	Ihn magst du, entrinn' ich, erwürgen.'	If I fail, then hang him.'
(3)	Da lächelt der König mit arger List,	The king smiled with evil cunning,
	Und spricht nach kurzem Bedenken:	And after reflecting awhile spoke:
	'Drei Tage will ich dir schenken.	'I will grant you three days,
	Doch wisse! wenn sie verstrichen	But know this: if the time runs out
	die Frist,	
	Eh' du zurück mir gegeben bist,	Before you are returned to me
	So muss er statt deiner erblassen,	He must die instead of you
	Doch dir ist die Strafe erlassen.'	But you will be spared punishment.'
(4)	Und er kommt zum Freunde:	He went to his friend. 'The king decrees
	'Der König gebeut,	
	Dass ich am Kreuz mit dem Leben	That I am to pay on the cross with my life
	Bezahle das frevelnde Streben;	For my attempted crime.
	Doch will er mir gönnen drei Tage Zeit,	But he is willing to grant me three days' grace.
	Bis ich die Schwester dem Gatten gefreit;	Until I have freed my sister to her husband
	So bleibe du dem König zum Pfande,[1]	Stand surety with the king
	Bis ich komme, zu lösen die Bande.'	Until I return to redeem the bond.'

[1] Schiller writes 'So *bleib* du dem König zum Pfande'.

(5) Und schweigend umarmt ihn der treue Freund	Silently his faithful friend embraced him,
Und liefert sich aus dem Tyrannen,	And gave himself up to the tyrant.
Der and're zieht von dannen.[2]	Möros departed.
Und eh' noch das dritte Morgenrot erscheint,[3]	Before the third day dawned
Hat er schnell mit dem Gatten die Schwester vereint,	He had quickly married his sister to her betrothed
Eilt heim mit sorgender Seele,	He now hastened home with troubled soul
Damit er die Frist nicht verfehle.	Lest he should fail to meet the appointed time
(6) Da giesst unendlicher Regen herab,	Then rain poured down ceaselessly;
Von den Bergen stürzen die Quellen herab,[4]	Torrents streamed down the mountains
Und die Bäche, die Ströme schwellen	Brooks and rivers swelled.
Und er kommt an's Ufer mit wanderndem Stab,	When he came to the bank, staff in hand,
Da reisset die Brücke der Strudel hinab,	The bridge was swept down by the whirlpools
Und donnernd sprengen die Wogen	And the thundering waves destroyed
Des Gewölbes krachenden Bogen.	Its crashing arches.
(7) Und trostlos irrt er an Ufers Rand,	Disconsolate, he trudged along the bank.
Wie weit er auch spähet und blicket,	However far his eyes travelled,
Und die Stimme, die rufende schickt,[5]	And his shouts resounded
Da stösst kein Nachen vom sichern Strand,	No boat left the safety of the banks
Der ihn setze an das gewünschte Land,	To carry him to the shore he sought.
Kein Schiffer lenkt die Fähre,	No boatman steered his ferry,
Und der wilde Strom wird zum Meere.	And the turbulent river became a sea.
(8) Da sinkt er ans Ufer und weint und fleht,	He fell on to the bank, sobbing and imploring,
Die Hände zum Zeus erhoben:	His hands raised to Zeus:
'O hemme des Stromes Toben!	'O curb the raging torrent!
Es eilen die Stunden, im Mittag steht	The hours speed by, the sun stands
Die Sonne, und wenn sie niedergeht,	At its zenith, and when it sets
Und ich kann die Stadt nicht erreichen,	And I cannot reach the city,
So muss der Freund mir erbleichen.'	My friend will die for me.'
(9) Doch wachsend erneut sich des Stromes Toben,[6]	But the river grew ever more angry
Und Welle auf Welle zerrinnet,	Wave upon wave broke.

[2] Schiller writes 'Der *andere* zieht von dannen'.
[3] Schiller writes 'Und *ehe* das dritte Morgenrot erscheint'.
[4] The second 'herab' is Schubert's.
[5] Schiller writes 'schic*ket*' and 'stö*sset*' in the next line.
[6] Schiller's original reads 'Stromes Wut' to rhyme with lines 4 and 5 of this strophe.

Und Stunde an Stunde entrinnet.
Da treibt ihn die Angst, da fasst er
    sich Mut
Und wirft sich hinein in die brausende
    Flut,
Und teilt mit gewaltigen Armen
Den Strom, und ein Gott hat Erbarmen.

And hour upon hour flew by
Gripped by fear he took courage

And flung himself into the seething flood.

With powerful arms he clove
The waters, and a god had mercy on him.

(10)   Und gewinnt das Ufer und eilet fort,
Und danket dem rettenden Gotte,
Da stürzet die raubende Rotte
Hervor aus des Waldes nächtlichem Ort,
Den Pfad ihm sperrend, und schnaubet
    Mord
Und hemmet des Wanderers Eile
Mit drohend geschwungener Keule.

    He reached the bank and hastened on
Thanking the god that saved him.
Then a band of robbers
Stormed from the dark recesses of the forest
Blocking his path and threatening death.

They halted the traveller's swift course
With their menacing clubs.

(11)   'Was wollt Ihr?' ruft er vor Schrecken
    bleich,
'Ich habe nichts als mein Leben,
Das muss ich dem Könige geben!'
Und entreisst die Keule dem nächsten
    gleich:
'Um des Freundes willen erbarmt euch!'
Und drei, mit gewaltigen Streichen,
Erlegt er, die andern entweichen.

    'What do you want?' he cried, pale with terror,

'I have nothing but my life
And that I must give to the king!'
He seized the club of the one nearest him:

'For the sake of my friend, have mercy!'
Then with mighty blows, he felled three of them,
And the others escaped.

(12)   Und die Sonne versendet glühenden
    Brand,
Und von der unendlichen Mühe
Ermattet sinken die Knie:
'O hast du mich gnädig aus
    Raübers hand,
Aus dem Strom mich gerettet ans
    heilige Land,
Und soll hier verschmachtend verderben
Und der Freund mir, der liebende,
    sterben!'

    The sun shed its glowing fire

And from their ceaseless exertion
His weary knees gave way,
'You have mercifully saved me from the hands of
    robbers.
You have saved me from the river and brought
    me to sacred land.
Am I to die of thirst here,
And is my devoted friend to perish?'

(13)   Und horch! da sprudelt es silberhell
Ganz nahe, wie rieselndes Rauschen,
Und stille hält er zu lauschen,
Und sieh, aus dem Felsen, geschwätzig,
    schnell,
Springt murmelnd hervor ein lebendiger
    Quell,
Und freudig bückt er sich nieder
Und erfrischet die brennenden Glieder.

    But hark, a silvery bubbling sound
Close by, like rippling water.
He stopped and listened quietly;
And lo, bubbling from the rock,

A living spring gushed forth,

Joyfully he stopped
To refresh his burning body.

(14)   Und die Sonne blickt durch der
    Zweige Grün,

    Now the sun shone through green branches,

Und malt auf den glänzenden Matten
Der Bäume gigantische Schatten,
Und zwei Wand'rer sieht er die Strasse ziehn,[7]
Will eilenden Laufes vorüber fliehn,

Da hört er die Worte sie sagen:
'Jetzt wird er ans Kreuz geschlagen.'

(15)   Und die Angst beflügelt den eilenden Fuss,
Ihn jagen der Sorge Qualen;
Da schimmern in Abendrots Strahlen
Von Ferne die Zinnen von Syrakus,
Und entgegen kommt ihm Philostratus,

Des Hauses redlicher Hüter,
Der erkennet entsetzt den Gebieter.

(16)   'Zurück! du rettest den Freund nicht mehr,
So rette das eigene Leben!
Den Tod erleidet er eben.
Von Stunde zu Stunde gewartet' er
Mit hoffender Seele der Wiederkehr,
Ihm konnte den mutigen Glauben
Der Hohn des Tyrannen nicht rauben.'

(17)   'Und ist er zu spät und kann ich ihm nicht
Ein Retter willkommen erscheinen,
So soll mich der Tod mit ihm vereinen.[8]
Des rühme der blut'ge Tyrann sich nicht,
Dass der Freund dem Freunde gebrochen die Pflicht—
Er schlachte der Opfer zweie
Und glaube an Lieb' und Treue.'

(18)   Und die Sonne geht unter, da steht er am Tor
Und sieht das Kreuz schon erhöh't,[9]
Und die Menge gaffend umstehet;[10]
Und an dem Seile schon zieht man den Freund empor,
Da zertrennt er gewaltig den dichten Chor:

And upon the radiant fields
The trees' gigantic shadows
He saw two travellers on the road

And with rapid steps was about to overtake them
When he heard them speak these words:
'Now he is being bound to the cross.'

Fear quickened his steps;

He was driven on by torments of anxiety;
Then, in the sun's dying rays
The towers of Syracuse glinted from afar,
And Philostratus, his household's faithful steward,
Came towards him.
With horror he recognized his master.

'Turn back! You will not save your friend now,
So save your own life!
At this moment he meets his death.
From hour to hour he awaited
Your return with hope in his soul;
The tyrant's derision could not weaken
His courageous faith.'

'If it is too late, if I cannot

Appear before him as his welcome saviour,
Then let death unite us.
The bloodthirsty tyrant shall never gloat
That one friend broke his pledge to another—

Let him slaughter two victims
And believe in love and loyalty.'

The sun set as he reached the gate

And saw the cross already raised,
Surrounded by a gaping throng.
His friend was already being hoisted up by the ropes
When he forced his way through the dense crowd.

[7] Schiller writes 'Und zwei Wan*derer*'.
[8] The 'mit' in this line is Schubert's own addition.
[9] Schiller writes 'Und sieht das Kreuz schon er*hohet*'.
[10] Schiller writes '*Das* die Menge gaffend umstehet'.

'Mich, Henker!' ruft er, 'erwürget!',	'Kill me, hangman!' he cried.
Da bin ich, für den er gebürget!'	'It is I for whom he stood surety.'

(19)   Und Erstaunen ergreift das Volk umher,

The people standing by were seized with astonishment;

In den Armen liegen sich beide
Und weinen vor Schmerzen und Freude.
Da sieht man kein Auge tränenleer,
Und zum König bringt man die Wundermär',
Der fühlt ein menschlich Rühren,[11]
Lässt schnell vor den Thron sie führen.

The two friends were in each other's arms,
Weeping with grief and joy.
No eye was without tears;
The wondrous tidings reached the king;

He was stirred by humane feelings,
And at once summoned the friends before his throne.

(20)   Und blickt sie lange verwundert an;[12]
Drauf spricht er: 'Es ist euch gelungen,
Ihr habt das Herz mir bezwungen,—
Und die Treue ist doch kein leerer Wahn—
So nehmt auch mich zum Genossen an,[13]
Ich sei, gewährt mir die Bitte,
In eurem Bunde der Dritte.'

He looked at them long, amazed,
Then he spoke: 'You have succeeded,
You have conquered this heart of mine.
Loyalty is no vain delusion—

Then take me, too, as a friend.

Grant me this request: Admit me
As the third in your fellowship.'

FRIEDRICH VON SCHILLER (1759–1805); poem written 27–30 August 1798

This is the thirteenth of Schubert's forty-four Schiller solo settings (1811–24). See the poet's biography for a chronological list of all the Schiller settings.

This is one of the most famous of all Schiller's ballads. German-speakers of earlier generations learned it by heart as schoolchildren and were able to recite it until their dying day. It is a Teutonic equivalent perhaps of Browning's (admittedly much shorter) *How they brought the Good News from Ghent to Aix*. Both poems depend on speed and suspense, the struggle against the clock being of the essence. Schiller fashioned the poem from an existing story: the source was a collection of *Fabulae*, Latin tales and anecdotes from the second century AD, gathered under the name of Hyginus and published in Amsterdam in 1670. The story is told in Chapter 257 of the collection under the heading 'Qui inter se amicitia junctissimi fuerunt' ('Those who have been most closely linked together by friendship'). Schiller's ballad was written with remarkable speed; the poet seems to have been inspired by his own friendship with Goethe, and by less happy memories of the tyranny of Duke Karl Eugen (*see* biography of the poet). Schiller amplified the Latin original, suppressing some details (for example, the name of the hostage, Selinuntius, is never mentioned) and adding others.

    It is significant that the ballad was written after the Reign of Terror in France, a world-shattering event that had shocked and grieved the poet, not least perhaps because it was said at the time that some of his earlier plays and anti-authoritarian attitudes had helped to fuel the catastrophe. In fact Schiller was out of sympathy with the mob. The poem opens by inviting our sympathy for an assassin prepared to risk his life in order to rid his city of a tyrant. This betokens impeccable revolutionary credentials, but then the story takes a quirky and

---

[11] Schiller's metre for 'menschlic*hes* Rühren' is better than Schubert's.
[12] Schiller writes 'Und *blicket* sie lange verwundert an'.
[13] Schiller writes 'So *nehmet* auch mich zum Genossen an'.

individualistic turn. The assassination fails and instead of immediate execution the would-be tyrannicide is permitted to travel to a distant wedding, leaving in his place a friend as trusting hostage. As Bertolt Brecht rather wryly points out in his sonnet *Über Schillers Gedicht 'Die Bürg-schaft'*, the tyrant was never a true tyrant in having the patience to wait for his revenge – 'Am End war der Tyrann gar kein Tyrann!'. Schiller is saying here that a state is made up of individual people, and that the goodness of the body politic is dependent on the foundation of one-to-one relation-ships. The honour of a nation depends on the trust between its individual citizens. At the end of the story the oligarch is touched by behaviour hitherto outside his experience; he is healed in the presence of love. Schiller believed that if each person took care of his own integrity, the state could not fail to become as enlightened as its individual members. The poem's ubiquitousness in the schoolrooms of Germany, even during the Third Reich, was subtly subversive and a complete contrast to the much-prized Norse-inspired ballads of Aryan heroism.

The story must have appealed to Schubert greatly – it is the only one of his songs that gave rise to an opera with the same subject and title. It is not known who wrote the libretto of this unfinished work (*Die Bürgschaft* D435, May 1816), an operatic fragment of sixteen numbers. It is fascinating to see Schubert returning to his piano-accompanied work for inspiration: no. 10 of the opera (an extended storm entr'acte and aria) takes its cue from bb. 127–214 of the ballad; see also this commentary for Verse 13.) It would not be unreasonable to suppose that Johann Mayrhofer (whom the composer had met at the end of 1814) played some part in directing Schubert's attention to a story rich in features close to his own heart. Mayrhofer was enthusiastic about classical antiquity: as a frustrated censor secretly highly critical of Metternich's regime, he would have appreciated the poem's politically subversive undertones. Above all the poet would have recognized that the ballad could be read as a hymn to the exalted male friendship of classical times. Although the point is scarcely laboured in the story, the death of the hostage is unthinkable to Möros not only because he has given his word that he will return, but because he loves his friend, as it were, better than himself. In classical terms this is related to the stories of the Theban Sacred Band, to Homer's Achilles and Patroclus, and to the story of Nisus and Euryalus in Virgil's *Aeneid*. In Schubert's opera the hostage (whose name becomes Theages in that context) has a wife and two children, extra characters to avert the potential box-office catastrophe of an all-male cast. Unfortunately, the libretto of this work (derived from Schiller's ballad without using his words) is generally held to be one of the worst that the composer ever attempted to set. In 1822 it was mooted that Beethoven should share the composition of an opera on this subject (the libretto was by F. L. Karl). This came to nothing, and six years later Schubert's friend, Franz Lachner, applied successfully to take over the project. The premiere of this opera took place in Pest scarcely three weeks before the death of Schubert who had hoped to travel to Hungary for the occasion.

There are those who see Schubert's *Die Bürgschaft* as a superior achievement to *Der Taucher* D77 because of its tighter formal structure. There is here a tremendous sense of pace, as if the performer is excitedly reciting the ballad with little time to luxuriate in vocal matters. At times we are hardly conscious of the music but remain involved with what is happening in the story. Much of the action in the poem is telescoped into the minimum number of words, and the composer follows suit with the minimum number of notes – both sung and played. The relent-less abbaacc rhyming structure also plays its part in winding up the tension.

Verse 1: The marking 'Schnell' stands at the top of the piece, as does a key signature of two flats (although it is not until b. 18 that we arrive decisively in G minor). If it is the aim of the ascending chromatic scales of the introduction to terrify the listeners, they fail in their purpose: the murderous approach of the conspirator and his arrest (bb. 1–6) are over in a flash, an abortive coup. Within seconds of the opening, Möros (re-named Damon in later editions of the poem) is clapped in irons and we hear him briefly interrogated by the tyrant (a mean little recitative full of slithery chromaticism bb. 16–18). Möros's simple answer (bb. 19–22) is immediately followed by the proclaiming of the death sentence, in this case crucifixion. The words and music are offhand enough to suggest that this is something of no more importance to the tyrant than is the crushing of a fly.

Verses 2–3: There is no change of pulse here, only an expansion of note values to allow Möros to sing a very reasoned (under the circumstances) aria in D minor to the King (from b. 27). He accepts the verdict with stoic courage, but asks for time to attend his sister's wedding. This is an age where 'family values' are taken seriously. He offers up his best friend as a hostage. The solid long lines and reliable harmonies of his set piece contrast with the devious chromatics of Dionysus' reply (a recitative from b. 59 in B minor). The tyrant will take a sadistic, voyeuristic, pleasure in monitoring the outcome of what seems to him an untenable bargain. He speaks peremptorily and emerges in Schubert's music as a petulant, even lightweight, figure.

Verse 4: This section is prefixed by the word 'Ruhig' ⅜. Möros goes to his friend (a bridge passage in G major, modulating into D major) and addresses to him an aria of noble simplicity (marked Mässig, from b. 78). This is music of almost preternatural calm and tenderness. The long succession of semibreve chords accompanying this aria (bb. 78–89) signify a strong and supportive character, rendered mute by the speed of Schiller's pen, but whose constancy is the mainspring of the action. A speechless embrace between the two men (described in the recitative bb. 107–9) must suffice. This is the type of friendship that Schiller envisaged between Posa and Don Carlos, and which Verdi was to depict in the noble duetting for baritone and tenor, the voices often a third a part; Schubert uses thirds in the piano writing for Verse 19 of this work to illustrate a similar friendship.

Lithograph by Josef Hyrtll after Monitz von Schwind, for Verse 8 of *Die Bürgschaft*.

Verse 5: The Wedding. The first two lines of this strophe are recitative, quickly dispatched. Schubert marries off Möros's sister with an interlude of old-fashioned courtly wedding music in B flat major, ⅜, marked 'Lieblich' (bb. 112–21). Two days of the three that the tyrant has allowed Möros for the conduct of his affairs have passed. A further recitative (bb. 122–7) places the traveller on his way homewards to face his sentence.

Verses 6–9: The Flood. The four verses that make up this episode are joined together in one large musical structure, more or less in D minor. The patter of non-stop semiquavers ('Geschwind') in the pianist's right hand (and jabbing quavers in octaves in the left) throughout verses 6 and 7 paint the relentless fall of rain. This is relatively gentle at first but gathers force apace, encouraged by crescendo markings. A description of the hero's calls of distress resounds on a long line of Ds (bb. 153–6) in the vocal line supported by the piano's strident sforzando chords on the offbeats. The rhythmic cell of Beethoven's 'Fate' motif (from the Fifth Symphony) appears in the pianist's left hand after 'Die Ströme schwellen' in Verse 6 (bb. 138–9), and again in the small interlude after Verse 7 (bb. 166–7). Verse 8 starts in the same hurried way, but the mood changes with the shift to imploring recitative at 'und fleht die Hände zum Zeus erhoben' (bb. 172–3), a prayer to the gods. The rain has caused a flood. Heavy chords in flowing quavers, a river swollen with water, contrast with the rainfall in lighter semiquavers of the previous verses. Bass octaves climb in semitones (bb. 185–92) as the river overflows. The effort of the swim for survival is mirrored by a vocal line that also climbs ever higher until it reaches a high G flat on the word 'Gott' (b. 206) – a god who mercifully allows a moment of respite. However, more trouble is afoot.

Verses 10–11: The Robbers. No sooner are the last words of Verse 9 sung (b. 210) than Verse 10 begins, two beats later. The traveller's trials now come thick and fast as the music is marked 'Geschwinder' and then 'Noch geschwinder'. It seems that Schubert is more in the mood to respond to natural disasters than man-made ones; this episode engages his attention least in terms of illustrative detail. The felling of three villains is effected without much vocal, or pianistic, effort. At least the story is quickly told and the retreat of the defeated hooligans is amusingly commented on by the piano after 'die andern entweichen' (the scurrying descending scale at b. 240). The quick dispatch of this part of the story benefits the pace of the whole.

Verse 12: The Sun. Goethe, in a letter to Schiller, wondered whether it was likely that the hero would be in danger of dying of thirst only a few hours after a dousing in rain and river. The first three lines are weary recitative drugged by heat, supported by a haze of tremolandi. At the fourth line ('O hast du mich gnädig aus Räubers Hand') there is a set piece arioso-prayer of great humility (marked 'Langsam, mit Ausdruck' and with a change of key signature to E minor, bb. 248–52). We also glimpse the tenderness felt for the friend in the setting of 'der liebende'. After a great deal of hectic music this seems the right time for a moment of repose.

Verse 13: The Stream. It is the music from this section that Schubert chose to use again in his opera of the same name a year later. In Number 14 of the operatic Die Bürgschaft at the 'Poco andante' section we find a reappearance of this aria note for note, the strings weaving the piano's watery accompaniment and the oboe playing the beautiful melody at 'Und horch! da sprudelt es silberhell'. It is little wonder that the baritone in the opera sings in counterpoint to the main tune rather than being entrusted with the D major melody itself which is in a most uncomfortable high-lying tessitura. Nevertheless this little moment of respite in the ballad (marked 'Etwas geschwinder', bb. 253–68) is a notable pre-echo of that immortal hymn to love – 'O Bächlein meiner Liebe' from Der Neugierige in Die schöne Müllerin. In the cycle, and in the opera (as well as in this ballad) this stream has a magical quality; it bubbles forth with holy water – holy at least to Schubertians.

Verses 14–17: The key signature changes from D major to B flat major, and the marking is once again 'Langsam'. The music at 'Und die Sonne blickt' (from b. 269) seems almost too leisurely for someone who needs to hurry at all costs. However, the solemn moment that registers the beauties of nature is soon over. (Could there ever have been more confusing climatic conditions within a space of a day, and within a few miles, than in this story? Let us be charitable and put everything down to the changeable island weather of Sicily which Goethe, if not Schiller, knew at first hand!) From 'Und zwei Wand'rer sieht er' the key signature is naturalized into C major and we return to a substantial fast movement (marked 'Geschwind', *alla breve*, from b. 276) that balances the storm music earlier in the piece. Möros overhears two travellers talking of the imminent crucifixion of his friend (bb. 289–92), and tension mounts as we move into the final lap always pushed forward by urgent quavers in the accompaniment. There is a little scene with the majordomo Philostratus, a confrontation between master and retainer that is often found in Greek theatre. We almost want to shake the old man as he slowly recounts his news ('Etwas langsamer' b. 323) when every second now counts, but there is a touching melody describing the indomitable faith of the hostage at 'Von Stunde zu Stunde' (b. 331). Our hero is determined to return even if he is too late and whatever the consequences. The statements of Verse 17 are the ultimate articles of the faith of friendship (b. 347). The piano interlude after 'und glaube an Lieb' und Treue' (bb. 364–79) is of a tempestuous, Beethovenian, turn of phrase. The music is very directional; it bears down on the key of E flat, as if pushing aside any onlookers and following a narrowing road into a city.

Verses 18–19: In a final burst of energy, Möros approaches the site of the dreadful crucifixion and of course he is just in time. Schubert manages to save one of the most powerful moments in the piece for the heartfelt cry of '"Mich, Henker!" ruft er, "erwürget!"' (bb. 391–4). It seems to hit exactly the right note of distress and self-sacrifice; this is accompanied by the same great-hearted semibreves that we remember from the twelve bars (bb. 78–89) of Verse 4. After this outburst, the hushed piano interlude – bare octaves between the hands – leads effectively into the dumbstruck music of the astounded crowd of Verse 19 (from b. 405). The euphonious thirds of friendship in the accompaniment (from b. 411, and especially under 'Da sieht man kein Auge tränenleer') are harmonic balm on emotional wounds. They presage the reconciliation that is about to take place.

Verse 20: Schubert keeps one masterstroke for the last page of the work. These are the four blocks of chords, in regal dotted rhythm and separated by rests (bb. 431–5) that depict the conversion of the tyrant – juxtapositions of fortissimo harmonies that reflect the power of initial revelation, as well as astounded disbelief. John Reed finds this music prophetic of Scarpia's chords in Puccini's *Tosca*. If this is so, one has to imagine here a converted Scarpia, or rather a Saint Paul on the road to Damascus. The G major final aria for Dionysus ('Mässig' ⅜) is genial, and suddenly humanized. Fischer-Dieskau says that this has 'too much Viennese Gemütlichkeit in it to be wholly effective'. But the point is that the tyrant has become a civilized *Mensch* in the miraculous twinkling of an eye, and for the young Schubert this means that his musical style can now embrace the urbane and forgiving. Like many other ballads (including the longest of all, *Adelwold und Emma* D211) the work ends with such a tiny postlude that it almost seems unworthy of the preceding song. Perhaps Schubert thought it sufficiently significant that these two final bars should contain Beethoven's 'Fate' motif in an unexpectedly warm metamorphosis.

In 1822 Moritz von Schwind made a design for the publication of the song that was never used.

Autograph:	Missing or lost
First edition:	Published as Book 8 of the *Nachlass* by Diabelli, Vienna in 1830 (P254)

Die Bürgschaft.

Zu Dionys, dem Tyrannen, schlich
Möros, den Dolch im Gewande;
Ihn schlugen die Häscher in Bande.
Was wolltest du mit dem Dolche, sprich!
Entgegnet ihm finster der Wütherich.
„Die Stadt vom Tyrannen befreien!"
Das sollst du am Kreuze bereuen.

„Ich bin, spricht Jener, zum Sterben bereit,
Und bitte nicht um mein Leben:
Doch willst du Gnade mir geben,
Ich flehe dich um drei Tage Zeit,
Bis ich die Schwester dem Gatten gefreit;
Ich lasse den Freund dir als Bürgen,
Ihn magst du, entrinn' ich, erwürgen."

Illustration by Hermann Plüdermann from *Deutsches Balladenbuch* (1861).

Subsequent editions: Peters: Vol. 5/11; AGA XX 109: Vol. 3/11; NSA IV: Vol. 8/153
Discography and timing: Fischer-Dieskau I 4[23] 16'24
                           Hyperion I 16[10-11]
                           Hyperion II 8[17-18]   16'30   Thomas Allen

←*Winterlied* D242a   *Das Geheimnis* D250→

BUNDESLIED   Song of fellowship
(GOETHE) **D258** [H144]
B♭ major   4 or 19 August 1815

In al - len gu - ten Stun - den, er - höht von Lieb' und Wein,

(20 bars)

In allen guten Stunden,   Whenever times are good,
Erhöht von Lieb' und Wein,   Enhanced by love and wine,
Soll dieses Lied verbunden   Let us together
Von uns gesungen sein!   Sing this song.
Uns hält der Gott zusammen,   The god, who brought us here,
Der uns hierher gebracht.   Binds us together,
Erneuert unsre Flammen,   And rekindles the flames
Er hat sie angefacht.   He first lit for us.

So glühet fröhlich heute,   Then glow with happiness today,
Seid recht von Herzen eins,   Be truly united in your hearts.
Auf! trinkt erneuter Freude   Come, drink this glass of purest wine

Dies Glas des echten Weins!	To our renewed joy.
Auf, in der holden Stunde	Come, at this sweet hour
Stosst an, und küsset treu,	Clink your glasses and, with a kiss,
Bei jedem neuen Bunde,	At each new meeting
Die alten wieder neu!	Renew our old bonds.

Wer lebt in unserm Kreise,	He who lives among us –
Und lebt nicht selig drin?	And merrily too –
Geniesst die freie Weise	Enjoys our free and easy ways
Und treuen Brudersinn!	And a true sense of brotherhood.
So bleibt durch alle Zeiten	So for all time
Herz Herzen zugekehrt;	Let our hearts be joined together,
Von keinen Kleinigkeiten	And let no pettiness
Wird unser Bund gestört.	Disturb our fellowship.

[. . .]	[. . .]

Mit jedem Schritt wird weiter	With each step we move further
Die rasche Lebensbahn,	Along life's rapid course
Und heiter, immer heiter	And, ever cheerful,
Steigt unser Blick hinan.	Our eyes are raised heavenwards.
Uns wird es nimmer bange,	We shall never grow fearful,
Wenn alles steigt und fällt,	Though all things rise and fall;
Und bleiben lange! lange!	And long may we remain thus,
Auf ewig so gesellt.	Eternally united.

JOHANN WOLFGANG VON GOETHE (1749–1832); poem written by 10 September 1775

This is the twenty-fifth of Schubert's seventy-five Goethe solo settings (1814–26). See the poet's biography for a chronological list of all the Goethe settings.

Goethe wrote this epithalamium for the wedding celebration of friends in Switzerland in September 1775, which explains the fifth line of the first strophe that refers to the god, possibly Eros or Cupid, who has brought the company together. It is very much a drinking song of good fellowship streaked with the exploration of metaphysical issues that these texts habitually require (though not in this case death and the hereafter). Schubert's music is jolly and hearty, prophetic of his 1826 setting of Shakespeare's *Trinklied* where the vocal line is often doubled by both hands of the piano (here this unison appropriately mirrors the meaning of 'Uns hält der Gott zusammen'). The reference to flames ('Erneuert unsre Flammen') is introduced by a flickering contrary-motion arpeggio in semiquavers in the accompaniment (b. 12) and prompts a downward arpeggio in the voice on a dominant seventh on 'Flammen' (b. 14) – the only sign of temperament in an otherwise rather stolid vocal line. Schubert allows this flickering motif to return in b. 16, and the postlude is rendered relatively tricky by spluttering semiquavers (b. 18). In the Hyperion Schubert Edition this song about sharing was distributed between three different male singers who sang the last strophe together and in unison.

There are five strophes in Goethe's poem, one of Schiller's favourites incidentally, all of which are printed in the AGA. Given here are 1, 2, 3 and 5. Despite the distinction of the poet, three or four strophes seem more than enough in performance.

Autographs:	Wienbibliothek im Rathaus, Vienna (fair copy made for Goethe)
First edition:	Published as part of *Bisher unbekannte und unveröffentlichte Compositionen von Franz Schubert, Heft II* by Weinberger & Hofbauer, Vienna in 1887 (P490)
Subsequent editions:	Not in Peters; AGA XX 115: Vol. 3/38; NSA IV: Vol. 8/196
Further settings:	Johann Friedrich Reichardt (1752–1814) *Bundeslied* two settings: for solo voice and piano (1781); for 3 voices and piano (1809)
Discography and timing:	Fischer-Dieskau I 5[4] 1'45

Hyperion I 24[10]
Hyperion II 9[5]   2'24   John Mark Ainsley, Simon
                                   Keenlyside & Michael George

←*Heidenröslein* D257   *An den Mond* D259→

Schubert at the age of seventeen, pencil drawing ascribed to Franz von Schober.

C

CANTATE ZUM GEBURTSTAG DES SÄNGERS JOHANN MICHAEL VOGL

Cantata for the birthday of the singer Johann Michael Vogl

Trio, STB

(STADLER) **D666** [H431]
C major   Composed for 10 August 1819

Sänger, der von Herzen singet
Und das Wort zum Herzen bringet,
Bei den Tönen deiner Lieder
Fällt's wie sanfter Regen nieder,
Den der Herr vom Himmel schickt,
Und die dürre Flur erquickt!

Diese Berge sah'n dich blühen,
Hier begann dein Herz zu glühen,
Für die Künstlerhöhn zu schlagen,
Die der Wahrheit Krone tragen;
Der Natur hast du entwandt,
Was die Kunst noch nicht verstand.

Da saht ihr Orestes scheiden,
Jakob mit der Last der Leiden,
Saht des Arztes Hoffnung tagen,
Menschlichkeit am Wasserwagen,
Saht, wie man sich Lienen sucht,
Bräute holt aus Bergesschlucht.

In der Weihe deiner Würde
Stehst du, aller Sänger Zierde,
Auf Thaliens Tempelstufen,
Hörst um dich des Beifalls Rufen,
Doch ein Kranz, ein Sinngedicht,
Ist der Lohn des Künstlers nicht.

Singer, you who sing from the heart
And bring your words to the heart,
The sounds of your songs
Are like gentle rainfall
Which the Lord sends from heaven
To refresh the parched fields.

These mountains saw you blossom;
Here your heart began to glow,
To beat for the heights of artistry
Which bear the crown of truth;
You have wrested from Nature
What Art has not yet understood.

There you saw Orestes depart,
And Jacob with his burden of sorrow;
You saw the dawning of the physician's hopes,
And human kindness at the water cart;
You saw them seeking out Lina
And taking brides from mountain gorges.

You stand in the consecration of your merits,
Glory of all singers,
Upon the steps of Thalia's temple;
You hear around you shouts of applause,
Yet a garland, an epigram,
Is not the artist's reward.

Wenn dich einst in greisen Tagen	If in your old age
Deines Lebens Mühen plagen,	The cares of life trouble you,
Willst du nicht zur Heimat wandern?	Will you not travel to your homeland?
Lass die Helden einem Andern,	Leave heroes to someone else;
Nur von Agamemnons Sohn	From Agamemnon's son
Trag die treue Brust davon.	Take only the faithful heart.
Gott bewahr' dein teures Leben,	May God preserve your precious life,
Heiter, spiegelklar und eben,	Happy, crystal, clear and even,
Wie das Tönen deiner Kehle	Like the sounds from your throat,
Tief herauf aus voller Seele;	Welling from the depths of your soul;
Schweigt dann einst des Sängers Wort,	If ever the singer's voice falls silent,
Tönet doch die Seele fort.	Then his soul will still sound forth.

ALBERT STADLER (1794–1888)

Schubert's occasional music in honour of special people in his life, including dedications of works to friends (one thinks of the touching little song written for Schober as he left Vienna and the comic letter to Josef von Spaun in Linz) could be the subject of a small treatise. The composer was not slow to thank those who had been good to him. The most substantial works composed specifically in honour of individuals are in cantata form, a type of musical homage reserved for father figures. The first of these, naturally enough, was for the father himself: Franz Theodor Schubert's name day in October 1813 was celebrated with *Zur Namensfeier meines Vaters* D80 for two tenors, bass and guitar accompaniment (with a text by Schubert himself). Next, a work that honoured Schubert's composition teacher, the *Beitrag zur fünfzigjährigen Jubelfeier* D407, was written in 1816 for the fiftieth anniversary of Antonio Salieri's arrival in Vienna. Again Schubert was probably the poet of the occasional text. Later in the same year Schubert composed a cantata for soloists, chorus and orchestra entitled *Prometheus* (D451) with a text by Philipp Dräxler von Carin. Admittedly this was a commission (the composer's first), but it honoured the name day of Heinrich Josef Watterroth, a professor of liberal views at the University of Vienna who was held in great esteem by the Schubertians. Sadly this work has long been lost. Still later in 1816 there was another orchestral cantata (D472) in honour of Josef von Spendou, an important man in the Austrian school system who was the patron and supporter of Schubert *père*, and a longstanding friend of the Schubert family.

Johann Michael Vogl was the last to be honoured with a cantata, this time for soprano, tenor and baritone. In 1817 Schubert had won the singer's interest in his songs. Although Vogl was at first distant and grand, not immediately convinced of Schubert's importance, he very soon became a devotee and spent more and more time with the composer. Continual and ever closer musical contact led to an invitation for Schubert to spend the summer of 1819 in Steyr, Upper Austria, a town some ninety miles west of Vienna. The cantata for Vogl was written during this holiday to celebrate the singer's fifty-first birthday. (Vogl liked to return to Steyr, his home town, for the summers. It was also the home town, incidentally, of Johann Mayrhofer and Albert Stadler, poet of the cantata.)

In introducing the composer to his circle, Vogl created an instant network of new Schubertians. Thus we hear a number of names for the first time which will continue to weave their way through the biography: the Schellmanns – Albert, father and son; Josef and Josefine Koller, father and daughter (the *Namenstaglied* D695 was written for Josef in 1819, and Josefine was the dedicatee of the Piano Sonata D664, composed during the same holiday, or perhaps on a later visit in 1825); the well-to-do Silvester Paumgartner, later to be the host of Vogl and

Schubert during their Steyr visits in 1823 and 1825 and the man for whom the *Forellenquintett* D667 was composed. Like Graz later in Schubert's career, Steyr became a centre of interest in the composer's music, and a place where he felt he could return (he did so in 1823 and 1825), confident of a warm and affectionate reception.

Josef and Josefine Koller were the hosts on the evening of this work's first performance, and Josefine (sometimes called Josefa) herself sang the soprano part. The middle line was taken by Bernhard Benedict, a local tenor. These two shared the extended solo passages in the cantata, and it is notable that the bass line sings only in the ensembles. This is because Schubert had fashioned this part for himself. Whether or not he sang as he accompanied is a contested point. One witness claims that he did, but Deutsch tells us categorically that, on this occasion, Albert Stadler played the piano. The work is divided into three main movements. The first of these is in C major and begins very much in the ceremonial manner of a Mozart opera overture. *Pomposo* dotted chords in the bass (forte) are echoed in the treble (piano). After four bars an elegant little solo tune emerges (b. 5) as if written for clarinet; this descends, and then re-ascends the stave and leads to an interrupted cadence which in turn takes us back to C major. Conventional stuff this, but crafted in impeccable classical style, and very much to the singer's taste. These opening eight bars are repeated and now serve as accompaniment to the first two lines of text that address the singer in a manner which charmingly combines the breadth and grandeur due to a famous personage with a certain intimate affection. After this, where the sound of songs is compared to rainfall, the piano writing quickens (b. 17); the glinting and plashing of these semiquavers, both hands in the treble clef (at 'Fällt's wie sanfter Regen nieder'), could have come from a Mozart piano concerto. The idea of something being sent from heaven ('Den der Herr vom Himmel schickt') inspires a piano trill suggestive of a small bolt of divine lightning (b. 22). Various elaborations and repetitions of these first strophe words extend the movement. The word 'erquickt' (refreshes) gives rise to a charming four-bar interlude for the piano (bb. 28–31) in gently wafting quavers, as if to suggest relaxed satiation. The repeat of 'Sänger, der von Herzen singet' occasions a quasi-canonic imitation between the voices as if to imply a resonance echoing outwards and spreading through the world.

The second movement (from b. 55, marked Allegretto) is in F major, and duple time changes to triple. This is the soprano solo and in gentle pastoral style, ideal for a salute to the singer's beginnings in the homeland mountainous region of Steyr. There is just a hint of an Alpine yodel in 'Diese Berge sahn dich blühen, Hier begann dein Herz zu glühen' (and also at the repeat of the words later in the movement). One of Vogl's friends who was at this performance recalled many years later that the singer seemed to be especially moved at this passage. All of this music is written in an unashamedly old-fashioned manner, almost demure in its effect, although there are more romantic expressive touches (the chromatic darkening of 'glühen', b. 62, and the majestic extended cadence of 'der Wahrheit Krone tragen', bb. 64–8).

When the tenor takes over (the poem's third strophe), and as Vogl gets into his professional stride in this biography-in-song, the musical mood changes from gently reflective to something that suggests hard work and activity. This is the only rather awkward passage in the piece as melodic invention cedes to a sort of narrative arioso. A lot of information has to be imparted, and some of it needs explanation to the modern listener: 'Da saht ihr Orestes scheiden' (bb. 122–4) refers to Vogl's assumption of the role of Orest in Gluck's *Iphigenia in Tauris* (the section is introduced by ominous pacing quavers with a left hand plunging towards the bottom of the keyboard – music appropriate for this restless and tragic character); 'Jakob mit der Last der Leiden' to the role of Jakob in Méhul's *Joseph*; 'Saht des Arztes Hoffnung tagen' to the role of the regimental doctor in Adalbert Gyrowetz's *Der Augenarzt*; 'Menschlichkeit am Wasserwagen' to the role of Micheli in Cherubini's *Deux journées* (in German *Der Wasserträger*). 'Saht, wie man sich Lienen sucht, / Bräute holt aus Bergesschlucht' is more obscure: Emeline (or Liene) is a character in Joseph Weigl's *Die Schweizerfamilie* where Vogl played the role of her suitor, Jakob Friburg.

The soprano returns for the fourth strophe and, as the poem emerges from its biographical phase and begins a reflection on the singer's fame, the accompaniment changes to suggest the celebration of something grand and sacred. It is exactly this rhythmic cell (minim + dotted quavers and semiquavers, from b. 144) that opens *Lied eines Schiffers an die Dioskuren* D360, so it is no surprise to see that there is a classical reference in this verse – Thalia was one of the Graces whose name is associated with festivity. Over this rhythm the vocal line continues in arioso mood – something between the dryness of recitative and the melodic flowering of melody. The tenor takes over for the fifth strophe with a veiled hint. Although Vogl was to retire fully only in 1822 (and an appearance in Schubert's opera *Die Zwillingsbrüder* lay ahead of him) there is reference here to a new phase in life – something which must have been talked about for some time in Vienna where it was generally felt that his powers were on the wane, at least as an opera singer. Leave the heroes to someone else (although what artist wants to be told this?) says the poet. If you have to stop playing the role of Orestes ('Agamemnons Sohn') you will still retain his great heart. The whole of this passage was probably inserted because Vogl planned to live in Steyr following his retirement, and his friends looked forward to his return there. This was never to be; the singer unexpectedly married in 1826 and from then on his links with his former circle were considerably weakened.

The third section marked 'Moderato' returns to the common time, as well as the C major, of the opening. This is a typical Schubertian peroration, often to be found in the part-songs, in that it employs a canon by way of musical envoi. This is justified in the text by the use of the phrase 'spiegelklar' – 'crystal clear' in translation, but literally 'mirror-clear'. This music is not just the suggestion of a canon, but the real thing – an eight-bar phrase heard first in the soprano line, then tenor, then bass. On the bass entry the soprano is given a charming descant as an instrumental obbligato; this emphasizes the 'heiter', or happy and carefree, nature of the envisaged retirement. The accompaniment to this section has begun in rather solemn fashion in quavers, but these turn to more liquid right-hand triplets, and by the time all three voices are singing together we have a party atmosphere with dance-like triplets between the hands. The revels are interrupted by the inevitable spectre of mortality ('Schweigt dann einst des Sängers Wort') which is announced by a shift from C to A flat major (b. 201). At this point one is reminded of how lucky we are in our own century that a great singer's art will never be lost to us, resounding on shellac, vinyl, CD and the downloaded music file across the centuries. Schubert's contemporaries were never to know this fact, but Stadler hits upon the idea of a resounding soul ('Tönet doch die Seele fort'). Is it not this very thing that *does* remain in the disembodied recorded tones we hear of the great artists no longer with us? We remember a great singer of the past not as a corporeal presence, but precisely because something belonging to that individual alone, call it a soul if you will (and it is perhaps easier for a voice to take on a spiritual quality when not allied to a visible body), remains resounding in the ether. This idea is beautifully caught by Schubert's closing music where cleverly layered repetitions of the words conjoin (as if gathering their expressive resources) in the six final bars. These few bars are high in tessitura for all three singers, and the music seems to trail off into infinity. It is as if sound waves were being gently beamed into the unknown future – especially for us, perhaps.

When this piece was first published in 1849, Vogl was little more than a forgotten singer; his reputation as one central to the Schubert story had not yet assured his worldwide fame. Accordingly, new words to do with a spring morning were added by the firm of Diabelli that fell away only with the publication of the AGA. In June 1980 the Songmakers' Almanac gave a concert at the Aldeburgh Festival to celebrate the seventieth birthday of Sir Peter Pears (1910–1986) – a twentieth-century Vogl to Benjamin Britten's Schubert. A new text to be sung in English to the music of Schubert's cantata was commissioned from Eric Crozier, librettist of Britten's *Albert Herring* and *Billy Budd*, taking its cue from the German original. This praised Pears's operatic career as well as his establishment of a new school for musicians in Snape. The name 'Peter' fitted the opening salutation 'Sänger' perfectly. Crozier's replacement for 'Der Natur hast du entwandt / Was die Kunst noch nicht verstand' ingeniously entwined the English singer's early fame with the contemporary growing renown of Britten's operas: '*Peter Grimes* and Peter Pears / Shared synonymous careers.'

Autograph:	Wienbibliothek im Rathaus, Vienna
First edition:	Published with altered text under the title of 'Der Frühlingsmorgen' as Op. post. 158 in 1849 (P364)
	Published with the original text as part of the AGA in 1892 (P522)
First known performance:	10 August 1819, at the house of Josefine von Koller. Performers: Josefine von Koller, Bernhard Benedict and Franz Schubert, accompanied by Albert Stadler
Subsequent editions:	AGA XIX 3: p. 37; NSA III: Vol. 2a/77

Discography and timing:	Deutsche Grammophon		Peter Schreier, Horst
	Schubert Terzette	10'30	Laubenthal & Dietrich Fischer-Dieskau
	Hyperion I 34[14]	9'50	Lynne Dawson, Michael Schade & Gerald Finley
	Hyperion II 22[6]		

⟵ *Der 13. Psalm* D663   *Beim Winde* D669 ⟶

CANTATE ZUR FEIER DER GENESUNG DER IRENE KIESEWETTER *see* AL PAR DEL RUSCELLETTO D936

IGNAZ FRANZ CASTELLI (1781–1862)

THE POETIC SOURCES

S1   *Selam, ein Almanach für Freunde des Mannigfaltigen*, ed. Castelli, Wien 1815

A setting by Antonio Salieri of Castelli's poem *Trinklied* is included as a supplement in this publication.

S2   *Selam, ein Almanach für Freunde des Mannigfaltigen*, ed. Castelli, Wien 1813

S3   *Poetische Kleinigkeiten*, erstes Bändchen, Anton Strauss, Wien, 1816

S4   *Aglaja, Taschenbuch für das Jahr 1826*, gedruckt und im Verlage bei Joh. Bap. Wallishausser, Wien

S5   *I.F. Castelli's Gedichte*, Duncker und Humblot, Berlin, 1835 (Vols 1, 2, 6)

THE SONGS

February 1815   *Trinklied* D148 [S1: pp. 297–301 with the inscription 'Mit Musik von Herrn Salieri, erstem k.k. Hofcapellmeister'] [S3, pp. 61–7, and S5, Volume 1 pp. 54–8, both too late to be Schubert's source and differing in many details]

January 1817   *Frohsinn* D520 [S2: pp. 207–9 with the inscription '*Gesellschaftslied*, Musik von Herrn Himmel. kön Preuss. Kapellmeister', certainly Schubert's source. Also to be found in S5: Volume 2 pp. 34–6].

1826–8   *Das Echo* D990C (in D1 D868) [S4: pp. 157–9 (Schubert's source). Also to be found in S5: Volume 6 pp. 99–102]

Castelli was born in Vienna on 6 March 1781. As a young man he played in theatre orchestras in order to see the plays, and remained an enthusiast for every branch of the stage. He worked as a civil servant, editor of journals and playwright. He had a typically Viennese career of the period – one where ceaseless literary activity was combined with a number of official appointments in government service. His first success was in 1802, during the Wars of Liberation, with a poem, *Kriegslied für die österreichische Armee*, printed and distributed to the troops in 1809.

He had his first hit as an opera librettist in 1810 with *Die Schweizerfamilie* of Joseph

Ignaz Castelli, lithograph by Josef Kriehuber.

Title page for the almanac *Aglaja* for 1826.

Weigl, a *Singspiel* that greatly influenced the young Schubert, not least because it included important parts for his favourite singers, Anna Milder and Michael Vogl. Castelli's interest in music, as well as his lively personality (he was a member of numerous drinking and artists' 'societies') led to his being dubbed 'The Austrian Anacreon'. He wrote songs, ballads, fairy tales, legends, fables, anecdotes, puzzles, drinking songs and so on, quite apart from his plays, of which there were almost two hundred, many of them in dialect, or translations from the French. He left one of the most important libraries of the period, and his volumes of memoirs are indispensable in their depiction of Biedermeier Vienna. In 1823 Castelli was to be Schubert's librettist for the ill-fated comic opera *Die Verschworenen*. The poet published this text with a famous challenge to German-speaking composers to set it to music, to which Schubert responded. Castelli was by all accounts a jovial and approachable man whose good works included the foundation of the Austrian Society for the Protection of Animals in 1847. He was much more important and influential in the literary life of Vienna than the somewhat insubstantial nature of the three Schubert settings of his poems might suggest. Indeed, unlike many of his poet-countrymen, Castelli had a literary reputation outside Vienna: according to the critic Julius Seidlitz, his light-hearted Anacreontic poetry was taken to be indispensably Viennese by the North Germans who tended to think that all poetry from Austria 'had a piece of Castelli in it'. Seidlitz clearly believed that this false perception had long delayed the proper appreciation of more serious Austrian literature.

Whether Schubert and Castelli were on close personal terms is to be doubted. In Castelli's *Memoiren meines Lebens* (1861) very little space is given to Schubert. When Franz von Schober wrote to Schubert from Breslau on 2 December 1824, he bemoaned the fact that Castelli was not more vocal on Schubert's behalf in the press: 'You have set one of his libretti, he should open his mouth.' This is perhaps not entirely fair, although when Castelli did praise he did not use his own name. Under the pseudonym 'Höhler' the poet was the Viennese correspondent of the *Dresdner-Abendzeitung*, and there he penned a dozen or so reviews of Schubert's works that would probably have been read with some interest by, among others, Carl Maria von Weber who worked in Dresden. For example, in January 1821 he praised Schubert's ability to 'paint with musical tones' and he greeted the publication of *Gretchen am Spinnrade* and *Die Forelle* as 'surpassing, in terms of truthful characterization, anything that had already been achieved in the realm of the lied'. The poet died in Vienna on 5 February 1862. By then he had truly outlived his period (Seidlitz rather unkindly pointed this out as early as 1836). The 'truthful characterization' that Castelli praised in Schubert had never been his own strongest suit. Nevertheless, Castelli's lyrics had been typical of the partly mythical 'easy-living' of the Biedermeier Viennese in Schubert's time. Perhaps the strongest influence exerted on Schubert by Castelli, although indirect, was that the poet was editor of the Viennese almanac *Selam* ('for friends of diverse interests'). Schubert found song texts in the issues of 1813, 1814 and 1815 of Castelli's anthology, and Walther Dürr even believes that a cycle was envisaged by Schubert from a sequence of unrelated poems in the 1814 issue (*see* the article on SELAM).

Bibliography: Clive 1997, pp. 26–7
Pohansl 1995, p. 101
Seidlitz [Jeitteles] 1837, Vol. 1, pp. 55–8

CAVATINE *see ALFONSO UND ESTRELLA* D732/2

HELMINA (WILHELMINE CHRISTIANE) VON CHÉZY (1783–1856)

THE POETIC SOURCE
There is no surviving printed source for the libretto to the play with music *Rosamunde, Fürstin von Zypern* with lyrics as Schubert set them. (See below for later five-act version.)

THE SONGS
December 1823   *Romanze* aus *Rosamunde* D797/3b
                 Hirtenchor aus *Rosamunde* D797/7
                 Jägerchor aus *Rosamunde* D797/8

Helmina von Chézy (a French name pronounced in German as an English-speaker may say 'Shate-si') was born in Berlin on 26 January 1783. Despite the fact that she came from a distinguished literary dynasty, she was raised in straitened circumstances and her life seems to have been a succession of turbulent incidents. She was brought up by her mother and grandmother, and her first marriage to a German baron was a short-lived disaster. When living in Paris she was a protégée of Friedrich and Dorothea Schlegel. In 1805 she married the French orientalist Antoine Léonard de Chézy (1773–1832) but this relationship lasted only five years. Helmina was left with two young sons, Maximilian and Wilhelm (1806–1865), whom she raised in Germany and Austria. She settled in Dresden in 1817 where she met Tieck and worked with Weber. She was perhaps best known as the librettist of that composer's *Euryanthe*, the production of which in October 1823 brought her to Vienna, and thus into the Schubert circle.

Deutsch believed it likely that at some point Weber warned Schubert against getting involved artistically with Madame von Chézy. She was nevertheless co-opted by Ignaz Castelli and Josef Kupelwieser, librettist of Schubert's opera *Fierabras*, to provide a libretto for *Rosamunde, Fürstin von Zypern* D797. This was organized as a benefit for the actress Emilie Neumann with whom Kupelwieser had a relationship. Accordingly, the work was produced in a great hurry at the Theater an der Wien in December 1823 with only two performances. Schubert's incidental music (nine numbers of which four were vocal) is immortal – especially as far as the *Entr'acte* (No. 5) and the *Ballett* (No. 9) are concerned – but *Rosamunde* was a disaster from a theatrical point of view.

Having written *Rosamunde*, Chézy was not easily to give up hopes of its success – if not in Vienna, then elsewhere. There was a second production in the Vorstadt Theater am Isartor in Munich in 1824 (a revised version) where the music was by the composer Phillip Jacob Roth (1779–1850). Chézy later revised the play again, this time into five acts (parts of this have survived and have been published by Till

Helmina von Chézy, an anonymous drawing.

Gerrit-Waidelich) but bringing Schubert's music back into play proved difficult because the composer had sold some of the vocal items to Viennese publishers. Her efforts to establish *Rosamunde* as a regular part of the German-speaking theatrical repertoire failed utterly. After 1828 her sons Wilhelm, a writer, and Max, a painter, became enthusiastic members of the Schubert circle. In 1830 the Chézy caravan settled in Munich where she importuned the King of Bavaria on behalf of *Rosamunde*, but to no avail. Chézy spent the last years of her life in Geneva where she died on 28 January 1856.

Both Chézy's mother and grandmother had been recognized poets (Karoline von Klenke – qv – and the celebrated Anna Luise Karsch (1722–1891), known as 'Die Karschin'). Helmina's life, and her travels throughout Europe, all betoken an ultimately fruitless quest to live up to her vision of herself as a great writer, third in a family line of poetesses. She numbered Adelbert von Chamisso (poet of Schumann's *Frauenliebe und -leben*) among her lovers. Schubert's friend Bauernfeld described her as 'extremely good-natured, somewhat ridiculous; cleanliness not her cardinal virtue'. Her own memoirs are in two volumes and were issued posthumously: *Unvergessenes. Denkwürdigkeiten aus dem Leben von Helmina von Chézy von ihr selbst erzählt*, Leipzig, Brockhaus, 1858 (*Never to be forgotten. Memorable Events in the Life of H. von C. recounted by herself*). Chézy makes mention of Schubert in these pages ('Schubert's wonderful music was esteemed and crowned with thunderous applause' Vol. 2, p. 261) only when it concerns her work with him on *Rosamunde*. Unable to blame herself for the failure of *Rosamunde*, and clearly unable to blame Schubert's music (which she acknowledged to be 'a majestic flow of melody' and 'a stream of harmony' that 'swept majestically over every obstacle'), Chézy came up with another excuse – apart from blaming the actors. This was none other than Schubert's quarrel with Weber about *Euryanthe* (qv COMPOSERS: Weber): she put forward the theory in her autobiography that Weber's fans were enraged with Schubert over his low opinion of *Euryanthe* and had either stayed away in droves from *Rosamunde* to punish him, or had prejudiced as much as possible the work's success by their non-appearance.

Bibliography: Waidelich 1997, pp. 46–57

The CHRONOLOGY OF SCHUBERT'S SONGS

This is one of the most tantalizing problems faced by the Schubert scholar and performer. Schubert dated his manuscripts with varying degrees of detail: sometimes, mostly in the year 1815, he wrote down everything we could ask for – day, month and year, and on one occasion even the time of day. We are often left with a month and a year, sometimes only a year – decidedly better than nothing, but on occasion nothing is what we get – particularly when an autograph is missing or lost and we must rely on a copy, as is often the case. There is sometimes a breakthrough – there have been many over the last half-century since the first Deutsch catalogue – and scholars have argued persuasively, song by song, for a revision of dates that have hitherto been accepted. Paper studies – what manuscript paper Schubert used and when – have applied twentieth-century technology to the problem without by any means answering all the questions. A study of Schubert's orthography in different phases of his career has also been helpful.

The ten volumes of the Breitkopf & Härtel edited by Mandyczewski [*see* SCHOLARS] offer a song chronology that was based on the best available information at the end of the nineteenth

century. The first edition of the Deutsch catalogue (1951) revised this in the light of half a
century's scholarship. By 1978 and the second edition of Deutsch, the actual catalogue numbering
of the songs was often different from the accepted dates of composition. It follows that the order
of Deutsch's numbering (still used as a basis of the listing of songs in the New Grove and MGG
for example) now departs in rather a large number of instances from the current thoughts on
chronology. A decision was taken, probably wise, and certainly understandable, that the musical
creations of Schubert could not be separated from the (by now) famous numbers that Deutsch
assigned to them. In any case, this would mean that the Deutsch catalogue would need to be
constantly revised when a scholar made a new discovery (and a theory is often not a discovery);
a single change of number would alter all the other numbers, and the resulting chaos is
unthinkable.

It thus follows that a definitive and foolproof order for the songs is impossible: Maurice
Brown [see SCHOLARS] set about making a catalogue (he died before he could finish it) and
Walther Dürr has written a provisional list. Dürr's work on the *Neue Schubert Ausgabe* has
highlighted a serious question in the matter of determining a chronology: is the song to be dated
according to the time it was begun, or the time when it was finished? Mandyczewski took the
former view; but he must have realized that before Schubert submitted his songs to publishers
(from 1821 on) he revised them and spruced them up for their journey into the public world.
Thus many a song could be said to be 'finished' only when a fair copy of a revised version was
sent to the publishers – sometimes years after its composition. From what we know of Schubert's
working methods, the composer was incapable of simply writing down a song from an earlier
manuscript when he saw room for improvement.

Dürr solves (or rather sidesteps) this problem by printing separately the opus numbers issued
in Schubert's lifetime in the NSA (Volumes 1–5 and in the Bärenreiter Edition Volumes 1–4).
For details of these, *see* OPUS NUMBERS. From NSA Volumes 6 to 14 the songs appear in chronological order according to the Deutsch Catalogue – although since these volumes began to
appear in the late 1960s various new discoveries have been made. In terms of accuracy, the
situation improves song by song, and argument by argument, but until hundreds of questions
have been sorted out, any list can only be provisional.

The desire to comprehend the composer in simple chronological terms (more Mandyczewski
than Dürr) remains a part of human nature. Goethe once asked the young Mendelssohn to take
him on just such a tour of musical history so that he could understand the growth and development of the art. Many people feel the same about Schubert the song composer. With the issuing
of the second Hyperion Edition of Schubert's songs on thirty-seven CDs, an order was established for practical purposes and for the pleasure and edification of the listener who had never
before been able to hear all the songs and part-songs from 1810 to 1828 in anything like a
chronological sequence.

When it comes to arranging the songs on disc as performed by some sixty different singers,
certain programme-planning considerations came into play. These were hardly ever allowed to
contradict the chronological evidence of the dates themselves (when available), but when the
only indication was a month or a year (often accompanied by a question mark) the song in
question was placed in a performing sequence that represented the best programme-planning
option – this often involved grouping together settings of a poet.

In the closing pages of this book a catalogue has been created with H (or Hyperion)
numbers, corresponding to the order to be heard on these thirty-seven discs. This list is for
practical use and is designed to facilitate the beginnings of a chronological awareness among
students and programme planners. No claims of infallibility are made on behalf of this
composite listing of songs, and part-songs, with piano. But it does permit searching and
comparison within the vocal output, and in terms of overall context, that has hitherto only

been available by turning back and forth the pages of the large Deutsch catalogue which naturally lists all Schubert's works, not only the songs; this is at least an easier and quicker means of looking for neighbouring songs and same-text settings. Furthermore, a glance at the 'H' number of any song listed in the main body of the present work will give an immediate idea of its approximate place within the corpus of piano-accompanied vocal works. Armed with this 'H' number, and having found its position within the list at the end of the third volume of this book, the reader will be able to see any song at a glance within the context of Schubert's life and output – a kind of bird's-eye view. If this is an exercise that can be achieved only with reasonable accuracy, the observation must be made that each succeeding generation of Schubert performers has had to make do with a picture of the composer and his work that has gradually become firmer and better defined over the years since his death. It is almost impossible to imagine a time when all the remaining problems will be solved, short of a dramatic discovery such as a catalogue of the works in Schubert's own hand, as was kept by Mozart. Scholars will, and must, continue with their forensic research, but in the meantime the songs must be sung and programmes must be planned both to delight and enlighten audiences, and some part of that delight lies in chronological juxtapositions or contrasts.

COLLEY CIBBER (1671–1757)

THE POETIC SOURCES
S1   *The British Musical Miscellany* (Walsh, London 1734–6) Volume 1 p. 84.

In this anthology the words attached to an anonymous tune are attributed to 'Mr Cibber, Poet Laureat' [*sic*]. Another setting from the same period by John Stanley (1712–1786) appeared as a single-sheet song and was also printed in such anthologies as *The Musical Entertainer* (1737) Volume 1 p. 12 and *The Muses' Delight* (1754) p. 182. A third setting of the poem, by Richard Leveridge (1670?–1758) appeared in *Calliope* (1746) Volume 1 p. 49.

   In theory any of these anthologies may have been the source used by Craigher de Jachelutta. A much more likely source however, is the second edition of the anthology listed as S2 below.

S2   Joseph Ritson: *A Select Collection of English Songs* (1783).

The second edition of this three-volume anthology was published as: *A Select Collection of English Songs* with their original airs and A Historical Essay on the Original and Progress of National Song by the late Joseph Ritson Esq. The Second Edition with Additional Songs and Occasional Notes by Thomas Park F.S., London Printed for F. C. and J. Rivington; Longman, Hurst, Rees; Orme and Brown; Lackington, Allen and Co.; Cadell and Davies; C. Law; S. Bagster; J. Booker; Black, Parry, and Co.; J. M. Richardson; J. Booth; R. Priestley; R. Scholey; Cradock and Joy; R. Baldwin; and J. Major 1813

   Joseph Ritson – a contraction of 'Richardson' (1752–1803) was an antiquary famous for his venomous criticisms and attacks on such luminaries as Dr Johnson and Bishop Percy. It was said that the only man he could get on with was Walter Scott. He eventually went mad and burned all his manuscripts. His fame as both a scrupulous scholar and an eccentric was known abroad and his work might well have attracted the attention of a writer with an international perspective like Craigher de Jachelutta.

THE SONG

1825   *Der blinde Knabe* D833 [S2: Volume II, Miscellaneous Songs No. XXIII, *The Blind Boy*
        with a footnote: 'Written for, and set by the celebrated Mr. Stanley, late organist of St.
        Andrews, Holborn. See the music in Volume III'] [The entry for *Der blinde Knabe*
        prints the complete text in English]

Colley Cibber was born in London on 6
November 1671, the son of the well-known
Danish sculptor, Caius Gabriel Cibber (1630–
1700), whose work can still be seen here and
there in the capital city. He was both an actor
and playwright of some significance and
became one of the very first actor-managers
(he was a great success as Lord Foppington in
Vanbrugh's play *The Relapse*) and worked at
Drury Lane between 1710 and 1733. He was
created Poet Laureate in 1730. Cibber made
many enemies through his social climbing and
ill-concealed vanity. He was the object of Alexander Pope's derision and is the antihero of the
Dunciad. It is probably because he had such a
reputation for being both poseur and clown
that Richard Capell, well versed in the literary
reputations of obscure authors, was so harsh
about *The Blind Boy* in his book on Schubert
songs. Cibber's *An Apology for the Life of Colley
Cibber* (1740) is a treasure trove of theatrical
anecdote and gossip of the theatre in the
middle of the eighteenth century. His son
Theophilus Cibber was married to the famous
singer and tragic actress who worked under
the name Susanna Cibber (1714–1766), the
sister and singing pupil of Thomas Augustine
Arne. Cibber died on 12 December 1757.

Colley Cibber, coloured plaster bust by Roubiliac.

CLÄRCHENS LIED *see* Die LIEBE D210

CLAUDINE VON VILLA BELLA

JOHANN WOLFGANG VON GOETHE (1749–1832); text written 1787/8 **D239**
Begun 26 July 1815

Goethe wrote *Claudine von Villa Bella* (1775) in the hope that it would be set to music. It was
published as *Ein Schauspiel mit Gesang* in 1776. Apart from the musical numbers, the play in
this version is in prose. This work was revised in Rome in 1787–8; at this point it became a
Singspiel with spoken interludes in verse. The two *ariette* discussed here are to be found only in
this second version. The poet aimed to comply with Italian style and conventions at the same

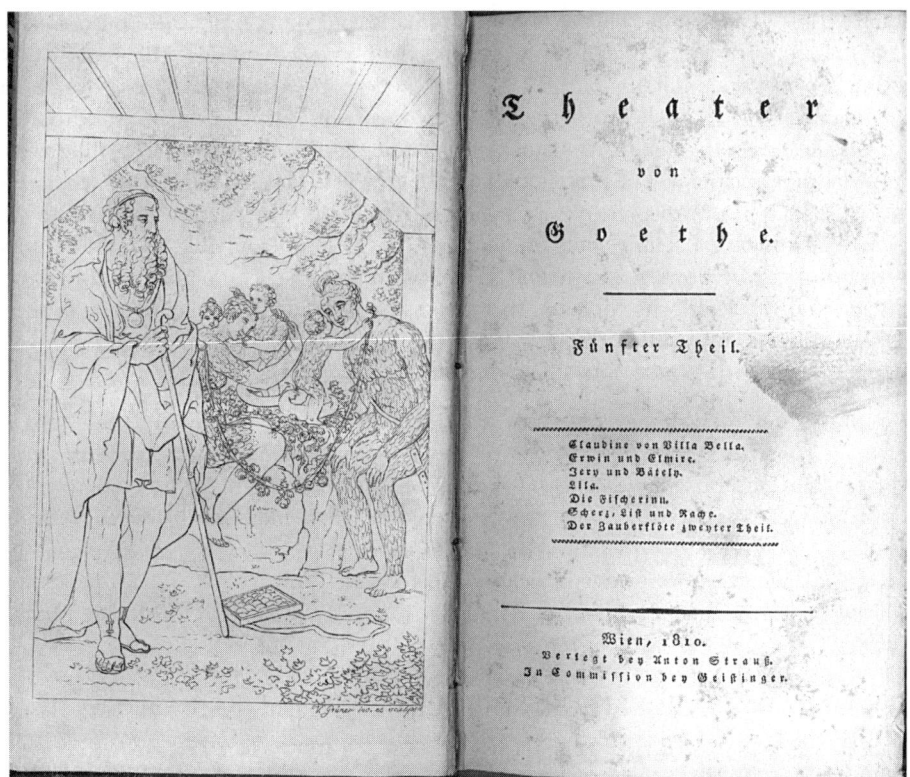

Viennese edition of *Claudine von Villa Bella* (1810).

time as turning his back on his *Sturm und Drang* past. (This despite the fact that the plot with its two estranged brothers bears some resemblance to Schiller's *Die Räuber*, published 1781, an archetypical *Sturm und Drang* work.) He also aimed to provide a libretto that would make composers, producers and singers happy, but in many ways he was an amateur in this field, and had no experience of musical theatre in places like Paris, London or Vienna. A number of the poet's friends and contemporaries – Beeke, Schickendorf, Reichardt – attempted its composition without conspicuous success. Some of the performers ended up being unwilling to speak verse, which meant that Goethe temporarily scrapped the poetry and rewrote the spoken sections in prose; the whole project, meant to be as light and carefree as air, caused him much trouble. Schubert worked from the 1788 version published in the complete edition of the poet's works published in Vienna by Anton Strauss (1810).

The story is set in Sicily. Claudine is the daughter of Alonzo, Lord of Villa Bella, and Lucinde is her cousin. Lucinde is wooed by the disinherited Carlos von Castelivecchio, alias Rugantino, a leader of a group of Sicilian bandits – and she returns his love without being aware of his identity. During Act I Claudine falls in love with Pedro, the younger brother of the estranged Carlos/Rugantino. Later in the opera there is a touch of *Così fan tutte*-like confusion between the identity of the now disguised lovers (and who loves whom), but everything works out in the end. Eight orchestrated numbers by Schubert for Goethe's Act 1 have survived – as well as copies of the voice parts of nos 9 and 10 from Act 2 – all delectably delicate and concise. Piano-accompanied arrangements of two numbers found their way into Friedlaender's edition for the publishing house of Peters (Vols 1 and 7), and they are included in this book because of their familiarity to generations of lieder singers.

Acts Two and Three of the *Singspiel* contain dramatic confrontations, heated misunderstandings and final reconciliations. We can only dream of Schubert's lost music for these more bracing scenes. In contrast the unfolding of Act 1 is relatively demure. After a substantial overture in E major (Adagio followed by Allegro vivace) the work opens with a trio for Lucinde, Pedro, Alonzo (No. 1, 'Das hast du wohl bereitet', C major, Allegro moderato) that depicts the bustling preparation for Claudine's birthday. The presentation of the birthday flowers (No. 2, 'Fröhlicher, seliger, herrlicher Tag', G major, Allegretto) is a pastoral movement in § that contrasts solo with choral episodes. The knowing Lucinde spots immediately that Claudine only has eyes for Pedro who has presented her with flowers, and that he is equally smitten. In encouraging Claudine to admit her fascination with Pedro she confesses that, down-to-earth and practical girl though she may be, she has fallen in love with a stranger who is also an adventurer ('Abenteurer').

Goethe's words for Lucinde, introducing her aria, are as follows:

Höre mich! Genug,	Enough, I tell you!
Es nenne niemand frei und weise sich	Let no one call themselves independent and wise
Vor seinem Ende! Jedem kann begegnen,	Before their end! There can be a union
Was Erd' und Meer von ihm zu trennen	Between people who seem separated by land
scheint.	and sea.
Du siehst den Fall, und du verwunderst dich?	This amazes you?
Das klügste Mädchen macht den dümmsten	The cleverest girl can play the stupidest tricks.
Streich.	

I HIN UND WIEDER FLIEGEN PFEILE — To and fro the arrows fly
D239/3 [H138+]
F major

Hin und wieder fliegen Pfeile;	To and fro the arrows fly
Amors leichte Pfeile fliegen	Cupid's light arrows fly
Von dem schlanken goldnen Bogen,	From the slender golden bow.
Mädchen, seid ihr nicht getroffen?	Maidens, are you not smitten?
Es ist Glück! Es ist nur Glück.	It is chance! It is just chance!
Warum fliegt er so in Eile?	Why does he fly with such haste?
Jene dort will er besiegen;	He desires to conquer that maiden there;
Schon ist er vorbei geflogen;	Already he has flown by;
Sorglos bleibt der Busen offen;	The heart remains open and carefree;
Gebet Acht! Er kommt zurück!	Take heed! He will be back!

As an aria from a Schubert opera with a piano part arranged from the orchestral score, this song does not figure in the list of official Goethe solo settings

This music, no. 3 of Schubert's *Singspiel*, is as slender and elegant as the golden bow, as light as love's arrows. At his (alas, only imaginary) disposal Schubert has two flutes, two oboes, two clarinets (in A), two bassoons, two horns, two trumpets, timpani and strings. The song is scored for strings alone with touches of cello pizzicato, and the composer is clearly keeping his powder dry for the more dramatic arias that will follow in later acts. Despite Lucinde's assurances that she is practical and not easily blown away by foolish enthusiasms, the music, poised high in the stave with gently cascading vocal triplets, suggests enraptured flightiness. In this miniature version of the Italian *da capo* aria, the deployment of clumsy left-hand octaves in the accompaniment makes it obvious that Schubert did not himself arrange these songs for piano.

Claudine now has a somewhat pensive solo *da capo* aria (No. 4 *Alle Freuden, alle Gaben, / Die mir heut' gehuldigt haben'*, C major, ⅜, Allegretto) in which she confesses that all her birthday gifts mean little to her in comparison with the bouquet of flowers presented to her by Pedro. The next aria, for the enamoured Pedro torn between love and duty, is very different (No. 5, *Es erhebt sich eine Stimme*, B flat major, ⅜, Maestoso). As if to reflect the character's indecision, the mood veers between music of a military character and a sensual central section (from b. 79) where he declares his love for Claudine and his desire to marry her. The end of his aria propels him off the stage. Claudine's reaction is the link between Pedro's aria and her own celebrated *Ariette*:

Er flieht! Doch ist es nicht das letzte Wort;	He's rushed off! But that's not the last word;
Ich weiss, er wird vor Abend nicht verreisen.	I know he won't leave before evening.
O werter Mann! Es bleiben mir die Freunde,	Dear man! My friends, the cherished couple,
Das teure Paa; zu meinem Trost zurück,	Remain behind; I am comforted by
Die holde Liebe mit der seltnen Treue.	Sweet love and rare constancy.
Sie sollen mich erhalten, wenn du gehst,	They will sustain me when you go,
Und mich von dir beständig unterhalten.	And keep on telling me of you.

As Lorraine Byrne writes, 'Lucinde's lied celebrates the *coup de foudre*, the bolt out of the blue, which suggests how the onset of love lies beyond one's control . . . the flirtatious mood of the setting convey's Schubert's understanding of a character who is not unlike the wanton Philine in *Wilhelm Meisters Lehrjahre*.

Autograph:	Gesellschaft der Musikfreunde, Vienna
First edition:	Published in orchestral version as part of the AGA in 1893; version for piano accompaniment published as part of *Nachgelassene, bisher ungedrückte Lieder von F Schubert* by Peters, Leipzig in 1885 (subsequently incorporated into Vol. 7 of Friedlaender's edition for Peters); see also Byrne/Farrelly 2002 (P480)
Subsequent editions:	Peters: Vol. 7/16; AGA XV: Vol. 7/56 (original orchestral version); NSA II: Vol. 14 (original orchestral version)
Discography and timing:	Fischer-Dieskau —
	Hyperion I 9[4]
	Hyperion II 8[23] 1'20 Arleen Auger

← *Punschlied (Im Norden zu singen) D253*   *Liebe schwärmt auf allen Wegen D239/6* →

II LIEBE SCHWÄRMT AUF ALLEN WEGEN   Love roves everywhere
D239/6 [H138++]
D major (C major in Peters)

Liebe schwärmt auf allen Wegen;	Love roves everywhere;
Treue wohnt für sich allein.	Constancy lives alone
Liebe kommt euch rasch entgegen;	Love comes rushing towards you;
Aufgesucht will Treue sein.	Constancy must be sought.

As an aria from a Schubert opera with a piano part arranged from the orchestral score, this song does not figure in the list of official Goethe solo settings

This song, no. 6 of Schubert's *Singspiel*, is often heard in recitals because of its inclusion in two volumes of the Peters Edition. Without any knowledge of the context of Goethe's story Claudine may be erroneously typecast as an excitable little minx who finds love wherever she goes. In fact, the poem says the opposite, and the 'Andante quasi allegretto' is a corrective to the many excitable and over-fleet interpretations often to be heard on the concert platform. There should be nothing hectic about this music; Claudine has decided to stand firm and wait for Pedro. In its own modest way this music should have the visionary steadfastness of Fiordiligi's *Come scoglio* with none of the exaggerated or bathetic overtones. Schubert conjures something exquisite from this slender quatrain. Lucinde's aria had been accompanied by strings alone, here Schubert adds the combination of oboe and bassoon, and these two instruments introduce the aria on their own, in a simple two-bar phrase, almost a horn-like motif. It is the plangent timbre of this instrumentation that is the clue to Claudine's emotional dilemma.

There are two further extant and completed numbers by Schubert. The first of these is a Bandit's Chorus (no. 7) for Rugantino and chorus. Between 1790 and 1792 Beethoven set this text for bass solo and orchestra (*Mit Mädeln sich vertragen* WoO90). Like Schubert's two songs it sometimes appears with piano accompaniment in earlier printings of volumes of Beethoven's lieder. The Act closes with no. 8, a rousing ensemble for Rugantino and his deputy Basco (like Alonso, a baritone) and male chorus. This is in effect a quarrel between Rugantino and some of his bandits; he wishes to abduct Lucinde, but his colleagues in crime are not convinced this is a good idea.

The fact that Schubert's operatic career was shadowed by an unhappy star is amply demonstrated in the case of *Claudine von Villa Bella*. Unlike his other stage works, the libretto is by a great poet (Körner's *Der vierjährige Posten* admittedly also boasts Körner as a famous author), and it may well have been among his most accessible and often-performed works. The whole *Singspiel* survived intact (and unpublished) until 1848. In that year of revolution and turmoil in Vienna the second and third acts were burnt as fuel in the home of Josef Hüttenbrenner, brother of the composer Anselm Hüttenbrenner, who was elsewhere at the time. Some years later Josef blamed the disappearance of two-thirds of the opera's manuscript on the incompetence of a domestic (one is reminded of the burning of the manuscript of Carlyle's *The French Revolution* by Leigh Hunt's similarly careless servant). This incident, as well as their silent guardianship of the 'Unfinished' (and as yet unperformed) Symphony, are indications of the unfortunate, if not deliberate, role played by the Hüttenbrenner family in Schubert's affairs after his death. The composer's ever-growing posthumous fame, in comparison with Anselm's fading reputation, seems to have ignited the family's collective jealousy.

Autograph:	Gesellschaft der Musikfreunde, Vienna
First edition:	Published in orchestral version as part of the AGA in 1893; version for piano accompaniment published as part of *Nachgelassene, bisher ungedruckte Lieder von F. Schubert* by Peters, Leipzig in 1885 (subsequently incorporated into Vol. 7 of Friedlaender's edition for Peters and subsequently also Vol. 1); see also Byrne/Farrelly 2002 (P479)
Subsequent editions:	Peters: Vol. 1/258 and Vol. 7/13; AGA XV: Vol. 7/72 (original orchestral version); NSA II: Vol. 14 (original orchestral version)
Bibliography:	Byrne/Farrelly 2002 Byrne 2003, pp. 387–96 McKay 1991, pp. 120–24
Discography and timing:	Fischer-Dieskau — Hyperion I 9^5 Hyperion II 8^{24} 1'16 Arleen Auger

⟵ *Hin und wieder fliegen Pfeile* D239/3   *Die Spinnerin* D247 ⟶

MATTHIAS CLAUDIUS (1740–1815)

THE POETIC SOURCE
In the absence of a contemporary Viennese edition of Claudius's works it seems likely that Schubert used a German edition, and possibly the first:

S1 *ASMUS omnia sua SECUM portans ['Asmus Carrying All His Things'], oder Sämmtliche Werke des Wandsbecker Bothen.* Parts I – IV, Hamburg und Wandsbek

Parts I and II, bound together, and paginated as one volume (1775); Part III (1778), and Part IV (1783). Schubert made no settings from Parts V to VIII (1790–1812) of the work.

THE SONGS

1815	*Klage um Ali Bey* D140 (Trio, TTB) [S1: Part I pp. 48–9]
End of 1815, early 1816	*Am ersten Maimorgen* D344 [S1: Part I p. 194] *Zufriedenheit* (first setting) D362 [S1: Part I p. 97]
November 1816	*Zufriedenheit* (second setting) D501 [S1: Part I p. 97] *Bei dem Grabe meines Vaters* D496 [S1: Part I p. 231] *Klage um Ali Bey* D496A [S1: Part I pp. 48–9] *An die Nachtigall* D497 [S1: Part I p. 56] *Abendlied* D499 [S1: Part IV p. 91] *Phidile* D500 [S1: Part I pp. 54–5]
4 November 1816	*Am Grabe Anselmos* D504 [S1: Part I pp. 21–2 as 'Bey dem Grabe Anselmos']

February 1817   *An eine Quelle* D530 [S1: Part I p. 154]
                       Der Tod und das Mädchen D531 [S1: Part I p. 199]
                       Das Lied vom Reifen D532 [S1: Part IV p. 7]
                       Täglich zu singen D533 [S1: Part III p. 128]

Matthias Claudius was a native of Holstein (born in Reinfeld on 15 August 1740) and his writing remained strongly connected to his North German stamping ground. He studied theology and law and came into contact with Klopstock and his circle in Copenhagen where as a young man he was employed as a private secretary. From 1768 he worked as a journalist in Hamburg where he met Herder, Lessing and C. P. E. Bach. As private tutor to the children of Johann Georg Jacobi he encountered other poets from the Göttingen Hainbund. Between 1771 and 1775 Claudius achieved a unique celebrity as the editor of *Der Wandsbecker Bote* (The Wandsbek Courier), a newspaper with which he became completely identified, and to which he was the principal contributor under the pseudonym of 'Asmus'. (Among other writers enlisted to the cause of the 'Bote' were Lessing, Klopstock, Herder and even Goethe). Claudius created a cosy, intimate literary style for the readership of his newspaper, with writing that was popular without being cheap, and religious without being rigid or dour. In cultivating this conversational tone with his readers he was one of the pioneers of popular journalism in Germany; a number of his poems were adopted by the German public as folksongs. He was an extremely happy family man, and he was never as contented as in Wandsbek – in modern-day Hamburg this is the name of the borough that lies to the northeast of the city. Claudius was in touch with the greatest writers of the age, but he lived extremely simply and avoided the honours and the trappings of public life enjoyed by many of his less talented contemporaries.

Claudius was one of Schubert's most important and lovable poets. As the son of a pastor, the poet's delight in the small things of life (including domestic harmony and tolerance) and a celebration of the beauties of everyday existence, chimed well with Schubert and released some of the composer's most endearing musical ideas. Not every Claudius poem is as dramatic as *Der Tod und das Mädchen* D531, yet the interchangeability of life and death were always in the forefront of the poet's mind (he nicknamed Death 'Freund Hain' and placed him as the frontispiece of his writings); this is perhaps the literary equivalent of the ambivalence between major and minor tonalities on Schubert's part. Composer and poet shared a non-sentimental awareness of the transience of life; in almost all of his thirteen Claudius settings Schubert matches the tenderness and simplicity, as well as the gentle ache and pathos, of the verse. The poet died in Hamburg on 21 January 1815. While admiring the uniquely human qualities of Claudius's writing, Oscar Wolff (1846) criticized his by

Matthias Claudius, an oil painting by Leisching.

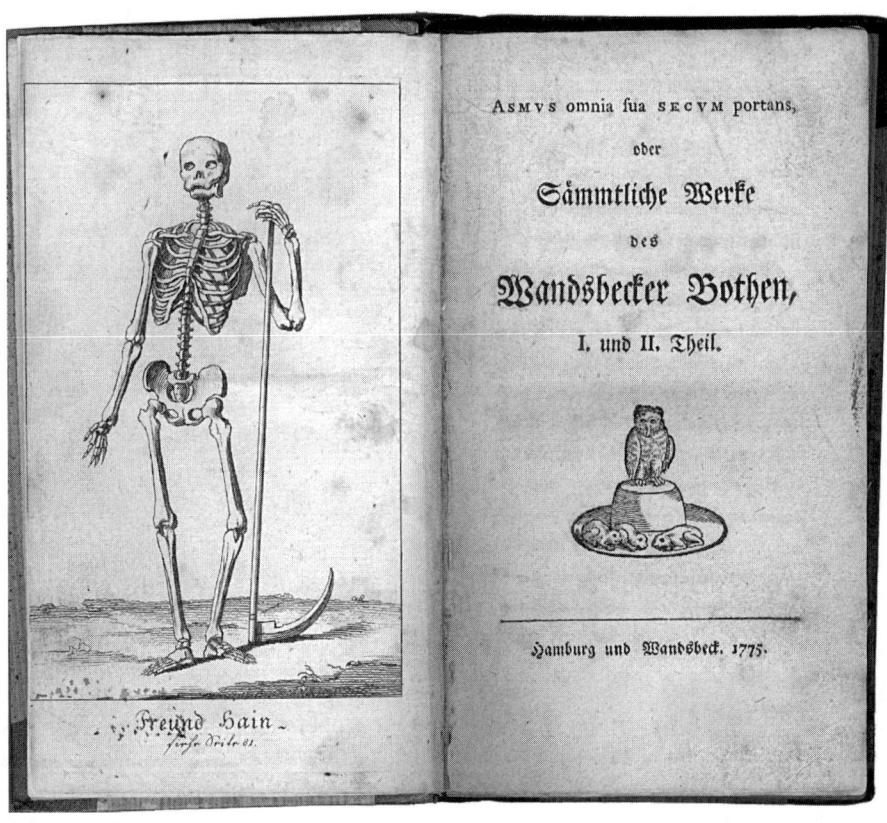

Title page of Volume One of the Complete Works of Claudius ('Asmus omnia sua secum portans', 1775) with frontispiece, 'Freund Hain'.

no means faultless grammar and style, the result of trying to achieve a literary 'Volkston' – the writing of poetry in a tonality for ordinary people. We know that Schubert's patron and poet, Matthäus von Collin (qv) was a devotee of Claudius from the articles he contributed to Schlegel's *Deutsches Museum* in 1812. Later admirers like Schopenhauer, Thomas Mann and Samuel Becket have remarked on Claudius's childlike piety and a tendency to mysticism and atheism – the latter during older age when he was much less productive. Today's reader of the 'Asmus' collection (there are eight issues of the collected works gathered in seven volumes) is struck by the multitude of small literary forms assembled in what seems a very modern manner. As Herbert Rowland puts it, 'reviews, essays, narratives, epistles, various prose reflections, epigrams, dialogues, verse tales, fables, lyric poetry and more – as well as a wide range of sacred and profane themes and reverent and satiric tones, all under the watchful eye of Freund Hain'. When Claudius died Christian Stolberg wrote a poem, *Andenken des Wandsbecker Boten*, in honour of the poet, with his trademark hat and walking stick, who had become an iconic figure, not only in German literature, but also in the home life of all Germans who were capable of reading:

Er sprach bei den Frommen gar freundlich ein,
Bat freundlich die Andern, auch fromm zu sein,
Und sah'n sie sein redliches ernstes Gesicht,
So zürnten auch selbst die Thoren ihm nicht.

Doch wussten nur Wenige, denen er hold,
Dass im hölzernen Stabe gediegenes Gold,
Dass heimliche Kraft in dem hölzernen Stab,
Zu erhellen mit Lichte des Himmels das Grab.

(He spoke kindly among the pious,   But only a few, those he was fond of, knew
And kindly bade the others be pious likewise;   That there was pure gold in the wooden staff,
And when they saw his eloquent, serious face,   That in the wooden staff was a secret power
Even the fools did not rage at him.   To illuminate the grave with the light of heaven.)

Bibliography: Rowland 2000, pp. 193–5

HEINRICH JOSEPH VON COLLIN (1771–1811)

THE POETIC SOURCE
Gedichte von H. J. von Collin, Anton Strauss, Wien, 1812

THE SONGS
December 1816   *Leiden der Trennung* D509 [p. 26, translation from Metastasio]
December 1818(?)   *Kaiser Max [sic] auf der Martinswand in Tyrol 1493*, fragment D990A
                   [p. 186]

Heinrich (born in Vienna on 26 December 1771) was the elder brother of Matthäus von Collin (1779–1824). They were the sons of a distinguished Viennese doctor and the family was ennobled in 1803. Matthäus inspired Schubert to five settings, all masterpieces, and played a significant part in the composer's life as friend and patron, but Schubert never met Heinrich, who died in Vienna on 28 July 1811 at the age of forty (apparently of 'Nervenfieber', the same official reason for Schubert's death) when the composer was still a schoolboy. In his foreword to the edition of the poems cited above, Matthäus calls Heinrich 'ein geliebter Bruder' and writes of him with reverence. These *Gedichte* are dedicated to Graf Moritz von Dietrichstein, the Viennese grandee and patron, who was also the dedicatee of Schubert's *Erlkönig*.

Heinrich, who rose to the highest echelons of the Austrian civil service, was celebrated above all as a man of the theatre (he was nicknamed 'the Austrian Corneille') and it was Collin's play *Coriolan* (1802) that inspired Beethoven to his Overture of 1807 (it is a common misconception that Beethoven's model for this work was Shakespeare). The elder Collin was a humanitarian idealist: his play *Balboa* – (1805), about the Spanish conquistadors, included the line, 'Human beings remain human beings, no matter what colour

Heinrich von Collin, painting by Lange.

they may be.' Like Theodor Körner he gained a reputation as a patriotic poet – he too did not live to see the victorious conclusion of the Napoleonic wars, but his *Wehrmannslieder,* stirring the Austrians to action against the French, brought his writing to Napoleon's attention.

Apart from his works for the theatre (where his characters are criticized for being more intellectual than feeling) Collin wrote occasional verse (for example, in honour of the performance of Haydn's *Die Schöpfung* in 1809, with Salieri and Beethoven in the admiring audience) but he was also a respected writer of historical ballads. Collin's *Kaiser Maximilian auf der Martinswand* inspired Schubert to make a sketch (D990A) but too little of the music was written to make a performance feasible.

MATTHÄUS KARL, FREIHERR VON COLLIN (1779–1824)

THE POETIC SOURCES
S1   *Selam Ein Almanach für Freunde des Mannifaltigen auf das Jahr 1813.* Von I. F. Castelli, Wien. Gedruckt und im Verlage bey Anton Strauss

The title page of this almanac also contains a quotation from the Goethe poem *An die Günstigen*: 'Und das Alter wie die Jugend, / Und der Fehler wie die Tugend / Nimmt sich gut in Liedern aus' (*To the favourable ones:* 'And age, as well as youth, / Error as well as virtue / Sound well in song')

S2   *Dramatische Dichtungen von Matthäus von Collin,* Erster Band, Konrad Adolph Hartleben, Pesth, 1813. (This volume contains two plays, the first of which is the five-act tragedy *Der Tod Friedrich des Streitbaren – ein Trauerspiel in fünf Aufzügen.*)

S3   *Matthäus Edler von Collin's nachgelassene Gedichte,* ausgewählt und mit einem biographischen Vorwort begleitet von Joseph von Hammer. I u 2 Bändchen. Wien. Gedruckt und im Verlage bey Carl Gerold, 1827

Schubert clearly used manuscripts of texts given to him by the poet; these were later published, sometimes in earlier versions, in this posthumous edition of the poet's works.

About three-quarters of these two volumes of *Nachgelassene Gedichte* are given over to dramatic works: the whole of Vol. 1 is an Elizabethan play entitled *Essex*; Vol. 2 contains three further dramas: *Fortunats Abfahrt von Cypern* (*see* below), *Die Liebeswerbung* (extract) and *Die Rückkehr.*

THE SONGS
1816(?)   *Licht und Liebe* D352, duet [S2: *Der Tod Friedrich des Streitbaren,* Act IV Scene 2 pp. 95–6]
1822–3   *Herrn Josef Spaun, Assessor in Linz* D749 [there are no printed sources of this poem which was written informally within the Schubert circle]
　　　　 Der Zwerg D771 [S1: pp. 68–9 with the title 'Treubruch'] [S3: Volume 2 pp. 140–41]
　　　　 Wehmut D772 [S1: p. 203] [S3: Volume 2 p. 133, with the title 'Naturgefühl']
　　　　 Nacht und Träume D827 [S3: Seemingly a compilation of 'Nacht und Träume', Volume 1 p. 134, and 'Nachtfeyer' Volume 2 p. 149. The *Nacht und Träume* poem is very similar (though not identical) to the *Gesang* for the Graf von Flandern in Collin's dramatic fragment *Fortunats Abfahrt von Cypern.* Volume 2 p. 65].

Matthäus von Collin (born in Vienna on 3 March 1779) was a cousin of Josef von Spaun, the schoolfriend who was a benign presence in many of the more fortunate aspects of Schubert's life. Collin was a poet and dramatist, a good eighteen years older than the composer, but a kindly and cultured host of considerable means (from 1815 he was tutor to Napoleon's young son, the Duke of Reichstadt, who was a virtual prisoner at Schönbrunn). Collin was something of an intellectual heavyweight, having held the professorship of philosophy at the University of Cracow, and the professorship of history of philosophy in Vienna. Admired for his taste, kindness and ability as a critic rather more than for his poetry, Collin's conversation must have bewitched Schubert on his visits (sometimes with the singer Vogl) to his household. At his home (Teinfaltstrasse 67 in the inner city) he held musical gatherings to which such literary luminaries as Pyrker, Caroline Pichler (qqv) and the great orientalist Hammer-Purgstall (*see* WEST-ÖSTLICHER DIVAN) were invited. It was on one of these occasions that Schubert and Anselm Hüttenbrenner as piano-duettists performed the *Variationen über ein französisches Lied* D624.

Collin was a disciple of the Schlegel brothers, and those poets' considerable influence on Schubert in the early 1820s probably went back to inspiring conversations with Collin. His editorship of the *Jahrbücher der Litteratur* produced some of the most important critical writing in Austria in the Biedermeier age, but he withdrew from that position on account of tightening state censorship. Fervent catholic and patriot though he was, Collin was clearly far less reactionary than the majority of those who worked in the higher echelons of the Metternich administration, and this would not have gone unnoticed by Schubert and his friends. It is possible that the composer hoped to interest Collin in writing an opera libretto for him. Schubert's *Der Zwerg* and *Wehmut*, two great Collin settings, were published in May 1823 as Op. 22 and dedicated to the poet. It is also possible that Collin was present at the first performance of *Der Zwerg* at an evening concert at the Gesellschaft der Musikfreunde in March of the same year. His death from a gastric infection at the age of forty-five on 23 November 1824 (his brother Heinrich died even younger) was a shock to the Schubert circle.

M. von Collin, oil painting by Leopold Kupelwieser.

Bibliography: Youens 2002, pp. 1–92

COLMAS KLAGE *see* KOLMAS KLAGE D217

COMPOSERS IN SCHUBERT'S WORLD

The following is a sequence of short biographical outlines of the other important composers in Schubert's life and career, especially those who influenced him and his songs and those who, in turn, were influenced by him. The composers appear here in the chronological order of their birth. There has been no attempt to provide biographical information regarding the greater and better-known composers (Gluck, Haydn, Mozart, Beethoven, Weber) who are listed here only in so far as they have some bearing on Schubert.

Early Music

Thanks to Schubert's friendship from 1823 with the musicologist and amateur singer Raphael Georg Kiesewetter von Wiesenbrunn (1773–1850) and his daughter Irene (*see* PIANISTS) it is very possible that the composer was given access to Kiesewetter's celebrated library of early vocal scores. The catalogue of this vast collection (*Galerie der alten Contrapunctisten*, Vienna 1847) includes Dufay, Ockeghem, Josquin des Prés, Isaak, Orlando di Lasso, Tallis, Praetorius, Palestrina, Vittoria, Monteverdi, Cavalli and so on. Kiesewetter's library also included all the works of Bach that were in print at that time.

Johann Sebastian Bach (1685–1750)

According to Spaun, Schubert worked through Bach and Handel thoroughly. Hüttenbrenner on the other hand claims that Schubert knew little of Bach. This may have been true of the earlier part of his career, but he seems to have studied the composer more assiduously as he got older. At Kiesewetter's home he heard, among other works, Bach's *Magnificat* BWV 283. On his summer visit to Zseliz in 1824 he took *Das wohltemperierte Clavier* with him. The Conspirators' Chorus in *Alfonso und Estrella* D732 (No. 17) suggests a knowledge of the *Christmas Oratorio* BWV 248. The opening of the Heine setting *Der Doppelgänger* D957/13 (*see Schwanengesang*) suggests the adoption of a Bachian motif, as do several passages in the piano music and the *Agnus Dei* from the E flat Mass D950.

George Frederick Handel (Georg Frideric Händel) (1685–1759)

Several of Schubert's contemporaries attest to his knowledge of Handel's music and the fact that he read through scores of Handel's operas and oratorios. The influence of this composer's style is to be heard as early as 1815 in the *Benedictus in C* D184. Anselm Hüttenbrenner recalled that when reading through Handel's music at the piano, Schubert turned to him and said, 'Oh the daring of these modulations! Things like that do not occur to the likes of us, even in a dream.' It seems likely that the composer also took part in a performance of *Messiah* in 1819 at the home of Anton von Pettenkoffer. It was well known that Beethoven had an edition of Handel's complete works; after Beethoven's death it is possible that Anton Schindler may have allowed Schubert to peruse some of the folio volumes. The composer's study of the Handel oratorios led to his desire to take further counterpoint lessons from Simon Sechter in the last months of his life. Schubert's enthusiasm for Handel's music is most clearly to be heard in the cantata for soprano, chorus and piano, *Mirjams Siegesgesang* D942.

Christoph Willibald Gluck (1714–1787)

From his teenage years Schubert was aware that this great opera composer (who had died in Vienna) was the teacher of his own teacher, Salieri (*see* p. 364); in a manner of speaking Gluck was Schubert's musical grandfather. Schubert made a four-hand version of the overture to *Iphigenia in Aulis* (D Anhang II, 1) when he was about thirteen years old and, three years later (1813), he attended a performance of *Iphigenia in Tauris*; according to Spaun, Schubert was moved to tears (Deutsch 1958, p. 129). He clearly fell in love with both the music and its performers, Milder and Vogl [qv SINGERS]. Although this is the only documented occasion where he attended a Gluck opera, it is highly likely that Schubert heard many other performances on later occasions; Josef von Spaun tells us (Deutsch 1958, p. 363) that 'all Gluck's operas he could play almost from memory' and Anton Holzapfel (Deutsch 1958, p. 59) remembers that Schubert 'went through the whole of Gluck from whose works he often played things to us, which I still remember, especially a hair-raising and moving scene from *Orfeo*, the like of which I have never heard before'. In 1816 Schubert made two piano-accompanied arrangements of arias from Gluck's *Echo et Narcisse* (qv). In the songs, and above all in his treatment of recitative, Schubert's knowledge of this composer's music seems to have been extensive. When it comes to the treatment of ancient subjects it is clear that Schubert could summon in his own music a monumental and classically proportioned grandeur that stemmed from his knowledge of Gluck's works. Schubert's own enthusiasm for harmonic variety and copious detail was tempered by Gluck's noble and statuesque example where 'less was always more'. This kind of control and sparseness of texture no doubt influenced Schubert's enthusiasm for beautifully crafted strophic songs with understated accompaniments.

Joseph Haydn (1732–1809)

Haydn was the most famous musical inhabitant of Vienna in Schubert's childhood, Beethoven notwithstanding. His example and influence in Schubert's life were pervasive – this despite the fact that Hüttenbrenner claimed that Schubert received little 'musical nourishment' from Haydn. Schubert had known Haydn's works from the very beginning: the string quartets, and the symphonies arranged for quartet, were performed in the family circle, and the religious music, including the *Nelson* Mass, was to be heard regularly at the Lichtenthal parish church. When Schubert was a student at the Imperial Konvikt, some thirty symphonies were part of the regular repertoire of the school orchestra. The young composer made a copy of a large and imposing song for bass voice, *Die Teilung der Erde* (D Anhang III, 2) which he took to be by Haydn. The text, one of Schiller's finest, imagines Zeus making a special dispensation for artists; these impractical beings are permitted to visit the god in heaven whenever they wish as compensation for being left out of his allocation of earthly riches. (The song is in fact by Franz de Paula Roser, 1779–1830, a one-time pupil of Mozart.) In terms of its abundant use of illustrative imagery *Die Schöpfung* (*The Creation*) was a particularly influential work; this was performed at the orchestral concerts held at the home of Pettenkoffer in 1819, as was *The Seven Last Words of Christ Our Saviour on the Cross*. The latter work may well have been the inspiration for Schubert's own cantata, *Lazarus* D689. According to the baritone Karl von Schönstein, excerpts from Haydn's oratorios and vocal quartets were performed with piano accompaniment at Zseliz in the summers of 1818 and 1824. Apart from several solo songs in baroque or rococo style, it is perhaps in Schubert's music for vocal ensemble that Haydn's influence is to be heard most. A short while before he died, Schubert went on a walking expedition with friends to Eisenstadt to view Haydn's grave at the Esterházy palace. This was a relatively recent installation as Haydn's body (without the head) had only been reclaimed from Vienna by the Esterházy family in 1820.

Michael Haydn (1737–1806)

The younger brother of the great composer was no less admired by Schubert – above all for his achievements in the genre of music for male vocal quartet. The still extant library of scores in the Lichtenthal parish church is an indication of how often the young composer would have heard Michael Haydn's music in his childhood. In 1810, when Schubert was a student at the Imperial Konvikt, he copied out a selection of Haydn's canons. Schubert's three-part settings of Schiller for male voices, exercises for Salieri, were modelled on the same composer as Schubert

Michael Haydn, lithograph by Franz Eybl.

Abbé Maximilian Stadler, engraving of J. B. Pfizer, 1813.

himself admitted with the words 'Imitatio ad Haydni consuetudinem'. Many years later, in 1825, while on holiday in Upper Austria, Schubert took the trouble to visit Michael Haydn's grave in Salzburg; in a letter to his brother Ferdinand the composer refers to Haydn's 'peaceful, clear spirit' – saying that no one on earth reveres Haydn more than he does, and that he only regrets that he himself cannot be equally 'ruhig und klar'. This strongly expressed admiration for someone who had lived and worked in the shadow of his more celebrated brother seems to have been influenced by Schubert's fellow feeling for a composer who had scarcely received the musical recognition he deserved.

Abbé Stadler (1748–1833)

Johann Karl Dominik Stadler, later Pater Maximilian, was born in Melk where he became known, when still a boy, as an organist and improviser in the Benedictine abbey. He went on to become a novice and priest there, and then studied further in Vienna at the Jesuit college. In 1784 he became abbé in Lilienfeld and following a promotion to Linz in 1796 he moved to Vienna and lived there permanently from 1815. He was a friend of both Haydn and Mozart and he must have known many of the Linz families whose sons were members of Schubert's intimate circle. He composed vocal music (including some lieder), church and organ music, piano sonatas, an oratorio entitled *Die Befreiung von Jersusalem* (with a text by the Collin brothers, Heinrich and Matthäus), a large cantata for voices and orchestra and *Die Frühlingsfeier* to words of Klopstock. There seems to have been some undocumented relationship between Schubert and the abbé, and Stadler's music had been known to the younger composer since his early years at the Lichtenthal parish church. Schubert possessed a copy of Stadler's *Der 8. Psalm* and made an arrangement of it for Vogl (see Psalm 8). Both composers wrote settings of psalms 23 and 92, and both used the translations of Moses Mendelssohn. Other poets the two composers had in common were Klopstock, Stolberg and Kuffner. After Schubert died Stadler wrote an organ fugue in memory of the composer, who was nearly fifty years his junior, weaving Schubert's name into the musical structure. The abbé made this homage to no other composer, and he had met most of his famous contemporaries in a long and prosperous life.

There is a possibility that Schubert met Stadler through the young composer Franz Lachner (*see* p. 384) who was the abbé's pupil.

Antonio Salieri (1750–1825)

Antonio Salieri, after a portrait of S. von Treuberg.

At one time the role of Antonio Salieri in Schubert's life was undervalued, but it is now known how important his guidance was to the younger composer, how thorough Salieri was as a teacher and how much Schubert owed to his supervision. It is easy to see why the Italian composer used to be given a minimal role in the Schubert story. He had been vilified by Pushkin's play *Mozart and Salieri*, written in 1826 when the composer was hardly cold in his grave; this was later turned into an opera by Rimsky-Korsakov, and then into a play, *Amadeus* (1979), by Peter Schaffer. Far from being responsible for Mozart's death, it is likely that Salieri's continuing success on the Viennese scene insulated him from any need to concern himself overmuch with his greater contemporary. In any case – and this is a flaw behind the psychology of Schaffer's play – if Salieri had had the perception and self-awareness to be tortured by such feelings of inferiority, he would almost certainly have been a greater, or at least a more imaginative, composer. He had arrived in Vienna at the age of seventeen and modelled himself on his revered master, Gluck. International success followed as a composer of operas (works like *Axur* and *Die Danaïden*), and he was created Hofkapellmeister in Vienna three years before Mozart's death in 1791, a post he held for thirty-six years. As a craftsman he was exemplary, which is why he seems to have been an effective teacher. By the time of Salieri's own death in 1825, Mozart had become a god among the Viennese, but the Italian was a survivor, and he numbered countless students among his flock who owed him various degrees of gratitude. Among these were seven important composers apart from Schubert himself: Beethoven, Hütten-brenner, Hummel, Liszt, Meyerbeer, Randhartinger and Weigl. Schubert took part in the cele-bration of Salieri's fiftieth jubilee celebrations in Vienna and composed a set of vocal pieces for the great occasion (*see Beiträge zur Funfzigjährigsten Jubelfeier des Herrn von Salieri* D407). Schubert also dedicated his Op. 5 set of Goethe settings to his teacher (*see* DEDICATEES).

Johann Friedrich Reichardt (1752–1814)

Johann Friedrich Reichardt was born in Königsberg in North Germany. He began life as a lawyer on the recommendation of Immanuel Kant. Eventually he became the greatest song composer of his day, as well as a busy journalist and talented writer. His *Vertraute Briefe aus Paris* (1804) is one of the best books ever written by a musician. At the age of twenty-three (1775) he was appointed Hofkapellmeister in Potsdam, a post he held for fifteen years until his radical political beliefs led to his dismissal. Little deterred, he moved to Halle where his home in nearby Giebichenstein became a focal point for musicians and poets such as Tieck, Novalis, Brentano and Arnim. Reichardt began to set Goethe's poetry as early as 1772, and in 1790 he planned to

J. F. Reichardt, engraving by B. H. Bendix, 1796.

issue a six-volume collection entitled *Musik zu Goethes Werken*; he visited Goethe in 1789, taking with him a setting of the *Singspiel, Claudine von Villa Bella* (set by Schubert in 1815). Goethe could not approve of Reichardt's sympathy for the French Revolution and this eventually led to an estrangement between the men; the composer was attacked in the *Xenien* (1797) as an ostrich, a half-bird who was unable to fly, always on the move and accomplishing little. By 1804 Zelter had became Goethe's preferred musical adviser, and the poet's relationship with Reichardt came to a decisive end in 1810. Reichardt composed some 150 Goethe settings; other poets that feature in his 1,500 lieder include Schiller, Hölty, Claudius and Klopstock. In fact the range of texts he set, and the sheer number of his chosen poets, far exceeds Schubert's tally, or that of any other song composer. His song collections (issued with such titles as *Lieder der geselligen Freude*) are often very beautiful publications, exquisitely produced with poem and music printed side by side (and impossibly expensive for the present-day collector).

Schubert was well aware of Reichardt's importance and would have eagerly read through any music by this composer that came his way, and the first book of *Oden und Lieder* (1779) and the *Lieder der Liebe und Einsamkeit* (1804) were certainly known to him. In the latter collection Schubert found the texts for *Die Liebe* D210 and *Kolmas Klage* D217; he was so impressed with Reichardt's *Monolog aus Iphigenia* for soprano and piano (D Anhang III, 7) in the same publication that he wrote out a copy for himself (now in the Fitzwilliam Museum in Cambridge). The plight of Iphigenia, who feels herself enslaved in her marriage to Thoas must have appealed to a young composer who admired Gluck's treatment of the theme and who had already responded sympathetically to another heroine, Gretchen, *in extremis*. Reichardt sets the very beginning of the first act (before the entrance of Arcas) where Iphigenia stands in front of the temple of Diana. Goethe mentions nothing about a chorus but Reichardt introduces supplementary voices to echo her words. This recitative was very much a subject of study for the younger composer; Schubert's contemporary interest in declamation supplemented by chorus is shown by his wonderfully adventurous setting of the *Szene aus* Faust D126 at the end of 1814.

Felix Mendelssohn, despite his strong link with his teacher Zelter (*see* p. 367) remained convinced that Reichardt was the greater musical figure – he stayed in contact with the composer's widow – and he seems to have valued Reichardt as a song composer over Schubert. That Reichardt is almost forgotten in modern times cannot obscure his status as a great pioneer of the lieder repertoire – Schubert certainly valued him as such.

Adalbert Gyrowetz (1753–1850)

This highly prolific composer was Bohemian-born. He had experience of the world that Schubert might have envied – he seemed to be everywhere at the right time: he met Mozart (who performed one of his symphonies) in Vienna, Goethe in Rome, Haydn in London (where Gyrowetz lived for three years in the 1790s) and, purportedly, Napoleon in Prague. He was created second Kapellmeister in Vienna in 1804 and composed a large number of operas in Italian, and also *Singspiele*. In August 1819, while on holiday in Steyr, Schubert composed a *Kantate* to celebrate the fifty-first birthday of the singer Johann Michael Vogl (D666). In the text by Albert Stadler there is the following line celebrating one of Vogl's great operatic roles: 'Saht des Arztes Hoffnung tagen'. This refers to the romantic hopes of the regimental doctor in Gyrowetz's celebrated *Der Augenarzt* (1811), a work that Schubert, a great fan of Vogl's since his youth, no doubt knew very well. Gyrowetz outlived Schubert by many years.

Adalbert Gyrowetz, lithograph by M. Bisenius.

The two composers met when they were both pall-bearers at Beethoven's funeral, and had perhaps encountered each other on earlier occasions.

Wolfgang Amadeus Mozart (1756–1791)

It is no surprise, and an understatement, to say that Mozart was Schubert's ideal; for the younger composer, Mozart's music represented the innocence of a vanished age. The fragile beauty of the opening of *Frühlingstraum* from *Winterreise* D911/11 is one of many examples of Schubert's lifelong debt to this composer, an artist whom he put on a pedestal.

On one of the few surviving pages (13 June 1816) of the composer's diary, we read the following:

> *A light, bright, fine day this will remain throughout my whole life. As from afar the magic tones of Mozart's music still gently haunt me. How unbelievably vigorously, and yet again how gently was it impressed deep, deep into the heart by Schlesinger's masterly playing [the work was one of the Mozart string quintets] . . . O Mozart, immortal Mozart how many, oh how endlessly many such comforting perceptions of a brighter and better life have you brought to our souls!*

Many years after Schubert's death, Spaun exaggeratedly insisted that there was probably not a note of Mozart (or Beethoven and Haydn) that Schubert did not know. There are certain works of Mozart that seem to have influenced the lieder (such as the song *Abendempfindung* K523). The relationship between this work and *Abendbilder* D650 and *Der Lindenbaum* D911/5 is mentioned in more detail in the commentaries. Above all it was *Die Zauberflöte* that was an absolutely seminal work for Schubert. Other operas were also capable of inspiring powerfully allusive Schubertian reactions. *Don Giovanni, La Clemenza di Tito, Così fan tutte* (a work that Schubert was asked to coach during his short employment with the Kärntnertortheater in 1822), *Idomeneo* and the *Requiem* were all known to him. The comic trio for Osmin, Belmonte and Pedrillo from *Die Entführung aus dem Serail* moved Schubert to such an extent that he placed his hands to his mouth in a mute expression of delight. This is wonderfully illustrated in a drawing by Martha Griebler entitled *Wie schön* (How beautiful).

In terms of Schubert's chamber and piano music, the Mozartian net spreads even wider, but in the songs there are sometimes allusions to Mozart's solo piano music, such as the Rondo in A minor K511.

Carl Friedrich Zelter (1758–1832)

Zelter was born in Berlin and remained a Berliner all his life – with the gruff, outspoken but nevertheless good-hearted characteristics of that city's inhabitants. His father was a Saxon mason who moved to Prussia; Zelter inherited the family building business and ran it until 1815 at the same time as developing his musical career. He began as an orchestral violinist, and eventually took over the Berlin-Singakademie which specialized in performances of sacred music by older composers including Handel and Bach. It was through the influence of Zelter that his composition pupil Mendelssohn conducted the first performance of the *Matthäus-Passion*. Zelter became a pioneer figure in musical education and was the teacher not only of Mendelssohn but also Meyerbeer and Nicolai. A man of the world, he was both practical and aesthetic; his gruff exterior masked a sensitive and highly thoughtful personality, and he had amazing reserves of physical energy for all his self-appointed tasks. Goethe admired this concentration and dedication, and the strength of his friendship with Zelter is reflected in 850 letters over nearly thirty years (between 1799 and 1828). During this period they spent a surprising amount of

C. F. Zelter, from an oil painting by Begas, 1827.

time together – some twenty weeks in total – in Weimar, Karlsbad, Teplitz, Wiesbaden and so on. In 1812, when the composer's son committed suicide, the poet proposed, by way of consolation, that they should exchange the familiar 'Du' – an unheard-of honour for the musician. It was Zelter who introduced the young Felix Mendelssohn into the Goethe circle, and the boy prodigy was a source of delight and wonder to the great poet. The frank exchange of views between the two men permitted Goethe to keep up with the cultural life of Berlin with Zelter as his faithful guide. The composer was of a conservative disposition, most at home with the music of the past that was his stock-in-trade as a conductor. He had an equivocal attitude to Beethoven, and disapproved of Weber and Berlioz. Largely thanks to Goethe's encouragement and support he had become a composer late in life – too late, perhaps, as he said himself, and there is a clumsiness in Zelter's music where technique is outweighed by feeling. And yet the best of his songs show a surprising melodic gift, devotion to his texts and a musical engagement that still speaks to us – even more eloquently when it is combined with a wilful endearing quirkiness.

Schubert clearly studied as much as he could find of Zelter's output, relatively slender in comparison with Reichardt's or Zumsteeg's: Zelter's style, a curiously ornate, and often melodically appealing, mixture of Bach and Mozart, would have fascinated Schubert, above all on account of the older composer's close connection to Goethe.

Johann Rudolf Zumsteeg (1760–1802)

Johann Rudolf Zumsteeg was born in Stuttgart and spent his whole life there. Stuttgart is in the south-west; Vienna, equally southern, is situated no little way to the east, with Berlin, home of Reichardt and Zelter, between them both, the northern apex. This is the geographical triangle of the early nineteenth-century German lied. Zumsteeg attended the Carlsschule, the military academy founded by the notoriously dictatorial Duke Carl Eugen of Württemberg. The poet Friedrich Schiller knew Zumsteeg when they were boys together at school, and the two artists remained in close contact – a friendship sealed by the shared adversity of their miserable upbringing. Zumsteeg, who was a cellist by training (he wrote ten cello concertos), provided the first incidental music for Schiller's *Die Räuber* in 1782; after this he gradually turned his attentions to song. Zumsteeg rose to the post of Konzertmeister in charge of court music; there

J. R. Zumsteeg (1799), after a painting by Hiemer.

was a great revival of Mozart's operas in Stuttgart and he enjoyed moderate success as an opera composer. Goethe met Zumsteeg once in Stuttgart, and Schiller persuaded the poet to mount a performance of one of Zumsteeg's operas in Weimar for the benefit of the composer's widow after her husband, still a young man, had died of a heart attack. A great deal of his music remains unprinted. Like Reichardt, who had a song-composing daughter Luise (1779–1826), Zumsteeg had a daughter, Emilie (1796–1857), who was later a song composer of note.

There is a contemporary account from Schubert's schoolfriend Anton Holzapfel that describes how Schubert busied himself with Zumsteeg's *Kleine Balladen und Lieder* (seven volumes published between 1791 and 1805, 170 settings in all) and was enthralled with them. The use of recitative, the explorations of mediant key relations and enharmonic modulations, the attempt to find a musical unity for the setting of an extended text, all these things Schubert took to heart. Like a young painter attempting to copy a famous painting, he set out to compose a number of ballads with Zumsteeg's version opened before him as a model. It goes without saying that his achievements quickly outstripped Zumsteeg's, not so much in matters of declamation and technique (Schubert often followed the older composer's choice of key and his time signatures) but in the adventurousness of the piano writing and the creation of a dramatic atmosphere. The Schubert songs with close Zumsteeg connections are *Hagars Klage* D5, *Lied der Liebe* D109, *Nachtgesang* D314, *Ritter Toggenburg* D397, *Die Erwartung* D159 and *Skolie* D507. Zumsteeg's influence on Schubert was strongest between 1811 and the spring of 1816 when Schubert made his second version of *Die Erwartung* D159. It is this setting that both defines what he had learned from Zumsteeg, and how the younger composer had excelled the older.

Luigi Cherubini (1760–1842)

Although this famous Italian composer of operas and church music lived in Paris from 1784 (where he achieved success as the protégé of Grétry), he spent time in Vienna in 1805–6 and in Schubert's youth Cherubini's reputation as a composer of religious and chamber music was still enormous in the Austrian capital. His most famous opera *Médée* was composed in 1797 and he composed *Faniska* for the very young Anna Milder in 1806. During his time in Vienna, Cherubini composed *Les Deux Journées* and Schubert heard a performance in 1819. This opera, in its German version, *Der Wasserträger*, gave the baritone Vogl one of his great successes in the role of Micheli. There is a reference to a 'Wasserwagen' in the *Cantate* for Vogl's birthday D666 composed in 1819.

Josef Weigl (1766–1846)

Weigl was born in Eisenstadt where his father, a distinguished cellist, held a position in the orchestra; young Weigl was the godson of Eisenstadt's presiding genius, Joseph Haydn. He came to Vienna and studied with Albrechtsberger, and with Salieri who took him under his wing. As a repetiteur at the Kärntnertortheater he rehearsed Mozart's *Le nozze di Figaro* (1786), *Don Giovanni* (1788) and possibly *Così fan tutte* in the composer's presence. In his autobiography Weigl wrote, 'To hear Mozart playing through the most difficult scores with his unique fluency, and at the same time singing and correcting the mistakes of others could not but excite the greatest admiration.' By the time he was in his late twenties Weigl was Kapellmeister at the Kärntnertor and he had written a number of successful operas. He spent some time in Italy but returned to Vienna in 1808; his greatest successes of the time were *Das Waisenhaus* of that year, and *Die Schweizerfamilie* (1809). Both these works were *Singspiele*, and were known to Schubert from his early years; he had already played numerous Weigl overtures in the school orchestra. In January 1821 Weigl, together with Salieri, signed a testimonial praising Schubert's musical abilities (paperwork that failed to help the composer obtain employment). In 1827 Weigl himself, whose operas were out of fashion, had fallen on harder times and he and Schubert competed

Josef Weigl, lithograph by Johann Putz.

for the same position of Vice-Kapellmeister at the Hofkapelle. Weigl won the appointment and Schubert apparently approved the choice – he had nothing against Weigl who was, after all, more than twice his age. The Viennese publisher Thaddäus Weigl, Josef Weigl's brother, later issued a number of Schubert songs under his own imprint.

Wenzel Müller (1767–1835)

Müller, for fifty years the house composer of the Leopoldstadt Theatre, was the most successful composer of comic operas in Schubert's Vienna. The diary that he kept up for thirty years is a valuable source of theatrical life of the time. Whenever Schubert attempted to write works in a lighter vein (such as the *Vier Refrain-Lieder* D866) he tried to model himself on Müller who effortlessly commanded the common touch – though with nothing like Schubert's depth, of course. Together with Josef Hüttenbrenner, Schubert attended a performance of Müller's *Aline, oder Wien in einem anderen Erdteil*; soon afterwards, according to Hans Koeltzsch, he incorporated material from a duet from this work into his *Wanderer-Fantasie* for piano D760. In 1826 Schubert pronounced Müller's operetta *Herr Joseph und Frau Baberl* to be 'unübertrefflich' (unsurpassable). There are many people who mistakenly imagine that Schubert's music was 'typically Viennese'; it was not, but Wenzel Müller's compositions were, and Schubert admired them for this very reason.

Franz Anton Schubert (1768–1827)

This composer was a member of a large family of Dresden musicians. He was a double bass player and the brother of Anton Schubert who played the double bass in the Dresden orchestra between 1790 and 1840. Franz became director of the Italian opera in 1808 and royal church composer in 1814. He was a colleague of Weber's when that composer worked in Dresden. Sadly he is remembered chiefly for a letter he wrote in April 1817 to the publishers Breitkopf & Härtel who had been sent a manuscript of *Erlkönig* by the Viennese Schubert, and had returned it as not interesting enough to publish. (How can we blame Goethe, a musical amateur, for ignoring Schubert, when Germany's foremost music publisher was also blind to his talents?) Unfortunately Breitkopf sent the music back to the wrong Franz Schubert who, in turn, wrote them a blistering letter: 'I beg to state the cantata was never composed by me. I shall retain the same in my possession in order to learn, if possible, who sent you that sort of trash in such an impolite manner, and also to discover the fellow who has thus misused my name.' The two Schuberts were paired in 1821 in an almanac publication [*see* WIDERSCHEIN D639]. The son of this Schubert, also a composer, Franz Schubert the younger (1808–1878) is, according to Jurij Chochlow (Chochlow 1995, p. 107), the possible composer of *Mein Frieden*, a song of little worth that has been falsely attributed to the 'real' Schubert in recent years, notably by Van Hoorickx [*see* DUBIOUS, MISATTRIBUTED AND LOST SONGS].

Ludwig van Beethoven (1770–1827)

Beethoven was a lodestar who was a continuing and constant influence on Schubert – even to the point of discomfort and occasional depression. The opera *Fidelio* was clearly in Schubert's mind as he wrote *Des Teufels Lustschloss* D84 as a sixteen-year-old in 1813 (the *Fidelio* vocal score had appeared in 1810), and Beethoven's Mass in C Op. 86 was, according to Hüttenbrenner, one of the works that Schubert most admired. In 1817 he began to write out Beethoven's Symphony no. 4 as a means of learning from it (compare his earlier method of copying from Zumsteeg scores), and the Symphonies nos 2 and 7 were enduring favourites – the dactylic rhythm of the hypnotic second movement ('Allegretto' in A minor) of the latter symphony is to be heard time and again in the songs. It is likely that Beethoven's String Quartet Op. 95 was the model for Schubert's in C minor, D703, just as Beethoven's Septet Op. 20 influenced Schubert's Octet D803. Beethoven's piano sonatas were constantly in Schubert's mind as he wrote his own, and so on and on.

In 1816 the publication of Beethoven's song cycle *An die ferne Geliebte* Op. 98 must have astonished Schubert, coming like the eruption of a volcano at the least expected time. Beethoven's most recent song-composing phase had been 1809–10 and included a number of significant Goethe settings. Since then there had been only Beethoven songs of little significance scattered here and there in the occasional almanac. Schubert would have had every right to believe that he had built for himself, during his incredibly fecund year of 1815, a fortress where his achievement, in song at least, was untouchable by anyone else, past or present. And then suddenly, as if out of nowhere, Beethoven published an opus, the like of which had never appeared before. This was a set of six songs. But whereas other people had published songs in sets, this was a set of six *connected* songs which belonged together as a single large musical construction. Beethoven had more or less invented the song cycle and, without knowing it of course, had stolen a march on Schubert in the one field where the younger composer had felt he had the right to consider himself pre-eminent.

A constant theme of the remainder of Schubert's career was the planning of a fitting response to *An die ferne Geliebte* – a search for the solution to the problem of the song cycle. Beethoven had clearly sought out a text suited to his purposes, and the doctor-poet Alois Jeitteles had provided it (the custom-made text is printed in no book or periodical). The three wonderful Harper's Songs of September 1816 by Schubert were actually composed in the month *before* Beethoven's Jeitteles cycle was published. Soon afterwards Schubert might well have asked his friend Mayrhofer for a similarly extended poem, and the result was the cantata-like *Einsamkeit* D620 where the music subdivides into six definite sections at the same time as remaining all-of-a-piece. This was in 1818. There is a copy in Schubert's hand (D Anhang III, 13, March 1820) of a Beethoven song. This is *Abendlied unterm gestirnten Himmel* (Goeble) WoO150 transposed from its original key of E major into D (perhaps for performance with Vogl).

Ludwig van Beethoven, drawing by Moritz von Schwind, *c.* 1820.

In 1823 and 1827 Schubert wrote two song cycles to the poems of Wilhelm Müller – the immortal *Die schöne Müllerin* and *Winterreise*. Here were two versions of his solution to the idea of a cycle, implied narratives where the musical numbers depended on each other without actually being glued together with music. In 1828, for the first public concert which featured Schubert's music entirely (and which was planned to mark the first anniversary of Beethoven's death), he wrote a piece for voice, horn and piano, *Auf dem Strom* D943, with many Beethovenian resonances (including a quotation from that composer's 'Eroica' Symphony). And at the end of his life he wrote a set of Rellstab songs, the texts of which had been on Beethoven's work desk when he died, and which Schubert possibly envisaged as a new homage to the idea of the Distant Beloved – in fact every song in the so-called *Schwanengesang*, including the Heine settings, is an exploration of this theme where the lover herself is absent and at a distance. There is no doubt that Schubert experienced a kind of release on the death of Beethoven; for one year only (before his own death) he was able to think of himself as the world's greatest composer and the inheritor of the Beethovenian mantle.

Václav Jan Tomášek (Wenzel Johann Tomaschek) (1774–1850)

Tomášek was the leading composer in Prague during Schubert's lifetime. Born in Bohemia but educated in Germany, his influence spread far beyond the borders of his home country. He was in touch with Haydn and Beethoven at different times of his life, and he corresponded with, and met, Goethe in the early 1820s. This was in connection with the nine volumes of settings of the poet's poems that he had privately published thanks to the support of his patron Georg Graf von Buqouy. There were forty-one songs in all (he worked on them between 1815 and 1820) with twenty-one of the texts also set by Schubert, although the composers would have been unaware of each other's work at the time of composing. It was a crowning moment of Tomášek's life to be able to perform his songs to Goethe himself in Eger, West Bohemia, in August 1822, as both singer and pianist. Goethe would have been fascinated to meet Tomášek – a similarly Renaissance man who had devoted himself to maths, history, aesthetics, philosophy and law. Thus Tomášek was able to bask in the great man's approbation that Schubert longed for, and never received. Tomášek's piano music, published simultaneously in Leipzig and Vienna, which concentrated on smaller musical forms (*Eklogen*, *Rhapsodien*, *Dithyramben*) and their artful construction, and contrast of major and minor tonalities, must have influenced Schubert's *Impromptus*. Schubert's link in Vienna with Czech music and musical personalities was probably Jan Václav Voříšek (Worzichek), a composer colleague of Tomášek's whom he certainly met on several occasions. Voříšek published two sets of *Impromptus* in 1822 and 1824, some time before the appearance of the Schubert works of that title.

Friedrich August Kanne (1778–1833)

Kanne's name has all but vanished to posterity, but his support of Schubert as a critic probably meant more to the composer than the good opinions of anyone else writing in Vienna. He was born in Saxony and in his twenties, having studied medicine and theology, made quite a name for himself as a composer in Leipzig and Dresden where several of his operas reached the stage. In 1806 this young polymath was invited to Vienna by Prince Lobkowitz; there he experienced the tail end of the kind of sumptuous aristocratic patronage that existed before the Napoleonic wars and enabled an artist to live comfortably, even luxuriously, as part of a retinue. In the early Vienna years Kanne had considerable success as an opera composer, almost always writing his own libretti. Although he took up employment elsewhere (notably as the Kapellmeister in Pressburg) he found himself unable to live outside Vienna and its ever-tempting hostelries. He had a serious drink problem combined with a depressive streak that made him both fiercely independent and pathetically lacking in willpower; this illness eventually ruined his life, and obliterated his reputation as a composer.

Friedrich Kanne, unsigned drawing.

By 1817 Kanne found himself working as music journalist and then editor of the *Allgemeine musikalische Zeitung* where it fell to him to write articles (usually anonymously) on the latest concerts and publications. His entertaining and revealing reviews, in which his insider knowledge of the nuts and bolts of music is clearly superior to most critics of the time, fearlessly berate the worst in Viennese taste and the passion of Italianate inanities. On the other hand he was clearly aware of Schubert's stature: in a review of 12 May 1821 he declared his admiration for the unity of conception of *Erlkönig* but showed he was an experienced performer when advocating that some of the triplets should have been transferred to the pianist's left hand to avoid tiring the right. Kanne thereby anticipated (and encouraged) the thousands of informal rearrangements and redistributions that pianists over the ages have adopted to get through the piece unscathed. The first extensive appraisal of Schubert's songs was almost certainly written by Kanne and published on 19 January 1822 (see Waidelich/Hilmar Dokumente I No. 142). In this article, one of several by this unequivocal admirer of Schubert, the recently published songs are praised as exemplary, and their composer is referred to as 'der geniale Tonsetzer' – 'the composer of genius'. Three months after this, in March 1822, the *Wiener Zeitschrift für Kunst, Literatur, Theater und Mode* dared to publish a similarly favourable leading article by Friedrich von Hentl ('Blick auf Schuberts Lieder'), and publishers (including the hitherto-sceptical Anton Diabelli) began to look on Schubert in a new light as a potentially good investment. It is clear that the admiring article by Kanne, a writer known to be capable of withering spleen when dealing with the second rate, was taken very seriously.

Vienna was a small enough city for Schubert to be aware of who was writing these favourable reviews – a fellow song composer who was free from any competitive jealousy, and able to greet new success wholeheartedly despite his own failures. There is some evidence that Schubert valued Kanne as a satirical writer and read his biting and pithy verses on the Viennese musical scene with some pleasure. At the end of Kanne's crucial review of January 1821 he writes that he knows other Schubert songs in manuscript; this suggests that there may even have been a personal link between the two composers, or at least between mutual friends. Moreover Kanne's one critical jibe is a complaint that in *Antigone und Oedip* D542 Schubert had needlessly altered a line of poetry (not yet in print) to the detriment of the metre. This would surely indicate a connection with Mayrhofer, or perhaps that the poet had earlier sent handwritten copies of his poems to other highly regarded Viennese composers – like the critic himself. Increasingly giving himself up to drink, Kanne fell back on writing occasional poetry for very little money, a sad existence where he was the despair of doctors and friends alike. He died in inevitably straitened circumstances on 16 December 1833.

Sigismund Ritter von Neukomm (1778–1858)

Neukomm, born in Salzburg, was related by marriage through his mother to one of Schubert's favourite composers, Michael Haydn. He lived in Vienna between 1797 and 1804 as a student of Joseph Haydn. He worked as a music assistant to the great composer and prepared the vocal score of *Die Schöpfung*. He also gave singing and piano lessons; his most celebrated students were Anna Milder and Franz Xaver Mozart, son of Wolfgang Amadeus. He then spent four years in St Petersburg as the Kapellmeister of the German theatre in that city. After a spell in Paris he returned to Vienna for the famous Congress (1814) in the musical entourage of Prince Talleyrand and was duly investigated by the Austrian secret police. The following year his *Requiem in C minor* in memory of Louis XVI, performed in St Stephan's Cathedral in Vienna, earned him his French knighthood. He spent four years in Rio de Janeiro as a music master at the court of the Portuguese king (where he performed the music of Haydn and Mozart tirelessly) and later returned to Talleyrand in Paris. This meant that Neukomm was away from the European musical scene during the years of Schubert's maturity. After Talleyrand's death there were further journeys and projects including the Mozart Memorial erected in Salzburg in 1842 when Neukomm directed all the music. He was particularly at home in England and claimed to have set more English words than any other foreign composer. His output remains largely unknown and unexplored in modern times. Neukomm was a friend of Mendelssohn, and of the important Leipzig critic Rochlitz (also one of Schubert's poets, qv). His achievements were rewarded with numerous honours and decorations.

Neukomm's *Sechs Gesänge* Op. 10 were written and published between 1808 and 1809 when the frenetically active composer returned to Vienna from St Petersburg to make daily visits to his ailing master, Haydn. It is possible that the Rochlitz *Klaglied*, published as part of this group, was set (albeit very differently) by the fifteen-year-old Schubert in 1812 (D23) straight from this edition of Neukomm's songs. How else Schubert might have discovered this particular isolated text is difficult to imagine. To find exact parallels between the two composers is impossible, but there is something Schubertian *avant la lettre* about Neukomm's music. In the naturalness of his musical invention and touching melodic gift there is neither any rigidity, nor a Berlin-schooled formula; he feels free to use coloratura, melisma and sequences where appropriate (thus demonstrating an awareness of the Italian style, similar to that in Schubert). In short, this is very sophisticated song-composing for its time.

Moritz Von Dietrichstein
(1775–1864)

Dietrichstein was praised to the skies by Frances Trollope (the novelist Anthony's mother) in her *Vienna and the Austrians* (1838) and it is easy to see why. He was one of the most powerful and influential men in public service, he was charming, cultured, formidably intelligent and always able to act judiciously to help others – an equivalent of that great Edwardian civil servant Sir Edward Marsh. Together with his subordinate Matthäus von Collin, he was tutor to the Duc de Reichstadt, Napoleon's son by his second marriage who lived under guard in Schönbrunn; The composer had first encountered Dietrichstein in his early schooldays through the aristocrat's support of Anselm Hüttenbrenner, and had reason to thank him on a number of occasions during his school career and

Moritz Graf von Dietrichstein, lithograph by Josef Kriehuber (1828).

adolescence. We have the impression that the civil servant had spotted Schubert early on and, with the instinctive prescience possessed by very few men in power, recognized talent when he saw it. His testimonial for Schubert on 24 January of 1821 talks of 'innate genius'. Dietrichstein, together with Leopold von Sonnleithner, played an important role in developing the scheme whereby Schubert's songs were printed for the first time and published on commission. As a mark of his gratitude, Schubert dedicated his Op. 1, *Erlkönig*, to this remarkable man.

Dietrichstein, like a number of the highly educated aristocracy of the time, was a decent amateur composer. In 1811 he published *XVI Lieder von Göthe* and sent them to the poet who replied with the genial civility due to someone of the composer's station. If only Schubert had been so lucky! Dietrichstein's music is in undemanding style but it shows cultivated taste. It is likely that the spaciousness and tempo of his setting of *Wonne der Wehmut*, as well as the repetition of the opening words, owe something to the famous Beethoven setting of this text that was published in 1810.

Ludwig Berger (1777–1839)

Berger was born into a family that was comfortably off. He soon showed signs of promise during his musical training in Berlin and was already a prolific composer in his twenties. He moved to Dresden where his closest friend was the painter Philipp Otto Runge. Soon afterwards he met his mentor Muzio Clementi and went on a tour to St Petersburg where he settled for a while as a piano teacher. He returned to Berlin and, having seriously injured his arm (Berger seems to have been dogged by one personal problem after another), he gave his last public concert in 1814. After this he taught the piano for twenty-five years, numbering Felix and Fanny Mendelssohn among his pupils.

In 1816, Berger came into a circle of people who were rather younger than his own thirty-eight years. In a quiet house in the Bauhofstrasse am Kupfergrahen in Berlin there was a regular salon in the home of Friedrich August von Stägemann, a civil servant; both he and his wife were published poets. Their salon was frequented by Achim von Arnim, Chamisso and Fouqué. Among the younger house guests were Wilhelm Hensel (destined to be one of the foremost

artists of the period and later to marry Fanny Mendelssohn), and a twenty-two-year-old poet from Dessau, Wilhelm Müller. Berger was rudely critical of Müller's work at the time, but his set of songs uses five Müller poems (all familiar to the Schubert lover) and five by other members of the *Liederspiel* cast. It was only some time afterwards, in 1821 and long after he had left Berlin, that Müller completed his own cycle using his poems and sketches from 1816 as the basis for a new cycle of twenty-three poems, as well as a prologue and epilogue. It is this work that Schubert encountered in print in 1823. (For the story of the genesis of *Die schöne Müllerin*, see the commentary on that cycle.)

Berger's mostly simple songs are clearly meant for amateur performance. Nevertheless, they have a terse effectiveness and greater sophistication than a preliminary reading reveals. *Des Baches Lied* (set by Schubert as

Des Baches Wiegenlied D795/20) is an exception: from the beginning of this song there is something profound in the oscillations of the highly unusual piano writing – hardly Schubertian, but moving.

Johann Nepomuk Hummel (1778–1837)

This virtuoso pianist has been re-evaluated in fairly recent years as a composer of considerable importance – his piano concertos, ultra-demanding in terms of virtuosity, bear comparison in some respects with Beethoven's. He was appointed Kapellmeister in Weimar in 1819. He set so little of Goethe's poetry, only a masonic chorus, that we imagine that neither man was convinced of the greatness of the other. Goethe was polite, Hummel was even more polite, all the niceties of their respective positions in Weimar were observed, but they never became friends. The overbearing figure of Zelter in the background, and Goethe's tendency to allow the Berlin composer to arbitrate on all musical matters, must have been irritating to a performer, as well as a composer, who was more famous than Zelter. On the other hand, Hummel and Schubert seem to have taken to each other immediately when they met in Vienna in 1827 at the home of Katharina von Lászny (by this time Schubert had long given up both setting Goethe and trying to contact him). Hummel had come to Vienna to pay his last respects to the dying Beethoven. Schubert and Vogl performed song after song for Hummel and his student Ferdinand Hiller (*see* p. 386). Tears rolled down the older composer's face at hearing this music, as well as this new kind of singing and accompanying. Spaun attests that Hummel then improvised on Schubert's song *Der blinde Knabe* D833, thus paying Schubert the greatest of compliments.

Johann Nepomuk Hummel.

Nikolaus Freiherr Von Krufft (1779–1818)

Krufft was Schubert's nearest model as a contemporary Viennese lieder composer. Unlike Schubert, Krufft was born into a noble family of considerable means. He studied with Albrechtsberger who rivalled Salieri as a teacher of composition at the time. He confined himself to church music, a certain amount of chamber music, music for solo piano and songs. He was a co-founder of the *Wiener allgemeine musikalische Zeitung* and died at the age of thirty-eight. The reason for his early demise was given as overwork – according to his obituary he dedicated all his time, including his nights, to his Muses. It would not be hard to imagine that such an ambiguous explanation might also conceal a case of the illness that ruined Schubert's health. Krufft's first collection of songs appeared in print in 1798 when he was nineteen. The most famous set was probably *Sammlung deutscher Lieder*, seventeen settings published in 1812 in Vienna. His poets include Schiller, Kotzebue, Matthisson, Voss, Hölty, Salis-Seewis and Goethe.

Conradin Kreutzer (1780–1849)

Less internationally travelled than Neukomm, Kreutzer nevertheless had a career that astonishes in terms of its changes and upheavals. He was born in Swabia and his early career as an instrumentalist was in this region, as well as in Switzerland. He was twenty-four when he moved to Vienna, and a performance of Salieri's opera *Palmyra* opened his eyes to the possibility of music for the theatre. Kreutzer spent six years in Vienna where he studied with Albrechtsberger and performed as pianist and clarinettist at all the great salons. He left the city after an altercation with Joseph Weigl and returned to Stuttgart where he married and was appointed Hof-kapellmeister. It was at this time that he met the poet Ludwig Uhland in Tübingen who remained his favourite poet when it came to songs. Out of a total of 180 lieder he composed ninety-two settings of Uhland. (It was per-haps because of his respect for this well-known partnership that Schubert confined himself to only one Uhland setting – the famous *Frühlingsglaube* D686). Constantly writing operas, chamber music, church music and piano music, Kreutzer was led in a round-about manner back to Vienna where he became the Kapellmeister of the Hofoper in

Conradin Kreutzer, lithograph by Johann Lanzedelly.

1822 and where he was partly responsible for considering Schubert's operas *Alfonso und Estrella* and *Fierabras* for production (these works were not taken up). His own opera *Libussa* left Schubert cold according to a contemporary source, but Schubert took part in performances of Kreutzer's male voice quartets. After Schubert's death Kreutzer became music director at the Josephstadt Theater in Vienna where he had his greatest successes with his light-hearted operas *Das Nachtlager in Granada* and *Der Verschwender*. He continued to work on and off in Vienna until 1840, and then moved to Cologne. He was active until the end of his life in a constant round of musical positions, all the while lobbying on behalf of (as well as accompanying) his two daughters who had decent careers as singers.

It is documented that Schubert himself admired Kreutzer's *Neun Wanderlieder* Op. 34, songs with titles including *Winterreise*, *Abreise* and *Heimkehr*. They were composed in 1817 and published in the early 1820s. When they were imperiously dismissed as rubbish ('Zeug') by Anselm Hüttenbrenner, Schubert replied, 'I wish I had composed them.' There is a directness and simplicity about this music, as if pared down to the bone, a true combination of romanti-cism and the minimalist discipline of the Berlin lieder school. It is this characteristic that links Kreutzer's style with the later Schubert. If Schubert was influenced by these songs in thinking about his own *Winterreise*, the influence was probably the other way round in the Müller songs (*Der Lindenbaum* and *Frühlingstraum*) from Kreutzer's *Ländliche Lieder* Op. 80. Whether these were written before or soon after Schubert's *Winterreise* is uncertain. The choice of poetry in the collection (which includes the same poem that opens *Der Hirt auf dem Felsen* D965) suggests that it was Kreutzer who was following a path already trodden by Schubert. If it is the other way round, Schubert owes to Kreutzer something as fundamental as his choice of E major for the tonality of *Der Lindenbaum*. The fact that Kreutzer's setting of Müller's *Die Post* (a crucial *Winterreise* text) was published as a supplement in the *Wiener Zeitschrift für Kunst, Literatur,*

Theater und Mode in 1826, long before Schubert began his own cycle, signals the possibility that Kreutzer came to all this poetry first. Schubert himself had been acquainted with the work of Müller since *Die schöne Müllerin* (1823) but he was only to discover the first half of the *Winterreise* poems in the almanac *Urania* in early 1827. He came across the more complete edition containing *Die Post* for the first time later in the same year.

Anton Fischer (1782–1808)

Fischer was born in Augsburg 'around 1782' (according to Schilling and Fétis) and journeyed to Vienna in his teens in order to make his fortune. He experienced terrible penury in the Imperial capital and became a member of the chorus at the Josephstadt theatre to make ends meet. He was the possessor of a pleasant tenor voice and in 1800 he became a member of Schikaneder's team at the Theater an der Wien and took on increasingly important roles, as well as polishing his abilities as a conductor. Impressed by the success of the operas and lighter works of such composers as Cherubini and Méhul, he was able to imitate their compositional styles to such an extent that when he presented his own works he was accused of plagiarism – Fétis lists one of his operas as being 'after the score of Grétry, modernized'. This is indeed ironic considering that Schubert's publication of the comic trio *Die Advokaten* D37 is the only occasion in his entire career when the great composer might have been accused of plagiarism himself. As Fischer died in 1808 (aged twenty-six) there was presumably no-one to object to the fact that in December 1812 Schubert adapted Fischer's *Die Advokaten* of 1804, and naturally improved it, if only to a degree. Even more surprisingly, the trio was published in May 1827 – perhaps without the composer's knowledge and at Schwind's behest – as Schubert's Op. 74. By then, scarcely anyone would have remembered the unfortunate Fischer. Fétis lists fourteen of Fischer's operas, mostly on fantastic or fairy-tale subjects, as well as an operetta for children. All of them were swept away by the vogue in Vienna for Italian opera in the years following his untimely death.

Louis Spohr (1784–1859)

This composer, one of Schubert's more famous contemporaries, had a Viennese dimension to his multi-faceted career. When Schubert was still a teenager, Spohr was Music Director of the Theater an der Wien (1813–15) during which time he was in contact with Beethoven who was an enduring inspiration. Because Spohr's name remained well known in Vienna after his departure, Schubert was accustomed to hearing his fellow composer's music in various concerts (sometimes his work shared the billing with Spohr's) and he might well have met the older composer on one of his later visits to Vienna. We know that Schubert's operatic hopes were mentioned in the Kreutzer–Spohr correspondence in 1822, and that long after Schubert's death Spohr conducted a performance of the 'Great' C major Symphony.

Carl Maria Von Weber (1786–1826)

It is almost certain that Schubert met Weber personally in late February or early March 1822, when that composer was in Vienna to conduct performances of *Der Freischütz*. They got on well enough at the time for Schubert to arrange for the influential Weber, Music Director in Dresden, to be sent a score of his recently composed opera *Alfonso und Estrella*. It seems that the two composers even corresponded over this matter, although the letters are lost. Weber returned to Vienna in October 1823 to conduct the first performances of his *Euryanthe*. Schubert was present at the premiere. Three days later the two composers went together to try a new instrument at the piano factory of Goll (Kreutzer was also there). These were very stressful times for Schubert: he was soon to enter hospital in the hope of curing his syphilis, and he might have felt far too ill and edgy to be diplomatic. On being asked his opinion of *Euryanthe* he said he preferred *Der Freischütz* and that there was not enough melody in the new opera. According to

Spaun, this ruptured the friendship between the two men, and Weber made no effort to further Schubert's operatic hopes in Dresden.

Simon Sechter (1788–1867)

Sechter was born in Bohemia. He studied in Vienna with his countryman Koželuh (Kozeluch) and went on to be the music teacher at the Institute for the Blind in Gumpfendorf. In 1824 he was appointed organist to the Hofkapelle. Only later in his life (in 1851) was he appointed to the teaching staff of the Konservatorium where he taught such composers as Vieuxtemps and Bruckner. He took the ground bass theory of Rameau as the starting point of his own theoretical writings. Schubert had wanted to study with Sechter as early as 1824 but had been warned by a friend not to allow himself to be infected by the 'leathery' quality of Sechter's own music. Schubert, together with a fellow composer of his own age, Johann Wolfgang Lanz, eventually visited Sechter on 4 November 1828 for an hour's lesson in fugue. This was exactly two weeks before Schubert's death and there was no opportunity to return, although the composer faithfully sketched the eighteen fugal exercises assigned to him (D965B). There has been much speculation as to why he enrolled with Sechter, including the possibility that he needed to be seen to undertake this kind of study to be eligible for an official position. It is more likely that he felt attracted to the music of Handel and Bach (like Beethoven at the end of his life), and simply wanted some supervision in the intricacies of counterpoint.

Simon Sechter, lithograph by Josef Kriehuber (1840).

Giacomo Meyerbeer (1791–1864)

He played no personal part in Schubert's career, but his star was on the ascendant in Austria in the last years of Schubert's life. In early September 1827, during his stay in Styria, Schubert heard a performance of Meyerbeer's tenth opera, *Il Crociato in Egitto*. The original libretto had been reworked into German by Josef Kupelwieser, who was the librettist of Schubert's opera *Fierabras*, so Schubert probably attended the performance at the Graz county theatre out of loyalty. According to Anselm Hüttenbrenner (who had not seen the composer for a long time) Schubert was thoroughly displeased with the work. He had probably heard excerpts from Meyerbeer's opera *Margarita d'Anjou* at a concert in Vienna in 1826.

Gioachino Rossini (1792–1868)

Schubert would have known Rossini's name from about 1816, although his first experience of a Rossini opera is likely to have been *Tancredi* in 1817. He was so delighted with this new kind of music that he wrote two overtures 'in the Italian style' (D591 and D592) but one can also see traces of the Italian composer in the Sixth Symphony D589, *Die Zwillingsbrüder* D647 and in the finales to the acts of *Alfonso und Estrella* D732. Schubert was delighted by *Il Barbiere di Siviglia* and thought that *Otello* was a greater piece than *Tancredi*. As he said to Hüttenbrenner, 'You can't deny the man his extraordinary genius . . . the instrumentation is highly original, as is sometimes the vocal line.' By 1822 the Rossini craze was no longer such fun: it had come to threaten the chances of Schubert's own theatrical compositions; the publishing market was flooded with arrangements of the latest hits, and even the concert life of the city was dominated by Rossini. In the evening concerts of the Musikverein alone there were excerpts performed from some twenty Rossini operas, and Schubert was present at many of these occasions. Of Schubert's songs, Rossini's influence is to be heard in such a parody as *Herrn Josef von Spaun, Assessor in Linz* D749 (with a touch of the malign that dissolves into frank delight) and in the three adorable Op. 83 Italian settings (Marschner's criticism of them is preposterous) written for Lablache, the *Drei Gesänge* D902. It is possible that the huge success in Vienna of Rossini's Walter Scott opera *La Donna del Lago* in 1823 and 1824 goaded Schubert into a riposte in lieder – the seven Walter Scott settings from *The Lady of the Lake* composed in 1825. The ambitious scale of this collection of songs suggests a deliberate challenge to the world of Italian opera from the younger and fast-developing realm of the lied.

Anselm Hüttenbrenner (1794–1868)

Hüttenbrenner, (*see also* FRIENDS AND FAMILY) three years older than Schubert, was also a student of Salieri. Schubert was shy of approaching and befriending Beethoven, but Hüttenbrenner had the confidence to do so. Of the two young composers he was the more fluent pianist (he often accompanied Schubert's songs in public), and he was certainly better looking, as well as very charming when he wished to be. He seems always to have believed that he was one of the elite and that he deserved to succeed. He was closest to Schubert on a daily basis in the years up to 1819 when Schubert wrote a nostalgic letter concerning the many happy hours they had spent together. A mark of Schubert's affection was the *13 Variationen über ein Thema von Anselm Hüttenbrenner* D576, dedicated to 'his friend and schoolfellow'. This theme in A minor has a Schubertian charm of its own, as has much of Hüttenbrenner's music – there are passages which really sound as if they might have been written by the great composer.

Hüttenbrenner's life was, in many ways, a disappointment. Not nearly as prolific or hard-working as his unassuming friend, he had to leave Vienna for family reasons in 1824 and from then on his artistic life, such as it was, was largely confined to the provincial precincts of Graz and Steiermark – a pleasant existence, but one in which he was distinctly marginalized. His letters give the impression of someone touchy and self-important, and at the same time subject to depression. In 1823 Schubert sent the auto-graph of the 'Unfinished' Symphony, care of Anselm Hüttenbrenner, to the Graz Musik-verein as a sign of his gratitude for having been elected an honorary member. It never reached its destination and remained in Hüttenbrenner's possession for forty-two years – his brother Josef (1796–1882) was Schubert's secretary and quasi business manager at the time Schubert made this gift. The effect of this was entirely to withhold a major masterpiece from the public. There has been much speculation as to why the score never reached its rightful owners – from outright accusations of stupidity and jealousy to rationalizations that Hüttenbrenner never pushed his own music forward and naturally did not push Schubert's either. In a harsh light both Hüttenbrenner brothers might be accused of working on Schubert's behalf only when there was an advantage to their own family in the offing. Gore Vidal's admission that 'Whenever a friend succeeds, a little something in me dies' seems to have applied to Anselm Hüttenbrenner as he contemplated Schubert's growing posthumous fame.

Anselm Hüttenbrenner, watercolour by Josef Teltscher.

Hüttenbrenner wrote about 250 songs, the great majority of them, perhaps not surprisingly, after Schubert's death. His choice of a poet was very different: there are only two Goethe settings, two of his own poems, six of Bürger (a poet more or less ignored by Schubert) and two each of Uhland and Schubart. There are thirty settings of Carl von Leitner (also an important Schubert poet) and no fewer than 160 by Ferdinand von Rast who wrote poetry under the pseudonym 'Hilarius' (Rast lived in Marburg and was a patron of the composer's later years).

Carl Loewe (1796–1869)

This composer, also a talented singer, was only one year older than Schubert, the nearest to an exact contemporary that one can find among accomplished song composers. He was North German by birth; his Pietist father was against the theatre and Loewe never wrote for the stage – although he had a highly developed instinct for drama that emerges in his ballads. He spent most of his career as Music Director at Stettin, now Poland. His career as a composer of songs and ballads more or less began in 1818 with three settings that included his masterful *Erlkönig*, considered superior to Schubert's by numerous nineteenth-century commentators, including Wagner. As someone who could accompany his own singing, Loewe had the advantage of being able to go on tour without other artists: he visited many towns in Germany, Austria, Italy and France. It is just possible that his reputation had reached Vienna by the time of Schubert's death, although he certainly paid no visit to the city in Schubert's lifetime. He visited Goethe in Weimar in September 1820, and also had contact with such figures as Zelter, Weber, Hummel and Marschner.

Loewe made fifty Goethe settings, although he often set extended ballads, such as *Der Zauberlehrling*, the kind of poem that Schubert avoided, certainly in his maturity. There are

Carl Loewe.

Loewe versions of both *Wandrers Nachtlied* poems (Schubert's D768 and D224), *Nähe des Geliebten* (Schubert's D162) and *Gretchen am Spinnrade* (Schubert's D118). Loewe's *Edward* is much more famous than Schubert's (*Eine altschottische Ballade*, D923), his *Fischermädchen* (Heine, Schubert's D957/10) almost unknown. He set *Gesang der Geister über den Wassern* as a quartet for SATB. An astounding link between the two composers is that Loewe wrote his own setting of the cantata *Lazarus* in 1835, a relatively obscure text by Niemeyer; Schubert's oratorio of 1820 (D689) was first printed, and then only in part, in 1865. This is one more detail in an uncanny catalogue of two artistic careers running on parallel lines – a result of remarkably similar tastes in literature – without either of the two composers being aware of the fact. The one sphere in which Loewe excelled Schubert was in the field of comic songs – many of his vocal works show an enormous sense of humour.

Jeanette Antonie Bürde (b. 1799)

Two years younger than Schubert, Jeannette Bürde (née Milder) was born in Vienna. She was the younger sister (by fourteen years) of Anna Milder Hauptmann, one of the greatest sopranos of the age. Anna Milder, who married Peter Hauptmann in 1810, was a pupil of Neukomm and Haydn; she was admired by Mozart's librettist, Schikaneder, by Salieri, Beethoven and Schubert (who saw her as Gluck's Iphigenia, and as Emmeline in Weigl's *Die Schweizerfamilie*). When Milder Hauptmann moved from Vienna to Berlin in 1815 (she was in a huff with the Kaiserstadt), the sixteen-year-old Jeanette followed her. She had studied singing with Tomaselli and Liverati, and she built a small career in Berlin as a singer. She turned to composition in 1823 and studied with Rungenhagen. Her husband was a professor at the Academy of Arts; after his death she worked as a piano teacher.

Jeanette must have realized that ageing singers, like her sister, tend to recycle their former successes. Anna's most famous role in Weigl's *Die Schweizerfamilie* included a certain amount of quasi-yodelling, in particular in the Cavatine with clarinet obbligato from that opera beginning 'Wer hörte wohl jemals mich klagen?' In 1823 Anna had commissioned Carl Blum to write her a Swiss *scena* entitled *Gruss an die Schweiz*. In 1829 Bürde's *Der Berghirt* and *Liebesgedanken* (the two Müller texts used in *Der Hirt auf dem Felsen*) were published in Berlin. Because he had seen Anna as Emmeline in *Die Schweizerfamilie*, it is possible that Schubert dreamed up the idea of a piece with clarinet obbligato, cast in the same B flat major tonality as the Weigl Cavatine. But it is highly likely, however, that Anna Milder suggested these texts to Schubert only because they had already been set by her younger sister, and she found that their subject matter resonated comfortably with her operatic past.

Benedict Randhartinger (1802–1893)

Randhartinger was certainly an acquaintance of the composer and socialized with him regularly in the 1820s. He claimed to have been a schoolfriend, but he actually came as a student to the Imperial Konvikt only after Schubert had left. He also claimed that he was the first to sing *Erlkönig* – he would have been thirteen at the time – but this is almost certainly self-serving nonsense of a very Viennese kind. The older Randhartinger got, the more he exaggerated his closeness to Schubert as there were fewer people still living to contradict him. He even claimed to have been a direct witness of Schubert's chance encounter with the Müller texts for *Die schöne Müllerin*: according to him Schubert pocketed the texts after having found them simply lying around. He was a pupil of Salieri (after Schubert had left him as a teacher) and he worked as a secretary for Count Széchényi whose poems had been set by Schubert; he received a manuscript of *Erlkönig* from Schubert in 1817. He had a long life in which to climb the greasy pole of Viennese musical endeavour. He was court Kapellmeister from 1862 to 1865; in this position it was remarked on at the time that he did less than he might to further Schubert's neglected church music. He composed over two thousand works among which are four hundred songs. He set many of the poets that Schubert chose, but he broadened his horizons to include younger writers like Nikolaus Lenau and Johann Nepomuk Vogl.

Despite the reissue of a selection of Randhartinger's lieder in a modern edition, we have to guess the dates of their composition. It is significant that his setting of 'Suleika's second song' is cast in B flat major, a strong link with Schubert's setting of the same text. There is no doubt that Randhartinger, on his best form, was a highly skilled composer. This sumptuous music, still framed by a certain classical rigour, suggests the 1830s when Schubert's example was still alive, rather than the 1840s when Viennese song composing dipped in quality at the same time as yielding to perfumed sentimentality – something that would be termed 'Victorian' in the context of English musical history. The languid, ornamented tendrils of the accompaniment suggest something suitably oriental for Goethe's *West-*

Benedict Randhartinger, lithograph by Josef Kriehuber (1844).

östlicher Divan – an exoticism in which Schubert was a pioneer. Both of Schubert's *Suleika* songs were written for Anna Milder Hauptmann to whom Randhartinger might also have sent his own *Suleika* song. Neither she nor her composers knew that the real author of the words was Marianne von Willemer, Goethe's 'Suleika' in real life.

Randhartinger's song *Rastloses Wandern* (the same poem set by Schubert as *Über Wildemann* D884), probably written in the 1830s, is a marvellous example of what Randhartinger learned from Schubert. It has a broad sweep, an ongoing impulse that has the momentum of a movement of a sophisticated sonata or chamber music work. The interplay between major and minor keys is entirely Schubertian, and completely worthy of the highly charged atmosphere of that composer's own Schulze settings. The restless pace of a song like *An mein Herz* D860, or indeed *Über Wildemann* itself, is transplanted to another composer's orbit with the greatest confidence. If *Rastloses Wandern* is not highly original, it is one of the best Schubert imitations ever penned. In writing this song Randhartinger, who shares the Schubertian *Zeitgeist*, proves his closeness to the composer far more convincingly than did any invented anecdotes.

Franz Lachner (1803–1890)

Lachner was the most successful composer of
the Schubert circle, the only one of Schubert's
younger musical friends to become a full-time
musical celebrity in later life. In the same way,
Moritz von Schwind, Lachner's close friend as
he had been Schubert's, made his career in
Munich and became a celebrated visual artist.
Lachner is the 'missing' link between Schubert
and Schumann, and there are some promising
signs today of a revival of interest in his music.
He was born in Bavaria, and he was to return
there as a favourite son. In the intervening
years, which one may call his 'Schubert
period', he lived in Vienna where he was a
pupil of Simon Sechter and the Abbé Stadler.
He was a friend of the composer from about
1823, although we have no idea how he was
introduced to the Schubert circle. In 1826
Lachner was appointed to a post at the Kärntnertor theatre. He was with Schubert on many
occasions in the last years of the composer's

Franz Lachner, lithograph by Andreas Staub (c. 1830).

life, but his memoirs of the time are not always reliable. He seems to have been more interested
than many of his contemporaries in Schubert's instrumental works. He claimed to have often
discussed his current compositions with Schubert, and that the two men showed their sketches
to each other. This must have been something rare indeed: after his break with Mayrhofer,
Schubert had no-one among his friends, apart from Schober perhaps, with whom he might
have had this kind of discussion. It seems that Schubert took Lachner under his wing, not
exactly as a pupil, but as something of a protégé. An indication of this is the publication of
Lachner's *Der Schmied* in the *Wiener Zeitschrift* of 25 September 1827. This short song is
smuggled into the tail end of a supplement where Schubert's *Der blinde Knabe* D833 only takes
up one and a half of the two available pages. One can imagine Schubert persuading his friend
Johann Schickh, editor of the *Zeitschrift*, to give the younger composer a boost. Lachner
returned to Munich in 1836 and he played an increasingly dominant part in the musical life
of that city.

On the twenty-fifth anniversary of Lachner's return to Munich, Moritz von Schwind dedicated to him the 'Lachner roll', 12.5 metres of remarkably witty drawings on a roll of paper
34 cm high. This depicted Lachner's career from its beginnings, and included several drawings
of Schubert surrounded by his friends. Schwind's own close position to Schubert, and
the integrity of his memories, verifies the strength of the connection between the two
composers.

Even more than Randhartinger's, Lachner's songs are the clearest audible evidence of closeness to Schubert and absorption of the Schubert style. His best songs were not composed in
Schubert's lifetime but many were written in Vienna two or three years after the death of the
composer. Lachner was audacious enough to set texts from Schubert's *Schwanengesang*, perhaps
in conscious homage, but his *Ständchen* and *Das Fischermädchen* are beautiful songs in their
own right, as is the Rellstab setting *Herbst* with the additional colour, ideal for an autumnal
evocation, of an obbligato cello. Perhaps the most Schubertian Lachner song of all is *Die*

Nachtigall, with a text by Grillparzer; it has a sweet melancholy in the major key that seems entirely influenced by Schubert's harmonic world.

Johann Freiherr Vesque von Püttlingen (1803–1883)

Unlike Lachner, Vesque was an entirely Viennese figure. He wrote his earlier songs under the name of Johann Hoven. People said he was claiming to be half a Beethoven, but the pseudonym is the name of a family property in Alsace where the composer spent an idyllic childhood. He was a remarkably talented man – a gifted tenor, an extraordinary linguist and one of the most successful lawyers of the period. By 1827, shortly before he met Schubert, he had already published a commentary on legal textbooks, *Darstellung der Literatur des Österreichischen allgemeinen bürgerlichen Gesetzbuches*, and in 1864 he wrote a definitive book on Austrian copyright. As a composer he was a pupil of Sechter and Moscheles, but it was through Vogl, his singing teacher, that the twenty-five-year-old Vesque came into contact with Schubert in the last year of the composer's life. He was present when singer and composer tried out new songs together, and his impeccably kept diaries testify to, but never exaggerate, his link with Schubert. As with his contemporary, Lachner, the proximity of Schubert and conversation with him about music must have been inspiring. Vesque dedicated his life to vocal music, writing three hundred songs and at least five operas that were produced in Vienna, also in Leipzig and Weimar. He was in personal contact with Mendelssohn and Loewe; he had known Schumann since the winter of 1838–9 when the Saxon composer had greatly benefited from his kindness in Vienna. He visited Schumann in Dresden in 1846 at a time when Randhartinger was also there. He became a revered Viennese figure whose songs were seen as the link between Schubert and Loewe, and even between Schubert and Wolf. The sheer number of songs in each of Vesque's Heine cycles might have encouraged Wolf towards the epic scale of his own single-poet collections.

It is curious that someone who was so highly thought of in Vienna is completely unknown today. Like Lachner's, his songs need reappraisal; unlike the far more conservative Bavarian, Vesque was drawn to greater modernity and greater irony of expression. He was aware that it was not possible to bask in the technical certainties of the golden days of his youth. Some of his later music seems to be straining towards an acknowledgement of such composers as Wagner, without renouncing the relationship of words to music, and that of voice to accompaniment, that had been nurtured by Schubert.

Johann Vesque von Püttlingen.

Felix Mendelssohn (1809–1847)

The critic (and future Schubert poet) Ludwig Rellstab wrote a review of the singer Carl Bader's performance of Schubert's *Erlkönig* in Berlin's Singakademie on 1 December 1827. The eighteen-year-old Felix Mendelssohn was Bader's accompanist, and Rellstab singles him out for praise because of his mastery of the difficult accompaniment. This occasion seems to have made no lasting impression on the young Mendelssohn; on the contrary, he seems to have decided that it was inappropriate for Goethe's text to be set in this way. There was no word of approbation from Mendelssohn at any time concerning Schubert's songs. Twelve years later Schumann won over his famous colleague to the cause of Schubert's symphonies, at first with some difficulty, but once convinced of Schubert's stature Mendelssohn conducted the 'Great' Symphony in C major (D944) in Leipzig with the greatest enthusiasm. He even attempted (without success) to have the work performed in London. It is worth mentioning that Mendelssohn's setting of the Goethe poem *Die Liebende schreibt* (Op. 86/3, 1831) is usually considered more successful than that of Schubert or Brahms.

Robert Schumann (1810–1856)

How different to Mendelssohn's were Schumann's first reactions to Schubert's music! Also in 1827, and with the same piece, *Erlkönig*, performed by a tenor from Dresden, Schumann found another idol to join his beloved author Jean Paul in his discoveries of that year. There was another song on the programme, in G flat major, according to Schumann – either *Wandrers Nachtlied I* D224 or *Nähe des Geliebten* D162. From then on, he made every effort to hear all the Schubert works he could; he was particularly enraptured by the piano duets. As a music critic he would constantly compare Schubert to Beethoven, and there is no doubt of the enormous role Schumann played in the broadening of Schubert's fame. As recognition of this, in 1838 the publisher Diabelli dedicated to Schumann the posthumous publication of Schubert's last three piano sonatas. His active proselytizing on Schubert's behalf might have waned in later years, but his love for the composer's music did not; in Zwickau one can see a large Schubert portrait inscribed by Clara Schumann as a gift to her husband for Christmas 1848. It is tempting to think that it was Schumann's destiny to unite the strands of Schubert's legacy with Mendelssohn's and, from his central geographical position in Leipzig, create a synthesis of what both

Vienna and Berlin offered the modern song composer. In fact, apart from the initial *coup de foudre* of *Erlkönig*, there is surprisingly little detailed critical reaction on Schumann's part to the flood of Schubert's lieder that was published between 1830 and 1850; his main engagement was with the composer's larger works for piano (or piano duet), the chamber music and the symphonies. Johannes Brahms, as yet unborn when Schubert died, was the first great song composer (*pace* Liszt) to have a thorough knowledge of Schubert's lieder.

Ferdinand Hiller (1811–1885)

This conductor, composer and teacher (born in Frankfurt, and for many years the Music Director in Cologne) was a close boyhood friend of Mendelssohn who advised him to study the piano with Hummel in Weimar. This led to encounters with Goethe (1827) and the composition of a handful of settings of that poet. In the same year the sixteen-year-old Hiller travelled with his master to visit Beethoven on his deathbed. During these

Ferdinand Hiller.

weeks teacher and pupil heard Schubert and Vogl (*see* Hummel, p. 376). Hiller's memories were written down over thirty years later:

> Schubert had but little technique. Vogl had but little voice, but they both had so much life and feeling, and were so completely absorbed in their performances, that the wonderful compositions could not have been interpreted with greater clarity and, at the same time, greater vision. One thought neither of piano playing, nor of singing, it was as though the music needed no material sound, as though the melodies, like visions, revealed themselves to spiritualized ears ... my master was so deeply moved that tears glistened on his cheeks ... When I visited [Schubert] in his modest dwelling, he received me so kindly, but with such respect, that I felt extremely embarrassed. To my self-conscious, pointless question as to whether he wrote much he replied: 'I compose every morning – when one piece is finished I start another'. It was clear that he really did nothing but music – and lived by the way, as it were.

Franz Liszt (1811–1886)

Liszt's role in the reception of Schubert's lieder was crucial. The composer had been a known name in Liszt's life from his teens, and it is likely that Schubert was aware of the young prodigy's growing reputation in Vienna. Liszt accompanied such singers as Nourrit, Schönstein and Tietze in recitals and in 1837 began making piano transcriptions of the lieder (*see* TRANSCRIPTIONS). Diabelli dedicated to him the posthumous edition of Schubert's *Impromptus*. Liszt showed a lifelong devotion to Schubert and his work. His secretary and travel companion during the 1850s was Franz von Schober, qv, who had probably been Schubert's closest friend, the poet of twelve solo songs by the composer, and the librettist of *Alfonso und Estrella*. This opera was performed in 1854 in Weimar thanks to Liszt's enthusiasm as much as Schober's self-interested persuasion.

CORA AN DIE SONNE
(BAUMBERG) **D263** [H150]
E♭ major   22 August 1815

Cora to the sun

(14 bars)

Nach so vielen trüben Tagen	After so many gloomy days
Send' uns wiederum einmal,	Take pity on our plaint,
Mitleidsvoll für unsre Klagen,	And send us once more
Einen sanften milden Strahl.	A soft, gentle ray of light.

Liebe Sonne! trink den Regen,	Dear sun, drink up the rain
Der herab zu stürzen dräut,	That threatens to pour down:
Deine Strahlen sind uns Segen,	Your rays are a blessing to us;
Deine Blicke – Seligkeit.	Your glances bliss.
Schein', ach, scheine, liebe Sonne!	Shine, ah, shine, dear sun!
Jede Freude dank' ich dir;	All delight I owe to you;
Alle Geists- und Herzenswonne,	Every joy of the spirit and the heart,
Licht und Wärme kommt von dir.	All light and warmth come from you.

GABRIELE VON BAUMBERG (1775–1839)

This is the fourth of Schubert's seven Baumberg solo settings (1809–1810 and 1815). See the poet's biography for a chronological list of all the Baumberg settings

This song belongs to the group of Baumberg settings from August 1815 which have a style of their own: old-fashioned, ceremonial, somewhat Haydnesque. Even the names of the women who are the stars of these songs (Lina and Cora) have a courtly grace. The original key is E flat, which in the wake of his enthusiasm for *Die Zauberflöte* seems to have become Schubert's special tonality for solemn invocations of this kind, with a touch of priestly ceremonial. The first setting of Goethe's *An den Mond* D259, *Der Morgenkuss* D264, *An die Sonne* D270 (both Baumberg) and Tiedge's *An die Sonne* D272 were all hymn-like settings composed within the same August week of 1815, and all in E flat major. As always within an apparent formula for a classical song of this type, Schubert leaves room for expressive manoeuvre. The opening is fairly conventional with its dotted rhythm upbeat, but mention of gloomy and sunless days pulls the song into A flat via the appropriately darkening effect of a D flat on 'trüben <u>Tagen</u>' (b. 2). It is a clever touch that the song should shy away from its home tonality so early in the piece. This enables the composer to return to the sunlit glories of the bright tonic (although only in first inversion) on 'Mitleidsvoll für uns're Klagen' (bb. 6–7) where the first note of the phrase is also the highest in the song. We reach the root position of the chord only with the last word of the strophe. The effect is of a prayer answered and of the clouds clearing.

At this time of the early morning the rays are as yet tentative and gentle. In the staccato accompaniment under '<u>einen</u> sanften milden Strahl', (bb. 9–11) and in the detached chords that form the upbeat to the postlude, we hear the beginnings of the Schubertian piano writing that depicts the working of the celestial dynamo that governs the heavens – the dactylic rhythms that will reach their apotheosis with Leitner's *Die Sterne* D939. The last four bars of piano writing describe a beautiful curve that reaches its high point on a B flat[7] chord in first inversion (the middle of b. 12) and then descends with elegance and grace to a languid feminine cadence worthy of Cora's longing for radiance and enlightenment.

In volume 9 of the NSA (p. 6) the opening of another version is printed with a short piano introduction that appeared only with the first edition of the song in 1848. Whether this variant goes back to Schubert himself is doubtful.

Autograph:	Library of Congress, Washington
First edition:	Published as Book 42 no. 3 of the *Nachlass* by Diabelli, Vienna in 1848 (P361)
Subsequent editions:	Peters: vol. 6/33; AGA XX 123: vol. 3/50; NSA IV: vol. 9/6
Bibliography:	Youens 1996, pp. 40–41

Arrangements:	Arr. Tilman Hoppstock for guitar accompaniment, in *Franz Schubert: 110 Lieder* (2009)
Discography and timing:	Fischer-Dieskau —
	Hyperion I 22[18]
	Hyperion II 9[11] 1'44 Catherine Wyn-Rogers

CORONACH (Totengesang der Frauen und Mädchen) *see SIEBEN GESÄNGE AUS WALTER SCOTT'S FRÄULEIN VOM SEE* NO. 4 D836

ABRAHAM COWLEY (1618–1667)

THE POETIC SOURCE
The Mistress; or several copies of Love-Verses written by A. Cowley, Humphrey Moseley, London, 1656

THE SONG
[n.d.]   *Der Weiberfreund* D271. The poem *The Inconstant* (No. 66 in *The Mistress*) seven strophes of six lines each, was the source of the translation by Joseph Franz von Ratschky (qv)

Cowley, born in London in 1618, was a child prodigy and a famously loyal Royalist poet during the English Civil War. At one time he was part of Queen Henrietta Maria's court in French exile. He rejoiced in the Restoration of the monarchy, died in Chertsey on 28 July 1667 and is buried in Westminster Abbey. The answer to Alexander Pope's famous question, 'Who now reads Cowley?' ('Who now reads Cowley? if he pleases yet / His moral pleases, not his pointed wit; / Forget his Epic, nay Pindaric Art, / But still I love the language of the Heart': *Imitations of Horace*, 1737) must be 'the enthusiastic Schubertian' – if only occasionally. Cowley was at his best in lighter material; his unfinished epic about King David, the *Davideis* (1656), and his *Select Discourses* (1658) make for heavy reading. Despite having written *The Inconstant*, Cowley seems to have been extremely timid in the company of women.

Abraham Cowley, frontispiece to *The Mistress* (1684).

JAKOB NICOLAUS CRAIGHER DE JACHELUTTA (1797–1855)

THE POETIC SOURCES

S1   *Poetische Betrachtungen in freyen Stunden von Nicolaus.* Carl Gerold, Wien, 1828

This modest and partially anonymous collection of poetry has a foreword by Friedrich von Schlegel

S2   Joseph Ritson: *A Select Collection of English Songs* with their original airs and A Historical Essay on the Original and Progress of National Song by the late Joseph Ritson Esq. The Second Edition with Additional Songs and Occasional Notes by Thomas Park F.S., London Printed for F. C. and J. Rivington; Longman, Hurst, Rees; Orme and Brown; Lackington, Allen and Co.; Cadell and Davies; C. Law; S. Bagster; J. Booker; Black, Parry, and Co.; J. M. Richardson; J. Booth; R. Priestley; R. Scholey; Cradock and Joy; R. Baldwin; and J. Major 1813

THE SONGS

1824/early 1825   *Die junge Nonne* D828 [S1: from section headed '1822', p. 58]

Early 1825   *Lied der Anne Lyle* D830 [now that it has been ascertained that Sophie May did not translate this Walter Scott text, it seems likely that Craigher was the author of this text from the English]

April 1825   *Der blinde Knabe* D833 [no printed source of the translation from Colley Cibber's poem available] Craigher's source for the original English poem was very probably S2 Volume II p. 121 where the poem was printed without music (for a fuller description of this source *see* the entry for Colley CIBBER)
                    Totengräbers Heimwehe D842 [S1 with title 'Gräbers Heimweh', p. 59]

The 'Imperial Baron' Craigher de Jachelutta was born in Ligosullo, Friuli, on 17 December 1797. Schubert clearly set Craigher's texts from the poet's manuscript three years before their publication in book form. Craigher was also almost certainly responsible for the Italian singing versions that were printed beneath the original German texts in the first editions of Bruchmann's *An die Leier* D737 (after Anacreon), Bruchmann's *Im Haine* D738, Sauter's *Der Wachtelschlag* D742 and Goethe's *Willkommen und Abschied* D767. It has been suggested that Craigher provided the German translations of the three Italian *Canzone* D902 written for Luigi Lablache in 1827: *L'incanto degli occhi* (*Die Macht der Augen*), *Il traditor deluso* (*Der getäuschte Verräter*) and *Il modo di prender moglie* (*Die Art, ein Weib zu nehmen*). This theory has been contested by Walther Dürr who points out that Craigher was a native Italian-speaker and, had he been shown these songs, he would have corrected

Schubert's faulty Italian accentuation. In fact these corrections post-date the German translations.

Craigher was born a Venetian subject of the occupying Austrian monarchy. He came from a poor family (the validity of his title is in doubt) but at a youthful age he had already succeeded in business and as an entrepreneur; he was typical of a new breed of the upwardly mobile and multilingual citizens of post-Napoleonic Europe. He made his home in Vienna from 1820 and was drawn to the circle of the Redemptorist priest, Klemens Maria Hofbauer, and Zacharias Werner. He seems to have had a genuine interest in poetry and music, despite a certain air of opportunistic charlatanism that clings to his literary endea-vours. He was a fervent Roman Catholic (as the poem of *Die junge Nonne* makes clear) and as such was part of the convert Friedrich von Schlegel's circle in Vienna. As an original poet (as opposed to a translator) Craigher was a

Nikolaus Craigher de Jachelutta, ink drawing by Thugut Heinrich, 1831.

the composer with a number of translations of French, Italian, Spanish and English classics (retaining the metre of the original language) that could be set to music and printed both in German and the original. There is no record of the financial implications of this plan, but it was a logical extension of Schubert's decision to print his Walter Scott settings, from earlier in the year, in both German and English.

Craigher's scheme was one of the greatest Schubertian pipe dreams – it might have been a body of song representative of the best of western literature, a forerunner of Wolf's Italian and Spanish Songbooks perhaps. Whether Craigher was the right man for such an enter-prise is highly doubtful, judging from the quality of his own original poems, two of which Schubert set to music, perhaps as a starting point for the so-called 'Accord'. The only thing that is miraculous about these texts is that Schubert transcended such overblown reli-gious effusions to create two songs of genius. In his later years Craigher published a fascinating memoir, *Erinnerungen an den Orient*, about his travels in Greece, Egypt and Palestine (in 1843, long after he knew Schubert). He reached Cairo and the Pyramids without venturing far enough south to visit Luxor where he might have encountered the statue of Memnon that inspired Schubert's Mayrhofer setting of that name. Craigher's main concern on this reli-giously-inspired journey was to visit the Holy Land and its biblical sites. He died in Cormons near Görz on 17 May 1855.

disciple of the already outmoded Göttingen Hainbund, a group of poets that had included Klopstock, Hölty and Voss.

In October 1825 Craigher had a meeting with Schubert (whom in his diary entry he describes as a 'splendid person') and his friend the painter Schwind. He made an agreement ('Accord') with Schubert that as an expert in various European languages he would provide

CRONNAN   Cronnan
('OSSIAN'–MACPHERSON) **D282** [H168]
This song exists in two versions, the second of which is discussed below:[1]
(1)   5 September 1815; (2) No date

(1)   'Langsam'   C minor $\frac{3}{4}$ [130 bars]

---

[1] In the absence of the relevant NSA publication, the AGA was used for the Hyperion recording. The AGA offers a composite of the first and second versions: in musical terms the second version (as published in the *Nachlass*) but from the point of view of text, nearer the first version (not published separately in the AGA). Mandyczewski changed the verbal 'improvements' of Sonnleithner and Diabelli back to the original Harold translation as found in the first version.

(2)   C minor

(130 bars)

The English translation given here is Ossian's original, despite tiny variations.

Shilric: Ich sitz' bei der moosigten Quelle; am Gipfel des stürmischen Hügels. Über mir braust ein Baum. Dunkle Wellen rollen über die Heide. Die See ist stürmisch darunter. Die Hirsche steigen vom Hügel herab. Kein Jäger wird in der Ferne geseh'n. Es ist Mittag, aber Alles ist still. Traurig sind meine einsamen Gedanken. Erschienst du aber, o meine Geliebte, wie ein Wand'rer auf der Heide, dein Haar fliegend im Winde, hinter dir;[2] dein Busen hoch aufwallend, deine Augen voll Tränen, für deine Freunde, die der Nebel des Hügels verbarg: dich wollt' ich trösten, o meine Geliebte, dich wollt' ich führen zum Hause meines Vaters! Aber ist sie es, die dort wie ein Strahl des Lichts auf der Heide erscheint? Kommst du, o Mädchen, über Felsen, über Berge zu mir, schimmernd, wie im Herbste der Mond, wie die Sonn, im Sturme des Sommers?[3] Sie spricht; aber wie schwach ist ihre Stimme! Wie das Lüftchen im Schilfe der See.

Vinvela: Kehrst du vom Kriege unbeschädigt zurück?[4] Wo sind deine Freunde, mein Geliebter? Ich vernahm deinen Tod auf dem Hügel; ich vernahm ihn und betrauerte dich![5]

Shilric: Ja, meine Schönste, ich kehre zurück, aber allein von meinem Geschlecht. Du sollst jene nimmer erblicken,[6] 'ich hab' ihre Gräber auf der Fläche errichtet. Aber warum bist du am Hügel der Wüste? Warum allein auf der Heide?

Shilric: I sit by the mossy fountain on the top of the hill of winds. One tree is rustling above me. Dark waves roll over the heath. The lake is troubled below. The deer descend from the hill. No hunter at a distance is seen. [. . .]

It is mid-day, but all is silent. Sad are my thoughts alone. Didst thou but appear, O my love! As a wanderer on the heath! thy hair floating on the wind behind thee, thy bosom heaving on the sight, thine eyes full of tears for thy friends whom the mist of the hill had concealed. Thee I would comfort my love, and bring thee to thy father's house! But is it she that there appears, like a beam of light on the heath? Bright as the moon in autumn, as the sun in a summer storm, comest thou, lovely maid, over rocks, over mountains to me? She speaks: but how weak her voice! Like the breeze in the reeds of the pool.

Vinvela: Returnest thou safe from the war? Where are thy friends, my love? I heard of thy death on the hill. I heard and mourned thee, Shilric.

Shilric: Yes, my fair, I return, but I alone of my race. Thou shalt see them no more. Their graves I raised on the plain. But why art thou on the desert hill? Why on the heath alone?

---

[2] The second version cuts the words 'hinter dir' after 'Winde'. It is open to question whether this change is actually Schubert's revision or one that stems from Diabelli.

[3] Harold's original translation reads: 'wie die Sonne *in einem Sturme* des Sommers' ('like the sun in a summer storm'). Schubert omits 'einem' but the Diabelli edition substitutes the word 'Glut'.

[4] The Diabelli edition changes this to 'Kehrst du vom Kriege *schadlos* zurück'.

[5] Harold's translation adds 'Shilric' after 'betrauerte dich' – a phrase which the Diabelli edition changes to '*beweinte* dich'. The composer also avoids having Shilric address the wraith directly as '*Vinvela*' later in the song, saving it up for the closing section.

[6] In the Diabelli edition this is changed to '*Jene* sollst *du nicht mehr* erblicken'.

Vinvela: O Shilric, ich bin allein, allein in der Winterbehausung. Ich starb vor Schmerz wegen dir. Shilric, ich lieg' erblasst in dem Grab.

Vinvela: Alone I am, O Shilrik; alone in the winter house. With grief for thee I expired. Shilric; I am pale in the tomb.

Shilric: Sie gleitet, sie durchsegelt die Luft wie Nebel vorm Wind. Und willst du nicht bleiben? Bleib' beschau' meine Tränen! zierlich erscheinst du, im Leben warst du schön.

Ich will sitzen bei der moosigten Quelle, am Gipfel des Hügels.[7] Wenn Alles im Mittag herum schweigt, dann sprich mit mir, o Vinvela! komm auf dem leichtbeflügelten Hauche! auf dem Lüftchen der Einöde komm! lass mich, wenn du vorbeigehst, deine Stimme vernehmen, wenn Alles im Mittag herum schweigt!

Shilric: She flees, she sails away as grey mist before the wind! And wilt thou not stay, my love? Stay and behold my tears! Fair thou appearest, Vinvela! Fair thou wast, when alive!

By the mossy fountain I will sit, on the top of the hill of winds. When mid-day is silent around. Converse, o my love, with me!

Come on the wings of the gale! On the blast of the mountain, come!

Let me hear thy voice, as thou passest, when mid-day is silent around!

JAMES MACPHERSON ('OSSIAN') (1736–1796), translated by EDMUND, BARON VON HAROLD (1737–1800) in 1782

Cronnan is a musical dialogue between two characters who never sing simultaneously (a performance for a single singer taking both male and female roles would thus be a possibility). This work is accordingly listed here as the fourth of Schubert's ten Ossian–Macpherson solo settings (1815–17). See the poet's biography (under Macpherson) for a chronological list of all the Ossian settings

This long song, half ballad and half aria, is one of the masterpieces of 1815. The sonorous, doom-laden majesty of the Celtic twilight is a familiar feature of the settings of Ossian, apocryphal bard of yore, but *Cronnan* has a rare symphonic sweep, a sense of musical unity, that places it in the front rank of the composer's longer songs. *Die Nacht* D534, the last of the Ossian ballads, is the only one that might be considered to be finer in its range of detail; but it is a fragment. Diabelli published that work as Book 1 of the *Nachlass* (at the same time as providing a spurious conclusion adapted from a Schubert choral setting); it is no surprise that *Cronnan* was published as Book 2 of a series that aimed to reveal the undreamed-of glories of Schubert's song legacy. Those who know the song only from the Peters Edition (a reprint of Diabelli's *Nachlass* version of 1830) will be astonished, on studying the first version as printed in the NSA, how many textual changes the publisher and his ashamed accomplice, Leopold von Sonnleithner, took it upon themselves to make (some of these are listed in the footnotes). Mandyczewski's AGA had made different changes to the text which also attempted to improve Harold: for example 'unbeschädigt' becomes the smoother 'schadlos' (b. 74) while altering the rhythm of Schubert's vocal line. It was the AGA version that was recorded for Hyperion. The NSA prints the partially corrupt Diabelli version as a second version. Walther Dürr believes that at least some of the musical details (the pianist's mordents in b. 5, for example) go back to Schubert himself and that Diabelli had access to an autograph of the song that is no longer extant.

The word 'Cronan' in Gaelic means 'a low, murmuring sound' or 'a pathetic ode'. Macpherson uses Cronnan as the name of the Gaelic bard who recounts the story of Shilric and Vinvela while

[7] Harold's 'am Gipfel des *stürmischen* Hügels' is here shortened by Schubert.

allowing them to speak their own words in direct speech. We have already met these star-crossed lovers from Ossian's (or rather Macpherson's) *Carric-Thura* in Schubert's duet *Shilrik und Vinvela* (D293, 20 September 1815). He composed *Cronnan* a fortnight earlier but it is in fact a continuation of the Shilric and Vinvela story, and a much more important work. In *Shilrik und Vinvela* it is the latter who doubts that her lover will return from battle. He asks her to bury him with honour, and she vows to remember him always. As Cronnan continues their story in this new episode, Shilric has returned safely from battle, the only one of his clan to survive; he finds that in the meantime Vinvela has died from grief, believing that he is dead (there is a touch of *Romeo and Juliet* about all this), and he sees her only as a ghost.

The introduction is not dissimilar to that of *Die Nacht* in terms of mood and nocturnal atmosphere; the successive gliding sixths in that work find their counterpart here in murmuring thirds. In *Cronnan* a full seven bars of prelude (marked *Langsam, schauerlich* – 'Slow, eerily') give the pianist ample time to establish the sombre mood of the forlorn hero 'at the peak of the stormy hill'. Water (the mossy fountain), the first of the elements mentioned in *Cronnan*, inspires a gently undulating background. The singer begins on a monotone, raising the pitch with each bar but nevertheless conserving the feeling of this being accompanied recitative. At 'Über mir braust ein Baum' (b. 11) semiquavers in the right hand are supplemented by the shuddering demisemiquavers of the left, appropriate to branches caught up in a gale. When the picture widens to include the sea, there is *forte* storm music in which angry waves pound in the inner voices of the accompaniment (b. 14) while accented crotchets, like tolling bells, resound in the hands' extremities. As the hero shifts his gaze from sea to forest, the agitated music subsides and melts into a gentle fermata (b. 22).

A new section marked *Geschwind* produces piano music, capriciously staccato and flighty, that seems a preparatory study for the music for deer, both stag and hind, which Schubert wrote in *Die Nacht*. To introduce the recitative at b. 28 for 'Die Hirsche steigen vom Hügel herab' ('The deer descend from the hill') delicate scales twitch between the hands, as if the movement of a single deer in the right is nervously mirrored by the rest of the herd (companionable thirds as opposed to single notes) in the left. For 'Kein Jäger wird in der Ferne geseh'n' (b. 30) the music is marked 'Im Takt' to change recitative into the discipline of measured time; stentorian chords in sixths evoke the horn calls of the hunter. After this, a tiny interlude made up of a descending figure is repeated in sequence, the harmony all the while flattening (and thus giving the impression of a dying-down or withdrawal) until we reach a chord of D flat that announces in curfew-like tones 'Es ist Mittag, aber Alles ist still' ('It is mid-day, but all is silent'). The accompanied recitative ('Langsam') of 'Alles ist still', and the following poignant echo for piano (b. 38) are worthy of Mahler in their depth of romantic longing; we are left in no doubt as to how deeply Shilric misses his beloved. This recitative ends in A flat minor (after 'Traurig sind meine einsamen Gedanken'). The enharmonic change between C flat and B natural conjures a B^7 chord, a transition into the next section.

This is a set piece: Shilric's E minor aria 'Erschienst du aber, o meine Geliebte' (marked 'Mässig geschwind' from b. 41). The agitation of this section, the height of its tessitura and its refusal to settle into any key for longer than a bar, suggest the panic of a desperate search. The line 'dein Haar fliegend im Winde', bb. 44–45 has inspired an appropriate accompaniment: groups of three right-hand semiquavers are attached to left-hand crotchets like floating strands of hair flowing behind the elusive Vinvela. From b. 47 ('deine Augen voll Tränen') the piano writing changes to a panting motif between the hands, each note like a drop of tears that will result in a flood. There is an operatic eloquence at 'dich wollt' ich trösten, o meine Geliebte' (bb. 49–50), a forte outburst that dies down to a whimper in a three-bar interlude for piano.

It is then that Shilric sees Vinvela. At first she seems real (a loud chord to accompany 'Aber ist sie es?' – 'But is that she?', from b. 56) but then, when he notices that she is as insubstantial as a beam of light, the dynamic of the accompaniment retreats to mezzo forte, and thence to an even more uncertain piano. After 'auf der Heide erscheint' a tiny phrase of four quavers introduces a miniature aria (it is perhaps more accurately an *arioso*), marked *Etwas langsam*, of ravishing effect. All the tenderness of his love for her seems encapsulated in these Mozartian phrases ('Kommst du, o Mädchen') accompanied by a succession of thirds that suggest a physical embrace, as if the beautiful girl is cradled in Shilric's arms. Double thirds have already established themselves as a feature of the piece, and John Reed sees in them a motif suggesting Vinvela's loyalty as well as her beauty. At the next recitative, 'Sie spricht' ('She speaks', bb. 67–8), we are aware of the sheer euphony of these thirds (and euphony is surely a musical analogue for beauty) in ethereal semiquaver pulsations that decorate a C^7, and then an F^7, chord. These upwardly arched figurations seem to stretch out towards something that is not really there; we can almost *see* Shilric's straining to catch the sound of Vinvela's voice. We can only wonder at Schubert's ability to mirror, infallibly, a complicated dramatic notion like this with the most simple of musical means. Needless to say, these bars set up the entrance of Vinvela in a way worthy of the music to come.

Vinvela now sings an *arioso* of rare beauty ('Kehrst du vom Kriege unbeschädigt zurück?' b. 73). The piano doubles the voice as if to coax a frail spirit into vocal life, and to guide her through the musical straits. The left hand stays almost entirely in the treble clef, an early use of a Schubertian sleight of hand in which, by minimizing the power of the bass line, the voice seems to dematerialize and come from another world. Vinvela speaks in some celestial guise; the dactylic rhythm of her vocal line prophesies such songs as *Der Tod und das Mädchen* D531 and the Senn setting *Schwanengesang* D744, songs of death and transfiguration.

There is a clever return to reality as Shilric's reaction to this music is brought back into a sharper focus; at b. 83, a G^7 chord (all naturals) seems to cut a swathe across the chromatic complexities of Vinvela's plaint. Shilric's short account of the death of his comrades (from b. 84, marked 'Langsam') is an eloquent arioso of grief and manly stoicism. The insidious descent of the phrase 'ich hab' ihre Gräber auf der Fläche errichtet' (bb. 86–7) lays bodies to rest with stately majesty. His next question to Vinvela ('Aber warum bist du am Hügel der Wüste?') seems almost offhand, straightforwardly accompanied by a chord or two. Once her spirit has been re-summoned, those wafting thirds associated with her loyalty and beauty make a reappearance (b. 91) as an introduction to her parting words. It would be difficult to find a better illustration than this in all Schubert of the richness of the composer's *arioso*, and how infinitely touching it can be. The setting of 'Shilric, ich lieg' erblasst in dem Grab' (b. 95) is a masterstroke. The phrase begins in chromatic disorientation, but the last four words (set to a simple dominant–tonic cadence) find their repose in a poised classical style more heartbreaking than romantic emotion. As a result we can almost hear her fade before our eyes; she retreats into the musical elegance of another age, and from thence into the infinite.

The piano now has an interlude (marked *Etwas langsam* from b. 98) that is one of the glories of the piece. 'Sie gleitet' ('She glides away') says Shilric, and the piano illustrates this process with stunning ingenuity, and *before* we hear the words. These four bars start in the middle of the keyboard and float upwards, seeming to evaporate as they do so. Built into the tender cadence just before 'sie gleitet' is also Shilric's longing, and the ache of his bereaved heart. A further interlude of triplets then mirrors the words about Vinvela sailing away. He begs her to stay. Another severely classical cadence ('Im Leben warst du schön' – 'Fair thou wast', bb. 107–8) encapsulates his grief in terms that are heartbreaking in their understatement.

This is followed by something of a recapitulation of the C minor opening section. The music is far from the same – no facile repeat this – but it evokes the same mood. We find the hero back at the mossy fountain; those murmuring watery semiquavers give this song a feeling of completion and wholeness rare in the longer ballads. The text must take the credit for this; whether or not Ossian was a genuine historical figure, and whether Schubert truly believed him to be, is immaterial to the effect that these words had on Schubert's imagination. As in many of the composer's *da capo* passages, the life of the narrator has been changed for ever by what has happened in the middle section. Thus do memories of Vinvela enliven and warm the song's conclusion. He begs her spirit to reappear. The setting of 'Komm auf dem leichtbeflügelten Hauche' ('Come on the wings of the gale', bb. 117–18) is enchantingly delicate, with piano writing that whispers and dances, beguiles and sings. We soon lose this feminine presence, however; it is, after all, only a chimera. We return to the sombre accompaniment in thirds which lead the song to its melancholy conclusion. *Cronnan* is a masterpiece that deserves a permanent place in the repertoire. The role of Vinvela can be assigned to a soprano in the spirit of a Schubertiad, but the song is just as suitable for a single male singer. One of Macpherson's footnotes to *Carric-Thura* implies that the singers Cronnan and Minona performed the story of Shilric and Vinvela at the court of Fingal, but there is no indication that Schubert believed that two singers were necessary for his own setting.

Autograph:	In private hands (first version, bb. 1–113)
	Wienbibliothek im Rathaus, Vienna (first version, bb. 114 to end)
First edition:	Published as Book 2 no. 1 of the *Nachlass* by Diabelli, Vienna in 1830 (P241)
Publication reviews:	Rellstab 'Ueberlick der Erzeugnisse', *Iris im Gebiete der Tonkunst* (Berlin), No. 39 (12 November 1830) [Waidelich/Hilmar Dokumente II No. 784b]
Subsequent editions:	Peters: vol. 4/174; AGA XX 188: vol. 4/21; NSA IV: vol. 9/36 (first version) & 46 (second version)
Bibliography:	Capell 1928, p. 94
	Clerk 1870, Vol. 1, p. 180

Discography and timing:			
	Fischer-Dieskau	—	
	Deutsche Grammophon	10'27	Janet Baker & Dietrich
	Schubert Duette		Fischer-Dieskau
	Hyperion I 22[26]	9'47	Simon Keenlyside &
	Hyperion II 10[3]		Lorna Anderson

← *Das Mädchen von Inistore* D281   *An den Frühling* D283 →

D

DA QUEL SEMBIANTE APPRESI *see VIER CANZONEN* D688/3

DANKSAGUNG AN DEN BACH *see Die SCHÖNE MÜLLERIN* D795/4

DAPHNE AM BACH
(STOLBERG) **D411** [H247]
D major   April 1816

Daphne by the brook

(19 bars)

Ich hab' ein Bächlein funden
  Vom Städtchen ziemlich weit,
Da bin ich manche Stunden
  In stiller Einsamkeit.
Ich tät mir gleich erkiesen
  Ein Plätzchen kühles Moos;
Da sitz ich, und da fliessen
  Mir Tränen in den Schoss.

Für dich, für dich nur wallet
  Mein jugendliches Blut;
Doch leise nur erschallet
  Dein Nam' an dieser Flut.
Ich fürchte, dass mich täusche
  Ein Lauscher aus der Stadt;
Es schreckt mich das Geräusche
  Von jedem Pappelblatt.

Ich wünsche mir zurücke
  Den flüchtigsten Genuss,
In jedem Augenblicke
  Fühl' ich den Abschiedskuss.
Es ward mir wohl und bange
  Als mich dein Arm umschloss,
Als noch auf meine Wange
  Dein letztes Tränchen floss!

I have found a little brook
  Quite far from the town;
There I pass many an hour
  In my quiet solitude.
I immediately chose
  A patch of cool moss;
There I sit, as my tears
  Flow down into my lap.

My young blood pulses
  For you, for you alone;
Yet your name echoes but softly
  By these waters.
For I fear lest some eavesdropper
  From the town should betray me;
I shudder at the rustling
  Of every poplar leaf.

I long for the return
  Of the most fleeting pleasure
Every moment
  I feel your parting kiss.
I was happy and yet sad
  As your arms embraced me.
As your last tears
  Fell on my cheeks.

Von meinem Blumenhügel	Long did I gaze after you
Sah' ich dir lange nach;	From my flower-decked hillside;
Ich wünschte mir die Flügel	I yearn for the wings
Der Täubchen auf dem Dach;	Of the doves on the roof;
Nun glaub' ich zu vergehen	Now I feel as if I am fading away
Mit jedem Augenblick.	With each moment.
Willst du dein Liebchen sehen,	If you wish to see your beloved,
So komme bald zurück!	Come back soon!

FRIEDRICH LEOPOLD, GRAF ZU STOLBERG-STOLBERG (1750–1819); poem written in 1775

This is the fourth of Schubert's nine Stolberg solo settings (1815–23). See the poet's biography for a chronological list of all the Stolberg settings

'The dullest of Schubert's brook songs' is how Capell glumly sums up this lovely little pastorale. It is certainly a forerunner of the celebrated *Wohin?* from *Die schöne Müllerin*; the water music's modulations in that song, and the charm of the miller lad, make it all too easy for Daphne to be found lightweight in comparison. It might be fairer to call Zumsteeg's setting of the same poem dull, a song that shows how far Schubert had improved on his erstwhile model. Zumsteeg's accompaniment hugs the vocal line without so much as a suggestion of water music; each verse ends with a pianistic flourish that has nothing to do with Daphne's character – suitably abject in Schubert as she contemplates her past. Little wonder that the mood of Schubert's music for her cannot be placed side by side with a song for a miller boy whose whole future lies in front of him.

In *Daphne am Bach* the brook remains in the background of a delicate and feminine evocation of solitude. Stolberg the classicist would have known that Daphne was one of the daughters of the river-god Peneius; something of that immortal nymph's poise has been inherited by her shepherdess namesake who is fading away in her grief but is brave enough to sing her song in the major key. In the miller's song *Wohin?* various modulations inform us that the singer is on the move, walking beside the brook and glancing in different directions. Daphne, on the other hand, sits still as she withdraws into her private world. This is an example of how vividly Schubert allows even the most modest of his characters to live within a believable dramatic framework. This was undoubtedly helped by a fine poem – in Raymond Joly's words, 'a rare instance of naïveté without condescension, simplicity without sham, a Greuze without the pose and the prurience'.

Autograph:	In private possession
First edition:	Published as Vol. 7 no. 37 in Friedlaender's edition by Peters, Leipzig in 1887 (P498)
Subsequent editions:	Peters: Vol. 7/87; AGA XX 209: Vol. 4/81; NSA IV: Vol. 10/138
Further settings and arrangements:	Johann Rudolf Zumsteeg (1760–1802) *Daphne am Bach* (published 1803)
	Luise Reichardt (1779–1826) *Daphne am Bach* (1819)
	Arr. Tillman Happstock (b. 1961) for guitar accompanient in *Franz Schubert: 110 Lieder* (2009)
Discography and timing:	Fischer-Dieskau —
	Hyperion I 9[9]
	Hyperion II 13[23] 2'23 Arleen Auger

←— *Der Herbstabend* D405   *Stimme der Liebe* D412 —→

DAS WAR ICH (I)

(KÖRNER) **D174** [H81]

D major   26 March 1815

That was me

Jüngst träumte mir, ich sah auf lichten Höhen ein Mädchen sich

(17 bars)

Jüngst träumte mir, ich sah auf lichten Höhen	Recently I dreamt I saw on sunlit hills
Ein Mädchen sich im jungen Tag ergehen,	A maiden wandering in the early morning,
So hold, so süss, dass es dir völlig glich.	So fair, so sweet, that she resembled you.
Und vor ihr lag ein Jüngling auf den Knien,	Before her knelt a youth.
Er schien sie sanft an seine Brust zu ziehen,	He seemed to draw her gently to his breast;
Und das war ich.	*And that was me.*
Doch bald verändert hatte sich die Szene,	But soon the scene had changed.
In tiefen Fluten sah ich jetzt die Schöne,	I now saw that fair maiden in the deep flood;
Wie ihr die letzte, schwache Kraft entwich,	Her frail strength was deserting her.
Da kam ein Jüngling hülfreich ihr geflogen,	Then a youth rushed to her aid;
Er sprang ihr nach und trug sie aus	He plunged after her and bore her from
den Wogen,	the waves.
Und das war ich!	*And that was me.*
So malte sich der Traum in bunten Zügen,	The dream was painted in bright colours;
Und überall sah ich die Liebe siegen,	Everywhere I saw love victorious,
Und alles, alles drehte sich um dich!	And everything was centred on you!
Du flogst voran in ungebund'ner Freie,	You sailed on, free and unfettered.
Der Jüngling zog dir nach mit stiller Treue,	The faithful youth followed you, silently,
Und das war ich!	*And that was me.*
[. . . 2 . . .]	[. . . 2 . . .]
Und als ich endlich aus dem Traum erwachte,	And when at length I awoke from my dream,
Der neue Tag die neue Sehnsucht brachte,	The new day brought new longing.
Da blieb Dein liebes, süsses Bild um mich.	Your dear, sweet image was still with me.
Ich sah dich von der Küsse Glut erwarmen,	I saw you warmed by the fire of his kisses;
Ich sah dich selig in des Jünglings Armen,	I saw you blissful in that youth's arms.
Und das war ich!	*And that was me.*
[. . . 2 . . .]	[. . . 2 . . .]

THEODOR KÖRNER (1791–1813)

This is the eighth of Schubert's sixteen Körner solo settings (1815–18). See the poet's biography for a chronological list of all the Körner settings

1815 was the year of Schubert's ill-fated love for Therese Grob. It is easy to see that this poem, a series of cinematic scenarios worthy of the derring-do fantasies of Walter Mitty, would have appealed to a young man without the real means to win his lady. The song is marked 'erzählend' ('telling a story') and there is a whimsical freedom here as though words and music are invented on the spot by a daydreamer whose actions scarcely match the boldness of his thoughts. The sucession of sequences in the second half of the song (from b. 10 of each strophe) is noteworthy: pulsating chords in semiquavers propel these ideas forward in the keys of D minor – A minor – C minor – G minor, each shift representing a new link in the chain of consequences that enlivens the narrator's tale – whether kneeling in obeisance, rushing in to the rescue or blissfully kissing the fair maiden. In each case this leads to a statement of 'And that was me'. The two-bar postlude confirms this assertion with just the right trace of self-satisfaction, and to humorous effect. This is Schubert experimenting with the dramatization of the narrator's art. There is also much tenderness in this charming little song. The singer can vary the final cadence of each verse so as to suggest anything from timid politeness to reckless bravery. The Peters Edition, following Diabelli as always, prints the song as through-composed (with some adjustment to the linking interlude), the AGA and NSA print it as a strophic song.

   There are six strophes in Körner's poem – these are all printed in the AGA. Given here are verses 1, 2, 3 and 6. In the fifth and sixth strophes Körner skilfully changes the wistful nature of vicarious longing into a triumphant hymn to reciprocated love. Although Walther Dürr (NSA Vol. 8, p. XX) avers that the sixth strophe might make a more convincing end to this narrative (because it ends with the conclusive 'Ja, das war ich'), one feels that the rueful standpoint of the onlooker – some would say someone rather like Schubert himself – is built into the shy charm of this song.

Autograph:	Pierpont Morgan Library, New York
First edition:	Published as Book 39, no. 2 of the *Nachlass* by Diabelli, Vienna in 1845 (P355)
Subsequent editions:	Peters: Vol. 6/22; AGA XX 56: Vol. 2/84; NSA IV: Vol. 8/22; Bärenreiter: Vol. 6/118
Bibliography:	Black 2003, pp. 48–9 (This song, with implications regarding the private lives of both Körner and Schubert, occasioned a borrowing from the *Benedictus* in Schubert's Mass in G major D167) Youens 1996, pp. 127–30
Discography and timing:	Fischer-Dieskau I 3[8] 2'51
	Hyperion I 4[4]
	Hyperion II 5[21] 3'08 Philip Langridge

← *Der Morgenstern* D172   *Die Sterne* D176 →

DAS WAR ICH (II)   That was me
(KÖRNER) **D174A/D450A** [H281]
D major   (Fragment) 1816?

See previous entry for poem and translation

THEODOR KÖRNER (1791–1813)

This is the fifteenth of Schubert's sixteen Körner solo settings (1815–18). See above

We must assume that Schubert was not entirely satisfied with his first setting of the poem as he made a rather half-hearted start on a second, probably in 1816. Only six bars of the vocal line were completed and all that exists of the original Schubert is five bars of voice line, written out without accompaniment or text. This encompasses the first two lines of the text, ending with 'ergehen', as printed above in the first setting. These, moreover, are crossed out. This is to be found under the heading 'Das war ich. Körner', at the back of an autograph fair copy for *Fragment aus dem Aeschylus* D450, a song written in 1816. (There is thus some confusion about a Deutsch catalogue number for this work: should it rightfully be paired with the song's first setting – thus D174A? – or should it be paired with the Mayrhofer setting as D450A?) The fragment was completed by Reinhard Van Hoorickx who made a remarkable stab at finishing this meagre material. We are grateful not to have lost these five hurriedly written bars, music typical of the open-hearted melodies that Schubert alone was able to write. Even when penning a tune he was never fully to develop, the composer strews melodic riches in the path of his listeners.

In the Hyperion recording of this version of the song, strophes 1, 2 and 4 were performed.

Autograph:	Conservatoire collection, Bibliothèque Nationale, Paris
First edition:	Published as part of the AGA in 1897; fragment subsequently completed by Reinhard Van Hoorickx; subsequently published as part of the NSA in 2009 (p. 857)
Subsequent editions:	Not in Peters; AGA: Revisionsbericht XX, p. 16; NSA IV: Vol. 8/205
Discography and timing:	Fischer-Dieskau — Hyperion I 32[17] 2'14 Daniel Norman Hyperion II 15[8]

← *Fragment aus dem Aeschylus* D450   *Grablied anf einen Soldaten* D454 →

DASS SIE HIER GEWESEN
(RÜCKERT) OP. 59 NO. 2, **D775** [H520]
C major   1823?

That she has been here

(67 bars)

Dass der Ostwind Düfte	The east wind
Hauchet in die Lüfte,	Breathes fragrance into the air,
Dadurch tut er kund,	And so doing it makes known
Dass du hier gewesen.	That you have been here!
Dass hier Tränen rinnen,[1]	Since tears flow here
Dadurch wirst du innen,	You will know,
Wär's dir sonst nicht kund,	Though you are otherwise unaware,
Dass ich hier gewesen.	That I have been here!
Schönheit oder Liebe,	Beauty or love:
Ob versteckt sie bliebe?	Can they remain concealed?
Düfte tun es und	Fragrant scents and
Tränen kund,	Tears proclaim
Dass sie hier gewesen.	That she has been here!

FRIEDRICH RÜCKERT (1788–1866); poem written in 1819/20

This is the second of Schubert's six Rückert solo settings (1822–3). See the poet's biography for a chronological list of all the Rückert settings

No matter how many times one hears this song, it always comes as a surprise. It seems astoundingly modern, prophesying the Wagner of *Tristan und Isolde,* or perhaps French impressionism (which was what Alfred Einstein heard in it). The opening 'ambiguous elevenths' remind Richard Capell of *Herr, was trägt der Boden hier*, from Hugo Wolf's *Spanisches Liederbuch*. Franz Liszt was clearly thinking of by *Dass sie hier gewesen* when he set Hebbel's *Blume und Duft* in 1862. Verbal imagery of scarcely moving breezes ('Nicht ein Lüftchen regt sich leise') inspired Richard Strauss to similar chromatic chords phrased in pairs of minims in *Ruhe, meine Seele!* (another C major song that begins far away from its home tonality). Not for the first time in the Rückert settings, as well as in the Goethe songs from the *Westöstlicher Divan*, the oriental background encourages Schubert to experiment with something new and exotic.

It is unusual, even in the word-order of German language, for a song lyric to begin with a clause that starts in mid-air – 'That the east wind breathes fragrance . . .'. (We may observe, however, that if a clause describes the permeation of fragrance, mid-air is a very logical place for it to start.) Something indefinite comes before concrete information; in the same way, an indefinable feminine fragrance carried by the east wind precedes the realization that 'she' has recently been there in person.

To put this idea to music, Schubert starts in harmonic limbo with diminished sevenths decorated with accented passing notes whereby the emotions of sexual longing are squeezed and pressed like perfume atomizers. The chords are phrased away in the same delicate, sighing-swooning way that we have encountered in *Geheimes* D719. Schubert has imagined the wind as coming from the East, as much as simply from the east: no merry sea breeze but something heavy with the fragrance of 'östliche Rosen' (the 'eastern roses' that Rückert gave to the title of his collection of verse, 1822). The music feels its way, as if depicting the blind, the awe-struck, those who are emotionally isolated. The straining eye or ear is relatively common in lieder, but here, uniquely in song, we have the sentient nostril. At 'Dadurch tut er kund' (bb. 9–12) the

---

[1] Rückert's original reads '*Weil* hier Tränen rinnen'

haze of harmony turning around on itself and stopping the music in its tracks seems confused, the lack of harmonic orientation a metaphor for something in the air, something not yet identified; the halting gait of the word-setting depicts the effort involved in identifying the intruder. And suddenly, oh sweet delight, the scents make sense.

It is miraculous that Schubert has found a means to create a musical analogue for something as nebulous, yet emotionally engaging, as the fragrance of the beloved. Yes, of course, it is her, for her fragrance is unique. Now that the mystery is solved, the world of chromaticism is temporarily abandoned in favour of the diatonic lyricism of C major; the arrival of the long-awaited tonic chord at 'gewesen' (bb. 15–16) is prepared by a bar of G^7 harmony. The phrase 'Dass du hier gewesen', a dreamy descent followed by a rapturous rise, is repeated like a magic incantation. After that, the vocal line is complemented by the accompaniment which imitates it at a distance of two bars (b. 13 in the vocal line, 15 in the piano). The lover and the object of his love are still separated; the piano interlude stops in its tracks, interrupted by a whole bar's rest (b. 18), as if the singer has been struck by another thought. His delight in his perfumed discovery has made him forget his disturbed state of mind.

The second verse is an exact musical repeat of the first. Now the returning diminished harmonies represent anguish as he realizes that his tears can have no fragrance, and that the beloved will never know that *he* has been there after she has left. As for the sight of teardrops on the ground, one person's look very much like another's. There is no reciprocity in this one-way olfactory experience, and that poignant realization is the subject of this verse. Schubert modifies and extends the imitative piano interlude (bb. 35–7). This does not fade away as before; instead it grows and climbs, a sequence of quavers in octaves beginning first on C, then E, then G – an eloquent crescendo in the pianist's right hand. The beginning of the poem's third verse is set as part of an interlude rather than as a new musical verse. Now it is the turn of the voice to imitate the piano in those eloquent descending scales, each one beginning higher than the one before as emotion piles on emotion (bb. 38–40). The entry of the voice ('Schönheit oder Liebe') creates between singer and piano the cosseting and caressing thirds and sixths that approximate a lover's touch, a four-bar phrase which ends with a questioning cadence on 'bliebe?' (b. 41).

There is a sense of release and a new openness in the seventh chords, gentler and no longer in diminished harmony, that begin the next section (at 'Düfte tun es und Tränen' bb. 44–50), a final musical verse fashioned out of the poem's two final lines. The extraordinarily elongated setting of '<u>Dü</u>fte' (five and a half beats) sends the fragrances wafting out into the world, and at 'Tränen' (tears) the sighing motif of crotchet quaver (b. 48) in the accompaniment is darkened into the minor. This is a real moment of 'Lachen und Weinen', made more eloquent by an expressive vocal mordent on 'Tränen', the only one in the piece.

In *Du bist die Ruh* D776 Schubert saves up his biggest harmonic surprise for the last verse, and here too, at almost the last moment, he lifts the song into new heights by harmonic sleight of hand. When the words 'Dass <u>sie</u> hier gewesen' occur (a repeated phrase that encompasses bb. 51–4) there is no comfortable return to C major. Instead of beatific calm, we hear a lover's desperation. The direction of the melody is now in reverse: 'dass sie hier' is upwardly inflected, and 'gewesen' droops. For the first time we hear that past participle 'has been' as indicative of a love affair that was, and is no longer. But Schubert, the lover-in-song, is an eternal optimist and memories of love nourish him almost as much as the real thing, a noticeable trait of some of the songs of *Winterreise* that look back to past happiness. A tiny interlude, two bars of those sighing chords, a flat turning into a natural (b. 58), and suddenly we find ourselves, as if by magic, back where we began: the same fragmented tune supported by diminished chords, and the same C major 'Dass sie hier gewesen' with the piano imitating the voice at a distance of two bars. This time the echo of the melody is completed with a feminine cadence of the utmost delicacy. The use of 'sie' (she) rather than the more immediate 'du' (you) of the first strophe emphasizes the valedictory nature of the poem's ending.

Schubert has somehow spun a song out of air. Not even in *Winterreise* do we encounter such deep expression conjured by such slender and economical means, and yet the song remains neglected. Singers who sniff at it should be encouraged to inhale deeply.

Autograph:	Missing or lost
First edition:	Published as Op. 59 no. 2 by Sauer & Leidesdorf, Vienna in September 1826 (P106)
Publication reviews:	*Allgemeine musikalische Zeitung* (Leipzig), No. 17 (25 April 1827), col. 219f. [Waidelich/Hilmar Dokumente I No. 486; Deutsch Doc. Biog. No. 866]
Subsequent editions:	Peters: Vol. 3/30; AGA XX 453: Vol. 8/2; NSA IV: Vol. 3/98; Bärenreiter: Vol. 2/128
Bibliography:	Adelhold 2002, p. 69
	Capell 1928, pp. 200–201
	Fischer-Dieskau 1977, p. 196
Further settings:	Giacomo Meyerbeer (1791–1864) *Sie und Ich (Elle et moi)* (1835)
Discography and timing:	Fischer-Dieskau II 6[8] 3'00
	Hyperion I 35[5]
	Hyperion II 27[8] 2'51 Philip Langridge

⟵ *Auf dem Wasser zu singen* D774   *Lachen und Weinen* D777 ⟶

DEDICATEES

Of the opus numbers assigned to songs published in Schubert's lifetime, twenty-five are without dedicatee, including *Winterreise*. The composer used dedications broadly in two different ways – to acknowledge gratitude (personal, musical and literary) and to make money. On certain occasions these distinctions are blurred, particularly in the case of those people who were rich and in a position to give the composer a grant in return for the dedication – even if Schubert had genuine reason to be grateful to them for their interest and support. In the flowery language accompanying dedications, the use of antiquated, courtly words like 'hochgebohrnen' (for high-born aristocrats) and 'wohlgebohrnen' (for well-born, upper-middle-class Viennese) was care-fully nuanced. The most simple and heartfelt dedications are those where the word 'Freund' (friend) appears on the title page.

Apart from appearances in various almanacs and periodicals, Schubert's songs were not published until 1821, and then, in the beginning at least, only 'on sale or return' (otherwise known as 'on commission'), sparing the publisher any financial risk. It was important to raise funds and this was no doubt achieved through dedications to important movers and shakers in the Viennese establishment who were admirers of Schubert's talent such as Dietrichstein (Op. 1), Fries (Op. 2) and Mosel (Op. 3). The prelate Pyrker (Op. 4) was another enormously impor-tant and generous patron; he was just as important some years later (but less generous) when Schubert's arm was probably more or less twisted to set Pyrker's poems for the two songs of Op. 79. From the musical point of view Schubert owed a debt of gratitude to his former composition teacher Salieri (Op. 5), and to the singer Vogl (Op. 6) who had become his tireless interpreter. Neither man would have been expected to make a present in return for dedications. Széchényi (Op. 7) was the first poet to be honoured with a dedication of settings of his own work, but he was both rich and influential enough to show his gratitude. Esterházy (Op. 8) had been a former employer of Schubert's, and would be so again – except in much better social conditions. He was probably the first of the bread-and-butter dedications for hospitality accepted. This certainly also applied to Franz von Schober's contact, Dankesreither (Op. 12) who may have been nevertheless gracious enough to send the composer a small gift.

In the midst of these important dignitaries Schubert could not forget his own friends and close colleagues. Thus the tenor Barth (Op. 11) was remembered with the dedication of part-songs that he sang superbly, albeit with less publicity than Vogl. The friendship and kindness of Spaun is rewarded with Op. 13, and in the case of Schober, the dedication of Op. 14 is a sign of affectionate devotion. The dedication to Goethe (Op. 19) is the most altruistic of all – the result of pure literary gratitude with no expectation of personal contact or financial reward. There was probably a financial element in the dedication of the songs to Justina von Bruchmann (Op. 20); she was the mother of a friend and was well-to-do – although Schubert had been a frequent guest in her home and may not have expected any money in return. The same is certainly true of Mayrhofer (Op. 21) where the dedication seems to be the discharging of a large debt both of personal and literary gratitude, and an olive-branch between friends who were no longer as close as they once had been. Matthäus von Collin (Op. 22) was rich and in a position to be able to reward Schubert for having conferred on him musical immortality at a stroke with two settings of undeniable greatness. The Opus 23 songs (a song each of Platen and Schober and two settings of Johann Senn) have no dedicatee. It seems that Schubert had wanted to offer these to his friend Senn in the Tyrol but was forbidden to do so by the Censor's Office (the poet was a political exile and was banned from Vienna).

Apart from Vogl and Barth, Schubert was to dedicate three further sets of songs to singers: Schönstein (Op. 25) and Milder (Op. 31) in 1824 and 1825 and the Italian bass Lablache (Op. 83) in 1827. These bows in the direction of gifted colleagues were surely regarded as being free of any element of financial expectation, although Schönstein was wealthy enough to have made Schubert a handsome present for *Die schöne Müllerin*. Of all the society hostesses Schubert visited, he seems to have been fondest of Katharina Lászny (Op. 36) and it is possible to believe that the work dedicated to her, the erotic *Der zürnenden Diana*, was an out-and-out gift. The only painter in this elite group of dedicatees, Schnorr von Carolsfeld (Op. 37), is there due to artistic fellow-feeling and admiration. Similarly, the dedication to Kenner (Op. 38) was made as a result of friendship and was an acknowledgement of a bond between poet and composer that went back to their adolescence. It was meant to make Kenner proud, and it did just that – his pleasure in this gesture lasted a lifetime.

The ideal hostess was someone like Sophie Weissenwolf (Op. 52), a serious music lover whom Schubert rather liked, who was also able to pay for her position, next to Schubert, on a title page (*see* STADLER). The dedication to Mathilde Schwarzenberg (Op. 62), like that to Josephine von Franck (Op. 92) and Maria Kinsky (Op. 96) were almost certainly straightforward financial arrangements negotiated by the publisher, an indication of Schubert's rising star among the public, and the willingness of musical ladies from high society to establish their roles as enlightened *mécènes*. There is no doubt that later in his career Schubert lost the taste for making personal dedications. Perhaps he had too many friends and was loath to insult members of his circle by omission. Important Schubertians like Sonnleithner, Kupelwieser, Bruchmann, Stadler, Ottenwalt, Schwind and Bauernfeld were never song dedicatees. Josef Hüttenbrenner (Op. 116) did manage to acquire a dedication posthumously, but one suspects some sleight of hand on his part (as indeed on the part of Anselm Hüttenbrenner for the dedication of the piano variations D576). If the publisher Haslinger insisted that the Op. 81 songs should be dedicated to the powerful Leipzig critic and poet Rochlitz, Schubert seems to have been unwilling to accede; Haslinger, most unusually, had to dedicate the songs on his own account ('gewidmet vom Verleger'). One feels that the Pinterics (Op. 56) dedication and also the Witteczek (Op. 80) were for services good and true rendered to the composer's cause. Schubert might have recognized in these generous and open-hearted supporters men who were devoted to his music and its future dissemination. Who knows whether they were in a financial position to return the compliment?

The dedication to the poet Seidl (Op. 95) has some of the hallmarks of pleading or friendly duress; this poet was not particularly close to Schubert personally but he was publicity conscious and acutely aware of his reputation and standing. This leaves Schubert's very last dedication, the one to Marie Pachler (Op. 106) of Graz who enchanted the composer with her friendship, hospitality and musical gifts during the summer of 1827. This was at least a dedication in the true sense of the word and a heartfelt 'thank you'. Schubert's dedicatees are now considered in alphabetical order.

Josef Barth (1781–1865) (*see also* SINGERS)
The Czech tenor, choral director and sometime clarinettist was the dedicatee ('Dem Hrn Joseph Barth K. K. Hofsänger gewidmet von seinem Freunde Franz Schubert') of three piano-accompanied male quartets.
Op. 11, advertised for sale on 22 April 1822: *Das Dörfchen* D598, *Die Nachtigall* D724 and *Geist der Liebe* D747

Justina von Bruchmann (1774–1840)
The mother of the poet Franz von Bruchmann, Justina von Bruchmann (née Weis) was the dedicatee ('gewidmet der Wohlgebohrnen Frau Justina Edlen von Bruchmann') of the three songs, perhaps in connection with the death in 1820 of her daughter Sybille.
Op. 20, advertised for sale on 10 April 1823: *Sei mir gegrüsst* D741, *Frühlingsglaube* D686 and *Hänflings Liebeswerbung* D552

Johann Nepomuk von Dankesreither, lithograph by J. Lanzedelly.

Matthäus von Collin (1779–1824) qv
The poet of five Schubert settings was the dedicatee ('dem verfasser derselben Herrn Mathaeus Edlen von Collin gewidmet') of two of them.
Op. 22, advertised for sale on 20 February 1826: *Der Zwerg* D771, *Wehmut* D772

Johann Nepomuk von Dankesreither (1750–1823)
The Bishop of St Pölten was said by Kreissle to have been a relative of Schober's but there is no evidence for this. He was a great admirer of Schubert, and in September 1821 was the host of Schober and Schubert at his Schloss at Ochsenberg not far from St Pölten, while the two friends were intensively at work on their opera *Alfonso und Estrella*. Dankesreither was the dedicatee ('Seiner bischöflichen Gnaden, dem Herrn,

Joh: Nep: Ritter von Dankesreither, Bischof zu St. Pölten . . . in tiefer Ehrfucht gewidmet') of the three Goethe settings known as *Gesänge des Harfners* D478.

Op. 12, advertised for sale on 13 December 1822: *Wer sich der Einsamkeit ergibt, Wer nie sein Brot mit Tränen ass* and *An die Türen will ich schleichen*

Moritz von Dietrichstein (1775–1864) [*see also* COMPOSERS]

Director of the Hoftheater and then Director of the Hofbibliothek, Dietrichstein was an enthusiastic supporter of Schubert's genius from early on. Schubert probably met him first at the home of the playwright Heinrich von Collin. Dietrichstein, also a passable composer of Goethe settings, was the dedicatee ('Seiner Exzellenz dem hochgebohrnen Herrn Moritz Grafen von Dietrichstein in tiefer Ehrfurcht gewidmet') of Schubert's first properly published composition.

Op. 1, advertised for sale on 2 April 1821: *Erlkönig* D328

Johann Karl Esterházy von Galántha (1777–1834)

The count was the employer of Schubert during two summers at his country house at Zseliz during the summers of 1818 and 1824. He was the father of two musical daughters, Marie and Karoline, whom Schubert taught. Esterházy had a bass voice and was pleased to sing Schubert's songs and ensembles. He was the dedicatee ('dem hochgebohrnen Herrn Joh. Carl Grafen Esterházy von Galántha ehrfurchtsvoll gewidmet') of four songs.

Op. 8, advertised for sale on 9 May 1822: *Der Jüngling auf dem Hügel* D702, *Sehnsucht* D516, *Erlafsee* D586, *Am Strome* D539

Josephine von Franck (b. 1789)

She was the wife of Josef von Franck who was a prominent wholesale dealer (Franck & Co.) and also a famous collector of portraits of actors and musicians that her husband had commissioned. She was the dedicatee ('der wohlgebornen Frau Josephine von Franck gewidmet') of the three Goethe settings.

Op. 92 (initially numbered Op. 87), advertised for sale on 11 July 1828: *Der Musensohn* D764, *Auf dem See* D543 and *Geistes-Gruss* D142

Moritz von Fries (1777–1826)

Scion of a powerful business family, Fries was counted the wealthiest man in Austria. He was an avid collector of paintings, drawings and books. He was a patron of Haydn and Beethoven (the dedicatee of the Seventh Symphony). Such was Fries's fame that Schubert's friend Leopold von Sonnleithner thought it important to furnish Schubert with a letter of introduction to Fries with a request that a work might be dedicated him. A gift of 20 ducats (with which Schubert was delighted) was the result of the dedication ('dem Hochgebohrnen Herrn Herrn Moritz Reichsgrafen von Fries . . . gewidmet').

Op. 2, advertised for sale on 30 April 1821: *Gretchen am Spinnrade* D118

Johann Wolfgang von Goethe (1749–1832) qv

Otto Biba has pointed out that because Austrian publishing law made it necessary for a publisher to receive permission for such dedications, Goethe must have given his assent for the one attached to the publication of Op. 19. If so, any evidence of a late flowering of contact between poet and composer has been lost. Despite his disappointments regarding futile attempts to make himself known to the great poet (in 1816 and again in 1821) with consignments of songs, Schubert dedicated ('dem Dichter verehrungsvoll gewidmet') three songs to Goethe.

Op. 19 advertised for sale on 6 June 1825: *An Schwager Kronos* D369, *An Mignon* D161, *Ganymed* D544

Josef Hüttenbrenner (1796–1882) (*see also* FRIENDS AND FAMILY)
The brother of Anselm (the composer), and Heinrich Hüttenbrenner (the poet, qv) was a tenor, a minor composer and a collector of Schubert autographs. In 1818, before Hüttenbrenner left Graz to live in Vienna, Schubert wrote out a copy of *Die Forelle* for him 'as evidence of my profound friendship'. In the early 1820s Josef was something of a secretary and factotum for Schubert who was said to have been irritated by his uncritical devotion and sometimes clumsy (and mostly unsuccessful) attempts to further the Schubertian cause. Nevertheless, Hütten- brenner had been one of the quartet of supporters who had agreed to underwrite the costs of publishing Schubert's first songs in an arrangement that spared the firm of Cappi & Diabelli any financial risk. *Die Erwartung*, an extended Schiller setting, was a work composed in May 1816 but revised much later for publication, appearing in print posthumously. Whether or not the dedication ('Seinem Freunde Josef Hüttenbrenner gewidmet') was actually attached to the (lost) autograph, and whether it represented the composer's intentions, is a matter of speculation. The work appeared posthumously.
Op post. 116, advertised for sale on 13 April 1829: *Die Erwartung* D159

Josef Kenner (1794–1868) qv
This poet was a schoolfriend of Schubert. He does not seem to have continued his work as a writer of verse into his more mature years. It was a sign of exceptional loyalty and friendship on Schubert's part that the publication of the work, an extended ballad that had once been illustrated with seven drawings by Moritz von Schwind, was dedicated ('dem Dichter gewidmet') to Kenner a full decade after it had first been composed.
Op. 38, advertised for sale on 9 May 1825: *Der Liedler* D209

Maria Karolina, Fürstin von Kinsky
The formality of this dedication seems deliberately to distance the composer from the recipient of his gift: ('Ihrer fürstl. Gnaden der Frau Fürstin v. Kinsky . . . in tiefester Ehrfurcht geweiht'), the 'deepest reverence' due entirely to the princess's rank. In fact there is a surviving letter from Princess Kinsky to Schubert (7 July 1828) that charmingly acknowledges Schubert's presence at one of her soirées as well as the dedication (the intermediary role of Karl von Schönstein is made clear). Money is enclosed as 'a poor token of my gratitude'. This graciousness from a high- born aristocrat is surely a sign of Schubert's increasing fame towards the end of his life.
Op. 96 was ready for sale in the summer of 1828: *Die Sterne* D939, *Jägers Liebeslied* D909, *Wandrers Nachtlied* D768 and *Fischerweise* D881

Luigi Lablache (1794–1858) (*see also* SINGERS)
This Italian singer was a member of the opera company at the Kärntnertortheater in Vienna put together by Domenico Barbaia (Barbaja) and was to become the most celebrated bass in Europe with first performances of Bellini and Donizetti to his credit – he was the first Don Pasquale. Schubert, who probably met the singer at the home of Georg Kiesewetter, seems to have struck up a friendship with Lablache, to whom he dedicated ('Herrn Ludwig Lablache gewidmet') three Italian songs.
Op. 83, advertised for sale on 12 September 1827: *L'incanto degli occhi* D902/1, *Il traditor deluso* D902/2 and *Il modo di prender moglie* D902/3

Katharina Lászny, engraving by J. Blaschke

Katharina Lászny von Folkusfálva
(1789–1828)

She was a gifted singer (a famous Susanna in Mozart's *Figaro*) and an equally acclaimed actress under the name of Catinka Buchwieser. In the heady days of the Congress of Vienna she became celebrated as a 'grande horizontale', distributing her favours liberally among the great and the not so good. In 1825 the twenty-one-year-old Moritz von Schwind was astounded to feel himself strongly attracted to the thirty-six-year-old Lászny, and mentions in his diary that Schubert has known her a long time. Schwind adds, almost admiringly, that Lászny is 'held in ill repute throughout the city'. Katharina and her husband Ludwig Lászny, a wealthy Hungarian nobleman, held musical soirées in their home in the Wieden suburb, and Schubert seems to have been a frequent visitor. He dedicated his piano piece, *Divertissement à la Hongroise* D818 to her in 1826. He also dedicated two Mayrhofer settings to her – 'der Frau Katharina von Lacsny gebornen Buchwieser gewidmet'.

Op. 36, advertised for sale on 11 February 1825: *Der zürnenden Diana* D707 and *Nachtstück* D672

Johann Mayrhofer (1787–1836) qv

The poet had been one of Schubert's closest friends and mentors until 1821. Despite an estrangement between the two in the later years of his life, Schubert's dedication ('dem Verfasser der Gedichte gewidmet von seinem Freunde Franz Schubert') indicates a continuing admiration for Mayrhofer's work (the three songs are all settings of the poet) and perhaps even a gesture of reconciliation.

Op. 21, advertised for sale on 19 June 1823: *Auf der Donau* D553, *Der Schiffer* D536 and *Wie Ulfru fischt* D525

Anna Milder (1785–1838) (*see also* SINGERS)

Milder was a great soprano who was often known as Milder-Hauptmann after her marriage. A famous Leonora in Beethoven's *Fidelio* she excited Schubert's admiration as the eponymous heroine of Gluck's *Iphigenia in Tauris* when he was still a stage-struck teenager. Schubert (in a letter of 8 September 1818 to Schober) thought that Milder was 'irreplaceable . . . she sings more beautifully than anyone else – and trills worse than anyone'. He never met Milder but corresponded with her and it is almost certain that he composed *Der Hirt auf dem Felsen* D965 with her in mind – a work without vocal trills! When the second of his *Suleika* songs was published the dedication was 'der wohlgebornen Frau Anna Milder Königl. preuss. Hof Opern Sängerin gewidmet'.

Op. 31, advertised for sale on 12 August 1825: *Suleika II* D717

Ignaz von Mosel, lithograph by Josef Kriehbuber, 1830

Ignaz von Mosel (1772–1844)

Mosel was a distinguished and highly placed civil servant, a friend of Dietrichstein (who was his senior in the administration of the court theatres) and a cultivated amateur musician and composer. He wrote a life of Antonio Salieri and became a great Schubert enthusiast, having more or less monitored the composer's progress from his school days. He was a fervent admirer of the lieder and Schubert was in touch with him regarding *Alfonso und Estrella*. Mosel outlived Schubert by over fifteen years, and in 1843 the older man wrote an important article defining Schubert's musical significance. The dedication ('dem Wohlgebohrnen Herrn Herrn Ignaz Edlen von Mosel . . . hochachtungsvoll gewidmet') of four of Schubert's best-known Goethe settings is an indication of Mosel's high standing in Schubert's mind as a powerful supporter.

Op. 3, advertised for sale on 29 May 1821: *Schäfers Klagelied* D121, *Meeres Stille* D216, *Heidenröslein* D257 and *Jägers Abendlied* D368

Marie Leopoldine Pachler (1794–1855)

Marie Pachler was a sufficiently accomplished pianist to have attracted the admiration of Beethoven in 1817. But it was as Schubert's charming and thoughtful host in Graz in the summer of 1827 that she will always be remembered. Schubert was a guest in the Pachler household between 3 and 20 September of that year and he seems to have been completely taken by the warmth and kindness of the family, including their young son, Faust (1819–1891). It was Marie Pachler who re-introduced Schubert to the poetry of Karl von Leitner which partially accounts for the dedication ('der Wohlgebornen Frau Marie Pachler gewidmet') of an opus number that contained two Leitner settings. The inclusion of Shakespeare's *An Silvia* was a last-minute substitute for a song that had been composed in Graz: *Eine altschottische Ballade*.

Op. 106, issued in the spring of 1828: *Heimliches Lieben* D922, *Das Weinen* D926, *Vor meiner Wiege* D927, *Gesang (An Silvia)* D891

Karl Pinterics (1778–1831)

Pinterics was a high-ranking official and private secretary to Prince Josef Franz Pálffy. He was a good amateur pianist, friend of Beethoven and became an admirer of Schubert and a collector of his music. In his lodgings near the Karlskirche he often gave parties where Schubert's music was to be heard. He seems to have been something of an adviser to Schubert; apparently it was Pinterics who in 1824 counselled him against taking counterpoint lessons from Simon Sechter, considering this inappropriate for such a well-established composer. In 1828, Schubert went to Sechter nevertheless, although only on this one occasion at the end of his life. The dedication to Pinterics ('Herrn Carl Pinterics von seinem Freunde Franz Schubert') is a clear indication that he was something more to Schubert than a well-placed aristocratic sponsor.

Op. 56, advertised for sale on 14 July 1826: *Willkommen und Abschied* D767, *An die Leier* D737 and *Im Haine* D738

Johann Ladislaus von Pyrker (1772–1857) qv
This famous and powerful cleric, Patriarch of Venice, was uniquely the dedicatee of two sets of Schubert songs. In the first instance, Op. 4, the songs were dedicated to him ('Sr Excellenz dem hochgebohrnen und hochwürdigsten Herrn Herrn Johann Ladislav Pyrker v. Felsö-Eör in tiefer Ehrfurcht gewidmet') because he had expressed an interest in *Der Wanderer* D489 after a performance at the home of Matthäus von Collin. The second set of songs, Op. 79, composed in Gastein, was two settings of Pyrker's own poems that were more or less set at the poet's behest. (The dedication's wording was exactly the same as that of the Op. 4.) Apparently Schubert received a satisfactory monetary gift after the first dedication, but not after the second.
Op. 4, advertised for sale on 29 May 1821: *Der Wanderer* D489, *Morgenlied* D685, *Wandrers Nachtlied* D224
Op. 79, advertised for sale on 16 May 1827: *Das Heimweh* D851, *Die Allmacht* D852

Antonio Salieri (1750–1825) (*see also* COMPOSERS)
The famous opera composer, and Schubert's composition teacher between 1812 and 1816, was the dedicatee ('dem Wolhgebohrnen Herrn Anton Salieri . . . hochachtungsvoll gewidmet') of five of Schubert's finest Goethe settings.
Op. 5, advertised for sale on 9 July 1821: *Rastlose Liebe* D138, *Nähe des Geliebten* D162, *Der Fischer* D225, *Erster Verlust* D226, *Der König in Thule* D367

Ludwig Ferdinand Schnorr von Carolsfeld (1788–1853)
Schnorr is the only visual artist to be honoured among Schubert's dedicatees. (It seems extraordinary that neither Schubert's close friend Leopold Kupelwieser nor Moritz von Schwind, Schnorr's pupil and the person who brought Schnorr into the Schubert circle, were honoured thus.) Schnorr was a member of the Friedrich von Schlegel circle and a Catholic convert. He attended the reading circle of Schober in 1822 and it is almost certainly here that Schubert came to know him. Otherwise, there is no documented link between the composer and painter, but in an old art history book there is mention of a painting by Schnorr (now disappeared) that shows Schubert in the company of the painter, together with Schwind and Bauernfeld. The dedication of two Schiller settings ('Seinem Freunde L. F. Schnorr von Karolsfeld gewidmet') is perhaps a sign of the painter's partiality to this poet.
Op. 37, advertised for sale on 28 February 1825: *Der Pilgrim* D794 and *Der Alpenjäger* D588

Franz von Schober (1796–1882) qv
It is a measure of the closeness of friendship between Schubert and Schober that the poet was the dedicatee ('Seinem Freunde Franz Ritter von Schober gewidmet') of one of Schubert's finest works, the first *Suleika* setting. It is very likely that at some point Schober had expressed an admiration for this great song. The singer's mood in *Geheimes*, charming as well as secretive, might have chimed with Schober's behaviour regarding his clandestine engagement to Justina von Bruchmann.
Op. 14, advertised for sale on 13 December 1822: *Suleika I* D720 and *Geheimes* D719

Carl Baron von Schönstein (1796–1876) (*see also* SINGERS)
A Hungarian-born lawyer by training who became an important civil servant, Schönstein was also an extremely gifted amateur singer – a high baritone. At the beginning of his career he loved Italian music above all, but after his meeting with Schubert in the summer of 1818

(through the Esterházy family) he became absorbed in German lieder, Schubert's songs in particular. He was second only to Johann Michael Vogl in Schubert's estimation, and Schönstein who was Schubert's exact contemporary, modelled his interpretations on those of the older singer. The music that was most associated with him was *Die schöne Müllerin*, the major cycle of twenty songs that was dedicated to him ('dem Carl Freyherrn von Schönstein gewidmet') and published in five volumes.

Op. 25, advertised for sale on 17 February 1824 (Vol. 1), 24 March 1824 (Vol. 2) and 12 August 1824 (vols 3–5): *Die schöne Müllerin* D795

Mathilde Therese Walpurgis Franciska Fürstin zu Schwarzenberg (1804–86)

It is not certain whether Schubert had any direct contact with this highly musical aristocrat, daughter of the patron of Haydn and Beethoven and sister of a future Austrian prime minister. She had been crippled until the age of seventeen when she was miraculously cured by a controversial healer. The tenor Josef Barth was employed in her father's household and this may have been a link between her and the composer. The dedication of this important opus number ('der Fürstin Mathilde zu Schwarzenberg ehrfurchtsvoll zugeeignet') was almost certainly rewarded financially.

Op. 62, advertised for sale on 2 March 1827: *Gesänge aus* Wilhelm Meister D877 (i) *Mignon und der Harfner* ('Nur wer die Sehnsucht kennt' as a duet); (ii) *Lied der Mignon* ('Heiss mich nicht reden'); (iii) *Lied der Mignon* ('So lasst mich scheinen); (iv) *Lied der Mignon* ('Nur wer die Sehnsucht kennt')

Johann Gabriel Seidl (1804–75) qv

Schubert wrote greater Seidl settings than the light-hearted and slightly banal *Vier Refrain-Lieder*, but it was these that were dedicated ('dem Dichter freundschäftlichst gewidmet') by Schubert and published a few months before his death. The dedication may have been in recognition of the fact that Seidl had probably done a great deal of work to acquire the commission for these songs from the publisher. Seidl may also have earlier made his possible displeasure known to Schubert that the Op. 80 songs, three settings of his poems published in 1827, had not been dedicated to him. It is clear that Schubert felt himself closer to their dedicatee Witteczek (p. 414).

Op. 95, advertised for sale on 13 August 1828: *Refrain Lieder* D866 (i) *Die Unterscheidung*; (ii) *Bei dir allein!*; (iii) *Die Männer sind mechant*; (iv) *Irdisches Glück*

Johann Senn (1795–1857) qv

This poet was obviously meant to be the dedicatee of Schubert's Op. 23 which appeared in August 1823 and included two setting of Senn's poems. The poet had been a political pariah, since 1820. He had been jailed for sedition in Vienna and then exiled to his hometown of Innsbruck in the Tyrol. The appearance of his name on a title page would not have been permitted (preceding opus numbers were dedicated to Schubert's poets and friends Mayrhofer and Collin). Mayrhofer, who worked at the censor's office, might have persuaded his colleagues to overlook the fact that Senn was clearly named as the poet of two songs.

Op. 23 appeared without dedication and Senn remained an invisible dedicatee.

Josef von Spaun (1788–1865) qv (*see also* FRIENDS AND FAMILY)

This most faithful and reliable of all Schubert's friends was the dedicatee ('seinem Freunde Jos: Edlen von Spaun, k.k. Bankal Assessor gewidmet') of a set of songs by miscellaneous poets. Schubert's setting of Spaun's own words, *Der Jüngling und der Tod* D545 was not published in the composer's lifetime. The dedication refers to Spaun's position in Linz, a post that is part of the title of Schubert's musical joke *Herrn Josef Spaun, Assessor in Linz* D749.

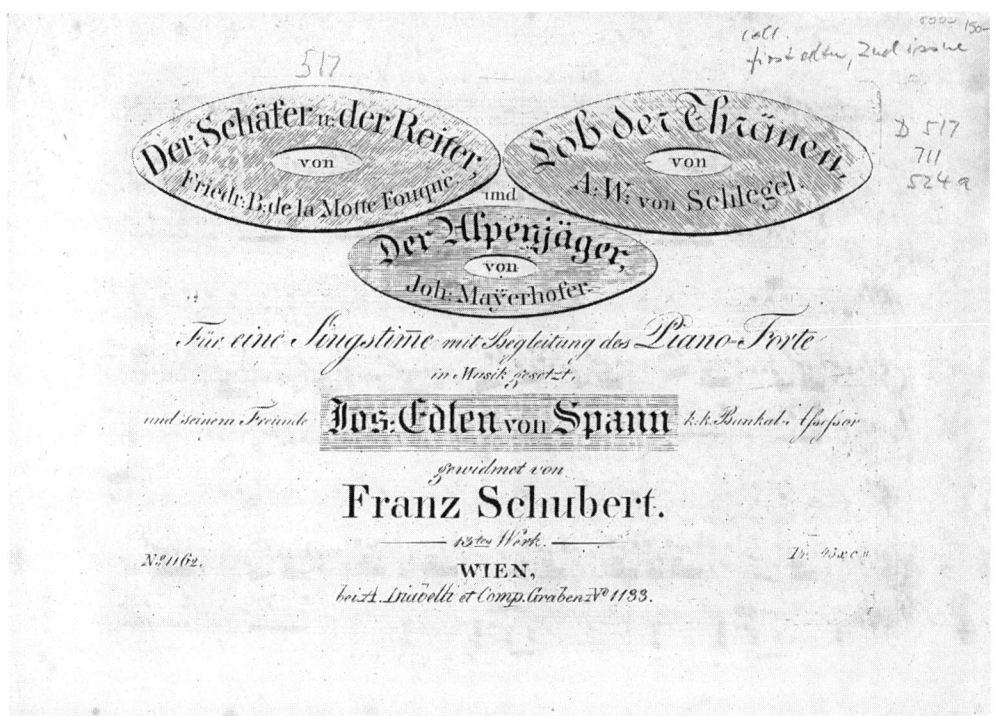

Three songs Op. 13 dedicated to Josef von Spaun.

Op. 13, advertised for sale on 13 December 1822: *Der Schäfer und der Reiter* D517, *Lob der Tränen* D711 and *Der Alpenjäger* D524

Ludwig von Széchényi (1781–1855) qv
This high-ranking noble and civil servant was an amateur poet and important official of the Musikverein. Schubert set two of his songs with a dedication to the poet ('dem hochgebohrnen Herrn Herrn Grafen Ludwig Széchényi von Sarvári-Felsö-Vidék . . . hochachtungsvoll gewidmet') alongside a setting by Matthäus von Collin. The latter would thoroughly eclipse the two Széchényi settings.
Op. 7, advertised for sale on 27 November 1821: *Die abgeblühte Linde* D514, *Der Flug der Zeit* D515, *Der Tod und das Mädchen* D531

Johann Michael Vogl (1768–1840) (*see also* SINGERS)
The famous opera singer who became a devoted supporter of the Schubertian cause through countless performances of Schubert's songs was the dedicatee ('dem Wohlgebohrnen Herrn Michael Vogl, Mitglied und Regisseur des k.k. Hofoperntheaters hochachtungsvoll gewidmet') of a set of songs that included two Mayrhofer settings on classical subjects.
Op. 6, advertised for sale on 23 August, 1821: *Memnon* D541, *Antigone und Oedip* D542 and *Am Grabe Anselmos* D504

Sophie Gräfin von Weissenwolf (1794–1847)
The Weissenwolffs were musical aristocrats who lived at Castle Steyregg (seven kilometres from Linz) in the summers and gave frequent musical parties there. They were acquainted with Schubert's friends, Albert Stadler and Josef von Spaun, and Schubert may have met the couple during his visit to the region in the summer of 1823. Sophie sang songs from *Die schöne Müllerin* hot off the press in 1824 and Schubert stayed as a guest at Steyregg several times in the summer

Sophie von Weissenwolff.

and autumn of 1825. Schubert wrote to his parents that 'the countess . . . is a great admirer of my humble self, has all my songs and sings them most prettily'. He had with him the Walter Scott settings in manuscript. In the same letter he wrote that the countess 'even made it clear that it would by no means displease her if I were to dedicate them to her'. The composer did just this ('der Hochgebornen Frau Frau Sophie Gräfin v. Weissenwolff geboren Gräfin v. Breunner hochachtungsvoll gewidmet') and probably received a welcome financial gift in return.

Op. 52, in two volumes, advertised for sale on 5 April 1826: *Sieben Gesänge aus Walter Scott's Fräulein vom See* Vol. 1 (i) *Ellens Gesang I* D837; (ii), *Ellens Gesang II* D838; (iii) *Bootgesang* D835; (iv) *Coronach* D836; Vol. 2 (v) *Normans Gesang* D846; (vi) *Ellens Gesang III* ('Ave Maria') D839; (vii) *Lied des gefangenen Jägers* D843

Josef Wilhlem Witteczek (1787–1859) (*see also* AUTOGRAPHS, ALBUMS AND COLLECTIONS)

He was a civil servant (Schubert met him through Josef von Spaun) and a passionate music lover. He became a fervent admirer of Schubert and hosted various Schubertiads in his apartment, both before and after the composer's death. In 1831 he took over the collection of copies of Schubert's songs that had been owned by Karl Pinterics and added to it with copies of all the

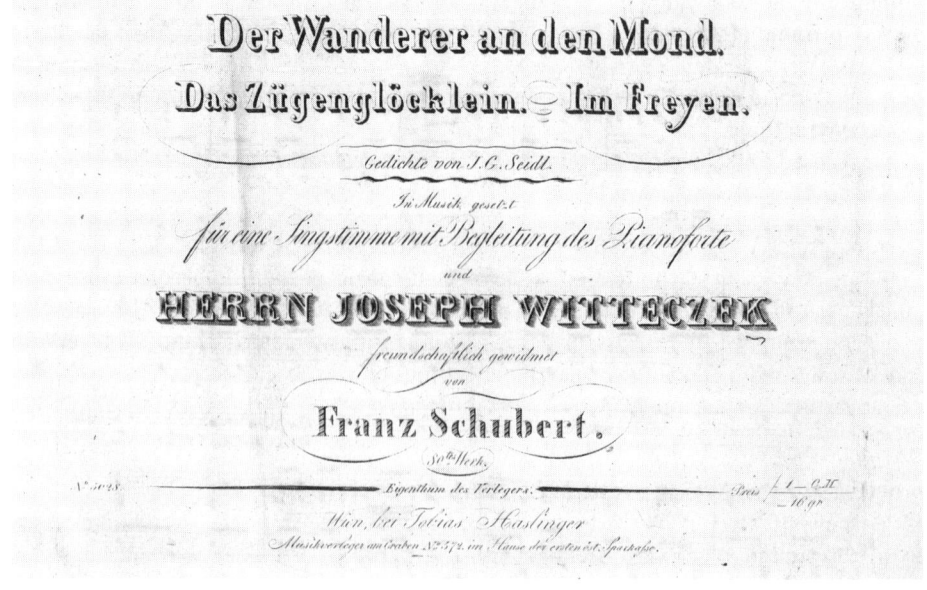

Three songs Op. 80 dedicated to Joseph Witteczek.

Schubert printed material up until 1850, taking great care to obtain copies of songs not yet published. The collection, left to Josef von Spaun at Wittezcek's death, also included other material – reviews, portraits, ephemera – that made the collection perhaps the most important of all Schubertian sources. On Spaun's death this 'Witteczek–Spaun' collection was left to the Musikverein in Vienna and was to prove invaluable in the preparation of the *Gesamtausgabe* of the composer's works that was issued at the end of the nineteenth century. The three Seidl settings were dedicated to Witteczek ('Herrn Joseph Witteczek freundschaftlich gewidmet') in recognition of his devotion to the composer's cause.

Op. 80, advertised for sale on 25 May 1827: *Der Wanderer an den Mond* D870, *Das Zügenglöcklein* D871, *Im Freien* D880

JOHANN LUDWIG FERDINAND, FREIHERR VON DEINHARD-DEINHARDSTEIN (1794–1859)

THE POETIC SOURCE
S1 *Selam, Ein Almanach für Freunde des Mannigfaltigen*, ed. Castelli, Anton Strauss, Vienna, 1814

THE SONG
15 October 1815   *Skolie* D306 [S1 p. 208]

Deinhard-Deinhardstein carved out an impressive career in Metternich's Vienna as a civil servant and writer. Castelli, another important Viennese figure in something of the same mould, referred to the poet's 'geniale Keckheit' ('brilliant cheekiness'). This highly talented bon viveur changed his job many times, bettering his position with each new appointment; he taught aesthetics at the university, worked as a censor and became vice-director of the Burgtheater. He was editor of various publications, the most notable of which was the *Jahrbuch der Litteratur* (from 1829 until 1849 – a previous editor had been the poet Matthäus von Collin qv) which put forward the government's 'patriotic' viewpoint. The innocuous poem of his set by Schubert (containing the seemingly de rigueur nineteenth-century Germanic link between death and drinking) pre-dates Deinhard-Deinhardstein's rise to prominence; it was published in the annual *Selam* for 1814 (of which Castelli was the editor, incidentally) when the poet was twenty-four years old. It is not printed in his collected works. Deinhard-Deinhardstein's greatest achievements were in the theatre; his

J.L. Deinhardstein, lithograph by Josef Kriehuber (1830).

Hans Sachs (1827) is counted one of his notable successes.

Schubert had some personal dealings with Deinhardstein although it is not certain when. Through Leopold von Sonnleithner Schubert was commissioned to compose *Am Geburtstage des Kaisers* D748, a hymn for soloists, chorus and orchestra, to a text of Deinhardstein honouring the Emperor Franz I. Diabelli published this as *Constitutionslied* in 1849. Deinhard-Deinhardstein died on 12 July 1815.

DELPHINE *see* *ZWEI SZENEN AUS DEM SCHAUSPIEL LACRIMAS* D857/1

DIDONE ABBANDONATA *see* VEDI QUANTO ADORO D510

DITHYRAMBE (I)   Dithyramb   Soloists TB
(SCHILLER) **D47** [H21]   & choir (SATB)
D major   (Fragment) 29 March 1813

(89+82 bars)

Nimmer, das glaubt mir, erscheinen die Götter,	Never, believe me, do the gods
Nimmer allein.	Appear alone.
Kaum dass ich Bacchus, den lustigen, habe,	No sooner is jolly Bacchus with me
Kommt auch schon Amor, der lächelnde Knabe,	Than Cupid comes too, the smiling boy,
Phöbus der Herrliche findet sich ein.	And glorious Phoebus arrives.
Sie nahen, sie kommen, die Himmlischen alle,	They approach, they are here, all the deities;
Mit Göttern erfüllt sich die irdische Halle.	This earthly abode is filled with gods.
Sagt, wie bewirt ich, der Erdegeborne,	Tell me, how shall I, earth-born,
Himmlischen Chor?	Entertain the heavenly choir?
Schenket mir euer unsterbliches Leben,	Bestow on me your immortal life.
Götter! Was kann euch der Sterbliche geben?	O gods! What can a mortal give you?
Hebet zu eurem Olymp mich empor!	Raise me up to your Olympus!
Die Freude, sie wohnt nur in Jupiters Saale,	Joy dwells only in the hall of Jupiter;
O füllet mit Nektar, o reich mir die Schale!	Fill the cup with nectar and pass it to me!
Reich ihm die Schale! O schenke dem Dichter,	Pass him the cup!
Hebe, nur ein; schenke nur ein!	Hebe, give the poet to drink!
Netz ihm die Augen mit himmlischem Taue,	Moisten his eyes with celestial dew,
Dass er den Styx, den verhassten, nicht schaue,	That he may not behold the hateful Styx;
Einer der Unsern sich dünke zu sein.	That he may deem himself one of us.
Sie rauschet, sie perlet, die himmlische Quelle,	It murmurs, it bubbles, the heavenly spring,
Der Busen wird ruhig, das Auge wird helle.	The heart grows calm, the eye grows bright.

FRIEDRICH VON SCHILLER (1759–1805); poem written in 1796

By the spring of 1813 Salieri seems to have been willing to allow his young student Schubert to prepare some of his composition exercises using German poetry. Sketches for unaccompanied voices with texts excerpted from Schiller's *Elysium* (D51, 53, 54, 57, 58) date from April and May 1813. In the same period there are five settings with different texts from the poet's *Der Triumph der Liebe* (D55, 61, 62, 63, 64). A fragment of Schiller's *Gruppe aus dem Tartarus* (otherwise known through the famous solo song D396) was also used for an exercise (D65). D67 is a fragment from Schiller's *Der Flüchtling* (D402). The same poet's *Spruch des Konfuzius* is set twice in July 1813 (D69, D70) followed by *Die zwei Tugendwege* (D71). In October 1813 there was a brief return to *Elysium* (D60). These sixteen exercises, plus a *Sanctus* (D56) and an *Alleluja* in F (D71A) were all devoted to the writing of unaccompanied three-part harmony, mostly for two tenors and bass. So much for Holzapfel's slur on Salieri for not being a very thorough teacher!

The setting of *Dithyrambe* for tenor, bass and chorus is contemporary with this period of exercises. Although there is nothing to prove a link with Salieri's lessons, it seems possible that the ageing Italian master decided to allow Schubert his head and see what he could do with a larger project. The manuscript has survived only in a fragmentary form, but there is enough of the piano writing to give a clear idea of its style. It is also possible that the work was written for a real performance within the school or home, and that a piano part was provided simply because it was unrealistic for a young composer to conceive something with orchestral accompaniment.

The work opens in D major with an ascending arpeggio (sometimes known as a 'Mannheim rocket') that shoots to the top of Olympus. This straightaway gives the work a symphonic feel and there is little throughout the piece to suggest intimate interaction of voice and piano. Neither should there be: this is a Bacchanal on a grand scale, a real public occasion. The idea of happiness (Bacchus, *der lustige*) is conveyed by upbeats consisting of smiling little semiquaver gruppetti reminiscent of the figuration that pervades Mozart's 'Rondo alla turca'. The vocal line goes into semiquavers only once, for a delightful little melisma on 'Knabe'. The entrance of the SATB chorus with its panting accompaniment on the fifth line of the strophe ('Sie nahen, sie kommen') is an inspired touch: everyone wants to rush to this party, and the build-up suggests the approach of the heavenly throng from afar. The monolithic choral writing in long note values supported by restlessly pulsating quavers is pure Gluck. At the second appearance of the phrase 'Die Himmlischen alle' the vigorous syncopations between the pianist's hands suggest the introduction to *Divinités du Styx* from *Alceste*, as if Schubert, when writing music for the gods, thinks of Olympus as a higher form of Hades. After a great deal of loud choral music the final two appearances of 'Himmlischen alle' are marked piano. These lofty chords in minims and semibreves are accompanied by soft, rippling arpeggios: the effect is somewhat ethereal, as if the upper reaches of Olympus are swathed in mists of sound. The energetic setting of 'Mit Göttern erfüllt sich die irdische Halle' recalls features of the opening music almost like a development section leading to a recapitulation of the D major of the opening. The banal piano interlude before this, a series of turns ascending the keyboard, is, surprisingly enough, genuine Schubert.

The second verse has the bass singing a variant of the tenor solo, less florid and ending with a short recitative ('Hebet zu eurem Olymp mich empor!') which introduces the chorus. With these forces and this poet, one cannot help thinking of the bass solo that follows the vocal quartet in launching the *Ode to Joy* in Beethoven's Ninth Symphony, but we have to remind ourselves that Beethoven's masterpiece was composed eleven years later.

The chorus takes over the rest of the verse; the fluency of the part writing shows that the composer benefited from his tutorials with Salieri. Where the music moves from the home key of D to B flat major, and later to G minor, Schubert seems to have had fun with the weaving of inner textures, and the oscillations that playfully suggest drunkenness among the gods (cf. the Shakespeare *Trinklied* – 'Bacchus, feister Fürst des Weins' D888, with its similar depiction, in the accompaniment particularly, of the inebriation caused by the same god). The setting breaks off towards the end of the second verse. There is no surviving music to the third verse, and we do not even know whether the composer intended to set it in the first place.

   This choral piece could not be more different from the famous solo version of this song, *Dithyrambe* D801 with its cheeky and disrespectful irony. Much later in his career Schubert was not afraid to laugh at the ridiculous posturing of the gods. In 1813, however, the dwellers on Olympus seemed worthy of much more serious treatment.

Autograph:	Wienbibliothek im Rathaus, Vienna
First edition:	Completed, arranged and published privately by Reinhard Van Hoorickx from manuscripts in the Vienna Stadtsbibliothek; subsequently published as part of the NSA in 1982 (P783)
Subsequent editions:	Not in AGA; NSA III: Vol. 2b/295
Discography and timing:	Hyperion I 33[13] James Gilchrist, Brandon Velarde & The Hyperion II 2[17] 4'21 London Schubert Chorale (dir. Stephen Layton)

← *Totengräberlied* D44   *Die Schatten* D50 →

DITHYRAMBE (II)   Dithyramb
(SCHILLER) OP. 60 NO. 2, **D801** [H602]

The song exists in two versions, the second of which is discussed below.
(1) Date unknown; (2) 1824? or 1826?

(1)   'Geschwind und feurig'   A major   §   [33 bars]

(2)   A major

(35 bars)

See previous entry for poem and translation

FRIEDRICH VON SCHILLER (1759–1805); poem written in 1796

This is the last of Schubert's forty-four Schiller solo settings (1811–24). See the poet's biography for a chronological list of all the Schiller settings

The dithyramb originated in Greece in the seventh century BC. It was a hymn of praise in honour of Dionysius (Bacchus), the wine god, one of whose surnames was Dithyrambus. The writer Archilochus observed that the lead singer at the banquet should be 'wit-stricken by the thunderbolt of wine'. Simonides, Pindar and Bacchylides all composed dithyrambs. In a later period the form became so ornate and overblown that the word became a synonym for 'bombast'.

Schubert had first attempted to set this text in March 1813. Two pieces of a fragment exist for tenor and bass solo with SATB chorus (*see* above). Thirteen years later he returned to the poem to make his last complete Schiller setting, perhaps the most popular. It continues the jollifications initiated in *Elysium* D584, with the same sense of unreality and amusement that one relishes in that work. These gods are awfully cheery people; wreaths of grapes replace grapes of wrath, and even Prometheus would be invited for a conciliatory drink if his liver were able to stand the pace. The cast list is impressive: all the top people are there in the manner of an old Hollywood biopic – 'Brahms meet Liszt; Liszt this is Showpan' – but old J. S. Bacchus, well-tempered as ever, comes first, as is correct and proper in a form dedicated to his honour. The date of the song is not certain; paper studies suggest 1826 when Schubert made a copy for the publisher. John Reed puts forward the interesting idea that the piece may have been written in the summer of 1824 for Count Esterházy, who was a bass, during Schubert's stay in Zseliz. This music seems rather racy, however, for the count's somewhat grave temperament (cf. *Das Abendrot* D627, a song that was definitely written for him).

In ancient Greek times, fifty men and boys danced a dithyramb to reed flute accompaniment, and the composer makes a rollicking dance that depicts an equally impressive throng. There is a bibulous exaggeration to this music which implies that the gods are no better behaved than the young men who might have sung it in a university refectory, rather than at a heavenly banquet. There is great strength in the rolling oscillations and thundered dotted triplets of b. 1 (A major – C sharp minor), a rhythmic conjunction that is repeated in b. 2 (F sharp minor – C sharp major) that leads, in turn, to a bar of staccato quavers (heavy rather than graceful, like a dancing Elektra) that land firmly in the dominant (b. 5). The vocal line zestfully takes up the dotted rhythm that has been a feature of the introductory piano music. There are large stretches of harmony here, solid as chunks of marble, underpinned by the important pedal notes A and E, tonic and dominant. From b. 14 there is a four-bar D pedal; the subdominant here means the less-than-dominant deities – Phöbus in Verse 1, Hebe in Verse 2 – and a sideways glance in their direction. It sounds as if Zeus/Jupiter himself is commanding Hebe in a peremptory tone of voice (bb. 8–9, third strophe), but in fact it is the poet – the narrative voice, Schiller himself. At 'Sie nahen, sie kommen, die Himmlischen alle' the dance music takes on a lilting Viennese charm; at bb. 19–20 left-hand quavers are plucked as deliciously as if pizzicati on a double bass. In their carousings even the gods are not immune to nudges and winks, slap and tickle. If the gods were Christian they would be expected to set an example to mankind; in this music there seems to be a definite sense of relief that they are not. *Dithyrambe* was first performed in Vienna on the day after Schubert's death; the song was rediscovered by Schubertians in the late 1930s when Elena Gerhardt recorded it. In the Peters Edition the vocal line is printed in the treble clef, but in both the AGA and NSA it is in the bass. The version printed as definitive in the AGA (the only surviving autograph) appears as the first version in the NSA (Volume 3b). This has a shorter postlude than the version prepared by Schubert for publication in July 1826. Beyond this date there is no information about when the song may have been composed – although speculation points to a date between 1824 and 1826.

Autograph:	Schiller National-Museum, Marbach am Neckar, Germany (first version)
Publication:	AGA Vol. 8 in 1895 (P693A) (first version)
	Published as Op. 60 no. 2 by Cappi & Czerny, Vienna in 1826 (P101) (second version)
First known performance:	20 November 1828 (the day after Schubert's death), *Abend-Unterhaltung* of the Gesellschaft der Musikfreunde, Musikverein, Vienna. Soloist: Wenzel Nejebse (see Waidelich/Hilmar

	Dokumente I No. 643 for full concert programme); according to an entry in Franz von Hartmann's diary, the piece was also performed at a Schubertiad on 21 April 1827 (see Deutsch Doc. Biog. No. 855)
Publication reviews:	*Berliner allgemeine musikalische Zeitung*, no. 11 (14 March 1827), p. 81ff. [Waidelich/Hilmar Dokumente I No. 461; Deutsch Doc. Biog. No. 826]
Subsequent editions:	Peters: Vol. 2/128; AGA XX 457: Vol. 8/14; NSA IV: Vol. 3a/110 & 3b/214; Bärenreiter: Vol. 2/140
Bibliography:	Capell 1928, pp. 203–4 Fischer-Dieskau 1977, pp. 189–90
Further settings:	J. F. Reichardt (1752–1814) *Dithyrambe*, No. 43 from *Schillers lyrischte Gedichte* Zweites Heft (1811)
Discography and timing:	Fischer-Dieskau II 6¹² 2'49

Discography and timing: Fischer-Dieskau II 6^{12} 2'49

Hyperion I 11^{18}

Hyperion II 32^{8} 2'40   Brigitte Fassbaender

← *Über Wildemann* D884   *Trinklied* D888 →

DOCH IM GETÜMMEL DER SCHLACHT *see ALFONSO UND ESTRELLA* D732 NO. 8

Das DÖRFCHEN
(BÜRGER) OP. 11 NO. 1, **D598** [H394]
D major   December 1817

The hamlet

Quartet TTBB

(158 bars)

Ich rühme mir	I take pride
Mein Dörfchen hier!	In my hamlet here,
Denn schön're Auen,	For nowhere else
Als rings umher	Do fairer meadows bloom
Die Blicke schauen,	Than the eye can see
Blüh'n nirgends mehr.	All around.
[(. . . 4 lines . . .)]	[(. . . 4 lines . . .)]
Dort Ährenfelder	Behold the fields of corn
Und Wiesengrün,	And the green pastures,
Dem blaue Wälder	Bordered
Die Grenze zieh'n!	By blue woods

An jener Höhe	On yonder hill
Die Schäferei,	The sheep farm,
Und in der Nähe	And nearby
Mein Sorgenfrei!	My 'Free from Care'.
So nenn' ich meine	For that is what I call
Geliebte, meine kleine[1]	My beloved little
Einsiedelei,	Retreat
Worin ich lebe,	Where I live
Zur Lust erweckt,[2]	In joy,
Die ein Gewebe	And which a network
Von Ulm' und Rebe	Of elms and vines
Grün überdeckt.	Drapes in green.
Dort kränzen Schlehen	There sloes adorn
Die braune Kluft,	The brown crevasse,
Und Pappeln wehen	And poplars sway
In blauer Luft.	In the blue air.
Mit sanftem Rieseln	A limpid brook
[(. . . 1 line . . .)]	[(. . . 1 line . . .)]
Auf Silberkieseln	Steals unhurriedly
Ein heller Bach;	Over silver pebbles.
Fliesst unter den Zweigen,[3]	Now it flows beneath the branches
Die über ihn	That arch
Sich wölbend neigen,	Shyly
Bald schüchtern hin;	Above it;
Lässt bald im Spiegel	Now it mirrors
Den grünen Hügel,	On its bed
Wo Lämmer geh'n,	The green hillside
Des Ufers Büschchen	Where lambs frisk,
Und alle Fischchen	The little bushes on the bank
Im Grunde seh'n.	And all the little fish.
Da gleiten Schmerlen	There loach glide
Und blasen Perlen,	And pearls bubble;
Ihr schneller Lauf	Their rapid course
Geht bald hernieder,[4]	Goes now down,
Und bald herauf	Now up again
Zur Fläche wieder;	To the surface.
[(. . . 69 lines . . .)]	[(. . . 69 lines . . .)]
O Seligkeit!	O bliss!
Dass doch die Zeit	May time
Dich nie zerstöre!	Never destroy you!
Mir frisches Blut,	Grant me ever anew

[1] The addition of *meine* is Schubert's.
[2] Bürger's original verb in this line is 'versteckt'.
[3] The addition of *den* is Schubert's.
[4] Bürger writes *hinnieder*.

Und frohen Mut[5]	Fresh blood
Stets neugewähre.[6]	And a joyful heart!
[(. . . 12 lines . . .)]	[(. . . 12 lines . . .)]
O Seligkeit, o Seligkeit.[7]	O bliss!

Gottfried August Bürger (1747–1794)

This and another male voice quartet, *Die Nachtigall* D724, were among the great successes of Schubert's career during his lifetime; they spread the composer's name in Austria almost as effectively as *Erlkönig*. There was something about these works that was immediately attractive to *Männerchor* singers, and to the public. It is par for the course that *Das Dörfchen* waited some two years for its first public performance on 19 November 1819. There was another important performance on 7 March 1821 at the Kärntnertortheater. At the same concert *Erlkönig* was sung by Johann Michael Vogl, accompanied by Anselm Hüttenbrenner. The quartet of singers was a mixture of professional and semi-professional artists; they were well known as an ensemble, and their skill and musicality encouraged the composer to write other beautiful (and demanding) four-part songs for these forces. (For biographical details about Barth, Umlauff, Nejebse, Götz and Nestroy *see* SINGERS.)

Some time before *Das Dörfchen* came to be published in June 1822, Schubert added a piano part; the first version is unaccompanied (this was originally D598 in the first edition of the Deutsch catalogue where the second version, the one discussed here, was D641; now *both* are D598). The version with piano is vocally very similar (though not identical). The accompaniment, almost as if it were conceived for rehearsal purposes, is seldom other than a doubling of the vocal lines and plays little part in the setting of musical atmosphere that depends on the shape and sweep of the melody. Like some other extended vocal quartets, this piece is in three movements. The first of these ('Allegretto') is an ABA construction where the generous, open-hearted tune of the opening returns at 'So nenn' ich meine / Geliebte, kleine / Einsiedelei'. The bright key of D major is made to resound to a melody that progresses in a rolling $\frac{3}{8}$, full of health and countrified happiness. But at the same time it is tinged with the authentic Schubertian ache (as at the suspension at 'rings umher die Blicke schauen' b. 8) which betokens a fragile passing moment of almost unbearable beauty. ('Go not happy day' is Tennyson's plea in similar spirit.) 'May time never destroy you' says Bürger at the end of the song. Time, and the Industrial Revolution, would change the landscape of this 'Dörfchen' irrevocably, and it is as if Schubert knew and wept, even as he smiled, aware that life in rural Austria, (as described in English terms in Oliver Goldsmith's *The Deserted Village*), would soon change also.

The panorama described by the eighteenth-century German poet is of picture-book perfection. But Schubert writes music for the jaded city dweller idealizing country life and his exaggeration is understandable. The top line of the vocal score at 'Dem blaue Wälder die Grenze zieh'n' (bb. 13–14) slips into upper regions, a tessitura characteristic of this medium where a lack of soprano voice means that the first tenor must rise to the challenge of giving the piece lightness and brightness. The word 'Einsiedelei' occurs not infrequently in Schubert songs, the concept of hermitage so beloved of the poets of an earlier generation.

The second section ('Andante con moto') changes gear: the key signature is A major and the time signature is $\frac{2}{4}$. The dotted rhythms of the first tenor seem as decorative as so many tendrils

---

[5] Bürger's line is '*Ihr treuen* Mut'.
[6] Bürger's line is '*Und Reiz* gewähre'.
[7] This is simply Schubert's own elaboration of the opening line of the final strophe.

of greenery, or as flexible as poplars gently bending in the breeze. And now Schubert has his chance to write water music. First of all we see the limpid brook from the point of view of the observer: smooth and gliding thirds and sixths of the two tenors entwine with a bass line that moves at the bottom of the stave in contrary motion. This is genial play with the idea of a mirror effect ('Lässt bald im Spiegel / Den grünen Hügel' from b. 56) where the frisking lambs and green hillside are visible on the riverbed. This optical illusion is given a musical analogue by the distance between the parts (to this end the composer silences the first bass for twelve bars) where broad vistas of sky are separated from expanses of water, the whole effect accentuated by the reflecting stream. When we are allowed to glimpse *under* the water (from 'Da gleiten Schmerlen' b. 69) the first tenor, at last free from the piano doubling his every note, begins his aquatic acrobatics, all flashing fin and glinting scales. The second tenor attaches himself, limpet-like, to his colleague for the hocketing ascent in thirds up the stave at 'Und bald herauf / Zur Fläche wieder' bb. 78–9; the basses are also allowed their own flourish at the repeat of these words. Schubert is having such a happy time, like a child splashing around in a paddling pool, that these water features are presented for a second time.

The final section ('Andante con moto' C alla breve) heralds a return to the home key. Schubert makes of this a bracing exercise in canon where each singer is allowed a separate appearance, as if standing in a spotlight for a curtain call. The lead tenor sets off accompanied by sturdy quavers, a moto perpetuo in D major that is prophetic of *Mein!* from *Die schöne Müllerin*. The second tenor takes his turn in the round, followed by the two basses. The four-bar coda is marked 'Adagio', an elongated setting of the address to bliss that has opened the song's final section, a more soulful setting of the words 'O Seligkeit'. The repeat of these words at the end is Schubert's idea, not the poet's. Here the tessitura of the first tenor part adds the expressive edge to the music that was to become one of the sentimental clichés of the barbershop quartet.

Why Schubert should have wished to set a poem by Bürger for the only time in his career has never been clear. The relatively recent research of Rita Steblin has attempted to throw new light on the so-called *Unsinnsgesellschaft* – a kind of male club to which Schubert belonged between 1817 and 1818 along with his friend Leopold Kupelwieser, where a freemasonry of nonsense and fun held sway, including all manner of parody and obscenity. This was an environment in which the elected brotherhood could let their hair down and have a good time in any number of charades and party games. There was also a newsletter with illustrations.

Two of the members enjoyed dressing up as women. One was the seemingly effeminate 'Nina Wurtzel' (pseudonym of Johann Carl Smirsch); the other 'Elise von Antifi Gagarnadl', in reality a masculine and happily married man – a bookkeeper and former soldier by the name of Ferdinand Dorflinger (1780–1818) who died suddenly at the age of twenty-eight. The dialect slang 'Antifi' refers to endive leaves, and 'Gagarnadl' is a composite word that unites the clucking of hens with eggs. The *Unsinnsgesellschaft* met at the 'Red Rooster Inn' in Vienna, and chicken allusions were therefore very popular with the members.

According to Steblin (who has uncovered what seems to be a never-ending web of allusions and interconnecting threads), the name Elise was selected by Dorflinger as a lampoon of the 'grande horizontale', Elise Hahn (whose surname also relates to roosters). She had been the third wife of the unfortunately cuckolded poet, Gottfried Bürger, who became an immense figure of fun with the younger generation. It seems that the poem *Das Dörfchen*, appropriately by Bürger, had enough in common with the surname Dorflinger for Schubert to have written a quartet in leg-pulling honour of his fellow society member. Steblin also accounts for the differences between the two versions of *Das Dörfchen* by pointing out that the earlier version contains references (such as to Elise's glowing face) that were more appropriate for the parody version than for the serious quartet with accompaniment that was accordingly shortened before publication. For discussion of a different kind regarding the musical subtleties of *Das Dörfchen*, see Gülke 1991.

Autograph:	Missing or lost; sketch in Schubert-Bund, Vienna
First edition:	Published as Op. 11 no. 1 by Cappi & Diabelli in June 1822 (P25)
Dedicatee:	Joseph Barth
First known performance:	Without piano: 19 November 1819, *Abend-Unterhaltung* of the Gesellschaft der Musikfreunde, Vienna. Performed by Joseph Kesaer, Johann Hutschenreiter, Johann Nestroy and Ignaz Sonnleithner (see Waidelich/Hilmar Dokumente I No. 26 for full concert programme)
	With piano: 8 September 1822, concert held by the Steyermärkischer Musikverein in the Redoutensaal, Graz. Performers unknown (see Deutsch Doc. Biog. No. 308 and Waidelich/Hilmar Dokumente I No. 170 for full programme)
Performance reviews:	With piano: *Grazer Zeitung* No. 111 (14 September 1822) [Waidelich/Hilmar Dokumente I No. 173; Deutsch Doc. Biog. No. 309]
Subsequent editions:	AGA XVI 4: p. 41; NSA III: Vol. 3
Bibliography:	Gülke 1991, pp. 159–73
	Steblin 1998
	Steblin 1999, pp. 33–43
Discography and timing:	Fischer-Dieskau —

Hyperion I 34[7]   4'20   John Mark Ainsley, Jamie MacDougall,
Hyperion II 20[3]   Simon Keenlyside & Michael George

← *Thekla: Eine Geisterstimme* D595   *Die Geselligkeit (Lebenslust)* D609 →

DON GAYSEROS
(FOUQUÉ) **D93**
c. 1814

In Chapter XIX of the first book of Fouqué's *Der Zauberring* ('The Magic Ring', 1812) there is a gathering of knights at the castle of Herr Folko. Each of these contributes a story, and Don Hernandez, a good-looking sunburnt Spaniard, asks permission to sing, rather than speak, his contribution. He asks for a guitar and accompanies himself 'with noble Castilian seriousness'. Afterwards he apologizes for the depressing nature of the story and is absolved by his colleagues from many lands who have no objection to darker blooms being included in their garland of stirring tales. The character Don Gayseros clearly owes something to Fouqué's reading of Cervantes: in *Don Quixote* the hero attends a puppet play in which Don Gayferos attempts to rescue his wife Melisendra, Charlemagne's daughter, from the churches of the moors of Saragossa. This is also the subject matter of Manuel de Falla's theatre piece *El retablo de Maese Pedro* (1922). It seems possible that Fouqué (or perhaps his typesetter) mistook the 'f' of the Spanish name for an 's' – in any case the two letters are very similar in printed German.

This little song cycle, the first of its kind in Schubert's output, has long been one of the great mysteries of the canon. A number of distinguished Schubert scholars, Maurice Brown among them, have seriously doubted its authenticity, and Einstein refers to it as a 'foreign body among the rest of [Schubert's] songs'. The extant manuscripts of the work are in the composer's own hand, but the fact that Schubert wrote out these songs is not absolute proof that he composed them; we have to assume that he did in the absence of evidence to the contrary (*see* DUBIOUS, MISATTRIBUTED AND LOST SONGS). On the other hand, if it were discovered that *Don Gayseros* had been originally set by someone else, and had been reworked by Schubert (as was the case with *Die Advokaten* D37 and the works modelled on Zumsteeg), many Schubertians would not be in the least surprised. The date of composition is also controversial. From the internal evidence of the music, Deutsch placed the songs some time in 1814; the second edition of his catalogue (1978) moved them to 1815. The watermark expert Robert Winter avers that they were composed as late as 1816–17 because they were written on the same type of paper as a copy of *Szene aus 'Faust'* D126; but there is disagreement as to when this copy was made.

There is no real performing practice tradition of *Don Gayseros*; Fischer-Dieskau left the work out of his complete song survey of the 1970s. Part of his reasoning must have been the long stretches of the music where a male singer would have to impersonate the character of Donna Clara in direct speech, and where a female singer would have to do the reverse with the music of the eponymous hero.

Autograph: Staatsbibliothek Preussischer Kulturbesitz, Berlin
First edition: Published as part of the AGA in 1894 (P535–7)

I ('Don Gayseros, Don Gayseros')
D93/1 [H30]

F major – A♭ major

(238 bars)

'Don Gayseros, Don Gayseros,
Wunderlicher, schöner Ritter,
Hast mich aus der Burg beschworen,
Lieblicher, mit deinen Bitten.

'Don Gayseros, Dir im Bündnis,
Lockten Wald und Abendlichter.
Sieh mich hier nun, sag' nun weiter,
Wohin wandeln wir, du Lieber?'

'Donna Clara, Donna Clara,
Du bist Herrin, ich der Diener,

'Don Gayseros, Don Gayseros,
Strange, fair knight,
Have you lured me from my castle
With your entreaties?

'Don Gayseros, the forest and the evening light,
In league with you, enticed me.
Behold me here now, and tell me
Dearest, where we are to go?'

'Donna Clara, Donna Clara,
You are the mistress, I the servant.

Du bist Lenk'rin, ich Planet nur,
Süsse Macht, o wollst gebieten!'

'Gut, so wandeln wir den Berghang
Dort zum Kruzifixe nieder;
Wenden drauf an der Kapelle
Heimwärts uns, entlängst den Wiesen.'[1]

'Ach, warum an der Kapelle,
Ach, warum bei'm Kruzifixe?'—
'Sprich, was hast Du nun zu streiten?
Meint ich ja, Du wärst mein Diener.'

'Ja, ich wandle, ja ich schreite,[2]
Herrin ganz nach Deinem Willen.'—
Und sie wandelten zusammen
Sprachen viel von süsser Minne.

'Don Gayseros, Don Gayseros,
Sieh, wir sind am Kruzifixe,
Hast Du nicht Dein Haupt gebogen
Vor dem Herrn, wie andre Christen?'

'Donna Clara, Donna Clara,
Konnt' ich auf was anders schauen,
Als auf Deine zarten Hände,
Wie sie mit den Blumen spielten?'

'Don Gayseros, Don Gayseros,
Konntest Du denn nichts erwidern,
Als der fromme Mönch Dich grüsste,
Sprechend: Christus geb' Dir Frieden?'

'Donna Clara, Donna Clara,
Durft' ins Ohr ein Laut mir dringen
Irgend noch ein Laut auf Erden,
Als Du flüsternd sprachst: Ich liebe?'

'Don Gayseros, Don Gayseros,
Sieh' vor der Kapelle blinket
Des geweihten Wassers Schale!
Komm und tu' wie ich, Geliebter.'

'Donna Clara, Donna Clara,
Gänzlich musst' ich jetzt erblinden

You guide my course, I am but your planet.
Sweet ruler, give your command!'

'Good, then let us walk down the mountainside
To yonder crucifix.
When we come to the chapel
Let us turn homewards, crossing the meadows.'

'Ah, why to the chapel,
Why to the crucifix?'
'Tell me, why do you argue now?
I thought you were my servant.'

'Yes, mistress, I shall walk there,
Just as you wish.'
And they strolled together
Talking much of sweet love.

'Don Gayseros, Don Gayseros,
See, we have reached the crucifix.
Have you not bowed your head
Before the Lord, like other Christians?'

'Donna Clara, Donna Clara,
How could I look at anything
But your delicate hands,
Playing with the flowers?'

'Don Gayseros, Don Gayseros,
Could you not reply then
When the holy monk greeted you
With the words "May Christ bring you peace"?'

'Donna Clara, Donna Clara,
How could any other sound on earth
Penetrate my ears,
As you whispered: "I love you"?'

'Don Gayseros, Don Gayseros,
Look, the basin of holy water
Glistens in front of the chapel!
Come and do as I do, beloved.'

'Donna Clara, Donna Clara,
I must now be completely blind,

---

[1] Fouqué writes 'entlängst *die* Wiesen'.
[2] Schubert reverses the order of Fouqué's verbs in this line.

Denn ich schaut' in Deine Augen,	For I gazed into your eyes,
Konnt' mich selbst nicht wiederfinden.'	And could not find myself again.'

'Don Gayseros, Don Gayseros,	'Don Gayseros, Don Gayseros,
Tu mir's nach, bist Du mein Diener,	Do as I do, if you are my servant.
Tauch' ins Wasser Deine Rechte,	Dip your right hand into the water
Zeichn' ein Kreuz auf deine Stirne.'	And make the sign of the cross on your brow.'

Don Gayseros schwieg erschrocken,	Don Gayseros, in horror, kept silent;
Don Gayseros floh von hinnen;	Don Gayseros fled from there;
Donna Clara lenkte bebend	And Donna Clara, trembling,
Zu der Burg die scheuen Tritte.	Turned her timid steps back to the castle.

FRIEDRICH HEINRICH CARL BARON DE LA MOTTE FOUQUÉ (1777–1843)

This is the first of Schubert's five Fouqué solo settings (c. 1814–17). See the poet's biography for a chronological list of all the Fouqué settings

This song is an unashamed experiment in trying to build musical tension by the use of modulation: the cat and mouse game between Donna Clara and her mysterious paramour is mirrored by a whole chain of key changes. Schubert gives the pianist so little to do that this alone would raise questions of its authenticity. The entire 'role' of Donna Clara is doubled note for note by the piano. It is almost as if Schubert (if it is indeed he) is demonstrating the art of modulation to one of his friends, or has made a wager on how many times he can change key in a single piece. This type of modulation has become so much a part of the vocabulary of modern popular music, each modulation capping the last as the story unfolds, that Schubert's experiments sound somewhat banal. The author Fouqué himself sets the mood for these modulatory changes by mentioning that Don Hernandez, the narrator, 'changes to another, darker tone' for the second song (p. 152) and that he once again 'changes the tone' (or tonality) for the third song (p. 154).

In the beginning, each musical unit – the exchange between the two characters – lasts for three strophes. The first of these progresses from F (Donna Clara, bb. 1–32) to B flat (Don Gayseros, bb. 33–49). Then E flat (Donna Clara, bb. 50–65) to A flat and D flat (both Don Gayseros, bb. 66–81 and bb. 82–114). The screw then begins to turn by using only two verses for each exchange, and modulations follow thick and fast: G flat to B major, G to C, F to B flat and finally F to A flat. There are no fewer than eleven changes of key signature in the piece. Apart from this juxtaposition of tonalities which effectively paints the mounting suspicion of Donna Clara that her lover is not a Christian, the musical characterization of the would-be lovers is rhythmically wooden. The only thing that interests the composer here, it seems, is the tonal scheme.

Collected editions:	Not in Peters; AGA XX 13: Vol. 1/132; NSA IV: Vol. 7/167; Bärenreiter: Vol. 6/21
Bibliography:	Einstein 1951, p. 66
Discography and timing:	Fischer-Dieskau —

Hyperion I 12[8]	4'14	Nancy Argenta, John Mark Ainsley &
Hyperion II 3[2]		Adrian Thompson

← *Der Taucher* D77   *Don Gayseros II* D93/2 →

II ('Nächtens klang die süsse Laute')
D93/2 [H31]

F major – C major

(85 bars)

Nächtens klang die süsse Laute	By night the sweet lute sounded
Wo sie oft zu Nacht geklungen,	Where it had so often echoed;
Nächtens sang der schöne Ritter,	By night the handsome knight sang,
Wo er oft zu Nacht gesungen.	As he had so often sung.
Und das Fenster klirrte wieder,	The window rattled once more
Donna Clara schaut' herunter,	And Donna Clara looked down.
Aber furchtsam ihre Blicke	But her fearful gaze
Schweiften durch das tau'ge Dunkel.	Swept through the dewy darkness,
Und statt süsser Minnelieder,[1]	And instead of sweet songs of love,
Statt der Schmeichelworte Kunde	Instead of coaxing words,
Hub sie an ein streng Beschwören:	She solemnly conjured him:
'Sag, wer bist Du, finstrer Buhle?	'Say, who are you, dark lover?
'Sag, bei Dein' und meiner Liebe,	'Say, by your love and mine,
Sag, bei Deiner Seelenruhe,	Say, upon the peace of your soul,
Bist ein Christ Du, bist ein Spanier?	Are you a Christian, are you a Spaniard?
Stehst Du in der Kirche Bunde?'	Do you stand within the family of the church?'
'Herrin, hoch hast Du beschworen,	'Mistress, you have conjured nobly;
Herrin, ja, Du sollst's erkunden.	Mistress, you shall indeed discover.
Herrin, ach, ich bin kein Spanier,	Alas, mistress, I am no Spaniard,
Nicht in Deiner Kirche Bunde.	Nor do I belong to your church.
'Herrin, bin ein Mohrenkönig,	'Mistress, I am a Moorish king,
Glüh'nd in Deiner Liebe Gluten,	Glowing with the fires of love for you;
Gross an Macht und reich an Schätzen,	I am great in power, rich in treasures,
Sonder gleich an tapferm Mut.	And equally courageous.
'Rötlich blühn Granadas Gärten,	'The gardens of Granada bloom red,
Golden stehn Alhambras Burgen,	The turrets of the Alhambra are golden,
Mohren harren ihrer Königin—	The Moors await their queen –
Fleuch mit mir durch's tau'ge Dunkel.'	Fly with me through the dewy darkness.'

[1] Fouqué's original refers to 'Minnereden' ('sweet words of love').

'Fort, Du falscher Seelenräuber,	'Away with you, false plunderer of souls,
Fort, Du Feind!' – Sie wollt' es rufen,	Away, Evil One!' – She tried to call out,
Doch bevor sie Feind gesprochen,	But before she had uttered the words 'Evil one',
Losch das Wort ihr aus im Munde.	They died on her lips.
Ohnmacht hielt in dunkeln Netzen,	Powerless, her fair body,
Ihren schönen Leib umschlungen.	Was held in his dark clutches.
Er alsbald trug sie zu Rosse,	At once he bore her to his horse,
Rasch dann fort im mächt'gen Flug.	And then swiftly away in powerful flight.

FRIEDRICH HEINRICH CARL BARON DE LA MOTTE FOUQUÉ (1777–1843)

This is the second of Schubert's five Fouqué solo settings (c. 1814–17). See the poet's biography for a chronological list of all the Fouqué settings

The opening of this song seems the most genuinely Schubertian of the three in terms of melody and shape. The implacable duple time of the previous piece yields to the lilt of ⅜. There is an attempt to bring to the music the feel of a serenade in the warm south, with a fragrantly blossoming vocal line. This is interrupted by an effective change of mood when Donna Clara confronts the knight (from b. 22). His answer begins in G major (Verse 5, b. 34) and in the Spanish serenade fashion of the opening, but when he reveals his true Moorish colours the flowing triplets dry up: the key changes to A flat major, and stark minim chords underpin the confession. The modulation game begins again as he attempts to woo her to his side, and one is tempted to credit Schubert with the idea that the two characters' backgrounds are so out of key with each other that conflicting tonalities are used as an analogue for alien creeds – as if different key signatures were symbolic of opposing religious rites. The final verse where Donna Clara is carried away, an 'Entführung' in a burst of very conventional piano passage work (the postlude, bb. 82–5) seems both hackneyed and unconvincingly abrupt. There may have been a more extended ending that has not survived.

Subsequent editions:	Not in Peters; AGA XX 14: Vol. 1/137; NSA IV: Vol. 7/173; Bärenreiter: Vol. 6/21
Discography and timing:	Fischer-Dieskau —

Hyperion I 12[9]   3'22   Nancy Argenta, John Mark Ainsley &
Hyperion II 3[3]   Adrian Thompson

← *Don Gayseros I* D93/1   '*Don Gayseros III* D93/3 →

III ('An dem jungen Morgenhimmel')
D93/3 [H32]
C major – E♭ major

(69 bars)

An dem jungen Morgenhimmel	The sun shines pure and brightly
Steht die reine Sonne klar,	In the youthful morning sky;
Aber Blut quillt auf der Wiese,	But blood flows in the meadow,
Und ein Ross, des Reiters baar,	And a horse without its rider,
Trabt verschüchtert in der Runde,	Trots, frightened, in a circle.
Starr steht eine ries'ge Schaar.	A band of mounted mercenaries stands motionless;
Mohrenkönig, bist erschlagen	Moorish king, you have been slain
Von dem tapfern Brüderpaar,	By the two brave brothers
Das Dein kühnes Räuberwagnis	Who observed your bold abduction
Nahm im grünen Forste wahr!	In the green forest.
Donna Clara kniet bei'm Leichnam	Donna Clara kneels by the corpse,
Aufgelöst ihr goldnes Haar,	Her golden hair undone,
Sonder Scheue nun bekennend,	Now confessing freely
Wie ihr lieb der Tote war,	How dear the dead man was to her.
Brüder bitten, Priester lehren,	Her brothers plead, the priests exhort;
Eins nur bleibt ihr offenbar.	Only one thing is apparent to her.
Sonne geht, und Sterne kommen,	The sun disappears, the stars come out,
Auf und nieder schwebt der Aar,	The eagle soars up and down.
Alles auf der Welt ist Wandel	Everything in this world is in flux;
Sie allein unwandelbar.	She alone is unchanging.
Endlich bau'n die treuen Brüder	At length the faithful brothers
Dort Kapell' ihr und Altar,	Build a chapel and an altar for her there;
Betend nun verrinnt ihr Leben,	Now her life passes in prayer;
Tag für Tag und Jahr für Jahr,	Day after day, year after year,
Bringt verhauchend sich als Opfer	She pines away, offering herself as a sacrifice
Für des Liebsten Seele dar.	To the soul of her beloved.

FRIEDRICH HEINRICH CARL BARON DE LA MOTTE FOUQUÉ (1777–1843)

This is the third of Schubert's five Fouqué solo settings (c. 1814–17). See the poet's biography for a chronological list of all the Fouqué settings

The four bars of piano introduction to this song could have been the beginning of an extended piece of a Spanish dance pastiche. The cycle is so full of musical sequences that they sometimes sound mechanical, but here the ear cries out for them. It seems possible that this fandango (scarcely long enough to make an impression that is sufficiently Spanish) was meant to be much longer, and that the music is lost. The recitative in E flat (from b. 5) that covers developments in the story does little to characterize the implausible newcomers to the scene, including brothers conveniently placed to rescue Donna Clara, a neurotic horse and a band of mercenaries. The composer passes over these as quickly as possible, and he was probably right to do so.

As soon as Donna Clara kneels beside the corpse (from b. 23, marked 'Etwas geschwind, doch kraftvoll') the song begins in earnest, in A minor. John Reed finds the 'fast and determined' tempo the composer asks for here inappropriate for depicting Donna Clara's remorse. This might be true for a German heroine in distress, but Schubert is surely attempting to invent music that seems to him to be genuinely Sevillian; the remorse has the dark temperament of Spain, and the harmonies, suggestive of an old passacaglia, are driven forward by guitar chords and a dance rhythm that encompasses both anger and grief. The striding left hand of this passage is the most Spanish thing in the entire cycle. It is as if Donna Clara has entered temporarily into the barbarian world that Don Gayseros wanted her to inhabit with him. Sure enough, with

'Endlich baun die treuen Brüder / Dort Kapell' ihr und Altar' the sense of the words is reflected by a shift back to the 'Christian' tonality of E flat (from b. 45), with its trinity key signature of three flats. The barbaric intensity of chords splayed across the bar line is softened by the reversion to hymn-book harmonies hugging and following the vocal line with a duty worthy of a nun's vows. But the thrust of that striding left-hand rhythm (transferred to the right in a six-bar coda) permeates the remainder of the song as an echo of the passion, the chance, now lost, whereby Donna Clara might have lived her life another way.

Subsequent editions:	Not in Peters; AGA XX 15: Vol. 1/141; NSA IV: Vol. 7/177; Bärenreiter: Vol. 6/21
Discography and timing:	Fischer-Dieskau —
	Hyperion I 12[10]
	Hyperion II 3[4] 2'41 Adrian Thompson

← *Don Gayeros II* D93/2   *Adelaide* D95 →

Der DOPPELGÄNGER *see SCHWANENGESANG* D957/13

DRANG IN DIE FERNE   Longing to escape
(LEITNER) Op. 71 **D770** [H510]
A minor   Early 1823

(77 bars)

(1) Vater, du glaubst es nicht,
    Wie's mir zum Herzen spricht,
    Wenn ich die Wolken seh',
    Oder am Strome steh';

Father, you would not believe
How it touches my heart
When I see the clouds,
Or stand by the river.

(2) Wolkengold, Wellengrün
    Ziehen so leicht dahin,
    Weilen im Sonnenlicht,[1]
    Aber bei Blumen nicht,

Golden clouds, green waves
Drift along so effortlessly,
Lingering in the sunshine
But not by the flowers.

(3) Zögern und rasten nie,
    Eilen, als wüssten sie,
    Ferne und ungekannt,[2]
    Irgend ein schön'res Land.

They never tarry or rest,
Hastening as if they knew
Of some fairer land,
Distant and undiscovered.

---

[1] Leitner's lines from the *Gedichte* (1825) are: 'Wandern von Ort zu Ort / Weit in die Ferne fort'.
[2] Leitner's lines from the *Gedichte* are: 'Irgend ein schönres Land / Was noch kein Schiffer fand'. The first of these appears as the fourth, not the third, line of this setting.

(4)	Ach! von Gewölk und Flut	Ah, from clouds and streams
	Hat auch mein wildes Blut[3]	My hot blood, too,
	Heimlich geerbt den Drang,	Has secretly caught the urge
	Stürmet die Welt entlang!	To storm through the world.
(5)	Vaterlands Felsental	The rocky valley of my native land
	Wird mir zu eng, zu schmal,	Is too narrow and confined,
	Denn meiner Sehnsucht Traum[4]	For my yearning dreams
	Findet darin nicht Raum.	Cannot be contained there.
(6)	Lasst mich! ich muss, ich muss	Let me go! I must
	Fordern den Scheidekuss.	Ask for the parting kiss.
	Vater und Mutter mein!	Father and mother,
	Müsset nicht böse sein!	You must not be angry!
(7)	Hab euch ja herzlich lieb;	I love you dearly,
	Aber ein wilder Trieb	But a wild urge
	Jagt mich waldein, waldaus,	Drives me to the forest and beyond,
	Weit von dem Vaterhaus.	Far from home.
(8)	Sorgt nicht, durch welches Land[5]	Do not worry about where
	Einsam mein Weg sich wand;	My lonely, tortuous path may lead;
	Monden- und Sternenschein	There too
	Leuchtet auch dort hinein.	The moon and stars will shine.
(9)	Überall wölbt's Gefild	Over all the earth
	Sich den azurnen Schild,[6]	Arches the azure shield
	Den um die ganze Welt	Which the Creator holds
	Schirmend der Schöpfer hält.	To protect the whole world.
(10)	Ach! und wenn nimmermehr	Ah, and if I never
	Ich zu euch wiederkehr',	Return to you, my loved ones,
	Lieben, so denkt: Er fand	Then you must think that I have found
	Glücklich das schön're Land.	Happiness in a fairer land.

KARL GOTTFRIED VON LEITNER (1800–1890); poem written in 1821

This is the first of Schubert's eleven Leitner solo settings (1822–3 and 1827–8). See the poet's biography for a chronological list of all the Leitner settings

Schubert was asked to set this poem by Johann Schickh, editor of the *Wiener Zeitschrift für Kunst*, that idiosyncratic thrice-weekly periodical that included poetry, reviews of various kinds, beautifully coloured illustrations of the latest fashions and sometimes a musical supplement. The song was one of eleven lieder by Schubert that were issued in the *Zeitschrift* in the composer's lifetime.

[3] Leitner writes 'junges Blut' ('young blood').
[4] Leitner's line is 'Ahnung und Wunsch und Traum' ('Intimation, desire and dream').
[5] The first two lines of Leitner's strophe are: 'Sorget nicht! Welch Gehäg / Einsam durchirrt mein Weg' ('Do not worry through which terrain / My lonely path will meander').
[6] The first two lines of Leitner's strophe are: 'Ueber ein jed Gefild / Wölbt sich der blaue Schild'.

It was very unusual for the composer to accept suggestions as to what he should set to music (the critic Rochlitz tried, and failed, as did the poet Seidl) so perhaps the subject matter of the poem immediately appealed to Schubert. After all, it was only after great opposition from his father that the composer was permitted to abandon his schoolteaching and was able to leave home. 'Father and mother do not be angry with me,' says the boy, 'I love you *but* . . .' The composer could undertake this setting with a certain amount of background experience.

Either Schubert was feeling very poetically creative on the day that he set this text (there are many changes to Leitner's poem as printed in the 1825 edition of the *Gedichte*, some of them significant improvements), or he had been given a handwritten earlier version which he set especially for the *Wiener Zeitschrift*. Schubert was seldom shy of altering the words of a text, but such major revisions as these seem unlikely under the circumstances. It is more probable that the poem as printed in the *Gedichte* (1825) and reprinted in Schochow 1974 (vol. 1, pp. 278-9) represented Leitner's later versions, and the poem as set by Schubert was an earlier version, revised for publication two years later by Leitner himself.

The prevailing mood is one of wanting to fly free, to be in the swim, to be able to join the dance of Life to which the rest of the world is twirling in giddy waltz rhythm. The word 'Drang' implies an urgency in this longing for escape to distant lands. The poem's numerous end-stopped lines induce a breathy haste in which one idea seems to tumble over the other. The poet's thoughts surge forward in such a way that it would be impossible for anyone else to get a word in edgeways; there is scarcely a chink in his flow of justifications to allow the parental listener to raise a word of objection. All the while in the background there is intoxicating waltz music, as if the boy, Cinderella fashion, is saying, 'Can I, too, go to the ball?' The words of the poem talk of the great outdoors, but the music murmurs also of company and wine, women and song – the sensuality denied to those with a strict upbringing. This music is prophetic of another highly strung A major Ländler about an outsider looking in, *Täuschung* from *Winterreise*.

Verses 1-3: The mood of the waltz song is set in the three bars of introduction – a rising A minor figure that sidles upwards for an octave before descending more slowly in a sigh of longing. The first vocal entry ('Vater, du glaubst es nicht') is fashioned after the tune of the introduction, and is accompanied by the left hand alone, marking time in dance rhythm. For the next bar ('Wie's mir zum Herzen spricht' b. 5) the voice repeats the pattern of the previous bar, this time a third higher; underneath it the piano plays the notes of 'Vater, du glaubst es nicht', thus setting up a pattern of canonic imitation between voice and piano that pervades the whole song. It is this which adds a special urgency to the young man's case, for it suggests the physical movement of facial and body language; it is as if he is reinforcing his words with pleading expressions and imploring gestures. Verse 1 is in A minor and runs directly into Verse 2, which switches suddenly into C major (b. 10), modulating at 'Aber bei Blumen nicht' (bb. 13–14) into G major. Then, after an ingratiating bar of interlude, back to C major for Verse 3 (b. 15) which seems at first to be more or less a repeat of Verse 2 until a sudden shift into A major (bb. 17–18). As ever with Schubert, the juxtaposition of A minor and major is a metaphor for romantic *Sehnsucht*.

Verses 4-6: Except for a tiny change of one note, dictated by word-setting considerations, the music for Verse 4 is a repeat of Verse 1. Without pause for thought, Verse 5 switches into new music in the subdominant (D minor, from b. 26) and leads straight into Verse 6. This is the central emotional pivot point of the piece and the verse with the most vehement word repetitions until the protracted coda. The almost hysterical tone (achieved by a highly strung operatic repetition of 'Ich muss' at b. 30) and the dwelling on the implications of parting, raise the song's temperature considerably; F major and its related chromatic territory is explored up hill and down dale (bb. 32-7, from 'Fordern den Scheidekuss'). The effect of this is remarkably expressive, partially because of the heightened vocal tessitura; it is as if the young man is coun-tering parental objections with increased intensity and louder voice. This does not last for long. At the repeat of 'Vater und Mutter mein, / Müsset nicht böse sein' we land in the dominant of C major (b. 39), and as frustration gives way to gentle affection, a few reconciliatory bars of interlude lead us into the calmer waters of that key for the beginning of Verse 7.

Verses 7–10: verses 7 and 8 are exact musical repeats of verses 2 and 3; Verse 8 modulates to A major (in the same manner as Verse 3) but instead of immediately softening into the tonic minor it remains in A major. At b. 39 there is an official change of key signature into three sharps; Verse 9 begins with a bar of piano music that is similar in shape to the introduction of the song, only now in A major. A tonic pedal for five whole bars gives the music for this section a moment of quietude, as if we were being lifted away from human problems to see the world in a less troubled (and thus less harmonically changeable) perspective. The repeat of the words 'Den um die ganze Welt [schirmend] der Schöpfer hält' (bb. 54–6) engineers a triumphant excursion into the domi-nant that praises the glory of creation. And then, sudden emptiness: the singer has realized that he might never return home. For six bars (bb. 57–62) thoughts of mortality prompt the piano's right hand to chime the passing bell, das Zügenglöcklein, for those who have died. But such thoughts are soon thrown off. The boy tells his parents to be confident that he has found the promised land. 'Lieben, so denkt: Er <u>fand</u> / Glücklich das schön're Land.' Schubert seizes on the word 'fand' to launch the final fantastic pipe dream; the music is derived from Verse 6 of course because it is there we heard of the 'parting kiss'. The leave-taking is therefore accomplished in the music, although the actual words sung at this point are of 'das schön're Land'.

The final vocal peroration (repeats of those words at bb. 68–72) takes the voice into the heights, as if it is a bird flying off into freedom. The piano in its postlude also takes wing, at first in the confident A major of the singer's parting, but staying to voice more doubtful feelings (those of the parents perhaps) in the minor key. In the last three bars the young man disappears, together with the piano's etiolated triplets, over the top of the keyboard's horizon while the pianist's left hand descends into the abyss of the bass. The void between, and the final rolled chord, sound an ominous warning that everything may not, after all, turn out for the best. Perhaps our traveller is destined for Elysian fields, rather than greener pastures. This song was written at more or less the time that the composer was suffering with symptoms of syphilis. His hard-won freedom to be his own master had resulted in greater independence and maturity, but in the enjoyment of that freedom he had contracted an illness that was to change his life for ever.

Autograph:	Missing or lost
First edition:	Published as a supplement to the *Wiener Zeitschrift für Kunst* on 25 March 1823 and as Op. 71 by Diabelli, Vienna in March 1827 (P118)
First known performance:	19 February 1829, *Abend-Unterhaltung* of the Gesellschaft der Musikfreunde, Vienna. Soloist: Ludwig Tietze (see Waidelich/ Hilmar Dokumente I No. 697 for full concert programme)
Subsequent editions:	Peters: Vol. 2/136; AGA XX 424: Vol. 7/91; NSA IV: Vol. 3a/136; Bärenreiter: Vol. 2/160
Bibliography:	Capell 1928, p. 183
	Fischer-Dieskau 1977, p. 254
Discography and timing:	Fischer-Dieskau II 5[22] 4'07
	Hyperion I 18[11]
	3'39 Peter Schreier
	Hyperion II 26[17]

← *Die Verschwornenen* D787/2   *Der zürnende Barde* D785 →

DREI GESÄNGE FÜR BASS-STIMME MIT KLAVIER
(METASTASIO: I & II) (ANONYMOUS/UNKNOWN; formerly attributed to Metastasio)
III: Anonymous/Unknown (formerly attributed to Metastasio)
OP. 83, **D902/1–3**
1827

The three songs of Op. 83 are associated with the name of the celebrated bass, Luigi Lablache (1794–1858). Lablache was at his height as a performer when Edward Holmes visited Vienna in 1827 and recorded his impressions (none of which includes Schubert) in *A Ramble among the Musicians of Germany*. Holmes saw the bass as Uberto in Paer's *Agnese*: 'Lablache as the distracted father astonished me by the feeling of his singing, and the truth of his acting, and showed a wonderful change from the prodigious folly and bombast of his demeanour and singing as an Indian cacique.' Holmes also noted that although the singer was a master of 'the arts of grimace and face-making' with 'elaborate contortions of body and dexterous pirouettes', he never once forgot the seriousness of his part. This blending of tragedy and comedy, as noted in the commentary for *Il traditor deluso*, seems to have been typical of the period in Italian opera.

A member of Domenico Barbaia's Italian company in Vienna since 1824, Lablache was, in a sense, a 'member of the opposition' – Schubert's own hopes for a career as an opera composer had been dashed when Barbaia took over the management of the Kärntnertortheater. But as Josef von Spaun pointed out in his *Notes on my association with Franz Schubert* (1858), the composer was not one to bear a grudge:

> *A splendid characteristic of Schubert's was his interest and pleasure in all the successful creations of other people. He did not know what it meant to be envious and he by no means overrated himself . . . Although absolutely German in tendency, he by no means agreed with the abuse of Italian music, and especially of Rossini's operas, which was usual at that time. The Barbiere di Sevilla he found delightful and he was enchanted by the third act of* Otello; *in the operas given at that time . . . Lablache's singing captivated him. The latter took a great liking to Schubert, and*

Drei Gesänge Op. 83 dedicated to Luigi Lablache.

once when the four-part song, Der Gondelfahrer, *was sung at a party he liked it so much that he asked for it to be repeated and then sang the second bass part himself.*

Lablache probably met Schubert at the home of Raphael Kiesewetter whose daughter Irene was the dedicatee and subject of a Schubert cantata (*Al par del ruscelletto* D936) that celebrated her return to health after an illness. The three songs of Op. 83 (Schubert's last in Italian) were certainly dedicated to Lablache, but it is also likely that they were written especially for him. It is possible that he sang them some time before they appeared in print, and that he played some part in the correction of the Italian accentuation before the work was handed on to the publisher. The songs were published simultaneously with a German text; these are still to be found in the Peters Edition where they are listed in Volume 6 under their German titles *Die Macht der Augen, Der getäuschte Verräter* and *Die Art, ein Weib zu nehmen*. The translator's name is not known. Walther Dürr points out that it is unlikely to have been Schubert's erstwhile collaborator Craigher de Jachelutta; Craigher was a native Italian-speaker and would almost certainly have corrected the mistakes in Schubert's Italian prosody before providing the German translation. In fact the corrections were made only after the translation was added.

Opus 83 as a whole is typical of the publications issued by Tobias Haslinger who was ever aware of musical politics and market forces. He must have found these pieces ideal for his purposes: the dedicatee was a celebrity, songs in the Italian language were all the rage and the style of the music was accessible. At least one critic, G. W. Fink of the Leipzig *Allgemeine musikalische Zeitung*, agreed. In an enthusiastic review (30 January 1828) he refers to Schubert as 'the generally lauded and favoured composer' and to all three songs as 'well suited to social entertainments'. He predicts that 'Signor Luigi Lablache, to whom these three numbers are dedicated, is sure to cause a furore with them.' The composer Heinrich Marschner, on the threshold of his own success as an opera composer, was less impressed. Writing in the Berlin *Allgemeine musikalische Zeitung* (19 March 1828), he criticized the songs for being neither fish nor fowl – not sufficiently colourful and vital enough to be truly Italian, not expressive enough to be real German lieder. 'The flow of his melodies is too intermittent, too heavy-handed; it is no glowing lava stream but only a somewhat cold, murmuring northern brooklet . . . Herr Schubert has thus not yet succeeded with these songs in bringing about an alliance, however desirable, between German and Italian music.' Of course Schubert had no such grandiose aim, and the listener of today is able to delight in the mixture of styles that is the inevitable result of such a work. We can only agree with Capell: 'Schubert is here working outside his natural style, but he does it uncommonly well.'

First edition:	Published as Op. 83 by Tobias Haslinger, Vienna in 1827 (*see also* 'Il traditor deluso' for variant version) (P134–136)
Dedicatee:	Luigi Lablache
Publication reviews:	*Allgemeine musikalische Zeitung* (Leipzig), No. 5 (30 January 1828), col. 77f. [Waidelich/Hilmar Dokumente I No. 574; Deutsch Doc. Biog. No. 1023]
	Berliner allgemeine musikalische Zeitung, No. 12 (19 March 1828), p. 90f. [Waidelich/Hilmar Dokumente I No. 599; Deutsch Doc. Biog. No. 1060]
	Allgemeiner musikalischer Anzeiger (Vienna) No. 32 (8 August 1829), p. 125f. [Waidelich/Hilmar Dokumente I No. 741]
Further setting:	Arr. Paul Angerer (b. 1927) *Drei Gesänge von Metastasio*, for baritone and strings (1981)

I L'INCANTO DEGLI OCCHI (II) The enchantment of eyes
Op. 83 no. 1, **D902/1** [H630]
C major

(122 bars)

Da voi, cari lumi,	On you, beloved eyes,
Dipende il mio stato;	Depends my life;
Voi siete i miei Numi,	You are my gods;
Voi siete il mio fato.	You are my destiny.
A vostro talento	At your bidding
Mi sento cangiar,	My mood changes.
Ardir m'inspirate,	You inspire me with daring
Se lieti splendete;	If you shine joyfully;
Se torbidi siete,	If you are overcast
Mi fate tremar.	You make me tremble.

This is the thirteenth of Schubert's fourteen Metastasio solo settings (1812–27). See the poet's biography for a chronological list of all the Metastasio settings

Of all Schubert's Italian settings, *L'incanto degli occhi* sounds the most Schubertian. This is not to denigrate the charm of *La pastorella* in either the solo (D528) or choral version; the fire and passion of the aria from *Didone abbandonata* D510 is as fine a piece of drama as the musical epistle *Herrn Josef Spaun, Assessor in Linz* D749 is a rollicking piece of Italian pastiche. It is just that this particular cavatina radiates that extraordinary sense of Mediterranean well-being that suggests (appropriately in this case) a twinkling eye and a tapping foot. In the introduction the right hand's repeated quavers have something of *Der Einsame* D800 about them, but it is the placing of the left-hand octaves (on the first beat as well as on the last quaver of each bar) that cheekily enlivens the music and transforms what could have been very banal in other hands into Schubertian gold. This music makes us smile, but it is far from being comic; it is both beautiful and raffish, and we somehow know that someone (Schubert) is quietly having fun at another's expense (Rossini's and the whole world of Italian opera) without having a malicious bone in his body.

To write music that pulls both leg and heartstring is an utterly Schubertian achievement. There is something irresistibly *buffo* about this music, but the moderate pulse of the kindly Allegretto betokens the gallantry and sagacity of a gentleman. The piano dynamics of the first page suggest a Don Pasquale (or Quixote) or a retired *Hidalgo*. The music is so downright genial that we can only assume that this song, like much of the music Schubert wrote with Vogl in mind, amounts to a portrait of its intended singer. If Luigi Lablache was really like his music it is little wonder that Schubert got on with him, and that he was said to have liked Schubert in return.

The entire first verse pootles amiably between tonic (C major) and dominant, but is a miracle of charm where every unexceptional change of chord is placed with consummate elegance. The voice blossoms into emollient semiquavers at 'Mi sen<u>to cangiar</u>' (bb. 21–2), a foretaste of what is to come in the third musical verse when the composer reworks the first four lines of the poem. These acciaccatura-led roulades are once again reminiscent of *Der Einsame*. In that song we see the outline of the flickering flame in the hearth; in *L'incanto degli occhi* the same figuration is prompted by similar imagery – the flashing of a lover's eyes. A new mood emerges for lines five to ten of the poem (from b. 38): to depict the idea of daring ('Ardir m'inspirate') the music moves into the key of A flat major, and the piano dynamic gives way to a more dramatic *forte*. Schubert lovingly recycles all the Italian clichés: sudden changes of dynamic, leaps between the bottom and top of the voice, the use of pathos that changes easily and shamelessly to equally opportunistic flirtation. But as this is not real Italian music there is a sophistication of modulation that is not easily found in Rossini's own miniatures – for example the shift from G major to B major, leading to the dominant of that key (F sharp major at b. 63) which, in turn, deliciously slides up a semitone to a chord of G^7 under the first repeat of the words 'Da voi, cari lumi' (b. 64) and acts as an irresistible, and beautifully timed, upbeat to the return of the tonic.

The song is really ABA in structure, where the repeat of A is an embroidered variation of what we have heard in the first section. There is many an old-fashioned set of variations by composers like Paisiello and Mayr which opens with a theme unadorned and progresses with ever quicker and more exacting divisions. The rondo finale of Rossini's *La cenerentola* comes to mind. Added to this there is a coda to the Italian manner born that allows the music to trail away to a whisper. Schubert puts Lablache through his paces in a rather more relaxed way than Rossini, and this aria is much less glittering than the Italianate virtuoso music he himself wrote for Anna Milder at the end of *Der Hirt auf dem Felsen* D965 – a work that was designed as a show-off piece. The low and rumbling coloratura writing of *L'incanto degli occhi*, when well done, sounds less like one of those exacting *bel canto* roles and more like the purring of a well-tuned Rolls Royce. And all the time the piano continues with its unchanging quavers and its mock-lugubrious left-hand interjections, an accompaniment which could be vamped by almost any singing teacher but at the same time one of the wittiest that Schubert ever wrote. Parody, pastiche, call it what you will, this work is no put-down; it ranks with Liszt's Petrarch Sonnets and Britten's *Seven Sonnets of Michelangelo* as an affectionate Italian stylization which outranks the genuine article. And like those works that pay inspired homage to Italy, it distils the country's musical manner, albeit with the exaggeration of a foreigner's bemused observation. All this, and a bonus: Schubert remains his inimitable, lovable self throughout.

The text is the 'Aria di Licinio' from Act II Scene 5 of Metastasio's *Attilio Regolo* (1740). The story is set in ancient Rome at the time of the Carthaginian wars. The hero, the Roman consul Regulus who eventually gives up his life by returning to Carthage to face a death sentence, has a daughter Attilia. In the second act of the opera she plots to save her father's life with the help of her beloved Licinio who is a slave to her every wish – as is attested by his aria.

See *L'incanto degli occhi* D990e for Schubert's earlier setting of this text as an exercise for Salieri.

Autograph:	British Library, London
Subsequent editions:	Peters: Vol. 6/146; AGA XX 579: Vol. 10/54; NSA IV: Vol. 4a/28; Bärenreiter: Vol. 3/19
Discography and timing:	Fischer-Dieskau II 9³ 3'17
	Hyperion I 36⁵
	Hyperion II 34¹ 2'48 Gerald Finley

⟵ *Ständchen* D920   *Il traditor deluso* D902/2 ⟶

II IL TRADITOR DELUSO

Op. 83 no. 2, **D902/2** [H631]

The traitor deceived

The song exists in two versions, the second of which is discussed below:

(1) 'Allegro'   E minor   𝄴   [195 bars]

(2) E minor

(157 bars)

Recitativo
Ahimè, io tremo, io sento
Tutto inondarmi, il seno
gelido sudor . . . Fugassi . . . Ah quale . . .
Qual è la via? Chi me l'addita? Oh Dio,
Che ascoltai? Che m'avvenne! Ove son io?

Recitative
Alas, I tremble!
I feel a cold sweat upon my brow
I must flee . . . but whither?
Where is the way? Who will show it to me
O God, what do I hear? What is happening
to me? Where am I?

Aria
Ah l'aria d'intorno
  Lampeggia, sfavilla;
  Ondeggia, vacilla
  L'infido terren!
Qual notte profonda
  D'orror mi circonda!
  Che larve funeste,
  Che smanie son queste!
  Che fiero spavento
  Mi sento nel sen!

Air
The air around me
  Flashes and sparkles;
  The perfidious earth
  Shakes and trembles!
The deep night
  Surrounds me with horror!
  What baleful creatures,
  What furies are these?
  What raging terror
  I feel in my breast!

Poem written in 1735

This is the last of Schubert's fourteen Metastasio solo settings (1812–27). See the poet's biography for a chronological list of all the Metastasio settings

L'incanto degli occhi, the first of three songs written for Luigi Lablache, had allowed the singer to portray himself as a latter-day Don Quixote singing to Dulcinea, all gentleness and charm. The famous bass now dons another, more formidable, costume, more attuned to his success as the father in Paer's *Agnese* which included a mad-scene (for further details of Lablache's career see the introduction to the commentary on this cycle). It is as well to note, however, that *Agnese* was an opera *semiseria*, and the participation of a *buffo* bass in a mad-scene of this period shows that, like almost all male madness depicted in eighteenth-century opera, the role had a strong element of comedy – as Edward Holmes's account of the performance makes clear. There is a similar ambiguity in Schubert's *Il traditor deluso*: it is full of dramatic postures but it is ultimately not serious, a certain ridiculousness being built into the music. As such, it is great fun to sing and play at the same time as being technically demanding. For all its superficially impressive bluster, it is not as musically rich as the preceding song which has an almost Mozartian grace.

The piece begins with a mighty *recitativo stromentato*. The key is E minor and the piano's left-hand tremolo suggests strings scrubbing away in great agitation. Over this background a dotted rhythm motif in right-hand octaves appears, rich in portent and absurdly melodramatic; for a moment it even sounds Wagnerian. This appears twice (once in the trombone register of the pianist's left hand bb. 5–8) before a modulation to B minor (b. 12) that is designed to twist the tension to a higher point. The motif then appears twice in this key (bb. 12–14 and bb. 14–16) as the music works itself up to a suitable pitch of panic (semiquaver oscillations, shuddering dotted rhythms) to reflect the disorientation of the character. The vocal line is dominated by short gasps and exclamations in a highly dramatic manner.

The aria (marked 'Allegro molto' at b. 32) is in E minor and *alla breve*. The main feature of the opening vocal melody is its unflinching insistence on a syncopation that throws the emphasis of nearly every bar on to the second crotchet. This characteristically Italian device is used so insistently as to make fun of it. The accompaniment swirls with arpeggio figurations; at the first repeat of 'Ah l'aria d'intorno' this changes to a series of right-hand chromatic scales (from b. 40) that are potentially hazardous for the pianist. In the hot seat, this seems much less fun, as are various other passages that call for darting dexterity and a dab-handedness at split octaves. At 'Qual notte profonda d'orror mi circonda!' (b. 53) the vocal line is smoothed out to ominous minims and semibreves as the piano shivers in oscillating quavers in the background; repeats of these words prompt other reactions such as sudden vocal leaps from the singer (for instance, b. 68), and the pitter-pat of awestruck quavers between the hands from the pianist (bb. 82–3 and 94–5). At 'Che fiero spavento', chromatic phrases, doubled in voice and piano, dig into the bottom of the bass stave in suitable woebegone desperation. This leads to the *da capo* recapitulation of the aria and a return of those jagged syncopated phrases (b. 99). And so it goes on, with Schubert using and re-using a short Italian verse, spinning it out and repeating it so that its meaning no longer matters. Having got the gist of what is being said, the listener is free to concentrate on assessing the vocal pyrotechnics. This remains a typical response of some, though not all, Italian audiences.

Schubert took a considerable amount of trouble here in both the vocal and pianistic detail. Of the three songs of this opus this is the one that pleased Marschner the best, probably because it works itself into a passable frenzy. As such it is a worthy companion to other tempestuous Italian arias by Schubert (*Son fra l'onde* D78, the closing sections of both *Didone abbandonata* D510 and *Herrn Josef Spaun, Assessor in Linz* D749). But this music engages the Schubertian's amused respect more, perhaps, than his affection.

The text is the 'Aria di Atalia' from Act II of Metastasio's *Gioas, Rè di Juda*. It does not seem to have concerned Schubert in the least that in the libretto's original context the murderess and usurper Athaliah (grandmother of Joash who eventually regains his rightful throne as King of Judah) is a female character.

Autographs:	British Library, London (vocal line only);
	Wienbibliothek im Rathaus, Vienna (first 64 bars)
Publication:	First published as part of the NSA in 1979 (P776) (first version)
	First published as Op. 83 by Tobias Haslinger, Vienna in 1827 (second version)
Subsequent editions:	Peters: Vol. 6/150; AGA XX 580: Vol. 10/58 (2nd version); NSA IV: Vol. 4a/35 (2nd version) & Vol 4b/250 (1st version); Bärenreiter: Vol. 3/23

Bibliography: Capell 1928, p. 226
                              Fischer-Dieskau 1977, p. 259
Discography and timing: Fischer-Dieskau II 9[4]   3'43
                              Hyperion I 36[6]
                              Hyperion II 34[2]   3'29   Gerald Finley

← *L'incanto degli occhi* D902/1   *Il modo di prender moglie* D902/3 →

III IL MODO DI PRENDER MOGLIE

How to choose a wife

Op. 83 no. 3, **D902/3** [H632]
C major

(163 bars)

Orsù! non ci pensiamo,	Now then, let's not think about it;
Coraggio e concludiamo,	Courage, let's get it over with.
Al fin s'io prendo moglie,	If in the end I have to take a wife
Sò ben perchè lo fò.	I know very well why I do it.
Lo fò per pagar i debiti,	I do it to pay my debts.
La prendo per contanti,	I take her for the money.
Di dirlo, e di ripeterlo,	I have no compunction telling you,
Difficoltà non ho.	And repeating it.
Fra tanti modi e tanti	Of all the ways of choosing a wife
Di prender moglie al mondo,	In the world,
Un modo più giocondo	I know of no happier way
Del mio trovar non sò.	Than mine.
Si prende per affetto,	One chooses a wife for love,
Si prende per rispetto,	Another out of respect,
Si prende per consiglio,	Another because he is advised to,
Si prende per puntiglio,	Another out of propriety,
Si prende per capriccio.	Another for a whim.
È vero, si o nò?	Is it true or not?
Ed io per medicina	And I,
Di tutti i mali miei	Why can't I take a little wife
Un poco di sposina	As remedy
Prendere non potrò?	For all my ills?

Ho detto e 'l ridico,	I've said it and I'll say it again:
Lo fò per li contanti,	I do it for the money.
Lo fanno tanti e tanti	So many do it,
Anch' io lo farò.	I do it too.

ANONYMOUS/UNKNOWN (FORMERLY ATTRIBUTED TO METASTASIO)

This is the last of Schubert's nineteen solo settings of an anonymous poet. See Anonymous/ Unknown for a chronological list of all the songs for which the poets are unknown

Although the text makes fun of the subject of marriage, we cannot forget that the subject is a sensitive one in the Schubert biography. According to some sources, Schubert in his late teens was seriously enough in love with Therese Grob, a local girl of the Lichtental parish who sang in the church choir, to have contemplated marriage. Money as always was a problem, and she made her life elsewhere. A Marriage Decree had been introduced early in 1815 that made it obligatory for anyone from the lower orders (including schoolteachers) to ask permission to marry only with proof that they could support any children of the union. This alone would have prevented the penniless Schubert from marrying. And it was always out of the question for him to dare to aspire to the hand of Karoline Esterházy who was out of his reach in terms of both money and birth. There are further stories (perhaps apocryphal) concerning the composer's marriage prospects: one was communicated by Ludwig Frankl, purportedly based on Schober's memoirs:

> *After the usual dance they almost always went to the coffee-house, Zum Auge Gottes. Schober persuaded him [Schubert] he ought to marry Gusti Grünwedel, a very charming girl of good family (she later married a painter and went to Italy), who seemed very well disposed towards him. Schubert was in love with her, but he was painfully modest; he was firmly convinced no woman could love him. At Schober's words he jumped up, rushed out without his hat, flushed with anger. The friends looked at one another in dismay. After half an hour he came quietly back and later related how, beside himself, he had run round St Peter's Church, telling himself again and again that no happiness was granted to him on earth. Schubert then let himself go to pieces. . . .*

The last sentence of this extract places this incident in 1821/2, preceding Schubert's infection. But the anecdote, if true, raises more questions than it answers: why did Schober's words make the composer angry? Why could no woman love him? Auguste Grünwedel was a real person, apparently beautiful, who passed briefly though the Schubertian orbit, but nothing further is known of her, certainly in relation to Schubert. It might have been a very good idea, all things being equal, for the composer to marry in 1822; his finances, thanks to Sonnleithner's intervention with the publishers, were on a solid footing, and 'Gusti' was well-to-do in her own right.

By 1827 the subject of marriage was so far in the past that the composer could almost certainly countenance this cynical Italian text without distress or distaste. The razor-sharp shade of Rossini's barber hovers over the music, an indication of how well Schubert loved that opera as the ever reliable Spaun informs us. Without the supporting context of an opera plot, as well as scintillating orchestration, Schubert is unable to work up the sparkle of a Rossini at his best; but the music, even if it is not quite *Largo al factotum*, is jolly and effective. The key is C major, and the bustling 'Allegro non troppo' in § creates an air of Italian busyness in just the right stirring manner to suggest a thickening plot. A contemporary lied unexpectedly comes to mind:

the Rochlitz setting *Alinde* D904. In that song the singer's search for Alinde seems similar to this search for a wife. This is most strongly to be noticed in the acciaccatura ornamentation of the piano writing (first at bb. 20–22) in a similarly playful §.

The poem's first three verses are accompanied by genial triplet configurations and a wide-ranging use of modulation – not perhaps as adventurous as if the style had been Schubert's own, but at least as inventive as is to be found in Rossini's music. The shifts of tonality are always towards the flat keys, and include the same move into the key of A flat major that we encounter in *L'incanto degli occhi*. Most of this music is governed by the ceaseless movement of triplets, but at the beginning of the fourth verse ('Si prende per affetto') semiquavers begin to make a teasing appearance in the accompaniment (from b. 72). This speeding-up of the note values in various stages is a typical trick for an Italian finale. At the final appearance of 'Un poco di sposina' (from b. 106) the vocal line is doubled with the piano to suggest guile and intrigue.

As is often the case with Italian texts of this era, it is the concluding verse of the poem (used again and again in whatever repeats are necessary) which is given over to a rousing finale. For these words of resolve the music moves into 'Allegro vivace' in common time. (Performers who attempt this music in too brisk an *alla breve* will have to pay the unplayable price on the next page when the music moves into semiquavers.) It is here perhaps that the melody fails to deliver that extra lift that we encounter in the great Rossini perorations. Its liveliness of effect depends more on the pianist, who suddenly discovers at the end of the piece a series of challenges to which there was no clue in the opening pages. Genial bouncing triplets are replaced by whirlwind roulades of semiquavers, mainly in C major but also encompassing chromatic shifts; not all of these lie easily under the fingers. Schubert makes of this music something diabolical, as if marrying for money were one of the most dastardly things one could do; his music in the song's final pages suggests a villain capable of murder at the very least. The vivacious postlude in semiquavers, an octave apart between the hands, is unlike anything else in the songs. It provides a rousing end to a work that gives delight to the Schubertian mainly because it is by Schubert and it is wonderful to see our hero in off-duty guise. If the promise of *L'incanto degli occhi* is not quite fulfilled in the second and third songs of the set it is only because the great is always the enemy of the good. And it is usually the case that the tender Schubert leaves a more lingering impression on the listener than when he is in barnstorming mood – such as here.

The text of this work is not to be found in Metastasio's work and remains one of the many small Schubertian mysteries still to be solved. The words almost certainly come from an opera by a minor composer; perhaps they had been sung by Lablache earlier in his career and he suggested that Schubert might re-use them.

Autograph:	British Library, London (fair copy)
Subsequent editions:	Peters: Vol. 6/157; AGA XX 581: Vol. 10/65; NSA IV: Vol. 4a/48; Bärenreiter: Vol. 3/30
Bibliography:	Capell 1928, p. 226
	Fischer-Dieskau 1977, p. 259
Discography and timing:	Fischer-Dieskau II 9[5] 4'36
	Hyperion I 36[7]
	Hyperion II 34[3] 4'16 Gerald Finley

← *Il traditor deluso* D902/2   *Heimliches Lieben* D922 →

Die DREI SÄNGER   The three minstrels

(Bobrik) **D329** [H205]

(Fragment) A major   23 December 1815

(119 bars)

In the text printed below, the lines in square brackets are those for which we do not have
Schubert's original music.

(1)   Der König sass beim frohen Mahle,   The king sat at his merry banquet
     Die Frau'n und Ritter um ihn her,   Surrounded by knights and ladies;
Es kreisten fröhlich die Pokale,   The goblets did their happy round,
     Und manches Becken trank man leer;   And many a glass was drained.
Da tönte Klang von goldnen Saiten,   Then came the sound of golden strings,
     Der süsser labt als goldner Wein,   Sweeter than golden wine,
Und sieh!—Drei fremde Sänger schreiten,   And lo! three strange minstrels
     Sich neigend, in den Saal hinein.   Entered the hall, bowing.

(2)   'Seid mir gegrüsst, ihr Liedersöhne!'   'Welcome, sons of song!'
     Beginnt der König wohlgemut,   Begins the king cheerfully,
'In deren Brust das Reich der Töne   'In whose hearts dwell the realm of music
     Und des Gesangs Geheimniss ruht!   And the secret of song.
Wollt ihr den edlen Wettstreit wagen,   If you care to engage in noble contest
     So soll es höchlich uns erfreu'n,   That would delight us greatly.
Und wer den Sieg davon getragen   And whoever is victorious
     Mag unsres Hofes Zierde sein!'   Shall adorn our court.'

(3)   Er sprichts – der erste rührt die Saiten,   Thus he spoke. The first minstrel touched
       the strings

  Die Vorwelt' öffnet er dem Blick,   And conjured up days past;
Zum grauen Anfang aller Zeiten   He drew his listeners' gaze
     Lenkt er der Hörer Blick zurück.   Back to the grey dawn of time.
Er meldet, wie sich neugeboren   He told how the new-created world
     Die Welt dem Chaos einst entwand.   Struggled free from chaos.
Sein Lied behagt den meisten Ohren   His song pleased most ears,
     Und willig folgt ihm der   And the *imagination* willingly followed him.
     V e r s t a n d .

(4)   Drauf mehr die Hörer zu ergetzen,   Then, to delight the listeners more,
     Erklingt des Zweiten lust'ge Mähr: The second minstrel struck up a merry tale
Von Gnomen fein und ihren Schätzen,[1]   Of cunning gnomes and their treasure,
     Und von der grünen Zwerge Heer: And a band of green dwarves.

[1] Bobrik's original reads 'Von Gnomen, Fei'in [= Feen, fairies] und ihre Schätzen'.

Er singt von manchen Wunderdingen,
   Von manchem Schwanke, schlau
   erdacht;
Da regt der S c h e r z die losen
   Schwingen,
   Und jeder Mund im Saale lacht.

He sang of many a wondrous thing,
   And of many a sly prank.

The *fun* was infectious,

   And everyone in the hall laughed loudly.

(5) Und an den Dritten kommt die Reih' –
   Und sanft aus tief bewegter Brust
Haucht er ein Lied von Lieb' und Treu'
   Und von der Sehnsucht Schmerz
   und Lust.
Und kaum dass seine Saiten klingen,
   Schaut jedes Antlitz [in den Schooss,
Und Tränen des G e f ü h l e s ringen
   Sich aus verklärten Augen los.]

Now it was the third one's turn.
   Softly, from the fullness of his heart,
He breathed a song of love and constancy,
   Of the pain and joy of longing.

And hardly had his strings sounded
   Than every gaze [was lowered,
And tears of *emotion* were wrung
   From transfigured eyes.]

(6) [Und tiefes Schweigen herrscht im Saale,
   Als seines Liedes Ton entschwand –
Da steht der König auf vom Mahle,
   Und reicht dem D r i t t e n seine
   Hand:
'Bleib bei uns, Freund! dir ist's gelungen,
   Du bist es, dem der Preis gebührt;
Das schönste Lied hat der gesungen,
   Der unser Herz zur Wehmut rührt.']

[Deep silence reigned in the hall
   When his song faded.
Then the king stood up from the table
   And gave the *third* minstrel his hand.

'Stay with us, my friend! You have won;
   To you the prize is due.
For he sang the most beautiful song
   Who moved our hearts to melancholy.']

FRIEDRICH BOBRIK (1781–1844); poem written in 1815

This is Schubert's only setting of a Bobrik text. See the poet's biography.

This song was probably once complete, but the last page of the autograph is missing and its 119 bars were buried in the section devoted to fragments in the AGA. Reasons for the song's neglect include the fact that more or less the same narrative ground was covered by the composer much earlier in the year with Goethe's *Der Sänger* D149, a ballad with a much better text.

Added to that, the music for this piece does not show Schubert at his most persuasive. John Reed dubs it 'a curiosity' with 'square four-bar phrases' and 'a very un-Schubertian air'. He compares it to the controversial *Don Gayseros* songs that show little of the composer's endlessly inventive mood and spirit. There are flashes of inspiration in *Die drei Sänger* but, like the *Gayseros* songs, it seems to be something of an experiment. One can perhaps understand why the composer was tempted by the challenge of depicting three different types of music for three different singers, but it is clear he was also set on avoiding recitative (a favourite device of 1815) and any extravagant use of modulation (likewise). All his life Schubert was told by critics, and even friends, that an excess of modulation spoiled his music. This may have been the composer's attempt to answer this criticism – a ballad in North-German style that makes a point of avoiding anything fancy and exaggerated.

The poem is in twelve verses. Unlike the Schiller ballads of 1815 there is no attempt to run sections into each other in a way that makes us scarcely conscious of the subdivisions of the text. Here there is a four-verse introduction that sets up the story; each of the minstrels is allocated two verses to state his case, and the final two verses (for which we do not have Schubert's music, but which have been set by Reinhard Van Hoorickx in order to complete the song) are reserved for the king's judgement.

Verse 1: The marking is 'Mässig geschwind'. This A major music is stately yet friendly, ideal for the court of an enlightened monarch. The vocal line (from b. 8) has an antique flavour, although this is not nearly as atmospheric as *Der König in Thule* D367, composed soon afterwards. The two songs share the imagery of goblets being drained dry: here this is achieved with a rather humorous trill on 'trank' (b. 16) with gurgling quaver accompaniment. For the strophe's fifth line ('Da tönte Klang') the marking is 'Singend' (b. 23). In F major, and with a switch to triple time, this is stately music in Mozartian manner (it may do for a wedding ceremony for example) as the three singers approach the king for an audience. The courtly dance encompasses a deferential approach to the throne, as the minstrels bow with old-world flourishes.

Verse 2: The marking is 'Etwas geschwind' (from b. 43). The king's aria ('Seid mir gegrüsst, ihr Liedersöhne') is in B flat with a return to common time. The modulation into A flat for 'des Gesangs Geheimniss ruht' (bb. 49–50) seems appropriate for entering into the secret realms of art and is a genuinely Schubertian touch. At this point the vocal line veers into a regal recitative: this monarch is sensible and wise, a change from the kings of the Schiller ballads who take hostages, or send divers to their death. However, there is always less scope for the musical depiction of good rather than evil.

Verse 3: The first singer's aria (from b. 60) is in D major and is marked 'Mässig, ernst', as well as 'alla breve'. The seriousness of this section borders on the dull, although at 'Die Vorwelt' öffnet er dem Blick' (bb. 63–4) we can detect a trace of the flowing quaver-accompanied melody in this key and metre that will one day turn into *An die Musik* D547 (it is significant that they are both pieces of music about music). The sixth verse begins in C major (bb. 70–71), a change of tonality that matches the new-born status of the world as mentioned in the poem.

Verse 4: The second singer is perhaps the most interesting, even though he does not win the prize. His aria (bb. 83–104) is in A major (𝄴), and is marked 'Lieblich, etwas geschwind'. The accompaniment paints the busy activity of pre-*Rheingold* gnomes, and the spinning of his tale suggests just that – the hum of the spinning wheel with the addition of the open fifths in the left hand which have been such an important feature of *Gretchen am Spinnrade*. We are meant to understand that this is showy and superficial in comparison with the noble and unadorned art of the third minstrel whose music is marked 'Wehmütig' and moves into A minor (b. 108).

Verse 5: The signal failure of this section is that Schubert does nothing to show us why the final singer's music is more beautiful or moving than that of the other two contestants. In fact his music in very plain style seems to be more anonymous than that given to either of the preceding artists. It was at this point that Schubert clearly lost heart although Walther Dürr points out in the NSA that the surviving autograph leaves it an open question as to whether Schubert completed the rest of the setting. If so, it was subsequently lost. After 'jedes Antlitz' (b. 119) the manuscript breaks off. Reinhard Van Hoorickx's completion sounds no more tentative than much of the original material. For Verse 6, the king's final aria, he returns to the B flat major of Verse 2, allowing himself an accompaniment of flowing triplets for the final cantilena.

| Autograph: | Wienbibliothek im Rathaus, Vienna (first draft) |
| First edition: | Published as part of the AGA in 1895 and subsequently completed by Reinhard Van Hoorickx (P714) |

Subsequent editions: Not in Peters; AGA XX 591: Vol. 10/97; NSA IV: Vol. 9/237
Discography and timing: Fischer-Dieskau   —
                         Hyperion I 22[9]
                         Hyperion II 11[18]   6'23   Catherine Wyn-Rogers

←— *Lorma D327*   *Das Grab D330* —→

DU BIST DIE RUH

You are rest and peace

(Rückert) Op. 59 no. 3, **D776** [H523]
Eb major   1823

(82 bars)

Du bist die Ruh,	You are repose
Der Friede mild,	And gentle peace.
Die Sehnsucht du,	You are longing
Und was sie stillt.	And what stills it.
Ich weihe dir	Full of joy and grief
Voll Lust und Schmerz	I consecrate to you
Zur Wohnung hier	My eyes and my heart
Mein Aug' und Herz.	As a dwelling place.
Kehr' ein bei mir,	Come in to me
Und schliesse du	And softly close
Still hinter dir	The gate
Die Pforten zu.	Behind you.
Treib andern Schmerz	Drive all other grief
Aus dieser Brust.	From my breast.
Voll sei dies Herz	Let my heart
Von deiner Lust.	Be full of your joy.
Dies Augenzelt	The temple of my eyes
Von deinem Glanz	Is lit
Allein erhellt,	By your radiance alone:
O füll' es ganz.	O, fill it wholly.

FRIEDRICH RÜCKERT (1788–1866); poem written 1819/20

*This is the third of Schubert's six Rückert solo settings (1822–3). See the poet's biography for a
chronological list of all the Rückert settings*

This is one of the most famous songs in the world, and also one of the most difficult to sing. The playing of it, whilst not requiring a virtuoso technique, calls for great control of colour and touch, as well as evenness of rhythm. As with *Lachen und Weinen* D777, composed at the same time, the song has become a classic and it is easy to forget the oriental inspiration behind the poem, something written into the music by a composer supremely sensitive to literary background. *Du bist die Ruh* has such inner poise that it suggests a transcendental religious experience unfolding in the solemn, meditative timescale that one associates with the rituals of the east. The song is extremely moving, but it sometimes seems not to move at all: this tempo (a slow ⅜) makes of the music something deliberately repetitive, even monotonous (though not at all dull). This is a litany that hymns long-lasting love, and the steady-breathed span of an enduring relationship. Rückert was not only an expert on eastern literature, he was an ardent spokesman for marriage and family life. Though the happiness of partnership was never to be Schubert's lot, in this heavenly music we glimpse the extent of his longing for emotional security, for the rapture and safety of a committed relationship. The poem unleashes a powerful gentleness in Schubert, a marriage of sensuality and idealism that recalls the sublime coda of the first *Suleika* D720 song, a miracle of eroticism married to idealism. Sadly, the composer's own recent experiences of love had brought him anything but peace and reassurance.

The extended seven-bar *Vorspiel* is an extraordinary achievement. The two hands of the pianist embark on their pilgrimage as they meet in the middle of the keyboard, the left marking out a gently pulsating rhythm in quavers, the right in evenly spaced semiquavers that oscillate back and forth (they must be handled with infinite care) as they trace the ghost of a melody. This music is the basis of the song's accompaniment; its slow-moving harmony suggests an opening flower, or perhaps the spreading before our gaze of a broad vista of emotional calm. The hands gradually move further apart; after three bars, two-part writing blossoms into three parts, and then five; the rocking semiquavers move to the left hand, and longer note values transfer to the right; dotted crotchets aspire heavenward as a sequence of lofty suspensions leads to a return to the E flat major of the song's opening. In these bars nothing much has happened on paper, and yet, in terms of sound and mood, and in typically Schubertian fashion, the composer has conjured up something visionary and sacred.

The poem is in five strophes. The music for the first two lines of the poem is almost identical (a single note is changed) to that of the third and fourth, and the same applies to the different music of the next verse. But it is these two strophes of poetry, taken together, which make the first complete musical verse of the song. This larger structure is in turn repeated, with its smaller internal repetitions, to make a second musical verse. It is this organic architecture, a perfectly balanced shape and symmetry, that makes everything in this music sound inevitable and pre-ordained. This is in turn a musical mirror of Rückert's remarkable rhyme scheme whereby in the poem's twenty lines there are only seven rhymes: ABAB, CDCD, CACA, DEDE, FGFG.

The first four bars of the vocal line, music of heavenly beauty, are a setting of the poem's first two lines. The composite mood of the three key words 'Ruh', 'Friede' and 'mild' is perfectly captured. The repetition of identical music for Rückert's third and fourth lines ('Die Sehnsucht du, / Und was sie stillt') seems an apt metaphor for unswerving constancy. A trace of unstilled 'Sehnsucht' is suggested by the diminished chord harmony under 'Ich weihe dir' (b. 16), a new fragment of melody this, where the lingering passing note on the word 'dir' (b. 17) is tenderness itself. The phrase for 'Voll Lust und Schmerz' (cf. a similar unity in contrast found in *Lachen und Weinen*) is once again a mixture of diminished and major key harmonies. The persistent movement of slowly flowing semiquavers is sometimes broken by dotted rhythms in the vocal line (at 'und Schmerz' for example, b. 18), a *bel canto* device which is here harnessed to suggest something far more restrained than an Italianate sob; rather a voice that momentarily hesitates, lingering on a note as if suddenly caught by emotion.

At first glance the music for 'Zur Wohnung hier Mein Aug' und Herz' (bb. 20–23) seems identical to that for the preceding phrase – 'Ich weihe dir Voll Lust und Schmerz' (bb. 16–19). The crucial difference is that 'voll' (b. 18) is sung on an A natural as part of a diminished chord, but the corresponding moment in the next phrase ('Mein Aug' und Herz', b. 22) is harmonized by the first inversion of the subdominant – A flat major. The change from that slightly unsettled A natural to the consolatory plagal A flat is an analogue for the solving of problems, the allaying of fears. An extra tag of two bars (bb. 24–5) repeats 'Mein Aug' und Herz' like a murmured blessing – a marvellous touch; the music's tessitura sinks, as if peacefully assuaged, and leads back to the tonic key. The drooping intervals we hear both times on the word 'Herz' (bb. 23 and 25) bow with reverence in the presence of the beloved.

The five-bar interlude (bb. 26–30) ponders the depth of these emotions. The tessitura of the piano writing goes deeper than anything so far, octaves between the hands are portentously introspective and add a suspicion of insecurity. This passage allows us to hear how unhappy and lost the singer would be without his or her beloved companion – along the lines of 'What have I done to deserve this luck?' Once again, the repetition of small musical cells is the secret of the music's strength: the interlude's third bar is a repeat of the first (thus bb. 26 and 28 are the same); the fourth bar (b. 29) is a reworking of the 'Mein Aug' und Herz' melody, transposed down a tone into the tonic key.

The next musical verse (the third and fourth of Rückert's strophes) is an almost exact repetition of the first. But Schubert had conceived his music for the opening words, and the subsequent text does not fit quite as well. Here it is not a question of mood but of such practicalities as breath control: the enjambment of the meaning of 'Und schliesse du', 'Still hinter dir' and 'Die Pforten zu' offers quite a challenge. Ideally, this sentence should be sung without a breath: 'closing . . . quietly behind you . . . the door' needs no interruption as a single thought, but it is all but impossible to achieve at this tempo (most singers compromise and breathe before the last three words of the phrase). There is a slight change of inflection for the word 'dies' (a D instead of a C) in the phrase 'Voll sei dies Herz' (b. 43). The punctilious word-setter in Schubert cannot resist heightening the note by one degree, as if to point out the singularity of this, the lover's heart. We then have another chance to hear the interlude (bb. 49–53) that has separated the two musical verses.

What Schubert now has up his sleeve is nothing short of miraculous. However beautiful the song has been up to this point, we are still astonished by the revelations of the third musical verse. For one bar (for the three syllables of 'Dies Augen . . .') we might be fooled into thinking that we have a repeat of what has gone before in the first two verses (and the song would still have been famous). But everything changes on 'Zelt' (tent), part of the compound noun 'Augenzelt', Rückert's newly minted oriental metaphor for a 'tent of eyes'. In this temple-like enclosure the beloved's gaze protects, cradles, enshrines and illuminates the life of the enraptured singer. The syllable 'zelt' moves to a C flat, (b. 55): in this way E flat major cedes to a first inversion of C flat major. It is as if we have embarked on an excursion to the moon, our magic carpet irradiated by starlight. The vocal line rises in steady degrees up the stave, a journey of some peril for the singer where the poem's heartfelt aspiration is built into the technical challenge. The sumptuous harmonic progression is through ever flatter keys – G flat major for 'deinem' (b. 56), the root position of C flat major for 'Glanz' (b. 57) and back to B flat major for 'allein' (b. 58). All through this passage the piano writing is made ever more heartfelt by telling suspensions in the inner voices of the right hand. This musical wonder is crowned by one of the composer's most famous top notes. The word 'erhellt', thoroughly in keeping with the brightness of its meaning, is set to a high F (b. 58) moving to a G (b. 59), a full dotted crotchet. Even this is not testing enough. Without a further breath the singer must encompass another, even higher, dotted crotchet as the syllable 'hellt' slips up a semitone to a high A flat (b. 60). The quiet, introspective mood of the song is flooded with grandeur, as if by the light of religious revelation. A whole bar of silence (b. 61) is now called for – an unforgettable, somewhat eerie effect – and for 'O füll' es ganz' we return to the music of blessing that has concluded each of the previous two verses, despite the fact that we are only halfway through this one.

Rückert has provided five strophes, and Schubert needs six to complete his musical structure. No matter; he simply repeats the words of the fifth strophe to round off his third musical verse. But what a repetition, in a song of many repetitions! The words are the same as before, as is the music (with the exception of a higher variant on 'deinem' (b. 60) which, despite Mandyczewski's opposition in the AGA, has become accepted performing practice, largely because it is printed in the ubiquitous Peters Edition). The slowly ascending scale (bb. 68 to 74) is just as moving and majestic as before. But the second brave high A flat on the same word ('erhellt' bb. 72–4) is not so much famous as notorious. This is because the composer appears to write a diminuendo on the held note, in contrast to the continuing forte of the first time. But has Schubert really asked for it? His flamboyant way of writing an accent is uncomfortably similar to the hairpin sign for a diminuendo, and leaves open the question of whether or not this taxing change of colour high in the stave is really a requirement. The *Neue Schubert-Ausgabe* opts for a simple accent, the *Gesamtausgabe* marks both high notes in the same way, but so familiar is this diminuendo, fixed for more than a century in the Peters Edition, that most singers still attempt it. It is, in any case, if successfully brought off, an interesting contrast and a beautiful effect.

After another bar's silence (b. 75) the 'blessing' music returns for a fervent repetition of 'O füll' es ganz' (b. 76). This time this music is enriched by beautiful echoes of the vocal line in the accompaniment, first high in the stave (b. 77) and then, as the song comes to its peaceful end, an octave lower. The composer has seemed to save up this felicitous effect until the last moments, but at this level of inspiration he has no need to be thrifty with his ideas. There is no poverty of invention here, only fascination with the challenge of making the most out of the least: the whole of this song seems to have sprung from a single seed. If 1823 was the year of the cycle (*Die schöne Müllerin*), the composer here shows himself master of organic recycling within a single song.

Autograph:	Missing or lost
First edition:	Published as Op. 59 no. 3 by Sauer & Leidesdorf, Vienna in September 1826 (P107)
Publication reviews:	*Allgemeine musikalische Zeitung* (Leipzig), No. 17 (25 April 1827), col. 291f. [Waidelich/Hilmar Dokumente I No. 486; Deutsch Doc. Biog. No. 866]
Subsequent editions:	Peters: Vol. 1/212; AGA XX 454: Vol. 8/4; NSA IV: Vol. 3a/100; Bärenreiter: Vol. 2/130
Bibliography:	Adelhold 2002, p. 68
	Capell 1928, pp. 201–2
	Fischer-Dieskau 1977, pp. 196–7
Further settings and arrangements:	Friedrich Curschmann (1805–1841) *Ruhe der Liebe* Op. 16 no. 2 (1837)
	Fanny Mendelssohn (1805–1847) *Du bist die Ruh* Op. 7 no. 4 (1848)
	Arr. Franz Liszt (1811–1886) *Lieder von Schubert* no. 3 arrangement for solo piano (1837–8) *See* TRANSCRIPTIONS
	Arr. Max Reger (1873–1916) for voice and orchestra (1913–14). *See* ORCHESTRATIONS

Arr. Anton Webern (1883–1945) for voice and orchestra (1903).
See ORCHESTRATIONS

Discography and timing: Fischer-Dieskau II 6[9] 4'14
Hyperion I 35[8]
Hyperion II 27[11]   4'17 Lynne Dawson

← *Greisengesang* D778   *Die Wallfahrt* D778a →

DU LIEBST MICH NICHT   You love me not
(PLATEN) OP. 59 NO. 1, **D756** [H488]

The song exists in two versions, the second of which is discussed below:
(1) July 1822; (2) appeared September 1826

(1) 'Mässig'   G♯ minor   ¾   [57 bars]

(2) A minor

(56 bars)

Mein Herz ist zerrissen, du liebst mich nicht!	My heart is broken; you do not love me.
Du liessest mich's wissen, du liebst mich nicht!	You gave me to know that you do not love me.
Wie wohl ich dir flehend und werbend erschien,	Though I appeared before you, entreating, wooing,
Und liebebeflissen, du liebst mich nicht!	Zealously loving, you do not love me.
Du hast es gesprochen, mit Worten gesagt,	You told me so, you said it in words,
Mit allzugewissen, du liebst mich nicht!	All too explicitly: you do not love me.
So soll ich die Sterne, so soll ich den Mond,	Would I miss the stars, the moon
Die Sonne vermissen? du liebst mich nicht!	The sun as much? You do not love me.
Was blüht mir die Rose, was blüht der Jasmin?	What is it to me that the rose blooms?
Was blühn die Narzissen? du liebst mich nicht!	The jasmine and the narcissus? You do not love me.

AUGUST GRAF VON PLATEN (1796–1835); poem written in February 1821

This is the second of Schubert's two Platen solo settings (1822). See the poet's biography for a chronological list of the Platen settings

There is nothing quite like this song elsewhere in the Schubert repertory, but there are three other songs it brings to mind, all of them based on a similar rhythmical figure (either a dotted crotchet and three quavers in a ¾ bar, or three quavers as an upbeat to a dotted crotchet, also in ¾): *Suleika I* D720, one of Schubert's greatest romantic songs, where the two lovers are separated by distance; *Abendstern* D806, where the star of love stays apart, alienated from its companions; and *Fülle der Liebe* D854 which is love transfigured by suffering into something sublime. It seems that this rhythm came into the composer's mind when a text spoke of suffering for love, or of surmounting the obstacles of passion. *Du liebst mich nicht* is the dark side of this triumph, the tortured survival of love despite a lack of reciprocation. Another dark song with similar quaver upbeats, in common time rather than ¾, is *Der Zwerg* D771 – and this describes how love can lead to murder.

In the accompaniment the motif of dotted crotchet and three quavers (or a close variant, where the dotted crotchet separates into quaver and accented crotchet) dominates forty-five out of fifty-six bars. Thus Schubert hammers home the idea of an unbending fixation. Instead of the sad, resigned acceptance familiar to the Schubertian – the trace of a tear hidden in a smile, or a smile through tears – we encounter out-and-out panic, and hysteria suggestive of suppressed rage. The form of the poem is the Persian ghazal, a ten-line form where the endings of the first, second, fourth, sixth, eighth and tenth lines are the same. Thus we hear the words 'Du liebst mich nicht' no fewer than ten times during the song, allowing that the composer adds his own repetitions to Platen's. As in *Fülle der Liebe*, the sameness of the rhythm is tempered by constant changes of harmony that here border on the deranged. The composer uses every shift and modulation at his disposal, a dizzy and gut-wrenching display of harmonic legerdemain. Weaving in and out of the home key is normally a pleasurable pastime for Schubert; but the restless shifting of *Du liebst mich nicht* makes for uncomfortable listening. This is a desperate man searching for an escape, a way out of the maze. Nevertheless he is trapped – each pathway leads to the same conclusion: 'From every viewpoint, and from whichever way I look at it, you do not love me.' There is nothing quite as bitter as this litany in all the lieder repertoire.

At the beginning the song seems to be a soliloquy, addressed to a memory of the person who has abandoned the poet; but in the passage beginning 'So soll ich die Sterne, so soll ich den Mond' (b. 29) there is a modulation and we move into a more intimate confrontation: the singer seems to look his lover in the face, a real close-up this, as he tearfully enumerates the full extent of his loss and predicament. Here the words 'Sterne' and 'Mond' are set to mournful minor thirds (bb. 30 and 31) that droop like stifled sobs. At the repeat of this line we have the same words set to rising major thirds (bb. 41 and 42), as expressive a use of the 'pathetic' major as anywhere in the Schubert songs and, strange to say, even more tearful than the minor-key inflections.

Very few singers who are used to the Schubert style can fathom the song's unfamiliar emotional contours. It is often performed too slowly which denies the work its vehemence. It is no surprise to learn that the composer reserved a tonality for this music, G sharp minor (this earlier version is published in both AGA and NSA), that is not found elsewhere in his songs apart from the first version of *An Mignon* D161. The orthography of all those harmonic changes in this key, bristling with accidentals, is as tortured as the poem itself – the complicated expression of a complicated passion. When the work came to be published in 1826 the composer seems to have revised and simplified it, perhaps under pressure from the publisher Leidesdorf. The postlude is shortened and the key is changed to a more pianistically accessible A minor.

This key brings the song closer to Mayrhofer's *Abendstern*, mentioned above, which has the same tonality and rhythmic impulse, as well as a related masochism, albeit more quietly expressed. This leads one to suppose that Schubert possibly had thought of A minor all along as the song's real tonality, suitable only for high baritones because of the awkward nature of the F sharps at the top of the stave at bb. 42 and 51 (F naturals would be far easier for most baritones).

Schubert shows an astonishingly deep understanding of Platen's nature in *Du liebst mich nicht*. As in its companion piece, *Die Liebe hat gelogen* D751, there is a scrupulous avoidance of any pronoun to fix the sex of the object of affection. The diary entries concerning the poet's love for his 'Adrast' (which Schubert could not have possibly known) display a similar self-lacerating tone of abandonment, loneliness and inner turmoil. Despite the fact that Capell dismisses this poem as having been written to a formula, and states that the poet was only interested in metrical virtuosity, this is a love poem unlike most others, which the composer turns into music unlike any other.

The meaningful and lengthened setting of 'Narzissen' (bb. 47–8) in the poem's last line, an unlikely climactic point for an impassioned fortissimo if taken at face value, shows a classicist's understanding of the background to the flower's name: 'A Grecian lad, as I hear tell, / One that many loved in vain, / Looked into a forest well / And never looked away again' as A. E. Housman put it, and as George Butterworth and John Ireland set it. In the outburst at the floral display, culminating with the narcissus, the poet dismisses these decorative flowers; the real man he has loved is irreplaceable, and the possibility of effete youths as replacements will not do. This emphasis on the flower of male beauty, is even more marked in Schubert's musical reaction than in Platen's poem. In *Du liebst mich nicht* there is a tension, a sense of panic and a hopelessness that speaks of a secret world and a dangerous one, of fantasy and of misplaced hope. Many people knew how Johann Winckelmann had been murdered in 1768 by an Italian pick-up, and Platen wrote an eloquent sonnet in honour of the great art historian. In setting these two poems the composer has somehow entered an alternative sexual world with unerring accuracy, leaving us a searing musical portrait of an important German poet.

Autograph:	Wienbibliothek im Rathaus, Vienna
Publication:	First published as part of the AGA in 1895 (P689) (first edition)
	First published as Op. 59 no. 1 by Sauer & Leidesdorf, Vienna in September 1826 (P105) (second edition)
Publication reviews:	*Allgemeine musikalische Zeitung* (Leipzig), No. 17 (25 April 1827), col. 291f. [Waidelich/Hilmar Dokumente I No. 486; Deutsch Doc. Biog. No. 866]
Subsequent editions:	Peters: Vol. 2/120; AGA XX 409a & b: Vol. 7/24 (first version) & 26 (second version); NSA IV: Vol. 3a/95 (second version) & 3b/202 (first version); Bärenreiter: Vol. 2/126
Bibliography:	Black 2003, p. 151 n. 4
	Capell 1928, p. 179
Discography and timing:	Fischer-Dieskau II 5[8] 3'18
	Hyperion I 28[13]
	Hyperion II 25[14] 3'19 Maarten Koningsberger

← *Die Liebe hat gelogen* D751   *Gott in der Natur* D757 →

DUBIOUS, MISATTRIBUTED AND LOST SONGS
(INCLUDING WORDLESS SONG FRAGMENTS)

Adieu!   Farewell

This once-popular song was attributed to Schubert for much of the nineteenth century. The music (in C minor, in common time, and with the marking of 'Andante') was composed by August Heinrich von Weyrauch 1788–1865. The French text in four quatrains, a deathbed farewell, begins:

Voici l'instant suprême,	Here is the supreme moment,
L'instant de nos adieux	The moment of our farewells.
O toi, seul bien que j'aime!	You, my sole love,
Sans moi retourne aux cieux!	Return to the heavens without me!

Adieu! attributed to Schubert.

Weyrauch was in fact a literary figure rather than a composer, and this accounts for the amateur nature of the composition from a musical point of view. Born in Riga and educated in St Petersburg, he was a linguistics professor at Dorpat and later went on to work in Dresden. He published poetry under the pseudonym of Heinrich von der Myrrhen and issued five books of lieder among his writings. Everything about this song, from the exclamation mark of the title to the appalling poem and impoverished piano writing, is testament to the fact that it is not authentic Schubert. It was published as *Adieu!* in Paris, *c.* 1835. The title page mentioned 'Mr. F Schubert' as the composer with 'paroles françaises' by Mr. Bélanger, and dedicated to Mr. A Nourrit (the famous tenor who did so much to advocate Schubert's lieder in France, *see* SINGERS). The song actually dates from 1824, and it was privately published by its composer with the title *Nach Osten*, and a poem by Karl Friedrich Gottlob Wetzel (1738–*c.* 1800).

We do not know whether Weyrauch played any part in the original falsification, or its eventual discovery. The music was re-imported to Germany in 1843 under Schubert's name as a solo piano piece. No doubt on account of its popularity the song was reprinted in Volume 6 of the Peters Schubert Edition (p. 130) together with a warning that the song had been incorrectly attributed to Schubert. As the only song in French by even a phoney 'Schubert', and a lyrical manner that suited the contemporary taste for the *cavatina*, it received many performances – and Schubert's name was usually given, willy-nilly, as the composer. The German text ('Lebe wohl') is a translation of the French text by Bélanger and has no connection with the original Wetzel poem. In this music one can hear a prophecy of the long-breathed melodies of Gounod (said to be influenced by Schubert); songs like Fauré's *Après un rêve* were the most significant flowering of a particularly French genre of *romance* initiated by *Adieu!* Franz Liszt accorded the song the honour of a transcription (under the title *Lebe wohl!*) as the first of his *Sechs Melodien von Franz Schubert* S563 (1844) (*see* TRANSCRIPTIONS).

Albumblatt   Album Leaf

This page of music is in E major, in common time, with the marking 'Moderato'. The autograph is in the Gesellschaft der Musikfreunde, Vienna. The unattributed text begins:

Auf dem Pfad, der dich durchs Leben leite,	On the path that leads you through life
Sollen immer viele Rosen blühn,	May roses bloom in abundance,
Und der Bach des Erdenlebens gleite	And may the silver stream of your earthly life
Silbern dir ins Meer der Zeit dahin.	Glide along into the sea of time.

This single page, literally an 'Albumblatt' because it was taken from an autograph album belonging to the writer Bertha Pelican, was privately printed by Reinhard Van Hoorickx who usually erred on the side of the optimistic when it came to the discovery of new Schubertian material. It had already been examined in November 1922 by Mandyczewski who noted that the handwriting was not Schubert's. Elsewhere on the leaf is the following: 'Laibach am 16. May 1825. Franz Schubert'. As far as we know Schubert never visited Laibach (the present-day Ljubliana in Slovenia) although he applied unsuccessfully for a job there in 1816.

An den Mond D311 (sketch without text)   To the Moon

This fragment of twelve-bar melody is to be found on the autograph shared by *Schwangesang* (Kosegarten) D318 and *Luisens Antwort* D319 (also Kosegarten), and dated 19 October 1815 (autograph in Wienbibliothek im Rathaus, Vienna). The title *An den Mond* is in the composer's hand, but there is no mention of a poet, and no verse. The key is A major, the time-signature ⅜, the marking 'Lieblich'.

An Gott D863

(Christoph Christian Hohlfeldt, 1776–1819)   To God

Hohlfeld's text (the third poem as printed in *Lieder für Blinde und von Blinden,* the 1827 anthology published to raise money for the blind in Vienna) begins:

Kein Auge hat Dein Angesicht geschaut,	No eye has beheld Your countenance,
Auf ew'gen Höhen ist Dein Thron gebaut.	Your throne stands on the eternal heights,
Dein Herold ist der Morgensonne Pracht;	The morning sun in all its splendour is Your
Von deinem Ruhm erzählen Tag und Nacht.	herald. Day and night tell of Your glory.
D'rum hebt der Mensch die Blicke himmelwärts,	Thus man turns his gaze heavenwards,
Dich fühlt das Herz.	And senses You in his heart.

There are two further strophes. (The full text of the poem is printed in Schochow 1974 vol. 1, p. 195.) Under the title of this poem in the *Lieder für Blinde* anthology are printed the words 'Musik von Franz Schubert', something that has tantalized many a Schubertian. Because Hohlfeldt was a poet particularly linked with Dresden one might imagine that a different composer was meant here, the Dresden Franz Schubert [*see Mein Frieden* below and COMPOSERS]. In 1991 there emerged in Hamburg (among the papers of a deceased antiquarian bookseller) a copy of a setting of this poem for tenor and piano, with horn obbligato and female chorus, a combination, thus, of the musical characteristics of *Auf dem Strom* D943 for tenor and piano, and the Grillparzer *Ständchen* D920 for mezzo voice and female chorus. This copy had been made in Christmas 1943 'for his brave comrades' by an officer in the German navy who was stationed as a watch and member of the marine artillery in Brunsbüttelkoog. This 'Kapitän Vierengel' was clearly not the composer himself (biographical investigation shows he lacked the musical education on his own account) and he had used a manuscript or printed source to make the copy of the music that has come down to us. There is no information as to what that 'original' might have been apart from the fact that either it came from the nineteenth century, or was deliberately made to appear as though it had. It is perfectly possible that the man who assiduously (and extremely neatly) made this copy while spending many hours on military duty believed he was writing out a genuine piece of Schubert. This manuscript has been recently published and it ranks as a highly effective piece of Schubertian pastiche; it is a pity we do not know who made it in the first place, and when; this composer–arranger would have been able to complete various song fragments with greater flair than Van Hoorickx for example.

The music is in the key of E flat (the tonality of *Auf dem Strom* as published in the Peters Edition) and the opening horn solo clearly derives from a knowledge of that work. There is a felicitous Schubertian feel about the leisurely unfolding of the whole piece (the echoing effects of the chorus are nicely observed) but a notable restriction of harmonic resources and certain grammatical mistakes in the voice-leading betray the hand of an enthusiastic admirer of the composer rather than Schubert himself. The author–composer must have known that this poem was a missing piece of the Schubertian jigsaw, and gone to considerable trouble to unearth the correct text in order to lend his or her efforts greater credence. The piece was clearly composed some time before 1943, but Vierengel's copy may have been taken from a relatively modern source (from the 1920s or 1930s) that had cleverly adopted nineteenth-century notational practices. As everyone knows, it is not easy to 'invent' Schubert with any accuracy, particularly Schubert writing in the glorious final years of his creative life; this effort is better than most – good enough at least to convince many a casual listener.

Bibliography: Brügemann 1998, p. 75

Augenblicke in Elysium   Moments in Elysium
D2990B (D1582)
(Schober)
Schober's sonnet (*Gedichte* p. 174) begins:

Vor der in Ehrfurcht all mein Wesen kniet,	You, before whom my whole being kneels in reverence,
Jetzt schweb' hernieder, Urbild ew'ger Schöne!	Float down, archetype of eternal beauty!

There is no mention in the first edition of the Schober poems (1842) of any connection with Schubert, but in the second edition (1865) occur the words 'Von Franz Schubert in Musik gesetzt' presumably inserted by the poet himself who may very well have known of a work that has been lost to us. No song or aria (*see Die Wolkenbraut* below) with this text has been discovered.

Begleitung für Klavier in B D988A   Keyboard accompaniment in B flat
This fragment consists of thirty-six bars in B flat major (with an *alla breve* time-signature) composed after 1820, and probably connected with a composition for a work for more than one voice (thus its appearance in Series III, Volume 3 of the NSA). The autograph is in the Wiener Männergesang-Verein. The slightly baroque musical character of this introduction (legato right hand and a bass in separated quavers) is reminiscent of the introduction to *An den Mond in einer Herbstnacht* D614.

Don Gayseros **D93/1,2,3** (qv)   Don Gayseros
(Fouqué)
Die Erde D579B (qv)   The Earth,
(Matthisson)
Die Vollendung D989 (qv)   Fulfilment
(Matthisson)
There is a full commentary on these five songs in the alphabetical body of this book. This is because the de la Motte Fouqué *Don Gayseros* songs, and the much more recently discovered Matthisson settings, have all been safely authenticated by the editorial team of the NSA. However, even if a copy of the music exists in Schubert's hand, there is nothing to prove beyond doubt that he himself had composed every song he penned – after all there are songs by Gluck and Beethoven that he wrote down or transposed and the same must have applied to other composers, and songs by friends such as Hüttenbrenner. These five songs seem to have passed all the neces-

sary musicological tests as regards their authenticity, but I am only one of several performers who remain unconvinced that this music was actually composed by Schubert. This is as much a question of stylistic intuition as anything else, but Schubertian performers live by their instincts – and the more Schubert they have sung or played the more developed are those reactions. In the case of *Don Gayseros* the accompaniments and harmonic world seem restricted (even impoverished) to the point of being completely atypical; the Matthisson songs feel uncomfortable under the fingers for different reasons – a deployment of resources that simply feel unfamiliar and 'foreign'. These reservations are insufficient to prevent the songs being considered a legitimate part of the canon, but this paragraph may be regarded as the raising of a doubt shared (on account of *Don Gayseros* at least) with Alfred Einstein and Maurice Brown and my colleague Robert Holl, and the expression of a politely dissenting opinion.

Heimweh D33A   Homesickness

This is one of Reinhard Van Hoorickx's least convincing 'additions' to the Schubert repertoire. He combines a fragment of unaccompanied melody from October 1812, in triple time and in D major, with a poem entitled *Schweizer Heimweh* by Johann Rudolph Wyss the younger – a poem originally in Bern dialect. At least the poem dates from 1811: it is authentic only in that it chronologically precedes Schubert's vocal line. This was no doubt a fragment of a composition exercise for Salieri. Van Hoorickx self-catalogues his unlikely little concoction as D33a.

Kaiser Ferdinand II   Emperor Ferdinand II
(Unknown poet) D Anhang 1,29

The unidentified poem begins:

Was reget die Stadt sich in fröhlicher Hast?	Why is the town seething with happy activity?
Was rennet das Volk durch die Gassen?	Why are people rushing through the streets?
Es strömet hinein in den Kaiserpalast;	They are streaming into the emperor's palace,
Von dort durch das Thor auf die Strassen;	And from there through the gate onto the open roads.
Und weit hin an Fenstern, auf Wällen, auf Wegen,	Far and wide, at windows, on the ramparts, on paths,
Harrt Alles kommenden Freuden entgegen.	Everyone awaits impending joy.

The music is in common time, the key is A major and the marking 'Freudig und staunend'. The poem has seventeen strophes in all. This is a companion ballad to the other two extremely lengthy, and extremely uneventful (in musical terms at least) ballads that Ferdinand Schubert published under his own name in his pedagogical vocal anthology, *Der kleine Sänger*, in 1853. If we can believe that *Der Graf von Habsburg* D990 (qv) and *Kaiser Maximilian auf der Martinswand* D990A – also destined for school performance – are genuine Schubert, then there is no reason to doubt that this is also by the same hand. The other two songs are authenticated by an autograph that this one lacks – which explains why this one, officially dubious, has not been assigned a D number. It seems that when writing songs on behalf of his brother, Schubert in a sense *became* his brother and wrote music in a way that Ferdinand would have done if he had been quicker and more industrious, but not necessarily more talented. Of course Ferdinand's instruction to Franz would have been to 'keep it simple for the children', but when Schubert put himself into his 'Ferdinand mode' he ensured that his brother's deception was not exposed by music of an unlikely high quality (everyone must have known that Ferdinand had a famous brother), while somehow preserving his own compositional integrity.

Klage   Lament

(Unknown poet) D₂ Anhang 1,28 (D₁512)

For the text of this song (beginning 'Nimmer trag' ich länger dieser Leiden Last') *see Der Leidende* D432. The key is G minor, the time-signature ²₄, and the marking 'Unruhig und etwas schnell'. This was the second item in the Therese Grob songbook, but it seems to have been added some time after Schubert made a gift of the album – now thought to have been firstly in the possession of Heinrich Grob, Therese's brother – chiefly because the handwriting is not Schubert's, and there is already an authentic setting of the same words as explained above. The chromatic descent of the vocal line (and its ascent in the other direction from b. 18) is something that might have appeared clever (and even heartfelt) to an inferior composer but it, and the banality of the accompaniment, are unworthy of Schubert himself. The poem was initially attributed to Hölty, but it is nowhere to be found in his works.

Liedentwurf D555   Song sketch without words in A minor

This is a substantial fragment of some twenty-six bars written out on the final side of the autograph (in the Wienbibliothek im Rathaus) of the Kosegarten setting *An die untergehende Sonne* D457. It therefore seems probable that it dates from May 1817; it is likely that there was originally more music that has now been lost. The sketch consists of a wordless vocal line (with no clue as to who the author was), as well as a fully worked out, if simple, accompaniment. The composer was clearly working from a volume of verse; unfortunately there is no longer any chance of discovering what that might have been. The music begins with an *alla breve* time signature (the marking is 'Unruhig') but this changes in b. 17 to ⁶₈ as the music slips, via a chromatic slide of three notes, into A major. From a purely musical point of view there is every possibility that this would have turned into a delightful song (as far as one can tell when there is no text) if Schubert had seen fit to continue to work on it. The fragment appears in NSA 11/228.

Liedentwurf D916A   Song sketch without words in C major

The sketch was written in an empty space in the first draft of the four-part quartet for male voices, *Das stille Lied* D916 (autograph in the Wienbibliothek im Rathaus, Vienna). The fragment that breaks off after thirty-three bars probably dates from May 1827. The key is C major and the music is written in common time. In bb. 17–19, and again from b. 27 to the end, chords that clearly refer to the accompaniment are sketched in on the treble stave. The character of the music with its intermediary fanfares and hints of polonaise rhythm is decisive and determined, even military. It may well be a sketch for a choral song for solo voice, chorus and piano. It is printed in NSA 14b/283.

Mein Finden   My Find

For a discussion of the way in which the song title *Mein Finden* was confused with *Mein Frieden*, *see* below.

Mein Frieden   My Peace

(Christian Berberich Heine – or Heyne) D Anhang 1,30

The poem begins:

Ferne, ferne, flammende Sterne,	Far, far away, the stars burn brightly,
Gehen nieder, kommen wieder,	They sink and reappear,
Blicken auf mich traulich nieder,	They gaze tenderly down on me;
Weit aus blauer Ferne	From the far blue distance
Schimmern nur die Sterne.	The stars only shine.

The music for this rather banal little song in E flat major was first unearthed in the archive of the Seitenstetten Abbey in Lower Austria where it was found among the papers of Peter Leopold Puschl (*see* AUTOGRAPHS, ALBUMS AND COLLECTIONS). It was ascribed to Schubert by Reinhard Van Hoorickx in 1980 who pleaded optimistically for its authenticity, even when the music sounded nothing like the composer to whom he had devoted his life. More than a century earlier Kreissle had mentioned a song with the title *Mein Finden* and with a text by C. Heine in his *Verzeichnis*, so that when the first thematic catalogue was published (1951) Deutsch assumed the song of this title was simply lost, or possibly confused by Kreissle with the Kosegarten setting *Das Finden* D219. This seems strange when Kreissle had already listed *Das Finden* as an extant composition.

In fact the title of the song is *Mein Frieden* (My Peace, rather than My Find or Discovery) to the poem by C. Heine (or Heyne). It was printed, not later than 1834, in the third volume of an anthology of miscellaneous vocal music entitled *Die Minnesänger*. Once we understand that this anthology was produced in Dresden, and that Heyne was a Saxon poet, it makes sense to think of a composer who is also from that part of the world. In Dresden there was a celebrated family of musicians named Schubert. 'Franz Schubert of Dresden' had the distinction both of writing the silliest letter ever when disavowing authorship of *Erlkönig* D328 (mistakenly ascribed to him, *see* COMPOSERS), and also having one of his weak compositions appear as a supplement to the same Leipzig almanac where *Widerschein* D639 by 'Franz Schubert of Vienna' was also a publisher's extra. The composer of *Mein Frieden* is very likely Franz Schubert junior of Dresden (1808–1878), the son of Schubert's contemporary. So we have here a rather simple case of mistaken identity – the wrong Franz Schubert! As a final irony it should be noted that Franz von Schober moved to Dresden years after the Viennese Schubert's death and became a good friend of the Dresden Schubert.

Bibliography: Schochow 1995, p. 107
                 Hoorickx 1980, p. 97

Nach Osten   Eastwards
The German title for the Weyrauch song *Adieu!* (*see* above).

'O So Lasst Euch Froh Begrüssen'   O, let me greet you joyfully
In Kreissle von Hellborn's biography of Schubert (p. 605) a separate song is listed with this title 'in the possession of Johannes Brahms'. This is an example of how easy it was to make mistakes with Schubert's autographs before Mandyczewski began his massive work for the AGA in tidying up what had become an almost unmanageable situation. In fact the song listed above is the last page of the long Schiller setting *Klage der Ceres* D323. The last forty-four bars of the work form a self-contained aria-like hymn of gratitude in B flat major (marked 'Etwas bewegt').

Die Schiffende D990D   The Boat Girl
(Hölty)
The Hölty text of this title written in 1774 begins:

Sie wankt dahin! die Abendwinde spielen	She glides along, with rocking motion. The evening breezes
Ihr Apfelblüthen zu,	Waft her apple blossom,
Die Vögelein, so ihre Gottheit fühlen,	The little birds, sensing her divinity,
Erwachen aus der Ruh.	Awake from their slumber.

In his catalogue of unpublished Schubert compositions, the composer's first biographer Kreissle von Hellborn mentions *Die Schiffende* as a Schubert song. Such a work has never emerged or been found, and Deutsch made the suggestion that there may have been some confusion with the song *Der Liebende* D207. Van Hoorickx, here clearly torn between his enthusiasm to publish new Schubertian material and his musicological conscience, privately published a G minor version of this song with the words 'not authentic!' printed by way of apology on the cover.

Das Totenhemdchen D864   The Little Shroud
(Bauernfeld)

The Bauernfeld poem (*Album österreichischer Dichter*, Wien 1850 p. 195 and *Gedichte*, Brockhaus, Leipzig, 1852 p. 98) is as follows:

Starb das Kindlein.	The child died.
Ach, die Mutter	Ah, its mother
Sass am Tag und weinte, weinte,	Sat day and night,
Sass zur Nacht und weinte.	Weeping.
Da erscheint das Kindlein wieder,	Then the child appears again
In dem Totenhemd, so blass;	In its shroud, so pale,
Sagt zur Mutter: 'Leg' dich nieder!	And says to its mother: 'Lie down!
Sieh, mein Hemdchen	See, your loving tears
Wird von deinen lieben Thränen	Have made my shroud
Gar so nass,	So wet,
Und ich kann nicht schlafen, Mutter!' –	And I cannot sleep, mother!'
Und das Kind verschwindet wieder,	And the child vanishes again,
Und die Mutter weint nicht mehr.	And its mother weeps no more.

Such was the importance of Bauernfeld's friendship with Schubert that Otto Erich Deutsch assigned this 'lost' song a D number in his catalogue merely on the evidence of the rubric 'Musik von Schubert' in the two poetic publications of 1850 and 1852 listed above – both issued more or less at the same time. It is difficult to imagine a late Schubert setting (the composer was only a friend of Bauernfeld from 1825) of a poem that is simultaneously sentimental and brutal in its epigrammatic practicality. The poem has a touch of the terse anguish of the *Knaben Wunderhorn* poems about death and ghosts that so appealed to Gustav Mahler. The addition of empathetic music would be bound to underline the almost ironic pathos at the expense of the lyric's borderline black humour and to obscure Bauernfeld's Heine-like impatience with the ever-weeping mother. It is clear that the poet does not believe in the possibility of an apparition, but only in the good sense of a mother who wants to see her child lie, dead or not, in a dry bed.

Bauernfeld probably remembered that Schubert had set one – and only one – of his original poems (this apart from the two Shakespeare translations) – but which one? The setting *Der Vater mit dem Kind* D906 had been published in Diabelli's *Nachlass* in 1832, twenty years earlier; by 1850 Bauernfeld was a very busy and famous man in the theatre who inhabited the musical milieu a great deal less assiduously than many others in the Schubertian circle. The fact that the poem *Der Vater mit dem Kind* (*Gedichte*, p. 25) is not headed by any mention of Schubert is perhaps evidence of Bauernfeld's faulty memory. It is likely that either the poet or one of his assistants remembered a musical setting of *Das Totenhemdchen* and came to the conclusion that this was the Schubert lyric in question. In fact, there had indeed been a setting of this

Das Totenhemdchen by Randhartinger.

lyric by Schubert's younger contemporary Benedict Randhartinger (*see* COMPOSERS). This had appeared at some time in the 1830s, the second of three songs (the first was *Erloschene Liebe*, a Zedlitz setting, the third *Elfengesang* to a poem by Ernst Schulze, another of Schubert's poets). Randhartinger's *Das Totenhemdchen* is rather Schubertian in its shift from a gloomy D minor to a consolatory D major, although he has to resort to awkward tremolo figurations for those difficult repeats of 'weinte'. It seems likely that the poet wrongly ascribed Randhartinger's setting to his old friend Schubert, and forgot entirely about *Der Vater mit dem Kind*.

Die Wolkenbraut D683
(Schober)

The Cloud-bride

Schober's poem (*Gedichte* p. 57) begins:

Der Jäger ruhte hingegossen	The huntsman lay stretched out
Gedankenvoll im Wiesengrün,	In the green meadow, deep in thought,
Da trat, vom Abendlicht umflossen,	When, bathed in the evening light,
Die schönste Jungfrau zu ihm hin.	The fairest maiden came up to him.

With the exception of one change (Mädchen replaces Jungfrau) in line 4, this is identical to the libretto of *Alfonso und Estrella* at the opening of the Second Act, No. 11 of the opera. After a short recitative for Alfonso there is a G minor aria in ⅛ for his father Froila. The musical material of this aria was to reappear some years later in *Täuschung* from *Winterreise* D957/19.

In the first edition of Schober's *Gedichte* (1842) the poem is printed without any mention of the fact that it is an excerpt from the libretto that was written for Schubert, set to music in October 1821. In the second edition of the poems of 1865 there is mention of Schubert setting these words to music ('Musik von Franz Schubert') – but not in an operatic context. Schubert had indeed set the words to music of course, but not, as has sometimes been assumed, as a solo song.

E

AUGUST GOTTLOB EBERHARD (1769–1845)

THE POETIC SOURCE
Das Feuerwerk printed in *Zeitung für die elegante Welt*, Leipzig, 1807

THE SONG
1812? *Viel tausend Sterne prangen* D642, quartet for SATB with piano

Eberhard was born in Belzig in Brandenburg on 12 January 1769, and died in Dresden on 13 May 1845. He studied theology, and then painting in Halle. At first he scratched a living engraving illustrations for botanical works, but he soon became known as a novelist. He also ran a bookshop in Halle which published the famous *Urania* by Christoph August Tiedge in 1801. Eberhard the author is best remembered for his poem in hexameters, *Hanchen und die Küchlein* (1823), a celebrated children's book that was also meant to be read by adults. The complete edition of Eberhard's works (1830) ran to twenty volumes. *Das Feuerwerk* appeared in the 1807 Leipzig almanac, *Zeitung für die elegante Welt*. Alfred Orel doubted whether such a publication would have been available to a schoolboy; he believed it likely that Schubert took over this text from a choral setting of the words by another Viennese composer, Leonhard von Call (1767–1815), imagining the poem to be anonymous. It was certainly unusual for the composer to fail to acknowledge the name of a poet if it was known to him.

Das ECHO   The echo
(CASTELLI) D₂990C (D₁868) [H668]
B♭ major   1826–8?

(31 bars)

Herzliebe, gute Mutter!
  O grolle nicht mit mir,
Du sahst den Hans mich küssen,
  Doch ich kann nichts dafür,
Ich will dir Alles sagen,
  Doch habe nur Geduld,
Das Echo drauss' am Hügel

Dearest mother,
  Do not be angry with me.
You saw Hans kiss me,
  But it was not my fault.
I will tell you everything,
  But have patience;
The echo on yonder

Beim Bügel,
Das ist an Allem Schuld.

Ich sass dort auf der Wiese,
   Da hat er mich gesehn,
Doch blieb er ehrerbietig
   Hübsch in der Ferne stehn,
Und sprach: 'Gern trät' ich näher,
   Nähmst du's nicht übel auf;
Sag, bin ich dir willkommen?'
          'Kommen!'
Rief schnell das Echo drauf.

Dann kam er, – auf die Wiese
   Zu mir hin setz' er sich,
Hiess mich die schöne Liese,
   Und schlang den Arm um mich,
Und bat, ich möcht' ihm sagen,
   Ob ich ihm gut kann sein?
Das wär' ihm sehr erfreulich.
          'Freilich!'
Rief schnell das Echo drein.

[(. . .)]

Dies hört' er, und hat näher
   Zu rücken mir gewagt,
Er glaubte wohl, ich hätte
   Das Alles ihm gesagt:
'Erlaubst du', sprach er zärtlich:
   'Dass ich als meine Braut
Dich recht vom Herzen küsse?'
          'Küsse!'
Schrie jetzt das Echo laut.

Nun sieh, so ist's gekommen,
   Dass Hans mir gab den Kuss,
Das böse, böse Echo,
   Es macht mir viel Verdruss,
Und jetzo wird er kommen,
   Wirst sehen, sicherlich,
Und wird von dir begehren
         In Ehren
Zu seinem Weibe mich.

Ist dir der Hans, lieb Mutter,
   Nicht recht zu meinem Mann,
So sag', dass ihm das Echo
   Den bösen Streich getan.

Hillside
Is to blame for everything.

I was sitting out in the meadow;
   There he saw me.
But he remained respectfully
   At a distance,
Saying: 'I should gladly come nearer
   If you would not take it amiss.
Say, would you welcome me?'
          'Come!'
Resounded the echo quickly.

Then he came to the meadow
   And sat down beside me;
He called me his fair Liese,
   Put his arm around me,
And asked me to tell him
   If I could love him,
For that would please him very much.
          'Of course!'
Resounded the echo quickly.

[(. . .)]

Hearing this he ventured
   Closer to me,
For he thought that I
   Had spoken these words.
He said tenderly: 'Be my bride,
   And let me kiss you
With all my heart'.
          'Kiss!'
Called the echo loudly.

So you see how it came about
   That Hans gave me that kiss;
That wicked, wicked echo
   Has caused me such trouble.
And now he will come for certain,
   As you will see,
And he will ask you
         With due deference
For my hand in marriage.

Dear mother, if you think
   That Hans is not the right husband for me,
Then tell him that the echo
   Has played this trick on him.

Doch glaubst du, dass wir passen,	But if you think
Zu einem Ehepaar,	That we make a fit wedding pair,
Dann musst du ihn nicht kränken,	Then you must not upset him.
Magst denken,[1]	You can think
Dass i c h das Echo war.	That *I* was the echo.

IGNAZ FRANZ CASTELLI (1781–1862)

This is the second of Schubert's two Castelli solo settings (1817 and ?1826–8). See the poet's biography for a chronological list of all the Castelli settings.

The fact that this song was once relatively popular is proved by its position in Volume 2 of the Peters Edition. Today a song like *Das Echo* would be less likely to find its way on to a concert programme. This is partly because of its length; the song does not make sense without all six of its composed strophes (Schubert leaves out the fourth of Castelli's seven verses because this does not advance the already lengthy narrative). Schubert's consciously simplified songs are something of an embarrassment for the modern recitalist; he seems to be holding back the best of his expressive abilities in order to pander to the market as perceived by the publishers of the time. Castelli's poem in the French style is from another age where the text derives from a formula (however clever the echo effect) rather than romantic feeling, and it must also be said that exploiting comic effects was hardly Schubert's métier.

Nevertheless, only Schubert could have written *Das Echo*. It may be made of lighter stuff than most of the lieder, but there are many authentic touches. The introduction is elegant and charming, as is the idea of the echo introduced in b. 4 (a repeat of b. 3) in a quieter dynamic. There is a similar repetition of the final cadence at the end of the introduction (bb. 5–6). The voice part displays, hardly surprisingly, a talent for melody. Who but Schubert would have so artfully flattened the vocal line at 'grolle' (b. 9) to depict the anger of the mother, a singular feature that remains (less convincingly) throughout all the other strophes? The spacing of the accompaniment, with its graceful ornamentation, is also in the composer's best eighteenth-century manner, the whole capturing the mood of a pastoral song or *bergerette*, a style beloved of Haydn who wrote any number of songs in this slightly saucy fashion.

It is by no means certain when *Das Echo* was written because the autograph is lost. The publisher was Thaddäus Weigl who issued it in 1830 as the first of six humorous songs seemingly promised by the composer. Only this one was forthcoming. Schubert's heirs concluded an exclusive contract with the firm of Diabelli to issue the *Nachlass*, and Weigl had clearly delayed publication in the hope that five further songs in a lighter vein would emerge from the archives. *Das Echo* is not as blatantly commercial in intent or execution as some of Seidl's *Vier Refrain-Lieder* of 1828, and as Schubert was first in touch with Weigl in 1826 it is possible that the song is from this time. That Weigl did not publish it immediately may have been a sign of his disappointment with a single song when he had been expecting a consignment of six. The problem with *Das Echo* is the same for the performer as it was for its first publisher: it falls between two stools, being neither a serious lied nor a popular song.

Autograph:	Missing or lost
First edition:	Published as Op. post. 130 by Thaddäus Weigl, Vienna in July 1830 (P249)

---

[1] In Castelli (*Aglaja*, 1826) '*Mag* denken'.

Subsequent editions:	Peters: Vol. 2/204; AGA XX 513: Vol. 8/258; NSA IV; Vol. 14a/182;
	Bärenreiter: Vol. 4/190
Further setting:	Erik Meyer-Helmund (1861–1932) *Das Echo* (1886-8)
Discography and timing:	Fischer-Dieskau —
	Hyperion I 26[11]
	Hyperion II 36[8] 6'05 Christine Schäfer

← *Irdisches Glück* D866/4   *Der 92. Psalm* D953 →

ECHO ET NARCISSE
By Christoph Willibald, Ritter von Gluck (1714–87)
(Jean Baptiste Louis Théodore, Baron de Tschudi)
1779

This *drame lyrique* in three acts with a libretto by Jean Baptise Louis Théodore, Baron de Tschudi (1734–1784) was modelled on Ovid's *Metamorphoses*. It is Gluck's last opera and was counted a failure, receiving very few performances in the eighteenth and nineteenth centuries. The original version of this 'drame lyrique en trois actes' was composed for Paris in 1779, but the revised version with a prologue (from which the first of these arias comes) dates from 1780. When it was a flop in Paris, Gluck returned to Vienna (for the last time, as it happened) intending to mount a production there. This never happened, and no one knows why exactly. Schubert no doubt had access to the original full score that was almost certainly in Vienna, possibly in Salieri's safekeeping.

In March 1816 Schubert made two arrangements in piano score of arias from this opera (D Anhang II, 3 nos 1 and 2).

In *Lebenstraum* D1A the influence of Gluck (*see* Composers) on the young Schubert can clearly be heard. The autograph of that work contains a fragment (twenty-nine bars) of Schubert's piano-duet arrangement of the Overture to *Iphigenia in Aulis* (D Anhang II, 1: beginning of 1810). Although we do not know whether Schubert had the opportunity to attend the opera house as early as 1810, it would have been possible for him to have seen a production of *Alceste* in that year. The only Gluck opera we are certain that Schubert actually saw was the other Iphigenia opera (*en Tauride* or '*in Tauris*' in German translation) in January 1813. From 1769 Gluck was Antonio Salieri's friend, teacher and mentor. Schubert was thus, in a way, a grand-pupil of the composer he referred to (on the title page of these song arrangements) as the 'Chev. Gluck'.

We have no idea why, and for whom, the composer made these arrangements. It is possible that they had something to do with his job application in April of that year to be Kapellmeister in Laibach (now Ljubljana, in Slovenia). Presumably the ability to make a vocal score from a full orchestral 'Partitur' was one of the skills required of a music director. Schubert may have made these arrangements at the end of May and included them with his application as a sample of his work; they are certainly among the neatest of his manuscripts. But it is equally possible that this music was prepared for a private performance within his own circle: the celebrations of Salieri's golden jubilee in Vienna took place in June 1816, and these arias may have been intended as a homage to the teaching lineage.

The arrangements themselves are kept simple and easily playable – model vocal score reductions for rehearsal purposes with the pianistic textures light and bright. These pieces are a reminder that Schubert's accompaniments were influenced by the vocal scores of theatrical works by Gluck and Mozart. Hugo Wolf's accompaniments were influenced in the same way by the piano reductions of Wagner's operas.

First Known   24 September 1779 at the Opéra, Paris; revised version 8 August
Performances: 1780 also at the Opéra, Paris

I RIEN DE LA NATURE   Nothing in all nature
Deutsch Anhang II, 3 no. 1 H243+
A major   Arranged March 1816

(71 bars)

Rien de la nature n'échappe à mes traits;   Nothing in all nature escapes my arrows;
ni le guerrier, couvert de son armure,   Not the warrior, clad in armour,
ni le chasseur léger qui fuit dans les forêts.   Nor the fleet-footed huntsman darting through
                                                        the forests.

Rien de la nature n'échappe à mes traits is sung by Cupid, or Amour, in the prologue to the opera. He is determined to make Narcissus fall in love again after his unsuccessful infatuation with Echo whom Apollo means to keep for himself.

Autograph: Wienbibliothek im Rathaus, Vienna
First edition: To be published as part of the NSA
Subsequent editions: Not in Peters; Not in AGA; NSA VIII: Vol. 1
Discography and timing: Fischer-Dieskau   —
                               Hyperion I 33^2
                               Hyperion II 13^{18} 2'00   Ann Murray

← *Lebensmelodien* D395   'O combats, o désordre extrême' D Anhang IIa →

II O COMBATS, O DÉSORDRE EXTRÊME   What conflict, what
Deutsch Anhang II, 3 no. 2 H243++   extreme confusion
C major   Arranged March 1816

(84 bars)

O combats, o désordre extrême,	What conflict, what extreme confusion,
ô trouble affreux et confus!	What dreadful, chaotic turmoil!
Hélas! je ne sais plus ce que je hais ou ce que j'aime,	Alas, I no longer know what I hate or what I love;
je sens au dedans de moi un long frémissement	I feel within me a prolonged shivering
qui me glace d'effroi.	which fills me with chill dread.
Je ne me connais plus moi-même;	I no longer know myself; my friend,
ô mon ami, je m'abandonne à toi!	I abandon myself to you!

O combats, o désordre extrême is the aria of Narcissus in the opera's second act. Apollo has put him under a spell: the reflection by which he is enraptured is not his own, but what appears to be, by magic, that of a beautiful water-goddess. This aria tells of Narcissus' confusion and passion and is sung just before he is restored to his senses by a clap of Apollo's thunder.

Autograph:	Wienbibliothek im Rathaus, Vienna
First edition:	To be published as part of the NSA
Subsequent editions:	Not in Peters; Not in AGA; NSA VIII: Vol. 1
Discography and timing:	Fischer-Dieskau —
	Hyperion I 33^3
	Hyperion II 13^{19} 1'24 Ann Murray

←— 'Rien de la nature' D Anhang IIb   *Die verfehlte Stunde* D409 —→

EDONE   Edone

(KLOPSTOCK) **D445** [H273]
C minor (without flats in the key signature)   June 1816

(37 bars)

Dein süsses Bild, Edone,	Your sweet image, Edone,
Schwebt stets vor meinem Blick;	Forever hovers before my eyes;
Allein ihn trüben Zähren,	But they are clouded by tears,
Dass du es selbst nicht bist.	For it is not you.
Ich seh' es, wenn der Abend	I see it when evening falls,
Mir dämmert, wenn der Mond	I see it when the moon shines,
Mir glänzt, seh' ich's, und weine,	And I weep,
Dass du es selbst nicht bist.	For it is not you.
Bei jenes Tales Blumen,	By the flowers in yonder valley,
Die ich ihr lesen will,	Which I would gather for her,

Bei jenen Myrtenzweigen,	By those myrtle stems,
Die ich ihr flechten will,	Which I would plait for her,

Beschwör' ich dich, Erscheinung,	I call you up, apparition;
Auf, und verwandle dich!	Arise, and transform yourself!
Verwandle dich, Erscheinung,	Transform yourself, apparition,
Und werd' Edone selbst!	And become Edone herself!

FRIEDRICH GOTTLOB KLOPSTOCK (1724–1803); poem written in Autumn 1767

This is the last of Schubert's thirteen Klopstock solo settings (1815–16). See the poet's biography for a chronological list of all the Klopstock settings.

The name Edone derives from Aëdon, according to Homer the wife of Zethus, king of Thebes and the mother of Itylus. Jealous of the twelve children of Niobe she plans to slay the eldest of these, but mistakenly kills her own son instead. To relieve her grief, Zeus changes her into a nightingale whose melancholy song reflects Aëdon's plaint for her child. The twilight imagery of Klopstock's poem about a presence that flits in and out of his life suggests he was well aware of this classical link. This beautiful little song reminds us of the shy beauties of the first Klopstock setting, *Das Rosenband* D280. The poet is capable of great lyrical tenderness when not tempted to patriotic historical epics (*Hermann und Thusnelda* D322) or religious hymns (*Dem Unendlichen* D291 and *Die Gestirne* D444). This song was included in the songbook for Therese Grob (*see* FRIENDS AND FAMILY) and stood at the head of the collection. It is perhaps no coincidence that 'Edone', like 'Therese', is a name in three syllables, or an amphibrach scanned ∪ – ∪. Any composer as literary as Schubert would surely have wished the first song in a specially assembled birthday album to serve as a dedication.

The music is chaste and wistful. As in *Der Leidende* D432, the accompaniment is a see-saw that oscillates between the left hand and the right's off-beat quavers. The vocal line has the quality of a flute or clarinet melody judiciously accompanied by strings. Is it too much to suppose that Schubert was also aware of the provenance of Edone's name and imagined some kind of birdsong in this high tessitura? Reed calls this the composer's 'woodwind' style, and notes that it is not only a feature of the 1816 songs but that it is also to be found in the middle section of the slow movement of the Symphony no. 4 (the 'Tragic').

The second strophe of this *durchkomponiert* setting is perhaps the most interesting and the most eventful harmonically. At 'wenn der Abend / Mir dämmert' (b. 12) the imagery of twilight prompts a shift to the remote shores of ever flatter keys; the moon (a symbol of virginity) encourages a flight of tenor-tessitura fancy where we can almost see the silver orb moving through the heavens (at 'Mir glänzt, seh ich's und weine', bb. 15–17), a chromatic arch of sound. The myrtle mentioned in the third strophe (b. 24) is of course the German symbol of virginity, worn by brides on their wedding day. (Schumann called his 1840 songs *Myrten* because they were dedicated to his Clara as a wedding present.) The poet will only make a garland for Edone if he can claim her as his own. The poem is about a dream that is thwarted. Perhaps Schubert saw reflected in it the impossible dream of making Therese Grob his wife.

Autographs:	Gesellschaft der Musikfreunde, Vienna;
	In private possession (part of the Therese Grob album)
First edition:	Published as Book 28 no. 4 of the *Nachlass* by Diabelli, Vienna in 1837 (P318) transposed into B minor

Subsequent editions:	Peters: Vol. 5/161; AGA XX 230: Vol. 4/116; NSA IV: Vol. 10/170
Bibliography:	Capell 1928, p. 119
	Reid 2007, p. 136
Further settings and	Josef Antonin Stepan (1726–1797) *Edone* (1778–9)
arrangements:	Johann Rudolph Zumsteeg (1760–1802) *Lida* (1783)
	Ludwig van Beethoven (1770–1827) Sketch (1809)
	Arr. Tilman Hoppstock (b. 1961) for guitar accompaniment, in
	Franz Schubert: 110 Lieder (2009)
Discography and timing:	Fischer-Dieskau —
	Hyperion I 23[17]
	Hyperion II 14[28] 1'17 Christoph Prégardien

←— *Die Gestirne* D444   *Die Liebesgötter* D446 —→

EDWARD *see* EINE ALTSCHOTTISCHE BALLADE D923

BERNHARD AMBROS EHRLICH (1765–1827)

THE POETIC SOURCE
S1 *Erstlinge unserer einsamen Stunden, von einer Gesellschaft*, Band 1, Prag, 1791

THE SONG
10 February 1815   *Als ich sie erröten sah* D153 [S1: p. 22]

Ehrlich was a German-speaking Czech, born in 1765 in Bärnsdorf who lived in Prague, and was in high-ranking government service there for most of his life. He was one of four brothers, all writers, who wrote poems in praise of various members of the Clam Callas family; powerful patrons of the arts in Bohemia. Ehrlich was in touch with Leon and Ratschky (qqv) who were the publishers of the *Wiener Musenalmanach*, to which he was a contrib-utor. Ehrlich was well known for his patriotic poetry in praise of the Emperor; he also wrote a celebratory poem welcoming Czar Alexander I of Russia to Prague in 1805 (who sadly never arrived in that city). Ehrlich also published 'a collection of prayers for ladies' entitled *Der Dienst des Herrn, oder die fromme Jungfrau. Ein Gebetbuch für Frauenzimmer* (1820). He died in Prague on 22 August 1827.

EIFERSUCHT UND STOLZ *see DIE SCHÖNE MÜLLERIN* D795/15

EIN FRÄULEIN SCHAUT VOM HOHEN TURM *see* BALLADE D134

EIN JUGENDLICHER MAIENSCHWUNG

EIN JUGENDLICHER MAIENSCHWUNG	May's youthful impulse	Trio, TTB Unaccompanied

(Schiller) **D61** [H24+]
B♭ major   8 May 1813

(50 bars)

Ein jugendlicher Maienschwung
Durchwebt, wie Morgendämmerung,
    auf das allmächt'ge W e r d e,
Luft, Himmel, Meer und Erde.

Like the dawn,
May's youthful impulse suffuses,
    In an all-powerful *burgeoning*,
The air, sky, sea and earth.

FRIEDRICH VON SCHILLER (1759–1805)

This is a straightforward student exercise, set by Salieri, in the writing of a canon. The venerable composer made Schubert compose many exercises in Italian, but he also assigned him German texts. Salieri composed a number of lieder (including a setting of Matthisson's *Andenken* which Schubert set, D99, as had Beethoven before him). This Schiller text, an extract from a long poem, *Der Triumph der Liebe – Eine Hymne*, was inspired by the opening chapter of Genesis (1:3 and 1:6). It was composed in the appropriate month of May: whether this was the teacher's or the pupil's sense of occasion (Schubert may have been allowed to find his own text), or merely a coincidence, we do not know. The music has a robust, cheery quality that is reminiscent of the domestic vocal chamber music of earlier composers. This song brings to mind Haydn's quartet *Alles hat seine Zeit* published in 1803, with its refrain of 'Lebe, liebe, trinke, lärme'.

Autograph:	Missing or lost
First edition:	Published as part of the AGA in 1897
Subsequent editions:	AGA XXI 39: p. 333; NSA III: Vol. 4/20
Discography and timing:	Hyperion I 12[6] 1'29 Adrian Thompson, John Mark Ainsley &
	Hyperion II 2[21] Richard Jackson

← *Verklärung* D59   *Thekla: Eine Geisterstimme* I D73 →

EINE ALTSCHOTTISCHE BALLADE

EINE ALTSCHOTTISCHE BALLADE	An old Scottish ballad	Duet

(Herder) **D923** [H634]

The song exists in three versions, the first of which is mainly discussed below:
(1) Graz, September 1827; (2) Graz, September 1827; (3) April 1828

(1)   G minor

(28 bars)

(2) 'Etwas geschwind'   G minor   §   [28 bars]

(3) 'Etwas geschwind'   G minor   §   [60 bars]

'Dein Schwert, wie ist's von Blut so rot?[1]
    Eduard! Eduard![2]
Dein Schwert, wie ist's von Blut so rot
    Und gehst so traurig da! – Oh!'
'Ich hab geschlagen meinen Geier tot,
    Mutter! Mutter!
Ich hab geschlagen meinen Geier tot
    Und das, das geht mir nah, – oh!'

'Deines Geiers Blut ist nicht so rot!
    Eduard! Eduard!
Deines Geiers Blut ist nicht so rot,
    Mein Sohn, bekenn mir frei, – oh!'
'Ich hab geschlagen mein Rotross tot!
    Mutter! Mutter!
Ich hab geschlagen mein Rotross tot!
    Und's war so stolz und treu, oh!'

'Dein Ross war alt und hast's nicht not!
    Eduard! Eduard!
Dein Ross war alt und hast's nicht not,
    Dich drückt ein and'rer Schmerz, oh!'
'Ich hab geschlagen meinen Vater tot,
    Mutter! Mutter!
Ich hab geschlagen meinen Vater tot,
    Und das, das quält mein Herz! Oh!'

'Und was wirst du nun an dir tun?
    Eduard! Eduard!
Und was wirst du nun an dir tun?
    Mein Sohn, bekenn mir mehr! Oh!'
'Auf Erden soll mein Fuss nicht ruhn
    Mutter! Mutter!
Auf Erden soll mein Fuss nicht ruhn,
    Will wandern über's Meer! Oh!'

'Und was soll werden dein Hof und Hall,
    Eduard! Eduard!
Und was soll werden dein Hof und Hall?
    So herrlich sonst und schön, oh!'
'Ach! immer steh's und sink und fall!
    Mutter! Mutter!

'Why does your brand so drop wi' blood,
    Edward, Edward?
Why does your brand so drop wi' blood,
    And why so sad gang ye, O?'
'O, I have killed my hawk so good,
    Mother, mother,
O, I have killed my hawk so good,
    And I had no more but he, O.'

'Your hawk's blood was never so red,
    Edward, Edward:
Your hawk's blood was never so red,
    My dear son I tell thee, O.'
'O, I have killed my red-roan steed,
    Mother, mother!
O, I have killed my red-roan steed,
    That erst was so fair and free, O.'

'Your steed was old, and ye have got more,
    Edward, Edward:
Your steed was old, and ye have got more,
    Some other dole ye dree, O!'
'O, I have killed my father dear,
    Mother, mother;
O I have killed my father dear,
    Alas, and woe is me, O!'

'And what penance will ye dree for that,
    Edward, Edward?
And what penance will ye dree for that?
    My dear son, now tell me, O.'
'I'll set my feet in yonder boat,
    Mother, mother:
I'll set my feet in yonder boat,
    And I'll fare over the sea, O.'

'And what will ye do with your towers and your hall,
    Edward, Edward?
And what will ye do with your towers and your hall,
    That were so fair to see, O?'
'I'll let them stand till they down fall,
    Mother, mother:

---

[1] The punctuation used has been taken from the *zweite Fassung* of the song as printed in the NSA IV Vol. 14, pp. 64–6.
[2] Schubert changed Herder's spelling of the name, 'Edward', to the German 'Eduard'.

Ach! immer steh's und sink und fall,
   Ich werd es nimmer sehn – Oh!'

'Und was soll werden dein Weib und Kind,
   Eduard, Eduard?
Und was soll werden dein Weib und Kind,
   Wenn du gehst über's Meer, oh!'
'Die Welt ist gross, lass sie betteln drinn,
   Mutter! Mutter!
Die Welt ist gross, lass sie betteln drinn,
   Ich seh sie nimmermehr, oh!'

'Und was soll deine Mutter tun?
   Eduard! Eduard!
Und was soll deine Mutter tun?
   Mein Sohn, das sage mir, oh!'
'Der Fluch der Hölle soll auf euch ruhn,
   Mutter! Mutter!
Der Fluch der Hölle soll auf euch ruhn,
   Denn ihr, ihr rietet es mir! Oh!'

I'll let them stand till they down fall,
   For them never more will I see, O.'

'And what will ye leave to your bairns and your wife,
   Edward, Edward?
And what will ye leave to your bairns and your wife,
   When ye gang o'er the sea, O?'
'The world's room, let them beg thro' life,
   Mother, mother:
The world's room, let them beg thro' life,
   For them never more will I see, O.'

'And what will ye leave to your own mother dear,
   Edward, Edward?
And what will ye leave to your own mother dear?
   My dear son, now tell me, O.'
'The curse of hell from me shall she bear,
   Mother, mother!
The curse of hell from me shall she bear,
   Such counsels she gave to me, O.'

Folk poem from PERCY's *Reliques of Ancient English Poetry*, trans. JOHANN GOTTFRIED HERDER (1744–1803)

This is the second of Schubert's two solo settings of Herder translations (1813 and 1827). See the poet's biography for a chronological list of all the Herder settings.

Thomas Percy (1729–1811), Bishop of Dromore (qv), was an important collector of ancient literature from many cultures; he translated works into English from Icelandic, Portuguese, Hebrew and Spanish. He is best remembered, however, for the *Reliques of Ancient English Poetry*, a three-volume collection published in 1765 containing poems from mainly British sources from the earliest times to the reign of Charles I. This ballad which appears in the *Reliques* in archaic form ('Quhy dois zour brand sae drop wi' bluid, Edward?') found its way in 1773 into Johann Gottfried Herder's *Von deutscher Art und Kunst* and thence eventually into *Stimmen der Völker in Liedern* – an anthology of songs translated from the old literature of many lands, and published in various forms between 1778 and 1807.

   This was an epoch when German philosophers led the way in the understanding of, and tolerance for, the diversity of the different races of the world. Herder was one of the first to foster the idea of a culturally based, non-aggressive nationalism. In 1773 he had written a major essay on 'Ossian and the Songs of Ancient Peoples' and as both philosopher and translator he helped bring Scottish culture to the attention of the German-speaking world. The stage was set for the international triumphs of Walter Scott, himself a scholar of German literature and much influenced by Thomas Percy's anthology. Walter Scott's *The Lady of the Lake* explores what he called 'the ancient manners, the habits and customs of the aboriginal race by whom the Highlands of Scotland were inhabited'. The backward Scots seemed to have a strength and integrity that pointed to spiritual virtues long forgotten by nations with easier histories. Numerous travellers – including Felix Mendelssohn – journeyed through Scotland. It seemed a richly worthwhile pursuit for those who had read their Ossian and Scott, and thrilled to Schiller's *Maria Stuart*.

This poem is known best in Loewe's celebrated setting that dates from 1818, nine years before Schubert's song. It is fascinating that the versions of the text as set by Schubert and Loewe are almost identical; they are both different in various details from the 1773 printing of Herder's translation. The Brahms duet, Op. 75 no. 1, was written fifty years afterwards. Schubert's song is much the simplest of the three settings, and it is probably because of this that it has been all but dismissed by commentators. At first glance it seems to have little in common with the great songs of the composer's last years, but the hypnotic repetition of, say, the four verses of *Des Fischers Liebesglück* D933 reminds us that the composer was showing a renewed interest in the challenges of the strophic song at this time. Some of the songs of *Winterreise* from the same year are also strophic and achieve the distilled simplicity which is the main characteristic of *Eine altschottische Ballade*. The setting is among the most phlegmatic the composer ever wrote from the point of view of notes (or lack of them); Schubert's response to murder most foul, with the twist of a *Hamlet*-like complication between mother and son, is to lay bare the bones and allow the interpreters to do the rest.

The simple introduction (pulsating Ds making a single octave between the hands) ends with what we might term the 'O' motif, a dotted minim that rises V–I in the key of G minor. It is the pianist's task somehow to make this pregnant with foreboding. The mother's music is marked 'Weibliche Stimme' – woman's voice – with vocal line doubled by the piano almost throughout. Diminished-seventh harmony ushers this music into B flat with a twist of E flat minor (she sings her 'O' on a held B flat while the cadence underneath falls a semitone rather than rises, bb. 13–14). Edward's music ('Männliche Stimme') echoes his mother's but in the key of B flat minor. His 'O' (on a held G) is also supported by a falling cadence (C minor to G major, bb. 25–6). The only interlude between the verses is a single dotted minim chord in D major that rises to the home key of G minor. This formula is repeated for all the verses, the contrast between the falling and the rising cadences suggesting a game of cat and mouse between the protagonists, also the listener. Schubert resists the dramatic approach of Loewe and opts instead for a hollow shock and revulsion – as if the music were echoing through an abandoned house. It is a song that seems ineffective on paper, but which can generate a sinister excitement in performance.

Loewe's *Edward* was published in 1824, and it is not impossible that Schubert was shown this setting, and perhaps challenged to equal it, by the pianist Marie Pachler with whom he was staying in Graz in September 1827. Maurice Brown thought so; Walther Dürr thinks it unlikely. But it was undoubtedly Pachler who re-introduced Schubert to the poems of Karl von Leitner, and to the Klenke poem *Heimliches Lieben* D922. By coincidence, Josef Abel, whose nativity scene so appealed to Schubert at an art exhibition in 1816 (Doc. Biog. No. 88) had painted a portrait of Marie Pachler in 1817. The picture in which Marie is depicted as a Biedermeier muse with harp in rather a seductive pose appears on p. 469 of Deutsch's iconographical volume. The link is rendered more curious by the fact that Frau Pachler was the mother of a little boy, Faust (for whom Schubert wrote a charming piano duet, *Kindermarsch* D928), and that the Scottish ballad set in Graz, at Marie's behest (so Faust's memoirs tell us), shows a family caught up in a web of twisted evil. *Eine altschottische Ballade* is a grisly antithesis to the idealized Christian relationship of mother and child.

There are three versions printed in the NSA. The first was used for Op. 165 and Peters. The second version is almost identical, apart from the disposition of the 'O' exclamations which occur before, not with, the cadential chords. The AGA prints these two versions in the reverse

Illustration of *Edward* (Eine altschottische Ballade) (1861).

order. In 1971 a third version was discovered in Budapest. This substituted the word 'Weh' for 'O' and directs the two voices to sing together in unison for the last thirteen bars of the song (this is at the passage beginning 'Der Fluch der Hölle soll auf *mir* ruhn'). The female voice sings this altered line, as if contemplating in horror the curse just placed upon her, while Edward repeats his own line. At the very end of the song the two sentiments are sung at the same time with their clashing 'mir' and 'euch' as well as 'Eduard' and 'Mutter' – a deliberate piling-up of words often to be found in the duets by Schumann inspired by Bach's vocal writing. The final 'Weh' is an octave higher than the 'O' in both the other versions – a sudden high G difficult for both singers to bring off without sounding like a blood-curdling yowl, perhaps the intention.

Autographs:	Pierpont Morgan Library, New York (first version);
	Hungarian National Library, Budapest (third version)
Publication:	First published as Op. post. 165 no. 5 by C. A. Spina, Vienna in 1862 (P400; first version)
	First published as part of the AGA in 1895 (P702; second version)
	First published in Budapest in 1971 by István Kecskeméti (with a facsimile of the autograph) and subsequently as part of the NSA in 1988 (P798; third version)

Subsequent editions:	Peters: Vol. 6/94; AGA XX 545a & b: Vol. 9/102 (given as first version, recte second & 104 (given as second version, recte first); NSA IV: Vol. 14/61 (first version), 64 (second version) & 67 (third version); Bärenreiter: 4/95 (third version) & 200 (second version)
Bibliography:	Brown 1955, pp. 260–4
	Capell 1928, pp. 243–4
	Fischer-Dieskau 1977, p. 249
	Kecskeméti 1969, pp. 564–8
Further settings:	Josef Antonin Stepan (1726–1797) *Edward* (1778–9)
	Carl Loewe (1796–1869) *Edward* Op. 1/1 (1818)
	Johannes Brahms (1833–1897) *Edward* Op. 75/1, duet for alto and tenor (1877)
Discography and timing:	Fischer-Dieskau —
	Hyperion I 13[8] 5'44 Marie MacLaughlin &
	Hyperion II 34[5] Thomas Hampson

← *Heimliches Lieben* D922   *Winterreise Part 2; Die Post* D911/13 →

Der EINSAME   The solitary
(LAPPE) Op. 41, **D800** [H555]

The song exists in two versions, the second of which is discussed below:
(1) Early 1825; (2) Published in June 1826

(1)   'Mässig, ruhig'   G major   **C**   [79 bars]

(2)   G major

(79 bars)

Wenn[1] meine Grillen schwirren,	When my crickets chirp
Bei Nacht, am spät erwärmten Herd,	At night, by the late-glowing hearth,
Dann sitz' ich mit vergnügtem Sinn,	I sit contentedly,
Vertraulich zu der Flamme hin,	Confiding to the flame,
So leicht, so unbeschwert.	So light-hearted and untroubled.
Ein trautes, stilles Stündchen	For one cosy, peaceful hour
Bleibt man noch gern am Feuer wach,	It is pleasant to stay awake by the fire,
Man schürt, wenn sich die Lohe senkt,	Kindling the sparks when the blaze dies down,

---

[1] Schubert changes Lappe's 'wrann' to 'wenn' throughout the poem.

Die Funken auf, und sinnt und denkt:	Musing and thinking,
Nun abermal ein Tag!	Well, yet another day!
Was Liebes oder Leides	What joy or grief
Sein Lauf für uns daher gebracht,	Its course has brought us
Es geht noch einmal durch den Sinn;	We run once again through our mind.
Allein das Böse wirft man hin.	But the bad is discarded
Es störe nicht die Nacht.	Lest it disturb the night.
Zu einem frohen Traume	We gently prepare ourselves
Bereitet man gemach sich zu,	For pleasant dreams.
Wenn sorgenlos ein holdes Bild	When a sweet image
Mit sanfter Lust die Seele füllt,	Fills our carefree soul with gentle pleasure
Ergibt man sich der Ruh.	We succumb to rest.
Oh, wie ich mir gefalle	Oh, how happy I am
In meiner stillen Ländlichkeit!	With my quiet rustic life.
Was in dem Schwarm der lauten Welt	What in the bustle of the noisy world
Das irre Herz gefesselt hält,	Keeps the heart fettered
Gibt nicht Zufriedenheit.	Does not bring contentment.
Zirpt immer, liebe Heimchen,	Chirp on, dear crickets,
In meiner Klause eng und klein.	In my narrow little room.
Ich duld' euch gern: ihr stört mich nicht,	I like to hear you: you don't disturb me.
Wenn euer Lied das Schweigen bricht,	When your song breaks the silence
Bin ich nicht ganz allein.	I am not completely alone.

KARL LAPPE (1773–1843)

This is the second of Schubert's two Lappe solo settings (1825–?6). See the poet's biography for a chronological list of all the Lappe settings.

This delightful evocation of the cricket on the hearth could not be more thoroughly Schubertian: here we find charm and delicacy, modulations perfectly attuned to the text and a gratefully insinuating vocal line. There is a grounded simplicity here that is an attribute of those who enjoy the earth and its straightforward pleasures. This song is a companion piece to another indoor evening reverie, *Der Winterabend* D938, which also clothes the thoughts of a simple and solitary man in music of uncommon refinement and sophistication. In both these songs the protagonists have come to terms, in different ways, with being on their own. According to Kreissle, Schubert's first biographer, the composer was in hospital at the time that he wrote this song. If this was the

Title page of *Der Einsame* Op. 41.

case it was because of some temporary relapse in his health. Nevertheless, with Schubert's help the resilience of the human heart overcomes loneliness, and the thoughts of the homespun philosopher take wing in music of a higher power. This finds a depth of emotion in the words that would perhaps have astonished the poet who penned the lines. In these and many other songs the composer gives a voice to those who seem unremarkable and ordinary; people are capable of deeper emotions than they are able to articulate. Schubert gently reminds his sophisticated listeners that the life of the 'little people' is not devoid of interest.

It so happens that Dickens wrote eloquently of the eponymous *Cricket on the Hearth* (1845) in one of his Christmas books where the characters feel the same gratitude to the house cricket – *Gryllus domesticus* or *acheta domestica* – as the singer of this song: 'There are not, in the unseen world, voices more gentle and more true, that may be so implicitly relied on, or that are so certain to give none but the tenderest counsel, as the Voices in which the Spirits of the Fireside and the Hearth address themselves to human kind.' This is a different species from the cicada, the rampant songsters immortalized in Chabrier's *Les Cigales* who 'sing better than violins', a cacophony turned into music with continually thrumming octave chords. Even Ravel's *Le Grillon*, with its more fastidious chirrupings, lives outdoors and is a different type of cricket, *acheta campestris*. Unlike the unceasing song of massed cicadas in the summer heat, the domestic cricket of Lappe's poem (written on the northerly Island of Rügen) chirps only from time to time; it can fall into silence, or it can suddenly begin a concerto (in Dickens's story it is the humming of the kettle that sets it off in competition).

From the very beginning Schubert's version of the unremitting chirp of the cricket is characterized by those ever-stationary repeated chords (marked mezzo staccato) in quavers in the accompaniment's right hand. These steady pulsations are the background to the whole song (and signify the presence of the cricket in the background too); in this case, however, the composer seems to have imagined the insect breaking the silence when these right-hand chords combine with staccato or semiquaver activity in the left hand. At the start of the song we hear a dry little chirp on the first and third beats of the bar where both hands play together – this is in the left hand, a motif of a rising fifth, G up to D. This seems to imitate splendidly the sound of the scraping of one tiny forewing against the other, as left hand grates against right – a warm-up before an instrumental solo. There follows a gentle shudder of four semiquavers preceded by a grace note, also in the left hand (b. 2), while the right hand continues with its comparatively bland mezzo staccato chords. This is no doubt meant to be a continuation or an elaboration of the cricket's song. But, as is often the case in Schubert, the motif does service for a number of ideas: it is echoed in the vocal line on the words 'erwärmten Herd' and 'Flamme hin', suggesting music for the fire in the hearth, the acciaccaturas hinting at sparks and a lick of flame. There is a delicious complicity in the way that this semiquaver figure is bounced between voice and piano (the end of b. 7, the start of b. 8).

At the beginning of the second verse, the 'cosy, peaceful hour' adds a crucial F natural to the chord of G (b. 17), the suspended animation of the seventh chord. The semiquaver figure here certainly represents the kindling of flame ('am Feuer wach'), the vocal line dropping a third for 'Lohe senkt' and rising a fourth for 'Funken auf'. The rhyming of the word 'Tag' with 'wach' in this strophe reminds us that Lappe, as a North German, would have pronounced 'Tag' without the hard 'g', a sound nearer to 'Tach'. It is astonishing how Schubert can always incorporate the most picturesque and appropriate word-setting into a song like this without disturbing its overall shape. An example of the seamless incorporation of a new idea is the phrase 'Allein das Böse wirft man hin' (b. 34) where throwing away bad thoughts allows a tiny moment of drama, and a jump of an octave that incorporates a dismissive gesture. At the repeat of 'Es störe nicht die Nacht' (bb. 36–7) the vocal line touches a high G (in the song's second, published version) where we can hear the smile on the poet's lips.

The fourth verse, like the second, begins with the dream-like ambiguities of the seventh chord (from b. 36). At 'sorgenlos ein holdes Bild / Mit sanfter Lust die Seele füllt' (bb. 41–3) the semi-quavers of voice and piano coincide for the only time in the song, as if the filling of the soul with pleasure requires an exact lining up of source and recipient, a docking station of the spirit. There has been a shift to the subdominant here (C major); as we wander further from the home key (into A minor for 'Ergibt man sich der Ruh'), we feel ourselves pulled deeper and deeper into a private world of restful contemplation. The fifth verse stays away from the tonic and gives the composer the opportunity to make the contrast of a forte passage: at 'Was in dem Schwarm der lauten Welt' (bb. 50–52) there is a strutting canonic effect as the left hand, in strident octaves, chases the vocal line at the distance of a crotchet. The semiquavers of contentment are momentarily banished. Thus is depicted the stress and hassle of town life. The way the composer has engineered the return to the tonic at 'Zirpt immer, liebe Heimchen, / In meiner Klause eng und klein' (from b. 56) is nothing short of masterly; how clearly we hear in this the poet's sigh of delight at returning to the place where all is right with the world.

The final verse has a surprise: after 'Wenn euer Lied das Schweigen bricht' the left hand crosses up into the treble reaches of the piano (b. 67) and the silence is broken with a cadenza for the cricket soloists who prove their versatility by singing in a different register. This magical peroration includes a vocal line in a higher tessitura in the final printed version than in the song's original appearance as a supplement of the *Wiener Zeitschrift*. The tenor Ludwig Tietze sang the song at one of the Gesellschaft der Musikfreunde gatherings at the end of 1826, and this may have been when Schubert recast it for a real tenor as opposed to the high baritone of Vogl. Accordingly the second version has high notes not found in the first. (The AGA prints this first version of the song separately, the NSA as *ossia* variants above the score; these are still a useful option for baritones who do not wish to transpose the whole song down into F major.) This touching of top notes in *mezza voce* adds to the singer's (and listener's) heady delight in the pleasures of such duetting. As Dickens put it: 'To have a Cricket on the Hearth is the luckiest thing in all the world!'

Autograph:	Missing or lost
Publication:	Published as a supplement to the *Wiener Zeitschrift für Kunst, Literatur, Theater und Mode* on 12 March 1825 (first version) Issued as Op. 41 by Diabelli, Vienna in January 1827 (P112; second version)
First known performance:	23 November 1826, *Abend-Unterhaltung* of the Gesellschaft der Musikfreunde, Musikverein, Vienna. Soloist: Ludwig Tietze (see Waidelich/Hilmar Dokumente I No. 416 for full concert programme)
Subsequent editions:	Peters: Vol. 2/92; AGA XX 465a & b: Vol. 8/36 & 41; NSA IV: Vol. 2/172; Bärenreiter: Vol. 2/59
Bibliography:	Black 2003, p. 32 Capell 1928, p. 206 Fischer-Dieskau 1977, p. 236
Further settings:	Georges Bizet's song *Le Grillon*, a Lamartine setting of 1866 best suited to coloratura soprano, is based on Schubert's cricket's motif of shuddering semiquavers. It is worth noting that the large volume of selected Schubert songs, issued more or less at the same time by Pauline Viardot and published by Hamelle, placed this song (translated as *Le Grillon*) at the beginning of the collection.

Discography and timing: Fischer-Dieskau II 6[19]   4'16
                         Pears-Britten 2[3]   4'21
                         Hyperion I 26[1]
                                                     4'34   Richard Jackson
                         Hyperion II 29[10]

← *Im Abendrot* D799   *Die junge Nonne* D828 →

EINSAMKEIT   Solitude
(Mayrhofer) **D620** [H401]
B♭ major – G major   July 1818

(410 bars)

(1) 'Gib mir die Fülle der Einsamkeit!'[1]   'Give me my fill of solitude!'
     Im Tal, von Blüten überschneit,   In the valley, bedecked with snowy blossom,
     Da ragt ein Dom, und nebenbei   A cathedral soars up, and nearby
     In hohem Stile die Abtei: The abbey in the gothic style,
     Wie ihr Begründer, fromm und still,   Devout and calm, like its founder,
     Der Müden Hafen und Asyl,   Haven and refuge of the weary.
     Hier kühlt mit heiliger Betauung,   Here unending contemplation
     Die nie versiegende—Beschauung.   Brings sacred refreshment to the spirit.

(2)   Doch den frischen Jüngling quälen   But the young man,
         Selbst in gottgeweihten Zellen   Even in his consecrated cell, is tortured
         Bilder, feuriger verjüngt;   By ever more ardent longings.
         Und ein wilder Strom entspringt   A wild torrent pours forth
         Aus der Brust, die er umdämmt   From his breast. He seeks to stem it,
         Und in einem Augenblick   But in a single moment
         Ist der Ruhe zartes Glück   His fragile, tranquil happiness
         Von den Wellen weggeschwemmt.   Is swept away by the flood.

(3) 'Gib mir die Fülle der Tätigkeit!'   'Give me my fill of activity!'
     Menschen wimmeln weit und breit,[2]   Everywhere there are throngs of people;
     Wagen kreuzen sich und stäuben,[3]   Coaches pass each other, throwing up dust;
     Käufer sich um Läden treiben,   Customers crowd around shops;
     Rotes Gold und heller Stein[4]   Red gold and dazzling stones

---

[1] Schochow 1974 Vol. 1, p. 347 lists nearly forty deviations from Mayrhofer's text, including many details of orthography and punctuation. For an explanation of the background to these alternative Mayrhofer readings see Editorial Note at the beginning of Johann Mayrhofer. Some of Mayrhofer's 1824 variants are shown in the following footnotes.
[2] Mayrhofer has '*Sieh, Menschen wimmeln weit und breit*'.
[3] Mayrhofer has '*Gewühl der Wagen braust und stäubt*'.
[4] Mayrhofer has '*Es locket* Gold und heller Stein'.

Lockt die Zögernden hinein,—[5]   Tempt the hesitant inside.
Und Ersatz für Landesgrüne[6]   Masked balls and plays
Bieten Maskenball und Bühne.[7]   Are a substitute for the green countryside.

(4)   Doch in prangenden Palästen,   But in the magnificent palaces,
       Bei der Freude lauten Festen,   Amid noisy, joyful banquets,
       Spriesst empor der Schwermut Blume[8]   The flower of melancholy springs up,
       Senkt ihr Haupt zum Heiligtume[9] And lowers her head towards the sanctuary
       Seiner Jugend Unschuldslust,—   Of his happy, innocent youth,
       Zu dem blauen Hirtenland[10]   To the blue land of shepherds
       Und der lichten Quelle Rand.[11]   And the edge of the sparkling stream.
       Ach, dass er hinweg gemusst![12]   Alas, that he had to depart!

(5)   'Gib mir das Glück der Geselligkeit!'   'Give me the pleasure of good company!'
       Genossen, freundlich angereiht   Friends, cheerfully seated
       Der Tafel, stimmen Chorus an   At table, strike up a song
       Und ebenen die Felsenbahn!   To smooth life's rocky path.
       So geht's zum schönen Hügelkranz   Up we go to the fair hills,
       Und abwärts zu des Stromes Tanz,   And down to the dancing river;
       Und immer mehr befestiget sich   Our affection grows ever stronger,
           Neigung
       Mit treuer, kräftiger Verzweigung. And other firm, devoted attachments are formed.

(6)   Doch, wenn die Genossen schieden,   But when friends have parted
       Ist's getan um seinen Frieden!   His peace is gone.
       Ihn bewegt der Sehnsucht Schmerz,[13]   Pierced by the pain of longing
       Und er schauet himmelwärts: He gazes heavenwards;
       Das Gestirn der Liebe strahlt.   There the star of love shines.
       Liebe—ruft die laue Luft   Love calls in the balmy air;
       Liebe—atmet Blumenduft   Love wafts from the fragrant flowers,
       Und sein Inn'res Liebe hallt.   And his inmost being is vibrant with love.

(7)   'Gib mir die Fülle der Seligkeit!'   'Give me my fill of bliss!'
       Nun wandelt er in Trunkenheit   Now he walks, enraptured,
       An ihrer Hand in schweigenden   Holding her hand in silent communion,
           Gesprächen,[14]
       Im Buchengang, an weissen Bächen   Along the avenue of beech trees, beside the
                                              clear brook;
       Und muss er auch durch Wüsteneien, And even if he has to walk through deserts
       Ihm leuchtet süsser Augen Schein; Her sweet eyes will shine for him.

[5] Mayrhofer has '*Den Unentscheidenen* hinein'.
[6] Mayrhofer has '*Entschädigung* für Landesgrüne'.
[7] Mayrhofer has '*Verheissen* Maskenball und Bühne'.
[8] Mayrhofer has '*Wird er ernst und trüb und stumm*'.
[9] Mayrhofer has '*Sehnt sich nach dem* Heiligtum'.
[10] Mayrhofer has '*Wünscht zurück sein* Hirtenland'.
[11] Mayrhofer has '*Mit der Quelle Silberband*'.
[12] In his autograph Schubert replaces the originally written word 'hingemusst' with 'hinweggemusst' without providing a new underlay (see NSA Vol. 12/23).
[13] Mayrhofer has 'Ihn *ergreift* der Sehnsucht Schmerz'.
[14] Mayrhofer has 'In ihrer Hand, in *Lust*gesprächen'.

Und in der feindlichsten Verwirrung	Amid the most hostile confusion
Vertrauet er der Holden Führung.	He trusts his fair guide.

(8) Doch die Särge grosser Ahnen,   But the tombs of his great forebears,
Siegerkronen, Sturmesfahnen   The crowns of conquerors, the ensigns of war,
Lassen ihn nicht fürder ruhn: Allow him no further peace.
Und er muss ein Gleiches tun,   He must do as they,
Und wie sie unsterblich sein.   And like them become immortal.
Sieh, er steigt auf's hohe Pferd,   See, he mounts his noble steed,
Schwingt und prüft das blanke   Tests his shining sword with a flourish,
  Schwert—
Reitet in die Schlacht hinein.   And rides into battle.

(9) 'Gib mir die Fülle der Düsterkeit.[15]   'Give me my fill of gloom!'
Da liegen sie im Blute hingestreut,   There they lie, stretched out in their own blood,
Die Lippe starr, das Auge wild   Who first defied terror,
  gebrochen—[16]
Die erst dem Schrecken Trotz   Their lips rigid, their eyes wild with death.
  gesprochen.
Kein Vater kehrt den Seinen mehr,   No father comes back to his family;
Und heimwärts kehrt ein ander Heer,   A quite different army returns home;
Und denen Krieg das Teuerste   And those who have lost their dearest in the war
  genommen,[17]
Begrüssen nun mit schmerzlichem   Now bid that army a sorrowful welcome.
  Willkommen.

(10) So däucht ihn des Vaterlandes Wächter   So, he sees that the Fatherland's guardian
Ein ergrimmter Bruderschlächter,[18]   Is but the raging murderer of his own brother,
Der der Freiheit edel Gut   Nurturing noble freedom
Düngt mit rotem Menschenblut.[19]   With the red blood of mankind.
Und er flucht dem tollen Ruhm   And he curses giddy fame,
Und tauschet lärmendes Gewühl   Exchanging noisy tumult
Mit dem Forste, grün und kühl,   For the cool, green forest;
Mit dem Siedlerleben um.   For a hermit's life.

(11) 'Gib mir die Weihe der Einsamkeit!'   'Give me the consecration of solitude!'
Durch dichte Tannendunkelheit   Through the darkness of dense pines
Dringt Sonnenblick nur halb und halb,   The sun only half penetrates,
Und färbet Nadelschichten falb.   And paints the beds of needles with a dusky hue.
Der Kuckuck ruft aus Zweiggeflecht,[20]   The cuckoo calls from the thicket,
An grauer Rinde pickt der Specht,   The woodpecker pecks at the grey bark,

---

[15] Mayrhofer has 'Düsterkeit' while Schubert writes 'Düsterheit', surely an unintentional change as every other strophe has nouns ending in 'keit'.

[16] The word 'wild' in this line seems to be Schubert's addition.

[17] Mayrhofer has 'Das Liebste hat der Krieg genommen!'

[18] Mayrhofer has 'Ein ergrimmter *Menschenschlächter*'.

[19] Mayrhofer has 'Düngt mit seiner *Brüder* Blut'.

[20] Mayrhofer has 'Guckuck' as the word for cuckoo. In Schubert's autograph he spells it 'Gukguk'. The modern singer should probably sing 'Kukuk'.

Und donnernd über Klippenhemmung   And the bold torrent
Ergeht des Giessbachs kühne Strömung.   Thunders over the barrier of rocks.

(12)   Was er wünschte, was er liebte,   Whatever he desired, whatever he loved,
        Ihn erfreute, ihn betrübte,—[21]   Whatever brought him joy and pain
        Schwebt mit sanfter Schwärmerei[22]   Floats past with gentle rapture,
        Wie im Abendrot vorbei.   As if in the glow of evening.
        Jünglings Sehnsucht – Einsamkeit—,   Solitude, the young man's longing,
        Wird dem Greisen nun zu teil,   Is now the old man's lot,
        Und ein Leben rauh und steil   And a harsh, arduous life
        Führte doch zur Seligkeit.   Has finally led to happiness.

JOHANN MAYRHOFER (1787–1836)

This is the thirty-first of Schubert's forty-seven Mayrhofer solo settings (1814–24). See the poet's biography for a chronological list of all the Mayrhofer settings.

This long and important song first saw the light of day in 1818, but the composer continued to tinker with it for a number of years. Leo Black is right to remind us that 'Einsamkeit' can mean both 'loneliness' and something much more positive in terms of being solitary. The fair copy of the autograph is dated 1822, and this was probably made only after a number of adjustments and rewrites which could have originated any time between 1818 and 1822. It is one of the first, and probably the most significant, of the numerous songs that belong to the composer's 'philosophical' phase. This is not to say the majority of Schubert's great songs do not have a philosophical component; he was a deep thinker, in his own way, throughout his life. But during the period 1818 to 1820 he enlarged (some would say strained) the boundaries of the lied by choosing to set contemporary texts for songs that were designed for more than narrative excitement or melodic beauty – in short, for something other than mere musical entertainment. The Friedrich Schlegel settings in particular were meant to be heard as something of a credo, underlining the composer's sympathy for pantheism and the world of the spirit as glimpsed through the workings of Nature. As romanticism took hold of Vienna in those watershed years it became almost obligatory for artists to nurture the unashamed 'Ich' of their creative personalities. The second word of the text of *Einsamkeit* is 'mir' – 'Give *me* my fill of solitude', says Mayrhofer, allowing himself a large measure of autobiographical licence. (The second and third strophes in particular seem taken directly from the poet's seminary experiences and his early years in Vienna.) However 'me' now also refers to the composer himself. In his early twenties Schubert had the confidence, and the need, to stake his claim as a thinker and to identify with poetry that attempted to make the world a place whose mysteries were interpreted and enriched by both words and music.

In 1818 Schubert had been invited to be music master for the two young Esterházy countesses at Zseliz. Among the books and papers he took with him for this five-month (June to November) soujourn was almost certainly a long poem by Mayrhofer, in manuscript. This was in six strophes with six answering antistrophes in the manner of an antique ode. (It is just possible that the poem was sent to Schubert *during* his Hungarian visit, but this is unlikely as the letters between the composer and Mayrhofer at the time do not mention such a consignment.) In early August Schubert was able proudly to report to his friends that the work was

---

[21] Mayrhofer has 'Ihn *entzückte*, ihn betrübte'.
[22] Mayrhofer has 'Schwebt *gelinder* Schwärmerei'.

finished; it seems that everyone close to him knew he was working on the project. The composer's letter begins:

> Zelez [*sic*] the third August, *1818*
>
> *Best and dearest friends,*
>
> *How could I forget you, you who mean everything to me? How are you Spaun, Schober, Mayrhofer, Senn? Are you well? I am quite well. I live and compose like a god, as though it was all meant to be so.*
>
> *Mayrhofer's* Einsamkeit *is ready, and I believe it's the best thing I've done [mein Bestes, was ich gemacht habe], for I was without a care in the world [ich war ja ohne Sorge].*

Schubert had every right to be proud of the piece, but his belief that it was his best yet deserves some explanation, quite apart from the fact that we know that he continued to revise it. The publication of Beethoven's song cycle *An die ferne Geliebte* in 1816 had almost certainly both fascinated and, to a certain extent, needled him. Just when Schubert thought that he was building a unique reputation for himself as a song composer, Beethoven came up with a surprising and successful work: six songs linked together to make a continuous piece, the cumulative effect of which was greater than any one of its sections would have led one to suppose. Beethoven was a famed innovator of musical form, and this work was proof of his continuing mastery. This must have been seen as a challenge by Schubert who had written many a ballad longer than *An die ferne Geliebte*, but never a piece linked together in this way. It seems entirely likely that Schubert asked Mayrhofer to write a poem especially for the purpose (just as Beethoven had almost certainly commissioned *An die ferne Geliebte* from the amateur poet Jeitteles). Thus *Einsamkeit* is divided into six sections to match Beethoven's ground plan. The two cycles, written within a short time of each other, represent different standpoints of the new zeitgeist – in Beethoven's case classicism tinged with Romantic ardour, in Schubert's, romanticism tempered by classical models. *Einsamkeit* is longer than the Beethoven cycle and, in its attempt to create something like a Seven Ages of Man survey, much more ambitious. Schubert's pleasure in the completion of such an extended piece is understandable: because the work was in a new and different form from any he had written before, he considered it his best. It was also his lifelong tendency to favour recently completed music over older work. The editors of the *Neue Schubert-Ausgabe*, when pondering why the composer failed to deliver *Einsamkeit* to a publisher, came to the conclusion that Schubert was dissatisfied because the piece ended in a different key from the one in which it had begun. (Beethoven's cycle begins, and ends, in E flat major.) There is no manuscript of *Einsamkeit* extant from 1818, only one from 1822. This may indicate that by that time the piece had already undergone considerable revision. Another reason for the composer's diffidence in submitting the work to a publisher is that he would have had to deliver the work to the censor at the same time: the political slant of Verse 10 might not have gone down well with the authorities.

Verse 1 (bb. 1–54): The opening is in B flat, with the marking 'Langsam'. The introduction is seven bars of semibreves, one chord per bar. In orchestral terms these would be for brass, a fate motif perhaps, as part of an operatic overture. On the printed page these empty rings of black-encircled stave lines give the music a bleak and ascetic look, and their effect is the same aurally. At the entry of the voice ('Gib mir die Fülle der Einsamkeit!' b. 8) we are introduced to our protagonist who immediately strikes us as serious and noble, if somewhat gloomy. The following piano interlude (bb. 12–15) contains a truly Schubertian turn of phrase: the right hand of the piano descends in a long musical sigh and then jumps a seventh so eloquently (b. 14) that we immediately hear the humanity, and the humility, of the singer's quest. The idealized picture of life at the abbey that follows is directly from Mayrhofer's youth. His father had wanted him to be a priest, and in 1806 he had gone to the famous St Florian monastery as a novice. He spent three years there (from the age of nineteen), and studied theology and philology. At the age of twenty-three he decided to change to law but it is obvious that much of the strength of the man (and some of the problems, no doubt) were formed by monastic life. This is perhaps the most difficult section of the work to sing because it lies rather high and requires a peaceful mood and the utmost poise. The accompaniment is little more than calm minims betokening the order and regularity of everyday life at the abbey. This was written before Schubert had visited Upper Austria and its monasteries with Vogl (in 1819 and 1825) but he must have heard about life in these great institutions from a number of his friends, including Mayrhofer himself.

Verse 2 (bb. 54–96): The music for the second strophe (the so-called 'antistrophe' to the first) is marked 'Geschwind'. Here, perhaps, we have an autobiographical explanation from Mayrhofer about why he could not endure the existence of a monk: unable to settle down to the cloistered life, he was too attracted by the excitements of the big city. In stark contrast to the first verse the music becomes driven with pulsating semiquavers and throbbing off-beat quavers that paw the ground as restlessly as a steed before a race. Mayrhofer's use of metaphor ('ein wilder Strom entspringt' bb. 71–3) allows the composer to indulge in his favourite water-music illustrations, an opportunity perhaps deliberately set up for him by the poet. We hear echoes of the whirlpool music of *Der Taucher* D77 and, at the other end of his career, prophecies of works like *Mirjams Siegesgesang* D942 with its Red Sea music. The fortissimo diminished chords that frame 'Und in einem Augenblick' (bb. 80–81 and 83–4) and the tremolo shudder at 'Ist der Ruhe zartes Glück' (marked 'Langsamer' bb. 85 and 86) are over the top in the grand manner; memories are stirred – of gruesome moments in earlier ballads. We can also detect the breadth and audacity of Vogl's artistic personality, and who better to champion this work than that soon-to-retire singing actor? The happiness of a sheltered life is swept away like so much flotsam and jetsam, and the water-music interlude in semiquavers (bb. 90–96) makes this clear. The whole of this section is harmonically unsettled and passes through many flat keys, eventually settling on E flat^7; the first words of the next strophe ('Gib mir die Fülle der Tätigkeit!') are accompanied by a loud G sharp minor chord – a sharply dramatic wrench.

Verse 3 (bb. 97–155): This section seems obviously influenced by the third song of Beethoven's *An die ferne Geliebte* – 'Leichte Segler in den Höhen'. The stately declamatory recitative-like bars that mark the beginning of every new section in this piece ('Gib mir' this or that) have occasioned the first change of key signature in the piece, a naturalization of the two flats of the opening. With a further change into the four sharps of E major, darting, mercurial triplets invade the piano writing (marked 'Geschwind' from b. 100); these feel remarkably familiar under the hands of those pianists who have played the Beethoven cycle. The clouds and streams of *An die ferne Geliebte* are replaced by the bustle of the 'Tätigkeit' of contemporary city life; apart from a passing reference in *Der Goldschmiedsgesell* D560, shops (b. 112) are not otherwise mentioned in Schubert's lieder, and the drumming-up of custom through window displays makes the reference even more modern. The shock of these mundane allusions is deliberately meant as a sudden contrast to the other-worldly peace of the opening. (The biblical story of the prodigal son and the progress of Hogarth's rake can be added to the seven ages of man as sources for Mayrhofer's survey.) The incessant triplets seem illustrative of babble and gossip, and a life empty of interior contemplation. This leads naturally into the entertainment of city life. The words 'Maskenball und Bühne' introduce an interlude-commentary (marked 'Geschwinder' bb. 133–54) where Schubert provides music with rhythmic energy, but which is devoid of any interesting harmonic content. All that prancing about palls before long, and the merriness of E major is replaced by a switch into E minor (two bars, bb. 153–4) leading into a bar of disillusioned silence.

Verse 4 (bb. 156–79): This is a soulful section beginning in C major (⁴₄ changes to ³₂) where introspection once again replaces mindless merrymaking. The syncopated rhythm denotes unease and the ache of nostalgia. There is a change of key signature into D major at 'Seiner Jugend Unschuldlust' (bb. 166–7), a passage which depicts the green pastures of youth as an idealized landscape of shepherds and shepherdesses. The blue 'Hirtenland' is painted with horn-like motifs of thirds and sixths in the accompaniment (Beethoven's 'Pastoral' Symphony comes to mind), and a short passage of unaccompanied recitative ('Ach, dass er hinweg gemusst!' bb. 178–9) expresses regret at leaving this idyllic life.

Verse 5 (bb. 180–231): Once again we have the expansive recitative phrase (in this case 'Gib mir das Glück der Geselligkeit!') that is the recurring feature of this song – slightly faster than usual, to go with the words (the marking for these two bars is 'Frisch'). The key of A minor moves into F major via C major. Schubert has a happy time with the *Ländler* music here which is marked 'Ziemlich geschwind'. A very Viennese and 'gemütlich' atmosphere is created, one that suggests communal singing ('Genossen . . . stimmen Chorus an'), foaming flagons of beer and thigh-slapping good humour. This is heartier music than, say, *Seligkeit* D433, but it is not without subtlety: particularly piquant is the twang of bare fourths in the right-hand accompaniment (first heard after 'Und ebenen die Felsenbahn!', thus bb. 196–7). This is clearly rustic outdoor music, probably a Heuriger band, a conviviality that is set up to be knocked down of course. In the version printed in the AGA the words 'Und immer mehr befestiget sich Neigung / Mit treuer, kräftiger Verzweigung' are set only once. In fact the repeat of these words in the NSA (bb. 214–25) is something quite new for Schubertians since Volume 12 of that edition appeared in 1996. It seems that Mandyczewski did not have access to the original manuscript for the AGA. The restoration of this passage in the NSA indicates that it was Diabelli who, not for the first time, had decided to 'edit' Schubert by cutting what he saw as twelve unnecessary bars from the piece. In the interlude following 'Mit treuer, kräftiger Verzweigung' (bb. 226–31) those same fourths sounds empty and forlorn, and Schubert constructs a splendid decrescendo effect, like someone sinking into depression after the party is over.

Verse 6 (bb. 232–56): 'Doch, wenn die Genossen schieden' (marked 'Recit') is unaccompanied and sung into a void, with faint echoes and fragments of the *Ländler* music punctuating the poet's thoughts and coming back to haunt him. This is truly a film-music technique. The mood changes to something much more lyrical as snatches of melody give way to flowing triplets (bb. 240–41), a transition to the next musical section that, on this occasion, does not coincide with the beginning of a new strophe. It is clear that Cupid's dart has pierced the singer's heart, and that the cheerful company of the many is no substitute for that of the preferred one. This initiates one of Schubert's florid songs of rapt devotion typical of the period: ornate and difficult-to-breathe vocal lines, markedly Italianate in character, and accompanied by triplets. *Blondel zu Marien* D626 was composed only a few weeks later and has many of the same characteristics: the ¹²₈ time signature and the E flat minor key signature (of bb. 244–56). Both songs yearn for idealistic love in a religious way. The word 'Liebe' is set pianissimo high in the vocal line (four times in bb. 248–52) as if the word were being whispered by the breezes. E flat minor shifts to G flat major and then, via the common pivotal note of G flat/F sharp, the music melts into D major (with a change of key signature) at 'Und sein Inn'res Liebe hallt' (bb. 253–5). Such a metamorphosis, typical of Schubert's ability to illustrate the deeper meaning of words with the use of harmonic relationships, takes us as if by magic into the innermost being of the narrator.

Verse 7 (bb. 257–84): 'Gib mir die Fülle der Seligkeit!' is the only one of these grand opening statements that shows any rapture or ecstasy, the curve of the phrase rising and falling in the arch of a seventh that contains the song's highest (and thus most aspiring) note, a G sharp at the top of the stave. The aria which follows (marked 'Langsam' with the key signature of B major) is even more tricky than the preceding one – a real vocal challenge in terms of *bel canto*. The walk with the beloved 'an weissen Bächen' is another perfect excuse for water music, and Schubert chooses the tonality of Mayrhofer's *Am Strome* (1817) and the future *Der Neugierige* from *Die schöne Müllerin* for this sumptuous *cavatina*. The long and demanding phrases require considerable vocal dexterity in order to negotiate all the corners and turns, but this use of melisma describes the state of being drunk with rapture. At the passage 'Und muss er auch durch Wüsteneien' (bb. 270–71) the voice feels its way, suspended on the top of the stave as if walking on a tightrope; the bass chords offer support, pointing the harmonic way. This coincides with the imagery of course.

Verse 8 (bb. 284–320): The B major signature is cancelled into naturals, and the marking is 'Feurig'. This antistrophe transports the scene from loving peace to war, and it is perhaps the most contrived part of the poem. It is here, if anywhere, that one agrees with Capell when he writes that 'Mayrhofer's hero is, after all, only an abstraction. We can take no personal interest in him'. There are many points in the poem where we feel that the poet is writing from the heart and from real experience (the opening section about abbey life, for instance) but mention of 'great forebears' and immortality is the flimsiest of painted cardboard. Schubert's music is nearest to the blood and thunder of the early years – a work like *Adelwold und Emma* D211 for instance. In the battle music at 'Sieh, er steigt auf's hohe Pferd', the composer reverts to his teenage manner, and the piano interlude is reminiscent of *Die Nonne* where the slighted nun tramples on her faithless lover's heart (after digging up his body). In performance this section is brief enough to sound passingly impressive, particularly the wrenched harmonic sequences in the interlude of bb. 313–20. Hammered F sharp major chords and arpeggios at the bottom of the keyboard (bb. 319–20) have only to slip a few internal semitones to change into the held D^7 chord that announces the next section.

Verse 9 (bb. 321–39): 'Gib mir die Fülle der Düsterkeit.' This is rather a strange thing to ask for, but it is nearer the poet's own character than other requests in the song. This section contains some of the most unusual words that Schubert ever set. There are a number of warrior's songs in the Schubert repertoire (the most moving of them *Kriegers Ahnung* from *Schwanengesang* where a soldier struggles with presentiments of death) but there is none that paints the devastation of the battlefield as vividly as this. (This chimes with the anti-war feelings that we read in the composer's letter to his brother Ferdinand on 21 September 1825.) The musical manner is grandiose and *pomposo* – after a three-bar 'Recit' the passage is marked 'Sehr langsam' and is made up of double-dotted figuration in the manner of Handel. The use of insistent dotted rhythms in an ironic manner, grimly triumphant and pitiless in its depiction of the ranks of the dead, is astonishingly prophetic of Musorgsky's *Commander-in-Chief*, the last of his *Songs and Dances of Death*.

Verse 10 (bb. 340–65): The marking is 'Geschwind'. This strophe is a cleverly managed recitative. The right-hand piano writing climbs a scale of minims a semitone apart (the left hand provides agitated shudders and interjections) and the image of gradually heightening perception, scales falling from the protagonist's eyes, is vividly conveyed. Gradually he sees that the fatherland's guardians are really only murderers, using the catchword of freedom as an excuse for bloodshed and the greed of political advantage. Between bb. 353–4 there is a change of tempo to 'Etwas langsam'. This little aria of withdrawal, prompted by disillusionment and distress, is built on a recurring E sharp pedal where the music is pivoted around the key of B major, a tonality that Schubert always used as harmonic balm. This meditative cantilena places the protagonist back in the cool of the forests. Here Mayrhofer's own political beliefs are confirmed: anti-state, anti-xenophobic, almost pacifist; a composer like Britten might gladly have set these words to music in the 1930s. This song was written only five years after the *Befreiungskrieg*, the war that rid Austria of French domination. A work that dismissed the 'Vaterlandes Wächter' as nothing more than 'Brüderschlächter' – 'brother murderers' – would be controversial with many an old soldier and patriot (the whole concept of *Bruderschaft* had, in any case, dangerous political connotations). This bridge passage (bb. 354–66) enables *Einsamkeit* to come full circle, in literary terms at least, for Mayrhofer is determined that his hero should end up a loner.

Verse 11 (bb. 367–90): This is arguably the most beautiful section of the piece. The B major of the preceding passage allows a magical change into G major for the final 'chapter heading' of the work, 'Gib mir die Weihe der Einsamkeit!' This music denotes self-discovery and revelation. In *Nacht und Träume* D827 the same key change between sections betokens a deepening of sleep and a sharpening of perception. Schubert does not disappoint in making this last request the calmest and the most full of human experience. If this song, composed in the spirit of the *Bildungsroman*, is to make its point, we need a closing section of this quality: Schubert's satisfaction with his new work is never more understandable than here. The setting of 'Weihe' (b. 368) seems to contain the holy feeling of a pilgrim receiving a blessing at the end of a long journey: apart from a softening of harmony (less block-like) there is also a tiny moment at the end of this bar where the bass is ornamented with demisemiquavers. In this full collaboration between the hands it is as if we have a coming together of a whole personality at last. The sun has come out and is visible through the trees. In this section of the song is one of Schubert's most lovely creations; based on an ever-recurring triplet figuration (mostly, but not always, in the right hand), the effect is that of the variations of a passacaglia. The voice spins a long melody with spacious and contented line. From b. 379 the call of the cuckoo in the pine forest is introduced ('Der Kuckuck ruft aus Zweiggeflecht') with the pianist's right hand gently imitating birdsong in falling minor thirds. The woodpecker also makes a tiny appearance (in split right-hand octaves) at bb. 382–3. To crown the richness of this strophe there is a powerfully evocative passage (bb. 384–90) where right-hand triplets are accompanied by left-hand tremolandi. This conveys the mournful majesty of a waterfall high in the mountains, and the music thunders gently, quite unlike any other of the composer's water evocations. This leads through various keys until there is an exquisitely judged, and gradual, return to G major for 'Was er wünschte, was er liebte'.

Verse 12 (bb. 385–410): The accompaniment for the poem's final strophe recycles this water motif; the left-hand tremolo is replaced with calm quavers, and the gently lulling triplets which will bring the entire song to a close now emerge. This is the first time that the so-called anti-strophe has completely harmonized with its companion, and there is no one better than Schubert at depicting floating and ethereal rapture. The way that the constant triplets change subtly through the conjunctions and piquant clashes of inner voices (at 'dem Greisen nun zu teil' bb. 400–401, for example) is one of the Schubertian pleasures appreciated most by the pianist who has the joy of observing such ingenuity at close quarters. Schubert does nothing by rote: even when he has arrived in the home stretch of a long piece he cannot resist adding and adapting as he goes. There are always tiny inflections to enrich the music: note the tiny left-hand shudders that are almost inaudible echoes of 'ein Leben rauh und steil', bb. 402–3. There is no doubt that this final section appears more effective as a result of the upheaval that has gone before; the theatrical disadvantage of ending a long song such as this with such deep introspection is balanced by the rewarding sense of peace and fulfilment. Both composer and poet have implicitly advised us, like Voltaire's Candide, to find happiness in cultivating our garden. So ends a remarkable piece of music that succeeds in chronicling a journey, not yet the winter traveller's but, rather more ambitiously, an entire lifespan. Following the frantic activity of a life of striving,

the solitude of old age at last brings wisdom; in this way Mayrhofer's words prophesy the theme
of the second part, as yet unknown, of Goethe's *Faust*.

Autograph:	Library of Congress, Washington, DC (antograph copy)
First edition:	Published as Book 32 of the *Nachlass* by Diabelli, Vienna in 1840 (P335)
Subsequent editions:	Peters: Vol. 5/175; AGA XX 339: Vol. 5/196; NSA IV: Vol. 12/16
Bibliography:	Black 2003, p. 81
	Capell 1928, pp. 140–41
	Einstein 1951, pp. 183–4
	Fischer-Dieskau 1977, pp. 109–10
Orchestration:	Detlev Glanert (b. 1960), *Einsamkeit* (2010). *See* ORCHESTRATIONS
Discography and timing:	Fischer-Dieskau II 2[2] 17'52
	Hyperion I 29[9–14]
	Hyperion II 20[10–15] 19'04 Nathan Berg

← *Sing-Übungen* D619   *Der Blumenbrief* D622 →

EINSAMKEIT *see* WINTERREISE *D911/12*

Die EINSIEDELEI (I)   The hermitage
(SALIS-SEEWIS) **D393** [H238]
A major   March 1816

(21 bars)

Es rieselt, klar und wehend,
Ein Quell im Eichenwald;
Da wähl' ich, einsam gehend,
Mir meinen Aufenthalt.
Mir dienet zur Kapelle
Ein Gröttchen, duftigfrisch;
Zu meiner Klausnerzelle
Verschlungenes Gebüsch.

Zwar düster ist und trüber
Die nahe Wüstenei;
Allein nur desto lieber
Der stillen Fantasei.
Da ruh' ich oft im dichten,
Beblümten Heidekraut;

In the oak wood flows a stream,
Clean and rippling.
Wandering alone, I choose there
My resting place.
A grotto, cool and fragrant,
Serves as my chapel;
Entwined bushes
Are my hermit's cell.

This nearby wilderness
Is dark and gloomy,
Yet all the more welcome
For silent musing.
Often I lie there in the dense
Flowering heather;

Hoch wehn die schwanken Fichten,	The tall, slender spruces sway,
Und stöhnen Seufzerlaut.	Moaning and sighing.
[. . .]	[. . .]
Nichts unterbricht das Schweigen	Nothing disturbs the silence
Der Wildnis weit und breit,	Of the woods far and wide,
Als wenn auf dürren Zweigen	Save when on dry branches
Ein Grünspecht hackt und schreit,	A woodpecker pecks and calls,
Ein Rab' auf hoher Spitze	A raven caws high on the top
Bemoster Tannen krächzt,	Of a mossy fir tree,
Und in der Felsenritze	And in the rocky crevice
Ein Ringeltäubchen ächzt.	A ring-dove moans.
Wie sich das Herz erweitert	How the heart is elated
Im engen, dichten Wald!	In the thick dense forest!
Den öden Trübsinn heitert	Gloomy melancholy is soon cheered
Der traute Schatten bald.	By its friendly shade.
Kein überleg'ner Späher	Here no disdainful eye
Erforscht hier meine Spur;	Spies on my steps.
Ich bin hier frei und näher	Here I am free, and closer
Der Einfalt und Natur.	To simplicity and to nature.
O blieb' ich von den Ketten	Would that I were free from the fetters
Des Weltgewirres frei!	Of the world's tumult!
Könnt ich zu dir mich retten,	Would that I could find salvation in you,
Du traute Siedelei!	Beloved hermitage!
Froh, dass ich dem Gebrause	Glad to escape the din
Des Menschenschwarms entwich,	Of the swarming throng,
Baut' ich hier eine Klause	I should build here a retreat
Für Liebchen und für mich.	For my love and me.

JOHANN GAUDENZ VON SALIS-SEEWIS (1762–1834); poem written in 1787

This is the fifth of Schubert's thirteen Salis-Seewis solo settings (1816–?21). See the poet's biography for a chronological list of all the Salis-Seewis settings.

The poet prefaces his verses with lines from Horace: 'Amat nemus et fugit urbes'. The full quotation begins with the words 'scriptorium chorus' – thus '[the whole band of writers] loves the woods and flees the city'. Perhaps the same applies to composers. Schubert set this poem more than once; in much the same way he composed two versions of the same poet's *Fischerlied* (D351 and D562), each of which derives its overall character from a different strophe of the same poem. In this setting of *Die Einsiedelei* the opening line of the poem gave the composer all the encouragement he needed to write a piece of water music. The brook babbles in the most enchanting manner throughout the song. (As pretty as this music is, the composer relegated the watery semiquavers to the inner parts of the accompaniment in the 1817 setting where they exert a more subliminal influence on the song's atmosphere.) The drawback of this constantly flowing accompaniment is that it makes it difficult for the listener to remember that the poem is about a quasi-religious experience. Perhaps the flowing of a friendly brook (an idea that would reach its apotheosis in *Die schöne Müllerin*) is too companionable for a true hermit, and the music needs to be tinged with introspection. On the other hand there is a very real sense of elation here which accords with the sentiments of the strophe beginning 'Wie sich das Herz erweitert'. The key is A major, the same as for the most celebrated of Salis-Seewis settings, *Der Jüngling an der Quelle* D300.

The vocal line, which is mostly independent of the accompaniment (a subtle way of showing perhaps that the hermit is not dependent on the brook), is constructed in Schubert's best folksong manner. In fact it rather resembles the tune of another piece of water music, the celebrated *Die Forelle* D550, which is also built around the rise and fall of a simple triadic figure in the tonic before it shifts to the dominant. It is the type of tune that we all imagine would be very easy to compose, so obviously does it seem to lie within the compass of an improvising hand, waiting to be discovered by anybody. It is notable that the tune of the well-loved *Der Jüngling an der Quelle* is also built around the major triad in deliberately naive fashion, as is the vocal line of *Wohin?* from *Die schöne Müllerin*. What all these songs have in common of course is water, and the use of the major triad is an analogue for transparency; we can see through water just as we can see through the evenly spaced fingers of a pianist's hand playing the notes of the common chord. Schubert set only the first verse of the poem, but repeat marks indicate he wished all six verses of the song to be performed, if the singer so wished. Accordingly both the AGA and the NSA print all six verses. The five printed here (1, 2, 4, 5 and 6) are more than enough for any concert performance – in fact only 1, 2, 4 and 5 are sung in the Hyperion recording. There is also an earlier, G minor, setting of these words for unaccompanied men's chorus (TTBB, D337) which has a different character from either of the solo versions.

Autograph:	Missing or lost
First edition:	Published as Book 38 no. 1 of the *Nachlass* by Diabelli, Vienna in 1845 (P351)
Subsequent editions:	Peters: Vol. 6/14; AGA XX 198: Vol. 4/60; NSA IV: Vol. 11/148
Discography and timing:	Fischer-Dieskau I 6²¹ 1'25 (Strophes 1 & 4 only)
	Hyperion I 17⁶
	Hyperion II 13¹² 3'16 Lucia Popp

← *Pflügerlied* D392   *An die Harmonie* D394 →

Die EINSIEDELEI (II)   The hermitage
(SALIS-SEEWIS) **D563** [H373]
A minor   May 1817

See previous entry for poem and translation

Johann Gaudenz von Salis-Seewis (1762–1834); poem written in 1787

This is the thirteenth of Schubert's thirteen Salis-Seewis solo settings (1816-?21). See the poet's biography for a chronological list of all the Salis-Seewis settings.

This gentle little song dates from a period in 1817 when Schubert revisited some of the Salis-Seewis texts that had been set, not always to his satisfaction, the year before. The first solo setting of *Die Einsiedelei* (D393), with its merry cascading introduction in descending triplets, is a charming water song, an open-hearted declaration of independence in a sparkling A major. A year later Schubert probably realized that this setting was rather too bubbly for the mood of the poem as a whole.

The 1817 setting is also simple, but is more serious in tone, though far from earnest. The poet rejoices in his solitary life and is happy to remain on his own. In this setting there is a bar of tonal ambivalence: the opening bar of music ('Es rieselt, klar und') is in A minor, and we reach the home key of C major only at the second full bar, on 'we<u>hend</u>'. The song is written for a string quartet texture where the first violin takes the vocal line, the second violin the piano's right hand and the cello the left-hand bass. At the heart of the music, buried within the crotchets and quavers of melody and harmony, there is a line, in gentle and sinuous semiquavers, that might have been written for a viola. This is the gentle stream, the purling flow of a thriving inner life and the contentment of an existence given over to nature. If this song is a distant relative of *Das Wandern*, the opening of *Die schöne Müllerin* (the same $\frac{2}{4}$ time signature, the same strophic simplicity), the miller's youthful vigour is replaced by a more mature taste for home-spun philosophy, far from the stress of the big city.

A fetching and unusual feature of the oscillating vocal line is to be heard at 'Mir die<u>net</u> zur <u>Ka</u>pelle' (b. 9) where two flattened sixths (D flats within the key of F major, the subdominant of the home key of C) replace the D naturals that would have been expected. This touch of flattened harmony is heard again at 'Zu mei<u>ner</u> Klaus<u>ner</u>zelle' (b. 13). The hermit of *Die Einsiedelei* lives in a calm world where these tonal adjustments denote contemplation rather than depression. The postlude (bb. 15–18), with a right-hand upper melody that has rather more character than the rest of the piano writing of the song, is quietly thoughtful; the tessitura of these closing bars, in the muted middle of the keyboard, hardly encourages performer or listener to rejoice. This is music where the soul is at peace with itself and has no need for the trappings of celebration. Like a number of the songs of 1816–17, and like so much else in Schubert's life and music, the unspoken theme seems to be 'moderation in all things'.

Of the poem's six strophes (*see* the first setting above), 1, 5 and 6 are performed on the Hyperion recording.

Autograph:	Staatsbibliothek Preussischer Kulturbesitz, Berlin (first draft)
First edition:	Published as Vol. 7 no. 31 in Friedlaender's edition by Peters, Leipzig in 1885 (P495)
Subsequent editions:	Peters: Vol. 7/72; AGA XX 322: Vol. 5/120; NSA IV: Vol. 11/152
Discography and timing:	Fischer-Dieskau —
	Hyperion I 34[5]
	Hyperion II 19[7] 1'41 Philip Langridge

← *Fischerlied* D562   *Gretchen im Zwinger (Gretchens Bitte)* D564 →

ELLENS GESÄNGE (I–III) *see SIEBEN GESÄNGE AUS WALTER SCOTT'S FRÄULEIN VOM SEE* nos 1, 2 & 6 D837–9

ELYSIUM   Elysium
(SCHILLER) **D584** [H386]
E major – A major   September 1817

(301 bars)

(1)	Vorüber die stöhnende Klage!	Cease all plaintive moaning!
	Elysiums Freudengelage	Elysian banquets
	Ersäufen jegliches Ach—	Drown all suffering.
	Elysiums Leben	Elysian life
	Ewige Wonne, ewiges Schweben	Is eternal bliss, eternal lightness,
	Durch lachende Fluren ein flötender Bach.	A melodious stream flowing through smiling meadows.

(2)	Jugendlich milde	Eternal May,
	Beschwebt die Gefilde	Young and tender,
	Ewiger Mai;	Hovers over the landscape;
	Die Stunden entfliehen in goldenen Träumen,	The hours fly past in golden dreams,
	Die Seele schwillt aus in unendlichen Räumen.	The soul expands in infinite space.
	Wahrheit reisst hier den Schleier entzwei.	Here truth rends the veil.

(3)	Unendliche Freude	Endless joy
	Durchwallet das Herz.	Fills the heart.
	Hier mangelt der Name dem trauernden Leide	Here grieving sorrow has no name;
	Sanftes Entzücken nur heisset man Schmerz.	And rapture that is but gentle seems like pain.

(4)	Hier strecket der wallende Pilger die matten	Here the pilgrim stretches his weary,
	Brennenden Glieder in säuselnden Schatten,	Burning limbs in the murmuring shade,
	Leget die Bürde auf ewig dahin—	And lays down his burden for ever.
	Seine Sichel entfällt hier dem Schnitter,	The reaper's sickle falls from his hand;
	Eingesungen von Harfengezitter	Lulled to sleep by quivering harps
	Träumt er, geschnittene Halme zu sehn	He dreams he sees blades of mown grass.

(5)	Dessen Fahne Donnerstürme wallte,	He whose standard raged with violent storms,
	Dessen Ohren Mordgebrüll umhallte,	Whose ears rang with murderous cries,
	Berge bebten unter dessen Donnergang,	And beneath whose thunderous steps mountains quaked,
	Schläft hier linde bei des Baches Rieseln,	Sleeps gently here by the babbling stream
	Der wie Silber spielet über Kieseln;	That plays like silver over the pebbles.
	Ihm verhallet wilder Speere Klang.	For him the violent clash of spears grows faint.

(6)   Hier umarmen sich getreue Gatten,   Here faithful couples embrace
        Küssen sich auf grünen samt'ven Matten,   And kiss on the green velvet sward
          Liebgekost vom Balsamwest;   Caressed by the balmy west wind.
        Ihre Krone findet hier die Liebe,   Here love finds its crown;
        Sicher vor des Todes strengem Hiebe   Safe from the cruel stroke of death
          Feiert sie ein ewig Hochzeitfest.   It celebrates an eternal wedding feast.

FRIEDRICH VON SCHILLER (1759–1805); poem written by 1781

This is the thirty-second of Schubert's forty-four Schiller solo settings (1811–1824). See the poet's biography for a chronological list of all the Schiller settings.

Schubert had known these words since his schooldays. He had set all but the second strophe for six separate unaccompanied vocal trios (TTB) in April and May 1813, as composition exercises for Salieri (D51, 53, 54, 57, 58 and 60). Only a few tiny rhythmical ideas from these early essays seem to have survived in this ballad, which is contemporary with two mythologically inspired masterpieces – Schiller's *Gruppe aus dem Tartarus* D583 (Schubert had also known that poem for years) and Mayrhofer's *Atys* D585. Having composed a mighty song about the Inferno (D583), Schubert fixed his eyes on Olympus. Capell was probably right when he said, 'Hell has been found by all artists from Dante downwards to be a more manageable subject than heaven.' Schubert is at his most inventive and original in *Gruppe aus dem Tartarus*, for hell is a milieu where every tortured composer must fight for himself.

In describing the delights of the Elysian fields Schubert needed a model; after all, in those lofty regions, homage is the order of the day. Beethoven had not yet composed the Ninth Symphony with its Schiller text (first performed in May 1824), but the influence of the older composer is evident in *Elysium*: this extended cantata is perhaps Schubert's lieder counterpart to Beethoven's 'Pastoral' Symphony, itself an evocation of heavenly fields for the mortals of Vienna. One of the most delightful things about *Elysium* is its succession of bucolic dances; it is rare that Schubert's genius as a composer of dance music is reflected thus in his more imposing vocal works.

Verse 1: The opening words – 'Cease all plaintive moaning' – set the tone of the entire piece. The lost souls in *Gruppe aus dem Tartarus* must now desist from their perpetual groaning and serious business is swept aside. There is a chorale tune for the opening three lines of text (bb. 3–10), a skipping dance for the fourth and fifth lines (bb. 11–15) and delightful water music for the last (bb. 16–23). In this key one notices the resemblance between the piano writing for bb. 20–23 (an upper pedal on B) and the music for the brook's lullaby for the drowned miller boy (*Des Baches Wiegenlied*) at the end of *Die schöne Müllerin*. All in all, this is a guided tour of heaven for the benefit of a new arrival. The interlude (a passage better suited to clarinets, bassoons and horns rather than the piano) leads to a recapitulation of the opening idea (bb. 23–33). The pianistic interlude that ends this section (bb. 31–3), a flourish of triplets including some inner-part writing in euphonious sixths, is lifted entirely from the end of the first movement of the fragmentary Piano Sonata in E major D459 that dates from August 1816.

Verse 2: The second musical section (bb. 34–77) is marked 'Ziemlich geschwind' $\frac{2}{4}$. This is the one strophe that Schubert had never set in his youth, and it contains the work's most original pianistic ideas. There is a sudden change of key signature, and we find ourselves in A major. Cascading arpeggios depict hovering May breezes and the dance of the hours. Left hand crosses over right, and the texture is that of a one-man piano duet. The music of the passing of time is distantly related to the falling figurations of *Auf dem Wasser zu singen* D774. The pace and feel of this verse are the same as that of the 'Pastoral' Symphony's first movement. Another Beethovenian association is certainly that composer's *An die ferne Geliebte* cycle, composed and published in 1816. In the fifth song of that cycle May-time imagery ('Es kehret der Maien, es blühet die Au') produces a similar tempo, and similarly dactylic rhythm with piano writing in thirds and sixths. This homage of the younger composer to the older is too obvious to be missed.

Verse 3: 'Unendliche Freude' says the poem, and this concept is quite a challenge for a composer. How on earth to depict endless heavenly joy? Another dance of course, and another, a marathon and orgy of dancing, the same idea repeated in different keys. This passage (bb. 78–144) cancels the sharps of the preceding section for five bars of excited tremolandi. At b. 83 there is a change into D flat major, and a piano figuration that is reminiscent of the accompaniment for a song written six months earlier: Goethe's *Ganymed* D544, bb. 31–46, at the section beginning 'Dass ich dich fassen möcht' . . . Lieg ich und schmachte'. Ganymed ascends to Elysium at the end of that setting so it should be no surprise to find him here under a different guise. At b. 94 the key signature of D flat is cancelled and a different idea takes over. This is a gently breathless move-ment of tripping quavers in alternating hands (until b. 109). Schubert cannot resist depicting a touch of 'grieving sorrow', although the poet assures us at the same time that all such pain is banished. In this heavenly locale where most people are on a real high, this is a bad trip, the merest imitation of Ecstasy. And then on with the dance! The Ganymed figuration reappears a semitone higher, with a switch into D major (from b. 112). Euphoria pulsates through this music, speed flowing through the veins: the joy is somewhat artificially induced. We begin to suspect that perhaps there is something rather grim about being condemned to have this much fun for all eternity.

Verse 4: There have already been astonishing shifts of tonalities a major third apart: A to F to D flat. Our pilgrimage around these realms continues with a further shift from G to E flat (from b. 144, marked 'Etwas langsam'). It is now the compound-time triplets of the 'Pastoral's second movement (the *Szene am Bach*) that are evoked. The traditional horn-like thirds and sixths of traveller's music (the opening of Beethoven's *Les Adieux* sonata in the same key) paint the burning-limbed pilgrims stretching out in the shade (no doubt exhausted after dancing). The little harvest hymn in A flat major that follows (beginning 'Seine Sichel entfällt'), with sighing silences, interruptions suggesting a scythe dropping from the pianist's hands (bb. 158 and 160), has tiny and unusual felicities, such as the accompaniment's hemiolas (bb. 162, 164). These, as well as the strumming chords in the left hand, put the listener in mind of quivering harps.

Verse 5: Now there is battle music, marked 'Lebhaft geschwind', and once again in the key of C major. The stridency of the thrice-repeated dotted rhythm motif (bb. 174–7) has a Beethovenian confidence in its refusal to modulate. A menacing chromatic scale of rising octaves, beneath a long note held high in the voice (bb. 179–80) uses hackneyed means to achieve a thrilling effect. This provides a foil for more water music, this time in E flat major (from b. 193) and prophetic of the stream's upbeat music in *Mein!* from *Die schöne Müllerin*. This section of *Elysium* is treated like a miniature sonata, with a recapitulation arranged to bring us back to the key of the opening fanfares. As it happens, an old-fashioned approach to form (Schubert usually allows his *durch-komponiert* ballads to follow the progress of the words without repetitions of complete sections) is wholly in keeping with the work's ultra-classical theme. As in most recapitulations there is a modification of the original material – changes in the harmony at the section beginning b. 220 are very telling; what has been accompanied the first time by bare chords (from b. 190) is now filled out with the rolling figurations of water music (from b. 223).

Verse 6: It takes Schiller's erotic imagery to summon from Schubert the most sensuous and deeply felt music of the piece. The grass is definitely greener on the other side. The music is marked 'Herzlich' and we return to the A major tonality of the second strophe. Accompanied by this gracious minuet (in ¾ of course), couples disport themselves; intertwined thirds and sixths smoothly flow in quavers, or swoon in rhapsodic triplets (bb. 234–50). The word 'Balsam' occasions a couple of attractive melismas. The finale (the last three lines of the poem, from b. 250, marked 'Feurig') is worked into a magnificent set piece where martial and triumphant fanfares are balanced by an ominous three-bar motif for the tread and threat of death (bb. 257–9). The piano, as such, has ceased to be of interest in Elysium; in this land of ceaseless bounty the horn of plenty furnishes the wedding feast, and an expensive orchestra, horns aplenty, accompanies the priapic revelry. The concept of eternity is illustrated by asking the singer (picturesquely and unreasonably) to stay seemingly interminably on the word 'ewig' (bb. 285–94 – no fewer than ten bars). Such an idea can work splendidly on paper, but has no thought for the capacity of real human lungs. (Beethoven was rarely kind to singers, and Schubert is here in his Beethovenian mode.) The last six bars of piano postlude hammer away at various inversions of the tonic key (not, by the way, in the E major of the very opening, but the new tonic of A). This over-the-top passage confirms that Schubert's debt to the older composer lies somewhere between imitation (both conscious and unconscious) and affectionate parody.

Mention of parody raises the possibility, however unlikely it may at first seem, that the whole of this song, including its almost comically unsingable ending, was written as a massive skit, all in a spirit of burlesque. It was composed during the period (1817–18) when Schubert was a member of the *Unsinnsgesellschaft*, a brotherhood of irreverent and sometimes obscene roguery and nonsense where like-minded pranksters met to sing and dance and poke fun at each other. The researches of Rita Steblin, in which she has attempted to decipher a freemason-like web of verbal references and hidden puns, have linked *Elysium* with the bookkeeper and former soldier Ferdinand Dorflinger (1780–1818) who (a happily married man) loved to dress up as a woman (code name: Elise von Antifi Gagarnadl). Famous texts were taken up and altered in a spirit of parody, and no poet fell victim to this more regularly than Schiller. For more on this Society of Misrule *see* the commentary on the male quartet *Das Dörfchen* – also apparently written for Dorflinger.

Autograph:	Wienbibliothek im Rathaus, Vienna (first draft, missing opening 19 bars)
First edition:	Published as Book 6 of the *Nachlass* by Diabelli, Vienna in 1830 (P248)
Subsequent editions:	Peters: Vol. 4/215; AGA XX 329: Vol. 54/149; NSA IV: Vol. 11/174
Bibliography:	Black 2003, p. 179 n. 23
	Capell 1928, pp. 130–31
	Fischer-Dieskau 1977, p. 100
	Steblin 1999[2], pp. 33–43
Discography and timing:	Fischer-Dieskau II 1 1[14] 8'42
	Hyperion I 11[17]
	Hyperion II 19[20] 8'38 Brigitte Fassbaender

← *Atys* D585   *Erlafsee* D586 →

EMMA *see* AN EMMA D113

KARL AUGUST ENGELHARDT (1768–1834) [PSEUDONYM: RICHARD ROOS]

THE POETIC SOURCE
Taschenbuch zum geselligen Vergnügen auf das Jahr 1822, Neue Folge, Gleditsch (Leipzig), Gerold (Wien), 1822

THE SONGS
[Schubert took the text, and much of the music, directly from Anton Fischer's 1804 setting of this comic trio]

25–7 December 1812	*Die Advokaten* D37 [no known source]
?1822	*Ihr Grab* D736 [p. 91]

Title page of *Taschenbuch zum geselligen Vergnügen* (1822).

Engelhardt (sometimes spelled Engelhart) was born in Dresden on 4 February 1768 (or 1769 according to Goedeke). His father was a confectioner who was descended from an impoverished branch of Hungarian nobility, and who died when the poet was a boy. It is possible that it is for this reason that the poet styled himself 'Baron von Engelhardt' from early on. He studied theology and rose through the Saxon civil service, first as a librarian, then as an archivist and eventually as War Secretary. He was ennobled in 1805 – the comic trio *Die Advokaten* boasted 'Baron von Engelhardt' as its author; it is typical of the large number of skits, parodies and humorous sketches he published in his lifetime. He was known in Vienna at the turn of the century thanks to Viennese reprints of works for children first published in Leipzig – a series of books entitled *Neuer Kinderfreund*. He first published his more serious poetry under the pseudonym 'Richard Roos' and was a friend and colleague of Theodor Winkler, qv (whose pseudonym was Theodor Hell), and also Friedrich Kind, qv. All three poets lived and worked in Dresden at more or less the same time and, by strange coincidence, each contributed one solo song to the Schubert canon. Engelhardt was editor for some years of the Dresden *Abendzeitung* and died in Dresden on 28 January 1834. Uniquely, this poet appears in the Schubert canon once under his real name and once under his pseudonym.

Bibliography: Goedeke 1910, Vol. 9, p. 274

Die ENTFERNTE GELIEBTE *see* ALS ICH SIE ERRÖTEN SAH D153

Der ENTFERNTEN
(Salis-Seewis) **D350** [H235]
E♭ major   Spring 1816

To the distant beloved

Wohl denk_ ich al - lent - hal - ben, o du Ent - fern - te, dein,_____

(20 bars)

Wohl denk' ich allenthalben,[1]
O du Entfernte, dein!
Früh, wenn die Wolken falben,
Und spät im Sternenschein.
Im Grund des Morgengoldes,
Im roten Abendlicht,
Umschwebst du mich, o holdes,
Geliebtes Traumgesicht!

Es folgt in alle Weite
Dein trautes Bild mir nach,
Es wallt mir stets zur Seite,
In Träumen oder wach;
Wenn Lüfte sanft bestreifen
Der See beschilften Strand,
Umflüstern mich die Schleifen
Von seinem Busenband.

[. . . 2 . . .]

Wo durch die Nacht der Fichten
Ein Dämm'rungsflimmer wallt,
Seh' ich dich zögernd flüchten,
Geliebte Luftgestalt!
Wenn sanft dir nachzulangen,
Der Sehnsucht Arm sich hebt,
Ist dein Phantom zergangen,
Wie Taugedüft verschwebt.

Everywhere I think of you,
Beloved, so far away!
Early in the morning, when the clouds grow pale,
And late at night, by starlight;
On the earth, gilded by the light of dawn,
And in the red glow of evening,
You haunt me,
Sweet, beloved vision.

Your beloved image
Follows me far and wide.
Whether I am dreaming or awake
It is always beside me.
When breezes gently brush
The reeds on the seashore,
The ribbons of your bodice
Flutter around me.

[. . . 2 . . .]

Where the twilight gleam of the pines
Flickers through the night,
I see your beloved, ethereal form
Skimming hesitantly through the air.
When my longing arms are raised
To touch you gently,
Your phantom image has dissolved,
Dispelled like the dewy mist.

---

[1] Text printed here as in Volume 10 of the NSA. In the AGA, Mandyczewski changed the autograph text back to the Salis-Seewis original.

JOHANN GAUDENZ VON SALIS-SEEWIS (1762–1834); poem written in 1789

This is the third of Schubert's thirteen Salis-Seewis solo settings (1816–?21). See the poet's biography for a chronological list of all the Salis-Seewis settings.

Schubert was lucky with this poem of Salis-Seewis. It provided him with the material for two marvellous pieces of music about the distant beloved; this was, by chance, in the same year that Beethoven composed his *An die ferne Geliebte*. The solo setting, D350, is a magical song in E flat major, too little known and absolutely typical of the best Schubert of 1816. The version for unaccompanied four-part male chorus (D331, H235+) is mood music of abstract sensuality and longing. Although the Deutsch catalogue allocates this choral version an earlier number (it is therefore officially designated the first setting), the exact date of either composition is not certain.

The solo song personalizes the poem in that its feelings belong to a single voice; it is a work of the purest enchantment. If Papageno had been a slightly more literate creature, and had been gifted with a more reflective nature, he might have sung this (the key of E flat is appropriate to *Die Zauberflöte* of course) to describe his dream of a perfect wife. The poem (written in 1789) is contemporary with Mozart, and Reed points out that it is an early version of the pervasive 'Ich denke dein' theme in German poetry of the period. The song's rhythm is a flowing 𝄴, and the accompaniment ripples along in even triplets, except for the frisson of semiquaver figurations at the end of each strophe. A note of longing and melancholy is injected into the song almost at the very beginning by the addition of a passing D flat into the harmony that temporarily pulls the song into a darker, flatter tonal region in the first full bar. Note the pretty little tonal shift on 'Morgen<u>goldes</u>' in the middle section (bb. 9–10): an A natural, instead of an A flat, in the piano part, an F[7] chord moving to B flat major, allows in a beam of morning light. The setting of 'Umschwebst du mich' (bb. 12–14), time standing still while the singer is entranced, is also a happy inspiration. In the vocal line, flowing quavers give way to four dotted crotchets poised first high, and then low, on the stave; 'Umschwebst' is set on two notes a drop of a seventh apart, as if to trace the flight path of the floating vision. This is followed, almost in the Italian style, by a veritable stream of quavers (on 'o holdes / Geliebtes Traumgesicht', repeated, bb. 14–18) that depict the ecstasy the singer feels in fancying that he sees love's apparition. Simplicity and unanswerable charm are hallmarks of the Salis-Seewis settings of which this song is a fine example. On the grounds of its purely melodic merits one can see why J. P Gotthard, its first publisher, succumbed to the temptation to issue *Der Entfernten* as a piano piece, instead of a song (1876).

There are five strophes in Salis-Seewis's poem – these are all printed in the AGA. Given here are 1, 2 and 5. Three verses seem sufficient in performance.

Autograph:	Stiftelsen Musikkulturens främlande, Stockholm
First edition:	Published as Vol. 7 no. 18 in Friedlaender's edition by Peters, Leipzig in 1885 (P470)
Subsequent editions:	Peters: Vol. 7/40; AGA XX 203: Vol. 4/69; NSA IV Vol. 10/10
Discography and timing:	Fischer-Dieskau I 6[26] 1'38
	Hyperion I 23[3]
	Hyperion II 13[8] 2'12 Christoph Prégardien

← *Der Flüchtling* D402   *Der Enfernten* D331 (first setting) →

ENTRA L'UOMO ALLOR CHE NASCE

Abraham's air

No.1 for high voice
No. 2 duet

(ARIA DI ABRAMO) (METASTASIO)
D33 [H13 & H13A]

Composition exercises, September–October 1812
Solo and duet numbers (1 and 2) from 6 exercises for Salieri (No. 3, trio; Nos 4–6, quartets)

(1)   G major

(2)   G minor (with a single flat as key siguature)

(24 bars)

(20 bars)

Entra l'uomo allor che nasce	From the moment man is born
In un mar di tante pene,	He enters on a sea of so much pain
Che si avezza dalle fasce	That he is accustomed from the cradle
Ogni affanno a sostener.	To endure all suffering.
Ma per lui si raro è il bene,	But good comes so rarely to him,
Ma la gioia è così rara,	And so rare is joy,
Che a soffrir mai non impara	That he never learns how to bear
Le sorprese del piacer.	The surprise of pleasure.

PIETRO METASTASIO (1698–1782); poem written in 1740

These two items constitute the second of Schubert's fourteen Metastasio settings, solo and duet (1812–27). See the poet's biography for a chronological list of all the Metastasio settings.

On this occasion the exercise sheet for Salieri contains six exercises (rather than the nine of *Quell'innocente figlio* D17). The task that was set for the fifteen-year-old Schubert is very similar to that of D17: one setting for soprano, one for female duet, a trio and three quartets. All the pieces are in ⅜ with the exception of the duet which is in common time. The solo is cast in E minor, the duet in G minor and the trio in D minor. Two of the quartets are in G minor and one in G major. It is clear that part of the young composer's brief was to ring the tonal changes.

The surprisingly cynical text is taken from another part of the same Metastasio oratorio text from 1740, *Isacco*, which had been used for D17. This is the so-called 'Aria di Abramo' which is the reason why the solo version was cast for tenor on the Hyperion recording. Schubert seems almost uninterested in the subtleties of word-painting in this music, a marked contrast to his passionate concern when he sets his own language. But the purpose of these studies was an important one: to encourage the young composer to think in long lines of coherent melody. He had such a developed feeling for drama, and the excitement of recitative-like passages, that it would have been easy for him to be satisfied with making music in fits and starts. In slaving away at exercises referring to a 'sea of pain', Schubert seems to have been making himself ship-shape, preparing his own vessel to sail for distant shores undreamed of by his teacher.

Autograph: Wienbibliothek im Rathaus, Vienna
Publication: Published in Alfred Orel's *Der junge Schubert* (1940); additional
                    piano accompaniments by Reinhard Van Hoorickx. Subsequently
                    issued as part of the NSA in 1986 (P796)

| Subsequent editions: | Not in Peters; Not in AGA; NSA VIII: Vol. 2/196 |
| Discography and timing: | Fischer-Dieskau   — |

Hyperion I 33[8-9] } Philip Langridge (solo 0'58") &
Hyperion II 2[8-9] } Ann Murray (duet 1'04")

← *Der Jüngling am Bache* D30   *Serbate, o Dei custodi* D35/3 →

Der ENTSÜHNTE OREST   Orestes purified

(MAYRHOFER) **D699** [H453]

C major   September 1820

(31 bars)

Zu meinen Füssen brichst du dich,[1]
O heimatliches Meer,
Und murmelst sanft: 'Triumph, Triumph!'[2]
Ich schwinge Schwert und Speer.[3]

M y c e n e ehrt als König mich,
Beut meinem Wirken Raum,
Und über meinem Scheitel saust
Des Lebens goldner Baum.[4]

Mit morgendlichen Rosen schmückt
Der Frühling meine Bahn,
Und auf der Liebe Wellen schwebt
Dahin mein leichter Kahn.

D i a n a naht! o Retterin,
Erhöre du mein Fleh'n:
Lass mich—das Höchste wurde mir,[5]
Zu meinen Vätern geh'n!

You break at my feet,
Sea of my homeland,
And softly murmur: 'Triumph! Triumph!'
I wield my sword and spear.

Mycenae honours me as King,
Offers me freedom for my actions;
And above my head rustles
The golden tree of life.

Spring adorns my path
With fresh roses,
And my boat glides lightly along
On waves of love.

Diana approaches; my saviour,
Hear my prayer!
Let me know the highest joy:
Let me return to my fathers.

[1] Mayrhofer has 'Zu meinen Füssen *wiegst* du dich'. For an explanation of the background to these alternative Mayrhofer readings see Editorial Note at the beginning of Johann MAYRHOFER.
[2] Mayrhofer has '*Ich rufe dir*: Triumph, Triumph!'
[3] Mayrhofer has 'Und schwinge *Schild* und Speer'.
[4] Mayrhofer has 'Des Lebens *reicher* Baum'.
[5] Mayrhofer has 'Lass mich – das Höchste *ward mir ja* – / Nun zu den Vätern geh'n!'

Johann Mayrhofer (1787–1836)

This is the thirty-eighth of Schubert's forty-seven Mayrhofer solo settings (1814–24). See the poet's biography for a chronological list of all the Mayrhofer settings.

In Greek mythology, Orestes was the son of Agamenon and Clytemnestra. On reaching manhood he avenged his father's murder by killing his mother and her lover, Aegisthus. For the crime of matricide he was haunted by the Furies and driven mad. In the *Oresteia* of Aeschylus, Orestes sought refuge from the Furies at Delphi; under the protection of Apollo he went to Athens to plead his case at the court on the Areopagus. He was narrowly acquitted by Athena's casting vote. (The Furies were appeased by being given the title 'Eumenides', a sign of their mercy.) We know from the song *Fragment aus dem Aeschylus* D450 (which is a translation from the *Eumenides* of Euripides) that Schubert and Mayrhofer knew this version of the mythological story. Nevertheless the re-telling of the story via Gluck's opera (*Iphigénie en Tauride*), would have been equally familiar to poet and composer in the German version, *Iphigenia in Tauris*. The singer Johann Michael Vogl was a famous Orestes – indeed, in that role he had been a musical hero of Schubert's teenage years. In the Euripides version of the tale, Orestes remains unforgiven by the Furies; he has to earn his release from the torments of madness by journeying across the Black Sea to Tauris, his 'mission impossible' to bring back to Athens the statue of Diana. His arrival on the island of the Scythians is the subject of the first Schubert–Mayrhofer collaboration on this subject, *Orest* D548 (1817) – published in 1831 as *Orest auf Tauris*, and incorrectly titled ever since. In Tauris Orestes narrowly escapes ritual sacrifice at the hands of his sister Iphigenia; the goddess Diana intervenes; the Scythians are vanquished and Orestes' remorse has absolved his guilt. This is as near to a happy ending in human affairs as is to be found in Greek mythology. He is appointed King of Mycenae (Argos) and takes Iphigenia with him back to Greece. Freed of his old guilt and from madness, he arrives on the shores of his father's realm. This is the literary cue for this song.

The trials of Orestes are over at last, and Mayrhofer envisages the moment of his triumphant return to his homeland which is bathed in a glow of spring beauty. The music of the opening, a motif that continues for ten spacious bars, sets the scene at a beach where the newly absolved monarch has recently landed; one feels the tug of the tide in these rumbling sextuplets, and the mighty ocean of life has deposited him once again in Mycenae against all expectations. With the tessitura of the arpeggios placed beneath the vocal line, the sea swirls around his feet. This is a unique and unusual image and there is no water music in Schubert quite like it.

The song represents an awakening from a long and terrible nightmare. It was doubtless written for the retired Vogl to use as a pendant to *Orest*, a type of 'Before and After' of mythology, and a happy ending to a grisly tragedy. The key is a regal C major, a purified tonality without sharps and flats, clear of accidental or blame. Orestes is elated and grateful; the voices of nature whisper of a new chapter in his destiny, but he is aware that he owes this release to the mercy of Diana, his 'Retterin'. From bb. 11–14 the pulsating sextuplets, grounded in blocks of harmonic marble, surely pay tribute to Gluck; how Vogl must have enjoyed delivering this arioso as he clung to those vestiges of grandeur that he could still muster from his operatic past. With Verse 3 (from b. 15) the shift into A flat major allied to the idea of a boat gliding on the water seems to prophesy the rocking sextuplet figurations of the accompaniment for *Auf dem Wasser zu singen* D774. Added to this there is the imagery of spring; under the pianist's fingers, *Frühlingsglaube* D686 comes to mind, an A flat major song that also dates from September 1820. John

Reed's incorrect contention that *Der entsühnte Orest* dates from 1817, alongside its mythological fellows, was made before the rediscovery of the long-lost manuscript in 1999 and its purchase for the Wienbibliothek im Rathaus. The musical style is more sumptuously experimental for the piano than in *Orest*, and the NSA (1996) argued convincingly that the 1820 date was correct before Schubert's own dated autograph came once more into view.

Orestes' heart is full to overflowing, yet Mayrhofer (who later proved himself capable of taking his own life) has Orestes beg the goddess to end his life on this note of release. His plea to Diana (whose approach we detect in the revelatory modulations in bb. 22–3) is a small aria on its own (bb. 25–31). These dotted rhythms tread a fine line between majestic self-confidence and god-fearing awe. Gluckian ceremonial establishes itself in the music once again. The last years of Orestes' life (he reputedly died at ninety) were given up to ruling his kingdoms peacefully. He succeeded Menelaus to the throne of Sparta, and established new settlements in Asia Minor to replace the cities destroyed during the Trojan War. When he died he was accorded divine honours.

Autograph:	Wienbibliothek im Rathaus, Vienna (first draft)
First edition:	Published as Book 11 no. 2 of the *Nachlass* by Diabelli, Vienna in 1831 (P271)
Subsequent editions:	Peters: Vol. 5/42; AGA XX 383: Vol. 6/121; NSA IV: Vol. 12/80
Bibliography:	Capell 1928, pp. 162–3
	Fischer-Dieskau 1977, p. 199
Discography and timing:	Fischer-Dieskau II 4[3] 3'27
	Hyperion I 14[14]
	Hyperion II 23[11] 3'31 Thomas Hampson

← *Des Fräuleins Liebeslauschen* D698   *Freiwilliges Versinken* D700 →

ENTZÜCKUNG   Rapture
(Matthisson) **D413** [H251]
C major   April 1816

(55 bars)

Tag voll Himmel! da aus Lauras Blicken	Heavenly day! When from Laura's gaze
Mir der Liebe heiligstes Entzücken	Love's most sacred rapture
In die wonnetrunkne Seele drang!	Pierced my soul in its ecstasy
Und, von ihrem Zauber hingerissen,	And, carried away by her magic,
Ich der Holden, unter Feuerküssen,	I sank, amid ardent kisses,
An den süssbeklommnen Busen sank!	On my fair one's sweetly trembling breast!

Goldner sah ich Wolken sich besäumen,	I saw the clouds fringed with a richer gold;
Jedes Blättchen auf den Frühlingsbäumen	Every tiny leaf on the trees of springtime
Schien zu flüstern: 'Ewig, ewig dein!'	Seemed to whisper: 'For ever yours!'
Glücklicher, in solcher Taumelfülle,	I shall scarcely be happier, or in such joyful delirium,
Werd' ich, nach verstäubter Erdenhülle,	In the myrtle groves of Eden,
Kaum in Edens Myrthenlauben sein!	When this mortal frame has turned to dust.

FRIEDRICH VON MATTHISSON (1761–1831); poem written in 1776/8

This is the twenty-first of Schubert's twenty-nine Matthisson solo settings (1812–17). See the poet's biography for a chronological list of all the Matthisson settings.

Although this song is not in the same category of difficulty as the juvenile *Des Mädchens Klage*, D6 (where the high-lying passages for soprano would be comical were they not so lethally hard to sing), it is still a trapeze-act of a song. It is not possible to sing the opening and closing verses of *Entzückung* with a heady falsetto as it is the high-lying tenor passages in Matthisson's *Naturgenuss* D188. Here the rapture is too substantial for pussyfooting and the forte dynamic markings in the score too unequivocal. The tempo is 'Nicht zu geschwind': all those notes high in the stave have to be filled with vibrant sound in a steady tempo, without cheating or skimping.

By 1816 Schubert knew a great deal more about singing than in 1811. The tessitura of this music is not the result of miscalculation, only perhaps misguided enthusiasm. He seems to have really wanted the heroic effect produced when the tenor voice is stretched to the limit. Substantial chords in the piano, often doubled strongly in both hands, abet this sense of extrovert determination. The key is C major, the tonality of light and openness, as well as of ceremonial. The opening bars recall the melody of Mozart's famous C major Sonata K545, but Mozart seems an inappropriate reference point in a song that is almost Wagnerian in its sweep and scope – music for an infant Lohengrin. Daring chromaticism reinforces this impression: note the descent in semitones at 'An den süssbeklommnen Busen sank!' (bb. 17–20.) This is a textbook example of chromatic harmony as a symbol of eroticism – on this day in April 1816 Schubert seems to have been in a hot and bothered state of mind.

In reality the song calls for two singers of different abilities. At the start of the second verse (b. 11) the music requires a light-voiced tenor of flexible movement and delicate sensibility. But then, as piano triplets change from sylvan rustle to cavalry charge, the vocal line shifts into a higher gear: the repetitions of 'flüstern' (bb. 27–8) in this high tessitura could never sound anything like a whisper. By the time we have reached the triumphant 'Ewig dein' in high and taxing minims, we need a voice of a quite different mettle.

The recitative (marked 'Declamirt') for the last two lines of the second verse (beginning 'Glücklicher, in solcher Taumelfülle' b. 33) is a disappointment – this passage is rather wooden, just when we would have expected Schubert to paint the images with a greater extravagance. It is as if the composer were losing interest in the project. The song ends with a repeat of the first two lines of Matthisson's poem (marked 'Wie oben' from b. 38). The opening ten bars are recycled, as the song returns from its middle section excursions into the safe haven of C major. Only a very clever performance can avoid the sense that there is something stilted and theatrical about the *da capo* aria which this song has suddenly become.

Autograph:	In private possession (USA)
First edition:	Published as part of the AGA in 1895 (P631)
Subsequent editions:	Not in Peters; AGA XX 211; Vol. 4/84; NSA IV: Vol. 10/144

Discography and timing: Fischer-Dieskau I 7[2]   2'03
                         Hyperion I 32[13]
                         Hyperion II 14[2]   2'17   Toby Spence

← *Lied in der Abwesenheit* D416   *Geist der Liebe* D414 →

Die ENTZÜCKUNG AN LAURA (I)   Delight in Laura

(SCHILLER) **D390** [H230]

A major   March 1816

(43 bars)

Laura, über diese Welt zu flüchten	Laura when your shimmering eyes are reflected in mine,
Wähn' ich—mich in Himmelsmaienglanz zu lichten,	I imagine I am fleeing this world
Wenn dein Blick in meine Blicke flimmt;	To bathe in the light of some heavenly May.
Ätherlüfte träum' ich einzusaugen,	I dream I am breathing ethereal air:
Wenn mein Bild in deiner sanften Augen	When my image floats
Himmelblauem Spiegel schwimmt.	In the sky-blue mirror of your gentle eyes.
Leierklang aus Paradieses Fernen,	I burn to draw to my intoxicated ears
Harfenschwung aus angenehmern Sternen	The sound of lyres from distant Paradise,
Ras' ich, in mein trunknes Ohr zu ziehn;	The flourish of harps from more pleasurable stars;
Meine Muse fühlt die Schäferstunde,	My muse senses the hour of love
Wenn von deinem wollustheissen Munde	When from your warm, sensual lips
Silbertöne ungern fliehn.	Silvery notes reluctantly escape.
Amoretten seh' ich Flügel schwingen,	I see cupids flap their wings;
Hinter dir die trunknen Fichten springen,	Behind you the drunken spruce trees dance
Wie von Orpheus' Saitenruf belebt;	As if brought to life at the call of Orpheus' strings.
Rascher rollen um mich her die Pole,	The poles revolve more swiftly around me
Wenn im Wirbeltanze deine Sohle	When in the whirling dance your feet
Flüchtig, wie die Welle, schwebt.	Slide, as fleeting as the waves.
Deine Blicke – wenn sie Liebe lächeln,	Your glances, when they smile love,
Könnten Leben durch den Marmor fächeln,	Could stir marble to life
Felsenadern Pulse leihn;	And make the veins of rocks pulsate.

Träume werden um mich her zu Wesen,	Around me dreams become reality;
Kann ich nur in deinen Augen lesen,	If I can only read in your eyes:
Laura, Laura mein!	Laura, my Laura!

FRIEDRICH VON SCHILLER (1759–1805); poem written by 1781

This is the twenty-fourth of Schubert's forty-four Schiller solo settings (1811–24). See the poet's biography for a chronological list of all the Schiller settings.

The poems that Schiller wrote about 'Laura' continue the tradition of Petrarch's Laura sonnets. Schiller was not the only German poet of the time to follow in the great Italian's footsteps: names like Gleim, Hölty and Lessing come to mind – as well as Matthisson whose poems on this theme are discussed elsewhere in this book. In 1781, the twenty-two-year-old Schiller lived in Stuttgart. No doubt something of a lonely, and certainly very intense, young man, he found himself enamoured of his landlady, Luise Dorothea Vischer, a military captain's widow who rented rooms in a house in Eberhardstrasse. The poet confessed to Minna Körner (later the mother of Theodor Körner) how attracted he had been to this older woman (she was eight years his senior) and how, unbeknown to her, she had briefly become his personal 'Laura'. He was drawn to her less on account of beauty than because she was kind-hearted and vivacious. This affinity was no doubt strengthened by what Schiller describes as Luise Dorothea's accomplished piano-playing and her ability to make 'ein vortreffliches Glas Punch' (an excellent bowl of punch). This poem was also later published under the title *Die seligen Augenblicke*.

There are nine verses, of which the AGA prints the first four. For this setting Schubert uses two strophes per musical verse, which calls for a single repeat of the song's forty-four bars – a remarkably organic melodic effusion, and one of the most ingratiating of the Schiller settings. The composer does not seem to be trying very hard to illustrate his distinguished poet; instead he allows himself to dream on a deliciously meandering, triplet-wafted, magic carpet of sound. The theme of this setting seems to be Laura herself, not the various ardently romantic reactions she arouses. Schiller's hyperbole is ironed out as the singer murmurs his admiration: the imagery is all about action, the music contemplative. This approach works well here; the details of the poet's hectic journeys heavenwards are ignored because he is already in heaven when he sees Laura. The music is written in a tessitura in which most tenors find it well-nigh impossible to float in ethereal rapture; this writing suits a soprano voice better where the vocal line sounds an octave higher, adding to a sense of disembodied rapture. The text of course is very much spoken by a man, but this has not discouraged women from singing this song from time to time.

There is a quasi-religious side to this worship of female beauty in Schubert's work. In Verse 1 the line 'in meine Blicke flimmt' (bb. 11–13) prophesies the famous *Ave Maria – Ellens dritter Gesang* at 'aus diesem Felsen starr und wild' (bb. 6–7 and similarly in later verses of that song). If the contemporary *Laura am Klavier* D388 points back to the age of Mozart, this song points forward to the *bel canto* art of Bellini. Salieri should have been delighted with *Die Entzückung an Laura* (if he ever saw it), for there is a languid sensuousness in this music that is Italianate to the core. The harmony changes no more frequently than is absolutely necessary and the melody is heartfelt, and utterly Schubertian, in its lyrical simplicity. For once the composer is not tempted to search beneath the surface of a Schiller poem to find a meaning. But the fact that he did not feel quite happy about this solution is evident from his decision to compose another, utterly different, setting in 1817.

Autograph:	In private possession
First edition:	Published as part of the AGA in 1895 (P625)

Subsequent editions:	Not in Peters; AGA XX 195: Vol. 4/54; NSA IV: Vol. 10/60
Further setting:	J. F. Reichardt (1752–1814) *Die Entzückung an Laura*, No. 34 of *Schillers Lyrische Gedichte*, Zweites Heft (1811)
Bibliography:	Capell 1928, p. 114
Discography and timing:	Fischer-Dieskau I 6[18] 2'00 (first two strophes only)
	Hyperion I 16[4]
	Hyperion II 13[3] 3'40 Thomas Allen

← *Des Mädchens Klage* D389   *Die vier Weltalter* D391 →

Die ENTZÜCKING AN LAURA (II)   Delight in Laura
(SCHILLER) **D577** [H379]
(Fragments) A major – G major   August 1817

Lau - ra! Lau - ra, ü - ber die - se Welt

(36 bars)

The poem printed below is more or less the same as for the first setting of this song, although the composer leaves out almost an entire line of the first strophe. In this second setting Schubert's music is missing (if indeed it was ever composed) for those words within square brackets. There is an extant vocal line (but no accompaniment) for the words underlined in Verse 4.

First fragment

Laura, über diese Welt zu flüchten	Laura I imagine I am fleeing this world
Wähn' ich—(. . .)	
Wenn dein Blick in meine Blicke flimmt;	When your shimmering eyes are reflected in mine
Ätherlüfte träum' ich einzusaugen,	I dream I am breathing ethereal air
Wenn mein Bild in deiner sanften Augen	When my image floats
Himmelblauem Spiegel schwimmt.	In the sky-blue mirror of your gentle eyes.

Leierklang aus Paradieses Fernen,	I burn to draw to my intoxicated ears
Harfenschwung aus angenehmern [Sternen	The sound of lyres from distant Paradise,
Ras' ich, in mein trunknes Ohr zu ziehn;	The flourish of harps from more pleasurable stars;
Meine Muse fühlt die Schäferstunde,	My muse senses the hour of love
Wenn von deinem wollustheissen Munde	When from your warm, sensual lips
Silbertöne ungern fliehn]	Silvery notes reluctantly escape.

Second fragment

Amoretten seh' ich Flügel schwingen,	I see cupids flap their wings;
Hinter dir die trunknen Fichten springen,	Behind you the drunken spruce trees dance
Wie von Orpheus' Saitenruf belebt;	As if brought to life at the call of Orpheus' strings.

Rascher rollen um mich her die Pole,	The poles revolve more swiftly around me
Wenn im Wirbeltanze deine Sohle	When in the whirling dance your feet
Flüchtig, wie die Welle, schwebt.	Slide, as fleeting as the waves.
Deine Blicke—wenn sie Liebe lächeln,	Your glances, when they smile love,
Könnten Leben durch den <u>Marmor fächeln,</u>	Could stir marble to life
<u>Felsenadern Pulse</u> [leihn;	And make the veins of rocks pulsate.
Träume werden um mich her zu Wesen,	Around me dreams become reality;
Kann ich nur in deinen Augen lesen,	If I can only read in your eyes:
Laura, Laura mein!]	Laura, my Laura!

FRIEDRICH VON SCHILLER (1759–1805); poem written by 1781

This is the thirtieth of Schubert's forty-four Schiller solo settings (1811–24). See the poet's biography for a chronological list of all the Schiller settings.

Schubert was probably dissatisfied with his first attempt at setting this lyric (if music so ravishing as D390 could be labelled merely an attempt) because he had made no effort to differentiate between the different moods and impulses of Schiller's strophes. Perhaps his conscience had been pricked by recalling Zumsteeg's setting that had appeared in Volume 6 of the *Kleine Balladen und Lieder* in 1803. This is one of Zumsteeg's most ambitious and complex works. It follows the contours of Schiller's poem to such an extent that there are no less than twenty-two changes of tempo in its nine pages. It uses an earlier and longer version of the poem. Zumsteeg changes at whim between aria and recitative; at one point when the metre defies musical setting, he even uses melodrama – spoken word with musical accompaniment: the word 'Schäferstunde' in Verse 2 prompts a delightful Pastorale honouring shepherds in a bucolic §, and mention of Orpheus striking up inspires a long and showy piano interlude.

The Schubert returns to the drawing board seemingly determined to write a more 'important' song than his setting of the year before, and starts promisingly. The lover rides to heavenly realms on Pegasus; in the accompaniment the composer captures the idea of a steed winging his way through the ethereal skies. This is no thundering steed in the manner of *Erlkönig*; its hooves make no contact whatever with the earth. The elated singer's vocal line soars above the galloping piano in the manner of Frank Bridge's 1914 warhorse of a song, *Love went a-riding*. A short piano introduction (from b. 13) to the second half of the verse ('Ätherlüfte träum' ich') changes character suddenly. The idea is ingenious; mention of a mirror image in the last two lines of the strophe prompts the use of a gently teasing canonic device between voice and piano. The unison dotted rhythms in A minor seem prophetic of the A minor Piano Sonata (Op. 143, D784) from 1823. Harps and lyres at the beginning of Schiller's second verse bring forth a rather more conventional and euphonious arpeggio figure (there is a change of key signature into A flat major from b. 28) with only two complete extant phrases, attractive without being revelatory. It is at this point that the first part of the manuscript breaks off.

The second fragment begins with the concluding two bars of this last section, still in A flat. This is a firm indication that Schubert meant Verse 2 to be all in the same vein and key, and Reinhard Van Hoorickx followed suit in his completion of this middle section. When we return to authentic Schubert we hear a modification of the 'Pegasus' motif, this time in D flat (with a new key signature). Instead of a winged steed we have winged cherubs with the music, depicting cheeky little putti, suddenly taking on an eighteenth-century flavour. This is Schiller in his 'return' to the world of classical antiquity as well as Mediterranean vegetation and climate mode. Mention of Orpheus (b. 48 – these numberings from the NSA, and not from the Hoorickx completion) prompts a change to B flat major, and the 'Wirbeltanz' whirls into G major just as suddenly. The whole of this section is in tempestuous dance rhythm driven into a frenzy of ⁶⁄₈ after the rococo elegance of the cupids' ²⁄₄. For the opening of Verse 4 the key changes to E major-minor for a recitative, but the dancer is already exhausted and Schubert has tired of the piece-meal approach. His instincts are leading him further and further away from the prolix ways of the Zumsteeg setting. We do not know whether Schubert had it in mind to wind up this song with a recapitulation of the music for the second verse. Reinhard Van Hoorickx chooses to do just this; his performing version wisely draws on Schubert's own music wherever possible.

The autograph of this version has the strange heading – perhaps, according to Dürr, in another hand – 'Entzückung eines Lauras Abschied' (The Rapture of a Laura's Farewell) and this is expressed in German grammatical terms 'eines', suggesting that this Laura is male. This strange alteration of Schiller's title is discussed by Rita Steblin in her article about the Schubert *Unsinns-gesellschaft* – the society of nonsense and fun to which Schubert belonged between 1817 and 1818. It is Steblin's contention that the song was written with some humorous intent for the farewell of 'Elise', the pseudonym of Ferdinand Dorflinger (1790–1818), a cross-dressing fellow member of the society. For further explication see the commentary on the quartet *Das Dörfchen*. The other solution, offered by Uri Liebrecht, is that 'eines' refers to the protagonist, the narrator of the poem, and his departure heavenward. The translation of this piece of German telegraphese would then read 'Enchantment (of a Man by Laura) and (His) Departure'.

Autographs:	Split into two: the first and second strophes in the Staatsbibliothek Preussischer Kulturbesitz, Berlin; the third and fourth strophes in Wienbibliothek im Rathaus, Vienna
First edition:	Published as part of the AGA as two fragments in 1895 and subsequently linked and completed by Reinhard Van Hoorickx (P719)
Subsequent editions:	Not in Peters; AGA XX 597: Vol. 10/119; NSA IV: Vol. 10/255
Bibliography:	Steblin 1999², pp. 33–43
Discography and timing:	Fischer-Dieskau —
	Hyperion I 16⁵
	Hyperion II 19¹³ 3'40 Thomas Allen

← *Iphigenia* D573   *Abschied (Lebe wohl! Du lieber Freund!)* D578 →

EPISTEL: 'AN HERRN JOSEF VON SPAUN' *see* HERRN JOSEF SPAUN, ASSESSOR IN LINZ D749

Die ERDE   The earth
(MATTHISSON) **D579B (D₁989A)** [H383]
E major   September or October 1817

Wenn sanft ent - zückt mein Au - ge sieht,

(36 bars)

Wenn sanft entzückt mein Auge sieht,	When with tender rapture my eyes behold
Wie schön im Lenz die Erde blüht;	How fair the earth blooms in spring,
Wie jedes Wesen angeschmiegt	How every creature nestles
An ihren Segensbrüsten liegt;	At her bountiful breasts
Und wie sie jeden Säugling liebt,	And how she loves each infant,
Ihm gern die milde Nahrung gibt,	And gladly gives it gentle nourishment
Und so in steter Jugendkraft	And thus, with constant youthful strength,
Hervorbringt, nährt und Wachstum schafft:	Brings forth, nurtures and creates growth;
Dann fühl' ich hohen Busendrang	Then I have an ardent, heartfelt longing
Zu rühmen den mit Tat und Sang,	To praise in deed and song Him
Des wundervoller Allmachstruf	Whose wondrous omnipotence
Die weite Welt so schön erschuf.	Made this vast world so beautiful.

FRIEDRICH VON MATTHISSON (1761–1831); poem written in 1778

This is the last of Schubert's twenty-nine Matthisson solo settings (1812–17). See the poet's biography for a chronological list of all the Matthisson settings.

It was always suspected that Schubert had written a lied of this name. Otto Erich Deutsch placed its title at the end of his monumental catalogue, along with all the other Schubertiana of doubtful or unknown origin; this accounts for its original late Deutsch number (the catalogue proper ends at D965). When the song came to light in 1969, it was authenticated by Christa Landon and squeezed into place in the second edition of the catalogue with a Deutsch number that was more appropriate to its probable date of composition. It is clear that *Die Erde* is in Schubert's handwriting, but it is not impossible that it is the work of someone else (*see* DUBIOUS, MISATTRIBUTED AND LOST SONGS).

This jaunty little E major song has echoes of the rusticity of *Erntelied* D434, and something of the charm of *Seligkeit* D433, two Hölty settings that incidentally share this song's tonality. And yet the cast of the accompaniment is unlike any other, and it simply feels un-Schubertian 'under the fingers'. For example, the cliché of a descending chromatic figure in thirds followed by trills in the introduction (bb. 7–8) suggests the style of one of Schubert's Viennese contemporaries, Conradin Kreutzer. The awkward two-octave leap for the pianist's right hand (between bb. 22 and 23, and even more awkwardly at bb. 26–7) is uncharacteristically bumpy; the crossing of hands, right over left, is more usually to be found in the songs of Schubert's friends Anselm Hüttenbrenner (e.g. *Die Seefahrt* bb. 29–32) and Benedict Randhartinger (e.g. *Rastloses Wandern* bb. 81–4) rather than those of Schubert himself, although the crossing of hands in the contemporary *Elysium* (bb. 34–77), albeit in the opposite direction, goes against this argument. The dotted rhythms of b. 19 are banal, and the spacing of the left-hand chords at b. 34 is peculiarly graceless, and unfamiliar to hands used to the composer's music. The fact that the poem is not to be found in the editions of Matthisson's works otherwise used by Schubert adds a further question mark to the attribution. If the manuscript is in Schubert's hand, it is surely not impossible that this is a copy of, say, a Hüttenbrenner song.

On the other hand, study of Schubert's unknown and undervalued lieder reveals that no song is quite like any other; each has a thumbprint, and sometimes a quirk, which is all its own. Schubert has an endless capacity to surprise us. And there are certainly many accompanimental patterns that occur only once in his entire oeuvre. Another rebuttal for a doubting Thomas is that *Die Erde* sets many a listener's foot merrily a-tapping.

Autograph:	Missing or lost
First edition:	Published the second of *Zwei Lieder* ed. Christa Landon by Bärenreiter, Kassel in 1960 (P731)
Subsequent editions:	Not in Peters; Not in AGA; NSA IV: Vol. 11/172
Bibliography:	Landon 1970, p. 200
Discography and timing:	Fischer-Dieskau —
	Hyperion I 5[6]
	Hyperion II 19[17] 2'17 Elizabeth Connell

← *Vollendung* D579a   *Atys* D585 →

ERINNERUNG (Kosegarten) *see* Die ERSCHEINUNG D229

ERINNERUNG (Todtenopfer)   Remembrance
(MATTHISSON) **D101** [H36]
E minor – E major   April 1814

(55 bars)

Kein Rosenschimmer leuchtet dem Tag zur Ruh!	No rosy shimmer lights the day to rest!
Der Abendnebel schwillt am Gestad empor,	The evening mist rises on the shore,
Wo durch verdorrte Felsengräser	Where, through dried-up grasses on the cliff,
Sterbender Lüfte Gesäusel wandelt.	Dying breezes whisper.
Nicht schwermutsvoller tönte des Herbstes Weh'n	The breath of autumn was not more melancholy than this,
Durch's tote Gras am sinkenden Rasenmal,	Quivering through the dead grass on the sinking sward,
Wo meines Jugendlieblings Asche	A memorial that marks the spot where the ashes of the beloved friend of my youth
Unter den trauernden Weiden schlummert.	Slumber beneath weeping willows.
Ihm Tränen opfern werd' ich beim Blätterfall,	I shall sacrifice tears to him when leaves fall
Ihm, wenn das Mailaub wieder den Hain umrauscht,	And when May's leaves again rustle in the grove,
Bis mir, vom schönern Stern, die Erde	Until, from a fairer star, the sweet earth
Freundlich im Reigen der Welten schimmert.	Shines upon me in the dance of the spheres.

FRIEDRICH VON MATTHISSON (1761–1831); poem written in 1793

This is the ninth of Schubert's twenty-nine Matthisson solo settings (1812–17). See the poet's biography for a chronological list of all the Matthisson settings.

This is an astonishingly accomplished song for its date of composition. The warmth and flexibility of the vocal line, the passion and intensity under control, stem from Schubert's developing feel for a new Italian style, or rather a style whereby the brooding vocal sensuality of the South was reconciled with the intellectual heights of the North. A few months later *Gretchen am Spinnrade* would burst into existence thanks to this meeting of two worlds. For now, the accompaniment is less developed and less dramatic than Gretchen's, but the singer must spin a line, *molto patetico*, that suggests a careworn aria. For this we must thank the influence of Salieri.

The dry bareness of the opening of this song, the staccato accompaniment and the key of E minor, bring to mind the future desolation of *Trockne Blumen* from *Die schöne Müllerin*. With the third line of the poem (at b. 9) we hear another song prefigured, this time the yearning cantilena of the Mayrhofer setting *Atys*, with its rocking § semiquaver accompaniment. In speaking this elegy for a close friend of his youth, the singer seems too absorbed in the depths of memory to essay a wider vocal range; a seamless vocal line turns in on itself, introspection reflected in the tessitura, as the piano evokes the sound of rustling grasses. At b. 28 mention of the friend's ashes dislocates the reverie into the first inversion of the flattened supertonic; in this distant key of F major we hear the unanchored bewilderment of bereavement, unfinished business, a life cut short. In the third verse (from b. 32) the modulation from E minor to E major is a little miracle of seasonal evocation, with musings of both autumn and spring. For nine serene bars the semiquaver accompaniment is taken over by the quaver movement of a *Wiegenlied*, anchored on the tonic for a full six bars – a tenacious loyalty unto death reflected in music. This is music of the most touching eloquence and it leads to a measure of consolation. The semiquavers return to evoke the planetary motions of the earth (from b. 41), the round dance of the spheres. The poet swears to honour the memory of his friend until his own death, after which he too will look back at the beautiful world from the faraway starry realms of heaven. When given the chance to praise the beauty of the earth, Schubert grasps it with both hands. There are aspects of this poem that the music does not encompass; the song comes too early in Schubert's career, and too early in the history of the lied, to be the complete masterpiece it might have been. Nevertheless, this is one of the finest of the Matthisson settings – its maturity and economy show a great composer in the making.

The poem, in Alcæic strophes, is one of Matthisson's best, traversing as it does a wide range of emotion and experience in a very short span. In a note in the 1810 edition published by Franz Haas in Vienna and Prague, the poet tells us that the 'Jugendlieblings Asche' referred to in the second strophe are the remains of the poet's dear schoolfriend, Jakob Friedrich Rosenfeld, who died in Dessau in 1782 after an unlucky fall on the ice. The song is published under the title *Todtenopfer* in the AGA. This follows Matthisson's renaming of the poem for the 1802 edition of his poetry printed in Zurich. This collection was Schubert's source for a number of his Matthisson songs, but he may have known either of the older Viennese editions of the poems (R. Sammer, 1803 and the Haas edition named above) where the poem is also printed as 'Erinnerung'. The song's autograph is lost, but both titles are found in contemporary copies. The Deutsch catalogue and the NSA follow this title.

Autograph:	Missing or lost
First edition:	Published as part of the AGA in 1894 (P540)
Subsequent editions:	Not in Peters; AGA XX 18: Vol. 1/151; NSA IV: Vol. 7/18; Bärenreiter: Vol. 5/116 (high voice), 110 (medium/low voice)

Discography and timing: Fischer-Dieskau I 1[12]   2'23

                             Hyperion I 5[10]
                                            2'29   Elizabeth Connell
                             Hyperion II 3[8]

← *Andenken* D99   *Geisternähe* D100 →

ERINNERUNGEN   Memories
(MATTHISSON) **D98** [H44]

This song exists in two versions, the second of which is discussed below:
(1) and (2) Autumn 1814

(1)   'Andante moderato'   B♭ major   § [fragment, 28 bars]

(2)   B♭ major

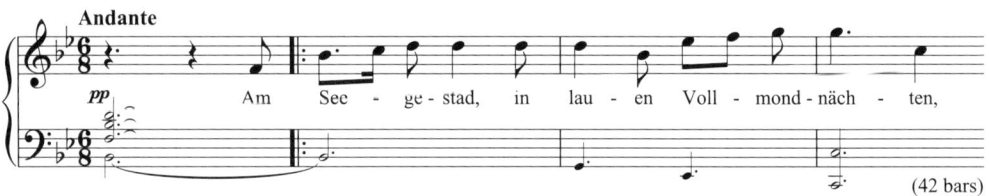

(42 bars)

Am Seegestad', in lauen Vollmondnächten,	By the shores of the lake, on warm nights with full moon,
Denk' ich nur dich!	I think only of you;
Zu deines Namens goldnem Zug verflechten	The stars intertwine
Die Sterne sich.	To spell your name in gold.
Die Wildnis glänzt in ungewohnter Helle,	The wilderness gleams with unwonted brightness,
Von dir erfüllt;	Filled with you:
Auf jedes Blatt in jede Schattenquelle	On every leaf, in every shady spring,
Malt sich dein Bild.	Your image is painted.
Gern weil' ich, Grazie, wo du den Hügel	I gladly linger, fair one,
Hinabgeschwebt,	As you glide down the hillside,
Leicht, wie ein Rosenblatt auf Zephyrs Flügel	Light as a passing roseleaf
Vorüberbebt.	Quivering on the zephyr's wings.
Am Hüttchen dort bekränzt' ich dir, umflossen	There, by the little hut
Von Abendglut,	Bathed in evening light,
Mit Immergrün und jungen Blütensprossen	I garlanded your straw hat
Den Halmenhut.	With evergreens and fresh blossoms.
Bei jedem Lichtwurm in den Felsenstücken,	Watching the glow-worms
Als ob die Feen	Dance among the rocks like fairies,

Da Tänze webten, riefst du voll Entzücken:	You would cry out with delight:
'Wie schön! wie schön!'	'How lovely!'

Wohin ich blick' und geh', erblick' ich immer	Wherever I look, wherever I go,
Den Wiesenplan,	I always see the meadow
Wo wir der Berge Schnee mit	Where we once saw the mountain snow
Purpurschimmer	
Beleuchtet sahn.	Tinged with crimson.

Ihr schmelzend Mailied weinte Philomele	Philomel sighed her melting May song
Im Uferhain;	In the grove by the shore.
Da fleht' ich dir, im Blick die ganze Seele:	There I implored you, with my whole soul in your gaze:
Gedenke mein!	Remember me!

FRIEDRICH VON MATTHISSON (1761–1831); poem written in 1792

This is the sixth of Schubert's twenty-nine Matthisson solo settings (1812–17). See the poet's biography for a chronological list of all the Matthisson settings.

This is not as innovative a song as, for example, the same poet's *Geisternähe* D100, but it has genuinely Schubertian moments. The composer employs a juxtaposition of strophic song (the first three verses) and recitative (the fourth verse); the fifth verse is an arioso combination of the two, and the final two verses return to the strophic pattern. It is fascinating that Matthisson's poem is cast in exactly the same metre and prosodic scheme as Goethe's *Nähe des Geliebten* (Schubert's D162) three years before the more famous lyric appeared. This poem has the narrator afloat in a sea of memories as he endeavours to explore and savour the fragile and unattainable past. The vocal line sounds improvised, and the result is a tune as if half-remembered that does not quite blossom into complete melody. The wistful atmosphere reminds us of the elusive nature of happiness, and the song has a sense of unresolved longing. These words are admirably suited to the rambling indecisiveness of the musical structure. At this stage of his career, Schubert seems especially keen to experiment with settings that enable him to conjure a hidden musical unity from disparate musical patterns.

The first three of the poet's strophes (bb. 1–14 repeated thrice) are set as a $\frac{6}{8}$ *sicilienne*, a familiar feature of the Matthisson songs of this period. The gently rippling piano writing is rather wanly supportive; it does service as wafting breezes, but it takes a deliberately background role. The sense of vocal awkwardness is caused by the high tessitura; there is scarcely a break in the vocal line that refuses to separate into singable paragraphs. The composer struggles to make the poet's long phrases (with clinching verbs sometimes as distant as lights at the end of the tunnel) sound musically natural. The recitative at the fourth verse (from b. 15) is despatched as quickly, and simply, as possible. Schubert was probably correct in thinking that the garlanding of a straw hat ('den Halmenhut') was not the best subject for tenorial cantilena. Neither, for that matter, is the subject matter of the fifth verse; but the pictorial temptations were too much for the young composer to resist. Fairy-like glow-worms occasion a fleeting and delightful elfin dance (marked Tempo I, from b. 20) and the enthusiasm of the girl is given voice in no fewer than three rising exclamations of 'Wie schön!' (bb. 24–6) (the poet only allows for two), the last of which reaches a high A flat, and then falls, wiltingly, to the C flat below. Schubert is faithful to Matthisson's inverted commas, but this sudden note of femininity has to be treated with caution by male performers – it can easily sound silly.

The song concludes with two strophic verses that bring the work full circle. There is a touching setting of the final 'Gedenke mein!' which suggests that the composer has already thought about these words when composing the earlier strophes, and planned ahead accordingly. Schubert is slowly mastering the main problem of writing songs of this kind: finding music that will be relevant not only to the first strophe, but to all the others as well. Although *Erinnerungen* is not a song for the lieder enthusiast to whistle on the way to work, Schubert's experiments with form are a valuable addition to his armoury. It would be some years before the composer hit on the idea (*Im Frühling* D882) of using variation form for a rather more modern set of lover's memories.

Autograph:	Wienbibliothek im Rathaus, Vienna (sketch)
Publication:	First published as part of the NSA in 1968 (P737; first version)
	First published as part of the AGA in 1894 (P545; second version)
Subsequent editions:	Not in Peters; AGA XX 24: Vol. 1/166 (second version); NSA IV:
	Vol. 7/8 (second version) & 180 (first version); Bärenreiter: Vol.
	5/107 (high voice) & 101 (medium/low voice)
Further settings:	Felix Mendelssohn (1809–1847) *Am Seegestad* (1823)
Discography and timing:	Fischer-Dieskau I 2[6] 2'15
	Hyperion I 33[23]
	Hyperion II 3[16] 3'42 Philip Langridge

← *Romanze* D114   *Die Betende* D102 →

ERLAFSEE   Lake Erlauf
(MAYRHOFER) OP. 8 NO. 3, **D586** [H387]
F major   September 1817

(86 bars)

Mir ist so wohl, so weh'	I am so happy, and yet so sad,
Am stillen Erlafsee.	By the calm waters of Lake Erlauf.
Heilig Schweigen	A solemn silence
In Fichtenzweigen.	Amid the pine-branches;
Regungslos	Motionless
Der blaue Schoss,[1]	The blue depths.
Nur der Wolken Schatten flieh'n	Only the clouds' shadows flit
Überm dunklen Spiegel hin,[2]	Across the dark surface.

[1] In Sartori's almanac of 1818 this line is as Schubert set it; it was later changed by the poet to 'Der *dunkle* Schoss'.
[2] In Sartori's almanac this line reads as 'Über *glatten* Spiegel hin'.

[(. . . 6 lines . . .)]	[(. . . 6 lines . . .)]

Frische Winde	Cool breezes
Kräuseln linde	Gently ruffle
Das Gewässer	The water,
Und der Sonne	And the sun's
Güld'ne Krone	Golden corona
Flimmert blässer.	Grows paler.

[(. . . 16 lines . . .)]	[(. . . 16 lines . . .)]

Mir ist so wohl, so weh'	I am so happy, and yet so sad,
Am stillen Erlafsee.	By the calm waters of Lake Erlaf.

JOHANN MAYRHOFER (1787–1836)

This is the thirtieth of Schubert's forty-seven Mayrhofer solo settings (1814–24). See the poet's biography for a chronological list of all the Mayrhofer settings.

Mayrhofer's role in shaping Schubert's literary and artistic tastes was considerable, but the composer was of independent mind. There are thirty-six lines to Mayrhofer's *Erlafsee*, and Schubert chose to set only fourteen of these (Verses 1 and 3), repeating the first two lines to make an ABCA structure. Schubert's first Mayrhofer setting (*Am See* D124) begins with a lake-side description, and grows into extended musings on a historical episode; here the composer seems to have determined to write a much more concise song.

The Erlauf is a tributary of the Danube in Lower Austria; Schubert's song has immortalized the old spelling. Lake Erlauf is situated on the northern border of Steiermark, near the town of Mariazell with its thirteenth-century church, famous as a place of pilgrimage, a holy site possibly related to another Mayrhofer setting, *Abschied* D475, purportedly inspired by a pilgrims' song. Mayrhofer's complete poem uses the lake as a backdrop for the fanciful appearance of a fairy-like image 'from the land of the shepherds'. This 'Wunderfrau' is momentarily upset by the mini-storm at 'Frische Winde' (the second of the two verses set by Schubert) but the poet comforts her. Mayrhofer's last verse seems to have been influenced by Goethe's *Der Musensohn* (it ends with a similar rhetorical question) which suggests that this visitation is perhaps the poet's muse and inspiration. This part of the poem was rather too obscure to encourage musical setting; in any case, mention of a sawmill on the Erlauf river at the end of the fifth strophe grates on the idyllic watery mood of the whole. (Clara Schumann was later brave enough to write a song on this subject, *Die Sägemühle*, to a poem of Kerner.) What Schubert seems to have liked best about Mayrhofer's poem (apart from the contrast of 'wohl' and 'weh' that was at the heart of his tonal response to so much poetry) was the chance to contrast a cantilena for the glassy surface of the lake with a *cabaletta* and a puff of wind.

The tune is enchanting; the drop of a sixth (b. 2) and an octave (b. 4) suggests languid though pensive relaxation. There is a smile in this music with a cloud behind it, or perhaps it's the cloud that is prevalent, the silver lining glinting in the distance. The differences between 'wohl' and 'weh' ('happy' and 'sad') are not emphasized in the harmony the first time round; for the last repeat of the words (b. 81) Schubert allows himself to flatten the D on '<u>so</u> weh' in order to paint sadness. The accompaniment glides underneath the tune like currents of meandering thought. At 'Heilig Schweigen / In Fichtenzweigen' (bb. 11–14) the majesty of the pine trees prompts a shift into the relative minor and a noble and decorative melody; for a moment the music has the grandeur of *Auf der Donau* D553. The accompaniment at 'Regungslos' (two quavers followed by a rest, bb. 15–16) is a familiar analogue for stillness or suspense. At the passage beginning 'Nur der Wolken Schatten flieh'n', the flitting clouds, and the dark mirror of the lake that reflects them, are represented by a dialogue in quasi-canon between voice and piano (bb. 16–24). At b. 21 the repeat of the words 'dunklen Spiegel' prompts the semiquavers of singer and pianist to move in mirror-image contrary motion, at least on the melismatic setting of the word 'dunklen'.

The vocal *fioriture* of this song, as well as the accompaniment in triplets, are a nod in the direction of the Italian style. This characteristic is even more pronounced in the middle section (marked 'Geschwinder', from b. 28) in which the composer seems to have been so delighted to find this congenial tune that he repeats words at will in order to keep the melody going. The presence of a Lydian B natural in the vocal line shakes the tonal equilibrium of F major; the water's glass-like surface is ruffled and it glints, just as it is made to do in the accompanimental figurations of *Die Forelle* D550 – these also break the surface of the water by insinuating a sharpened fourth (in that case a G natural) into the tonic D flat major triad. The repetition of words makes more musical than poetic sense on 'Das Gewässer' (bb. 34–5, 40–41), but the falling sequences on 'Flimmert blässer' (bb. 50–53) are ideal for painting the sun's gradually waning powers. The last time these words occur (bb. 73–4) they set up a haunting modulation back into F major for the recapitulation of 'Mir ist so wohl, so weh'. Schubert's careful cutting of the poem ensures that mention of the paling sun leads us back without any fuss into the contemplative mood that Lake Erlauf has inspired. The three-bar postlude with its highly ornamented cadence (b. 85) allows the accompaniment briefly to display the *bel canto* characteristics of the vocal line.

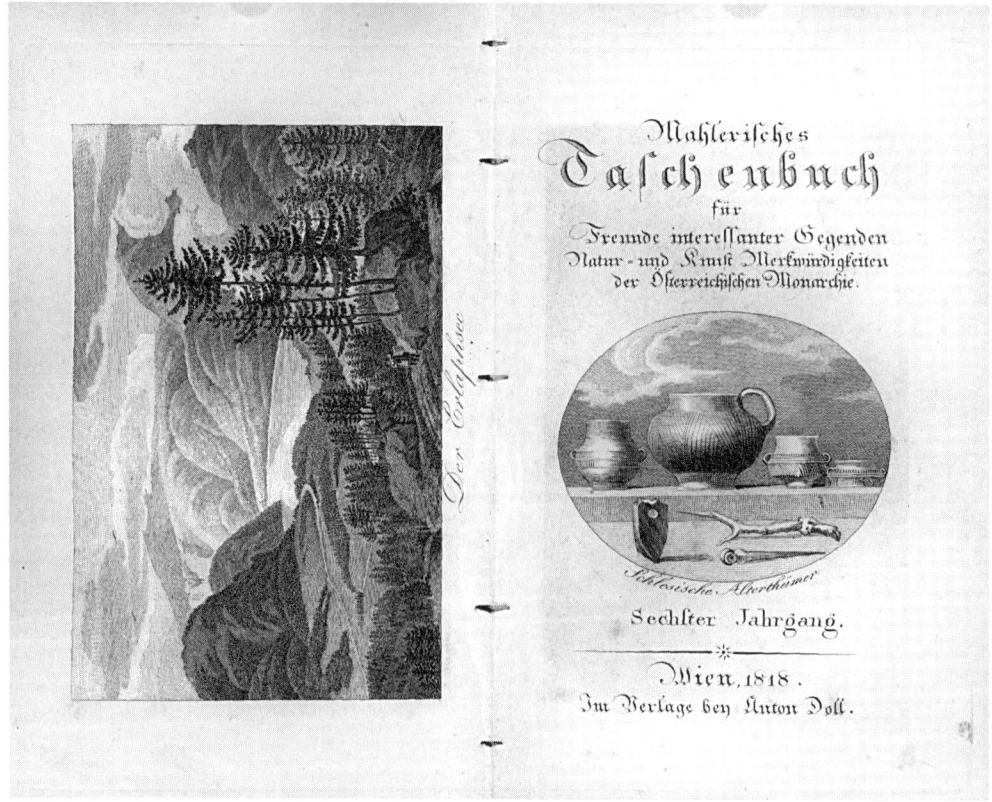

Mahlerisches Taschenbuch (1818) with engraving of Lake Erlauf.

This song has the distinction of being the first by Schubert to be printed, albeit only as a supplement to an almanac. The red-letter day for the composer was 6 February 1818, and the book was Franz Sartori's *Mahlerisches Taschenbuch* (Pictorial Pocket-Book), a tourist guide for 'friends of the noteworthy aspects of nature and art in the Austrian realm'. Schubert's setting (printed as a fold-in supplement) was part of a tripartite tribute to the Mariazell area that also included Mayrhofer's verse and an engraving by Johann Blaschke printed as the almanac's frontispiece. Indeed it seems likely that Mayrhofer wrote the poem specifically to illustrate the engraving in which we see the pine trees and clouds mentioned in the poem, as well as the river (the Erlauf) that powers the rather unpoetic sawmill in the original lyric's penultimate verse. Mayrhofer's poem *Auf der Donau* (set as D553) is printed elsewhere in this anthology.

Autographs:	Wienbibliothek im Rathaus, Vienna (first draft)
	In private possession (incomplete fair copy)
First edition:	Published as a supplement to *Mahlerisches Taschenbuch für Freunde interessanter Gegenden Natur- und Kunst-Merkwürdigkeiten der Österreichischen Monarchie* in February 1818 and subsequently as Op. 8 no. 3 by Cappi & Diabelli, Vienna in May 1822 (P23)
Dedicatee:	Johann Karl Grafen Esterházy von Galántha
Subsequent editions:	Peters: Vol. 2/19; AGA XX 331: Vol. 5/164; NSA IV: Vol. 1/78; Bärenreiter: Vol. 1/63
Discography and timing:	Fischer-Dieskau II 1[16] 4'04
	Hyperion I 21[17]
	Hyperion II 19[21] 3'41 Edith Mathis

← *Elysium* D584   *An den Frühling* D587 →

ERLKÖNIG
(GOETHE) OP. 1, **D328** [H179 & H201A]

The Erlking

The song exists in four versions, the fourth of which is discussed below:
(1) October? 1815; (2) April? 1816; (3) 1816?; (4) appeared end of March 1821

(1) 'Schnell'   G minor   **C**   [145 bars]

(2) 'Schnell'   G minor   **C**   [Accompaniment in duplets, 145 bars]

(3) 'Schnell'   G minor   **C**   [145 bars]

(4)   G minor

(148 bars)

Wer reitet so spät durch Nacht und Wind?	Who rides so late through the night and wind?
Es ist der Vater mit seinem Kind;	It is the father with his child;
Er hat den Knaben wohl in dem Arm,	He has the boy in his arms,
Er fasst ihn sicher, er hält ihn warm.	He holds him safely, he keeps him warm.
'Mein Sohn, was birgst du so bang dein Gesicht?'—	'My son, why hide you your face in fear?
'Siehst, Vater, du den Erlkönig nicht?	'Father, can you not see the Erlking?
Den Erlenkönig mit Kron und Schweif?'	The Erlking with his crown and tail?'
'Mein Sohn, es ist ein Nebelstreif.'—	'My son, it is a streak of mist.'
'Du liebes Kind, komm, geh mit mir!	'Sweet child, come with me!
Gar schöne Spiele spiel ich mit dir;	I'll play wonderful games with you;
Manch bunte Blumen sind an dem Strand,	Many a pretty flower grows on the shore,
Meine Mutter hat manch gülden Gewand.' –	My mother has many a golden robe.'
'Mein Vater, mein Vater, und hörest du nicht,	'Father, father, do you not hear
Was Erlenkönig mir leise verspricht?'—	What the Erlking softly promises me?'
'Sei ruhig, bleibe ruhig, mein Kind:	'Calm, be calm my child;
In dürren Blättern säuselt der Wind.'—	The wind is rustling in the withered leaves.'
'Willst, feiner Knabe, du mit mir gehn?	'Won't you come with me, my fine lad?
Meine Töchter sollen dich warten schön;	My daughters shall wait upon you;
Meine Töchter führen den nächtlichen Reihn	My daughters lead the nightly dance,
Und wiegen und tanzen und singen dich ein.'	And will rock and dance and sing you to sleep.'
'Mein Vater, mein Vater, und siehst du nicht dort	'Father, father, can you not see
Erlkönigs Töchter am düstern Ort?'	Erlking's daughters, there in the darkness?'
'Mein Sohn, mein Sohn, ich seh es genau:	'My son, I can see clearly:
Es scheinen die alten Weiden so grau.'	It is the old grey willows gleaming.'
'Ich liebe dich, mich reizt deine schöne Gestalt;	'I love you, your fair form allures me,
Und bist du nicht willig, so brauch ich Gewalt.'—	And if you don't come willingly, I'll use force.'
'Mein Vater, mein Vater, jetzt fasst er mich an!	'Father, father, now he's seizing me!
Erlkönig hat mir ein Leids getan!'—	The Erlking has hurt me!'
Dem Vater grauset's, er reitet geschwind,	The father shudders, he rides swiftly,
Er hält in Armen das ächzende Kind,	He holds the moaning child in his arms;
Erreicht den Hof mit Müh' und Not:[1]	With one last effort he reaches home;
In seinen Armen das Kind war tot.	The child lay dead in his arms.

JOHANN WOLFGANG VON GOETHE (1749–1832); poem written in 1782

This is the twenty-ninth of Schubert's seventy-five Goethe solo settings (1814–26). See the poet's biography for a chronological list of all the Goethe settings.

---

[1] Schubert's only change to this text is 'Müh' instead of Goethe's 'Mühe'.

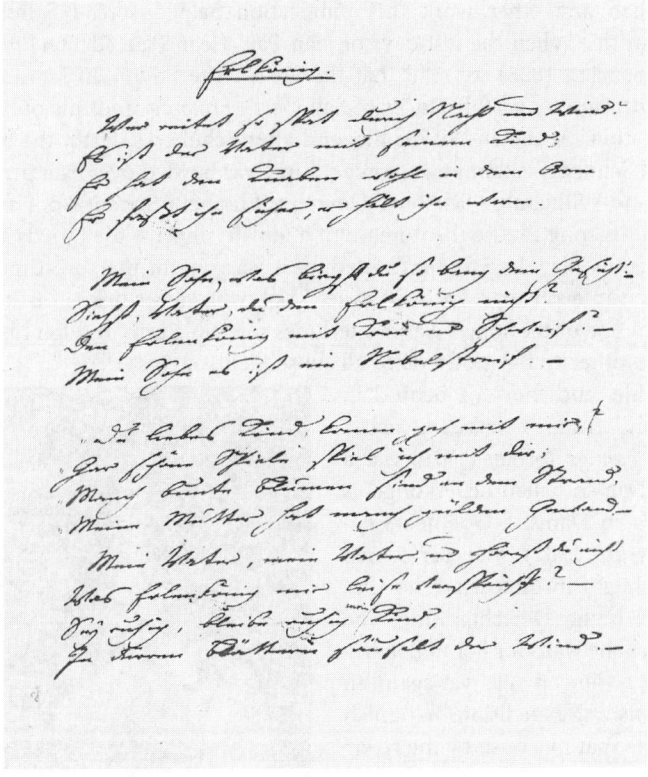

Goethe's autograph of *Erlkönig* (strophes 1–4).

Beethoven's attempt to set this song dates from 1796. His 'extended fragment' in D minor (Reid 2007, p. 144) is numbered as WoO 131. Schubert was already something of an old hand at setting Goethe's poetry when he composed *Erlkönig* in 1815; it is certainly his most famous song, and arguably the best known of all lieder. Josef von Spaun in his usually reliable memoirs remembers visiting Schubert's home in the company of the poet Mayrhofer where they found the composer reading the poem aloud and glowing ('ganz glühend') with enthusiasm. He apparently sat down and composed the song there and then; after which the small party went to the Imperial Konvikt to try it out as there was no piano in Schubert's home. That very evening it was sung at the Konvikt to immediate enthusiasm, and was also examined in detail by Schubert's former teacher, the old organist Wenzel Ruzicka (1757–1823). Ruzicka commented on the clashes between Ds and E flat when the boy cries out against the advances of the Erlking (in bb. 72–6) and pronounced the dissonances necessary for the text and beautifully resolved. Thus someone of the older generation immediately saw the point of the song despite its startling modernity. Soon it became a legend, an article of faith, within the circle. Schubert's friend Spaun sent it to Goethe as part of the ill-fated consignment of 1816 and attempted, without success, to get it published as early as 1817; at that stage it had been performed informally a number of times, stirring all listeners to enormous enthusiasm.

The composer published it proudly as his Opus 1 (1821). This was some six years after the song had been written, and the arrangement with Cappi & Diabelli was 'on commission', thus minimizing the financial risk to the publishing firm which was headed by that doubting Thomas, Anton Diabelli, gifted in business matters but no musical visionary. The deal had to be carefully overseen by Schubert's friends, in particular Leopold von Sonnleithner, but it was worth the trouble: more than any other work this publication helped spread Schubert's reputation throughout the world. When the last days of Jean Paul (Jean Paul Richter) were described by his biographer (Spazier, 1826) we read that the great writer, dying in faraway Bayreuth, was moved beyond measure by performances of Schubert's *Erlkönig*, and this only four years after the song's publication. At the end of his life, and after Schubert's death, the wary old Goethe, who had ignored Schubert's attempts to contact him, was bowled over by a performance by the formidable soprano Wilhelmine Schröder-Devrient; Elisabeth Schwarzkopf and Sarah Walker also proved that this song can be the domain of a female singer – the lyric is, after all, sung by a woman in Goethe's play. In Schubert's lifetime it was one of the sure-fire successes of the composer's chosen interpreter, Johann Michael Vogl, who nevertheless insisted that a bar be inserted (b. 41) in one of the song's piano interludes to enable him to catch his breath (this bar remains in place, rather to the gratitude of all subsequent singers).

Dortchen in *Die Fischerin*, engraving by Joseph von Hempel.

The poem's title, and the idea behind it, derived probably from Goethe's teacher Herder whose *Erlkönigs Tochter* (1779) was a translation of a Danish ballad ('ellerkonge' is 'king of the elves' in Danish). Goethe's *Singspiel*, *Die Fischerin* (1782) was performed outdoors by torchlight in Tiefurt an der Ilm. In this open-air drama Dortchen sings the ballad to herself as she waits for her father and her fiancé Niklas – they are late, yet again, in returning from a fishing expedition. To punish them she hangs her hat in a bush by the riverbank and hides. Niklas returns singing an old ballad (by Herder) about a girl who drowns, having been lured from church by the 'Wassermann'. Seeing Dortchen's hat and abandoned bucket Niklas assumes that she has also drowned in the river. After all this terrible consternation Dortchen reappears and ruefully agrees to marry Niklas the next day.

The musical versions of the poem started off in a humble way. The first Dortchen, the actress Corona Schröter (who was also Goethe's mistress), sang the words to her own music (No. 17 of her collection of *Fünf-undzwanzig Lieder*, published in Weimar in 1786). The ever-faithful Reichardt, when still Goethe's favoured composer, set it with alacrity (a breathless scherzo in G minor, 1794). The poem is perfect for music; it tells a spell-binding and suspenseful story with the greatest economy of means. The rhythm rolls along, and the characters spring to life with the intensity of folksong and the sophistication of great art. We are not certain whether Schubert knew Zelter's setting (in D major, 𝄵, with the most frightening of climaxes of any setting for the words 'Erlkönig hat mir ein Leids getan'). He certainly did not know Loewe's song, composed in 1818, and published also only in 1821. Loewe's setting is a magnificent achievement in its own right, and the only real competition that the Schubert version has ever faced; in comparison, the Spohr setting is musically pedestrian, despite its ferociously difficult violin obbligato.

Erlkönig drawn by Hermann Plüddemann, 1861.

Schubert sweeps aside the time-honoured mixture of recitative and arioso (the formality of ballad composition) in favour of an uncanny organic unity. In the pianist's right hand thundering triplets in pitiless octaves are almost unceasing, and they bind the piece together in the same way that the whirling of Gretchen's spinning wheel had inaugurated a new chapter in lieder history in 1814. In the left hand a triplet motif punctuates the repeated octaves, suggesting something malign and dangerous that creeps up on you at night, even if you are riding at full gallop. For this idea Schubert probably added equestrian impetus to a Beethovenian inspiration – a similar disposition of triplets in 'Nur hurtig fort' from *Fidelio*, a duet between Leonore (disguised as a man) and the jailer Rocco where Florestan's is the innocent life at stake in another three-way battle of wills. The vocal characterization is astonishing: the concerned yet controlled tone of the narrator, as if Goethe himself; the fear that has been generated from the beginning of the song is intensified with the father's first question (bb. 36–40) where a phrase rises within the interval of a fourth – often used by Schubert to illustrate fear; the much more obvious panic of the boy; and the carefree, if sinister, pronouncements of the Erlking who here sings a song as if within a song. The latter is accompanied at each of its appearances (bb. 57–71 and again at bb. 87–96) by triplets shared between the hands (the left playing the first on the beat, the right supplying the second and third) rather than the otherwise habitual single-handed triplets. This change of texture gives these passages a feeling of treading water, of being suspended in time or, as Walther Dürr hears it, of being sung from behind a veil. The thundering horse-hooves return only when the triplets re-establish themselves entirely in the right hand, as quickly as if two separate parts of a film had been invisibly spliced together. Apart from these oases of eerie calm when the Erlking speaks, the accompanist is given no respite, but the physical effort involved in playing this music is also somehow a commentary on the father's superhuman effort to save the life of his sick child. In all editions supervised by Goethe the words to describe this are 'Mühe' and 'Not' which Schubert changes to 'Müh' und 'Not'. In the poet's mind, at least, this extra syllable on Mühe might have implied an emphatic, exhausted slowing down.

Only at the end of the song does Schubert make use of recitative, and to most devastating effect in the last three bars. This is a masterstroke; the arrival at the destination on a helplessly stranded first inversion chord is immediately illustrated as being pointless. In the freedom of a sudden recitative (bb. 145–6) we feel the child's body crumple; up to this time there has been something living held in the father's firm grip, now it is simply a corpse – Schubert sets the word 'tot' unaccompanied. Elisabeth Schwarzkopf made that empty vowel sound like wind blowing over a graveyard. (In Goethe's own time there were complaints about English copies of the poem where the father is made to hold his 'eighteenth' – achtzehnte – child rather than his moaning – 'ächzende' – one!)

The boy's fevered terror and the father's stoic attempts to hide his own worst fears are remarkable enough. Much of the splendour of this role-playing is to do with Schubert's cunning use of tessitura. The father's voice lies deep in the stave, the boy's high. In between is the narrator. Also in the middle is the voice of the Erlking (of all the characters he is the least stressed, the most controlling) but the accompaniment aids the interpreter to make something horribly beguiling of his music. The depiction of sweetly reasonable and honeyed evil is something new and sinister in song. This is not the voice and demeanour of a conventional villain, but that of a torturer with exquisite manners. The Erlking's vocal line is in the major key (as in Loewe's chilling version), empty of joy and devoid of truth. This civilized façade is maintained until, literally, the last second of the passage (bb. 116–23) when the Erlking speaks for the third time. This 'Ich liebe dich, mich reizt deine schöne Gestalt' is marked pianissimo thanks only to Schubert's second thoughts – the first version (NSA Volume 1b p. 178) is marked forte. The phrase beginning 'Und bist du nicht willig, so brauch ich Gewalt' is sung quietly and seductively (albeit to a melodic line in descending steps that eerily recalls the final words of condemnation by the Commendatore at the end of Mozart's *Don Giovanni*). Only on the second syllable of the last word, Ge<u>walt</u>, does the marking change to fortissimo. If this dynamic is scrupulously observed, a monster is suddenly revealed, a trickster who has concealed the iron fist in the velvet glove until the terrifying and fatal moment when he mercilessly delivers the *coup de grâce*.

Erlkönig drawn by Eugen Neurether, 1829.

The earliest printed illustration of Erlkonig, by Ramberg (1821).

Erlkönig is a song that defies age (the composer's, particularly) and one that defines an age. Like Beethoven's Fifth Symphony it appeals to all levels of musical sophistication in equal measure – to those who see something deeply symbolic in the poem and to those who simply love a rattling good yarn excitingly told. It was that rare thing: a popular hit that absolutely deserves to be. The four versions printed in AGA and NSA (in a slightly different order) vary in this and that detail. We love Schubert all the more that in the second of these he rewrites the fiendish piano triplets as simple duplets in quavers. He found it hard for his own piano technique to keep pace with his demands as a composer. There were, however, certain compensations: the composition of this song was certainly the moment when he knew that no mere virtuoso pianist could ever hope to match his genius, or play a stronger musical hand. Mention must be made nevertheless of Franz Liszt's astonishing performance of a solo arrangement of *Erlkönig* (*see* TRANSCRIPTIONS). There is a documented occasion (17 March 1840) when half the audience stood on their chairs to hear and see him play this song.

Collectors of old records will recall a performance of *Erlkönig* (a Columbia '78', LFX 336) sung as *Le Roi des aulnes* in French translation with a cast of characters – the tenor Georges Thill as the narrator and Erlking, the bass H. B. Etcheverry as the father and 'Claude Pascal (12 ans)' as the boy. Such a distribution of roles might seem highly questionable but for the fact that we know that it happened not only with the composer's consent, but on one occasion with his participation. Albert Stadler, poet and schoolfriend of Schubert, wrote out his Schubertian recollections in 1858. One of his most vivid memories was of the summer of 1819 in Steyr when Schubert was on holiday with the singer Vogl. They spent a good deal of time at the home of the merchant Josef von Koller and his family:

The very talented daughter of the house, Josefine, Schubert, Vogl and I enjoyed the pleasantest hours there, alternating performances of Schubert's songs with performances of his pianoforte pieces as well as many pieces from the operas of Vogl's hey-day. An odd effect was made, I still remember, by the attempt (only among ourselves of course) to sing Erlkönig as a trio. Schubert sang the father, Vogl the Erlkönig, Josefine the child and I played. – After the music we sat down to supper and then remained together enjoying ourselves for another hour or two.

Such was the popularity of this song that it was subjected to more daring arrangements than this. Less than eighteen months after his brother's death, Ferdinand Schubert made an orchestral arrangement of *Erlkönig* for voices and mixed choir. Friedlaender also notes an orchestral arrangement without voices where solo passages were given to flute (narrator), clarinet in C (child), horn in B flat (Erlking) and bass trombone (father).

Autographs:	First draft missing or lost; Staatsbibliothek Preussischer Kulturbesitz, Berlin (fair copy for Goethe); Pierpont Morgan Library, New York (fair copy made for Breitkopf & Härtel)
Publication:	First published as part of the AGA in 1895 (P614–616; first, second and third versions) First published as Op. 1 by Cappi & Diabelli in 1821 (P1; fourth version)
Dedicatee:	Moritz von Dietrichstein
Publication reviews:	*Der Sammler* (Vienna), No. 39 (31 March 1821), p. 156 [Waidelich/ Hilmar Dokumente I No. 79; Deutsch Doc. Biog. No. 218] *Allgemeine musikalische Zeitung* (Vienna), No. 38 (12 May 1821), col. 299f. [Waidelich/Hilmar Dokumente I No. 98; Deutsch Doc. Biog. No. 234] F. von Hentl 'Blick auf Schubert's Lieder', *Wiener Zeitschrift für Kunst, Literatur, Theater und Mode* No. 36 (23 March 1822), p. 289f. [Waidelich/Hilmar Dokumente I No. 146; Deutsch Doc. Biog. No. 278]
First known performance:	1 December 1820, *Abend-Unterhaltung* of the Gesellschaft der Musikfreunde, Vienna. Soloist: August Ritter von Gymnich (see Waidelich/Hilmar Dokumente I No. 65 for full concert programme)
Performance reviews:	Although there are no reviews of this first performance, several papers reported on the first public performance of Johann Michael Vogl, which also took place in an *Abend-Unterhaltung* of the Gesellschaft der Musikfreunde on 8 March 1821 (see Waidelich/ Hilmar Dokumente I No. 72 for full concert programme): *Wiener allgemeine Theaterzeitung* No. 31 (13 March 1821), p. 122f. [Waidelich/Hilmar Dokumente I No. 74] *Allgemeine musikalische Zeitung* (Vienna), No. 23 (21 March 1821), col. 183 [Waidelich/Hilmar Dokumente I No. 75; Deutsch Doc. Biog. No. 211] *Der Sammler* (Vienna), No. 37 (27 March 1821), p. 148 [Waidelich/Hilmar Dokumente I No. 76]
Subsequent editions:	Peters: Vol. 1/170; AGA XX 178a–d: Vol. 3/202 (first version), 208 (given as second version, recte third), 214 (given as third version, recte second) & 219 (fourth version); NSA IV: Vol. 1a/3 (fourth version), Vol. 1b/173 (first version), 180 (second version) & 187 (third version); Bärenreiter: Vol. 1/2 (first version) & 204 (second version)
Bibliography:	Brown 1958, pp. 45–7 Brown 1968, pp. 122–34 Capell 1928, pp. 107–12 Einstein 1951, pp. 112–14 Gibbs 1994, pp. 33–48 Friedlaender 1902, Vol. 2, p. 184 Newbould 1997, pp. 149–50 Reid 2007, pp. 143–5 Stein 1971, p. 64

Sternfeld 1979, pp. 127–9

Further settings and arrangements:	Johann Friedrich Reichardt (1752–1814) *Erlkönig* (1784)
	Carl Friedrich Zelter (1758–1832) *Erlkönig* (1807)
	Václav Jan Tomášek (1774–1850) *Erlkönig*, Op. 59 no. 1 (1815)
	Anselm Hüttenbrenner (1794–1868) *Erlkönig* (1829)
	Carl Loewe (1796–1869) *Erlkönig* (1815)
	Arr. Hector Berlioz (1803–1869) *Le Roi des aulnes* for tenor and orchestra (1860)
	Arr. Franz Liszt (1811–1886) for solo piano (1837–8) and for voice and orchestra, no. 4 of *Sechs Lieder von Schubert* (1860)
	Arr. Max Reger (1873–1916) for voice and orchestra (1915)
	Arr. Percival Garratt (1877–1953) *Erlkönig* for two pianos (1937)
	Hans Werner Henze (b. 1926) *Erlkönig, Orchesterfantasie über Goethes Gedichte und Schuberts Opus 1* (1996)
	Arr. Tilman Hoppstock (b. 1961) for guitar accompaniment, in *Franz Schubert: 110 Lieder* (2009)

Discography and timing:	Fischer-Dieskau I 6[8]	4'19	Sarah Walker (solo version)
	Hyperion I 8[18] & 24[11]		John Mark Ainsley, Christine
		4'14	Schäfer & Michael George (trio version)
	Hyperion II 10[15] & 11[14]		John Mark Ainsley, Christine
		4'22	Schäfer & Michael George (trio version)

← *Dem Unendlichen* D291   *Liane* D298 →
← *Hermann und Thusnelda* D322   *Klage de Ceres* D323 →

ERMIN *see* JOHANN GOTTFRIED KUMPF

ERNTELIED   Harvest song
(HÖLTY) **D434** [H261]
E major   May 1816

(15 bars)

Sicheln schallen,	Sickles echo,
Ähren fallen	Ears of corn fall
Unter Sichelschall;	To the sound of the sickles.
Auf den Mädchenhüten	On the girls' bonnets
Zittern blaue Blüten,	Blue flowers quiver;
Freud' ist überall.	Joy is everywhere.

Sicheln klingen,   Sickles resound,
Mädchen singen   Girls sing
Unter Sichelklang,   To the sound of the sickles;
Bis, vom Mond beschimmert,   Until, bathed in moonlight,
Rings die Stoppel flimmert,   The stubble shimmers all around,
Tönt der Erntesang.   And the harvest song rings out.

Alles springet,   All leap about,
Alles singet,   All who can utter a sound
Was nur lallen kann.   Sing out.
Bei dem Erntemahle   At the harvest feast
Isst aus einer Schale   The farmer and his labourer
Knecht und Bauersmann.   Eat from the same bowl.

[. . .]   [. . .]

Jeder scherzet,   Then every man teases
Jeder herzet   And hugs
Dann sein Liebelein.   His sweetheart.
Nach geleerten Kannen,   When the tankards are empty
Gehen sie von dannen,   They go off,
Singen und juchhein!   Singing and shouting with joy.

LUDWIG CHRISTOPH HÖLTY (1748–1776); poem written in 1773. Adapted for publication in
1804 by JOHANN HEINRICH VOSS (1751–1826).

*This is the twenty-first of Schubert's twenty-three Hölty solo settings (1813–16). See the poet's
biography for a chronological list of all the Hölty settings.*

This must be one of the most delightful of all the Hölty settings. It is, as Einstein points out, 'no
longer an *Arbeitslied* designed for a particular purpose', but a song 'raised to the highest level of
art'. It might not have been written for a specific band of workers during their harvest, but hard
work, and joy in the physical outdoor life are writ large in this music. The key is E major (a
favourite Hölty tonality, as in *Blumenlied* D431) and we can almost smell the flowers or, in this
case, the newly harvested corn fields. The accompaniment is particularly fascinating; an imaginary woodwind orchestra of clarinets and flutes is underpinned by bassoons that flit about in
staccato semiquavers. This gives an old-fashioned air to the proceedings, and in some ways this
music suggests the songs of C. P. E. Bach or the counterpoint of the sixteenth-century Italian
madrigalists.

All this weaving of textures (the piece is a type of four-part invention) splendidly portrays a
bustling atmosphere where each has his or her job to do, and where joyful cooperation with
one's fellow workers is the order of the day. When played on the piano the bass line has to do
service in the first four bars as the sound of sickles whirring in the cornfield and, rather more
delicately, flowers trembling on girls' bonnets. Eric Sams has pointed out that these semiquavers,
tripping delicately in pastoral fashion, are related to the shepherdess's music in Mozart's *Das
Veilchen*, almost certainly a seminal influence on Schubert's work. On the words 'Freud' ist
überall' (bb. 8–11) the bass line is doubled into striding octaves appropriate for general jubilation. We fancy that we are hearing the slightly ponderous and hearty village dance music that
was such a feature of the evenings during the harvest festivities. Schumann was to evoke similar

rustic jubilation in his *Das ist ein Flöten und Geigen* from *Dichterliebe*, albeit darkened by Heine's more complicated sub-plot. The postlude of Schubert's song is a joy; staccato triplets, a double-dotted ascending fanfare and rumbustious mordents all combine to paint a picture of the high spirits and well-being that come after the completion of a hard job well done. As the pianist comes to the end of a performance of this song there is a feeling of tidiness, even in the turning of those slightly tricky mordents, a certain pride in the accomplishment of order. It is seldom that an inveterate city dweller such as Schubert has entered into the rituals of country life with such imaginative empathy. The introduction printed in the Peters Edition (and in neither the AGA nor the NSA) is almost certainly spurious, but nothing could be more heartwarmingly genuine than the song itself.

The striking similarity of Schubert's vocal line to the tune for the English hymn *We Plough the Fields and Scatter* (minus the upbeat to the hymn's melody) is perhaps not as coincidental as it might first seem. This celebrated harvest hymn is a translation of lines taken from a longer poem, *Das Bauernlied*, by Matthias Claudius (*Amus omnia sua secum portans, oder Sämmtliche Werke des Wandsbecker Bothen*, 1783, Part IV p. 68). It became customary to leave out the first two strophes of the poem and begin with the third verse (beginning 'Wir pflügen und wir streuen / Den Samen auf das Land') about ploughing and seed-sowing. This shortened version of the poem had also been composed by Johann Abraham Peter Schulz (1747–1800) and his simple yet stirring setting was published in 1800 in the second edition of his *Melodien für Volksschulen*. It is not inconceivable that this collection might have been used as a textbook in the family school where Schubert worked as a teacher. Schulz's music appeared with Claudius's words in various German songbooks and hymnals, and it was the Schulz setting of these words that was translated in 1861 by Jane Montgomery Campbell and taken into the English hymnals later in the nineteenth century. If Schubert had been fond of the same tune still heartily sung to this day by many an English-speaking churchgoer, it would be easy to imagine that his subconscious reconstructed echoes of Schulz's melody in honour of Hölty's secular harvest celebrations.

Autograph:	Missing or lost
First edition:	Published as Book 48 no. 2 of the *Nachlass* by Diabelli, Vienna in 1850 (P381)
Subsequent editions:	Peters: Vol. 6/60; AGA XX 226: Vol. 4/109; NSA IV: Vol. 10/164
Further settings:	Felix Mendelssohn (1809–1847) *Sicheln schallen* (1823–4)
Discography and timing:	Fischer-Dieskau I 7[16] 1'17
	Hyperion I 18[6] 1'50 Peter Schreier
	Hyperion II 14[13]

⟵ *Seligkeit* D433   *Klage (An den Mond)* D₂436 ⟶

Die ERSCHEINUNG   The apparition
(ERINNERUNG)
(KOSEGARTEN) OP. 108 NO. 3, **D229** [H120]
E major   7 July 1815

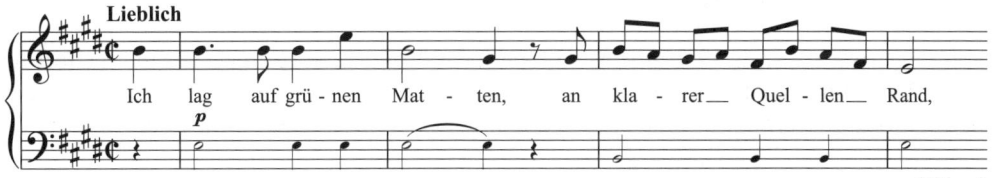

(19 bars)

Ich lag auf grünen Matten,	I lay in green meadows
An klarer Quellen Rand.	By the edge of the clear spring;
Mir kühlten Erlenschatten	The shade of alders
Der Wangen heissen Brand.	Cooled the fire of my cheeks.
Ich dachte diess und jenes,	I thought of this and that,
Und träumte sanft betrübt,	And dreamed with gentle sorrows
Viel Gutes und viel Schönes,[1]	Of many a good and lovely thing
Das diese Welt nicht gibt!	Which this world does not yield.
Und sieh, dem Hain entschwebte	And lo, from the grove there arose
Ein Mägdlein sonnenklar.	A maiden, as bright as the sun.
Ein weisser Schleier webte	A white veil flowed
Um ihr nussbraunes Haar.	Around her nut-brown hair.
Ihr Auge feucht und schimmernd,	Her moist, shining eyes
Umfloss' ätherisch Blau,	Were flooded with heavenly blue,
Die Wimper nässte flimmernd	And on her eyelashes glistened
Der Wehmut Perlentau.	Dewy pearls of sadness.
[. . .]	[. . .]
Ich auf, sie zu umfassen!	I stood up to embrace her,
Und ach, sie trat zurück.	And, alas, she receded;
Ich sah sie schnell erblassen,	I saw her quickly pale,
Und trüber ward ihr Blick.	And her gaze grew more sorrowful.
Sie sah mich an so innig,	She looked upon me so fervently,
Sie wies mit ihrer Hand,	And with her hand she gestured
Erhaben und tiefsinnig,	Solemnly and pensively towards heaven,
Gen Himmel und verschwand.	And vanished.
Fahr wohl, fahr wohl, Erscheinung!	Farewell, farewell, vision!
Fahr wohl, dich kenn' ich wohl!	Farewell, I know you well,
Und deines Winkes Meinung	And understand as I should
Versteh' ich, wie ich soll . . .	The meaning of your sign.
Wohl für die Zeit geschieden,	'Though we are parted for a time,
Eint uns ein schön'res Band.	A fairer bond unites us;
Hoch droben, nicht henieden	High above, not here below,
Hat Lieb' ihr Vaterland!	Love has its home!'

LUDWIG KOSEGARTEN (1758–1818); poem written in July 1787

This is the fourth of Schubert's twenty-one Kosegarten solo settings (1815–17). See the poet's biography for a chronological list of all the Kosegarten settings, as well as a discussion of Morten Solvik's Kosegarten Liederkreis and this song's place within it.

This song has real charm, although one must perform all four verses printed here for the story to make sense, and the tune is in danger of outstaying its welcome after so many repetitions. There is a link with *Die Forelle* D550 (composed some eighteen months later) through the shape of its

---

[1] The original has 'Viel *Süsses mir und* Schönes'.

The Apparition in Kosegarten's *Poesieen* (1798).

melody. At the very opening, 'Ich lag auf grünen Matten' (bb. 1–3), as well as 'Mir kühlten Erlenschatten' (bb. 4–7), the tune is a pre-echo of that famous angling phrase 'In einem Bächlein helle'. Towards the end of the verse the similarities become stronger: the melody at 'Ich dachte diess und jenes' (bb. 8–10), and later also at 'Viel Gutes und viel Schönes' (bb. 12–14) is exactly the same as 'Ich stand an dem Gestade' in the song of the trout.

It is almost certain that these similarities came about in a deeper way than simple self-quotation. They give us an insight into the composer's creative process, of how particular images and situations prompted musical shapes, or tonal analogues, that arose from his unconscious. Both poems (in the same metre, incidentally) deal with stories that are inspired by the sight of water. Thus the 'Bächlein helle' of *Die Forelle* and the 'An klarer Quellen Rand' of *Die Erscheinung* are related, despite the fact that *Die Erscheinung*, strictly speaking, is not a water song: the apparition appears from the grove and is no water nymph or Lorelei. There is also a tinge of melancholy in both poems; lessons are learned from the observation of events that the narrator would have wished otherwise in a more perfect world. The crucial thing from the composer's point of view is that the narrator has been put into a dreamlike condition by the sound of the lapping water, and is in the right state of mind to welcome such a vision. (One commentator suggested that the apparition appeared as a result of too much alcohol!) Water runs through much of the song like a gentle accompanying leitmotif in pianistic double thirds. The postlude is particularly successful in this regard: gentle cascades in thirds and sixths in three different registers of the piano (with a succession of Es in the left hand which drop an octave for each successive bar) murmur their impartial commentary on this beguiling dream. Is it fanciful to hear in this piano writing an echo from the vocal score of Mozart's *Così fan tutte*? *Soave sia il vento*, that matchless trio for Don Alfonso with Fiordiligi and Dorabella (who imagine that they are bidding their lovers farewell) is a musical feast of sighing thirds in E major (compare bb. 16–18). The emotional agenda of this poem is curiously related to the situation in Da Ponte's libretto, particularly the words of Kosegarten's final strophe.

There are five strophes in Kosegarten's poem – these are all printed in the AGA. Given here are 1, 2, 4 and 5. Four seem sufficient in performance although the third strophe adds a more detailed description of the apparition. The full poem is translated in Wigmore 1988.

Autograph: In private possession (first draft)
First edition: Published in an 'Album musicale' by Sauer & Leidesdorf, Vienna in December 1824 and subsequently as Op. 108 no. 3 with the title 'Erinnerung' by M. J. Leidesdorf, Vienna in 1829 (P195)

Subsequent editions:	Peters: Vol. 6/117; AGA XX 92: Vol. 2/175; NSA IV: Vol. 5/134; Bärenreiter: Vol. 4/44
Further settings and arrangements:	Sophia Maria Westenholz (1759–1838) *Die Erscheinung* (1806) Johann Rudolf Zumsteg (1760–1802) *Ich lag auf grünen Matten* (1801) Arr. Tilman Hoppstock (b. 1961) for guitar accompaniment, in *Franz Schubert: 110 Lieder* (2009) under title *Erinnerung*
Discography and timing:	Fischer-Dieskau I 4[10] 2'24
	Hyperion I 22[10]
	Hyperion II 8[3] 3'18 Jamie MacDougall

← *Von Ida* D228   *Die Täuschung* D230 →

ERSTARRUNG *see WINTERREISE* D911/4

Die ERSTE LIEBE   First love
(FELLINGER) **D182** [H86]
C major   12 April 1815

(53 bars)

Die erste Liebe füllt das Herz mit Sehnen	First love fills the heart with longing,
Nach einem unbekannten Geisterlande,	For an uknown enchanted land.
Die Seele gaukelt an dem Lebensrande,	The soul flutters on the edge of life,
Und süsse Wehmut letzet sich in Tränen.	And sweet melancholy dissolves in tears.
Da wacht es auf, das Vorgefühl des Schönen,	Now dawns the intimation of beauty;
Du schaust die Göttin in dem Lichtgewande,	You behold the goddess in her robe of light;
Geschlungen sind des Glaubens leise Bande,	The gentle bonds of faith are sealed,
Und Tage rieseln hin auf Liebestönen.	And the days flow by in songs of love.
Du siehst nur sie allein im Widerscheine,	Her alone you see reflected,
Die Holde, der du ganz dich hingegeben,	The fair one to whom you have surrendered yourself;
Nur sie durchschwebt deines Daseins Räume.	She alone pervades your whole being.
Sie lächelt dir herab vom Goldgesäume,	She smiles down on you from heaven's golden fringes
Wenn stille Lichter an den Himmeln schweben,	When silent lights hover in the sky.
Der Erde jubelst du: S i e i s t d i e M e i n e !	Joyfully you cry to the world: *She is mine!*

JOHANN GEORG FELLINGER (1781–1816); poem written in 1812

This is the second of Schubert's three Fellinger solo settings (1815). See the poet's biography for a chronological list of all the Fellinger settings.

The Styrian poet Fellinger provides Schubert with a similar challenge to that posed by Kosegarten in *Geist der Liebe* D233: the advent of love is depicted as a holy experience. Fellinger's beloved, it seems, has a similar effect on him to a visitation from the Queen of Heaven. This was not an uncommon reaction among young Roman Catholic artists of the period; there are a number of Schubert songs addressed to the Virgin Mary which contain music of sensuous delight. Although there is no doubt that Kosegarten is the better poet, and that Fellinger's conflation of sacred and profane is somewhat kitsch, Schubert was seemingly unabashed at the challenge of setting the latter's verses in exalted mood. His confidence is all the more exceptional in that this poem is in fact a sonnet – the first that Schubert set to music. Later in his career, 1818–19, he went on to set sonnets of Petrarch and Goethe successfully after shying away from completing a sonnet to *Die Macht der Liebe* by Kalchberg in October 1815 (D308), selected from the same literary anthology, *Selam* 1814 in which he found the text of *Die erste Liebe*. It is generally felt that putting a poem of this kind to music is a real challenge, but Schubert makes light of the problem and the listener is unaware of any tussle between word and music.

On the contrary, *Die erste Liebe*, through-composed and of daring intensity, is one of the truly remarkable achievements of 1815, a real tenor song which, among other things, shows the composer's increasing awareness of how to write effectively, albeit demandingly, for singers. Diabelli chose to publish the song in B flat (rather than C) in the *Nachlass*, and a contemporary copy exists a third lower, in the key of A flat. The whole of the first verse exists in a world of enchantment, an impression reinforced by the height of the tessitura (the 'Nach einem *unbekannten Geisterlande*' in b. 8 soars up to an A) and the almost total absence of a tonic chord in the root position to bring the fluttering soul to earth. (Note the triplets in the piano when this image is first broached at 'Die Seele gaukelt', b. 10.)

The second verse arrives as if it embodies a solution to the soul's wanderings: a grandiose fanfare motif in the piano at b. 16 (we are in the presence of a goddess, after all) is then taken up by the voice as if in canon, b. 17. (Berlioz used the same interval and rhythm for his 'Reviens, reviens' in *Absence* from *Les Nuits d'été*.) At b. 17 there is a root position C major chord in the left hand: it is as if the first verse has been mere introduction, and the real song could only begin with the dawning of the intimation of beauty and the tonal certainty of this motif. As if to remind us that such beauty is an immortal constant, this dotted rhythm pervades the accompaniment of the second verse, no doubt inspired by the word 'Lichtgewande', b. 21. Just as Schubert often obsessively repeats certain motifs in his accompaniments associated with the workings of nature – and the shining of stars in particular – the repetition of octave Es high in the accompaniment (bb. 23–5) here signifies a quality of light, and vestal garments a-shimmer. The verse ends with a flowing triplet accompaniment to illustrate the days flowing by in songs of love (bb. 26–30).

The third verse inhabits the vocal stratosphere, underpinned by those pulsating triplets that composers from Schubert to Wolf have taken to be a musical analogue for religious (or erotic) devotion and awe. As Einstein points out, the climax of the song at the end is 'passionately exuberant'; it has a maturity and mastery that belies the youth of its creator. Robert Schumann would not have considered these final bars (the repetition of 'Sie ist die Meine!', bb. 46–50) as old-fashioned (cf. the conclusion of his own setting of Eichendorff's *Frühlingsnacht*). The final cadence, and the postlude of triplets, murmuring their adoration in dying falls, are worthy of a fully fledged composer of the Romantic age. This music is also strongly prophetic of the end of Schumann's duet *Er und sie*: there the words 'einen/eine' echo in the piano postlude as if still

reverberating in the minds of the performers after the singing has finished. *Die erste Liebe* closes
with similar pianistic musings on the words 'die Meine!' (bb. 50–4).

Autograph: Missing or lost
First edition: Published as Book 35 no. 1 of the *Nachlass* by Diabelli, Vienna in
                              1842 (P341)
Subsequent editions: Peters: Vol. 5/202 (B♭ major); AGA XX 61: Vol. 2/94; NSA IV: Vol.
                              8/36
Discography and timing: Fischer-Dieskau I 3[13]   2'27
                              Hyperion I 20[11]
                              Hyperion II 6[5]   2'57   John Mark Ainsley

← *Sehnsucht der Liebe* D180   *Trinklied* D183 →

ERSTER VERLUST   First loss
(GOETHE) OP. 5 NO. 4, **D226** [H117]
A♭ major – F minor   5 July 1815

(22 bars)

Ach, wer bringt die schönen Tage,[1]	Ah, who will bring back those fair days,
Jene Tage der ersten Liebe,	Those days of first love?
Ach, wer bringt nur eine Stunde	Ah, who will bring back but one hour
Jener holden Zeit zurück!	Of that sweet time?
Einsam nähr' ich meine Wunde,	Alone I nurture my wound
Und mit stets erneuter Klage	And, forever renewing my lament,
Traur' ich ums verlorne Glück.	Mourn my lost happiness.
Ach, wer bringt die schönen Tage,	Ah, who will bring back those fair days,
Jene holde Zeit zurück!	That sweet time?

JOHANN WOLFGANG VON GOETHE (1749–1832); poem written in 1785

*This is the eighteenth of Schubert's seventy-five Goethe solo settings (1814–26). See the poet's
biography for a chronological list of all the Goethe settings.*

This song belongs to that elite group of single-page Schubertian masterpieces that this poet was
almost solely able to inspire: *An den Mond* D259, *Der König in Thule* D367, *Liebhaber in allen*

---

[1] Goethe places exclamation marks after each appearance of the word 'Ach'. These were not adopted in the song's
publication.

Gestalten D558, *Meeres Stille* D216, *Nähe des Geliebten* D62 and the two *Wandrers Nachtlieder*, D224 and D768. The first four of these are extended by repetitions of the verses; the final three depend on a single shattering strophe – the listener experiences something as devastatingly compact as is the music on the page. Collin's *Wehmut* (D772) is another potent song that can be printed on a single page, but the kind of powerful musical miniature Schubert was able to write owed everything to Goethe's powers of compression. In music like this every note, every syllable, tells; there is not a note too many, nor an expressive opportunity lost. The result is a small jewel, perfection of a kind that is less obvious in larger musical structures.

From the beginning there is an ambivalence between minor and major tonalities. Thus the opening of the rueful entreaty is accompanied by F minor chords in root position, but the word 'schönen' (b. 2) launches the second inversion of A flat major. Throughout the song the major-key pleasure in the beauty of love's memory contends with the minor-key pain of its loss. The setting of the word 'Liebe' (b. 5), a three-note melisma, is a case in point: is this happy or sad? The voice rises a fourth, from C to F, as if lifting in rapture, but this confidence is undermined by the flattened harmony that supports and darkens the F, momentarily poised before it slips down a tone, a resolution on a simple chord of E flat major. There surely could never have been a finer musical illustration of 'bitter-sweet'; the excitement of remembering love is combined with a realization of its loss, and finally an acceptance of that loss, the latter a state of grace that seems particularly Schubertian – not a dominant part of the poet's psyche, perhaps, but of the composer's, certainly. That such an eloquent hymn to the past should come from the pen of an eighteen-year-old boy, without a past of his own to speak of, is one of the miracles of music.

The ardent cantilena presses forward in bb. 6–7; the repeated notes in the vocal line (a succession of four D flats in b. 6) brings a tenacious quality to the music, a dignity in struggle, a determination to hold on to memory. The descending phrase of 'Jener holden Zeit zurück' (b. 8) is accompanied by off-beat quavers in the pianist's right hand – this writing suggests something precious and beautiful slipping out of a lover's hands. The vocal line at 'Einsam nähr' ich meine Wunde' (bb. 10–12) is doubled by the piano, a gesture of solidarity that only emphasizes

Erster Verlust, vignette for Czerny's arrangement of the Schubert song for solo piano, 1838–9.

the solitary plight of the protagonist; the word 'Wunde' occasions the most individual moment in the accompaniment – a dotted figure in the treble (b. 12) that sounds like the commiseration of a plangent oboe. We are reminded of how classical this music is. The harp-like arpeggiated chords in the pianist's right hand that accompany 'Und mit stets erneuter Klage' (bb. 12–14) might be played on a lyre belonging to Gluck's Orpheus. Indeed, the understated dignity of many a Gluck aria seems more of a model here than anything written by Mozart. The vocal line for 'Traur' ich ums verlorne Glück' descends to the lowest note of the song (bb. 15–16), an emotional nadir, at the same time an exquisite bridge passage into a modified recapitulation of the song's opening five bars (the decision to repeat the first and fourth lines of the opening strophe is Goethe's). This time the phrase 'Jene holde Zeit zurück' ends unequivocally on an A flat major chord. The grateful ear accepts this as might a jilted lover who struggles to maintain a shred of optimism. But this slender hope is utterly extinguished by the piano, a single-bar postlude that returns to F minor in five soft but inexorable notes. The final taste is bitter rather than sweet.

It seems churlish to point out that Schubert adds the word 'wer' to the last line of Goethe's poem to allow himself the musical shape he wanted (b. 19). He included *Erster Verlust* in the book of sixteen songs he sent to the great poet in 1816. Did the composer perhaps wonder whether Goethe's failure to reply to this consignment had something to do with this lese-majesty? If so, he should not have felt any guilt: the setting of this text by Goethe's friend Zelter adds the words 'süsse, liebe' to the final 'holde' to facilitate an extravagant vocal peroration. Zelter's setting of these words (1807) is not to be disparaged, but Schubert's is far more profound. The poem incidentally was originally an aria assigned to the character of the Baroness in Goethe's *Singspiel, Die ungleichen Hausgenossen* (The Dissimilar Lodgers). This in turn was

Schubert's autograph of *Erster Verlust* from the album sent to Goethe in 1816.

inspired by a Carlo Gozzi comedy translated by Friedrich Wilhelm Gotter (qv) in 1781. Another source of the text was the libretto of Mozart's opera *Le Nozze di Figaro*. One only has to read the poem of *Erster Verlust* to see that it has some relationship with the mood of the soprano arias *Porgi amor* and *Dove sono* where the Countess looks back on the happier times she had once enjoyed with her estranged husband, the Count. This link may also account for the exceptionally Mozartian mood of Zelter's setting mentioned above.

Schubert, in a heartfelt letter to Schober from Zseliz (21 September 1824) quotes the poem's third and fourth lines. Nine years after setting it, *Erster Verlust* evoked memories of a different kind of loss, of a vanished time of 'united striving after the highest beauty', of sitting cosily with close friends who shyly shared their latest work with each other while awaiting approval or criticism.

Autograph:	Staatsbibliothek Preussischer Kulturbesitz, Berlin (fair copy made for Goethe)
First edition:	Published as Op. 5 no. 4 by Cappi & Diabelli, Vienna in 1821 (P13)
Dedicatee:	Antonio Salieri
Publication review:	F. von Hentl 'Blick auf Schubert's Lieder', *Wiener Zeitschrift für Kunst, Literatur, Theater und Mode* No. 36 (23 March 1822), p. 289f. [Waidelich/Hilmar Dokumente I No. 146; Deutsch Doc. Biog. No. 278].
Subsequent editions:	Peters: Vol. 2/11; AGA XX 89: Vol. 2/172; NSA IV: Vol. 1/44; Bärenreiter: Vol. 1/36
Bibliography:	Byrne 2003, pp. 400–402
	Capell 1928, pp. 52 & 102
	Einstein 1951, p. 109
Further settings:	Johann Friedrich Reichardt (1752–1814) *Erster Verlust* (1794)
	Hans Georg Nägeli (1773–1836) *Erster Verlust* (1797)
	Felix Mendelssohn (1809–1847) *Erster Verlust* Op. 99 no. 1 (1841)
	Hugo Wolf (1860–1903) *Erster Verlust* Op. 9 no. 3 (1876)
	Nikolai Medtner (1880–1951) *Erster Verlust* Op. 6 no. 8 (1904–5) [also set in Russian]
	Alban Berg (1885–1935) *Erster Verlust* (1904)
	Othmar Schoeck (1886–1957) *Erster Verlust* Op. 15 no. 5 (1908)
	Pierre Octave Ferroud (1900–1936) *Erster Verlust* (1932)
Discography and timing:	Fischer-Dieskau I 4[9] 1'58
	Hyperion I 1[10]
	Hyperion II 7[17] 2'04 Janet Baker

⟵ *Der Fischer* D225   *Idens Nachtgesang* D227 ⟶

∿∽∿∽∿∽∿∽∿∽

Die ERWARTUNG   Anticipation
(SCHILLER) **D159** [H267]

This song exists in two versions, the second of which is discussed below:
(1) May 1816; (2) date unknown

(1)   'Langsam'   B♭ major – G major   **C**   [183 bars]

(2)   B♭ major

(194 bars)

(1)	Hör' ich das Pförtchen nicht gehen?	Did I not hear the gate?
	Hat nicht der Riegel geklirrt?	Was that not the bolt creaking?
	Nein, es war des Windes Wehen,	No, it was the wind
	Der durch die Pappeln schwirrt.[1]	Blowing through the poplars.

(2)	O schmücke dich, du grünbelaubtes Dach,	Adorn yourself, leaf-clad roof,
	Du sollst die Anmutstrahlende empfangen;	You are to receive her in all her radiant beauty;
	Ihr Zweige! baut ein schattendes Gemach,	Branches, build a shady bower
	Mit holder Nacht sie heimlich zu umfangen,	To envelop her secretly in sweet night,
	Und all ihr Schmeichellüfte, werdet wach	And all you caressing breezes, be awake,
	Und scherzt und spielt um ihre Rosenwangen,	Play and dally about her rosy cheeks
	Wenn seine schöne Bürde, leicht bewegt,	When her delicate foot lightly bears
	Der zarte Fuss zum Sitz der Liebe trägt.	Its fair burden to the seat of love.

(3)	Stille, was schlüpft durch die Hecken	Hush, what is that darting through the hedge,
	Raschelnd mit eilendem Lauf?	Rustling and scurrying?
	Nein, es scheuchte nur der Schrecken	No, it was only a startled bird
	Aus dem Busch den Vogel auf.	Frightened from the hedge.

(4)	O! lösche deine Fackel Tag! Hervor,	Extinguish your torch, day!
	Du geist'ge Nacht, mit deinem holden Schweigen,	Draw on, contemplative night, with your sweet silence,
	Breit' um uns her den purpurroten Flor,	Spread your purple veil around us,
	Umspinne uns mit geheimnisvollen Zweigen.	Enfold us with your secret boughs!
	Der Liebe Wonne flieht des Lauschers Ohr,	The rapture of love shuns both the listening ear
	Sie flieht des Strahles unbescheidnen Zeugen!	And the immodest witness of the sun's rays!
	Nur Hesper, der Verschwiegene, allein	Hesperus alone, the silent one,
	Darf still herblickend ihr Vertrauter sein.	Looking calmly on, may be its confidant.

(5)	Rief es von ferne nicht leise,	Was that not a faint call,
	Flüsterndcn Stimmen gleich?	Like whispering voices?
	Nein, der Schwan ist's, der die Kreise	No, it is the swan, tracing circles
	Zieht durch den Silberteich.[2]	Over the silvery lake.

[1] Schiller writes 'Der durch *diese* Pappeln schwirrt'.
[2] Schiller writes 'Zie*het* durch den Silberteich'.

(6) Mein Ohr umtönt ein Harmonienfluss,
Der Springquell fällt mit angenehmem
Rauschen,
Die Blume neigt sich bei des Westes Kuss,
Und alle Wesen seh' ich Wonne tauschen,
Die Traube winkt, die Pfirsche zum Genuss,

Die üppig schwellend hinter Blättern
lauschen,
Die Luft, getaucht in der Gewürze Flut,
Trinkt von der heissen Wange mir die Glut.

Flowing harmonies fill my ears,
The spring murmurs sweetly,

The flower bows at the west wind's kiss,
And I see all creatures united in bliss.
The grape beckons, the peach is ripe to be
relished,
Swelling lusciously, hidden among leaves.

The air, bathed in spicy scents,
Drinks the glow from my burning cheeks.

(7) Hör' ich nicht Tritte erschallen?
Rauscht's nicht den Laubgang daher?
Die Frucht ist dort gefallen,[1]
Von der eignen Fülle schwer.

Do I not hear footsteps,
Something rustling in the leafy walk?
A fruit has fallen there,
Heavy with its own ripeness.

(8) Des Tages Flammenauge selber bricht
In süssem Tod, und seine Farben blassen,
Kühn öffnen sich im holden Dämmerlicht
Die Kelche schon, die seine Gluten hassen.
Still hebt der Mond sein strahlend
Angesicht,
Die Welt zerschmilzt in ruhig grosse
Massen,
Der Gürtel ist von jedem Reiz gelöst,
Und alles Schöne zeigt sich mir entblösst.

The flaming eye of day perishes
In sweet death, and its colours fade,
In the beauteous dusk the flower-bells,
Which loathe day's fire, open boldly.
Silently the moon raises its radiant
countenance,
The world dissolves in vast, calm shapes,

The girdle is released by that spell,
And all beauty is revealed to me.

(9) Seh' ich nichts Weisses dort schimmern?
Glänzt's nicht wie seidnes Gewand?
Nein, es ist der Säule Flimmern
An der dunkeln Taxuswand.

Do I not see a shimmer of white,
The glistening of a silver garment?
No, it is the column gleaming
Against the row of dark yew trees.

(10) O! sehnend Herz, ergötze dich nicht mehr,
Mit süssen Bildern wesenlos zu spielen,
Der Arm, der sie umfassen will, ist leer

Kein Schattenglück kann diesen Busen
kühlen,
O! führe mir die Liebende daher,
Lass ihre Hand, die zärtliche, mich fühlen,
Den Schatten nur von ihres Mantels Saum,
Und in das Leben tritt der hohle Traum.[2]

Yearning heart, delight no longer
In toying with sweet, airy images,
The arms that desire to embrace them are
empty,
No, joy in shadows can cool this breast.

O, bring my beloved to me,
Let me feel her delicate hand,
The bare shadow of her mantle's hem,
And the hollow dream will come to life!

---

[1] Schiller writes 'Nein, die Frucht ist dort gefallen'.
[2] In later Schiller editions this is 'der *holde* Traum' but (*pace* NSA) 'hohle' is correct according to Schubert's source (*Gedichte*, Vienna, 1810)

(11)   Und leis' wie aus himmlischen Höhen   And softly, as if from celestial heights,
         Die Stunde des Glückes erscheint,   The hour of bliss arrives,
           So war sie genaht, ungesehen,   Thus she had come, unseen,
           Und weckte mit Küssen den Freund.   Waking her beloved with kisses.

FRIEDRICH VON SCHILLER (1759–1805); poem written in September 1799

This is the twenty-ninth of Schubert's forty-four Schiller solo settings (1811–24). See the poet's biography for a chronological list of all the Schiller settings.

This long and beautifully crafted poem recalls an episode when Schiller was awaiting a visit from his fiancée, Charlotte von Lengefeld; by the time the poem appeared in print she had already been his spouse for nine years. The form of the poem is ingenious: in the shorter, four-lined verses (1, 3, 5, 7, 9, 11) two expectant lines of dactylic trimeter are followed by two in less energetic trochaic quadrimeter. From a rhyming point of view this is ABAB. The longer strophes (2, 4, 6, 8, 10) are cast in spacious ottava rima (CDCDCDEE). The shorter verses are terse with expectation and bring the poet sharply down to earth after the expansive reveries of the longer strophes. This scheme gives the composer an ideal opportunity to alternate excited recitative with lofty arioso. Schubert's song is a serenade to twilight in several movements with interludes that remind us of the excited nature of the vigil.

Schubert modelled his setting on Zumsteeg's tidy, and not inconsiderable, ballad composed in 1800. In the first version (May 1816) Schubert begins and ends his piece in different keys (B flat and G) but Zumsteeg began and ended his setting in F major. It is uncertain when Schubert returned to this work to revise it; it could well have been towards the end of his life, as John Reed suggests (the dedication to Josef Hüttenbrenner of this posthumous publication is no real help in fixing the date). In any case, this second version, like Zumsteeg's, begins and ends in the same tonality.

Schubert's musical plan follows Schiller's division of his poem into eleven sections.

Verse 1: 'Langsam' in **C** time. A gracious four-bar introduction conjures the delight of being in a deliciously secluded arbour as the breezes play in the late afternoon – these are reflected by capricious semiquaver triplets that dance over the keyboard (bb. 2–3). Secrecy, discretion, delicate expectancy, all is on tiptoe. A tremor of repeated mezzo staccato chords (b. 4) is taken to be the sound of the creaking gate. As the poet ponders whether this is the case, the rustle of poplars blowing in the breeze is combined with horn calls of longing in the piano's left hand (bb. 6–7). A short recitative dismisses the creak as a false alarm, the first of several.

Verse 2: Without further ado, and still in the key of B flat major, the music embarks on a tender section in dotted rhythm (from b. 10). The piano writing on the page looks like a gently billowing canopy lovingly constructed by the right hand in order to shelter the left. Schubert also uses visual roof imagery in his Seidl setting *Im Freien* D880 – although in that song the music's ceiling is flat and fixed (bb. 70–72 of that work). The night air is at first languorous and then playfully teasing. The gently swirling arpeggios of bb. 18–20 stroke the beloved's cheek, while mention of the words 'scherzt und spielt' inspires a prancing figure in the right hand that is skilfully harmonized with a return to the swaying dotted rhythms (bb. 23–9) This is the first of the set piece arias in this anthology of night pictures, and perhaps the most inventive.

Verse 3: 'Geschwind' (b. 30). We hear the sudden rustling in impetuous semiquavers, but it is after all only the movement of a bird. Everything is kept to perfect scale: we are aware that the disturbance is a tiny one, and audible only to the listener who strains for any sound of his

Die Erwartung, illustration by Wilhlem von Kaulbach for Strophe 11.

lover's arrival. Do we hear a bird's wings fluttering out of fear in the eight repeated semiquavers followed by a slightly ominous seventh chord? (bb. 35–6). This little flurry of nature is once again understood and dismissed. The interlude of bb. 38–40 is beautiful music for startled wildlife, like deer caught in eighteenth-century headlights (cf. a similar passage about startled deer in the opening section of the Ossianic *Cronnan* D282).

Verse 4: The marking 'Feierlich', and a change of time signature to ³⁄₄ (b. 41), introduces a high-flown overture to night, double-dotted and in the grandiose key of C minor. This is one of Schubert's ceremonial invocations, and one is reminded of the Baumberg setting *An die Sonne* D270 where another poet with an assignation is similarly impatient for sunset. For the first time the singer is required to produce an imposing vocal line. The classical allusion of Hesperus or Venus (in b. 57),

the so-called evening star, has clearly made Schubert think of the operas of Gluck whose style is echoed throughout this section, particularly at the dramatic pulsations (as if conceived for brass) that accompany bb. 52–6. At b. 58 (for 'Hesper, der Verschwiegene') the time signature changes to **C**.

Verse 5: 'Etwas bewegt' (b. 62). The interruptions of deluded expectancy are now given more sophisticated treatment, although still in recitative form. The swan, gliding in a circle, is suavely depicted in music appropriate to a big and mysterious bird (bb. 67–70). (Cf. the music for the swan in that magisterial song for bass, *Das Abendrot* D627.) After 'Silberteich' Schubert cannot resist giving us a fish-eye view of the depth and stillness of the lake (bb. 69–70) with layers of dark water and slime in the piano writing. This sudden close-up detail, as if a camera were following the swan in its habitat and taking a shot of it from the bottom of the lake, is typical of what might be termed Schubert's extraordinarily cinematic mind.

Verse 6: This central panel of the work (bb. 71–91 – marked 'Majestätisch, nicht zu langsam') is in the key of E major. The accompaniment consists of ceaseless semiquaver triplets, the ideal means to suggest harmonies that flow and fill the ear, as the poet directs. In this great hymn to nature there is little verbal imagery to hang on to, so the composer provides a generalized canvas, an aria of the broadest kind. The slowly changing harmony, and the long span of the vocal line, once again brings Gluck to mind. The piano writing, however, is something completely Schubertian. The *Lindenbaum*-like E major triplets are not all that unusual, but the rustling major seconds in alternating octaves of the piano (bb. 77–8 and 85–6) are especially delicious. They put the pianist's fingers in mind of Schumann's *Frühlingsnacht* from the Eichendorff *Liederkreis.*

Verse 7: Another recitative, this time marked 'Etwas geschwind' (b. 92, still in E major) and showing chromatic resourcefulness. As the ingenious chord progressions spiral upwards in contrary-motion quavers (bb. 92–5) we could be hearing the sound of running feet – or are we just feeling the poet's pulse? As the same pianistic tongue-twister sidles downwards (bb. 99–100) we realize it is nothing more than the fall of ripe fruit – the 'Pfirsche zum Genuss' of the previous strophe perhaps? After such an appropriate illustrative flourish, Schubert cannot bring himself to set the poet's '*Nein*' that precedes 'Die Frucht ist dort gefallen'; this ruins the poet's troachaic tetrameter that Zumsteeg faithfully observes (Schubert's word-changes also alter the metre in Verses 1 and 5). In any case, the increasingly anxious narrator has little time for the plucking and gathering of fruit. Two dejected bars of chords (marked 'Langsam', but only in the first version) lead to an F minor chord in the first version, a C major one in the second.

Verse 8: This is another aria (marked 'Langsam', in the key of C minor/E flat major, and in ⅜). It is at this point that the earlier and later versions of the song begin to differ significantly in terms of tonality, the second transposed sometimes a semitone, sometimes a tone lower than the first. The words are in the grand style, already old-fashioned in 1816, so at first Schubert calls on the shades of Gluck and the Mozart of *opera seria* to provide him with inspiration for another set-piece aria, one of several blocks of musical marble in the imposing structure of this song. This music for a sunset becomes much more interesting from b. 114 at the heralding of the exquisite entry of the moon into the picture. The melismatic setting of the word 'Mond' (b. 119) is enchantingly delicate. At bb. 121–5, with the image of 'Die Welt zerschmilzt in ruhig grosse Massen', we encounter words about the dissolving of the world that sound more like Novalis than Schiller. The canonic writing between voice and piano is marvellous here. The trills that resonate in the bass (bb. 122–4) are prophetic of the song *Auf der Donau* D553, the Mayrhofer setting composed the following year; in that case these left-hand rumblings represent the sunset of medieval civilization, and the evaporation of the powers of former tyrants – another kind of dissolving world.

Verse 9: All sorts of deceptive sounds have already been illustrated, but now we have music (marked 'Mässig geschwind' from b. 133) to mirror the tricks of glinting and refracted light. The key signature changes to B flat major (C major in the earlier version). It is in this section particularly that the comparative poverty of Zumsteeg's invention is revealed. He deemed one staccato chord sufficient to depict the deceptive gleam; Schubert's glinting motif is light years ahead. And then he cleverly uses the same motif, now down in the mouth, for three bars, to paint the lover's disillusionment (bb. 146–8). Will the beloved never come?

Verse 10: This is an aria (b. 148, marked 'Etwas bewegt', with no change of key, but with a reversion to a **C** time signature) that at last addresses the vulnerability of the narrator's feelings. The music is more inward-looking, and as a result more touching. Here we can detect the influence of Mozart and *Die Zauberflöte*, rather than the music of Gluck. The harmonic excursions of this heartfelt plea (bb. 148–67) take us as far afield as G flat major (b. 157). At the end of this aria, which contains just the right suggestion of exhaustion and disillusionment, we assume that the narrator falls asleep.

Verse 11: The marking is 'Etwas langsamer' (b. 167). Time passes. Do we hear the ticking minutes measured by the tread of quaver chords; or is this the entry of the beloved who comes at last on tiptoe to wake the poet? There is a radiance and assurance to this straightforward music. In the most remarkable manner Schubert here introduces a feminine presence; Schiller's change of metre (four dactylic trimiters with *Auftakt*) aids a change of mood. Everything is fragrant and delicate, the footfall light and confident. She has been delayed, and he has been silly to imagine that anything is wrong. The words require the narrator to be awoken (and kissed) more than once. This paragon of female virtue cannot be 'ungesehen' twice, and her unexpected kiss can only be a surprise the first time. But musical convention dictates otherwise: the tiny rush of male excitement after the first mention of a kiss (an upward scale of triplets at b. 180) is held back to enable a second recounting of the story with a held high note (five beats) on 'leis' (bb. 182–3). Both these details and those following pertain only to the second version; in the first the composer does not repeat the last strophe of the text. The music becomes giddy with rapture without losing a sense of eighteenth-century grace. The postlude of the second version (Op. 116) is a great improvement on the song's first. Arpeggiated chords at bb. 191–2 (symbolizing kisses, surely) are followed by a falling legato line in triplets. With this tender embrace we can hear, just as Schubert imagines, that the beloved is drawn down to the level of the couch on which the poet has been slumbering. It would be comforting to think that sometime between May 1816 when Schubert composed the first version, and when he perfected the second (perhaps as many as twelve years later), there had been a few moments of such intimate tenderness in his own life. Sadly, the phrase 'Schubert imagines' seems of the essence.

Autograph:	Bibliotheca Bodmeriana, Geneva-Cologny (first draft)
Publication:	First published as part of the NSA in 1968 (P736; first version)
	First published as Op. post. 116 by M. J. Leidesdorf, Vienna in 1829 (P203; second version)
Dedicatee:	Josef Hüttenbrenner
Subsequent editions:	Peters: Vol. 3/84; AGA XX 46: Vol. 2/47 (second version); NSA IV: Vol. 7/141 (first version) & 153 (second version); Bärenreiter: Vol. 6/144 (first version) & 89 (second version)
Further settings:	J. F. Reichardt (1752–1814) *Die Erwartung*, No. 10 of *Schillers Lyrische Gedichte*, erstes Heft (1810)
	J. R. Zumsteeg (1760–18102) *Die Erwartung* from *Kleine Balladen und Lieder*, zweites Heft (1800) (printed in NSA, Vol. 7/203–10)
Bibliography:	Capell 1928, p. 90
	Fischer-Dieskau 1977, p. 140
	Newbould 1997, pp. 148–9
Discography and timing:	Fischer-Dieskau I 3[2] 10'44
	Hyperion I 1[7] 13'09 Janet Baker
	Hyperion II 14[19]

← *Winterlied* D401   *Beitrag zur funfzigjährigsten Jubelfeier des Herrn von Salieri, erstem k.k. Hofkapellmeister in Wien* D407 →

EVANGELIUM JOHANNIS   The gospel according to St John
(BIBLE) **D607** [H398]
E major   Spring 1818

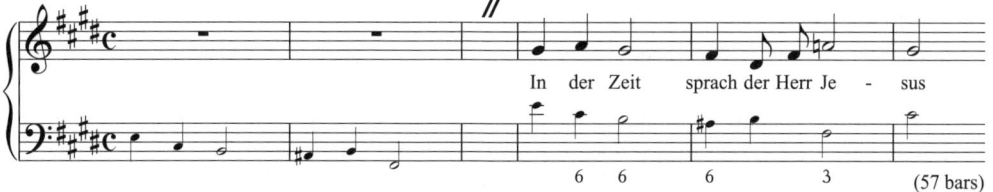

In   der   Zeit   sprach der Herr Je - sus

6   6   6   3   (57 bars)

In der Zeit sprach der Herr Jesus zu den
Scharen der Juden: Mein Fleisch ist wahrhaftig
eine Speis, mein Blut ist wahrhaftig ein Trank!
Wer mein Fleisch isset und trinket mein Blut,
der bleibt in mir und ich in ihm. Wie mich
gesandt der lebendige Vater, und ich lebe um
des Vaters Willen: also wer mich isset, wird
auch leben um meinetwillen. Dieses ist das Brot
das vom Himmel kommen ist. Nicht wie eure
Väter haben Himmelbrot gegessen, und sind
gestorben. Wer von diesem Brot isst, der wird
leben in Ewigkeit.

In those days the Lord Jesus spoke to the
multitude of Jews. 'For my flesh is meat indeed,
and my blood is drink indeed. He that eateth
my flesh, and drinketh my blood, dwelleth in
me, and I him. As the living Father hath sent
me, and I live by the Father; so he that eateth
me, even he shall live by me. This is that bread
which came down from heaven; not as your
fathers did eat manna, and are dead; he that
eateth of this bread shall live forever.'

ANONYMOUS TRANSLATION FROM THE GOSPEL ACCORDING TO ST JOHN, 6:53–8

This is the first of Schubert's two solo biblical settings. See entry under 'Bible' for a list of all songs setting texts either directly drawn from, or inspired by, the Bible.

Twenty-six years after Schubert's death, his friend Anselm Hüttenbrenner wrote a short memoir which contained the following passage:

I once asked Schubert whether he did not also want to try setting prose to music and chose, for this purpose, the text from St John, Chapter VI verse 59 . . . He solved this problem wonderfully in 24 bars which I still possess as a very precious souvenir of him. He chose for it the solemn key of E major and the verse for a soprano voice with figured bass accompaniment.

For some reason Hüttenbrenner's autograph copy of the work contains only the last twenty-four of the piece's fifty-seven bars. This is the second of the work's two pages. The first page (thirty-three bars) is in the British Library (Zweig collection), and there is another copy of the second part. Hüttenbrenner's suggestion called into being one of the strangest of the Schubert songs, if song it may be called. It serves as some proof that only poetry was able to bring forth the purest melody in the composer's mind. Prose, on the other hand, moved him to a type of arioso, half recitative with an occasional outbreak of melody. The accompaniment suggests the organ, and the harmonic language sometimes evokes church music of the past. At other times it looks forward to the future, and the word-setting technique of Wagner, governed as that is by the flexibility of speech. The overall effect is rather timeless, which is perhaps appropriate for the words of Christ. If anything, the sense of freedom of this accompanied recitative reminds us of Schubert's most pioneering religious work, the cantata *Lazarus* D689, composed in 1820. The story of Lazarus was also taken from St John's Gospel and reworked by the poet August Hermann Niemeyer. Deutsch incorrectly states that the text of this extract from the *Evangelium Johannis* is based on Luther's translation of the Bible; this is a completely different translation of St John's Gospel, 6:54–8. Reinhard Van Hoorickx, who realized the work from its figured bass (as recorded on the Hyperion Edition), discovered that the complete text, including the introductory sentence, is contained in the Gospel pericope for the Mass for the Feast of Corpus Christi. The original Greek text of this passage is reprinted in Schochow 1974 Volume 1, p. 205.

John Reed suggests the work might have been used for worship. The great Schubertian bass-baritone Robert Holl has arranged for this piece to be liturgically performed (in his own realization with organ) in the context of Schubert's *Deutsche Messe* D872. This version has been fully reprinted in *Schubert und das Biedermeier* (Holl 2002). In this instance it occupied the penultimate place before the last movement of the mass itself.

Autographs:	British Library, London (first 33 bars)
	Wienbibliothek im Rathaus, Vienna (last 24 bars)
First edition:	Vocal line with figured bass first published in 1902 in Heuberger's *Franz Schubert*; realized and privately printed by Reinhard Van Hoorickx
Subsequent editions:	Not in Peters; Not in AGA; NSA I: Vol. 8
Bibliography:	Holl 2002, pp. 45–51
Discography and timing:	Fischer-Dieskau —
	Hyperion I 21^{19}
	Hyperion II 20^{7} 3'05 Edith Mathis

←— *An den Mond in einer Herbstnacht* D614   *Grablied für die Mutter* D616 —→

A portrait from 1813 by Leopold Kupelwieser of a young man long thought to be Schubert
(now a discredited attribution).

FAHRT ZUM HADES

Journey to Hades

(Mayrhofer) **D526** [H339]
D minor – F major   January 1817

(91 bars)

Der Nachen dröhnt, Zypressen flüstern –	The boat moans, the cypresses whisper;
Horch, Geister reden schaurig drein;	Hark, the spirits add their gruesome cries.
Bald werd' ich am Gestad', dem düstern,	Soon I shall reach the shore, so gloomy,
Weit von der schönen Erde sein.	Far from the fair earth.
Da leuchten Sonne nicht, noch Sterne,	There neither sun nor stars shine,
Da tönt kein Lied, da ist kein Freund.	No song echoes, no friend is nigh.
Empfang die letzte Träne, o Ferne!	Distant earth, accept the last tear
Die dieses müde Auge weint.	That these tired eyes will weep.
Schon schau' ich die blassen Danaiden,[1]	Already I see the pale Danaïdes,
Den fluchbeladnen Tantalus;	And curse-laden Tantalus.
Es murmelt todesschwangern Frieden,	Your ancient river, Oblivion,
Vergessenheit, dein alter Fluss.	Breathes a peace heavy with death.
Vergessen nenn' ich zwiefach Sterben,	Oblivion I deem a twofold death;
Was ich mit höchster Kraft gewann,	To lose that which I won with all my strength,
Verlieren—wieder es erwerben—	To strive for it once more –
Wann enden diese Qualen? wann?	When will all these torments cease? O when?

JOHANN MAYRHOFER (1787–1836)

This is the eighteenth of Schubert's forty-seven Mayrhofer solo settings (1814–24). See the poet's biography for a chronological list of all the Mayrhofer settings.

This marvellous song has never achieved the popularity of its Schiller counterpart *Gruppe aus dem Tartarus* D583 in which the singer views the horrors of the underworld, as in Dante's *Inferno* where Virgil takes the younger poet on a guided tour of hell. *Fahrt zum Hades* is less explosive

[1] The adjective 'blassen' is Schubert's addition to Mayrhofer's poem, as is the 'o' of 'o Ferne' in Verse 2, line 3. For an explanation of the background to these alternative Mayrhofer readings see Editorial Note at the beginning of Johann MAYRHOFER.

but far more chilling: Schiller has simply observed the sufferings of the damned, but Mayrhofer believes himself already doomed to be one of their number. *Gruppe aus dem Tartarus* is a flurry of sextuplet semiquavers but *Fahrt zum Hades* is powered by triplets that are less rumbustious but just as lethal. Taken at a funereal pace, and ignoring the all-important *alla breve* marking (a danger for inexperienced Schubertians), this music can seem lifeless and complacent. In fact this song should rage eloquently against the dying of the light. D minor is a favourite Schubert key for depicting epic travel: in this key the first song in *Winterreise* launches another ill-omened journey, and the old coachman Kronos drives a path through life with inescapable force; it is also in D minor that Death invites the Maiden to cross the threshold into his domain. The music of the Commendatore from Mozart's *Don Giovanni* (the Don also travels to Hades) must have played a part in Schubert's feeling for this tonality; the Commendatore is sung by a bass, and Schubert wrote the vocal part of *Fahrt zum Hades* in the bass clef.

The ineluctable descent of the piano's left hand is a strong feature on the song's first page. In the right hand the power of the triplets is merciless; they are ominous, but also very quiet. This is a journey across the river Styx, and Schubert who usually revels in the crystalline, sparkling qualities of water here depicts something heavier with thick chords – Lethean ooze, denser than the Dead Sea, 'heavy with death' as Mayrhofer says. In the midst of this journey the gentle inflection reserved for the echo of the words 'Weit von der schönen Erde' (bb. 15–7) is heart-breaking. The narrator had not wanted to die; the music that Schubert gives him is reason enough to want to cling on to life. This theme of bittersweet regret is expanded in a new section marked 'Mässig' where although there is no change of key signature the music is now in F major.

'The "curse-laden Tantalus"', from *Der Mythos alter Dichter*, Vienna (1815).

Schubert almost certainly intended that the speeds of the crotchets in these juxtaposed sections should match.

The modulation to the relative major ('Da leuchten Sonne nicht') gives rise to music which is a hymn to earth's beauties rather than a description of their absence, as in the poem. It is extremely difficult, after all, to write a song using words that negate music's existence ('Da tönt kein Lied'). The most famous musical visitor to these realms was Orpheus, and the influence of Gluck is discernible in the nobility of the vocal line at 'Empfang die letzte Träne, o Ferne!' (bb. 32–6). With the return of triplets (b. 46) we glimpse King Danaus's fifty daughters, the Danaïdes, who were betrothed to the fifty sons of Aegyptus and compelled by their father to kill them on their wedding night. Their collective punishment in Hades was everlastingly to fill leaking buckets – Schubert himself added the adjective 'pale' to Mayrhofer's poem to describe them. Among the many punishments traditionally ascribed to the wretched Tantalus (who had divulged secrets entrusted to him by Zeus) was eternal hunger (laden fruit trees withdrew their branches as soon as he stretched out his hand to eat from them), eternal thirst (although surrounded by water) and the suspension over his head of a huge rock ever threatening to crush him. The idea that peace can be 'todesschwanger', literally 'pregnant with death', is one of Mayrhofer's darkest and strangest coinages. As the music falls from B flat minor to the remote reaches of D flat minor (bb. 46–58) the black depths of the ancient river Lethe are revealed; the vocal line here falls to its nadir.

There is now a short recitative. D flat minor becomes A major, pivoting on the C sharp that the two root position chords have in common. In an ascent of wild chromatic chords (the passage is marked 'schnell') the poet resists the idea of oblivion; it is as if he is struggling to climb his way out of a pit. This chromatic scramble colours an essentially fruitless recitative. It is the artist in Mayrhofer speaking, the poet who would wish to leave something behind for posterity, when the narrator states that being forgotten is really two-fold death: immortality is only possible for writers if their work is remembered. Regaining his composure in an arioso of great classical dignity (marked 'Langsam' bb. 64–8), the poet asks when his suffering will end. The unspoken answer is of course, 'It will never end'; we are spared the gruesomely triumphant repetitions of 'Ewigkeit' that are intoned at the climax of the Schiller setting *Gruppe aus dem Tartarus* D583. For a moment we might imagine that Mayrhofer is asking this question in real life, as if he considers that he is inhabiting a living hell of his own, a world where all the hard-won achievements of the Enlightenment – broad-minded tolerance and freedom of speech – have been irrevocably lost. This is the climax and end of his poem, but Schubert, rather like a film director, ensures that his song does not end with a portrait of the poet in close-up, but rather with further footage of the Stygian journey. Mayrhofer's first strophe is dredged up and once more put through its paces. From the musical point of view matters are a little more complicated: bb. 4–7 are heard again at bb. 69–72, and bb. 11–7 equate to bb. 76–82 after which there is new material for a coda that ends the journey unequivocally, with no right of appeal. The whole device of a modified *da capo* aria gives the music a shape which seems appropriate to its classical subject and epic emotional scale. We are reminded that the suffering will be endless and eternal and another ferry-load sets off, carrying its victims to eternal damnation.

Autograph:	Missing or lost
First edition:	Published as Book 18 no. 3 of the *Nachlass* by Diabelli, Vienna in 1832 (P291)
Subsequent editions:	Peters: Vol. 5/94; AGA XX 297: Vol. 5/20; NSA IV: Vol. 11/79
Bibliography:	Fischer-Dieskau 1977, pp. 96–7
	Youens 1996, pp. 183–7
Discography and timing:	Fischer-Dieskau I 9[14] 5'16
	Hyperion I 2[5]
	Hyperion II 17[17] 4'16 Stephen Varcoe

← *Wie Ulfru fischt* D525   *Augenlied* D297 →

FAUST

This, perhaps the most famous of Goethe's works, encompasses every aspect of his gifts and activities – as dramatist, philosopher, statesman, novelist, mythologist, scientist and theatre manager. Goethe's use of the age-old story of Faust, a querulous scholar, hungry and impatient to comprehend all human experience, has an autobiographical edge: in *Dichtung und Wahrheit* (published in 1814) the poet confessed that he had 'wandered into every department of

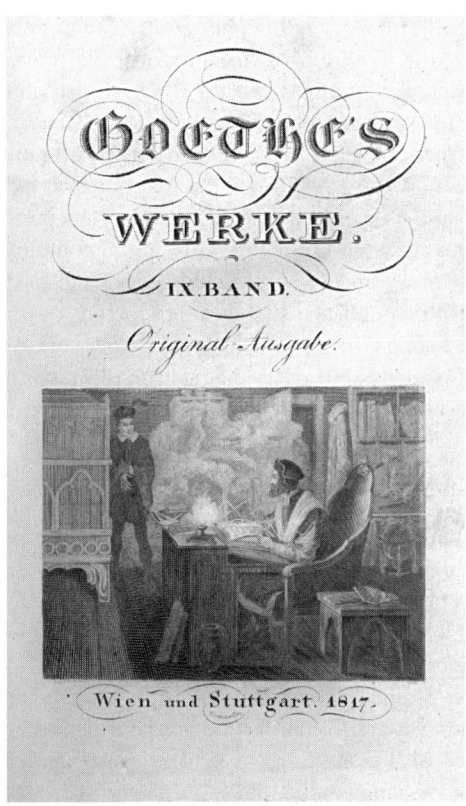

Faust (Volume 9 of Goethe's complete works, Vienna 1817), drawing by Schnorr von Carolsfeld.

knowledge, and returned early enough satisfied with the vanity of science; and life, too, I had tried under various aspects, and always came back sorrowing and unsatisfied'.

Johann Faust or Dr Faustus (the first name of Goethe's Faust is Heinrich) was a genuine historical figure who lived in Germany in the late fifteenth and early sixteenth centuries; he studied divinity and medicine and then, trading on the credulity of a superstitious age, became known as a magician and astrologer; his meddling in the occult arts made him notorious and an Elizabethan tract refers to Faust's 'damnable life and deserved death'. There was a 'Volksbuch' about Faust published in Frankfurt in 1587 where the Devil strangles his erstwhile protégé. Other writers attempted Faust plays, notably Marlowe and Calderón, but the result of Goethe's lifelong engagement with the subject was a compendium of his art, an *omnium gatherum* (a phrase invented, though not for *Faust*, by Samuel Taylor Coleridge, the first translator of Goethe's play into English). It is little wonder that in writing a work of this range and ambition, and over such a long period of time, the poet occasionally lost sight of the plot: to some commentators *Faust* has seemed an unmanageable succession of scenes with a narrative that merely provides an excuse to establish a forum for Goethe's latest ideas, and to display his mastery of every kind of German verse. But the play has triumphed over such cavilling. According to George Henry Lewes, Goethe's first English biographer, 'it has every element: wit, pathos, wisdom, farce, mystery, melody, reverence, doubt, magic and irony; not a chord of the lyre is unstrung, not a fibre of the heart untouched'. It is easy to see how a reading of *Faust* must have affected Schubert, aged seventeen. No one knows who first encouraged him to read *Faust*. He had not yet met Mayrhofer, so perhaps it was the poet Theoder Körner who was such an enthusiast that he wrote a poem 'To Goethe' describing his emotions on reading *Faust*. These were also perhaps the feelings of Schubert on encountering the masterpiece: 'Take wing my song, fly up as does the sun / On high! Through all the heavens' heights / The earth ascends, darkness has ebbed away. / I'm bathing in the source of all delights'. The incandescence of Schubert's Goethe setting, *Gretchen am Spinnrade*, was clearly fuelled by the rolling power of the play's preceding scenes. He never saw a production of *Faust* in the theatre, and for that matter neither did its author – although excerpts were played in Berlin and Breslau in Goethe's lifetime. The work has remained an almost insuperable challenge to any theatrical director, the more abstract second part rather more so than the first. The impracticability of Thomas Hardy's monumental verse drama, *The Dynasts*, some would say his greatest work, poses a similar problem. Radio performances of both works have been one solution.

Goethe's avid interest in Faust lasted for more than seventy years – from his early boyhood to the year of his death. He first encountered the story, already 200 years old, as a play for puppets during his childhood in Frankfurt: 'This marionette fable', he wrote, 'murmured with many voices in my soul.' Goethe's earliest version of the play, the so-called *Urfaust* from 1773–5, was rediscovered as late as 1887. Later scenes were added in 1788 during his sojourn in Italy, and his first publication of the play (ending at the cathedral scene between the 'Böser Geist' and Gretchen that was later set to music as Schubert's D126) appeared in 1790 under the title *Faust. Ein Fragment*. With Schiller's urging and encouragement Goethe returned to the task with new energy and *Faust, Der Tragödie erster Teil* appeared at last in 1808. It was the Austrian-printed edition of this version (Anton Doll, Vienna, 1810) that the seventeen-year-old Schubert encountered in the late autumn of 1814. The composer was never to know the rather more complex second part of the tragedy. The continuation of the story and the protracted genesis of *Faust* Part Two (begun in 1816 and finished only in time to be published shortly after Goethe's death in 1832) is of no concern to a study of the Schubert songs, though it is central to the work of Robert Schumann whose *Szenen aus Goethes Faust* (WoO3g 1849) is based largely on this second part of the drama. Hector Berlioz's *La Damnation de Faust* (1846) is inspired by Part One alone.

SYNOPSIS OF PART ONE, a context for Schubert's five musical settings from *Faust*.

The play is preceded by a Dedication ('Zueignung') and two prologues, the first for the theatre inspired by *Sakuntala* of Kalidasa, the second a Prologue in Heaven inspired by the *Book of Job*, a conversation between the Devil and God who graciously gives permission to His adversary to attempt to lead Faust astray, believing that Mephistopheles will not be able to achieve this.

NACHT: The play proper begins with 'Night', a mighty monologue for Heinrich Faust who also converses with a Spirit, and with his young apprentice, Wagner. The aged and disillusioned scholar resolves to commit suicide by drinking a potion but draws back from this action on hearing Easter bells and a chorus of angels – 'Christ is arisen'. The recording of this scene spoken by Alexander Moissi (one of the most famous of Burgtheater actors in Vienna in the 1890s) is a powerful evocation of the grandeur of nineteenth-century theatre. (***Chor der Engel* D440 – 'Christ ist erstanden'**) [An unaccompanied chorus for SATB, this chorus falls outside the scope of this book.]

VOR DEM TOR: The next scene takes place in front of the city gates, a scene of Easter celebration that serves to emphasize Faust's alienation from his fellow citizens. Back in his study (STUDIERZIMMER) Faust first encounters Mephistopheles who has disguised himself as a black dog, his 'Pudel', who has long kept company with the old philosopher.

AUERBACHS KELLER and HEXENKÜCHE: Faust and his devilish mentor drink among students in Auerbach's Cellar in Leipzig. It is during this gathering that the Flea song is sung by Mephistopheles ('Es war einmal ein König'), famous in settings by Beethoven and Musorgsky. After this they visit the Witches' Kitchen where Faust drinks an elixir that will make him a good-looking young man once again. In this way a deal is struck (the original Faustian pact) whereby Faust will be allowed to experience all he could possibly wish; however, if he feels even one moment of true contentment he will forfeit his soul.

STRASSE: The newly emboldened and rejuvenated Faust lusts after the beautiful young Gretchen; he takes her arm in the street but she pulls away, embarrassed. Faust asks Mephistopheles to obtain her for him by whatever means necessary; the Devil confesses that she is so pure that he has no power over her – careful planning will be required to seduce this blameless girl.

ABEND: Later the same evening Gretchen is in her bedchamber; she briefly recalls the man who suddenly burst into her life on the street. She is certain that someone so confident and good looking must be a member of the nobility. As soon as she leaves her room Faust and Mephistopheles enter; Faust, smitten with Gretchen, rejoices in the spirit of 'abundance and order' that he feels in her room. Mephistopheles places a stolen casket of jewels on the table, an attempt to corrupt the girl with worldly riches. After Faust and Mephistopheles have left, she returns to her room and, as she undresses, sings an old ballad with a strange sense of foreboding; its opening line 'Es war ein König in Thule' is an innocent counterpoint to Mephistopheles' song in Auerbach's cellar, 'Es war einmal ein König'. (*Der König in Thule* **D367**)

Gretchen then notices the casket and excitedly tries on the jewels. In Gounod's operatic version of *Faust* (1859) the famous *cabaletta*, 'Ah! je ris de me voir', is sung at this point.

SPAZIERGANG: During a short walk with Faust, Mephistopheles recounts, with some relish, how Gretchen's mother, believing that 'unrighteous wealth ensnares the soul', has handed the jewels over to an acquisitive priest. Faust commands Mephistopheles to obtain more jewels for Gretchen.

DER NACHBARIN HAUS: The scene shifts to the home of Gretchen's neighbour Marthe to whom Gretchen, in a state of confusion, brings a second, even more resplendent, box of jewels. She asks the older woman's advice. Marthe offers to keep the treasures for Gretchen: she can try them on in front of the mirror if she is scared of going out in them. Mephistopheles enters the house under the cruel pretext of bringing news of the death of Marthe's profligate husband in Italy. While speaking with Marthe he admires Gretchen's beauty and presses her to take a lover – the real point of his visit. He offers to return that evening bringing a friend (Faust of course) who had been witness to the death of Marthe's husband.

STRASSE: In a short scene in the street Faust airs qualms about bearing false witness to the death of Marthe's husband. Mephistopheles mocks what remains of Faust's attachment to the truth.

GARTEN: In the scene in Marthe's garden, Mephistopheles engages their hostess in conversation, leaving Faust free to woo Gretchen who, for her part, is very worried about what her mother would think of her receiving such attention from a man. She tells Faust something of her background and how, when her mother was very ill, she nursed and brought up her little sister who had since died. She is clearly a creature of pure goodness and he is enchanted by her. She starts to pluck a flower in a game of 'He loves me, he loves me not'. The outcome indicates 'He loves me' and Faust does indeed declare his love for her. He takes her in his arms: 'Let this look, this pressure of the hand say to you what is unutterable! – to give ourselves up wholly, and feel a bliss which must be eternal! Eternal! – its end would be despair. No, no end! No end!' Gretchen presses his hand and then breaks away and runs from him. Schumann sets this scene (*Szenen aus Goethes Faust*, No. 1).

EIN GARTENHÄUSCHEN: Gretchen, excited and confused, takes refuge in a summerhouse in Marthe's garden and Faust follows her there. They are alone at last and they kiss passionately. Mephistopheles knocks on the door and he and Marthe intrude on this intimate moment. The two men depart and Gretchen is left alone, confused at the way she has said 'yes to everything . . . I am but a poor silly girl; I cannot understand what he sees in me'.

WALD UND HÖHLE: In forest and cavern, during one of their increasingly fantastical journeys, Faust and Mephistopheles discuss the developing love affair with Gretchen, the Devil cynical and cruel, impatient with emotion or tenderness. Faust is disgusted by this reptilian attitude to the poor girl and it is clear that he has fallen in love with her. The awakening of any real affection between Faust and Gretchen had not been part of Mephistopheles' plan and throughout the play he fears that Gretchen's ability to influence Faust is greater than his own. Faust sees that undermining her peace of mind will have disastrous consequences for Gretchen – 'Let her fate fall crushing upon me, and both of us perish together!' It is this vision of incipient doom that clearly coloured Schubert's setting of Gretchen's following monologue.

GRETCHENS STUBE: Alone in her room and working at her spinning wheel Gretchen agonizes over the loss of her equilibrium. In love for the first time she should be happy, yet something is terribly amiss. Despite a passionate nature and a loving heart, she has always thought herself chaste and able to resist temptation. It disturbs her that she is addicted to Faust's presence, obsessed by him, and this quite apart from any sorcery at work – Mephistopheles has already admitted to having limited influence over her. Gretchen is ecstatically in love with Faust, certainly and, despite his initial unworthy motives, he with her. The composer was all too aware of the catastrophic nature of this sudden and unexpected attachment: guilt was something that Schubert had been brought up to feel, and in his setting, Gretchen's falling in love is underlaid by the reader's awareness of the impending tragedy. (*Gretchen am Spinnrade* **D118**)

MARTHENS GARTEN: Faust and Gretchen discuss religion in Marthe's garden. She affection-ately accuses him of lacking Christianity, expressing her fears for his soul; he parries with agnostic and pantheistic rationalizations. She also confesses her deep antipathy for Mephistoph-eles – with his 'repulsive face . . . It is written on his forehead that he can love no living soul.' Faust longs to sleep with her; 'I would gladly leave the door unbolted for you tonight' says Gretchen, 'but my mother would catch us.' Faust responds by giving her a phial containing a sleeping draught to quieten her mother, assuring her that it will do no harm. When Gretchen later gives it to her mother it kills the older woman. Only Gretchen knows that her mother has not died from natural causes.

AM BRUNNEN: Gretchen and her friend Lieschen gossip by the village well. They talk of their erstwhile friend Bärbelchen (Barbara) who was seduced and has subsequently been abandoned. She now 'feeds two when she eats and drinks' and will have to do penance at church wearing a white smock. Afterwards Gretchen reflects to herself that once she would have been the first to condemn such behaviour, but now she herself has fallen prey to sin, even if the man who drove her to it was 'so sweet, so dear!'

ZWINGER: Gretchen prays to the Virgin in a shrine that is erected in the wall of the city ramparts. She is pregnant and in desperate trouble. Her mother is dead and she has no one to whom she can turn – *see also* Schumann, *Szenen aus Goethes Faust*, No. 2 (**Gretchen im Zwinger (Gretchens Bitte) D564**).

NACHT, STRASSE VOR GRETCHENS TÜRE: This powerful scene is an outburst from Gretchen's brother Valentin, a professional soldier who has long been proud of his sister's spotless reputa-tion. He now vociferously bemoans the fact that her dalliance with Faust will lead to her becoming a whore. He stands outside Gretchen's door, waiting for Faust whom he is determined to kill. On his arrival Faust engages Valentin (whose hand Mephistopheles has paralysed) in a duel, fatally wounding him. Faust, now liable to prosecution for murder, flees before Gretchen descends to find her dying brother. With his last breath Valentin berates Gretchen for having renounced her honour; he warns her that she will live among beggars and cripples and be one of the cursed of the earth.

DOM. AMT, ORGEL UND GESANG: In Frankfurt cathedral an Evil Spirit, unseen by others, whispers in Gretchen's ear; whether this is Mephistopheles himself or simply her own guilty conscience is not clear. The Evil Spirit taunts Gretchen about her dead mother and the 'fore-boding presence' of her unborn baby. The congregation and choir sings 'Dies Irae', words that conveniently mirror Gretchen's torment and plight. Now entirely abandoned and heavily preg-nant, Gretchen loses consciousness. This is the last we see of her until the final scene of the play – *see also* Schumann, *Szenen aus Goethes Faust*, No. 3 (**Szene aus 'Faust' D126**).

WALPURGISNACHT: HARZGEBIRG: This section is devoted to the May-Day Night celebrations of the witches and supernatural spirits on the Harz mountains, a wild orgy of dissipation that is the exact opposite of Gretchen's selfless love. The 'Intermezzo', 'Walpurgisnachtstraum', a set-piece entertainment, depicts Oberon and Titania's golden wedding feast. Before this begins, Faust has a vision of Gretchen in prison. She has drowned her newborn child to save it from being mistreated by society, and is condemned to execution for murder.

TRÜBER TAG. FELD: On a gloomy day in open country Faust vents his rage on Mephistopheles for having concealed Gretchen's suffering from him. To Faust's cries of 'Save her! or woe to thee' Mephistopheles triumphantly replies 'Save her! – Who was it that plunged her into ruin? I or you?' Nevertheless, anxious to retain Faust's confidence, he offers to confuse Gretchen's jailer, allowing Faust to effect Gretchen's release; the pair will make their escape on magic horses provided by Mephistopheles.

KERKER: The last scene of *Faust* Part One is set in the prison for condemned criminals where Gretchen is due to be beheaded the following morning. Faust and Mephistopheles have come to help her escape. Her chains magically dissolve but she refuses to go with Faust and, despite his desperate pleas, remains behind to face her sentence. It is a mad scene of a kind, but this woman, a deranged infanticide, is also saintly, far more sinned against than sinning. It is a magnificent role for a fine actress and perhaps the most moving in all Goethe's plays. At the same time as repenting her criminal deeds, Gretchen's love for Faust has remained constant; she has succeeded, to the Devil's consternation, in awakening his better self. This will be a deciding factor in his own redemption at the end of Part Two of the play. As Faust and Mephistopheles make off without Gretchen, their rescue mission a failure, Mephistopheles cruelly rejoices in the fact that she has been judged ('gerichtet'); a heavenly voice from above retorts that she has also been saved ('gerettet'). The last sound in Part One is a voice from within the prison calling out 'Heinrich! Heinrich!' Gounod's opera ends in a different way: Gretchen's soul ascends into heaven as Faust kneels in prayer. There is a similar apotheosis in Berlioz's *La Damnation de Faust* (1846).

JOHANN GEORG FELLINGER (1781–1816)

THE POETIC SOURCES

S1   *Selam, ein Almanach für Freunde des Mannigfaltigen auf das Jahr 1814*, ed. Ignaz Castelli, Anton Strauss, Wien, 1814

S2   *Johann Georg Fellinger's Poetische Schriften*, in two volumes, ed. Johann Gottfried Kumpf, Gelb, Klagenfurt, 1819.

This is the first published edition of Fellinger's poems.

THE SONGS

6 April 1815   *Die Sterne* D176 [S1: p. 214] [S2: p. 19]

12 April 1815   *Die erste Liebe* D182 [S1: p. 40] [S2: p. 63]

15 October 1815   *Die Sternenwelten* D307 [S1: pp. 313 & 315]
                             In *Selam*, 1814, the Slovenian original of the poem by Urban Janik entitled
                             'Svesdifhe' is printed on parallel pages pp. 312 and 314. 'Die Sternenwelten'
                             was also published (with Urban Jarnik's Slovenian original) in *Carinthia, ein
                             Wochenblatt zum Nutzen und Vergnügen*, No. 25, Klagenfurt, 1812.

Fellinger was born on 3 January 1781 in Peckau, Styria. He started life as a law student and a private tutor, and then became a professional soldier, wounded at the Battle on the Piave in May 1809, and taken as a prisoner of war to Frankfurt. Unlike Theodor Körner he did not die for his country, but he lost an eye and this disability made it difficult for him to make a new career. Like Mayrhofer, Fellinger eventually took his own life – on 27 November 1816. He was a great lover of music, and wrote a touching poem about Mozart's *Don Giovanni*; there is also an admiring poem dedicated to Schubert's friend and contemporary, the

Fellinger's *Poems*, 1819, frontispiece engraving of the poet by A. Tepplar.

composer Anselm Hüttenbrenner in the second volume of his *Gedichte*. This edition was edited by Johann Kumpf (qv) who published poems under the pseudonym 'Ermin'. Schubert set two of Kumpf's poems. Fellinger was admired by an important Styrian poet of the younger generation – Karl Gottfried von Leitner (this is another link with Schubert who just failed to meet Leitner personally through their mutual friends the Pachlers who lived in Graz). Among Leitner's posthumous papers was preparatory work for a second edition of Fellinger's work; this was never published.

FELS AUF FELSEN HINGEWÄLZET *see* HELIOPOLIS II D754

FERNE VON DER GROSSEN STADT *see* LIED (FERNE VON DER GROSSEN STADT) D483

Das FINDEN

(Kosegarten) **D219** [H113]
Bb major   June 1815

The find

Etwas langsam, unschuldig

Ich hab' ein Mäd - chen fun - den, sanft, e - del, deutsch und gut.

pp

(18 bars)

Ich hab' ein Mädchen funden,	I have found a maiden
Sanft, edel, deutsch und gut.	Gentle, noble, kind and German.
Ihr Blick ist mild und glänzend,	Her gaze is as tender and radiant
Wie Abendsonnenglut,	As the glow of the evening sun.
Ihr Haar wie Sommerweben,	Her hair is like gossamer
Ihr Auge veilchenblau.	Her eyes are violet-blue.
Dem Rosenkelch der Lippen	From the rosy chalice of her lips
Entquillt Gesang wie Tau.	Pours song like the dew.
[. . . 4 . . .]	[. . . 4 . . .]
Sie wandte sich, sie säumte,	She turned and hesitated,
Sie winkte freundlich mir;	Then beckoned me sweetly.
Froh ihres Blicks und Winkes,	Gladdened by her gaze and her beckoning
Flog ich entzückt zu ihr.	I flew to her in delight.
Erhaben stand und heilig	Before me, sublime and saintly,
Vor mir das hohe Weib.	Stood the noble maiden.
Ich aber schlang vertraulich	But I tenderly wrapped my arm
Den Arm um ihren Leib.	Around her waist.
Ich hab' das edle Mädchen	I took the noble maiden
An meiner Hand geführt;	By the hand;
Ich bin mit ihr am Staden	I walked with her
Des Bachs hinab spaziert.	Beside the brook.
Ich hab' sie liebgewonnen,	I fell in love with her.
Ich weiss, sie ist mir gut,	I know she is fond of me.
Drum sei mein Lied ihr eigen,	Therefore let my song be hers,
Ihr eigen Gut und Blut.	Her very own.

Ludwig Theobul Kosegarten (1758–1818)

*This is the first of Schubert's twenty-one Kosegarten solo settings (1815–17). See the poet's
biography for a chronological list of all the Kosegarten settings, as well as a discussion of Morten
Solvik's Kosegarten Liederkreis and this song's place within it.*

This song has the musical charm of the best of the Kosegarten settings, all of which date from 1815, apart from *An die untergehende Sonne* D457 which was completed in 1817. The poem itself is not the best that Kosegarten ever penned, although it is not impossible that, tongue in cheek, he was parodying the folksong style. One commentator has called this text 'shallow and bombastic', but no one has accused Schubert of these faults. He seems content to ignore the narrator's somewhat nationalistic tone and to concentrate on the girl instead; he puts 'unschuldig' ('innocent') at the top of his score and the music reflects her purity. The accompaniment to the first four lines of the strophe remains in the treble clef in both hands, a dainty ladylike tessitura, and pianissimo to boot. The texture of the piano writing is transparent with a suggestion of hunting horn harmonies which may well be intended to remind us that courtship shares its delights with the chase. The second half of the strophe introduces delicately pulsating semiquavers, a transparent piano texture at the mention of hair like gossamer (from b. 9). From time to time, at appropriate words, the vocal line departs from its masculine swagger and yields to teasingly feminine ornamentation. The two-bar postlude postulates the meeting of feminine and masculine, one girlish bar in the treble, the other in the mellow regions of the bass clef. From the sheerly melodic point of view this song lives up to its title: it is something of a find. Performers should be discouraged from using the spurious and banal bar of introduction printed in the Peters Edition. There are seven strophes in Kosegarten's poem – these are all printed in the AGA. Given here are 1, 6 and 7; three seem sufficient in performance.

Part of the melody of this song reappears as part of the theme for the second movement (a set of variations marked 'Andante con moto') of the piano-duet Sonata in B flat major D617, written in Zseliz in 1818 during the first of Schubert's Hungarian summers as music tutor to the two Esterházy countesses. With Schubert's quoting himself in this manner it is tempting to imagine he is telling us (or himself) something about a 'find' – a rare girl of modesty and beauty with whom he has fallen in love. Beyond his general remarks concerning a pretty chambermaid, we know rather little in detail about this aspect of Schubert's stay in Zseliz, but it was long bandied about that the composer must have had a relationship with a girl who worked in the house, one Josefine ('Pepi') Pöckelhofer. If she was something of a lady of easy virtue she seems hardly to merit the description of *Das Finden*. It is surely far more likely that Schubert was already taken, smitten even, by the maidenly qualities of his pupil, Countess Karoline Esterházy, still only thirteen years old. It was with her, after all, that he would have played the duets composed at Zseliz. If the composer already felt the kind of admiration for this girl that Kosegarten expresses here (the poet Novalis famously fell in love with his Sophie when she was even younger than thirteen), it was wise (and ingenious) to refer back to this song, and its sentiments, via a wordless piece for piano duet.

Autographs:	Österreichische Nationalbibliothek, Vienna (first draft and fair copy)
First edition:	Published as Book 42 no. 2 of the *Nachlass* by Diabelli, Vienna in 1848 (P360)
Subsequent editions:	Peters: Vol. 6/32; AGA XX 85: Vol. 2/67; NSA IV: Vol. 8/10
Discography and timing:	Fischer-Dieskau I 4⁶ 1'13 (Strophes 1 & 3 only)
	Hyperion I 18¹
	Hyperion II 7¹³ 2'14 Peter Schreier

←— *Grablied* D218   *Lieb Minna* D222 —→

Der FISCHER   The fisherman

(GOETHE) OP. 5 NO. 3, **D225** [H116]

The song exists in two versions, the second of which is discussed below:
(1) July 1815; (2) April? 1816

(1)   'Mässig'   B♭ major $\frac{2}{4}$ [18 bars]

(2)   B♭ major

(18 bars)

Das Wasser rauscht', das Wasser schwoll,	The waters murmured, the waters swelled,
Ein Fischer sass daran,	A fisherman sat on the bank;
Sah nach dem Angel ruhevoll,	Calmly he gazed at his rod,
Kühl bis ans Herz hinan.	His heart was cold.
Und wie er sitzt und wie er lauscht,	And as he sat and listened
Teilt sich die Flut empor:	The waters surged up and divided;
Aus dem bewegten Wasser rauscht	From the turbulent flood
Ein feuchtes Weib hervor.	A water nymph arose.
Sie sang zu ihm, sie sprach zu ihm:	She sang to him, she spoke to him:
'Was lockst du meine Brut	'Why do you lure my brood
Mit Menschenwitz und Menschenlist	With human wit and guile
Hinauf in Todesglut?	Up into the fatal heat?
Ach wüsstest du, wie's Fischlein ist	Ah, if you only knew how contented
So wohlig auf dem Grund,	The fish are in the depths,
Du stiegst herunter, wie du bist,	You would descend, just as you are,
Und würdest erst gesund.	And at last be made whole.
Labt sich die liebe Sonne nicht,	'Do not the dear sun and moon
Der Mond sich nicht im Meer?	Refresh themselves in the ocean?
Kehrt wellenatmend ihr Gesicht	Do not their countenances emerge doubly beautiful
Nicht doppelt schöner her?	From breathing the waters?
Lockt dich der tiefe Himmel nicht,	Are you not enticed by the heavenly deep,
Das feuchtverklärte Blau?	The transfigured, watery blue?
Lockt dich dein eigen Angesicht	Are you not lured by your own face
Nicht her in ew'gen Tau?'	Into this eternal dew?'
Das Wasser rauscht', das Wasser schwoll,	The waters murmured, the waters swelled,
Netzt' ihm den nackten Fuss;	Moistening his bare foot;
Sein Herz wuchs ihm so sehnsuchtsvoll	His heart surged with such yearning,
Wie bei der Liebsten Gruss.	As if his sweetheart had called him.
Sie sprach zu ihm, sie sang zu ihm;	She spoke to him, she sang to him,

Da war's um ihn geschehn;   Then it was all over;
Halb zog sie ihn, halb sank er hin   She half dragged him, he half sank down
Und ward nicht mehr gesehn.   And was never seen again.

JOHANN WOLFGANG VON GOETHE (1749–1832); poem probably written in 1778

This is the fifteenth of Schubert's seventy-five Goethe solo settings (1814–26). See the poet's biography for a chronological list of all the Goethe settings.

Schubert had a seemingly endless ability to invent different types of water music. In the first song (*Das Wandern*) of *Die schöne Müllerin* he finds a motif which serves both to suggest the happily trudging miller lad *and* the water doing its work, driving the millstones. Inventing versatile accompaniments is the secret of writing a good strophic song, and Schubert took pride in perfecting the strophic song as no one else has done before or since. *Der Fischer* is in the same key of B flat as *Das Wandern*, and is also water music that serves more than one purpose. The constant semiquavers which enliven the second-violin tessitura of the piano writing glisten and plash; there are swirling but distinctly undramatic eddies of the tide within the accompaniment, but there is little here that suggests the drama of seduction and death by drowning which is recounted in the denouement. One is reminded of Brueghel's depiction of Icarus falling into the sea (memorably commented on in W. H. Auden's poem, *Musée des Beaux Arts*) where the boy's catastrophe is pictured in the far distance. The poet takes note of the 'torturer's horse' in the foreground of the picture as it 'Scratches its innocent behind on a tree'; Brueghel's masterpiece is largely taken up with the banality of everyday domestic life – the only reality.

The song is clearly a masterpiece of its type, but if it fails to excite great passion in some modern Schubertians it is surely because of the composer's decision to write a strophic song within old-fashioned parameters. Goethe thought it wrong that a 'false interest in detail' should be 'demanded and aroused' in song composition. This dogmatic statement placed *durchkomponiert* (through-composed) songs in the realm of something approaching musical pornography. This poem was almost untouchable it was so famous, held up by Herder as a model for other poets. In a

Der Fischer drawn by Eugen Neureuther, 1829.

Der Fischer by Ramberg, from the almanac *Minerva* (1821).

conversation with Eckermann in November 1823 Goethe rails against painters who have taken the poem as their theme; his lyric is nothing more than a simple and charming expression, he says, of how water tempts us to bathe on a summer day.

Schubert seems to be somewhat in agreement. His tune is a sturdy one; the accompaniment stirs up a storm but avoids controversial tempests. The singer is relied upon to present the Lorelei's words with the correct combination of reproof and erotic allure while, with the help of a few mordents, emotive horn-calls, and expressive bass lines, accompanists can do their best to suggest the mermaid's blandishments. There is a very German strength and sweetness in all this simplicity, and Schubert faithfully matches Goethe in his folksong vein. The fisherman's disappearance at the end is as peremptory as the all-purpose postlude. Lorraine Byrne sees something more significant: 'The angler's immersion in water signifies a return to the preformal state, with a sense of death and annihilation on one hand, but of rebirth and regeneration on the other.'

The overambitious settings of this lyric by three young composers, Robert Schumann (1828), Hugo Wolf (1875, incomplete) and Richard Strauss (1877), all in a very grand and histrionic manner, show beyond doubt that Schubert's strophic simplicity was a wiser solution than their youthful hubris in attempting to storm the expressive heights of this elusive text. Better than any of these neophyte efforts is a setting by the composer Vesque von Püttlingen, a friend of Schubert's in the composer's last years.

The music that Schubert sent to the publisher in the summer of 1821 was a second version cleaned and modified in small details, spruced up as it were, for the work's proud public appearance as part of Op. 5. The NSA publishes the song's first version (which made its first printed appearance in Volume 1 of that edition in 1970), and a side-by-side comparison with the second version shows how six years of experience have refined Schubert's notation and presentation. With the music itself written in 1815 there was almost nothing to be improved, but the composer was now much more sophisticated in how he made his performing wishes known in terms of articulation and clarity of instruction to his performers. Volume 1b of the NSA (p. 279) also includes an ornamented version of the Op. 5 version where the vocal decorations of the singer Johann Michael Vogl are preserved. The key is G major as befits a baritone of Vogl's range. There are a number of added appoggiature, a mordent and changes of rhythm on 'sprach zu ihm' (b. 21) and 'die liebe Sonne nicht' (bb. 39–40) and a more extravagant roulade on 'schöner' (b. 45) – the latter written out in full by the NSA editors. All this provides a fascinating insight into how a singer born in the eighteenth century embraced a new art form while incorporating long-established performing practices. Schubert is always said to have permitted such embellishments from Vogl without necessarily approving of them.

Autograph:	British Library, London
Publication:	First published as part of the NSA in 1970 (P749; first version)
	First published as Op. 5 no. 3 by Cappi & Diabelli, Vienna in 1821
	(P12; second version)
Dedicatee:	Antonio Salieri
Publication review:	F. von Hentl, 'Blick auf Schubert's Lieder', *Wiener Zeitschrift für*
	Kunst, Literatur, Theater and Mode No. 36 (23 March 1822),
	p. 289f. [Waidelich/Hilmar Dokumente No. 146; Deutsch Doc.
	Biog. No. 278]
Subsequent editions:	Peters: Vol. 2/9; AGA XX 88: Vol. 2/171 (second version); NSA IV:
	Vol. 1a/42 (second version) & Vol. 1b/213 (first version);
	Bärenreiter: Vol. 1/34
Bibliography:	Byrne 2003, pp. 215–22
	Capell 1982, pp. 104–5
	Fischer-Dieskau 1977, p. 43
	Gülke 1991, p. 73
Further settings and	Sigmund Seckendorff (1744–1785) *Der Fischer* (1779)
arrangements:	Johann Friedrich Reichardt (1752–1814) *Der Fischer* (1781)
	Carl Friedrich Zelter (1758–1832) *Der Fischer* (1809)
	Václav Jan Tomášek (1774–1850) *Der Fischer* Op. 59 no. 3 (1815)
	Carl Loewe (1796–1869) *Der Fischer* Op. 43 no. 1 (1835)
	Johann Vesque von Püttlingen (1803–1883) *Der Fischer* (1865)
	Robert Schumann (1810–1856) *Der Fischer* (1828)
	Hugo Wolf (1860–1903) *Der Fischer* Op. 3 no. 3 (1875)
	Richard Strauss (1864–1949) *Der Fischer* WoO 33 (1877)
	Arr. Tilman Hoppstock (b. 1961) for guitar accompaniment (2
	versions), in *Franz Schubert: 110 Lieder* (2009)
Discography and timing:	Fischer-Dieskau I 4[8] 2'32
	Hyperion I 1[9]
	2'10 Janet Baker
	Hyperion II 7[16]

 ← *Wandrers Nachtlied I D224*   *Erster Verlust D226* →

FISCHERLIED (I)   Fisherman's Song
(SALIS-SEEWIS) **D351** [H236]
D major   1816?

(24 bars)

Das Fischergewerbe   The fisherman's trade
Gibt rüstigen Mut!   Gives us a cheerful heart.

Wir haben zum Erbe
Die Güter der Flut.
Wir graben nicht Schätze,
Wir pflügen kein Feld;
Wir ernten im Netze,
Wir angeln uns Geld.

Wir heben die Reusen
Den Schilfbach entlang.
Und ruhn bei den Schleusen,
Zu sondern den Fang.
Goldweiden beschatten
Das moosige Dach;
Wir schlummern auf Matten
Im kühlen Gemach.

Mit roten Korallen
Prangt Spiegel und Wand.
Den Estrich der Hallen
Deckt silberner Sand.
Das Gärtchen daneben
Grünt ländlich umzäunt
Von kreuzenden Stäben
Mit Baste vereint.

Im Antlitz der Buben
Lacht mutiger Sinn,
Sie meiden die Stuben
Bei Tagesbeginn;
Sie tauchen und schwimmen
Im eisigen See,
Und barfuss erklimmen
Sie Klippen von Schnee.

[. . .]

Oft rudern wir ferne
Im wiegenden Kahn;
Dann blinken die Sterne
So freundlich uns an;
Der Mond aus den Höhen,
Der Mond aus dem Bach,
So schnell wir entflöhen,
Sie gleiten uns nach.

Wir trotzen dem Wetter,
Das finster uns droht,
Wann schöpfende Bretter
Kaum hemmen den Tod.

Our inheritance
Is the wealth of the waters.
We dig for no treasure,
We plough no fields;
We harvest with our nets,
We fish for money.

We lay the fish traps
Along the reed-covered stream,
And rest at the locks
To sort our catch.
Golden willows shade
The mossy roof;
We sleep on mats
In the cool chamber.

Mirror and wall
Are resplendent with red corals;
Silver and sand covers
The floors of the halls.
Close by the little garden blooms,
Ringed by a rustic fence
Of criss-crossed stakes
Mingled with bast.

On the boys' faces
A bold spirit laughs;
They slip from their rooms
At break of day.
They dive and swim
In the icy sea,
And, barefoot, climb
Cliffs of snow.

[. . .]

Often we row far
In the rocking boat;
Then the stars shine
So kindly upon us;
The moon from the heights,
The moon from the brook,
No sooner have we escaped
Than they glide after us.

We defy the storm,
That darkly threatens us
When heaving timbers
Barely fend off death.

Wir trotzen auch Wogen	We defy the waves, too,
Auf krachendem Schiff,	On the groaning ship,
In Tiefen gezogen,	Drawn into the depths,
Geschleudert ans Riff!	Hurled against the reef!
Der Herr, der in Stürmen	The Lord, whose thunderbolts flash
Der Mitternacht blitzt,	In midnight storms,
Vermag uns zu schirmen,	Can protect us
Und kennt, was uns nützt.	And knows what we need.
Gleich unter dem Flügeln	Beneath the wings
Des Ewigen ruht	Of the Eternal One
Der Rasengruft Hügel	Rest both the mound of the grassy tomb
Das Grab in der Flut.	And the grave beneath the waters.

JOHANN GAUDENZ VON SALIS-SEEWIS (1762–1834); poem written in 1791

This is the second of Schubert's thirteen Salis-Seewis solo settings (1816–?21). See the poet's biography for a chronological list of all the Salis-Seewis settings.

Schubert, the only great composer to be born in Vienna (as distinct from making a home there), was an inveterate town dweller. He loved the amenities that only a town could offer, and became rather bored in the country; on one country holiday, according to his friend Stadler, he preferred to stay in bed in the morning rather than go walking. The dramatic countryside of the Salzkammergut, which he visited with the singer Vogl in 1825, moved him to write rapturous letters home, but most of his songs about nature were written in urban surroundings. Distance lends enchantment, and like many of the poets of his day (the pastoral tradition was old-fashioned but by no means dead), Schubert idealized the country and the people who lived and worked in it. Just as Shakespeare's plays have interludes in which rustics bring a change of colour and pace to the proceedings, Schubert's output is sprinkled with *Singspiel* songs worthy not only of Mozart's Papageno but also of the Bard's clowns and gravediggers. Almost all of Schubert's Viennese friends were would-be intellectuals and artists, and if anyone was cast unwittingly as the clown of the group it was the composer himself whose nickname was 'Schwammerl' – 'Little Mushroom'.

It is little wonder that the composer empathized with the miller and the hunter, the fisherman and poacher, the carpenter and goldsmith, and depicted them all affectionately in song. The apotheosis of this deceptively simple music is *Die schöne Müllerin* where a façade of genial working-class equanimity is undermined to reveal the profound personal crisis of a hyper-sensitive soul. In that cycle Schubert blurs the boundaries of comedy and tragedy: he alone of his contemporaries brings universal significance to Biedermeier tableaux in the same way that Shakespeare could animate temporal Tudor political propaganda with immortal verbal music. There is much of the humanity of the miller's music in many of the 'work songs' from Schubert's earlier years. This *Fischerlied*, for example, is sung by a spirited and lifelike character and has a wonderful swing to it. The strength and simplicity of such a melody (the accompaniment is among the most simple he wrote) was often imitated by that ardent Schubertian, Arthur Sullivan. Unlike later settings of this poem (D562, and another for men's chorus, D364), each of the verses ends with jolly 'tra-la-las' which are the composer's invention, not the poet's. The key is D major which seems to suggest to Schubert the activity and preoccupations of working folk, particularly when water is part of the picture (Schlegel's *Der Schiffer* D694, *Fischerweise* D881 and Schober's *Jägers Liebeslied* D909 come to mind). The poem has eight strophes as printed in the AGA. All except Verse 5 are printed above. In the Hyperion performance of this first setting, D351, stro-phes 1, 4, 6 and 7 of the original poem were recorded.

Autograph:	Stiftelsen Musikkulturens Främjande, Stockholm
First edition:	Published as part of the AGA in 1895 (P630)
Subsequent editions:	Not in Peters; AGA XX 204: Vol. 4/70; NSA IV: Vol. 11/145
Discography and timing:	Fischer-Dieskau I 6²⁷ 1'24 (1, 2 and last only)

Discography and timing: Fischer-Dieskau I 6^{27} 1'24 (1, 2 and last only)
Hyperion I 2^1
Hyperion II 13^{10} 2'22 Stephen Varcoe

← *Der Entfernten* D350 (second setting)   *Pflügerlied* D392 →

FISCHERLIED (II)   Fisherman's song
(SALIS-SEEWIS) **D562** [H372]
F major   May 1817

See previous entry for poem and translation

JOHANN GAUDENZ VON SALIS-SEEWIS (1762–1834); poem written in 1791

This is the twelfth of Schubert's thirteen Salis-Seewis solo settings (1816-?21). See the poet's biography for a chronological list of all the Salis-Seewis settings.

The perennial difficulty with all but the greatest strophic songs is that the music is more appro-priate to some verses than to others. When Schubert returns to certain elusive texts it suggests an artistic conscience haunted by this very problem. The first *Fischerlied* of 1816 is quite different from that of a year later. Schubert now eschews merry tra-la-las in favour of a setting in the key of F major, a tonality he often associates with pastoral music and with sleep. The mood of the first *Fischerlied* takes its cue from the upbeat first line of the poem; this setting grows from the last lines of the second and eighth verses. The tra-la-las of D351 are a particularly inappropriate sequel for descriptions of slumber and the watery grave. In the first setting we hear splashing and wading, but here deeper currents are at work. The alto line of the accompaniment sways gently like fish swimming in the depths. If the first setting depicts with humour and sympathy a merry worker, the second reveals what lies beneath the surface in him, and for him. It is impossible to say which setting is 'the better version': the poem needs both in order to encom-pass its range. There are eight verses as printed in the AGA. All except Verse 5 are printed before the commentary for *Fischerlied I* D351 above. In the Hyperion performance of D562, strophes 1, 2, 3 and 8 of the poem were recorded. These strophes seemed marginally more appropriate for the music of this second setting.

Autograph:	Staatsbibliothek Preussischer Kulturbesitz, Berlin (first draft, cancelled)
First edition:	Published as part of the AGA in 1895 (P674)
Subsequent editions:	Not in Peters; AGA XX 321: Vol. 5/118; NSA IV: Vol. 11/146
Discography and timing:	Fischer-Dieskau II 1[7] 2'04 (1, 2 and last only)
	Hyperion I 2[2]
	Hyperion II 19[6] 3'34 Stephen Varcoe

← *Die Blumensprache* D519   *Die Einsiedelei* D563 →

Das FISCHERMÄDCHEN *see SCHWANENGESANG* D957/10

Des FISCHERS LIEBESGLÜCK   The fisherman's luck in love
(LEITNER) **D933** [H653]
A minor   November 1827

(21 bars)

(1)   Dort blinket   Yonder light gleams
      Durch Weiden,   Through the willows,
      Und winket   And a pale
      Ein Schimmer   Glimmer
      Blassstrahlig   Beckons to me
      Vom Zimmer   From the bedroom
      Der Holden mir zu.   Of my sweetheart.

(2)   Es gaukelt   It flickers
      Wie Irrlicht,   Like a will o' the wisp,
      Und schaukelt   And its reflection
      Sich leise   Sways
      Sein Abglanz   Gently
      Im Kreise   In the circle
      Des schwankenden See's.   Of the undulating lake.

(3)   Ich schaue   I gaze
      Mit Sehnen   Longingly
      In's Blaue   Into the blue
      Der Wellen,   Of the waves,
      Und grüsse   And greet
      Den hellen,   The bright
      Gespiegelten Strahl.   Reflected beam.

(4) Und springe
Zum Ruder,
Und schwinge
Den Nachen
Dahin auf
Den flachen,
Krystallenen Weg.

And spring
To the oar,
And swing
The boat
Away on
Its smooth,
Crystal course.

(5) Fein-Liebchen
Schleicht traulich
Vom Stübchen
Herunter,
Und sputet
Sich munter
Zu mir in das Boot.

My sweetheart
Slips lovingly
Down
From her little room,
And joyfully
Hastens to me
In the boat.

(6) Gelinde
Dann treiben
Die Winde
Uns wieder
See-einwärts
Vom Flieder
Des Ufers hindann.

Then the breezes
Gently
Blow us
Again
Out into the lake
From the lilac tree
On the shore.

(7) Die blassen
Nachtnebel
Umfassen
Mit Hüllen
Vor Spähern
Den stillen,
Unschuldigen Scherz.

The pale
Evening mists
Envelop
And veil
Our silent,
Innocent dallying
From prying onlookers.

(8) Und tauschen
Wir Küsse,
So rauschen
Die Wellen
Im Sinken
Und Schwellen,
Den Horchern zum Trotz.

And as we exchange
Kisses,
The waves
Lap,
Rising
And falling,
To foil eavesdroppers.

(9) Nur Sterne
Belauschen
Uns ferne,
Und baden
Tief unter
Den Pfaden
Des gleitenden Kahn's.

Only stars
In the far distance
Overhear us,
And bathe
Deep down
Below the course
Of the gliding boat.

(10) So schweben
Wir selig,

So we drift on
Blissfully,

Umgeben	In the midst
Vom Dunkel,	Of darkness,
Hoch überm	High above
Gefunkel	The twinkling
Der Sterne einher.	Stars.

(11)	Und weinen	Weeping,
	Und lächeln,	Smiling,
	Und meinen,	We think
	Enthoben	We have soared free
	Der Erde,	Of the earth,
	Schon oben,	And are already up above,
	Schon drüben zu sein.	On another shore.

KARL GOTTFRIED VON LEITNER (1800–1890); poem written in 1821

This is the ninth of Schubert's eleven Leitner solo settings (1822–3 and 1827–8). See the poet's biography for a chronological list of all the Leitner settings.

With the composition of *Winterreise*, Schubert's mastery of strophic song had deepened immeasurably. Like a Michelin-starred chef he could take pride in the quality and intensity of his reductions, the essences of different tastes distilled in the heat of inspiration. With deceptive ease this eventful poem is encompassed in a strophic song. The accompaniment and the shape of the vocal line seem supremely all-purpose: they are equally appropriate for flickering light, dancing waves, caressing breezes, the floating of mists and the glinting of stars.

Some scholars belittle Leitner as a country bumpkin of a poet (the word 'hindann' in Verse 6 is very old German, its use provincial) yet this ingenious rhyme scheme (AXABXBX) could only have been written by a very sophisticated boatman, Styrian or even Stygian. As Raymond Joly writes, 'The rhymes glimmer and vanish unpredictably like stars mirrored in a lake.' In earlier years Schubert might have attempted a number of strophic settings of this text (cf. the two very different *Fischerlieder* D351 and D562), or perhaps a *durchkomponiert* song mirroring the rich sequence of events. But here, at the height of his powers, he gives us a mere two pages (at least in Peters, four in the NSA), a kind of sheltered *Auf dem Wasser zu singen*, and a masterpiece of hovering enchantment. The four-bar *Vorspiel* introduces a motif of six lapping semi-quavers alternating with a dotted crochet (b. 1, repeated in b. 2) which depicts the undulations of a boat at its moorings. The more or less stationary left-hand harmonies of the introduction suggest the steadying influence of anchor or rope. The vocal line continually tries to find its balance: for example, two bars with $\frac{3}{8}$ length-of-phrase (in b. 11) are succeeded by a $\frac{6}{8}$ phrase (b. 12), then two further $\frac{3}{8}$ phrases (b. 13), another $\frac{6}{8}$ in b. 14 and a $\frac{3}{8}$ length-of-phrase as b. 15 enjambs with b. 16. The rocking motion that is implicit in the accompaniment reveals the fisherman singing in his vessel as he watches and waits, and dreams of his beloved.

The vocal line looks back unashamedly to the first twelve *Winterreise* songs: in the poem's second verse (b. 11 of the song) the word 'Irrlicht' brings back that cycle's will-o'-the-wisp, the dancing light caused by the ignition of gases in marshy areas. The fact that the vocal line of this Leitner song is written in this very unusual notation (semiquavers and dotted semiquavers) owes everything to this famous *Irrlicht* D911/9, written nine months earlier. That song of delusive fantasy gives us an important clue to the nature of *Des Fischers Liebesglück*. The descriptions of happy events (the rowing of the boat, the meeting of the lovers, their making love under the stars) may very well have been meant to be real narrative as far as Leitner was concerned, but Schubert puts a different gloss on them. For the composer this is not a real story at all – from beginning to end it is the reverie of a dreamer who fantasizes about these actions as he watches, and longs for, his inaccessible beloved who remains firmly inside her house. Of course, as the story unfolds in his mind, he lives it with appropriate fervour (as must the singer), but the fisherman's progress towards fulfilment and happiness is not really happening. If it were, the music would have had to be *durchkomponiert*; as long as everything remains in the imagination of the protagonist, the strophic form, and a preponderance of the minor key, is the ideal medium.

The key is A minor, always special with Schubert, and hardly the tonality of fulfilment – it is more often associated with loneliness and isolation, as in *Abendstern* D806. The change to the major key (at b. 20) is jealously guarded for the end of each musical verse (which consists of three verses of Leitner's poetry); as always the juxtaposition of major and minor in this tonality betokens the deepest, and possibly hopeless, longing. The tiniest details (like the frisson of a single mordent in the piano's introduction, b. 3) are especially telling. The vocal line requires great breath control from the singer, and there are heady excursions into the stratosphere (high As touched in bb. 17 and 19, the second of these harmonized in the major key). The song requires a fine and daring sense of rubato, never better (or more boldly) handled than by the tenor Karl Erb in his celebrated pre-war recording where he audaciously transposes the song into B minor. After hearing what Erb does with this song it seems impossible to revert to the earthbound tyranny of the bar line; in fact the same rubato and freedom that are necessary to make *Irrlicht* a song of random uncertainty are necessary here. The fact that Leitner wrote eleven strophes, not twelve, does not exactly suit Schubert's musical scheme whereby each of his musical verses uses three verses of the poem. The composer must accordingly repeat Leitner's penultimate verse (bb. 31–7 in the NSA) to achieve the symmetry he requires.

Autograph:	Wienbibliothek im Rathaus, Vienna (first 4 bars)
First edition:	Published as Book 27 no. 3 of the *Nachlass* by Diabelli, Vienna in 1835 (P314)
Subsequent editions:	Peters: Vol. 2/234; AGA XX 550: Vol. 9/116; NSA IV: Vol. 14/79; Bärenreiter: Vol. 4/105
Bibliography:	Capell 1928, p. 245
	Dittrich 2007, p. 256
	Fischer-Dieskau 1977, pp. 255–6
	Newbould 1997, pp. 308–9
	Youens 2002, pp. 273–84
Further settings:	Detlef Kraus (1919–2008) 'Variationen über *Des Fischers Liebesglück* D933 für Streichquartett' (1995)
Discography and timing:	Fischer-Dieskau II 9[11] 5'15 (Strophes 1–3 & 7–11 only)
	Hyperion I 6[12] 7'19 Anthony Rolfe Johnson
	Hyperion II 35[6]

← *Vor meiner Wiege* D927   *Der Wallensteiner Lanzknecht beim Trunk* D931 →

⁓⁓⁓⁓⁓⁓

FISCHERWEISE   Fisherman's Ditty
(SCHLECHTA) OP. 96 NO. 4, **D881** [H598]

The song exists in two versions, the second of which is discussed below:
(1) March 1826; (2) April 1828

(1)   'Ziemlich bewegt'   D major   ¢   [92 bars]

(2)   D major

(92 bars)

Den Fischer fechten Sorgen	The fisherman is not plagued
Und Gram und Leid nicht an;	By cares, grief or sorrow.
Er löst am frühen Morgen	In the early morning he casts off
Mit leichtem Sinn den Kahn.	His boat with a light heart.

Da lagert rings noch Friede
   Auf Wald und Flur und Bach,
Er ruft mit seinem Liede
   Die gold'ne Sonne wach.

Round about, peace still lies
   In meadows and in streams
With his song the fisherman
   Bids the golden sun awake.

Er singt zu seinem Werke
   Aus voller frischer Brust,
Die Arbeit gibt ihm Stärke,
   Die Stärke Lebenslust!

He sings at his work
   From a full, vigorous heart.
His work gives him strength,
   His strength exhilarates him.

Bald wird ein bunt' Gewimmel
   In allen Tiefen laut,
Und plätschert durch den Himmel
   Der sich im Wasser baut–

Soon a bright multitude
   Will resound in the depths,
And splash
   Through the watery heavens.

[(. . .)]

[(. . .)]

Doch wer ein Netz will stellen,
   Braucht Augen klar und gut,
Muss heiter gleich den Wellen
   Und frei sein wie die Flut;

But whoever wishes to set a net
   Needs good, clear eyes,
Must be as cheerful as the waves,
   And as free as the tide.

Dort angelt auf der Brücke
   Die Hirtin–schlauer Wicht,
Gib auf nur deiner Tücke
   Den Fisch betrügst du nicht.

There, on the bridge, the shepherdess
   Is fishing. Cunning minx,
Leave off your tricks!
   You won't deceive *this* fish!

FRANZ XAVER VON SCHLECHTA (1796–1875)

This is the last of Schubert's six Schlechta solo settings (1815–26). See the poet's biography for a chronological list of all the Schlechta settings.

This is a universally popular song that sparkles with merry bravado thanks to the brilliance of yet another variation on Schubert's favourite water-music theme. In fact the accompaniment could be thought of as a speeded-up version of that remarkable Goethe setting *Am Flusse* D766, also in D major and powered by right-hand oscillations. Until the last strophe (where the music is audibly wrong-footed) it celebrates a man's world in which women are allowed to play little part. The bouncing counterpoint between the solo line and the accompaniment gives a strong impression of comradely collusion. Just as in a sea shanty, it is as if a soloist has been elected (in this case a baritone) to lead the proceedings. The left hand of the piano part is like a veritable chorus of assorted men's voices: gruff basses sing wordlessly at bb. 3–4 of the piano's introduction, while the tenors take over at bb. 5–6; a whistled obbligato is a charming touch as the left hand crosses to the treble at bb. 38–9, and again at bb. 42–3, the only moment when the accompaniment dares to enter the dangerous domain of the soprano register. The advantage of having the percussive piano stand-in for a vocal ensemble is that the left-hand tunes, when combined with the energetic motor rhythms of the right, create an irresistible illusion of splashing waves and glinting sunlight.

The composer's mastery of the male part-song is here given pianistic expression in solo song; it is significant that the key of D major is a favourite Schubertian tonality for this kind of music. The music glows with the vigour of a healthy occupation fruitfully pursued in the great outdoors – part of the tradition of the Viennese *Singspiel* that goes back to Schikaneder's Papageno, and one of the reasons (apart from his imagination) that Schubert, the Viennese town dweller, was able to empathize with the simplicities of country life. At the same time the composer's evocation is limited by the skills of his poet whose protagonist – at the height of his powers, both in terms of his fishing skills and as a Lothario – is no authentic working man, but Schlechta himself wearing fisherman's fancy-dress at a costume ball. Young, good-looking, over-confident (what the Viennese might call 'ein fescher Kerl' – a dashing young man), the song's hero is everything that the composer is not. The fisherman has yet to meet his match, someone who will make him settle down and land him as her husband. This encounter (with the shepherdess) takes place in the song's final strophe; he has always employed a certain amount of guile to make his catch (and his amatory conquests), but the rather hearty harmonic progressions also suggest that our hero's thought processes are elemental, rather than Machiavellian. A reading of the biographical note on Schlechta will confirm that the poet too was a simple-hearted man.

Schubert has no compunction in leaving out one of the poet's printed stanzas to make a neat structure of two verses of text for each one of music. The poem that is printed in Schlechta's *Dichtungen* (1824) has seven strophes. Schubert's musical design entailed the using of two

Fischerweise, vignette for Czerny's arrangement of the Schubert song for solo piano (1838–9).

strophes of verse to make a single musical strophe. With an odd number of verses in the original poem the composer had to leave out the following, fifth, verse:

Und schlüpft auf glatten Steinen   And slither on the slippery stones,
    Und badet sich und schnellt,   And swim, and dart up.
Der Grosse frisst den Kleinen   The big one devours the little ones,
    Wie auf der ganzen Welt.   As throughout the world.

In musical terms the song is strophic apart from the all-important adjustment in the final verse in which the shepherdess is spotted on the bridge. The rhythmic displacement (depicting the surprise of the *coup de foudre*) on 'schlauer Wicht' (b. 69) is all the more noticeable for being unique in the song. Up until this point the fisherman's catch has practically landed in his lap; but this skill has depended on a clear eye and a clear head, a free mind and heart. Robbed of this equanimity (and the beauty of the shepherdess might do just this) perhaps he will be the one to take the bait and be left dangling.

In fact, and rather to our surprise, the shepherdess is cast as the schemer of the piece. To describe her the poet uses the masculine noun 'Wicht' (surely related to the old English word 'wight') and the masculine adjective 'schlauer' and yet she has done nothing to deserve being addressed at in such a way. Why should she be accused of playing tricks? It would make more sense, surely, if the poet were addressing the fisherman, letting *him* know that he won't be able to land this catch, refering to him, with mock disapproval, as a 'schlauer Wicht'? The musical tug at the heartstrings on 'die Hirtin' b. 68 suggests affectionate engagement: either the fisherman has fallen for her – or is at least not insensible to her good looks – or she is smitten with him.

By the time the poem was republished in Schlechta's posthumous collection, *Ephemeren* (1876), the lyric, now entitled *Fischerlied*, was scarcely recognizable as the one that Schubert had set to music. There are five strophes instead of the original seven. Here is the last of them:

Dort angelt voll Verlangen   There the shepherdess is fishing,
    Die Hirtin. Ei, du Wicht!   Filled with desire. Hey, you little minx,
Den du begehrst zu fangen   This fish you're intent on catching
    Den Fisch berückst du nicht!   Is one you *won't* bewitch.

The importance of this revision is that it makes the poet's original thoughts a little clearer as regards who is fishing for whom. We learn that the shepherdess is 'voll Verlangen' and thus she could be landed with little angling skill; the use of the masculine accusative pronoun, 'Den', in the second-last line (as opposed to 'die') makes it clear that the shepherdess is indeed the 'Wicht' or 'imp' who is attempting to trap the fisherman, here also referred to in the accusative as 'Den Fisch'. The removal of the perjorative adjective 'schlauer' is also revealing. The anti-women twist to this ditty about male freedom and the fisherman's refusal to be tied down has become less vehement over the years. Schlechta has watered down the misogyny: the girl, still addressed with the familiar knockabout 'du', now 'enchants' (berückst) rather than deceives (betrügst). Schlechta, like almost all the boys in Schubert's circle, went to school in a monastery where the dangers of the daughters of Eve would have been daily impressed on him; he had also been a disciple of Johann Mayrhofer whose Odysseus-like boatman, *Der Schiffer* D536, was never going to be susceptible to the siren calls of women's voices. We are reminded how much the young men in Mayrhofer's circle were influenced by that poet's *Beyträge zur Bildung für Jünglinge* (1817–18) which advocated masculine independence unsullied by sensual thoughts. They would also have read de la Motte Fouqué's *Undine* (published in Vienna in 1814), where the water sprite (better known in her French incarnation as Ondine) traps those who live on land; this 'Hirtin' is an Ondine in reverse, a sprite on dry land who has set out to trap a fisherman who lives on the water. Did Schlechta realize he was overturning the tradition of hundreds of years of pastoral poetry (where women are courted rather more gallantly) by changing the hapless Shepherdess into something of a Lorelei?

The NSA publishes an earlier version of *Fischerweise* in Volume 5b. This is marked 'Ziemlich bewegt'. The passage high in the voice (beginning 'Dort angelt auf der Brücke', b. 76) is specifically marked 'leise', an indication of the head voice that is needed by the singer to give this music a sufficently light touch. Walther Dürr, in his introduction to Volume 5 of the NSA, points out the very real possibility that the song dates from as early as 1817, and that the extant manuscripts (dated 1826 and 1828) are copies of a much earlier one. In light of the fact that *Fischerweise* seems an ideal (if more light-hearted) companion piece for *Der Schiffer*, composed in 1817, this theory deserves serious consideration.

Autograph:	Wienbibliothek im Rathaus, Vienna (first version, draft)
	National Library, Budapest (second version, fair copy)
Publication:	First published as part of the AGA in 1895 (P696; first version)
	First published as Op. 96 no. 4 by Schober's Lithographisches Institut, Vienna in Summer 1828 (P168; second version)
Dedicatee	Maria Karolina Fürstin von Kinsky
First known performance:	Otto Erich Deutsch has the date of first performance of this piece as 26 March 1828, as part of the Schubert 'Privatkonzert' at the Musikverein, Vienna. However, it has since been shown that this work, which was present on early drafts of the programme, was removed in favour of *Der Wanderer an den Mond* D870, probably at Johann Michael Vogl's request. The only paper to report on the concert containing *Fischerweise* was the *Allgemeine musikalische Zeitung* (Leipzig), which perhaps had an early copy of the programme before the change was made (the critic was clearly not present). See Waidelich/Hilmar Dokumente II Nos 599a, 602, 603 and 603a
Subsequent editions:	Peters: Vol. 2/186; AGA XX 495a & b: Vol. 8/190 (first version) & 194 (second version); NSA IV: Vol. 5a/67 (second version) & Vol. 5b/223 (first version); Bärenreiter: Vol. 3/198
Bibliography:	Capell 1928, p. 214
	Einstein 1951, p. 304
	Fischer-Dieskau 1977, p. 239
	Jestremski 2003, pp. 115–24
	Kohlhäufl 1999, p. 185
	Panofka 1991, p. 15
	Racek 1956, p. 100
Discography and timing:	Fischer-Dieskau II 8^4 3'13
	Hyperion I 2^3
	Hyperion II 32^4 3'27 Stephen Varcoe

← *Sehnsucht* D879   *Im Frühling* D882 →

FLORIO *see ZWEI SZENEN AUS DEM SCHAUSPIEL LACRIMAS* D857/2

Der FLÜCHTLING   The fugitive
(SCHILLER) **D402** [H234]
B♭ major   March 1816

Ziemlich langsam, feierlich

Frisch at - met des Mor-gens le - ben - di - ger Hauch,

(114 bars)

Frisch atmet des Morgens lebendiger Hauch,	The lively morning breeze blows fresh;
Purpurisch zuckt durch düstrer Tannen Ritzen	The young light flickers crimson between the dark pines
Das junge Licht und äugelt aus dem Strauch,	And glints from the bushes,
In goldnen Flammen blitzen	The cloud-capped mountain peaks
Der Berge Wolkenspitzen,	Blaze with golden flames,
Mit freudig melodisch gewirbeltem Lied	Warbling their happy, melodious song
Begrüssen erwachende Lerchen die Sonne,	The awakening larks greet the sun
Die schon in lachender Wonne	Which, with joyful laughter,
Jugendlich schön in Auroras Umarmungen glüht.	Glows young and fair in the dawn's embrace.
Sei Licht mir gesegnet!	I bless you light!
Dein Strahlenguss regnet	Your rays stream down
Erwärmend hernieder auf Anger und Au.	To warm meadow and pasture.
Wie flittern die Wiesen,[1]	See how the fields glitter,
Wie silberfarb zittern	And a thousand silvery suns
Tausend Sonnen im perlenden Tau!	Glisten in the pearly dew!
In säuselnder Kühle	In the whispering coolness
Beginnen die Spiele	Young nature
Der jungen Natur,	Begins her games,
Die Zephyre kosen	The Zephyrs caress
Und schmeicheln um Rosen,	And fondle the roses,
Und Düfte beströmen die lachende Flur.	And sweet scents pervade the smiling meadows.
Wie hoch aus den Städten die Rauchwolken dampfen,	How high the clouds of smoke rise from the town,
Laut wiehern und schnauben und knirschen und strampfen	Horses and bulls neigh loudly, snort,
Die Rosse, die Farren,	Stamp and gnash their teeth,
Die Wagen erknarren	Creaking carts
Ins ächzende Tal.	Roll along the valley,
Die Waldungen leben,	The woods are alive,

---

[1] Schubert here transposes verbs in two of Schiller's lines, originally 'Wie silberfarb flittern / Die Wiesen wie zittern'.

Und Adler und Falken und Habichte schweben, Eagles, falcons and hawks hover,
Und wiegen die Flügel im blendenden Strahl. And move their wings in the dazzling light.

  Den Frieden zu finden,   To find peace
  Wohin soll ich wenden   Where shall I turn
  Am elenden Stab?   With my wretched staff?
  Die lachende Erde   The smiling earth,
  Mit Jünglingsgebärde,—   With youthful countenance,
  Für mich nur ein Grab?   Is but a grave for me!

Steig empor, o Morgenrot, und röte Rise up, o dawn,
 Mit purpurnem Kusse Hain und Feld, And with your crimson kiss tinge grove
            and field,

Säusle nieder, o Abendrot, und flöte[3] Descend with a whisper, o sunset,
 In sanften Schlummer die tote Welt![4] And lull the dead world to gentle sleep.
  Morgen—ach, du rötest   Morning, you tinge with red
  Eine Totenflur,   A land of death,
Ach und du, o Abendrot, umflötest Ah, and you, o sunset,
 Meinen langen Schlummer nur.   Merely warble around my long sleep.

FRIEDRICH VON SCHILLER (1759–1805); poem written before 1781

This is the twenty-eighth of Schubert's forty-four Schiller solo settings (1811–24). See the poet's biography for a chronological list of all the Schiller settings.

This song has had something of a bad press from the commentators because it contains contradictory messages: the joy in nature in the first section and the pessimism of the last seem ill-reconciled by the music. There is even some discussion of the composer's flagging inspiration. Making the whole cohere into a single entity is the singer's task, and it depends on how convincingly the excitable and quixotic character of the fugitive is put across. From that point of view it is not so sure to be a success on the concert platform as many other Schubert songs. The poem dates from the same epoch as Schiller's play *Die Räuber* (1780), and as Reed says, 'reflects a sympathy for the outcast fashionable in the *Sturm und Drang* period'.

 The song opens with music for a measured early morning walk. The key is B flat major, and the pace of this hymn of thanksgiving to nature is expansive enough to suggest a protagonist of some *gravitas*. Like many other songs of the period the tessitura is challenging – a passage like bb. 9–11, for example, sits uncomfortably high. At b. 13 the accompaniment changes to caroling triplets to accompany the dawn chorus of the lark. The vocal line is grandly expansive at this point while glancing chromaticisms in the piano writing (particularly at bb. 17–21) suggest the darting rays of the newly risen sun and their glinting refraction. A genial four-bar postlude brings this section (Schiller Verse 1) to an end.

 At b. 24 the key signature changes to D major, and the marking to 'Ruhig'. This is a statuesque, and rather old-fashioned, hymn of praise to light (the contrast of light and shade is a feature of this poem). From bb. 24–9 the accompaniment shadows the vocal line in simple crotchets and quavers. Robert Holl has pointed out the melodic similarity of this passage to closing sequences of Haydn's Imperial hymn, 'Gott, erhalte Franz den Kaiser'. From b. 30 the imagery of fields that glitter and glisten inspires throbbing semiquavers. The pattern of the piano writing changes to

---

[3] The addition of 'o' in this line is Schubert's.
[4] Schiller's original line here is 'Sanft in Schlummer, die *erstorb'ne* Welt'.

something more conspiratorial at mention of Nature's games (from b. 33); the playful caresses between voice and piano at 'In säuselnder Kühle' are pre-echoes of Zuleika's interaction with the billowing east wind in D720 (b. 33 has also marked the beginning of Schiller's third strophe which the composer incorporates without fuss into this second musical section). At bb. 40–2 the repetition of the words 'Und Düfte beströmen die lachende Flur' is marked by a decoration of the vocal line (written by Schubert as an ossia in the score) which would be worthy of a great opera singer of the time. This reinforces the impression that *Der Flüchtling* owes more to Gluck than to any other composer. There is much about this poem which might have suggested the character of Orestes (in Vogl's incarnation of the role) in *Iphigenia in Tauris*, a firm favourite of the composer's ever since his youthful visits to the opera.

The scherzo movement that follows (marked 'Geschwind' in $\frac{3}{8}$, from b. 44) is a setting of Schiller's fourth strophe. The music, with its rather minimal accompaniment, looks playful on paper, an echo of *Der Geistertanz* D116 perhaps, but the tempo of this section implies pursuit, in the same way as Orestes is pursued by the Furies. The sounds of mankind are threatening ones (is this the first reference in song to a horror of traffic and urban development?) and the eagle and falcon are predatory birds. An eight-bar postlude of rippling semiquavers (bb. 78–84) illustrates the dazzling light referred to in Schiller's poem. This is a very early attempt on Schubert's part to depict at least an element of madness in one of his protagonists, although we are still far away from the power of the traveller's reactions to the circling crow in *Winterreise*. If this section is performed with sufficient angst (so that the next strophe is not a completely unexpected change of mood) the song as a whole is more believable. It is as if the fugitive's mask of stoicism (as demonstrated in the earlier strophes) has slipped as a result of his unwilling contact with unfriendly civilization.

The poet's fifth strophe is a noble recitative marked 'Unruhig'. The D major of the previous section yields to G minor, and a return to common time. Each of the two rhetorical questions asked by the narrator moves from the minor key back into D major, an unashamed use of the so-called 'pathetic' possibilities of the brighter tonality. The succession of dactyls is accompanied by chords alternating ruefully between the hands. Once again this 'Wanderstab' (walking stick) is light years away from that taken up by the winter traveller at the end of *Das Wirtshaus* (D911/21), but we can see that the composer is already attracted by a character who is tragically alienated from society.

The concluding apostrophe to morning (without change of marking or key signature) is something of a musical recapitulation of the opening in B flat major, but it is much modified in colour and mood; the poem is now shot through with images of sunset, death and sleep. Once again it is the singer's far-from-easy task to register, and convey, the difference between the two states of mind as coming from the same tortured individual. An exquisite final cadence ('Meinen langen Schlummer nur' bb. 108–11) is very reminiscent of Vinvela's music from the grave ('Shilric, ich lieg, erblasst in dem Grab') in *Cronnan* D282 bb. 95–6. This is followed by a four-bar postlude, mourning music on a B flat pedal that also signifies the muffled beat of a death march. In comparison with many other Schubert songs the music may seem underwritten, even perfunctory, but one must remember that 1816 was, on the whole, a year of purification for him as he studied the rigours of strophic song composition. In the hands of a great artist much can be made of this music. Janet Baker had the vocal and interpretative means to make *Der Flüchtling* a song of great eloquence, all the more moving because of its spare texture.

Schubert had already set the first verse of this poem as an exercise for Salieri in May 1813: *Frisch atmet des Morgens lebendiger Hauch* D67 is for unaccompanied male trio, TTB. It is thus possible that Salieri was shown this song as it was composed when Schubert was just still working with the Italian maestro. The old boy would have been pleased by the Gluckian overtones of the piece. Gluck, after all, was Salieri's teacher, thus Schubert's grand-teacher.

Autograph:	Wienbibliothek im Rathaus, Vienna (first 22 bars)
First edition:	Published as No. 36 of *Neueste Folge nachgelassener Lieder und Gesänge* by J. P. Gothard, Vienna in 1872 (P461)
Subsequent editions:	Not in Peters; AGA XX 192: Vol. 4/35; NSA IV: Vol. 10/100
Bibliography:	Capell 1928, p. 114
Discography and timing:	Fischer-Dieskau I 6[16] 4'38
	Hyperion I 1[15]
	Hyperion II 13[7] 5'24 Janet Baker

← *Gruppe aus dem Tartarus* D396   *Der Entfernten* D350 (first setting) →

Der FLUG DER ZEIT   The flight of time

(Széchényi) Op. 7 no. 2, **D515** [H332]

A major   1817?

(67 bars)

Es floh die Zeit im Wirbelfluge	Time flew past like a whirlwind,
Und trug des Lebens Plan mit sich.	And bore with it the plan of life.
Wohl stürmisch war es auf dem Zuge,	It was stormy on the journey;
Beschwerlich oft und widerlich.	Often arduous and unpleasant.
So ging es fort durch alle Zonen,	Thus it went through each age,
Durch Kinderjahre, durch Jugendglück,	Through childhood years and youthful happiness;
Durch Täler, wo die Freuden wohnen,	Through valleys wherein joys dwell,
Die sinnend sucht der Sehnsucht Blick.	Sought by longing's reflective gaze.
Bis an der Freundschaft lichtem Hügel	Until, flying more gently and calmly,
Die Zeit nun sanfter, stiller flog,	Time came to the shining hill of friendship,
Und endlich da die raschen Flügel	And there at last folded its fleet wings
In süsser Ruh' zusammenbog.	In sweet repose.

Ludwig von Széchényi (1781–1855)

This is the second of Schubert's two Széchényi solo settings (1817?). See the poet's biography for a chronological list of the Széchényi settings.

Schubert, master of water music, sees the passing of time (in this song at least) as so much water under the bridge. This setting is cast as a brisk barcarolle, though far less ornate than *Auf dem Wasser zu singen* D774 which is also a depiction of time on the move. The softly bouncing rhythm of *Der Flug der Zeit* is too gentle for the force and drama of the first part of Széchényi's text (there is no whirlwind here, one has to go to *Rastlose Liebe* D138 for that) but the music is suited to the sweetness of friendship's power lauded at the end. It is interesting that the most majestic of Schubert's songs about the passage of time, the very different *An Schwager Kronos*

D369, was also cast in $\frac{6}{8}$ rhythm. There was something about compound time used in this way which seems to have suggested to the composer inexorable pre-ordained movement – the swing of the pendulum, the tick of the clock, as well as the movement of sure-footed horses whipped into a gallop by Time, the old coachman. And then one remembers that the immortal *Auf dem Wasser zu singen* itself is also cast in the $\frac{6}{8}$ of a barcarolle.

Another completely different song that comes to mind is *Der Strom* D565; the tortured and restless harmonic changes of that work describe life's downstream journey in coruscating detail. In the far more detached *Der Flug der Zeit*, harmonic changes are kept to a minimum, resulting in a generalized panorama filled in with blocks of relatively unadventurous harmony. The song is in three strophes, a kind of ABA structure, except that A is much modified the second time around. The four-bar prelude also serves as a postlude. The opening four bars of the vocal line (bb. 4–7) are built around an arpeggio in the home key; this shifts into A minor and thence to E major (a very decisive cadence at bb. 10–12). There is an extended switch into C major (from 'Wohl stürmisch war es auf dem Zuge', bb. 13–20). This phrase includes a mild and kindly setting of the rather unpleasant word 'widerlich' (bb. 18–19). The B section ('So ging es fort', from b. 20) is an extended transition, a condensed life story: a chronicle of the childhood years is unfolded more or less on an E pedal (bb. 21–8), the later stages on an F sharp pedal (bb. 29–36). This leads to the recapitulation of the opening music, this time marked 'Etwas langsamer'. The image of 'sweet repose' is illustrated by the harmony slipping gently into A major in second inversion (bb. 51–2, and again bb. 59–60).

The song is unpretentiously simple – too simple perhaps. One cannot help feeling that Schubert was concerned to write music that would appeal to the rather conservative tastes of the poet and dedicatee, the influential Count Széchényi. It seems extraordinary that the two Széchéyni settings (this, and *Die abgeblühte Linde* D514, admittedly a more original song) should have been hurried into print in 1821 alongside other opus numbers crammed with real masterpieces. This alone suggests that there was an element of musical politics in the composer's decision to set this poetry in the way that he did. It would be some years before Schubert wrote another barcarolle, *Das Fischermädchen* from *Schwanengesang*, that has a similar introduction, rooted in the tonic key, and with a melody which suggests folksong. This Heine setting (where the composer used many of the same melodic and harmonic tools as in *Der Flug der Zeit*) has enchanted thousands of listeners. Eleven years' experience, and a greater poem, made all the difference in the world.

Autograph:	Missing or lost
First edition:	Published as Op. 7 no. 2 by Cappi & Diabelli in November 1821 (P19)
Dedicatee:	Ludwig Szézchényi von Sarvári-Felsö-Vidék
Publication reviews:	*Allgemeine musikalische Zeitung* (Vienna), No. 6 (19 January 1822), col. 43ff. [Waidelich/Hilmar Dokumente I No. 142; Deutsch Doc. Biog. No. 270]
Subsequent editions:	Peters: Vol. 4/10; AGA XX 301: Vol. 5/33; NSA IV: Vol. 1/63; Bärenreiter: Vol. 1/52
Bibliography:	Capell 1928, p. 143
Discography and timing:	Fischer-Dieskau I 9[18] 2'28
	Hyperion I 21[6]
	Hyperion II 17[10] 2'15 Edith Mathis

← *Die abgeblühte Linde* D514   *Frohsinn* D520 →

Der FLUSS

The river

(F. VON SCHLEGEL) **D693** [H448]

B major   March 1820

(35 bars)

Wie rein Gesang sich windet	Just as pure song winds its way
Durch wunderbarer Saitenspiele Rauschen,	Through the wondrous intoxicating music of the strings,
Er selbst sich wieder findet,	So does the river find itself;
Wie auch die Weisen tauschen,	And as the melodies change,
Dass neu entzückt die Hörer ewig lauschen.	Those who listen will for ever by captivated anew.
So fliesset mir gediegen	So flows, steadfast,
Die Silbermasse, schlangengleich gewunden,	The silver band, twisting snake-like
Durch Büsche, die sich wiegen,	Through swaying bushes,
Vom Zauber süss gebunden,	Sweetly spellbound
Weil sie im Spiegel neu sich selbst gefunden.	Because they have found themselves anew in the mirror.
Wo Hügel sich so gerne	Where hills and bright clouds
Und helle Wolken leise schwankend zeigen,	Gladly reveal themselves, gently rolling,
Wenn fern schon matte Sterne	When in the distance faint stars
Aus blauer Tiefe steigen,	Already rise from the blue depths
Der Sonne trunkne Augen abwärts neigen.	And the sun's drunken eyes sink downwards.
So schimmern alle Wesen	So all things shimmer
Den Umriss nach im kindlichen Gemüte,	In outline in the childlike mind
Das, zur Schönheit erlesen,	Which, chosen for beauty
Durch milder Götter Güte,	By the goodness of the kindly gods,
In dem Krystall bewahrt die flücht'ge Blüte.	Preserves the fleeting blossom in the crystal waters.

FRIEDRICH VON SCHLEGEL (1772–1829); poem written in 1800/01

This is the eleventh of Schubert's sixteen Friedrich von Schlegel solo settings (1818–25). See the poet's biography for a chronological list of all the Friedrich von Schlegel settings. See also the article about the cycle of which this song is part – Abendröte.

Admirers of the Mayrhofer setting from 1817, *Am Strome* D539, here find another *bel canto* aria in B major, no less beautiful and, arguably, more ambitious in terms of its expressive and philo-sophical range. Schlegel's image of 'rein Gesang', pure song, free of intellectual adornment, is here identified with the Italian aria style. We remember that the naive musical exercises of Schubert's student years were for Antonio Salieri, and all in the Italian language. He must often have been told by the old master that the Italian style was the most natural and comfortable for the voice, that German music was too intellectual. Schubert wrote for at least one great Italian singer, Luigi Lablache, and he understood that the mindset of opera stars from the south was utterly different from that of German artists. This river, which Schubert casts in the role of an Italian singer, is 'chosen for beauty' by the 'kindly gods', but confesses to a 'childlike mind'. Perhaps Schubert found Italian singers similarly childlike, but he prized them for their stream of beautiful tone nevertheless.

The long-lined cantilena may seem *bel canto* pastiche on the page, but it is the purest Schubert: no self-indulgent sobs of emotion are permitted, no swooning rubato and not even one *furtiva lagrima*. The left-hand accompaniment is an unending flow of undulating quaver triplets in ⅛ in the future manner of Chopin's *Barcarolle*. There is sensuality in this *Bewegung*, as well as a hint of indolence. The music has a passive quality throughout, as if the river simply awaits the imprint of outside images: the clouds, the stars and the sun understand themselves better when they see themselves mirrored in the glassy surface. The sweet vulnerability of the river's open-hearted nature is heard in the music, the 'childlike mind' ready to receive whatever comes its way. Of course there is a veiled eroticism in this receptiveness, and in this regard the key of B major, always a special Schubertian tonality, brings *Suleika I* (D720) to mind. There are also parallels with another B major song, *Nacht und Träume* D827; the idea of moonlight floating through space can be equated with the river winding through the landscape. The silent hearts of men in *Nacht und Träume* who listen with delight ('Die belauschen sie mit Lust') have their equivalent in *Der Fluss* in the singer's captivated audience, and the viewers spellbound by their watery reflections ('die Hörer ewig lauschen' as Schlegel's first strophe has it).

The curve of the vocal line shadows the words, winding through the stave. The murmuring of the wondrous strings ('wunderbarer Saitenspiele Rauschen') is given to a tiny oscillating figure in semiquavers in the right-hand accompaniment (first heard at b. 5) that continues gently to vibrate throughout the first verse. An absolutely Schubertian touch is the setting of 'die Hörer ewig lauschen' (bb. 14–15) where an unexpected E sharp on 'Hörer' briefly lifts the vocal line above the piano's supporting chord to suggest a straining ear, the extra effort of deep listening.

The second of Schlegel's strophes is divided into sections for Schubert's purposes. Having painted an extensive musical metaphor in the first verse the composer now lets us hear the river itself, its flow depicted in both hands of the accompaniment, at first an octave, then a tenth apart (from b. 18). The chromaticism of this section depicts the 'twisting, snake-like' progress of the river; in the suddenly murky textures (with no more right-hand octaves to brighten the picture) we are briefly reminded of the triplet-accompanied passage in *Fahrt zum Hades* D526, and its description of the ancient river of Oblivion. This passing cloud is soon banished by the charm of Schubert's setting of the strophe's remaining four lines. The swaying of the bushes inspires dancing semiquavers in the accompaniment after 'die sich wiegen' (b. 25). The last line of the verse includes a descending passage for the voice (the repeat of 'neu sich selbst gefunden' bb. 30–31) which is matched by dotted crotchets simultaneously ascending in the piano. Mirror fashion, object and reflection meet each other at the end of this contrary-motion scale, the gathering point of the final cadence.

Schubert uses two of Schlegel's verses for one of his own. This river sings in a strophic fashion suitable to its simple temperament, but the new words perfectly fit the repeat of the music. The rustling string motif of the first verse now admirably conveys the gently rolling clouds ('helle Wolken leise schwankend') and the quavers under 'So schimmern alle Wesen' convey the idea of shimmer as the harmonies imperceptibly change beneath the words and add to them a chromatic glint. Because of its absence from the Peters Edition, *Der Fluss* probably has not received the number of performances it deserves, but even if it had been more easily available to singers its difficulties are obvious. It requires a highly placed voice with a superb technique and an ability to spin an endless line. These skills are given to many an opera singer, but to sing this song in an operatic manner (it is marked 'piano' and 'pianissimo' throughout) would be to misunderstand it completely. Like Schlegel's *Die Sterne*, it requires a rare blend of formidable *bel canto* technique with lieder-singing sensibility.

Autograph:	Wienbibliothek im Rathaus, Vienna (first 12 bars missing)
First edition:	Published as No. 27 of *Neueste Folge nachgelassener Lieder und Gesänge* by J. P. Gotthard, Vienna in 1872 (P453)
Subsequent editions:	Not in Peters; AGA XX 375: Vol. 6/91; NSA IV: Vol. 12/162
Bibliography:	Capell 1928, p. 165
	Fischer-Dieskau 1977, pp. 199–200
Discography and timing:	Fischer-Dieskau II 3^{17} 4'38
	Hyperion I 27^{11}
	Hyperion II 23^{6} 4'50 Matthias Goerne

← *Die Vögel* D691   *Der Knabe* D692 →

Die FORELLE   The trout
(SCHUBART) OP. 32, **D550** [H391]

The song exists in five versions, the fourth and fifth of which are discussed below:
(1) Early 1817?; (2) Early 1817?; (3) 21 February 1818; (4) Appeared 9 December 1820;
(5) October 1821

(1)	'Mässig'	D♭ major	$\frac{2}{4}$	[53 bars]
(2)	'Nicht zu geschwind'	D♭ major	$\frac{2}{4}$	[53 bars]
(3)	'Etwas geschwind'	D♭ major	$\frac{2}{4}$	[53 bars]

(4)   D♭ major

(5)   D♭ major

In einem Bächlein helle	In a limpid brook
Da schoss in froher Eil'	The capricious trout
Die launische Forelle	In joyous haste
Vorüber wie ein Pfeil.	Darted by like an arrow.
Ich stand an dem Gestade	I stood on the bank
Und sah in süsser Ruh'	In blissful peace, watching
Des muntern Fischleins Bade	The lively fish swim
Im klaren Bächlein zu.	In the clear brook.
Ein Fischer mit der Rute	An angler with his rod
Wohl an dem Ufer stand,	Stood on the bank
Und sah's mit kaltem Blute,	Cold-bloodedly watching
Wie sich das Fischlein wand.	The fish's contortions.
So lang dem Wasser Helle,	As long as the water
So dacht' ich, nicht gebricht,	Is clear, I thought,
So fängt er die Forelle	He won't catch the trout
Mit seiner Angel nicht.	With his rod.
Doch endlich ward dem Diebe	But at length the thief
Die Zeit zu lang. Er macht	Grew impatient. Cunningly
Das Bächlein tückisch trübe,	He made the brook cloudy,
Und eh ich es gedacht,	And in an instant
So zuckte seine Rute,	His rod quivered,
Das Fischlein zappelt dran,	And the fish struggled on it.
Und ich mit regem Blute	And I, my blood boiling,
Sah die Betrogne an.	Looked on at the cheated creature.

[(. . .)]   [(. . .)]

CHRISTIAN FRIEDRICH SCHUBART (1739–1791); poem written in 1782

This is the third of Schubert's four Schubart solo settings (1816–17). See the poet's biography for a chronological list of all the Schubart settings.

This is certainly among the most celebrated of all Schubert's lieder; there are many songs (even well-known and much loved ones) that are far more profound and moving than *Die Forelle*, but it is easy to understand its pride of place in a list of Schubertian hits. There is a freshness, a zest, an innocence about this music which has hooked its listeners since the song was composed. It has the memorability of a folksong, a type of melodic inevitability that only the greatest tune-smiths can achieve; the piano writing adds a dash of sophistication and a touch of virtuosity. (This accompaniment is by no means easy to play in the original key of D flat major, but it is even more difficult in other tonalities, the medium-voice transpostion, B major, in particular.) Schubert in the guise of open-hearted country lad has always been especially irresistible, particularly to those who like their composers sunny and uncomplicated, and this song (despite its anachronistic flirtation with animal-rights concerns) neither offends nor challenges those who might be perplexed by the composer's deeper and darker sides.

It is just possible that someone else might have thought of the idea of the rippling arpeggio which accompanies the beginning of the vocal line (at 'In einem Bächlein helle', b. 1) and which depicts the flight of an arrow or the merry upward movement of the fish through an octave and

Vignette by F. Sorrieu for *La Truite*, French translation by Bélanger of *Die Forelle*, published by Charles Richault in Paris (*c.* 1840).

a half's stretch of water. It is inconceivable, however, that what follows could have been thought of by anyone other than Schubert. At 'Ich stand an dem Gestade' (b. 9) the pattern of the accompaniment changes: instead of a sextuplet built around the chords of D flat and A flat[7], the composer devises a little rush of notes, an ornamentation of the main motif, which contains at its centre four linked semitones – F, G flat, *G natural*, A flat. With this, the trout is brought to life at a stroke. The glint of adjacent semitones sparkles in the musical stream as the fish breaks the pattern of a normal arpeggio and, at the same time, the water's smooth surface. With this chromatic gleam we hear a visible ripple of sparkling white water. There is something about the sheer cheekiness of this motif which conveys utter delight – the joy in being free and full of energy. In conjunction with the marvellously memorable tune it energizes the listener, and sets the foot tapping and the eyes dancing, as if we are at one with that trout in the sheer pleasure of being alive. Those who know the outcome of the story might add, as so often with Schubert, 'Enjoy it while you can, it might not last long.'

The vocal line is in Schubert's best tradition of saluting the wonders of nature: here the composer seems to identify the movement of even quavers in $\frac{2}{4}$ with the effortless perfection of flora and fauna. Examples of this are the openings of *Heidenröslein* D257, and of the Schlegel settings *Der Schmetterling* D633 and *Der Knabe* D692, where butterfly and bird are given voice in measured quavers, and in the same carefree folksong mode. The melody is remarkably similar to the opening of *Blumenlied* (Hölty, D431), as well as *Die Erscheinung* D229, a Kosegarten song from 1815 which is also set at the water's edge. Leo Black has pointed out the similarity of this tune to the opening chorus of the opera *Fierabras* (Act 1 No. 1, at the words 'Der runde Silberfaden läuft sinnig durch die Hand') where the description of the silver threads of the princess at her spinning might also serve to describe the watery milieu of the trout.

Die Forelle is in modified strophic form which adds a dash of dramatic variety to the charm of the whole. Dirty work afoot at 'Er macht das Bächlein tückisch trübe' (bb. 29–31) is splendidly represented by triplets in the dark middle register of the piano, and the intrusion of muddy F flats into the clear waters of the major key. The astonishment and suspense of the onlooker is brilliantly displayed in a passage which slips into recitative without our even noticing the change ('Und eh' ich es gedacht' bb. 31–3). Note the splendid effect of the piano's staccato accompaniment in the bar of 'zuckte seine Rute' (b. 34); with this explosive consonant the fishing rod jerks its prey out of the water. The last convulsive movements of the fish are wonderfully painted by the vocal line at 'Das Fischlein zappelt dran' (bb. 35–8) with its repeat of 'das Fischlein' as if the trout's fate hangs in the balance before it is landed. This is the only moment in the song's accompaniment when we hear a succession of sixteen semiquavers (bb. 36–7): pulled out of its element, and thrashing around all a-quiver, the trout can no longer move within its former rhythm of graceful sextuplets.

The last verse can be rendered rueful or furious according to the singers' sympathies, but this should not be allowed to get out of hand (having expressed regret at the sight of an animal run over on a country road by a previous motorist, how many of us allow the pang of compassion to linger longer than a few seconds?) The postlude, which seems to recede and die away as if the observer were walking on, is almost as delicious as the meal which now awaits the fisherman. The species is clearly the native European brown trout (*Salmo trutta*) found in rivers and lakes, the 'Bachforelle' or 'Seeforelle' rather than the 'Meerforelle' – sea trout. The American rainbow trout was introduced into European rivers long after this time. Schubart's original intention with this poem was to warn girls against masculine wiles. The composer chose to ignore the poet's last verse which pointed out this very moral:

Die ihr am goldnen Quelle	You girls who tarry at the fountain
Der sichern Jugend weilt,	Of confident youth,
Denkt doch an die Forelle;	Just remember the trout:
Seht ihr Gefahr, so eilt!	If you see danger, escape quickly!
Meist fehlt ihr nur aus Mangel	Most of you err only because
Der Klugheit. Mädchen, seht	You're not shrewd enough. Look out, girls,
Verführer mit der Angel!	For seducers with their rods,
Sonst blutet ihr zu spät.	Or else you'll bleed too late!

According to the testament of Johann Leopold Ebner, when Schubert first played through *Die Forelle* to his Konvikt circle, Anton Holzapfel claimed to hear a similarity between a passage in the accompaniment and Beethoven's *Coriolan* overture. Perhaps he had in mind the accompanying figure in the cellos that begins in b. 52 of that work, but this is hardly plagiarism. Schubert wanted to destroy his composition then and there, but the composer's friends persuaded him otherwise. There are five versions of this song, none of them significantly different from the others in the main body of the song, but differing in terms of the introduction (or lack of it) and length of postlude. The first version probably dates from early 1817; its tempo marking is 'Mässig'. The piece was soon so popular that the composer was often obliged to make copies. The second version (also perhaps from 1817) is marked 'Nicht zu geschwind' and was written out for Franz Kandler's album. On one famous occasion in February 1818 Schubert, in an attempt to dry the manuscript of the third version (marked 'Etwas geschwind', a copy made at the request of Josef Hüttenbrenner) sprinkled ink on it, rather than sand. The fourth version was prepared for publication in the *Wiener Zeitschrift*; it is this version that is published as Op. 32 in the NSA, and from which the bar numbers quoted in this commentary are taken.

It is notable that none of these four autographs boasts an introduction. The final manuscript copy was prepared by the composer in 1821 with four introductory bars. This is the only authentic version of the prelude, but it is not the version that is well known. After its appearance in the *Wiener Zeitschrift*, the song was taken over by the firm of Diabelli in 1825; in 1827 it was given the opus number of 32. In 1829 Diabelli added another bar to the extant introduction of version five, and it was this that was published in Peters Volume 1, and subsequently played by thousands of pianists. In comparison to many of Diabelli's spurious introductions, this one has an acceptably authentic ring. It is, in any case, hallowed and time-honoured by countless performances; in the very first bar, authentic or not, we hear the crucial swimming motif in adjacent chromatic semitones in the right hand; one might argue this sets the scene for the trout rather better than the piano writing of the fifth version.

The song was given a new lease of life in 1819 when, at the behest of his patron, Silvester Paumgartner in Steyr, Schubert used it as the theme for variations in the fourth movement of the so-called 'Trout Quintet' D667 for piano, two violins, cello and double bass. In repeating the music 'by popular demand', and in another form, the composer seems to acknowledge with pleasure how well known his song had become. Brian Newbould also points out that with the composition of the quintet Schubert removed any sense of worry concerning whether or not he had successfully encompassed the purpose of Schubart's lyric: 'He left a curious enigma comfortably behind – with the discarded text.' The writer Franzpeter Goebels suggests that Schubert took the poem from another setting of Schubart's poem – that of Friedrich August Baumbach (1753–1813) that had appeared in Johann Peter Milchmayer's *Klavierschule*.

Autographs:	In private possession (second and fourth versions)
	Library of Congress, Washington, DC (fifth version, fair copy)
Publication:	First published as part of the AGA in 1895 (P676–678; first, second and third versions)
	First published as a supplement to the *Wiener Zeitschrift für Kunst, Literatur, Theater und Mode* in December 1820; subsequently issued by Diabelli, Vienna in January 1825, and designated Op. 32 in the third issue in 1827 (P74; fourth version)
	First published as part of the NSA in 1975 (P760; fifth version
Publication reviews:	*Abend-Zeitung* (Dresden), No. 26 (30 January 1821) [Waidelich/Hilmar Dokumente I No. 69; Deutsch Doc. Biog. No. 199]
First known performance:	13 January 1825 in a 'Grosses Vocal- und Instrumental-Concert' organized by Anna Milder, Königliches Schauspielhaus, Berlin. Soloist: Anna Milder (see Waidelich/Hilmar Dokumente I No. 302 for full concert programme)
Performance reviews:	*Königlich privilegirte Berlinische Zeitung* No. 15 (19 January 1825) [Waidelich/Hilmar Dokumente I No. 307]
	Allgemeine musikalische Zeitung (Leipzig), No. 7 (15 February 1825), col. 118 [Waidelich/Hilmar Dokumente I No. 316]
Subsequent editions:	Peters: Vol. 1/197; AGA XX 327a–d: Vol. 5/132 (first version), 135 (given as second version, recte third), 148 (given as third version, recte second) & 141 (fourth version); NSA IV: Vol. 2a/109 (fourth version) & Vol. 2b/194 (first version), 198 (second version), 202 (third version) & 206 (sixth version); Bärenreiter: Vol. 2/12
Bibliography:	Black 1998, p. 22
	Black 2003, p. 16
	Kohlhäufl 1999, p. 184

	Newbould 1997, p. 161		
	Shackleton, 2012		
Arrangements:	Arr. Franz Liszt (1811–86) for solo piano (1838) and for solo piano, no. 6 of *Sechs Melodien von Schubert* (second version, 1844)		
	Arr. Leopold Godowsky (1870–1938) for solo piano, *The Trout* (1927, second rev. edition, 1937) [*see* TRANSCRIPTIONS]		
	Arr. Benjamin Britten (1913–76) for voice, 2 clarinets and strings (1942)		
Discography and timing:	Fischer-Dieskau II 1[12]	2'02	
	Hyperion I 21[4]		
	Hyperion II 19[25]	2'15	Edith Mathis

⟵ *Lied eines Kindes* D596   *Der Kampf* D594 ⟶

FRIEDRICH HEINRICH DE LA MOTTE FOUQUÉ (1777–1843)

THE POETIC SOURCES

S1 *Der Zauberring, ein Ritterroman* von Friedrich Baron de la Motte Fouqué, Johann Leonhard Schrag, Nürnberg, 1812

S2 *Undine, eine Erzählung* von Friedrich Baron de la Motte Fouqué, Franz Haas'schen Buchhandlung, Wien 1814

S3 *Gedichte* von Friedr [*sic*] Baron de la Motte Fouqué, Neueste Auflage. Wien 1816–19. Bey B. Ph. Bauer, 3 Theile

S4 *Gedichte* von Friedrich Baron de la Motte Fouqué, Erster Band, *Gedichte aus dem Jünglings-alter*, in der J. G. Cotta'schen Buchhandlung, Stuttgart und Tübingen, 1816

S5 *Gedichte* von Friedrich Baron de la Motte Fouqué, Zweiter Band, *Gedichte aus dem Manns-alter*, in der J. G. Cotta'schen Buchhandlung, Stuttgart und Tübingen, 1817

THE SONGS

c. 1814	*Don Gayseros* D93
	I (Don Gayseros, Don Gayseros') D93/1 [S1: Chapter XIX, pp. 150–52]
	II ('Nächtens klang die süsse Laute') D93/2 [S1: Chapter XIX pp. 152–4]
	III ('An dem jungen Morgenhimmel') D93/3 [S1: Chapter XIX pp. 154–5]
15 January 1816?	*Lied (Mutter geht durch ihre Kammern)* D373 [S2: Chapter XI p. 97]
April 1817	*Der Schäfer und der Reiter* D517 [S3: Erster Theil (*Gedichte aus dem Jünglingsalter*), p. 77 with the title *Schäfer und Reiter*]
September 1824	*Gebet* D815 quartet SATB [S3: Zweiter Theil (*Gedichte aus dem Mannesalter*), p. 55 with the title *Gebeth 1809*]

Fouqué was born in Brandenberg an der Havel on 12 February 1777. He came from a rich Huguenot family that was originally from Normandy. His family was military, and the poet began as a soldier, serving with distinction in the Napoleonic wars and achieving high military rank. The most financially successful work of de la Motte Fouqué's career, the novel entitled *Der Zauberring* – 'The Magic Ring' was published in 1812 and became an

Friedrich Baron de la Motte Fouqué after a painting by
Wilhelm Hensel.

immediate best-seller. Perhaps Schubert was lent a copy of it by his schoolfriend Josef von Spaun. As happens so often in picaresque novels, various characters are called upon to tell stories from their native lands. Don Hernandez who is 'a man of very tall stature, with a dark sunburnt visage' (thus in the novel's English translation of 1825) is requested to tell a tale from his own 'wonderful and romantic country, especially something of the long and fearful conflicts between the Christians and Moors'. The theme of the work is reconciliation between these warring religions, a subject that was to re-emerge in Schubert's work in

1823 in the opera *Fierabras*. It is notable that Fouqué's play *Eginhard und Emma* was one of Josef Kupelwieser's sources when he came to fashion the libretto for the same Schubert opera, and Heinrich Heine was much later to model his famous poem *Donna Clara* on Fouqué's *Don Gayseros*. The Heine version gives the Christian versus Moor conflict another twist: at a suitably triumphant moment, the virtuous and good-looking hero reveals himself to the anti-semitic Donna Clara (who is much taken with his charm and looks) as the son of the Rabbi Israel of Zaragoza.

Fouqué came into the orbit of August Schlegel whose translations of Calderón led the younger man to an interest in Spain and its history. In his turn, Fouqué encouraged Kleist and Eichendorff in their work. His fairy-tale romance *Undine* inspired E. T. A. Hoffmann, Ravel's famous piano piece (via Aloysius Bertrand), Giradoux in his play *Ondine* in 1939, and Henze and Ashton in their ballet of 1958. Fouqué's dramatic trilogy *Der Held des Nordens* was an important inspiration to Wagner in the fashioning of *Der Ring des Nibelungen*. The earlier part of Fouqué's career was far more successful than the later. By the middle of the nineteenth century he seemed merely a remote, out-of-touch aristocrat with a mannered style that veered between medievalism and romanticism. It is only since the publication of Arno Schmidt's biography (1958) that the idea of Fouqué as an essential figure in German Romantic literature has re-emerged. For his ability to spin yarns built upon myth and shot through with a philisophical significance, he has been seen by more recent critics as a forerunner of J. R. R. Tolkien. The poet died in Berlin on 23 January 1843 shortly after having been invited to live there as a pensioned and honoured guest by King Friedrich Wilhelm IV.

Das FRÄULEIN IM THURME *see* ROMANZE D114

Das FRÄULEIN VOM SEE *see SIEBEN GESÄNGE AUS WALTER SCOTTS FRÄULEIN VOM SEE* D835–9, D843, D846

Des FRÄULEINS LIEBESLAUSCHEN   The young lady's serenade

(SCHLECHTA) **D698** [H452]

A major   September 1820

(137 bars)

Hier unten steht ein Ritter[1]
　Im hellen Mondenstrahl,
Und singt zu seiner Zither
　Ein Lied von süsser Qual:

'Lüfte, spannt die blauen Schwingen
　Sanft für meine Botschaft aus,
Rufet sie mit leisem Klingen
　An dies Fensterlein heraus.

'Sagt ihr, dass im Blätterdache
　Seufz' ein wohlbekannter Laut,
Sagt ihr, dass noch Einer wache,
　Und die Nacht sei kühl und traut.

'Sagt ihr, wie des Mondes Welle
　Sich an ihrem Fenster bricht,
Sagt ihr, wie der Wald, die Quelle
　Heimlich und von Liebe spricht!

'Lass ihn leuchten durch die Bäume,
　Deines Bildes süssen Schein,
Das sich hold in meine Träume
　Und mein Wachen webet ein.'

Doch drang die zarte Weise
　Wohl nicht zu Liebchens Ohr,
Der Sänger schwang sich leise
　Zum Fensterlein empor.

Und oben zog der Ritter
　Ein Kränzchen aus der Brust;

A knight stands down below
　In the bright moonlight,
And sings to his zither
　A song of sweet suffering:

'Breezes, gently spread your blue wings
　And bear my message;
With soft strains call her
　To this window.

'Tell her that beneath the canopy of leaves
　A familiar voice is sighing;
Tell her that someone is still awake,
　And that the night is cool and intimate.

'Tell her how the wave of moonlight
　Breaks upon her window;
Tell her how the grove and the fountain
　Speak secretly of love.

'Let the sweet light of your image
　Shine through the trees,
Your image which is gently woven
　Into my dreams and my waking hours.'

But the tender melody could not have reached
　His sweetheart's ear,
For the singer swung himself softly
　Up to her window.

And once up there the knight
　Drew a garland from his breast

[1] For passages of alternative text in this song, see NSA IV Volume 12, pp. 174–9. This version of the poem beginning 'Da unten steht ein Ritter / Im weissen Mondenschein' ('A knight stands down below / In the white moonlight') is taken by the editor of the NSA to be more authentic than the version printed above, and recorded on Hyperion long before the publication of NSA Volume 12.

Das band er fest am Gitter
  Und seufzte: 'Blüht in Lust!'

                                    And bound it fast to the grille,
                                      Sighing 'Bloom in joy.'

'Und fragt sie, wer euch brachte,
  Dann, Blumen, tut ihr kund.'
Ein Stimmchen unten lachte:
  'Dein Ritter Liebemund.'

                                    'And if she asks who brought you,
                                      Then, flowers, tell her.'
                                    A voice below laughed:
                                      'Your knight, Liebemund!'

FRANZ XAVIER VON SCHLECHTA (1796–1875)

This is the third of Schubert's six Schlechta solo settings (1815–26). See the poet's biography for a chronological list of all the Schlechta settings.

For over a hundred years this song has been known simply as *Liebeslauschen*. It was first published under this title by Diabelli in 1832, and so it remained in the Peters Edition where it was sung from time to time by the more enthusiastic Schubertian tenors. Schubert's original title was *Des Fräuleins Liebeslauschen* and for good reason – it is the Fräulein, believe it or not, who is the one in control for the duration of the song. To understand this we have to look into the work's provenance and, as with every song with a Schlechta text (the poet was a constant reviser of his work, not always for the best), the background is rather complicated.

Schnorr von Carolsfeld (1788–1853) was an artist who stood on the periphery of the Schubert circle; he may have attended Schubertiads. He was a close friend of Friedrich von Schlegel and was celebrated for his genre painting. Schnorr was the teacher of Schubert's artist friend, Moritz von Schwind, and was also the dedicatee of the Op. 37 songs. In early 1820, before Schubert knew Schwind, an oil painting by Schnorr entitled 'Des ritterlichen Jägers Liebeslauschen' was exhibited at the Akademie der vereinigten bildenden Künste in Vienna; this institution shared a building in the Annagasse with the Normalhauptschule where Ferdinand Schubert taught.

The work (to be found on p. 192 of Deutsch's iconographical volume) depicts a scene dominated by a large tree that grows next to a building of Gothic design. Through one of the building's windows we can see into a gently lit bedroom where a young woman is seated writing a letter; she is deep in concentration and supports her head in her left hand. In the foreground of the picture, concealed in the branches, is a young man in a tunic with a hunting horn slung over his shoulder. Viewers of the picture see the scene from his vantage point of an upper branch as, clasping the trunk of the tree, he twists his head round at an awkward angle in order to look into his lady's chamber. This act of peeping or spying,

Des ritterlichen Jägers Liebeslauschen, oil painting by Schnorr von Carolsfeld, burnt in 1931.

ungallant at best, and a felony at worst, is made to appear charming in Schnorr's picture; we are reminded of the young miller standing importunately at his beloved's window in *Morgengruss* D795/8.

Inspired by the painting, Franz von Schlechta wrote a poem (beginning, in its final version at least, 'Das Fräulein schreibt noch munter') that turns Schnorr's scenario into a lyric. Schlechta has the young lady write a letter which she folds, ready for dispatch; she sighs that she does not know who will deliver it to her beloved. Like the sounds of a gentle flute come the words, 'Trust the message to me, o beautiful one, I will be your messenger.' He will go to no end of trouble, he whispers to himself, to find the right recipient. It is by no means certain that the hunter reveals himself to his beloved at this point; one might have imagined he would jump into the bedchamber, Errol Flynn-like, to present his compliments in person, but this would be to transgress the rules of courtly love. It is more likely that he shins down the tree having gained a great deal of vicarious pleasure.

We have no idea whether this poem was an accurate reflection of Schnorr's own scenario, but it is very probable that poet and painter discussed the work at some point. Schlechta now decided to write a pendant to his own poem giving the maiden a chance to have *her* say. The poet seems to have realized that the practice of climbing trees to look into bedroom windows was worthy of reproof, however gentle. In this scenario (the one set to music by Schubert) it is the lady who pulls the strings (although we only discover this right at the end of the poem). The title *Des Fräuleins Liebeslauschen* (which has been restored and adopted by the NSA, and should now be used for performances of this song) makes this clear. Here, the same knight sings a serenade to his beloved, but there is no response to his musical offering because she is not in her bedroom, rather she is in the garden spying on *him*. He has climbed up the tree outside her window (as has been his wont) and attempts to fix a garland to her window, a precarious business. As he confides a fanciful message to the flowers, instructing them to tell the beloved his own name, he has no idea that he is being watched and overheard in the same way as he himself did the watching and overhearing in Schnorr's first picture, and Schlechta's first poem. A voice from below, that of his beloved, pipes up with the missing information in a gently mocking tone: 'Your Knight, Liebemund.' The name might be translated as 'Sugar mouth' or 'Lover-in-Words'. This particular young man has been all talk and no action, and his habit of spying on the lady and sending her exquisite love messages and flowers has been unveiled. Fortunately he is good-looking, well-born and presumably not the voyeur he would be deemed in a later age. We can only assume

Des Fräuleins Liebeslauschen, lithograph by Schnorr von Carolsfeld

that unless he flees the scene in disarray there is a happy ending to the story, with the young lady in question holding the upper hand in a relationship where fantasy has turned into reality.

Having written the second poem Schlechta arranged to have both poems published as a pair in the 1821 edition of *Conversationsblatt – Zeitschrift für wissenschaftliche Unterhaltung*. The editor of this journal, Franz Gräffer (1785–1852), himself destined to become a Schubert poet in 1825 (of the part-song *Trinklied aus dem 16. Jahrhundert* D847), had the happy idea of uniting poetry and art by commissioning Schnorr to make a lithograph that illustrated Schlechta's *second* poem. The order of inspiration, therefore, was first a painting – then a poem – then a second poem followed by a second illustration, this time a lithograph – and only then, music by Schubert. It is not impossible that Gräffer also commissioned Schubert's musical response (perhaps urged by Schlechta to do so) but if this was the case, the idea came to nothing, at least in terms of the *Conversationsblatt*. But Schnorr's lithograph *Des Fräuleins Liebeslauschen* did appear. It shows the same tree and the same window but a different view of the knight – this time more side than back – as he attempts to fix his floral wreath to the grille covering the windowpane. Strapped to his belt is a lute. At the bottom of the tree (possibly poised on some of its lower branches – it is difficult to tell) stand two women, one younger than the other. The younger beloved looks slightly alarmed and flustered, her abundant hair in disarray, an erotic hint that she is in a state of déshabillé. Schnorr has added a wimple-wearing chambermaid or confidante to underline the essential repectability of the scene. This picture is to be found in Volume 12 p. XXVII of the song series of the NSA. For some reason it was not published in Deutsch's volume of 1913 (only Schnorr's first painting is to be found there) and this has been a source of confusion ever since.

When it came to publishing his *Dichtungen* in 1824 Schlechta published both serenades under the general title *Liebeslauschen*: the first was headed *Ritter* (Knight), the second *Fräulein* (Maiden). In 1832, after Schubert's death, the publisher Diabelli initially planned to reproduce Schnorr's lithograph so that the possessor of the music would be able to see a story illustrated in word, picture and tone. According to Hilmar, planning for this conjunction of creativities was advanced enough to allow for extra space for the lithograph in the music's pagination, but for some reason it never came about. The poet, a real fusspot when it came to his own work, had no doubt exasperated Diabelli enough; he made the publishing history of the song impossibly difficult by insisting on changing the underlay of his own text for this posthumous publication (thus the two lines of slightly different text in the NSA, the first following Schubert's manuscript, the second, in italics, taking into account what are probably Schlechta's own changes to the manuscript). It is this second version (beginning 'Hier unten steht ein Ritter') that was printed in the Peters Edition, and has been sung by generations of singers. When Schlechta's poems were reprinted in *Ephemeren* in 1876, the text is changed yet again, not improving it to any degree. The lack of the correct illustration – the appearance in 1913 of the first (rather than the second) painting in Deutsch's sumptuous volume of pictures was a red herring – and the change of title to the more simple *Liebeslauschen*, were both unhelpful when it came to explaining what was happening in the text.

Certain songs rely almost entirely on their melodies to carry them through: tune is more important than psychological commentary. *Des Fräuleins Liebeslauschen* is just such a song, not a lied in the usual Schubertian sense, but a picture of a song – or more exactly a song of a picture. Schnorr's picture is set in romanticized Gothic times and here is an ideal picture-book serenade. The music, in Schubert's most expansive and leisurely vein, looks forward to the *Ständchen* of *Schwanengesang*, especially in the use of piano interludes (bb. 36–9 and bb. 72–5) which echo the vocal line. As always the piece is alive with illustrative touches: the wafting movement of the music from b. 21 seems to blow the vocal line this way and that in the most gentle of breezes. In b. 29 the distance between the serenader and his beloved is depicted in the emphasis of octave jumps in the voice, both downwards and upwards. The change into A minor from b. 42 is sweetly affecting. Sometimes one senses that words are being made to fit the tune: the dotted crotchets on 'wie' and 'auf' in bb. 58 and 61 are far from ideal, and it takes a clever performance to make the emphasized 'und' in b. 70 convincing; in bb. 61–3 the original phrase 'ihr Fenster streut sein Licht' is clearly superior to the amended 'an ihrem Fenster bricht'. When sung with Schlechta's revised text 'ihrem' awkwardly takes up an entire bar and the dotted rhythm of b. 63 is clearly more illustrative of the joyous verb in 'streut sein Licht', as opposed to 'Fenster bricht'. (At times like this one wishes to shake Schlechta for his scant awareness of Schubert's musical intentions.) The ghost of Mozart's Pedrillo (from *Die Entführung aus dem Serail*) emerges in the § 'Allegretto' section from b. 96 (verses 6 and 7 of the text).

The last couplet has always been a puzzle. In the absence of the correct picture it has been all but impossible to identify who is speaking beneath the tree-climber. In earlier years I even fancied that it was the flowers themselves who speak, as in other Schubert songs (*Der Blumen Schmerz* D731 for example). But it is the girl depicted in the painting who supplies an ironic name for her serenader. Schubert makes her lisp this 'Ritter Liebemund' in the manner of a talking flowerlet (the music becomes extremely feminine and flirtatious at b. 120 with bell-like pianistic oscillations that look forward to the accompaniment of the second *Suleika* song). The postlude contains music of delicious whimsy, and new melodies even at this late stage, with a delight in the delicacy of the smallness of voice and bloom which makes one think of Wolf's *Auch kleine Dinge* in the same key. It is not impossible also to imagine in this music and its final, wilting cadence, the shamefaced reaction of the knight who must now climb down from his high tree and renounce his boyish pranks in favour of pastimes rather more to a lady's liking.

Autograph:	Wienbibliothek im Rathaus, Vienna (fair copy)
First edition:	Published as Book 15 no. 2 of the *Nachlass* by Diabelli, Vienna in 1832 (P281)
Subsequent editions:	Peters: Vol. 3/151; AGA XX 381: Vol. 6/113; NSA IV: Vol. 12/174
Bibliography:	Capell 1928, p. 168
	Orel 1930
Discography and timing:	Fischer-Dieskau II 4[1] 3'51
	Hyperion I 4[14]
	Hyperion II 23[10] 4'52 Philip Langridge

← *Namenstagslied* D695   *Der entsühnte Orest* D699 →

FRAGMENT AUS DEM AESCHYLUS   Fragment from Aeschylus
(Mayrhofer after Aeschylus) **D450** [H280]

The song exists in two versions, the second of which is discussed below:
(1) June 1816; (2) June 1816

(1) 'Mässig'   A♭ major   ¢   [52 bars]

(2) A♭ major

So wird der Mann, der son-der Zwang ge-recht ist,

(52 bars)

So wird der Mann, der sonder Zwang gerecht ist,	Thus the man who is by nature just
Nicht unglücklich sein,	Will not be unhappy;
Versinken ganz in Elend kann er nimmer;	He can never sink completely into misery.
Indess der frevelnde Verbrecher	Whereas in the river of time
Im Strome der Zeit gewaltsam untergeht,	The wicked criminal
Wenn am zerschmetterten Maste	Is swept under violently when the storm tears the sails
Das Wetter die Segel ergreift.	From the shattered mast.
Er ruft, von keinem Ohr vernommen,	He cries out, but no ear hears him;
Kämpft in des Strudels Mitte, hoffnungslos.	He struggles hopelessly in the midst of the maelstrom.
Des Frevlers lacht die Gottheit nun,	Now the gods mock the evildoer,
Sieht ihn, nun nicht mehr stolz,	And behold him, no longer proud,
In Banden der Not verstrickt,	Enmeshed in the toils of distress,
Umsonst die Felsbank fliehn;	Fleeing in vain the rocky reef;
An der Vergeltung Fels scheitert sein Glück,	On the cliffs of vengeance his fortune is wrecked,
Und unbeweint versinkt er.	And unmourned he sinks.

JOHANN MAYRHOFER (1787–1836)

This is the third of Schubert's forty-seven Mayrhofer solo settings (1814–24) and his only setting of a text after Aeschylus. See Mayrhofer's biography for a chronological list of all the Mayrhofer settings, and Aeschylus' biography for further information about the poet.

Aeschylus successfully introduced certain important reforms in the staging of his plays which incorporated the use of realism. The Greek public was apparently struck with terror at the entry of the Furies (a group of twelve actors in chorus) in the third of Aeschylus' *Oresteia* plays, *The Eumenides*. This song, in Johann Mayrhofer's translation, is a fragment of that choral passage (lines 540–55). Schubert casts the lines for solo voice, but the *Vorspiel* would be entirely believable as an introduction for a grand chorus and is certainly grand enough to prepare the singer Vogl's entrance in full Greek costume as it were. This, however, is neither particularly frightening nor atmospheric music, and the composer's forebearance gives the song a kind of courtroom impartiality – the impassiveness of 'the writing on the wall' – rather than seeming as a thunderbolt personally delivered by an angry Zeus.

The song as a whole is as uncompromising as its sentiments. Bb. 6–7 of the introduction, as well as the two-bar interlude (bb. 13–14) have a certain punctiliousness about them, as if misdeeds were being recorded in some giant musical ledger. The opening recitative allows no time to smile upon the man who has lived his life well; instead we pursue the 'wicked criminal' through the storm of retribution. Some of Mayrhofer's own poems, later set by Schubert, use similar water imagery, either for sailing against the tide of life (*Der Schiffer* D536) or being borne along on a watery path to death – surrounded by Austrian scenery (*Auf der Donau* D553) or with mythological backdrop (*Fahrt zum Hades* D526). The words 'Er ruft, von keinem Ohr vernommen' (bb. 19–23) sound desperate enough as cries for help when accompanied by churning staccato triplets; but their repeat (at bb. 27–31) prompts a passage reminiscent of the terrified boy in *Erlkönig*, with similar seventh and ninth clashes between the voice, and an accompaniment pulsating with harsh and merciless triplets. In this music the gods seem to be laughing at the man's plight, and poet and composer take no small part in the grim glee. The great striding left-hand basses with off-beat quavers in the right (bb. 38–44) are straight out of Gluck, and deliver a death sentence as if pronounced by the 'divinités du Styx'. The villain who has once been so proud is utterly humbled. The words 'scheitert sein Glück' (bb. 48–9) are echoed in the piano's tumbling bass line in a way that betokens the depths of his reversal of fortune. A vocal arpeggio, harmonized first in A flat major, then in A flat minor, pronounces him 'unbeweint'. It is rare to find anything as vindictive as *Schadenfreude* in Schubert's songs, but here the composer's natural compassion for life's losers is scarcely evident, for the very reason that these people are usually 'gainers' in the short term and feather their nests at everyone else's expense. The final vocal cadence ('versinkt er') sinks to the bottom of the stave, but inconclusively ends on the major third of the scale. This allows the piano to add two miniature cadences that sound like dying gasps (there is only one of these in the song's first version): the punished man goes under only at the very last chord of the song. That this is in the major key is an indication of a just punishment – a terrible end for the criminal is a blessing for society. What sort of public enemy did Mayrhofer have in mind for such retribution? Whom did he wish to be brought low by divine justice? Could the poet have meant that modern oligarch, his employer and the nation's tormentor, Prince Clemens Metternich – or perhaps, the notorious Austrian chief of police, Josef, Count Sedlnitsky?

The song dates from exactly the same time as *Prometheus* (D451), not the Goethe song, but Schubert's first paid commission, a cantata for voices and orchestra in honour of Heinrich Josef Watteroth, and a work sadly lost to posterity. Was it the classical subject of this work that led Schubert to compose *Fragment aus dem Aeschylus*, his first song on a classical setting? The song (published in two slightly different versions in the NSA) had an exceptionally rich performing history in the composer's own time, especially considering the work was not published until after his death. Apart from the many occasions when it was performed informally within the composer's circle, it was sung at the home of the actress Sophie Müller (in March 1825); and at a Schubertiad at the home of Josef von Spaun (21 April 1827). On both these occasions Johann Michael Vogl was the singer, Schubert himself the pianist.

Although he studied Greek at school, it is doubtful whether Mayrhofer was sufficiently versed in ancient Greek to make his own version of this Aeschyclus poem from scratch – he needed a model. This he undoubtedly found in Friedrich Stolberg's *Vier Tragödien des Aeschylos*, published in Hamburg bei Friedrich Perthes in 1802 with line drawings after Flaxman. (A diary entry of Franz von Hartman from December 1826 informs us that Schober, Schwind and Bauernfeld viewed these Flaxman illustrations with delight.) In the section of the book devoted to *Die Eumeniden* this chorus fragment is printed in a separate paragraph on p. 268. It is significant that *Fragment aus dem Aeschylus* was not published among Mayrhofer's works in 1824, and neither does it appear in the posthumous edition of 1843. The Stolberg translation is printed below; the similarities between this and Mayrhofer's version (marked in italics) are unlikely to have been coincidental:

> Wer sonder *Zwang*
> *Der Gerechtigkeit pflegt,*
> *Unglücklich* wird der *nicht sein,*
> Versinken im Wehe nicht der!
> Ein kühner Uebertreter,
> Der gesezlos [sic] Recht und Unrecht vermischt,

Wird gewaltsam scheitern
Wenn *an zerschmettertem Maste*
Das Wetter die Segel ergreift!

Er ruft, die Götter hören ihn nicht;
Ihn sieht in unbändigem Strudel ein Gott,
Und lacht ob des vermessnen,
Nicht mehr trötzenden
Unauflösbar verstickten
Welcher der Klippe nicht entrann.
Er zerschellte selbst sein voriges Glück
An den Stein der *Vergeltung*!
Unbeweinet
Schwindet und nichtig er dahin!

Autographs:	Österreichische Nationalbibliothek, Vienna (first version) Conservatoire collection, Bibliothèque Nationale, Paris (second version)
Publication:	First published as part of the AGA in 1895 (P644; first version) First published as Book 14 no. 2 of the *Nachlass* by Diabelli, Vienna in January 1832 (P279; second version)
First known performance:	Following the two private performances listed above, the song's first public outing took place on 26 March 1828 at the Musikverein, Vienna as part of the Schubert 'Privatkonzert'. Soloist: Johann Michael Vogl
Performance reviews:	*Allgemeine musikalische Zeitung* (Leipzig) No. 19 (7 May 1828), col. 307f. [Waidelich/Hilmar Dokumente I No. 613; Deutsch Doc. Biog. No. 1067] *Abend-Zeitung* (Dresden), No. 141 (12 June 1828), p. 564 [Waidelich/Hilmar Dokumente I No. 620; Deutsch Doc. Biog. No. 1068] *Berliner allgemeine musikalische Zeitung* No. 27 (2 July 1828), p. 215 [Waidelich/Hilmar Dokumente I No. 624; Deutsch Doc. Biog. No. 1069]
Subsequent editions:	Peters: Vol. 5/78; AGA XX 236a & b: Vol. 4/128 (first version) & 131 (second version); NSA IV: Vol. 10/184 (first version) & 187 (second version)
Discography and timing:	Fischer-Dieskau I 7[24] 2'29 Hyperion I 14[8] 2'29 Thomas Hampson Hyperion II 15[7]

← *Gott der Weltschöpfer* D986   *Das war ich* D174a/450a →

FREIWILLIGES VERSINKEN

Voluntary oblivion

(Mayrhofer) **D700** [H454]

D minor   September 1820

(44 bars)

Wohin, o Helios? In kühlen Fluten[1]	Whither, o Helios? In cool waters
Will ich den Flammenleib versenken,	I will immerse my burning body,
Gewiss im Innern, neue Gluten	Inwardly certain that I can bestow
Der Erde feuerreich zu schenken.	New warmth upon the earth's fires.

Ich nehme nicht, ich pflege nur zu geben;[2]

Und wie verschwenderisch mein Leben,

Umhüllt mein Scheiden goldne Pracht,

Ich scheide herrlich, naht die Nacht.

I do not take; I am wont only to give.

As prodigal as my life,

My parting is bathed in golden splendour;

I depart in glory when night draws near.

Wie blass der Mond, wie matt die Sterne![3]

So lang ich kräftig mich bewege;

Erst wenn ich auf die Berge meine Krone lege,

How pale the moon, how faint the stars,

As long as I move on my powerful course;

Only when I lay down my crown upon the mountains

Gewinnen sie an Mut und Kraft in weiter Ferne.

Do they gain strength and courage in the far distance.

Johann Mayrhofer (1787–1836)

This is the thirty-ninth of Schubert's forty-seven Mayrhofer settings (1814–24). See the poet's biography for a chronological list of all the Mayrhofer settings.

Helios, the sun god, was the son of Hyperion and Thera, brother of Selene the moon goddess, and of Eos, goddess of the dawn. He is usually represented as a young man of great beauty with a mass of golden hair. Homer describes Helios as bringing light to both gods and men, and in Greek mythology he is quite distinct from the character of Apollo – although this separate identity became blurred during the Roman era. The representation of Apollo with rays around his head, to characterize him as identical with the sun is something that dates only from Virgil and the Roman Empire. With his starting point as Oceanus, the river that encircles the world, he climbs the heavens from the East in a chariot drawn by four horses, and reaches the highest point at noon. At eventide, with his journey done, the chariot descends in the West and the weary horses bathe and refresh themselves in a large golden bowl. Out of sight of mortals Helios

[1] The adjective 'kühlen' is Schubert's addition here, as is the word 'feuerreich' in line 4. For an explanation of the background to these alternative Mayrhofer readings see Editorial Note at the beginning of Johann Mayrhofer.
[2] Mayrhofer's original phrase is '*gewohnt* zu geben'.
[3] Schubert replaces Mayrhofer's 'bleich' with 'blass'. The phrase 'auf die Berge' is the composer's addition; and the word 'Kraft' in the poem's last line replaces the poet's 'Glanz' ('radiance').

Apollo rides across the sky, after C. F. Hartmann's *Apollo und die Horen [Horae] über Dresden* (1808).

is carried back to his starting point on Oceanus (in some versions of the story he sails around half the world in a golden boat). Ovid describes a magnificent palace in the East containing a throne occupied by the god and surrounded by the personifications of the different divisions of time; other writers describe a second palace in the West where his horses feed upon herbs growing in the islands of the blessed.

The majesty and scope of this great song is one of the miracles of the Schubert canon; because of its difficulty in performance, for the singer especially, it is also one of its best-kept secrets. Within forty-four bars of music, sunset and moonrise are depicted – this happens in many a lied of course, but never on such a gigantic scale. Einstein says that the song would 'probably be dated not 1820 but 1900 – if there had still existed in 1900 a German composer of such abandon and freedom as Schubert'. Fischer-Dieskau avers that Alban Berg had this song in mind when, in a radio interview in the 1930s, he defended the 'unvocal' leaps of atonal music by citing similar examples from past centuries. For all its modernity, *Freiwilliges Versinken* is hewn in the giant marble blocks of an antique civilization, even if, like the mighty temple of Karnak in Luxor, it defies chronology and, like Karnak, seems to have more to do with Moonman or Martian than ancient history.

The song starts with two bars of portentous trills embedded deep within mighty chords. These bars are repeated quietly as the singer, hushed with reverence, addresses the sun god. The repeat of 'Wohin?' (bb. 5–6) is Schubert's own. The word 'Helios' (b. 4) had dropped to a low A beneath the stave, and this second 'Wohin?' is a full tenth higher: as if answering this question at the same time as asking it, the trajectory of the sun's journey for the day can be traced between these two points on the stave. That semibreve 'Wohin?' ('Whither?'), a question thrown into the void of space, aches with mortal longing to understand the divine mysteries. (The listener is equally in awe of Schubert's ability to weave a cosmic spell in a handful of bars.)

The remainder of the poem is in inverted commas as Helios honours Mayrhofer with a reply to his question. This is one of the few occasions in Schubert's lieder where his music is sung by a deity, and the surrounding accompanimental panoply, and the strangeness of the articulation, simultaneously passionate and remote, would be worthy of the oracle at Delphi. In actual fact, the inverted commas are Mayrhofer himself, speaking in the role of Helios; the metaphor is that of the poet who, daily, must shine in public service and then die in a return to the darkness of oblivion where, undisturbed in his cramped room in the Wipplingerstrasse, he can nurture his desires and ideals. It is little wonder that this oblivion is voluntary; the poet's desire to escape from the singeing heat of life is equally evident in *Auflösung* D807.

Schubert's insertion of the adjective 'kühlen' (b. 8) subverts Mayrhofer's metre and rhyme scheme – a price worth paying when the cool balm of evening, immediately audible, is the ideal foil to the impassioned curiosity of the song's opening line. Schubert's Friedrich Schlegel style (especially as we hear it in the very recent song *Abendröte* D690) is evident in bb. 7–12, but there is an additional grandeur in this music that is reserved for evocations of antiquity. In order to put the sun to bed, trills and measured ornamentation (cf. the quasi-baroque dotted rhythms of the introduction to *Nachtstück* D672) invoke the spirit of Handel and the double-dotted baroque overture. The ghost of a Heine setting, not yet composed, *Der Doppelgänger* D957/13, is already present in the guise of a demisemiquaver shudder at 'Ich nehme nicht' (bb. 15–16) and, more significantly, at 'Wie blass der Mond' (bb. 28–9). This is an example of how Schubert's mind translated images into music: the pale moon is also the sun's ghostly double, its 'Doppelgänger', and an idea from 1820 rises again in the Schubertian firmament in 1828, not because Schubert is quoting himself, but because a similar poetic image calls it forth from his mind. A single rumbling trill in the bass under 'versenken' (b. 10) echoes the crumbling ruins of castles of *Auf der Donau* D553 (1817). When we hear similar trills in the first movement of the B flat Piano Sonata D960 (1828) we might be excused for identifying them as the shudders of abandoned hopes and dreams.

Schubert had made other songs about the setting sun (*An die untergehende Sonne* D457) where the vocal line seems to sink in a descending spiral; but the perilous leaps at 'scheide' and 'herrlich' (bb. 23–4, also 'Krone' and 'lege' bb. 36–7) are something new, and it is these intervals that Alban Berg must have had in mind. The last lines of the second and third verses (bb. 26–7 and bb. 40–41) are harder still for the singer; they look easy enough on paper, but most baritones quake at this demand for a smooth *mezza voce* entry into the *passaggio* at the end of a long breath, and at the end of an ever-climbing line. The successful negotiation of this passage (particularly at 'weiter Ferne', the singer's closing phrase) is the prerogative of a master of the vocal mysteries. (Fischer-Dieskau, in his only recording of a live Schubert recital with Benjamin Britten, never sounded more god-like than at the end of this song.) The music for the rising of the moon and the emergence of the stars (at bb. 27–8) spirits this song heavenwards, into the realms of the sublime. The even more transcendental postlude (bb. 41–4) is mournful yet soothing, radiant yet muted, the birth of a new kind of light after the extinguishing of the sun's brilliance.

Helios now goes underground, far from the sight of mortal man, to replenish his powers. Having had their performances, artists go home to reckon the private costs. They must face the daily challenge of renewing their song, and prepare to survive another day in the heat and glare of public scrutiny. This double life, half of it lived in the unnatural intensity of the spotlight, the other in the underworld full of tortured doubt, is the lot of the artist. When Helios says 'Ich nehme nicht, ich pflege nur zu geben' ('I do not take, I am wont only to give'), one thinks of an epitaph, not only for the sad, complicated poet who wrote these words, but for Schubert himself.

Mention must be made here of the song's first edition (as printed in Peters) for which Diabelli sanctioned a radical repositioning of some of the vocal line (in bb. 3, 4, 15, 28 and 29) probably to render the song more accessible for performance by higher voices. This changes the majestic character of the song's opening by transposing a portion of the invocation to Helios a third higher but it fails to adapt many of the equally challenging low notes later in the song, and, for no apparent reason, the rhythm in bb. 26 and 30 is changed. This ranks as one of the more pointless and mismanaged of the Diabelli corruptions.

Autograph:	Wienbibliothek im Rathaus, Vienna (first draft)
First edition:	Published as Book 11 no. 4 of the *Nachlass* by Diabelli, Vienna in April 1831 (P273)
Subsequent editions:	Peters: Vol. 5/47; AGA XX 384: Vol. 6/124; NSA IV: Vol. 12/184
Bibliography:	Black 2003, p. 98
	Capell 1928, pp. 163–4
	Einstein 1951, pp. 192–3
	Fischer-Dieskau 1977, p. 97
	Kohlhäufl 1999, p. 298
	Youens 1996, pp. 202–5
Discography and timing:	Fischer-Dieskau II 4[4] 3'50
	Hyperion I 14[16]
	Hyperion II 23[12] 4'25 Thomas Hampson

← *Der entsühnte Orest* D699   *Frühlingsglaube* D686 →

FREUDE DER KINDERJAHRE   Joys of childhood
(KÖPKEN) **D455** [H283]
C major   July 1816

Freude, die im frühen Lenze[1]
  Meinem Haupte Blumen wand,
Sieh, noch duften deine Kränze,
  Noch geh' ich an deiner Hand;
Selbst der Kindheit Knospen blühen
  Auf in meiner Fantasie;
Und mit frischem Reize glühen
  Noch in meinem Herbste sie.

Früh schon kannt' ich dich! Du wehtest
  Froh bei jedem Spiel um mich,
Sprangst in meinem Balle, drehtest
  Leicht in meinem Kreisel dich:
Liefst mit mir durch Gras und Hecken
  Flüchtig Schmetterlingen nach,
Rittest mit auf bunten Stecken
  Wirbeltest im Trommelschlag.

Joy which in early spring
  Wove flowers around my head,
See, your garlands are still fragrant
  And I still walk holding your hand.
Even the buds of childhood bloom
  In my imagination,
And still shine with fresh charm
  In my autumn.

From early childhood I knew you! You fluttered
  Happily around me whenever I played,
You bounced with my ball, spun
  Easily in my top,
You ran swiftly with me through grass and hedgerow,
  Chasing butterflies.
You rode with me on bright-painted hobby horses,
  And rolled when I played the drum.

[1] In the Voss almanach of 1795, this reads 'in *frühem* Lenze'.

[. . .]   [. . .]

Kamen auch zuweilen Sorgen;   At times, too, there were cares;
  Kindersorgen sind nicht gross!   A child's cares are not great.
Früh hüpft' ich am andern Morgen,   Early the next morning I would skip about,
  Schaukelte die Sorgen los;   And swing away my cares.
Kletterte dir nach auf Bäume,   I would climb trees, following you,
  Wälzte müd' im Grase mich;   And roll in the grass when tired;
Und entschlief ich: süsse Träume   And when I fell asleep sweet dreams
  Zeigten mir im Bilde dich!   Would reveal your image.

FRIEDRICH VON KÖPKEN (1737–1811); poem written before 1801

This is Schubert's only setting of a Köpken text. See the poet's biography.

Nostalgia for childhood is a recurring theme in the songs of 1816. As his diary entries for the year show, the young composer, hardly out of his own childhood, was inclined to wax philosophical about his past. He was certainly not yet in his own autumn, as Köpken claims to be. The song is merry and breezy and not at all easy to sing in its original key of C (transposed into A major, as in the Peters Edition, it is far more accessible). After smooth beginnings, the second half of the song has a notable succession of dotted rhythms in the accompaniment (bb. 11, 13–14, 17–18). These are doubtless meant to depict the excited stirrings of the childlike imagination; they put the listener in mind of *Aus alten Märchen*, the song from *Dichterliebe*, about the power of children's fairy tales where Schumann's music evokes a rocking horse cantering through the terrain of childhood. The opening tune, for those connoisseurs of the Gilbert and Sullivan operettas, has the lilt of the police sergeant's song, 'When a felon's not engaged in his employment', from *The Pirates of Penzance*. Arthur Sullivan was a great Schubertian after all.

    Schubert wrote out only one verse; when this song was first printed in the Peters Edition, Max Kalbeck, at Max Friedlaender's invitation, added a second verse (of appalling sentimentality). At that time (1887) the poem had not been traced. Mandyczewski, in preparing the AGA (1895), obviously had it to hand as he was able to print five verses. The NSA states that the textual source is not known but this is corrected in the *Revisionsbericht*: it is in fact *Musen Almanach für 1795, ed. J. H. Voss, Bohn Hamburg, 1794* [p. 9].

Autograph:	Sibley Music Library, University of Rochester, New York (first draft)
First edition:	Published as Vol. 7 no. 35 in Friedlaender's edition by Peters, Leipzig in 1887 (P496)
Subsequent editions:	Peters: Vol. 7/84 (A major); AGA XX 240: Vol. 4/142; NSA IV: Vol. 10/192
Further setting:	J. F. Reichardt (1752–1814) *Freude der Kinderjahre*, No. 24 of *Neue Lieder geselliger Freude* (1804) with a different version of the poem taken from Köpken's *Episteln*, 1801
Discography and timing:	Fischer-Dieskau I 7[27] 1'58
	Hyperion I 23[20]
	Hyperion II 15[10] 2'16 Christoph Prégardien

← *Grablied auf einen Soldaten* D454   *Das Heimweh* D456 →

FRIENDS AND FAMILY – A CALENDAR

Schubert's life and productivity were singularly dependent on the affectionate support of his contemporaries. Those who were lucky enough to be selected as his poets are listed alphabetically under their own names in this book, and singers, pianists and fellow composers are discussed in three separate articles. There were nevertheless important figures in Schubert's life who fall under none of these convenient categories. The student of the composer's songs and the reader of these commentaries may wish to have a bird's-eye view of the people – mostly young men – who were part of Schubert's inner circle.

The differentiation between being a friend and a good colleague is not always easy to make. Not everyone in Vienna who met and worked with Schubert became his friend – although on occasion it may seem as if the opposite were the case and that the Schubert circle was a rolling wave that swept everyone into one happy, music-making community. There are many instances of poets, singers and other artists with whom Schubert worked happily enough on a professional basis, but with whom he never became at all intimate. In terms of contemporary poets alone this includes such names as Ignaz Castelli, Helmine von Chézy, Nicolaus Craigher de Jachelutta, Johann Mailáth, Karoline Pichler, Adolf von Pratobevera, Ladislaus Pyrker, Friedrich Reil, Friedrich von Schlegel, Johann Gabriel Seidl, Ludwig Count von Széchényi, Zacharias Werner, Alois Zettler. A name like Franz Grillparzer remains an enigma: he knew a lot about Schubert and saw him often, he also attempted to honour the composer's posthumous memory appropriately – but there is no direct record of any dealings between them.

Josef von Spaun by Moritz von Schwind.

In geographical terms there were three main groupings of friends, the first of which was the circle in Vienna, beginning with those who had been Schubert's schoolfriends at the Stadtkonvikt. The second group was the circle from Upper Austria in the west of the country. This was subdivided into three somewhat overlapping categories: those who came from Linz, those who were first educated at the Kremsmünster Konvikt before coming to the Vienna Konvikt and those, like Vogl, who were from Steyr. Thirdly, there were those who came from Graz (Styria) in the south.

A profession is only mentioned for those listed below when it is neither lawyer nor civil servant, as it is in a majority of cases. The friends – a selective list only of those who played some part in the composer's life as a song composer – are here arranged in the chronological order in which Schubert made their acquaintance.

1808–1813: The School Years

Josef von Spaun (1788–1865) (one of Schubert's poets, qv, *see also* DEDICATEES) was Schubert's Ur-Freund at the Imperial Konvikt (1808–1813) and perhaps the most faithful of the composer's associates thereafter. His recollections of the composer are perhaps the most ordered and reliable among the memoirs of Schubert's friends. Many of Schubert's social connections stem from Spaun; it is almost impossible to imagine the composer's life without his benign and kindly interventions. In 1821 Spaun left Vienna, clearly with rather a heavy heart, in pursuit of his civil-service career (Linz and a year in Lemberg, *see Herrn Josef Spaun, Assessor in Linz* D749). He returned in 1826 in time to host the great Schubertiads. Josef's younger brother **Max von Spaun** (1797–1844, with the nickname Spax) was also a student at the Konvikt from 1813. He was perhaps closest to Schubert only from 1826 on, and it was through him that the Hartmann brothers came into the Schubert circle (*see* 1824 below).

Leopold Ebner (1791–1870) probably met Schubert only after the composer left the Konvikt, but he claimed that he went there to visit friends and to hear Schubert's music. He was an early collector of copies of the composer's songs (*see* AUTOGRAPHS, ALBUMS AND COLLECTIONS).

Anton Holzapfel (1792–1868) was a close friend of Schubert's at the Imperial Konvikt (1808–1813). Holzapfel was later a source of many valuable memories regarding the composer's early years, and possibly a provider of song texts at the time, including the poems of Ossian. He was a member of Schubert's circle until about 1818, after which their paths rarely crossed.

Josef Kenner (1794–1868) (one of Schubert's poets, qv, *see also* DEDICATEES) was introduced to Schubert by Spaun. He was a fellow student at the Konvikt by 1813, having first been to school (like Schober much earlier, and Vogl) at the Konvikt at Kremsmünster.

Albert Stadler (1794–1888) (one of Schubert's poets, qv) was a schoolfriend of the composer at the Imperial Konvikt from 1812. His early collection of copies of Schubert's manuscripts (now in Lund, Sweden) is an invaluable source for the songs. Stadler left Vienna in August

Anton Holzapfel, unsigned watercolour.

1817, but he remained in personal contact with Schubert until 1825 when they were together for the last time in Stadler's native city of Steyr in Upper Austria.

    The Spaun brothers, Holzapfel, Kenner and Stadler were all from Linz in Upper Austria. Thanks to the benign influence of Josef von Spaun, Schubert was to have a special link with this so-called 'Linzer Kreis' for the rest of his life.

Michael von Rueskäfer (1794–1862) was a close friend of Schubert at the Konvikt. He was expelled for disciplinary offences in 1813, but he kept in touch with the composer. Both Rueskäfer and his brother Friedrich are mentioned in the documents in the later 1820s.

Johann Senn (1795–1875) (one of Schubert's poets, qv), born in the Tyrol, met Schubert as a fellow pupil at the Imperial Konvikt, although a close friendship seems to have developed between poet and composer only from 1815. This gifted and unfortunate young man never saw Schubert after 1820 when he was imprisoned for political reasons and then exiled to the Tyrol. He was visited in the Tyrol by Bruchmann (*see* below) in 1822.

Franz von Schlechta (1796–1875) (one of Schubert's poets, qv) went to school in Kremsmünster with Schober (*see* below) and Max and Anton von Spaun. He was a pupil to the Imperial Konvikt in 1813 where he met Schubert and became a member of his inner circle.

Other friends from this period were **Josef Streinsberg** (1798–1862), **Maximilian Weisse** (1798–1863) and **Anton Hauer** whose brother **Josef Hauer** (1802–71) later shared Schubert's Handelian enthusiasms.

Therese Grob (1798–1875) was the daughter of a local family well known to the Schuberts; she eventually married a baker. She was the first Schubert singer (as soprano at the Liechtental church) and is celebrated as the composer's first love. The album of Schubert songs long associated with her name, and more recently with that of her brother, is discussed in AUTOGRAPHS.

Benedict (also Benedikt) **Randhartinger** (1802–1893) (*see also* COMPOSERS) was a well-known Viennese musical figure. His account of his close relationship with Schubert first at school and later in life, as communicated to Kreissle (*see* SCHOLARS), is almost certainly self-servingly exaggerated. His birthdate is often given as 1797 as if to place him as Schubert's direct contemporary. Although he was certainly a pupil at the Imperial Konvikt he was probably there only after Schubert left.

1814

Johann Mayrhofer (1787–1836) (one of Schubert's most important poets, qv) met Schubert through the good offices of Josef von Spaun with whom he had lodged in Vienna. He was almost an exact contemporary of Spaun, worked as an Imperial book censor, and was the intellectual leader of the Linz circle that was responsible for the educational and philosophical periodical *Beyträge zur Bildung für Jünglinge*. The composer was to share a small room in a lodging house with Mayrhofer from November 1818 to the end of 1820.

1815

Josef Witteczek (1787–1859) was a generous patron of the arts and later the first punctilious Schubert collector. He was introduced to Schubert by Spaun. Witteczek's Schubertiads were legendary and continued after the composer's death (*see* AUTOGRAPHS, ALBUMS AND COLLECTIONS, SCHOLARS and DEDICATEES).

Karl von Enderes (1788–1860) was introduced to Schubert by Spaun probably at the end of 1815 or the beginning of 1816. Enderes was a botanist and he became, like Witteczek, an avid host of Schubertiads at his home in the Neuburgerstrasse. These were most celebrated in 1825 when Vogl was a regular guest as a singer. In 1839, when Vogl sang a complete performance of *Winterreise*, it was at Enderes's home in the Hoher Markt. Enderes was loved for his gentle personality and his humanity.

Franz von Schober (1796–1882) (one of Schubert's poets qv, *see also* DEDICATEES) was born in Sweden and partially educated in Germany. He was a student at Kremsmünster and a friend of the Spaun family in Linz where he saw Schubert's song manuscripts as early as 1813. It is not certain when he met Schubert personally, but it was certainly no later than 1815. He quickly became one of his closest friends and a central figure in the composer's life.

Anselm Hüttenbrenner (1794–1868) (*see* COMPOSERS) was born in Graz and as a promising young composer was sent to Vienna to study with Antonio Salieri. From April 1815 he was very close to Schubert (he was the accompanist of the first public performance of *Erlkönig*) until family obligations drew him back to Graz, first in 1818–19, and then more permanently from 1821. The story of his guardianship of the score of the 'Unfinished' Symphony until it was first performed in 1865 by Herbeck (*see* SCHOLARS) would cast him as a jealous rival of Schubert, but this is contested by other versions of events. Hüttenbrenner's music played no small part in Schubert's life.

Josef von Gahy (1793–1864), the gifted pianist, was introduced to Schubert by Josef von Spaun (*see* PIANISTS). There were many other instrumentalists in Schubert's life – violinists, cellists, horn players and so on, but of all these Gahy was the nearest to being a friend.

1816

Anton von Spaun (1790–1849) was the elder brother of Josef von Spaun, and Mayrhofer's colleague in the publication of *Beyträge für Jünglinge* (1816–17); he met Schubert personally no later than 1816. In April of that year he wrote to his fiancée that he had been knocked sideways by hearing Schubert play the piano at Schober's home. He later organized a private concert in Linz in honour of his daughter Henriette's birthday, where Vogl was accompanied by Schubert himself.

Leopold von Sonnleithner (1797–1873) was the eldest son of Ignaz von Sonnleithner (1770–1831). He made Schubert's acquaintance at the performance of the orchestrally accompanied cantata *Prometheus* D451 (a work now lost) at the home of the Watteroth family (July 1816) and became an enthusiastic collector of copies of the songs. His collection is sadly lost. It was Sonnleithner who, together with Josef Hüttenbrenner (*see* below) initiated the publication of Schubert songs in 1821 – at first attempting unsuccessfully to find a publisher, and then proposing the ingenious business arrangement of selling the songs on commission (*see* PUBLISHERS). Sonnleithner's remarks on the performances of Schubert's songs remain invaluable (*see* RUBATO). He later regretted assisting Diabelli in revising the Ossian settings.

Leopold von Sonnleithner, unsigned oil painting.

1817

Johann Michael Vogl (1768–1840) (*see* DEDICATEES and SINGERS) was the principal interpreter of Schubert's songs in his lifetime. He met the composer (thanks to Spaun and Schober) in the summer or autumn of 1817.

Josef Hüttenbrenner (1796–1882), brother of the composer Anselm, first met the composer in the summer of 1817. He took an immediate interest in Schubert, and particularly the songs (*see* *Die Forelle* D550). He moved from Graz to Vienna in 1818 and was involved with Sonnleithner in arranging for the first publication of the songs to be sold on commission. In the period 1822–3 he became a kind of secretary and factotum for the composer, dealing with the publishers and

Josef Hüttenbrenner, watercolour by Josef Danhauser (?).

Leopold Kupelwieser, pencil drawing by Josef von Hempel.

attempting, without success, to interest opera intendants in Schubert's dramatic work. Hüttenbrenner's useful activity on Schubert's behalf was not without a healthy dose of self-interest. Years after the composer's death the admiring description of Hüttenbrenner by the Beethoven scholar Alexander Thayer as 'Schubert's prophet, singer, friend and pupil' seems the result of a successful public-relations exercise. (*See* AUTOGRAPHS, ALBUMS and COLLECTIONS and DEDICATEES).

Leopold Kupelwieser (1796–1862), born in Vienna, met Schubert in 1817 at the latest when both artists were fellow members of the *Unsinnsgesellschaft* – a jolly club or brother-hood of joyous misrule and contained anarchy; and there is a comic drawing to prove it. At the same time Schubert met Leop-old's older brother **Josef Kupelwieser** (1791– 1866) who was not as close to the composer, but who was his librettist for *Fierabras* D796, and possibly other earlier operas.

If not quite as famous an artist as Schwind, 'Kuppel', as Leopold was known to his friends, had precocious success as a member of the Nazarene school: some of the most beautiful pencil portraits of members of the Schubert circle (of Schwind, Bruchmann, Vogl, Senn, Schober – also an oil painting of the latter) come from his expert hand. Apart from these there is the full-faced Schubert portrait, signed and dated 10 July 1821 by the composer himself, and the watercolours of the Schubertians' party games at Atzenbrugg (Schubert seated at the piano with a dog under the seat) and the 'Land party of the Schubertians', an image dominated by a Landauer and horses (where the composer is depicted in the distance at the far left of the picture). It seems that Kupelwieser, and later his fiancée and wife **Johanna Lutz** (1803–

1883) came to be among the most trusted of the composer's friends. He was instrumental in helping the artistic career of Moritz von Schwind who was eight years younger and, like Schwind, was an admirer of Schober – for a time at least. From the end of 1823 until 1825 Kupelwieser was in Italy on a study tour; this was when the composer was ill. The most desperately unhappy letter Schubert ever wrote, in which he compares himself with the afflicted Gretchen ('Meine Ruh' ist hin . . . Mein Herz ist schwer'), was addressed to Kupel-wieser in Rome on 31 March 1824. In the late 1850s the artist was one of those who declined to furnish Ferdinand Luib with further biographical information on the composer. On his return from Rome Kupelwieser became famous as a painter of religious pictures. One senses that he took friendship, and the obligations of confidences, very seriously.

1818

In the summer of this year Schubert travelled to Zseliz (then in Hungary, now in Slovakia) as music teacher to the two young Esterházy countesses. His noble employers are discussed in the commentary on the song *Gebet* D815, but his two young teenage pupils were more to be counted as friends – **Marie Esterházy** (1802–1837) and **Karoline Esterházy** (1805–1831). The latter was only thirteen at this time, but she and Schubert subsequently spent the summer of 1824 as pupil and teacher, and the composer was said to have been in love with her. It was also in the summer of 1818 that Schubert first made the acquaintance of the singer **Karl von Schönstein** (1797–1876) for whom the song cycle *Die schöne Müllerin* D795 was written. (*See* DEDICATEES and SINGERS.)

1819–1820

Anton Ottenwalt (1789–1845) (one of Schubert's poets, qv) married the sister of Josef von Spaun, Marie (1795–1847), in this year. The couple lived in Linz where Ottenwalt met Schubert, also in 1819. He had earlier played a considerable role in the Anton Spaun-Mayrhofer collaboration on the *Beiträge zur Bildung für Jünglinge*.

There is disagreement about when Schubert first met the gifted, bright young spark of a Viennese-born painter, **Moritz von Schwind** (1804–1871): already as a fifteen-year-old boy in March 1819 according to Dürr, or in 1821 – as a result of his friendship with Kupelwieser – according to Hilmar's *Schubert-Enzyklopädie*. Of all Schubert's artistic friends it was Schwind who went on to enjoy the most distinguished career in his own right as a painter with an international reputation. (It was the separate study of the work of Schwind that initially led the art historian Otto Erich Deutsch to become interested in Schubert.) Schwind, given to a youthful enthusiasm that was considered over the top, even by the

Karoline Esterházy, watercolour by Anton Hähnlich, 1837.

Moritz von Schwind, lithograph by Josef Kriehuber, 1827.

standards of the time, idolized Schober almost more than Schubert. He was delighted to count himself the third of a very special triumvirate, the other two members of which were Schober and Schubert himself. In return, Schubert was known at times to refer to Schwind as 'his beloved' – with what degree of humour or seriousness is a moot point. Bauernfeld records him saying of Schubert, 'I wish I could paint as well as he composes.' The young artist, although only in his late teens, seems to be have been completely au fait with the ups and downs of Schubert's illness. Two year later, when the composer went to live in the Frühwirthhaus near the Karlskirche (he lodged there between February 1825 and October 1826), Schwind wrote to Schober in Breslau with all the details of the move solicitously expressed: 'As far as I can, I share his whole life with him.' Schubert now found himself right next door to the Schwind family residence, the so-called 'Schwindien', in the 'Mondscheinhaus'; in these last three years of the composer's life the two men spent a lot of time together with Schubert regularly sharing with Schwind his latest work.

'Schubert's room', ink drawing by Moritz von Schwind, 1821.

Over many years of activity Schwind made a number of drawings with Schubertian resonances, although he was not a portraitist like his teacher Kupelwieser, or Teltscher and Rieder (*see* below). His drawing of Schubert's room (1821) seems more eloquent for the composer's absence. *Der Spaziergang vor dem Stadttore* shows a young man reading in the foreground, while Schubert is just to be discerned (mainly by his glasses) walking with a group of friends in the background. Schwind was very interested in illustrating the composer's work: he made a number of title-page vignettes and illustrated the Kenner ballad *Der Liedler* D209 with a series of drawings; several Schubert song publications were graced with Schwind vignettes.

Devastated by Schubert's unexpected death in 1828 and the failure of his own engagement to Anna Hönig in 1829 (*see* below), Schwind moved to Munich where he made a fine career, finally settling there permanently in 1847. As he got older he seems to have been drawn increasingly to memorializing his links with Schubert: firstly as part of the *Lachner Roll* (1862), a series of drawings (on a roll of paper that was the width of a frieze) in honour of his friend the composer Franz Lachner (*see* COMPOSERS) where Schubert makes a number of guest appearances, cartoon fashion; and then in the painting *A Schubert Evening at Josef von Spaun's* (1868). In this famous work, Schwind's astonishing memory, almost Proustian in visual terms, recreates the personalities of a vanished era, with the seated Vogl and the piano-playing Schubert at the centre of a large room where almost everybody of importance in the circle (including the elusive Mayrhofer) makes an exquisite cameo appearance. Some of Schwind's most lively drawings of the composer in profile also date from the 1860s. It seems to have been Schwind's lifelong ambition to decorate a room, or a concert hall, with a series of images based on Schubert's songs. A number of the sketches for such a project survive and show the sumptuous nature of an imagined shrine to the composer's lieder that was never completed.

Franz von Bruchmann (1798–1867) (one of Schubert's poets, qv), one of the more problematical figures in the Schubert circle, was introduced to the composer by Josef von Streinsberg.

His mother Justina (*see* DEDICATEES) was the recipient of three of Schubert's songs, his sister Sybilla died young and was the subject of one of the songs (*Schwestergruss* D762) and his other sister Justina was the object of Schober's unwelcome affections, at least as far as Bruchmann himself was concerned. Bruchmann, a sometime friend of August von Platen (qv) was very close to the poet, Johann Senn who was exiled for political reasons.

c. 1820

Matthäus von Collin (1779–1824) (one of Schubert's poets, qv, and DEDICATEES) was a cousin of Josef von Spaun. An enthusiast of Schubert's music from the time he met the composer (about 1820), Collin gave a number of Schubertiads in his home. He was one of several powerful men within the Viennese establishment who worked on behalf of the Schubertian cause. He was older and more distinguished than the other members of the circle, but his family relationship to Spaun, and his participation in writing a joke poem to be sent to Spaun in Linz (*see Herrn Josef Spaun, Assessor in Linz* D749) qualifies him as a friend.

Josef Huber (1794–1870) was a friend of Mayrhofer and probably met Schubert around 1820. He was famous for his height and long nose and was sometimes caricatured in drawings by Moritz von Schwind. Schubert's Goethe-influenced poem *Der Geist der Welt* (*see* SCHUBERT AS POET), scribbled on the back of a menu card, was perhaps dedicated to Huber. Thanks to 'tall Huber' we have an account of the first-ever Schubertiad that took place on 26 January 1821 at Schober's home:

> *Last Friday I enjoyed excellent entertainment . . . in the evening Franz [Schober] invited Schubert and fourteen of his close acquaintances. So, with him playing, many of Schubert's splendid songs were sung and this went on until after 10 o'clock in the evening. After that we had some punch which had been brought by one of the guests and, as it was very good and plentiful, the party, which was already in high spirits, became even merrier. So it was 3 o'clock in the morning before we left. You may imagine how agreeable it was for me to enjoy the company of so many cultivated men, something I had missed for so many years.*

The composer lodged with Huber in the Stubenbastei between the autumn of 1823 and the spring of 1824, a period when Schubert was particularly ill and was sometimes in hospital – evidence enough of the friendship between the two men.

It was Leopold von Sonnleithner who introduced Schubert to both the formidable **Anna Fröhlich** (1793–1880) and her much younger sister **Josefine Fröhlich** (1803–1878). It was for Anna Fröhlich, an excellent musician and pianist, that Schubert composed a remarkable work for mezzo and chorus, *Ständchen* (*Zögernd, leise*) D920, with words by Grillparzer (*see* SINGERS).

1823

Franz Lachner (1803–1890) was a young composer from Munich who met Schubert first in 1823. He soon befriended the older composer who became an admired mentor. According to Lachner the two men showed each other their compositions and various important instrumental works were tried out in Lachner's lodgings, including the F minor *Fantasie* for piano duet D840. At this point in his life Lachner seems to have been more interested in instrumental rather than vocal music – something of an exception in the Schubert circle, and a possible reason for Schubert's delight in the young man's company. In later years Lachner was better known as a composer of lieder (*see* COMPOSERS) but it was lucky for him that he had an opera, *Die*

Bürgschaft, accepted for production in Prague. Schubert was invited by Schindler to attend in October 1828, but he was too ill even to answer the invitation. The other young composer and singer with whom Schubert was on friendly terms towards the end of his life (from the summer of 1827) was **Johann Vesque von Püttlingen** (1803–1883) who became one of the foremost song composers in Vienna, setting every single one of Heine's *Heimkehr* poems. He was also a friend of Robert Schumann. Vesque recalled spending time in the company of Schubert, Vogl and Grillparzer in 1828, and the young man sang Schubert songs accompanied by the composer. Vesque's pseudonym was Johann Hoven. (*See* COMPOSERS)

Raphael Kiesewetter von Wiesenbrunn, lithograph by Anton Hänisch, 1847.

Raphael Kiesewetter (1773–1850) was a distinguished and well-to-do civil servant who was a passionate amateur musician and leading member of the Musikverein. His collection of music (chiefly what today would be termed early music) grew into one of the most wide-ranging and important anywhere; in the decade before his death he published a number of ground-breaking books which were based on his collection (including a history of Arabian and Persian music) which marked him out as a pioneer of musicology of this kind. He came into Schubert's ken as an amateur singer, and as part of a quartet of male voices that performed *Geist der Liebe* D747 at the Gesellschaft der Musikfreunde on 9 January 1823. The pianist Jenger and the composer Anselm Hüttenbrenner were also in contact with Kiesewetter, and for the last five years of his life Schubert counted Kiesewetter a friend and admirer and was invited to the concerts that took place in the councillor's home. At the same time he would have been no doubt granted access to Kiesewetter's collection and would have been able to study rare works, including the more difficult to obtain compositions of J. S. Bach. Kiesewetter's daughter Irene (1811–1872), was an amateur pianist of some ability as well as an enthusiastic accompanist of Schubert's songs. She went through a period of illness and the piano-duet accompanied cantata *Al par del ruscelletto* D936 was composed as a celebration of her return to health. It is possible that the vocal quartet *Der Tanz* D826 was also composed in connection with her recovery.

1824

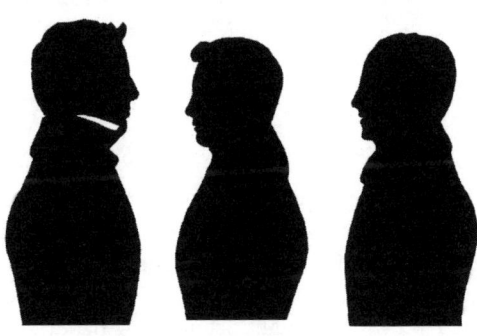

The three von Hartmann brothers – Franz, Ludwig and Fritz, unsigned silhouettes.

The presence of the two brothers **Fritz von Hartmann** (1805–1850) and **Franz von Hartmann** (1808–1875) was fortunate for our knowledge of the Schubert *Freundekreis*. These musically receptive young men had been born into a cultured family that moved to Linz in 1820 and became friendly with the Spaun family. In 1824, when the two boys came to Vienna to study law, they were welcomed into the Schubert circle and began to document all sorts of occasions in their diaries: Schubertiads with Spaun and Witteczek, breakfast meetings where Gahy played the piano, the meetings of the Reading circle, and so on. By 1825 the Hartmann brothers had become closer to Schubert and to Schwind. Their innate musicality and their reverence for Schubert's songs is touching: 'I first understood many Müller and other songs that I knew already almost by heart through the singing of Vogl.' Thanks to the Hartmanns, many details that otherwise would have been lost – which songs and pieces were performed, which works of literature were read aloud – have come down to us. We are also informed about the names of the inns and hostelries that were visited, and when the parties began and ended – all in all an invaluable snapshot of the Schubert circle in its later phase when younger men were beginning to replace the older members who had married or moved away.

Wilhelm August Rieder (1796–1880) was the son of the composer Ambros Rieder who was resident in Hugo Wolf's future haunt of Perchtoldsdorf, not far from Vienna. Rieder's *Präludien und Fughetten* for organ or piano were published in 1826 by Diabelli with a dedication to 'the valued composer Herr Franz Schubert' – the only musical dedication that Schubert ever received during his lifetime. Ambros's son, the painter Wilhelm Rieder, produced the most widely known (and according to Deutsch 'the best') of all Schubert pictures. The famous three-quarter pose has Schubert sitting rather casually with his right arm (to the left of the picture) around the back of a chair. The composer holds in his hand a volume of poetry, the cover visible with its inner border, as if he had been momentarily distracted from a text. The picture was painted in the second half of 1825, the shape of the volume and the ornamental border visible on its cover matches that of Johann Gabriel Seidl's *Dichtungen* (*Lieder der Nacht*), officially published in 1826, but advertised in the *Wiener Zeitschrift* and available in October 1825. A coat with a velvet collar is buttoned up and barely disguises the composer's corpulence: the whole effect is utterly natural and shows a man of great dignity and concentration. Rieder was actually a friend of Schubert's; he often attended Schubertiads, and the composer sometimes went to his home to play on his Anton Walter piano.

The name of **Anna Hönig** (1804–1888, with the nickname of 'Netti' or 'Nettl') has already been mentioned in connection with Moritz von Schwind, whose fiancée she was, and who drew her portrait. She was apparently not very pretty, but an extraordinarily sweet woman, and Schubert enjoyed her company (his first visit to the Hönig home was in 1824 or 1825). There was a short period of strain in their relationship when the composer took umbrage at something Anna had said (might he have been jealous of Schwind's adoration of her?) but Schwind smoothed things over and Schubert renewed his visits. In 1832 Anna married **Ferdinand Mayerhofer von Grün-bühel** (1798–1869) who was a close friend of Bauernfeld (*see* below). Mayerhofer assisted that poet in the translation of *Antony and Cleopatra* (*Trinklied* D888) that appeared as part of the Viennese edition of Shakespeare's works in 1826.

1825

Eduard von Bauernfeld (1802–1890) (one of Schubert's poets, qv), the famous Viennese drama-tist, was a school contemporary of Moritz von Schwind, but a relatively late addition to the circle of Schubert's close friends. He had attended a Schubertiad as early as 1822, and had been well educated musically, but he lacked the overwhelming enthusiasm of Schwind and the latter's ability to push himself forward. In February 1825 Schwind brought Schubert to Bauernfeld's lodgings; he recited some of his poems, Schubert played and sang, and the young men then repaired to the nearest tavern. By March he and Schubert had exchanged the familiar 'Du'.

Bauernfeld was at all the important later Schubertiads and saw Schubert two days before his death to discuss the libretto of the opera they were writing together, *Der Graf von Gleichen*. This had run into trouble with the censors on account of its subject – bigamy. Like Schwind, it was later in his life that Bauernfeld returned to Schubert as subject matter for artistic creativity; many of his verse reminiscences attempt to reconstruct the atmosphere of his youth in the company of the composer who, posthumously, was becoming increasingly celebrated.

Johann Baptist Jenger (1793–1856) (*see also* PIANISTS) was just old enough to have served in the War of Liberation against Napoleon. Stationed in Graz, he stayed in the military for some years afterwards, first as a protégé of Prince Karl Philipp Schwarzenberg, and then in the War Office. In Graz he became friendly with Marie Pachler (*see* below) and with the Hüttenbrenner family. A fine pianist – his speciality was working with singers – he was a member of the Styrian Musical Society. At the end of 1825 he moved back to Vienna, and this brought him into the orbit of the Schubert circle – although it is said that he knew Schubert from as early as 1817. With the composer and the singer Vogl, he visited the actress Sophie Müller (1803–1830, *see* SINGERS) in late 1825 and early 1826. Jenger became active in the affairs of the *Gesellschaft der Musikfreunde* in Vienna and was in demand as an accompanist. He must have been a superb diplomat – friendly, outgoing, supportive. A friend of the painter Teltscher (*see* below), he was instrumental in arranging Schubert's successful visit to Graz in September 1827.

Born in Prague, **Josef Eduard Teltscher** (1801–1837) is the fourth of Schubert's celebrated painter friends – the others are Schwind, Kupelwieser and Rieder. It was Jenger, that ever-charming conduit, who introduced Teltscher to the Schubert circle. He had lived in Vienna from

Jenger, Hüttenbrenner and Schubert, pastel by Josef Teltscher, 1827.

1820 and we know that he must have encountered Schubert from 1825 at the latest: in Sophie Müller's diary for January 1826 she mentions the fact that Teltscher had visited her, and brought with him a lithograph of Schubert. (**Sophie Müller** (1803–1830), a friend of both Schubert and Vogl is discussed under SINGERS.) The portrait that was printed thus is now sadly lost, but it must have been executed shortly before. Teltscher became a regular at Sophie Müller's and was there on several occasions with Schubert. Jenger had hoped that both Teltscher and Schubert would visit Marie Pachler (*see* below) in the summer of 1826. Teltscher painted the charming triple portrait of Schubert, Hüttebrenner and Jenger – perhaps at the behest of Karl von Schönstein – as well as another portrait of Schubert that was praised after the composer's death for having captured his 'guileless, childlike, pious and upright nature'. Teltscher also painted Karoline Esterházy, Sophie Müller, Marie Pachler, Schönstein himself and Ignaz von Sonnleithner. He drowned in Piraeus while on holiday in Greece with Jenger.

1827

Jenger initiated a new circle of friends for Schubert in Graz. **Marie Leopoldine Pachler** (1794–1855) was Schubert's hostess in the Styrian capital, and perhaps the last person with whom he made a new and intimate friendship. It was Jenger who brought the meeting about; he had actually attempted to do so in 1826 (and again in 1828 when Schubert had already enjoyed the Pachlers' hospitality) but the composer was unable to afford the journey in those years. The visit of 1827, however, was idyllic – as Schubert wrote to Marie Pachler, 'I shall never forget the welcoming house with its charming hostess, the sturdy Pachleros [Marie's husband Karl, 1789–1850] and little Faust [1819–1891, eight years old at the time] where I spent the happiest days I have known for a long time.' Schubert wrote a piano duet, *Kindermarsch* D928, his only piece of music for children, for Faust and his mother to play to Karl Pachler on his name-day.

Marie was a fine enough pianist for Beethoven to have been fascinated by her playing ('You are the true nurturer of my spiritual children'), and in her home she entertained any number of artists, poets and musicians. Among these was **Karl Gottfried von Leitner** (1800–1890) (one of Schubert's poets, qv) who was sadly not able to meet Schubert personally in the summer of 1827. He is surely one of Schubert's 'almost' friends. Marie gave Schubert a volume of Leitner's poems (*Gedichte*, Graz, 1825), and he set seven texts from it. He also set *Eine altschottische Ballade* D923 and *Heimliches Lieben* D922 in Graz. To Marie Pachler Schubert dedicated the four songs of Op. 106 (*see* DEDICATEES).

Schubert's Family

Schubert's father, **Franz Theodor Schubert** (1763–1830), was born in Neudorf, today Vysoka/Sumperk in the Czech republic. In 1783 he had come to Vienna to better his fortunes in the footsteps of his brother Karl,

Franz Theodor Schubert, unsigned oil painting.

also a teacher, and worked in the same Carmelite school for three years. In 1786 he began to teach at the elementary school in the Himmelpfortgrund which was eventually made over to him, although he had to spend his inheritance on improving conditions there. In 1785 he married **Elisabeth Katharina Vietz** (1756–1812). Seven years older than her husband, she too was born in the present-day Czech republic (Zuckmantel, now Zlaté Hory). Her family, originally more well-to-do than Schubert's, had fallen on hard times: her father, a locksmith, had come to Vienna in 1772 after being found guilty of appropriating guild funds, and died shortly thereafter. The shame of this incident hung over the family; Elisabeth worked as a maid and must have regarded Franz Schubert's proposal as a godsend. In the sixteen years of their marriage she bore him fourteen children. Nine of these died in infancy or early childhood (*): Ignaz (1785–1844); Elisabeth (1786–1788*); Karl (1787–1788*); Franziska (June to August 1788*); Magdalena (1789–1792*); Franz (August to September 1790*); Anna Carolina (lived 18 days in July 1791*) and Peter (1792–1793*). Up to this point, and apart from the first son, there had been seven consecutive child deaths; the same illness seems to have carried off Franziska and Elisabeth within a day of each other in August 1788. Four healthy births followed: Joseph (1793–1798*); Ferdinand (1794–1859); Karl (1795–1855) and Franz Peter (1797–1828). There followed two girls, the thirteenth and fourteenth children, who were born after the composer-to-be: Aloysia Magdalena (who lived only for two days in December 1799*) and Maria Theresia (1801–1878).

Franz Peter was the youngest surviving son of Elisabeth Schubert, born to her at the age of forty-one and apparently her favourite – a compensation perhaps for the probably unexpected loss of her five-year-old son Joseph in 1798. The surviving siblings of the composer, save Maria Theresia, were all older than him: Ignaz, Ferdinand and Karl (*see* below). Elisabeth Schubert died in 1812 (worn out it would seem by the demands of motherhood), and Franz Schubert senior remarried Anna Kleyenböck (1783–1860), not yet thirty. From this marriage came a further five children – Schubert's half-brothers and sisters Maria Barbara Anna (1814–35); Josefa Theresia (1815–1861); Theodor Cajetan Anton (December 1816 to July 1817); Andreas Theodor (1823–1893) and Anton Eduard (1826–1892).

Schubert seems to have got on well with his step-mother; his relationship with his father was much more contentious. Vater Schubert had many good points: he was upright and hard-working, supposedly kind with his many pupils in the school with a fine reputation as a teacher in the vicinity, and very musical – string quartets were played in the school holidays (brothers Ferdinand, Ignaz and Franz with Schubert senior). Schubert received violin lessons from his father, and had a musical upbringing of which he had no reason to be ashamed, although the authoritative influence of the Imperial Konvikt in terms of his general education is not to be underestimated (the letter-writing of brother Ferdinand, who had not been schooled at this institution, was a good deal less fluent). That the composer loved his father is beyond doubt, but one feels he also feared him. Franz Theodor was a paterfamilias, typical of the time and of a deeply Catholic Austria, who did not brook dissent from family subordinates. He was a go-getter with a limited outlook, clearly with a high sex drive (this perhaps inherited by his sons) and iron willpower, but his own upbringing had been provincial and in the years spent surviving the vicissitudes of the Napoleonic wars his outlook had by-passed the Enlightenment. He bettered himself by climbing gradually higher in terms of civic eminence, but mostly within the narrow boundaries of his parish – although he was given the Freedom of the City in 1826. It seems obvious that once Franz had met people from a different walk of life, and of a different class, there would be grounds for conflict – not only about his future career but about his lifestyle in general. There are many psychological interpretations of the dream Schubert wrote down on 3 July 1822 ('Mein Traum', qv Schubert the composer as Poet) but at its centre stands the father who is disappointed in some respects with his son, and the self-exiling Schubert who is unable to take up his father's invitations to partake in the feast prepared for him – whatever that may signify – and who finds it repellent.

Schubert was born in the schoolhouse at 54 Nussdorfer Strasse in the ninth district, today a *Geburtshaus* museum. In 1801 the family moved around the corner into Säulengasse 10, the house known as 'Zum schwarzen Rössl'; it was in this house, the present-day unlikely site of the Schubert-Garage instead of a national monument, that Schubert wrote many of the great songs of 1814 and 1815 during the summers and school holidays.

The composer's eldest brother **Ignaz Schubert** (1785–1844) was twelve years his senior. He had been put in charge of teaching Franz to play the piano and was astounded by the boy's quick progress which rapidly overtook his own pianistic abilities. He was a freethinker and hated the authoritarianism of both church and state – institutions revered by Schubert *père*. Ignaz was rather envious of the freedom that Schubert enjoyed, both as a pupil at the Konvikt and with his bohemian friends. He was never able to break out of the daily grind of being a schoolteacher and he took over his father's school at Rossau on Franz Theodor's death in 1830.

Ferdinand Lukas Schubert (1794–1859) was the composer's favourite brother. He was perhaps the most musical member of the family apart from Franz himself, taught by some of the same teachers. Like all the family he started out as a school assistant but soon branched out and became an organist and an indefatigable writer (of copious editions of school textbooks) and a composer. Gradually his teaching positions became grander than anything his father would have dreamed of, and he ended up as honorary music professor at the Conservatorium where he taught the organ. On 1 September 1828 Franz Schubert moved into Ferdinand's newly built apartment outside the city walls (now the *Sterbehaus* at Kettenbrückenstrasse 6), on advice from doctors that it would be a healthier alternative to living in the inner city. The walls of the building had not yet dried out and the state of the house exacerbated the composer's ill health. The plumbing in these apartments was not finished and the drinking water was probably polluted. The composer died under Ferdinand's roof on 19 November 1828. Ferdinand's ineptitude vis-à-vis his brother's health and well-being is implicit in these ill-managed events; it seems also typical of much of Ferdinand Schubert's life. In the summer of 1824, when he was music master to the Esterházy countesses in Schloss Zseliz, the composer had left Ferdinand in charge of his affairs. It fell to Ferdinand to proofread *Die schöne Müllerin* which was being published by Sauer & Leidesdorf, a task which was carried out with insufficient care. As Schubert's surviving relative, a lot depended on Ferdinand's ability to manage what he could of his brother's legacy – a task he undertook willingly, but with varying success. He disposed unwisely of some of the extraordinary musical material in his charge – although in his defence it must be admitted he was a tireless copyist. His hasty and sometimes opportunist reactions to selling material probably had something to do with his need to support his eight children (as Robert Schumann wryly remarked of him), survivors of the twenty born to his two marriages. As a composer (he confined himself mainly to

Photograph of Ferdinand Schubert later in life.

church music) his achievements lay so far beneath those of his brother as to be almost risible. But Ferdinand seems to have been genuinely devoted to Franz. He was not above asking for Schubert's help in composing music for important occasions, sometimes (more or less) passing it off as his own, and this apparent plagiarism was clearly effected with the composer's tacit consent, so keen was Franz to advance his brother's less distinguished career. Ferdinand later made a speciality of arranging Schubert's songs for voice and orchestra (*Erlkönig* D328, *Der Hirt auf dem Felsen* D965, *Die junge Nonne* D828, *Der Taucher* D77, *Ave Maria* D839 and *Gott im Ungewitter* D985, among others). Some of these arrangements received critical brickbats at the time and have not survived into modern use. Ferdinand's daughter Emma, Schubert's niece, died in Vienna in 1927 at the age of eighty-one.

Karl Schubert (1795–1855) is the forgotten brother who has only received scholastic attention in relatively recent years. He was the only Schubert not to show an interest in music; instead he was an artist who held his first successful exhibition in 1822. In 1823 he married Therese Schwemminger. Schubert referred to Karl as his brother 'twice-over' – both in blood and as a brother-in-art. Karl executed some very attractive drawings including vedute of Vienna and its surroundings (and even as far afield as Gmunden); after his brother's death he even made a point of making drawings that followed in the composer's footsteps as it were. Nevertheless, his attempts to better himself with an appointment outside Vienna came to nothing: he remained based in the area in which he was born, albeit not in the schoolhouse itself. On one occasion Schubert attempted to help him get a position in Graz and asked for the help of Anselm Hüttenbrenner, influential in that part of the world – sadly to no effect. It is thought that Karl designed the vignette on the second edition of *Der Wanderer* D489.

Schubert's younger and only surviving sister, **Maria Theresia** (1801–1878), married Matthias Schneider. Their son was Eduard Schneider (1827–1889). After Ferdinand's death in 1859, Eduard inherited the *Nachlass* of papers and manuscripts that had remained in the family. These were eventually sold to Nikolaus Dumba (*see* Autographs, Albums and Collections).

FRÖHLICHES SCHEIDEN
A cheerful parting
(Leitner) **D896** [H649]
(Fragment) F major   Autumn 1827 or later

Gar fröh-lich kann ich schei-den, ich hätt' es nicht ge - meint,
(90 bars)

Gar fröhlich kann ich scheiden,	I can depart happy,
Ich hätt' es nicht gemeint;	Though I would never have thought it;
Die Trennung bringt sonst Leiden,	Separation usually brings sorrow,
Doch fröhlich kann ich scheiden;	But I can depart happy;
Sie hat um mich geweint.	She wept for me.
Wie trag' ich dies Entzücken	How can I bear this rapture
In stummer Brust vereint?	Gathered within my silent breast?
Es will mich fast erdrücken,	It almost stifles me.

Wie trag' ich dies Entzücken?	How can I bear this joy?
Sie hat um mich geweint!	She wept for me.
Ihr Alpen, See'n und Auen,	Mountains, lakes and meadows,
Du Mond, der sie bescheint,	And the moon that shines on her,
Euch will ich mich vertrauen:	I shall confide in you:
Ihr Alpen, See'n und Auen!	Mountains, lakes and meadows,
Sie hat um mich geweint.	She wept for me.
Und sterb' ich in der Fremde,	And if I die in a foreign land
Mir dünkt nicht fürchterlich	I shall not fear
Der Schlaf im Leichenhemde;	That beshrouded sleep;
Denn, sterb' ich in der Fremde,	For if I die in a foreign land
So weint sie wohl um mich.	She will weep for me.
Drum fröhlich kann ich scheiden,	So I can depart happy,
Ich hätt' es nicht gemeint;	Though I would never have thought it;
Die Trennung bringt sonst Leiden,	Separation usually brings sorrow.
Doch fröhlich kann ich scheiden;	But I can depart happy:
Sie hat um mich geweint.	She wept for me.

KARL GOTTFRIED VON LEITNER (1800–1890); poem written in 1821

This is the second of Schubert's eleven Leitner solo settings (1822–3 and 1827–8). See the poet's biography for a chronological list of all the Leitner settings.

All three of the Leitner song fragments have been assigned the Deutsch number of D896 (*Sie in jedem Liede* is D896A, and *Wolke und Quelle* is D896B). This is the only one that has a Leitner poem attached to the vocal line written in Schubert's hand. In Van Hoorickx's realization (recorded for Hyperion) the tempo is 'Etwas bewegt', and the accompaniment is in amiably flowing quavers that are reminiscent of another 1827 song, *Das Lied im Grünen* D917. (Van Hoorickx takes his cue from the fact that in bb. 73–5 of this sketch the composer has suddenly chosen to fill in the empty piano staves with just this kind of piano writing.) The vocal line suggests a high tenor even more than the less decisive *Wolke und Quelle*. Where else in the songs of this period do we find a high A flat held as a semibreve (b. 27), and a high B flat on a dotted crotchet (b. 64) on the word 'in'? It seems unlikely that awkward corners such as these would have survived a further revisionary stage on Schubert's part. Other details are more convincingly Schubertian: at the change of key at the beginning of the second verse the long semibreve for 'trag'' (b. 18) suggests an unbearable eternity ('how can I bear this rapture') in a novel manner.

In this autograph we have the opportunity to see the composer react to a text early on in the compositional process; manuscripts of this type were mostly destroyed when the song reached a more complete form. It seems certain that Schubert tidied up such details as vocal practicalities and refinements of prosody at a later stage of revision; what was important was to put down on paper his initial response to a poem – warts and all. For example, there are rather too many plodding crotchets in this sketch to have survived in a later *Fassung*; Schubert would probably have varied the declamation to make it more subtle, at the same time as keeping the best aspects of the felicitously shaped melody.

It would seem that Schubert was rarely able to jot down a work in a perfectly finished form, and it is more than likely that he did much more revision and polishing than his reputation for easy spontaneity suggests. But he alone had the ability to move the music into its next stage of sophistication and perfection. Anyone attempting a completion or realization of the music as it stands has their hands tied; the reconstructive scholar must stick scrupulously to the very imperfections which the composer himself would have brushed aside at the next stage of revision. Having a few songs left to us in such a rough and ready condition is salutary. We would almost certainly be surprised beyond measure to see the very earliest sketches for *Winterreise*, music that probably started life in a similarly embryonic state.

Autograph:	Wienbibliothek im Rathaus, Vienna (incomplete sketch)
First edition:	Published as part of the NSA in 1988; performing version by Reinhard Van Hoorickx (P803)
Subsequent editions:	Not in Peters; Not in AGA; NSA IV: Vol. 14b/269
Bibliography:	Brown 1954, p. 93
Discography and timing:	Fischer-Dieskau —

Hyperion I 36^9
Hyperion II 35^2 3'08   Michael Schade

← *Wolke und Quelle* D896b   *Sie in jedem Liede* D896a →

Die FRÖHLICHKEIT   Cheerfulness
(PRANDSTETTER) **D262** [H148]
E major   22(?) August 1815

(22 bars)

Wess Adern leichtes Blut durchspringt,	The man whose blood surges lightly
Der ist ein reicher Mann;	Through his veins is rich.
Auch keine goldnen Ketten zwingt	He is not fettered by the golden chains
Ihm Furcht und Hoffnung an.	Of fear and hope.
Denn Fröhlichkeit geleitet ihn	For gaiety guides him
Bis an ein sanftes Grab	With its magic wand
Wohl durch ein langes Leben hin	Through a long life
An ihrem Zauberstab.	To a gentle death.
[. . . 2 . . .]	[. . . 2 . . .]
Wohin sein muntrer Blick sich kehrt,	Wherever he turns his cheerful gaze
Ist alles schön und gut,	All is fair and good.

Ist alles heil und liebenswert	All is well, worthy of love
Und fröhlich wie sein Mut.	And as blithe as his heart.
Für ihn nur wird bei Sonnenschein	For him alone sunshine
Die Welt zum Paradies,	Makes the world a paradise;
Ist klar der Bach, die Quelle rein,	The brook is clear, the spring pure,
Und ihr Gemurmel süss.	And its murmur sweet.
[. . .6 . . .]	[. . .6 . . .]

MARTIN JOSEF PRANDSTETTER (1760–1798)

This is Schubert's only setting of a Prandstetter text. See the poet's biography.

This merry little song is one of the many cheeky ditties which Schubert places into the mouths of working-class philosophers who put us in mind of Shakespeare's comic characters. Such homespun wisdom was often to be heard from the comical characters of popular Viennese revue. Unlike their intellectual betters in the serious theatre, many music hall artists dared to lampoon the ruling order in satire which, because it was too genial and lowbrow to be considered truly subversive, was tolerated by the authorities. The immortal master of this kind of entertainment, great art disguised as farce, was the playwright Johann Nestroy (1801–1862), also one of Schubert's ensemble singers.

The marking is 'Lebhaft' and the piano writing of the introduction with its oscillation between single notes and thirds (something which suggests folksong and Ländler) is reminiscent of the Schubertian dance. The verb 'durchspringen' has given the composer all the encouragement he needs to find music which springs and bounces along as if the singer's blood is being pumped from head to toe at a hearty rate. It may also be said that the tune seems ever to be moving in an upward direction which is very appropriate for a singer who is on a permanent 'high' (at least in the first verse) right up to the two final loud chords of the postlude. After the first two lines of poetry, octave leaps in the piano interlude (bb. 9–10) seem to describe a great big grin; details in the accompaniment (perky staccati and gurgling trills) suggest uncomplicated high spirits. The words 'goldnen Ketten' (b. 15) prompt sparkling chains of notes – vocal melismas of great geniality. The strophes printed here are 1, 2, 5 and 6 of the poem in twelve verses (printed complete in the AGA and the NSA). A rather more chastened mood emerges in the subsequent strophes as thoughts of the 'gentle grave' render the narrator more philosophical, and non-stop quavers in the vocal line reflect the soft murmurings of the brook.

Autograph:	Missing or lost
First edition:	First published as part of the AGA in 1895 (P579)
Subsequent editions:	Not in Peters; AGA XX 134: Vol. 3/64; NSA IV: Vol. 9/2
Discography and timing:	Fischer-Dieskau I 5[17] 1'04 (First two strophes only)
	Hyperion I 20[7]
	Hyperion II 9[9] 2'34 Ian Bostridge

‹   *Wer kauft Liebesgötter* D261   *Lob des Tokayers* D248 ⟶

FROHSINN

Cheerfulness

(CASTELLI) **D520** [H333]

The song exists in two versions, both of which are discussed below:
(1) January 1817; (2) January 1817

(1) F major

(19 bars)

(2) F major

(20 bars)

Ich bin von lockerem Schlage,	I'm a happy-go-lucky fellow,
Geniess' ohne Trübsinn die Welt,	And enjoy the world without melancholy;
Mich drückt kein Schmerz, keine Plage,	No sorrow, no care worries me,
Mein Frohsinn würzt mir die Tage;	My cheerfulness adds spice to my days;
Ihn hab' ich zum Schild mir gewählt.	I have chosen it as my shield.
Ich grüsse froh jeden Morgen,	I greet each morning cheerfully,
Der nur neue Freuden mir bringt,	And it brings me only new joys.
Fehlt Geld mir, muss ich wohl borgen,	If I'm short of money, then I have to borrow some;
Doch dies macht niemals mir Sorgen,	But this never worries me,
Weil stets jeder Wunsch mir gelingt.	Since my every request is always granted.
Bei Mädchen gerne gesehen,	Though girls like to see it,
Quält Eifersucht niemals mein Herz;	Jealousy never plagues my heart;
Schmollt eine, lass ich sie stehen,	If a girl sulks, I walk off and leave her;
Vor Liebesgram zu vergehen,	To die of the pangs of love
Das wäre ein bitterer Scherz.	Would be a bitter joke.

IGNAZ FRANZ CASTELLI (1781–1862)

This is the first of Schubert's two Castelli solo settings (1817 and 1826–8?). See the poet's biography for a chronological list of all the Castelli settings.

This song is the metropolitan equivalent of Mayrhofer's *Der Alpenjäger* D524; it is in the same key and rhythm, and the sentiments are those of a Viennese who is determined to enjoy life, and refuses to get involved in the tribulations of the grand and important. The character's single-mindedness is shown by the composer's sticking to a conventional and well-trodden harmonic plan; there is not an unusual modulation in sight. Schubert found the Castelli poem in the almanac *Selam* (1813) where there are eleven verses. Before these were discovered in modern times by Dietrich Berke, it had seemed possible that the composer did not regard this as a strophic song, but simply a small and jolly exposition of Papageno-like wit and wisdom. Castelli notes that the words had been set to music by the Berlin composer Friedrich Heinrich Himmel (1765–1814) and this setting (in D major, 𝄴) was published as a musical supplement in *Selam* without appearing to influence Schubert in the least.

We often notice with admiration how adept the composer is at constructing Italianate melodies in the *bel canto* manner; here he shows that he is just as skilled at creating a more muscular German equivalent, a vocal line that is less smooth and unctuous, made to accommodate explosive consonants and a different kind of emotional inflection.

There are two versions available to the performer, both printed in the NSA (1999). The old *Gesamtausgabe* prints the autograph (with a marking of 'Heiter' – 'Merry' – and a four-bar introduction that the NSA convincingly argues is spurious). The Peters Edition prints Diabelli's doctored version (marked 'Lebhaft') with a new introduction that is certainly inauthentic, with changed figurations in the accompaniment. There must have been another manuscript that reflected the composer's original thoughts. The earlier version (also seemingly by Diabelli) is so plain and unadorned, however, that when this song was recorded for the Hyperion Edition (before the publication of the NSA), features from both versions were incorporated, a fact that will scarcely be noticeable to even the most highly trained Schubertian ear.

The text is another matter, however. The first verse as printed above is authentic Castelli, but the second and third were added to the first edition by Diabelli and are nowhere to be found in Castelli – hack work no doubt by a hired poetaster of the time. The industrious Mandyczewski ditched these two further verses for the AGA, but failed to identify both the poet and the fact that the almanac *Selam* 1813 was the source of the words. For those performers who wish to substitute the words printed above for real Castelli, we provide two further authentic strophes – 3 and 5 of the poet's original:

Das Glück treibt elende Künste,
   Steht öfters mit Schurken im Bund;
Lohnt sie mit reichem Gewinnste,
Das kränkt den Mann vom Verdienste:—
   I c h seh' es mit lachendem Mund.

Fortune plays wretched tricks
   And is often in league with rogues;
When it richly rewards them
The man of means is outraged.
   But *I* view it with a smile.

Cupido mag auf mich zielen,
   Ich lache nur seiner Gewalt;
Mit Weibern will ich nur spielen:—
Mir bleibt doch Eine aus Vielen,
   Auf diese Art tröst' ich mich bald.

Cupid may aim his darts at me,
   But I merely mock his power;
I wish only to toy with women;
But if one out of many remains for me,
   I shall console myself soon enough.

Autograph:	Gesellschaft der Musikfreunde, Vienna (first draft)
Publication:	First published as part of the AGA in 1895 (P665; first version)
	First published as Book 45 no. 1 of the *Nachlass* by Diabelli,
	Vienna in 1850 (P370; second version)
Subsequent editions:	Peters: Vol. 4/44; AGA XX 289: Vol. 5/2 (first version); NSA IV:
	Vol. 11/70 (first version) & 71 (second version)
Bibliography:	Berke 1969, p. 485

Discography and timing: Fischer-Dieskau I 9[7] 0'38 (first strophe only)
Hyperion I 34[3]
Hyperion II 17[11] 1'46 Stephan Loges

← *Der Flug der Zeit* D515

Jagdlied D521 →

Die FRÜHE LIEBE
(HÖLTY) **D430** [H257]

Early love

The song exists in two versions, the first of which is discussed below, and is dated May 1816. The authenticity of the second version is in doubt.

(1) E major

Schon im bun - ten Kna - ben-klei - de pfleg-ten hüb-sche Mäg - de-lein

(14 bars)

(2) E major

Schon im bun - ten Kna-ben-klei - de

(18 bars)

Schon im bunten Knabenkleide,	When I was still a lad in bright clothes
Pflegten hübsche Mägdelein	I would rather feast my eyes
Meine liebste Augenweide,	On pretty girls
Mehr als Pupp' und Ball zu sein.	Than on a doll or ball.
Ich vergass der Vogelnester,	I forgot about birds' nests,
Warf mein Steckenpferd ins Gras,	And threw my hobby-horse on the grass
Wenn am Baum bei meiner Schwester	When a pretty girl sat beside my sister
Eine schöne Dirne sass;	Under a tree.
Freute mich der muntern Dirne,	I delighted in the lively girl,
Ihres roten Wangenpaars,	Her red cheeks,
Ihres Mundes, ihrer Stirne,	Her mouth, her brow,
Ihres blonden Lockenhaars;	Her blond curly hair.
Blickt' auf Busentuch und Mieder,	I would gaze at her shawl and bodice
Hinterwärts gelehnt am Baum;	As she leant against a tree;

Streckte dann ins Gras mich nieder,	Then I would stretch out in the grass
Dicht an ihres Kleides Saum.	Close to the hem of her dress.
[(. . .)]	[(. . .)]

LUDWIG HÖLTY (1748–1776); poem written 15 February 1773. Adapted for publication in 1804 by JOHANN HEINRICH VOSS (1751–1826).

This is the eighteenth of Schubert's twenty-three Hölty solo settings (1813–16). See the poet's biography for a chronological list of all the Hölty settings.

Perhaps Schubert returned to Hölty's lyrics in 1816 because of Josef von Spaun's plan at that time to publish songs grouped by their authors which meant that more settings of this poet's work were needed to make a convincing collection of them. This new engagement with Hölty's poetry has nothing forced or dutiful about it. Admittedly among this second group of poems there is nothing like the famous *An den Mond* D193, neither are there experimental songs that can easily outclass *An die Apfelbäume* D197; by 1816 Schubert seems to have decided what he likes most about this poet, and that is open-hearted simplicity. He also composed melancholy settings (*Klage an den Mond* D436 and *An den Mond* II D468) but he was more drawn to Hölty's pictures of youth and domesticity, happiness and hard work. Freshness and spontaneity are exactly what these songs have in abundant quantity.

This little scherzino bubbles with childlike high spirits, as if the composer is laughing at one of his younger siblings, or indeed himself. The piano writing in a bustling $\frac{2}{4}$ is laid out like the sort of Clementi sonatina which a boy of this age would be playing in his piano lessons; the hands are close together without leaps and jumps but there is a roguish complicity between the various strands of melody. In the manner of a Haydn song the voice part doubles the piano's right hand except at the final cadence where it is freed for a last flourish (bb. 15–19). The song is a mock apology for over-amorous behaviour and Schubert takes great delight in this little Don Juan in the bud. The key of the song is E major, the quintessential Hölty tonality for scenes in field or garden which are flooded with sunlight from a happier, less complicated time. In that sense the song is nostalgic, like many Schubert settings of this poet.

The version printed in the AGA is the first of two printed in the NSA: this is without a piano introduction. The second version in the NSA (marked 'Heiter') has a four-bar introduction that is simply taken from the postlude. Hölty's poem has five strophes and Schubert omits the last of these. The AGA prints it in brackets. A reference to the adult man sleeping in the grave of his fathers must have seemed too morbid an ending for a song of this light-hearted mood.

Autograph:	In private possession (first draft, auctional 2001)
Publication:	First published as part of the AGA in 1895 (P639; first version)
	First published as part of the NSA in 2002 (P836; second version)
Subsequent editions:	Not in Peters; AGA XX 222: Vol. 4/104 (first version); NSA IV: Vol. 10/156 (first version) & 157 (second version)
Discography and timing:	Fischer-Dieskau I 7[12] 1'32
	Hyperion I 23[15]
	Hyperion II 14[8] 1'36 Christoph Prégardien

←— *Minnelied* D429   *Blumenlied* D431 —→

Die FRÜHEN GRÄBER

(KLOPSTOCK) **D290** [H176]
A minor   14 September 1815

The early graves

(16 bars)

Willkommen, o silberner Mond,
Schöner, stiller Gefährte der Nacht!
Du entfliehst? Eile nicht, bleib,
  Gedankenfreund!
Sehet, er bleibt, das Gewölk wallte nur hin.

Des Maies Erwachen ist nur
Schöner noch, wie die Sommernacht,
Wenn ihm Tau, hell wie Licht, aus der
  Locke träuft,
Und zu dem Hügel herauf rötlich er kommt.

Ihr Edleren, ach, es bewächst
Eure Male schon ernstes Moos!
O wie war glücklich ich, als ich noch mit euch
Sahe sich röten den Tag, schimmern die Nacht!

Welcome, silvery moon,
Fair, silent companion of the night!
You flee? Do not hasten away, stay, friend of
  contemplation.
See, she stays; it was only the clouds passing.

May's awakening
Is lovelier even than the summer's night,
When dew, glistening brightly, drips from his
  locks,
And he rises red above the hills.

Nobler spirits, alas, your tombstones
Are already overgrown with gloomy moss.
Ah, how happy I was then, when with you,
I watched the day dawn and the night sky glitter!

FRIEDRICH GOTTLOB KLOPSTOCK (1724–1803); poem written in 1764

*This is the seventh of Schubert's thirteen Klopstock solo settings (1815–16). See the poet's
biography for a chronological list of all the Klopstock settings.*

The poem is one of Klopstock's 'Odes to my dead friends'. This kind of simple setting is easily
overshadowed by its more outgoing neighbours, but it is a small gem – a perfect example of
Romantic feeling illuminating a text from the previous century. The poet's contemplations on
death included the loss of his first wife, Meta – the celebrated 'Cidli' – to whom he had only
been married for four years. The melody is beautiful and haunting, tinged with regret, even
anguish – the second line of the verse modulates in an unexpected and disconsolate manner,
the colouring on 'Gedankenfreund' full of pathos – but it maintains a poise appropriate to a
poet who had attained a philosophical calm through a study of the classics. Gluck's famous C
major setting of the words (and scrupulously respecting their prosody, unlike Schubert) dates
from 1773. The dactylic rhythm of the first part of the verse is typically Schubertian. In the
manner of the eighteenth-century lied, the vocal line is almost completely doubled by the piano
– something that seems only to aid the depiction of translucent moonlight, and the creation of
an atmosphere that transcends earthly reality. The poet has highlighted the masculine gender
of the handsome self-renewing month of May (through the use of 'des', 'ihm' and 'er') as a
contrast to the beauty lost to the world with the death of young men in the springtime of their

lives, the patriotic noble souls, who now lie dead and buried. The phrase despised as 'The old Lie' by Wilfred Owen, but no doubt well known to the nationalistic Klopstock, comes to mind: *Dulce et decorum est pro patria mori.*

The publisher Diabelli clearly considered the original key of A minor too high for commercial viability; accordingly the song was issued in G minor with a spurious four-bar introduction. Mention should be made of Fanny Mendelssohn's unusual and beautiful setting of these words, composed in November 1828, a month before Schubert died, where both the pianist's hands remain in the sombre reaches of the bass clef. This is all the more poignant when one considers that Schubert himself was one of those young men, heroic too in his way, who went to an early grave. Another song from quite another time and place comes to mind: Ravel's Greek folksong setting about buried war heroes, *Là-bas vers l'église.*

Autograph:	Gesellschaft der Musikfreunde, Vienna (first draft)
	Pierpont Morgan Library, New York (fair copy of the last four bars)
First edition:	Published as Book 28 no. 5 of the *Nachlass* by Diabelli, Vienna in April 1837 (P319)
Subsequent editions:	Peters Vol. 5/192; AGA XX 144: Vol. 3/84; NSA IV: Vol. 9/71
Bibliography:	Gülke 1991, pp. 76–9
	Reid 2007, pp. 124–5
Further settings and arrangements:	Christoph Willibald von Gluck (1714–1787) *Die frühen Gräber* (1786)
	Christian Gottlob Neefe (1748–1798) *Die frühen Gräber* (1785)
	Johann Friedrich Reichardt (1752–1814) *Die frühen Gräber* (1779)
	Ludwig van Beethoven (1770–1827) Sketch (1815)
	Fanny Mendelssohn (1805–1847) *Die frühen Gräber* Op. 9 no. 4 (1828)
	Ernst Krenek (1900–1991) *Die frühen Gräber* Op. 19 no. 5 (1923)
	Arr. Tilman Hoppstock (b. 1961) for guitar accompaniment, in *Franz Schubert: 110 Lieder* (2009)
Discography and timing:	Fischer-Dieskau I 5[23] 1'49
	Hyperion I 8[5]
	Hyperion II 10[11] 2'26 Sarah Walker

← *Die Sommernacht* D289   *Dem Unendlichen* D291 →

FRÜHLINGSGESANG   Spring song   Quartet, TTBB
(SCHOBER) OP. 16 NO. 1, **D740** [H483]
D major   January–April 1822

(155 bars)

Schmücket die Locken mit duftigen Kränzen	Adorn your tresses with fragrant garlands
Und folget der Freude beglückendem Drang!	And follow your joyful impulses;
Begrüsset den Frühling mit heiteren Tänzen,	With merry dances welcome spring,
Den Sieger, der Alles in Liebe bezwang.	The victor, who has conquered all for love.
Der Winter bedroht ihn mit schauriger Kälte,	Winter threatens him with dread cold;
Der Sommer verfolgt ihn mit flammendem Speer;	Summer pursues him with flaming spear;
Aber er schwebt unter blauem Gezelte	But beneath the blue firmament he glides along
Sorglos und lächelnd auf Düften daher.	On sweet scents, carefree and smiling.
Und die treue Erde	And the true earth
Mit Liebes-Geberde	With a loving gesture
Eilt ihm entgegen,	Hastens to meet him,
Es heben und regen	A thousand powers
Sich tausend Kräfte in ihrer Brust	Surging in her breast,
Und künden der Liebe selige Lust.	And proclaiming the blissful pleasures of love.
[(. . .)]	[(. . .)]
Drum schmücke die Locken mit bräutlichen Kränzen,	So if vital energy pulsates in your breast,
Wem schaffende Kraft noch den Busen durchdringt,	Adorn your tresses with nuptial garlands
Und huld'ge dem Sieger in heiteren Tänzen,	And honour in merry dances the victor
Der Alles mit schaffender Liebe bezwingt.	Who conquers all with the creative power of love.

Franz von Schober (1796–1882)

After the success of first *Das Dörfchen* D598, and then *Die Nachtigall* D724, Schubert was almost certainly pressed to write another male-voice quartet along the same lines – there was obviously a market for such music. Like both those works, *Frühlingsgesang* is in the key of D major, and like *Die Nachtigall* it consists of a bewitching dance-like opening, which contrasts well with the closing jollification where lyricism is more or less abandoned in favour of hearty communal singing, presumably accompanied by the clinking of foaming tankards. It is natural that the composer should have turned to his close friend Schober to furnish the words – the two were working together as librettist and composer on the opera *Alfonso und Estrella* at the time.

It is more than likely that the lead tenor part was written for the same artist who sang the first performance of *Die Nachtigall*, Josef Barth. The time signature ($\frac{2}{4}$) is the same for both songs, and a somewhat rigid rhythmic template provides the lead tenor with the stable framework he needs later to launch into his rich embroidery of the vocal line. These quartets were written with an unashamed desire to cater for public taste, and in the coloratura of the first tenor line we glimpse the influence of fashionable Italian vocal pyrotechnics.

None of this is to deny that the piece is thoroughly Schubertian. As always when this composer launches into musical dactyls (and there can be few pieces more insistently grounded in dactylic rhythm than this) we are swept along by the irresistible momentum of it all. Spring is here depicted as a real life force, like the stars (cf. the similar rhythm of *Die Sterne* D939).

Mankind, aided by Schubert's vision, can only regard these natural phenomena with wonder, and join in the dance.

The melody of *Frühlingsgesang* is a delight – a trippingly ingratiating tune eight bars long which is good enough to repeat immediately, words and all. And we hear this phrase, or variants of it, throughout the piece – never tiring of it. At 'Begrüsset den Frühling mit heiteren Tänzen' (from b. 18) there is a contrasting four-bar phrase with a high-lying tessitura for the lead singer: the setting of 'Begrüsset', with a gentle accent placed high in the tenor line and then falling in obeisance to the triumphant new visitor. These four bars too, in the spirit of round dance, we hear more than once.

The second verse (from b. 58) shifts into B minor at mention of winter ('Der Winter bedroht ihn mit schauriger Kälte'), and the change is chilling. We are suddenly in the region of frozen wastes and blizzards – but not for long, as the return of spring is inevitable. At the third verse ('Und die treue Erde / mit Liebes-Geberde' from b. 75) there is a contemplative passage in A major, open fifths in the bass accompaniment, which is hauntingly prophetic of *Pause* from *Die schöne Müllerin*. This leads us back to a final repeat of the principal melody, now gracefully ornamented. The composer has here written out the type of free 'improvement' of the music (at 'Und künden der Liebe selige Lust' bb. 86–94) which might just have been spontaneously added as a *da capo* by a contemporary singer with some musical initiative, whether or not Schubert had included these capricious extras in the score.

The final verse (marked 'Heiter doch nicht zu schnell') is obviously inspired by the words 'schaffende Kraft' and is very effective, if somewhat disappointing after the ravishing music of the opening. As in *Die Nachtigall*, Schubert gives the first tenor a substantial (and technically difficult because high-lying) solo in § (bb. 105–16) before introducing the second tenor in quasi canon. The first bass enters in the subdominant for his solo (b. 124), and a duet ensues with the second bass (from b. 128). All four voices join together for the peroration which includes a reminder of the coloratura abilities of the lead tenor. The music whips itself up into a bucolic dance, but the piece ends with a coda where a significant word like 'Liebe' is elongated (a high B for Tenor I, b. 156) to soulful effect. It is a formula that had worked before: the sensitivity of the first section is balanced by the manly back-slapping of the second.

There are two versions of this piece. The first, D709, is without piano accompaniment, and this was performed at the Kärntnertortheater on 7 April 1822. The work (sometimes known as *Frühlingslied*) was published in October 1823 with a piano part, but this is more or less a reduction of the vocal parts. It remains a moot point whether it was provided merely for the convenience of rehearsal, and to keep the singers in tune, or whether the composer actually preferred to hear this music with an accompaniment. The addition of the piano adds a certain weight and colour to the piece which is not unattractive, and the decision concerning the piano's inclusion remains, then as now, a matter of taste and convenience.

Autograph:	Conservatoire collection, Bibliothèque Nationale, Paris
First edition:	Published as Op. 16 no. 1 by Cappi und Diabelli, Vienna in October 1823 (P48)
First known performance:	7 April 1822 in a benefit at the Kärntnertortheater, Vienna. Performers: Franz Rosner, Ludwig Tietze, Wenzel Nejebse and Johann Michael Weinkopf (see Waidelich/Hilmar Dokumente I no. 147 for full concert programme)
Performance reviews:	*Wiener allgemeine Theaterzeitung* no. 47 (18 April 1822), p. 186f. [Waidelich/Hilmar Dokumente I no. 149]
	Allgemeine musikalische Zeitung (Leipzig), no. 22 (29 May 1822), col. 357 [Waidelich/Hilmar Dokumente I no. 160]

Subsequent editions: AGA XVI 7: p. 65; NSA III: Vol. 3
Discography and timing: Hyperion I 28⁹   Paul Agnew, Jamie MacDougall, Simon
                                                          4'03
                           Hyperion II 25⁹   Keenlyside & Michael George

← *Herrn Josef Spaun, Assessor in Linz D749*   *Nachtviolen D752* →

FRÜHLINGSGLAUBE   Faith in spring
(UHLAND) OP. 20 NO. 2, **D686** [H455]

The song exists in three versions, the third of which is discussed below:
(1) September 1820; (2) Autumn 1820?; (3) November 1822

(1)   'Mässig'   B♭ major $\frac{2}{4}$ [51 bars]

(2)   'Mässig'   B♭ major $\frac{2}{4}$ [51 bars]

(3)   A♭ major

(51 bars)

Die linden Lüfte sind erwacht,	Balmy breezes are awakened;
Sie säuseln und weben Tag und Nacht,	They stir and whisper day and night,
Sie schaffen an allen Enden.	Everywhere creative.
O frischer Duft, o neuer Klang!	O fresh scents, O new sounds!
Nun, armes Herze, sei nicht bang!	Now, poor heart, do not be afraid.
Nun muss sich Alles, Alles wenden.	Now all must change.
Die Welt wird schöner mit jedem Tag,	The world grows fairer each day;
Man weiss nicht, was noch werden mag,	We cannot know what is still to come;
Das Blühen will nicht enden.	The flowering knows no end.
Es blüht das fernste, tiefste Tal:	The deepest, most distant valley is in flower.
Nun, armes Herz, vergiss der Qual!	Now, poor heart, forget your torment.
Nun muss sich Alles, Alles wenden.	Now all must change.

LUDWIG UHLAND (1787–1862); poem written 21 March 1812

This is Schubert's only setting of an Uhland text. See the poet's biography.

The tune is as accessible and memorable as a hymn, and there is a hint of the march of spring in the piano's dotted rhythm (cf. 'Der Mai ist gekommen, der Winter ist aus' from *Trockne Blumen* in *Die schöne Müllerin*). But there is nothing triumphant about the music which floats, glides and insinuates itself into the senses. The song is in strophic form with slight variations, and in two verses. The key is A flat major (changed at publication stage by the composer from B flat major after a gestation of more than two years). In the left hand the accompaniment consists mainly of sextuplets; the right is a mixture of smooth quavers and semiquavers, incorporating that little dotted motif suggestive of the frisson of spring awakening. The legato vocal line wends its way between the trellis-like lines of the stave like a seamlessly woven garland.

Everything is here graceful undulation; the melody climbs as it aspires to its goal on 'Sie schaffen an allen Enden' (bb. 9–13) and then shyly subsides. The sound of fragrance, the fragrance of sound, hangs in the air at 'O frischer Duft, o neuer Klang!' (bb. 13–15). We hear this 'Klang' in a tiny piano interlude (b. 16) where an E flat minim is picked out by the little finger of the right hand, while the sextuplets, the concern of the other fingers, seraphically go on their way. All this is supported by left-hand thirds which provide an ache of longing at the heart of the music. (In the second verse this passage even more effectively mirrors the resonance of sound, and the glimpse of spring colours in the deepest and most distant of valleys – 'Es blüht das fernste, tiefste Tal'.) A diminished seventh at 'Nun, armes Herz' (b. 17) gives us a hint of the pains of the past. The performers pull themselves together for 'Nun muss sich Alles, Alles wenden' in the home key (bb. 20–24); this borders on the ecstasy which accompanies a vision of unreasonable hope. Here the remaining energy of those who have been rebuffed countless times is marshalled to convince the listeners (and themselves) that yes, everything will be all right. The flowering of the final phrase, the second 'Nun muss sich Alles, _Alles_ wenden' (the repeat of 'alles' is the poet's own, the repeat of the entire line Schubert's) has something even more visionary about it: in its melisma (b. 23) – extravagant for Schubert – we hear the echo of the song of the nightingale as it presses its heart to the rose thorn, or perhaps the swansong of a creature _in extremis_ and on the threshold of transfiguration.

This, by common consent, is one of Schubert's great songs, much loved and performed (though not often well). It is his only setting of the important Swabian poet Ludwig Uhland, and although these lines are famous and adequate for Schubert's needs they are not the poet's greatest literary achievement. Walther Dürr believes that Schubert's recent brush with the authorities (and the exile of the poet Johann Senn) played a part in his choice of text – a longing for a change of season equates with a desire for regime change. This is a moot point. The song however shines with the inner glow that seems far removed from political considerations, a rhapsodic _Innigkeit_, which we have come to recognize as an inherently Schubertian quality. The quiet and gentle optimism that life will surely get better, that happiness lies just around the corner, seems appropriate to (and prophetic of) what we know of the composer's own later stoicism in the face of failed hopes and personal tragedy. Even when he wrote, in the years of his illness, of his disappointment and desperation, his music continued to flow, unadulterated by bitterness and rancour. The belief, expressed in this song, that springtime has come and, with it a conviction, that better times will follow, has the bright-eyed radiance of a dying yet sublimely optimistic child – Little Nell in _The Old Curiosity Shop_, or Beth in _Little Women_. The essential goodness and innate resilience of these characters does not seem all that far away from Schubert himself as we have come to perceive him through his music. Hermann Hesse in Chapter One of _Glasperlenspiel_ (1943) writes of _Frühlingsglaube_ that,

> _the first chords of the piano accompaniment assailed me like something already familiar. Those chords had exactly the same fragrance as the sap of the young elder, just as bittersweet, just as strong and compressed, just as full of the coming spring. ... As soon as the first chord is struck I immediately smell the tartness of the sap, and both together mean to me 'spring is on the way'. This private association of mine is a precious possession I would not willingly give up._

There is danger in this bittersweet mixture of emotions. Like all songs where we sense the narrator has suffered a great deal, *Frühlingsglaube* teeters precariously on the borders of sentimentality and, if performers are determined to milk it for all its possibilities of pathetic expression, it can easily take on the characteristics of a lachrymose Victorian ballad. The secret of a truly moving performance lies in the tempo. Schubert's marking 'Ziemlich langsam' means 'rather slow', and it is the interpretation of the 'rather' which is the nub. The time signature is $\frac{2}{4}$ and it is the crotchet, not the quaver, which is the main beat. Performers who favour four slow quavers in the bar, rather than two flowing crotchets, will lose the fragrant lightness of the 'linden Lüfte' which 'säuseln und weben'; the song becomes leaden and sad, rather than a floating vision of hope eternal.

Frühlingsglaube is indeed, at its heart, a sad song, but it is not for the performers to promote the work's inherent pathos. This shines through the music of its own accord, together with an inbuilt awareness of the frailty of human hopes and of life itself. The emotional power is engendered by the difference in viewpoint between the performer who is confident that everything will change for the better ('Nun muss sich Alles, Alles wenden'), and those listening who know that spring will never arrive for this singer, nor for Schubert for that matter. Thus the singer and the text rejoice while the music itself leads the listener to a different conclusion entirely: we hear so much gratitude for so little reward, all of it so soon to be betrayed, and the effect is almost unbearably poignant. How different this is from Mendelssohn's breezy and energetic song (Op. 9 no. 8, 1830) which reflects Uhland's words perfectly – but on one level. This was a twenty-one-year-old composer who had not yet known a significant setback. And there is no clue in the music to suggest that Mendelssohn knew Schubert's setting, although the printed song would have been available to him.

This song reflects the Schubert's astonishing and humbling ability to rejoice in the beauty of the world, in the here and now. He gave out love (in both musical and personal terms) and expected little, if anything, in return. The greatest of his songs seem to incorporate an element of the man himself: naive sophistication, charming directness, graceful earthiness, unsparing, even painful, honesty – a simple joy in being alive in the present. These things animate *Frühlingsglaube* with a breath of life against all the odds; why a seemingly simple work like this can vibrate with humanity when grander works by lesser composers remain lumps of musical clay is one of the mysteries of music.

Volume 1b of the NSA prints two further versions: the first from September 1820, the second from later in the autumn of the same year. The marking of both is 'Mässig'; the key is B flat major. Although it would be uncomfortably high for many singers it is easy to believe that these versions reflect the composer's original choice of tonality – a key for the heady unreality of dreams and unfounded hopes. This first version as it appears in the AGA is from a copy of the song made by Ferdinand Schubert and is also in A flat.

Autographs:	Vatican Library (in B flat major) (first version)
	Bayerische Staatsbibliothek, Munich and Staatsbibliothek zu Preussicher Kulturbesitz, Berlin (second version)
Publication:	First published as part of the NSA in 1970 (P753 & P754; first and second versions)
	First published as Op. 20 no. 2 by Sauer & Leidesdorf, Vienna in April 1823 (P37; third version)
Dedicatee:	Justina von Bruchmann
Subsequent editions:	Peters: Vol. 1/94; AGA XX 300a & b: Vol. 6/108 (given as first version, recte second) & 110 (given as second version, recte third); NSA IV: Vol. 1a/141 (third version) & Vol. 1b/252 (first version) & 256 (second version); Bärenreiter: Vol. 1/112

Bibliography:	Black 2003, p. 193 (for a discussion of the political aspects of Uhland's verse)
	Capell 1928, p. 168–9
	Einstein 1951, p. 193
	Fischer-Dieskau 1977, p. 138
	Kohlhäufl 1999, p. 320
Further settings and arrangements:	Conradin Kreutzer (1780–1849) Op. 33 no. 2 (1812)
	Felix Mendelssohn (1809–1847) Op. 9 no. 8 (1830)
	Arr. Franz Liszt (1811–1886) for piano, no. 7 of *Lieder von Schubert* (1837–8)
Discography and timing:	Fischer-Dieskau II 3²² 2'53
	Hyperion I 29¹⁹
	Hyperion II 23¹³ 3'30 Marjana Lipovšek

← *Freiwilliges Versinken* D700   *Der Jüngling auf dem Hügel* D702 →

FRÜHLINGSLIED   Spring song
(HÖLTY) **D398** [H263]
G major   13 May 1816

(16 bars)

Die Luft ist blau, das Tal ist grün,	The sky is blue, the valley green,
Die kleinen Maienglocken blühn,	The lilies of the valley are in bloom,
Und Schlüsselblumen drunter;	With cowslips among them;
Der Wiesengrund	The meadows
Ist schon so bunt	Are already so colourful,
Und malt sich täglich bunter.	And grow more so each day.
Drum komme, wem der Mai gefällt,	Come, then, if you love May,
Und schaue froh die schöne Welt	Behold with joy the beautiful world
Und Gottes Vatergüte,	And God's fatherly kindness
Die solche Pracht	That brought forth
Hervorgebracht,	Such splendour,
Den Baum und seine Blüte.	The tree and its blossom.

LUDWIG CHRISTOPH HÖLTY (1748–1776); poem written 17 February 1773. Adapted for publication in 1804 by JOHANN HEINRICH VOSS (1751–1826).

This is the thirteenth of Schubert's twenty-three Hölty solo settings (1813–16). See the poet's biography for a chronological list of all the Hölty settings.

This is the first of a new wave of Hölty songs begun in 1816. The poet's original title was 'Mailied', and it was composed on a May day in 1816 that may well have been as wonderful as the one here evoked by the poet. It is the purest Schubert and impossible to analyse: to think too hard as to how the composer achieved this freshness would be like stripping away a flower's petals to find out how it grows. The accompaniment ripples deliciously, here and there making delightful intervals of thirds and sixths with the vocal line; there is one charming *Zwischenspiel* (bb. 7–8) and a postlude which touches the relative minor just long enough to suggest gratitude and awe amidst all the high spirits. Everything here is freshly minted and utterly natural – as miraculous as the tree mentioned in the second verse which brings forth its blossom thanks only to the kindness of God. There are spring songs of greater profundity in the Schubert canon (the Uhland setting *Frühlingsglaube* for instance D686) but there is no song which better captures the bright, airy aspect of that season, and the light-heartedness, the lifting of the spirits, that comes with its onset. Schubert had already set these Hölty words in 1815 for male trio (TTB, D243). The tempo is *Langsam* in that work; it is quite a different kind of tribute to spring, conveying a sense of wonder in a solemn hymn of gratitude, rather than in a carefree paean of praise.

Autograph:	Library of Congress, Washington, DC
First edition:	Published as Vol. 7 no. 39 in Friedlaender's edition by Peters, Leipzig in 1887 (P500)
Subsequent editions:	Peters: Vol. 7/89; AGA XX 217: Vol. 4/97; NSA IV: Vol. 10/88
Arrangement:	Arr. Tilman Hoppstock (b. 1961) for guitar accompaniment, in *Franz Schubert: 110 Lieder* (2009)
Discography and timing:	Fischer-Dieskau I 7[7] 1'13
	Hyperion I 17[9]
	Hyperion II 14[15] 1'16 Lucia Popp

← *Klage (An den Mond)* D₂436   *Auf den Tod einer Nachtigall* D399 →

FRÜHLINGSLIED   Spring song
(POLLAK) **D919** [H612]
A♭ major   Between April and June 1827; solo song reworking of quartet for TTBB D914

(86 bars)

Geöffnet sind des Winters Riegel,	Winter's bolts are opened;
Entschwunden ist sein Silberflor;	His silver veil has vanished;
Hell blinken der Gewässer Spiegel,	The mirrors of the water sparkle brightly;
Die Lerche schwingt sich hoch empor;	The lark soars aloft.
Wie durch Salomos Zaubersiegel[1]	As if awakened by Solomon's magic seal,
Geweckt ertönt der Freude Chor.	The chorus of joy resounds.

[1] In the choral version of this piece the line has been changed to 'Wie durch des weisen Königs Siegel'.

Der Frühling schwebt auf die Gefilde	Spring hovers over the fields
Und lieblich wehet Zephir nur,	And zephyrs blow softly.
Der Blumendüfte süsse Milde	The gentle sweetness of fragrant flowers
Erhebt sich in der Luft Azur,	Rises into the azure air.
In der Verklärung Wunderbilde	In its magical transfiguration,
Empfängt uns lächelnd die Natur.	Smiling nature receives us.
Schon prangen goldgeschmückt Sylphiden	Already sylphs are resplendent in gold array,
Und Florens Reich erblüht verschönt,	And Flora's realm blooms with enhanced beauty.
Rings waltet Lust und stiller Frieden,	All around there is joy and tranquil peace.
Der Hain ist nun mit Laub bekrönt,	The grove is now crowned with leaves,
Wer fühlet, ihm ist Glück beschieden,	And happiness is granted to all who have feelings,
Weil Eros' süsser Ruf ertönt.	Since the sweet call of Eros resounds.
Empfanget denn mit trautem Grusse	So receive with a heartfelt greeting
Den holden Lenz, den Schmuck der Welt,	Fair spring, the jewel of the world,
Der weihend uns mit leisem Kusse	Who with a soft kiss consecrates
Des Daseins Rosenbahn erhellt,	And brightens the rosy path of our existence,
Der hold uns winkt zum Hochgenusse	Sweetly beckons us to the highest pleasures
Und jedes Herz mit Wonne schwellt.	And fills every heart with bliss.

Aaron Pollak (1764–1829)

This is Schubert's only setting of a Pollak text. See the poet's biography.

This is one of only two instances when Schubert's unaccompanied choral works re-emerge as piano-accompanied songs. The first was the Seidl setting *Widerspruch* D865, originally conceived as a four-part male chorus with optional piano accompaniment, which was published in November 1828 as both quartet and solo song (Op. 105 no. 1). In that case nothing special was done to deck the music out for its new guise: the solo part is identical to the first tenor line in the quartet; the accompaniment is also unchanged and doubles the vocal line throughout. In the case of *Frühlingslied*, however, the presence of the piano transforms what had been originally conceived for unaccompanied male quartet (D914) into a beautiful solo song, personable and containing authentic Schubertian detail.

The publisher Tobias Haslinger had commissioned the quartet to be included in his choral anthology *Die deutschen Minnesänger*. The wonderful Seidl quartet *Grab und Mond* D893 appeared in this series, as did *Wein und Liebe* D901, but for some reason *Frühlingslied* for TTBB (in C major, rather than the A flat major of the solo version) was never published. In this form the manuscript was dated April 1827. Schubert made some adjustments to the word underlay in the quartet seemingly *after* the solo song had been written.

This piece is one of the most rarely heard in the Schubert repertory, not because of its lack of quality, but because of the strange circumstances of its composition and publication. A copy of the song was found in the 1890s among the papers of Rudolf Weinwurm who had been choirmaster of the Wiener Männergesang Verein and in close contact with Schubert's nephew Eduard Schneider. It was such a late discovery that *Frühlingslied* is not to be found in the Peters Edition (a historic disadvantage for a Schubert song's progress through the world) and it was only just in time to be included in the Supplement volume (1897) of the AGA. Its inclusion in Bärenreiter Vol. 4 is a boon for those without access to either this tome or to Volume 14 of the NSA (1988).

Scholars are still discussing the arrangement's authenticity. At least Schubert's hand in melody and harmony is uncontested; it is only the piano accompaniment that comes into question. At times this seems dully chained to the vocal line, and there are untypical moments of pianistic awkwardness. But if someone other than Schubert made this arrangement, they are by far the most gifted of the many who have attempted to impersonate the composer's style. There is also a freedom in adapting the work for its new form (the first example is that the work begins forte in the choral version, pianissimo in the solo) which indicates the confident hand of the work's original creator. Another possibility of course was that it was done by a Schubert disciple (Franz Lachner perhaps?) guided in general, if not in every last detail, by the composer himself. This would explain both the felicitous and uncharacteristic aspects of the piano writing.

A flat major is a key that we already associate with Schubertian spring music because of the song *Frühlingsglaube* D686. In Weinwurm's copy, the composer's use of the word 'Voce' to designate the vocal line is typical of works of this period, and there is an appropriately Italianate feel about the weaving triplets of this purling cantilena. The lambent triplet accompaniment is similar to that of another 1827 song, *Heimliches Lieben* D922. In *Frühlingslied* the softly rippling arpeggios are enlivened by a touch of spring-like energy in the left hand's dotted rhythms, semiquavers that have to line up with the right-hand triplets to avoid sounding grotesquely clipped (this is as good an indication as any in Schubert's work of the performing practice of the time regarding triplets and dotted rhythms). In Verse 1 (bb. 10–12), there is a reference to King Solomon ('durch Salomos Zaubersiegel') which perhaps gives us a second clue (the first is his name) to Aaron Pollak's Jewish background. In the choral version Schubert himself changed these words to refer less specifically to a wise king, and we must assume he would have done so for the solo version as well if he had had the manuscript to hand (the NSA changes it, and adds a footnote).

The music for Verse 2 (from b. 32) changes into D flat major, and the accompaniment moves into gently throbbing triplets, appropriate for the imagery of 'Der Frühling schwebt auf die Gefilde'. There is no attempt to include in this arrangement the beautiful contrapuntal touches between tenors and baritones that can be heard at this point in the choral version. Instead, the right hand of the piano is given some moments of counter-melody and some effective harmonic suspensions. As elsewhere in this song, the melody and harmony are unquestionably by Schubert, so the music sounds genuine; but it seems a pity that the piano doggedly shadows the vocal line to such an extent. The music for Verse 3 is an exact repeat of Verse 2.

At 'Empfanget denn mit trautem Grusse' (Verse 4) the music returns to the home key of A flat major, changes time signature to ⅜, and takes on more of a celebratory swing. We are reminded of how *Der Hirt auf dem Felsen* D965 also ends with an invocation to spring and an upbeat change of time and mood. The dotted rhythm of the vocal line is echoed at a distance of a crotchet by a similarly cheeky piano figuration, an idea that is adopted from the dialogue between the tenors and basses in the choral version. At 'Der hold uns winkt zum Hochgenusse', semiquavers, indicative of rising sap and new flowerings (from b. 59) begin to enter the accompaniment. The vocal line (at 'Wonne schwellt' b. 68) is decorated with a turn like a garland at a spring festival. The piano writing in this coda is not typical of Schubert the lieder composer, but it does recall the keyboard layout to be found in some of the chamber music, in particular the works for violin and piano that are such a feature of 1827. The progress from pianissimo to forte at 'Der weihend uns mit leisem Kusse / Des Daseins Rosenbahn erhellt' (bb. 67–71) is achieved in a thoroughly instrumental manner, as is the coda where the final lines for the voice are accompanied by gently swirling semiquaver arpeggios high in the keyboard. In the postlude these cascade downwards from the top of the piano to the very bottom, all on an unchanging chord of A flat major. This makes a charming general effect, something which may also be said of the song as a whole – a potpourri of salon fragrances. The text, flowery in every sense, is somewhat to blame for this, but then *Heimliches Lieben* makes a similar impression. Indeed, it is the presence of that very song in the authentic Schubert catalogue for 1827 that seems to confirm that this arrangement of *Frühlingslied* came from Schubert's hand in the same year.

| Autograph: | Missing or lost |
| First edition: | Published as part of the AGA in 1897 (P729) |

Subsequent editions:	Not in Peters; AGA XXI 36b: Supplement, p. 325; NSA IV: Vol. 14/53; Bärenreiter: Vol. 4/89
Discography and timing:	Fischer-Dieskau —
	Hyperion I 36[4]
	Hyperion II 32[19] 4'36 Juliane Banse

← *Der Vater mit dem Kind* D906   *Gute Nacht* D911/1 →

FRÜHLINGSSEHNSUCHT *see SCHWANENGESANG* D957/3

FRÜHLINGSTRAUM *see WINTERREISE* D911/11

FÜLLE DER LIEBE   Unbounded love
(F. VON SCHLEGEL) **D854** [H573]
A♭ major   August 1825

(104 bars)

(1)	Ein sehnend Streben	A yearning desire
	Teilt mir das Herz,	Pierces my heart,
	Bis alles Leben	Till all life
	Sich löst in Schmerz.	Is dissolved in sorrow.
(2)	In Leid erwachte	The youthful spirit
	Der junge Sinn,	Awoke in suffering,
	Und Liebe brachte	And love brought me
	Zum Ziel mich hin.	To my goal.
(3)	Ihr edle Flammen,	You, noble flames,
	Wecktet mich auf;	Aroused me;
	Es ging mitsammen	Everything surged
	Zu Gott der Lauf.	To God.
(4)	Ein Feuer war es,	It was a fire
	Das alles treibt;	Driving it all;
	Ein starkes, klares,	A strong, clear fire
	Das ewig bleibt.	That remains for ever.
(5)	Was wir anstrebten,	What we strove for
	War treu gemeint;	Was truly meant;
	Was wir durchlebten	What we lived through
	Bleibt tief vereint.	Remains profoundly united.

(6)	Da trat ein Scheiden	Then a parting
	Mir in die Brust;	Entered my heart;
	Das tiefe Leiden	The deep sorrow
	Der Liebes Lust	Of love's joy.
(7)	Im Seelengrunde	In the depths of my soul
	Wohnt mir Ein Bild;	Dwells an image.
	Die Todeswunde	The fatal wound
	Ward nie gestillt.	Was never healed.
(8)	Viel tausend Tränen	Many thousand tears
	Flossen hinab;	Flowed down;
	Ein ewig Sehnen	An eternal longing
	Zu Ihr ins Grab.	For her in the grave.
(9)	In Liebes Wogen	The spirit surges
	Wallet der Geist,	In waves of love
	Bis fortgezogen	Until, when it has departed,
	Die Brust zerreisst.	The heart breaks.
(10)	Ein Stern erschien mir	A star appeared to me
	Vom Paradies;	From Paradise;
	Und dahin flieh'n wir	And there, united,
	Vereint gewiss.	We shall assuredly escape.
(11)	Hier noch befeuchtet	Here my gaze is still moist
	Der Blick sich lind,	With gentle tears
	Wenn mich umleuchtet	When around me shines
	Dies Himmelskind.	This heavenly child.
(12)	Ein Zauber waltet	A magic spell
	Jetzt über mich,	Now holds me in thrall,
	Und der gestaltet	Fashioning all this
	Dies all' nach sich.	In its own way,
(13)	Als ob uns vermähle	As if a spiritual power
	Geistesgewalt,	United us
	Wo Seele in Seele	Where soul surges
	Hinüberwallt.	Into soul.
(14)	Ob auch zerspalten	Although my heart
	Mir ist das Herz;	Is torn in two
	Selig doch halten	I will consider
	Will ich den Schmerz.	My sorrow a blessing.

FRIEDRICH VON SCHLEGEL (1772–1829); poem written after 1809?

This is the last of Schubert's sixteen Friedrich von Schlegel solo settings (1818–25). See the poet's biography for a chronological list of all the Friedrich von Schlegel settings.

This, in some ways, is the most problematic of the Friedrich von Schlegel settings. The poet of *Fülle der Liebe* was a very different man from the liberal creator of the *Abendröte* poems. He had renounced pantheism in favour of an increasingly orthodox Roman Catholicism; the writer who once acclaimed the French Revolution had become a supporter of the Metternich regime.

The composer had also changed; since the break-up of his friendship with Mayrhofer, and the onset of his illness, he had moved on from the enthusiasms (including a flirtation of his own with pantheism) that had resulted in the innovative songs (settings of Schlegel and Mayrhofer) of 1820. Nevertheless, there is nothing to show us that Schubert underwent a major change of political or religious sympathy. There is no sign of a softening of scepticism, or a hardening of the arteries, in a young man who was still only in his late twenties.

It was perhaps a personal contact with Friedrich Schlegel (or *von* Schlegel, as he was entitled to style himself in his Viennese years) that reawakened the composer's interest in the poetry of the famous literary brothers. At the Viennese home of the painter Ludwig Schnorr von Carolsfeld there were regular seances, and it is known that Schlegel took part in these. Schubert's music was played afterwards, and Schubert himself took part on 20 March 1825. It is entirely possible that Schubert had met Schlegel on other occasions, but if the two were involved together in something of a mystical experience, it might have made a strong impression. Later in 1825 the composer turned his gaze on two further lyrics by August von Schlegel (who, as it happened, felt little sympathy for his 'reformed' brother's views).

Fülle der Liebe was composed during that wonderful summer of 1825 when Schubert was on holiday with Vogl in Upper Austria. It was at this time that the composer was working on the 'Great' C major Symphony, D944. Vocal creations of the period include settings of Wilhelm von Schütz (*Delphine* and *Florio* D857) and the songs *Das Heimweh* D851 and *Die Allmacht* D852. The latter two works, among Schubert's finest inspirations, were settings of Ladislaus Pyrker, Patriarch of Venice (that city was still an Austrian possession) who was in Bad Gastein at the same time as Schubert and Vogl – in fact Pyrker was the owner of the spa facilities there.

During this holiday Schubert composed songs suitable for his friend's voice and rather particular performing manner. The grandeur of *Die Allmacht*, if not in its original key, fitted Vogl like a glove and was in all probability written for him. *Fülle der Liebe* has the hallmarks of a Vogl piece for it is a dramatic monologue which depicts the protagonist in the most noble, yet tortured light; we detect here shades of a classical hero who has suffered much, and has been transfigured in the process. There is a gestural quality in this music, at times almost melodramatic, which perhaps more than any other Schubert song suggests the grand manner of Vogl in performance. This rather old-fashioned theatricality was roundly criticized by some of Schubert's friends as affectation, but it was at the heart of the singer's undoubted power as an interpreter. If we were to ask where Schubert found this text (for the composer was far from his normal sources of books in Vienna, and the poem does not appear in the collection which he had used for his other Schlegel settings) it is possible that he brought it with him from Vienna. But it is also possible that it was suggested by Pyrker who must have known Schlegel well; both of the last-named men moved in circles close to Metternich himself. Unlike fans of the poet's earlier work, the Patriarch of Venice must have rejoiced in the circumstances of Schlegel's conversion, his closeness to Rome and his increasingly conservative political stance.

Here is a love poem with a strong religious gloss, the pain of bereavement lessened by assurance of an afterlife, the sensuality of passion sublimated by religious conviction. And the death of the beloved moves the poet from the path of temptation; indeed, in her death he is saved from besmirching himself with earthly sensuality. All of this has a lofty evangelical tone in which we can glimpse Schlegel's self-dramatizing self-regard – the poem's hyperbole strikes a completely different note from any of Schubert's other Schlegel settings. But one must admit that some of these images seem to echo the composer's own struggles. After all, he too was suffering from a terminal 'Todeswunde'; perhaps one of the reasons for taking the holiday in Upper Austria was connected with the possibly beneficial effects of the healing waters of Gastein. Schubert was also no stranger to renunciation, and to unbounded love and its sufferings. In any case he fashions from this poem a powerful, if unusual masterpiece. Once he has decided to set a poem, it is very rare for him not to serve it with his whole heart.

The pervading rhythm is that of a dotted crotchet followed by three quavers. These quavers are sometimes dotted also, as in the introductory bars where a passage of four loud ascending chords (suggestive of the grandeur of stoic suffering – how Vogl must have loved this) is answered and balanced by four hushed chords, still *pomposo* in their rhythm, but suggestive of humility, albeit in a rather staged manner. The hint of double-dotting makes this very 'public' music, suitable for a Handelian hero, or even a Rossinian heroine – is it too irreverent to notice that there is more than a little similarity here to the introduction to Rosina's 'Una voce poco fa' from *Il barbiere di Siviglia*? Much of this music is written without the disruption of jagged dotted rhythms and much of the song features the plainer version of the rhythm mentioned above: a dotted crotchet followed by three quavers. When Schubert uses this rhythm it suggests irreversible fate (the final setting of Mignon's *So lasst mich scheinen* D877/3), obsession (the Platen song *Du liebst mich nicht* D756) or otherworldly radiance (Mayrhofer's *Abendstern* D806). There is a lone and noble struggle in all these songs, where the weak and disadvantaged show that they have a tenacious power of their own. Fate, obsession and transfiguration all play their part in *Fülle der Liebe*, and the composer sticks mercilessly to the motif throughout. He balances the risks of rhythmic monotony with an ever-changing (and sometimes bewildering) harmonic agenda. What seems like the rambling progress of the song (particularly when at too slow a tempo, or sung by a less than expert singer) is more skilfully organized than at first it seems to be.

Schubert has fourteen verses to set to music, each one of them rather short-breathed. Schlegel's rhyme scheme is an unbending ABAB and is not helpful to the building of long musical structures. The short lines and density of cadences give a rather breathy and impatient feel to the poem, probably intentionally, but we might have hoped for fewer banal rhymes from a writer of Schlegel's literary acumen. The dominating musical refrain is dispersed through the song, and heard three times in all; it moves from the home key of A flat major to F major, and back to A flat. Its first appearance (bb. 5–23) unites Schlegel's first three strophes. We hear a modified repeat of this refrain in strophes 6, 7 and 8, which are also cobbled together (beginning 'Da trat ein Scheiden' bb. 34–54). The vocal line is artfully ornamented and changed in detail (note the added pathos of the harmonization of 'Todeswunde') but this is essentially the same music. The final appearance of this refrain occurs at Verse 12 ('Ein Zauber waltet', b. 75) where it is even more varied, but nevertheless provides a strong feeling of a return to the home base. This scheme leaves Schubert free for the remaining five verses of the poem (4 and 5 as well as 9, 10 and 11) to wander, and wander he does in a manner extravagant even by his standards. At the section beginning 'Ein Feuer war es' (Verse 4, b. 24) we move suddenly into C major, and veer between that key and E major for eight lines of the poem, including a shift into C minor which sets up the return to the A flat major of the second refrain at Verse 6.

The most extraordinary music is reserved for the heart of the poem, verses 9 to 11. The move into the grandeur of C major at 'In Liebeswogen / Wallet der Geist' (from b. 54) is already familiar from Verse 4 ('Ein Feuer war es') but the sideways shift in harmony from G major to the first inversion of E flat minor at 'fortgezogen' (bb. 56–7) is a new and shattering detail which illustrates love slipping out of the poet's life as surely as one harmony slips to another under the pianist's hands. Verse 10 (from b. 63) is a jewelled moment of relative repose, the still centre of a work otherwise remarkable for its restlessness. We move into Schubert's beloved A major, and mention of a star from paradise conjures reminiscences of Mayrhofer's *Abendstern* written the year before. How naturally and unselfconsciously Schubert moves into upwardly floating semiquavers at the repeat of 'Und dahin fliehn' (b. 67) to paint the twinned souls' ascent into paradise. We then return, via Verse 11, to the third and final refrain.

Of course Schubert reserves something special for the end. At 'Ob auch zerspalten / Mir ist das Herz' (from b. 93) the movement between A flat major and E minor (in first inversion) is perhaps the most heated moment in a song remarkable for its incendiary emotional flourishes. Each note of the tonic chord moves only a semitone either up or down to reach a region of heart-rending, and almost gruesome, contrast. Of this moment in the song Newbould remarks: 'Was ever the expressive value of harmony, or Schubert's absorption in its power, more tellingly illustrated?' Even if the poet's pain seems to degenerate dangerously into self-pity and posture, the beauty of the music carries the day. In the *Abendröte* songs Schlegel is reflected as a true visionary; in *Fülle der Liebe* he emerges as something more contrived and stagey, a latter-day Oedipus or Orestes perhaps. This must have suited Vogl, a famous Orestes in the theatre, down to the ground. But it is surely interesting that when these melodic and harmonic ideas are found again in the sublimely beautiful slow movement of the D major Piano Sonata (D850) there is no trace of grandeur and bluster, only the deepest and most gentle feeling. The solo piano music, stripped of the noble yet superfluous robes of grandee and cleric, suggests something written for the composer himself rather than for Vogl, and perhaps Pyrker. That *Fülle der Liebe* is nevertheless a most remarkable and affecting song, and that it repays performance by a singer of great presence, is not in doubt.

Autograph:	Staatsbibliothek Preussischer Kulturbesitz, Berlin
First edition:	Published as a supplement to the *Wiener Zeitschrift für Literatur, Kunst und Mode* in September 1830; subsequently published as Book 25 no. 1 of the *Nachlass* by Diabelli, Vienna in October 1835 (P309)
Subsequent editions:	Peters: Vol. 3/193; AGA XX 480: Vol. 8/132; NSA IV: Vol. 13/163
Bibliography:	Black 2003, pp. 144–5
	Capell 1928, pp. 217–18
	Dobersberger 1997, p. 271
	Einstein 1951, pp. 305–6
	Newbould 1997, p. 238
Discography and timing:	Fischer-Dieskau II 7[10] 5'27
	Hyperion I 27[21]
	Hyperion II 30[10] 6'48 Matthias Goerne

← *Die Allmacht* D852   *Wiedersehn* D855 →

FURCHT DER GELIEBTEN   The lover's fear (To Cidli)
('An Cidli')
(KLOPSTOCK) D285 [H171]

The song exists in two versions, both of which are discussed below:
(1) 12 September 1815; (2) no date

(1)   No tempo indication   A♭ major   ¢   [18 bars]

(2)   A♭ major

(18 bars)

Cidli, du weinest, und ich schlummre sicher,   Cidli, you weep, and I slumber safely
Wo im Sande der Weg verzogen fortschleicht;   Where the path winds through the sand;
Auch wenn stille Nacht ihn umschattend decket,   Even when the silent night shrouds that path
Schlummr' ich ihn sicher.   In shadow, I shall slumber safely.

Wo er sich endet, wo ein Strom das Meer wird,   Where it ends, where the river becomes sea,
Gleit' ich über den Strom, der sanfter aufschwillt;   I shall glide upon the current which flows
Denn, der mich begleitet, der Gott gebots ihm!   More gently, for God, who accompanies me,
Weine nicht, Cidli.   Bids it flow thus. Do not weep, Cidli.

FRIEDRICH GOTTLOB KLOPSTOCK (1724–1803); poem written in Autumn 1752

This is the second of Schubert's thirteen Klopstock solo settings (1815–16). See the poet's biography for a chronological list of all the Klopstock settings.

The original key for this beautiful little song is A flat, a favourite Schubertian tonality in this period for intimate utterances which are nevertheless constrained by an element of classical discipline and poise. There is an added religious element in this poem, as there is in much of Klopstock's work, but he was also a man of vigorous action. We might imagine that it is perhaps because of all this physical activity that Cidli fears for Klopstock's safety when he is on his travels, and weeps accordingly. Cidli, incidentally, was Klopstock's nickname for his beloved Meta (Margarethe) Moller from Hamburg whom he met in Copenhagen and later married. Klopstock loved to imagine that he was writing poems as a voice from the grave, and Meta Moller, also an accomplished writer, used to do the same thing. An eighteenth-century literary game, ghoulish even by the standards of the nineteenth, this was an ardent literary dialogue in anticipation of the couple's future heavenly status, and possibly a means of rendering more holy what might have seemed to be an inappropriately ardent exchange of love poems prior to the couple's marriage. (*Das Rosenband*, on the other hand, also a 'Cidli' poem, revels in a much more open sensuality, and as a result does not appear in some earlier editions of the poet's *Oden*.) In light of the events to come, the kind of preparatory practice for death represented by *Furcht der Geliebten* seems to have been a direct challenge to fate; in fact it was not Cidli who would need to be comforted from the grave, but Klopstock himself when Meta died in 1758 giving birth to a stillborn son. The name 'Cidli' (pronounced 'Kidli' rather than 'Sidli', and sometimes spelled as such) reappears in his great epic religious poem *Messias* (begun in 1749 and completed twenty-eight years later) where she is the daughter of Jairus and the loving wife of Gedor. Cidli dies in the fifteenth canto of the poem, a part of the work that was written many years after Meta's death. This is no doubt Klopstock's way of honouring his first wife's memory. Whether Schubert knew this background information is doubtful, although there was no name more revered than Klopstock's in German literature, and someone like Mayrhofer might have been aware of these biographical details.

Klopstock is still very much alive as he reassures his beloved that there is no need to worry about him, for he is safely in the hands of God. The song is in the same tonality as *Das Rosenband* D280, a setting of a much more celebrated poem about the same woman. The most exceptional musical characteristic of the piece (apart from the ravishing melody) is the succession of unfolding left-hand quavers which meander through the sand at 'Wo im Sande der Weg verzogen' (bb. 6–10), a drifting accompaniment singularly appropriate to the words. This music is equally suitable for the gliding effect of the second verse at 'Gleit' ich über den Strom'. The harmonies at 'Auch wenn stille Nacht ihn umschattend' (bb. 11–12) take us into the distant regions of G flat major, but the effect of adding flats to the serene A flat harmony is precisely right for what the poet describes as the shadowy night-shrouded paths. Despite all this expressive detail, the feeling of a chorale is preserved, and the result is a beautiful blend of styles where the hymn book merges with the sensuously romantic lied. The final sentence for the voice, the tender and simple 'Weine nicht, Cidli', is a touching conclusion to the song which has begun with the equally simple 'Cidli, du weinest'. The poet has explained his faith to her and, beguiled by music of this charm and quiet inner conviction, we can really believe that she is reassured.

There are two versions, both published in both the AGA and the NSA, but they are differentiated only by the smallest details. The marking 'Sanft' is printed only in the second of the two versions. The first version of the song is entitled *Furcht des Geliebten*, but both the preliminary sketch and the second version (to be found in the Stadler Lieder album – a copy that probably goes back to a vanished autograph) are headed *An Cidli*. The NSA thus accords two different titles to side-by-side versions of essentially the same song.

Autograph:	In private possession, Vienna (sketch)
Publication:	First published as part of the AGA in 1895 (P581; first version)
	First published as Vol. 7 no. 10 in Friedlaender's edition by Peters, Leipzig in 1885 (P482; second version)
Subsequent editions:	Peters: Vol. 7/24; AGA XX 138a & b: Vol. 3/70 (first version) & 71 (second version, *An Cidli*); NSA IV: Vol. 9/58 (first version, *Fürcht der Geliebten*), 59 (second version) & 220 (sketch, *An Cidli*)
Further settings and arrangements:	Gottfried Emil Fischer (1791–1841) *An Cidli* (1820)
	Arr. Tilman Hoppstock (b. 1961) for guitar accompaniment, in *Franz Schubert: 110 Lieder* (2009)
Discography and timing:	Fischer-Dieskau I 5[19] 1'38
	Hyperion I 22[16]
	Hyperion II 10[6] 1'48 Simon Keenlyside

← *Lied (Es ist so angenehm, so süss)* D284   *Selma und Selmar* D286 →

Leopold Kupelwieser, *Das Kaleideskop und die Draisine*. Drawing of the artist with Schubert, as members of the Unsinngesellschaft (July 1818) (*see* p. 601).

G

GANYMED
(GOETHE) OP. 19 NO. 3, **D544** [H357]
A♭ major – F major   March 1817

Ganymede

Wie im Morgenglanze
Du rings mich anglühst,
Frühling, Geliebter!
Mit tausendfacher Liebeswonne
Sich an mein Herze drängt[1]
Deiner ewigen Wärme
Heilig Gefühl,
Unendliche Schöne!

Dass ich dich fassen möcht'[2]
In diesen Arm!

Ach, an deinem Busen
Lieg ich und schmachte,[3]
Und deine Blumen, dein Gras
Drängen sich an mein Herz.
Du kühlst den brennenden
Durst meines Busens,
Lieblicher Morgenwind!
Ruft drein die Nachtigall
Liebend nach mir aus dem Nebeltal.
Ich komm', ich komme!
Ach wohin, wohin?[4]

Hinauf strebt's hinauf![5]
Es schweben die Wolken

How your glow envelops me
In the morning radiance,
Spring, my beloved!
With love's thousandfold joy
The hallowed sensation
Of your eternal warmth
Floods my heart,
Infinite beauty!

O that I might clasp you
In my arms!

Ah, on your breast
I lie languishing,
And your flowers, your grass
Press close to my heart.
You cool the burning
Thirst within my breast,
Sweet morning breeze,
As the nightingale calls
Tenderly to me from the misty valley.
I come, I come!
But whither? Ah, whither?

Upwards! Strive upwards!
The clouds drift

[1] Goethe has 'Herze'.
[2] In later editions 'Dass ich *diesem* fassen möcht'.
[3] The connective 'und' in this line is Schubert's addition to Goethe.
[4] Goethe has 'Wohin? Ach, wohin?'.
[5] Goethe has 'Hinauf! Hinauf strebt's'.

Abwärts, die Wolken	Down, yielding
Neigen sich der sehnenden Liebe.	To yearning love,
Mir! Mir!	To me, to me!
In eurem Schosse	In your lap,
Aufwärts!	Upwards,
Umfangend umfangen!	Embracing and embraced!
Aufwärts an deinen Busen,	Upwards to your bosom,
Alliebender Vater!	All-loving Father!

JOHANN WOLFGANG VON GOETHE (1749–1832); poem written by early 1774

This is the forty-ninth of Schubert's seventy-five Goethe solo settings (1814–26). See the poet's biography for a chronological list of all the Goethe settings.

The published marking is 'Etwas langsam' in common time and, as a result, slow and lugubrious tempi have dogged this song over many generations. The autograph is missing but there are two other copies of this work, one belonging to Josef Hüttenbrenner, and the other the Spaun family; in both of these the marking is 'Etwas geschwind', and the tempo marking is 'Alla breve'. Any musician who has worked on this song for any length of time will know that a two-in-a-bar tempo is vital both for the music and for the singer's breath. From the very beginning we sense the transformative powers of spring; the piano's left-hand staccato notes underpin the sensuous melody of the right hand. In the NSA the indication 'simile' is printed under bb. 3 and 9, a sign that these left-hand staccati are meant to continue throughout the song's first page; this enlivening articulation is either ignored by most pianists or negated by over-use of the pedal. The right-hand tune begins with an unremarkable ascent of an A flat arpeggio, and then a quick three-note descent to the chord of the dominant seventh. There is nothing very unusual about this formula, the alternation of a forward thrust with a downward sigh, but it perfectly depicts questing curiosity at the same time as vulnerability. After an eight-bar introduction, the voice enters in slower note values. The very first 'Wie' is rather too long to be ideal from the point of view of prosody, but with this deliberate pull against the piano music's flow, a feeling of lingering longing in the midst of spring's awakening is immediately established.

There is everything ambivalent in this music: repose and agitation, innocence and, yes, a certain eroticism, though not of an overheated kind. From b. 19 the melodic line gambols with delight. The rapturous setting of the phrase 'Unendliche Schöne', and the modulation into C flat major that it encompasses, is one of the song's glories. There is a touch of sultry languor suggested by the opulence of this rich tonality. At 'Lieg ich und schmachte' desire is dormant in the bud of the music, but sheer musical delight outweighs any sense of seductive coyness, a trait that can too easily be imposed on the music by a performer determined to play the vamp. After a little interlude of staccato crotchets (bb. 48–9) there is suddenly a breath of fresh air. The hot-house tonality of flats is replaced by more bracing sharps. (The setting of the phrase 'Du kühlst' reflects the refreshment inherent in the words to an astonishing degree.) The trills from b. 36 are like wind rippling through a field of barley, and Jove plays his flute in the guise of a nightingale. Suddenly with bouncing, nervy quavers (from b. 68) we have the music of transfiguration; we hear the singer's trepidation and excitement as the whole song seems to move upwards, lifted into new realms, a staccato passage into another world. When the legato lines in voice and piano intertwine after this, there is a remarkable musical analogue for the key words in this passage 'Umfangend umfangen' – embracing and embraced: the tiny little motif in adjacent tones heard on the words 'schweben die Wolken' (D-C-B-C, b. 79) is taken up by the piano and played underneath a second tune on the second appearance of 'Wolken' (b. 81). This is a subtle modification of the first motif with only the third note changed (D-C-F-C) where the F is a fourth above the C. In b. 84 it is the piano that plays this second variant underneath a repeat of the first option (D-C-B-C) by the voice.

This reciprocal playfulness, as each takes up the other's music, represents an equality of initiative in kiss or embrace: clearly, consensual music. At bb. 85–91, and again at bb. 100–105 there are two agitated passages, pulsating quavers alternating in the pianist's hands, that suggest all the fun of the chase. From b. 106 ('Alliebender Vater') voice and piano are in rapturous unison, an inseparable unity. At the end of the song (the singing of bb. 110–16 in one breath is the famous Olympian challenge for the singer) we have reached the heavenly key of F major. There is no going back for Ganymede, and a recapitulation of the opening tonality is out of the question. The postlude (six bars of ascending minims) crowns the youth in his new divine incarnation. In an amazingly short time this work has moved from the longings of mortals to the achievement of god-like serenity.

It is extraordinary that many years later, when he composed *Die junge Nonne* D828, Schubert penned a descending phrase in F major ('Glut- / Der ewigen Liebe getraut') that matches at pitch, and with the same bass note, the descending shape of 'Alliebender Vater' in *Ganymed*. There was something about this motif, in this tonality, that represented for Schubert the erotic and mystical unification of the supplicant (whether male or female) with God and the gods.

The Greek legend has it that Zeus turns himself into an eagle in order to snatch the beautiful Trojan prince Ganymede and take him to heaven as a cup-bearer to replace Hebe. In Goethe's poem there is no question of a surprise attack, and certainly no rapacious eagle. It is clear that in these lines the love and attraction between the boy (sometimes depicted as a shepherd) and the beguiling forces of the god are entirely mutual. The poem has often been called pantheistic, as if Goethe believed that Nature and God were in fact the same thing – a Spinozan interpretation of the poem where Ganymede's willing surrender is to winds and clouds, rather than to the god in person.

Nicholas Boyle has pointed out, however, that in this case the poet was more influenced by Gottfried von Leibniz (1646–1716). Far from believing that God and Nature are one, Leibniz postulated that every identity has the single task of representing all the universe from its own point of view. As Boyle writes, 'Ganymede remains throughout the poem an independent individual whose "strength of soul" is always equal to that of the surrounding world, never subordinate.' This confirms Schubert's acuity in casting Ganymede as very much his own man, rather than a plaything of the gods; the young Trojan prince steers his music with plucky openness, and seems to make his own choice both to embrace, and be embraced – 'Umfangend umfangen!' This mirrors the strength of mind of the poem's creator. Goethe is telling us that he himself is in love with the beauties of spring, and so delighted at the

Ganymedes, engraving from *Der Mythos alter Dichter* (Vienna, 1815).

thought of becoming at one with nature that he is as enraptured as a Ganymede. If one imagines the poet himself saying the words, the journey from earth to heaven is infinitely more believable for being an imaginative metaphor. It seems that Goethe's vision of himself as a Ganymede was nothing to do with beauty and sex and rather more to do with a mortal who, at the height of his career, felt himself destined for immortality because of his services to the Muses.

This is not to say that Schubert was unaware of the homo-erotic implications of the ancient legend. There is a sign that even Goethe was a touch embarrassed about this aspect, or rather that he made an important change to make his meaning clearer: this concerns the poem's ninth line, 'Dass ich dich fassen möcht'. In later editions (from about 1812) he changed this to 'dass ich <u>diesen</u> fassen möcht', so that the relationship between Ganymed and Zeus is more distant, and making it possible for the poet to be embracing various aspects of nature, rather than a single person or god. This modification matches 'In eurem Schosse' at the end of the poem, a phrase which makes it clear that the boy is referring to the lap of the clouds rather than the lap of Zeus; in an earlier manuscript version of the poem this had been the much more daring 'In deinem Schosse' (in *your* lap, all-loving father). It seems likely that it was Mayrhofer who drew Schubert's attention to the text, probably in *Goethes Schriften*, Volume 8 (1789), with the original wording – i.e. 'dass ich <u>dich</u> fassen möcht'.

For the twenty-year-old Schubert, joy in the beauties of the present was being matched by his deepening knowledge of the past. His fascination with sex was well documented by his friends; but equally obvious to every Schubertian is the composer's inexhaustible ability to pour the purest of love into his music. Sadly the integration of love and sex in a long-term relationship was something that he failed to achieve in his short life; but the transparent and almost artless way in which this poem has been set indicates Schubert's ability to perceive love and sex on the same idealistic plane. Those who criticize *Ganymed* and find it wanting (in comparison to Wolf's setting, for example) are clearly dismayed by its lack of explicit eroticism; in fact it is the wide-eyed innocence of this song that is its special glory. As James Davidson has pointed out, the role of Ganymede in heaven is a serious and holy one – he serves ambrosia (that drink whose meaning is 'without mortality') to the gods and is granted immortality because of his services to them. Prurience has bedevilled the Ganymede myth from the very beginning with its sacred and religious aspects much underplayed. If Goethe, as Lorraine Byrne suggests, 'infuses Ganymede's passionate abandon with a spiritual interpretation' it is an indication of what a great Goethe composer Schubert already was that he should find exactly the right music for the poet, music that effortlessly combines these two sides of the myth. Byrne also points out that 'for Schubert as well as Goethe, the existence of the ideal loving father remained problematic', as evidenced by the composer's yearning for fatherly love in contrast with a rebellion against the father (as in the later song *Prometheus* D674, another Goethe setting). It is this very 'dialectical irony' that is expressed by Hugo Wolf when he juxtaposes his settings of the two poems in his *Goethelieder* of 1889.

Autograph:	Missing or lost
First edition:	Published as Op. 19 no. 3 by Diabelli, Vienna in June 1825 (P82)
Dedicatee:	Johann Wolfgang von Goethe
Subsequent editions:	Peters: Vol. 1/244; AGA XX 311: Vol. 5/75; NSA IV: Vol. 1a/132; Bärenreiter: Vol. 1/104
Bibliography:	Byrne 2003, pp. 89–95
	Capell 1928, pp. 132–3
	Davidson 2007, pp. 170–200
	Fischer-Dieskau 1977, pp. 89–90
	Gülke 1991, pp. 117–23

Further settings: Carl Loewe (1796–1869) *Ganymed* Op. 81 no. 5 (1842)
                           Hugo Wolf (1860–1903) *Ganymed* (1889)
Discography and timing: Fischer-Dieskau I 9[26]   4'13
                           Hyperion I 5[7]   4'07   Christine Schäfer
                           Hyperion I 24[24]   4'11   Elizabeth Connell
                           Hyperion II 18[8]   4'11   Elizabeth Connell

← *Auf dem See* D543   *Mahomets Gesang* D549 →

GEBET   Prayer   Quartet, SATB
(Fouqué) **D815** [H552]
A♭ major   September 1824

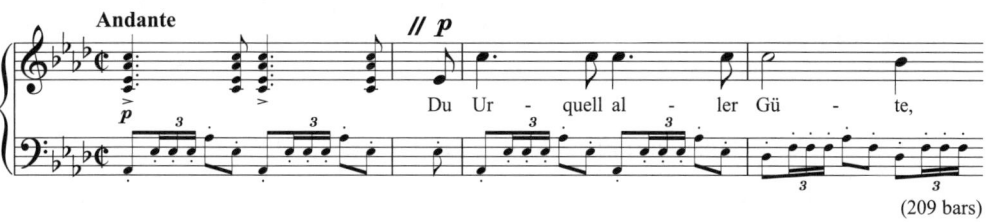

(209 bars)

Du Urquell aller Güte,	Primal source of all goodness,
Du Urquell aller Macht,	Primal source of all power,
Lindhauchend aus der Blüte,	Breathing fragrantly from blossoms,
Hochdonnernd aus der Schlacht,	Thundering mightily from battle,
Allwärts ist dir bereitet	Everywhere a temple and a feast
Ein Tempel und ein Fest,	Are prepared for you;
Allwärts von dir geleitet,	Everywhere you lead those
Wer gern sich leiten lässt.	Who are willingly led.

Du siehst in dies mein Herze,	You look into this heart of mine,
Kennst seine Lust und Not,	You know its pleasure and its pain;
Mild winkt der Heimat Kerze,	Gently the candle of my homeland beckons,
Kühn ruft glorwürd'ger Tod.	Boldly a glorious death summons.
Mit mir in eins zusammen schlingt	Here a child's grace is entwined
Hier sich Kindleins Huld,	With me as one,
Und draussen leuchten Flammen	And outside flames glow,
Abbrennend Schmach und Schuld.	Burning away shame and guilt.

Bereit bin ich zu sterben	I am prepared to die in battle,
Im Kampf der Ahnen werth,	Worthy of my forefathers,
Nur sichre vor Verderben	As long as my wife and child at home
Mir Weib und Kind am Herd.	Are safe from ruin.
Dein ist in mir die Liebe,	Your love is within me,
Die diesen beiden quillt,	Flowing to these two;
Dein auch sind mut'ge Triebe	Yours, too, are the courageous urges
Davon die Brust mir schwillt.	That swell my breast.

Kann es sich mild gestalten,	If it can come about mercifully,
So lass es, Herr, gescheh'n,	Then, Lord, let it happen:
Den Frieden fürder walten	Let peace reign again,
Und Sitt' und Ruh bestehn.	And order and calm prevail.
Wo nicht, so gib zum Werke	If not, then give us light for our task
Uns Licht in Sturmesnacht,	On stormy nights;
Du ew'ge Lieb' und Stärke,	You who are eternal love and strength,
Dein Wollen sei vollbracht.	May your will be done.

Wohin du mich willst haben,	Wherever you would send me, Lord,
Mein Herr! ich steh bereit.	I stand prepared;
Zu frommen Liebesgaben	Whether for gifts of devoted love
Wie auch zum wackern Streit.	Or for the valiant fight.
Dein Bot' in Schlacht und Reise,	Your messenger in battle and journey,
Dein Bot' im stillen Haus,	Your messenger in the tranquil home,
Ruh'ich auf alle Weise	Whatever comes to pass,
Doch einst im Himmel aus.	I shall one day rest in heaven.

FRIEDRICH DE LA MOTTE FOUQUÉ (1777–1843)

The story behind the composition of this quartet (during Schubert's second summer stay in Hungary) can be told in the words of someone who was there when it was written – Karl von Schönstein, the singer to whom the work was dedicated. The distinguished amateur tenor communicated this information to Ferdinand Luib, Schubert's prospective biographer, in 1857:

> *The four-part song in question,* Gebet *by Fouqué, was composed by Schubert in Zseliz, in September 1824, as I can prove from the manuscript, which I have . . . every member of the very musical Esterházy family sang. The count sang bass, the countess and the younger daughter, Karoline, sang contralto; the latter's voice was charming but weak and so, when there was general music-making, she occupied herself solely with accompanying, at which she excelled. The elder daughter, Marie, sang soprano most beautifully. My humble self, for I was frequently at the Esterházy's, completed the quartet, as a high baritone . . .*
>
> *Countess Esterházy invited Meister Schubert during breakfast, which we all took together, to set to music for our four voices a poem of which she was particularly fond; it was the above-mentioned* Gebet. *Schubert read it, smiled inwardly, as he usually did when something appealed to him, took the book and retired forthwith, in order to compose. In the evening of the same day we were already trying through the finished song at the piano from the manuscript. Schubert accompanied it himself. If our joy and delight over the Master's splendid work were already great that evening, these feelings were still further enhanced the next evening, when it was possible to perform the splendid song with greater assurance and certainty from the vocal parts, which had now been written out by Schubert himself, the whole thereby gaining in intelligibility. It is understandable that anyone familiar with this opus and its not exactly small dimensions will feel sceptical of the truth of what I have said, when he realizes, in addition, that Schubert produced this work in barely ten hours. After all, Schubert was the man for that kind of thing, this heaven-inspired clairvoyant who, as it were, simply shook his most glorious things out of his sleeve (to use a colloquial expression).*

Although one wonders whether Schubert was ever actually addressed as 'Meister' when he was at Zseliz (he was unknown in 1824 and world famous by the time Schönstein wrote this memoir), it is unsurprising that people were astounded that he had finished this rather substantial work – twenty-six pages long in the NSA – in the course of a single day. It must have taken the composer some time even to work out how he should best subdivide and allocate the long poem between the voices. One can hardly imagine him selecting this text himself (the mature Schubert was no admirer of religious patriotism), but once the request had been made, that 'inward smile' must have been the realization that he could make something out of the poem appropriate to the circumstances.

A court composer like Haydn could hardly have been more considerate and accommodating; every decision concerning this setting was taken in relation to the social and musical hierarchies of count and countess, the daughters of the household (one of them at least) and their singing guest. For example, the passage where the poet hopes that he will be found worthy of his ancestors was naturally allocated to the noble paterfamilias. The piece is hard enough to have challenged the Esterházys and Schönstein without tripping them up. And Schubert was kind enough to have played the piano himself, sparing Karoline the task of sight-reading a score of some difficulty (those ever-recurring left-hand semiquaver triplets are tricky). It is curious that the performance of the best documented work to be composed in Zseliz should exclude only one member of the family, the very one with whom Schubert was said to be deeply in love.

In the Schubertian world of tonality the key of A flat major is appropriate for prayers and meditations. The introduction sets the scene where noble tranquillity is combined with a frisson of movement in the bass line, a figure as appropriate for the bubbling brook of the 'Urquell' in a piano dynamic, as for the forte rolling of battle-drums. One wonders whether it was those insinuating semiquaver triplets in the left hand, at first gentle and then military, which made Schönstein say that Schubert 'shook his most glorious things out of his sleeve'. In playing this music the pianist has that very sensation.

The poem's first verse is given over to music for all four voices combined; at first this is gentle and pious, but to illustrate the two-sided aspect of God's powers, 'Güte' (goodness) and 'Macht' (power), it progresses to a broad pomposo section for the imagery of battles and feasts. Schubert uses the poem's next two strophes to introduce the singers one by one; each singer is allocated four lines of the poem as a solo. Of the three singers of the Esterházy family, the young countess Marie had the greatest vocal virtuosity and a voice with a dramatic edge to it. Accordingly she is given a twelve-bar solo (beginning 'Du siehst in dies mein Herze' from b. 27), replete with an ornamented vocal line and a sustained high B flat. Piano triplets nicely depict the flickering of candles at 'Mild winkt der Heimat Kerze' (bb. 32–3). Elsewhere the accompaniment in dotted rhythms suggests Italian opera; certainly these fervent words are worthy of Rossini's 'Giovanna d'Arco'. Obviously Marie, aged twenty-two, was a figure of some temperament who expected the composer in residence to arrange for her to shine in this line-up. Her passage ends on D flat major and is followed by a much gentler solo for her mother in B flat minor (beginning 'Mit mir in eins zusammen schlingt' from b. 40); again the change of tessitura exactly caters for the countess's expressive, but not particularly wide-ranging, alto voice.

An interlude of drum rolls announces the count whose words, and the martial manner of their setting, suggest an experienced man of war ('Bereit bin ich zu sterben' from b. 51). The 'Weib und Kind' (wife and child) of whom he speaks are standing next to him in the quartet line-up, and one can imagine the smiles of complicity exchanged in this piece of family music-making. Finally it is time for the honoured guest, Baron von Schönstein, whose abilities are practically in the professional class. He called himself a 'high baritone', a term that can also be a euphemism for a tenor without much of a top. Schubert knows this and keeps his part, strictly speaking the tenor line, within the bounds of his range – no higher than a G. But Schönstein was an accomplished musician, and the rhythm he is made to tackle is more complex, and the ornamentation of his part more profuse than that of the others. His passage (from b. 59) is heroic within limits, but does not upstage the grandeur of Count Esterházy's simpler and more stoic utterances. The return of the opening left-hand triplet rhythms in this section (from b. 70) shows the hand of the composer at work as he cleverly crafts this disparate cantata into a convincing unity.

The poem's fourth verse is a varied repetition of the first and Schubert, hard pressed to finish his task, saved himself a little time. Fortunately the new words fit the music extremely well. The last verse of the poem changes to $\frac{3}{4}$ with a new tempo marking of 'Andantino' (from b. 97). Here the lead is taken by the tenor voice – Baron von Schönstein. That he should have been given this discreetly starring role at the conclusion of the piece once again shows Schubert's sense of social niceties. The Baron was after all the guest of the house, and it was acknowledged that his links with the musical world were the strongest. The three other singers echo each of his phrases, sometimes joining him in four-part harmony, but mostly allowing him a moment of glory. This strophe is then enjambed with a repeat of Fouqué's opening verse set in a grandly baroque-oratorio manner with all the trappings: a pile-up of voices, churning semiquavers in the accompaniment and a touch of imitative part-writing. A lesser composer might have ended here in a blaze of glory, but not Schubert, even if he was in a hurry to get the piece ready by dinner time. We return to the poem's closing verse for a gently lyrical soprano solo (from b. 154; Schubert's singing pupil Marie has been a little neglected since the opening) and now it is the other three parts that echo *her* musical phrases. The accompaniment is at this point in amiably purling semiquavers. This leads to the quartet's final pages; perhaps the work's most beautiful passage are the fifth and sixth repeats of the 'Ruh' ich auf alle Weise / Doch einst im Himmel aus' (bb. 194–206). The mood here is reminiscent of a gentle cantilena from an Italian *bel canto* opera. The piano writing becomes simpler, slower and more transparent; an A flat major arpeggio wafts first up (bb. 192–3), then down (bb. 198–9) both piano staves. The vocal lines at last settle, every one, on different notes in an A flat major chord, the words slowed down to muted dotted minims. 'Mezzo staccato' chords in the piano magically convey the ascension of souls, reaching the top of the keyboard with the singer's dying breath. We are reminded of the postlude to *Ganymed* D544.

Robert Schumann in a rare written comment on Schubert's vocal music referred to *Gebet* in its classical poise and purity as a German equivalent of Palestrina ('unsere Palästrinagesänge'). Although composed only some twenty years earlier, this music in its deliberately devout simplicity seemed to Schumann to encapsulate the classical poise and purity of a vanished musical age, while Schubert's status was already that of a revered old master who had lived in an entirely different epoch.

Autograph:	Wienbibliothek im Rathaus, Vienna
First edition:	Published as Op. post. 139 by Diabelli, Vienna in 1840 (P331)
Dedicatee:	Karl Baron von Schönstein (dedicated by Diabelli)
First known performance:	23 February 1837 at the Musikverein, Vienna. Performers unknown
Subsequent editions:	AGA XVII: p. 198; NSA III: Vol. 2a/109

Discography and timing:	Deutsche Grammophon *Schubert Quartette*	10'33	Elly Ameling, Janet Baker, Peter Schreier & Dietrich Fischer-Dieskau
	Hyperion I 35[12] Hyperion II 29[7]	10'40	Patricia Rozario, Catherine Wyn-Rogers, Jamie MacDougall & Michael George

← *Wandrers Nachtlied II* D768   *Lied eines Kriegers* D822 →

GEBET WÄHREND DER SCHLACHT

Prayer during battle

(KÖRNER) **D171** [H79]

The song exists in two versions, the second of which is discussed below:
(1) 12 March 1815; (2) Date unknown

(1) 'Etwas Langsam' B♭ major **C** [32 bars]

(2) G major

(59 bars)

Vater, ich rufe dich!	Father, I cry unto You!
Brüllend umwölkt mich der Dampf der Geschütze,	The smoke of roaring guns envelops me;
Sprühend umzucken mich rasselnde Blitze.	Explosive flashes dart all around me.
Lenker der Schlachten, ich rufe dich!	Lord of battles, I cry unto You!
Vater du, führe mich!	Father, guide me!
Vater, du führe mich!	Father, guide me!
Führ' mich zum Siege, führ' mich zum Tode:	Lead me to victory; lead me to death.
O Herr, ich erkenne deine Gebote;	Lord, I acknowledge Your commands;
Herr, wie du willst, so führe mich.	Lead me, Lord, where You will.
Gott, ich erkenne dich!	God, I acknowledge You!
Gott, ich erkenne dich!	God, I acknowledge You!
So im herbstlichen Rauschen der Blätter,	In the autumnal rustling of leaves,
Als im Schlachtendonnerwetter,	As in the thunder of battle;
Urquell der Gnade, erkenn' ich dich!	Source of Grace, I acknowledge You!
Vater du, segne mich!	Father, grant me Your blessing!
Vater du, segne mich!	Father, grant me Your blessing!
In deine Hand befehl' ich mein Leben,	Into Your hands I commend my life;
Du kannst es nehmen, du hast es gegeben;	You may take it, for You gave it.
Zum Leben, zum Sterben segne mich!	Whether for life or death, grant me Your blessing!
Vater, ich preise dich!	Father, I praise You!
Vater, ich preise dich!	Father, I praise You!
'S ist ja kein Kampf für die Güter der Erde;	This is no battle for the riches of this earth;
Das Heiligste schützen wir mit dem Schwerte:	With the sword we defend that which is most sacred;
Drum, fallend und siegend, preis' ich dich!	Therefore, whether dying or victorious, I praise You.
Gott, dir ergeb' ich mich!	God, I surrender myself to You!

Gott, dir ergeb' ich mich!	God, I surrender myself to You!
Wenn mich die Donner des Todes begrüssen,	If the thunder of death greets me,
Wenn meine Adern geöffnet fliessen:	If my open veins flow,
Dir, mein Gott, dir ergeb' ich mich!	To You, my God, I surrender myself!
Vater, ich rufe dich!	Father, I cry unto You!

THEODOR KÖRNER (1791–1813); poem written in 1813

This is the sixth of Schubert's sixteen Körner solo settings (1815–18). See the poet's biography for a chronological list of all the Körner settings.

There is nothing quite like this song in all Schubert, certainly from the pianist's point of view. The tremolo accompaniment of *Der Atlas* (Heine, D957/8) from *Schwanengesang*, written at the other end of the composer's song-writing career, is the nearest comparison. In this *Gebet* a similar tremolo in the right hand shivers and rumbles underneath the voice and provides an almost orchestral background to the noble tune – half prayer, half battle-cry – of the vocal line. In trying to identify a possible model for the song from an older composer one need go no further than Friedrich Heinrich Himmel (1765–1814) whose setting of these words was certainly the best-known in the nineteenth century, even appearing in Victorian songbooks as *Father I call on thee!* The tremolo accompaniment is very much a feature of Himmel. In terms of the mood of apprehension before a battle (and the warrior's brave grandeur, even tenderness, in the face of certain death) another song from *Schwanengesang* comes to mind – *Kriegers Ahnung* D957/2 – this time a Rellstab setting.

The first page of music (which contains the poem's first verse) is the most inventive. It begins with the main tune with which we are to become familiar (perhaps too familiar) throughout the song. After this initial statement ('Vater, ich rufe dich!'), a description of the sights and noises of battle prompts Schubert into exceptionally excited activity. In the left hand there are rushing demisemiquavers and ominous trills (bb. 2–3); after 'der Dampf der Geschütze' a cannonball of a scale rushes up the treble stave (b. 5). The repeated leaps of an octave in obsessive dotted figuration (marked 'geschwinder werdend') under 'Sprühend umzucken mich rasselnde Blitze' (bb. 6–7) are nothing less than convulsive; they have an eccentric insistence and instrumental impracticality that puts us briefly in mind of Beethoven. After this tumult, four bars of recitative bring this curtain-raising (and hair-raising) section to a close. At b. 10 the mood of 'Vater, du führe mich!' is suddenly an oasis of calm – slow and religious; a short piano interlude of solemn chords ending on a cadence in the dominant prepares us for the song proper.

The music is now strictly strophic, and it is this perhaps that makes Capell level the charge of monotony against the setting. One cannot leave out a strophe without doing violence to a poem that depends on an *enchaînement* of ideas whereby the last line of each section is repeated to provide the opening of the next – a type of poetic relay race. This repetition gives the whole song the air of a religious litany; the comfort of such ritual in moments of strife is obvious, and the composer has every good reason to conceive the setting in such a manner. Continuing illustrative diversity (for which the opening strophe has whetted our appetite) is the only thing lacking. The tremulous oscillations that support the first six notes of melody yield to a more controlled throb of semiquavers that are a constant factor in the setting, like the ceaseless vibration of pounding cannonfire in the distance. The accompaniment stays in the lower register of the piano and this contributes to the darkness of the mood, as if the whole landscape inhabited by the song is obscured by swirling gun smoke.

Fischer-Dieskau declined to record *Gebet während der Schlacht* in his 1970s survey of the Schubert lieder. It is difficult to ascribe this only to the fact that it does not belong in the first rank of the young composer's creations; indeed the great singer recorded many songs less musically interesting than this. It seems obvious that German-speaking artists of Fischer-Dieskau's generation found distasteful the jingoism inherent in poems of this kind, and the intensity with which Körner greets thoughts of battle and death with something approaching the zeal of a *Liebestod*. The collection *Leyer und Schwert* from which the poem comes was a favourite present for German boys who were born in the first quarter of the twentieth century. (Plenty of sabre-rattling war poems were anthologized for young Britons with the same 'educative' purpose.) The modern listener may still find the dark emotions stirred up by this song disturbing. The historical situation in March 1815 (Napoleon had just escaped from Elba and was on the loose again) seems to have pushed the young composer into a patriotic mood. Weber's response to this poem, with its ceaseless, virtuosic accompaniment (Op. 41 no. 1, 1814, recorded in the Hyperion collection *Songs by Schubert's Friends and Contemporaries*), was even more extravagant.

In Volume 8 of the NSA, issued in 2009, a first version of this song was published for the first time. This is in the higher tonality of B flat major – a tenor key. A telling difference between the versions is the lack of the indication 'tremolo' for the accompaniment in the first version, particularly pertaining to bb. 13 and 22. The second version may go back to a lost Schubert authograph or it may be a Diabelli adaptation, as its tonality would infer.

Autograph:	Houghton Library, Harvard University, Cambridge, MA (first version)
Publication:	Published as part of the NSA in 2009 (P851; first version)
	Published as Book 10 no. 7 of the *Nachlass* by Diabelli, Vienna in April 1831 (P268; second version)
Subsequent editions:	Peters: Vol. 2/214; AGA XX 55: Vol. 2/80; NSA IV: Vol. 8/16 & 19; Bärenreiter: Vol. 6/116 (first version) & 156 (second version)
Bibliography:	Youens 1996, pp. 100–102
Further settings:	Friedrich Heinrich Himmel (1765–1814) *Gebet während der Schlacht* (1814)
	Carl Maria von Weber (1786–1826) *Gebet während der Schlacht* Op. 41 no. 1 (1814)
Discography and timing:	Fischer-Dieskau —
	Hyperion I 22²² 3'51 Simon Keenlyside
	Hyperion II 5¹⁹

← *Schwertlied* D170   *Der Morgenstern* D172 →

Die GEBÜSCHE   The thicket
(F. von Schlegel) **D646** [H416]
G major   January 1819

(71 bars)

Es wehet kühl und leise	The breeze blows cool and soft
Die Luft durch dunkle Auen,	Through dark meadows,
Und nur der Himmel lächelt	And only the heavens smile
Aus tausend hellen Augen.	From a thousand bright eyes.
Es regt nur eine Seele	Only one soul stirs
Sich in des Meeres Brausen,	Amid the roaring ocean,
Und in den leisen Worten,	And in the soft words
Die durch die Blätter rauschen.	That whisper through the leaves.
So tönt in Welle Welle,	Thus wave echoes wave
Wo Geister heimlich trauren;	Where spirits secretly mourn;
So folgen Worte Worten,	Thus words follow words
Wo Geister Leben hauchen.	Where spirits breathe life.
Durch alle Töne tönet	Through all the sounds
Im bunten Erdentraume,	In the earth's many-coloured dream,
E i n leiser Ton gezogen,[1]	*One* faint sound echoes
Für den, der heimlich lauschet.	For him who secretly listens.

FRIEDRICH VON SCHLEGEL (1772–1829); poem written in 1800/1801

This is the third of Schubert's sixteen Friedrich von Schlegel solo settings (1818–25). See the poet's biography for a chronological list of all the Friedrich von Schlegel settings. See also the article about the poetic cycle of which this song is part – Abendröte.

This poem is among the most fascinating that Schubert ever set, and the song, a masterpiece of the deepest feeling and harmonic daring, is a match for the words. Robert Schumann, who knew his Schlegel (although he was drawn first and foremost to the poet's critical work), places the last section of the poem (beginning 'Durch alle Töne tönet') as a motto for his *Fantasie* Op. 17 for piano (1836/8). Schlegel's lines here refer to the ability of the select few to hear and understand what seems incomprehensible to others, like the chosen of a religious order who have 'seen the light'. Johann Wilhelm Ritter (1776–1810), one of the Schlegel circle in Jena, wrote that 'every one of our spoken words is a secret song, for music from within continuously accompanies it'. In the poem for *Sprache der Liebe* D410, August von Schlegel, Friedrich's older brother, tells us that music is the language of love and can surmount barriers: 'love *thinks* in sweet music'.

Nearly twenty years before the composition of Schumann's *Fantasie*, Schubert grasped the message of *Die Gebüsche*; indeed it was specifically this poem that seems to have attracted the composer to the work of the younger Schlegel in the first place. In 1819 the Schubertians saw Schlegel's pantheism as an alternative to organized religion. This nocturne is thus a sequel to the aubade of Goethe's *Ganymed* D544; the breeze blowing through the meadows is a counterpart to that poem's 'Lieblicher Morgenwind', where Zeus is omnipresent in each manifestation of nature. But Schumann's future view of the poem as a charter for secret initiates might also have occurred to Schubert whose friends were a kind of Davidsbund *avant la lettre*, a band against the Philistines. This even extended to a secret resistance to the repressive Metternich regime. In a town of secret societies and secret liaisons, Schlegel's words, written long before the poet had become a conservative pillar of Metternich's regime, had an urgent significance.

Both Einstein and Reed have commented on the music's similarity to the Impromptu (D899 no. 3) in G flat (an autograph in G major – the original key of *Die Gebüsche* – also exists). The song opens in similar tempo, and with a similar accompaniment of flowing arpeggios.

---

[1] Schubert sets this line as 'Ein, *nur* ein leiser Ton gezogen'.

The *Vorspiel* begins with two beats of sextuplets in the tonic key; in b. 2 the introduction of a D sharp as the bass note, as well as in the right hand figurations, produces the augmented chord that we find elsewhere in the Schlegel settings, not to mention elsewhere in this song. This leads to a bar in E minor and a return to the tonic chord before the entry of the voice. In some ways this is a fairly conventional introduction, but it already displays a harmonic quirkiness difficult to define. The augmented chord mentioned above seems to imply the opening of a door into a secret harmonic world; in *Die Gebüsche* doors open, one after another, on to a dazzling succession of vistas. As in other Schlegel settings, there is more than a suggestion of Italianate melismata for the singer, and the cooling breezes are depicted by the delightful wafting of the vocal line across the stave. This is part of an overlay of various voices, each a constituent thread of the whole. Additionally a succession of literary assonances play their part: Auen, Augen, Brausen, rauschen, trauren, hauchen – as if one word or idea were seamlessly 'morphing' into the next.

We now launch into an extraordinary journey that takes us over hill and dale in a way that can only be compared to the deceptive technique of Fauré seventy years later: seemingly calm and beatific, but seething with harmonic invention in the inner voices. The piquant word-setting and restless series of modulations leave the listener puzzled, delighted and elated – reactions that are utterly appropriate to the poem and the passionate mood behind it. Unlike in *Der Strom* D565, however, there is not a trace of storminess here, and no change of dynamic; the hushed nocturne achieves its impact by other means. There are countless beautiful touches, and each line deserves a comment: for example, the rising and brightening sequence of 'Und nur der Himmel lächelt' (bb. 13–15); the way that 'tausend hellen Augen' is underpinned by the augmented chord, and pricks out its starry brightness with a D sharp ornamenting an A minor arpeggio (on the word 'hellen' in b. 17). In b. 18 there is an important variance between the NSA and other editions of the song: in the second beat of the bar, under the word 'Augen', the first and fourth of the right-hand semiquavers should be A sharps, rather than A naturals. This is taken directly from the manuscript by Walther Dürr, and was obviously 'corrected' by earlier editors. It adds only a momentary exotic colouring to the line, but the sharpening of the pitch seems to indicate eyes that are striving to see beyond their innate ability.

In the second quatrain of the poem the setting of 'Es regt nur eine Seele' is full of longing and a weird and wonderful harmonic journey takes us from the second inversion of D minor at the beginning of the phrase (b. 20) to the E major at the end of the verse ('die Blätter rauschen', b. 33) via a rainbow of successively flatter keys. The melodic line of the third strophe is much more static. Four variants of nearly the same tune are harmonized somewhat, though not very, differently; this provides a moment of relative stasis to the structure. This admirably illustrates the repetitiveness of nature, and the idea of wave echoing wave, word following word.

The third quatrain ends in D flat major (b. 44). In a *Zwischenspiel* (b. 41), the right hand changes only one note and we slip imperceptibly into C sharp minor, then also by changing only one note, into the first inversion of A major, and so on. This metamorphosis of tonality is positively Goethean in its subtlety, each newly minted arpeggio unfolding like a freshly opening bud as in the *Die Metamorphose der Pflanzen* ('A new one at once links to the circle that's closed / That the chain may extend into the ages for ever / And the whole be infused amply with life, like the part'). The first words of the final strophe produce a moment of absolute magic: 'Durch alle' is supported by an A^7 chord in first inversion (bb. 46–7); the left hand C sharp ascends a semitone and we find ourselves at 'Töne tönet' in the second inversion of G major (b. 48), a tantalizing sideways glance at the home key. Instead of leading us to repose, this simply opens another of those doors into realms ever more heady. Nothing has prepared us for the spectacular setting of 'Ein, nur ein leiser Ton gezogen'. Here Schubert has added the word 'nur', but a glance at Schlegel's poem shows that the poet had also meant to emphasize the word (it reads 'E i n' in the German manner of printed emphasis) and Schubert obeys the spirit of the poet's demand at the expense of the metre. The setting of 'Ein' is on an F, elongated to three and a half beats, and underpinned by a descending scale of crotchets (bb. 52–3). This is followed by Schubert's 'nur', still on the same F, as loving an anacrusis as he ever wrote. Underneath, we pass through a succession of diminished-seventh chords in flat keys to emerge radiantly from darkness on to the second 'ein', an F sharp high in the voice and harmonized by a D major chord in second inversion. We seem here to have entered ethereal spheres, so magical is this music, so completely in tune with Schlegel's imagery. The words rapturously repeated, which refer to the chosen listener – 'Für den, für den' – are excused chromatic inflection, and accorded the almost religious aura of the subdominant (C major) which suggest the truly understanding soul has finally been encountered in a holy moment. Gently leaning accidentals in the vocal line at 'heimlich lauschet' (bb. 64–5) are prophetic of *Der Fluss* D693 where similar chromatic distortion at 'die Hörer ewig lauschen' makes the ears prick up as if during the act of intent listening, and as if trying to break a code. The song's postlude is an exact repeat of its introduction.

Die Gebüsche is a great song, but it has not always been regarded as such. It is not easy to sing, particularly at the quiet dynamic and relatively slow speed ('Langsam') requested by the composer, but it repays close study, and is one of the high points of what might be termed Schubert's 'experimental' years. The magical quality of this piece, as well as of the equally visionary song *Abendröte*, the twin pillars that enclose the group, encourages present-day performers to attempt to make a unity of the Friedrich von Schlegel songs. An added incentive is to be able to introduce the listener to the rapturous world of Schlegel as a younger poet, one of the links that bind together the work of Schubert and Schumann, and not altogether by chance.

Autograph:	In private possession (USA)
First edition:	Published as Vol. 7 no. 1 in Friedlaender's edition by Peters, Leipzig in 1885 (P476)
Subsequent editions:	Peters: Vol. 8/3; AGA XX 350: Vol. 6/1; NSA IV: Vol. 12/65
Bibliography:	Black 2003, pp. 65–6
	Einstein 1951, p. 187
	Youens 2007[2], pp. 166–77
Discography and timing:	Fischer-Dieskau II 2[12] 2'41
	Hyperion I 27[18]
	Hyperion II 21[10] 3'19 Matthias Goerne

← *Die Berge* D634   *Der Wanderer* D649 →

Die GEFANGENEN SÄNGER   The captive songsters
(A. VON SCHLEGEL) **D712** [H462]
G major   January 1821

Hörst du von den Nachtigallen	Do you hear the bushes echoing
Die Gebüsche widerhallen?	With the nightingales' song?
Sieh', es kam der holde Mai.	See, fair May is here.
Jedes buhlt um seine Traute,	Every creature woos his sweetheart;
Schmelzend sagen alle Laute,	Every sound sweetly declares
Welche Wonn' im Lieben sei.	What bliss there is in love.
And're, die im Käfig leben,	Others, who live in cages,
Hinter ihren Gitterstäben,	Behind bars,
Hören draussen den Gesang;	Hear the song outside;
Möchten in die Freiheit eilen,	They would dearly like to fly to their freedom,
Frühlingslust und Liebe teilen:	To share in love and the joys of spring:
Ach! da hemmt sie enger Zwang.	But, alas, force keeps them closely confined.
Und nun drängt sich in die Kehle	And now, bursting from their grief-stricken souls,
Aus der gramzerrissnen Seele	The power of their song
Schmetternd ihres Lieds Gewalt,	Wells up in their throats;
Wo es, statt im Weh'n der Haine	But, instead of soaring amid the swaying trees,
Mit zu wallen, an der Steine	It rebounds from the hard stone
Hartem Bau zurücke prallt.	Of the walls.
So, im Erdental gefangen,	Thus, captive in this vale of earth,
Hört der Menschen Geist mit Bangen	Man's spirit hears with longing
Hehrer Brüder Melodie;[1]	The songs of his noble brothers;
Sucht umsonst zu Himmelsheitern[2]	He seeks in vain to expand this earthly life,
Dieses Dasein zu erweitern,	To embrace the serene joys of heaven.
Und das nennt er Poesie.	And he calls this Poetry.
Aber scheint er ihre Rhythmen	But, if he appears to dedicate its rhythms
Jubelhymnen auch zu widmen,	To hymns of praise,
Wie aus lebenstrunkner Brust:	As from a heart intoxicated with life,
Dennoch fühlen's zarte Herzen,	Yet do tender hearts feel
Aus der Wurzel tiefer Schmerzen	That the flower of his joy
Stammt die Blüte seiner Lust.	Springs from the root of deep suffering.

AUGUST WILHELM VON SCHLEGEL (1767–1845); poem written in 1810

This is the seventh of Schubert's ten August von Schlegel solo settings (1816–25). See the poet's biography for a chronological list of all the August von Schlegel settings.

Die gefangenen Sänger shows every sign of the judicious exercise of the composer's craft where a number of ideas are thriftily nursed, elaborated and recycled to link the five verses of a long poem into an impressive musical unity. At first glance it might not seem to furnish the ideal material for a complex *durchkomponiert* song, but Schubert took a great deal of trouble with it, and we might ask ourselves why.

The poem dates from 1810, so it is anachronistic for the Schubertian to imagine that during a time of French invasion, August von Schlegel equated his caged birds with the victims of

[1] Schlegel's original line is '*Hoher* Brüder *Harmonie*', but Schubert gives preference in this case to 'Melodie'.
[2] Schlegel's original line is '*Strebt* umsonst zu Himmelsheitern'.

Metternich's secret police. August (unlike his brother Friedrich who became a Viennese resident) lived in Switzerland and Germany and his poetry did not encompass Austrian politics. But Metternich's regime was not the only oppressive one in Europe, and August (unlike Friedrich) remained a lifelong liberal; he had been close friends with Mme de Staël whose *De l'Allemagne* had been banned by Napoleon in 1810. Schlegel had lived through that crisis with her and had himself been banned from France. There are reasons enough to find political echoes in this poem without bringing up Metternich, but if the cap fits let the great man wear it. The reference to the singers' (or poets') caged confinement must surely have seemed apposite to the case of the poet Johann Senn who had been arrested in March 1820 at an incident when the composer, subsequently also questioned by the police, was present. This was the one direct brush with the repressive state authorities experienced by Schubert. He got away with a caution, but Senn was detained and imprisoned, an ordeal that dragged on for fourteen months before he was finally deported to the Tyrol, his career in ruins and his prospects blighted. When this song was composed in January 1821, Senn's fate was still undecided, and the poet was behind bars, as much a captive as the birds in Schlegel's poem.

The drooping figuration, a crotchet phrased away to a quaver, and almost obsessively repeated, is prophetic of another 1821 song accompaniment written a few months later – *Geheimes* D719. There the theme is of the frisson experienced between two lovers that can only be expressed in meaningful glances. Similarly, the birds communicate with each other as if in code; those who are imprisoned draw sustenance from secret communication with their free brothers. The invention of a musical language to describe a secret language (if we believe that birds actually can speak to each other) is what is achieved here. The vocabulary is small, repetitive and immediately recognizable. That lilting, rocking little motto pervades the song, refusing to develop into extended melody and preferring to reflect the tiny, cell-like structures of birdsong. With these unpromising beginnings Schubert performs miracles.

The first strophe is in G major. The outdoor nightingales sing in freedom in the May breezes. The sinuous melody in § darts and wafts; the vocal line, when it imitates the drooping figurations of the accompaniment, approximates to a cooing sound, as if doves and nightingales belonged to the same family of birds. The aerial atmosphere is enhanced by the fact that both staves of the accompaniment are in the treble clef. To add to a feeling of unearthly joy, the composer uses the tonic chord in root position extremely sparingly until the interlude in the song's thirteenth bar. The rise and fall of the vocal line on 'Sieh, es kam der holde Mai' is delightful (bb. 9–10); it is even more appropriate at 'Welche Wonn' im Lieben sei' (bb. 21–3) and the melismas on 'holde' and 'Lieben' are especially gracious. What other song has the same happy (yet somehow disturbingly nostalgic) § gait, a mention of birdsong, a reference to May? Hölty's *Mailied* D503 perhaps? Certainly, but we must not overlook this song's most famous descendant, *Frühlingstraum* from *Winterreise*, where the same criteria also apply. And, like *Frühlingstraum*, this song has a dark side. In that case there is a time shift away from the happy past (the major key) to the bitter present (the minor); in *Die gefangenen Sänger* the shift is of space rather than time: from the free outdoors to incarceration.

For the second verse (from b. 25) the same motif that has begun the song is adapted to the minor key. The prosody of 'And're, die im Käfig leben' is masterly, with the quaver-rest gap after 'And're' which suggests that even speaking of the plight of these poor 'others' has produced a lump in the throat. The setting of the passage beginning 'Möchten in die Freiheit eilen' right up to the 'Ach' on a high G that drops a diminished fifth in expressive plaint, is extraordinary (bb. 31–5). Whoever has seen a bird caught within a confined space, attempting to escape but only succeeding in colliding, time after time, with the barrier that holds it captive, will understand this passage. There is something unbearably poignant about the fruitless mission of the piano's airborne triplet (we hear this three-note pattern repeated no fewer than eight times with unchanging harmony, bb. 13–14) as it strives for resolution; the unsuccessful quest for the root position of the chord is the longing for release. The desolate 'Ach' on a diminished chord (b. 35, and again at b. 38) signifies failure.

The key signature of the third verse changes from two to five flats as we find ourselves, rather unexpectedly, in B flat minor for the darkest strophe of the song (from b. 44). The vocal line is fashioned out of the same materials, and the accompanying motifs are similar, but there are new details. The vocal melody at 'Schmetternd ihres Lieds Gewalt' (and even more appropriately at 'an der Steine / Hartem Bau zurücke prallt' where Schlegel, sympathetic to the French Revolution, must have though of the Bastille) bounces back and forth within the range of a sixth and seventh as if sound were reflected harshly back on itself within too small a space, an acoustical effect described precisely in the text. The piano adds to this impression of harshness with semiquaver triplets in the right hand, wing-flapping oscillations in octaves. Where will we hear this in a more familiar song? In *Frühlingstraum* of course, where the early morning cockerel arouses the sleeper from his dreams (bb. 16, 18 and 20). The two works are united by distress: the sound of imprisoned birdsong sends shivers down the spine in much the same way as the winter traveller is awoken not only by cock-a-doodle-doo ('Und als die Hähne krähten'), but by the harsh cawing of ravens ('Es schrieen die Raben vom Dach'). In *Die gefangenen Sänger* the stone walls of the prison make even the most beautiful birdsong seem ugly and grating. At the end of the verse there is a seven-bar interlude that leads the music back to G minor. For the first time in the song the bass clef makes an appearance, pulling the work's specific gravity earthwards. We have heard the ill-effects of imprisonment; now it is time for a moral to be drawn.

The philosophical envoi is never a particularly easy thing to set to music. When it has to be included it is best to keep it simple and unadorned. Accordingly, the fourth verse of the poem is the shortest. It contains the moral, the key to the allegory, but Schubert sets this to music derived from earlier melodic and rhythmic patterns, gently floating along in the barcarolle rhythm that may seem rather frivolous here. There are no elaborate melismas or decorations, and no repetitions of text. It is clear that man the creator has more options than the birds of nature. Inspired by the song of our fellow artists, we seek in vain to find a bit of heaven in this earthly life. The second-strophe music for the birds trying to escape (a constantly repeating circle of triplets) reappears in a lower register where the addition of bass clef harmonies illustrates mankind's weightier destiny. And this time there *is* a way out. Poetry is the key that opens all doors, and Schubert introduces it in such a way that the concept seems to be created and named before our very ears. The ravishing modulation back to G major that coincides with the last syllable of 'Poesie' (bb. 50–51) surrounds the precious word with an aura of calm and peace.

And so we have come full circle. Earlier agitations are now settled in the calm of a world view. Even if a poet's work (or a composer's) appears to be the result of jubilant enjoyment of life, the roots of creativity stem from deep suffering. This is a concept with which Schubert clearly identifies; the gentle swinging gait of the song is not much enlivened by the words 'Jubelhymnen' and 'lebenstrunkner Brust'. The truth behind the mystery of creativity lies deeper than hearty celebration, and the minor-key colouring of 'Aus der Wurzel tiefer Schmerzen' acknowledges this. The Schubertian duality inherent in 'Lachen und Weinen' is summed up by the setting of the phrase 'Blüte seiner Lust'. The diminished seventh of 'Blüte' opens, like a beautiful flower, into an unambiguous G major and the expansive melisma of 'seiner Lust' (bb. 92–6).

Autograph: Wienbibliothek im Rathaus, Vienna (first draft on the back of
                              sketches of the A flat major Mass)
                              Pierpont Morgan Library, New York (complete draft)

First edition:	Published as Book 33 no. 2 of the *Nachlass* by Diabelli, Vienna in 1842 (P338)
Subsequent editions:	Peters: Vol. 5/193; AGA XX 389: Vol. 6/164; NSA IV: Vol. 13/2 & 198 (sketch)
Bibliography:	Black 2003, p. 72 (ideas for this song and the A flat Mass D678 appear on the same piece of manuscript paper)
	Capell 1928, p. 169
	Fischer-Dieskau 1977, pp. 296–7
	Kohlhäufl 2002, pp. 173–84
Discography and timing:	Fischer-Dieskau II 4[9] 4'15
	Hyperion I 34[17]
	Hyperion II 24[4] 5'21 Matthias Goerne

← *Sehnsucht* D636   *Die Nacht* (not in Deutsch) →

GEFRORNE TRÄNEN *see WINTERREISE* D911/3

GEHEIMES   A secret

(GOETHE) OP. 14 NO. 2, **D719** [H467]
A♭ major   March 1821

Über meines Liebchens Äugeln	Everyone is astonished
Stehn verwundert alle Leute;	At the eyes my sweetheart makes;
Ich, der Wissende, dagegen,	But I, who understand,
Weiss recht gut, was das bedeute.	Know very well what they mean.
Denn es heisst: ich liebe diesen	For they are saying: he is the one I love,
Und nicht etwa den und jenen.	Not this one or that one.
Lasset nur, ihr guten Leute,	So, good people,
Euer Wundern, euer Sehnen!	Cease your wondering and your longing!
Ja, mit ungeheuren Mächten	Indeed, she may well look about her
Blicket sie wohl in die Runde;	With a mightily powerful eye,
Doch sie sucht nur zu verkünden	But she seeks only to give him a foretaste
Ihm die nächste süsse Stunde.	Of the next sweet hour.

JOHANN WOLFGANG VON GOETHE (1749–1832); poem written 31 August 1814

This is the fifty-ninth of Schubert's seventy-five Goethe solo settings (1814–26). See the poet's biography for a chronological list of all the Goethe settings.

The enchanting elegance of this little song ensures its place as one of the jewels of the repertoire. It has a beautiful and ingratiating vocal melody but so strong is the character of the accompaniment, which is made up of repetitions of a single rhythmical idea, that the piano writing is the most memorable feature. A crotchet chord is phrased away to a quaver, followed by a quaver rest – a wilting little figure on tiptoe that is secretive, cheeky, full of longing, like the inward groan of a frustrated lover who can scarcely wait for the next time. This music is as suggestive as a wink, and as delicate as a blush – in Richard Stokes's words 'a miracle of complicity'. We hear not only the singer's feelings; we are also somehow able to see his lover's visual responses. This figure governs all but five bars of the song. An over-exquisite and over-phrased performance from the singer can, on occasion, make for cloying preciousness. These constantly repeated little sighs are a daring notion on Schubert's part: seldom in an accompaniment does he harvest a single idea with such determination. It takes some nerve on the part of the pianist to observe the phrasing and all those rests, again and again; it also takes a great control of touch at the keyboard to make the diminuendo effective in each bar as the crotched falls to the quaver. For the pianist it is like walking a tightrope, and for the singer also: the danger is of falling into parody, where this music can acquire all the worst mannerisms of 'arty' lieder-performance.

We should not be embarrassed by this borderline flirtation with preciosity; it is possible to carry off this song by negotiating that danger with the help of good legato singing. The more one looks into this song, the more one admires it, for the word-setting alone is a miracle of inventiveness. The special accentuation of 'meines' (b. 8) implies a proprietary pride; the ache of 'Liebchens' (b. 9) is conveyed by a longer note that falls into a graceful quaver descent for the word 'Äugeln' and perfectly paints the vivacity of her glance, with a flutter of the eyelashes perhaps. The upward rise on 'Stehn verwundert' (bb. 12–13) makes everyone else stand on tiptoe in their admiration for those legendary eyes. The word 'Ich' (b. 17) is separated from the rest of the phrase ('der Wissende, dagegen') with a crotchet rest; this conveys either a sharp intake of breath from a besotted suitor, or the swagger of satisfaction from someone who knows himself to be the preferred one. (Either interpretation can be successfully encompassed by singers of different temperaments.) At the major/minor alternation of the repeated phrase 'Weiss recht gut' (bb. 25–8 and bb. 30–36) another song in A flat major comes to mind, also of oriental inspiration – *Lachen und Weinen* from the summer of 1822. *Geheimes* is another textbook example of Schubert's creative use of the juxtaposition of bright and dark harmonic mood: the change into the minor seems to mean a frown of concentration as the singer carefully scans the face of his *inamorata* the better to read the meaning of her glance. The momentary shift into A flat minor is nothing to do with sadness: the flattening of the third degree of the scale implies something that goes deeper, as in a search for greater understanding. The melismatic second setting of 'bedeute' (bb. 33–6) is a curvaceous turn of phrase, which seems emblematic of secrecy and covert romantic activity, pregnant with hidden meanings. At 'Denn es heisst: ich liebe diesen / Und nicht etwa den und jenen' (bb. 42–50) there is another alternation of major and minor tonalities, this time between E flat major and minor – 'I love *this* one' (major-key radiance) 'not *that* one!' (minor-key disdain).

As in *Versunken* and *Ganymed*, two other settings of erotic texts by Goethe in the key of A flat, there is Schubert's favourite excursion into C flat major in the middle section (at 'Lasset nur, ihr guten Leute / Euer Wundern, euer Sehnen!' bb. 52–61). On this occasion the modulation betokens an aside in which the singer inwardly challenges, and mocks, the curious onlooker as he notices the futile glances of longing directed towards someone whom he knows belongs to him. The return to A flat (the musical recapitulation at the words 'Ja, mit ungeheuren Mächten' b. 63) has been engineered by a simple yet divine chain of chords under the elongated setting of 'Sehnen' (bb. 59–61). This seems simultaneously to paint the meaning of the word, and cheekily to mock the longing of the outsider who can never hope to experience such love as this. There is another major/minor juxtaposition with the repeated phrase 'Ihm die nächste süsse Stunde'. The C flat on the second 'Ihm' (b. 86) emphasizes a sense of mystery about the identity of the secret 'him'; he is of course the singer himself, but no one knows this. The elongation of the second 'nächste' (bb. 87–8) is also masterful, for it implies the bittersweet agony of waiting for that happy hour when the two can be alone together at last.

For this poem from Goethe's *West-östlicher Divan* Schubert seems to have thought himself into the oriental background of a seraglio. Perhaps the young suitor is dallying with the sultan's wife, and there is danger that they might be discovered. Despite the protagonist's boasts to his audience, the relationship is a thing of discretion and secrecy. Leo Black suggests a less happy scenario; he maintains that the minor key comes exactly when the singer says 'ihm' because he is not in a position to say 'mir'. This is to imagine an older admirer longingly looking at the object of his affections and masochistically forced to watch her flirting with others. This is another kind of secret of course. Seldom has a song been truer to its title. The added frisson of forbidden love is heard everywhere as the constantly repeated motif in the accompaniment engenders a tension, as if the breath is held while playing it. At the heart of *Geheimes* is the confession of a liaison unknown to others; one could not begin to guess how many times this state of affairs existed among the young (and not so young) in Schubert's Vienna.

It should not surprise us that the song was dedicated to the most romantically active member of the composer's circle, Franz von Schober, who was to become secretly engaged to Justina von Bruchmann a few years later (much to the horror of her brother Franz when he eventually found out). There is no example of a song of this erotic intensity being dedicated to any other of the composer's male friends. When the songs of Op. 14 were being prepared for publication, the composer was staying with Schober; he had earlier completed the opera *Alfonso und Estrella* to his friend's libretto. At the very least, the dedication of these particular songs shows an enormous complicity between the two as if Schubert knew all the details of Schober's private life, and vice versa. *Geheimes* depicts an intimacy that can only be expressed in public by fleeting eye contact, that exchange of glances between two people that no one else understands.

Like *Versunken* D715 the poem for this song appears in Goethe's *West-östlicher Divan* as part of the 'Uschk Nameh' – 'The Book of Love'. The first poem in this section, *Musterbilder* ('Exemplars') lists famous examples of lovers in eastern lore and legend: Rustan and Rodawu, Jussuph and Suleika, Ferhad and Schirin, Sheba and Solomon. After *Geheimes* comes another lyric in the same metre, the last poem in 'The Book of Love', entitled *Geheimstes* ('Most secret'). Here it is clearly the same enchanted lover who has sung *Geheimes* who fends off the curiosity of a group of 'Anekdotenjäger' – gossip mongers – who long to know the identity of his lover. He assures them that they will be awestruck if, and when, they face her and stand in her radiance. In the last strophe he maintains that his love for the mysterious unknown girl is like that of Medshnun for Leila, Goethe's reference to an ancient legend, an eastern version of *Romeo and Juliet* renowned through many Muslim countries. (Leila is best known to singers as a passing mention in Fauré's song *Les Roses d'Ispahan*.) The fact that this story of separated lovers has a tragic outcome is perhaps an indication that the two lovers of *Geheimes* are involved in a forbidden liaison – or maybe the young man is merely brandishing these famous comparisons in hyperbolic fashion to indicate the strength of his devotion.

Measured metronomically, that is to say setting a metronome mark per crotchet, the song is often performed far too fast, as if the vocal line had been written in quavers and there were half the number of bar lines. With the marking 'Etwas geschwind' (only 'rather fast' as opposed to 'very fast') applied to crotchets, the pianist is cautioned to avoid the sense of headlong frenzy often experienced in performances of this song. A steadier tempo elongates the longing, makes the outcome less certain. There are two versions of the song but they are so similar that even the NSA does not print both of them, preferring to notate the few differences (for example a mordent on *ver*wundert in the poem's second line) as an ossia above the stave of the definitive version (the text of the first edition).

Autograph:	Österreichische Nationalbibliothek, Vienna (first draft)
First edition:	Published as Op. 14 no. 2 by Cappi & Diabelli in December 1822 (P35)
Dedicatee:	Franz von Schober
Subsequent editions:	Peters: Vol. 1/232; AGA XX 392: Vol. 6/183; NSA IV: Vol. 1/118; Bärenreiter: Vol. 1/93
Bibliography:	Fischer-Dieskau 1977, p. 145
Arrangment:	Arr. Johannes Brahms (1833–1897), for voice and orchestra (1862) [*see* ORCHESTRATIONS]
Discography and timing:	Fischer-Dieskau II 4^{12} 1'50
	Hyperion I 28^4
	Hyperion II 24^9 1'55 John Mark Ainsley

← *Grenzen der Menschheit* D716   *Suleika I* D720 →

Das GEHEIMNIS (I)
(SCHILLER) **D250** [H135]
A♭ major   7 August 1815

The secret

(17 bars)

Sie konnte mir kein Wörtchen sagen,	She could not speak one word to me,
Zu viele Lauscher waren wach;	There were too many listening;
Den Blick nur durft' ich schüchtern fragen,	I could only shyly question the look in her eyes,
Und wohl verstand ich, was er sprach.	And well understood what it meant.
Leis' komm' ich her in deine Stille,	Softly I approach your silence.
Du schön belaubtes Buchenzelt,	Leafy beech grove;
Verbirg in deiner grünen Hülle	Beneath your green cloak
Die Liebenden dem Aug' der Welt!	Conceal the lovers from the eyes of the world.
Von ferne mit verworrnem Sausen	Far away, in whirring confusion,
Arbeitet der geschäf'tge Tag,	The bustling day is at work,
Und durch der Stimmen hohles Brausen	And through the empty buzz of voices
Erkenn' ich schwerer Hämmer Schlag.	I discern the beat of heavy hammers.
So sauer ringt die kargen Lose	Thus man toils to wrest his meagre lot
Der Mensch dem harten Himmel ab;	From a cruel heaven
Doch leicht erworben, aus dem Schosse	Yet happiness is easily won.
Der Götter fällt das Glück herab.	Falling from the lap of the gods.

Dass ja die Menschen nie es hören,	May people never hear
Wie treue Lieb' uns still beglückt!	How happy our true love makes us.
Sie können nur die Freude stören,	They can only mar our joy,
Weil Freude nie sie selbst entzückt.	Since they have never tasted joy themselves.
Die Welt wird nie das Glück erlauben,	The world will never permit happiness,
Als Beute nur wird es gehascht;[1]	It can only be snatched;
Entwenden musst du's oder rauben,	You must seize it
Eh' dich die Missgunst überrascht.	Before envy catches you unawares.
Leis' auf den Zehen kommt's geschlichen,	It steals in on tiptoe
Die Stille liebt es und die Nacht,	Cherishing silence and the night.
Mit schnellen Füssen ist's entwichen	With rapid steps it flees
Wo des Verräters Auge wacht.	Where the traitor lurks.
O schlinge dich, du sanfte Quelle,	Gentle fountain, envelop us
Ein breiter Strom um uns herum,	Like a broad stream,
Und drohend mit empörter Welle	And with angrily threatening waves
Verteidige dies Heiligtum!	Defend this sanctuary.

FRIEDRICH VON SCHILLER (1759–1805); poem written in 1797

This is the fourteenth of Schubert's forty-four Schiller solo settings (1811–24). See the poet's biography for a chronological list of all the Schiller settings.

This song is the seed from which a grander setting grew eight years later. That neglected song (D793) is sadly not yet a star in the repertoire, but it is better known than this simple strophic one which is all but completely neglected. The final section of *Die Erwartung* (D159) has something in common with the secrecy of this lover's tryst, and their music which feels to be on tiptoe. The staccato quavers of the left hand accompaniment add to this impression, as does the highly strung vocal tessitura. For a singer able to spin a radiant vocal line this is a wonderful exercise in the depiction of tremulous emotion; the need for secrecy reins in overt expressions of excitement and any temptation to take too fast a tempo. This sense of control can brew considerable intensity in performance. The secret for singer and pianist is not to indulge in the kind of rubato that accommodates and indulges the difficulties of negotiating the rhythm – the detached left-hand quavers must be as implacable, the progress of the song as determined, as a carefully hatched plot. This music is surely better suited to the soprano voice than to the tenor. The song shares its A flat major tonality with *Das Rosenband* D280, a similarly intimate setting. A drawback is that the complete scope of Schiller's marvellous poem is not ideally served by an unmodified strophic song, and in the Hyperion Edition only the first two verses are performed (the NSA prints all strophes other than the first in italics).

In bb. 11–12, as printed in the NSA, Schubert writes 'Buchengrün' instead of 'Buchenzelt': this of course destroys Schiller's rhyme with 'Aug' der Welt'. In a case like this, we have to admit that the composer was sometimes a careless copyist, and the performer should reinstate the original poetry. The word 'grünen' appears in the line beneath; it is so easy to see how, in the twinkling of an eye, this mistake may have been made by glancing over to Schiller's text and taking in the wrong part of the strophe – thus Schubert's invention of 'Buchengrün'. The poem is one of those that Schiller wrote for his wife, Charlotte von Lengefeld. The couple had already been married for seven years and this lyric is a window on the enduring intensity of their rela-

---

[1] Schiller has 'Als Beute *wird es nur* gehascht'.

tionship. In recent years Charlotte's importance as a writer and literary personality in her own right has been thoroughly reassessed.

Autograph:	Wienbibliothek im Rathaus, Vienna (first draft)
First edition:	Published as No. 28 of *Neueste Folge nachgelassener Lieder und Gesänge* by J. P. Gotthard, Vienna in 1872 (P454)
Subsequent editions:	Not in Peters; AGA XX 105: Vol. 3/2; NSA IV: Vol. 13/120
Discography and timing:	Fischer-Dieskau I 4[21] 2'49
	Hyperion I 1[13]
	Hyperion II 8[19] 3'02 Janet Baker

← *Die Bürgschaft* D246   *Hoffnung* D251 →

Das GEHEIMNIS (II)   The secret
(SCHILLER) D793 [H517]
G major   May 1823

(100 bars)

See previous entry for poem and translation

FRIEDRICH VON SCHILLER (1759–1805); poem written in 1797

This is the forty-second of Schubert's forty-four Schiller solo settings (1811–24). See the poet's biography for a chronological list of all the Schiller settings.

This is one of the few Schiller settings that is a product of Schubert's maturity, but it has its roots in the past. At first glance the versions of *Das Geheimnis* appear to be different songs altogether but it is soon clear that the twenty-six-year-old composer respected the basic ideas and inspirations of his younger self and attempted to rework and amplify these original ideas rather than start again from scratch – though he often did that too. Far from forgetting music as soon as he had written it, Schubert was much less vague about these matters than legend has it. It is unlikely that he was always able to put his hands on manuscripts from the past with ease, but he seems to have had his own mental filing system and was able, when he chose, to recall past work with incredible clarity.

This song is one of the most beautiful of all the Schiller settings. Einstein calls it 'a flower of melodic exuberance in which even suggestions of an Italian style are not out of place'. The melody is more or less based on the earlier version, but it blossoms profusely under the nurturing hand of a gardener of melody at the height of his powers. If D250 is a shy and delicate rosebud of a song, beautiful in its own understated way, D793 is in full bloom with a heady perfume; Einstein no doubt sees the Italian style in the tendrils of vocal melisma which luxuriate in the vocal line. The accompanimental idea of the earlier version is retained at first – quavers that alternate with rests to suggest complicity. This idea is delicately established with a prelude of four hushed bars (D250 is without an introduction) which continues to support the vocal line for the first four lines of the poem. It is in the second half of the verse that Schiller gives a locale for the lovers' tryst, and it is the description of the 'leafy beech grove' (bb. 16–17) with its 'green cloak' of vegetation (bb. 18–20) that inspires Schubert to a new type of accompaniment. The heady intoxication of love *en sourdine* prompts a piano part in pendulous triplets – the very look of them on the printed page like leafy branches extending their shade over the lovers; the tie marks in both staves, strands of musical string, securing the flowering arpeggios to the arboreal trellis. We hear the branches' music in the right hand but, thanks to the left, the trees themselves are also firmly planted in the earth. So splendid is the melody that one scarcely notices that for nine bars the music is rooted on a dominant pedal (bb. 13–21). It is this that makes time stand still for the lovers. The piano's interlude, on a tonic pedal (bb. 48–52), then seems to be the work's crowning glory. There is nothing quite like it in all Schubert – sensual and ahead of its time in its heavily perfumed romantic languor, this sybaritic music would not sound out of place in a piano piece by Chopin. We hear this interlude four times in all, between each of the strophes, and for the last time as the song's postlude.

The words of the second verse call for a different accompaniment and a modified vocal line, and Schubert gives us a sextuplet figure in the piano that can be made to whirr, bustle and buzz (from b. 29). In bb. 33–5 the beat of the hammers is depicted by left-hand crotchets, each one preceded by the crunch of a grace note. In the second half of the verse the word 'sauer' (b. 38) prompts a flattening of pitch into the minor tonality, a semitone lower than the corresponding passage in the first verse. Other tiny details are changed here (and throughout the song) in the vocal line in order to accommodate perfectly the scansion of Schiller's words. The second half of Verse 3 is also in the minor key, an apt illustration of the contrast between the happiness of the lovers in the first four lines and the unhappiness of the rest of the world in the remainder of the strophe. The accompaniment to Verse 4 is modified slightly into a patter of breathless quavers to illustrate the words 'Mit schnellen Füssen' (from b. 81). It is a measure of the versatility of the composer's 'tree' motif from Verse 1 that these mellifluous bowered triplets of the second half of the verse (and of the postlude, of course) can easily be pressed into service as the most liquid of water music (from b. 85).

Only close examination of the music reveals how much work the composer has done to individualize each stanza of this setting without disturbing the overall flow of an apparently seamless work of art. This is the modified strophic song par excellence. Written at the same time as *Die schöne Müllerin* D795, *Das Geheimnis* stands to one side of the celebrated cycle, but not entirely in its shadow; it is a fine example of Schubert's vein of creativity in that crucial year of 1823 when the composer's musical motto appears to have been *multum in parvo*.

Autograph:	Staatsbibliothek Preussischer Kulturbesitz, Berlin (first draft)
First edition:	Published as Op. post. 173 no. 2 by C. A. Spina, Vienna in 1867 (P408)
Subsequent editions:	Peters: Vol. 6/109; AGA XX 431: Vol. 7/125; NSA IV: Vol. 13/123
Bibliography:	Einstein 1951, p. 255
Further setting:	J. F. Reichardt (1752–1814) *Das Geheimnis*, No. 2 of *Schillers Lyrische Gedichte, erstes Heft* (1810)
Discography and timing:	Fischer-Dieskau II 6[6] 4'40
	Hyperion I 16[9]
	Hyperion II 27[5] 5'55 Thomas Allen

← *Vergissmeinnicht* D792   *Der Pilgrim* D794 →

GEHEIMNIS (An Franz Schubert)   A mystery (to Franz Schubert)
(MAYRHOFER) **D491** [H310]
B♭ major – F major   October 1816

Sag an, wer lehrt dich Lie - der,

(60 bars)

Sag an, wer lehrt dich Lieder,	Tell us, who teaches you
So schmeichelnd und so zart?	Such tender, flattering songs?
Sie rufen einen Himmel	They evoke a heaven
Aus trüber Gegenwart.	From these cheerless times.
Erst lag das Land verschleiert	First the land lay veiled
Im Nebel vor uns da —	In mist before us —
Du singst — und Sonnen leuchten,	Then you sing, and the sun shines,
Und Frühling ist uns nah.	And spring is near.
Den schilfbekränzten Alten,[1]	You do not see
Der seine Urne giesst,	The old man, crowned with reeds,
Erblickst du nicht, nur Wasser,	Emptying his urn;
Wie's durch die Wiesen fliesst.	You see only water flowing through the meadows.
So geht es auch dem Sänger,	So too it is with the singer.
Er singt, er staunt in sich;[2]	He sings, he marvels inwardly;
Was still ein Gott bereitet,	He wonders, as you do,
Befremdet ihn, wie dich.	At a river god's silent creation.

JOHANN MAYRHOFER (1787–1836)

This is the tenth of Schubert's forty-seven Mayrhofer solo settings (1814–24). See the poet's biography for a chronological list of all the Mayrhofer settings.

Haydn made a marvellous piece of music out of a valedictory poem written in his honour by Mrs Anne Hunter at the end of his second London visit, the song *O tuneful voice*. If a friend takes the trouble to write a eulogy, the least a composer can do, by way of returning the compliment, is to set it to music. Mayrhofer probably wrote this *Geheimnis* in gratitude for the songs that Schubert had already made from his texts, and in hopeful anticipation of many more. In this he was not to be disappointed.

Mayrhofer praises the composer's unforced naturalness, and Schubert immediately seems to respond to such a salute with gratitude in turn to his forbears Mozart and Haydn. He begins with a tiny piano prelude that quite unashamedly makes an elegant descent from the heights in a decorated B flat major arpeggio, an analogue for inspiration from heaven in its simplest form;

---

[1] Mayrhofer's word order is 'Den alten Schilfbekränzten'. For an explanation of the background to these alternative Mayrhofer readings see Editorial Note at the beginning of Johann MAYRHOFER.
[2] Mayrhofer's text (*Gedichte*, 1824) reads 'Er singt *und* staunt in sich'.

this is followed by a tiny phrase (b. 2) which seems to quote from the theme of the slow movement of Mozart's last Piano Concerto, K595 in B flat. The use of turns and mordents in the accompaniment to the first two lines of the poem (bb. 4, 5 and 7) reinforces the impression of Mozartian elegance. 'You have conjured something from nothing,' Mayrhofer is saying, and Schubert now evokes the Haydn of *Die Schöpfung* to describe the miracle of his own creation. The 'Land verschleiert / Im Nebel' (bb. 13–15), accompanied in darkly turbulent quavers, is a tiny lieder equivalent of the Chaos evoked in Haydn's oratorio; the emergence of the 'Sonnen leuchten' (bb. 19–20) has a touch of the splendour of 'Und es ward Licht', the words that signal the creation of light in that great work. The bouncing staccato quavers confirm the slightly old-fashioned and *galant* atmosphere of this bow in Haydn's direction.

Classicism has been duly saluted; what we hear next is surely its replacement by romanticism. There have been various attempts to identify the 'schilfbekränzten Alte' (from b. 29 in the music) who empties his urn, and who is unregarded by Schubert. Reed believes that Mayrhofer was chiding Schubert for not sharing his own preoccupation with classical themes – a gentle rebuke that perhaps signalled Mayrhofer's intention to take in hand the composer's classical education. (Certainly by the following year Schubert knew a great deal more about mythology.) Perhaps the composer takes the culture and learning of modern times too much for granted, without realizing how much inspiration the poets of the day owed to the ancients.

Even for Mayrhofer, however, it would seem very curious to criticize Schubert's shortcomings in the middle of a poem of praise, and the solution to this puzzling poem is rather more straightforward than Reed believes. With his crown of reeds and urn (through which pour the waters of a river), Mayrhofer evokes the traditional figure of a river god (there were very many of them in Greek mythology), a mainstay of classical decoration and statuary to be found throughout Europe in the work of such artists such as Tiepolo, Michelangelo and Rubens among many others. (This explains the line 'Was still ein Gott bereitet' at the end of the poem where the silent workings of the river god are compared to those of a god of music, Apollo perhaps.) Schubert delights in the stream flowing through the meadows, irrespective of its distant, mightier source as personified by the old man with the urn. In similar fashion, a Schubert song is another natural wonder, a gift from the gods. Mayrhofer thus acknowledges the unfathomable and secret origins of Schubert's output, as hidden from everyday human understanding as the secret working of nature. For all the river god's efforts in feeding one of his tributaries, Schubert values the stream in its own right, irrespective of its impressive source; and for all the composer's miraculous inspiration, not to mention hard work at his desk, the listener gratefully hears only a beautiful song seemingly conjured out of thin air. There is no need to source Schubert's genius, an impossible task even should one want to and the poet does not really expect a response to the rhetorical question at the beginning of the poem.

All this is very different from Johann Michael Vogl's patronizing contention that Schubert was a somnambulist, little aware of how he had composed his masterpieces, and that he created them in an inspired but dreamlike state; Mayrhofer knew better than to suggest that Schubert was unaware of the technical aspects of his craft. This water imagery also pays tribute to the composer's special musical connection with this medium – something well established even by 1816, and long before the definitive water music of *Die schöne Müllerin*. There is already a deluge of new ideas in Schubert's work and the songs are awash with musical delights; indeed in paying less attention to the classical origins of the river god, the composer stands on the threshold of the Romantic era. The change from A flat minor to E major in this section (bb. 35–8) is a marvellous illustration of the enharmonic means of turning the water of the ancients into the wine of artistic inspiration. One can almost hear the musical colour change as dull flats cede to sparkling sharps.

The River God by John Bacon the Elder, based on a drawing by William Blake.

The final lines (from 'So geht es auch dem Sänger') are also a source of confusion. As an introduction to this section there is an extraordinary shift from E major to F (bb. 42–4) that suggests a change of subject matter or perspective. Who exactly is the singer referred to in the fifth line of the second verse? In his commentary, Fischer-Dieskau assumes that Mayrhofer is referring to Schubert who is astounded at his own creativity. Yet Mayrhofer himself seems to be the subject of the sentence, and the singer of Schubert's songs. After all, it is known that the poet was an amateur vocalist and guitar player, and in 1816 Schubert had not yet met Johann Michael Vogl who was to be his definitive interpreter. After the words 'Er singt' there is an upward arpeggio (bb. 47 and 49) as if Schubert is casting Mayrhofer in the bardic role of Orpheus doing his warming-up exercises. This may also account for the slightly over-dramatized way that 'er staunt in sich' is set. ('Did *my* poetry really inspire music as beautiful as this?') The final two lines of the poem, and the vocative 'dich', bring Schubert back into the picture after Mayrhofer has described his own emotions. As explained above, the reference to 'ein Gott' here refers to the river god with his urn who has prepared the stream that delights Schubert, as well as to whichever other god or muse has attended the birth of his songs. Poet and composer both marvel at their joint creation, something more than the sum of its parts; it should be no surprise to realize that the prickly Mayrhofer plays a considerable role in the scenario, and is not just a passive hagiographer.

As it happens, the key of F major in which this *Geheimnis* ends is shared by the final section of *Ganymed* D544, a song that is also about the working of a miracle. The postlude there comprises a sequence of chords that rises heavenward as the boy is assumed into the realms of Olympus. The postlude of *Geheimnis* moves in the opposite direction; the god of music sends a rainbow of chords that falls to earth (and the tonic) in a gentle arc of sound.

Elizabeth McKay has suggested that the imagery of the 'trüber Gegenwart' and the description of a land veiled in mist may be a topical reference to the exceptionally bad European weather throughout the summer of 1816 due to a volcanic eruption in Indonesia.

Autograph:	Missing or lost
First edition:	Published as Vol. 7 no. 21 in Friedlaender's edition by Peters, Leipzig in 1887 (P491)
Subsequent editions:	Peters: Vol. 7/46; AGA XX 269: Vol. 4/223; NSA IV: Vol. 11/18
Bibliography:	Black 2003, pp. 56–9 & 61
	Fischer-Dieskau 1977, p. 82
	McKay 2001, pp. 65–78
Discography and timing:	Fischer-Dieskau I 8[17] 2'20
	Hyperion I 17[16]
	Hyperion II 16[12] 2'42 Lucia Popp

← *Der Hirt* D490   *Zum Punsche* D492 →

GEIST DER LIEBE   Spirit of love
(KOSEGARTEN) **D233** [H124]
E major   15 July 1815

(20 bars)

Wer bist du, Geist der Liebe,	Who are you, spirit of love,
Der durch das Weltall webt?	Who are at work throughout the universe,
Den Schoss der Erde schwängert,	Sowing the seed in the earth's womb,
Und den Atom belebt?	And giving life to the atom?
Der Elemente bindet,	Who are you, who bind the elements,
Der Weltenkugeln ballt,	Fashion the spheres,
Aus Engelharfen jubelt	Rejoice with angels' harps,
Und aus dem Säugling lallt?	And lisp from the infant's mouth.
[. . . 2 . . .]	[. . . 2 . . .]
Nur der ist gut und edel,	He alone is good and noble
Dem du den Bogen spannst.	Whose bow is drawn by you;
Nur der ist gross und göttlich,	He alone is great and godlike
Den du zum Mann ermannst.	Who through you attains true manhood.
Sein Werk ist Pyramide,	His work is a pyramid,
Sein Wort ist Machtgebot.	His word a mighty command;
Ein Spott ist ihm die Hölle.	He mocks hell
Ein Hohn ist ihm der Tod.	And scorns death.

LUDWIG KOSEGARTEN (1758–1818); poem written in 1787

This is the seventh of Schubert's twenty-one Kosegarten solo settings (1815–17). See the poet's biography for a chronological list of all the Kosegarten settings, as well as a discussion of Morten Solvik's Kosegarten Liederkreis and this song's place within it.

This poem aims at a philosophical breadth of expression which distinguishes *Geist der Liebe* from a number of charming pieces of the period, despite sharing the key of E major with many of them. Kosegarten was a professor of theology, and the love apostrophized here treads a fine line between heaven and earth. In consequence the song is something of a hybrid – a religious poem in a way but, unlike the rigorously devout works of Klopstock, it leaves open the possibility that the love between man and maid is as valid as that between Man and his Creator. The spirit of Love impregnates Mother Earth, the poet tells us, but we cannot help but be reminded that everyday man, though somewhat less ambitious in his choice of partner, has his own means of doing the same thing on a smaller scale. The Kosegarten settings are at their best when they depict intimate moments of rapt communication between amatory mortals. Here mention of universe and atom, elements and spheres, seems overpowering in comparison to the slender musical language that characterizes the composer's Kosegarten style. The same problem is evident in 1816 in the Schiller setting *Laura am Klavier* D388 – how to reconcile devotion to a young lady playing the piano in the drawing room (and the delicate music this inspired) with references to 'the giant arm of Chaos' and so on.

In *Geist der Liebe* the direction 'Mit Kraft' is insufficient to solve a similar problem of a slender musical style over-parted by the grandeur of the words. Schubert was successfully to find his epic voice two months later for Klopstock's *Dem Unendlichen* D291; indeed, in the second half of *Geist der Liebe* (from 'Der Elemente bindet') dotted rhythms in the left hand (bb. 10–12) provide pre-echoes of the fanfare motifs of that masterpiece, as if played by celestial brass. It is interesting too that we see here an early manifestation of the right-hand triplets (from b. 8) that are to be found in so many religious songs: *Der gute Hirt* D449 (also in E major) and the choral *Der 23. Psalm* D706. Walther Dürr (NSA Vol. 8 p. XXVI) points out that this song is on the obverse side of the autograph of another Kosegarten setting, *Der Abend* D221, a song with a majesty of its own, and that the two works were almost certainly composed on the same day. For those singers tempted to include the poem's third verse (not printed here) 'Oriflam' refers to the flag of St Denis, said to exert a terrifying power on non-believers.

Autograph:	Wienbibliothek im Rathaus, Vienna (fair copy)
First edition:	Published as Op. post. 118 no. 1 by Josef Czerny, Vienna in 1829 (P222)
Subsequent editions:	Peters: Vol. 4/144; AGA XX 96: Vol. 2/180; NSA IV: Vol. 8/124
Discography and timing:	Fischer-Dieskau I 4[13] 1'23
	Hyperion I 20[10]
	Hyperion II 8[7] 1'41 Ian Bostridge

← *Hymne an den Unendlichen* D232   *Der Abend* D221 →

GEIST DER LIEBE (I)
(MATTHISSON) **D414** [H252]
G major   April 1816

Spirit of love

(14 bars)

Der Abend schleiert Flur und Hain	Evening veils meadow and grove
In traulich holde Dämmrung ein;	In sweet, friendly dusk;
Hell flimmt, wo gold'ne Wölkchen ziehn,	Brightly, amid passing golden clouds,
Der Stern der Liebeskönigin.	The star of Venus shines.

Die Wogenflut hallt Schlummerklang,   The waves murmur lullabies,
Die Bäume lispeln Abendsang,   The trees whisper evensong,
Der Wiese Gras umgaukelt lind   With delicate kisses the spring breeze
Mit Sylphenkuss der Frühlingswind.   Plays gently in the meadow grass.

Der Geist der Liebe wirkt und strebt,   The spirit of love is busy at work
Wo nur ein Puls der Schöpfung bebt;   Wherever the pulse of creation beats;
Im Strom, wo Wog' in Woge fliesst,   In the torrent, where wave flows into wave,
Im Hain, wo Blatt an Blatt sich schliesst.   In the grove, where leaf clings to leaf.

O Geist der Liebe! führe du   O spirit of love, lead the youth
Dem Jüngling die Erkorne zu!   To his chosen one!
E i n Minneblick der Trauten hellt   *One* tender glance from his beloved
Mit Himmelsglanz die Erdenwelt!   Will fill this world with heavenly radiance.

FRIEDRICH VON MATTHISSON (1761–1831); poem written in 1776/7

This is the twenty-second of Schubert's twenty-nine Matthisson settings (1812–17). See the poet's biography for a chronological list of all the Matthisson settings.

This is a delicate little song in the Mozartian manner. The melody at the beginning ('Der Abend schleiert Flur und Hain') is almost childlike; in his opera *Die Bürgschaft* D435 (also from 1816), Schubert used it for a *Romance* (an Andantino, also in G major, No. 7 of that work) in which Anna, the wife of Theages, sings a little song to her children concerning a lamb that has strayed from its home. The following sequence ('In traulich holde Dämmrung ein' bb. 3–4) adds to the nursery-rhyme impression. However, all suspicion of banality vanishes with what follows: the tune takes off on a genuinely Schubertian harmonic expedition. The melody modulates into D (at 'Hell flimmt, wo gold'ne Wölkchen ziehn' at b. 4) and back into G in the next bar before the vocal line is capped by a succession of semiquavers that pay homage to the 'Liebeskönigin' with a hand (and a tessitura) pointing up to the stars of the heavens (bb. 9–11). The little postlude to each verse (based on the song's opening) is the equivalent of a courtly bow that sweeps the ground in its gallantry. As Reed points out, the song is related in tonality and folksong simplicity to *Heidenröslein* D257 without achieving the memorability of that masterpiece. But Schubert obviously liked the poem well enough to use it again six years later for the very different four-part male chorus setting D747.

Autograph:	In private possession (USA)
First edition:	Published as part of the AGA in 1895 (P632)
Subsequent editions:	Not in Peters; AGA XX 212: Vol. 4/87; NSA IV: Vol. 10/146
Discography and timing:	Fischer-Dieskau I 7³ 1'31
	Hyperion I 23¹⁰
	Hyperion II 14³ 1'51 Christoph Prégardien

← *Entzückung* D413   *Klage (Die Sonne steigt)* D415 →

GEIST DER LIEBE (II)   Spirit of love   Quartet, TTBB
(MATTHISSON) OP. 11 NO. 3, **D747** [H481]
C major   January 1822

Etwas bewegt

Der A - bend schlei - ert Flur_ und Hain_ in_ trau - lich hol - de Dämm-'rung ein,

(90 bars)

See previous entry for poem and translation

FRIEDRICH VON MATTHISSON (1761–1831); poem written in 1776/7

A poem like Matthisson's *Naturgenuss* provided the composer with a solo setting in 1815, D188, as well as an unaccompanied quartet many years later. Similarly, Schubert had already set *Geist der Liebe* as a solo song in 1816, D414. One can understand why he returned to the poem in 1822: there are certain images in *Geist der Liebe* that can be wonderfully illustrated with the resources of four-part vocal harmony, particularly in the second and third verses. There is no doubt that this setting of the words achieves a sumptuous expressiveness that is not to be found in D414.

   The key is C major, with a flowing ('Etwas bewegt') tempo in §. The first verse, though undoubtedly heartfelt, borders on the sentimentality of the male-voice glee; the close harmony, with its leaning little chromatic inflections, is suggestive of a place 'Way down upon the Danube river'. An anachronistic response on the part of this commentator is not Schubert's fault of course; just a few of his works (no doubt fresh and unspoiled in his own time) seem, with hindsight, to be haunted by the hackneyed commonplaces of a later epoch. Very occasionally, especially when he wishes to write for popular taste, we could mistake Schubert for a composer from the Victorian age. The beginning of this song is an example of this.

   On the other hand, the second verse contains music that is as ravishingly beautiful as any he wrote. From b. 14 a gentle drone of an open fifth in the bass, music to lull us to sleep, is the foundation for an exquisite solo from the first tenor; this filigree vocal embroidery, descriptive of lapping water and wafting breezes, is built on the chord of G^7, and time is made to stand still with the deliciously suspended harmony. At 'Der Wiese Gras umgaukelt lind' (b. 20) we return to C major and the pastoral idyll achieves new heights with the tenor's response to the concept of a 'Sylphenkuss', the repeat of the word surrounded with a golden glow by a shift to the first inversion of D flat major (b. 27). This leads to a cadence in A flat major at the end of the strophe. The challenging tessitura that other composers have often employed merely to impress or astonish is here completely responsive to the expressive demands of the poetry.

The music for the third verse – the heart of the poem – is perhaps the most remarkable. It begins in A flat major (an undulating barcarolle-like phrase that depicts the pulse of creation, no less) and then moves to C flat major (from b. 34). This is one of the composer's favourite modulations when he is in the key of A flat and erotic love is on the agenda. From here there is a shift to D major via B minor (which is the enharmonic minor of C flat). As if to illustrate that the spirit of love is everywhere, we have the impression that it has seeped into every nook and cranny of the keyboard, and thus has the power to move effortlessly through every key. The setting of 'Im Strom, wo Wog' in Woge fliesst, / Im Hain, wo Blatt an Blatt sich schliesst' (pivoted around A major) is a simply enchanting reverie (from b. 37), a succession of vocal caresses. If we have been bewitched by the composer's setting of these words first time round, we are not prepared for the masterstroke that accompanies the repeat of these two lines: the gently rocking 'Im Strom, wo Wog' in Woge fliesst' is in F sharp minor (bb. 43–7), but the setting of the 'Im Hain' phrase is a falling sequence in the major, a tone lower, which stops the heart (bb. 46–9). It is as if we have reached to the very depths of the grove where we might hope to learn the secrets of Mother Nature herself. With the delicate semiquaver triplets on 'wo Blatt an Blatt', sung by the lead tenor, we can almost see the growth of fresh greenery: Schubert's botanist microscope enables us to watch it unfurling tentatively as it aspires to the sunlight.

After music which achieves a magical mood of this kind, the danger is anticlimax, and so it proves here. The poem moves from tender natural imagery – where Schubert is an unrivalled master – to rather ordinary romantic hyperbole. (A return to the 'open' key of C major seems ideal for this, although for a moment we believe that we are in A minor.) The resulting music is a merry and effective but unexceptional song in ¾ – certainly no match for what has gone before. The same formula is followed which governs many other vocal quartet perorations: a solo for the lead tenor; the repeat of that tune for the second tenor while the first provides a descant; and then it is the turn of the basses who have a brief solo passage before the forces gather for the final page. There is no more coloratura for Tenor I, but there is the almost statutory final high note on 'Himmelsglanz' with a soulful swell (bb. 88–90), and a decisive cadence. Manly honour has been satisfied with this hearty finale, but for moments of true Schubertian magic, one has to listen to the second and third verses.

Autograph:	Gesellschaft der Musikfreunde, Vienna (draft without piano)
First edition:	Published as Op. 11 no. 3 by Cappi & Diabell, Vienna in June 1822 (P27)
Dedicatee:	Joseph Barth
First known performance:	Without piano: 3 March 1822, concert of the Gesellschaft der Musikfreunde at the Redoutensaal, Vienna. The names of performers are not listed on the programme, but since this performance was followed by several others in the space of a few short months, the ensemble probably consisted of Joseph Barth, Ludwig Tietze, Johann Nestroy and either Carl Reissiger or Wenzel Nejebse. Deutsch suggests that Peter Lugano might have been involved instead of Tietze (see Waidelich/Hilmar

Dokumente I No. 145 for full concert programme; see also Deutsch Doc. Biog. No. 275)

With piano: 26 May 1822 in a benefit concert at the Kärntnertortheater, Vienna. Performers: Joseph Barth, Ludwig Tietze, Wenzel Nejebse and Johann Nestroy (see Waidelich/Hilmar Dokumente I No. 159 for full concert programme)

Performance reviews: Without piano: *Allgemeine musikalische Zeitung* (Leipzig), No. 19 (8 May 1822), col. 305 [Waidelich/Hilmar Dokumente I No. 156]

With piano: *Allgemeine musikalische Zeitung* (Vienna), No. 48 (15 June 1822), col. 379f. [Waidelich/Hilmar Dokumente I No. 164; Deutsch Doc. Biog. No. 291]

Allgemeine musikalische Zeitung (Leipzig), No. 28 (10 July 1822), col. 465f. [Waidelich/Hilmar Dokumente I No. 166]

Subsequent editions: AGA XVI 6: p. 59; NSA III: Vol. 3

Discography and timing: Hyperion I 28[11]   4'30   John Mark Ainsley, Jamie MacDougall,
Hyperion II 25[7]   Simon Keenlyside & Michael George

← *Naturgenuss* D422   *Herrn Josef Spaun, Assessor in Linz* D749 →

GEISTERCHOR *see ROSAMUNDE, FÜRSTIN VON ZYPERN* D797/4

GEISTERNÄHE
(Matthisson) **D100** [H37]
E♭ major   April 1814

Nearby spirits

(55 bars)

Der Dämm'rung Schein
Durchblinkt den Hain;
Hier, beim Geräusch des Wasserfalles,
Denk' ich nur dich, o du mein Alles!

Dein Zauberbild
Erscheint, so mild
Wie Hesperus im Abendgolde,
Dem fernen Freund, geliebte Holde!

Er sehnt wie hier
Sich stets nach dir;
Fest, wie den Stamm die Epheuranke[1]
Umschlingt dich liebend sein Gedanke.

The light of dusk
Glimmers through the grove;
Here, by the murmur of the waterfall,
I think only of you, who are everything to me!

Your magical image
Appears, so gentle,
Like Hesperus in the gold of evening,
To your distant friend, my beloved!

He yearns for you always,
As he does here.
His loving thoughts embrace you
As tightly as the ivy embraces the tree trunk.

[1] Matthisson has 'die Eppichranke' – another poetic term for 'ivy'.

Durchbebt dich auch	Do you, too, quiver
Im Abendhauch	In the evening breeze
Des Brudergeistes leises Weh'n	With the faint breath of a kindred spirit,
Mit Vorgefühl von Wiederseh'n?	A presentiment of our reunion?
Er ist's, der lind	It is this, sweet child,
Dir, süsses Kind,	Which gently
Des Schleiers Silbernebel kräuselt,	Weaves a silver veil of mist
Und in der Locken Fülle säuselt.	And ruffles your abundant curls.
Oft hörst du ihn,	Often you hear it
Wie Melodien	Like wistful melodies
Der Wehmut aus gedämpften Saiten	From muted strings,
In stiller Nacht vorübergleiten.	Wafting past in the silent night.
Auch fesselfrei	Although unfettered,
Wird er getreu,	This spirit will faithfully
Dir ganz und einzig hingegeben,	Devote himself to you alone,
In allen Welten dich umschweben.	And hover over you throughout the universe.

FRIEDRICH VON MATTHISSON (1761–1831); poem written in 1792/3

This is the eighth of Schubert's twenty-nine Matthisson solo settings (1812–17). See the poet's biography for a chronological list of all the Matthisson settings.

In the spring of 1814 we encounter the poet Matthisson for the first time since the youthful 'gothick' settings of *Der Geistertanz* D15 and D15A, and the more mellifluous *Die Schatten* D50. The fetching *Andenken* D99, also from April 1814, is a song in the cantilena style of earlier Beethoven lieder – tuneful and shapely. But *Geisternähe* is something altogether more modern – a ground-breaking prototype that was only possible after the young composer's thorough initiation into the world of Italianate lyricism. Einstein sums up the song as 'seven verses set to a single melody, with deep feeling and a wealth of musical imagination'. Leo Black thinks it 'perhaps the best of Schubert's very early songs' and Peter Gülke has called it Schubert's first nocturne – an early contribution to a nascent genre – sung by a troubadour. It is likely that the teaching of Salieri played an important part in this new phase of song-writing. The world of the spirits is completely different from D15; this ghost is meant to console rather than terrify, and he (or it) has has all the suavity of an Italian *cavaliere servente*.

The rolling E flat major triplets of the introduction are timelessly linked with the opera world. Admittedly, part of the purpose of such neutral undulations is the preparation of hospitable ground and fallow soil in which melody is able to sink its roots, and blossom. But Schubert is seldom merely an efficient gardener; his song landscapes incorporate many a decorative feature. In the third line of the poem we read of the 'Geräusch des Wasserfalles' (bb. 6–7) and it is this imagery that instigates the incessant background murmur of the waterfall. These descriptive, and far from neutral, triplets bind the song into a satisfying whole from the musical point of view; at the same time the musings of the lonely spirit are focused into unified expression.

There is a rising four-note scale at 'Hier, beim Geräusch des Wasserfalles'; this, a two-bar phrase (bb. 6–7), is repeated to encompass the rest of the strophe (bb. 7–8), one of the song's unifying thumbprints. For the second strophe (from b. 12) the music modulates into the dominant (B flat major) and Schubert constructs another melodic line that depends on repetition for

its effect. Here the composer is so intent on pursuing the continuing sense of the words that he
has failed to take into account the singer's need to breathe. It seems that Salieri's lessons have
been too well learned and that the vocal line here is rather too seamless.

The poet's longing (at 'Er sehnt wie hier' bb. 19–20) occasions a shift into F minor with
triplets entering the left hand for the first time, like pulsating heartbeats. The appearance of
diminished-seventh arpeggios adds to the pathos. The climbing four-note motif from the first
strophe reappears, this time a fourth higher (b. 22). The song is beginning to sound like a
genuine tenor piece; and now, at the heart of it, Schubert introduces recitative to follow aria, a
reversal of the time-honoured operatic procedure. But first, arioso: from b. 28 the accompanying
triplets continue to support a vocal line ('Durchbebt dich auch / Im Abendhauch') that abandons
melody in favour of something nearer the inflections of speech. And then, at 'Er ist's, der lind
/ Dir, süsses Kind', safely settled in the holy reaches of the subdominant (from b. 31), there is a
clearing in the music, a peaceful grove in the landscape. The triplets yield to the stillness of
minims and semibreves; the poet directly addresses his beloved with a sensual intimacy where
the ruffling effects of the evening breeze are mirrored in the gentle movement of the singer's
semiquavers. It is clear from this that it is a spirit who touches and caresses his former lover.
We are not aware of a break in the song, only the momentary suspension of time. This had been
part of the young Schubert's careful plan.

For the poem's sixth verse the aria resumes in C minor (from b. 37); the waterfall is no longer
part of the scenery, but the accompaniment's triplets depict, equally suitably, the mysterious,
and slightly restless, movement of the spirit companion who is forever at his beloved's side.
Although this section is cast as melody, the words move swiftly by in the manner of recitative
(apart from the held tempo of the strophe's last line, suddenly in gliding crotchets – 'In stiller
Nacht vorübergleiten'). The role of this section is to set up the final verse that will bring the
various strands of the song together. A bar of accompaniment (b. 43) returns the music to the
home key of E flat major in conventional manner. The last strophe is musically modelled on
the first with various adaptations. We have heard a simple ABA structure, but Schubert's architecture has a way of appearing more subtle. The climactic cadence at 'In allen <u>Welten</u>' (b. 51)
brings a moment of impassioned dalliance on a diminished seventh. It is as if the composer has
imagined his music fixed in the heavens, as if caught in unresolved space, alongside the ghostly
narrator. The elongation of the second, and final, 'umschweben' (bb. 53–4) is more imaginative
than a stock-in-trade Italianate melisma; the vocal line holds its ground on a held B flat, a
metaphor for the narrator's unearthly steadfastness, and the changes of harmony underneath,
in the accompanying triplets, signify movements of time and place within the ever-shifting
universe – 'I will be with you *wherever* you are'.

Autograph:	Missing or lost
First edition:	Published as part of the AGA in 1894 (P539)
Subsequent editions:	Not in Peters; AGA XX 17: Vol. 1/147; NSA IV: Vol. 7/14;
	Bärenreiter: Vol. 5/113 (high voice) & 107 (medium/low voice)
Bibliography:	Black 2003, pp. 24–5 (on the links between *Geisternähe* and the
	second *Salve Regina* in E flat D106)
	Einstein 1951, p. 67
Discography and timing:	Fischer-Dieskau I 1[11] 3'40
	Hyperion I 33[19]
	Hyperion II 3[9] 3'50 Philip Langridge

← *Erinnerung (Todtenopfer)* D101   *Die Befreier Europas in Paris* D104 →

Der GEISTERTANZ (I & II)   The ghost dance

(MATTHISSON) **D15** & **D15A** [H7 & H8]

(Fragments)

(D15) C minor, *c.* 1812

(51 bars)

(D15A) F minor, *c.* 1812

(101 bars)

Die bretterne Kammer	The boarded chamber
Der Toten erbebt,	Of the dead trembles
Wenn zwölfmal den Hammer	When midnight twelve times
Die Mitternacht hebt.	Raises the hammer.
Rasch tanzen um Gräber	Quickly we airy spirits
Um morsches Gebein	Strike up a whirling dance
Wir luftigen Schweber	Around graves
Den sausenden Reih'n.	And rotting bones.
Was winseln die Hunde	Why do the dogs whine
Beim schlafenden Herrn?	As their masters sleep?
Sie wittern die Runde	They scent from afar
Der Geister von fern.	The spirits' dance.
Die Raben entflattern	Ravens flutter up
Der wüsten Abtei,	From the ruined abbey,
Und fliehn an den Gattern	And fly past
Des Kirchhofs vorbei.	The graveyard gates.
Wir gaukeln und scherzen	Jesting, we flit
Hinab und empor,	Up and down
Gleich irrenden Kerzen	Like will-o'-the-wisps
Im duntigen Moor.	Over the misty moor.
O Herz! dessen Zauber	O heart, whose spell
Zur Marter uns ward,	Was our torment,

Du ruhst nun in tauber	You rest now,
Verdumpfung erstarrt;	Frozen in a numb stupor.
Tief bargst du im düstern	You have buried our grief
Gemach unser Weh;	Deep in the gloomy chamber;
Wir Glücklichen flüstern	Happy we, who whisper you
Dir fröhlich Ade!	A cheerful farewell!

FRIEDRICH VON MATTHISSON (1761–1831); poem written in 1797/8

These are the first and second of Schubert's twenty-nine Matthisson solo settings (1812–17). See the poet's biography for a chronological list of all the Matthisson settings.

The complete solo-song setting of this poem, D116, was composed in October 1814, a few days before *Gretchen am Spinnrade*. About two years before, Schubert had twice attempted to conquer Matthisson's lyric which has a superscription from Horace: 'Pulvis et umbra sumus' – 'We are dust and shadows' (Book IV, ode vii). Both versions break off in the middle of piano passage work, as if Schubert had lost heart, or patience – or both. The two unsuccessful versions illustrate the dangers the young composer faced when he allowed the poem to lead him up the churchyard path without any idea of where he was going. He relished the luxury of line-by-line illustration, but he soon recognized that a pithy and elegant lyric such as this would become unwieldy and top-heavy without a plan to make sense of the whole. These attempts must have brought home to him the value of the strophic song for certain lyrics, as opposed to these sprawling, ad hoc, piano-dominated fantasias. His eventual solution in D116 was a modified strophic structure with room for an ingenious recitative between the verses.

The marking for D15, the first version, is 'Allegro'. The fragment is in the key of C minor and in 𝄴 time. Both these attributes survived in the final version, D116. The shuddering of the coffin, the 'bretterne Kammer' of the poem, is achieved with two jabbed chords loud enough to shake the piano, itself something of a coffin on wheels. The stroke of midnight is depicted by the bass notes in dotted minims, rather sweetly numbered one to twelve on the music, in case we miss the point, although somewhat strangely changing pitch, as if the clock tower was invaded by gremlins. Before the words of Verse 5, there is rather a wrenched modulation from E flat to E major. By the time the piano has had a lengthy comment on jesting and flitting, the spirits have become heavy-handedly corporeal and beyond a joke; they are stopped dead in their tracks.

D15A starts off in F minor and in common time. The marking is 'Allegro presto'. After five bars (marked 'Midnight' as if a stage direction) the music shifts to the dominant, and illustrates 'the howling wind' (another specific stage direction) with a ghostly, but unnervingly loud accompaniment, with echoes from the first movement of Beethoven's 'Pathétique' Piano Sonata, Op. 13. Fourteen bars of bone-rattling yield to a short section marked 'Feierliche Stille' – 'Solemn silence' (b. 21). The twelve strokes of the midnight bell are now left to our imagination; the composer realizes that to illustrate them literally fails to chime with the fleeting nature of the poem. The dance of the spirits, this time in 𝄴 and duly labelled 'Tanz' (from b. 49) lopes along in a lugubriously humorous manner; at b. 65 the words of Verse 2 are repeated with the words 'Und morsches Gebein' left out in order to justify a huge leap of a thirteenth between the graves ('Gräber', b. 71) and the whirling dance ('sausenden Reih'n', b. 72). Nowhere in all Schubert is the gap between low and high spirits so graphically mapped on the stave. The whining of the dogs is effectively painted in mournful suspensions (Schubert shows off newly acquired skills by using the tenor clef in the left hand of the piano part here, from b. 80). This is something also encountered in Salieri's songs with piano. The piano writing in the last bars is loud but empty: having shot his bolt the composer realizes with horror how much more of the poem there is to set, and quits the scene with a puff of pianistic smoke (bb. 99–100 where the fragment ends).

Autograph:	Wienbibliothek im Rathaus, Vienna
First edition:	Both fragments published in the 'Fragmente' section at the end of Series XX of the AGA in 1895 (P712 & P713)
Subsequent editions:	Not in Peters; AGA XX 590: Vol. 10/92 & 94; NSA IV: Vol. 7/188 & 190
Discography and timing:	Fischer-Dieskau —

Hyperion I 12^2 & 12^3 1'31
Hyperion II 2^1 & 12^2 2'48   Adrian Thompson

⟵ *Das Mädchens Klage* D6   *Quell'innocente figlio (Aria dell' angelo)* D17/1 ⟶

Der GEISTERTANZ (III)   The ghost dance
(MATTHISSON) **D116** [H47]
C minor   14 October 1814

(50 bars)

See previous entry for poem and translation

FRIEDRICH VON MATTHISSON (1761–1831); poem written in 1797/8

This is the sixteenth of Schubert's twenty-nine Matthisson solo settings (1812–17). See the poet's biography for a chronological list of the all Matthisson settings

The black humour of this song is all the more remarkable because the three other settings emphasize different aspects of the poem. Schubert's first two (incomplete) attempts, the fragments D15 and 15A from about 1812 (*see* above), are ghoulish pieces of programme music, influenced by Beethoven. The piano plays a major role in these works. At the other extreme the fourth and last setting, the unaccompanied quintet for men's voices D494 (H311+, 1816) abandons this exaggeration for ghosts of a friendlier, more genial persuasion. The wistful wraiths of the male chorus are nothing like the diabolically chuckling, white-sheeted spirits of this song. The dotted rhythms and the conspiratorial doubling of the voice part with the piano create a kind of Halloween atmosphere, without a serious threat. There is great glee in this music, and the ghosts seem proud of any terror felt by those gullible enough to believe in them. An unlikely influence seems to be Mozart who had always haunted Schubert and whose C minor Fantasia K475 provides the skeleton outline for the opening phrase in the same key.

   The song was written only five days before *Gretchen am Spinnrade* D118, and it is a sign of the composer's blossoming maturity that he declines the temptation to give us what had been an obvious solution two years earlier: twelve chords for the strokes of midnight. Instead he maps out the shape of the whole with skill, and keeps the song on the move. The first two strophes are set as a scherzo. The third strophe (from b. 13) is a recitative where the whining of dogs (with suitably whingeing piano harmony) is contrasted with fragments of dotted rhythm to suggest ghostly flashes in the far distance. At b. 20 the music is marked 'Geschwinder'; the scurrying scales of a four-bar piano interlude illustrate the ravens' flight. This passage show the well-learned lesson of Haydn's *Die Schöpfung* where musical zoological illustrations *precede* the appearance of the animals that they describe. Another recitative passage (Strophe 4, b. 23) follows, and there is more piano music for ornithological strafing and dive-bombing (bb. 26–7); as so often with Schubert's early music, one imagines that had he been born a century later he could have been a wonderful pianist for the silent cinema. It is then back to the ghosts for a reprise of their scherzo (marked 'Wie oben', b. 28); theirs seems to be the longest-running musical at the Abbey. They make a timely exit before dawn, and we realize that the composer has not tried at all hard to write music to frighten us. Indeed, in comparison to the horror ballads of his earlier years (which can take such descriptions in deadly earnest), this song marks a new stage in his development: we are aware of a new urbanity; he doubts that such things as ghosts really exist.

Autograph:	Boston Public Library, Mass. (first 30 bars only)
First edition:	Published as Book 31 no. 2 of the *Nachlass* by Diabelli, Vienna in 1840 (P333)
Subsequent editions:	Peters: Vol. 2/237; AGA XX 29: Vol. 1/186; NSA IV: Vol. 7/52; Bärenreiter: Vol. 5/152 (high voice) & 146 (medium/low voice)
Bibliography:	Einstein 1951, p. 69
	Fischer-Dieskau 1977, pp. 30–31
Discography and timing:	Fischer-Dieskau I 2[11] 1'26
	Pears-Britten 2[4] 1'47
	Hyperion I 11[8]
	Hyperion II 4[3] 1'37 Brigitte Fassbaender

←— *An Laura, als sie Klopstocks Auferstehungslied sang* D115   *Das Mädchen aus der Fremde* D117 —→

GEISTES-GRUSS   A spirit's greeting
(GOETHE) OP. 92 NO. 3, **D142** [H59 & H59A]

The song exists in six versions, the sixth of which is discussed below:
(1) March 1816; (2) March or April 1816; (3) 1820 or 1821?; (4) November 1821; (5) between 1821 and 1823; (6) appeared July 1828

(1)   Recit; 'Mit Majestät, etwas langsam'   E♭ major – E♭ minor   C   [25 bars]

(2)   Recit; 'Mit Majestat'   E♭ major – E♭ minor   C   [25 bars]

(3)   Recit; 'Mit Kraft'   D major – F major   C   [25 bars]

(4)   Recit; 'Kräftig'   E♭ major – G♭ major   C   [26 bars]

(5)   'Kraftvoll'   E♭ major – G♭ major   C   [26 bars]

(6)   E major – G major

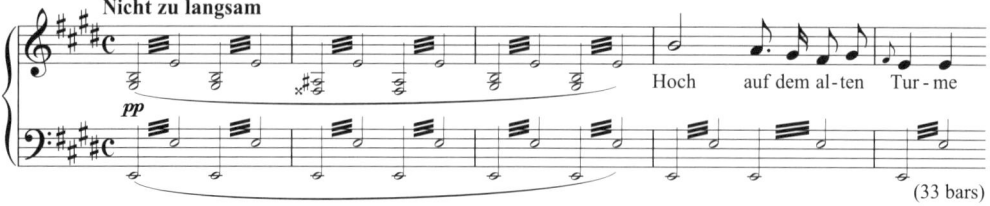

(33 bars)

Hoch auf dem alten Turme steht	High on the ancient tower
Des Helden edler Geist,	Stands the hero's noble spirit;
Der, wie das Schiff vorüber geht,	As the ship passes
Es wohl zu fahren heisst.	He bids it a safe voyage.
'Sieh, diese Senne war so stark,	'See, these sinews were so strong,
Dies Herz so fest und wild,	This heart so steadfast and bold,
Die Knochen voll von Rittermark,	These bones full of knightly valour;
Der Becher angefüllt;	My cup was overflowing.
'Mein halbes Leben stürmt' ich fort,	'Half my life I sallied forth,
Verdehnt' die Hälft' in Ruh,	Half I spent in tranquillity;
Und du, du Menschen-Schifflein dort,	And you, little boat of mankind,
Fahr' immer, immer zu!'	Sail ever onward!'

JOHANN WOLFGANG VON GOETHE (1749–1832); poem written 18 July 1774

This is the thirty-sixth of Schubert's seventy-five Goethe solo settings (1814–26). See the poet's biography for a chronological list of all the Goethe settings.

This lyric dates from a memorable day in July 1774 when Goethe, accompanied by a group of friends including the famous Swiss pastor and scientist Lavater, took a boat trip from Ems down the Lahn towards the Rhine. Goethe improvised the poem on board and dictated it to Lavater as they passed the dramatically situated ruins of Castle Lahneck on the way to Coblenz. What cost the poet very little trouble to write seems to have caused the composer a great deal of trouble to set to music, judging by the number of versions in his hand – six in all which share the same Deutsch number. Four of these are printed in the old *Gesamtausgabe*, while the *Neue Schubert-Ausgabe* has uncovered two more. The differences between the first five 'Fassungen' are minuscule. The sixth version (published as Op. 92 no. 3) is another matter.

The first two versions that date either from 1815 or March/April 1816 are almost identical. They both start in E flat (the marking is 'Recit') with the second section – the voice of the ghost – in G flat major ('Mit Majestät' from b. 6). The second version was part of the lieder album of 1816 that was sent to Goethe. The third version was written out in 1818 according to Reed, 1820 or 1821 according to the NSA (on the grounds that Schubert's way of writing a natural sign changed in 1820). This is written in the F clef and in the keys of D and F major, thus a semitone lower than the original keys. The beginning of the ghostly pronouncement is marked 'Mit Kraft'. It was copied out by Schubert for Count Esterházy who was a bass, and who was Schubert's employer for two summers (1818 and 1824) in Zseliz in Hungary. The fourth version reverts to E flat; certain chords are arpeggiated and the vocal line is ornamented twice. This version and its date seem to point to the influence of Schubert's baritone Johann Michael Vogl (the version in D would have been a trifle too low for him). The fifth version has the direction 'Kraftvoll' ('With strength') at the very beginning and the ghost's music is marked 'Mässig'; tiny details and note values have been changed, but it is difficult to see why.

The sixth and final version is substantially different, at least on the first page. It was published in the last months of the composer's life and he made a complete revision of the first section, at the same time as essentially conserving the shape and skeleton of the piece from the old times – an appropriate procedure when one considers the subject matter of the song. The key is recast into E major; what had been a recitative in all the other versions is now a slow measured tune that differs rhythmically, rather than melodically, from the earlier songs. The ineffably peaceful unfolding of melody with a completely new tremolando accompaniment is reminiscent of the ethereal opening of the violin *Fantaisie* D934 or the opening of the overture to the opera *Fierabras* D796 (1823). This type of shimmering and shuddering pianistic effect is very much a thumbprint of the last five years of the composer's career: it is also to be used in certain passages in the Heine settings – *Am Meer* and *Der Atlas* from *Schwanengesang* D957. At last Schubert has found the ghostly atmosphere for the opening that had eluded him for so long. This first section of the song (bb. 1–13) is marked 'Nicht zu langsam'. The second section (marked 'Stark, im ersten Zeitmasse' – 'Strongly, in the first tempo') is completely unchanged from earlier versions apart from the fact that it is a semitone higher than most of them. One can see why Schubert retained the setting of 'Mein halbes Leben stürmt' ich fort' (strong activity suggested by the dotted rhythms – bb. 21–3), followed by the more languid antithesis of 'Verdehnt' die Hälft' in Ruh' – bb. 23–5. This is not only a melodic curve that rises and falls symmetrically, but the perfect realization of the meaning of the words. The soft repetitions of 'du' (bb. 26 and 27) bring *Wandrers Nachtlied II* D768 to mind. The whole song creates a similar mood of inscrutable grandeur as man communes with nature.

Autographs:	Staatsbibliothek Preussicher Kulturbesiztz, Berlin (second version)
	Goethe Museum, Weimar (fouth version)
	Fitzwilliam Museum, Cambridge (fifth version)
Publication:	First published as part of the AGA in 1895 (P611 & P612; first and fourth versions)
	First published as Vol. 7 no. 4 in Friedlaender's edition by Peters, Leizpig in 1885; subsequently removed from this volume for the 1887 reprint, and then published as part of the NSA in 1985 (P788; second version)
	First published as part of the NSA in 1985 (P789 & P790; third and fifth versions)
	First published as Op. 87 no. 3 (later corrected to Op. 92 no. 3) by M. J. Leidesdorf, Vienna in 1828 (P164; sixth version)
Dedicatee:	Sixth version dedicated to Josephine von Franck
Publication reviews:	Sixth version reviewed in *Münchener Musikzeitung* No. 14 (3 January 1829), col. 209ff. [Waidelich/Hilmar Dokumente I No. 680]
Subsequent editions:	Peters: Vol. 4/82; AGA XX 174a–d: Vol. 3/189 (first version), 190 (second version), 191 (given as third version, recte fifth) & 192 (given as fourth version, recte sixth); NSA IV: Vol. 5a/14 (sixth version), Vol. 5b/192 (first version), 184 (second version), 196 (third version), 198 (fourth version) & 200 (fifth version); Bärenreiter: Vol. 3/154 (sixth version) & 230 (second version)
Bibliography:	Capell 1928, p. 103

Further settings and arrangements:	Johann Friedrich Reichardt (1752–1814) *Geistesgruss* (1795 and 1809)
	Karl Friedrich Zelter (1758–1832) *Geistes-Gruss* (1809)
	Nicolas Medtner (1879–1951) *Geistesgruss* Op. 15/12 (1905–7)
	Arr. Tilman Hoppstock (b. 1961) for guitar accompaniment, in *Franz Schubert: 110 Lieder* (2009)
Discography and timing:	Fischer-Dieskau I 6⁴ 2'01
	Hyperion I 24³ & 24⁴ 1'30 Michael George
	Hyperion II 4¹⁵ & 4¹⁶ 2'05 (third and sixth versions)

← *Der Mondabend* D141   *Genügsamkeit* D143 →

GEISTLICHE LIEDER – The collection of religious songs published together as *Nachlass* (qv) Book 10 (1830) *see* individual entries for Dem UNENDLICHEN D291; Die GESTIRNE D444; Das MARIENBILD D623; VOM MITLEIDEN MARIÄ D632; AM TAGE ALLER SEELEN ('LITANEI') D343; PAX VOBISCUM D551; GEBET WÄHREND DER SCHLACHT D171; HIMMELSFUNKEN D651

GEISTLICHES LIED ('Marie')   Sacred Song ('Mary')
(NOVALIS) **D658** [H425]
D major   May? 1819

(21 bars)

Ich sehe dich in tausend Bildern,	I see you in a thousand pictures,
Maria, lieblich ausgedrückt,	Mary, sweetly portrayed;
Doch keins von allen kann dich schildern,	Yet none of them can depict you
Wie meine Seele dich erblickt.	As my soul has seen you.
Ich weiss nur, dass der Welt Getümmel	I only know that since then
Seitdem mir wie ein Traum verweht	The world's tumult has drifted away from me like a dream,
Und ein unnennbar süsser Himmel	And an ineffably sweet heaven
Mir ewig im Gemüte steht.	Is forever in my heart.

NOVALIS (pseudonym of FRIEDRICH VON HARDENBERG) (1772–1801); poem written in 1799

This is the first of Schubert's six Novalis solo settings (1819–20). See the poet's biography for a chronological list of all the Novalis songs.

The Schubert songs to the texts of Novalis are an underestimated part of the canon but, for many reasons, a vitally important one. Schubert's perfect page of music is a hymn tune that borders on a love song. Exquisite in vocal and accompanimental detail, the postlude a mirror of the prelude, it seems to be a setting that reconciles the two eternal warring themes of love – spiritual control and sensuality, idealism and reality; in short, sacred and profane. In November 1794, Novalis met the twelve-year-old Sophie von Kühn who was to remain his Beatrice and Laura, the focal point of the poet's life even after her death at the age of fifteen. After this unexpected catastrophe, Novalis wrote in his notebook: 'I have religion for Sophie – not love. Absolute love, independent of the heart, grounded in faith, is religion.'

It seems clear that Marie, the Madonna, had become interchangeable in Novalis's mind with Sophie, and this despite the fact that he was brought up as a Protestant and thus outside the Marian cult. Both poet and composer are attuned to that spiritual eroticism which is part of the artist's struggle to reconcile sexuality with religion. The many pictures Novalis has seen of the Virgin Mary can never equal the inner picture he has of her. After Sophie's death, the idealized lover and the humanized mother of God became one, just as in the poet's mind the profane life of the artist is at one with the sacred love of the priest. Perhaps Schubert, who despised the hypocritical hellfire-threatening clerics he came across, would have agreed with what Novalis wrote about the coming together of two worlds: 'Poet and priest were one in the beginning – only later times have separated them. The true poet is however always a priest, just as the true priest has always remained a poet. Ought not the future bring back this ancient condition of things?' The title of the poem is something of a mystery; Schubert had never called the mother of God anything other than 'Maria'. It seems that Schubert's heading on the manuscript led to the misunderstanding. There is no title to this song, only the roman numerals for XV that refer to the poem's numbering in the *Novalis Schriften*, Zweiter Teil, p. 42. At the top of the music Schubert dates the song with the words 'May' (an old way of writing 'Mai' in German) and 'Auf Mitte' – in the middle of the month. Perhaps an early reader of this autograph took this hastily written word May to be 'Mary'? A compromise was somehow reached that avoided the English word in favour of the French version 'Marie' which, when pronounced in the German way, produces the same number of syllables as Maria.

Autograph:	In private possession (Switzerland)
First edition:	Published as part of the AGA in 1895 (P685)
Subsequent editions:	Not in Peters; AGA XX 364: Vol. 6/53; NSA IV: Vol. 12/90
Bibliography:	Capell 1928, p. 159
	Fischer-Dieskau 1977, pp. 126–7
Further settings:	Luise Reichardt (1779–1826) *An Maria* (1819)
	Max Reger (1873–1916) *Ich sehe dich in tausend Bildern* (1907)
	Joseph Marx (1882–1964) *Marienlied* (1909)
	Othmar Schoeck (1886–1957) *Marienlied* (1905–7)
Discography and timing:	Fischer-Dieskau II 3[7] 1'12
	Hyperion I 13[15]
	Hyperion II 21[21] 1'33 Marie McLaughlin

← *Sehnsucht (Mignon)* D656   *Hymne* D659 →

GEISTLICHES LIED (Hymne II)   Sacred song (Hymn II)

(NOVALIS) **D660** [H427]

B♭ minor – B♭ major   May 1819

(17 bars)

Wenn ich ihn nur habe,	If only I have Him,
Wenn er mein nur ist,	If He is mine alone,
Wenn mein Herz bis hin zum Grabe	If my heart never forsakes its trust
Seine Treue nie vergisst:	Unto the grave:
Weiss ich nichts von Leide,	Then shall I know no suffering,
Fühle nichts, als Andacht, Lieb' und Freude.	Feel nothing but devotion, love and joy.
Wenn ich ihn nur habe,	If only I have Him,
Lass ich alles gern,	I shall gladly forego all else,
Folg an meinem Wanderstabe	And with my pilgrim's staff
Treugesinnt nur meinem Herrn;	Follow my Lord, true to Him alone,
Lasse still die Andern	Quietly letting all others
Breite, lichte, volle Strassen wandern.	Walk through the wide, bright, crowded streets.
Wenn ich ihn nur habe,	If only I have Him,
Schlaf ich fröhlich ein,	I shall fall joyfully asleep;
Ewig wird zu süsser Labe	His heart's flow
Seines Herzens Flut mir sein,	Will for ever be my sweet comfort;
Die mit sanftem Zwingen	With gentle force
Alles wird erweichen und durchdringen.	It will soften and pervade all things.
Wenn ich ihn nur habe,	If only I have Him
Hab ich auch die Welt;	I have the whole world,
Selig, wie ein Himmelsknabe,	Blissful as a cherub
Der der Jungfrau Schleier hält.	Holding the Virgin's veil,
Hingesenkt im Schauen	Deep in contemplation,
Kann mir vor dem Irdischen nicht grauen.	Nothing in this earthly life can make me afraid.
Wo ich ihn nur habe,	Wherever I have Him
Ist mein Vaterland,	There is my homeland;
Und es fällt mir jede Gabe	And every gift falls into my hand
Wie ein Erbteil in die Hand;	As an inheritance:
Längst vermisste Brüder	In His disciples I find again
Find ich nun in seinen Jüngern wieder.	My long-lost brothers.

NOVALIS (pseudonym of FRIEDRICH VON HARDENBERG) (1772–1801); poem written in 1799

This is the third of Schubert's six Novalis solo settings (1819–20). See the poet's biography for a chronological list of all the Novalis settings.

After the relative sophistication of *Hymne* D659 (qv) the three further sacred songs of Novalis (not including the glorious song titled *Nachthymne* D687) seem almost embarrassingly naive in terms of their musical means. Both *Hymne* (formerly designated *Hymne I*) and the *Nachthymne* are through-composed, but for the other texts, some of the most profound words the composer ever set, Schubert chose the simplest musical formula – the strophic song. Perhaps when he came to set Novalis Schubert identified with Beethoven and his *Sechs Lieder von Gellert* (1803), which are statuesque and strophic with the exception of the concluding *Busslied*. The rigours of these words produced psalm-like settings of great economy and power, bare on the printed page but packing an enormous rhetorical punch. Like Novalis, Gellert was Protestant, and Beethoven (who was born into a Roman Catholic family, but whose teacher Christian Gottlob Neefe was Protestant) was aware of the evangelical tradition of church music, including C. P. E. Bach's settings of such writers as Gellert and Carl Friedrich Cramer. It follows that Schubert was also, in his turn, aware of what had gone before in terms of religious songs with piano.

It cannot be claimed, however, that these Novalis hymns rival, or even parallel, the Gellert settings of Beethoven. The words of Novalis are infinitely more demanding and subtle, and Schubert is unable to exploit the grandiose harmonic simplicity that makes Beethoven's confident way with Gellert especially memorable. Nevertheless, these hymns (and this one in particular) had their adherents in the Schubert circle. Refuting Kreissle von Hellborn's low opinion of the Novalis hymns, no less important a Schubertian than Josef von Spaun tells us that Hofsekretär Josef Gross, who was a most gifted musician, valued this song as 'the most beautiful of all the songs that Schubert ever wrote'. Spaun also tells us that the singer Vogl placed an extraordinarily high value on the Novalis songs. It is difficult enough for modern-day performers to think themselves into the conventions of strophic song; regaining contact with the pious world of eighteenth-century church lieder is a similarly challenging task.

Some of these Novalis poems made their way into contemporary evangelical church song-books (with music other than by Schubert of course) with the 'difficult' strophes simply left out. The third strophe of this song shows the influence on Novalis of his teacher Abraham Gottlob Werner and that learned man's theory of 'Neptunismus', the concept of a gigantic ocean ('Urmeer') which dates from the time of the Creation. This produces water and geological metaphors that are combined with eschatological imagery of the last hours on earth. In the fourth verse (not recorded in the Hyperion performance) Novalis veers towards Roman Catholic imagery, as is often the case with this poet; these words stem from the years spent in Jena during which he visited Dresden and viewed the Sistine Madonna of Raphael. Naturally, neither of these verses found their way into the contemporary Protestant hymn books.

The most exceptional thing about this music is that half of each strophe is in the key of B flat minor, a tonality seldom used by Schubert, but usually associated (as in *Gretchen im Zwinger* D564, *Der 13. Psalm* D663 and *Ihr Bild* D957/9) with deep and contemplative devotion. The second half (from b. 9) reverts to B flat major where all the conditional clauses and 'ifs' of the earlier lines melt into the certainties of redemption. The melody, accompanied by discreet chords, is in the hymn-tune style with a succession of tuneful sequences. The conviction with which the words are sung makes a great difference to the song's effect. The postlude is attractive without being especially profound, but that is perhaps to judge it unfairly in comparison to a religious song like *Am Tage Aller Seelen* ('Litanei') D343 composed in a less esoteric and more openly emotional mood.

Autograph:	Bibliotheca Bodmeriana, Geneva-Cologny
First edition:	Published as no. 38 *Neueste Folge nachgelassener Lieder und Gesänge* by J. P. Gotthard, Vienna in 1872 (P463)
Subsequent editions:	Not in Peters; AGA XX 361: Vol. 6/49; NSA IV: Vol. 12/22
Bibliography:	Capell 1928, p. 159
Further settings:	Luise Reichardt (1779–1826) *Geistliches Lied* (1819)

Carl Loewe (1796–1869) *Wenn ich ihn nur habe* (1821)
Reinhard Schwarz-Schilling (1904–1987) *Wenn ich ihn nur habe*
(1949)
Discography and timing: Fischer-Dieskau II 3⁴   1'59   (Strophes 1, 2 & 5 only)
Hyperion I 29⁵
Hyperion II 22²   2'37   Marjana Lipovšek

⟵ *Hymne D659*   *Geistliches Lied ('Wenn alle untreu werden') D661* ⟶

GEISTLICHES LIED (Hymne III)   Sacred song (Hymn III)
(Novalis) **D661** [H428]
B♭ minor – B♭ major   May 1819

(23 bars)

Wenn alle untreu werden,	If all men should prove faithless
So bleib ich dir doch treu;	Yet will I remain true to You,
Dass Dankbarkeit auf Erden	Lest gratitude should die out
Nicht ausgestorben sei.	On this earth.
Für mich umfing dich Leiden,	For my sake suffering enveloped You;
Vergingst für mich in Schmerz;	For my sake You died in pain.
Drum geb ich dir mit Freuden	Therefore I joyfully give You
Auf ewig dieses Herz.	My heart for ever.
Oft muss ich bitter weinen,	Often I must weep bitterly
Dass du gestorben bist,	That You are dead,
Und mancher von den Deinen	And that many of your loved ones
Dich lebenslang vergisst.	Forget You throughout their lives.
Von Liebe nur durchdrungen	Inspired by love alone
Hast du so viel getan,	You have done so much,
Und doch bist du verklungen,	And yet, now You have departed,
Und keiner denkt daran.	No one thinks about it.
Du stehst voll treuer Liebe	Filled with true love
Noch immer jedem bei,	You stand by every man,
Und wenn dir keiner bliebe,	And if no one stayed true to You,
So bleibst du dennoch treu;	Yet would You remain true;
Die treueste Liebe sieget,	The truest love triumphs,
Am Ende fühlt man sie,	In the end men feel it,
Weint bitterlich und schmieget	And weep bitterly, nestling
Sich kindlich an dein Knie.	Like children at Your knee.

Ich habe dich empfunden,	I have known You
O! lasse nicht von mir;	O do not forsake me!
Lass innig mich verbunden	Let me be inwardly
Auf ewig sein mit dir.	United with You for ever.
Einst schauen meine Brüder	One day my brothers will look
Auch wieder himmelwärts,	Once more towards heaven,
Und sinken liebend nieder,	And swoon with love,
Und fallen dir ans Herz.	And sink upon Your heart.

NOVALIS (pseudonym of FRIEDRICH VON HARDENBERG) (1772–1801); poem written in 1799

This is the fourth of Schubert's six Novalis solo settings (1819–20). See the poet's biography for a chronological list of all the Novalis settings.

This hymn, like the second of the *Geistliche Lieder* D661 (formerly known as *Hymne II*), is in the key of B flat minor. It contrasts the dark-hued opening lines of each strophe (accompanied by conventionally voice-doubling chords in the minor key) with a shift to the major – in this case a dance-like motif in semiquavers (the change is at 'Drum <u>geb</u> ich dir mit Freuden' from bb. 12–13) which is rather merry and in eighteenth-century style. It would be far too easy to write off this music as uninspired: it is clearly the composer's attempt to find a religious styliza-tion that he thought appropriate to the poet. By all accounts many of his contemporaries found the music both moving and effective. Longing for the Saviour and gratitude for His love is fairly uncontroversial in a superficial reading of this poem, but our knowledge of the Novalis story and the death of his beloved Sophie (*see* biographical article of the poet) reveals the fine line between conventional praise of God as the love object, and the way in which Novalis brings thoughts of her into the centre of his meditations on the Passion.

The Novalis hymn has four strophes, all of which are translated above. For the Hyperion recording, Strophe 4 was omitted.

Autograph:	Bibliotheca Bodmeriana, Geneva-Cologny
First edition:	Published as No. 39 of *Neueste Folge nachgelassener Lieder und Gesänge* by J. P. Gotthard, Vienna in 1872 (P464)
Subsequent editions:	Not in Peters; AGA XX 362: Vol. 6/50; NSA IV: Vol. 12/102
Further settings:	Carl Loewe (1796–1869) *Wenn alle untreu werden* (1822); later reissued for 4 voices (1855)
Discography and timing:	Fischer-Dieskau II 3[5] 1'47 (first two strophes only)
	Hyperion I 29[6]
	Hyperion II 22[3] 2'30 Marjana Lipovšek

⟵ *Geistliches Lied ('Wenn ich ihn nur habe') D660*   *Geistliches Lied ('Ich sag es jedem, dass er lebt') D662* ⟶

GEISTLICHES LIED (Hymne IV)   Sacred song (Hymn IV)

(NOVALIS) **D662** [H429]

A major   May 1819

(23 bars)

Ich sag es jedem, dass er lebt	I tell everyone that He lives
Und auferstanden ist,	And is risen,
Dass er in unsrer Mitte schwebt	That He hovers in our midst
Und ewig bei uns ist.	And is for ever with us.
Ich sag es jedem, jeder sagt	I tell everyone, and everyone
Es seinen Freunden gleich,	At once tells his friends
Dass bald an allen Orten tagt	That the new kingdom of heaven
Das neue Himmelreich.	Will soon dawn.
Jetzt scheint die Welt dem neuen Sinn	Only now, with our new understanding,
Erst wie ein Vaterland;	Does the world seem like home;
Ein neues Leben nimmt man hin	Joyfully we receive a new life
Entzückt aus seiner Hand.	From His hand.
Hinunter in das tiefe Meer	The fear of death has sunk
Versank des Todes Graun,	Into the deep ocean,
Und jeder kann nun leicht und hehr	And everyone can now look to his future,
In seine Zukunft schaun.	Elated and carefree.
Der dunkle Weg, den er betrat,	The dark path He trod
Geht in den Himmel aus,	Leads to heaven,
Und wer nur hört auf seinen Rat,	And all those who heed His counsel
Kommt auch in Vaters Haus.	Shall also enter the Father's house.
Nun weint auch keiner mehr allhie,	Now no one will weep here on earth
Wenn Eins die Augen schliesst,	When eyes are closed;
Vom Wiedersehen, spät oder früh,	This sorrow will be sweetened,
Wird dieser Schmerz versüsst.	Soon or late, by heavenly reunion.
Es kann zu jeder guten Tat	For every good deed
Ein jeder frischer glühn,	Another can burn still more brightly;
Denn herrlich wird ihm diese Saat	For this seed will flower gloriously
In schönern Fluren blühn.	In fairer fields.
Er lebt, und wird nun bei uns sein,	He lives, and will be with us
Wenn alles uns verlässt!	When all else forsakes us!
Und so soll dieser Tag uns sein	Therefore let this day be
Ein Weltverjüngungs-Fest.	A celebration of the reborn world.

NOVALIS (pseudonym of FRIEDRICH VON HARDENBERG) (1772–1801); poem written in 1799

This is the fifth of Schubert's six Novalis solo settings (1819–20). See the poet's biography for a chronological list of all the Novalis settings.

Here Schubert uses two of Novalis's strophes to make one musical verse. As in two of the other Novalis *Geistliche Lieder* (*see* above) the form is absolutely strophic. The composer might have given in to the temptation to provide musical illustrations for verbal imagery along the way had he been less attuned to the purity of these extraordinary texts. There are no tempo markings for these Novalis *Geistliche Lieder*, but the writing of this one, with its throbbing quaver accompaniment, implies an urgency lacking in D660 and D661. The listener has to be convinced that the singer, having seen the light, is anxious to impart his or her faith in a blaze of inner conviction. Once again the manner of musical expression is determinedly and deliberately antiquated; the Germans call this style 'schlicht' – simple and unpretentious. Poems that offer this degree of elevated feeling, unless they are given a musical incarnation of inarguable sublimity (as with Novalis's *Nachthymne* D687), must surely be set in exactly this straightforward way – rather like the great Protestant congregational hymns. The awkward key juxtaposition of this song's A major tonality with the B flat minor of the previous number, D661, seems to refute the idea that these little works were meant to be performed as a cycle of any kind.

A recital would in any case seem to be the wrong milieu for this music. The bass-baritone Robert Holl has overseen the performance of all of these four Novalis settings (that is *Hymne* D659 and the three *Geistliche Lieder* D660–2 – formerly known as *Hymne* II, III and IV) where they were interpolated in a church service; each song, accompanied by organ, was sung by a different singer and from a different position in the church – as if various members of the congregation were standing up to give spontaneous testimony to their faith. Holl found this an extremely convincing way of presenting these works; it may be that they need such a quasi-liturgical setting for us to hear them as the composer imagined them.

This poem glows with Novalis's belief in an afterlife, but some music lovers might argue that these words have not exactly set this composer's mind on fire. It seems likely that Schubert's own melodic muse had briefly chosen to suppress itself in favour of the music inherent in the poet's language, and there can surely be no doubt that Schubert's encounter with the work of Novalis moved him profoundly. Leo Black offers the thought that 'the texts of these "hymns" invoke and worship a male Saviour, something that came perhaps less naturally to Schubert than his reaction to the feminine principle in the *Salve Regina* hymn'. It is true that the composer's various *Salve Regina* settings seem sensual by comparison, but Schubert clearly perceives a great difference between liturgical texts in Latin and the poetry of Novalis.

This *Geistliches Lied* has eight strophes, all of which are translated above. For the Hyperion recording strophes 5 and 6 were omitted (thus a single musical verse).

Autograph:	Bibliotheca Bodmeriana, Geneva-Cologny
First edition:	Published as No. 40 of *Neueste Folge nachgelassener Lieder und Gesänge* by J. P. Gotthard, Vienna in 1872 (P465)
Subsequent editions:	Not in Peters; AGA XX 363: Vol. 6/52; NSA IV: Vol. 12/104
Bibliography:	Black 2003, p. 67
Discography and timing:	Fischer-Dieskau II 3[6] 1'21 (first four strophes only)
	Hyperion I 29[7] } 1'48 Marjana Lipovšek
	Hyperion II 22[4]

← *Geistliches Lied* ('Wenn alle untreu werden') D660   *Der 13. Psalm* D663 →

GENÜGSAMKEIT

(SCHOBER) **D143** [H60]

C♯ minor   1815

Simple needs

(17 bars)

'Dort raget ein Berg aus den Wolken her,	'There a mountain rises nobly above the clouds;
Ihn erreicht wohl mein eilender Schritt.	My rapid steps approach it.
Doch ragen neue und immer mehr,	But new peaks, more and more, tower up
Fort, da mich der Drang noch durchglüht.'	As I am inspired to press onwards.'
Es treibt ihn vom schwebenden Rosenlicht	He is urged on by the shimmering rosy light
Aus dem ruhigen heitern Azur.	From the calm, serene azure.
Und endlich waren's die Berge nicht	But in the end there were no mountains;
Es war seine Sehnsucht nur.	It was only his longing.
Doch nun wird es ringsum öd' und flach,	All around it is desolate and flat,
Und doch kann er nimmer zurück.	And yet he can never turn back.
'O Götter, gebt mir ein Hüttendach	'Gods, give me a hut
Im Tal, und ein friedliches Glück!'	In the valley, and tranquil good fortune!'

FRANZ VON SCHOBER (1796–1822)

This is the first of Schubert's fourteen Schober solo settings (1815–17, 1821–3 and 1827). See the poet's biography for a chronological list of all the Schober settings.

There is little in this simple and unpretentious music (in that sense it is worthy of its title) to foreshadow the strong working relationship between composer and poet that would produce a masterpiece like *Am Bach im Frühlinge* D361 the very next year, much less the glories of *An die Musik* (D547, 1817) and *Viola* (D786, 1823). Fischer-Dieskau writes of the 'sheer incomprehensibility of the text'. There is nothing original in Schober's treatment of the theme of the traveller who finds his goal ever shifting with the horizon. This was doubtless copied from Schiller's *Der Pilgrim* D794, or a number of other poets who used the same idea to similar effect. The sudden two-line conclusion proposing a cottage in the valley is banal in the extreme. There was never a young artist less likely to want to live in poverty-stricken circumstances than the worldly Schober, although he may be excused, perhaps, for adopting the Romantic pose of Franciscan simplicity that thousands of well-to-do young men took up in this period. Schubert clothes the whole in the manner of a quasi-⅜ *Ländler* or waltz, rather in the manner of *Seligkeit* (D433, 1816), also in four sharps. It is perhaps significant that the composer chooses the rather unusual key of C sharp minor – the tonality of *Der Wanderer* (D489, also 1816), the traveller who is at home nowhere in the world, and whose plight resembles that described in *Genügsamkeit*. The music for these two wanderers is utterly different, however. The rather merry postlude in octaves (bb. 13–17) reminds us that the composer often uses ⅜ rhythm, and a flowing tempo, for journeys in which the traveller is swept along as if by a dancing throng that surrounds him (cf. *Drang in die Ferne* D770, or the Mayrhofer *Sehnsucht* D516). This conflict between *Bewegung* and the willpower of the singer results in a flippancy – grim determination combined with humour.

Autograph:	Missing or lost
First edition:	Published as Op. post. 109 no. 2 by Diabelli, Vienna in July 1829 (P233)
Subsequent editions:	Peters: Vol. 4/122; AGA XX 181: Vol. 3/230; NSA IV: Vol. 7/88; Bärenreiter: Vol. 6/46
Discography and timing:	Fischer-Dieskau I 6[11] 1'48
	Hyperion I 22[12]
	Hyperion II 4[17] 2'10 Catherine Wyn-Rogers

← *Geistes-Gruss* D142   *Der Sänger* D149 →

(GEORG) FRIEDRICH (KONRAD LUDWIG) GERSTENBERGK
(1780–1838)

THE POETIC SOURCE
S1   *Gabriele, Ein Roman von Johanna Schopenhauer.* In drei Theilen. Dritter Theil. Leipzig F. A. Brockhaus, 1821

THE SONG
July 1826   *Hippolits Lied* D890 [S1: p. 146]

If Schubert thought that the poem of *Hippolits Lied* was by Johanna Schopenhauer (1766–1838), it was because he had not bothered to read the introduction in the novel where Schopenhauer freely admits that she could not claim to be gifted as a poet, and names her friend Friedrich von Gerstenbergk (with copious thanks) as the author of the four lyrics that adorned her novel. Both the AGA and the Peters editions (following the first edition of the song published by Diabelli in the seventh volume of the *Nachlass*) ascribed the text to Schopenhauer herself. The writer and critic Friedrich Gerstenbergk (not to be confused with the more famous writer Heinrich Wilhelm von Gerstenberg, 1737–1823) was born in Ronneburg, Saxony in 1780, the son of a lawyer named Müller who died early. The boy was adopted by his uncle on his mother's side and took the name of Gerstenbergk, reserving his original name, Friedrich Müller, for his published work. After studying law in Jena and Leipzig he worked first as an archivist in the services of the duke of Weimar (coming into contact there with Goethe) and then in Eisenach. It was while he was working in Weimar that he encountered Johanna Schopenhauer who lived in that city between 1806 and 1828. Gerstenbergk's (or rather Müller's) best-known publication was *Kaledonische Erzählungen* (Tübingen, 1814) a series of sagas (*Ragnhild und Audna* for example) which achieved great popularity as a kind of modernized Ossian in prose – though there was no question of claiming that these stories were anything but fiction. Gerstenbergk died in Rautenberg bei Altenburg in 1838.

See also Johanna SCHOPENHAUER.

GESÄNGE AUS WILHELM MEISTER
(GOETHE) Op. 62, **D877** nos 1–4
January 1826

For the definitive D877 [H585–588] version of Mignon's cycle, *see* below. For a guide as to where the earlier settings of the lyrics may be found in this book *see* entry under MIGNON LIEDER. For a list of all the Schubert songs inspired by the novel WILHELM MEISTERS LEHRJAHRE *see* entry under that name.

Autographs: Wienbibliothek im Rathaus, Vienna (sketches of three D877 songs); Sächsische
               Landesbibliothek, Dresden (fair copy of four D877 songs, five pages; the sixth in
               Wienbibliothek im Rathaus, Vienna)
First edition: Published as Op. 62 by Diabelli, Vienna in March 1827 (P114–117)
Dedicatee: Mathilde Therese Fürstin zu Schwarzenberg

I MIGNON UND DER HARFNER   Mignon and the Harper   Duet
OP. 62 NO. 1, **D877/1** [H585]
B minor   January 1826

(50 bars)

Nur wer die Sehnsucht kennt	Only those who know longing
Weiss, was ich leide!	Know what I suffer.
Allein und abgetrennt	Alone, cut off
Von aller Freude,	From all joy,
Seh' ich an's Firmament	I gaze at the firmament
Nach jener Seite.	In that direction.
Ach! der mich liebt und kennt	Ah, he who loves and knows me
Ist in der Weite.	Is far away.
Es schwindelt mir, es brennt	I feel giddy,
Mein Eingeweide.	My vitals are aflame.
Nur wer die Sehnsucht kennt	Only he who knows longing
Weiss, was ich leide!	Knows what I suffer.

Poem written in June 1785

This is the seventy-second of Schubert's seventy-five Goethe settings (1814–26). Although the piece is strictly speaking a duet, as a piano-accompanied piece with significant solo passages it is listed here as one of the lieder rather than as an ensemble item. See the poet's biography for a chronological list of all the Goethe settings.

Goethe surprises the reader of *Wilhelm Meisters Lehrjahre* by printing this immortal lyric at the end of a short chapter (Book 4, Chapter 11) where the eponymous hero of the novel is rescued from a band of robbers by a beautiful lady and her companions. As he recovers from gunshot and sabre wounds he dreams of this unknown champion without realizing that she will one day be his wife. During his convalescence Wilhelm is visited by the Harper and Mignon who have come into his life earlier in the novel and who now sing in the background. Thus the lyric captures Wilhelm's emotions as much as those of the two characters that sing the lyric: 'He [Wilhelm] fell into a dreamy longing; and his feelings were in sympathy with the song which at that moment Mignon and the Harper began to sing, with a passionate expression, in the form of an irregular duet'. For the first time Schubert takes account of what Goethe writes in the novel (the poem appeared on its own in countless anthologies and collections of Goethe's work) and composes a duet. He also seems to have imagined Wilhelm listening to it somewhat feverishly and at a distance; there is a musical haze around this song that is as much about Wilhelm's 'dreamy longing' as the two singers' feelings.

The key is B minor, the tonality of some of Schubert's most profound utterances. During the *Vorspiel* we are introduced to some of the song's strongest features: the shift between tonic and subdominant (as between b. 1 and b. 2 of the music, as well as the first and second song in the set – *Heiss mich nicht reden* is in E minor); the mezzo staccato repeated notes in the bass that give an obsessive 'tolling bell' effect; the 'Neapolitan' key of C major in b. 3 that is harmonically distant from the tonic and serves to heighten the sense of distance and alienation in the poem. The two characters are also somehow separated, despite the fact that they sing at close quarters and often in quasi-canonic imitation. They are not looking at each other, rather they are both gazing out into the distance, completely wrapped up in their own thoughts and problems. Schubert has built into this music a somewhat distracted quality, a restlessness which is exacerbated by the interplay between the voices.

Mignon enters in b. 5 and leads the way, the Harper following her at the distance of a bar. The rise and fall of the intertwined voices has an elegiac quality, a wail that suggests exotic music from a faraway land. At 'Allein und abgetrennt / Von aller Freude' (b. 14) the singers' lines move closer together, only half a bar apart, the canonic effect tighter than before. In contrast, the wide spacing of the accompaniment between the hands is significant: chords in the right hand are in the middle of the treble stave, but on the opposite side of the keyboard they are thirds deep in the bass clef. The distance between the hands seems to emphasize the breadth of the horizon, or the vast sweep of sky between heaven and earth. We hear something similar at the end of *Totengräbers Heimwehe* D842, from the previous year, and Wolf in his *Ganymed* has learned this lesson well. At 'Ach! der mich liebt und kennt' (b. 23) the voices unite at last, and the euphonious move into C major shows a glimpse of the homeland ideal 'in der Weite', ineffably dear, but unattainable and thus strangely bereft in effect. This section shifts into E minor (bb. 29–30) as a preparation for the explosive outburst of 'Es schwindelt mir' (from b. 33), skilfully bounced between the voices as quasi-recitative. In this stormy section, no sooner is one diminished seventh resolved than it is mercilessly followed by another. This squall of sudden emotion is followed by a modified recapitulation of the opening, a technique already familiar from many of Schubert's instrumental slow movements. The move back into B minor for the last verse (at b. 37) reverses the roles of father and daughter (not that this pair is aware that this is their relationship). The Harper now begins the plaint (b. 38) and Mignon follows. Underneath this, the pianist is required to provide a rustling tremolando accompaniment in the bass which adds to a slightly ominous background shimmer, as if lower strings were playing *sul ponticello*. The postlude (bb. 47–50) has a rocking figuration that rises through the stave, and seems to ask a question: 'Is there a way out of this tragedy for us?' The answer is not slow in coming. Eight repeated semiquavers played mezzo staccato on a succession of Bs deep in the left hand give the answer: mezzo staccato repeated notes were to be a feature of *Winterreise*, notably in *Der Wegweiser* where they insist on the inexorable journey to the grave of the winter traveller. Here the repetitions underline that these Italian refugees are earthed and grounded on German soil, trapped in the web of their sad destinies.

It is only at the end of Goethe's novel (Book 8, Chapter 7), and shortly before Mignon's death, that she reveals what the old Harper, her father (a fact she never discovers), had actually meant to her (in Book 5, Chapter 15 the Harper had gone mad and had been quietly entrusted by Wilhlem to the care of a kind country pastor):

> 'I long for him every hour of the day' she said. 'I did not notice you were so attached to him while he was still living with us' said Wilhelm. 'I was afraid of him when he was awake, I could not bear to look into his eyes' she said 'but when he was asleep, I would sit by his bedside, warding off the flies and could never see enough of him. He gave me support in moments of terror. No one will ever know how much I owe him. If I had only known the way, I would have run to him before now.'

Subsequent editions:	Not in Peters; AGA XX 488: Vol. 8/166; NSA IV: Vol. 3a/113; Bärenreiter: Vol. 2/142
Further settings:	There are very many solo settings of this lyric (*see* IV below) but no other well-known duet settings
Discography and timing:	Fischer-Dieskau —

Discography and timing:		
Fischer-Dieskau	—	
Deutsche Grammophon *Schubert-Duette*	3'54	Janet Baker & Dietrich Fischer-Dieskau
Hyperion I 26[6] Hyperion II 31[8]	3'51	Christine Schäfer & John Mark Ainsley

←— *Die Allmacht* D875a   *Heiss mich nicht reden* D877/2 —→

II LIED DER MIGNON   Mignon's song
Op. 62 no. 2, **D877/2** [H586]
E minor   January 1826

(42 bars)

Heiss mich nicht reden, heiss mich schweigen,   Do not bid me speak; bid me be silent,
Denn mein Geheimnis ist mir Pflicht;   For my duty is to keep my secret;
Ich möchte dir mein ganzes Innre zeigen,   I long to reveal my whole soul to you,
Allein das Schicksal will es nicht.   But fate does not permit it.

Zur rechten Zeit vertreibt der Sonne Lauf	At the appointed time the sun in its course
Die finstre Nacht, und sie muss sich erhellen;	Drives away the dark night, and day must break;
Der harte Fels schliesst seinen Busen auf,	The hard rock opens its bosom
Missgönnt der Erde nicht die tiefverborgnen Quellen	And ungrudgingly bestows on the earth its deep-hidden springs.
Ein jeder sucht im Arm des Freundes Ruh,	Every man seeks peace in the arms of a friend;
Dort kann die Brust in Klagen sich ergiessen;	There the heart can pour out its sorrows.
Allein ein Schwur drückt mir die Lippen zu,	But an oath seals my lips,
Und nur ein Gott vermag sie aufzuschliessen.	And only a god can open them.

Poem written *c.* 1785

This is the seventy-third of Schubert's seventy-five Goethe solo settings (1814–26). See the poet's biography for a chronological list of all the Goethe settings.

Goethe tells us at the end of Book 5, Chapter 6, that this was 'a poem that Mignon had recited once or twice with great expressiveness and which the haste of so many singular occurrences prevented us from inserting sooner'. It thus seems, as Capell says, merely 'appended' to the story. What is it that Mignon knows and is not prepared to tell? As far as we can surmise, she is not aware of her relationship to the Harper that renders her the fruit of an incestuous union. The lyric merely adds to Mignon's general air of mystery, and Goethe has been characteristically shrewd in introducing it in a seemingly offhand way. At this point the reader has only reached the end of Book 5 of the novel; it seems probable that this lyric refers to Mignon's love for Wilhelm Meister who has clearly never thought of her in any romantic capacity. The poor girl, still a child in years though laden with tragic experience, lives in Wilhelm's proximity and is witness to his passionate attachments to other older, and more beautiful, women. She will never confess to this unreciprocated love, and this is her secret – or at least one of them.

In fact Goethe contrives an explanation towards the end of the novel (Book 8, Chapter 3) that shows Mignon's vow of silence in a new light. Here the doctor takes Wilhelm aside and tells him what he has learned about Mignon's past by piecing together fragments of information learned from Wilhelm's beloved, Natalie, as well as songs and 'childish indiscretions' on the part of the unfortunate girl. When she was kidnapped as a child, the band of acrobats that had taken her laughed and joked and, thinking she was asleep, decided that she should never be allowed to find her way back to her home. A young girl in the hands of such rogues might have been subject to sexual abuse, and there is nothing to say that this ignominy, impossible to describe in a nineteenth-century novel, was not part of Mignon's sad fate. Goethe, like Dickens in similar instances, would expect his audience to read between the lines. What the doctor says next about Mignon is surprising:

The poor creature was overcome by utter despair, in the midst of which the Mother of God appeared to her and promised to take care of her. So she swore a sacred oath that she would never again trust anyone, never tell anyone her story, and live and die in the expectation of direct divine sustenance.

The doctor informs Wilhelm that Mignon is motivated by only two things: the longing to see her motherland again, and a longing for Wilhelm himself. For the first time Wilhelm realizes the depth and intensity of Mignon's attachment to him. On one occasion she had been about to surprise Wilhelm in his bedroom, hoping for a night of 'fond, peaceful, nestling', but this plan was dashed with the amorous arrival of the actress Philine, a turn of events that sent her into convulsions of jealousy. She rushed to the room of the Harper and spent the night at his feet. Any explanation of these feelings has been rigorously suppressed by Mignon as part of her vow to the Virgin.

Schubert's setting has a hieratic quality that implies ritual and obsession, with Mignon as guardian-priestess of her own cult. The use of dactylic rhythm in Schubert's music usually implies something sacred or inexorable – the footfall of death, the movement of the stars in their heavens, a fixed and unalterable given. And so it is with Mignon and her vow of silence. The key is E minor, the subdominant of the B minor of the preceding duet, and the plagal, and thus religious, relationship between the two songs seems completely appropriate. The music itself has a deceptive simplicity with the accompaniment hugging much of the vocal line. As in *Mignon und der Harfner*, the time signature is an *alla breve* $\frac{3}{2}$ that moderates the tempo indication of 'langsam' and adds the lilt of a solemn dance to the plaint. We are reminded of Mignon's fragility and the vulnerable femininity behind her boyish appearance. After two bars of the melody there is a courtly little dying fall, like a curtsey (bb. 7–8) that seems to apologize for intransigence, and this is repeated at the end of the next two-bar phrase, and throughout the song. The second verse (from b. 14 with upbeat) moves into the key of C major. An ascent up the stave (with the singer nudged heavenward with support, note for note, from the piano) depicts the glory of a sunrise: 'und sie muss sich erhellen' is a majestic cadence made out of very little more than the elongation of the word 'erhellen' in b. 17 (with the addition of an echoing phrase in the accompaniment) but it illuminates that corner of a dark song with a burst of light. The second and third lines of this strophe are set to similar music, but notable is the singer's plunge down to the bottom of the stave for 'die tiefverborgnen Quellen' (b. 21), followed by a trickle of playful semiquavers as the stream bubbles forth from its hiding place. A tiny yet eloquent interlude (bb. 22–5) takes us from C major to a B major chord – the dominant of what we expect to be E minor. The third verse begins in E major however, to infinitely touching effect. The intimacy and peacefulness of friendship are portrayed in music which is balm to the ear. The meaning of the phrase 'in Klagen sich ergiessen' is beautifully illustrated at its repetition in bb. 29–30: the falling vocal line, each note accompanied by a different chord, tumbles gratefully to the tonic, a perfect analogue for the pouring out of troubles.

The song ends with the poem's final two lines set as fervent recitative, accompanied by portentous minims and semibreve chords. Here Mignon no longer seems to be a little girl but rather a figure of almost Wagnerian grandeur. The dactylic rhythm has evaporated in favour of a blazing intensity and confrontation with fate. The final bar of the vocal line ('vermag sie aufzuschliessen', bb. 39–41) is a musical repeat of 'Allein das Schicksal will es nicht' in the first strophe (bb. 11–12). This is Schubert's means of unifying the song after its digression into recitative. For the singer this line is like walking a tightrope, so high is the tessitura and so great the temptation to make a gratuitous ritardando. This final obstacle in itself seems to sum up Mignon's battle to control her life in the face of setbacks and tragedy. The tiny two-bar postlude leaves the song feeling, and sounding, unfinished – the addition of a few more chords in the final bar, rather than a simple semibreve, would have perhaps provided a more convincing conclusion and made the pianist's life easier.

Subsequent editions:	Peters: Vol. 2/130; AGA XX 489: Vol. 8/169; NSA IV: Vol. 3/117; Bärenreiter: Vol. 2/146
Bibliography:	Byrne 2003, pp. 272–8
	Panofka 1991, p. 14
Further settings:	Johann Friedrich Reichardt (1752–1814) *Das Geheimnis* (1795–6)
	Carl Friedrich Zelter (1758–1832) *Geheimnis* (1811)

Johann Rudolf Zumsteeg (1760–1802) *Aus Wilhelm Meisters Lehrjaren* (1805)

Robert Schumann (1810–1856) *Heiss mich nicht reden* Op. 98a no. 5 (1849)

Pyotr Il'yich Tchaikovsky (1840–1893) *Ne sprashivay* (1884)

Hugo Wolf (1860–1903) *Mignon I* (1888)

Discography and timing: Fischer-Dieskau —

Hyperion I 26[7]

Hyperion II 31[9]   2'57   Christine Schäfer

⟵ *Mignon und der Harfner* ('Nur wer die Sehnsucht kennt') D877/1   *So lasst mich scheinen* D877/3 ⟶

III LIED DER MIGNON   Mignon's song
Op. 62 no. 3, **D877/3** [H587]
B major   January 1826

So lasst mich schei-nen, bis ich wer-de,

(47 bars)

So lasst mich scheinen, bis ich werde,	Thus let me seem till thus I become.
Zieht mir das weisse Kleid nicht aus!	Do not take off my white dress!
Ich eile von der schönen Erde	I shall swiftly leave the fair earth
Hinab in jenes dunkle Haus.[1]	For that dark dwelling place below.
Dort ruh' ich eine kleine Stille,	There, for a brief silence, I shall rest;
Dann öffnet sich der frische Blick;	Then my eyes shall open afresh.
Ich lasse dann die reine Hülle,	Then I shall leave behind this pure raiment,
Den Gürtel und den Kranz zurück.	This girdle and this rosary.
Und jene himmlischen Gestalten	And those heavenly beings
Sie fragen nicht nach Mann und Weib,	Do not ask who is man or woman,
Und keine Kleider, keine Falten	And no garments, no folds
Umgeben den verklärten Leib.	Enclose the transfigured body.
Zwar lebt' ich ohne Sorg' und Mühe,	True, I lived free from care and toil,
Doch fühlt' ich tiefen Schmerz genung.	Yet I knew much deep suffering.
Vor Kummer altert' ich zu frühe;	Too soon I grew old with grief;
Macht mich auf ewig wieder jung!	Make me young again forever!

[1] For this version of the song (but not D469), Schubert changes Goethe's 'jenes feste Haus' to 'jenes *dunkle* Haus'.

Poem written in June 1796

This is the seventy-fourth of Schubert's seventy-five Goethe solo settings (1814–26). See the poet's biography for a chronological list of all the Goethe settings.

This poem occurs in Book 8, Chapter 2, of the novel. Natalie, whom Wilhelm has named 'die schöne Amazone' and whom he will eventually marry, tells him her concerns for Mignon's health:

> *She spoke to him in general terms about Mignon's illness, telling him that the girl was becoming more and more the prey of strong emotions and, highly sensitive as always, concealed the fact that she often suffered violent cramps around the heart, but so dangerously severe that sometimes this prime organ of life stopped beating suddenly when she was unexpectedly excited, and there seemed to be no sign of life in the dear child's body.*

It seems that there has been a change in Mignon's character. She now only wears women's clothes which she had formerly despised. Natalie then recounts to Wilhelm the story of a children's party that she had organized. She had promised the children that an angel would bring them presents:

> *I chose Mignon to play the part of the angel, and on the appointed day she was clothed in a long, thin white garment with a girdle of gold around her chest and a golden crown in her hair. I first thought I would omit the wings, but the women who dressed her insisted on a pair of big golden wings with which they could demonstrate their skill. And so this miraculous vision appeared, a lily in one hand and a little basket in the other, right in the midst of the girls, and surprised me as well. 'Here comes the angel!' I said. All the children made as if to withdraw, but then finally shouted 'It's Mignon!' though still not venturing any closer to the wondrous sight.*
>
> *'Here are your presents' she said, handing them the basket. They gathered around her, gazed, touched her, and then one of them asked: 'Are you an angel?' 'I wish I were', Mignon replied. 'Why are you holding a lily?' 'My heart should be open and pure as a lily, then I would be happy.' 'What are the wings for? Let me see!' 'They stand for lovelier wings which are not yet opened.'*
>
> *She continued to give these remarkable answers to their simple questions. When their curiosity was satisfied and the first impressions of her appearance began to fade, they wanted to undress her. But she would not allow this. She took up her zither, climbed up on this high desk, and sang with unbelievable grace and appeal this song.*

Schubert's music for this lyric is perhaps the greatest of his 'Mignon' songs. The key is B major, a carefully planned counterbalance to the B minor of the opening duet of the cycle. The change to triple metre after the strict *alla breve* duple rhythm of the two previous songs seems to free the music to slip into another world, far away from earthly pain. For much of the first verse there is a repeated F sharp hidden within the texture of the accompaniment (sometimes as the bass note) that puts us in mind of *Die liebe Farbe* from *Die schöne Müllerin* where the miller boy, like Mignon, faces the prospect of death. Unlike the miller boy, we hear no anger here and no self-pity. Even 'resignation' would be the wrong word; rather we hear a transcendental acceptance of the consequences of living and dying, a terrible sweetness and wisdom born of suffering. The music takes us beyond sorrow and into a luminous vision of 'das mildre Land'. Mignon expects to die 'in the expectation of direct divine sustenance' (*see* p. 691) and her music expresses her quiet radiant confidence in this outcome. It is at times like this that one understands Brahms's comment about Schubert being able to inhabit regions that are beyond the reach of other composers. At the beginning of the third verse, when we hear the words 'Und jene himmlischen Gestalten, / Sie fragen nicht nach Mann und Weib' ('And those heavenly beings do not ask who is man or woman'), we feel ourselves transfigured, alongside Mignon, in a world where the distinction between the sexes is as irrelevant as food and clothing and all human ailments. During the novel Mignon has displayed clairvoyant abilities. Byrne states that Goethe imputes to Mignon 'the same insight, the same prophetic preternatural character as the androgynous Greek gods. As in classical mythology, her embodiment of male and female qualities invests her with greater power.'

There are some technical means to describe the magic of this passage (the music of the opening is built on the second inversion of the tonic chord that makes it seem unanchored and floating free of reality) but this is inadequate to explain the song's strength: of course Goethe's words play no little part in its potency.

Mignon dressed as an angel by Wilhelm von Kaulbach.

The key of B major is one of Schubert's favourite tonalities for music of this mood, and the pianist should not be afraid to follow the composer's demands for a mezzo-staccato articulation where marked. It is this that gives the accompaniment its essential transparency and its feeling of gentle lift-off – as if Mignon were already floating some inches off the ground, on her way to being a hovering spirit. We know how much she has longed for a mother's love, and the other-worldly rapture of this song reminds us of the transcendental B major passage in *Vor meiner Wiege* D927 where the poet remembers being cradled in the arms of a loving mother.

The form of the song is simplicity itself: it is almost completely strophic and the composer uses two of Goethe's verses to make one musical verse. The second and fourth verses of the poem allow Mignon more dramatic utterance: the ascending vocal line at 'Dann öffnet sich der frische Blick' (bb. 17–19) is suddenly forte and doubled by octaves in the piano, the tessitura is higher and the vocal decoration on 'frische' in b. 18 (and later on 'Schmerz genung' in the fourth verse at b. 38) adds a moment of recitative-like rhetoric to the proceedings and allows us to see an echo of Mignon's strength and resolve, however undermined by illness. The composer allows himself one change of harmony on this 'Schmerz genung': here D minor is a poignant contrast to the D major of the corresponding earlier passage. Despite the subtlety and sophistication of the musical imagination at work, we might believe that the song was simple enough to be sung to children, as indeed it is in Goethe's novel. The accompaniment attempts nothing fancy, and dutifully hugs the vocal line for much of the time. Schubert sets 'jenes dunkle Haus' in the first verse (bb. 12–13) instead of Goethe's 'jenes feste Haus'. This seems to have been the composer's own alteration, and even if this was lese-majesty, how beautiful the word 'dunkle' (dark) sounds at the bottom of the stave and in this register of the soprano voice! Apart from this, Goethe himself might have been pleased with a song that embraces many of the ideals of the older masters of lieder, while achieving a depth of expression utterly beyond their reach.

Subsequent editions:	Peters: Vol. 2/132; AGA XX 490: Vol. 8/172; NSA IV: Vol. 3a/120; Bärenreiter: Vol. 2/148
Further settings:	Johann Friedrich Reichardt (1752–1814) *Mignons letzter Gesang* (1796)
	Robert Schumann (1810–1856) *So lasst mich scheinen* Op. 98a no. 9 (1849)
	Hugo Wolf (1860–1903) *Mignon III* (1888)
Discography and timing:	Fischer-Dieskau —
	Hyperion I 26[8]
	Hyperion II 31[10] 3'09 Christine Schäfer

← *Heiss mich nicht reden* D877/2   *Nur wer die Sehnsucht kennt* D877/4 →

IV LIED DER MIGNON   Mignon's song
Op. 62 no. 4, **D877/4** [H588]
A minor   January 1826

(46 bars)

Nur wer die Sehnsucht kennt	Only those who know longing
Weiss, was ich leide!	Know what I suffer.
Allein und abgetrennt	Alone, cut off
Von aller Freude,	From all joy,
Seh' ich an's Firmament	I gaze at the firmament
Nach jener Seite.	In that direction.
Ach! der mich liebt und kennt	Ah, he who loves and knows me
Ist in der Weite.	Is far away.
Es schwindelt mir, es brennt	I feel giddy;
Mein Eingeweide.	My vitals are aflame.
Nur wer die Sehnsucht kennt	Only he who knows longing
Weiss, was ich leide!	Knows what I suffer.

Poem written in June 1785

This is the last of Schubert's seventy-five Goethe solo settings (1814–26). See the poet's biography for a chronological list of all the Goethe songs.

After such a cycle of songs which follows Mignon's career in the order of the novel – a cycle moreover that has been planned to make perfect sense in terms of its key progressions (B minor – E minor – B major) – it seems strange to revert to the Mignon of an earlier part of the book with another *Nur wer die Sehnsucht kennt*. The key of A minor moreover does not easily follow the preceding B major. It seems clear from the manuscript that Schubert had already planned the three songs in the cycle before he decided to publish his sixth, and last, setting of *Nur wer die Sehnsucht kennt* as an alternative to the opening duet, and almost as an afterthought. He must have realized that it was not the easiest thing in the world for a soprano to have a tenor at her disposal, a tenor who would be willing moreover to fade into the background for the remaining two songs in the set. Here is an alternative which, if placed at the beginning of a solo cycle of three Mignon songs, also makes some kind of sense in terms of an ascending progression of tonalities: A minor – E minor – B major.

The music for this song is world-famous, the simplicity and potency of the melody a perfect mirror of Mignon's plight. It is therefore something of a surprise to discover that Schubert decided to recycle an old song, a Salis-Seewis setting he had composed ten years before (*Lied (Ins stille Land)*, D403) and to graft on new words to a melody that already existed. Of course he made changes to the shape of the tune, and the Mignon setting, with its impassioned middle section, is a much grander creation than *Lied (Ins stille Land)*. But the key of that song (A minor in its later versions) and the gently undulating accompaniment, as well as the overall shape of the melody, have been absorbed unashamedly into the Goethe setting. Leo Black also points out that the songs *Atys* D585 and *An die Türen will ich schleichen* D478/3, also the opening of the Arpeggione Sonata D821 (other works in A minor), all begin similarly with the same three rising notes – A, B, C. The Salis-Seewis poem has much in common with Mignon's lyric – it asks imploring questions about who will lead us to the land of rest. The longing of Mignon and the Harper to be reunited with a distant beloved seems very similar. Both songs are about 'crossing the bar' in one way or another, and both songs are sung to the open heavens. In fact Mignon's longing is for Wilhem Meister and her body burns passionately for the kind of embraces she will never receive from him; he may as well live in the far distance because he is so unavailable to her.

The piano introduction is new. This is inspired by the opening vocal melody, but it is not merely a pre-echo of what we will hear sung; the second half of the *Vorspiel*, with its plangent chromatic stab of pain on the flattened supertonic (b. 3) belongs to the piano alone. This sets the scene with grandeur and eloquence as mournful right-hand octaves (which challenge any pianist's ability to play a meaningful legato) draw us into Mignon's world, and left-hand triplets propel the song gently forward in the manner of an Italian aria. Perhaps Schubert remembered that Mignon might express herself in the musical manner of her homeland; the vocal line seems the purest *bel canto*, and the modulation into the relative major on the repeat of 'Weiss, was ich leide' (bb. 13–14) and the little ornament on 'was' seem almost Bellini-esque. The middle section of the song is something that only Schubert could have written. The tune for the words 'Allein und abgetrennt / Von aller Freude, / Seh' ich an's Firmament / Nach jener Seite' has been directly lifted from *Lied (Ins stille Land)*. The accompaniment, however, has become much more sophisticated: rather banal quavers in the earlier setting are replaced with right-hand crotchets accented off the beat like little stabs of pain (from b. 16). From b. 23 the music for the phrase 'Ach! der mich liebt und kennt / Ist in der Weite' is an illustration of Schubert's ability at this stage of his career to spin the most profound magic out of the slenderest resources. The accompaniment slowly alternates between a third inversion of an E^7 chord (the bass a mezzo staccato dotted crotchet on a low D) with the first inversion of A minor with a low C in the bass. As in the duet setting, the distance between left hand and right somehow suggests the broad sweep of the firmament, as well as the unattainability of he who lives 'in der Weite'.

This relatively simple device conjures up an extraordinary atmosphere: a deep stillness descends on the song in a matter of seconds, and the voice (marked 'sehr leise' at b. 23) floats above the piano as if lost in the stars. The bass C falls to a low B flat and a darkness deeper yet is ushered in together with an a tempo marking (b. 27): a shudder of sextuplets in the right hand on a diminished seventh, the first of a chain of such chords, introduces the 'Es schwindelt mir' section that had given Schubert such trouble in earlier settings. Here he gets it exactly right: the passage is searing and exciting, but it is contained within the frame of the whole. There is a brief moment of forte for b. 29, but the frisson of shock and palpitation is accomplished mainly within piano. This leads to a recapitulation which is by and large a repetition of the opening. The postlude repeats the introduction. Schubert has pared down his creation to the most economical form where every note, every dynamic mark, every beautifully set word, tells to the fullest effect. This is one of those masterpieces that appears always to have been a part of the song repertory. One cannot imagine a single note differently.

Subsequent editions:	Peters: Vol. 1/214; AGA XX 491: Vol. 8/174; NSA IV: Vol. 3a/122; Bärenreiter: Vol. 2/150
Further settings:	Johann Friedrich Reichardt (1752–1814) *Sehnsucht* (1795 and 1805–6)
	Carl Friedrich Zelter (1758–1832) *Sehnsucht* (1795, 1812, 1821)
	Ludwig van Beethoven (1770–1827) *Sehnsucht* (4 versions) WoO 134 (1807–8)
	Carl Loewe (1796–1869) *Sehnsucht* (1818)
	Fanny Mendelssohn (1805–1847) *Mignon* (1826)
	Robert Schumann (1810–1856) *Nur wer die Sehnsucht kennt* Op. 98a no. 3 (1849)
	Pyotr Il'yich Tchaikovsky (1840–1893) *Net, tol'ko tot, kto znal* (1869)
	Hugo Wolf (1860–1903) *Mignon II* (1888)
	Nicolas Medtner (1879/80–1951) *Mignon* (1908–9)
	Volker Schütz 'Nur wer die Sehnsucht kennt' Version für Jazz (1999)
Discography and timing:	Fischer-Dieskau —
	Hyperion I 26⁹
	Hyperion II 31¹¹ 2'52 Christine Schäfer

← *So lasst mich scheinen* D877/3   *Lebwohl, du schöne Erde*
                                                    (*Abschied von der Erde*) D829 →

GESÄNGE DES HARFNERS AUS WILHELM MEISTER
(Goethe) Op. 12, **D478**
September 1816, revised Autumn 1822, second set, nos 1–3

For the definitive version [H492–494] of the Harper's cycle, *see* below. For a guide as to where to find the earlier settings of the lyrics in this book *see* entry under HARPER'S SONGS. For a list of all the Schubert songs inspired by the novel WILHELM MEISTERS LEHRJAHRE *see* entry under that name.

First edition:	Published as Op. 12 by Cappi & Diabelli, Vienna in March 1822 (P28–30)
Dedicatee:	Johann Nepomuk von Dankesreither
Bibliography:	Gülke 1991, pp. 79–83

I (Wer Sich der Einsamkeit Ergibt)
Op. 12 NO. 1, **D478** second set NO. 1 (D₁478B) [H492]

The song exists in two versions, the second of which is discussed below:
(1) September 1816; (2) Published 1822

(1)   'Langsam'   A minor   ¢   [51 bars]

(2)   A minor

(52 bars)

Wer sich der Einsamkeit ergibt,	He who gives himself up to solitude,
Ach, der ist bald allein;	Ah, he is soon alone;
Ein jeder lebt, ein jeder liebt,	One man lives, another loves
Und lässt ihn seiner Pein.	And both leave him to his suffering.
Ja! lasst mich meiner Qual!	Yes, leave me to my suffering!
Und kann ich nur einmal	And if I can just once
Recht einsam sein,	Be truly lonely,
Dann bin ich nicht allein.	Then I shall not be alone.
Es schleicht ein Liebender lauschend sacht,	A lover steals softly, listening:
Ob seine Freundin allein?	Is his sweetheart alone?
So überschleicht bei Tag und Nacht	Thus, day and night,
Mich Einsamen die Pein,	Suffering steals upon me,
Mich Einsamen die Qual.	Torment steals upon me in my solitude.
Ach, werd' ich erst einmal	Ah, when I lie lonely
Einsam im Grabe sein,	In the grave,
Da lässt sie mich allein!	Then my torment will leave me alone.

Poem written by 1783

This is the forty-fifth of Schubert's seventy-five Goethe solo settings (1814–26). See the poet's
biography for a chronological list of all the Goethe settings.

The Harper is a repentant sinner who lives on the fringes of society and on the edge of sanity. He has drifted into the circle of actors surrounding Wilhelm Meister, who knows nothing about this enigmatic figure. The reader of the novel discovers later that as a younger man (and a monk) he has had an affair with a woman, Sperata, who turned out to be the sister hidden from him by his family. A child was born of this union – in fact this was Mignon. He does not speak readily and his best way of communication is to break into song where he is able to confess his pain and wrong-doing in an enigmatic manner. In Goethe's novel Wilhelm Meister visits the

Wilhelm Meister visits the Harper, an illustration by Naeke from the larger format edition of Goethe's *Ausgabe Letzer Hand.*

Harper, overhears him sing a song from outside the door (actually no. 2 in Schubert's set, *see* below) and then goes into the room and speaks to him. He encourages him to sing something else. One should note how carefully Schubert read the introduction to 'Wer sich der Einsamkeit ergibt': 'Der Alte blickt auf seine Saiten, und nachdem er sanft präludiert hatte, stimmte er und sang' ('The old man looked down at the strings and after he had softly played a prelude struck up and started to sing'). Schubert writes a prelude that fits this description like a glove. The introduction sounds improvised, tentative certainly, perhaps even a little absent-minded; it is played not by a young minstrel but an old man heavy with care. Throughout the song (and except for an astonishing outburst towards the end) Schubert is careful to ask for soft dynamics that reflect the frailty and the inward nature of the Harper's suffering, and yet this simple four-bar introduction which leads us to an A minor chord is somehow invested with towering grief.

The opening words ('Wer sich der Einsamkeit ergibt') climb an arpeggio with a crescendo; they are tight with an emotion hitherto suppressed and which now breaks out in song. The whole of this section seems improvised as a motto; it applies to all mankind, and the song proper that particularizes the Harper's own fate has not yet begun. This quality of recitative is brilliantly shown in the composer's setting of 'Ein jeder lebt' (bb. 8–9) and 'ein jeder liebt' (bb. 9–10). Each phrase has a pause after it and we understand the implied gesture – 'on one hand. . . and then on the other hand'. Those who live and those who love are differentiated not only by a vowel (in 'lebt' and 'liebt') but are given a separate place in the mind's eye of the Harper. He then tells us that *both* these types of people turn their back on those who give themselves up to solitude. The ornamentation of the vocal line is not found in the 1816 copy and was added when the work was prepared for publication in 1822. We detect here the hand of the singer Johann Michael Vogl who might have added decorations in performance, some of which the composer (unusually) liked well enough to adopt permanently. (Ornamented versions of the Harper's songs going back to Vogl and transposed into lower keys for baritone are printed in the NSA Volume 1b pp. 292–303).

With the word 'Ja!' (upbeat to b. 14) we are pulled from the general into the particular. Having uttered something like an aphorism or maxim, the Harper is pierced to the heart to realize how truly it applies to him. At b. 20 the setting of '<u>bin</u> ich nicht allein' places the verb poignantly high in the tessitura with an accented grace note. The floridity of the vocal writing is supported by an almost anonymous accompaniment in triplets. It seems obvious that Schubert gave this music the character of an Italian cantilena precisely because the Harper is an Italian; like Mignon he comes

Title page of *Gesänge des Harfners*, Op. 12 (1822).

from the land 'wo die Zitronen blühn'. The sinister and furtive quality of 'Es schleicht ein Liebender lauschend sacht' (bb. 21–3) is brilliantly caught. In Einstein's view, only Schubert among the great composers understood these words fully. Here we have the obsessive side of human nature where sexual impulses are paramount and the jealousy that flows from them is ruinous. Sex rules this man – or has done; his predicament and guilt are the result. The lover slinks past (the left-hand accompaniment now in furtive legato crotchets) because he fears that his *inamorata* is with someone else. This is the utterance of someone whose belief in love has been blighted, who feels himself unworthy of fidelity. Certain of betrayal, he feels he deserves it too.

Schubert repeats the last four lines of the poem to make a song of five rather than four quatrains. It seems to be in the nature of a grand summing-up although the marking 'mit leiserer Stimme' shows that the composer requires vocal restraint. The tessitura of 'im Grabe sein' burrows right down to the bottom of the tenor's range as befits mention of the grave (bb. 34–5), and the first 'Da lässt sie mich allein', suddenly high in contrast at the end of b. 35, is marked with a fortissimo of frightening vehemence. This passage, as well as the postlude, is rendered even more eloquent by sinking octaves in the left-hand accompaniment (bb. 32–7) in the manner of Purcell's great aria for Dido, 'When I am laid in earth'. Schubert was still (although only just) a pupil of Antonio Salieri. Perhaps it was Salieri who made his young pupil aware of the conventions of the Italian *lamento* with its bass line falling within a tetrachord.

The first version of this setting is published in NSA Volume 1b p. 220. This dates from September 1816 and shows the state of the song before Schubert prepared it for publication in 1822. It is essentially the same music but the more experienced and sophisticated composer (by now six years older) has revised it. The comparison of the two versions shows how Schubert allows his original inspiration to stand, but dresses it up a little more smartly for its definitive presentation to the world.

Autograph: Österreichische Nationalbibliothek, Vienna (fair copy)
First known performance: Semi-public *Musikalische Unterhaltung* in the Abbey of
St Florian, Linz at the beginning of October 1826. Soloist:

	Antonie Adamberger, accompanied by the organist Anton Kattinger in this song and selections from *Die schöne Müllerin*.
Subsequent editions:	Peters: Vol. 2/27; AGA XX 254: Vol. 4/189; NSA IV: Vol. 1a/85 & Vol. 1b/220; Bärenreiter: Vol. 1/68
Bibliography:	Capell 1928, pp. 121–2
	Dürr 1982, pp. 15–20
	Einstein 1951, p. 141
	Fischer-Dieskau 1977, p. 78
Further settings and arrangements:	Johann Friedrich Reichardt (1752–1814) *Einsamkeit* (1795–6)
	Carl Freidrich Zelter (1758–1832) *Einsamkeit* (1795)
	Fanny Mendelssohn (1805–1847) *Harfners Lied* (1825)
	Robert Schumann (1810–1856) *Wer sich der Einsamkeit ergibt* Op. 98a no. 6 (1849)
	Hugo Wolf (1860–1903) *Harfenspieler I* (1888)
	Arr. Max Reger (1873–1916) *Wer sich der Einsamkeit ergibt* for voice and orchestra (1915) [*see* ORCHESTRATIONS]
	Arr. Tilman Hoppstock (b. 1961) for guitar accompaniment, in *Franz Schubert: 110 Lieder* (2009)
Discography and timing:	Fischer-Dieskau I 8[6] 4'25
	Hyperion I 23[21]
	Hyperion II 25[18] 3'47 Christoph Prégardien

⟵ *Selige Welt* D743   *Wer nie sein Brot mit Tränen ass* D₂472/2 ⟶

II (Wer nie sein Brot mit Tränen Ass)
Op. 12 NO. 2, **D478** second set NO. 2 (D₁480/3) [H493]
A minor   Autumn 1822

(66 bars)

Wer nie sein Brot mit Tränen ass,[1]	Who has never eaten his bread with tears,
Wer nie die kummervollen Nächte	Who, through nights of grief,
Auf seinem Bette weinend sass,	Has never sat weeping on his bed,
Der kennt euch nicht, ihr himmlischen Mächte!	Knows you not, heavenly powers.
Ihr führt ins Leben uns hinein,	You bring us into life;
Ihr lasst den Armen schuldig werden,	You let the poor wretch fall into guilt,
Dann überlasst ihr ihn der Pein:	Then you abandon him to his agony:
Denn alle Schuld rächt sich auf Erden.	For all guilt is avenged on earth.

[1] This poem was originally published with the old-fashioned spelling for 'Brot', thus 'Brod'.

Poem written by 1783

This is the sixty-sixth of Schubert's seventy-five Goethe solo settings (1814–26). See the poet's biography for a chronological list of all the Goethe settings.

This is the only song in the *Gesänge des Harfners* that does not date from 1816 although Schubert set the poem twice that year (D478/2 and D478/2b). Both songs are in A minor and both have a great deal to commend them, but it is clear that the composer was not completely satisfied with his work. When he came to prepare the Harper's songs for publication as his Opus 12 in 1822 he composed this text afresh. He seems to have made an effort to unify the three songs and he matches his new setting to the style of the first. As a whole then, and despite various cosmetic changes in the outer songs, the cycle is an 1816 work with a new central panel.

In Goethe's novel *Wilhelm Meisters Lehrjahre* this is the first song that the eponymous hero hears when he visits the Harper's lodgings – an attic room in a shabby inn in a remote part of the town:

> *The sombre, deeply moving music was accompanied by anguished melancholy singing. Wilhelm crept up to the door. The old man was rhapsodizing, repeating stanzas, half singing, half reciting . . . The mournful, heartfelt lament affected the listener deeply. It seemed to him as if the old man was at times prevented by tears from continuing to sing, and the strings of the harp resounded until the voice came in again, softly and with broken sounds.*

It is astonishing how faithfully Schubert responded to these lines when he came to write the music. The introduction is a pendant to the prelude of the first song – seemingly improvised, distracted, related perhaps to some of the openings of the Müller settings (*Winterreise* is always mentioned in connection with the Harper songs, but this is surely a minor-key variant of *Pause* from *Die schöne Müllerin*, the harp related to the miller boy's lute with a similarly dotted and graced accompanying figure). This opening phrase of two bars is repeated; for Schubert has taken that aspect of Goethe's description to heart ('rhapsodizing, repeating stanzas'), and indeed both strophes of this poem are set twice – not at all a common feature in Schubert's output. The vocal line is extraordinary; it manages to be both grand (as befits a tragic figure) and utterly broken. Falling in frail steps from an E at the top of the stave (an especially plaintive note in the *passaggio* of the tenor voice), the phrase 'Wer nie sein Brot mit Tränen ass' has great pathos; its descent paints a picture of infinite weariness. The dotted rhythms of 'kummervollen Nächte' (b. 11) once again seem Italianate with a discreet trace of a sob. From halfway through b. 12 flowing triplets take over the accompaniment. At bb. 16–17 their meanderings seem to threaten to modulate at 'himmlischen Mächte' but we return safely to the home key (A minor momentarily softened into the major) for an interlude (bb. 18–21) that will also form the basis of the postlude.

From b. 20 the same words are set to quite different music that is tinged with the pathetic major which emphasizes the Harper's sadness. There is an extraordinary modulation into F major at 'himmlischen Mächte' (bb. 28–30) – the heavenly powers lead us into new tonal realms, something that has only been hinted at first time round. 'This cadence is strangely marked with a diminuendo so difficult as to be almost impracticable' (Capell). Perhaps – but when it *is* achieved how vividly does it suggest the Harper choking back tears that almost prevent him from singing. The lower strings of the harp resound in a fragment of tune in the piano's left hand (bb. 30–34); this is a remnant of a noble melody, now ruined and lacking a counterpoint, a glimpse of the singer's erstwhile dignity. This leads us into a new strophe (from b. 35 with upbeat) and the key of B flat major which is related to the main key in Neapolitan fashion. Summoning all his strength the Harper thrums grandiose and static chords that accompany a declamatory passage ('Ihr führt ins Leben uns hinein') – 'half singing, half reciting' (as Goethe directs). He is now fully in his stride with the wounded eloquence of an Oedipus; anger and bitterness spur him on to feats of vocal strength of which he had not thought himself capable. This strophe is repeated (from b. 44 with upbeat) where 'Ihr führt ins Leben uns hinein' is in B flat minor. The floodgates of emotion have been opened and high in the tessitura of the voice the vocal line is punched with the dotted rhythms of anguish. One vowel held for five and a half crotchets on the word 'alle' (all) sits astride an ascending bass line in bb. 51–2 that mercilessly tightens the harmonic screws. The note is so long that it encompasses *all* guilt, even the unimaginable enormity of the Harper's guilty secret. This is the nearest he comes to confessing. Passion spent, a further repeat of the last three lines of the strophe (from 'Ihr lasst den Armen', b. 54) is pianissimo. The way the final word 'Er<u>den</u>' slips into A major at bb. 60–61 is heartbreaking. Schubert's favourite and most eloquent change of key is A minor to major and in his hands it is unfailingly magical. Here it signifies mercy. It shows the composer's compassion for the plight of the Harper and that he at least has forgiven the old man his trespasses. This complex and tormented piece is a worthy forerunner of other great songs of alienation and loneliness in *Winterreise*. Byrne points out a possible source of Goethe's initial poetic idea: the hymn 'Wie lange soll ich jammervoll mein Brot mit Tränen essen' of Paul Gerhardt (1607–1676).

Autograph:	Missing or lost
Subsequent editions:	Peters: Vol. 2/30; AGA XX 258: Vol. 4/192; NSA IV: Vol. 1a/89; Bärenreiter: Vol. 1/71
Bibliography:	Byrne 2003, p. 304
	Capell 1929, pp. 120–21
	Einstein 1951, p. 141
Further settings and arrangements:	Carl Friedrich Zelter (1758–1832) (1795 and 1816)
	Robert Schumann (1810–1856) *Wer nie sein Brot mit Tränen ass* Op. 98a no. 4 (1849)
	Franz Liszt (1811–1886) *Wer nie sein Brot mit Tränen ass*, 2 versions (1845, rev. 1859 & 1860 and 1848, rev. 1860 & 1862)
	Hugo Wolf (1860–1903) *Harfenspieler III* (1888)
	Arr. Max Reger (1873–1916) *Wer nie sein Brot mit Tränen ass* for voice and orchestra (1915) [*see* ORCHESTRATIONS]
	Arr. Tilman Hoppstock (b. 1961) for guitar accompaniment, in *Franz Schubert: 110 Lieder* (2009)
Discography and timing:	Fischer-Dieskau I 8[7] 5'02
	Hyperion I 23[22]
	Hyperion II 25[19] 4'15 Christoph Prégardien

← *Wer sich der Einsamkeit ergibt* D478/1   *An die Türen will ich schleichen* D478/3 →

III (An die Türen Will Ich Schleichen)
Op. 12 NO. 3, **D478** second set NO. 3 (D₁479B) [H494]

The song exists in two versions, the second of which is discussed below.
(1) September 1816; (2) Pubished 1822

(1) 'Mässig' A minor 𝄵 [52 bars]

(2)   A minor

Mässig, in gehender Bewegung

pp

sempre legato

An die Tü - ren will ich schlei- chen,

(50 bars)

An die Türen will ich schleichen,	I shall steal from door to door
Still und sittsam will ich stehn,	And stand there, silent and humble;
Fromme Hand wird Nahrung reichen,	A kind hand will offer food
Und ich werde weiter gehn.	And I shall go on my way.
Jeder wird sich glücklich scheinen,	Each will deem himself happy
Wenn mein Bild vor ihm erscheint,	When he sees me before him.
Eine Träne wird er weinen,	He will shed a tear;
Und ich weiss nicht was er weint.	And yet I know not why he should weep.

Poem written in 1785

This is the forty-sixth of Schubert's seventy-five Goethe solo settings (1814–26). See the poet's biography for a chronological list of all the Goethe settings.

The third song in the *Gesänge des Harfners* cycle comes from Book 5, Chapter 14 of Goethe's *Wilhelm Meisters Lehrjahre*. It follows a dramatic incident where the Harper has attempted to kill the child Felix with a knife, 'as if he were going to sacrifice him'. There has also been a fire that Wilhelm suspects the Harper of having started. The enigmatic character disappears from view, but a little while later Wilhelm finds him in a garden singing a fragment of a song which shows his distracted state of mind, the song of someone 'who feels himself quite close to madness'. This is music of someone trapped in his own world; his former brooding introspection and self-awareness have vanished. All that remains is the empty landscape of an uncertain future. He is now the denuded archetypal figure outlined by Byrne: 'Der Wanderer, Der Harfner, Der Alte . . . Like Orestes, the Harper endures the harsh discipline of seeking expiation and his madness represents largely unconscious and conflicting feelings regarding responsibility and guilt.' Byrne later compares this music to the monotonous plaint of Orpheus mindlessly bemoaning the loss of his Eurydice as he haunts the Thracian landscape. The rhetorical text repetitions of the other two songs in the set have disappeared; the Harper's tragic role in the story is reduced to a whimper, all the more deranged for its lack of musical emphasis. The piece is ineluctable in the unremitting monochrome of its mood (it glides in even crotchets without a trace of operatic convention) and in its sad and barren simplicity. Only at the very end of the novel does the Harper learn of his relationship to Mignon (who has meanwhile died) and he takes his own life as a consequence.

There is a vaguely contrapuntal baroque style to the setting (cf. the Schlegel setting *Vom Mitleiden Mariä* D632) that adds to its sense of being lost in time. The last line of the poem holds the key: those who give him alms will shed a tear, but the Harper does not know why they should weep. He no longer feels sorry for himself; his madness is our problem and no longer his. There is something here of the weird self-contained world of *Der Leiermann* from *Winterreise*. John Reed has pointed out that the composer's tempo direction 'Mässig, in gehender Bewegung' was also used at the start of that great cycle (at the head of the first version of *Gute*

Nacht) to launch the winter traveller on his journey. It was perhaps here in 1816 that Schubert first acquired a taste for the subtle idea of ending a song cycle enigmatically and unresolved. It is significant that the composer set that poem once and for all (there are no other settings apart from a copy ornamented by Vogl in a lower key – that version in F minor is printed in Volume 1b of the NSA).

The first version of this setting is published in NSA Volume 1b p. 224. This dates from September 1816 and shows the state of the song before Schubert prepared it for publication in 1822. It is essentially the same music with a different tempo indication and a shortened postlude. Schubert allows his original inspiration more or less to stand, a compliment to his younger self, but he cannot resist revising it slightly for its journey into the world at large.

Autograph:	Fragment of first draft (bb. 41–52) in Wienbibliothek im Rathaus, Vienna
Subsequent editions:	Peters: Vol. 2/33; AGA XX 255b: Vol. 4/196; NSA IV: Vol. 1a/93 & Vol. 1b/224; Bärenreiter: Vol. 1/74
Bibliography:	Black 2003, p. 174 (a comparison between this music and the Sanctus of the Mass in E flat D950)
	Byrne 2003, pp. 320–26
	Capell 1928, p. 122
	Einstein 1951, p. 141
Further settings and arrangements:	Johann Friedrich Reichardt (1752–1814) *Letztes Lied des Harfenspielers* (1809)
	Carl Freidrich Zelter (1758–1832), *An die Turen will ich schleichen* Op. 98a no. 8 (1818)
	Robert Schumann (1810–1856) *An die Türen will ich schleichen* Op. 98a no. 8 (1849)
	Modest Mussorgsky (1839–1881) *Pesn' startsa: stanu skromno u poroga* [Old Man's Song] (1863)
	Hugo Wolf (1860–1903) *Harfenspieler II* (1888)
	Nickolai Medtner (1879/80–1951) *Aus* Wilhelm Meister Op. 15 no. 2 (1907–8)
	Arr. Max Reger (1873–1916) *An die Türen will ich schleichen* for voice and orchestra (1915) [see ORCHESTRATIONS]
	Arr. Tilman Hoppstock (b. 1961) for guitar accompaniment, in *Franz Schubert: 110 Lieder* (2009)
Discography and timing:	Fischer-Dieskau I 8[8] 2'08
	Hyperion I 23[23]
	Hyperion II 25[20] 1'47 Christoph Prégardien

← *Wer nie sein brot mit Tränen ass* D478   *Sei mir gegrüsst!* D741 →

GESANG AN DIE HARMONIE *see* AN DIE HARMONIE D394

GESANG (An Silvia)   To Silvia
(SHAKESPEARE/BAUERNFELD)
OP. 106 NO. 4, **D891** [H605]
A major   July 1826

(30 bars)

A literal translation of Bauernfeld's translation is given here.
Shakespeare's original text is printed below in italics.

Was ist Silvia, saget an,
   Dass sie die weite Flur preist?
Schön und zart seh' ich sie nah'n,
   Auf Himmels Gunst und Spur weist,
Dass ihr Alles untertan.

What is Silvia, tell me,
   That the wide meadows laud her?
I see her draw near, fair and tender,
   It is a mark of heaven's favour
That all are subject to her.

Ist sie schön und gut dazu?
   Reiz labt wie milde Kindheit;
Ihrem Aug' eilt Amor zu,
   Dort heilt er seine Blindheit,
Und verweilt in süsser Ruh'.

Is she fair and kind as well?
   Her charms refresh with child-like gentleness;
Cupid hastens to her eyes,
   There he cures his blindness
And lingers in sweet peace.

Darum Silvia, tön', o Sang,
   Der holden Silvia Ehren;
Jeden Reiz besiegt sie lang,
   Den Erde kann gewähren:
Kränze ihr und Saitenklang!

Then to Silvia let our song resound,
   To fair Silvia's glory!
She has long acquired every charm
   That this earth can grant:
Bring her garlands, and the music of strings!

Who is Silvia? What is she,
That all our swains commend her?
Holy, fair, and wise is she.
The heaven such grace did lend her,
That she might admired be.

Is she kind as she is fair?
For beauty lives with kindness.
Love doth to her eyes repair,
To help him of his blindness;
And, being helped, inhabits there.

Then to Silvia let us sing
That Silvia is excelling;
She excels each mortal thing
Upon the dull earth dwelling.
To her let us garlands bring.

WILLIAM SHAKESPEARE (1564–1616), translated by EDUARD VON BAUERNFELD (1802–1890);
published in Vol. 2 of the *Wiener Shakespeare Ausgabe* in 1825

*This is the last of Schubert's three Shakespeare solo settings (1826) and the second of three
Bauernfeld solo settings (1826–7). See both poets' biographies.*

From the Library Shakespeare, *Two Gentlemen of Verona*.

This lyric is from the play *The Two Gentleman of Verona* which is difficult to date. It is taken by many scholars to be an early Shakespeare play, but it was first published in the 1623 Folio, and there is no record of a pre-Restoration performance. It features two lovers (Valentine and Proteus), two ladies (Silvia and Julia) and two servants (the quick-witted Speed and the bumpkin Launce). This shows a debt to the writing of the Bard's predecessor John Lyly, but there is also a strong *commedia dell' arte* influence. The plot concerns the wooing of the lady Silvia, daughter of the duke of Milan, by three suitors: Valentine, the preferred lover; Proteus, his rival; and Thurio, a poltroon. This song is heard in Act IV Scene 2. The true lover Valentine has been banished from Milan, his plans to elope with Silvia betrayed to the duke by Proteus. Thurio has also been duped by Proteus into believing that he has a chance to win Silvia's hand. At Proteus's suggestion, Thurio engages musicians to serenade Silvia in front of her bedroom window; thus this lyric is sung by neither of Silvia's serious suitors, rather by a small men's chorus. Curiosity concerning Silvia's finer qualities is expressed by this motley crew of singers who have been hired for this unusual gig; in this context the lyric has a humorous edge that recalls the artistic efforts of the mechanicals in *A Midsummer Night's Dream*. Capell writes that the piano here is 'idealization of a rustic music'.

Capell also rightly says that 'Schubert has ousted the gentlemen of Verona and made Silvia his own'. It is clear that the composer is enchanted by the lyric. As he composed this piece in the Schober family house at Währing, outside Vienna, his thoughts were with Eduard von Bauernfeld who was on holiday in Upper Austria, the same part of the world where Schubert had spent such a wonderful summer the year before. Bauernfeld's literary skills rekindled the composer's newly awakened operatic hopes; Schubert waited impatiently for the libretto of *Der Graf von Gleichen* to which Bauernfeld was putting the finishing touches. A setting of his newly published translation from the new Viennese edition of Shakespeare's works was no doubt meant as a homecoming present to the composer's future collaborator.

The strummed-lute accompaniment of the right hand in quavers is already familiar from the song *Florio* D857/2. The mood here is utterly different, however. Instead of enraptured melancholy, merry geniality holds sway. The composer has decided to give the tenor 'lead' to a single voice, but he is true to Shakespeare's scenario in that the accompaniment suggests more than one musician. The left-hand figurations are those of a born comedian, a jazz player plucking his double bass, expert in cheeky interjections that add that essential ingredient of 'swing' to a hit. The first syllable of the phrase 'Who is Silvia?' (b. 5) is elongated by the voice in languid rapture; beneath this gallant vocal phrase the bass asks 'Who is Silvia?' in dotted-rhythm diminution, nudging the music forward as if to say, with a winking staccato, 'Go on, tell me, who is she?' From time to time the pianist's left hand is put to more legato use: the words 'Flur preist' are echoed in the soprano register as the left hand crosses the right (b. 11) on a swooning suspension. There is another echo after 'Auf Himmels Gunst und Spur weist', although its most touching appearance is in the second strophe after the words 'Dort heilt er seine Blindheit'. Here, as the balm-like chord of the ninth resolves on a dominant seventh (b. 18, second strophe), the pianist's fingers, left hand crossing over right, seem to apply the very magical remedy that heals Cupid's blindness. The melody itself is a miracle of inevitability; the octave jumps in minims at 'Dass ihr Alles' (bb. 23–4) seem eccentric on paper (and are not the best German word-setting), but they are unarguable. After taking a lot of trouble to make certain that his Scott songs could be made to fit the English originals, Schubert seems to have completely underestimated the potential of this song (and that of *Ständchen* ('Hark, hark! The lark' D889) as far as the English market was concerned. It says something for Bauernfeld's skill that both songs can easily be sung to Shakespeare's original texts, but it seems unlikely that Schubert had access to these in Währing.

The autograph of this song, written in a small book of pocket size with staves ruled by the composer himself, came to light in Hungary as recently as 1969. The legend that the Shakespeare songs were written on menu cards was apocryphal, although a casual observer might have mistaken this small book for something about the size of a menu. Schubert seems to have written the song down as both first draft and finished copy. On looking at the manuscript we can see that the echo effects, as the pianist crosses hands, were added as charming afterthoughts. This is typical of the way that Schubert sometimes amplified the detail in his accompaniments at a relatively late stage of a song's composition. The later dedication of the song by Schubert to his charming and talented Graz hostess, Marie Pachler, must have seemed something deliciously apt but it was an inspired second thought: the gruesome Herder ballad *Eine altschottische Ballade* was removed from the original Op. 106 line-up at a late stage in order to make way for the hymn to Sylvia – so much more appropriate in these circumstances.

Autographs:	Wienbibliothek im Rathaus, Vienna (first draft)
	Hungarian National Museum, Budapest (fair copy)
First edition:	Published as Op. 106 no. 4 by Schober's Lithographisches Institut,
	Vienna in early 1828 (P161)
Dedicatee:	Marie Pachler
Subsequent editions:	Peters: Vol. 2/202; AGA XX 505: Vol. 8/232; NSA IV: Vol. 5/118;
	Bärenreiter: Vol. 4
Bibliography:	Capell 1928, p. 225
	Fischer-Dieskau 1977, p. 233
Further settings:	Gooch-Thatcher 1991 lists 157 settings in Shakespeare's original
	English. Of these best known are:
	Roger Quilter (1877–1953) *Who is Silvia?* (1926)
	Gerald Finzi (1901–1956) *Who is Sylvia?* (1929, rev. 1942)
Discography and timing:	Fischer-Dieskau II 8[14] 2'45
	Hyperion I 26[12]
	Hyperion II 32[11] 2'55 John Mark Ainsley

← *Ständchen* D889   *Hippolits Lied* D890 →

GESANG DER GEISTER ÜBER DEN WASSERN (I)

The song of the spirits over the waters

(GOETHE) **D484** [H307]

(Fragment) G major – A minor   September 1816

In the text printed below, the lines in brackets are those
not set by Schubert in this fragment.

[Des Menschen Seele	[The soul of mankind
Gleicht dem Wasser:	Is like the water:
Vom Himmel kommt es,	From heaven it comes;
Zum Himmel steigt es,	To heaven it rises;
Und wieder nieder	And again
Zur Erde muss es,	To earth it must descend,
Ewig wechselnd.	Eternally fluctuating.
Strömt von der hohen,	When the pure jet
Steilen Felswand	Gushes from the high,
Der reine Strahl,	Steep rock-face,
Dann stäubt er lieblich	It sprays gratefully
In Wolkenwellen	Its misty waves
Zum glatten Fels,	Against the smooth rock,
Und leicht empfangen,	And when lightly gathered
Wallt er verschleiernd,	Surges like a veil,]
Leisrauschend] dann	Softly hissing,
Zur Tiefe nieder.	Down into the depths.
Ragen Klippen	If cliffs loom up
Dem Sturz' entgegen,	In the path of its fall,
Schäumt er unmutig	It foams angrily,
Stufenweise	Step by step,
Zu dem Abgrund.	Into the abyss.
Im flachen Bette	In its level bed
Schleichet er das Wiesental hin,	It meanders through the meadow valley,
Und in dem glatten See	And in the glassy lake
Weiden ihr Antlitz	All the stars
Alle Gestirne.	Delight in their own countenance.
Wind ist der Welle	The wind is the waves'
Lieblicher Buhler;	Sweet lover;

Wind mischt von Grund aus	The wind thoroughly stirs up
Schäumende Wogen.	The foaming billows.
Seele des Menschen,	Soul of mankind,
Wie gleichst du dem Wasser!	How like the water you are!
[Schicksal des Menschen,	[Fate of mankind,
Wie gleichst du dem Wind!]	How like the wind!]

JOHANN WOLFGANG VON GOETHE (1749–1832); poem written 9/10 October 1779

This is the forty-seventh of Schubert's seventy-five Goethe solo settings (1814–26). See the poet's biography for a chronological list of all the Goethe settings.

This is one of Goethe's most celebrated lyrics. Some literary experts have found its philosophical tone facile; Schubert and other composers (Loewe and Reutter among them) have found it irresistibly moving. The poem was written on 9 October 1779 during a holiday in which the poet explored western Switzerland; it commemorates his visit to the Staubbach and the Riesenbach at Lauterbrunnen where some twenty waterfalls plunge down the rock face from a great height, giving the impression of a single shimmering, transparent veil. The poem, originally cast as a dialogue between the spirits of the title, was sent to Charlotte von Stein, the poet's muse in Weimar. She was apparently unmoved ('not entirely my religion'), but countless readers since have been on Goethe's wavelength, and found clear and deep resonances in these noble free-verse rhythms.

Schubert attempted this lyric four times. He completed two settings which both fall outside the scope of this book – an unaccompanied chorus for TTBB (D538, the second setting), and the third setting (D714) for eight male voices accompanied by violas, cellos and double basses. This beautiful piece receives occasional performances despite the fact that it calls for a mixture of forces that is impractical in concert-giving terms. The other two settings are with piano accompaniment; they were left as fragments by the composer, and both have been completed with considerable skill by different people.

Engraving by Moritz von Schwind for the first edition (1858) of the choral and orchestral *Gesang der Geister* D714.

This setting for solo bass was almost certainly complete at some stage, and the opening and closing pages have simply been lost. John Reed postulates that the autograph was broken up during the composition of one of the later versions. This setting poses a problem rare in Schubert studies, for this is a substantial and important fragment that begins in the middle of the poem, and peters out just before the end; only a re-composition of the outer sections can make the surviving rump of the music accessible to a listening public. Reinhard Van Hoorickx's completion ranks as perhaps his most successful major reconstruction of a fragment. He took his inspiration for the opening music from the last four bars of Schubert's surviving music – 'Seele des Menschen / Wie gleichst du dem Was . . .'. Prompted by the direction 'Wie oben' ('As above') Van Hoorickx assumes that 'Seele des Menschen' is a recapitulation of the music that had originally opened the piece. The first seven lines of the poem (bb. 1–26 of the Hoorickx version) is set to a majestic 'Langsam' in A minor. The melody supported by spread chords, reminiscent of the mood of *Meeresstille* D215 and D216, is lifted from the last section of the piece and elaborated.

The second section 'Strömt von der hohen' moves into G major; the time signature is ⅜ with a demisemiquaver accompaniment to depict the clouds of spray. All this is dictated by how the surviving fragment begins, and it is to Van Hoorickx's great credit that there is no discernible bump when Schubert's own music emerges mid-stream at 'dann / Zur Tiefe nieder', twenty-two bars later. Admittedly, when Schubert himself takes over, the accompaniment descends with great daring and effect into the lower regions of the piano to paint these words effectively.

The next section is in E minor and marked 'Geschwind' (b. 12 of the fragment); this begins with four bars of energetic interlude before the words 'Ragen Klippen / Dem Sturz' entgegen'; from b. 16 it contains some of the most extraordinary vocal writing in all Schubert. To comply with the words, the voice plunges and leaps 'step by step into the abyss'. Only a bass could do justice to this. The time signature changes to ⁴⁄₄, and the music storms through a number of sequences (rattling semiquavers in the right hand) with downward leaps, sometimes of a ninth (always doubled in stentorian manner by the pianist's left hand) in the vocal line. On the word 'Abgrund' (b. 20) the voice is asked to touch low E, the same low note that concludes *Grenzen der Menschheit* D716. The piano, as well as the voice, is taken through all its registers (bb. 30–35) and ends on a deep rumble in the bass clef.

When the river moves into flat country, so does the music, in ⁶⁄₈ now and in a serenely flowing C major. Van Hoorickx has noted that the first two bars of the piano writing (bb. 16–17), taken together with the gentle little melody of 'Im flachen Bette / Schleichet er' (bb. 17–19) outline the same melody, albeit transposed, as the three opening choral bars of the Kyrie of the composer's first Mass (in F, D105). Whether this is a conscious quotation or not is open to question, but this is gentle water music in lilting Schubertian manner, perhaps with some inner acknowledgement of the divinity of Nature. A wide range is expected of the singer who is asked to sing a high G at 'Lieblicher Buhler' (b. 52) and a G two octaves lower, at 'Wind mischt von Grund' (b. 56). This demanding change of tessitura renders the piece unperformable by most singers. And thus we find ourselves back in the A minor of the opening for four bars of genuine Schubert that break off just as the music modulates to C major. Van Hoorickx adds eight bars of completion, doubt-lessly less inspired than the composer, but a service to those singers who, despite the setting's challenges, wish to bring a substantial amount of unknown Schubert to the listening public.

Schubert would have been amazed to know that Beethoven was also grappling with this song in 1816. There are seven extant bars in the so-called Scheide sketchbook.

Autograph: Wienbibliothek im Rathaus, Vienna (fragment)
First edition: Published as part of the AGA in 1895 and subsequently completed
                        by Reinhard Van Hoorickx (P716)

Subsequent editions: Not in Peters; AGA XX 594: Vol. 10/106; NSA IV: Vol. 11/210
Bibliography: Hilmar 1993, p. 7
                        Reid 2007, p. 172
Discography and timing: Fischer-Dieskau   —
                        Hyperion I 24²⁶
                        Hyperion II 16⁹   4'44   Michael George

← *Lied ('Ferne von der grossen Stadt') D483*   *Der Wanderer D489* →

GESANG DER GEISTER ÜBER DEN WASSERN (II)

The song of the spirits over the waters

Chorus, TTBB

(GOETHE) **D705** [H459]

(Fragment) C♯ minor   December 1820

(139 bars)

Schubert composed a vocal line for this entire piece (though not the entire poem as set in the first version). Much of the accompaniment is lacking however. The text and interludes underlined in this poem are the passages where Schubert's own piano writing is to be heard. When not underlined, Schubert's original vocal line is accompanied by a piano part composed by Eugene Asti especially for the recording in the Hyperion Edition.

[Introduction]
Des Menschen Seele
Gleicht dem Wasser:

The soul of mankind
Is like the water:

[Interlude] (3 bars)

Von Himmel kommt es,
Zum Himmel steigt es,
Und wieder nieder
Zur Erde muss es,
Ewig wechselnd.

From heaven it comes;
To heaven it rises;
And again
To earth it must descend,
Eternally fluctuating.

[Interlude] (4 bars; right hand only of piano part)

Strömt von der hohen,
Steilen Felswand
Der reine Strahl,
Dann stäubt er lieblich
In Wolkenwellen
Zum glatten Fels,

When the pure jet
Gushes from the high,
Steep rock face,
It sprays gratefully
Its misty waves
Against the smooth rock,

Und leicht empfangen,	And when lightly gathered
Wallt er verschleiernd,	Surges like a veil,
Leisrauschend dann	Softly hissing,
Zur Tiefe nieder.	Down into the depths.

[Interlude] (3 bars; harmonic skeleton only of piano part)

Ragen Klippen	If cliffs loom up
Dem Sturz' entgegen,	In the path of its fall,
Schäumt er unmutig	It foams angrily,
Stufenweise	Step by step,
Zum Abgrund.	Into the abyss.

[Interlude] (5 bars; harmonic skeleton only of piano part)

Im flachen Bette	In its level bed
Schleicht er das Wiesental hin,	It meanders through the meadow valley
Und in dem glatten See	And in the glassy lake
Weiden ihr Antlitz	All the stars
Alle Gestirne.	Delight in their own countenance.

Schubert's vocal line finishes here and Asti adds a postlude of eight bars.
For the rest of the original poem see the previous setting above.

JOHANN WOLFGANG VON GOETHE (1749–1832); poem written 9/10 October 1779

This remarkable setting has long stood as a tantalizingly incomplete fragment in the supplement of the old *Gesamtausgabe*. The state in which Schubert left the manuscript provides a fascinating glimpse at his way of working. Although most of the autograph is sketchy in every sense, Schubert lays down the basis of his thoughts with great precision. He starts with being very exact about the piano part, a marvellous inspiration of semiquavers in each hand, two octaves apart and in unison, and he takes the trouble to write out the first section to establish that this type of figuration is to be the template for the whole piece. The key is C sharp minor; the accompaniment flows evenly and mysteriously for four bars (it is clear that this is no mere miller boy's stream, but rather the broad River of Life) until two portentous minim chords set up the entry of the men's voices. Here we have a mood of the greatest contemplative tranquillity. The piano's semiquavers betoken the movement of water, but the singers who murmur their vocal line of pianissimo minims and semibreves over this undulating texture speak for the dignity and nobility of the soul. The modulation into C sharp major at 'Gleicht dem Wasser' (b. 12) seems to affirm, with quiet inward rejoicing, the immortality assured by these words. The interlude which now gently leads us upwards from the depths to the headier regions of 'Von Himmel kommt es' (bb. 13–15) is the composer's own.

It was here (at the beginning of b. 16 and the words 'Von Himmel kommt es') that Schubert abandoned the piano staves, and Eugene Asti took over responsibility for the accompaniment in the version recorded for Hyperion. He did so with great imagination, yet with the tact of the true Schubertian who prefers simplicity to the overambitious pastiche that invariably strikes a false note. Schubert left us the choral parts intact (although it is not always clear what he intended in terms of word underlay) so there is at least a skeleton of the work's basic harmony. Nevertheless it took someone with Asti's skill as both accompanist and composer to devise a piano part that is convincing in reflecting the varying moods of water (as dictated by the words), but which also follows Schubert's hastily erected signposts concerning pianistic layout. Asti is not afraid to move high in the piano register when light, glistening textures are required, nor to abandon semiquavers altogether when the strength of 'Ragen Klippen / Dem Sturz' entgegen' calls for a Beethovenian Fifth Symphony motif (three upbeat quavers and hammered first beat of the bar), dramatic runs and stirring chords of longer note value. The bass line of the accompaniment does not slavishly follow the choral bass line (which would have been a temptingly safe option) but achieves a convincing, and at times delightful, independence. Among the numerous felicitous details there is a particularly effective bass trill before the last 'Schäumt er unmutig' (b. 99) which reminds us how Schubert used this device in the first movement of the B flat major Piano Sonata, D960.

Extremely lovely is Schubert's move to a contemplative D flat major at the end of this setting ('Im flachen Bette schleicht er' at b. 109). Here Asti follows Schubert's hints for a pedal D flat in the piano's left hand; the dactylic rhythm that gradually emerges in the accompaniment to this section, and which is the governing feature of the postlude, imparts an appropriate radiance (cf. *Die Sterne* D939) to the image of the stars mirrored in the surface of the lake. The composer's vocal line ends here despite the fact that there are two verses of Goethe's poetry left. Asti decided not to attempt a completely new composition of these final eight lines. He nevertheless made a Schubertian masterpiece accessible to choral singers. Because the voice part left to us is fully sketched, together with crucial clues concerning the harmonic direction of the interludes, this setting of *Gesang der Geister über den Wassern* may be more confidently performed as a piece of genuine Schubert than most other completions of a major vocal fragment.

Autograph:	Memorial Library of Music, Stanford, CA (fragment)
First edition:	Published as part of the AGA in 1897 and subsequently completed by Eugene Asti (b. 1962) in 1994 (unpublished) (P730)
Subsequent editions:	AGA XXI: Supplement, p. 313; NSA III: Vol. 3
Further settings:	Carl Loewe (1796–1869) *Gesang der Geister über den Wassern* for SATB and piano Op. 88 (*c.* 1840)
	Hermann Reutter (1900–1985) *Chorphantasie* for soloists, chorus and orchestra (1939)
Discography and timing:	Hyperion I 24²⁷ 7'50 The London Schubert Chorale
	Hyperion II 23¹⁷ (dir. Stephen Layton)

← *Der zürnenden Diana* D707   *Der 23. Psalm* D706 →

GESANG DER NORNA   Norna's song
(Scott trans. Spiker) Op. 85 no. 2, **D831** [H558]
F minor   Early 1825

A literal translation of Spiker's translation is given here.
Scott's original poem is printed below in italics.

Mich führt mein Weg wohl meilenlang	My course leads me for many a mile
Durch Golf und Strom und Wassergrab.	Through gulf and stream and moat;
Die Welle kennt den Runensang	The waves know the Runic lay
Und glättet sich zum Spiegel ab.	And grow mirror-smooth.
Die Welle kennt den Runensang,	The waves know the Runic lay,
Der Golf wird glatt, der Strom wird still;	The gulf grows smooth, the stream is still;
Doch Menschenherz, im wilden Drang,	But the heart of man, in its wild impulse,
Es weiss nicht, was es selber will.	Does not know its own desires.
Nur eine Stund' ist mir vergönnt,	I am granted only one hour in the year
In Jahresfrist, zum Klageton,	To sing of my woes;
Sie schlägt, wenn diese Lampe brennt—	It strikes when this lamp burns –
Ihr Schein erlischt—sie ist entflohn.	When its gleam dies the hour has fled!
Heil, Magnus Töchter, fort und fort!	Hail, daughters of Magnus, forever hail!
Die Lampe brennt in tiefer Ruh';	The lamp burns in deep peace;
Euch gönn' ich dieser Stunde Wort,	To you, at this hour, I tell my tale.
Erwacht, erhebt Euch, hört mir zu!	Awake, arise, hear me!

For leagues along the watery way
Through gulf and stream my course has been;
The billows know my Runic lay,
And smooth their crests to silent green.

The billows know my Runic lay –
The gulf grows smooth, the stream is still;
The human hearts, more wild than they,
Know but the rule of wayward will.

One hour is mine, in all the year,
To tell my woes – and one alone;
When gleams this magic lamp, 'tis here –
When dies the mystic light, 'tis gone.

Daughters of northern Magnus, hail!
The lamp is lit, the flame is clear –
To you I come to tell my tale,
Awake, arise, my tale to hear!

SIR WALTER SCOTT (1771–1832), translated by SAMUEL HEINRICH SPIKER (1786–1858);
poem written in 1821

This is the second of Schubert's eight Scott solo settings (1825–6) and the only setting of a Spiker translation. See Scott's biography for a chronological list of all the Scott settings, and Spiker's biography for further information about the translator.

Walter Scott wrote *The Pirate* in 1821. Set in Shetland (Zetland) and the Orkneys, it is one of the author's most successful and imaginative novels. No less a critic than William Hazlitt waxed lyrical about its qualities. When Scott is gone, he exclaims, 'Ah! who will call the mist from the hill? Who will make the circling eddies roar? . . . Who will summon the spirits of the northern air from their chill abodes, or make gleaming lake or hidden cavern teem with wizard or with elfin forms? There is no one but the Scottish Prospero, but old Sir Walter, can do the trick aright.'

The story is set around 1700. The hero is Clement Cleveland, a buccaneer who is shipwrecked on the Shetland coast. He is rescued and brought ashore, but his exotic presence wreaks havoc on the tightly knit community to which chance has brought him. Ulla Troil, or Norna of the Fitful-head as she is known because of the towering sea-cliff where she dwells as a recluse, believes she possesses supernatural powers. She meddles in the lives of the superstitious islanders with her bogus spells and prophecies; this leads to fateful results for both Norna and her son, whom she eventually discovers to be Cleveland himself.

The song occurs in Chapter XIX of the novel. Brenda and Minna, daughters of Magnus Troil, both have nightmares in which they hear 'some wild runic rhyme, resembling those sung by the heathen priests of old, when the victim (too often human) was bound to the fatal altar of Odin or of Thor'. They awake to find Norna sitting in their room and singing 'in a slow, sad, and almost unearthly accent'. She has come in the middle of the night to recount a complex narrative of woes. These portentous comings and goings somehow remained convincing to Scott's readers in his own epoch; today they would be the stuff (and nonsense) of high comedy.

Schubert endows Norna with more than a hint of hocus pocus, but he allows this character to be taken seriously by her gullible captive audience. The song is set in the mezzo or contralto range, taking its cue from Brenda's dreams of 'deep tones and wild and melancholy notes'. As befits an incantation, the music is strophic (except for a new departure in the vocal line at 'Ihr Schein erlischt', bb. 51–3). The § rhythm sways from side to side; this chimes with Scott's description of Norna 'who moved her body slowly to and fro over the pale lamp, as she sung'.

The bottom-heavy accompaniment opaquely hugs the vocal line and suggests darkness, and the smoke of the flickering lamp by which Norna sings. In gait and mood *Gesang der Norna* is reminiscent of the closing passages of two melodramatic ballads from much earlier in the composer's career. In the last two verses of Matthisson's *Romanze* D114 the ghost of Rosalia von Montanvert haunts 'the ruins of the tower by the sea' in a loping § rhythm. In *Die Nonne* D208 (Hölty) there is even more of a similarity, and in the same key of F minor: a mysterious tune, marked 'Mässig mit Grauen' (very much in the alto register, and doubled by the piano), describes the ghost of the nun who, having killed her unfaithful lover, each night emerges to stamp on his heart torn from his body, her eyes glowing red beneath the white of her veil. This was the kind of scenario very familiar to Scott from his readings of early German

NORNA'S TALE, *page* 440

Norna's Tale, the title page of the 1891 edition of Scott's *The Pirate*.

Romantic writers. In *Gesang der Norna* Scott transplants this kind of scenario to a Scottish milieu; it is triumphantly re-exported to German lands in Spiker's translation (published in Berlin; the song is in Chapter VI of the second book).

The song was apparently sung by the actress Sophie Müller, a friend of Schubert and Vogl. She records in her diary of March 1825 that she was visited by the pair who brought 'new songs from *The Pirate*'. As Schubert set only this one song from that novel this firmly places its composition in early 1825.

Autograph:	Missing or lost
First edition:	Published as Op. 85 no. 2 by Diabelli, Vienna in March 1828 (P154)
Subsequent editions:	Peters: Vol. 4/66; AGA XX 542: Vol. 9/82; NSA IV: Vol. 4/66; Bärenreiter: Vol. 3/42
Discography and timing:	Fischer-Dieskau —
	Hyperion I 13¹⁰
	Hyperion II 29¹³ 3'48 Marie MacLaughlin

← *Lied der Anne Lyle* D830   *Des Sängers Habe* D832 →

GESANG DES HARFNERS D478/2A and 2B *see* WER NIE SEIN BROT MIT TRÄNEN ASS

'GESANG IN c' *see* LEBENSTRAUM D1A

Die GESELLIGKEIT	Zest for life	Quartet, SATB
(Lebenslust)	(Conviviality)	
(UNGER) **D609** [H395]		
D major January 1818		

(38 bars)

Wer Lebenslust fühlet,	He who feels zest for life
Der bleibt nicht allein,	Will never be alone.
Allein sein ist öde	Being alone is tedious,
Wer kann sich da freun?	And who can enjoy that?
Im traulichen Kreise,	To live together
Beim herzlichen Kuss,	In an intimate circle

Beisammen zu leben,	Amid fond kisses
Ist Seelengenuss!	Is the soul's delight.
Das lehrt uns der Tauber	The turtle-dove teaches us:
Für Liebe und Lust,	For love and pleasure
Erhebt sich dem Täubchen	He raises his silken breast
Die seidene Brust,	To his mate,
Es girret für Wonne,	Who coos with happiness.
Es lehret im Kuss:	Her kiss teaches us
Beisammen zu leben	That to live together
Sei Herzensgenuss.	Is the heart's delight.
[. . .]	[. . .]
Dem folget, ihr Guten,	Follow her, good friends,
Und singet nicht mehr:	And no longer sing
Die Einsamkeit wäre	That solitude is not
Nicht öde, nicht leer;	Tedious and empty.
Allein sein erzeuget	Being alone creates
Nur Sehnsucht und Schmerz,	Only longing and pain.
Beisammen zu leben	To live together
Befriedigt das Herz.	Assuages the heart.

Johann Karl Unger (1771–1836)

Johann Karl Unger, professor at the Theresianum in Wiener-Neustadt (a type of finishing school for young men of noble birth) had been a signatory to Schubert's unsuccessful application for a post in Laibach (now Ljubliana in Slovenia) in 1816. In 1817 Schubert met the great singer Vogl who quickly became an advocate for Schubert's songs; Vogl was later to be the teacher of Unger's daughter Karoline (1803–1877) who became a famous singer (and also a composer, writing under her married name of Sabatier). Vogl may have encouraged Unger to renew contact with Schubert. Early in 1818, at a time when money was a continuing problem for the composer, Unger pulled strings with his former pupil Count Esterházy and put the composer's name forward as a suitable music teacher for the count's two young daughters. Thus came about the first (and longer) of the two summer sojourns when Schubert took up residence at Zseliz, the Landschloss – more mansion than castle – which was the count's Hungarian summer residence.

Unger was a many-sided man who fancied himself as a poet (his *Gedichte* were issued in 1797); he was also a contributor to almanacs in one of which a version of this poem appeared in 1804. (This fact was only discovered by Dietrich Berke as recently as 1969.) Until that time the quartet was known by its old title of *Lebenslust* (as it was published in the AGA) and the poet was unknown. The editorial commentary of the NSA mentions the puzzling differences between the text as printed in the almanac, and the composer's manuscript. The editors even conjecture that Schubert set the quartet from an anonymous source. In 1818 Schubert's friend Anselm Hüttenbrenner also set an Unger poem as a vocal quartet – *Der Abend*.

The answer to this puzzle lies in a slim volume of manuscripts in my possession (fifty-six pages) entitled *Carl Ungers Lieder, Nachgeahmt oder von ihm selbst gedichtet und in Musick* [sic] *gesetzt*. The book is not dated but it contains numerous simple solo song settings, many apparently by Unger, others where his words are made to fit arrangements of music by Paer, Haydn and Pleyel. In almost all cases, however, the poems are by Unger. The music for *Die Geselligkeit*, for example, is marked 'by an unknown' (a simple F major song in ¾ without very great merit), but the verses are identical to the text in Schubert's manuscript. It seems likely that this volume was assembled much earlier than 1818 (one of the pieces refers to the *Befreiungskrieg* of 1813) and that it was used as Schubert's source for *Die Geselligkeit*, as well as *Die Nachtigall* D724, and by Hüttenbrenner for his *Der Abend*.

As for the music itself, there are touches of Schubertian subtlety here and there; but it was made to appeal to a jollier, less complicated, common denominator than much of the composer's work for SATB (compare the magisterial *Gebet* D815 from 1824). The introduction is obviously authentic because it sounds so much better than the leaden musical tags that Diabelli was wont to place in front of original Schubert songs that he published in the *Nachlass*. The tricky little semiquaver flourish before the entry of the voices (b. 3) encapsulates the mood of merry high spirits that are at the heart of this poem. This is one of the composer's *Ländler*-like waltzes in ⅜, and it is kept deliberately simple. There is a telling change from D major to an ominous D minor to paint the repeat of the word 'öde' (b. 12); at this point the cosy and rollicking accompanying semiquavers change to quavers, an octave apart between the hands, that rise and fall within a two-octave range like an icy wind on a forsaken plain. At 'Im traulichen Kreise, Beim herzlichen Kuss' (from b. 18) canonic technique is employed between the voices; the composer obviously felt that this was a good way to give the important first tenor (whose music is almost always more demanding than the other three singers) a short moment to be heard on his own. The third time we hear 'Ist Seelengenuss' it is accompanied by a gleeful ascending scale culminating in a contrary-motion A major arpeggio decorated by acciaccature (bb. 26–8).

In the performance for Hyperion, three of the four verses of the poem were recorded. They are all published in the NSA.

Autograph:	Conservatoire collection, Bibliothèque Nationale, Paris (headed *Quartetto 1818*)
First edition:	Published as No. 7 of *Neueste Folge nachgelassener, mehrstimmiger Gesänge mit und ohne Begleitung von Franz Schubert* by J. P. Gotthard, Vienna in 1872 (P516)
Subsequent editions:	AGA XVII 13: p. 225; NSA III: Vol. 2a/64

Discography and timing:	Fischer-Dieskau	—	
	Deutsche Grammophon		Elly Ameling, Janet Baker, Peter
	Schubert-Quartette	1'18	Schreier & Dietrich Fischer-Dieskau
	Hyperion I 34[9]		Patricia Rozario, Catherine
	Hyperion II 20[4]	3'46	Denley, Ian Bostridge & Michael George

⟵ *Das Dörfchen* D598   *Auf der Riesenkoppe* D611 ⟶

Die GESTIRNE

(Klopstock) **D444** [H272]

F major   June 1816

The constellations

(37 bars)

Es tönet sein Lob Feld und Wald,
　Tal und Gebirg,
Das Gestad' hallet, es donnert das Meer
　dumpf brausend
Des Unendlichen Lob, siehe des Herrlichen,
Unerreichten von dem Danklied der Natur!

Es singt die Natur dennoch Dem, welcher
　sie schuf,
Ihr Getön schallet vom Himmel herab,
　lautpreisend
In umwölkender Nacht rufet des Strahls
　Gefährt
Von den Wipfeln, und der Berg' Haupt
　es herab!

[. . . 7 . . .]

Wer gab Melodie, Leier, dir? zog das Getön

Und das Gold himmlischer Saiten dir auf?
　Du schallest
Zu dem kreisenden Tanz, welchen, beseelt
　von dir,
Der Planet hält in der Laufbahn um dich her.

[. . . 3 . . .]

Ich preise den Herrn! preise den, welcher
　des Monds
Und des Tods kühlender, heiliger Nacht,
　zu dämmern,
Und zu leuchten! gebot. Erde, du Grab,
　das stets
Auf uns harrt, Gott hat mit Blumen
　dich bestreut!

[. . .]

Field and forest, valley and mountain
　sound his praise;
The shore resounds, the sea thunders with a dull
　roar
The praise of the Infinite Being, the Glorious One
With whom nature's song of thanksgiving cannot
　compare!

Yet nature sings to him who created her;

Her song resounds down from heaven; in the
　cloud-veiled
Night light's companion loudly echoes his praises

From the treetops and the mountain peaks.

[. . . 7 . . .]

Lyre, who gave you melody? Did the golden
　music
Of heavenly strings just come to you? You play

For the whirling dance that, inspired by you,

The planet holds on its course all around you.

[. . . 3 . . .]

I praise the Lord! I praise him who bade
　glimmer
And gleam the sacred, cooling night of the moon

And of death. Earth, you are a grave that forever

Awaits us; God has strewn you with flowers!

[. . .]

FRIEDRICH GOTTLOB KLOPSTOCK (1724–1803); poem written in early 1764

This is the twelfth of Schubert's thirteen Klopstock solo settings (1815–16). See the poet's biography for a chronological list of all the Klopstock settings.

The most glorious and extravagant of the Klopstock settings was *Dem Unendlichen* D291 and here the composer, less than a year later, tackles another work from the same poet and seems content to give it a rather more modest musical garb. The poem has all the textual ingredients necessary for a blockbuster – roaring seas, resounding thanksgiving, whirling dance and spinning planets. This is intoxicating stuff, and *Dem Unendlichen* from 1815 is Schubert's enthusiastic response to this side of Klopstock. In 1816, however, the boldness and sheer exuberance of the previous year yielded to something different: the music is stirring in its own way, but it is more intimate and displays greater economy of means. As the achievements of 1815 are consolidated, there seems to be a conscious and successful attempt to find the concision and lucidity apparent in the (admittedly less ambitious) lieder of the North German masters.

At a different time the poem's opening might have been cast as a stirring recitative. Instead Schubert, intent on conquering the strophic form, launches into a melody that makes the greatest possible effect using the simplest possible means. Even the two-bar preamble, heard only once, is expressive. Pulsating right-hand triplets combine with a purposeful and strongly etched bass line. The oscillation between the tonic and the German sixth was to become hackneyed in music of portentous mood, but this is an early use of the device and it is fresh and original. Trumpet-like, the voice climbs an F major arpeggio on 'Es tönet sein Lob' (bb. 2–3), a dotted quaver plus semiquaver on the second beat emphasizing the determination with which the narrator is intent on praising God. This dotted figure for the voice is echoed in the accompaniment on the fourth beat of the bass line, a quasi-canonic imitation that adds just a hint of *pomposo* grandeur to the proceedings. The strength of the part-writing is a feature of the Schubert songs of this period: the vocal line meshes splendidly with the pianist's left hand which is energized here and there with rumbling trills and resonant octaves. The music passes restlessly through various tonalities (F minor, D flat major, A flat major) and it is interesting to see how cunningly Schubert handles Klopstock's rolling hexameters – he allows himself varying amounts of musical time to encompass the prosody of each of these. As the strophe moves to its central point he constructs a vast musical arc that covers nearly three lines of poetry; this begins on F major (at 'es donnert das Meer' bb. 7–8) and only returns there, in root position, at the very end of the verse ('Danklied der Natur!' bb. 14–15). In between we seem lost in space, one harmonic constellation opening after another before our ears. We reach the home straight with a sense of breathless relief. For Schubert to have arrived in F major any sooner, however, would have earthed this music in mid-flight. This song packs an unexpected punch; its modest musical means are somehow sufficient to match the grandeur of *Dem Unendlichen* without resorting to the pomp and ceremony of that work. It is not the only strophic song from 1816 to look ordinary on paper and to touch sublimity in performance.

Schubert only wrote out one verse of the song with repeat marks. The NSA accordingly prints only one verse. The AGA prints the poem's fifteen verses, and for the *Nachlass* Diabelli (eventually followed by the Peters Edition) selects five of these (1, 3, 6, 10, 14) and prints the music as if the song were *durchkomponiert*. In the performance for the Hyperion Edition four verses were selected from the *Gesamtausgabe* (1, 2, 10, 14 – translated above) and some tiny adjustments made to the prosody of the vocal line to make the music fit the words. Schubert admittedly left this aspect of the song incomplete; he would have had to address this issue had the song been published in his lifetime. *Die Gestirne* is chiefly remarkable as an early study for the stentorian *Die Allmacht* D852 of 1825; it seems to be the missing musical link between that song and *Dem*

Unendlichen and it achieved great popularity, no doubt partly on account of Liszt's imposing transcription for solo piano.

   Maurice Brown tells us that *Die Gestirne* was highly valued by the great French tenor Adolphe Nourrit, someone whose singing was especially important for the broadening of the composer's reputation in France (and thus for the development of the French *mélodie*). When Nourrit was buried in Marseilles on 8 March 1839, this song was played on the organ of that town's cathedral by his friend Frédéric Chopin.

Autograph:	Staatsbibliothek Preussischer Kulturbesitz, Berlin
First edition:	Published as Book 10 no. 2 of the *Nachlass* by Diabelli, Vienna in April 1831 (P263)
Subsequent editions:	Peters: Vol. 5/35; AGA XX 229: Vol. 4/114; NSA IV: Vol. 10/170
Arrangement:	Arr. Franz Liszt (1811–1886) for solo piano, no. 3 of *Franz Schuberts geistliche Lieder* (1840) [*see* TRANSCRIPTIONS]
Discography and timing:	Fischer-Dieskau I 7[18] 0'51 (first strophe only)
	Hyperion I 31[7]
	Hyperion II 14[27] 2'48 Christine Schäfer

← *Schlachtgesang* D443   *Edone* D445 →

Das GESTÖRTE GLÜCK
(KÖRNER) **D309** [H189]
F major   15 October 1815

Thwarted bliss

(19 bars)

Ich hab' ein heisses junges Blut,	I'm young and hot-blooded,
Wie ihr wohl alle wisst,	As you all know,
Ich bin dem Küssen gar zu gut,	And very fond of kissing,
Und hab' noch nie geküsst;	Yet I've never kissed;
Denn ist mir auch mein Liebchen hold,	For although my maiden cares for me
'S war doch, als wenn's nicht werden sollt':	It seems as though it will not happen:
Trotz aller Müh und aller List,	In spite of all my efforts, all my cunning,
Hab ich doch niemals noch geküsst.	I have never kissed her.
Des Nachbars Röschen ist mir gut:	Rosie, our neighbour's daughter, is fond of me
Sie ging zur Wiese früh,	One morning she went to the fields,
Ich lief ihr nach und fasste Mut,	I ran after her, took courage
Und schlang den Arm um sie:	And put my arm around her;
Da stach ich an dem Miederband	But then I pricked my hand

Mir eine Nadel in die Hand;	On a pin in her bodice.
Das Blut lief stark, ich sprang nach Haus,	The blood gushed out, I rushed home,
Und mit dem Küssen war es aus.	And that was the end of kissing.
Jüngst ging ich so zum Zeitvertreib,	The other day I was strolling to pass the time,
Und traf sie dort am Fluss,	And met her by the river;
Ich schlang den Arm um ihren Leib,	I slipped my arm around her
Und bat um einen Kuss;	And begged for a kiss;
Sie spitzte schon den Rosenmund,	She quickly puckered her rosy lips,
Da kam der alte Kettenhund,	But along came her old watchdog
Und biss mich wütend in das Bein!	And bit me angrily on the leg!
Da liess ich wohl das Küssen sein.	So I let kissing alone.
[. . . 2 . . .]	[. . . 2 . . .]
Und allemal geht mir's nun so;	Every time it's the same;
O! dass ich's leiden muss!	How I suffer!
Mein Lebtag werd' ich nimmer froh,	I shall never in my life be happy
Krieg' ich nicht bald 'nen Kuss.	If I don't get a kiss soon.
Das Glück sieht mich so finster an,	Fate is so unkind to me.
Was hab' ich armer Wicht getan?	What have I, poor wretch, done?
Drum, wer es hört, erbarme sich,	So whoever hears this, take pity on me;
Und sei so gut und küsse mich.	Be kind and kiss me.

THEODOR KÖRNER (1791–1813)

This is the thirteenth of Schubert's sixteen Körner solo settings (1815–18). See the poet's biography for a chronological list of all the Körner settings.

This is an eighteenth-century vignette, and very much a ditty for a rueful Papageno. The melodic line is not always comfortably written (a high A for the unimportant word 'und', b. 6), but the falling musical sequences are charming (bb. 8–10) and the little flourishes in the accompaniment delightful (a fleet arpeggio in b. 8, and saucy triplets from b. 10). The protagonist is a rogue, but not a serious villain – he is in love with love in a Cherubino-like way, something that may be indulged in the young and ardent, especially in the light of his continuing gaucherie. As Walther Dürr points out, this youthful clumsiness is wonderfully conveyed in a rhythm which resembles a ⅜ *Ländler* with mid-bar accentuations rather more than the written ⅚. This is the type of song where Schubert, like Shakespeare, chooses rustics for his clowns. It is hardly surprising that the song is simple – on this single day in October 1815 the composer set seven others to texts by five poets. There are six verses of *Das gestörte Glück* of which four were selected for the Hyperion recording (1, 2, 3 and 6 of Körner's lyric). The narrator's adventures with an angry father and a broken ladder (not included here) compound the lad's misery; there is certainly a danger in music of this simplicity that the listener's patience can be tried by too many verses. Although this song was composed on 15 October 1815 (alongside seven others, written down in a single book) it was written on a separate piece of paper; thus it does not belong to the *Selam* cycle (qv) of seven songs posited by Walther Dürr (NSA Vol. 9 p. XVI).

Autograph:	In private possession in Austria (first draft)
First edition:	Published as No. 8 of *Neueste Folge nachgelassener Lieder und Gesänge* by J. P. Gotthard, Vienna in 1872 (P434)

Subsequent editions:	Not in Peters; AGA XX 157: Vol. 3/124; NSA IV: Vol. 9/146
Bibliography:	Youens 1996, pp. 138–40
Discography and timing:	Fischer-Dieskau I 5^{33} 1'51 (Strophes 1, 2 & 4 only)
	Hyperion I 4^8
	Hyperion II 10^{25} 2'20 Philip Langridge

← Die Macht der Liebe D308   *Nur wer die Sehnsucht kennt* D310 →

GLAUBE, HOFFNUNG UND LIEBE	Faith, hope	Male quartet,
(REIL) **D954** [NOT IN HYPERION]	and love	chorus, SATB
B♭ major Before 2 September 1828		& piano

Gott, lass die Glocke glücklich steigen,	Lord, may the bell safely rise up,
Die Töne schallen in der Luft,	May its peals ring brightly in the air
Dass hell sie von der Andacht zeugen,	That they bear witness to the devotion
Zu der uns unser Glaube ruft.	To which our faith calls us.
An Dich, o Schöpfer, glauben wir,	Creator, we believe in You,
Die Glockentöne hallen dir!	The bells peal out for You!
Von dir tönt alles Heil hernieder.	All our salvation descends resoundingly from You,
O nimm zu deinem Lob und Ruhm	Accept the sound of our thanks,
Auch unsers Dankes Töne wieder	Praising and glorifying You
Aus deines Hauses Heiligtum!	From the sanctuary of Your house!
Auf deine Gnade hoffen wir,	We hope for Your mercy,
Die Feiertöne jubeln dir.	The festive sounds celebrate Your glory.
O Gottes Friede nur frohlocke,	May God's peace and our love alone
Nur Liebe uns von diesem Turm!	Ring out joyously from this tower.
Und nie bewege sich die Glocke	And may the bell's chimes never be rung
Zum Unglück, Jammer, Brand und Sturm!	To mark misfortune, misery, fire and storm!
Zur Liebe, Liebe läutet sie!	May they ring for love alone,
Aus Liebe nur klingt Harmonie.	Harmony can only sound from love.

FRIEDRICH REIL (1773–1843)

This is a curious (and unique) case: two adjacent items in the Deutsch catalogue, D954 and D955, with the same title of *Glaube, Hoffnung und Liebe*, were written for different forces, and composed with different texts. The subject matter of both works was inspired by the phrase from St Paul's epistle to the Corinthians (1:13); this chapter of the Bible is also the source for *Wenn ich mit Menschen*, the last of Brahms's *Vier ernste Gesänge* Op. 121.

The first song, D954, in its original piano-accompanied version is for male quartet (TTBB) with a few bars at the end of each strophe where the SATB chorus joins in. The orchestrated version is for small wind band – oboes, clarinets, bassoons, horns and trombones. This has a male four-part chorus with the addition of sopranos and altos at the end of each verse. The piece was composed for the consecration of the new bell at the Church of the Holy Trinity (the Dreifaltigkeitskirche) in the Alsergrund in Vienna on 2 September 1828. It was there that Beethoven's body was taken in procession on the day of his funeral in March 1827; Schubert was one of the torch-bearers. It was also for the so-called 'Alserkirche' that the Mass in E flat major D950 was conceived; the composer was well known there through the 'Regens chori', Michael Leitermayer, who was a fellow pupil of Schubert's first teacher Michael Holzer, and a friend of Ferdinand Schubert.

The biggest of the bells had cracked twenty-three years previously, and was replaced as a result of public subscription. There was a great deal of interest in the inauguration of the new bell. John Reed refers to D954 as written in Schubert's 'best Haydn manner'. The combination of horns and bassoons with the male voices is particularly effective; the $\frac{6}{8}$ *Bewegung* depicts the bell swinging from side to side. The word *hell* (bright) announces the addition of oboes to the accompanying texture as clarinets paint a bright metallic ping on off-beat accents. The poem, in three strophes, is by Friedrich Reil (who wrote the text for *Das Lied im Grünen* D917). It is likely that Schubert prepared the piano part as a kind of rehearsal score for the orchestral version. This was published a few months after the composer's death to raise money for the church. It was possible to buy the wind parts along with the piano accompaniment if desired.

Autograph:	Österreichische Nationalbibliothek, Vienna
First edition:	Published by Tranquillo Mollo, Vienna in December 1828 (P515)
First known performance:	2 September 1828 at the consecration of the new bell at the Dreifaltigkeitskirche, Vienna. Performers unknown
Performance reviews:	*Wiener allgemeine Theaterzeitung* No. 117 (27 September 1828), p. 468f. [Waidelich/Hilmar Dokumente I No. 638; Deutsch Doc. Biog. No. 1144]
Subsequent editions:	AGA XVII 5: p. 152 (orchestral & piano version printed together); NSA III: Vol. 2b/264 (piano version) & Vol. 1 (orchestral version)
Bibliography:	Black 2003, pp. 182–3
Discography and timing:	Hyperion I
	Hyperion II

GLAUBE, HOFFNUNG UND LIEBE   Faith, hope and love

(KUFFNER) OP. 97, **D955** [H669]

E♭ major   August 1828

The following versification is how Kuffner's poem appears in Selam (1813); it is subdivided in a different way in Lieder für Blinde und von Blinden (1827). The NSA contends, not altogether convincingly, that the poem has long suffered from being transcribed from musical sources and that it should be versified in five four-line strophes with a final verse in six lines.

Glaube, hoffe, liebe!	Have faith, hope and love.
Hältst du treu an diesen Dreien,	If you hold constantly to these three
Wirst du nie dich selbst entzweien,	You will never be divided within yourself,
Wird dein Himmel nimmer trübe.	And your skies will never be darkened.
Glaube fest an Gott und Herz!	Have steadfast faith in God and in your heart.
Glaube schwebet himmelwärts.	Faith soars heavenwards.
Mehr noch als im Sternrevier,	The Lord dwells within your breast
Lebt der Gott im Busen dir.	Still more than among the stars.
Wenn auch Welt und Menschen lügen,	Though this world and mankind may lie,
Kann das Herz doch nimmer trügen.	The heart can never deceive.
Hoffe dir Unsterblichkeit,	Hope for immortality,
Und hienieden bessre Zeit!	And for better days here on earth.
Hoffnung ist ein schönes Licht	Hope is a fair light
Und erhellt den Weg der Pflicht.	Illuminating the path of duty.
Hoffe, aber fordre nimmer!	Hope, but never make demands.
Tag wird mählig, was erst Schimmer.	Gradually the first glimmer becomes daylight.
Edel liebe, fest und rein!	May your love be noble, strong and pure.
Ohne Liebe bist du Stein.	Without love you are as stone.
Liebe läut're dein Gefühl,	Let love purify your feelings;
Liebe leite dich an's Ziel!	Let love lead you to your goal.
Soll das Leben glücklich blühen,	If life is to flower in happiness
Muss der Liebe Sonne glühen.	The sun of love must glow warmly.
Willst du nie dich selbst entzweien,	If you would never be divided within yourself,
Halte treu an diesen Dreien!	Hold constantly to these three.
Dass nichts deinen Himmel trübe:	Lest anything should darken your skies,
Glaube, hoffe, liebe.	Have faith, hope and love.

CHRISTOPH KUFFNER (1780–1846)

This is Schubert's only setting of a Kuffner text. See the poet's biography.

It is a mystery why Schubert should have written a very different piano-accompanied song (D955), this time to a text of Christoph Kuffner, with exactly the same title as the Reil choral setting discussed above. The manuscript is dated August 1828 (as is the *Schwanengesang* D957), so the song could easily have been composed before the instrumental work that shares its title (this despite the later Deutsch number). The fact that the song was published so quickly after its composition suggests, as John Reed puts it, 'some topical interest'.

The text was printed in Kuffner's works in 1817, but it is likely that the composer had known it for some years as it was published in Castelli's almanac *Selam* in 1813 – the source of other Schubert settings. The poem was also to be found in the anthology, *Lieder für Blinde und von Blinden* (Wien, 1827). This poetry collection was the brainchild of the pedagogue Johann Wilhelm Klein (1765–1848) who had established a remarkable institute in Vienna (opened in 1825) for the teaching of blind people – a concept that was emulated in various other German cities. The anthology by blind people, for blind people, about blind people – including a poem in honour of those afflicted poets Homer, Ossian and Milton, as well as an alternative translation of Colley Cibber's *The blind boy* by Mailáth (qv) – was clearly meant to be linked to a musical supplement of some kind that was probably never published. Of the seventy poems printed, fifty are linked with composers' names. Most constantly recurring of these is Simon Sechter, later to be Schubert's instructor in counterpoint; other composers include Conradin Kreutzer, Schubert's friends Franz Lachner and Benedict Randhartinger, as well as Schubert himself: he is assigned *An Gott* D863 (qv), the poem by 'Hohlfeld' *recte* Holfeldt, a work that is lost, if indeed it was ever written (*see* DUBIOUS, MISATTRIBUTED AND LOST SONGS). The Kuffner poem here under discussion (printed on pp. 50–51 of the anthology) is headed with the phrase 'Musik von Abbé Stadler'. Schubert had known and admired Maximilian Stadler (1748–1833) (*see* COMPOSERS) from his earliest years and made an arrangement of his *Der 8 Psalm*; Stadler, a well-known composer and musicologist, wrote a fugue in Schubert's memory.

It is possible that for the consecration of their new bell in 1828 the organizers of the ceremony at the Trinity Church originally required the composer to set a text that emphasized a trinity of virtues. The Kuffner poem, republished the previous year, would have seemed an ideal choice: the opening of the passage of St Paul which includes 'Glaube, Hoffnung und Liebe' (and which inspired Kuffner's poem) also refers to a 'klingende Schelle', or tinkling bell. The *Wiener allgemeine Theaterzeitung* refers to the 'Dreyeinigkeit geweihte Glocke' – the bell dedicated to the Trinity. Schubert might have set this Kuffner text in response to that commission in short score (thus piano-accompanied); he might even have envisaged an organ accompaniment.

But what if the planners of the ceremony suddenly became more ambitious, and asked Friedrich Reil to write a new, and more topical, text where their new bell was specifically mentioned? If Schubert was then asked to set this second set of words to music, he could have done so at great speed, and scored the work for a number of singers and instruments.

The Kuffner setting D955 seems like an oratorio aria in piano-accompanied reduction, rather than a convincing piano-accompanied song. If this *Glaube, Hoffnung und Liebe* was already completed when D954 was mooted, it is possible that Schubert offered it to Diabelli. The publisher, knowing the great public interest in the bell, and that there was always a 'niche market' for religious songs, contrived to bring it out by 6 October, an astonishingly quick turnaround for those days.

The music takes its inspiration from Mozart's Masonic music, particularly Sarastro's prayers and pronouncements in *Die Zauberflöte*. The key of E flat (a trinity of accidentals) is also *Magic Flute*-inspired. Its cantata-like style, and its solemn division into separate sections according to the title, were encouragement to share the song between three tenors in the recording for the Hyperion Edition. A short four-bar introduction leads to three different commands. 'Glaube', 'hoffe' and 'liebe!' The restless striding basses (from b. 7) seem suited to organ pedals; this sixteen-bar section is by way of introduction to the three strophic verses which apostrophize faith, hope and love, one by one.

The tempo changes to 'Etwas geschwinder' (b. 17) and the first of three identical little arias expounds on 'Glaube' – faith. This verse, like the others, starts in the key of E flat minor, progresses to G flat major and thence to C flat major. This thicket of flats makes the music appear Romantic on paper, but it still sounds old-fashioned in manner, as if written for church performance. The use of diminished-chord harmony appropriate for the lies of mankind ('Wenn auch Welt und Menschen lügen' bb. 26–8) strikes an oddly modern note, as does the opening up of the flats into naturals (like lies brushed aside with enormous willpower, from b. 31) when the vocal line climbs chromatically up the stave traversing the friendlier flat-free clearings of G^7 on its way back to E flat. It reaches this key of the Trinity as if the true faith has been rediscovered after a struggle.

The music for hope (beginning 'Hoffe dir Unsterblichkeit') is the same as for the preceding verse, but one notices different details because of the new words. The gradual dawning of day depicted at the end of the strophe is also well served by the opening out of the harmony. For the verse mentioning love ('Edel liebe, fest und rein!') the strophic music in E flat minor has a lecturing tone that seems rather unmagical for a text that talks of love flowering in a glow of happiness. The triumphal note inherent in 'Muss der Liebe Sonne glühen' from b. 31 (the chromatically ascending phrase back to the cadence in E flat major) is much more convincing as word-setting.

At b. 35 we return to Tempo I for the closing bars of the homily. This is the same music that had begun the song, a grave little aria where C minor shifts into A flat major and then to D flat major. These turns of the tonal screw suggest a pastor warming to the theme of his Sunday sermon. The song's conclusion repeats the opening exhortations of 'Glaube, hoffe, liebe', the latter word lovingly set as a higher, longer and more lingering note than before (bb. 43–4). This 'liebe' has taken us into the heady regions of G flat major. If we have glimpsed the world of musical romanticism in the settings of these words we return to a classical mood for the final repeat of them with a switch back to E flat major. We hear once again 'Glaube, hoffe, liebe' in a lower tessitura, this time ornamented by a mordent on the final word. This music has the piety of a public event about it, but it is hardly Schubert the composer of lieder as we know him in 1828. This untypical homily, rushed into print within two months by Diabelli, was the last of Schubert's songs to be printed in his lifetime. The writing of D954 was clearly the result of a commission; if D955 was also written as a result of a link with the Alserkirche, it would explain a great deal.

Autograph:	Österreichische Nationalbibliothek, Vienna (first draft)
First edition:	Published as Op. 97 by Diabelli, Vienna in October 1828 (P173)
Subsequent editions:	Peters: Vol. 2/190; AGA XX 462: Vol. 8/28; NSA IV: Vol. 5/71; Bärenreiter: Vol. 3/202
Bibliography:	Black 2003, pp. 182–3
Discography and timing:	Fischer-Dieskau II 6[17] 3'55
	Hyperion I 37[13] Anthony Rolfe Johnson,
	Hyperion II 36[10] 4'59 Michael Schade & John Mark Ainsley

← *Der 92. Psalm D953* *Schwanengesang: Liebesbotschaft D957/1* →

JOHANN WOLFGANG VON GOETHE (1749–1832)

THE POETIC SOURCES

The specific literary source of many of Schubert's Goethe settings is impossible to identify with certainty. The following books are the most likely sources, and may have been available to the composer at different times of his life, mainly through the good offices of friends (the small library of Johann Mayrhofer for example, as well as the expansive collections of the Schober, Bruchmann or Spaun families and others). Schubert was not usually one of those composers (like Hugo Wolf, for example) who returned faithfully to the same carefully cherished copies of books that he owned, but the Anton Doll edition of the Goethe *Gedichte* (1810) seems to have been an honoured exception. Schubert used it for over forty settings – for the first time on 30 November 1814 for

Nachtgesang D119, and for the last time in December 1822 for *Willkommen und Abschied* D767. He had clearly been led to the *Gedichte* (Volume 7 of Goethe's *Werke*) having first been enraptured by *Faust* (the first volume of the collection). It is reasonable to suppose that the local Viennese editions of most poems would come more readily to hand than the German, and that for the sake of convenience Schubert might have preferred to slip a small paperback volume into his pocket from the Goethe edition published by Bauer (S6), a series of books which was familiar to him from the works of poets such as Jacobi, Salis-Seewis, Hölty, Schreiber, the Schlegel brothers and several others.

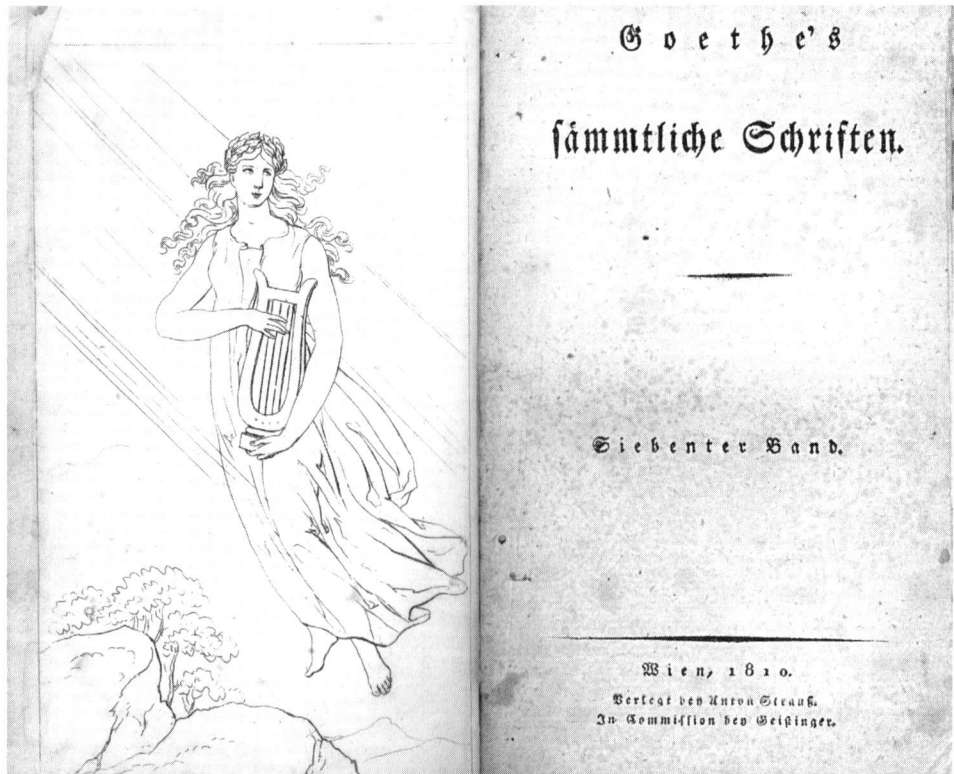

Frontispiece and title page of Volume 7 – *Lyrische Gedichte* – of the twenty-six-volume Viennese edition of Goethe published by Anton Strauss in 1810.

S1   *Goethes Schriften*, Göschen, Leipzig, 1789, in eight volumes (Volume 8 *Vermischte Gedichte*)

S2   *Wilhelm Meisters Lehrjahre*, Unger, Berlin, 1795 (in four volumes with Reichardt's eight musical settings folded in)

S3   *Goethes Werke*, Cotta, Tübingen, 1806, in twelve volumes (Volume 1 *Gedichte* and Volumes 2 and 3 *Wilhelm Meisters Lehrjahre*)

S4   *Goethes Sämmtliche Schriften*, Anton Strauss, Wien, 1810, in twenty-six volumes (Volume 1 *Faust*, Volume 7 *Lyrische Gedichte*, Volumes 10 and 11 *Wilhelm Meisters Lehrjahre*)

S5   Theater von Goethe, Vierter Theil, *Egmont*, Wien 1810, verlegt bei Anton Strauss, In Commission bei Gesitlinger (Viennese reprint of *Goethes Schriften* Band IV)

S6   Goethes Werke, Cotta, Tübingen, 1815–19 in twenty volumes (Volume 1 *Gedichte*, Volume 2 *Vermischte Gedichte* – including *Aus Wilhelm Meister*)

S7   *Gedichte von Goethe*, Bauer, Wien, 1815 (three small paperback volumes)

S8   *West-östlicher Divan von Goethe*, Cotta, Stuttgard [*sic*], 1819

S9   *Goethes Werke*, Kaulfuss and Armbruster, Wien, 1816–22, in twenty-six volumes (Volume 2 *Gedichte*, Volume 9 *Faust*, Volume 21 *West-östlicher Divan*, 1820)

S10   Johann Friedrich Reichardt: *Lieder der Liebe und der Einsamkeit*, Zweiter Teil, Gerhard Fleischer der Jüngere, Leipzig, 1804

This volume of Reichardt songs was certainly in Schubert's possession in 1815. He took from it the texts for *Die Liebe* ('Freudvoll und leidvoll') D210 and *Kolmas Klage* D217.

THE SONGS

19 October 1814	*Gretchen am Spinnrade* D118 [S4: Volume 1 – containing the First Part of *Faust* pp. 166–7 where the words 'Gretchen (am Spinnrade)' are printed directly above the poem and beneath the usual heading 'Gretchens Stube']
30 November 1814	*Nachtgesang* D119 [S4: Volume 7 p. 78] *Trost im Tränen* D120 [S4: Volume 7 pp. 76–7] *Schäfers Klagelied* D121 (first version) *Schäfers Klagelied* D121 (second version) [for both versions of the song S4: Volume 7 p. 75]
3 December 1814	*Sehnsucht* D123 [S4: Volume 7 pp. 79–80]
12 December 1814	*Szene aus 'Faust'* D126 [S4: Volume 1 – containing the First Part of *Faust* pp. 187–9]
February 1815	*Der Sänger* D149 [S4: Volume 7 pp. 274–5] [S3: Volume 1 pp. 219–20, or perhaps S7: Volume 2 p. 5]
27 February 1815	*Am Flusse* (first setting) D160 [S4: Volume 7 p. 32] *An Mignon* D161 (first version) [S4: Volume 7 pp. 81–2] *An Mignon* D161 (second version) [S4: Volume 7 pp. 81–2] *Nähe des Geliebten* D162 [S4: Volume 7 p. 30] [S6: Volume 1 p. 58] [S3: Volume 1 p. 32; or perhaps S7: Volume 11 pp. 30–31]

19 May 1815	*Rastlose Liebe* D138 [S4: Volume 7 p. 7] [possibly S6: Volume 1 p. 85]
3 June 1815	*Die Liebe* D210 ('Freudvoll und leidvoll') [S5: Act III Scene 2 (Clärchens Wohnung), p. 58] [S10: p. 14, where the title of Reichardt's setting is *Liebe* – thus explaining Schubert's title which is nowhere to be found in the Goethe sources]
20 June 1815	*Jägers Abendlied* (first setting) D215 [S4: Volume 7 p. 88; or perhaps S7: Volume 1 p. 79]
21 June 1815	*Meeres Stille* (first version) D215A [S4: Volume 7 p. 37; or perhaps S7: Volume 1 pp. 35–6] [S3: Volume 1 p. 39] *Meeres Stille* (second version) D216 [S4: Volume 7 p. 37] [S6: Volume 1 p. 66] [S3: Volume 1 p. 39; or perhaps S7: Volume 1 p. 36]
5 July 1815	*Wandrers Nachtlied I* D224 [S4: Volume 7 p. 87] [S6: Volume 1 p. 99; or perhaps S7 Volume 1 pp. 78–9] *Der Fischer* D225 [S4: Volume 7 pp. 279–80] [S6: Volume 1 pp. 171–2; or perhaps S7: Volume 2 p. 11] *Erster Verlust* D226 [S4: Volume 7 p. 28] [S6: Volume 1 p. 57] [S3: Volume 1 p. 31; or perhaps S7: Volume 1 p. 29]
15 July 1815	*Tischlied* D234 [S3: Volume 1 pp. 54–5] [S4: Volume 7 pp. 56–8] [S6: Volume 1 p. 123; or perhaps S7: Volume 1 pp. 49–51]
August 1815	*Die Spinnerin* D247 [S4: Volume 7 pp. 293–4] [S6: Volume 1 pp. 187–8; or perhaps S7: Volume 2 pp. 25–6]
18 August 1815	*Der Gott und die Bajadere* D254 [S4: Volume 7 pp. 328–81] [S3: Volume 1 pp. 276–80] [S6: Volume 1 pp. 231–5; or S7: Volume 2 pp. 60–64]
19 August 1815	*Der Rattenfänger* D255 [S4: Volume 7 p. 103] [S6: Volume 1 p. 186; or perhaps S7: Volume 1 p. 94] *Der Schatzgräber* D256 [S4: Volume 7 p. 103; or perhaps S7: Volume 2 pp. 25–6] *Heidenröslein* D257 [S4: Volume 7 p. 7; or S3: Volume 1 p. 7; or perhaps S7: Volume 1 p. 7] *Bundeslied* D258 [S4: Volume 7 p. 54] [S3: Volume 1 pp. 52–3] [S6: Volume 1 pp. 119–20]
20 August 1815	*Wonne der Wehmut* D260 [S4: Volume 7 p. 87] [S6: Volume 1 p. 98] [perhaps S7: Volume 1 p. 78]
21 August 1815	*Wer kauft Liebesgötter?* D261 [S4: Volume 7 pp. 23–4] [S6: Volume 1 pp. 41–2] [S3: Volume 1 p. 25; or perhaps S7: Volume 1 pp. 24–5]
October(?) 1815	*Erlkönig* D328 [S4: Volume 7 pp. 277–8] [S6: Volume 1 pp. 169–70] [S3: Volume 1 pp. 224–5; or perhaps S7: Volume 2 p. 10]
18 October 1815	*Sehnsucht (Mignon)* (first version of first setting) D310A [S6: Volume 2 p. 81 – 'Dieselbe'] *Sehnsucht ('Mignon')* (second version of first setting) D310B [S6: Volume 2, p. 81 – 'Dieselbe']

23 October 1815	*Mignon (Kennst du das Land?)* D321 [S6: Volume 1 p. 163]
13 November 1815	*Wer sich der Einsamkeit ergibt* (first setting) D325 [S6: Volume 2 p. 82 – 'Harfenspieler'. (It does not appear in S4 in the *Gedichte* volumes, only in *Wilhelm Meister*.) The early dating of this version precludes S9: Volume 2 (1816) as a source for the Harper songs]
1815? (possibly 1819?)	*Hoffnung* D295 [S4: Volume 7 p. 91] [S6: Volume 1 p. 103] [perhaps S7: Volume 1 p. 82] *An den Mond* (second setting) D296 [S4: Volume 7 pp. 89–90] [S6: Volume 1 pp. 101–2]
March 1816	*Geistes-Gruss* D142 [S4: Volume 7 p. 85; or perhaps S7: Volume 1 pp. 76–7]
Early–middle 1816	*Sehnsucht (Mignon)* (second setting) D359 [S6: Volume 2 p. 81 – 'Dieselbe (only *Heiss mich nicht reden* carries the title 'Mignon')] *Der König in Thule* D367 [S4: Volume 7 p. 281] [S6: Volume 1 pp. 173–4; or perhaps S7: Volume 2 p. 13] *Jägers Abendlied* (second setting) D368 [S4: Volume 7 p. 88] [S6: Volume 1 p. 100] *An Schwager Kronos* D369 [S6: Volume 2 pp. 44–5] [S3: Volume 1 pp. 127–8; or perhaps S7: Volume 1 pp. 117–19]
September 1816	*So lasst mich scheinen* (first setting, fragment) D469A [S6: Volume 2 p. 82 'Dieselbe'] *So lasst mich scheinen* (second setting, fragment) D469A [S6: Volume 2 p. 82 'Dieselbe'] *Sehnsucht (Mignon)* (third setting) D481 [S6: Volume 2 p. 81 – 'Derselbe'] *Wer nie sein Brot* (first setting) D478/2 [S6: Volume 2 p. 83 – 'Derselbe'] *Wer nie sein Brot* (second setting) D478/2b [S6: Volume 2 p. 83 – 'Derselbe'] *Wer sich der Einsamkeit ergibt* (second setting) D478/1 [S6: Volume 2 pp. 82–3 – 'Harfenspieler'] *An die Türen will ich schleichen* (second version) D478/3 [S6: Volume 2 p. 83 – 'Derselbe'] *Gesang der Geister über den Wassern* (first setting, fragment) D484 [S6: Volume 2 pp. 38–9]
1817	*Gesang der Geister über den Wassern* (unaccompanied chorus) (second setting) D538 [S6: Volume 2 pp. 38–9] [S3: Volume 1 pp. 118–19]
March 1817	*Auf dem See* D543 [S4: Volume 7 p. 69] [S6: Volume 1 p. 78] *Ganymed* D544 [Sources like S6 (pp. 54–5) and S9 have 'Dass ich *dich* fassen möcht' instead of '*diesen*'. Mayrhofer may have owned a copy of the prized S1: pp. 210–11] *Mahomets Gesang* (first setting, fragment) D549 [S5: Volume 7 pp. 190–92] [S3: Volume 1 pp. 115–17) [S6: Volume 2, pp. 36–8]
May 1817	*Liebhaber in allen Gestalten* D558 [S6: Volume 1 pp. 32–4] *Schweizerlied* D559 [S6: Volume 1 pp. 155–6] *Der Goldschmiedsgesell* D560 [S6: Volume 1 pp. 35–6] *Gretchen im Zwinger* (fragment) D564 [S9: Volume 9 p. 212]

April 1819	*Sehnsucht ('Mignon')* (choral setting) D656 [S6: Volume 2 p. 81; although S2 and S4 pp. 10–11 are also possible]
October 1819	*Die Liebende schreibt* D673 [S6: Volume 2 p. 6, no. VIII of the *Sonette* inspired by Minna Herzlieb] *Prometheus* D674 [S6: Volume 2 pp. 52–4] [S3: Volume 1 pp. 133–4; or perhaps S7: Volume 1 pp. 124–6]
1820	*Gesang der Geister über den Wassern* (for chorus and piano) (second setting, fragment) D705 [S6: Volume 2 pp. 52–3] *An den Mond* (first setting) D259 [S4: Volume 7 pp. 78–80] [S6: Volume 1 pp. 101–2] [perhaps S7: Volume 1 pp. 80–81]
1821	*Im Gegenwärtigen Vergangenes* (vocal quartet) D710 [S9: Volume 21 pp. 22–3] [S8: pp. 22–3 also possible]
February 1821	*Gesang der Geister über den Wassern* (chorus and strings) D714 (third setting) [S6: Volume 2 pp. 38–9]
February–March 1821	*Versunken* D715 [S9: Volume 21 p. 52] [S8: p. 52 also possible]
March 1821	*Grenzen der Menschheit* D716 [S4: Volume 7 pp. 213–14; or perhaps S7: Volume 1 pp. 128–30] [S6: Volume 21 pp. 55–6] *Geheimes* D719 [S9: Volume 21 p. 59] [S8: p. 60 also possible] *Suleika I* D720 [S9: Volume 21 pp. 152–3] [S8: p. 161 also possible] *Suleika II* D717 [S9: Volume 21 pp. 157–8] [S8: pp. 166–7 also possible] (possibly 1824?) *Mahomets Gesang* (second setting, fragment) D721 [S4: Volume 7 pp. 190–92] [S6: Volume 2 pp. 36–8]
April 1821	*Heiss mich nicht reden* (first setting) D726 [S6: Volume 2 p. 81 – 'Mignon'; although S2 and S4 Volumes 10–11 also possible] *So lasst mich scheinen* D727 (third setting) [S6: Volume 2 p. 82 – 'Dieselbe'; although S2 and S4 Volumes 10–11 also possible] *Johanna Sebus* (fragment) D728 [S4: Volume 7 pp. 332–4] [S6: Volume 1 pp. 23–4]
August 1822	*Wer nie sein Brot* (third setting) D478/2 [S6: Volume 2 p. 83 – 'Derselbe'; although S2 and S4 Volumes 10–11 also possible]
December 1822	*Der Musensohn* D764 [S4: Volume 7, pp. 9–10; or perhaps S7: Volume 1 p. 11] *An die Entfernte* D765 [S4: Volume 7 p. 31] [S3: Volume 1 p. 33; or perhaps S7: Volume 1 pp. 31–2] *Am Flusse* (second setting) D766 [S4: Volume 7 p. 32] [S3: Volume 1 p. 34; or perhaps S7: Volume 1 p. 33] *Willkommen und Abschied* D767 [S4: Volume 7 pp. 39–40] [S6: Volume 1 pp. 68–9] [S4: Volume 7 pp. 39–40; or perhaps S7: Volume 1 pp. 37–8] *Wandrers Nachtlied II* D768 [S6: Volume 1 p. 99 – 'Ein gleiches']
January 1826	*Mignon und der Harfner* ('Nur wer die Sehnsucht kennt') (fifth setting, duet) D877/1 [S6: Volume 2 p. 81 – 'Dieselbe'; although S2 and S4 Volumes 10–11 are also possible]

Heiss mich nicht reden (second setting) D877/2 [S6: Volume 2
p. 81 – 'Mignon'; although S2 and S4 Volumes 10–11 are also possible]
So lasst mich scheinen (fourth setting) D877/3 [S6: Volume 2
p. 82; although S2 and S4 Volumes 10–11 are also possible]
Lied der Mignon ('Nur wer die Sehnsucht kennt') (fourth setting) D877/4
[S6: Volume 2 p. 81; although S2 and S4 Volumes 10–11 are also possible]

Mention should also be made of other Goethe settings for unaccompanied voices that are outside the scope of this book: *Gesang der Geister über den Wassern* D538 for Quartet (TTBB) March 1817; *Gesang der Geister über den Wassern* D714 for vocal Octet (4 Ten 4 Bass) with strings

Goethe's achievements as a poet, playwright, artist, scientist and philosopher are awe-inspiring. A necessarily abbreviated biography of the poet, tailored to the narrower concerns of the lieder enthusiast, is printed below; this is an essay in which the poems set to music by Schubert are placed within the chronological context of Goethe's life. The large number of composers who have set Goethe to music (Hugo Wolf is perhaps the most distinguished of Schubert's successors in this respect) would merit a much longer study, outside the scope of this book.

'I was born at Frankfurt on the 28th August 1749, at midday, on the stroke of twelve. The position of the stars was favourable; the sun was in the sign of Virgo . . . Jupiter and Venus were friendly, Mercury not in opposition.' Thus begins Goethe's autobiography *Dichtung und Wahrheit* ('Poetry and Truth'), although it would be dangerous for our limited purposes to allow him to continue his own tale, so embroidered and revised is truth with inevitable poetry. The grandfather was a tailor who had done well enough to enable his son, Goethe's father, to buy a civic title and a comfortable house. From his father the poet inherited a tendency to formulate and theorize, and a passion for collecting – a love of order. From his mother's side he had practical good sense and humour, and above all her sense of fantasy. Her fairy stories were part of a haphazard education that was luckily attuned to his unique gifts. Painting and drawing, experiments with a puppet theatre and the study of various languages were all to bear fruit, but cello and piano lessons were never to give him an intimate understanding of music.

Nevertheless, Goethe was proud to have seen the child prodigy Mozart perform in Frankfurt in 1763; Mozart was seven, Goethe fourteen.

At the age of sixteen Goethe was sent to Leipzig University to study law. His first poems were published anonymously; they appeared in the same issue of a Leipzig newspaper that announced Telemann's death, and his replacement in Hamburg by C. P. E. Bach. It was also in Leipzig that the poet's friend, Bernhard Breitkopf, composed the first Goethe settings. An innkeeper's daughter, Annette Schönkopf, was the first of the many love affairs that were to divide the poet's life into chapters. As Richard Capell writes, 'Goethe's career is rather like Henry VIII's, in that it is chronicled according to the brief reign of a succession of queens.' Nicholas Boyle has pointed out that for Goethe in his early life 'the fixity of a commitment was incompatible with the only poetry he could write, a poetry of continuing desire'.

In 1768 Goethe, seriously ill, returned to Frankfurt. During his recuperation, drawings of nudes by Boucher were removed from his room on doctor's orders. He took up alchemy and theology instead. Father Goethe was losing patience with these dilettante whims – little could he know that it was all these various interests that were turning his son into a visionary polymath. From this period dates the poem *Am Flusse* (D160 and D766).

In 1770, the year of Beethoven's birth, Goethe was packed off to the University of Strasbourg. It was there that he met Johann Gottfried Herder who introduced him to the works of Homer, Shakespeare and Ossian – and above all to folk poetry. Herder, who was the first writer of comparable intelligence that Goethe had befriended, taunted the young poet into thinking more deeply. From the very beginning of his career, especially after he began to meet important literary figures and read widely (literature from many epochs and in various languages, including English), it is remarkable how many of Goethe's lyrics are parodies and brilliant reworkings of the work of other people – often unattributed folksongs and anonymous texts from old collections of poetry. Like Shakespeare it seems that Goethe sometimes felt less inclined to outright invention than to the process of appropriating and adapting material, including metrical patterns and ideas, and turning someone else's dross into his own gold. It is often noted in these commentaries that the idea for a Goethe poem came from another literary source, sometimes one that seems rather unlikely. Who would have guessed, for example, that the inspiration for *Der Goldschmiedsgesell* was Henry Carey's *Sally in our Alley* or that *Kennst du das Land* was inspired by Thomson's *The Seasons*? It is also no surprise that the subject of Faust went back in literature to long before the time of the Elizabethan playwright Christopher Marlowe.

The famed relationship with the country pastor's daughter, Friederike Brion, who lived in Sesenheim (today Sessenheim) some thirty miles north-east of Strasbourg, dates from this time. This gave rise to the poems *Mailied* and *Mit einem gemalten Band* set by Beethoven, as well as Schubert's *Heidenröslein* D257 and *Willkommen und Abschied* D767. The Strasbourg idyll lasted only ten months and, with what would be something of a pattern in his emotional life, the poet took flight before he became too deeply involved, leaving Friederike heartbroken. In 1772, after a short period studying at Wetzlar where he met Charlotte Buff (who was to inspire *Die Leiden des jungen Werthers*), Goethe returned to Frankfurt and established his reputation as a young firebrand in the *Sturm und Drang* manner. From this time dates his play *Götz von Berlichingen*. Plays and novels about medieval knights and ladies became all the rage, but the young poet aspired to even bigger canvases; Mohammed, Socrates,

Portrait of Goethe in 1773.

Caesar, Christ were all grist to his imaginative mill. *Mahomets Gesang* (D549 and D721) is surprisingly contemporary with the much shyer poem *Das Veilchen* set by Mozart. The poems for *Ganymed* D544, *Prometheus* D674, *An Schwager Kronos* D369, *Bundeslied* D258 and *Wonne der Wehmut* D260 were all written in these four Frankfurt years. André Gide describes the young Goethe (at the time of his writing *Ganymed*) as being a godly man for whom religious rites and duties counted for nothing. He was already an astonishingly free spirit whose enormous personality lay at the heart of his greatness: 'The only God he recognizes merges with nature: the All, of which he, Goethe is a part. And it is because he is part of this divine All that Goethe honours and esteems himself. His individualism is part of his worship, and his duties towards himself are derived from his duties towards God, whom he seeks and finds everywhere in the Cosmos, and not by shutting his eyes to the outside world.'

The poem for *Geistes-Gruss* D142 was written during a holiday journey down the Rhine in 1774 during which Goethe became close friends with the brother of the poet Jacobi, seven of whose poems were to be set by

Schubert. It was also during this Frankfurt period that Goethe began to get to grips with turning the Faust legend into verse-drama. In their *Urfaust* versions the poems for *Gretchen am Spinnrade* D118, *Gretchen im Zwinger* D564, *Der König in Thule* D367 and *Szene aus 'Faust'* D126 all date from this time – slightly less than forty years before Schubert was to set them. The love affair of this period was with Lili Schönemann to whom Goethe even became engaged. She was of high birth and her parents thought the match unsuitable; in any case he displayed his habitual fear of commitment. A visit to Switzerland was a temporary escape (the poem for *Auf dem See* D543 was written there in 1775) but the poet knew that he had to be on the move once more. He was at the height of his creative powers, but pirated editions of his works cheated him of money and he felt the need for financial security. Princes from all over Germany were on the lookout for advisers and gifted, interesting men who would be a credit to them. A way out of his problems, both personal and financial, was an invitation to the court of Karl August, duke of Weimar. Goethe arrived in Weimar in November 1775. One of the first poems he wrote there, remembering Lili Schönemann at the same time as thinking of the new object of his affection Charlotte von Stein (*see* below), was *Jägers Abendlied* D215 and D368.

Weimar was to be the poet's home for the rest of his life. It was not a rich state, nor a big one, but thanks to the duke's mother, Duchess Anna Amalia (who was, among other things, a composer), foundations had been laid for a remarkably cultural court of which Goethe himself was to be the star attraction. Within six months of coming to Weimar he was a privy councillor. Although he wrote poetry continually – the *Harzreise im Winter* written at this time was to be the source of Johannes Brahms's *Alto Rhapsody* Op. 53 (1869) – he published nothing for the next ten years; his energies were given over to a list of administrative tasks that no ivory-tower artist could ever have contemplated, and which led to his well-deserved reputation as both artist and scientist. Goethe's work on behalf of the state's

mining industry, for example, was to deepen his life long interest in geological and mineralogical studies.

Charlotte von Stein, wife of the duke's Master of Horse, was among the few at the court who almost immediately perceived Goethe's greatness. Half Scottish by birth, she was already a mature, married woman by the time she met the young poet. With her serious nature and great sense of decorum, she deplored the rowdy side of his character. 'Make something worthy of me', he wrote to her, and she educated, groomed and governed him. She taught him how to dance, and equipped him with the social graces needed for a life of mixing with princes. In return he put her on a pedestal; he courted her as a knight might have wooed a paragon of medieval virtue. Goethe wrote over 1,700 letters to Charlotte that were as likely to be accompanied by the latest produce from his garden as by an immortal

Portrait of Charlotte von Stein with her signature.

lyric written for her alone. Protected and guided by her love, the fiery young poet grew up and found, for a number of years at least, a core of inner tranquillity. He became much occupied with the court theatre (some of the lyrics we know as songs are actually taken from small plays) and began work on his novel *Wilhelm Meisters Lehrjahre* that was also to be a rich mine of song lyrics for Schubert, and others. Here is a chronological list of the Goethe poems written in those eleven Weimar years that were later to be set by Schubert: *Hoffnung* D295, *Wandrers Nachtlied I* D224, *Rastlose Liebe* D138, *An den Mond* D259 and D296, *An die Entfernte* D765, *Der Fischer* D225, *Grenzen der Menschheit* D716, *Gesang der Geister über den Wassern* D484, D538, D705, D714, *Liebhaber in allen Gestalten* D558, *Wandrers Nachtlied II* D768, *Wer sich der Einsamkeit ergibt* D325, D478/1, *Erlkönig* D328, *Der Sänger* D149, *Wer nie sein Brot mit Tränen ass* D478/2, D478/2b, *Mignon (Kennst du das Land?)* D321, *Erster Verlust* D226, *Nur wer die Sehnsucht kennt* D310, D359, D481, D877/1.

After more than a decade in Weimar Goethe experienced what would now be termed a midlife crisis. He had been ennobled in 1782; he was famous and respected, but he felt that his life in Germany was stultifying. Once again he needed to escape. The idealism and refinement of Charlotte von Stein had to be replaced by something more vital and earthy. Like his character Mignon he looked to the south, and there he sought rejuvenation and artistic rebirth. On 3 September 1786 he slipped away from Karlsbad where he had been visiting Charlotte; without telling her, he left with only a knapsack and an assumed name.

Whilst in Italy (1786–8) Goethe 'discovered himself'; some scholars even believe that he lost his virginity there, and that his former exploits with women had been cerebral at the expense of physical release. (Judging from the *Römische Elegien* it would be more accurate to say that his poetry lost its virginity.) This turning point in Goethe's creative and emotional life was rich in poetry inspired by classical metre, largely unsuitable for musical

setting. He was particularly busy as a playwright during this period. *Egmont* – from which the text 'Freudvoll und leidvoll' (*Die Liebe* D210) is taken – was completed in Italy, also the final version of his 'Schauspiel mit Gesang', *Claudine von Villa Bella* D239 that Schubert and a number of other composers were to turn into opera.

A return to Weimar in 1788 (very much on the poet's terms, with fewer responsibilities at court) marked the end of Goethe's relationship with Charlotte who had been mortified that the Italian adventure was planned without her knowledge. This intellectual relationship was replaced by something utterly different: the poet set up house with a twenty-three-year-old girl (he was nearly sixteen years older) named Christiane Vulpius. She was scarcely literate, but her simple joyful earthiness provided Goethe with the background he needed to work calmly and productively. The after-effects of the French Revolution meant that the poet was forced to visit the battlefield in the duke's entourage from time to time (*Der Rattenfänger* D255 and *Die Spinnerin* D247 were written during this period). However most of this phase of Goethe's life (1788–93) was given over to his re-awakened interest in scientific research. He took particular issue with Newton's laws, and had his own very different

Portrait of Goethe in middle age.

(and misguided) theories about the nature of colour and light. At more or less the same time he met the poet Schiller who had moved to Jena some time before. What might have been a relationship of deadly rivalry turned into the most fruitful collaborative friendship in Goethe's life; it was just what he needed to return his energies to poetry. Schiller galvanized Goethe into finishing such works as *Wilhelm Meister*, and it was also thanks to Schiller that work on *Faust* was resumed. In return Goethe encouraged Schiller in his writing of *Wallenstein* and *Wilhelm Tell*. They soon saw each other as ideal colleagues, fighting for the same lofty ideals of classicism in art. After the tell-it-all style of the *Venetianische Epigramme*, a new mood of Arcadian euphemism can be found in Goethe's writing. The two poets collaborated together on various collections (notably the *Musenalmanache* – Almanacs of the Muses – of 1797 and 1798) where new poems, ballads and epigrams appeared, some of them ideally suited for musical setting. Dramatic or barnstorming poems now appear less often than lyrics of antique poise and pastoral delight. The following is a chronological list of poems (later set by Schubert) which were written in the 'Schiller years' between 1794 and 1805: *Meeres Stille* D215A and D216, *Heiss mich nicht reden* D726 and D877/2, *An die Türen will ich schleichen* D478/3, *Nähe des Geliebten* D162, *Wer kauft Liebesgötter?* D261, *So lasst mich scheinen* D469, D727, D877/3, *Der Schatzgräber* D256, *An Mignon* D161, *Der Gott und die Bajadere* D254, *Der Musensohn* D764, *Tischlied* D234, *Schäfers Klagelied* D121, *Nachtgesang* D119, *Sehnsucht* D123, *Trost in Tränen* D120. The sudden death of Schiller in 1805 robbed Goethe of his greatest colleague, the only man whom the poet regarded as a literary equal.

In 1806 the Napoleonic wars made a stark impact on Weimar. After the defeat of the Prussians at Jena, marauding French troops broke into Goethe's house and threatened him. Christiane bravely repelled them, and in gratitude Goethe married her after sixteen years of life together. By this time the poet was a celebrity, and visitors came from all over the world

Portrait of Goethe as an older man.

to pay him court: he met Napoleon twice, as befitted a man of his renown. The pushy Bettina von Arnim pursued him and wished to have his child. Christiane was determined to be the only mother of the poet's children and Bettina was summarily put in her place (whilst cultivating a relationship with the older Frau Goethe, the poet's mother). She did, however, manage to engineer a famous, if not entirely successful, meeting between Goethe and Beethoven in Teplitz. Song texts from this period are: *Die Liebende schreibt* D673, *Der Goldschmiedsgesell* D560, *Johanna Sebus* D728 and *Schweizerlied* D559.

Goethe was now to turn his gaze towards the east. Soldiers from Weimar had been stationed in Spain and brought back exquisite examples of Arabic calligraphy. A Russian regiment of Bashkirs was stationed in Weimar, and the hall of the Protestant grammar school resounded with the Koran. The newly translated works of Hafiz inspired the poet to enter into the spirit of oriental love poetry. He invented a new persona for himself – the sage and potentate, Hatem. In this game of oriental symbolism Goethe cast Marianne von Willemer, a young woman who lived outside Frankfurt with an older husband, his friend Jakob von Willemer, as his Zuleika. It is almost certain that their relationship was purely literary and the highly gifted Marianne wrote poetry in reply to his which was so skilful, so much like Goethe's own, that he absorbed it unacknowledged into his writings. Schubert was never to know of the part that Marianne had played in the poetry of the *West-östlicher Divan* as it was only revealed long after the composer's death. The poems written in 1814 and 1815 in the eastern manner were the last of Goethe's lyrics, in terms of the chronology of the poet's life, that Schubert was to set. They were: *Versunken* D715, *Im Gegenwärtigen Vergangenes* D710, *Geheimes* D719 and the two *Suleika* songs D720 and D717.

Franz Schubert was never to set any Goethe lyrics that date from after 1819 – most of

Schubert's Goethe settings are to poems written long before 1815. Paradoxically, just as the ageing poet had finished writing the works that Schubert was destined to set, the composer, a seventeen-year-old boy in Vienna, was only beginning to make his contribution to the musical immortalization of Goethe as a poet of rare humanity and wisdom. Goethe was to live seventeen more years. Indeed, he was to outlive Schubert by four years although he was nearly half a century older. For the purposes of this essay the Goethe story is over. The poet's friendship with Mendelssohn (the pupil of the poet's beloved friend, the composer Carl Friedrich Zelter), the conversations with Eckermann (Goethe's Boswell), the *Marienbader Elegie* (commemorating the poet's last love, Ulrike von Levetzow), the composition of the second part of *Faust* do not belong here.

In August 1831 the poet spent his last birthday, his eighty-second, with his grandchildren in Ilmenau. In the fir-woods of that mountainous region there was a lonely wooden hut. On the wall of the hut fifty-one years before (in September 1780) he had written 'Ein gleiches' ('Über allen Gipfeln ist Ruh'), the text that Schubert set as *Wandrers Nachtlied II*. According to the memoirs of Berginspektor Mahr, Goethe, confronted by the handwriting of his younger self, read these few lines and tears ran down his cheeks. He slowly drew his handkerchief from the pocket of his coat, dried his eyes and said in a sad and gentle voice: 'Yes: wait, you too shall rest before long.' How could Goethe have known that the man, whose name would be bracketed with his for the rest of time, had died four years earlier, having made those very words immortal in a way undreamed of by him?

Fortunately it took Schubert some time to realize that his eager attempts to establish a personal contact with the poet were to be extinguished by the great man's indifference. In October 1814 the meeting of minds (on Schubert's side at least) took on the character of a wild new passion. It so happened that the publication of Goethe's poetry in Austria was permitted only a few years before the composer set it (*see* Source 4, above). Instead of regarding

Portrait of Goethe at seventy-seven with signature.

the ageing Goethe as a well-established classic (which was his status in Germany by 1814), the young Austrian composer's relationship with the poet had all the intensity of a meeting of contemporaries.

A collaboration that exploded into life with *Gretchen am Spinnrade* was followed by various experiments in the last months of 1814 – quiet strophic songs (*Nachtgesang* and *Trost in Tränen*), a modified strophic song (*Schäfers Klagelied*), a through-composed song of various disparate sections (*Sehnsucht*) and the operatic *scena* with chorus, *Szene aus 'Faust'*. None of these recaptures the raw energy and drama of *Gretchen am Spinnrade*.

It is 1815 of course which was the *annus mirabilis* – not only for song in general (for Schubert set many poets in this year) but particularly for the composer's relationship (albeit at a distance) with his new-found poetic mentor. Some of the most famous songs of the period are through-composed (*Rastlose Liebe*, *Erster Verlust*, *Erlkönig*, perhaps the most famous of all) but most of them are strophic. The majority of these are highly successful creations. In certain cases such as *Nähe des Geliebten*, *Die Spinnerin* and *Heidenröslein*, the strophic nature of the setting immeasurably enhances the culminative effect of the music and the power of the narrative. One should also mention here Schubert's unmatched ability to take some of Goethe's single verses and make of them brief and magical musical utterances (*Wandrers Nachtlied I*, *Meeres Stille*, *Wonne der Wehmut*). Schubert also wrote a three-act *Singspiel* to the Goethe play *Claudine von Villa Bella*; sadly only one of the three acts originally composed has survived. What remains of this work is elegant, charming and tuneful, without immediately suggesting the same natural affinity with the poet that is shown in the lieder. Two of the arias have survived in the recital repertoire thanks to arrangements for voice and piano (not the composer's own) published by Edition Peters in 1885 at the instigation of Max Friedlaender – one for Lucinde (*Hin und wieder fliegen Pfeile*) and one for Claudine (*Liebe schwärmt auf allen Wegen*).

In 1816, the year in which the composer first attempted to contact the poet and make him aware of the existence of his music, the Goethe list is much smaller. There are two marvellously intense and compact strophic songs (*Der König in Thule* and *Jägers Abendlied*) as well as a thundering masterpiece (*An Schwager Kronos*) in the *Erlkönig* manner, but it is the lyrics from Goethe's novel *Wilhelm Meister* that seem to have fascinated and tested the composer. Two of the three celebrated *Gesänge des Harfners* were composed, but not without earlier attempts to find the right tone for the Harper's lyric *Wer nur sein Brot*. For the first time Schubert applied himself to Goethe's *Gesang der Geister über den Wassern*, and came to the conclusion that this philosophical poem needed a choral rather than solo setting.

It is then that something changes in the composer's relationship with the poet. Schubert's desire to conquer the world of music with Goethe at his side seems to die for lack of nourishment. Having written out a book of songs for the poet (with a covering letter from his friend Josef von Spaun outlining an ambitious scheme of song publication with the Goethe songs as the high point of the projected series), it must have been hurtful in the extreme to have the book returned without a word of acknowledgement. A second volume of twelve Goethe settings had been assiduously prepared by the composer, but this was never sent. Schubert's cause was probably not helped by the fact that Spaun's uncle, Franz Seraphicus von Spaun, was a strong opponent of the great poet – a single glance at the name 'von Spaun' on the covering letter might have caused the contents of the parcel to be ignored. There is another possible reason that has never before been raised: in a letter written on 24 February 1816 (some six weeks before Schubert's parcel was sent) Goethe gives vent to his frustration on account of his shocking treatment by the composer Eberwein in connection with a recent performance of one of his plays (*Des Epimenides Erwachen*). He had made a vow ('ein Gelübde') not to allow any new composition of his texts 'hiersobald' – 'for the time being' – as he has not received the respect he felt was his due. It was clearly the wrong time, a couple of months later, for a new book full of songs to arrive from Vienna. Goethe was no fan of Austria, a country he never visited, nor of its capital city, with a reputation for intrigue. He was also extremely worried at this time by the illness of his wife (she died in June 1816). The old poet received, like all famous men, a voluminous amount of unsolicited mail. One wonders how many other composers of the time sent their songs to Goethe in manuscript; in 99 per cent of cases its tactful disposal was accomplished without history offering the slightest reproach. If we are to believe Goethe's letter of February 1816, his rejection of Schubert was part of a blanket policy decision, dogmatically adhered to, at least for a time, to ignore *all* composers who applied to him for recognition. In *Gespräche mit Eckermann* (21 January 1827) Goethe explained to his Boswell that he would sooner not reply at all to a letter rather than send a superficial acknowledgement.

Goethe can be accused of treating his priceless postal consignment carelessly, impolitely, but not with calculated philistinism. It seems very unlikely that Goethe was offended by listening to Schubert's music itself. The *Rastlose Liebe* settings of Reichardt and Zelter bring home to the listener that Schubert's *Rastlose Liebe* (included in Goethe's parcel) is less 'extreme' in many ways than theirs. If Goethe could live with these settings by composers he knew and respected, it was unlikely that he would have taken instant exception to the subtle musical differences and discoveries embodied in the particular group of Schubert songs that was sent to him. In any case, he would have been delighted by the strophic simplicity of *Heidenröslein*. Schubert has more in common with his predecessors than has generally been recognized; to judge this effectively one needs to know something about the contemporary music in circulation at the time, and few Schubert enthusiasts have taken the trouble to do so. If the *Erlkönig* settings of Reichardt and Zelter are not the equal of Schubert's, neither are they boring and negli-

gible. These are fine compositions that hold the listener's attention. Songs like these doubtless held Schubert's attention too.

In any case, it hardly surprises that in 1817 Schubert is very much more selective as far as Goethe is concerned. This was the year when the composer warmed to the classically inspired texts of his Viennese friend Mayrhofer – what is perhaps the most important Goethe setting of the year tackles a mythological subject (*Ganymed*) that Mayrhofer may have brought to the composer's attention. There are also tiny humorous songs, a setting of a poem from one of the poet's Swiss holidays when he was on the run from emotional commitment (*Auf dem See*) and two substantial fragments relating to larger-than-life characters – Mohammed and Gretchen, the latter no longer at the spinning wheel but on her knees before a statue of the Madonna (*Gretchen im Zwinger*). Perhaps significantly, both of these songs on the broadest of emotional and poetic canvases were left unfinished.

The year 1818 (much less productive of songs in any case than other years) is Goethe-free. By 1819 it is clear that the composer no longer regards the poet as 'his' Goethe, but simply as a great writer whose work claims his attention alongside the work of other more recent discoveries such as Friedrich von Schlegel and Novalis. There are four Goethe settings from this year including a choral setting of the famous *Nur wer die Sehnsucht kennt*, a blockbuster on a classical theme (*Prometheus*) and a delightfully feminine setting of *Die Liebende schreibt*. Sometime after February 1820 he composed *An den Mond* D296, a poem revisited with moving success. Right at the end of that year there is another attempt at the *Gesang der Geister über den Wassern*, this time for chorus with piano accompaniment; the piece was once again left as a fragment.

Schubert's enthusiasm was renewed when he read a new series of Goethe poems published in Germany in 1819, and receiving their Viennese publication in the following year. These poems had been written by Goethe more or less at the same time that the music for *Gretchen am Spinnrade* had been composed. The new volume opened the whole exotic world of the *West-östlicher Divan* to the composer – *Geheimes, Versunken*, the *Suleika* poems. He grappled with a text that he probably had known for a long time and made of it a musical masterpiece – *Grenzen der Menschheit*. Dating from this year there is also a second version of *Mahomets Gesang* (left incomplete, as was the ballad *Johanna Sebus*) as well as further inconclusive attempts to solve the problem of the *Mignon* lyrics. Despite a number of songs not brought to fruition, the years 1821 and 1822 find Schubert back to the best Goethian form since 1815. Two of the *Gesänge des Harfners* were slightly revised from 1816 and brought together for publication with a newly composed middle song in the set of three. Some of the best-loved masterpieces date from this period, including *Der Musensohn* and *Willkommen und Abschied*, not to mention the sublime *Wandrers Nachtlied II*. An important setting from early 1821 lies outside the scope of this series – *Gesang der Geister über den Wassern* for men's chorus and low strings. This Goethe renaissance was not to last, for 1823 is the year of *Die schöne Müllerin* (Wilhelm Müller was to be the favoured poetic companion of Schubert's later life). Unless *Suleika II* was written to order and dates from 1824 as John Reed conjectures, there were no new Goethe works written for three years.

On 20 October 1822 a young Viennese traveller by the name of Max von Löwenthal was granted an audience by the great poet in Weimar (*Goethes Gespräche* V, Biedermann p. 130). Löwenthal, on his way back home after visiting London and Paris, was proud of his home city, particularly for its music, and he commented on the fact that Goethe had never visited it. The grand old man explained that all the extra duties of his old age accounted for a lack of time to undertake such expeditions, but that Vienna must be a wonderful city for music considering the beautiful instruments built there. This occasion was almost certainly the first time that Goethe heard Schubert's name fall from someone else's lips; Löwenthal brought up the subject of the composer's settings of Goethe's poetry, but Goethe said

that he did not know these songs, and he had quite clearly forgotten the name of the man who had sent him a parcel of lieder six years earlier. Unless the poet was extremely forgetful, he would have registered the name of Schubert from then on.

Schubert made one more attempt at personal contact with Goethe. He had been nineteen when Spaun wrote to the poet on his behalf, but in June 1825 at the age of twenty-eight he was not unknown; indeed he stood on the threshold of the renown which he would have lived to see and enjoy if he had only been given another decade. Schubert's note to the great man (he no longer needed his friend Spaun as an intermediary) consists of one long, ornate sentence where the formality (and a certain clumsiness) of language scarcely masks the depth of feeling: 'If I should succeed in giving evidence of my unbounded veneration of Your Excellency by the dedication of these compositions of your poems, and possibly in gaining some recognition of my insignificant self ["meine Unbedeutenheit"], I should regard the favourable fulfilment of this wish as the fairest event of my life.' But this was no longer a schoolboy writing, and it was no longer a schoolboy musical crush that prompted his enthusiasm. Instead of a handwritten volume, Schubert was able to send Goethe printed songs which were dedicated to the poet and published as Op. 19. Two special presentation copies with gold lettering on satined paper were specially ordered from the printer, almost certainly at the composer's expense. The songs were *An Schwager Kronos*, *An Mignon* and *Ganymed*. Despite the fact that he had every reason to hope that such a handsome parcel would receive some acknowledgement, we somehow feel that the composer fully expected to be ignored again, and he was right. This time Goethe kept the volume in his library, and noted its receipt in his diary (mis-spelling Schubert's name as Schubart), but did not bother to send an acknowledgment. Schubert's songs had the misfortune to arrive in the same post as a consignment of quartets from the young Felix Mendelssohn by whom the old poet was greatly charmed. By this time Schubert was on holiday in Upper Austria with

Vogl, and was taken up with setting Walter Scott.

The last Goethe settings are a result of unfinished business brought triumphantly to a close. Once Schubert had embarked on the texts from *Wilhelm Meister* he worried at them until they were right. He had definitively set the Harper's songs and published them in 1822 (it had taken him from 1815 to get them to his satisfaction), but he was still not happy with the three great lyrics of Mignon. In 1826 Schubert no longer had the burning enthusiasm of the youth who had first discovered Goethe; instead there was the mature understanding of a human being who, in his own way, had been through as much pain as Goethe's waif. The Op. 62 songs published in 1827 begin and end with settings of *Nur wer die Sehnsucht Kennt* (the first for tenor and soprano duet, the second for soprano solo) which are summits of Schubert's achievement with this poet. The man who composed the final version of *Heiss mich nicht reden* and *So lasst mich scheinen* was a sadder and more experienced individual than the boy who had written *Erlkönig*. At the beginning of the story of two artists, one young and passionate, the other well established and venerable, we feel that the composer is in the poet's debt, that he has been raised to a higher musical power by the words. (Schubert admitted as much himself: on 14 June 1816 he noted in his diary, 'I sang Goethe's *Rastlose Liebe* and Schiller's *Amalia*. Unanimous applause for the former, less for the latter. Although I myself think that my *Rastlose Liebe* is better than *Amalia*, I cannot deny that Goethe's musical poet's genius ["musikalisches Dichter-Genie"] contributed much to the success.') By the time the last *Mignon* songs were written the composer's debt to the poet is fully repaid. Schubert, we feel, should now be thanked for the reverence in which Goethe's name is held in the hearts of a million music lovers. Although the relationship was nurtured only by one-sided admiration, there is a link between Schubert and Goethe that lies too deep for words. This coming-together of word and tone is a continuing source of wonder, admiration and gratitude. Whatever his formidable reputation in the non-German-speaking world as a sage, philosopher and man of great culture, in whatever high respect he is held by English-speaking writers and dramatists, it is we musicians who, regardless of whether German is our mother tongue, are lucky enough to be able to *love* Goethe, mainly thanks to Schubert and his song-composing successors. The music lover is exasperated that Schubert's attempts to establish a connection with the poet were all in vain, but the more one studies Goethe's works and life, the more one is able to agree with Heine (in *Die romantische Schule*) that the poet represents 'that perfect union of personality and genius such as we wish to have in remarkable men'.

Goethe died in Weimar on 22 March 1832. The poet, whose capacity for growth and self-improvement was legendary, had by then at least some awareness of the importance of the Viennese composer. In 1826 he heard a performance of *Erlkönig* which impressed him as an exciting depiction of a horse-ride. In 1830 the same song was performed for him by the soprano Wilhelmine Schröder Devrient and he kissed the singer on the brow, claiming to have understood the totality of the composer's conception for the first time. The poet's views on song, first formulated some sixty years earlier, had clearly deepened as he got older, side by side with music, an art form that had changed immeasurably as an expressive language. It was not in Goethe's remarkable nature to resist development and change once he had understood how it worked. The same man who was in correspondence with Carlyle about the building of the latest British railways was almost certainly capable of saluting the greatness of Franz Schubert – but the chance to do so never came up at the right time of his life. How different all of this might have been if he had visited Vienna in the 1820s.

Bibliography: Byrne 2003
                 Gide 1942, p. xv
                 Moser 1949

Die GÖTTER GRIECHENLANDS *see* STROPHE AUS 'DIE GÖTTER GRIECHENLANDS' D677

CARLO GOLDONI (1707–1793)

THE POETIC SOURCE

S1 *Il filosofo di campagna, dramma per musica* in Volume 43 of *Opere teatrali del Sig. avvocato Carlo Goldoni Veneziano. Con rami allusivi.* Antonio Zatta e figli, Venezia, 1788–95

THE SONGS

1817?   *La pastorella al prato* D513 (TTBB) [from Act II Scene 16 of *Il filosofo di campagna*, S1: Volume 43 pp. 103–4]

January 1817   *La pastorella al prato* D528 [*see* above]

It is unlikely that Schubert took the text of *La pastorella* directly from the complete works of Goldoni. The music had already been set by Galuppi; and Schubert's contemporary Karl Freiherr von Doblhoff, a fellow pupil of Salieri, also set it to music as a quartet (1820, dedicated to Salieri). This suggests that both Schubert and Doblhoff were given (or perhaps assigned) the text by their teacher.

Carlo Goldoni was born in Venice on 25 February 1707, and was both a playwright and librettist. Almost as important and prolific a figure as Metastasio (qv), he is credited with a new freedom in mid-eighteenth-century Italian theatre (and thus opera). Goldoni's plays were appealing to look at, with fast-moving action and relatively easy-to-follow plots; in opera this meant a reduction in the amount of recitative. He collaborated a great deal with Galuppi and countless others, but he lived in an era where the fame of the librettist still outweighed that of any composer. In 1761, as a result of a feud with the playwright Carlo Gozzi, Goldoni's style was parodied and reviled in a famous *commedia dell' arte* classic, *La Fiaba dell'amore delle tre melarance* – 'The Love for three oranges' – that became the basis of Prokofiev's opera more than 150 years later. Goldoni beat a retreat to Paris where he spent the last thirty years of his life, ending up as Italian tutor to the daughters of Louis XV at Versailles. He died in poverty in Paris on 7 February 1793, a victim of the reversals of the French Revolution.

CHARLES GOLDONI
né a Venise en 1707.

Goldoni.

Der GOLDSCHMIEDSGESELL   The goldsmith's apprentice
(GOETHE) **D560** [H369]
F major   May 1817

Es ist doch mei - ne___ Nach - ba - rin ein___ al - ler - lieb - stes___ Mäd - chen!

(14 bars)

Es ist doch meine Nachbarin
Ein allerliebstes Mädchen!
Wie früh ich in der Werkstatt bin,
Blick' ich nach ihrem Lädchen.

[(Zu Ring und Kette poch' ich dann
Die feinen goldnen Drähtchen.
Ach! denk ich, wann? und wieder, wann?
Ist solch ein Ring für Kätchen?)]

[(. . .)]

Ich feile; wohl zerfeil' ich dann
Auch manches goldne Drähtchen.
Der Meister brummt, der harte Mann!
Er merkt, es war das Lädchen.

Und flugs wie nur der Handel still,
Gleich greift sie nach dem Rädchen,
Ich weiss wohl, was sie spinnen will:
Es hofft das liebe Mädchen.

Das kleine Füsschen tritt und tritt;
Da denk' ich mir das Wädchen,
Das Strumpfband denk' ich auch wohl mit,
Ich schenkt's dem lieben Mädchen.

Und nach den Lippen führt der Schatz
Das allerfeinste Fädchen.
O wär' ich doch an seinem Platz,
Wie küsst' ich mir das Mädchen!

My neighbour is
An enchanting girl.
In the morning, at my workbench,
I gaze across at her little shop.

[(Then I beat the fine gold threads
Into ring and chain.
Ah! When? I think, and again, when
Will such a ring be for Kätchen?)]

[(. . .)]

I file away, and at times I file right through
Many a golden thread.
My master grumbles, unfeeling man!
He sees it was that little shop.

And as soon as her work is finished
She reaches for her spinning wheel.
I well know what she intends to spin.
She has her hopes, the darling girl.

As her little foot keeps on working
I think of her dainty calves
And of her garter;
I gave it to the darling girl.

My sweetheart takes
The finest thread to her lips.
Ah, if only I could be in its place,
How I should kiss her!

JOHANN WOLFGANG VON GOETHE (1749–1832); poem written 12 September 1808

This is the fifty-third of Schubert's seventy-five Goethe solo settings (1814–26). See the poet's biography for a chronological list of all the Goethe settings.

The original of this pretty neighbour was none other than Sally, heroine of Henry Carey's well-known ballad *Sally in our Alley*. The English poem was parodied by Johann Wilhelm Ludwig

Gleim (1719–1803) among others, and Goethe quotes the first line of Gleim's *Die Nachbarin* at the beginning of his poem, before branching off with his own tale of an apprentice in love. Goethe's English was perfectly good enough to have taken Carey's text as his direct model.

In March 1817 Schubert was fascinated by Goethe texts that encompassed large philosophical issues – the first setting of *Ganymed* D544 and *Mahomets Gesang* D549 both date from this time. In May of the same year we encounter another Schubert, and another Goethe. Three unassuming poems were selected, and three delightful and unpretentious small songs were the result. *Liebhaber in allen Gestalten* D558, *Schweizerlied* D559 and *Der Goldschmiedsgesell* D560 form a happy musical trio of folksong-like simplicity, although their poems were written at very different times in Goethe's life. The music for all three songs was written out on a folded sheet of paper that became separated into two. Of these three songs *Der Goldschmiedsgesell* is the least popular; it might even rank as the least known of Schubert's Goethe settings. A baritone given to singing the heavier Goethe songs would do well to include it in a group for lightness and contrast. The music is in Schubert's best Papageno manner. A cheery vocal line is sparsely punctuated by chords in the piano; these represent the apprentice at work as he hammers and files the precious metal at his workbench, singing the while. The goldsmith's apprentice is one of Schubert's team of lively (and usually sexually aware) working-class characters; like Shakespeare, the composer had a soft spot for earthy, uncomplicated people.

The AGA prints all seven of Goethe's strophes; for the Hyperion recording six of these were chosen (leaving out Verse 3 as printed in the AGA). The NSA (published in 1999) prints five strophes, leaving out the second verse as printed above; these five were chosen by Schubert himself for inclusion in his autograph. The introduction as printed in the Peters Edition (and in smaller print in the AGA) is spurious, but with its wistful cadence it is far from the worst of the kind provided by Diabelli and his cohorts.

Der Goldschmiedsgesell illustrated by Eugen Neureuther (1829)

Autograph: Conservatoire collection, Bibliothèque Nationale, Paris (first draft)
First edition: Published as Book 48 no. 6 of the *Nachlass* by Diabelli, Vienna in 1850 (P385)

Subsequent editions:	Peters: Vol. 6/66; AGA XX 122: Vol. 3/49; NSA IV: Vol. 11/142
Bibliography:	Byrne 2003, pp. 200–203
Further settings and arrangements:	Ludwig Berger (1777–1839) *Der Goldschmiedsgesell*, Op. 33 no. 5
	Arr. Tilman Hoppstock (b. 1961) for guitar accompaniment, in *Franz Schubert: 110 Lieder* (2009)
Discography and timing:	Fischer-Dieskau I 5[8] 2'06 (three strophes only)
	Hyperion I 24[25]
	Hyperion II 19[3] 2'02 Simon Keenlyside

← *Schweizerlied* D559   *Nach einem Gewitter* D561 →

GONDELFAHRER (I)   The gondolier
(MAYRHOFER) **D808** [H549]
C major   March 1824

(40 bars)

Es tanzen Mond und Sterne	Moon and stars dance
Den flücht'gen Geisterreih'n;	The fleeting round of the spirits:
Wer wird von Erdensorgen	Who would be forever fettered
Befangen immer sein!	By earthly cares!
Du kannst in Mondesstrahlen	Now, my boat, you can drift
Nun, meine Barke, wallen;	In the moonlight;
Und aller Schranken los,	Free from all restraints
Wiegt dich des Meeres Schoss.	You are rocked on the bosom of the sea.
Vom Markusturme tönte	From the tower of St Mark's
Der Spruch der Mitternacht;	Midnight's decree tolled forth.
Sie schlummern friedlich Alle,	All sleep peacefully;
Und nur der Schiffer wacht.	Only the boatman wakes.

JOHANN MAYRHOFER (1787–1836)

*This is the last of Schubert's forty-seven Mayrhofer solo settings (1814–24). See the poet's
biography for a chronological list of all the Mayrhofer settings.*

Schubert never saw the sea (his water music is largely about brooks, rivers and lakes) and he
certainly never had the chance to visit Venice in the footsteps of so many other German-

speaking travellers, Goethe among them. The Queen of Cities had been part of Napoleon's empire since 1797. After Napoleon's defeat (and until 1866) it was reduced to being a province of the Habsburg Empire, and was filled with German-speaking administrative staff, and even clergy. Ladislaus Pyrker (1772–1847) (qv), the Patriarch of Venice and effectively the Austrian emperor's Venetian viceroy, was hardly a popular figure among the locals, but he made a number of essential reforms in terms of the efficiency of public institutions. He was also one of Schubert's poets.

The link with Pyrker was Schubert's only connection with Venice. *Gondelfahrer* was composed without even so much as an invitation to stay with the Patriarch in the Doge's palace. It is one of three songs of 1824 to texts of Johann Mayrhofer in which the composer bids his farewell to the poet whose intellectual influence and friendship meant so much to him in his late teens and early twenties. The solo setting of *Gondelfahrer* is not as merry as the version for four men's voices and piano (D809) written at more or less the same time (*see* commentary below) but on first hearing, in marked contrast to the other 1824 Mayrhofer songs, it seems to paint a light-hearted picture – a musical postcard from the Adriatic. The harmonic blueprint of the three-bar introduction, undulating between C major and A flat major is perhaps, from the point of view of harmony textbooks, veering more towards the Neapolitan than the Venetian; from far away Vienna this bow to Italiante harmony must have seemed an appropriate enough gesture.

The tune dances in ⁶⁄₈ as charmingly as the reflection of moonlight on water, but this water is darker and deeper than a rippling German brook; although the doubling of the vocal line in this song – also noticed by Leo Black – suggests an affinity with *Wohin?* from *Die schöne Müllerin* D795 where the voice is similarly doubled by the accompaniment's left hand. For Black this is appropriate for music of a 'well-nigh hedonistic passivity'. One hears throughout the murky depth of a bass line that underlines the age-old mystery of Venice. The vocal line is supported with a texture that matches the opaque lagoon; long before the age of the *vaporetto* these are still waters that are only disturbed by the rippling passage of the occasional gondola. The mordents in the piano's left hand (bb. 16 and 20) hint at a touch of Italian capriciousness; at the same time, in doubling the vocal line, they seem to suggest the guttural break in a gondolier's voice. Perhaps Mayrhofer had deliberately chosen to write a twelve-line poem because it describes a midnight scene. Schubert could not resist mirroring the sound image of the campanile of St Mark's as it strikes midnight. Between bb. 23 and 28 we hear twelve rolled A flat major chords, two per bar. In the autograph the composer carefully numbers these chimes under the left-hand octaves, 1–12 as, in 1812, he had gleefully numbered the strokes of midnight in *Der Geistertanz* D15 (bb. 15–26). Walther Dürr makes the point that the bell-like sonority of these chords would have better suited the pianos of Schubert's time. As soon as the campanile falls silent the music magically slips back into the C major of peaceful dreams ('Sie schlummern friedlich'). The suitably extended long watch of the gondolier is represented by the drawn-out E on 'wacht' (bb. 33–4), eventually resolving on to an F – this is the hardest effect to achieve successfully from the singer's point of view (cf. the famous rising phrase in *Du bist die Ruh* D776). *Gondelfahrer* is one of the very few Schubert songs (*Nacht und Träume* D827 is another – and the two songs are related in atmosphere) where the accompaniment throughout is in the bass clef for both hands. There is an audible distance between high voice and piano; the cupola of a night sky that seems to lie between the song's two participants gives a certain sombre majesty to the music, although the tune is light and graceful enough.

Mayrhofer's gondola is perhaps a more ominous vessel than Schubert chose to take on board. Could it be that the truculent gondolier, the figure of death who rows a floating coffin in Thomas Mann's *Death in Venice*, is prefigured here, and Mayrhofer's waiting gondolier is also waiting to ferry his charges across the Styx? The words 'aller Schranken los' (bb. 18–19) perhaps suggest death as a release from the cares of the world – although they are not set this way by Schubert.

We should perhaps also remember that 'Mitternacht' was the nick-name of Austria's chancellor, Clemens Metternich, and that bells tolled as liberals were being executed and Vienna danced.

Autograph:	Staatsbibliothek Preussischer Kulturbesitz, Berlin
First edition:	Published as No. 2 of *Neueste Folge nachgelassener Lieder und Gesänge* by J. P. Gotthard, Vienna in 1872 (P428)
Subsequent editions:	Not in Peters; AGA XX 461: Vol. 8/26; NSA IV: Vol. 13/148
Bibliography:	Black 2000, p. 89
Arrangement:	Arr. Tilman Hoppstock (b. 1961) for guitar accompaniment, in *Franz Schubert: 110 Lieder* (2009)
Discography and timing:	Fischer-Dieskau II 6[16] 1'59
	Hyperion I 15[10]
	Hyperion II 29[4] 1'57 Margaret Price

← *Auflösung* D807   *Gondelfahrer* (II) D809 →

GONDELFAHRER (II)   The gondolier   Quartet, TTBB
(MAYRHOFER) OP. 28, **D809** [H550]
C major   March 1824

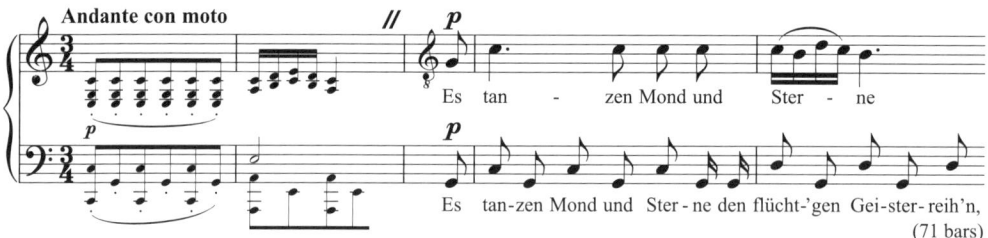

See previous entry for poem and translation

JOHANN MAYRHOFER (1788–1836)

At the time this quartet was written, poet and composer were supposedly estranged, but it is clear that Schubert, even after he had left Mayrhofer's lodgings in 1821 to make an independent life for himself, received handwritten copies of new poems. *Gondelfahrer* appeared in the privately printed *Gedichte* of October 1824 to which Schubert was not a subscriber, but the composer had set it much earlier in the year. There is no hint of any dark cloud in this enchanting music to poetry that the composer clearly set because he liked it – not (as one suspects with some of the settings of his friends' work) because he was on cordial terms with the poet. The solo setting is cast as a barcarolle in §, a gliding and lilting nocturne where we sense the romantic mystery of Venice. This quartet on the other hand is more open, less private, but no less enchanting. Communal music-making implies a 'night out with the boys' rather than a secretly hatched plot involving all the sexual game-playing for which Venice is famous. This quartet is starlit and romantic; it requires four male singers of sensitivity and poetic spirit, jolly enough to enjoy more than one glass of *prosecco*.

As in the solo song, Schubert chooses C major as his key, but the time signature is ¾ rather than §. The delightful tick-tock of the mezzo staccato quaver accompaniment initiates a

Bewegung that runs throughout the piece as if it were bathed in the reflection of moonlight dancing on the surface of the waters. (In his most famous song in ⅜, the *Ständchen* from *Schwanengesang*, the composer uses a similar device, this time to approximate the plucking of lute or guitar, and it makes a delightful effect in a work also lit by the moon.) The six-bar introduction strolls insouciantly through various keys before returning to home base. The four voices enter together, and from the beginning the first tenor is cast as *primus inter pares*, the glittering star responsible for the song's various flights of fancy. (The commentary for *Das Dörfchen* discusses the various singers who sang these quartets during Schubert's lifetime.)

The words begin with 'Es tanzen Mond und Sterne'. It is the word 'Sterne' (stars) that initiates a graceful little roulade of four dancing semiquavers that suddenly invades the top vocal line (b. 9). This is a tiny explosion of melismatic nonchalance, a devil-may-care wink translated into sound. It is more than ornamentation, however; rather part of a spun melody – one of those carefree Schubertian miracles where we feel that all's well with the world. This little turn of phrase also encapsulates the mystery and intrigue of the phrase 'Den flücht'gen Geisterreih'n' (bb. 10–11). The expressive harmonic squeeze on the word 'Erden*sorgen*' (bb. 12–13) is another delight of the first verse. So enraptured is the composer with the imagery of Mayrhofer's first four lines that he immediately repeats them; here the second tenor is allowed a stab at the semiquaver motif (b. 16), and the phrase is lobbed back and forth between him and the first tenor. The undulations in the music and these little ruffles on its surface tell us, even before the words of the second verse confirm it, that we are drifting in a boat, probably a gondola, that rocks gently up and down in the swell of the current.

The music for the section beginning 'Du kannst in Mondesstrahlen' (from b. 26) was clearly conceived by the composer who had written *Auf dem Wasser zu singen* D774 the year before. In that song cascading semiquavers formed a dialogue between voice and piano; here a similar effect is created between first and second tenors in hocketing thirds. The harmonic foundation is a simple one: we have moved to the subdominant (G major) and these enchanting flurries alternate between this key and its dominant seventh on D. Once again the strophe is repeated to elongate the musical delight, and once again Schubert pleases himself with various subtle variations in the interplay between the two top lines of the vocal score.

When it comes to depicting the striking of St Mark's (from b. 47), Schubert does the same as he did for the solo setting: he moves a semitone up from the dominant (G) to A flat major, a Neapolitan shift. The effect of this shift is suitably mysterious. In both the solo version and the quartet the campanile is allowed to strike within six repeated bars grounded in A flat major (bb. 47–52), a moment of harmonic repose. In the solo version we hear the clock strike twelve, twice per bar; in the choral version the effect is less literal because it is impossible to subdivide a bar neatly into two when it is in ⅜. Instead there is a curious syncopation in the piano writing, a two-note chime unevenly spaced. We are delighted by the slide back to C major for the atmospheric 'Sie schlummern friedlich' (bb. 52–3). The composer does not use all the words of this third strophe again; the striking of midnight can happen only once per song. Swooning elaborations on the last two lines of the verse continue to work their magic, for here it is not snoring that is depicted, but rather the flickering of happy dreams. The best effect of all is reserved for the very last two repetitions of 'Und nur der Schiffer wacht' (from b. 65). For once the vocal line abandons its contrapuntal exchanges in semiquavers in favour of closer harmonies in slower note values. The sweet yet mournful chords evoke a gondolier's warning call across the expanses of the lagoon, a magically poetic coda worthy of this perfect little masterpiece.

Autograph: Missing or lost
First edition: Published as Op. 28 by Sauer & Leidesdorf in August 1824 (P73)

First known performance:	9 May 1824, in a concert given by Friedrich Wranitzky at the kleinen Redoutensaal, Vienna. Performers: Anton Haizinger, Jacob Rauscher, Joseph Seipelt and Herr Ruprecht (see Waidelich/ Hilmar Dokumente I No. 274 for full programme). The quartet is not identified by name in either the programme or the reviews – but it seems probable that *Der Gondelfahrer* was performed on this occasion (see also Waidelich/Hilmar Dokumente II No. 274 and Deutsch Doc. Biog. No. 469)
Performance reviews:	*Wiener allgemeine Theaterzeitung* No. 66 (1 June 1824), p. 264 [Waidelich/Hilmar Dokumente I No. 279] *Allgemeine musikalische Zeitung* (Vienna), No. 37 (2 June 1824), p. 145f. [Waidelich/Hilmar Dokumente I No. 280]
Subsequent editions:	AGA XVI 9: p. 83; NSA III: Vol. 3
Arrangements:	Arr. Franz Liszt (1811–1886) for solo piano (1838) [*see* Transcriptions] Arr. G. Hausmann (fl. 1840) *Der Gondelfahrer* for chorus and orchestra Arr. Hermann Kretzschmar (1848–1924) *Der Gondelfahrer* for chorus und orchestra Arr. Michael Raucheisen (1889–1984) for two high voices (Maria Ivogün & Karl Erb) and piano (1927) [*see* Transcriptions] Arr. Hans Zender (b. 1936) *Coronach, 23. Psalm und Der Gondelfahrer* for choir and orchestra [*see* Orchestrations]
Discography and timing:	

			John Mark Ainsley, Jamie
Hyperion I 35[10]			MacDougall, Simon
Hyperion II 29[5]		3'27	Keenlyside & Michael George

← *Gondelfahrer* D808   *Wandrers Nachtlied II* D768 →

GOTT DER WELTSCHÖPFER
(Uz) **D986** [H279]
C major   1816?

God, creator
of the world

Quartet, SATB

(54 bars)

Zu Gott, zu Gott flieg' auf, hoch über
  alle Sphären!
Jauchz ihm, weitschallender Gesang,
Dem Ewigen! Er hiess das alte Nichts gebären;
Und sein allmächtig Wort war Zwang.

Fly up to God, high above all the spheres,

Wide-echoing song, rejoice in Him!
The Eternal! He bade the ancient void give birth,
And His almighty word was law.

Ihm, aller Wesen Quelle, werde
Von allen Wesen Lob gebracht,
Im Himmel und auf Erde
Lob seiner weisen Macht!

[(. . . 20 . . .)]

To Him, source of all beings,
Let all beings give praise;
In heaven and on earth
Praise be to His wise power.

[(. . . 20 . . .)]

JOHANN PETER UZ (1720–1796); poem written between 1763 and 1767

For a note concerning the background to the publication of Op. 112, see the commentary for the first quartet in the sequence, *Gott im Ungewitter* D985. *Gott der Weltschöpfer*, the second piece in the triptych, is altogether simpler than what has gone before. The music eloquently speaks for dating this quartet to as early as 1816. If the blazing C major of triumphant religious conviction reminds us of the later grandiose choral setting of *Die Allmacht* D875A, this piece is much less ornate; it is nevertheless typical of the mature Schubert to modulate from C major to C flat major within the space of ten bars. The accompaniment is scarcely more than a doubling of the vocal parts relieved by only a handful of more adventurous pianistic details. The three chords of introduction are almost painfully plain; in the absence of the original autographs it is not even certain whether these are genuine Schubert or were inserted by the publisher Czerny. There are signs, here and there, of the old-style striding basses, reminiscent of *Das grosse Halleluja* from 1816, but on the whole this effective music eschews fussy chromaticism. The plunging basses which move the music from C major to F before the repeat of the words 'flieg' auf, zu Gott' suggest the movement of flight. But even illustrative touches such as this are rare. The purpose of this music is to convey a sort of religious immensity. In this mood, Schubert draws on block harmonies rather than resorting to the harmonic wiles more typical of his art. Haydn, Mozart and Beethoven achieve blazing moments like this in the finales of their religious works. Schubert's teacher Salieri would have claimed to have learned such powerful simplicity from Gluck, whose operas were, of course, also a great influence on the young Schubert.

Of the poem's twenty-one strophes, Schubert sets only the first. This is a contrast to the previous song (*Gott im Ungewitter*) where Schubert sets all seven of Uz's quatrains.

Autograph:	Missing or lost
First edition:	Published as Op. post. 112 no. 2 by Josef Czerny, Vienna in March 1829 (P201)
Publication reviews:	*Allgemeiner Musikalischer Anzeiger* (Vienna), no. 14 (4 April 1829), p. 55 [Waidelich/Hilmar Dokumente I no. 718] *Wiener Zeitschrift für Kunst, Literatur, Theater und Mode* no. 93 (4 August 1829), p. 772 [Waidelich/Hilmar Dokumente I no. 740]
Subsequent editions:	AGA XVII 7: p. 164; NSA III: Vol. 2a/54

Discography and timing:	Deutsche Grammophon		Elly Ameling, Janet Baker,
	Schubert-Quartette	2'22	Peter Schreier & Dietrich Fischer-Dieskau
	Hyperion I 32[23]		Patricia Rozario, Catherine
	Hyperion II 15[6]	2'06	Wyn-Rogers, Jamie MacDougall & Michael George

←— *Gott im Ungewitter* D985   *Fragment aus dem Aeschylus* D450 —→

GOTT, HÖRE MEINE STIMME *see Der VIERJÄHRIGE POSTEN* D190

GOTT IM FRÜHLINGE
(Uz) **D448** [H275]

God in springtime

The song exists in two versions, the first of which is discussed below:
(1) June 1816; (2) November 1816?

(1) E major

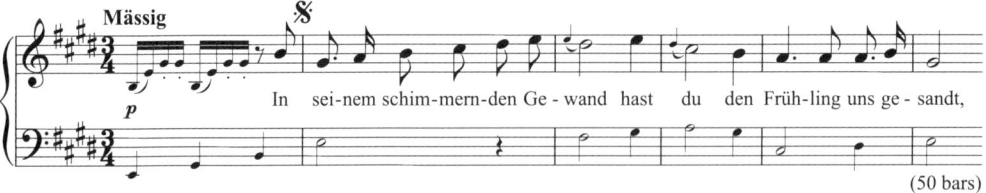

In sei-nem schim-mern-den Ge - wand hast du den Früh-ling uns ge - sandt,

(50 bars)

(2) 'Langsam mit Gefühl'   E major   ¾   [46 bars]

In seinem schimmernden Gewand	You have sent us spring
Hast du den Frühling uns gesandt,	In his shimmering robes
Und Rosen um sein Haupt gewunden.	And entwined roses about his head.
Holdlächelnd kömmt er schon!	Already he comes, sweetly smiling;
Es führen ihn die Stunden,	The hours lead him
O Gott, auf seinen Blumenthron.	To his throne of flowers, O Lord.
Er geht in Büschen, und sie blühen;	He walks among bushes, and they bloom;
Den Fluren kömmt ihr frisches Grün,	The meadows acquire their fresh green,
Und Wäldern wächst ihr Schatten wieder,	And shade returns to the woods;
Der West, liebkosend, schwingt	Caressingly the west wind
Sein tauendes Gefieder,	Waves its dewy wings
Und jeder frohe Vogel singt.	And every happy bird sings.
Mit eurer Lieder süssem Klang,	Birds, with the sweet notes of your songs
Ihr Vögel, soll auch mein Gesang	Let my song also
Zum Vater der Natur sich schwingen.	Soar up to the Father of Nature.
Entzückung reisst mich hin!	I am filled with rapture!
Ich will dem Herrn lobsingen,	I will sing praises to the Lord
Durch den ich wurde, was ich bin!	Who made me what I am.
[(...4...)]	[(...4...)]

JOHANN PETER UZ (1720–1796); poem written between 1763 and 1767

This is the fourth of Schubert's five Uz solo settings (1816). See the poet's biography for a chronological list of all the Uz settings.

All five of the Uz songs belong to the productive month of June 1816. Schubert has fitted out an eighteenth-century poem with music that suggests an earlier epoch: all is rococo elegance with little outward show of Romantic introspection. The stylistic 'e' on a dative, masculine or neuter, noun – as in *Frühlinge* – is an archaism that lasted well into the nineteenth century, as we know from the Schober setting recently renamed by the NSA – *Am Bach im Frühlinge* D361. The vocal line sails above one of those moto perpetuo accompaniments that the composer invents to illustrate the ceaseless workings of nature (e.g. *Die Sterne* of Leitner D939). A figure made up of four semiquavers (two phrased together and two staccato) occurs 140 times and generates elated yet contained tension to suggest the unwinding of the vernal coil. Capell writes that this figure was inspired by the poet's opening words about 'shimmering robes', but it also depicts the energy of spring's rising sap and the joyful state of mind of the singer. Schubert contributed a second version of the song, marked 'Langsam mit Gefühl' (as opposed to 'Mässig'), to the lieder album for Therese Grob. The accompanying figure, technically tricky for the first version, is less distinctive and easier to play in the second.

The form of the song is a simple ABA with art concealing art when the composer returns to the music of the first strophe with a tiny bridge passage (a single bar, b. 16) of delicate ingenuity. There are delicious touches throughout: the exotic introduction of A sharp in the bass (the key is E major) on the perfumed word 'Rosen' (b. 7), thus slyly initiating a brief move to the dominant; the use of triplets in the vocal line to paint green shoots ('frisches Grün', b. 21) cheekily emerging, as well as the caressing west wind and the singing of birds; the sudden rapturous semiquavers on 'reisst mich hin' (bb. 10–11 for the second time). The beautiful little postlude where the semiquavers go into the left hand, while the tune in the right suggests gratitude and piety, exists in only one of the copies of the song.

Schubert selected the first three of Uz's seven strophes, and the song is the perfect length for the open-hearted and simple pantheistic hymn the composer makes of it. It reflects his own religious conviction in the absence of a commitment to the church of his fathers – that intuition accompanied by strong emotion that Spinoza called 'the intellectual love of God', which acknowledges the dependence of all things on the wholeness of nature.

Autograph:	Pierpont Morgan Library, New York (first version, first draft)
	In private possession in Switzerland (second version, part of the Therese Grob album)
Publication:	First published as Vol. 7 no. 43 in Friedlaender's edition by Peters, Leipzig in 1887 (P504; first version)
	First published as part of the NSA in 2002 (P839; second version)
Subsequent editions:	Peters: Vol. 7/94; AGA XX 233: Vol. 4/121 (first version); NSA IV: Vol. 10/176 (first version) & 178 (second version)
Bibliography:	Capell 1928, pp. 115–16
	Fischer-Dieskau 1977, p. 72
Discography and timing:	Fischer-Dieskau I 7^{21} 2'12
	Hyperion I 19^2
	Hyperion II 15^2 2'06 Felicity Lott

← *Die Liebesgötter* D446   *An den Schlaf* D447 →

GOTT IM UNGEWITTER   God in the tempest   Quartet, SATB
(Uz) **D985** [H278]
C minor   1816?

(108 bars)

Du Schrecklicher, wer kann vor dir	Awesome One, who can stand before you
Und deinem Donner steh'n?	And your thunder?
Gross ist der Herr! was trotzen wir?[1]	Great is the Lord; why do we defy Him?
Er winkt, und wir vergeh'n.	When He gives a sign we perish;
Er lagert sich in schwarzer Nacht;	When He rests in the black night
Die Völker zittern schon:	The nations tremble:
Geflügeltes Verderben wacht	Winged destruction watches
Um seinen furchtbarn Thron.	Around His fearful throne.
Rothglühend schleudert seine Hand	Glowing red, His hand
Den Blitz aus finstrer Höh':	Hurls lightning from the dark heights,
Und Donner stürzt sich auf das Land	And thunder bursts upon the land
In einer Feuersee:	In a sea of fire.
Dass selbst der Erde fester Grund	So that even the earth's solid foundations
Vom Zorn des Donners bebt,	Quake at the thunder's wrath,
Und was um ihr erschüttert Rund	Together with all that dwells on its shaken surface
Und in der Tiefe lebt.	And in its depths.
Den Herrn und seinen Arm erkennt	Trembling nature recognizes
Die zitternde Natur,	The Lord and His arm,
Da weit umher der Himmel brennt	As far and wide the heavens
Und weit umher die Flur.	And the fields blaze.
Wer schützt mich Sterblichen, mich Staub,	Who will protect me, a mortal, mere dust,
Wenn, der im Himmel wohnt	If He who dwells in heaven
Und Welten pflückt, wie dürres Laub,	And plucks the whole world like withered leaves
Nicht huldreich mich verschont?	Will not spare me in His mercy?
Wir haben einen Gott voll Huld,	We have a gracious God,
Auch wenn er zornig scheint:	Even when He seems angry.
Er herrscht mit schonender Geduld,	He rules with gentle patience,
Der grosse Menschenfreund!	The mighty friend of mankind.

JOHANN PETER UZ (1720–1796); poem written between 1763 and 1767

In the absence of the original manuscripts, Eusebius Mandyczewski in the AGA followed the first edition of Op. 112, publishing the three quartets *Gott im Ungewitter* (Uz) D985, *Gott der Weltschöpfer* (Uz) D986 and *Hymne an den Unendlichen* (Schiller) D232 as if they were three movements of a cantata, separated only by their titles that appear to mark subsections of the same piece. The quartets were first published in this way by the firm of Czerny in 1829, the year after the composer's death. Schubert had certainly been in touch with Czerny in the last year of his life, so there is a possibility that this sequence had been agreed between them; Ferdinand Schubert may also have played a part in this posthumous assemblage. There is no real evidence to suggest that Schubert had envisaged one large work beginning in C minor (*Gott im*

---

[1] In Uz's original, 'Der Herr ist gross'.

Ungewitter) attached to another short quartet in C major (*Gott der Weltschöpfer*) and returning to C minor for *Hymne an den Unendlichen*. And yet the idea of such a sequence is not unattractive, and is typical of how the composer would sometimes arrange his works for publication. The first two works in the sequence certainly have a poet in common, and almost certainly date from June 1816 when Schubert was occupied with his solo settings of Uz. In all these poems, Uz looks to the natural world, and the weather, for evidence of God's ubiquity. The *Hymne an den Unendlichen* dates from 1815; it is possible that Schubert envisaged combining this Schiller setting with the two Uz quartets as early as 1816. At the time he was still in touch with Salieri, and this work might have derived from his contrapuntal exercises with the Italian maestro.

Like *An die Sonne* D439, another Uz setting for SATB, this is a fine example of Schubert's antique style where shades of Handel and C. P. E. Bach conjoin with those of Haydn, himself influenced by the older masters. As the date is uncertain, Deutsch consigned it to the outward region of Schubert's catalogue – the late 900s where the problematic works are to be found. That someone as experienced as Deutsch could come to no conclusion about the dating of this music shows that Schubert in this mood gives us almost no clues or thumbprints typical of his song-composing style. Despite the work's grandeur and skill, it is strangely anonymous. Both Leopold von Sonnleithner and Schubert's brother Ferdinand orchestrated the piano accompaniment. The piece found favour with the publisher Czerny soon after Schubert's death, possibly because there was then an appetite in Vienna for religious music of this kind – as indicated by Franz Lachner's orchestration of *Mirjams Siegesgesang* D942.

There could scarcely be a word in the German language more suggestive of dotted rhythm, when spoken, than 'Schrecklicher'. It is the shudder inherent in this word that pervades the first section of this song. The key of C minor seems the obvious choice for religious music with an element of divine vengeance. After the invocation (the bass sings 'Du Schrecklicher' as a solo, and is twice echoed by his colleagues) the music moves to and fro between the staves in ever-inventive interchange and imitation. The question 'Wer?' is tossed between the top and bottom pairs of voices (bb. 10–11). 'Gross ist der Herr! was trotzen wir?' initiates a fugato at b. 12 that lasts only eight bars, but which displays a working knowledge of fugal technique; it moves convincingly between alternating subject and counter-subject in ascending order up the four staves, from bass to soprano. The peremptory setting of 'Er winkt' (bb. 20–21) is appropriately gestural, and at 'und wir vergeh'n' the bass line swoons in the bottom regions as if giddily over-awed (bb. 23–4).

At 'Er lagert sich in schwarzer Nacht' (from b. 24) there is a switch to the later musical language of *Sturm und Drang*. The piano writing, rumbling octave basses, suddenly looks like Beethoven on the page, an illustrative response to the idea of trembling ('Die Völker zittern schon' bb. 26–8). There is more contrapuntal interchange and imitation at 'Geflügeltes Verderben wacht / Um seinen furchtbarn Thron', music for the indictment of a potentate whose punishment is a foregone conclusion. This repetitive section moves without pause into a moto perpetuo of storm music. This takes its musical direction from the thunder-and-lightning words 'Blitz aus finstrer Höh'' (bb. 35–6) and the following 'Donner stürzt sich auf das Land', as well as the image of 'Die zitternde Natur'. An onslaught of concerted voices sweeps aside layered part-writing, and banishes all pretence at old-fashioned counterpoint. The look of the incessant dotted rhythms on the page is similar to that of the horse-ride battle music of *Normans Gesang* D846. This music of the Last Judgement brings to mind the Klopstock setting by C. P. E. Bach on the same subject – *Der Tag des Weltgerichts* – which is also based on a moto perpetuo of jangling dotted rhythms. The section ends in B flat major – a six-bar postlude fades away, diminuendo, as it moves through different harmonies on a B flat pedal (from b. 62) and returns to a hushed B flat major.

The younger Bach and Klopstock were content to leave the world quaking before the terror of divine reprisal. But Uz provides a consolatory get-out clause for the righteous, and Schubert sets this as a benign *Andante con moto* in E flat major (from b. 70). The wrath of God is tempered by His mercy, and the relative major shows the other side of His character. The music still remains rather simple and old-fashioned, as is often the case with this composer when he portrays the devout, but occasionally an inimitably Schubertian touch emerges in the details: he cannot, for example resist dry quavers separated by rests at 'pflückt', wie dürres Laub' (bb. 74–6). The word 'zornig' occasions off-beat dramatic emphasis (b. 83) but the elongation of the word 'grosse' (bb. 87–8 and 97–8) reaffirms God's friendship with mankind. Overall this music is remarkable for its seamless legato, in line with the text's insistence that God is gentle and patient, despite appearing angry.

Autograph:	Missing or lost
First edition:	Published as Op. post. 112 no. 1 by Josef Czerny, Vienna in March 1829 (P200)
Publication reviews:	*Allgemeiner musikalischer Anzeiger* (Vienna), no. 14 (4 April 1829), p. 55 [Waidelich/Hilmar Dokumente I no. 718]
	Wiener Zeitschrift für Kunst, Literatur, Theater und Mode no. 93 (4 August 1829), p. 772 [Waidelich/Hilmar Dokumente I no. 740]
First known performance:	29 November 1829 in the first *Gesellschafts-Concert* of the Gesellschaft der Musikfreunde at the Redoutensaal, Vienna. The work was performed in an arrangement for orchestra by Leopold von Sonnleithner (who is only identified as 'a member of the Gesellschaft' in the programme). Performers unknown. (See Waidelich/Hilmar Dokumente I no. 754 for full concert programme.)
Performance reviews:	*Wiener Zeitschrift für Kunst, Literatur, Theater und Mode* no. 149 (12 December 1829), p. 1228 [Waidelich/Hilmar Dokumente I no. 755]
	Allgemeine musikalische Zeitung (Leipzig), No. 51 (23 December 1829), col. 845ff. [Waidelich/Hilmar Dokumente II no. 756]
	Berliner allgemeine musikalische Zeitung no. 5 (30 January 1830), p. 40 [Waidelich/Hilmar Dokumente I no. 763]
Subsequent editions:	AGA XVII 6: p. 156; NSA III: Vol. 2a/20
Bibliography:	Black 2000, p. 32
Discography and timing:	Deutsche Grammophon *Schubert-Quartette* 5'19 Elly Ameling, Janet Baker, Peter Schreier & Dietrich Fischer-Dieskau
	Hyperion I 32²² Patricia Rozario, Catherine Wyn-Rogers, Jamie 4'46 MacDougall & Michael George
	Hyperion II 15⁵	

← *Der gute Hirt* D449   *Gott der Weltschöpfer* D986 →

GOTT IN DER NATUR

(KLEIST) **D757** [H489]

C major   August 1822

God in nature   Quartet, SSAA

Gross ist der Herr, gross ist der Herr!

(118 bars)

Gross ist der Herr! Die Himmel ohne Zahl	Great is the Lord! The heavens without number
Sind Säle seiner Burg,[1]	Are rooms in His palace,
Sein Wagen Sturm und donnerndes Gewölk'	Storms are His chariot;
Und Blitze sein Gespann.	Thunderclouds and lightning His horses.
Die Morgenröt' ist nur ein Widerschein	The dawn is but a reflection
Von seines Kleides Saum;	Of His garment's hem;
Und gegen seinen Glanz ist Dämmerung[2]	And compared with His radiance
Der Sonne flammend Licht.	The sun's blazing light is but dusk.
Er sieht mit gnäd'gem Blick zur Erd' herab,[3]	He looks graciously down
Sie grünet, blüht und lacht.	Upon the blooming, flowering, smiling earth.
Er schilt; es fähret Feuer von Felsen auf,	At His reproach fire rises from the rock,
Und Meer und Himmel bebt.	And sea and sky tremble.
Lobt den Gewaltigen, den grossen Herrn,[4]	Praise the Almighty, the great Lord.
Ihr Lichter seiner Burg,	Lights of His citadel,
Ihr Sonnenheere! flammt zu seinem Ruhm!	Hosts of His suns, blaze to His glory!
Ihr Erden singt sein Lob!	Worlds, sing His praise!
[(. . . 13 . . .)]	[(. . . 13 . . .)]

CHRISTIAN EWALD VON KLEIST (1715–1759)

The following extract is from the memoirs of Gerhard von Breuning (1884) who recounts his conversations with the Fröhlich sisters who were acquainted with Schubert in their youth. The formidable Anna Fröhlich had encouraged the composer to compose choral music for her female singing pupils at the Konservatorium:

---

[1] Kleist's line (as printed in *Sämmutliche Gedichte* (Vienna, 1816)) is 'Sind seine Wohnungen' followed by 'Sein Wagen sind die donnernden Gewölk''.
[2] The third and fourth lines of this strophe read 'Und gegen seinen Glanz ist alles Licht / Der Sonne, Dämmerung'.
[3] The third strophe is printed thus: 'Er sieht mit gnäd'gem Blick von seiner Höh / Zur Erd' herab; sie lacht. / Er schilt; es fähret Feuer von Felsen auf / Des Erdballs Axe bebt.'
[4] Kleist writes 'den gnäd'gen Herrn'.

On 8 October 1876, the Vienna Men's Choral Society had performed Schubert's Gott in der Natur *with resounding success. When I told this to Anna the next day she broke in excitedly 'He wrote that for me'. Surprised and sceptical I replied 'But it is for chorus and orchestra' whereupon she said, 'But originally it was written for quartet. It happened like this. It was shortly after Schubert had been introduced to us and was coming to the musical evenings which I used to give at that time at our house; we had just sung the trios and other things from* Die Zauberflöte *and he said over and over again: Bless my soul! (I can see him still, folding his hands together as if in prayer, because he was so moved, and pressing them against his mouth, as he used to do when he heard something beautiful – Heavens! How beautiful that is. . . . and then suddenly "But I know just what I shall do" – And then in a few days he brought me the quartet "Gott ist mein Hirt" [Psalm 23] and soon after that the quartet* Gott in der Natur *. . . But apart from these he only wrote the* Ständchen *for me and, later on,* Mirjams Siegesgesang *. . .'. Kathi added . . . 'Yes indeed, our poor Schubert, his was a wonderful nature. Never was he envious and jealous, as so many others are. On the contrary, if something beautiful in the way of music was performed, he would put his hands together, against his mouth, and sit there quite enraptured. The innocence and simplicity of his nature were quite indescribable. Very often he would sit with us on the sofa, joyfully rubbing his hands, and say "Today I think I have done something which is really good". Ah well, our poor Schubert! Only a fortnight before his illness, or rather before his death, he was at our house.'*

The Fröhlich memories, even if filtered through other sources and embroidered with hindsight, have the ring of truth. Two of the four women, Anna and Josefine, lived until 1878, and the other two, Babette and Katharina until 1879, so they survived to see their former friend become a world-famous figure. Breuning's long account of their conversation bristles with their bossy energy and enthusiasm; it exactly captures the tone of the Viennese senior citizen who has done, seen and known it all, and is prepared to talk about it as a special favour. It is clear that Schubert also found the Fröhlichs irresistible, not only because three of them were wonderful musicians, but because they were the type of life-enhancing women from whom no one can refuse a request. Usually Schubert was notoriously uncooperative in providing music to order, but Anna was clearly a special case. Having written the *Ständchen* D920 for mezzo soprano and male (instead of female) chorus, he meekly corrected his mistake, and immediately provided another version of the piece for the correct forces.

Four-part writing for four female voices (two sopranos and two altos) is not the easiest musical combination. It is hardly surprising that the piece was re-scored for men's chorus with orchestra (typical of the sort of arrangement sanctioned by Ferdinand Schubert after his brother's death) and that is how Breuning first heard it in Vienna. Apart from that *Ständchen* chorus, Schubert wrote only two works for four-part female chorus. The other piece (as Anna tells us) is *Der 23. Psalm* D706. On the whole that is more successful than *Gott in der Natur* because it is gentle and exploits the euphonious combination of voices without drawing attention to the main drawback of the format: a lack both of a strong bass line and the type of punchy force and energy that is possible in a mixed quartet, or a quartet of men's voices. Nevertheless, the composer seems to have been inspired by *Die Zauberflöte* where there is a lot of ingenious part-writing for ensembles of higher voices in the music for the three ladies and three boys.

There are a few *Magic Flute*-like passages in *Gott in der Natur*; even the words might have been intoned by a Sarastro. The text by Christian Ewald von Kleist (not by Gleim; this mistake goes back to Schubert's autograph, and was perpetuated by the AGA) is old-fashioned enough to summon up a feast of pomposo baroque pastiche. Schubert sets the first four of the poem's seventeen verses. The key is ceremonial C major, and the 'Maestoso' opening movement is made up of scales, ominous trills appropriate for divine thunder, and double-dotted figurations.

Schubert seems to have changed the poet's words to include a 'Sturm' not in the original: this gives him an opportunity to provide exciting figurations of bristling demisemiquavers in the piano, the left hand a rolling tremolo. The image of lightning ('Und Blitze') sets off antiphonal exchanges between the voices (b. 12) while the accompaniment's dotted rhythm seems electrically charged.

The poem's second strophe inspires quieter and more gentle music; the lead soprano is cast as a soloist floating a descant over a lyrical and hushed description of the dawn where the other three vocal parts are supported by the piano's chords gently throbbing off the beat (from b. 22). The image of 'Glanz', like starlight in *Nachthelle* D892, prompts accompanying semiquavers pulsating on banks of held chords (from b. 25), a radiance that is as awe-struck as awe-inspiring. Then there is a return to the milder music as God looks benignly down on earth ('Er sieht mit gnäd'gem Blick zur Erd' herab'). The choral version of these words is echoed in an almost operatic solo by the first soprano (bb. 33–4); the tessitura here plunges down the stave as the all-seeing Almighty gazes down from a higher vantage point. Dotted rhythms and a fortissimo dynamic return at 'Er schilt; es fähret Feuer von Felsen' (from b. 38), a reaction to the phrase 'Meer und Himmel bebt' – a shaking also depicted in left-hand tremolandi octaves (from b. 40). This device is found more in Schubert's later music than his earlier work, and is an early indication of the Romantic style.

The piece's second movement is an 'Allegro giusto' in ¾ (from b. 46) in the grand manner of a closing movement of a religious cantata where praise to God in the highest draws the threads of all that has preceded it into a mighty peroration. The key remains C major, now less clouded by illustrative chromatic harmonies. Although there are thirteen more verses in Kleist's poem (entitled *Hymne*), Schubert prefers to repeat the words of the same verse in order to achieve a majestic conclusion. The sopranos are first pitted antiphonally against the altos, the voices underpinned by a typically baroque bass – quavers in striding octaves. The addition of right-hand music to this signals all four voices uniting in block harmony (from b. 70), but only for a short while; Schubert enjoys himself too much with lobbing the vocal line between the parts for that unanimity to last long.

At the fourth repetition of the words (from b. 80), in a really orchestral touch, the accompaniment breaks out into a ceaseless slew of sewing-machine semiquavers in the best baroque manner. This energizes the texture in the absence of louder vocal sound – something which is made impossible by the absence of men's voices. This semiquaver moto perpetuo continues almost to the end, at first accompanied by striding left-hand quavers, and then by broad chords that thicken the bass line. The final bars insist on the triad of the home key in a bold manner worthy of a large symphonic work by Beethoven. Anna Fröhlich's young lead singer is given a challenging high C (b. 111), and double octaves ascend the piano to bring the piece to a close in a suitably stirring way. The whole thing is a shining example of Schubert's ability to write to order, and of his ability to assimilate the manner and style of older composers. Before it was fashionable to write for children, or for schools, he gives no quarter to the young ladies of the Konservatorium; he writes for them as seasoned professionals. Only an insistence on a suitably religious text and the absence of love poetry show that the prospective performers are still of an age to require chaperones.

Autograph:	Männergesang-Verein, Vienna (incomplete sketch)
First edition:	Published as Op. post. 133 by Diabelli, Vienna in November 1839 (P327)
First known performance:	8 March 1827, *Abend-Unterhaltung* of the Gesellschaft der Musikfreunde at the Musikverein, Vienna. Performed by twelve students of the Vienna Conservatoire (see Waidelich/Hilmar

	Dokumente I no. 459 for full concert programme; see also Deutsch Doc. Biog. no. 822)
Performance reviews:	*Berliner allgemeine musikalische Zeitung* No. 23 (6 June 1827), p. 182 [Waidelich/Hilmar Dokumente I no. 506; Deutsch Doc. Biog. No. 849]
Subsequent editions:	AGA XVIII 3: p. 10; NSA III: Vol. 3
Discography and timing:	Hyperion I 35[1] Hyperion II 25[15] 6'38 Patricia Rozario, Lorna Anderson, Catherine Denley & Catherine Wyn-Rogers

← *Du liebst mich nicht* D756   *Schwanengesang* D744 →

GOTT IST MEIN HIRT *see* Der 23. PSALM D706

Der GOTT UND DIE BAJADERE   The god and the dancing-girl
(Goethe) **D254** [H140]
E♭ major   18 August 1815

(26 bars)

Mahadöh, der Herr der Erde,	Mahadeva, Lord of the Earth,
Kommt herab zum sechstenmal,	Descends a sixth time
Dass er unsers gleichen werde,	That he might become one of us
Mit zu fühlen Freud' und Qual.	And with us feel joy and sorrow.
Er bequemt sich hier zu wohnen,	He deigns to dwell here
Lässt sich alles selbst geschehn.	And experience all things himself.
Soll er strafen oder schonen,	If he is to punish or forgive
Muss er Menschen menschlich sehn.	He must see mortals as a mortal.
Und hat er die Stadt sich als Wandrer betrachtet,	And having viewed the town in the guise of a traveller
Die Grossen belauert, auf Kleine geachtet,	Watching the great, observing the lowly,
Verlässt er sie Abends, um weiter zu gehn.	He leaves it in the evening to journey onwards.
Als er nun hinaus gegangen,	When he had walked out
Wo die letzten Häuser sind,	To where the last houses are,
Sieht er, mit gemalten Wangen,	He encounters a lovely, forlorn girl
Ein verlornes schönes Kind.	With painted cheeks.
'Grüss' dich, Jungfrau!' – 'Dank der Ehre!	'Greetings to you, maiden!' – 'I thank you for this honour!
Wart', ich komme gleich hinaus —'	Wait, I shall come straight out.'
'Und wer bist du?' – 'Bajadere,	'And who are you?' – 'A dancing-girl,
Und dies ist der Liebe Haus.'	And this is the house of love.'

Sie rührt sich, die Cimbeln zum Tanze
   zu schlagen;
Sie weiss sich so lieblich im Kreise zu tragen,
Sie neigt sich und biegt sich, und reicht ihm
   den Strauss.

   Schmeichelnd zieht sie ihn zur Schwelle,
   Lebhaft ihn ins Haus hinein.
   'Schöner Fremdling, lampenhelle
   Soll sogleich die Hütte sein.
   Bist du müd', ich will dich laben,
   Lindern deiner Füsse Schmerz.
   Was du willst, das sollst du haben,
   Ruhe, Freuden oder Scherz.'
Sie lindert geschäftig geheuchelte Leiden,
Der Göttliche lächelt; er siehet mit Freuden,
Durch tiefes Verderben, ein menschliches
   Herz.

[. . . 2 . . .]

   Spät entschlummert, unter Scherzen,
   Früh erwacht, nach kurzer Rast,
   Findet sie an ihrem Herzen
   Tod den vielgeliebten Gast.
   Schreiend stürzt sie auf ihn nieder;
   Aber nicht erweckt sie ihn,
   Und man trägt die starren Glieder
   Bald zur Flammengrube hin.
Sie höret die Priester, die Totengesänge,
Sie raset und rennet, und teilet die Menge.
'Wer bist du? was drängt zu der Grube
   dich hin?'

   Bei der Bahre stürzt sie nieder,
   Ihr Geschrei durchdringt die Luft:
   'Meinen Gatten will ich wieder!
   Und ich such' ihn in der Gruft.
   Soll zur Asche mir zerfallen
   Dieser Glieder Götterpracht?
   Mein! er war es, mein vor allen!
   Ach, nur Eine süsse Nacht!'
Es singen die Priester: 'Wir tragen die Alten,
Nach langem Ermatten und spätem Erkalten,
Wir tragen die Jugend, noch eh' sie's gedacht.'

[. . .]

   So das Chor, das ohn' Erbarmen
   Mehret ihres Herzens Not;

She hastens to begin the dance with a clash of
   cymbals.
She knows how to circle round so charmingly;
She dips and turns, and hands him a posy.

   She coaxes him to the threshold
   And vivaciously draws him into the house.
   'Fair stranger, this humble abode
   Shall at once be bright with lamplight.
   If you are weary, I shall refresh you,
   And soothe your sore feet.
   You shall have whatever you desire:
   Rest, pleasure or play.'
Assiduously she soothes his feigned pains.
The immortal smiles; joyfully he beholds,
Through her deep corruption, a human heart.

[. . . 2 . . .]

   Falling asleep late while dallying,
   Waking early after brief rest,
   She finds the beloved guest
   Dead at her side.
   Screaming, she falls upon him,
   But she cannot revive him.
   And soon his rigid limbs
   Are borne to the funeral pyre.
She hears the priests and the funeral chants;
In her frenzy she rushes and pierces the crowd.
'Who are you? What drives you to this grave?'

   By the bier she throws herself down,
   And her cries echo through the air:
   'I want my husband back!
   And I shall seek him in the tomb.
   Shall these limbs in their divine glory
   Fall to ashes before me?
   He was mine, mine alone,
   Alas, for but one sweet night!'
The priests chant: 'We bear away the old,
For long exhausted, lately grown cold;
Take the youth to you in flames!'

[. . .]

   Thus chants the choir, mercilessly
   Deepening the pain within her heart.

Und mit ausgestreckten Armen	And with outstretched arms
Springt sie in den heissen Tod.	She leaps into the burning death.
Doch der Götter-Jüngling hebet	But the divine youth rises up
Aus der Flamme sich empor,	From the pyre
Und in seinen Armen schwebet	And his beloved soars aloft
Die Geliebte mit hervor.	In his arms.
Es freut sich die Gottheit der reuigen Sünder;	The godhead rejoices in penitent sinners;
Unsterbliche heben verlorene Kinder	With arms of fire immortals raise
Mit feurigen Armen zum Himmel empor.	Lost children up to heaven.

JOHANN WOLFGANG VON GOETHE (1749–1832); poem written 6–9 June 1797

This is the twenty-first of Schubert's seventy-five Goethe solo settings (1814–26). See the poet's biography for a chronological list of all the Goethe settings.

This important poem (subtitled 'Indische Legende') was a rare excursion into the East for Goethe in the years before his *West-östlicher Divan* period (cf. *Mahomets Gesang* D549 and D721 where the poem is even earlier). This 'Indian legend' was written in 1797, and published in

Illustrated *Der Gott und die Bajadere* from *Der Dichter des Deutschen Volkes* (1846).

Schiller's *Musenalmanach* for 1798 with Zelter's melody as part of the supplement provided in a pocket at the back of the book. The idea for the text came from a story recounted rather dryly in Sonnerat's *Journey to East India and China* (1783) but marvellously fashioned by Goethe into a tale about the redemptive power of love. The practice of *suttee*, where a Hindu widow immolates herself ith her husband's body, incomprehensible and repulsive to Christians, was treated by Goethe with a characteristic respect for other religions and customs.

The word 'Bajadere' is the German version of the French *bayadère* (meaning a Hindu dancing girl, particularly at a Southern Indian temple) and derives from the Portuguese *bailadiera* or dancer. It was Goethe's idea to introduce the god Shiva into the poem under the name of Mahadöh or Mahadeva – the great god. The story was made into an opera by Auber and a ballet by Minkus. It is the only song in the repertoire before the time of Weill and Eisler (with the possible exception of *Die Männer sind mechant* D866/3) which is about prostitution – a sore point in Schubert's later history when he was to discover the terrible consequences of love at a price. The young composer's selection of this text seems to show a tolerance and freedom from convention that would almost certainly not have reflected his father's religious views, for example, despite the fact that Hegel had already compared this saga to the Christian story of Mary Magdalene.

Schubert's setting is controversial in its unambitious simplicity. Capell favours it and John Reed does not, considering the composer to have been completely led astray by his decision to treat the poem strophically. Similarly, Fischer-Dieskau finds the poem intractable for musical setting; for him Schubert's solution is too simple and Othmar Schoeck's too descriptive. It might be added that Carl Loewe's setting, not his greatest, is also episodic and attempts to reflect the text strophe by strophe. 'The poem', writes Capell, 'makes no call at all for music; but if music there was to be, Schubert's unobtrusive hymn-like tune was better than an elaborate setting which would for a certainty have been tiresome.' In agreeing with Capell, one is reminded of Schubert's 1828 setting of *Edward* (*Eine altschottische Ballade* D923) which, in its strophic simplicity, seems a failure on paper but is riveting in performance. Like the story of Edward and his terrible mother, *Der Gott und die Bajadere* is not the sort of strophic song where the performer can leave out a number of verses; the story requires almost all of them. Having embarked on the long journey with trepidation, both performer and listener find that the repetitive quality of the music has something hypnotic and mantra-like about it; one is tempted to give the composer credit for having imagined the chants of a faraway land with its exotic religious rites. The tune at first hearing seems merely hymn-like; mention of Mahadöh, Lord of the Earth, in the opening seems to have put Schubert in mind of Haydn's *Emperor's Hymn* Hob. XXVIa: 43. But the piece has hidden beauties, particularly in the second half where Goethe's metre (a tricky one) requires flowing dactyls to offset the foursquare opening. We are caught up in the grave dignity and concision of the story and, as Capell suggests, are somehow grateful that gratuitous musical illustration does not interrupt its flow. Loewe makes the girl dance trippingly, which adds nothing to the intensity of the story.

On the manuscript Schubert wrote: 'In these verses as well as in the others the content must determine the dynamics.' This is an indication that in this case Schubert was, for once, worried about the expressive limits of strophic form, even in his own increasingly masterful hands. In the Hyperion Edition we extended this implied freedom to the allocation of certain lines to other characters in Schubertiad fashion: the main voice of the narrator (Christine Schäfer) was supplemented by that of Mahadöh (John Mark Ainsley) in the opening, and the voices of the temple priests (John Mark Ainsley and Michael George) in the final strophes. Goethe's poem has nine strophes: for the Hyperion recording, 1, 2, 3, 6, 7 and 9 were performed – as translated above. Strophes 4 and 5 are not essential to the narrative but expand on the erotic relationship between Mahadöh and the dancer. Wigmore 1988 translated all nine strophes. That Schubert himself thought highly of this setting is shown by the fact that it was part of the second Lieder album prepared for Goethe (though never sent) in the summer of 1816.

Autograph:	Conservatoire collection, Bibliothèque Nationale, Paris (fair copy made for Goethe)
First edition:	Published as part of *Bisher unbekannte und unveröffentlichte Compositionen von Franz Schubert, Heft II* by Weinberger & Hofbauer, Vienna in 1887 (P489)
Subsequent editions:	Peters: Vol. 7/106; AGA XX 111: Vol. 3/32; NSA IV: Vol. 8/186
Bibliography:	Capell 1928, p. 105
	Fischer-Dieskau 1977, p. 45

Further settings:	Carl Friedrich Zelter (1758–1832) *Der Gott und die Bajadere* (1812)
	Carl Loewe (1769–1896) *Der Gott und die Bajadere: Indische legende* Op. 45 no. 2 (1835)
	Othmar Schoeck (1915–1986) *Der Gott und die Bajadere* Op. 34 (1921)

Discography and timing:	Fischer-Dieskau	—	
	Hyperion I 24⁶	9'01	Christine Schäfer with John
	Hyperion II 9¹		Mark Ainsley & Michael George

⟵ *Die Spinnerin* D247   *Der Rattenfänger* D255 ⟶

FRIEDRICH WILHELM GOTTER (1746–1797)

THE POETIC SOURCES
S1 *Gedichte von Friedrich Wilhelm Gotter*, bei Karl Wilhelm Ettlinger, Gotha, 1787, in 2 volumes. There was a Viennese reprint of this publication issued by Rudolf Gräffer, Wien, 1787

S2 *Gedichte von Friedrich Wilhelm Gotter*, bei Ch. Kaulfuss und C. Armbruster, Wien, 1816

It is possible that Schubert set the poem from either of these two editions. It seems more likely, however, that he used a Viennese edition, and more probably the recently published one of Gotter's works which is in a more portable format than either the Ettlinger or Gräffer volumes

THE SONG
August 1816   *Pflicht und Liebe* D467 [S2: pp. 14–15; or S1: Volume 1 pp. 8–9]

Portrait of Friedrich Gotter with signature.

Gotter was born in Gotha on 3 September 1746. After legal studies at the University of Göttingen he moved to Wetzlar in 1767 and spent a year in Austria as a teacher to two young noblemen. On his return to Wetzlar he came into contact with the young Goethe who was studying there at the University and courting Charlotte Buff in his 'Werther' phase. He remained in contact with Goethe for the rest of his life. Gotter was a specialist in French literature and he translated a number of French plays for performance in Germany, but was also interested in English poetry: his 1771 translation of Gray's *Elegy written in a country churchyard* had a considerable influence on the poets of the Göttingen Hainbund (qv Hölty). With his friend Christian Boie he founded the celebrated *Göttinger Musenalmanach* based on the French 'Almanac des Muses'. This idea alone, the transplanting of the Almanac from its French beginnings to its first real German-speaking manifestation, places Gotter as a hugely influential figure in the history of German literature. He was very much interested in working with composers and provided the libretto for Benda's melodrama *Medea*, as well as adapting Shakespeare's *The Tempest* for Friedrich von Einsiedel's *Die Geisterinsel*. Gotter was a much more significant figure in German literature and operatic history (as a sought-after librettist) than the small role he played in Schubert's output suggests. He was a frail individual from his boyhood, always much loved; he had a special gift for declamation and improvisation, and his so-called recited 'impromptus' were received with amazement by those who heard them. The last twenty-five years of his life were spent as an archivist and civil servant in his home town where he died on 18 March 1797.

Bibliography: Baumann 1992, p. 493

Das GRAB (I–V)   The grave
(Salis-Seewis) **D329a, D330, D377, D569, D643a** [H206, H225 & H377]

(D329a) for SATB, unaccompanied, C minor, 28 December 1815

(12 bars)

(D330) for TTBB, C minor, 28 December 1815

(8 bars)

(D377) for TTBB, C minor, 11 February 1816

(9 bars)

(D569) for unison male chorus, C♯ minor, June 1817

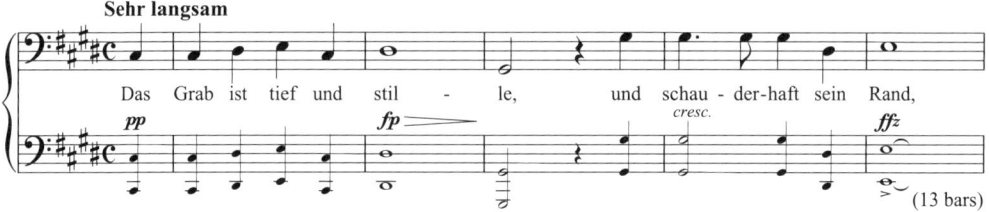

(13 bars)

(D643A) for SATB, unaccompanied, E♭ major, 1819

(10 bars)

Das Grab ist tief und stille,	Deep and silent is the grave,
Und schauderhaft sein Rand,	Terrible its brink;
Es deckt mit schwarzer Hülle	With its black shroud it covers
Ein unbekanntes Land.	An unknown land.
Das Lied der Nachtigallen	The nightingales' song
Tönt nicht in seinem Schoss.	Does not sound in its depths.
Der Freudschaft Rosen fallen	Only friendship's roses fall
Nur auf des Hügels Moos.	On the mossy mound.
[. . . 2 . . .]	[. . . 2 . . .]
Das arme Herz, hiernieder	Here below, the poor heart,
Von manchem Sturm bewegt,	Tossed by many a storm,
Erlangt den wahren Frieden	Only attains a true peace
Nur wo es nicht mehr schlägt.	When it beats no more.

JOHANN GAUDENZ VON SALIS-SEEWIS (1762–1834); poem written in 1783

There were ten solo-song settings of the poetry of Salis-Seewis composed in 1816, and some stray settings in 1817 and 1821. The last of these is the immortal *Der Jüngling an der Quelle* D300. *Das Grab* is not one of these solo settings, but it is an important poem in terms of the composer's assiduous sense of duty in regard to the work of a poet: Schubert set this text as a part-song no fewer than five times. The lyric is wrapped in a shroud of imagery: it features nightingales and friendship's roses at the same time as forsaken brides and the wailing of orphans. And he was not the only composer to be fascinated: this poem became an extremely fashionable text of the period (the Austrian musicologist A. Weinmann called it a 'literarisch-musikalischer Bestseller') and it appears many times in the work-lists of composers now largely forgotten. Schubert never seems to have thought of the poem as suitable for a solo song; this view of death emphasizes the fact that it is something that affects us all – a communal, and thus a choral, concern.

The first sketch for this poem (D329A) is a fragment that dates from 28 December 1815. This is an unaccompanied four-part canon in C minor (SATB) which breaks off after thirteen bars and is crossed out by the composer. For the second version, D330, Schubert abandons the idea of a canon. The setting, on the other side of the same manuscript, is dated 28 December 1815, for male voices. This TTBB setting has a piano accompaniment, and is in the key of G minor. Notable are the flattened harmonies for 'tief und stille' and the radiant transition into the tonic major for 'unbekanntes <u>Land</u>'.

Two months later, in February 1816, Schubert sets the poem again (D377). It is in C minor this time but it is also for piano-accompanied male chorus (TTBB). The tune is more static and ritualistic, and deliberately less expressive in terms of melody. This setting is the most austere of the five different versions; it seems almost drained of feeling in its graveside grief.

More than a year later, in June 1817, Schubert composed the most impressive of all his settings of this poem (D569). It is for unison male chorus with piano. For some reason Mandyczewski published the song as part of Series XX of the AGA (the solo song series) rather than in the choral series (XVI and XVII) where it belonged. This is no doubt why Fischer-Dieskau included it in his recorded survey of Schubert lieder in the 1970s. But *Das Grab* D569 is ideally for unison chorus with piano, and achieves its full impact with these forces. The key is C sharp minor, the tempo 'Sehr langsam'. The dark mood of the music, a majesty of utterance bordering on the lugubrious, puts one in mind of the great C sharp minor setting of the year before, *Der Wanderer* D493. The piece begins in the minor key, and slides into the major towards the conclusion of each strophe. This change of tonality is something of a Schubertian thumbprint.

If there are high points in a song as deep in every way as *Das Grab*, these are the elongated cadences, cavernous in their musical effect, on the second to third full bars on the word 'stille', and again at the end of the strophe on 'Ein unbekanntes Land'. The vocal part of the song remains in minims and crotchets, often in unison with the piano, a simplicity that enhances, rather than diminishes, the grandiose effect of the music. But it is the postlude that finds the composer at his most individual. Here decorative demisemiquavers follow on from double-dotted crotchets in such a way as to be prophetic of the great Mayrhofer setting *Freiwilliges Versinken* D700 (1820). In that song Schubert conjures a vast, unexplored solar system in musical space with dotted rhythms that constitute a slow processional, a cosmic pavane. In *Das Grab* D569 the equivalent phrase is 'Ein unbekanntes Land' at the end of the first strophe, and the piano writing that follows it. The afterlife, if indeed there is one, is terra incognita, like the wide open space of the uncharted galaxies. Once again we marvel at how this composer's imagination responds to related ideas as if he were speaking a musical language of synonyms, his response to verbal imagery also linking up songs from earlier periods. In this 'Schubert-speak', music for the limitless depths of the grave was to be recycled in *Freiwilliges Versinken* to describe the fathomless descent of the sun in the heavenly firmament as well as its corollary, the ascent of the moon in the heavens.

The fifth setting, D643A, was discovered relatively recently in the Austrian monastery of Seitenstetten, and dates from 1819, an unaccompanied four-part song for mixed voices (SATB) in E flat major. It is the only setting in the major key, and it is an obvious attempt to emphasize the peace of the afterlife rather than the terrors of death.

Autographs:	University Library of Lund, Sweden (second setting)
	In Wienbibliothek im Rathaus, Vienna (third and fourth settings)
Publication:	First published as part of the AGA in 1895 (first, second and
	fourth settings; the second and fourth settings are P617 and P675
	respectively)

First published as No. 5 of *Neueste Folge nachgelassener,*
mehrstimmiger Gesänge mit und ohne Begleitung von Franz
Schubert by J. P. Gotthard, Vienna in 1872 (P426; third setting)
First published by Doblinger, Vienna in 1972 (fifth setting)

Subsequent editions: AGA XX 182: Vol. 3/231 (II) & XX 186, Vol. 4/6 (IV); NSA III:
Vol. 2b/308 (I), Vol. 3 (II–IV) & Vol. 2a/75 (V)

Discography and timing: Fischer-Dieskau II 1[8] 2'23 Version 4

(II) John Mark Ainsley,
Jamie MacDougall, Simon

Hyperion I 22[28] (II);   Keenlyside & Michael George
23[2] (III); 34[4] (IV)   2'04   (III & IV) The London
Hyperion II 12[1](II);   2'03   Schubert Chorale
12[20](III); 19[11] (IV)   3'08   (dir. Stephen Layton)

← *Die drei Sänger* D329   *Zufriedenheit* D330 →
← *Lorma* D376   *Morgenlied* D381 →
← *Der Jüngling and der Quelle* D300   *Iphigenia* D573 →

GRABLIED   Song of the grave
(KENNER) **D218** [H112]
F minor   24 June 1815

Er fiel den Tod für's Vaterland,   He met his death for the Fatherland,
Den süssen der Befreiungsschlacht;   A sweet death in the battle for freedom.
Wir graben ihm mit treuer Hand,[1]   With loyal hands we bury him
Tief, tief den schwarzen Ruheschacht.   Deep in the dark tomb of peace.

Da schlaf', zerhauenes Gebein!   Sleep there, splintered bones!
Wo Schmerzen einst gewühlt und Lust,   Where sorrows and desires once gnawed
Schlug wild ein tötend Blei hinein   A deadly bullet struck savagely
Und brach den Trotz der Heldenbrust.   And broke the hero's resistance.

Da schlaf' gestillt, zerriss'nes Herz,   Shattered heart, once so rich in hopes,
So wunschreich einst, auf Blumen ein,   There may you sleep peacefully upon the flowers
Die wir im veilchenvollen März   Which we scatter on your cool grave
Dir in die kühle Grube streu'n.   In March, with its blooming violets.

Ein Hügel hebt sich über dir,   A mound rises above you,
Den drückt kein Mal von Marmelstein,   Weighted down by no marble monument,

---

[1] Friedländer in Peters Edition changes this to 'Wir graben *ihn*'.

Von Rosmarin nur pflanzen wir	We plant a sprig of rosemary
Ein Pflänzchen auf dem Hügelein.	Upon that mound.
Das sprosst und grünt so traurig schön,	It sprouts, mournful and lovely in its green,
Von deinem treuen Blut gedüngt;	Fertilized by your faithful blood;
Man sieht zum Grab ein Mädchen gehn,	A girl is seen walking to the grave,
Das leise Minnelieder singt.	Softly singing songs of love.
Die kennt das Grab nicht, weiss es nicht,	She knows not the grave, and knows not
Wie der sie still und fest geliebt,	How he loved her, silently and steadfastly;
Der ihr zum Kranz, den sie sich flicht,	He who has given her the rosemary
Den Rosmarin als Brautschmuck giebt.	To fashion into a bridal chaplet.

JOSEF KENNER (1794–1868); poem written 18 July 1813

This is the last of Schubert's three Kenner solo settings (1815). See the poet's biography for a chronological list of all the Kenner settings.

Josef Kenner was one of the composer's schoolfriends and the poet of the ballad *Der Liedler* D209. The gothic horror of this piece, werewolves and all, gives us some idea of how the impressionable young men of the Imperial Seminary thrilled to a *Jurassic Park* scenario of the day. But *Grablied* leaves this innocent camp and marches into the serious pitched battle of the Austrian soldier. At the time of the 'Befreiungsschlacht' against the French, the patriotic young men of the Schubert circle regarded the death of a war hero as a personal tragedy. References to 'splintered bones' and 'deadly bullets' show a fascination with the gory details of violence; the poet and his comrades had been spared a similar fate because of a few years' difference in age. It is easy to see in this poem a specific lament for Schubert's admired acquaintance, the poet Körner (qv) who was an artist as well as a man of action. He had fallen in battle some two years before the song was written, but Napoleon's unexpected return from Elba, and the frantic military activity of the 'Hundred Days', made the Viennese return to thoughts of war and the bravery of the fallen. *Grablied* was written two days after the composer had penned *Kolmas Klage* D217, an Ossianic elegy for the death of the female narrator's father and brother in battle. Four days later the whole of Europe's fate was decided at the Battle of Waterloo.

The music is typical of Schubert's elegies of the period – Kosegarten's *Schwangesang* D318 (also in F minor) comes to mind. There are the usual sensitive touches one can all too easily take for granted: the chromatic setting of the word 'süssen' is ornamented with a lingering appoggiatura, and mention of the 'Befreiungsschlacht', the War of Liberation, elicits regret rather than self-satisfied jingoism. The semi-staccato chords in the accompaniment (bb. 6–7) under 'Wir graben ihm' (the sound of a shovel doing its grim work, iron against earth) classify *Grablied* as one of the composer's gravedigger songs. It seems the singer is not only present at the funeral, but actually doing the spade work – often the sad lot of a fellow soldier in the field. The tomb-like depth of the piano in the remarkable little four-bar postlude, as well as the ominous basses tolling in octaves, is prophetic of the greatest of all burial songs, written a decade later, and without mention of war, *Totengräbers Heimwehe* D842. This song is in F minor; the composer's feeling for appropriate tonality does not change greatly over the years – in 1815, F minor was already his key for graveyard ritual.

The two-bar introduction printed in the Peters Edition is spurious but inoffensive and effective enough to be used in performance. The poem has six verses in the AGA, and five in Peters. The first three printed here were recorded in the Hyperion Edition. It would no doubt be difficult for performers to sustain the listener's interest over six verses. Nevertheless, the complete poem is given here, not least because of the way it strays unwittingly into the future poetic world of Wilhelm Müller's (much later) *Die schöne Müllerin* where 'Rosmarin' also features (*Die liebe Farbe*), and where the miller's fantasy that the girl may pass his grave (*Trockne Blumen*) occasions an important musical climax as the flowers at his graveside spring back into full bloom. Kenner's final twist (that the fallen soldier's grave should provide the garland of flowers for the girl's marriage to another man) is worthy of A. E. Housman's *A Shropshire Lad*. There is some evidence (discussed by Walther Dürr in NSA Vol. 8 p. XXV) that this song was highly prized in the Schubert circle, also because of Kenner's poem. That it appeared in print in the *Oberösterreichisches Jahrbuch für Literatur* as late as 1844 is an indication that it must have seemed a worthy reminder of the patriotism of an earlier age.

Autograph:	Österreichische Nationalbibliothek, Vienna
First edition:	Published as Book 42 no. 4 of the *Nachlass* by Diabelli, Vienna in 1848 (P362)
Subsequent editions:	Peters: Vol. 6/34; AGA XX 84: Vol. 2/166; NSA IV: Vol. 8/108
Discography and timing:	Fischer-Dieskau I 4[5] 1'45 (two strophes only)
	Hyperion I 20[22]
	2'48 Michael George
	Hyperion II 7[12]

← *Kolmas Klage* D217   *Das Finden* D219 →

GRABLIED AUF EINEN SOLDATEN   Dirge for a soldier
(SCHUBART) **D454** [H282]
C minor   July 1816

Zieh hin, du braver Krieger du!   Depart hence, brave warrior!
Wir g'leiten dich zur Grabesruh,   We accompany you to a peaceful grave,
Und schreiten mit gesunkner Wehr,   And with lowered weapons,
  Von Wehmut schwer   Heavy with sorrow,
Und stumm vor deinem Sarge her.   Walk silently before your coffin.

Du warst ein biedrer, deutscher Mann.   You were an upright German.
Hast immerhin so brav getan.   You fought so bravely.
Dein Herz, voll edler Tapferkeit,   Your heart, full of noble courage,
  Hat nie im Streit   Never in battle
Geschoss und Säbelhieb gescheut.   Feared the bullet and the sword.

[...]   [...]

Du standst in grauser Mitternacht,	You kept watch at dread midnight,
In Frost und Hitze auf der Wacht,	In frost and heat;
Ertrugst so standhaft manche Not	You steadfastly endured many hardships,
Und danktest Gott	And gave thanks to God
Für Wasser und für's liebe Brot.	For water and for bread.
Wie du gelebt, so starbst auch du,	You died as you lived,
Schlosst deine Augen freudig zu.	Willingly closing your eyes,
Und dachtest: Aus ist nun der Streit	And reflecting: The battle
Und Kampf der Zeit.	And struggle of Time is past.
Jetzt kommt die ew'ge Seligkeit.	Now comes eternal bliss.
[. . . 3 . . .]	[. . . 3 . . .]

CHRISTIAN FRIEDRICH SCHUBART (1739–1791); poem written in 1784

This is the second of Schubert's four Schubart solo settings (1816–17). See the poet's biography for a chronological list of all the Schubart settings.

This song presented one of the few problems encountered when programming the Hyperion Schubert Edition. The German singer of a younger generation, to whom it had originally been assigned, was uncomfortable about having to sing the praises of a German soldier, a son of the fatherland – 'ein biedrer, deutscher Mann'. Fischer-Dieskau also omits the song from his complete survey. It is a historical irony that an English singer should have found it easier to declaim these words.

In the wake of the Napoleonic War, Germany and Austria were regarded by the larger powers as plucky little countries that had been violated by the French. Vienna had been an occupied city, and suffered many casualties. By the middle of 1816 the aftershocks of war could still be felt; former soldiers, often to be seen in the city's streets, were still dying of the long-term effects of wounds and injuries untreatable by the medicine of the time. In 1816 there was every reason for Schubert to be patriotic.

This may account for the fact that this setting suggests occasional music – as if composed in honour of a bereaved friend, or family, of the composer's acquaintance. If a soldier had died in 1816, some time after his return from the front, such a page of music would have been a welcome and thoughtful mark of respect. The marking 'Ernst' ('serious') is appropriate for a song that does not relay deep personal involvement, only a sad and dignified response to the death of someone who had done his duty. The point of the poem, surely, is that this is no national hero, only a typical German man and patriot. In fact the poem had a less than glorious beginning. The poet Schubart, a long-term prisoner of the cruel and capricious Karl Eugen, Duke of Württemberg, observed the funeral of a soldier, one day in 1784, from the window of his cell, with the dead march and muffled drums of the burial ceremony. This led the poet in dark and ironic mood to reflect bitterly on the tragic conditions of his own imprisonment, and on how the honoured corpse was at least now spared the pain and horror that must be endured by the living, both on the battlefield and elsewhere. That these words were written by someone who was a victim of contemporary German totalitarianism removes, surely, the fear that they may be taken to be jingoistic. The final lines (in Schubert's song if not in Schubart's longer poem) show that the poet, formerly anti-religious, had embraced Christianity while in captivity. It is doubtful, of course, whether Schubert was aware of this background; this gloss was published only in 1825 in a Frankfurt edition of the poems that included a sketch of Schubart's life.

If this is not a great song, it is full of genuinely Schubertian details, some of them thumbprints of the 1816 songs: at the opening, the voice doubled by piano at 'Zieh hin, du braver Krieger du!' signifies both solemn ceremonial and manly determination; there is a notable softening from G minor to a yielding G major at the phrase ending 'Grabes<u>ruh</u>' (bb. 4–5); the expressive jump of a fifth on 'Wehmut' (b. 8); the elongated setting of 'stumm' (b. 9) sung first in an unaccompanied void, then joined by a muted diminished chord in the piano. The most personal and beautiful part of the song, however, is the seven-bar postlude, long by Schubertian standards. Quavers fall in gently melancholic sequences – haunting music that seems to ponder the sadness of the human condition at the moment of valediction, marking an inexorable descent into the grave. There are eight verses of Schubart's poem printed in the AGA of which 1, 2, 4 and 5 are translated above. The music works well for some of the subsequent strophes, particularly for Verse 5 that ends with a promise of eternal bliss.

Autograph: Sibley Music Library, University of Rochester, New York
First edition: Published as no. 6 of *Neueste Folge nachgelassener Lieder und Gesänge* by J. P. Gotthard, Vienna in 1872 (P432)
Subsequent editions: Not in Peters; AGA XX 239: Vol. 4/140; NSA IV: Vol. 10/190
Bibliography: Porhansl 1993, pp. 72–3
Discography and timing: Fischer-Dieskau   —
                       Hyperion I 32^{15}
                       Hyperion II 15^{9} 3'43   Stephen Varcoe

← *Das war ich* D174a/450a   *Freude der Kinderjahre* D455 →

GRABLIED FÜR DIE MUTTER   A mother's funeral song
(ANONYMOUS) **D616** [H399]
B minor   June 1818

(37 bars)

Hauche milder, Abendluft,	Breathe more gently, evening breeze;
Klage sanfter, Philomele,	Lament more softly, Philomel;
Eine schöne, engelreine Seele	A beautiful, pure, angelic soul
Schläft in dieser Gruft.	Sleeps in this grave.
Bleich und stumm, am düstern Rand,	The father stands, pale and silent,
Steht der Vater mit dem Sohne,	With his son at the gloomy graveside;
Denen ihres Lebens schönste Krone	With her the fairest crown of their lives
Schnell mit ihr verschwand.	Has suddenly vanished.
Und sie weinen in die Gruft,	And they weep upon the grave.
Aber ihrer Liebe Zähren	But their tears of love
Werden sich zum Perlenkranz verklären	Shall be transfigured to a wreath of pearls
Wenn der Engel ruft.	When the angel calls.

ANONYMOUS/UNKNOWN

This is the seventeenth of Schubert's nineteen solo settings of an anonymous poet. See
Anonymous/Unknown for a chronological list of all the songs for which the poets are unknown.

The key of B minor (and a melting change into B major) points to music of deep emotion; this
is a companion piece to the much later song in the same tonality, *Vor meiner Wiege* D927, where
that song closes as the poet Leitner contemplates the death of his mother. Because the composer
lost his own mother at the age of fifteen it is tempting to see the song as having an autobiographical element; at least one scholar has suggested that the words are by Schubert himself.
Whether or not this is the case, there is still the question as to why he should choose to write a
song of this kind more than six years after his mother's death.

The answer is found in Deutsch's volume of *Memoirs* by Schubert's friends. Maria Anna
Streinsberg, mother of Schubert's friend Josef Ludwig von Streinsberg, had died on 26 June 1818.
This *Grablied* was clearly composed (shortly before Schubert's departure for his first sojourn in
Zseliz) in her memory. Schubert had known Streinsberg, a year his junior, since his schooldays;
he was a good friend of Josef von Spaun, and was later to marry into the Bruchmann family.
Streinsberg had been involved on that frightening evening in 1820 when the poet Senn and his
circle, Schubert among them, had been arrested. The literary style of the poem, with its high-
flown reference to 'Philomele', suggests a poet from the time of Matthisson or Salis-Seewis. The
presence of the father and the son (Streinsberg himself) at the graveside was perhaps easier to
find in an extant poem during a period when (rather undistinguished) occasional verse reflected
family bereavement as an everyday occurrence.

A melodic line of this kind with an expressive tune cast in $\frac{6}{8}$ summons powerful comparisons
to both earlier, and later, songs: the mood of *Lied* (*Ins stille Land*) D403 (Salis-Seewis) comes to
mind, as does the melody of *Winterlied* D401, also from 1816. The shape of this rising and falling
vocal line has been recycled by Schubert not because of wintry conditions at the funeral, but on
account of the coldness of death and the grave where nothing grows – 'Keine Blumen blühn' as
Hölty says in *Winterlied*. The solemnity and pain of the famous last setting of Mignon's *Nur wer
die Sehnsucht kennt* D877/4 is also prefigured in this music. Underneath 'Bleich und stumm' (b.
13) we have two quavers followed by a rest to describe paleness and silence, also used in *Erlafsee*
D586 to illustrate the still depths of the lake. Father and son stand at the graveside, two generations united in their grief by parallel sixths (b. 16), an idea that is announced in the first bar of
the song's introduction. A note of resentment against fate is heard at the recitative-like outburst
of 'Schnell, schnell mit ihr verschwand' (bb. 20–1). The transformation into B major, just before
the angel's call, is a typically Schubertian touch (cf. *Vor meiner Wiege*), and the little consolatory
postlude is simple, yet highly expressive. Schubert's compassion and his kindness shine through
this music. Instead of a subjective lament for the composer's own mother, pain felt at first hand,
we hear a recollection of that bereavement, softened by time, and offered as the composer's gift
of concerned and affectionate support for a friend. In NSA (Volume 12 p. XVII) Walther Dürr
points out that the song must have been sent to Streinsberg immediately after his mother's death
as a spontaneous expression of fellow-feeling (the composer remembering the death of his
own mother) rather than as a result of any commission or request. The autograph shows signs
of haste and the music paper had been used by someone else. This makes it impossible for
Streinsberg himself to have been the poet as John Reed suggests.

Autograph:	Wienbibliothek im Rathaus, Vienna (first draft)
First edition:	Published as Book 30 no. 3 of the *Nachlass* by Diabelli, Vienna in 1838 (P326)

Subsequent editions:	Peters: Vol. 5/170; AGA XX 338: Vol. 5/194; NSA IV: Vol. 12/14
Bibliography:	Black 2003, pp. 64–5
	Deutsch 1958, p. 167 (Memoir by Streinsberg)
	Fischer-Dieskau 1977, p. 111
	Porter 1961, p. 104
Discography and timing:	Fischer-Dieskau II 2[1] 2'43
	Hyperion I 21[21]
	Hyperion II 20[8] 2'26 Edith Mathis

← *Evangelium Johannis* D607   *Sing-Übungen* D619 →

GRAB UND MOND   Grave and moon   Quartet, TTBB
(SEIDL) **D893** [H607+]   (Unaccompanied)
A minor   September 1826

(46 bars)

Silberblauer Mondschein	Silver-blue moonlight
Fällt herab;	Shines down,
Senkt so manchen Strahl hinein	Sinking many a beam
In das Grab.	Into the grave.
Freund des Schlummers, lieber Mond,	Dear moon, sleep's friend,
Schweige nicht	Do not keep it secret
Ob im Grabe Dunkel wohnt,	Whether darkness or light
Oder Licht!	Dwells in the grave
Alles stumm?! Nun stilles Grab,	It is mute?! Well, you speak then,
Rede du!	Silent grave!
Zogst du manchen Strahl hinab	You have drawn so many a beam
In die Ruh;	To rest.
Birgst gar manchen Mondenblick,	You hide so many a moon's glance,
Silberblau;	Silver-blue;
Gib nur einen Strahl zurück—	Give back just one beam!
'Komm und schau!'	'Come and see!'

JOHANN GABRIEL SEIDL (1804–1875)

The unaccompanied choral music of Schubert fell outside the scope of the Hyperion Schubert Edition – just as it falls, strictly speaking, outside the remit of this book. However, exceptions have been made for works that have some bearing on the solo lieder – such as the choral setting of *Sehnsucht (Mignon)* D656, the only one of Schubert's six settings of the lyric without piano. This setting of Seidl is one of the most important and astonishing part-songs in the Schubert canon. Its poet played an important part as the co-creator of some of Schubert's finest mature lieder, including his very last song *Die Taubenpost* D965A. In the almost brutal emotion of *Grab und Mond* we glimpse another, deeply pessimistic, side of a Biedermeier poet, better known for *gemütlich* lyrics that idealize friendship and extol the beauties of nature. Seidl was perfectly capable of adopting a fashionably religious tone for texts such as *Das Zügenglöcklein* D871 and *Am Fenster* D878 (he was ambitious for preferment in the civil service, and would never have been openly atheistic) but in writing this text, and in choosing to set it in such a dark fashion, neither poet nor composer shows much confidence in an afterlife, to say the least. This music seems like preparation for *Winterreise*, and the half-tragedy and half-mockery of the Heine settings (as Maurice Brown observed) had its beginnings in the composition of this part-song.

The poet addresses the moonlight that has illuminated a grave and asks whether there is darkness or light down there. The answer (or lack of one) is silence; a remarkable passage, shifting from A minor to A flat major (bb. 17–22) contains a dry and ghostly setting of the words 'Alles stumm? . . . stumm? stumm?' At b. 23 the music slips down into A flat minor, with a change of key signature to four flats. In failing to find a response the poet now begs the grave for a moonbeam of solace. So many moonbeams have been drawn to the depths, is it not possible that the grave can give back a gleam of moonlit hope? The grave itself now answers in a single phrase, the poem's concluding line, 'Come and see'. One could argue that the poem by Seidl, ever the diplomat, leaves the question open – it may be that his grave will comfortingly confess to being lit by heavenly moonbeams. Schubert's setting, however, creates a mood of fear and horror; the stentorian, four-part voice of a yawning chasm taunts the listener with its grim and mocking invitation: 'Come and see! – What do you think? – Do you see heavenly light shining back at you? – Look for yourself!'

The first 'Komm und schau' is in C flat major (bb. 38–9); the second, now within the context of a naturalization of all flat signs, moves enharmonically to a wild outburst of sound in D minor. It is seldom that Schubert summons such vehemence; the timbre of the piano with its civilized, indoor overtones would seem out of place here. The third time we hear these words (there is a change from fortissimo to pianissimo) the music settles into a cadence that leads to the closing A major chord. If the earlier outburst was an expression of the finality of death, this ending offers the solace of acceptance and an end to suffering. As Schubert wrote to his family when on holiday in 1825, in connection with the hypochondria of his brother Ferdinand: 'As though dying is the worst that can happen to humans . . .'

Autograph:	Staatsbibliothek Preussischer Kulturbesitz, Berlin
First edition:	Published as no. 1 of *Die deutschen Minnesänger, Neueste Sammlung von Gesängen für vier Männerstimmen* by Tobias Haslinger, Vienna in October 1827
Publication reviews:	*Münchener Allgemeine Musik-Zeitung* no. 24 (15 March 1828), col. 370f. [Waidelich/Hilmar Dokumente II no. 596a] *Allgemeine musikalische Zeitung* (Leipzig), no. 15 (9 April 1828), col. 249f. [Waidelich/Hilmar Dokumente I no. 610; Deutsch Doc. Biog. no. 1075]
First known performance:	6 April 1827, in a concert given by Joseph Merk at the Kleiner Redoutensaal, Vienna. Peformers: Joseph Eichberger, Herr Ruprecht, Wenzel Krall and Franz Borschitzky (see Waidelich/

	Hilmar Dokumente I no. 470 for full concert programme). The quartet is not identified by name in either the programme or the reviews – but it seems probable that *Grab und Mond* was performed on this occasion (see also Waidelich/Hilmar Dokumente II No. 470 and Deutsch Doc. Biog. no. 845)
Performance reviews:	*Wiener allgemeine Theaterzeitung* no. 44 (12 April 1827), p. 179 [Waidelich/Hilmar Dokumente I no. 473] *Wiener Zeitschrift für Kunst, Literatur, Theater und Mode* No. 47 (19 April 1827), p. 383f. [Waidelich/Hilmar Dokumente I no. 479]
Subsequent editions:	AGA XVI 41: p. 197; NSA III: Vol. 4/148
Discography and timing:	Hyperion I 26[18] Hyperion II 32[14] 3'12 The London Schubert Chorale (dir. Stephen Layton)

← *Nachthelle* D892   *Zur guten Nacht* D903 →

Der GRAF VON HABSBURG   The Earl of Habsburg
(SCHILLER) **D990** [NOT IN HYPERION]
G major   1818?

Zu Aa-chen in sei - ner__ Kai-ser-pracht, im al - ter-tüm - li-chen Saa - le,

(24 bars)

Zu Aachen in seiner Kaiserpracht
   Im altertümlichen Saale,
Sass König Rudolphs heilige Macht
   Beim festlichen Krönungsmahle.
Die Speisen trug der Pfalzgraf des Rheins,
Es schenkte der Böhme des perlenden Weins,

   Und alle die Wähler, die Sieben,
Wie der Sterne Chor um die Sonne sich stellt,
Umstanden geschäftig den Herrscher der Welt,
   Die Würde des Amtes zu üben.

[. . . 11 . . .]

In Aachen, in the imperial splendour
   Of his ancient hall,
King Rudolph in his holy majesty
   Sat at his coronation feast.
Count Palatine of the Rhine carried in the food,
The Count of Bohemia poured the sparkling
   wine.
   And the seven electors,
Ranged like a choir of stars about the sun,
Stood solicitously around the lord of the world,
   To demonstrate the nobility of his office.

[. . . 11 . . .]

FRIEDRICH VON SCHILLER (1759–1805); poem written in 1803

This is the thirty-sixth of Schubert's forty-three Schiller solo settings (1811–24). See the poet's biography for a chronological list of all the Schiller settings.

Printed here is only the first strophe of Schiller's twelve-strophe poem about the foundation of Austria's ruling family – a dynasty apparently blessed from the beginning as a result of a very

Illustration of *Der Graf von Habsburg* from *Album für Deutschlands Töchter* (1863).

early Habsburg's chivalric and God-fearing generosity, the gift of a steed to a friar. There can scarcely have seemed a better argument for the non-separation of Church and State. Schiller's source was Aegidus Tschudi's *Chronicon Helveticum*, encountered during his researches for *Wilhelm Tell*. The poem, a story within a story, has something in common with Goethe's *Der Sänger* in that a minstrel plays the role of narrator. As Walther Dürr remarks in the preface to Volume 12 of the NSA, this song and its companion piece *Kaiser Maximilian auf der Martinswand* D990A, are a most unlikely addition to the corpus of Schubert's ballads. Nowhere else has Schubert attempted to set texts of this length as pure strophic songs (the nearest is Goethe's *Der Gott und die Bajadere* D254 in 1815). Even Reichardt's simple setting changes tempo and melody for verses 6 to 10, and again for the final strophes.

Both these works that deal with Austrian imperial history were included in an anthology for schoolchildren by the composer's brother, Ferdinand Schubert, *Der kleine Sänger* (1853). In that book there is a large section of patriotic material; *Der Graf von Habsburg* is No. 25 of these, and there is no acknowledgement of Franz Schubert's authorship (the pages of that book taken up by this hymn-like setting are reproduced in facsimile at the back of the separate *Kritischer Bericht* volume that expands the commentary printed in Volume 14 of the NSA). Also in *Der kleine Sänger* there are much better-known Schubert songs (such as *Heidenröslein* D257); these are also arranged for more than one voice, and again without mention of Schubert. Indeed, the title page of *Der kleine Sänger* implies that all the music that lies therein is the work of Ferdinand himself. (Schubert agreed to ghost for his less talented sibling on a number of occasions; Ferdinand seems to have availed himself of this subterfuge rather shamelessly.)

It seems likely that Schubert undertook these harmonizations of Schiller's ballad (and the even longer one by Heinrich von Collin) as a favour to his brother; it is also probable that the whole thing was accomplished very speedily. There is no attempt to develop an accompaniment as such, and the piano writing is sketchy, as if it were only a rough first draft. Dürr points out that public performance of this extremely simple material would not have been possible;

Schubert helped his brother (who from 1816 held a musical position at the Imperial orphanage in Vienna) by making an arrangement that was meant specifically for school use (there is an underlay of text for the first verse only, but there are repeat marks). On feast days such institutions were expected to come up with music that honoured the royal family.

Paper studies point to the date of this song as being late 1818. Theories about the music being by Ferdinand himself have been ruled out because there is no other instance of Ferdinand's music in his brother's handwriting. On the other hand there is quite a lot of Franz Schubert's music written out in Ferdinand's script. Needless to say *Der Graf von Habsburg* is in stark contrast stylistically to other vocal music written by Schubert at the same time. The two songs mentioned in this commentary were not recorded in the Hyperion Schubert Edition. It seemed pointless to record only one strophe of an ongoing narrative and, as Dürr implies, a complete performance of the poem with this music would be an inspiring experience for neither listeners nor performers.

Autograph:	Wienbibliothek im Rathaus, Vienna
First edition:	Published in an arrangement for two voices and piano as no. 25 of *Der kleine Sänger* by A. Schweigers Buchdruckerei Vienna, an anthology of school music by Ferdinand Schubert, in 1853 (P392)
Dedicatee:	Dedicated to Andreas Grafen von Hohenwart by Ferdinand Schubert
Subsequent editions:	Not in Peters; Not in AGA; NSA IV: Vol. 14/169
Bibliography:	Hilmar 1978, p. 81
	Hoorickx 1969, p. 118
	Hoorickx 1977, p. 274
Subsequent settings:	Johann Friedrich Reichardt (1752–1814) *Der Graf von Habsburg* (1809)
	Carl Loewe (1796–1869) *Der Graf von Habsburg* Op. 98 (1843–4)
Discography and timing:	Fischer-Dieskau —
	Hyperion I —
	Hyperion II

Der GREISE KOPF *see* WINTERREISE D911/14

GREAT BRITAIN AND BRITISH LITERATURE

The impact on German literature of Shakespeare, Ossian, Scott, Byron and many other British authors (such as James Thomson of *The Seasons*, Samuel Richardson of *Pamela* and *Clarissa* and Laurence Sterne of *Tristram Shandy*) was immense. In the wake of the Napoleonic Wars Great Britain was a beacon of new industrial technologies and the coming world power. Haydn's celebrated and financially advantageous visits to England thirty years earlier, and the Scottish publisher George Thomson's links with Haydn, Beethoven and Weber as a purveyor of folksong arrangements, encouraged German-speaking composers to treat the English musical market with financial, if not necessarily artistic, respect. If England was a gold mine in mercantile terms, Scotland, the former home of the bard Ossian, had since the 1770s established itself as one of the seats of romanticism; its misty allure was still powerful at the end of the 1820s when Mendelssohn visited the Hebrides, calling on Sir Walter Scott en route.

Schubert's acquaintance with the poetry of Ossian (in the second edition of Edmund von Harold's translation) came about thanks to the chance gift from Anton Holzapfel. The composer's friend remembered buying this 'miserable translation' for a few pence at a second-hand book store in Vienna. This would have been in 1815 or earlier. It is possible that Schubert had already read Goethe's *Werther* and knew the name of the Celtic bard from those pages but he would only have been aware of the Scottish name Macpherson, the writer who had brought a re-created Ossian to the public in 1762 (and under whose name Ossian is discussed in this book) if he had read the Harold translation's introduction. Macpherson's name fails to appear on the title page and, moreover, he is referred to as 'der Engländer Macpherson' which the feisty Scot would have regarded as an insult.

Johann Michael Vogl, part of Schubert's intimate circle from 1817, was an enthusiastic reader of English literature in the original. It might have been Vogl who introduced the composer to the works of Walter Scott, but in the mid-1820s the craze for this poet, fed by the runaway success of Rossini's opera *La Donna del Lago*, would have been difficult to escape in Vienna, where dresses made from Scottish plaids featured in the fashion plates of the *Wiener Zeitschrift*. It was probably either Vogl or the poet and polyglot translator Nikolaus Craigher de Jachelutta who helped the composer prepare the alternative English underlay for the first edition of songs from Scott's *The Lady of the Lake* as his Op. 52. Of these seven settings, six were published with an optional version using the original English text (this was not possible for *Normans Gesang* because the translator, D. Adam Storck, had employed an entirely different metre). These English versions are all reproduced in the NSA. This relatively costly publishing ploy, however, did nothing to secure Schubert a foothold in the English musical market.

Wilhelm Müller, poet of *Die schöne Müllerin* and *Winterreise*, was deeply and widely read in English literature – his first publication was a German translation of Edward Marlowe's *Doctor Faustus*. There is a reference to a poem by Edmund Spenser and also possibly Shakespeare in *Ungeduld* from the first cycle, and the imagery of *Die Nebensonnen* in the second might have been inspired by Shakespeare's *Richard II*. Müller's almost idolatrous enthusiasm for Byron and that poet's *Childe Harold's Pilgrimage* influenced the conception of the poems for *Winterreise*. The composer was probably unaware of all these literary cross-currents.

Schubert's musical encounters with Shakespeare in 1826 were the result of his close friendship with the young playwright Eduard von Bauernfeld who was part of a team of writers commissioned to produce a specifically Viennese edition of Shakespeare's works – *William Shakspeare's saemtliche Dramatische Werke*.

Schubert was an avid reader of the novels of James Fenimore Cooper (1789–1851) in German translation. On 12 November 1828, a week before he died, the composer wrote to his friend Schober, begging him to find further titles by the same author. At this time there was very little awareness, certainly among Austrians, that North Americans writing in English were part of a separate literary culture (everyone was an 'Engländer') but it was to American adventure stories and folklore that Schubert turned for entertainment in the last days of his life. He had already read a number of Cooper novels: *The Pilot* (1824), a sea-tale set in England, and *The Spy* (1821) with Westchester County, New York, as its background. Of the series of novels that featured Natty Bumppo (nicknamed 'Leather-Stocking' or 'Hawk-Eye'), friend of the Delaware Indians, Schubert had read the first, *The Pioneers* (1823), as well as the most famous, *The Last of the Mohicans*, penned only two years earlier in 1826 and available almost instantly in German. As far as we know the composer never received an extra consignment of Cooper's novels from Schober.

The following is a list of the Schubert songs with texts translated from poems or prose originally in English. Each of these titles has a commentary in this book and all the poets and translators mentioned in the list of songs are subjects of biographical articles:

4 May 1813	*Verklärung* (Alexander Pope, from the *Odes*, translated J. G. Herder) D59
22 June 1815	*Kolmas Klage* ('Ossian'/James Macpherson, from *Carric-Thura*, translation unknown, taken from Reichardt setting) D217
25 August 1815	*Der Weiberfreund* (Abraham Cowley, from *The Mistress*, translated by J. F. von Ratschky) D271
1815	*Ossians Lied nach dem Falle Nathos* ('Ossian'/James Macpherson from *Darthula*, translation by Edmund, Baron von Harold) D278
September 1815	*Das Mädchen von Inistore* ('Ossian'/James Macpherson from *Fingal* translated by Edmund, Baron von Harold) D281
5 September 1815	*Cronnan* ('Ossian'/James Macpherson from *Carric-Thura*, translated by Edmund, Baron von Harold) D282
20 September 1815	*Shilrik und Vinvela* ('Ossian'/James Macpherson from *Carric-Thura*, translated by Edmund, Baron von Harold) D293
28 November 1815	*Lorma* (first setting) ('Ossian'/James Macpherson from *The Battle of Lora*, translated by Edmund, Baron von Harold) D327 fragment
17 January 1816	*Lodas Gespenst* ('Ossian'/James Macpherson from *Carric-Thura*, translated by Edmund, Baron von Harold) D150
February 1816	*Der Tod Oskars* ('Ossian'/James Macpherson, separately printed as *Der Tod Oskars*, translated by Edmund, Baron von Harold) D375
10 February 1816	*Lorma* (second setting) ('Ossian'/James Macpherson from *The Battle of Lora*, translated by Edmund, Baron von Harold) D376
February 1817	*Die Nacht* ('Ossian'/James Macpherson from *Croma*, translated by Edmund, Baron von Harold) D534 fragment
1825	*Der blinde Knabe* (Colley Cibber, translated by Craigher de Jachelutta) D833, Op. 101/2
Beginning of 1825	*Lied der Anne Lyle* (Andrew Macdonald/Walter Scott, from *The Legend of Montrose*, translated by ?Craigher de Jachelutta) D830, Op. 85 no. 1 *Gesang der Norna* (Walter Scott, from *The Pirate*, translated by Samuel Spiker) D831, Op. 85 no. 2
April–July 1825	*Sieben Gesänge aus Walter Scotts* Fräulein vom See Op. 52 (Walter Scott, from *The Lady of the Lake*, translated by D. Adam Storck): (i) *Ellens Gesang I* D837 (solo soprano); (ii) *Ellens Gesang* II D838 (solo soprano); (iii) *Bootgesang* D835 (male chorus, TTBB); (iv) *Coronach* D836 (female chorus, SSA); (v) *Normans Gesang* D846 (tenor solo); (vi) *Ellens Gesang* III – 'Ave Maria' D839; (vii) *Lied des gefangenen Jägers* D843 (baritone solo)
March 1826?	*Romanze des Richard Löwenherz* (Walter Scott, from *Ivanhoe*, translated by Karl Methusalem Müller) D907, Op. 86
July 1826	*Trinklied* (William Shakespeare, from *Antony and Cleopatra*, translated by Ferdinand Mayerhofer von Grünbühel and Eduard von Bauernfeld) D888 *Ständchen* (William Shakespeare, from *Cymbeline*, translated by August von Schlegel) D889 *Gesang (An Silvia)* (William Shakespeare, from *The Two Gentleman of Verona*, translated by Eduard von Bauernfeld) D891

September 1827   *Eine altschottische Ballade* (translated by J. G. Herder from *Reliques of Ancient English Poetry* by Thomas Percy) D923

Schubert's songs first received mentions in the English press in 1825 and 1827, thanks to the Viennese correspondent of *The Harmonicon*. In his 1827 review he wrote: 'In our Society of Music were given two new songs composed by the favourite Schubert, which excited general musical interest. The first was *Die* [sic] *zürnende Diana* . . . the second, the Forester's song, from Sir. W. Scott's *Lady of the Lake*.' The composer's death went unnoticed in the English press but his reputation as a song composer grew thanks to visiting singers. Wilhelmine Schröder Devrient in 1832 and 1837, and Josef Staudigl (*see* SINGERS) performed Schubert in their British recitals. Favourites were such songs as *Ungeduld* D795/7, *Die junge Nonne* D828, *Ellens dritter Gesang* (*Ave Maria*) D839 and the Rellstab *Ständchen* D957/4. *Der Hirt auf dem Felsen* D965 was performed in the Hanover Square Rooms by the soprano Ann Bishop and the clarinettist Thomas Willmann in June 1836. The German-born British publisher Christian Wessel brought out editions of songs, printed in the original German, as supplements to his almanac *The Cadeau*. That Schubert's songs were performed as interludes at concerts of the Philharmonic Society (the Rellstab *Ständchen* in 1839, *Der Wanderer* D489 in 1843) shows that he was accepted in Britain as a song-writer long before he was valued as a composer of any great importance. Mendelssohn attempted in vain to organize a public performance through the Philharmonic Society of the 'Great' C major Symphony D944 in England (he managed to arrange one, however, for the Queen and Prince Consort at Windsor Castle). When he attempted instead a performance of the overture to *Fierabras* D796 he encountered hostility from the orchestra. The critic of *Musical World* (and later *The Times*), James Davison (1813–1885) immortalized himself, after a fashion, with the following review on 13 June 1844: 'The Overture of Schubert is literally beneath criticism, perhaps a more overrated man than this Schubert never existed. He has certainly written a few good songs, but what then? Has not every composer written a few good songs? And out of the thousand and one with which he deluged the musical world it would indeed be hard if some half-dozen were not tolerable. And when that is said, all is said that can justly be said of Schubert.'

The amends made to the composer by later generations of British musicians, beginning with the work of Sir George Grove, are outlined in the SCHOLARS article, the British contribution to lieder performance in the two separate articles SINGERS and PIANISTS.

GREISENGESANG   Song of old age
(RÜCKERT) OP. 60 NO. 1, **D778** [H522]

The song exists in three versions, the third of which is discussed below:
(1) Beginning to middle of 1823?; (2) 1826?; (3) B minor, appeared June 1826

(1) 'Mässig'   B minor   ¢   [102 bars]

(2) 'Mässig'   B minor   ¢   [102 bars]

(3) B minor

(102 bars)

Der Frost hat mir bereifet
Des Hauses Dach;
Doch warm ist mir's geblieben
Im Wohngemach.

Der Winter hat die Scheitel
Mir weiss gedeckt;
Doch fliesst das Blut, das rote
Durchs Herzgemach.

Der Jugendflor der Wangen,
Die Rosen sind
Gegangen, all gegangen
Einander nach.

Wo sind sie hingegangen?
Ins Herz hinab.
Da blühn sie nach Verlangen,
Wie vor so nach.

Sind alle Freudenströme
Der Welt versiegt?
Noch fliesst mir durch den Busen
Ein stiller Bach.

Sind alle Nachtigallen
Der Flur verstummt?
Noch ist bei mir im Stillen
Hier eine wach.

Sie singet: 'Herr des Hauses!
Verschleuss dein Tor,
Dass nicht die Welt, die kalte,
Dring' ins Gemach.

Schleuss aus den rauhen Odem
Der Wirklichkeit,
Und nur dem Duft der Träume
Gib Dach und Fach!'

[(. . . 2 . . .)]

The frost has covered
    the roof of my house,
But I have kept warm
    in my living room.

Winter has whitened
    the top of my head,
But the blood flows red
    in my heart.

The youthful flush of my cheeks,
    the roses
Have gone,
    one by one.

Where have they gone?
Down into my heart;
There, as before,
    they bloom as desired.

Have all the rivers of joy in this world
    run dry?
A silent stream still flows
    through my breast.

Have all the nightingales
    in the meadows fallen silent?
Within me, secretly,
    one still stirs.

She sings: 'Master of the house,
    bolt your door
Lest the cold world
    should penetrate the parlour.

Shut out the harsh breath
    of reality
And give shelter
    only to the fragrance of dreams!'

[(. . . 2 . . .)]

FRIEDRICH RÜCKERT (1788–1866); poem written in 1819/20

This is the fifth of Schubert's six Rückert solo settings (1822–3). See the poet's biography for a chronological list of all the Rückert settings.

This oriental evocation is from Rückert's *Östliche Rosen*, as are all Schubert's settings of that poet. The old man, still capable of summoning memories of love, is surely Rückert's tribute to the semi-autobiographical character that the ageing Goethe created for himself in the *West-östlicher Divan*: Hatem, the celebrated aged poet who, despite the fullness of his years, was the mentor and ardent lover of Zuleika. A sage's pronouncements on life and love suggest the wisdom of the East. There could be no better voice for this character than the bass with its ripe and rumbling tessitura, although any singer of this song must also be a master of *mezza voce*. The autograph of *Greisengesang* is in the bass clef; the Peters Edition, following the first edition, prints it in the treble.

Mention of Goethe's Hatem is apposite. In choosing the key of B minor for this song, Schubert perhaps conceived it as a companion piece for the first *Suleika* setting ('Was bedeutet die Bewegung?' D720) in the same key. There was something about this tonality that struck the composer as oriental or exotic; in the same way, the afterlife is an exotic and unknown region. John Reed, commenting on Schubert's use of B minor/major, says that 'many songs associated with the idea of death move towards a climax in B major, as in *Grablied für die Mutter*, *Vor meiner Wiege* and *An die untergehende Sonne* signifying an apotheosis of "das mildre Land"'. Here, if the old man is near death, all signs of commiseration in the minor key are contradicted by the life-enhancing answering phrases in B major: death is not his pathway to paradise, and he relishes his ability to cherish memories of earthly pleasures. Not for him the pessimism of *Der greise Kopf* from *Winterreise* where the singer, whose head is covered in frost, is bitterly disappointed not to be white-haired – he must continue to endure life. It is clear, however, that the head and heart of the protagonist of *Greisengesang* are still in good working order. Leo Black points out that the title Rückert later added to this poem – *Künftiges Alter* – 'Future Old Age', not 'Present Old Age' – implies that this 'Greise' is livelier than we may think. Far from being depressive, he appears to radiate mental health. This is partly because Schubert – also for formal reasons – chose to leave out the final two strophes of Rückert's poem; the final 'Liebesach' places the protagonist in rather a different, less contented, light:

Ich habe Wein und Rosen	I have wine and roses
In jedem Lied,	In every song,
Und habe solcher Lieder	And have thousands more
Noch tausendfach.	Such songs.
Vom Abend bis zum Morgen	From evening till morning
Und Nächte durch	And through the night
Will ich dir singen Jugend	I will sing to you of youth
Und Liebesach.	And the pangs of love.

The introduction consists of portentous forte chords, first in minims and then quickening into crotchets, all marked *ben marcato*. The tempo is 'Alla breve', so this makes an active, even vigorous, introduction; this man is a fighter and has no intention of fading away. Fischer-Dieskau finds this prelude 'surprisingly severe and rather loud for the text'. A possible explanation is that Schubert sees this old man as no ordinary individual and wishes to introduce him to the listener with a touch of oriental pomp, as if he were a prince or king. Anton von Spaun heard the baritone Johann Michael Vogl sing this song at the monastery of St Florian in June 1823 during a holiday break in Upper Austria that was arranged for Schubert by his friends in the wake of his sickness. If the song was conceived for Vogl in the first place (it seems likely that it was) we must take into account the singer's well-known sense of self-importance, and his taste for music that cast him in a dramatic light – surely the characteristic of an opera performer accustomed to singing regal roles. And so the curtain rises on this 'ageing amorist' (as Capell calls him) with a majestic flourish.

The opening vocal melody (from b. 6) is determined without being exactly agile. The voice is accompanied in octave unisons in the lower reaches of the piano which expand into unusually low-lying harmonies at the end of the phrase. This unison device is prophetic of another celebrated Schubert song about another, probably, old, man – *Totengräbers Heimwehe* D842 from 1825. In the middle of that song (bb. 40–48) there is a similar shape to the vocal line (also accompanied in octaves between the hands in a similar tessitura) with the words 'Von allen verlassen, / Dem Tod nur verwandt' ('By all forsaken, kin to death alone'). This is near enough to *Greisengesang* (with its imagery of frost and winter, and the final season of a man's life) for us to see the parallels: not only in the words themselves but in the situations, as well as the ages, of the protagonists at the edge of the grave. Such portentous unisons represent the inexorable workings of fate, loneliness and, perhaps more mundanely, the creaking of old limbs. We also hear traces of this ominous music in the first movement of the A minor Piano Sonata D845 (also 1825). In the case of *Greisengesang* such dark doubts are set up only to be knocked down.

The drooping phrase with which the song opens (bb. 5–9) is immediately mirrored by an answer (bb. 9–12), this time in the major key, and rising to D sharp, more or less the top of the singer's range where he is required to use a *mezza voce*. Thus the song's form throughout, following the words, is 'first the bad news, then the good'. The poem's second verse (beginning 'Der Winter hat die Scheitel' from b. 13) is an exact repeat of the music that has gone before. As in all these Rückert settings, repeats play a vital part in the architecture.

The poem's third and fourth verses are harnessed to make a less lyrical middle section (beginning 'Der Jugendflor der Wangen', from b. 21) which begins firmly in B minor with unison octaves once again, this time ornamented with acciaccaturas that drag slightly behind the vocal line in such a way as to suggest doddering or stuttering. After 'Gegangen, all gegangen / Einander nach' there is a brief piano interlude (bb. 27–9) that plunges deeper into the bass clef with funeral music, in solemn octaves, for fading bloom and withered stem. At the end of this passage we reach an F sharp major semibreve chord, the dominant of B minor. The ensuing stillness adds to the grandeur of the song, its singer engrossed in deepest thought. Another semibreve follows where the bass note changes from F sharp to G (b. 30); this small but dramatic shift initiates a brief recitative. 'Where have youth's roses gone?' the singer asks in a phrase – 'Wo sind sie hingegangen?' – music that would not have been out of place in the celebrated *Der Wanderer* D489. There is anguish in this question that climbs the stave in slow semitones (bb. 31–2). The cadence settles on 'hinge<u>gegangen</u>?' – two minims suspended over a pair of tied semibreves. For a moment there is stasis; the answer to the conundrum lies poised just beyond us in a held chord on the first inversion of F sharp major[7]. What follows is inevitable enough, for we are expecting a resolution on a chord of B of some kind. But when the answer comes, supported by a B *major* chord under the emotive word 'Herz' (b. 34), soothed by gentle tonal balm, we are reminded that the workings of the heart lie at the centre of all the great Schubert songs. The full answer is 'Ins Herz hinab' (down into my heart) and, true to the meaning of the words, the vocal line descends in semibreves and dotted minims, arriving on a chord of G sharp minor (b. 36).

This interrupted cadence also comes as a surprise, for we would have been quite satisfied for the strophe to end on a beatific B major chord. But no, there is life in the old boy yet and what follows is extraordinary. From the stony earth of G sharp minor, both voice and piano open outwards and upwards and reach towards the kinder, milder reaches of B major. It is as if the roots of those dying roses, in going down into the heart of the singer, have received miraculous new nourishment; what has been barren ground becomes, in a matter of moments, a garden of blossoming tendrils rising to meet the sunlight. This, of course, exactly reflects the meaning of the poem, for these imaginary flowers grow instantly, and the name of the gardener is Memory. The contrast between the sturdy, and slightly plodding, crotchets of reality and these vibrant phrases of the past in dreamy coloratura quavers is extremely moving. This requires of the bass voice an unusual mobility, and delicacy, something that adds to the impression of youthful fantasy being re-created in a context where no one would suspect it could flourish.

Greisengesang is a proper strophic song written in the year of *Die schöne Müllerin* where the form reached its apotheosis in Schubert's hands. The composer simply uses Rückert's next four strophes and sets them in almost identical manner. This meant that he had to dispense with two further strophes, the eight lines of poetry that are printed earlier in this commentary. The introduction returns as an interlude (bb. 49–53). The sombre B minor passages are just as effective with new words, and images of silent stream and singing nightingale grace the B major passages. The nightingale's extended advice to the old man (the seventh and eighth strophes of the poem) takes the song to its conclusion. This is not set in the manner or tessitura of birdsong, but this detail can be overlooked. The insubstantial floating of dreams is perfectly caught in the ornate roulade setting of 'Träume' (bb. 87–8) despite the fact that the most extended use of coloratura occurs on the inessential word 'und' (first in b. 89, and then b. 94).

Not everyone admires this passage. Mandyczewski disliked the fact that in both the first and second musical verses unimportant words were accorded emphatic melismatic extravagance. As late as the 1960s another version of the manuscript came to light; this is now considered the first version and is published as such in the NSA. Here the vibrant blossoming of the vocal line does not take place – all is unornamented semibreves and minims; the last section of the song as we usually know it seems reduced to a simpler form, shrunk and contracted almost as if by Schenkerian analysis. On the other hand, the second version, a copy in the Spaun–Cornaro collection (also in the NSA), has all the coloratura additions we have already described, and then some. This was doubtless Vogl's copy (as we may guess by these extra grace notes and mordents) which not only paints the rose, but also the gilds the lily.

When Schubert came to publish the song himself in June 1826 he chose a compromise. He rejected Vogl's extra variants (the so-called 'second version') but the coloratura passage that concludes each of the two musical verses is retained, suggesting that, to start with, he had envisaged the song without them. It seems probable that Vogl first encountered the song in this simpler version and began to insert his own ornaments to replace those arguably noble and phlegmatic semibreves. Vogl's 'improvements' were probably not entirely to his taste, and Schubert decided to write in *some* of the ornamentation of these passages himself; he had come to like his revisions for the very reasons outlined above – the extra movement and vitality of those wafting quavers seem to rejuvenate the old man before the listeners' ears. There seems no reason to doubt that the song as published represents Schubert's final thoughts.

In 1834 Rückert entitled his poem 'Vom künftigen Alter' ('A prospect of old age') and it is under this heading that Richard Strauss (a major Rückert composer) wrote a setting of these words in 1929, using all ten strophes of the poem (Op. 87 no. 1). But he seems to have been influenced by Schubert nevertheless: the Strauss song is written for exactly the same type of bass voice with similar demands in terms of flexibility and *mezza voce*. Strauss, however, does allow himself a bird-like trill and flourish in the piano part to introduce the nightingale's homily. He was in his middle sixties when he wrote this song, and still had twenty more years to live. Schubert, in his late twenties, had only five.

Autographs:	Staatsbibliothek Preussischer Kulturbesitz, Berlin (first draft)
	Wienbibliothek im Rathaus, Vienna (fair copy)
Publication:	First published as part of the NSA in 1982 (P781 & P782; first and
	second versions)
	First published as Op. 60 no. 1 by Cappi & Czerny, Vienna in June
	1826 (P100; third version)
Publication reviews:	*Berliner allgemeine musikalische Zeitung* No. 11 (14 March 1827),
	p. 81ff. [Waidelich/Hilmar Dokumente I No. 461; Deutsch Doc.
	Biog. No. 826]
Subsequent editions:	Peters: Vol. 2/124; AGA XX 456: Vol. 8/10 (third version); NSA
	IV: Vol. 3a/106 (third version), Vol. 3b/206 (first version) & 210
	(second version); Bärenreiter: Vol. 2/136 (third version)
Bibliography:	Adelhold 2002, pp. 64–5
	Capell 1928, pp. 202–3
	Fischer-Dieskau 1977, pp. 184–5
Arrangements:	Arr. Johannes Brahms (1833–1897) for voice and orchestra (1862)
	Richard Strauss (1864–1949) *Vom künftigen Alter* Op. 87 (1929)
	Arr. Max Reger (1873–1916) for voice and orchestra (1913–14)
Discography and timing:	Fischer-Dieskau II 6[11] 5'39
	Hyperion I 35[7]
	Hyperion II 27[10] 5'42 Neil Davies

← *Lachen und Weinen* D777   *Du bist die Ruh* D776 →

GRENZEN DER MENSCHHEIT   Human limitations
(GOETHE) **D716** [H466]
E major   March 1821

(159 bars)

Wenn der uralte,	When the age-old
Heilige Vater	Holy Father,
Mit gelassener Hand	With a calm hand,
Aus rollenden Wolken	Scatters beneficent thunderbolts
Segnende Blitze	Over the earth
Über die Erde sä't,	From the rolling clouds,
Küss' ich den letzten	I kiss the extreme hem
Saum seines Kleides,	Of His garment,
Kindliche Schauer	With childlike awe
Tief in der Brust.[1]	Deep in my heart.

[1] Goethe writes '*Treu in der Brust*'.

Denn mit Göttern	For no mortal
Soll sich nicht messen	Shall measure himself
Irgend ein Mensch.	Against the gods.
Hebt er sich aufwärts	If he reaches upwards
Und berührt	And touches the stars
Mit dem Scheitel die Sterne,	With his head
Nirgends haften dann	Then his unsure feet
Die unsichern Sohlen,	Have no hold,
Und mit ihm spielen	And clouds and winds
Wolken und Winde.	Sport with him.
Steht er mit festen,	If he stands firm
Markigen Knochen	With vigorous limbs
Auf der wohlgegründeten	On the solid,
Dauernden Erde;	Enduring earth,
Reicht er nicht auf,	He cannot even reach up
Nur mit der Eiche	To compare himself
Oder der Rebe	With the oak tree
Sich zu vergleichen.	Or the vine.
Was unterscheidet	What distinguishes gods
Götter von Menschen?	From men?
Dass viele Wellen	Before them many waves
Vor jenen wandeln,	Roll onwards,
Ein ewiger Strom:	An eternal river;
Uns hebt die Welle,	But the wave lifts us up;
Verschlingt die Welle,	The wave swallows us
Und wir versinken.	And we sink.
Ein kleiner Ring	A narrow ring
Begrenzt unser Leben,	Bounds our life,
Und viele Geschlechter	And generations
Reihen sich dauernd	Forever succeed one another
An ihres Daseins	In the infinite chain
Unendliche Kette.	Of their existence.

JOHANN WOLFGANG VON GOETHE (1749–1832); poem written in 1780?

This is the fifty-eighth of Schubert seventy-five Goethe solo settings (1814–26). See the poet's biography for a chronological list of all the Goethe settings.

This is as grand a poetic hymn as Goethe ever wrote. The four mighty strophes which precede the envoi (the marvellous lines about the ring, that age-old symbol of completion) traverse the whole range of universal experience and aspiration. The first verse is perhaps the most remarkable. The rest of the poem flows from this – an imposing picture presided over by a mighty figure who stands somewhere between Zeus and the Judeo-Christian God of the frescoes of the Sistine Chapel. In the words of Lorraine Byrne, 'The God of Goethe's pantheistic universe takes the form of a good and wise father who provokes traditional Christian feelings of gratefulness, love and awe.' The first strophe concerns immortal fire; the second, air; the third, earth; and the fourth, water, the most Schubertian of the four elements, although the composer avoids the tempting diversions of scene-painting in favour of forging, as if chain by chain, a symphonic whole. In *Grenzen der Menschheit* we find a composer who has emerged from the song experiments of 1819 and 1820 (the Schlegel and Novalis settings, as well as some of the most challenging Mayrhofer) with a command of form whereby symphonies can be songs, and songs symphonies – the contemporary first song of *Suleika* D720 is evidence enough of this.

Schubert made certain important decisions when he looked at the poem on the printed page. There are five strophes; the first two are the longest (ten lines each) and the shortest is the last (six lines). Verses 3 and 4 have eight lines each. In order to arrange a recapitulation that comes full circle (true to the idea of the 'ring' that underlies the whole conception) Schubert divides the first strophe into two sections (six and four lines respectively). This enables him to set the work effectively in six musical strophes where the last incorporates most of the features of the first, and some of the second – thus ABCDEA.

Like the immediately preceding Goethe setting, *Versunken* D715, the music begins far from the home key, in that case A flat major and E major here. The majestic C major chord (with an upbeat B) that starts the whole work seems to denote a blank canvas, a universe not yet created (Haydn's *Creation* affected every composer who followed him). Schubert has actually borrowed this progression (a short upbeat which rises a semitone and opens out to a longer chord) from the accompaniment to the *Prometheus* of 1819 (D674) – the turbulent music of that song that triggers the outburst 'Ich dich ehren? Wofür?' (bb. 65–6). Einstein calls this 'the iambic motif of defiance', and it pervades and unites the song in such a way that we forget that *Grenzen der Menschheit* is a succession of slow-motion variations on this fragment of Promethean music. Whether this is a conscious borrowing or not is uncertain, but it seems to be. 'Why should we honour the gods?' Prometheus asked; and *Grenzen der Menschheit* ruminates on the same question and comes up with a famously cogent response. In the introduction, every shift of chord denotes a new contour as if contemplating different ways of solving a timeless conundrum. The eventual arrival into E major at b. 11 introduces the long-awaited G sharp that signifies the arrival of the home key (not yet in root position, however); this appears like a shaft of light that floods the dark landscape with colour. Throughout this section the harmonic shifts vividly convey the 'gelassener Hand' of the great Creator as it moves first here, then there. There is a textbook (but highly effective) use of the subdominant (the plagal relationship always serves to illustrate a religious point) in the shift to A major after 'Heilige Vater' (bb. 20–1). Here the composer signals his awe in the divine presence, but at 'rollenden Wolken' (bb. 25–7) the abrupt change to G sharp major (the dominant of C sharp minor) is a cosmic shift as the clouds are parted as if with the casual turn of an all-controlling hand. The most tempestuous storms below are caused by the mildest of movements above; it is as if Paul Bunyan were absent-mindedly creating the Grand Canyon with a trailing hoe. Accordingly the thunderbolts, seen from the gods' point of view, are given gentle music only slightly ruffled with semiquavers on 'Blitze' (b. 29) and 'Erde sä't' (b. 31). The music is also marked 'pianissimo', pointedly contrary to the normal musical depiction of thunder and lightning.

The change to Schubert's favourite dactylic rhythm (long-short-short) at b. 33 ('Küss' ich den letzten / Saum seines Kleides') is most effective. This is the 'Kindliche Schauer' also experienced by the maiden in *Der Tod und das Mädchen* D531, and which we later encounter in Mignon's *Heiss mich nicht reden* D877/2. In that song, the young girl, locked into her fate, keeps a dark secret that only a god could allow her to reveal. Schubert usually reserves this rhythm for something cosmic (cf. *Die Sterne* D939) and this is no exception. The sweet gentleness and the vulnerable sense of surrender in this passage are remarkably caught in this dance-like music of the spheres.

The music to the next verse is the most active. The vocal line (from b. 53) has a number of quavers, even a dotted quaver-semiquaver. This sign of agitation denotes the crime of hubris. The progression of semibreves before 'Denn mit Göttern' is ornamented by an ominous trill reminiscent of the opening of *Freiwilliges Versinken* D700, a song about the immutable laws of nature and the movements of the sun god Helios. The accompaniment under 'Hebt er sich aufwärts / Und berührt / Mit dem Scheitel die Sterne' is an unambiguous use of the 'Prometheus' motif, describing, as it does, someone equally ill-advised and unwise. This phrase has risen in chromatic steps (beginning at 'Hebt er sich aufwärts') and the consequent plunging descent of the vocal line (at 'Nirgends haften dann / Die unsichern Sohlen') depicts the fall from grace; the vocal line seems to lose its foothold and slip in successive sequences to ever lower regions where 'Wolken und Winde' will sport with the unfortunate climber. Clouds and wind are normally depicted aloft, above mankind; but here they are seen in the bass clef as if from the perspective of the even higher heavenly stars, and Schubert has imagined the drop between the two layers of existence as a vast one. Accordingly these words are set to some of the lowest notes in the piece. This passage (bb. 68–71) and others in the song are singled out by Leo Black as being an example of Schubert's voice-doubling-bass as a 'symbol of passivity and submission'. The nine-bar interlude (from b. 79, again a *Prometheus* variant) is made of crotchet upbeats, semibreves and minims; it moves the music from F major back to E major, and is a miracle of modulation where each sequence seems to encapsulate a thought or perception too profound to be expressed in human words.

True to its meaning, the music for 'Steht er mit festen, / Markigen Knochen' is more secure and grounded. We have moved into the dominant key (B major). The vocal line aspires upwards for 'Oder der Rebe' as if we are witnessing man's attempt to measure himself with the vine. A simple interlude oscillating between D major and G minor chords introduces the question at the heart of the piece – what is the difference between gods and men? The ongoing melody (which throughout, in its grandeur and flexibility, is prophetic of Wagnerian word-setting in, appropriately enough, the *Ring* tetralogy) yields to the repeated notes of a phrase that sounds like a ritualistic chant, something that might be intoned by priest or shaman: 'Was unterscheidet / Götter von Menschen?'

The answer to this eternal question is the song's crowning glory. The waves that both lift us up, and then swallow us as we sink, are not depicted in anything like rolling water music – in this respect Hugo Wolf was a lot more graphic. It is the empty and dismal intervals of this section, hollow thirds and grating fourths, which illustrate the wretchedness of man's fate. We have already encountered intervals like these in connection with another 'ewiger Strom' – the river Styx in *Gruppe aus dem Tartarus* D583 (at 'Schmerz verzerret / Ihr Gesicht!'). The enharmonic changes (E sharps = F naturals in the vocal line, and in the piano C sharps = D flats) at 'Verschlingt die Welle, / Und wir versinken' matter only from the point of view of notation. But they show how strongly Schubert was engaged in the deepest aspects of the text. As life cedes to death, this enharmonic spelling reflects man's altered state, the same yet not the same, and nature's ability to absorb and recycle her own. The descents in the vocal line at 'versinken' may seem obvious, but they are hugely effective. The interlude closing this section (bb. 130–34) is the only one where there is a direct quotation from *Prometheus* where the same notes of the accompanying figure in bb. 72–3 of that song's accompaniment are elongated into semibreves with a crotchet upbeat.

We wonder how it is that this sprawling song seems so much of an organic entity, despite the fact that we have traversed a universe during its weighty progress. Schubert's success lies in his flair for musical organization and bringing the lessons he has learned in his symphonic writing to the lied. The final verse returns to the music of the opening; at the end it also uses the dactylic music that Schubert employs for the last four lines of Goethe's first strophe. It is entirely appropriate that the elevated tone of the opening (not that the whole song has not been elevated, but the addition of subdominant harmony makes it feel even more sacred) should see this mighty song to its conclusion. In employing semibreves and minims (notes that look like rings on paper), Schubert, like Hugo Wolf when setting this poem, engages in the visual punning that we sometimes find as composers transfer their thoughts to paper almost in the manner of draughtsmen. But the song as a whole has been written as a symphonic hymn and only its great difficulty (the bass tessitura where the singer has a low E) has prevented it from being better known and performed with greater regularity.

It is just possible that, like the Schreiber setting *Das Abendrot*, *Grenzen der Menschheit* was conceived for Count Esterházy whose voice was of this range. The music is slow-moving (which seems to have suited his technique) and the text is lofty enough to have satisfied his tastes, although he might have preferred a song about God, rather than the gods. It would almost certainly have been too hard for him, however. Although it is likely that Schubert and the Esterházys kept in touch between the first visit to Zseliz (1818) and the second in 1824, there is no firm evidence to link the family with *Grenzen der Menschheit*.

Autograph:	In private possession (last seen 1992)
First edition:	Published as Book 14 no. 1 of the *Nachlass* by Diabelli, Vienna in January 1832 (P278)
First known performance:	According to the diary of Franz von Hartmann, this song was first performed at a Schubertiad at the house of Josef von Spaun on 21 April 1827 (see Deutsch Doc. Biog. No. 855)
Subsequent editions:	Peters: Vol. 3/144; AGA XX 393: Vol. 6/185; NSA IV: Vol. 13/22
Bibliography:	Black 2000, p. 89
	Black 2003, pp. 94–8
	Byrne 2003, pp. 131–5
	Capell 1928, pp. 152–4
	Einstein 1951, pp. 217–18
	Fischer-Dieskau 1977, pp. 143–4
Further settings:	Hugo Wolf (1860–1903) *Grenzen der Menschheit* (1889)
	Alban Berg (1885–1939) *Grenzen der Menschheit* (1902)
	Wolfgang Fortner (1907–1987) *Grenzen der Menschheit*, cantata for baritone, chorus and orchestra (1930)
Discography and timing:	Fischer-Dieskau II 4^{13} 8'11
	Hyperion I 34^{18}
	Hyperion II 24^{8} 7'09 Michael George

← *Versunken* D715   *Geheimes* D719 →

GRETCHEN AM DOM *see* SZENE AUS 'FAUST' D126

GRETCHEN AM SPINNRADE   Gretchen at the spinning wheel
(GOETHE) OP. 2, **D118** [H49]

The song exists in two versions, the second of which is discussed below:
(1) 19 October 1814; (2) 1816

(1)   'Etwas schnell'   D minor   §   [120 bars]

(2)   D minor

Nicht zu geschwind (M.M. ♩. = 72)

pp

Mei-ne Ruh__ ist hin,__ mein Herz__ ist schwer,

(120 bars)

Gretchen (Am Spinnrade allein)[1]

Meine Ruh' ist hin,	My peace is gone,
Mein Herz ist schwer,	My heart is heavy,
Ich finde sie nimmer	I shall never, never again
Und nimmermehr.	Find peace.
Wo ich ihn nicht hab'	Wherever he is not with me
Ist mir das Grab,	Is my grave,
Die ganze Welt	The whole world
Ist mir vergällt.	Is turned to gall.
Mein armer Kopf	My poor head
Ist mir verrückt,	Is crazed,
Mein armer Sinn	My poor mind
Ist mir zerstückt.	Is shattered.
Meine Ruh' ist hin,	My peace is gone,
Mein Herz ist schwer,	My heart is heavy,
Ich finde sie nimmer	I shall never, never again
Und nimmermehr.	Find peace.
Nach ihm nur schau' ich	I look out of the window
Zum Fenster hinaus,	Only to seek him,
Nach ihm nur geh' ich	I leave the house
Aus dem Haus.	Only to seek him.
Sein hoher Gang,	His fine gait,
Sein' edle Gestalt,	His noble form,
Seines Mundes Lächeln,	The smile of his lips,
Seiner Augen Gewalt,	The power of his eyes.
Und seiner Rede	And the magic flow
Zauberfluss,	Of his words,
Sein Händedruck,	The pressure of his hand
Und ach, sein Kuss!	And, ah, his kiss!
Meine Ruh' ist hin,	My peace is gone,
Mein Herz ist schwer,	My heart is heavy,

---

[1] This is the heading in Schubert's source, *Theater von Goethe*, erster Teil, Wien 1810, bei Anton Strauss.

Ich finde sie nimmer	I shall never, never again
Und nimmermehr.	Find peace.
Mein Busen drängt sich	My bosom yearns
Nach ihm hin,	For him.
Ach dürft' ich fassen	Ah, if only I could grasp him
Und halten ihn.	And hold him.
Und küssen ihn!	And kiss him
So wie ich wollt',[2]	As I would like,
An seinen Küssen	I should die
Vergehen sollt'!	From his kisses!

JOHANN WOLFGANG VON GOETHE (1749–1832); poem written before 1775

This is the first of Schubert's seventy-five Goethe solo settings (1814–26). See the poet's biography for a chronological list of all the Goethe settings.

The name Gretchen makes an appearance elsewhere in the Schubert songs: in *Die Unterscheidung* D866/1 (1828), she is the girl with whom the boy Hans will dance to make his lover jealous; she is little Margaret alias Peggy, Maggie, the archetypal girl, anyone and everyone. Mahler in his song *Hans und Grethe* writes of the round dance of life and sex – boy meets girl, Jack has his Jill. In Goethe's *Faust* (qv), Gretchen is the typically good, lower middle-class German girl, with rough hands from hard work, who is seduced, made pregnant and abandoned. She kills her child and is sentenced to death. In the final scene of Part One of the play, Faust attempts to spirit her from prison with the help of Mephistopheles, but she refuses to go with him. In rejecting an easy escape route at the moment of her deepest abasement she wins for herself a spiritual reprieve and a holy voice announces that she is saved – 'gerettet'. During Goethe's student days in Leipzig, one Catherina Maria Flindt was sentenced to death for killing her illegitimate child; she was rescued from prison by her lover but, tormented by her conscience, returned to face her execution. In Frankfurt in 1772, soon after Goethe had parted from his lover Friederike Brion, and at a time when he was feeling guilty about his treatment of her, another girl by the name of Susanna Margareta Brandt, was publicly executed for killing her baby. Goethe's own doctor attended Brandt, and the poet also knew the executioner.

    A study of Schubert's early songs confirms that many signs and touches of genius existed in his lieder well before 19 October 1814. But these earlier works, often overtly influenced by other composers, pale beside the *coup de maître* that is *Gretchen am Spinnrade*. To emerge from what had been a most distinguished apprenticeship into the realm of mastery, Schubert needed to find the right poet to set him on creative fire. It was Shakespeare who had liberated the young Goethe from the narrow precepts of his predecessors, and it was Goethe who performed the same service for Schubert. *Gretchen* is his first Goethe setting and it was love at first sight. There had been dalliances with the idealized Elisa, Adelaide and Laura of Matthisson, but in comparison to Goethe's creation these are cardboard cut-outs; in Gretchen, who is on the brink of being engulfed by her own turbulent emotions and the strictures of a cruel world, the composer recognized the new frank reality of the Romantic age, his own reality perhaps, and the full implications of his song-writing destiny. This most auspicious of days in the lieder calendar was preceded, on 18 October 1814, by one of the biggest open-air celebrations ever known in Vienna,

---

[2] Schubert adds '*O könnt ich ihn küssen / So wie ich wollt*' to the repeat of these words.

a thanksgiving and Volksfest in the Prater to mark the first celebration of Napoleon's defeat at the Battle of Leipzig and the freeing of the German nations from the French yoke. Offerings of gratitude were made on specially constructed altars to celebrate German-Austrian cooperation. A feeling that he was living in great and stirring times perhaps helped encourage Schubert, the next day, to compose the first of many immortal collaborations between Weimar and Vienna, German word and Austrian tone.

It would have taken him only a few hours to read the scenes of *Faust* that precede the celebrated lyric 'Meine Ruh' ist hin'. There is something in the raw energy of this music that suggests that the composer is right inside the drama; he had clearly been transported into new and uncharted realms by the cumulative power of the scenes in the play, stirred by the magical worlds evoked by Faust and Mephistopheles, and was in a spin of his own as he set about composing Gretchen's song. It is as if he and his heroine, both vulnerable teenagers, are reacting at the same time to verbal sorcery – both have been subject to a magic stream of words, Schubert on paper and Gretchen in the flesh ('seiner Rede / Zauberfluss'). The unassuaged desires that burn behind the shyness of inexperienced adolescence, the confusion of sexual awakening – these feelings belong as much to Schubert as to Gretchen herself. No amount of musical genius can free a strictly brought-up young man from guilt about something that was also exciting and beautiful – and this is also Gretchen's dilemma. In this song she is no abandoned woman; the anguish of her reaction to Faust's advances (she has not yet been to bed with him, unlike the scenario in Gounod's *Faust*) reflects the perennial battle between Christian shame and sexual arousal. That such a piece should have been written by a boy of seventeen is one of the wonders of musical history; equally amazing is the emotional maturity that enabled Schubert to empathize with Gretchen in such a manner.

As the stage directions demand, Schubert places the scene in Gretchen's room; we hear the constriction of the enclosed space in the repetitiveness of the vocal line. The accompaniment represents the spinning wheel, with the click-clack of the bobbin in the left hand, counterpointing the rotation of the wheel, but it is a spinning wheel capable of mirroring orchestral sonority, a big dipper following the ups and downs of the human heart. The piano's notes, trapped within a small space on the stave, transcend the original intent of their imagery: they seem like Gretchen's confused thoughts hammering in her brain, momentarily stalled by desire, and are suggestive of something diabolical rather than just the wooden wheel and the spinner's foot-pedal. From the musical and structural point of view it is the movement of this spinning dynamo that pulls together all the strands in the song and weaves them into an imperishable yarn. This accompaniment, and the way it animates and enriches both the musical and psychological texture of the song, identifies *Gretchen am Spinnrade* as being one of the key staging posts in the history of the lied.

Gretchen from the *Minerva* almanac (1829).

Goethe has set out his verse in short lines – simplicity and desperation all in one – and Schubert has found a musical means to mirror that structure: each line is followed by a rest, a short gasp between statements. The piece starts in low gear, veering between stretches of D minor, drained of expression, and a shift to an unexpected C major (b. 7) which gives an archaic modal twist to the harmony. At b. 8 the intensity of the girl's emotions is shown by the unexpected diminished chord harmony under 'ich <u>finde sie</u> nimmer' and then '<u>nimmermehr</u>' – the latter moment (b. 10) reaching for an F at the top of the stave, a cry of despair that, contained though it is, must have thoroughly alarmed the song's early audiences. In this way Gretchen, who has started the song in a depressed daze, gradually warms into vehement life. At 'Die ganze Welt / Ist mir vergällt' (bb. 17–19) the tessitura is suddenly lower, and most sopranos, in competition with a mezzo-forte accompaniment, place this phrase in the chest register. This music seems wrenched from the gut, while the heartstrings are set a-jangling by the sudden shift up an octave in 'Mein armer Kopf / Ist mir verrückt' (bb. 21–5). Schubert does not shy away from the wail of hysteria inherent in this line; the voice is challenged to sit around E, F and G – the soprano's perilous passaggio – to marvellous effect. The composer now inserts a reprise of Goethe's opening verse (from b. 31); the poem does not need this repeat to establish a sense of obsession, but the music does, and each time we hear the refrain it is deployed in a subtly different way.

The music for Goethe's fourth strophe (beginning 'Nach ihm nur schau' ich' bb. 42–50) is a variant of the music for the second; it is refashioned to encompass the erotic compulsion behind the despair. The music for lines three and four of the strophe is the same as for lines one and two, a whingeing repetition that emphasizes poor Gretchen's obsessive dependence on Faust. The thought of how handsome and good he is prompts the music to move into F major (the relative major of the tonic key) from b. 51; this seems like the application of a balm to a fevered brow. (The dreamlike quality of this passage suggests the use of pedal here, to be used only sparingly in the rest of the song.)

This section (verses 5 and 6) is a miniature *Frauenliebe und -leben*; it starts as idealistically and demurely as that Schumann cycle and, as in *Er, der Herrlichste von allen*, progresses to a description of the beloved's best points. Schumann's heroine is eventually happily married, but the stories of the two women dramatically diverge as fleeting key-shifts trace Gretchen's whirlwind courtship. The descending chromatic scale for 'Zauberfluss' (b. 61) is a marvellous detail, suggesting, as it somehow does, a slew of artfully seductive words. All through this recitation concerning Faust's smile, eyes and voice there has been a long crescendo. But it is only when the relationship becomes physical, with the actual touch of his hand on Gretchen (depicted by the sforzato octave B flat in the left hand, b. 63), that matters spiral out of control, and there is a flurry of breathless sexual excitement indicated by the accelerando marked at that point (performers often spoil this riveting moment by speeding up too soon). The pianist's left hand continues with relentlessly hammered octaves in the bass, one dotted minim per bar, and it is clear that Faust's hand, wherever it plays, is mercilessly insistent. Poor Gretchen shudders in ecstasy, the accompaniment's swirling semiquavers and the insistence of the left hand are indicative of flailing limbs and plundered petticoats. Goethe speaks only of a kiss, but Schubert's setting of 'ach, sein Kuss' exceeds anything in the song repertoire in terms of daring. 'Ach' is set on an F, a minim of desperate ecstasy high on the stave; the accompanying chord is B flat major (b. 66) and the music seems to quiver with uncertainty. The piano chord re-positions itself with a B natural in the bass (b. 67) as a launching pad for the singer's next high note. As Gretchen's phrase 'sein Kuss' leaps upwards into a part of the stave that is as yet beyond her experience (in reality no higher than a G prolonged with a fermata) the piano pounces onto a chord (b. 68) that quickly expands a semitone at the top, A to B flat, so that what has begun as a tightly closed dominant seventh harmony is prised open, an accented appoggiatura of baleful harmonic effect.

This is an extraordinary tonal analogue for the sudden loss of innocence, and it is powerfully underlined by the throbbing anguish of the singer's depiction of that 'Kuss'. The bass-line harmonies leading up to this point (a rise of B flat, to B natural to C sharp) have suggested Faust stalking his prey. The energy of this as depicted in the accompaniment exactly coincides with the singer's effort to place and support her climactic top note; the combined effect is overwhelmingly physical. A searing memory, both painful and sweet, is thrown into the void created by Faust's absence. And then a moment of silence before the pianist seeks to find a way out of the emotional impasse.

The four remarkable piano solo bars of emotional hiatus and uncertainty (bb. 69–72) in the accompaniment are grounded on an A pedal. These are traditionally played with a hesitant rubato as if it is an effort for Gretchen to catch her breath and to get the spinning wheel back into action. They also brilliantly convey the limbo of uncertainty in which Gretchen finds herself. Nevertheless, she is governed by mechanical habit for the wheel is her work and her drudgery. Drawn once more into D minor, Gretchen sets it turning again. There is another repeat of the opening refrain (bb. 73–82), and once again this is Schubert's decision rather than Goethe's. A lesser composer would have been lost as to what to do next.

Gretchen from Düntze's edition of Goethe's *Werke* (1882).

The simple change from D minor to B flat major for 'Mein Busen drängt sich' (bb. 84–6) is positively wanton in its effect: as the vocal line lifts a semitone, A to B flat, it is as if Gretchen, utterly in love with Faust, offers up her entire body to him. In the earliest version of the play Goethe meant something at least as strong as this – his original lines in his *Urfaust* were 'Mein Schoss! Gott! Drängt / Sich nach ihm hin' – 'God! My womb longs for him.' (These were unknown to Schubert of course.) Goethe later modified the words for publication, probably so as not to shock his reading public, but also because they were unsuitable for a girl of Gretchen's inexperience. For thirty seconds we hear a force of nature unleashed; she wants to kiss Faust *as she would like* ('Und küssen ihn / So wie ich wollt'). The music has moved into a higher and more dramatic gear, sequence by mounting sequence, B flat[7] bass to E flat, then C to F, D to G minor and finally settling on a pedal E (b. 91). Just before this, at b. 90, the composer has marked a slowly unfolding accelerando that will govern the *Bewegung* of the rest of the song, or at least until the ritardando of b. 113. Passion such as this was unheard of in German song, perhaps more revolutionary than the invention of a wheel. The home stretch of the piece begins at b. 101. With 'O könnt ich ihn küssen' Schubert adds two words to Goethe's poem, though no one seems to care. (When the composer sent the song to the poet as part of the fruitless 1816 consignment, it is clear that he hoped this lese-majesty would not be discovered.) One cannot blame Schubert for this adaptation: this 'könnt ich' places the strength of Gretchen's increasingly compulsive needs strongly to the fore. Sforzato bass notes in dotted minims underpin a quickening pace where the performers should feel the rhythm as one in a bar, the swinging of a giant pendulum of panic and desire.

The gathering momentum culminates in two top As (at 'Vergehen sollt' at b. 107, and again at b. 111). The singer is most tested here, the first of the top notes infinitely easier to achieve than the second that comes too soon afterwards for comfort. (It is rather easy to believe that by writing *vergehen* here Goethe implied orgasm – perhaps occasioned by the friction of the turning of the spinning-wheel next to the thigh.) In any case, suddenly all passion is spent. After a single bar of the familiar spinning accompaniment in D minor, we hear once more the quiet desperation of a very abbreviated recapitulation of 'Meine Ruh' ist hin' (b. 114). The only flaw in this masterpiece is one of vocal practicality: most singers would be extremely grateful for just one more bar of spinning interlude to come down from the 'high' of hysterical passion and make the transition to the bereft return of the refrain. Johann Vogl asked for a similar mercy in a passage in *Erlkönig* and Schubert made the necessary alteration.

The song had first appeared as Op. 2 (printed on commission with Cappi und Diabelli) in April 1821. There are two autograph versions. The first of these is surprisingly not printed separately in Volume 1a (an early volume) of the NSA where the differences between the two are designated merely with above-the-stave ossias. There is a different tempo marking for the versions (as can be seen at the head of this article) and in the opening of the first version the upper stave is marked 'sempre legato' while the left hand (referring to the quavers rather than the dotted minims), is 'sempre staccato'. Schubert made the second version, revised in tiny details, in 1816 for the sadly ignored album for Goethe; it was this copy that was eventually handed over to the printer in 1821 for publication as Op. 2.

It is astonishing to discover that Beethoven was occupied in making sketches for a setting of this poem as early as 1803 or thereabouts. These veer between G major and G minor and there is no indication of any idea concerning an accompaniment, the very element that was so crucial to Schubert's song.

Autograph:	Wienbibliothek im Rathaus, Vienna (fair copy)
First edition:	Published as Op. 2 by Cappi & Diabell, Vienna in 1821 (P2)
Dedicatee:	Moritz von Fries
Publication reviews:	*Abend-Zeitung* (Dresden), No. 29 (30 January 1821) [Waidelich/ Hilmar Dokumente I No. 69; Deutsch Doc. Biog. No. 199] This review is particularly unusual for having been issued *before* the work was printed – the author reviews several of Schubert's songs based on manuscript copies of the pieces that he knows to be in circulation, and comments that they have not yet been engraved *Der Sammler* (Vienna), No. 52 (1 May 1821), p. 208 [Waidelich/ Hilmar Dokumente I No. 93; Deutsch Doc. Biog. No. 232] *Wiener allgemeine Theaterzeitung* No. 54 (8 May 1821), p. 219 [Waidelich/Hilmar Dokumente I No. 97] *Allgemeine musikalische Zeitung* (Vienna), No. 6 (19 January 1822), col. 43ff. [Waidelich/Hilmar Dokumente I No. 142; Deutsch Doc. Biog. No. 270] F. von Hentl 'Blick auf Schubert's Lieder', *Wiener Zeitschrift für Kunst, Literatur, Theater und Mode* No. 36 (23 March 1822), p. 289f. [Waidelich/Hilmar Dokumente I No. 146; Deutsch Doc. Biog. No. 278]
First known performance:	2 March 1821, *Abend-Unterhaltung* of the Gesellschaft der Musikfreunde, Vienna. Soloist: Sophie von Linhart (see Waidelich/Hilmar Dokumente I No. 71 for full programme)
Subsequent editions:	Peters: Vol. 1/176; AGA XX 31: Vol. 1/911; NSA IV: Vol. 1/10; Bärenreiter: Vol. 1/8
Bibliography:	Black 2003, p. 53 (a Jungian view of the song) Byrne 2003, pp. 329–32

Capell 1928, pp. 84–6
Einstein 1951, pp. 104–5
Fischer-Dieskau 1977, pp. 35–6
Gülke 1991, pp. 79–83
Reid 2007, pp. 174–6

Further settings and
arrangements:

Carl Friedrich Zelter (1758–1832) *Lied der Margarethe aus* Faust
(1809)
Louis Spohr (1784–1859) *Gretchen am Spinnrade* (1809)
Carl Loewe (1796–1869) *Meine Ruh ist hin* (1822)
Hector Berlioz (1803–1869) 'D'amour, L'ardent flamme' from *La
Damnation de Faust* (1846) [a very free adaptation of the text]
Mikhail Glinka (1804–1857) *Tyashka pechal' i grusten svet* (1848)
Arr. Franz Liszt (1811–1886) for solo piano, no. 8 of *Lieder von
Schubert* (1837–8)
Richard Wagner (1813–1883) *Gretchen am Spinnrade* (1832)
Giuseppe Verdi (1813–1901) *Perduta ho la pace*, no. 5 of 6
Romanze (1838)
Charles Gounod (1818–1893) 'Il ne revient pas' from *Faust* Act
IV (1859) [a very free adaptation of the text]
Arr. Max Reger (1873–1916) for voice and orchestra (1915)
Arr. Hans Werner Henze (b. 1926) *Richard Wagnersche
Klavierlieder*, orchestration of Wagner's setting for solo voices,
chorus and orchestra (1998–9)
Luca Lombardi (b. 1945) 'La canzona di Greta' for soprano and
string quartet

Discography and timing:

Fischer-Dieskau — —
Hyperion I 13[4]
Hyperion II 4[5]   3'56   Marie McLaughlin

← *Das Mädchen aus der Fremde* D117   *Nachtgesang* D119 →

GRETCHEN IM ZWINGER
(Gretchens Bitte)
(GOETHE) **D564** [H374]
(Fragment) B♭ minor – C major   May 1817

Gretchen within the ramparts
(Gretchen's prayer)

Sehr langsam

Ach nei-ge du Scher-zen-rei-che,

(43 bars)

In the text printed below, the lines in italics are those not set by Schubert in this fragment.

Ach neige,
Du Schmerzenreiche,
Dein Antlitz gnädig meiner Not!

You who are laden with sorrow,
Incline your face graciously
To my distress.

Das Schwert im Herzen,	With the sword in your heart,
Mit tausend Schmerzen	And a thousand sorrows,
Blickst auf zu deines Sohnes Tod.	You look up at your dying son.
Zum Vater blickst du,	You gaze up to the Father,
Und Seufzer schickst du	And let a sigh rise up
Hinauf um sein' und deine Not.	For His affliction and your own.
Wer fühlet,	Who can feel
Wie wühlet	How the pain
Der Schmerz mir im Gebein?	Gnaws away in my bones?
Was mein armes Herz hier banget,	What my poor heart fears,
Was es zittert, was verlanget,	What it dreads, what it craves,
Weisst nur du, nur du allein!	Only you can know!
Wohin ich immer gehe,	Wherever I go,
Wie weh, wie weh, wie wehe	How it hurts, how it hurts
Wird mir im Busen hier!	Here in my breast!
Ich bin, ach, kaum alleine,	Alas, no sooner am I alone
Ich wein', ich wein', ich weine,	Than I weep, I weep,
Das Herz zerbricht in mir.	And my heart breaks within me.

Die Scherben vor meinem Fenster — *Ah, I sprinkled with dewy tears*
Betaut' ich mit Thränen, ach! — *The flower-pots at my window!*
Als ich am frühen Morgen — *When early this morning*
Dir diese Blumen brach. — *I plucked these flowers for you.*

Schien hell in meine Kammer — *When the early sun shone brightly*
Die Sonne früh herauf, — *Up into my room*
Sass ich in allem Jammer — *I, in all my misery,*
In meinem Bett' schon auf. — *Was already sitting up in bed.*

Hilf! rette mich von Schmach und Tod! — *Help! Save me from shame and death!*
Ach neige, — *You who are laden with sorrow,*
Du Schmerzenreiche, — *Incline your face graciously*
Dein Antlitz gnädig meiner Not! — *To my distress!*

JOHANN WOLFGANG VON GOETHE (1749–1832); poem written in 1771/5

*This is the fifty-fourth of Schubert's seventy-five Goethe solo settings (1814–26). See the poet's
biography for a chronological list of all the Goethe settings.*

In the narrative storyline of Goethe's *Faust* (qv), this scene comes between two other Faust texts
composed by Schubert – *Gretchen am Spinnrade* D118 and *Szene aus 'Faust'* D126. Formerly
known as *Gretchens Bitte*, it is chronologically the last of Schubert's five *Faust* compositions
which also include *Der König in Thule* D367 and *Chor der Engel* D440. The *Stabat Mater* image
of the mother of God, her heart pierced with a sword as she regards the agony of her son, comes
from Luke 2:35.

In the previous scene of the play, Gretchen has met her friend Lieschen at the town well. She hears the gossip about the shameful fate of one Bärbelchen, and the ignominy brought about by her pregnancy. Bärbelchen's lover has abandoned her, and now she will have to repent in public for her sin. Faust has not yet abandoned Gretchen (he will do so after the murder of her brother Valentin) but Gretchen realizes that she is pregnant and that she has inadvertently killed her mother by giving her the sleeping draught that has enabled Faust's nocturnal visits. Desperate and ashamed, she visits the shrine of the Virgin, a statue of Mary placed in a niche 'im Zwinger' – built into the city ramparts, remnants of the medieval walls that had surrounded many European cities long after there was a need for any kind of fortification. (Vienna itself had such ramparts, the so-called 'Bastei' – demolished for the construction of the Ringstrasse later in the century – and for a time in 1823/4 Schubert himself lodged in an apartment built into the structure of these now largely demolished city walls.) In the poet's stage directions Gretchen places fresh flowers in a jug at the foot of the Virgin's shrine which makes sense of a part of the poem that Schubert did not set. Clearly Goethe has the ramparts of Frankfurt in mind.

Goethe gives over the whole of the scene to a single lyric of operatic scope and intensity, justly famous and complete in itself. More than two and a half years after Schubert had composed his first Gretchen song in October 1814, it is obvious that he is now in the mood to write a through-composed aria. This may account for the fact that the piano, for all the richness of the accompaniment's texture, is reduced to a supporting role. Almost all psychological interest in the song is concentrated in the vocal line, and this may have been one of the reasons why the composer abandoned the work after setting only five of the eight verses.

The marking is 'Sehr langsam'. The opening flow of accompanying semiquavers in B flat minor, a tonality Schubert employed only a handful of times, is reminiscent of *Auf der Donau*

Illustration for *Gretchen im Zwinger* by Ramberg, frontispiece to the almanac *Minerva* (1829).

D553 written the month before, a song not dissimilar in its general dark mood. But that poem, pessimistic as it is, sightsees on its way up the Danube; Gretchen's plight on the other hand is static. There is no spinning wheel here to keep the song on the move. The first nine lines of the poem, grouped into three strophes of three lines each, seem to be part of a litany, a formal prayer which Gretchen knows by heart. The piano ornamentation at b. 5 reminds us of another song addressed to the Virgin, *Blondel zu Marien* D626 that is also fashioned as a *bel canto* aria in the darker reaches of the flat keys. At b. 6 mention of the Holy Mother's tribulations occasions an accompaniment of mourning semiquavers palpitating between alternating hands (once again reminiscent of *Auf der Donau*) and a piano interlude in the unusual key of D flat minor (bb. 10–12). At b. 13 there is a change of key to A major; the effect of this is like a sudden ray of hope as Gretchen envisages Mary gazing up at God.

Having completed her sacred salutation Gretchen allows her continuing entreaties to relate to her own personal plight. At 'Wer fühlet, / Wie wühlet' (b. 18) the liturgical metre is abandoned and the music moves into another dimension – the most arresting and original part of the fragment. The tonality of A major yields to the minor in a remarkable passage for the bottom half of the voice – as if a viola solo in a string quartet texture, burrowing painfully deep into the bone. By b. 22 ('Weisst nur du') this sobbing effect yields to a broader legato cantilena that seems openly influenced by an Italian operatic model. At b. 29 there is a switch to *alla breve* time, and the marking changes to 'Etwas geschwind'. The first three lines of Verse 5 tighten the screws of tension with a sequence of modulations, a tactic used in the final climactic pages of *Gretchen am Spinnrade*. Instead of rolling semiquavers this accompaniment has pizzicato quavers alternating between the hands. The last three lines of the verse, after some tearful repetition of words, dissolve, like all Gretchen's courage, into a broken-hearted C major. The composer then placed four flats on a new stave and abandoned the composition.

After many public performances of this work I believe it to be one of the very few Schubert fragments that can be presented successfully to the public in its present form without the need to search for a version with a modern-day completion. Ending with a C major chord following b. 43 (the last bar of the fragment as printed in NSA) seems to me better than the sudden C major chord to be found in the Peters Edition. Of course, leaving the song at this point means that a large and important part of the poem is unperformed, and there is an understandable temptation to adopt one of the completions of the work. Of these, the young Benjamin Britten's is the only one by a composer of genius and a great Schubertian, and can thus be taken seriously. It was recorded for the Hyperion Schubert Edition (the remainder of Goethe's poem, unset by Schubert, is printed above in italics).

As one would expect from a composer of this rank, Britten carefully recycles Schubertian material. The music for Verse 6 is taken from Verse 2 and transposed to the A flat tonality suggested by Schubert's final key signature. Verse 7 artfully recalls the rising major-key arpeggio of 'und störe, störe nimmer' from *Auflösung* D807, a song with which Britten and Peter Pears were very well acquainted. The manner in which the twentieth-century composer meets the challenge of 'Hilf! Rette mich von Schmach und Tod' – surely the heart, and point, of Goethe's poem – is more original. Perhaps it could also be said that in its originality it no longer sounds like Schubert. Conceived for the veteran opera singer Joan Cross, this music loses sight perhaps of Gretchen's essentially adolescent vulnerability. Britten has Gretchen repeat 'Hilf!' three times in the same high tessitura that she uses when she sings 'Weh! Weh!' in Schubert's *Szene aus 'Faust'* D126, and Britten underpins this passage with similar shifting progressions, exploring various possibilities of enharmonic modulation. (It is possible that Britten was influenced by Schumann's setting of this passage in *Szenen aus Goethes 'Faust'*, a work the English composer was later to conduct and record with distinction.) These lead the piano to a climactic B flat minor chord in second inversion, over which the voice plummets from one end of its range to the other. Equally daringly, Britten invents a transition and inserts the words 'Ach, rette mich' twice – rhetorical additions to Goethe's poem, phrases that are supported by echoes of the opening semiquavers of the accompaniment. These prepare a touching recapitulation of the opening prayer, unaltered Schubert as is right and proper. The last of these lines is repeated with different harmonies leading to a newly invented and convincing final cadence for the piano. The less well-known (and out of print) completion by Ivor Keys is far less daring, but it more successfully preserves a Schubertian harmonic vocabulary, *circa* 1817, while making ingenious use of existing material.

Autograph:	Goethe Museum, Frankfurt am Main (first draft, fragment)
First edition:	Published as a fragment as Book 29 no. 3 of the *Nachlass* by Diabelli, Vienna in 1838 (P322)
Subsequent editions:	Peters: Vol. 5/166; AGA XX 596: Vol. 10/116; NSA IV: Vol. 11/230
Bibliography:	Byrne 2003, pp. 345–9
	Capell 1928, pp. 133–4
	Einstein 1951, p. 165
Further settings and arrangements:	Bernhard Klein (1793–1832) *Ach neige, du Schmerzenreiche* (*c.* 1820)
	Carl Loewe (1796–1869) *Szene aus 'Faust'* (1835)
	Robert Schumann (1810–1856) *Gretchen vor dem Bild der Mater dolorosa*, No. 2 of *Szenen aus Goethes 'Faust'* WoO3 (1849)
	Richard Wagner (1813–83) *Melodram* (1831)
	Giuseppe Verdi (1813–1901) *Deh, pietoso, oh Addolorata* (1838)
	Hugo Wolf (1860–1903) *Gretchen vor dem Andachtsbild der Mater Dolorosa* (1878)
	Hans Pfitzner (1869–1949) from *Das dunkle Reich* Op. 38, choral fantasy for soprano and baritone solo, chorus, organ and orchestra (1929–30)
	Arr. Benjamin Britten (1913–1976) completion of Schubert's fragment for voice and piano (1943)
	Arr. Ivor Keys (1919–1995) completion of fragment (*c.* 1950)
	Arr. Hans Werner Henze (b. 1926) *Richard Wagnersche Klavierlieder*, orchestration of Wagner's setting for solo voices, chorus and orchestra (1998–9)
Discography and timing:	Fischer-Dieskau —
	Hyperion I 13⁶
	Hyperion II 19⁸ 3'56 Marie McLaughlin

← *Die Einsiedelei* D563   *Der Strom* D565 →

GRETCHENS BITTE *see* GRETCHEN IM ZWINGER D564

JOHANN DIEDERICH GRIES (1775–1842)

THE POETIC SOURCES

S1 *Blumensträusse, Italienischer, Spanischer und Portugiesischer Poesie von August Wilhelm Schlegel*, Berlin in der Realschulbuchhandlung, 1804

This book contains a majority of translations by August Wilhelm Schlegel. In the Petrarch section *Or che 'l ciel e la terra e 'l vento tace* is translated as 'Nunmehr, da Himmel, Erde schweigt' and signed GRIES. Three further Petrarch translations (on pp. 52, 56 & 67) are similarly attributed but they were not set by Schubert. Notes at the back of the book identify this as being Petrarch's Sonnet 130.

S2 *Gedichte und poetische Übersetzungen von J. G. Gries,* mit königlich Würtembergischem Privilegio. Stuttgart, F. C. Löflund und Sohn, 1829

'Sonette von Francesco Petrarca' make up the fifth section of this collection. Fourteen of Petrarch's sonnets are translated in all, but there is no evidence to support John Reed's contention (*Schubert Companion* p. 466) that the other Petrarch sonnets set by Schubert might also be Gries translations. A footnote identifies this as being Petrarch's Sonnet No. 131 (cf. above).

THE SONG
September 1818   *Sonett III* D630 [S1: p. 51, listed as Sonett XVIII] [S2: p. 94, listed as Sonnet VI]
On the autograph Schubert identifies the poet as Dante.

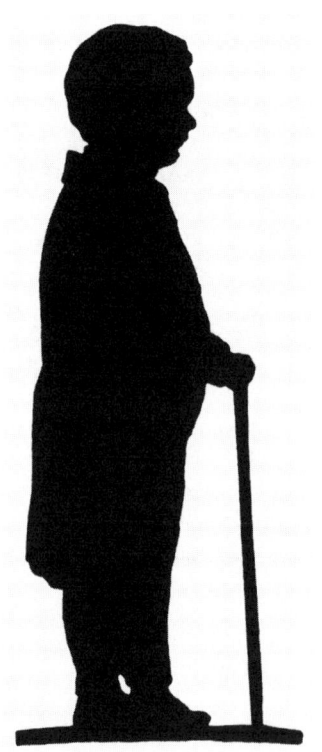

Gries was born on 7 February 1775 in Hamburg to a wealthy family. He was later to lose his fortune, and much of his translation work was undertaken out of financial necessity. During his studies in Jena he met Goethe, Wieland, Herder and Schiller, and his first poems were printed in almanacs edited by these influential patrons. He seems to have been friends with almost everyone of importance of the time – August von Schlegel, Novalis, Brentano, Eichendorff and Uhland. He wrote some original poetry, but his main interest was translating Italian and Spanish texts, for which he was much admired. The 1829 edition of his works contains translations from Pulci, Poliziano, Bojardo, Sannazaro, Machiavelli, Tassoni, Salvator Rosa, Fulvio Testi and Metastasio. The Gries translation set by Schubert as D360 is considered (by Einstein among others) to be particularly fine. Gries died in Hamburg on 9 February 1842.

Johann Gries silhouette by C. F. Duttenhofer.

FRANZ GRILLPARZER (1791–1872)

THE POETIC SOURCES
S1   *Janus, Zeitschrift herausgeben von Friedrich Wähner,* Wien 3 Oktober 1818

S2   *Monatbericht der Gesellschaft der Musikfreunde des Oesterreichischen Kaiserstaates,* ed. Leopold con Sonnleithner, Wien, März 1829

S3   *Gedichte von Grillparzer*, Stuttgart, Verlag der J. G. Cotta'schen Buchhandlung, 1872

S4   *Gedichte von Franz Grillparzer, Jubiläums Ausgabe zum hundertsten Geburtstag des Dichters (1791–1891)*, Stuttgart, Verlag der J. G. Cotta'schen Buchhandlung, 1891

THE SONGS

February 1819   *Bertas Lied in der Nacht* D653 [S1: p. 3 – the poem was originally written to be sung in the 'Urfassung' of Grillparzer's play *Die Ahnfrau* (1816) and then discarded; the first and second printed editions of the play (1817 and 1819) do not contain this lyric (*see* song commentary)] [S4: p. 150]

July 1827   *Ständchen* D920, D921 [S3: p. 335, the two versions of this work for alto soloist and first (mistakenly) male, then female, chorus were undoubtedly composed to a copy of the poem in Grillparzer's own hand]

March 1828   *Mirjams Siegesgesang* D942 [S2: pp. 41–6 – first printing of the poem; also S3: p. 339. Schubert composed this poem from a copy of the poem in Grillparzer's own hand]

Franz Grillparzer was one of Schubert's most famous and celebrated contemporaries. His plays still hold the stage, particularly in his native Austria. Like Schubert, he was born in Vienna (on 15 January 1791) but, unlike the composer, he moved in a milieu of well-connected aristocratic privilege: on his mother's side he was a member of the distinguished Sonnleithner family. Despite his work in the Court Library Service he was, however, never a great favourite with the Establishment, and was capable of enraging the powers-that-were with his writings, some of which were deemed to be anti-Catholic. His relationships with women were turbulent and manifold, but the most important of them was his lifelong friendship (never quite extended to marriage) to Kathi Fröhlich who had the nickname of 'die ewige Braut'; Kathi was sister of Anna and 'Pepi', who feature strongly in Schubert's story. It was in connection with the shared friendship of poet and composer for the Fröhlich sisters that *Ständchen* D920 for alto soloist and chorus was composed. A few years after Schubert's death Grillparzer studied composition with the organist and contrapuntalist Simon Sechter (who had given Schubert lessons at the end of the composer's life). There is an extant setting by Grillpzarzer of Heine's *Das Fischermädchen*.

Although Schubert and Grillparzer were in friendly contact quite early on through the offices of the poet's cousin Leopold von Sonnleithner, they seem to have been little more than amiable acquaintances. The poet was reclusive, hypochondriacal and not easy company. He was quite a close friend of Beethoven (this is the reason that Fischer-Dieskau puts forward for Schubert's wariness in the relationship). Although primarily known

Franz Grillparzer.

worldwide as a man of the theatre Grillparzer wrote a number of *Novellen*, as well as a good deal of poetry. Only a handful of his plays can be mentioned here apart from *Die Ahnfrau* (1817), that is linked to a Schubert song: *Sappho, Der Traum ein Leben, König Ottokars Glück und Ende, Ein treuer Diener seines Herrn, Ein Bruderzwist in Habsburg, Libussa, Die Jüdin von Toledo*. He had a full and distinguished life; he was in contact with almost every important German man of letters including Goethe (who received him in 1826, although the second meeting was not a success due to Grillparzer's shyness), and he was widely travelled and much honoured. He told the composer Ferdinand Hiller that Schubert lacked any talent for the stage and he wrote the somewhat controversial epigram on Schubert's tombstone, 'The art of music here entombed a rich possession, but even fairer hopes'. Although well meant, this facile phrase suggests a lack of inside knowledge of the composer's output, but it was, after all, a viewpoint shared even by those who knew Schubert better. It has fairly recently emerged that in the preparation of this inscription Grillparzer simply added a poetic gloss to sentences in this vein that were prepared for him by the composer's friends Josef von Spaun and Josef Blahetka. Einstein suggests that despite the poet's fame, Schubert was not impressed by his work either: 'Grillparzer was one of those not unusual German poets . . . in whose poetry the ideas scarcely ever achieve complete purity of form.' Mayrhofer, it seems, although struggling and unknown, was another matter. Who could possibly say that in literary matters, Schubert was not his own man?

After Schubert's death, however, and with the passing of the years, Grillparzer became increasingly fascinated by the composer. This is reflected in a number of his writings, particularly in the Novelle, *Der arme Spielmann*. He possessed a bust of Schubert in his study and was active on various committees which believed that Schubert should be honoured with a memorial statue in Vienna. In the *Gedichte* (on p. 154) there is a poem about Schubert that appears to celebrate the composer as a remarkably independent *savant* – hugely gifted and productive (perhaps over-productive) but completely unworldly and unable to function effectively within the highly politicized world of Viennese musical life. This is wildly to exaggerate the composer's naivety: Schubert was always more aware and in control of his career than he seemed to be at first glance, even admitting his lack of business acumen. Nevertheless, the poem does capture an important aspect of the composer's seeming indifference to success, and the fact that nothing was allowed to deflect him from his work.

Franz Schubert

Schubert heiss ich, Schubert bin ich,
Und als solchen geb' ich mich.
Was die Besten je geleistet,
Ich erkenn' es, ich verehr' es,
Immer doch bleibt's ausser mir.
Selbst die Kunst, die Kränze windet,
Blumen sammelt, wählt und bindet,
Ich kann ihr nur Blumen bieten,
Sichte sie und – wählet ihr;
Lobt ihr mich – es soll mich freuen,
Schmäht ihr mich – ich muss es dulden,
Schubert heiss ich, Schubert bin ich,
Mag nicht hindern, kann nicht laden,
Geht ihr gern auf meinen Pfaden,
Nun wohlan, so folget mir!

Franz Schubert

Schubert is my name, Schubert am I,
And present myself as such.
Whatever the finest men have achieved
I recognize and revere,
But it always remains something above and beyond me.
Even the art that weaves garlands
And gathers flowers, chooses and binds them:
I can offer it mere flowers.
I sift through them and – you choose.
If you praise me, I am delighted.
If you revile me, I must endure it.
Schubert is my name, Schubert am I,
I don't want to prevent you, but I cannot invite you.
If you are happy to walk on my paths
Well then, follow me!

Grillparzer died in Vienna on 21 January 1872, shortly before his *Gedichte* were published for the first time. With such figures as Heinrich von Kleist and Friedrich Hebbel, his reputation as one of the most important of nineteenth-century dramatists writing in German has endured.

Bibliography: Berke 1999, p. 203

Das GROSSE HALLELUJA
(Klopstock) **D442** [H270]
E major   June 1816

The great Hallelujah

Solo voice or chorus

(66 bars)

Ehre sei dem Hocherhabnen, dem Ersten, dem Vater der Schöpfung!	Glory be to the Exalted One, the First, The Father of Creation,
Dem unsre Psalmen stammeln,	To whom we stammer our psalms
Obgleich der wunderbare Er	Although He, the wondrous One,
Unaussprechlich, und undenkbar ist!	Is ineffable and unthinkable.

Eine Flamme von dem Altar an dem Thron
Ist in unsre Seele geströmt!
Wir freun uns Himmelsfreuden,
Dass wir sind, und über Ihn erstaunen können!

A flame from the altar at the throne
Has entered our souls.
We taste the joys of heaven,
For we exist and can wonder at Him.

Ehre sei Ihm auch von uns an den Gräbern hier,
Obwohl an seines Thrones letzten Stufen
Des Erzengels niedergeworfene Krone
Und seines Preisgesangs Wonne tönt!

Glory be to Him also from us among the graves,
Although the archangel has set his crown
On the lowest steps of His throne,
And joyous songs hymn His praise.

Ehre sei, und Dank, und Preis dem Hocherhabnen, dem Ersten,
Der nicht begann, und nicht aufhören wird!
Der sogar des Staubs Bewohnern gab,
Nicht aufzuhören!

Glory, thanks and praise be to the Exalted One, the First,
Who had no beginning, and will have no end,
Who granted that even the creatures of the dust
Shall have no end.

Ehre Dir! Ehre! Ehre Dir!
Hocherhabner Erster!
Vater der Schöpfung!
Unaussprechlicher, o Undenkbarer!

Glory be to You,
Exalted One, the First,
Father of Creation!
Ineffable, Unthinkable One!

FRIEDRICH GOTTLOB KLOPSTOCK (1724–1803); poem written in 1766

Das grosse Halleluja is almost always performed as a choral piece, but the work's designation is 'for single voice or chorus'. Accordingly it is listed here as the tenth of Schubert's thirteen Klopstock solo settings (1815–16). See the poet's biography for a chronological list of all the Klopstock settings.

This is one of a number of Schubert works from 1816 that looked to the musical techniques of the past for inspiration. It is a one-off, an experiment which was not repeated. The music is written out on two rather than three staves with the text placed above the piano part. This was the standard practice with earlier composers of lieder (Haydn and Reichardt for example) where it was assumed that the vocal line simply followed the right hand of the accompaniment. *Das grosse Halleluja* and its companion piece *Schlachtgesang* D443 are the only two occasions in Schubert's lieder on which we find this old-fashioned means of notation revived. But here there is a further complication. Instead of a melodic line in single notes on the top stave, we find chords, mainly in three parts, but sometimes in two or four parts. These are easy enough to play on the piano, but it is not really clear if they are the composer's shorthand notation of a part-song. The publisher Diabelli certainly thought so: when the work appeared nineteen years after Schubert's death it was printed for three-part women's chorus. On the other hand, *Das grosse Halleluja* appears in the solo-song series of the AGA, probably because the manuscript makes no mention of it being a choral work, and Mandyczewski followed the autograph scrupulously.

Too scrupulously perhaps. A single voice singing this song would make of it a weak affair – it seems reasonable to suppose that such a subject as the 'great Hallelujah' implies the use of a chorus. The existence of *Schlachtgesang*, another Klopstock setting from June 1816, and obviously choral, reinforces this notion. The marking here is 'Feierlich', and as so often in his settings of eighteenth-century poets, the composer summons the solemn musical ghosts of the past to suggest old music. The setting is firmly based on the portentous 'walking basses' of a composer like C. P. E. Bach whose own lieder settings of Klopstock were famous and probably well known to Schubert. (Not surprisingly, Schubert easily outdoes Bach *fils* in the broad sweep of the music, and in harmonic subtlety.) Mozart was also capable of writing in the 'antique' style when he wanted to depict ceremonial and age-old tradition. As we listen to *Das grosse Halleluja*, with its solemn melody sustained over a pacing bass line, we can hear Schubert's admiration for the contrapuntal music of the two armed guards in the second act of *Die Zauberflöte*.

The Mozartian connection is the reason why the Hyperion recording opted – *pace* Diabelli – for a male, rather than female, chorus. The grandeur of the poem suggests a weightier sound than could be provided by women's voices in this vocal range. Male voices sound an octave lower than written, and are thus heard in the same tessitura as the left-hand accompaniment. The right-hand chords in the piano sound an octave higher than the singers instead of simply doubling them at pitch. The musical texture is thus much richer than it might seem on the printed page. The close part-writing between tenors, baritones and bass (five singers in all on the recording) adds to the impression of an imposing wall of stentorian sound, thoroughly appropriate to the idea of a paean of God-fearing praise. The supporting bass line, ceaselessly inventive and always on the move, propels the music forwards and is the secret of its vigour. If this line had been remotely singable (and it is not) it might have seemed that Schubert's autograph was a short score for four-part chorus. Because matters are not as simple as that, care was taken to allocate the five available voices to two, three and occasionally four parts in the most effective way for the singers concerned.

Autograph:	Missing or lost
First edition:	Published as a trio (SSA) as Book 41 no. 2 of the Nachlass by Diabelli, Vienna in *c.* 1847 (P358)
Subsequent editions:	Not in Peters; AGA XX 227: Vol. 4/110; NSA IV: Vol. 10/272
Discography and timing:	Fischer-Dieskau I 7[17] 2'43

Hyperion I 32[14]

Hyperion II 14[25]   2'29   Daniel Norman, Toby Spence, Christopher Maltman, Stephan Loges & Neal Davies

⟵ *An die Sonne* D439   *Schlachtgesang* D443 ⟶

GRUPPE AUS DEM TARTARUS (I)   Scene from Hades
(Schiller) **D396** [H233]
(Fragment) C minor   March 1816

Horch – wie Murmeln des empörten Meeres,
Wie durch hohler Felsen Becken weint ein Bach,

Stöhnt dort dumpfigtief ein schweres – leeres,
  Qualerpresstes Ach!
Schmerz verzerret . . .

Hark! Like the angry murmuring of the sea,
Or a brook sobbing through pools in hollow
  rocks,
From the depths arises a muffled groan,
  Heavy, empty and tormented!
Pain distorts . . .

Friedrich von Schiller (1759–1805); poem written by 1781

This is the twenty-sixth of Schubert's forty-four Schiller solo settings (1811–24). See the poet's biography for a chronological list of all the Schiller settings.

This fragment was written down on a spare empty page of the manuscript of Schubert's D major Violin Sonata D384. Schubert had known the poem for at least three years; in 1813 he had set the second strophe (*Schmerz vezerret ihr Gesicht* D65) for male voices (TTB) as an exercise for Salieri. There is nothing wrong with the musical inspiration behind this first attempt to set Schiller's mighty poem; indeed there are progressions here that are audacious and prophetic of the semiquaver excitement of *Im Walde* D708. Nevertheless it is easy to see why the composer lost heart, having used up too much of the poem too quickly to place the final result on a canvas imposing enough for the song's subject. In the second setting of these words (D583, 1817, discussed below) Schubert takes twenty-three bars to reach the point in the poem covered by only fourteen here. The harmonic sequence, changing once in each bar, is effective, but it fails to plumb the depths of the underworld. It is just possible that more of this setting existed once and has been lost, but when we compare it with the second version we have every reason to suppose that Schubert knew he could do better.

Autograph:	Newberry Library, Chicago
First edition:	Published as part of the NSA in 1975 (P765)
Subsequent editions:	Not in Peters; Not in AGA; NSA IV: Vol. 2b/271
Bibliography:	Brown 1954, pp. 93–102
Discography and timing:	Fischer-Dieskau —
	Hyperion I 14³
	Hyperion II 13⁶ 0'28 Thomas Hampson

← *Ritter Toggenburg* D397   *Der Flüchtling* D402 →

GRUPPE AUS DEM TARTARUS (II)   Scene from Hades
(SCHILLER) OP. 24 NO. 1, **D583** [H384]
C minor   September 1817

Horch—wie Murmeln des empörten Meeres,
  Wie durch hohler Felsen Becken weint ein
    Bach,
Stöhnt dort dumpfig tief ein schweres, leeres,
  Qualerpresstes Ach!

    Schmerz verzerret
Ihr Gesicht, Verzweiflung sperret
  Ihren Rachen fluchend auf.[1]
Hohl sind ihre Augen-ihre Blicke
Spähen bang' nach des Cocytus Brücke,
  Folgen tränend seinem Trauerlauf.

Fragen sich einander ängstlich leise:
  Ob noch nicht Vollendung sei?—
Ewigkeit schwingt über ihnen Kreise,
  Bricht die Sense des Saturns entzwei.

Hark! Like the angry murmuring of the sea,
  Or a brook sobbing through pools in
    hollow rocks,
From the depths arises a muffled groan,
  Heavy, empty and tormented!

    Pain distorts
Their faces, in despair
  Their mouths open wide, cursing.
Their eyes are hollow – their frightened gaze
Strains towards Cocytus' bridge,
  Following as they weep that river's
    mournful course.

Anxiously, softly, they ask one another
  If the end is yet nigh.
Eternity sweeps in circles above them,
  Breaking Saturn's scythe in two.

FRIEDRICH VON SCHILLER (1759–1805); poem written by 1781

*This is the thirty-first of Schubert's forty-four Schiller solo settings (1811–24). See the poet's
biography for a chronological list of all the Schiller settings.*

The poem shows the ease with which Schiller could draw on his classical education. Although the
first literary work that comes to mind by way of influence is Dante's *Inferno*, where Virgil guides
Dante through the underworld, the lack of a Christian slant in Schiller's poem suggests that his source

[1] Schiller (*Gedizche*, Doll, Vienna, 1810) has 'Ihre Rachen fluchend auf.'

is the same as Dante's: Book VI of Virgil's *Aeneid* where Aeneas, guided by the Sybil, travels in search of his father Anchises. On the way to the Elysian fields he passes by the Tartarus, ablaze and emanating a terrible noise. The Sybil explains that the tortured souls within are those that have dared to rival the gods. The song was composed at the height of Schubert's Mayrhofer-inspired enthusiasm for classical mythology in music. It is an astonishing achievement not only because it so perfectly finds the key to Schiller's poem (it is arguably the greatest of all the Schubert settings of this poet) but because it refutes the notion that it was only 'modern' declamation in the Wagnerian manner (as in the songs of Hugo Wolf) that was able to upstage or replace 'old-fashioned' melody.

The song even looks extraordinary on paper, the introduction a cut-away map of the under-world: at street level we see only a bank of repeated Cs, their nodding heads above the stave, while rising semitones, undermining the foundations of hope in the afterlife, heave in the subter-ranean depths. The pianist's tremolandi (the marking is 'Etwas geschwind') begin on C, an octave apart; the insistent rising chromaticism squeezes the hands closer together as mercilessly as a thumbscrew, until a plateau of pain is reached with the crunch of an A flat seventh chord (b. 3). (Pianists should note that there is no decrescendo here; the entire bar, just like bb. 6 and 9, is fortissimo.) The process then begins again, this time on C sharp (b. 4), and yet again on D (b. 7), the pitch on which the voice enters and where it stays in mesmerized horror, transfixed for seven notes. By the time the singer changes to E flat and the word 'Meeres' (b. 10) we realize that this is Schubertian water music, opaque with Stygian sludge. It might seem that the sinister scales of the accompaniment belong to a nest of writhing serpents, but Schiller tells us that the groans of the damned sound like the sea, and Schubert provides waves of sound to illustrate the analogy. It is a measure of the epic scale of this setting (very unlike the first version in much tamer semiquavers) that by this time we have only reached the end of the poem's first line.

After the word 'Meeres', there is an extended pedal on E flat as the harmony moves in and out of A flat minor in second inversion (bb. 10–14) in waves of oscillating semiquavers; after this the basses in the accompaniment begin to rise in semitones, one bar at a time, and this inexorable progress adds to the effect of panic and claustrophobia. The distance between the E flat bass of b. 10 and the A natural bass of b. 20, the last bar of this section, is the interval of a tritone, a metaphor for the devil in music. The tension built up by this unnaturally prolonged upbeat and its relentless approach to the next section (it is as if we were hurtling towards an abyss) makes us both fear, and long for, the moment of reckoning that will end the suspense. When, at the word 'Ach' (b. 21), the music finally snaps into D minor like a spring-loaded trap this exclamation is nothing less than a desperate gasp of emotion. This is also the moment where the time signature changes from ₁₂⁄₈ to **C**, and where the tempo marking changes to 'Allegro'.

The words 'Schmerz verzerret / Ihr Gesicht, Verzweiflung sperret / Ihren Rachen fluchend auf' had been set to music, also in C minor, as early as 1813 by Schubert; in an exercise for Salieri that remained a fragment (D65) two unaccompanied tenors and a bass lob these menacing words at each other in fugal imitation. Four years is a long time in the life of a great composer and Schubert now only needs one voice to make a much more terrifying effect. At b. 22 of D583 these lines initiate a merciless catalogue of woes within a tiny span of vocal intervals. Martial dotted rhythms of this kind usually denote armed struggle – indeed the dotted motif of struggle in D minor in *Gruppe aus dem Tartarus* prefigures its use in another D minor Schiller setting, *Der Kampf* D594 from two months later. Here is also a musical prophecy of the sense of spiritual conflict in the Pyrker setting *Das Heimweh* D851 where these dotted rhythms pervade the song. In *Gruppe aus dem Tartarus*, however, the motif denotes desperate struggle to little effect. In the treble stave the pianist holds on to minims as if clutching at a raft in the midst of swirling rapids. These anchor notes rise in half steps from F to the high-water mark of A (bb. 21–9). Is it the doomed who are attempting to escape their fate, or are the performers fighting to get a better look at the alarming vista of suffering that now spreads before them? From b. 32 the poet's imagery of hollow eyes gazing towards the bridge over Cocytus, the river of lamentation, prompts cavernous harmonies with the voice now taking its turn in chromatic duty; as if reading a damning indictment its pitch gradually rises over seven bars (bb. 32–8) from E flat to F sharp, then settles in F sharp minor at 'Folgen tränend'. This section (from b. 40) is the nearest we get in this song to the sound of compassion, but F sharp is another tritone in relation to the song's home key of C, and there is to be no mercy. Performers should be warned that the whole of this Allegro section (from b. 21 until the end) should be in one implacable tempo.

The music for Schiller's next verse is introduced by an interlude (b. 46) where the piano moves in two stalking bars from the tonic, F sharp minor to its dominant, a chord of C sharp major that is suddenly surrounded (from b. 48) by ominous, throbbing activity. These repeated quavers with both hands placed in the bass clef begin to build tension in the manner of a Rossini crescendo – a reworking of the idea of ascending chromatic scales that has pervaded this piece. Instead of watery rumblings we now hear urgent pulsations, and soon these will be hammerings. It is as if an entire imprisoned chorus is whispering urgent imprecations. There is scarcely a vocal line here at all, only a succession of quasi parlando rising intervals as the damned are asking whether there will be an end to all this suffering; so strong is the tonal scheme that we scarcely notice the lack of conventional melody. In the meantime the repeated quavers in the piano writing have risen from C sharps to two bars of Ds, two of E flat (the notes always climbing to their new position before the predictability of the bar line), E natural, F and G. These movements are harmonized with changing chords driven by punching left-hand dotted rythms where the fourth beats of the bar moving to the next downbeat form a chain of eery, ever-rising, plagal cadences.

After an interlude (bb. 61–3) that encompasses a frightening crescendo for the pianist who can scarcely play the instrument loudly enough, these doomed souls receive their answer. From the perspective of the damned, the normally comforting word 'Ewigkeit' is not a promise of release to better realms but a horrible taunt – a sentence of eternal death and torment. This word is declaimed (rather than sung) in triumphant exultation, first in C major (bb. 64–5) and then in A minor (bb. 66–7). After both these outbursts the piano's answering chordal arpeggios echo the terrible word as if hammering home the sentence. Time will no longer be measured, and to emphasize this, the scythe of Saturn is symbolically broken by a succession of jagged chords (bb. 68–86). The clinching words of the poem are repeated to music of unforgiving grandeur; sforzati in the piano writing are aggressive and vehement. Only in the piano postlude as we leave the scene (from b. 86) do the scales reverse their direction and descend; it is as if we have summoned a ghoulish nightmare that now returns to the depths from whence it came. The final C minor chord of banked semibreves is the image of Saturn, an ancient version of the Grim Reaper, who coldly presides over this endless tragedy. On the page the semibreves, and the rippling line making a spread chord of them, resemble the ring-surrounded planet named after the god.

More authentic than any themed opus-number grouping is the fact that Schubert set *Elysium* D584 by the same poet as a kind of heavenly pendant to the dark pessimism of *Gruppe aus dem Tartarus*. Although they belong together, the two songs are hardly ever heard on the same programme, probably because *Elysium* is a much longer and perhaps even more challenging piece of music.

Autograph:	Missing or lost
First edition:	Published as Op. 24 no. 1 by Sauer & Leidesdorf, Vienna in October 1823 (P50)
Publication reviews:	*Allgemeine musikalische Zeitung* (Leipzig), No. 26 (24 June 1824), cols 425–8 [Waidelich/Hilmar Dokumente I No. 282; Deutsch Doc. Biog. No. 479] This negative review describes Schubert's songs as suffering from a 'Modulations-manie'
First known performance:	8 March 1821, *Abend-Unterhaltung* of the Gesellschaft der Musikfreunde at the Musikverein, Vienna. Soloist: Josef

	Preisinger (see Waidelich/Hilmar Dokumente I No. 73 for full programme)
Subsequent editions:	Peters: Vol. 2/61; AGA XX 328: Vol. 5/144; NSA IV: Vol. 2/13; Bärenreiter: Vol. 1/142
Bibliography:	Capell 1928, p. 130
	Fischer-Dieskau 1977, pp. 99–100
	Newbould 1997, p. 155
Arrangements:	Arr. Johannes Brahms (1833–1897) for voice (or chorus) and orchestra (1871) (*see* ORCHESTRATIONS)
	Arr. Max Reger (1873–1916) for voice and orchestra (1915) (*see* ORCHESTRATIONS)
	Fartein Valen (1887–1952) *Gruppe aus dem Tartarus* (1939)
Discography and timing:	Fischer-Dieskau II 1[13] 3'18
	Hyperion I 14[4]
	Hyperion II 19[18] 2'57 Thomas Hampson

← *Die Erde* D579b   *Atys* D585 →

GUARDA, CHE BIANCA LUNA *see VIER CANZONEN* D688/2

~◈~◈~◈~◈~◈~

GUITAR

By the time that Brahms arrived to live in Vienna in 1862, a piano in the home was considered a *sine qua non* by most well-educated and well-to-do families. Forty-five years earlier, in Schubert's time, a prosperous and cultivated middle class was still a developing social stratum and far fewer people were in a position to own their own piano. It was not only a question of money, but of space in their small apartments. At this time the guitar was the favourite means to accompany vocal music in the home and it became known as the 'Biedermeierinstrument'. Domestic music-making was not confined indoors however. The countryside, within easy reach of the city, was the backdrop to outdoor parties and summer gatherings (sometimes called 'Landpartien') where music was an essential accompaniment to dancing. This is where the guitar came into its own among the Schubertians. There is an etching by the artist Ludwig Mohn entitled *Ballspiel in Atzenbrugg*, an outdoor scene *circa* 1821, where the virtuoso pianist Josef von Gahy, seated next to Schubert, is depicted in the centre of the scene with a guitar. A standing violinist is providing music for the dancers, or perhaps (it is difficult to see from the picture) the two instruments are playing together. At about this time, Schubert's *Sechs-und-dreissig Originaltänze* Op. 9 (D365) had been published, thirty-six dances for piano that were issued with an alternative arrangement for violin (or flute) and guitar. A work such as this would have sounded particularly well in the open air.

We assume that Gahy was an able guitarist because this versatility seems not to have been uncommon among keyboard players of the time. Both Hummel and Moscheles were accomplished guitarists; in an age when the presence of a piano could not be relied upon, the guitar was an indispensable substitute. In a letter to Schober (9 November 1823) Moritz von Schwind mentions the guitar also making an appearance among the Schubertians at a Viennese hostelry where, once again, it was partnered with the violin to provide party music in the absence of the piano. Schubert himself probably played the guitar reasonably well – it seems more than likely that on many an occasion when he wished to share one of his new songs with friends or family he reached for this portable and companionable instrument and sang to his own accompaniment. However there is no proof of this: he never said anything about the instrument, and nothing has come down to us regarding his opinion of it. There is something about this silence which implies it was thoroughly taken for granted and, as an accepted part of everyday musical life, it was not especially worthy of comment.

Landpartie with guitar.

At the beginning of the nineteenth century there were a number of well-known professional guitarists in Vienna such as Simon Molitor and Alois Wolf, but the arrival in 1806 of the Italian virtuoso and composer Mauro Giuliani (1781–1829) transformed the status of the instrument in Austria. Not only did Giulani become Vienna's most famous guitarist but he was a prolific composer and he also played the cello in the first performance of Beethoven's Seventh Symphony. It is highly likely that, at some time in the 1820s or even earlier, Schubert heard Guilani play. German composers such as Weber, Marschner and Spohr, as well as Conradin Kreutzer in Vienna, wrote songs specifically for guitar accompaniment. Anton Diabelli, more famous as a publisher, composed songs with guitar, as did Schubert's young protégé Franz Lachner (qv Composers). One can be sure that publishers considered it commercially desirable to offer an alternative guitar accompaniment for songs whenever possible.

Schubert's only work that officially includes guitar accompaniment is the vocal trio *Zur Namensfeier meines Vaters* D80, composed in 1813 (there was no piano in the Schubert household at the time). It is possible that a much later song, *Die Nacht* (qv), the first setting of Caroline Pichler's *Der Unglückliche* (relatively recently discovered and not assigned a Deutsch number) was written for guitar accompaniment. In 1918 the autograph of a quartet for flute, violin, guitar and cello was discovered that was at first enthusiastically identified as a lost work by Schubert. In 1931 this was identified as a *Notturno* by Wenzel von Matiegka (1773–1830), a trio for flute, violin and guitar to which Schubert had added a cello part (D$_2$, Anhang II, 2). Only a second trio and variation added to Matiegka's score were found to be original Schubert, and the work tells us nothing new about the composer's relationship to the guitar.

When the amateur tenor Johann Carl Ritter von Umlauff (1796–1861) was resident in Vienna (1821–26) he is said to have performed songs by Schubert, with guitar accompaniment, with the composer himself as a member of his audience. Umlauff claimed to have made Schubert a present of a guitar by Bernard Enzensperger – an instrument that is still in existence although there is some doubt as to the authenticity of its link with the composer. The Viennese luthier Georg Staufer (who also built the Arpeggione for which the Sonata D821 was composed, an instrument described at the time as a 'Guitare-Violoncell') made a guitar which was said to have been in the composer's possession at his death. This instrument, part of the 1978 Schubert Exhibition in Vienna and the property of the Wiener Schubertbund, is also of doubtful provenance.

Performances of the vocal quartets *Die Nachtigall* D724 (on 27 August 1822) and *Geist der Liebe* D747 (on 24 September 1822) with guitar accompaniment are documented. These arrangements were certainly not Schubert's own work, and the decision to provide these accompaniments certainly went back to Anton Diabelli who clearly had an affinity with the instrument and was an excellent guitarist in his own right. Diabelli was also the kind of shrewd businessman who saw the point of publishing music with an eye to the popular market and for people who were not wealthy enough to own a piano. Diabelli was untrammelled by the finer points of copyright that would affect modem-day publishers. We have no idea whether Schubert was ever given the chance to approve, or disapprove, of the guitar accompaniments issued in his name, much less whether he played any direct part in their arrangement.

In September 1822 there was an advertisement in the *Wiener Zeitung* for a collection of songs published by Diabelli. This was *Pholomele. Eine Sammlung der beliebesten Stucke für Singstimme mit Begleitung der Guitarre.* In this collection was to be found guitar-accompanied arrangements of *Erlkönig* D328, *Der Wanderer* D489, *Morgenlied* D685 and *Schäfers Klagelied* D121.

This was followed by published guitar arrangements of Op. 20 (*Sei mir gegrüsst!* D741, *Frühlingsglaube* D686, *Hänflings Liebeswerbung* D552), Op. 21 (*Auf der Donau* D553, *Der Schiffer* D536, *Wie Ulfru fischt* D525), Op. 22 (*Der Zwerg* D771, *Wehmut* D772) and Op. 43 (*Die junge Nonne* D828, *Nacht und Träume* D828). All of these were Diabelli publications.

As early as 1824 three songs with alternative guitar accompaniment from *Die schöne Müllerin* D795 were published by the periodical *Lyra* in Frankfurt. These were *Mit dem grünen Lautenbande* D795/13, *Der Müller und der Bach* D795/19 and *Morgengruss* D795/8. There were further advertisements for publications of guitar-accompanied songs by Diabelli, including the complete *Die schöne Müllerin*, but it is by no means certain that these were ever issued. Guitar accompaniments to the Op. 23 songs (*Die Liebe hat gelogen* D751, *Selige Welt* D743, *Schwanengesang* D744, *Schatzgräbers Regehr* D761) were similarly advertised with no surviving evidence that these arrangements ever became available. However in 1822 there were guitar accompaniments published of the three vocal quartets of Op. 11 (*Das Dörfchen* D598, *Die Nachtigall* D724 and *Geist der Liebe* D727). In 1823 the Op. 16 quartets (*Frühlingsgesang* D740 and *Naturgenuss* D422) were issued with 'accompaniment of pianoforte or guitar'.

After Schubert's death there were any number of guitar accompaniments issued for the Schubert songs – as in 1833 when Diabelli issued four songs from *Die schöne Müllerin: Das Wandern* D795/1, *Wohin?* D795/2, *Ungeduld* D795/7 and *Morgengruss* D795/8. In the first decades of the twentieth century an important renaissance of the classical guitar led to an increased interest in the instrument's ability to accompany for Schubert's songs. Richard Schmid, a Viennese guitarist whose father Anton (b. 1844), also a guitarist, published twenty effective arrangements, *circa* 1910. Ferdinand Schubert, who had been one of Anton's teachers, told him that Franz Schubert's guitar-playing enthusiasm had been spurred on by the poet Theodor Körner (this must have been in 1813) who was himself a keen guitarist. In the present day there is a great interest amongst guitarists in accompanying Schubert songs, particularly as there is a clear historical justification for doing so. Modern guitarists are more ambitious than ever to provide accompaniments that incorporate as much as possible of the detailed subtlety of the piano originals. In the recording made of *Die schöne Müllerin* by Peter Schreier and the guitarist Konrad Ragossnig (b. 1932) in 1980, for example, the accompaniments were especially arranged by Ragossnig in collaboration with John Duarte. Ragossnig claimed that four of these arrangements were among the most difficult pieces ever conceived for guitar – an indication of the kind of challenge faced by modem guitarists when attempting to accompany Schubert songs with the kind of detail to be found in the original piano parts. In more recent years the German guitarist Tilman Hoppstock (b. 1961) has arranged and published *110 Schubert Lieder* (2009). He selected the works that suit the instrument best, making careful decisions regarding vocal range and transposition, enabling voice and guitar to sound well together. Hoppstock's arrangements include three volumes dedicated to selections from each of the song cycles, two Goethe volumes, a volume of Klopstock and Schiller settings, two volumes of miscellaneous poets and a Mayrhofer volume. The present-day guitarist is better equipped to become a Schubert song accompanist than ever before.

Bibliography: 10 Schubert Lieder zur Gitarre, mit einer musikhistorischen Skizze Franz Schubert als Gitarrist von Richard Schmid Op. 75, Leipzig, Hoffmeister, *c.* 1910.

Der GUTE HIRT

(Uz) **D449** [H277]

E major   June 1816

The good shepherd

(70 bars)

Was sorgest du? Sei stille meine Seele!	Why are you troubled? Be calm, my soul!
Denn Gott ist ein guter Hirt,[1]	For God is a good shepherd;
Der mir, auch wenn ich mich nicht quäle,	Even if I do not rack myself with exertion
Nichts mangeln lassen wird.	He will let me want for nothing.
Er weidet mich auf blumenreicher Aue,	He feeds me in flower-filled meadows,
Er führt mich frischen Wassern zu,	He leads me to fresh waters,
Und bringet mich, im kühlen Taue,	And in the cool dew
Zur sichern Abendruh'.	Brings me to safe evening rest.
Er hört nicht auf, mich liebreich zu beschirmen,	He does not cease to protect me lovingly,
Im Schatten vor des Tages Glut.	In shade from the heat of day,
In seinem Schosse vor den Stürmen	In his bosom from tempests
Und schwarzer Bosheit Wut.	And from the rage of black evil.
Auch wenn er mich durch finstre Täler leiten,	Even when he leads me through dark vales,
Mich durch die Wüste führen wird,	Or through the wildemess,
Will ich nichts fürchten! mir zur Seiten	I shall fear nothing; at my side
Geht dieser treue Hirt,	Walks the faithful shepherd.
[(. . . 2 . . .)]	[(. . . 2 . . .)]
Ich aber will ihn preisen und ihm danken!	But I will praise Him and thank Him!
Ich halt an meinem Hirten fest;	I shall hold fast to my shepherd,
Und mein Vertrauen soll nicht wanken	And my faith shall never waver
Wenn alles mich verlässt.	When all else forsakes me.

JOHANN PETER UZ (1720–1796); poem written between 1763 and 1767

This is the last of Schubert's five Uz solo settings (1816). See the poet's biography for a chronological list of all the Uz settings.

The poem is a paraphrase, if not a translation, of Psalm 23. The key of E major is often associated in Schubert with joy and innocence, particularly in a religious context. Everything in this

[1] Uz's original line is 'Denn Gott ist ein *getreuer* Hirt'.

music is calm and placid; the music is unusually marked 'Vertrauensvoll' – trustingly. It has a homespun quality (the accompaniment is entirely in triplets without a single moment of rest from beginning to end) that suggests the harmonium and prayer meetings. In fact, as always with Schubert, the sophistication of the harmony rescues the song from the commonplace. It is a companion piece to the work in which Schubert was to give definite expression to his flowing-triplet seraphic style, *Der 23. Psalm* D706 (in the translation of Felix Mendelssohn's grandfather, Moses) for women's voices from December 1820. Schubert's other Uz setting of the time (*Gott im Frühlinge* D448) is similarly in E major and is also a hymn of praise to God in His vernal manifestation. That little jewel was included in the book of seventeen songs that Schubert made in 1816 for the birthday of his sweetheart Therese Grob, and it is very likely that *Der gute Hirt* was also written with her voice and demeanour in mind.

The music is fashioned as a *da capo* aria. The poet's first and last verses are set to exactly the same music apart from a suggested variant (a higher ossia) in b. 10 for the second verse. The middle three strophes are through-composed. The 'Fine' printed after the *da capo* repeat is not found on Schubert's hastily written manuscript (taken by the NSA to be the only definitely original version), and there is indeed no indication to the pianist as to how the song is to be brought to a close. There is moreover no introduction. However Volume 10 of the NSA (p. 278) prints an interesting variant (or 'Veränderung') of this song in the transposed key of C major. This is a copy from the Witteczek collection that probably goes back to the baritone Johann Michael Vogl. It contains a four-bar introduction that is based on the opening melody of the song, and a spacious postlude following the song's last bar over which is written a giant fermata – an indication of a ritenuto over all six notes in the vocal line. There are also various interesting, if somewhat awkward and rather unnecessary, ornaments that were almost certainly added by Vogl himself some time after the song was written. Both the first edition of the song (Gotthard, 1872) and the AGA print the song in E major. There is no sign of Vogl's ornaments, but they do include the prelude and postlude of the song (as in the NSA C major version) and it is possible that these go back to Schubert himself.

Autograph:	Wienbibliothek im Rathaus, Vienna (first draft)
First edition:	Published as No. 7 of *Neueste Folge nachgelassener Lieder und Gesänge* by J. P. Gotthard, Vienna in 1872 (P433)
Subsequent editions:	Not in Peters; AGA XX 234: Vol. 4/124; NSA IV: Vol. 10/181 & 278 (ornamented version)
Discography and timing:	Fischer-Dieskau I 7[22] 3'06
	Hyperion I 9[19]
	Hyperion II 15[4] 3'12 Arleen Auger

← *An den Schlaf* D447   *Gott im Ungewitter* D985 →

GUTE NACHT *see* WINTERREISE D911/1

HÄNFLINGS LIEBESWERBUNG   The linnet's wooing

(KIND) OP. 20 NO. 3, **D552** [H363]

The song exists in two versions, the second of which is discussed below:
(1) April 1817; (2) appeared April 1823

(1)   'Lieblich'   A major   §   [26 bars]

(2)   A major

(26 bars)

Ahidi! ich liebe.	Chirp, chirp, I am in love!
Mild lächelt die Sonne,	The sun smiles gently,
Mild wehen die Weste,	The west wind blows mild,
Sanft rieselt die Quelle,	The stream murmurs softly,
Süss duften die Blumen.	The flowers' scent is sweet!
Ich liebe, Ahidi!	I am in love, chirp, chirp!
Ahidi! ich liebe.	Chirp, chirp, I am in love!
Dich lieb' ich, du Sanfte,	I love you, my tender one,
Mit seidnem Gefieder,	With your silken feathers,
Mit strahlenden Äuglein,	And your radiant little eyes.
Dich, Schönste der Schwestern!	Fairest among your sisters!
Ich liebe, Ahidi!	I am in love, chirp, chirp!
Ahidi! ich liebe.	Chirp, chirp, I am in love!
O sieh, wie die Blumen	See how the flowers
Sich liebevoll grüssen,	Lovingly greet one another,
Sich liebevoll nicken!	Lovingly nod to each other!
O liebe mich wieder!	Love me in return!
Ich liebe, Ahidi!	I am in love, chirp, chirp!
Ahidi! ich liebe.	Chirp, chirp, I am in love!
O sieh, wie der Epheu	See how the ivy
Mit liebenden Armen	Embraces the oak tree
Die Eiche umschlinget.	With loving arms.
O liebe mich wieder!	Love me in return!
Ich liebe, Ahidi!	I am in love, chirp, chirp!

JOHANN FRIEDRICH KIND (1768–1843); poem written in 1793

This is Schubert's only setting of a Kind text. See the poet's biography.

In writing the 'Trout' Quintet D667, Schubert used a popular song as the basis of a piece of instrumental music. In composing this song, it is probable that he used what must have been a popular piece of dance music for piano (the third of the *Deutsche* D972, an undated set of dances) as an accompaniment. If this is so, it is possibly a unique instance of music preceding word in Schubert's song output (this may also have been the case in *Die Macht der Liebe* D308). Of course it might be that the song came first and its piano part was popular enough to find an echo on the dance floor, but it seems more likely that the poem by Kind has been made to fit the music as a type of obbligato (the vocal line uncharacteristically sounds like one). So we have an example of the tail wagging the dog or, in this case, the wing flapping the bird. The runs of the accompaniment are written in semiquavers (rather than the quavers we find in the dance) and the time signature is ⁶⁄₈, not ³⁄₄, but the first six bars of the melody are the same in both song and dance. This puts us in mind of Brahms's *Liebeslieder Walzer*, written as piano duets with optional vocal parts. Kind's anthropomorphic poem with its echoes of Hölty cleverly captures the characteristics of birdsong with its short-spanned repetitions. The excursion into B flat major for the fourth and fifth lines of the poem (bb. 16–19) is a winsome touch (providing relief from the insistent A major of the home key) that we do not find in the dance music. The first version of the song has a tempo marking of 'Lieblich'; the second (almost identical and used as the basis for the Op. 20 publication) is marked 'Etwas geschwind'.

The sheer cosiness and sweetness of this song mirrors the best family values of the Biedermeier period. There is no attempt specifically to describe any of the characteristics of the linnet – *Carduelis cannabina*. *Hänflings Liebeswerbung* is almost a definition of Viennese *Gemütlichkeit*. The same may be said for Brahms's *Das Mädchen spricht* (also in A major) which explores more or less the same theme with swallows rather than linnets. There is a good deal of genre painting of the period that has the same quality that borders on kitsch. The song is nevertheless enchanting in the right performers' hands, and Schubert and his friends seem to have been fond of it. His placing of this song as the third of the Op. 20 group (the others were the much more serious *Sei mir gegrüsst* and *Frühlingsglaube*) seems a judicious exercise in pleasing the ordinary listener. This was the first of the composer's song sets to be published by the house of Sauer & Leidesdorf and they no doubt wanted a hit. And the poet was, after all, the famous librettist of Weber's *Der Freischütz*.

Autograph:	Wienbibliothek im Rathaus, Vienna
Publication:	First published as part of the NSA in 1970 (P755; first version)
	First published as Op. 20 no. 3 by Sauer & Leidesdorf, Vienna in April 1823 (P38; second version)
Dedicatee:	Justina von Bruchmann
Subsequent editions:	Peters: Vol. 4/12; AGA XX 316: Vol. 5/90 (second version); NSA IV: Vol. 1a/145 (2nd version) & Vol. 1b/260 (first version); Bärenreiter: Vol. 1/116
Discography and timing:	Fischer-Dieskau II 1³ 1'33 (first two strophes only)
	Hyperion I 21¹³
	Hyperion II 18¹⁴ 2'27 Edith Mathis

← *Pax vobiscum* D551　　　　　　　　　　　　*Der Schäfer und der Reiter* D517 →

HAFIZ (MAHOMED SHAMS UD-DIN) (*c.* 1300–1389)

Persian poet, inspiration behind Goethe's poems for his *West-östlicher Divan* (1819). *See:* WEST-ÖSTLICHER DIVAN and also separate entries for *Geheimes* D719; *Im Gegenwärtigen Vergangenes* D710 and *Versunken* D715.

HAGARS KLAGE	Hagar's lament

HAGARS KLAGE   Hagar's lament

(SCHÜCKING) **D5** [H3]
C minor – A♭ major   30 March 1811

(369 bars)

(1)   Hier am Hügel heissen Sandes[1]
      [(. . .)]
      Sitz' ich, und mir gegenüber
         Liegt mein sterbend Kind!

Here I sit, on a mound of burning sand,
[(. . .)]
and before me
Lies my dying child!

(2)   Lechzt nach einem Tropfen Wasser,
      Lechzt und ringt schon mit dem Tode,
      Weint, und blickt mit stieren Augen
         Mich bedrängte Mutter an!

He thirsts for a drop of water;
He thirsts, and already struggles with death;
He weeps, and with vacant eyes
Looks upon me, his distressed mother.

(3)   Du musst sterben, armes Würmchen,
      Ach, nicht eine Träne,
      Hab' ich in den trocknen Augen,
         Wo ich dich mit stillen kann!

You must die, poor mite;
Alas, not a single tear do I have
In my dry eyes
To soothe you.

(4)   Ha! säh' ich eine Löwenmutter[2]
      Ich wollte mit ihr kämpfen,
         Kämpfen mit ihr um die Eiter.[3]
      [(. . .)]

If I saw a lioness
I would fight with her,
Fight with her for her milk.
[(. . .)]

(5)   Könnt' ich aus dem dürren Sande
      Nur ein Tröpfchen Wasser saugen!
         Aber ach, ich muss dich sterben
           sehn![4]

If only I could suck
But one drop of water from the parched sand!
But alas, I must watch you die!

---

[1] Schücking's second line is 'In der menschenlosen Wüste'.
[2] Schubert transfers the 'Ha' from the second to the first line of the strophe.
[3] Schücking's fourth line is 'Dass ich löschte deirem Durst!'
[4] Schubert here conflates two lines of Schucking: 'Aber ach, so musst du sterben / Und ich muss dich sterben sehn!'

(6) Kaum ein schwacher Strahl des Lebens
     Dämmert auf der bleichen Wange,
     Dämmert in den matten Augen,
          Deine Brust erhebt sich kaum.

Scarcely a feeble ray of life
Glimmers on your pale cheeks
And in your dull eyes;
Your little chest scarcely rises.

(7) Hier am Busen komm' und welke!
     Kömmt ein Mensch dann durch die Wüste,
     So wird er in den Sand uns scharren,
          Sagen: 'Das ist Weib und Kind!'

Come to my breast and perish there!
If a man then comes through the wilderness
He will bury us in the sand,
Saying: 'Here is a woman and her child!'

(8) Ich will mich von dir wenden,
     Dass ich dich nicht sterben seh',[5]
     Und im Taumel der Verzweiflung
          Murre wider Gott!

I shall turn away from you
Lest I see you die,
And in the frenzy of despair
Cry out against God!

(9) Ferne von dir will ich gehen,
     Und ein rührend Klaglied singen,
     Dass du noch im Todeskampfe
          Tröstung einer Stimme hörst.

I shall go far away from you
And sing a touching lament,
So that in the throes of death
You will still hear a comforting voice.

(10) Noch zum letzten Klaggebete
     Öffn' ich meine dürren Lippen,
     Und dann schliess' ich sie auf immer,
          Und dann komme bald, o Tod![6]

I shall open my parched lips
In one last grieving prayer;
Then I shall close them for ever,
Then, o Death, come soon.

(11) Jehova! blick' auf uns herab,[7]
     Jehova, erbarme dich des Knaben!
     Send' aus einem Taugewölke
          Labung uns herab!

Look down on us, Jehovah!
Take pity on the child!
From dewy clouds
Send us refreshing rain!

(12) Ist er nicht von Abrams Samen?
     Er weinte Freudentränen,
     Als ich ihm dies Kind geboren,
          Und nun wird er ihm zum Fluch!

Is he not of Abraham's seed?
He wept tears of joy
When I bore him this child,
And now the child has become a curse to him!

(13) Rette deines Lieblings Samen,
     Selbst sein Vater bat um Segen,
     Und du sprachst: 'Es komme Segen
          Über dieses Kindes Haupt.'[8]

Save the seed of your chosen one
His father asked for your blessing,
And you spoke: 'Let this child's head
Be blessed.'

(14) Hab' ich wider dich gesündigt,
     Ha! so treffe mich die Rache,
     Aber, ach, was tat der Knabe,
          Dass er mit mir leiden muss?

If I have sinned against you
May vengeance strike me!
But what has the boy done
That he must suffer with me?

---

[5] Schücking writes 'sehe'.
[6] Schücking writes 'Und dann konne bald *der Tod*'.
[7] Schubert here shifts 'Jehova!' to the beginning of the line rather than having it at the end. In the following line he adds another 'Jehova' instead of the poet's 'Und'.
[8] Schücking writes 'Über dieses *Knabem* Haupt'.

(15)   Wär' ich doch in Sir gestorben,   Would that I had died in Syria
       Als ich in der Wüste irrte,   When I was walking in the wilderness,
       Und das Kind noch ungeboren   And the child lay unborn
              Unter meinem Herzen lag!   Under my heart!

(16)   Nein; da kam ein holder Fremdling,   No! A fair stranger came to me,
       Hiess mich rück zu Abram gehen,   Bade me return to Abraham
       Und des Mannes Haus betreten,   And enter the house of the man
              Der uns grausam jetzt verstiess.   Who now cruelly rejects us.

(17)   War der Fremdling nicht ein Engel?[9]   Was the stranger not an angel?
       Denn er sprach mit holder Miene: For he spoke with gracious mien:
       'Ismael wird gross auf Erden,   'Ishmael will be great on earth,
              Sein Samen zahlreich sein!'[10]   And his seed will multiply!'

(18)   Nun liegen wir und welken,[11]   Now we lie dying,
       Unsre Leichen werden modern   And our bodies will rot
       Wie die Leichen der Verfluchten,   Like the corpses of the accursed
              Die der Erde Schoss nicht birgt.   Which the earth's womb does not conceal.

(19)   Schrei zum Himmel, armer Knabe!   Cry unto heaven, my poor boy!
       Öffne deine welken Lippen!   Open your parched lips!
       Gott, sein Herr! verschmäh' das Flehen   God, his Lord, do not scorn
              Des unschuld'gen Knaben nicht.   The pleas of this innocent boy.

CLEMENS AUGUST SCHÜCKING (1759–1790)

This is Schubert's only setting of a Schücking text. See the poet's biography.

This is the song that stands at the very beginning of Mandyczewski's sumptuous ten-volume *Gesamtausgabe*. There are, in fact, unfinished settings of Gabriele von Baumberg that are earlier still, but this is essentially Schubert's first complete vocal work, more of a ballad, or *scena*, than a lied. There is a copy in the Witteczek-Spaun collection which has the following inscription: 'Schubert's first song composition, written in the Konvikt at the age of fourteen, 30 March, 1811', but the first draft of the work could be some time earlier. The earlier settings of Baumberg's *Lebenstraum* D1a and D39 are both fragments.

Schubert's model was a ballad by the Swabian composer Johann Rudolf Zumsteeg (1760–1802), *Hagars Klage in der Wüste Bersaba*. This was published in 1797, the year of Schubert's birth. In the manner of young art students who visit galleries in order to copy their favourite painters' work, Schubert set about a similar process. He placed the Zumsteeg score before him and reworked it bar by bar. Schubert is guided by great respect for the original and in the first part of the piece chooses the same key and time signatures, as well as the same points for piano interludes. As the work progresses he departs from his model and becomes increasingly adventurous, although not always to good effect. A few years later, setting Schiller's poem *Die*

---

[9] Schücking writes 'dein Engel'.
[10] Schücking writes 'Und sein Samen zahlreich sein!'.
[11] Schücking writes 'Ha, wir liegen und welken'.

Hagar in the desert from the almanac *Aglaja* (1828). From the painting by Giacomo Bassano (1510–1592).

Erwartung, the younger composer would inadvertently wipe the floor with Zumsteeg, but here the fourteen-year-old Schubert's departures from his model are those of an ambitious and inexperienced tearaway, not yet fully knowledgeable about the capabilities of the human voice. (His regular visits to the opera only began later.) In terms of understanding vocal *Stimmfach* the older composer is a sober professional and Schubert an irresponsible joyrider. (Any soprano singing *Hagars Klage* has reason to chastise this teenager for making her suffer on the tessitura tightrope!) On every other level, however, where raw talent is a more exciting commodity than good judgement, the depth of Schubert's feeling and the wily strength of his imagination announce the arrival of rare genius.

It would be some time before Schubert had regular access to the poetry libraries of friends, so it is not surprising that this text was lifted from another song. But this is not the only work by Zumsteeg he could have considered, and it is fascinating that he chose *this* story for his debut. Schücking, admittedly a poet of no importance or renown, here gives centre stage to slaves and outcasts, the bondwoman and her illegitimate son about whom St Paul is so scathing in Galatians 4:21–31. It is clear from an impartial reading of the story (Genesis 16:1–16 – the first exile of Hagar into the desert when pregnant, and 21:8–21 – the second banishment with her son Ishmael) that Hagar is scarcely to blame for her plight. After she was purchased as a slave in Egypt, she became Abraham's concubine because Sarah, his wife, was unable to conceive. During her pregnancy, in Sarah's eyes at least, Hagar became insufferably arrogant, but in matters of sexual rivalry ill-feeling stemmed from both sides. Hagar, fearing Sarah's wrath, fled to the desert where she was told by an angel of the Lord to return to bear her son Ishmael who would have many descendants and be in constant struggle with all other men. Some fourteen years after the birth of Ishmael, Sarah gave birth to Isaac, the son with whom God promised Abraham to make a covenant. Sarah saw the two boys playing together and, fearing for Isaac's inheritance, once again insisted that Abraham should exile Hagar, this time together with Ishmael. Abraham frees them from slavery and sends them into the desert of Beer-sheba. The song opens with the bondwoman's distress in the wilderness; the water bottle Abraham has given her is now empty. The boy is fourteen years old (Schubert's age at the time of writing the work) but for the purposes of the poem it seems that Schücking has taken Ishmael to be a helpless infant.

Throughout his life Schubert's greatest family difficulties were with his father. We know too, from the composer's account of a dream ('My Dream', *Documentary Biography*, p. 226) among other things, that the patriarch was disappointed in Franz who longed for a reconciliation with his father. The recurring theme of other early ballads such as *Leichenfantasie* D7 and *Der Vater-mörder* D10 is difficult father-and-son relationships. As he grew older there was a battle of wills between the two men regarding Franz's future career. How easy it would be for Schubert to project his situation onto Hagar and Ishmael, placed in the desert of their husband's or father's affections. And how comforting to imagine that great things were in store for the outcasts despite all their suffering: Ishmael was to be accepted as an ancestor by the Arab peoples, perhaps as a forefather of Mohammed himself, and Franz Peter Seraphicus Schubert was also to be immortal. It is likely that selecting an appropriate text and writing music quietly in his room was empowering for the young composer in more ways than one: an act of subtle and concealed defiance, a way of assuaging the pain of those awkward teenage years.

Alfred Einstein points out how much Zumsteeg owed (and thus Schubert too, without realizing it) to the example of *scene* with orchestra by the forgotten master Georg Benda (1722–1795). His melodramas, such as *Ariadne* and *Medea* (1775), were extended monologues where the heroine tells of her plight through a variety of vocal techniques ranging from recitative to cantilena, supported by instrumental commentary reflecting her changing emotions. Mozart admired these groundbreaking works, and Zumsteeg latched onto the crucial idea that replacing orchestra with piano altered the form into something more mercurial and flexible; the suggestive power of the piano, and the intimate musical details revealed by an attentive accompanist's fingers, liberated rather than constricted the listener's imagination. It is for this reason, Einstein points out, that orchestrations of Schubert songs are 'almost always a simultaneous coarsening and weakening of the original'.

Verses 1–3 'Largo': At the very opening of the work, and elsewhere, we hear the presence of Haydn, a master by whom Zumsteeg seems less influenced than his young imitator. The power of the slowly unfolding introduction (the key is C minor, as in Zumsteeg) owes its mood to the spatial grandeur of *Die Schöpfung*; the moonscape emptiness of outer space is analogous to that of the desert. John Reed detects in these opening bars a seminal motif or thematic cell that recurs in many of Schubert's instrumental works, and which was to be the basis of the 'Adagio molto' of his 'Tragic' Symphony D417. Both song and symphony are in C minor, and hearing the introductions of the works one after the other highlights a genuine Schubertian thumbprint. The composer omits Schücking's line 'In der menschenlosen Wüste' ('In the unpeopled desert') either because it did not appeal to him or, in his enthusiasm to begin his great work, he left it out unintentionally; such mistakes happen during the act of copying. This is probably why the first strophe has only three lines whereas it is likely that the elisions in verses 4 and 5 were deliberate and made for reasons of dramatic fluidity. As Hagar begins to sing, the portentous crotchets of the introduction yield to more lively quavers, and from the beginning of the second strophe (b. 15) the voice is accompanied by pulsating semiquavers. Whatever one may say about the awkwardness of the vocal line, there is no doubt that Schubert here depicts a woman of the fiercest temperament. In Zumsteeg she is much more contained and Germanic. Perhaps Schubert has imagined Hagar's smouldering Egyptian looks; certainly the music is touched by something dark and exotic. The words 'sterbend Kind' (b. 12) descend to the bottom of the voice, whereas 'schon mit dem Tode' (bb. 15–16) climbs to a fortissimo wail.

The interlude between the second and third strophes (bb. 22–6) is meant to denote the mute pleading of the child's eyes. Here Schubert does not improve on Zumsteeg. After the intensity of the voice part the music suddenly reverts to eighteenth-century commonplace, cadential trill and all; it is the power of words that brings the most intense reactions from the young composer. 'Du musst sterben' (b. 26) is a case in point. While Zumsteeg sounds a suitably pathetic note, Schubert responds to this phrase with an exciting venom, as if he himself were in a rage at the unfairness of it all. This is not only an exhausted mother at the end of her tether, but also a glowering Medea, threatening death. Schubert repeats the words, intoxicated with the power of a descending harmonic sequence (bb. 27–8). The third verse has a broad and impressive sweep to it, the plashing semiquavers descriptive of the tears that refuse to come. Zumsteeg, choosing to illustrate the absence of tears rather than the idea of them, is justified in his drier approach.

Verses 4–5 'Allegro': The new section begins with a seventeen-bar *Zwischenspiel* for piano in the stormy key of D minor (bb. 43–59). Here the taut rhythms of Beethoven in *Sturm und Drang* mood seem to be the inspiration. What might have appeared empty dramatic gesture is made clear by the words: Schubert imagines the rippling muscles and feline guile of the hunting lioness. The power of nature lurking in the bushes is wonderfully conveyed; crotchet rests punctuating the music (bb. 51–2) are crucial to the build-up of tension. A sudden outbreak of semiquavers rushing upwards (b. 55) seems to be launched by the animal's powerful leap; this springing surprise is followed by pounce and kill as forte split octaves descend the keyboard (bb. 56–7). Schubert shifts the poet's lines so that Hagar's first word is the dramatic (and unintentionally comical) 'Ha!' – a precursor of Thusnelda who begins her bloodthirsty ballad

(*Hermann und Thusnelda*, D322) in similar fashion. It is here that the vocal writing becomes almost impossible for most singers (happily not for Christine Brewer on the Hyperion recording). The force of the young composer's conviction somehow carries this otherwise ludicrous passage that imagines a tussle between Hagar and the lioness. She must be tough to take on such a challenge, and so must the singer to take the high notes on impossible vowels. In Zumsteeg's song the fourth line of the poet's strophe ('so that I may quench your thirst') explains why Hagar, herself a lioness defending her young, fights the animal; but here Schubert omits the line, probably because it holds up the action.

The fifth strophe inspires obsessive repetitions of drooping seconds in the piano writing on diminished-seventh chords (from b. 72). These suggest the pursing of lips and a quick intake of breath – desperate and unsuccessful attempts to suck water from the sand, one of the earliest signs of Schubert's aptitude for tonal analogue. Although not the most elegant of his illustrative touches, it shows an ability to respond to words on quite another level from that of Zumsteeg.

Verses 6–7 'Largo': This is one of the most effective sections of the piece. From b. 88 we revert to Zumsteeg's example of repeated quavers in music that is suddenly of hushed stillness. These switches of tempo are at the heart of the drama. As at the very beginning of the song, a Haydn-inspired chromaticism carries far more emotional weight than Zumsteeg's opening. The same may be said here of that composer's rather ordinary dominant sevenths in comparison to Schubert's other-worldly harmonic explorations. All this is in the spirit of Schubert's aim, as later revealed by his friend Josef von Spaun, to 'modernize Zumsteeg's song form'. These rapt quavers with their inner moving parts seem taken from a memory of a Haydn string quartet, or perhaps one by Mozart. The drooping sequences successfully convey the idea of colour draining from the cheeks of the dying child. The dryly alternating quavers beneath 'Dämmert auf der bleichen Wange' (bb. 94–5) seem distant ancestors of the staccato quavers at the beginning of *Auf dem Flusse* in *Winterreise* D911 where the river's icy surface and Ishmael's cheek pale with death have inspired a similar musical response. The music of the next strophe could be written for a Gluck heroine (from b. 99): grand and noble, statuesque but still decorated by runs and turns of phrase that recall the eighteenth century. On the other hand, the final phrase 'Sagen: "Das ist Weib und Kind!"' and the three bars of piano writing following it use every chromatic turn at the young Schubert's disposal. This reference to mother and child seems to touch him to the quick.

Verses 8–9 'Geschwind': Note Schubert's momentary reversion to a German tempo marking; for once he uses the same word as Zumsteeg, and in the same language. He appears here to have remembered that he is writing a song related to a biblical figure. Accordingly there is an outbreak of quasi-fugal music in the 'old style' (bb. 118–32) and *Hagars Klage*, from the very beginning of Schubert's career, joins hands with *Mirjams Siegesgesang* D942 from the end of it. This passage lasts some fifteen bars, an obvious attempt to improve on Zumsteeg's six. Once the words begin again we revert to non-contrapuntal music; this is like an allegro movement of a piano sonata with vocal obbligato. Hagar writhes in her torment, a great deal of which relates to the uncomfortable tessitura. The pianist uses every trick in the book: rattling right-hand semiquavers and striding left-hand basses (bb. 142–3); and scale passages of some virtuosity (bb. 144–7). It is as if Schubert is trying to outdo Zumsteeg at every turn: if the older man sets 'Verzweiflung' to a diving diminished seventh, Schubert plunges the entire octave on the same word (bb. 146–7). The whole of the ninth strophe is a miscalculation, however. Schubert should have adopted Zumsteeg's quietly dignified approach, but instead we have an embarrassingly inappropriate accompaniment with chirpy grace notes and banal harmonies (from b. 152). The composer's energy is out of control and he loses the musical mood suited to a despairing mother.

Verse 10 'Adagio': As if to compensate for this unintentional frivolity we move from A flat major to a section in D flat major (from b. 194). This occasions a heartfelt, though hardly very original, piano interlude of nine bars. The vocal line is doubled by the accompaniment, and the most interesting section of this strophe (bb. 214–16) is the simplicity and bareness of the words 'Und dann komme bald, o Tod!' ('Then, o Death, come soon'). This bleak statement is followed by three bars of piano chordal writing, fortissimo (bb. 217–19), and three bars pianissimo (bb. 220–22), the latter a simple descending F minor scale with the hands an octave apart. John Reed points out that these bass octaves would become a familiar Schubert death theme. The last semibreve F slips down a semitone to an octave E (b. 223) and a dotted rhythm in the right hand establishes the unexpected key of E major. This transition is a presentiment of the voice of the authentic adult Schubert.

Verse 11 'Largo', followed by 'Allegro': It is now that we hear, arguably for the first time ever, the unmistakable sound of Schubert's genius as opposed to his talent. He seizes on the word 'Jehova!' which in the original Schücking is at the end of the line ('Blick' auf uns herab, Jehova!'–'Look down upon us, Jehovah!') and places it at the forefront, both of the sentence and of the drama. Hagar repeats it three times as she calls to God, twice in a descending arpeggio figure (bb. 225–7) and for the last time in an upward curve (b. 228) that directs the supplicant's gaze heavenward. The dotted accompaniment evokes heavenly trombones and the shiver of fear before the Almighty. The effect is gigantic, like a fresco by Tiepolo (who painted Hagar and the angel on a ceiling of the Palazzo Patriarcale in Udine), with the heavens depicted in vast receding perspectives. For 'blick' auf uns herab', and the subsequent repetitions of 'Jehova!', slowly oscillating quavers in both hands with thickly spaced basses (from b. 230) rumble with mighty grandeur. Hagar's cries of 'Jehova' at the top of her voice, allied with a darkly grounded low C pedal in the piano (bb. 233–5), make for something quite extraordinary – simultaneously agonized and exultant. Zumsteeg's expressive little mordent on the word seems risibly inadequate by comparison. Schubert has taken eighteen bars to cover words that the older man set to music in five. The rest of the strophe cannot match this level of inspiration. The fast music (from b. 242) for 'Send' aus einem Taugewölke / Labung uns herab!' ('From dewy clouds / Send us refreshing rain!') sounds peremptory, and almost banal. Zumsteeg's extended (and rather effective) melisma on 'Labung', a rare extravagance, is not taken up as a model.

Verses 12–14: From here on Schubert more or less abandons the older composer's disciplined approach and substitutes a slew of his own experiments. This makes the remainder of the song patchy and there is a noticeable deterioration in its flow. Thus Verse 12 is set very quickly as a recitative with an all-purpose yearning piano interlude. Abraham's tears of joy at Ishmael's birth are given short shrift indeed (bb. 258–9) – perhaps significantly, in regard to the adolescent composer's own feelings about his father; this is a much more tender moment in Zumsteeg. Verse 13 (Allegretto) switches moods in an uneasy way and strikes an inappropriately rococo note, the doubling of vocal coloratura with piano (b. 269) merely sounds awkward and coy. Obviously unhappy with this, the composer launches into a swinging G minor § (*Allegro*) for Verse 14 (from b. 280). This metre does not suit the words and gives undue prominence to further expostulations of the comic-sounding 'Ha!' Schubert may have hoped to create a suitable background for the idea of vengeance and a sense of Hagar's derangement at this point. As this mood suits only the first two lines of the strophe, another rather makeshift recitative is tacked on to cover the lines 'Aber, ach, was tat der Knabe, / Dass er mit mir leiden muss?' ('But what has the boy done / That he must suffer with me?'), bb. 306–10.

Verses 15–17: The piece recovers somewhat at this point as Schubert reverts to Zumsteeg's key of A flat and provides an old-fashioned, but nevertheless beautiful, set-piece aria for Hagar (from

b. 312). The composer provides a sustained melody (Andante alla breve), realizing that after all these ups and downs the ear longs for something more settled. This reflective piece takes up two of the poet's strophes (15 and 16) and ends dramatically on a high A flat on the word 'verstiess' (b. 328). After this the piano provides three little sighing phrases that peter out, leaving Hagar alone with her fears and her memories of her first desert exile. Verse 17 begins with the vocal phrase 'War der Fremdling nicht ein Engel?' ('Was the stranger not an angel?') which is almost melody, not quite recitative. This is left to resound unaccompanied in the empty expanse of the wilderness (bb. 331–3). Her question receives no answer, and it is indeed the poet's ploy to finish the poem before the point where God intervenes to save the unfortunate pair. Only knowledge of the Bible could calm doubts about the eventual safety of mother and son. In music that veers between arioso and recitative, Hagar gathers her strength and recovers some grasp on the memories of the angel's first visitation and his sweeping promise about Ishmael's future.

Verses 18–19: As the long piece draws to a close it is clear that Schubert, later the pupil of Antonio Salieri, is attempting to add a sort of Italianate operatic gloss to Zumsteeg's Germanic simplicities and decencies. (Indeed it is said that it was this piece that first aroused Salieri's interest in the young Schubert.) What Zumsteeg lacks is *extravagance*, and Schubert, despite his veneration for the older composer's achievements, finds him worthy but dull, slow to exploit the less obvious, but deliciously dramatic, aspects of a poem. And it is clear that to be Viennese in 1811 was to be closer to an Italianate sense of drama, even via Mozart's operas, than to be a composer in Zumsteeg's Stuttgart or Reichardt's Berlin. The music for Verse 18 (Largo from b. 342) is reasonably perfunctory and treated as a transitional passage to the work's concluding aria (Adagio from b. 353). Before this, however, there is an exceptional and suitably ominous use of the diminished-seventh chord on 'Leichen werden modern' ('our bodies will rot', bb. 347–8). At 'Schrei zum Himmel, armer Knabe!' (Verse 19 from b. 353) we have reached the work's peroration, and Schubert does not disappoint. Hagar reverts to the grand Gluckian figure who has called out to Jehovah earlier in the piece. A broad and dramatic vocal line is supported by rippling left-hand semiquaver triplets, and the effect is regal and larger than life. Melismas on several words play their operatic part in expanding this section so that its breadth is worthy of Hagar's plight, and worthy too of the amplitude of voice that is required to sing the piece in the first place. Zumsteeg ensures that he returns to the key of C minor with which he began his song, but Schubert ignores this nicety and finishes in A flat. The meltingly gentle postlude has a dignity that suggests that the composer was already thinking of Hagar's imminent rescue from doom by the hand of God: 'and God opened her eyes, and she saw a well of water; and she went and filled the bottle with water, and gave the lad drink' (Genesis 21:19). Ishmael and Hagar settled in the Desert of Paran where Ishmael took an Egyptian wife.

It is clear that this piece became a great favourite with the young Schubert's schoolfellows at the Imperial Konvikt. It seems that a performance was arranged at some time fairly soon after the work's composition with an alternative text, some of which has survived in fading and partially illegible pencil on the autograph fair copy. This 'Kontrafaktur' seems to have been made up of a literary patchwork: the passage at b. 60 is from Isaiah 34:8 ('Es ist der Tag der Rache des Herrn') and from b. 132 there is another distinctly non-biblical text about Zeus, nectar, hunting and bathing (the superscription 'Arcadia p. 16' has not helped to identify the source). The piano writing is unchanged throughout. It seems that this was meant as a joke for an in-crowd at the Imperial Konvikt who already knew the original well enough to laugh at departures from it. One wonders what Schubert's young friends, in party mood, would have made of W. C. Handy's *Aunt Hagar's Blues* (1920), which pays tribute to the fact that the biblical Hagar was considered the mother of African-Americans.

Autograph:	In private possession, London (fair copy, with alternative text in pencil)
First edition:	Published as part of the AGA in 1894 (P527)
Subsequent editions:	Not in Peters; AGA XX 1: Vol. 1/1; NSA IV: Vol. 6/3; Bärenreiter: Vol. 5/1
Bibliography:	Capell 1928, pp. 30 & 70
	Einstein 1951, pp. 43–4
	Fischer-Dieskau 1977, p. 18
	Schnapper 1937, p. 83
Discography and timing:	Fischer-Dieskau —
	Hyperion I 31²
	Hyperion II 1³ 16'19 Christine Brewer

← *Lebenstraum* D39   *Leichenfantasie* D7 →

HALT! *see Die SCHÖNE MÜLLERIN* D795/3

FRIEDRICH LEOPOLD FREIHERR VON HARDENBERG *see* NOVALIS

HARFNERLIEDER (THE HARPER'S SONGS) FROM *WILHELM MEISTER*: AN OVERVIEW

For a complete chronological list of the songs from this novel (including Mignon's songs) *see* WILHELM MEISTERS LEHRJAHRE; for details of individual numbers from Schubert's published sets of the Harper's songs and Mignon's songs, *see* MIGNON LIEDER FROM WILHELM MEISTER and GESÄNGE AUS WILHELM MEISTER.

The Harfner, or Harper – even Harpist in some translation – is one of the most mysterious of Goethe's creations. This character is above all an artist – a gifted singer and instrumentalist – and as such a modern personification of Orpheus. Although he is mentally unstable and often described as 'the bitter old harper' (and he is indeed half-crazed with guilt), he has the capacity to charm and educate with music-making that is both profound and moving. Like Orpheus he has a tragic destiny and Goethe's reinvention of the myth allows for a combination of the Orpheus of the Greeks and Virgil, and a more modern role as a star-crossed musician and lover, as well as a tragic father figure. Byrne comments that in Goethe's novel 'the Harper oscillates between the power of form to master intense passion, and the power of intense passion to engulf form'.

The Italian monk Augustin – for this is the Harper's name – had fallen in love with his neighbour Sperata without realizing that she was his sister. Sperata, an embarrassingly late fruit of his own parents' marriage, had been

The Harper and Wilhelm Meister by Ferdinand Piloty, 1877.

concealed from her older siblings. Augustin is thus very much older than Sperata when they have a child of their own, later named Mignon. When it is discovered that the couple have been guilty of incest they are forcibly separated. The gullible Sperata is never told the truth; instead she is made to feel guilty for having stolen Augustin away from the Church. ('The confessor was proud of the skill with which he had contrived to break the poor creature's heart.') Sperata gives up her daughter for adoption and becomes unhinged and delusional. Augustin, imprisoned in a cloister, first refuses to believe that Sperata is his sister, then attempts to justify their relation-ship, arguing that in other cultures marriage between siblings is permitted. Defiant defence of his actions alternates with guilt, and his mental anguish is exacerbated by his enforced separation from Sperata whom he loves dearly. His torment is thus based on the Church's cover-up of the tragedy as much as on the act of incest itself, an unintentional crime that Goethe clearly views as being less culpable than dogmatic bigotry and cruelty. Sperata dies insane and, by a quirk of fate, is revered as a saint (another Goethean sideswipe at the Italian Church). Augustin escapes from the cloister, undetected in a band of pilgrims, and bids her corpse farewell, convincing himself that she is only sleeping. He then sets off on his travels. As fate, and Goethe, would have it, Augustin finds himself in Germany where he becomes attached to a theatrical troupe (headed by the young Wilhelm Meister, eponymous hero of the novel) with whom Mignon has taken refuge. Although he is unaware of who she is (like Sperata he believes that his daughter has been drowned in a lake), there is an intimation that Mignon recognizes his importance in her life. His lyrics, threaded through the novel, create a sequence that is independent from hers. Unlike Schumann in his Op. 98a, Schubert makes no attempt to combine Mignon and the Harper in a single quasi-narrative work, although their voices are heard together in the duet *Mignon und der Harfner* D866/1 that opens the Op. 62 songs, a set otherwise given over to Mignon.

Outside the sphere of his sung lyrics the Harper plays a complicated role in the novel as an unstable force liable to violent and unreasonable action, but he is always treated with compas-sion and understanding, no doubt on account of his towering artistic gifts. At the end of his final, mad, song (*An die Türen will ich schleichen*) he is handed over to a kind pastor and makes a partial recovery. However, he remains a danger to others and, after starting a fire, tries to sacrifice the boy Felix (actually Wilhelm's natural son by his first love, Marianne), Abraham-and-Isaac fashion. At the end of the novel, on hearing of Mignon's death and learning her identity, the Harper attempts suicide by drinking laudanum (he has long carried a flask of this substance with him for the purpose). But when Felix supposedly drinks the prepared potion by mistake the Harper slits his throat and he survives once more by dint of medical intervention and the staunching of the wound. He later rips the bandages off and dies. We learn that Felix has not drunk the poison after all but it is too late to save the Harper. His character has been an alter ego, a tragic doppelgänger for Wilhelm Meister himself who has to master certain nega-tive traits of his own, above all the destructive power of his imagination. Both Mignon and the Harper cease to play a part in the narrative when Wilhelm's eventually successful struggle for enlightenment and self-knowledge render their largely symbolic presence superfluous.

The *Gesänge des Harfners*, published in 1822 as Op. 12 (D478), are Schubert's definitive settings of the three Harper lyrics, just as the four *Gesänge aus Wilhelm Meister* D877 are his final and definitive settings of Mignon's texts from Goethe's novel. For eleven years (from 1815) he had been trying to find the right music for Mignon's poems, as well as those of the Harper. The following is a list of the various Harper settings from Goethe's novel and their dates.

Der Sänger ('Was hör ich draussen vor der Tür'), D149. February 1815
There are two versions of this song, differing in details and length, but essentially the same composition. This was the first of the *Wilhelm Meister* settings, and one of two poems from the

novel that Schubert set only once (the other was *Mignon* (*Kennst du das Land?*) D321 from 23 October 1815).

The other Harper song-setting from 1815 is the only one not catalogued under D478, namely **Wer sich der Einsamkeit ergibt**, sometimes known as *Harfenspieler*, D325. 13 November 1815 The seven remaining settings of the Harper's songs are all grouped in the second Deutsch catalogue under the number D478. This is divided between first 'Fassung' (an earlier version of the cycle *Gesänge des Harfners* from 1816) and the second 'Fassung' which is the Harper's cycle in Schubert's revised version (prepared for publication in 1822 as Op. 12), as it is always performed today. Each of these two 'versions' is in turn subdivided. The first from 1816 consists of four songs – the lyric 'Wer nie sein Brot' appearing twice. Neither the first nor last of this 1816 cycle (D478 [first version] no. 1 'Wer sich der Einsamkeit ergibt' and D478 [first version] no. 3 'An die Türen will ich schleichen') is given a separate commentary in this book, nor were they recorded separately in the Hyperion Schubert Edition as they are almost identical to the 1822 versions.

It was the poem 'Wer nie sein Brot mit Tränen ass' that gave Schubert the most trouble. Two settings of this text (both confusingly numbered D478/2) are included in the first version of the cycle from September 1816, and both were dropped in 1822:

Wer nie sein Brot mit Tränen ass *(I)*, D478/2. First setting

Wer nie sein Brot mit Tränen ass *(II)*, D478/2. Second setting

Finally, in 1822, Schubert published his Harper cycle, minimally revising old material for the two outer songs, and composing a new central panel, thus:

Gesänge des Harfners, D478 (Second version, Autumn 1822)

   (I)   *Wer sich der Einsamkeit ergibt*, D478/1. September 1816, revised 1822
  (II)   *Wer nie sein Brot mit Tränen ass*, D478/2. Third setting, Autumn 1822
 (III)   *An die Türen will ich schleichen*, D478/3. September 1816, revised 1822

Mignon und der Harfner D877/4 (1826) 'Nur wer die Sehnsucht kennt' duet setting for soprano and tenor, the fifth of Schubert's setting of these words (*see* MIGNON'S LIEDER FROM WILHELM MEISTER)

HARK, HARK THE LARK *see* STÄNDCHEN D889

EDMUND FREIHERR VON HAROLD (1737–1800)

Edmund Baron von Harold (or de Harold as he sometimes, more honestly, styled himself), translator of the poems of Ossian into German, was born in 1737 in Limerick. His family claimed descent from a son of King Harold II (last Anglo-Saxon king of England who lost his life at the Battle Hastings), who fled to Ireland in the wake of the Norman Conquest. Minor Irish nobility, especially those whose lineage was manufac- tured for the purpose, often became professional soldiers, putting their services for hire as they sought their fortunes. Harold set his sights on Germany and entered the Bavarian service. By 1787 he was a colonel in command of the Königsfeld regiment and a Gentleman of the Bedchamber to the Elector Palatinate. He was a member of the Royal Society of Antiquaries in London as well as of the Düsseldorf Academy.

Harold's questionable noblility is only one of the mysteries about his life but he was obviously an adventurer who liked to dabble in literature and who had kissed the Blarney stone to great advantage. The poems of Ossian (in reality the elaborations of James Macpherson, qv) were an ideal field in which he might be held to have special authority as someone who claimed to speak Gaelic. The trouble was Harold's German – learned late in life and only in the course of soldiering. He was not the first to translate passages of Ossian into that language, but he was the first writer to translate the complete works of Ossian for a German-speaking readership in the kind of rolling poetic prose that characterizes the original. The translation appeared in Düsseldorf in 1775 in three volumes with the title *Die Gedichte Ossian's eines alten celtischen Helden und Barden.* Harold's translation was roundly criticized, not least on account of his lack of German style. In the foreword to the second edition (1782, two volumes, with the more convincing title of *Die Gedichte Ossians des Celtischen Helden und Barden*) the publishers claimed that since the first appearance of the book Harold had broadened his knowledge of the German language, taken note of critical suggestions and completely revised the translations. It was these that fell into Schubert's hands. The second edition is less beautifully printed than the first and compressed in size and layout.

According to Schubert's schoolfriend Anton Holzapfel it was he who was responsible for giving the composer this 'miserable translation' published, 'if I remember rightly in Hanover or Brunswick' (actually Mannheim), bought for a few pence from a second-hand bookshop. He refers to a 'rather thick volume' – his gift to Schubert seems to have been the two 1782 volumes of Harold's translations bound together as one.

It seems that Harold was not content merely to translate Macpherson, he had to go one step further. According to the foreword to the 1782 edition, as a fellow-Celtic countryman of Ossian's, Harold had begun to gather fragments by the poet that he had heard recited as a child and, 'supported by his relatives and learned

friends', had 'discovered' many more Ossian poems. The fruit of this is to be seen in '*Neu entdeckte Gedichte Ossians*, Düsseldorf, bei Johann Christian Dänzer, 1787'. Far away from the controversies in London surrounding the authenticity of Macpherson's work, Harold was free to pursue his own line of fabrication (although G. C. Lichtenberg in Germany had joined Dr Johnson in London in denouncing the literary fraud). In the foreword to *Neu entdeckte Gedichte Ossians* Harold claimed to have uncovered new evidence that Ossian was Irish rather than Scottish. Moreover, the poems he discovered show Ossian to have had hitherto unexplored religious interests explained by the noble poet's instinctive revulsion towards atheism. Reading through Harold's preposterous *Lieder von Tara, Sulmora* (later turned into a five-act play), *Kinfena und Sira, Bosmina, Sulima* (!) and *Sitrick,* one is reminded how very talented James Macpherson was by

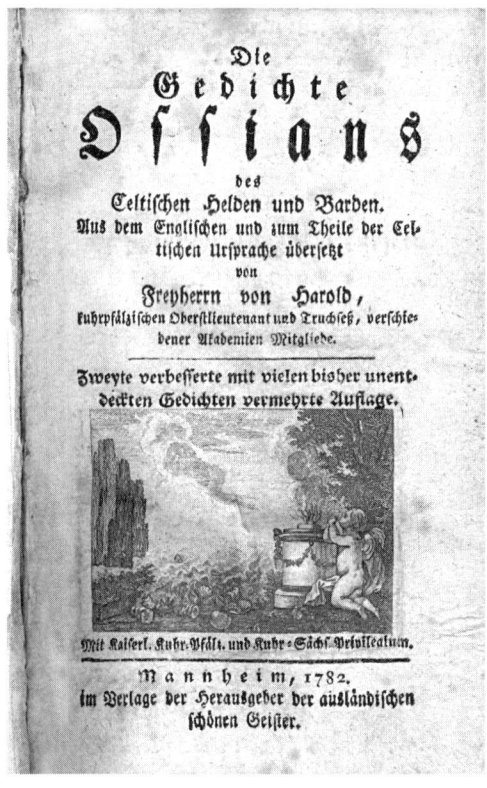

Ossian's *Gedichte* (second edition) translated by Edmund von Harold (1782).

comparison as a writer of atmospheric prose, and how fortunate Schubert was to have discovered the earlier Harold efforts – derived at least from Macpherson – rather than the later ones.

Harold died on 28 June 1800. His son was naturalized into the Bavarian nobility and became Freiherr von Harold – a case perhaps of his father's aristocratic fantasy as Baron de Harold turning into reality. The title died out in Germany in 1884.

For the sources of Harold's translations of Ossian *see* James MACPHERSON.

HEIDENRÖSLEIN

The wild rose

(GOETHE) OP. 3 NO. 3, **D257** [H143]
G major   19 August 1815

(16 bars)

Sah ein Knab' ein Röslein stehn,	A boy saw a wild rose
Röslein auf der Heiden,	Growing in the heather;
War so jung und morgenschön,	It was so young, and as lovely as the morning.
Lief er schnell, es nah zu sehn,	He ran swiftly to look more closely,
Sahs mit vielen Freuden.	Looked on it with great joy.
Röslein, Röslein, Röslein rot,	Wild rose, wild rose, wild rose red,
Röslein auf der Heiden.	Wild rose in the heather.
Knabe sprach: Ich breche dich,	Said the boy: I shall pluck you,
Röslein auf der Heiden!	Wild rose in the heather!
Röslein sprach: Ich steche dich,	Said the rose: I shall prick you
Dass du ewig denkst an mich,	So that you will always remember me.
Und ich wills nicht leiden.	And I will not suffer it.
Röslein, Röslein, Röslein rot,	Wild rose, wild rose, wild rose red,
Röslein auf der Heiden.	Wild rose in the heather.
Und der wilde Knabe brach	And the impetuous boy plucked
's Röslein auf der Heiden;	The wild rose from the heather;
Röslein wehrte sich und stach,	The rose defended herself and pricked him,
Half ihm doch kein Weh und Ach,	But her cries of pain were to no avail,
Musst' es eben leiden.	It simply had to be borne.
Röslein, Röslein, Röslein rot,	Wild rose, wild rose, wild rose red,
Röslein auf der Heiden.	Wild rose in the heather.

JOHANN WOLFGANG VON GOETHE (1749–1832); poem written in 1771

This is the twenty-fourth of Schubert's seventy-five Goethe solo settings (1814–26). See the poet's biography for a chronological list of all the Goethe settings.

This song is one of those Schubertian miracles for which there is no real explanation beyond the genius of its creator. As Einstein wrote, 'Schubert does not imitate the folksong tradition. He creates it or provides an occasion for it.' The simplicity and innocence of the music is not born of inexperience, but rather of an ever-deepening familiarity with Goethean ways and means. It was proudly included in the collection of songs sent to the poet in April 1816, and if Goethe had bothered to have it played through to him he might have realized that it represented the summit of his own ideal of what a song with keyboard accompaniment should be – simple, uncluttered, allowing the words to be heard with the most transparent clarity.

The poem, itself a parody of the folk style, was written in 1771 when Goethe was a law student at the University of Strasbourg. There he came under the powerful influence of J. G. Herder (only five years his senior) who encouraged him to study the simple beauties of folksong texts in pursuit of freshness and spontaneity in his writing. This was the period of the poet's love affair with Friederike von Brion. Both Herder and Goethe made versions of an old German folksong about a wild rose (which goes back to a poem written in 1602 by Paul von der Aelst), but it is Goethe's poem with its sexual overtones that has survived the moralizing stance of Herder's – more suited to the schoolroom than the open fields.

Reichardt composed a setting of the poem simply in G major (this was so admired by Zelter that in 1807 he declined to make one of his own), and one cannot forget that the other celebrated flower song with a Goethe text, Mozart's *Das Veilchen* K476, is also in G major and ⅔. As so often in 1815, Schubert began his groundbreaking work by bowing to the past and acknowledging his forbears but, after fixing his own song in G major and in ⅔, similarities and obeisances were at an end. Schubert's tune is unforgettable whereas the melody of the Reichardt song is frankly unmemorable.

Schubert takes us outdoors ('the bucolic air might be thought to have been born of one mind with the poem', writes Capell) whereas Mozart's mini-opera on two pages is peopled by shepherds and shepherdesses clothed in the silk costumes of a court *bergerette*. The alternation between the hands of light quaver chords (it might be called a 'vamp' in the language of popular music) suggests the light-hearted cheeky gait of a young man with eyes and heart a-roving. At the same time these chords, in their very proper economy, suggest the demure innocence of the rose, and in the various strophes the pianist can slightly vary the articulation and dynamics to throw the emphasis on one or other of the song's protagonists. The semiquavers that flower on the vocal line are an absolutely integral part of the tune rather than extraneous decoration. At the same time the curvaceous melody suggests luxurious and alluring beauty, as if the visual simplicity of the rose is complemented by its fragrance – a scent carried into the air on these wind-borne vocal semiquavers, and playing no little part in the boy's delight. Behind the deceptive charm of the two and a half bars of interlude between the verses (a sequence of two groups of quavers – ascending thirds separated by a falling fifth and ornamented by cheeky acciaccaturas bb. 15–16) lies an illustration of the selfish and callous attitude of the flower-picker, rather too cocky for his own good. At the same time we are made aware of the dangerous power of revenge in the flower's prickly thorn – thus the piano's staccato and the composer's accents. Schubert marks the refrain ('Röslein, Röslein, Röslein rot') 'nachgebend' (from b. 11), which means giving way or yielding; hence the small *ritardando* required for the beautiful ascending phrase of quavers (bb. 11–12). The effect of this refrain is of the utmost wistfulness, as if kissing a childhood dream of innocence goodbye as it floats off into the ether. After the lingering

Heidenröslein by Eugen Neureuther, 1829.

fermata at the end of b. 12 (and every singer is challenged to show his or her *mezza voce* mettle here) this musing is peremptorily cancelled by a return to tempo at bb. 13–14 ('Röslein auf der Heiden'). This is marked 'wie oben', ('as above') which nicely negates any suggestion of sentimentality and returns the setting to the earthy folksong domain.

It takes no great leap of imagination to see in this poem a scenario for the contraction of a wounding disease, sexually transmitted between lovers. Like all the best folk material, however, the poem works on a number of levels, from the light-hearted to the sinister. The merriment of Schubert's astonishing setting is underscored by a mood utterly typical of some of his seemingly happy works: a streak of gentle melancholy in the major key suggests deeper layers of meaning, unspoken and potentially heartbreaking.

This is one of the few Schubert songs (*Der Lindenbaum* from *Winterreise* is another) to have achieved the status of anonymously composed folksong in German-speaking culture. It is interesting, however, that Erk's *Liederschatz* (a compendium of the most often-sung German folksongs in the nineteenth century) prefers a setting from 1827 by Heinrich Werner. Although Beethoven never completed a setting of these words he was absorbed in the poem on and off between 1796 and 1822. A completion of his fragment was published in 1898.

The work did not take Schubert a great deal of time: four other songs were composed on the same day. For those who might like to imagine the heat of creativity in the Schubertian workshop on 19 August 1815, those settings (all of Goethe poems) were *Der Rattenfänger* D255, *Der Schatzgräber* D256, *Bundeslied* D258 and the first version of *An den Mond* D259.

Autographs:	University Library of Lund, Sweden (first draft)
	Staatsbibliothek Preussischer Kulturbesitz, Berlin (fair copy for Goethe)
First edition:	Published as Op. 3 no. 3 by Cappi & Diabelli, Vienna in 1821 (P5)
Dedicatee:	Ignaz von Mosel
Publication reviews:	*Wiener allgemeine Theaterzeitung* No. 61 (22 May 1821), p. 244 [Waidelich/Hilmar Dokumente I No. 101; Deutsch Doc. Biog. No. 238]
	F. von Hentl 'Blick auf Schubert's Lieder', *Wiener Zeitschrift für Kunst, Literatur, Theater und Mode* No. 36 (23 March 1822), p. 289f. [Waidelich/Hilmar Dokumente I No. 146; Deutsch Doc. Biog. No. 278]
Subsequent editions:	Peters: Vol. 1/182; AGA XX 114: Vol. 3/37; NSA IV: Vol. 1/24; Bärenreiter: Vol. 1/18
Bibliography:	Capell 1928, pp. 103–4
	Einstein 1951, p. 110
	Fischer-Dieskau 1977, pp. 62–3
	Reid 2007, pp. 178–80
Further settings and arrangements:	Johann Friedrich Reichardt (1752–1814) *Heidenröslein* (1809)
	Václav Jan Tomášek (1774–1850) *Heidenröslein* Op. 53 no. 1 (1815)
	Johann Christoph Kienlen (1783–1829) *Heidenröslein* (1810)
	Robert Schumann (1810–1856) *Heidenröslein*, no. 3 of *Romanzen und Balladen* for SATB, Op. 67 (1849)
	Johannes Brahms (1833–1897) *Heidenröslein*, no. 6 of *Volks-Kinderlieder* WoO 31 (1857)

Franz Lehár (1870–1948) *Heidenröslein* from *Friederike* (1928)
Arr. Leopold Godowsky (1870–1938) for solo piano as *Hedge Rose*
(1927, second revised edition 1937) [*see* TRANSCRIPTIONS]
Arr. Tilman Hoppstock (b. 1961) for guitar accompaniment (2
arrangements), in *Franz Schubert: 110 Lieder* (2009)

Discography and timing: Fischer-Dieskau I 5³   1'45

Hyperion I 20¹⁵

Hyperion II 9⁴   2'01   Patricia Rozario

← *Der Schatzgräber* D256   *Bundeslied* D258 →

HEIMLICHES LIEBEN   Secret love
(KLENKE) OP. 106 NO. 1, **D922** [H633]

The song exists in two versions, the second of which is discussed below:
(1) Graz, September 1827; (2) April 1828

(1)   'Mässig'   B♭ major   **C**   [86 bars]

(2)   B♭ major

(85 bars)

O du, wenn deine Lippen mich berühren,[1]	When your lips touch me,
So will die Lust die Seele mir entführen;	Desire all but bears away my soul;
Ich fühle tief ein namenloses Beben	I feel a nameless trembling
Den Busen heben.	Deep within my breast.
Mein Auge flammt, Glut schwebt auf meinen Wangen;	My eyes flame, a glow tinges my cheeks;
Es schlägt mein Herz ein unbekannt Verlangen;	My heart beats with a strange longing;
Mein Geist, verirrt in trunkner Lippen Stammeln,	My mind, lost in the stammering of my drunken lips,
Kann kaum sich sammeln.	Can scarcely compose itself.
Mein Leben hängt in einer solchen Stunde	At such a time my life hangs
An deinem süssen, rosenweichen Munde,	On your sweet lips, soft as roses,
Und will, bei deinem trauten Armumfassen,	And, in your beloved embrace,
Mich fast verlassen.	Life almost deserts me.

[1] Klenke's *Gedichte* (1788) has *Myrtil* instead of 'O du'. The poem is entitled *An Myrtil* not 'Myrtill' as Faust Pachler supposed.

O! dass es doch nicht ausser sich kann fliehen,	Oh that my life cannot escape from itself,
Die Seele ganz in deiner Seele glühen!	With my soul aflame in yours!
Dass doch die Lippen, die voll Sehnsucht brennen,	Oh that lips ardent with longing
Sich müssen trennen!	Must part!
Dass doch im Kuss' mein Wesen nicht zerfliesset,	Oh that my being may not dissolve in kisses
Wenn es so fest an deinen Mund sich schliesset,	When my lips are pressed so tightly to yours,
Und an dein Herz, das niemals laut darf wagen,	And to your heart, which may never dare
Für mich zu schlagen!	To beat aloud for me!

Karoline Louise von Klenke (1754–1802)

This is Schubert's only setting of a Klenke text. See the poet's biography.

For many years this poem was thought to be by Karl von Leitner, author of so many other masterpieces associated with Schubert's visit to Graz in 1827 where his hostess was the gifted pianist Marie Pachler. Faust Pachler, Marie's son, who was aged eight at the time of Schubert's visit (and for whom the composer wrote the piano duet *Kindermarsch* D928 in the autumn of 1827), described in a letter of 1876 to Konstantin von Wurzbach his search for this song's poet:

> *In the catalogue of Schubert's works, apart from the one compiled by G. Nottebohm, who was enlightened by me, the poem of the composition* Heimliches Lieben *is listed as being by the Graz poet K. G. von Leitner. But it has for its authoress the well-known daughter of Karschin, Frau von Klenke, and starts 'Myrtill, wenn deine Lippen mich berühren' and has the title* An Myrtill. *I myself have seen a song composed to this latter, original, text among the estate of the Court actor, Heinrich Anschütz. My mother's teacher, Professor Julius Schneller, sent it to her, with the title and the opening altered, together with some others which he had particularly liked, and he either forgot to name the authoress or did not know himself who the words were by. My mother thought it so very well suited to composition that she sent it, with many others, to Schubert. I first discovered the original title and opening through a sheet of music offered me for sale (it too was from Anschütz's estate); and from some biographical notes in* Deutschlands Dichterinnen, *an album of poetry, I found the name of the poet or rather the poetess.*

It seems that without realizing it Schubert had composed a song to a text by Karoline Klenke, daughter of the 'Naturdichterin' Anna Luise Karschin (1722–1791) and mother of Helmina von Chézy who in 1823 had collaborated with Schubert on *Rosamunde* D797 – a theatrical debacle despite the beautiful music written for it. The text for *Heimliches Lieben* seems to have been one of Marie Pachler's particular favourites. In placing it at the beginning of the collection of songs dedicated to her the composer acknowledges this as *her* lied, composed under her roof and at her suggestion. The memoirs of Leitner's mentor, the history and philosophy professor Julius Schneller (1840) imply, very discreetly, that the poem might have had a shared secret significance for him and Marie. (Perhaps it was Schneller who first substituted 'O du' for Klenke's original 'Myrtil'.) The companionship of the worthy brewer Karl Pachler might have been insufficiently stimulating for such a gifted musician and artist as Marie Pachler, but the tenor of the poem makes clear that whatever might have passed between Julius Schneller and his student, respectability was maintained by a veil of discretion.

John Reed writes of the Leitner style exemplified by this song as being 'tinged with *Gemüt-lichkeit*' but he is not uncritical of the piece as a whole. Richard Capell's view is equally ambivalent:

> *It is not a very characteristic piece. Nothing cries out 'Schubert' when the page is opened. The song is in the nature of a period piece, but the elegance and the sentiment are charming. Behold Schubert in the drawing-room! He must have heard much young ladies' music at* biedermeierisch *parties; and now, perhaps, he said he would show how, with just as thin a texture, the thing might be done delightfully. The song [. . .] has the merit of preserving the atmosphere of the drawing-rooms of the 1820s with some poetic idealisation; and moreover, it is most gratefully vocal. The melody that sails above the piano's undulations is an irresistible invitation to the singer.*

This is certainly modified rapture – it is rare to read such phrases as 'period piece' and 'thin texture' in connection with a song which is then described as irresistible, particularly to the singer. In my student years, in the midst of many singers' enthusiasm for this piece, I also felt uncomfortable with it. The great accompanist Gerald Moore once mentioned in the 1970s that his 'bugbear', his least favourite song by the master, was the Rückert setting *Sei mir gegrüsst* D741 I confessed to him that my least favourite was *Heimliches Lieben* because it employs a vein of drawing-room sentimentality to be found almost nowhere else in Schubert's songs. The pathos of those pivoting oscillations between the third of the scale, the sharpened supertonic and the mediant (D to C sharp back to D and then drooping to B flat on the words 'du, wenn deine Lippen mich berühren') to me suggested seasickness. Such swooning-in-tone became the stuff of sugary salon valentines, and a commonplace of Victorian musical vocabulary. One has only to compare another work from 1827, the celebrated G flat Impromptu for Piano D899/3, to know how Schubert can use a similarly triplet-accompanied melody to spin music of the deepest and purest emotion. *Auf dem Strom* D943 with horn obbligato also uses an Italianate melody accompanied by ceaseless triplets – without suggesting the salon.

But what Capell says in praise of *Heimliches Lieben* is equally true: it is indeed 'most gratefully vocal' in a way that implies an intimate knowledge of Italian cantilena. The unceasing triplets, encompassing a range of a tenth and more in the left hand, support the voice in a way that Bellini would have understood and applauded. This left-hand stretching is hardly typical of Schubert's song accompaniments, and one wonders whether the pianistic technique, including the delicately turned trills and the singing right-hand melody, might have been fashioned especially for Marie Pachler's playing style.

It is clear that the composer was able to make a salon stylization as easily as an Italian one. He may well have intended to poke gentle fun at the type of music admired by young ladies at their '*biedermeierisch* parties', as Capell calls them. In doing so he seems effortlessly to ennoble an empty genre with touches of genuine magic. Exactly the same is true of some of the pieces that Schubert wrote to make fun of the Rossini style – he made such beautiful music out of them that their power to enchant exceeds their talent to amuse. In view of this I have come to see that my earlier aversion to this piece was unfair to the composer. The secret of a good and ardent performance is to keep going and not to take the 'Mässig' marking as an excuse to drag and over-luxuriate.

Just as Schubert cultivated a deliberately rustic style for songs about fishermen, farmers, hunters – working ditties sung by honest working folk – he was able to create a 'Graz style' in honour of the good-hearted musical provinces. This is less rustic than cosy and trusty – a portrait of a safe and innocently domesticated life away from the metropolis. Schubert's bread-and-butter letter to Marie Pachler makes clear that he regarded 'cordiality' and 'openness' as

Heimliches Lieben, vignette from Czerny's arrangement for solo piano (1838).

typical of Graz, and not of Vienna. 'At Graz I soon recognized an artless and sincere way of being together.' In that recognition there was also born a sympathy for Leitner's verse: the full-hearted widower of *Der Winterabend* D938, the courting fisherman of *Des Fischers Liebesglück* D933, the genuinely philosophical monk of *Der Kreuzzug* D932, the starry-eyed observer of the heavens of *Die Sterne* D939 all have an innocence and artlessness about them. They come from a place where people are not spoiled, where they still believe in old-fashioned values and live accordingly. With hindsight, and knowing something of the poet Leitner who was later to become a paragon of marital devotion (*see* his biography) we realize that *Heimliches Lieben* has an entirely different character from Leitner's verse.

The long piano introduction (bb. 1–6) announces the opening vocal melody in embellished and extended form. This 'sentimental' tune has been cleverly shaped to reflect the meaning of the words: the dip in the melody (from repeated Ds to C sharps) at 'deine <u>Lippen mich ber</u>ühren' (bb. 8–9) implies a glancing brush of a kiss, fleeting enough to disturb the equilibrium of the vocal line only by a semitone. Other words and phrases are painted with equal aptitude: the more decisive dotted rhythms (sensitive to the prosody) of 'die Seele mir entführen' (bb. 10–11), the emotional jump of a seventh for 'Beben' (b. 14) and so on. And all the while the melody is accompanied by unceasing triplets, seraphically supportive.

A yearning interlude (bb. 17–19) leads to a second verse that shifts into D flat major for the glowing colours of its more passionate sentiments. If these words were truly reflected in song the result would be wild indeed but, as Reed says, 'Klenke's Sapphic ode has had the raw passion drained out of it' and the triplets remain as angelic as ever. Verse 3 (from b. 34) is a rondo-like repetition of the first strophe; here the perilous nature of a life hanging on a thread is once again admirably suited to that sentimental vocal line where the singer rocks between semitone intervals like a tightrope-walker judging every tiny footstep.

Verse 4 (from b. 46) embarks on an orgy of chromaticism. The composer must have amused himself constructing a vocal line for the first half of the strophe which is effectively set as a chromatic scale rising from A (the minim in b. 47) up to F (b. 50). Once more the relationship of F major and D flat major is exploited, as if with a wry smile, for all its worth. This emotionally heated music is repeated for Verse 5 (from b. 55) and then the words are used again for a coda of new material, perhaps the most beautiful section of the song. This is introduced by a dotted-rhythm motif in the left hand (b. 64) that subtly helps to steer the singer's softly enraptured musings. The repeat of the words first heard on the song's previous page come to an end with a vocal climax on 'Für mich zu schlagen' (at bb. 73–5); another composer might have ended the song here, but if Schubert is set on writing a salon song then it must have a typically lingering farewell. This cliché is wonderfully redeemed by the musical quality of this envoi: a striking cello-like counter-melody deep in the bass entwines with the treble to suggest the male hero singing in secret duet with the female. The whole nature of this postlude is a study for the ending of *Auf dem Strom* D943 composed for voice, horn and piano the following year.

Schubert, like Richard Strauss, occasionally wrote music to please others. There was a group of people in his life, whether intimate friends or powerful patrons, for whom he wrote songs: Therese Grob; his brother Ferdinand; friends and hosts like Mayrhofer, Schober, Bruchmann and Pyrker; members of the Esterházy family; the great singers Milder, Vogl and Lablache; and the redoubtable Anna Fröhlich. It says a great deal for the charm of Marie Pachler, with whom Schubert was in personal contact for less than two weeks, that she joined this select list.

Autographs:	Pierpont Morgan Library, New York (first draft)
	Hungarian National Library, Budapest (fair copy)
Publication:	First published as part of the AGA in 1895 (P701; first version)
	First published in the spring of 1828 by Schober's Lithographisches Institut, Vienna without opus number and subsequently as Op. 106 no. 1 (also by the Lithographisches Institut) (P158; second version)
Dedicatee:	Marie Pachler
Subsequent editions:	Peters: Vol. 4/104 ; AGA XX 544 a & b: Vol. 9/92 (first version) & 97 (second version); NSA IV: Vol. 5a/102 (second version) & Vol. 5b/234 (first version); Bärenreiter: Vol. 4/20
Bibliography:	Capell 1928, pp. 244–5
	Fischer-Dieskau 1977, pp. 249–50
Further setting:	J. F. Reichardt (1752–1814) *An Myrtil* (1780)
Discography and timing:	Fischer-Dieskau —
	Hyperion I 36[12]
	Hyperion II 34[4] 4'33 Juliane Banse

⟵ *Il modo di prender moglie* D902/3   *Eine altschottische Ballade* D923 ⟶

HEIMWEH D33a *see* DUBIOUS, MISATTRIBUTED AND LOST SONGS

Das HEIMWEH   Longing for home
(HELL) **D456** [H284]
F major   July 1816

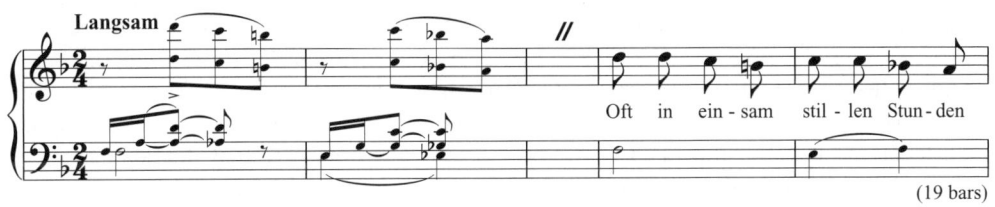

(19 bars)

Oft in einsam stillen Stunden	Often, in quiet, solitary hours,
Hab' ich ein Gefühl empfunden,	I have experienced a feeling,
Unerklärbar, wunderbar!	Inexplicable, marvellous,
Das wie Sehnsucht nach der Ferne	Like a yearning for the far distance,
Hoch hinauf in bess're Sterne,	High above, on a better star,
Wie ein leises Ahnen war.	Like a soft presentiment.

Jetzt, wo von der Heimat Frieden	Now, in a distant foreign land,
Ich so lang' schon abgeschieden,	Having left so long ago
Und in weiter Fremde bin,	The peace of my homeland,
Fühlt ein ängstlich heisses Sehnen	I feel a fearful, burning longing
Unter sanften Wehmutstränen	Beneath tears of gentle sadness
Tief bewegt mein innrer Sinn.	Deep in my troubled heart.
Wenn in Stunden sel'ger Weihe	If only, in hours of blissful solemnity,
Sich der frühern Wonnen Reihe	My spirit could dimly experience
Dunkel wär' mein Geist bewusst,	My former joys in turn;
Wenn sich neue Sinne fänden,	If only I could discover new senses
Die das Höhere verständen	Which might divine the higher Truth
In der tiefbewegten Brust!	In my sorely troubled heart!

THEODOR HELL (PSEUDONYM OF KARL GOTTFRIED WINKLER) (1775–1856)

This is Schubert's only setting of a Hell text. See the poet's biography.

John Reed rightly calls this song a minor masterpiece. It is from 1816, a year of triumphs in miniature form. It was also a year when the virtues of musical control were clearly among the young composer's *desiderata*: the poems of the lieder are often clothed in musical garb as deliberately modest as is ideally suited to their purpose. It is possible to detect in this the guiding hand of Antonio Salieri whose influence over the young composer was probably at its height that summer – Schubert's diary entry for Salieri's anniversary celebrations reveals a young man in thrall to his teacher. By December of that year the composer had stopped taking lessons and the venerable Italian's star was setting in the Schubertian firmament. However, after the heady and more extravagant creativity of 1815, the composer seems to have concentrated on creating expressive and flexible vocal lines, and discovered the means of moving his listeners with the least overt display. *Das Heimweh* is a fine illustration of this 1816 art of *multum in parvo*.

   The introduction, one wilting forlorn bar succeeding another, puts one in mind of the heady chromaticism of the much later Rückert setting *Dass sie hier gewesen* D775; unfulfilled longing is what the two songs have in common, as well as a rhetorical use of a motif traced in right-hand octaves. Another comparison can be made with the neighbouring work in the Deutsch catalogue, *An die untergehende Sonne* D457, also first sketched in July 1816 and where the musical sequences in the introduction move ever downwards. In that work the sun sinks to the horizon; in *Das Heimweh* the traveller looks longingly towards his homeland on the other side of it. The descending pattern of the introduction is mirrored by the vocal line that depicts both sadness and passionate eloquence; the latter is achieved by the rhythm's departure from the bereft opening quavers of 'Oft in einsam stillen Stunden' at bb. 8–9 where 'Hab' ich ein Gefühl empfunden' suddenly takes on a quasi-operatic sweep. In a similar way the demandingly high tessitura (at 'Hoch hinauf in bess're Sterne' bb. 15–16) ensures that the voice is at full stretch. There is something highly strung in this music utterly appropriate to the feeling it describes.

   Schubert wrote out only one verse and then added repeat marks. When this song received its first publication in 1887 in Volume VII of the Peters Edition, the editor Max Friedlaender commissioned two extra verses from Max Kalbeck. Eight years later the editor of the *Gesamtausgabe*, Eusebius Mandyczewski took the trouble to track down the original poem, and three of the six verses printed there (and subsequently in the NSA) were chosen (1, 2 and 5) for the performance by Peter Schreier on Hyperion. Unfortunately Mandyczewski made no note at the time of the source of the poem which thus became lost to modern scholarship. It was still unknown for the printing of Volume 10 of the NSA in 2002; I have identified two possible sources, one from 1795 and the other from 1816, which are listed in the article under the poet's name, Winkler.

Autograph:	Conservatoire collection, Bibliothèque Nationale, Paris
First edition:	Published as Vol. 7 no. 28 in Friedlaender's edition by Peters, Leipzig in 1887 (P492)
Subsequent editions:	Peters: Vol. 7/64; AGA XX 241: Vol. 4/144; NSA IV: Vol. 10/196
Bibliography:	Youens 2002, pp. 168–75
Discography and timing:	Fischer-Dieskau I 7[28] 1'25 (first strophe only)
	Hyperion I 18[8]
	Hyperion II 15[11] 3'00 Peter Schreier

← *Freude der Kinderjahre* D455   *An die untergehende Sonne* D457 →

Das HEIMWEH   Homesickness
(Pyrker) Op. 79 no. 1, **D851** [H571]

The song exists in two versions, the second of which is discussed below:
(1) Bad Gastein, August 1825; (2) appeared May 1827

(1)   'Ziemlich langsam'   A minor   **C**   [250 bars]

(2)   G minor

(205 bars)

(1) Ach! der Gebirgssohn hängt mit kindlicher Lieb' an der Heimat; / Wie den Alpen geraubt[1] hinwelket die Blume, So welkt er / Ihr entrissen dahin!—	Ah, the son of the mountains clings with a childlike love to his homeland. As the flower wilts when plucked from the Alpine meadow, So he wilts when he is torn away.
(2) Stets sieht er die trauliche Hütte, / Die ihn gebar, im hellen Grün umduftender Matten; / Sieht das dunkele Föhrengehölz, Die ragende Felswand / Über ihm, und noch Berg' auf Berg'	Always he sees the cosy cottage Where he was born amid fragrant, bright green meadows; He sees the dark pine copse, The rock face looming above him and mountain upon mountain

[1] Pyrker writes '*Und* wie den Alpen geraubt'.

in erschütternder Hoheit /	towering up in fearful majesty,
Aufgetürmt, und glühend	And glowing
im Rosenschimmer des Abends. /	in the rosy light of evening.
Immer schwebt es ihm vor,	Constantly they hover before his eyes.
verdunkelt ist alles um ihn her. /	all else around him is obscured.

(3)	Ängstlich horcht er; ihm deucht,[2]	He listens anxiously; he thinks
	er höre das Muhen der Kühe / Vom nahen Gehölz,[3]	he hears the lowing of cattle In the nearby copse,
	und hoch von den Alpen herunter /	and bells tinkling
	Glöcklein klingen;	From high on the alps.
	Ihm deucht: er höre das Rufen der Hirten, /	He thinks he hears the call of shepherds
	Oder ein Lied der Sennerin,[4]	Or the song of a cowgirl who,
	die mit umschlagender Stimme[5] /	with yodelling voice,
	Freudig zum Widerhall aufjauchzt	Joyfully sings her melodies
	Melodien des Alplands. /	To the echoing mountains.
	Immer tönt es ihm nach;	always it sounds in his ears.

(4)	ihn fesselt der lachenden Ebnen / Anmut nicht;	The charm of the smiling plains Cannot keep him;
	er fliehet der Städt' einengende Mauern /	All alone, he flees from the constricting walls of the town,
	Einsam, und schaut aufweinend vom Hügel	And, weeping, looks up from the hills
	die heimischen Berge; /	towards his native peaks;
	Ach! es zieht ihn dahin[6]	Ah, he is drawn there
	mit unwiderstehlicher Sehnsucht!	with irresistible longing!

JOHANN LADISLAUS PYRKER (1772–1847); poem written before 1819

This is the first of Schubert's two Pyrker solo settings (1825). See the poet's biography for a chronological list of all the Pyrker settings.

The poem as it appears above does not reflect the poet's original metre, although the original line-breaks are indicated. In his versification in hexameters it is printed in seventeen uninterrupted lines beginning thus:

Ach! der Gebirgssohn hängt mit kindlicher Lieb' an der Heimat;
Und wie den Alpen geraubt, hinwelket die Blumen, so welkt er
Ihr entrissen, dahin!— Stets sieht er die trauliche Hütte
Die ihn gebar, im hellen Grün umduftender Matten; . . .

For the convenience of the reader and listener, Pyrker's long hexameters have here been broken up to facilitate the printing of parallel translation, and the poem is divided into four sections which correspond to the shape of Schubert's setting.

[2] Pyrker writes 'ihm *däucht*' (also later in the same strophe).
[3] Pyrker writes 'Von *dem* nahen Gehölz'.
[4] Pyrker writes 'Oder *der Sennerin Lied*'.
[5] Pyrker writes 'mit *über*schlagender Stimme'.
[6] Pyrker writes 'Ach! *denn es* zieht ihn dahin'.

The Pyrker songs (the other is *Die Allmacht* D852) date from Schubert's spectacularly successful holiday with the singer Vogl in Upper Austria in the summer of 1825. The composer and singer were in Bad Gastein between the middle of August and 4 September. The powerful cleric Ladislaus Pyrker, Patriarch of Venice, was there at the same time and almost certainly handed to the composer the two poems in handwritten form. The poet was an important member of the establishment and someone whom we are told Schubert greatly admired, having already met him in Vienna.

Verse 1: Schubert's mind must have been full of the 'Great' C major Symphony D944, a work that is generally considered to have been written at this time. *Das Heimweh* has a long introduction (bb. 1–11), symphonic in scope, and it uses motifs which suggest gritty symphonic development. The dotted rhythms convey embattlement and struggle (in the manner of the earlier Schiller setting *Der Kampf* D594); the pathetic falling sequences of bb. 5–8 (reminiscent of the other *Das Heimweh* D456) and the wilting chromatic harmonies of anguish (the plaintive 'So welkt er' for example at bb. 21–2) combine to paint a bleak but powerful picture. The homesick singer finds himself in an arid place, and this is confirmed by the spartan two-part harmony where the vocal line is doubled by the piano. Some of the other harmonic implications are nearer to home. In Schubert's day Austrians considered themselves part of the greater Germany. The use of the augmented sixth known as 'German' (first beat of bars 3 and 4 and *passim*) is a brilliant musical pun, telling us wordlessly, again and again, the name of the land for which the narrator obsessively pines. Perhaps Pyrker had mentioned to Vogl and Schubert how much he missed the mountains of German-speaking lands during his time working in Venice as its governor and regent.

Verse 2: A single bar (b. 34) of six staccato triplets and two crotchets followed by a fermata on the bar line introduces the relative major. There is scarcely a more effective use of this time-honoured change in all Schubert. The shift of camera angle (we might imagine flashback technique in the cinema) is transporting; it allows us to look into the singer's past and homeland. At 'Stets sieht er die trauliche Hütte' (from b. 35) the music takes on a tenderness as melting as the opening has been uncompromisingly harsh. The pianist's beguiling triplets contain a tiny bell rung in the right hand that seems to resound through the valley (bb. 40–42 and 45–6) and the wide intervals in the vocal line suggest the yodel of the mountain shepherd. During this whimsical music we have moved gently from B flat major to G major (b. 39) to D major (b. 40) and then to F major (b. 45). The sudden shift to C major, the dominant of F minor, with an *angstvoll* bass line at 'Sieht das dunkele Föhrengehölz' (b. 47), signals bigger thoughts and images. As it gathers power the song reveals its relationship to its sibling work, *Die Allmacht*, and we are reminded of the awe-inspiring splendours of nature surrounding the composer as he was writing this song. There is a mountain-conquering momentum as we climb over the flats of this scenery to emerge triumphant astride five sharps on 'Aufgetürmt' (b. 53). This stentorian B major also reveals its lyrical side; after 'Im Rosenschimmer des Abends' (bb. 55–8) we hear in the accompaniment the theme of the woebegone prelude transposed into this key (from b. 62). We move to G major (b. 67) via B minor (b. 69) as the singer muses over the words. Schubert even throws in his own spontaneous repeat of 'ach! die trauliche Hütte' (b. 69, the 'ach!' being Schuberts' own addition), permitting it to glow in the rosy light of evening. We grope our way over a misterioso bridge passage ('Verdunkelt ist alles', from b. 75) that takes us through a dark and precarious mountain pass; our destination is another hidden copse of memory.

Verse 3: After an extended D pedal upbeat containing the ghost of the song's opening melody (bb. 82–5), we emerge into G major sunlight (from b. 86, marked 'Geschwind') where Heidi meets Haydn: we can almost see the flaxen-headed milkmaid, as well as hear her, and we can smell the country air. Schubert the city slicker allows himself some amusement at the yokel and yodel. The left hand provides the onomatopoeic mooing (from bb. 87–8) on an ascending sixth (a good German cow, the harmony tells us) and even this comic gesture adds to the song's motivic unity where so much is based on this harmonic feature. We are given a glimpse of Schubert the composer of dance music: a crazy little *Ländler* in the pianist's right hand (from bb. 126–7) adds to the sense of wild rejoicing as the singer clutches at straws of fantasy and memory. The bounce of the music is not unlike that of *Die Post* in *Winterreise* where joyful hopes, soon to be dashed, are also momentarily aroused by the sound of the distant post-horn. John Reed points out similarities between this passage and the Trio from the Scherzo of the 'Great' C major Symphony. The symphonic passage is in A major and we are reminded that A minor/major was the original tonality of the song (*see* below). An interlude of dotted rhythms (bb. 145–55) winds us down (the music that introduces 'Die Post bringt keinen Brief für dich' comes to mind, albeit written out in crotchets rather than triplet quavers) and prepares us for the return to G minor.

Verse 4: There is a skilful sense of recapitulation here (from b. 158, with the marking Tempo 1). The motifs are the same, but the harmonic movement is completely different: a more practical solution to homesickness must be sought – languishing is not enough. There is an attempt to break away from the shackles: twice the music escapes briefly and passionately into remote keys only to be pulled back into the doleful reality of G minor. The first 'unwiderstehlicher Sehnsucht' (bb. 171–2) is hammered home dramatically, the second (bb. 177–8) is a melancholy little conversation between piano and voice, and the last at the song's close (bb. 196–9) has the poignancy of a solo violin line, a melisma that must be the definitive setting of the German word for longing.

The culminative effect of this song is of a piece of symphonic or chamber music, and the first movement of the String Quintet comes powerfully to mind. (Even more powerful pre-echoes of the immortal D956 occur in *Die Allmacht* D852.) This 'larger than lied' quality is precisely what Schubert had in mind to honour a poet whose reputation for his achievements as Patriarch of Venice (whether or not deserved) rendered him larger than life. This appointment from the emperor took Pyrker away from his native Austria, and he seems to have selected the text (the background to which is fully explained under the poet's biography) for musical setting for autobiographical reasons – and Schubert knew it.

Fischer-Dieskau (following Deutsch) mistakenly avers that Pyrker wrote the poem especially for the composer. It would be nearer the truth to say that *Das Heimweh* was probably written *out* especially for Schubert. The lines come from the sixth canto of a much longer epic poem from 1820 entitled *Tunisias*. This is the tale of Emperor Charles V's military expedition to North Africa in 1535 and is one of several texts associated with Schubert that describes the battle between the Christian and Muslim worlds. The emperor arrives in Tunis with troops from the Alpine mountains who groan with discomfort and homesickness in the terrible heat of the desert. The sixth canto is set in the encampment under Rogendorf's command and, in selecting lines 607–23 of his poem, Pyrker clearly chose a passage that reflected his mood at the time. He probably made the composer a gift of an autograph specially prepared for that purpose.

There are two versions of *Das Heimweh*, and the first is substantially different from the second precisely because the best way to make a musical structure of this poem was not clear to the composer at first. It is as if Schubert were a sculptor searching for a way to release the images trapped within a block of marble. The first version (in Volume 5b of the NSA) is in A minor and has only three sections; there is no 'Tempo 1' recapitulation in the tonic (Verse 4, above) and the much lengthier third section ('Geschwind') incorporates all the remaining words of the poem, sung at a spanking pace, with passionately extended, almost unhinged, settings of 'Sehnsucht' (bb. 174–6, 208–11, 226–30) that go all the way back to the Körner song *Sehnsucht der Liebe* D180. There is a kind of mad exaltation in this section where the composer's fervour seems to border on mountain fever. The twenty-bar postlude includes a recapitulation of both the yodelling *Ländler* and the song's 'Ziemlich langsam' introduction. When Schubert came down to earth and returned to Vienna he realized that this was not the right shape for the work; he cut and recast the final section and inserted a substantial new slow movement – Tempo I in the tonic key – beginning with the words 'Ihn fesselt der lachenden Eb'nen / Anmut nicht'. This created a convincing ABCA form with a weight and depth of feeling appropriate to 'unwiderstehlicher Sehnsucht'. A poet's strophes are usually a Schubertian unit, a demarcation of melody, and it seems that on first encountering this poem the composer was momentarily lost without their guidance. The composer drew on his experience with the modified strophic song to make a structure that contained a convincing recapitulation – a type of sonata form in vocal terms.

The AGA (unlike the NSA) prints both versions of the song in A minor. At some point it is clear that Schubert agreed that the work (perhaps to suit Vogl) should be published in G minor and, as is implied by the NSA printing, we have to take this key as the composer's final thought on the matter. Nevertheless the A minor version as printed in Volume 8 p. 120 of the AGA is a useful resource for tenors who prefer this key on the grounds of its tessitura; there is some justification for choosing to sing this song in the tonality of Schubert's first inspiration where it seems linked to a character with similar unassuaged longings to return home across the seas (Atys D585).

Autograph:	Staatsbibliothek Preussischer Kulturbesitz, Berlin
Publication:	First published as part of the AGA in 1895 (P695; first version)
	First published as Op. 79 no. 1 by Tobias Haslinger, Vienna in May 1827 (P123; second version)
Dedicatee:	Johann Ladislaus Pyrker von Felsö-Eör
Publication reviews:	*Allgemeine musikalische Zeitung* (Leipzig), No. 4 (23 January 1828), col. 49ff. [Waidelich/Hilmar Dokumente I No. 569; Deutsch Doc. Biog. No. 1014]
	Allgemeine Musik-Zeitung (Offenbach), No. 26 (29 March 1828), col. 208 [Waidelich/Hilmar Dokumente I No. 607; Deutsch Doc. Biog. No. 1070a]
Subsequent editions:	Peters: Vol. 2/142; AGA XX 478a & b: Vol. 8/112 (first version) & 120 (second version, printed in A minor); NSA IV: Vol. 3a/149 (second version) & Vol. 3b/239 (first version); Bärenreiter: Vol. 2/169
Bibliography:	Black 2003, pp. 124–5
	Capell 1928, pp. 212–13
	Fischer-Dieskau 1977, pp. 215–16
	Youens 2002, pp. 175–90
Discography and timing:	Fischer-Dieskau II 7[8] 7'11
	Hyperion I 18[12] 7'26 Peter Schreier
	Hyperion II 30[8]

← *Lied des gefangenen Jägers* D843   *Die Allmacht* D582 →

HEINRICH HEINE (1797–1856)

THE POETIC SOURCES

S1   *Reisebilder* von H. Heine. Erster Theil. Hamburg bey Hoffmann und Campe, 1826

This slim and compact volume, first of a set of four, opens with eighty pages given over to the poems of *Die Heimkehr* from which Schubert probably selected his six settings.

S2   *Buch der Lieder* von Heinrich Heine. Hamburg bei Hoffmann und Campe, 1827

Die Heimkehr 1823–1824, dedicated to Friederike [Rahal] Varnhagen von Ense 'in light-hearted homage', is the third section of this famous publication and begins on p. 177. Schubert would have had to bypass many an interesting (and settable) poem before settling on the six he discovered. For this reason it seems more likely that the composer discovered the texts in the *Reisebilder*.

THE SONGS

August 1828   *Der Atlas* D957/8 [S1: p. 28 *Die Heimkehr* no. XXVI] [S2: p. 202 no. XXIV: In neither of these two publications is there any printed title apart from the poem's first line 'Ich unglücksel'ger Atlas']

Ihr Bild D957/9 [S1: p. 27 *Die Heimkehr* no. XXV] [S2: p. 201 no. XXIII: In neither of these two publications is there any printed title apart from the poem's first line 'Ich stand in dunkeln Träumen']

Das Fischermädchen D957/10 [S1: p. 12 *Die Heimkehr* no. VIII] [S2: p. 186 no. VIII: In neither of these two publications is there any printed title apart from the poem's first line 'Du schönes Fischermädchen']

Die Stadt D957/11 [S1: p. 21 *Die Heimkehr* no. XVII] [S2: p. 195 no. XVI: In neither of these two publications is there any printed title apart from the poem's first line 'Am fernen Horizonte']

Am Meer D957/12 [S1: p. 19 *Die Heimkehr* no. XVI] [S2: p. 193 no. XIV: In neither of these two publications is there any printed title apart from the poem's first line 'Das Meer erglänzte weit hinaus']

Der Doppelgänger D957/13 [S1: p. 24 *Die Heimkehr* no. XXII] [S2: p. 198 no. XX: In neither of these two publications is there any printed title apart from the poem's first line 'Still ist die Nacht, es ruhen die Gassen']

Heinrich Heine was born Harry Heine in Düsseldorf on 13 December 1797 (although he later claimed that his year of birth was 1799). His father was a kindly but ineffectual merchant; to fund his education Heine relied on the largesse of his millionaire uncle, Salomon Heine of Hamburg, something of a domestic tyrant who, in return for subsidy, attempted to control his nephew's life. Efforts to interest young Harry in banking and retailing failed, so he was packed off to the universities of Bonn, Göttingen and Berlin and obtained an undistinguished legal degree which he never used. There is little reliable information about Heine's life in this early phase, but he is said to have fallen in love with his cousins, Salomon's daughters, neither of whom were at all interested in their impecunious young relative. In this way, Hamburg and its inhabitants are forever linked with poetry concerning Heine's unhappiness. But we shall never know to what extent the desolate lyrics of the *Buch der Lieder* are founded on autobiographical incident, and how much simply on the poet's imagination and tendency to self-dramatization.

Heine's first volume of poetry (now a great bibliophilic rarity) was published in 1822. It

Title page of Heine's *Reisebilder* (1826).

Title page of Heine's *Buch der Lieder* (1827).

included lyrics (later assembled under the headings *Junge Leiden* and *Lyrisches Intermezzo*) that re-emerged with the *Buch der Lieder* in 1827. In the same year he journeyed to Poland, and in 1823 he entered into the circle and salon of Rahel Varnhagen von Ense in Berlin. He went on a walking holiday in the Harz mountains in 1824 and paid a not-too-successful visit to Goethe in Weimar. (He had the temerity to tell the great man that he, too, was working on a *Faust*.) In 1825, in order to widen the scope of his career opportunities, he converted to Protestantism. This was arguably something that was necessary at the time, but Heine later felt he had betrayed his Jewish roots. (Felix Mendelssohn resented his father's decision to have his children baptized, giving them no say in the matter; Heine's choice was his own.)

In 1826 the poet visited England, and in 1828 Italy. Both countries were described in his inimitable, often hilarious, but unforgiving style. The *Reisebilder* ('Pictures of Travel') were issued in four volumes between 1826 and 1831. The first of these contained the group of eighty-eight poems known collectively as *Die Heimkehr* ('The Homecoming'), the *Harzreise* with its mixture of prose and poetry, as well as the poems that make up the first two parts of *Die Nordsee*. It was this small but potent volume that delighted Schober and his reading circle, and was read aloud at the beginning of 1828. The humour of *Die Harzreise* made a particularly happy impression, and it remains amusing to this day. Deutsch averred that Schubert's Heine songs were probably conceived at this time but there is no proof that this is the case. There is a theory (going back to the memoirs of the singer Karl von Schönstein) that the composer had read Heine much earlier, and that his settings date from before 1828. Of course he *could* have read the *Reisebilder* earlier; he could also, theoretically, have had a copy of the *Buch der Lieder* in his possession since 1827. But the date and condition of the *Schwanengesang* autograph, as well as other circumstantial evidence, point to these Heine songs being among the composer's last.

Schubert's selectivity in choosing the texts is evident from their order in the published editions. There is no reason to suppose that his own reordering of the poems was not deliberate. The poems appear in quite a different order in terms of their publication:

'Du schönes Fischermädchen' [*Das Fischer-mädchen*] (*Reisebilder* VIII);
'Das Meer erglänzte weit hinaus' [*Am Meer*] (XIV);
'Am fernen Horizonte' [*Die Stadt*] (XVI);
'Still ist die Nacht, es ruhen die Gassen' [*Der Doppelgänger*] (XX);
'Ich stand in dunkeln Träumen' [*Ihr Bild*] (XIII);
'Ich unglücksel'ger Atlas' [*Der Atlas*] (XXIV)

On 18 November 1830 (almost exactly two years after Schubert's death), Heine wrote to Eduard Marxsen (later the teacher of Brahms) thanking him for a consignment of small songs set to his poetry. The poet continues, 'apparently, shortly before his death, Schubert is said to have set my lieder to very good music which unfortunately I do not yet know'.

In 1831, attracted by the new political freedom brought about by the revolution that had swept Louis-Philippe to power, Heine moved to Paris. This brought him into contact with such figures as Meyerbeer, Hugo, Dumas and Balzac. His later writings were banned in Germany in 1835 for being politically seditious, and he returned to his homeland only twice, in 1843 and 1844. It was said that his role in life was to explain the Germans to the French, and vice versa. Heine's French period was notable for the development of his career as a critic, cultural historian, polemicist and so on; the lyricist beloved of lieder enthusiasts almost disappears from view. In 1843, in a review in the journal *Lutezia*, Heine wrote: 'Schubert's popularity in Paris is very great and

his name is exploited in the most shameless way . . . Poor Schubert! And what words are foisted on his music. It is particularly the Heinrich Heine songs, composed by Schubert, which are favourites here . . .' Heine goes on to complain about the translations into French of these lyrics, and how the publishers cheated him of his copyright fees. But of a musical appreciation of Schubert's songs, not a word. The French influence on Heine's life and work is not to be underestimated. As Alexander Stillmark puts it:

> The deep affinities between beauty and pain, the fickleness of women, the sweet torments of the wounded heart, the satedness of the voluptuary, or the interconnection of pain and pleasure are all further refinements of Romantic sensibility which Heine explored more fully than his predecessors: this made him a predecessor of Baudelaire and Rimbaud.

The comparison with Baudelaire extends to their suffering from the same illness (another link with Schubert of course). Incapacitated for years in what he called his *Matratzengruft* (Mattress Grave), paralysed and blind as a result of venereal infection, Heine died in Paris in on 17 February 1856. Vilified by the right (including of course the Nazis) and idolized by the left who still see him as a proto-critic of the evils of fascism and capitalism, he remains a controversial figure to this day. Some detractors (like Karl Kraus) claimed that Heine's populist streak had prostituted the German language. Certainly the lyrics that were set to music are no longer considered the most interesting side of his poetic output – but musicians will always beg to differ.

Heine's verse can embrace sentimentality to the point of cliché. At the same time the poet profoundly distrusts sentiment, and does everything he can to deflate it. This dichotomy is at the heart of the bittersweet irony of his verse. Hundreds of composers found his poetry touching and accessible – which indeed it is on one level. But he loved to play with the tension between 'poesy', as he called it, and discordant

German literature as a poet both Romantic and anti-Romantic:

Despite my exterminatory campaigns against Romanticism, I myself always remained a Romantic – and to a greater extent than I ever realized. After I had delivered the deadliest blows to the notion of Romantic poetry in Germany, I was once more assailed by the endless longing for the Blue Flower in the dreamland of Romanticism, and I took up the enchanted lute and sang a song in which I abandoned myself to all the wondrous exaggeration, all the moonlit intoxication, all the blossoming nightingale insanity of a melody I had once adored. It was I know 'the last unfettered forest song of Romanticism', and I am Romanticism's last poet.

Heinrich Heine by Charles Gleyre for *Deutscher Musenalmanach* (1854).

reality, and this was much harder for Romantic composers to capture in musical terms. Although Schubert was arguably unable (or unwilling) to follow Heine down every ironic pathway, the powerful and bleak *Schwanengesang* songs are a far cry from the effusive, and ultra-Romantic, settings of many a later composer. Robert Schumann will go down in history as Heine's composer par excellence, but even he never created a Heine setting as frightening and imposing as *Der Doppelgänger*.

In his *Geständnisse* ('Confessions', 1854), Heine explained his own special position in

It was this romanticism allied to a streak of anti-romanticism that was to fascinate Robert Schumann when he came to compose *Dichterliebe*, and surely it is this same ambivalence that attracted a composer like Schubert who had been born into the classical tradition, who had been young and impressionable at the birth of romanticism (the Blue Flower Heine mentions above is the invention of the poet Novalis, and is referred to in the Schober setting *Am Bach im Frühlinge* D361). At the end of his life Schubert seems to have been ready to enter into more modern realms of poetry with Heine as his guide. This journey was possible and exciting precisely because Heine, Janus-like, had one eye on the future and one on the past.

Bibliography: Stillmark 2000, p. 435
Youens 2007, pp. 1–88

HEISS MICH NICHT REDEN *see GESÄNGE AUS WILHELM MEISTER:* LIED DER MIGNON D877/2; MIGNON I D726; MIGNON LIEDER FROM *WILHELM MEISTER:* AN OVERVIEW

HEKTORS ABSCHIED   Hector's farewell   Duet
(SCHILLER) OP. 58 NO. 1, **D312** [H191]

The song exists in two versions, the second of which is discussed below:
(1) 19 October 1815; (2) appeared April 1826

(1)   'Langsam'   F minor   ¢   [131 bars]

(2)   F minor – A♭ major

(135 bars)

Andromache:	*Andromache:*
Will sich Hektor ewig von mir wenden,	Will Hector for ever turn away from me,
Wo Achill mit den unnahbaren Händen	While Achilles, with proud hands
Dem Patroklus schrecklich Opfer bringt?	Makes a terrible sacrifice for Patroclus?
Wer wird künftig deinen Kleinen lehren	Who, in the future, will teach your son
Speere werfen und die Götter ehren,	To hurl the javelin and revere the gods,
Wenn der finstre Orkus dich verschlingt?	When black Hades engulfs you?

Hektor:	*Hector:*
Teures Weib, gebiete deinen Tränen!	Dear wife, stem your tears!
Nach der Feldschlacht ist mein feurig Sehnen,	I long ardently for battle;
Diese Arme schützen Pergamus.	These arms shall protect Pergamus.
Kämpfend für den heil'gen Herd der Götter	I shall fall fighting for the sacred home
Fall ich, und des Vaterlandes Retter	Of the gods, and descend to the Stygian river
Steig' ich nieder zu dem styg'schen Fluss.	As the saviour of my fatherland.

Andromache:	*Andromache:*
Nimmer lausch' ich deiner Waffen Schalle	Never again shall I hear the clang of your arms;
Müssig liegt das Eisen in der Halle,	Your sword will lie idle in the hall.
Priams grosser Heldenstamm verdirbt.	Priam's great heroic race will perish.
Du wirst hingeh'n, wo kein Tag mehr scheinet,	You will go where no daylight shines,
Der Cocytus durch die Wüsten weinet,	Where Cocytus weeps through the wastelands;
Deine Lieb' im Lethe stirbt.	Your love will die in the waters of Lethe.

Hektor:	*Hector:*
All mein Sehnen will ich, all mein Denken,	I would drown all my longing, all my thoughts
In des Lethe stillen Strom versenken,	In the silent waters of Lethe,
Aber meine Liebe nicht.	But not my love.
Horch! der Wilde tobt schon an den Mauern,	Hark! The wild mob already rages at the walls.
Gürte mir das Schwert um, lass das Trauern!	Gird on my sword, cease your grieving.
Hektors Liebe stirbt im Lethe nicht.	Hector's love will not perish in Lethe.

FRIEDRICH VON SCHILLER (1759–1805); poem written in 1777/80

*Hektors Abschied is a musical dialogue between two characters who never sing simultaneously
(a performance for a single singer taking both male and female roles would thus be a possibility).
This duet is accordingly listed here as the twentieth of Schubert's forty-four Schiller solo settings
(1811–24) rather than as an ensemble. See the poet's biography for a chronological list of
all the Schiller settings.*

Although Schubert almost certainly found this text in Schiller's *Gedichte* (Anton Doll, Vienna,
1810), the poem first appears in Act II Scene 2 of *Die Räuber*, the poet's first play. This
concerns the fortunes of the brothers Karl and Franz Moor, and Karl's beloved Amalia. We
learn that Karl and Amalia have often sung this duet together with lute accompaniment, and
in the play she sings it to comfort the boys' father, Maximillian, who believes himself to be
dying. In the context of the play it highlights Amalia's resolution and bravery in times of
turbulent danger.

Capell is right to call the music 'formal and stately'. No music of the common people this,
rather an aria for doomed royalty. Propelled by grandiose triplets it rolls with a dignity denied
the love stories of mere mortals. For Andromache's opening utterance Schubert discovered,
prophetically, a vein of what was one day going to be known as Italian grand opera style. The
cleverness of this would be more easily analysed if this piece were from the Italian-obsessed
1820s, rather than 1815. In the introduction, pregnant and pulsating F minor chords ache to
support a *bel canto* imprecation, and they are not disappointed; the opening vocal lines look
forward to the young Verdi in their portent. Brian Newbould hears an intimation of 'the
harmonic structure in the same key to launch the Fantasy in F minor for piano duet'. The idea
of the little boy soon to be fatherless brings a flute or oboe solo in the relative major (bb. 9–10),
and again the formulae of Italian opera suit the grandiose formality of the ancients – as Bellini

Hektors Abschied from the Schiller *Jubiläums-Ausgabe* (1859).

was soon to demonstrate in his opera about a priestess in Roman times, *Norma*. Hector's music (from b. 23) is less inspired and slightly wooden, as if he had things on his mind other than trying to placate his wife. A sudden change of harmony (with 'Teures Weib', sharps of the real world replacing underworld flats) ushers in music of heroic resolve with the type of rising sequences used to greater effect elsewhere in the mythological songs. Pergamus, the citadel of Troy, fails to sound redoubtable (bb. 31–2) although by then it was on the verge of annihilation. Hector repeats his words (from b. 49) and his vocal line sounds no more convincing second time round, even if it does bathe itself deeper in the Stygian stream with a mordent shudder ('ich nieder <u>zu</u> dem styg'schen Fluss).

Andromache follows with an aria in A minor ('Nimmer lausch' ich', from b. 70). This is chiefly remarkable for its modulations in the repetition of its last line ('Deine Lieb' im Lethe stirbt') where Hector's love for her undergoes an audible sea change in the waters of Lethe (bb. 95–100). His closing aria ('All mein Sehnen') changes key (into A flat major) and tempo marking (to 'Nicht zu schnell'). This is as much of a *cabaletta* as Andromache's opening was *cavatina*. It is a generously open-hearted tune with a clever chromatic descent on 'In des Lethe stillen Strom versenken' (bb. 104–6) and the obligatory recitative (bb. 103–6) to mark the tumult outside. There is a touching moment (b. 116) where a sudden 'Langsam' briefly shifts the warrior's attention away from the braying crowd to the distraught Andromache. Nevertheless, Schubert was much more comfortable with Andromache's wifely grief – Schiller's words do not enable the young composer to invest the son of Priam, and Troy's greatest hero, with believable human feelings. The success of *Gretchen am Spinnrade* (and this was already in Schubert's past) should explain why the music of Andromache in this song seems more connected to real emotion than Hector's brave posturings.

The small differences between the two versions indicate how the Schubert of 1826 took a song from 1815 and, without changing its essence or attempting to recompose it, dusted it down and sharpened its contours in preparation for its new life as a published work.

Autograph:	Conservatoire collection, Bibliothèque Nationale, Paris
Publication:	First published as part of the AGA in 1895 (P598; first version)
	First published as Op. 58 no. 1 by Thaddäus Weigl, Vienna in
	April 1826 (P97; second version)
Publication reviews:	*Allgemeiner musikalischer Anzeiger* (Frankfurt), No. 33 (10
	February 1827), p. 317f. [Waidelich/Hilmar Dokumente I no. 452;
	Deutsch Doc. Biog. No. 798]
Subsequent editions:	Peters: Vol. 4/53; AGA XX 159a & b: Vol. 3/130 (first version) &
	136 (second version); NSA IV: Vol. 3a/84 (second version) & Vol.
	3b/178 (first version); Bärenreiter: Vol. 2/117
Bibliography:	Newbould 1997, p. 47
Further setting:	J. F. Reichardt (1752–1814) *Hektors Abschied*, No. 19 of *Schillers Lyrische Gedichte*, erstes Heft, 1810

Discography and timing:	Deutsche Grammophon		Janet Baker & Dietrich
	Schubert Duette	4'50	Fischer-Dieskau
	Hyperion I 14⁶		Marie McLaughlin &
	Hyperion II 11³	5'01	Thomas Hampson

← *Sehnsucht (Mignon)* D310a   *Die Sterne* D313 →

HELIOPOLIS I
(MAYRHOFER) OP. 65 NO. 3, **D753** [H485]
E minor – E major   April 1822

Heliopolis I

(68 bars)

Im kalten, rauhen Norden	In the cold, harsh north
Ist Kunde mir geworden	I learnt
Von einer Stadt, der Sonnenstadt.	Of a city, the city of the sun.
Wo weilt das Schiff, wo ist der Pfad,	Where is the ship, where the path
Die mich zu jenen Hallen tragen?[1]	That will take me to its courts?
Von Menschen konnt' ich nichts erfragen,—	Men could tell me nothing,
Im Zwiespalt waren sie verworren.[2]	For they were entangled in conflict.
Zur Blume, die sich H e l i o s erkoren,	I then turned to the flower chosen by *Helios*,
Die ewig in sein Antlitz blickt,	That forever gazes into one's face,
Wandt' ich mich nun—und ward entzückt:	And was enchanted.
'Wende, so wie ich, zur Sonne	'Like me, turn your eyes
Deine Augen! Dort ist Wonne,[3]	To the sun! There is bliss,
Dort ist Leben;	There is life;
Treu ergeben,	In true devotion
Pilg're zu und zweifle nicht:	Make your pilgrimage, and do not doubt.
Ruhe findest du im Licht;	In the light you will find peace.
Licht erzeuget alle Gluten—	Light creates all ardour,
Hoffnungspflanzen, Tatenfluten!'	Begets flowers of hope and torrents of deeds!'

JOHANN MAYRHOFER (1787–1836); poem written September–October 1821

*This is the forty-second of Schubert's forty-seven Mayrhofer solo settings (1814–24). See the
poet's biography for a chronological list of all the Mayrhofer settings.*

This is the fifth poem of a sequence of twenty, *Heliopolis*, written by Mayrhofer in September–
October 1821. It was probably conceived as a cycle for Schubert – there is a theme of journeying
in these words that prefigures *Winterreise* – but it was never completed as such. In the late
autumn of 1821 Mayrhofer sent a copy of the poems to St Pölten where Schubert was working
with Schober on the opera *Alfonso und Estrella*. Schubert set three of them in 1822: *Nachtviolen*
D752, *Heliopolis* D753 and the second *Heliopolis* song, D754. *Lied eines Schiffers an die Dioskuren*
was also part of the poet's cycle under Mayrhofer's original title, *Schiffers Nachtlied*; whether
Schubert's setting (D360) also dates from 1822 or was written much earlier (as stated in the

[1] Mayrhofer writes 'Die mich zu *ihren* Hallen tragen?'. For an explanation of the background to these alternative
Mayrhofer readings see Editorial Note at the beginning of Johann MAYRHOFER.
[2] Later changed by Mayrhofer to 'In Zwiespalt waren sie *verloren*'.
[3] Later changed by Mayrhofer to 'Deine *Blicke*! Dort ist Wonne'.

NSA) remains debatable. The *Heliopolis* cycle as such was not published in Mayrhofer's *Gedichte* (1824), although the poems for D752, D754 and D360 were included there separately. The second collection of Mayrhofer poems published posthumously in 1843 contains *Heliopolis* as a cycle of seventeen poems (p. 195), beginning with the text of D753, but not including the three poems already published in 1824.

The longing for the warmth of the south has always figured in German literature. It is an old theme as Mayrhofer himself acknowledges in a four-line preface to this poem that Schubert chose not to set to music:

Ein altes Thema, vorgetragen	Let us vary an old story,
In grauen Zeiten, lass uns variieren!	One related in grey times!
Wir dürfen, wenn wir auch Ikarisieren –	Even though we suffer the same fate as Icarus
Uns öfters noch zur Sonne wagen!	We should once in a while dare to approach the sun!

Goethe's Mignon gives voice to this in her immortal *Kennst du das Land?* The warm and tolerant south lured Thomas Mann's Gustav von Aschenbach to Venice, where he met with self-discovery and death. Similarly, Mayrhofer in this poem seems to say, 'Fly towards the sun, live dangerously . . . fight for what you believe in whatever the consequences, journey to the place where you belong.' Heliopolis was the Greek name for the ancient Egyptian city of Iunu or Onu, centre of the priapic cult of the sun god Re, the Osiris hymned by Sarastro in *Die Zauberflöte*. In Cairo it is the name of a suburb established at the end of the nineteenth century where the wealthy reside in surroundings more elegant and salubrious than elsewhere. Mayrhofer surely imagined a mystical Utopia where art and the artist were venerated in an atmosphere of Platonic idealism. In *Calamus* (1860) Walt Whitman wrote, 'I dreamed in a dream I saw a city invincible to the attacks of the rest of the world . . . the new city of Friends' – this was clearly *his* Heliopolis. The famous classicist A. E. Housman (an atheist who who hated 'the laws of man' as much as Mayrhofer) employed biblical analogy for 'the country far away / Where I shall never stand / The heart goes where no footstep may / Into the promised land' (No. 2 of *More Poems*, 1936).

As in the Mayrhofer setting *An die Freunde* D654, the introduction consists of a sparse line of left-hand accompaniment. These unisons and steady crotchets have long suggested to Schubertians the opening of the Piano Sonata in A minor D845. For John Reed the opening of the Andante con moto of the 'Great' C major Symphony also comes to mind. Schubert associates the tonality of *Heliopolis* with dryness (*Trockne Blumen* from *Die schöne Müllerin*), freezing cold (*Auf dem Flusse* from *Winterreise*) and dark despair and exclusion (*Tiefes Leid* D876). As the song progresses it warms to its theme; the accompaniment fills out, as if the poet has gathered adherents to his cause as he continues his journey in search of the legendary city. The march to that destination in the implacable rhythm of even crotchets recalls the Schiller setting *Der Pilgrim* D794; there are intimations of danger and a grim determination in the sequences of falling diminished seventh harmony beginning at 'Von Menschen konnt' ich nichts erfragen' (bb. 17–19).

The poet, disillusioned with mankind, decides to seek enlightenment elsewhere. A change to E major (b. 24) signals this new direction; suddenly we are in the tonality of *Elysium* D584, at one with the gods of Olympus. William Blake also memorably addressed a sunflower in his *Songs of Experience*, wishing to follow it to 'that sweet golden clime, / Where the travellers journey is done'. The reply of Mayrhofer's own flower ('Wende, so wie ich, zur Sonne / Deine Augen', from b. 34) inspires music of almost unearthly simplicity, a chorale of a kind that could come from a Delphic source. The vocal line here limits itself, with some exceptions, to the interval of a fourth between B and E on the treble stave, resulting in a childlike purity, the artlessness that one may expect from the voice of nature. The repetition of the musical material within this constricted vocal compass is tiring and tiresome in the hands of a less than accomplished singer, hypnotic when sung beautifully. In itself this is not the composer's most memorable melody (and this may account for the scarcity of performances of this song) but it has a very special atmosphere. Towards the end the piano marking is abandoned in favour of a heroic forte for the idea of 'Tatenfluten' (bb. 57–9). The effect is slightly awkward: it is as if Mayrhofer's veiled advocacy of flower power in a piano dynamic has slipped during the song, leaving him revealed as the vehement propagandist for his own imaginary Heliopolis.

If we were to attempt to find anyone within the Schubert circle who might have been personified as this alluring flower, it would be Franz von Schober – of Swedish origin, blond, good-looking and powerfully charming. In the eyes of some of Schubert's friends he was a hedonist, untrammelled by the restrictions of Biedermeier morality. But Mayrhofer seems to have admired his independent spirit, in the same way that Socrates permitted himself to admire and love the beautiful and undisciplined Alcibiades. The subtitle of the poem is the dedicatory 'An Franz'; this was taken by Feuchtersleben, Mayrhofer's friend and biographer, to refer to Schober, although some have seen Franz Schubert as the dedicatee (*see* commentary on the second *Heliopolis* song D754 below). A short while after Schubert's death, Mayrhofer wrote a moving poem (Documentary Biography, p. 832) where he envisages the composer as a bird flying from the cold north to the realms of the sun. Mayrhofer could do no better than wish his recently departed friend safe passage to Heliopolis at last.

Autograph:	Oslo University Library, Norway (incomplete fragment)
First edition:	Published as Op. 65 no. 3 by Cappi & Czerny, Vienna in November 1826 (P111)
Publication reviews:	*Berliner allgemeine musikalische Zeitung* No. 11 (14 March 1827), p. 81ff. [Waidelich/Hilmar Dokumente I No. 461; Deutsch Doc. Biog. No. 826]
Subsequent editions:	Peters: Vol. 3/33; AGA XX 404: Vol. 7/8; NSA IV: Vol. 3/128; Bärenreiter: Vol. 2/156
Bibliography:	Capell 1928, p. 177
	Fischer-Dieskau 1977, p. 120
	Kohlhäufl 1999, p. 293
Discography and timing:	Fischer-Dieskau II 5[4] 3'55
	Hyperion I 11[14]
	Hyperion II 25[11] 3'21 Brigitte Fassbaender

← *Nachtviolen* D752   *Heliopolis II* D754 →

HELIOPOLIS II   Heliopolis II
(Mayrhofer) **D754** [H486]
C minor   April 1822

(59 bars)

Fels auf Felsen hingewälzet,	Rock piled upon rock,
Fester Grund und treuer Halt;	Firm ground and steady foothold;
Wasserfälle, Windesschauer,	Waterfalls, blasts of wind,
Unbegriffene Gewalt—	Uncomprehended power.
Einsam auf Gebirges Zinne	Solitary, on the mountain peak,
Kloster=wie auch Burg=Ruine;	Stands a monastery and a ruined castle;
Grab' sie der Erinn'rung ein!	Etch them in the memory,
Denn der Dichter lebt vom Sein.	For the poet lives through existence.
Atme du den heil'gen Äther,	Breathe the holy aether,
Schling die Arme um die Welt;	Clasp the world in your arms;
Nur dem Würdigen, dem Grossen	Boldly consort
Bleibe mutig zugesellt.	Only with the worthy and the great.
Lass die Leidenschaften sausen	Let the passions seethe
Im metallenen Accord;	In brazen harmony.
Wenn die starken Stürme brausen,	When fierce tempests rage
Findest du das rechte Wort.	You will find the right word.

JOHANN MAYRHOFER (1787–1836); poem written September–October 1821

This is the forty-third of Schubert's forty-seven Mayrhofer solo settings (1814–24). See the poet's biography for a chronological list of all the Mayrhofer settings.

The poem is the twelfth in a group of twenty lyrics that Mayrhofer probably intended to be set as a cycle by his friend Schubert. It is published separately in the poet's *Gedichte* (1824, p. 178) where the title is 'Im Hochgebirge' (In the High Mountains). The cycle as a whole had been dedicated simply 'To Franz'. It was sent in manuscript form by Mayrhofer to St Pölten where Schubert and Schober were working together on the opera *Alfonso und Estrella*. When it appeared in altered form in 1843 in the posthumous edition of the *Gedichte*, Ernst von Feuchtersleben, editor of the volume, had no doubt that this 'Franz' referred to Franz von Schober – and the dedication is printed thus. There have been some dissenting voices, however, including Diestrich Fischer-Dieskau, who claim that 'Franz' was Schubert himself. 'Just what effect Mayrhofer hoped to have on Schubert', writes Fischer-Dieskau, 'is made particularly clear in *Heliopolis II* where [he] speaks directly to his younger friend'.

If this is indeed a lecture from an older and more experienced poet to a younger composer it must have its roots in Mayrhofer's knowledge of Greek philosophy, and the ideal of Platonic love – the older man as spiritual guide, inspiring in the younger the loftiest behaviour. The desire of a poet to shape the personality of a younger musician had its twentieth-century equivalent in the extraordinarily fruitful (non-sexual) relationship of W. H. Auden and Benjamin Britten from about 1935–40 (although that friendship failed to survive the poet taking on the role of self-appointed life-counsellor). The parallels are far-reaching. The poet in each pairing was the more articulate, intellectual and bossy; each generously broadened the younger colleague's mental and literary horizons. In both cases an intense (but almost certainly non-romantic) friendship cooled when the composer felt the need to escape from the poet's influence in order to establish a modus vivendi more congenial to his own nature. Be that as it may, it still seems more likely that Mayrhofer is addressing these words to Franz von Schober, not Franz Schubert: the use of the closing phrase 'das rechte Wort' sounds like an older poet giving advice to a younger one.

Schubert set this *Heliopolis* poem with demonic energy; it is among his most vehement outbursts. The brief but explosive Senn setting *Selige Welt* D743 comes to mind, as does Mayrhofer's *Der Schiffer* D536. All three songs are almost over-idealized portraits of manly strength, without any sign of the 'lineaments of gratified desire' (would Mayrhofer have understood what William Blake was talking about?) The Austrian poet seems to have attempted the high-minded abstinence counselled by Socrates in *Phaedrus* and *The Symposium*, his whole life a struggle between the spirit and the flesh or, as in Plato's analogy, between the white and black horses of the charioteer. Schubert knew Mayrhofer well enough to be able to think himself into the exaltation of the poet's would-be heroic nature (the self-abnegating heroism Mayrhofer sought to foster in his younger, easy-living friends, whether Schober, Schubert, or both). The composer finds the right tone for the song: this second *Heliopolis* setting is significantly written in the bass clef, and Schubert imagines his singer climbing up the sheer rock face to that monastery of abstinence. This requires the brandished fist of a Beethoven (the singer must summon this defiance while the overworked pianist's fists are otherwise engaged) and one is reminded that C minor is Beethoven's favourite key for this kind of music – and that it is also the relative minor of Mayrhofer's *Der Schiffer* D536, a boatman who probably climbs mountains on his days off.

The pianist holds on to the keyboard for dear life, the doubling of all these growling octaves a sign of determination and willpower. The safe grip of hand and foot, the climber's treble and bass as it were, is thus secured inch by inch. Leo Black has pointed out the strong relationship of this song with both the moods and the challenges of the *Wandererfantasie* D760 for solo piano, a link that has been largely overlooked in favour of commentary on that work's musical connection to the Schmidt von Lübeck setting *Der Wanderer* D489. John Reed writes that 'the relentless drive, and in particular the C major climax, anticipate the finale of the "Great" C major Symphony'.

The repeat of 'Grab' sie' (the identical bb. 17–18) ensures that these etchings are scratched deep enough into the mind, like climbing spikes lodged in the cracks. The harmonic progressions are astonishing, rising a semitone and then slipping back a notch. This is among the most chromatic of Schubert's lieder, an impression strengthened by the fact that all these shifts occur within so short a time (almost inducing a kind of musical vertigo). At b. 27 the music pauses in the home key for the climber to look at the view and recover his breath (the singer is not so lucky). At b. 37 there is at last a victorious modulation into C major, although no hint of a smile greets the exhausted mountaineer's hard-won triumph. Finding the 'right word' for Schubert was seldom the self-conscious struggle that this text and its music provoked in him; the song portrays the determination of the poet in exultant mood, and the song induces our respect rather than our affection.

Autographs:	Österreichische Nationalbibliothek, Vienna (first draft)
	Staatsbibliothek Preussischer Kulturbesitz, Berlin (fair copy)
First edition:	Published as Book 37 no. 1 of the *Nachlass* by Diabelli, Vienna in June 1842 (P346)
Subsequent editions:	Peters: Vol. 3/204; AGA XX 405: Vol. 7/10; NSA IV: Vol. 13/46
Bibliography:	Black 2003, pp. 59–60 & 116
	Capell 1928, p. 177
	Einstein 1951, p. 253
	Fischer-Dieskau 1977, p. 120
Discography and timing:	Fischer-Dieskau II 5⁵ 2'06
	Hyperion I 11¹⁵
	Hyperion II 25¹² 1'59 Brigitte Fassbaender

← *Heliopolis* I D753   *Die Liebe hat gelogen* D751 →

THEODOR HELL *see* KARL GOTTFRIED THEODOR WINKLER

HERBST

(Rellstab) **D945** [H662]
E minor   April 1828

Autumn

(26 bars)

Es rauschen die Winde	The wind blows
So herbstlich und kalt;	With an autumnal chill;
Verödet die Fluren,	The meadows are bare,
Entblättert der Wald.	The woods leafless.
Ihr blumigen Auen!	Flowering meadows;
Du sonniges Grün!	Sunlit green!
So welken die Blüten	Thus do life's blossoms
Des Lebens dahin.	Wilt.
Es ziehen die Wolken	The clouds drift by,
So finster und grau;	So sombre and grey;
Verschwunden die Sterne	The stars have vanished
Am himmlischen Blau!	In the blue heavens.
Ach, wie die Gestirne	Ah, as the stars disappear
Am Himmel entflieh'n,	In the sky,
So sinket die Hoffnung	So does life's hope
Des Lebens dahin!	Fade away.
Ihr Tage des Lenzes	You days of spring,
Mit Rosen geschmückt,	Adorned with roses,
Wo ich die Geliebte	When I pressed
An's Herze gedrückt!	My beloved to my heart.
Kalt über den Hügel	Winds, blow cold
Rauscht, Winde, dahin!	Over the hillside!
So sterben die Rosen	So do the roses
Der Liebe dahin!	Of love die.

LUDWIG RELLSTAB (1799–1860); poem written before 1825

This is the third of Schubert's ten Rellstab solo settings (1827–8). See the poet's biography for a chronological list of all the Rellstab settings.

This wonderful song about old memories – springtime experiences yellowed, like the falling leaf, with the passage of time – bristles with new musical procedures. It is surely one of the most potent indications of how Schubert's songwriting might have developed had he been granted a longer lifespan. What is particularly thrilling is how he combines the age-old form of the strophic song with music that is in the new Schubert style of the *Schwanengesang* – economical and lean, yet full of powerful and condensed expression. Another ⅞ dramatic song comes to mind, *Die junge Nonne* D828 of 1825, but how portentous and old-fashioned is that beloved but lumbering accompaniment when compared to this! In *Herbst* the piano staves seem as thinly foliated as trees on a blustery autumn day – another strophe and one feels that all the remaining semiquavers would be blown away to silence. Everything here is for maximum effect with minimum pianistic fuss, and the vocal line is free to range across the stave in long arcs of eloquent expression. We hear the same music three times without tiring of it in the least.

The autumn winds are set in motion by oscillating right-hand semiquavers in minor thirds. This stark murmuring sound brings the chill of foreboding into the music. And then quavers on adjacent tones and semitones (an E minor scale beginning on the leading note) insinuate themselves into the bass clef. In counterpoint with the wind this motif creeps into the body of the song and, without warning, seizes the heart in an icy grip. This unfurling figure rises to a dotted crotchet on C, the sixth degree of the E minor scale, before it changes direction and takes a bar to fall to an A at the bottom of the bass stave. One of the intervals in this descent is a major third (B–G): only a Schubert or a Beethoven could know how such a tiny adjustment can change a commonplace scale into a unique melody. Once this left-hand scale has bottomed out on that low A the right-hand harmonies change on the second beat of the bar: the thirds that make up the tremolo (E and G) slither up to F natural and A and the result is a first inversion of the flattened supertonic, a sidestep into all the desolation of autumn. This low, left-hand A lasts three beats before rising to A sharp and then to the dotted semibreve B over which the music briefly moves into the dominant before a return to E minor and the entry of the voice.

The singer's melody is strong and purposeful with a touch of dramatic rhetoric. The pianist's right hand continues its oscillations while the main musical conversation takes place between the singer and the piano's bass line. The effect of a serious colloquy is heightened by the suggestion of a canon – the second bar of the vocal phrase ('herbstlich und kalt') remains on a fixed note as the bass line echoes and answers the first. (Here the music seems prophetic of another great autumn song, Fauré's *Automne* with its plunging octave basses in the related key of B minor.) Once again we note the creation of *multum in parvo*: the melody of 'Es rauschen die Winde / So herbstlich und kalt' (bb. 4–6) is nothing more than an E minor arpeggio moving down, and then up the stave, and the following phrase ('Verödet die Fluren / Entblättert der Wald' bb. 6–8) is a D minor sequence of this sturdy, but hardly original, idea. No matter, the effect is magical, and typical of a number of similar sequences in the Rellstab songs of *Schwanengesang*.

What follows is much more unusual; indeed Johannes Brahms could have incorporated the next few bars into his songs without our noticing an intrusion. The dislocations of the syncopated vocal line in the middle of a word ('Ihr blumigen Auen' and 'Du sonniges Grün' in the first verse, bb. 9 and 11) are to be found nowhere else in Schubert's songs. This mournful melisma, somewhere between a wail and a sob, exhales the towering and dolorous tenor of late romanticism as yet unknown to the musicians of Schubert's epoch – in comparison the harrowing lacerations of *Winterreise* seem grounded in the classics. The vocal line harmonized in the woeful regions of the submediant seems drawn downwards by the weight of its distress, and the inner-voice harmonies of the accompanying semiquavers rise against it in contrary motion, each beat registering a subtle change of harmony. It is this grinding clash of notes and rhythms, signifying the deepest engagement of feeling, that prophesies Brahms. Note the heavy bank of left-hand crotchets and quavers in b. 10 ascending the stave before 'Du sonniges Grün'. (It is now the piano's turn to lead in the overlapping exchanges between voice and accompaniment.) In the previous phrase the left hand had settled on a C major chord (under 'blumigen'), but now (under 'sonniges') the same harmony is 'decorated' (although hardly the appropriate word for so sad an effect) by a magnificent accented passing note in the left hand (a dotted crotchet B leaning on the C that resolves it). This emphasizes the pain of bidding farewell to life's green summer. It is little wonder that Brahms went to the trouble of copying out this song when he saw the autograph shortly after its rediscovery. His own style was by then fully formed but the song must have made his own debt to Schubert in this late mode all the clearer. Brahms had incidentally written a *Herbstgefühl* in 1867 to a poem by Adolf von Schack (Op. 48 no. 7) with a similar (though less agitated) autumnal mood that is much influenced by Schubert and includes a quotation from *Der Doppelgänger*.

Schubert uses a single Rellstab strophe for each musical verse. He moves rather swiftly through the first six lines of poetry, but uses the words 'So welken die Blüten / Des Lebens dahin' twice (bb. 12–16 and 16–21) in order to reach a conclusion. This occasions a vocal line of the broadest sweep, imposing and melancholic, and ringing with the flattened harmonies (the chord of F major in b. 14 makes a wonderfully mournful impression in the context of the key of E minor) with which Schubert casts a pall over this seasonal depiction. Note the sad downward movement of the scale for the withering of 'welken' and the sudden, desperate leap upwards for 'dahin'. This last word is supported by a dotted semibreve pedal on C that underpins four different right-hand harmonies in the course of a bar (b. 16) – a metaphor for the changing and restless nature of time. But this is only the first appearance of these words. Their repeat occasions something more intense: the addition of a B flat in the second 'welken' (b. 17) further darkens the mood and the final 'Blüten' is set to a rising octave on an F minor chord (b. 18) that seems to stretch out in a vain effort to touch the past. The doleful turn on a dotted semibreve for '<u>Lebens</u> dahin' twists the concluding cadence into bitter expressiveness. This is reminiscent of the written-out turn with which *Der Doppelgänger* D957/13 ends to the words – 'in alter Zeit' – which also emphasize the ravages of time.

The song's extraordinary prelude serves as an interlude between the verses. (Little changed, it will also serve as a coda.) One can only marvel at the genius of Schubert when it comes to strophic songs. His very best examples manage to allow the music to be both equally expressive, and appropriate, for each of the poet's verses.

There has been much speculation as to why *Herbst* was not included as part of the *Schwanengesang*, and why it languished for years in obscurity. The tiny flaw in the word-setting is a possible cause of its suppression. After a magnificent opening strophe Schubert might have been less than happy with how Rellstab's words fitted the remaining two. In terms of musical mood there is no problem at all, and a fine performer can gloss over any rough corners, but there are one or two details that would have struck Schubert as unacceptably imperfect in this year of matchless creations. The phrase 'Ach, wie die Gestirne' (bb. 8–10) contains a long expressive melisma on the unimportant word 'wie', and in the third verse a similarly incongruous emphasis of the non-crucial word 'über'. At the beginning of the poet's sixth verse (in the third musical strophe of the song) the enjambment of the two lines 'Kalt über den Hügel / Rauscht, Winde, dahin' makes for a long (and unbridgeable) gap between 'Hügel' and 'Rauscht', with 'Rauscht' uncomfortably snatched. (The wail of 'Winde' is, however, a perfect expressive fit.) Brahms (much to the exasperation of people like Hugo Wolf) sometimes allowed this sort of imperfection into his word-setting, and we also find it in a song like Schumann's *Die Lotosblume*; but such awkwardness is hardly ever found in the songs of Schubert's maturity. The first verse is so perfect in every respect, however, that *Herbst* did not deserve to be suppressed completely, or sidelined into a friend's autograph album.

Another factor may be the song's similarities to *Aufenthalt* from *Schwanengesang* (*see* the commentary on that song). Schubert might simply have felt that *Herbst* was a study for the later song, and that it was impossible for both works to appear in the same group or cycle. In any case, *Herbst* was 'lost' for many years in an autograph album belonging to Heinrich Panofka

(1807–1887) who was born in Breslau but spent much of his life in France, Italy and England. A violin student in Vienna at the time and a friend of the poet Hoffmann von Fallersleben, Panofka met Schubert in 1827, and he must have made something of an impression for the composer to have written (or at least copied) an entirely original song in his autograph album, adding the words 'Zur freundlichen Erinnerung'. Perhaps Panofka, later to become a critic and a celebrated singing teacher, was already sufficiently fascinated by Schubert's songs to have moved the composer to take this amount of trouble. The album contains a stunning array of contributions from Beethoven (via Schindler), Weber, Schumann, Brahms, Liszt, Berlioz et alia. It is the only autograph or copy of *Herbst* in existence and was unknown to Friedlaender when he prepared the seventh volume of his Schubert Edition for Peters. The song was unearthed just in time to appear in the very last volume of the old Mandyczewski *Gesamtausgabe* in 1895 (AGA). Panofka went on to write a significant appreciation of Schubert's work in the *Revue et gazette musicale* in 1838. This had a crucial effect on the composer's reception in France: it was from about this time that the early *mélodie* composers (also impressed by performances by the tenor Adolphe Nourrit) began to take notice of Schubert's songs.

Autograph:	Kongelige Bibliotek, Copenhagen (Heinrich Panofka album)
First edition:	Published as part of the AGA in 1895 (P711)
Subsequent editions:	Not in Peters; AGA XX 589: Vol. 10/90; NSA IV: Vol. 14/93; Bärenreiter: Vol. 4/118
Bibliography:	Fischer-Dieskau 1977, pp. 274–5
Further settings:	Franz Lachner (1803–1890) *Herbst* for voice and piano with cello or horn obbligato, no. 1 of *Deutsche Lieder* (1831?) Franz Liszt (1811–1886) *Es rauschen die Winde* (1845–56, rev. 1860)
Discography and timing:	Fischer-Dieskau II 9^{14} 4'22 Hyperion I 37^2 Hyperion II 36^2 3'21 John Mark Ainsley

← *Mirjams Siegesgesang* D942   *Lebensmut* D937 →

Der HERBSTABEND   Autumn evening
(Salis-Seewis) **D405** [H246]

The song exists in two versions, the first of which is discussed below:
(1) 27 March 1816; (2) November 1816?

(1)   F minor

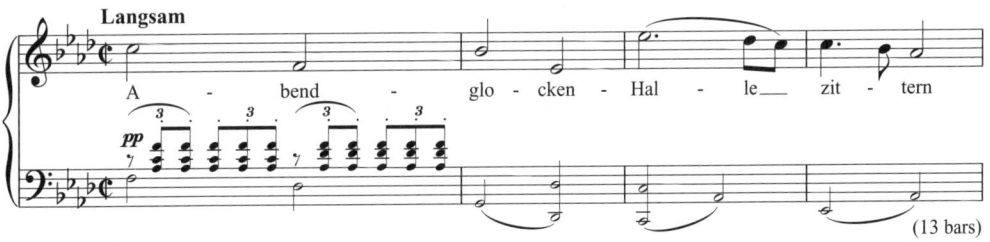

(13 bars)

(2)   'Langsam'   F minor   ¢   [15 bars]

Abendglocken-halle zittern	Evening bells chime, dull and tremulous,
Dumpf durch Moorgedüfte hin;	In the marshland breeze;
Hinter jenes Kirchhofs Gittern	Behind those churchyard railings
Blasst des Dämmerlichts Karmin.	The crimson glow of twilight fades.

Abendglocken-halle zittern
   Dumpf durch Moorgedüfte hin;
Hinter jenes Kirchhofs Gittern
   Blasst des Dämmerlichts Karmin.

Aus umstürmten Lindenzweigen
   Rieselt welkes Laub herab,
Und gebleichte Gräser beugen
   Sich auf ihr bestimmtes Grab.

[. . .]

Wenn schon meine Rasenstelle
   Nur dein welker Kranz noch ziert,
Und auf Lethe's leiser Welle
   Sich mein Nebelbild verliert.

Lausche dann! Im Blätterschauer
   Wird es dir vernehmlich wehn:
Jenseits schwindet jede Trauer;
   Treue wird sich wiedersehn!

Evening bells chime, dull and tremulous,
   In the marshland breeze;
Behind those churchyard railings
   The crimson glow of twilight fades.

From storm-tossed linden branches
   Withered leaves stream down,
And blanched grasses bend
   Over their appointed graves.

[. . .]

When only your withered wreath still adorns
   The grass where I lie,
And my misty image is lost
   On Lethe's gentle waves:

Listen then! In the shower of leaves
   This message shall be wafted to you:
In the world beyond, all sorrow shall vanish;
   Constant lovers shall be reunited!

JOHANN GAUDENZ VON SALIS-SEEWIS (1762–1834); poem written in 1787/92

This is the tenth of Schubert's thirteen Salis-Seewis solo settings (1816–?1821). See the poet's biography for a chronological list of all the Salis-Seewis settings.

This beautiful song is one of the unaccountably neglected little masterpieces of 1816. It looks uninterestingly simple in print, and because it takes only a modest single page in the *Gesamtausgabe* and was never published in the Peters Edition it is perhaps destined to languish in obscurity. Fischer-Dieskau rightly avers that it is a song for lovers of *bel canto*. The constant throbbing triplets of the accompaniment suggest something Italian in its atmosphere, and the widely ranging vocal line (a sighing drop of a fifth in each of the first two bars, followed by an upward leap of an octave) implies a vocal virtuosity and flexibility associated with opera singers. But because this is Schubert, the song goes beyond mere technical display – it is wonderfully 'innig', a characteristic of the composer's intimate night songs.

   The first image the poet provides is of evening bells resounding over the marshes, muted by the breezes but also trembling – the acoustical phenomenon of metallic sounds heard at a distance. The brightness of the vocal line in minims is underpinned by minims in the bass; the sound of both together plus the piano's background triplet shimmer perfectly illustrate the image. The strength of the bass line and its skilful support of the somewhat wayward vocal line should have earned Salieri's highest praise; it is a textbook case of how a good piece of music is written by assuring both the independence and inter-dependence of the outer parts. The spookiness of a churchyard is conveyed by the chromatic descent of 'Hinter jenes Kirchhofs Gittern' (bb. 8–9). It is obvious from the setting of the word crimson ('Karmin') with an ornate gruppetto of semiquavers that Schubert considered this a splendidly exotic colour. He thought enough of this song to include a copy in the Therese Grob Songbook (from November 1816), where he adds a two-bar prelude. This version, long available only in a private printing of Reinhard Van Hoorickx, is now available in the NSA. There is a surviving sketch for this song that shares a page with the first version of *Lied (Ins stille Land)* D403.

Like *Trockne Blumen* from *Die schöne Müllerin* this poem by Salis-Seewis is what Dürr refers to as a 'Tumba Gedicht' where the beloved calls out from his place of burial with a final message for the beloved. There are five strophes of which 1, 2, 4 and 5 were recorded for the Hyperion Edition and translated here. The third strophe beginning 'Freundin! wankt, im Abendwinde' would be suitable for performance by a male singer. In the NSA, however, only the first three strophes are printed.

Autographs:	Staatsbibliothek Preussischer Kulturbesitz, Berlin (first draft, first version)
	Wienbibliothek im Rathaus, Vienna (fair copy, first version)
	In private possession in Switzerland (Therese Grob songbook; second version)
Publication:	First published as part of the AGA in 1895 (P629; first version)
	First published as part of the NSA in 2002 (P832; second version)
Subsequent editions:	Not in Peters; AGA XX 202: Vol. 4/68 (first version); NSA IV: Vol. 10/120 (first version) & 121 (second version)
Further settings:	Johann Vesque von Püttlingen (1803–1883) *Der Herbstabend* Op. 8 no. 2 (1831)
Discography and timing:	Fischer-Dieskau I 6[25] 1'37 (first two strophes only)
	Hyperion I 17[5]
	Hyperion II 13[22] 2'45 Lucia Popp

← *Sprache der Liebe* D410   *Daphne am Bach* D411 →

HERBSTLIED   Autumn song
(SALIS-SEEWIS) **D502** [H321]
G major   November 1816

(20 bars)

Bunt sind schon die Wälder,	The woods are already brightly coloured,
Gelb die Stoppelfelder,	The fields of stubble yellow,
Und der Herbst beginnt.	And autumn is here.
Rote Blätter fallen,	Red leaves fall,
Graue Nebel wallen,	Grey mists surge,
Kühler weht der Wind.	The wind blows colder.
Wie die volle Traube	How purple shines
Aus dem Rebenlaube	The plump grape
Purpurfarbig strahlt!	From the vine leaves!
Am Geländer reifen	On the espalier
Pfirsiche mit Streifen	Peaches ripen
Rot und weiss bemalt.	Painted with red and white streaks.

Sieh, wie hier die Dirne	Look how busily the maiden here
Emsig Pflaum' und Birne	Gathers plums and pears
In ihr Körbchen legt;	In her basket;
Dort, mit leichten Schritten	Look how that one there,
Jene goldne Quitten	With light steps,
In den Landhof trägt!	Carries golden quinces to the house.
Flinke Träger springen,	The lads dance nimbly
Und die Mädchen singen,	And the girls sing;
Alles jubelt froh!	All shout for joy.
Bunte Bänder schweben	Amid the tall vines
Zwischen hohen Reben	Coloured ribbons flutter
Auf dem Hut von Stroh.	On hats of straw.
Geige tönt und Flöte	Fiddles and flutes play
Bei der Abendröte	In the glow of the evening
Und im Morgenglanz;	And by the moon's light
Junge Winzerinnen	The girls who gather grapes
Winken und beginnen	Wave, and begin
Deutschen Ringeltanz.	A German round-dance.

JOHANN GAUDENZ VON SALIS-SEEWIS (1762–1834); poem written in 1782

This is the eleventh of Schubert's thirteen Salis-Seewis solo settings (1816–?21). See the poet's biography for a chronological list of all the Salis-Seewis settings.

This simple little song has a charm and strength of its own; indeed of all those relatively unknown Salis-Seewis miniatures it has an increasingly secure place on the concert platform (if it had been printed in the Peters Edition it would already have been much better known). The music is in $\frac{2}{4}$ with those mezzo staccato quavers in the accompaniment that are associated with much greater songs (*Gute Nacht* and *Der Wegweiser* from *Winterreise*) from Schubert's maturity. Like those works there is something ambulatory about *Herbstlied*; it is a little too casual perhaps to be a march (it may be sung by harvesters or fruit pickers as they saunter off to work) but the simplicity of the writing also suggests a chorale as if these workers may break into four-part harmony. The hearty country folk reflected in this music are upstanding, hard-working and religious; there was always a side of Schubert that took delight in the activities of the common people, and his down-to-earth style, a little comically rough, recalls Shakespeare's way with some of his porters, clowns and mechanicals. In mood and subject matter this music is related to the Hölty *Erntelied* D434 from May 1816. Like the Claudius setting *An die Nachtigall* D497 it is a G major song that is launched from the subdominant. The sequences are delightfully effective: two upward phrases at the beginning (bb. 1–4) describe the brightly coloured woods, and two falling phrases (bb. 9–12) the tumbling leaves and the mist. This may seem obvious enough in terms of word painting, but how many real folksongs (and this truly has the air of one) would show feeling for such detail? Note how the word 'Wind' at the end of the first verse sweeps upwards in melisma (b. 16), and 'Kühler' (b. 17) wafts downwards from an E minor chord, nicely suggesting an autumn chill in the air. This is Schubert at his best in 1816: music in unpretentious garb encompassing astonishing mastery. Once heard in a fine performance this *Herbstlied* is never forgotten.

Of the five strophes of the poem by Salis-Seewis, 1, 2, 3 and 4 were recorded for the Hyperion Edition. It has pride of place in the poet's *Gedichte*, printed at the beginning of the collection.

Autograph: Missing or lost
First edition: Published as No. 24 of *Neueste Folge nachgelassener Lieder und
                        Gesänge* by J. P. Gotthard, Vienna in 1872 (P450)
Subsequent editions: Not in Peters; AGA XX 282: Vol. 4/248; NSA IV: Vol. 11/48
Arrangements: Arr. Tilman Hoppstock (b. 1961) for guitar accompaniment, in
                        Franz Schubert: 110 Lieder (2009)
Discography and timing: Fischer-Dieskau I 9[1]   1'26
                        Hyperion I 17[21]
                        Hyperion II 16[25]   1'47   Lucia Popp

← *Am Bach im Frühlinge* D361   *Mailied* D503 →

Die HERBSTNACHT

Autumn night

(SALIS-SEEWIS) **D404** [H242]

The song exists in two versions, the second of which is discussed below:
(1) March 1816; (2) April 1816

(1)   No tempo indication   F major   **C**   [16 bars]

(2)   F major

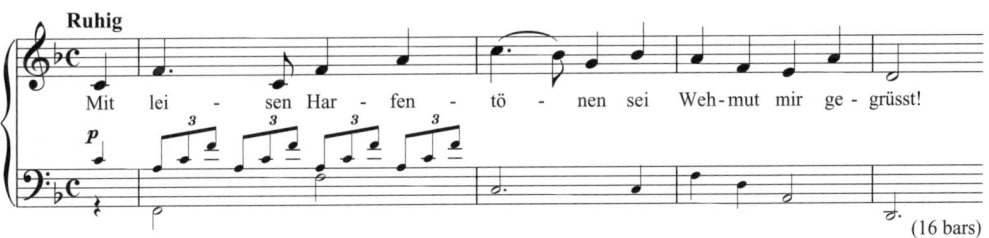

Mit leisen Harfentönen	To the soft strains of a harp
Sei, Wehmut, mir gegrüsst!	I greet you, Melancholy!
O Nymphe, die der Tränen	O nymph, you who lock
Geweihten Quell verschliesst!	The hallowed source of tears,
Mich weht an deiner Schwelle	On your threshold.
Ein linder Schauer an,	I feel a gentle shudder,
Und deines Zwielichts Helle	And your dusky light
Glimmt auf des Schicksals Bahn.	Glimmers on the path of destiny.

[...4...]   [...4...]

Der Leidenschaften Horden,   Thronging passions,
Der Sorgen Rabenzug,   Black, teeming cares
Entfliehn vor den Akkorden,   Disperse at the chords

Die deine Harfe schlug;	From your harp.
Du zauberst Alpensöhnen,	For the sons of the mountains,
Verbannt auf Flanderns Moor,	Banished to Flanders' plains,
Mit Sennenreigentönen	You conjure images of home
Der Heimat Bilder vor.	With strains of Alpine dances.
In deinen Schattenhallen	In your shadowy groves
Weihst du die Sänger ein;	You reveal your secret to singers;
Lehrst junge Nachtigallen	You teach young nightingales
Die Trauer-melodei'n;	Their sorrowful melodies;
Du neigst, wo Gräber grünen,	Where graves grow green
Dein Ohr zu Hölty's Ton;	You bend your ear to Hölty's song;
Pflückst Moos von Burgruinen	And with my Matthisson
Mit meinem Matthisson.	You gather moss from castle ruins.
[. . .]	[. . .]

JOHANN GAUDENZ VON SALIS-SEEWIS (1762–1834); poem written in 1794/8

*This is the eighth of Schubert's thirteen Salis-Seewis solo settings (1816–?1821). See the poet's
biography for a chronological list of all the Salis-Seewis settings.*

The poet's title was *Die Wehmut* – 'Melancholy' (as we find it listed in AGA) but Schubert's own title is *Die Herbstnacht* – actually the title of another Salis-Seewis lyric. One may think, looking at the poem, that *Die Wehmut* would be more suitable for a text where autumn is merely a backdrop to an ode to Melancholy, but Schubert interprets 'Wehmut' in this case as something much lighter than despair, an emotional cloud that can be painted well enough in tiny minor-key departures from the major tonality. The shape of the vocal line, built on the tonic triad, is very reminiscent of *Die Einsiedelei* D393; it is as if the composer is consciously trying to create a style of folksong appropriate to this particular poet. Even if the music on its single page is not as memorable as that of *Der Herbstabend* (in the same key of F minor, and also with triplet accompaniment) there are a number of characteristic delicious harmonic touches in response to tiny fluctuations in the text's mood. A small example is the setting of 'Wehmut' in the poem's first line; in the context of a tune in the major key, the second syllable of that one sad word is effortlessly limned in the minor without disturbing the generally genial equilibrium of the whole. A similar effect comes at the end of the first verse when 'auf des Schicksals Bahn' (b. 15) gently touches the minor as a warning as to what fate might have in store for us. Also typically Schubertian is the switch from F major into A flat major at the phrase 'der Thränen / Geweihten Quell verschliesst!' (bb. 5–8). Capell cites this particular key-shift as evidence of the composer's 'gift of musical epigram'. It certainly helps to suggest the opening of a door onto a new threshold of experience as the nymph is directly addressed.

The NSA prints two versions of the song, the first from March 1816, the second from April. The second has a tempo marking of 'Ruhig' and several dynamic markings not in the first; there are also a few musical differences (the bass of b. 9, for example). The performer would be justi-fied in taking the 'Zweite Fassung' (NSA Volume 10 p. 118) as the composer's final thoughts.

The poem by Salis-Seewis has eight strophes. The sixth of these refers to Swiss soldiers under General Theodor von Reding who fought with great valour in Flanders under the Spanish flag during the Napoleonic wars. For the Hyperion recording were chosen 1, 6 and 7, the last because it seemed indicative of the generous nature of the poet for him to have saluted two fellow-writers, Hölty and Matthisson, alongside imaginary 'young nightingales'.

Autographs:	Curtis Institute, Philadelphia (first draft)
	Wienbibliothek im Rathaus, Vienna (fair copy)
Publication:	First published by C. A. Spina, Vienna in 1860, although no copies of this publication seem to have survived. It then appeared as Vol. 7 no. 4 in Friedlaender's edition by Peters, Leipzig in 1885 under the title *Die Wehmut* (P394; first version)
	First published as part of the NSA in 2002 (P831; second version)
Subsequent editions:	Peters: Vol. 7/12; AGA XX 200: Vol. 4/64 (first version); NSA IV: Vol. 10/116 (first version) & 118 (second version)
Discography and timing:	Fischer-Dieskau I 6²³ 2'02
	Hyperion I 17⁷
	Hyperion II 13¹⁶ 2'26 Lucia Popp

← *Abschied von der Harfe* D406   *Lebensmelodien* D395 →

JOHANN GOTTFRIED HERDER (1744–1803)

THE POETIC SOURCES

S1   *Zerstreute Blätter von J. G. Herder*, Zweite Sammlung. Zweite vebesserte Ausgabe, Gotha, 1796 bey Carl Wilhelm Ettinger

S2   *Von deutscher Art und Kunst.* Einige fliegende Blätter, Hamburg, Bode, 1773

THE SONGS

4 May 1813   *Verklärung* D59 [S1: pp. 387–8: The song is taken from Part V of of S1: *Wie die Alten den Tod gebildet? Ein Nachtrag zu Lessings Abhandlung desselben Titels und Inhalts* (How did the Ancients depict death? An appendix to Lessing's treatise of the same title and content). The title of the translation is *Popes sterbende Christ an seine Seele* (Pope's 'The Dying Christian to his soul'). Herder's translation had been printed in London (Corr and Dussek, 1787) side by side with Pope's original.]

September 1827   *Eine altschottische Ballade* D923 [S2: pp. 25–7: This translation was made from *Percy's Reliques* (qv Percy). In the Herder source it is to be found in the first section entitled 'Auszug aus einem Briefwechsel über Ossian und die Lieder alter Völker (Excerpt from a correspondence concerning Ossian and the songs of the ancients).]

Herder, one of the giant intellects of eighteenth-century German literature, was born on 25 August 1744 in Mohrungen in East Prussia. In his student years at Königsberg University he was acquainted with Immanuel Kant as well as J. G. Hamann. At the age of twenty he moved to Riga where he taught as well as preached at the cathedral. From early on it was clear that his genius lay in commenting on the thoughts of others through the medium of literary criticism as a means of airing his own ideas – as in his commentaries on Winckelmann and Lessing's *Laokoon*. A devotee of the writing of J. J. Rousseau, Herder went to France in 1769 but was lured back to Germany by the offer of an appointment as tutor to a prince of Holstein-Eutin. It was at this time that he met Claudius and Lessing. In

J. G. Herder from a painting by J. F. A. Tischbein.

folksong – the *Stimmen der Völker in Liedern* (1778–9) was to have an enormous influence in this field for decades to come. Several of these texts were set by Brahms some eighty years later, including his riveting duet using *Edward* – the same poem also set by Loewe and by Schubert for his *Eine altschottische Ballade* D923, and which had found itself a home in *Stimmen der Völker* instead of, *Von deutscher Art und Kunst*. Also written in Weimar was Herder's enormously influential *Ideen zur Philosophie der Geschichte der Menschheit* (1784–91).

After an unsuccessful trip to Italy (he felt little of the country's profound humanizing powers as experienced by the far more intuitive Goethe), Herder turned his attention to political reflections (the French Revolution inspired *Briefe zur Beförderung der Humanität*) and theological writings. With a reputation for being touchy at the best of times, he became ever more unsettled and argumentative in later years, falling out with the Duke of Weimar as well as Goethe himself whose increasingly close friendship with Schiller alienated Herder. He continued to write and translate, often espousing the opinion that his translations of folksong and foreign literature were far more noteworthy than the originals. He died on 18 December 1803.

Darmstadt (where he found himself with his charge as part of a three-year tour) he met Caroline Flachsland whom he married. An extended stay in Strasbourg for medical reasons (Herder suffered from extremely poor eyesight) dissolved the contract with his aristocratic employer and brought him into contact with the young Goethe who was studying there. It was Herder who introduced Goethe to Shakespeare, one of his enthusiasms (others were the Bible, Homer and Ossian). The essays of *Von deutscher Art und Kunst* (*see* S2 above) were largely the work of Goethe and Herder in collaboration.

In 1776 Herder moved to Weimar at Goethe's invitation. He lived there happily and productively for twelve years; particularly fruitful in this period was his research into

Herder's powerful mind and eloquent writing were to change and influence many aspects of German thought. He encouraged his colleagues to embrace a concept of world literature and to show respect for the achievements of other cultures. This is still a characteristic of Germany today where there is a strong tradition of translation from many languages, and an open-minded welcome among the reading public for the work of writers from other countries and cultures. It is significant that Herder's two contributions to the Schubert song canon were both translations from English.

HERMANN UND THUSNELDA
(KLOPSTOCK) **D322** [H201]

Hermann and Thusnelda 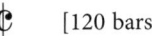   Duet

The song exists in two versions, the second of which is discussed below:
(1) 27 October 1815; (2) Spring 1816(?)

(1) 'Mit Majestät'   E flat major – B flat major   ¢   [120 bars]

(2) E flat major – B flat major

(138 bars)

Thusnelda:
Ha, dort kömmt er, mit Schweiss, mit
    Römerblut,
Mit dem Staube der Schlacht bedeckt!
    So schön war
    Hermann niemals! So hat's ihm
        Nie von dem Auge geflammt.
Komm, o komm, ich bebe vor Lust, reich'
    mir den Adler
Und das triefende Schwert! Komm,
    athm' und ruh'
    Hier aus in meiner Umarmung
        Von der zu schrecklichen Schlacht.
Ruh' hier, dass ich den Schweiss von der
    Stirn' abtrockne
Und der Wange das Blut! Wie glüht
    die Wange!
    Hermann, Hermann, so hat dich
        Niemals Thusnelda geliebt!
Selbst nicht, als du zuerst im Eichenschatten
Mit dem bräunlichen Arm mich wilder
    umfasstest!
    Fliehend blieb ich und sah dir
        Schon die Unsterblichkeit an,
Die nun dein ist! Erzählt's in allen Hainen,
Dass Augustus nun bang' mit seinen Göttern
    Nektar trinket! Erzählt es in allen Hainen,
        Dass Hermann unsterblicher ist!

Hermann:
Warum lockst du mein Haar? Liegt nicht
    der stumme

Thusnelda:
Ah, there he comes, covered with sweat, with
    Roman blood,
And with the dust of battle.
    Never was Hermann
    so fair!
        Never did his eyes flame so!
Come! I tremble with desire! Hand me the eagle

And the dripping sword! Come, breathe
    and rest here
    In my embrace
        From the dread battle.
Rest here that I may wipe the sweat from
    your brow
And the blood from your cheeks! How your
    cheeks glow!
    Hermann! Hermann! Never has Thusnelda
        Loved you so!
Not even when in the shade of the oak tree
Your swarthy arms first embraced me wildly!

    As I fled I remained there, already
        Glimpsing the immortality
Which is now yours! Proclaim it in every grove
That Augustus is now uneasy as he drinks
    Nectar with his gods! That Hermann
        Is more immortal than he!

Hermann:
Why do you coil my hair? Does not
    my father

Tote Vater vor uns? O, hätt' Augustus	Lie dead and silent before us! Oh, if only
Seine Heere geführt, er	Augustus had led his armies, he would be
	lying there
Läge noch blutiger da!	Still more bloodied!
Thusnelda:	*Thusnelda:*
Lass dein sinkendes Haar mich,	Let me gather up your lank hair, Hermann,
Hermann, heben,	
Dass es über dem Kranz in Locken drohe!	That it may fall in menacing locks over the laurel
	wreath!
Siegmar ist bei den Göttern!	Siegmar is with the gods!
Folge du, und wein' ihm nicht nach!	You shall be his successor, and not mourn him!

FRIEDRICH GOTTLOB KLOPSTOCK (1724–1803); poem written in spring 1752

Hermann und Thusnelda is a musical dialogue between two characters who never sing
simultaneously (a performance for a single singer taking both male and female roles is thus a
possibility). This duet is accordingly listed here as the ninth of Schubert's thirteen Klopstock solo
settings (1815–16) rather than as an ensemble. See the poet's biography for a chronological list
of all the Klopstock settings.

Klopstock was one of the precursors of German nationalism. That Schubert should have chosen
to set this poem which was over sixty years old (it was written in 1752) is surely indicative of
the nationalist feeling that swept German-speaking lands in the wake of Napoleon's final defeat
at Waterloo. Too short and short-sighted for military service, the composer was no doubt
surrounded by the nationalistic enthusiasms of his young contemporaries, the former students
of the Imperial Konvikt to whom he played much of his new work and who made up the core
of his first spellbound audiences. Schubert would have known this poem from his early teens:
it was printed in the second volume of *Sammlung Deutscher Beyspiele zur Bildung des Styls*, a
school textbook of the time which the young composer used as a source for three or four of his
earliest settings. Perhaps he had also read the epic stage work by Klopstock, *Hermanns Schlacht*,
in which this theme is broadened, extended and developed to infinitely more subtle effect; that
work appears at the end of double-volume 7–8 of *Klopstocks Werke* (1804) which must have
been in the composer's hands when he set the two Klopstock choruses, *Nun lasst uns den Leib
begraben* D168 and *Jesus Christus unser Heiland* D168A.

    The appeal of the poem to young patriots is obvious. It imagines the jubilant aftermath of the
so-called *Hermannschlacht*, the battle in AD 9 during the reign of the Emperor Augustus, in which
the legions of the Roman general Quintillius Varus were defeated by Arminius who was also
known as 'Hermann der Cherusker' (Chief of the Cherussi). The continuing significance of this
event was indicated by the considerable celebrations in Germany in 2009 for its two thousandth
anniversary – German patriotism free of its twentieth-century connotations. Hermann had
fought for a time in the Roman army but on his return to his homeland led a revolt that culminated in a battle in the Teutoburg Forest in which the Roman occupiers were annihilated. This
was the first famous victory of the German 'race' against a foreign invader. 'If we could beat them
then we can beat them now' is the message that young men in 1815 would derive from the tale.
Hermann survived a later defeat by Germanicus (although his wife Thusnelda was taken to Rome
in captivity) and continued to rule until his assassination in AD 21. His exploits were celebrated
by German writers (Ulrich von Hutten and Daniel von Lohenstein) in the sixteenth and seventeenth centuries, and the middle of the eighteenth century saw a real revival of interest in this

historical episode thanks to a play by J. E. Schlegel (uncle of August and Friedrich), and above all to Klopstock who penned not only this poem but also a trilogy of plays dealing with different episodes in the life of Arminius. Goethe's gifted friend Angelika Kauffmann (born in Schwarzen-berg in the Vorarlberg, now an important centre of Schubertian performance) painted an imposing canvas of Hermann being greeted and crowned by Thusnelda and surrounded by flower-throwing maidens and the trophies of his victory against the Romans (*Hermann von Thusnelda gekrönt*, 1785). For many years this canvas was in the Kunsthistorisches Museum in Vienna from where it was removed, on Hitler's orders, in 1944 and hung in the Reichskanzlei – evidence enough of its potent subject matter in terms of German military history. The painting was destroyed by fire in 1945 – a symbolic reminder perhaps that Thusnelda's jingoistic joy was short lived, and that she was later to be vanquished and captured by the Roman enemy. The painting survives now only in a smaller preparatory oil and prints.

Schubert's setting comes between *Die Hermannschlacht*, a play written by Kleist in 1809 (bitterly critical, by historical analogy, of the squabbling Prussian and Austrian factions who failed to unite in time against Napoleon) and de la Motte Fouqué's play *Hermann* written in 1818. Such writers as C. D. Grabbe and Otto Ludwig continued to embroider the Hermann theme until the middle of the nineteenth century. It is sometimes suggested that the sixteen-year-old Schubert was the author of the text for his *Auf den Sieg der Deutschen* D81 (qv), a miniature paean to the allied victory over Napoleon, for voice and accompaniment of string trio, composed in 1813. If this is indeed the case, the young Austrian was content to write of himself as one of the 'Deutsche', and to regard himself in the poem's second verse as one of noble Hermann's sons who had risked being gobbled up by the French hyena.

Hermann and Thusnelda opens with a twenty-seven-bar prelude, a triumphal march for the victor of the battle in the Teutoburger Wald. The ceremonial key of E flat is used, which the composer seems to favour for pagan or Ossianic ritual. Dotted rhythms and triplet semiquavers suggest trumpets and drums. An adventurous shift to C flat major (b. 15) introduces a surging quaver figuration that depicts an overflowing of joy on the part of the onlookers, Hermann's wife Thusnelda among them. In the earlier setting by Christian Gottlob Neefe (1748–1798), the whole of the poem (with the exception of Strophe 6) is a military march, but as usual Schubert has something more elaborate in mind.

The vocal line opens with an unaccompanied and free recitative for Thusnelda (from b. 28), punctuated by fragments of the march tune as if

Engraving of Hermann by H. C. Müller (*Frauentaschenbuch*, 1820).

offstage. It is hardly easy for a singer to start a song with an explosive 'Ha', but it gives us an idea of Thusnelda's character. We experience her bloodthirsty enjoyment of all the evidence of carnage and her seeming indifference to the death of Hermann's father; she also admits to feeling more attracted than ever to Hermann in his bloodstained state. This gruesome model of the ideal German heroine is probably derived from the stories of the women of Sparta who preferred their loved ones to return dead on their shields rather than alive and defeated.

At b. 43 Thusnelda's outpourings become more lyrical, and the composer employs arioso (marked *Im Takte* – 'In time') which has the melodic curves of aria while retaining the function and feeling of recitative. At 'Komm, o komm, ich bebe vor Lust' we are still in the home key of E flat as flowing quavers, tremblings of pleasure that seem to jump off the page, underpin the vocal line, while right-hand crotchets echo the singer's words. At 'Ruh' hier, dass ich den Schweiss von der Stirn' abtrockne' there is a change of key signature to A flat. This rather more gentle section is in ⅜ and marked *Nicht zu langsam*; the rippling semiquavers set up an expectation of an aria that is never fulfilled. The restful tenderness of 'Ruh' hier' lasts only for a few lines. The accents in the piano's left hand (bb. 61 and 62), phrased away in crotchets, perfectly depict the act of gently wiping the hero's forehead. After six relaxed and tender bars (bb. 61–6) the music again becomes agitated and opens out into a veritable paean of passionate adoration. This reaches its climax as it veers into an elaborate cadence in G flat for 'so hat dich / Niemals Thusnelda geliebt!' (bb. 72–6). Sweeping sextuplets and stentorian basses remind us that Schubert's most recent Klopstock setting had been *Dem Unendlichen*

Engraving of Thusnelda by H. C. Müller (*Frauentaschenbuch*, 1820).

D291, very different in its religious viewpoint, of course, but similar in grandeur and scale. Thusnelda's wild enjoyment of Hermann's bloody exploits to the point of erotic excitement is conveyed with pulsating demisemiquavers added to the accompaniment under 'Wie glüht die Wange!' bb. 68–9. The enthusiasm of this, if not the actual music, puts us in mind of the Wilde/Strauss Salome as she contemplates the beauties of Jokanaan's severed head.

At b. 77 we return to recitative for a brief resumé of the couple's earlier courtship (if so it may be called), another part of the Arminius story altogether and also famous in German legend. Hermann had carried off Thusnelda as his bride in a famous 'Entführung'. She here admits that she went with him willingly, having glimpsed his future greatness. The transformation between *then* and *now* is conveyed by the long note on 'Die nun dein ist' accompanied by staccato chords (bb. 81–2). The seal of immortality is the florid setting of 'dein', ornamented in the voice and accompanied by a mighty A flat[7] chord (b. 84). We are certainly in the presence of a formidable character from German folklore, a precursor of Wagner's Ortrud or the Valkyries.

At b. 84 there is a change of metre (to triple time) and a change of key (D flat major). The marking is *Etwas langsam, mit heiligem Jubel* (rather slowly with sacred exultation). Once again we are denied a real aria in favour of arioso. The accompaniment, one of the composer's most distinguished ostinato inspirations, was recycled ten years later as the basis for Ellen's first song (*Ellens erster Gesang*) from *The Lady of the Lake* settings, D837. In that remarkable rondo the king of Scotland, disguised as a hunter, is serenaded to the words 'Raste Krieger, Krieg ist aus'. The accompaniment is there marked piano and seems expressive of a faraway battle or even distant elfin horns in an enchanted forest. Here the writing is forte, but the theme in common for the two works is the majesty of kings in ancient realms and the role of their women in administering post-battle comforts. It was unusual for the composer at the height of his maturity in 1825 to lift an idea intact from earlier work, but it is not surprising given this motif's buoyancy and happy combination of pomp and tenderness. Needless to say the beautiful counter-melody that Schubert invents for Ellen is far superior to Thusnelda's vocal line.

After this set piece for Thusnelda, Hermann himself speaks at last – with some impatience, certainly without the heroic distinction that we might have expected from the build-up given him by his wife. His recitative (from b. 112) is short and to the point, and eminently believable as the words of someone weary from battle and who has witnessed the slaughter of his father. He would naturally have preferred to do battle with Augustus himself than with Varus. He has the least to say of all the male heroes in this conversational form of two-voiced dialogue (the other settings in this vein are *Antigone und Oedip* D542, *Hektors Abschied* D312 and *Shilrik und Vinvela* D293). Schubert favoured this form invented by the North German ballad composers over the conventional (and more Italian) duet form where the singers' voices intertwine.

Undaunted by Hermann's negative feelings, Thusnelda embarks on the song's final section, marked *Mässig langsam, mit hoher Würde* ('Moderately slow with great dignity'). Here the key is B flat (from b. 121) and, as in many of the Schubert ballads, there is no attempt to return to the tonality of the opening. The accompaniment is formed from another ostinato based on a proud, almost dance-like rhythm. The most exceptional moment here is the musical depiction of the ascent of Siegmar (Hermann's slain father) into Valhalla. The phrase 'Siegmar ist bei den Göttern!' (b. 129) begins on a B flat and rises chromatically to D flat whereby the accompaniment underneath 'Göttern' (b. 130) engineers a modulation to G flat major. The final phrases ('Folge du') are imperious and built on descending B flat major arpeggios in the voice, although a touch of compassion is allowed (despite Thusnelda's hard-hearted injunctions *not* to weep) in the plaintive chromatics of 'wein' ihm nicht'. The piano postlude of two and a half rather peremptory bars is an echo of this vocal line. Unfortunately in both the poem and its setting the valiant Hermann comes across as something of a henpecked husband.

'Ludicrous' is how Fischer-Dieskau describes the song; 'Hardly interesting' says Capell; 'It leads nowhere' says Reed. On balance, the piece deserves a little better than these verdicts that have been influenced, one feels, by distaste for the poem's jingoistic subject matter. Nothing in this *scena* stretches belief any more than some of Wagner's scenarios, and Schubert has the advantage of brevity (even by his own ballad standards). In Thusnelda he created a larger-than-life Amazonian character, infinitely more formidable than Hermann and loosely based on history – her strength of purpose and independence of spirit admirable, her bloodthirsty nature less so. Had she been allowed to take part in the battle herself one feels that the Romans would have been even more soundly beaten. It is clear that the song can only achieve relative success if sung by a magnificently voiced Thusnelda, while the 'role' of Hermann can be sung by a less exceptional singer.

The NSA prints two versions. The second, from 1816, is an expanded revision of the 1815 first draft (twenty-seven bars of introduction rather than eight). The more elaborate second version was published in the *Nachlass* and subsequently in the Peters Edition.

Autographs:	Wienbibliothek im Rathaus, Vienna (first version)
	Pierpont Morgan Library, New York (second version)
Publication:	Published as Book 28 no. 1 of the *Nachlass* by Diabelli, Vienna in
	1837 (P315) (second version) and in Vol. 9 of the NSA (first version)
Subsequent editions:	Peters: Vol. 5/154; AGA XX 169: Vol. 3/159; NSA IV: Vol. 9/185
	(first version) & 191 (second version)
Further settings:	Christian Gottlob Neefe (1748–1798) *Hermann und Thusnelda*,
	no. 4 of *Oden von Klopstock mit Melodien* (1776)

Discography and timing:

Deutsche Grammophon	5'25	Janet Baker & Dietrich
Schubert Duette		Fischer-Dieskau
Hyperion I 22²³	5'30	Lorna Anderson & Simon
Hyperion II 11¹³		Keenlyside

← *Mignon (Kennst du das Land?)* D321   *Erlkönig* D328 (trio version) →

HERRN JOSEF SPAUN, ASSESSOR IN LINZ

(M. von Collin) **D749** [H482]
F minor – C minor   January 1822

To Mr Josef von Spaun,
taxman in Linz

(108 bars)

Recitativo	*Recitative*
Und nimmer schreibst du?	And do you never write?
Bleibest uns verloren,	Are you lost to us
Ein starr Verstummter,	For all time,
Nun für ew'ge Zeit?	Struck dumb?
Vielleicht, weil neue Freunde du erkoren?	Perhaps because you have found new friends?
Wardst du Assessor denn am Tisch so breit,	Or have you become a taxman, sitting at a vast desk,
Woran beim Aktenstoss seufzt Langeweile,	Sighing with boredom at your heap of files,
Um abzusterben aller Freudigkeit?	In order to forgo all joy?
Doch nein, nur wir sind's.	Of course not, it's just us.
Nur uns ward zuteile	Only we have been granted
Dies Schweigen, dies Verstummen und Vergessen.	This silence, this muteness, this forgetfulness.
Armut und Not selbst an der kleinsten Zeile!	There is a dire lack of even the smallest line.
Für jeden bist du schriftkarg nicht gesessen;	Not for everyone have you been miserly with your pen;

Für manchen kamen Briefe angeflogen,	Letters have streamed in, for many,
Und nach der Elle hast du sie gemessen;	And you have surely measured them by the yard.
Doch uns, Barbar, hast du dein Herz entzogen!	But from us, barbarian, you have withdrawn your heart!

Aria	*Aria*
Schwingt euch kühn, zu bange Klagen,	Anxious plaints, soar boldly
Aus empörter Brust hervor,	From our incensed hearts
Und, von Melodien getragen,	And, borne aloft by melodies,
Wagt euch an des Fernen Ohr!	Dare to approach his distant ear.
Was er immer mag erwidern,	Whatever he may retort
Dieses hier saget doch:	Tell him this:
'Zwar vergessen, jenes Biedern	'Though we are forgotten,
Denken wir in Liebe noch!'	We still think lovingly of the good fellow!'

MATTHÄUS VON COLLIN (1779–1824); poem written in January 1822

This the second of Schubert's five Matthäus von Collin settings (1816 and 1822–3). See the poet's biography for a chronological list of all the Matthäus von Collin settings.

This piece preserves something of the pranks and camaraderie of the Schubert circle in a unique way. Josef von Spaun, Schubert's oldest and most faithful friend, had been named assessor with the Excise Revenue Office of Upper Austria at its headquarters in Linz on 23 September 1821. Spaun packed up his belongings, left Vienna and was undoubtedly preoccupied with settling in to his new home in the late autumn of that year. Schubert wrote to him on 2 November, Schober on 4 November, but neither received a reply. Matthäus von Collin, Spaun's cousin (who was perhaps also an unanswered correspondent) then wrote a poem addressed to Spaun that was designed to tease him into making contact with his old friends who were anxious to discover how he was getting on. It is surely likely that Collin wrote the letter specifically for Schubert to set to music and, in the light of the craze for Italian music in Vienna at the time, almost certainly conceived it as a libretto for an aria of tragic betrayal in the dramatic manner. This gave Schubert the ideal opportunity to imitate the style of Italian opera, or at least Italian-influenced opera seria. The result is that very rare thing in Schubert's output – a piece of music with humorous intent. The small manuscript of the song, exquisitely penned, seems once to have been folded and sent through the post. There is no record of the addressee's reply to these imprecations.

Schubert lacked the malicious wit and cynicism to write a biting parody or even a genuine comic song (how easily this came to the mordant sensibilities of Hugo Wolf). Perhaps Capell is right when he says that the composer possessed nothing nearer to humour than good humour, and perhaps this lack of worldly wit and opportunism was his Achilles heel when it came to success in the opera house. Schubert loved music almost too much to joke about it; sarcasm and loathing, the trademarks of the real parodist, were foreign to him. In the month that this piece was written, the main musical talking point in Vienna was the takeover of the Kärntnertortheater by the Italian impresario Domenico Barbaia. The consequent ascendancy of Italian opera thus ruined Schubert's hopes of success in the opera house; German opera was a dead duck in this period. The singer Vogl had resigned from the Court Opera and many of Schubert's friends were dismissed by the new regime. If there is any real anger in this music it is not directed at Spaun or Rossini but at the unfair turn of events. The pastiche, so good in its own right, gives the impression that Schubert the chameleon has temporarily changed his national colours, paying genuine homage (with an affectionate smile) to the flair and vigour of music from the south.

The song, with the marking 'Allegro furioso', opens with an impassioned recitative. The key signature betokens F minor but the naked ear would never be able to discern the tonality through all the chromatic writhings and permutations. Scrambling semiquavers, an octave apart in the hands, rise crab-like up the keyboard and punching staccato quavers launch the voice in its mock-accusatory question, 'And do you never write?' For the purposes of the musical joke the pose is that of jealous lover confronting treachery. This pattern is repeated in a higher pitch in bb. 3–4 with the voice plunging dramatically down an octave into the chest register for 'ew'ge Zeit' b. 6. The belligerence of the pianistic writing continues unabated; via a descending D flat^7 figuration in semiquavers the music moves into F sharp minor for the wounded, quasi-jealous observations regarding new friends. The vocal line is deliberately turned into a feast of appoggiaturas that squeeze the harmonies relentlessly. A shift into D minor (b. 10) and thence E^7 (b. 11, ornamented by more scrambling semiquavers) prepares the way for an A minor portrait of Spaun (from b. 12) with a pile of tax files. Spaun's table is so broad, and his work as a tax assessor so boring, that the harmony does not change for three bars. At b. 16 the vocal line and sighing harmonies are illustrative of the yawns of a civil servant chained to his desk. After a remarkably convoluted bar of chromatic harmony (b. 21) we return to the discombobulated semiquavers of the song's opening (Tempo I, b. 22). The purpose of these is to launch music less of anger than of pathetic self-pity. It is no surprise that the most peaceful passage so far has been 'Dies Schweigen, dies Verstummen und Vergessen' where the piano is content simply to hold an A minor chord. The soothing Andantino section (from b. 28) in undulating thirds and sixths seems ideal for a mad scene where the heroine, caught up in the tragedy of her situation, can only murmur a few words at a time. The sequence of modulations at the next 'A tempo' (from b. 36) sounds curiously like a recording that is gradually speeded up. This is perhaps the most subtle of Schubert's comic effects in the piece. At the same time, feelings purportedly hurt by Spaun's cruel disregard of his friends are made to reach a climax in a high C on the word 'Barbar' and a cadenza on a descending chromatic scale, the final result of this breathless wind-up. With this accusatory flourish we are are ready for the aria.

The key changes to C minor. If one thinks of the fury of the first movement Allegro of Beethoven's Sonata Op. 111 in the same key which it resembles, it is curious to realize that this music was being written at the same time. In bb. 47–9 Schubert has a keen eye and ear for the commonplaces of such set-piece operatic introductions. The vocal line from b. 50, with its widely spaced arpeggios up the stave (note the leaps in bb. 54–5 at 'Schwingt euch kühn, zu bange Klagen'), is deliberately over the top. In this context the sheer banality of the little interlude for piano that will deliver us into the relative major (from b. 62) is breathtaking. Another great composer who has mocked the clichés of Italian opera in this way is Benjamin Britten in the final act of *A Midsummer Night's Dream*. And yet Schubert does not dare (or wish) to make his music truly as bad as some he must have heard under the heading of Italian opera. Once this aria gets under way it is so effective that it is easy to forget that the intention is to make fun. Of course, it needs a marvellous singer to achieve its full effect – one able to deal with the triplet coloratura of bb. 94–6, and the slew of semiquavers starting on a high C at bb. 100 and 101 – and with such a singer even the 'ridiculous' last page of the piece with its senselessly repeated words (and these in tessituras where no words can be heard) is almost certain to reap the enthusiastic applause of the audience. This is often the case with Italian music generally – the pyrotechnics of the performer can make us forget the composer's limitations. The result here is a piece of music designed to be ridiculous, but the sheer accomplishment needed to sing it well and present it to the public (high Cs and all) will always be admired and applauded in a way that will inevitably undermine intentions of parody. The text remains somewhat exaggerated and silly (as Collin intended), but since when did a silly text prevent an Italian aria from becoming part of the repertoire?

The Peters Edition gives the version (under the title *Epistel, Musikalischer Schwank*) that was printed by Diabelli in Volume 46 of the *Nachlass*. This cuts bb. 18–19 (as printed in both AGA and NSA) and gives an *ossia* for those singers unable to encompass the high C of b. 43.

Autograph:	Wienbibliothek im Rathaus, Vienna
First edition:	Published as Book 46 of the *Nachlass* by Diabelli, Vienna in 1850 (P374)
Subsequent editions:	Peters: Vol. 6/47; AGA XX 588: Vol. 10/82; NSA IV: Vol. 13/34
Discography and timing:	Fischer-Dieskau II 4[17] 4'55
	Hyperion I 4[15]
	Hyperion II 25[8] 4'46 Philip Langridge

← *Geist der Liebe* D747   *Frühlingsgesang* D740 →

HIMMELSFUNKEN
Intimations of heaven

(SILBERT) **D651** [H420]

G major or B♭ major   February 1819

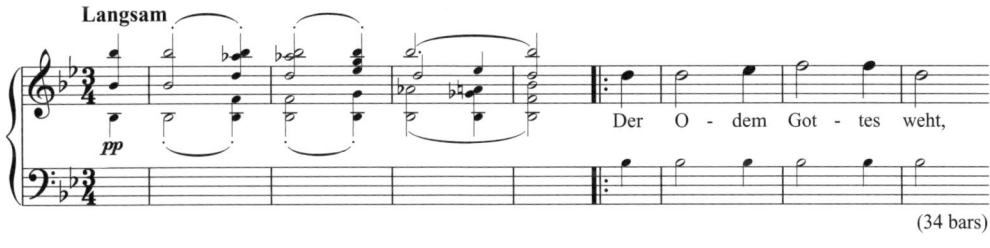

(34 bars)

Der Odem Gottes weht!	God's breath is felt.
Still wird die Sehnsucht wach;	Silently longing awakens.
Das trunkne Herz vergeht	The ecstatic heart
In wundersüssem Ach!	Swoons in sweet suffering.
Wie löst sich äthermild	The earth's oppressive bonds
Der Erde schweres Band,	Dissolve in the mild air.
Die heil'ge Träne quillt,	Sacred tears flow
Ach! nach des Himmels Land.	As we yearn for the heavenly land.
[...2...]	[...2...]
Und das verwaiste Herz	And the orphaned heart
Vernimmt den stillen Ruf,	Hears the soft call
Und sehnt sich heimatwärts	And longs to return home
Zum Vater, der es schuf!	To the Father, its Creator.

JOHANN PETRUS SILBERT (1772–1844)

This is the second of Schubert's two Silbert solo settings (1819). See the poet's biography for a chronological list of all the Silbert settings.

Despite its simple strophic form, this remarkable little song in metaphysical mode is one of Schubert's most potent single-page settings. It perhaps lacks the concision and clarity of the great Goethe miniatures from 1815 but this is hardly surprising – Silbert is no Goethe. To match the poet's ecstatic metaphysical musings inspired by the Redemptorist pastor, saintly Clemens Maria Hofbauer (1751–1820), Schubert writes a song that is half hymn and half romantic effusion, clothed in a chromatic musical language where longing borders on eroticism. There could be nothing more suitable than this music – it is as if a Bach chorale were transfigured by the Romantic zeitgeist – to illustrate Silbert's claim that his whole being is overcome 'In wundersüssem Ach'. The opening phrase mentions the breath of God and we are wafted into a world where His presence floats in the musical ether much in the manner of the fragrance of the beloved in *Dass sie hier gewesen* D775. With different words, the music of *Himmelsfunken* could easily be a love song, swooning for an earthly rather than a heavenly love. It is Schubert's natural inclination to acknowledge the divine immanence in all things beautiful.

   At this time in particular it seems that Schubert (no doubt much encouraged by the discussions of the reading circle, and the earnest aspirations of friends like Senn, Bruchmann and Spaun to embrace the true) attempted to reconcile distrust of religious hypocrisy and empty ceremonial with a comprehension of the great issues of life, death and the Infinite. God moves in mysterious ways, and a feature of this song is the subtlety of the harmonies that gently shift beneath its surface, which is to say the searching progress of the inner voices that glide into every chromatic nook and cranny. This is apparent from the *Vorspiel* where the top and bottom notes of the chords are in unison two octaves apart but where the alto and tenor voices of the hymn-like chords add ethereal and piquant accidentals. The harmonic changes that occur under 'Still wird die Sehnsucht wach' (bb. 8–13), where the words 'wird' and 'Sehnsucht' are both elongated to five beats, seem remarkably appropriate to depict the stirrings and deepest aspirations of the soul. (This passage works less well with the words of the subsequent verses.) Leo Black points out that a modified quotation of the musical material for this song reappears in Schubert's opera *Fierabras* – first in the Overture to that work (from b. 9) and then in Act 1 No. 14, for the knights' chorus with the words 'O teures Vaterland' (it was clearly Schubert's intention to preview the knights' chorus in the work's overture). We are reminded that the concept of 'Fatherland' in Schubert's time could take on almost sacred significance in a country that was all but religiously loyal to the ruling Habsburgs.

   There is a great temptation for many performers to take this song too slowly; but although marked 'Langsam', it seems lugubrious and endless when three slow crotchets are deliberately eked out in each bar. The breath and air mentioned are liquid media, and despite its rather solid look on the printed page this song can also be surprisingly fluid if not bogged down in portentousness. The spirit of the words calls for a celestial dance, and a gliding dotted minim to be counted more or less one-in-a-bar. The loping gait (for this is one of Schubert's moto perpetuo songs where everything is dominated by one rhythm) is quite hypnotic if a flowing tempo enables the singer to negotiate the long phrases without sounding laboured.

   Himmelsfunken has always been known to Schubertians in the key of G major. It was first published as such by Diabelli (and thus by Friedlaender in the Peters Edition). Mandyczewski in the *Gesamtausgabe* also published the song in G, and the first edition of the Deutsch catalogue lists the song in this key. The second edition of Deutsch chooses, however, to follow the tonality of a copy of the song made by Schubert's brother Ferdinand. This is in B flat, and it is this version that is published in Volume 12 of the NSA. When heard a minor third higher, the song seems light and ethereal and more closely related to the visionary Mayrhofer setting *Die Sternennächte* D670 composed in the same period. The editors of this new edition suggest that Schubert might have envisaged that the first verse of the poem, only, be performed. If this were so it would explain why this strophe alone seems perfectly tailored to the music (in later verses long note values fall on obviously inessential words like 'zu' and 'wie').

In fact Silbert's poem has five strophes of which 1, 2 and 5 were recorded for the Hyperion Edition and are translated here.

Autograph:	Missing or lost
First edition:	Published as Book 10 no. 8 of the *Nachlass* by Diabelli, Vienna in April 1831 (P269)
Subsequent editions:	Peters: Vol. 2/218; AGA XX 169: Vol. 6/14; NSA IV: Vol. 12/80
Bibliography:	Black 1997, p. 9
	Black 2003, pp. 66 & 148–9 (The connection of this song with both *Winterreise* and the opera *Fierabras* is noted.)
	Einstein 1951, p. 189
Arrangements:	Arr. Franz Liszt (1811–1886) for solo piano, no. 2 of *Franz Schuberts geistliche Lieder* No. 2 (1840) [*see* TRANSCRIPTIONS]
Discography and timing:	Fischer-Dieskau II 2^{15} 2'52
	Hyperion I 29^2 3'16 Marjana Lipovšek
	Hyperion I 31^4 3'34 Christine Brewer
	Hyperion II 21^{15} 3'16 Marjana Lipovšek

← *Abendbilder* D650 *Das Mädchen* D652 →

HIN UND WIEDER FLIEGEN PFEILE *see CLAUDINE VON VILLA BELLA* D239/3

HIPPOLITS LIED
(GERSTENBERGK) **D890** [H606]
A minor July 1826

Song of Hippolytus

(37 bars)

Lasst mich, ob ich auch still verglüh',	Let me be, though I waste silently,
Lasst mich nur stille geh'n;	Let me go quietly;
Sie seh' ich spät, sie seh' ich früh'	I see her in the evening, I see her in the morning,
Und ewig vor mir steh'n.	Forever standing before me.
Was ladet ihr zur Ruh' mich ein?	Why do you bid me find repose?
Sie nahm die Ruh' mir fort;	She took away all my repose,

Und wo sie ist, da muss ich sein,	And wherever she is, there must I be,
Hier sei es, oder dort.	Either here, or there.
Zürnt diesem armen Herzen nicht,	Do not be angry with this poor heart,
Es hat nur einen Fehl;	It has only one failing:
Treu muss es schlagen, bis es bricht,	It must beat faithfully until it breaks,
Und hat dess' nimmer Hehl.	And has never concealed that.
Lasst mich, ich denke doch nur sie;	Let me be, I think only of her,
In ihr nur denke ich:	And in her;
Ja, ohne sie wär' ich einst nie	Without her I should not one day
Bei Engeln ewiglich.	Hope to be with the angels for evermore.
Im Leben denn und auch im Tod,	In life and in death,
Im Himmel, so wie hier,	In heaven, as here below,
Im Glück und in der Trennung Not	In joy and in the grief of parting,
Gehör' ich einzig ihr.	I belong to her alone.

FRIEDRICH GERSTENBERGK (1780–1838); poem published in 1821 in a novel by JOHANNA SCHOPENHAUER (1766–1838)

This is Schubert's only setting of either a Gerstenbergk or Schopenhauer text. See both biographies.

The poem occurs in Volume 3 of Johanna Schopenhauer's three-part novel *Gabriele* (1821), although the words are by the author's close friend Friedrich Gerstenbergk (qv). He seems to have written the poem, spoken by the character Hippolit, at Schopenhauer's special request (she thought of herself as a novelist, and not at all as a poet). This bulky novel enjoyed considerable success in its time and made its author a great deal of money.

The plot of *Gabriele*, a work that Goethe read with approval in June 1822 ('Gut. Sehr gut' was his verdict in a letter to his son August) is long and complicated. It is a so-called 'Entsagungs-roman' where the eponymous heroine is spiritually and physically transfigured as a result of the renunciation of her own happiness, and by always doing right. The more she accepts her fate and does her duty, the more beautiful and remarkable she becomes. Gabriele is the daughter of Baron Aarheim, a Frankenstein-like character, a homicidal alchemist who lusts after power and spends all his time in his laboratory in search of the philosopher's stone. He is evil, completely lacking in scruples and in stark contrast to his daughter.

In the course of the novel Gabriele has to undergo various trials of the spirit. She enters a society dominated by men and repeatedly sacrifices herself out of a sense of duty. The first of these trials concerns her deep love for Ottokar who, at first unbeknown to Gabriele, is promised to another woman, Aurelia. When Gabriele admits her love for him and discovers that her feelings are reciprocated, she will not allow him to break his oath to Aurelia and renounces him – her first step on the pathway to radiant beauty and a kind of sainthood.

Next, Gabriele's wicked father insists that she marry his elderly cousin, the ghastly buffoon, Moritz. Although she finds Moritz repugnant she obeys the wishes of her father (who threatens to poison her if she does not). On learning that her father has died just after the ceremony (from taking poison), Gabriele faints, realizing that her self-sacrifice has been entirely in vain. After her recovery from this bitter news, she seems more radiant than ever.

She discovers that her childhood friend Hippolit loves her when he, too, considers poisoning himself with the contents of a vial found in Aarheim's laboratory. Gabriele persuades him not to, convincing him that this course of action is the easiest, and most cowardly, thing to do – that it is harder to live than to die, and the greatest gift (even if a painful one) he can give her is his continuing existence. As a married woman she is unable to continue her friendship with Hippolit and sends him away to his inconsolable grief. It is at this point of the novel that Johanna Schopenhauer inserts Gerstenbergk's poem. Eventually Gabriele realizes that she returns Hippolit's affections. In the culminating pages of the book she confesses her love to him and, as she does so, dies. In the complicated double narrative of a novel full of symbolism and hidden parallels, this is taken to be a kind of empowering suicide – the most positive thing that Gabriele has ever done in that it frees her from the strictures of the world. A woman who has always followed the patriarchal behests of society achieves her independence at last. The grief of Hippolit as he sinks to his knees in front of her body is hardly to be borne.

It is quite possible that Schubert read the entire novel during his stay with the Schobers in Währing in the summer of 1826. By strange coincidence *Gabriele* opens with a description of a rehearsal for Shakespeare's *Antony and Cleopatra*, a work that also engaged Schubert's attention at this time in connection with his setting of *Trinklied* D888. If Schopenhauer's novel was capable of moving Goethe, it is not unlikely that Schubert, if hopelessly enamoured of Karoline Esterházy, was also touched by this complicated story of impossible love. The novel could easily be read by a struggling artist as a comforting parable of life going wrong in every direction except for a deepening spiritual (and in Schubert's case, musical) awareness brought about by each successive turn of misfortune.

Hippolits Lied is often thought to be of classical Greek inspiration, and the novel is so full of literary allusion that Schopenhauer must have given Gabriele's ardent suitor this name for a reason. Hippolytus was the son of Theseus with whom the ill-fated Phaedra fell in love. In Jean Racine's version of this story (*Phèdre* (1677) Act V, sc. 2) Hippolyte is still pursued by Phèdre, but it is Aricie, a princess held captive at Thésée's court, who is the object of his own hopeless love:

Je l'adore; et mon âme, à vos ordres   I adore her, and my soul, . . . defying your
   rebelle,   command,
Ne peut ni soupirer, ni brûler que pour elle.   Can only sigh and burn for her alone.

There is a mood to these words that reflects the Gerstenbergk poem printed above. Schopenhauer's Hippolit, like Racine's Hippolyte, is caught in a web of forbidden love. Both characters are wan and mournful, and go around in circles without finding an exit from the moral maze; in Schubert's song the accompaniment also seems to describe circles – to such an extent that it brings to mind, with its A minor tonality, the distressed and circular movement of the hurdy-gurdy handle turned aimlessly by *Der Leiermann* from *Winterreise*. This is music that seems stuck in an emotional groove.

Part of the continuing challenge of playing Schubert's song accompaniments is the never-ending variety of pianistic invention created especially for each poem and situation. Once the composer has such an accompanimental figure, he seldom uses it in the same way for another song. In *Hippolits Lied* the flow of quavers is decorated by an insistently repeating mordent that Fischer-Dieskau finds 'charming' but which sounds more like a nervous tic, a sign of emotional shock and numbness. This musical twitch is the central motif in the accompaniment and is to be found nowhere else in the lieder. Unlike many other songs in the key of A minor, this lacks the healing balm of the major key and, apart from an eloquently turned miniature postlude, is entirely strophic. Leo Black, in conversation with me, has compared the song to the *Menuetto* in the A minor String Quartet D804. The dotted rhythm that permeates that remarkable movement (derived in turn from the opening of the Schiller setting *Strophe aus 'Die Götter Griechenlands'* D677) has abbreviated and compressed itself into a mere mordent by the time it reaches *Hippolits Lied*, but the way the music pivots on the dominant is a striking link between the two songs and the piece of chamber music – all in the key of A minor. Each of these works seems to be an elegy for something that has come before and is irretrievably lost. In the Schiller setting this refers to the entire civilization of the ancient Greeks (and with it, the innocence of mankind); in the Gerstenbergk setting Gabriele herself is forever lost to the distraught Hippolit. The string quartet was written in March 1824, the same month that Schubert, stricken with syphilis, wrote an agonized letter to Kupelwieser in Rome in which he compares his fate to that of Gretchen in *Faust* ('Meine Ruh' ist hin / Mein Herz ist schwer'). In this case it is tempting to connect this music, and the fate of Hippolit, with the loss of the composer's own peace of mind and the evaporation of all his hopes for the future.

First edition: Published as Book 7 no. 2 of the *Nachlass* by Diabelli, Vienna in
                          1830 (P251)
Subsequent editions: Peters: Vol. 5/5; AGA XX 504: Vol. 8/ 230; NSA IV: Vol. 14a/20
Discography and timing: Fischer-Dieskau II 8[13]   2'15
                          Hyperion I 14[5]
                          Hyperion II 32[12]   2'41   Thomas Hampson

←— *Gesang (An Silvia)* D891   *Nachthelle* D892 —→

Der HIRT   The shepherd
(Mayrhofer) **D490** [H309]
D minor   8 October 1816

(26 bars)

Du Turm! zu meinem Leide	Bell-tower, to my grief
Ragst du so hoch empor,	You soar so high,
Und mahnest grausam immer	And forever remind me cruelly
An das, was ich verlor.	Of what I have lost.

Sie hängt an einem Andern,	She is devoted to another,
Und wohnt im Weiler dort.	And lives in the hamlet there.
Mein armes Herz verblutet,	My poor heart bleeds,
Vom schärfsten Pfeil durchbohrt.	Pierced by the sharpest arrow.

In ihren schönen Augen	In her beautiful eyes
War keiner Untreu Spur;	There was no trace of faithlessness,
Ich sah der Liebe Himmel,	I saw in them only heavenly love,
Der Anmut Spiegel nur.	The mirror of grace.

Wohin ich mich nun wende –	Now wherever I turn
Der Turm, er folget mir;	The bell-tower follows me.
O sagt' er, statt der Stunden,	Would that, instead of telling the hours,
Was mich vernichtet, ihr!	It told her what is destroying me.

JOHANN MAYRHOFER (1787–1836)

This is the ninth of Schubert's forty-seven Mayrhofer solo settings (1814–24). See the poet's biography for a chronological list of all the Mayrhofer settings.

This is not one of the great Mayrhofer settings and is one of the least known of this poet's songs. It was written at about the same time as the enchanting *Alte Liebe rostet nie* D477 and *Geheimnis (An Franz Schubert)* D491 in which the poet pens his personal eulogy to the composer's genius. There is something about this music, however, which suggests that Schubert attached special significance to it. The key of D minor, the marking of *Mässig* and the mezzo staccato accompanying quavers at the opening are strongly prophetic of no less distinguished a song than *Gute Nacht* in *Winterreise*. Our first impression of the shepherd is that he is a tragic figure, a feeling that fades as strophe follows strophe and as the song reveals itself to be of eighteenth-century inspiration rather than a Romantic creation. This is rather a bizarre poem. The shepherd is half pastoral (reflected in the song's simplicity and mention of such stilted conceits as love's arrow) and half modern man. The significance of the soaring bell-tower and love's arrow might not have been lost on Freud. It is tempting to connect this song to the story of Schubert's love for Therese Grob – it was composed a month before he put together an album of songs that has been named after her, and also at about the time when the relationship, such as it was, is said to have quietly dissolved. Leo Black has pointed out that in a picture such as Schnorr von Karolsfeld's *Am Nemi-See* (1821), a man takes his leave of a tower (suggesting both safety and imprisonment), and that crucial scenes from Schubert's opera *Fierabras* are played out in a tower where the Frankish knights and Florinda are besieged. Schubert-*père* could be seen as an immovable structure blocking his son's ambitions to be a full-time composer. It is otherwise difficult to say what drew Schubert to this particular text. Mayrhofer seems ill at ease in this mixture of baroque and his own special brand of expressionism. Perhaps he had been inspired by Goethe's poem *Die wandelnde Glocke* where it is a bell rather than a bell-tower that stalks the unfortunate protagonist. An unusual feature of the song is that it seems to be in D minor throughout but the ritornello that opens each strophe (and also closes the song) ends in F major (bb. 5 and 26). This tonal twist adds to the work's awkward sense of mystery.

Autograph:	Gesellschaft der Musikfreunde, Vienna
First edition:	Published as part of the AGA in 1895 (P660)
Subsequent editions:	Not in Peters; AGA XX 267: Vol. 4/220; NSA IV: Vol. 11/16
Discography and timing:	Fischer-Dieskau I 8[15] 2'10 (Strophes 1, 2 & 4 only)
	Hyperion I 23[24]
	Hyperion II 16[11] 3'02 Christoph Prégardien

← *Der Wanderer* D489   *Geheimnis (An Franz Schubert)* D491 →

Der HIRT AUF DEM FELSEN   The shepherd on the rock[1]

(MÜLLER/VARNHAGEN VON ENSE) **D965** [H683]

B♭ major   October 1828

(349 bars)

Text by Wilhelm Müller:

Wenn auf dem höchsten Fels ich steh',	When I stand on the highest rock,
In's tiefe Tal hernieder seh',	Look down into the deep valley
Und singe,	And sing,
Fern aus dem tiefen dunkeln Tal	The echo from the ravines rises up
Schwingt sich empor der Widerhall	From the dark depths
Der Klüfte.	Of the distant valley.
Je weiter meine Stimme dringt,	The further my voices carries,
Je heller sie mir wieder klingt	The clearer it echoes back to me
Von unten.	From below.
Mein Liebchen wohnt so weit von mir,	My sweetheart dwells so far from me,
Drum sehn' ich mich so heiss nach ihr	And thus I long so ardently
Hinüber.	For her.

Text by Karl Varnhagen von Ense:

In tiefem Gram verzehr ich mich,[2]	I am consumed by deep sorrow;
Mir ist die Freude hin,	My joy has gone.
Auf Erden mir die Hoffnung wich,	My hope on this earth has vanished;
Ich hier so einsam bin.	I am so alone here.
So sehnend klang im Wald das Lied,	So fervently the song resounded through the forest,
So sehnend klang es durch die Nacht,	So fervently it resounded through the night;
Die Herzen es zum Himmel zieht	It drew hearts heavenwards
Mit wunderbarer Macht.	With its wond'rous power.

Text by Wilhelm Müller:

Der Frühling will kommen	Spring will come
Der Frühling, meine Freud',	Spring, my delight;
Nun mach' ich mich fertig	Now I shall prepare
Zum Wandern bereit.	To go a-wandering.

[1] This title would be better translated as 'The Shepherd on the Cliff' but it seems rather too late to change the time-honoured English title.

[2] These verses appear as strophes 2 and 3 (the order of the verses was switched by Schubert) of Varnhagen von Ense's *Nachtlicher Schall* in his *Vermischte Gedichte* (1816).

WILHELM MÜLLER (1794–1827). From Schubert's death the authorship of verses 5 & 6 was unknown until 2010 when the poet was identified as KARL AUGUST VARNHAGEN VON ENSE (1785–1858)

This is the forty-fifth and forty-sixth of Schubert's forty-six Müller solo settings (1823, 1827 and 1828). See the poet's biography for a chronological list of all the Müller settings. This is Schubert's only setting of of a Varnhagen von Ense text. See also that poet's biography.

In some ways (and not only because it was the last work he wrote) *Der Hirt auf dem Felsen* is the culmination of Schubert's attempts to achieve a synthesis between the musical manners of north and south. A few years after this work was written, Rossini published a song in his *Serate musicale* entitled *La pastorella delle Alpi* that makes fun of the bumptious Tyrolean yodellers and provides a good soprano with a character piece of rollicking fun. It is all something of a laugh (as is often the way with Rossini) at the expense of the folksong style and the gauche musical manners of Tyrolean Italians who, in the manner of their music, were as good as uninitiated foreigners. Schubert was much less materially successful than Rossini, but fame and money have a way of stopping the ear to new experiences. Schubert knew, and learned from, Rossini's music, but the Italian maestro was quite ignorant of Schubert's. This gave the Viennese composer an advantage. In *Der Hirt auf dem Felsen* the sounds of Italian vocal display resound in a German-speaking setting of dramatic hills and valleys, and the folksong style native to his own country is suffused with the vocal virtuosity native to Rossini's. Those incompatible beasts, the mawkish Alpine yodel and the clichéd Italian cantilena, are shorn of their more clumsy attributes and shepherded into the fold of profound music-making; their gambolling together in playful interchange is the happy achievement of this marvellous work.

The song was was written for Anna Milder [*see* SINGERS], the soprano whom Schubert had admired throughout his artistic life. Ferdinand Schubert sent her the manuscript a year after his brother's death, and she performed the work in Riga in 1830, although there is some dispute as to whether this was a first performance. Schubert conceived the idea of writing something for a soprano in 1828 (almost certainly with Milder in mind) that was more overtly operatic, with a suggestion of a plot and a little larger than life. Or it may have been Milder herself who came up with the idea, including the furnishing of suitable texts. She too was a straddler of traditions and generations. She fancied herself as a yodeller and Swiss mountain music was something of a trademark for her. This went back to Joseph Weigl's opera of 1809, *Die Schweizerfamilie*, in which she had played the role of Emmeline, complete with a yodelling song (a winsome *Cavatine* in B flat beginning 'Ich hüpfe und singe, ich tanze und springe') that had made her the darling of Vienna in her twenties. In later life she loved to revisit the triumphs of her youth: mountain-inspired music to rejuvenate her popular connection with Weigl's Emmeline was always welcome.

Milder's younger sister, Jeanette Bürde [*see* COMPOSERS], provided uncomplicated songs for her entitled *Der Berghirt* and *Der Frühling*, using the same Müller poems with which this cantata opens and closes. It remains a moot point as to whether these preceded Schubert's *Der Hirt auf dem Felsen* (in which case he took over the poems and set them more sumptuously) or whether Bürde set the texts after they had been selected by Schubert. When the composer came to write something for Milder in the last weeks of his life, the result was a cantata with these same texts by Wilhelm Müller (the poet of *Die schöne Müllerin* and *Winterreise*) appearing in its first and third movements; the middle movement had words by Karl Varnhagen von Ense, a biographer and historian, more famous in Berlin but with strong Viennese connections and known personally to Milder as the husband of the world-famous salonnière Rahel Varnhagen.

Einstein calls this concoction a 'scena in concertante style', and this of course refers to the crucial role of the clarinet as an obbligato instrument. Ignaz von Mosel, an admirer of Schubert since the composer's school days, and the dedicatee of Op. 3, had described Milder's voice in *Der Sammler* as early as 1812, as 'metallreich und clarinetähnlich' (richly metallic and like a clarinet). Perhaps Schubert thought so too. Here the noble precedent of the obbligato to Sextus's aria 'Parto, Parto' in Mozart's opera seria *La Clemenza di Tito* may have been an influence. As early as 1815 Schubert had composed an *Offertorium* in C (D136) that combines the soprano voice with clarinet. In some of his own most beautiful opera arias and duets he had already discovered how this instrument was especially suited to shadow and echo singers. These factors pointed to the character of the work for Milder: something both old-fashioned and new, partially grounded in Italian eighteenth century *bel canto* but also related to the German simplicity of the *Singspiel*, the whole tailored to the skills of a virtuoso clarinettist and a great German singing actress. Here Milder did not disappoint. She was an authoritative artist, no blushing soubrette; her voice suggested someone in charge, the right voice to imply that, as soon as winter is over, the young shepherd will rush across the valley and take his shepherdess in his arms. Mozart's Sextus is a famous trouser-role and *Der Hirt auf dem Felsen* is a trouser cantata – it is no wilting or shy Daphne or Chloe who heralds the priapic arrival of spring. Milder, after all, created Beethoven's Leonore (or Fidelio), the most famous *Hosenrolle* of all.

In the piano's six-bar overture in an Andantino (the double-dotted Ds a microcosm of dramatic overture style) sound and sight are briefly obscured by swirling mist. Suddenly this is pierced by a sunlit beam, a single ethereal note (also a D) played by the shepherd standing on his cliff (b. 6). This note blossoms into descending and ascending arpeggios thrown into the void, the guttural yodel of the mountain dweller transfigured into a call from the heart by the generous echo of the open spaces. Could Schubert have known that the natural notes of the alphorn, as Thea King has pointed out, follow the shape of this tune? It is quite possible that he had heard these instruments on his extended holiday in Upper Austria in 1825. Certainly the clarinet seems more appropriate to depict the rich mooing of the alphorn than the flute and oboe which are time-honoured in pastoral music as stand-ins for the reedier shepherd's pipe. In this mountain scenario the clarinet with its rich bottom register comes into its own: Thea King observed that the bouche fermée muted sound of the instrument's lower range, when played pianissimo, resembles the deep moo of a mother cow. The German word 'Hirt' covers a keeper both of herds and flocks (nothwithstanding the separate German words 'Schäfer' and 'Senne').

Unsigned vignette for the first edition of *Der Hirt auf dem Felsen* (1830).

The music suggests the shepherd's position, high in the mountains. It is as if the melodic line itself has eyes to sweep the vista; even the rise and fall of the printed music traces the shape of mountains on the page. We can almost smell the pure sweet air in the rarefied stratosphere of the clarinet's tessitura. As we follow the shepherd's glance (he both sees and feels through his clarinet) the music plunges into the valleys below, thanks to the chalumeau register. Down he looks, and then up again in an ascending arpeggio of eyes sweeping the horizon. The piano throbs in sympathy, guiding the shepherd's searching gaze into this or that harmonic corner of the mighty picture before him. With the entry of the voice (b. 38) we may momentarily wonder whether instrumentalist and vocalist are two lovers singing to each other across the void, but it soon becomes apparent that in his loneliness the shepherd projects his voice into the mountainous spaces and is comforted by the echo. We hardly notice how difficult the vocal part is, so naturally does it seem to follow the clarinet up and down the wide-ranging vista. There is a beautiful excursion into G flat (from b. 64), a different region of the shepherd's thoughts and the dwelling place of his beloved. The clarinet interlude back into B flat via D major is one of those Schubertian middle-section miracles (bb. 86–95) by which the reprise can be no mere repetition, suffused as it seems to be with an added dimension of longing.

The middle 'movement' is in G minor, always a favourite key for Schubert to express the pain of love after hearing, as a boy, Pamina's 'Ach, ich fühl's' from Mozart's *Die Zauberflöte*. The cast of the accompaniment looks back to the very recent composition of the famous *Ständchen* from *Schwanengesang*. This music is an enormous challenge to the singer's breath control, but a subtle one, for a perfect performance sounds easy. The modulation from G minor to major on the words 'Die Herzen es zum Himmel zieht' (the magical moment is on the barline of b. 183) adds a spiritual dimension to the shepherd's devotion; it is as if he has found an answer to a long-puzzling question about the nature of love, an answer that is related to the transformative power of music. At the very moment of the modulation it dawns on him that the heart itself will ever resiliently and miraculously survive the pain of separation. In order to make this passage work in musical terms, Schubert reverses the printed order of Varnhagen's stanzas. The words 'Mit wunderbarer Macht' (originally at the end of the opening strophe of Varnhagen's poem) thus form the radiant culmination of this middle section. The last section brightens to embrace the slap and tickle of a young man's earthier needs although Schubert is careful, for Milder's sake, to avoid any part of Müller's *Liebesgedanken* (*Ländliche Lieder*, No. 6) that openly refers to a 'Mädchen'. The beautiful clarinet cadenza had the protagonist lost in higher thought (bb. 217–18) but as the sap rises he/she descends to musings in the springtime key of B flat – the same key and time signature in which another young man in another Müller poem, *Das Wandern* from *Die schöne Müllerin*, had gone a-wandering. The pianist takes a holiday here in an undemanding accompaniment (apart from one exposed passage in suddenly slippery terrain, bb. 259–62 that has caused many an unwary mountaineering accompanist to lose his grip) but it is his sense of rhythm that keeps the shepherd's thoughts and hopes dancing. After this, three lines from the first section are recapitulated (from 'Je weiter meine Stimme dringt') and these words (and echoes from the first movement) intertwine with the wander-music to bring the proceedings to a joyous conclusion. Schubert had provided Madame Milder with a showpiece – high and low, slow and sustained, fast and agile – without sacrificing a jot of his integrity. Only the piano part seems denuded, as if a conscious reflection of the customary Italianate lack of invention in that sphere. Or is it because Schubert knew there was not much chance of his playing this piano part himself and he also understood all too well that Madame Milder was the *prima donna assoluta*?

Autographs:	Gesellschaft der Musikfreunde, Vienna (fair copy)
	Wienbibliothek im Rathaus, Vienna (sketch)
First edition:	Published as Op. post. 129 by Tobias Haslinger, Vienna in 1830 (P239)
Publication reviews:	Rellstab 'Ueberblick der Erzeugnisse', *Iris im Gebiete der Tonkunst* (Berlin) No. 39 (12 November 1830) [Waidelich/Hilmar Dokumente II No. 784b]
First known performance:	March 1830, in a concert given by Anna Milder at the Schwarzhäuptersaale, Riga. The exact date of the concert, and the names of the clarinettist and pianist, are not known. For details

of the first Viennese performance of the piece, given on 21
March 1830 by Karoline Achten, see Waidelich/Hilmar
Dokumente I No. 768

Subsequent editions: Peters: Vol. 6/134; AGA XX 569: Vol. 10/16; NSA IV:
Vol. 14b/300

Bibliography: Capell 1928, p. 247
Fischer-Dieskau 1977, pp. 283 & 299–300
Hilmar-Voit 1991, p. 53
Newbould 1997, pp. 315–17

Discography and timing: Fischer-Dieskau   —
Hyperion I 9[21]
Hyperion II 37[14]   12'19   Arleen Auger & Thea King (clarinet)

← *Schwangengesang* (13): *Der Doppelgänger* D957/13   *Schwangengesang* (14)
Die Taubenpost D965a →

HIRTENCHOR *see ROSAMUNDE*, FÜRSTIN VON ZYPERN D797/2

HOCHZEIT-LIED   Wedding song
(Jacobi) **D463** [H289]
E♭ major   August 1816

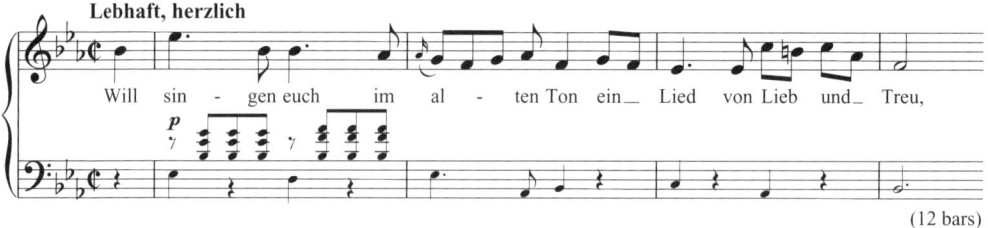

(12 bars)

Will singen euch im alten Ton   I will sing you a song in the old style,
Ein Lied von Lieb' und Treu;   A song of love and constancy.
Es sangen's unsre Väter schon,   Our fathers once sang it.
Doch bleibt's der Liebe neu.   But it remains ever new for lovers.

Im Glücke macht es freudenvoll,   In good times it brings joy,
Kann trösten in der Not: In times of distress it can comfort:
'D a s s   n i c h t s   d i e   *'Let nothing part these hearts,*
    H e r z e n s c h e i d e n s o l l,
N i c h t s s c h e i d e n, a l s d e r T o d :   *Nothing, save death.*

Dass immerdar mit frischem Mut   Let the man protect his bride
Der Mann die Traute schützt,   Evermore with new heart,
Und alles opfert, Gut und Blut,   And sacrifice everything, his wealth and his blood
Wenn's seinem Weibchen nützt;   For the good of his wife.

Dass er auf weiter Erde nichts   Let him desire nothing on this wide earth
Als sie allein begehrt,   But her alone,

Sie gern im Schweiss des Angesichts	And with the sweat of his brow
Für ihren Kuss ernährt;	Joyfully support her, for her kisses.

Dass, wenn die Lerch' im Felde schlägt,	When the lark sings in the field
Sein Weib ihm Wonne lacht,	Let his wife's laughter bring him joy;
Ihm, wenn der Acker Dornen trägt,	When the land is strewn with thorns
Zum Spiel die Arbeit macht,	May she lighten his work.

Und doppelt süss der Ruhe Lust,	The delights of rest shall be doubly sweet,
Erquickend jedes Brot,	Every meal shall refresh;
Den Kummer leicht an ihrer Brust,	His cares shall be eased on her breast,
Gelinder seinen Tod.	His death shall be gentler.

Dann fühlt er noch die kalte Hand	Then he shall feel his cold hand
Von ihrer Hand gedrückt,	Pressed by her hand;
Und sich in's neue Vaterland	He shall be borne from her arms
Aus ihrem Arm entrückt.'	To his new homeland.'

JOHANN GEORG JACOBI (1740–1814); poem written between 1775 and 1782

This is the third of Schubert's seven Jacobi solo settings (1816). See the poet's biography for a chronological list of all the Jacobi settings.

The music is in E flat major and a celebratory two in the bar. The marking is 'Lebhaft, herzlich' and Schubert clearly obeys the hint in the first verse about the music being 'im alten Ton'. The work belongs culturally and stylistically with those philosophizing drinking songs that occupy a modest if not infrequent place in Schubert's canon. The poet lectures the married man as if he were a benign priest or a well-behaved best man (no jokes). This is hearty music, earthy in its German simplicity, the type of village marriage that we hear about in Heine's *Das ist ein Flöten und Geigen*. The composer ignores the poet's deepening seriousness in the second strophe where the words are printed widely spaced to denote special significance. There is a strength and security in this deliberate good-hearted directness that also encompasses on this day of celebration a glimpse of death – though hardly an alarming one in the context of this music. Carl Loewe, already writing splendid songs in not-so-faraway Germany, often achieved a style like this in his ballads where the melodic inspiration is not startling but is pleasant enough. The autograph is lost but the NSA prints five of Jacobi's seven strophes in italics. In the performance for the Hyperion Edition, six of the seven strophes were performed, leaving out no. 4.

Two different ideas for performing the five Jacobi songs as a set are discussed in the commentaries for *An Chloen* D462 and *Trauer der Liebe* D465.

Autograph:	Missing or lost
First edition:	Published as part of the AGA in 1895 (P647)
Subsequent editions:	Not in Peters; AGA XX 245: Vol. 4/150; NSA IV: Vol. 10/202
Discography and timing:	Fischer-Dieskau I 7[31] 0'56 (first two strophes only)
	Hyperion I 8[10]
	Hyperion II 15[16] 2'33 Sarah Walker

← *An Chloen* D462   *In der Mitternacht* D464 →

Der HOCHZEITSBRATEN   The wedding roast   Trio, STB

(SCHOBER) **D930** [H647]
G major   November 1827

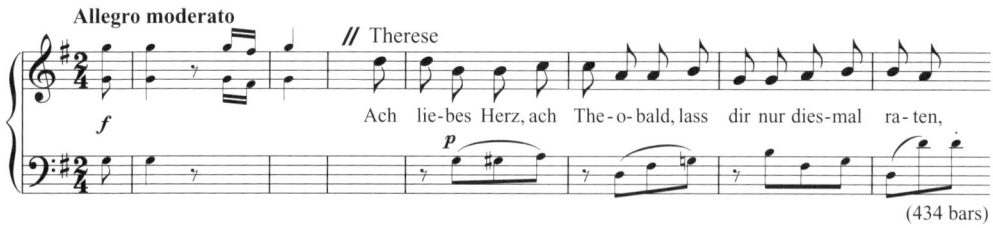

(434 bars)

Therese:
Ach liebes Herz, ach Theobald,
Lass dir nur diesmal raten,
Ich bitt' dich, geh nicht in den Wald,
Wir brauchen keinen Braten.

Theobald:
Der Stein ist scharf, ich fehle nicht,
Den Hasen muss ich haben,
Der Kerl muss uns als Hauptgericht
Beim Hochzeitschmause laben.

Therese:
Ich bitt' dich, Schatz –

Theobald:
Ich geh allein.

Therese:
Sie hängen dich.

Theobald:
Was fällt dir ein!

Therese:
Allein kann ich nicht bleiben.

Theobald:
Nun gut, so magst du treiben.

* * * * *

Therese:
Wo steckt er denn?
Gsch! gsch! prr, prr.

Therese:
Oh dear heart, Oh Theobald,
Just listen to me this time:
I beg you, don't go into the woods.
We don't need any meat!

Theobald:
My flint is sharp, I won't miss.
I must have that hare:
The fellow will be the main course
At our wedding feast!

Therese:
I beg you, dear –

Theobald:
I'll go alone.

Therese:
They'll hang you!

Theobald:
What nonsense!

Therese:
I can't stay here alone.

Theobald:
All right, you do the beating!

* * * * *

Therese:
Where's he hiding then?
Gsch! Gsch! prr, prr.

Theobald:
Hier ist der Ort,
Jetzt treibe fort,
Jetzt hier im Kraut,
Jetzt im Gebüsch.

Therese:
Nur immer frisch!

Theobald:
Nur nicht so laut!

Kaspar:
Horch! horch!

Theobald:
Nur still! nur still!

Kaspar:
Potz Blitz, was soll das sein?
Ich glaub sie jagen.
Da schlag der Hagel drein!
Potz Blitz!

Theobald:
Still! Still!

Therese:
Nur aufgepasst!

Kaspar:
Potz Blitz!

Theobald:
Da sprach ja wer?

Therese:
Was du nicht hörst!

Kaspar:
Der kommt nicht aus, den sperr ich ein.

Theobald:
Es wird der Wind gewesen sein.

Therese:
O Lust, ein Jägersmann zu sein.
Ein Has, ein Has!

Theobald:
Here's the place.
Now go on beating –
Now in the undergrowth,
Now in the bushes.

Therese:
That's the way!

Theobald:
Not so loud!

Kaspar:
Listen! Listen!

Theobald:
Quiet! Quiet!

Kaspar:
Confound it, what's going on here?
They must be hunting.
I'll rain some bullets on to them.
Confound it!

Theobald:
Shut up!

Therese:
Keep concentrating!

Kaspar:
Confound it!

Theobald:
Who spoke then!

Therese:
Your imagination!

Kaspar:
He won't escape. I'll trap him.

Theobald:
It must have been the wind.

Therese:
What fun it is to be a huntsman.
Look – a hare!

Theobald:
Da liegt er schon!

Kaspar:
Nun wart, Hallunk, dich trifft dein Lohn!
Du Galgenstrick, du Enakssohn,
Du Haupthallunk, dich trifft dein Lohn!

Theobald:
Welch Meisterschuss,
Grad in die Brust!
O Lust, o süsse Jägerlust!

Therese:
O sieh! den feisten Rücken,
Den will ich trefflich spicken.
O Lust, o süsse Jägerlust!

* * * * *

Kaspar:
Halt Diebsgepack!

Therese & Theobald:
Nun ist es aus.

Kaspar:
Den Hasen gebt, die Büchs heraus!

Theobald:
Ich muss . . .

Therese:
Ich will . . .

Kaspar:
Ins Loch, ins Arbeitshaus!

Therese & Theobald:
O weh! oh weh! Mit uns ists aus.

Kaspar:
Ich treib euch schon das Stehlen aus.

Therese & Theobald:
Herr Jäger, seid doch nicht von Stein,
Die Hochzeit sollte morgen sein!

Kaspar:
Was kümmerts mich!

Theobald:
There he is – dead!

Kaspar:
Just wait, you scoundrel, you'll get what's coming!
You wicked good-for-nothing,
You arch-fiend, you'll get what's coming!

Theobald:
What a great shot –
Right in the heart!
Oh, the pleasures of hunting!

Therese:
Oh what a plump, meaty hare.
I'll grease it really well!
Oh, the pleasures of hunting!

* * * * *

Kaspar:
Stop, you pack of thieves!

Therese & Theobald:
Now we've had it!

Kaspar:
Give me the hare, and the gun.

Theobald:
I really must . . .

Therese:
I want to . . .

Kaspar:
Go to jail – to the workhouse!

Therese & Theobald:
Oh dear, now we've had it!

Kaspar:
I'll cure you of poaching!

Therese & Theobald:
Sir, don't be so hard –
We're getting married tomorrow!

Kaspar:
What do I care!

Theobald:
Mit Most will ich euch reich versehn.

Theobald:
I'll give you lots of new wine.

Therese:
Und ich, ich strick euch einen Beutel.

Therese:
And I could stitch you a haversack.

Therese & Theobald:
O hört, o hört, er sei euer Dank!

Therese & Theobald:
Please listen! Accept our gifts!

Kaspar:
(Das Mädchen ist verzweifelt schön.)
Nein, nein, 'sist alles eitel!

Kaspar:
(The girl's deuced pretty!)
No, that won't do you any good!

Therese & Theobald:
Und dieser Taler weiss und blank,
Lasst ihr uns gehn, er sei euer Dank.

Therese & Theobald:
And these gleaming new coins –
Accept them and let us go.

* * * * *

* * * * *

Therese & Theobald:
Ach! statt den Hasenrücken
Muss ich den Jäger spicken!

Therese & Theobald:
Oh dear! Instead of greasing the hare
We must grease up to the gamekeeper!

Kaspar:
Sie ist doch zum Entzücken,
Ich muss ein Aug zudrücken.
Nun wohl, weil ernstlich ihr bereut,
Und's erstemal im Forste seid,
Mag Gnad für Recht heut walten,
Ihr möget Hochzeit halten.

Kaspar:
But she's charming!
I'll have to turn a blind eye.
All right, as you're truly sorry,
And it's your first time in the forest,
Let justice be ruled by mercy.
You may have your wedding.

Therese & Theobald:
O tausend Dank! O lieber Herr!
Gebt uns zur Hochzeit doch die Ehr!

Therese & Theobald:
A thousand thanks! Dear kind Sir!
Please honour us with your presence!

Kaspar:
Es sei, ich komme morgen,
(Für'n Braten will ich sorgen.)

Kaspar:
Agreed. I'll come tomorrow –
(And I'll see to the wedding dish.)

Alle:
Lebt wohl, lebt wohl bis morgen.

All:
Goodbye until tomorrow.

* * * * *

* * * * *

Therese & Theobald:
Das Herz ist frei von seiner Last,
Wir haben Hochzeit und 'nen Gast,
Und Obendrein den Braten,
So sind wir gut beraten!
La la la . . .

Therese & Theobald:
Our hearts are freed from care;
We've got our wedding, and a guest,
And on top of that a wedding dish,
So we are well provided for!
La la la . . .

<table>
<tr><td>Kaspar:</td><td>Kaspar:</td></tr>
<tr><td>Hol euch der Fuchs, ich wäre fast</td><td>The devil take them, I wish I were</td></tr>
<tr><td>Der Bräutgam lieber als der Gast,</td><td>The groom and not the guest!</td></tr>
<tr><td>Sie ist kein schlechter Braten,</td><td>She's not a bad wedding dish.</td></tr>
<tr><td>Der Kerl ist gut beraten!</td><td>The fellow's well provided for!</td></tr>
<tr><td>La la la . . .</td><td>La la la . . .</td></tr>
</table>

Franz von Schober (1796–1882)

This is one of the very few Schubert pieces that was intended to make people laugh. If we wish to imagine the atmosphere of a typical Schubertiad (after the serious songs had already been performed, of course, and only when everyone was in the mood for a musical dessert or *Nachspeise*) we may find it in this music. It is likely that the text contains private jokes and allusions now lost to us. The plot, involving a flirtatious woman and two men, one her fiancé and the other in a position of authority, is reminiscent of the Susanna–Figaro–Count triangle in Mozart's *Le nozze di Figaro*. The sexual innuendo and fascination concerning the link between sex and power – a reworking of the question of *droit de seigneur* – are typical of Franz von Schober; that the girl is probably forced to grant the gamekeeper her favours seems to have struck a chord of fantasy with him. The darker side of the story is hardly apparent at first, however, and its conclusion is left hanging tactfully in the air. The whole piece is clothed in delightful music where the yodel of the yokel is given a rare musical elegance. Both Schubert and Schober clearly dashed the piece off quickly and without fuss, probably with a deadline for a party in mind; the text appears nowhere in the poet's printed works.

There is no reference in the documents to the date of this work's first performance, but it must have been heard some time in the winter of 1827–8. (Deutsch in his original catalogue mentions a performance *circa* 1 January 1828, although this cannot be substantiated.) By February 1828 Schubert felt able to offer the 'Komisches Terzett' to the publisher Schott in Mainz with the assurance that it had already been 'performed to applause'. Perhaps it had started life as a one-off, a *pièce d'occasion*, similar to the various playlets and literary party pieces (to be found in the Documentary Biography) written by the members of the Schubert circle such as Bauernfeld. Maybe one of them was getting married and this piece, both text and music, was cooked up in his honour; what began as a joke might have been so well received ('mit Beyfall aufgeführt' as Schubert wrote to Schott) that its commercial possibilities became apparent. Or its composition may have been as a sequel to Schubert's other comic cantata for three singers – *Die Advokaten* D37 for two tenors and bass that had been published in May 1827 as Opus 74. Although that 1812 song by the fifteen-year-old Schubert is not even entirely original, having been modelled on a work by Anton Fischer, it is another pleasant *jeu d'esprit* in the early Schubert style, very probably taken up by Diabelli in the belief that it would appeal to the music-buying public. The same business considerations may have been behind the writing of *Der Hochzeitsbraten* although it took some time to reach the printer. It was eventually published in 1829 with a vignette by Moritz von Schwind on the cover.

The three characters of *Der Hochzeitsbraten* are Therese (soprano), her fiancé Theobald (tenor), and the gamekeeper, Kaspar (baritone) who appears only in the middle of the piece. The setting is presumably some rural part of Austria in earlier times where the only way a young couple can afford a wedding roast is to poach a hare, risking imprisonment and even death in doing so.

The opening of this cantata is in G major, instantly recalling the bustle and energy of the G major duet at the beginning of Mozart's *Figaro* (also sung, incidentally, by two characters soon to be married). This 'Allegro moderato' episode in $\frac{2}{4}$ takes up a full eight pages in the NSA, and is a marvel of Schubertian invention and dramatic pacing. The melody of Therese's opening vocal line ('Ach, liebes Herz, ach Theobald') is announced in a piano prelude made up of dancing quavers and bustling semiquavers in the manner of a tiny overture. The vocal writing is in mock-folksong style; these lovebirds are country folk designed to be laughed at by sophisticated townies. The accompaniment ducks and bobs to suggest any number of things – the pouting soubrette whimsy of Therese, the busy Theobald cleaning his gun (his sharp stone, 'Stein', is here an abbreviation of 'Feuerstein' for flint) and the girl's Susanna-like determination to have her own way. In this section, right-hand semiquavers embark on many a tonal excursion as the pianist's fingers struggle to avoid tripping over themselves. This passage is strikingly similar to the weaving semiquaver figuration that features (from b. 9) in the comic trio, 'Marsch! Marsch! Marsch!' (ending 'Platz! Platz!') from Mozart's *Die Entführung aus dem Serail* which, according to Gerhard von Breuning, Schubert wished to hear sung again and again. In that ensemble Belmonte and Pedrillo are pitted against the malevolent Osmin in much the same way that Therese and Theobald sing in counterpoint with the corrupt gamekeeper – but this is to get ahead of the story. Theobald's determination to go out alone is eventually worn down by Therese's insistence. The exasperated 'Nun gut' as he succumbs to her wheedling strikes a familiar chord with all victims of nagging. Theobald reluctantly agrees that Therese should come with him in search of game, but only if she makes herself useful by beating the hare out of the undergrowth.

Suddenly we are in the woods (from b. 95). There is no need to allow time for this scene-change – Schubert is infinitely happier with this type of 'opera' where such considerations of the unities do not have to be taken into account. The piano writing now evokes breathless suspense with pregnant gaps in the music's flow, and measured trills in adjacent semitones in the accompaniment. The mood here is sheer comic-opera melodrama – note the rise of a semitone in the piano figurations after 'Hier ist der Ort' (b. 100), denoting that dirty work is afoot. This turning of the harmonic screw in stages is a continuing feature of the piece, surely the nearest the Schubertian lied ever comes to the high jinks of pantomime.

What follows is unlike anything else in this composer's vocal music. Therese encourages the hare out of hiding by beating the ground (the onomatopoeic 'gsch! gsch!' is spoken in rhythm, from b. 107) at the same time as making encouraging noises as one might to a pet ('prr, prr', intoned on various notes). The combined effect of these sounds, together with the piano accompaniment chugging away in various patterns of semiquavers, is rather like an impression of an early steam train. The modulations in this section are masterfully handled to suggest the couple's rovings through various different parts of the forest. The long crescendo over the comically inappropriate words 'Nur nicht so laut!' ('only not so loud!') is in the tradition of Rossini (bb. 131–6).

Suddenly we hear (as if offstage) a third voice – the gamekeeper Kaspar whose interjections of 'Horch! horch!' are like a Captain Hook spoiling the innocent fun of Wendy and Peter. The music lifts another semitone, from D major (the dominant of the home key of G major) to E flat major (from b. 145). Kaspar becomes the hunter of humans, his music combining with Therese's hare-beating noises and Theobald's cautionary admonitions. A complex trio is built up in this way between the three characters, two of whom are unaware of the other's presence. There is little in Schubert's many operas as witty and effective as this trio where each of the three characters has feelings distinct from the others whether it is the gamekeeper's outrage as he swears to bag the criminals; Theobald's dogged determination to bag his hare; or Therese's ill-advised exaltation in the fun of it all. At Theobald's first inkling that he hears another voice ('Da sprach ja wer?' bb. 179–80) the tonal axis moves from the flat keys (E flat and B flat) to the sharp (B major as the dominant of E minor). When the hare is actually shot ('Ein Has, ein Has!' bb. 205–6) the music shifts from broken octaves on B to the triumphal key of C major a

Der Hochzeitsbraten, first edition (1829) with vignette by Schwind.

semitone higher. In this way a real sense of mounting melodramatic suspense is built into the music.

A C major arpeggio high on the keyboard followed by a solitary low staccato C in the bass represents gunshot and the thump of a carcass (bb. 207–10). (In various modern-day Schubertiads in which I have taken part, a toy rabbit has sometimes been thrown into the performing circle to synchronize with these pianistic gestures.) It is in C major that the hunting scene comes to its climax: the gamekeeper prepares to pounce, Theobald is mightily pleased with his shooting skill and Therese is overjoyed with the prospect of cooking the hare for the wedding feast. The gamekeeper's insults for Theobald, his own prospective prey, include the curious word 'Enakssohn'. This is a reference to the legendarily tall sons of the biblical tribe named Anak in the Authorized Version (Numbers 13:33), suggesting that the role of Theobald might originally have been conceived for a tall tenor – perhaps Josef Barth (qv SINGERS).

The piano interlude, five bars in tiptoe quavers on rising semitones (bb. 233–7) implies Kaspar's approach as he surprises the couple and arrests them. At the vivid change of musical mood for 'Halt Diebsgepack!' (a switch to 'Allegro', the key of A minor, and to $\frac{6}{8}$) we can almost feel Kaspar's grip and the tightening noose around Theobald's neck. In this tumultuous passage, by far the most dramatic of the piece, Kaspar threatens jail for the man and workhouse for the girl, but they tearfully appeal to his better nature with the news that they are going to get married. The musical style quickly changes into a seductive barcarolle (from b. 256 at 'Herr Jäger, seid doch nicht von Stein') reminiscent of *Das Fischermädchen* from *Schwanengesang*. At first Kaspar dismisses these entreaties ('Was kümmerts mich!', accompanied by an insouciant arpeggio bb. 267–8). The pair are reduced to offering bribes of various kinds, the most effective of which is 'dieser Taler weiss und blank'. It seems unlikely that Therese and Theobald should have money to bribe the gamekeeper (if they had, why on earth would they have had to poach their wedding feast in the first place?) No, these white, round proferred 'coins' are currency of a different kind – Therese's breasts – and a live performance taking place far from the censor's eyes could have made this clear by gesture or visual innuendo. Kaspar now observes that the girl is 'verzweifelt schön' – deuced pretty. Compromise and corruption are clearly in the air. This section that has veered between A minor and major ends on the dominant – a chord of E major (bb. 300–301).

There follows a short Allegretto section in $\frac{2}{4}$ (beginning 'Ach! statt den Hasenrücken') where all the characters reflect separately on their options. This is cast in the form of a canon in E minor. First Therese acknowledges that she has no choice but to grease up to the gamekeeper rather than greasing the hare; three and a half bars later Theobald ruefully agrees that this is what she will have to do; Kaspar's entry is appropriately lascivious. He is now prepared to turn a blind eye to the crime, and as the music moves into recitative mode he agrees, with the greatest pomposity, that the marriage should go ahead. Therese and Theobald chortle their thanks as if they were Susanna and Figaro paying lip service to the count, but it is clear that there is a price to be paid: Kaspar's phrase 'ich komme morgen, / (Für'n Braten will ich sorgen)' is full of oily menace, crowned by a suggestive trill on 'sorgen' (bb. 351–2) that veritably shakes with lust. He makes clear, without saying as much (and we always have to remember the hand of the censor) that on the morrow he will not hesitate to exercise his newly exacted *droit de seigneur*. His importunate impatience to get his hands on Therese is brilliantly, and subtly, emphasized by his final 'Lebt wohl', held longer than anything sung by the bridal couple and thus both more suggestive and more ominous. One recalls Josef Kenner's remarks about the 'completely unscrupulous' Schober having 'no respect for Mine and Thine in marriage'.

The final movement in $\frac{3}{4}$ – an Andantino in G major from b. 368 – is the musical high point of the work. The preceding sections have been masterfully written, and Schubert's narrative technique, when he does not have to worry about stagecraft as such, is exemplary. But here we have a rare example of the Tyrolean yodel built into a Schubertian vocal line (the most famous Schubertian yodel is to be found in *Der Hirt auf dem Felsen* D965) and what he does with it is marvellous. The audience's laughter, in my experience, is now replaced by the sort of seraphic smiles that are reserved for genuine Schubertian felicities. Therese and Theobald sing of being let off the hook in duple rhythm while the gamekeeper embroiders leering triplets around them which rise suggestively from the bottom of the stave, an obbligato of pantomime lust. With the open-hearted yodel-like 'La la la' figurations the couple also move into triplet rhythm; these artlessly delightful undulations are mocked by the gun-wielding lecher (the marking in the music is 'spottend') who imagines himself at the morrow's wedding as the bridegroom rather than the guest. Three-part writing for voices, mellifluous but enlivened by the cutting edge of the bass line, this is music beyond praise.

By the end of the piece nothing has been truly resolved. We are reminded that there are moments in *Figaro* where the count is certain that he is about to have his way with Susanna and she always manages to escape him. Kaspar has been such a ridiculously pompous and corrupt figure that one would be delighted to see him trounced. In any case, a discreet Biedermeier veil is drawn over the final outcome of this titillating little drama. What remains is Schubert's geniality and his unique ability to touch us, even in the middle of a farrago of nonsense such as this.

Autograph:	Österreichische Nationalbibliothek, Vienna		
First edition:	Published as Op. post. 104 by Diabelli, Vienna in 1829 (P231)		
Subsequent editions:	AGA XIX 2: p. 14; NSA III: Vol. 2/135		
Discography and timing:	Deutsche Grammophon	10'35	Elly Ameling, Peter Schreier
	Schubert Terzette		& Dietrich Fischer-Dieskau
	Hyperion I 36[16]	11'17	Lynne Dawson, Michael Schade
	Hyperion II 34[18]		& Gerald Finley

← *Der Leiermann* D911/24   *Wolke und Quelle* D896b →

LUDWIG CHRISTOPH HEINRICH HÖLTY (1748–1776)

THE POETIC SOURCES

S1 *Gedichte von Ludwig Heinrich Christoph Hölty*, Besorgt durch seine Freunde Friedrich Grafen zu Stolberg und Johann Heinrich Voss, Wien, Gedruckt für F.W. Schrämbl bey Ign. Alberti, 1790

Missing from this collection are the texts for *Die Knabenzeit* D400, *Minnelied* D429, *Seligkeit* D433. These are all to be found in S3.

S2 *Gedichte* von Ludewig [*sic*] Heinrich Christoph Hölty. Neu besorgt und vermehrt von Johann Heinrich Voss. Hamburg, bei Carl Ernst Bohn, 1804 (expanded reprint of 1783 edition)

S3 *Gedichte von L. H. Ch. Hölty*. Neu besorgt und vermehrt von Johann Heinrich Voss. Wien 1815, bey Chr. Kaulfuss und C. Armbruster. Gedruckt von Anton Strauss.

S4 *Sammlung Deutscher Beyspiele zur Bildung des Styls*, Zweyter Band, Wien, im Verlagsgewölbe des k.k. Schulbücher-Verschleisses bey St. Anna in der Johannis-Gasse, 1808

Hölty, *Gedichte*, Vienna (1815).

All the Schubert songs are included in the cheap Viennese reprint (S3) of the Hölty poems. It is clear that this could not have been the edition that Schubert used for *Totengräberlied* D44 in 1813. For this he might have used the Schrämbl edition of 1790, the Viennese edition of Degen or indeed the Hamburg Edition of 1804. It is far more likely, however, that he found the poem in a Viennese-printed school textbook, an anthology of poetry for the teaching of literary style (S4). The same book contains possible sources for Schiller's *Dithyrambe* and Matthisson's *Die Schatten*, all songs from the first months of 1813. Schubert might equally well have started off with one of the eighteenth-century Viennese editions of Hölty, and acquired the new and inexpensive 1815 edition of the poems in time for his later settings of the poet in 1816. On the other hand he may have been in possession of the 1804 Hamburg edition (S2) throughout. This was certainly the most popular of all Hölty editions and the one used by Johannes Brahms for his six settings of the poet.

THE SONGS

19 January 1813	*Totengräberlied* D44 [S1: pp. 41–2] [S2: pp. 214–15 in the 'Oden und Lieder' section, 'Zweites Buch'] [S3: pp. 176–7] [S4: p. 67]
1815	*Winterlied (Trinklied im Winter)* D242a, Trio (TTB) [S1: pp. 62–3] [S2: pp. 216–18] [S3: pp. 178–9]
17 May 1815	*An den Mond* D193 [S1: p. 70] [S2: pp. 207–8 in the 'Oden und Lieder' section, 'Zweites Buch'] [S3: p. 170] *Die Mainacht* D194 [S1: pp. 150–51] [S2: pp. 103–4 in the 'Oden' section] [S3: p. 86]

22 May 1815   *An die Nachtigall* D196 [S1: p. 141] [S2: p. 158 in the 'Oden und Lieder' section,
               'Erstes Buch'] [S3: p. 128]
               An die Apfelbäume, wo ich Julien erblickte D197 [S1: p. 161] [S2:
               pp. 115–16 in the 'Oden' section] [S3: p. 95]
               Seufzer D198 [S1: p. 166] [S2: pp. 193–4 in the 'Oden und Lieder' section,
               'Zweites Buch'] [S3: p. 158]

25 May 1815   *Auf den Tod einer Nachtigall (I)* D201 [S1: pp. 12–13] [S2: pp. 141–2 in the
               'Oden und Lieder' section, 'Erstes Buch'] [S3: pp. 114–15]

29 May 1815   *Die Liebende* D207 [S1: pp. 162–3] [S2: pp. 247–8 in the 'Oden und Lieder'
               section, 'Zweites Buch'] [S3: pp. 201–2]
               Die Nonne D208 (first version) and D212 (second version) [S1: pp. 54–7] [S2:
               pp. 41–5 in the 'Balladen' section] [S3: pp. 35–8]

17 June 1815   *Der Traum* D213 [S1: p. 95] [S2: pp. 46–7 in the 'Balladen' section] [S3:
               pp. 39–40]
               Die Laube D214 [S1: pp. 148–9] [S2: pp. 186–7 in the 'Oden und Lieder' section,
               'Erstes Buch'] [S3: pp. 153–4]

12 May 1816   *Klage (An den Mond)* D436 and D437 [S1: p. 90] [S2: pp. 168–9, as *Klage* in the
               'Oden und Lieder' section, 'Erstes Buch'] [S3: p. 138]

13 May 1816   *Frühlingslied* D398 [S1: p. 119] [S2: p. 172 in the 'Oden und Lieder' section,
               'Erstes Buch'] [S3: p. 141]
               Auf den Tod einer Nachtigall (II) D399 [S1: pp. 12–13] [S2: pp. 141–2 in the
               'Oden und Lieder' section, 'Erstes Buch'] [S3: pp. 114–15]
               Die Knabenzeit D400 [S2: pp. 139–40 in the 'Oden und Lieder' section, 'Erstes
               Buch'] [S3: pp. 112–13]
               Winterlied D401 [S1: pp. 124–5] [S2: pp. 173–4 in the 'Oden und Lieder' section,
               'Erstes Buch'] [S3: pp. 142–3]

May 1816   *Minnelied* D429 [S2: pp. 175–6 in the 'Oden und Lieder' section, 'Erstes Buch']
               [S3: pp. 145–6]
               Die frühe Liebe D430 [S1: pp. 128–9] [S2: pp. 177–8 in the 'Oden und Lieder'
               section, 'Erstes Buch'] [S3: pp. 145–6]
               Blumenlied D431 [S1: p. 136] [S2: p. 179 in the 'Oden und Lieder' section,
               'Erstes Buch'] [S3: p. 147]
               Seligkeit D433 [S2: pp. 191–2 in the 'Oden und Lieder' section, 'Zweites Buch']
               [S3: p. 157]
               Erntelied D434 [S1: pp. 26–7] [S2: pp. 209–10 in the 'Oden und Lieder' section,
               'Zweites Buch'] [S3: pp. 171–2]

7 August 1816 *An den Mond* D468 [S1: pp. 78–9] [S2: pp. 222–3 in the 'Oden und Lieder'
               section, 'Zweites Buch'] [S3: pp. 182–3]

November 1816 *Mailied* D503 [S1: p. 21] [S2: pp. 159–60 in the 'Oden und Lieder' section,
               'Erstes Buch'] [S3: p. 129–30]

Mention should also be made of other Hölty settings for unaccompanied voices that are outside the
scope of this book: *Totengräberlied* D38, Trio for two tenors and bass, 1813?; *Mailied* D129 (first
setting), Trio for two tenors and bass, 1815?; *Der Schnee zerrinnt* D130, Canon for three voices, 1815?
[using part of the text of *Mailied*]; *Mailied* D199 (second setting), Duet for two voices or two horns,
24 May 1815; *Mailied* D202 (second version of above) 26 May 1815; *Trinklied im Winter* D242, Trio

for two tenors and bass, August 1815?; *Frühlingslied* D243 (first version), Trio for two tenors and bass, August 1815?; *Willkommen, lieber schöner Mai* D244, Canon in two parts for three voices, August 1815?; *Trinklied im Mai* D426, Trio for two tenors and bass, May 1816; *Liebe säuseln die Blätter* D988, Canon for three voices, date unknown

Ludwig Christoph Heinrich Hölty was born in Mariensee near Hanover on 21 December 1748. At school he showed great aptitude for the English language, and later learned Italian and Spanish. His looks put people off: he was tall and ungainly of stature with a stooping, awkward walk that suggested he was somewhat simple, and had an almost frighteningly pale complexion. As a youth he had been good-looking but an attack of smallpox shortly after the death of his mother robbed him of this advantage. However those who knew him well were attracted to his shining blue eyes, his roguish laugh and wit, his capacity for unending hard work and his burning feel for what was right and wrong. He studied theology at Göttingen where he became a member of the Göttinger Hainbund, an artistic brotherhood that came into being on a moonlit walk through the woods in September 1772 when six undergraduate poets, inspired by the beauty of their surroundings, joined hands, danced round an oak tree and swore eternal friendship. Thus it was that Johann Heinrich Voss, Johann Martin Miller and Johann Friedrich Hahn among others vowed allegiance to the emotional poetry of Klopstock, and enmity to the artificial poetry of Wieland. This eighteenth-century version of what might be called a 'Living Poets' Society' (the Stolberg brothers were later members, as were Haugwitz and Leisewitz) was opposed to rationalism and convention. Hölty's poetry is often in classical metres, but his theme is May and springtime, and he is always aware that death is never far away. There is something in his genial and gentle work, ambivalent in both joy and sadness, that perfectly matches Schubert's own temperament and which strongly appealed to later poets such as Hölderlin, Novalis and Mörike. Hölty died at the age of twenty-seven from tuberculosis, on 1 September 1776, over twenty years before Schubert's birth.

Ludwig Hölty by Chodowiecki from Voss's *Musenalmanach* (1778) by J. H. Voss.

The disparity between many of the poet's originals and the versions Schubert set goes back to the fact that after Hölty's death several editions of the poems were edited by his friends and colleagues, some of them, notably Johann Heinrich Voss, more accomplished than others. The first of these, a most unreliable edition bungled by Geisler in 1782, was quickly followed in 1783 by an unsatisfactorily rushed version by Friedrich Grafen zu Stolberg-Stolberg in collaboration with Voss. The most famous of these 'improved' editions, definitive in its way, is that of 1804 (in fact S2), this time edited by Johann Heinrich Voss alone. This was the basis of the Viennese reprint used by Schubert, and the edition owned by Brahms. The great lieder composers were in fact setting, without being aware of it, a posthumous collaboration between Hölty and Voss. The original and unadulterated Hölty texts first came to light in a critical edition from 1914–18. These versions are printed in Schochow 1974, vol. 1: 'An die Nachtigall, die vor meinem Kammerfenster sang' (original version of *An die Nachtigall*) pp. 172–3; 'Elegie auf eine Nachtigall' (original version of *Auf den Tod einer Nachtigall*) pp. 182–3; 'Die Knabenzeit' (original version of *Die Knabenzeit*) p. 183; 'Minnelied' (original version of *Minnelied*) pp. 185–6; 'Minnehuldigung' (original version of *Die frühe Liebe*) pp. 187–8; 'Minnelied' (original version of *Blumenlied*) pp. 188–9; 'Minnelied' (original version of *Seligkeit*) pp. 189–90; 'Maylied' (original version of *Mailied*) pp. 193–4. Voss's alterations were made with the best and most sophisticated of intentions, but they tend to iron out the true authorial voice of Hölty with its quaint naiveté and sometimes quirky turn of phrase.

HOFFNUNG   Hope
(GOETHE) **D295** [H212][1]

The song exists in two versions, both of which are discussed below:
(1) and (2) After February 1820

(1) 'Langsam'   F major   ₵   [34 bars]

(2) E major

Schaff', das Tagwerk meiner Hände,
Hohes Glück, dass ich's vollende!
Lass, o lass mich nicht ermatten!
Nein, es sind nicht leere Träume:
Jetzt nur Stangen, diese Bäume
Geben einst noch Frucht und Schatten.

O Fortune, let me complete
My hands' daily task!
Let me not, O let me not grow weary!
No, these are not vain dreams;
Though now but saplings, these trees
Will one day yield fruit and shade.

JOHANN WOLFGANG VON GOETHE (1749–1832); poem written in November 1776
at the earliest

This is the thirty-fourth of Schubert's seventy-five Goethe solo settings (1814–26). See the poet's biography for a chronological list of all the Goethe settings.

---

[1] The 2012 re-dating of this song obviously affects its place in the chronology. Had this information been published in 2003, both this song and *An den Mond* D291 would have been placed between H450 and H470.

One of the secrets of Goethe's success was what the Germans term 'Fleiss' – hard work and diligence. There is no doubt that the poet had an extraordinary ability to work long and hard, and it was this, allied to his intuition and genius, that made him what he was. The poem dates from Goethe's early Weimar years when he was given enormous responsibility in the governing of the state.

Admittedly Weimar was only a tiny dukedom, but the poet's hands were full in a vigorous programme of reform and modernization, including the inspection of the local mines (which gave rise to his *Harzreise im Winter*) and the replanning of the ducal gardens and planting of trees. However, the composition of *Hoffnung* was occasioned by something rather more personal. In April 1776, Carl Augustus, duke of Weimar, placed a house and garden in the Ilm valley at Goethe's disposal. Proud of his new property, the ever-practical poet set about creating an agreeable landscape. In a letter to Charlotte von Stein (8 November 1777) he describes his excitement at the arrival of thirty fruit trees; he needed to plant these quickly, and ring them around with thorns in order to protect them from marauding rabbits. In his later years in Weimar, Goethe could survey his practical handiwork with a measure of satisfaction. As an old man he could share the sentiments of Thomas Hardy (set by Britten in *At Day-Close in November*):

> I set every tree in my June time,
> And now they obscure the sky.

Compare these words to Goethe's diary notes for his second Swiss journey in 1776:

> Portentous dreams I planted
> Are still saplings, yet some day
> These trees will shade me.

Schubert finds a remarkably moving tone for this song considering that it is so like a chorale or hymn tune. There is no religious feeling here, however; only the sense that work and responsibility are in themselves sacred. Old-fashioned virtues summon up old-fashioned music. The staccato left-hand accompaniment beautifully conveys the idea of daily tasks accomplished with precision and discipline. The right hand, which doubles the vocal line a great deal of the time, traces a melody that has all the gravity of a pilgrim's chorus. The vocal line climbs high on the stave towards the end of the song, a metaphor for hope and aspiration; the ascent to the forte of the last line signifies a heart swelling with well-deserved pride. Although among the least known of Schubert's single-page masterpieces to Goethe texts, this song with the brevity of a motto or epigram has the self-contained perfection of *Erster Verlust* D226 and *Wandrers Nachtlied* D768. The song exists in two almost identical autographs, the first in F (in Berlin), the second in E (in Washington) with a more comfortable and practical tessitura. The date of the song has always been contentious. The AGA placed it in 1815; Reed suggested a date of 1819 (concluded from Winter's paper studies); in 2011 the NSA, on account of Schubert's handwriting as well as the music paper, placed both versions of the song 'After February 1820'. Indeed *Hoffnung* may belong with the other Schubert Goethe settings of April 1821, or even December 1822. Leo Black pointed out a link between this song and the 'walking' rhythm and harmonies of a chorus in the 1823 opera *Fierabras* (Act 2 No. 11) where there is hope of peace between two great military commanders (Fierabras and Charlemagne).

Autographs:	Staatsbibliothek Preussischer Kulturbesitz, Berlin (first version)
	Library of Congress, Washington (second version)
Publication:	First published as No. 14 of *Neueste Folge nachgelassener Lieder und Gesänge* by J. P. Gotthard, Vienna in 1872 (P440; first version)
	First published as part of the AGA in 1895 (P613; second version)

Subsequent editions:	Peters: Vol. 7/62; AGA XX 175 a & b: Vol. 3/193 (first version) & 194 (second version); NSA IV: Vol. 9/110 (first version) & 111 (second version)
Bibliography:	Black 1998, p. 29
	Black 2003, p. 80
	Winter 1978, p. 500
Discography and timing:	Fischer-Dieskau I 6[5] 1'38
	Hyperion I 24[22] Michael George
	Hyperion II 12[7] 1'28

← *Sehnsucht (Mignon)* D359   *An den Mond* D296 →

HOFFNUNG (I)   Hope
(Schiller) **D251** [H136]
G♭ major   7 August 1815

(18 bars)

Es reden und träumen die Menschen viel	Men talk and dream
Von bessern künftigen Tagen,	Of better days to come.
Nach einem glücklichen goldenen Ziel	You see them running and chasing
Sieht man sie rennen und jagen,	After a happy, golden goal.
Die Welt wird alt und wird wieder jung,	The world grows old, and young again,
Doch der Mensch hofft immer Verbesserung!	But man forever hopes for better things.
Die Hoffnung führt ihn ins Leben ein,	Hope leads man into life.
Sie umflattert den fröhlichen Knaben,	It hovers around the happy boy;
Den Jüngling lockt ihr Zauberschein,	Its magic radiance inspires the youth,
Sie wird mit dem Greis nicht begraben;	Nor is it buried with the old man.
Denn beschliesst er im Grabe den müden Lauf,	For though he ends his weary life in the grave,
Noch am Grabe pflanzt er—die Hoffnung auf.	Yet on that grave he plants his hope.
Es ist kein leerer schmeichelnder Wahn,	It is no vain, flattering illusion,
Erzeugt im Gehirne des Toren.	Born in the mind of a fool.
Im Herzen kündet es laut sich an,	Loudly it proclaims itself in men's hearts:
Zu was Besserm sind wir geboren,	We are born for better things.
Und was die innere Stimme spricht,	And what the inner voice tells us
Das täuscht die hoffende Seele nicht.	Does not deceive the hopeful soul.

FRIEDRICH VON SCHILLER (1759–1805); poem written in 1797

This is the fifteenth of Schubert's forty-four Schiller solo settings (1811–24). See the poet's biography for a chronological list of all the Schiller settings.

Schiller was one of the most important inspirational figures of Schubert's early years. His lyrics were well suited to the stirring times of the Napoleonic wars; his works advocated both action and contemplation, and countless young men took his patriotism to heart. The poet's bracing lack of self-pity and his boundless determination made him a natural pioneer of *Sturm und Drang*. By 1815 it was well known that in later life he had backed away from the revolutionary principles of his youth (his anti-tyrannical stance and early sympathy for the principles of the French Revolution had made him seem subversive as a young man) and in Schubert's teenage years Schiller's exhortations were conservative enough to appeal to Metternich and the Austrian establishment. With the poet's historical dramas, such as the great *Wallenstein* trilogy, the public was transported to another period (during the Thirty Years War) when Germany was struggling for existence. Schiller's status as a classic in Austria was confirmed in 1809 by the authorized publication of a Schiller edition by the Viennese publisher Anton Doll.

In musical terms, this little song is the paradigm of tuneful simplicity. Much less well known than, say, *Heidenröslein* D257, it has the same catchy inevitability that distinguishes the composer's folksong-like lieder. Schubert has scanned the words of the first verse and found two images that are the clues to the character of the setting – 'rennen' (to run, b. 7) and 'jagen' (to hunt, b. 8). Accordingly the music runs in delightful ascending flights of fancy, not only in the tripping vocal line but also in the piano; note the exultant little interlude (b. 13) after the first 'Verbesserung'. The chase after happiness is suggested by the accompaniment's hunting horns echoing in alternating thirds and sixths, particularly in the penultimate bar (b. 17) of the postlude. For all its charm, however, this song is too lightweight to match the universal scope of Schiller's sentiments. Schubert must have thought so too; he returned to the poem at a later date and made another setting of greater harmonic complexity (D637) which is less carefree and optimistic, more evocative of impossible dreams than of breezy certainties. Nevertheless, who else but Schubert with his whole life ahead of him, and everything to hope for, could have composed such an open-hearted little gem?

Autograph:	Wienbibliothek im Rathaus, Vienna (first draft)
First edition:	Published as No. 23 of *Neueste Folge nachgelassener Lieder und Gesänge* by J. P. Gotthard, Vienna in 1872 (P449)
Subsequent editions:	Not in Peters; AGA XX 106: Vol. 3/4; NSA IV: Vol. 4b/216; Bärenreiter: Vol. 3/210
Discography and timing:	Fischer-Dieskau — Hyperion I 20[24] Hyperion II 8[20] 1'54 Patricia Rozario

← *Das Geheimnis* D250   *Das Mädchen aus der Fremde* D252 →

HOFFNUNG (II)

Hope

(Schiller) Op. 87 no. 2 **D637** [H412]
B♭ major   1817? or April 1819?

(26 bars)

See previous entry for poem and translation

Friedrich von Schiller (1759–1805); poem written in 1797

This is the thirty-eighth of Schubert's forty-four Schiller solo settings (1811–24). See the poet's biography for a chronological list of all the Schiller settings.

This is Schubert's second attempt at this poem. The first dates from 1815, a chirrupy and tuneful ditty that reflects the youthful optimism of a teenager. Although it is not certain that this second setting dates from 1819, it is likely that Schubert returned to the poem about then. He was now able to give it a much deeper appraisal with a fuller understanding of the philosophical issues that interested his contemporaries. The second setting does, however, have something in common with another 1815 song, the Schober *Genügsamkeit* D143 which is also in a sturdy § and displays a similar stoical determination.

The introduction to *Hoffnung (II)* shows a preoccupation with subtly moving inner parts. The chromaticism of the opening four bars is a musical metaphor for life's habit of moving the goalposts without notice. Circumstances change as quickly as a chord in the hand which (just when you think you have recognized it) evolves under the fingers into something else. To continue to hope through thick and thin takes resolution, quiet determination and courage, not merely a breezy *esprit*. Note for example, in a song whose key is B flat major, the setting of 'künftigen Tagen' ('days to come') in B flat minor (bb. 7–8), underlining that 'what's to come is still unsure', as Shakespeare puts it.

John Reed is correct to point out that Capell's characterization of the song as 'racy – a wilder kind of drinking song' is one of that writer's misjudgements. Of course the music could be pushed into a rollicking tempo, but this is to misunderstand its essential introspection – a side of the German character that the Englishman Capell found stodgy and self-indulgent. The song in its pastoral manner is a forerunner of the Schlegel setting *Abendlied für die Entfernte* D856 (also in §) that reflects on the same issues ('the heart remains constant, hoping faithfully unto the grave'). Both songs share an earnest and touching desire not only for better circumstances in life but also for self improvement. At the elongated setting of 'Verbesserung' at the end of the first verse (bb. 19–21) the breadth of the note values seems to imply the opening up of new vistas of perception as much as windows of opportunity. All this is in line with the shared hopes and aspirations of the *Bildung* circle that was particularly active in 1819 before Johann Senn (qv) was exiled to the Tyrol. It is significant that the manly and quietly heroic qualities advocated here do not explicitly mention God or religion. Nevertheless it seems self-evident that this song was composed by the same hand that wrote the Silbert and Novalis settings, rich in metaphysical imagery, and at about the same time.

Autograph:	Missing or lost
First edition:	Published as Op. 84 no. 2 (later corrected to Op. 87 no. 2) by A. Pennauer, Vienna in 1827 (P132)
Subsequent editions:	Peters: Vol. 4/75; AGA XX 358: Vol. 6/36; NSA IV: Vol. 4a/88; Bärenreiter: Vol. 3/58
Bibliography:	Capell 1928, pp. 157–8
	Fischer-Dieskau 1977, p. 41
	J. F. Reichardt (1752–1814) *Hofnung* from *Schillers Lyrische Gedichte*, zweites Heft (1811)
Arrangements:	Arr. Tilman Hoppstock (b. 1961) for guitar accompaniment, in *Franz Schubert: 110 Lieder* (2009)
Discography and timing:	Fischer-Dieskau II 3[1] 2'57
	Hyperion I 29[3]
	Hyperion II 21[6] 2'41 Marjana Lipovšek

← *Vom Mitleiden Mariä* D632   *Widerschein* D639 →

HORCH, HORCH! DIE LERCH *see* STÄNDCHEN D889

HEINRICH HÜTTENBRENNER (1799–1830)

THE POETIC SOURCES

There is no printed source to Hüttenbrenner's poems. Schubert set the song from an autograph no doubt given to him by Josef Hüttenbrenner.

THE SONG

November 1820   *Der Jüngling auf dem Hügel* D702, Op. 8 no. 1

Mention should also be made of one other Hüttenbrenner setting that falls outside the scope of this book: *Wehmut* D825, Quartet for TTBB, Summer? 1826

Heinrich was the youngest of four Hütten-brenner brothers (there were also apparently sisters in the family). All of them were born in Graz – Anselm the composer and close friend of Schubert in 1794; Josef, Schubert's sometime secretary and factotum in 1796; Andreas (who became a famous lawyer and was ennobled) in 1797; and Heinrich who was born on 9 January 1799. He first went to university in Graz but as a result of a letter he received in May 1819 from his brother Josef he continued his legal studies in Vienna where Schubert's star, Josef assured him, was in the ascendant. Josef's hope was that Heinrich would become Schubert's librettist but it was not to be. There must have been some social contact between the aspiring poet and the composer (we know that Schubert and three of the brothers were together at the funeral of the poet Karl Schröckinger on 23 December 1819) but there is no evidence of friendship. It was almost certainly Josef who placed his brother's work where Schubert was sure to see it. Heinrich returned to Graz where he became professor of Roman and ecclesiastical law. He was a contributor to various periodicals and he continued to write poetry, though not in great quantity. Some of his poetry was set by his brother Anselm. He died suddenly on 29 December 1830, his brothers outliving him by many decades. Schubert set one other poem by Heinrich, the lovely quartet for unaccompanied male voices, *Wehmut* ('Die Abendglocke tönet') D825. For much of the song the first bass adheres to minims on a fixed pitch like a chiming bell. It was published as part of Op. 64 in 1828 by Pennauer, six weeks before Schubert's death. The music, however, was almost certainly written a great deal earlier.

HULDIGUNG
(Kosegarten) **D240** [H131]
E major   27 July 1815

Homage

(20 bars)

Gar verloren, ganz versunken	Lost and absorbed

Gar verloren, ganz versunken
In dein Anschaun, Lieblingin,
Wonnebebend, liebetrunken,
Schwingt zu dir der Geist sich hin.
Nichts vermag ich zu beginnen,
Nichts zu denken, dichten, sinnen.
Nichts ist, was das Herz mir füllt,
Huldin, als dein holdes Bild.

Süsse, Reine, Makellose,
Edle, Theure, Treffliche,
Ungeschminkte rote Rose,
Unversehrte Lilie,
Anmutreiche Anemone,
Aller Schönen Preis und Krone,
Weisst du auch, Gebieterin,
Wie ich ganz dein eigen bin?

[...6...]

Und wie bald ist nicht verschwunden
Jenes Schlummers kurze Nacht!
Horch, es jubelt: Überwunden!
Schau, der ewge Tag erwacht!
Dann du Theure, dann du Eine,
Bist du ganz und ewig Meine!
Trennung ist das Loos der Zeit!
Ewig einigt Ewigkeit!

Lost and absorbed
In contemplation of you, my darling,
Trembling with ecstasy, drunk with love,
My spirit flies to you.
I can do nothing,
I cannot think, or write or plan.
Nothing fills my heart, beloved lady,
But your sweet image.

You are sweet, pure and spotless,
Noble, beloved and sublime,
Unadorned red rose,
Unblemished lily,
Gracious anemone,
Prize and crown of all beauty.
Do you know, fair lady,
That I am utterly yours?

[...6...]

And how soon does that brief night
Of slumber vanish!
Hark, rejoicing! Victory!
See, the eternal day awakens!
Now, my one and only love,
You are all mine, for ever!
Separation is the lot of time;
Eternity unites eternally!

LUDWIG KOSEGARTEN (1758–1818)

This is the twelfth of Schubert's twenty-one Kosegarten solo settings (1815–17). See the poet's biography for a chronological list of all the Kosegarten settings, as well as a discussion of Morten Solvik's Kosegarten Liederkreis and this song's place within it.

It is the courtly old-fashioned title and some of the language (the beloved is addressed as 'Huldin' and 'Gebieterin', exalted words even by Kosegarten's eighteenth-century standards) that are the real key to the music. In Schubert's favourite Kosegarten tonality of E major, the vocal line and the accompaniment are full of the deep bows of obeisance – a distinguished gentleman's homage to a high-born lady. There is something that suggests the singer is an older man, a German Don Ottavio perhaps who is paying formal court to a Donna Anna. The first bar of the vocal line ('Gar verloren') consists of a five-note figure; the second bar ('ganz versunken') is a sequence that caps the first phrase, as if the singer were doffing his, and searching for a more extravagant (and thus higher in tessitura) verbal gesture to describe his admiration. This is followed by a two-bar phrase (bb. 3–4) in which the music bows low while sweeping downwards in an E major arpeggio. The same formula is followed in the next four bars, this time with an even more florid bow as the cadence moves briefly into the dominant. The middle section (from 'Nichts vermag ich zu beginnen', b. 9) is another pair of two-bar phrases, each of them ending with a gracious and adoring appoggiatura – yet more obeisances. These cadences that divide the piece into a number of courtly gestures give the song a somewhat stilted quality, as if it is framed by inverted commas; the music seems scrupulously constructed rather than born of spontaneous passion. Nevertheless, the vocal line is extremely gratifying to sing. From b. 13 the coda ('Nichts ist, was das Herz mir füllt, / Huldin, als dein holdes Bild') makes a final dip into the middle of the vocal tessitura, dallies on another appoggiatura (supported by a chromatic swoon in the accompaniment under the extended setting of 'holdes', b. 16) before standing tall on the return to the tonic. The piano's postlude (bb. 19–20) is an ingratiating chromatic scale and an exquisite feminine cadence. This song gives the impression of a suitor approaching his lady-love in measured steps so as not to alarm her; passion is everywhere moderated by eighteenth-century manners.

The title of Kosegarten's poem in the 1824 edition of the *Gedichte* is *Minnesang*. The poet was such a Romeo in his youth that his heirs quite possibly wanted to suggest that a poem as ardent as this could only have been written for his wife. As the reader progresses through the poem it is clear that it is an elegy for the fictional Ellwina (her name is mentioned in Strophes 7 and 8). *Huldigung* has nine strophes – in the performance for the Hyperion Edition, 1, 2 and 9 were recorded and these strophes are translated here.

Autograph:	Österreichische Nationalbibliothek, Vienna
First edition:	Published as part of the AGA in 1895 (P570)
Subsequent editions:	Not in Peters; AGA XX 103: Vol. 2/210; NSA IV: Vol. 8/146
Discography and timing:	Fischer-Dieskau I 4[19] 0'48 (first strophe only)
	Hyperion I 20[14]
	Hyperion II 8[14] 2'18 John Mark Ainsley

← *Die Mondnacht* D238   *Alles um Liebe* D241 →

HYMNE (Hymne I)   Hymn
(NOVALIS) **D659** [H426]
A minor – F major   May 1819

(167 bars)

Wenige wissen
Das Geheimnis der Liebe,
Fühlen Unersättlichkeit
Und ewigen Durst.
Des Abendmahls
Göttliche Bedeutung
Ist den irdischen Sinnen Rätsel;
Aber wer jemals
Von heissen, geliebten Lippen
Atem des Lebens sog,
Wem heilige Glut
In zitternde Wellen das Herz schmolz,
Wem das Auge aufging,
Dass er des Himmels
Unergründliche Tiefe mass,
Wird essen von seinem Leibe
Und trinken von seinem Blute
Ewiglich.

Wer hat des irdischen Leibes
Hohen Sinn erraten?
Wer kann sagen,
Dass er das Blut versteht?

Einst ist alles Leib,
Ein Leib,
In himmlischem Blute
Schwimmt das selige Paar.–

O! dass das Weltmeer
Schon errötete,
Und in duftiges Fleisch
Aufquölle der Fels!
Nie endet das süsse Mahl,
Nie sättigt die Liebe sich.
Nicht innig, nicht eigen genug
Kann sie haben den Geliebten.
Von immer zärteren Lippen
Verwandelt wird das Genossene
Inniglicher und näher.
Heissere Wollust
Durchbebt die Seele.
Durstiger und hungriger
Wird das Herz:

Und so währet der Liebe Genuss
Von Ewigkeit zu Ewigkeit.
Hätten die Nüchternen
Einmal nur gekostet,

Few know
The secret of Love,
Few feel its insatiability,
Its endless thirst.
The divine meaning
Of the Last Supper
As a riddle to earthly minds.
But he who has drawn
The breath of life
From ardent, beloved lips;
He whose heart has melted in trembling waves
Of sacred passion,
He who has opened his eyes
To measure the fathomless depths
Of heaven,
Will eat of His body
And drink of His blood
Eternally.

Who has guessed the lofty meaning
Of that earthly body?
Who can say
That he understands the blood?

One day all will be body,
One single body;
The blessed pair
Shall swim in heavenly blood.

O that the world's oceans
Might now turn red,
And the rock spring up
As fragrant flesh!
The sweet meal never ends;
Love is never satisfied.
It can never possess the beloved
Profoundly and exclusively.
With ever more tender kisses
The beloved is transformed,
Possessed more inwardly and more closely.
Desire still more ardent
Pierces the soul.
Thirstier, hungrier
Grows the heart;

Thus the pleasure of Love
Endures throughout eternity.
If only the sober
Once tasted it,

Alles verliessen sie,	They would abandon all else
Und setzten sich zu uns	And sit with us
An den Tisch der Sehnsucht,	At the table of longing,
Der nie leer wird.	Which is never empty.
Sie erkennten der Liebe	They would see Love's
Unendliche Fülle,	Infinite richness,
Und priesen die Nahrung	And extol the nourishment
Von Leib und Blut.	Of body and blood.

NOVALIS (pseudonym of FRIEDRICH VON HARDENBERG) (1772–1801); poem written in 1799

This is the second of Schubert's six Novalis solo settings (1819–20). See the poet's biography for a chronological list of all the Novalis settings.

Because this music comes from the most richly experimental period of the composer's life, and because the poem is itself highly unusual, there is no other Schubert song quite like it. The poem is printed in short lines that are not rhymed; indeed it could easily have been written as prose. What is most striking is that, although the song was composed at a time when much of Schubert's writing for piano is demandingly florid, the look of this music on the page is decidedly plain, as if the composer had imagined it printed in a Pietist songbook or hymnal with the simplest of keyboard accompaniments. All is economical to the point of severity but the result is impressively direct, if not gratifyingly melodious for its own sake. The music is arioso – not quite recitative and not quite aria, but somewhere between the two. In this we hear the beginnings of the great unfinished cantata *Lazarus* which is as far as can be imagined in musical style from, say, the Mass in A flat D678, a public piece, overtly dramatic in style and content. The essential plainness of the composer's musical solution to this *Hymne* somehow chimes with the earnest Saxon Protestant background of Novalis himself, and we see something of a portrait of the poet emerging in the demeanour of the music.

Novalis writes out his hymn in one long strophe, but the divisions in the poem are printed here to allow the listener to see how Schubert divided the work into distinct sections. The first of these (marked 'Mit Andacht', 'With devotion') approximates the naturalness of speech in the way it weaves in and out of melody, stopping briefly (with cadence and fermata) to draw breath and consider the next point. It is obviously a matter of priority for the composer that the text should be understood. The effect is of something spoken from the pulpit, with passion and accompanying rhetorical gestures, some vehement, others calm.

At 'Wer hat des irdischen Leibes / Hohen Sinn erraten?' (from b. 75) there is a short seven-bar recitative (marked as such, with a change of key from C major to A flat major), followed by another question ('Wer kann sagen, / Dass er das Blut versteht?' from b. 79). Then comes the most striking and grandiose section – searing music for the words of a seer, and an appropriate match for the unusual and mystical imagery (from b. 82 marked 'Langsam, feierlich' and *alla breve*). The accompaniment is not complicated, consisting of a succession of mighty chords, spaced evenly as if to herald and punctuate a pronouncement of some import. Reed considers that this section of the song only narrowly escapes pomposity.

The section beginning 'O! dass das Weltmeer / Schon errötete' (from b. 99, in ⅜) is less successful. Schubert finds himself at a loss to do justice to the words while retaining the simple overall style. The accompaniment surges (or, if the pianist is not careful, plods) in a quasi-Italianate manner; the energy this should generate might be considered to approximate to the drives of thrusting desire, but falls short of the mark. The words 'Durstiger und hungriger /

Wird das Herz' call forth a tremolo-accompanied phrase (from b. 125) that is both melodramatic and something of a rarity.

The final section of the piece recovers the momentum with an ingenious 'circular' melody (accompanied by triplets) for 'Und so währet der Liebe Genuss' (from b. 129). This two-bar phrase is heard twice but when the vocal line adds a sixth in the chord of B flat major (b. 132) the harmony seems unanchored and free to float in space – this phrase is going nowhere in particular, and could be listened to again and again. It is thus an exact musical analogue for the words that describe the pleasure of love lasting through all eternity. A return to the 'Italian'-accompanied music (at 'Hätten die Nüchternen' b. 137) is followed by the B flat^6 arpeggios (from b. 153), this time representing the infinite richness of that love.

The music for the whole of this piece, somewhat stiff, not particularly melodic and thus not enormously memorable, is hardly the stamping ground of the average Schubertian. But it has qualities that are a fascinating indication of a young composer attempting to look into his own soul. Schubert seems drawn to texts that reflect the reconciliation of sexual desire with a search for spiritual growth. Plato in his *Symposium* (a work also studied in the *Bildung* circle) referred to these conflicting desires as the black and white horses of the charioteer. By all accounts, the frolicking of the black horse of sensuality was an important part of Schubert's make-up. Novalis avers that even erotic feelings are holy and uplifting and that the artist who addressed these issues was himself Christ-like. One remembers that Schubert had just set these lines of Schlegel (himself Novalis-influenced at the time) in the song *Die Gebüsche*:

Durch alle Töne tönet	Through all the sounds
Im bunten Erdentraume	In the earth's many-coloured dream,
E i n leiser Ton gezogen,	*One* faint sound echoes
Für den, der heimlich lauschet.	For him who secretly listens.

Also in *Abendröte* D690:

Und das All ein einzig Chor,	And the whole world becomes a single choir,
Manches Lied aus Einem Munde.	Singing many a song with one voice.

If the flesh was important to Schubert, so were the workings of the heart and brain; his instinct at this time was to find a philosophy that could harmonize all three. There is every indication that at least for a while he was nourished by the fearless poetic syntheses of Novalis which, through the magic of poetry, made a glowing unity out of many shadowy issues. It is said that the poet was inspired to write this poem in the Easter week of 1799 following a visit to the grave of his beloved fiancée Sophie. [*See also* GEISTLICHES LIED I, II and III (D660–62), originally published as Hymne II, III and IV]

Autograph:	Bibliotheca Bodmeriana, Geneva
First edition:	Published as no. 37 ('Der Hymnen von Novalis' no. 1) of *Neueste Folge nachgelassener Lieder und Gesänge* by J. P. Gotthard, Vienna in 1872 (P462)
Subsequent editions:	Not in Peters; AGA XX 360: Vol. 6/42; NSA IV: Vol. 12/91
Bibliography:	Black 2003, p. 63
	Capell 1928, p. 159
	Einstein 1951, pp. 190–1
	Fischer-Dieskau 1977, pp. 124–5 & 127

Further setting:	Alma Schindler Mahler (1879–1964) *Hymne*, no. 1 of *Fünf Gesänge* (1924)
Discography and timing:	Fischer-Dieskau II 3[3] 5'52
	Hyperion I 29[4]
	Hyperion II 22[1] 7'09 Marjana Lipovšek

← *Geistliches Lied ('Marie')* D658   *Geistliches Lied ('Wenn ich ihn nur habe')* D660 →

HYMNE II *see* GEISTLICHES LIED ('Wenn ich ihn nur habe') D660

HYMNE III *see* GEISTLICHES LIED ('Wenn alle untreu werden') D661

HYMNE IV *see* GEISTLICHES LIED ('Ich sag es jedem, dass er lebt') D662

HYMNE AN DEN UNENDLICHEN   Hymn to the eternal   Quartet, SATB
(SCHILLER) **D232** [H123]
C minor   11 July 1815

Zwischen Himmel und Erd', hoch in der
  Lüfte Meer,
In der Wiege des Sturms trägt mich
  ein Zackenfels,
    Wolken thürmen
    Unter mir sich zu Stürmen,
Schwindelnd gaukelt der Blick umher,
  Und ich denke dich, Ewiger!

Deinen schauernden Pomp borge
  dem Endlichen,
Ungeheure Natur! du der Unendlichkeit
    Riesentochter!
    Sei mir Spiegel Jehovahs!
Seinen Gott dem vernünft'gen Wurm
  Orgle prächtig, Gewittersturm!

Between heaven and earth, high in the
  surging winds,
In the cradle of the storm I stand upon a
  jagged rock;
    Storm clouds
    Bank below me,
My gaze darts around giddily,
  And I think of You, Eternal God!

Lend your fearful splendour to all things finite,

Immense nature,
    Mighty daughter of infinity!
    Hold a mirror to Jehovah!
Tempest, in your majestic thunder
    May the decent common worm know its God.

Horch! er orgelt – den Fels wie
    er herunterdröhnt!
Brüllend spricht der Orkan Zebaoth's
    Namen aus.
        Hingeschrieben
        Mit dem Griffel des Blitzes:
K r e a t u r e n, e r k e n n t i h r m i c h ?
Schone, Herr! wir erkennen dich!
	Hark! Thunder! How it rumbles down
	    the rock!
	The hurricane roars Jehovah's name,
	
	        Engraved
	        With the lightning's pencil:
	'Creatures, do you know me?'
	'Spare us, Lord, we know you!'

FRIEDRICH VON SCHILLER (1759–1805)

This piece is usually considered together with the vocal quartets *Gott im Ungewitter* D985 and *Gott der Weltschöpfer* D986 (both poems by Uz) where it is heard as the third of a three-part pillar of quartets in C minor, C major and C minor. This goes back to the three pieces being published together by Josef Czerny in 1829 as Op. 112 (post.). It is not known when Schubert set the two Uz poems (hence their high numbers in that part of the Deutsch catalogue reserved for works of uncertain date) but Dietrich Berke in the preface to Series III of the NSA argues persuasively that they are probably also from 1815. It is quite possible that Schubert himself suggested to Czerny that these three works taken together would make a single opus fit for publication.

Although the music of *Hymne an den Unendlichen* is not quite as grand as *Gott im Ungewitter*, it is a four-part setting that is evidence of a Beethovenian (rather than a Mozartian) frame of mind. Another influence is Haydn. In the grand manner of *Die Schöpfung*, the crackling arpeggio in the piano in b. 5 precedes the mention of lightning in b. 8 (that is if the reading of 'Blitz' is sustained: the NSA, in deference to the original Schiller, prints 'Blick', citing 'Blitz' – in the AGA – as a misreading, rather than a deliberate change on the composer's part). Typical of Haydn is the quasi-canonic 'pile-up' of vocal parts beginning in the bass (doubled by a 'cello' line in the accompaniment) at 'Schwindelnd gaukelt der Blick umher' (from b. 7); this builds upwards as the tenor and alto add the same words in different note values, and the soprano makes the last entry on top of a sumptuous bank of sound supported by throbbing semiquavers in the pianist's right hand. As is common in the composer's choral writing of the time, the piano doubles the vocal line more or less until the middle of the song, but this is more than a convenient tack for rehearsing the voices – the grandeur of the poem needs the support of the most effulgent piano sound. Schubert fills out the chords in the piano part, allowing himself (from 'ich denke dich, Ewiger' b. 11) a whole page of demisemiquaver arpeggios that leave the upper parts to float free of doubling. The bottom line is written for a true bass; it touches low F (b. 12) and is not, as in a good deal of the composer's part-song writing, suitable for baritone.

One can only wonder if Schubert conceived this song for performance in church where there were singers (including the sweetheart of his adolescence Therese Grob) who would have been able to tackle it. The song certainly seemed to have been a way of thinking of God – out of the pulpit and into the open air – that appealed to Schubert at the time, but it was only one aspect of his devotional music. A few months later he composed the Klopstock setting *Dem Unendlichen* D291 which lays the foundation of his epic song style in religious mode; this was to reach its fullest flowering with *Die Allmacht* D852.

Autograph:	Missing or lost
First edition:	Published as Op. post. 112 no. 3 by Josef Czerny, Vienna in 1829 (P202)
Publication reviews:	*Allgemeiner Musikalischer Anzeiger* (Vienna), No. 14 (4 April

	1829), p. 55 [Waidelich/Hilmar *Dokumente I* No. 718] *Wiener Zeitschrift für Kunst, Literatur, Theater und Mode* No. 93 (4 August 1829), p. 772 [Waidelich/Hilmar *Dokumente I* No. 740]	
First known performance:	28 February 1836, Redoutensaal, Vienna. Performers unknown	
Subsequent editions:	AGA XVII 8: p. 167; NSA III: Vol. 2a/40	
Discography and timing:	Deutsche Grammophon *Schubert Quartette*	3'19	Elly Ameling, Janet Baker, Peter Schreier & Dietrich Fischer-Dieskau
	Hyperion I 22²⁷ Hyperion II 8⁶	3'30	Patricia Rozario, Catherine Denley, Jamie MacDougall & Michael George

⟵ *Das Sehnen* D231 *Geist der Liebe* D233 ⟶

HYMNE AN DIE JUNGFRAU *see SIEBEN GESÄNGE AUS WALTER SCOTT'S FRÄULEIN VOM SEE* D839/6 (ELLENS GESANG III)

Leopold Kupelwieser, detail of Kupelwieser with Schubert from *Landpartie der Schuberlianer* (1820).

I

ICH SAG ES JEDEM, DASS ER LEBT *see* GEISTLICHES LIED D662

ICH SASS AN EINER TEMPELHALLE *see* LEBENSTRAUM D1A & D39

ICH SCHLEICHE BANG UND STILL HERUM *see Die*
VERSCHWORENEN D787

ICH SEHE DICH IN TAUSEND BILDERN *see* GEISTLICHES LIED
('Marie') D658

IDENS NACHTGESANG   Ida's song to the night
(KOSEGARTEN) **D227** [H118]
B♭ major   7 July 1815

(15 bars)

Vernimm es Nacht, was Ida dir vertrauet,	Hear, night, what Ida confides to you;
Die satt des Tags in deine Arme flieht.	Sated with the day, I fly to your arms.
Ihr Sterne, die ihr hold und liebend auf	Stars, gazing down sweetly and lovingly
mich schauet,	upon me,
Vernehmt süsslauschend Idens Lied.	Listen fondly to Ida's song.
Den ich geahnt in liebevollen Stunden,	O night, o stars, I have found him,
Dem schlummerkrank mein Herz entgegen	Whom I dreamed of in hours of bliss,
schlug,[1]	
O Nacht, o Sterne, hörts, ich habe ihn	For whom my sleep-sick heart beat,
gefunden,	
Des Bild ich längst im Busen trug.	And whose image I have long carried
	within me.

[1] Kosegarten writes 'Dem *sehnsucht*krank mein Herz entgegen schlug'.

[...3...]   [...3...]

Freund, ich bin dein, nicht für den	My beloved, I am yours, not for the sands
Sand der Zeiten,	of time
Der schnellversiegend Chronos Uhr entfleusst,	That swiftly run dry from Chronos' hourglass,
Dein für den Riesenstrom heilvoller Ewigkeiten,	But for the mighty river of healing eternity
Der aus des Ew'gen Urne scheusst.	That gushes from the urn of the Eternal One!

LUDWIG THEOBUL KOSEGARTEN (1758–1818)

This is the second of Schubert's twenty-one Kosegarten solo settings (1815–17). See the poet's biography for a chronological list of all the Kosegarten settings, as well as a discussion of Morton Solvik's Kosegarten Liederkreis and this song's place within it.

Between June and October 1815, Schubert composed twenty settings of the poems of Kosegarten. Afterwards he returned only once to this poet, in 1817, for *An die untergehende Sonne* D457, which is the only Kosegarten song that is not strophic. The 1815 settings thus form a school of strophic composition and they have a uniformly classical simplicity and dignity. Their somewhat archaic style shelters a number of shy and unspectacular beauties, and the textures and moods vary considerably. Compare this ecstatic hymn and its four-part accompaniment with a song written on the same day, the exquisitely modal and palely translucent three-part invention *Von Ida* D228. The impassioned *Das Sehnen* D231 from 8 July is different again.

Behind the name Ida, and its genitive Idens, lies an unusual textual puzzle in Kosegarten's *Gedichte*. In the first edition of the poems (Leipzig, 1788) and the last (Greifswald, 1824), the name of the poet's beloved is Agnes, but in the edition used by Schubert (Heinrich Gräff, Leipzig, 1802), as well as the preceding one (Leipzig, 1798), this name is replaced by 'Ida'. The name 'Agnes' is thus written out of the poet's story at the turn of the century only to make a posthumous return in 1824. (In fact both names were meant to disguise the identity of a young girl called Karoline; for an explanation of this *see* KOSEGARTEN.) Fortunately in terms of musical setting the two names, Agnes and Ida, are interchangeable, both being duo-syllabic, but Ida is definitely the more singable.

The marking is 'Zart, langsam'. There is an introductory B flat major chord in the AGA and NSA, but in the Peters Edition the first chord is D minor. Although the style is classical enough to suggest an eighteenth-century setting, there is an exemplary freedom in the vocal line: the way 'flieht' is set in b. 6 – a drooping interval of a seventh accompanied by demisemiquavers, exquisitely fleet of foot with the chord resolving only after the singer has finished singing the word – is remarkable. The staccato right-hand accompaniment (with a legato bass) for pinpricks of starlight in b. 8 is an augury of much similar writing to come, as is the mezzo staccato writing for the piano in the song's eight final bars. There are six strophes in the poem by Kosegarten which is hardly one of his most convincing in terms of imagery or atmosphere – these are all printed in the AGA and NSA. Given here are 1, 2 and 6 as recorded in the Hyperion Edition. Three seem sufficient in performance.

Autographs:	British Library, London
	Österreichische Nationalbibliothek, Vienna (fair copy)
First edition:	Published as no. 8 in Friedlaender's edition by Peters Edition, Vol. 7, Leipzig in 1885 (P481)
Subsequent editions:	Peters: Vol. 7/22; AGA XX 90: Vol. 2/173; NSA IV: Vol. 8/116
Bibliography:	Solvik 1999

Discography and timing: Fischer-Dieskau   —
Hyperion I 7[11]
Hyperion II 8[1]   2'04   Elly Ameling

←— *Erster Verlust* D226   *Von Ida* D228 —→

IDENS SCHWANENLIED   Ida's swan song
(Kosegarten) **D317** [H196]

The song exists in two versions, the second of which is discussed below:
(1) 19 October 1815; (2) Undated

(1)   'Traurig'   F minor   ¢   [12 bars]

(2)   F minor

(13 bars)

Wie schaust du aus dem Nebelflor	O sun, how pale and weary
O Sonne, bleich und müde!	You gaze from your misty veil!
Es schwirrt der Heimchen heis'rer Chor	The hoarse chorus of crickets
Zu meinem Schwanenliede.	Chirrups to my swan song.
Es girrt die scheidende Natur	Departing nature coos
Ihr Lebewohl so traurig;	Its sad farewell.
Es stehen Busch und Wald und Flur	Bushes, woods and meadows
So trostlos und so schaurig.	Stand so desolate, so eerie.
Entblättert steht der Erlenhain,	The alder grove stands leafless
Entlaubt der graue Garten,	The bleak garden stripped of greenery
Wo Er und ich im Mondenschein	Where he and I in the moonlight
Einander bang' erharrten;	Anxiously awaited one another.
Wo Er und ich im Mondenblitz,	Where, in the moon's rays, he and I
Im Schirm der Linden sassen,	Sat beneath the canopy of the linden tree,
Und auf des Rasens weichem Sitz	And on the soft lawn
Der öden Welt vergassen;	Forgot the dismal world
Wo ich, gelehnt an seine Brust,	Where, leaning against his breast,
In süsse Träume nickte,	I drifted into sweet reverie,
Und holder Wahn und Edens Lust	Where blissful delirium and the pleasures of Eden
Die Träumende durchzückte.	Thrilled through me as I dreamed.

[...6...]   [...6...]

  Ach, klagt um eure Schwester, klagt   Mourn for your sister, mourn,
Ihr Rosen und ihr Nelken!   Roses and carnations!
Wie bald, und hin ist meine Pracht,   How quickly my splendour is gone,
Und meine Blüten welken!   And my blossoms fade.

[...]   [...]

  Der Wandrer, der in meiner Zier   The wanderer who looked upon me in my finery,
In meiner Schönheit Schimmer   In my shimmering beauty,
Mich schaute, kommt und forscht nach mir, Comes by and seeks me out;
Und sieht mich nimmer, nimmer!   But he will never see me again.

  Es kommt der Traute, den ich mir   He comes, whom I have chosen
Erkoren einzig habe,—   As my only love.
Ach fleuch, Geliebter, fleuch von hier; Fly beloved, fly from here.
Dein Mädchen schläft im Grabe.   Your sweetheart sleeps in the grave.

[...]   [...]

  Triumph! Auf Herbstesdämmerung   Rejoice! After the dusk of autumn
Folgt milder Frühlingsschimmer.   Comes spring's gentle radiance.
Auf Trennung folgt Vereinigung,   After separation comes reunion,
Vereinigung auf immer!   Eternal reunion!

LUDWIG THEOBUL KOSEGARTEN (1758–1818)

This is the eighteenth of Schubert's twenty-one Kosegarten solo settings (1815–17). See the poet's biography for a chronological list of all the Kosegarten settings, as well as a discussion of Morton Solvik's Kosegarten Liederkreis and this song's place within it.

This setting is very much in the mould of the Ida songs from July 1815. An air of quiet grace and classical control, not to mention elegiac melancholy (the marking is 'Traurig') is achieved by the sparest of piano writing with some delicate and unusual illustrative touches like the chirping of the crickets in the triplet accompaniment of the first verse (oscillating triplets from b. 5). In the second half of b. 5 this oscillation is between the very same notes of F and B natural that Schubert used to depict the song of the crickets in the vocal line of the first verse of Matthisson's *Stimme der Liebe* D187, written the preceding May. The composer had a tendency to notate the sounds of nature exactly as he heard them. Grimm's indispensable dictionary of the German language with its countless examples of early usages of words and imagery informs us that the chirping of crickets forebodes death which explains their presence in Kosegarten's poem, and in this song. The falling sequences at bb. 5–7, and the way the vocal line demurely descends the stave by degrees, indicate the restrained and feminine pathos of Ida's farewell. The postlude is a little work of art: in each of three consecutive bars, triplets, dotted quavers and semiquavers briefly ascend the stave and then settle onto a rueful diminished chord (this happens twice, bb. 9 and 10). In b. 11 this figuration leads to a D flat major chord with an accented passing note in a fortissimo dynamic. This stab of anguish is followed by resolution and the resigned melancholy of bb. 12 and 13 leads us back to F minor.

There are seventeen strophes in Kosegarten's poem – these are all printed in the AGA and the NSA. For the Hyperion recording verses 1, 12, 14, 15 and 17 were selected by Elly Ameling (all printed here) which permits the singer to concentrate on Ida's valediction, as befits a swansong. The earlier verses (also printed above) describe the blissful nature of the love once enjoyed by Ida. The loss of this relationship has taken away her desire to live, and leads her to sing this miniature 'Liebestod'. Unless a performer is willing to undertake a lengthy strophic song it is impossible to reflect the full scope of Kosegarten's poem in a single performance. The second version of the song differs from the first in that it has a two-quaver upbeat at the opening instead of a crotchet, and a more elaborate, and longer, postlude. It is as if the musical rendition of the swansong itself is being left to the piano.

Autograph:	Moldenhauer Archive, Library of Congress, Washington (first version)
	Music Deposit 21, Irving S. Gilmore Music Library, Yale University (second version)
Publication:	Published as part of the NSA in 2012 (first version)
	Published as part of the AGA in 1895 (P603; second version)
Subsequent editions:	Not in Peters; AGA XX 164: Vol. 3/148; NSA IV: Vol. 9/159 (first version) & 160 (second version)
Discography and timing:	Fischer-Dieskau —
	Hyperion I 7[19]
	Hyperion II 11[8] 3'03 Elly Ameling

← *An Rosa II* D316   *Schwangesang* D318 →

IHR BILD *see SCHWANENGESANG* D957/9

IHR GRAB   Her grave
(Roos) **D736** [H478]
E♭ major   End 1822 or January 1823

(60 bars)

Dort ist ihr Grab –	There is her grave,
Die einst im Schmelz der Jugend glühte,	Who once glowed with the lustre of youth;
Dort fiel sie – dort – die schönste Blüte,	There she fell, the fairest blossom,
Vom Baum des Lebens ab.	From the tree of life.
Dort ist ihr Grab –	There is her grave;
Dort schläft sie unter jener Linde.	There she sleeps beneath that linden tree.
Ach, nimmer ich ihn wiederfinde	Ah, never again shall I find
Den Trost, den sie mir gab!	The consolation she gave me.

Dort ist ihr Grab –	There is her grave;
Vom Himmel kam sie, dass die Erde	She came from heaven, that the earth
Mir Glücklichem zum Himmel werde –	Might turn to heaven for me in my happiness.
Und dort stieg sie hinab.	And there she sank down.
Dort ist ihr Grab	There is her grave,
Und dort in jenen stillen Hallen, –	And there in those silent vaults,
Bei ihr, lass ich mit Freuden fallen	At her side, I too shall joyfully
Auch meinen Pilgerstab.	Lay down my pilgrim's staff.

RICHARD ROOS (PSEUDONYM OF KARL AUGUST ENGELHARDT) (1768–1834)

This is Schubert's only Engelhardt solo setting. See the poet's biography.

The commentators agree that this is one of Schubert's better graveside meditations. It is in gently melancholic and reflective mood but, as in so many of his songs of this type, death is a calming and releasing presence rather than something terrifying. The Claudius setting *Bei dem Grabe meines Vaters* D496 is also in E flat, as is the same poet's *Am Grabe Anselmos* D504, and so, too, is Schubert's most famous graveside song, *Am Tage Aller Seelen (Litanei)* D343. This ceremonial key with its trinity of flats, and, in Schubert's music its associations with Mozart's *Die Zauberflöte*, is 'indicative of awe and devotion' (Reed, 1985).

At this point in his life Schubert was close to Franz von Bruchmann whose sister Sybilla had died in 1820. The great Bruchmann setting *Schwestergruss* D762 about Sybille was composed in November 1822, and it is surely possible that the infinitely less complex song *Ihr Grab* was written more or less at the same time and relates to the same person. Schubert also dedicated his Rückert setting *Sei mir gegrüsst* D741 (a message of love across the boundaries that separate the dead from the living) to Bruchmann's mother who no doubt continued to suffer for some years on account of her daughter's early death. The constant repetition of 'Dort ist ihr Grab' (it stands at the beginning of each verse) puts us in mind of Rückert's repetitions of 'Sei mir gegrüsst', typical of the Orient-inspired ghazal favoured by this poet and by Platen. As a one-off setting of a poem from an almanac (perhaps belonging to Frau von Bruchmann) entitled *Taschenbuch zum geselligen Vergnügen* ('Pocket-book of sociable pleasures'), *Ihr Grab* has very much the air of a *pièce d'occasion*, a song composed to please or comfort. Anniversaries of the death of a beloved family member were often marked by gatherings where music might be performed in their honour.

The opening of the song is perhaps its most arresting feature: a G major chord slides upwards to a keening A flat passing note in the right hand while deep in the bass four quavers seem to depict a yawning, dark chasm. This disorientated bar is expressive of an inward stab of pain; it is repeated in b. 2, and returns to the safety of G major in the third bar. From here it is a short distance to the first inversion of E flat major for 'Dort ist ihr Grab' (b. 4). The avoidance of the tonic in root position brings an other-worldly feel to the announcement that there will never be consolation. The vocal line seems weighted downwards as if to show, in the wilting shape of the melody, that the poor girl's life has bent to the forces of nature like a drooping flower. Schubert leads us through a number of keys during the song, the chromatic inflections always serving the expressiveness of the plaint. The first strophe ends in D flat major (b. 14) and the second passes through C flat major (b. 16), E flat minor (b. 25) and G flat major (b. 28). The third begins in B flat major (b. 32). There is a brief reminiscence of earthly happiness where G minor melts into G major, but the climactic phrase 'Dort, dort, stieg sie hinab', a fermata on the second 'dort', returns the song to mourning mood. The last verse is in the home key of E flat major

(b. 45). In both the third and fourth verses the vocal line is supported by flowing quavers rather than statuesque minim chords. Even at the end, the chord of E flat major in root position is avoided almost entirely. It is only in the final two bars of postlude (bb. 59–60) that the song is allowed to come to rest in the security and warmth of the bass clef, as if to say 'home at last, deep in the earth'.

The continual repetition of the word 'dort' implies a numbness, as if the significance of the loss can still not be properly grasped. The unsettled harmonic world of this song, the repetitive rehearsal of the sad story leading to eventual resolution, is a perfect musical metaphor for the struggle of coming to terms with bereavement. Those painful, exploratory left-hand quavers that have underpinned the clash of discords in the opening bars are tamed into acceptance only in the postlude where they fit at last into the harmonic scheme of the home key. The sadness and misery are relatively muted and the expression of grief is kept firmly under control.

Autograph:	In private possession (Cornaro Collection, Vienna)
First edition:	Published as Book 36 no. 3 of the *Nachlass* by Diabelli, Vienna in 1842 (P345)
Subsequent editions:	Peters: Vol. 6/8; AGA XX 402: Vol. 7/4; NSA IV: Vol. 13/28
Discography and timing:	Fischer-Dieskau II 5[2] 4'33
	Hyperion I 28[16]
	Hyperion II 25[4] 3'55 Maarten Koningsberger

← *Die Rose* D745   *Der Wachtelschlag* D742 →

IL MODO DI PRENDER MOGLIE & IL TRADITOR DELUSO *see DREI GESÄNGE FÜR BASS-STIMME MIT KLAVIER* D902/2 & 3

IM ABENDROT   Sunset glow
(Lappe) **D799** [H554]

The song exists in two versions, the second of which is discussed below:
(1) February 1825; (2) Summer–autumn 1827

(1) 'Sehr Langsam, mit gehobener Dämpfung' A♭ major   𝄵   [36 bars]

(2) A♭ major

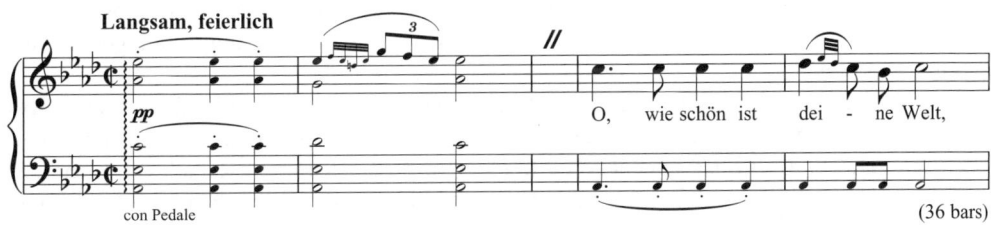

O wie schön ist deine Welt,	How lovely is your world,
Vater, wenn sie golden strahlet!	Father, in its golden radiance
Wenn dein Glanz herniederfällt,	When your glory descends

Und den Staub mit Schimmer malet;	And paints the dust with glitter;
Wenn das Rot, das in der Wolke blinkt,	When the red light that shines from the clouds
In mein stilles Fenster sinkt!	Falls silently upon my window.
Könnt' ich klagen, könnt' ich zagen?	Could I complain? Could I be apprehensive?
Irre sein an dir und mir?	Could I lose faith in you and in myself?
Nein, ich will im Busen tragen	No, I already bear your heaven
Deinen Himmel schon allhier.[1]	Here within my heart.
Und dies Herz, eh' es zusammenbricht,	And this heart, before it breaks,
Trinkt noch Glut und schlürft noch Licht.	Still drinks in the fire and savours the light.

KARL LAPPE (1773–1843)

This is the first of Schubert's two Lappe solo settings (1825). See the poet's biography for a chronological list of all the Lappe settings.

When Vogl sang this song at a Schubertiad at the home of Josef von Spaun in January 1827, the assembled company insisted on hearing it again – and little wonder. Here is the very essence of Schubertian greatness in its maturity: the ability to write a song that looks as simple on paper as it is emotionally complex and musically rewarding. This hymn contains the world in a grain of sand, or a ray of evening sunlight. Although it is a paean of joy and gratitude it moves us to tears: earthly beauty seems terribly fragile simply because of our own mortality. It is an intimate song, but it is also a vast proclamation of 'faith', a loose enough word to embrace the beliefs of most of mankind, including those who might not share the religious convictions of the devout poet. Lappe himself was undoubtedly devout, but Dietrich Fischer-Dieskau is eloquent in his understanding of the song as the product of a pantheistic, rather than a strictly Christian, impulse: 'The religious spirit underlying the music is that of a child's nature, whose gods are the stars, the mountains, the seasons and the flowers.' These enormous ideas are contained in a small autograph which is, as Mandyczewski describes it, 'extraordinarily neat and most lovingly written'.

The song bears Schubert's imprint, if not quite from the opening chords, then from the second bar of the introduction: three E flats, the top notes of what we have taken to be strummed tonic chords, reveal themselves as the beginning of a glorious melody that unfolds, in *alla breve* tempo, over the four bars of the introduction. At the beginning of the second bar there is the first of a number of Schubertian revelations. Who else, while moving from A flat major to an E flat^7, would choose to keep the low A flat exactly where it is, resounding as a tonic pedal point beneath the dominant harmony? The turn that follows that chord (b. 2) uses a decorative commonplace to establish an aura of wonder and devotion. The third bar moves into the second inversion of the subdominant: two melting cadences, each followed by tiny moments of silence, fall to the tonic in awestruck worship. How right John Reed is to say that the composer has an 'ability to give to the most familiar chord sequences a new inflection and an altogether new expressive power'.

Even in Schubert's lifetime his tendency to modulation was discussed by the critics. It was often seen (or heard) as a weakness and distraction, and he was reproved for it on more than one occasion. The world has since learned to glory in such discursive escapades, and there is no one like Schubert for leading us gently astray into hidden pathways of unexpected harmonic delight. But this song, in company with a handful of other masterpieces, reminds us that the composer at his greatest depends on neither 'heavenly length' (Schumann's phrase) nor diversity of harmony to leave his imprint on the soul. The song passes as imperceptibly as the sunset it

---

[1] Lappe writes 'Deinen Himmel schon *dahier*'.

describes, and like a sunset it changes at the same time as appearing to stand still. This somehow discourages our curiosity to analyse what is happening. And then, suddenly, it is gone. This could be a metaphor for life itself: we imagine it will last for ever but it is as ephemeral as those few moments when the sun hangs in the sky before slipping gently over the horizon. Leo Black, quoting Peter Gülke, says that the music gives the impression of being prayed rather than performed.

The poet's first verse is mirrored in a huge musical arc, moving between the tonic key and variously decorated versions of the dominant, with pedal points on both. The simplicity of the grand design, essentially built on two harmonies, gives the picture its amplitude and its space – the way those two basic harmonies are given new life by subtle modifications adds depth and humanity. The second verse is introduced by a shortened version of the prelude (from b. 18) that began the song. Because we have been lulled into a mood of quiet contemplation, the harmonic changes in the next four bars, all unfolding within a time frame of about twenty seconds, feel cosmic. The song's equilibrium is suddenly disturbed by the question 'Könnt' ich klagen, könnt' ich zagen?' ('Could I complain? Could I be apprehensive?') The shadow of doubt looms for a moment only. After the restlessness of 'Irre sein an dir und mir?' ('Could I lose faith in you and in myself?' bb. 23–4) a small interlude in the piano climbs tenuously towards the light of clarification in b. 25. With the word 'Nein' (b. 27) all doubt is stilled, as reassuring as a parent's hand on the arm of a frightened child. We revert to the world of security and beauty, sustained by these wonderful pedal points which are, in turn, supported by the sustaining pedal that, unusually for Schubert, is a specific requirement in the score (the song's marking in its first version is 'Sehr langsam, mit gehobener Dämpfung' – mention of dampers that can only be raised by use of the pedal).

There is, however, one more surprise in store. Schubert reserves this for the moment when the poet tells us that heaven is something that he bears within his own heart ('Deinen Himmel schon allhier' b. 27). Here we move briefly into D flat major, that most personal and heartfelt of Schubert's harmonic realms, the subdominant. It is this moment that was prefigured in the introduction. Thus in the midst of the narrator's humility before the wonders of God and nature, he allows himself a brief moment of self-revelation. After this we return to the familiarity of the great hymn and of the vocal line itself, hovering around the mediant, wafting on the horizon and refusing to sink to the tonic. Even if we finally reach A flat major on 'schlürft noch <u>Licht</u>' (b. 32), the repeat of 'Licht', the final note of the song (b. 34), returns to a C that seems to vibrate endlessly into the ether. In fact the piano has the last word, and that extraordinary seventh chord, the slowly uncoiling turn, and the final mezzo staccato triplets, are even more haunting than when we heard them first.

Tomorrow is another day, and tomorrow the sun will set once again – perhaps without us. It is this realization that adds a typically Schubertian bittersweet note to what is otherwise a hymn of praise. In music of this height and depth we hear both the towering permanence of nature and the inevitability of its loss to all human beings who are given the privilege of looking on its marvels, and rejoicing in them, for a limited time only. We have travelled with Schubert as our guide in all seasons and in every mood. It is as if, at his death, he has quietly slipped ahead of us, singing the while, perhaps a song like *Im Abendrot*. He shows us that to celebrate being alive and to accept death are different sides of the same coin, the cost of life itself. Mozart, Beethoven and a few others are capable of revealing the unfathomable, but it is Schubert who seems always willing to take us by the hand as we breach the chasm.

The main difference between the two versions of the song is fewer rolled chords in the second, the replacement of 'mit gehobener Dämpfung' with 'Con pedale' and the tempo indication. The *alla breve* indication of the later version seems to be a wise alteration – the 'Sehr langsam' in 4 of the first edition (rather than 2) has led many performers astray.

Autograph:	Pierpont Morgan Library, New York (fair copy)
First edition:	Published as Book 20 no. 1 of the *Nachlass* by Diabelli, Vienna in December 1832 (P294)
Subsequent editions:	Peters: Vol. 2/219; AGA XX 463: Vol. 8/30; NSA IV: Vol. 13/132 & 134
Bibliography:	Capell 1928, pp. 205–6
	Fischer-Dieskau, p. 236
Arrangements:	Arr. Max Reger (1873–1916), for voice and orchestra (1913–14) [*see* ORCHESTRATIONS]
Discography and timing:	Fischer-Dieskau II 6[18] 4'13
	Hyperion I 31[6]
	Hyperion II 29[9] 3'34 Christine Brewer

← *Lied eines Kriegers* D822   *Der Einsame* D800 →

IM DORFE *see WINTERREISE* D911/17

IM FREIEN   In the open
(SEIDL) OP. 80 NO. 3, **D880** [H595]

The song exists in two versions, the second of which is discussed below:
(1) Undated; (2) March 1826

(1)   'Mässig'   E♭ major   ¾   [132 bars]

(2)   E♭ major

Drausen in der weiten Nacht

(132 bars)

Draussen in der weiten Nacht	Now once more I stand outside
Steh ich wieder nun,	In the vast night;
Ihre helle Sternenpracht	Its bright, starry splendour
Lässt mein Herz nicht rühn!	Gives my heart no peace.
Tausend Arme winken mir	A thousand arms beckon to me
Süss begehrend zu,	With sweet longing;
Tausend Stimmen rufen hier,	A thousand voices call:
'Grüss dich, Trauter, du!'[1]	'Greetings, dear friend!'
O ich weiss auch, was mich zieht,	Oh, I know what draws me,
Weiss auch, was mich ruft,	What calls me,

[1] Seidl writes 'Grüss dich, *Schwärmer*, du'.

Was wie Freundes Gruss und Lied	Like a friend's greeting, a song,
Locket, locket durch die Luft.	Floating enticingly through the air.
Siehst du dort das Hüttchen stehn,	Do you see the cottage there
Drauf der Mondschein ruht.	On which the moonlight lingers?
Durch die blanken Scheiben sehn	From its shining windows
Augen, die mir gut!	Fond eyes gaze out.
Siehst du dort das Haus am Bach,	Do you see the house there by the brook,
Das der Mond bescheint?	Lit by the moon?
Unter seinem trauten Dach	Beneath its cosy roof
Schläft mein liebster Freund.	Sleeps my dearest friend.
Siehst du jenen Baum,	Do you see that tree,
Der voll Silberflocken flimmt?	Glittering with silver flakes?
O wie oft mein Busen schwoll,	Oh, how often did my heart swell
Froher dort gestimmt!	With joy there!
Jedes Plätzchen, das mir winkt,	Every little place that beckons
Ist ein lieber Platz,	Is dear to me,
Und wohin ein Strahl nur sinkt,	And wherever a moonbeam falls,
Lockt ein teurer Schatz.	Cherished treasure entices.
Drum auch winkt mir's überall	So everything here beckons to me
So begehrend hier,	With longing,
Drum auch ruft es, wie der Schall	And calls to me with the sounds
Trauter Liebe mir.	Of true love.

JOHANN GABRIEL SEIDL (1804–1875)

This is the fifth of Schubert's twelve Seidl solo settings (1826–8). See the poet's biography for a chronological list of all the Seidl settings.

Fischer-Dieskau states that this long and marvellous song anticipates the style of Schumann. In the sense that many a Schumann song started life as an embryonic piano piece rather than with a fully conceived vocal line, this may be a just observation, but it is only half the story. *Im Freien* is of course a piano impromptu of very special character (hardly anywhere else in Schubert's vocal music does the accompaniment venture so high into the keyboard stratosphere for example) but the singer's line is far from an afterthought. The most powerful impression made in this song are the ideas of communing with nature, communing with memories of the past and, above all, of the performers 'communing' with one another. Voice and piano move in parallel motion so that what emerges is the idea of 'being of a like mind'. The pianist's octaves throughout could be a tonal analogue for the perfectly tuned chiming of souls, the idea that pervades the Brahms song *Wir wandelten* Op. 96 no. 2. The vocal line also suggests reciprocity: some of the poem's phrases ('Lässt mein Herz nicht rühn' in Verse 1 and 'Grüss dich, Trauter' in Verse 2, for example) are repeated in musical phrases that would be incomplete one without the other. It is as if two people, in rapt conversation, echo each other's words or complete each other's sentences; the effect is one of close and comfortable friendship rather than amatory passion. The marking 'Mässig, mit Innigkeit' says it all.

Sometimes, in order to perform a piece imaginatively, an artist will invent a scenario about what is happening in the poem, a story that cannot be proved one way or the other. Here the poet is possibly in the company of a friend to whom he wishes to point out the beauties of a favourite village (topography was a Seidl speciality). It has been a long time since he visited this place, but nothing has changed. Everything is as it was. Because the travellers have arrived at night, no one yet knows they are there. It is a perfect opportunity to stand above the town which nestles in a valley and point out all the landmarks that have become cocooned in a golden glow of memory. Schubert has written the vocal line and accompaniment in such an intimate way as to suggest that all the questions along the lines of 'Do you see this or that?' are not merely rhetorical but are addressed to someone specific at the poet's elbow. So overwhelming is the sense of sharing in this music, so intimate and heartfelt the communication, that love seems to flow in all directions – love for the *Heimat* and its beauty in the moonlight, love between the narrator and the objects of his affections, and thus love between voice and piano. Leo Black has written of 'the serene awareness of security through friendship' in this song.

The accompaniment reflects not only 'the moon-flecked river ripples and the glistening willow leaves' (Capell, 1928) but also 'an abundant fullness of heart' (Einstein, 1951). The piano writing swells and surges at certain moments, and at others is as sensitive to the tiniest inflection of an ever-changing mood as if it were mirroring all the nuances of a silver-bromide photographic plate. After words like 'Sternenpracht' (Verse 1, b. 14) and 'wie der Schall' (Verse 8, b. 107) the piano echoes the notes of the vocal line – B flat, E flat and back to B flat – in close imitation and shy diminution; the siren song floats through the air after the last line of Verse 3 ('locket durch die Luft' bb. 41–3) and suddenly becomes even more alluring by abandoning (though only for three beats, bb. 45–6) octaves in favour of euphonious sixths. In one of the comparatively rare visual puns in Schubert's lieder, the roof of the friend's house (Verse 5) is depicted in the printed score by a succession of repeated Fs as tightly and evenly packed as black thatch (bb. 65–9). Underneath this ceiling of notes is sheltered a left-hand accompaniment that sounds as though it was written for somnolent horns (the only time the left hand moves in quavers and dotted quavers rather than semiquavers), and whose music rises and falls as gently as a sleeping man's chest.

At the beginnings of verses 4, 5 and 6 (each opening with the narrator's finger pointing out something new) the composer uses changes of harmony as if he were a film director, varying camera shot and angle while zooming in on a new detail in the panorama. The final verse as it returns to the home key of E flat gathers up the energy of the preceding seven ('Drum auch winkt' – as if to say 'That is why and how I've been drawn back here'). At the very end, the sounds of true love (those beguiling right-hand sixths make a final appearance at bb. 125–8) cause the the poet to refocus his gaze from the distance and look to someone much nearer, the only ornamentation in the vocal line being a tender turn at the last moment (b. 128). The singer seems to realize that this picture of nature has become even more beautiful and meaningful because of the tender empathy he has found by his side – and yes, this closeness is represented by the presence of his ever-faithful accompanist.

The incessant flow of semiquavers in this accompaniment puts us in mind of *Der Winterabend* D938. Both pieces are about memory and nostalgia, and both tug at the heartstrings. A state of contentment and comfortable accommodation with life pours out of this music; to have reached this stage there must have been much learning, and some tears, along the way. As in *Der Wanderer an den Mond* D870 there is a strong suggestion of healing, of rediscovering truths or values that have hitherto been obscured by greed and ambition, or perhaps the stress of life in the city. A passage from the end of Dickens's *Great Expectations* comes to mind:

*I thought all that countryside more beautiful and peaceful by far than I had ever known it to be
yet. Many pleasant pictures of the life that I would lead there, and the change for the better that
would come over my character . . . beguiled my way. They awakened a tender emotion in me . . .
I felt like one who was toiling home barefoot from distant travel, and whose wanderings had lasted
many years.*

There are two versions of the song: two autographs of the first version and the printed first
edition (for which the autograph is lost) which counts as the second version. Only the latter is
printed in the NSA with ossias printed above the stave for the small number of differences in
the autograph versions.

Autographs:	Wienbibliothek im Rathaus, Vienna (first version, first draft)
	Kolbenheyer Gesellschaft, Nürnberg (first version, fair copy)
Publication:	Published as Op. 80 no. 3 by Tobias Haslinger, Vienna in May 1827
	(P127; second version; the first version remains unpublished)
Dedicatee:	Joseph Witteczek
Publication reviews:	*Wiener allgemeine Theaterzeitung* no. 82 (10 July 1827), p. 336
	[Waidelich/Hilmar Dokumente I no. 512]
	Münchener allgemeine Musik-Zeitung no. 1 (6 October 1827), col.
	8 [Waidelich/Hilmar Dokumente I no. 530; Deutsch Doc. Biog.
	No. 955]
	Allgemeine musikalische Zeitung (Leipzig), no. 4 (23 January
	1828), col. 49ff. [Waidelich/Hilmar Dokumente I no. 569;
	Deutsch Doc. Biog. no. 1014]
	Berliner allgemeine musikalische Zeitung no. 20 (14 May 1828),
	p. 157f. [Waidelich/Hilmar Dokumente II no. 613a]
	Allgemeiner musikalischer Anzeiger (Vienna), no. 19
	(9 May 1829), p. 74 [Waidelich/Hilmar Dokumente I
	no. 726]
First known performance:	6 May 1827, Grosser Universitätssaal, Vienna as part of a
	fundraising event for the widows and orphans of the Viennese
	University legal faculty. Soloist: Ludwig Tietze, accompanied by
	Franz Schubert
Performance reviews:	*Der Sammler* (Vienna), no. 77 (28 June 1827), p. 308 [Waidelich/
	Hilmar Dokumente I no. 509]
Subsequent editions:	Peters: Vol. 3/39; AGA XX 494: Vol. 8/184; NSA IV: Vol. 4/11;
	Bärenreiter: Vol. 3/8
Bibliography:	Capell 1928, pp. 221–2
	Fischer-Dieskau 1977, p. 246
	Youens 2002, pp. 395–404
Discography and timing:	Fischer-Dieskau II 8³ 4'35
	Hyperion I 15¹³
	Hyperion II 32¹ 6'18 Margaret Price

⟵ *Der Wanderer an den Mond* D870   *Am Fenster* D878 ⟶

IM FRÜHLING
(SCHULZE) **D882** [H599]

In spring

The song exists in two versions, the second of which is discussed below:
(1) March 1826; (2) appeared September 1828

(1)   'Langsam'   G major   ¢   [50 bars]

(2)   G major

Still sitz ich an des Hügels Hang, der Him-mel ist__ so__ klar,

(50 bars)

Still sitz ich an des Hügels Hang,	I sit silently on the hillside.
Der Himmel ist so klar,	The sky is so clear,
Das Lüftchen spielt im grünen Tal,	The breezes play in the green valley
Wo ich beim ersten Frühlingsstrahl	Where once, in the first rays of spring,
Einst, ach, so glücklich war.	I was, oh, so happy.
Wo ich an ihrer Seite ging	Where I walked by her side,
So traulich und so nah,	So tender, so close,
Und tief im dunkeln Felsenquell	And saw deep in the dark rocky stream
Den schönen Himmel blau und hell,	The fair sky, blue and bright,
Und sie im Himmel sah.	And her reflected in that sky.
Sieh, wie der bunte Frühling schon	See how the colourful spring
Aus Knosp' und Blüte blickt!	Already peeps from bud and blossom.
Nicht alle Blüten sind mir gleich,	Not all the blossoms are the same to me:
Am liebsten pflückt' ich von dem Zweig,[1]	I would like most of all to pluck them from the branch
Von welchem sie gepflückt.	From which she had plucked.
Denn alles ist wie damals noch,	For all is still as it was then,
Die Blumen, das Gefild;	The flowers, the fields;
Die Sonne scheint nicht minder hell,	The sun shines no less brightly,
Nicht minder freundlich schwimmt im Quell	And no less cheerfully,
Das blaue Himmelsbild.	The sky's blue image bathes in the stream.
Es wandeln nur sich Will und Wahn,	Only will and delusion change,
Es wechseln Lust und Streit,	And joy alternates with strife;
Vorüber flieht der Liebe Glück,	The happiness of love flies past,
Und nur die Liebe bleibt zurück,	And only love remains;
Die Lieb' und ach, das Leid!	Love and, alas, sorrow.

[1] Schulze writes 'Am liebsten *pflück'* ich von dem Zweig'. This subtly changes the meaning. In Schubert's subjunctive (which happen to be the same as the past tense) the narrator would like to pick blossoms together with his girl; but Schulze picks flowers a year later, in his solitary state and in the present tense, from the same branches that she once picked from.

<table>
<tr><td>

O wär ich doch ein Vöglein nur
Dort an dem Wiesenhang!
Dann blieb' ich auf den Zweigen hier,
Und säng ein süsses Lied von ihr,
Den Ganzen Sommer lang.

</td><td>

Oh, if only I were a bird,
There on the sloping meadow!
Then I would stay on these branches here,
And sing a sweet song about her
All summer long.

</td></tr>
</table>

ERNST SCHULZE (1789–1817); poem written 31 March 1815

This is the eighth of Schubert's ten Schulze solo settings (1825–6). See the poet's biography for a chronological list of all the Schulze settings. An outline of a suggested performing version for a Schulze cycle is listed under 'Auf den wilden Wegen'.

This is one of the best loved of the Schubert songs. If Ernst Schulze had penned nothing else, his posthumous reputation would be ensured (at least among musicians) as the poet of *Im Frühling*. The poem was written 'On 31 March 1815' (the poem's title in the *Poetisches Tagebuch*), two years after Schulze had set his sights on Adelheid Tychsen and when he still believed that he had some hope of winning her. He does not claim here that she reciprocated his passion; strictly speaking it is only he who is 'so tender, so close' in the second verse. We do not notice this detail at first; we assume the two already to have been lovers, and we are meant to. Schulze was not beyond being economical with the truth and it was ambiguities of this kind that enabled Friedrich Bouterwek, who edited Schulze's works, to construct a fictitious scenario for the *Poetisches Tagebuch* in which his Muse was a dead 'fiancée' (Cäcilie Tychsen) and where mention of her sister Adelheid (who was still alive at the time) was more or less suppressed.

Memory of and nostalgia for past moments of happiness ('alte unnennbare Tage', 'old unnameable days' as Mörike called them in his *Im Frühling*) are some of the trickiest of ideas to turn into art. To revisit a place where one has been happy with someone else stirs mixed emotion: 'Halb ist es Lust, halb ist es Klage' ('half pleasure, half lament') as Mörike wrote. There is much that has changed, but there are certain constants that have not. The river banks look unaltered but one can never step into the same water a second time. The vocal line of *Im Frühling* is subtly modified strophe by strophe, but this is nothing new in Schubert's output. The accompaniment, however, has a life of its own, and it was a stroke of genius on the composer's part to call on a form he used only once in his songs, that of theme and variations. What could be more perfect to express the concept of 'the same, yet not the same'?

In *Im Frühling* is a sophisticated metamorphosis of a theme for variations that had run like a thread through Schubert's life for the previous twelve years. Variation form was a Schubertian speciality. In his book devoted to the subject, Maurice Brown has sixteen chapters on different instrumental works. The first of these concerns the set of variations that constitute the second movement of the Symphony no. 2 in B flat, D125. Listen again to this and you will hear a tune and variations, in E flat major, with a lilt and a gait that are unmistakably prophetic of *Im Frühling*. The symphony was written at the end of 1814, a few months after the first performance of Schubert's Mass in F in which the soprano soloist had been Therese Grob, the girl with whom Schubert was said to have been in love. The next appearance of a reworking of this musical theme was in 1815, at the height of the relationship: in the twelfth number of the opera *Die Freunde von Salamanka* D326, Diego and Laura sing a love duet in C major, 'underneath a roof of trees by the silver stream, the shepherd longs for his beautiful girl and moans in enraptured tones'. By 1824 Therese had long been married to someone else, but the tune from this opera was used again, this time as a basis for the variations of the second movement of the Octet for winds and strings, D803. Perhaps Schubert was already weaving this melody into that web of allusion and emotional cross-reference where certain tunes bring back our pasts as infallibly as

Proust's moistened madeleine evoked his. Schulze's poem might have brought to mind the springtime of Schubert's own life, together with the pain of recognition that so much had now changed for the worse. But as the poet says, much also remains the same, or almost the same. Perhaps Schubert's old tune, an echo of the golden days of 1814, came to his mind's ear. If so, John Reed points out that it is a theme that continues to haunt the composer's mind, beyond the composition of the song itself; the Allegretto Rondo finale of the A major Piano Sonata D959 (1828) marks the final appearance of this recurring Schubertian thumbprint.

For the piano the song is a set of variations, but vocally it is in modified strophic form where two of the poet's verses are used to make one of Schubert's musical strophes. Thus as far as the voice is concerned, 1 + 2 is the same as 3 (slightly modified) + 4 which is related to 5 (in the minor) + (after a bridge passage) 6. The piano's theme is heard in an introduction that is the epitome of the happy/sad in Schubert, subtle and searching with a streak of melancholy (no conventional springtime paean this), yet also warmed by a gentle smile and a lift to the rhythm. At the entry of the voice the piano momentarily abandons its theme in order to aid and abet the magical workings of the vocal line. Did ever breezes play so lovingly in music ('Lüftchen spielt im grünen Tal' b. 7)? Was there ever more eloquent use of the supertonic than in the sidestep return (b. 8) to the past of 'ich beim ersten Frühlingsstrahl'? Was ever a repeated phrase like 'Einst ach, so glücklich war' ('I was, oh, so happy' bb. 8–10) more appropriately set, the pulse quickening in the minor mode as the memory of love returns in a rush of pain/pleasure, followed by rueful acceptance, in the major, that nothing can last for ever?

The second section (Verses 3 and 4) is the first of the piano's variations – pearly semiquavers rippling high in the treble (from b. 17), underpinned by staccato left-hand quavers. The effect is quite delicious and timeless; indeed the charm of the piano writing (with its stride basses *avant la lettre* suggesting a slightly languid yet cheeky 'swing') has become common currency. At its best, the tiniest of details brings pleasure here: at 'Am liebsten pflückt' ich von dem Zweig' (b. 24), the explosive consonant and the ongoing staccato bass (often ignored by pianists) suggest the sound of a flower snapped from a branch; the picture of the heavens reflected in the stream (at 'Das blaue Himmelsbild') is fleetingly blurred by a mordent as the pianist's right hand (b. 31) skims the surface of the water.

From b. 33 it is a time for a *minore* movement, conventionally placed near the end of a set of variations in the major key. The previous variation is turned on its head: for the first time semiquavers in the left hand stir the dark emotional waters, and quavers in agitated syncopation are to be found in the right. The reign of the tonic minor is disturbed at b. 38 by an aching reminiscence in the Neapolitan key of A flat on 'Und nur die Liebe bleibt zurück', the key that Reed associates in Schubert with 'secure and reciprocated love' and which here holds sway for less than two bars.

The sudden advent of a middle section storm was to be a pattern of some of the greatest slow movements of Schubert's maturity (in the A major Piano Sonata D959, for example, and the String Quintet D956). In such works, when calm returns, an echo of the catastrophe remains behind to cast a warning shadow over the recapitulation; we have learned too much to go back to our old ways, and nothing now can be the same. So it is in this song. After a bar of modulation that returns us to G major, the right hand semiquavers of the first variation return (b. 41), but the leaping basses of the left hand are subverted by the storm syncopations. This belies the would-be optimism of the last verse, warning us that what follows is sheer fantasy. At the words 'and sing a sweet song about her', the voice jumps a seventh, full of a yearning at b. 45 which is prolonged by a fermata. This has happened three times in the song on different words. This vocal leap is wonderful for the bright clarity of 'hell' (Verse 2), and also for 'Quell' (Verse 4), which is brightest by reflection; but most of all, heartbreakingly appropriate in the last verse for 'von ihr' where 'she' is put on a pedestal high in the voice. Schubert shortens Schulze's last two lines for a rapt coda; as the singer pauses on 'Ganzen Sommer lang' in b. 49 the pianist aspires to the highest note in the whole accompaniment but cannot tarry there. It is all an evanescent dream, fleetingly conjured and dying with the last wistful notes of the postlude. Schubert's use of modified strophic form was seldom so virtuosic, and the lied has seldom attained such perfection.

There are two versions of the song printed in the NSA. The first of these, a preparatory copy, has the tempo marking 'Langsam'. The second version was the one published three times in all: in the *Wiener Zeitschrift* in 1828, in the posthumous Op. 101, and as part of Book 25 of the *Nachlass*. Singers should beware the famous misprint in the Peters Edition: six bars from the end the word 'Lied' is printed as an A instead of C. This error goes back to the song's first printing as a supplement to the *Wiener Zeitschrift*.

Autograph:	Conservatoire collection, Bibliothèque Nationale, Paris (first draft)
Publication:	First published as part of the NSA in 1985 (P787; first version)
	First published as a supplement to the *Wiener Zeitschrift für Kunst, Literatur, Theater und Mode*, 16 September 1828; subsequently published as Op. post. 101 no. 1 by H. A. Probst, Leipzig in December 1828 (P178; second version)
Subsequent editions:	Peters: Vol. 2/227; AGA XX 497: Vol. 8/202; NSA IV: Vol. 5a/170 & 176; Bärenreiter: Vol. 4/58 & 61
Bibliography:	Capell 1928, pp. 216–17
	Einstein 1951, pp. 328–9
	Fischer-Dieskau 1977, p. 228
	Newbould 1997, pp. 298–9
	Youens 1996, pp. 287–92
Discography and timing:	Fischer-Dieskau II 8[6] 4'08
	Pears-Britten 1[1] 4'36
	Hyperion I 18[19]
	Hyperion II 32[5] 4'24 Peter Schreier

← *Fischerweise* D881 *Lebensmut* D883 →

~~~~~~~~~~~~~~~~

IM GEGENWÄRTIGEN VERGANGENES
(Goethe) **D710** [H470]
D♭ major   March 1821

The past in the present

Quartet, TTBB

(155 bars)

Ros' und Lilie morgentaulich
Blüht im Garten meiner Nähe,
Hinten an, bebuscht und traulich,

Roses and lilies, moist with morning dew,
Blossom in the nearby garden;
Beyond it, covered in bushes,

Steigt der Felsen in die Höhe.	The familiar rock-slope rises.
Und mit hohem Wald umzogen,	And ringed with a tall forest,
Und mit Ritterschloss gekrönet,	Crowned by a knight's castle,
Lenkt sich hin des Gipfels Bogen,	The mountain peak curves down
Bis er sich dem Tal versöhnet.	Until it is at one with the valley.
Und da duftet's wie vor Alters,	And there the air is as fragrant as it was long ago,
Da wir noch von Liebe litten,	When we still suffered with love,
Und die Saiten meines Psalters	And the strings of my psaltery
Mit dem Morgenstrahl sich stritten.	Vied with the sun's morning rays;
Wo das Jagdlied aus den Büschen	When from the bushes the hunting-song
Fülle runden Tons enthauchte,	Echoed in full, rounded tones
Anzufeuern, zu erfrischen,	To inspire and refresh us
Wie's der Busen wollt' und brauchte.	As the heart, in its need, desired.
Nun die Wälder ewig sprossen,	Take courage
So ermutigt euch mit diesen,	From the eternally burgeoning forests;
Was ihr sonst für euch genossen	The joy you once tasted for yourselves
Lässt in andern sich geniessen.	Can now be found in others.
Niemand wird uns dann beschreien,	No one will then reproach us
Dass wir's uns alleine gönnen,	For begrudging it to anyone else.
Nun in allen Lebensreihen	Now you must be able to savour joy
Müsset ihr geniessen können.	In every stage of life.
Und mit diesem Lied und Wendung	And at this turn in our song
Sind wir wieder bei Hafisen:	We come back to Hafiz;
Denn es ziemt des Tags Vollendung	For it is fitting to enjoy the day's fullness
Mit Geniessern zu geniessen.	With connoisseurs of enjoyment.

JOHANN WOLFGANG VON GOETHE (1749–1832)

This is the most obscure of all Schubert's excursions into quasi-oriental poetry, and certainly one of his least known Goethe settings. It is also the most unusual of his part-songs, a hybrid with a much more independent piano part than is usual in this genre. It begins with a long and beautiful tenor solo, and the listener who hears these forty bars, without realizing what is to come, can only assume that 'Ros' und Lilie' is an enchanting and unaccountably neglected solo song. (Tiana Lemnitz recorded it as such in the thirties, ditching the remainder of the work, and few people were any the wiser.) The second section (marked 'Allegretto') is a duet for two tenors where the addition of the second voice is a real surprise for the innocent ear; the third section ('Allegro moderato') blossoms into a male quartet (TTBB); and the final 'Andantino quasi allegretto' gives prominence once again to the solo tenor, before he is joined by the first bass, then the second tenor, and finally the second bass – all in quasi-fugal manner. No other part-song has this formula, and one feels that it was composed for a specific occasion where the first tenor was something of a star attraction.

On this basis it seems likely that the main part was written for the high tenor Ludwig Tietze (or Titze) (1797–1850). He was the most accomplished of a group of singers in Schubert's circle who performed the four-part choral songs in various ensembles that changed from time to time depending, then as now, on the individual singers' availabilities. His voice was of beautiful quality and he was accustomed to being treated as something of a star. Indeed Tietze's work as a singer of male-voice quartets was overtaken by his position as one of Schubert's chosen soloists.

There seems to have been a jovial band of ensemble singers in Vienna at the time with more or less the same background, the best-documented members of the vocal quartets all being Czech-born. Tietze, though educated in Vienna, came originally from what is nowadays the Czech Republic. The other tenors were Johann Umlauff (1796–1861), a pupil of Vogl, and Josef Barth (1781–1865). The basses for this ensemble which made regular appearances in 1821/2 were Josef Götz (1775–1842) and Wenzel Nejebse (1796–1865). The native Viennese, Johann Nepomuk Nestroy (1801–1862) also took part as a bass in some performances of Schubert's quartets between 1819 and 1822; he was to become one of Austria's greatest writers of comic plays and farces, with over eighty stage works to his credit (qqv SINGERS where Tietze and these five ensemble vocalists are discussed in more detail).

Schubert's flirtation with the Orient (in this case courtesy of Goethe's *West-östlicher Divan*, qv) dated back to Goethe's Indian ballad, *Der Gott und die Bajadere* D254 (1815). The opera fragment *Sakuntala* was composed in 1820 but it was only in 1821 that Schubert began to set Orient-inspired texts in earnest. These works with obvious Eastern subject matter included poetry by Platen and Rückert written in Persian ghazal form. Hérold's opera *Das Zauberglöck-chen* had an oriental plot, and Schubert contributed some numbers to the Viennese production of this work. Schubert's own operas, *Fierabras* and the incomplete *Der Graf von Gleichen* have storylines based on the conflict between Christendom and Islam.

And this leads naturally back to Mozart's Singspiel, *Die Entführung aus dem Serail*, a work that Schubert adored. Surely a great deal of his enthusiasm for oriental evocation derives from Mozart, who wrote such works as the famous *Rondo alla turca* for piano (from K331) although Schubert would probably not have known anything of Mozart's unfinished opera *Zaide* set in Turkey, *Il re pastore* set in Lebanon and his incidental music for the play *Thamos, König in Ägypten* (K345).

The ⁶⁄₈ movement of *Im Gegenwärtigen Vergangenes* owes something to Pedrillo's *Romance* 'Im Mohrenland gefangen war' from *Die Entführung*: it is obviously set in a seraglio garden where the flowers are a metaphor for beautiful girls; it has the same time signature, a similar easy melodic flow, and the accompaniment suggests that the singer is strumming a lute or guitar. The opening of the song-aria in D flat major begins gently and lyrically. At 'Und mit hohem Wald umzogen' (b. 15) it becomes more dramatic as the accompaniment turns to triplets and stabbing left-hand octaves – we have already encountered this glowering mood to describe the similar imagery of castles built on high precipices in the middle section of *Auf der Donau* D553. Schubert has enjoyed the ingratiating melody of 'Ros' und Lilien' so much that he now engineers a repeat of the opening words and music (from b. 29), an ABA structure that is not to be found in Goethe's poem. A short bridge passage (bb. 39–41) modulates to A major, playing on the fact that D flat (C sharp) is the third of the new key.

And here we have our surprise, accompanied by a new tempo marking – 'Allegretto' – and a key-signature change to A major. Can it be a new voice that begins a gentle melody with the words 'Und da duftet's wie vor Alters'? Before we can decide, another tenor (actually our soloist, Tenor I) joins in a contrapuntal weave – the same melody a fourth higher. So this is a part-song after all – or at least a duet! The mingling of these voices creates the effect of the same voice singing against itself. The old poet is singing with an alter ego – or doppelgänger – of himself when young. The poem, as can be seen from the title, is about past and present, and this music is suffused not only with the fragrances of the garden, but also heady memories of the glories of youth. The tug at the heartstrings, with the regretful little melisma of 'Alters', (b. 23, then b. 44) says it all as the figure is gently exchanged between the two voices. It is difficult to analyse how this music seems to make time stand still, but it is a metaphor that exactly relates to the poem's intent. The change from ⁶⁄₈ to ⁴⁄₄ plays a part in the magical effect, as does the extended pedal on A, while the piano imitates the psaltery in right-hand triplets with plucked left-hand chords. This music expands the idea of Goethe's poem in a unique way: by setting these lines for two voices, Schubert rounds out the literary idea with an extra dimension that could only have been realized in music.

At 'Wo das Jagdlied aus den Büschen' (b. 59) we are suddenly introduced to a much heartier evocation of youthful energy; this hunting music is strenuous and in unison. A two-bar bridge passage (bb. 68–9) reintroduces 'Und da duftet's wie vor Alters' and its reappearance is like a gentle balm on older ligaments exhausted with too much exercise. As with the opening cantilena, this music is far too good to be heard only once, and Goethe is accordingly adapted and repeated.

Between bb. 89 and 116 (with the new marking of 'Allegro moderato') we return to D flat major from A major, and revert to 𝄴, for the third – and perhaps the most conventional – section of the piece. This is for four-part male chorus, TTBB. The extraordinary words about the ever-renewing nature of life should be taken to heart by artists apprehensive about being replaced by those from the younger generation. Goethe is saying, with a wisdom characteristic of his later years, that we cannot begrudge our juniors the pleasure and success that we ourselves once had – it is all as inevitable as the new season's growth in the forests. Indeed, by living through the pleasures of those who replace us, we are capable of re-experiencing our former achievements. Anyone who has seen a great artist who is happy in the role of teacher knows how true this can be.

The final section (from b. 117) is an epilogue, played, as it were, in front of the curtain. The four singers come one by one on to the stage for this envoi, which is all the more delicious for the way the introduction of each voice approximates a fugal entry. Schubert here permits himself mention of the Persian poet Hafiz, whose name he excised from the end of *Versunken* D715. Richard Stokes points out that Goethe took the conjunction of 'Ros' und Lilie' directly from Rückert's teacher, Hammer-Purgstall of Vienna, the first of the German-speaking Persian scholars. As for the music, it is once again Tenor I who is given a position of *primus inter pares*. Goethe's strophe (beginning 'Und mit diesem Lied und Wendung') is heard three times, the last time with a more rhythmically taut accompaniment in dotted rhythms (from b. 140). There is a modulation back to the home key of D flat major for the closing phrase where the contrapuntal weaving cedes to block-chord harmony, as in a chorale of acceptance and gratitude. Right at the end, the important word 'geniessen' (to enjoy) is given an almost religious significance by its extended setting (bb. 152–4) – half loving salute, half regretful farewell – as well as the solemnity of the plagal cadence that is the final harmonic colour to be heard in this unusual and beautiful work.

Autograph:	Wienbibliothek im Rathaus, Vienna (first draft)
First edition:	Published as Book 43 of the *Nachlass* by Diabelli, Vienna in 1849 (P365)
Subsequent editions:	AGA XVI 15: p. 119; NSA III: Vol. 3
Discography and timing:	Hyperion I 28² 6'47 John Mark Ainsley & The London Hyperion II 24¹² Schubert Chorale (dir. Stephen Layton)

←— *Suleika II* D717   *Mahomets Gesang* D721 —→

IM HAINE

In the wood

(Bruchmann) Op. 56 no. 3, **D738** [H505]
A major   1822 or 1823

(20 bars)

Sonnenstrahlen	As rays of sunlight
Durch die Tannen,	Fall
Wie sie fallen	Through the fir trees
Ziehn von dannen	All sorrow
Alle Schmerzen,	Drifts away
Und im Herzen	And in our hearts
Wohnet reiner Friede nur.	Dwells only peace.
Stilles Sausen	Balmy breezes
Lauer Lüfte,	Murmuring softly,
Und im Brausen	And the whispering
Zarte Düfte,	Delicate scents
Die sich neigen	That float down
Aus den Zweigen,	From the branches
Atmet aus die ganze Flur.	Caress every meadow.
Wenn nur immer	If only
Dunkle Bäume,	Dark trees,
Sonnenschimmer,	Shimmering sunlight
Grüne Säume	And the edge of green woods
Uns umblühten	Were to flower
Und umglühten,	And glow about us for ever,
Tilgend aller Qualen Spur!	Wiping away all traces of pain!

FRANZ VON BRUCHMANN (1798–1867)

This is the second of Schubert's five Bruchmann solo settings (1822–3). See the poet's biography for a chronological list of all the Bruchmann settings.

Very little is known about the background to this song; the date is not even certain. Deutsch placed it in 1822 based on the likelihood that it belongs to the same period as the other four Bruchmann songs. The poet's works were never published, and they have only survived in Schubert's settings which must have been composed from Bruchmann's handwritten copies. Despite the questions hanging over its provenance, this song is gloriously and uncomplicatedly Schubertian, and it boasts a melody that could have been written by no other master. As in so many of his vocal works he can involve a suggestion of an Italianate style – as here – without being one whit less Schubert *pur sang*. Each of Bruchmann's short lines of four syllables inspires fragments of a tune that stop on a dotted crotchet on the second beat of a ⅜ bar; the miracle is that these sequences add up to a melody that is an organic whole and which somehow joins the end-stopped lines into a coherent sentence. Not content with this legerdemain, Schubert repeats the last four lines of the seven-line strophe (the tune now ornamented by exquisite little excursions into semiquaver melismas at bb. 13 and 14) and as a *coup de grâce* repeats for a second time the final line of the strophe for good measure. All in all this makes an outrageously long melody of fifteen bars' duration, uninterrupted by a single rest in the vocal line.

Another breathless waltz song from more or less the same period comes to mind – *Drang in die Ferne* D770. While this Leitner setting is undoubtedly more complex than the Bruchmann waltz, it is interesting that both works share the tonality of A major/minor and time signature of ⅜. Schubert was no stranger to the writing of *Ländler* or waltzes for piano in conventional ¾, a form that was soon to be recognized as quintessentially Viennese with the enormous success of Lanner and Johann Strauss I.

The publication of *Im Haine* included an Italian singing translation, probably by Nicolaus Craigher de Jachelutta, printed on a separate stave above the original German. The title was translated as *Nel boschetto* and the Italian (beginning 'Se dall' Etra, / Feboi i raggi / Ei penetra, / in mezzo à' faggi') has some curiously awkward accentuations. (As well as appearing in the NSA, it is reprinted in Schochow 1974 Volume 1, p. 48.) This was part of a scheme apparently cooked up between Craigher and Schubert (as well as the publisher A. W. Pennauer) in an attempt to broaden the international appeal of the composer's songs. The catchy tunefulness of this waltz in Italian *arietta* guise might well have captured the public's imagination but unfortunately we do not have the sales figures.

Autograph:	Missing or lost
First edition:	Published as Op. 56 no. 3 by A. Pennauer, Vienna in July 1826 (P104)
Dedicatee:	Karl Pinterics
Publication reviews:	*Allgemeiner musikalischer Anzeiger* (Frankfurt), No. 2 (8 July 1826), p. 10f. [Waidelich/Hilmar Dokumente I No. 395]
Subsequent editions:	Peters: Vol. 2/114; AGA XX 415: Vol. 7/46; NSA IV: Vol. 3/74; Bärenreiter: Vol. 2/108
Bibliography:	Capell 1928, pp. 175–6
Discography and timing:	Fischer-Dieskau II 5¹³ 2'40
	Hyperion I 19³
	Hyperion II 26¹¹ 2'31 Felicity Lott

← *Am See* D746   *An die Leier* D737 →

IM JÄNNER 1817 (Tiefes Leid)   January 1817 (Deep sorrow)
(Schulze), **D876** [H582]
E minor – E major   January 1826

(36 bars)

Ich bin von aller Ruh geschieden
Ich treib' umher auf wilder Flut;[1]
An e i n e m Ort nur find' ich Frieden,
Das ist der Ort, wo alles ruht.
Und wenn die Wind' auch schaurig sausen,
Und kalt der Regen niederfällt,
Doch will ich dort viel lieber hausen,[2]
Als in der unbeständ'gen Welt.

   Denn wie die Träume spurlos schweben,
Und einer schnell den andern treibt,
Spielt mit sich selbst das irre Leben,
Und jedes naht und keines bleibt.
Nie will die falsche Hoffnung weichen,
Nie mit der Hoffnung Furcht und Müh;
Die Ewigstummen, Ewigbleichen
Verheissen und versagen nie.

   Nicht weck' ich sie mit meinen Schritten
In ihrer dunklen Einsamkeit.
Sie wissen nicht, was ich gelitten,
Und keinen stört mein tiefes Leid.
Dort kann die Seele freier klagen
Bei Jener, die ich treu geliebt;
Nicht wird der kalte Stein mir sagen:
Ach, dass auch sie mein Schmerz betrübt!

All peace has forsaken me;
I am tossed upon the stormy waters.
In *one* place alone I shall find peace:
The place where all things rest.
Though the wind may whistle eerily
And the rain fall cold,
I would far rather dwell there
Than in this fickle world.

   For as dreams float away without trace,
As one swiftly succeeds another,
So life is a dizzy whirl:
Everything draws near, nothing remains.
False hope never fades,
Nor with that hope fear and toil;
The ever-silent, the ever-pale
Never promise, and never deny.

   I shall not waken them in their dark solitude
With my footsteps.
They do not know what I have suffered;
My deep sorrow disturbs none of them.
There my soul can lament more freely
With her whom I have truly loved;
There no cold stone will tell me,
Alas, that my suffering distresses her too.

ERNST SCHULZE (1789–1817); poem written 17 January 1817

This is the seventh of Schubert's ten Schulze solo settings (1825–6). See the poet's biography for a chronological list of all the Schulze settings. An outline of a suggested performing version for a Schulze cycle is listed under 'Auf den wilden Wegen'.

The title of this song in the Peters Edition, *Tiefes Leid*, is not Schubert's own; it was written in an anonymous hand at the top of the manuscript, and uses a tag found in the third verse of the poem. It is not impossible that this was the title by which the song was known in the Schubert circle. The date of the poem is the 'official' title in the Deutsch catalogue. In terms of the chronology of Schulze's *Poetisches Tagebuch* this is the ninety-fifth poem, written a month before the poet, already a dying man, brought the work to a close with the hundredth, which he wrote on the birthday of his first love, Cäcilie Tychsen (who had died just over four years previously). Of all the Schulze poems set by Schubert, *Im Jänner 1817* gives us the clearest autobiographical picture of the poet's circumstances at the time of writing. Adelheid Tychsen, Cäcilie's surviving sister, had forbidden him to enter her house but in the last months of his life he chose to revisit in verse (if not in fact) the grave of Cäcilie, who of course was unaware of his suffering at her sister's hands. There is a feeling here that Schulze is playing one sister off against the other, but

---

[1] Schulze writes '*Und* treib' umher auf wilder Flut'.
[2] Schulze writes 'Doch *mag* ich dort viel lieber hausen'.

he seems to have a real grasp of how desperate his own situation is. In Capell's words the song is 'pathetic in a kind of humbled way'. The poet, who elsewhere is determined to follow the twisted logic of his own misconceptions, here seems utterly helpless. He freely admits that 'false hope never fades' and in doing so is unusually perceptive about his own obsessive nature. For the only time in the Schulze settings the music turns away from the certainties of duple time to paw the ground restlessly in a disorientated triple metre (the E minor section), or to float eerily with the spirits in E major 'in some gently, hypnotically swaying other-world, no longer earth-bound' (Susan Youens).

As is appropriate to a graveside hymn (if a hymn can have the marking 'Mässig, unruhig'), the song is in simple strophic form. In each of the three verses (which are composed of two rhyming quatrains) the first six lines make up the *minore* section and the final two lines move into the major key and are repeated (with slight variations) to make a symmetrical musical structure. The effect of this strophic symmetry is the impression of the morbid and compulsive revisiting of old burial grounds, all to no avail. Because there are six lines of words to cover in E minor (versus only two with the same amount of music in the major), life's tumult in a torrent of words is in vivid contrast to the peace of the grave. In the opening, accents on the third beat betoken jagged nerves, the detached quavers of the accompaniment short gasps. There is an eerie impression of wind over graveyards at 'Und wenn die Wind' auch schaurig sausen' (bb. 13–15): right-hand octaves look like level tombstones separated only by the decency of a patch of rest on the printed page. These octaves on repeated Bs on the offbeat (bb. 14–22) leave the left hand to shift beneath with changing harmonies. This effect carries over the double bar line of a change from minor to major (at b. 18) uniting the two very different sections of the song. Such an effect was to reappear in *Winterreise*: in the song *Rückblick* D911/8 a bank of As, repeated and off the beat, is underpinned by the left hand, on all the strong beats, floundering in harmonic quicksand at 'Kömmt mir der Tag in die Gedanken, / Möcht ich noch einmal rückwärts sehn'. Capell (echoed by Fischer-Dieskau) has already commented on the similarity between 'du Stadt der Unbeständigkeit!' in that song and the setting of the words 'in der unbeständ'gen Welt' in *Im Jänner 1817*.

The whole of this major-key section is remarkable for a vocal line that lies in the middle of the song's texture, with the piano singing an obbligato line above it. This brings to mind the solemn wind and brass music that accompanies burials and is known as 'Blaskapelle'. This music is also to be found represented in *Das Wirtshaus* in *Winterreise* D911/21 where the pianist's little finger sings a descant over the verse beginning with the words 'Ihr grünen Totenkränze / Könnt wohl die Zeichen sein'. There are similarities too between *Im Jänner 1817* and another E minor song of 1826, Mignon's *Heiss mich nicht reden* D877/2 which also deals with a burden that is carried to the grave.

Autograph	Bodleian Library, Oxford
First edition:	Published as Book 30 no. 1 of the *Nachlass* by Diabelli, Vienna in 1838 (P324)
Subsequent editions:	Peters: Vol. 3/202 (as 'Tiefes Leid'); AGA XX 487: Vol. 8/164; NSA IV: Vol. 14a/8
Bibliography:	Youens 1996, pp. 282–4
Discography and timing:	Fischer-Dieskau II 7[16] 2'40 (first two strophes only)
	Hyperion I 18[17]
	Hyperion II 31[5] 3'44 Peter Schreier

⟵ *O Quell, was strömst du rasch und wild*
        (Die Blume und der Quell) D874

                                            Mondenschein D875 ⟶

IM KALTEN, RAUHEN NORDEN *see* HELIOPOLIS I D753

'IM NORDEN ZU SINGEN' *see* PUNSCHLIED D253

IM WALDE (Waldesnacht)   In the forest
(F. VON SCHLEGEL), **D708** [H457 & H460+]
E major   December 1820

(214 bars)

Windes Rauschen, Gottes Flügel,	The rushing of the wind, God's own wings,
Tief in kühler Waldesnacht,	Deep in the cool night of the forest,
Wie der Held in Rosses Bügel,	Like the hero mounted on his steed,
Schwingt sich des Gedankens Macht.	So does the power of thought soar.
Wie die alten Tannen sausen,	As the old pine-trees rustle,
Hört man Geistes Wogen brausen.	So we hear the surging waves of the spirit.
Herrlich ist der Flamme Leuchten	Glorious is the flame's glow
In des Morgenglanzes Rot,	In the red light of morning,
Oder die das Feld beleuchten,[1]	Or the flashes that light up the fields,
Blitze, schwanger oft von Tod.	Often pregnant with death.
Rasch die Flamme zuckt und lodert,	Swiftly the flame flickers and blazes,
Wie zu Gott hinauf gefordert.	As if summoned upward to God.
Ewig's Rauschen sanfter Quellen,	The eternal murmuring of gentle springs
Zaubert Blumen aus dem Schmerz;	Conjures flowers from sorrow;
Trauer doch in linden Wellen	Yet sadness beats alluringly against our hearts
Schlägt uns lockend an das Herz;	In gentle waves.
Fernab hin der Geist gezogen,	The spirit is borne far away
Die uns locken, durch die Wogen.	By those waves that allure us.
Drang des Lebens aus der Hülle,	Life's urge to be free of its fetters,
Kampf der starken Triebe wild,	The struggle of strong, wild impulses,
Wird zur schönsten Liebensfülle	Are turned to love's fair fulfilment,
Durch des Geistes Hauch gestillt.	Stilled by the breath of the spirit.
Schöpferischer Lüfte Wehen	We feel the creative breath
Fühlt man durch die Seele gehen.	Pervade our souls.

[1] Schlegel writes 'Oder die das Feld *befeuchten*'.

Windes Rauschen, Gottes Flügel,	The rushing of the wind, God's own wings,
Tief in kühler Waldesnacht![2]	Deep in the dark night of the forest;
Frei gegeben alle Zügel,	Free from all restraints
Schwingt sich des Gedankens Macht,	The power of thought soars;
Hört in Lüften ohne Grausen	Without fear we hear the song of the spirits
Den Gesang der Geister brausen.	Echoing in the breezes.

FRIEDRICH VON SCHLEGEL (1772–1829); poem written *c.* 1802

This is the thirteenth of Schubert's sixteen Friedrich von Schlegel solo settings (1818–25). See the poet's biography for a chronological list of all the Friedrich von Schlegel settings.

This poem is to be found in Schlegel's *Gedichte* (1809) next to his *An Novalis*. It is not the last of the Schlegel settings but it is certainly the largest and the most astonishing. It was written at a time when the enthusiasm of Schubert and his circle for the pantheism of the poet was at its height. This is young man's music, not because it lacks mastery (on the contrary, Capell calls it 'assuredly one of Schubert's greatest inspirations') but because it expends energy in the grand and lavish manner that is the hallmark of a young genius in full flower. In it we hear a young man with everything to hope for. The doors of the opera houses are still open to him, it seems; he has found in Vogl the greatest of interpreters and he is free from the burdens of the schoolroom.

To this period of Schubert's life belongs some of his most avant-garde work. The composer is in experimental mode, above all in his use of arioso and subtle word-setting that approaches the naturalness of speech. Some of the music of this period, lacking conventional tunes, such as the cantata *Lazarus* D689, still feels remote to the average Schubertian. Not so *Im Walde* where the composer's audacity in matters of form and length does not preclude a succession of melodies that make up one long uninterrupted paean, a flood of thrilling sound to sweep the listener away. The hastily scrawled autograph indicates Schubert's excitement and exhilaration.

The song was published posthumously in E flat major to make it more accessible to the average mezzo or baritone, but Schubert's key is E major, suitable for a fine high baritone (Matthias Goerne recorded it in this tonality for Hyperion). The marking is 'Geschwind' ('Fast') but the composer moderates this with a restraining **C** – four in the bar, as opposed to cut-time *alla breve*. There are interpretations of this song that make of it a relative of *Erlkönig* D328, *Willkommen und Abschied* D767 or *Auf der Bruck* D853, where the excitement of a horse-ride pounds throughout the music. The image of the hero's horse comes early in the Schlegel poem (bb. 25–6), and it might be argued that the music is driven forward in a similar way to the Goethe and Schulze masterpieces. It seems to me, however, that there is no steed in this forest, only the magical rustling of what Wagner would later call 'Forest Murmurs' (*Siegfried*, Act II) and the frissons of the imagination. The singer fancies that he is in deepest communion with nature and this is above all a song about the power of thought. The poem does not belong to the *Abendröte* cycle, but it might well be part of that set – a magnified and extended *Die Gebüsche* D646 where the songs of many bushes and trees combine to give the forest a musical voice.

There are nearly ten bars of piano introduction, and it is clear from the beginning that Schubert is in adventurous mood. Two bars of excited oscillations, a moto perpetuo of rippling semiquavers that will form the accompaniment in one shape or another almost without interruption, are in the home key of E major. These lead (via a bass that sidles downwards) to two

---

[2] Schlegel writes 'Tief in *dunkler* Waldesnacht'. In b. 169 Schubert clearly prefers to use the adjective 'kühler', as at the beginning of the song (b. 15). But in the work's closing pages (bb. 198–208) the composer reverts to Schlegel's text with the repetition of the lines 'Windes Rauschen, Gottes Flügel / Tief in dunkler Waldesnacht'. The word 'dunkler' is here set to a pair of minims on low B.

Im Walde ('Waldesnacht'), first edition (1832).

bars in C sharp major no less (bb. 3–4), remote and dramatic with a touch of the sinister. Another drop in the bass line takes us to A^7 (b. 5), and from there we climb back up to two further bars on a dominant pedal that returns us to the E major murmurings of the opening. The stage has been set, and the grand scale of the song established.

The entry of the voice provides a dramatic jolt with the sudden move to D sharp major at 'Windes Rauschen' (b. 11). Leo Black points out that the composer Egon Wellesz used to quote this passage apropos Schubert's violent originality. This drop of half a step is only to a curiously written E flat major of course, but Schubert somehow makes us hear it as a rising harmony because the vocal line climbs from G sharp to A sharp; thus tension mounts as the harmonic ground gives way beneath our feet. This short phrase is complemented by a sequence – 'Gottes Flügel' – a bar later (bb. 12–13) and a tone higher. We thus have two separate dramatic exclamations before we enter the secret and intimate world of the subdominant (in first inversion) for 'Tief in kühler Waldesnacht' (bb. 15–16), clearly somewhere awesome and mysterious. The final word of the phrase ('Waldesnacht') returns to the tonic key and is ornamented by a grace note, suggesting a shudder of excitement. Within a bar the whole process of this first section is repeated, the same words now set higher in the voice for the poem's first line, and returning to exactly the same notes for 'Tief in kühler Waldesnacht'. Mention of the hero's steed ('Wie der Held in Rosses Bügel') prompts the pianist's left hand to abandon semiquavers in favour of octaves in the manner of *Auf der Bruck* D853. The old pine trees ('die alten Tannen' bb. 28–30) rustle splendidly at first hearing with a leap upwards, and then a drop of an octave (the same intervals serve 'Geistes Wogen brausen'). At the repeat of the words their music takes on an almost military precision as it marches up the stave in thirds in E major (bb. 32–4), followed by 'Geistes Wogen' (b. 35) which plunges down in the opposite direction, this time in E minor. This long-arched structure in the vocal line is very Schlegelian: it is as if the forest itself inhales and exhales, a living thing suddenly animate. Leo Black notes Schubert's tendency in this strophe, and throughout the song, to double voice and piano, a device 'prompted by ideas of inmost feelings, of an inner voice, of being overtaken by forces beyond one's control, or of submission to a superior force', the superior force on this occasion being 'the power of thought' or, as Black puts it, 'the power of the Idea'.

In the second strophe ('Herrlich ist der Flamme Leuchten', b. 51) flashes of lightning are brilliantly depicted in the exchange of staccato left-hand quavers with the dancing arpeggio figurations of the vocal line, which bristles with the electricity of consonants sung at high speed (a test for any singer's diction). Thunder finds musical voice in the forceful bass notes, reinforced with a slew of acciaccaturas, under 'Tod', b. 57, occurring a full bar after the plunging octaves of 'Blitze' in b. 56, just as thunder follows lightning. It is a stroke of genius to use this phenomenon of nature to add, with perfect timing, an ominous rumble to the setting of the word 'death'. Schubert is then faced with the challenge of capping this effect for the even more evocative 'Rasch die Flamme zuckt und lodert', bb. 60–61, and here he astonishes us even more. Once again the vocal line climbs as the bass line falls and the capricious nature of the sparking flame is caught in three dazzling arpeggios in the piano with basses on D (first inversion of B flat major), D flat (a diminished seventh chord) and C (second inversion of F minor). These are followed by triumphant quaver chords that break through from B flat minor to major, bb. 62–3, and thence to F major, the only place in the whole song where the pianist is given any respite from pulsating semiquavers. Above this passage (reminiscent of the 'Ewigkeit' section of *Gruppe aus dem Tartarus* D583) the vocal line, suddenly ecstatic with a vision of the godhead, expands into dotted minims and semibreves (bb. 63–4). To balance this music the passage is heard again (bb. 66–71) (the song is made up of repeated phrases throughout): the vocal line is the same for 'Rasch die Flamme zuckt und lodert', but the piano harmonizes those particular words with glittering arpeggios of completely different harmonies. This Schubertian legerdemain, where the composer demonstrates his ability to conjure St Cecilia's 'immortal fire' (as Auden calls it), shows us that a flame never flickers twice in exactly the same way.

With the third strophe we are led into regions of peaceful enchantment; it is as if we have come to a clearing in the forest that is other-worldly in its beauty. Schubert emphasizes this by allowing the four-bar interlude (bb. 72–5) to dematerialize before our ears, like mist lifting to reveal a vision of loveliness. First the bass notes thin out, then they rise, coaxing the right hand up into more ethereal regions of the piano. The harmonic progression is from F major via G^7 to C major, a major third away from the tonic of E and one of Schubert's favourite key relationships. Most singers find the vocal placement here (from b. 75) perilously high, and it was this passage that no doubt persuaded the publisher Diabelli to transpose the whole song down a semitone. And yet this heady texture, as if the singer were spiritually intoxicated by what he sees, was surely the composer's intention. At first the pianist's left hand doubles the vocal line, but at 'Trauer doch in linden Wellen' (b. 83) a delightful dialogue begins, as between voice and cello, where their paths diverge. The whole mood of this section is pastoral. The flower imagery of 'Zaubert Blumen aus dem Schmerz' (bb. 81–3) prompts music prophetic of the 'Rose nahet, Lilie schwankt' section of the ballad *Viola* D786, another instance of a left-hand melody flowering in support of the voice beneath a seraphic flow of right-hand semiquavers. We move into D flat major by a remarkable twist of harmony, giving the highly placed setting of 'lockend an das Herz' (bb. 85–6) an element both of delight and pain; the idyll is over, and we return to more galvanizing areas of the forest. At 'Fernab hin der Geist gezogen' (b. 90) there is a quickening of the mood as the song is again invaded by spiritual electricity, the beginning of a long build-up to the music of the fourth strophe. The left hand returns to the bass regions, and the second and third times we hear the words 'Fernab hin der Geist gezogen' we are rewarded with a sumptuous phrase based on the subdominant of D flat major. A G flat octave deep in the bass supports a yearning drop of a fifth on 'Fernab hin' as if to emphasize the distance between us and the spirit, and the longing of mortals to follow where it leads (bb. 94–5).

Everything has been leading to Schlegel's fourth strophe, the vibrant heart of the poem and the lines which must have meant the most to Schubert, uniting as they do the ideas of unfettered freedom, the fulfilment of love and the spiritual nature of creativity. The composer introduces these words by providing a breathing space, an interlude of six bars of gentle semiquavers where the performers gather their strength for what is to follow, and the listener is given a moment of respite. We are in the key of D flat until the entry of the voice, where a sudden enharmonic change to C sharp major (at b. 110) is a sign of the roller-coaster of heightened emotions and quickly changing harmonies which is to follow. The piano writing takes on a ferocious difficulty in its layout, as if the simple wrist movement that has been required up to now is insufficiently taxing to reflect the idea of 'Drang des Lebens', as if the very playing of the accompaniment should be a battle, a 'Kampf der starken Triebe wild'. The vocal line is here divided into short phrases punctuated by rests, in a similar way to the opening of the song, but significantly there is now less time between vocal exclamations as the screws of tension are tightened. At 'schönsten Liebensfülle' (bb. 117–18) the vocal line becomes ethereal and quiet (to illustrate 'Geistes Hauch' – 'breath of the spirit') and gently lyrical. The accompaniment has a new figure in the left hand, quavers phrased in ascending fifths and sixths (from b. 117), suggestive of unappeased longing or pounding heartbeats. All these words are now repeated to similar melodies, but in different keys; the ear is bewildered by the speed with which the harmonic scenery shifts and we feel as if we are in Schubert's hands on a dangerous joyride and can only hang on for dear life. Even by the high standards of excitement and virtuosity generated by this song, the setting of the passage beginning 'Schöpferischer Lüfte Wehen / Fühlt man durch die Seele gehen' (b. 140) is spectacular. The pianist's left hand falls in chromatic steps (from b. 140) and the right hand ascends in semitones in wrist-torturing swirls of semiquavers, bearing the voice upwards with it. The virtuosity of this passage suggests a searing strength and muscularity. The feeling of being shaken deeply, penetrated with a shattering emotion, is caught in some of the most extraordinary music that Schubert ever wrote. This is the voice of romanticism, as far away as can be imagined from the established formulae of the Viennese classics. The words are repeated in a higher sequence (from b. 145) where the tessitura of the piano writing suggests even more strongly the lightning flashes of divine inspiration. The section ends with a more reflective setting of 'Fühlt man durch die Seele gehen', a phrase we hear twice (bb. 147–54).

A three-bar interlude (bb. 154–7) leads to a vocal bridging passage that is a means of disguising the recapitulation in the manner of Haydn and Beethoven, and is used to tease the listener accustomed to the rules of sonata form. Thus in two juxtaposed passages we hear Schubert's vision of the future, as well as his debt to the past. 'Windes Rauschen, Gottes Flügel' is set ominously low in the voice, with a rise of a ninth and then an octave drop. This is not the music that we have associated with these words at the beginning of the piece, and we expect yet another episode in an already long song. It soon becomes clear, however, that Schubert is using this phrase to engineer a return to the music of the beginning; we arrive at 'Tief in Kühler Waldesnacht' with a brilliantly plotted landing into the home key of E major (from b. 163). We have come full circle and survived a journey through the forest; spared the Lorelei and Erlking who have no place in Schlegel's universe, we have encountered spirits of a more uplifting kind. This music is essentially a shortened and varied recapitulation of the first strophe, and there is a coda section using the first two lines of the last strophe again. It is as if we are gradually receding from the picture that has been conjured; the forest is allowed to return to its natural state as it no longer interacts with man. In the same key of E major Robert Schumann created a postlude to his song *Waldesgespräch* Op. 39 no. 3 (the poem by Schlegel's admirer Eichendorff) where the fading piano lines evoke the forest folding its supernatural secrets deep into its bosom. Here Schubert returns the voice to the depths of low Bs ('Tief in dunkler Waldesnacht') as dark as the forest itself. Six bars of ever-softening and receding piano music (still articulated in rustling semiquavers) conclude this towering masterpiece, one of the most miraculous of all Schubert's longer songs, and a fitting high point of his Schlegel settings.

The song was entitled *Waldesnacht* on publication in the *Nachlass*, presumably to differentiate it from the Schulze setting *Im Walde* Op. 93 no. 1. Some meddling hand has excised bb. 180–83 in that edition. This cut is adopted by Peters Edition where the editors of the time, clearly uncomfortable with some of Schlegel's imagery, misguidedly invited Ludwig Stark to modernize parts of the poem, including the Loewe-like addition of elves and forest spirits. It is these which are now laughably old-fashioned. The original Schlegel is printed in smaller print above Stark's unfortunate adaptation.

Autograph:	Gesellschaft der Musikfreunde, Vienna (first draft)
First edition:	Published as Book 16 of the *Nachlass* by Diabelli, Vienna in March 1832 (P283) where the title is *Waldesnacht*
Subsequent editions:	Peters: Vol. 3/159; AGA XX 388: Vol. 6/149; NSA IV: Vol. 12/186
Bibliography:	Black 2000, p. 89
	Black 2003, pp. 45 & 92–3 (description of surprise harmonies; comparison with Scriabin)
	Capell 1928, pp. 166–7
	Einstein 1951, p. 216
	Fischer-Dieskau 1977, pp. 123–4
Discography and timing:	Fischer-Dieskau II 4[8] 6'46
	Hyperion I 27[22] 7'09 Matthias Goerne
	Hyperion I 29[21] 6'18 Marjana Lipovšek
	Hyperion II 23[15] 6'18 Marjana Lipovšek
	Hyperion II 24[2] 7'09 Matthias Goerne

⟵ *Der Jüngling auf dem Hügel* D702   *Der zürnenden Diana* D707 ⟶
⟵ *Der 23. Psalm* D706   *Sehnsucht* D636 ⟶

IM WALDE   In the forest
(SCHULZE) OP. 93 NO. 1, **D834** [H561]

The song exists in two versions, the second of which is discussed below:
(1) March 1825; (2) September 1827?

(1) 'Nicht zu schnell'   G minor   **C**   [176 bars]

(2) B♭ minor

Ich wandre über Berg und Tal	I wander over hill and dale,
Und über grüne Heiden,	And over green moorland,
Und mit mir wandert meine Qual,	And my suffering wanders with me,
Will nimmer von mir scheiden.	Never leaving me.
Und schifft' ich auch durch's weite Meer,	And were I to sail across the wide sea
Sie käm' auch dort wohl hinterher.	It would still follow me there.
Wohl blühn viel Blumen auf der Flur,	Though many flowers bloom in the meadow
Die hab' ich nicht gesehen.	I have not seen them,
Denn e i n e Blume seh' ich nur	For I see but *one* flower
Auf allen Wegen stehen.	On every path I tread.
Nach ihr hab' ich mich oft gebückt	I have often stooped down towards it
Und doch sie nimmer abgepflückt.	But have never plucked it.
Die Bienen summen durch das Gras[1]	The bees hum through the grass
Und hängen an den Blüten;	And linger on the blossoms;
Das macht mein Auge trüb' und nass,	At this my eyes grow clouded and moist;
Ich kann mir's nicht verbieten.	I cannot help it.
Ihr süssen Lippen, rot und weich,	Sweet lips, so red and soft,
Wohl hing ich nimmer so an euch!	Never did I linger so on you.
Gar lieblich singen nah und fern	Far and near the birds sing sweet
Die Vögel auf den Zweigen;	On the branches.
Wohl säng' ich mit den Vögeln gern,	I should dearly love to sing with them,
Doch muss ich traurig schweigen.	But I must keep a mournful silence.
Denn Liebeslust und Liebespein,	For the joy and the pain of love
Die bleiben jedes gern allein.	Prefer to remain alone.
Am Himmel seh' ich flügelschnell	I watch the clouds wing their way
Die Wolken weiter ziehen,	Swiftly across the sky;
Die Welle rieselt leicht und hell,	The waves ripple softly and bright.
Muss immer nahn und fliehen.	They must ever come and go.
Doch haschen, wenn's vom Winde ruht,	Yet when the wind dies down,
Sich Wolk' und Wolke, Flut und Flut.	In play, cloud catches cloud, and wave catches wave.
Ich wandre hin, ich wandre her,	I wander here and there,
Bei Sturm und heitern Tagen,	Through storm and fine weather,
Und doch erschau' ich's nimmermehr	Yet I shall never again behold it,
Und kann es nicht erjagen.	Shall never find it.
O Liebessehnen, Liebesqual,	O longing and torment of love,
Wann ruht der Wanderer einmal?	When will the wanderer find rest?

ERNST SCHULZE (1789–1817); poem written 22 July 1814

This is the first of Schubert's ten schulze solo settings (1825–6). See the poet's biography for a chronological list of all the Schulze settings. An outline of a suggested performing version for a Schulze cycle is listed under 'Auf den wilden Wegen'.

[1] Schulze writes 'Die Bienen *sumsen* durch das Gras'.

Schulze's *Poetisches Tagebuch* entry reads, 'In the forest behind Falkenhagen, 22 July 1814.' This places the poet in the area around Göttingen three days before his horse-ride across country and the composition of *Auf der Bruck* D853. It is a bone of contention whether Schubert deliberately changed the title of that song to *Auf der Brücke*, 'On the bridge' (thus removing any reference to Bruck, a lookout point near Göttingen), but it is certain that he removed Falkenhagen as a locale from this song's title. He preferred to place his protagonist simply 'in the forest'.

Just as in *Auf der Bruck*, the song is driven tempestuously forwards and the recurrence of a ritornello gives the impression of going around in self-defeating circles, as if lost in a forest. Capell detects here 'a single over-mastering impulse that never relaxes' which is perhaps a way of saying that the work is irrigated by a scarcely concealed flood of sexual energy where the composer is more than a match for the poet. Women tended to back away from Schulze when he became emotionally involved with them, but he was handsome enough to have enjoyed a host of conquests. Indeed he must have been well aware that his good looks were not only part of his appeal as a Don Giovanni, but also part of his armour that shielded him from real intimacy. The Tychsen sisters, Cäcilie and Adelheid of whom he was enamoured at different times, had both been able to see through his looks; they set this inherited advantage at nought, and the passionate young man realized that he doubly desired those whom he could not have. Talk of flowers in this poem refers to a woman; there are thousands available for plucking but he wants only one, even if he has to stoop to pick it (note the imagery, for he believes that this woman is not really on his level). But Adelheid Tychsen will not permit him into her Garden, and he is stung by the audacity of the bees who fly in where poets fear to tread. He also talks of finding 'it' (neuter gender) in the last verse; presumably he means happiness – 'das Glück' – which he seemed to value as a commodity. The wanderer asks when he will find 'rest' but he means quietus; thus did an earlier generation of poets refer to the moment of orgasmic release as related to death.

The first version of the song was composed in March 1825 in G minor; the NSA prints this version in Volume 5b with ornaments that almost certainly go back to the baritone Vogl. It seems that Schubert wrote out a fair copy in a higher key during his visit to Graz in 1827 and left this (as well as a fair copy of *Auf der Bruck*) in the care of his friend Anselm Hüttenbrenner to hand over to a local publisher, Kienreich. (It was stated on the title page of Kienreich's publication that Schubert had composed these two songs during his Graz visit although he almost certainly had not.) The pairing of the two songs seems to have been something Schubert effected deliberately. For the fair copy of *Im Walde* he selected the key of B flat minor – not a common tonality in his work and shared by Gretchen in her anguished prayer to the mater dolorosa (*Gretchen im Zwinger* D564) and by Heine in confronting a portrait of his beloved in *Ihr Bild* (D957/9) from *Schwanengesang*. Gretchen has lost her innocence, and both Heine and Schulze their peace of mind. Even in the new higher key, the texture of the music is more bottom-heavy than is usual (especially the piano writing between bb. 57 and 65 and bb. 140–47), the forest paths muddy with unclear thoughts and emotions. Susan Youens has pointed out that there is much in *Im Walde* that is related to the triplet-accompanied passages in Beethoven's *An die ferne Geliebte*, but she makes the point, as do other commentators, that in terms of its shape and constant triplet movement, it is most strongly related to another anguished song of search, *Erstarrung* (D911/4) from *Winterreise*. Note how the pianist's left hand in that masterpiece plays an eloquent heartfelt melody in single notes in the undergrowth of the score as it tries to search for traces of the beloved with delicate and supple fingers, however frostbitten. In *Im Walde* the search is less specific: at first the triplets are in the left hand instead of the right, and the right-hand melody is robbed of melodic finesse by being in double octaves. Nevertheless it is clear that there is more than a coincidental similarity between the two songs and that *Im Walde* was something of a study for *Erstarrung*. This is clearer still when one compares the structure of the two works: in each the first and fourth of the strophes are related, as are the second and fifth. The touching, lyrical episodes from both songs (the winter traveller's 'Wo find ich eine Blüte', from b. 47 of *Erstarrung*, and Schulze's 'Wohl blühn viel Blumen auf der Flur', from b. 34 of *Im Walde*) are very similar in atmosphere.

This interleaving of material strengthens and buttresses the structure; there is a strong impression of repetition and recapitulation but in a slightly unpredictable way. As in the *Winterreise* song, Schulze seems to be wandering in an erratic manner. In *Im Walde* there are marvellous passages in the tonic 'pathetic' major that relate to the bees and the birds (from bb. 66 and 92). The idea of hanging on to the thought of someone, almost clinging in a physical sense, is wonderfully captured by the doubling of voice and piano in obsessively rising octaves in bb. 75–80 – as if the pianist is hanging on to the staves by his fingernails. It is remarkable how individually tailored to their poets the two songs remain. Müller's hero is more refined and aware, dealing with an emotional crisis in which a real relationship (or one that we believe to be real) has foundered. The plight of Schulze, whose rather aggressive self-pity is combined with self-delusion (the vocal line is somehow suffused with both these attributes), inspires less sympathy. That Schubert should have responded so accurately to this aspect of Schulze's personality without being aware of all the details of the poet's biography reveals his uncanny ability to read between the lines. (In fact, Schulze's poems came from a real story of emotional upheaval, Müller's did not, at least nothing contemporary with the writing of *Die Winterreise*.) Until he found that rare combination of drama and sincerity in Müller, both heart-wrenching and underplayed, Schubert was content to experiment, via Schulze's poems, with this kind of overheated narrative confessional.

Autograph:	In private possession
Publication:	First published as Op. 93 no. 1 by Diabelli, Vienna in 1835 (P307; first version)
	First published as Op. 90 no. 1 by J. A. Kienreich, Graz in 1828; subsequently corrected to Op. 93 in 1835 (P156; second version)
First known performance:	5 February 1829, *Abend-Unterhaltung* of the Gesellschaft der Musikfreunde, Musikverein, Vienna. Soloist: Anton Obermüller (see Waidelich/Hilmar Dokumente I No. 694 for full concert programme)
Subsequent editions:	Peters: Vol. 3/57; AGA XX 476: Vol. 8/96; NSA IV: Vol. 5a/16 & Vol. 5b/202; Bärenreiter: Vol. 3/156
Bibliography:	Capell 1928, p. 215
	Fischer-Dieskau 1977, pp. 225–6
	Youens 1996, pp. 263–7
Discography and timing:	Fischer-Dieskau II 7[6] 5'23
	Hyperion I 18[18]
	Hyperion II 29[16] 5'42 Peter Schreier

←*Auf der Bruck (Auf der Brücke)* D853   *Der blinde Knabe* D833 →

IMPROMPTU *see* NUR WER DIE LIEBE KENNT D513A

IN DER FERNE *see* SCHWANENGESANG D957/6

IN DER MITTERNACHT   At midnight
(JACOBI) **D464** [H290]

E♭ major   August 1816

(9 bars)

Todesstille deckt das Tal	Deathly silence lies over the valley
Bei des Mondes falbem Strahl;[1]	Beneath the moon's pale beams;
Winde flüstern dumpf und bang	Winds whisper, dull and troubled,
In des Wächters Nachtgesang.	Mingling with the watchman's night song.
Leiser, dumpfer tönt es hier	Softer, duller, are the sounds
In der bangen Seele mir,	Within my troubled soul;
Nimmt den Strahl der Hoffnung fort,	They eclipse my ray of hope
Wie den Mond die Wolke dort.	As the clouds eclipse the moon.
Hüllt, ihr Wolken, hüllt den Schein	Clouds, conceal the light
Immer tiefer, tiefer ein!	Ever more deeply!
Vor ihm bergen will mein Herz	My heart would hide from him
Seinen tiefen, tiefen Schmerz.	Its deep, deep pain.
Nennen soll ihn nicht mein Mund;	My lips shall not name him;
Keine Träne mach' ihn kund;	No tear shall make him known;
Senken soll man ihn hinab	One day they shall lower him
Einst mit mir in's kühle Grab.	Into the cool grave, to lie with me.
[. . .]	[. . .]
An des Todes milder Hand	Guided by death's gentle hand
Geht der Weg in's Vaterland;	My path leads home.
Dort ist Liebe sonder Pein;	There is love without pain;
Selig, selig werd' ich sein.	There shall I find bliss.
O der schönen langen Nacht,	O for the long, lovely night
Wo nicht Erdenliebe lacht,	When earthly love does not smile,
Wo verlassne Treue nicht	When faith betrayed
Ihren Kranz von Dornen flicht!	Does not plait its wreath of thorns.

JOHANN GEORG JACOBI (1740–1814); poem written between 1775 and 1782

This is the fourth of Schubert's seven Jacobi solo settings (1816). See the poet's biography for a chronological list of all the Jacobi settings.

This is probably the finest of the shorter Jacobi settings with the exception of *Am Tage aller Seelen* (*Litanei*) D343 and is perhaps the earliest of the lied's celebrated midnight confessionals.

[1] Jacobi writes 'Bei des Mondes *halben* Strahl'.

Even Zelter's song *Um Mitternacht* (1818) to Goethe's famous autobiographical poem post-dates this. Other midnight songs include the Schulze setting *Um Mitternacht* D862 and Mahler's Rückert setting of the same name. With its marking of 'Sehr langsam' and its three flats, *In der Mitternacht* shares some of the attributes (though not the triple metre) of *Litanei*, but there is infinitely less consolation in this private mini-tragedy. Whenever Schubert doubles his vocal line with the piano we know that something portentous is being said, but the enigmatic drama behind this poem is difficult to explain.

In its own right (and it should be considered as such, independently of the other Jacobi poems) this night meditation is deeply poetic and unjustly neglected. Its weary guarding of a secret brings Goethe's Mignon, and her song *Heiss mich nicht reden*, to mind. *In der Mitternacht* is a fine example of many of the songs that Schubert strove to write in 1816; some of them may not be immediately memorable, but they are conceived within their own limitations with a carefully calculated perfection of utterance. Everything about this song is a gentle understatement. For example, the first five notes of piano doubling voice might make us believe we have moved into the minor key but we remain in the serenity of the major – an ambivalence that is one of Schubert's most searching ways of expressing sorrow.

There are six strophes in Jacobi's poem – these are all printed in the AGA. In the Hyperion performance Strophe 5 was omitted, as reflected in the translation above. Two different suggestions for performing the five Jacobi songs as a set are discussed in the commentaries for *An Chloen* D462 and *Trauer der Liebe* D465.

Autograph:	In private possession
First edition:	Published as part of the AGA in 1895 (P648)
Subsequent editions:	Not in Peters; AGA XX 246: Vol. 4/151; NSA IV: Vol. 10/204
Discography and timing:	Fischer-Dieskau I 7^{32} 1'53 (first two strophes only)
	Hyperion I 8^{11}
	Hyperion II 15^{17} 4'26 Sarah Walker

← *Hochzeit-Lied* D463   *Trauer der Liebe* D465 →

INITIALS AND SIGNATURES

The German word *Paraphe* (plural *Paraphen*), also known as a *Kontrollnummer* or *Kontrollvermerk*, denotes some kind of official certification involving initials or part of a signature. It is the term used by musicologists for the handwritten initials that are often to be found on the back of the printed copies (bottom right-hand corner) of Schubert songs published on commission by Cappi and Diabelli in 1821. For the songs of Opp. 1–7 this is 'Sch' and for Opp. 12–14

Two examples of the *Paraphe* 'Schbt', the first on the back of Op. 12, the second, written in haste, on the back of Op. 13.

'Schbt', often accompanied by some other numbered reference. Schubert was not renowned for his efficiency regarding financial matters and without some kind of housekeeping of this kind it might have been possible for dishonest subscribers to claim more than one copy of the song against a prepayment. For more than a century it was accepted that the composer himself had signed (or half-signed) some of these copies as part of a process of controlling sales; of course this added enormously to the value of these editions. In 1986, to the dismay of antiquarians and collectors who clearly had most to lose, Ernst Hilmar averred that these markings were not from Schubert's own hand but were the annotations of Leopold von Sonnleithner and Josef Hütten-brenner who had been the moving spirits behind the publication of the songs. Hilmar took as his evidence a previously discounted remark of the Fröhlich sisters reported to Gerhard von Breuning that is to be found on p. 250 of Deutsch's *Schubert, Memoirs by his Friends* (1958): 'One hundred copies [of the songs] had been produced by Diabelli, and as a precaution against fraud ("zur Kontrolle gegen Unterschleif"), Sonnleithner wrote an "S" in his own handwriting on the back of every copy.' The matter has been hotly contested ever since with counter-arguments, the evidence of handwriting experts and so on. It has been argued that in the cases of Opp. 1–7 and Op. 96 Schubert had indeed proudly signed copies of his publications in imitation of that fellow composition pupil of Salieri, J. N. Hummel. Brahms firmly believed that his own copy of Schubert's Op. 4 songs had been signed by Schubert himself.

Two examples of 'Paraphen' are given above (from the back of Opp. 12 and 13) and, to the right, Schubert's full signature. The *Kurrentschrift* used by all German speakers at the time can be illegibly confusing for those not used to it: capital 'S' looks nearer to a capital 'O' (at least as written by Schubert); 'c' is a simple perpendicular line, like an undotted 'i'; 'h' is looped very much like a florid English 'f'; 'b' and 't' are similar to English letters.

Bibliography: Hilmar 1988[2], pp. 145–54

Schubert's full signature.

IPHIGENIA   Iphigenia
(MAYRHOFER) OP. 98 NO. 3, **D573** [H378]

The song exists in three versions, the third of which is discussed below:
(1) July 1817; (2) *c.* 1825; (3) 1828

(1)   'Nicht zu langsam'   G♭ major – D♭ major   𝄵   [35 bars]

(2)   'Langsam'   E♭ major – B♭ major   𝄵   [35 bars]

(3)   F major – C major

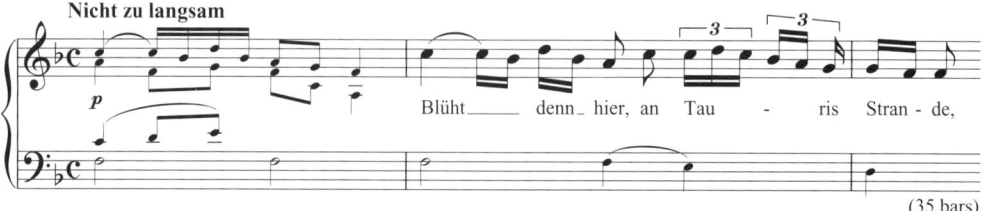

(35 bars)

Blüht denn hier an T a u r i s Strande	Here on the shore of *Tauris*
Aus dem teuren Vaterlande[1]	Does no flower bloom
Keine Blume? Weht kein Hauch[2]	From my beloved homeland?
Aus den seligen Gefilden,	Does no breeze blow from the blessed fields
Wo Geschwister mit mir spielten? –	Where my brothers and sisters played with me?
Ach, mein Leben ist ein Rauch!	Ah, my life is but smoke!
Trauernd wank' ich in dem Haine, –	Sadly, hesitantly, I walk through the grove;
Keine Hoffnung nähr' ich – keine,	I cherish no hope – none,
Meine Heimat zu erseh'n,	Of ever seeing my homeland.
Und die See mit hohen Wellen,	And the sea, with its mighty waves
Die an Klippen sich zerschellen,[3]	Crashing against the cliffs,
Übertäubt mein leises Fleh'n.	Drowns my soft pleas.
Göttin, die du mich gerettet,	Goddess who rescued me
An die Wildnis angekettet, –	And chained me in this wilderness,
Rette mich zum zweitenmal;	Rescue me a second time;
Gnädig lasse mich den Meinen,	Mercifully grant, o goddess,
Lass' o Göttin! mich erscheinen	That I may appear before my own people
In des grossen Königs Saal!	In the hall of the great king!

Johann Mayrhofer (1787–1836)

This is the twenty-eighth of Schubert's forty-seven Mayrhofer solo settings (1814–24). See the poet's biography for a chronological list of all the Mayrhofer settings.

The poem has its beginnings in the first act of Goethe's *Iphigenia in Tauris*: compare for example the last three lines of Mayrhofer's second strophe with Goethe's 'Und gegen meine Seufzer bringt die Welle, / Nur dumpfe Töne brausend mir herüber'. As in a number of his poems, Mayrhofer's way of paying homage to a favourite author (Sophocles, Catullus, Jean Paul) is to write a paraphrase of their work. It is fitting, therefore, that this Mayrhofer song has its musical genesis in two of Schubert's Goethe settings. In *Mignon* (*Kennst du das Land?*) D321 the waif Mignon longs to return to her Italian homeland; *Gretchen im Zwinger* D564 contains an ardent plea for help from a desperate Gretchen to the Virgin Mary – a sacred parallel to Iphigenia's prayer to the pagan goddess Diana to allow her to leave Tauris and return to the court of her father Agamemnon. *Gretchen im Zwinger* was composed in B flat minor only a few months earlier, and the first version of *Iphigenia* ends in that song's relative major of D flat. These two songs are closely related in the quasi-operatic nature of their music, and the manner of their word-setting.

Schubert's earliest theatrical visits in 1813 had been to hear Gluck's Iphigenia operas (sung in German) with Anna Milder Hauptmann in the title role and Johann Michael Vogl as Orestes. In the Fitzwilliam Museum, Cambridge, there is a copy in Schubert's hand (from 1815) of Johann Friedrich Reichardt's *Monolog aus Goethes Iphigenie* for solo soprano, chorus of women's voices and piano. This substantial song (recorded in the Hyperion collection *Songs by Schubert's Friends and Contemporaries*) clearly impressed the young composer, one suspects as much for its subject matter as for its musical content. The background to the Greek legend, the woes of the archetypal

---

[1] Mayrhofer (as in *Gedichte*, 1843) writes an entirely different line: 'Keine Blume' aus H e l l a s Lande'. For an explanation of the background to these alternative Mayrhofer readings see Editorial Note at the beginning of Johann Mayrhofer.
[2] For lines 3 and 4 of the poem Mayrhofer writes 'Weht kein *milder Segenshauch* / Aus den *lieblichen* Gefilden'.
[3] Mayrhofer writes 'Die an Klippen *kalt* zerschellen'.

dysfunctional family, would have been well known to Schubert: Agamemnon, father of Iphigenia, has been slain by her mother, Clytemnestra, who has in turn died at the avenging hand of her brother Orestes. It was the type of dramatic classical subject that appealed to Mayrhofer, and Schubert was clearly keen to write songs that demonstrated his enthusiasm for the Gluck operas. As a pupil of Salieri who had himself studied with Gluck, Schubert could consider himself a grand-pupil of that great composer, and it is hardly surprising that there are Gluckian echoes in *Iphigenia*.

Like 'Che farò senza Euridice' from *Orfeo ed Euridice*, this song on a tragic subject begins unashamedly in the major key. The slightly florid vocal line launches music that is regal enough for a princess, but ornate enough in leaps and melismas to suggest a noble soul *in extremis*. The yearning vocal line over the dominant pedal (from b. 6) on 'Wo Geschwister mit mir spielten?' with playful music in skipping thirds signals a retreat into memories of the innocence of childhood. (If this music were to be orchestrated, as it perhaps was in Schubert's mind, this passage would be allocated to the woodwind.) The syncopations of b. 9 ('Ach, mein Leben ist ein Rauch!'), something of an operatic commonplace, lead to an aria in G minor (bb. 10–15) where the accompanying triplets shudder as the down-at-heart Iphigenia makes her way through the sacred grove. Mayrhofer, as if keen to provide every illustrative opportunity for his young protégé, now shows a glimpse of the sea, a new perspective that provides the excuse for a shift into D major. Between bb. 16 and 20 the bass line, in rumbling demisemiquavers (with an ominous crescendo), goes through every possible harmonic permutation between D and E natural, three semitones on which are built a flurry of stormy left-hand oscillations. The interlude at bb. 21–2 seems conceived as clarinet music.

The prayer to the goddess is in the new key of C major. Before this impassioned plea Diana has in fact done Iphigenia a kindness by spiriting her away to Tauris; the hapless princess was due to be sacrificed to appease the gods when the Greeks were delayed on their way to Troy by contrary winds. We suddenly hear less of a victim and more of a regal princess. The tessitura in the song's first version in G flat major encompasses high A flats, an option for voices of some amplitude (a sense of scale and perspective remains necessary – this is, after all, a lied with piano). The postlude (bb. 34–5) where Iphigenia imagines herself once again in her father's palace, conjures up the pomp due to an ancient king. It is unusual for Mayrhofer's poetry to concern itself with female emotions, and although *Iphigenia* fails adequately to compete with Goethe's Gretchen and Mignon, or Scott's Ellen, this song should be heard more often on the concert platform. It is noteworthy that Mayrhofer chose not to publish this poem in his *Gedichte* of 1824, and that it only appeared in print posthumously in the *Gedichte* of 1843 edited by Ernst von Feuchtersleben.

There are three versions of the song. The first of these ('Nicht zu langsam') is the one in G flat major. This is printed in the NSA in

Iphigenia by Ramberg from the almanac *Minerva* (1827).

Volume 5b, p. 238. If a singer is capable of singing it in this high, almost heroic, key it must remain the performing preference. The second version is in E flat major, a copy from the Spaun Cornaro collection. This transposition for mezzo seems to have been made with Schubert's approval. When the piece was finally published posthumously in 1829 the second version was transposed up into F major to make it suitable for soprano performance. We must assume that Schubert had given the publisher permission to issue the song in this compromise tonality, and that he had agreed the opus number of 98 before his death. Even if artists wish to perform the song in the original G flat, they should study the F major version (NSA Volume 5a) for the definitive articulation and dynamic markings prepared by Schubert for the song's publication.

Autograph:	Österreichische Nationalbibliothek, Vienna
Publication:	First published as part of the NSA in 1985 (P791; first version)
	First published as part of the NSA in 1985 (P792; second version)
	First published as Op. 98 no. 3 by Diabelli, Vienna in 1829 (P230; third version)
Subsequent editions:	Peters: Vol. 4/97; AGA XX 325: Vol. 5/127; NSA IV: Vol. 5a/77 & Vol. 5b/228 & 231; Bärenreiter: Vol. 3/206
Bibliography:	Capell 1928, p. 137
	Kohlhäufl 1999, p. 162
Discography and timing:	Fischer-Dieskau —
	Hyperion I 3[5]
	Hyperion II 19[12] 3'16 Ann Murray

← *Das Grab* D573   *Abschied* D578 →

IRDISCHES GLÜCK *see VIER REFRAIN-LIEDER* D866/4

IRRLICHT *see WINTERREISE* D911/9

ITALY AND ITALIAN LITERATURE

The setting of Italian poetry was almost second nature to Schubert, although he was far from fluent in the language. Vienna was the most southern German-speaking metropolis and had a link with Italian culture that was not shared by Berlin or Leipzig. The Schubert lied (as noted by Franz von Schober) combines the best of the North and the South – the great poetry and *Innigkeit* of the German tradition married with the sensuality of vocal melody, and inherent drama, associated with Italian.[1] Vienna was considered a feasible refuge by Italian artists like Salieri and Metastasio in a way that the northern German cities would not have been. The Veneto and Venice itself were in Austrian possession and Italian was one of the many languages in daily use in the Habsburg Empire. Mozart had been similarly at ease with Italian, and Schubert's familiarity with Mozart's Italian operas from the scores themselves, as well as performance, was an important part of his development. One of the greatest influences on his musical life was his composition teacher Antonio Salieri who set numerous composition exercises in Italian and almost certainly expected his pupils to understand his own spoken Italian, including the

---

[1] 'Hier [Vienna] konnt' allein er nord'sche Tiefe einen / Mit Gluth und Melodie aus Südens Hainen' ('Here alone could he unite Northern profundity with the glow and melody from southern groves'). From *An Franz Schubert* in Schober's *Gedichte*, 1842, p. 110.

quondam choirboy, 'Francesco' Schubert, whom he had auditioned for a place in the Hofkapelle and Imperial Konvikt in 1808. The ascendancy of Italian opera in Vienna, and of the impresario Domenico Barbaia (1778–1841) during the years of Schubert's maturity, was a fatal blow to the composer's own operatic hopes, but Schubert was still able to appreciate the best of the genre and to value Rossini especially highly. In 1827, during a visit to Graz, he walked out of a performance of Meyerbeer's *Il crociato in Egitto*; this 'melodramma eroico' was hardly a tuneful Italian opera and, in Schubert's eyes, clearly the worse for it.

For the second editions of Schubert's Opp. 56 and 68 songs it was probably Nicolaus Craigher de Jachelutta who provided Italian translations of four German poems, clearly in an effort to widen their appeal from a marketing point of view. Thus *Willkommen und Abschied* D567 (Goethe) became *Felice arrivo e congedo*; the Italian alternative for *An die Leier* D737 (Bruchmann) was *Alla cetra*; *Im Haine* D738 (Bruchmann) was *Nel boschetto*, and *Der Wachtelschlag* D742 (Sauter), *Il canto della quaglia*. This was an idea that failed to take root for the remainder of Schubert's song publications. These versions are printed in the NSA and have been recorded in modern times by Cecilia Bartoli.

The composer's friendship with and admiration for the genial bass Luigi Lablache [qv SINGERS] brought about a wonderful late flowering of his music in the Italian manner, but for these three songs of course the Italian text was original.

The following are the titles of Schubert's songs in Italian, and of songs with Italian resonances. The titles in bold denote an alphabetical article in this book. Each of the poets mentioned here is the subject of an alphabetical article. Salieri, Mozart, Beethoven and Rossini are discussed in relation to their influence on Schubert in the article on COMPOSERS:

1812(?)	***Quell'innocente figlio*** D17 (Metastasio). Composition excercises for Antonio Salieri: No. 1 (soprano solo); No. 2 (duet, 2 soprani); No. 3 (terzet, SAT); No. 4 (quartet, SATB); No. 5 (terzet, SAT); No. 6 (terzet, SAT); No. 7 (quartet, SATB); No. 8 (quartet, SATB); No. 9 (quartet, SATB)
September–October 1812	***Entra l'uomo allor che nasce*** D33 (Metastasio). Composition exercises for Salieri: No. 1 (soprano solo); No. 2 (duet, SA); No. 3 (terzet, SAT); No. 4 (quartet, SATB); No. 5 (quartet, SATB); No. 6 (quartet, SATB)
5 November 1812	*Te solo adoro* D34 (Metastasio). Composition exercise for Salieri (quartet, SATB)
October–December 1812	***Serbate, o dei custodi*** D35 (Metastasio). Composition excercises for Salieri: No. 1 (quartet, SATB); No. 2 (chorus, SATB); No. 3 (tenor solo with instrumental accompaniment)
1813?	***Misero pargoletto*** D42 (Metastasio). Arias for soprano and piano, two different settings
7–13 September 1813	***Pensa, che questo istante*** D76 (Metastasio). Aria for bass voice
18 September 1813	***Son fra l'onde*** D78 (Metastasio). Aria for soprano and piano
24 May–19 July 1815	Symphony No. 3 in D, D200, with a final Presto Vivace movement that irresistibly suggests a *Tarantella*. There are of course other Schubert symphonies and chamber music pieces that suggest the Italian style, especially in the use of the 'Scherzo' and in the *buffa*

character of final movements. These Italianate mannerisms are seamlessly woven into Schubert's own style with an ease that is reminiscent of Mozart's, and even Beethoven's, adoption of similar influences – although neither of these older masters had Rossini to deal with as a rival.

29 May 1815	***Die Nonne*** D208 (Hölty). This bloodthirsty story of a betrayed nun's terrible revenge on her lover has an unequivocal Italian setting. From the first line of the poem we are told that the nun lived in 'Welschland', a name designating 'foreign parts' that the Germans always thought of as synonymous with Italy. In temperament she is also very much of her race; the poet describes her as 'filled with Italian fury' ('voll von welscher Wut').
20 June 1815	***Meeres Stille*** D215a and D216 (Goethe). The poet had spent six weeks in Sicily with the landscape artist Christoph Kniep (1755–1825). Their return journey from Messina to the mainland (13/14 May 1787) was on a French vessel with numerous passengers. The ship was becalmed at the entrance to the Gulf of Naples and currents carried it dangerously near the rocks of Capri. The poem was written some years after this incident which is described in Goethe's *Italienische Reise*.
Begun 26 July 1815	**Claudine von Villa Bella** D239 (Goethe) is a *Singspiel* set in Sicily. Only the first act survives, but both Lucinde who sings the *Ariette* 'Hin und wieder fliegen die Pfeile' and Claudine who sings the *Ariette* 'Liebe schwärmt auf allen Wegen' are warm-hearted Italian girls.
August 1815	*Lacrimoso son io* D131 (unknown). Canon for three unaccompanied voices; the second version is changed to 'Lacrimosa' as if this had been envisaged for female voices. Mozart set the same text as a four-part canon, K555. ***Die Bürgschaft*** D246 (Schiller) is set in the ancient Greek polis of Syracuse, present-day Sicily, ruled by the tyrant Dionysius. The extremes of heat described in the poem, as well as the sudden rainstorms, seem rather more believable in this geographical context.
23 October 1815	***Mignon (Kennst du das Land?)*** D321 (Goethe). Though not in Italian for the purposes of the German reader, the song of the Italian-born Mignon from the novel *Wilhelm Meisters Lehrjahre*, qv, is supposedly sung in Italian and contains nostalgic descriptions of the landscape and Palladian architecture familiar to her. The character of the 'Harfner', the old harper from the novel (Mignon's father) is also Italian; some aspects of his volatile temperament may be ascribed to his nationality.
December 1816	***Vedi quanto adoro*** D510 (Metastasio), Aria of Dido, queen of Carthage for soprano and piano (also known as *Didone abbandonata*), four versions
1817(?)	***La pastorella al prato*** D513 (Goldoni). Quartet TTBB, with piano
January 1817	***La pastorella al prato*** D528 (Goldoni), for soprano and piano
November 1817	Schubert's two 'Overtures in Italian style' (in D, D590, and in C, D591)

November–December 1818	***Sonett I*** D628, ***Sonett II*** D629, ***Sonett III*** D630. Three sonnets of Petrarca ('Petrarch') in translations of August von Schlegel (the first and second) and J. D. Gries (the third).
January 1820	**Vier Canzonen** D688 (Vittorelli and Metastasio). Four songs for voice and piano: (i) *Non, t'accostar all'urna*; (ii) *Guarda, che bianca luna*; (iii) *Da quel' sembiante appresi*; (iv) *Mio ben ricordati*
January 1822	***Herrn Josef Spaun, Assessor in Linz*** D749 (Matthäus von Collin). A 'musical joke' and letter to the absent Josef von Spaun (qv) composed as a parody of the pathos and drama of Italian opera, including a high C and cadenza with sliding chromatic scale.
March 1824	***Gondelfahrer*** D808 (Mayrhofer) (solo song) and **Der *Gondelfahrer*** D809 (quartet, TTBB) have Venice as their setting
Before September 1827	**Drei Gesänge für Bass-Stimme mit Klavier** D902 (Metastasio and unknown). Written for the great Italian bass Luigi Lablache [*see* SINGERS]: (i) *L'incanto degli occhi*; (ii) *Il traditor deluso*; (iii) *Il modo di prender moglie*
26 December 1827	***Al par dei ruscelletto*** D936 (Unknown). Also known as 'Kantate für Irene Kiesewetter' [*see* FRIENDS AND FAMILY]. Choral piece for male quartet (TTBB) and chorus (SATB) with piano-duet accompaniment.

FRANZ SCHUBERT – THE COMPLETE SONGS

FRANZ SCHUBERT
THE COMPLETE SONGS
VOLUME TWO
J–SCHULZE

GRAHAM JOHNSON

translations of the song texts by Richard Wigmore

YALE UNIVERSITY PRESS
NEW HAVEN AND LONDON

The publisher acknowledges the generous sponsorship of the Guildhall School & Music Drama, London, without which the publication of this work would not have been possible.

Deepest gratitude also to the Marilyn Horne Foundation, a US nonprofit organization devoted exclusively to the art of song, for its support and encouragement of this publication.

For information about this and other Yale University Press publications, please contact:

U.S. office: sales.press@yale.edu   www.yalebooks.com
Europe Office: sales@yaleup.co.uk   www.yalebooks.co.uk

Set in 10/12 pt Minion by Toppan Best-set Premedia Limited
Printed in Great Britain by TJ International Ltd, Padstow, Cornwall

Library of Congress Control Number: 2013931540

ISBN   978-0-300-11267-2

A catalogue record for this book is available from the British Library.

Published with assistance from the Annie Burr Lewis Fund

10 9 8 7 6 5 4 3 2 1

J

JOHANN GEORG JACOBI
(1740–1814)

THE POETIC SOURCES

S1 *Gedichte von Johann Georg Jacobi*, Zweyter Theil, Wien 1816, bey Chr. Kaulfuss und C. Armbruster. Gedruckt von Anton Strauss (Meisterwerke deutscher Dichter und Prosaisten, 17tes Bändchen)

S2 *Gedichte von Johann Georg Jacobi*, Erster Theil, Wien 1816, bey Chr. Kaulfuss und C. Armbruster. Gedruckt von Anton Strauss (Meisterwerke deutscher Dichter und Prosaisten, 16tes Bändchen)

The Jacobi poems had only recently appeared in this handy, pocket-sized Viennese edition, hot off the press as it were. Schubert was unlikely to have bought the set for himself, probably borrowing it (one volume at a time) from Schober who would have had a budget that enabled him to buy books. It seems likely that in August 1816 Schubert was in possession of Volume 2 only – this begins with *Litanei* (Schubert's autograph is headed *Am Tage aller Seelen*), continues with *Hochzeit-Lied* and contains all the other settings of the month. In September he appears to have borrowed Volume 1 and found the poem for

Jacobi's *Gedichte*, Volume 2, Vienna (1816), from which six of the seven settings were taken.

Lied des Orpheus D474 therein. There is a third volume in this edition of Jacobi's works, but Schubert did not set any poems from it. He seems to have been too taken up by Mayrhofer and Goethe poems in September 1816 to retrace his steps to the summer idylls of Jacobi.

THE SONGS

August 1816 *Am Tage aller Seelen (Litanei)* D343 [S1: pp. 7–9 where the title is *Litaney auf das Fest aller Seelen*][1]
An Chloen D462 [S1: pp. 18–19]
Hochzeit-Lied D463 [S1: pp. 10–11]

---

[1] A footnote to the poem states: 'On this religious festival Roman Catholics visit the graves of their loved ones, light candles and pray for the departed.'

In der Mitternacht D464 [S1: pp. 112–13]

Trauer der Liebe D465 [S1: pp. 46–7]

Die Perle D466 [S1: pp. 48–9]

September 1816   *Lied des Orpheus (Als er in die Hölle ging)* D474 [S2: pp. 75–6]

Johann Georg Jacobi, engraving after a portrait of
Josef Zoll.

Johann Georg Jacobi was born near Düsseldorf on 2 September 1740. He studied various
disciplines at the Universities of Göttingen,
Helmstedt, Marburg, Leipzig and Jena. By the
age of twenty-six he was a professor of philosophy at Halle University and had converted
to Catholicism. He later taught at Freiburg
and was versed in English, French and Italian
literature. Much influenced by the classics,
particularly the odes of Anacreon, he published
his *Die Winterreise* in 1769 (influenced by the
writings of Lawrence Sterne) and *Die Sommerreise* in 1770. Perhaps the much younger poet
Wilhelm Müller read these poems long before
he wrote his own *Die Winterreise* in 1821–3.
Jacobi founded the periodical *Iris* in which
Goethe (whom he had met in 1774) published
a number of important poems for the first
time. Jacobi was a great admirer of Goethe's
achievements, an admiration that was scarcely
reciprocated by the greater poet. Raymond
Joly describes Jacobi's poetry as 'very firmly
rooted in the 18th century: *aufgeklärte
Empfindsamkeit* (the sensibility of the Enlightenment), Golden Mean *cum* Bible, with a dash
of shepherdese'. Although Jacobi was highly
regarded by his contemporaries, his reputation
did not endure. He died in Freiburg im
Breisgau on 4 January 1814. In Vienna the
Jacobi poems were published only posthumously in 1816 – almost certainly as a mark of
respect to their recently deceased creator.

Jacobi was the elder brother of the rather
more famous philosopher Friedrich Heinrich
Jacobi (1743–1819), a disciple of Spinoza and
opponent of Kant and fellow-editor of *Iris*.
This Jacobi enjoyed a famously close relationship with Goethe and his philosophical writings were of special interest to the circle of
intellectuals around Anton von Spaun in Linz;
these were quoted in the *Beyträge zur Bildung
für Jünglinge*, the educational almanac that
appeared in two consecutive years (Vienna,
1817–18) and to which one of its main instiga-
tors, Johann Mayrhofer, made poetic contributions (*see Der Schiffer* D536).

Der JÄGER *see DIE SCHÖNE MÜLLERIN* D795/14

JÄGERCHOR *see ROSAMUNDE, FÜRSTIN VON ZYPERN* D797/4

JÄGER, RUHE VON DER JAGD *see SIEBEN GESÄNGE AUS WALTER
SCOTT'S FRÄULEIN VOM SEE* OP. 52 NO. 2

JÄGERS ABENDLIED (I)
(GOETHE) **D215** [H109]
F major   20 June 1815

Huntsman's evening song

Im Felde schleich' ich, still und wild,	I stalk through the fields, grim and silent,
Gespannt mein Feuerrohr.	My gun at the ready.
Da schwebt so licht dein liebes Bild,	Then your beloved image,
Dein süsses Bild mir vor.	Your sweet image hovers brightly before me.
Du wandelst jetzt wohl still und mild	Perhaps you are now wandering, silent and gentle,
Durch Feld und liebes Tal,	Through field and beloved valley;
Und ach mein schnell verrauschend Bild,	Ah, does my fleeting image
Stellt sich dir's nicht einmal?	Not even appear before you?
Des Menschen, der die Welt durchstreift	The image of the man who roams the world,
Voll Unmut und Verdruss,	Sullen and frustrated,
Nach Osten und nach Westen schweift,	Who wanders east and west
Weil er dich lassen muss.	Because he must leave you.
Mir ist es, denk' ich nur an dich,	Whenever I think of you
Als in den Mond zu sehn;	It is as if I were gazing at the moon;
Ein stiller Friede kommt auf mich,	A silent peace descends upon me,
Weiss nicht wir mir geschehn.	I know not how.

JOHANN WOLFGANG VON GOETHE (1749–1832); poem written in 1775

This is the thirteenth of Schubert's seventy-five Goethe solo settings (1814–26). See the poet's biography for a chronological list of all the Goethe settings.

As with *Schäfers Klagelied* D121, Schubert treats this as a poem of rueful separation – a window into the emotions of those whose duties take them far from their loved ones. Goethe wrote this poem soon after he had parted from his erstwhile fiancée, Lili Schönemann and when Charlotte von Stein was already beginning to take a central role in his life. The beloved addressed here is perhaps a combination of both women, and the hunter the poet himself. It is possible that he cast himself in this role because of the various field exploits in which he was expected to take part with his new friend and patron, Carl August, Duke of Weimar. As Nicholas Boyle has written: 'In *Jägers Abendlied* memories of Lili Schönemann mingle uncertainly with thoughts of the distant Charlotte, so that the restless poet's own identity seems to lose its fixity.'

Schubert has caught the mood of someone hope-lessly enamoured and emotionally inexperienced. The idea of the beloved's image hovering seems to suggest to the composer the long-spun melodies of *bel canto* (this version is an indication of how strongly Salieri has passed on a feel for the Italian style to his pupil). The music is prophetic of *Blondel zu Marien* of 1818 D626 in which the same idea of a distant and magical beloved summons up an ornate aria full of melisma and affectionate orna-mentation. The accompaniment is supportive rather than atmospheric: arpeggiated chords in the opening yield to anonymous flowing triplets. As

Jägers Abendlied, vignette from Czerny's arrangement for solo piano (1838).

appropriate to an aria of this genre, it is the melody and harmony (there is an adventurous modula-tion to A flat from the home key of F at 'ach mein schnell verrauschend Bild' at bb. 12–13) that carry the song. The tempo marking is 'Sehr langsam' but this is sensibly moderated by the *alla breve* time signature. After all, the first verb of the song suggests unsettled, if surreptitious, movement.

Goethe's poem contains four strophes. In this setting Schubert uses the first two of these to make one verse of music (as recorded for the Hyperion Edition). It is likely that the composer was aware that the third strophe, the plaint of a well-travelled man of the world, was written in the voice of the poet himself rather than in that of the humble hunter. That he omitted this strophe in the second setting he prepared for Goethe (*see* below) suggests that he preferred to focus on the geographical boundaries of the hunter, the man in the field, rather than the broader vistas of the great poet's emotional insecurities. He had probably come to judge this first setting of the words as being too ornate, too musically fussy, to fit its stolid singer. In order to jettison an awkward strophe Schubert would have had to invent a musical structure that used only one of Goethe's verses at a time, and he did exactly this for his second setting. The NSA (and Bären-reiter) print the third and fourth verses of the Goethe poem in italics; they are both given in the translation above. This first setting of Goethe's poem did not surface in time to be published in the AGA and only became available in the NSA in 1970.

Autograph:	Wienbibliothek im Rathaus, Vienna
First edition:	Published as a supplement to *Die Musik* in 1907 and subsequently as part of the NSA in 1970 (P746)
Subsequent editions:	Not in Peters; Not in AGA; NSA IV: Vol. 1b/198; Bärenreiter: Vol. 1/211
Discography and timing:	Fischer-Dieskau —
	Hyperion I 24^{12}
	Hyperion II 7^8 1'33 Simon Keenlyside

← *Die Laube* D214   *Meeres Stille* D215a →

JÄGERS ABENDLIED (II)   Huntsman's evening song
(GOETHE) OP. 3 NO. 4 **D368** [H221]
D♭ major   Early 1816?

(13 bars)

See previous entry for poem and translation

JOHANN WOLFGANG VON GOETHE (1749–1832); poem written in 1775

This is the thirty-ninth of Schubert's seventy-five Goethe solo settings (1814–26). See the poet's biography for a chronological list of all the Goethe settings.

Schubert's return to this poem shows that he was not satisfied with his first setting, and it is easy to see why. He had invented an Italianate melody in wafting triplets that failed to suggest the robust German figure of the hunter. The composer's melismas, musical tracery for the floating image of the beloved, had made the protagonist sound rather too much like a courtly troubadour. Of course the poem describes Goethe at an emotional crossroads in his life, but in this second setting Schubert preferred to take the word 'Jäger' at face value, inventing a musical context for the hunter as a down-to-earth man of the people. The vocal line is both simple and dignified. The Italianate floridity of the first setting has given way to something more stolid, at least in the song's opening. The accompaniment is placed in exactly the same part of the keyboard as for *Nacht und Träume* D827 and *Wandrers Nachtlied II* D768, the softly resonating lower notes of the piano providing gravitas and humanity while supporting the dreamy contemplation of the text. This combination of masculine and feminine elements is ideal in a song where a man dreams of a woman while he is parted from her. A more expansive vocal line allows the composer to add crucial detail in the accompaniment that was lacking in the first setting. The sliding sixths of the opening five bars were no doubt inspired by the slinking imagery of the key words 'schleich' ich, still', but they also serve to depict someone wary and watchful and, at the same time, the mournful chromatic ascent of each pianistic phrase suggests tenderness in a bear of a man. Schubert has thus invented an accompaniment that sets out to illustrate something physical, the hunter's move-ment through the fields in pursuit of his prey, but which is then pressed into service as an emblem of the emotions. As the song progresses we hear the narrator's lugubrious demeanour warmed into greater emotional vivacity by the power of love. (In a similar way the music invented for the whirring of Gretchen's spinning wheel soon becomes identified with her racing pulse and anguished sexual longing.) The lift of a semitone high in the vocal line at 'Da schwebt so licht dein liebes Bild' (bb. 7–8) takes us into the inner world of the hunter's imagination. It is all the more touching that a simple man, when transported by longing and suddenly awkwardly eloquent, should break into a more ornate vocal style at 'Dein süsses Bild mir vor' (bb. 10–11). In this way the ghost of Schubert's first setting hovers over this passage, and the emergence of melisma, a rare unbuttoned moment for the usually prosaic hunter, is a touchingly ardent flowering.

Goethe had very strong ideas about how the poem should be read. In 1814 he wrote: 'The first and third verses have to be recited energetically with some fire, while the second and fourth must be gentle, because here a new emotion has appeared.' Schubert was probably not aware of these instructions, but it is interesting that his first setting had attempted the kind of AB structure that the poet had in mind. His second setting (where the music is the same for each verse) is a far greater song, however, and more than a match for the text. The composer was sufficiently proud of it to place it right at the beginning of the lieder album sent (in vain) to Goethe in 1816 – and this despite the fact that he had the temerity to leave out the third of the poet's four verses. (In an earlier version of this second setting all four verses of the poem were included so it is rather difficult to guess Schubert's final thoughts on the matter.) Till Gerrit Waidelich points out in the *Schubert Liedlexikon* (2012) that this omission was probably a quite deliberate choice on Schubert's part because the third strophe scarcely fits into the 'Ich und Du' dialogue of the rest of the poem.

Autograph:	Staatsbibliothek Preussischer Kulturbesitz (fair copy made for Goethe)
First edition:	Published as Op. 3 no. 4 by Cappi & Diabelli, Vienna in 1821 (P6)
Dedicatee:	Ignaz von Mosel
Publication reviews:	*Wiener allgemeine Theaterzeitung* No. 61 (22 May 1821), p. 244 [Waidelich/Hilmar Dokumente I No. 101; Deutsch Doc. Biog. No. 238]
	F. von Hentl 'Blick auf Schubert's Lieder', *Wiener Zeitschrift für Kunst, Literatur, Theater und Mode* No. 36 (23 March 1822), p. 289f. [Waidelich/Hilmar Dokumente I No. 146; Deutsch Doc. Biog. No. 278]
Subsequent editions:	Peters: Vol. 1/228; AGA XX 262: Vol. 4/203; NSA IV: Vol. 1a/25; Bärenreiter: Vol. 1/19
Bibliography:	Capell 1928, p. 123
	Fischer-Dieskau 1977, p. 80
	Gülke 1991, pp. 74–5
Further settings and arrangements:	Johann Friedrich Reichardt (1752–1814) *Jägers Nachtlied* (1781)
	Philipp Christoph Kayser (1755–1823) *Jägers Nachtlied* (1777)
	Carl Friedrich Zelter (1758–1832) *Jägers Abendlied* (1807)
	Friedrich Heinrich Himmel (1765–1814) *Jägers Abendlied* (1807)
	Václav Jan Tomášek (1774–1850) *Jägers Abendlied* (1815)
	Nikolay Medtner (1880–1951) *Jägers Abendlied* Op. 18/6 (1908–9)
	Arr. Tilman Hoppstock (b. 1961) for guitar accompaniment (2 arrangements), in *Franz Schubert: 110 Lieder* (2009)
Discography and timing:	Fischer-Dieskau I 8[10] 2'41
	Hyperion I 24[13]
	Hyperion II 12[16] 2'35 Simon Keenlyside

← *Der König in Thule* D367   *An Schwager Kronos* D369 →

JÄGERS LIEBESLIED
(Schober) Op. 96 no. 2 **D909** [H625]
D major   February 1827

Huntsman's love song

(66 bars)

Ich schiess' den Hirsch im grünen Forst,
Im stillen Tal das Reh,
Den Adler auf dem Klippenhorst,
Die Ente auf dem See.
Kein Ort, der Schutz gewähren kann,
Wenn meine Flinte zielt;
Und dennoch hab' ich harter Mann
Die Liebe auch gefühlt! –

Hab oft hantiert in rauher Zeit,
In Sturm und Winternacht,
Und übereist und eingeschneit
Zum Bett den Stein gemacht.
Auf Dornen schlief ich wie auf Flaum,
Vom Nordwind ungerührt,
Doch hat der Liebe zarten Traum
Die rauhe Brust gespürt.

Der wilde Falk war mein Gesell,
Der Wolf mein Kampfgespann;
Mir fing der Tag mit Hundgebell,
Die Nacht mit Hussa an.
Ein Tannreis war die Blumenzier
Auf schweissbeflecktem Hut,
Und dennoch schlug die Liebe mir
Ins wilde Jägerblut.

O Schäfer auf dem weichen Moos,
Der du mit Blumen spielst,[1]
Wer weiss, ob du so heiss, so gross
Wie ich die Liebe fühlst.
Allnächtlich überm schwarzen Wald,
Vom Mondenschein umstrahlt,
Schwebt königshehr die Lichtgestalt,[2]
Wie sie kein Meister malt.

I shoot the stag in the green forest
And the roe in the silent valley;
The eagle in its eyrie on the cliffs,
The duck on the lake.
No place can give protection
When my gun is aimed,
And yet I, though a hard man,
Have also felt love.

I have often worked in harsh conditions,
In storms and winter nights,
And, covered with ice and snow,
Have made a bed of stones.
I have slept on thorns as on down,
Untroubled by the north wind.
Yet my rough breast has also felt
Love's tender dream.

The fierce hawk was my companion;
The wolf my adversary in battle;
My day began with the baying of hounds,
My night with the cry of tally-ho.
A sprig of fir was the flower
That adorned my sweaty hat,
And yet love penetrated
My wild huntsman's blood.

O shepherd on the soft moss,
Playing with flowers,
Who knows if you feel love
As much and as ardently as I do?
Every night, above the dark forest,
Its radiance hovers, bathed in moonlight,
With a regal splendour
That no master could paint.

[1] In *Gedichte* (1842) Schober writes 'Der du mit *Blüthen* spielst'.
[2] In *Gedichte* (1842) Schober writes 'Schwebt *Königsgross* die Lichtgestalt'.

Wenn sie dann auf mich niedersieht,	When she looks down upon me,
Wenn mich der Blick durchglüht,	When her gaze burns through me,
Da weiss ich, wie dem Wild geschieht,	Then I know how the wild animals feel
Das vor dem Rohre flieht.	When they flee from my gun.
Und doch! mit allem Glück vereint	And yet that feeling is united
Das nur auf Erden ist;	With all the happiness on earth,
Als wenn der allerbeste Freund	As if my dearest friend
Mich in die Arme schliesst!	Held me in his arms.

Franz von Schober (1796–1882)

This is the thirteenth of Schubert's fourteen Schober solo settings (1815–27). See the poet's biography for a chronological list of all the Schober settings.

There are a number of hunters' songs in the Schubert canon. The most famous of them is *Der Jäger* D795/14 at the heart of *Die schöne Müllerin*. Then there are the two versions of *Jägers Abendlied* D215 and D368 (the Goethe poem) and two different songs, both from 1817, with the title of *Der Alpenjäger* – the first to a poem by Mayrhofer and the second to a Schiller poem. *Lied des gefangenen Jägers* D843 is a Walter Scott setting from 1825. In addition, there are various guest appearances by hunters in the Ossian settings. Of all these songs, Schober's *Jägers Liebeslied* has received the worst press. Capell dismisses it as 'insignificant' (a dangerous verdict on any of the songs of Schubert's maturity, particularly one that was written at exactly the same time as the first part of *Winterreise* D911). The song was very popular with singers at one time which explains its inclusion in Volume 1 of the Peters Edition, but of all the works in that otherwise populist collection it is the least performed today.

The reasons for this are more understandable when scanning the poem, which is unusual to say the least. Walther Dürr has rightly called it a 'hymn to friendship', something that is also true of *Schiffers Scheidelied* D910. This hunter, a Biedermeier Clint Eastwood, hardly paints himself as a sympathetic character – although there is more than a touch of macho pride in a self-portrait that might have been inspired by one of the Fenimore Cooper novels popular in Vienna at the time and eagerly read by Schubert in 1828. Details like battling with wolves and the sweat-soaked hat are images worthy of frontier land and that later famed writer of Westerns in German, Karl May. Capell takes a thorough dislike to this seemingly hard and aggressive man for 'shooting at every living thing he sets eye on'. And yet the hunter, susceptible to love, wonders whether shepherds (like the lovesick swain of the Goethe setting *Schäfers Klagelied* D121, perhaps) feel anything like the same thing. This is a moot point. The fourth strophe mentions a 'Lichtgestalt', literally a shape, or being, of light, but here translated as 'its radiance' – i.e. the radiance of love itself. We are not told anything about the object of the hunter's affection.

The fifth verse in this translation introduces the word 'she' to the poem, not entirely with justification: 'sie' seems here to refer back to the feminine noun 'Lichtgestalt', the presence of the burning light of love itself which shines down upon the hunter, filling him with unfamiliar emotion. He is disturbed by the feeling, and confesses as much, finding himself as cornered as one of the animals on which he preys. If this ambiguity of gender is intentional (and it is not easily translatable into English), the crucial 'sie' ensures a respectability to the first half of the strophe that allows the song to end with a vision of a male friend's embrace. There are two types of love in this man's life, and he feels safer and more familiar with close male friendship than with the frightening new emotion he now experiences. Why it should be so alarming is another matter for consideration.

There is something about this lyric that reminds us of Walt Whitman's poetry, as well as A. E. Housman's *A Shropshire Lad*, where themes of comradeship have erotic overtones that can easily be ignored by readers disinclined to notice them. Generations of British soldiers loved Housman's poems without concerning themselves with the subtext. In a similar way *Jägers Liebeslied* was later incorporated into a students' songbook and became quite well known in its own right to the hearties of the time. Even if one delves deeper into the words, they can be written off as a not particularly distinguished attempt to praise the ideal of platonic friendship in the tradition advocated in Mayrhofer's anthology *Beiträge für Jünglinge*. Nevertheless, this poem, as well as *Schiffers Scheidelied*, confirms that Schubert and Schober were very special friends at a time when the label of friendship could safely incorporate a generous margin of affection between men without encompassing questions of sexual desire. (Whether or not this was the case here is a moot point – *see* LETTERS AND DIARIES nos 12 and 13.) It is surely significant that of all the manuscripts of Schubert's songs left at the Schobers' home on the composer's death, this was the only one the poet chose to retain in his possession.

For Schober, Schubert was the genius that he himself could never be; he knew that his composer friend possessed gifts that marked him out for immortality. In Schubert's eyes, Schober was everything *he* could not be: elegant, good-looking, affably articulate and a target for the ladies. They both longed to be the other, if only for a moment – to explore each other's destinies, to experience what each felt he lacked in himself. From this yin and yang sprang a genuine devotion and affection – as incomprehensible to some of the composer's other friends as it is to later generations who fancy they can see through the charlatan that Schober, to some degree, undoubtedly was. The friendship was subject to strain, and waxed and waned with the years, but in 1827 they seem to have come to a point where a reaffirmation of their bond struck them as appropriate. In the 1827 comic trio *Der Hochzeitsbraten* D930 Schober delights in the somewhat lascivious concept of the poacher's girl becoming the gamekeeper's booty. In *Jägers Liebeslied* there are similar metaphors of the chase. Schober could well be referring to himself as someone who has, in Capell's words, shot 'at every living thing he sets eye on', a Don Giovanni hunting for a succession of sexual partners (both stag and roe the poem says, whether or not significantly) while acknowledging that there now is something more important to him than all these encounters. He has been the heartless seducer, rampaging through the forests and taking what he wishes; now he finds himself more vulnerable. And he loves this new person so much that it feels as good as if he were being embraced by his special friend. The poem's overall message is that old friendships matter a good deal: the hunter's recently awakened feelings of love (almost certainly towards a woman) are so beautiful that they are comparable to being held in the arms of 'der allerbeste Freund'. Schubert returns the compliment by setting poems (this and *Schiffers Scheidelied*) that cast Schober in two very gallant and dramatic roles (Schumann glamorizes Heine in a similar way). The composer allowed the songs to be published by the Lithographic Institute of which Schober was then the director – despite the fact that the firm was a clearly precarious business enterprise.

As if to emphasize the unadorned and truthful nature of the affection described (both the new love and the old friendship) the song is almost entirely strophic, with some changes for the fifth verse. The music is cast in a barcarolle rhythm in §; the key is D major and the introspective dynamic markings suggest a lovelorn serenade more than a celebration of the outdoor life, although the distant sound of hunting horns is built into the rise and fall of the music. This, with its slightly restless, utterly Schubertian modulations, is reminiscent of the contemporary Rochlitz setting *Alinde* D904 and Heine's *Das Fischermädchen* D957/10 of 1828, both wistful love songs cast in the same wafting § rhythm ('Mässig geschwind') that suggests unstilled longing. The introduction begins with unisons in D major; in the second bar these are filled out into B flat major chords that rock to F major and back, followed by the same pattern on G minor/D minor. This in turn leads to A major/D minor and back to the home key of D major – a lovely descending sequence that, simple as it is, could only have been written by Schubert. Heartfelt simplicity is order of the day whenever he writes music for real working-class characters – or upper middle-class poets like Schober who are pleased to play at this role. The old-fashioned form of the music allows the words to be heard, and concentrated upon, with admirable clarity.

This is one of those songs that needs sympathetic performance. There are certain turns of phrase in the music, gracefully fitting the words of different verses with the practised skill of this master of strophic songs, that will give the true Schubertian moments of gentle delight. However, like *Romanze des Richard Löwenherz* D907, the song can appear as banal as the performer believes it to be, or as touching. There has always been a separate class of Schubert songs whose personal or biographical significance perhaps outweighs their importance in terms of absolute music – the Schober setting *Pilgerweise* D789 is one of these, and *Jägers Liebeslied* also clearly belongs in this category.

Autograph:	Sächsische Landesbibliothek, Dresden
First edition:	Published by Schober's Lithographisches Institut, Vienna in the summer of 1828 as No. 2 of *Vier Lieder*; subsequently issued as Op. 96 no. 2 by Diabelli, Vienna in 1829 (P166)
Dedicatee:	Maria Karolina, Fürstin von Kinsky
Subsequent editions:	Peters: Vol. 3/70; AGA XX 515: Vol. 8/264; NSA IV: Vol. 5a/60; Bärenreiter: Vol. 3/192
Bibliography:	Capell 1928, p. 225
Discography and timing:	Fischer-Dieskau II 9[1] 3'56 (strophes 1, 2, 4 & 5 only)
	Hyperion I 36[2]
	Hyperion II 33[13] 5'27 Gerald Finley

← *Einsamkeit* D911/11   *Schiffers Scheidelied* D910 →

JAGDLIED   Hunting song   Solo song or
(Werner) **D521** [H334]   unison chorus
F major   January 1817

(32 bars)

Trarah, trarah! Wir kehren daheim –	Tara, tara! We are returning home,
Wir bringen die Beute der Jagd! –	Bringing the spoils of the chase!
Es sinket die Nacht,	Night is falling,
Drum halten wir Wacht;	So we keep watch;
Das Licht hat über das Dunkel Macht!	Light has power over darkness!
Trarah, trarah. Auf, auf!	Tara, tara! Up, up!
Das Feuer angefacht!	Fan the flames!

Trarah, trarah! Wir zechen im Kreis!	Tara, tara! We drink in a circle;
Wir spotten des Dunkels der Nacht![1]	We mock the darkness of the night!
Des Menschen Macht,	The might of man,
In freudiger Pracht,	Joyous and glorious,
Die Qual verhöhnt, des Todes lacht! –	Scorns pain and laughs at death!
Trarah, trarah! Auf, auf!	Tara, tara! Up, up, up!
Die Glut ist angefacht!	The fire is ablaze!

ZACHARIAS WERNER (1768–1823); poem written *c.* 1807

Diabelli's decision (with Leopold von Sonnleithner's help) to append this song to the incomplete Ossian fragment *Die Nacht* D534 (for its first appearance in print as *Nachlass* Volume 1 in July 1830) has rendered this inoffensive piece somewhat notorious. For this posthumous publication Diabelli printed the chorus unaltered in musical terms, but there were changes made to Werner's words, probably by Sonnleithner himself, in order to render it more appropriate as an ending to the Ossian ballad. This spurious coda can be seen in the Peters Edition and in the AGA (see below). It is this version that was recorded as part of *Die Nacht* for Hyperion. In 1860 Johann Herbeck (*see* SCHOLARS) arranged and published the piece for four-part chorus, still using the altered text.

The original words as printed above are taken from Werner's *Wanda, Königin der Sarmaten, Eine romantische Tragödie mit Gesang* (1810) where a chorus of knights and cavalry ('Gesang-Chor der Reiter und Reisigen') break into song at the end of the first Act. The first and second strophes are separated by Prince Rüdiger's address to his men. The work was not printed in the choral series of the AGA (no doubt because of its inclusion, albeit in a corrupt version, in the solo song series) and at the time of writing it has not yet appeared in Series III of the NSA where the chorus will appear in print for the first time with Werner's words.

Jagdlied is fairly typical of the merry carousing that Schubert would often provide for men's chorus, in this case in unison. The marking is 'Feurig' and there are some pleasing changes of key (C to A major at bb. 17–18), slightly unusual for sturdy music of this kind. At 'Das Licht hat über das Dunkel Macht!' (bb. 14–16, words that appear in both the original and corrupt versions) the passage on a pedal C in § rhythm is prophetic of the midnight music in *Gondelfahrer* D808.

Autograph:	Gesellschaft der Musikfreunde, Vienna
First edition:	First published (with different words) as part of *Die Nacht*, Book 1 of the *Nachlass* by Diabelli, Vienna in 1830; published in this version as part of the AGA in 1895 (P666)
Subsequent editions:	Peters: Vol. 4/172–3 (as part of *Die Nacht*); AGA XX 290: Vol. 5/51–3 (as part of *Die Nacht*); NSA III: Vol. 3
Discography and timing:	Fischer-Dieskau —
	Hyperion I 6³
	Hyperion II 17¹² 1'34 Anthony Rolfe Johnson & male chorus

←— *Frohsinn* D520   *Die Liebe* D522 —→

---

[1] In Werner's original, there is a comma after 'Dunkels', thus 'We mock darkness, *and* night' rather than 'the darkness of the night'.

URBAN JARNIK (1774–1844)

THE POETIC SOURCE
S1: *Selam, ein Almanach für Freunde des Mannigfaltigen auf das Jahr 1814*, ed. Ignaz Castelli, Anton Strauss, Wien, 1814

'Die Sternenwelten' was also published in a different, non-rhyming, translation (again with Urban Jarnik's Slovenian original) in *Carinthia, ein Wochenblatt zum Nutzen und Vergnügen*, No. 25, Klagenfurt, 1812. The poem is printed in Slovenain in Schochow Volume 1 pp. 88–9.

THE SONG
October 1815   *Die Sternenwelten* D307 [Jarnik's Slovenian poem *Svésdishzhe* is printed on S1: pp. 312 and 314 opposite Johann Georg Fellinger's German translation on pp. 313 and 315]

The Slovenian poet and priest Urban Jarnik (Jarnigg in German) was born on 11 May 1784 in Nadižar in Potoka, in the Zillerthale region of the Steiermark. Slovenia, at that time part of the Habsburg Empire, only occasionally encroaches on the history of song – Schubert unsuccessfully applied in 1816 for a post in Laibach (the present-day Ljubljana) and Hugo Wolf was born and brought up in a German-speaking enclave of Slovenia, the reason perhaps for his heightened sense of devotion to poetic achievements in his mother tongue. In Schubert's time the Slovenians were a fragmented people subject to the administrations of Styria, Carinthia, Istria, Lombardy, Trieste and so on; there was even an area known as Venetian Slovenia. The cause of Slovenian nationalism was best served by such literary figures as Jarnik who saw their language as a powerful unifying factor in the struggle for national recognition. It is clear that the Carinthian poet Fellinger (qv), a liberal idealist, had some sympathy with Jarnik's cultural objectives which included research into Slovenian-influenced Carinthian dialect and the creation of a Slovenian dictionary. Jarnik also translated German poetry into Slovenian. He died on 11 June 1844 in Moosburg (Blatograd) where he was the resident priest.

| JESUS CHRISTUS UNSER HEILAND (Osterlied) (KLOPSTOCK) **D168A** [H76] E♭ major   9 March 1815 | Jesus Christ our Saviour (Easter song) | Choir, SATB |

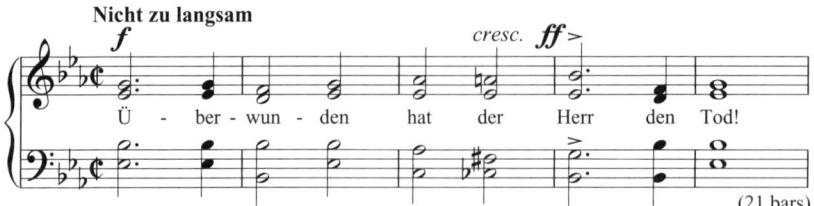

(21 bars)

Überwunden hat der Herr den Tod!   The Lord has vanquished death!
Des Menschen Sohn und Gott   The son of man and the son of God

Ist auferstanden!	Is arisen,
Ein Sieger auferstanden!	Arisen and victorious.
Halleluja!	Alleluja!
[(. . . 2 . . .)]	[(. . . 2 . . .)]

FRIEDRICH GOTTLOB KLOPSTOCK (1724–1803)

This little Klopstock setting illustrates well the strong Austrian link between Church and State, and above all between religion and patriotism. In the middle of a series of songs about fallen heroes, Schubert wrote a setting about the resurrection of Christ with no more or no less seriousness than his laments for Körner and his compatriots. It seems that just as Christ is designated a 'Sieger' – a warrior victor – the fallen warrior has achieved an almost Christ-like status. The work appears in the first edition of the Deutsch catalogue as D987 (among works of uncertain date) because the autograph had disappeared. This came to light only in 1967. Hindsight makes it rather easy to link this piece with *Begräbnislied* D168 and, in fact, both manuscripts share the same date. The key of *Jesus Christus unser Heiland* is E flat, the relative major of the C minor of *Begräbnislied*, and the mood of each work is a mirror image of the other. Furthermore, they were both written to Klopstock texts, and for SATB with piano, something of an unusual format for the composer in 1815. They are thus fitting companion pieces, the first chorus burying the dead, the next promising resurrection. The most effective moment in this single page is the word painting of 'auferstanden' (bb. 10–12) which stays dramatically high in the air for a tied minim in graphic illustration of its meaning.

Autograph:	Scottish Record Office, Edinburgh (Ogilvy of Inverquharty Collection)
First edition:	Published as No. 9 of *Neueste Folge nachgelassener, mehrstimmiger Gesänge mit und ohne Begleitung von Franz Schubert* by J. P. Gotthard, Vienna in 1872 and subsequently as part of the AGA in 1892 (P520)
Subsequent editions:	AGA XVII 17: p. 244; NSA III: Vol. 2a/18
Discography and timing:	Hyperion I 20²³ Hyperion II 5¹⁶ 0'52 Patricia Rozario, Catherine Denley, Ian Bostridge & Michael George

← *Nun lasst uns den Leib begraben (Begräbnislied)* D168   *Trinklied vor der Schlacht* D169 →

JOHANNA SEBUS   Johanna Sebus
(GOETHE) **D728** [H475]
(Fragment) D minor   April 1821

(81 bars)

Der Damm zerreisst, das Feld erbraust,	The dam bursts, the fields roar,
Die Fluten spülen, die Fläche saust.	The waters surge in, the plain howls.
'Ich trage dich, Mutter, durch die Flut,	'I'll carry you, mother, through the flood;
Noch reicht sie nicht hoch, ich wate gut.' —	It's not yet high, I'll manage to wade.'
'Auch uns bedenke, bedrängt wie wir sind,	'Think of us, too, in our distress,
Die Hausgenossinn, drei arme Kind!	The frail woman who lodges with you
Die schwache Frau! . . . sie eilt davon!' —[1]	And her three poor children . . . She is hurrying away!'
Sie trägt die Mutter durch's Wasser schon.	Already she is carrying her mother through the water.
'Zum Bühle da rettet Euch! harret derweil;	'Get to the hill over there and wait.
Gleich kehr' ich zurück, uns allen ist Heil.	I'll soon be back and we shall all be safe.
Zum Bühl ist's noch trocken und wenige Schritt';	It's still dry on the hill, and it's only a few steps away;
Doch nehmt auch mir meine Ziege mit!'	But take my goat with you.'
Der Damm zerschmilzt, das Feld erbraust.	The dam crumbles, the fields roar,
Die Fluten wühlen, die Fläche saust.	The waters seethe, the plain howls.
Sie setzt die Mutter auf sichres Land,	She sets her mother down on safe ground,
Schön Suschen, gleich wieder zur Flut gewandt.	Fair Susie, and immediately returns to the flood.
'Wohin? Wohin? Die Breite schwoll;	'Where are you going? The distance has grown;
Des Wassers ist hüben und drüben voll.	The water is high on both sides.
Verwegen in's Tiefe willst du hinein!' —	Will you be so rash as to plunge into the depths?'
'Sie sollen und müssen gerettet sein!'	'They must and shall be rescued!'
([. . . 3 . . .])	([. . . 3 . . .])

JOHANN WOLFGANG VON GOETHE (1749–1832); poem written 11/12 May 1809

This is the sixty-fifth of Schubert's seventy-five Goethe solo settings (1814–26). See the poet's biography for a chronological list of all the Goethe settings.

This, like *Mahomets Gesang* D721, is a heroic fragment. It was composed at about the time that Vogl first performed *Erlkönig* publicly, and it seems that Schubert was inspired by that song's success to return to Goethe in epic mood, with a crowd-pulling virtuoso piano accompaniment to match. The subject matter is not altogether promising and the composer lost heart quite early in proceedings. The subtitle of Goethe's poem reads 'In memory of the virtuous and beautiful seventeen-year-old girl [Johanna Sebus] from the village of Brienen who, on 13 January 1809, during the freezing of the Rhine and great collapse of the dam at Cleverham, died while bringing help.' This brings to mind a much earlier Schubert song (1814), the first of all the Mayrhofer settings, *Am See* D124. That poem was written in honour of Duke Leopold of Brunswick who had lost his life in 1785 while attempting to rescue his subjects from drowning; in *Johanna Sebus* Schubert returns to the same theme of a gallant rescuer overcome by the enemy – in this case water. In terms of mood, tonality and metre (D minor in 4/4) it is strikingly reminiscent of the churning semiquavers of the final pages of *Der Taucher* D77, the gigantic Schiller ballad that

---

[1] Goethe writes 'Die schwache Frau! . . . *Du gehst* davon!'

Johanna Sebus by Theobald von Oer, *Deutsches Balladenbuch* (1861).

occupied Schubert at the age of sixteen, and which describes the bravery of an intrepid youth who eventually dives to his death. Likewise, in Goethe's *Der Fischer* D225 (1815) the fisherman is lured to a watery grave by the Lorelei; in *Der Zwerg* D771 (1822) the eponymous anti-hero sinks his boat and, by implication, himself with it (like Peter Grimes); and in the final song of *Die schöne Müllerin* the young protagonist dies in the millstream.

The tempo marking for *Johanna Sebus* is 'Schnell' (fast), which is relatively unusual for Schubert. The piece achieves a piano-generated thundering impetus rare in his lieder, and it simply does not suit his style. The song begins on a melodramatic 'high', and in consequence has almost nowhere to go – although it is grim fun for the pianist while it lasts. One noteworthy point is the repeat of the opening D minor music for 'Der Damm zerschmilzt' (from b. 50), this time transposed to E minor in an attempt to heighten tension. Each time the words 'Der Damm' appear (followed either by the verbs 'zerreisst', 'zerschmilzt' or 'verschwindet') the composer treats them in a similar structural way. The piece has a highly strung hysterical flavour that does not preclude comedy, and there is something unintentionally funny about Johanna (whom Goethe also calls 'Schön Suschen') worrying about her goat! (Goethe – in strophes not set by Schubert – goes on to describe how Johanna, having successfully saved her mother, returns to rescue the neighbours and perishes in the attempt.)

Although the incident actually happened there is an air of unreality about the story, and Schubert no doubt abandoned the piece because not even he could engender sympathy for the heroine; she fails to live as a character, at least in the way the composer chose to set the music. The last we hear of Johanna in this song is an outburst of heroic intent: 'Sie sollen und müssen gerettet sein!' (bb. 75–80). We are almost in the world of Brünnhilde, and it is here that Schubert breaks off, somewhat prudently. Goethe's final lines, which moralize in folk-like manner, would have made an embarrassing end to a song with these dramatic aspirations. For his performing edition, Reinhard Van Hoorickx completed the nine bars of music derived from the earlier accompaniment that bring the fragment to a stormy, but inevitably peremptory, close.

Autograph:	Wienbibliothek im Rathaus, Vienna
First edition:	Published as part of the AGA in 1895 and subsequently completed by Reinhard Van Hoorickx (P722)
Subsequent editions:	Not in Peters; AGA XX 601: Vol. 10/128; NSA IV: Vol. 13/213
Further settings:	Johann Friedrich Reichardt (1752–1814) *Johanna Sebus* (1809–11) Carl Friedrich Zelter (1758–1832) *Johanna Sebus* for soloists, chorus and piano (1810)
Discography and timing:	Fischer-Dieskau —
	Hyperion I 28^5
	Hyperion II 25^1 2'29 John Mark Ainsley

← *Die Nachtigall* D724   *Der Blumen Schmerz* D731 →

Der JÜNGLING AM BACHE (I)   The youth by the brook
(SCHILLER) **D30** [H12]
F major   24 September 1812

(88 bars)

An der Quelle sass der Knabe,	By the stream sat a youth,
Blumen wand er sich zum Kranz,	Weaving flowers into a wreath;
Und er sah sie fortgerissen,	He saw them carried off
Treiben in der Wellen Tanz.	And swept along in the dancing waves.
'Und so fliehen meine Tage	'Thus my days speed by,
Wie die Quelle rastlos hin!	Relentlessly, like the stream!
Und so bleichet meine Jugend,	And my youth pales,
Wie die Kränze schnell verblühn!	As quickly as the wreaths wilt!
Fraget nicht, warum ich traure	'Do not ask why I mourn
In des Lebens Blütenzeit!	when life is in full bloom!
Alles freuet sich und hoffet,	All is filled with joy and hope
Wenn der Frühling sich erneut.	When spring returns.
Aber diese tausend Stimmen[1]	But all these thousand voices
Der erwachenden Natur	Of burgeoning nature

---

[1] The word 'diese' in Schiller's poem is absent from D30, but is present in the later two settings of the poem, D192 and D638.

Wecken in dem tiefen Busen	Awaken deep in my heart
Mir den schweren Kummer nur.	Only heavy grief.
Was soll mir die Freude frommen,	'What good to me is the joy
Die der schöne Lenz mir beut?	Which the fair spring offers me?
Eine nur ist's, die ich suche,	There is only one I seek,
Sie ist nah und ewig weit.	She is near and yet eternally distant.
Sehnend breit' ich meine Arme	Yearningly I stretch out my arms
Nach dem teuren Schattenbild,	Towards that beloved shadowy image,
Ach, ich kann es nicht erreichen,	Ah, I cannot reach it,
Und das Herz ist ungestillt![2]	And my heart is unquiet.
Komm herab, du schöne Holde,	'Come down, gracious beauty,
Und verlass dein stolzes Schloss!	and leave your proud castle!
Blumen, die der Lenz geboren,	Flowers, which the spring has borne,
Streu ich dir in deinen Schoss.	I shall strew on your lap,
Horch, der Hain erschallt von Liedern,	Listen! The grove echoes with song
Und die Quelle rieselt klar!	And the brook ripples limpidly,
Raum ist in der kleinsten Hütte	There is room in the tiniest cottage
Für ein glücklich liebend Paar.'	For a happy, loving couple.'

FRIEDRICH VON SCHILLER (1759–1805); poem written in 1803

*This is the third of Schubert's forty-four Schiller solo settings (1811–24). See the poet's biography
for a chronological list of all the Schiller settings.*

If it is a poisonous libel (fancifully promoted by Pushkin, for example) to claim that Antonio
Salieri had something to do with the death of Mozart, there is no doubt that the venerable
Italian composer had a good deal to do with the birth of Schubert's career. Salieri was Schubert's composition teacher at the Imperial Choir School in Vienna, and he insisted that his
pupils' wrote vocal lines in Italian – musical shape taking precedence over the meaning of the
words. On the other hand, the older German composers whom Schubert admired (Zumsteeg
and Reichardt especially) made a point of subjugating their compositional fancy to the poets'
texts. For the composers from Stuttgart and Berlin, song was akin to recitation; meaning and
nuance in declamation were the *raison d'être* for the vocal line, which was untainted by 'frivolous' Italian *bel canto*. Schubert was mightily fascinated by the dramatic austerity of this
approach, but even more powerful was the young composer's genius for melody which blossomed with Mozart's example and became more expert under Salieri's tutelage. This provided
what serious German song had hitherto lacked – the Italianate warmth and flexibility of a
touching vocal line. The German lied as Schubert conceived it was created by balancing the
musical and poetic demands of north and south to achieve a truly European synthesis of intellectuality and heart.

   One of the numerous composition exercises Salieri gave to the teenage composer was to set
Metastasio's *Quell'innocente figlio* for various vocal combinations. The first of these exercises
(D17/1) bears a strong resemblance to this setting of *Der Jüngling am Bache* which is in effect
Schubert's first song like this, putting aside the lengthier ballads. Schubert had already used
Schiller texts to make a couple of highly successful Zumsteeg-like narratives, but here the poet

---

[2] 'Ist' is replaced by Schiller's 'bleibt' ('remains') in the later two settings of the poem, D192 and D638.

provides him with a lyric for a song with no real story attached. It is not strictly strophic in the rigid North German sense; Schubert varies the treatment of the second half of each verse because, as Einstein puts it, he is 'drawn irresistibly to find a means of expressing himself'. The whole is like a rondo with interludes; recitative leads back to enchanting arioso. This is not to say that within that overall scheme there was not room for illustrative detail learned from the art of ballad composition: perhaps the call of quail in dotted rhythm (via Beethoven's song *Der Wachtelschlag* of 1803) is deliberately introduced at bb. 20–22 and 66–8, and a much slower dotted rhythm shuddering (a sudden 'sehr langsam' at bb. 38–41) is contrasted with an enchanting bridge passage that returns us to the main key. At the end of the song from b. 79 there are horn calls in the piano's left hand which, in John Reed's words, 'lift the heart'.

Two and a half years later the composer adjusted the setting (D192 – the tune remains very similar but is transposed to the minor key) and in 1819 there was a third attempt (D638 – completely new musically, but still strophic). Schiller's verses thus fascinated and challenged Schubert over a period of seven years. This is perfect evidence of his artistic conscience when attempting to find his way into a poem. If he decided on a strophic setting it was no easy option; the challenge was always to find music that encapsulated the whole poem, with no sense of jarring disappointment in one or other of the verses.

This first setting has a lot to commend it – youthful ardour and innocence, a bow in Mozart's direction (the younger composer's idol) but at the same time a definite announcement of the coming Schubert. The poem, on the other hand, was written in 1803 by Schiller, already ill and with not long to live – a lyric for a Weimar production of a French play by Louis-Benoît Picard, *Der Parasit*, sung in the fourth act by the pivotal character of Charlotte. There was nothing to indicate this in Schiller's *Gedichte*, but Schubert somehow knew the words had been made for music.

Autograph:	Wienbibliothek im Rathaus, Vienna (fair copy)
First edition:	Published as part of the AGA in 1894 (P531)
Subsequent editions:	Not in Peters; AGA XX 5: Vol. 1/45; NSA IV: Vol. 4b/218; Bärenreiter: Vol. 3/212
Discography and timing:	Fischer-Dieskau I 1[3] 3'30
	Hyperion I 1[1]
	Hyperion II 2[7] 3'46 Janet Baker

←— *Klaglied* D23   *Entra l'uomo allor che nasce (Aria di Abramo)* D331 —→

Der JÜNGLING AM BACHE (II)   The youth by the brook
(SCHILLER) **D192** [H93]
F minor   15 May 1815

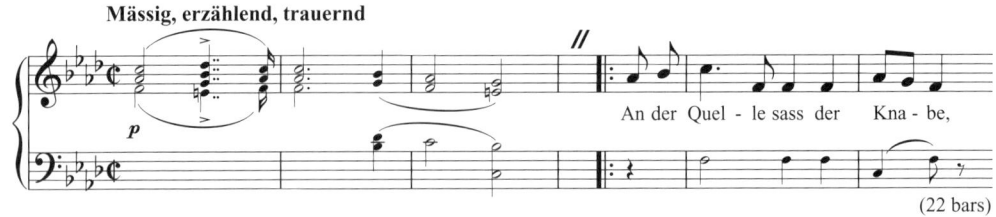

An der Quel - le sass der Kna - be,

(22 bars)

See previous entry for poem and translation

FRIEDRICH VON SCHILLER (1759–1805); poem written in 1803

This is the eleventh of Schubert's forty-four Schiller solo settings (1811–24). See the poet's biography for a chronological list of all the Schiller settings.

There are three settings of this text. The first of them (D30) dates from 1812, the third, D638, from 1819. This song is sandwiched almost equidistantly between the other two. It owes a great deal to the 1812 version; indeed it is a minor-key modification of the earlier work, rather than a totally new conception. Schubert, contrary to popular legend, was not so forgetful about his songs that he was unable to recall one of them from three years previously. The first version was a marvel for a boy of fifteen to have written and owes more to Salieri's teaching than any first-hand knowledge of the emotions described. The composer, by 1815 able to number *Gretchen am Spinnrade* D118 among his achievements, returned to the poem, chastened perhaps by those experiences that inevitably separate a fifteen-year-old adolescent from someone of eighteen. There are those who see this song as falling between two stools, lacking both the uninhibited freshness of the first version and the masterful melodic invention of the (completely different)

Der Jüngling am Bache by Wilhelm von Kaulbach.

third. Nevertheless, taken on its own terms the song has a Mozartian poise and control. It could be said that the music in this mood suits the first verse better than the others, but the well-schooled elegance of the whole reflects the pastoral nature of the text. It could also be said to mirror accurately the emotional diffidence of someone in their late teens, old enough to be hurt, but not experienced enough to be able to do anything about it.

Autograph:	Wienbibliothek im Rathaus, Vienna (first draft)
First edition:	Published as Vol. 7 no. 40 in Friedlaender's edition by Peters, Leipzig in 1887 (P501)
Subsequent editions:	Peters: Vol. 7/90; AGA XX 68: Vol. 2/108; NSA IV: Vol. 4b/224; Bärenreiter: Vol. 3/216
Discography and timing:	Fischer-Dieskau I 3^{18} 2'57
	Hyperion I 7^{2}
	Hyperion II 6^{13} 2'57 Elly Ameling

⟵ *Des Mädchens Klage* D191   *An den Mond (Geuss, lieber Mond)* D193 ⟶

Der JÜNGLING AM BACHE (III)   The youth by the brook
(SCHILLER) OP. 87 NO. 3 **D638** [H424]

The song exists in two versions, the second of which is discussed below:
(1) April 1819; (2) published in August 1827

(1)   No tempo indication   D minor $\frac{2}{4}$ [28 bars]

(2)   C minor

(33 bars)

See Der Jüngling am Bache (I) *for poem and translation*

FRIEDRICH VON SCHILLER (1759–1805); poem written in 1803

This is the thirty-ninth of Schubert's forty-four Schiller solo settings (1811–24). See the poet's biography for a chronological list of all the Schiller settings.

Schiller's poem was first published in *Taschenbuch für Damen auf das Jahr 1805*. It is a late product of his poetic art at a time when he was aware that he did not have long to live. The narrative 'I' of the poem (after the first four lines have set the scene) shows a touching desire to re-experience the freshness, and even the unsettling pain, of youth. In this, at least, there is the joy of being alive. The young man's melancholy at the return of spring is reminiscent of

Schiller's own feelings (as described to Goethe) – that this time of year brought forth in him 'ein unruhiges und gegenstandsloses Sehnen', an unsettled and groundless longing. The French poet Verlaine was also to write of a 'deuil' which is 'sans raison'. This ambivalence of feeling, the duality of happiness in sadness and sadness in happiness, is a Schubertian hallmark – his speciality even. A perfect illustration of this would be the Collin setting *Wehmut* D772, with a line like 'Es wird mir dann so wohl so weh' (the spring song *Im Frühling* D882 is another) – a smile through the tears, or the tears behind the smile. It is perhaps because *Der Jüngling am Bache* offered this type of challenge, found often enough in the Romantic poets but rare for Schiller, that Schubert attempted to set the lyric three times, in 1812, 1815 and finally 1819.

The first setting of these words (D30) is a beautiful song of Mozartian grace, but despite an effectively dramatic passage at 'Wecken in dem tiefen Busen / Mir den schweren Kummer nur' (bb. 37–41) there is perhaps too open a smile here fully to reflect Schiller's words. Nevertheless, John Reed is not alone in preferring this first version to the later attempts. The second setting (D192) applies the minor tonality to a melody that is still based on the first. It might be argued that this 'improvement' loses the freshness of the original inspiration without offering anything new in its place, apart from a somewhat darker mood.

The third setting, 'Mässig' in C minor, is Schubert's final attempt at solving the problem, and even this did not come easily. In regard to this lyric Einstein rightly praises the composer's 'artistic sense of responsibility'. There are two versions, the first of which (in D minor, dating from April 1819, and printed in the NSA, Volume 4b, p. 226) has an accompaniment that changes character halfway through and introduces joyous sextuplets (from b. 18) to enliven the accompaniment's texture. When the composer came to prepare the song for publication eight years later, having already composed the first part of *Winterreise*, he clearly decided that integration and unity (traditionally the highest ideals for a successful strophic song) were best served by a moderate but implacable flow of semiquavers through each strophe; he also lengthened and deepened the significance of the prelude and postlude. The new vocal line is tinged with melancholy to reflect the poet's sadness but it still has enough melismatic energy to suggest that the singer is young. The introduction replaces the plaintive mood of the earlier settings with something more insistent and driven; dotted rhythms in the left hand, as if muted timpani, add an undertone of menace. Particularly haunting is the modulation into D minor at 'Treiben in der Wellen Tanz' (bb. 13–15) with the tormented awkwardness of the augmented second on the first syllable of 'Wellen' and a similar passage at the end of each strophe that paves the way for the return of the tonic. This third setting of the poem seems far more troubling than the first two. Perhaps this is because, as in such songs in the first part of *Winterreise* as *Erstarrung* D911/4 und *Einsamkeit* D911/12, the relentless gait of the accompaniment, driven by obsession, seems impervious to the voice – it no longer has the patience to indulge the singer in any trace of *bel canto* rubato, the situation has become far too serious for such charming niceties.

Autograph:	Wienbibliothek im Rathaus, Vienna
Publication:	Published as Op. 84 no. 3 by A Pennauer, Vienna in 1827; subsequently changed to Op. 87 no. 3 (P133; first version) Published as part of the AGA in 1895 (P684; second version)
Subsequent editions:	Peters: Vol. 2/158; AGA XX 359a & b: Vol. 6/38; NSA IV: Vol. 4a/90 & Vol. 4b/226; Bärenreiter: Vol. 3/60
Bibliography:	Capell 1928, p. 158 Einstein 1951, p. 48
Arrangements:	Arr. Tilman Hoppstock (b. 1961) for guitar accompaniment in *Franz Schubert: 110 Lieder* (2009)

Discography and timing: Fischer-Dieskau II 3[2]   4'17

Hyperion I 16[12]

Hyperion II 21[19]   4'22   Thomas Allen

← *An die Freunde* D654   *Sehnsucht (Mignon)* D656 →

Der JÜNGLING AN DER QUELLE   The youth by the spring
(SALIS-SEEWIS) **D300** [H376]
A major   1816? or 1821?

(29 bars)

Leise, rieselnder Quell, ihr wallenden, flispernden Pappeln!	Softly rippling brook, swaying, whispering poplars,
Euer Schlummergeräusch wecket die Liebe nur auf.	Your slumbrous murmur only awakens love.
Linderung sucht' ich bei euch, und sie zu vergessen, die Spröde;	I sought consolation in you, wishing to forget her, she who is so aloof.
Ach! und Blätter und Bach seufzen: Luise, dir nach!	But alas, the leaves and the brook sigh for you, Louise!

JOHANN GAUDENZ VON SALIS-SEEWIS (1762–1834); poem written between 1800 and 1806

The dating of this song is so uncertain that it could possibly be the first, possibly the last, of Schubert's thirteen Salis-Seewis solo settings (1816–?21). See the poet's biography for a chronological list of all the Salis-Seewis settings.

The commentators wax lyrical over this song and with reason. This is water music ('Etwas langsam') of the gentlest kind; the spring tinkles rather than bubbles, and nowhere is there a hint of gush. And yet this music paints a personal picture rather than the rococo allegory that we are used to in settings of texts of this kind (by Haydn for example) where one shepherd and shepherdess can always stand in for another. The pianist's hands are both placed in the airy regions of the treble clef throughout and the music glistens with the dew of the new romanticism without giving in to a deluge of emotion. This was what it was like for Schubert to be writing songs circa 1816: the roots of the setting are certainly in the classical tradition, but who could deny that this is a new and tender flowering? All is poise and tender restraint; the love described is not heated by a darker, more complicated passion, but is heartfelt nevertheless. Although the date of the song is contested (John Reed believes it may have been written in 1821) it is likely that it belongs with the other Salis-Seewis settings of 1816 or 1817 that have a similar limpid clarity and simplicity.

The accompaniment is constructed in three layers like a string trio. At the bottom in the viola register are long-held pedal notes. These are dotted minims on A or E with a brief passing visit to F natural (at b. 21) towards the end; the little finger of the left hand sustains these for a bar at time, and it is the fixed nature of the bass line that gives the feeling of time standing still in a fine performance of this song. In the middle register are quavers (also played with the left hand) that lie at the heart of the piano part, and which intertwine with the vocal line in sensual duet. And then the right hand plays the purest and most transparent of water music, purling semiquavers that rise and fall within the cusp of a hand that remains almost stationary at the keyboard. There is a little melody that is traced within these burbling notes, a gently rising scale that is in contrary motion with the left hand's quavers, and which suggests the mirror imagery associated with the reflecting powers of water. In addressing the stream so intimately perhaps the youth can also see himself? This accompaniment might have been inspired in the first instance by the word 'Schlummergeräusch' (slumbrous murmur, b. 9) but its treble register also adds a touch of sparkle to the song, like flecks of water glinting here and there in the sunlight. It is possibly for this reason that Einstein regards Der Jüngling an der Quelle as an early example of impressionism or musical pointillism.

The vocal line is repetitive and largely based on arpeggios, but somewhere in this folksong naivety lies the magic ingredient that weaves a hypnotic spell. A number of tiny details contribute to the effect of the whole. As the whispering beauties of the environs kindle in the youth painful feelings of the love that he had hoped to forget, the vocal line on 'wecket die Liebe nur auf' leaps an octave from E to E (bb. 10–12). We have a sense of the lad's heart in his mouth as, almost against his will, memories of Luise (the Nachlass and Peters Edition have 'Louise') flood his thoughts. Never could there have been an accented passing note with a more tender ache in it than on 'Spröde' at b. 16 (we understand immediately that she has primly been refusing his advances, and that he is dying of frustration), nor a more sensuously arched phrase than the second 'Ach! und Blätter und Bach' (bb. 19–20).

For the final three words of the poem Salis-Seewis had originally written 'Elisa! mir zu' rather than 'Luise, dir nach'. Although the poem is not written in rhyme, it seems that Schubert was pleased to suggest something of an assonance in the final couplet where the original final words 'mir zu' were changed to 'dir nach', seemingly to rhyme with 'Bach'. In musical terms the vowel in 'Bach' is lengthened and in 'nach' shortened, an almost-rhyme that adds to the sense of exquisite closure in bb. 22–3. (In the AGA Mandyczeswki restored the poet's original 'mir zu'.) That 'Luise' should be repeated twice at the end (the name's second syllable elongated on minims) and then made to die on the singer's breath as if carried away by wind and water (bb. 21–7) is also probably the composer's inspiration, and a very happy one. It may be that Schubert was working from Albert Stadler's written-out anthology of song texts, or even a copy of the Salis-Seewis poem unknown to us (and Walther Dürr in the NSA regards both of these as possibilities). On the other hand Schubert might simply have realized that the clipped and neutral first syllable of 'Elisa' would not make for sensuality as a sung vowel, whereas the 'Lu' of 'Luise' rolls languidly off the tongue and gives the singer a plaintive colour at the beginning of the word. As for the postlude, two bars of unadorned A major oscillation at the very end (bb. 27–8) are exquisite as the brook is restored to nature, no longer ruffled by the singer's gaze and breath. The combination of its A major tonality and gently unfolding timelessness suggests a mystical link with Auch kleine Dinge, the opening song of Wolf's Italienisches Liederbuch (1891). There is a similar sense of unrufflable perfection in both songs.

Autograph:	Missing or lost
First edition:	Published as Book 36 no. 1 of the Nachlass by Diabelli, Vienna in 1842 (P343)
Subsequent editions:	Peters: Vol. 6/3; AGA XX 398: Vol. 6/208; NSA IV: Vol. 9/128
Bibliography:	Capell 1928, p. 170
	Einstein 1951, p. 220
	Fischer-Dieskau 1977, p. 152

Discography and timing: Fischer-Dieskau II 4[14]   1'37
Hyperion I 23[6]
Hyperion II 19[10]   1'35   Christoph Prégardien

← *Der Strom* D565   *Das Grab* D569 →

Der JÜNGLING AUF DEM HÜGEL   The youth on the hill
(HÜTTENBRENNER) OP. 8 NO. 1, **D702** [H456]
E minor – G major   November 1820

(92 bars)

Ein Jüngling auf dem Hügel	A youth sat on the hill
Mit seinem Kummer sass;	With his sorrow;
Wohl ward der Augen Spiegel	His eyes grew dim
Ihm trüb' und tränennass.	And moist with tears.
Sah frohe Lämmer spielen	He watched lambs gambolling happily
Am grünen Felsenhang,	On the green hillside,
Sah frohe Bächlein quillen	And brooks rippling merrily
Das bunte Tal entlang;	Through the bright valley.
Die Schmetterlinge sogen	Butterflies sipped
Am roten Blütenmund,	At the red mouth of the flowers;
Wie Morgenträume flogen	Clouds scudded about
Die Wolken in dem Rund;	Like morning dreams.
Und Alles war so munter	And everything was so cheerful,
Und Alles schwamm in Glück,	Bathed in happiness;
Nur in sein Herz hinunter	His heart alone
Sah nicht der Freude Blick.	Was untouched by the light of joy.
Ach! dumpfes Grabgeläute	Ah, just now the muffled death-knell
Im Dorfe nun erklang,	Sounded in the village,
Schon tönte aus der Weite	And in the distance
Ein klagender Gesang;	A mournful song echoed.
Sah nun die Lichter scheinen,	Then he saw the lights shining,
Den schwarzen Leichenzug,	And the black cortège;
Fing bitter an zu weinen,	He began to weep bitterly,
Weil man sein Röschen trug.	For they were bearing his little Rose.

Jetzt liess den Sarg man nieder,	Then they lowered the coffin;
Der Totengräber kam,	The gravedigger came
Und gab der Erde wieder,	And restored to the earth
Was Gott aus selber nahm.	What God once took from it.
Da schwieg des Jünglings Klage,	Then the youth ceased lamenting,
Und betend ward sein Blick,	And his eyes were fixed in prayer;
Sah schon am schönen Tage	Already he saw that fair day
Des Wiedersehens Glück.	When they would be reunited in joy.
Und wie die Sterne kamen,	And as the stars came out
Der Mond heraufgeschifft,	And the moon sailed heavenwards,
Da las er in den Sternen	He read in those stars high above
Der Hoffnung hohe Schrift.	The holy writ of Hope.

HEINRICH HÜTTENBRENNER (1799–1830)

This is Schubert's only setting of a Hüttenbrenner text. See the poet's biography.

Here is the classic instance of Schubert setting a poem by a friend in order to please or repay an obligation. The imposing classical poems of Mayrhofer were occupying his attention at the time and there is nothing in this little graveside *scena* that would have seemed to him indispensable. In 1817 he had set *Der Jüngling und der Tod* D545 to a poem by his oldest school friend Josef von Spaun, and *Der Jüngling auf dem Hügel* seems to have been planned as a pendant to that work. But planned by whom? Some of Schubert's friends were canny enough to realize that it would only be a matter of time before their hard-working friend was very famous indeed, and around great artists there have always been factions of hangers-on who specialize in glory-by-association. The Hüttenbrenners of Graz – the brothers Anselm, Josef and Heinrich – were just such a family. The eldest, Anselm, was a fellow-pupil of Salieri, and a rival composer who thought himself at least as gifted as Schubert, if not more so. As the years progressed, the rivalry got the better of the friendship, and although the whole family valued their closeness to Schubert and often engaged in useful work to broaden Schubert's reputation and advance his interests, there seems always to have been an ulterior motive. Why the Hüttenbrenners kept the manuscript of the 'Unfinished' Symphony away from the eyes of the world for some forty years remains a mystery, but it probably had something to do with the resentment that endured after Schubert's death.

Josef Hüttenbrenner (1796–1882) in 1817 had received an ink-stained copy from Schubert of *Die Forelle* D550 with an inscription betokening intimate friendship. He went on to fulfil a unique, if not always comfortable, role in Schubert's life as secretary, publicist, book-keeper and factotum. He was much involved with the first publications of the Schubert songs from 1821. In late 1820 (when the composer was still sharing an apartment with Mayrhofer) Josef almost certainly presented his brother Heinrich's poem for Schubert's attention and, once it was composed, ensured both its public performance and its relatively speedy publication (in 1821 and 1822 respectively). It was one of Josef Hüttenbrenner's tasks to liaise with the publishers and it is difficult to imagine the composer himself wishing to rush this song into print when far better ones lay in a drawer. The fact that it stands at the head of an opus number otherwise devoted to Mayrhofer settings, and which perhaps should have been solely given over to this poet, suggests nepotism at work. Schubert eventually came to regard Josef Hüttenbrenner as a nuisance.

There is no record of the composer's opinion of Heinrich himself; we know very little about the poet apart from the fact that he was a law student in Vienna and was the youngest and the shortest-lived of the brothers. It is likely that Schubert was fond of all of them for old times' sake. But the song, as observed by Capell, shows traits of something hastily done. Of all Schubert's 'Jüngling' songs, a genre that calls for charm, this is the least personable. The affection that Schubert had for Josef von Spaun shines through *Der Jüngling und der Tod* D545, although it is not a great poem. In setting this Hüttenbrenner 'Jüngling', however, the composer finds himself faced with an intractable assembly of wooden clichés in pastoral mode (thus the opening § time signature), melodramatic, tear-jerking and sentimentally pious to boot. The very young Schubert might have handled it with better conscience – the preposterous (and equally stiff) funeral scenario of Schiller's *Leichenfantasie* (D7, 1811) comes to mind.

The original key is E minor, and the marking 'Nicht zu langsam'. The composer does his best to paint the youth sitting pensively on the hill, but one has only to compare a later song of a lovelorn young man in a similar location ('Still sitz' ich an des Hügels Hang' – Schulze's *Im Frühling* D882) to hear the difference when the composer is fully involved in a poem's imagery. Nevertheless, because Schubert is Schubert, he does his considerable best under the circumstances. The harmonies in the Hüttenbrenner setting, slightly portentous, suggest the old-fashioned minstrelsy and archaic harmonies of a work like *Der König in Thule* D367. The two-part writing between voice and piano at 'der Augen Spiegel', bb. 15–16, is an ingenious reflection of the words. There will be a comparable interplay of voice and accompaniment with similar imagery in *Tränenregen* from *Die schöne Müllerin* D795/10.

At b. 21 the second section ('Mässig') moves into C major as the lambs gambol happily in the fields, like so many four-legged cousins of *Die Forelle*; their movements are captured in a triplet accompaniment, much less fluid than the sextuplets reserved for the trout. There are other works from this period (the Schlegel songs *Der Knabe* D692, *Der Schmetterling* D633 and *Die Vögel* D691) where the artless natures of bird and butterfly express themselves in the simplicity of dancing arpeggios built around common chords. And yet this music is not as straightforwardly happy as it may seem; the pastoral idyll is designed to pull at the heartstrings in the manner of Italian opera with its use of the 'pathetic major'. A year later Schubert was to remember this music when he came to compose an aria for King Mauregato in *Alfonso und Estrella* D732, 'Wo find ich nur den Ort' no. 32 where this vocal melody in wafting thirds re-occurs from b. 46 of that aria. The king, once villainous and now to be reformed, describes a vision whereby songs of joy have resounded in his halls – '. . . es war ein schöner Traum' he says – it was all a beautiful dream. The B flat major music of the opera makes a later reappearance, in turn, in a song, also in B flat, about a blind boy, *Der blinde Knabe* D833. The poetic image that prompts this similar response in all three works is seeing something at a distance, something imagined, unreal and unattainable. The boy described by Hüttenbrenner is unable to share in the joy of the gambolling lambs. There now follows a transitional passage in C minor (bb. 41–8) that leads into the funeral-cortège music which lies at the heart of this song.

For the section beginning 'Ach! dumpfes Grabgeläute / Im Dorfe nun erklang' (G minor, 'Langsam' from b. 49) one admires another ingenious Schubertian experiment, one of several in the canon, with the resonance of bell music, here deeper and more sonorous than elsewhere (cf. *Das Zügenglöcklein* D871 – the passing-bell tolled when a Catholic dies; *Abendbilder* D650 – vesper bells; *Viola* D786 – snowdrops as bells; *Das Heimweh* D851 – cowbells, and so on). For six bars the pianist's hands alternate with unchanging tolling sounds, a bleak open twelfth apart, crotchets in the left hand, and crotchets off the beat in the right. This pedal effect conjures a very dark and ominous atmosphere, and the dramatic screws are tightened as the bass line rises ineluctably in gradual semitones, like grief welling to the surface. There is a moment of great tenderness at the mention of 'Röschen', b. 59; for this 'little Rose' there is a tiny echo of the dactylic motif of *Der Tod und das Mädchen* D531. The central mystery of the poem is why the youth is not at the funeral himself instead of observing this sad event from the hill. Has he been Rose's forbidden lover, or has she been his secret passion? In any case he is barred from being at her side. So indistinct is the poet's scenario that one could also take this funeral to be an event recalled in memory, or even a prophetic fantasy of what will take place in the future. After the cortège we begin the burial music (bb. 61–8) in which the lie of the vocal line and the piano collaborate in digging deep into the nether reaches of the stave. When faced with the melodramatic setting of 'Der Totengräber kam' (b. 63), the listener is inevitably reminded of the sublimity of which Schubert was capable, with a similar scenario, in the closing pages of *Totengräbers Heimwehe* D842.

For the final musical section ('Da schwieg des Jünglings Klage') the music is marked 'Etwas geschwinder' and we sense that Schubert has tired of the poem. At another moment he might have come up with something more interesting than this straightforward change from G minor to G major, and a return to the § of the opening (from b. 69). However, the extended G pedal where the piano's right hand intertwines with the vocal line in the manner of a charming obbligato instrument is simply effective. All this brings about a seraphic sense of contentment. But it comes too soon, and too automatically, after the ridiculously high drama of the burial scene for us to believe in its spiritual import. The religiosity of the Silbert settings, for example, is a good deal more convincing. The postlude (bb. 89–92) ascends skywards while contemplating hope's 'hohe Schrift', but the music remains earthbound. Unless Schubert is on a high and able to lift poets like Craigher or Pyrker to the headier regions on his own shoulders, he needs a specially gifted imagist, a Klopstock or a Novalis, truly to inspire him when it comes to poetry of a religious bent.

Autograph:	Gesellschaft der Musikfreunde, Vienna
First edition:	Published as Op. 8 no. 1 by Cappi & Diabelli, Vienna in May 1822 (P21)
Dedicatee:	Johann Karl Grafen Esterházy von Galántha
First known performance:	30 March 1821, Gesellschaft der Musikfreunde, Vienna. Soloist: Sophie Linhart (see Waidelich/Hilmar Dokumente I No. 78 for full concert programme)
Subsequent editions:	Peters: Vol. 2/16; AGA XX 385: Vol. 6/126; NSA IV: Vol. 1/68; Bärenreiter: Vol. 1/56
Bibliography:	Capell 1928, p. 168
Discography and timing:	Fischer-Dieskau II 4[5] 5'06
	Hyperion I 29[20]
	Hyperion II 23[14] 5'05 Marjana Lipovšek

← *Frühlingsglaube* D686   *Im Walde* D708 →

Der JÜNGLING UND DER TOD   The youth and death
(SPAUN) **D545** [H359]

The song exists in two versions, both of which are discussed below:
(1) March 1817; (2) March 1817

(1) 'Sehr langsam'   C# minor – B♭ major   ¢   [33 bars]

(2) C# minor – F major

Der Jüngling:	The Youth:
Die Sonne sinkt, o könnt' ich mit ihr scheiden,	The sun is sinking; O that I might depart with it,
Mit ihrem letzten Strahl entfliehen!	Flee with its last ray:
Ach diese namenlosen Qualen meiden	Escape these nameless torments,
Und weit in schönre Welten ziehn!	And journey far away to fairer worlds!
O komme, Tod, und löse diese Bande!	O come, death, and loose these bonds!
Ich lächle dir, o Knochenmann,	I smile upon you, skeleton;
Entführe mich leicht in geträumte Lande!	Lead me gently to the land of dreams!
O komm und rühre mich doch an!	O come and touch me, come!

Der Tod:	Death:
Es ruht sich kühl und sanft in meinen Armen,	In my arms you will find cool, gentle rest;
Du rufst, ich will mich deiner Qual erbarmen.	You call. I will take pity on your suffering.

JOSEF VON SPAUN (1788–1865)

This is Schubert's only setting of a Spaun text. See the poet's biography.

The popularity of the Claudius setting *Der Tod und das Mädchen* D531 in the Schubert circle was such that it achieved an almost iconic status. For some time the authorship of the poem for *Der Jüngling und der Tod* was a mystery; these words, a poetic pendant to Claudius's masterpiece, inverted the maiden's distraught pleas for mercy into the fashionable death-wish of a younger generation of males brought up on the Romantic poses of Goethe's *Werther*. The text was ascribed to Anton von Spaun who was a distinguished historian but hardly a poet. It was only in the 1860s that Josef von Spaun, brother of Anton, admitted that the poem was his. He seems to have been embarrassed by it (it is certainly not the work of a professional) and perhaps he regretted the youthful rush of enthusiasm that had led him to write it, no doubt after a hearing of Schubert's *Der Tod und das Mädchen*, as a mark of homage. It is likely that he never expected his close friend to respond to these verses with a musical setting. That the composer did set

Spaun's words to music was surely an indication of the very special affection that he felt for an old friend who had always played the role of benign guardian.

The key is C sharp minor, also the tonality of the heavy-hearted song *Der Wanderer* D489/493. The opening of the slow movement of the piano Fantasy (D760), inspired and named after that celebrated song, irresistibly reminds us of the introduction to *Der Jüngling und der Tod*. There are a number of other Schubert songs (*An die untergehende Sonne* D457, *Freiwilliges Versinken* D700) that deal with the majesty of sunset, the vocal line falling by degrees, the accompaniment stately and portentous. Although the opening of this song is an early example of that tradition, the grandiose workings of nature quickly yield to a touching human drama where the youth begs for death in words that deliberately reverse the pleas of Claudius's maiden ('rühre mich doch an' – bb. 21–2 – instead of 'rühre mich nicht an'). There is no attempt to make the youth's music manly, brave or nonchalant (as the words might suggest). Though more expansive, his pleas are every bit as musically delicate and subtle as the girl's; the vocal line palpitates and sighs on many a melting appoggiatura and dying fall. 'O komme, Tod, und löse diese Bande' (bb. 15–17) is an extremely beautiful passage of arioso indicative of a style that switches easily between recitative-like intensity and snatches of memorable melody. Although it might be argued that Schubert meant this song to be sung by a woman, he is always less concerned than some composers to paint stereotypes. He knows that at a crucial moment of life or death, a man is likely to be every bit as vulnerable, child-like and afraid as a woman (who might well, in her turn, be strong and defiant). There is a good deal of trepidation mixed in with this masochistic, even erotic, desire for union with Death, and the music pulling in two directions at once makes the poem more believable.

The final section illustrates the maxim that those ideas that seem most inevitable with hindsight do not always spring immediately to the creator's mind. Both versions of the song share a single manuscript. The first version (D545A, printed on p. 108 of Volume 10 of NSA) has Death ('Der Tod' marked above the stave) singing in the depths of G minor (bb. 26–32). Schubert here returns to the bass tessitura he had used for the words of Death in his famous Claudius setting. But surprisingly enough, the appearance of Death is not prefaced by an interlude which uses the famous rhythmic and harmonic motifs from *Der Tod und das Mädchen*; neither is there a postlude to put us in mind of that masterpiece. It is only in the second version that this seemingly inevitable self-quotation takes place, as if somewhat reluctantly. For this the key changes to D minor (Death has always spoken easily in this key since the demise of Mozart's *Don Giovanni*) and the tread of the predator/liberator is the familiar one in solemn dactyls. The incorporation of this self-quotation was swiftly accomplished, perhaps as a result of urgings within the Schubert circle after a play-through of the first version. Another change, perhaps occasioned by a singer's request, is the most important difference between the two versions of the song. The first seems cast for two singers of different tessituras – high on the stave for the young man, low for Death. The song is not officially designated as a duet within the Schubert canon, but it is the nearest thing to that genre, simply because it would be an exceptional singer capable of encompassing the vocal range of both characters. The second version (where the second half of the song takes a completely different harmonic direction from that of the first version) can easily be sung by a single singer, probably a tenor or soprano.

For those (almost everyone) who feel tempted to take the slow-looking death pronouncement of the related Claudius setting at a funereal pace, it is instructive to see that in *Der Jüngling und der Tod* Schubert has written out this interlude in notes of half the value – crotchets and quavers rather than minims and crotchets. The Grim Reaper's scythe has cut time into a gliding two-in-a-bar. The speed of the passages in both songs is certainly meant to be the same – and so it will be if performers have the courage to obey Schubert's controversial $\bemol = 54$ metronome mark of the Claudius setting.

Autograph:	Pierpont Morgan Library, New York (first and second drafts)
Publication:	Published as part of the AGA in 1895 (P671; first version)
	Published as No. 18 of *Neueste Folge nachgelassener Lieder und Gesänge* by J. P. Gotthard, Vienna in 1872 (P444; second version)
Subsequent editions:	Peters: Vol. 7/56; AGA XX 312a & b: Vol. 5/80; NSA IV: Vol. 11/108 & 110
Bibliography:	Einstein 1951, p. 161
	Kohlhäufl 1999, p. 170
	Porter 1961, pp. 108–9 & 114
Discography and timing:	Fischer-Dieskau I 9[27] 4'03
	Hyperion I 3[1]
	Hyperion II 18[10] 4'13 Ann Murray

← *Mahomets Gesang* D549   *Trost im Liede* D360 →

EIN JUGENDLICHER MAIENSCHWUNG *see* EIN JUGENDLICHER MAIENSCHWUNG D61

JULIUS AN THEONE   Julius to Theone
(MATTHISSON) **D419** [H255]
G minor   30 April 1816

(94 bars)

Nimmer, nimmer darf ich dir gestehen,
  Was beim ersten Drucke deiner Hand,
  Süsse Zauberin, mein Herz empfand!
Meiner Einsamkeit verborg'nes Flehen,
Meine Seufzer wird der Sturm verwehen,
Meine Tränen werden ungesehen
  Deinem Bilde rinnen, bis die Gruft
  Mich in ihr verschwieg'nes Dunkel ruft.

Ach! du schautest mir so unbefangen,
  So voll Engelunschuld ins Gesicht,
  Wähntest den Triumph der Schönheit nicht!
O Theone! sahst du nicht den bangen
Blick der Liebe an deinen Blicken hangen?
Schimmerte die Röte meiner Wangen
  Dir nicht Ahnung der verlornen Ruh'
  Meines hoffnungslosen Herzens zu?

Never, never can I confess to you
  What my heart felt, sweet enchantress,
  When I first pressed your hand.
My sighs, the hidden entreaties of my loneliness,
Will be blown away by the storm;
My tears will flow unseen
  For the image of you, until the grave
  Calls me to its secret darkness.

Ah! You gazed into my face so candidly,
  So full of angelic innocence,
  Not suspecting the triumph of your beauty.
O Theone! Did you not see the anxious
Loving glance hanging on your glances?
Did not my flushed cheeks give
  A hint of the lost peace
  Of my hopeless heart?

Dass uns Meere doch geschieden hätten	Would that oceans had separated us
Nach dem ersten leisen Druck der Hand!	After that first soft touch of hands!
Schaudernd wank' ich nun am Rand	Shuddering, I now totter on the brink
Eines Abgrunds, wo auf Dornenbetten,	Of an abyss where, on beds of thorns
Tränenlos, mit diamantnen Ketten,	With diamond chains and without tears,
Die Verzweiflung lauscht! Mich zu retten,[1]	Despair lies in wait. To save me,
Holde Feindin meines Friedens, beut	Fair enemy of my inner peace,
Mir die Schale der Vergessenheit!	Hand me the cup of forgetfulness!

FRIEDRICH VON MATTHISSON (1761–1831); poem written in 1779

This is the twenty-fifth of Schubert's twenty-nine Matthisson solo settings (1812–17). See the poet's biography for a chronological list of all the Matthisson settings.

Occasionally in his songs Schubert betrays his ambitions as an operatic composer and writes something that is more aria than lied. An infallible test as to whether this is the case is how the accompanist feels: 'Am I making a difference; am I really a part of the proceedings; or am I simply supporting a vocal line?' In a *real* song the piano part takes on a life of its own from the very first note, intertwining with the voice in equal partnership. In an aria there is a definite feeling that the pianist is standing in for something grander but less personal, and the relationship between voice and accompanist takes place over the chasm of the orchestral pit.

There is something of this divide between singer and pianist in *Julius an Theone*. Even the title suggests an operatic drama – Shakespeare with a touch of the German (*Julius und Julia* perhaps). The poem is taken from a novel or 'an unfinished romance', as Matthisson puts it (commentary to *Gedichte*, 1811), and from the opening chords it is clear that Schubert is treating the poem in the grand manner as a bleeding chunk from an imaginary larger work. The words are extravagant and, unlike the majority of Matthisson's poetry, seem to discourage more intimate treatment. The introduction veritably propels Julius onto the stage as if he is escaping from a previous scene. In the best tradition of an aria excerpt the music begins midstream; the opening four bars are curtain raisers in the *Sturm und Drang* manner, setting up the arrival of the tonic key and entry of the voice. This is all exciting and passionate but somehow rather ordinary. The accompaniment throbs orchestrally, and the vocal line has a broad-brushed sweep that sets it apart from the finer nuances of the lieder tradition. Similarly, the soaring long lines of Tamino's 'Dies Bildnis ist bezaubernd schön' from Mozart's *Die Zauberflöte* K620 have a quite different appeal from the close-up refinements of the same composer's song *Abendempfindung* K523. Schubert's touching diary entry in praise of Mozart ('O Mozart, immortal Mozart, how many, oh how endlessly many comforting perceptions of a brighter and better life have you brought to our souls?' – see LETTERS AND DIARIES No. 1), penned in 1816, makes it clear that the earlier composer's work in the theatre was much in Schubert's mind at the time.

The first one and a half strophes of the poem are set in the operatic manner. At b. 15 the second strophe begins comfortably in B flat (the relative major of the opening G minor) but from 'Wähntest den Triumph der Schönheit nicht' (b. 43) the music moves into a type of accompanied recitative rich in passionate chromaticism; some of the key shifts (at the two exclamations of 'O Theone' for example) are astonishing (bb. 47–9). Here the music moves away from the mode of the set piece into something much more individual. The opening of the third strophe returns to aria, but the composer changes tack again for the last two lines. As if somewhat alarmed by the theatrical excesses of the piece so far, the time signature changes to ¾ at b. 81,

---

[1] Matthison (*Gedichte*, 1811) writes 'Ha! mich zu retten'.

and at 'Holde Feindin meines Friedens' we have music of immense constraint and modesty (marked *Mässig*, the vocal line largely doubled by the piano). Perhaps Schubert is attempting to write music that has already tasted the effects of the 'cup of forgetfulness' – an almost suicidal classical reference Matthisson borrowed, surely, from Hölty whose poem *Die Schale der Vergessenheit* became a seldom performed Brahms song (Op. 46 no. 3, 1868). The sombre postlude, drained of all passion, sinks into oblivion before our ears with its drooping ending in thirds and sixths. The severe classical poise of this final section could not be more of a contrast to the opening bars. Although it has a beauty of its own we ask ourselves whether it is a successful conclusion to a song-aria that has promised us more of a blistering peroration. *Julius an Theone* belongs to the same experimental class as the poet's *Klage* D415. In allowing the words to dictate the form, the composer is thinking only of his delight in following the poet wherever he may lead, to the possible detriment of its overall musical shape.

Autograph:	Missing or lost
First edition:	Published as part of the AGA in 1895 (P635)
Subsequent editions:	Not in Peters; AGA XX 215: Vol. 4/91; NSA IV: Vol. 10/150
Discography and timing:	Fischer-Dieskau I 7[5] 3'28
	Hyperion I 23[12]
	Hyperion II 14[6] 3'31 Christoph Prégardien

⟵ *Stimme der Liebe* D418   *Minnelied* D429 ⟶

Die JUNGE NONNE   The young nun
(CRAIGHER) OP. 43 NO. 1, **D828** [H556]
F minor   1824/early 1825

(94 bars)

Wie braust durch die Wipfel der heulende Sturm!	How the raging storm roars through the treetops!
Es klirren die Balken, es zittert das Haus!	The rafters rattle, the house shudders!
Es rollet der Donner, es leuchtet der Blitz! —	The thunder rolls, the lightning flashes,
Und finster die Nacht, wie das Grab! — — —	And the night is as dark as the grave.
Immerhin, immerhin!	So be it!
So tobt' es auch jüngst noch in mir!	Not long ago a storm still raged in me.
Es brauste das Leben, wie jetzo der Sturm!	My life roared like the storm now,
Es bebten die Glieder, wie jetzo das Haus!	My limbs trembled like the house now,
Es flammte die Liebe, wie jetzo der Blitz! —	Love flashed like the lightning now,
Und finster die Brust, wie das Grab! —	And my heart was as dark as the grave.
Nun tobe, du wilder, gewalt'ger Sturm!	Now rage, wild, mighty storm;
Im Herzen ist Friede, im Herzen ist Ruh! —	In my heart is peace, in my heart is calm.

Des Bräutigams harret die liebende Braut,	The loving bride awaits the bridegroom,
Gereinigt in prüfender Glut —	Purified in the testing flames,
Der ewigen Liebe getraut. —	Betrothed to eternal love.
Ich harre, mein Heiland, mit sehnendem Blick;	I wait, my Saviour, with longing gaze!
Komm, himmlischer Bräutigam! hole die Braut!	Come, heavenly bridegroom, take your bride.
Erlöse die Seele von irdischer Haft! —	Free the soul from earthly bonds.
Horch! friedlich ertönet das Glöcklein vom Turm;	Listen, the bell sounds peacefully from the tower!
Es lockt mich das süsse Getön	Its sweet pealing invites me
Allmächtig zu ewigen Höh'n.	All-powerfully to eternal heights.
'Alleluia!'	'Alleluia!'

JACOB NICOLAUS CRAIGHER DE JACHELUTTA (1797–1855); poem written in 1823

This is the first of Schubert's three Craigher solo settings (1825). See the poet's biography for a chronological list of all the Craigher settings.

'After lunch Schubert came and brought a new song, *Die junge Nonne*; later Vogl came, and I sang it to him; it is splendidly composed.' Thus wrote the soprano Sophie Müller in her diary on 3 March 1825, and it is because of this that we are able to ascribe the song, with some certainty, to the early spring of 1825; in any case it is highly likely that *Die junge Nonne* was written in the same period as the other Craigher settings, *Der blinde Knabe* D833 and *Totengräbers Heimwehe* D842. This was a year of mighty songs like Pyrker's *Die Allmacht* D852 and Schulze's *Auf der Bruck* D853, that period between the composition of the two great Müller cycles when Schubertiads were frequent and all the newly composed lieder were 'events' – the works of a mature master at ease with his genius with even the fear and tension Schubert suffered because of his illness seeming to be in a state of remission. After the crucial experience of writing *Die schöne Müllerin* D795, the composer no longer appeared to need 'heavenly length' in order to make his dramatic point. Sophie Müller was right: 'Splendidly composed' the song most certainly is. Indeed, it has such a symphonic feel (German musicologists term such a song a 'lyrische Szene') that Liszt orchestrated it and Schubert's brother Ferdinand arranged it, after his brother's death, for large orchestra and female chorus. The slightly uncomfortable thought of this commercial exploitation of a great piano-accompanied lied brings to mind the Nuns' Chorus from Ralph Benatzky's operetta *Casanova*. Schubert's own *Ave Maria* (a setting of Scott's words) was soon to suffer a similar fate. Long before Rogers and Hammerstein's 'Climb ev'ry mountain', staging music in the cloister was imperilled by the threat of kitsch.

The figure of the nun herself was possibly loosely modelled by Craigher on the legend of St Agnes Eve when young women, after following a certain ritual, are supposedly able to experience a vision of their future husbands. In *The Eve of St Agnes* by Keats (1820) the girl, Madeline, is not a nun, and her elopement with her lover has no religious motives; in Tennyson's *St. Agnes' Eve* (1833) the character has acquired the veil, but this was some years after Craigher's poem. There is no evidence that Schubert was schooled by Craigher into following a scenario in musical terms that included the actual arrival of Christ, followed by the death of the nun as she is assumed into heaven in the arms of the Heavenly Bridegroom. It seems more likely that the composer simply took these words on their own terms (see Hirsch for a different view). The title, after all, seems simply to suggest a novice discarding earthly passions as she finds her true vocation. Schubert had grown out of supernatural balladry by this stage of his career although, in the rumble of the tremolando of the accompaniment and supporting octave triplets, the music recalls *Kolmas Klage* D217 from a decade earlier; this too was music written for a larger-than-life heroine facing stormy weather.

The key of F minor is established with the broadest of brushes although the dynamic does not rise above *piano* for thirty-six bars. Howling wind and ringing bell (possibly the passing bell if we are to believe the young nun is dying) are both introduced by a motif that is heard again and again in various guises (including the vocal line, itself a variant of this theme). The left hand beneath the rustlings of the right does its storm work, and then crosses over (a most eloquent gesture in this context) to sound the angelus in dotted crotchets (bb. 2, 4 and 6). It is as if we are seeing, and hearing, both the diabolical and the divine in the human condition – a Jekyll and Hyde juxtaposition where both roles are played side by side by the pianist. The tension rises and the screw is mercilessly turned by a semitone rise to the key of F sharp minor (b. 16). It is here, as Capell so aptly puts it, that 'every listener is aware that some powerful spirit is at work'. G sharp in the bass (under the first 'Und finster die Nacht', b. 22) pushes pitch and excitement higher (a D in the vocal line) but the voice now descends by semitones (D flat – b. 24 – and then C, b. 27) from where (on the dominant of the home key) the hollow incantation of 'wie das Grab' makes its eerie effect as it returns to F minor (b. 28). To be faithful to Schubert's markings, all of this drama has to be encompassed within a hushed dynamic range.

At the third verse ('Nun tobe, du wilder, gewalt'ger Sturm', b. 52) the music brightens into F major, and the change of key is as if a cloud has cleared in the nun's understanding rather than in nature, for the storm continues to rage outside. A miracle has taken place and her prayer has been answered. She now has 'a recognition of the essential benignancy of the forces of the wild night' (Capell again, who is splendid on this song) and she carries us with her in the sweep of her conviction and new-found insight. Her fear of the storm, both nature's and life's, has been banished; instead we hear a type of visionary ecstasy that in lesser musical hands would have been maudlin but here we are transfixed by the transformation: the hypnotic rhythm of the music, both repetitive and ever changing, would make us follow her anywhere. The glorious descent in bb. 59–60 on the words 'Glut — / Der ewigen, ewigen Liebe' seems a direct quote, note for note, of Ganymede's cry 'Alliebender Vater' written seven years earlier (D544). The music in both songs is united by the imagery of an erotic and mystical unity with the godhead. A remarkable turning point in the music is the passage that is most difficult to sing at 'Horch! friedlich ertönet das Glöcklein vom Turm'. The high F on 'friedlich' is a brute for almost all singers (particularly in this pianissimo marking) but it gloriously instigates the song's coda. The effect of the final bell music throughout this passage is of the greatest imaginable Romantic grandeur and at the same time gently moving. The storm motif continues but it has forever lost its power to intimidate. What has started out as a force of potential danger and evil is now seen to be yet another facet of the workings of God's omniscient plan.

In a few minutes, and not even helped by a poem of the first rank, Schubert has conjured a scene of Shakespearean dimensions in which confrontation and struggle finally resolve into acceptance and reconciliation. The song's span and structure suggest the experiences of a lifetime rather than a single night, so powerfully does the music recreate the poetic symbolism of past passions in terms of the thunderstorm, and final peace of mind in the ringing of the morning angelus. Thus a poem of neo-Gothic extravagance has been transformed into a song about a real woman. No composer has ever surpassed Schubert's ability to bring warmth and life to what might so easily have remained, in other hands, a cardboard cut-out of *Sturm und Drang*.

It is worth noting that the publishing of this song in 1825 by the Viennese firm of Pennauer occasioned, on 27 July, a long and interesting letter to Schubert from one of the firm's senior employees – the emollient Franz Hüther. He admits that there have been some mistakes in the books of songs already issued – some twenty copies of Op. 43 were sold before these errors could be rectified. Whether or not all the misprints were found and corrected is impossible to say in the absence of Schubert's autograph. But it is possible that the typesetter found the composer's writing difficult to read. For this reason there has long been discussion as to whether the left-hand B sharps in bb. 16 and 39 are correct, or whether they should be B naturals (to conform to the answering vocal line at bb. 18 and 40). The NSA opts for leaving the piano and vocal lines differently inflected, arguing that the B natural is easier for performers to sing, and Schubert had taken the difference into account.

Autograph:	Missing or lost
First edition:	Published as Op. 43 no. 1 by A. Pennauer, Vienna in July 1825 (P83)
First known performance:	28 December 1826, *Abend-Unterhaltung* of the Gesellschaft der Musikfreunde at the Musikverein, Vienna. Soloist: Karoline Schindler (see Waidelich/Hilmar Dokumente I No. 431 for full concert programme)
Subsequent editions:	Peters: Vol. 1/201; AGA XX 469: Vol. 8/62; NSA IV: Vol. 2/178; Bärenreiter: Vol. 2/64
Bibliography:	Black 2003, p. 114
	Capell 1928, pp. 207–8
	Fischer-Dieskau 1977, pp. 205–6
	Hirsch 1993, pp. 117–25
	Newbould 1997, pp. 297–8
Arrangements:	Arr. Franz Liszt (1811–1886) for solo piano as no. 6 of *Lieder von Schubert* (1837–8) [*see* TRANSCRIPTIONS]
	Arr. Leopold Godowsky (1870–1938) for solo piano as *The Young Nun* (1927, 2nd revised edition 1937) [*see* TRANSCRIPTIONS]
Discography and timing:	Fischer-Dieskau —
	Hyperion I 15^{17}
	Hyperion II 29^{11} 4'50 Margaret Price

← *Der Einsame* D800   *Lied der Anne Lyle* D830 →

Drawing of Franz Schubert, *c.* 1827, formerly ascribed to Josef Teltscher.

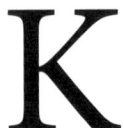

K

KAISER FERDINAND II *see* DUBIOUS, MISATTRIBUTED AND LOST
SONGS

KAISER MAXIMILIAN AUF DER	Emperor Maximilian on
MARTINSWAND	Martin's cliff

(H. VON COLLIN) D₂990A [NOT IN HYPERION]
B♭ major   December 1818?

(40 bars)

Hinauf! Hinauf!

In Sprung und Lauf!

Wo die Luft so leicht, wo die Sonne so klar,

Nur die Gemse springt, nur horstet der Aar;

Wo das Menschengewühl zu Füssen mir rollt;

Wo das Donnergebrüll tief unten grollt;

Das ist der Ort, wo die Majestät

Sich herrlich den Herrschertron erhöht!

Die steile Bahn

Hinan! hinan!

Dort pfeifet die Gemse! Ha, springe nur vor;

Nachsetzt der Jäger und fliegt empor.

[. . . 25 . . .]

Upwards! Upwards!

In vigorous bounds,

To where the air is so light and the sun so bright;

There only the chamois leaps and the eagle nests;

There humanity seethes at my feet,

And thunder rumbles deep below.

This is the place where his majesty

Magnificently sets up his victor's throne.

Up the steep path!

Upwards! Upwards!

There the chamois whistles, ah leap ahead,

For the huntsman is hot on the trail.

[. . . 25 . . .]

HEINRICH VON COLLIN (1772–1811); poem published in 1812

This is the second of Schubert's two Heinrich von Collin solo settings (1816 and 1818). See the poet's biography for a chronological list of all the Heinrich von Collin settings.

The story about the Emperor Maximilian is to be found in one of the first German travel books, Stephan Winands Pighius's *Hercules Prodicius, seu principis inventutis vita et peregrinatio* (1587). It was reworked by Heinrich Collin into a long ballad at a time when Austrian patriotism was at its height and Schubert's friend, the poet Franz von Schlechta, also published a verse-drama entitled *Max auf der Martinswand Abendteuer* in his *Dichtungen* of 1824 – the incident is thus described as an 'adventure'. The Martinswand is a steep cliff with a 100-metre drop in the Hechenbergmassiv, north-west of Innsbruck in the Tyrol. The story takes place in the 1490s (1493

Kaiser Maximilian auf der Martinswand by Adolf Ehrhardt. From *Deutsches Balladenbuch* (1861).

according to Heinrich Collin, 1490 according to the heading of Schubert's autograph). Carried away by the excitement of the hunt, the emperor decides to pursue his prey by taking a short cut up the sheer face of the Martinswand. He alights on a rock from which he can climb neither up nor down. He is trapped and has resigned himself to death (even the priest is summoned to give him the last blessing) when a young man appears who shows him a way of escape. The rescuer then disappears and Maximilian realizes that his life has been saved by an angel. Only the first verse of the ballad is printed above. There are twenty-six strophes in all, each essential to the ongoing narrative.

The song, or ballad, is a real puzzle for the Schubertian. It is one of the pieces of music that Schubert's brother Ferdinand (1794–1859) asked him to compose for various reasons, most of them connected with Ferdinand's work as a teacher or, later, trainer of teachers. On this occasion Ferdinand must have asked his brother for a simple melody that could be learned by rote in class so that the youngsters could sing in patriotic admiration of the Habsburg monarchy. There can be no other explanation for the banal effect of the music that was quickly sketched out in Schubert's hand and later published in Ferdinand's book for the training of musical school-children entitled *Der kleine Sänger* (published in 1853 in Vienna). For this publication Ferdinand was not above arranging some famous Schubert songs (like *Heidenröslein* D257) as part-songs and passing them off as his own music.

The other song in this mould was an almost stultifyingly simple setting of the equally patriotic Schiller poem *Der Graf von Habsburg* D990 (qv), included in the same book by Ferdinand as his own work. As the autographs of both songs exist in Schubert's hand it is scarcely tenable that this music really was by Ferdinand Schubert. Because both ballads are continuous narratives it is a case of 'all or nothing' in performance. This song in duple time takes up eight pages of the NSA and scarcely strays from the tonic, subdominant and dominant of B flat major. The accompaniment doubles the vocal line throughout. To give a complete performance of the ballad a singer or choir (or a combination of both) would have to sing those eight pages six times through, all at rather a stately, hymn-like tempo. The decision was taken for this reason not to include these two songs in the Hyperion Schubert Edition. It is unthinkable that Schubert himself would have considered such works suitable for public performance, much less commercial publication. That the work is included by Walther Dürr in the Bärenreiter reprint of the NSA seems to posit an opposite view. Nevertheless, not even the most avid Schubertian is holding his or her breath for a live performance.

Autograph:	Wienbibliothek im Rathaus, Vienna
First edition:	Published in an arrangement for two voices and piano as no. 26 of *Der kleine Sänger* by A. Schweigers Buchdruckerei, Vienna, an anthology of school music by Ferdinand Schubert, in 1853 (P393)
Dedicatee:	Dedicated to Andreas Grafen von Hohenwart by Ferdinand Schubert
Subsequent editions:	Not in Peters; Not in AGA; NSA IV: Vol. 14/174; Bärenreiter: Vol. 4/182
Bibliography:	Hoorickx 1977, p. 274
Discography and timing:	Fischer-Dieskau —
	Hyperion I —
	Hyperion II

JOHANN NEPOMUK RITTER VON KALCHBERG (1765–1827)

THE POETIC SOURCE
S1 *Selam, ein Almanach für Freunde des Mannigfaltigen auf das Jahr 1814*, von I. F. Castelli, Wien, Gedruckt und im Verlage bey Anton Strauss

THE SONG
15 October 1815   *Die Macht der Liebe* D308
[S1: p. 38: this poem is the second of three *Sonnette* in this periodical – the first by J. G. Meinert and the second and third by Kalchberg whose other sonnet is entitled *An die Ruhe*]

Kalchberg was perhaps the most important literary figure from the Steiermark region of Austria (he lived and worked in Graz) between the Enlightenment and the Romantic period. He was born in Pichl im Mürzthal on 15

J. N. von Kalchberg from *Deutsch-Österreichische Literaturgeschichte* (1914).

March 1765. His work was well known in Vienna through plays like *Wülfing von Stubenberg* and *Die Ritterempörung: Eine wahre Begebenheit der Vorzeit.* These were highly successful between 1790 and the turn of the century. Perhaps it was on account of the poet's local renown that the young composer tackled a sonnet by him (printed in the almanac *Selam*) despite its unsuitability for musical treatment. Schubert found the work of another Styrian poet, Johann Fellinger, in the same volume and set it on the same day (*Die Sternenwelten* D307). Twelve years later, during his visit to Graz as a guest of the Pachler family, he experienced Styrian cultural life at first hand and became acquainted with the poetry of Karl von Leitner (qv), Kalchberg's sometime protégé. Kalchberg died in Graz on 3 February 1827, only a few months before Schubert's visit to the Styrian capital. Despite the poet's conservative background and anti-revolutionary credentials he was a bitter and eloquent opponent of the Metternich regime. Schubert might have enjoyed meeting him. *See also* SELAM.

Der KAMPF   The struggle
(SCHILLER) **D594** [H392]
D minor   November 1817

(178 bars)

(1) Nein, länger werd' ich diesen Kampf nicht
        kämpfen,
      Den Riesenkampf der Pflicht.
      Kannst du des Herzens Flammentrieb nicht
        dämpfen,
      So fordre, Tugend, dieses Opfer nicht.[1]

No! I shall fight this battle no longer,

   This mighty battle of duty.
If you cannot cool the fierce ardour within
   my heart,
   Then, Virtue, do not demand this
     sacrifice.

(2) Geschworen hab ich's, ja, ich hab's
        geschworen,
      Mich selbst zu bändigen;
      Hier ist dein Kranz, er sei auf ewig mir
        verloren,
      Nimm ihn zurück und lass mich sündigen!

I took a vow, yes, I took a vow

   To master myself.
Here is your crown; let it be lost to me
   for ever.
Take it back and let me sin.

(3) Zerrissen sei, was wir bedungen haben;
        Sie liebt mich – deine Krone sei verscherzt!
      Glückselig wer, in Wonnetrunkenheit
        begraben,
      So leicht wie ich den tiefen Fall verschmerzt.

Let us tear up the bond we have made:
   She loves me – your crown shall be forfeit.
Happy he who, drunk with ecstasy,

   Takes his precipitous fall as lightly as I.

[1] Schiller's original reads 'So *fodre*...'

(4)   Sie sieht den Wurm an meiner Jugend   She sees the worm gnawing at the flower
          Blume nagen   of my youth;
       Und meinen Lenz entfloh'n;   She sees the spring of my life slip by;
       Bewundert still mein heldenmütiges   She silently admires my heroic renunciation,
          Entsagen,
       Und grossmutsvoll beschliesst sie   And generously decides on my reward.
          meinen Lohn.

(5)   Misstraue, schöne Seele, dieser Engelgüte!   Fair soul, distrust this angelic kindness!
          Dein Mitleid waffnet zum Verbrechen mich.   Your compassion armed me for my crime.
       Gibt's in des Lebens unermesslichem Gebiete,   Is there in life's vast realm
          Gibt's einen andern schönern Lohn –   A fairer reward than *you*?
             als dich?

(6)   Als das Verbrechen, das ich ewig fliehen   Than the crime which I sought to flee for
          wollte?   ever?
       Tyrannisches Geschick!   Tyrannical fate!
       Der einz'ge Lohn, der meine Tugend   The sole reward which was to crown my
          krönen sollte,   virtue
       Ist meiner Tugend letzter Augenblick!   Is my virtue's final moment.

FRIEDRICH VON SCHILLER (1759–1805); poem written 1784–5

This is the thirty-fifth of Schubert's forty-four Schiller solo settings (1811–24). See the poet's
biography for a chronological list of all the Schiller settings.

This is a real set piece, an aria in Schiller's grand manner that might have been conceived to
conclude an operatic act, written at a time when the friendship of Schubert and Mayrhofer was
at its height. We know that this work became one of the favourites of Johann Michael Vogl, the
retired opera baritone who had taken up the cause of Schubert's songs, but was it actually written
for him? The composer, often in collaboration with Mayrhofer, created classically inspired material for the mutually admired singer who had become a champion of Schubert's songs, but
Spaun's memoirs state that Vogl sang *Der Kampf* at his first musical meeting with Schubert
towards the end of 1817. There is nothing to say, however, that Schubert might not have written
it with Vogl in mind shortly *before* they met. It is doubtful whether Schubert needed help from
Mayrhofer when it came to selecting Schiller. He had set this poet from the earliest days, and
Der Kampf is to be found in this six-strophe version in the *Sämmtliche Werke* (Anton Doll,
Vienna 1810), the source of many of the composer's Schiller settings. On the other hand, the
subject of the poem – the mastering of the physical passions by willpower and heroic struggle
– was something of a Mayrhoferian theme.

    There is an earlier version of the poem in the almanac *Thalia* (1786) entitled *Freigeisterei der*
Leidenschaft. Als Laura vermählt war im Jahre 1782. Der Kampf seems to have been written some
years after the internal struggle it describes; by the time the text was published it was probably
Schiller's wish to obscure its slightly embarrassing biographical origins, if indeed the whole
episode was not 'erdichtet', or invented, as he claimed in some editions of the poem. Commentators tell us of the poem's connection with Charlotte von Kalb (1761–1843) who was unhappily
married to an older husband long before she met Schiller (the poet was certainly not at the
couple's wedding as the subtitle of *Freigeisterei der Leidenschaft* suggests). The Kalbs arrived in
Mannheim in 1784 and Charlotte found in Schiller a willing guide to the town and a fellow

Shakespeare enthusiast. The two were instantly mutually attracted and her loveless marriage might have made an affair inevitable. This was to reckon, however, without Schiller's highly developed sense of integrity, which made him even more attractive to Charlotte and who, as a result, might have yielded to him all the more readily (the paradox of this situation is well described in the poem). We shall never know what happened, if anything. This was not the first time that Schiller met someone whom he cast as his Laura. An older woman, Luise Fischer, had been the inspiration behind *Laura am Klavier* (set as D388, qv). Neither of these 'Lauras' is to be confused with Friedrich von Matthisson's imagined *inamorata* of the same name – the Laura of Petrarch being the inspiration for both poets, as well as for many other writers.

In *Der Kampf* it seems likely that the narrator of the poem will be permitted to consummate his relationship with his married friend. But in this victory is also defeat: in order to requite the passion she feels for him he will have to be party to an immoral act. We are expected to feel horror with him in his predicament, but we are merely reminded that, despite his talent for drama, Schiller's ivory tower of high moral ideals sometimes houses characters who are not convincingly flesh and blood. Nevertheless *Der Kampf*, nearly forty-five years after the poem was written, seems to have met some opposition from the Viennese censor's office: there was a long delay in the granting of permission to publish the song in 1829 after the composer's death. Perhaps they disliked the title on political grounds. It is scarcely possible today to hear in these words the lasciviousness that might have troubled those guardians of public morals. The complete poems of Schiller were openly available in Vienna, but the authorities clearly believed that words set to music were more likely to influence the public than if they remained within the pages of a book. This is incidentally the only Schubert song we know of that had a brush with the censor; there were possibly others, but the Palace of Justice in Vienna containing all the relevant records burnt down in 1927.

The Vogl songs were not usually written in the bass clef and they rarely explore the lower reaches of the stave in the way of *Der Kampf*. Perhaps Schubert had Johann Karl Graf Esterházy in mind as a possible singer. The composer was in contact with the Esterházy family early in 1818 with a view to taking up summer employment at Zseliz as music-master to the count's two daughters. Esterházy was an able amateur bass, and it is just possible that Schubert wrote *Der Kampf* the preceding November as a type of audition piece. For this theory, however, the choice of text is rather racy: Esterházy, a prospective employer whom the composer had not yet met, was a religious family man.

On the other hand *Der Kampf* would have been eminently suitable for Vogl or someone else with an operatic background. What makes it stiff and old-fashioned for modern audiences is exactly what would have appealed to the singing actor of Schubert's time. It has *attitude* – it strikes a musical pose as surely as Vogl was capable of striking one (he was accordingly ridiculed as a ham by some of the younger members of the Schubert circle). One can hear in this music many moods that are neatly parcelled and skilfully varied: military determination; soulful desperation; lyrical cantilena which bends to temptation; the contrast between recitative and a legato line. The narrator presents himself as a person moral enough to insist on rectitude, but human enough at least to *contemplate* adultery. All of this was grist to the mill for the singer-cum-tragedian in a century when performers were expected to be larger than life. *Der Kampf* is a cantata where soulful depression and joy are counterpointed as cleverly as high and low, fast and slow. And all calculated to bring the public to its feet at the end of the performance.

Verse 1: It is said that the second part of the first *Marche héroïque* in D major for piano duet D602 had originally served as the introduction to *Der Kampf* but the autographs of both works have dissappeared. The opening is marked 'Feurig' (fiery) and this movement is an early Schubertian essay in symphonic song-writing, which is to say an ongoing musical structure; the motifs of the accompaniment (here announced in the dotted rhythms of the opening, unison octaves that bounce up the stave, full of nervous energy) are developed in a symphonic way. This technique is noticeable in some of the greatest songs of the composer's maturity (*Suleika I* D720, *Der Zwerg* D771, *Die junge Nonne* D828); here the manner in which the vocal line is carried forward by the energy and development of the accompaniment is prophetic of things to come. After eight stormy bars in, and around, D minor, the voice's entry on an emphatic 'Nein' is a textbook beginning in operatic manner. We are so swept up with the clever musical development of the motif that we do not notice a lack of a real tune. The whole introductory passage is really a glorified recitative, as is much of the song. After 'dieses Opfer nicht' (bb. 22–3) there is a spacious fermata on a G major chord (b. 24). This sets up the ceremonial C major of the following section.

Verse 2: The second strophe is preceded by the sort of manly gestural tune that we associate with many of the Schiller settings, for this poet usually brought out Schubert's Beethovenian streak. This is music for the swearing of an oath, with solemn octave leaps, from high to low, in the vocal line. The chromatic rises beginning at 'Hier ist dein Kranz' (bb. 35–6) echo a similar passage (also accompanied in dotted rhythms) in *Gruppe aus dem Tartarus* D583, another Schiller setting, composed a few months earlier. The words there deal with faces in hell distorted with pain; the implication here is that the singer is undergoing self-inflicted torture. The vocal line continues to rise until, at the end of the strophe, we hear a marvellous shift from F major to F sharp major at 'und lass mich sündigen!' (bb. 40–43). There is something irresistibly sensual about this change of key, as if a monk had suddenly decided to abandon the contemplative life in favour of wine and women.

Verse 3: At the beginning of the third strophe the F sharp major chord is an obvious bridge to a change of key and time signature (B major, $\frac{3}{4}$). The dotted rhythm prompted by the first word 'Zerrissen', the violent image of tearing, is prophetic of a song from 1821, the final section of *Der Unglückliche* D713, where the words 'Zerrissen sind nun alle süssen Bande' inspire similar sequences of rhythmic shuddering derived from the pomposo manner of baroque oratorio. The piano writing continues in the octaves between the hands established from the beginning, a familiar Schubertian metaphor for courage and determination. As this falters, a tender six-bar interlude appears in sighing crotchets (as if an oboe solo, bb. 53–8): this begins with 'Sie liebt mich' – a phrase that stretches to a higher note (bb. 60–61) on its repetition, as if to emphasize the singer's disbelief. The composer's response to someone who claims to be 'drunk with ecstasy' is to provide a waltz, the lilt provided by the single bass note in the left hand, followed by the second and third beats phrased away in the right (from b. 65). This sweetness is ironic, the same type of disorientation illustrated by *Täuschung* in *Winterreise* D911/19. The words depicting a fall from grace – 'den tiefen Fall' bb. 78–81 – are set to a downward jump of a tenth, a chance for a singer with a bass voice to show off his bottom register. The final 'verschmerzt' in this section (bb. 92–3) descends to a low E, one of the few occasions in Schubert's lieder when this note is required. Here, and throughout the song, Schubert seems to be allowing for one of Vogl's main technical weaknesses: shortness of breath. The vocal line is replete with rests that are made to work towards the overall dramatic effect. The bottom E is the last of a four-note phrase with two full crotchet rests before it; anyone who has worked with singers will know that such a descent is preferably preceded by a full and generous preparatory breath. This passage ends in E major, paving the way for a change of key signature into that very tonality, and a change of tempo – Langsam.

Verse 4: A melody at last! Here Schubert is ingenious in writing a rather beautiful *bel canto* tune where no single phrase lasts longer than two bars before a quaver rest, when the singer is able to take another breath. As always there is a literary reason for the snaking elegance of the vocal line – in this case mention of the worm gnawing away at the flower of the singer's youth. This passage is a gift for a singer proud of his legato, full of *Affekt* and pathos, much aided by references to life's vanished springtime. This is the Italianate section of the piece, where gently gliding triplets in the accompaniment are subservient to the shaping of a moving melody. But even here, promise of a full-scale aria does not materialize. The triplets yield to recitative (from b. 103) at 'Bewundert still mein heldenmütiges Entsagen', although there is a sudden return to the tune at 'Misstraue, schöne Seele' (from b. 112). This is a clever elision, disguising as it does the beginning of the fifth strophe in a song where there have already been too many divisions between sections.

Verse 5: The mood of sensual ruefulness lasts for one line of the fifth strophe. Mention of military arms ('Dein Mitleid waffnet zum Verbrechen mich', from b. 116) brings those familiar dotted rhythms back – this time suggesting not so much strides and bounds as a knight on a galloping charger (cf. the accompaniment for *Normans Gesang* D846). This emphasizes the singer's opinion that winning a fair lady requires less of a faint heart and rather more daring. It is a nice touch that this jangling militarism disappears and melts into lyricism at the rhetorical question, 'is there in life a fairer reward than you?' This seems a backward glance at the poet's threatened virtue, and the word '<u>einen</u>' (in the phrase 'Gibt's einen andern schönern Lohn') is highlighted with diminished-seventh chords (at bb. 124 and 127) dallying on expressive minims emphasizing both the sweetness and the anguish of the dangerous primrose path.

Verse 6: The 'Recitative' marking above the phrase 'das ich ewig fliehen wollte' (from b. 131) seems superfluous. More or less the whole song has been an exercise in accompanied recitative, including the blustering, and rather hackneyed, section accompanied by rumbling bass octaves at 'Tyrannisches Geschick!' (bb. 133–7). Schubert is always at his weakest when the poet does not pull his weight with inspiring imagery. This is the type of derring-do passage that the composer revelled in when dashing off ballads like *Der Taucher* D77, but by 1817 he was growing out of such spear-shaking and becoming more of a musical Shakespeare. A double bar line, and a return to the D minor of the opening at b. 149, announces the song's coda, everything that Vogl might have relished in terms of an imposing finale. There are moments of subtlety: the jump of a fourth at '<u>Der einz'ge Lohn</u>' is mirrored, in canon style, in the piano's bass octaves (bb. 149–50). In this skirmish between lust and conscience, one stalking the other, the forte phrase is repeated quietly, the jump of a fourth this time initiated in the accompaniment (b. 159). We might have expected a noisy and decisive end to this scena, but apart from the two loud final chords, Schubert provides a get-out clause whereby the question is unresolved. Perhaps the tortured lover will do the right thing after all, and not yield to temptation. The vacillating minims of the postlude, marked pianissimo from b. 173, signify the internal struggle more eloquently than stormy tremolandi. One can imagine what a singing actor of the old school would have made of these bars in terms of facial expression and by-play. This song reminds us that a formidable operatic midwife was present at the birth of the lieder recital, a long time before a restrained stage etiquette had been formulated for the new medium taken up by Vogl's pioneering advocacy.

Autograph:	Missing or lost
First edition:	Published as Op. post. 110 by Josef Czerny, Vienna in January 1829 (P196)
First known performance:	6 December 1827, *Abend-Unterhaltung* of the Gesellschaft der Musikfreunde at the Musikverein, Vienna. Soloist: Schoberlechner (see Waidelich/Hilmar Dokumente I No. 542 for full concert programme)

Publication reviews:	*Abend-Zeitung* (Dresden), No. 26 (30 January 1821), n. pag. [Waidelich/Hilmar Dokumente I No. 69; Deutsch Doc. Biog. No. 199]
Subsequent editions:	Peters: Vol. 6/174; AGA XX 33: Vol. 5/171; NSA IV: Vol. 11/200
Bibliography:	Capell 1928, pp. 130–31
	Fischer-Dieskau 1977, pp. 98–9
Discography and timing:	Fischer-Dieskau II 1[18] 5'15
	Hyperion I 34[8]
	Hyperion II 20[1] 5'26 Neal Davies

← *Die Forelle* D550   *Thekla: eine Geisterstimme* D595 →

KANTATE ZUM GEBURTSTAG DES SÄNGERS JOHANN MICHAEL VOGL *see* CANTATE ZUM GEBURTSTAG DES SÄNGERS JOHANN MICHAEL VOGL D666

KANTATE ZUR FEIER DER GENESUNG DER IRENE KIESEWETTER *see* AL PAR DEL RUSCELLETTO D936

KEHR EIN BEI MIR *see* DU BIST DIE RUH D776

JOSEPH KENNER (1794–1868)

THE POETIC SOURCE
S1 *Selam. Ein Almanach für Freunde des Mannigfaltigen auf das Jahr 1815.* Von I. F. Castelli, Wien gedruckt und im Verlage bey Anton Strauss

There is a handwritten copy of *Der Liedler* in the possession of Frau Prof. Dr Hedwig Kenner in Vienna. This was used by the editorial team of the NSA to point out a considerable number of differences from the version of the poem set by Schubert, a comparison that was made before the discovery of the literary source.

Also printed in the *Balladen und Romanzen* section of this issue of *Selam* is Kenner's *Pant's Krönungsfest* (reprinted in Mayrhofer's *Beiträge zur Bildung für Jünglinge* in 1817) and *Das Brautbett* by Aloys Jeitteles, poet of Beethoven's *An die ferne Geliebte*.

THE SONGS
1815	*Ballade* D134
January? July? 1815	*Der Liedler* D209 Op. 38 [S1: pp. 42–6 in 'Balladen und Romanzen' section, signed only with the letter 'K']
24 June 1815	*Grablied* D218

Joseph Kenner was born in Vienna on 24 June 1794 but brought up in Linz. He never knew the identity of his father the shame of which may have rendered him touchy on matters of morality. Like Vogl and Schober he belonged to that select band of gifted boys from Lower Austria who were educated at Kremsmünster. In 1811 he came to study at the Imperial College in Vienna where he encountered the fourteen-year-old Schubert as a fellow student. The composer's three Kenner settings date from early 1815, the time at which Schubert

Silhouette of Kenner as a student in Kremsmünster.

was enduring a life of schoolteaching and Kenner was continuing his studies to be a lawyer. There was no doubt that Kenner's poetic and drawing talents were admired by his contemporaries as something very special. Together with Josef von Spaun, Anton Stadler and Josef Holzapfel, Kenner often heard Schubert play and sing on the composer's visits to his old school. Thirty years after Schubert's death, Kenner described to Ferdinand Luib those extraordinary times in the freezing cold piano room of the Imperial College:

It was there that his earliest compositions were first tried out and discussed and it was there that I was surprised by the dedication of the 'Liedler', which was presented to me. You cannot possibly imagine how humble I felt at this mark of distinction, at this dedication, and at the truly friendly way in which it was done, because you know neither my admiration for Schubert's artistic greatness nor my opinion of my own very humble merits. I did indeed know that Schubert craved merely for words which were fairly

manageable and that therefore I had no reason to be in the least conceited because mine were chosen.

Kenner was devoted to the memory of those golden days for the rest of his life even if, as the years wore on, poet and composer had less and less in common. Although a published poet (*Der Liedler* had appeared in Ignaz Castelli's Viennese-published almanac *Selam* in 1815) it seems that from early on Kenner had doubts about his ability to become a full-time artist. In 1816 he went back to Linz to take up an appointment in government service; he kept in touch with the Schubert circle through Spaun and others, though there are no surviving letters between composer and poet. Schubert probably saw Kenner on the occasions when he visited Linz. The publication of *Der Liedler* D209 as Op. 38 in 1825, and Schubert's honouring of the original dedication to him, must have given Kenner particular pleasure.

Moritz von Schwind's illustrations for the work from 1823 show that Kenner's own talents (certainly in combination with Schubert's music) were highly regarded in the

Josef Kenner by Max von Chézy.

composer's circle. On a visit to Linz in October 1823, Schwind wrote to Franz von Schober describing Kenner's delight in these pictures, mentioning that the erstwhile poet could scarcely tear himself away from them. However, there is something of the provincial puritan in Kenner's attitude in later years. His rather acerbic memoirs are particularly hard on Franz von Schober whom he blamed for encouraging the composer along pathways that led to his final illness. In writing to his brother Anton in 1858 he spoke of Schubert's soul as having been split in two, one half of which aspired heavenwards, and the other that was bathed in slime ('im Schlamme badete'). This seems rather an exaggerated denunciation of the morals of the composer who caught syphilis, according to legend, after straying only once, and with the greatest misfortune. It is a moot point whether this remark refers to other aspects of the composer's sexual behaviour.

In later years, Kenner had no interest in climbing onto the Schubert bandwagon. His was a disciplined and four-square personality, inclined to self-criticism and censoriousness regarding others. Unlike other writers who were certainly no more gifted than he (Franz von Schlechta comes to mind), he made relatively few appearances as a poet in almanacs or printed publications and in later life limited these to technical articles on historical and topographical issues connected with his native Linz, and his job as a civil servant. He spent his retirement (after 1857) in Bad Ischl and died there on 20 January 1868. Thanks to the careful copies made by the poet's sons, a good deal of the correspondence between members of the Upper Austrian circle surrounding Schubert has survived and remains in the archives of the Kenner family.

Bibliography: Dürhammer 1999, p. 160

KENNST DU DAS LAND? *see* MIGNON (KENNST DU DAS LAND?) D321

JOHANN FRIEDRICH KIND (1768–1843)

THE POETIC SOURCES
S1 *Gedichte von Friedrich Kind* (mit einem Kupfer), Leipzig bei Johann Friedrich Hartknoch, 1808

S2 *Friedrich Kind's Gedichte, Erster Theil, Neueste Auflage*, Wien 1816, bey B. Ph. Bauer. (This is the first of three booklets of this edition devoted to Kind's work, the second and third dated 1818 and 1820 respectively.)

It is possible that Schubert used either of these sources, but bearing in mind the composer's familiarity with the Viennese pocket editions of poets like Hölty, Jacobi and Schlegel, it is likely that he found this poem in S2.

THE SONG
April 1817   *Hänflings Liebeswerbung* D552 Op. 20 no. 3 [S1: pp. 132–3] [S2: pp. 120–21]

Friedrich Kind, son of one of the first German translators of Petrarch, was born in Leipzig on 4 March 1768. Always true to his Saxon roots, he spent most of his long and distinguished working life in Dresden where he began by practising law. He numbered Kotzebue and La

Fontaine among his models and was one of the first dramatists to write a play about a painter's life, *Van Dycks Landleben* (1816). He was enormously prolific and soon became important in the distinguished literary life of the city (*see* biographical note on his colleague Karl

J. F. Kind after a miniature by Moritz Michael Daffinger.

Kind to commission a second musical supplement for this same publication from the well-known but minimally talented Franz Schubert of Dresden (*see* COMPOSERS). It no doubt appealed to his sense of humour to have *two* musical supplements folded-in to this almanac, the first composed by 'Franz Schubert aus Wien', the second by 'Franz Schubert aus Dresden'. Carl Maria von Weber was Music Director of the Dresden opera at the time, and Kind provided him with the libretto for his opera *Der Freischütz*. This alone was sufficient to make Kind a famous man in the eyes of Schubert's contemporaries; his *Gedichte* were accorded a three-volume edition by Bauer of Vienna in 1816. It is a pity that the single poem set by Schubert was unrepresentative of Kind's scope and abilities. Schubert's German song-composing rival, Conradin Kreutzer, who spent many years in Vienna, also made a successful opera from a Kind play (*Das Nachtlager von Granada*) in 1834. Kind's career was a success story of a very German kind – he scarcely ventured outside Dresden but exerted a nationwide influence. The poet died in that city on 25 June 1843, a short time before Robert Schumann moved there.

Winkler who wrote under the pseudonym Theodor Hell). Kind wrote poems and plays and eventually became editor of various publications and newspapers including the almanac, W. G. Becker's *Taschenbuch zum geselligen Vergnügen*, that published Schubert's *Widerschein* D639 as a supplement in the 1821 issue. It was mischievous and quirkily imaginative of

KLÄRCHENS LIED *see* Die LIEBE D210

KLAGE (An den Mond)   Lament (to the moon)
(HÖLTY) **D436** [H262]

The song exists in two versions, the first of which is discussed below:
(1) 12 May 1816; (2) November 1816?

(1)   F major

Dein Sil - ber schien durch Ei - chen-grün, das Küh - lung gab, auf mich her-ab,

(29 bars)

(2)   'Mässig'   F major – D minor   §   [29 bars]

Dein Silber schien	Your silver
Durch Eichengrün,	Shone down on me
Das Kühlung gab,	Through the green oaks
Auf mich herab,	That gave cool shade,
O Mond, und lachte Ruh	O moon, and, smiling, shed peace
Mir frohem Knaben zu.	On me, a happy youth.
Wenn jetzt dein Licht	When now your light
Durch's Fenster bricht,	Breaks through the window,
Lacht's keine Ruh	No peace smiles on me,
Mir Jüngling zu,[1]	Now a young man;
Sieht's meine Wange blass,	It sees my cheeks pale,
Mein Auge tränennass.	My eyes moist with tears.
Bald, lieber Freund,	Soon, dear friend,
Ach bald bescheint	Soon your silver light
Dein Silberschein	Will shine
Den Leichenstein,	On the tombstone
Der meine Asche birgt,	That hides my ashes,
Des Jünglings Asche birgt!	The young man's ashes.

LUDWIG HÖLTY (1748–1776); poem written 15 February 1773

This is the twelfth of Schubert's twenty-three Hölty solo settings (1813–16). See the poet's biography for a chronological list of all the Hölty settings.

Apart from the celebrated *Seligkeit* D433 and the justly famous *An den Mond* D193 by the same poet, this is the gem of the Hölty settings, although relatively seldom performed. It was named simply *Klage* by Schubert, but later publishers added three qualifying words – An den Mond – to differentiate it from other songs in the canon entitled *Klage*. The poem has a remarkable density of expression; the first verse refers to the past, the second to the present and the third to the tragedy of the future, as if the poet (if Hölty has cast himself as the narrator) knows he does not have long to live. In remarkably few words we read the entire emotional history of a young man who was happy in his youth, but now, chastened by experience, is no longer so; the inevitable end is his death. The one constant factor is the moon who has been his companion through all these phases of his story. Wilhem Müller's lines 'Es zieht ein Mondenschatten / Als mein Gefährte mit' come to mind from the first song of *Winterreise* D911/1, and indeed this *Klage* is a type of *Winterreise* reduced to miniature proportions.

The tempo marking is 'Mässig' and the key is F major; the lilting vocal line is harmonized quite simply, the whole thing as ethereal as a dancing moonbeam. The first verse, a lovely inspiration indeed, leads to a piano interlude of haunting tenderness (bb. 8–12). The vocal line is the same for the second verse, but a song of innocence has yielded to a song of experience and the tune seems partially reharmonized with glinting chromaticisms and thereby rendered sadder and more complicated. Second-guessing Schubert in strophic mood, we await expectantly a similarly modified repeat of the piano interlude. But no. We have finished with the major key

---

[1] In the second version of the song this is changed by Schubert to 'Mir *Knaben* zu'.

and all nostalgic reminiscences, and we plunge suddenly into D minor (from b. 20) and the dark unknown of future oblivion. Once again *Winterreise* comes to mind, for this is the key of the cycle's first song *Gute Nacht*. 'The sudden shift to D minor, the repeated staccato As in the pianist's right hand, and we are brought to the edge of the infinite', writes John Reed. Susan Youens in her book *Retracing a Winter's Journey* (1991) sees something even more significant in those repeated semi-staccato notes. She argues persuasively that 'the grouping of four non-legato repeated pitches or chords' is a motivic device for the idea of journeying; this figure makes its appearance in the opening bar of the great song cycle, and thereafter (particularly in that other travelling song *Der Wegweiser* D911/20) plays a subtle but crucial part in providing something of a subliminal unifying force in the work. If this is so, the device is heralded eleven years earlier in the last verse of this *Klage*, itself a remarkably aphoristic song about journeys and experience. Despite its brevity this song shows us the astonishing future potential of our composer when *Winterreise* was only a moongleam in his eye.

Later on in 1816 Schubert was to use this musical idea of repeated notes in another plaint. This time it is the vocal line where the notes are held, as if spellbound, on the same pitch: this is the repeated phrase 'Nachtigall, ach!' in bb. 30–33 of the Claudius setting *An die Nachtigall* D497.

The NSA prints a second version of the song (probably from November 1816) as it is included in the Therese Grob album. There are some interesting variants of phrasing and articulation, and the tiny postlude is somewhat contracted. There is another variant of the first version in NSA Volume 10 p. 270; this appeared in the Nachlass in 1850 as the first edition of this setting, and it was thereafter adopted by Edition Peters. There are not many differences in the main body of the song, but the rather tasteless introduction is sufficient evidence of an editorial hand (Diabelli's probably) that understood little of Schubert's style.

Paul Reid points out that Beethoven's little-known, yet very significant setting of Hölty's poem was written when the composer was nineteen, exactly Schubert's age when he tackled the same text.

Autograph:	Missing or lost (first version)
	In private possession in Switzerland (second version; Therese Grob songbook)
Publication:	Published as Book 48 no. 3 of the *Nachlass* by Diabelli, Vienna in 1850 (P382; first version)
	Published as part of the NSA in 2002 (P838; second version)
Subsequent editions:	Peters: Vol. 6/62; AGA XX 216: Vol. 4/95; NSA IV: Vol. 10/166, 168 & 270
Bibliography:	Gruber 1999, p. 317
	Reid 2003, pp. 192–5
Further settings:	Johann Friedrich Reichardt (1752–1814) *An den Mond* (1789)
	Johann Rudolf Zumsteeg (1760–1802) *An den Mond* (1803)
	Ludwig van Beethoven (1770–1827) *Klage* WoO 113 (1790, two versions)
	Jan Bedřich Kittl (1806–1868) *Klage* Op. 16 no. 2 (1844)
Discography and timing:	Fischer-Dieskau I 7[6] 1'33
	Hyperion I 15[3]
	Hyperion II 14[14] 1'45 Margaret Price

← *Erntelied* D434   *Frühlingslied* D398 →

KLAGE   Lament
(Matthisson) **D415** [H253]
C major   April 1816

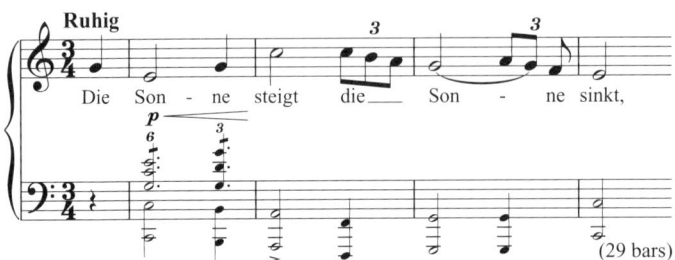

(29 bars)

Die Sonne steigt, die Sonne sinkt,	The sun rises, the sun sinks,
Des Mondes Wechselscheibe blinkt,	The moon's ever-changing disc gleams,
Des Aethers Blau durchwebt mit Glanz	The blue aether is shot through
Der Sterne goldner Reihentanz;	With the brilliant, golden dance of the stars.
Doch es durchströmt der Sonne Licht,	But the sun's light,
Des Mondes lächelndes Gesicht,	The moon's smiling countenance,
Der Sterne Reigen, still und hehr,	The dance of the stars, silent and sublime,
Mit Hochgefühl dies Herz nicht mehr!	No longer flood this heart with elation.
Die Wiese blüht, der Büsche Grün	The meadow blooms, the green bushes
Ertönt von Frühlingsmelodien,	Echo with spring melodies;
Es wallt der Bach im Abendstrahl	In the evening sunlight the brook
Hinab ins hainumkränzte Tal:	Gushes down into the wooded valley.
Doch es erhebt der Haine Lied,	But the song of the woods,
Die Au, die tausendfarbig blüht,	The meadow, blooming with a thousand colours,
Der Erlenbach im Abendlicht	The alders by the brook in the twilight,
Wie vormals meine Seele nicht!	Do not uplift my soul as they once did.
[…]	[…]

FRIEDRICH VON MATTHISSON (1761–1831); poem written in 1778

This is the twenty-third of Schubert's twenty-nine Matthisson solo settings (1812–17). See the poet's biography for a chronological list of all the Matthisson settings.

Throbbing triplets are an important feature of the accompaniment – a rhythmic impulse often heard in Schubert's music when the beauties of nature are ordered by God's hand. On top of this rolling carpet of effulgent sound (with the bass line in sonorous octaves) unfolds a broadly arched vocal line, adding a touch of the sublimity suggested by the words. But the point of the song is that because the singer is without his beloved (the title of the originally much longer poem is *Liebespein* – the pain of love), he is no longer moved by this heavenly harmony. Accordingly, Schubert follows the first half of the song with a new section (beginning 'Doch es durchströmt der Sonne Licht' from b.18) marked 'Ziemlich geschwind' and in the relative minor. Here is the real 'Klage' – the plaint of the title. The music, now bare and woebegone, has lost its motivation. The poet, who has described nature's beauties, tells us that in his present state of mind they no longer exist for him. The surging current of elated feeling has been set up at the beginning simply so that its absence can be felt at the heart of the song.

Schubert's attempt to mirror the thrust of the poet is praiseworthy, but it is also a salutary demonstration that music can far more readily reflect things as they *are* rather than as they are not. We are both brought down to earth and earthed: common time replaces the swing of triple metre and the music loses its magic and frisson. In the autograph the three-stave score is reduced to two, and the song is continued in a kind of shorthand – it is printed thus in the NSA. For the AGA Mandyczewski simply transcribed this passage and completed the song (this realization is also printed in the NSA).

The autograph is crossed out, which almost certainly means that the composer felt that it was an experiment that had failed.

Autograph:	In private possession
First edition:	Published as part of the AGA in 1895 (P633)
Subsequent editions:	Not in Peters; AGA XX 213: Vol. 4/88; NSA IV: Vol. 10/266
Discography and timing:	Fischer-Dieskau I 7[4] 2'40
	Hyperion I 23[11]
	Hyperion II 14[4] 2'33 Christoph Prégardien

← *Geist der Liebe* D414   *Stimme der Liebe* D418 →

KLAGE (NIMMER LÄNGER TRAG' ICH) *see* DUBIOUS, MISATTRIBUTED AND LOST SONGS

KLAGE   Lament
(ANONYMOUS) **D371** [H216]

(1) (Sketch) Date unknown; (2) January 1816

(1)   No tempo indication   B minor   ¢   [19 bars]

(2)   B minor

Trauer umfliesst mein Leben,	Sorrow floods my life,
Hoffnungslos mein Streben,	My endeavours are in vain,
Stets in Glut und Beben	In unremitting ardour and trembling
Schleicht mir hin das Leben;	My life slips by;
O nimmer trag' ich's länger!	I can endure it no longer!

Leiden und Schmerzen wühlen	Grief and suffering gnaw away
Mir in den Gefühlen,	At my feelings;
Keine Lüfte kühlen	No breezes cool
Banger Ahndung Schwülen;	My feverish, anxious foreboding.
O nimmer trag' ich's länger!	I can endure it no longer!
Nur ferner Tod kann heilen	Only distant death can cure
Solcher Schmerzen Weilen;	The presence of such suffering;
Wo sich die Pforten teilen,	When the gates open
Werd' ich wieder heilen;	I shall be cured;
O nimmer trag' ich's länger!	I can endure it no longer!

ANONYMOUS/UNKNOWN

This is the seventh of Schubert's nineteen solo settings of an anonymous poet. See Anonymous/
Unknown for a chronological list of all the songs for which the poets are unknown.

This neglected and relatively unknown setting has a number of the hallmarks of more famous songs; it starts with the dactylic rhythm so dear to the composer (as in *Der Tod und das Mädchen* D531), and has a depth of feeling quite out of proportion with its modest strophic form. Of the twenty-one songs that Schubert wrote in the key of B minor, there is scarcely one that it is not of significance; *Zuleika* and *Mignon*, the miller boy and the winter traveller are all made to express some of their strongest feelings in the tonality later chosen for the 'Unfinished' Symphony D759. This song is an early example of the composer's special affinity for this key.

   Although there is something hymn-like and simple, almost sedate, about this *Klage* on the printed page, its use of chromatic harmony and syncopation depicts considerable inner anguish. The rhythm of the phrase 'Schleicht mir hin das Leben', bb. 12–16, is displaced and goes askew as semibreves slide down the stave, a convincing analogue for life running out of the sufferer's control. John Reed has suggested there is some autobiographical link with the composer's unsuccessful relationship with Therese Grob. The song is closely related to *Der Leidende* D432 which was part of the Therese Grob Songbook and also dates from 1816; that song too is in B minor and paints similarly desperate emotions. *Klage* has something of an archaic atmosphere, a deliberate evocation of an earlier musical style, which is part of Schubert's harmonic vocabulary in some of his religious works such as *Vom Mitleiden Mariä* D682. The poems of both *Klage* and *Der Leidende* D432 were attributed by Schubert's contemporaries to Ludwig Hölty (1748–1786), but neither poem has been found in that poet's collected works. There was probably a handwritten anthology, a 'Liederbuch' belonging to the composer's friend Anton Stadler, which contained poems like this, sometimes incorrectly ascribed. The name 'Hölty' written on Schubert's autograph suggests he was simply following the attribution in this source.

Autograph	Wienbibliothek im Rathaus (sketch; first version)
	Österreichische Nationalbibliothek, Vienna (fair copy; second version)
Publication:	Published as part of the AGA in 1895 (P620; first version)
	Published as No. 21 of *Neueste Folge nachgelassener Lieder und Gesänge* by J. P. Gotthard, Vienna in 1872 (P447; second version)

Subsequent editions:	Not in Peters; AGA XX 185a & b: Vol. 4/4; NSA IV: Vol. 10/21 & 246
Discography and timing:	Fischer-Dieskau I 6¹³ 2'46
	Hyperion I 17³
	Hyperion II 12¹¹ 2'17 Lucia Popp

← *Am ersten Maimorgen* D344   *An die Natur* D372 →

KLAGE DER CERES   The lament of Ceres

(SCHILLER) **D323** [H202]
G major – B♭ major   November 1815/June 1816

(463 bars)

(1)   Ist der holde Lenz erschienen?
Hat die Erde sich verjüngt?
Die besonnten Hügel grünen,
Und des Eises Rinde springt.
Aus der Ströme blauem Spiegel
Lacht der unbewölkte Zeus,
Milder wehen Zephyrs Flügel,
Augen treibt das junge Reis.
In dem Hain erwachen Lieder,
Und die Oreade spricht:
Deine Blumen kehren wieder,
Deine Tochter kehret nicht.

(2)   Ach, wie lang' ist's, dass ich walle
Suchend durch der Erde Flur,
Titan, deiner Strahlen alle
Sandt' ich nach der teuren Spur,
Keiner hat mir noch verkündet
Von dem lieben Angesicht,
Und der Tag, der alles findet,
Die Verlorne fand er nicht.
Hast du, Zeus! sie mir entrissen,
Hat, von ihrem Reiz gerührt,
Zu des Orkus schwarzen Flüssen
Pluto sie hinabgeführt? ·

Has fair spring appeared?
Has the earth grown young again?
The sunny hills turn green,
The ice's crust cracks.
From the blue mirror of the rivers
Unclouded Zeus laughs,
The Zephyrs' wings beat more gently,
The young shoots push forth buds.
Song awakens in the grove,
And the Oread speaks:
Your flowers return
But your daughter does not.

Ah, how long have I been wandering,
Through the earth's meadows, searching,
Titan, I sent all your rays of light
To seek out my dear one;
No one has yet brought me word
Of her beloved countenance,
And day, that finds all things,
Has not found my lost daughter.
Have you, Zeus, snatched her from me,
Has Pluto, touched by her charms,
Carried her
Down to the black rivers of Orcus?

(3)   Wer wird nach dem düstern Strande   Who will convey the tidings of my grief
         Meines Grames Bote sein?   To the sombre shore?
         Ewig stösst der Kahn vom Lande,   The boat forever pulls away from land,
         Doch nur Schatten nimmt er ein.   But it takes only shades on board.
         Jedem sel'gen Aug' verschlossen   The fields of night remain closed
         Bleibt das nächtliche Gefild',   To the eyes of every immortal,
         Und so lang der Styx geflossen,   And so long as the Styx has flowed
         Trug er kein lebendig Bild.   It has borne no living creature.
         Nieder führen tausend Steige,   A thousand paths lead downwards,
         Keiner führt zum Tag zurück,   But none leads back to the light.
         Ihre Träne bringt kein Zeuge   No witness evokes the daughter's tears
         Vor der bangen Mutter Blick.   Before the eyes of the anxious mother.

(4)   Mütter, die aus Pyrrhas Stamme   Mothers, born mortal
         Sterbliche geboren sind,   Of Pyrrha's race,
         Dürfen durch des Grabes Flamme   May follow their beloved children
         Folgen dem geliebten Kind,   Through the flames of the grave.
         Nur was Jovis Haus bewohnet,   Only they that dwell in the house of Jove
         Nahet nicht dem dunkeln Strand,   May not approach the dark shore.
         Nur die Seligen verschonet,   Your stern hand, O Fates,
         Parzen, eure strenge Hand.   Spares only the immortals.
         Stürzt mich in die Nacht der Nächte   Plunge me from the golden halls of heaven
         Aus des Himmels goldnem Saal,   Into the night of nights!
         Ehret nicht der Göttin Rechte,   Do not respect the rights of the goddess;
         Ach! sie sind der Mutter Qual!   Alas, they are a mother's torment!

(5)   Wo sie mit dem finstern Gatten   Where she is joylessly enthroned
         Freudlos thronet, stieg ich hin,   With her gloomy spouse, I would descend,
         Und träte mit den leisen Schatten[1]   And with the soft shadows
         Leise vor die Herrscherin.   Tread softly before the queen.
         Ach, ihr Auge, feucht von Zähren,   Ah, here eyes, moist with tears,
         Sucht umsonst das goldne Licht,   Seek in vain the golden light;
         Irret nach entfernten Sphären,   They stray to far-off spheres,
         Auf die Mutter fällt es nicht.   But do not alight on her mother –
         Bis die Freude sie entdecket,   Until, to her joy, she discovers her,
         Bis sich Brust mit Brust vereint,   Until their bosoms are united,
         Und, zum Mitgefühl erwecket,   And even harsh Orcus,
         Selbst der rauhe Orkus weint.   Aroused to pity, weeps.

(6)   Eitler Wunsch! Verlorne Klagen!   Vain wish! Forlorn laments!
         Ruhig in dem gleichen Gleis   The trusty chariot of day
         Rollt des Tages sich'rer Wagen,   Rolls calmly on its even course;
         Ewig steht der Schluss des Zeus.   The decree of Zeus stands for ever.
         Weg von jenen Finsternissen   He has turned his august head
         Wandt' er sein beglücktes Haupt,   Away from those black realms.
         Einmal in die Nacht gerissen,   Snatched into the night,
         Bleibt sie ewig mir geraubt,   She remains forever lost to me,

[1] The 'Und' at the beginning of this line in Schubert's addition.

Bis des dunkeln Stromes Welle	Until the waves of the dark river
Von Aurorens Farben glüht,	Glow with the colours of the dawn,
Iris mitten durch die Hölle	And Iris draws her fair bow
Ihren schönen Bogen zieht.	Through the midst of hell.

(7) Ist mir nichts von ihr geblieben,	Is nothing of her left to me,
Nicht ein süss erinnernd Pfand,	No sweet pledge to remind me
Dass die Fernen sich noch lieben,	That, though far distant, we still love one another?
Keine Spur der teuren Hand?	No trace of her beloved hand?
Knüpfet sich kein Liebesknoten	Is there no bond of love
Zwischen Kind und Mutter an?	Between mother and child?
Zwischen Lebenden und Toten	Is there no alliance
Ist kein Bündnis aufgetan?	Between the living and the dead?
Nein! Nicht ganz ist sie entflohen,	No, she is not completely lost to me,
Wir sind nicht ganz getrennt!²	We are not completely separated!
Haben uns die ewig Hohen	For the eternal gods
Eine Sprache doch vergönnt!	Have granted us a language!

(8) Wenn des Frühlings Kinder sterben,	When the children of spring die,
Wenn von Nordes kaltem Hauch	When leaves and flowers fade
Blatt und Blumen sich entfärben,	At the north wind's cold breath,
Traurig steht der nackte Strauch,	And the bare bushes stand mournful,
Nehm ich mir das höchste Leben	I take the highest life
Aus Vertumnus' reichem Horn,	From Vertumnus's cornucopia,
Opfernd es dem Styx zu geben,	And sacrifice the seed's golden corn
Mir des Samens goldnes Korn.	To the Styx.
Trauernd senk' ich's in die Erde,	Lamenting, I plant it in the earth,
Leg' es an des Kindes Herz,	Laying it on the heart of my child,
Dass es eine Sprache werde	That it may become a language
Meiner Liebe, meinem Schmerz.	Of my love and my sorrow.

(9) Führt der gleiche Tanz der Horen	Then, when the unchanging dance of the hours
Freudig nun den Lenz zurück,	Brings back joyous spring,
Wird das Tote neu geboren	What was dead is born anew
Von der Sonne Lebensblick!	Under the sun's life-giving gaze!
Keime, die dem Auge starben	Seeds which the eye took for dead
In der Erde kaltem Schoss,	In the earth's cold womb,
In das heitre Reich der Farben	Struggle joyfully free
Ringen sie sich freudig los.	Into the bright realm of colours.
Wenn der Stamm zum Himmel eilt,³	As stems surge towards the sky,
Sucht die Wurzel scheu die Nacht,	Roots shyly seek the night,
Gleich in ihre Pflege teilt	The powers of the Styx and those of the aether
Sich des Styx, des Äthers Macht.	Are equally divided in their cultivation.

(10) Halb berühren sie der Toten,	They exist half in the regions of the dead
Halb der Lebenden Gebiet,	And half in those of the living –

---

² Schiller's original line reads 'Nein, wir sind nicht ganz getrennt!'. Schubert declines to repeat the word as Schiller does.
³ Schiller writes 'eilet', and two lines later, 'teilet'.

Ach! sie sind mir teure Boten,	Ah, to me they are dear messengers,
Süsse Stimmen vom Cozyt!	Sweet voices from Cocytus!
Hält er gleich sie selbst verschlossen	Though it holds her captive
In dem schauervollen Schlund,	In the gruesome abyss,
Aus des Frühlings jungen Sprossen	Her beloved mouth speaks to me
Redet mir der holde Mund,	Through spring's young shoots,
Dass auch fern vom goldnen Tage,	It tells me that, though far from the golden day,
Wo die Schatten traurig ziehn,	Where the shades wander mournfully,
Liebend noch der Busen schlage,	Her breast still beats lovingly,
Zärtlich noch die Herzen glühn.	And hearts still glow tenderly.

(11)	O! so lasst euch froh begrüssen,	O, let me greet you joyfully,
	Kinder der verjüngten Au,	Children of the reborn meadows,
	Euer Kelch soll überfliessen	Your cup shall overflow
	Von des Nektars reinstem Tau.	With the purest dew of nectar.
	Tauchen will ich euch in Strahlen,	I shall bathe you in sunbeams,
	Mit der Iris schönstem Licht	I shall paint your leaves
	Will ich eure Blätter malen,	With the rainbow's fairest light,
	Gleich Aurorens Angesicht.	Like Aurora's countenance.
	In des Lenzes heiterm Glanze	In the serene radiance of spring,
	Lese jede zarte Brust,	In the faded wreath of autumn,
	In des Herbstes welkem Kranze	Every tender heart may discern
	Meinen Schmerz und meine Lust.	My sorrow and my joy.

FRIEDRICH VON SCHILLER (1759–1805); poem written in June 1796

This is the twenty-first of Schubert's forty-four Schiller solo settings (1811–24). See the poet's biography for a chronological list of all the Schiller settings.

This poem first appeared in the *Musen-Almanach für das Jahr 1797*, a collaboration between Goethe, eminent contributor, and Schiller, editor and moving spirit. At the end of this small but highly influential volume were published the notorious *Xenien*, epigrammatic verses in which Goethe and Schiller attacked and parodied their enemies. *Klage der Ceres* was one of the non-Xenien successes of the collection, although Schiller wrote to his friend Christian Körner, who had complimented him on it, 'I was pleased to hear my poem gave you pleasure, but in comparison to Goethe in poetry, I am, and remain, a bungler.' The poem tells of the grief of Ceres – known to the Greeks as Demeter – whose daughter Proserpine (Persephone) has become the underworld consort of Pluto. Zeus is sufficiently moved by Ceres' grief, and worried by the earth's resultant sterility, to allow Proserpine to divide her life between the darkness and the light. Schiller does not actually spell out this final arbitration, preferring to suggest the workings of the god with the seasonal emergence of long-buried spring flowers. In this way the poem is related to Goethe's *Ganymed* (D544), where the will of Zeus is implemented by the intervention of a *deus ex machina*, suggested by the movement of wind and clouds.

Verse 1: The story is set just at that turning point of the year, when the eagerly awaited arrival to spring is in doubt, a favourite Schubertian period of joy mingled with apprehension. The opening music, a piano prelude in G major (bb. 1–7), is deceptively light-hearted and somewhat Haydnesque with just a few chromaticisms to show Schubert as a young composer of the modern generation. Classical subjects often inspired in the composer a deliberately old-

Pluto kidnaps Proserpine from *Der Mythos alter Dichter*, Vienna (1815).

fashioned response. It was possibly the charming, but rather conventional, interludes in the piano (between the recitatives depicting the rippling breezes of Zephyr at bb. 22, 25, 28 and 30) that prompted Fischer-Dieskau to describe the piece as 'a five-finger exercise'. The grim news of Proserpine's disappearance announced by the Oread turns the song in a tragic direction at the end of the first verse; in order for that change to be effective the composer has had to start the piece on a lighter note.

Verses 2–3: This section (from b. 43 with the marking 'Mässig langsam') begins as a conventional aria in B flat but soon roams around the keyboard in a crazed chromatic search for Proserpine. In a set-piece aria for a grieving mother Ceres even blames Zeus for the loss of her daughter. Legend has it that Ceres searched the entire world for nine days and nights without eating, drinking, bathing or changing her clothes. The controlled levity of the opening pages has disappeared.

Anyone who can address Zeus in such imperious terms is to be reckoned with, and the scope of the music proclaims a goddess, and a vocalist, of some substance. The vocal range of this cantata is problematic: too high for a mezzo soprano in passages that look heavenward, it also requires the voice to plunge from time to time into the depths of the underworld. The third verse (*alla breve* from b. 74) first settles into G minor and then ranges through every key imaginable (favouring G flat major) as Ceres contemplates the horror of her daughter's fate. The eventual return to G minor is achieved by means of tortured piano interludes of chromatic double thirds (from b. 129). At this point (on 9 November 1815) Schubert decided that he had had enough of Ceres for the time being, turning his attention instead to writing his Mass in B flat, D324.

Verses 4–5: As carefully noted on the autograph, work was resumed (on a G minor chord, b. 143) seven months later in June 1816, a period rich in songs. Schubert was also preoccupied at this time with another classical subject, the cantata *Prometheus* (tragically the music is lost to us). The recitative of the fourth verse (Ceres' reflections on a mother's love) is notable for the contrast of the depths of 'the night of nights' (bb. 157–8) with the height of 'the golden halls of heaven' (bb. 160–2). It is the fifth verse that perhaps has the most astonishing music in the piece: the words are driven by a relentless panting ostinato towards the climax of 'Bis die Freude sie entdecket' (bb. 196–9) and thereafter, as Orcus weeps, the completely dislocated juxtaposition of harmonies (swivelling between F major and A major) suggests a contortion of the facial muscles never before seen or heard (bb. 205–9), even in the tortured realms of Hades – a fine preparation for *Gruppe aus dem Tartarus* D583 that would be composed in 1817. In this passage marked 'Langsam, quasi Recit', compassion is squeezed from Pluto as blood from a stone.

Verse 6: The fight seems to go out of Ceres here. From b. 213 an aria in A minor with ravishing and touching changes of harmony shows a softer side of maternal grief. A recitative ushered in by a fanfare in B flat at b. 225 (incidentally the single most important key in the work and the tonality that subtly binds the ballad together) heralds a triplet-accompanied plaint, water music of the broadest grandeur (depicting that dark river the Styx), from b. 232. The extended chromatic ascent of the word 'Ewig' (bb. 230–31) is especially magisterial.

Verse 7: The theme of this verse is the reciprocity of love between mother and child. The tiny piano fragment (bb. 245–6) before the words 'Ist mir nichts von ihr geblieben' evokes with astonishing directness the empty nursery, a child's musical box no longer used, the primal communion between mother and infant daughter. One never ceases to be amazed by Schubert's genius at finding the most apt and simple musical analogues for feelings and situations of great complexity. But he has bought this moment of repose and beauty at considerable cost (something he also tends to do in the operas when overall dramatic tension can be sacrificed to extending the sybaritic enjoyment of the moment). Ceres' rhetorical questions, no fewer than four of them, steer the piece in a completely new direction; optimism replaces the despair of earlier pages and we are ill-prepared in musical terms for this sudden change.

Verses 8–9: This passage, in F minor, 'Ziemlich geschwind', from b. 269 with its fleeting staccato quavers in the accompaniment, is almost flippant; however reassured about her daughter Ceres may be. It is followed by a dance of the hours ('Tanz der Horen') in A flat (from b. 341) where there is something about the ⅜ metre that seems short-breathed and flighty for an Olympian who, only moments earlier, has been in the depths of despair. The listener is reminded of the competitive miller boys in *Am Feierabend* from *Die schöne Müllerin* D795/5. At the end of this passage the upwardly aspiring plant stems ('Wenn der Stamm zum Himmel eilt' bb. 374–7) and the night-seeking roots ('Sucht die Wurzel scheu die Nacht' bb. 380–86) are juxtaposed in vocally commanding terms, exploring first the upper, then the lower, regions of the stave – and of the earth itself.

Illustration for *Klage der Ceres* from Schiller's *Jubiläums-Ausgabe* (1859).

Verses 10–11: A recitative in A major (from b. 390) leads us back via a circuitous route, and for only a short while, to the G major (from b. 415) of the opening. The music regains its classical poise (including mordents in the piano part under 'Herzen glühn'). It is as if Ceres has awakened from a nightmare and all memories of maternal hysteria are banished. The final verse, an aria in B flat beginning at b. 420 with the marking 'Etwas bewegt', finds the goddess once more smilingly fit to frequent Olympus. This is graceful and grateful music. In vocal terms it still commands the grand style, but the fact is that at this stage of his life Schubert finds it easier to retain our attention in his ballads with the pain and anger of melodramatic poems than with contemplative texts.

In certain patches of this work, one of the last modelled on the style of Zumsteeg, Schubert finds Schiller's classical allusions a shade too pedantic to bring to life in a vibrant way. Nevertheless the character of Ceres, when she is mad with grief, is a magnificent portrait of a formidable mother who will fight for her child at any cost. The young composer could hardly have imagined anyone other than Anna Milder (*see* Singers) singing this music, conceived as it is for an artist of the first rank. It is here that Schubert, who had the luck in his student years to hear great performances of opera, had the edge on many of his non-Viennese contemporaries. Mandyczewski believed that the composer intended to make a second draft of the work but never found the time to do so – his interest in the ballad form was in any case waning. *Klage der Ceres*, championed by the pianist Irwin Gage, has been adopted by such singers as Gundula Janowitz and Cheryl Studer in modern times.

In the NSA Vol. 9 (p. XXVIII) Walther Dürr discusses Johannes Brahms's ownership of a fragment of the autograph (the final section) of this song, a fragment that has now disappeared. Because Schubert interrupted work on the setting in November 1815 (resuming in June 1816) there are three separate autograph sources. There are also two variant versions of the work, printed in parallel by the NSA (Vol. 9/228–36), neither of which is in Schubert's own hand. The first of these is from the album of Franziska Tremier (in the Wienbibliothek) [*see* Autographs, Albums and Collections] and the other is in the possession of Otto Biba in Vienna. These versions avoid the high tessitura of the original and also offer ornamentations that suggest the hand, or at least the influence, of the singer Johann Michael Vogl.

Autographs:	Wienbibliothek im Rathaus, Vienna (first draft and revisions; three manuscripts in all)
First edition:	Published as part of the AGA in 1895 (P609)
Subsequent editions:	Not in Peters; AGA XX 172: Vol. 3/171; NSA IV: Vol. 9/196, 225 (variant for bb. 142–203) & 228 (ornamented & adapted versions)
Bibliography:	Capell 1928, p. 90
	Fischer-Dieskau 1977, p. 41
Discography and timing:	Fischer-Dieskau —
	Hyperion I 5[11]
	Hyperion II 11[15] 17'43 Elizabeth Connell

← *Erlkönig* D328   *Wer sich der Einsamkeit ergibt (Harfenspieler)* D325 →

KLAGE UM ALI BEY (I)   Lament for Ali Bey   Trio, TTB
(Claudius) **D140** [H208]
E♭ minor   1815 or 1816?

(11 bars)

Lasst mich! lasst mich! ich will klagen,	Leave me! Leave me! I wish to lament,
Fröhlich sein nicht mehr!	And never again be joyful!
A b o u d a h a b hat geschlagen	*Abu Dahab* has slain
Ali und sein Heer.	Ali and his army!
So ein muntrer kühner Krieger	Such a bold and cheerful warrior
Wird nicht wieder sein;	There will never be again;
Über alles ward er Sieger,	He vanquished all,
Haut' es kurz und klein.	Hacking them to pieces.
Er verschmähte Wein und Weiber,	He scorned wine and women,
Ging nur Kriegesbahn,	Pursuing only the path of war,
Und war für die Zeitungsschreiber	And was beloved
Gar ein lieber Mann.	By the journalists.
Aber, nun ist er gefallen,	But now he has fallen!
Dass er's doch nicht wär!	Would that he had not.
Ach, von allen Bey's, von allen	Ah, of all the Beys
War kein Bey wie er.	There was no Bey like him.

Jedermann in Sirus saget:	Everyone in Syria is saying:
'Schade, dass er fiel!'	'What a pity that he has fallen!'
Und in ganz Egypten klaget	And throughout all Egypt
Mensch und Crocodil.	Men and crocodiles lament.
Daher sieht im Geist, wie's scheinet,	With horror Daher imagines
Am Serail mit Graus	His friend's head
Seines Freundes Kopf und weinet	Displayed in the harem,
Sich die Augen aus.	And weeps his eyes out.

MATTHIAS CLAUDIUS (1740–1815); poem written in 1773

This vocal trio, one of Schubert's very rare attempts at comedy, was recorded in the Hyperion Edition in its solo version first published in 1968. The piece was composed in either 1815 or 1816 and we now know that its original form was almost certainly as a trio. The rather obscure fragment of Egyptian history that is the background to the Claudius poem (*see* commentary below) has prompted Schubert to imagine three courtiers who make their plaint with elaborate ritual and patent insincerity; the death of a Mamluk (or Marmeluke as it used to be spelled) some forty years earlier could not have expected to register genuine grief with Schubert. The idea of a trio of courtiers bemoaning the misfortunes of their sovereign reminds us of the Three Ladies in *Die Zauberflöte*. Did Mandyczewski perhaps have this precedent in mind when he assigned this ensemble to female voices in the AGA in 1897?

Autograph:	Missing or lost
First edition:	Published as Book 45 no. 3 of the *Nachlass* by Diabelli, Vienna in 1850 (P372)
Subsequent editions:	AGA XVIII 6: p. 32; NSA III: Vol. 3
Discography and timing:	Hyperion I 20²⁶ 2'50 John Mark Ainsley, Jamie MacDougall
	Hyperion II 12³ & Michael George

← *Zufriedenheit* D362   *An Chloen* D363 →

KLAGE UM ALI BEY (II)   Lament for Ali Bey
(CLAUDIUS) **D496A** [H313A]
E♭ minor   November 1816

(8 bars)

See previous entry for poem and translation

MATTHIAS CLAUDIUS (1740–1815); poem written in 1773

This is the fifth of Schubert's thirteen Claudius solo settings (1816–17). See the poet's biography
for a chronological list of all the Claudius settings.

Here is a rare example of a Schubert comic song. Our composer was never short of genial high spirits, as a work like the light-hearted trio *Der Hochzeitsbraten* D930 shows, but he was never very comfortable with malicious *Schadenfreude* (very much a Hugo Wolf speciality).

In this case, however, the enemy is distant enough to be a cardboard cut-out of a character, and so easier to lampoon. Most Austrians of Schubert's generation would still to some extent have regarded Muslims as 'the enemy' because of long-standing altercations with Islam that had come to a head with the Turkish siege of Vienna in 1683. This gives the setting a certain Viennese drollery which had clearly not been the North German poet's intention. Certainly Mozart wrote a number of Turkish parodies in his operas and instrumental music, and even a song, *Meine Wünsche* K539, which celebrates the victory of Kaiser Josef II over the 'Muselmänner'.

Ali Bey Al-Kabir was not Turkish but an Egyptian Mamluk (born *c.* 1728). He had come to Egypt as a slave and by 1760 had worked himself up to become de facto leader ('Sheikh El Balad') of the country which was nominally controlled by the pashas appointed by the Ottoman Empire. Ali Bey, together with his ally Sheikh Daher (mentioned in the last verse of Claudius's poem), battled to expand the Mamluk ascendancy and drove the Turks, weakened by a war with Russia, out of Palestine and Damascus. He met his end on 8 May 1773, his downfall the result of competitive ambition within his own ranks: he was either stabbed or poisoned on the orders of his former subordinate, the double-dealing Mohamed Bey Abu-El-Dahab who pretended fealty to his Turkish overlords then took control of Egypt. The head of Sheikh Daher was sent as a trophy to Constantinople some years later. The Mamluks continued to rule Egypt until Napoleon's invasion of that country in 1798. Ali Bey was considered a far more honourable man than his savage murderer. To that extent the consternation expressed by Claudius regarding his death might have been at least partially sincere.

It is unlikely that Schubert was aware that Ali Bey and the seventeenth-century citizens of Vienna had been the common enemies of the Ottoman Empire. Instead the poem provided the composer with an excuse to write a piece in the playful spirit of Mozart's *Die Entführung aus dem Serail* K384. The mourning E flat minor tonality used perfectly seriously in the Claudius setting *Am Grabe Anselmos* D504 is here employed in parody as a graveside melancholy. The music has something of an exotic oriental character without achieving the wit and perspicacity of Mozart's evocations. This piece (with its squeezebox chords requiring exaggerated crescendo and diminuendo on the strong beats) was originally conceived as a vocal trio D140 (*see above*); this piano-accompanied solo version appears to have been made by the composer, perhaps for rehearsal purposes.

Autograph:	Missing or lost
First edition:	Published as part of the NSA in 1968 (P735)
Subsequent editions:	Not in Peters; Not in AGA; NSA IV: Vol. 7/84; Bärenreiter: Vol. 6/42
Discography and timing:	Fischer-Dieskau —
	Hyperion I 17[19]
	Hyperion II 16[17] 1'48 Lucia Popp

← *Bei dem Grabe meines Vaters* D496   *An die Nachtigall* D497 →

KLAGLIED   Lament
(Rochlitz) **D23** [H11]

The song exists in two versions, the second of which is discussed below:
(i) 1812; (ii) 1812

(1)   'Adagio con espressione'   G minor   §   [21 bars]

(2)   G minor

Meine Ruh' ist dahin,	My peace is gone,
Meine Freud' ist entfloh'n,	My joy has fled;
In dem Säuseln der Lüfte,	In the rustling of the breezes,
In dem Murmeln des Bach's	In the murmuring of the brook
Hör' ich bebend nur Klageton.	I, trembling, hear only the sound of lament.
Seinem schmeichelnden Wort,	His flattering words
Und dem Druck seiner Hand,	And the press of his hand,
Seinem heissen Verlangen,	His ardent desire,
Seinem glühenden Kuss,	His burning kisses –
Weh' mir, dass ich nicht widerstand!	Alas, that I did not resist!
Wenn ich von fern ihn seh',	When I see him from afar
Will ich ihn zu mir zieh'n,	I long to draw him to me;
Kaum entdeckt mich sein Auge,	No sooner does his eye discern me,
Kaum tritt näher er mir,	No sooner does he approach me
Möcht' ich gern in mein Grab entflieh'n.	Than I desire to escape to my grave.
Einmal, ach einmal nur	Ah, if once, but once
Möcht' ich ihn glücklich seh'n	I might see him happy
Hier am klopfenden Herzen,	Here upon my beating heart,
An der sehnenden Brust:	Upon my yearning breast,
Wollte dann lächelnd untergehn!	I could then die with a smile!

JOHANN FRIEDRICH ROCHLITZ (1769–1842)

This is the first of Schubert's four Rochlitz settings (1812–27). See the poet's biography for a chronological list of all the Rochlitz settings.

Nestling among the early ballads and composition exercises, this jewel of a song stands out at a glance as quintessential Schubert. The first thing to notice about it is that the opening words are familiar: 'Meine Ruh' ist dahin, / Meine Freud' ist entfloh'n'. Any Schubert lover will connect that phrase to 'Meine Ruh' ist hin, / Mein Herz ist schwer'. Of course this is a rather flagrant reworking of Gretchen's lament at her spinning wheel, and it is surely meant as Rochlitz's homage to Goethe. Schubert must, therefore, have known the imitation before the 'real thing'; – *Gretchen am Spinnrade* D118, the work that would place his songs on the world map, dates from October 1814, and he had a lot of ground to cover, and a lot of books to read, between the two songs. If one wonders how the young Schubert found the words of Rochlitz before those of Goethe, the answer may well be that a setting of the same text by the Viennese composer Sigismund Neukomm (1776–1858) fell into the student composer's hands.

The Italianate influence in this music is evident, the result of long hours spent with Salieri exercises, musical training that made the shapely vocal lines both muscular and flexible. The opening appears culled from the middle of a vocal score of an opera, the statutory two bars played as an introduction by the repetiteur before an audition excerpt. And then that florid little melisma on 'Meine Ruh'' (in the second version only) that brings to a German lyric the temperamental flourish of Italian ornamentation. This device occurs once again at the beginning of one of the earliest Goethe settings, *Nachtgesang* D119 of 1814. The accompaniment – a crotchet in the left hand followed by two anonymous quavers – nurses and nudges the vocal line along in the best tradition of the solicitous opera conductor. In some ways this is an Italian aria in all but name but, because the language is German, other influences come into play: the Teutonic strength of the consonants gives the music a word-allied seriousness, a grandeur that the young Schubert could only achieve in his own language. At 'In dem Säuseln der Lüfte' (bb. 8–10) the *Bewegung* of the accompaniment quickens into semiquavers, and the vocal line, singing of the breezes, floats above it with (bb. 9–10) a heartbreaking little fragment of tune that seems imprinted on the memory from somewhere else. Indeed, in the cello melody at the opening of the slow movement of the Piano Trio in B flat D898 (the third and fourth bar of that heart-stopping solo), the same creative hand can be detected   the child as father to the man. And if we have already looked into Schubert's future, we can equally visit his past: in *Lebenstraum* D39, composed when he was only thirteen, we hear something similar on the phrase 'Kein Lüftchen wehte' (bb. 26–9 of that song). In *Klaglied* the interrupted cadence on the first 'Klageton' (bb. 15–16) followed by a clinching repeat of the strophe's last line is also the purest Schubert.

For a long while this was known as 'Schubert's first song', and this rubric graces one of the contemporary manuscript copies. It is certainly not Schubert's first vocal composition; Mandyczewski preferred to think of *Der Jüngling am Bache* D30, a charming little Mozartian scena and part pastiche, as Schubert's earliest song creation, *pur sang*. But quite apart from the dates (D30 was written in September 1812 and this song could well have dated from earlier in the same year) it is understandable that the composer's friends thought of *Klaglied* as the first Schubert *lied*: it has an eloquent seriousness that defies analysis, and an emotional depth disproportionate to its brevity. It is also cast in strophic mould, the traditional form for German lieder (although words from later verses fit the music only with difficulty). Above all, the song is magical in a way that is already 'Schubertian', with its long-arched vocal lines that stretch time and make it stand still, as if the music were held within a vast inner stillness.

There are so few differences between the two versions that the NSA preferred to give these in ossias above the stave of the published version. It is notable that in the first version Schubert had originally written 'Sehr langsam, mit Ausdruck'. Was it perhaps at Salieri's behest, during a lesson, that he crossed this out and substituted Italian wording, only to change it back to German for the second version?

Autograph:	Wienbibliothek im Rathaus, Vienna (first version, first draft)
First edition:	Published as Op. post. 131 no. 3 by Josef Czerny, Vienna in 1830 (P257)

Subsequent editions:	Peters: Vol. 4/160; AGA XX 6: Vol. 1/52; NSA IV: Vol. 6/56; Bärenreiter: Vol. 5/48
Bibliography:	Capell 1928, p. 80
	Einstein 1951, pp. 48–9
	Fischer-Dieskau 1977, pp. 18–19
Arrangements:	Arr. Tilman Hoppstock (b. 1961) for guitar accompaniment, in *Franz Schubert: 110 Lieder* (2009)
Discography and timing:	Fischer-Dieskau —
	Hyperion I 33[7]
	Hyperion II 2[6] 2'28 Marie McLaughlin

← *Viel tausend Sterne prangen* D642   *Der Jüngling am Bach* D30 →

CHRISTIAN EWALD VON KLEIST (1715–1759)

THE POETIC SOURCES
S1 *Des Herrn Christian Ewald von Kleist Sämmtliche Werke*, Erster Theil, Wien bey Johann Edlen v. Trattnern K. K. Hofbuchdruckern und Buchhändlern, 1765

S2 *Die sämmtlichen Werke des Herrn Ewald Christian von Kleist*, Wien, gedruckt für F. Schrambl bey Ignaz Albert, 1780

S3 *Ewald Christian Kleist's sämmtliche Werke*, Neueste Auflage, Wien, 1816, Bey B. Ph. Bauer

THE SONG
August 1822   *Gott in der Natur* D757 [S1: pp. 7–11, under the title *Hymne*] [S2: pp. 6–9, under the title *Hymne*] [S3: p. 84 under the title *Hymna auf dem Marsch nach Hoff*]. Hof is in Oberfranken where the Austrian troops were defeated in battle in 1758. In the quartet's autograph and contemporary copies, as well as the first edition, the text is falsely ascribed to Johann Wilhelm Ludwig Gleim (1719–1803). The name of this 'less dangerous' poet was possibly substituted for that of the distinguished Prussian soldier Kleist in some Austrian publications (although Gleim was also known for his patriotically Prussian *Preussiche Kriegslieder*). Perhaps the source used by Schubert was an unidentified anthology, as yet unknown to us, in which the text was in fact ascribed to Gleim.

Christian Ewald von Kleist is not to be confused with his great-nephew Heinrich von Kleist (1777–1811) whose *Die Marquise von O* was read by the Schubert reading circle in 1827 and whose *Penthesilea* (1883–5) was the basis of Hugo Wolf's ill-starred if impressive tone poem. This earlier and lesser-known Kleist was a Pomeranian nobleman, born in Zeblin in Pomerania on 7 March 1715. Most of his adult life was spent in military service – first with the Danish forces and then the Prussian army where he had attained the rank of major by the beginning of the Seven Years War. He wrote a great deal of patriotic poetry and epics based on the classics, but his most famous poem is probably *Der Frühling*, based on James Thomson's *The Seasons*. Kleist's literary friends included such figures as Gleim, Nicolai and,

Ewald Christian von Kleist.

above all, Lessing. The character of Tellheim in Lessing's *Minna von Barnhelm* is modelled on Kleist. He died of his wounds on 12 August 1759 after fighting at Kunersdorf where the Prussians were defeated by the Russians and Austrians. Another of the eighteenth-century poets set by Schubert, Christoph August Tiedge, wrote a celebrated poem about this battle. The manner of Kleist's death cast him as a national German hero, a parallel figure to Theodor Körner who was to die valiantly for his country some fifty-four years later. Although Kleist's poetic gifts were exaggerated at the time due to his personal standing and his valiant demeanour, Oskar Wolff counts him as one of the first German poets to have been gripped by the 'new spirit' – the very first stirrings of the Romantic movement. Kleist's descendant, Ewald Heinrich von Kleist (1922–2013) was one of the group who plotted unsuccessfully against Hitler in 1944.

Bibliography: De Clercq 1991, p. 124
                 Porhansl 1990, pp. 11–13
                 Wolff 1846, vol. 2, p. 357

KAROLINE LUISE VON KLENKE (1754–1802)

THE POETIC SOURCE
S1 *Gedichte von C. L. von Klenke geb. Karschin*, Berlin 1788

THE SONG
September 1827   *Heimliches Lieben* D922, Op. 106 no. 1 [S1: pp. 193–4, where the title is *An Myrtil*]

Karoline Klenke, born on 21 June 1754 in Fraustadt in Posen (now Poland), is one of those figures, like Abraham Mendelssohn, who is renowned for having been the child of a more famous parent, and the parent of a more famous child. Her mother, Anna Luise Karsch (1722–1791), known as 'die Karschin' or 'die deutsche Sappho', a nickname given to her by the well-meaning Gleim, was a poet of considerable renown who nevertheless struggled to make her way in Berlin in a male-dominated literary world. Karoline was aware

as a child of the precarious circumstances in which writers lived, having to rely on constant handouts from patrons and the fickle support of condescending royalty. She had nothing of her mother's reputation, and less of her talent. Her first marriage at the age of fifteen (at her mother's insistence) was to her step-uncle (or, according to another source, her step-brother), the rough and uneducated lottery secretary Hempel. The marriage ended in divorce after ten bitterly unhappy years, although Karoline enjoyed some success in

'Die Karschin' (Anna Luise Karsch), mother of Karoline von Klenke.

(qv). The scant mention that her mother receives in Chézy's memoirs is indicative of an unhappy childhood spent in desperate poverty, a condition that Karoline's slender literary talents could do little to alleviate although she did at least ensure that the child received a good literary education. Karoline Klenke died, at the age of forty-eight, in Berlin on 21 September 1802, outliving 'die Karschin', her famous mother, by only eleven years. Her death was a liberation for young Helmina who set out for Paris, in fact beginning a career that would make her an international literary name.

It is very unlikely that Schubert saw the volume of poetry associated with *Heimliches Lieben*. He was almost certainly given the text in handwritten form by Marie Pachler, his hostess in Graz in the summer of 1827. She in turn had been given the poem by one of her ardent musical admirers (and perhaps lover), Julius Schneller, a left-wing poet who had been

Berlin with a play entitled *Der ehrliche Schweizer* in 1786. Freed from Hempel's control Karoline turned to writing poetry, although the enormous subscription list for her *Gedichte* publication of 1788 was an indication of her mother's fame rather than her own reputation. At the age of twenty-eight she married the twenty-two-year-old Baron Karl von Klenke from Bremen whose mother was vehemently opposed to the match. When this marriage, initially blissfully happy, also failed, Karoline threw herself on her mother's mercy, taking her daughter Wilhelmine (Helmina) to Berlin with her. An ambitious and unmanageable girl, Helmina had something of her grandmother's talent and a good deal more audacity in terms of public relations. She eventually published and edited Klenke's *Leben und Romantische Dichtungen* (Frankfurt, 1805) under her married name Helmina von Chézy

The cover of Hermann Kletke's anthology *Deutschlands Dichterinnen* (1855).

exiled from Graz because of his liberal views. It seems that Schneller had adapted the Klenke poem, removing the name 'Myrtil', probably so that it fitted his romantic agenda of wooing Marie Pachler. It is a strange coincidence that Schubert had already collaborated with Chézy in 1823 on the music for *Rosamunde*. It was Faust Pachler, Marie's son (for whom Schubert wrote the piano duet *Kindermarsch* D928) who discovered the identity of the poet when he came across Klenke's name and a mention of the 'Myrtil' poem in a small anthology entitled *Deutschlands Dichterinnen* (Germany's woman poets). The anthologist was Hermann Kletke (1813–1876), a poet famous for *Der Sandmann* set to music by Schumann. Thus the name of Karoline Klenke, like that of his female poets Marianne von Willemer and Ernestine von Krosigk (qqv), was never known to the composer himself.

FRIEDRICH GOTTLOB KLOPSTOCK (1724–1803)

THE POETIC SOURCES
S1 *Klopstocks Oden, Erster Band*, Leipzig, bey Georg Joachim Göschen, 1798

The first volume of *Klopstocks Oden* was issued both separately and bound together with *Klopstocks Oden, Zweyter Band*, Leipzig, bey Georg Joachim Göschen, 1798 (which was itself also issued separately). If Schubert's source was the 1798 Göschen Edition it seems he possessed only the first of the two volumes of Klopstock's *Oden*. Schubert's possible use of the *Oden* published in Vienna by Trattner in 1784 is ruled out by the absence of *Das Rosenband* from this edition.

S2 *G. F. Klopstocks Oden, Erster und Zweiter Band*, Wien, gedruckt und verlegt bey B. Ph. Bauer, 1816

On the face of it this Viennese *Oden* (in three volumes) was published too late to be Schubert's source, but an edition such as this was often issued in the preceding autumn of its official publication date to enable the sales to benefit from the Christmas market. If this was the case here, Schubert may have regarded the Klopstock Odes (as opposed to the *Geistliche Lieder* set earlier in the year – *see* S3) as a brand new discovery with the volumes of poetry hot off the press in September 1815.

S3 *Klopstock's Werke Siebenter Band Oden, Geistliche Lieder, Epigramme* Leipzig, Bey Georg Joachim Göschen, 1804.

This is the seventh volume of Klopstock's complete works in twelve volumes (1789–1817) of which S1 is the first.

THE SONGS

9 March 1815	*Nun lasst uns den Leib begraben (Begräbnislied)* SATB with piano D168 [S3: p. 237, in section 'Veränderte Lieder'] *Jesus Christus unser Heiland, der den Tod überwand (Osterlied)* SATB with piano D168A [S3: p. 224, in section 'Veränderte Lieder']
12 September 1815	*Das Rosenband* D280 [S1: p. 123] [S2: Erster Band p. 136] In earlier sources this poem, one of Klopstock's Odes to Cidli, was entitled *Das schlafende Mädchen*. In the 1784 'Göttinger Musenalmanach' (where the poem is accompanied by a musical setting) the title is simply *Cidli*. *Furcht der Geliebten* D285 [S1: p. 131] [S2: Erster Band p. 144]

14 September 1815   *Selma und Selmar* D286 [S1: p. 244] [S2: Zweiter Band p. 40]
                    Vaterlandslied D287 [S1: pp. 300–301 as 'Zum Singen für Johanna Elisabeth
                    von Winthem'] [S2: Zweiter Band pp. 101–2]
                    An Sie D288 [S1: pp. 124–5] [S2: Erster Band pp. 137–8]
                    Die Sommernacht D289 [S1: p. 234] [S2: Zweiter Band p. 29]
                    Die frühen Gräber D290 [S1: p. 223] [S2: Zweiter Band p. 18]

                    In the Viennese edition the apostrophe in 'Gefährt' der Nacht!' possibly
                    suggested Schubert's variant 'Gefährte der Nacht!' At the end of the second
                    verse the Viennese edition has 'rötlich er kommt' (as in Schubert) rather
                    than 'rötlich er kömt' as in S1.

15 September 1815   *Dem Unendlichen* D291 [S1: pp. 191–2] [S2: Erster Band pp. 208–9]

27 October 1815   *Hermann und Thusnelda* D322 [S1: pp. 112–13] [S2: Erster Band pp. 125–6]

                    In S2 the poem's last line is printed as 'Folg' du' as opposed to the 'Folg du'
                    of S1. This may have inspired Schubert's variant 'Folge du'.

June 1816   *Das grosse Halleluja* D442 [S1: pp. 227–8] [S2: Zweiter Band pp. 22–3]
                    Schlachtlied (Schlachtgesang) D443 [S1: pp. 255–7] [S2: Zweiter Band pp.
                    51–3] This poem was also set for unaccompanied double chorus in February
                    1827 as D912 (Op. post. 151)
                    Die Gestirne D444 [S1: pp. 186–90] [S2: Erster Band pp. 203–7]
                    Edone D445 [S1: p. 311] [S2: Zweiter Band p. 112]

Friedrich Gottlob Klopstock was born in Quedlinburg near Hamburg on 2 July 1724 and brought up with a sound classical training influenced by Pietistic thought. As a boy his first acquaintance with the epics of Homer and Virgil initiated his resolve to do something equivalent in his own language, with the subject taken from German history. In 1745 he enrolled at Jena University where he achieved his first, and perhaps greatest, success, *Der Messias*. Klopstock's enthusiasm for the works of Milton, and in particular *Paradise Lost* (translated by Bodmer), led to the writing of this acknowledged masterpiece, the first part of which appeared in print in the poet's twenty-fourth year and which was eventually translated into seventeen languages. The work quickly won Klopstock a huge reputation, although it would be another twenty-eight years before it was finished to his satisfaction. In 1747 he began to write a series of Odes, a free-verse form he was to pursue all his life. His metrical experiments were continued by Hölderlin who regarded Klopstock as the supreme German poet and knew all his Odes by heart.

An unrequited passion for his cousin Sophie Schmidt (the 'Fanny' of his verses) was followed by time spent in Zurich and Braunschweig. In 1751, at the invitation of the King of Denmark, he moved to Copenhagen where he was charged to finish *Der Messias*. In Hamburg he had met Margarethe (Meta) Moller (the 'Cidli' of a number of love poems, three of which Schubert set) and he married her in 1754. Meta, an accomplished poet in her own right, was commemorated following her death in childbirth in 1758 by the two poems *Die Sommernacht* and *Die frühen Gräber*, set to music by Gluck in 1770 and by Schubert as D289 and 290. After experimentation in the fields of patriotic historical drama and religious poetry, Klopstock returned to Germany where he was influential in the group around the young Goethe at Strasbourg University and more so, in the circle of poets known as the 'Göttinger Hainbund' (qv Hölty). Schiller was equally smitten by the poet's work. It has always been a moot point among Germanists as to whether Klopstock was an innovator or the final flowering spirit of the Baroque. He

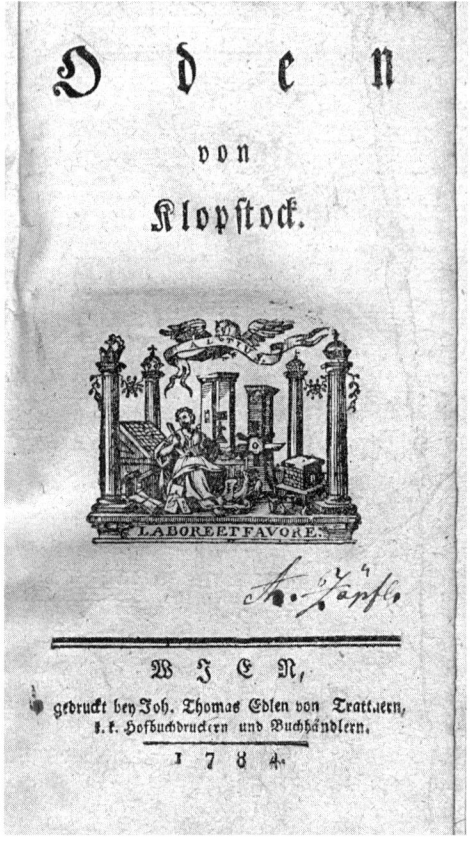

Klopstock's *Odes*, Viennese edition of 1784.

Klopstock aged seventy-four (1798) from a painting by
Anton Hickel.

seems to have been poised between the two: on one hand he greeted the French Revolution with joy (he was awarded honorary citizenship of the new French Republic) but then, after the execution of Louis XVI, he denounced the new regime with equal vehemence.

His later writings include a tract on spelling reform. He was an enthusiast of Teutonic mythology and wrote three plays about the early German hero Arminius who successfully fought the Roman invader and entered German mythology as Hermann. Fischer-Dieskau's short pen portrait of the man does him justice: 'Klopstock founded an entirely new style of German poetry in the eighteenth century by employing Greek metres and, later, free rhythms. Along with this revolution in poetic style he sought to bring about a new lifestyle that laid great emphasis on physical activity, on skating, walking and riding.' In 1792 he was

happily married for the second time. He was revered by his artistic colleagues as well as by high society: this was the man to whom Coleridge and Wordsworth paid their respects in 1798 and on whom Lord Nelson and Lady Hamilton called in 1800. The poet died in Hamburg on 14 March 1803 and was accorded a lavish funeral with huge public participation, something that would hitherto have been imaginable only for a famous statesman. In this respect Klopstock as great artist and celebrity had more in common with Ludwig van Beethoven than his nearer contemporary Joseph Haydn. He was happier and luckier than Beethoven though, and in personal terms Haydn's hard-working equanimity and long-lived productivity provide a fairer comparison.

Schubert was acquainted with Klopstock's work from his schooldays, mainly through the use of the textbook *Institutio ad eloquentiam* that quoted extensively from the poet's work (Klopstockius) and raised him to the level of exemplar in terms of use of language. Schubert's thirteen solo song settings were supplemented by the two choral settings listed above as well as a *Stabat Mater* to Klopstock's words (from

February 1816, D383) and a surprisingly late *Schlachtgesang* for double choir (February 28 1827, D912). Such was Schubert's enthuasiam for this poet that when Josef von Spaun wrote to Goethe in 1816 with a prospectus of the composer's plans, the publication of two volumes of Klopstock song settings was envisaged.

Der KNABE   The boy
(F. von Schlegel) **D692** [H449]
A major   March 1820

(90 bars)

Wenn ich nur ein Vöglein wäre,	If only I were a bird,
Ach, wie wollt' ich lustig fliegen,	Ah, how joyfully I would fly,
Alle Vögel weit besiegen.	Far outstripping all other birds.

Wenn ich nur ein Vöglein wäre,
Ach, wie wollt' ich lustig fliegen,
Alle Vögel weit besiegen.

Wenn ich so ein Vogel bin,
Darf ich alles, alles haschen,
Und die höchsten Kirschen naschen;
Fliege dann zur Mutter hin.
Ist sie bös in ihrem Sinn,
Kann ich lieb mich an sie schmiegen,
Ihren Ernst gar bald besiegen.

Bunte Federn, leichte Flügel
Dürft' ich in der Sonne schwingen,
Dass die Lüfte laut erklingen,
Weiss nichts mehr von Band und Zügel.
Wär' ich über jene Hügel,
Ach, dann wollt' ich lustig fliegen,
Alle Vögel weit besiegen.

If only I were a bird,
Ah, how joyfully I would fly,
Far outstripping all other birds.

If I were a bird
I could get everything
And nibble the highest cherries.
Then I'd fly back to mother.
If she were angry
I could nestle sweetly up to her
And soon overcome her sternness.

Coloured feathers, light wings,
I could flap them in the sunlight,
So that the air resounded loudly,
I would no longer be curbed and shackled.
If I were beyond those hills,
Ah, how joyfully I would fly,
Far outstripping all other birds.

FRIEDRICH VON SCHLEGEL (1772–1829); poem written in 1800/1801

This is the tenth of Schubert's sixteen Friedrich von Schlegel solo settings (1818–25). See the poet's biography for a chronological list of all the Friedrich von Schlegel settings. See also the article about the cycle of which this song is part - Abendröte.

The original key of this song is A major, the same tonality in which the birds sang their chirpy melodies in *Die Vögel* D691. If the composer thought of birds in this tonality it is perhaps natural

that this song should also be in A major, for it is as much about the birds as about the anonymous boy who gives the song its title. Perhaps if Friedrich von Schlegel had been a Shakespearean like his brother August, he might have written about a schoolboy who was less the
aspiring high-flyer, rather someone with 'shining morning face, creeping like snail /
Unwillingly to school' (Jaques's speech in Shakespeare's *As You Like It*). In fact Schlegel launched his poem
(published in the *Musenalmanach* of 1802) with a nod in the direction of one of Herder's *Volkslieder* (1778) beginning 'Wenn ich ein Vöglein wär / Und auch zwei Flüglein hätt'; this lyric also
appeared in *Des Knaben Wunderhorn* in 1806.

Despite the fact that *Der Knabe* and *Die Vögel* share a tonality and a lively tempo (and are
perhaps the jolliest of the *Abendröte* (qv) settings), they are in fact very different. The birds
merrily cruise the heavens in ⅜ time, but this boy is grounded in ²⁄₄. We hear his impatience
throughout: the vocal line aspires unsuccessfully heavenward on 'Wenn ich nur ein', only to bend
earthward in disappointment in the conditional tense of 'Vöglein wäre' (bb. 5–6). The accompaniment, oscillating staccato thirds in the left hand, mezzo staccato semiquavers off the beat
in the right, paws the earth like a Pegasus with clipped wings. The phrase 'Alle Vögel weit
besiegen' inspires an outbreak of the thirds and sixths of hunting music (bb. 11–14) which
Schubert takes to be emblematic of male competitiveness. The jaunty little interlude that ends
this section (before 'Wenn ich so ein Vogel bin', thus bb. 15–18) suggests an imagination running
riot with images of tilting at rivals, like a junior Don Quixote; it is a battle-music of sorts, but
one where the weapons are wooden swords.

Until now we have heard an unusually limited harmonic vocabulary – the alternation between
tonic and dominant. Indeed, the introduction is nothing more than a four-bar elaboration of
an arpeggio in the tonic key, with a crescendo to forte as the boy grows high and mighty in his
thoughts. It is something of a relief then to enter the subdominant at 'Wenn ich so ein Vogel
bin' (from b. 19) where notions of cherry-picking adventures are linked to thoughts of the boy's
mother. After much schoolboy bravado the music adopts a new tone of intimacy and tenderness.
It is the high tessitura of this passage, plus its soft dynamic marking, which suggests, in the
original key, a light soprano voice rather than a tenor; on the other hand there is something
very male about this song – one imagines it sung by a bit of a ragamuffin with his heart in the
right place. The next passage (in B minor, the relative minor of the subdominant key of D,
beginning 'Ist sie bös in ihrem Sinn', from b. 32) reinforces this boyish slant. In this music we
hear his ability to charm his way out of trouble in a way that would be impossible for his sisters.
The sprung accompaniment, the second beat phrased away in a winsomely yearning drop of an
octave, suggests both wheedling and cheek, the mother's softening anger (forgiveness is neither
instantaneous nor easily won) depicted by the change of harmony under the elongated setting
of 'gar bald besiegen' (bb. 38–41). This little fantasy soon yields to thoughts of birds as we return
to the middle section's first idea, namely bouncing quavers in the subdominant (from b. 45).
Here the high tessitura is especially suited to the idea of 'Dass die Lüfte laut erklingen'. We then
return to B minor, but for a much shortened section encompassing the words 'Wär' ich über
jene Hügel' (from b. 59). This phrase in the conditional ('*wär ich*'), with a touching little piano
echo after 'Hügel' – evocative of a sad sigh (b. 62) – ushers in a recapitulation of the boy's
fantasy.

With a lesser composer we might have had a perky repeat of the same carefree opening lines,
but Schubert is too clever for that. His music enables us to hear the boy's words again, this time
crestfallen, in the context of reality. The difference between animals and humans, it has been
said, is that animals do not weep for what might have been; it is the unique capacity of human
beings to dream of what they cannot have, and to bemoan a loss. The final strophe of *Der Knabe*
is unique in Schubert in that it replays an already-established melody at half speed (crotchets
instead of quavers) as a means of depicting the wistful tones of 'if only'. The fight and flight have

gone out of the lad; he no longer has the mad energy required to cruise the heavens. The music, though still in the same tempo, seems to slow down and the hunting motifs from b. 75 are no longer abrasive; instead we hear the sad, far-off echoes of human longing, like distant horns in a dark forest. The little interlude that had been indicative of imaginary battles in the opening section is here transformed into the song's postlude, the jauntiness still there, but momentarily deflated. Thus has many a youngster's dream to play for Manchester United vanished into thin air with a rueful smile as his gaze turns toward the realities of life at its more mundane. Within a few bars Schubert has transformed a headstrong boy into a thoughtful young man. Tomorrow's mental excursions 'beyond those hills' will bring new dreams and new rebuffs. Schlegel's point here is that human beings cannot transcend their given roles in life, and be more, or less, than human. The son of Daedalus failed to understand this, and in attempting to be a high-flyer his wings melted in the sun. Schubert's song portrays a would-be nineteenth-century Icarus with rare musical charm.

Autograph:	Staatsbibliothek Preussischer Kulturbesitz, Berlin (first draft)
First edition:	Published as No. 22 of *Neueste Folge nachgelassener Lieder und Gesänge* by J. P. Gotthard, Vienna in 1872 (P448)
Subsequent editions:	Not in Peters; AGA XX 374: Vol. 6/88; NSA IV: Vol. 12/158
Bibliography:	Capell 1928, p. 165
	Einstein 1951, p. 188
Discography and timing:	Fischer-Dieskau II 3[16] 1'57
	Hyperion I 27[12] 2'24 Matthias Goerne
	Hyperion II 23[7]

← *Der Fluss* D693   *Der Schiffer* D694 →

Der KNABE IN DER WIEGE   The boy in the cradle (Lullaby)
(Ottenwalt) **D579** [H381]

The song exists in two versions, the first of which is discussed below:
(1) Autumn 1817; (2) November 1817

(1)   C major

(66 bars)

(2)   'Etwas bewegt'   A♭ major   §   [38 bars]

Er schläft so süss, der Mutter Blicke hangen	He sleeps so sweetly. His mother's gaze
An ihres Lieblings leisem Atemzug,	Hangs on the soft breathing of her darling,
Den sie mit stillem sehnsuchtsvollem Bangen	Whom, with silent, anxious yearning,
So lange unterm Herzen trug.	She carried for so long beneath her heart.

Sie sieht so froh die vollen Wangen glühen	With joy sees his full cheeks glowing,
In gelbe Ringellocken halb versteckt,	Half-hidden in yellow curls,
Und will das Ärmchen sanft herunter ziehen,	And gently tucks in the little arm
Das sich im Schlummer ausgestreckt.	That had stretched out in sleep.
Und leis' und leiser schaukelt sie die Wiege	Ever more gently she rocks the cradle,
Und singt den kleinen Schläfer leis' in Ruh;	And softly sings the infant to sleep;
Ein Lächeln spielet um die holden Züge,	A smile plays around his fair features,
Noch bleibt das Auge friedlich zu.	Though his eyes stay peacefully closed.
Erwachst du Kleiner, o so lächle wieder,	When you awake, little one, smile once more,
Und schau ihr hell ins Mutterangesicht:	And look brightly into your mother's face.
So lauter Liebe schaut es auf dich nieder,	With pure love she looks down upon you,
Noch kennest du die Liebe nicht.	Though you do not yet know what love is.

[. . . 6 . . .]   [. . . 6 . . .]

ANTON OTTENWALT (1789–1845)

This is Schubert's only setting of an Ottenwalt text. See the poet's biography.

All the commentators call this piece a lullaby (the autograph in Paris is headed *Wiegenlied*) which on reading the poem it may seem to be. But Schubert is always able to find a deeper musical key to a poem than is at first obvious, and in this case the main emotion is one of sheer paternal delight. The marking 'Etwas lebhaft', the two in a bar time signature, and the phrasing of the right-hand quavers, ending each group of three notes with a staccato, suggest the joy of parenthood as a father gazes at a child who is safely asleep. Most cradle songs are rather somnolent affairs, but the major clue in determining the mood and speed of this music is to do with the singing of it. Take the phrase 'An ihres Lieblings leisem Atemzug' (bb. 8–12): there is nowhere where one may interrupt this phrase with a breath (as it happens, the words concern the child's breathing). However, in this tessitura, and at conventional lullaby tempo, no singer could encompass the whole phrase in one breath. Schubert's marking of 'Etwas lebhaft' is to be taken to heart.

The inspiration for the accompanying rhythm is certainly the rocking of a cradle (no more than once in every bar at this tempo) but we are also made aware of the elation of a proud prospective father and his participation in the new adventure of parenthood. Ottenwalt was not yet a father when he wrote these words but, in his late twenties, his longing for a wife and family is apparent. (For his observations of life in general and of Schubert in particular, we are grateful for, and indebted to, his letters). It would not be surprising if the composer had been deeply moved by this real-life outburst of would-be paternal affection of a kind that he might himself have longed to receive as a child. This seems also to apply to the much later Bauernfeld setting, *Der Vater mit dem Kind* D906. A certain jauntiness in Schubert's piano accompaniment hints at a nascent complicity between father and son, and all the boyish fun in store for them in the future. (The beautiful Seidl *Wiegenlied* D867 where the poetry seems written for a girl-child has quite different music.) As a foil to the masculine side of the music we hear the father's infinitely tender concern in the smoothness and sweetness of the vocal line. His adoration of the child's mother is equally evident, as well as his pleasure in the contemplation of her unique role in the family's triptych. The smile of the parents, the smile of the child, the simplicity of the harmony mirroring one of life's primal pleasures (the key is simple C major and the harmonic adventures are equally innocent), all combine to make a song which in lesser hands would have fallen into a honeypot of Biedermeier sentimentality. Schubert avoids this by a wide margin. He was certainly courting danger when he chose to limit the harmonic vocabulary of the song to this extent, but what the music lacks in harmonic variety it makes up for in melodic charm and an unusual accompanying texture. The phrase 'lange unterm Herzen trug' (bb. 25–8) is remarkably similar in terms of melody and key to a phrase ('Hab' ich nicht geliebet und gelebt?') in the second version of *Thekla* D595. The common themes are love, trust, closeness and safety, the blood-line between parent and child. It must be added that the opening of the Ottenwalt song's vocal line has been lifted, almost note for note, from the second setting of *Sängers Morgenlied* (Körner) D165, also in C major. Here the connection between the birth of new day and the radiance of a new young life, both reflected in the purity of a tonality as yet unsullied by accidentals, is easy enough to imagine.

For the Hyperion Edition four of Ottenwalt's ten verses were recorded (two verses of the poem make up one of the song), and on sheerly musical grounds it is doubtful if Schubert intended more to be performed. Nevertheless, the other verses of the poem have their own interest: the end of the fourth verse printed here leads on to the fifth in an unusual kind of enjambement, raising a topic at the end of one verse that is dealt with in the next. The ending of the fourth strophe is not completely understandable without this fifth verse that describes how the child learns to love at his mother's breast. If this verse is performed the musical structure also requires the sixth. And then it might seem a pity not to bring the father into the story of the child's development, and the beginning of the child's cognitive abilities (Verses 7 and 8). Ottenwalt has been careful to envisage the growth of his child from a helpless infant into a rational human being. It was not for nothing that he was a close colleague of Mayrhofer's in that poet's contemporary *Bildung für jünglinge* project to educate young men in a fitting way.

For those singers and pianists who feel it their duty to perform more of this song, the NSA has printed out the entire musical underlay for Ottenwalt's poem in the first version (September 1817), presumably because Schubert may have intended his music to encompass all the verses. At the time of the song's composition the composer was not yet a personal friend of the poet; they eventually met in Linz in 1819 when Schubert himself sang this song to Ottenwalt. The second version is in A flat (November 1817) with the marking 'Etwas bewegt'. The music breaks off at b. 38 and there are some interesting indications that Schubert was beginning to think of varying the vocal line for the different strophes (bb. 36 and 38). (He may have done so – it is possible that this second version was lost after it was completed.) The song was transposed down a major third possibly at the earnest request of singers in the Schubert circle, but there is no doubt that the original key conveys better the heady emotion of first-time parenthood. Dürr makes the point that Schubert, most unusually, mentions this song three times in his own letters – once in 1819 after meeting Ottenwalt in Linz and singing the song to him personally, and in 1821 and 1822 as he attempted to track down the autograph for his own collection of manuscripts.

Autograph:	Conservatoire collection, Bibliothèque Nationale, Paris (incomplete draft of second version)
Publication:	Published as No. 16 of *Neueste Folge nachgelassener Lieder und Gesänge* by J. P. Gotthard, Vienna in 1872 (P442; first version) Published as part of the AGA in 1897 (P727; second version)
Subsequent editions:	Not in Peters; AGA XX 335: Vol. 5/180; NSA IV: Vol. 11/162 & 234

Discography and timing: Fischer-Dieskau II 1[19]   2'33   (first two strophes only)
                          Hyperion I 6[7]
                          Hyperion II 19[15]   3'50   Anthony Rolfe Johnson

← *Abschied (Lebe wohl! Du lieber Freund!) D578*   *Vollendung D579a* →

Die KNABENZEIT   Boyhood
(HÖLTY) **D400** [H265]
A major   13 May 1816

(24 bars)

Wie glücklich, wem das Knabenkleid   Happy he around whose shoulders
   Noch um die Schultern fliegt!   A boy's coat still flaps.
Nie lästert er der bösen Zeit,[1]   He never curses the bad times;
   Stets munter und vergnügt.   He is always cheerful and content.

Das hölzerne Husarenschwert   The wooden hussar's sword
   Belustiget ihn jetzt,[2]   Delights him now;
Der Kreisel, und das Steckenpferd,   The top, and the hobby-horse
   Auf dem er herrisch sitzt.   On which he sits proudly.

[. . . 2 . . .]   [. . . 2 . . .]

O Knabe, spiel' und laufe nur,   Play, child, and run about
   Den lieben langen Tag,   The whole day long
Durch Garten und durch grüne Flur   Through garden and green meadow,
   Den Schmetterlingen nach.   Chasing butterflies.

Bald schwitzest du, nicht immer froh,   Soon you will be sweating, not always happily,
   Im engen Kämmerlein,   In the cramped classroom
Und lernst vom dicken Cicero   Learning fusty Latin
   Verschimmeltes Latein!   From a fat tome of Cicero.

[1] Hölty's original reads 'Nie lästert er *die* bösen Zeit'.
[2] Hölty used the archaic 'itzt' for 'jetzt', which rhymes with 'sitzt'.

LUDWIG HÖLTY (1748–1776); poem written in early 1771. Adapted for publication in 1804 by JOHANN HEINRICH VOSS (1751–1826).

This is the fifteenth of Schubert's twenty-three Hölty solo settings (1813–16). See the poet's biography for a chronological list of all the Hölty settings.

This song expresses a delightful moment of nostalgia for childhood. If this setting lacks the melodic charm of the contemporary Hölty setting *Die frühe Liebe* D430 it nevertheless has a similar freshness enhanced by its breezy A major tonality as well as a tricky high-lying tessitura. It is as if the composer had an unbroken voice in mind when he wrote the music. (Schubert seems to have associated the key of A major with the vivacity of boyhood, as in *Der Knabe* D692.) The composer was still a teenager in 1816, but there is no one so nostalgic for lost youth as a nineteen-year old who imagines himself already old and experienced beyond measure. The warning for the younger generation is entirely apposite coming from a composer so recently freed from the 'cramped classroom' and 'a fat tome of Cicero'. It seems that Johann Heinrich Voss, in 'editing' the poetry of his friend Hölty, felt free to add various strophes to poems such as this. These give ample opportunity to performers to vary the mood from games of soldiers, chasing butterflies and sweating over Latin. The accompaniment is in running semiquavers that flutter after the running boy, just like his coat, at 'um die Schultern fliegt'. The dive-bombing interlude at bb. 16–20 is particularly indicative of the tireless energy of children. The postlude dancing up and down the right-hand stave can be playfully phrased in light-hearted manner but its four-square structure can also be made to suit the pedantry (the wagging of a school-masterly finger) implied by the last verse. Schubert's schoolboy seems incapable of 'whining' in the manner Shakespeare describes in his 'Seven Ages of man' speech from *As You Like It*. The same is true of the composer himself.

Schubert made some corrections in pencil to the autograph; these were printed as an alternative in the AGA but adopted definitively by the NSA. The most important of these concerns the melody of the three opening bars of the song plus upbeat. In the version printed in the AGA (and recorded in the Hyperion Edition) the vocal line of *Die Knabenzeit* bears an uncanny resemblance to an aria, also in A major, from Mozart's *La Clemenza di Tito*: the opening of Sextus' aria, 'Deh, per questo istante solo'. (This is such a famous tune that the poet Mörike, in his *Ach nur einmal noch im Leben!* claimed his garden gate creaked, in a soprano voice, the same refrain on opening.) It seems possible that Schubert had spotted this similarity (or had it pointed out to him) and, embarrassed by unconscious plagiarism, changed the vocal line with a stroke of the pencil. One may see the original cast of the tune in a footnote in the NSA, Volume 10 p. 94.

There are six strophes in Hölty's poem, all conveniently printed in the NSA as underlay to the song. The strophes printed above are those recorded in the Hyperion Edition – 1, 2, 5 and 6.

Autograph: Library of Congress, Washington
First edition: Published as part of the AGA in 1895 (P637)
Subsequent editions: Not in Peters; AGA XX 219: Vol. 4/100; NSA IV: Vol. 10/94
Discography and timing: Fischer-Dieskau I 7⁹   1'52
                                Hyperion I 23¹⁶
                                                      2'05   Christoph Prégardien
                                Hyperion II 14¹⁷

← *Auf den Tod einer Nachtigall* D399   *Winterlied* D401 →

Der KÖNIG IN THULE

(GOETHE) OP. 5 NO. 5, **D367** [H220]

The king of Thule

D minor   Early 1816

(34 bars)

Es war ein König in Thule	There was a king in Thule
Gar treu bis an das Grab,	Faithful unto the grave,
Dem sterbend seine Buhle	Whose dying beloved
Einen goldnen Becher gab.	Gave him a golden goblet.
Es ging ihm nichts darüber,	Nothing was more precious to him;
Er leert ihn jeden Schmaus;	He drained it at every feast.
Die Augen gingen ihm über,	His eyes filled with tears
So oft er trank daraus.	Whenever he drank from it.
Und als er kam zu sterben,	And when he came to die
Zählt' er seine Städt' im Reich,	He counted the towns in his realm,
Gönnt alles seinen Erben,	Bequeathed all to his heirs,
Den Becher nicht zugleich.	Except for that goblet.
Er sass beim Königsmahle,	He sat at the royal banquet,
Die Ritter um ihn her,	His knights around him
Auf hohem Vätersaale,	In the lofty ancestral hall
Dort auf dem Schloss am Meer.	In his castle by the sea.
Dort stand der alte Zecher,	The old toper stood there,
Trank letzte Lebensglut,	Drank life's last glowing draught,
Und warf den heilgen Becher	And hurled the sacred goblet
Hinunter in die Flut.	Into the waves below.
Er sah ihn stürzen, trinken	He watched it fall and drink
Und sinken tief ins Meer.	And sink deep into the sea.
Die Augen täten ihm sinken;	His eyes, too, sank;
Trank nie einen Tropfen mehr.	He drank not one drop more.

JOHANN WOLFGANG VON GOETHE (1749–1832); poem written in 1773/4

This is the thirty-eighth of Schubert's seventy-five Goethe solo settings (1814–26). See the poet's biography for a chronological list of all the Goethe settings.

It was the Greek writer Pytheas who first mentioned Thule in the 4th century BC; for him it was an island some way north of Britain. By the seventeenth century it was a byword for a mysterious realm in the frozen north at the top of the world. The composer Thomas Weelkes published a madrigal in 1600 entitled *Thule, the Period of Cosmographie*. The author of the words is unknown (perhaps Weelkes himself). Schubert could not possibly have known it but it sets a scene that is not unworthy of Goethe's remarkable poem:

Thule, the period of cosmography,
Doth vaunt of Hecla, whose sulphurious fire
Doth melt the frozen clime and thaw the sky . . .

Der König in Thule from *Die Dichter des deutschen Volkes* (1846).

Hecla is Iceland's most active volcano, and Iceland is more or less where Thule was situated according to Tudor imaginings – or even Goethe's imagination come to that. The word 'period' implies the furthest limit, the end, of geographical imaginings – which is the origin of the word's meaning as 'full stop'.

In Hans Pfitzner's extraordinary song, *Stimme der Sehnsucht* Op. 19 no. 1 (Carl Busse) the indefatigable voice of longing is a 'dark, confused sound' from distant Thule that penetrates the soul.

For Goethe (according to Lorraine Byrne) Thule represents 'longing for, and awareness of, the furthest bounds of what is, by its own nature restricted . . . in terms of space, but also in terms of time and love.' Schubert's song was included in the selection of songs that the composer sent the great poet via the good offices of Josef von Spaun in 1816. The music would almost certainly have pleased Goethe a great deal, had he asked someone to play and sing it for him. This was one of the poems that Goethe liked personally to recite to an audience and he took a lot of trouble with it. It was conceived as part of the *Urfaust* in 1774. The small but telling verbal differences between that earlier version and the one Schubert set is analogous with the kind of musical changes that Schubert himself often made in his songs when preparing them for publication: the outward shape remains the same but small internal alterations bring the work into sharper focus.

The song seems to have been modelled to an extent on Zelter's 1812 similarly strophic setting in A minor, deliberately archaic with a modal touch to summon up the Gothic world of *Faust* and the simplicity of Gretchen, the girl who sings it as she muses on her first meeting with the eponymous hero (or anti-hero) (*see* FAUST). Schubert's setting eclipses Zelter's, but not so resoundingly that we fail to hear the careful, and no doubt sincere, homage to the elderly Berliner. These strophic verses are originally more or less in the 'Death' key of D minor, but there is a harmonic ambiguity (the opening eight-bar phrase, for example, starts on the subdominant and ends on the dominant without the sharpened leading note) that disguises the real tonality. This seems an appropriate musical language in which to describe kings who never can believe, and are never openly told, that they are going to die. The tune is extraordinarily simple, but mournfully and hypnotically beautiful, a timeless folksong collected fresh from the fields of Schubert's imagination.

The song can be interpreted in many ways. In its original context Gretchen is artless and hums an old ballad, but who would now care to perform the ballad *Erlkönig* in the phlegmatic spirit of its original context of a ditty sung while mending nets on the seashore? *Der König in Thule* concentrates on a man's last and desperate link with love, an object of sentimental value that cannot be taken beyond the grave. The song is seen here as a heart-rending commentary on constancy and the king's attachment to the memory of someone ineffably dear to him, almost certainly his mistress rather than his queen. (Although Faust has begun to groom Gretchen for his nefarious purposes, he will eventually achieve redemption only through his enduring love for her.) The poem evokes the loneliness of bereavement, and the uselessness of wealth and power once love is no longer part of life. Despite its simplicity the setting is on the same transcendental level of creative inspiration as Goethe's lyric.

Autograph:	Missing or lost
First edition:	Published as Op. 5 no. 5 by Cappi & Diabelli, Vienna in July 1821 (P14)
Dedicatee:	Antonio Salieri
Publication reviews:	F. von Hentl 'Blick auf Schubert's Lieder', *Wiener Zeitschrift für Kunst, Literatur, Theater und Mode* No. 36 (23 March 1822), p. 289f. [Waidelich/Hilmar Dokumente I No. 146; Deutsch Doc. Biog. No. 278]

Subsequent editions:	Peters: Vol. 2/12; AGA XX 261: Vol. 4/202; NSA IV: Vol. 1a/45; Bärenreiter: Vol. 1/37
Bibliography:	Byrne 2003, pp. 335–9
	Capell 1928, pp. 122–3
	Fischer-Dieskau 1976, pp. 79–80
Further settings and arrangements:	Johann Friedrich Reichardt (1752–1814) *Der König von Thule* (1805–6)
	Carl Friedrich Zelter (1758–1832) *Der König von Thule* (1811)
	Hector Berlioz (1803–1869) *Le Roi de Thulé* from *La Damnation de Faust* (1846)
	Robert Schumann (1810–1856) *Der König von Thule*, op. 67 no. 1, for SATB choir
	Franz Liszt (1811–1886) *Es war ein König in Thule* (1842 & 1856), subsequently arranged for piano solo in 1843
	Charles Gounod (1818–93) *Il était un Roi de Thulé* from *Faust* Act III (1859)
	Arr. Tilman Hoppstock (b. 1961) for guitar accompaniment (2 arrangements), in *Franz Schubert: 110 Lieder* (2009)
Discography and timing:	Fischer-Dieskau I 8[9] 3'02
	Hyperion I 11[6] 3'05 Brigitte Fassbaender
	Hyperion II 12[15]

← *Lodas Gespenst* D150   *Jägers Abendlied II* D368 →

FRIEDRICH VON KÖPKEN (1737–1811)

THE POETIC SOURCES
S1 *Musen-Almanach fürs Jahr 1795*, Herausgegeben von Johann Heinrich Voss, verlegt von J. H. Voss, Hamburg, bei Carl Ernst Bohn

This tiny almanac in pink cardboard covers is also the source (p. 177) of Friederike Brun's *Ich denke dein*, the poem that became the model for Goethe's *Nähe des Geliebten* (qv D162) later in 1795.

S2 *Episteln. Zum Anhange vermischte Gedichte. Abdrücke für Freunde*, Magdeburg 1801

In comparing the two versions of this poem it is clear that Schubert's source was S1. For Volume 7 of the Peters Edition (p. 84) Max Friedländer invited Max Kalbeck to add another verse of this own.

THE SONG
July 1816   *Freude der Kinderjahre* D455 [S1: p. 9] [S2: pp. 130–31]

Friedrich von Köpken was born in Magdeburg on 9 December 1737 where he trained as a lawyer. He was a poet, an expert in the French theatre, a literary critic and translator, and was at the centre of literary life in his home city as well as an important member of the political establishment. In 1764 he spent three weeks in Klopstock's company and in 1788 dedicated what he regarded as his most important work, *Hymnus auf Gott* to the older

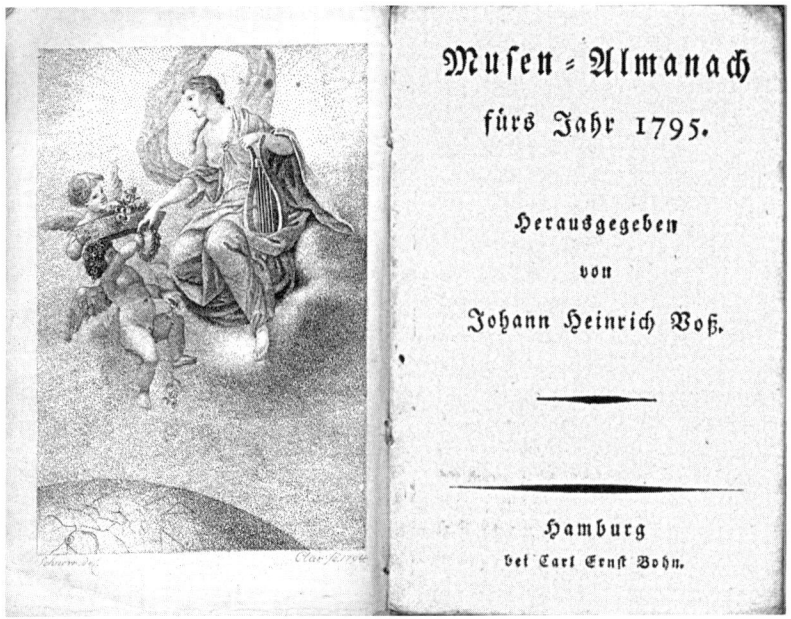

Title page of Voss's *Musenalmanach* (1795).

poet. He was friendly with Uz and later on with Friedrich von Matthisson, also a native of Magdeburg. The first six of Matthisson's diverting travel letters (in *Briefe von Friedrich von Matthisson*, 1795) were addressed to Köpken. The poet's *Versuch über die Manier unserer bekannteren Dichter* (1796) is a biographical survey of eighteenth-century German poetry that shows how alarmed he was by more recent literary developments. Köpken was exceedingly shy about publishing his poems which he wrote for his own personal enjoyment and his first collection of lyrics was printed as late as 1792. He was elevated to the nobility in 1786 and died on 4 October 1811.

THEODOR KÖRNER (1791–1813)

THE POETIC SOURCES
S1 *Körners Gedichte*, Erster Theil, Bey B. Ph. Bauer, Wien (1815)

The presence of every Körner text set by Schubert within a single slim volume of a Viennese reprint makes it overwhelmingly likely that the composer was in possession of this edition in 1815, and perhaps returned to it in 1818 for his last setting.

S2 *Knospen* von Theodor Körner, Leipzig, bei Georg Joachim Göschen, 1810

The absence of *Der Morgenstern* in any other collection of Körner's poetry raises the possibility that unless Schubert was in possession of the Viennese Bauer edition of 1815 (S1 above), he used this volume of poems as one of his Körner sources; Josef von Spaun might have lent the composer his copy, although it would be pleasant to imagine Körner presenting a volume of the poems to the young Schubert as a gift in 1813.

S3 *Leyer und Schwert von Theodor Körner, Lieutenant im Lützow'scher Freykorps*. Von dem Vater des Dichters veranstaltete Ausgabe, Wien 1814

This edition is a contemporary Viennese reprint of the Berlin edition ('In der Nicolaischen Buchhandlung') of 1814.

S4 *Theodor Körners vermischte Gedichte und Erzählungen nebst einer Charakteristik des Dichters von C. A. Tiedge und biographischen Notizen über ihn von dem Vater des Verewigten*. Leipzig 1815

This is the rare second volume of Körner's *Poetischer Nachlass*.

S5 Stephan Franz: *Sechs Gedichte von Körner*, Op. 10, Vienna, L Maisch, 1814

Franz (1785–1855) was one of Vienna's most distinguished song composers in Schubert's youth. Of the six Körner poems set by Franz, only the last, *Abschied von Wien Anno 1813*, was not set by Schubert. This volume of songs was also a possible source of texts for Schubert.

S6 *Dramatische Beyträge von Theodor Körner*, Wien 1815, Zweiter Band: *Der vierjährige Posten* [and four other dramas]

THE SONGS

27 February 1815	*Sängers Morgenlied* D163 [S1: pp. 77–8] [S2: pp. 101–3][S5: Franz's Op. 10 no. 1]
March 1815	*Liebesrausch* (I) D164 [S1: pp. 79–80] [S2: pp. 104–5] [S5: Franz's Op. 10 no. 4]
1 March 1815	*Sängers Morgenlied* D165 [S1: pp. 77–8] [S2: pp. 101–3] [S5: Franz's Op. 10 no. 1]
1 March 1815 ('In 5 hours')	*Amphiaraos* D166 [S1: pp. 70–72] [S2: pp. 91–3] [S4: pp. 31–3]
12 March 1815	*Trinklied vor der Schlacht* D169 [S1: pp. 161–2] [S3: p. 81] *Schwertlied* D170 [S1: pp. 163–6] [S3: p. 83] *Gebet während der Schlacht* D171 [S1: pp. 139–40] [S3: p. 55] *Der Morgenstern* D172 [S1: pp. 61–2] [S2: pp. 78–9]
26 March 1815	*Das war ich* (I) D174 [S1: pp. 74–5] [S2: pp. 96–8][S4: pp. 33–4]
8 April 1815	*Liebesrausch* D179 [S1: pp. 79–80] [S2: pp. 104–5] [S5: Franz's Op. 10 no. 4] *Sehnsucht der Liebe* D180 [S1: pp. 81–3] [S2: pp. 108–10] [S4: pp. 36–8]
26 May 1815	*Liebeständelei* D206 [S1: pp. 72–3] [S2: pp. 94–5] [S5: Franz's Op. 10 no. 3]
15 October 1815	*Wiegenlied* D304 [S1: pp. 169–70] [S4: pp. 62–3] [S5: Franz's Op. 10 no. 1] *Das gestörte Glück* D309 [S1: pp. 214–15] [S4: pp. 81–3] [S5: Franz's Op. 10 no. 5]
1815?	*Gott! Gott! höre meine Stimme* (from *Der vierjährige Posten*) D190/5 [S6: pp. 10–11]
1816?	*Das war ich* (II) D174 [S1: pp. 74–5] [S2: pp. 96–8] [S4: pp. 33–4] The second setting of this lyric adopts the D number of the first setting (see above). It is a six-bar fragment without verbal underlay that probably dates from June 1816. A performing edition of the song was made by Reinhard Van Hoorickx.

March 1818   *Auf der Riesenkoppe* D611 [S1: pp. 89–90] [S2: pp. 117–18] [S4: pp. 44–5, no. 6
                  of 'Erinnerungen aus Schlesien']

Mention should also be made of other Körner settings for unaccompanied voices that are outside the
scope of this book; all poems are to be found in S1: *Der Morgenstern* (second version) D203, Duet
for voices or horns, 26 May 1815; *Jägerlied* D204 Duet for voices or horns, 26 May 1815; *Lützows
wilde Jagd*, D205, Duets for voices or horns.

English writers have called Theodor Körner
the Rupert Brooke of his time because he was
a gifted and good-looking poet and fell tragically young in action. In fact Körner's galvanizing effect on the generations of young men
who came after him far outweighed that of
Brooke. The Saxon poet and playwright was
six years older than Schubert; young enough
to appear something of a contemporary, precocious and daredevil enough to inspire the
teenage composer, and many others, to a type
of hero worship. Unlike the vast majority of
Körner's admirers, Schubert enjoyed a brief
personal connection with the poet and never
forgot his encouragement.

Karl Theodor Körner, born on 23 September
1791, came from a literary family in Dresden;
both his father Christian Gottfried Körner
(1756–1831) and his mother were close friends
of Schiller. A remarkable man in his own right,
as well as a wise and devoted parent, Christian
Körner wrote the biographical note on his son
that is printed at the beginning of S3. The
younger Körner studied in Freiberg and Berlin.
An enthusiastic participant in the student

Theodor Körner, *c.* 1808, by an anonymous artist.

societies of the time, his *Burschenschaft* alle-
giances showed him to have been something
of a hothead and already a young patriot
enraged by the French occupation of Germany.
He was sent down from Leipzig University in
1811 for fighting a duel and fled the city to
escape imprisonment. He arrived in Vienna on
26 August 1811 and decided to stay there to
study Greek, but soon fell in with a group of
actors (rather like the eponymous hero of
Goethe's *Wilhelm Meister*) for whom he began
to write. These plays were so successful that
they were accepted for immediate production
and, in January 1812, he wrote to his father to
tell him that he had found his vocation as
a playwright. In the course of rehearsals at

the Burgtheater (where he was eventually
appointed house dramatist) he met the young
actress Antonie Adamberger who became his
fiancée [*see* SINGERS]. Although the poet was
killed in battle before she could marry him,
her name adds another dimension to Körner
(and Schubert) studies. After her marriage to
Josef Cales von Arneth, assistant curator of the
emperor's collection of coins and antiques, she
became a reciter of poetry to the empress at
the recommendation of Ladislaus Pyrker (qv).
Antonie attended many a Schubertiad and
became a wonderful interpreter of Schubert
songs in the last years of the composer's life –

Theodor Körner in 1810, painting by Gerhard von Kügelgen.

As we left the theatre we met the poet Körner with whom I was on very friendly terms. I presented the little composer to him, of whom he had already heard a certain amount from me. He was glad to make his acquaintance and encouraged Schubert to live for art, which would make him happy.

Later that evening in a restaurant Körner and Schubert almost got involved in a brawl in defence of the singers Anna Milder and Johann Michael Vogl whose performances as Iphigenia and Orestes were being criticized at the next table. Like the young Schumann's single personal encounter with Heine in 1828, this evening spent in Körner's company was sufficient to make the composer fall under the poet's spell. On that night in Spaun's and Körner's company, Schubert must have felt very much an artist, part of a community with shared ideals. His determination to resist parental pressure and to abandon schoolteaching was strengthened. This must have been shortly before the call to arms from the Prussian king and it was not long before Körner's native Saxony was drawn into the fight also. Körner decided to enlist in a glamorous but exacting Prussian regiment of volunteers (they wore famous black and gold uniforms) led by the charismatic soldier Adolph von Lützow. The poet left Vienna for ever on 15 March 1813 and was soon a member of the *Lützowischer Korps der Freiwilligen*. The portrait reproduced overleaf showing Körner in the Lützower uniform was made by his sister Emma during a visit to Dresden when the poet saw his family for the last time. He was very nearly killed in a mid-June engagement with the French when the enemy commander had a personal agenda against him on account of his (by now well-known) anti-French diatribes. On 26 August 1813 he was shot, possibly by friendly fire, and died during a skirmish at Gadebusch along the banks of the Elbe.

Körner left five tragedies, five comedies, short stories and a certain amount of poetry: the early *Knospen* was published in Leipzig in 1810, further material was published posthumously in 1815 (*see* S3 above) and the patriotic

an enduring link with one of the idols of his adolescence.

Körner was deliriously happy in Vienna, where he lived in the apartment in the Wipplingerstrasse that was later to be occupied by Mayrhofer and shared by Schubert. He came into contact with Karoline Pichler (qv) (April 1812), who marvelled at his literary facility, and he wrote *Der vierjährige Posten*, a light-hearted play that Schubert was to set to music as a *Singspiel* in 1815 (D190). The growth of Körner's career coincided with the unravelling of Napoleon's and the disastrous Russian campaign of 1812. The Germans and the Austrians began to see the possibility of freeing themselves from French domination and the young men of the time could scarcely wait to fight for their country.

Sometime in early 1813 Josef von Spaun took his younger friend Schubert (then very much his protégé) to the opera to see Gluck's *Iphigenia in Tauris*. Many years later Spaun remembered:

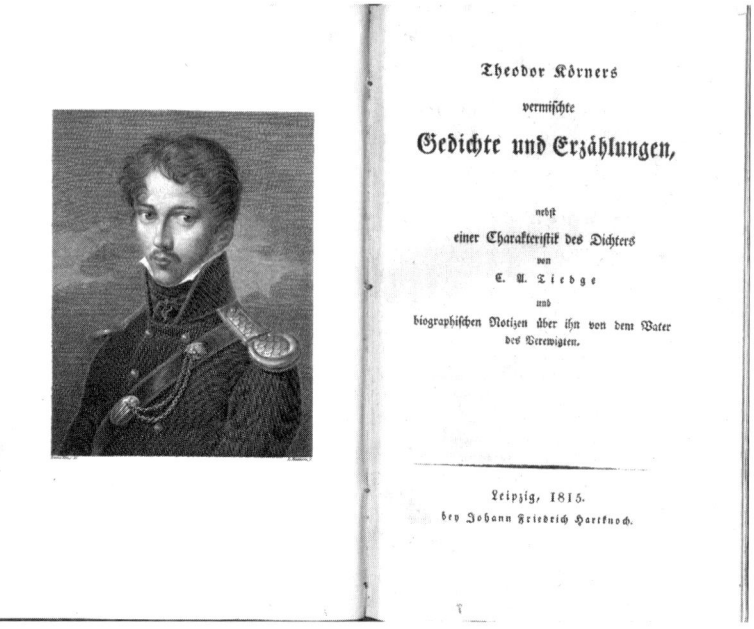

Title page of Körner's *Vermischte Gedichte* (1815).

poems *Leyer und Schwert*, the impact and popularity of which were much enhanced by the manner of his death, in 1814. Körner's patriotism was rediscovered by the German nationalists at the end of the nineteenth century, and countless printings of his works were circulated to inspire young men to commit brave acts on behalf of the kind of leaders and administrations that the poet himself would have abhorred. Between 8 and 19 May 1815 Schubert composed a one-act *Singspiel, Der vierjährige Posten* D190 using as his libretto Körner's play of the same name. His literary source was no doubt the precocious Körner's *Dramatische Beiträge* published in Vienna by Wallishausser in two volumes between 1813 and 1815.

The pace at which Körner worked, and his impatience to achieve great things without delay (as if he were already aware that he did not have a long life ahead of him), must have been extraordinarily inspiring for a young composer whose own creative fervour in 1815 (when most of the Körner settings were composed) fully matched that of his role model. It is tempting to speculate on what kind of person Körner might have become had he been granted a fuller lifespan; his political views and unquestioning patriotism would almost certainly have changed.

Johann Mayrhofer wrote a poem in Körner's honour, *Am Grabe Körners*, that Schubert must have known, and which encapsulates the admiration of the Schubert circle for this poet:

Nicht ihn, der in dem Kampfgewühl
Für seine Heimath streitend fiel,
Beklaget! selig ist sein Loos,
Und friedlich in der Erde Schoss.

Es wachsen Veilchen über ihn,
Und deuten an ein mildes Blühn:
Blüht Liebe ihm und Freiheit nun –
Wer möchte nicht im Grabe ruh'n?

Do not mourn him
Who fell in the tumult of battle
Fighting for his homeland! Blessed is his lot
As he lies at peace in the bosom of the earth.

Violets grow above him,
Intimations of a gentle flowering;
Love and freedom now flower for him.
Who would not wish to rest in the grave?

Was sehnsuchtsvoll das Herz begehrt,	What the heart ardently yearns for
Hienieden wird es nicht gewährt;	Is not granted here on earth.
Und eine steile Felsenwand	And a steep rock face
Verwehret uns das Blüthenland.	Bars us from the land of blossom.
Und wer sich auch, im kühnen Drang	And whoever, in a bold impulse,
Und keuchend, auf die Felsen schwang,	Has leapt with a gasp on to the rocks
Erblickt vor sich die See – und nur	Beholds the sea before him – and the meadows
Umflort die Hesperidenflur.	Of the Hesperides only grow misty.
Nur Fittiche, sie tragen hin,	Wings alone can bear us
Wo tausend goldne Früchte glühn.	To where a thousand golden fruits grow.
Uns drängt der schwere Leib zurück	Our heavy bodies drag us back
Vom reinen, fernen Geisterglück.	From the pure, far-off bliss of the spirits.

This poem makes us realize how deeply Mayrhofer would have appreciated, and understood, A. E. Housman's lines about the good fortune of those who die young, 'The lads in their hundreds . . . The lads that will die in their glory and never be old'.

Bibliography: Youens 1996, pp. 51–150

KOLMAS KLAGE   Colma's lament
(Macpherson after Ossian) **D217** [H111]
C minor   22 June 1815

Ziemlich langsam

Rund um ... mich Nacht, ich irr' al - lein,

p   *cresc.*   (119 bars)

The anonymous translation is a free verse adaptation of Macpherson. A literal rendering of the German is given here. Macpherson's prose original is printed below in italics

(1)	Rund um mich Nacht,	Around me is night.
	Ich irr' allein,	I wander alone,
	Verloren am stürmischen Hügel;	Lost on the stormy hill;
	Der Sturm braust vom Gebirg,	The storm roars from the mountains,
	Der Strom die Felsen hinab,	The torrent pours down the rocks;
	Mich schützt kein Dach vor Regen,	No roof shelters me from the rain.
	Verloren am stürmischen Hügel,	Lost on the stormy hill,
	Irr' ich allein.	I wander alone.

(2) Erschein', o Mond,   Appear, o moon!
     Dring' durch's Gewölk;   Pierce through the clouds!
     Erscheinet, ihr nächtlichen Sterne,   Appear, stars of the night!
     Geleitet freundlich mich,   Lead me kindly
     Wo mein Geliebter ruht.   To the place where my love rests.
     Mit ihm flieh' ich den Vater,   With him I would flee from my father;
     Mit ihm meinen herrischen Bruder,   With him, from my overbearing brother.
     Erschein', o Mond.   Appear, o moon!

(3) Ihr Stürme, schweigt,   Be silent, storms;
     O schweige, Strom,   Be silent, stream!
     Mich höre, mein liebender Wanderer,   Let my loving wanderer hear me!
     Salgar! ich bin's, die ruft.   Salgar! It is I who call.
     Hier ist der Baum, hier der Fels,   Here is the tree, here the rock.
     Warum verweilst du länger?   Why do you tarry longer?
     Wie, hör' ich den Ruf seiner Stimme?   Do I hear the cry of his voice?
     Ihr Stürme, schweigt!   Be silent, storms!

(4) Doch, sieh, der Mond erscheint,   But lo, the moon appears,
     Der Hügel Haupt erhellet,   The tips of the hills are bright,
     Die Flut im Tale glänzt,   The flood sparkles in the valley,
     Im Mondlicht wallt die Heide.   The heath is bathed in moonlight.
     Ihn seh' ich nicht im Tale,   I do not see him in the valley,
     Ihn nicht am hellen Hügel,   Nor on the bright hillside;
     Kein Laut verkündet ihn,   No sound announces his approach.
     Ich wand'le einsam hier.   Here I walk alone.

(5) Doch wer sind jene dort,   But who are they,
     Gestreckt auf dürrer Heide?   Stretched out there on the barren heath?
     Ist's mein Geliebter, Er!   It is he, my love,
     Und neben ihm mein Bruder!   And beside him my brother!
     Ach, beid' in ihrem Blute,   Ah, both lie in their blood,
     Entblösst die wilden Schwerter!   Their fierce swords drawn!
     Warum erschlugst du ihn?   Why have you slain him?
     Und du, Salgar, warum?   And you, Salgar, why?

     [(. . .)]   [(. . .)]

(6) Geister meiner Toten,   Ghosts of my dead,
     Sprecht vom Felsenhügel,   Speak from the rocky hillside,
     Von des Berges Gipfel,   From the mountain top;
     Nimmer schreckt ihr mich!   You will never frighten me!
     Wo gingt ihr zur Ruhe,   Where are you gone to rest?
     Ach, in welcher Höhle   Ah, in what cave
     Soll ich euch nun finden?   Shall I find you now?
     Doch es tönt kein Hauch.   But there is no sound.

(7) Hier in tiefem Grame   Here, in deep grief,
     Wein' ich bis am Morgen,   I shall weep until morning;

Baut das Grab, ihr Freunde,	Build the tomb, friends;
Schliesst's nicht ohne mich.	Do not close it without me.
Wie sollt' ich hier weilen?	Why should I remain here?
An des Bergstroms Ufer	On the banks of the mountain stream,
Mit den lieben Freunden	With my dear friends
Will ich ewig ruh'n.	I shall rest for ever.

[(. . .)] [(. . .)]

It is night – I am lone, forlorn on the hill of storms. The wind is heard in the mountains. The torrent shrieks down the rock. No hut receives me from the rain; forlorn on the hill of winds.

Rise moon! from behind thy clouds; stars of the night appear! Lead me, some light, to the place where my love rests from the toil of the chase! His bow near him unstrung; his dogs panting around him. But here I must sit alone, by the rock of the mossy stream. The stream and the wind roar; nor can I hear the voice of my love.

[At this point a six-line paragraph of the original English text – beginning 'Why delays my Salgar' is omitted.]

Cease a little while, O wind! Stream, be thou silent a while! Let my voice be heard over the heath; let my wanderer hear me, Salgar! It is I who call. Here is the tree, and the rock. Salgar, my love! I am here. Why delayst thou thy coming?

Lo! The moon appeareth. The flood is bright in the vale. The rocks are grey on on the face of the hill. But I see him not on the brow; his dogs before him tell not that he is coming. Here I must sit alone. But who are there that lie beyond me on the heath? Are they my love and my brother? – speak to me, O my friends! They answer not. My soul is tormented with fears. – Ah! They are dead. Their swords are red from the fight. O my brother! My brother! Why hast thou slain my Salgar? Why, o Salgar! Hast thou slain my brother? . . .

[Five lines are here excised by the German translator.]

Oh! from the rock of the hill; from the top of the windy mountain, speak ye ghosts of the dead! speak, I will not be afraid. – Whither are you gone to rest? In what cave of the hill shall I find you? No feeble voice is on the wind; no answer half-drowned in the storms of the hill.

I sit in my grief. I wait for morning in my tears. Rear the tomb, ye friends of the dead, but close it not till Colma come. My life flies away like a dream; why should I stay behind? Here shall I rest with my friends, by the stream of the sounding rock . . .

JAMES MACPHERSON ('OSSIAN') (1736–1796); TRANSLATOR UNKNOWN

This is the first of Schubert's ten Ossian–Macpherson solo settings (1815–17). See the poet's biography (under Macpherson) for a chronological list of all the Ossian settings.

The young Schubert of 1815–17 was mightily taken by the poetry of Ossian; along with most of his contemporaries he believed that these prose poems were the work of a famous Gaelic hero from the 4th century AD, translated into English by James Macpherson. The cult of Ossian became a worldwide phenomenon. To what extent Macpherson based his poems on original sources is still hotly disputed; in his own century Samuel Johnson, among others, denounced the poet and politician as a literary fraud.

Kolmas Klage was the first of Schubert's 'Ossian' settings and one of the best. Like every German-speaker of the time Schubert was aware of Goethe's *Die Leiden des jungen Werthers* (1774). Towards the end of that influential novel, Werther, contemplating suicide, has his last meeting with his beloved Charlotte:

> *'Have you brought nothing to read?' she enquired. He had nothing. 'There in my drawer,' she continued 'is your own translation of some of the songs of Ossian. I have not read them yet. I always hoped to hear you recite them; but it never seemed possible to arrange it.' He smiled, and fetched the manuscript. A tremor ran through him as he took it in his hand, and his eyes were filled with tears as he looked at it. He sat down and read.*

Werther reads aloud none other than the story of Colma in which the heroine discovers the bodies of her lover and brother who have slain each other in mortal combat. Goethe continues: 'Werther and Charlotte felt their own fate in the misfortunes of Ossian's heroes – felt this together, and merged their tears.' In the novella Colma's tragedy unfolds in Goethe's own translation which uses a more complete rendering of Macpherson's narrative than we find in Schubert's song.

We cannot be certain that Schubert had read Goethe's *Werther*. We do know, however, that he was familiar with the narration of Colma from a musical setting by Johann Friedrich Reichardt (1752–1814), also entitled *Kolmas Klage*, the ninth song in the second book of *Lieder der Liebe und der Einsamkeit* (1804) with accompaniment for piano or harp. That setting is divided into three songs, separately titled – *Rund um mich Nacht*; *Doch sieh, der Mond erscheint* and *Geister meiner Toten* – but it is meant to be performed in continuous sequence. The younger composer must have taken Reichardt's music as his model – running the three strophic songs together – using the same key signature of three flats (though turning major tonality into minor), opening the piece in common time as does Reichardt (although Schubert changes to ¾ time for the fourth strophe) and using the same translation of Macpherson's prose. This disproves the theory put forward by Anton Schindler, and subsequently Deutsch, that a certain Franz von Hummelauer had arranged the words for Schubert from Harold's translation, turning the prose into poetry as a kindness to the composer. The result is a song in an old-fashioned style, a way of composing songs, ironically, that Schubert's own musical experiments had already consigned to the annals of the musical past. However, Schubert was also perfectly capable of changing five or six words in Reichardt's text as the poetic fancy took him (or perhaps simply as a result of haste while copying). There are two strophes fewer in Schubert's setting than in Reichardt's.

This type of imitation (and improvement, for the young master's inspiration almost always eclipses the original) is to be found often enough when Schubert encounters the ballads of Zumsteeg and reworks them in a spirit of what might be termed back-handed homage; this work shows that Reichardt, king of the Berlin school of lieder composition, was an equally powerful influence on him. Incidentally, Carl Friedrich Zelter's *Colma, ein Altschottisches Fragment* is a veritable mad-scene for soprano (also in C minor) and one of his best pieces. Schubert seems to have been unaware of this work at the time.

Schubert's initially stormy ballad, at one time thought important enough to warrant inclusion in Volume 2 of the Peters Edition, is now almost totally neglected. It has certain curious features not typical of Schubert's songs – the lack of any piano introduction, for example, is very unusual for a work of this size. Its most unsettling aspect, however, and one that has probably kept it out of the concert hall, is its tripartite form. A rousing opening song in three verses (C minor, 'Ziemlich langsam' in *alla breve* time) is followed by two slow movements. These two fail to live up to the momentum and impact of the opening. If Schubert had conceived a more grief-stricken finale perhaps the song would have held the stage; but he preferred to leave Colma with the downbeat setting of the phrase 'Will ich ewig ruh'n' – which one cannot deny is very beautiful in its own way.

Verses 1–3: Influenced by the no-frills directness of an earlier age, Schubert has the voice plunge immediately into the fray, and a tremendous whirlwind is whipped up in the accompaniment by 'mezzo staccato' triplets throbbing in the right hand accompanied by rumbling sextuplets in the left. For the vocal line there is just the right amount of grandeur to suggest druidic incantation – this is not a song for a small voice. The idea of a woman alone in the threatening night summons up ominous left-hand octaves in ascending triplets, marked staccato (bb. 8 and 10), a full decade before the definitive appearance of this motif in *Die junge Nonne* D828. Much of this strength of purpose is to be found in Reichardt's music, but it is Schubert's affecting modulations, for example the semitone rise in the vocal line between 'Der Sturm' (b. 8) and 'Der Strom' (b. 10), that outclass the older composer's efforts. The way the sixth and seventh lines of the poem are counterpointed with a dying fall on the word 'Regen' in F minor (b. 13) followed by an ascending answering sequence and a cadence in A flat on 'Hügel' is stirringly effective. The seventeen bars that comprise the first verse are deemed good enough to be heard three times. The composer merely indicates in the score that the mood of the second verse should be lighter (the marking is 'durchgehends leichter') as the moon is called on for assistance (at bb. 17–18) and that the third strophe should be more stormy ('desto stürmischer'). Schubert's autograph (NSA Vol. 8 p. XXXVI) shows that he copied exactly what Reichardt offered in his printed edition, right down to the words 'gleich weiter' (the same again) appended to a single verse of music on three staves, while the words of the second and third strophes are written out at the foot of the page.

Verses 4–5: From b. 52 there is a beautiful but rather more conventional fourteen-bar cantilena in A flat which, like the opening C minor movement, is strophically repeated. One might have expected that Colma's discovery of the bodies would prompt new music, but Schubert remains true to the spirit of his predecessors: he makes the pathetic chromatic sequences of 'Ist's mein Geliebter, Er' and 'Und neben ihm mein Bruder' (Verse 5, where they are heart-rendingly apt) also do service for the earlier 'Die Flut im Tale glänzt' and 'Im Mondlicht wallt die Heide' (Verse 4) where they seem a lot less appropriate. There can be no doubt that the sentiment of the gruesome later verse has inspired this music. The way that Colma encounters the bodies of her lover and brother as she moves betweeen the strophes with scarcely a gasp for breath (and with the words 'Doch wer sind jene dort?' b. 65) is surprisingly wooden. The singer has to make the discovery of the bodies sound like a shocking surprise, and Schubert's music is little help in this respect.

Verses 6–7: Once again each of the two verses has the same music (F minor, 'Langsam, trauernd' from b. 80) repeated without variation or interlude. Here it is the questioning inflection of 'Ach, in welcher Höhle / Soll ich euch nun finden?' (b. 92, followed by an 'empty' bar of piano writing, b. 93, as the question goes unanswered) that has obviously governed the vocal line, and the later verse that makes do with music conceived for the earlier. The simplicity and eloquence of this section is very telling, but Schubert has miscalculated the amount of vocal stamina necessary to switch tessituras between sections in a work of this length and intensity. The final pages of the song, so different from the powerful opening, and placed in the *passaggio* of the voice, are unexpectedly demanding; what is easiest for the pianist is often hardest for the singer. This may also account for the infrequent appearance of *Kolmas Klage* in the concert hall. It is nevertheless a remarkable work with touches of real Schubertian genius tempered by the guiding example of a former age. It is possible that this work was conceived as something of a tribute to the memory of Johann Friedrich Reichardt a few days before the first anniversary of that composer's death on 27 June 1814.

Autograph:	Gesellschaft der Musikfreunde, Vienna
First edition:	Published as Book 2 no. 2 of the *Nachlass* by Diabelli, Vienna in 1830 (P242)
Publication review:	Rellstab 'Ueberblick der Erzeugnisse', *Iris im Gebiete der Tonkunst* (Berlin) No. 39 (12 November 1830) [Waidelich/Hilmar Dokumente II No. 784b]
Subsequent editions:	Peters: Vol. 2/207; AGA XX 83: Vol. 2/161; NSA IV: Vol. 8/104
Bibliography:	Capell 1928, p. 93
Discography and timing:	Fischer-Dieskau —

Hyperion I 15[8]

Hyperion II 7[11]   6'26   Margaret Price

← *Meeres Stille* D₂216   *Grablied* D218 →

LUDWIG THEOBUL KOSEGARTEN (1758–1818)

THE POETIC SOURCES

S1 *Ludwig Theobul Kosegarten's Poesieen.* Erster und Zweyter Band, Leipzig, bei Heinrich Gräff. 1798

This edition (dedicated 'To his friend Schiller') in two generous and beautifully illustrated volumes contains a copious list of subscribers: these include Theodor Körner's father in Dresden, the poet Gleim in Halberstadt, Friedrich Schiller and August Wilhelm von Schlegel in Jena, Angelika Kaufmann in Rome, Moritz Arndt, Karl Droysen and Karl Lappe in Rügen, Herder in Weimar and many more literary celebrities of the time.

S2 *Ludwig Theobul Kosegarten's Poesieen.* Erster und Zweyter Band Neue verbesserte Ausgabe. Leipzig bey Heinrich Gräff, 1802

This was the edition from which Schubert worked for his 1815 Kosegarten settings. Schochow worked with the 1788 edition of the poems and found hundreds of deviations from the poet's texts that were incorrectly laid at Schubert's door. Equally, the first version of the 1798 edition (S1 above) could not possibly have been Schubert's source. This 1802 edition is thought to have been the source by the editors of the NSA, but *see* notes for S3 below.

S3 *Ludw.Theob. Kosegarten's Poesieen*, Erster, Zweyter und Dritter Theil, Neueste Auflage, Wien 1816, bey B. Ph. Bauer

This Viennese edition, a reprint of the 1802 Leipzig edition, appeared only after Schubert had completed most of his Kosegarten settings in 1815. Volume 1 (Erster Theil) is perhaps the source of *An die untergehende Sonne* (begun in July 1816) with its reading of 'Sinkst du den Äther hinab' (if Schubert used the 1802 edition he would have had to take note of the errata printed at the beginning of the volume to find these words). There is a possibility, however, that the Bauer edition of 1816 was already available in 1815 – in which case it is possible that Schubert had this set of three Viennese paperbacks for more of his Kosegarten settings.

THE SONGS

25 June 1815   *Das Finden* D219 [S2: Volume 1 pp. 289–91] [S3: Zweyter Theil pp. 40–42] [Kosegarten Cycle (Morten Solvik) no. 5, sung by Wilhelm]

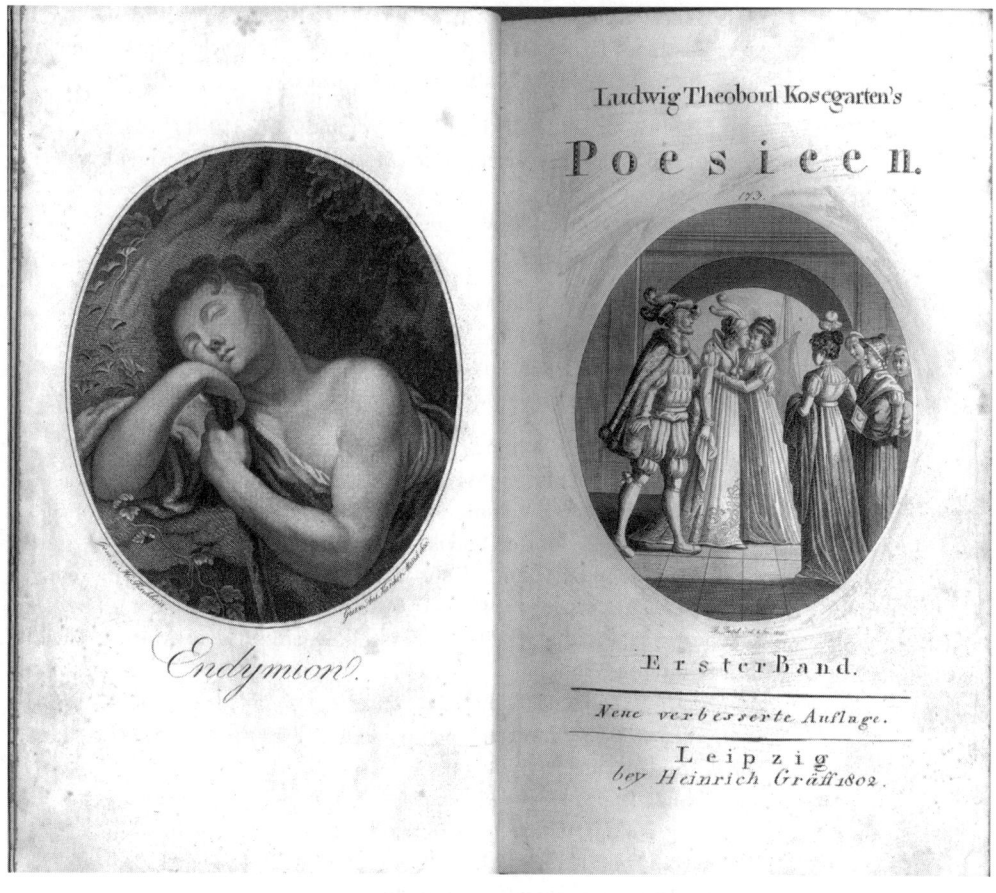

Title page of Kosegarten's *Poesieen* (1802).

7 July 1815	*Idens Nachtgesang* D227 [S2: Volume 1 pp. 347–8] [S3: Zweyter Theil pp. 86–7] [Kosegarten Cycle (Morten Solvik) no. 6, sung by Ida] *Von Ida* D228 [S2: Volume 1 pp. 354–5] [S3: Zweyter Theil pp. 91–2] [Kosegarten Cycle (Morten Solvik) no. 3, sung by Ida] *Die Erscheinung* D229 [S2: Volume 2 pp. 39–41] [S3: Zweyter Theil pp. 157–9] [Kosegarten Cycle (Morten Solvik) no. 4, sung by Wilhelm] *Die Täuschung* D230 [S2: Volume 2 pp. 42–3] [S3: Zweyter Theil pp. 159–61] [Kosegarten Cycle (Morten Solvik) no. 9, sung by Wilhelm]
8 July 1815	*Das Sehnen* D231 [S2: Volume 2 pp. 132–4] [S3: Dritter Theil pp. 12–14] [Kosegarten Cycle (Morten Solvik) no. 10, sung by Ida]
15 July 1815	*Geist der Liebe* D233 [S2: Volume 2 pp. 130–31] [S3: Dritter Theil pp. 11–12] [Kosegarten Cycle (Morten Solvik) no. 14, sung by Wilhelm] *Der Abend* D221 [S2: Volume 2 pp. 159–61] [S3: Dritter Theil pp. 36–7] [Kosegarten Cycle (Morten Solvik) no. 15, sung by Wilhelm]
24 July 1815	*Abends unter der Linde* (I) D235 [S2: Volume 2 pp. 310–11] [S3: Dritter Theil pp. 162–3]

20 July 1815	*Das Abendroth* D236 Trio for two sopranos, bass and piano [S2: Volume 2 pp. 162–4] [S3: Dritter Theil pp. 38–9] [Kosegarten Cycle (Morten Solvik) no. 13, sung by Wilhelm, Luisa and Ida as a trio]
25 July 1815	*Abends unter der Linde* (II) D237 [S2: Volume 2 pp. 310–11] [S3: Dritter Theil pp. 162–3] [Kosegarten Cycle (Morten Solvik) no. 12, sung by Wilhelm] *Die Mondnacht*, D238 [S2: Volume 2 pp. 165–6] [S3: Dritter Theil pp. 40–41] [Kosegarten Cycle (Morten Solvik) no. 11, sung by Wilhelm]
27 July 1815	*Huldigung* D240 [S2: Volume 2 pp. 135–8] [S3: Dritter Theil pp. 15–18] [Kosegarten Cycle (Morten Solvik) no. 1, sung by Wilhelm] *Alles um Liebe* D241 [S2: Volume 2 pp. 139–41] [S3: Dritter Theil pp. 18–20] [Kosegarten Cycle (Morten Solvik) no. 2, sung by Wilhelm]
19 October 1815	*Die Sterne* D313 [S2: Volume 1 pp. 243–6] [S3: Erster Theil pp. 227–9] [Kosegarten Cycle (Morten Solvik) no. 7, sung by Wilhelm] *Nachtgesang* D314 [S2: Volume 1 pp. 247–8] [S3: Erster Theil pp. 229–30] [Kosegarten Cycle (Morten Solvik) no. 8, sung by Luisa] *An Rosa I* D315 [S2: Volume 1 pp. 320–21 – designated here as *An Rosa, zweytes Lied* because of the long *An Rosa* poem pp. 302–19, not set by Schubert] [S3: Zweyter Theil pp. 65–6] [Kosegarten Cycle (Morten Solvik) no. 19, sung by Wilhelm] *An Rosa II* D316 [S2: Volume 1 pp. 322–3 – designated as *An Rosa, Drittes Lied, see* above] [S3: Zweyter Theil pp. 66–7] [Kosegarten Cycle (Morten Solvik) no. 20, sung by Wilhelm] *Idens Schwanenlied* D317 [S2: Volume 1 pp. 360–63] [S3: Zweyter Theil pp. 93–8] [Kosegarten Cycle (Morten Solvik) no. 16, sung by Ida] *Schwangesang* D318 [S2: Volume 1 pp. 386–8] [S3: Zweyter Theil pp. 116–18] [Kosegarten Cycle (Morten Solvik) no. 17, sung by Ida] *Luisens Antwort* D319 [S2: Volume 2 pp. 57–63] [S3: Zweyter Theil pp. 172–8] [Kosegarten Cycle (Morten Solvik) no. 18, sung by Luisa]
July 1816–May 1817	*An die untergehende Sonne* D457 Op. 44 [S3: Erster Theil pp. 211–13] [S2: Vol. 1 p. 224–6]

Kosegarten was born in Mecklenburg on 1 February 1758. He was baptized Gotthard Ludwig Kosegarten but later removed the Gotthard and substituted Theobul as his middle name. He was the son of a pastor and became a preacher and schoolteacher. After a period of study at Greifswald University the nineteen-year old became a live-in tutor at Bergen on the island of Rügen not far from Greifswald. Much of his poetry, like that of his friend and colleague Karl Lappe (qv), is associated with this region. At the time Rügen was part of Swedish-ruled Pomerania; the island came under Prussian control only after the Congress of Vienna in 1814. Kosegarten's

teaching post was at the home of the provincial governor Carl August von Wolffradt. There he fell in love with Karoline, the thirteen-year-old daughter of the household. There was a secret correspondence, the exchange of embraces during piano practice and nocturnal meetings in her bedroom. When one of Kosegarten's letters was found he was expelled from the house (May 1778) and the scandal spread through the island. Nevertheless, he went on to take holy orders and eventually took up the chair of theology at his old university.

In 1785 Kosegarten took a post working as a teacher in Wolgast (until 1792), where the future painter Philipp Otto Runge was among

Theobul Kosegarten, painted by Jany Weström, frontispiece to first volume of *Poesieen*, Leipzig (1798).

'Tellow', was published by a Berlin publisher, Himburg, who specialized in erotica and paid well. In the first edition of his poems (*Gedichte*, 1788) it is clear that Kosegarten wanted no one to connect the name 'Ida' with the heroine of this anonymous memoir; the love poems in this collection are thus addressed to 'Agnes'. By 1798, twenty years after the Karoline/Ida incident, the poet clearly felt that enough time had elapsed since his former disgrace, and in the second edition of the poems (now entitled *Poesieen*) the name reverts to Ida. Schubert set three of these lyrics from the third edition of 1802 (D227, D228, D317).

Kosegarten had a flirtation with *Sturm und Drang* and wrote most of his poems before he was thirty. He contributed to Schiller's *Musenalmanach* and the same poet's *Horen*, although neither Schiller nor Goethe were admirers of the third edition of the *Poesieen* (1798–1802), so many of which inspired Schubert. Kosegarten's mildly erotic novel *Ida von Plessen* (1804) was another work clearly influenced by the love of his life. In later years he was famous for two epics in sentimental style written in

his charges. There he began to write poems, these addressed to various girls, perhaps students, perhaps relatives of his wife Katharina (who is sometimes referred to as 'Emma') and perhaps entirely fictitious characters – Odalia, Rosa, Molly, Sulvina, Minona, Fredegunde, Fanny and Hyppolyta. The poems Schubert set as *An Rosa I* and *An Rosa II* (D315 and D316) were penned in this period. In 1790 Kosegarten translated Samuel Richardson's *Clarissa* and dedicated it to the queen of England (Charlotte, consort of George III), who invited him to London to be her court preacher – an invitation he declined.

In 1791 Kosegarten wrote a fictional autobiography of his early years entitled *Ewalds Rosenmunde* in which the young Karoline, his former beloved, is disguised as 'Ida'. He did not dare put his own name to this work, in view of its highly contentious subject matter, so he created the name Ewald for himself and the book, supposedly edited by someone named

Kosegarten in 1800, drawing by Hyölstrom, 1800.

hexameters. His *Legenden* were said to have influenced the work of the Swiss poet Gottfried Keller. He was also an expert on English poetry (*Brittisches Odeon*, 1800 complied with the help of Lappe (qv)). The 1798 edition of his poetry contains translations of Dryden's *Alexander's Feast* and Thomas Gray's *Elegy written in a Country Churchyard*.

The poet's later years were blighted by difficulties brought about by the politics of warfare and nationalism. The French invasion of Rügen in 1807 led to his taking up a university professorship in Greifswald, but he had acquired the reputation of being too conciliatory with the occupying enemy. With the defeat of Napoleon and the sharp rise of an aggressive brand of French-hating German nationalism, Kosegarten found himself ranged against his former pupil Ernst Moritz Arndt, as well as the inventor of modern gymnastics, Friedrich Ludwig Jahn. Both these younger men, particularly the proto-racist Jahn, promoted a punitive stance towards the French, while Kosegarten advocated a pan-European attitude of forgiveness and rapprochement. This culminated in a shocking incident at Wartburg Castle near Eisenach in 1817, orchestrated by Jahn, when Kosegarten's so-called unpatriotic works were among books publicly burned. Eisenach was some fifty miles away from Weimar and news of this event disgusted Goethe who, like Kosegarten, could not bring himself to hate the French. The ultra-Protestant student societies that organized this incident were detested by the Austrian chancellor Metternich and the authorities in Vienna had no objections whatever to Kosegarten's writings. In the same year Schubert composed *An die untergehende Sonne*, the last and probably greatest of his settings of this poet – a fact not known of course to the beleaguered creator of the poem.

Kosegarten died on 26 October 1818. He is often accused of bombast and pretentiousness, and of aspiring to elevated poetic characteristics that conflicted with the increasingly naturalistic tendencies of the times; however, he does not emerge as such for the lover of Schubert's lieder. His son Johann Gottfried Ludwig (1792–1860) was a gifted orientalist who advised Goethe on aspects of the *West-östlicher Divan*; Goethe became godfather to the younger Kosegarten's children and even provided a gravestone epitaph for his fellow-poet:

> Lasst nach viel geprüftem Leben
> Hier den edlen Pilgrim ruhn!
> Ehrt sein Wollen und sein Streben,
> Wie sein Dichten und sein Tun!

> After a life of trials
> May the noble pilgrim rest here.
> Revere his ideals and endeavours
> As much as his writings and achievements.

This inscription was never used. It must have taken a lot of nerve to decline Goethe's tribute but the family was very Christian and felt Goethe was damning Ludwig Theobul with faint praise ('intention' and 'endeavour') as well as failing to give God His due. Instead, an old-fashioned hymn-stanza was used that firmly linked Kosegarten with his religious roots and placed him 'ins Haus der ew'gen Wonne' with a certainty of salvation far beyond Goethe's own beliefs. Kosegarten's son, who supervised the posthumous edition of his father's work, reinstated the name Agnes in the Ida poems; it is clear that he wanted no one to connect the facts of his late father's life to the work of the anonymous Ewald or *Ida von Plessen*. His own biography of his father (in Volume 12 of the *Dichtungen*, 1824) expunges all reference to the work of 'Ewald'. His editing caused some confusion in Schochow (see *Schuberts Liedertexte*, Volume 1 p. 243).

THE KOSEGARTEN 'CYCLE'

In 1998 the American musicologist Morten Solvik proposed the idea of a Kosegarten cycle made up of twenty of the twenty-two Kosegarten Schubert settings, excluding the first version of *Abends unter der Linde* D235 and the 1817 song *An die untergehende Sonne* D457. Between 1997 and 1999 this 'cycle' received performances in Chicago, Vienna and Oxford (the latter performance introduced by Elizabeth Norman McKay and reviewed by her in *Schubert durch die Brille*, no. 24, 2000).

The order for this 'cycle' is based on the fact that circa 1860 the archivist of the publishing firm of Spina, Johann Wolf, made an ordering of fair copies of the Kosegarten songs numbered 1 to 20. This is a sequence that Solvik believes goes back to Schubert himself – a different order from that of their composition. This 'Reinschrift' was broken up a long time ago and is now divided into nine different 'instalments' as shown below, each of which has long been sold and collected as a separate autograph item containing, variously, one, two, three or four songs. Some of these fair copies came into the possession of the Wienbibliothek im Rathaus: (a) D240, 241, 228, 229; (b) D219, 227; (c) D313, 314; (d) D230, 231; (e) D238, 237, 236; (f) D233, 221; (g) D317, 318; (h) D319; (i) D315, 316.

Reassembling these nine sources into a single 'Reinschrift', or fair copy, and conserving the order of the songs as printed above, is complicated by the fact that some (though not all) of the manuscripts show evidence of yet another numbering in red crayon. Solvik suggests that the fair-copy sequence assembled by Wolf was designed by Schubert himself. From this, and after a lot of hypothesizing, a cycle or *Liederspiel* emerged with a complicated plot, nicknamed by Elizabeth McKay as *Four Weddings and Two Suicides*. This was performed by three fictional characters – Wilhelm (twelve songs), Ida (five songs) and Luisa (two songs) plus a single trio for all three singers. (Their names are mentioned in five songs of the cycle.) The songs were not composed in the order of the fair copy (see dates of composition above), and Kosegarten himself wrote the poems over a period of thirteen years; they appear in different parts of the sources S2 and S3, as a glance at their page numbers above will demonstrate.

Walther Dürr points out (NSA Vol. 8 p. XVII) that Schubert set Kosegarten songs on 8, 15 and 27 July 1815 by concentrating on the works printed on pp. 132 and 141 of the second volume of the poems (1802). On another occasion (7 July) his choice of poem lay between pp. 39 and 43, and on 20 and 25 July he set to music the poems that appear between pp. 162 and 166. This conscientious and thorough attitude to the perusal of the collection suggests someone who is selecting texts as he goes along, rather than a composer with a storytelling agenda. Apart from this, there was no thriving *Liederspiel* tradition in Vienna that might have given rise to such an event in the Schubert circle. If Schubert and his friends had indeed taken part in something as novel as this, it is extraordinary that none of the people who might have been involved in the enterprise (including the singers) left any account of it in their writings. In Berlin of course it was a different matter entirely: a well-documented history of the *Liederspiel* existed in that city – an invention of the composer Johann Friedrich Reichardt whose *Lieb' und Treue* was staged there in 1800. This format gave rise to the poems for the *Liederspiel* entitled *Die schöne Müllerin* which developed as a collaboration between the composer Ludwig Berger and various poets (Wilhelm Müller being the foremost) in Berlin during 1816 and 1817.

Solvik's plot, purportedly reassembled as Schubert and his friends of 1815 had once known it, is somewhat convoluted. The key relationships between the songs are either awkward (the juxtaposition of F sharp major and F major for example in nos 11 and 12), or tiring on the ear (three successive songs in B flat major, 5–7, these following on, rather awkwardly, from a song in E major). It also seems bad planning that one male singer should sing twelve out of twenty songs, and that the female interest should be so marginal with Luisa performing only two songs. This issue was addressed in the Oxford performance by taking songs 14 and 15 away from Wilhelm and allocating them to the female voices; the tenor clearly found the bass line of *Das Abendrot* too low for comfort, and the music was presented as a duet. In Oxford, unlike for Solvik's original casting plan, Elwina appeared as a new mezzo soprano character. Despite these small details, the audience was enthusiastic once they had cottoned on to the idea and the story – after all, they had the chance of hearing songs by Schubert that are seldom sung and certainly underestimated.

Such events as the Kosegarten-Schubert evenings in Oxford and elsewhere need no academic excuse to justify them, nor the imprimatur of authenticity. It has always been the privilege of performers (as well as their challenge) to gather together songs in garlands carefully woven for different occasions and for different programmatic reasons. The present-day song recital, infinitely more flexible and economical than opera, has the capacity for endless exploration and variation. This includes the possibility of planning newly conceived *Liederspiele* – song-narratives that have little to do with the composer's original intentions, and which follow a scenario designed to entertain and instruct. We should be grateful to Morten Solvik for creating a framework whereby neglected songs by Schubert are performed for an audience that is engaged by a new-found dramaturgy.

Bibliography: Holmes 2004
                 McKay 2000, p. 141
                 Solvik 1999, pp. 169–82

Die KRÄHE *see* *WINTERREISE* D911/15

Der KREUZZUG   The crusade
(Leitner) **D932** [H655]
D major   November 1827

Ein Münich steht in seiner Zell	A monk stands in his cell
Am Fenstergitter grau,	At the grey window-grating;
Viel Rittersleut' in Waffen hell	A band of knights in shining armour
Die reiten durch die Au.	Comes riding through the meadows.
Sie singen Lieder frommer Art	They sing holy songs
Im schönen ernsten Chor,	In fine, solemn chorus;
Inmitten fliegt, von Seide zart,	In their midst the banner of the Cross,
Die Kreuzesfahn' empor.	Made of delicate silk, flies aloft.
Sie steigen an dem Seegestad'	At the shore they climb
Das hohe Schiff hinan.	Aboard the tall ship.
Es läuft hinweg auf grünem Pfad',	It sails away over the green waters,
Ist bald nur wie ein Schwan.	And soon seems but a swan.
Der Münich steht am Fenster noch,	The monk still stands at the window,
Schaut ihnen nach hinaus:	Gazing out after them:
'Ich bin, wie ihr, ein Pilger doch,	'I am, after all, a pilgrim like you,
Und bleib ich gleich zu Haus'.	Although I remain at home.

'Des Lebens Fahrt durch Wellentrug
Und heissen Wüstensand,
Es ist ja auch ein Kreuzeszug
In das gelobte Land.'

'Life's journey through the treacherous waves
And the burning desert sands,
Is also a crusade
Into the Promised Land.'

KARL GOTTFRIED VON LEITNER (1800–1890); poem written in 1824

This is the eighth of Schubert's eleven Leitner solo settings (1822–3 and 1827–8). See the poet's biography for a chronological list of all the Leitner settings.

This is by far the most successful of the simpler Leitner settings. It has a vivid storyline, something lacking in the meditations of *Das Weinen* D926, and it has more musical and dramatic focus than *Der Wallensteiner Lanzknecht beim Trunk* D931. The poem is set during one of the composer's favourite historical periods, the Crusades (two operas, *Fierabras* D796 and the unfinished *Der Graf von Gleichen* D918, are set in this epoch, as well as the Walter Scott *Ivanhoe* setting *Romanze des Richard Löwenherz* D907). That Schubert was pleased with at least two of his Leitner settings is shown by the fact that this song was chosen, together with *Die Sterne*, as part of the programme for the only public concert devoted entirely to his works in his lifetime (26 March 1828 in the Musikverein building in the Tuchlauben). The singer was Vogl and one can only imagine how that great old thespian would have assumed the role. It was clearly one of his more famous 'party pieces'. No doubt every aspect of his operatic past would have been employed to give life to the noble aspects of the monk's renunciation of foreign travel in favour of journeys of the spirit.

The music is written in what Capell calls Schubert's evensong style – solemn and elevated in mood, the marking 'Ruhig und fromm'. The piano introduction is a fragment of melody, related to the vocal line without being identical, which also serves as an interlude between the second and third verses and as a postlude. This moves from D major to B minor (b. 2) and

Der Kreuzzug, a drawing by Peter Fendi.

back to D major via a bar of quavers (b. 3) that are phrased in pairs, wafting gently in the middle of the keyboard until they climb at the last moment to the high D of the baritone tessitura. This figuration is never taken up by the voice (as is a similar phrase in *Das Weinen* D926) but it nicely illustrates the Crusaders' silk pennant flying aloft at the end of Verse 2, as well as the soul's ascension to a better place after a life of religious contemplation at the end of the song.

When the voice enters it is doubled by the piano; there is a very special reason for this, as we shall discover later. This music, which might on first hearing seem to come from the pages of a hymn book, manages a turn of phrase that is still thoroughly Schubertian: the earnest sense of purpose of these Crusaders is combined with an elegiac wistfulness appropriate to the monk's subjective view – his life could have been so much more eventful if he had opted for a different path. The protagonist is clearly not one of those provincial priests whom the composer is known to have loathed because of their cant and hypocrisy (this was his reaction to the clergy in Zseliz during his Hungarian sojourn in 1818); Schubert also accepts Leitner's notion that the soldiers in the processional are not the normal bunch of adventurers and ruffians but rather a group of young idealists motivated by the most radiant belief in their divine mission. In the composer's mind these knights must have come from a better and more noble place than Vienna – the grass of Graz seems infinitely greener in the Leitner settings. The whole scene is fit to be painted in glowing colours by an artist of the Nazarene school (Kuplwieser perhaps), each of the Crusaders a fresh-faced would-be pilgrim. The shift into the plagal reaches of G major at 'Sie singen Lieder frommer Art' (from b. 14) emphasizes the holy nature of the songs. Sudden mention of the Crusaders' pennant is musically painted by a touch of chromatic colour in the harmony as A sharps are introduced into chords which, from 'von Seide zart' (bb. 19–20) move into the key of B minor.

After a repeat of the four-bar introductory music there is completely new music for the poem's third verse. These are the harmonies of change and departure. Thus at 'Sie steigen an dem Seegestad' / Das hohe Schiff hinan' (from b. 28) both melody and harmony rise a number of steps up the stave, as if climbing a gangplank; the sudden shift to B flat major for 'Es läuft hinweg auf grünem Pfad'' (b. 32) cuts the music momentarily adrift from the D major jetty for this magical journey, a medieval version of *L'Embarquement pour Cythère*. The way that B flat major recedes into A major in the course of the words 'Ist bald nur wie ein Schwan' (bb. 34–6) is Schubert at his masterly best – within this decrescendo the ship becomes a tiny swan-like shape on the horizon as the singer's line rises in exploratory semitones as if straining to catch sight of the distant vessel. The music for 'bald nur wie ein Schwan' (Leitner's unwitting prophecy of *Lohengrin*) is repeated as a tiny interlude (bb. 37–8).

And now for the song's masterstroke: the pious pilgrims' march continues to resonate in the air after the Crusaders' departure (they are heard in the piano from b. 38, exactly the music that has accompanied the first verse) while the monk hums only the ghost of the melody. Of course the words of the poem's fifth strophe tell us he is lost in contemplation of the dangers the soldiers will face, and how he himself is also on a spiritual journey of a different kind. But by the brilliant device of allowing the piano to take over the main melody while the monk 'sings along', as it were, in the bass line, we are told everything about both the pain and the joy of having to play a background role. The singer supports the Crusaders with his prayers, and the solid bass line tells us that he represents the rock of their faith. But we are also aware that there is a large element of renunciation in this song, and that he has been prepared to put aside the melodies of life in exchange for harmony of a more celestial kind. In the bare bones of that bass line (which stays at home as much as the monk himself) there is nothing so luxurious as a memorable tune to be heard, emphasizing the austerity of his vocation. After we have heard the whole piece, those wafting quavers of the piano postlude (identical to the introduction) in the second-last bar seem especially affecting – *Der Kreuzzug* finishes with the monk's tear-filled eyes turned heavenward.

Autograph:	Wienbibliothek im Rathaus, Vienna
First edition:	Published in Vienna in January 1832 as a supplement to the *Wiener Allgemeiner musikalischer Anzeiger*, and subsequently as Book 27 no. 2 of the *Nachlass* by Diabelli, Vienna in 1835 (P313)
First known performance:	26 March 1828 at the Musikverein, Vienna as part of the Schubert 'Privatkonzert'. Soloist: Johann Michael Vogl (see Waidelich/Hilmar Dokumente I No. 603 for full concert programme)
Contemporary reviews:	*Allgemeine Musikalische Zeitung* (Leipzig), No. 19 (7 May 1828), col. 307f. [Waidelich/Hilmar Dokumente I No. 613; Deutsch Doc. Biog. No. 1067] *Abend-Zeitung* (Dresden), No. 141 (12 June 1828), p. 564 [Waidelich/Hilmar Dokumente I No. 620] *Allgemeine Musikalische Zeitung* (Berlin), No. 27 (2 July 1828), p. 215 [Waidelich/Hilmar Dokumente I No. 624; Deutsch Doc. Biog. No. 1069]
Subsequent editions:	Peters: Vol. 2/232; AGA XX 549: Vol. 9/114; NSA IV: Vol. 14/76; Bärenreiter: Vol. 4/103
Bibliography:	Youens 2002, pp. 232–6
Discography and timing:	Fischer-Dieskau II 9[10] 3'39 Hyperion I 36[15] Hyperion II 35[8] 3'56 Gerald Finley

← *Der Wallensteiner Lanzknecht beim Trunk* D931   *Al par del ruscelletto (Cantate für Irene Kiesewetter)* D936 →

KRIEGERS AHNUNG *see SCHWANENGESANG* D957/2

ERNESTINE VON KROSIGK (1767–1843)

THE POETIC SOURCE
Taschenbuch für das Jahr 1805, Egeria, herausgegeben von Karl Müchler, Berlin. Bei Johann Friedrich Unger, 1805

THE SONG
30 July 1816   *Aus 'Diego Manazares'* [Manzanares], *Ilmerine* [Almerine] D458 [pp. 70–71]

The character in Krosigk's short story is *Diego Manzanares* who is in love with *Almerine*. With both these misspellings it is highly unlikely that Schubert came into first-hand contact with the almanac containing Krosigk's story; it seems probable that he set the poem from an incorrectly transcribed handwritten source. It is a curious fact that when the song was published for the first time (by J. P. Gotthard, Vienna in 1872) the name 'Diego Manzanares' was spelled correctly. Whether Schubert's song should now be retitled according to its correct literary source is a question for the editors of a third edition of the Deutsch catalogue.

Ernestine von Krosigk (née Ernestine Krüger, and sometimes known under her *nom de plume* of 'Emma') is one of the two new poets to have been recently identified with Schubert (the other is Karl Varnhagen von Ense, qv). She was born on 21 October 1767 in Berlin to a family of senior civil servants and she received a particularly enlightened literary education; her brother's tutor guided her reading of all the great German poets and she wrote her first poem at the age of nine. In her late teens she came into contact with Ramler (who was the anthologist for the volume of poetry – the *Lyrische Bluhmenlese* of 1778 – from which Haydn took the majority of his German lieder texts) and Karl Philipp Moritz whose work on Greek and Roman mythology was probably known to Mayrhofer. She married the Prussian lieutenant Krosigk in 1790. Her *Gedichte* were published with great success in 1792 at a time when there was a definite Enlightenment vogue for women poets such as Anna Luise Karsch (the famous 'Die Karschin', grandmother of Helmina von Chézy (qv)), Chézy's mother Karoline Klenke (qv) and Gabriele von Baumberg (qv). The death of her children and other misfortunes led to the end of what had, anyway, been an unhappy marriage. In 1803 she opened a school for governesses and achieved some renown as an educationalist. She was encouraged to return to literary work by Karl Müchler who edited the almanac named above, and who was a poet set to music by Weber. Krosigk published *Das Dörfchen Larcy, oder Edelmuth und Liebe* (in 1805). *Stunden* followed in 1806. She lived and worked productively in the difficult wartime conditions of the Napoleonic invasion of Germany. She had a long but not particularly productive career in Berlin between 1814 and her death. She died on 10 May 1843, no doubt completely unaware that Schubert, by then increasingly famous in Germany, had set her words to music. It is very doubtful whether Schubert ever knew her name either; it is much more likely that an unattributed handwritten copy of this poem came into his hands rather than a printed copy of Müchler's 1805 almanac.

CHRISTOPH KUFFNER (1780–1846)

THE POETIC SOURCES
S1 *Selam. Ein Almanach für Freunde des Mannifaltigen von I. F. Castelli. Vierter Jahrgang 1815.* Wien, gedruckt und im Verlage bey Anton Strauss.

There are several indications that this was Schubert's source – he was clearly in possession of the almanac for several settings in 1815, and he may have rediscovered the volume to re-use in 1828. In Vs. 1 this printing has 'Hältst du treu', as in the music; S2 has 'Hältst du fest'. The most important line is, however, in Vs. 4 where 'Ohne Liebe bist du Stein', as in the music, is only to be found in S1; the line in S2 is the rather more subtle 'Ohne Liebe gibts nur Schein' – undoubtedly a later thought.

S2 *Lieder für Blinde und von Blinden.* Gesammelt und herausgeben von Johann Wilhelm Klein, Direktor des k.k. Blinden-Instituts in Wien. Wien 1827, Auf Kosten des Herausgebers zum Besten der Blinden.

The words 'Edel Liebe' (Vs. 4) are found here, as in the music, while in S1 we find 'Liebe edel'. There are other reasons (*see* above) for thinking that Schubert composed the song from S1. The musical director of the Institute for the Blind was Simon Sechter with whom Schubert briefly studied in 1828. Underneath the poem *Glaube, Hoffnung und Liebe* are printed the words 'Musik von Abbé Stadler'.

S3 *Gedichte von Christoph Kuffner*, Pesth, bei Konrad Adolph Hartleben 1817

Schochow wrongly dates this edition from 1818.

THE SONG
August 1828   *Glaube, Hoffnung und Liebe* D955 Op. 97 [S1: pp. 269–70] [S2: pp. 50–51] [S3: pp. 87–8]

Christoph Kuffner (sometimes written Kueffner) was born into a cultured Viennese family on 28 June 1780. As a young man he studied music and came into contact with Mozart and Haydn whom he entertained at his father's house in gatherings that were celebrated for the literary and musical distinction of their guests. For both of these masters he wrote oratorio texts that were never used. His third wife was the sister of the piano virtuoso Leo, Edler von Meyer. He studied philosophy and spent his entire working life in the civil service, eventually rising to high rank. Like the infinitely more talented Johann Mayrhofer he worked for a period as censor. This leisurely activity gave him a great deal of time for a second life in literature. He translated the Latin plays of Plautus and wrote many comedies, dramas (for example *Cervantes in Algier*, 1820) and novels. His first collection of *Gedichte* appeared in 1817 and includes the one poem by him that was set by Schubert – although this was almost certainly not the composer's source. It is probable that Kuffner provided the text for Beethoven's Choral Fantasy Op. 80. In this case he would probably have used his musical experience to write words to fit an existing melody. His collected works, published at the end of his life, went into twenty volumes. Julius Seidlitz, in a withering article in his revue of modern Austrian literary life (1836), refers to the 'odourless spice' of Kuffner's huge output of poetry. If Kuffner were dead, the critic went on, it might at least have been said of him that he was not quite the worst poet of his epoch – but the fact that he was still working as a poet negated anything that might have been said in his favour. Kuffner lasted another ten years and died in Vienna on 7 November 1846.

Bibliography: Seidlitz [Jeitteles] 1837, Vol. 1, pp. 113–14

JOHANN GOTTFRIED KUMPF ('ERMIN') (1781–1862)

THE POETIC SOURCES
S1 *Selam. Ein Almanach für Freunde des Mannifaltigen auf das Jahr 1814. Herausgegeben von I. F. Castelli, Dritter Jahrgang 1814.* Wien, gedruckt und im Verlage bey Anton Strauss.

S2 *Selam. Ein Almanach für Freunde des Mannifaltigen von I. F. Castelli. Vierter Jahrgang 1815.* Wien, gedruckt und im Verlage bey Anton Strauss.

J. G. Kumpf ('Ermin'), unsigned portrait.

THE SONGS

1815   *Der Mondabend* D141 [S2: pp. 288–9]
15 October 1815   *Mein Gruss an den Mai* D305 [S1: pp. 200–201]
                       Schochow, 1974, mentions another printing of this poem in *Becker's Taschenbuch*
                       zum geselligen Vergnügen für 1808 where it does not in fact appear

Johann Gottfried Kumpf, who wrote under the pseudonym 'Ermin', was born in Klagenfurt on 9 December 1781. He studied medicine in Vienna from 1805, and from there went on to practise in Pesth and Trieste, returning to Klagenfurt in 1811. He was a friend and biographer of the Styrian poet and war hero Fellinger, qv (three times set by Schubert), whose poems he edited with a biographical introduction in 1819. A doctor of medicine by profession (he wrote a textbook on cholera in 1831), Kumpf/ Ermin was one of countless part-time writers of the period whose work was published in some of the numerous pocket-book almanacs that found their way to members of the Schubert circle, and thus no doubt to the composer himself. That Schubert found Ermin's poems in a Viennese almanac is some indication of the poet's standing in the Austrian capital. Kumpf died in Klagenfurt on 21 February 1862.

Drawing of Schubert by Moritz von Schwind.

L

LA PASTORELLA AL PRATO (I)
(GOLDONI) **D513** [H344]
C major 1817?

The shepherdess
in the meadow

Quartet, TTBB

La pastorella al prato
Contenta se ne va,[1]
Coll'agnellino a lato[2]
Cantando in libertà.
Se l'innocente amore[3]
Gradisce il suo pastore[4]
La bella pastorella
Contenta ognor sarà.

The shepherdess in the meadow
Wanders happily,
The lambs at her side,
And sings blithely.
If her innocent love
Is rewarded by her shepherd,
The fair shepherdess
Will always be happy

CARLO GOLDONI (1707–1793)

Schubert's second setting of this poem, a solo song, is much better known (*see* below). The young composer had tackled a number of Metastasio lyrics for his numerous composition exercises, but of Goldoni's countless verses (this one is from the little-known *Il filosofo di campagna*) *La pastorella* is the only one that engaged Schubert's attentions. It is hard to imagine how the composer would have come across such a text without a lead from Salieri. Further evidence of a possible Salieri connection is the setting of the verse as a vocal quartet by one of Schubert's fellow students, Karl Freiherr von Doblhoff. This setting was dedicated to their revered teacher and was part of *Sei Divertimenti Campestri* published in 1820. Schubert's version remained unpublished in his lifetime and we can only conjecture that it dates from 1817 because of the second version, D528, which is dated January of that year. A further complication is that this work, marked *Quartetto*, shares a manuscript with the undated song fragment *Nur wer die Liebe kennt* D513A.

On stylistic grounds there is an argument for the piece to be dated earlier than 1817. The music here is far from the sophisticated norm of the majority of Schubert's works for male

[1] Goldon writes (in *Opere teatrali*, 1795) 'Col gregge, se ne va'.
[2] Goldoni writes 'Con agenelline allato'.
[3] Goldoni writes 'Se l'innocente *amante*'.
[4] Goldoni writes '*Gradisce* il suo pastor'.

quartet, TTBB. The piano writing is in flowing semiquavers – these well enough convey the ambling and relaxed nature of the text – but the accompaniment rarely shows any independence from the vocal line, and there is no sign of the illustrative pianistic detail that enlivens and illuminates the later works in this vein. The smoothness of the *bel canto* writing is pleasing and euphonious but nothing new: Schubert had achieved this sort of melodic ease with Italian texts as early as 1813. More individual is the delightful vocal interplay, lobs in a tennis game of musical counterpoint, between the voices (the first tenor and first bass) at 'Cantando in libertà' (bb. 12–15), and the moment of freedom enjoyed by the lead tenor three bars from the end, like a tiny cadenza, with the flourish of the final 'libertà'. Otherwise everything about this piece is straightforward, including its unexceptional ABA form. The middle section (beginning 'Se l'innocente amore / Gradisce il suo pastore') contains an echo (or perhaps a prophecy, depending on the dates): the tiny little decorative figure of two demisemiquavers on 'am*ore*' and 'pa*store*' (bb. 18 and 20), the culmination of a line of repeated notes in the vocal line, is possibly a link with *Der Wanderer* D489 (at the line 'Die Sonne dünkt mich').

The threefold repetition of 'Contenta ognor sarà' (from b. 21), a phrase initially decorated with dotted rhythms and then with excursions to high Gs for the first tenor, passes muster as a convincing operatic cliché. The conventional modulation from dominant to tonic, soupily achieved by the sliding chromatic movement of the first bass (b. 28), similarly relishes an Italianate commonplace and borders on knowing parody. It is the composer's smile behind this music that reinforces the possibility that this work dates from as late as 1817; there is little here of the adolescent earnestness to be found in the composition exercises of 1813.

Autograph: Wienbibliothek im Rathaus, Vienna (headed *Quartetto*)
First edition·   Published as part of the AGA in 1891 (P513)
Subsequent editions: AGA XVI 19: p. 134; NSA III: Vol. 3
Discography and timing: Hyperion I 34²   John Mark Ainsley, Jamie
                         Hyperion II 17²²   MacDougall, Simon
                                         1'45   Keenlyside & Michael George

← *La pastorella al prato* (II) D528   *An eine Quelle* D530 →

LA PASTORELLA AL PRATO (II)   The shepherdess in the meadow
(GOLDONI) **D528** [H343]
G major   January 1817

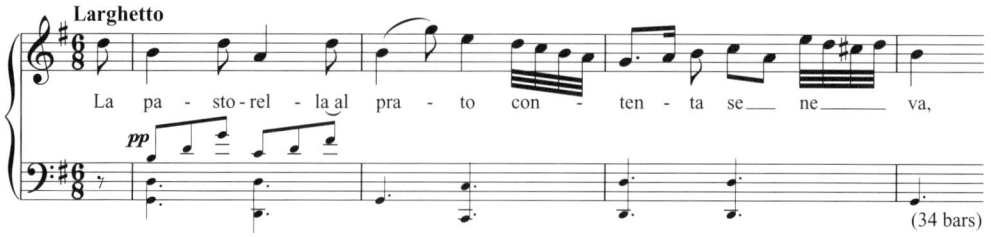

(34 bars)

See previous entry for poem and translation

CARLO GOLDONI (1707–1793)

This is Schubert's only Goldoni solo setting. See the poet's biography.

This is the second Schubert setting of Goldoni's little poem. The first (D513) is a charming and undemanding quartet for men's voices, with appropriate canonic flourishes on the words 'Cantando in libertà' (*see* commentary above). The text is taken from Carlo Goldoni's opera libretto *Il filosofo di campagna* (Act II Scene 16) and is the final strophe of an aria sung by the minor character Lena. There is a town girl versus country girl rivalry at work here. Lena is the niece of the rich farmer Nardo (the homespun philosopher of the text) and she is mocked for her ambition, despite her not even having a suitor, to better her position in society. Her aria is in defence of the true and simple heart of the country dweller. The libretto had been set by Baldassare Galuppi in 1754 who created with it one of the most successful and popular operas of the eighteenth century. Schubert was almost certainly still taking advice from Salieri at the time he wrote the quartet, and the corrections on the autograph of the solo song are most likely those of the Italian master. It is probable that this song marks the end of their teacher–pupil relationship.

The solo aria is infinitely more Italian in flavour and style than D513. Like a number of his other songs in this language it is as if the composer began setting the words in a spirit of pastiche and parody but fell in love with the style that he had set out to mock. In this conflict of Prater versus prato is defined Schubert's ambivalence towards the crowd-pleasing music that so threatened his own prospects as a composer of German operas, but which, in the final analysis, he could not bring himself truly to dislike. As he himself admitted, it was impossible to deny Rossini's genius. The richly ornamented vocal line of *La pastorella* is reminiscent of the embellishments added to some of the Schubert songs by the singer Vogl, an artist old-fashioned enough to ornament all his music in eighteenth-century Italian style. The beautifully varied settings of the word 'libertà' (bb. 7–8, 11–12, 28–9) show that Schubert's delight in word-painting was not confined to the German language.

Autograph:	Staatsbibliothek Preussischer Kulturbesitz, Berlin (headed *Ariette*)
First edition:	Published as No. 19 of *Neueste Folge nachgelassener Lieder und Gesänge* by J. P. Gotthard, Vienna in 1872 (P445)
Subsequent editions:	Not in Peters; AGA XX 574: Vol. 10/46; NSA IV: Vol. 11/84
Bibliography:	Monson 1992
Discography and timing:	Fischer-Dieskau —
	Hyperion I 9[17]
	Hyperion II 17[21] 2'07 Arleen Auger

← *Schlaflied D527*   *La pastorella al prato* (I) D513 →

LABETRANK DER LIEBE   The cordial of love
(Stoll) **D302** [H182]
F major   15 October 1815

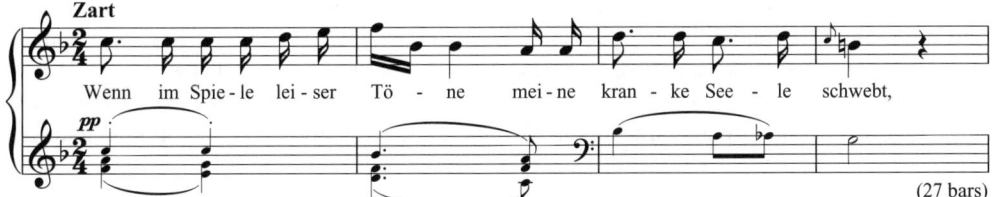

Wenn im Spie-le lei-ser Tö - ne mei-ne kran - ke See - le schwebt,

(27 bars)

Wenn im Spiele leiser Töne	When, amid the strains of soft music,
Meine kranke Seele schwebt,	My suffering soul hovers,
Und der Wehmut süsse Träne	And sweet tears of sadness
Deinem warmen Blick entschwebt:[1]	Flow from your warm gaze:
Sink' ich dir bei sanftem Wallen	I sink down silently
Deines Busens sprachlos hin;	On your gently heaving breast
Engelmelodien schallen,	Angelic melodies sound
Und der Erde Schatten fliehn.	And the earth's shadows take flight.
So in Eden hingesunken,	Thus, immersed in paradise,
Lieb' mit Liebe umgetauscht,	Exchanging love with love,
Küsse lispelnd, Wonnetrunken,	Whispering kisses, drunk with ecstasy,
Wie von Seraphim umrauscht:	As if seraphim played about us:
Reichst du mir im Engelbilde	You gave me, in the form of an angel,
Liebewarmen Labetrank,	A reviving potion, warm with love,
Wenn im schnöden Staubgefilde	As my languishing soul
Schmachtend meine Seele sank.	Sank in the hateful, dusty wastes.

JOSEPH LUDWIG STOLL (1778–1815)

This is the second of Schubert's three Stoll solo settings (October 1815). See the poet's biography for a chronological list of all the Stoll settings. See also the article for Selam.

This ravishingly beautiful song is absolutely unhymned by the commentators. It has become lost in the welter of music written on the exceptional day in October 1815 that saw its birth. Schubert's flirtation with Stoll's poetry was brief but gently fruitful – the other Stoll song, *An die geliebte* D303, was also written on the 15th. Kumpf's *Mein Gruss an den Mai* D305 and Fellinger's *Die Sternenwelten* D307 were written on this day, as were two settings of Körner (including *Das gestörte Glück* D309) and one each by Deinhardstein and Kalchberg. While in possession of the poetic source that unites most of these songs, the almanac *Selam* for 1814, Schubert seems to have been in unstoppable creative form. For a text that called for music to accompany sweet suffering and the music of the seraphim, Schubert matched the poet, if not image by image, then in the poem's general Elysian tenor. As is often the case in music that describes heavenly radiance, the composer avoided the F clef for much of the setting. Nevertheless, the magic of the song depends on the interaction of the vocal line with the bass; in this way the reciprocated nature of the encounter is built into the fabric of the music. After the rarefied opening bars, a delicate accompaniment in mezzo staccato semiquavers pushes the music forward with a *Bewegung* that suggests both the stirrings of masculine passion and the rise and fall of the bosom as described in the text. 'Deinem warmen Blick entschwebt' (bb. 6–8), with the 'schwebt' decorated with a heady little melisma, is a marvel. The music on the words 'Engelmelodien schallen' (bb. 15–17), with its heart-stopping suspensions, is at once erotic and pure. The reviving potion is of course a kiss, and Schubert somehow finds the means to suggest neither a peck, nor a passionate lunge, but rather a lingering, sensual exchange. We are many years away from the sacred-erotic atmosphere of *Du bist die Ruh* D776 but *Labetrank der Liebe* is clearly created by the same hand. With its rising tetrachord in the vocal line, followed

---

[1] Stoll's original verb here is 'entbebt'.

by a falling fifth, as well as the use of suspensions in the piano writing, the opening of this song seems prophetic of Schumann's famous Eichendorff setting, *Mondnacht* Op. 39 no. 5. Walther Dürr believes it possible that this song was part of an intended cycle created from the poems Schubert found in the almanac *Selam*, on 15 October 1815 (*see* SELAM CYCLE).

Autograph:	Österreichische Nationalbibliothek, Vienna (first draft)
	New York Public Library (fair copy)
First edition:	Published as part of the AGA in 1895 (P590)
Subsequent editions:	Not in Peters; AGA XX 150: Vol. 3/114; NSA IV: Vol. 9/132
Discography and timing:	Fischer-Dieskau I 5[27] 2'42
	Hyperion I 10[17]
	Hyperion II 10[18] 3'20 Martyn Hill

← *Lambertine* D301   *An die Geliebte* D303 →

LACHEN UND WEINEN   Laughter and tears
(Rückert) Op. 59 no. 4, **D777** [H521]
A♭ major   1823?

(83 bars)

Lachen und Weinen zu jeglicher Stunde	When you're in love, laughter and tears
Ruht bei der Lieb' auf so mancherlei Grunde.	Can come at any time, and for so many reasons.
Morgens lacht' ich vor Lust;	In the morning I laughed for joy;
Und warum ich nun weine	And why I'm crying
Bei des Abendes Scheine,	Now that it's evening,
Ist mir selb' nicht bewusst.	I don't even know myself!
Weinen und Lachen zu jeglicher Stunde	When you're in love, tears and laughter
Ruht bei der Lieb' auf so mancherlei Grunde.	Can come at any time, and for so many reasons.
Abends weint' ich vor Schmerz;	In the evening I cried with pain;
Und warum du erwachen	And how you can wake up
Kannst am Morgen mit Lachen,	Laughing this morning:
Muss ich dich fragen, o Herz.	This I must ask you, my heart!

Friedrich Rückert (1788–1866); poem written in 1819/20

This is the fourth of Schubert's six Rückert solo settings (1822–3). See the poet's biography for a chronological list of all the Rückert settings.

This is certainly the most famous, as well as the most pithy, of Schubert's philosophical songs. It has always been loved by Schubertians because of its easy, winsome charm, and because the title and text encapsulate the composer's special ability to depict two emotions simultaneously. Much of Schubert's music is poised between major and minor, between dark and light. His major-key music is often suffused with an undercurrent of sadness: he is painfully aware that the blessed state of joy must end all too soon. On the other hand, in the darkest tragedy there is always a consoling beam of light, in the midst of the coldest season there is always a 'Frühlingsglaube' – a belief that spring breezes will soon soothe the frozen ravages of winter.

In *Lachen und Weinen* we hear of a love affair in full bloom, and have no real fears for the eventual happiness of the protagonist. If introspection is detected, it is momentary. Friedrich Rückert, in writing his collection entitled *Östliche Rosen*, was deeply influenced by Goethe's sybaritic *West-östlicher Divan*, and *Lachen und Weinen* has much in common with Schubert's setting from that collection, *Geheimes* D719. Both songs are in A flat major, and both are animated by the ardent energy of youthful love; both suggest a world of lovemaking where formality is underscored by complex amatory intrigue; sexual licence lies close to the surface but is hidden by a veneer of etiquette.

Vignette for this poem in Rückert's *Östliche Rosen* (1822).

The composer uses the poem's first words as a title. In a later edition of Rückert's poems (which Schubert never saw) the poem appears as *Lachens und Weinens Grund* ('The reason for laughter and tears'). Although there is nothing in Rückert's text to confine the song to a female singer (and it is sometimes sung by male artists) the music suggests feminine capriciousness, the characteristics perhaps of an imagined eastern girl, younger sister to Zuleika. (Richard Capell writes of 'the fling of some tempestuous petticoat'.) The nimble piano introduction contains a pair of turns (bb. 2 and 4), challenging figurations that are executed by the accompanist's fingers like pirouettes. These alone suggest femininity. The weaving of this music, where each note of these little roulades has to be clearly heard, the pianistic equivalent of a dancer turning on the head of a pin (particularly tricky for pianists with large hands), is superbly descriptive of emotions darting back and forth, in and out of a lovers' maze. The third and fourth bars are a repeat of the first two, encapsulating the 'either/or' mood of the singer's dilemma as first one emotion is tried out and then another. The perfection in the part-writing is notable: the left hand is made up of a gentle melody that is singable in its own right; the two staves, which delicately intermesh as if they were gears of the tiniest watch mechanism, might have been scored for clarinet and bassoon, winds tenderly blowing in the same direction. In b. 5 (which leads back to the cadence in the home key) there is piquant use of a miniature upper pedal: beneath a roof of mezzo staccato E flats, the ascending scale in thirds between the hands suggests something deliciously clandestine – the nursing of a lover's secret emotions. It is not the only time in the song that E flat is a pivot of ambivalence.

The melody of the opening four-bar phrase ('Lachen und Weinen zu jeglicher Stunde') rolls gently down the stave, incorporating an upward inflection for 'Lachen' and a downward one for 'Weinen'. So successful are bb. 9–12 that the next line of the poem is set to four bars (bb. 13–16) of exactly the same music and accompaniment. This repetition is typical of the delightful symmetry built everywhere into the song's plan: laughter and tears are weighed, one against the other, and found to be of equal importance.

With talk of sunrise and sunset ('Morgens lacht' ich vor Lust' b. 18) Schubert introduces the dactylic rhythm (long-short-short) which he often uses (as in *Der Tod und das Mädchen* D531 and *Der Wanderer* D489 for example) to depict cosmic matters: starlight, the turning of the world and the immutable aspects of living and dying. Here the rhythm is used to paint the dynamic nature of love itself and the perky character of the singer whose 'Lust' is set as a merry melisma that jumps a fourth from B flat to an E flat (at b. 20) which is held over the bar line. Suddenly, the suspended note changes colour as the accompanying chord slips from A flat major to A flat minor (b. 21). Another song from the same period – the Stolberg setting *Auf dem Wasser zu singen* D774 – is built on exactly this conjunction of harmony and on the same device of a held E flat in the vocal line that seems to change colour and mood with the intervention of the piano's harmonies.

The next line of poetry and the following vocal phrase ('Und warum ich nun weine') stays poised on E flat (with the exception of an expressive appoggiatura pushing 'weine' up to an exotic F flat at b. 25). Underneath this, the piano pulsates for some five bars on chords in dactylic rhythm that remain rooted on E flat[7], as if to emphasize that here is an open question awaiting an answer. The result is a cleverly engineered pause in the harmonic content of the music, despite its continuing rhythmic impetus. The singer no longer feels like laughing; now being in love makes her weep. This new-found insecurity (to the words 'Bei des Abendes Scheine' bb. 27–30) takes place over the accompanist's descent in minim chords (F flat major – C flat major – D flat minor – A flat minor), a slow sunset slide, visually strengthened by sweeping phrase marks. The lack of any propulsion from the piano – no dancing quavers or dactylic rhythm in this passage – adds to this sudden seriousness. With the final word of the line we find ourselves once more in A flat minor (b. 30), but this *minore* moment is soon to be contradicted.

The singer has a crotchet rest (plus a fermata) to ponder this anomaly – why is she happy in the morning yet sad at night? Just when we might have expected a soulful answer, we experience one of the most famous shrugs in song literature. In major-key music which is once again animated by snappy dactylic rhythm she tells us twice that she does not know the answer ('Ist mir selb' nicht bewusst' bb. 31–5). There is something about the setting of these words ('quick and voluble . . . light and girlish' as Capell puts it) that suggests she no longer cares about the answer, that prolonged introspection is not her forte. And generations of listeners have loved her all the more for her disinclination to search her soul. This singer knows that love, for all its complexity and paradoxes, should be more enchantment than burden. The piano echoes the vocal line's repetition of 'Ist mir selb' nicht bewusst' (bb. 36–9) and, following this, the music of the ritornello that served as *Vorspiel* is now the interlude bridging the two halves of the song.

The text of the second verse reverses the word-order to 'Weinen und Lachen' and, although for eight bars the music is the same as for the corresponding eight bars in the first verse, the dactylic section begins this time in A flat *minor*. It seems as if the whole song has been planned as something of a musical palindrome. 'Abends weint' ich vor Schmerz' (bb. 57–60) is, not surprisingly, sung in the minor key, and this time it is the word 'Schmerz' that leaps up a fourth and holds on to the E flat tied across the bar line. Here it is once again the piano's role to be contradictory: underneath that ambiguous E flat, it insists on A flat *major* (at b. 60) to cancel out the minor key mood of 'Schmerz'. The most important difference between the first and second strophes is at 'Und warum du erwachen / Kannst am Morgen mit Lachen' bb. 61–5 where the music has to be lively enough to mirror the idea of morning laughter. To achieve this, Schubert lifts the tessitura of the vocal line and underpins it by tightening the harmonic screw: E flat[7] is followed by A flat[7], and the music arrives in D flat major for the highest, brightest phrase in the piece – 'Morgen mit Lachen' (bb. 64–5). This is followed by a whole bar's rest, as well as a fermata. This time to ponder proves more than long enough for the patience of the singer. Her question to her heart ('Muss ich dich fragen, o Herz') receives no reply, nor is she expecting one. She is prepared to write the whole thing off as one of life's inscrutable mysteries.

Again the piano echoes the music of what has just been sung before repeating the enchanting ritornello (we hear those dancing ornamental turns for the third time in far fewer than that number of minutes) which leads the song to its conclusion. We are left with the experience of an intricate and perfect musical mechanism which is totally at the service of the poet and the poem's simple paradox. At this stage of his life Schubert knew exactly how much (or how little) was necessary to match the poet's intention. It is also a perfect character piece of a lover who glimpses, if only for a moment, the seriousness of being in love, but that moment is not enough to deflect her from enjoying the present and in that moment is the song's greatness.

Autograph:	Missing or lost
First edition:	Published as Op. 59 no. 4 by Sauer & Leidesdorf, Vienna in September 1826 (P108)
Publication reviews:	*Allgemeine musikalische Zeitung* (Leipzig), No. 17 (25 April 1827), col. 291f. [Waidelich/Hilmar Dokumente I No. 486; Deutsch Doc. Biog. No. 866]
Subsequent editions:	Peters: Vol. 2/122; AGA XX 455: Vol. 8/7; NSA IV: Vol. 3/103; Bärenreiter: Vol. 2/133
Bibliography:	Capell 1928, p. 202
	Fischer-Dieskau 1977, p. 197
Discography and timing:	Fischer-Dieskau II 6[10] 1'48
	Pears-Britten 1[5] 1'34
	Hyperion I 35[6]
	Hyperion II 27[9] 1'56 Lynne Dawson

← *Dass sie hier gewesen* D775   *Greisengesang* D778 →

LACRIMAS *see ZWEI SZENEN AUS DEM SCHAUSPIEL LACRIMAS* D857

'LADY OF THE LAKE' SONGS *see SIEBEN GESÄNGE AUS WALTER SCOTT'S FRÄULEIN VOM SEE* Op. 52 D837–8, D835–6, D846, D839, D843

LAMBERTINE   Lambertina
(Anonymous) **D301** [H181]
E♭ major   12 October 1815

(43 bars)

O Liebe, die mein Herz erfüllet,	O love, that fills my heart,
Wie wonnevoll ist deine Seligkeit!	How sweet is your bliss!

Doch ach! wie grausam peinigend durchwühlet	But ah, how cruelly, how painfully
Mich Hoffnungslosigkeit.	I am consumed by despair.

Er liebt mich nicht, er liebt mich nicht, verloren	He does not love me, he does not love me;
Ist ohne ihn des Lebens süsse Lust.	Without him life's sweet pleasure has vanished.
Ich bin zu einem Leiden nur geboren,	I am born only to bitter suffering;
Nur Schmerz drückt meine Brust.	Sorrow alone oppresses my heart.

Doch nein, ich will nicht länger trostlos klagen!	But no, I shall no longer lament inconsolably!
Zu sehen ihn gönnt mir das Schicksal noch;	Fate still permits me to see him.
Darf ich ihm auch nicht meine Liebe sagen,	Though I may not declare my love to him,
G'nügt mir sein Anblick doch.	Yet the very sight of him is enough for me.

Sein Bild ist Trost in meinem stillen Kummer,	His image is a comfort in my silent grief,
Hier hab' ich's mir zur Wonne aufgestellt;	I have set it up here to bring me joy;
Dies soll mich laben, bis dass ew'ger Schlummer	This will console me until eternal slumber
Mein mattes Herz befällt.	Overcomes my weary heart.

ANONYMOUS/UNKNOWN (FORMERLY ATTRIBUTED TO JOSEPH LUDWIG STOLL)

*This is the sixth of Schubert's nineteen solo settings of an anonymous poet. See Anonymous/
Unknown for a chronological list of all the songs for which the poets are unknown.*

This is a characteristically brave experiment from that *annus mirabilis* of song, 1815. It is also something of an experiment on the part of the poet: the lyric is mostly a model of metric regularity (lines 2 to 16 are pentameters, every fourth line a trimeter) but the opening of the poem is an isolated tetrameter. The start of the piano introduction is a pre-echo of the Goethe setting *An die Entfernte* D765 from 1822. *Lambertine*, which manages to sound new and at the same time be in the old Haydnesque cantata style, is divided into three clear sections. The opening strophe (in E flat with the marking 'Langsam, mit Ausdruck') is prefaced by a remarkably sophisticated and extended six-bar *Vorspiel*. The top line of this has all the temperament of an impassioned violin solo and the vocal line, with its ornate duplets and decorative triplets, has an Italian cast to it. At b. 9 this is thrown into a mood of minor-key grieving: left-hand trills (unusual in this period of Schubert's song-writing) undermine the girl's happiness like worms in the bud. The setting of 'Hoffnungslosigkeit' (bb. 12–13) in E flat minor occasions an accompaniment in part-writing of richly layered sophistication that, again, is scarcely typical of the period. There is no doubt that Schubert took more than usual care with this setting.

   For the middle section in F minor the marking is 'Bewegt'. The four flats and the change of speed are reminiscent of the middle section of Hölty's *An den Mond* D193 from earlier in the year. The music surges forward, adrift in a sea of all the disorientated key changes that flow from the realization that 'He loves me not'. After this, all seems set for a recapitulation of the beautiful music of the first verse (as happens in *An den Mond*) but it is not to be. We return to the key of E flat and the last two verses of the poem are set to new music entirely. Gone are the restless sextuplets; their sprawling despair is replaced by luminous poise, heartfelt and chaste. Lambertina has made a stoical decision to continue loving without there being any reciprocation; the music of these last two verses suggests a struggle for abstinence, and thereby a sort of spiritual liberation (the time signature moves to $\frac{3}{8}$ from the straitjacket of duple time). That the last verse is a musical repeat of the third only adds to this feeling of resolve. The last section of the song lies high, radiant and calm, a challenge for any singer. It is a fine example of how Schubert can movingly depict the progress of a character from one point in her life to another, even in a song as short as this.

There are two mysteries about this piece: the first is the identity of the poet (the text is almost certainly not by Stoll, an attribution that still persists); the second is why Schubert should have chosen on the song's autograph to notate the theme and beginning of the second variation (pulsating sextuplets) of his *Zehn Variationen* in F, D156, his first really important work for piano from February 1815.

Autograph:	Library of Congress, Washington
First edition:	Published as Book 36 no. 2 of the *Nachlass* in 1842 (P344)
Subsequent editions:	Peters: Vol. 6/5; AGA XX 149: Vol. 3/112; NSA IV: Vol. 9/130
Discography and timing:	Fischer-Dieskau —
	Hyperion I 9[10]
	Hyperion II 10[17] 3'19 Arleen Auger

← *Liane* D298   *Labetrank der Liebe* D302 →

Der LANDENDE OREST *see* OREST [AUF TAURIS] D548

KARL LAPPE (1773–1843)

THE POETIC SOURCES
S1 *Blätter von Karl Lappe. Erstes Heft. Lied and Leben*. Stralsund, 1824. Gedruckt in der Königl. Regierungs-Buchdruckerei

S2 *Karl Lappe's Sämmtliche poetische Werke*. Mit dem Bildniss des Verfassers. Erster Theil. Rostock, Verlag von J. M. Oeberg, 1836

THE SONGS
January 1825   *Im Abendrot* D799 [S1: p. 24] [S2: p. 17]
          Der Einsame D800 [S1: pp. 88–9] [S2: pp. 65–6]

Mention should also be made of another Lappe setting for unaccompanied voices that is outside the scope of this book: *Flucht* D825B Op. 64 no. 3. Quartet (TTBB)

Karl Lappe, schoolmaster and farmer, was born into a preacher's family in Wusterhausen, near Wolgast in Pomerania on 24 April 1773. He was of sickly appearance and never enjoyed good health. His literary career is typical of nineteenth-century Germany where poets often achieved a regional celebrity. His *Gedichte* were published in two instalments in 1801 and 1811 (*Der Einsame* makes its first appearance in the 1811 volume, p. 49) and his complete works in 1836, without his being taken seriously by the literati of the big cities. The publication of two of his poems in Schiller's *Musenalmanach* of 1796 was probably due to the intervention of his teacher and mentor Kosegarten. Deutsch pronounces him

Karl Lappe, unsigned portrait as frontispiece for his
Sämmtliche poetische Werke (1840).

source of their inspiration. These locales were also beloved of the painter Caspar David Friedrich whose *Kreidefelsen auf Rügen* (Chalk Cliffs on Rügen) (1818) depicts three travellers looking out onto a sun-drenched sea. This painting suggests the panorama, if not exactly the time of day, described in *Im Abendrot*. Lappe's collection *Blätter* (1824) was Schubert's source; it was enthusiastically reviewed in the *Wiener Zeitschrift* on Christmas Day 1824 (the poetry was compared to that of Uz), and the editor of that journal, Johann Schickh, a friend of the composer, almost certainly passed on to Schubert the copy of the poems that had been sent to his office. I was fortunate enough to acquire Lappe's *Blätter*, inscribed by the poet to Schickh and possibly used by the composer. On the subscriber list printed at the beginning of the volume Schickh is down for two copies, and two Viennese booksellers have ordered one each; the surprise is that no less a luminary than Ignaz Castelli (qv) had put his name down for twenty – as if he intended to make a gift of the book to friends, something that suggests a personal link between the two men. On the other hand this gesture from the well-to-do Castelli might be explained by the fact that this volume of poetry was printed with the purpose of raising money for Lappe whose home in Pütte ('Die Hütte in Pütte') had been destroyed by fire, a terrible catastrophe for the poet and his large family. The *Wiener Zeitschrift* review had mentioned the straitened circumstances of the poet and Schubert could not have failed to feel sympathetic. Lappe's simplicity of approach, and his homely naturalness, were clearly attractive to the composer. Lappe died on 28 October 1843 in Stralsund, the mainland town across the water from the island of Rügen.

'unimportant', but Lappe provided the texts of two of Schubert's most beloved songs and his poem *So oder So* achieved national celebrity through the setting of K. Klage (1788–1850). Beethoven also set this lyric as a song in 1817 (WoO148) and the same poem was used by Schumann for his choral setting Op. 59 no. 1 with the title *Nord oder Süd!* Lappe's debt to the pantheistic poetry of Goethe is obvious in *Im Abendrot*, but he was also influenced by Kosegarten. The two poets share the seascapes of the island of Rügen (a favourite holiday destination for Germans), and in particular the northernmost peninsula of Wittow, as a

Die LAUBE
(HÖLTY) **D214** [H108]
A♭ major   17 June 1815

The arbour

(19 bars)

Nimmer werd' ich, nimmer dein vergessen,	Never shall I forget you,
Kühle grüne Dunkelheit,	Cool, green darkness,
Wo mein liebes Mädchen oft gesessen,	Where my beloved often sat
Und des Frühlings sich gefreut.	And delighted in the spring
Schauer wird durch meine Nerven beben,	My nerves will shudder
Werd ich deine Blüten sehn,	When I see your blossoms,
Und ihr Bildnis mir entgegenschweben,	See her image float towards me,
Ihre Gottheit mich umwehn.	And her divine radiance envelop me.
[. . . 2 . . .]	[. . . 2 . . .]
Wenn ich auf der Bahn der Tugend wanke,	When I totter on the path of virtue,
Weltvergnügen mich bestrickt;	Tangled in earthly pleasures,
Dann durchglühe mich der Feurgedanke,	Then let the thought burn through me
Was in dir ich einst erblickt:	Of what I once beheld in you.
Und, als strömt' aus Gottes offnem Himmel,	And when virtue streams down upon me
Tugendkraft auf mich herab,	From God's open heaven
Werd' ich fliehen, und vom Erdgewimmel	I shall flee, and remove my pilgrim's staff
Fernen meinen Pilgerstab.	From this earthly throng.

LUDWIG HÖLTY (1748–1776); poem written in early April 1773. Adapted for publication in 1804 by JOHANN HEINRICH VOSS (1751–1826).

This is the eleventh of Schubert's twenty-three Hölty solo settings (1813–16). See the poet's biography for a chronological list of all the Hölty settings.

On 17 June 1815 Schubert, in earthy and cheeky mood, composed the risqué *Der Traum* D213, immediately followed by another Hölty setting, a lyric of the highest idealism, *Die Laube*, where the poet mourns his dead beloved and swears abstinence from the dross of earthly pleasures. In 1815, this most fecund of song years, the composer was able to embrace the sacred and the profane in the span of a single day. A fortnight later he was to compose another song in A flat, the incomparable Goethe setting *Erster Verlust* D226; *Die Laube*, also in four flats, appears to be a study for that masterpiece. There are similarities to the Kosegarten *Ida* songs from the same period. Although the voice part hugs the accompanimental line for some of the time, all is not quite stoic simplicity. In bb. 3–7 the descending vocal line is enhanced with a tiny kick of syncopation which suggests past delight. The accompaniment changes to semiquavers at b. 13 (when appropriate to depict the narrator's quivering nerves). The setting (with a fermata) of 'schweben' in b. 17 is harmonically adventurous, preceding a return to a rather more conventional final cadence. There are times such as this when the baroque, Viennese and Italian influences that shaped much of Schubert's endlessly inventive nature are combined with the German manner associated with Reichardt and Zelter. Melody and sentiment are brought under control in a way that seems more appropriate to the Protestant north than the Catholic south, and extraneous musical show is kept to a minimum. Nevertheless, the rather high tessitura adds a vocal ardour in performance that is far less evident when the piece is simply studied on the page. Reichardt's setting of these words, the seventh song in his *Oden und Lieder von Klopstock, Stolberg, Claudius und Hölty* (E flat major, in ⅜, Berlin, 1779) also has a northern feel in its understatement, though very different from Schubert's song. Schubert also placed the enormously long ballad *Adelwold und Emma* D211, composed in the same month, in an austere northern milieu. The influence of that work (and Hölty) hang over this arbour despite the Italianate influence of Petrarch and his Laura.

There are six strophes in Hölty's poem – these are all printed in the AGA and are all translated in Wigmore 1988. Given here are those recorded for the Hyperion Edition: Verses 1, 2, 5 and 6.

Autograph:	Missing or lost
First edition:	Published as Op. post. 172 no. 2 by C. A. Spina, Vienna in 1865 (P402)
Subsequent editions:	Peters: Vol. 6/98; AGA XX 81: Vol. 2/159; NSA IV: Vol. 8/102
Discography and timing:	Fischer-Dieskau I 4³ 1'49 (four strophes)
	Hyperion I 10¹⁵
	Hyperion II 7⁷ 2'20 Martyn Hill

 *Der Traum* D213   *Jägers Abendlied* D215

LAURA AM KLAVIER
(Schiller) **D388** [H228]

Laura at the piano

The song exists in two versions, both of which are discussed below:
(1) March 1816; (2) March 1816?

(1)   E major – B♭ major

(87 bars)

(2)   A major

(106 bars)

Wenn dein Finger durch die Saiten meistert—	When your fingers hold sway over the strings, Laura
Laura, jetzt zur Statue entgeistert,	I stand there now dumbfounded, as if turned into a statue,

Jetzt[1] entkörpert steh' ich da.
Du gebietest über Tod und Leben,
Mächtig, wie von tausend Nervgeweben
 Seelen fordert Philadelphia.

 Now disembodied
You have command over life and death,
As mighty as Philadelphia,
 Drawing the souls from a thousand sensitive beings.

Ehrerbietig leiser rauschen
Dann die Lüfte, dir zu lauschen;
 Hingeschmiedet zum Gesang
 Stehn im ew'gen Wirbelgang,
Einzuzieh'n die Wonnefülle,
Lauschende Naturen stille.
 Zauberin! mit Tönen, wie
 Mich mit Blicken, zwingst du sie.

In reverence the breezes whisper more softly,
So as to listen to you:
 Riveted by the music,
 Nature listening silently,
Stops in her whirring course
To take in the abundant delights.
 Enchantress! With sounds you enthral her,
 As you enthral me with your eyes.

Seelenvolle Harmonien wimmeln,
 Ein wollüstig Ungestüm,
Aus ihren Saiten, wie aus ihren Himmeln
 Neugebor'ne Seraphim;
Wie, des Chaos Riesenarm entronnen,
Aufgejagt vom Schöpfungssturm, die Sonnen
 Funkelnd fuhren aus der Nacht,
 Strömt der Töne Zaubermacht.

Soulful harmonies
 Sensual and impetuous,
Teem from her strings, like new-born seraphim
 From their heaven.
As the flashing suns shot from the night,
Escaping the giant arm of Chaos
 Driven away by the storm of creation
 So the magic power of music pours forth.

Lieblich jetzt, wie über glatten Kieseln
Silberhelle Fluten rieseln,—
 Majestätisch prächtig nun
 Wie des Donners Orgelton,
Stürmend von hinnen jetzt, wie sich
 von Felsen

Sweetly now, as clear, silvery water
Ripples over smooth pebbles;
 Now with majestic splendour,
 Like the thunder's organ-tones;
Now raging forth like rushing, foaming
 torrents

---

[1] Schiller writes 'Itzt', but the Viennese edition used by Schubert (Doll, 1810) changes this to the modern 'Jetzt'. See also Verse 4.

Rauschende, schäumende Giessbäche wälzen,	Surging from rocks;
Holdes Gesäusel bald,	Now sweetly murmuring,
Schmeichlerisch linde,	Gently coaxing,
Wie durch den Espenwald	Like wooing breezes
Buhlende Winde,	Wafting through the aspen woods.
Schwerer nun und melancholisch düster	Now heavier, dark with melancholy,
Wie durch toter Wüsten Schauernachtgeflüster,	Like fearful nocturnal whisperings through dead wastes
Wo verlornes Heulen schweift,	Where the howls of lost, wandering souls echo,
Tränenwellen der Kozytus schleift.	And Cocytus drags waves of tears.

Mädchen sprich! Ich frage, gib mir Kunde:	Maiden speak! I beg you tell me:
Stehst mit höhern Geistern du im Bunde?	Are you in league with divine spirits?
Ist's die Sprache, lüg' mir nicht,	Do not lie to me: is this the language
Die man in Elysen spricht?	They speak in Elysium?

[(. . . 2 . . .)]   [(. . . 2 . . .)]

FRIEDRICH VON SCHILLER (1759–1805); poem written by 1781

This is the twenty-second of Schubert's forty-four Schiller solo settings (1811–24). See poet's biography for a chronological list of all the Schiller settings.

After graduating from the military academy where he had studied as a doctor, Schiller took a job as a non-commissioned medical officer to a Stuttgart regiment. This was a miserable, poorly paid appointment with no prestige and it is hardly surprising that he sought to divert himself with his considerable powers of imagination. In Stuttgart he succumbed to the charms of women for the first time, fixing his attentions on the wife of a captain in whose home he was a lodger. This woman, Luise Fischer, was the Laura of a cycle of eight poems (some of them long and complex) that date from 1781 and are more or less contemporary with the composition of Schiller's first great play, *Die Räuber*. It is certain that nothing happened between the poet and his piano-playing landlady, and it is unlikely that she ever knew that she was the object of such intense literary worship. Laura was a name of Petrarch's beloved and, despite the debt Schiller's odes owe to Klopstock and Wieland, there is in this set something of a homage to the manner of early Italian literature. The poet with his rather elevated standards of self-control might have compared his feelings to those of Dante for Beatrice, a cerebral celebration, at a distance, of the feminine ideal. Time brought greater self-knowledge: Schiller was later to write that while the set of Laura poems were unified by 'burning imagination and deep feeling', he could also detect here and there 'suggestively sensual expressions disguised as Platonic rhetoric'.

   After periods of enthusiasm for the work of Schiller in May and August 1815, Schubert's interest in the poet was rekindled in March 1816 when, among a number of other Schiller settings, two poems from the 'Laura' cycle were composed. This coincides with the end of the two-year period during which Schubert was said to have been in love with Therese Grob, and it is not fanciful to compare the composer's idealized and impractical affection with the poet's for 'Laura' nearly thirty-five years earlier. Schiller's muse played the piano, Therese had a beautiful singing voice; cantabile piano playing is an extension of the vocal arts, and for both the young Schubert and Schiller (in this poem at least) the power of music explained and rationalized tempestuous attraction to the opposite sex. The first verse of Schiller's poem describes

Laura am Klavier from Schiller's *Jubiläums-Ausgabe* (1859).

prodigies of prestidigitation and compares them to the supernatural achievements of Philadelphia, a famous conjuror and spiritualist of the time. To give musical voice to this analogy in our century one would need the composing fire of a Prokofiev and the fingers of Martha Argerich. However, Schubert seems to place Schiller in a historical context and Laura is a gifted amateur of the 1780s. The song thus becomes an exercise in the polarity between the shy femininity of Laura's playing and the poet's effusive response, between the exquisite manners and music of the pre-revolutionary era and Schiller's seething intensity.

There are two versions of this song, dating from the same month. In the first (p. 46 of Volume 10 of the NSA) the piano prelude is only six bars long and there is no postlude. Various other differences between the versions (often arising because the key of the first, E major, dictates a different vocal range to that of the second, A major) show how hard Schubert was prepared to work at adapting and refining his initial musical ideas when tussling with Schiller. Perhaps the most memorable thing about this song (and we shall now discuss its second version) is its thirteen-bar *Vorspiel*, a fragment from a rococo piano sonata, including some nimble descending passage-work in semiquavers at bb. 9 and 10. The first verse is given over to alternation between recitative (from b. 13) and solo piano strains (bb. 18–21) where the little sonata continues on its way as if the poet during his impassioned interruption has pressed a pause button, freezing the music in time. Verses 2 and 3 ('Etwas langsamer') are in the home key; the section begins modestly: a graceful vocal line is accompanied by flowing quavers and eventually blossoms into a quasi-Italian cantilena propelled along by pulsating triplet chords (from b. 46). In the middle of Verse 3 ('Wie, des Chaos Riesenarm' from b. 54) there is a recitative that, not surprisingly, is unequal to the cataclysmic images of the text. Here, as elsewhere in this poem, Schiller uses metre in a virtuosic way to paint the turbulence he describes, and a reciter could probably make more of this passage than a singer. The water music of Verse 4 (the marking is 'Sanft, beinahe die vorige Bewegung' from b. 62) encompasses a shift to E major without a change of key signature. This begins gently enough ('Lieblich jetzt, wie über glatten Kieseln'), becoming more violent (from b. 67) as is required by the words. Here is the nearest thing to pianistic bravura in the song. The dotted rhythm and downward leaps of 'Rauschende, schäumende Giessbäche wälzen' (bb. 73–5) are eerily prophetic of the vocal line of a far more famous song from twelve years later – *Aufenthalt* ('Rauschender Strom / Brausender Wald') from *Schwanengesang* D957/4. Mention of Cocytus (at bb. 86–7) reminds us that the underworld river makes an appearance in the map of another Schiller work, the infinitely more famous *Gruppe aus dem Tartarus* D583. Perhaps the most effective vocal music in *Laura am Klavier* is the genuinely eloquent questioning recitative of Verse 5 (bb. 89–93) to which an enigmatic repeat of Laura's wordless piano refrain ('Wie oben' from b. 94) is the only acceptable answer. The remaining two strophes of Schiller's poem go unset. The song feels like a somewhat forced marriage between word and tone, as awkward a conjunction as between the poet (whose verbal command outstripped, as yet, his knowledge of real people and the ways of the world) and his inspiration, the captain's wife, who had retreated from her unhappy marriage into her music.

According to Fischer-Dieskau it was the Mozartian cast of this song that enraged Antonio Salieri, prompting the break between him and his pupil. This theory (that aligns itself with the Pushkin/Schaffer scenario of Salieri's hatred for Mozart) begs the question as to why Schubert was such an enthusiastic participant in the celebrations in honour of his teacher later in 1816, and why he should have published a set of songs dedicated to Salieri (Op. 5) five years later. It is worth noting that Schubert's only other song about playing a keyboard instrument, *An mein Klavier* (D342), also dates from 1816 and is also in A major.

Autograph:	Wienbibliothek im Rathaus, Vienna (first version, last three bars only)
Publication:	Published as part of the AGA in 1895 (P623; first version)
	Published as part of the AGA in 1895 (P624; second version)
Subsequent editions:	Not in Peters; AGA XX 193a & b: Vol. 4/41; NSA IV: Vol. 10/46 & 52
Bibliography:	Capell 1928, pp. 113–14
	Fischer-Dieskau 1977, pp. 70–71
Discography and timing:	Fischer-Dieskau I 6[17] 5'41
	Hyperion I 16[3] 5'16 Thomas Allen
	Hyperion II 13[1]

← *Abendlied* D382   *Des Mädchens Klage* D389 →

LEB' WOHL, DU SCHÖNE ERDE   Farewell to the earth
(Abschied von der Erde)
(Pratobevera) **D829** [H589]
F major   Written for 17 February 1826

(33 bars)

Leb' wohl, du schöne Erde!   Farewell, beautiful earth!
Kann dich erst jetzt verstehn,   I can understand you only now,
Wo Freude und wo Kummer   When joy and sorrow
An uns vorüber weh'n.   Pass away from us.

Leb' wohl, du Meister Kummer!   Farewell, Master Sorrow!
Dank dir mit nassem Blick!   I thank you with moist eyes!

Mit mir nehm' ich die Freude,	Joy I take with me,
Dich lass' ich hier zurück.	You I leave behind.
Sei nur ein milder Lehrer,	Be a kindly teacher
Führ' alle hin zu Gott,	And lead all men to God;
Zeig' in den trübsten Nächten	In the darkest nights
Ein Streiflein Morgenrot!	Reveal a gleam of dawn!
Lasse sie Liebe ahnen,	Let them know what love is
So danken sie dir noch,	And they will be thankful;
Der früher und der später,	Some sooner, others later
Sie danken weinend doch.	Will thank you with tears.
Dann glänzt das Leben heiter,	Then life will be radiantly happy;
Mild lächelt jeder Schmerz,	Every sorrow will smile gently,
Die Freude hält umfangen	And joy will hold in its embrace
Das ruhige, klare Herz.	The pure, tranquil heart.

ADOLF VON PRATOBEVERA (1806–1875)

This is Schubert's only setting of a Pratobevera text. See the poet's biography.

This touching and unusually haunting piece of music for reciter and piano was entitled *Abschied* when it first appeared in print as a supplement to Reissman's Schubert biography of 1873. *Abschied von der Erde* was probably Max Friedlaender's title for the Peters Edition in 1885, and this was adopted by Mandyczewski in the AGA. The NSA prefers *Leb' wohl, du schöne Erde*.

This melodrama (a spoken recitation with musical commentary) was written as a result of the closeness of the Pratobevera family to the Schubert circle. Franziska Pratobevera (later Franziska Tremier) was a soprano, described as 'our little nightingale' by her family. No doubt inspired by private concerts where she had heard Johann Michael Vogl perform Schubert songs, she was among the first singers to learn songs from *Winterreise* D911. She had an important song album incorporating several Schubert manuscripts in her possession.

Adolf von Pratobevera had written a verse drama entitled *Der Falk* ('The Falcon'). In honour of the birthday of his father, Karl Josef von Pratobevera (1769–1853), this was performed on 17 February 1826 with a musical ending specially composed by Schubert. (Whether money changed hands for this 'commission' is disputed – Deutsch thought it likely.) Peter Branscombe reminds us in a chapter on 'Schubert and the Melodrama' (in *Schubert Studies*, 1982) that the composer was interested in this medium (with orchestral accompaniment) throughout his career, from *Des Teufels Lustschloss* to *Fierabras*. No other composer of Schubert's stature wrote so many melodramas as parts of his operas. This is the composer's only piano-accompanied work of this kind. Kreissle von Hellborn, Schubert's first biographer, tells us that the words were spoken in the play by Mechthild, the daughter-in law of Ritter Hugo who has requested her to sing him a pilgrim's song as he dies. In view of the fact that Kreissle was to be Pratobevera's brother-in-law, it is disappointing that he fails to provide more details. It would be interesting to know, for example, whether Schubert himself took part in the first performance of the melodrama. Ritter Hugo's squire, Kuno, went under the nickname Meister Kummer which explains the reference to this character in the second stanza, although 'Meister Kummer' has usually been taken as a metaphor for overwhelming sorrow.

The piano-writing flows gently in non-stop triplet movement. Although simple, it has an unexpectedly powerful effect because the words seem effortlessly wedded to the rise and fall of the music. The great tenor Sir Peter Pears used to perform it most memorably when, as a result of a stroke, he could no longer sing.

An interesting musicological detail is to be found in bb. 20, 30 and 31 of the piano music: in the right hand a triplet with downward stalks is bracketed with a dotted quaver + semiquaver with upward stalks, the latter two-note figuration taking over the first and third notes of the triplet notated underneath. Here is proof in Schubert's own hand that a triplet could sometimes be thought of as dotted quaver + semiquaver. This has long been a matter of discussion in terms of performing practice in such songs as *Wasserflut* in Schubert's *Winterreise* D911/6.

Autograph:	Gesellschaft der Musikfreunde, Vienna
First edition:	Published as part of August Reissmann's *Franz Schubert: Sein Leben und seine Werke* (pp. 15–18 of *Notenbeilagen*), in 1873 (P469)
First known performance:	The first performance of this piece is thought to have taken place in a semi-private production at the home of Adolf von Pratovebera on 17 February 1826. The programme is now lost. See Waidelich/Hilmar Kommentar I No. 373a
Subsequent editions:	Peters: Vol. 7/109; AGA XX 603: Vol. 10/136; NSA IV: Vol. 13/150
Bibliography:	Branscombe 1982, pp. 139–40 Fischer-Dieskau 1977, pp. 110–11 Winter 1978, p. 498
Discography and timing:	Fischer-Dieskau II 9^{16} 3'13 Hyperion I 26^{20} Hyperion II 31^{12} 2'44 Richard Jackson

← *Nur wer die Sehnsucht kennt* D877/4   *Widerspruch* D865 →

Das LEBEN IST EIN TRAUM   Life is a dream   Trio, SSA
(WANNOVIUS) **D269** [H159]

The song exists in two versions, the second of which is discussed below:
(1) August 1815; (2) 25 August 1815

(1) 'Ruhig'   B♭ major   **C**   [5 bars]

(2)   B♭ major

(7 bars)

Das Leben ist ein Traum,	Life is a dream,
Man merkt, man fühlt ihn kaum;	Hardly noticed, hardly felt;
Denn schnell wie Wolken ziehn,	For swift as the clouds
Ist dieser Traum dahin.	The dream is gone.
Wohl dem, der gut geträumt,	Happy he who has dreamed well;
Wohl dem, dess Saat hier keimt	Happy he whose seed ripens here
Zur Ernte für die Zeit	To harvest
Der Unvergänglichkeit.	For eternity.
Das Leben ist der Blick	Life is a glimpse
Auf einer Zukunft Glück,	Of future bliss
Das jeder haben kann,	Which everyone can attain
Der hier es wohlgetan.	Who has here done good.
Wohl dem, der nach der Nacht	Happy he who after the grave's night
Des Grabes froh erwacht,	Wakens joyfully,
Den nicht die Stimme schreckt,	Who is not frightened by the voice
Die aus dem Schlummer weckt.	That wakes him from his sleep.
Wer bei der Arbeit Schluss	He who must fear the reckoning
Die Rechnung fürchten muss,	When his work is ended
Hat wahrlich keinen Blick	Will in truth have no glimpse
Auf einer Zukunft Glück.	Of future bliss.

CHRISTOPH WANNOVIUS (1753–1814)

This is the only setting made by Schubert of the poetry of Wannovius. See the poet's biography.

This slight piece in the manner of a musical exercise is one of two three-part choral settings with piano accompaniment written by Schubert. The other is *Das Abendrot* D236 from July 1815. The unusual deployment here of Soprano I, Soprano II and Alto (*Das Abendrot* includes a bass in its forces) suggests that it was written for a specific musical gathering in that hectic and highly creative August of 1815. The work is reminiscent of Haydn, even to the extent that the older composer wrote a solo song on the same theme with the same title. Haydn was given to writing semi-philosophical vocal ensembles of this sort, and in more or less this harmonic style. The accompaniment, apart from the single bar of introduction, is merely a short score of the three vocal lines. The quasi-contrapuntal form is suited to the words: the dreamlike and ever-shifting quality of life is reflected by the echo effect between the three parts that shadow each other with just a suggestion of canonic imitation.

Autograph:	Wienbibliothek im Rathaus, Vienna
Publication:	Unpublished, due to appear in NSA III, Vol. 3 (first version)
	Published as Book 44 no. 4 of the *Nachlass* by Diabelli, Vienna in 1849 (P369; second version)
Subsequent editions:	AGA XVIII 5: p. 31; NSA III: Vol. 3
Discography and timing:	Hyperion I 22[8] 1'58 Patricia Rozario, Lorna Anderson &
	Hyperion II 9[20] Catherine Wyn-Rogers

←— *An die Sonne* D272   *Lilla an die Morgenröte* D273 —→

Des LEBENS TAG IST SCHWER *see* LIED (DIE MUTTER ERDE) D788

LEBENSLIED

Song of life

(MATTHISSON) **D508** [H324]
C major   December 1816

Mässig geschwind

Kom - men und Schei - den, Su - chen und Mei - den,

(29 bars)

Kommen und Scheiden,	Arriving and departing,
Suchen und Meiden,	Seeking and shunning,
Fürchten und Sehnen,	Fearing and yearning,
Zweifeln und Wähnen,	Doubting and guessing,
Armut und Fülle, Verödung und Pracht	Poverty and abundance, desolation and splendour
Wechseln auf Erden, wie Dämmrung und Nacht!	Alternate on earth like dusk and night.
Fruchtlos hinieden	In vain you strive
Ringst du nach Frieden!	For peace here below!
Täuschende Schimmer	Will-o'-the-wisps
Winken dir immer;	Forever beckon to you;
Doch, wie die Furchen des gleitenden Kahns,	But, like the furrows ploughed by the gliding boat,
Schwinden die Zaubergebilde des Wahns!	These magic creations of illusion vanish!
Auf zu der Sterne	Let faith bravely
Leuchtender Ferne	Gaze up from the dust
Blicke vom Staube	To the stars
Mutig der Glaube:	Shining in the distance;
Dort nur verknüpft ein unsterbliches Band	Only there does an undying bond
Wahrheit und Frieden, Verein und Bestand!	Unite truth and peace, fellowship and permanence!
Günstige Fluten	Favourable tides
Tragen die Guten,	Bear the virtuous,
Fördern die Braven	Carry the brave
Sicher zum Hafen,	Safely to harbour,
Und, ein harmonisch verklingendes Lied,	And to the noble spirit life closes
Schliesst sich das Leben dem edlen Gemüt!	As a harmonious, dying song!
Männlich zu leiden,	To suffer manfully,
Kraftvoll zu meiden,	To avoid resolutely,
Kühn zu verachten,	To despise boldly:
Bleib' unser Trachten!	Let us make this our endeavour!
Bleib' unser Kämpfen! in eherner Brust	And our striving,
Uns des unsträflichen Willens bewusst!	Conscious of a spotless will within our iron breast!

Friedrich von Matthisson (1761–1831); poem written in 1786/7

This is the twenty-seventh of Schubert's twenty-nine Matthisson solo settings (1812–17). See the poet's biography for a chronological list of all the Matthisson settings.

The manuscript of this work is solemnly (or triumphantly) marked with the words 'In the house of Herr von Schober', an inscription shared by the Heinrich von Collin setting *Leiden der Trennung* D509 also written in December 1816. Schubert had moved to the Schober apartment and found himself for the first time in his life (apart from his years as a student at the Imperial Konvikt) living away from his family. Much had changed for Schubert during 1816. From a diary entry of 8 September we know that a visit to the poet Mayrhofer had inspired him to a small flood of philosophical reflections; in that same autumn he had turned his back on any possibility of marriage to Therese Grob and left Salieri as a teacher. He was determined to make a life of his own, surrounded and supported by friends of similar tastes and ideals. It is hardly surprising then that he should have been attracted to this poem of Matthisson's – *Lebenslied* reads something like the succession of noble (if rather unoriginal) aphorisms that Schubert attempted to record on the night of 8 September before sleep overtook him.

There is great strength and resolve in this music; it is in C major but full of subtle little chromatic highways and byways as wide ranging as Matthisson's invocations. The vocal line is doubled by ominous staccato octaves at 'Armut und Fülle, Verödung und Pracht' (bb. 8–11). The repeated phrase 'Wechseln auf Erden wie Dämmrung und Nacht' is masterfully handled: when it is heard for the first time (bb. 13–16), the dark suspensions depict the uncertainty of the half light leading to a cadence in E flat; on the second occurrence (bb. 17–20) it moves triumphantly back into C major with the feeling of a question answered. The five bars of postlude are of the utmost determination. They stride forward partially inflected in the minor key, a rising phrase in the piano's left hand, with the air of a man with a mission. The spurious prelude (as printed in the *Nachlass* and Volume 6 of the Peters Edition) is derived from this passage.

This little-known song, neglected by singers and scholars alike, shares something of the mood of the Senn setting *Selige Welt* D743, as well as that poem's image of a ship coming into harbour after a dangerous voyage. There are five strophes in Matthisson's poem as printed above. For the Hyperion Edition the last strophe, not very appropriate for a female singer, was left out – but it is this strophe that probably spoke to Schubert with the greatest force. The song seems to have been written by the composer in order to stiffen his resolve and he appears to have found a kind of Dutch courage in Matthisson's lyric for a new and exciting phase of his life. At this stage Schubert could not know that a Schober family emergency (the illness of Axel Schober for whose expected return to Vienna Schubert had to vacate his room) would force him to move back home the following August.

Autograph:	Wienbibliothek im Rathaus, Vienna (fair copy)
First edition:	Published as Book 38 no. 2 of the *Nachlass* by Diabelli, Vienna in 1845 (P352)
Subsequent editions:	Peters: Vol. 6/16; AGA XX 284: Vol. 4/250; NSA IV: Vol. 11/53
Arrangements:	Arr. Tilman Hoppstock (b. 1961) for guitar accompaniment, in *Franz Schubert: 110 Lieder* (2009)
Discography and timing:	Fischer-Dieskau I 9[3] 1'00 (first two strophes only)
	Hyperion I 17[22]
	Hyperion II 17[2] 2'32 Lucia Popp

← *Skolie* D507   *Leiden der Trennung* D509 →

LEBENSLUST *see* Die GESELLIGKEIT D609

LEBENS-MELODIEN
(A. von Schlegel) **D395** [H243]
G major – E♭ major   March 1816

Melodies of life

(33 bars)

Der Schwan:

Auf den Wassern wohnt mein stilles Leben,
Zieht nur gleiche Kreise, die verschweben,
Und mir schwindet nie im feuchten Spiegel
Der gebogne Hals und die Gestalt.

Der Adler:

Ich haus' in den felsigen Klüften,
Ich braus' in den stürmenden Lüften,
Vertrauend dem schlagenden Flügel
Bei Jagd bei Kampf und Gewalt.[1]

[...8...]

Der Schwan:

Ahndevoll betracht' ich oft die Sterne
In der Flut die tiefgewölbte Ferne,
Und mich zieht ein innig rührend Sehnen
Aus der Heimat in ein himmlisch Land.

Der Adler:

Ich wandte die Flügel mit Wonne
Schon früh zur unsterblichen Sonne,
Kann nie an den Staub mich gewöhnen,
Ich bin mit den Göttern verwandt.

[...2...]

Die Tauben:

In der Myrten Schatten
Gatte treu dem Gatten
Flattern wir und tauschen
Manchen langen Kuss.
  Suchen und irren,
  Finden und girren,
  Schmachten und lauschen,
  Wunsch und Genuss!

The Swan:

My tranquil life is on the waters,
Drawing equal circles that ripple away to nothing;
And in the damp mirror my curved neck
And my figure never disappear.

The Eagle:

I dwell in the rocky crevasses;
I race in the stormy winds,
Trusting my beating wings
In the hunt, in battle and in attack.

[...8...]

The Swan:

Often, filled with intuition, I behold the stars
In the deep-vaulted, distant flood,
And I am drawn by a fervent longing
From my home to a heavenly land.

The Eagle:

In early youth I turned my wings
With joy towards the immortal sun;
I can never accustom myself to the dust;
I am related to the gods.

[...2...]

The Doves:

In the shade of the myrtles,
Spouse true to spouse,
We flutter, and exchange
Many a long kiss.
  We seek and rove,
  Find and coo,
  Languish and listen,
  With desire and pleasure.

[1] Schlegel writes 'Bey Jagd *und* Kampf und Gewalt'.

Venus Wagen ziehen	We draw the chariot of Venus,
Schnäbelnd wir im Fliehen,	Billing in our flight;
Unsre blauen Schwingen	Our blue wings
Säumt der Sonne Gold.	Are fringed by the gold of the sun.
O wie es fächelt,	How we stir
Wenn sie uns lächelt!	When she smiles upon us!
Leichtes Gelingen!	Easy success,
Lieblicher Sold!	A charming reward!
Wende denn die Stürme,	Then avert your storms,
Schöne Göttin! Schirme	Fair goddess! Shield
Bei bescheidner Freude	Your pair of doves
Deiner Tauben Paar!	In their modest pleasure!
Lass uns beisammen!	Let us be together,
Oder in Flammen	Or sacrifice us both
Opfre uns beide	In flames
Deinem Altar.	Upon your altar!

August Wilhelm von Schlegel (1767–1845); poem written in 1797

This is the first of Schubert's ten August von Schlegel solo settings (1816–25). See the poet's biography for a chronological list of all the August von Schlegel settings.

This is the only August von Schlegel poem set by Schubert that even vaguely resembles *Abendröte*, the cycle of poems by August's younger brother Friedrich from which the composer was later to set twelve songs (1819–20). August's fanciful evocations of speaking swan, eagle and doves date from 1797, the year of Schubert's birth, and are prophetic of Friedrich Schlegel's cycle where animals, humans, trees, rivers and mountains sing 'many a song with one voice', all speaking of their different natural characteristics, all part of a vast universal plan. These are the melodies of life, hidden from most people but audible for 'him who secretly listens' (*see Die Gebüsche* D646). The practice of ascribing human feelings to animals and other living things such as trees and flowers was dubbed 'the pathetic fallacy' by Ruskin in the middle of the nineteenth century. There is no doubt however that here the Schlegels were using nature to make a point about the follies of mankind when compared to the innocence and grace of the natural world. Animal behaviour was a rebuke to humans who might imagine themselves to be above their station. Each species has a *raison d'être* and the natural order of things is illustrated in the inevitability of a swan's graceful glide across a lake (the narcissistic, self-obsessed Romantic artist), or an eagle's flight through the heavens (symbol of adventure, longing and freedom). Unlike overambitious human beings, the animals rejoice in their natures and their given part in the divine plan (the doves represent domesticity and dreams of marital bliss).

It is easy to see why the Schubert of 1816 was tempted by this poem. It starts with the words 'Auf den Wassern' and this phrase alone set his imagination working with water music. The idea of contrasting the mellifluous musings of the swan with the craggy vocal line of the eagle prompted the young Schubert to his Mozartian and Beethovenian styles, as if these two great composers were also archetypes and natural phenomena in his mind. The swan is of course Mozartian in its unruffled elegance and beauty, the powerful eagle animated by Beethovenian *Sturm und Drang*. But the poem is in three parts, and, after the royal beasts, Schubert speaks with his own voice in the music for the doves: cosier, more domestic creatures, neither beautiful nor strong but full of love, as the marking 'Lieblich' at the head of their music confirms.

Even a work as simple as this shows touches of mastery in terms of word-setting; indeed the text prompts a deliberate limitation to the musical language. The song opens with the music of a rippling stream, in this tempo ('Mässig, ruhig') prophetic of *Der Neugierige* from *Die schöne Müllerin*. Written at the top of the stave are the words 'Der Schwan' to show us who is singing. At the end of the second line ('verschweben', bb. 7–8) the ear expects a cadence to take the music away from the home key but, somewhat disappointingly, it returns full circle, like the gliding swan itself, to its harmonic point of origin. This gives the music a rather short-breathed quality, but it perfectly defines the limited geographical boundaries of the bird's life. Then with the line 'Und mir schwindet nie im feuchten Spiegel' (bb. 9–12) the depth of the lake is sounded with the movement of the bass from G to F natural (bb. 10–11), and thence at 'Spiegel' to a C major chord on the bass note of E (the first inversion of the subdominant, b. 12). The downward jump of an octave on 'Spiegel' in the vocal line at b. 12 suggests the same watery mirror.

For the next section, devoted to the eagle (it is 'Der Adler' who now speaks, the golden eagle – *Aquila chrysœtos* or *Steinadler*) we move from G major to a bustling Beethovenian scherzo in C minor and ⅜ time ('Geschwind'). Figurations in semiquavers suggest the flapping of the eagle's wings (bb. 19 and 21). There is a long dominant pedal point (from b. 25) on 'Ich haus' in den felsigen Klüften, / Ich braus' in den stürmenden Lüften' where rumbling octaves in the bass support surging right-hand chords in quavers, like the flight of a bird tossed hither and thither by turbulent air currents.

Uncertainty reigns as to how many strophes the composer intended to be sung. The most recent decision, that of the NSA, gives the singer only one verse each for swan, eagle and doves, each sung one after the other. The AGA on the other hand has a repeat marking at the end of the eagle's first solo that guides the singer back to the swan, then once again to the eagle. After this there is a change of time signature and new music for the doves to strophic repetitions of three further verses of poetry. The Hyperion Edition followed the AGA; the NSA had not yet been published. The Peters Edition, following Josef Czerny's posthumous first edition, is the most confusing. It prints the same music as the AGA but without a repeat marking, leaving the performers wondering whether the first music for the doves should be performed *before* returning to the swan; clearly not what Schubert could have intended.

The swan and eagle are creatures with great aspirations, but the doves of the final section (in E flat major, the marking is 'Lieblich') are less ambitious. Schlegel's mention of 'blue wings' identifies them as members of the *Columba* species perhaps the domestic pigeon or stock dove. They are content with 'easy success' and 'a charming reward' – a quiet life, protected by Venus. The splendid and lonely life of swan or eagle is not for them. And here Schubert comes into his own with music of a broader melodic line (in ¼ as opposed to the ⅔ of the swan) and affectionate turns of phrase suggesting that he identifies more with the plump doves than the other creatures. The setting of 'Suchen und irren, / Finden und girren' (b. 38) delightfully hints at the cooing of birds: tripping dactyls alternate with the trochees of 'irren' and 'girren', the double r in each word onomatopoeic. There is a domesticity about this music that brings to mind another 1816 song, *An mein Klavier* D342, particularly at the cadence with the first appearance of the words 'Wunsch und Genuss'. The moral of the poem is that happiness with a beloved partner, in the manner of the birdcatcher Papageno perhaps, with his Papagena, is the most blessed thing that life has to offer.

There are fourteen strophes provided by Schlegel for the alternation between 'Der Schwan' and 'Der Adler'. The first two of these are placed by Schubert under the vocal lines, as printed in the NSA. It would be theoretically possible (but surely artistically unwise) to sing the song's opening pages no fewer than six times! (Fischer-Dieskau omitted this song altogether from his

Schubert survey.) Matthias Goerne chose Strophes 9 and 10 in order to repeat the music for swan and eagle before going on to sing all three strophes assigned to the doves. For a printing of Schlegel's complete poem see pp. 311–12 of Volume 10 of the NSA. If they opt for a repeat at all, singers may prefer to select another pair of Schlegel's verses (Strophes 3 and 4 for example, instead of 9 and 10) when performing *Lebensmelodien*.

Autograph:	Missing or lost
First edition:	Published as Op. post. 111 no. 2 by Josef Czerny, Vienna in February 1829 (P198)
Publication reviews:	*Allgemeiner musikalische Anzeiger* (Vienna), No. 5 (31 January 1829), p. 19 [Waidelich/Hilmar Dokumente I No. 688]
Subsequent editions:	Peters: Vol. 4/128; AGA XX 205: Vol. 4/72; NSA IV: Vol. 10/72
Bibliography:	Shackleton 2012
Discography and timing:	Fischer-Dieskau —
	Hyperion I 27²
	Hyperion II 13¹⁷ 4'15 Matthias Goerne

⟵ *Die Herbstnacht* D395   *Rien de la nature* D Anhang IIa [*see* under *Echo et Narcisse*] ⟶

LEBENSMUT   Courage for living
(SCHULZE) **D883** [H600]
B♭ major   March 1826

O wie dringt das junge Leben
Kräftig mir durch Sinn und Herz!
Alles fühl' ich glühn und streben,
Fühle doppelt Lust und Schmerz.
Fruchtlos such' ich euch zu halten,
Geister meiner regen Brust!
Nach Gefallen mögt ihr walten,
Sei's zum Leide, sei's zur Lust.

Lodre nur, gewalt'ge Liebe,
Höher lodre nur empor!
Brecht, ihr vollen Blütentriebe,
Mächtig schwellend nur hervor!
Mag das Herz sich blutig färben,
Mag's vergehn in rascher Pein;
Lieber will ich ganz verderben,
Als nur halb lebendig sein.

How vigorously young life
Pulses through my mind and heart!
I feel everything is glowing, aspiring;
I feel pleasure and pain doubly.
In vain I seek to restrain you,
Spirits of my quickened breast!
You rule at will
For sorrow or for pleasure.

Blaze on, mighty love,
Blaze higher.
Burst open, ripe, blossoming desires,
Swelling abundantly;
Let my heart be tinged with blood;
Let it perish swiftly in pain;
I would rather be completely ruined
Than be only half alive.

Dieses Zagen, dieses Sehnen,	This hesitation, this longing
Das die Brust vergeblich schwellt,	That swells my breast in vain;
Diese Seufzer, diese Tränen,	These sighs, these tears
Die der Stolz gefangen hält,	Which pride holds captive,
Dieses schmerzlich eitle Ringen,	This painful, futile struggle,
Dieses Kämpfen ohne Kraft,	This fighting without strength,
Ohne Hoffnung und Vollbringen	Without hope, without fulfilment,
Hat mein bestes Mark erschlafft.	Has sapped my whole being.
Lieber wecke rasch und mutig,	Rather let the quick, bold battle cry
Schlachtruf, den entschlafnen Sinn!	Awaken my sleeping mind!
Lange träumt' ich, lange ruht' ich,	Long have I dreamt, long have I rested,
Gab der Kette lang mich hin;	Long have I yielded to the chain;
Hier ist Hölle nicht, noch Himmel,	Here there is neither hell nor heaven,
Weder Frost ist hier, noch Glut;	Neither frost nor warmth;
Auf in's feindliche Getümmel,	Up, into the hostile tumult,
Rüstig weiter durch die Flut!	Briskly beyond it through the flood!
Dass noch einmal Wunsch und Wagen,	So that once more desire and daring,
Zorn und Liebe, Wohl und Weh	Anger and love, weal and woe
Ihre Wellen um mich schlagen	Pound me with their waves
Auf des Lebens wilder See,	On life's stormy sea,
Und ich kühn im tapfern Streite	And I, boldly, bravely struggling,
Mit dem Strom, der mich entrafft,	Steer my boat with the current
Selber meinen Nachen leite,	That sweeps me along,
Freudig in geprüfter Kraft.	Happy in my well-tried strength.

Ernst Schulze (1789–1817); poem written 1 April 1815

This is the ninth of Schubert's ten Schulze solo settings (1825–6). See the poet's biography for a chronological list of all the Schulze settings. An outline of a suggested performing version for a Schulze cycle is listed under 'Auf den wilden Wegen'.

In his *Poetisches Tagebuch* Schulze's hymning of Adelheid Tychsen as gently as a bird singing in the branches (*Im Frühling* D882) was not to last for long. Memories of past springtime happiness seem to have worked him up into a lather of optimism and self-confidence. Only the day after he had penned that text of lovelorn nostalgia, Schulze wrote this poem which seems to reflect a more violent vernal rite, a young man's acknowledgement of the rising sap. The two songs stand adjacent in the Deutsch catalogue, as if Schubert had set one poem and then turned over a page to find the next. *Lebensmut* was originally entitled 'On 1 April 1815'. Knowing the poet's story, such a display of madcap energy in less than propitious circumstances seems uncomfortably appropriate for April Fool's Day, but the third verse is an accurate assessment of his tale; he acknowledges the 'painful, futile struggle . . . without hope, without fulfilment'. He tells us that he has dreamt and rested (*Im Frühling*) but he remains in the thrall of the forces of 'gewalt'ge Liebe'; he would rather perish in a type of cataclysmic *Liebestod* than be only half alive.

Schubert was quite used to brandishing his fist in Beethovenian manner and it would be wrong to suppose that *Sturm und Drang* was uncongenial to him. One thinks of songs like *Selige Welt* D743 and *Der Schiffer* D536 (which contain similar nautical imagery to that found in the last of Schulze's verses for *Lebensmut*), as well as *Heliopolis* II D754 with its demonic energy and vehemence. These works have a political significance, an angry response to injustice and repression in an unfair society. There were times when the composer needed to shout and hammer and bristle, the dark reverse of the familiar coin of empathy and gentleness. This was not merely a product of Schubert's 'angry young man' phase: there are passages in the last piano sonatas and in *Schwanengesang* that show that the composer, at the end of his life, still had a taste for musical rhetoric and the grand defiant gesture.

Following the poet's example, *Lebensmut*, however, whistles at the wind with a great deal of bluster, and ultimately no great substance. If the pathos of *Im Frühling* is echoed in the immortal *Frühlingstraum* from *Winterreise* D911/11, *Lebensmut* finds its parallel in that cycle in the sudden outburst of energy in *Mut!*, which shows us that depression, at its black heart a listless thing, can rear its ugly head in different guises and at varying speeds. These include, as in *Lebensmut*, the brightest of forced smiles in the major key, the manic depressive suffering from a sort of perverse happiness, where laughter and high spirits take on a tinny and unrealistic note. This knowledge renders *Lebensmut* hellishly sad; indeed Susan Youens has pointed out that the song's prelude is reminiscent of Orpheus' descent into the underworld at the opening of *Lied des Orpheus* D474.

There are five verses in the song. In musical terms Verses 1, 2, 4 and 5 are the same. Verse 3 sandwiched between two gigantic pillars of word and tone, is a variant in the tonic minor and the key signature changes to five flats (at b. 26); the weighty words of confessional insight here are given short shrift, as if the poet is describing someone else's feelings. A dilemma, by now familiar, faces us when considering Schubert's response to some of these Schulze texts; either he has not understood the words well enough, or only too well. The thundery interludes, a kind of obsessive *marche militaire* of the spirit, grind forward mirthlessly, their jolting patterns more banal in repetition than they seem at first hearing. At various points they promise modulations and relief from the poet's harping on one string, but once again we find ourselves caught in a repetitive and compulsive pattern. If this is not one of Schubert's greatest songs, it has a triumph of a different kind: it is a superb portrait of Schulze, for better or worse, in manic mood.

In the absence of an autograph the NSA consulted a copy of the song that comes from Graz that was in the possession of the Pachler family. This version varies in tiny details from the ones that appear in either Peters (the *Nachlass* first edition) or AGA. These discrepancies are more crucial perhaps to singer and pianist than to the listener, but a study of the Graz version is recommended for those intending to perfom this song.

Autograph:	Missing or lost
First edition:	Published as Book 17 no. 1 of the *Nachlass* by Diabelli, Vienna in 1832 (P285)
Subsequent editions:	Peters: Vol. 5/80; AGA XX 498: Vol. 8/206; NSA IV: Vol. 14/10
Bibliography:	Capell 1928, p. 217
	Youens 1996, pp. 292–7
Discography and timing:	Fischer-Dieskau II 8[7] 2'56 (strophes 1, 3 & 4 only)
	Hyperion I 18[20]
	Hyperion II 32[6] 4'57 Peter Schreier

← *Im Frühling* D882   *Über Wildemann* D884 →

LEBENSMUT   Courage for living
(RELLSTAB) **D937** [H663]
(Fragment) B♭ major   1827? Spring or summer 1828?

Fröh-li-cher Le-bens-mut   braust in dem ra-schen Blut,

(24 bars)

Fröhlicher Lebensmut	Joyful courage for living
Braust in dem raschen Blut;	Surges in the quick blood;
Sprudelnd und silberhell	The fountain of life flows
Rauschet der Lebensquell.	Bubbling and silver-bright.
Doch eh' die Stunde flieht,	But before the hour flies,
Ehe der Geist verglüht,	Before the spirit's ardour fades,
Schöpft aus der klaren Flut	Draw joyful courage for living
Fröhlichen Lebensmut!	From the clear waters.
Mutigen Sprung gewagt;	Dare the bold leap;
Nimmer gewinnt, wer zagt;	He who hesitates never wins;
Schnell ist das Wechselglück,	Fortune changes rapidly;
Dein ist der Augenblick.	The moment is yours.
Wer keinen Sprung versucht,	He who does not venture the leap
Bricht keine süsse Frucht,	Will reap no sweet fruit.
Auf! Wer das Glück erjagt,	Come! He who chases fortune
Mutigen Sprung gewagt.	Must dare the bold leap.
Mutig umarmt den Tod!	Embrace death with courage
Trifft's Euch sein Machtgebot,	When his mighty command touches you.
Nehmt Euer volles Glas,	Take your full glass
Stosst an sein Stundenglas;	And clink it against his hourglass.
Des Todes[1] Brüderschaft	Death's brotherhood
Öffnet des Lebens Haft,	Unlocks life's prison;
Neu glänzt ein Morgenrot;	A new dawn shines.
Mutig umarmt den Tod!	Embrace death with courage.

LUDWIG RELLSTAB (1799–1860); poem written before 1825

*This is the first of Schubert's ten Rellstab solo settings (1827–8) according to Deutsch,
but it is also perhaps the last. See the poet's biography for a chronological list of
all the Rellstab settings.*

A reading of the poem shows how the composer was inspired to new musical solutions by
unusual imagery. He had written songs about manly courage before (the striding Schulze
Lebensmut D883 of 1826 is in the same key and shares some of this song's characteristics), but

---

[1] 'Thanatos' Bruderschaft' as printed in the Peters Edition Volume 7.

Rellstab's words about the 'quick blood' being pumped through the body in joyful surges, as well as the imagery of a gushing fountain of life, give rise to a unique accompaniment and a vocal line of the utmost energy. Blood is liquid after all, but thicker than water. Thus the similarity to the pianistic formulae of *Auf dem Wasser zu singen* D774 is noticeable without being exact. Rellstab's surges of nature are not to be heard rippling on the edge of a lake in undulating watery cascades; heavier and more viscous chords circulate through *Lebensmut* like a whirring musical illustration of blood itself. The pianist's hands leap up the keyboard as a metaphor for a rush of blood to the head. The speed and the waltz-time signature may encourage the listener to think of this piece as a dance, but it is almost impossible to dance to with its emphasis on the second half of the third beat (marked forte) of so many bars in a deliberate offbeat fashion. This music disrupts the free and easy rhythms of dancing – it is rather about leaping, endless endeavour and *carpe diem*, exertion that is heartbreaking or, more likely, heart-stopping.

The first verse is the only one to be set, and the postlude is lacking. This is both good and bad. Good because the fragment left to us means that it can be performed, convincingly enough, as a strophic song (the translation of all three verses is provided here for that reason) simply using the introduction as a postlude (this is how the Peters Edition has printed it for more than a hundred years); bad because a completely strophic version of this song for all three verses is probably not what Schubert had in mind. The last verse of Rellstab's poem calls for some change of mood – as from major to minor – at the mention of death. (This is certainly the case with the varied harmonic colours of the Schulze *Lebensmut* D883 which was written in modified strophic form.) Schubert, possibly looking ahead to problems in the later verses that he did not care to solve, abandoned the sketch after composing only one verse.

But what a verse it is, certainly in terms of unflagging energy! And there is a need to keep the momentum going – as in *In der Ferne* from *Schwanengesang* D957/6 a convincing musical flow is threatened by the poet's choice of metre. In *Lebensmut* a heavy syllable at the end of each line ('Lebens<u>mut</u>', 'Blut' and so on) makes for an end-stopped effect despite the fact that some of the lines must enjamb in order to make sense. This problem is not entirely solved by Schubert where the last beat of almost every bar is a crotchet with a suggestion of an involuntary musical full stop (another reason, perhaps, why he did not continue with the music for later verses). This makes it doubly important for the accompaniment to push forward for fear of leaving sentences in mid-air.

There are some wonderfully piquant harmonic moments that are probably noticed less than they should be in the onrush of music. In the first strophe's sixth line ('Ehe der Geist verglüht') the last syllable, 'ver<u>glüht</u>', is set to a high G flat harmonized by a pulsating diminished-seventh chord (bb. 11–12). The singer must hold this heroic note for four whole beats; across the bar line the 'spelling' of that G flat changes to an F sharp (within a tied note) as the harmony beneath it transforms itself into D^7. This chord opens out into G minor as the top note nudges a semitone higher and becomes a silvery G (specifically marked piano in the singer's stave) at '<u>Schöpft</u> aus der klaren Flut'. The effect of this change to a new key is of a great difficulty successfully surmounted. There are similar progressions, all designed to reinforce the sense of elation.

This is one of Schubert's highest and least comfortable songs in terms of vocal tessitura – comparable to the Leitner fragments composed in 1827 (*Fröhliches Scheiden* D896 and *Sie in jedem Liede* D896A) – and the high A on the word 'Flut' and the two B flats on '<u>Fröh</u>lichen Lebensmut' would discourage most singers. All these songs suggest the range of the tenor Ludwig Tietze. As with the Leitner settings mentioned above this song may have been abandoned on account of a falling-out between the singer and the composer. It may be that if *Lebensmut* had gone on to the next stage of creative refinement its tonality would have been modified.

Autograph:	Gesellschaft der Musikfreunde, Vienna
First edition:	Published as No. 17 of *Neueste Folge nachgelassener Lieder und Gesänge* by J. P. Gotthard, Vienna in 1872 (P443)
Subsequent editions:	Peters: Vol. 7/58; AGA XX 602: Vol. 10/134; NSA IV: Vol. 14b/284; Bärenreiter: Vol. 4/108
Bibliography:	Capell 1928, pp. 69 & 247
Discography and timing:	Fischer-Dieskau —
	Hyperion I 37[5]
	Hyperion II 36[3] 1'58 Michael Schade

← *Herbst* D945   *Die Unterscheidung* D866/1 →

LEBENSTRAUM (I) (Gesang in c)   Dream of life
(BAUMBERG) **D1A** [H1]
(Fragment) C minor – C major   Before 1810

(394 bars)

(1) Ich sass an einer Tempelhalle[1]
    Am Musenhain,
    Umrauscht vom nahen Wasserfalle,
    Im sanften Abendschein.
    Kein Lüftchen wehte; – und die Sonn' im
      Scheiden
    Vergüldete die matten Trauerweiden.

In the soft light of evening,
Surrounded by cascading water,
I sat at the portals of a temple
In the grove of the Muses.
No breeze stirred, and the sun in parting
Gilded the weary weeping willows.

(2) Still sinnend sass ich lange da,
    Das Haupt gestützt auf meine Rechte.
    Ich dachte Zukunft und Vergangenheit;
      und sah
    Auf einem Berg, dem Thron der Götter nah,
    Den Aufenthalt vom heiligen Geschlechte
    Der Sänger alt' und neuer Zeit,
    An deren Liede sich die Nachwelt noch
      erfreut.
    Tot, unbemerkt, und längst vergessen
      schliefen
    Fern in des Tales dunkeln Tiefen
    Die Götzen ihrer Zeit, –
    Im Riesenschatten der Vergänglichkeit.

I sat there in long contemplation,
Resting my head in my right hand.
I pondered the future and the past,

And on a hill, close to the gods' throne,
I saw the abode of the holy race
Of singers, from times both old and new,
In whose songs posterity still delights.

Dead, unheeded, long forgotten,

The idols of their day
Slept far away in the valley's dark depths,
In the giant shadow of evanescence.

[1] In Baumberg's *Gedichte* (1805) the opening line is: 'Ich sass *vor eines Tempels Halle*'. This is a considerable change from Baumberg's *Gedichte* (1800): 'Mir träumt, ich sass an einem Wasserfalle' ('I dreamt I sat by a waterfall') where the poem is called *Ein Jugendtraum*.

(3) Und langsam schwebend kam aus jenem   Then from that dark valley,
         dunkeln Tale,

     Entstiegen einem morschen Heldenmahle,   Arising from a heroes' decaying feast,

     Jetzt eine düstere Gestalt daher,   A murky form came gliding slowly along,

     Und bot (in dem sie ohngefähr   And as it vaguely passed me,

     Vorüberzog) in einer mohnbekränzten   In a chalice garlanded with poppies
         Schale

     Aus Lethe's Quelle mir – Vergessenheit!   It offered me oblivion from Lethe's stream.

(4) Betroffen, wollt' ich die Erscheinung   In my consternation I was about to ask the
         fragen: apparition

     Was dieser Trank mir nützen soll?   How this draught could avail me,

     Doch schon war sie entflohn: ich sah's mit   But it had already vanished: I contemplated it
         stillem Groll,   in silent anger

     Denn meinen Wünschen—konnt' ich nicht   For I could not renounce my longing.
         entsagen.

     Da kam in frohem Tanz, mit   Then, blithely dancing with zephyr-light steps,
         zephyrleichtem Schritt,

     Ein kleiner Genius gesprungen,   A small spirit came bounding up,

     Und winkt' und rief mir zu: 'Komm mit!   Waving and calling to me: 'Come with me!

     Entreisse dich den bangen   Tear yourself from this fearful half-light
         Dämmerungen,—

     Sie trüben selbst der Wahrheit   Which dulls even the sunlight of truth.
         Sonnenschein!

     Komm mit! Ich führe dich in jenen   Come with me; I will take you into yonder
         Lorbeerhain,   laurel-grove

     Wohin kein Ungeweihter je gedrungen.   Where the uninitiated have never entered.

     Ein unverwelklich schöner Dichterkranz   A poet's lovely wreath that will not fade,

     Blüht dort für Dich im heitern   Blooms for you there in the bright spring
         Frühlingsglanz   radiance,

     Mit einem Myrtenzweig umschlungen.'   Entwined in a myrtle branch.'

(5) Er sprach's, und ging mir schnell voran.   Saying this, he quickly led the way.

     Ich folgte, voll Vertrauen, dem holden   Full of trust I followed the kindly boy,
         Jungen,

     Beglückt in meinem süssen Wahn.   Happy in my sweet delusion.

(6) Es herrschte jetzt die feierlichste Stille   The most solemn silence now reigned

     Im ganzen Hain. Das lang-ersehnte Ziel,   Throughout the grove. The prize I had long
                                                             desired

     Hellschimmernd sah ich's schon in ferner   I saw, shimmering brightly in vague, distant
         Schattenhülle,   outline,

     Und stand, verloren ganz im Lustgefühl.   And stood, quite lost in rapture.

     'Nimm' (sprach er jetzt) 'es ist Apollons   He now spoke: 'Take it, for it is Apollo's will;
         Wille.

     Nimm hin dies goldne Saitenspiel!   Take this golden lyre.

     Es hat die Kraft in schwermutsvollen   With its magic tones it has the power,
         Stunden

     Durch seinen Zauberton zu heilen all' die   In melancholy hours, to heal all the wounds
         Wunden,

Die Missgesschick und fremder Wahn dir schlug.'	That misfortune and alien madness have inflicted on you.'
Mit zärtlich rührenden Akkorden,	Its tender, touching chords
Tönt es vom Süd bis zum Norden,	Resound from south to north
Und übereilt der Zeiten schnellen Flug	More swiftly than time's rapid flight.
Sei stolz, sei stolz auf dein Besitz! Und denke:	Be proud of your possession, and reflect:
'Von Allem, was die Götter Sterblichen verleihn,	'Of all that the gods bestow on mortals,
Ist d i e s das höchste der Geschenke!	*This* is the highest gift.
Und Du wirst es nicht entweihen.'	And you will not abuse it.'
[(. . . 3 lines . . .)]	[(. . . 3 lines . . .)]

(7) Noch nicht vertraut mit ihrer ganzen Macht,   Not yet familiar with its full power,

Sang ich zuerst nur kleine Lieder;   At first I sang only small songs
Und Echo hallte laut und fröhlich wieder.   Whose echo rang loudly and joyfully . . .

[(. . . 135 lines . . .)]   [(. . . 135 lines . . .)]

GABRIELE VON BAUMBERG (1775–1839)

This is the first of Schubert's seven Baumberg solo settings (1809–10 and 1815). See the poet's biography for a chronological list of all the Baumberg settings.

The honour of being D1, the first work by Schubert listed in the Deutsch catalogue, belongs to the Fantasie in G for piano duet. As we leaf through this tome (the second – 1978 – edition of which is much weightier than the first of 1951) we find the first vocal work with piano: *Hagars Klage* D5, which dates from March 1811. Those lucky enough to own the AGA, Eusebius Mandyczewski's spacious lieder *Gesamtausgabe*, an edition that aimed to be chronological, can see this biblical ballad printed right at the beginning of the ten-volume set.

Since the publication of the revised Deutsch *Werkverzeichnis* in 1978, performing versions of two splendidly resourceful settings of a poem by Gabriele von Baumberg have emerged, albeit still only available in privately printed editions. These are certainly Schubert's first surviving songs, and they may well pre-date anything else we possess from the hand of the composer.

A considerable amount of music has been discovered since Mandyczewski's edition (1897), and there are substantial differences between the two editions of the Deutsch catalogue. These include countless adjustments of opinion regarding matters such as the dating of manuscripts and the interpretation of problematic fragments. The *Gesang in c* (Song in C minor) is just such a case: it should now surely be re-classified as the first setting of Baumberg's *Lebenstraum* (the second setting is D39), and the argument for it to be listed as such in a third edition of the Deutsch catalogue is a strong one. However, I must make clear that after many years this is not an opinion shared by the editors of the NSA or *Schubert Liedlexikon* who are unconvinced that this fragment has anything to do with Gabriele von Baumberg, or a first setting of *Lebenstraum*.

Gesang in c is a fragment of 394 bars with a vocal line and fully worked-out accompaniment. There are, however, no words on the autograph, and this has been an obvious stumbling block to its inclusion in the canon. (There is a similar mystery, still to be solved, in the much shorter wordless song sketch from May 1817, D555.) Various criteria show that the manuscript of D1A dates from before 1810, so it is probably the work of Schubert at the age of thirteen or younger. That he had some sort of poetic text in front of him is obvious, but until relatively recently there was no clue as to what it was. The mystery only began to unravel with the discovery of the origin of the text for D39 that was long known simply as *Ich sass an einer Tempelhalle*. This manuscript dates from about 1810 and is also a fragment – this time of 231 bars. The composer wrote out the text for the first six bars of the vocal line (beginning with 'Ich sass an einer Tempelhalle'), but the poem itself remained unidentified when the first Deutsch catalogue was published (where it is erroneously ascribed to 1813, thus being allocated the late number of D39). In the 1970s Dr Heinz Sichrovsky of Vienna discovered that in composing this song Schubert had set the first twenty-nine lines of *Lebenstraum* (a poem of 221 lines printed over thirteen pages) by Gabriele von Baumberg. This discovery, duly acknowledged in the second edition of the Deutsch catalogue (1978), was not made in time for the first printing of the song fragment (1969) in the *Neue Schubert-Ausgabe*.

The piecing together of D39 had its own difficulties which are examined in the commentary on that song. The text for D1A remained even more prob-

Ein Jugendtraum.

Mir träumt', ich fafs an einem Wafferfalle
Von Wünfchen matt; — vorüber flog die Zeit
Und both', indem fie einen Augenblick verweilt',
In einem grünumwundenen Pokale
Aus Lethens Quelle mir — Vergeffenheit.
Ich wollte danken — wollte fragen,
Wie diefs Gefchenk zu brauchen fey?
Doch fchnell war fie entflohn, *Vergeffen* war
                                        mir *neu*,
Ich konnte nichts als ihre Flucht beklagen.
                        A

Baumberg's *Ein Jugendtraum* from *Gedichte* (1800).

lematic; because there was no text attached to it most scholars were prepared to leave it as an unsalvageable fragment – something perhaps to be hummed, or sung to 'la' at the more fanatical of Schubert seminars. For some time scholars have suspected that D1A was an earlier attempt at setting the text of D39, but it took the indefatigable Reinhard Van Hoorickx, encouraged by John Reed, to grapple with the Baumberg poem and come up with a reasonable performing edition. Reed sent Hoorickx a suggested underlay for the first seventeen bars of the piece. At first Van Hoorickx busied himself with making the text fit D39 (remember, Schubert had written in the words only under the first twelve bars); after this he turned his attentions to the *Gesang in c*, D1A.

This is a much longer fragment: Schubert sets double the number of Baumberg's lines (fifty-eight instead of twenty-nine for D39). In both songs, where words are lacking, the problem is in guessing correctly which of the poet's words (or even whole phrases) Schubert had repeated, omitted or changed altogether. That the composer was cavalier with texts in his early youth is proven by how much he altered such poems as Schücking's *Hagars Klage*, and, when it suited him, freely adapted the words that were copied from the printed edition of the Zumsteeg setting. There is no reason to suppose that in the case of both versions of the Baumberg poem he had not been similarly 'inventive'. Unfortunately, these alterations were carried in his head and he did not bother to write them under the vocal line. For this reason Van Hoorickx had to make small adjustments to both words and musical stresses in order to prepare workable performing editions. But the interesting point is that adjustments were necessary for *both* songs, the second of which (D39) is undeniably a setting of Baumberg's poem.

Although there was a dissenting voice from Dr Walther Dürr of the *Neue Schubert-Ausgabe* (who was not convinced by the Reed/Hoorickx thesis), this seems an entirely feasible, indeed inspired, solution to an old problem. As the listener follows the words and music together, the musical illustration of the verbal imagery shows the young Schubert already in possession of many of the qualities that were characteristic of his genius. In the numerous instances where words and music appear well matched, the young composer's intense and felicitous response to dramatic situations is notable, as well as his taste for unusual modulation. Less developed as yet is his talent for melody; it seems that this eventually came to fruition after his introduction to Italian music and as a result of his ongoing tuition with Antonio Salieri.

This work boasts one of the longest introductions of the early songs, as if the composer had the equivalent of an orchestral overture in mind, reminding us that the origins of the Schubertian lied are operatic in inspiration. The manuscript shares the closing section of the composer's piano-duet arrangement of Gluck's overture to *Iphigenie in Aulis*. Only part of this arrangement survives, but an examination of the beginning of the Gluck overture reveals the use of ominous falling fourths that Reed has identified as a Schubertian 'thumbprint'. The same falling motif introduces this song, also based on a mythologically inspired theme, and attempts to paint the grandeur and silence of the sacred grove in which the poet finds herself. Nothing in these thirty-three introductory adagio bars quite blossoms into memorable melody, but they are rich in atmosphere. The most unusual effect is the use of quasi-orchestral textures – singing dotted minims in the right hand and caressing quavers placed unusually high for left-hand accompanying figurations. It is notable that the descending fourths 'theme' is something of a leitmotif for the entire work: there are seven subsequent appearances in the vocal line and accompaniment of the snaking musical shape announced at the very beginning.

Verse 1: No sooner has the voice come in than there is a beautiful, albeit strange and awkward, modulation (on 'Tempel<u>halle</u>' b. 14): an F natural slides up to an F sharp as a B flat^7 shifts into D major. This suggests a changed state, the frisson of entering a sacred grove. Three bars later (at 'Umrauscht vom nahen Wasserfalle') we hear running semiquavers in the accompaniment (bb. 40–42) – Schubert's first water music. Other nice touches are the entirely appropriate downward inflexion of the vocal line at 'Im sanften Abendschein' (more recitative than melody, bb. 43–5) and the sudden oppressive texture in contrary motion between voice and piano at 'Kein Lüftchen wehte' (bb. 46–8). The phrase 'die Sonn' im Scheiden / Vergüldete', that rises in b. 49 only so that it may fall on the portentous interval of the diminished seventh in b. 51, has just a hint of the sunset grandeur that we will encounter ten years later (cf. the passage 'Umhüllt mein Scheiden goldne Pracht, / Ich scheide herrlich') in the Mayrhofer masterpiece *Freiwilliges Versinken* D700. The idea of sunset is continued in the descending figurations in the piano interlude at bb. 55–64.

Verse 2: 'Andante' (from b. 65). The crotchet movement quickens, and again one notices how thoroughly Schubert has learned his lesson from Gluck who builds musical grandeur with repetitive figuration and blocks of sound, as if carved from marble. The gap of two bars between the words 'sass ich lange' (bb. 68–9) and the clinching 'lange da' (bb. 72–3) is both bold and descriptive. The piano writing rumbles and trundles in the background, now crotchets, and then increasingly strident quavers for the appearance of the throne of the gods. The juxtaposition of the rising 'Zukunft' ('future', b. 81) and the falling 'Vergangenheit' ('past', bb. 82–3) is the mark of a young composer who understands, as if by second nature, the inner significance of words and their musical analogues. The second time we hear 'Vergangenheit' it slides down to the murkiest of bass textures (bb. 86–7). The awe felt for the gods is expressed in the heavenward octave leap on the second 'Götter' (b. 102), and the sense of panic, skilfully engendered by the rhythm, as the stillness of the grove is invaded by the divine presence. 'Tod' (b. 137) is set as a sad and solitary minim, and it can be no coincidence that the phrase 'in des Tales dunkeln Tiefen' (bb. 146–7) descends to the depths of the stave.

Verse 3: 'Adagio' (from b. 160). This verse is a strange one from the poet's point of view. She is offered the drink of oblivion, suicidal for the ambitious artist. For an eighteenth-century woman, the abandonment of her wish to be a writer and shunning of her struggle for greatness within a male environment would offer her a stress-free ride to oblivion. It is fascinating to see how beguiling Schubert makes this passage. The image of 'eine düstere Gestalt' does not bring forth music that is in the least bit ominous. (How different this is in the second setting.) Indeed, this music shows us how *easy* it is to give up and yield to the voices offering you the 'mohnbekränzte Schale' – 'the poppy-garlanded chalice'. The key here is a suave and euphonious A flat major, with gently undulating thirds pricked out in the sweetest register of the treble. The composer imagines the poet momentarily tempted by these blandishments; then she comes to her senses on the sudden diminished chord which emphasizes 'mir' on 'Aus Lethe's Quelle _mir_' (bb. 180–3). 'Vergessenheit!', the strophe's last word at bb. 184–5, prompts another portentous downward plunge.

Verse 4: 'Allegro'. Schubert makes much of the word 'Betroffen' (dazed, bb. 193–4). The falling fourths of the opening overture make a brief reappearance (from b. 195). The poet wants to ask the spirit a question, and this is marvellously suggested by the vocal line sticking, transfixed, on one pitch, with words separated into syllables over three bars, as if in a stutter of fright. When the question is at last uttered, it comes out unaccompanied and Adagio (from b. 217), phrased in the falling fourths of Gluckian doom: 'Was dieser Trank mir nützen soll?' The spirit hurries away, and with it the piano writing, suddenly in fleet semiquavers (from b. 220). The words 'Ich sah's mit stillem, stillem Groll' are set on repeated Ds (from b. 228) despite the harmonic changes in the piano – a perfect depiction of tenacity and steadfastness when faced by a stormy crisis.

At b. 245 the tempo marking changes to 'Allegro Moderato'. It was the G major music of this section, identical to the concluding melody and accompaniment of the D39 fragment, that alerted John Reed to the fact that this wordless conundrum may have been an earlier setting of the Baumberg poem. Suddenly the spirit of Mozart enters the music, perhaps because he is everybody's idea of a musical genius disguised as a young boy. And what better than Mozart's example to guide the young Schubert towards the groves of Apollo and the prospect of immortality? Although graced with a pleasing little melody, this passage is rather banal. The importance of the gift on offer ('Ein unverwelklich schöner Dichterkranz') seems little suited to this cherubic frolic.

Verse 5: At the end of this section the recitative ('Er sprach's, und ging mir schnell voran', from b. 304) announces the little genie's flight and the piano follows suit with an ornate and flurried 'Allegro' progress across two octaves of keyboard (bb. 306–8).

Verse 6: This section is given over to recitative, ranging from arioso passages that are almost melodic to statuesque Gluckian passages: at 'Hellschimmernd sah ich's schon in ferner Schattenhülle' the voice makes an impressive, and descriptively appropriate, descent to a low E (bb. 324–7). The invitation to take up Apollo's lyre is made in stentorian terms in the bass clef, something at odds with the boyish and playful characterization (and much higher tessitura) of the Amor-like figure earlier introduced. It is as if Schubert has temporarily forgotten who is speaking to whom. By now it is clear that the young composer has lost the thread although he struggles manfully on, principally because he owes it to himself to continue with the poem up to the point where it has the greatest significance for someone who also intends to dedicate his life to Apollo. (The situation summons memories of Swinburne's *Hymn to Proserpine* – 'Yea, is not even Apollo, with hair and harpstring of gold / A bitter God to follow, a beautiful God to behold?') The genie continues his lecture, and he does so in Sarastro vein: the music suddenly takes on the tone of the high moral seriousness of *Die Zauberflöte*. A little C minor aria (from b. 346, marked Andante) begins with a long piano introduction (until b. 352). The music for the words 'Mit zärtlich rührenden Akkorden' is gentle and effective in its way, showing more of a developed sense for melody than anything else in the piece. But it must have been clear to Schubert that something had gone badly awry with his plan to follow Baumberg's itinerary for the remainder of her mind-journeys (later in the poem she is carried aloft on Pegasus, no less – a type of eighteenth-century equivalent of Frank Bridge's *Love went a-riding*).

Verse 7: The last of the verses set (incomplete) is framed in terms of a gently reflective C major aria marked 'Adagio' (from b. 386). In these words the poetess, not yet endowed with Apollo's entire strength, realizes that she is at first only able to sing small songs. Perhaps Schubert was reproached by this and felt that he was running before he could walk; there is nothing at all small about this, his very first song. It is a pity that only three bars before he breaks off, and for the first time in this work, he betrays his inexperience with vocal tessitura by assigning an entirely gratuitous (and unreasonable) high A to a bass voice (b. 391) otherwise required to plumb the depths. For his performing edition Reinhard Van Hoorickx added three bars of piano postlude to bring the piece to a close.

It is startling enough that a boy of twelve could have been moved by a poem like this, and able to grasp its central message: 'I will be an artist, no matter what any one else says or thinks, because it is my right and my destiny.' There is a strong feeling of 'otherness' throughout, – Schubert (like Gabriele von Baumberg) clearly realizing that he is not like most people, and knowing that it is his right to belong to an elite group as a specially selected servant of Apollo. Baumberg's lines are the stuff of high-flown fantasy, but they are also unmistakably a *cri de cœur*. She was destined to experience the oblivion that she most feared, and part of the tragedy of her life was that she was a woman of spirit attempting to fight the male-dominated world on its own terms. Her words identify a female artist's plight in a hostile world. Here we see the young composer, at twelve or thirteen, already identifying with the female psyche; it would be another four years before he went on to compose *Gretchen am Spinnrade*.

We do not know whether Schubert, at the age of thirteen or younger, had already encountered parental hostility at the prospect of his being a professional musician (this would certainly come later), but the texts of a number of his early songs seem to have been chosen for their relevance to his own life. If his ability to express his deeper feelings in eloquent terms was confined to music (particularly at this vulnerable age), the alliance between word and tone was here nothing less than a survival mechanism. More importantly, this song of dedication and commitment seems to set the pattern of a lifetime: songs were about things that were of crucial importance – personally, emotionally, philosophically; even the light-hearted songs were composed with a seriousness and dedication that was a matter of musical life and death for Schubert. That the young musician should have felt at one with outpourings of this kind tells us a great deal about his sense of childhood isolation, and that he was already experiencing certain defensive feelings against domestic and political injustice. In this way he proved himself ready to throw down the gauntlet for battle. It also shows us that even at this prepubescent age (Schubert's voice broke in 1812) he could feel within himself the greatness of his destiny.

Autograph:	Männergesang-Verein, Vienna
First edition:	First published as a fragment without the Baumberg underlay as part of the NSA in 1969; subsequently arranged and completed by Reinhard Van Hoorickx and published privately (P741)

Subsequent editions:	Not in Peters; Not in AGA; NSA IV: Vol. 6/157 (as 'Gesang in c')
Bibliography:	Brown 1961, pp. 296–7
	Hoorickx 1974[2], pp. 373–4
	Hoorickx 1977, p. 95
	Landon 1970, p. 216
	Youens 1996, pp. 29–33
Discography and timing:	Fischer-Dieskau —
	Hyperion I 33[1]
	Hyperion II 1[1] 12'46 Stephen Varcoe

Lebenstraum D39 →

LEBENSTRAUM (II)   Dream of life
(BAUMBERG) **D39** [H2]
(Fragment) C major – G major   Before 1810

(231 bars)

See previous entry for poem and translation; for this piece, the text is set as far as Verse 4,
line 72: 'Ein kleiner Genius . . .'

GABRIELE VON BAUMBERG (1775–1839)

This is the second of Schubert's seven Baumberg solo settings (1809–10 and 1815). See the poet's
biography for a chronological list of all the Baumberg settings.

The flurry of activity from circa 1810 suggests that as soon as Schubert, aged thirteen or so, had abandoned Gabriele von Baumberg's *Lebenstraum* (I) after setting fifty-nine lines of it (D1A, the so-called *Gesang in c*), he determined to try again. The autograph of D1A contains a small section of this second setting – also without an underlay of words. This means that *Hagars Klage*, hitherto acknowledged as Schubert's first song, has been displaced by *two* songs (albeit both incomplete fragments) which were possibly written somewhat earlier than anything else that has survived from Schubert's hand. If the Deutsch catalogue were to be completely reordered (something that is now hardly practical), D1A and D39 would be strong candidates for D1 and D2. At the very least they are contemporary with the music for piano duet that we have always taken to be Schubert's earliest surviving works.

Quite apart from the problem of textual underlay, the scholarly reconstruction of this work was made difficult by the fact that the manuscript was divided between three different sources. This no doubt prevented the piece from becoming better known at an earlier time. Correct identification of the text was also delayed. The work was only partly reassembled (without full text or identification of poet, and lacking another few bars later unearthed in Vienna) in the

Neue Schubert-Ausgabe in 1969. Only since Dr Heinz Sichrovsky's discovery of the poem and Van Hoorickx's reconstructions of both songs has it been possible for performers to compare these two settings of the Baumberg text.

It is fascinating to imagine the tone of the composer's youthful self-criticism in this, the first instance of what was to be a lifelong penchant for returning to poems that had eluded him. Schubert was hopelessly overambitious in wishing to set the Baumberg poem in its entirety (in the first version – already a long piece – only a quarter of the poem had been set) but it seems that when he began this second attempt he intended still to do just that. If the work was to be kept to a manageable length he would have to cover more ground with less discursive illustration and he now aimed for a tighter construction that kept the story on the move. There is a reflection here of the war that was being waged by the spirits of the past and present for the possession of the young man's musical soul. In D1A he had given his wholehearted allegiance to Gluck, but he obviously now felt that he should embrace the lucidity and elegance of something less dramatic and more modern. The very look of the music on the page of D39 suggests the marshalling of another set of musical influences: in the opening, a hint of watered-down Mozart (the overture to Joseph Weigl's opera *Die Schweizerfamilie* begins in a similarly anodyne manner in C major); in the recitatives, the newly discovered world of the ballads of Johann Rudolf Zumsteeg.

Verse 1: The introduction is reduced to a mere ten bars (as opposed to the thirty-three bars of D1A). These comprise a modest right-hand melody (decorated by turns or mordents, bb. 5 and 8) and a flowing pattern of left-hand semiquavers suggesting the *galant* style with Alberti bass. The sense of mystery and wonder at being in the grove of the gods in D1A is sacrificed to an elegant opening section where the 'Tempelhalle' is made of the coolest marble, pleasing in its proportions rather than imposing. The cascading waters of 'Umrauscht vom nahen Wasserfalle' are suggested by the singer's tripping melismas (b. 16). The sense of ongoing unity in the vocal line is not interrupted by pianistic illustration, which is a pity, for this was one of D1A's impressive moments. 'Im sanften Abendschein' is similarly suave, but the murmuring accompaniment beneath 'Kein Lüftchen wehte' illustrates the very thing that the text denies – the sense of airborne rustlings. (The atmosphere of a later ballad, Ossian's *Cronnan* D282, comes to mind.) On the other hand, for 'die Sonn' im Scheiden / Vergüldete' the Adagio recitative (which takes over the end of the phrase from b. 28) effectively mirrors the sun's descent over the horizon. It is awkwardly cut in two, however, by the insertion of a three-bar dramatic pianistic flurry (bb. 30–2) which separates the verb ('vergüldete') from its object ('die matten Trauerweiden'). This is a rare example of Schubert disrupting grammatical sense. The inexperienced composer had become carried away by the task of painting the glint of sunlight on the weeping willows and imagined an extravagant and imperious gesture from the sun god. (This assumes that Reed and Van Hoorickx proposed the correct word underlay for this passage.)

Verse 2: The act of quietly musing ('Still sinnend sass ich lange da') inspires a recitative that includes the most outlandish modulation of the piece. The rise of a semitone in tonality (C major to D flat minor) has a sudden gear-change at 'lange' that might suggest the elapse of years spent in thought, rather than minutes, or perhaps a radical shift of consciousness. In this piece it is occasionally difficult to tell the difference between inspired (and deliberate) eccentricity, and youthful ineptitude. The solemn insistence on the repetition of 'auf meine Rechte' within the relatively unimportant phrase 'Das Haupt gestüzt auf meine Rechte' seems unjustified. The contrast between future and past ('Ich dachte Zukunft und Vergangenheit') is more effectively depicted in D1A; here there is too much bluster. On the other hand, the repetitions of 'dem Thron der Götter nah' emphasize the poet's awe at being in the presence of the throne of the gods (bb. 68–75). The whole of this 'scene' in F minor (there has been a change of key signature at b. 61) is impressively majestic despite (or because of) its repetitions of the text, as if the spirit of Gluck has returned to give this section, with its pulsing quaver accompaniment, his blessing. A new 'Andante' section beginning in the distant key of B minor (from b. 94), and settling into D major with the entrance of the voice, introduces the idea of hymning the singers of olden and newer times. The musical rise and fall of the phrases for the two appearances of 'Der Sänger alt' und neuer Zeit' (bb. 101–12) has a mellifluous and singer-friendly quality, with a hint of graceful coloratura. We find writing of this kind (also in D major) in the Goethe ballad *Der Sänger* D149 of 1815, another work that examines the nature of a singer's calling. All of this is gently lyrical and civilized, and very much in the *galant* style. Perhaps this harmonic continuity (a pedal grounded on D for thirty-five bars, bb. 118–52) is Schubert's way of trying to emphasize that singers, old and new, are united in one great spiritual aim, in one greater tonality although this is probably reading too much into a section in which the sense of drama, a necessary element in keeping works like this glued together, falters and dies. The recitative of the rest of this verse is full of good ideas: the dramatic but eccentric setting of 'Tod' – a single crotchet introduced by two keyboard flourishes in contrasting dynamics (bb. 153–6) – isolates death in just the right way for it to be 'unbemerkt, und längst vergessen' (unheeded and long forgotten); the settings of 'Riesenschatten der Vergänglichkeit' are suitably ominous (the words are heard twice, as if echo and shadow come from the same bag of musical imagery, the first time with the piano stalking the voice in octaves).

Verse 3: The new tempo marking from b. 173 is Adagio in ¾ and the key is C minor. It is one of the most effective passages in this setting, depicting the entry of the dark spirit and its attempt to offer the poet the poppy-drink of oblivion. In complete contrast to D1A, Schubert sets these words in a way that suggests the rumblings of the underworld: here we glimpse the hand that was destined to create *Fahrt zum Hades* D526 and *Gruppe aus dem Tartarus* D583 – slowly pulsating right-hand quavers are pushed forward by a shuddering motif in the pianist's left hand. This shows how at ease Schubert already was in the playing fields of the new romanticism where Gothic horror danced hand in hand with classical mythology. The lolloping triplets under 'Entstiegen einem morschen Heldenmahle' (bb. 184–5) are splendidly grotesque and prophetic of *Der Geistertanz* D116. Now the sinister purpose of the spirit's appearance is revealed, and the poet panics at the prospect. The sleeping draught is pressed on the narrator, first with undue haste and menace – a Presto vivace recitative is accompanied by scurrying piano scales (from b. 192) – and then (from b. 196) with persuasive charm – a mini aria in ¾, marked 'Allegro' and 'dolce' with a sudden, unearthly shift from G minor to A flat major. (Here is a further indication that the *Gesang in c* shares the same text as D39 in that Schubert had already discovered this key relationship for these words in the equivalent section of D1A.) This hypnotic little aria promising relief from pain seems briefly to suspend time, although the horrified diminished seventh on 'Lethe' proves that the composer, already well versed in the classics, knew how to provide a suitably frightened response to the idea of Hades. The temptation to yield to this dangerous wooing is broken by the sound of the terrible word 'Vergessenheit', separated from the rest of the sentence by a piano interlude (bb. 206–9), and resounding, unaccompanied (bb. 209–10) in the poet's ears. After this, the sudden harsh diminished chord shudders with shock at the possibility of any true artist willingly accepting oblivion. The poet fights back as if to save her life, or at least her art.

Verses 4–5: The rest of the song does not rise to this challenge. Indeed one can sense the waning of the young Schubert's interest in the project. The recitative beginning 'Betroffen, wollt' ich die Erscheinung fragen' (from b. 213) is simpler than the setting of the same words for D1A, and less effective. There is insufficient resentment and disdain in the refusal of the sleeping draught. The recitative marked 'Vivace' (beginning with oscillating semiquavers to introduce 'Doch schon war sie entflohn') is the passage of fifteen bars which was the last piece of the manuscript jigsaw to be put in place. There is nothing very exceptional about this music either, perfectly effective though it is. The dancing entrance of the 'kleiner Genius' is already familiar to us from D1A. Schubert lifted it from the earlier setting but, after copying out ten bars he put a strong line through the passage. His dissatisfaction with the whole enterprise seems reflected (as is the case in a famous crossing-out in the *Winterreise* manuscript) by the graphical vigour of the deletion. It is unlikely that the composer continued with this setting on manuscript sheets now lost to us – although this is always possible.

The dating of Schubert's early songs, particularly fragments such as these, is always fraught with difficulties. Given that that D1A and D39 are probably the earliest of all his works, it is difficult to be absolutely certain which came first. The presence of a fragment for D39 on the autograph for D1A suggests that we have got the order correct. But for a while, Reinhard Van Hoorickx believed that D39 *pre*-dated D1A, and it is easy to see why, based on the quality of the music. Schubert gave full rein to his responses to words and images in D1A where he was schooled by Gluck's example, but not yet inhibited by it. In D39 he attempted something different, more controlled and faster-moving: he aimed for concision and classical lucidity, but achieved this at the expense of expressiveness. He had not yet mastered what Zumsteeg had to teach him.

The fact is that both settings have their problems. And in both cases the composer reached a certain point and felt unable to continue. The stage was now set for a new type of approach to song composition. Schubert now took Zumsteeg's ballads and modelled his own settings on them, bar for bar, section by section. This was his self-improvement scheme as he composed his next song, *Hagars Klage*, and his decision to work like this was no doubt influenced by his failure to complete the two *Lebenstraum* songs.

Autographs:	Conservatoire Collection, Bibliothèque Nationale, Paris (up to b. 140); in private possesssion (up to b. 226); Männergesang-Verein, Vienna (final sheet)
First edition:	Published as 'Ich sass an einer Tempelhalle' as part of the NSA in 1969 with only partial verbal underlay. A performing version by Reed and Hoorickx was published privately (P740)
Subsequent editions:	Not in Peters; Not in AGA; NSA IV: Vol. 6/171 without complete verbal underlay
Bibliography:	Brown 1961, pp. 296–7
	Hoorickx 1974², pp. 373–4
	Hoorickx 1977, p. 95
	Landon 1970, p. 216
Discography and timing:	Fischer-Dieskau —
	Hyperion I 33⁴
	Hyperion II 1² 6'36 Stephen Varcoe

← *Lebenstraum (Gesang in c)* D1A   *Hagars Klage* D5 →

LEBEWOHL *see* ABSCHIED (LEBE WOHL! DU LIEBER FREUND!) D578

LEICHENFANTASIE   Funereal fantasy
(SCHILLER) **D7** [H4]
D minor – G minor   *c.* 1811

(453 bars)

(1)	Mit erstorb'nem Scheinen	With dim light
	Steht der Mond auf totenstillen Hainen,	The moon shines over the death-still groves
	Seufzend streicht der Nachtgeist durch	Sighing, the night spirit skims through the
	die Luft—	air —
	Nebelwolken trauern,	Mist-clouds lament,
	Sterne trauern	Pale stars shine down mournfully
	Bleich herab, wie Lampen in der Gruft.	Like lamps in a vault.
	Gleich Gespenstern, stumm und hohl	Like ghosts silent, hollow, gaunt
	und hager,	
	Zieht in schwarzem Totenpompe dort	In black funeral pomp
	Ein Gewimmel nach dem Leichenlager	A procession moves towards the graveyard
	Unterm Schauerflor der Grabnacht fort.	Beneath the dread veil of the burial night.

(2)   Zitternd an der Krücke,
        Wer mit dusterm, rückgesunknem Blicke
            Ausgegossen in ein heulend Ach,
        Schwer geneckt vom eisernen Geschicke,
            Schwankt dem stumm getragnen Sarge
            nach?
        Floss es 'Vater' von des Jünglings Lippe?
            Nasse Schauer schauern fürchterlich
        Durch sein gramgeschmolzenes Geripple,
            Seine Silberhaare bäumen sich—

        Who is he who trembling on crutches
        With sombre, sunken gaze,
            Pouring out his misery in a cry of pain,
        And harshly tormented by an iron fate
            Totters behind the silently borne coffin?
        Did the boy's lips say 'Father'?
            Damp, fearful shudders run through
        His frame, racked with grief;
            His silver hair stands on end.

(3)   Aufgerissen seine Feuerwunde!
        Durch die Seele Höllenschmerz!
            'Vater' floss es von des Jünglings Munde,
        'Sohn' gelispelt hat das Vaterherz.
        Eiskalt, eiskalt liegt er hier im Tuche,
            Und dein Traum, so golden einst, so süss!
        Süss und golden, Vater, dir zum Fluche!
        Eiskalt, eiskalt liegt er hier im Tuche!
            Deine Wonne und dein Paradies.—

        His burning soul is torn open
        Throughout his soul, hellish pain!
            'Father' uttered the boy's lips
        'Son' spoke the father's heart in a whisper.
        Ice-cold, he lies here in his shroud,
            And your dream, once so golden, so sweet,
        Sweet and golden, now a curse on you, father!
        Ice-cold he lies here in his shroud,
            Your joy and your paradise!

(4)   Mild, wie umweht von Elysiumslüften,
            Wie, aus Auroras Umarmung geschlüpft,

        Gently, as if stroked by Elysian breezes,
            As if slipping from Aurora's embrace

Himmlisch umgürtet mit rosigten Düften, Wreathed in the heavenly fragrance of roses
 Florens Sohn über das Blumenfeld hüpft, Flora's son dances over the flowery fields,
Flog er einher auf den lachenden Wiesen, He flew across the smiling meadows,
 Nachgespiegelt von silberner Flut, Mirrored by the silver waters;
Wollustflammen entsprühten den Küssen, Flames of desire sprang from his kisses
 Jagten die Mädchen in liebende Glut. Driving maidens to burning passion.

(5) Mutig sprang er im Gewühle der Menschen, Bravely he leapt amid the swarm of humanity,
  Wie ein jugendlich Reh,[1] Like a young deer
 Himmelum flog er in schweifenden With his restless longings he flew around the
  Wünschen, heavens.
  Hoch wie der Adler in wolkigter Höh':[2] As high as the eagle, soaring in the clouds;
 Stolz wie die Rosse sich sträuben und Proud as the steeds as they rear, foaming,
  schäumen,
  Werfen im Sturme die Mähne umher[3] Tossing their manes in the storm,
 Königlich wider den Zügel sich bäumen, And regally resisting the reins
  Trat er vor Sklaven und Fürsten daher. Did he walk before slaves and princes.

(6) Heiter wie Frühlingstag schwand ihm His life slipped by, as bright as a spring day
  das Leben,
  Floh ihm vorüber in Hesperus' Glanz, Flying past him in the glow of Hesperus.
 Klagen ertränkt' er im Golde der Reben, He drowned his sorrows in the golden vine;
  Schmerzen verhüpft er im wirbelnden He tripped away his grief in the whirling
  Tanz. dance.
 Welten schliefen im herrlichen Jungen, Whole worlds lay dormant in the fine youth
  Ha! wenn er einsten zum Mann gereift— Ah! When he matured into a man—
 Freue dich, Vater! – im herrlichen Jungen Rejoice father, in the boy,
  Wenn einst die schlafenden Keime When, one day, the latent seeds are ripened!
  gereift.

(7) Nein doch, Vater— Horch! die But no, father hark! the churchyard gate is
  Kirchhoftüre brauset, rattling,
  Und die ehr'nen Angel klirren auf— And the iron hinges are creaking open
 Wie's hinein ins Grabgewölbe grauset! How terrifying it is to peer into the grave!
  Nein doch lass den Tränen ihren Lauf!— But no let the tears flow!
 Geh, du Holder, geh im Pfade der Sonne[4] Go, gracious youth, in the sun's path,
  Freudig weiter der Vollendung zu, Joyfully onwards to perfection,
 Lösche nun den edlen Durst nach Wonne, Quench your noble thirst for joy,
  Gramentbundner, in Walhallas Ruh— Released from pain, in the peace of Valhalla!

(8) Wiedersehn—himmlischer Gedanke!— To see him again – heavenly thought!
  Wiedersehn dort an Edens Tor! To see him again at the gates of Eden!
 Horch der Sarg versinkt mit dumpfem Hear the dull sound of the swaying coffin
  Geschwanke,[5] as it goes down,

---

[1] Schiller's line here is 'Wie *auf Gebirgen* ein jugendlich Reh'.
[2] In Schiller, '*die* Adler'.
[3] In Schiller, 'die *Mahnen* umher'.
[4] In Schiller, 'geh in *Pfad* der Sonne'.
[5] In Schiller, '*dumpfigem*' – in the repeat of the phrase, Schubert reverts to Schiller's original.

Wimmernd schnurrt das Totenseil empor!	The ropes whirr upwards with a whine!
Da wir trunken um einander rollten, Lippen schweigen, und das Auge sprach—	As we staggered about each other Our lips were silent, but our eyes spoke:
'Haltet! haltet!' da wir boshaft grollten— Aber Tränen stürzten wärmer nach.— —	'Stop! Stop!' as we grew angry— But afterwards tears fell more warmly.

(9) Mit erstorbnem Scheinen,
    Steht der Mond auf totenstillen Hainen,
      Seufzend streicht der Nachtgeist durch die Luft.
      Nebelwolken trauern,
      Sterne trauern[6]
    Bleich herab, wie Lampen in der Gruft,
    Dumpfig schollerts überm Sarg zum Hügel,
      O um Erdballs Schätze nur noch einen Blick!
    Starr und ewig schliesst des Grabes Riegel,
    Dumpfer—dumpfer schollerts über'm Sarg zum Hügel,
      Nimmer gibt das Grab zurück.

With dimmed light
The moon shines over the death-still groves;
    Sighing, the night spirit skims through the air—
    Mist-clouds are mourning,
    Pale stars shine down mournfully,
Like lamps in a vault.
The clods pile over the coffin with a dull thud.
    Oh, for just *one* more glimpse of the earth's treasure!
The grave's bolts close, rigid and eternal;
The thud of the clods grows duller as they pile over the coffin
The grave will never yield up!

FRIEDRICH VON SCHILLER (1759–1805); poem written in 1780/81

This is the first of Schubert's forty-four Schiller solo settings (1811–24). See poet's biography for a chronological list of all the Schiller settings.

Schiller, 'imprisoned' in his military academy, wrote this poem in 1780 in a state of high emotion and despair. A fellow student by the name of August von Hoven had died and the poet wrote to the young man's father enclosing this work. The letter of condolence that accompanied the poem is a fascinating indication of Schiller's general state of mind at the time: 'I am not yet twenty-one years old, but I can tell you the world has no more joys for me . . . the nearer I get to maturity, the more I wish I had died as a child.' Richard Capell exaggerated somewhat when he wrote that 'the humanity of the case . . . is not the poet's subject. It is an exercise in the macabre.' Whilst this may be truly said of Pfeffel's *Der Vatermörder* D10 set by Schubert at the end of the same year, *Eine Leichenfantasie* (Schiller's title; the composer omitted the indefinite article) was a heartfelt response to a father's bereavement (and the poet's own sense of loss). It may also have been a kind of oblique reproof to Hoven's father for not caring sufficiently about his late son's welfare. The poem is influenced on one hand by the religious poetry of Klopstock, and on the other by the graveside scenes in Goethe's *Der Leiden des jungen Werthers* that had appeared six years before and changed the course of German literature. Goethe's tragic hero was buried by night, as is the unnamed corpse in this poem. This mixture of genres, old and new, sometimes engendered a stilted type of *Sturm und Drang* which is bound to seem almost comically ghoulish to our ears. It is important to remember, however, that in order to escape from an appallingly restrictive routine, the young Schiller's imagination worked overtime, his emotions running amok in the confines of his hated academy. The poem is contemporary with his *Die Räuber*, a highly charged play if there ever was one, but both were written with the greatest seriousness.

[6] Schiller writes 'Nebelwolken *schauern* / Sterne trauern'. The repetition of 'trauern' is probably a copying error on the composer's part.

There is also no doubt that Franz Schubert took the poem seriously, and he was not the first musician to do so. There was a setting by the Czech composer Václav Tomášek dating from 1805, and probably earlier settings as well. Underneath the heading of the printed poem are the words 'In Musik zu haben beim Herausgeber' ('available from the publisher in a musical setting'). There are other Schubert graveyard songs (the settings of Matthisson's *Der Geistertanz* for example, D15 and D116) in which the composer partakes of the glee typical of all boys when confronted with a tale of ghosts or witches. By contrast, he seems to be aiming at something quite different here.

The three biggest 1811 songs, *Hagars Klage* D5, *Leichenfantasie* and *Der Vatermörder* D10, are united by a thematic thread of parenthood – the father-son relationship. It has been said that Schubert's early ballads are drawing-room operas, but at this time they tend also to be about the dramatic ups and downs in family life. In *Hagars Klage* (the fourteen-year-old composer's first ballad) Hagar, concubine of Abraham and mother of Ishmael, begs for mercy for her son: 'Ah, He wept tears of joy when I bore this child, and now the child has become a curse to him ... What has the boy done that he must suffer with me? ... Do not scorn the pleas of this innocent boy.' It is interesting that, according to the Bible, Ishmael was fourteen years old when he and his mother were cast into the desert, and that Abraham preferred his other son, Isaac. At this time Schubert's mother was still alive (though possibly ailing) and it is not hard to imagine her favouring Franz among her children, and feeling protective of him against his father's choleric outbursts. The young composer was later to dream that his own father banished him to the wilderness, and that his brothers' actions found more favour with their father. *Der Vatermörder* is about a son who murders his father. This is one way to resolve what might have been termed, in a later age, Oedipal conflict. The other way is for the son to die instead of the father, offered up as a sacrifice in the manner of an Isaac rather than an Ishmael. In *Leichenfantasie* it is as if Schubert sees himself in the role of the dead son reconciled at last to a father who, at the graveside, is able to love his child unconditionally. He seems to be saying those immortal words of childish self-dramatization, 'If I died, you'd be sorry.'

Verse 1: The opening music (Adagio, in D minor) is astonishingly mature even if it is in the manner of Haydn's more ornate solo piano music. A repeat, more or less, of the ten-bar introduction serves as the accompaniment for the first four lines of the poem, and it is clear that the piano opening was planned to mirror the words. The music's upward impetus suggests that all eyes sweep heavenwards to the moon; the night spirit's sighs are painted in clashing minor seconds (b. 19) and a fleeting scale passage gives musical expression to a line from the Book of Job later quoted by Thomas Hardy at the head of one of his poems, *The Clock of the Years*: 'A spirit passed before my face; the hair of my flesh stood up.' This ascending airy scale makes expressive use of an instrumental figure in demisemiquavers that has already appeared in the openings of the teenage composer's Ouvertüre in D (D2A), the Sinfonie in D fragment (D2B) and in one of the six Minuets for wind (D2D). 'Nachtgeist durch die Luft' is a splendid piece of word-setting first time round (b. 18) but the sequential repetition of the same words (at b. 20 the voice is suddenly asked to sing a high A) betrays the composer's inexperience in one important way: as yet Schubert has no idea about the limitations of the human voice. The vocal demands of *Leichenfantasie* would be better shared between a trio of artists: high tenor, baritone and bass and it is all too obvious that the young composer has had little opportunity to hear real singers. Not long afterwards Salieri offered specific guidance on this very point, and Schubert began visiting the opera where he would learn from Mozart's example among others.

The A minor cantilena section beginning 'Sterne trauern / Bleich herab' (from b. 24) is reminiscent of the writing in Mozart's A minor Rondo for piano. There is an appropriate sense of a heavenly void in the empty bar of left-hand accompaniment (b. 27) before the melody, star-like, shines through in the right. But the continued doubling of voice and piano is awkward, and apart from a deliberately jarring change of harmony on 'Totenpompe' (b. 32) the rest of the verse makes do with conventionally portentous tremolando rumblings.

Verse 2: After such a strong opening it is disappointing that Schubertian inspiration quickly flags. Either the task of depicting the shattered form of the grief-stricken father is too much for the teenage composer, or he has little sympathy for him. This strophe (from b. 45) is the low point in a piece full otherwise of interesting things. The most that could be said about 'Zitternd an der Krücke' (Andante) is that the feebleness of invention paints, perhaps deliberately, a figure too exhausted to move or get the words out in any believable way; the music really does 'totter behind the coffin'. From 'Schwer geneckt vom eisernen Geschicke' (Adagio, C minor, b. 60) Schubert attempts to use the bass register of the voice to depict the gravitas of an older man but the word-setting is uninspiring and the section seems to have been planned only as a transitional movement to . . .

Verse 3: Presto, in C minor, (from b. 83); for the first two lines of the verse, we are treated to a display of *Sturm und Drang*. After a Mannheim rocket in reverse (a downward-plunging arpeggio figure), quavers rattle away in the right hand as ascending arpeggios in the left lead the way to a number of sudden and unexpected key juxtapositions. This gives the section a wild Beethovenian quality that owes at least some of its eccentricity to the composer's inexperience rather than avant-garde inspiration. The words are awkwardly set, mostly with a dotted minim per syllable; the whole of this outburst seems to have been conceived orchestrally. The words '"Vater" floss es von des Jünglings Munde' initiates a new section (Allegretto in F minor, from b. 114). To reflect the dialogue between father and son Schubert creates a canon between voice and piano. The idea is a touching one, only spoiled by the banality of the rhythm and the way that the words are locked into a pattern where they (and the singer) scarcely have time to breathe. The young composer's word-setting has not yet become free of conventional instrumental rhythmic patterns, although his shivering setting of 'Eiskalt' (bb. 124 and 125) is effective enough. The music for 'Und dein Traum, so golden einst' suffers from being a repeat of the '"Vater" floss es' theme. The most original passage in this verse is the setting of 'Deine Wonne und dein Paradies' (from b. 142) which rises heavenward and melts into a visionary cadence in C major, the dominant of F minor.

Verse 4: The next three verses (in dactylic metre in contrast to the funereal trochees) consist of flashbacks to the golden youth of the boy whose life has been cut short. Schubert's music places him in Schiller's era, which is to say it is in a *galant* eighteenth-century mood. At first (Verse 4, Allegretto in F major, from b. 149) the model is certainly Mozart. There are elegant turns of phrase and some effective ornamentation, but rather too much of the vocal line is doubled by the piano. The exception is the rippling accompaniment that weaves around the vocal phrase 'Nachgespiegelt von silberner Flut' (bb. 180–3). The composer is already adept at illustrating the movement of water. It was to be a recurring theme in his songs for the rest of his life.

Verse 5: Allegro, D minor, from b. 194. In this miniature biography of Schiller's hero the boy ages sufficiently to display a more self-consciously masculine (or Beethovenian) profile. John Reed has pointed out that the rhythmic cell of this section has already been used in the Fantasie in G for piano duet (D1B, 1810). It is true that the verb 'springen' (to leap) was the inspiration behind the use of this motif that unleashes its power like a tightly coiled spring, but once again the gabbled setting of 'Mutig sprang er' (b. 203) is suspect, and there is the distinct impression that words are being grafted on to instrumental ideas. This musical movement is certainly developed at the expense of repeating words in the manner of an eighteenth-century cantata, and the leaping gazelle takes on the character of a battering ram (bb. 222–3). Schubert apparently realizes that the lithe image of the deer has been lost in the fray and an ascending scale passage with a diminuendo at bb. 225–6 briefly re-establishes an impression of delicacy. Comparisons with beasts of the air and field continue: the eagle flies high (bb. 231–3) and the vocal line is accordingly placed in the stratosphere; the tessitura fails to make singers crow with delight. Foaming steeds thunder away in octave leaps for the voice part (bb. 237–8) as the harmony hoofs downwards in semitones and there is much sub-Beethovenian musical rhetoric when Schiller's hero steps out in front of slaves and princes and shakes an all-purpose defiant fist at them (an action suggested at bb. 247–9 at the repetition of 'Sklaven und Fürsten').

Verse 6: Andante, F major, from b. 249, reverts to the manner of a courtly eighteenth-century minuet – not exactly a 'wirbelnder Tanz' (no matter how many left-hand semiquavers are added to stir things up) but a deliberately antique piece of music for flashback purposes. These lines are perhaps the rigidly self-controlled Schiller's indirect criticism of the deceased whose propensity for drink and a good time is duly explained away as a fault of youth, soon to be rectified by the fruits of maturity. The manly determination of 'Welten schliefen im herrlichen Jungen' (Allegro, D minor, from b. 268) sounds like the announcement of a fugue that never materializes, a good enough metaphor for the failure of the arrival of maturity. This section only lasts for two lines before the miniature Mozartian movement of 'Freue dich, Vater' (Allegretto, F major, from b. 279) captures a real *Zaüberflöte* jauntiness and aphoristic simplicity.

Verse 7: The music for the remaining three verses is significantly more original than the majority of the ballad's middle verses. A brief Andante in F major (from b. 296) begins with a motif that shivers with horror – four repeated staccato semiquavers. The words 'Nein doch, Vater' are genuine arioso – a melodic line with the true intonation of recitative. It is as if Schubert has momentarily stepped into the song's frame to sing those words to his own father; the music wants to placate the patriarch as much as comfort him. The picture of creaking gates is effectively painted (bb. 308–9); swiftly descending scales at b. 312 precede a downward look into the grave – a beautiful Haydnesque passage for the piano (bb. 316–17) smoothly ascending and ornamented, illustrates the free flow of tears before the singer mentions them. There follows a passage (from b. 320) as if written for brass, marked 'Maestoso' and in D major, which is nothing less than prophetic of the music of Wagner. A hero is announced as if he were as important as Siegfried. This section (beginning, after the piano introduction, with 'Geh, du Holder', b. 328) even ends with a repeated reference to Valhalla ('in Walhallas Ruh', bb. 344–8). The gently ascending chromatic setting of that word second time around implies a less imposing resting place than the famous edifice depicted in Wagner's *Ring*.

Verse 8: The setting of the opening lines (Allegro moderato, A flat) has a seraphic quality that might be termed Mozartian if the melodic invention were somewhat superior. All young composers find it easier to depict hell rather than heaven and the fourteen-year-old Schubert is no exception; the gates of Eden are dull in comparison with the portals of the eternal abyss. Now that we have come to the moment of burial, the imagination works overtime. The descent of the coffin in stages ('der Sarg versinkt', bb. 363–5) is graphically done, and even the vocally ungratifying repetition of 'mit dumpfigem Geschwanke' (b. 366) lurches appropriately as if the bier sways from side to side. Schubert had had little first-hand experience of much he describes in this piece (eagles, steeds, beautiful maidens, the golden grape) but with the death of so many of his siblings he was certainly no stranger to the sight of coffins being lowered into the ground. The bars of 'Wimmernd schnurrt das Totenseil' (bb. 368–70) comprise a supremely appropriate use of a passage between voice and piano in contrary motion: the left-hand coffin plunges by semitone degrees deep into the ground as, by a law of physics, the supporting ropes, and the vocal line, are propelled upwards. This is followed by an Allegro moderato in F major (from b. 371) where tremolando passages in the piano roll drunkenly, and the doubling of voice and piano at 'Lippen schweigen' (b. 374) is made to represent lips locked in silence. As tears begin to flow at the graveside the vocal line becomes freer (at 'Tränen stürzten wärmer', bb. 378–81); the final cadence, despite its impossible tessitura, is touchingly eloquent.

Verse 9: The recapitulation of the opening music is a triumph made possible by Schiller's repetition of the poem's opening six lines. This device has the effect of drawing together all the disparate strands of the piece, giving the impression that it has almost been a coherent whole. The reappearance of this nocturnal music has a calm majesty and a long span that is a welcome respite from the fragmented preceding sections. After six lines of this recapitulation, Schubert follows Schiller's new words with new music. The section beginning 'Dumpfer schollerts' (b. 413) is magnificent in the way the spade, grimly mechanical in its dreadful task, does its work with a menacing series of left-hand flourishes followed by the hollow staccato of clay falling on the wood of the coffin. The piano interlude after the third 'noch einen Blick' (bb. 427–9) creates an imposing atmosphere of rhetorical anguish. The final section, 'Starr und ewig schliesst des Grabes Riegel' (Andante, D minor, from b. 431 leading to a conclusion in G minor), is perhaps the best part of the whole work. After the reappearance of the shivering four-note motif (this time in demisemiquavers) heard at the beginning of Verse 7, the left-hand digging motif resumes at b. 436. The repeat of 'Nimmer gibt das Grab zurück' (at b. 448) points forward to the end of *Der Wegweiser* D911/20 from *Winterreise*. There the words are 'Die noch Keiner ging zurück'. The idea in the cycle that the road to the grave is a one-way street is remarkably similar to the finality of Schiller's closing image. Moreover, both passages are in G minor with repeated throbbing chords in the right hand underpinned by a strong bass line. In this way a powerful image from 1827, world-famous as part of a much-performed masterpiece, can be heard in embryonic form in a work from 1811.

Autograph:	Wienbibliothek im Rathaus, Vienna
First edition:	Published as part of the AGA in 1894 (P529)
Subsequent editions:	Not in Peters; AGA XX 3: Vol. 1/22; NSA IV: Vol. 6/22; Bärenreiter: Vol. 5/18
Bibliography:	Capell 1928, p. 79
	Einstein 1951, pp. 44–5
	Fischer-Dieskau 1977, p. 19
	Schnapper 1937, pp. 116–25
Discography and timing:	Fischer-Dieskau I 1[1] 19'16
	Hyperion I 16[1–2] 19'17 Thomas Allen
	Hyperion II 1[4–5]

← *Hagars Klage* D5   *Der Vatermörder* D10 →

LEIDEN DER TRENNUNG   The sorrow of separation
(H. von Collin) **D509** [H325]

The song exists in two versions, the second of which is discussed below:
(1) December 1816; (2) December 1816

(1)   No tempo indication   G minor   **C**   [18 bars]

(2)   G minor – B♭ major

Etwas langsam

p

Vom Mee - re trennt sich die Wel - le,

(26 bars)

The text is a translation by Heinrich von Collin of Arbace's aria in Act III Scene 1 of Metastasio's Artaserse. The original Italian text is printed below in italics.

Vom Meere trennt sich die Welle,	The wave breaks free from the sea
Und seufzet durch Blumen im Tal,	And sighs amid the flowers in the valley;
Und fühlet, gewiegt in der Quelle,	It feels cradled by the spring,
Gebannt in dem Brunnen, nur Qual!	But captive in the well, nothing but torment.
Es sehnt sich die Welle	In the whispering spring,
In lispelnder Quelle,	In the murmuring brook,
Im murmelnden Bache,	In the well-chamber,
Im Brunnengemache	The wave longs
Zum Meer, von dem sie kam,	For the sea from which it came,
Von dem sie Leben nahm,	From which it drew life,
Von dem, des Irrens matt und müde,	From which, faint and weary with wandering,
Sie süsse Ruh' verhofft und Friede.	It hopes for peace and sweet repose.

L'onda dal mar divisa
Bagna la valle e 'l monte;
Va passeggiera
In fiume,
Va prigioniera
In fonte,
Mormora sempre e geme
Fin che non torna al mar.
Al mar, dov'ella nacque,
Dove acquistò gli umori,
Dove da lunghi errori
Spera di riposar.

HEINRICH VON COLLIN (1771–1811), AFTER METASTASIO

This is the first of Schubert's two settings of Heinrich von Collin (1816 and 1818). See the poet's biography for a chronological list of the Heinrich von Collin settings. See also entry for Metastasio.

Schubert's achievement (and how clever he had become during the course of 1816 in handling verse of every metrical kind) is that the song seems to be a single flowing unity despite the verses of the poem being in anapaestic, dactylic and iambic rhythms respectively. Of course this is water music, and very charming it is too; we have the feeling that the vocal line is charting the course of the river, sometimes flowing in a straight line (and thus remaining on one note), sometimes moving in a more circuitous course. In this way the song is comparable to *Der Strom* (D565) where, in the middle of the song, the vocal line stays on the same note while the river flows through the quiet valley and the green fields; elsewhere it rises and falls with the terrain. Much of *Leiden der Trennung* is built around repeated Ds in the vocal line; one is reminded here of the phrase 'Nachtigall, ach' (also repeated Ds in G minor) in *An die Nachtigall* D497, composed a few weeks earlier. As the sea is mentioned in the last verse (at b. 16) the intervals in the voice widen and plunge ever onwards; only at the end where the river finds quietus as it once again becomes part of the sea from which it came, does the music move into the relative major. These closing bars (the coda really begins as early as b. 17 and continues to the end of the song) are exceptionally calm and radiant.

Like *Lebenslied* D508, the autograph carries the inscription 'At the house of Herr von Schober', and the choice of text seems no less appropriate than that Matthisson setting for the beginning of a new and independent phase in Schubert's life. The move to Schober's dwelling at the end of 1816 must have seemed like a blissful return to the artistic milieu to which the composer felt he belonged. Heinrich von Collin's translation of Metastasio's little poem (from the libretto for *Ataserse*) depicts a displaced and unhappy wave at last reunited with its fellows. In physical terms the text could be said to mirror Schubert's move southwards, from the Säulengasse in Vienna's ninth district to the elegant first, his happier stamping ground. The 'peace and sweet repose' for which the composer yearned was simply the continuation of his life as a full-time artist. It is hard not to see in this little song the celebration of changed circumstances, and in the inscription of the composer's new address on the autograph a sign of his grateful relief to be back in the day-to-day company of a kindred spirit.

As Fischer-Dieskau writes, this is 'a song that awaits re-discovery'. It has long been over-looked, perhaps because Max Friedlaender chose not to include it in the Peters Edition. Its wide range would seem impractical to some singers: high Gs in b. 14 and a final plunge to a low B flat in the final bar of the vocal line.

Autographs:	New York Public Library (first draft)
	Gesellschaft der Musikfreunde, Vienna (fair copy)
Publication:	Published as part of the NSA in 1999 (P816; first version)
	Published as No. 32 of *Neueste Folge nachgelassener Lieder und Gesänge* by J. P. Gotthard, Vienna in 1872 (P458; second version)
Subsequent editions:	Not in Peters; AGA XX 285: Vol. 4/251; NSA IV: Vol. 11/54 & 56
Bibliography:	Capell 1928, p. 126
	Fischer-Dieskau 1977, p. 88
Discography and timing:	Fischer-Dieskau I 9⁴ 1'18
	Hyperion I 17²³
	Hyperion II 17³ 1'20 Lucia Popp

← *Lebenslied* D508   *Licht und Liebe (Nachtgesang)* D352 →

Der LEIDENDE (Klage)   The sufferer
(ANONYMOUS) **D432** & **D432B** [H259 & H259A]

The song exists in three versions, the first of which is discussed below:
(1) May 1816; (2) November 1816? (3) Date unknown

(1)   B minor

Nim-mer trag ich län - ger die-ser Lei - den Last,

(26 bars)

(2)   'Unruhig' A minor $\frac{2}{4}$ [26 bars]

(3)   'Unruhig' B minor $\frac{2}{4}$ [26 bars]

Nimmer trag' ich länger dieser Leiden Last!	No longer can I bear the burden of this suffering;
Nimm den müden Pilger bald hinauf zu dir.	Take this weary pilgrim to you soon.
Immer, immer enger wird's in meinem Busen,	Ever more oppressed grows my heart;
Immer, immer trüber wird der Augen Blick.	Ever dimmer grows my gaze.
Nimmer trag' ich länger dieser Leiden Last!	No longer can I bear the burden of this suffering.
Öffne mir den Himmel, milder, güt'ger Gott!	Open your heaven for me, kind and merciful God!
Lass mich meine Schmerzen senken in das Grab!	Let me bury my sorrows in the grave.
Allzu viele Qualen wüten mir im Innern,	All too many torments rage within me;
Hin ist jede Hoffnung, hin des Herzens Glut.	Gone is all hope, gone my heart's ardour.
Öffne mir den Himmel, milder, güt'ger Gott!	Open your heaven for me, kind and merciful God!

AUTHOR UNKNOWN (ATTRIBUTED TO LUDWIG HÖLTY)

*This is the tenth of Schubert's nineteen solo settings of an anonymous poet. See Anonymous/
Unknown for a chronological list of all the songs for which poets are unknown.*

This melody will seem maddeningly familiar to many listeners – seven years later Schubert transposed it into B flat minor and used it as the basis for the *Minore II* episode in the Entr'acte (No. 5) after the third act of *Rosamunde* (D797, 1823). John Reed plausibly suggests that the composer was in the middle of his health crisis at this time (he had every right now to see himself as 'The Sufferer') and might have recalled this song because of the poem's opening line. There is no doubt that for a small song *Der Leidende* made a big impression in the Schubert circle. There are no fewer than three copies printed in the NSA (two in the AGA). The version printed in Peters (taken directly from the *Nachlass*) has a spurious bar of vamping introduction. Schubert wrote the song out twice, once in the first version, and again for the Therese Grob album where he transposed it down a tone into A minor. Using red pencil he later altered the shape of the vocal line in the original version. This was perhaps an attempt to make it easier to sing for a lower voice, but he might also have thought that the first setting had too much charm for its own good and when it came to the meaning of the words. These changes represent a variation of the first version but the effect almost equates to a total recomposition of the piece, with much of the whimsy of the original setting suppressed. Commentators have missed the fact that this third version of the song also has a *Rosamunde* connection: in the *Minore I* (G minor) section of the same Entr'acte (*Minore II* is a variation of *Minore I* in any case) the second bar of the tune, as in this version of *Der Leidende*, falls rather than rises.

The song, especially as Schubert first conceived it, is a magical combination of nagging unhappiness (all versions are marked *Unruhig* – restless) and the brave acceptance of an emotional predicament. This duality is reflected in a minor-key melody that unwinds sinuously to the accompaniment of pizzicato left-hand quavers, the ideal indication of a light Schubertian touch, and the hope of some light at the end of the tunnel. The song thus remains delicate, suitable for insouciant whistling, despite its stark text and dark colours. One of the reasons for this touch of optimism is the upward lift of the tune (in the first version at least) at line ends – on the words 'länger' (b. 6) and 'Pilger' (b. 18).

This same anonymous text was set in the song *Klage* (also included in the Therese Grob album) that was initially catalogued as D512 but was exiled to the back of the second edition of the catalogue (Anhang 1, 28) when it was decided the song was not by Schubert after all. The poem was initially ascribed to Hölty, no doubt because he had penned so many of the lyrics that the composer was working on at the time.

Autograph:	Österreichische Nationalbibliothek, Vienna (first version)
	In private possession (part of the Therese Grob album; second
	version) (*see* DUBIOUS, MISATTRIBUTED AND LOST SONGS)
Publication:	Published as Book 50 no. 2 of the *Nachlass* by Diabelli, Vienna in
	1850 (P390; first version)
	Published as part of the AGA in 1895 (P640; second version)
	Published as part of the NSA in 2002 (P837; third version)
Subsequent editions:	Peters: Vol. 6/79; AGA XX 224a & b: Vol. 4/106; NSA IV: Vol.
	10/159, 160 & 161
Bibliography:	Capell 1928, p. 116
Discography and timing:	Fischer-Dieskau I 7[14] 1'45
	Hyperion I 23[13] & 23[14] 1'47 Christoph Prégardien
	Hyperion II 14[10] & 14[11] 1'59 (first and third versions)

← *Blumenlied* D431   *Seligkeit* D433 →

Der LEIERMANN *see* WINTERREISE D911/24

KARL GOTTFRIED VON LEITNER (1800–1890)

THE POETIC SOURCES

S1 *Gedichte von Karl Gottfried Ritter von Leitner.* Wien bey J. P. Sollinger, 1825

S2 *Gedichte von Karl Gottfried Ritter von Leitner. Zweite sehr vermehrte Ausgabe.* Hannover Viktor Lohse, 1857

THE SONGS

1823?   *Drang in die Ferne* D770 Op. 71 [a handwritten copy of the poem was passed to Schubert by Johann Schickh, editor of the *Wiener Zeitschrift für Kunst, Theater, Literatur und Mode*. Schubert then composed a musical supplement to that publication which appeared on 25 March 1823] [S1: pp. 10–12 – in a much revised version] [S2: pp. 3–4]

c. 1827   *Fröhliches Scheiden* D896 [S1: p. 154] [S2: p. 97]
Sie in jedem Liede D896A [S1: pp. 160–62] [S2: pp. 102–3]
Wolke und Quelle D896B [S1: pp. 165–6] [S2: pp. 106–7]

October (?) 1827   *Das Weinen* D926 Op. 106 no. 2 [S1: pp. 76–7] [S2: pp. 23–4]
Vor meiner Wiege D927 Op. 106 no. 3 [S1: pp. 50–51] [S2: p. 22]

November 1827   *Der Wallensteiner Lanzknecht beim Trunk* D931 [S1: pp. 17–18] [This poem is not to be found in S2]
Der Kreuzzug D932 [S1: pp. 30–31] [S2: p. 264]
Des Fischers Liebesglück D933 [S1: pp. 110–13] [S2: pp. 44–6]

January 1828   *Der Winterabend* D938 [S1: printed as 'Winterabend' pp. 198–9] [S2: pp. 122–3]
Die Sterne D939 Op. 96 no. 1 [S1: pp. 19–21] [S2: pp. 28–9]

The life and career of Karl Gottfried Ritter von Leitner were inextricably bound up with his native Styria. He was born in Graz on 18 November 1800 into an aristocratic family from the Steiermark; like the poet Eichendorff his earliest memories were of living in a castle set in a magical landscape, the home of his kindly stepfather. As a schoolboy in Graz he witnessed at first hand the French invasion of 1809. He studied law at university (1820–4) but he never took to it as a profession; more important was the encouragement of Julius Schneller, one of his university professors in Graz. Schneller was a former teacher of Josef von Spaun, an admirer of Schubert's songs (he wrote a poem on the subject in 1826), and a close friend, perhaps lover, of Marie Pachler (qv. *Heimliches Lieben* D922). Schneller's enthusiasm for Schubert's music (without actually knowing the composer) may have contributed to the celebrity welcome the composer received from Marie Pachler on his first and only visit to Graz; her solicitous hospitality in the summer of 1827 gave Schubert one of the happiest times of his life. The composer had set a Leitner poem in 1823 (*Drang in die Ferne* D770, published in the *Wiener Zeitschrift* as a fold-out supplement) at

the behest of Johann Schickh, the proprietor of that influential publication and a supporter of Leitner's work since 1820. With various people so enthusiastic about Leitner's poems recently published in Vienna (*Gedichte*, 1825) it was unlikely that Marie Pachler had to work very hard to persuade Schubert to read them.

It is possible that Schubert composed, or at least sketched, some of his new Leitner songs when he was in Graz and it is almost certain that a copy of Leitner's verse accompanied the composer back with him to Vienna. In the unusual foreword to these *Gedichte* Leitner addresses his own book (he referred to it as a 'Liederbuch') as if it were a person embarking on a journey: 'wherever you come across someone with an open, innocent nature, salute him modestly and tell him in friendly songs about the beautiful Alpine countryside from which you come, and of the sorrows and joys, of the life and loves, of the young man who sent you out into the world'. It seems that in Franz Schubert this little book had found just such a sympathetic reader and all but the first of the poems for Schubert's eleven Leitner songs (some of them masterpieces, others only fragments) were taken from it. In many ways – in terms of personal modesty, political

Carl Gottfried von Leitner as a young man.

Leitner as an older man, lithograph by Johann Haller, 1857.

sympathy and hidden depths of artistic inspiration – Leitner was something of a Schubertian soulmate, at least in this early stage of his career. Sadly the poet was not in Graz at the time of Schubert's visit – it seems he was visiting Cilli, now Celje in Slovenia, where he had earlier been a teacher at the Gymnasium for a year – and the two never met.

It is also possible that at this time Leitner was in no mood to meet visitors. In 1827 his literary aspirations had suffered a humiliating setback: a volume of his novellas (including his tormented and unsettling masterpiece about the state repression of artists, *Meister Kunbert*) had been condemned in threatening manner by the censors in Vienna. Much later he wrote *Schmerz in Lenze*, a poem about this time in his life ending with the lines 'My mouth . . . is barred with an iron padlock, and a world of song dies in custody'. Like his friend Anastasius Grün (Graf von Auersperg), another

outspoken critic of the regime, Leitner's aristocratic status probably spared him further punishment. The fate of Schubert's friend and poet Johann Senn (qv) had been very different. Following this incident Leitner's confidence as a writer was undermined and he abandoned prose. (His teacher, the left-leaning Julius Schneller, a distinguished historian, had also fallen foul of the Austrian censors for praising the Enlightenment and the rule of Emperor Josef II.) Sponsored by the poet Kalchberg (qv) and the famous orientalist Hammer Purgstall (*see* WEST-ÖSTLICHER DIVAN), Leitner was appointed to a position in the provincial legislature in Graz and began to specialize in narrative poetry, some of it horror-balladry (*Schauerballaden*). This was a darker side of Leitner's art that Schubert was never to know.

Writing in 1836 Julius Seidlitz gave an interim verdict on the poet, based on the 1825 *Gedichte* and Leitner's publications in various almanacs – he clearly had no idea about the poet's altercation with the Austrian censors. Seidlitz wrote that if Leitner lived outside Austria he would be treated with as much respect as the most distinguished of the Berlin poets of the younger generation. The critic bemoans the fact that even in Vienna Leitner was known only to the literati, and compares his poetry to a beautiful and gentle maiden, lost in contemplation and dreaming her inmost thoughts. Seidlitz finds Leitner's talent to be genuine and true – the only thing that hampers him is the lack of self-confidence and an ability to make the most of his achievements in the outside world. These words might almost have been written about Schubert himself – and they echo what the singer Vogl said about the composer after their first meeting in 1817. They also massively underestimate the strength of Leitner's personality, his contrary political convictions and the emotional range of his poetry that encompasses tougher and stranger realms than Seidlitz ever realized. Schubert of course was similarly undervalued by many of his contemporaries, and for some of the same reasons.

In 1846 Leitner married Karoline Beyer. The marriage was childless but the poet was utterly devoted to his wife; in his holiday periods he enjoyed travelling with her as far afield as Belgium and London. With the fall of the Metternich regime in 1848 his gifts as a reforming politician came to the fore and he worked so hard in this legislative role that he retired exhausted in 1854. In the same year Leitner and Karoline travelled to Italy; she had fallen ill, probably with tuberculosis, and he had clearly hoped that her health would improve in a warmer climate. The moving five-part poem *In Pisa* describes her death, a shattering experience recounted in eloquently bitter quatrains. The poet accompanied his wife's coffin on its journey from Pisa back to Graz where she had wished to be buried. The second edition of the *Gedichte* (1857), published more than thirty years after the first and containing much new material, was dedicated to her memory ('Dem Andenken Karolinens'). The introspection of the widower

living alone while recalling his conjugal happiness had been prophesied years earlier in the poem for *Der Winterabend* D938. Following his bereavement Leitner was drawn into the circle of mystic and spiritualist Jakob Lorber (also a musician) whose biography Leitner wrote, and left among his posthumous papers. He claimed that with Lorber's help Karoline had appeared to him during séances and he reconciled this with his staunchly Catholic piety – just as he managed to remain a patriot and royalist while despising the Metternich government. The poem for *Der Wallensteiner Lanzknecht beim Trunk* D931 shows Leitner's admiration for Schiller's Wallenstein, a patriot betrayed by the duplicity of Vienna. The poet's establishment of the Austrian branch of the German Schiller Society in 1859 showed his admiration for a great writer who had been both a high-minded radical and a rigid conservative.

A timely invitation from Johann, Archduke of Styria (whose biography was written by Leitner in 1860) gave a new impetus to the poet's career – he was appointed one of the curators of the newly founded *Joanneum* (National Museum). Once more in public service, he spent much of the remainder of his long life as an editor, librarian, historian, lecturer and curator – all posts that benefited from his vast knowledge of the history and cultural traditions of Steiermark. He became known as a 'vaterländischer Dichter', celebrated for writings that took their background and inspiration from his own corner of Austria. There was a third edition of poetry, *Herbstblumen*, in 1870 and, in 1880 as part of his eightieth birthday celebrations, a volume of *Novellen und Gedichte* in which the short stories that had roused the censors' ire were printed for the first time. The literary critics were bemused by these tales; few people understood their significance in relation to the political circumstances of more than fifty years earlier.

Leitner is now acknowledged as the foremost Styrian poet of the Biedermeier epoch, and he was nicknamed the 'Austrian Uhland', an indication of his debt to the Swabian school of poetry (including such figures as Mörike,

Kerner and Schwab) whose work is also built around local legends and culture. His personal connections with such Viennese poets as Bauerneld, Castelli, Grillparzer and particularly Seidl had drawn him into a close relationship with the surviving members of the Schubert circle. In 1832 Albert Stadler (qv) had written to Leitner: 'I have read your poems, but more than read them I have felt them'; perhaps Stadler felt qualified to speak also for his close friend Schubert whose Leitner settings dated from only five years earlier. Leitner's memoirs concerning his own peripheral relationship to Schubert are a model of accuracy, probity and modesty. As late as 1881 the poet was expressing his appreciation of Schubert's musical settings of his poems, saying that on hearing the music he re-experienced the emotions he felt when first writing the texts. Schubert's friends Franz Lachner and Anselm Hüttenbrenner (qqv COMPOSERS) also wrote Leitner songs, and the poet provided the latter composer with a libretto for his opera

Lenore as well as writing Hüttenbrenner's obituary in three instalments in successive issues of Graz's *Tagespost* in June 1868.

Leitner died on 17 June 1890, an old man honoured on every side. Even during his lifetime he was always convinced that he would be among the 'half-forgotten'. His fears were justified; on a visit to Graz (2007) I met a local antiquarian book-seller who sorrowfully told me that Leitner's gravestone had been peremptorily removed from the local cemetery to make way for a new pathway. Even the plaque erected in his honour in the Rathaus is no longer viewable, as it has become part of a private office. Karl von Leitner, even without his connections to Franz Schubert, deserves better of posterity (and the city of his birth) than this.

Bibliography: Schlossar 1906
                    Seidlitz [Jeitteles] 1837,
                    vol. 1, p. 116
                    Youens 2002, pp. 202–300

GOTTLIEB VON LEON (1757–1832)

THE POETIC SOURCE
Selam, Ein Almanach für Freunde des Mannigfaltigen auf das Jahr 1813. Herausgegeben von I. F. Castelli, Wien, Anton Strauss

The poem also appeared in an anthology printed in Basel in 1803: *Neue Allemannische Gedichte* ed. Ignaz Felner (1754–1805).

THE SONG
January 1817   *Die Liebe* D522 [p. 240]

Gottlieb von Leon, born in Vienna on 17 April 1757, became one of the most important literary men of Austria's capital city. He was forty years older than Schubert (whom he was to outlive) and it is scarcely surprising that the composer chose to clothe Leon's words in the musical manner of an earlier age. Leon published his *Gedichte* in 1788. In 1816 he was named Kustos (curator) of the Hofbibliothek,

an appointment that was a tribute to his deep knowledge of the collection of autographs and printed books in the Imperial collection. He was a great admirer of Klopstock and Hölty, and wrote Anacreontic odes in their manner as well as *Minnelieder* in the style of Bürger and Gleim. Indeed his poems contributed to the awakening of a taste for medieval literature in Austria. Although he was not a very original

poet, Leon was a fine translator (from Latin, French and Spanish) and he was involved in several important publishing ventures including the editing of the *Wiener Musenalmanach* (1795 and 1796) and *Apollonia* (with Ratschky, poet-translator of Schubert's *Der Weiberfreund* D271). One of his most significant later publications was the pro-Jewish *Rabbinische Legenden* (1821). He retired from public life in 1827 and died on 17 September 1832. The poem set by Schubert does not appear in the volume of Leon's *Gedichte* published in Vienna in 1788.

Silhouette of Gottlieb Leon by Hieronymus Löschenkohl, 1789.

LETTERS AND DIARIES
Schubert's songs reflected in his own words

Ernest Newman (1868–1959), Wagner's biographer and a great critic (though not one usually associated with Schubert's music), wrote an introduction to *Franz Schubert's Letters and Other Writings* (London, Faber and Gwyer, 1928) edited by Otto Erich Deutsch:

> *Schubert's letters are the true counterpart of his music: the style is simple – melodic and diatonic, we may call it, without any involutions or complexities either of structure or of thought, expressing in the directest possible way only the broad fundamentals of things (though often, in spite of the artlessness of the prose, with something of the beauty of touch that makes his musical expression of the fundamental simplicity of feelings so magical), without anything whatever of self-consciousness or the desire to produce an effect. From his letters, as from his music, we get the impression of a nature of the utmost sweetness and simplicity, – the latter, of course, not being synonymous with superficiality; the simplicity of a Schubert or a Mozart may go deeper than the sophistications of many a more intellectual composer.*

The following article includes extracts from the Schubert letters, surprisingly few in number, which pertain to the composition, publication or performance of his songs.

1. From Schubert's Diary [Tagebuch] 13 June 1816
    ... All my life I shall remember this fine, clear, lovely day. I still hear softly, as from a distance, the magic strains of Mozart's music. With what unbelievable power, and yet again how gently, did the masterly playing of Schlesinger [the violinist] impress it deep, deep into one's heart ... O Mozart, immortal Mozart, how many, how infinitely many inspiring suggestions of a finer, better life have you left in our souls! This quintet is, so to speak, one of the greatest of his lesser works – On this occasion I too had to make my appearance. I played variations from Beethoven and sang Goethe's **Rastlose Liebe** *[D138] and Schiller's* **Amalia** *[D195]. Unanimous applause for the first, less for the second. I too felt that my rendition of* Rastlose Liebe *was more successful than that of* Amalia, *yet it cannot be denied that the essential musicality of Goethe's poetic genius was largely responsible for the applause.*

2.   From Schubert's Diary [Tagebuch] 16 June 1816
It must be fine and inspiring for a musician to have all his pupils gathered around about him, to see how each strives to give of his best in honour of the master's jubilee, to hear in all their compositions the simple expression of Nature, free from all that eccentricity which tends to govern most composers nowadays, and for which we are indebted – almost wholly – to one of our greatest German musicians . . . after fifty years spent in Vienna and nearly as long in the Emperor's service, Herr Salieri celebrated his jubilee . . . with a big gathering of his scholars of both sexes.

See **Beitrag zur funfzigjährigsten Jubelfeier des Herrn von Salieri, erstem k.k. Hofkapellmeister in Wien** D407. The youthful sideswipe in this diary entry is aimed at Salieri's bugbear Beethoven (*see* Composers) of whom Schubert was at heart, a fervent admirer.

3.   From Schubert's Diary [Tagebuch] 8 September 1816
Now I cannot think of anything more. Tomorrow I shall certainly think of something else. How is that? Is my mind duller today than tomorrow because I am sleepy and full-fed? – Why does the mind not go on thinking when the body is asleep? – It surely goes a-wandering? – It cannot sleep too?

Sonderbare Fragen,	What strange questions
Hör' ich alle sagen?	Do I hear folk say?
Es lässt sich hier nicht wagen	They cannot be answered,
Wir müssen dulend tragen	We must patiently bear it
Nun gute Nacht	Now good night
Bis ihr erwacht	Until you awake.

The connection with **Gute Nacht** D911/1 from *Winterreise*, composed nine years later is, of course, only coincidental.

4.   Letter to Josef Hüttenbrenner (see Friends and Family), Vienna, 21 February 1818, 12 o'clock at night
Dearest friend,
    I am exceedingly pleased that you like my songs. [the formal 'Sie' rather than the 'Du' form is used, unlike with Josef's brother Anselm.] *As a proof of sincerest friendship I am sending you yet another, which I have just written at midnight at Anslem Hüttenbrenner's. I wish that we could pledge our friendship in a glass of punch.* Vale!
    Just now when I wanted to sprinkle sand over the thing I took up instead, half drunk with sleep, the ink-stand and poured it all over. What a disaster!

The ink-stained autograph enclosed in this letter was one of the surviving manuscript copies of **Die Forelle** D550.

5.   Letter to Schober (qv) and other friends, Zseliz, 3 August 1818
Dearest and best friends,
    How could I possibly forget you – you who are everything to me! Spaun, Schober, Mayrhofer, Senn, how are you all? I am in the best of health. I live and compose like a god, as though indeed nothing else in the world were possible. Mayrhofer's **Einsamkeit** [D620] *is finished, and I think it is the best thing I have done, for I was care-free when writing it. I hope you are all as well and happy as I am.*

6.   Letter to Anselm Hüttenbrenner (*see* Composers) in Graz, Vienna 21 January 1819
. . . what has become of all those supremely happy hours that we once spent together? Perhaps you do not think of them any more. But how often do I!

The reference, somewhat oblique, is to the Goethe poem (**Erster Verlust** D226) which Hütten-brenner almost certainly knew.

7.   Letter to Josef von Spaun (qv), Vienna, 2 November 1821
Dear friend,
. . . I must tell you that my dedications have not missed their mark: namely the Patriarch [Ladislaus Pyrker qv, *see* Dedicatees] *has been good for 12 ducats and Friess* [sic] [Moritz von Fries, *see* Dedicatees] *on Vogl's intervention for 20, which is splendid for me. So you must be good enough to conclude your correspondence with the Patriarch with an expression of thanks suitable to his position and to mine . . . Your friend, Franz Schubert. Write soon to the Patriarch and to us. NB. Send me Ottenwald's* [sic, qv Ottenwalt] *Wiegenlied* [**Der Knabe in der Wiege** D579].

This letter showing Schubert in a mood, rare for him, to engage in musical politics, was written in connection with his dedication to Pyrker of the songs of Op. 4 (**Der Wanderer** D489, **Morgenlied** D685, **Wandrers Nachtlied** D224, and to Fries of Op. 2, **Gretchen am Spinnrade** D118).

8.   Letter to Josef Hüttenbrenner, Vienna, 31 October 1822
. . . As I have to make some very important alterations in the songs which I handed over to you, do not give them yet to Herr Leidesdorf [see Publishers], *but bring them back to me here instead. Should they already have been sent to him, they must be fetched back as soon as possible.*

This letter was written in connection with the three songs of Op. 20 (**Sei mir gegrüsst** D741, **Frühlingsglaube** D686 and **Hänflings Liebeswerbung** D552). Deutsch points out that making such last-minute changes to his compositions was rare for the composer. This was probably in connection with his decision to publish *Frühlingsglaube* in A flat, rather than B flat, major.

9.   Letter to Josef von Spaun (qv), Vienna, 7 December 1822
Dear Spaun,
I hope the dedication of these three songs will give you a little pleasure. You deserve so much more for all that you have done for me that I really ought to give you, ex officio, *something infinitely greater* ['ein ungeheure'], *and I would too if only I were in a position to do so. You will be satisfied with the selection, for I have selected those songs which you yourself specified. Two other sets are appearing at the same time; one is already printed, and I have put aside a copy for you, and the other is actually in the printer's hands. The first set* [**Gesänge des Harfners**, Op. 12 D478] *contains, as you will see, the* Three Songs of the Harper *of which the second 'Wer nie sein Brot mit Tränen ass' is new and has been dedicated to the Bishop of St Pölten, and the other contains, as you will* not *see,* **Suleika** [D720] *and* **Geheimes** [D719] *and is dedicated to Schober . . . I have also set to music some more of Goethe's poems, for instance* **Der Musensohn** [D764], **An die Entfernte** [D765] *and* **Willkommen und Abschied** [D767].

This letter refers to the dedication of three songs, Op. 13, to Spaun, **Der Schäfer und der Reiter** D517, **Lob der Tränen** D711 and **Der Alpenjäger** D524, works for which Schubert's most faithful friend must have earlier expressed his admiration. The letter was almost certainly written at about the same time Schubert discovered he was seriously ill.

10.   Letter to the publisher Anton Diabelli (Schubert writes 'von Diabelli', an ironically flat-tering touch perhaps), Vienna, 21 February 1823
Herr von Diabelli,
     I enclose the quartet together with the pianoforte accompaniment.
     The appearance of the two books of Waltzes has somewhat surprised me, as their publication is not in complete accordance with the agreement. A suitable remuneration ['Eine angemessene Vergütung'] *would not be out of place.*
     Furthermore I should like to ask you kindly to let me see the account for the last three books [Opp. 12–14] *for I intend to draw my balance and will let you have them, if you wish, for 300 florins.*

This letter refers to the male quartet (TTBB) ***Naturgenuss*** D422 which had probably been furnished with a piano accompaniment at the publisher's request. Schubert is clearly angry about his business dealings with Cappi & Diabelli which led to a temporary break in dealings with the firm [*see* PUBLISHERS]. He had already received 800 florins for the publisher's rights to Opp. 1–7 (throwing away the opportunity, carefully crafted by Leopold von Sonnleithner, to retain his copyright and earn more money from his music) and the further sum of 300 florins referred to here (which seems to have been a figure to which he was beaten down) is for the songs of Op. 12 (***Gesänge des Harfners*** D478), Op. 13 (***Der Schäfer und der Reiter*** D517, ***Lob der Tränen*** D711 and ***Der Alpenjäger*** D524) and Op. 14 (***Suleika I*** D720 and ***Geheimes*** D719). The letter coincides of course with the early stages of the composer's illness when he was uncertain of his future and in desperate financial straits.

11.   Letter to the publishing firm Cappi & Diabelli, Vienna, 10 April 1823
     . . . there can be no question whatever of your publishing any more of my songs whose worth you could never estimate cheaply enough ['nicht wohlfeil genug taxieren konnten'], *though I now receive 200 florins a volume for them. Herr von Steiner too has made me several offers of publica-tion for my works. In conclusion I must ask you to send me back all my manuscripts, the engraved as well as the unengraved works.*

Schubert's ill-feeling against Diabelli (and his partner Cappi) had clearly not been assuaged. The composer, despite his threats, published nothing with Steiner who was at that time the partner of Tobias Haslinger who eventually became Schubert's publisher (after Steiner had retired) towards the end of the composer's life.

12.   Letter to Franz von Schober, Steyr, 14 August 1823
Dear Schober,
     Although I am rather late in writing I hope, nevertheless, that this letter, may still find you in Vienna . . . I am in fairly good health, though I rather doubt ever becoming perfectly well again. I lead here a very simple life in every way, take plenty of exercise, work hard at my opera, and read Walter Scott.
     I get on admirably with Vogl. We were together in Linz where he sang a great deal and very well. Bruchmann, Sturm and Streinsberg visited us in Steyr a few days ago, and were sent off too with a fresh load of songs. I shall hardly see you before your return, so I must now again wish you all luck in your undertaking and assure you of my never-failing love, which will suffer unspeakably in your absence ['versichere Dich meiner ewig währenden Liebe, die Dich auf das schmerzlichste vermissen wird']. *Let me hear something from you from time to time wherever you may be . . .*

This letter was written on the recuperative holiday in Upper Austria arranged for Schubert by the singer Vogl. This is the first time that Schubert refers to his illness. The letter shows that his reading of the poetry and novels of Walter Scott predated by some eighteen months his settings of this poet's works. At this time Schober (qv) was in the process of moving to Breslau where he spent two years attempting to establish himself as an actor. In none of his other letters, with the exception of letter 13 below, also to Schober, does Schubert express such a passionate attachment to a fellow human being.

13. Letter to Franz von Schober, Vienna, 30 November 1823
    ... *Vogl is here, and has sung once at Bruchmann's and once at Witteczek's. He interests himself almost exclusively in my songs. Writes out the vocal lines for himself and makes, so to speak, a living out of it* ['Schreibt sich selber die Singstimmen heraus, und lebt so zu sagen, davon']. *For this reason he is extremely polite and deferent* ['manierlich und folgsam'] *towards me ... I hope I am now in a fair way to recover my health, and this new-found blessing will make me forget many another trouble; but you dear Schober, you I can never forget, for no one else can ever be to me, alas, what you once were* ['Denn was Du mir warst kann mir leider neimand anderer sein']. *And now farewell and do not forget your ever loving friend* ['und vergesse nicht / Deines Dich ewig liebenden / Freundes'] *Franz Schubert.*

The laconic reference to Vogl's writing out the vocal line of Schubert's songs is ambiguous; many singers write out the music in order to learn and memorize it, but here it could also mean the rewriting or the unwelcome ornamentation of the vocal lines [*see* ORNAMENTATION], suggested, perhaps, by Schubert's somewhat wry tone.

14. From Schubert's lost Diary [Tagebuch], undated, circa 30 March 1824, at 2 a.m.
    Enviable Nero! You were strong enough to destroy a corrupt people with the sound of stringed instruments and with song! ['bei Saitenspiel und Gesang ekles Volk zu verderben!']

This late-night diary entry is a rare instance of a verbal expression of bitterness and rage on Schubert's part, almost certainly on account of his illness.

15. Letter to Leopold Kupelwieser in Rome, Vienna, 31 March 1824
    Dear Kupelwieser,
        I have been longing to write to you for a long time, but could never hit upon the when and where. Now ... at last I am able to pour out my whole heart to someone again. You are so good and so faithful, you are sure to forgive me things that others would only take very much amiss. – to be brief, I feel myself to be the most unfortunate and the most wretched man in the whole world. Picture to yourself someone whose health is permanently injured, and who, in sheer despair, does everything to make it worse instead of better; picture to yourself, I say, someone whose brilliant hopes have come to nothing, someone to whom love and friendship are at most a source of bitterness, someone whose inspiration (whose creative inspiration at least) for all that is beautiful threatens to fail, and then ask yourself if that is not a wretched and unhappy being.
        'Meine Ruh' ist hin, mein Herz ist schwer, ich finde sie nimmer und nimmermehr' [**Gretchen am Spinnrade** D118]. *That could be my daily song now, for every night when I go to sleep I hope never to wake again, and each morning I am only recalled to the griefs of yesterday. So I pass my days, joyless and friendless, except when Schwind comes now and again to see me and brings with him a ray of light from those sweet days that are no more* [cf. **Erster Verlust** D226] ...

> *Our reading society* ['Lesegesellschaft'] *as you will already know has dealt itself its own death-blow by swelling its ranks with a rowdy chorus of beer-drinkers and sausage-eaters and it is being dissolved in two days* ['denn ihre Auflösung erfolgt in 2 Tagen'] *– though I have scarcely attended it since you went away . . .*
>
> *Leidesdorf* [see PUBLISHERS] *whom I have got to know very well, is a really earnest and good-hearted man, but of such a melancholy disposition* ['von so grosser Melancholie'] *that I am afraid his company in this respect may have influenced me rather too much. Things are going badly with him as with me, and therefore we never have any money . . . I have written very few new songs . . .*

This most celebrated of all Schubert letters quotes the texts of two famous Goethe settings (the second indirectly). Schubert also uses in this letter the rather unusual word 'Auflösung', the title of a Mayrhofer song he had composed earlier in the same month (cf. **Auflösung** D807).

16.   Letter to the composer's brother Ferdinand Schubert, Zseliz, 18 July 1824
Beloved Brother,
> *You can take my word for it that I was really hurt at not receiving news either from home or from you for such a long time. Leidesdorf gives no sign of life either . . . Do go and look him up in the music shop: he really might send me what I have already written to him about.* [Schubert's footnote: *You must be really energetic with him though, for he is rather negligent by nature –* 'er ist etwas lässiger Natur'.] *You could also find out about the publication of the 3rd set of the* 'Müllerlieder' [**Die schöne Müllerin** D795/10–12, thus **Tränenregen, Mein!** and **Pause**]. *I see nothing in the paper about it . . .*
>
> *To be sure that blessed time is over when everything appeared to us in a nimbus of youthful glory, and we have to face instead the bitter facts of existence, which I try to beautify, however, as far as possible with my own imagination (for which God be thanked!). One turns instinctively to a place where one found happiness before, but in vain, for happiness is only to be found within ourselves . . .*
>
> *I console myself about the songs made over to Mohn for only a few of them seem to me to be good – for example the songs included with* **Das Geheimnis** [D793], **Wandrers Nachtlied** [D768] *and the absolved, not abducted Orestes (**Der entsühnte** – nicht entführte – **Orest**)!* [D699]. *This mistake made me laugh very much. Try to get these at any rate back as soon as possible.*

During Schubert's absence in Hungary Ferdinand Schubert had been charged with reading the proofs of *Die schöne Müllerin* published by Leidesdorf, a task he performed in dilatory fashion. Further songs forming part of the manuscript of *Das Geheimnis* D793 may have been **Der Pilgrim** D794 and the Schober flower-ballad **Vergissmeinnicht** D792. The song autographs which Ferdinand (according to his letter to the composer of 3 July 1824) had rather over-generously handed to the painter Ludwig Mohn, were numbered thus in Ferdinand's letter: 1. **Geheimnis** of Schiller (1823) [D793]; 2. **An den Frühling** (1817) [D587]; 3. **Lebensmelodien** (1816) [D395]; 4. **Beim Winde** of Mayrhofer (1819) [D669]; 5. **Frohsinn** [D520]; 6. **Wandrers Nachtlied** II [D768]; 7. **Trost** (1817) [D671]; 8. **Frühlingslied** (1816) [D398]; 9. **Der entführte** [*sic*] **Orest**, recte **Der entsühnte Orest** (1820) [D699]; 10. **Sprache der Liebe** of Schlegel (1816) [D410]. The inference to be drawn from Schubert's letter is that provided the autographs of 1, 6 and 9 were returned to him, he could live without the others – not the case of course for later Schubertians.

17.   Letter to Moritz von Schwind, Zseliz, August 1824

. . . Before everything else I must ask you to make it a matter of conscience to make a real fuss with Leidesdorf ['scandaleuse auszumachen'] *for neither answering my letter nor sending me what I have asked for. The Müllerlieder* [**Die schöne Müllerin** D795] *are making very slow progress too: a volume comes out every three months . . .*

18.   Letter to Franz von Schober, Zseliz, 21 September 1824

Dear Schober,

I hear you are unhappy? That you have had to get over a bad attack of despair? . . . Although I am exceedingly grieved to hear this, I am not at all surprised, that being the fate of most intelligent people in this miserable world . . .

I want to cry out with Göthe [Schubert's spelling here of Goethe]: *Wer bringt nur eine Stunde jener holden Zeit zurück!* [the third and fourth lines – without the prefatory 'Ach!' – of the first strophe of **Erster Verlust** D226]. *That was when in our intimate circle each showed the other, with motherly diffidence, the children of his Art, and waited, not without apprehension, for the verdict that Love and Truth would pronounce upon them: that time when each inspired the other with a common striving towards the Ideal that animated one and all . . .*

Since you went away I have written scarcely any songs . . .

19.   Letter to Johann Wolfgang von Goethe, early June 1825

Your Excellency,

Should I succeed with the dedication of these settings of your poems in expressing my boundless admiration of Your Excellency, and at the same time earning perhaps something of respect for my unworthy self, the gratification of this wish would be for me the happiest moment of my life.

With the greatest respect,

Your most humble servant,

Franz Schubert

Letter sent with the published dedication copy of three Goethe settings Op. 19 (**An Schwager Kronos** D369, **An Mignon** D161 and **Ganymed** D544).

20.   Letter to Josef von Spaun, Linz, 21 July 1825

. . . Vogl and I went on to Gmunden where we spent very pleasantly six whole weeks. We lodged with Traweger, who possesses a splendid pianoforte and is, as you know, a great admirer of my humble self. My life there was delightfully free and easy. There was frequent music at Hofrat von Schiller's, and amongst other things some of my new songs from Walter Scott's Lady of the Lake *were heard* [**Sieben Gesänge aus Walter Scott's Fraulein vom See** Op. 52), *the Hymn to the Virgin* [**Ellens Gesang III** D839] in particular being generally approved.

21.   Letter to the composer's father and step-mother, Steyr (Schubert's spelling is Steyer), 25 July 1825

. . . My new songs from Walter Scott's Lady of the Lake *in particular had a great success. There is a great deal of surprise too at my piety* ['Frömmigkeit'] *which found expression in a Hymn to the Blessed Virgin* [**Ellens Gesang III** D839] *which seems to have moved all hearts and created quite a devotional atmosphere. I fancy that is because my religious feeling is never forced* ['weil ich mich zur Andacht nie forcire'], *and I never compose hymns or prayers of this sort unless I am involuntarily overcome* ['unwillkürlich übermannt'] *by a sense of devotion, and then the feeling is, as a rule, genuine and heartfelt . . .*

In Steyreck we stayed with Countess Weissenwolf [see DEDICATEES] *who is a great admirer of my humble self, possesses everything I have written, and sings many of the things very prettily too. The Walter Scott songs made such an extremely good impression that she made it clear that she would be by no means displeased were I to dedicate them to herself. But in connection with these I mean to break from the usual publishing procedure which brings in so little profit. I feel that these songs, bearing as they do the celebrated name of Scott, are likely to arouse more curiosity* ['mehr Neugierde errgen könnten'], *and – if I add the English text – should make my name better known in England too . . .*

With regard to the letter from Milder [see SINGERS], *I am very pleased about the good reception accorded to* **Suleika** [D720] *although I wish I could have a look at the* critique ['Recension'] *myself to see if there were anything to be learned from it. A review, however favourable, can be at the same time ridiculous, if the critic lacks reasonable intelligence, as is not seldom the case . . .*

The Variations from my new Sonata for two hands [the 'Andante poco mosso' of the A minor Sonata, D845] *met with special enthusiasm. These I played alone and not unsuccessfully, for several people assured me that under my fingers the keys were transformed into singing voices which, if true, pleases me very much as I cannot abide that cursed chopping* ['das vermaledeyte Hacken'] *of the instrument to which even first-class pianists are addicted: it pleases neither the ear nor the heart . . .*

22.   Letter to Ferdinand Schubert, Gmunden, 12 September 1825
. . . [in Salzburg] *we obtained an introduction to Count Platz, President of the Provincial estates, whose family, being already acquainted with our names, received us with all possible kindness. Vogl sang some of my songs, whereupon we received a pressing invitation to perform the seven items of our programme again before a specially chosen audience on the following evening. On this occasion the Ave Maria [***Ellens Gesang III*** D839] *mentioned in my first letter met with particular favour and touched all hearts. The way in which Vogl sings and I accompany him, so that we seem to be fused for the moment into a single being, is something new to these people, unheard of.* ['Die Art und Weise, wie Vogl singt und ich accompagnire, wie wir in einem solchen Augenblicke *Eins* zu sein scheinen, ist diesen Leuten etwas ganz Neues, Unerhörtes.']

Schubert uses the same word, 'accompagnire', that Schumann later uses for a pianist working with singers. It certainly would not have occurred to him to use the verb 'kollaborire'.

23.   Letter to Ferdinand Schubert (continuation of Letter 22) Steyer (*sic*), 21 September
       1825
. . . *The Untersberg or rather, highest mountain. With its own squadron and the rest of the mountainous mob, shone and sparkled magnificently in – or rather close to – the sun. We drove through the valley already described as through Elysium (cf.* **Elysium** D584), *though our paradise had this advantage over the other, that we were seated in a delightfully comfortable carriage, a luxury unknown to Adam and Eve. Instead of encountering wild beasts we met with many a charming girl . . .*

24.   To the publisher Bernard Schott in Mainz, Vienna, 21 February 1828
Dear Sir,
   I am much honoured by your letter of February 8th, and am very pleased to enter into closer association with a firm of such repute, and one that is in a position to give publicity to my works abroad. I have the following compositions on hand . . .

(a) *Trio for pianoforte, violin and violoncello which was performed with great success here* [Piano Trio in E flat major, D929]

(b) *Two string quartets (in G major* [D887] *and D minor* [D820, 'Der Tod und das Mädchen'])

(c) *Four impromptus for pianoforte alone, which could be published either separately or together* [Op. post. 142, D935]

(d) *Fantasia* [in F minor] *for the pianoforte arranged for four hands, dedicated to the Countess Caroline Esterházy* [D940]

(e) *Fantasia for piano and violin* [D934]

(f) *Songs for a single voice with pianoforte accompaniment. Poems by Schiller, Goethe, Klopstock etc. etc. and Seidl, Schober, Leitner, Schulze, etc. etc.* [Schubert had a choice of about 400 songs available]

(g) *Quartets for male and female voices with pianoforte accompaniment, of which two contain solo parts, poems by Grillparzer and Seidl* [this list includes **Der 23. Psalm** D706, **Ständchen** D920 and **Nachthelle** D892]

(h) *A five-part song for male voices by Schober* [**Mondenschein** D875]

(i) **Schlachtgesang** [D912] *by Klopstock, double chorus for eight male voices*

(j) *Humorous trio* **Der Hochzeitsbraten** [D930] *by Schober for soprano, tenor and bass, which has already been performed with success* . . .

This is the list of my published compositions, excepting three operas, a Mass and a symphony. These last compositions I mention only to make you acquainted with my efforts in the highest forms of musical art.

Should you care to consider for publication anything from the above list, I should be pleased to send it in return for a moderate remuneration . . .

Nothing by Schubert was published by Schott. The Leipzig publisher Probst to whom the composer wrote in similar terms on 10 April 1828 eventually published only the E flat major Piano Trio.

25.   Letter to the poet Johann Gabriel Seidl (qv), Vienna, 4 August 1828
Esteemed Herr Gabriel!

Enclosed I send back to you [the 'Sie' form is used, not the 'Du'] *these poems – nowhere in them can I discover anything poetical or useable in terms of musical setting. I take this opportunity to ask you whether you have in your possession my music for your poems* **Widerspruch** [D865] *and* **Wiegenlied** [D867], *if this is the case please send them to me as soon as possible as I intend to publish them.*

26.   Letter to Johann Baptist Jenger (*see* Friends and Family *and* Pianists), Vienna, 25 September 1828
. . . *I have already given Haslinger* [the publisher] *the second part of* **Winterreise** [D911]. *This year I will have to give up the journey to Grätz* [Graz], *for lack of money and bad weather are wholly against it.*

This letter, signed 'Dein Freund Schubert', is written to one of the few pianists, other than himself, to whom the composer gladly entrusted his song accompaniments.

27.   Letter to the publisher Probst in Leipzig, 2 October 1828
Dear Sir,

I am wondering if the trio will ever appear? Are you still without its number. It is Opus 100. I am anxiously awaiting its publication. I have composed among other things three Sonatas for pianoforte alone which I want to dedicate to Hummel [*see* Composers]. *I have also set to music* *several lyrics by Heine [**Schwanengesang** D957/8–13] which have had an extraordinarily good reception here, and finally I have written a Quintet for 2 violins, 1 viola and 2 violoncelli. I have played the Sonatas in several places with great success, but the Quintet will be tried out only during the coming days. Should any of these compositions commend themselves to you, please let me know . . .*

LETZTE HOFFNUNG *see* WINTERREISE D911/16

LIANE   Liane
(Mayrhofer) **D298** [H180]
C major   October 1815

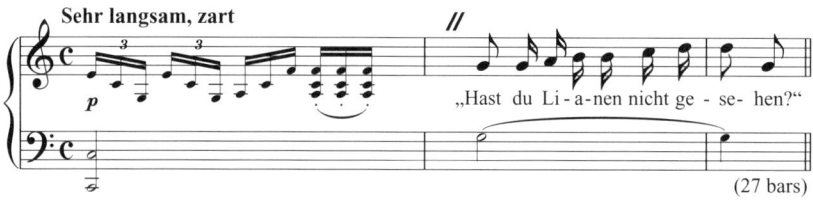

(27 bars)

'Hast du Lianen nicht gesehen?'[1]   'Haven't you seen Liane?'
'Ich sah sie zu dem Teiche gehn.'   'I saw her walking to the pond.'
Durch Busch und Hecke rennt er fort,[2]   He runs off, through bush and hedgerow,
Und kommt an ihren Lieblingsort.[3]   Until he reaches her favourite spot.

Die Linde spannt ihr grünes Netz,   The lime tree spreads out its green net,
Aus Rosen tönt des Bachs Geschwätz;   The brook babbles among the roses;
Die Blätter rötet Sonnengold,   Golden sunlight tinges the leaves,
Und alles ist der Freude hold.   And everything is touched with joy.

Liane fährt auf einem Kahn,   Liane glides along in a boat,
Vertraute Schwäne nebenan.   Her beloved swans accompany her.
Sie spielt die Laute, singt ein Lied,   She plays her lute, and sings
Wie Liebe in ihr selig blüht.   Of the blissful love that blossoms within her.

Das Schifflein schwanket, wie es will,   The boat rocks as it pleases,
Sie senkt das Haupt und denket still   She lets her head sink, and thinks silently
An ihn,—der im Gebüsche ist,[4]   Of him who is in the bushes,
Sie bald in seine Arme schliesst.   And who will soon enfold her in his arms.

---

[1] Mayrhofer writes '*geseh'n*' which Schnbert changes, notwithstanding the rhyme with 'gehn'. For an explanation of the background to these alternative Mayrhofer readings see Editorial Note at the beginning of Johann Mayrhofer.
[2] Mayrhofer writes 'Busch und *Hecken*'.
[3] Mayrhofer writes 'Und kommt *zu ihrem* Lieblingsort'.
[4] Mayrhofer writes '*Nur ihn* – der im Gebüsche ist'.

Johann Mayrhofer (1787–1836)

This is the second of Schubert's forty-seven Mayrhofer solo settings (1814–24). See the poet's biography for a chronological list of all the Mayrhofer settings.

Schubert's fascination with Mayrhofer's poetry began gradually. His first setting was *Am See* D124 from 1814, the year he was introduced to the poet; *Liane* is the sole Mayrhofer work of 1815. The output of Mayrhofer song thus began as a modest stream (there were nine lieder in 1816) and turned into a flood with twenty settings in 1817. *Liane* has long been something of a mystery, but its background may well be explained by Mayrhofer's avowed sympathy with the writing of Jean Paul (the pseudonym of Jean Paul Richter, 1763–1825). Jean Paul's vast and complicated novel *Titan* was published in Berlin in three parts between 1800 and 1803. The hero Albano (heir to the principality of Hohenflies without realizing it) encounters the beautiful Liane in Pestitz, the princely residence of the principality. This is only a sub-plot but the character of Liane, inspired, no doubt, by Goethe's Mignon, ethereal in such a way as to appear half mortal and half faerie, and given to singing to lute accompaniment, was one of the most famous in German literature at the beginning of the nineteenth century. She is also blind, an affliction borne lightly but one that separates her from worldliness. Jean Paul had at first intended Albano and Liane to plight their troth, but he was as merciless as Dickens, who often felt impelled to extinguish his most saintly heroines, and countless intrigues and calamities prevent her and Albano from coming together, culminating in Liane's death. This caused floods of tears in Jean Paul's readership, which doubtless included Mayrhofer as an impressionable teenager and, some years afterwards, Robert Schumann.

After Liane's death, on the striking of each hour, Albano knelt in fervent prayer saying, 'Liane, appear and give me peace!' Mayrhofer's poem seems to answer this prayer as if it were a poetic sequel or addendum to the novel, a scenario where Albano and a transfigured Liane meet at last, whether in an improved version of the story's events or perhaps in indeterminate heavenly regions. This way of viewing literary events in an alternative light was not new. The *Thekla* poem of Schiller, set twice by Schubert (D73 and D595), is a kind of ghostly sequel to the same poet's *Wallenstein* trilogy, and Mayrhofer more than once took the Greek plays (or in the case of *Atys* D585, Catullus) and elaborated his own poems from their storylines. Goethe too did this in writing poems such as *Ganymed* and *Prometheus*. Jean Paul's vulnerable and unearthly Liane and Albano, the unwitting heir to the kingdom of Hohenflies, are here allowed to claim what is rightfully theirs – although the poet wisely refrains from describing the actual moment of their coming together. Instead he sets up a meeting between two ghost-like figures who are seen to be awaiting each other in a moment of expectant bliss that will perhaps last an eternity. (In fact in *Titan* Albano, having been in love with his sister, eventually marries the beautiful Idione and rules over Hohenflies.) These women in his later life never attracted the fame or following of Liane who achieved something of the celebrity of Mignon. Note that at the end of the Mayrhofer poem Liane is only able to sink her head and think of her lover; because she is blind she is unable to look for, or see, him approaching when he emerges from the bushes.

It is likely that Schubert himself read the Jean Paul source; at the very least Mayrhofer must have explained something of the background to him. (The 1824 setting *Der Sieg* D805 mentions – in Schubert's original version – a 'Sphinx' that seems also to have derived from a reading of *Titan*.) Within a marking 'Sehr langsam, zart' Schubert creates in *Liane* a world that suggests dreamlike unreality. The introduction has all the cushioned euphony of thirds and sixths in C major, that white-key tonality of artless innocence;[5] after semiquaver triplets have climbed

---

[5] Performers are referred to NSA Vol. 9/298–300 for different readings of the song's opening bars.

towards a masculine G major at b. 3 there is a conversational exchange treated as recitative. In this music we can plainly hear the influence of the Schiller setting *Die Erwartung* D159 from earlier in the year; that ballad also opens with a question in a mood of tender impatience. Having received the information he needs, the poet (or Albano) runs towards Liane's favourite spot. This is conveyed by the rush of triplets in b. 5. The music begins to settle down in b. 7 with a return of the gently throbbing triplets in thirds and sixths and a vocal line that has all the flexibility and sinuous grace available to those schooled in *bel canto*. With two remarkable bars of interlude and transition (bb. 15–16) the song prepares to focus its attention on Liane herself. This is stately water music framed by ceremony, like a sumptuous *Embarquement pour Cythère* with its retinue of mythological swans. Limpid sextuplets and the anchored harmonies with long stretches of pedal points suggest that the vessel is bobbing gently up and down in the water, or even swimming in space. This music also recalls *Die Erwartung* D159 and the wonderful passage marked 'Majestätisch' that begins 'Mein Ohr umtönt ein Harmonienfluss'. There is much in *Die Erwartung* – subject, style and detail – that seems to have derived from this song. Liane's music is majestic in a dreamlike way. Looking forward to the lovers' reunion never occasions a hint of accelerando or human passion; it is as if she remains inviolate, dreaming of her lover and, wraith-like, caught in a web of time. In any case it is clear that Schubert is describing something more imposing (and mysterious) than a casual tryst between boy and girl. It has been suggested that Liane was a real girl whom Mayrhofer loved as a young man, but it is more likely that her purity and stoical bravery in the face of death and lack of romantic fulfilment are modelled on Jean Paul's character. We cannot doubt that Mayrhofer himself suffered considerably at various times of his life with romantic feelings that were never permitted to flower.

This oblique connection between Schubert and Jean Paul, a writer normally associated exclusively with Schumann, is an unexpected and happy one. Jean Paul's nephew Richard Otto Spazier (1803–1854) published in 1826 *Jean Paul Friedrich Richter in seinen letzten Tagen*, an account of his uncle's last days. According to his young secretary and carer, the blind and dying poet was particularly moved by listening to lieder. The Berlin composer Zelter was one of his favourites, but there were others: 'Above all he was gripped by that passage in Schubert's splendid song *Erlkönig* – "Du liebes Kind, komm geh mit mir," and "Sie wiegen und tanzen und singen dich ein". The mysterious promise of happiness [the Erlking's beguiling words to the boy], secretly conveyed through the voice and the accompaniment, transported him with a magical power to a transfigured and more beautiful existence.' *Erlkönig* had been published only four years earlier in Vienna; that it was being performed in faraway Bayreuth to a dying invalid is a sign that Schubert was already making more friends in German-speaking lands than he could possibly have realized.

Autograph:	Gesellschaft der Musikfreunde, Vienna
First edition:	Published as part of the AGA in 1895 (P607)
Subsequent editions:	Not in Peters; AGA XX 170: Vol. 3/165; NSA IV: Vol. 9/125
Discography and timing:	Fischer-Dieskau I 6² 2'42
	Hyperion I 7¹⁸
	Hyperion II 10¹⁶ 3'16 Lucia Popp

←— *Erlkönig* D328   *Lambertine* D301 —→

LICHT UND LIEBE (NACHTGESANG)
(M. VON COLLIN) **D352** [H326]
G major 1816? 1822?

Light and love (Nocturne) Duet, ST

(76 bars)

Männliche Stimme:	Male voice:
Liebe ist ein süsses Licht.	Love is a sweet light.
Wie die Erde strebt zur Sonne,	Just as the earth aches for the sun
Und zu jenen hellen Sternen	And those bright stars
In den weiten blauen Fernen,	In the distant blue expanses,
Strebt das Herz nach Liebeswonne:	So the heart aches for love's bliss,
Denn sie ist ein süsses Licht.	For love is a sweet light.

Weibliche Stimme:	Female voice:
Sieh! wie hoch in stiller Feier	See, high in the silent solemnity,
Droben helle Sterne funkeln:	Bright stars glitter up above:
Von der Erde fliehn die dunkeln	From the earth flee the dark
Schwermutsvollen trüben Schleier.	Heavy baleful mists.
Wehe mir, wie so trübe	Alas! Yet how sad I feel
Fühl ich tief mich im Gemüte,	Deep in my soul;
Das in Freuden sonst erblühte,	Once I brimmed with joy;
Nun vereinsamt, ohne Liebe.	Now I am abandoned, unloved.

Beide Stimmen:	Both voices:
Liebe ist ein süsses Licht.	Love is a sweet light.
Wie die Erde strebt zur Sonne,	Just as the earth aches for the sun
Und zu jenen hellen Sternen	And those bright stars
In den weiten blauen Fernen,	In the distant blue expanses,
Strebt das Herz nach Liebeswonne:	So the heart aches for love's bliss,
Denn sie ist ein süsses Licht.	For love is a sweet light.

MATTHÄUS VON COLLIN (1779–1824); poem written in 1808/13

This is the first of Schubert's five Matthäus von Collin settings (1816, 1822–3). Although the piece is strictly speaking a duet, as a piano-accompanied work with significant solo passages it is listed here as one of the lieder rather than as an ensemble item. See the poet's biography for a chronological list of all the Matthäus von Collin settings.

Why did Schubert not compose more duets for voices and piano? There are only two that are really worthy of the name (i.e. where two voices actually sing together): *Licht und Liebe* and *Mignon und der Harfner* D877/1. The choice of title for the first of these is something of a puzzle.

The poem's opening line might have logically suggested *Liebe ist ein süsses Licht*, but Schubert possibly remembered another poem by Matthäus Collin entitled *Licht und Liebe* that was published in the almanac *Selam* for 1813 (edited by Castelli, pp. 201–2), although this poem, beginning 'Voll von Sternen ist der Himmel! / Voll von lieben hellen Sternen!', is entirely different from the song extract from a play that is considered here.

The text of the poem used by Schubert is taken from Act IV Scene 1 of Collin's epic drama *Der Tod Friedrichs des Streitbaren* (1813) where the eponymous hero, Duke Friedrich the Valiant, reflects on past happiness. In the distance he hears first the sound of a man's singing voice, then a woman's, and finally the two together. The male voice in the play has no role beyond that of an anonymous fisherman, but the female voice is that of Agnes von Meran to whom Friedrich has once been married. They have parted because Agnes was unable to present him with an heir, but Friedrich still loves her. The stage directions are the following: 'A valley near Lunz, Austria . . . in the background a lake. On a hill near the bank there is a fisherman's hut hidden by trees. A moonlit night'. In *Licht und Liebe* Schubert follows this scenario to the letter, even though it means that the soprano spends the first half of the song waiting to sing. This stage direction links *Licht und Liebe* with the Mayrhofer setting *Abschied, nach einer Wall-fahrtsarie* D475: *Lunz* is the poet's published title for that lyric, and it refers to the town of Lunz am See, near Mariazell in Lower Austria, which in turn is the site of yet another Mayrhofer song, *Erlafsee* D586.

It is interesting that the composer needed Collin's specific instructions in the play as an excuse to cast a song with piano as a duet; how different this is from Mendelssohn, for example, who seems to have regarded any love poem as suitable for duet setting – 'ich' poems as well as those voiced by the plural 'wir'. Mendelssohn was especially fond of combined women's voices; the inspiration for this sisterly collaboration goes back to Mozart's Fiordiligi and Dorabella but it now seems more Victorian in effect. Schumann elaborated on Mendelssohn's example and took matters several steps further: with his *Spanisches Liederspiel* Op. 74 the song cycle for four voices was born, where the lied has a quasi-operatic cast (in both senses) all of its own. Perhaps the singing of duets seemed too operatic and stagey to Schubert and he, like Hugo Wolf, preferred to keep the lied form reserved for separate soloists.

The four-bar introduction to this song, printed in smaller type in the AGA, has long been considered spurious for this reason, but in the absence of an autograph the NSA takes Diabelli's first edition at face value and prints it as part of the song. We launch immediately into one of Schubert's most gracious and pleasing melodies in that gently undulating triple time ('Langsam' perhaps, but better understood as a slow one per bar) that is the ancestor of the waltz. This is tenor music par excellence, and we can detect the hand of the master who was to compose the *Ständchen* from *Schwanengesang*: a similar heady sweetness, a rise and fall that seems inevitable, and a certain dramatic context appropriate for a set piece from a play. The key is G major, and it is not especially daring in harmonic terms. When 'In den weiten' (bb. 12–13) is followed by the beautiful falling sequence 'blauen Fernen' (bb. 13–14), and when 'Strebt das Herz nach Liebeswonne' is repeated in a higher tessitura (bb. 16–18), we realize that the composer is able to take the operatic commonplaces of this kind of serenade and turn sentimentality into real feeling.

For the second verse the music modulates (suggesting the entrance of a new character) from G major into E major (change of key signature at b. 25). The accompaniment throbs in gentle syncopations supporting a noble, but rather less inspired, vocal line for the soprano. The purpose of this is to act as a foil to the big tune of the opening that will reappear at the recapitulation. E major cedes to E minor, and from 'Wehe mir, wie so trübe' (bb. 35–6) the quasi-recitative is underpinned by harmonies falling in bass-line semitones to find temporary quietus in C major

(b. 40). As the vocal line is caught and pinned on a murmured B natural (at 'Nun ver<u>einsamt,</u> <u>ohne Liebe</u>', from b. 41) something delectable happens in the accompaniment which is suddenly gently animated by semiquavers that cradle this fixed note and pass it back and forth between harmonizations in E minor and B major, and thence to B minor. This is a picturesque pathway back to the home key of G major (where we arrive at b. 45).

This modulation coincides with the inevitable reappearance of 'Liebe ist ein süsses Licht' where the tenor's return is surreptitiously accomplished with the gentle change back into the home key: a most artfully prepared and winning moment. After this, the two voices dovetail in lambent rapture where passion is moderated by moonlight and memory. The voices echo each other at first, then join forces in euphonious thirds and sixths. At the end of this intimate conversation, the piano's semiquavers are stilled for a final section (repeats of 'Liebe ist ein süsses Licht' bb. 64–68). This is very much part of the musical structure but, at the same time, suggests the freedom and release of a joint *bel canto* cadenza for the singers, no matter how strictly the music has been notated. Performers have been known to make a meal of this with much slowing down in an unashamed operatic, valedictory, spirit. But the music works better when followed to the letter – the feeling of a quasi-operatic peroration is built in without the performers needing to add to it. The accompanimental details in these final twelve bars are telling, particularly the cello-like fragment of melody which is presented, in the bass clef, in counterpoint to the final 'ein süsses Licht' (bb. 71–2). At moments like this one can easily imagine that this beautiful nocturne had been orchestrated in the composer's mind, just in case Collin should ever want to use it in the theatre.

The dating of this work is contested. In the absence of a manuscript, John Reed believes that it was written much later than 1816; he places it with the other Collin songs in 1822 or 1823. Although it is a tidy idea to place all the Collin settings in the same period, there is, as Otto Erich Deutsch also thought, something about *Licht und Liebe* that suggests the younger Schubert. It is true that the magical world of Collin's *Nacht und Träume* is prophesied by that high-lying vocal line and those oscillating accompanying semiquavers, but this duet, delightful as it is, is not in the same exalted class as that masterpiece. And there is one further point concerning another, much longer, duet by Schubert in G major with an E minor middle section: *Auguste jam coelestium* D488, for soprano and tenor, accompanied by strings, with oboes and bassoons, was composed in October 1816. *Licht und Liebe* possibly represents a contemporary attempt to write secular music for the same vocal forces.

Autograph:	Missing or lost
First edition:	Published as Book 41 no. 1 of the *Nachlass* by Diabelli, Vienna in *c.* 1847 (P357)
Subsequent editions:	Not in Peters; AGA XX 286: Vol. 4/253; NSA III: Vol. 2b/270
Bibliography:	Youens 2002, pp. 69–83

Discography and timing:			
Deutsche Grammophon *Schubert Duette*	5'05	Janet Baker & Dietrich Fischer-Dieskau
Hyperion I 32³		
Hyperion II 17⁴	4'11	Michael Schade & Lynne Dawson

← *Leiden der Trennung* D509   *Vedi quanto [t]adoro (Didone abbandonata)* D510a →

LIEB MINNA. ROMANZE   Darling Minna
(STADLER) **D222** [H114]
F minor   2 July 1815

'Schwüler Hauch weht mir herüber,
Welkt die Blum' an meiner Brust.
Ach, wo weilst du, Wilhelm, Lieber?
Meiner Seele süsse Lust!
  Ewig Weinen,
  Nie Erscheinen!
Schläfst wohl schon im kühlen Schoosse,
Denkst auch mein noch unterm Moose?'

Minna weinet, es verflogen
Mählig Wang- und Lippenrot.
Wilhelm war hinausgezogen
Mit den Reihn zum Schlachtentod.
  Von der Stunde
  Keine Kunde!
Schläfst wohl längst im kühlen Schoosse,

Denkt dein Minna unterm Moose.

Liebchen sitzt im stillen Harme,
Sieht die gold'nen Sternlein ziehn,
Und der Mond schaut auf die Arme
Mitleidsvollen Blickes hin.
  Horch, da wehen
  Aus den Höhen
Abendlüftchen ihr herüber:
Dort am Felsen harrt dein Lieber.

Minna eilt im Mondenflimmer
Bleich und ahnend durch die Flur,
Findet ihren Wilhelm nimmer,
Findet seinen Hügel nur.
  'Bin bald drüben
  Bei dir Lieben,
Sagst mir aus dem kühlen Schoosse:
"Denk' dein, Minna, unterm Moose." '

'A sultry breeze wafts across to me,
The flower at my breast withers.
Ah, where do you linger, Wilhelm dearest,
My soul's sweet delight?
  I weep eternally,
  You never appear!
Perhaps you already sleep in the earth's cool womb;
Do you still think of me beneath the moss?'

Minna wept; gradually the crimson drained
From her cheeks and lips.
Wilhelm had departed
With the ranks to death in battle.
  From that hour
  There was no news.
Your Minna thinks: perhaps you have long been
  sleeping
Beneath the cool moss.

The sweet maiden sits in silent grief,
Watching the motion of the golden stars,
And the moon looks upon the poor creature
With compassionate gaze.
  Hark, evening breezes
  Waft across her
From the heights:
Your beloved is waiting there by the cliff.

Pale and filled with foreboding, Minna hastens
Across the meadows in the shimmering moonlight.
But she does not find her Wilhelm;
She finds only his grave.
  'Soon I shall be there
  With you, beloved,
If from the cool womb you tell me:
"I am thinking of you, Minna, beneath the moss." '

Und viel tausend Blümchen steigen	And many thousands of flowers spring
Freundlich aus dem Grab herauf.	Tenderly from the grave.
Minna kennt die Liebeszeugen,	Minna understands this testimony of love,
Bettet sich ein Plätzchen drauf.	And makes a little bed upon them.
'Bin gleich drüben	'Very soon I shall be there
Bei dir Lieben!'	With you, beloved!'
Legt sich auf die Blümchen nieder	She lies down upon the flowers
Findet ihren Wilhelm wieder.	And finds her Wilhelm again.

ALBERT STADLER (1794–1888)

This is the first of Schubert's two Stadler solo settings (1815–20). See the poet's biography for a chronological list of all the Stadler settings.

This text may be typical of the amateur versifying that was the stock-in-trade of the Schubert circle, but no one can deny the industry and ambition of young poets like Albert Stadler who delivered an entire opera libretto to Schubert at more or less the same time as handing over the poem for *Lieb Minna*. By the beginning of July 1815 the composer completed his one-act *Singspiel* to Stadler's text: *Fernando* D220 is a story that might have fascinated Britten had Stadler been a better librettist. It encompasses the search of a twelve-year-old boy, Philipp, for his mother as well as his lost father – revealed in time to be the eponymous hero, a hermit who shelters Philipp from the storm.

Stadler's poem, *Lieb Minna*, has a fortuitous connection with Kenner's *Der Liedler* D209 in that both texts feature someone called Wilhelm and two heroines whose names are so similar – Milla and Minna – that one is tempted to believe that Stadler was attempting to write a sequel to Kenner's ballad. In fact, Till Gerrit Waidelich's contention that the scenario of Stadler's poem owes a great deal to Johann Peter Hebel's famous tale *Unverhofftes Wiedersehen* of 1811 (a bride awaits her beloved and fades away in the certainty that he has died) is a far more plausible explanation of the poem's genesis.

The composer was not naively unaware of the literary limitations of poems like this; he was prepared to set poetry that was less than perfect as part of the unwritten contract that enabled the Schubertians, a group of ambitious, temperamental and opinionated young men, to go from strength to strength. Schubert declined to play the genius surrounded by disciples (this would never have worked); instead he allowed his fondness for his friends to translate into a supportive attitude towards their creative endeavours, a give and take that guaranteed the survival of the circle. Of course this was no conscious decision on Schubert's part, merely the result of his affectionate and essentially democratic nature.

Lieb Minna was composed only three days before two Goethe settings: the miraculous *Wandrers Nachtlied* D224 ('Der du von dem Himmel bist') and *Erster Verlust* D226. Indeed *Lieb Minna* (in F minor) seems something of a study for the ambiguity between F minor and its relative major of A flat found in *Erster Verlust*. There is an extraordinary similarity between the one-bar postlude of *Erster Verlust* (which in five notes seems to encapsulate all the pain in the world) and the two-bar conclusion to *Lieb Minna*. Both songs are about loss, but in three days in 1815 Schubert was able to progress from Minna's somewhat melodramatic fate to a single distilled page of universal significance. *Lieb Minna* is, nevertheless, a skilful piece of work that depends on its performers for variety. Because it is a narrative it is not possible to sing fewer than all five strophes – if the singer is brave enough to follow the marking of 'Sehr langsam, schmerzlich', the song is a long one. The opening vocal line – supported by tentative mezzo staccato quavers in the piano and never straying far from the security of the home key (visits to A flat major notwithstanding) – depicts fragility and dependency. What emerges from the song (and poem) is a portrait of Minna as a Dickensian-type heroine of somewhat one-dimensional femininity. The reticence of the music paints a portrait of an exquisitely tear-bedewed face; the slow progress to Wilhelm's graveside is made with the most delicate foot-steps. Unable to bear the burden of bereavement Minna fades away, a tiny, muted *Liebestod* in musical terms, and joins her lover in a better world. It is not a song that stands high in priorities for a recital, but when taken up by a really fine singer it can make an unexpectedly touching impression.

Autograph:	Wienbibliothek im Rathaus, Vienna
First edition:	Published as Vol. 7 no. 14 in Friedlaender's edition by Peters, Leipzig in 1885 (P485)
Subsequent editions:	Peters: Vol. 7/31; AGA XX 86: Vol. 2/168; NSA IV: Vol. 8/114
Discography and timing:	Fischer-Dieskau —
	Hyperion I 3[8]
	Hyperion II 7[14] 5'04 Ann Murray

← *Das Finden* D219   *Wandrers Nachtlied I* D224 →

Die LIEBE   Love (Joyful and sorrowful)
(GOETHE) **D210** [H104]
B♭ major   3 June 1815

(21 bars)

Freudvoll	Joyful,
Und leidvoll,	Sorrowful,
Gedankenvoll sein;	Thoughtful;
Langen	Yearning
Und bangen	And grieving
In schwebender Pein;	In lingering pain;
Himmelhoch jauchzend	Touching the heavens in joy,
Zum Tode betrübt;	Despairing unto death;
Glücklich allein	Happy alone
Ist die Seele, die liebt.	Is the soul that loves.

JOHANN WOLFGANG VON GOETHE (1749–1832); poem written before 1788

This is the twelfth of Schubert's seventy-five Goethe solo settings (1814–26). See the poet's biography for a chronological list of all the Goethe settings.

Goethe's play *Egmont* (completed in 1787) is a stirring tale set in Brussels in the time of the Counter-Reformation. It concerns Egmont's attempts to secure for his beleaguered people a measure of religious toleration from the Spanish, at that time masters of Flanders. His beloved, Klärchen (whose name, Clara, means brightness and clarity), although fragile in appearance, is a tough and independent girl, an emancipated spirit. When Egmont is sentenced to die at the end of the play she poisons herself, but not before putting up a fight and attempting to stir the people to rebel on his behalf. This lyric occurs in Act III Scene 2. Klärchen's mother wants her daughter to marry Brackenburg, a wealthy citizen's son. However Klärchen now confesses that she is fully committed to Egmont. Responding to her mother's questioning she hums the two last lines of this poem before singing the complete lyric. Her mother dismisses it as a 'Heiopopeio' – a lullaby. Klärchen admits to having sung this music to rock a 'big child' (Egmont) to sleep, thus audaciously admitting that her relationship with him is intimate. A moment later her beloved appears in a cloak adorned with the Order of the Golden Fleece and Klärchen is joyfully proud – 'freudvoll' indeed. The 'leidvoll' emotions are experienced in full later in the play.

This poem has fascinated a number of composers: Reichardt and Beethoven before Schubert, and Franz Liszt (in three settings) in later years. The Beethoven setting (Op. 84 no. 4 from

Klärchen and Egmont depicted in the almanac *Urania* (1815).

1809–10), paired with Klärchen's other song in *Egmont, Die Trommel gerühret*, is a more dramatic affair and, being orchestrally accompanied, intended to be used in the theatre. Unlike the Beethoven and Liszt settings, Schubert's little song disdains to repeat words to elongate the musical structure. In a letter to Goethe of August 1804 Zelter complains that he has to repeat the word 'Freudvoll' in his setting because the 'eu' diphthong in the word made an expressive melisma impossible. Schubert attempts neither elongation of the diphthong nor repetition; his song conveys a harmonically subtle message from the heart that contains the ambiguity of the feelings that love inspires, and is quickly over. He always had the knack of using the major key in a way that suggests doubt and pathos. The very nature of the conflicting words 'Freudvoll und leidvoll' are conveyed within the simple and unrepeated musical setting of these words. This duality is an apt reflection of Klärchen's words to Egmont in Act III: 'Let me look into your eyes; find everything in them, comfort and hope, and joy and grief.'

The marking is 'Sehr langsam'. Triplets in measured semiquavers pervade the song's structure. 'Freudvoll' (b. 1) is harmonized to a simple B flat major chord, but 'leidvoll' (b. 2) occasions a diminished chord harmony with B natural at the top but still grounded on the B flat bass. 'Langen' (b. 5) and 'bangen' (b. 6) are similarly contrasted. The voice lies high in a tessitura that brings a sense of drama and tension to music that could otherwise easily sound uneventful. In the second half of the piece Schubert returns to the play's military background. 'Himmelhoch jauchzend' (b. 9) is joyously accompanied by a series of tiny fanfares in a forte dynamic, while 'Zum Tode betrübt' (bb. 10–12) reverts to pianissimo. This is a life and death situation. Klärchen's belief that love is the answer to all life's problems is clearly allied to her desire to fight the good fight, in a man's doublet and hose if necessary. On the words 'Glücklich allein' (b. 15, beginning on a perilously high B flat) fanfare-like triplets alternate between the pianist's hands, and there is a tenaciously held note on the word 'allein' (b. 16); all this adds to the impression that the singer-heroine is a woman of great strength and determination. The postlude (bb. 18–20) seems to be the composer's own more gentle and rueful meditation on the import of the words. There is also an ominous hint of suspense in the left-hand triplets (from b. 18), as if celli were playing a miniature drum roll, a ghostly echo of a complementary setting of *Die Trommel gerühret* that Schubert was never to compose. One cannot help feeling that this ominous little muffled heartbeat is telling us something of Klärchen's future fate.

Walther Dürr points out that the adoption of *Die Liebe* as a title for this song is an indication that Schubert's source was the 1804 volume of Reichardt's song publication *Lieder der Liebe und der Einsamkeit*. The young composer also copied the Ossian text for *Kolmas Klage* D217 from this collection, and in it Reichardt's title for this setting of the *Egmont* lyric is *Liebe*; Schubert followed suit, adding the definite article.

Autograph:	Gesellschaft der Musikfreunde, Vienna (first draft)
First edition:	Published as Book 30 no. 2 of the *Nachlass* by Diabelli, Vienna in 1838 (P325)
Subsequent editions:	Peters: Vol. 2/236; AGA XX 78: Vol. 2/130; NSA IV: Vol. 8/68
Bibliography:	Byrne 2003, pp. 357–9
	Capell 1928, p. 101
	Reid 2007, pp. 150–52
Further settings and arrangements:	Johann Friedrich Reichardt (1752–1814) *Liebe* from *Lieder der Liebe und der Einsamkeit* (1804)
	Carl Friedrich Zelter (1758–1832) *Clärchen* (1804)
	Ludwig van Beethoven (1770–1827) *Freudvoll und leidvoll*, part of incidental music to *Egmont*, Op. 84 no. 4 (1809–10)
	Johann Christoph Kienlen (1783–1829) *Klärchens Lied, aus Egmont* (1810)
	Franz Liszt (1811–1886) *Freudvoll und leidvoll*, solo song (1844 & 1848–9); *Andantino*, piano transcription of Schubert's setting (1847) [*see* TRANSCRIPTIONS]
	Anton Rubinstein (1829–1894) *Klärchens Lied* Op. 57 no. 4 (1864)
Discography and timing:	Fischer-Dieskau —
	Hyperion I 7⁹
	Hyperion II 6²⁴ 1'28 Elly Ameling

←— *Der Liebende* D207   *Adelwold and Emma* D211 —→

Die LIEBE

Love

(LEON) **D522** [H335]

G major   January 1817

Wo weht der Lie - be ho-her Geist?

(17 bars)

Wo weht der Liebe hoher Geist?	Where does love's noble spirit breathe?
Er weht in Blum' und Baum,	It breathes in flower and tree,
Im weiten Erdenraum,	In the wide world
Er weht, wo sich die Knospen spalten	It breathes wherever the buds burst open
Und wo die Blümlein sich entfalten.	And the flowers unfold.
Wo weht der Liebe hoher Geist?	Where does love's noble spirit breathe?
Er weht im Abendglanz,	It breathes in the glow of evening,
Er weht im Sternenkranz,	It breathes in the circle of stars;
Wo Bien' und Maienkäfer schwirren	Wherever bees and cockchafers hum,
Und zart die Turteltauben girren.	And turtle doves coo tenderly.
Wo weht der Liebe hoher Geist?	Where does love's noble spirit breathe?
Er weht bei Freud' und Schmerz	It breathes in joy and sorrow
In aller Mütter Herz,	In every mother's heart,
Er weht in jungen Nachtigallen,	It breathes in young nightingales
Wenn lieblich ihre Lieder schallen.	When their sweet songs sound forth.
Wo weht der Liebe hoher Geist?	Where does love's noble spirit breathe?
In Wasser, Feuer, Luft	In water, fire and air,
Und in des Morgens Duft.	And in the morning's fragrance;
Er weht, wo sich ein Leben reget,	It breathes wherever life stirs
Und wo sich nur ein Herz beweget.	And wherever even a single heart beats.

GOTTLIEB VON LEON (1757–1832)

This is Schubert's only setting of a Leon text. See the poet's biography.

This charming little strophic song deserves to be better known. The music is eighteenth century in character; for the sake of appearances and decorum there is a philosophical turn of phrase to the deliberations about love, but there is also a core of Schubertian sensuality that makes the song a living thing despite the lofty imagery. The interrogative gestures of the *Vorspiel* (a pair of question marks in music) puts us in mind of *Alles um Liebe* D241, another song in ⅜, where the question is 'Was ist es, das die Seele füllt'?' ('What is it that fills the soul?') The answer in that case is hardly surprising: 'the soul is filled with love'. In *Die Liebe* questions of this kind are purely rhetorical, a game between lovers played half in earnest and half in teasing jest. Interpreted by a singer with charm the music makes it plain that, esoteric sightings notwithstanding, love's spirit is alive and flourishing in the human heart. Some might identify with the poem's circumlocutions and higher thought, but Schubert's music also encompasses intimations of physical pleasure.

And yet the music is not typically Schubertian; it avoids modulation and harmonic experiments, and the deliberate and robust song style of Beethoven seems to have been an inspiration. (At the time the song was written there is more than a hint of Beethoven in Schubert's piano sonatas.) The introduction has something of a keyboard sonata about it with two descending figures, each moving with a tiny flourish from the home key of G major to the dominant seventh. From apparently innocuous figurations of this type Beethoven could construct castles in the air, and Schubert was himself now already a master builder. The prelude brings to mind other Schubert songs with eighteenth-century backgrounds, particularly the Baumberg settings (*Der Morgenkuss* D264 and *Abendständchen an Lina* D265, for example).

The last two lines of each strophe seem awkward, even perverse, until one realizes that Schubert has created, with some ingenuity, a hemiola: from b. 10 the last eight bars of the piece (in ⅜) might easily be rearranged as twelve bars in ²⁄₄, or four in ⅜. This gives a jaunty, slightly quirky, edge to the word-setting – a determined angularity that again brings Beethoven to mind. There is a curious charm to the postlude that takes some delight in wrong-footing the listener's rhythmic expectations: love is always surprising, never to be taken for granted.

Autograph:	Missing or lost
First edition:	Published as part of the AGA in 1895 (P667)
Subsequent editions:	Not in Peters; AGA XX 291: Vol. 5/4; NSA IV: Vol. 11/76
Discography and timing:	Fischer-Dieskau I 9⁸ 1'40 (first two strophes only)
	Hyperion I 21³
	Hyperion II 17¹³ 3'23 Edith Mathis

← *Jagdlied* D521   *Trost* D523 →

Die LIEBE FARBE *see Die SCHÖNE MÜLLERIN* D795/16

Die LIEBE HAT GELOGEN   Love has lied to me
(PLATEN) OP. 23 NO. 1, **D751** [H487]
C minor   Before 17 April 1822

(18 bars)

Die Liebe hat gelogen,	Love has lied;
Die Sorge lastet schwer,	Care weighs heavily upon me.
Betrogen, ach, betrogen	Alas, I am deceived, deceived
Hat alles mich umher!	By all around me!

Es fliessen heisse Tropfen	Hot tears flow
Die Wange stets herab,	Ceaselessly down my cheek.
Lass ab, mein Herz, zu klopfen,	Heart, beat no more;
Du armes Herz, lass ab.	Poor heart, beat no more!

AUGUST GRAF VON PLATEN (1796–1835); poem written in 1819(?)

This is the first of Schubert's two Platen solo settings (1822). See the poet's biography for a chronological list of the Platen settings.

This ranks as one of Schubert's single-page masterpieces, in the same extraordinary aphoristic class as *Erster Verlust* D226 and *Wandrers Nachtlied* D768. The pace and metre are those of *Der Tod und das Mädchen* D531 – a dactylic rhythm that, in Schubert's motivic language, underlines the harsh and irreversible sentence of Fate. To lose one's love is to die a little, and in this song we sense that the loss of love is as inevitable as death itself, a terrible shock and yet somehow expected as part of the sufferer's life sentence. In the beginning we sense a frozen dignity, the vehemence of feelings concealed under a façade of icy self-control – the principal dynamic is piano, and not until the end of the middle section is there an outburst where the emotional catastrophe is matched by a sustained forte dynamic. Until then this is music of stiff upper lip and iron will. Schubert had never met Platen, but that the poet of this lyric was an aristocrat seems not to have been lost on him.

The tonality is C minor. The poet and musicologist Christian Friedrich Schubart described this as the key of unhappy love, and we have only to think of Mozart's *Als Luise die Briefe* K520, another C minor song where slighted passion is the theme, to take Schubart's point. In *Die Liebe hat gelogen* the mood is of the highest drama, and yet everything is reined in by the implacable dactyls. The two bars of introduction announce the gravity of the situation, and on the third beat there is a momentary shift to a forte chord (the first inversion of D flat major, the flattened supertonic). Schubert uses exactly this juxtaposition of tonalities in the introduction to the ominous *Die Krähe* from *Winterreise* D911/15. This stab of pain, the twisting of a harmonic knife, subsides, and another bar of chords, muted and heavy like a dead march, return us to the dominant – a springboard for the singer's plaint. The words are intense and bitter, the articulation of them lofty. Only in the height of the tessitura do we detect an inward wail, the sound of someone trapped in an emotional situation from which there is no escape. At 'Betrogen, ach, betrogen' (bb. 4–5) there is a sudden shift into C major and, hot on its heels, another to A major. The change sounds majestic and *pomposo*, as if a king is trumpeting the betrayal in a proclamation to the heavens, but there is a subtext to this grandeur. Here is the major key of self-laceration. This is a triumphantly masochistic assertion of the fact that life remains as bleak as ever, and that one has been hurt again is somehow just punishment. After this sustained passage, high in the stave, the descent of the vocal line at 'alles mich umher!' (b. 6) and the way the cadence dissolves into the pathetic major seem to describe the crumbling of the poet's world, the crumpling of a proud spirit.

In the second verse it is as if we have been led into an inner chamber of Platen's heart. Following the public announcement of the rift, he is able to show the private side of his feelings. This extraordinary music is once again prophetic of *Winterreise*, above all the song *Einsamkeit* D911/12. The first two lines of the verse are repeated in a heart-wrenching sequence and no sooner has one spate of tears been wiped away than another flood begins. This passage is full of passing notes, appoggiature that lean distractedly on 'fliessen', 'Tropfen' and 'Wange'; at the repeat of these words, the turning of the harmonic screws – from C minor (bb. 8–9) up to C sharp minor (bb. 9–10) – is exceptionally powerful. The mezzo staccato syncopations in the right hand illustrate the dropping tears (as in *Gefrorne Tränen* from *Winterreise* D911/3) and, in the next line of the poem ('Lass ab, mein Herz, zu klopfen'), these same quavers are pressed into service to depict the knocking heartbeats of distress and desperation (bb. 12–13). Here the music reaches fortissimo and, as Capell notes, 'The singer may, if his voice is properly controlled, allow himself an almost operatic vehemence of expression.' Forty years later this passage (bb. 8–11) would inspire Johannes Brahms in the writing of *Sind es Schmerzen sind es Freuden* in *Die schöne Magelone* Op. 33 no. 3. In the central section of that great song, Brahms's setting of the words 'Ach es fällt die Träne nieder / Ist es dunkel um mich her' clearly evoke Schubert's mezzo staccato accompaniment (falling tears) in *Die Liebe hat gelogen*; the heartbreaking harmonic sequences Brahms engineers for 'Es fliesse heisse Tropfen / Die Wange stets herab' also go back to Schubert's song.

It was an inspiration on Schubert's part to repeat the first verse of this eight-lined poem. A return to the opening music shows a recovery of self-control. We have glimpsed the inner torment of the poet; indeed there has been an astonishing outburst of feeling at 'Du armes Herz, lass ab', but now we return to the elevated gravity of a figure who is doomed, like a character from Greek tragedy. The music at first glance looks the same, but it is modified in certain subtle ways. There is a flattening of the harmony and a discord at 'Sorge lastet schwer' (b. 15), and this leads to a more muted setting of 'Betrogen, ach, betrogen' where the bright surprise of the major key first time around is exchanged for a dominant-seventh chord that sounds more regretful, more unresolved and emotionally at sea. The depth of feeling of the closing bars is reinforced by an eloquent bass line in the piano which contains a shudder of apprehension: 'What next? [first beat, b. 17] What is there to live for?' The closing bar, by way of postlude, ends in the major key and with piano dynamic. This tiny song has traversed a number of emotions ranging from bitter anger to hysterical weeping. We now reach the shores of noble resignation as the door closes on what we sense is only one unhappy chapter in an altogether unhappy life.

And yet this is also a portrait of great sympathy and understanding – a remarkable delineation of a poet whom Schubert never met. Of all the people with whom Schubert was even vaguely connected, Platen was the only one whom we know beyond doubt to have been homosexual. His diaries from 1818 reveal an unreciprocated obsession with a young fellow officer, whom he nicknamed 'Adrast', when he was in the Bavarian army. He suffered from the pain of this emotional débâcle for some years, and it is possible that the two Schubert settings (particularly *Du liebst mich nicht* D756) refer to Platen's thwarted feelings for 'Adrast'. Coincidentally, the name of the opera that Schubert wrote in 1818–19 in collaboration with Mayrhofer is also *Adrast*, D137. At the centre of that story is the passionate affection of Adrast for his charge, the younger Atys (a name with further Schubert–Mayrhofer resonances).

Platen spent some time in Vienna in 1820, and it is interesting to speculate on whether he came into contact there with Schubert's friend Franz von Bruchmann. He travelled on to Erlangen, near Nuremberg, where he attended the lectures of his friend Friedrich Schelling. Was it merely coincidence that Bruchmann (very much against the edicts of the time which forbade Austrian students to attend universities in foreign countries) also went to Erlangen for the same purpose? Before he returned to Vienna from Erlangen, Bruchmann was presented with a signed copy of Platen's recently published *Ghaselen*, a collection that displayed the poet's virtuosity in handling oriental verse forms. The flyleaf contained a dedicatory sonnet in which Bruchmann is addressed in the 'Du' form. On p. 199 of the 1834 edition of the Platen poems, this sonnet is titled 'An F. von B'. At this stage of their friendship Platen was charmed by Bruchmann's gruff contrariness and sorry to see him leave Erlangen. The poem on the facing page in this edition is addressed to Shakespeare and posthumously comforts the bard who, like Platen himself, is enamoured of a 'soulless' young man who cares nothing for his suffering. The juxtaposition of the two sonnets, deliberate or not, shows us that Platen at least partly identified his own masochistic attraction to unavailable young men with Shakespeare's seemingly one-sided love for the 'master-mistress' of his passion.

Platen's writings reached Schubert via Bruchmann at more or less the same time that the composer discovered the *West-östlicher Divan* texts of Goethe. When Bruchmann returned to Vienna he sent to Platen Schubert's first published settings of Goethe (including *Erlkönig* and *Gretchen am Spinnrade*) and these were enthusiastically received by the poet. Sometime in late 1821 Platen sent his *Die Liebe hat gelogen*, through Bruchmann, for Schubert's attention, which Schubert set to music. In April 1822 Bruchmann sent a manuscript copy of the song to Platen, and a note that said, 'Here you will find your poem set to music as desired. Thus I have done my part.' After the 'Du' of the sonnet written in Erlangen, Bruchmann's use of the 'Sie' form in this missive seems symptomatic of a ruptured relationship. What occasioned this cooling-off – Platen pushing his romantic luck with Bruchmann perhaps – we shall never know.

Platen was the only considerable poet outside the Schubert circle who had actively wished to see his own name linked artistically with the composer's. Schubert obliged with *Die Liebe hat gelogen* and *Du liebst mich nicht*, but why did Platen wish to have these particular, deeply personal, lyrics set to music, and why did Schubert acquiesce so swiftly? There is a curious sense of intrigue in the poet's sending such self-revelatory poems to a composer via a (temporarily) compliant middleman. Had Platen somehow gathered from Bruchmann that Schubert was sympathetic to the highly charged poetry of Mayrhofer with its agenda of 'Griechische Liebe' seen from a Platonic viewpoint (*see Uraniens Flucht* D554)? Even if Schubert did not share Platen's proclivities to any great degree, he certainly seems to have read between the lines. He seems to have tuned into the poet's highly strung and complex nature simply by reading his poetry. That he provided another unusual song a few months later, again tailored to Platen's personality, suggests that this empathy was not a one-off accident but part of Schubert's Shakespearian ability to encompass every aspect of the heart's affections.

Autograph:	Missing or lost
First edition:	Published as Op. 23 no. 1 by Sauer & Leidesdorf, Vienna in August 1823 (P44)
Publication reviews:	*Allgemeine musikalische Zeitung* (Leipzig), No. 26 (24 June 1824), cols 425–8 [Waidelich/Hilmar Dokumente I No. 282; Deutsch Doc. Biog. No. 479]
Subsequent editions:	Peters: Vol. 2/60; AGA XX 410: Vol. 7/28; NSA IV: Vol. 2/4; Bärenreiter: Vol. 1/136
Bibliography:	Capell 1928, p. 180
	Fischer-Dieskau 1977, pp. 155–6
	Youens 1985, pp. 19–34
Discography and timing:	Fischer-Dieskau II 5[9] 2'20
	Hyperion I 28[12]
	Hyperion II 25[13] 2'32 Maarten Konigsberger

← *Heliopolis II* D754   *Du liebst mich nicht* D756 →

LIEBE SCHWÄRMT AUF ALLEN WEGEN *see CLAUDINE VON VILLA BELLA* D239/6

Der LIEBENDE   The lover
(HÖLTY) **D207** [H103]
B♭ major   29 May 1815

(30 bars)

Beglückt, beglückt,	Blessed is he
Wer dich erblickt,	Who beholds you,
Und deinen Himmel trinket-	And drinks your heavenly beauty
Wenn dein Gesicht[1]	When your face,
Voll Engellicht	Bathed in angelic light,
Den Gruss des Friedens winket.	Bestows the greeting of peace.
Ein süsser Blick,	One sweet glance,
Ein Wink, ein Nick,	A sign, a nod,
Glänzt mir wie Frühlingssonnen;	Shines upon me like the spring sun.
Den ganzen Tag	The whole day long
Sinn' ich ihm nach,	I think of it,
Und schweb' in Himmelswonnen.	And float in heavenly bliss.
Dein holdes Bild	Your sweet image
Führt mich so mild	Leads me so tenderly along
An sanfter Blumenkette,	By a gentle chain of flowers
In meinem Arm	In my arms
Erwacht es warm,	It awakens warm
Und geht mit mir zu Bette.	And goes with me to bed.
Beglückt, beglückt,	Blessed is he
Wer dich erblickt	Who beholds you,
Und deinen Himmel trinket;	And drinks your heavenly beauty,
Wem süsser Blick[2]	Who is lured to sweeter kisses
Und Wink und Nick	By a sweet glance,
Zum süssern Kusse winket.	A sign, a nod.

[1] Hölty writes '*Wem* dein Gesicht'.
[2] Hölty writes '*Wen* süsser Blick'.

Ludwig Hölty (1748–1776); poem written in 1776. Adapted for publication in 1804 by
Johann Heinrich Voss (1751–1826)

This is the eighth of Schubert's twenty-three Hölty solo settings (1813–16). See the poet's
biography for a chronological list of all the Hölty settings.

Let us consider the state of affairs three days before the composition of this song. The day of 26 May 1815 was given over to the writing of vocal duets with horn accompaniment (D199, D202–5), occasional music to be sung outdoors on a warm late spring night, and probably specially requested by Schubert's friends. For these the composer enlisted the aid of Hölty's poems as well as those of Theodor Körner. At the end of this already full day there was another Körner flirtation: the delightful solo song *Liebeständelei* D206. It is easy to imagine a scenario where the shadowy figure of Schubert's beloved Therese Grob is linked to picnic frolics and music in the open air. If this were so, it would not be surprising that the texts chosen at this time veer between the idealism of romantic love and sheer sexual frustration. The continuation of this fantasy scenario is to imagine the composer, with this al fresco music under his arm, ready for performance, going into the country with friends for a couple of days' rest. The Deutsch catalogue is empty for 27 and 28 May, but it is certain that Schubert returned to work on 29 May with a light heart and in the mood to write what John Reed rightly calls a 'gem'. This is a poem of rapturous hope, perhaps encouraged by 'a sign, a nod', masquerading as certainty. The poet is led to the greatest optimism by the girl's affectionate teasing, intimations of pleasures to come, despite knowing that these may amount to little of substance.

There is no calm, assured knowledge of love given and received. On the contrary, the tempo marking ('Mit drängender Eile') encourages a fevered urgency, as if sounding jaunty will, in wish-fulfilment, earn the singer his prize. He is no experienced Casanova, more of a hopeful young Romeo. The playful little piano interludes are enchanting with their typically Schubertian interplay between major and minor. Such were his high spirits and confidence that on the same day the composer went on to write *Die Nonne* D208, one of the most Gothic and blood-soaked of all his horror stories. The villain of that piece seduces a nun from her life of purity and she exacts a terrible revenge. Despite the different storylines of the two songs, they are both products of those seemingly hot and bothered spring days of 1815 when sexual energy was making itself felt in any number of literary and musical guises.

Autograph:	Gesellschaft der Musikfreunde, Vienna
First edition:	Published as part of the AGA in 1895 (P564)
Subsequent editions:	Not in Peters; AGA XX 76: Vol. 2/123; NSA IV: Vol. 8/58
Discography and timing:	Fischer-Dieskau I 4[1] 1'52 (first three strophes only)
	Hyperion I 10[9]
	Hyperion II 6[23] 2'33 Martyn Hill

← *Liebeständelei* D206   *Die Liebe (Freudvoll und Leidvoll)* D210 →

Die LIEBENDE SCHREIBT   The lover writes
(GOETHE) **D673** [H435]

The song exists in two versions, the first of which is discussed below:
(1) October 1819; (2) October 1819

(1) B♭ major

(67 bars)

(2) 'Mässig, zart'   A major   ¾   [67 bars]

Ein Blick von deinen Augen in die meinen,	One glance from your eyes into mine;
Ein Kuss von deinem Mund auf meinem Munde,	One kiss from your lips upon mine;
Wer davon hat, wie ich, gewisse Kunde,	Can he who has certain knowledge of these, as I do,
Mag dem was anders wohl erfreulich scheinen?	Take pleasure in anything else?
Entfernt von dir, entfremdet von den Meinen,	Far from you, estranged from my loved ones,
Führ' ich stets die Gedanken in die Runde,	I let my thoughts rove constantly,
Und immer treffen sie auf jene Stunde,	And always they fix upon that one
Die einzige; da fang' ich an zu weinen.	And only hour; then I begin to weep.
Die Träne trocknet wieder unversehens;	Suddenly my tears are dried:
Er liebt ja, denk' ich, her in diese Stille,	He loves indeed, I reflect, here in this stillness;
O solltest du nicht in die Ferne reichen?	O, should you not reach out to me in the far distance?
Vernimm das Lispeln dieses Liebewehens;	Hear these whispered words of love;
Mein einzig Glück auf Erden ist dein Wille,	Your goodwill towards me is my sole happiness on earth,
Dein freundlicher zu mir; gib mir ein Zeichen!	Give me a sign!

JOHANN WOLFGANG VON GOETHE (1749–1832); poem written in 1807/8

This is the fifty-fifth of Schubert's seventy-five Goethe solo settings (1814–26). See the poet's biography for a chronological list of all the Goethe settings.

This is one of the least known of Schubert's Goethe settings, and perhaps the least successful. In comparison with other settings of this poet it seldom appears in recitals. It is in sonnet form – two quatrains and two tercets (or, to put it more musically, an octet and a sextet) – the sonnet being an aspect of Goethe's work that composers usually ignore. The poem dates from 1807, the time of Goethe's infatuation with Minna Herzlieb, eighteen-year-old ward (Goethe was fifty-eight at the time) of the Jena bookseller Carl Friedrich Ernst Frommann, a long-standing acquaintance of the poet. Silvie von Ziegesar is a name that has been more recently proposed by a Goethe scholar as the identity of the putative narrator of this sonnet; also Bettina von Arnim, although the proactive personality of the redoubtable Bettina seems a far cry from the vulnerable woman who pens this letter to her beloved.

This is no. 8 in the cycle of seventeen poems in this form written by Goethe. A new German translation of Petrarch's sonnets had just appeared (sold by From-mann of course) and for a brief time Minna became Goethe's Laura. Goethe confessed to Zelter (in a letter of 15 January 1813) that he had loved Minna 'mehr wie billig' – a phrase that implied he had enjoyed a physical rela-tionship with her. There is something about this music that recalls the dainty *Lieb Minna* D222 from 1815 (although it is a complete coincidence that Albert Stadler should have chosen this name for his poem). John Reed also notes the work's similarity (particularly in terms of its triplet-accompanied melody) to the first of the Schiller settings of *Die*

Minna Herzlieb from an oil painting by Luise Seidler.

Entzückung an Laura D390. Schubert's Petrarch sonnets in German translation (D628–630) date from the previous year.

As a message to the beloved the song is a rather less passionate counterpart to the dusky passions of the oriental Zuleika who, also parted from her paramour, attempts to communicate with him at a distance. (Schubert's settings of Marianne von Willemer's words were to be composed some years later.) Within the strict stylistic bounds of the sonnet there is an element of ladylike decorum, while Zuleika throws discretion, literally, to the winds. But that decorum, particularly when a male poet idealizes feminine behaviour (in the manner of Chamisso's *Frauen-liebe und -leben*), is part of the song's context, and thus its musical vocabulary. This poem appealed tremendously to Mendelssohn (Op. 86 no. 3, 1831) who threw his heart into a setting that outdoes Schubert's in the opinion of many lieder aficionados. Brahms also set the poem (Op. 47 No. 5, 1868) and in creating one of the few estimable sonnet settings in the German repertoire he seems not to have been at all intimidated by Schubert's slender song.

These are three wonderful composers, yet none of them has been inclined comprehensively to plumb the depths of a poem which is nothing less than a fervent plea from a young woman who has everything in life to lose, and who fears for her sanity. Perhaps the formality of the sonnet is to blame for a lack of histrionics. With its title we might have wished for something like the letter aria from Tchaikovsky's *Eugene Onegin*, but Schubert's Germanic figure is no match for Tatyana's Slavic temperament and musical language.

In Schubert's song we find ourselves in the Mozartian world of the letter duet from *Le nozze di Figaro* where Susanna and the countess compose a letter of entrapment for the count, also in B flat major (Schubert's original key for the song, although the *Nachlass*, and thus the Peters Edition, publishes it in A). The introduction proposes four bars made up of two phrases, one answering the other, as in 'Shall I write a letter?' (bb. 1–2), 'Yes, I shall!' (bb. 3–4). Question and answer is very much a part of the musical scheme. Thus the pauses here between musical phrases betoken the flourish of the pen (after Mozart's example) and the time taken to think of the next line. Directly after 'Ein Blick von deinen Augen in die meinen' the cello-like echoes in the tenor (and thus masculine) line (bb. 7–8) paint the idea of a reciprocated glance. This tender little reply-motif is a feature of the whole of the first section of the song – which is to say the first eight lines of the sonnet. In this muted rhapsody in B flat major, mention of searching in vain for joy in other things ('was anders wohl erfreulich scheinen', bb. 15–16) prompts a momentary modulation to D flat major, but this excursion strays beyond the current preoccupation with that one hour of bliss, and the vocal line returns quickly to the home key, unsatisfied with the glimpse of outside reality, and almost obsessively grounded in a little melody imprisoned within the narrow interval of a fifth. After this there is a much stronger switch of key (this time to G flat major). At 'da fang' ich an zu weinen' (bb. 30–31) we can hear tears welling up in the unusually engineered modulation. This is a link passage into the second section of the song marked 'Etwas bewegter'.

For the final six lines of the sonnet Schubert changes time signature from ¾ to ₵. He finds a delicate and fragile, almost palpitating mood for the girl's desperate longing for reassurance. Here we can also sense a hint of an operatic set piece as *cavatina* yields to *cabaletta*. Triplets are split between the treble and bass staves where only two notes in each group of three in any one hand can be heard. This highly uncommon feature in the accompaniment is to be found in *Sonett II* D629 (Petrarch) from 1818 (bb. 24–6), where the poet speaks of his abject adoration for Laura and feels himself lacking the wholeness of reciprocated love. In both songs the effect is the same: the unevenly distributed threes depict someone at sixes and sevens. The final 'gib mir ein Zeichen' (bb. 62–6) is affectingly done, though to say that 'it could not be more passionate' (Fischer-Dieskau) is an exaggeration. Here Mendelssohn certainly is Schubert's superior. Whether Schubert was entirely satisfied with the song is open to doubt; it was not one of the pieces that he published in his lifetime, and usually anything by Goethe was given priority when it came to work waiting to appear in print.

Lorraine Byrne calls the rediscovered fashion for sonnet writing Goethe's 'sonnet-rage'. She points out that it was mirrored by Schubert's circle with both Schober and Senn composing cycles in this form which took on a new lease of life and popularity after more than a century of neglect. The form is a particular challenge to composers, however, because of its change of metre and rhyme midstream; Schubert set five sonnet texts in all, in addition to this one: *Die erste Liebe* (D182 Fellinger), *Die Macht der Liebe* (D308, Kalchberg) and three Sonnets of Petrarca – *Sonett I* D628 and *Sonett II* D629 (both translated by August von Schlegel) and *Sonett III* D630 translated by Gries. *Die Liebende schreibt* was the last of Schubert's efforts with the form. Although the NSA prints two versions of the song the authenticity of the second is in doubt.

Autograph:	Missing or lost
Publication:	Published as part of the NSA in 1996 (P810; first version)
	Published as a supplement to the *Wiener Zeitschrift für Kunst, Literatur und Mode* on 26 June 1832 and then as Op. post. 165 No.1 in 1862 (P396; second version)
Subsequent editions:	Peters: Vol. 6/85; AGA XX 369: Vol. 6/68; NSA IV: Vol. 12/116 & 220
Bibliography:	Byrne 2003 pp. 360–67
	Capell 1928, p. 154
	Einstein 1951, p. 192
	Fischer-Dieskau 1977, p. 130

Further settings and arrangements:	Felix Mendelssohn (1809–1847) *Die Liebende schreibt* Op. 86 no. 3 (1831)
	Johannes Brahms (1833–1897) *Die Liebende schreibt* Op. 47 no. 5 (1858)
	Arr. Tilman Hoppstock (b. 1961) for guitar accompaniment, in *Franz Schubert: 110 Lieder* (2009)
Discography and timing:	Fischer-Dieskau —

Hyperion I 29[17]
Hyperion II 22[10]   2'20   Marjana Lipovšek

← *Trost* D671   *Prometheus* D674 →

LIEBESBOTSCHAFT *see SCHWANENGESANG* D957/1

Die LIEBESGÖTTER   The gods of love
(Uz) **D446** [H274]
C major   June 1816

(26 bars)

Cypris, meiner Phyllis gleich,	Cypris, like my Phyllis,
Sass von Grazien umgeben!	Sat surrounded by Graces;
Denn ich sah ihr frohes Reich;	For I saw her happy realm,
Mich berauschten Cyperns Reben.	Cypris' grapes made me euphoric.
Ein geweihter Myrthenwald,	A consecrated myrtle grove,
Den geheime Schatten schwärzten,	Darkened by mysterious shadows,
War der Göttin Aufenthalt,	Was the goddess's abode
Wo die Liebesgötter scherzten.	Here the gods of love frolicked.
[. . . 2 . . .]	[. . . 2 . . .]
Unter grüner Büsche Nacht,	Under cover of the green bushes
Unter abgelegnen Sträuchen,	In the far-off thicket,
Wo so manche Nymphe lacht,	Where many a nymph laughed,
Sah ich sie am liebsten schleichen.	I saw them steal most gladly.
Viele flohn mit leichtem Fuss'	Many shunned with light step
Allen Zwang betränter Ketten,	All restraints of tear-soaked fetters,
Flatterten von Kuss zu Kuss[1]	Flitted from kiss to kiss
Und von Blonden zu Brünetten.	And from blondes to brunettes.
[. . .]	[. . .]

---

[1] In the Peters Edition this line was bowdlerized as follows: 'Flatterten von *Fuss zu Fuss*'.

JOHANN PETER UZ (1720–1796); poem written in 1744

This is the third of Schubert's five Uz solo settings (1816). See the poet's biography for a chronological list of all the Uz settings.

'One of Schubert's lesser gems' is how Capell classified this song – which seems about right. It is certainly not as well known as it should be, but it has a limited emotional scope which allows it to delight us without pulling at our heartstrings. It is interesting how similar this is to some of the Hölty settings: the accompaniment purls happily between two hands never far apart (as if it were being played on an instrument of very modest compass); the mood is pastoral and perky, charming and elegant. And yet there is never any question of the Hölty settings being framed by such a self-consciously rococo style – they may evoke a sunlit Germany from long ago but Höltyland is full of real people. This Uz setting on the other hand is set in Elysium or Arcadia with a cast of gods and goddesses, nymphs and shepherds. Within this convention the peeping-Tom narrator, slightly drunk to boot, is allowed to express his pleasure in watching these cavorting heavenly nymphs without suffering the fate of Actaeon. The poetry is Anacreontic and the hand of artifice, however delightfully graceful, is never far away. It is as if Schubert has set out to write a gavotte rather than a lied.

The cheekily racy mood is thinly disguised by courtly euphemism; the decorations in the vocal line at 'umgeben' in the second line (b. 6) lend a period flavour to the proceedings. This is Schubert in a Watteau-esque 'Fêtes galantes' mode truly *avant la lettre*. The capricious setting of the final line of the first strophe ('Wo die Liebesgötter scherzten' from b. 18 to b. 21) is virtuosic for the singer (such fast passage-work with quick leaps can all too easily degenerate into a Swiss yodel) and utterly captivating for the audience. The composer also works his magic in Uz's fourth strophe where one wonders if there could be a more delectable musical incarnation of 'blondes and brunettes'. The postlude in semiquaver triplets, one hand chasing the other, is distinctly dance-like. And yet despite all this fun one feels a sense of modified rapture, even decorum, in this music. It is this which keeps it firmly in the pasticheur's domain. The NSA prints all five verses of the poem, Peters only two. The translations printed above, and sung for the Hyperion Edition, are of verses 1 and 4. The tessitura of the song is high and it is unsurprising that Witteczek had a copy of the song in the more comfortable A major. This was the period when Schubert was using a *Liederbuch* (a handwritten anthology of song texts) belonging to his friend Anton Stadler.

Autograph:	Missing or lost
First edition:	Published as Vol. 7 no. 45 in Friedlaender's edition by Peters, Leipzig in 1887 (P506)
Subsequent editions:	Peters: Vol. 7/98; AGA XX 231: Vol. 4/118; NSA IV: Vol. 10/172
Discography and timing:	Fischer-Dieskau I 7¹⁹ 2'01
	Hyperion I 23¹⁸
	Hyperion II 15¹ 1'31 Christoph Prégardien

⟵ *Edone* D445   *Gott im Frülinge* D448 →

LIEBESLAUSCHEN *see* Des FRÄULEINS LIEBESLAUSCHEN D698

LIEBESRAUSCH (I)   Love's intoxication
(KÖRNER) **D164** [H72]
(Fragment) G major   March 1815

Glanz des Gu - ten und des Schö-nen strahlt mir dein ho - hes Bild.

(6 bars)

Dir, Mädchen, schlägt mit leisem Beben	For you, maiden, my heart beats,
Mein Herz voll Treu' und Liebe zu.	Gently trembling, filled with love and devotion.
In Dir, in Dir versinkt mein Streben,	In you, in you, my striving ceases;
Mein schönstes Ziel bist Du!	You are my life's fairest goal.
Dein Name nur in heil'gen Tönen	Your name alone has filled my bold heart
Hat meine kühne Brust gefüllt;	With sacred tones.
Im Glanz des Guten und des Schönen	In the radiance of goodness and beauty
Strahlt mir Dein hohes Bild.	Your noble image shines for me.
Die Liebe sprosst aus zarten Keimen,	Love burgeons from tender seeds,
Und ihre Blüten welken nie!	And its blossoms never wither.
Du, Mädchen, lebst in meinen Träumen	You, maiden, live in my dreams
Mit süsser Harmonie.	With sweet harmonies.
Begeist'rung rauscht auf mich hernieder,	I am fired with the rapture of inspiration;
Kühn greif' ich in die Saiten ein,	Boldly I pluck the strings,
Und alle meine schönsten Lieder,	And all my loveliest songs
Sie nennen Dich allein.	Utter your name alone.
Mein Himmel glüht in Deinen Blicken,	My heaven glows in your eyes;
An Deiner Brust mein Paradies.	My paradise is upon your breast.
Ach! alle Reize, die Dich schmücken,	Ah, all the charms that adorn you
Sie sind so hold, so süss.	Are so fair, so sweet.
Es wogt die Brust in Freud' und Schmerzen,	My breast surges with joy and pain;
Nur eine Sehnsucht lebt in mir,	One desire alone dwells within me,
Nur ein Gedanke hier im Herzen:	One thought alone lies here in my heart:
Der ew'ge Drang nach Dir.	Eternal yearning for you!

THEODOR KÖRNER (1791–1813)

This is the second of Schubert's sixteen Körner solo settings (1815–18). See the poet's biography for a chronological list of all the Körner settings.

The second version of this song (D179 from April 1815, *see* below) is a passionate outburst – a real lyrical effusion accompanied by throbbing triplets – rather different from the composer's first version. This first is not negligible, and would have been entirely lost to us if it had not been for the indefatigable detective work of Reihnard Van Hoorickx who made an imaginative reconstruction of the song as it might have been. Walther Dürr (NSA Vol. 8, p. XX) is convinced that the surviving fragment comes from a once-complete work. All that is left to posterity is four bars of the vocal line (the music for the end of the song at the first strophe 'Glanz des Guten und des Schönen / Strahlt mir dein hohes Bild') and two bars of pianistic afterthought. As an introduction Van Hoorickx has simply used the most original music in the fragment (a shivering little postlude of semiquaver triplets descriptive of a rush of blood to the head in a moment of ecstasy). For the rest of the strophe he has crafted a credible vocal line supported by an accompaniment of flowing quaver triplets, also taking its cue from what remains of the autograph. This completion is not very ambitious, perhaps, but it works better than many a more sophisticated attempt to emulate the master's notoriously inimitable style. Van Hoorickx's work conserves what is special about the fragment, and one would have to know a great deal about Schubert to be able to denounce this song as an obvious impostor. On the other side of the autograph is the Theodor Körner setting *Das war ich* D174 (qv).

Autograph:	Pierpont Morgan Library, New York (Heineman Foundation Collection)
First edition:	Completed by Reinhard Van Hoorickx; facsimile of autograph subsequently published in 1928; subsequently published as part of the NSA in 2009 (P856)
Subsequent editions:	Not in Peters; Not in AGA; NSA IV: Vol. 8/205
Discography and timing:	Fischer-Dieskau —
	Hyperion I 20^{13}
	Hyperion II 5^{12} 2'44 Ian Bostridge

⟵ *An Mignon* D161   *Sängers Morgenlied* D165 ⟶

LIEBESRAUSCH (II)   Love's intoxication
(Körner) **D179** [H84]
G major   8 April 1815

(22 bars)

See previous entry for poem and translation

THEODOR KÖRNER (1791–1813)

This is the ninth of Schubert's sixteen Körner solo settings (1815–18). See the poet's biography for a chronological list of all the Körner settings.

This song, accompanied throughout in throbbing triplets, has some of the pulsating magic of *Nähe des Geliebten* (D162) written a few months earlier. Its glory lies in the impassioned and taut vocal line, and the chromatic vigour of the underpinning bass. At bb. 6–7, and again in rising sequence at bb. 8–9, the poet concentrates his energies on the beloved ('In Dir versinkt mein Streben'), fixing on her as his goal. This is brilliantly mirrored by the pincer movement of the rising bass line and the vocal line moving in the opposite direction, as if both staves were bearing down on the object of their pursuit. A feature of the song is the freedom and inventiveness of the accompaniment's chordal dispositions – sometimes it is the top voice in the right-hand chord that leads, sometimes the bass, and it is often the artfully placed inner voicings that guide the music's direction. This piano writing is all in support of a high-lying paean of rapturous praise that traverses a number of tonalities and reaches a climactic point in B major at b. 18. The return to the home key of G major is both clever and perfectly natural-sounding.

John Reed links this song with Schubert's love for Therese Grob, but it sounds rather too high-flown for her. Schubert has a crush certainly, but this poem reflects is an admiration that transcends both romantic inclination and the grave. On the lines 'Dein Name nur in heil'gen Tönen / Hat meine kühne Brust gefüllt' it is as if Schubert momentarily permits his music to refer to Körner, the fallen poet who had briefly been his friend and inspiration. The three-bar postlude brings *Nähe des Geliebten* to mind, as well as the noble opening of a much later song, *Memnon* D541, where there is a similar stately musical pendulum swinging between tonic and dominant in the inner voices of the accompaniment. There is rapture and pain here a-plenty and it remains, for all its skill, very much a young man's music. A picture of Körner himself in wooing mode is obviously the principal image in the composer's mind, together with an awareness that the poet's ability to feel, express and receive love is forever a thing of the past. Nevertheless, Schubert knew it was within music's power to give new life to those who had perished. Having captured the poet's essence, Schubert set about writing another song on the same day which is equally evocative of Körner's passionate and mercurial personality, *Sehnsucht der Liebe* D180.

Autograph:	Aoyama Junior College, Osaka
First edition:	Published as No. 29 of *Neueste Folge nachgelassener Lieder und Gesänge* by J. P. Gotthard, Vienna in 1872 (P455)
Subsequent editions:	Not in Peters; AGA XX 59: Vol. 2/90; NSA IV: Vol. 8/30; Bärenreiter: Vol. 6/124
Bibliography:	Youens 1996, pp. 130–32
Discography and timing:	Fischer-Dieskau I 3[11] 2'23 (first two strophes only)
	Hyperion I 4[6]
	Hyperion II 6[3] 3'06 Philip Langridge

← *Vergebliche Liebe* D177   *Sehnsucht der Liebe* D182 →

LIEBESTÄNDELEI   Flirtation
(KÖRNER) **D206** [H102]
E♭ major   26 May 1815

Süsses Liebchen! Komm zu mir! Tausend Küsse geb ich dir.

(15 bars)

Süsses Liebchen! Komm' zu mir!	My sweet love! Come to me!
Tausend Küsse geb' ich Dir.	I will give you a thousand kisses.
Sieh' mich hier zu Deinen Füssen.	You behold me here at your feet.
Mädchen, Deiner Lippen Glut	Fair maiden, the ardour of your lips
Gibt mir Kraft und Lebensmut.	Gives me strength and the courage for life.
Lass Dich küssen!	Let me kiss you!
Mädchen, werde doch nicht rot!	Fair maiden, do not blush!
Wenn's die Mutter auch verbot.	Even though your mother has forbidden it,
Sollst Du alle Freuden missen?	Are you to forgo all pleasures?
Nur an des Geliebten Brust	Only on your lover's breast
Blüht des Lebens schönste Lust.	Does life's fairest joy flower.
Lass Dich küssen!	Let me kiss you!
Liebchen, warum zierst Du Dich?	My love, why are you so coy?
Höre doch und küsse mich.	Listen, and kiss me.
Willst Du nichts von Liebe wissen?	Do you wish to know nothing of love?
Wogt Dir nicht Dein kleines Herz	Does your little heart not surge,
Bald in Freuden, bald in Schmerz?	Now with pleasure, now with pain?
Lass Dich küssen!	Let me kiss you!
Sieh', Dein Sträuben hilft Dir nicht;	See, your reluctance is to no avail;
Schon hab' ich nach Sängers Pflicht	Already, my duty as a singer done,
Dir den ersten Kuss entrissen!—	I have snatched the first kiss from you!
Und nun sinkst Du, liebewarm,	And now, warm with love, you sink
Willig selbst in meinen Arm.	Willingly into my arms.
Lass Dich küssen![1]	Let yourself be kissed!

THEODOR KÖRNER (1791–1813)

This is the eleventh of Schubert's sixteen Körner solo settings (1815–18). See the poet's biography for a chronological list of all the Körner settings.

This delightful *Singspiel* aria, Papageno-like, is reminiscent of some of the mildly risqué and erotic German songs of Haydn and has the nature of the Viennese *Singspiel* from Schubert's adolescence. Beethoven's *Der Kuss* Op. 128 also comes to mind. This song is utterly charming and it is only its absence from the Peters Edition that has prevented it from being performed by a great many singers. It has a cheeky piquant quality that has more to do with the eighteenth century (Hogarth and *Tom Jones*) than with German romanticism. The impatience of the flirtation is emphasized by two plaintive requests of 'Lass Dich küssen!' on the same diminished chord (bb. 10–11 and 11–12) after which the singer takes matters into his own hands and simply helps himself to what has hitherto been requested and refused. Schubert's sense of theatre is utterly faultless here: at bb. 12–13 the vocal line stays suspended on a held B flat (four and a half beats) on the word 'Lass'. It seems that the ardent young singer has temporarily immobilized the girl in his arms during which the piano accompaniment plants no fewer than four kisses on her lips (clipped quaver chords separated by rests). This is the springboard from which the

[1] Thus in the NSA and Bauer's 1815 Viennese reprint of Körner's *Gedichte*. In Körner's *Knospen* (1810) this line in the final verse is 'Lässt dich küssen'.

pouncing pianist is propelled into action (on the singer's behalf) by the rising arpeggio of the tiny postlude (bb. 14–15). This surely betokens the girl pushing him away (also at the end of the second and third verses) and, in turn, necessitating the renewed wooing of the subsequent verses where the lover's suave (actually rather naive) wheedling begins all over again.

The content of the poem's last verse is entirely different; by now the girl is a convert to the kisses and the final arpeggio at the end of the fourth verse denotes the singer's triumph. Körner was less than sixteen when he wrote this poem – it appeared in his first published collection, *Knospen* in 1810 – so it is more the text of a would-be Lothario than an accomplished wooer. The same aspect of schoolboy fantasy seems to apply to Schubert in the setting of it. At least it has none of the scarcely concealed chauvinism, some would even say sleazy misogyny, that comes across in many a performance of Beethoven's *Der Kuss*.

Autograph:	Library of Congress, Washington (first draft)
First edition:	Published as No. 11 of *Neueste Folge nachgelassener Lieder und Gesänge* by J. P. Gotthard, Vienna in 1872 (P437)
Subsequent editions:	Not in Peters; AGA XX 75: Vol. 2/122; NSA IV: Vol. 8/56
Bibliography:	Youens 1996, pp. 136–7
Discography and timing:	Fischer-Dieskau I 3[24] 1'19 (first three strophes only)
	Hyperion I 4[5]
	Hyperion II 6[22] 2'00 Philip Langridge

← *Auf den Tod einer Nachtigall* D201   *Der Liebende* D207 →

LIEBHABER IN ALLEN GESTALTEN

A lover in all guises

(GOETHE) **D558** [H367]
A major   May 1817

Ich wollt' ich wär' ein Fisch, so hur - tig und frisch,

(20 bars)

Ich wollt' ich wär' ein Fisch!	I wish I were a fish,
So hurtig und frisch;	So agile and fresh;
Und kämst Du zu angeln,	And if you came to catch me,
Ich würde nicht mangeln.	I would not fail you.
Ich wollt' ich wär' ein Fisch!	I wish I were a fish,
So hurtig und frisch.	So agile and fresh.
Ich wollt' ich wär ein Pferd!	I wish I were a horse,
Da wär ich Dir wert.	Then you would esteem me.
O wär' ich ein Wagen!	Would that I were a coach!
Bequem Dich zu tragen.	I should carry you in comfort.
Ich wollt' ich wär ein Pferd!	I wish I were a horse!
Da wär ich Dir wert.	Then you would esteem me.

Ich wollt' ich wäre Gold!	I wish I were gold,
Dir immer im Sold;	Always at your service.
Und tätst Du was kaufen,	And if you bought something,
Käm' ich wie gelaufen.[1]	I would come running back.
Ich wollt' ich wäre Gold!	I wish I were gold,
Dir immer im Sold.	Always at your service!

[(. . . 3 . . .)]   [(. . . 3 . . .)]

Wär' ich gut wie ein Schaf!	Would that I were as meek as a lamb
Wie der Löwe so brav;	And as brave as a lion;
Hätt' Augen wie's Lüchschen,	That I had the eyes of a lynx
Und Listen wie's Füchschen.	And the cunning of a fox!
Wär' ich gut wie ein Schaf!	Would that I were as meek as a lamb
Wie der Löwe so brav;	And as brave as a lion!

[(. . .)]   [(. . .)]

Doch bin ich wie ich bin,	But I am as I am;
Und nimm mich nur hin!	Just accept me like this.
Willst bess're besitzen,[2]	If you want a better man,
So lass Dir sie schnitzen.	Then have him made for you.
Ich bin nun wie ich bin;	I am as I am;
So nimm mich nur hin!	Just accept me like this.

JOHANN WOLFGANG VON GOETHE (1749–1832); poem written in summer 1810

This is the fifty-first of Schubert's seventy-five Goethe solo settings (1814–26). See the poet's biography for a chronological list of all the Goethe settings.

This is one of the more famous of Schubert's lighter songs, and a favourite encore of many a soprano. Peasants and princes alike have wished to be reincarnated into something that would bring them closer to the intimate charms of a beloved; the idea goes back to the myth of Proteus and the Ovidian concept of metamorphosis. It is typical of Goethe that he should effortlessly marry classical learning with the style of a cheeky and earthy folksong. However masculine some of these words might be, it is unusual on the concert platform today to hear this song sung by a man – surely because of Schubert's music. The song has become part of the soprano repertoire (Elisabeth Schumann and Irmgard Seefried sang it often) to the extent that Fischer-Dieskau chose not to include it in his giant Schubert survey of the 1970s. 'I can't get enough of you', the poem seems to say, 'and I will go to any lengths to get more.' The music bubbles and twinkles with goodwill and happiness and turns the predatory nature of the words into something harm- lessly gentle. Perhaps male singers are embarrassed by the song's whimsical coquetry; there is much in the turns of musical phrase (for example the piquant *acciaccature* in bb. 1 and 2 of the introduction) which suggests flirtatious femininity. Staccato notes in the left hand (from b. 5) and the cheeky little interplay between voice and piano (the echoing phrases at the end of each strophe at bb. 13–14, and 17–18) add to an impression of a teasing game of hide and seek.

[1] Goethe (*Werke*, 1815) writes 'Kam ich *wieder* gelaufen' ('I came running back again'). The NSA has 'wie gelaufen' in the underlay, the Peters Edition only 'gelaufen'.
[2] Goethe writes 'Willst *Du Bess're* besitzen'.

There are nine verses printed in the *Gesamtausgabe* (only three in Peters). The four that are printed in NSA – verses 1, 2, 3 and 9 of Goethe's poem – seem clearly selected by the composer himself in the autograph. In recording the song for Hyperion Edith Mathis flatly refused to include Goethe's second verse ('Ich wollt' ich wär ein Pferd', 'I wish I were a horse'); non German-speaking vocalists are unaware that 'Pferd' is slang for an over-stolidly built woman. This is one of the dangers of women singing texts where Goethe himself is the narrator. Printed above are the four verses selected by Schubert, as in the NSA, with the addition of the extra verse ('Wär ich gut wie ein Schaf') chosen by Mathis to replace the 'Pferd' strophe on the Hyperion recording. There are four further verses (Goethe's strophes 4, 5, 6 and 8) to be found in the AGA and in the *Quellen und Lesarten* of the NSA (Vol. 8, p. 276). Three of these can be made to fit Schubert's music if the singer is so inclined, but at least there is no doubt in this case which words most pleased the composer himself.

The song was written out on a double piece of paper containing three Goethe songs of similar lightness, if not quite equal delight. The other two are *Schweizerlied* D559 and *Der Goldschmieds-gesell* D560.

Autograph:	Conservatoire Collection, Bibliothèque Nationale, Paris
First edition:	Published as Vol. 7 no. 44 in Friedlaender's edition by Peters, Leipzig in 1887 (P505)
Subsequent editions:	Peters: Vol. 7/97; AGA XX 120: Vol. 3/46; NSA IV: Vol. 11/140
Further settings and arrangements:	Carl Friedrich Zelter (1758–1832) *Duettino: Ich wollt' ich wär ein Fisch* for two voices (1810) Arr. Tilman Hoppstock (b. 1961) for guitar accompaniment, in *Franz Schubert: 110 Lieder* (2009)
Discography and timing:	Fischer-Dieskau —
	Hyperion I 21^{15}
	Hyperion II 19^{1} 1'48 Edith Mathis

← *Uraniens Flucht* D554   *Schweizerlied* D559 →

Der LIEBLICHE STERN   The lovely star
(Schulze) **D861** [H579]
G major   December 1825

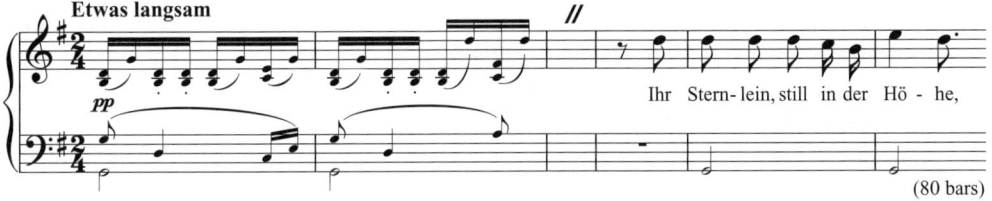

(80 bars)

Ihr Sternlein, still in der Höhe,	Little stars, so silent in the heavens,
Ihr Sternlein, spielend im Meer,	Little stars, playing upon the sea,
Wenn ich von Ferne daher	When from afar
So freundlich euch leuchten sehe,	I see you sparkling so delightfully,
So wird mir von Wohl und von Wehe	Then, for weal or woe,
Der Busen so bang und so schwer.	My heart grows troubled and heavy.

Es zittert von Frühlingswinden	The sky trembles in the spring breezes
Der Himmel im flüssigen Grün,	Above the watered meadows;
Manch Sternlein sah ich entblüh'n,	I saw many a star blossom,
Manch Sternlein sah ich entschwinden;	I saw many a star vanish.
Doch kann ich das schönste nicht finden,	But I cannot find the fairest star,
Das früher dem Liebenden schien.	That once shone for this lover.
Nicht kann ich zum Himmel mich schwingen,	I cannot soar to the heavens
Zu suchen den freundlichen Stern;	To seek that kindly star;
Stets hält ihn die Wolke mir fern.	Clouds forever conceal it from me.
Tief unten, da möcht' es gelingen,	Deep below, there I might succeed
Das friedliche Ziel zu erringen,	In reaching the peaceful refuge;
Tief unten, da ruh' ich so gern!	Deep below I would gladly find rest.
Was wiegt ihr im laulichen Spiele,	Breezes, why do you lull the rocking boat
Ihr Lüftchen, den schwankenden Kahn?	In gentle play?
O treibt ihn auf rauherer Bahn	Drive it along a rougher course,
Hernieder ins Wogengewühle!	Down into the whirlpool!
Lasst tief in der wallenden Kühle	Deep in the cool, turbulent waters
Dem lieblichen Sterne mich nah'n!	Let me draw near to that lovely star.

ERNST SCHULZE (1789–1817); poem written 28 April 1814

This is the fourth of Schubert's ten Schulze solo settings (1825–6). See the poet's biography for a chronological list of all the Schulze settings. An outline of a suggested performing version for a Schulze cycle is listed under Auf den wilden Wegen.

The song is 'a little pearl' according to Capell; in John Reed's words it is 'content to celebrate our love and longing'. And yet a song that raises the issue of suicide is more of a flawed pearl, and is surely less than 'content'. It's very presence in a group of Schulze songs, works written at the height of Schubert's expressive maturity, raises certain questions. Can it be true, as John Reed has written, that 'Schubert ignores the tragic hints in the last two verses of the poem'? Unlikely. For if the Schubert of 1825 ignores the 'tragic hints' it is because he decides that, at certain moments, a deliberate conflict of meaning between words and music is called for. If he had never written a song like *Täuschung* (No. 19 in *Winterreise*, where the waltz rhythm and the major key seem ironic and horribly incongruous with the traveller's plight) there might have been more room for doubt. But these Schulze songs are the precursors of the second Müller cycle, and *Der liebliche Stern* has an arguable claim to be considered the *Täuschung* of the group. Of course this presupposes the performance of the Schulze songs as a set. (Walther Dürr notes in the NSA that Schubert's addition of the Schulze setting *Über Wildemann* D884, March 1826, to the free pages left in the autograph of the earlier *Der liebliche Stern* implies that he at some stage thought of his Schulze settings as belonging together in a set.) They are, however, almost never performed as such (see '*Auf den wilden Wegen*').

In *Täuschung* the winter traveller's woe is framed by the rhythm of a naive Viennese waltz. He is powerless to change the light-hearted dance of humanity, a dance that is only distressing when contrasted with his own circumstances. (Robert Schumann twice wrote songs where the unhinged narrator is surrounded by cheerful dance music which is grotesquely inappropriate to his state of mind: *Das ist ein Flöten und Geigen* at the heart of his *Dichterliebe* cycle Op. 48 no. 9, and the Hans Andersen-inspired *Der Spielmann* Op. 40 no. 4.) Schubert used motor rhythms, less susceptible to rubato than music governed by human emotion, throughout the song canon. Nature therefore goes about her business if not quite regardless of man's presence, then at least as a given in his uncertain life – the setting of the sun, the rustling of the winds (in both *Suleika* songs for example), the blinking of the stars as a source of light and energy (Leitner's *Die Sterne* D939) and above all the flowing of water that stops for no one. In *Des Baches Wiegenlied* D795/20, the final song in *Die schöne Müllerin*, the most heartbreaking words relating to suicide and betrayal are sung quietly in the major key, in unvarying strophes. The tragedy of the miller boy is seen as part of the inscrutable workings of nature, and it is this which makes it unbearably moving.

In *Der liebliche Stern* the music of the gently twinkling stars carries on, and the poet is shown to be a small cog in the impartial workings of the universe, despite believing himself to be at its epicentre. The difference between Schulze and the winter traveller is clear: the protagonist of *Winterreise* is blessed (or cursed) with self-knowledge; the poet of *Der liebliche Stern* has little idea how obsessive his relationship with life and love has become. But the music makes it clear that if he were to drown in the search for a beautiful star, the stars would still shine and life would go on. Thus Schubert does not 'ignore the tragic hints' but comments on the puny human condition by counterpointing the poet and his environment.

But this music is subtly and deliberately distorted, precisely because it is seen through the poet's eyes. There is a confluence of musical motifs here – water music and starlight. For the introduction even the look of the music is unusual. In all Schubert there is nothing quite like those awkward figurations (Capell mistakenly called them 'dainty'!) of bb. 2 and 4 with their right-hand leaps. Think of how easily in comparison the water flows under the hand in *Wohin?* from *Die schöne Müllerin* D795/2. Here everything is in reverse: it is as if the accompaniment has been composed by holding up a mirror to a more conventional piece of water music. From the opening bar the left hand in the tenor register has a strangely beguiling tune that looks upside down, falling from its quaver anacrusis rather than rising. If this cantus firmus signifies the Lorelei-like song of the star, should this celestial melody not be made to shine in the treble? Of course not, because this song, almost uniquely in the canon, is all about reflection. For Schulze who scans the surface of the sea, the star can only be found beneath the water; the natural order of the universe is thus subverted. Schubert has created a topsy-turvy land through the looking glass which is all the more disturbing because it masquerades as reality. The singer accepts the mirror image as the truth, but Schubert knows differently. Most performers can make of this music something light-heartedly charming, but the 'Etwas langsam' marking is a warning against too facile an interpretation, and the phrase 'hidden depths' is especially applicable.

In most of the Schulze songs one-track-minded obsession, born of the most sophisticated use of strophic song, has been the order of the day: the unflinching returns of the ritornello in *Auf der Bruck* D853, the self-hypnotizing and repetitive choreography of *Um Mitternacht* D682. *Der liebliche Stern* continues the pattern. The song remains centred around the tonic chord of G major to a remarkable degree; it moves once to the minor key (from b. 13), once to a stentorian B flat (prophetic of the heroism of *Lebensmut* D883, from b. 30) and in the last verse to the elegiac subdominant of C major for 'Lasst tief in der wallenden Kühle' (from b. 70). But the poet's theme is himself, and he is repeatedly drawn back to the tonality of an unchanging view-point. The strophic form is skilfully and subtly modified, but always within the parameters of a world in which neither the stars nor the poet are able to change their courses. Seen in this light, *Der liebliche Stern* reveals itself as perhaps one of the most falsely prettified and least understood songs of Schubert's maturity.

Autograph: In private possession (from b. 67 to end)
First edition: Published as Book 13 no. 2 of the *Nachlass* by Diabelli, Vienna in
                            1832 (P277)

Subsequent editions: Peters: Vol. 3/140; AGA XX 486: Vol. 8/160; NSA IV: Vol. 13/192
Bibliography: Capell 1928, p. 216
                          Youens 1996, pp. 278–81
Discography and timing: Fischer-Dieskau II 7¹⁵   2'37
                          Hyperion I 18¹⁶ & 19⁸   2'44   Peter Schreier
                                                   2'58   Felicity Lott
                          Hyperion II 31²   2'44   Peter Schreier

← *An mein Herz* D860   *Um Mitternacht* D862 →

LIED (Brüder, schrecklich brennt dic Träne)   Song   Soprano & small orchestra
(Anonymous) **D535** [not in Hyperion]
G minor   February 1817

(29 bars)

Brüder, schrecklich brennt die Träne,   Brothers, terribly burn the tears
Die verschäute Armut weint;   Wept by the hapless poor.
Findet diese Jammerscene   Does this scene of woe
Unter uns wohl keinen Freund?   Find no friend among us?
Der Verzweiflung preisgegeben   A prey to despair,
Ringt die welken Hände sie;   She wrings her pale hands.
Kommt, erleichtert heut' ihr Leben   Come, lighten her life today
Durch des Mitleids Sympathie.   With compassionate sympathy.

ANONYMOUS/UNKNOWN

This is the fourteenth of Schubert's nineteen solo settings of an anonymous poet. See
Anonymous/Unknown for a chronological list of all the songs for which the poets are unknown.

So unusual is this piece of music, a 'lied' with orchestral accompaniment, that Mandyczewski published it at the end of the solo lieder series; the NSA prefers to place it in Series III. The accompaniment is scored for strings with oboes, bassoons and horns. The repeat markings indicate that the text to be found in the autograph is only a fraction of what was performed: one does not assemble orchestral resources like these with a soloist for a three-minute song. This writing seems typical of the music Schubert wrote for his infinitely less talented brother, Ferdinand, who often passed such works off as his own. The composer, in a spirit of fraternal kindness, realized this and cut his cloth accordingly – the music had to be well made and pleasant but not in any way so individual as to raise suspicions regarding its authorship. The composition, in quasi-hymnal style with a slightly Baroque flavour, seems to have been destined for performance at the Wiener Waisenhaus, the city's main orphanage, or the 'Verein für verschämte Arme' – organization for the humble poor. It is disturbing to think of these manipulative and embarrassing words actually being put into the mouths of orphans who were required to learn and sing them. It was published in 1853 in Ferdinand Schubert's pedagogical anthology *Der kleine Sänger*, appearing there as no. 14 and arranged for two voices with piano accompaniment. Its title there is 'Song of the poor schoolchildren to their patrons and well-wishers'. It took a William Blake (as in his lyric *Holy Thursday*) to depict the humbug of the rich whose charity (the 'Mitleids Sympathie' of the above poem) is dependent on its recipients begging for it in such servile and self-demeaning terms. When this song was written Blake was still very much alive in London, and raging against the exploitation of British children.

Autograph:	Wienbibliothek im Rathaus, Vienna (first draft)
First edition:	Published as part of the AGA in 1895 (P709)
Subsequent editions:	Not in Peters; AGA XX 585: Vol. 10/78; NSA III: Vol. 1
Discography and timing:	Hyperion I
	Hyperion II

LIED (Des Lebens Tag ist schwer und schwül) ('Die Mutter Erde')
Song ('Mother Earth')

(Stolberg) **D788** [H514]
A minor – A major   April 1823

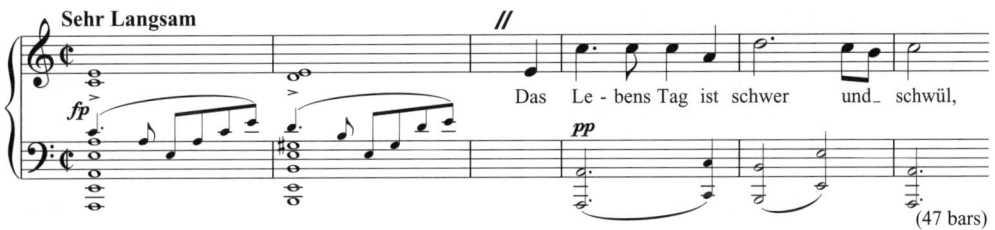

(47 bars)

Des Lebens Tag ist schwer und schwül;
Des Todes Atem leicht und kühl:[1]
Er wehet freundlich uns hinab
Wie welkes Laub in's stille Grab.

Es scheint der Mond, es fällt der Tau,
Auf's Grab wie auf die Blumenau;
Auch fällt der Freunde Trän' hinein,
Erhellt von sanfter Hoffnung Schein.

Uns sammelt alle, Klein und Gross.[2]
Die Muttererd' in ihren Schoss.
O säh'n wir ihr ins Angesicht;
Wir scheuten ihren Busen nicht!

Life's day is heavy and sultry,
The breath of death is light and cool;
Fondly it wafts us down,
Like withered leaves, into the silent grave.

The moon shines, the dew falls
On the grave as on the flowery meadow;
The tears of friends also fall,
Lit by the gleam of gentle hope.

Mother Earth gathers us all, great and small,
In her lap;
If we would only look upon her face
We should not fear her bosom.

[1] Stolberg (*Gedichte*, Vienna, 1818) writes 'Des Todes *Odem* leicht und kühl'.
[2] Stolberg writes '*Und* sammelt *Alle*, Klein und Gross'.

FRIEDRICH LEOPOLD, GRAF ZU STOLBERG-STOLBERG (1750–1819); poem written in 1780

This is the eighth of Schubert's nine Stolberg solo settings (1815–23). See the poet's biography for a chronological list of all the Stolberg settings.

The opening of this poem must have been known to Heinrich Heine whose lines 'Der Tod, das ist die kühle Nacht / Das Leben ist der schwüle Tag' from his *Buch der Lieder* were memorably set by Brahms (Op. 96 no. 1). Heine was no fan of Stolberg but he was fond of quotations and parody, either inimical or reverential, in the spirit of romantic irony. The lines also clearly resonated strongly with Schubert. In the summer of 1825 the composer, on holiday in the town of Steyr, wrote a letter home to his parents in which he regretted his brother Ferdinand's tendency to hypochondria and fear of death: 'If only he could once see these heavenly mountains and lakes, the sight of which threatens to crush or engulf us, he would not be so attached to puny human life, nor regard it as otherwise than good fortune to be consigned to the earth with its indescribable power to create new life.' Although this joyous holiday in Upper Austria was a time of remission rather than cure from the syphilis that had laid Schubert low in 1823, the fears of his brother must have resonated with his own diminished propects.

But the composer was a changed man. From that nightmare period of shame, fear of death and suicidal depression, Schubert had somehow emerged unscathed at the core. His health may have been fatally undermined, but his mental state ensured that his music would flow until the end of his life with ever richer and more profound meaning. The homily in his letter home sums up the content of Stolberg's poem – and little wonder, for the song dates from the bad times of 1823 when it was the cathartic power of creation, particularly in association with composing *Die schöne Müllerin* D795, that helped the composer face the realities of life and death. Apart from *Auf dem Wasser zu singen* D774, all the other Stolberg settings date from 1815. It would not be surprising if Schubert had returned to the poetry of Stolberg because he felt this particular poem had some relevance to his illness.

The composer's own beloved alternation between A minor and A major is here employed to marvellous effect with a new key signature at b. 14 so that the majority of the song benefits from the radiance of the major key – to both happy and sad effect, for no one was more gifted than Schubert at making the major key devastatingly poignant. The second verse of the poem is magically illuminated by musical moonlight highlighting dew on the grave; heart-stopping clashes and suspensions illustrate the tears of friends (bb. 25–8), showing an almost Wagnerian broadening of chromatic expression in the harmonic armoury (cf. the opening of the contemporary *Dass sie hier gewesen* D775). The song is bound together by a pianistic motif of quavers ascending in an arpeggio in various regions of the keyboard, giving the impression of the accompaniment for a through-composed sonata movement (for viola perhaps, one of the most motherly of instruments).

In the slowly rocking introduction (where whole bars seem to hang suspended from the held semibreve chords) there is a suggestion of the swinging to and fro of a cradle. A protective haven is woven by the intertwining embrace of voice and piano in thirds and sixths whereby the effulgence and depth of Brahms (as Capell points out) and Mahler seem to be prophesied. We forget, and perhaps even accept, that in burying ourselves in the lap of Mother Earth, we bid life farewell. Connoisseurs of Schubert's piano works will recognize in the accompaniment to the section beginning 'Es scheint der Mond, es fällt der Tau' (bb. 19–22) a strong reminiscence of the Andante of the A major Sonata, Op. 120 (D664). Leo Black has furthermore uncovered in the postlude a reference to the slow movement of the Beethoven Violin Concerto. In bb. 23–4 at the words 'wie auf die Blumenau' there is a remarkable echo of the Collin setting *Wehmut* D772 at 'In ihrer Schönheit Fülle schau' (bb. 10–12) – two matching phrases that end on the same dipthong.

There is a variant of the song (not another actual version) in A flat minor/major (*see* NSA Volume 13 p. XXVII and p. 258) where the vocal line is notated in full, as well as the piano interludes. This straightforward transposition was probably made for vocal reasons. The often-used title 'Die Mutter Erde' (as in Peters Edition for example) goes back to the song's publication in 1838 and does not appear to have had anything to do with Schubert himself.

Autograph: Wienbibliothek im Rathaus, Vienna (first draft)
First edition: Published as Book 29 no. 2 of the *Nachlass* by Diabelli, Vienna in
                         1838 (P321)
Subsequent editions: Peters: Vol. 5/164; AGA XX 427: Vol. 7/104; NSA IV: Vol. 13/92
Bibliography: Black 2003, p. 108
Further settings: Johann Adam Peter Schulz (1747–1800) *Lied im Volkston*
                         (1782–90)
Discography and timing: Fischer-Dieskau II 6³   3'41
                         Hyperion I 5⁵
                         Hyperion II 27²   3'46   Elizabeth Connell

← *Viola D786*   *Pilgerweise D789* →

LIED (Es ist so angenehm)   Song
(Schiller?) **D284** [H170]
G major   6 September 1815

(13 bars)

Es ist so angenehm, so süss,   It is so pleasant and so sweet
Um einen lieben Mann zu spielen,   To dally with a man you love,
Entzückend, wie ein Paradies,   And as delightful as paradise
Des Mannes Feuerkuss zu fühlen.   To feel the man's fiery kisses.

Jetzt weiss ich, was mein Taubenpaar Now I know what my pair of doves
Mit seinem sanften Girren sagte,   Were saying with their soft cooing,
Und was der Nachtigallen Schar   And what the host of nightingales
So zärtlich sich in Liedern klagte.   Were lamenting so tenderly in their songs.

Jetzt weiss ich, was mein volles Herz, Now I know what weighed upon my full heart
In ewig langen Nächten engte;   In long, never-ending nights;
Jetzt weiss ich, welcher süsse Schmerz Now I know what sweet sorrow so often
Oft seufzend meinen Busen drängte;   Oppressed my breast with its sighs.

Warum kein Blümchen mir gefiel,	And why no flower pleased me,
Warum der Mai mir nimmer lachte,	Why May never smiled upon me,
Warum der Vögel Liederspiel	Why the song of the birds
Mich nimmermehr zur Freude fachte.	Never aroused me to joy.

Mir trauerte die ganze Welt,	To me the whole world seemed in mourning,
Ich kannte nicht die schönsten Triebe,	I did not know fair desire.
Nun hab' ich was mir längst gefehlt,	Now I have what I lacked for so long:
Beneide mich, Natur – ich liebe!	Envy me, Nature, I am in love!

FRIEDRICH VON SCHILLER? (1759–1805); poem written 16 May 1786?

If this poem is indeed by Schiller, it is the nineteenth of Schubert's forty-four Schiller solo settings (1811–24). See the poet's biography for a chronological list of all the Schiller settings.

This song is typical of the shy treasures buried within the Schubert repertory – and particularly in this extraordinary year of 1815. The song (and its accompaniment in gently undulating semiquavers) may look run of the mill on the printed page, but this is music in *Singspiel* style and, like many arias of this genre, can be utterly enchanting in sympathetic performance. As sung by Janet Baker the fiery kisses of the first verse burn into the memory and the cooing doves of the second fly off the page. It takes a mistress of song to disguise the piece's only weakness – false accentuation. In the first verse the dangling hiatus in the meaning whereby the genitive 'des Mannes' is elongated on a high A (on the word's last syllable) is hardly a good example of prosody, and neither is the emphasis of the final syllable of 'zärtlich' in the same place in the second verse. There are other examples where unimportant syllables, particularly when set to the high notes in the first and seventh bars, have to be skilfully 'tucked in' to the line so that the listener does not notice.

Schiller's authorship of this poem has long been doubted. The poem can be found in the *Taschenbuch für Damen auf das Jahr 1809* where it is posthumously ascribed to him, and it is also printed in the source used by Schubert, the Schiller Ausgabe of Anton Doll (Vienna, 1810) in the tenth volume (or the second volume of the *Gedichte*) under the subheading 'written as an impromptu contribution to a Singspiel'. The young composer clearly believed the poem to be by Schiller. However, because it is not included in more reputable editions of Schiller's works, Deutsch suggested that the lyric may be by the poet's friend Karoline von Wolzogen. For the NSA Walther Dürr unearths evidence of a letter written by Schiller on 17 May 1786 to Ludwig Ferdinand Huber where the poet describes having written two arias and a trio for an operetta, the words already handed over to the composer. The text printed above may have been one of these occasional pieces.

All of the poet's strophes are printed above. For the Hyperion recording Janet Baker performed only the first two.

Autograph:	Missing or lost
First edition:	Published as part of the AGA in 1895 (P580)
Subsequent editions:	Not in Peters: AGA XX 137: Vol. 3/69; NSA IV: Vol. 9/56
Discography and timing:	Fischer-Dieskau —
	Hyperion I 1¹⁴
	Hyperion II 10⁵ 1'14 Janet Baker

← *An den Frühling* D283   *Furcht der Geliebten ('An Cidli')* D285 →

LIED (Ferne von der grossen Stadt)
(Pichler) **D483** [H306]
E major　September 1816

Song

(22 bars)

Ferne von der grossen Stadt,	Far from the great city,
Nimm mich auf in deine Stille,	Receive me into your stillness,
Tal, das mit des Frühlings Fülle[1]	O valley, which nature has adorned
Die Natur geschmücket hat!	With spring's abundance;
Wo kein Lärmen, kein Getümmel	Where no din, no turmoil
Meinen Schlummer kürzer macht,	Shortens my slumber,
Und ein ewig heitrer Himmel	And a serene sky smiles eternally
Über sel'gen Fluren lacht!	Upon happy meadows.
Freuden, die die Ruhe beut,	Here I shall savour undisturbed
Will ich ungestört hier schmecken,	The joys that tranquillity offers;
Hier, wo Bäume mich bedecken,	Here, where trees cover me
Und die Linde Duft verstreut,	And the linden scatters its sweet scent
Diese Quelle sei mein Spiegel,	Let this spring be my mirror,
Mein Parkett der junge Klee,	And the young clover my floor,
Und der frischberas'te Hügel	And the hill, fresh with grass,
Sei mein grünes Kanapee.[2]	My green couch.
Deiner mütterlichen Spur,	O Nature, I shall follow
Dem Gesetz, das ungerochen	Your maternal trail,
Noch kein Sterblicher gebrochen,	The law that no mortal
Will ich folgen, o Natur!	Has yet broken unavenged.
Aus dem dunkeln Schoss der Erden,	From the earth's dark womb
Will ich Freuden mir erzieh'n,	I shall garner delights;
Und aus Baum und Blume werden	And joys shall bloom
Seligkeiten mir erblüh'n.	On tree and flower.
[. . . 5 . . .]	[. . . 5 . . .]

KAROLINE PICHLER (1769–1843); poem written *c.* 1791

This is the second of Schubert's four Pichler solo settings (1816, a song of an unknown date, and 1821). See the poet's biography for a chronological list of all the Pichler settings.

This song should be sung, perhaps, before the Mayrhofer setting *Rückweg* D476 (also composed in September 1816) in which that poet, having enjoyed a wonderful time in the country, returns

[1] Pichler (Idyllen, 1803) writes 'Tal, das mit *der Frühlingsfülle*'.
[2] Pichler writes '*Kanapeh*'.

to Vienna with dragging steps. It is a cheery contribution to the eternal debate between the relative merits of country and town. The poetess published her *Idylle* (ten scenes in a country setting) in 1803, although Schubert appears to have used the 1813 edition. This text is the conclusion of the second of these idylls, *Der Sommerabend* or *The Summer Evening*, dedicated to Pichler's friend Josepha von Ravenet. The book as a whole is a succession of fantasy pastorals with Pichler taking on the role of Marie Antoinette (daughter of Maria Therese and recently decapitated) as she plays at being a *bergère*. One could count on such Viennese socialite authors as Pichler to be well behind the political times. The young maidens Lyda and Seline (described by Pichler as 'blühende Mädchen') compete with one another to praise the beauties of the countryside. Seline asks Lyda for her thoughts and Lyda coyly offers to recite a long poem on the subject – 'whether I wrote it myself, or whether I learned it, or whether a god whispered it to my soul I am not going to tell you, however plagued you are by curiosity'. The old-fashioned exchanges in hexameters between the two nymphs end at this point, and Pichler's lyric as set by Schubert, mostly in ABBACDCD form, begins. The mood is hymn-like with the accompaniment closely hugging the vocal line except for stentorian dotted rhythms to mirror the meaning of 'Lärmen' and 'Getümmel' in bb. 11 and 12.

There are eight verses of which the first three were recorded for the Hyperion Edition; all are printed in NSA. The fifth strophe gives a clue as to why there is an obvious quotation from Haydn's Imperial Hymn *Gott, erhalte Franz den Kaiser* Hob XXVIa: 43 in the song's closing phrases (from b. 14) and in the piano postlude (bb. 18–20). In her fifth verse Pichler likens her rural domain, with its apiary, to a Bee Republic. Perhaps Schubert parodies these pretensions to be ruler of an Arcadian paradise with a touch of imperial pomp? A simpler explanation may be that it was appropriate to quote a patriotic hymn for Austria in a poem that is full of descriptions of the beauties of the country itself, the emperor's Austria, *die Österreichische Monarchie*, as an equivalent of the king's England. Karoline Pichler herself was anything but a shy country recluse; her literary salon was at one time the most important in Vienna. It was a literary fashion for inveterate town dwellers to idealize and sentimentalize country life.

Autograph:	Pierpont Morgan Library, New York (first draft)
First edition:	Published as part of the AGA in 1895 (P658)
Subsequent editions:	Not in Peters; AGA XX 265: Vol. 4/212; NSA IV: Vol. 11/12
Discography and timing:	Fischer-Dieskau I 8[13] 1'00 (first strophe only)
	Hyperion I 5[1]
	Hyperion II 16[8] 3'08 Elizabeth Connell

⟵ *Der Sänger am Felsen* D482   *Gesang der Geister über den Wassern* D484 ⟶

LIED (Ins stille Land)   Song
(SALIS-SEEWIS) **D403** [H240]

The song exists in four versions:
(1) 27 March 1816; (2) April 1816; (3) November 1816?; (4) August 1823

(1) 'Mässig'   G minor   §   [23 bars]

(2) A minor

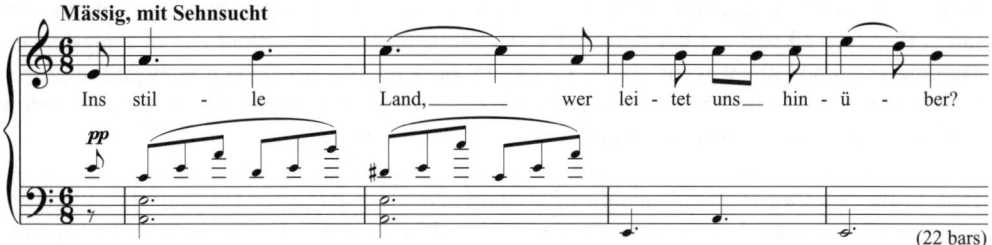

Mässig, mit Sehnsucht

Ins stil - le Land,_____ wer lei - tet uns_ hin - ü - ber?

pp

(22 bars)

(3) 'Langsam, mit Sehnsucht'   A minor   §   [24 bars]

(4) 'Mit Sehnsucht'   A minor   §   [29 bars]

Ins stille Land!	To the land of rest!
Wer leitet uns hinüber?	Who will lead us there?
Schon wölkt sich uns der Abendhimmel trüber,	Already the evening sky grows darker with cloud,
Und immer trümmervoller wird der Strand.	And the shore is ever more strewn with flotsam.
Wer leitet uns mit sanfter Hand	Who will lead us gently by the hand
Hinüber! ach! hinüber	Across, ah, across
Ins stille Land?	To the land of rest?
Ins stille Land!	To the land of rest!
Zu euch, ihr freien Räume	To the free, ennobling spaces!
Für die Veredlung! zarte Morgenträume	Tender morning dreams
Der schönen Seelen! künft'gen Daseins Pfand.	Of fine souls! Pledge of a future life!
Wer treu des Lebens Kampf bestand,	He who faithfully won life's battle
Trägt seiner Hoffnung Keime	Carries the seeds of his hopes
Ins stille Land.	To the land of rest.
Ach Land! ach Land!	O land
Für alle Sturmbedrohten.	For all those threatened by storms.
Der mildeste von unsers Schicksals Boten	The gentlest harbinger of our fate
Winkt uns, die Fackel umgewandt,	Beckons us, brandishing a torch,
Und leitet uns mit sanfter Hand	And leads us gently by the hand
Ins Land der grossen Toten,	To the land of the great dead,
Ins stille Land.	The land of rest.

JOHANN GAUDENZ VON SALIS-SEEWIS (1762–1834); poem written in 1800/1806

This is the seventh of Schubert's thirteen Salis-Seewis solo settings (1816–?1821). See the poet's biography for a chronological list of all the Salis-Seewis settings.

Death was a favourite theme of Salis-Seewis. The messenger of fate ('Schicksals Bote') mentioned in the third verse is Hermes whose torch illuminates the way to the land of rest where the 'great dead' ('die grossen Toten') reside ennobled and free. Judging by its four surviving autographs this haunting little song appears to have been a great favourite in the composer's lifetime – and little wonder. It has a power and emotional scope that are quite disproportionate to its length and musical means. In its third version the song was included in the collection of lieder made for Therese Grob, who was said to have been Schubert's beloved in his youth. The tune is, in

John Reed's words, 'characteristically poised between sorrow and hope'. Simple though it seems to be, there are all sorts of harmonic expressive touches that show the hand of a master; for example, the momentary intrusion of a grating D sharp into the accompaniment (in the second full bar of the piece, under the word 'Land') that reflects a passing twinge of fear and pain, gently resolved in the soul's otherwise smooth passage to the realms of peace.

This melody is a rare exception in that Schubert used it again, with certain alterations, in 1826 as the basis for the final version of Mignon's *Nur wer die Sehnsucht kennt* D877/4. That poem from Goethe's *Wilhelm Meister* had tantalized him for a number of years. He had already composed no fewer than four previous versions of the famous lyric and clearly felt he had failed to master it until the melody of *Lied* (*Ins stille Land*) insinuated itself into his mind (sufficient proof against the preposterous notion that the composer was capable of forgetting his own music the day after writing it). It is easy to see how this serene little song which gently bemoans, and at the same time accepts, the dictates of fate, should have seemed appropriate for the character of Mignon whose own lament about the suffering of longing is tempered, in the first section of the song at least, by calm and resignation. Schubert's reading of Mignon's 'Sehnsucht' seems to have been that she too longed for 'das stille Land' and the grave.

There are four versions of the song printed in Volume 10 of the NSA. The first of these (27 March 1816) is marked 'Mässig' and is in G minor. This was the version published by Diabelli in the *Nachlass*, and thus the one to appear in the Peters Edition. (It is also the version that was recorded with Margaret Price for Hyperion.) The second version is Schubert's fair copy (dated April 1816, marked 'Mässig, mit Sehnsucht') in A minor and it is logical to regard this version as definitive. Two further copies were written out in albums. The first of these (almost certainly in November 1816) was for the album dedicated to Therese Grob; the key is A minor, the marking 'Langsam, mit Sehnsucht' and a few thrummed tonic chords serve as an introduction. The last 'Fassung' ('Mit Sehnsucht') was written out in 1823 for an unknown friend; the opening bars of introduction are more ornate than in the third version (incorporating a second beat in subdominant harmony); there are added bars to enable breathing between phrases; and the final cadence is smoothed out by some added beats in the accompaniment. Singers may prefer this version which was published only in 2002. Diabelli was so bold as to add a four-bar introduction of his own to the first published edition (1845) of the G minor version; this is a notable failure, simultaneously banal and sentimental, and performers using the Peters Edition should omit it.

It is obvious that Schubert conceived his tune for the first verse of the poem with its majority of end-stopped lines. In the first strophe there is only one moment, between the fifth and sixth lines (bb. 16–17) where the meaning carries through from 'Hand' to 'Hinüber'. The second verse (and to a lesser extent the third) bristles with similar enjambments, however, and in order to make sense of the words the performer has to work out completely different phrasing and breathing at the same time as attempting to preserve the original melodic flow.

Autographs:	Staatsbibliothek Preussischer Kulturbesitz, Berlin (first version)
	Wienbibliothek im Rathaus, Vienna (fair copy, second version)
	In private possession in Switzerland (third version; Therese Grob songbook; as well as a fourth version)
	In private possession (fourth version)
Publication:	First published as Book 39 no. 3 of the *Nachlass* by Diabelli, Vienna in 1845 (P356; first version)
	First published as part of the AGA in 1895 (P628; second version)
	First published as part of the NSA in 2002 (P829; third version)
	First published as part of the NSA in 2002 (P830; fourth version)

Subsequent editions:	Peters: Vol. 6/25; AGA XX 201a & b: Vol. 4/66; NSA IV: Vol. 10/108, 110, 112 & 114
Bibliography:	Capell 1928, p. 117
Further settings:	Benedict Randhartinger (1802–1893) *Ins Stille Land* (quartet, SATB with piano, dedicated to Schubert)
	Jan Bedřich Kittl (1806–1868) *Ins Stille Land* Op. 4 no. 6 (*c.* 1830)
Discography and timing:	Fischer-Dieskau I 6[24] 1'09 (first strophe only)
	Hyperion I 15[9]
	Hyperion II 13[14] 3'00 Margaret Price

← *An die Harmonie* D394   *Abschied von der Harfe* D406 →

LIED (Mutter geht durch ihre Kammern)   Song
(Fouqué) **D373** [H218]
G minor   15 January 1816?

(11 bars)

Mutter geht durch ihre Kammern
Räumt die Sachen ein und aus,[1]
Sucht, und weiss nicht was, mit Jammern,
Findet nichts als leeres Haus.

Leeres Haus! O Wort der Klage,
Dem, der einst ein holdes Kind
Drin gegängelt hat am Tage,
Drin gewiegt in Nächten lind.

Wieder grünen wohl die Buchen,
Wieder kommt der Sonne Licht,
Aber, Mutter, lass' dein Suchen,
Wieder kommt dein Liebes nicht.

Und wenn Abendlüfte fächeln,
Vater heim zum Herde kehrt,
Regt sich's fast in ihm, wie Lächeln,
Dran doch gleich die Träne zehrt.

Mother goes through her rooms,
Moves the furniture here, then there
Seeks she knows not what, with sorrow
Finds nothing but an empty house.

Empty house! O words of grief
For one who once cosseted there
A sweet child in the daytime
And gently rocked it to sleep at night.

The beech-trees will grow green again,
The light of the sun will return,
But, mother, cease your searching,
Your beloved child will not return.

And when the evening breezes stir,
And the father returns home to the fireside,
There's a flicker of something like a smile
Within him, wasted straight away by tears.

[1] Fouqué writes 'Räumt die *Schränke* [cupboards] ein und aus'.

Vater weiss, in seinen Zimmern	Father knows that in his rooms
Findet er die Todesruh',	He will find the peace of death.
Hört nur bleicher Mutter Wimmern,	He will hear only the whimpering of the pallid mother,
Und kein Kindlein lacht ihm zu.	And no little child will gurgle at him.

FRIEDRICH DE LA MOTTE FOUQUÉ (1777–1843); poem written before 1811

This is the fourth of Schubert's five Fouqué solo settings (c. 1814–17). See the poet's biography for a chronological list of all the Fouqué settings.

This tiny strophic song was composed two days before the epic Ossian setting *Lodas Gespenst* D150 (also in the key of G minor), evidence, if any were needed, that Schubert's song-writing activity in 1816 was wide-ranging. Fouqué's words are from his famous novella *Undine* (1811), the tale of a water sprite (as *Ondine* later to inspire Ravel, among many others). In the manner of Hans Christian Andersen's little mermaid, Undine falls in love with a mortal, the knight Huldbrand. She marries him and acquires a soul, but Huldbrand is smitten with the beautiful Bertalda, thought to be the daughter of a duke. This song about the loss of a child leads up to

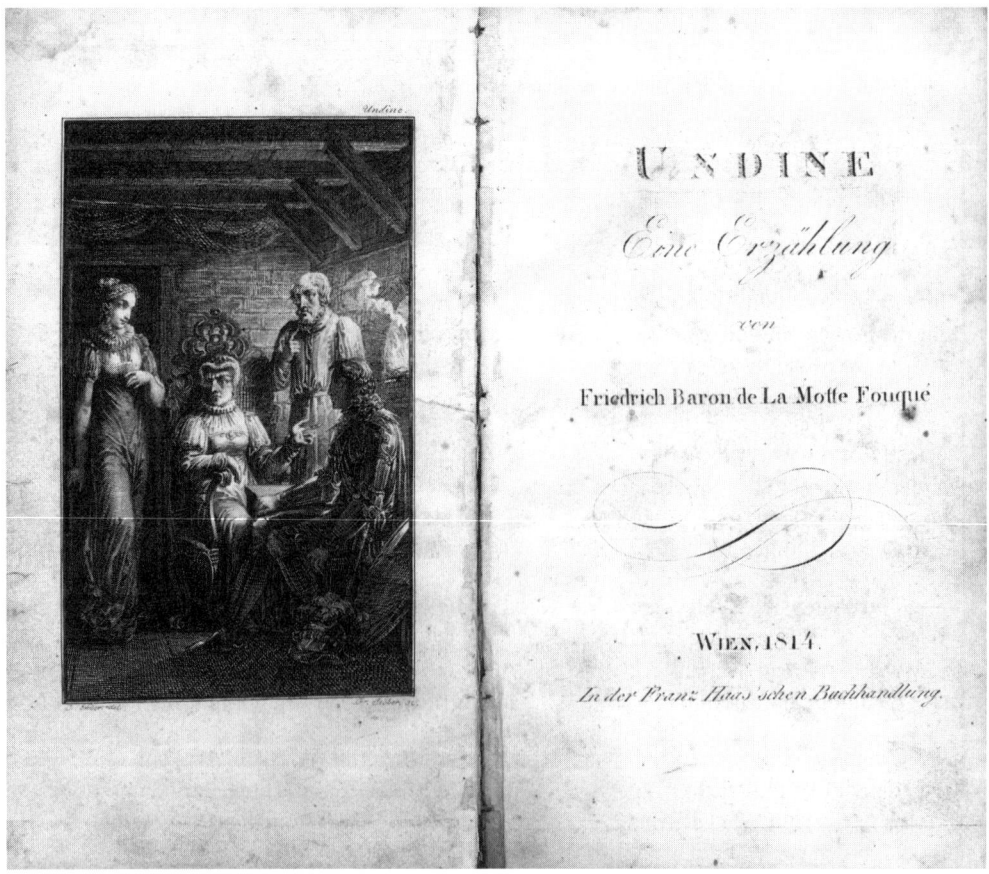

Title page of Fouqué's *Undine*, Viennese edition (1814).

the wayward water sprite's ingenuous but devastating revelation that the same poor fisher couple who gave her a home are also Bertalda's parents. Bertalda, who has long thought herself to be of noble birth, is horrified to be claimed by them. This little lute-accompanied ballad is sung by Undine in the book's eleventh chapter – 'Bertalda's Name Day'.

Schubert succeeds in giving this folksong-like music the character of a spell or incantation. It is much more memorable than a tune of such simplicity deserves to be, not to mention the accompaniment that presents no challenge to anyone with even a rudimentary ability to play the piano. There is no doubt that the composer would have read de la Motte Fouqué's short work from cover to cover (probably in the Franz Haas edition published in Vienna in 1814) and that he would also have been aware of the supernatural, Lorelei-like character of the singer. Although the words are actually about the loss of a child, rather than its death, Schubert was perhaps drawn to this text because of the many sad experiences of infant mortality in his parents' household. Visits to the graveyard must have been a regular occurrence for his family.

Autograph:	Wienbibliothek im Rathaus, Vienna (first draft)
First edition:	Published as part of the AGA in 1895 (P619)
Subsequent editions:	Not in Peters; AGA XX 184: Vol. 4/3; NSA IV: Vol. 10/24
Discography and timing:	Fischer-Dieskau —
	Hyperion I 17[1]
	Hyperion II 12[13] 1'49 Lucia Popp

← *An die Natur* D372   *Lodas Gespenst* D150 →

LIED (ZUFRIEDENHEIT) *see* ZUFRIEDENHEIT D362 & D501

LIED AN DEN TOD *see* AN DEN TOD D518

LIED AUS DER FERNE   Song from afar
(Matthisson) **D107** [H39]

The song exists in two versions, both of which are discussed below:
(1) July 1814; (2) November 1816?

(1) E major

(18 bars)

(2) 'Etwas geschwind'   D major   §   [18 bars]

Wenn, in des Abends letztem Scheine,	When in the dying light of evening,
Dir eine lächelnde Gestalt,	As you sit on the sward in the oak grove,
Am Rasensitz im Eichenhaine,	A smiling figure passes you,
Mit Wink und Gruss vorüberwallt,	Waving a greeting,
Das ist des Freundes treuer Geist,	That is the faithful spirit of your friend,
Der Freud' und Frieden dir verheisst.	Promising you joy and peace.
Wenn in des Mondes Dämmerlichte	When in the moon's dusky light
Sich deiner Liebe Traum verschönt,	Your dream of love grows fairer,
Durch Cytisus und Weimutsfichte	And a melodious rustling echoes
Melodisches Gesäusel tönt,	Through laburnum and pine,
Und Ahnung dir den Busen hebt:	And your breast swells with a presentiment,
Das ist mein Geist, der dich umschwebt.	It is my spirit which hovers about you.
Fühlst du, beim seligen Verlieren	If, lost in blissful contemplation
In des Vergangnen Zauberland,	Of the magic realm of the past,
Ein lindes, geistiges Berühren,	You feel a gentle, unearthly touch
Wie Zephyrs Kuss an Lipp' und Hand,	Like the kiss of Zephyr on your lips and hands,
Und wankt der Kerze flatternd Licht:	And if the wavering candlelight flickers:
Das ist mein Geist, o zweifle nicht!	That is my spirit, do not doubt it!
Hörst du, beim Silberglanz der Sterne,	If, by the silver light of the stars,
Leis' im verschwiegnen Kämmerlein,	In your secret chamber
Gleich Aeolsharfen aus der Ferne,	You hear, like soft, distant aeolian harps,
Das Bundeswort: Auf ewig dein!	The words of our bond: For ever yours!
Dann schlummre sanft; es ist mein Geist,	Then sleep sweetly; it is my spirit
Der Freud' und Frieden dir verheisst.	That promises you joy and peace.

FRIEDRICH VON MATTHISSON (1761–1831); poem written in 1792/3

This is the eleventh of Schubert's twenty-nine Matthisson solo settings (1812–17). See the poet's biography for a chronological list of all the Matthisson settings.

John Reed finds this delightful strophic song too light-hearted for its 'ghost-haunted poem'. And yet Schubert saw reflected in it the affectionate dabbling with the occult that was part of the Romantic spirit of the times. This is perfectly caught, for example, in a letter that Robert Schumann wrote to the young Clara Wieck in 1833: 'Tomorrow at the stroke of 11, I shall play the Adagio from Chopin's *Variations* and at the same time I shall think of you very hard; exclusively of you. Now, the request is that you should do the same, so that we may see each other and meet in spirit . . . If you do not, a piano string will break at 12 o'clock; it will be me.'

If one believes that both lovers are alive, and merely parted by distance, the teasing tone of this song is more understandable. The poem's subtext is 'Ich denke dein', and it is uncanny how the setting is reminiscent of the music Beethoven wrote for Matthisson's poem *Andenken* WoO136 (beginning 'Ich denke dein'): there is the same lilting $\frac{6}{8}$ rhythm, a similarity in the cast of the accompaniment and, in the second of the song's two versions, the same tonality of D major. The distance between the vocal line and the accompaniment, which is consigned to the upper reaches of the bass clef (the tenor register) for long stretches, is prophetic of a much greater song, also set in the countryside: when we hear the music for the words 'Am Rasensitz im Eichenhaine' (bb. 5–7), we can just make out the haunting shape, accompaniment and A major tonality of the opening passage of *Des Müllers Blumen* ('Am Bach viel kleine Blumen stehn') from the cycle *Die schöne Müllerin* D795/9. The two songs, composed almost nine years apart, also share a § time signature.

The manuscript of the first version of the song (from July 1814) is lost, but the NSA prints this version in E major, with the marking 'Allegretto'. The 'Zwischenspiel' and postlude here (bb. 35–6 and 52–3) is cheekier with its dotted rhythms, and the accompaniments to the second and third verses temporarily blossom into more active semiquavers (bb. 27–8). The E major version is the only one to be found in the AGA. It is significant that in 1816 Schubert wrote out the song in D major for the lieder album he prepared for Therese Grob. This version (the NSA's 'Zweite Fassung') is marked 'Etwas geschwind' with slightly more straightforward figurations in some of the accompaniment. The downward transposition and the smoothing out of the piano writing makes something more intimate of the song; as this represents Schubert's second thoughts, two years after he had first composed the song, this version is perhaps to be preferred.

Autograph:	Missing or lost (first version)
	In private possession (second version; part of the Therese Grob album)
Publication:	Published as part of the AGA in 1894 (P542; first version)
	Published as part of the NSA in 1968 (P733; second version)
Subsequent editions:	Not in Peters; AGA XX 21: Vol. 1/158; NSA IV: Vol. 7/26 & 29; Bärenreiter: Vol. 5/126 (first version, high voice), 120 (first version, medium/low voice), 129 (second version, high voice) & 123 (second version, medium/low voice)
Further settings:	Ferdinand Ries (1784–1838) *Lied aus der Ferne* Op. 35 no. 6 (1811)
	Mauro Guiliani (1781–1820) *Lied aus der Ferne* Op. 89 no. 2, with piano or guitar accompaniment (1817)
Discography and timing:	Fischer-Dieskau I 2³ 1'37 (first two strophes only)
	Hyperion I 12¹⁵
	Hyperion II 3¹¹ 2'54 Adrian Thompson

← *Die Befreier Europas in Paris* D104   *Lied der Liebe* D109 →

LIED DER ABWESENHEIT *see* LIED IN DER ABWESENHEIT D416

LIED DER ANNE LYLE   Annot Lyle's song
(Scott) Op. 85 no. 1, **D830** [H557]
C minor   Early 1825?

(62 bars)

Original lines from Love and Loyalty *by Andrew Macdonald, quoted by Sir Walter Scott in* The Legend of Montrose *(translator unknown, but possibly Craigher von Jachelutta). A literal rendering of the German version is given here. The character is 'Annot Lyle' in the original Scott story, a Highland variation that is not reflected in this German translation. Macdonald's original is printed below in italics. See also the biographical article on* MACDONALD.

Wärst du bei mir im Lebenstal,	If you were with me in life's valley,
Gern wollt' ich alles mit dir teilen;	I would gladly share everything with you;
Mit dir zu flieh'n wär' leichte Wahl,	It would be an easy choice to fly with you
Bei mildem Wind, bei Sturmes Heulen.	In gentle breezes, or in the howling storm.
Doch trennt uns harte Schicksalsmacht,	But the harsh power of fate separates us;
Uns ist nicht gleiches Loos geschrieben,	We are not granted the same destiny.
Mein Glück ist, wenn dir Freude lacht,	Happiness is mine when joy smiles upon you;
Ich wein' und bete für den Lieben.	I weep and pray for my beloved.
Es wird mein töricht' Herz vergeh'n,	My foolish heart will beat no more
Wenn's alle Hoffnung sieht verschwinden,	If it sees all hope vanish.
Doch soll's nie seinen Gram gesteh'n,	But it shall never admit its grief,
Nie mürrisch klagend ihn verkünden.	Nor proclaim it with sullen lament.
Und drückt des Lebens Last das Herz,	And if life's burden oppresses my heart,
Soll nie den matten Blick sie trüben,	It shall never cloud my weary eyes
So lange mein geheimer Schmerz	While my secret sorrow
Ein Kummer wäre für den Lieben.	May distress my beloved.

Wert thou, like me, in life's low vale, / With thee how blest, that lot I share; / With thee I'd fly wherever gale / Could waft, or bounding galley bear. / But parted by severe decree, / Far different must our fortunes prove; / May thine be joy – enough for me / To weep and pray for him I love.

The pangs this foolish heart must feel, / When hope shall be forever flown, / No sullen murmur shall reveal, / No selfish murmurs ever own. / Nor will I through life's weary years, / Like a pale drooping mourner move, / While I can think my secret tears / May wound the heart of him I love.

ANDREW MACDONALD (1757–1790) QUOTED AND ADAPTED BY SIR WALTER SCOTT (1771–1832); TRANSLATED BY (?) JACOB NICOLAUS CRAIGHER DE JACHELUTTA (1797–1855)

This is probably the first of Schubert's eight Scott solo settings (1825–6). See the poet's biography for a chronological list of all the Scott settings, and the biography of Macdonald for the original poem before Scott adapted it as above.

With the firm of Constable in Edinburgh, Jedediah Cleishbotham, schoolmaster and parish-clerk of Gandercleugh, published *Tales of my Landlord* (Third Series) in 1819. This was of course Sir Walter Scott's temporary pseudonym. The first two and a half volumes of the printed set of four are given over to *The Bride of Lammermoor*, the sad tale of Lucy Ashton, immortalized in Donizetti's opera as *Lucia di Lammermoor*. *The Legend of Montrose*, from which work this song is taken, occupies the remaining part of Volume 3 and all of Volume 4. As far as the plot concerns the Schubert-lover, Annot Lyle (named as 'the faery-queen of song and minstrelsy' on p. 233 of the novel's first edition, or 'the most beautiful little fairy certainly that ever danced upon a heath by moonlight' p. 257) was carried off in infancy (and in complicated Scott-plot fashion) by a savage tribe known as the Children of the Mist; later she was snatched away once again, this time during a raid by the M'Aulay clan who raised her as one of their own. At the time of the novel she is eighteen but 'she might have passed for four years younger ... Her hair was a dark shade of the colour usually termed flaxen, whose clustering ringlets suited admirably with her fair complexion' (pp. 272–3). Of almost saint-like disposition, she is given to singing with angelic voice and playing on the clairshach, or Scottish harp. In this respect she is related to Scott's other heroine, Ellen Douglas. Both of Scott's maidenly creations were inspired by Goethe's Mignon. Annot is torn between her true affections for the Earl Menteith and her loyalty to the choleric Allan M'Aulay.

Annot sings the lyric just after Allan M'Aulay has revealed his love to her; he berates her for continuing to love the Earl Menteith, for whom, in any case, she considers herself unworthy by birth. 'Her affection [for Menteith] was of that quiet, timid, meditative character, which sought rather a reflected share in the happiness of the beloved object, than formed more presumptuous or daring hopes.' Annot eventually discovers that she is the daughter of the noble Duncan Campbell of Ardenvohr;

Annot Lyle with Lord Monteith and Allan M'Aulay, drawing by W. E. Lockhart, 1877.

she is able to marry Menteith, of course, and thus effects a reconciliation (always a paramount theme in Scott's work), in this case between the factions of Cavalier and Presbyterian. The title of Scott's novel refers to a real historical character: James Graham, Earl of Montrose (1612–1650) who was hanged in Edinburgh for his loyalty to the Royalist cause. Such was the popularity of the character of Annot Lyle in German-speaking lands that one Georg Lotz wrote a novel 'frei nach Scott' ('loosely based on Scott'), published in Hamburg in 1822, entitled *Annot Lyle, die Harfnerin* in which the plagiarist concentrates on the love story and ignores Scott's complicated historical plot.

If we wish to find a musical clue to the character of Annot's song we have only to follow her progress through the book, which suggests that Schubert did the same. The music sounds as unaffectedly simple as a Scottish folksong. Einstein explains this by drawing parallels with the Andante of the E flat Piano Trio D929, in the same key and with a similar kind of C minor melody with throbbing staccato accompaniment that also switches suddenly to E flat major. It is said that that movement is modelled on a Swedish folksong, and a certain 'Nordic' character is common to both pieces. It is also possible that Schubert had studied some of the Beethoven folksong arrangements (settings of Burns among many others) where the lilt of the Caledonian muse sometimes survives that great master's adaptations. The harmonies and repetitions suggest the soft turning away of wrath – direct confrontation sidestepped by a small, well-turned ankle, for here is also the momentum of a slow, sad dance, perhaps a reflection of Scott's description of Annot as a fairy-like dancer in Chapter V of his novel. In a similar way, Mignon's *Heiss mich nicht reden* D877/2 has the air of a transcendental pavane. With the arrival of C major from b. 19 there are brave smiles through tears. The shyly insistent repeated thirds in the right hand of the opening of the piano's ritornello tug at the sleeve and the heartstrings. Together, voice and piano dare to dream of love, while miraculously mirroring Scott's description of a lack of presumption: legato cantilena alternates with staccato passages, where Annot steps forward in a boldness born of strong emotion, only to retreat in diffidence. Although it lacks the rounded immediacy and dramatic variety of Ellen's music (that other great Schubert–Scott heroine from *The Lady of the Lake*), this song is an unjustly forgotten gem in the Schubert catalogue.

In connection with the song and its German text, both the Deutsch catalogue and NSA mention Sophie May, the pseudonym of the Berlin authoress Sophie Mayer (1788–1827). She translated many novels of Scott, and O. E. Deutsch believed she was the translator of *Lied der Anne Lyle*, although scholarly sources assert that no translation of *A Legend of Montrose* can be traced to her. This is no doubt because her translation of that novel was published with the following title page: *Allan Mac-Aulay, der Seher des Hochlandes. Eine Legende aus den Kriegen von Montrose. Von Walter Scott aus dem Englischen übersetzt von Sophie May. Wien, Mausberger's Druck und Verlag, 1826.* Having discovered this two-volume edition, I was disappointed to find that the poem in question in Book II, Chapter 10 of the translation (beginning 'Wärst du wie ich im niedern Thal geboren / Wie selig, selig pries' ich dann mein Los!), bears no resemblance to Schubert's text.

The proximity of this song to *Die junge Nonne* D828 and *Der blinde Knabe* D833 suggests, however, that the translation might have been undertaken by Schubert's enthusiastic new colleague Nikolaus Craigher de Jachelutta (qv), perhaps as a kind of trial run for their collaboration. The Catholicism of the Highlands would have appealed to Craigher, and the related imagery of 'Wie braust durch die Wipfel der heulende Sturm!' in *Die junge Nonne* and 'bei Sturmes Heulen' in *Lied der Anne Lyle* may not be entirely coincidental, particularly as the words 'howling storm' are not to be found in Scott's (or Macdouald's) original English text. Schubert's autograph, had it survived, may well have included a mention of Craigher's name.

Autograph:	Missing or lost
First edition:	Published as Op. 85 no. 1 by Diabelli, Vienna in March 1828 (P153)
Subsequent editions:	Peters: Vol. 4/63 as *Lied der Anna Lyle*; AGA XX 541: Vol. 9/78; NSA IV: Vol. 4a/62; Bärenreiter: Vol. 3/38
Bibliography:	Capell 1928, p. 243
	Einstein 1951, p. 351
Discography and timing:	Fischer-Dieskau —
	Hyperion I 13[9]
	Hyperion II 29[12] 4'26 Marie McLaughlin

← *Die junge Nonne* D828   *Gesang der Norna* D831 →

LIED DER DELPHINE *see ZWEI SZENEN AUS DEM SCHAUSPIEL LACRIMAS* D857/1

LIED DER DIDONE *see* VEDI QUANTO [T']ADORO (DIDONE ABBANDONATA) D510

LIED DER LIEBE
(MATTHISSON) **D109** [H40]
B♭ major   July 1814

Song of love

(31 bars)

Durch Fichten am Hügel, durch Erlen am
   Bach,
Folgt immer dein Bildnis, du Traute! mir nach.
Es lächelt bald Liebe, es lächelt bald Ruh',[1]
Im freundlichen Schimmer des Mondes, mir zu.

Past spruces on hillsides, through alders by
   the brook
Your image, beloved, follows me always.
To me it smiles now love, now peace
In the kindly glimmer of the moon.

Den Rosengesträuchen des Gartens entwallt

Im Glanze der Frühe die holde Gestalt;
Sie schwebt aus der Berge bepurpurtem Flor
Gleich einem elysischen Schatten hervor.

In the brightness of early morning your fair
   form
Arises from the rose bushes in the garden;
It floats from the crimson-flowering mountains
Like an Elysian shadow.

Oft hab' ich, im Traume, die schönste der
   Feen,[2]
Auf goldenem Throne dich strahlen gesehn;

Oft hab' ich, zum hohen Olympus entzückt,

Als Hebe dich unter den Göttern erblickt.

Often in dreams I have seen you,

The loveliest of fairies, radiant on your golden
   throne;
Often I have glimpsed you, spirited to lofty
   Olympus,
As Hebe among the gods.

Mir hallt aus den Tiefen, mir hallt von
   den Höhn,
Dein himmlischer Name wie Sphärengetön.

Ich wähne den Hauch, der die Blüten umwebt,
Von deiner melodischen Stimme durchbebt.

From the depths, from the heights

I hear your heavenly name echo like music of
   the spheres;
I imagine the scent enveloping the blossom
Shot through with your melodious voice.

In heiliger Mitternachtstunde durchkreist
Des Äthers Gefilde mein ahnender Geist.
Geliebte! dort winkt uns ein Land, wo
   der Freund
Auf ewig der Freundin sich wieder vereint.

At midnight's holy hour my prescient mind
Floats through the realms of the ether.
Beloved! There a land beckons

Where lover and beloved are forever reunited.

---

[1] Matthisson writes 'Es lächelt bald *Wehmut*, es lächelt bald Ruh' ('It smiles now melancholy, now peace').
[2] Matthisson writes 'Oft hab' ich im Traume, *als* die schönste der Feen'.

Die Freude, sie schwindet, es dauert kein Leid;	Joy vanishes, no sorrow endures;
Die Jahre verrauschen im Strome der Zeit;	The years flow away in the river of time;
Die Sonne wird sterben, die Erde vergehn:	The sun will die, the earth perish:
Doch Liebe muss ewig und ewig bestehn.	But love must last for ever and ever.

Friedrich von Matthisson (1761–1831); poem written in 1792/3

This is the thirteenth of Schubert's twenty-nine Matthisson solo settings (1812–17). See the poet's biography for a chronological list of all the Matthisson settings.

The Matthisson songs provide a glimpse into the young composer's song workshop in 1814. In *Trost. An Elisa* D97 he had fashioned an elaborate recitative, in *Andenken* D99 a simple melody. In *Lied der Liebe* he combines both elements in a form that he was to make increasingly his own – the modified strophic song. But this song is not entirely Schubert's own. If one thought that Zumsteeg influenced Schubert only in the writing of ballads, a study of the older composer's setting of this poem offers a number of surprises: the B flat major tonality, the rhythmic shape of the entire vocal line and even some of the harmonic progressions stem from the Zumsteeg version from near the end of Volume IV of that composer's *Kleine Balladen und Lieder*, published in Leipzig between 1800 and 1805. Of course, much has been remodelled and given touches of Schubertian felicity, and the accompaniment is very different. Zumsteeg's tempo is 'Etwas langsam'. Schubert's 'Allegretto' suggests that he takes the poet's imagery, already rather old-fashioned for 1814, a mite less seriously.

After two bars of introduction, the jaunty tune begins, built with sequences of rising progressions that suggest the excitement of awaiting the beloved. In each strophe the accompaniment begins in quavers and overflows into semiquavers. It all seems gently suitable for the poem's meaning without providing particularly illuminating insights; the vivid concision of Goethe was soon to bring the best out of Schubert in this respect. For the treatment of the fifth verse there is a welcome change to recitative. Schubert draws on what he has learned earlier in his Matthisson settings, and what did not occur to Zumsteeg: the stroke of midnight (the sforzato at b. 22) inevitably reminds one of *Der Geistertanz* D15 (he has now learned that the midnight chime can be suggested without extending the illustration to a literal count of twelve) and the promise of reunion in the afterlife (bb. 27–30) goes straight back to the visionary tone of *Trost. An Elisa*. The problem of returning convincingly to the main melody after this is not entirely satisfactorily solved – the song's conclusion from the Tempo I of b. 30 is sudden and contrived – despite there being some excuse for this with the words 'Die Freude, sie schwindet'. Much of the blame for a certain awkwardness in this song lies at Matthisson's door; his lyrics are generally attractive, but they offer little scope for internal development in musical terms.

Autograph:	Missing or lost
First edition:	Published as part of the AGA in 1894 (P544)
Subsequent editions:	Not in Peters; AGA XX 23: Vol. 1/163; NSA IV: Vol. 7/33; Bärenreiter: Vol. 5/133 (high voice), 127 (medirem/low voice)
Further settings:	Johann Rudolf Zumsteeg (1760–1802) *Lied der Liebe* (1800) Johann Wenzel Kalliwoda (1801–1866) *Lied der Liebe* Op. 117 (1852) Felix Mendelssohn (1809–1847) *Durch Fichten am Hügel* (September 1823)

Discography and timing: Fischer-Dieskau I 2[5]   1'53   (strophes 1, 4, 5 & 6 only)
                          Hyperion I 12[14]
                          Hyperion II 3[12]   2'48   Adrian Thompson

←— *Lied aus der Ferne* D107   *Der Abend* D108 —→

LIED DER MIGNON *see: GESÄNGE AUS WILHELM MEISTER* D877/1–4;
MIGNON (Kennst du das Land?) D321; MIGNON (So lasst mich scheinen,
bis ich werde) D469 I & II; MIGNON I ('Heiss mich nicht reden') D726;
MIGNON II ('So lasst mich scheinen') D727; SEHNSUCHT ('Nur wer die
Sehnsucht kennt) (I) D310, (II) D359, (III) D481, (IV) D656; *See also:*
MIGNON LIEDER (MIGNON'S SONGS) FROM *WILHELM MEISTER*:
AN OVERVIEW

LIED DES FLORIO *see ZWEI SZENEN AUS DEM SCHAUSPIEL LACRIMAS*
D857/2

LIED DES GEFANGENEN JÄGERS *see SIEBEN GESÄNGE AUS WALTER
SCOTT'S FRÄULEIN VOM SEE* Op. 52 no. 7 D843

LIED DES ORPHEUS,   Song of Orpheus as he entered hell
ALS ER IN DIE HÖLLE GING
(Jacobi) **D474** [H295]

The song exists in two versions, both of which are discussed below:
(1) September 1816; (2) 1817 or 1818?

(1) 'Mässig mit Kraft'   G♭ major – D major   **C**   [132 bars]

(2) G♭ major – B♭ major

(1)   Wälze dich hinweg, du wildes Feuer!   Roll back, savage fire!
        Diese Saiten hat ein Gott gekrönt;   These strings have been crowned by a god;
        Er, mit welchem jedes Ungeheuer,   With whom every monster
        Und vielleicht die Hölle sich versöhnt.   And perhaps hell itself is reconciled.

(2)	Diese Saiten stimmte seine Rechte:[1]	His right hand tunes these strings;
	Fürchterliche Schatten, flieht!	Flee, dread shadows!
	Und ihr winselnden Bewohner dieser Nächte	And you, whimpering inhabitants of this darkness,
	Horchet auf mein Lied!	Listen to my song!
(3)	Von der Erde, wo die Sonne leuchtet	From earth, where the sun
	Und der stille Mond,	And the silent moon shine,
	Wo der Tau das junge Moos befeuchtet,	Where dew moistens fresh moss,
	Wo Gesang im grünen Felde wohnt;	Where song dwells in green fields;
(4)	Aus der Menschen süssem Vaterlande,	From the sweet country of mankind,
	Wo der Himmel euch so frohe Blicke gab,	Where the heavens once looked upon you with joyful gaze,
	Ziehen mich die schönsten Bande,	I am drawn by the fairest of ties
	Ziehet mich die Liebe selbst herab.	I am drawn down by love itself.
(5)	Meine Klage tönt in eure Klage;	My lament mingles with yours,
	Weit von hier geflohen ist das Glück;	Happiness has fled far from here;
	Aber denkt an jene Tage,	But remember those days,
	Schaut in jene Welt zurück!	Look back into that world!
(6)	Wenn ihr da nur einen Leidenden umarmtet,	If there you embraced but one sufferer,
	O so fühlt die Wollust noch einmal;	Then feel desire once more,
	Und der Augenblick, in dem ihr euch erbarmtet,	And may that moment when you took pity
	Lindre diese lange Qual.	Soothe my long torment.
(7)	O, ich sehe Tränen fliessen!	O, I see tears flowing!
	Durch die Finsternisse bricht	Through the darkness
	Ein Strahl von Hoffnung; ewig büssen[2]	A ray of hope breaks through; the good gods
	Lassen euch die guten Götter nicht!	Will not let you atone for ever.
(8)	Götter, die für euch die Erde schufen,	The gods who created the earth for you
	Werden aus der tiefen Nacht	Will call you from deep night
	Euch in selige Gefilde rufen,	Into the Elysian fields
	Wo die Tugend unter Rosen lacht.	Where virtue smiles amid roses.

JOHANN GEORG JACOBI (1740–1814); poem written *c.* 1770

This is the last of Schubert's seven Jacobi solo settings (1816). See the poet's biography for a chronological list of all the Jacobi settings.

When the three volumes of Jacobi's poems came hot off the press in their first Viennese edition in 1816 (probably passed on to Schubert by one of his literary friends) the composer must have

---

[1] Jacobi writes '*Meine* Saiten'.
[2] Jacobi writes '*Nun* ein Strahl von Hoffnung'.

been more than ready to put his own gloss on the Orpheus legend, a theme thoroughly familiar to him. The connection with Gluck's opera *Orfeo ed Euridice* is obvious enough. Schubert knew the score through Salieri, and during his time as a student at the Imperial Seminary he had once performed the scene in Hades from memory. What is rather less obvious is the link with Mozart; as Eric Sams has demonstrated, this is one of the 1816 songs that shows the direct influence of that master, and of *Die Zauberflöte* in particular. To prove this we need go no further than the introduction to *Lied des Orpheus*, a flourish of six bars in G flat which sets up the hero's command to the fires of hell to roll back: he has come to rescue his Eurydice. If we transfer our gaze to the finale of the first act of *Die Zauberflöte* we can see the similarities. Prince Tamino, like Orpheus, is a tamer of beasts through the magic of music and has come to rescue his bride.

In Mozart the offstage voices sing 'Zurück!' rather than Jacobi's nearly synonymous 'Hinweg'. In response (do not be fooled by the difference in dynamic between Schubert's fortissimo on the piano and Mozart's softer-grained strings) the musical substance is nearly the same: downward-moving arpeggii in groups of four staccato crotchets and the punctuation of loud chords rebuff the efforts of both Orpheus and Tamino to enter where they should not go. Even the trills that launch this figure (starting on F sharp in Mozart, G flat in Schubert) are of the same length (this enharmonic imitation is less plagiarism than hero-worship).

Mozart's responses to words had become for Schubert a private creed, a new mythology of allusion. He was so steeped in this that he used Mozartian quotation, in apposite places, as unselfconsciously as stringing together original sentences in an established language. This was the period when Schubert was forced to realize that his love for Therese Grob was impractical and hopeless. It is not hard to see him casting himself in the heroic role of Orpheus/Tamino and travelling (musically) to the ends of the earth to save an imperilled relationship.

Verses 1–2: The song has a ceremonial air, a highly costumed operatic approach that we find more in the Schiller settings for example, than in the more inward-looking Goethe works. This is a magnificent recitative in a theatrically grand manner. It is surprisingly thrilling when sung by a woman, not least because the character of Gluck's Orfeo is suggested by the mezzo soprano voice (hence the Hyperion recording with Brigitte Fassbaender). In the second verse (from b. 19) Orpheus, while threatening the shadows, turns his lyre's pegs in gradations of rising semitones, from D flat major up to E (shades of the unsuccessful tuning of the same recalcitrant instrument in *An die Leier* D737).

Verses 3–6: At b. 31 there are three important changes: to ⅜, a marking of 'Ziemlich langsam' and a new key signature of A major. This is for the main aria of Orpheus, the central panel of the work and the set piece where the gifted musician shows his mettle. It can surely be no coincidence that all the Harper's songs (from

Orpheus and Eurydice from *Der Mythos alter Dichter,*
Vienna (1815).

Goethe's *Wilhelm Meister*) were conceived at the same time (September 1816) and in the same tonality of A (minor rather than major). Orpheus is thus both the historical antecedent and the musical contemporary of the crazed old Harper who also faces a love-induced hell. That introverted music, however, has little in common with the stagily beguiling, heroic coloratura assigned to Orpheus, often uncomfortably high in the stave. The composer seems to have imagined a singer of suitably mythical powers: high As (bb. 60 and 62) are demanded as readily as the low A flat, two octaves beneath, of the introduction (b. 19). The beginning of Verse 5 (the dovetailing, mingled echoes between voice and piano at 'Meine Klage tönt in eure Klage' from b. 51) marks the start of the substantial differences between the first and second versions of the piece. It is clear that by the time the song was revised in 1817 or 1818, the composer had Johann Michael Vogl in mind, a great singer famously interested in mythology, but a baritone (and an ageing one) rather than a tenor. The hushed piano interlude after Verse 6 (from b. 67), where Orpheus' protestations cease in favour of lyrical, wordless sequences, is among the loveliest moments in the piece.

Verses 7–8: The interlude produces its required effect. As soon as Orpheus sees his first tears he knows he has won (at least for the time being). And from b. 71, with the marking 'Geschwind', and a marking of 'geschwinder werdend' (thus encouraging a general accelerando), we revert to the majestic devices of Gluck. Schubert never wrote anything more Gluckian than the accompaniment between bb. 75 and 89; the motor rhythm and bounce of these weaving quavers is exhilarating. The stage *finale* music of Verse 8 ('Geschwinder' from b. 91) is prophetic of the closing section of the Schiller setting *Sehnsucht* (D636) in terms of both words and music. The 'selige Gefilde' of this poem and Schiller's 'schönes Wunderland' are related territories of mythological imaginings. Here in the vocal line the physical distance between night (the F natural in b. 97) and the Elysian fields (the G at b. 101) is a ninth. Schubert shows something of the same delight in sudden changes between the Stygian depths of the chest register and the heaven of the head voice in that other ballad from the underworld from a few months earlier, *Klage der Ceres* D323. The partial rescue of Proserpine is accomplished in that song but we know that the story of Orpheus and Euridyce will not come to such a happy conclusion. Although we never encounter Eurydice herself, her eventual loss is surely implied by this song's less than triumphant conclusion – still in the major key, certainly, but very much in muted mood. At least this is the case with the first version.

Mention has already been made of the song's two versions. In the AGA Mandyczewski, who much preferred the first, went so far as to suggest that the second was a corrupt adaption made for publication by Diabelli. This does not tally with the facts as we know them. It seems that Schubert was prepared, for practical reasons, to temper his early ideas in order to bring the song into the vocal range of Johann Michael Vogl. This also involved giving the singer greater opportunities to take breaths, and providing him with a fortissimo conclusion. Instead of simply transposing the piece Schubert preferred to recast it, keeping the tonality of the opening intact, but deflecting the music into B flat major (rather than D major) for the closing section. This makes for a lower (and more comfortable) tessitura for a baritone. Usually the second version of a piece is taken as Schubert's last word on the subject, but here it seems clear that if there is a singer brave enough to take on *Lied des Orpheus* in its demanding first version, this would be preferable to the second – still a fine song for lower voices, but somewhat weakened by compromise.

Autograph: Wienbibliothek im Rathaus, Vienna (first version, first draft)
Publication: Published as part of the AGA in 1895 (P650; first version)
                    Published as Book 19 no. 1 of the *Nachlass* by Diabelli, Vienna in
                    1832 (P292; second version)

Subsequent editions:	Peters: Vol. 5/98; AGA XX 250a & b: Vol. 4/164; NSA IV: Vol. 10/226 & 234
Bibliography:	Capell 1928, p. 118
	Einstein 1951, p. 134
	Fischer-Dieskau 1977, p. 75
	Sams 1978, p. 947
Discography and timing:	Fischer-Dieskau I 8² 4'23
	Hyperion I 11¹²
	Hyperion II 15²² 4'30 Brigitte Fassbaender

← *An den Mond* D468   *Mignon ('So lasst mich scheinen')* D469 →

LIED EINES KINDES   A child's song
(Anonymous) **D596** [H390]
(Fragment) B♭ major   November 1817

(24 bars)

Lauter Freude fühl' ich,	I feel nothing but joy,
Lauter Liebe hör' ich,	I hear nothing but love,
Ich so überglücklich	I am such a lucky child,
Fröhlich spielend Kind.	Playing happily.
Dort der gute Vater,	There my good father,
Hier die liebe Mutter	Here my dear mother;
Rund herum wir Kinder	And around them we children
Froh und fröhlich sind!	*Are glad and merry!*

ANONYMOUS/UNKNOWN

This is the sixteenth of Schubert's nineteen solo settings of an anonymous poet. See Anonymous/ Unknown for a chronological list of all the songs for which the poets are unknown.

This jaunty little song fragment is an idealization of happy family life; it has a real Biedermeier quality to it. Fortunately the child is far too impish and roguish for the picture to be sickly sweet. The accompaniment stays in the treble clef for both staves (as if the bass clef is reserved for grown-ups and broken voices) with a range as short as the child itself. The 𝄴 time signature and the air of innocent modesty are reminiscent of Mozart's *Sehnsucht nach dem Frühlinge* K596, the tune of which figures in the final movement of that composer's last Piano Concerto K595, also in B flat. A curious feature is the cheekily perverse use of accents on the third and sixth of the accompanying triplets in bars 9–12. This gives an impression of a game where the child saunters along the road in lopsided manner, one foot on the pavement, the other off. In the Hyperion recording the first twenty-four bars are genuine Schubert, the last four (including the setting of the last line of the poem printed in italics) are by Reinhard Van Hoorickx. It was perhaps also Van Hoorickx who invented this final rhyme for this anonymous poem.

Autograph:	Missing or lost
First edition:	Published as part of the AGA in 1895; subsequently completed by Reinhard Van Hoorickx (P720)
Subsequent editions:	Not in Peters; AGA XX 598: Vol. 10/12; NSA IV: Vol. 11/236
Discography and timing:	Fischer-Dieskau —
	Hyperion I 21[18]
	Hyperion II 19[24] 0'56 Edith Mathis

← *Der Alpenjäger* D588   *Die Forelle* D550 →

LIED EINES KRIEGERS
(Anonymous) **D822** [H553]
A major   31 December 1824

Warrior's song   Bass solo
                & men's chorus

(81 bars)

Solo:
Des stolzen Männerlebens schönste Zeichen
Sind Flamme, Donner und die Kraft der Eichen.
Doch nichts mehr vom Eisenspiel und nichts vom Spiel der Waffen,

Chor:
Der ew'ge Friede ward uns zugewendet,
Dem Schlafe ward die Kraft der Faust verpfändet.

Solo:
Zwar jüngst noch haben wir das Schwert geschwungen
Und kühn auf Leben oder Tod gerungen.
Jetzt aber sind die Tage hohen Kampfs verklungen,
Und was uns blieb aus jenen Tagen,
Es ist vorbei, bald sind's, ach, nur noch Sagen.

Solo:
The finest tokens of proud manhood
Are flame, thunder and the strength of the oak.

But no more talk of the play of steel or the flash of weapons.

Chorus:
Everlasting peace has been granted to us,
And the power of the fist has been pledged to sleep.

Solo:
Not long ago we brandished the sword

And boldly struggled for life or death.
But now the days of high battle have faded away,

And what remained to us of those days
Has passed; soon, alas, there will be mere tales.

Chor:	Chorus:
Und was uns blieb aus jenen Tagen,	And what remained to us of those days
Es ist vorbei, bald sind's, ach, nur noch Sagen.	Has passed; soon, alas, there will be mere tales.

ANONYMOUS/UNKNOWN

We are not certain why Schubert composed this song for bass solo and chorus, but it is likely to have been in connection with the celebrations surrounding New Year's Eve 1824. If he had managed to compose the extended quartet *Gebet* D815 in a single day in September of that year, this must have been a mere hour's work. On first reading, the poem comes across as a rather undistinguished variant of Byron's *So we'll go not more a-roving* – old soldiers hanging up their arms in times of peace, regretting that their best exploits are over. But mention of everlasting peace could also imply that the soldiers are dead, closer to Hardy's ghosts in *Channel Firing* than to Byron's retired libertines. The only musical clue to this in Schubert's rumbustious setting is the male chorus singing (in unison) in the sombre minor key (bb. 31–40, and at the end of the setting).

Otherwise the tonality is an unambiguous A major. The opening left-hand octaves recall the flourishes of *Die Zauberflöte*, and they also have a fortuitous similarity to the introduction of *Una voce poco fa* from Rossini's *Il barbiere di Siviglia*, an opera of 1816 that Schubert almost certainly knew. But this is no song to remind one of Rosina's feminine teasing; on the contrary, all seems designed for the ultra-masculine sing-song. It is possible that the text was written by someone within the Schubert circle and was meant to cater for that rather lachrymose mood of nostalgia (exacerbated by drink) that overtakes the passing of one year into the next.

The incessant dotted rhythms in the solo section are part of Schubert's musical vocabulary for warriors, no doubt because professional fighters spend a lot of their time on horseback, occasioning these jolts and judders. Indeed, Schubert lieder accompanists will be reminded of the left-hand octaves that were soon to pulsate through *Auf der Bruck* D853. There are warlike passages in the quartet *Gebet* (already mentioned above) that employ the rhythmic vocabulary of *Lied eines Kriegers*, but this little party piece also looks to the future: it could be a study for passages in the Walter Scott settings of 1825, particularly *Normans Gesang* D846 (which is a moto perpetuo based on these militarized dotted rhythms) and the stomping of horses' hooves as Ellen attempts to sing the 'Krieger' to rest in *Ellens Gesang* I D837. Schubert, born and brought up at a time of military unrest, had something of a taste for soldiers' music throughout his life – one thinks of such songs as Körner's *Gebet während der Schlacht* D171 from 1815, and *Kriegers Ahnung* D957/2 from 1828, not to mention the *Marches Militaires* for piano duet. The military also features in a number of his operas: again, these range from the beginning of his career (*Der vierjährige Posten* of 1815) to *Fierabras* of 1821/2, and *Der Graf von Gleichen* from the end of his life. All these operas feature knights or soldiers.

Autograph:	Missing or lost
First edition:	Published as Book 35 no. 2 of the *Nachlass* by Diabelli, Vienna in 1842; and subsequently issued a second time as Book 41 no. 1 of the *Nachlass* in *c.* 1847 (P342)
Subsequent editions:	Peters: Vol. 5/204; AGA XX 464: Vol. 8/32; NSA III: Vol. 3
Bibliography:	Orel 1937, pp. 285–98
Discography and timing:	Hyperion I 35[13] Neil Davies with Toby Spence,
	Hyperion II 29[8] 3'06 Daniel Norman, Christopher Maltman & Stephan Loges

←— *Gebet* D815

Im Abendrot D799 —→

LIED EINES SCHIFFERS
AN DIE DIOSKUREN

Boatman's song to the Dioscuri

(Mayrhofer) Op. 65 no. 1, **D360** [H303]

A♭ major   1816?

Dioskuren, Zwillingssterne,
Die ihr leuchtet meinem Nachen,
Mich beruhigt auf dem Meere
Eure Milde, euer Wachen.

Wer auch fest in sich begründet,
Unverzagt dem Sturm' begegnet;
Fühlt sich doch in euren Strahlen
Doppelt mutig und gesegnet.

Dieses Ruder, das ich schwinge,
Meeresfluten zu zerteilen;
Hänge ich, so ich geborgen,
Auf an eures Tempels Säulen.

Dioscuri, twin stars,
Shining on my boat,
Your gentleness and vigilance
Comfort me on the ocean.

However firmly a man believes in himself,
However fearlessly he meets the storm,
He feels doubly valiant and blessed
In your light.

This oar which I ply
To cleave the ocean's waves,
I shall hang, once I have landed safely,
On the pillars of your temple.

JOHANN MAYRHOFER (1787–1836)

This is the eighth of Schubert's forty-seven Mayrhofer solo settings (1814–24). See the poet's biography for a chronological list of all the Mayrhofer settings.

The sons of Zeus, Castor and Polydeuces (Pollux is the Latin version of the name) were long known as the protectors of seamen; the electrical phenomenon now known as St Elmo's fire was taken by the ancients to be their appearance during storms at sea. Legend has it that Castor (a mortal) was killed in a battle; his immortal twin Polydeuces was so devoted to him that he asked Zeus to be permitted to die also. Zeus allowed them to spend alternate days in heaven and Hades together, and later legend identified them with the constellation of Gemini, the Twins. Mayrhofer's attraction to the concept of idealistic love and friendship between men, honoured by heaven (outside a Christian context), speaks for itself. It seems likely that the poet was inspired by a Catullus poem about Castor and Pollux (*see Atys* D585). On another level, exalted in a different way, it is clear that Mayrhofer's art was indebted to the work of those heavenly twins of German literature, Goethe and Schiller.

Analysis can scarcely explain why this modified strophic song touches all who hear it; much of its perennial appeal lies in its melody, the power of which is a Schubertian miracle, so perilously near does it lie to a four-square hymnbook commonplace. Like that other famous hymn *Am Tage Aller Seelen* (*Litanei*) D343 it gives the impression of being a distillation of the most elevated religious feeling, and it seems only natural that the faith of the pagan should be treated as seriously as Catholicism in Schubert's work. This 'Schiffer' is not a modern revolutionary like the boatman of another Mayrhofer song – *Der Schiffer* D536; neither is he the rustic voluptuary of the Schlegel song of the same title, D694. He is a genuine gods-fearing seafarer, such as might have served Odysseus, his calling acknowledged by the two spread chords that open the work like the ripple of water in the wake of a plied oar. Throughout the song, built on a generous and resonant bass line, is the feeling of contact with the currents and depths of the sea but, at the end of the second verse especially, the navigator's eyes and voice are turned heavenward with awe, and the vocal line seems bathed in starlit radiance. This is something to do with the distance between piano sound (both hands in the bass clef) and the voice, a magic-inducing musical span in cosmic space that prophesies *Nacht und Träume* D827. The key is A flat, which Schubert often used for evocations of the wonders of god-in-nature (*see Ganymed* D544). That the gods are kind and merciful is apparent from the beautiful softening of harmony on 'Eure Milde' (bb. 10–11) – merely the simple expedient of a seventh chord, but who but Schubert knows how to place an everyday harmonic standby as tellingly as this?

For the first two lines of the middle verse the piano doubles the vocal line (from b. 21), a simple but perfect way to reflect the meaning of 'Doppelt mutig'. The third verse, a repeat of the first as far as the vocal line is concerned, allows the boatman to resume his work and finish his prayer as he rows. The work is hard, the voyage long and perilous, the progress of the boat slow and arduous – all these things are felt in the depth and grandeur, the tidal tug, of the piano's left hand, as well as the effortful displaced accents of the postlude (bb. 38 and 39). The promise of an offering to the Dioscuri at the end of a voyage is as heartfelt and pious a vow as ever a Christian man made to his maker. The hazardous homebound journey of Odysseus, full of danger, rich in reward, again comes to mind.

There is a handwritten cycle of Mayrhofer poems dating from September–October 1821 entitled *Heliopolis* where this poem is the twentieth in a projected collection that remained incomplete in both literary and musical terms. As a result there is some discussion as to whether the song can truly date from as early as 1816. It is possible that for this new *Heliopolis* project the poet re-used a lyric he had crafted many years earlier – after all the Dioscuri poem, this time entitled *Schiffers Nachtlied*, appears again separately in the first printed edition of the the poems (*Gedichte*, 1824 Wien, Friedrich Volke). John Reed is happier with 1822 on stylistic grounds, and the above-mentioned similarity between vocal versus piano deployment in *Nacht und Träume* (also 1822) supports his thesis. On the other hand, the Witteczek–Spaun collection dates the song from 1816, and the usually reliable Josef von Spaun in his memories of Schubert's life written in 1858 vividly recalled the effect that *Lied eines Schiffers an die Dioskuren* had on the astonished Vogl at his first meeting with Schubert at the beginning of 1817. The question remains open to further discussion and scholastic debate.

Autograph:	Missing or lost
First edition:	Published as Op. 65 no. 1 by Cappi & Czerny, Vienna in November 1826 (P109)
Publication reviews:	*Berliner allgemeine musikalische Zeitung* No. 11 (14 March 1827), p. 81ff. [Waidelich/Hilmar Dokumente I No. 461; Deutsch Doc. Biog. No. 826]
Subsequent editions:	Peters: Vol. 3/32; AGA XX 268: Vol. 4/331; NSA IV: Vol. 3/124; Bärenreiter: Vol. 2/152
Bibliography:	Capell 1928, p. 127

Discography and timing: Fischer-Dieskau I 8[16]   2'31

Hyperion I 14[12]

Hyperion II 16[4]   2'43   Thomas Hampson

←— *Alte Liebe rostet nie D477*   *Wer nie sein Brot mit Tränen ass*
                                                                    D478/2 —→

Das LIED IM GRÜNEN   Song in the country
(Reil) **D917** [H628]
A major   June 1827

(158 bars)

(1)	Ins Grüne, ins Grüne!	To the green countryside!
	Da lockt uns der Frühling der liebliche Knabe,	Spring, that sweet youth, invites us there,
	Und führt uns am blumenumwundenen Stabe,	And leads us with his flower-entwined staff
	Hinaus, wo die Lerchen und Amseln so wach,	To where larks and blackbirds stir,
	In Wälder, auf Felder, auf Hügel, zum Bach	To woods and fields, over hills to the brook,
	Ins Grüne, ins Grüne.	To the green countryside!
(2)	Im Grünen, im Grünen!	In the green countryside,
	Da lebt es sich wonnig, da wandeln wir gerne,	Life is blissful, there we love to roam;
	Und heften die Augen dahin schon von ferne;	Even from afar we fix our eyes on it,
	Und wie wir so wandeln mit heiterer Brust,	And as we wander there with cheerful hearts,
	Umwallet uns immer die kindliche Lust,	A childlike joy envelops us,
	Im Grünen, im Grünen.	In the green countryside!
(3)	Im Grünen, im Grünen,	In the green countryside,
	Da ruht man so wohl, empfindet so Schönes,[1]	We find such peace, and sense such beauty;
	Und denkt behaglich an Dieses und Jenes,	We contentedly dwell on this and that,

[1] Reil writes '*und* empfindet so *Schönes*'.

Und zaubert von hinnen, ach! was uns bedrückt,	Conjure away our troubles,
Und alles herbei, was den Busen entzückt,	And conjure up our hearts' delight,
Im Grünen, im Grünen.	In the green countryside!

(4) Im Grünen, im Grünen,
Da werden die Sterne so klar, die die Weisen
Der Vorwelt zur Leitung des Lebens uns preisen.
Da streichen die Wölkchen so zart uns dahin,
Da heitern die Herzen, da klärt sich der Sinn,
Im Grünen, im Grünen.

In the green countryside,
The stars are so bright, those stars which the wise men
Of old extolled as our life's guidance.
The little clouds glide by so tenderly.
Our hearts are cheered, and our senses clear
In the green countryside!

(5) Im Grünen, im Grünen,
Da wurde manch Plänchen auf Flügeln getragen,
Die Zukunft der grämlichen Aussicht entschlagen.[2]
Da stärkt sich das Auge, da labt sich der Blick,
Leicht tändelt die Sehnsucht dahin und zurück[3]
Im Grünen, im Grünen.

In the green countryside
Many a little plan takes wing,
And the future sheds its gloomy aspect;
The eye is strengthened and the gaze refreshed,
Our longings play gently to and fro,
In the green countryside!

(6) Im Grünen, im Grünen
Am Morgen, am Abend in traulicher Stille
Da wurde manch Liedchen und manche Idylle
Gedichtet, gespielt, mit Vergnügen und Schmerz.[4]
Denn leicht ist die Lockung, empfänglich das Herz
Im Grünen, im Grünen.

In the green countryside,
Morning and evening, in the intimate stillness,
Many a song and many an idyll
Has been written and sung with fun and sorrow,
For temptation comes easy and the heart is receptive
In the green countryside!

(7) Ins Grüne, ins Grüne
Lasst heiter uns folgen dem freundlichen Knaben!
Grünt einst uns das Leben nicht förder, so haben[5]

Into the green countryside
Let us merrily follow the friendly youth.
And when, one day, life no longer blossoms for us,

---

[2] Reil writes 'Ansicht entschlagen'.
[3] Reil writes 'Da tändeln die Wünsche dahin und zurück'.
[4] Reil writes 'Gedichtet, gespielt, in Sehnsucht und Scherz'. In the Peters Edition we find a rewrite: 'Und Hymen oft kränzt den poetischen Scherz'.
[5] Reil writes 'Grünt einst uns das Leben nicht mehr, ey! so haben'. Schubert's simple adjustment seems a major improvement.

Wir klüglich die grünende Zeit nicht versäumt,	Then we shall have been wise enough not to miss the verdant years,
Und wann es gegolten, doch glücklich geträumt,[6]	And shall have dreamed happily when the time was right,
Im Grünen, im Grünen.	In the green countryside!

Friedrich Reil (1773–1843); poem written in 1827

This is Schubert's only Reil solo setting. See the poet's biography.

For a ramble through the highways and byways of springtime and spring thoughts, what could be better than this beloved song? It meanders gently through the green countryside modulating only at major crossroads; smaller country lanes are explored within the home key of A major. Only Schubert could devise such charming twists and turns within the compass of a pianist's hand. The form of this relaxed lied is masterful, however tempting it may be to imagine that Schubert made it up as he went along. There are three main melodies to this sublime Rondo and relaxed moto perpetuo. Verses 1 and 2 are set to the main A major tune (bb. 1–32). Verses 3 and 4 are set to the second tune in D major (from b. 36) with a momentary excursion into B flat major (from b. 45). (D and B flat major contrast in exactly the same way in *Mein!* from *Die schöne Müllerin* D795/11.) In classical rondo fashion Verse 5 of *Das Lied im Grünen* returns to the A major tune (from b. 91). Only in Verse 6 does a third tune appear, derived from the first (from b. 105), but this time with the added presence of the relative minor (from b. 111). It is this strophe that is repeated with new words – see below – in the corrupt but charming variant of the song that has so often been printed as definitive. The last verse appears to be an ordinary rondo repeat at first, but it goes into various keys and ends up in D minor (from b. 141) for momentary musings on mortality. The whole effect is like glimpsing a familiar and loved landmark from different angles in the course of a leisurely walk: once you get home you realize your stroll has taken you full circle. This makes it one of the most treacherous of all Schubert lieder to memorize; one can get as lost as is possible in a dense wood full of inviting little pathways. This is not helped by the apparent sameness of the accompaniment (it is not really at all the same on closer analysis) giving the singer no signposts on which to hang memory pointers in a forest of purling quavers. The first eight quavers of *Das Lied im Grünen* seem to be directly fashioned after the semiquavers of the first piano interlude-variation in *Im Frühling* D882 (from b. 17 of that famous song of spring greenery). Lovers of Schubert's solo piano music might recognize in both songs the tonality and mood of the last movement of the A major Sonata (D959).

Because Friedrich Reil was quite a literary personality in Vienna he is the only poet (apart from that obsessive reviser Franz von Schlechta) who managed to add more of his own words to a composition between Schubert's handing of the manuscript to the publisher and publication – possible only because the composer had died in the meantime. Thus repeat marks were added to the passage that lies between bb. 105 and 120 in the song, and the following verse inserted:

Das Lied im Grünen, vignette for Czerny's arrangement for solo piano (1838–9).

---

[6] Reil writes 'Und, *seit* es gegolten'.

O gerne im Grünen	How I loved being in the countryside
Bin ich schon als Knabe und Jüngling gewesen	Even as a boy and a youth.
Und habe gelernt, und geschrieben, gelesen,	There I learnt, and wrote, and read
Im Horaz und Plato, dann Wieland und Kant,	Horace and Plato, then Wieland and Kant,
Und glühendes Herzens mich seelig genannt	And with a glowing heart deemed myself blessed
Im Grünen, im Grünen.	In the green countryside.

The NSA leaves this verse out and makes clear that there is no scholastic authority whatever for this posthumous addition. The verse remains an option for those singers who believe they have not got enough words to master already, and who like the literary tone provided by the poets' names that trip off the tongue. This can be quite fun and does not seem to damage the musical architecture of the song – singer and pianist just take a slightly longer route home. The posthumous verse is included in the Peters Edition. For further versification by Reil concerning Schubert's untimely demise, as well as a description of the circumstances in which the poem was written in the first place, *see* the poet's biography.

Autograph:	Stanford University, CA (first draft)
First edition:	Published as Op. post. 115 no. 1 by M. J. Leidesdorf, Vienna in June 1829 (P218)
Subsequent editions:	Peters: Vol. 4/132; AGA XX 543: Vol. 9/85; NSA IV: Vol. 14a/45; Bärenreiter: Vol. 4/82
Bibliography:	Capell 1928, p. 244
	Fischer-Dieskau 1977, p. 246–7
	Youens 2002, pp. 309–24
Discography and timing:	Fischer-Dieskau II 9[6] 5'07
	Hyperion I 5[2]
	Hyperion II 33[16] 5'01 Elizabeth Connell

⟵ *Romanze des Richard Löwenherz D907*   *Ständchen D920* ⟶

LIED IN DER ABWESENHEIT   Song of absence
(Stolberg) **D416** [H250]
(Fragment) B minor   April 1816

Ach, mir ist das Herz so schwer!
Traurig irr' ich hin und her,
Suche Ruhe, finde keine,
Geh' an's Fenster hin, und weine!

Ah, my heart is so heavy!
Sadly I wander to and fro.
I seek peace, but find none.
I go to the window and weep!

Sässest du auf meinem Schoss,   If you were sitting on my lap
Würd' ich aller Sorgen los,   All my cares would vanish;
Und aus deinen blauen Augen   And from your blue eyes
Würd' ich Lieb' und Wonne saugen!   I would draw love and bliss!

Könnt' ich doch, du süsses Kind,   Sweet child, if only I could at once
Fliegen hin zu dir geschwind!   Fly swiftly to you!
Könnt' ich ewig dich *umfangen*,   If only I could *embrace* you for ever,
Und an deinen Lippen hangen!   *And hang on your lips!*

Friedrich Leopold, Graf zu Stolberg-Stolberg (1750–1819); poem written in 1775

This is the seventh of Schubert's nine Stolberg settings (1815–23). See the poet's biography for a chronological list of all the Stolberg settings.

John Reed states that 'Schubert's failure to complete this song has deprived us of a minor master-piece.' The first section is in the composer's 'important' key of B minor (before a modulation to G major at b. 9 for the second section, 'ziemlich geschwind') and the sad, weighty utterance of the opening nine bars certainly promises much. The contrast between these bars and the jolly rollicking section beginning 'Sässest du auf meinem Schoss' is so great, however, that it is likely that the composer was not happy with the result. We have here, in effect, two separate songs of such entirely different moods that we end up believing neither the tragic tone of the one (which seems to overstate the case made by the words) nor the rather saucy high spirits of the other.

That said, there is much to treasure here that is genuine Schubert. The B minor section could well be sung by a Mignon or a repentant Gretchen, and the stark prelude of doubled octaves with its dragging gait drained of energy and emotion (and which makes a reappearance before the change of mood) puts us in mind of Goethe's Harper (another creation of 1816). John Reed believed, as did Reinhard Van Hoorickx, that Schubert intended a tripartite form for this song and meant to end it with a repeat of the aria in the minor. The utterly delicious G major section is of such infectious gaiety (with something of a Moravian character that puts us in mind of Dvořák) that it is difficult to imagine how the composer intended to exit from it and return to the B minor mood at the end. Although it is reasonable to imagine the poet's pipe dream punctured, prompting a return to the music of the opening, this is easier said than done without Schubert's help. In the Hyperion recording we preferred to follow Eusebius Mandyczewski's completion (printed in NSA Volume 10 p. 367 ex. 22) with slight alterations in the final two bars. This does not attempt a recapitulation. Walther Dürr, in describing the state of the extant manuscript (in the collection of the famous Viennese tenor, the late Anton Dermota), believes that the song was in fact finished by Schubert, and that nothing very much is missing from the completed work.

It seems fairly obvious that the music for the Schlegel setting *Der Knabe* (D692, March 1820) had its beginnings in the second section of this song. The combined topics of childhood and flying summon up a tune of similar rhythmical shape, also in $\frac{2}{4}$. Both works have the same air of a pipingly repetitive ditty in a children's playground, and both share a merry and mischievous simplicity.

Autograph: In private possession
First edition: Published in *Moderne Welt*, Vienna in a special Schubert issue,
                        completed by Eusebius Mandyczewski and edited by O. E.
                        Deutsch, in 1925. Published in its original form as part of the NSA
                        in 2002 (P844)

Subsequent editions: Not in Peters; Not in AGA; NSA IV: Vol. 10/268
Discography and timing: Fischer-Dieskau   —
                            Hyperion I 17[8]
                            Hyperion II 14[1]   1'45   Lucia Popp

← *Romanze* D144   *Entzückung* D413 →

LIED NACH DEM FALLE NATHOS *see* OSSIANS LIED NACH DEM
FALLE NATHOS D278

Das LIED VOM REIFEN   The song of the hoar-frost
(Claudius) **D532** [H346]
A♭ major   February 1817

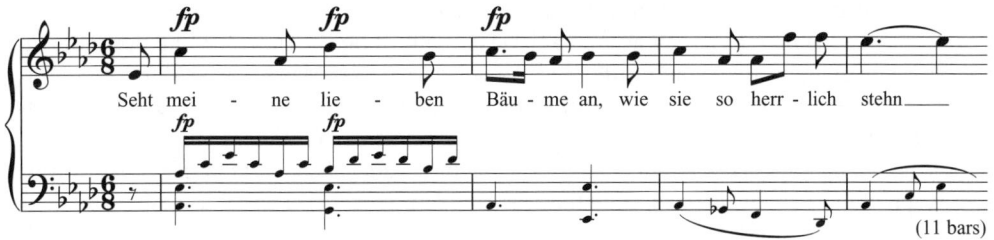

(1) Seht meine lieben Bäume an,   Look how splendid
        Wie sie so herrlich stehn,   My beloved trees are,
     Auf allen Zweigen angetan   Adorned on every branch
        Mit Reifen wunderschön!   With beautiful frost!

(2) Von unten an bis oben 'naus   From top to bottom
        Auf allen Zweigelein   It hangs on every twig,
     Hängt's weiss und zierlich, zart und kraus,   White and delicate, fragile and crisp.
        Und kann nicht schöner sein;   Nothing could be lovelier.

(3) Und alle Bäume rund umher,   And all the trees around,
        All' alle weit und breit,   Far and wide,
     Stehn da, geschmückt mit gleicher Ehr',   Stand arrayed in like dignity
        In gleicher Herrlichkeit.   And splendour.

     [(. . . 6 . . .)]   [(. . . 6 . . .)]

(10) Viel schön, viel schön ist unser Wald!   Our woods are so lovely;
        Dort Nebel überall,   Yonder all is veiled in mist;
     Hier eine weisse Baumgestalt   Here a white tree
        Im vollen Sonnenstrahl —   Is outlined in full sunlight.

(12) Wir sehn das an und denken noch   We look upon this scene
        Einfältiglich dabei: And naively reflect:
     Woher der Reif und wie er doch   Whence this frost?
        Zu Stande kommen sei?   How could it have got here?

(11)   Lichthell, still, edel, rein und frei,
            Und über alles fein!—
        O aller Menschen Seele sei
            So lichthell und so rein!
	Shining, silent, noble, pure, and free,
	            And exquisite beyond all else!
	        May the souls of all mankind
	            Be as shining and as pure!

[(. . . 3 . . .)]	[(. . . 3 . . .)]

MATTHIAS CLAUDIUS (1740–1815); poem written 7 December 1780

*This is the twelfth of Schubert's thirteen Claudius solo settings (1816–17). See the poet's
biography for a chronological list of all the Claudius settings.*

This is perhaps as near as Schubert ever came to writing a Christmas carol – and that in
February! Countless song programmes devised for the festive season would be richer for this
little song, half forgotten and not pressed into service because it failed to find a place in the
Peters Edition. The tune seems to call for community singing, although the surprisingly tricky
accompaniment, a sinuous line of semiquavers beneath the more straightforward vocal line,
requires more than a village-hall accompanist, especially at bb. 11 and 13 in the postlude. The
chromatic weaving of the piano writing recalls the style of Carl Maria von Weber.

The last five bars of this song were written on the reverse of the autograph of *Der Tod und das
Mädchen* D531, the most famous of the Claudius songs written at this time. This celebrated manuscript was cut up into pieces by one of the surviving members of Schubert's family so that various
autograph hunters could claim a part of the relic. *Das Lied vom Reifen* was thus desecrated alongside its more famous sibling, and so it has never been very clear what the composer wanted at the
end of the song. For the Hyperion Edition we performed here the four bars of postlude to be found
in the AGA, as well as adding another bar at the end which was discovered in the library of the
Gesellschaft der Musikfreunde. This is in fact what was printed in the NSA in 1999, after the
Hyperion recording was made in 1992. With these elements brought back together this song is no
longer, strictly speaking, a fragment. According to John Reed it is clear from Schubert's autograph
that the composer meant only three verses to be sung and the first three strophes are accordingly
printed in the NSA. The poem is an enchanting one, originally entitled *Ein Lied vom Reiffen*.
Claudius prefaces it with a quotation from the Apocrypha: Jesus Sirach, Chapter 43: 'Er schüttet
den Reifen auf die Erde wie Salz' ('He shakes frost on the earth like salt'). Fifteen verses are printed
in the AGA (also in Volume 11 p. 265 of the NSA). Edith Mathis chose to record a further three
of these (10, 12 and 11), preferring to end with the positive sentiments of Verse 11. These additional
words add a certain homespun philosophical point to a song that otherwise contents itself with
straightforward description. Walther Dürr suggests that it is possible that Schubert took the text
directly from the Reichardt setting listed below.

Autographs:	University Library of Lund, Sweden (first part) Gesellschaft der Musikfreunde, Vienna (second part) In private possession (third part)
First edition:	Published as part of the AGA in 1895 (P669)
Subsequent editions:	Not in Peters; AGA XX 303: Vol. 5/36; NSA IV: Vol. 11/88
Further setting:	Johann Friedrich Reichardt (1742–1814) *Ein Lied vom Reif* from *Lieder für Kinder*, Vol. 3 (1787)
Discography and timing:	Fischer-Dieskau I 9[20] 2'24 (four strophes)
	Hyperion I 21[9]
	Hyperion II 17[24] 3'01 Edith Mathis

← *An eine Quelle* D530   *Der Tod und das Mädchen* D531 →

LIEDENTWURF IN A MINOR *see* DUBIOUS, MISATTRIBUTED AND LOST SONGS

LIEDENTWURF IN C MAJOR *see* DUBIOUS, MISATTRIBUTED AND LOST SONGS

LIEDESEND   Song's end
(MAYRHOFER) **D473** [H299]

The song exists in two versions, both of which are discussed below:
(1) September 1816; (2) September 1816

(1) 'Majestätisch'   C minor – E major   **C**   [113 bars]

(2) C minor – E minor

(1) Auf seinem gold'nen Throne   On his golden throne
     Der graue König sitzt—   The grey king sits,
     Und starret in die Sonne,[1]   Staring into the sun
     Die rot im Westen blitzt.   That glows red in the west.

(2) Der Sänger rührt die Harfe,[2]   The minstrel strokes his harp,
     Sie rauschet Siegessang;   A song of victory resounds;
     Der Ernst jedoch, der scharfe,   But austere solemnity
     Er trotzt dem vollen Klang.   Defies the swelling tones.

(3) Nun stimmt er süsse Weisen,   Now he plays sweet tunes
     An's Herz sich klammernd an: Which touch the heart;
     Ob er ihn nicht mit leisen   To see if he can soothe the king
     Versuchen mildern kann.   With gentle strains.

(4) Vergeblich ist sein Mühen,   His efforts are in vain,
     Erschöpft des Liedes Reich—   The realm of song is exhausted,
     Und auf der Stirne ziehen   And, like storm clouds,
     Die Sorgen wettergleich.   Cares form upon the king's brow.

---

[1] Mayrhofer writes '*Er* starret'. For an explanation of the background to these alternative Mayrhofer readings see Editorial Note at the beginning of Johann MAYRHOFER.
[2] In the first version of the song, Schubert changes Mayrhofer's 'Der Sänger' to 'Der Barde'. Perhaps the poet had some say in the reinstatement of his original words; perhaps Schubert later realized that the words 'Der Barde' were in Verse 5 already.

(5)	Der Barde, tief erbittert,	The bard, sorely embittered,
	Schlägt die Harf' entzwei,[3]	Breaks his harp in two,
	Und durch die Lüfte zittert[4]	And through the air vibrates
	Der Silbersaiten Schrei.	The cry of the silver strings.
(6)	Und wie auch Alle beben,[5]	But, though all tremble,
	Der Herrscher zürnet nicht;	The ruler is not enraged;
	Der Gnade Strahlen schweben	The light of mercy
	Auf seinem Angesicht.	Lingers on his countenance.
(7)	'Du wolle mich nicht zeihen	'Do not reproach me
	Der Unempfindlichkeit:	With insensitivity;
	In lang verblühten Maien	In months of May long past
	Wie hast du mich erfreut!'	How you have gladdened me!'
(8)	'Wie jede Lust gesteigert,	'How you enhanced every joy
	Die aus der Urne fiel!	Which fell from fate's urn!
	Was mir ein Gott veweigert,	What a god denied me
	Erstattete dein Spiel.'	Your playing restored to me.'
(9)	'Vom kalten Herzen gleitet	'From a cold heart
	Nun Liedeszauber ab;	The magic of song now steals away,
	Und immer näher schreitet	And ever closer step
	Nun Vergänglichkeit und Grab.'[6]	Transience and the grave.'

JOHANN MAYRHOFER (1787–1836)

This is the fourth of Schubert's forty-seven Mayrhofer solo settings (1814–24). See the poet's biography for a chronological list of all the Mayrhofer settings.

There are two versions to this song, both from September 1816. Although they vary considerably in details (and some of the differences are worthy of discussion), taken as a whole there is no justification for considering them as two separate songs, much less as two different settings of the same text. They remain a striking example, when compared side by side, of Schubert's capacity for self-criticism and his endless ability to finesse his work, whether in the tiniest detail or overall concept.

Verse 1 (bb. 1–10): This is music of considerable pomp, fit for a king, and an old and mighty one at that. The dotted rhythms in C minor are the backdrop for a vocal line that sweeps regally down the stave. This downward movement is also descriptive of a magnificent sunset. In the first version there is a shift to E flat major at b. 5 and thence, via C flat major at b. 6, to G flat major, a tonality that establishes itself at b. 9. The second version is more or less the same for the opening five and a half bars, after which it takes a different harmonic direction. The vocal line implies that the king has looked upwards to the sun in the first version (bb. 6–7); the second version has his gaze, surely more correctly, following the downward path of the sunset. This version ends in C flat major.

---

[3] Mayrhofer writes '*seine* Harf''.
[4] Mayrhofer writes 'Durch *die Halle* zittert'.
[5] Mayrhofer writes '*Doch* wie auch Alle beben'.
[6] Schubert adds the word 'Nun' to Mayrhofer's original 'Vergänglichkeit und Grab' in the song's second version.

Verse 2 (from b. 11): Both versions of the song begin this new section in D major – the first marked 'Etwas geschwind', the second 'Feurig'. Schubert seems equally satisfied with both key juxtapositions (i.e. G flat to D major with a shared enharmonic F sharp, and C flat major to D major with the same F sharp acting as a slightly different kind of pivot). A rather conventional military interlude for the piano (bb. 11–26, more or less the same in both versions) sets up a formal-sounding verse of singing, as if the minstrel's heart is not in it. There is something mock-military about this music: Mozart's D major march 'Bella vita militar' from *Così fan tutte* comes to mind. The second half of this section varies: the first version ends in F major, the second in C major.

Verse 3 (from b. 33): This section in A flat major and in triple time is marked 'Sanft' in both versions. The courtliness and suavity of the substantial piano interlude is matched by an equally florid vocal line. One is reminded of the aria in *Der Liedler* D209, in the same key, as this first defines the art of minstrelsy and later buries the hero. The influence here is sheer *bel canto*, and Schubert does not spare his singer from an obstacle course of vocal difficulties – ornamentation, arpeggio figurations, the fine-tuning of chromatic juxtapositions and at b. 40 a most ungrateful descending phrase that starts with the word 'Ob' on a high A flat. This section negates therefore the impression of the song's opening that Schubert had a mezzo or baritone in mind. Curiously, the most challenging passages from a technical point of view are the same in both versions; whatever grounds Schubert had for his revisions, sparing the singer was not one of them (thus completely different from the contemporary *Lied des Orpheus* D474 where Schubert tailors the second version to the shorter voice of Vogl).

Verses 4–7 (from b. 47): This section begins in F minor and is marked 'Geschwind'. The wrenching chordal juxtaposition at the double bar line b. 52 (A flat minor to F sharp minor) mirrors the contortion of the king's brow. After having worked so hard in the preceding section, the fury (more of a tantrum really) of the musician at his lack of success is rather unlikely, a clear case of lese-majesty. The minstrel in *Der Liedler* D209 shattered his beloved harp using it to battle with a werewolf, but here the bard – clearly lacking the long-suffering patience of the professional accompanist – is provoked to destructiveness by nothing more dramatic than sheer ingratitude. Up to the moment of the harp's destruction (the rising arpeggio of b. 59) both versions of the song are more or less identical. At 'Und durch die Lüfte zittert' the music moves into F sharp major in preparation for the king's unexpectedly mild reaction to this outburst. In the second version this section is normalized with a new key signature in F sharp major; in the first, Schubert is content with adding a lot of accidentals. The whole of this section (bb. 63 and 78) is remarkable for its mood of lordly kindness – the monarch is regal and grave, unexpectedly tolerant, tired and very old.

Verses 8–9: By any standards the section begining at b. 79 (marked 'Ernst' in the first version, 'Mit Würde, doch herzlich' in the second) is exceptionally effective. The new markings are a key signature of B major and ¾ time. The composer switches to the bass clef in the first version (as if a new character in an opera were speaking) but in the second he retains the treble clef in the interests of unity. There is no question of this song being performed by any other than a single soloist, although it has been recorded (Fischer-Dieskau and Lipovšek) as a duet. The first version retains the regal dignity to the end but the second makes a significant change almost at the last minute. With the words 'Und immer näher schreitet' (b. 100, the marking is 'Etwas geschwinder') the accompaniment abandons the sedate security of crotchets and moves into ominously rustling quavers. Schubert monitors a quickening of fear, his hand on the royal pulse. The king's poise of utterance disintegrates and we realize that death will claim monarch and commoner alike. The ten-bar postlude with a pianissimo ending conserves the impression of Death, pitilessly stalking. It is a valuable second thought and would justify any performer's choice of this version over the first.

Mayrhofer's poem owes much to Goethe's *Der Sänger* and *Der König in Thule*, and to some of the Schiller ballads. He personalizes the poem by pointing out that a lack of response to music is a sign of illness of the spirit, while acknowledging that there are some states of mind that even his beloved music cannot reach. It is as if the poet regards death itself as a state of being indifferent to music. There are also biblical overtones: in one of the greatest of English songs *King David* (Herbert Howells/Walter de la Mare) the royal psalmist 'Called for the music of a hundred harps / To ease his melancholy'. There, as here, the king's inexplicable depression ('No cause for his sorrow had he') proves insusceptible to music. The idea of a minstrel's relationship to his royal master must have struck a chord with musicians like Schubert, who though spared Mozart's nightmares of noble patronage, was not in a position, as was Beethoven, to defy the hierarchical structures of rank and privilege. How many embittered and unappreciated musicians must there have been in Vienna who felt like breaking their metaphorical harps in fury? Franz von Bruchmann also provided Schubert with a text (*Der zürnende Barde* D785) about a defiant old minstrel; such poems honouring the practitioners of music over their employers were of course meant as a compliment to the composer. Then, as now, it was easier for artists to live a life of penury if they were able to continue in the belief that they played something of a sacred role in society. Schiller's ballad *Die Theilung der Erde* (not set to music by Schubert, but copied out by him *c.* 1810 in a setting by Franz de Paula Roser) makes this very point: the impractical poet (and by extension, all artists) has been left out of Zeus' allocation of the earth's resources and by the time he asks for his share, everything of material value has already been given away to the landowners, merchants, politicians and clergy. The only thing that Zeus can offer the poet (or in this case the musician) by way of compensation is a place in heaven at the god's side; Olympus will be open to him whenever he wishes to enter.

Autographs:	Wienbibliothek im Rathaus, Vienna (first draft of first version and fair copy of second version)
Publication:	Published as part of the AGA in 1895 (P649; first version)
	Published as Book 23 no. 2 of the *Nachlass* by Diabelli, Vienna in 1833 (P304; second version)
Subsequent editions:	Peters: Vol. 5/139; AGA XX 249a & b: Vol. 4/154; NSA IV: Vol. 10/213 & 219
Discography and timing:	Fischer-Dieskau I 8[1] 5'30
	Hyperion I 3[6]
	Hyperion II 15[26] 6'07 Ann Murray (second version)

⟵ *Sehnsucht (Mignon)* D481   *Abschied, nach einer Wallfahrtsarie* D475 ⟶

Der LIEDLER   The minstrel
(Kenner) Op. 38, **D209** [H62]
A minor – A♭ major   June–12 December 1815 (the date of Schubert's dedicatory inscription)

(383 bars)

(1) 'Gib, Schwester, mir die Harf' herab,   Sister, pass down my harp,
     Gib mir Biret und Wanderstab,   Hand me my hat and staff,
     Kann hier nicht fürder weilen!   I can no longer tarry here.
     Bin ahnenlos, bin nur ein Knecht,   I am but a servant, without forebears,
     Bin für die edle Maid zu schlecht,   I am too humble for the noble maiden
     Muss stracks von hinnen eilen.   And must at once hasten from here.

(2) Still, Schwester, bist gottlob nun Braut,   'Be calm, sister, you are now, praise God, a bride.
     Wirst morgen Wilhelm angetraut,   Tomorrow you will wed Wilhelm.
     Soll mich nichts weiter halten!   There is nothing more to keep me here.
     Nun küsse mich, leb', Trude, wohl!   So kiss me, Trude, farewell!
     Dies Herze, schmerz- und liebevoll,   This heart of mine, so full of pain and love –
     Lass Gott den Herrn bewalten.'   Let the Lord God guide it.'

(3) Der Liedler zog durch manches Land,   The minstrel travelled through many a land,
     Am alten Rhein- und Donaustrand,   On the banks of the old Rhine and Danube,
     Wohl über Berg und Flüsse.   Across mountains and rivers.
     Wie weit er flieht, wohin er zieht,   However far he journeyed, wherever he
                                                     wandered,
     Er trägt den Wurm im Herzen mit   He carried the worm in his heart,
     Und singt nur sie, die Süsse.   And sang only of her, his sweet love.

(4) Und er's nicht länger tragen kann,   And when he could bear it no longer
     Tät sich mit Schwert und Panzer an,   He girded on sword and armour,
     Den Tod sich zu erstreiten.   To seek death in battle.
     Im Tod ist Ruh, im Grab ist Ruh,   In death is peace, in the grave is peace;
     Das Grab deckt Herz und Wünsche zu;   The grave buries the heart and its desires.
     Ein Grab will er erreiten.   On horseback he sought a grave.

(5) Der Tod ihn floh, und Ruh' ihn floh!   Death eluded him; peace eluded him!
     Des Herzogs Banner flattert froh   The Duke's banner gaily waved
     Der Heimat Gruss entgegen,   A greeting from the homeland;
     Entgegen wallt, entgegen schallt   His friends' greetings resounded
     Der Freunde Gruss durch Saat   Through field and wood,
          und Wald
     Auf allen Weg' und Stegen.   On every road and bridge.

(6) Da ward ihm unterm Panzer weh!   Then he grew melancholy in his armour.
     Im Frührot glüht der ferne Schnee   The distant snow on his native mountains
     Der heimischen Gebirge;   Glistened in the dawn.
     Ihm war's als zög's mit Hünenkraft   It seemed as if, with titanic force,
     Dahin sein Herz, der Brust entrafft,   His heart were being drawn there, wrenched
                                                     from his breast;
     Als ob's ihn hier erwürge.   It was as if he were suffocating here.

(7) Da konnt er's fürder nicht bestehn: Then he could no longer resist:
     'Muss meine Heimat wiedersehn,   'I must see my homeland again,
     Muss sie noch einmal schauen!   I must behold it once more!
     Die mit der Minne Rosenhand   With the rosy hand of love

Ein Herz an jene Berge band,	It bound my heart
Die herrlichen, die blauen!'	To those mountains, blue and glorious!'

(8) Da warf er Wehr und Waffe weg,   He threw away his weapons,
Sein Rüstzeug weg ins Dorngeheg;   Cast his armour into the thorny hedge;
Die liederreichen Saiten,   His melodious strings,
Die Harfe nur, der Süssen Ruhm,   His harp, his sweetheart's eulogy,
Sein Klagepsalm, sein Heiligtum,   His threnody and his sacred hymn –
Soll ihn zurückbegleiten.   His harp alone would accompany him home.

(9) Und als der Winter trat ins Land,   When winter came to the country,
Der Frost im Lauf die Ströme band,   And frost congealed the flowing rivers,
Betrat er seine Berge.   He reached his mountains.
Da lag's, ein Leichentuch von Eis,   There lay his homeland, a shroud of ice,
Lag's vorn und neben totenweiss,   Deathly white all around,
Wie tausend Hünensärge!   Like a thousand Titans' coffins!

(10) Lag's unter ihm, sein Muttertal,   Beneath him lay his native valley,
Das gräflich Schloss im Abendstrahl,   And, in the sun's dying rays, the Count's castle
Wo Milla drin geborgen.   In which Milla was sheltered.
Glück auf! der Alpe Pilgerruh   Good luck! The Alpine pilgrim's rest
Winkt heute Ruh dir Ärmster zu;   Bids you pause today, poor boy;
Zur Feste, Liedler, morgen!   Tomorrow, minstrel, to the castle.

(11) Ich hab' nicht Rast, ich hab' nicht Ruh,[1]   I know no peace, I know no repose;
Muss heute noch der Feste zu,   This very day I must reach the castle
Wo Milla drin geborgen.   Where Milla is sheltered.
'Bist starr, bist blass!' Bin totenkrank,   'You are frozen, you are pale.' I am sick
                              unto death,
Heut ist noch mein! Tot, Gott sei Dank,   Today is still mine! Death, thank the Lord,
Tot find't mich wohl der Morgen.   Death will strike me tomorrow!

(12) Horch Maulgetrab, horch Schellenklang!   Hark mules' hooves, hark the jingling of bells!
Vom Schloss herab der Alp' entlang   Down from the castle, along the mountainside
Zog's unter Fackelhelle.   Rode a torchlit procession.
Ein Ritter führt, ihm angetraut,   A knight led his bride,
Führt Milla heim als seine Braut.   Led Milla home as his wife.
Bist, Liedler, schon zur Stelle!   You are already here, minstrel!

(13) Der Liedler schaut' und sank in sich.   The minstrel watched, overcome with gloom.
Da bricht und schnaubet wütiglich   But then a werewolf broke through the wood,
Ein Werwolf durch's Gehege,[2]   Snorting with rage.
Die Maule fliehn, kein Saum sie zwingt,   The mules fled from the path;
Der Schecke stürzt. Weh! Milla sinkt   The dappled pony fell.
Ohnmächtig hin am Wege.   Alas! Milla fainted by the wayside.

---

[1] In the surviving manuscript source of the poem (in private possession), Strophe 11 does not exist. Whether this strophe was later inserted by Kenner at Schubert's request or whether the cut version represents the poet's final thoughts is unclear.

[2] Kenner and Schubert in his autograph use the antiquated spelling 'Währwolf'.

(14) Da riss er sich, ein Blitz, empor,   Like lightning, he leapt forward
      Zum Hort der Heissgeminnten vor,   To his beloved's aid.
      Hoch auf des Untiers Nacken   High against the monster's neck
      Schwang er sein teures Harfenspiel,   He hurled his cherished harp,
      Dass es zersplittert niederfiel,   So that it shattered and fell to the ground.
      Und Nick und Rachen knacken.   But the monster's neck and jaw were crushed.

(15) Und wenn er stark wie Simson wär',   Had he been as strong as Samson
      Erschöpft mag er und sonder Wehr   He could not, exhausted and unarmed,
      Den Grimmen nicht bestehen,   Have resisted the raging beast.
      Vom Busen, vom zerfleischten Arm   From his breast, from his lacerated arm,
      Quillt's Herzblut nieder, liebewarm;   His heart's blood gushed down, hot with love;
      Schier denkt er zu vergehen.   He thought he was near to death.

(16) Ein Blick auf sie! und alle Kraft   One glance at her, and at once
      Mit einmal er zusammenrafft,   He summoned all the strength
      Die noch verborgen schliefe!   Which lay hidden within him.
      Ringt um den Werwolf Arm und Hand,   He gripped the werewolf with arms and hands,
      Und stürzt sich von der Felsenwand   And plunged with it from the rock face
      Mit ihm in schwindle Tiefe.   Into the giddy depths.

(17) Fahr', Liedler, fahr' auf ewig wohl!   Farewell, minstrel, farewell for ever!
      Dein Herze schmerz- und liebevoll,   Your heart, so full of pain and love,
      Hat Ruh im Grab gefunden   Has found rest in the grave!
      Das Grab ist aller Pilger Ruh',   The grave brings rest to all pilgrims;
      Das Grab deckt Herz und Wünsche zu,   The grave buries the heart and its desires,
      Macht alles Leids gesunden.   And heals all sorrows.

Josef Kenner (1794–1868); poem written in 1813

This is the second of Schubert's three Kenner solo settings (1815). See the poet's biography for a chronological list of all the Kenner settings.

How different in scale and density this music is from a ballad such as *Der Taucher* (D77) where Schubert depicts kingly pomp and circumstance with mighty flourishes for voice and piano. The comparative simplicity of *Der Liedler* is a conscious retreat from that ornate style, and a clear attempt to tell a story from a viewpoint appropriate to a simple youth. (Cappi & Co.'s advertisement for the sale of the published song a decade later refers to a ballad 'written in simpler and more comprehensible style than other compositions by Schubert' as if this were a selling point.) It was the composer's only extended ballad eventually to become available with guitar accompaniment. The poem evokes a world of more or less medieval minstrelsy – a popular setting for stories of the time, including the libretti of numerous *Singspiel* operas and more complex works like Weber's *Euryanthe*, yet to be composed. The melodramatic meanderings of the Celtic bard Ossian also influenced Kenner, just as settings of Ossian by Reichardt and Zumsteeg clearly influenced Schubert. The poem was famous in the Schubert circle some time before the composer set it to music and had been published in the Viennese almanac *Selam* (edited by Ignaz Castelli) for the year 1815 (which appeared for sale at the end of 1814). The author signed his contribution with the letter 'K' instead of his whole name. Although it was the high point of Kenner's literary career, more or less over before it had begun, such a

Der Liedler, I by Moritz von Schwind. The set of drawings that follows over the next few pages was inspired by Schubert's ballad, and was executed by Moritz von Schwind in 1822. This was the artist's earliest engagement with the illustration of Schubert's songs.

publication would have been considered a great honour for the twenty-year-old poet, and the entire Konvikt circle would have felt a kind of collective pride in his achievement (the first of Schubert's works to be printed appeared in an almanac in 1818). In setting the ballad to music at the end of 1815, Schubert was adding not only his own seal of congratulatory approval, but that of his school contemporaries as well. Moritz von Schwind, who was younger than both composer and poet and not part of the Schubert circle at the time, later illustrated the piece with twelve sepia drawings. *Der Liedler* was the only Schubert song to be so lavishly honoured by Schwind's art in the composer's lifetime. When the artist visited Linz in October 1823 he showed the drawings to Kenner who could not get enough of them.

Verses 1–2: The time signature is $\frac{2}{4}$, the key A minor. The poignant chromaticism, the grace notes of the second bar and the high placing of the left-hand chords suggest a work that Schubert undoubtedly knew – Mozart's Rondo for piano, K511, in the same key. The piano textures are as bare and simple as befits a humble lad who must consign his fate to the open road. Rather like a junior version of the winter traveller in *Winterreise*, the protagonist wastes no time in leaving the house. He feels himself unworthy of a certain beautiful and noble maiden (we later learn that her name is Milla) with whom he is clearly in love. He addresses his sister 'Trude' (Gertrude) and asks for the harp, hat and walking staff. We learn that Trude hopes to be married to Wilhelm on the morrow, but her brother, the eponymous hero, has no such happy expectations. As he consigns his heart to God's guidance, the music steers him to the remote key of E flat major (via bb. 83–4) signalling that his wanderings have begun. For the first verse the minstrel's voice has been heard in the first person; from now on his story (with the exception of a few lines) is assigned to a more impartial narrator. The first of Moritz von Schwind's seven surviving illustrations to the ballad (sepia drawings from 1823) depict the Liedler bidding his family farewell at the door of his home (*see* above).

Der Liedler, II by Moritz von Schwind.

Verse 3: At b. 99 the marking is 'Langsam, wehmütig' and the time signature is ⅜. This tender cantilena in A flat major is prophetic of many Schubert songs in which calm triplets underpin a seamless Italianate aria; the Hölty setting *An den Mond* D193, an almost contemporary work, comes to mind. In this case these travelling triplets depict the slow but dogged progress of the hero as he perambulates up hill and down dale. The music efficiently delineates his progress from land to land, encompassing Rhine and Danube. Deeply depressed, he can only sing music in praise of his beloved. The woeful expression on his face is clear from the second of Schwind's surviving seven illustrations to the ballad. The minstrel sits with his harp underneath a tree while his public listens to his singing with a mixture of enchantment and perplexity (*see* above).

Der Liedler, III by Moritz von Schwind.

Verse 4: This way of life is not satisfactory; the minstrel must bury his sorrows somehow and he chooses the life of a professional soldier. Frustration is shown by the passages marked 'Schnell' (at bb. 121 and 136) with the interpolation of a 'Sehr langsam' arioso from b. 129, where the death wish is expressed. This leads to a wrenching change from A flat major to F sharp minor and a series of scale passages (bb. 138 to 141), music that seems to chase its own tail. Battle music in clashing crotchet chords (bb. 142–52) recklessly courts death. The third of Schwind's illustration depicts the minstrel in full battle cry (*see* previous page).

Verse 5: At b. 156, and with the marking 'Zeitmass des Marsches', we change to a *marche militaire* in D major, music that must be related to the chorus 'Bella vita militar' from Mozart's *Così fan tutte*, and is in the same key. The canvas is suddenly peopled with an army of jaunty compatriots who awaken the minstrel's homesickness.

Verses 6–8: At b. 184 the tempo marking changes to 'Mässig' with three bars' worth of mournful music in §. At bb. 187–8 a recitative accompanied by undulating semiquavers on a dominant seventh chord eerily evokes the majesty of mountain tops from the homeland. At b. 194 the home key of A reappears, but this time nostalgia colours those distant pastures in the major tonality; the traveller's longing for home in the celebrated *Der Wanderer* D489 (the passage in that song with the words 'Wo meine Freunde wandeln gehn') is prophesied in this music marked 'Ziemlich geschwind' (from b. 196). The § rhythm and a touch of exoticism in the harmony (b. 199) bring Mozart to mind again, this time Pedrillo's Romanze from *Die Entführung aus dem Serail*.

The minstrel decides to abandon his military life. From now on only his harp will accompany him. The divesting of his arms and armour is accomplished with sparsely accompanied recitative. Schwind's fourth illustration shows the hero contemplating his homeland, still in his armour, but clearly dissatisfied with the life of the soldier (*see* below).

Der Liedler, IV by Moritz von Schwind.

Verses 9–11: When the minstrel returns to the wintry reality of home, the minor key re-establishes itself ('Mässig' from b. 214, now with a § time signature). The piano doubles the voice in bleak desolation; the arioso frets and worries. The C minor music at 'Ich hab' nicht Rast' ('Bewegt' from b. 238) echoes *Schäfers Klagelied* D121, a song in the same key that was written

Der Liedler, V by Moritz von Schwind.

the year before, also music of a man unhappily in love, standing on a mountain and looking down into the valley. The minstrel feels that he will die the next day (the pianistic shudders of bb. 248–9 underline this) but he takes comfort in the fact that today belongs to him. He still has something left to do in life, but he knows not what. The fifth of Schwind's illustrations has the Liedler in this darkest of moods contemplating the winter panorama of his homeland (*see* above).

Verse 12: The music is marked 'Geschwinder' from b. 265. Milla's wedding celebrations (to someone else of course) are noisily depicted in deliberately banal churning sextuplets in E flat major. Some of the simplest but most expertly paced music in the piece now depicts the wedding procession of Milla and the knight who will be her husband (miraculously but unhappily visible, it seems, from the minstrel's vantage point). The procession is coming his way. The minstrel's mounting realization that Milla can no longer be his is complemented by the feeling that, true to his earlier premonition, he is already in the grave.

Verse 13: The music has taken a rather remarkable sidestep into G flat major, and thence to A flat minor. The gently pulsating semiquaver accompaniment of the beautiful four-bar passage at bb. 283–6 contains a crucial line in the song – 'Der Liedler schaut' und sank in sich.' This music of heartbroken inactivity is the lull before the storm. The line is illustrated by Schwind in perhaps the most beautiful of his seven illustrations, the sixth of the sequence (*see* overleaf).

Verse 14: At b. 287 the marking suddenly changes to 'Schnell' for an outburst of silent-film heroism and implausibility. In the previous verse a blood-hungry werewolf, a *lupus ex machina*, has emerged snarling from the forest, and now livens up the story with dislocations of limb and tonality. The rushing passage-work in the accompaniment (bb. 287, 289 in an upward direction, and for bb. 293 and 294, downwards) is appropriate to a monster, scaly or hairy. Our hero uses the only weapon he has to hand, his precious harp, to crush the jaw of the werewolf, splitting the instrument in two. He thus sacrifices his dearest possession, the very thing that defines his role in life. The beautiful Milla has already fainted on a gently descending (or rather wilting) vocal line (bb. 296–300). There is no mention whatever of her consort, the minstrel's rival.

Der Liedler, VI by Moritz von Schwind.

Verses 15–16: From b. 301 there is a sudden change to fast narrative recitative. The piano writing hammers away in octaves as the monster lacerates the minstrel's arm. From b. 319 blood pours from his wounds, not as sensuously as in *Der zürnenden Diana* D707, but in limpid quaver chords. Mortally wounded, the minstrel realizes at b. 335 that Milla is still not safe from the werewolf. Fortissimo sextuplets in the pianist's right hand (bb. 337–40) form the wildest of arpeggios as the minstrel gets hold of the werewolf with both hands (mirroring the struggle that follows, the pianist simultaneously holds on to octaves as if a vicious animal were struggling within this compass) and plunges into the abyss (a topographical detail that has thus far not been mentioned), taking the monster with him. The last of three left-hand thumps (on the first beats of bb. 350, 351 and 352) is the E flat major chord that kills both man and beast, and prepares the way for the recapitulation of the A flat major music heard in Verse 3. The moment of the hero's plunge into the abyss, embracing the werewolf, is depicted by Schwind in the seventh and last of his illustrations.

Verse 17: It is a measure of Schubert's greatness that the song can survive the preceding episode without merriment, and it does so in performances by that great bass-baritone Robert Holl. The reprise of the Italianate *cantilena* for Verse 3 buries the lad and rescues the story from the depths, bringing the work to a touching close.

When he wrote this piece Schubert was in love with Therese Grob, a girl who sang at the parish church of Liechtenthal. There was some money in her family and Schubert, who had no prospects, was ineligible from every point of view. This poem about love until death, and supreme sacrifice (including in a sense the renunciation of music itself) must have made many a string resound sympathetically in the heart of the poor young minstrel of Vienna. Other members of the circle were moved by it too, for many years it seems. Of course Joseph Kenner was deeply touched by the setting (he had no illusions regarding the quality of his own writing) and he accepted the work's dedication in print in 1825, nearly a decade after it was composed, with undying gratitude.

Der Liedler, VII by Moritz von Schwind.

We know little about the background to Schubert's decision to publish this work in his lifetime, the only one of his longer narrative ballads to achieve this distinction. That it appeared in print at all may have been something to do with the desire of the newly established publishers Pietro and Carlo Cappi (recently shorn of their association with their former partner Diabelli) to offer something popular by Schubert that was not too musically difficult. The advertisement in the *Wiener Zeitung* of 9 May 1825 trades on the reputation of Zumsteeg's ballads (still popular with older music lovers of the time) and promises something better. It is true that Schubert, for whatever reason, seems to have made some conscious effort to create something considerably simpler than that of his other works in the genre. (Was he catering perhaps for Kenner's own abilities as a performer?) The vocal writing, though hardly easy to sing well, is less challenging than in many other works of this kind – and the relative simplicity of the piano writing is evident from the uncluttered texture of the music on the page.

Autograph:	In private possession
First edition:	Published as Op. 38 by Cappi & Co., Vienna in May 1825 (P79)
Dedicatee:	Joseph Kenner
Publication reviews:	Publication announcement and brief review in *Wiener-Zeitung* No. 105 (9 May 1825), p. 456 [Waidelich/Hilmar Dokumente I No. 331; Deutsch Doc. Biog. No. 552]
Subsequent editions:	Peters: Vol. 4/33; AGA XX 98: Vol. 2/184; NSA IV: Vol. 2/144; Bärenreiter: Vol. 2/37
Bibliography:	Kohlhäufl 1999, pp. 172–5
	Porhansl 1996, p. 111
Discography and timing:	Fischer-Dieskau I 4¹⁵ 13'23
	Hyperion I 4¹
	Hyperion II 5¹ 14'55 Philip Langridge

← *Der Sänger* D149   *Trinklied* D148 →

LILLA AN DIE MORGENRÖTE   Lilla to the dawn
(Anonymous) **D273** [H160]
D major   25 August 1815

Wie schön bist du, du güldne Morgenröte,
Wie feierlich bist du!
Dir jauchzt im festlichen Gesang der Flöte
Der Schäfer dankbar zu.

Dich grüsst des Waldes Chor, melodisch singet
Die Lerch' und Nachtigall,
Und rings umher von Berg und Tal erklinget
Der Freude Wiederhall

How beautiful you are, golden dawn,
How majestic!
With his flute's festive song
The shepherd offers you joyful thanks.

The chorus of the woods greets you,
Lark and nightingale sing sweetly,
And round about joy's echo
Resounds.

ANONYMOUS/UNKNOWN

*This is the fourth of Schubert's nineteen solo settings of an anonymous poet. See Anonymous/
Unknown for a chronological list of all the songs for which the poets are unknown.*

This is one of the six lieder and three part-songs that Schubert composed on 25 August 1815.
The source of the poem, probably an almanac, is unknown, as is the identity of the poet. Till
Gerrit Waidelich has pointed out (*Schubert Liedlexikon*) that Lilla was a popular name on
account of the farmgirl heroine of that name in Soler's opera *Una cosa rara*, libretto by da
Ponte and produced in Vienna in 1786. Despite the fact that the song was conceived on a day
of such frantic activity, it sounds as if Schubert had all the time and space in the world. The
house in the Säulengasse was probably stiflingly uncomfortable and humid in August, and yet
this music is so calm and poised that it might have been composed in the cool of the Greek
mountains before the onset of a summer day. The introduction is a typical horn motif rather
than the flute figurations suggested by the text, but restraint when it comes to elaboration
lends the music a statuesque Attic decorum. Lilla seems as much pagan priestess as Enlightenment shepherdess. The sense of echo anticipates the Mayrhofer setting *Abschied, nach einer
Wallfahrtsarie* D475 where a pilgrims' chorus resounds through the mountains. From early on
in his career it seems that Schubert was fascinated by the sound of musical echoes in open
spaces. The culmination of this kind of music was not the winsome *Das Echo* (D990C) but *Der
Hirt auf dem Felsen* D965 which was to be Schubert's definitive statement on the subject of
sound resonating in open spaces.

Autograph: In private possession (Basel)
First edition: Published as part of the AGA in 1895 (P576)
Subsequent editions: Not in Peters; AGA XX 130: Vol. 3/59; NSA IV: Vol. 9/19

Discography and timing: Fischer-Dieskau   —
                           Hyperion I 9[20]
                           Hyperion II 9[21]   1'39   Arleen Auger

← *Das Leben ist ein Traum D269*   *Tischlerlied D274* →

L'INCANTO DEGLI OCCHI (I)   The enchantment of eyes
(METASTASIO) **D990E** [H18]
B♭ major   (Song exercise without accompaniment) 1813?

Da voi,— ca - ri— lu - mi, di - pen - de il mi - o sta - to:

Da voi, cari lumi,	On you, beloved eyes,
Dipende il mio stato;	Depends my life;
Voi siete i miei Numi,	You are my gods;
Voi siete il mio fato.	You are my destiny.
A vostro talento	At your bidding
Mi sento cangiar,	My mood changes.
Ardir m'inspirate,	You inspire me with daring
Se lieti splendete;	If you shine joyfully;
Se torbidi siete,	If you are overcast
Mi fate tremar.	You make me tremble.

PIETRO METASTASIO (1698–1782)

This is the seventh of Schubert's fourteen Metastasio solo settings (1812–27). See the poet's biography for a chronological list of all the Metastasio settings.

This aria text is from Metastasio's *Attillo Regolo* of 1740. (For a fuller explication of the plot *see* the commentary on *L'incanto degli occhi (II)*, under *Drei Gesänge für Bass-Stimme* Op. 83 no. 1.) Of all the Italian poems set as exercises in his adolescence, Schubert returned to this one, and this one alone, in his maturity. The result was the beautiful canzona of 1827 (D902/1), a subtle and delectable *opera buffo* stylization for bass voice which is at the same time an inimitably Schubertian creation. Although the Rossini craze in Vienna was the principal stumbling block for Schubert's hopes of operatic success, this late piece, conceived for Luigi Lablache, is as much homage to the Italian composer as the gentlest of send-ups. Schubert's bemused smile fits a Rossini pastiche perfectly: after all, who was more inclined to mock the whole gallimaufry of operatic clichés than Rossini himself?

There is little comparable in terms of deliciously underplayed wit to this first setting of *L'incanto degli occhi*, the date of which is uncertain (perhaps between 1813 and 1817). It is the first of two songs written out on a double sheet of paper that came into the possession of the collector H. P. Wertitsch as late as 1988, a more complete version of the song than had hitherto been known. The companion song on this manuscript is *Ombre amene*, and for both pieces the vocal line is provided without accompaniment. So this is almost certainly a Salieri exercise, albeit one of the more extended and ambitious ones. The sophistication of the melodic inflexions, as well as the modulations (the key is B flat major but the song's central section is in D flat major), suggests that the composer had envisaged an accompaniment, and a reasonably elaborate one at that. As he almost always wrote down the vocal line first, there is nothing unusual in the lack of a piano part in an early sketch. An accompaniment has been provided by Reinhard Van Hoorickx for the earlier, and less complete, version of the exercise.

The whole of this work is more advanced than the earlier exercises that had been designed simply to foster a smooth sense of melodic flow and efficient part-writing. This is a fully fledged aria, displaying a feeling both for the capabilities of the human voice (it is reasonably grateful to sing apart from its final note, a high B flat) and for word-painting. The fourth appearance of the words 'Mi fate tremar' occasions five bars of coloratura flourishes in semiquaver scales on 'fate' (bb. 29–34) – an effective depiction of the trembling of the narrator. Such florid passage-work is relatively rare in Schubert's songs and, unlike other composers, he never used the Italian style as an excuse for gratuitous display – there is a real textual reason for this virtuosity. 'Mi fate tremar' is a phrase that Schubert also much enjoyed playing with in D902 although in a more subtle manner. Note how 'Voi siete i miei Numi' stays anchored on one note as if to give a prayer-like flavour to the passage (bb. 5–6). This tenacious stability of the vocal line, which mirrors faith in the gods, is not brought out in Van Hoorickx's arrangement, the best feature of which is, as usual, its refusal to indulge in the hubris of trying to be too clever. If Van Hoorickx is not quite able to conjure up magic from these simple ingredients, he allows us to enjoy what remains of Schubert himself. For the Hyperion recording, his piano introduction was retained; it is in the style of some of the genuine *Vorspiele* to be found in the Italian songs.

Autograph:	Wienbibliothek im Rathaus, Vienna
First edition:	Incomplete version of the vocal line (issued by the NSA in 1979 (P775)), realized by Reinhard Van Hoorickx and recorded for the Hyperion Edition. The complete vocal line issued by the NSA in 1999.
Subsequent editions:	Not in Peters; not in AGA; NSA IV: Vol. 4b/249 (in complete bare vocal line as realized and privately printed by Hoorickx, Vol. 11/214, the full vocal line discovered in 1988.)
Discography and timing:	Fischer-Dieskau —
	Hyperion I 33[18]
	Hyperion II 2[14] 2'33 Ann Murray

← *Misero pargoletto* D42 (first setting)   *Misero pargoletto* D42 (second setting) →

L'INCANTO DEGLI OCCHI (II) *see DREI GESÄNGE FÜR BASSSTIMME MIT KLAVIER* Op. 83 no. 1

LINDE WESTE WEHEN   Gentle west winds blow   Duet
(Anonymous) **D725** [not in Hyperion]
(Fragment) B minor   April 1821

(22 bars)

Linde Weste wehen,	Gentle west winds blow,
Atmen Balsamdüfte	Breathing sweet scents
Von Jasmingesträuche	Of jasmine bushes
Und von Veilchen.	And violets.

ANONYMOUS/UNKNOWN

There is disagreement between the Deutsch catalogue (D₂, 1978) and the NSA (2006) as to the title of this work. The earlier title is *Linde Lüften wehen* but is clearly supplanted by a more recent reading of the underlay. The fact that this song is a piece of only eleven bars is a real loss to the world of performing music. The printing of the fragment in the NSA suggests a perfectly formed duet that breaks off abruptly after one page of rather delicious music, as if the remainder might be lost. However this is unlikely as the surviving music takes up only part of a single page of manuscript. There are just two duets by Schubert, both masterpieces, where the voices sound together (as opposed to alternately), and a piece for mezzo-soprano and tenor such as this would have been a valuable addition to that tiny group of songs. The key of B minor is immediately reminiscent of the first *Suleika* song D720, and there is a sultry aspect to this piece that suggests further eastern inspiration. The semiquaver weave between the voices where the two singers are effectively a third apart (although the tenor, sounding an octave lower, seems higher on paper) is extremely sensual. All in all this tantalizing beginning promises much.

Autograph:	Gesellschaft der Musikfreunde, Vienna
First edition:	Published in *Festschrift für Johannes Wolf*, edited by Max Friedlaender, in 1929. Subsequently published as part of the NSA in 2006 (P847)
Subsequent editions:	Not in Peters; Not in AGA; NSA III: Vol. 2b/325
Discography and timing:	Fischer-Dieskau —
	Hyperion I
	Hyperion II —

Der LINDENBAUM *see WINTERREISE* D911/5

LITANEI *see* AM TAGE ALLER SEELEN D343

LOB DER TRÄNEN   In praise of tears
(A. von Schlegel) Op. 13 no. 2, **D711** [H406]

The song exists in two versions, the second of which is discussed below:
(1)   1818?; (2) appeared December 1822

(1)   'Andante'   D major   ¾   [27 bars]

(2)   D major

Laue Lüfte,
Blumendüfte,
Alle Lenz- und Jugendlust;
Frischer Lippen
Küsse nippen,
Sanft gewiegt an zarter Brust;
Dann der Trauben
Nektar rauben;
Reihentanz und Spiel und Scherz:
Was die Sinnen
Nur gewinnen:
Ach! erfüllt es je das Herz?

Wenn die feuchten
Augen leuchten
Von der Wehmut lindem Tau,
Dann entsiegelt,
Drin gespiegelt,
Sich dem Blick die Himmelsau.
Wie erquicklich
Augenblicklich
Löscht es jede wilde Glut!
Wie vom Regen
Blumen pflegen,
Hebet sich der matte Mut.

Nicht mit süssen
Wasserflüssen
Zwang Prometheus unsern Leim!
Nein, mit Tränen;
Drum im Sehnen
Und im Schmerz sind wir daheim.
Bitter schwellen
Diese Quellen
Für den erdumfangnen Sinn,
Doch sie drängen
Aus den Engen
An das Meer der Liebe hin.

Ew'ges Sehnen
Floss in Tränen,
Und umgab die starre Welt,
Die in Armen
Sein Erbarmen
Immerdar umflutend hält.
Soll dein Wesen
Denn genesen,
Von dem Erdenstaube los,

Warm breezes,
Fragrant flowers,
All the pleasures of spring and youth;
Sipping kisses
From fresh lips
Lulled gently on a tender breast;
Then stealing nectar
From the grapes,
Dancing, games and banter:
Whatever the senses
Can obtain:
Ah, does it ever satisfy the heart?

When moist eyes
Glisten
With the gentle dew of sadness,
Then, reflected in them,
The fields of heaven
Are revealed to the gaze.
How refreshingly,
How swiftly
Every fierce passion is quelled;
As flowers are revived
By the rain,
So do our weary spirits revive.

Not with sweet
Flowing water
Did Prometheus force our clay into life,
But with tears;
And so with longing
And with pain we are at home.
These springs
Well up bitterly
For the earthbound senses,
But they penetrate
Beyond their confines
To the ocean of love.

Eternal longing
Flowed in tears,
And encircled the motionless world
Which eternally holds
This act of mercy
In its watery arms.
If you
Are to be healed,
Free from earth's dust,

Musst im Weinen	You must in tears
Dich vereinen	Be united
Jener Wasser heil'gem Schoss.	With the sacred source of those waters.

August Wilhelm von Schlegel (1767–1845); poem written in 1807

This is the sixth of Schubert's ten August von Schlegel solo settings (1816–25). See the poet's biography for a chronological list of all the August von Schlegel settings.

This lilting, waltz-like setting has such a delightful melody that it was once a great favourite with audiences. It was selected to be in the first volume of the Peters Edition, a series that more or less published Schubert's output in the order of its popularity, the songs becoming more recherché with each successive volume. It is interesting that of all the songs in this volume, *Lob der Tränen* is now perhaps the least performed, its Italianate prettiness less tempting to the performer of today who prefers the composer in less generalized mood.

The song as a whole suffers from an imbalance between the weight of poetic content and the ingratiating tune, the shape of which was suggested by the poet's double rhymes. The fact that it is also an unmodified strophic song shows that the composer had no wish to attend to the fact that the poem's message deepens with each strophe. By the time we hear of Prometheus' painful creation of mankind in these lilting tones we can only smile at the incongruity. Perhaps this conflict of tears and smiles in poetic and musical imagery was intentional, in which case the composer was showing a most sophisticated irony. It is more likely, however, that Schubert by 1818 had not yet got the measure of the achievement of the Schlegel brothers.

Although the song teeters on the edge of sentimentality, a stylistic leaning towards what was later referred to as the musical taste of the Victorian drawing room, it has numerous touches of mastery: the 'Lachen und Weinen' kind of ambivalence between G minor and D major of the introduction; the eruption into dancing triplets at 'Reihentanz' (from b. 14); the glorious way in which the final (repeated) line of each strophe takes rapturous flight (and then rising basses achieving lift-off at bb. 20–21 at 'erfüllt es je das Herz'). We cannot help but admire melodic writing as natural and graceful as this. The song is also a masterclass in the question of how triplets should line up against a dotted quaver + semiquaver figuration. Should the semiquaver come *after* the last of the triplets (as is the practice in modern music-making) or *with* the last of the triplets (as was often the case in Schubert's time, and is surely so in a song like *Wasserflut* from *Winterreise*?) The answer is that the singer should use his or her discretion and allow the dotted rhythms either more or less elasticity according to the meaning of the words and their position in the score. For example, when the vocal line is triplet-accompanied it would seem pointless to insist on a punctiliously jerky dotted rhythm, but at other times the vitality of the meaning could require a slightly more clipped rhythm.

For the dating of this song we rely on something written in haste by Schubert at the bottom of the manuscript of the first version: 'Spaun! Don't forget Gahy and Rondo'. This refers to a piano duet, D608, written in January 1818. As the composer was away in Zseliz for the summer months, it is likely that this song was composed early in the year. It is sometimes ascribed to 1821 because that is when Schubert made a fair copy for the publisher. When the song was published in 1822 it was dedicated to Josef von Spaun who it seems had liked it so much that the composer let him keep the manuscript. The NSA also prints this first version of the piece with the marking Andante, and with a few different phrasings, dynamics and other small details. Schubert used this version of the song when he prepared *Lob der Tränen* for publication at the end of 1822 and it follows that the tiny tweakings and adjustments he made for the second (i.e. published) version represent his final thoughts on the song.

Autograph:	Wienbibliothek im Rathaus, Vienna (first version)
Publication:	Published as part of the NSA in 1970 (P751; first version)
	Published as Op. 13 no. 2 by Cappi & Diabelli, Vienna in December 1822 (P32; second version)
Dedicatee:	Josef von Spaun
Subsequent editions:	Peters: Vol. 1/187; AGA XX 294: Vol. 5/10; NSA IV: Vol. 1a/100 & Vol. 1b/229; Bärenreiter: Vol. 1/80
Bibliography:	Capell 1928, p. 143
	Fischer-Dieskau 1977, p. 67
Arrangements:	Arr. Franz Liszt (1811–1886) for solo piano (1838) [*see* TRANSCRIPTIONS]

Discography and timing:　Fischer-Dieskau I 9[11]　2'49　(first two strophes only)

Hyperion I 21[20] & 27[1]　4'43　Edith Mathis

2'49　Matthias Goerne

Hyperion II 20[20]　2'49　Matthias Goerne

← *Das Abendrot* D627　　　　　　　　　　　　　　　*Sonett I* D628 →

LOB DES TOKAYERS　　　　In praise of Tokay

(Baumberg) **D248** [H149]

B♭ major　August 1815

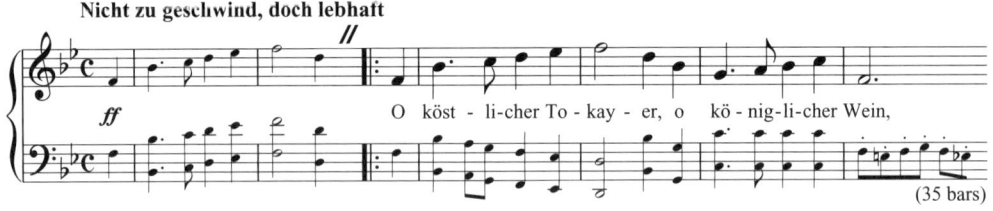

Nicht zu geschwind, doch lebhaft

ff

O köst - li-cher To - kay - er, o kö - nig-li-cher Wein,

(35 bars)

O köstlicher Tokayer!	Exquisite Tokay!
O königlicher Wein!	Prince among wines!
Du stimmest meine Leier	You inspire my lute
Zu seltnen Reimerei'n.	To rare flights of poetry.
Mit lang' entbehrter Wonne	With long-desired bliss
Und neuerwachtem Scherz	And newly awakened gaiety
Erwärmst du, gleich der Sonne,	You warm my half-frozen heart
Mein halberstorbnes Herz:	Like the sun.
Du stimmest meine Leier	You inspire my lute
Zu seltnen Reimerei'n,	To rare flights of poetry.
O köstlicher Tokayer!	Exquisite Tokay,
O königlicher Wein!	Prince among wines!
O köstlicher Tokayer!	Exquisite Tokay!
O königlicher Wein!	Prince among wines!
Du giessest Kraft und Feuer	You pour strength and ardour
Durch Mark und durch Gebein.	Through my whole being.

Ich fühle neues Leben	I feel new life
Durch meine Adern sprühn,	Sparkling in my veins,
Und deine Nektarreben	I feel your nectar grapes
In meinem Busen glühn.	Glowing in my breast.
Du giessest Kraft und Feuer	You pour strength and ardour
Durch Mark und durch Gebein,	Through my whole being
O köstlicher Tokayer!	Exquisite Tokay!
O königlicher Wein!	Prince of wines!
O köstlicher Tokayer!	Exquisite Tokay!
O königlicher Wein!	Prince among wines!
Dir soll, als Gramzerstreuer,	To you who allays sorrow
Dies Lied geweiht sein!	This song is dedicated.
In schwermutsvollen Launen	In melancholy moods
Beflügelst du das Blut,	You fire the blood;
Bei Blonden und bei Braunen	You give courage to the bashful,
Giebst du dem Blödsinn Mut.	To blonde and brunette alike.
Dir soll, als Gramzerstreuer,	To you who allays sorrow
Dies Lied geweiht sein,	This song is dedicated.
O köstlicher Tokayer!	Exquisite Tokay,
O königlicher Wein!	Prince among wines!

GABRIELE VON BAUMBERG (1775–1839)

This is the third of Schubert's seven Baumberg solo settings (1809–10 and 1815). See the poet's biography for a chronological list of all the Baumberg settings.

This rousing drinking song seems an unlikely poem to have been composed by a woman but Gabriele von Baumberg was no ordinary blushing violet of the Biedermeier era. Indeed in an English translation of her lyric it is hard to convey the uninhibited ecstasy in which she writes about 'tripping' on her favourite wine. Mention of a lyre places the timescale of the poem in antiquity; it was probably meant to be an imitation of the celebrated drinking songs of the Greek poet Anacreon, one of whose lyrics was translated by Schubert's friend Bruchmann for *An die Leier* D737. Baumberg herself posed in classical Greek garb with a lyre for a portrait as was customary for female poets who were considered descendants of Sappho, whatever their sexual inclinations. The only anachronism in this classical pastiche is of course specific mention of Tokay, which places the provenance of the poem very much within the Austro-Hungarian Empire. Baumberg had married the Hungarian radical poet Bacsányi and it is clear that her experience of the wine was in its country of origin. There is no doubt, however, that Tokay was freely available throughout the Empire and was considered almost a local drink in the Vienna of Schubert's time. It seems logical, in the absence of the autograph, to date this song with the other 1815 Baumberg settings. It is only the Esterházys' long association with the Tokay-producing vineyards of Hungary that might suggest a later date – 1818, for example, when Schubert was in the summer employ of a branch of this noble family.

Bearing in mind the unbuttoned nature of this paean to Tokay, it is hardly surprising that the eighteen-year-old Schubert's setting is suitable for a large number of people. It was published as a solo but its strong striding basses and powerful chords (much of the song calls for a loud accompaniment) encourage choral treatment. The tune is hearty and enjoyable and is not one of the composer's most subtle creations. As is often the case with drinking songs, the accompaniment bubbles with good spirits, and counterpoints the simplicity of the vocal line in order for it to be quickly assimilated by amateur musicians; the staccato quavers in this case represent *pétillant* (or more appropriately here, 'sprudelnd') high spirits. The middle section (from b. 12, 'Mit lang' entbehrter Wonne') is quieter and more lyrical with the touch of that philosophical observation characteristic of the German drinking song. When the voices finish, chords rise to the top of the stave in the accompaniment and descend in a scale in sixths to the

Wine label by Martha Griebler for the Schubertiade, Hohenems.

home key of B flat; the following five bars stay resolutely grounded in this tonality with dotted quaver/semiquaver figures embroidering the tonic chord in various registers of the keyboard. The jerkiness of all this hocketing and hicupping concludes the song in comically bibulous fashion.

It is said that some nineteenth-century drinkers drank Sauternes throughout meals, despite the fact that today something so sweet would generally appear as a dessert wine. The Hungarian taste for sweet wine must account for the enthusiasm for Tokay which, in Schubert's day, seems to have been considered a wine for all occasions. Everyday Tokay can be sweeter or drier according to the vintage, and it is likely that this *Tokay szamorodni* (literally 'Tokay as it comes') was the wine that the members of Schubert's circle would have been able to afford in Viennese hostelries. However Baumberg is referring to the picking of grapes in the poem's first verse when she speaks of her 'half-frozen heart' being warmed by the sun – half-frozen grapes are harvested to make what the Germans call 'Eiswein'. Her mention of a 'königlicher Wein' indicates that she was referring to the more expensive *Tokay aszu* that is aged in oak for a minimum of three years. In more modern times the wine has been praised in song by Noël Coward in the musical-operetta *Bitter Sweet* (1929): 'Wine of the sun that will waft you along, / Lifting you high on the wings of a song'. Coward has his chorus of officers pronounce the varietal in a very English way, however: 'The only call we all obey, / Tokay – Tokay – Tokay!'

Autograph:	Missing or lost		
First edition:	Published as Op. post. 118 no. 4 by Josef Czerny, Vienna in June 1829 (P225) with the poem falsely ascribed to Körner		
Subsequent editions:	Peters: Vol. 4/148; AGA XX 135: Vol. 3/66; NSA IV: Vol. 8/176		
Bibliography:	Youens 1996, pp. 45–6		
Discography and timing:	Fischer-Dieskau I 5[18]	1'14	(first strophe only)
	Hyperion I 22[20]	2'17	John Mark Ainsley, Jamie MacDougall, Simon Keenlyside & Michael George
	Hyperion II 9[10]		

←— *Die Fröhlichkeit* D262   *Cora an die Sonne* D263 —→

LODAS GESPENST   Loda's ghost

(Macpherson after 'Ossian') **D150** [H219]
G minor – B♭ major   17 January 1816

(277 bars)

*Instead of a translation of the German text Macpherson's original is printed below; it is divided
into eight sections to coincide with Schubert's musical treatment of the extract.*

(1) Der bleiche, kalte Mond erhob sich in Osten. Der Schlaf stieg auf die Jünglinge nieder! Ihre blauen Helme schimmern zum Strahl; das sterbende Feuer vergeht. Der Schlaf aber ruhte nicht auf dem König: er hob sich mitten in seinen Waffen, und stieg langsam den Hügel hinauf, die Flamme des Turms von Sarno zu sehn. Die Flamme war düster und fern; der Mond verbarg in Osten sein rotes Gesicht; es stieg ein Windstoss vom Hügel herab, auf seinen Schwingen war Lodas Gespenst. Es kam zu seiner Heimat, umringt von seinen Schrecken, und schüttelt' seinen düstern Speer. In seinem dunklen Gesicht glühn seine Augen wie Flammen; seine Stimme gleicht entferntem Donner. Fingal stiess seinen Speer in die Nacht und hob seine mächtige Stimme.

The wan, cold moon rose in the east. Sleep descended on the youths. Their blue helmets glitter to the beam; the fading fire decays. But sleep did not rest on the king: he rose in the midst of his arms, and slowly ascended the hill, to behold the flame of Sarno's tower. The flame was dim and distant; the moon hid her red face in the east. A blast came from the mountain, on its wings was the spirit of Loda. He came to his place in his terrors, and shook his dusky spear. His eyes appear like flames in his dark face; his voice is like distant thunder. Fingal advanced his spear in night and raised his voice on high.

(2) Zieh dich zurück, du Nachtsohn, ruf deine Winde und fleuch! Warum erscheinst du, vor mir, mit deinen schattigten Waffen? Fürcht' ich deine düstre Bildung, du Geist des leidigen Loda? Schwach ist dein Schild,[1] kraftlos das Luftbild, dein Schwert. Der Windstoss rollt sie zusammen; und du selber bist verloren;[2] fleuch von meinen Augen, du Nachtsohn! ruf deine Winde und fleuch!

Son of night, retire: call thy winds, and fly! Why dost thou come to my presence, with thy shadowy arms? Do I fear thy gloomy form, spirit of dismal Loda? Weak is thy shield of clouds: feeble is that meteor, thy sword! The blast rolls them together and thou thyself art lost. Fly from my presence, son of night! Call thy winds and fly!

[1] In Harold's translation, 'Schwach ist dein Schild *von Wolken*'.
[2] In Harold, 'und *du bist selber verloren*'.

(3)   Mit hohler Stimme versetzte der Geist, willst du aus meiner Heimat mich treiben? Vor mir beugt sich das Volk. Ich dreh die Schlacht im Felde der Tapfern. Auf Völker werf' ich den Blick,[3] und sie verschwinden. Mein Odem verbreitet den Tod. Auf den Rücken der Winde schreit' ich voran, vor meinem Gesichte brausen Orkane. Aber mein Sitz ist über den Wolken,[4] angenehm die Gefilde meiner Ruh.

Dost thou force me from my place? replied the hollow voice. The people bend before me. I turn the battle in the field of the brave. I look on the nations, and they vanish: my nostrils pour the blast of death. I come abroad on the winds: the tempests are before my face. But my dwelling is calm, above the clouds; the fields of my rest are pleasant.

(4)   Bewohn' deine angenehmen Gefilde, sagte der König: denk' nicht an Comhals Erzeugten. Steigen meine Schritte aus meinen Hügeln in deine friedliche Eb'ne hinauf? Begegnet ich dir[5] mit einem Speer, auf deiner Wolke, du Geist des leidigen Loda? Warum runzelst du denn deine Stirn auf mich? Warum schüttelst du deinen luftigen Speer? Du runzelst deine Stirn vergebens: nie floh ich vor den Mächtigen im Krieg. Und sollen die Söhne des Winds den König von Morven erschrecken? Nein, nein;[6] er kennt die Schwäche ihrer Waffen!

Dwell in thy pleasant fields, said the king: Let Comhal's son be forgot. Do my steps ascend from my hills, into the peaceful plains? Do I meet thee, with a spear, on thy cloud, spirit of dismal Loda? Why then dost thou frown on me? Why shake thine airy spear? Thou frownest in vain. I never fled from the mighty in war. And shall the sons of the wind frighten the king of Morven? No; he knows the weakness of their arms!

(5)   Fleuch zu deinem Land, versetzte die Bildung: Fass die Wunde,[7] und fleuch! Ich halte die Winde in der Höhle meiner Hand: ich bestimm den Lauf des Sturms. Der König von Sora ist mein Sohn; er neigt sich vor dem Steine meiner Kraft. Sein Heer umringt Carric-Thura, und er wird siegen! Fleuch zu deinem Land, Erzeugter von Comhal, oder spüre meine Wut, meine flammende Wut![8]

Fly to thy land, replied the form: receive the wind, and fly! The blasts are in the hollow of my hand: the course of the storm is mine. The king of Sora is my son, he bends at the stone of my power. His battle is around Carric-Thura; and he will prevail! Fly to thy land, son of Comhal, or feel my flaming wrath!

(6)   Er hob seinen schattigten Speer in die Höhe! er neigte vorwärts seine schreckbare Länge. Fingal ging ihm entgegen, und zuckte sein Schwert.[9] Der blitzende Pfad des Stahls durchdrang den

He lifted high his shadowy spear! He bent forward his dreadful height. Fingal, advancing, drew his sword. The gleaming path of the steel winds through the

---

[3] In Harold, 'werf ich *mein Aug*'.
[4] Harold has 'Aber mein Sitz ist *ruhig* über den Wolken'.
[5] Harold has '*Begegne* ich dir'.
[6] Harold is content with a single 'Nein'.
[7] This 'Wunde' is Schubert's hurried mistake for 'Winde'.
[8] Schubert inserts a 'meine Wut' here before Harold's 'meine flammende Wut'.
[9] Schubert cuts the phrase 'die Klinge des dunkelbraunen Luno' that follows 'zuckte sein Schwert'.

düstern Geist. Die Bildung zerfloss gestaltlos, in Luft, wie eine Säule von Rauch, welche der Stab des Jünglings berührt, wie er aus der sterbenden Schmiede aufsteigt. Laut schrie Lodas Gespenst, als es, in sich selber gerollt, auf dem Winde sich hob. Inistore bebte beim Klang. Auf dem Abgrund hörten's die Wellen. Sie standen vor Schrecken in der Mitte ihres Laufs!

gloomy ghost. The form fell shapeless into air, like a column of smoke, which the staff of the boy disturbs, as it rises from the half-extinguished furnace. The spirit of Loda shrieked, as rolled into himself, he rose on the wind. Inistore shook at the sound. The waves heard it on the deep. The waves stopped in their course, with fear:

(7) Die Freunde von Fingal sprangen plötzlich empor. Sie griffen ihre gewichtigen Speere. Sie missten den König: zornig fuhren sie auf; all ihre Waffen erschollen!

The friends of Fingal started, at once; and took their heavy spears. They missed the king: they rose in rage; all their arms resound!

(8) Der Mond rückt' in Osten voran. Fingal kehrt' im Klang seiner Waffen zurück. Gross war der Jünglinge Freude, ihre Seelen ruhig, wie das Meer nach dem Sturm. Ullin hob den Freudengesang. Die Hügel Inistores frohlockten. Hoch stieg die Flamme der Eiche; Heldengeschichten wurden erzählt.

The moon came forth in the east. Fingal returned in the gleam of his arms. The joy of his youth was great, their souls settled, as a sea from the storm. Ullin raised the song of gladness. The hills of Inistore rejoiced. The flame of the oak arose; and the tales of heroes are told.

JAMES MACPHERSON ('OSSIAN') (1736–1796), translated by EDMUND, BARON VON HAROLD (1737–1800)

This is the seventh of Schubert's ten Ossian–Macpherson solo settings (1815–17). See the poet's biography (under Macpherson, James) for a chronological list of all the Ossian settings.

The bard Ossian was the invention of James Macpherson, a Scottish student of Gaelic mythology who claimed to have discovered a treasure trove of ancient manuscripts which he rendered into English. Although Macpherson felt he needed to stand behind such a misty historical figure, his words are inventive and atmospheric enough to have earned him considerable renown in his own right. Thomas Chatterton, the celebrated literary hoaxer of the eighteenth century, was also talented enough to have achieved literary fame on his own account. It is true, though, that without the patina of historical authenticity German writers like Herder and Goethe would probably have been less interested in the fictional writings of a tribe of noble savages of impeccable honour and untainted naturalness. Macpherson's prose poems are heavily loaded with atmosphere, short on historical accuracy and rich in (sometimes hilarious) anachronism. Dr Johnson was one of those who scoffed from the first, much to the fury of Macpherson whose motives were not all dishonourable; he wished to draw attention to what he perceived to be a dying and neglected tradition of Celtic bardic poetry, using whatever means possible. Ossian's effusions were some of the best publicity that the Scottish nationalist cause has ever received.

Johann Wolfgang von Goethe, in his semi-autobiographical *Dichtung und Wahrheit* (Book III, Chapter 13) described the literary atmosphere during the period when he wrote his first successful novel, *Werther*: 'Ossian lured us off to Ultima Thule, where we roamed about on the

Fingal confronts Loda's ghost, painted by H. Singleton and engraved by James Fittler, published in *The Poems of Ossian*, London (1812).

infinite grey heath amidst protruding mossy gravestones, looking around us at the grass blown by a chill wind, and above us at the heavily clouded sky. Only by moonlight did this Caledonian night really become day: perished heroes and vanished maidens hovered about us, and we actually began to believe that we had seen the ghost of Loda in its fearsome form.' *Lodas Gespenst* describes the confrontation between Fingal the warrior king and the ghost of Loda (Odin in Norse mythology). In standing up to Loda, Fingal banishes the power of the god and superstition. Despite Capell's contention that the pages are 'singularly barren', this work is one of the most concise, fast-moving and exciting of the Ossian settings. The translation into German is by a figure almost as mysterious as Ossian himself – Baron Edmund von Harold (qv).

Section 1: The piece is headed 'Düster, mässig langsam' and the opening ritornello in G minor matches the sombre nature of this marking with mezzo staccato chords that are full of muted suspense. The recitative (beginning 'Der bleiche, kalte Mond erhob sich in Osten') is peaceful but with an undertow of unease. The gradually fading night-fire ('das sterbende Feuer', bb. 17–18) is illustrated, before the words are sung, by a series of harmonies in chromatic descent (bb. 15–17). A sudden 'Geschwind' (b. 20) shows us the restless state of the king whose climb up the hill to Sarno's tower is cleverly depicted by a wearily ascending vocal line (bb. 28–32). Recitative here, as throughout the piece, alternates with arioso and brief interludes for the piano. By the time the spirit of Loda appears ('es stieg ein Windstoss vom Hügel herab' bb. 46–7) we are in the key of D flat; the accompaniment doubles the vocal line in a passage heavy with portent (bb. 48–51). A martial phrase for the piano, in B flat minor (b. 55), depicts spear-shaking, and tremolandi (from b. 56) the flame-like flicker of the spirit's eyes. We seem to have arrived at this point in the story rather quickly, almost as if Fingal is already accustomed to the appearance of the god in this manner. In a confrontation that is reminiscent of that between Siegfried and Wotan, Loda attempts to dissuade Fingal from raising the siege of Carric-Thura.

Section 2: The key signature changes to F major, the time signature to ¾ and the marking is 'Ernst'. For the aria beginning 'Zieh' dich zurück, du Nachtsohn' sung by the brave and down-to-earth Fingal, fear is banished along with any complicated chromatic progressions. This passage, with its trills and striding basses, could have come from a Handel oratorio; there is even a brief suggestion of old-fashioned counterpoint between voice and piano (from b. 78). This is all appropriate for a warrior king of few words who is not afraid to defy the god and fulfil his destiny.

Section 3: Loda's reply begins with a recitative describing his voice ('Mit hohler Stimme versetzte der Geist', b. 97), but his principal utterance is a noble aria in B flat ('Vor mir beugt sich das

Volk' from b. 101), marked 'Mässig, kraftvoll'. Schubert succeeds in giving the aggrieved god a lofty tone. There is menace in the use of the piano to double the voice at 'Auf Völker werf' ich den Blick' (bb. 105–7) and considerable excitement is stirred up by the rather Beethovenian-sounding dotted rhythm (from b. 108) used to denote the god's revenge. The return to B flat major and simple chordal accompaniment for 'Aber mein Sitz ist über den Wolken' (from b. 120) lifts the mood of this section from unseemly bickering to dignified Olympian majesty, all the more effective for its pianissimo markings. Macpherson remarks in a footnote that 'there is a great resemblance between the terrors of this mock divinity, and those of the true God, as they are described in the 18th Psalm'. He is here referring to its eighth verse: 'There went up a smoke out of his nostrils, and fire out of his mouth devoured: coals were kindled by it.' It was Macpherson himself of course who was responsible for the seemingly mysterious similarities between the two texts, but he treated it as an imponderable thread that linked together the religions of the ages.

Section 4: The whole of this section (beginning at b. 130 with 'Bewohn' deine angenehmen Gefilde') is recitative, cleverly crafted with its rising sequences to depict Fingal summoning the courage to confront Loda once and for all. Fingal defends his actions and his own record of bravery in battle. From b. 141 the rhythm of the section 'Warum runzelst du denn deine Stirn' suggests a shaken fist or spear. Macpherson, with a semblance of great textual scholarship, explains Fingal's audacious blasphemy in the following note: 'Whether a proof could be drawn from this that Ossian had no notion of a divinity, I shall leave to others to determine: it appears, however, that he was of the opinion that superior beings ought to take notice of what passed among men.'

Section 5: Loda's riposte summons some of Schubert's best music for the piece. A memorable martial passage in C minor ('Fleuch zu deinem Land', from b. 154, with a change of time signature to ⅜) has an accompaniment that suggests the flourish of hunting horns. This builds up into an impressive aria aided by a series of rousing sequences, repeated after an interlude of recitative. Something in the military nature of this music prophesies warring clans, galloping horses and the pacing imprisoned nobility in the composer's Walter Scott settings of nine years later; we hear a ghostly presentiment of the polonaise style of *Lied des gefangenen Jägers*. Perhaps *Lodas Gespenst* marks the beginning of Schubert's Scottish style.

Section 6: A new section is marked 'Geschwind' from b. 182. Loda waves his spear ('Er hob seinen schattigen Speer in die Höhe') but it proves rather wooden. This section built on already familiar hunting horn motifs has nothing new to frighten Fingal, or us. The passage that shows Schubert's peerless musical imagination depicts the dematerialization of the ghost once Fingal has struck Loda's spear with his sword. The piano interludes both before and after 'Die Bildung zerfloss gestaltlos, in Luft' (bb. 196–9, and bb. 201–5) are remarkably descriptive of wreaths of smoke, disembodied and cleansed of the god's malevolent presence; the hushed euphony of thirds and sixths drains the music of the chromatics of conflict. Once again tremolandi are used (at b. 215 before 'Inistore bebte beim Klang'), now deep in the bass clef to suggest earthquake and the subverting of the order of the gods, and thus of nature itself. The very waves are too terrified to move. To mirror this phenomenon, rumbling oscillations cease in favour of detached or staccato crotchets (from b. 219) and a most startling shift from C minor to C sharp minor (bb. 221–3) illustrates the perverting of the laws of earthly harmony.

Section 7: Schnell – in A major – from b. 224. This is nothing more than a short section with a number of dramatic scale passages; it serves as music for the gathering of Fingal's clans and is a useful link to the recapitulation of the opening material at b. 248. There is an effective eleven-bar section at the end for the piano (bb. 237–47) which paints the upheaval in the world caused by Fingal's hubris: semibreve chords lead to snatched staccato crotchets, with portentous bars of rest to depict awestruck silence between. As Shakespeare once observed, 'The rest is silence.'

Section 8: This is the music come full circle. 'Der Mond rückt' in Osten voran' has the same music as the opening, but then follows a repeat of this refrain reharmonized in the relative major of B flat (b. 253) because the danger has been resolved by Fingal's bravery. The piano part on the final page of the work seems to have been conceived as a five-part choral piece without text. The effect is joyful enough without quite measuring up to the rest of the piece. The final five bars, a postlude for piano, seem almost deliberately banal (the marking is 'Bieder' which means honest or unsophisticated) and it may be, as Fischer-Dieskau contends, that the composer wanted to illustrate the tribe's return to normality after its brush with the fantastic world of the spirits. Fischer-Dieskau also notes that Carl Loewe used the same effect in *Prinz Eugen* where this tremendously rousing ballad has a strangely hushed single bar of piano postlude, although the effect there is rogueish rather than apologetic.

In 1830 Diabelli judged *Lodas Gespenst* to be unpublishable as Schubert had left it. He enlisted the help of Leopold von Sonnleithner (a friend of the composer since July 1816) to change the text and to adapt *Punschlied* D277, a drinking song to a Schiller text. This was grafted on to the Ossian setting and served as a rousing finale. This curious concoction was published as *Lodas Gespenst* in the *Nachlass* and subsequently the Peters Edition. Sonnleithner changed Schiller's bibulous words 'Vier Elemente / Innig gesellt' to 'Heil unserm König, tapfer und stark' . . . 'Heil ihm, der Morvens König ist', and so on. The incomplete but substantial fragment *Die Nacht* D534 suffered something of a similar fate with the addition of *Jagdlied* D521. According to his memoirs, Sonnleithner regretted the part he had played in tampering with Schubert's work.

Lodas Gespenst exactly as it was conceived by the composer can be an effective piece in performance (it has the advantage of being of comparatively manageable length) but it needs good dramatic timing and a cracking pace to make it, in Macpherson's own words, 'the most extravagant fiction in all Ossian's poems'.

Autograph:	Conservatoire Collection, Bibliothèque Nationale, Paris
First edition:	Published (with the addition of the music of *Punschlied* D277 as a finale) as Book 3 of the *Nachlass* by Diabelli, Vienna in 1830 (P243)
Publication reviews:	Rellstab 'Ueberblick der Erzeugnisse', *Iris im Gebiete der Tonkunst* (Berlin), No. 39 (12 November 1830) [Waidelich/Hilmar Dokumente II No. 784b]
Subsequent editions:	Peters: Vol. 4/181; AGA XX 44: Vol. 2/21; NSA IV: Vol. 7/105; Bärenreiter: Vol. 6/56
Bibliography:	Capell 1928, p. 93
	Fischer-Dieskau 1977, p. 55
Discography and timing:	Fischer-Dieskau I 2[22] 11'48
	Hyperion I 17[2]
	Hyperion II 12[14] 10'58 Lucia Popp

← *Lied (Mutter geht durch ihre Kammern) D373*   *Der König in Thule D367* →

LORMA (I)   Lorma
(MACPHERSON after 'OSSIAN') **D327** [H204]
(Fragment) A minor – B♭ major   28 November 1815

(47 bars)

The original English version from Fingal is given here as a translation. The lines in italics are those not set by Schubert in this fragment.

Lorma sass in der Halle von Aldo. Sie sass beim Licht einer flammenden Eiche. Die Nacht stieg herab, aber er kehrte nicht wieder zurück. Lormas Seele war trüb!

'Was hält dich, du Jäger von Cona, zurück? Du hast ja versprochen wieder zu kehren![1] Waren die Hirsche weit in der Ferne? Brausen an der Heide, die düstern Winde um dich! ich bin im Lande der Fremden, wer ist mein Freund, als Aldo? komm von deinen erschallenden Hügeln, O mein bester Geliebter!'

Sie wandte ihre Augen gegen das Tor. Sie lauscht zum brausenden Wind. *Sie denkt, dies seien die Tritte von Aldo. Freud steigt in ihrem Antlitz! aber Wehmut kehrt wieder, wie am Mond eine dünne Wolke, zurück.*

Lorma sat in Aldo's hall. She sat at the light of a flaming oak. The night came down, but he did not return. The soul of Lorma is sad!

'What detains, thee, hunter of Cona? Thou didst promise to return. Has the deer been distant far? Do the dark winds sigh round thee on the heath? I am in the land of strangers; who is my friend but Aldo? Come from thy sounding hills, O my best beloved!'

Her eyes are turned toward the gate. She listens to the rustling blast. She thinks it is Aldo's tread. Joy rises in her face! But sorrow returns again, like a thin cloud on the moon.

JAMES MACHPHERSON ('OSSIAN') (1736–1796), translated by EDMUND, BARON VON HAROLD (1737–1800)

This is the sixth of Schubert's ten Ossian–Macpherson solo settings (1815–17) See the poet's biography (under Macpherson, James) for a chronological list of all the Ossian settings.

The poem is a fragment from Edmund von Harold's translation of Macpherson's poem *The Battle of Lora*. Schubert was clearly attracted to the text with its evocation of a heroine who waits in vain for her beloved to return to her, the night scene illuminated by the flames of a burning oak tree. The heroine is Lorma who has left her husband Erragon and run away with her lover Aldo. Neither of the two Schubert settings encompasses the end of the story where Lorma sees Aldo's ghost (he has perished in battle) and dies soon afterwards in grief. Duparc's medieval evocation *Au pays où se fait la guerre* comes to mind where the woman waiting interminably in the tower for her paramour has her hopes falsely aroused only to be dashed a moment later. For

---

[1] The 'ja' in this line is Schubert's addition.

some reason the composer was at a loss as to how to finish the first setting of the poem, and the completion of the second has been lost. This is a pity because both fragments contain beautiful music.

They are both in A minor. One can see a relationship between the two settings as if the words inspired the same sort of response from the composer, even if the details and the shapes of the melodies are rather different. The 1816 version (D376) is in common time, but this first setting is in ⅜. There is a solemn introduction of seven bars built of a right-hand tune in sixths – something of a slow dance as if ceremonial music is being played in the hall of Aldo and is muffled by thick castle walls. These passages in sixths are in differing registers of the piano; together with a left hand that imitates their rhythm in quasi-counterpoint, they link together the various segments of the opening recitative. (Euphonious thirds and sixths in the accompaniment play an important part in other Ossian settings, notably *Cronnan* D282 and *Die Nacht* D534.) The second setting has music that is much more evocative of Lorma's disturbed emotions; here her distress is in counterpoint to the impersonality of the dance music.

With 'Was hält dich, du Jäger von Cona, zurück' (b. 19) Lorma begins to speak. This was to be the occasion of an impassioned C minor aria in the later version, but here the composer contents himself with a G minor arioso marked *Mässig langsam*. This sets Lorma's first two phrases (the second a musical sequence of the first) in terms of simple, almost phlegmatic speech, and her utterances are separated by short bursts of piano commentary. At b. 29 a new section begins (at 'Brausen an der Heide die düstern Winde'); here the dotted quaver plus semiquaver rhythms prophesy the fiery D minor opening of the Schiller setting *Der Kampf* D594, as well as the rumbustious middle section of *Gruppe aus dem Tartarus* D396. The arioso continues in more peaceful fashion at 'ich bin im Lande der Fremden' (bb. 31–2). Under the name 'Aldo' there is a chromatic scale in the accompaniment, a figuration that Schubert used no fewer than eight times in the remaining thirteen bars of the fragment. This rising scale in the alto line (played either by the left hand or the lower fingers of the right as the little finger sustains melodic minims) seems to be a leitmotif: Lorma can think of nothing but 'Aldo' whose motif denotes disappearance or evaporation.

The six bars (bb. 42–7) of recitative and interlude from '... gen das Tor' were discovered some forty years ago by Maurice Brown in the Stadtbibliothek in Vienna as he studied the manuscript of a piano sonata from 1817. It was quite common for the composer to return to old, unused pieces of manuscript paper; in this case works that stand two years apart in chronology are found side by side on the same written page. These forty-seven bars are as much as we have of the first setting of *Lorma*. (The 1816 version is only five bars longer.) Without attempting to complete the whole poem (surely an impossible task) Reinhard Van Hoorickx decided to work this fragment to the same point reached by the second setting. From 'Sie denkt, es seien die Tritte von Aldo' he achieves this with fairly modest unjarring means (recorded for the Hyperion Edition), and he uses the 'Aldo' motif, that inner-voiced chromatic scale, to useful effect. There is no doubt that this could have been a piece of real stature had Schubert completed it himself.

Autograph:	Wienbibliothek im Rathaus (first draft)
First edition:	Fragment published privately in Stuttgart in 1928; subsequently completed by Reinhard Van Hoorickx. First formally published as part of the NSA in 2002 (P842)
Subsequent editions:	Not in Peters; Not in AGA; NSA IV: Vol. 10/247
Bibliography:	Brown 1954, p. 93
	Hoorickx 1977, p. 285

Discography and timing: Fischer-Dieskau   —
                                         Hyperion I 22[25]   3'23   Catherine Wyn-Rogers
                                         Hyperion II 11[17]

← *Wer sich der Einsamkeit ergibt (Harfenspieler) D325*   *Die drei Sänger D329* →

LORMA (II)   Lorma

(MACPHERSON after 'OSSIAN') **D376** [H224]
Fragment A minor – A♭ major   10 February 1816

(52 bars)

See previous entry for poem and translation. N.B. italics pertain only to D327

JAMES MACPHERSON ('OSSIAN') (1736–1796), translated by EDMUND, BARON VON HAROLD
(1737–1800)

This is the ninth of Schubert's ten Ossian–Macpherson solo settings (1815–17) See the poet's biography (under Macpherson, James) for a chronological list of all the Ossian settings.

Schubert made two attempts to set the story of Lorma who waits in vain for her beloved (a type of Ossianic equivalent of Schiller's *Die Erwartung* D159 without the happy ending), the first of which dates from November 1815 (*see* previous entry). A few months later he tried again, recasting the song entirely, but apparently breaking off only three sentences later than in his first attempt. (Walther Dürr avers that Schubert probably *did* complete the song, and that the remainder of it somehow got lost.) We can only imagine how beautifully he would have set the description of Lorma a little later in the poem – 'she was as pale as a watery cloud that rises from the lake, to the beam of the moon'.

The music begins in a mournful A minor in the simple, rather old-fashioned folksong style (cf. the opening of *Lodas Gespenst* D150) which the composer seems to have thought appropriate for depicting the Scottish Highlands in primeval times. The opening recitative is most effective with its evocation of night. The cadence on 'Lormas Seele war trüb' has the feel of eighteenth-century oratorio. There follows (from b. 12) an impassioned ⅜ aria in C minor ('Was hält dich, du Jäger von Cona, zurück'), marked 'Mässig'. This has a repeated accompanying figure in gliding sixths that suggests the suitably 'ancient' music of Bach where an oboe might be the obbligato instrument sharing the vocal line with the singer. 'Wer ist mein Freund, als Aldo?' (from b. 32) is supported by a bass line that rises in chromatic semitones, adding Romantic anguish to a section that has a deliberately classical feel. The next section ('Mit Bewegung' from b. 43 with a change of key signature to A flat major) uses the same figure on the piano in different registers to depict, in rather conventional fashion, the click of a gate, the rustling of wind and the supposed tread of Aldo, the returning hero. The words of the final cadence ('wie am Mond eine dünne Wolke, zurück') are beautifully set, with a touching dying fall, as gentle as a moon-beam, which modulates to E flat. It is a great pity that the composer should seem to give up the ghost at this point. Perhaps he realized that the rest of the poem would require so much ethereal music for the spirit of Lorma (there are no more stirring battle scenes in this section) that the piece would lack the musical contrasts needed to hold the attention of the listener.

Autograph:	Wienbibliothek im Rathaus, Vienna (first draft)
First edition:	Published as part of the AGA in 1895 (P715)
Subsequent editions:	Not in Peters; Not in AGA; NSA IV: Vol. 10/251; Bärenreiter: Vol. 9
Discography and timing:	Fischer-Dieskau —
	Hyperion I 17[4]
	Hyperion II 12[19] 2'47 Lucia Popp

←— *Der Tod Oscars* D375   *Das Grab* D377 —→

MICHAEL LUBI (1757–1808)

THE POETIC SOURCE
S1 *Gedichte von Michael Lubi*, Graz 1804, gedruckt bey den Gebrüdern Tanzer

THE SONG
December 1814   *Ammenlied* D122 [pp. 167–8]

Lubi was born in Tüffer in the south Steiermark in 1757. He was a doctor of law and, like so many of his profession, an amateur poet. On being declared bankrupt he lost his qualifications to practise law and was imprisoned. He spent the rest of his days in penury in Graz. His poetry collection was dedicated to Joseph Edler von Sonnenfels in Vienna who also inspired Lubi to write a cantata libretto in his honour. Many of the poems in this volume are gracefully (if rather obsequiously) dedicated to members of the nobility, or to names from classical mythology (the inspiration was the Odes of Horace) such as Amint, Nice and Tyndaris. Lubi died on 7 June 1808 in Graz.

LUISENS ANTWORT   Louisa's answer
(Kosegarten) **D319** [H198]

This song exists in two versions, the second of which is discussed below:
(1) 19 October 1815; (2) 1816 (?)

(1) 'Klagend'   B♭ minor   ¢   [26 bars]

(2) B♭ minor

Klagend

p

Wohl wei - nen Got-tes En - gel,

(31 bars)

(1)   Wohl weinen Gottes Engel,
       Wenn Liebende sich trennen.
       Wie werd' ich leben können,
       Geliebter, ohne dich!
       Gestorben allen Freuden,
       Leb' ich fortan den Leiden,
       Und nimmer, Wilhelm, nimmer
       Vergisst Luisa dich.

God's angels weep
When lovers part.
How shall I be able to live
Without you, beloved?
Dead to all joys
I shall henceforth live for sorrow,
And never, William, never
Shall Louisa forget you.

(2)   Wie könnt ich dein vergessen!
       Wohin ich, Freund, mich wende,
       Wohin den Blick nur sende,
       Umstrahlt dein Bildnis mich.
       Mit trunkenem Entzücken
       Seh' ich es auf mich blicken.
       Nein, nimmer, Wilhelm, nimmer
       Vergisst Luisa dich.

How could I forget you?
Wherever I turn, beloved,
Wherever I cast my eyes,
Your image shines around me.
With heady rapture
I see it gaze upon me.
No, never, William, never
Shall Louisa forget you.

(3)   Wie könnt' ich dein vergessen!
       Gerötet von Verlangen,
       Wie flammten deine Wangen,
       Von Inbrunst nass, um mich!
       Im Widerschein der deinen,
       Wie leuchteten die meinen!
       Nein, nimmer, Wilhelm, nimmer
       Vergisst Luisa dich.

How could I forget you?
How your cheeks burned,
Flushed with desire,
Perspiring with ardour for me!
How my cheeks glowed
In the reflection of yours!
No, never, William, never
Shall your Louisa forget you.

[. . . 3 . . .]

[. . . 3 . . .]

(7)   Wie könnt' ich dein vergessen!
       Vergessen jener Stunden,
       Wo ich, von dir umwunden,
       Umflechtend innigst dich,
       An deine Brust mich lehnte,
       Ganz dein zu sein mich sehnte!—
       Geliebter, nimmer, nimmer
       Vergisst Luisa dich.

How could I forget you,
Forget those hours
When I was embraced by you,
When, clasping you ardently,
I leant upon your breast,
Longing to be wholly yours?
Beloved, never, never
Shall Louisa forget you.

[. . . 10 . . .]

[. . . 10 . . .]

(18)   Verachtet und vergessen,   If I were despised and forgotten,
         Verloren und verlassen,   Lost and forsaken,
         Könnt' ich dich doch nicht hassen;   I still could not hate you;
         Still grämen würd' ich mich,   I should grieve silently
         Bis Tod sich mein erbarmte,   Until death took pity on me
         Das Grab mich kühl umarmte—   In the grave's cool embrace.
         Doch auch im Grab, im Himmel,   But even in the grave, even in heaven
         O Wilhelm, liebt' ich dich!   I should still love you, William!

(19)   In mildem Engelglanze   I would bathe your bed
         Würd' ich dein Bett umschimmern   In a gentle, angelic radiance,
         Und zärtlich dich umwimmern: And murmur tenderly into your ear:
         'Ich bin Luisa, ich!   'I am Louisa:
         Luisa kann nicht hassen,   Louisa cannot hate you,
         Luisa dich nicht lassen,   Louisa cannot leave you.
         Luisa kommt, zu segnen,   Louisa comes to bless you,
         Und liebt auch droben dich.'   And still loves you up above.'

Ludwig Kosegarten (1758–1818); poem written in 1785

This is the twentieth of Schubert's twenty-one Kosegarten solo settings (1815–17). See the poet's biography for a chronological list of all the Kosegarten settings, as well as a discussion of Morten Solvik's Kosegarten Liederkreis and this song's place within it.

On the same day as composing Kosegarten songs about Rosa and Ida (the latter of these a coded reminiscence of a thwarted passion from the poet's early years) Schubert turned to a fictional Louisa. It was to be the last of his many Kosegarten settings for the year. The poem is a reply to a famous lyric by Klamer Eberhard Karl Schmidt, *Trennung und Wiedervereinigung*, which Mozart set in 1787 as *Das Lied der Trennung* K519, one of his most beautiful songs. Schmidt's poem begins with the lines 'Die Engel Gottes weinen, / Wo Liebende sich trennen!' and bemoans the parting of the lovers as seen from the man's point of view. Kosegarten here attempted to reply as if he were Louisa herself, caught up in the same romantic situation. The promiscuous poet invents the name of Wilhelm for the fellow protagonist; Kosegarten was fond of noms de plume and it is not impossible that he saw himself as Wilhelm in this scenario.

Although the accompaniment of Mozart's setting was in semiquavers and Schubert's in quavers, there is no doubt that the younger composer had the 'Bewegung' of Mozart's song in mind, and that his song is intended as a sort of companion piece. The spacing of the piano figurations in undulating sixths brings to mind another Mozart song, *Abendempfindung* K523, which Schubert seems to have known well; it is as if he is paying homage to two great Mozart songs at once. Even the melodic line of *Luisens Antwort* has something of the shape of *Lied der Trennung*, and the key of B flat minor (unusual for Schubert) is related, as if in fugal answer, to Mozart's key of F minor. There are no fewer than nineteen verses in both the AGA and the NSA (in the latter conveniently printed as underlay), exactly the same number as are printed in the Kosegarten sources. The NSA prints two versions, the first dated 19 October 1815, and the second almost certainly from 1816. For the Hyperion Edition recording Elly Ameling selected 1, 2, 18 and 19 (i.e. the first two verses of the poem and the last two). Two further strophes from the poem, 3 and 7, are printed above.

Autograph: Wienbibliothek im Rathaus, Vienna (first and second versions)
First edition: Published as part of the AGA in 1895 (P605; second version)
Subsequent editions: Not in Peters; AGA XX 166: Vol. 3/152; NSA IV: 9/166 (first
                        version) & 168 (second version)
Discography and timing: Fischer-Dieskau   —
                        Hyperion I 7[20]
                        Hyperion II 11[10]   3'45   Elly Ameling

← *Schwangesang* D318   *Der Zufriedene* D320 →

Drawing of Franz Schubert by Josef Teltscher, inscribed by the composer, 'Denken Sie möglichst oft an Ihren Franz Schubertmpia, Wien 1825' (Think as often as possible of your Franz Schubert [mpia = *manu propria*, signed with my own hand], Vienna 1825).

ANDREW MACDONALD (1757–1790)

THE POETIC SOURCE
S1 *Love and Loyalty* printed in *The miscellaneous works of A. M'Donald; including the tragedy of Vimonda, and those productions which have appeared under the signature of Matthew Bramble Esq. with various other compositions by the same author.* London, printed for J. Murray, 1791. pp. 237–93. (Opera libretto)

THE SONG
Early 1825?   *Lied der Anne Lyle* D830 (Walter Scott in *A Legend of Montrose* quotes from Macdonald's work) [S1: Act III Scene 2, AIR XXVII p. 289]

Macdonald's air is sung towards the end of *Love and Loyalty* by the opera's heroine Juliana as she modestly (and unsuccessfully) attempts to dissuade Alphonso, King of Bohemia, from ennobling her and raising her to the throne as his consort. She nevertheless becomes Queen Juliana. The air is preceded by these of her spoken lines:

> *I glory in the thought of being dear to you; but I will deserve it. You shall never blush for me. Go – pursue those nobler views your state points out. – Adorn your throne with some noble princess and leave me in my obscurity.*

The words in italics below represent Scott's changes to Macdonald's original when publishing his Anne Lyle lyric:

Wert though like me in life's low vale,
    With thee, how blest! that life [*lot*] I'd share:
With thee I'd fly as far as [*wherever*] gale
    Could waft, or swelling ocean [*bounding galley*] bear.
But parted by severe decree,
    Far different must our fortunes prove;
May thine be joy! enough for me
    To weep and pray for him I love.

The pangs this foolish heart may [*must*] feel,
    When hope must be for ever gone [*shall be forever flown*],
No fruitless sorrow [*sullen murmur*] shall reveal,
    No sullen murmur [*selfish murmurs*] ever own.
Not will I thro' my [*through life's*] weary years,
    As a [*Like a*] pale drooping mourner rove [*move*],
While I can think my secret tears
    Are not forgot by him [*May wound the heart of him*] I love.

Scott calls this 'a little Gaelic song' but it is in fact nothing of the sort, apart from the fact that it was written by a Scot. It was clearly taken by Scott directly from S1 above, and Scott's acknowledgement of the author spells the name, M'Donald, in the archaic Scottish manner.

Macdonald was born in Leith, the son of a gardener, and wrote under the name of Matthew Bramble. At one stage he was tutor to the children of the Oliphants of Gask – one of these was Caroline Nairne (1766–1845) who wrote the poems 'Will ye no come back again?' and 'Charlie is my darling'. Macdonald was an accomplished violinist and director of a Glasgow music club. He went to London hoping to make his fortune in the theatre but died at the age of thirty-three of consumption in miserable circumstances in Kentish Town. It is curious that Scott, usually a punctilious historian, is content to place words less than thirty years old, and by a clearly unfamiliar poet, in the mouth of his seventeenth-century heroine Annot Lyle. He must have been under pressure, as was often the case, to meet a publishing deadline.

See also LIED DER ANNE LYLE D830, WALTER SCOTT.

Die MACHT DER AUGEN *see* L'INCANTO DEGLI OCCHI D990E *and* DREI GESÄNGE FÜR BASS-STIMME MIT KLAVIER D902/1

Die MACHT DER LIEBE   The power of love
(KALCHBERG) **D308** [H188]
B♭ major   15 October 1815

Überall, wohin mein Auge blicket,
   Herrschet Liebe, find' ich ihre Spur;
   Jedem Strauch und Blümchen auf der Flur
Hat sie tief ihr Siegel eingedrücket.

Sie erfüllt, durchglüht, verjüngt und schmücket

   Stets das All der wirkenden Natur:
   Erd' und Himmel, jede Kreatur
Lebt und webt durch sie, von ihr beglücket.

[[. . . 2 (6 lines) . . .]]

Wherever my eyes turn
   Love reigns: everywhere I find its trace.
   On every bush and flower in the meadows
It has deeply imprinted its seal.

It forever pervades, warms, rejuvenates and adorns
   All that lives in productive nature.
   Heaven, earth and all creatures,
Live and find happiness through love alone.

[[. . . 2 (6 lines) . . .]]

JOHANN NEPOMUK VON KALCHBERG (1765–1827)

This is Schubert's only setting of a Kalchberg text. See the poet's biography.
See also the article for Selam.

Of the eight songs written on 15 October 1815, this is perhaps the most problematic. It has charm and melodic elegance but the composer failed to find a means to transfer Kalchberg's sonnet into a musical form. The poem is included in the almanac *Selam* for 1814, in a section entitled *Sonnette* (pp. 37–41 with a prominent title page) but Schubert was in such a hurry on that day that he seems not to have realized that the fourteen-line poem constituted a poetic entity. For the first quatrain (the only one he set) he followed the text exactly as he found it. Reed and Schochow knew only of a later edition of Kalchberg's works, which was also the only source available to Mandyczewski. This was the poet's *Gedichte*, published in Vienna in 1816 (Volume 1 p. 108), in which he had already revised the poem that Schubert found in *Selam*. Thus it appeared to earlier scholars that the composer had altered the words, but he had in fact been faithful to an earlier version of his poet's text.

Faithful up to a point. Schubert seems to have been content to set the first four lines and then treat the second quatrain of the sonnet as if it were merely the second verse of a strophic poem. ('Dazu eine Strophe' he wrote – 'add another strophe'.) In not writing the second strophe in his manuscript the composer left posterity with a problem: he could not have realized that an ephemeral publication like *Selam* would all but vanish from view and that the second verse would have to be retrieved much later, and in altered form, from the 1816 *Gedichte* volume.

The second verse as printed above is from *Selam*, and is thus different from that in the AGA and from the text used for the Hyperion Edition. At the time of recording the *Selam* source had not yet been discovered, and the original text was not yet available to performers. Kalchberg's lines as printed above fit the music much more easily than the printed alternatives with which Mandyczewski wrestled in order to make the second strophe work (he entirely rewrote the second line for that purpose). The closing sestet of the sonnet is completely unadaptable to Schubert's music. Those who have Volume 9 of the NSA at their disposal will find these puzzles definitively unravelled.

There are some illustrative touches that confirm the composer's musical inspiration was, as ever, guided by verbal imagery: the two vocal phrases that make up 'Überall, wohin mein Auge' are identical, leaving the impression of an image carefully scanned; the phrase 'der Flur / Hat sie tief ihr Siegel eingedrücket' moves to its lowest point on the word 'tief' in b. 15; the piano postlude (repetitions of the same two-beat phrase with the first note accented) is a good musical analogue for the imprinting of a seal ('ihr Siegel eingedrücket'), not once but thrice, just to be sure. Even if the song is hardly a success as a setting of a sonnet, the words and music provide enough of a positive ending to the group of seven songs (all from 15 October 1815) to support Walther Dürr's belief in the possibility of a *Selam* cycle (qv).

Autograph:	Österreichische Nationalbibliothek, Vienna (first draft)
First edition:	Published as part of the AGA in 1895 (P595)
Subsequent editions:	Not in Peters; AGA XX 156: Vol. 3/123; NSA IV: Vol. 9/145
Discography and timing:	Fischer-Dieskau I 5³² 1'41
	Hyperion I 20³⁰
	Hyperion II 10²⁴ 1'42 Patricia Rozario

⟵ *Die Sternenwelten* D306   *Das gestörte Glück* D309 ⟶

JAMES MACPHERSON ('Ossian') (1736–1796)

THE POETIC SOURCES

S1 *Fingal, An Ancient Epic Poem in Six Books: together with several other Poems, composed by Ossian, the Son of Fingal. Translated from the Galic* [sic] *language* London, printed for T. Becket and P. A. De Hondt, in the Strand, 1762

S2 *Die Gedichte Ossians des Celtischen Helden und Barden*. Aus dem Englischen und zum Theile der Celtischen Ursprache übersetzt von Freiherrn von Harold. Mannheim, 1782 im Verlage der Herausgeber der ausländischen schönen Geister [242 pages]. Dedicated to Karl Theodor, Kurfürst of Pfalzbayern.

S3 *Die Gedichte Ossians seines alten Celtischen Helden und Barden*. Zweyter Band, Mannheim 1782 im Verlage der Herausgeber der ausländischen schönen Geister [287 pages].

Schubert's copy of Harold's work had S2 and S3 bound together, as was often the case. The third part of Harold's book (mostly given over to the eight books of *Temora*) was sometimes bound in the same volume, sometimes sold separately. If Schubert was in possession of this substantially thicker version of Harold's 1782 text he found nothing in *Temora* to interest him.

S4 *Kolmas Klage* in *Lieder der Liebe und der Einsamkeit* II Theil, Johann Friedrich Reichardt, Leipzig, 1798 bei Gerhard Gleischer dem Jüngeren.

THE SONGS

22 June 1815	*Kolmas Klage* D217 [S1: from *The Songs of Selma* p. 210 beginning 'COLMA: 'It is night; I am alone, forlorn on the hill of storms''] [S4: almost certainly taken directly from Reichardt's setting of the poem] This is the only Schubert Ossian text that is not a translation by Harold. S3 pp. 21–4 offers a different translation entirely.
1815	*Ossians Lied nach der Falle Nathos* D278 [S1: p. 169 from *Darthula* beginning 'Bend forward from your clouds, I said, ghosts of my fathers! Bend.'] [S3: from *Darthula. Ein Gedicht*, pp. 241–2]
September 1815	*Das Mädchen von Inistore* D281 [S1: p. 14 from *Fingal* beginning 'Weep on the rocks of roaring winds, O maid of Inistore'] [S3: from Book 1 of *Fingal. Ein altes episches Gedicht in sechs Büchern*, pp. 62–3]
5 September 1815	*Cronnan* D282 [S1: p. 197 from *Carric-Thura* beginning 'I sit by the mossy fountain; on the top of the hill of the winds'] [S2: from *Carric-Thura. Ein Gedicht*, pp. 82–4]
20 September 1815	*Shilric und Vinvela* D293 [S1: p. 195 from *Carric-Thura* beginning 'My love is a son of the hill. He pursues the fleeing deer'] [S2: from *Carric-Thura. Ein Gedicht*, pp. 79–81]
28 November 1815	*Lorma* (I) D327 [S1: p. 118 from *Battle of Lora* beginning 'Lorma sat in Aldo's hall. She sat at the light of a flaming oak.'] [S3: from *Die Schlacht von Lora. Ein Gedicht*, p. 282]
17 January 1816	*Lodas Gespenst* D150 [S1: pp. 198–9 *Carric-Thura* beginning 'The wan, cold moon rose in the east'] [S2: from *Carric-Thura. Ein Gedicht*, pp. 86–9]
February 1816	*Der Tod Oscars* D375 [S1: p. 190 footnote to *Temora* beginning 'Why openest thou afresh the spring of my grief, O son of Alpin, inquiring how Oscar

fell?'] [S3: a complete setting of *Der Tod Oscars. Ein Gedicht*, pp. 287–8, continuing with a false numbering of pp. 283–7, thus *recte* 287–93]

10 February 1816   *Lorma* (II) D376 [S1: p. 118: *see Lorma* (I) above] [S3: from *Die Schlacht von Lora. Ein Gedicht*, p. 282]

February 1817   *Die Nacht* D534 [S1: p. 253 footnote to *Croma* beginning 'Night is dull and dark. The clouds rest on the hills'] [S2: from *Croma. Ein Gedicht*. pp. 181–3 (Erster Barde) and pp. 188–90.]

Mention should also be made of another 'Ossian' setting for unaccompanied voices that is outside the scope of this book: *Bardengesang* D147 Terzett (TTB) 20 January 1816

James Macpherson, born on 27 October 1736 in Ruthven, near Inverness in Scotland, was at the centre of one of the greatest disputes in British literary history. Educated in Aberdeen and Edinburgh, in 1758 he published a heroic poem in six cantos entitled *The Highlander*. The failure of this worthy work to achieve public success no doubt steeled the poet's determination to arrange his career in more fruitful ways. Under the influence of the Gaelic scholar John Home he produced his first Ossianic fragment, 'The Death of Oscar'. He was also encouraged by the literary cleric and Gaelic expert Hugh Blair (both Home and Blair remained warm supporters of Macpherson when his work was later surrounded by controversy). In 1760 Macpherson published *Fragments of Ancient Poetry Collected in the Highlands of Scotland and Translated from the Galic or Erse Language*. This book sowed the rumours that there was an important Scottish epic from the distant past that had been recently discovered after centuries of neglect. The eighteenth-century cult of Primitivism, or The Noble Savage, was at its height, and British readers (as well as French, Germans and Italians) were agog for material in this vein.

In 1762, after making much of travelling around Scotland gathering literary materials from ancient sources, Macpherson published *Fingal* (S1 above) which purported to be his translation of an epic by Ossian, son of Finn (or, as Macpherson has it, Fingal). Ossian was supposedly blind and as an old man lamented and celebrated the friends of his youth through epic poetry. The original Finn MacCoul, son of Comhal and father of Ossian the warrior

bard, is said to have dated from the third century AD when he led the Fianna (Fenians) to defend Ireland against the Norse. The fact that no Gaelic manuscripts survive from before the tenth century threw a shadow on the scholastic side of Macpherson's enterprise from the very beginning. The sequel to *Fingal*, entitled *Temora*, appeared in 1763, only a year afterwards, rather too quickly for the author to claim that he had undertaken further and deeper literary research. While *Temora* is now taken to be pure invention, *Fingal* is at least partly based on some genuine sources – Celtic texts, ballads and sagas of Irish origin going back to the twelfth century that had been current in Scotland since the sixteenth century. Few people now doubt that fragments of genuine poetry existed (many handed down from generation to generation by word of mouth) and that these were freely translated by Macpherson. But he was not satisfied with presenting fragments to the world and so created larger works – a kind of literary patchwork quilt with seemingly newly composed interconnecting material – all of it in a shape and form that appealed to the eighteenth-century literati and much of it anachronistic, to say the least. Macpherson's 'Ossian', arranged into books, each comprising an extended epic, generated fervent admiration but also vehement distrust.

Macpherson was something of a Gaelic scholar (though no real expert), an ardent nationalist and a gifted writer in his own right. He owed his worldly success (and eventual notoriety) to being an unwitting marketing genius: to the people of Europe he had given an

FINGAL,

AN

ANCIENT EPIC POEM,

In SIX BOOKS:

Together with feveral other POEMS, compofed by

OSSIAN the Son of FINGAL.

Tranflated from the GALIC LANGUAGE,

By JAMES MACPHERSON.

Fortia facta patrum.   VIRGIL.

LONDON:

Printed for T. BECKET and P. A. DE HONDT, in the Strand.

M DCC LXII.

Title page of *Fingal, an ancient epic poem* (1762).

James Macpherson, engraving (1775) by J. K. Sherwin,
after Sir Joshua Reynolds.

Cuthullin (the Irish Cuchulain) who, according
to legend, lived centuries apart (Gaelic scholars
in Ireland objected mightily to this) and the
kingdom of Morven in north-west Scotland
was invention grounded in actual topography
(prophetic of Thomas Hardy's Wessex). In a
spectacular telescoping of history Macpherson
had Fingal fighting both the Norwegians and
the Romans led by Caracalla. After a while his
literary embroidery (because he was so good at
it) became the woven fabric supporting the
whole enterprise.

The enthusiasm felt by some (and not
others) for Benjamin Britten's realizations of
Purcell songs can be seen as something similar
– 'more Britten than Purcell' detractors would
say, and some musicologists have dismissed
the works as outrageously anachronistic. But
the twentieth-century composer adds to the
authentic Purcellian melody an accompanying
frame that illuminates the inner spirit of his
seventeenth-century counterpart with a greater
sense of musical occasion than many a dry
and more 'correct' edition of Purcell's music.
On the cover of these works, published by
Boosey and Hawkes, the composer's name is
given simply as Henry Purcell; similarly everything that Macpherson wrote was credited
simply to Ossian.

If Macpherson had been content to use a
rubric like 'inspired by' or 'after' Ossian he
would have faced far less criticism, but the
stakes were too high and the European
public craved information about an ancient
warrior race that had actually existed. Thus
Macpherson, quickly driven into a corner,
insisted on the truth of the work's word for
word authenticity, and so began a mighty
cause célèbre.

Many of Macpherson's compatriots, enraptured by the prose poetry and the attention it
was bringing to Scotland, backed him to the
hilt. (This is not to subscribe to Dr Johnson's
conspiracy theory of members of an exclusively Scottish coterie supporting one of their
own in a concerted effort to deceive the English
'enemy'.) Intellectuals like David Hume and
Adam Smith were at first believers and later
sceptical. The lofty Edward Gibbon commented

exciting historical epic, to the downtrodden
community of Gaelic-speakers a glorious past
with which to confront the iniquities of the
present (the devastating 1746 rout of the Scots
by the English at Culloden was a relatively
recent event). The result was a public-relations
triumph for Scotland and Scottish nationalism:
at a stroke Macpherson had raised the profile of
a politically defeated people whose history and
substantial native literary heritage had been
undervalued or ignored. He no doubt sincerely
believed that everything he wrote was, broadly
speaking, in the spirit of Ossian (or what he
understood to be the bardic tradition of Gaelic
poetry), but his atmospheric prose showed
signs of too good an education: unmistakable
echoes of Homer, the Bible and Milton led to
accusations of falsification from the outset.

While parts of *Fingal* have their roots in real
Gaelic minstrelsy, Macpherson, more artist
than scholar, could not resist editing and elaboration. Thus he brought together Fingal and

The Dream of Ossian, frontispiece to *Ossians Gedichte* (1839).

on Ossian, contrasting the 'untutored Caledonians glowing with the warm virtues of nature' with the decadence of the Romans, but he later picked holes in Macpherson's historical chronology concerning the Roman invasion of Britain. Many people, the poet Thomas Gray among them, admired the Ossian poems without caring much about their provenance.

In 1815 Wordsworth wrote a wicked parody of the style: 'All hail, Macpherson! hail to thee Sire of Ossian! The Phantom was begotten by the smug embrace of an impudent Highlander upon a cloud of tradition – it travelled southward, where it was greeted with acclamation, and the thin Consistence took its course through Europe, upon the breath of popular applause.'

In 1866, long after Macpherson's death, Matthew Arnold wrote, 'Choose any of the better passages in Macpherson's *Ossian* and you can see even at this time of day what an apparition of newness and power such a strain must have been to the eighteenth century.' In this evaluation lies Macpherson's claim to a kind of greatness; it was no small talent that was able to attract the devoted attention of Klopstock and Schiller, Napoleon and Goethe, not to mention Franz Schubert and Felix Mendelssohn. The first German translation of Ossian appeared in 1764, awakening the interest of the German public in their own distant past. Through the mediation of Herder, folksong was recognized as stemming from the same fount of imaginative spontaneity as the poetry of wild, savage peoples. 'Ossian so kurz, stark, männlich, abgebrochen', wrote Herder – 'short, strong, manly, abrupt'.

Those who know Gaelic still tend to be on Macpherson's side – after all he gathered together authentic strands of the old, almost-forgotten tradition and presented them with a power and immediacy that served the cause to such an extent that 'authenticity' became something difficult to define. It was perhaps no worse than Britten's use of a modern tonal vocabulary to draw attention to the songs of an earlier composer, something that was in fact a spur to the Purcell renaissance and in a roundabout way a boost to the scholarship that complained most vociferously about such taking of liberties. It was unfortunate for Macpherson that Dr Samuel Johnson, famous for his probity and cutting wit (as well as his dislike of the Scots) turned his quizzical gaze on Ossian. As far as Johnson was concerned, Macpherson was a rogue responsible for an outrageous hoax. He demanded to see the original ancient Gaelic manuscripts but these were not immediately forthcoming. (According to *Fingal*'s London publisher, Becket, they had been available for viewing in his establishment in the Strand before the book had been published but no one had expressed any interest in seeing them.) Dr Hugh Blair, the above-mentioned Macpherson supporter and Regius professor of rhetoric and belles-lettres at the University of Edinburgh, encountered Johnson in London and asked him whether he really thought that 'any man of a modern age could have written such poems?' Johnson's celebrated reply was, 'Yes, Sir, many men, many women and many children.' Macpherson was given a pre-publication preview of his most famous critic's incendiary remarks against him in *Journey to the Western Islands*, 1775. By this time, twelve years after *Fingal* had first appeared, Macpherson had grown mightily proud of his literary status (even a supportive fellow Scot, Hume had commented on his 'absurd pride and caprice'[1]) and he rudely demanded a retraction. Johnson responded, 'I received your foolish and impudent note. Whatever insult is offered me I will

do my best to repel, and what I cannot do for myself the law will do for me. I will not desist from detecting what I think a cheat, from any fear of the menaces of a ruffian . . . I thought your book an imposture from the beginning . . . You may print this if you will.'

Johnson, in his accusations of a literary hoax of such scope, surely overestimated his opponent's talents, as if the whole world of Ossian had been the invention of a single writer. He had no understanding of the Ossianic tradition (his Scottish biographer James Boswell was far more sympathetic to the powers of 'Ossian') yet, during his subsequent visit to the Highlands with Boswell, Johnson describes himself sitting on a mossy bank ('such as a writer of Romance might have delighted to feign') with trees whispering over his head and 'a clear rivulet' streaming at his feet, feeling that 'all was rudeness, silence and solitude'. This Johnsonian idyll might perfectly describe the mood of the opening of Schubert's Ossian setting *Cronnan* D282.

Had Macpherson lived today he would have been a best-selling author with a cult following. The worldwide success of Tolkien's *Lord of The Rings* and the subsequent films are a pale echo of the tidal enthusiasm unleashed by Macpherson's work. The ripples of influence that he left behind on European literature comprise wave after wave of allusion, and not only in the world inhabited by Goethe and Schubert. J. M. Coetzee notes that Hazlitt placed Macpherson alongside Dante and Shakespeare and that 'the recovery of the Ossian epic in Scotland became a spur to the recovery – or invention – of other founding national epics: *Beowulf* in England, the *Kalevala* in Finland, the *Nibelunglied* in Germany, the *Chanson de Roland* in France, the *Lay of the Host of Igor* in Russia'. Over a hundred years after the appearance of *Fingal*, Arthur Rimbaud wrote of the London Underground in the prose poem 'Métropolitain' (from *Illuminations*) and conjured up the image of 'Du détroit d'indigo aux mers d'Ossian sur le sable rose et orange' ('From the indigo straits to the seas of Ossian on pink and orange sands'). Macpherson's work, thanks to its fantasy and resonant gran-

---

[1] David Hume, letter to Dr Hugh Blair, 19 September 1763, *The Letters of David Hume: Volume I*, ed. J. Y. T. Greig (1932, 2011).

deur, has survived all attempts to dismiss its significance. For him there was to be no Chatterton-esque suicide in a garret, but it is hard to imagine Thomas Chatterton's career as a hugely gifted literary forger (which led to his demise) without the example of the older poet.

In later life Macpherson made a very bad translation of the *Iliad* (1773) and wrote *A History of Great Britain* (1775), and from 1780 he was an MP at Westminster. He died in Belville, Inverness, on 17 February 1796, rich enough to secure himself a burial place in Westminster Abbey.

'Ossian' was apparently uniformly pronounced 'Oshen' by Highlanders (accented first syllable), with the second syllable connected to the Gaelic for 'to sing' – 'seinn'. The Irish pronunciation is 'Osheen' with an accent on the second syllable.

Bibliography: Clerk 1870, Vol. 1, p. 229
                    Coetzee 2012
                    Saunders 1894

Das MÄDCHEN (WENN MICH EINSAM LÜFTE FÄCHELN) *see* BLANKA D631

Das MÄDCHEN   The maiden
(F. von Schlegel) **D652** [H421]

The song exists in two versions, the first of which is discussed below:
(1) February 1819; (2) Authenticity uncertain (date unknown)

(1)   A major

(38 bars)

(2)   'Mit Innigkeit'   A major   ¾   [38 bars]

Wie so innig, möcht' ich sagen,	I should like to say that my beloved
Sich der meine mir ergibt,	Shows me such ardent devotion
Um zu lindern meine Klagen,	In order to still my complaints,
Dass er nicht so innig liebt.	That he does not love me ardently.

Will ich's sagen, so entschwebt es;	When I am about to tell him, the words float away;
Wären Töne mir Verliehen,	If the power of music were granted me
Flöss' es hin in Harmonien,	My feelings would pour out in harmonies,
Denn in jenen Tönen lebt es.	For they live in music.
Nur die Nachtigall kann sagen,	Only the nightingale can say
Wie er innig sich mir giebt,	What ardent devotion he shows me
Um zu lindern meine Klagen,	In order to still my complaints
Dass er nicht so innig liebt.	That he does not love me ardently.

FRIEDRICH VON SCHLEGEL (1772–1829); poem written in 1800/1

This is the fifth of Schubert's sixteen Friedrich von Schlegel solo settings (1818–25). See the poet's biography for a chronological list of all the Friedrich von Schlegel settings.

The cycle of poetry entitled *Abendröte* reflects the pantheistic philosophy of the younger Friedrich von Schlegel (before his conversion to Roman Catholicism) and was inspired by the poet's friendship with Novalis (qv). Schlegel's aim is typical of his Romantic *Weltanschauung*. At the moment of sunset, all things in nature are given voice by the poet: thus we have speaking (or singing) stars and mountains expressing their state of being, as well as smaller creations such as birds and butterflies. Human beings are included in this extraordinary line-up – a traveller, as well as a boy, and the girl of *Das Mädchen*. In this grand chorus (the various threads of which are brought together in the song entitled *Abendröte* D690) the poet explores the unity of all things in nature, hidden to most people but apparent to those with ears to hear and hearts to understand.

The inclusion of these forlorn lines in Schlegel's cycle seems puzzling at first, for this is the only poem from that important collection that refers to romantic love. It would seem that *Das Mädchen* is meant to be generically representative of all maidens, her plaint a familiar one since time immemorial. The contrast between this 'exquisite valentine' (as Capell calls it) and *Der Knabe* D692 could not be greater. The poet seems to be saying that women experience love more deeply than men, and that this is in the natural order of things. The maiden is aware that her lover's feelings are not similarly 'innig', that he is 'only after one thing' perhaps; her feelings are fundamentally different from his, but she has neither the words, nor the music, to explain her melancholy. Perhaps the poet is attempting to define the difference between the sexes. Despite all her lover's amorous protestations, the girl feels cheated by his lack of true reciprocation. As in *Der Knabe* (the boy who longs to fly with the birds), Schlegel acknowledges that human beings, unlike animals, are able to mourn for what might have been and can long for the unattainable.

Ever since *Gretchen am Spinnrade* D118, Schubert's ability to empathize with women and to depict the female condition has been a source of wonder and delight. Unlike some other great composers he does not patronize women, but rather invests their music, be it for Mignon or Ellen, Zuleika or Delphine, with the greatest sense of human reality. His music for the 'fairer sex' is seldom placed within the inverted commas of a staged femininity.

Nevertheless, Schubert was a nineteenth-century composer and his women occasionally display an exaggerated Dickensian delicacy (depending on the poet of course). In the short-breathed phrases of this music, its descending sequences seeming to wilt like a flower on a stem, we sense the maiden's appearance, slight of stature, exquisite of feature. The alternation of triplet semiquavers and quaver duplets gives the music a shy feel. As she searches for an explanation to her woes (she is surprised to be giving voice to them at all) the music carefully descends the stave in ladylike steps. The change to the tonic minor at 'Um zu lindern meine Klagen' (b. 8) comes in reticently on tiptoe; the music only momentarily darkens with a change of colour, like thoughts troubled by a passing cloud of doubt.

The girl's inability to express exactly what it is that disturbs her is perfectly caught by the music for 'Will ich's sagen, so entschwebt es' (bb. 14–16) where the two phrases are set in opposition, the first aspiring in its upward inflection, the second evaporating before our ears as the music falls away. The middle section suddenly finds its musical tongue as it were (from b. 16). An outbreak of fervent chromaticism lets us hear the girl absorbed in her dreams of being musically expressive; Schubert has here imagined her stronger and more eloquent, and for seven bars (until b. 22) he lends her the ability to give voice to her passionate nature. The courtship games played by man and maid are swept aside by a rising tide of liberated feeling as she finds the means to tell him the truth. This section is crowned by the triumphant forte setting in bb. 21–2, 'in jenen Tönen lebt es', but after this there is nowhere else to go and the phrase resonates in the void of unfulfilled hopes. We return to the reality of the tonic via an interlude (bb. 23–4) consisting of two bars of the dotted rhythm figure that has accompanied the maiden's plaint. (On its own it sounds like a skipped heartbeat, or a tiny shudder of apprehension.) Two further bars are taken up by a broad cadence in dotted crotchets (bb. 25–6), eloquent in its length and simplicity (cf. a similar cadence before the last strophe of *Der Schiffer* D694, as dreams cede to reality). Mention of the nightingale in the final section reminds us that another ⅜ setting, Claudius's *An die Nachtigall* D497, shares certain musical similarities with *Das Mädchen*: both songs are single-paged effusions, tiny and intimate, touching in their modesty, bejewelled by Schubert's ability to give to the weak an unexpectedly powerful musical voice.

There is another version of *Das Mädchen*, a 'zweite Fassung', published in the NSA (Volume 10, p. 210). The marking is 'Mit Innigkeit' which, as Walther Dürr points out has the ring of Schubertian authenticity because a mere copyist would never take it upon himself to invent such an interpretative direction, but it is a copy and not an autograph. The music is written out in ⅜ rather than ⅜ which seems somehow to coarsen Schubert's original intention. The ⅜ time signature with semiquaver triplets (rather than quavers) better suggests youthful emotion, delicate and contained, tremulous and vulnerable.

Autograph:	Gesellschaft der Musikfreunde, Vienna
Publication:	First published as Book 40 no. 1 of the *Nachlass* by Diabelli, Vienna in *c.* 1842 (P348; first version)
	First published as part of the NSA in 1996 (P812; second version)
Subsequent editions:	Peters: Vol. 3/211; AGA XX 354: Vol. 6/16; NSA IV: Vol. 12/82 & 210
Discography and timing:	Fischer-Dieskau —

	Hyperion I 27[16] & 34[13]	2'20	Marjana Lipovšek
		2'35	Christine Schäfer
	Hyperion II 21[16]	2'35	Christine Schäfer

←— *Himmelsfunken* D651   *Bertas Lied in der Nacht* D653 —→

Das MÄDCHEN AUS DER FREMDE (I) (Schiller) D117 [H48]
A major   16 October 1814

The maiden from strange parts

(53 bars)

In einem Tal bei armen Hirten
Erschien mit jedem jungen Jahr,
So bald die ersten Lerchen schwirrten,
Ein Mädchen, schön und wunderbar.

To poor shepherds in a valley
Appeared each spring
With the first chirruping larks,
A maiden, fair and wondrous.

Sie war nicht in dem Tal geboren,
Man wusste nicht, woher sie kam,
Doch schnell war ihre Spur verloren,[1]
Sobald das Mädchen Abschied nahm.

She had not been born in the valley.
No one knew from where she came.
But when the maiden departed
All trace of her vanished.

Beseligend war ihre Nähe,
Und alle Herzen wurden weit,
Doch eine Würde, eine Höhe
Entfernte die Vertraulichkeit.

Her very presence was blissful
And all hearts opened to her;
Yet a certain dignity, a loftiness
Precluded familiarity.

Sie brachte Blumen mit und Früchte,
Gereift auf einer andern Flur,
In einem andern Sonnenlichte,
In einer glücklichern Natur.

She brought flowers and fruit
Ripened in other fields,
Under another sun
In a happier countryside.

Und teilte jedem eine Gabe,
Dem Früchte, jenem Blumen aus,
Der Jüngling und der Greis am Stabe,
Ein Jeder ging beschenkt nach Haus.

She bestowed her gift on all,
Fruit on one, flowers on another;
The youth, the old man with his stick,
Each one went home enriched.

Willkommen waren alle Gäste,
Doch nahte sich ein liebend Paar,
Dem reichte sie der Gabe[n] beste,[2]
Der Blumen allerschönste dar.

All guests were welcome,
But if a loving couple approached
She would give them her finest gifts,
The fairest flowers of all.

Friedrich von Schiller (1759–1805); poem written in summer 1796

This is the eighth of Schubert's forty-four Schiller solo settings (1811–24). See the poet's biography for a chronological list of all the Schiller settings.

This poem, written in the summer of 1796, was published as the second item of a celebrated Schiller–Goethe collaboration, the *Musenalmanach* for 1797. The collection opened with *Alexis*

[1] Schiller writes 'Und schnell'.
[2] Schubert writes 'Gabe', rather than 'Gaben', almost certainly a copying mistake.

und Dora, a long poem that came to be regarded as one of the purest products of Goethe's classical phase. The Schiller miniature that follows it, *Das Mädchen aus der Fremde*, is no less pure, and radiates the calm of the poet's neoclassical style. Schubert uses all six verses and groups them in pairs to make a thrice-repeated strophic song of gentle sweetness. The time signature is §, traditional for pastoral songs of this type. Mention of a valley and shepherds in the first sentence is enough to inspire the composer to a softly undulating rhythm, a dance typical of the pastoral genre; the fifths in the bass represent the drone of shepherds' pipes, part of an ongoing tradition in this type of music that extends to Hugo Wolf's *Die Spröde* and beyond.

Das Mädchen aus der Fremde from the Jubiläums-Ausgabe of Schiller's *Gedichte* (1859).

The date of the song's composition (or at least the writing out of a fair copy) is significant – the day of the first performance of Schubert's Mass in F at the Lichtental church where the soprano soloist was Therese Grob. As Therese was said at the time to have been the composer's beloved, the presentation of a song referring to floral bouquets and 'a loving couple' would have been an appropriate gift. Not long after composing *Das Mädchen aus der Fremde* Schubert wrote music of the same character for *Schäfers Klagelied* D121 – indeed the melodic and rhythmic cell that gave that song life is prefigured here in b. 10. *Schäfers Klagelied* is an incomparably greater song because the Goethe poem, written within the same bucolic convention, is touching and real, right down to the mention of the shepherd's faithful dog. *Das Mädchen aus der Fremde* on the other hand is a more cerebral and stylized creation: the mysterious girl is obviously Flora, spring personified, but she never really comes to life. Like a German Mélisande, she holds the public at arm's length (perhaps Schubert felt himself to be similarly distanced by his irreproachable paramour). An interesting detail illustrating the difficulties of strophic song composition is the delicate piano music in the first verse underneath 'die ersten Lerchen schwirrten', deliciously evocative of chirping birdsong. This pianistic decoration sounds less convincing under the words 'Der Jüngling und der Greis am Stabe' in the fifth verse (a rather perky old man this, with a pogo stick intead of a walking staff!)

This was the last song Schubert wrote before he crossed, three days later, into song immortality with *Gretchen am Spinnrade* D118. For all its tuneful felicities there is nothing in *Das Mädchen aus der Fremde* to suggest the storm of musical emotion that was about to break with the immortal monologue from Goethe's *Faust*. But sympathetic listening to the Schiller setting reveals an *Innigkeit* – a feeling of tenderness, mystery and empathetic concern – which demonstrates clearly that the composer already had understanding and depth in plenty. Schubert was to attempt another setting of the same poem in 1815 (D252) where the music has a somewhat racier tone in *Zauberflöte* style.

Autograph:	Library of Congress, Washington
First edition:	Published as part of the AGA in 1894 (P547)
Subsequent editions:	Not in Peters; AGA XX 30: Vol. 1/189; NSA IV: Vol. 8/178
Bibliography:	Reid 2007, pp. 92–3
Further settings:	Ludwig van Beethoven (1770–1827) sketch for a setting (1809–10)

Discography and timing: Fischer-Dieskau I 2[12]   2'06
                          Hyperion I 16[8]
                                          2'24   Thomas Allen
                          Hyperion II 4[4]

← *Der Geistertanz* D116   *Gretchen am Spinnrade* D118 →

Das MÄDCHEN AUS DER FREMDE (II)   The maiden from strange parts
(Schiller) **D252** [H137]
F major   12 August 1815

(10 bars)

See previous entry for poem and translation

Friedrich von Schiller (1759–1805); poem written in summer 1796

This is the sixteenth of Schubert's forty-four Schiller solo settings (1811–24). See the poet's biography for a chronological list of all the Schiller settings.

For the background to the poem the reader is referred to the commentary on the first setting (D117) printed above. This is nothing like that setting in mood. It is not one of those instances where the composer has felt tempted to tinker with details in an earlier conception; rather he has decided to begin again in an entirely different vein. Reed finds this second setting more memorable, but other commentators such as Bauer prefer the first. Schubert opted second time around for a Papageno-like ditty that brings Mozartian *Singspiel* to mind. This is appropriate enough for the priapic nature of spring (the poem is an allegory about that season's arrival on the landscape) but it fails to capture the air of mystery about the first tentative stirrings of seasonal warmth and colour. The gliding barcarolle of the 1814 setting had admirably portrayed this important aspect of the poem.

Nothing is as simple as it seems, however, for the composer was in the business of marrying the Mozartian past and the Schubertian present. Here the tuneful simplicities of the vocal line (mostly doubled by the piano's right hand) are underpinned by a more adventurous left hand which disrupts the proceedings like a rogue cellist improvising interesting peripheral embroidery to enliven a staid string quartet (listen to the long descending chromatic scale underneath 'So bald die ersten Lerchen schwirrten' at bb. 4–6). That this concept was not foreign to the composer's musical nature is proved by the slow movement of the celebrated String Quintet of 1828 where the second cello is given exactly this task to sublime effect. To return to this rather more humble song, however, a trill in the viola register under 'Lerchen schwirrten' (b. 6) depicts the larks and continues in the ornate little three-bar postlude that carols joyously. This is appropriate enough in relation to birdsong but less suitable for some of the other verses.

Despite these stray felicities, the composer seems to have found this text elusive. Schubert's music always sounds slightly stilted when used to illustrate allegory; he was better off with the storytelling excitements of the longer Schiller ballads, and of course with the intensely human shorter lyrics of Goethe.

For the Hyperion Edition only the first three strophes were recorded.

Autograph:	In private possession
First edition:	Published as Vol. 7 no. 41 in Friedlaender's edition by Peters, Leipzig in 1887 (P502)
Subsequent editions:	Peters: Vol. 7/92; AGA XX 108: Vol. 3/10; NSA IV: Vol. 8/180
Further settings and arrangements:	Johann Friedrich Reichardt (1752–1814) *Das Mädchen aus der Fremde* (1809)
	Arr. Tilman Hoppstock (b.1961) for guitar accompaniment, in *Franz Schubert: 110 Lieder* (2009)
Discography and timing:	Fischer-Dieskau —
	Hyperion I 22⁴
	Hyperion II 8²¹ 1'28 Simon Keenlyside

← *Hoffnung D251*   *Punschlied (Im Norden zu singen) D253* →

Das MÄDCHEN VON INISTORE   The maid of Inistore
(MACPHERSON after 'OSSIAN') **D281** [H167]

The song exists in two versions:
(1) Date unknown; (2) September 1815

(1)   'Nicht zu langsam'   C minor   **C**   [23 bars]

(2)   C minor

(28 bars)

Instead of a translation of the German text, Macpherson's original is printed below

Mädchen Inistores, wein' auf dem Felsen der stürmischen Winde, neig' über Wellen dein zierliches Haupt, du, dem an Liebreiz der Geist der Hügel weicht; wenn er in einem Sonnenstrahl, des Mittags über Morvens Schweigen hingleitet. Er ist gefallen! Der Jüngling erliegt, bleich unter der Klinge Cuthullin's! nicht mehr wird der Mut deinen

Weep on the rocks of roaring winds, O maid of Inistore! Bend thy fair head over the waves, thou lovelier than the ghosts of the hills; when it moves, in a sunbeam, at noon, over the silence of Morven! He is fallen! Thy youth is low! Pale beneath the sword of Cuthullin! No more shall valour

Lieben erheben, dem Blut der Gebieter zu
gleichen. O Mädchen Inistores! Trenar, der
zierliche Trenar ist tot! In seiner Heimat heulen
seine Doggen, sie seh'n seinen gleitenden Geist.
In seiner Halle liegt sein Bogen ungespannt,
man hört auf dem Hügel seiner Hirsche keinen
Schall, man hört auf dem Hügel nun keinen
Schall!

raise thy love to match the blood of kings.
Trenar, graceful Trenar died, O maid of
Inistore! His dogs are howling at home! They
see his passing ghost. His bow is in the hall,
unstrung. No sound is in the hills of his hinds.

JAMES MACPHERSON ('OSSIAN') (1736–1796), translated by EDMUND,
BARON VON HAROLD (1737–1800)

*This is the third of Schubert's ten Macpherson solo settings (1815–17). See the poet's biography
(under Macpherson) for a chronological list of all the Ossian settings.*

At any mention of Ossian the Schubert enthusiast will immediately think of ballads like *Die
Nacht* D534 and *Cronnan* D282. But here is another setting which, like *Ossians Lied nach dem
Falle Nathos'* D278, is a real song, compact rather than discursive and diffuse. At first glance it
seems to be in conventional ABA form (there is a sense of recapitulation at b. 14 on the second
'O Mädchen Inistores!') but closer examination shows that it is through-composed and responds
imaginatively to a number of illustrative challenges in the text. Inistore in Ossianic (and Gaelic)
terms is *Innis-Torc* (or Thorc) which means 'Isle of Boars and Whales', said to be one of the
Orkney Islands.

The key is an eloquent C minor and the nature of the music is such that one cannot help
looking for an operatic model. *Die Zauberflöte* was the inspiration behind many of Schubert's
earlier ballads and songs, but in this case Ossian's 'ancient' text (and the composer might have
believed it to be genuinely ancient) seems to have called up an older musical shade. *Das Mädchen
von Inistore* has an elevated tone of mourning in the grand manner which recalls a musical style
both impassioned and statuesque, bringing to mind Gluck's *Orfeo ed Euridice*. Schubert was said
to have known that work from the score although he never saw it performed. The interval of a
minor third between C and E flat at the start of the tune recalls Eurydice's 'Che fiero momento'
in the third act of Gluck's opera. Schubert uses the mournful whine inherent in this interval to
suggest whistling wind, the weeping of the maiden and the howling of the dogs. In this early
use of a type of leitmotif technique, the piece achieves a formal unity rare in the Ossian settings.
The middle section beginning 'Er ist gefallen!' (b. 10) is in fact a recitative, but it is so masterfully incorporated into the whole that we do not notice the boundaries between one type of
writing and another. This was undoubtedly the composer's aim.

Particularly moving is the final section which begins 'In seiner Halle liegt sein Bogen'
(bb. 21–2). The music seems hopeless and empty. The hardest music to write is that which is
about silence, but Schubert manages it here. Mournfully pivoted around D flat, the flattened
supertonic, variations on the same phrase are repeated three times, each time quieter than
before. The melting effect of a D natural on the final 'keinen Schall!' (b. 27) is that Trenar
dematerializes before our very ears, as if he had never been. The bereft little piano postlude
(nothing more than a downward C minor arpeggio) is the antithesis of the grand air of dramatic
tragedy and bereavement that opened the piece, as if the pomp of public grief has ceded to the
reality of personal loss. Johannes Brahms was also attracted by this poem (albeit in a different
translation) which he set in 1862 as his Op. 17 no. 4, an extremely beautiful setting for women's
chorus, two horns and harp.

It is Trenar rather than Nathos who is mourned in this song, but the same theme of bereavement and admiration for those fallen in battle governs the music as in *Ossians Lied nach dem*

Falle Nathos D278. The background to the story (including a typically British concern for dogs' and horses' relationship to their masters) is provided by James Macpherson's footnote:

> *The maid of Inistore was the daughter of Gorlo, King of Inistore or Orkney islands. Trenar was brother to the King of Iniscon, supposed to be one of the islands of Shetland. The Orkneys and Shetland were at that time subject to the King of Lochlin. We find that the dogs of Trenar are sensible at home of the death of their master, the very instant he is killed. It was the opinion of the times that the souls of heroes went immediately after death to the hills of their country, and the scenes they frequented in the most happy times of their life. It was thought too that dogs and horses saw the ghosts of the deceased.*

The NSA prints two versions but there is only one extant autograph, that of the first version where the last five bars of the song are missing. The second version in the NSA (printed by Diabelli and Peters) is based on a copy of the song in the Albert Stadler album and which Walther Dürr believes goes back to a lost Schubert autograph.

Autograph:	Österreichische Nationalbibliothek, Vienna (first version)
First edition:	Published as Book 4 no. 3 of the *Nachlass* by Diabelli, Vienna in 1830 (P246)
Publication reviews:	Rellstab 'Ueberblick der Erzellgrisse', *Iris im Gebiete der Tonkunst* (Berlin), No. 39 (12 November 1830) [Waidelich/Hilmar Dokumente II No. 784b]
Subsequent editions:	Peters: Vol. 4/202; AGA XX 148: Vol. 3/110; NSA IV: Vol. 9/32 (first version) & 34 (second version)
Bibliography:	Clerk 1870, Vol. 1, p. 180
Further settings:	Johannes Brahms (1833–1897) *Gesang aus Fingal*, no. 4 of 4 *Gesänge* Op. 17 for female voices, horns and harp (1860)
Discography and timing:	Fischer-Dieskau I 5²⁶ 2'33
	Hyperion I 20³
	Hyperion II 10² 2'51 John Mark Ainsley

←*Das Rosenband* D280   *Cronnan* D282 →

Des MÄDCHENS KLAGE (I)   The maiden's lament
(Schiller) **D6** [H6]
D minor   1811 or 1812

Der Eichwald brauset,[1] die Wolken ziehn,[2]	The oak forest roars, the clouds scud by,
Das Mägdlein sitzet[3] an Ufers Grün,	The maiden sits on the verdant shore;
Es bricht sich die Welle mit Macht, mit Macht,	The waves break with mighty force,
Und sie seufzt hinaus in die finstere Nacht,	And she sighs into the dark night,
Das Auge vom Weinen getrübet.	Her eyes dimmed with weeping.
'Das Herz ist gestorben, die Welt ist leer,	'My heart has died, the world is empty,
Und weiter gibt sie dem Wunsche nichts mehr,	And no longer yields to my desire.
Du Heilige, ruf' dein Kind zurück,	Holy one, call back your child.
Ich habe genossen das irdische Glück,	I have enjoyed earthly happiness;
Ich habe gelebt und geliebet!'	I have lived and loved!'
Es rinnet der Tränen vergeblicher Lauf,	Tears run their course in vain;
Die Klage, sie wecket die Toten nicht auf;	Lamenting docs not awaken the dead;
Doch nenne, was tröstet und heilet die Brust	But tell me what can console and heal the heart
Nach der süssen Liebe verschwundener Lust,	When the joys of sweet love have vanished,
Ich, die Himmlische, will's nicht versagen.	And I, the heavenly maiden, will not deny you.
'Lass rinnen der Tränen vergeblichen Lauf,	'Let my tears run their vain course;
Es wecke die Klage die Toten nicht auf!	Let my lament not awaken the dead!
Das süsseste Glück für die trauernde Brust,	For the grieving heart the sweetest happiness,
Nach der schönen Liebe verschwund'ner Lust	When the joys of fair love have vanished,
Sind der Liebe Schmerzen und Klagen.'	Is Love's anguish and lament.'

Friedrich von Schiller (1759–1805); poem published in 1799

This is the second of Schubert's forty-four Schiller solo settings (1811–24). See the poet's biography for a chronological list of all the Schiller settings.

There is some doubt as to whether this song dates from 1811 or 1812, although Deutsch has assigned a catalogue number that suggests the earlier date. Either way, *Des Mädchens Klage* was composed as a result of the young Schubert's discovery of Schiller. It is an infinitely less mature debut than his first encounter with Goethe (*Gretchen am Spinnrade* D118) at the age of seventeen, but Schiller's poetry was more available than Goethe's in Vienna in 1811–12. When Wallenstein's daughter Thekla performs this lyric in Act III Scene 7 of Schiller's play *Die Piccolomini*, she sings only two verses, accompanying herself on the guitar. Schubert could not have copied the text from Zumsteeg's 1801 setting (titled *Thekla, aus dem Wallenstein*) because the latter composer wrote his song for a production of the play and used only these two strophes in his setting. For the four-strophe version Schubert would have had to consult an edition of Schiller's poems. German editions of contemporary writers were hard to come by in a country where books were rigidly censored. The publishing house of Anton Doll in Vienna issued their Schiller *Gesamtausgabe* in 1810, the ninth and tenth volumes of which were devoted to the poems. These books (also available as separate offprints) – *Gedichte* volumes 1 and 2 – were possibly loaned to Schubert (his family were unlikely to have been able to afford them) and they were undoubtedly the textual source of his many Schiller settings.

---

[1] 'braust' in both later settings of the text.
[2] 'ziehen' in both later settings of the text.
[3] 'sitzt' in both later settings of the text.

Once Schubert had discovered a poet, he tended to compose settings in batches. It is no surprise therefore that another Schiller ballad, *Leichenfantasie*, is the next song in the catalogue (D7). There is also a question mark on the dating of that ballad, although it too was probably written in 1811. It is just possible, however, that both D6 and D7 belong with that other Schiller setting, *Der Jüngling am Bache* (D30), which we can confidently assign to September 1812. The mood of that much shorter work is very different, however; it has perfect proportions, and is well written for the voice. These factors may be accounted for by the difference between the compositions of a fourteen- and a fifteen-year old.

If *Hagars Klage* D5 was composed at a time of teenage unhappiness, there is no reason to suppose that this song represents a change of text-selecting mood. Both texts would have appealed to someone who thought of himself as alone, or unfairly treated. Hagar, abandoned by Abraham, appeals to Jehovah for help; the maiden in *Des Mädchens Klage* appeals to 'die Himmlische'– the Virgin Mary. The word 'Klage' ('lament') is common to both songs and it also appears in the beautiful 1812 Rochlitz setting, *Klaglied* D23. Whatever Schubert's later religious convictions, or lack thereof, there is every reason to suppose that at this early stage of his life he was still a believer. On the back of the manuscript of this song he had planned a piece of religious music – a *Missa in Partitura* for chorus, strings and organ. He wrote the title and voice categories but never began the music itself. *Des Mädchens Klage* is, incidentally, the first of a number of Schubert songs that refer to the Virgin Mary: *Des Mädchens Klage* (second setting D191; third setting D389); *Gretchen im Zwinger* D564; *Das Marienbild* D623; *Blondel zu Marien* D626; *Vom Mitleiden Mariä* D632; *Marie* D658; *Ave Maria (Ellens dritter Gesang)* D839. Although Schubert later spoke up bitterly against the misuse of religious symbols, and that of the Cross in particular (letter to his brother Ferdinand, 21 September 1825), his attitude to the Virgin Mary seems to have remained sympathetic and susceptible. Some of his loveliest church music is to be found in his various settings of the *Salve Regina* and *Stabat Mater*.

Verse 1: The music begins in every way 'on a high'. The depths of contemplation and depression suggested by the two later settings of this song are entirely absent. Instead the young composer responds, perhaps overenthusiastically, to the descriptions of nature's stormy power. The key is D minor, important in Mozart's *Don Giovanni* as well as being Beethoven's 'Tempest' tonality. The tessitura of the voice part might be considered cruelly high, but Schubert was not deliberately punishing his singer, he simply lacked experience in appropriate vocal writing. The music has the air of being conceived in the style of an instrumental sonata (for violin perhaps) with words added later. Perhaps because he did not have the guiding example of Zumsteeg in front of him, Schubert was very cavalier with the poem. Right at the beginning, for example, he substitutes the emphatically explosive 'brauset' (b. 2) for 'braust', and repeats willy-nilly whichever phrases and words appeal to him. The poem's opening line inspires a small compendium of *Sturm und Drang* pianistic devices. As soon as the maiden is mentioned in the second line the word *dolce* is used (b. 10) and the music changes into D major. The effectiveness of this essentially Schubertian fingerprint is undermined, however, by the setting of the words on a D major arpeggio that soars up to a high tessitura, suggesting a Valkyrie rather than a vulnerable damsel. This is immediately followed by tempestuous water imagery (the poem's third line), the pianist's fingers working up a storm in short choppy scales, encompassing a fifth (bb. 14, 16 and 18), which pound the shore (and ear) mercilessly. The word 'seufzt' – 'sighs' (b. 20) – brings another change of mood: hectic quavers are replaced by longer notes in the vocal line. Underneath the singer's semibreves and minims the piano invokes pathos with pleading intervals and 'meaningful' scales. Mention of tears in the last line (from b. 28) freezes the action into crotchets enlivened by piquant chromaticisms.

Verse 2: The marking changes to 'Grave', the time signature to ⅜. This is undoubtedly the most interesting section of the song – a set piece for the maiden whom Schubert unconsciously casts as a larger-than-life diva. Schiller places this strophe in inverted commas to signify direct speech. The music cultivates an air of self-conscious pathos and the *rum-ti-tum* accompaniment occasions a smile. These things are still to be found in countless Italian operatic arias up to the time of Verdi, and beyond, but it is astonishing that this 'southern' style had, as early as 1811, seeped so deeply into Schubert's musical consciousness. Again the free repetitions of 'gestorben' (together with an inherent sob built into the music) seem almost comically theatrical; we are reminded that the German lied – at least as Schubert was soon to redefine it – incorporates the visceral responses of a young composer sitting open-mouthed with excitement in the opera house. The fluidity and uninhibited emotion of the vocal line in D minor, poised above, and meshing with, those incessantly rolling sextuplets in the accompaniment, seem strangely familiar. Here is a note of Mediterranean passion seldom to be found in Zumsteeg or Reichardt – or even Mozart in quite the same way. We are surely hearing the beginnings of music for another woman *in extremis*. It is not a long a journey from 'Das Herz ist gestorben' (Schiller) to 'Mein Herz ist schwer' (Goethe's *Gretchen am Spinnrade*); how appropriate it would be for Schubert to have sown the seeds of his first great Goethe song at the heart of his first Schiller setting.

This aria uses the strophe's first three lines; the remainder of the verse is set to an awkward 'Recitativo in tempo' (a misnomer that Walther Dürr takes as a sign that the teenage Schubert was not yet studying with Salieri). The high B flat on 'das <u>ir</u>dische Glück' (b. 53) merely confirms the strapping health of a character who is supposed to be fading away with grief. With such

disregard for logic, the young composer seems to have been an operatic natural. As in *Hagars Klage*, a moment of genuine inspiration is followed by a musical disappointment: the strophe's third and fourth lines are repeated in an allegretto tempo (from b. 59), together with a modulation into F major. This is again in an ungrateful tessitura, doubled note for note by the piano. Having treated the singer's line in the *Grave* section with great skill, Schubert returns to what appear to be violin studies.

Verses 3–4: The poem, as Schiller envisaged it, may be summed up thus: the narrator introduces the maiden in the first verse; she bewails her fate in the second; the third strophe introduces the voice of the Virgin; the girl speaks once again in the fourth. This shape seems not to have been understood by Schubert who elided the second and third strophes and paid no attention to potentially the most dramatic moment, the opening of the Virgin's statement. Only a change of tempo to Andante (b. 67) shows that a crucial new section of the poem is beginning mid-bar; and then the nondescript doubling of the vocal line by the piano seems particularly inept and anony-

Des Mädchens Klage from the Jubiläums-Ausgabe of Schiller's *Gedichte* (1859).

mous. The clue that it is the Virgin speaking is given only in the last line of the strophe ('Ich, die Himmlische') and it is likely that the young composer was not clear about what was happening. 'Ich, die Himmlische' is unequivocal, however. Just before that point there is a double bar line (at b. 77) and, interestingly, a modulation into C major, the key of so much of Schubert's later religious music. The Virgin, when finally introduced, is no other-worldly apparition; her outpourings are largely marked forte and inhabit the stratosphere. What is more, Schubert continues her aria into the next strophe (there is no gap at all in the music) instead of returning to the maid who has been chastened and instructed by the heavenly intervention of Verse 3 but who nevertheless persists stubbornly in her grief.

This is one of those truly rare occasions where Schubert seems to have got himself into a muddle over the dramatization of a poem. The music for the fourth strophe, with its undulating triplet accompaniment in the left hand, was no doubt meant to have had a radiant and comforting tone, but is instead possibly the most difficult-to-sing page in the composer's entire vocal output. It sits around high Gs and As (as at bb. 101–5) with a relentlessness born of Schubert's innocence and inexperience, rather than the Virgin's. Placing her words in the heavenly heights of the stave, Schubert must have wanted them to sound as if they were coming from another world. The result, however, is music that, because it lies in a part of the voice and across a break in the registers, is almost never performed. It takes the greatest skill to negotiate these hurdles, but on the recording for the Hyperion Edition, against all the odds, Christine Brewer did just this.

Autograph:	Staatsbibliothek Preussischer Kulturbesitz, Berlin
First edition:	Published as part of the AGA in 1894 (P528)
Subsequent editions:	Not in Peters; AGA XX 2: Vol. 1/16; NSA IV: Vol. 3b/188; Bärenreiter: Vol. 2/208
Bibliography:	Einstein 1951, p. 44
Discography and timing:	Fischer-Dieskau —
	Hyperion I 31[5]
	Hyperion II 1[7] 5'13 Christine Brewer

← *Der Vatermörder* D10   *Der Geistertanz* D15 →

Des MÄDCHENS KLAGE (II)   The maiden's lament
(Schiller) Op. 58 no. 3, **D191** [H92]

The song exists in two versions, the second of which is discussed below:
(1) 15 May 1815; (2) appeared April 1826

(1) 'Langsam'   C minor $\frac{2}{4}$ [16 bars]

(2) C minor

See previous entry for poem and translation

Friedrich von Schiller (1759–1805); poem published in 1799

This is the tenth of Schubert's forty-four Schiller solo settings (1811–24). See the poet's biography for a chronological list of all the Schiller settings.

Albericht von Wallenstein, a general in the Thirty Years War, was the subject of a trilogy of plays by Schiller, completed and first performed in 1799. In Act III of the second of these, *Die Piccolomini*, Wallenstein's daughter Thekla is parted from her beloved Max Piccolomini and the lovers, from opposing families, are caught up in a Romeo and Juliet situation. Thekla picks up a guitar and accompanies herself in a song (*Des Mädchens Klage*) 'after playing a melancholy prelude'. It is interesting that in the play the poem contains two verses, avoiding the complication of divine intervention from the Virgin Mary who is addressed in the second strophe.

Like a number of Schiller poems to which the composer was attracted, but which he found problematic, this text was set three times over a five-year period. A tempestuous and almost unsingable 'durchkomponiert' version dates from 1811 (*see* commentary above), and this 1815 strophic setting was first composed without the melancholy prelude described in *Die Piccolomini* (see the 'Erste Fassung' of the song in NSA Volume 3b p. 196, with its marking of 'Langsam' rather than 'Sehr langsam'). The matter of an introduction was rectified on publication, probably more for practical reasons than on grounds of fidelity to the play. The third version of 1816, which has more of a guitar-inspired accompaniment, is comparatively unknown (*see* commentary below).

There is something about the brooding intensity of this 1815 setting that has made it hugely popular with singers, aided by its privileged place in the first volume of the Peters Edition. As Brian Newbould has pointed out, the opening two bars with upbeat bear an uncanny resemblance to the *Lacrimosa* of the Mozart *Requiem*, a work that was much in Schubert's thoughts at the time. There is a great deal here, however, that is purest Schubert: the charming, almost pastoral turn of melody on 'an Ufers Grün' for example (b. 4), and the way in which the powerful left hand underpins and illustrates the words 'mit Macht, mit Macht' (bb. 5–6). The passionate grief-laden sweep of the vocal line (wonderfully crafted to accommodate Schiller's five-line strophe) made it a great favourite with those who like their lieder on the histrionic side, among whom could be numbered many a nineteenth-century Russian singer. Musorgsky was said to have played the four-bar introduction with spine-chilling intensity. To make this kind of impression it is essential that the marking of 'Sehr langsam' is understood to mean two slow crotchets in a bar rather than four slow quavers. A correct interpretation of this time signature speeds the music up and turns the song into something windswept and stormy rather than the ponderous plaint often heard on the concert platform.

Autograph:	Wienbibliothek im Rathaus, Vienna (first draft)
Publication:	First published as part of the AGA in 1895 (P561; first version)
	First published as Op. 56 no. 3 (later changed to Op. 58 no. 3) by Thaddäus Weigl, Vienna in 1826 (P99; second version)
Publication review:	*Allgemeiner musikalischer Anzeiger* (Frankfurt) No. 33 (10 February 1827), p. 317f. [Waidelich/Hilmar Dokumente I No. 452]
Subsequent editions:	Peters: Vol. 1/210; AGA XX 67a & b: Vol. 2/104; NSA IV: Vol. 3a/92; Bärenreiter: Vol. 2/124
Bibliography:	Fischer-Dieskau 1977, p. 41
	Newbould 1997, p. 152
	Porter 1961, p. 110

Arrangements: Arr. Franz Liszt (1811–1886) for solo piano, no. 2 of *Sechs*
                           Melodien von Schubert (1844) [*see* TRANSCRIPTIONS]
Discography and timing: Fischer-Dieskau —
                           Hyperion I 7⁵
                           Hyperion II 6¹²   3'12   Elly Ameling

←— *Die Verschworenen* D190/5   *Der Jüngling am Bache* D192 —→

Des MÄDCHENS KLAGE (III)   The maiden's lament
(Schiller) **D389** [H229]
C minor   March 1816

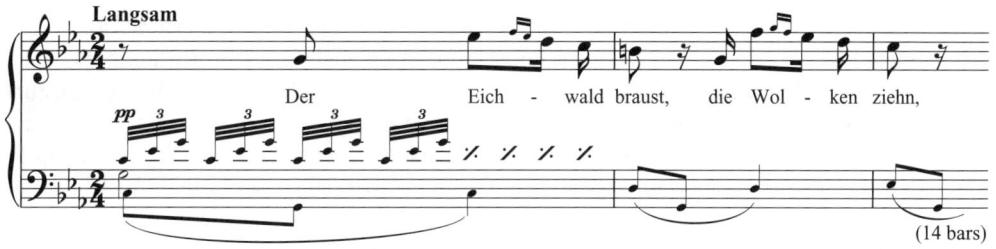

(14 bars)

See Des Mädchens Klage (I) for poem and translation

Friedrich von Schiller (1759–1805); poem published in 1799

This is the twenty-third of Schubert's forty-four Schiller solo settings (1811–24). See the poet's biography for a chronological list of all the Schiller settings.

It is unusual for a third, and final, Schubert setting to be less popular than the second. We almost always agree with the composer's verdicts on his own music: if he chose to return to a poem we can usually find a reason for his dissatisfaction with the previous encounter. We would never throw the earlier versions away, but the later songs are often distillations of all that had gone before, with added understanding and mastery.

That is not the case with this song, perhaps one of the least-known of Schubert's lieder for female voice. The second setting from May 1815 (D191) is enshrined in the first volume of the Peters Edition and has thus been accessible to generations of singers, and rightly so. The absence of this third setting in Peters has had a lot to do with its low profile, but the second setting with its brooding intensity is a great song in a way that the third is not; it has grandeur and space, and a noble pathos. Although it has a simple strophic structure, its effect (given a fine performance) is far from simple. The piano interludes can be played stormily or as a gentle throb, depending on the words, allowing performer and listener to reflect on the meaning of each verse, and to prepare for the next.

What we have here is completely different, and we must conclude that it is in the nature of an experiment, an attempt by means of vigorous pianistic activity to add something new, and more febrile, to the achievement of 1815. The vocal line is not dissimilar in range, stature and difficulty to D191, and the key is also C minor, but the piano part is a restless cauldron of incessant demisemiquaver triplets. The Schubert accompanist, accustomed to the feel of this composer's writing, can quickly detect the unusual; this piano part is clearly a one-off, toying with the manner of the virtuoso pianists of the time. (This type of writing, reminiscent of Hummel or Kalkbrenner, occasionally occurs in Schubert's chamber or solo piano music but is extremely rare in the lieder.) Musical energy is provided by the unrelenting blackness of pianistic texture – the sheer number of dragon's-teeth notes packed in the smallest space, and with no sign of a rest or of any respite for the wrist. In comparison to this, even Schubert's notoriously difficult moto perpetuo songs like *Erlkönig* are redeemed by the presence of light and space and air, and a demanding song like *Versunken* D715, with its incessant semiquavers, is a delightfully woven cascade of artfully developed thematic material. In this setting of *Des Mädchens Klage*, however, we have turbulent broken-chord scrubbing around the basic harmonies. The fingerwork is too automatic and predictable to be truly challenging, and while the pianistically engendered turbulence is effective in its way as a background for a soaring vocal line, it is just not convincingly Schubertian. The lack of an introduction and the almost peremptory ending also seem untypical.

So where does this style come from? In the absence of a complete modern edition of the songs of Carl Maria von Weber, whom Schubert knew personally later in his life, it has been difficult to assess the influence of that composer's songs on Schubert. It is fairly certain that Weber's settings of the war hero Theodor Körner would have interested Schubert (he had met the poet in Vienna, and admired him as man and artist). Weber's *Leyer und Schwert* songs to Körner's battle-inspired texts were published in Berlin in 1815. The first of the set had a Körner poem, *Gebet während der Schlacht*, that was also set by Schubert in 1815 with a most uncharacteristic and restless accompaniment. But it is surely the non-stop demisemiquavers of the Weber song (also in C minor) that seem to have temporarily diverted Schubert. All that scurrying about was new and impressive, but ultimately futile: a lied can never double as a piano étude without diminishing the expressiveness of the words – Liszt learned this lesson many years later. In the greatest songs, the rests between the notes are as eloquent as the notes themselves.

The first setting of this poem (D6) had been extreme and experimental in another way. The fourteen-year old's inexperience in writing vocal music is as evident from the very start (the unreasonable tessitura is almost comically difficult) as is his inherent dramatic flair and feeling for words. There is much that is interesting in this youthful indiscretion, but it is hardly a surprise that Schubert put the poem to one side and returned to it in 1815 to set it a second time. The third version from 1816, strophic in the same manner, seems to have been an attempt to combine the grand and magisterial vocal line of D191 with something of the wildness that characterized the through-composed (and very episodic) D6. Of course, there are marvellous touches like the voice's rise in wailing semitones on 'sie seufzt hinaus in die finstere Nacht' (bb. 8–9), an effect that recalls the ghostly 'Ade!' of the dancing spirits in the choral version of *Der Geistertanz*, but even the vocal line of D389 seems less inspired than D191.

None of the settings really comes to terms with the central problem of this text which is that the maiden's own voice is heard only in the second and fourth strophes (printed in inverted commas). The first strophe is scene-setting introduction, the third reveals the Virgin Mary ('Ich, die Himmlische') who speaks comfortingly to the desperately unhappy girl. In D6 the teenage composer seems not to have understood what is happening in the poem. In D191 and D389 the more mature young master leaves this differentiation in characterization to the performers, thus imposing on them an onerous task: it is all but impossible adequately to vary the mood between earthly plaint and heavenly consolation without more help from Schubert. If ever a text called for one of his magical changes from minor to major – a *modified* strophic song – this is it. On the other hand there is something darkly hypnotic and compulsive about the music in its rigidly strophic form. We are left with the impression that the composer has imagined the Madonna speaking *through* the girl herself, rather than addressing her in a heavenly visitation.

Autograph:	Wienbibliothek im Rathaus, Vienna (incomplete)
First edition:	Published in August Reissmann's *Franz Schubert: Sein Leben und Werke*, pp. 12–14 in 1873 (P468)
Subsequent editions:	Not in Peters; AGA XX 194: Vol. 4/52; NSA IV: Vol. 3b/198; Bärenreiter: Vol. 2/214
Bibliography:	Porter 1961, p. 110
Further settings:	Carl Friedrich Zelter (1758–1832) *Des Mädchens Klage* (1799)
	Johann Rudolf Zumsteeg (1760–1802) *Thekla* (1801)
	Nikolas von Krufft (1779–1818) *Des Mädchens Klage* (1812)
	Mikhail Glinka (1804–1857) *Dubrava shumit* (Russian translation by Zhukovsky) (1834)
	Fanny Mendelssohn (1805–1847) *Der Eichwald brauset* (1826)
	Felix Mendelssohn (1809–1847) *Des Mädchens Klage* (1847?)
Discography and timing:	Fischer-Dieskau —
	Hyperion I 32[2]
	Hyperion II 13[2] 2'44 Lynne Dawson

← *Laura am Klavier* D388   *Die Entzückung am Laura* D390 →

Die MÄNNER SIND MECHANT! *see VIER REFRAIN-LIEDER* D866/3

MAHOMETS GESANG (I)   The song of Mahommed
(GOETHE) **D549** [H358]
(Fragment) E major – C major   March 1817

(114 bars)

Seht den Felsenquell,	Behold the spring among the rocks,
Wie ein Sternenblick;	Bright and joyful
Freudehell,[1]	As a twinkling star;
Über Wolken	Above the clouds
Nährten seine Jugend	Its youth was nurtured
Gute Geister	By good spirits
Zwischen Klippen im Gebüsch.	In the bushes between the crags.
Jünglingfrisch	With the freshness of youth
Tanzt er aus der Wolke nieder[2]	It dances from the clouds

[1] For D549 only, Schubert reverses the order of lines 2 and 3 of Goethe's poem which reads: 'Seht den Felsenquell / Freudehell / Wie ein Sternenblick'. Schubert reverts to this for D721.
[2] The word 'nieder' was almost certainly added to the line as a result of an oversight – the composer's eyes jumping to line 3 of the verse by mistake. This does not happen in D721.

Auf die Marmorfelsen nieder,	Down on to the marble rocks,
Jauchzet wieder	And echoes jubilantly
Nach dem Himmel.	Heavenwards.
Durch die Gipfelgänge	Through gullies among the peaks
Jagt er bunten Kieseln nach,	It chases after brightly coloured pebbles,
Und mit frühem Führertritt	And with the precocious step of a leader
Reisst er seine Bruderquellen	Bears its brother springs
Mit sich fort.	Away with it.
Drunten in dem Tal[3]	Down in the valley
Unter seinem Fusstritt werden Blumen,[4]	Flowers appear beneath its tread,
Und die Wiese	And the meadow
Lebt von seinem Hauch.	Draws life from its breath.
Doch ihn hält kein Schattental,	But no shady valley can detain it,
Keine Blumen,	Nor the flowers
Die ihm seine Knie' umschlingen,	That embrace its knees,
Ihm mit Liebes-Augen schmeicheln:	And flatter it with lovelorn looks;
Nach der Ebne dringt sein Lauf	Winding like a snake
Schlangenwandelnd.	It rushes on its course towards the plain.
Bäche schmiegen	Streams merge with it
Sich gesellig an. Nun tritt er	Companionably. Now
In die Ebne silberprangend,	In silver radiance, it enters the plain,
Und die Ebne prangt mit ihm,	And the plain is equally radiant,
Und die Flüsse von der Ebne,	And the rivers of the plain
Und die Bäche von den Bergen,	And the streams from the mountains
Jauchzen ihm und rufen: Bruder!	Cry out to him jubilantly:
Bruder, nimm die Brüder mit,	Brother, take your brothers with you,
Mit zu deinem alten *Vater,*	With you to your ancient *father,*
Zu dem ew'gen Ocean . . .	*To the eternal ocean.*
[[. . . 3 (31 lines) . . .]]	[[. . . 3 (31 lines) . . .]]

Johann Wolfgang von Goethe (1749–1832); poem written in winter 1772/3

This is the fiftieth of Schubert's seventy-five Goethe solo settings (1814–26). See the poet's biography for a chronological list of all the Goethe settings.

At the time of writing *Götz von Berlichingen* (1772–3) Goethe was much occupied with theological themes. He wanted to write a play about the prophet Mahommed, but this was never completed apart from a few fragments of which this free-verse hymn is the most important. This was not meant to be sung by Mahommed himself, but by Ali and his wife Fatema, the prophet's daughter, as they trace the astonishing story of the growth of Islam. For this reason Lorraine Byrne has pointed out that the correct title of both poem and song should be *Mahomets-Gesang*, the hyphen clarifying that the text is not spoken by the prophet himself.

---

[3] Goethe's original line is 'Drunten wieder in dem Tal' ('Down in the valley again').
[4] 'Werden' is Schubert's own addition in this line.

Knowledge and reworking of sources such as the Koran and the Greek and Roman classics freed Goethe from the Christian conventions of his upbringing; in the story of Mahommed the poet was able to find a new context for the discussion of man's place in the universe and his relationship to Nature and a non-Christian god. Mahommed was a great revolutionary who, as this poem makes clear in Goethe's analogy, carried his supporters with him, like a river collecting its tributaries, to establish a new epoch in history. This sense of a brotherhood collaborating to found a new order chimed with Goethe's *Sturm und Drang* belief that his own genius was a pre-eminent factor in the future of German literature. He was right of course, but at this stage he still believed in a collective enterprise of which he was a part, and wanted to carry all his colleagues with him Mahommed-style. However much he desired to play the prophet, though, this was beyond even his powers. The poem, rich in water imagery, can be considered as a preparatory study for Goethe's later masterpiece, *Gesang der Geister über den Wassern*.

Schubert was immediately attracted to this poem which Nicholas Boyle describes as having been a 'magnificently controlled rhythmic crescendo'. Schubert failed at least once to reflect this in music, probably twice, but both settings are magnificent fragments and there is nothing else quite like them in all the song output. There is something of an epic struggle on Schubert's part to live up to Goethe – perhaps to make himself worthy of the poet with a work mighty enough to break down the doors of the poet's resistance. (In 1816 Schubert's efforts to alert the poet to his musical existence by sending him a volume of songs – which were duly returned – had been unsuccessful). It appears that the composer's salutary common sense had temporarily abandoned him, the poem having inspired in him a madness both divine and fatal. He was at the height of his powers, a moto perpetuo masterpiece like *An Schwager Kronos* D369 already under his belt, and here was another moto perpetuo poem with the added bonus that it required his already finely honed skills as a master of water music to convert spring, stream, river and ocean into musical imagery.

Schubert chooses E major as his key. The *Bewegung* is sextuplets in $\frac{2}{4}$ which represent the tiny spring at the beginning of the story. This movement brooks no change throughout the remainder of the piece, however. The fatal flaw of the setting is thus evident in the very first bar, for if six notes per beat represent a bubbling stream it will be beyond the capacity of a mere piano, not to mention a mere pianist, to render an ocean convincingly. Although the accompaniment starts off gently it is soon evident that we glimpse here a type of pianistic virtuosity which, though rare in Schubert's songs, emerges from time to time in his chamber music. It is a method of note-spinning favoured by Hummel and his inferiors and found more often in works of the North German lieder school, where the piano makes a dense weave of sound that whirrs away unstoppably, unpunctuated by even the suspicion of a rest.

The second verse ('Jünglingfrisch / Tanzt er' from b. 27) modulates into the relative minor and now the greatest pianistic difficulties appear in earnest. The accompaniment underneath the repeat of 'Jauchzet wieder / Nach dem Himmel', with its leaping left hand (from b. 39), is as tricky as anything in the lieder repertoire, but to no especially stirring effect. At the end of this thicket of notes we find ourselves in B major, softening to B minor for the beginning of the third verse ('Durch die Gipfelgänge', b. 47). This passage quickly passes through D minor and F minor ('Und mit frühem Führertritt / Reisst er seine Bruderquellen') to a long section in A flat for the fourth and fifth verses (from the double bar line and change of key signature at b. 56). At 'Nach der Ebne dringt sein Lauf' we move through A flat minor (b. 82) and lift into A minor (b. 88). In a way Schubert impressively gets into his stride. The harmonic scheme has the music turning the screw of tension with undeniable power, but we have to ask 'Wohin?', for we would now need five pianos and ten sets of hands to do justice to the scope of the narrative. The sixth verse has twenty-one lines but the composer does not quite reach the end of the ninth. He summons up all his energy and sets 'Und die Flüsse von der Ebne' most impressively in his thundering

Dem Unendlichen style (from b. 105) but then one of two things happened: either courage failed him or he continued the song, perhaps even finishing it, in a blaze of glory, and the music has been tragically lost to us (the manuscript may well have been longer than the fragment we possess, but how much longer is the question, and was it long enough to have encompassed this mighty poem?). Schubert was one of the many pilgrims who never reached Mecca, at least on this showing.

A setting of the tenth line of the verse (printed in italics above) has been added by Reinhard Van Hoorickx to bring the piece to an end, admittedly mid-strophe but with as little fuss as possible. This performing version was recorded for the Hyperion Edition. The poem has thirty-one lines that remain unset.

Autograph:	Wienbibliothek im Rathaus, Vienna (first draft)
First edition:	Published as part of the AGA in 1895; subsequently completed by Reinhard Van Hoorickx (P717)
Subsequent editions:	Not in Peters; AGA XX 595: Vol. 10/110; NSA IV: Vol. 13/201
Discography and timing:	Fischer-Dieskau —
	Hyperion I 24²³
	Hyperion II 18⁹ 3'50 John Mark Ainsley

⟵ *Ganymed D544*   *Der Jüngling und der Tod D545* ⟶

MAHOMETS GESANG (II)   The song of Mahommed
(GOETHE) **D721** [H471]
(Fragment) C♯ minor   March 1821

Mässig geschwind

Seht den Fel-sen-quell, freu - de - hell,

(39 bars)

See previous entry for poem and translation. Schubert set only the first eleven lines of Goethe's
poem in this fragment

Johann Wolfgang von Goethe (1749–1832); poem written in winter 1772/3

This is the sixty-second of Schubert's seventy-five Goethe solo settings (1814–26). See the poet's
biography for a chronological list of all the Goethe settings.

Goethe wrote this poem in the early 1770s as part of an unfinished verse drama on the life of the prophet. Schubert had attempted to set it before, in 1817. He must have been attracted to it partly because it offered a chance to write water music – to depict a stream turning into a river, then becoming a veritable flood – which was all a metaphor for the gathering force of Mahommed's followers. However the challenges of a song about the growth of the Muslim faith are considerable. There are two main differences between the settings: that of 1817 is for tenor, that of 1821 for bass; the 1817 song has a moto perpetuo accompaniment of triplets, the later attempt discussed here a plethora of semiquavers. There is a remote possibility that Schubert actually completed the earlier version; as it is it breaks off at the bottom of the page after 114 bars, and it may be that the continuation has been lost. Even if this were the case it is strange that Schubert should have embarked on setting the monumental text again. There is no doubt, however, that he lost heart with this second version as it breaks off after only thirty-nine bars.

The second setting owes a lot to the first, above all its constant, restless movement and the similarity of the prosody. Both works have a key signature with four sharps, but the tenor version starts rather gently with bubbling triplets in E major while that for bass voice is in a more ominous C sharp minor. In 1817 Schubert had taken the opening words about the joyful stream at face value, but there is much more of a sense of drama in the second setting. The composer was not of the generation that remembered the danger that Austria had faced with Turkish invasion, but by 1821 his knowledge of history would have improved significantly (probably thanks to his sojourn with Mayrhofer). There is in this second song a sense of momentous happenings, with threatening implications for the West. (From this point of view the earlier song had begun too genially, but that fragment stays the course much longer precisely because the composer does not play his hand all at once.) Goethe's admiration for Mahommed as a great historical figure is tempered fifty years later by a Viennese historical viewpoint, and we hear a stream of violence and inherent danger rather than the innocence of a merry little brook. The growth of Islam, Schubert seems to be saying, was an ominous turn of events – and far more so than comes across in his first setting. In both versions the size of the canvas is established by the virtuosity of the piano writing.

The most interesting music in this fragment is for 'Jünglingfrisch / Tanzt er aus der Wolke' (from b. 28) where Goethe develops a theme (in miniature) similar to the later *Gesang der Geister über den Wassern* – that of water coming from the skies and returning there as part of the great natural cycle. The idea of youthful energy is appropriately reflected in a bouncing hunting-horn motif in the left-hand accompaniment; the phrase 'Jauchzet wieder / Nach dem Himmel' (bb. 32–3) climbs the stave (the song is written in the bass clef), propelled upwards by relentless pianistic fingerwork. This traverses the keyboard in an impressive, if somewhat mechanical, manner and it seems that as soon as he found himself trapped into writing such clichés, the composer retreated, for it is here that the music breaks off.

The performing edition of Reinhard Van Hoorickx brings this fragment to a close by returning to the opening music to provide a four-bar postlude. This leaves everything that Schubert himself wrote intact, and takes us back to the dramatic mood of the *Vorspiel* in C sharp minor.

Autograph:	Pierpont Morgan Library, New York
First edition:	Published as part of the AGA in 1895; subsequently completed by Reinhard Van Hoorickx (P718)
Subsequent editions:	Not in Peters; AGA XX 600: Vol. 10/125; NSA IV: Vol. 10/209
Bibliography:	Byrne 2003, pp. 63–8
Further settings:	Carl Loewe (1796–1869) *Mahomets Gesang* Op. 85 (1840)
Discography and timing:	Fischer-Dieskau —

Hyperion I 28[3]

Hyperion II 24[13]   1'25   Michael George

← *Im Gegenwärtigen Vergangenes* D710   *Heiss mich nicht reden* D726 →

JOHANN [JÁNOS] NEPOMUK JOSEF MAILÁTH [also MAJLÁTH]
(1786–1855)

THE SOURCES
S1 *Gedichte von Johann Graf Mailáth*, Wien 1825. Bey Tendler und von Manstein

S2 *Leben der Sophie Müller, weiland K. K. Hofschauspielerinn, und nachgelasssene Papiere.*
Herausgegeben von Johann Grafen Mailáth. Wien 1832. Gedruckt bey Ferdinand Ullrich.

THE SONG
September 1821   *Der Blumen Schmerz* D731 [S1: pp. 60–61]

Johann (János) Mailáth was born in Pest on 5 October 1786 to a noble Hungarian family (his father József was a top-ranking court official). He studied philosophy in Erlau and law in Raab and became a civil servant in 1808, a position he was forced to leave because of eye disease. He was treated for this by the famous opthamologist Beer in Vienna. Mailáth took up residence in that city, now determined to follow a literary career, and also gradually becoming interested in historical studies. His recklessness with money, as well as his patriotic idealism, was shown by the gift of his family's jewellery to the Emperor Franz in 1808 to support the war against Napoleon. He was a member of the Schubert circle in the 1820s although there are no surviving documents that link him directly with the composer apart from the biography of Sophie Müller that he wrote and edited (S2) in which the composer and his songs feature. As a member of the Hungarian intelligentsia living in Vienna, Mailáth would have been acquainted with the Esterházy family who were Schubert's summer employers in 1818 and 1824.

Mailáth's *Leben der Sophie Müller*, a life of the talented actress who died in 1830 at the age of twenty-seven, was published in order to raise money for a monument to her memory. It seems she was mourned by the whole of Vienna. She was a friend of Schubert and Vogl (who was also her singing teacher) and the pair often went to her house to perform songs for her and with her. Mailáth's admiring biography of the beautiful Sophie contains entries from her diary for 1825 that detail

these visits [*see* SINGERS]. The work is thus of the highest interest to Schubertians. At the end of his book (S2 between pp. 197 and 214) Mailáth included poems in Müller's honour by, among others, Theodor Hell, Karl Gottfried von Leitner, August von Schlegel, Friedrich de la Motte Fouqué, Ladislav Pyrker, Ludwig Tieck, Caroline Pichler and Ignaz Castelli (all qv).

Mailáth was a skilled journalist and a fluent linguist who made it his mission to introduce the Austrians to Hungarian poetry. His love for the literature of his homeland (*Magyarische Sagen und Mährchen*, Brünn, 1825) was in conflict with his need to live in German-speaking countries in order to make a living. In 1825, the year of the appearance of a volume of his own *Gedichte* in German, the firm Cotta of Stuttgart published *Magyarische Gedichte*, his German translations of Hungarian lyrics. This is a valuable and lovingly assembled anthology of eighteenth-century literature and includes sections on such famous poets as Mihály Csokonai, the brothers Károly and Sándor Kisfaludy, Ferenc Kölcsey and Dániel Berzsenyi. It became increasingly difficult for Mailáth to reconcile fealty to the Habsburg emperors (he wrote a five-volume history of the Austrian Empire between 1834 and 1850) with a patriotic pride in his motherland; this divided loyalty caused him great mental stress. In 1832 he published a history of the city of Vienna, and, as editor of the almanac *Iris* in the 1840s he encouraged the work of important writers such as Grillparzer and Adalbert Stifter. He left Vienna after the upheavals of

1848, having sided neither with the revolutionaries nor the conservatives, and moved to Munich where he was accepted as a member of the Akademie. On 3 January 1855, nearing seventy and without any pension or financial security, he drowned himself in the Starnberger See ('the last refuge of many of the world-weary of that generation', says Fischer-Dieskau), tied together at the wrists with his daughter Henriette who had long been his secretary and with whom he had made a suicide pact. This sad ending was symptomatic of a temperament often given to despair and pessimism. Mailáth's poetry seems to have found no further resonance among musicians although there is an unpublished setting of his *Der Abendstern* by Fanny Mendelssohn.

MAILIED

(HÖLTY) **D503** [H322]
G major   November 1816

May song

(18 bars)

Grüner wird die Au,	The meadow grows greener,
Und der Himmel blau;	And the sky is blue;
Schwalben kehren wieder	Swallows return
Und die Erstlingslieder	And the little birds
Kleiner Vögelein	Warble their first songs
Zwitschern durch den Hain.	Throughout the grove.
Aus dem Blütenstrauch	The breath of love wafts;
Weht der Liebe Hauch:	From the blossoming bushes:
Seit der Lenz erschienen,	Since spring has appeared
Waltet sie im Grünen,	Love reigns over the verdant landscape,
Malt die Blumen bunt,	Painting the flowers bright colours,
Rot des Mädchens Mund.	And the lips of maidens red.
Brüder, küsset ihn!	Brothers, kiss them!
Denn die Jahre fliehn!	For the years fly past!
Einen Kuss in Ehren	No one can forbid you
Kann euch Niemand wehren!	One honourable kiss!
Küsst ihn, Brüder, küsst,	Kiss them, brothers, kiss them,
Weil er küsslich ist!	Since they are kissable.
Seht, der Tauber girrt,	See, the dove is cooing;
Seht, der Tauber schwirrt	See, the dove is billing
Um sein liebes Täubchen!	Around his beloved mate!
Nehmt euch auch ein Weibchen,	Like the dove,
Wie der Tauber tut,	You too should take a wife
Und seid wohlgemut!	And be happy!

LUDWIG CHRISTOPH HÖLTY (1748–1776); poem written in 1773. Adapted for publication in 1804 by JOHANN HEINRICH VOSS (1751–1826)

This is the last of Schubert's twenty-three Hölty solo settings (1813–16). See the poet's biography for a chronological list of all the Hölty settings.

This is one of the least known of all the Hölty settings (its original title was *Frühlingslied*) and one of the most appealing. It is also Schubert's farewell to Hölty. It appears in the Therese Grob songbook where it remained unnoticed until rescued by Maurice Brown who was the first to write about the song in 1954, and Reinhard Van Hoorickx who privately printed a facsimile of the Grob songbook. Had it been included in the Peters Edition it is inconceivable that it would not have been widely performed over the last hundred years. 'As sweet as a May morning', Reed writes with justification. The tune lifts heavenwards at the end of the first two phrases and is irresistible. The fledglings whistle their melodies outdoors and the piano comments in a veritable sinfonia (something like the Haydn *Toy Symphony*) of cheeky warblings. In the postlude these answer each other in different octaves (bb. 15–16) as if parents and children of the bird world are conversing. A horn figure in the accompaniment, at 'Schwalben kehren wieder' (b. 5), betokens music al fresco and is a sign that earlier Schubert settings of this poem were conceived for two voices (D129) or for two voices or two horns (D199). All three settings are in §. The solo setting with piano makes use of some of the earlier ideas but it is definitely the best of the three. A sense of well-being radiates from the song; there is joy here as well as peace, merriness as well as something indefinably touching. In short, the song is an entirely lovable, and surprisingly recent, addition to the mainstream Schubert repertoire.

Autograph:	In private possession (part of the Therese Grob album)
First edition:	Published privately by Reinhard Van Hoorickx and subsequently as part of the NSA in 1999 (P815)
Subsequent editions:	Not in Peters; Not in AGA; NSA IV: Vol. 11/50
Further settings:	Johann Friedrich Reichardt (1752–1814) *Mailied* (1779)
	Franz Köringer (1921–2000) *Hommage an Franz Schubert* (this song included in mixture of lieder) (1996)
Discography and timing:	Fischer-Dieskau —
	Hyperion I 23²⁷
	Hyperion II 16²⁶ 1'57 Christoph Prégardien

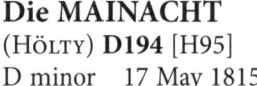 *Herbstlied* D502

Skolie D507 →

Die MAINACHT
(HÖLTY) **D194** [H95]
D minor   17 May 1815

May night

Ziemlich geschwind

Wann der__ sil - ber - ne Mond

(20 bars)

Wann der silberne Mond durch die Gesträuche blinkt,	When the silver moon shines through the bushes
Und sein schlummerndes Licht über den Rasen streut,	And casts its drowsy light over the grass;
Und die Nachtigall flötet,	When the nightingale warbles,
Wandl' ich traurig von Busch zu Busch.	I wander mournfully from bush to bush.
Selig preis ich dich dann, flötende Nachtigall,	Then I deem you blessed, fluting nightingale,
Weil dein Weibchen mit dir wohnet in e i n e m Nest,	Because your sweetheart dwells with you in a *single* nest,
Ihrem singenden Gatten	And gives a thousand loving kisses
Tausend trauliche Küsse gibt.	To her warbling mate.
Überhüllet von Laub, girret ein Taubenpaar	Concealed in foliage, a pair of doves
Sein Entzücken mir vor; aber ich wende mich,	Coo to me in delight; but I turn away
Suche dunklere Schatten,	In search of deeper shadows,
Und die einsame Träne rinnt.	And shed a solitary tear.
Wann, o lächelndes Bild, welches wie Morgenrot	O smiling image, that shines like the dawn,
Durch die Seele mir strahlt, find' ich auf Erden dich?	Through my soul, when shall I find you on this earth?
Und die einsame Träne	And the solitary tear, glistening,
Bebt mir heisser die Wang' herab.	Flows more warmly down my cheek.

LUDWIG CHRISTOPH HÖLTY (1748–1776); poem written in 1774. Adapted for publication in 1804 by JOHANN HEINRICH VOSS (1751–1826)

This is the third of Schubert's twenty-three Hölty solo settings (1813–16). See the poet's biography for a chronological list of all the Hölty settings.

The fact that Johannes Brahms set some of the poetry of Hölty (among other songs *Die Mainacht*, *An die Nachtigall* and *Minnelied* – all first set by Schubert) could be seen as a both a homage to the earlier composer and a tacit accusation that Schubert had not made the most of the poems' expressive possibilities. In the same way Hugo Wolf challenged Schubert's reputation with different conceptions of Goethe's *Ganymed*, *Prometheus* and *Grenzen der Menschheit* (all 1889) because he saw that there was a new way to set these lyrics using a recently minted harmonic vocabulary and a Wagnerian-inspired sense of prosody.

It is undeniable that Brahms's *Die Mainacht* Op. 43 no. 2 has moved more people than the Schubert setting but, as always in matters of taste and style, we have to ask ourselves whether the broad appeal of a Romantic lied (and *Die Mainacht* by Brahms is a quintessential product of mid-century romanticism) makes for a better song or simply a different one. Unlike Wolf, who was punctilious in matters of prosody, Brahms could not claim to treat poetry with more respect than Schubert: in *Die Mainacht*, for example, he cuts out Hölty's second strophe because in so doing he is able to build a powerful arched structure (ABA) with a contrasted middle verse and an effective *da capo* destined to bring more than a solitary tear to many an eye. Brahms uses the poem autobiographically, describing his own loneliness (as he often does in his quasi-confessional song diary) but it is arguable whether the gentle sensibility of these verses is able to support such portentous musical emotion.

Hölty's poem, influenced by Klopstock's *Die Sommernacht* (*see* D289) belongs incontrovertibly to the eighteenth century. A fastidious minority of music and poetry lovers perhaps will take comfort in the Schubert setting, because the modesty of the composer's conception seems to take into account the zeitgeist, and he does not make an effulgent drama out of Hölty's emotional crisis.

In fact it is the tempo ('Ziemlich geschwind' in alla breve time) that shows how differently the two composers understood the poem. The Brahms is all spacious introspection, the atmosphere taking its mood from the 'schlummerndes Licht' of the poem's second line. On the other hand, however drowsy the light, Schubert feels that his protagonist is far too unhappy and restless to melt into a soporific background of nature at rest. An urgent dactylic rhythm in the left hand of the accompaniment propels his search for a mate ever onward – there is more than a touch of impatience in his quest. Hölty himself, ardent and slightly awkward (as described in this book's biographical article) seems to materialize before our ears. At b. 11 the music modulates into the relative major (a minuscule change of direction of the figure in the right hand achieves this in a manner both simple and audacious), only to return to the minor key for the last three syllables of each strophe.

It is most felicitous that at the opening of the third verse the cooing of doves is beautifully suggested in the left hand by the dactylic figure where two staccato crotchets underpin the onomatopoeic rolled double r of the word 'girret' (Verse 3, b. 4). (This was of course also to be the rhythm of Death in *Der Tod und das Mädchen* D531, and in the same tonality.) Schubert was becoming such a sophisticated composer of strophic songs that it is possible that this detail came to his attention first and was his original inspiration for the pulsating little accompaniment figure.

The famous *An den Mond* by Hölty D193 was composed within the same twenty-four-hour period in which Schubert discovered this important poet.

Autograph:	Wienbibliothek im Rathaus, Vienna (first draft)
First edition:	Published as part of the AGA in 1895 (P562)
Subsequent editions:	Not in Peters; AGA XX 70: Vol. 2/112; NSA IV: Vol. 8/44
Further settings and arrangements:	Fanny Mendelssohn (1805–1847) *Die Mainacht* Op. 9 (1838)
	Arr. Tilman Hoppstock (b. 1961) for guitar accompaniment, in *Franz Schubert: 110 Lieder* (2009)
	Johannes Brahms (1833–1897) *Die Mainacht* Op. 43 no. 2 (1866)
Discography and timing:	Fischer-Dieskau I 3[20] 1'59
	Hyperion I 15[4]
	Hyperion II 6[15] 2'05 Margaret Price

← *An den Mond (Geuss, lieber Mond)* D193   *Rastlose Liebe* D138 →

MARIE *see* GEISTLICHES LIED ('MARIE') D658

Das MARIENBILD

(Schreiber) **D623** [H403]
C major   August 1818

Image of the Madonna

Mit heiliger Rührung

Sei ge-grüsst, du Frau der— Huld

(24 bars)

Sei gegrüsst, du Frau der Huld,	Hail, gracious Lady
Und der reinen, schönen Minne,	Of pure, fair love,
Ohne Makel, ohne Schuld,	Without blemish, without guilt,
Und von demutsvollem Sinne!	Humble in spirit.
Fromme Einfalt wölbte dir	In pious simplicity
Diese ärmliche Kapelle	This lowly chapel was raised to you
In den Stamm der Eiche hier	In the trunk of this oak,
Ohne Säulen, ohne Schwelle.	With neither pillars nor beams.
Vögelein auf jedem Ast	On every bough
Singen deinem Kindlein Lieder.	Birds sing their songs to your child;
Durchs Gezweig im goldnen Glast	Angels, bathed in golden radiance,
Steigen Engel auf und nieder.	Clamber up and down amid the branches.
Und dem Herzen wird so leicht,	And the heart, though oppressed with grief,
Wär es auch von Gram umsponnen,	Is made light;
Und dem Pilger wird gereicht	And the pilgrim receives refreshment
Labung aus dem Gnadenbronnen.	At the fount of grace.
Wohl ein Hüttlein baut ich gern	I would fain build a little hut
Hier im stillen Waldesgrunde,	Here in the silent forest,
Dass mir dieser Meeresstern	That this star of the sea
Leuchte nun um jede Stunde;	Might shine for me now and always;
Dass in diesem kleinen Raum	That in this small space
Mir der Himmel angehöre,	Heaven might be mine,
Dass kein banger, böser Traum	And that no troubled, evil dream
Meinen letzten Schlummer störe.	Might disturb my last sleep.

ALOYS SCHREIBER (1761–1841)

This is the third of Schubert's four Schreiber solo settings (1818). See the poet's biography for a chronological list of all the Schreiber settings.

It seems that Schubert discovered a volume of Schreiber's poetry in the spring of 1818. The poems had been published in 1817 in Vienna in pink paper covers, a handy pocket-sized volume ideal for the journey to Zseliz in Hungary where he took up residence in July as music master to the children of Count Esterházy. *Das Marienbild* is one of two Schreiber songs written at

Zseliz that summer. John Reed has suggested that they were composed 'by request', as Schubert was 'not at this time in sympathy with orthodox piety'. However another poem featuring Mary was composed in that summer (*Blondel zu Marien* D626) and if these Zseliz settings were not a reflection of the composer's own enthusiasm why should he return to the theme in Vienna with a compelling Stabat Mater in song, *Vom Mitleiden Mariä* (D632, December 1818), long after his employment had ended?

It seems that in the late summer of 1818 Schubert was going through a particularly introspective phase and that he continued to be as interested in Mary-in-music as he had always been. One has simply to look at a list of some very beautiful music devoted to the Madonna in Schubert's church music (*see* RELIGION AND RELIGIOUS MUSIC). If Novalis could believe that Marian resonances went far beyond specifically Roman Catholic belief (*see* commentary on *Geistliches Lied ('Marie')* D658 and the biography of Novalis), it is an easy step to see the significance of Mary for Schubert outside the dogma of conventional Christianity.

The original title of the poem adds the words 'in einem Baume' – in a tree. The improvised simplicity of the forest chapel, no more than an icon set in an oak tree, suggests a pagan shrine; on the other hand, the music for *Lied eines Schiffers an die Dioskuren* (Mayrhofer) D360, a heartfelt pagan hymn, would not have been out of place in a church. The words 'Ohne Säulen, ohne Schwelle' (bb. 20–21) bring to mind the star-struck veneration of this prayer to Castor and Pollux in *Lied einer Schiffers* where the boatman's oar is hung as an offering from the pillars of the temple dedicated to the heavenly twins ('Auf an eures Tempels Säulen', bb. 33–5). Both songs precede worship in the sacred precincts of a shrine, demonstrating that in Schubert's music Christian and pagan, sacred and profane, seem capable of interchange and reconciliation. The accompaniment to *Das Marienbild*, rich in thirds and sixths, is mostly in the piano's opulent tenor range, suggesting horn music, the sound one may hear from the distant hunt in the middle of a forest. The tender chromaticisms of the vocal line, which tell of a votary's tentative awe, weave around the unblemished C major tonality, a key that often implies clarity and purity. (Schubert chose this key for the last of his *Salve Regina* settings D811, an unaccompanied work for four men's voices that has much of the mellow mood and tessitura of the accompaniment of *Das Marienbild*.) The repetition of the last line of each verse leaves the supporting harmony more or less unchanged, but miraculously suggests a two-way exchange between supplicant and mother of God, a prayer answered simply by altering the shape of the vocal line and bringing it to the fulfilment of the cadence. There is also a courtly quality to this strophic song, which, in its simplicity of form and with a vocal line florid with ornamentation, suggests the art of the troubadour, and the Marian cult of the Crusades – a favourite epoch of Schubert's lieder and operatic imaginings. It is also a musical manifestation of the so-called Nazarene movement in painting of which Schubert's friend, Leopold Kupelwieser became a noted exponent.

Autograph:	In private possession
First edition:	Published as Book 10 no. 3 of the *Nachlass* by Diabelli, Vienna in 1831 (P264)
Subsequent editions:	Peters: Vol. 5/38; AGA XX 341: Vol. 5/214; NSA IV: Vol. 12/38
Bibliography:	Black 2003, pp. 65 & 161 (links this song and the E flat Mass D950)
	Capell 1928, p. 145
Discography and timing:	Fischer-Dieskau II 2[4] 3'29 (first four strophes only)
	Hyperion I 13[1]
	Hyperion II 20[17] 5'32 Marie McLaughlin

← *Der Blumenbrief* D622   *Blondel zu Marien* D626 →

FRIEDRICH VON MATTHISSON (1761–1831)

THE POETIC SOURCES

S1 *Gedichte von Matthisson*, Fünfte stark vermehrte Auflage, Zürich bey Orell, Füssli und Compagnie, 1802

S2 *Gedichte von Matthisson*, Erstes und Zweytes Bändchen, nach der fünften vermehrten Original-Ausgabe, Wien bey R. Sammer, Buchhändler, 1803

S3 *Gedichte von Friedrich von Matthisson* Erster und Zweiter Theil, Vollständige Ausgabe, Tübigen, bei Cotta, 1811

S4 *Sammlung Deutscher Beyspiele zur Bildung des Styls*, Zweyter Band, Wien, im Verlagsgewölbe des k.k. Schulbücher-Verschleisses bey St. Anna in der Johannis-Gasse, 1808

S5 *Wilhelmine, Ein Lesebuch für Mädchen von 10 bis 15 Jahren: Zur Bildung des Herzens und des Geschmacks*. Von dem Prof. Johann Genersich, Zweyter Theil, Wien, 1811. Im Verlag bey Anton Doll

For his 1811 and 1812 Matthisson songs Schubert may very well have used S1 (1802), but as *Der Geistertanz* and *Die Schatten* are printed next to each other in the second volume (Zweiter Theil) of S3 (1811), it is possible he acquired this volume hot off the press. On the other hand he might have found *Die Schatten* in a school textbook printed in Vienna (S4) where it is also possible he found poems for musical setting by Pfeffel, Hölty and Schiller (D10, D44, D47). The second part of S3 is not particularly rich in lyrics suitable for music, and this may be another argument pointing to Schubert's possession of the school anthology before the explosion of Matthisson settings in 1814, an event that was possibly occasioned by his discovery of another edition of the poet's works.

For his 1814 songs the NSA believes that Schubert used S1 (1802), but the use of a very small and handy pocket edition from Vienna (S2), a pirated reprint of S1, is equally likely. All the 1814 songs are contained in both S1 and S2, but only two of those texts composed in 1815 or 1816 are printed there. This suggests that in 1815 Schubert switched to S3 (1811) as a source, and in this period only used the first volume (Erster Theil) of that set. Perhaps he had mislaid the second volume (or returned it to its owner) after using it in 1812–13.

The Viennese paperback issue of Matthisson's poems (Bauer) was not published early enough to have been Schubert's source.

THE SONGS

1812	*Der Geistertanz* (I and II) D15 and D15A [S1: pp. 167–9] [S2: 2.Bändchen pp. 12–13] [S3: Zweiter Teil p. 104]
	In S1 this poem is headed with a Latin tag from Horace: 'Pulvis et umbra sumus'
12 April 1813	*Die Schatten* D50 [S1: pp. 64–5] [S2: 1.Bändchen p. 63] [S3: Zweiter Teil p. 103] [S4: p. 54]
1814	*Adelaide* D95 [S1: p. 61] [S2: 1.Bändchen p. 59] [S3: Erster Teil p. 144]

April 1814	*Trost. An Elisa* D97 [S1: p. 200] [S2: 2.Bändchen pp. 38–9] [S3: Erster Teil p. 90] *Erinnerungen* D98 [S1: pp. 201–2] [S2: 2.Bändchen pp. 40–41] [S3: Erster Teil pp. 266–7] *Andenken* D99 [S1: pp. 209–10] [S2: 2.Bändchen p. 46] [S3: Erster Teil pp. 266–7] *Geisternähe* D100 [pp. 207–8] [S2: 2.Bändchen p. 45] [S3: Erster Teil pp. 280–81] *Erinnerung (Todtenopfer)* D101 [S1: pp. 297–8] [S3: Erster Teil p. 290] In S1 the title of the poem is *Erinnerung* *Die Betende* D102 [S1: pp. 190–91] [S2: 2.Bändchen pp. 29–30] [S3: Erster Teil p. 6]
4 April [or July] 1814	*Lied aus der Ferne* D107 [S1: pp. 205–6] [S2: 2.Bändchen pp. 43–4] [S3: Erster Teil p. 274–5]
July 1814	*Der Abend* D108 [S1: pp. 213–14] [S2: 2.Bändchen p. 50] [S3: Erster Teil p. 29] *Lied der Liebe* D109 [S1: pp. 211–12] [S2: 2.Bändchen pp. 48–9] [S3: Erster Teil pp. 278–9]
29 September 1814	*Romanze* D114 [S1: pp. 283–6] [S2: 2.Bändchen pp. 98–100] [S3: Erster Teil pp. 101–4] In S3 the poem's title is *Das Fräulein im Thurme*. In Strophe 7 the heroine's surname is changed from Montanvert to Mortimer so S3 was certainly not the source of this poem for Schubert.
2–7 October 1814	*An Laura als sie Klopstocks Auferstehungslied sang* D115 [S1: pp. 188–9] [S2: 2.Bändchen p. 28] [S3: Erster Teil pp. 11–12]
14 October 1814	*Der Geistertanz* (III) D116 [S1: pp. 167–9] [S2: 2.Bändchen pp. 12–13] [S3: Zweiter Teil p. 104]
1815 (May?)	*Die Sterbende* D186 [S3: Erster Teil pp. 44–5]
May 1815	*Stimme der Liebe* (I) D187 [S3: Erster Teil p. 17] *Naturgenuss* D188 [S3: Erster Teil p. 42]
25 August 1815	*Todtenkranz für ein Kind* D275 [S1: p. 195] [S2: 2.Bändchen p. 34] [S3: Erster Teil p. 248]
April 1816	*Entzückung* D413 [S3: Erster Teil p. 7] *Geist der Liebe* D414 [S3: Erster Teil p. 39] *Klage* D415 [S3: Erster Teil pp. 51–2]
29 April 1816	*Stimme der Liebe* (II) D418 [S3: Erster Teil p. 17]
30 April 1816	*Julius an Theone* D419 [S3: Erster Teil pp. 58–9]
December 1816	*Skolie* D507 [S1: p. 176] [S3: Erster Teil p. 150] *Lebenslied* D508 [S3: Erster Teil pp. 109–10]
September or October 1817	*Vollendung* D579A or D989 [S1: pp. 186–7] [S2: 2.Bändchen p. 27] [S3: Erster Teil p. 60] *Die Erde* D579B or D989a [S5: p. 160]

1822?	*Naturgenuss* D422 Quartet for TTBB and piano [S3: Erster Teil p. 42]
January 1822	*Geist der Liebe* D747 Quartet for TTBB and piano [S3: Erster Teil p. 39]

Mention should also be made of other Matthisson settings for unaccompanied voices that are outside the scope of this book: *Goldner Schein* D357 Canon for three voices, 1 May 1816; *Andenken* D423 (second setting) Trio for two tenors and bass, May 1816; *Erinnerungen* D424 (second setting) Trio for two tenors and bass, May 1816; *Widerhall* D428 Trio for two tenors and bass, May 1816; *Der Geistertanz* (fourth setting) D494 Trio for two tenors and bass, November 1816; *Jünglingswonne* D983 Op. 17 no. 1 Quartet for TTBB, undated

One might have thought that Schubert first came across the poetry of Friedrich von Matthisson only through the settings of Zumsteeg and Beethoven. But Matthisson was already an established classic in Schubert's school years, a measure of the self-made poet's acceptability to the Austrian authorities when he was not yet fifty. Quotations from Matthisson's work were featured in the primer for literature and rhetoric entitled *Institutio ad eloquentiam* from which Schubert probably had to learn passages by heart. Apart from a very early brush with a text by Rochlitz in 1812, Schubert's encounter with Matthisson was his first with a completely contemporary writer, a living and working poet (who would survive Schubert by three years). While copying the ballads of Zumsteeg and recomposing them directly from the original scores, the young Schubert could not have failed to notice the Matthisson settings in that composer's *Kleine Balladen und Lieder*. He copied some of these too, and perhaps it was Zumsteeg's slender Matthisson settings that persuaded Schubert to take shorter lyrics seriously as vehicles for music.

F. Matthisson, *Gedichte* (1791) with an engraving of the poet from a drawing by Massot.

F. Matthisson, *Gedichte* (1802) with a frontispiece engraving of the older poet.

Matthisson was born in Hohendodeleben near Magdeburg on 23 January 1761. His father was a Prussian army chaplain who died before his son's birth, so he was educated by his grandfather and then at a seminary, the Klosterbergen in Magdeburg. He studied theology and philology at Halle and went on to a teaching post at the Philanthropin, a seminary in Dessau (1781–4). After this he accepted a travelling tutorship, initiating years of a peripatetic life in which he took the greatest pleasure. From early on Switzerland was an important centre of his inspiration. He had already published a volume of *Gedichte* (Mannheim, 1787) but after his arrival in Switzerland in the same year his reputation as a poet became international. The revised volume of *Gedichte* (Zürich, 1791) opens with a poem in praise of Lake Geneva. This part of Switzerland was the setting for what became an idyllic phase of his life. His close friendship with the wealthy writer Karl Viktor von Bonstetten (1745–1832) ensured an ongoing feast of lively hospitality, particularly at Nyon on Lake Geneva where Bonstetten lived for six years on a beautiful estate. This became a home from home for the younger poet. Bonstetten, an exceptionally charming

and educated man (later to be the travelling companion of Madame de Staël) was, and remained, Matthisson's most cherished friend. He was something of an elder-brother figure to the poet and had earlier been the object of the passionate affection of Thomas Gray, author of *Elegy Written in a Country Churchyard*, after the dazzlingly handsome Swiss writer, then in his middle twenties, had visited Cambridge in 1770. Matthisson's 1791 *Gedichte* is dedicated to Bonstetten and another close friend, the Swiss nobleman Salis-Seewis (qv), a poet also to be set by Schubert.

At the back of the *Gedichte* Matthisson prints two of Gray's, pathetically, smitten letters to Bonstetten (in English) – this is perhaps the most passionate writing within a volume of verse where poetic polish tends to be more prominent than human depth. Matthisson was proud of his connection, via Bonstetten, with Gray, and was prepared to risk being indiscreet in the interests of literary name-dropping. There was nothing that Matthisson valued more than hobnobbing with famous people. The 1791 volume places the beloved Bonstetten in the role of 'friend to the great writers' with Matthisson succeeding

Gray in that privileged position. Throughout a long and almost hyperactive life Matthisson was an inveterate collector of people, and it would probably be easier to list the celebrities he did not meet on his travels than the poets, musicans and aristocracy he encountered, almost daily it seems. It is indicative of his mindset that the turbulent events in France in the years of the Revolution should not have touched him to any degree, nor dimmed his delight in the company of high-born patrons. He had charm, and he knew how to use it. He married in 1793 but this was dissolved in 1797. A son, Ludwig, born in 1795 of this union, died in 1799. He married for a second time in 1810, but his bride, twenty-nine years his junior, predeceased him, and he also lost a young child from this marriage. In a different age Matthisson might have been quite happy to remain a bachelor.

Between 1795 and 1811 he was appointed companion and reader to Princess Louisa of Anhalt-Dessau, enabling him to travel around Europe in the finest style, meeting the greatest people. A relationship that he purportedly had with one of the princess's ladies-in-waiting is described in the commentary on *Adelaide* D95. His copious memoirs (*Erinnerungen* in five volumes, 1810–16), written when Schubert was busy setting Matthisson poems from years earlier, look back on the poet's life as a panorama of changing landscapes and personalities. They make interesting reading up to a point, but Oskar Wolff in 1846 found Matthisson's prose style 'unbearably mannered', and it seems to have been the consensus of the time that everything in this poet was calculated and planned to an extraordinary degree, leaving little room for spontaneity or naturalness. To compare Matthisson's writings about Italy to Wilhelm Müller's (not to mention Goethe's *Italienische Reise*) is to understand something of Matthisson's limitations as an observer of human nature, and thus as a poet. Nevertheless his unflagging industry is remarkable, as was his lifelong ability to turn almost every aspect of his experience into something fit for publication.

Friedrich von Matthisson, engraving after the portrait by Tischbein, 1798.

F. von Matthisson, *Gedichte* (1811).

Matthisson's work was praised early on by Schiller for its gentle melancholy and contemplative enthusiasm, but the style never developed to any degree and refused to change with the times. The poems became much imitated after 1815 (and not by the best poets) when political events were moving to the right in favour of the innocuous courtly styles of the *ancien régime*. Matthisson's homages to classical style and metre sometimes emerge as unintentional parodies, and they lack the strength of the best of his forerunners, his revered Klopstock for example. August von Schlegel had praised Matthisson in 1798 at the height of his success, but later wrote a biting epigram that compared his poetry to a proud and lifeless collection of marble statues. Beethoven, whose setting of *Adelaide* had done much to make Matthisson famous, was on the other hand a sincere fan; he wrote to the poet thanking him for the 'blessed pleasure that your poetry has always brought me and still will bring'. In return Matthisson, in the notes to the poem printed at the end of his *Gedichte*, mentions Beethoven's *Adelaide* as the best of all musical settings of his verse.

Matthisson had a marvellous life in many ways. His connections with the aristocracy bore fruit to which must be added, in all fairness, his love of life and people – an attractive zest that always carried his career forward as if under a lucky star. In 1812 he entered the service of the Duke of Württemberg and for sixteen years climbed the regal staircase of privilege, flourishing in a court that had in its past and on its conscience the dark echoes of Schubart's imprisonment and Schiller's unhappy adolescence. He was ennobled (the author of the 1811 edition of the *Gedichte* – S3 above – had become Friedrich *von* Matthisson) and appointed intendant of the court theatre in Stuttgart as well as chief librarian of the Royal Library. All these posts brought financial rewards and when Matthisson retired in 1828 and returned to his home territory, Wörlitz near Dessau, he was a revered and well-to-do poet, if not also a relic of a vanished age. His *Stammbuch* (a superior kind of autograph album, recently published in splendid facsimile) is a testament to a lifetime of successful networking: it contains contributions (and often poems) from such figures as Claudius, Klopstock and Pfeffel (1785), Schubart (1787), Salis-Seewis (1793), Schiller, Stolberg, Herder and Köpken (1794), Jacobi (1801), Goethe (1808), Johanna Schopenhauer and Gerstenbergk (1818), Hell (Winkler) and Kind (1824), Müller (1826) and Niemeyer (1827). This is simply to select those who happened to be Schubert's poets from a dazzling throng of Matthisson's friends and acquaintances. He kept in touch with Goethe in Weimar and in 1826 he read aloud a scene from *Faust* for his great contemporary who remarked, 'You read that as if you yourself had written it.' It is not impossible that there was a hidden barb in this comment but, if so, it went over Matthisson's head.

By 1814 his poems were already period pieces and the less reverent contemporary literary world treated him accordingly. This made not a jot of difference to Schubert who at seventeen was not yet ready for the poetry of Novalis or the Schlegels. Matthisson's elegance and sensibility served the composer's youthful purposes well in the spring and summer of 1814 as a pathway to his encounter with Goethe's poetry in October (*Gretchen am Spinnrade* D118). Schubert still had a great deal of time for Matthisson in 1816 and as late as 1822, particularly favouring these texts for the convivial occasions when unaccompanied male trios and quartets were to be sung. Almost certainly unaware that his poetry had found bountiful favour with another composer on a par with his admired Beethoven, Matthisson died in Wörlitz on 12 March 1831.

Bibliography: Wolff 1846, Vol. 3, p. 206
                 *Das Stammbuch Friedrich
                 von Matthissons*, facsimile,
                 2007

FERDINAND (FRANZ XAVER JOHANN) MAYERHOFER VON GRÜNBÜHEL (1798–1869)

For reference to this poet, who helped translate *Trinklied* D888 (Shakespeare) *see* EDUARD VON BAUERNFELD. (*See also* FRIENDS AND FAMILY.)

JOHANN BAPTIST MAYRHOFER (1787–1836)

EDITORIAL NOTE

Throughout this book Mayrhofer's poems are printed as Schubert set them between 1814 and 1824. There are many deviations (the more important of which are footnoted in the separate song articles) between the Schubert texts and the poems as printed in the poet's *Gedichte* of 1824. For this unique publication Mayrhofer probably revised many of the poems that had been passed to Schubert for composition in handwritten copies up to ten years earlier. As these copies have not survived (apart from the *Heliopolis* cycle), it is impossible for us to know when and whether Schubert's song texts faithfully represent earlier versions of the poems. It follows that many of Schubert's so-called deviations from the *Gedichte* (1824) are simply earlier versions of the poet's text. On other occasions, Schubert, as was his wont, certainly altered some of the poet's wording for reasons of his own (sometimes haste and carelessness also played a part in these changes). The Schubert enthusiast will be interested to see alternative versions of these well-loved and increasingly studied texts representing, as they do, either Mayrhofer's original intentions *before* Schubert made his own changes, or the poet's own amendments to the texts made *after* Schubert's songs had been composed.

THE POETIC SOURCES

S1 *Gedichte von Johann Mayrhofer*, Wien Bey Friedrich Volke, 1824

No fewer than forty of the forty-seven texts set by Schubert appear in this privately printed edition. Schubert set all of the Mayrhofer texts to music from handwritten sources. The five songs from 1824 (D805, D806, D807 and D808, with *Gondelfahrer* set a second time for vocal quartet as D809) were set before the publication of S1 in October 1824. This book was republished in facsimile in 1936, in itself an extremely rare publication.

S2 *Gedichte von Johann Mayrhofer. Neue Sammlung. Aus dessen Nachlasse mit Biographie und Vorwort herausgegeben von Ernst Freiherr von Feuchtersleben.* Wien, 1843. Verlag von Ignaz Klang, Buchhändler.

It says something about the extent of Mayrhofer's output that in this posthumously edited collection of poetry, a book of 296 pages, only five Schubert song texts (sometimes considerably different from the versions set to music) are to be found.

S3 *Mahlerisches Taschenbuch für Freunde interessanter Gegenden Natur-und Kunst Merkwürdig-keiten der Österreischischen Monarchie.* Sechster Jahrgang. Wien 1818 Im Verlage bey Anton Doll.

This source contains an engraving of the *Erlafsee* (Marianzell) as its frontispiece. Schubert's first ever song publication was *Erlafsee* D586, printed as a musical supplement that was given away with this Taschenbuch. The collection is prefaced by Mayrhofer's poem *Auf der Donau*, and closes with Mayrhofer's *Der Erlafsee*.

S4 *Beyträge zur Bildung für Jünglinge*, Franz Härter, Wien 1818

This is the second and final volume of the Mayrhofer-edited annual for young people.

S5 Handwritten text of poetic cycle *Heliopolis* (1821)

Once in Schober's possession, and now in the Wienbibliothek im Rathaus. Schubert set four of these poems, although it is by no means certain (particularly in relation to the dating of the composition of D360) that the composer used this manuscript as his source.

S6 *Huldigung der Frauen. Taschenbuch für das Jahr 1839*. Herausgegeben von I. F. Castelli. Siebzehnter Jargang. Wien bei Tendler und Schaefer

Printed in this volume: *Aus Joh. Mayrhofers Nachlasse.* Two poems, *Flora* and *Jung und Alt* (*see* D477)

THE SONGS

7 December 1814	*Am See* D124 [S1: pp. 6–8]
October 1815	*Liane* D298 [S1: p. 10]
June 1816	*Fragment aus dem Aeschylus* D450 [no known printed text, but *see* AESCHYLUS for Mayrhofer's probable source by Stolberg]
September 1816	*Liedesend* D473 [S1: p. 40] *Abschied. Nach einer Wallfahrtsarie* D475 [S1: pp. 15–16 – the title of the poem in this source is *Lunz*] *Rückweg* D476 [S1: p. 24] *Alte Liebe rostet nie* D477 [S2: p. 98] [S6: p. 323 where the title is *Jung und Alt*]
1816(?) or 1822(?)	*Lied eines Schiffers an die Dioskuren* D360 [S1: p. 183, the title in this source is *Schiffers Nachtlied*] [S5: No. 20 of the handwritten cycle]
October 1816	*Der Hirt* D490 [S1: p. 11] *Geheimnis* D491 [S1: p. 9] *Zum Punsche* D492 [S2: p. 84]
November 1816	*Abendlied der Fürstin* D495 [S1: p. 36]
1817?	*Der Schiffer* D536 [S1: p. 107 – the heading in this source is *Schiffer*] [S4: p. 325]
Early 1817	*Augenlied* D297 [S1: p. 59]
Spring(?) 1817	*Sehnsucht* D516 [S1: p. 100]
January 1817	*Der Alpenjäger* D524 [S1: p. 107 – the heading in this source is simply *Alpenjäger*] *Wie Ulfru fischt* D525 [S1: pp. 42–3] *Fahrt zum Hades* D526 [S1: p. 155] *Schlaflied* D527 [S1: p. 47]
March 1817	*Am Strome* D539 [S1: p. 58]

                    Philoktet D540 [S1: pp. 152–3]
                    Memnon D541 [S1: p. 160]
                    Antigone und Oedip D542 [S1: pp. 163–4]
                    Orest D548 [S1: p. 159 – the title in this source is *Der landende Orest*,
                    Schubert's song was published as *Orest auf Tauris* in the Nachlass]

April 1817   *Auf der Donau* D553 [S1: pp. 18–19] [S3: p. 1]
                    Uraniens Flucht D554 [S1: pp. 169–74]

May 1817   *Nach einem Gewitter* D561 [S1: p. 28] [S2: p. 127, title here *Nach dem
                    Gewitter*]

July 1817   *Iphigenia* D573 [S2: p. 287]

September 1817   *Atys* D585 [S1: pp. 156–7]
                    Erlafsee D586 [S1: pp. 94–5] [S3: pp. 185–6]

July 1818   *Einsamkeit* D620 [S1: pp. 135–9]

March 1819   *An die Freunde* D654 [S1: p. 50]

October 1819   *Beim Winde* D669 [S1: pp. 118–19]
                    Die Sternennächte D670 [S1: p. 141]
                    Trost D671 [no known published source]
                    Nachtstück D672 [S1: p. 12]

Autumn(?) 1819   *Über allen Zauber Liebe* D682 [S1: p. 53]

September 1820   *Der entsühnte Orest* D699 [S2: p. 288]
                    Freiwilliges Versinken D700 [S1: p. 175]

December 1820   *Der zürnenden Diana* D707 [S1: p. 158]

April 1822   *Nachtviolen* D752 [S1: p. 121 – the title in this source is *Nachtviolenlied*] [S2:
                    p. 214, as no. I of the eight-poem *Nachtviolen* cycle] [S5: no. 4 of the
                    handwritten cycle]
                    Heliopolis I D753 [S2: p. 195, as no. I of cycle *Heliopolis*] [S5: no. 5 of the
                    handwritten cycle]
                    Heliopolis II D754 [S1: p. 178 with the title of 'Im Hochgebirge'] [S2: p. 44 as
                    section 2 of poem in three parts: *An Franz*] [S5: no. 12 of the handwritten
                    cycle]

Early March 1824   *Der Sieg* D805 [S1: pp. 54–5]
                    Abendstern D806 [S1: p. 96]
                    Auflösung D807 [S1: p. 122]
                    Gondelfahrer D808 [S1: p. 112]
                    Gondelfahrer D809 Vocal quartet (TTBB) with piano accompaniment [S1:
                    p. 112]

Mayrhofer's influence on Schubert was literally incalculable and permeated every aspect of the composer's life and work. To describe what Schubert learned from Goethe, Schiller, Schlegel or Novalis is not easy, but at least we can read the same books that were available to him. Mayrhofer's printed words, however, were supplemented by countless conversations with Schubert that are forever lost to us. In terms of literature, history and aesthetics the poet shared everything he knew with the unformed, open-hearted youngster whose genius he had the perspicacity to recognize from early on. There is very little first-hand documentary evidence and no contemporary portrait of the poet; for his likeness we have only Moritz von Schwind's drawing, a profile of his head made over thirty years after his death. Josef von Spaun provided further clues: '. . . beautiful blue eyes, full of life, a delicate, well-formed nose and a charming mouth with a satirical cast . . . not exactly handsome, but intelligent and attractive'. For the life we rely on fragments of memoirs and posthumous descriptions. What follows in this article is also a mixture of known facts and speculation; but such is the importance in Schubert studies of this friendship and collaboration, that it is inevitable that Schubertians will attempt a fleshing out of the bare biographical bones.

Johann Mayrhofer was born in Steyr, Upper Austria, on 22 October 1787. The long-accepted date of 3 November, incorrectly adopted by the poet's early biographer Feuchtersleben, has recently been shown by Michael Lorenz to be a mistake that goes back to an inaccurate index to the baptismal register in Steyr. His father, an attorney, died when the boy was eleven. The poems *Alte Liebe rostet nie* and *Memnon* (and its sequel *Aurora*) suggest an extremely close relationship with his mother. In accordance with Mayrhofer *père*'s wishes he entered the seminary of St Florian to study theology and train for the priesthood; different sources allocate a different number of years to this phase of his life, which seems to have left him traumatized and decidedly anticlerical. He arrived in Vienna in 1807 to continue his theological studies, successfully concluding them before officially leaving the church in 1810. The big city where so many of his schoolfriends, members of the Linz *Freundeskreis* like Anton von Spaun and Johann Senn, had come to further their careers, must have been something of a shock to a young man from the provinces. He transferred to a study of law at Vienna University. After qualifying, like countless graduates of similar background, he was drawn into the vast and ramshackle Austrian civil service. He lodged for a time with his

Johann Mayrhofer by M. von Schwind (from *Ein Schubert-Abend bei Josef von Spaun*, 1868). The only available facial likeness, drawn from memory by Moritz von Schwind, as part of a large composite sepia drawing. In Schwind's tableau, Mayrhofer is depicted standing at the right-hand edge, perhaps a deliberately alienated positioning of the poet on the artist's part.

former professor Heinrich Joseph Watteroth (the dedicatee of Schubert's lost cantata *Prometheus* D451) and was said to have fallen unhappily in love with the daughter of the house, Wilhelmine, who eventually married Mayrhofer's fellow-lodger Joseph Witteczek, destined to become one of the great collectors of Schubert's works. Mayrhofer was appointed book censor in 1816, and was gradually promoted within the ranks to become one of the most senior officers in that bureau of state repression. This was one of the major paradoxes of the poet's life: he earned his wage enforcing illiberal, repressive and petty laws against his fellow-writers, while remaining in blazing political sympathy with liberals and free spirits. The stringent censorship that he rigidly practised, and of which he passionately disapproved, must have added to the burdens of a nature that seems to have been weighed down by depressive illness.

Schubert first met Mayrhofer at the age of seventeen, two years before he left home to reside with the Schober family. By this time he had already composed *Gretchen am Spinnrade* D118 (he probably showed this song to Mayrhofer at their first meeting) but he was still at his most impressionable. The young composer's enthusiasm for Goethe played a large part in the friendship. (In a letter of 3 July 1818, Anton von Ottenwalt recounts to Josef von Spaun how Mayrhofer 'spoke with fine enthusiasm of Goethe's songs and Schubert's melodies for them'.) In 1829, the year after Schubert died, the poet looked back to Schubert's first visit to his apartment in the Wipplingerstrasse in the company of Spaun (with whom Mayrhofer had been to school in Upper Austria):

> *Both the house and the room have felt the hand of time: the ceiling somewhat sunk, the daylight reduced by a large building opposite, a played out pianoforte, a narrow bookshelf: such was the room which, together with the hours spent in it, will never be effaced from my memory . . .*

The intensity with which this is expressed has something about it of Constantine Cavafy's poem of 1907 *One Night* ('The room was penurious and common')[1] where the Greek poet conjures the shadows of a past love by evoking the humble abode in which he had once experienced joy. Whether sexually charged (as was the case with Cavafy) or not, Mayrhofer's lines were clearly written with love. After this first meeting Schubert must have visited Mayrhofer often and talked long into the night about Goethe, as well as Schiller and Hölty, and all the other poets whose work was probably better known to Mayrhofer than anyone else in the composer's circle. Intellectual stimulation was clearly lacking from Schubert's home life, and such a highly educated man, though still only in his late

twenties, must have seemed like a sage to the seventeen-year old.

No one else in Vienna was as aware of Schubert's greatness, as *convinced* of it, as Mayrhofer. (Spaun's admiration, for example, was more down to earth.) The poet lacked musical erudition (although he loved opera – Gluck and Mozart – and played the guitar), but it was his intuition – that tortured yet insightful inner voice by which he led his life to an extraordinary degree – which led him to perceive Schubert's importance. Divorced from the everyday pleasures of a cosy and fulfilled existence, he had a way of seeing most of life's issues in starkly realistic terms and as part of a bigger, usually pessimistic, picture. Susan Youens quotes a key Mayrhofer attribute as perceived by his biographer Ernst von Feuchtersleben: 'dunkle Lebensangst' – dark anxiety about life. But it seems that Schubert offered the poet respite from that unremitting darkness. The trajectory of the young composer's achievement was not simply gradually rising, it was rocketing to the sky. Mayrhofer was among the few who could see this blazing comet and imagine the breadth of its future glory. His ability as a seer, whether mulling over his own sicknesses or diagnosing those of society, resulted in self-inflicted torment, but contemplation of Schubert's genius seems to have brought him joy. In writing poems for Schubert to set to music, the depressed poet, lifted by the collaboration beyond his usual boundaries, experienced the most meaningful times of his life.

He seems to have known that, with Schubert's help, the seeds of word and music – those same seeds that he so often bemoaned his inability to sow – would flower (*see Abendstern* D806). The rays of sunlight brought by Schubert's song (*see Geheimnis* D491) were for Mayrhofer not simply part of life's incidental sensual pleasures (as they were to many of the composer's friends), they represented his *raison d'être*, a chance to connect with unalloyed brightness. As Brahms said, Mayrhofer was the most serious of all Schubert's friends. Although the poet was not given to talking a great deal about other people, or even *to* other

---

[1] In the translation of John Mavrogordato.

people, he viewed what he said to the composer (quite apart from what he wrote for him) as a sacred responsibility, as if he were Socrates conversing with his pupil Plato. As head of the 'Bildung' circle (Elizabeth McKay's name for the group of men originally from Linz who aspired to common ideals of education based on classical principles), Mayrhofer's influence extended far beyond the composer himself. He was clearly fascinated, for example, by the handsome Franz von Schober, a headstrong Alcibiades to Mayrhofer's Socrates. The poet's perplexing mixture of assertiveness and reclusiveness at times must have intensely annoyed Schubert. He was clearly also irritated by Mayrhofer's hypochondria. In September 1818 Mayrhofer was one of the recpients of a letter written from Zseliz which Schubert addressed to various friends. He tells the poet that he too longs for November (when he will return to Vienna and share a lodging with him). 'Cease ailing', he adds, 'or at least, dabbling in medicines . . .' But the composer was clearly drawn to Mayrhofer because of what he was learning and feeling; their relationship was a two-way pact in which Schubert got a great deal in return for opening a musical door into regions otherwise unavailable to the poet.

Schubert only came to Mayrhofer's poetry gradually (there was no one who could force him to set what he did not like). There was one Mayrhofer setting in 1814 (*Am See* D124), and one in 1815 (*Liane* D298), a song that probably came about after a discussion concerning Jean Paul's novel *Titan*. At the end of 1815 (18 November to 31 December) Schubert composed a *Singspiel* to a Mayrhofer text, *Die Freunde von Salamanka* D326; it is a considerable loss to students of the collaboration between composer and poet that the spoken dialogue from this work has not survived. Mayrhofer's influence can be detected in some of Schubert's 1816 diary entries, one of which reads 'to a free man, matrimony is a terrifying thought . . . he exchanges it either for melancholy, or for crude sensuality'. This disapproval of marriage was no advert for sexual freedom. As an alternative to the world of Biedermeier uxoriousness, Mayrhofer introduced Schubert

to the high-minded world of Greek antiquity. Perhaps they visited the various state collections of treasures from Greek and Roman times that were on show in Vienna. The poet was probably responsible for introducing Goethe's *Ganymed* to Schubert (to be set as a song D544) and explaining the background of the text; *Strophe aus 'Die Götter Griechenlands'* D677 is a fragment of a much longer poem by Schiller, and its selection for setting has the hallmarks of a similar recommendation. It would also be naive to suppose that Schubert was not influenced by the poet's left-leaning political ideals which harked back to the Enlightenment and Freemasonry, making him an old-fashioned radical. That Schubert set *Frühlingsglaube* D686 by Ludwig Uhland, a poet whom he considered 'belonged' to the composer Conradin Kreutzer, probably reflects Mayrhofer's admiration for that great poet of liberty. (Mayrhofer wrote a complementary poem called *Lenzglaube*.)

The great year of the classical settings was 1817 when Schubert initiated a duo with the celebrated baritone Johann Michael Vogl, who had played Orestes in performances of Gluck's opera *Iphigenie auf Tauris*. The nobility of that character was something of which Mayrhofer approved: he penned a number of texts (including two involving Orestes) designed to interest Vogl, who was an aficionado of the classics. In this same year Mayrhofer was much involved with his friend from Linz, Anton von Spaun, in the publication of a yearbook, *Beyträge zur Bildung für Jünglinge*, which, through literature, aimed to encourage young men to embrace virtuous and uplifting lives as citizens within a just society. This short-lived almanac (there were only two issues, 1817 and 1818), inspired by Herder's theories of education, which were in turn influenced by Hellenic writers like Plato, mirrored the long-held beliefs among the members of the Linz circle. The poem *Der Schiffer* (set by Schubert as D536) about the boatman with his bracingly stoic view of the world was first published in these pages. The friends involved in this enterprise included a number of Schubert's poets (Kenner and Senn for example), and the group

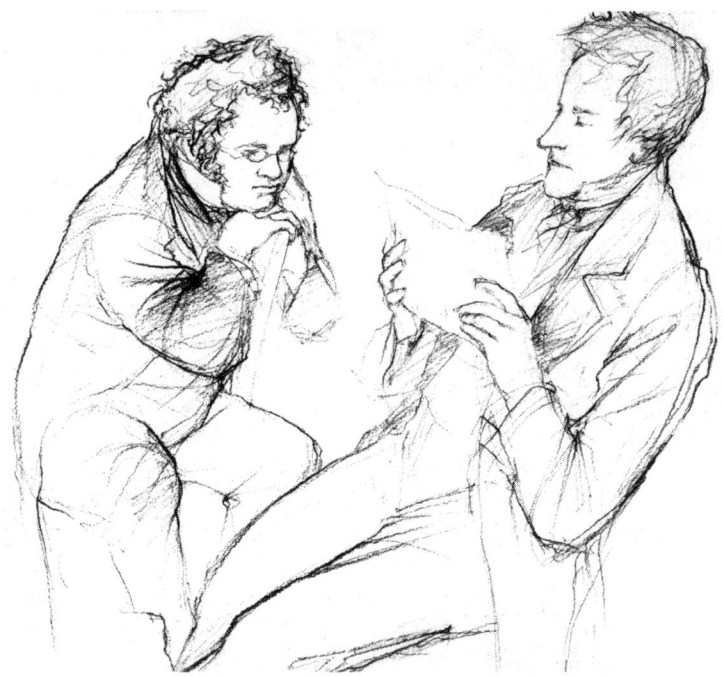

Gib mir die Fülle der Einsamkeit, pencil drawing, 2005, by Martha Griebler, depicting Schubert and Mayrhofer.

as a whole thought of itself as a *Tugendbund* – a band (if not exactly the 'Sacred Band' of Thebes) of manly virtue. Other members of the composer's circle – Josef von Spaun and particularly the sybarite Franz von Schober – seem to have distanced themselves from the high-minded idealism inherent in the project.

Schubert was a good deal younger than Spaun and Mayrhofer and if the *Beiträge für Jünglinge* were addressed to youth in general, one may take it that Mayrhofer believed that in Schubert he had found a 'Jüngling' in whom the group's theory of *Bildung* might be put into practice. He seems to have regarded Schubert as his special project, and with some justification. By 1817 there was an amount of shared experience between them with which no one else, with the possible exception of Franz von Schober, could compete. Mayrhofer was the kind of person who would have bolstered Schubert's modestly unexpressed beliefs that he had it in him to become a great composer. When the two created *Einsamkeit* D620 together in 1818 it was almost certainly as a silent riposte to the challenge of Beethoven's *An die ferne Geliebte* cycle of 1816.

Mayrhofer, immersed in Greek mythology, discerned in Schubert's music the gift and the voice of the gods. He knew all about the guilt of Orestes, as well as that character's selfless love for Pylades, and his willingness to give up his own life so that his friend's would be spared. Perhaps he hoped that his services to the young composer would expiate all that he regarded as unpalatable and failed about his own life. Mayrhofer is sometimes misleadingly referred to as Schubert's second father: the poet's financial difficulties (see Lorenz, 2000) meant that he was in no position to play a supportive role in Schubert's life other than in educational terms; never was the phrase 'moral support' more meaningful than here. On meeting Schubert, this man racked with depression and self-loathing had exactly the opposite reaction to the evil master-at-arms Claggart on encountering the radiant Billy Budd (in Melville's story of that name): instead of wishing to destroy the beautiful in Schubert, he sought to foster and protect it.

Mention of an opera by Benjamin Britten invites a twentieth-century comparison – the complicated collaboration between that composer and the poet W. H. Auden, six years his senior, from 1935 until the early 1940s (a period that almost exactly matches the time span of the closeness between Schubert and Mayrhofer). In this friendship the fathomless intellect of Auden was put at the disposal of a younger and much less educated musician; for a period this was the defining relationship in the life of the composer who found himself immersed in an entirely new cultural milieu. The thrill of collaboration with a creative talent on his own exalted level allowed Auden to forgive Britten's somewhat provincial awkwardness and lack of intellectual background. For Auden the attraction of creating a work of art together with someone whom he knew to possess an equal genius was always (at his own admission) the most powerful of incentives for falling in love and establishing a partnership. There were some remarkable works that came out of this friendship, but Auden's hopes for its future were dashed, and there was an estrangement exacerbated by the poet's proprietorial and controlling personality.

In Fritz Lehner's often remarkable film (1986) about Schubert entitled *Mit meinen heissen Tränen*, Mayrhofer is demeaningly depicted making sexual advances towards Schubert that are impatiently repelled. It is highly likely that Mayrhofer was homosexual by nature but with someone as complicated as this poet, inclination does not necessarily translate into practice. Schubert moved into Mayrhofer's lodging in November 1818. The poet lived in a single room on the third floor of a house in the Wipplingerstrasse belonging to one Maria Anna Sanssouci who owned a tobacco shop that sold lottery tickets. This room had been formerly occupied by the poet Theodor Körner who had lived there during his stay in Vienna in 1812/13. It was later described by Schober (1868) as 'a long, dark parlour' and, apart from his parental home, it was where Schubert lived for longer than anywhere else among his various addresses in Vienna. The thought of his laying a finger on Schubert in physical terms would probably have horrified Mayrhofer even more than it might have disturbed the composer. The inti-macy between the two (especially in the cramped quarters of the Wipplingerstrasse was rendered more claustrophic by arguments and Mayrhofer's violent temper. There was a certain amount of horseplay, and a story exists of Schubert having to soothe the 'savage author', as if an unruly dog, by reciting the incantation – 'Waldl, Waldl, wilder Verfasser'.

The unfolding of the Mayrhofer story is possible without necessarily making any inference regarding Schubert's sexuality. Given Schubert's musical talents Mayrhofer would have behaved in the same way, no matter what Schubert's sexual orientation, and given Mayrhofer's gift as a poet the same holds true for Schubert. That the composer went along with the 'pact' represented by the friendship may indicate a colloquy between two like-minded individuals, neither of whom was at ease with the cards that life had dealt them, both looking for a solution beyond the realms of sexualized intimacy. Schubert's easy-going nature, and a fascination with what he had to learn from Mayrhofer, enabled him to cement a close friendship with the poet despite any differences between them. In relation to Schubert, Stanley Wells's words come to mind: 'If Shakespeare himself, did not, in the fullest sense, love a man, he certainly understood the feelings of those who do.' (Wells 2002)

There were other important influences in Schubert's life, mainly the siren call of Franz von Schober, to whom Schubert was clearly attracted and devoted, and who encouraged a more permissive lifestyle than anything countenanced by Mayrhofer the ascetic. One can imagine the older poet as possessive, controlling and punctilious – almost over-aware of a responsibility to nurture and protect the young genius in the spirit of the *Beiträge für Jünglinge*. The composer moved out of Mayrhofer's apartment in the Wipplingerstrasse at the beginning of 1821 (some say at the end of 1820) and decided to live on his own. When the Mayrhofer chapter in Schubert's life came to a close, whether or not with acrimony, it must have represented a catastrophe for the Austrian poet, an excommunication from grace.

Mayrhofer's self-punitive personality was clearly formed by unknown circumstances and unhappinesses. Profound feelings of unworthiness and a chronic lack of self-esteem go so far back in a person's life that they cannot be laid at the door of school alone, much less a postgraduate institution, but it is likely that seminary life at St Florian brought matters to a head. The poet's fervent readings of the Greek classics, and of Plato's dialogues in particular, seem to have equipped him to accept his nature for what it was, while giving him a high-minded reason to abjure love in physical terms. Sex and lust were to be transcended by a Platonic interpretation of love that was above and beyond any physical expression. For decades the poet A. E. Housman, also a master of the classics, lived (and suffered) by these precepts and Mayrhofer would have understood well the romantic idealism and dark pessimism of *A Shropshire Lad*. A self-conscious manliness, a similar horror of effeminacy, prefigures the 'comradeship' hymned in *Leaves of Grass* by Walt Whitman, a poet who would have recognized a 'camerado' in Mayrhofer's sinewy sailor, *Der Schiffer*. In one version of his poem, entitled 'Ohne Liebe kein Glück', Mayrhofer writes, 'Mir leuchte Platons heilig Licht' – 'Let Plato's divine light shine on me'. This self-imposed renunciation permitted expression of both his misogyny and his admiration of male beauty (there are signs here and there in his poetry that he allowed himself this sensual luxury) provided he stringently abjured all sexual practice.

The self-control of abstinence is advocated by the Catholic Church to this day for those with homosexual inclinations. But once he had left the Church, Mayrhofer seems to have taken his cue not from the Bible but from the literature of the ancient world. He clearly preferred to face himself as the enemy rather than blame the devil, and there is no biblical equivalent of the Sacred Band of Thebes, lovers and national heroes sworn not to dishonour each other through cowardice or other unworthy behaviour. His Greek models were something positive to hold on to, although there was little practical difference between

Platonic proscriptions of 'unworthy' behaviour and those of the Church. Plato in *Phaedrus*, for example, describes the charioteer who must be firmly in control of both his horses, the obedient white steed in harness together with its unruly black neighbour champing at the bit to disrupt the equilibrium of the soul.

In certain Schubert songs based on classical literature such as *Memnon* D541 and *Atys* D585 (qv the commentaries on these songs), Mayrhofer rails against this kind of emotional abnegation and self-burial, giving voice to tribulations that seem autobiographically guilt-ridden and secretive. In others there is a kind of martyr's pride in having to carry a mighty burden. The long ballad *Uraniens Flucht* D554, based on the imaginary trials of the disappointed Venus-Urania (who appears in Plato's *Symposium* as the patron goddess of love between men), is most revealing of Mayrhofer's mental stance. In this work he and the distraught goddess bemoan the fact that all higher standards of behaviour have been subverted by banality, greed and lust. The bedraggled Urania, abused and manhandled when on earth, spots from her heavenly vantage point two of her votaries below, 'ein liebend Paar', 'a pair of lovers' (their gender or genders not specified) whose sacrifice at her shrine shows a pureness of heart. On account of this piety Zeus spares the whole of mankind, deflecting the heavenly thunderbolt that was about to wipe out both male and female, at the last minute. In this scenario of a classically reinterpreted destruction of Sodom, a 'loving pair' with the right sense of (self-) sacrifice ensures universal salvation; those men who have especially close friendships with their own sex are expected to display higher standards of morality than the married populace.

Uraniens Flucht may be superficially interpreted as a subversive celebration of the cult of Venus-Urania, and in favour of misunderstood and unfairly treated homosexuals, but it is in no way libertarian. The heavenly reprieve (for Mayrhofer at least) depends on these two votaries undertaking the kind of shiningly sexless life to which the poet aspired. Mayrhofer may have imagined himself and Schubert, joined in friendship and common endeavour, as able similarly to save mankind; at the very least it is likely that Mayrhofer revered Schubert because he came to believe that the composer stood as his gateway to The Good (everyone who has known and loved Schubert's music would understand how that kind of devotion might have blossomed). Nevertheless, it cannot be denied that the poet imposed a fruitless repression (above all on himself), requiring higher standards than most human beings could ever hope to attain. The penance of his working life, sweating daily in the Tartarus of the censor's office, could been seen as the punishment doled out to himself for failure, and for being unworthy of mercy – an indication of a dizzying degree of self-hatred, something confirmed by the extraordinary text for *An die Freunde* D654. In many ways Mayrhofer never really left the seminary; swathed as he may have been in studies of the classics, his self-mortification owed as much to the Rome of St Peter's as to the Athens of Pericles.

People convinced of their own ugliness and unworthiness often confine their sexual adventures to moments of drink-released abandon; Mayrhofer's reputation for abstemiousness makes one doubt whether he ever fell beneath the high standards he set himself. But there is a marvellous poem (partly modelled on truth and partly fantasy) by Eduard von Bauernfeld entitled *Ein Wiener Censor* (printed in full on pp. 171–4 of Youens 1996) where Mayrhofer, moved by the beauty of Schubert's improvisations, gets up from his accustomed corner, congratulates the composer and bolting down glass after glass of wine speaks at length to the astonishment of the gathered guests. They listen spellbound as he weeps tears of sorrow and becomes 'garrulous then and witty', talking about the good old Josephinan days of the Enlightenment, days of freedom and tolerance, the memory of which disgraces the present administration's small-minded vindictiveness. 'Foaming with clenched fists . . . raging . . . his wild speech laced with wit and sarcasm', he talks of the triumph of the light after prophesying, chillingly, that 'Bad times will come / And men of darkness / Will battle against light and truth'. Nevertheless, 'in the end / The new beautiful era will come / The spirit, freedom and the new / Teachings of equality will triumph'.

After Schubert moved out of the Wipplingerstrasse he composed two Mayrhofer settings in April 1822 and dedicated the three songs of Op. 21 to the poet – all settings of Mayrhofer. The heady years of 1821 to late 1822, under the influence of the loose-living Franz von Schober, almost certainly led to the disaster of Schubert's venereal illness, and we may be sure that Mayrhofer was aghast at this new direction in his protégé's life and its consequences. Mayrhofer's name appears spasmodically in the later 1820s as an occasional guest at Schubertiads (at Bruchmann's in 1823 and also at the famous party at Josef von Spaun's on 15 December 1826). According to Schober's later evidence, the composer and poet continued to speak of each other with the highest regard. But the old intimacy was gone for ever, and Mayrhofer seems to have kept in the background. The fact that Schubert failed

Gedichte by Johann Mayrhofer (1824), privately printed, and the rarest of all Schubert literary sources.

to subscribe to the 1824 printing of Mayrhofer's poems has been taken as evidence of a rift between them. The poet explained it thus after Schubert's death: 'The course of events, social attachments, illness and change in our attitudes to life kept us apart in later years.' Schubert was in Zseliz between May and October 1824; the *Gedichte* appeared in October 1824 (the poet's unanswered letter to Goethe in October 1824 enclosing a copy of his poems indicates this clearly) and the composer would not have been able to place himself on the subscribers list, even if he had wanted to. (Rita Steblin avers that the second of two copies reserved by Moritz von Schwind was possibly intended for Schubert.)

Throughout these later years Mayrhofer retained his enthusiasm for Schubert's music and his veneration for his friend's genius. Schubert's premature death came as a terrible shock. Adam Haller reported Mayrhofer's friend Ernst von Feuchtersleben as saying Mayrhofer's genius was drying up, for the harmony of his life had faded with Schubert's death. In 1831 the poet tried to drown himself in the Danube (in sympathy with the failed Warsaw uprising). He succeeded in killing himself on 5 February 1836 when, prompted by fear of a cholera epidemic, he jumped from a third-floor window in the censorship office and died in agony some forty hours later.

'Poetry with the terseness of a clenched fist' is how Susan Youens describes Mayrhofer's work. With its unconventional syntax and lack of smooth connecting tissue between disparate ideas, it can appear rough-hewn to the point of clumsiness. But a survey of the poetry as a whole, not just that set by Schubert, reveals a man of startling intelligence and originality who chose the granite-edged over the emollient as his means of expression. Some of his most astonishing passages concern nature. Worship of nature was part of the transference

that enabled Mayrhofer to avoid the sharing of emotions with other human beings, and some of his greatest lyrics are landscapes that omit all mention of people. Much of the time he lived in a world of abstraction and idealism unspoiled by human interference, giving him a certain freedom. He might be better understood as a forerunner of Expressionism; one senses that had he lived a hundred years later his strange individuality and refusal to conform would have marked him out as a valued member of the avant-garde. There were those, such as Grillparzer (qv), who had contempt for this poetry, but other fine critics realized that his work constituted something specifically Austrian, a special voice that needed to be encouraged. Julius Seidlitz (referring to Mayrhofer as 'one of the younger Viennese poets' in his *Die Poesie und die Poeten in Österreich im Jahre 1836*) described him as 'someone exceptional who, by concentrating his energies could ultimately construct an Austrian national poetry not dependent upon the German school'. Instead of 'concentrating his energies', Mayrhofer threw himself over a balcony and plunged to his death in the very year that Seidlitz made this observation. The critic's book was published in 1837 and Mayrhofer died unaware of these words of praise.

Over the last thirty years or so Mayrhofer's work has been considerably discussed and re-evaluated, and it is no longer possible simply to dismiss him patronizingly as 'one of the many bad poets indulged by poor Schubert, himself not much of a judge of literature'. In any case it is impossible to imagine the Schubert canon without the Mayrhofer settings; often when the composer is at his most daring and profound, often when the canvas is at its grandest and broadest, often when Schubert seems most engaged with issues that confront and defy the world of Biedermeier complacency, it is Mayrhofer who is standing by his side.

Bibliography: Dürhammer 1999, pp. 54, 91 & 221
                Lorenz 2000, pp. 21–50
                Seidlitz [Jeitteles] 1837, Vol. 1, pp. 140–41
                Youens 1996, pp. 151–227

MEERES STILLE (I)   Calm sea
(GOETHE) **D215A** [H110]
C major   21 June 1815

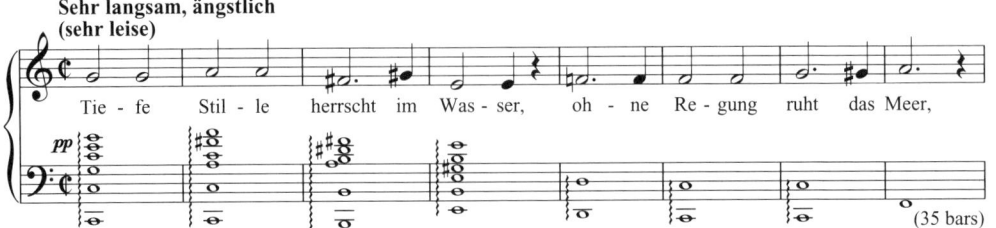

Tiefe Stille herrscht im Wasser,   Profound calm reigns over the waters,
Ohne Regung ruht das Meer,   The sea lies motionless;
Und bekümmert sieht der Schiffer   Anxiously the sailor beholds
Glatte Fläche rings umher.   The glassy surface all around.
Keine Luft von keiner Seite!   No breeze from any quarter!
Todesstille fürchterlich!   A fearful, deathly calm!
In der ungeheurn Weite   In the vast expanse
Reget keine Welle sich.   No wave stirs.

JOHANN WOLFGANG VON GOETHE (1749–1832); poem written between 1787 and 1795

This is the fourteenth of Schubert's seventy-five Goethe solo settings (1814–26). See the poet's biography for a chronological list of all the Goethe settings.

The more famous setting of this text (D216) was written on 21 June. It would be easy to mistake the earlier version, written the day before, for a preliminary sketch for that masterpiece. Indeed, without a very definite memory of the song, many a listener might even be seduced into thinking it is the same piece: apart from starting a third higher on the stave and more or less staying there, it shares the key, movement and much of the accompaniment of the well-known version. It is, however, quite different in a number of details and a masterpiece in its own right. As John Reed has pointed out, in lines three and four of the poem (bb. 9–16) there is a greater feeling of chromatically engendered fear and anxiety, appropriate for depicting a potentially dangerous, even fatal, becalming at sea. This setting is actually three bars longer, with two bars of interlude (bb. 26–7) and one of postlude (b. 35) absent in D216. After having written such a beautiful and arresting song, it is a wonder that Schubert felt the need to improve on it the next day, and is an indication of his tendency to intense self-criticism. For the second setting he mercilessly pruned every superfluous note (including the interlude and postlude), every inessential movement of the vocal line, reducing the element of fear, perhaps, but adding to the inexorable majesty of the stillness of the scene. The first version is perfection, the second perfection of a different kind. The only possible improvement (and a highly important one) is the utter inevitability of the vocal line that rises and falls with the least effort and the greatest effectiveness; it is this refining of the already ultimately refined that is the mark of the very greatest of song composers.

Meeresstille.

Tiefe Stille herrscht im Wasser,
Ohne Regung ruht das Meer,
Und bekümmert sieht der Schiffer
Glatte Fläche rings umher.
Keine Luft von keiner Seite!
Todesstille fürchterlich!
In der ungeheuern Weite
Reget keine Welle sich.

Meeres Stille from Düntzer's edition of Goethe's *Werke* (1882).

Autograph:	Wienbibliothek im Rathaus, Vienna (first draft, fragment)
First edition:	Published in *Schweizerische Musikzeitung*, edited by O. E. Deutsch, in 1952 and subsequently as part of the NSA in 1970 (P744)
Subsequent editions:	Not in Peters; Not in AGA; NSA IV: Vol. 1b/197; Bärenreiter: Vol. 1/210
Bibliography:	Byrne 2003, pp. 144–50
	Capell 1928, pp. 101–2
	Fischer-Dieskau 1977, p. 52
Discography and timing:	Fischer-Dieskau —
	Hyperion I 7^{10}
	Hyperion II 7^{9} 3'03 Elly Ameling

←— *Jägers Abendlied* D215   *Meeres Stille* D$_2$216 —→

MEERES STILLE (II)   Calm sea
(Goethe) Op. 3 no. 2, **D₂216** [H110a]
C major   21 June 1815

See previous entry for poem and translation

JOHANN WOLFGANG VON GOETHE (1749–1832); poem written between 1787 and 1795

This is the fifteenth of Schubert's seventy-five Goethe settings (1814–26). See the poet's biography for a chronological list of all the Goethe settings.

Goethe's poem dates from 1787 when, during his Italian journey, he travelled from Messina in Sicily to Naples; the dangerous circumstances of the return voyage that gave rise to this poem are described in the article ITALY AND ITALIAN LITERATURE (Vol. I, p. 957): on the outbound journey he struggled with seasickness during a storm. The great poet, born and brought up in Germany, had only glimpsed the sea for the first time when he climbed to the top of St Mark's Tower in Venice on 30 September 1786; a week or so later he visited the Lido and marvelled at

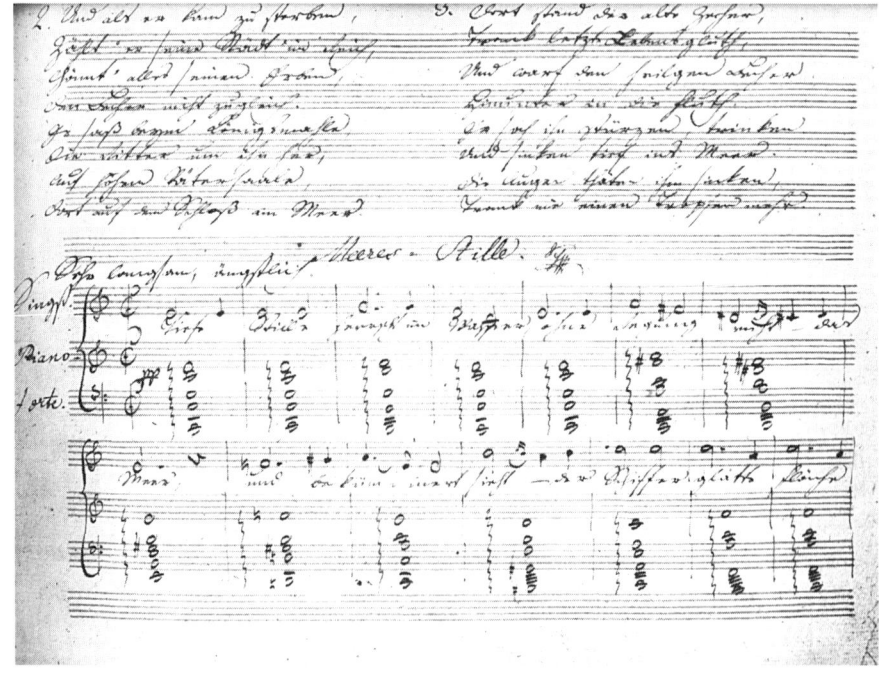

Schubert Autograph of *Meeres Stille* (II), from the album prepared for Goethe (the words at the top of the page are the second and third verses of *Der König in Thule* D367).

the vast expanse of water. Schubert on the other hand never saw the sea – Austrian lakes were all he ever knew.

The song is a marvel of impressionistic calm. The sea is motionless, but we are aware of the sinister implications of a becalmed voyage before the era of steam power. A tensely wrought melodic line is underpinned by breathless modulations – piano arpeggios roll stealthily upwards, almost imperceptibly, conveying stillness and fear at the same time. The song is only one page long but it somehow suspends time and place; the horizons are endless, the ship is cradled in dark waters, the piano part seems to measure the sea's depth, its chords vibrating like a sounding-line and lead. Above the vocal line there is no trace of wind in the sails. Fischer-Dieskau has written that 'the score of the song looks like a drawing' and indeed here is a map of motionless semibreves where the undulating lines denoting arpeggios seem almost nautically illustrative. The only undercurrent is one of human apprehension at the void created by Nature who has withdrawn her cooperation.

Beethoven also set the poem (chorally with orchestra) at more or less the same time, linking it with a happy ending – a setting of the pendant poem, *Glückliche Fahrt* (Prosperous Voyage) that Goethe insisted should be printed side by side with this one. Schubert preferred to leave the ship at sea, captured in music and set for ever, as if under glass, on the water's unruffled surface. The challenge faced by the singer is to convey a sense of the infinite calm of nature while also communicating human disquiet at the potentially baleful consequences (the music itself, calm and magisterial, does not easily lend itself to the depiction of fear). This side of the song, denoted by the marking 'ängstlich', is seldom brought out in performances. Perhaps this is to do with the zeitgeist and the fact that the first steam ship made its way up the Danube shortly after Schubert's death. A calm sea on a cruise today hardly threatens catastrophe from rogue currents, or death from thirst and starvation; singers on holiday disport themselves happily on deck while the ship's engines are on standby to ensure an unruffled continuation of the journey.

Autograph:	Gesellschaft der Musikfreunde, Vienna (first draft)
First edition:	Published as Op. 3 no. 2 by Cappi & Diabelli, Vienna in 1821 (P4)
Dedicatee:	Ignaz von Mosel
Publication reviews:	*Wiener allgemeine Theaterzeitung*, No. 61 (22 May 1821) p. 244 [Waidelich/Hilmar Dokumente I No. 101; Deutsch Doc. Biog. No. 238]
Subsequent editions:	Peters: Vol. 2/3; AGA XX 82: Vol. 2/160; NSA IV: Vol. 1/197; Bärenreiter: Vol. 1/17
Bibliography:	Brown 1954, pp. 94–5
	Byrne 2003, pp. 144–50
	Gülke 1991, pp. 117–23
Further settings and arrangements:	Johann Friedrich Reichardt (1752–1814) *Meeresstille* (1796)
	Arr. Franz Liszt (1811–1886) for solo piano, no. 5 of *Zwölf Lieder von Schubert* (1837–8) [*see* Transcriptions]
	Adolphe Martin Foerster (1854–1927) *Meeresstille*, Op. 6 (1878)
	Nikolai Medtner (1879–1951) *Meeresstille* (1905–7)
	Charles Griffes (1884–1920) *Meeres Stille* (*c*. 1903–11)
	Arr. Tilman Hoppstock (b. 1961) for guitar accompaniment (2 arrangements) in *Franz Schubert: 110 Lieder* (2009)
Discography and timing:	Fischer-Dieskau I 4[4] 2'25
	Hyperion I 1[5]
	Hyperion II 7[10] 2'05 Janet Baker

← *Meeres Stille* D215a   *Kolmas Klage* D217 →

MEIN! *see DIE SCHÖNE MÜLLERIN* D795/11

MEIN FINDEN *see* DUBIOUS, MISATTRIBUTED AND LOST SONGS

MEIN FRIEDEN *see* DUBIOUS, MISATTRIBUTED AND LOST SONGS

MEIN GRUSS AN DEN MAI   My greeting to May
(Ermin) **D305** [H185]
B♭ major   15 October 1815

(27 bars)

Sei mir gegrüsst, o Mai! mit deinem Blütenhimmel,	Welcome, May, with your canopy of blossom,
Mit deinem Lenz, mit deinem Freudenmeer;	With your spring, with your ocean of joy.
Sei mir gegrüsst, mit deinem fröhlichen Gewimmel[1]	Welcome, with your happy swarm
Der neubelebten Wesen um mich her.	Of newly awakened creatures around me.
[. . . 8 . . .]	[. . . 8 . . .]

Johann Gottfried Kumpf (pseudonym of Johann Gottfried Ermin) (1781–1862);
poem written *c.* 1808

*This is the second of Schubert's two Ermin settings (1815). See the poet's biography (under
Kumpf, Johann Gottfried) for a chronological list of all the Ermin settings. See also
the article for Selam.*

This is a charming little trifle with delightful piano interludes and a merry postlude in the
Haydnesque manner. The poem has nine verses; it compares the sensuous pleasures of the south
(olive trees, almonds, pomegranates) with the beauties of the Austrian fatherland where roses
are plucked by the poet's beloved Silli. Schubert wrote out the first verse and added the words
'eight more verses' under the stave. This is a rare miscalculation. Schubert (perhaps unintentionally) fiddled with the poet's words in the fifth line of the music, adding two extra syllables – *see*
footnote below (bb. 14–16). As he set the poem, did his eye perhaps stray up to the second line
of the text when he should have been looking at the third? The print of the almanac *Selam* (1814,
pp. 200–1), from which this song comes, is certainly small enough for a mistake like this to
occur. This amplification of the text works very well for the first verse – the composer makes it
fit of course – but it renders the other strophes unsingable as each has too few syllables for the

---

[1] Kumpf's original line is: 'Sei mir gegrüsst, du fröhliches Gewimmel'.

number of notes! The NSA considerately solves the problem of these missing syllables with a usefully adapted underlay for practical performance of all nine verses. For the recording on the Hyperion Edition (made some twenty years before the appearance of Volume 9 of the NSA) we opted simply to repeat the words of the first verse which is short and charming enough to warrant a second hearing.

    This is the fourth song in the possible cycle of seven that Schubert composed on 15 October 1815 (*see Selam* cycle).

Autograph:	Österreichische Nationalbibliothek, Vienna (fair copy)
First edition:	Published as part of the AGA in 1895 (P592)
Subsequent editions:	Not in Peters; AGA XX 153: Vol. 3/118; NSA IV: Vol. 9/137
Discography and timing:	Fischer-Dieskau I 5[29]
	Hyperion I 7[21]
	Hyperion II 10[21] 1'36 Elly Ameling

⟵ *Wiegenlied D304*   *Skolie D306* ⟶

MEMNON
Memnon

(MAYRHOFER) OP. 6 NO. 1, **D541** [H351]
D♭ major   March 1817

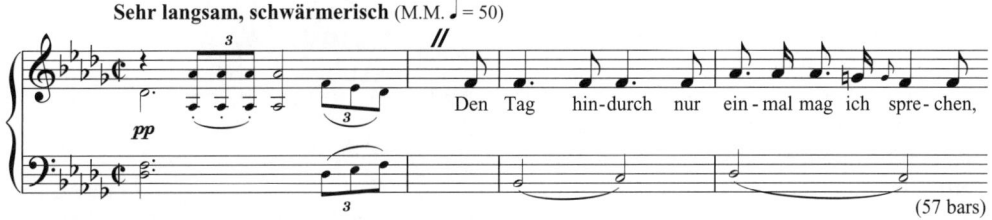

(57 bars)

Den Tag hindurch nur einmal mag ich sprechen,	Constant silence and grieving are my wont;
Gewohnt zu schweigen immer und zu trauern:	The whole day long I may speak but once:
Wenn durch die nachtgebor'nen Nebelmauern	When Aurora's tender crimson rays
Aurorens Purpurstrahlen liebend brechen.	Break through the night-begotten walls of mist.
Für Menschenohren sind es Harmonien.	To men's ears this is music.
Weil ich die Klage selbst melodisch künde	Since I proclaim my very grief in song,
Und durch der Dichtung Glut das Rauhe	And transfigure its harshness in the fire of
ründe,	poetry,
Vermuten sie in mir ein selig Blühen.	They imagine that joy flowers within me.
In mir—nach dem des Todes Arme langen,	Within me, to whom the arms of death stretch
	out,
In dessen tiefstem Herzen Schlangen wühlen;	As serpents writhe deep in my heart;
Genährt von meinen schmerzlichen Gefühlen—	Nourished by my anguished feelings –
Fast wütend durch ein ungestillt Verlangen:	And almost frenzied with unquiet longing.

Mit dir, des Morgens Göttin, mich zu einen,   Oh to be united with you, goddess of morning,
Und weit von diesem nichtigen Getriebe,   And, far from this vain bustle,
Aus Sphären edler Freiheit, aus Sphären   To shine down as a pale, silent star
    reiner Liebe,[1]
Ein stiller, bleicher Stern herab zu scheinen.[2]   From spheres of noble freedom and pure love.

JOHANN MAYRHOFER (1787–1836)

*This is the twenty-second of Schubert's forty-seven Mayrhofer solo settings (1814–24). See the
poet's biography for a chronological list of all the Mayrhofer settings.*

Memnon, son of Aurora and Tithonus, king of
Egypt and Ethiopia, was sent to Troy by his
father to help fight the Greeks. He slew Anti-
lochus, son of Nestor, but was in turn slain by
the vengeful Achilles (it was the love of Anti-
lochus that had consoled Achilles after the
death of Patroclus). The famous battle between
Achilles and Memnon was attended by their
goddess mothers, Thetis and Aurora (Dawn),
both of whom implored Zeus for victory on
behalf of their sons. Achilles won and the tears
shed by Dawn on the death of Memnon were
said to be the origin of early morning dew.
Aurora begged Zeus to resuscitate her son, and
he agreed to do this once a day. Every morning
Aurora caressed him with her warming rays;
he responded with disconsolate wailing. It is
this sound that connected the young warrior's
story to the mighty Colossi of Memnon, twin
statues of the Pharaoh Amenophis (Amen-
hotep) III, built as guardians of his burial
temple (nothing of which remains). They now
stand alone in a large empty plain on the west
bank of the Nile at Thebes, across the river
from modern-day Luxor. The sandstone
colossi are 18 metres high and placed 15

The statue of Memnon in Thebes (Luxor). The author
in Egypt, 1992.

metres apart. It was the north colossus, which had been damaged in an earthquake in 27 BC, to
which the legend is attached. The historians Strabo, Pausanias, Tacitus and Philostratus all testi-
fied that at dawn the statue gave forth a prolonged sound like mournful singing. Memnon's
ghostly speech seems to have been triggered by the sudden change of temperature at dawn,
when the sun's rays, scorching during Egyptian summers, hit the statue that had been chilled
by the desert temperatures at night. There is a Latin graffito on one of the statues that tells us
that 'Sabina Augusta, wife of Hadrian Caesar, heard Memnon twice during the first hour'. This
was during a visit to Egypt by the imperial family in AD 130. The statues remained a tourist
attraction until the third century AD when the Emperor Septimius Severus had the cracks
repaired, and Memnon sang no more.

---

[1] The repeat of 'aus Sphären' in this line is Schubert's own. For an explanation of the background to these alternative
readings *see* editional note at the beginning of JOHANN MAYRHOFER.
[2] Schubert reverses the order of Mayrhofer's adjectives here. The poet writes: 'Ein bleicher, stiller Stern . . .'

Schubert's masterpiece works both as a worthy depiction of a great classical legend and as a metaphor for Mayrhofer himself, trapped behind a stony mask with a destiny not of his choosing, creating his poems at painful cost, undreamed of by the reader. The key is D flat, a tonality used by the composer only half a dozen times and for some of his most rapt and magical songs, including *Ellens Gesang I* D837, *Am Bach im Frühlinge* D361 and *Die Sternennächte* D670, another Mayrhofer setting that also looks to the consoling perspective of a distant star.

The five-bar introduction has a marvellously sumptuous tune but, with its inner voice of staccato triplets (octave A flats in the right hand from b. 1), its texture is hollow, and we somehow hear notes resonating within a cavernous chamber. Slowly the statue warms into life, the vocal line (from b. 5) at first nursed within the smallest intervals, gradually widening its scope until the heavenly aspiration of 'Purpurstrahlen liebend brechen' (bb. 12–13). The heartbreakingly tender high F on 'liebend' at the end of the first verse is in response to a mother's comfortingly warm caress after a cold night of exile. The introductory ritornello is repeated in A flat in b. 14; the sun is five degrees higher in the tonal firmament, and Memnon warms to his theme. The pair of three-bar phrases beginning 'Für Menschenohren . . .' (b. 16) followed by 'Weil ich die Klage . . .' (b. 18) are among Schubert's loveliest sequential repetitions.

The colossus now takes us into his confidence. With a shift to the mediant key of F major (a change of key signature at b. 21) he opens a chink in his emotional armour that leads us closer to his heart. His quiet regret at man's misunderstanding of his grief ('Vermuten sie in mir ein selig Blühen', bb. 23–6) is that of a gentle giant, his massive size evident by the breadth and nobility of the vocal line, now spanning a ninth (for the word 'in' at bb. 24 and 27). In the third verse (marked 'Etwas geschwinder werdend') the knocking triplet figure of the introduction (now transferred to the left hand) is the foundation of a storm of emotions, leading us through many keys, within the stony breast. The writhing of these snaking sextuplets in semiquavers underpins a quite frightening power in the declamation; Memnon's awakening has been so cleverly paced that in hearing the full range of his vocal powers we fear that he will walk off his very pedestal in his rage and anguish.

But he is no Frankenstein's monster and, with the waxing daylight, his song, which thrives only in the moment of the cruellest contrast between cold and heat, gradually fades away. At b. 40 there has been a subtle return to a key signature of D flat major, and the last three lines of the poem are set to music of almost indescribable beauty and resignation as the colossus sees his dream as hopeless. He can only aspire to being reunited with his mother in the more noble realms of death. One would have to go far to find the spirit of Schubert's lieder from Greek antiquity better summed up in musical terms than by the magnificent phrase 'Ein stiller bleicher Stern herab zu scheinen' (bb. 47–50). In the hands of a great singer with a total command of *mezza voce* the repetition of this phrase (bb. 50–3) brings the song to a conclusion in a way that makes time stand still. The spirit of life evaporates from the unwieldy body of the colossus until the next dawn, his punishment to be rooted to the spot, weeping for what might have been had he been able to join his spirit in its heavenward aspirations. Schubert chose not to set the poet's sequel 'Aurora' which is a mother's reply, helpless to release her son's soul, 'fragmented into dreams and weary longing', from the weight of its grief (Schochow, 1974, prints this poem in full, Vol. 1 p. 335).

And so Memnon still looks down on the 'vain bustle' – in our age, hordes of tourists who seldom bother to go nearer than the 'photo opportunity' vantage point where the buses park. Some years ago I went to pay him closer homage and discovered that the ancient statue was covered in chiselled inscriptions, the graffiti of former ages, beginning with the Greeks. One of the most prominent of these marks was made by a visitor in 1817, the year engraved in a large rectangle on his right leg. So Memnon bears on his flesh, as it were, the mark of the very year in which he was assured by Mayrhofer and Schubert a second lease of musical immortality. The metaphor for someone trapped inside a body that is no longer a happy or natural habitat is clear.

The left foot of the staute of Memnon. Photographed in 1992.

The need for such misfits to guard their silence is emphasized in music of quiet grandeur which underlines the poet's own stoicism.

Perhaps Mayrhofer was aware of Clemens Brentano's poem *Nachklänge Beethovenscher Musik* (written in Vienna in 1814 as a reaction to the *Battle Symphony* Op. 91) in which 'Memons Bild, des Morgens erste Sonnen' is used in powerful imagery: the poet experiences Beethoven's music as if it were sunlight shooting on to Memnon's forehead, enabling him to give voice to feelings otherwise suppressed. In more modern times Memnon has appeared in Ibsen's *Peer Gynt* (Act IV Scene 2), in a play by Laurence Binyon and a song by Paul Bowles with a Cocteau text. Indeed, the French seem to have found the legend particularly appealing. Paul Valéry's prose poem *Chant cristallin de la statue de Memnon* was published posthumously in 1950. Guillaume Apollinaire writing in 1903 (in the poem *Avenir* from the collection *Le Guetteur mélancolique*) describes an uncertain future where 'les clartés de l'aube neuve / Ne feront plus vibrer la statue de Memnon' (the clarity of the new dawn, will no longer make the statue of Memnon resonate'). In another poem from the same collection Apollinaire writes of 'la voix de Memnon dans les tendres matins'. With such a description one might almost believe that the French poet knew Schubert's song.

Autograph:	Wienbibliothek im Rathaus, Vienna
First edition:	Published as Op. 6 no. 1 by Cappi & Diabelli, Vienna in 1821 (P15)
Dedicatee:	Johann Michael Vogl
Publication reviews:	*Allgemeine musikalische Zeitung* (Vienna) No. 6 (19 January 1822), col. 43ff. [Waidelich/Hilmar Dokumente I No. 142; Deutsch Doc. Biog. No. 270]
	F. von Hentl 'Blick auf Schubert's Lieder', *Wiener Zeitschrift für Kunst, Literatur, Theater und Mode* No. 36 (23 March 1822), p. 289f. [Waidelich/Hilmar Dokumente I No. 146; Deutsch Doc. Biog. No. 278]

Subsequent editions:	Peters: Vol. 3/4; AGA XX 308: Vol. 5/59; NSA IV: Vol. 1/46; Bärenreiter: Vol. 1/38
Bibliography:	Capell 1928, pp. 21 & 137–8
	Davidson 2007, pp. 271–7
	Fischer-Dieskau 1977, p. 95
	Kohlhäufl 1999, p. 167
Arrangements:	Arr. Johannes Brahms (1833–1897) for voice and orchestra (1862) [see ORCHESTRATIONS]
	Arr. Max Reger (1873–1916) for voice and orchestra (1913–14)
Discography and timing:	Fischer-Dieskau I 9²⁴ 4'36
	Hyperion I 14⁷
	Hyperion II 18² 5'42 Thomas Hampson

⟵ *Philoktet* D540   *Der Schiffer* D536 ⟶

MOSES MENDELSSOHN (1729–1786)

THE POETIC SOURCE
Die Psalmen Uebersetzt von Moses Mendelssohn. Mit allergnädisgten Freyheiten, Berlin bey Friedrich Maurer 1783

THE SONGS

June 1819   *Der 13. Psalm* 'Ach, Herr, wie lange willst du mein so ganz vergessen?' D663 [S1: 'XIII' 'Dem Sangmeister, ein Psalm Davids' pp. 23–4]

December 1820   *Der 23. Psalm* 'Gott ist mein Hirt' D706 [S1: 'XXIII' '1. Psalm Davids' pp. 47–8]

August 1823   *Der 8. Psalm* (Schubert's arrangement of a composition by Maximillian Stadler) [S1: 'VIII' 'Dem Sangmeister auf Gittith, ein Psalm Davids' pp. 14–15]

July 1828   *Der 92. Psalm* 'Lieblich ists, dem Ewgen danken' D953 [S1: 'XCIII' 'Psalmlied für den Sabbath' p. 220]

Schubert set *Der 92. Psalm* in Hebrew (although he is likely to have read the Mendelssohn translation at the same time). When the work was published with a German text in 1870 the Mendelssohn translation was used.

Die Psalmen translated by Moses Mendelssohn (1783).

It is difficult for English-speaking music lovers to appreciate that, because of his place in the history of philosophy and the development of German thought, Moses Mendelssohn is a figure of equal, if not greater, importance than his composer grandson, Felix. Abraham Mendelssohn, Moses Mendelssohn's business-man son, remarked ruefully that he was only well known for being his father's son or his son's father. Abraham baptized his children and brought them up as Protestants (hence the suffix Bartholdy added to the family name to identify conversion, still used in Germany but never considered necessary in England). As an adult, Felix Mendelssohn, justly proud of his grandfather's achievements, bitterly regretted that he had had no choice in the matter of his father's decision regarding the family's conversion.

Moses Mendelssohn, whom Felix never knew, had worked within the bounds of his ancestral faith to effect changes in Jewish life. He argued that the deism of the Enlighten-ment, which he had developed into a universal religion of reason, was identical with Judaism. Without in any way renouncing his faith he believed in a cultural and political union for Christians and Jews, separation of church and state, and civil equality for his people. For this he was reviled by both anti-Semites and conservative Jews. If Schubert identified with Goethe's pantheism, he owed a great deal to Mendelssohn, as did Goethe, via the great Jewish philosopher Spinoza.

Like the poet Wilhelm Müller, Mendels-sohn was born in Dessau, the son of Mendel Heymann, on 6 September 1729. His progress from a poor background to a position in the forefront of German intellectual life was the result of an astonishing autodidactic capacity for hard work. His home language was Yiddish and his first school was one of Talmudic and Hebrew studies. At the age of thirteen he left home and had to fend for himself. He followed his teacher David Fränckel to Berlin and studied Maimonides and other sacred writ-ings. From these beginnings he mastered not only German, but also Latin (he studied John Locke's *Epistola de Tolerantia*), French,

Moses Mendelssohn after the painting by J. R. Frisch.

English and Greek. In his early years he was a teacher, before becoming a part-time book-keeper to a silk manufacturer; in the midst of his tasks as thinker and writer he developed this business into an extremely prosperous one. Mendelssohn, noted for his moral authority and goodness as much as for his intelligence, became extremely famous on a number of levels – as a critic, aesthetician, philosopher, translator (from ten languages); he became known as the 'German Socrates'. In 1762 he married Fromet Gugenheim, a love match at a time when almost all Jewish marriages were arranged. In 1763 he was named a 'Schutzjude', a protected status that allowed a Jew to stay indefinitely in Prussia. His skill as a chess player brought him into contact with Gottfried Lessing whose exact contemporary he was and whose friend and protégé he became. It was well known that Mendelssohn was the playwright's model for *Nathan der Weise*, a work of gentle wit and noble serenity that reached the stage in 1783. This was also the year of two important Mendelssohn publications: the Psalm transla-tions and *Jerusalem oder über religiöse Macht und Judentum* – perhaps his most important book on the role of Judaism in society. In Germany, since the end of the Second World War, there has been renewed interest in Mendelssohn studies which had been harshly suppressed during the Nazi era. The philosopher died on 4 January 1786 in Berlin.

PIETRO ANTONIO DOMENICO BONAVENTURA METASTASIO (1698–1782)

THE POETIC SOURCES
S1 *Opere del Signor Abate Pietro Metastasio*. In Parigi Presso la Vedova Herissant, nella Via Nuova, di Nostra-Donna, alla Croco d'oro, 1780–82

It is impossible to say which of the many possible editions Schubert used or knew, but the most handsomely produced of them all was the twelve-volume Herissant Edition with thirty-seven plates, printed in Paris and dedicated to Marie Antoinette. This was the only complete works prepared with Metastasio's own collaboration and approval, and it remains the most important source to this day. As a composer of the Metastasio libretto for *Semiramide* (1782, Herissant Volume 7) and a disciple and friend of the poet, Salieri was likely to have been a proud owner of this edition, although his name does not appear on the subscribers' list. One can imagine a different volume of Metastasio being taken off the shelf each week so that Schubert could copy down the various Italian extracts carefully selected by the teacher for his pupil's exercises.

S2 *Opere Scelte dell'Abate Metastasio* da Romualdo Zotti, in two volumes, Londra, Schulze e Dean, Poland Street for sale at Presso R. Zotti, Broad Street, Golden Square, 1813

This selection of Metastasio's work is given here merely as an example of the many abridged editions available at about the time Schubert composed his settings.

THE SONGS

1812	*Quell'innocente figlio* D17 (*Aria dell' angelo* from *Isacco, Figura del Redentore*, Part I) [S1: Tomo Settimo p. 389] [S2: p. 221]: The aria from D17 (*Quell'innocente figlio*) is no. 1 of nine exercises that Schubert wrote on this text for Salieri. In this case a piano part was added by Alfred Orel and Reinhard Van Hoorickx to the solo soprano line. No. 2 is a duet for two sopranos; no. 3 is a trio for soprano, alto and tenor; no. 4 is a quartet (SATB); no. 5 is another trio for the same forces as no. 3, as is no. 6. Nos 7–9 are different arrangements for SATB quartet. All of these exercises are without piano accompaniment.
September–October 1812	*Entra l'uomo allo che nasce* D33 (*Aria di Abramo* from *Isacco*, Act II) [S1: 'Tomo Settimo' p. 410] [S2: Volume 2 p. 229]: The aria from D33 (*Entra l'uomo allo che nasce*) is no. 1 of six exercises that Schubert wrote in this text for Salieri. A piano part was added by Orel and Van Hoorickx. No. 2 is a duet for soprano and alto, no. 3 is a trio for soprano, alto and tenor and nos 4–6 are different arrangements for SATB quartet. *Te solo adoro* D34 (*Aria di Achior* from *La Betulia liberata*, Act II) dates from 5 November 1812 and is an arrangement for unaccompanied SATB quartet. The source for this was S1, 'Tomo Sesto', p. 358.

October–December 1812	*Serbate, o Dei custodi* D35 (Chorus from *La Clemenza di Tito*, Act I Scene 5) [S1: 'Tomo Terzo' p. 128] [S2: Volume 1 p. 58]: The accompanied solo aria for tenor from D35 (*Serbate, o dei custodi*) is the third of three exercises Schubert wrote for Salieri. The first of these is for unaccompanied SATB, the second for four-part chorus.
1813	*Misero pargoletto* D42 (Timante's lines from *Demofoonte*, Act III Scene 5) [S1: 'Tomo Quarto' p. 250] [S2: Volume 2 p. 131]: There are two arias for soprano and piano written D42, both settings of *Misero pargoletto*. The first version is unaccompanied (accompaniment added by Reinhard Van Hoorickx) and the second has a piano accompaniment.
September 1813	*Pensa che questo istante* D76 (*Aria di Fronimo* from *Alcide al Bivio* Act I Scene 1) [S1: 'Tomo Ottavo' p. 214]
18 September 1813	*Son fra l'onde in mezzo al mare* D78 (*Aria di Venere* from *Gli orti Esperidi*, Act I) [S1: 'Tomo Decimo' p. 64]
1816?	*L'incanto degli occhi* (I) (*'Da voi, cari lumi'*) D990 E (*Aria di Licinio* from *Attilio Regolo* Act II Scene 5) [S1: 'Tomo Ottavo' p. 57] [S2: Volume 2 p. 22] *Ombre amene* D990F (*Aria di Licori* from the 'Serenata' entitled *L'Angelica* Part One) [S1: 'Tomo Decimo' p. 207]
December 1816	*Leiden der Trennung* D509 (*Aria di Arbace* from *Artaserse* Act III Scene 2) translated by Heinrich von Collin [S1: 'Tomo Primo' p. 86] [S2: Volume 1 p. 39] *Vedi quanto* [*t'*]*adoro* D510 (*Aria di Didone* from *Didone Abbandonata*, Act II Scene 4) [S1: 'Tomo Terzo' p. 55]
January 1820	*Da quel sembiante appresi* D688/3 (*Aria di Lisinga* from *L'Eroe Cinese*, Act I Scene 3) [S1: Tomo Settimo' p. 193] *Mio ben ricordati* D688/4 (*Aria di Gandarte* from *Alessandro nell'Indie* Act III Scene 7) [S1: 'Tomo Quarto' p. 346]
1827	*L'incanto degli occhi* (II) (*'Da voi, cari lumi'*) D90/1 (*Aria di Licinio* from *Attilio Regolo* Act II Scene 5) [S1: 'Tomo Ottavo' p. 57] [S2: Volume 2 p. 22] *Il traditor deluso* (*'Aimè, qual forza ignota anima quelle voci!'*) D902/2 (*Aria di Atalia* from *Gioas, Rè di Guida*, Part II [S1: 'Tomo Sesto' pp. 319–20] [S2: p. 215] There are two surviving sketches for Schubert's opera *Rüdiger* D791 (begun in May 1823) with a libretto by Ignaz von Mosel. According to Mosel his libretto was based on Metastasio's *Ruggiero*.

Pietro Metastasio was born in Rome on 13 January 1698 as Antonio Bonaventura Trapassi, the son of Felice Trapassi, a grocer who had been a papal guard, and who was not averse to making money from his son's talents. At the age of eleven Antonio's ability for improvisation (he seems to have had the charm and insouciance of a modern street rapper) attracted the attention of the jurist and literary figure Gian Vincenzo Gravina who took over his education and taught him Greek and Latin. The name of Metastasio is Gravina's transliteration into Greek of the poet's real family name. In 1715 he took minor orders (it is for this reason that the poet is often referred to in publications of his work as Abate Metastasio). On the death of Gravina, Metastasio moved to Naples where lessons in singing and compostion with Nicola Porpora (1686–1768) led to his decision to devote his life to poetry and the stage. His first opera libretto for a full-length stage work was *Didone abbandonata* in 1724 (from which Schubert – among many others – set an aria, D510, in 1816).

Metastasio soon became the greatest librettist of his age, composing a new libretto for an *opera seria* every year from 1726. He authored twenty-seven of these (set by more than 300 composers), as well as over 800 shorter opera texts. The court librettist Apostolo Zeno named Metastasio his successor in Vienna in 1730; aged thirty-two, and at the invitation of the Emperor Charles Vl, the poet travelled to the Imperial City and remained there for the rest of his life. This invitation, made partly at the behest of one of his closest women friends whom he met in Naples and who was a lady-in-waiting to the Austrian empress, was something of a poisoned chalice: fashions changed and the *opera seria* found less favour with the Habsburg rulers. Nevertheless, almost every composer of note used Metastasio's libretti, including Handel, J. C. Bach, Pergolesi, Scarlatti, Gluck, Haydn, Cherubini and even Meyerbeer. Mozart used his words for seventeen concert arias, as well as for the oratorio *La Betulia liberata* K118 and the opera *La clemenza di Tito* K621. Metastasio had a special professional relationship with Salieri who owed his knowledge of the theatre to the guidance of the older man. Schubert was thus in a sense Metastasio's grand-pupil and was certainly weaned on a diet of Metastasio words to set as exercises for Salieri. The poet died in Vienna on 12 April 1782.

OPERE

DEL

SIGNOR ABATE

PIETRO

METASTASIO.

TOMO PRIMO.

IN PARIGI,

Preffo la Vedova HERISSANT, nella Via Nuova di Noftra-Donna, alla Croce d'oro.

M. DCC. LXXX.

Pietro Metastasio and his *Opere*, frontispiece after painting by Johann Steiner, and title page of complete edition, Paris (1780).

Metastasio was almost certainly the most successful and most prolific librettist of all time, the greatest years of his career being from early 1723 to 1740. Because of his musical education he was able to imagine his texts as he wrote them being sung in an operatic context. He possessed the ability to write verses that were concise, conveying deep and varied emotions with the smallest possible number of words, understanding that the addition of music lengthens verbal texts (sometimes at the expense of the narrative action); and his economy in these matters was an ideal asset. When he wrote arias for *da capo* settings that were to be ornamented, he was aware of the vowels that best suited high notes and also coloratura passages. Hundreds of composers, including Mozart, took Metastasio's libretti more or less as they were, ready made and ideal for composition. Later composers who thrashed out their libretti with their chosen writers would have been surprised by Metastasio's efficiency in foreseeing (and attempting to solve in advance) many of the word-to-music problems encountered in the theatre. Such a conveyor-belt approach lost favour in later times when the collaboration between composer and librettist became subject to more interaction and personal chemistry (as was the case, for instance, between Mozart and Da Ponte).

METRONOME MARKINGS *see* TEMPO AND EXPRESSION MARKINGS

MIGNON LIEDER (MIGNON'S SONGS) FROM *WILHELM MEISTER*: AN OVERVIEW

For a complete chronological list of the songs from this novel (including Mignon's songs) *see* Wilhelm Meisters Lehrjahre. All other cross references to both individual songs and grouped items are given in the article below.

In *Wilhelm Meisters Lehrjahre* (begun in 1777, published in 1795) the teenage waif known as Mignon (her real name is never mentioned) has been hopelessly in love with Wilhelm, the work's hero, since meeting him towards the beginning of the novel. At the end of the book, racked with physical and psychological afflictions, she dies of a seizure as she watches him embrace Therese, his fiancée. Mignon is accorded an elaborate, though secular, funeral. The background to her story is revealed to the reader only as she lies in her coffin (Book VIII, Chapter 9).

Thanks to a birthmark she is posthumously identified by the Marchese, a visiting Italian nobleman, as his long-lost niece. She had been born of an incestuous union between the Marchese's brother the Harper (whose real name was Augustin) and their sister, Sperata. At the time of the child's birth, and during Mignon's early childhood, Augustin and Sperata did not realize they were blood relatives. (For a fuller explanation of this episode *see* Harfnerlieder.) Goethe appears to have been aware of the genetical factors that might have affected the physical and mental health of a child born to siblings, although this aspect of Mignon's pathology is not openly broached in the novel. Augustin and Sperata were forcibly separated and Mignon, somehow made to feel guilty regarding her origins, was fostered by a rustic couple who lived far away from the city (which was 'possibly Milan' as we discover in the novel). The little tomboy rejoiced in roaming the countryside and several later episodes in the novel testify to her continuing love of nature. The child's rambling excursions had taken her into the grounds of a wonderful Palladian villa with a portico of columns and a garden full of statues. This image appears powerfully in the second strophe of *Mignon* (*Kennst du das Land?*) D321. After this the child was abducted by a group of acrobats, leading her grieving family (including her natural mother) to imagine that she had drowned in a lake. Mignon was taken over the Alps via a dangerous mountain pass (again an experience recalled in *Kennst du das Land?*) into Germany to work more or less as a slave performer in a circus troupe. It is under these circumstances that she is discovered and rescued by Wilhelm Meister, a young man of independent means who aspires to work in the theatre and has gathered around him a troupe of actors.

We first encounter Mignon in Book II, Chapter 4. To start with Wilhelm is uncertain of her gender because she is clothed in male attire (she remains unwilling to wear feminine clothes until the beginning of Book VIII). In Goethe's novel she is a 'Knabenmädchen' and in the earlier version of the novel, *Wilhelm Meisters theatralische Sendung*, she is referred to with both male and female pronouns. She is initially unwilling to talk to Wilhelm, evading his enquiries. Her dancing involves contorted and painful acrobatic postures. Wilhelm is fascinated by this enigmatic child who tells him that her name is Mignon, but when he asks her age she replies, 'Nobody has counted.' Wilhelm takes her to be about twelve or thirteen. He notes about her a taciturn air – a forehead that hides a secret, and a mouth that displays tight-lipped reticence.

Later the cruel Italian circus owner drags Mignon by the hair, threatening to beat her to death when she refuses to perform for the paying public. On witnessing this abuse Wilhelm buys Mignon out of captivity and she swears to serve him faithfully. She washes off her circus make-up to reveal brown skin. She speaks a mixture of Italian and French and leaps about energetically. She attempts to write down everything she knows by heart but her handwriting is scarcely legible. (At this point in the story the Harper makes his first appearance and also becomes a member of Wilhelm's entourage; neither he nor Mignon realize that they are father and daughter.)

Many of the novel's first English readers regarded Goethe's work as immoral because Wilhelm enjoys a number of relationships with attractive women (Mariane, Philine, Aurelie, Natalie and Therese). At the end of Book II Wilhelm takes Mignon in his arms and she is convulsed with spasms, seeming to melt away. It is just as well in terms of present-day mores that Wilhelm does not reciprocate the teenager's passionate feelings but regards himself instead as her protector and father figure.

Book III opens with Mignon's immortal lyric *Kennst du das Land?* (qv *Mignon* D321), encompassing some of her childhood experiences, her longing for Italy and her desire to share her beloved homeland with Wilhelm. (Goethe himself needed no such encouragement to visit the country – his *Italienische Reise* changed the direction of his life and art.) We are told that Mignon sings the words in Italian, that the performance was of an extraordinary freshness and artlessness and that the lyric was transcribed by Wilhelm into German. Mignon proves unexpectedly musical; she has found an old zither which the Harper restores to working order. When she plays the instrument she seems able to communicate her innermost emotions.

In Book IV Wilhelm becomes deeply fascinated by an enigmatic woman whom he names 'the Amazon', later identified as Natalie. As Mignon and the Harper perform *Nur wer die Sehnsucht kennt* (qv *Sehnsucht* – the different settings listed below – and as No. 1 and No. 4 of *GESÄNGE AUS WILHELM MEISTER* D877), Wilhelm is dreaming of 'the Amazon' and this mysterious lyric, full of unassuaged longing, harmonizes with his own feelings. Mignon's paroxysms of jealousy when she sees Wilhelm with other women are reflected by the words 'Es schwindelt mir, es brennt / Mein Eingeweide!'

A significant feature of Book V of the novel is the preparation and performance by the troupe of Shakespeare's *Hamlet*. At the celebratory dinner after the first night Mignon plays the tambourine and becomes over-excited and tipsy, performing a wild dance as if she were a maenad. As Wilhelm, rather drunk, climbs the stairs to his bedroom he feels a pain in his arm – Mignon has bitten him. That night a woman – whom we later learn is the vivacious actress Philine – steals into his bed and embraces him. Mignon, now undergoing the painful transition from childhood to sexual maturity, had planned to do so herself and, on seeing someone else get there first, seeks solace in the company of the Harper – without of course realizing that he is her father.

The next afternoon a fire breaks out and the focus of the narrative shifts to the Harper and the welfare of the little boy, Felix, who later turns out to be Wilhelm's son by his first love, Mariane (*see* HARFNERLIEDER). The actors' lodging house is set on fire by the Harper and burns down but the second performance of *Hamlet* is nevertheless a great success. Book V brings to an end the protagonist's engagement with his theatrical troupe – Wilhelm is now ready to embark on his next stage of 'Bildung'. The book closes with another Mignon lyric, *Heiss mich nicht reden* (D726 qv, and as No. 2 of GESÄNGE AUS WILHELM MEISTER D877) which we are told Mignon had once recited with deep feeling. The author admits that it was only the pressure of other events that prevented its earlier insertion into the narrative. We later discover (Book VIII, Chapter 3) that Mignon's vow of silence referred to in this song goes back to her childhood ordeal at the hands of her kidnappers who were planning to kill her. The Virgin Mary appeared to her to reassure her, or so she claimed, and as a result she took a holy vow of silence concerning all the details of her suffering. Mignon is also silent, of course, regarding her feelings for Wilhelm.

Mignon reappears only in Book VIII after Wilhelm's life has changed considerably; he has fallen in with the more elevated company of Lothario and his circle of enlightened aristocrats (Book VII). In the meantime Mignon, together with a number of younger children, has been given refuge at the home of Natalie, Lothario's sister (Wilhelm's 'Amazon'). Natalie informs Wilhelm of Mignon's fragility, both physical and mental, and the former tomboy's willingness at last to adopt female dress. Natalie also recounts an episode where Mignon has appeared to the younger children dressed as an angel. When challenged by them to set aside this disguise, Mignon sings the lyric *So lasst mich scheinen bis ich werde* (qv the different settings listed below – and as No. 3 of GESÄNGE AUS WILHELM MEISTER D877) in which she insists on the suitability of a costume which predicts the state of her future heavenly transfiguration. Natalie's rational explanation to her young charges that angels were not supernatural beings was considered so religiously contentious in England that Thomas Carlyle suppressed this entire episode in his 1824 translation of *Wilhelm Meister*, including one of Goethe's greatest lyrics. Nevertheless, Carlyle was one of the first commentators to realize that Mignon was unique. He wrote that 'The history of Mignon runs like a thread of gold through the tissue of the narrative, connecting with the heart much that were else addressed only to the head.' He refers to her as 'the daughter of enthusiasm, rapture passion, and despair, she is of the earth, but not earthly . . . we could almost fancy her a spirit so pure is she, so full of fervor, so disengaged from the clay of this world.'

Almost the earliest of Schubert's Mignon settings is a song which seems never to have figured in the composer's plans for a definitive group of Mignon Lieder:
Mignon (Kennst du das Land?) D321 [H200]. 23 October 1815.

A few days before composing this song, Schubert wrote the first of no fewer than six settings of *Nur wer die Sehnsucht kennt*, written over an eleven-year period. This catalogue item (D310) actually consists of two songs that are similar, but far from identical. They count as two versions (Fassungen) of the same setting (Bearbeitung). After this, each setting of the lyric has its own Deutsch number.
Sehnsucht (I) ('Nur wer die Sehnsucht kennt'), D310 [H190]. 1st setting, 1st version. 18 October 1815.
Sehnsucht (I) ('Nur wer die Sehnsucht kennt'), D310a [H190a]. 1st setting, 2nd version. 18 October 1815.
Sehnsucht (II) ('Nur wer die Sehnsucht kennt'), D359 [H211]. 2nd setting. 1816.

Sehnsucht (III) ('Nur wer die Sehnsucht kennt'), D481 [H298]. 3rd setting. September 1816.

Sehnsucht (IV) ('Nur wer die Sehnsucht kennt'), D656 [H424+]. 4th setting (for male-voice quintet). April 1819.

The fifth and sixth settings of this lyric are the first and last songs of D877 (Op. 62) (*see* GESÄNGE AUS WILHELM MEISTER), and date from 1826. Their titles are *Mignon und der Harfner* (a duet for soprano and tenor) and the solo *Lied der Mignon*.

The lyric 'Heiss mich nicht reden' was first composed in April 1821 as *Mignon I* D726. This went together with *Mignon II* ('So lasst mich scheinen'), also composed in April 1821, perhaps as the beginning of a planned new set of Mignon Lieder. The second and later setting of 'Heiss mich nicht reden' is part of D877 (no. 2, *Lied der Mignon*) (*see* GESÄNGE AUS WILHELM MEISTER).

The lyric 'So lasst mich scheinen' also achieves its definitive setting as D877/3 (*Lied der Mignon*) (*see* GESÄNGE AUS WILHELM MEISTER). The composer had set it twice, possibly three times, before, depending on whether the two fragments of D469 are to be considered as part of the same song, or as parts of two different (and now lost) settings:

Mignon (Fragments) ('So lasst mich scheinen'), D469 [H296 & H297]. Two fragments – the first beginning at the start of the poem, the second at 'eine kleine Stille'. September 1816.

Mignon II ('So lasst mich scheinen'), D727 [H473] April 1821.

The character of Mignon is one of the most powerful in European fiction. For a full discussion of the Mignon phenomenon in the broadest European context until the present day see Terence Cave's *Mignon's Afterlives*, 2011. The author refers to Mignon (p. 55) as 'fragmented into a micro-series of potential characters: she is boy–girl, a child acrobat, an aphasic child, a dancing puppet, a devoted page, a girl on the threshold of puberty, a wild maenad, a devout Catholic longing for her spiritual home, a precocious angel, a dead child who is given a secular funeral'.

Some indication of the fascination Goethe's Mignon exerted over later writers is given by a list of works that owe their inspiration, at least in part, to this character: in German – Brentano (*Godwi*); Eichendorff (*Ahnung und Gegenwart*); Mörike (*Maler Nolten*); Stifter (*Katzensilber*); Wedekind (*Lulu*); Rilke; Gerhard Hauptmann; Thomas Mann; in French – Mme De Staël (*Corinne*); Lamartine; Gautier; George Sand (*Consuelo*); Balzac (*Modeste Mignon*); Baudelaire (*L'Invitation au voyage*); Zola (*Nana*); Genet (*Notre Dame des Fleurs*); in English – Byron (*The Bride of Abydos*); Scott (*Peveril of the Peak*); Bulwer Lytton (*The Last Days of Pompeii*; *Zanoni*); Eliot (*Daniel Deronda*); Du Maurier (*Trilby*); James (*What Maisie Knew*); Nabokov (*Lolita*); Angela Carter (*Nights at the Circus*).

Goethe by Martha Griebler.

MIGNON (Kennst du das Land?)   Do you know the land?
(GOETHE) D321 [H200]

The song exists in two versions, the second of which is discussed below:
(1) 23 October 1815; (2) May–June 1816 (?)

(1)   'Mässig'   A major $\frac{2}{4}$ [77 bars]

(2)   A major

(81 bars)

Kennst du das Land, wo die Zitronen blühn,[1]	Do you know the land where lemon trees blossom;
Im dunklen Laub die Gold-Orangen glühn,	Where golden oranges glow amid dark leaves?
Ein sanfter Wind vom blauen Himmel weht,	A gentle wind blows from the blue sky,
Die Myrte still und hoch der Lorbeer steht,	The myrtle stands silent, the laurel tall:
Kennst du es wohl?	Do you know it?
Dahin! Dahin	There, o there
Möcht' ich mit dir, o mein Geliebter, ziehn.	I desire to go with you, my beloved!
Kennst du das Haus? Auf Säulen ruht sein Dach,	Do you know the house? Its roof rests on pillars,
Es glänzt der Saal, es schimmert das Gemach,	The hall gleams, the chamber shimmers,
Und Marmorbilder stehn und sehn mich an:	And marble statues stand and gaze at me:
Was hat man dir, du armes Kind, getan?	What have they done to you, poor child?
Kennst du es wohl?	Do you know it?
Dahin! Dahin	There, o there
Möcht' ich mit dir, o mein Beschützer, ziehn.	I desire to go with you, my protector!
Kennst du den Berg und seinen Wolkensteg?	Do you know the mountain and its clouded path?
Das Maultier sucht im Nebel seinen Weg;	The mule seeks its way through the mist,
In Höhlen wohnt der Drachen alte Brut;	In caves the ancient brood of dragons dwells;
Es stürzt der Fels und über ihn die Flut,	The rock falls steeply, and over it the torrent.
Kennst du ihn wohl?	Do you know it?
Dahin! Dahin	There, o there
Geht unser Weg! o Vater, lass uns ziehn!	Lies our way. O father, let us go!

Johann Wolfgang von Goethe (1749–1832); poem written in 1782–3

This is the thirty-second of Schubert's seventy-five Goethe solo settings (1814–26). See the poet's biography for a chronological list of all the Goethe settings.

---

[1] 'Zitronen' is spelled 'Citronen' in Goethe's *Gedichte* (1815).

This immortal lyric from Goethe's novel *Wilhelm Meisters Lehrjahre* has fascinated composers since it was written. Challier's *Liederkatalog* (1885) lists fifty-eight settings, and that is in addition to the famous versions listed on p. 348. It is extraordinary therefore that it was an English poet, James Thomson (1700–1748), who gave Goethe the idea for the poem, and that Goethe's lyric is a parody of an excerpt from *Summer*, part of the much longer *The Seasons* (1730) that was the basis of Haydn's oratorio of 1801:

> Bear me, Pomona! to thy citron grove
> To where the lemon and the piercing lime,
> With the deep orange, glowing through the green,
> Their lighter glories blend. Lay me, reclin'd,
> Beneath the spreading tamarind, that shakes,
> Fann'd by the breeze, its fever-cooling fruit.

Thomson's address to the Roman goddess Pomona places him at one with the plight of the waif Mignon who longs to return to her native land of Italy whence she was kidnapped long ago. Goethe's intervention demonstrates that side of the German spirit which itself yearned for the liberating sunshine of Italy as an antidote to the rigours of an over-organized and inhibiting lifestyle. More specifically, the poem reflects Goethe's longing to escape the bureaucratic duties of Weimar. The poet's own travels in Italy marked an important stage of his development, an essential part of his growth from German artist to world figure. Thanks to Italy he was able, in later years, to defy and mock the rigidities of his countrymen who were clearly in need of a humanizing dose of southern tolerance and laissez-faire. Hugo Wolf's setting transfers this poem to an imposing canvas of human significance and poignancy, but Schubert's is faithful to the idea of a young, vulnerable girl of Italian origin, excitable and passionate, freezing in the cold German climate and longing to return home. In Goethe's novel the song is supposedly sung in the girl's mother tongue, although we only ever learn of the German version since Wilhelm finds it difficult to translate the supposed originality and childishness of the Italian phrases. It is Wilhelm, a young man of good birth and means, whom Mignon addresses as beloved protector and father, although their relationship is innocent and idealistic. In the beginning of the Third Book of the novel Goethe describes Mignon's performance, and it is clear that he is giving a master class to future composers and singers of the lyric:

> *She began each verse with a certain gravity and stateliness as if she wanted to draw our attention to something special, to convey something important. At the third line the singing became heavier, darker; her expression at the words 'Kennst du es wohl?' was one of mystery and concern. Behind the words 'Dahin! dahin!' there lay a yearning that was overwhelming and 'Lass uns ziehn!' she was able to vary to such an extent each time it was repeated that it was first beseeching and urgent, then expressing energy and the promise of good things.*

Schubert's model here is clearly the Beethoven setting Op. 75 no. 1, composed in 1809 and published in 1810. This impression is confirmed by Schubert's setting of Reissig's *Der Zufriedene* D320, also on 23 October 1815, a song that appears in the same Beethoven opus. The younger composer's obedient adoption of Beethoven's tonality of A major for his Mignon song gets him into trouble because he begins his vocal line higher in the stave, and the result is a song that is in a perilously uncomfortable tessitura for all but the highest sopranos. Indeed, when the song was published in the *Nachlass* (and was adopted from there by the Peters edition) the key was changed to F major, and this has remained the tonality in which it is almost always performed today on the concert platform.

There is no introduction (as is also the case with the Beethoven setting), even though Schubert might have improvised one for the benefit of the singer. The marking is 'Mässig' and

Evocation of the poem *Kennst du das Land?* by Richard Püttner (1842–1913).

Kennst du das Haus? Auf Säulen ruht sein Dach . . . Villa Rotonda, Vicenza (1566), designed by Andrea Palladio,
probably Goethe's inspiration for the second verse of this poem.

the melody (with just the right amount of sleeve-pulling and wheedling inherent in the soulful
dip in the vocal line at 'Land') begins in crotchets and quavers shadowed by a hymn-like accompaniment. It is here particularly that the sombre sobriety of the Beethoven setting is unapolo-
getically emulated. In b. 4 we hear semiquaver triplets for the first time in the right hand (a bar
earlier than they appear in the Beethoven song in the left). This announcement of the 'gentle
wind' that wafts from the top of the vocal line in C major at the end of b. 8 frees the piano
writing from its chordal straitjacket. The two dream bars of interlude (bb. 15–16 with the piano
on a pedal F gently rocking between harmonies as if rooted to the spot) make Mignon appear
lost in enchanted reverie as she remembers the sumptuous vegetation of her native land. The
question 'Kennst du es wohl?' is unaccompanied and sung in the resonance of a gently spread
chord that will lead the voice to the dominant on 'wohl'.

For the next section ('Dahin! Dahin / Möcht' ich mit dir') Beethoven's marking is 'Geschwinder'.
Schubert's 'Etwas geschwinder' at b. 19 is usually played by pianists at double the speed, at least,
of the first section, a misinterpretation of the moderate 'etwas' – somewhat. These sextuplet
semiquavers lie comfortably enough beneath the pianist's hand and glide rather too easily under
the fingers; as a result Mignon's pleas to go thither, back to the imagined beauties of Italy, can
sound impossibly perky and banal, if too fast. Mignon is excited by her prospective journey (the
almost triumphant high note at the end of this section is evidence of this) but at a more moderate
tempo she retains something of the pathos she acquires in the first verse.

The second verse is a repeat of the first and the music fits the words perfectly well. Mignon
here remembers the beautiful Palladian villa in Italy she had chanced to visit as a child. In *Wilhelm
Meisters Wanderjahre* (the sequel to the *Lehrjahre*) we are told that this is in the region of Lake
Maggiore; in Goethe's *Italienische Reise* the district of Vicenza is referred to as her home. It is near
Vicenza of course that Palladio built his Villa Rotonda in the middle of the sixteenth century, a
building that Mignon might be describing here. It is significant that with the phrase 'du armes

Kind' the seemingly speaking statues avoid addressing the child in any manner that can identify her sex – although this expression of pity colloquially pertains to all ages and stations.

For the third strophe there is a change into the minor key. Beethoven had elected to stay in the major key throughout the song; he incorporated a change into the tonic minor at the eighth bar of *every* strophe so as to be harmonically equipped to emphasize the drama of the third (at 'In Höhlen wohnt der Drachen alte Brut'), at the same time as being able to say he had composed that Goethean ideal, a completely strophic song. Schubert here writes what came to be called a modified strophic song and the change of key signature at b. 41 simply switches the melody into A minor. Leo Black points out that Schubert is the only major composer to register a drastic change of mood at the beginning of the third strophe. At 'In Höhlen wohnt der Drachen alte Brut' the vocal line moves into F major (rather than C major) with a lower and more powerful tessitura for a singer who must now compete with a forte accompaniment. 'Es stürzt der Fels' at b. 52 occasions the doubling of voice and piano as if to describe the unforgiving bareness of a sheer rock face. The arpeggios at 'Flut' (b. 54) are deployed higher in the keyboard, but apart from this, until the song's third appearance of the 'Dahin!' section, Schubert reverts to exactly the same music as for the other two strophes. It seems that his aim was to heighten the effect of the Beethoven setting in manner rather than substance. This is a fine song, and well worth performing, but it does not come up to the exalted standard of the four Mignon settings of 1826 (D877). If Schubert had composed a new *Kennst du das Land?* at that time it might truly have rivalled Wolf's.

The NSA publishes two versions of the song, the first dated 22 October 1815, the second a revision probably from May/June 1816. The composer has expanded the 'Etwas geschwinder' section by elongating some of the 'Dahin' exclamations and lending greater sweep and excitement to the vocal line. It was the second version of course that was published in the *Nachlass*, albeit a major third lower than written.

See also MIGNON LIEDER (MIGNON'S SONGS) FROM *WILHELM MEISTER*: AN OVERVIEW, HARFNERLIEDER (THE HARPER'S SONGS) FROM *WILHELM MEISTER*: AN OVERVIEW

Autograph:	Österreichische Nationalbibliothek, Vienna (first version)
	Bibliothèque Nationale, Paris (fair copy made for Goethe) (second version)
First edition:	Published as Book 20 no. 3 of the *Nachlass* by Diabelli, Vienna in 1832 (P296)
Subsequent editions:	Peters: Vol. 2/221; AGA XX 168: Vol. 3/155; NSA IV: Vol. 9/177 (first version) & 181 (second version)
Bibliography:	Capell 1928, pp. 99–100
	Einstein 1951, pp. 114–15
	Fischer-Dieskau 1977, p. 54
Further settings:	Johann Friedrich Reichardt (1752–1814) *Italien* (1795)
	Carl Friedrich Zelter (1758–1832) *Kennst du das Land?* (1795)
	Ludwig van Beethoven (1770–1827) *Mignon*, Op. 75 no. 1 (1809)
	Gaspare Spontini (1774–1851) *Mignons Lied* (?1830)
	Louis Spohr (1784–1859) *Mignons Lied*, Op. 37 no. 1 (1815)
	Fanny Mendelssohn (1805–1847) *Sehnsucht nach Italien* (1822)
	Robert Schumann (1810–1856) *Mignon*, Op. 98a no. 1 (1849)
	Franz Liszt (1811–1886) *Mignons Lied* (1842, 1854 & 1860), four versions including one with orchestra; subsequently arranged for piano solo in 1843
	Pyotr Il'yich Tchaikovsky (1840–1893) *Pesn' Min'oni*, Op. 25 no. 3 (1874–5)

Hugo Wolf (1860–1903) *Mignon* (1890 & 1899), three versions
including two with orchestra
Alban Berg (1885–1935) *Mignon* (1907)

Discography and timing: Fischer-Dieskau —
Hyperion I 7²²
Hyperion II 11¹²   4'22   Elly Ameling

← *Der Zufriedene* D320   *Hermann und Thusnelda* D322 →

MIGNON (So lasst mich scheinen, bis ich werde)   Mignon fragments

(GOETHE) **D469 I** & **D469 II** [H296 & H297]

Fragments (Bruchstücke) of the first and second setting, September 1816

(1) A♭ major

(2) G major

These fragments share a manuscript with Wer nie sein Brot mit Tränen ass *D478/2b. The first fragment of D469 is a setting with right-hand accompaniment only, of the first two lines of the first strophe of Goethe's poem – this is completely crossed out, bar by bar:*

So lasst mich scheinen, bis ich werde,   Thus let me seem till thus I become.
Zieht mir das weisse Kleid nicht aus!   Do not take off my white dress!

On the same manuscript, directly underneath the first, the second fragment with a more complete accompaniment for both hands is a setting from the poem's second strophe. The surviving part of the setting is shown by the text that is not in italics below:

Dort ruh' ich eine kleine Stille,   There, for a brief silence, I shall rest;
Dann öffnet sich *der frische Blick;*   Then a fresh vista opens.

Ich lasse dann die reine Hülle,   Then I shall leave behind this pure raiment,
Den Gürtel und den Kranz zurück.   This girdle and this wreath.

Johann Wolfgang von Goethe (1749–1832); poem written in June 1796

This is the forty-first of Schubert's seventy-five Goethe solo settings (1814–26). See the poet's biography for a chronological list of all the Goethe settings.

There are a number of Schubert songs that exist only in fragments – sometimes because the composer never finished the settings, sometimes because manuscripts have been destroyed or lost. Although it was the policy of the Hyperion Edition to record fragments completed by a twentieth-century hand (usually that of Reinhard Van Hoorickx), some scraps of Schubertiana are so slight that they defy effective completion. The two fragments here are settings of a poem where Mignon, not long for this life, is dressed up like an angel. In this incomplete state they have a fragility and a mystery that is somehow appropriate to her character. The complete poem has four stanzas of which only parts of the first two are printed above. The reader is referred to the commentary below on the version from 1821, D727.

The Deutsch catalogue treats these two fragments as part of the same song and accords them a shared Deutsch number while also conceding the possibility that the first fragment (in A flat) was part of a song that was never completed, and that the second (in G major according to the key signature, although the fragment begins in C flat major) was part of the second verse of a much more sophisticated setting that has been lost. Both fragments together last less than a minute, yet the composer has found a musical key to the enigma of Mignon, her appearance reflected in the translucence of the music.

Autograph:	Wienbibliothek im Rathaus, Vienna (both fragments)
First edition:	Published as part of the *Revisionsbericht* of the AGA in 1897 (P726)
Subsequent editions:	Not in Peters; AGA: *Revisionsbericht*, note to 394, p. 86; NSA IV: Vol. 3/254
Further settings:	These fragments form part of a composite grouping of less well-known Mignon settings by Schubert, *Mignon* by Aribert Reimann (b. 1936), transcribed for soprano and string quartet (1995)
Discography and timing:	Fischer-Dieskau —
	Hyperion I 24[17] & 24[18] 0'25 Christine Schäfer
	Hyperion II 15[23] & 15[24] 0'37

← *Lied des Orpheus (als er in die Hölle ging)* D474   *Sehnsucht (Mignon)* D481 →

MIGNON I (Heiss mich nicht reden)   Mignon's song
(Goethe) **D726** [H472]
B minor   April 1821

(59 bars)

Heiss mich nicht reden, heiss mich schweigen,	Do not bid me speak; bid me be silent,
Denn mein Geheimnis ist mir Pflicht;	For my duty is to keep my secret;
Ich möchte dir mein ganzes Innre zeigen,	I long to reveal my whole soul to you,
Allein das Schicksal will es nicht.	But fate does not permit it.
Zur rechten Zeit vertreibt der Sonne Lauf	At the appointed time the sun in its course
Die finstre Nacht, und sie muss sich erhellen;	Drives away the dark night, and day must break;
Der harte Fels schliesst seinen Busen auf,	The hard rock opens its bosom and
	ungrudgingly bestows
Missgönnt der Erde nicht die tiefverborgnen	On the earth its deep-hidden springs.
Quellen.	
Ein jeder sucht im Arm des Freundes Ruh,	Every man seeks peace in the arms of a friend;
Dort kann die Brust in Klagen sich ergiessen;	There the heart can pour out its sorrows.
Allein ein Schwur drückt mir die Lippen zu	But an oath seals my lips,
Und nur ein Gott vermag sie aufzuschliessen.	And only a god can open them.

Johann Wolfgang von Goethe (1749–1832); poem written November 1782

This is the sixty-third of Schubert's seventy-five Goethe solo settings (1814–26). See the poet's biography for a chronological list of all the Goethe settings.

There is no doubt that if Schubert had not returned to this text in 1826 and composed a definitive *Lied der Mignon* ('Heiss mich nicht reden') D877/2, this earlier version of Mignon's plaint would now be much better known. The famous E minor setting that forms part of the composer's Op. 62 – the four settings from *Wilhelm Meister* published in March 1827 – has dominated the recital platform to the exclusion of the song discussed here. This is an example of an uncontested masterpiece overshadowing something only slightly less remarkable, and we find such an *embarras de richesse* more than once in the composer's work list.

Schubert chooses the key of B minor for this version, thus giving the same tonality to his two great female creations of 1821, Zuleika and Mignon, Goethe characters both. *Mignon II*, the first version of 'So lasst mich scheinen' (composed at the same time) is also in B minor, and the songs are a matching pair, particularly with regard to the similarity of their chromatically inflected postludes. (Schubert also uses B minor for *Mignon und der Harfner*, the duet from Op. 62, and B major for the final version of *Lied der Mignon* ('So lasst mich scheinen'), Mignon's third song.) As John Reed writes, 'B minor and B major stand at the ambivalent centre of Schubert's emotional world. Together they represent what may be called the passion (in every sense of that word) inherent in the human condition.' The fragility of the waif's existence (she will die at the end of the novel) is reflected in the use of the dactylic rhythm (long-short-short, or minim-crotchet-crotchet) that had been employed to chilling effect in *Der Tod und das Mädchen* D531 in 1817. Presumably this is because the composer interprets Mignon's fate – the 'Schicksal' of which she speaks – as implacable, like death itself. Characteristic Schubertian pathos is shown in the alternations between B major and B minor to underline the difference between the ideas of longing and fate in a type of counterpoint: for the first line of the strophe the key is B minor, changing to B major for the second (b. 9). The third and fourth lines alternate similarly, and the same pattern, one line of minor, one of major, governs the third strophe of the song. The major-key sections seem even sadder, perhaps because more vulnerable and child-like, than those in the minor. The second verse is the contrasting middle section of the poem. At 'sie muss sich erhellen' (bb. 25–7) the elongation of the word for 'illuminate' or 'brighten' (a semibreve on 'er<u>hell</u>en') depicts the imposing radiance of daybreak with a majestic modulation into G major (although it is still within a pianissimo dynamic). A tiny, but significant, detail is the ornamentation of the vocal line, a little turn of semiquavers following a dotted crotchet, at 'tiefverborgnen <u>Quellen</u>' (b. 35). True to the meaning of the words ('deep-hidden springs'), this motif is heard from within the piano part precisely a bar before its appearance in the voice (b. 36); it is as if Mignon has discovered the secret of the well-spring in the rock face, and conjured the water to the surface, a metaphor for the pouring forth of long-suppressed emotions. The third strophe is loosely modelled on the first, but this song does not quite have an ABA structure; the music takes on a dramatic and rhetorical turn at 'Und nur ein Gott vermag sie aufzuschliessen' (bb. 49–53) which leads to its conclusion.

Throughout the song the tessitura of the voice is poised high on the stave, and there is a significant distance between the vocal line and the accompaniment where the right hand is concentrated in the alto and tenor registers. This is prophetic of the layout of *Nacht und Träume* D287, perhaps Schubert's most famous song in B major, where there is a similar sense of the vast space between heaven and earth, as between the dreams of humanity and their realization. For further information concerning the text and its background *see Gesänge aus Wilhelm Meister* D877, Mignon Lieder: an overview and *Wilhelm Meisters Lehrjare*.

Autograph:	Wienbibliothek im Rathaus, Vienna (first draft)
First edition:	Published posthumously (without opus number) by J. P. Gotthard, Vienna in 1870 (P419)
Subsequent editions:	Not in Peters; AGA XX 394: Vol. 6/189; NSA IV: Vol. 3b/227; Bärenreiter: Vol. 2/228
Bibliography:	Capell 1928, pp. 156–7 Einstein 1951, p. 218
Further settings:	This song forms part of a composite grouping of less well-known Mignon settings by Schubert, *Mignon* by Aribert Reimann (b. 1936), transcribed for soprano and string quartet (1995)
Discography and timing:	Fischer-Dieskau　— Hyperion I 28[6]　2'41　Christine Schäfer Hyperion II 24[14]

←— *Mahomets Gesang* D721　　　　　　　　　　　　　　　　　*Mignon II* D727 —→

MIGNON II (So lasst mich scheinen)　Mignon's song
(Goethe) **D727** (first setting) [H473]
B minor　April 1821

(64 bars)

So lasst mich scheinen, bis ich werde,　　　　Thus let me seem till thus I become.
Zieht mir das weisse Kleid nicht aus!　　　　　Do not take off my white dress!

Ich eile von der schönen Erde	I shall swiftly leave the fair earth
Hinab in jenes feste Haus.[1]	For that secure dwelling place below.
Dort ruh' ich eine kleine Stille,	There, for a brief silence, I shall rest;
Dann öffnet sich der frische Blick;	Then my eyes shall open afresh.
Ich lasse dann die reine Hülle,	Then I shall leave behind this pure raiment,
Den Gürtel und den Kranz zurück.	This girdle and this rosary.
Und jene himmlischen Gestalten	And those heavenly beings
Sie fragen nicht nach Mann und Weib,	Do not ask who is man or woman,
Und keine Kleider, keine Falten	And no garments, no folds
Umgeben den verklärten Leib.	Enclose the transfigured body.
Zwar lebt' ich ohne Sorg' und Mühe,	True, I lived free from care and toil,
Doch fühlt' ich tiefen Schmerz genung.	Yet I knew much deep suffering.
Vor Kummer altert' ich zu frühe;	Too soon I grew old with grief;
Macht mich auf ewig wieder jung!	Make me young again for ever!

Johann Wolfgang von Goethe (1749–1832); poem written in June 1796

This is the sixty-fourth of Schubert's seventy-five Goethe solo settings (1814–26). See the poet's biography for a chronological list of all the Goethe settings.

This song, very much linked to the preceding *Mignon* D726, and in the same key, exemplifies the importance in Schubert's harmonic vocabulary of B minor/major as a tonality for those who are contemplating their own mortality – like Mignon in this setting, the ageing protagonist of *Greisengesang* D778, the narrator in *Vor meiner Wiege* D927, and so on. This is the poem that, according to Bettina von Arnim, most delighted Goethe's mother – and Bettina rejoiced in conveying this information to the poet. On hearing the lyric the elderly Frau Goethe was convinced that her famous son must have 'found religion' at last, so heartfelt was the sentiment, so shining Mignon's belief in the afterlife. The poem was also admired by that stern critic Schiller for different reasons. In a letter to his friend Christian Körner (the father of the poet Theodor Körner) he refers to this 'klein Gedichtchen' (small little poem) as 'himmlisch' (heavenly), remarking that it melts the heart to the deepest emotion, and that one cannot improve on it in terms of the art of poetry.

This is Schubert's second (and, as far as we know, first complete) attempt at setting 'So lasst mich scheinen'. Not included in the Peters Editon it has always languished in the shadow of Op. 62 no. 3 (D877) written five years later. There is nevertheless much to recommend in D727. The music has a simplicity and strength that is foreign to the etiolation of the later setting, and it could be argued that this is closer to the character of Mignon. Fascinatingly, Schubert seems to have made a point of relating this music to Mignon's relative, the old Harper, whom she does not realize is her father, a man driven to madness by the consequences of his daughter's birth and the death of his sister and lover, Mignon's mother. One has only to compare the opening of this song with the four-bar introduction to the Harper's *Wer sich der Einsamkeit ergibt* from 1816 (D478) and the family resemblance in terms of chords and pace is hugely clear. The *ambulante* character of D727, once under way, also recalls the Harper's *An die Türen will ich schleichen*

---

[1] In the later version of this song D877/3, Schubert changes Goethe's 'feste' to 'dunkle'.

D479. Schubert revised these 1816 Harper songs for publication in 1822; perhaps in 1821 when he composed this Mignon song he was thinking of a cycle that would combine the music of both *Wilhelm Meister* characters (just as Schumann combined them for his Op. 98a) instead of the separate opus numbers (Opp. 12 and 62) under which they finally appeared. (The Harper also makes a short guest appearance in Op. 62 to sing a duet with Mignon.) The rolled chords at bb. 20 and 48 of D727 suggest that the Harper might be accompanying the plaint of his unacknowledged daughter but the novel tells us that Mignon used the zither to accompany herself in this song as she was dressed like an angel – and this is no doubt what we are hearing here.

The song shares with *Nacht und Träume* D827 (a B major song about that little death, sleep) a high-lying vocal part supported by a low-lying accompaniment, the distance between voice and piano creating a certain exaltation and tension. This effect is heightened by changes into a B major key signature at bb. 20 and 48 where the euphony between the thirds and sixths, *molto patetico*, has a Mahlerian tinge to it *avant la lettre*. The four-bar postlude (bb. 61–4) is a moving little peroration and a gem in its own right.

For further information concerning the text and its background *see Gesänge aus Wilhelm Meister* D877, MIGNON LIEDER: AN OVERVIEW and WILHELM MEISTERS LEHRJAHRE.

Autograph:	Wienbibliothek im Rathaus, Vienna (first draft)
First edition:	Published as Book 48 no. 5 of the *Nachlass* by Diabelli, Vienna in 1850 (P384)
Subsequent editions:	Peters: Vol. 6/64; AGA XX 395: Vol. 6/191; NSA IV: Vol. 3/852; Bärenreiter: Vol. 2/230
Bibliography:	Capell 1928, pp. 156–7
	Einstein 1951, p. 218
Further settings:	This song forms part of a composite grouping of less well-known Mignon settings by Schubert, *Mignon* by Aribert Reimann (b. 1936), transcribed for soprano and string quartet (1995)
Discography and timing:	Fischer-Dieskau —
	Hyperion I 11[7]
	Hyperion II 24[15] 3'39 Brigitte Fassbaender

← *Mignon I* D726   *Die Nachtigall* D724 →

JOHANN CHRISTIAN MIKAN (1769–1844)

THE POETIC SOURCE
Der Sammler, June issue (appeared 14 June 1814)

The *Sammler*, a celebrated Viennese monthly, reviewed a poetry reading (*Zweytes Declamatorium*) given on 13 April 1814 by the actress Sophie Schröder, who ended her evening's entertainment with a poem by Mikan concerning the defeat of Napoleon Bonaparte and the arrival of the Allied troops in Paris. This was in honour of the birthday of Prince Karl von Schwarzenberg. The paper prints the six-strophe poem in its entirety, and this was doubtless the teenage Schubert's source.

THE SONG
16 May 1814   *Die Befreier Europas in Paris* D104 [p. 380]

Mikan was born in Teplitz on 5 December 1769, the son of a well-to-do professor of chemistry and botany at Prague University. He himself became professor of botany at the same university in 1812 and travelled to Brazil on a scientific expedition in 1817–18. He was an expert occasional versifier. His anthology of writings entitled *Kinder meiner Laune – ältere und jüngere, ernste und scherzhafte* (Prague, 1833) is a miscellaneous collection of poems, charades, witticisms and aphorisms as well as some more serious memoirs concerning his journey to Brazil. The book was issued to make money for the widows and orphans of the Bohemian cholera epidemic. The fact that the stirring poem that Schubert set to music is not reprinted in this anthology might have something to do with a certain amount of embarrassment concerning the premature triumphalism of the occupiers of Paris for, of course, Napoleon returned to fight another day, and the city was only recaptured again after his final defeat at Waterloo. Mikan died in Prague on 28 December 1844.

MINNELIED
(Hölty) **D429** [H256]
E major   May 1816

Love song

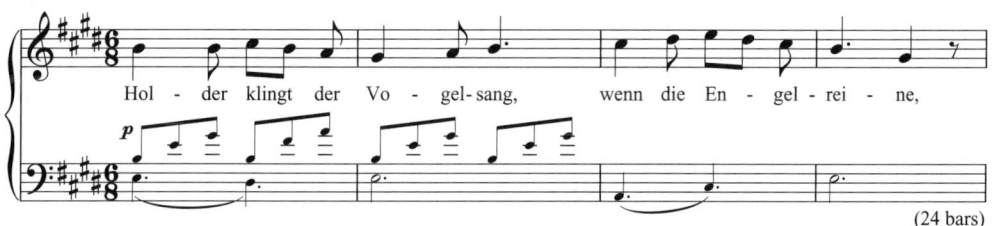

(24 bars)

Holder klingt der Vogelsang,	The birdsong sounds sweeter
Wenn die Engelreine,	When the pure angel
Die mein Jünglingsherz bezwang	Who has conquered my youthful heart
Wandelt durch die Haine.	Walks through the woods.
Röter blühet Tal und Au,	Valley and meadow bloom with a redder hue,
Grüner wird der Wasen,	The grass grows greener
Wo mir Blumen rot und blau[1]	Where her hands have gathered
Ihre Hände lasen.	Red and blue flowers.
Ohne Sie ist alles tot,	Without her all is dead,
Welk sind Blüt' und Kräuter;	Flowers and herbs wilt;
Und kein Frühlingsabendrot	And no spring sunset
Dünkt mir schön und heiter.	Seems beautiful or serene to me.

---

[1] Hölty's original first two lines here, changed by the unmarried Schubert, are 'Wo die Finger meiner Frau / Maienblumen lasen' ('Where my wife's fingers / Have gathered May flowers'). It seems he first wrote Hölty's words on the autograph and then crossed them out, substituting his own (or someone else's suggestion).

Traute, minnigliche Frau,	Dear, lovely lady,
Wollest nimmer fliehen;	Never leave me;
Dass mein Herz, gleich dieser Au,	And then my heart, like this meadow,
Mög' in Wonne blühen!	Will bloom in joy!

LUDWIG CHRISTOPH HÖLTY (1748–1776); poem written in 1773. Adapted for publication in 1804 by JOHANN HEINRICH VOSS (1751–1826)

This is the seventeenth of Schubert's twenty-three Hölty solo settings (1813–16). See the poet's biography for a chronological list of all the Hölty settings.

If it is true, as John Reed believes, that there was something of a crisis in the love affair (or non-affair) between Schubert and Therese Grob in May 1816, there could be no stronger musical evidence than the tone of this exquisite song – sweetness underscored by a gentle sadness, yet without a trace of self-pity. On first hearing it seems to be happy, but repeated hearings and subtle interpretative insight reveal a bravery combined with regret, the renunciation of a dream with a gallant smile; the sighs of the beautiful little postlude hardly betoken the happiness of possession and assured consummation. This is the stuff of daydreams and fantasy (at least from Schubert's point of view, if not Hölty's), the music of someone who idealizes the very type of relationship that he knows he cannot have.

The most touching verse in this setting is the third (the composer uses two of the poet's strophes to make each musical verse) which speaks of how dead everything seems without the beloved. As so often with this composer, lilting music in the major key does not necessarily paint unalloyed happiness. This setting has, of course, been overshadowed – somewhat unjustly – by Brahms's Op. 71 no. 5, a sumptuous and introspective song for lower voice in C major. Was Brahms too drawn to this poem less in celebration of a relationship than in gentle mourning for the lack of one? To avoid mention of a wife, Schubert changes the poet's words 'Wo die Finger meiner Frau / Maienblumen lasen' to 'Wo mir Blumen roth und blau / Ihre Hände lasen'. With the music for these substituted words (bb. 13–16) there is an echo, perhaps unconscious, of Haydn's Emperor's Hymn. Traces of this national anthem can also be found in the Matthisson *Lebenslied* D508, in the Schiller setting *Der Flüchtling* D402 and, most noticeably, in the piano postlude of the Pichler *Lied* 'Ferne von der grossen Stadt' D483, another work from 1816. The main theme of Mendelssohn's E flat String Quartet Op. 12 is also markedly influenced by the same fragment of the Haydn hymn. Incidentally, Mendelssohn's own setting of this Hölty text is also charming without plumbing the emotional depths of the Brahms, but neither of these later settings has the seemingly effortless multi-faceted profundity of Schubert's. His is one of those songs that can be taken as light-heartedly, or as much to heart, as the quality of the interpretation or the subjective state of mind of the listener allows.

The publication of the NSA has brought a new fact to light (with the autograph reproduced on p. XL of the introduction to Volume 10). After two strophes of the poem (making a single musical verse) Schubert added a repeat mark to the piano part and then scratched it out. Accordingly only two of the poet's four verses are printed in the NSA. Walther Dürr avers that this is because the composer realized that his music was not suitable for the verse that refers to death (the third) – not that the poet writes of any person's death, only of the lack of colour and life when his wife is absent. Be that as it may, a fine interpreter could surely incorporate this imagery into the music. The melody of the song is so delicious that to hear only a single musical verse is simply not enough.

Autograph:	In private possession
First edition:	Published as Vol. 7 no. 3 in Friedlaender's edition by Peters, Leipzig in 1885 (P478)
Subsequent editions:	Peters: Vol. 7/10; AGA XX 221: Vol. 4/203; NSA IV: Vol. 10/154
Further settings and arrangements:	Felix Mendelssohn (1809–1847) *Minnelied im Mai* Op. 8 no. 1 (1826)
	Johannes Brahms (1833–1897) *Minnelied* Op. 71 no. 5 (1877)
	Charles Ives (1874–1954) *Minnelied* (c. 1901)
	Arr. Tilman Hoppstock (b. 1961) for guitar accompaniment, in *Franz Schubert: 110 Lieder* (2009)
Discography and timing:	Fischer-Dieskau I 7[11] 2'01
	Hyperion I 17[11]
	Hyperion II 14[7] 1'57 Lucia Popp

←— *Julius an Theone* D419   *Die frühe Liebe* D430 —→

MINNESANG *see* HULDIGUNG D240

MINONA   Minona
(Bertrand) **D152** [H65]
A minor   8 February 1815

(240 bars)

(1)	Wie treiben die Wolken so finster und schwer	How the clouds, so dark and heavy,
	Über die liebliche Leuchte daher![1]	Scud across the sweet sun!
	Wie rasseln die Tropfen auf Fenster und Dach!	How the raindrops rattle on window and roof!
	Wie treibet's da draussen so wütig und jach,	How furious is the storm out there,
	Als trieben sich Geister in Schlachten!	As if spirits were locked in battle.
(2)	Und Wunder! Wie plötzlich die Kämpfenden ruhn,	And strange to tell! How suddenly the combatants cease,
	Als bannten jetzt Gräber ihr Treiben und Tun![2]	As if the grave now put an end to their conflict!
	Und über die Haide, und über den Wald—	And over the heath and the forest

[1] Bertrand's original line is '*Dort* über die liebliche Leuchte daher!'
[2] Bertrand employs the archaic 'itzt' rather than 'jetzt'.

Wie weht es so öde, wie weht es so kalt![3]   How desolate, how cold is the wind,
So schaurig vom schimmernden Felsen!   Blowing eerily from the shimmering rock!

(3)   O Edgar! wo schwirret dein   O Edgar! Where is your whirring arrow?
            Bogengeschoss?
        Wo flattert dein Haarbusch? wo   Where is your flowing mane of hair? Where is
            tummelt dein Ross?   your steed?
        Wo schnauben die schwärzlichen   Where are the black mastiffs romping around
            Doggen um dich?   you?
        Wo spähst du am Felsen Beute für mich?   Where among the rocks are you seeking game
                                                             for me?
        Dein harret das liebende Mädchen!   Your loving maiden awaits you!

(4)   Dein harret, o Jüngling! im jeglichen   Your anxious bride awaits you, young man,
            Laut,[4]   with every sound;
        Dein harret so schmachtend die   She awaits you with such yearning.
            zagende Braut;
        Es dünkt ihr zerrissen das liebliche   She imagines the bonds of love broken,
            Band,
        Es dünkt ihr so blutig das   She imagines your huntsman's clothes covered
            Jägergewand—   with blood.
        Wohl minnen die Toten uns nimmer!   For the dead love us no longer!

(5)   Noch hallet den moosigen Hügel   Yet still their love song echoes like whispering
            entlang   harps
        Wie Harfengelispel ihr Minnegesang.   Over the mossy hillside.
        Was frommt es? Schon blicken die   To what avail? Already the night stars
            Sterne der Nacht
        Hinunter zum Bette von Erde gemacht,   Gaze down upon the bed of earth
        Wo eisern die Minnenden schlafen!   Where the lovers sleep unshakeably.

(6)   So klagt sie; und leise tappt's draussen   Thus she laments; outside there is a soft
            umher,   tapping,
        Es winselt so innig, so schaudernd   And a low whine, urgent and fearful.
            und schwer;
        Es fasst sie Ensetzen, sie wanket zur Tür,[5] Seized with horror she staggers to the door;
        Bald schmiegt sich die schönste der   The finest of the mastiffs, her favourite,
            Doggen vor ihr,
        Der Liebling des harrenden Mädchens;   Nuzzles against the awaiting maiden.

(7)   Nicht, wie sie noch gestern mit   Not a message from her lover, as yesterday
            kosendem Drang,
        Ein Bote des Lieben, zum Busen   When it leapt at her breast with eager affection.
            ihr sprang—

[3] Bertrand's original line is 'Wie weht es herüber so öde, so kalt'.
[4] Bertrand writes '*in jeglichem* Laut'.
[5] Bertrand writes 'Es *greift* sie Eutsetzen'.

Kaum hebt sie vom Boden den trauernden Blick, | It barely lifts its mournful eyes from the ground,

Schleicht nieder zum Pförtchen, und kehret zurück,[6] | Creeps down to the door, and returns whence it came,

Die schreckliche Kunde zu deuten. | To indicate its terrible tidings.

(8) Minona folgt schweigend mit bleichem Gesicht, | Minona follows, pale-faced and silent,

Als ruft es die Arme vor's hohe Gericht— | As if, poor girl, she were summoned before the High Court.

Es leuchtet so düster der nächtliche Strahl – | The night sky shines with sombre gleam.

Sie folgt ihr durch Moore, durch Heiden und Tal | She follows the mastiff through bog, heath and valley

Zum Fusse des schimmernden Felsen. | To the foot of the shimmering rock.

(9) 'Wo weilet, o schimmernder Felsen, der Tod? | 'O shimmering rock, where does death lurk?

Wo schlummert der Schläfer, vom Blute noch rot?'[7] | Where does the sleeper slumber, still red with blood?'

Wohl war es zerrissen das liebliche Band, | The bonds of love were indeen broken;

Wohl hatt' ihm, geschleudert von tückischer Hand, | A fatal arrow, unleashed by an evil hand,

Ein Mordpfeil den Busen durchschnitten. | Had pierced his breast.

(10) Und als sie nun nahet mit ängstlichem Schrei, | And now, as she draws near with a fearful cry,

Gewahrt sie den Bogen des Vaters dabei. | She sees her father's bow nearby.

'O Vater, o Vater, verzeih es dir Gott! | 'O father, father, may God forgive you!

Wohl hast du mir heute mit frevelndem Spott | Today you have fulfilled your vow of vengeance

So schrecklich den Dräuschwur erfüllet! | So terribly, and with such cruel mockery!

(11) 'Doch soll ich zermalmet von hinnen nun gehn? | 'But am I now to leave here, crushed?

Er schläft ja so lockend, so wonnig, so schön! | He sleeps, so alluring, so happy, so handsome.

Geknüpft ist auf ewig das eherne Band; | The iron bond is tied for ever;

Und Geister der Väter im Nebelgewand | In misty garments the spirits of our fathers

Ergreifen die silbernen Harfen.' | Strike the silver harps.'

---

[6] Bertrand's original word here is 'Schleicht *wieder* zum Pförtchen' ('Creeps *again* to the door'). 'Nieder' is probably a copying error.

[7] Bertrand's original 'so rot' is rather less dramatic than Schubert's 'noch rot'.

(12)	Und plötzlich entreisst sie mit sehnender Eil	And suddenly, with passionate haste, she rips
	Der Wunde des Lieben den tötenden Pfeil;	The deathly arrow from her beloved's wound;
	Und stösst ihn, ergriffen von innigem Weh,[8]	Overcome by intense grief, she plunges it
	Mit Hast in den Busen so blendend als Schnee,	Swiftly into her breast, dazzling white as snow,
	Und sinkt am schimmernden Felsen.	And sinks down upon the shimmering rock.

FRIEDRICH ANTON BERTRAND (1787–1830?)

This is the first of Schubert's two Bertrand solo settings (1815). See the poet's biography for a chronological list of the Bertrand settings.

Bertrand's ballad, a setting of an Ossianic pastiche, is either ignored by the commentators or dismissed in damning terms. As far as it is possible to determine, the song had never been recorded before Elly Ameling sang it for the Hyperion Edition. It was left out of Fischer-Dieskau's mammoth compilation (as was the other Bertrand setting, the gigantic *Adelwold und Emma* D211) and this has not added to its chances. A number of Schubert's songs from the early period need the advocacy of living artists before they can come to life, for only a fine singer is able to recreate what Schubert himself heard in his imagination; more harm has probably been done to the Schubertian cause by snap judgements made at musicologists' pianos than by anything else. It has to be admitted that the Ossian-influenced poem for this ballad is not of the first rank, but it is nowhere near as ridiculous as Gothic fantasies by much more famous writers (Matthisson's *Romanze* and Hölty's *Die Nonne* for instance, set by Schubert in 1814 and 1815 respectively).

There is nothing like a blood-and-thunder poem from an unknown pen to get the critics shouting thud and blunder. However, *Minona* furnishes Schubert with a number of splendid pictorial opportunities and is much more concise, and thus suitable for performance, than some of its fellow ballads. As Brian Newbould noted in 1997, 'despite all odds, the song works'.

Verse 1: The piano's opening introduction in ominous minims is powerful and dramatic, a slow build-up with a suggestion of contrapuntal imitation like a bank of clouds obfuscating the harmony. Three strong octaves in the left hand announce the key of A minor, but we stride inexorably into B minor (b. 3) and then C sharp minor (b. 5) via right-hand suspensions – for suspense is the intention. The vocal recitative (from b. 11) is heavy with a premonition of doom. The piano's raindrop music (marked 'Schnell' from b. 13) uses a figure that Schubert may have remembered from the development section of the first movement of Mozart's A major Piano Concerto K488. The battle of the spirits (beginning at b. 17) is reflected by the kind of swirling piano music we will hear again in the Goethe setting *Rastlose Liebe* D138 written a few months later.

Verses 2–4: This is recitative of a high quality, initially more effective and spine-chilling because (from the end of b. 23) it is without pianistic support. The lines beginning 'Und über die Haide'

---

[8] Schubert here prefers to codify the suicidal ecstasy of Minona suggested by Bertrand's 'Sie stösst ihm, ergriffen von *Freuden und Weh*' ('... overcome by *joy and grief*'), thus his 'ergriffen von innigem Weh'.

(marked 'Etwas geschwind' with the piano doubling the voice) are underpinned by a similar harmonic sequence to that which opened the ballad. The key word here is 'öde', the empty barrenness of the texture ideal for musical illustration of a cold heath. There is a change of key signature (to B flat major) and a tempo change ('Langsam') at b. 43. If we were not sure from her name that Minona was a Scottish (or rather Celtic) heroine in the Ossianic mould, the invocation to someone called Edgar would confirm our suspicions. The heroine's name, incidentally, was taken by Bertrand from the Ossianic epic *Carric Thura* where it refers to a female singer. The original Gaelic ('Min-Fhonn') means 'sweet air or tune'. The use of simple B flat harmony over a two-bar stretch of piano writing is most effective: the flute solo of the right hand (b. 43 itself) suggests a touch of desolate (and potentially deranged) grief. This together with the name of the hero makes these bars a ghostly pre-echo of Donizetti's *Lucia di Lammermoor* and shows that a feeling for the deserted moor, and the ancestral hall, of Scotland was very much in the European air and ear. A not very serious attempt to illustrate the movement of arrows and snorting dogs (a piano interlude, bb. 47–9, marked 'Schnell') is followed by a magical snippet of a cantilena in B flat that again suggests the world of Italian *bel canto* (Schubert's debt to Salieri in this regard is seldom sufficiently acknowledged) with the words 'Dein harret das liebende Mädchen!' For this the piano's accompanying triplets begin at b. 56, and we find ourselves at a preview of Hölty's *An den Mond* D193. Further recitative paints Minona's worst nightmares of abandonment. At b. 70 (and a change of marking to 'Sehr langsam') we return to A minor on the words 'Wohl minnen die Toten uns nimmer'. The tune sung by the soprano here is repeated in a variant intermezzo for piano in bb. 89–94, as well as a closing leitmotif-like phrase at the very end of the piece (bb. 236–9). In this way Schubert shows that he regards this music, and its meaning, as the heart of the work. He had lost his mother and had a stormy relationship with his father and, in parallel, Minona defies the terrible vengeance of her father to love whom she pleases, even if such defiance will result in her death.

Verses 5–7: This recitative (b. 76) initiated by an A minor chord has some wonderful touches: the unexpected modulation on 'Was frommt es?' (bb. 78–9); the uncanny melodic and harmonic resemblance of 'Nacht / Hinunter' (bb. 81–2) to the second appearance of the word 'entschwindet' in the Collin setting *Wehmut* D772; and the nobility and sadness of the dying fall of the harmony on 'zum Bette von Erde gemacht' (bb. 82–4). The piano interlude in B minor (marked 'Klagend', bb. 89–94, with a change of key signature to two sharps) is among the most beautiful in all the ballads. As a variant of the 'Wohl minnen die Toten' phrase first heard in b. 70, it reflects Minona's anguished state of mind.

Now is the time to direct the listener's attention to the mastiff who plays a crucial part in the story. The Kupelwieser drawing of the Schubertiad at Atzenbrugg, with the dog Drago sitting comfortably under Schubert's piano, shows that the composer was at ease with canines. From time to time he depicted animals in music but nowhere more cleverly than here. The new marking for the hound's imploring music is 'Nicht zu geschwind, ängstlich', and the ⅜ time allows the mezzo staccato articulation between the pianist's hands to suggest the scratching of half-sharpened claws. The right fretful, imploring harmonies are found, going around in circles, appropriate for bad news in a dumb language. The only thing comparable is that tiny moment in *Der Geistertanz* D116, written a few months earlier, where whining hounds are momentarily given voice (the interlude at bb. 11–12 of that song).

Verses 8–10: As Minona follows the dog towards the revelation of her last tragic journey it is the spirit of Mozart that hovers over the music. The words 'Es leuchtet so düster' (bb. 161–8) seem to come straight from the 'Recordare' quartet of the *Requiem*, and it is significant that both Bertrand's text and the timeless Latin are about being summoned in judgement on the Day of

Wrath, no less (the 'hohe Gericht' of bb. 158–9). Verse 9 begins in questioning recitative and gathers pace as Minona realizes that dirty work is afoot, and that her own father is responsible for the death of her beloved. The moment when she approaches the body of Edgar (marked 'Schnell' b. 202) is superbly dramatic, the voice being forced higher and higher into a dramatic tessitura. One is reminded of the ballads of Schubert's earlier years that are sometimes almost unsingable in their vocal demands, but a singer who can touch on a high B in passing has little to fear from a passage where the musical inspiration, including the throbbing accompaniment, is that of Gluck's *Iphigenia*. The invocation to the father ('O Vater, o Vater, verzeih es dir Gott!', bb. 206–10) is blood-curdling. The word 'Dräuschwur' (vow of vengeance, b. 213) produces an instrumental flourish (bb. 214–17) in imitation of dramatic brass-writing that is worthy of the young Verdi.

Verses 11–12: The unlikely progression of the story from here has moments of banality, it is true, but there are also sublime touches. A fine performer can make much of the 'Mässig geschwind' passage (bb. 218–20) where Minona is drawn for one last time to the beauty of her murdered lover. The silver harps of the spirits (from b. 225) have a mystical breadth and majesty that prophesy the confidence of *Lohengrin*, or even *Das Rheingold*, in staying rooted unashamedly in unchanging harmonies for each of three rapturous bars. The death of Minona is rather beautifully underplayed, and the simplicity and eloquence of the final bars of piano writing have already been mentioned. The close of the work, like the opening of *Der Liedler* D209 composed the month before, clearly reveals the influence of Mozart's Rondo in A minor K511.

Autographs:	Gesellschaft der Musikfreunde, Vienna (first draft);
	Wienbibliothek im Rathaus, Vienna (fair copy)
First edition:	Published as part of the AGA in 1894 (P551)
Subsequent editions:	Not in Peters; AGA XX 40: Vol. 2/6; NSA IV: Vol. 7/124;
	Bärenreiter: Vol. 6/74
Bibliography:	Clerk 1870, Vol. 1, p. 180
	Newbould 1997, pp. 48–9
Discography and timing:	Fischer-Dieskau —
	Hyperion I 7[1]
	Hyperion II 5[4] 11'01 Elly Ameling

← *Auf einen Kirchhof* D151   *Als ich sie erröten sah* D153 →

MIO BEN RICORDATI *see VIER CANZONEN* D688/4

MIRJAMS SIEGESGESANG
(Grillparzer) **D942** [H661]
C major   March 1828

Miriam's song
of victory

Soprano & chorus

(486 bars)

(1) Rührt die Cymbel, schlagt die Saiten,
Lasst den Hall es tragen weit;
Gross der Herr zu allen Zeiten,
Heute gross vor aller Zeit.

Strike the cymbals, sound the strings,
Let them echo far and wide:
Great is the Lord always,
And greater today than ever.

Chor.
Gross der Herr zu allen Zeiten,
Heute gross vor aller Zeit.

Chorus.
Great is the Lord always,
And greater today than ever.

(2) Aus Ägypten vor dem Volke,[1]
Wie der Hirt den Stab zur Hut,
Zogst du her, dein Stab die Wolke
Und dein Arm des Feuers Glut.

Like the shepherd with his protecting staff,
You led your people out of Egypt;
Your staff was the clouds,
Your arm the fire's heat.

Chor.
Zieh, ein Hirt vor deinem Volke,
Stark dein Arm, dein Auge Glut.

Chorus.
Go forth, a shepherd leading your people,
With your mighty arm and your eyes blazing!

(3) Und das Meer hört deine Stimme,
Tut sich auf dem Zug, wird Land.
Scheu des Meeres Ungethüme,
Schaun's durch die kristallne Wand.

The sea hears your voice,
Opens up before the multitude, and becomes land.
Fearful of the monstrous sea,
We behold it through the crystal wall.

Chor.
Wir vertrauten deiner Stimme,
Traten froh das neue Land.

Chorus.
We have trusted your voice
And have joyfully entered the new land.

(4) Doch der Horizont erdunkelt,
Ross und Reiter löst sich los,
Hörner lärmen, Eisen funkelt,
Es ist Pharao und sein Tross.

But the horizon darkens,
Horse and rider break away;
Horns peal, swords flash:
It is Pharaoh and his baggage train.

Chor.
Herr, von der Gefahr umdunkelt,
Hilflos wir, dort Mann und Ross.

Chorus.
Lord, surrounded by darkness and danger
We are helpless. Yonder are men and horses.

(5) Und die Feinde, mordentglommen,
Drängen nach den sichern Pfad;[2]
Jetzt und jetzt– da horch, welch
 Säuseln,
Wehen, Murmeln, Dröhnen– Sturm!
's ist der Herr in seinem Grimme,
Einstürzt rings der Wasser-Thurm.

And our enemies, flushed with murder,
Throng towards the safe passage.
But hark now! What surging and whistling,

What plashing and groaning: a tempest!
It is the Lord in his wrath.
The towered waters collapse.

(6) Mann und Pferd,
Ross und Reiter
Eingewickelt, umsponnen,
Im Netze der Gefahr,[3]
Zerbrochen die Speichen ihrer Wagen,
Tot der Lenker, tot das Gespann.

Man and horse,
Steed and rider
Are enveloped and ensnared
In the net of danger;
The spokes of their chariots are shattered,
Driver and horses are dead.

[1] Grillparzer (*Gedichte* 1872) has '*Egypten*'.
[2] Grillparzer (*Gedichte* 1872) has 'Drängen nach *auf sich'rem* Pfad'.
[3] Grillparzer (*Gedichte* 1872) has '*Von* Netze der Gefahr'.

(7) Tauchst du auf, Pharao?   Are you coming up, Pharaoh?
     Hinab, hinunter,   Go down, down,
     Hinunter in den Abgrund,   Down into the abyss
     Schwarz wie deine Brust.   As black as your heart.

(8) Und das Meer hat nun vollzogen,   The sea has now done its work,
     Lautlos rollen seine Wogen,   Its waves roll silently;
     Nimmer gibt es, was es barg,   At once a wilderness, grave and coffin,
     Eine Wüste, Grab zugleich und Sarg. It will never yield what it has hidden.

              Chor.   *Chorus.*
     Tauchst du auf, Pharao?   Are you coming up, Pharaoh?
     Hinab, hinunter,   Go down, down,
     Hinunter in den Abgrund,   Down into the abyss
     Schwarz wie deine Brust.   Black as your heart.
(9) Schrecklich hat der Herr vollzogen, The Lord has done his terrible work,
     Lautlos ziehn des Meeres Wogen;   The sea's waves flow silently;
     Wer erräth noch, was es barg?   Who could guess what they hide –
     Frevlergrab zugleich und Sarg   That grave and coffin of the impious?

(10) Drum mit Cymbeln und mit Saiten   Then let the cymbals and the strings
     Lasst den Hall es tragen weit,   Echo far and wide.
     Gross der Herr zu allen Zeiten,   Great is the Lord always,
     Heute gross vor aller Zeit.   And greater today than ever.

              Chor.   *Chorus.*
     Gross der Herr zu allen Zeiten,   Great is the Lord always,
     Heute gross vor aller Zeit   And greater today than ever.

Franz Grillparzer (1791–1872); poem written in March 1828. *See also* Bible.

Schubert's Hebrew setting of *Der 92. Psalm* D953 was composed more or less in the same period as *Mirjams Siegesgesang* and shows a similar sensitivity to Jewish history and tradition. A few months later Schubert was to set six poems of Heinrich Heine who would soon become notorious in more conservative circles for being anti-establishment. Schubert's sympathy with the poet and his background is evident in those *Schwanengesang* songs; apart from this, the other Jewish-inspired works of 1828 raise the possibility that Cantor Salomon Sulzer's friendship with Schubert had brought about in the composer a new interest in Jewish culture and literature.

After the composer's death, Anna Fröhlich (1793–1880) revealed the background to this piece, explaining that Schubert had written the cantata for her sister Josefine ('Pepi', 1808–1878), a trained opera singer. The other Fröhlich sisters, all of whom were extremely musical, were Barbara ('Betti', 1798–1878) and Katharina ('Kathi', 1798–1879). Grillparzer's connection with the Fröhlich family was well known: he was in love with Kathi (he never married her and she became known as the eternal fiancée – the 'ewige Braut'). No doubt this theatrical lion could have been prevailed upon to write a poem for Schubert, especially if the musical result involved one or more of the Fröhlich sisters. Less believable, however, is the practical side of the casting. Josefine Fröhlich was a mezzo soprano for whom Schubert had written the solo part in another Grillparzer setting, the gentle and beguiling *Ständchen* D920. The tessitura of that work seems carefully crafted to the range of an amateur contralto – nowhere does the composer tax the voice with unreasonably operatic demands. The role of Miriam is quite another matter: it is larger than life in every way and, with the exception of some of the operatic music, is perhaps the most demanding of all Schubert's soprano roles. It requires considerable stamina and an opulent voice able to ride triumphantly over a large chorus. A resounding high C places it outside the range of many a lieder-singing soprano. If the solo part of *Ständchen* was conceived accurately for Josefine Fröhlich, there is no way she could also have sung Miriam. That said, the choice of subject matter (the prophetess Miriam was a strong and independent woman who, after the miracle recounted here, criticized Moses and confronted his authority) was, as Walther Dürr points out, very much in tune with the emancipated Fröhlich sisters who were, it seems, proto-feminists.

The work received its first performance in a private concert organized by Anna Fröhlich in Schubert's memory (and to raise money for a memorial) at the Musikverein on 30 January 1829, a few months after the composer's death. Anna accompanied this cantata (there is some evidence that the work was performed with *two* pianos on that occasion – the pianos of Schubert's time might have been drowned, alongside Pharoah, by the might of the choral singing) but her sister Josefine did not sing Miriam. Indeed, the concert organizers must have been at a complete loss to find a woman singer adequate for a role that would have suited Schubert's admired Anna Milder Hauptmann. In the end Miriam was sung by a tenor, the resilient Ludwig Tietze, admired for his ability in the vocal stratosphere. The music was so obviously conceived for the brilliance of a female voice, however, that this must have been one of the more demanding evenings of Tietze's career.

Leopold von Sonnleithner, a great connoisseur of the time and close to the composer, remarked that Schubert intended this work for a large orchestra. If this were so, the re-scoring would have been no easy task. There are arguably some unpianistic passages (notably in the concluding fugue), but this is an intricately written accompaniment with numerous pianistic effects, not merely a short score standing in for an orchestra. Franz Lachner (qv COMPOSERS) provided an orchestration as early as 1830, but this has not stood the test of time (although its promised reprinting in the NSA may spearhead a revival). Like so much else in this composer's vocal music, the clash of Miriam's timbrels sounds better at the keyboard. In a curious way, this hybrid work, somewhere between oratorio excerpt and choral ballad, joins hands with the early songs: we return to the Old Testament world of *Hagars Klage* D5 composed some seventeen years earlier, and we hear many an echo of the piano-generated drama of such ballads as *Der Taucher* D77 and *Die Bürgschaft* D246.

Mirjams Siegesgesang is a biblical epic worthy of Cecil B. DeMille: the raising of the waters of the Red Sea, the chase of Pharaoh's hordes at full gallop, and his destruction, were all featured in that director's *The Ten Commandments* (1923). Not for the first time we notice that narrative cinema of this type, with its exaggerated yet effective pathos, seems related to the mood of the early Schubert ballads as well as to this work from the end of his life.

Two other great composers hover in the background of this work's genesis – Ludwig van Beethoven and George Frideric Handel. It is likely that Schubert inherited the synagogue commission from Sulzer for *Der 92. Psalm* because Beethoven was out of the running; from the same composer's deathbed Schubert probably gained the Rellstab poems, later published as the first part of *Schwanengesang*. By 1828 he seems to have become closer friends with Anton Schindler, Beethoven's former factotum, and there are signs that Schindler was even preparing to take up the younger composer as his new protégé. (Whether Schubert would have played along with this, had he lived, we shall never know.) Schindler had taken possession of Beethoven's music library, and this contained at least one treasure not to be found easily else-where: the Samuel Arnold edition (1787–90) of the collected works of Handel which had been sent as a gift from England. It seems certain that Schubert perused these volumes, via Schindler, after Beethoven's death, with as much interest as the older composer, one effect of which was to make him want to return to his studies and begin counterpoint lessons with Simon Sechter. It is likely that *Mirjams Siegesgesang* is early fruit of Schubert's new enthusiasm for the Handelian oratorio tradition. Beethoven had once remarked that all composers bend the knee before Handel. Miriam and the tribes of Israel, unbending before mighty Pharaoh, are made to curtsey in like manner.

Grillparzer's poem is based on the episode of the Israelites' flight from Egypt. Mention of Miriam's song of victory occurs in Exodus 15:20/21: 'And Miriam the prophetess, the older sister of Aaron and Moses, took a timbrel in her hand; and all the women went after her with timbrels and with dances. And Miriam answered them, Sing ye to the Lord, for He hath triumphed gloriously; the horse and his rider hath He thrown into the sea.' Thus, as Miriam praises God she recounts a part of the story of Pharaoh's destruction. Taking his cue from this, Grillparzer adds to the celebratory aspect of the outer verses with a long central section, essential for Schubert's purposes, that tells the story of the flight from Egypt and the pursuit of Pharaoh in the historic present. As if the poet had also studied Handel's works, the words preserve the sort of narrative distance that distinguishes oratorio texts from operatic libretto or song lyric. Mention of 'we' confirms that Grillparzer was fully aware that portions of the poem were to be set for chorus (as is indicated in his *Gedichte*, 1872). Miriam's followers are referred to in the bible as 'All the women' but Schubert chooses to back the prophetess with a chorus of mixed voices. The versification of the poem is printed above as in Grillparzer; the verse numbers in brackets are inserted only for the convenience of discussing the music in sections as Schubert composed it.

Verse 1 'Allegro giusto': The very opening of the work proclaims its Handelian ancestry, with dotted rhythms setting it off to a grand start. This is music for a state celebration, the brilliance of C major being the time-honoured tonality for such jubilation. After the introductory six-bar fanfare the soprano begins her trumpet-like melody. Perhaps this loud and jangling introduction corresponds to the mention of the cymbal; in b. 10 the succession of sixths in the pianist's right hand is rather metallic too, but these chords probably refer to 'die Saiten' – the strings. The dotted rhythms of the left hand also suggest percussion of some kind. After the sibyl's 'Gross der Herr zu allen Zeiten Heute gross vor aller Zeit' (bb. 18–20) we suddenly hear the exciting entry of the massed chorus echoing the last phrase of the soloist in a manner as familiar in Handel or Bach as in Purcell or Gilbert and Sullivan. A piano interlude in the old style, *pomposo* and with a touch of canon (bb. 28–31), introduces the chorus's repeat of the words 'Rührt die Cymbel'; here Schubert has enormous fun with the imitation between the voice parts. This interweaving of snaking quavers, accompanied by rhythmically insistent crotchets in the piano, generates real energy – an intoxicating barefoot stomp such as might have been danced in biblical times. (Crowd scenes in Cecil B. de Mille epics come to mind.) The rest of the section repeats and develops these ideas with the same old-fashioned, symmetrical interaction between soloist and chorus.

Verses 2–3 'Allegretto' (from b. 78): Inspired, no doubt, by the image of a protecting shepherd, Schubert constructs the next section in a pastoral § in the comforting key of F major. All is classical symmetry: four bars of piano introduction announce the melody that is then taken up by the soloist and chorus in decorous turns. The heat of the fire, and of God's blazing eyes, is incorporated in this essentially flowing and peaceful music: with a modulation into E flat major (b. 93) the singer climbs to the ringing upper reaches of the stave followed by the interjection of dotted fanfare at b. 94. From b. 108 the setting of 'Stark dein Arm' is suitably muscular and strident with more fanfares, this time in D flat major. Here, as elsewhere, the rhetorical exchanges

Der Ägypter Untergang im Roten Meer und die Rettung der
Israeliten.

The Destruction of the Egyptians by Julius Schnorr von Carolsfield (1794–1872).

between solo voice and chorus are in a style that suggests music from another century. The first mention of the sea at the beginning of Verse 3 ('Und das Meer hört deine Stimme', b. 119) retains the § rhythm but introduces a note of turbulence into the music, an intimation of a tidal wave (from the interlude at b. 128) as God parts the waters. Some of the best and most original music in the piece (from 'Scheu des Meeres Ungethüme') now follows. The whispered fear and amazement of the chorus is accompanied on the piano by an edifice of suspensions in slowly moving dotted crotchets. The effect is of shimmering water (the chorus's moving semiquavers) held in check by a miraculous wall that is a dam restraining the sea's force. Low tremolos in G flat major (from b. 136) underpin a slow and ominous pianistic underswell; this is a perfect musical analogue for the miracle – the surging power of the sea held and parted, against all laws of gravity and nature, by a higher power. Schubert conveys both fear and danger, as well as the impermanence of this altered state where water glistens and moves even as it is held stationary. The music of the Good Shepherd (*Der 23. Psalm* D706, another Fröhlich-inspired work) returns raised to a higher power and dynamic, and the crossover into the promised land occasions a triumphant high C from Miriam (b. 161) at the final 'das neue Land'.

Verses 4–6 'Allegro agitato' (from b. 166): This section in C minor describes, with an admirable sense of excitement, Pharaoh giving chase. Scuttling semiquavers convey mounting panic and the raising of dust by a vast phalanx of Egyptian troops. The piano's left hand sounds a military bugle motif in dotted rhythm. The choral echoes of Miriam's increasingly breathless descriptions become shorter and more frequent, and this too adds to the tension. At 'Hörner lärmen' (bb. 177–8) the piano writing moves into the bouncing triplets of a cavalry charge. These alternate with semiquavers in writing that paints the swift movement of a large army over constantly changing terrain. This recalls part of the long Schober ballad *Viola* D786 when the abandoned flower in danger of extinction flees the forces of winter, propelled forward by semiquavers that stumble over many changing harmonies. A turning point is reached at the repetitive setting of 'Jetzt und jetzt' (from b. 213), a rhetorical device reminiscent of a cliff-hanging end to an episode of a soap-opera. A succession of hammered C flats (bb. 215–16) changes enharmonically to ominous triplets in B minor for 'da horch'!'(from bb. 218–19) and further single-word exchanges ('Wehen', 'Murmeln', 'Dröhnen') between soloist and chorus. Here one thinks of Bach's *St Matthew Passion* as much as of Handel, but Schubert could not have known that work. This is a bridge passage to a new section, and the return to C minor is cleverly managed with the most protracted and exciting build-up. With the word 'Sturm' Miriam, crossing the divide between dominant and tonic in a mighty cadence (bb. 229–30), announces the pummelling waves of the watery retribution visited upon the forces of Pharaoh. This new section is marked *Allegro moderato*. In this music of destruction the power of the piano is insufficient to convey the full force of the cataclysmic turn of events, particularly when the instrument's weaker middle register is pitted against the chorus at full throttle. Schubert abandoned the ballad *Johanna Sebus* D728 (also about disaster caused by water) because he had come to an impasse: the piano is capable of only so much violent sound, and there comes a point when it takes an orchestra in full flood to produce sufficient volume.

Verses 7–9 'Andantino' (from b. 270): The spirit of Handel returns to point the moral of the story in music of the greatest self-righteousness and pomp. 'You got what was coming to you, Pharoah' is the gist of Miriam's tirade in an E minor panoply of dotted rhythms and old-fashioned canonic entries and trills. The image of the enemy being sent down into the abyss ('Hinab, hinunter, / Hinunter in den Abgrund') prompts the doubling of singer and piano and a descent into the chest regions of the voice (bb. 283–4). The music here is so physical that one can almost see the prophetess striking a pose in the grand manner, her finger pointing imperiously down towards the watery grave. Some of the most gracious and original music is reserved for 'Und das Meer hat nun vollzogen' (from b. 298). These gently rolling phrases suggest quiet, rather than violent, movement of water (the poet gave Schubert the cue for the mood here with the word 'Lautlos' – 'soundless'). Here the sea is dead rather than red, its depths containing not only the bodies of the Egyptian army, but also the many imponderable mysteries of the Lord. Having delivered this extended solo, Miriam hands over to her implacable chorus. The imperious music and mockingly sarcastic words asking Pharoah whether he will emerge like a surfacing diver from the depths ('Tauchst du auf, Pharao?') are repeated from the beginning of Verse 7 (from b. 315); but instead of echoing Miriam's words in Verse 8, the chorus moves to the slightly different Verse 9 (from b. 337). Here a chorus proves even better able to depict the sinuous flow of water that gently obliterates all evidence of this great event: smoothly gliding counterpoint between the voices paints wave after wave of nescience, as if the Egyptians had never been. These doleful undulations, as well as the repetitions of 'Nimmer gibt es' at the end of the strophe (from b. 353), illustrate the eerie end of a once-powerful enemy. One is tempted to feel rather sorry for Pharaoh who has become, perforce, a deep-sea diver, but is obviously no match for a high C diva.

Verse 10: The story of the Egyptian rout having been told, it is now time to return to the celebration. From b. 369 (Tempo I) there is a stirring return to the music of the opening, beginning with the piano's C major fanfare. This represents a real clearing of the air after the long episode in E minor. Miriam sings 'Drum mit Zimbel und mit Saiten' – that crucial 'Drum' ('for that reason' or 'therefore') summing up in a single word the events recounted in the last ten minutes. This time we do not have to wait so long to hear the chorus mirror Miriam's phrases – they enter almost immediately (from b. 378). A lesser composer would have been satisfied with a simple repeat of the opening music, but for Schubert the fun is just beginning; indeed we now encounter one of his principal reasons for writing this work in the first place – he wishes to practise his fugal writing! Taking the final two lines of the last strophe, he creates as mighty a contrapuntal structure as is to be found in any of his vocal works with piano. The basses state the four-bar subject at b. 400 ('Gross der Herr zu allen Zeiten, / Heute gross vor aller Zeit'); the tenors enter a fourth above (b. 404) with the fugal answer, slightly altered as is permitted and required; then the altos and sopranos repeat the process in turn. The working out of the fugue arguably has a whiff of the schoolroom exercise about it but is nevertheless effective. Particularly stirring is the mighty stretto on a pedal G (b. 456) before the work abandons contrapuntal garb and ends in an outburst of punched-out chordal harmony and unanimous joy.

The unfolding and intermingling of all four voices (Miriam herself is silent, leaving this peroration to the masses) is mightily impressive, even if a little stiff and unwieldy in comparison with the real masterpieces of fugal writing. Indeed, one is reminded here of the sinewy and wilful writing of late Beethoven: the uncompromising fugue that ends the D major Cello Sonata, Op. 102 no. 2, was published as early as 1817 (it is likely that Schubert knew it) and feels similarly awkward and 'modern' under the pianist's fingers. The *Missa Solemnis* was also finally published in 1827 and Schindler would no doubt have let Schubert borrow a copy. Inspired now by the same Handelian source as the older composer, only in 1828 does Schubert seem to have welcomed the idea of acquiring old-fashioned contrapuntal mastery. Like Beethoven, this is an interest that belongs to his final period.

Mirjams Siegesgesang is one of a series of works that give us a fascinating hint of the directions Schubert might have taken had he lived. Other 'signpost' works are the starkly modern Heine settings from *Schwanengesang* D957/8–13 (unlike any other Schubert songs), the unfinished opera *Der Graf von Gleichen* D918, and of course the bold Romantic inventiveness of the sublime late piano sonatas and the String Quintet. It is as if we are standing on the threshold of something new and staring into an infinite horizon, the waters of the Red Sea having quietly removed all trace of former life and activity. The possibilities for the future are endless, but there is not enough detail visible to enable us to continue the journey alone.

Autograph:	British Library, London
First edition:	Published as Op. post. 136 by Diabelli, Vienna in 1839 (P329)
Dedicatee:	Joseph Witteczek (dedicated by Diabelli)
First known performance:	30 January 1829, Musikverein, Vienna. The concert was organized by Anna Fröhlich in order to celebrate Schubert's music and raise money to construct a monument in his memory, and was repeated on 5 March 1829 in the same venue. Soloist: Ludwig Tietze (See Waidelich/Hilmar Dokumente I No. 687 and Deutsch No. xxvi for full concert programme)
Performance reviews:	*Der Sammler* (Vienna) No. 23 (21 February 1829), p. 92 [Waidelich/Hilmar Dokumente I No. 698] *Monatbericht der Gesellschaft der Musikfreunde des Oesterreichischen Kaiserstaates* (Vienna, March 1829), pp. 41–6 [Waidelich/Hilmar Dokumente I No. 703]
Subsequent editions:	AGA XVII 9: p. 170; NSA III: Vol. 2b/196
Bibliography:	Berke 1999, p. 203
Discography and timing:	Fischer-Dieskau — Hyperion I 31[11] Hyperion II 36[1] 18'05 Christine Brewer

← *Auf dem Strom* D943   *Herbst* D945 →

MISERO PARGOLETTO (I)

(METASTASIO) **D42** [H17]

G minor   (Composition exercise) 1813?

Andante

Mi - se-ro par - go - let - to,

(90 bars)

Unhappy child

Misero pargoletto,	Unhappy child,
Il tuo destin non sai.	You do not know your fate.
Ah! non gli dite mai	Ah, never tell him
Qual era il genitor.	Who his father was.
Come in un punto, oh Dio,	O God, how in one moment
Tutto cangiò d'aspetto!	Everything changed its aspect!
Voi foste il mio diletto,	You were my delight
Voi siete il mio terror.	Now you make me afraid.

PIETRO METASTASIO (1698–1782); poem written in 1733

This is the fourth of Schubert's fourteen Metastasio solo settings (1812–27). See the poet's biography for a chronological list of all the Metastasio settings.

This aria is from Metastasio's libretto for *Demofoonte* (first set by Caldara and also the young Gluck) where it is sung by Timante in Act III. The settings of this poem almost certainly belong to the beginning of Schubert's intense period of vocal study with Salieri, 1812–13. It is significant that this is a male character, yet Schubert set the text for soprano voice. It seems likely that when Salieri allocated these texts he did not always (if ever) explain the context of the arias in terms of the libretto's overall plot. The NSA prints three pieces of music under this title. There is the fully worked-out aria with piano (discussed in the next commentary) and then two versions of a completely different setting, the first with a vocal line only (NSA volume 6 p. 180), the second (discussed here) with a certain amount of accompaniment sketched in, mainly bass lines. (Schubert was to adopt this as a permanent way of working – creating the vocal line first with only hints of the piano writing, and filling in the details later.) Reinhard Van Hoorickx created a song from this last fragment, carefully incorporating what remains of the genuine Schubert into his realization; for example the winsome left-hand pizzicato of the opening derives from the staccato figurations added to bb. 19–20, after 'Qual era il genitor'. This version was recorded for the Hyperion Edition.

When hearing the opening of this piece, the opera enthusiast experiences a sense of *déjà entendu*: 'Where have I heard that music before?' Schubert might well have asked himself the same thing. We know that Mozart's *Die Zauberflöte* was one of the operas the composer heard in 1812, and it seems to have left a huge impression – so much so that when he came to set this text about an unhappy child and the problems with its father (an *idée fixe* in the subject matter of the early ballads) he thought of the Pamina/Sarastro relationship. Schubert's mind worked like that: certain musical images and shapes were called upon, as if summoned from a database, as soon as he grasped the dramatic implications of any musical situation. In this way he had no need to look up one of his earlier works in order to quote it: if he were confronted with a similar set of literary stimuli, similar music would come to him afresh. This is possibly why he hardly noticed that the first four bars of this setting are entirely lifted from the tune (and partially the rhythm) of Pamina's great aria *Ach, ich fühl's*, the G minor tonality included in the unintentional plagiarism. In all likelihood Salieri acidly pointed out that the tune of *Misero pargoletto* lacked a certain originality, no doubt embarrassing his pupil. After all, we have failed to find any evidence of Schubert quoting unintentionally from Salieri's operas.

Apart from this little upset, the song is a beautiful one that deserves to be better known. It requires fine *bel canto* singing, and is rather more wiltingly wistful than the later setting that aims for greater drama. Or it may be that Reinhard Van Hoorickx has erred on the side of caution by keeping his version of the accompaniment less active and obtrusive. In this, he too seems to have been influenced by the gentle subtlety of Mozart's accompaniment for Pamina.

Autograph:	British Library, London
First edition:	Published as part of the NSA in 1969; subsequently completed for performance and privately published by Reinhard Van Hoorickx (P742)
Subsequent editions:	Not in Peters; Not in AGA; NSA IV: Vol. 6/181
Discography and timing:	Fischer-Dieskau —
	Hyperion I 33[11]
	Hyperion II 2[13] 3'55 Patricia Rozario

← *Ombre amene, amiche piante (La Serenata)* D990f   *L'incanto degli occhi* D990e →

MISERO PARGOLETTO (II)   Unhappy child
(Metastasio) **D42** [H19]
G minor   1813?

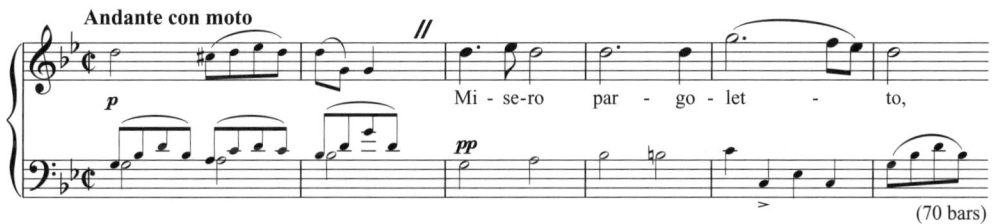

Mi - se-ro   par - go - let - to,

(70 bars)

See previous entry for poem and translation

Pietro Metastasio (1698–1782); poem written in 1733

This is the fifth of Schubert's fourteen Metastasio solo settings (1812–27). See the poet's biography for a chronological list of all the Metastasio settings.

It seems likely that the final version was composed only a few weeks after the first, and that Salieri had encouraged Schubert to go straight back to the drawing board. The old-style soprano clef had to be used, for Salieri was a stickler for the rules of the old order. The first version of the piece (unpublished until it appeared in 1969 in the NSA as 'Erste Bearbeitung') had consisted of two attempts at constructing a vocal line: the first is totally unaccompanied, the second has a tiny amount of piano writing sketched in. Perhaps Salieri recommended this as a safe means of constructing a singable tune, and it remained a habit with Schubert until the end of his life; a surviving sketch shows that his very last song *Die Taubenpost* was plotted in a like manner.

This second version takes an entirely different tack for the vocal line while retaining the key of G minor. Only the barest of Pamina's bones can be discerned here, but the piano introduction, bb. 1–13, remains a charming, and perhaps defiant, variation on Mozart's immortal aria for the 'misera Pamina'. The vocal line is initially a kind of obbligato to this piano music, the first four bars of which are repeated under the voice. The form of the piece is simple enough – a *da capo* aria with a middle section (from b. 31) that in dramatic tessitura, and the orchestral effect of the piano part, owes more to Gluck than Mozart. From b. 38 until a climactic high B flat on the word 'terror' the vocal line lies high and awkward. The desperation of the the mother is depicted at b. 45 with a shuddering diminished 7th chord that recalls the walking statue of the Commendatore in *Don Giovanni*, the most frightening moment in all opera. The artful hesitancy with which Schubert returns to the opening theme already shows a surprisingly sophisticated hand.

Autograph:	British Library, London
First edition:	Published as part of the AGA in 1895 (P703)
Subsequent editions:	Not in Peters; AGA XX 570: Vol. 10/31; NSA IV: Vol. 6/60; Bärenreiter: Vol. 5/42 (high voice edition)
Discography and timing:	Fischer-Dieskau —
	Hyperion I 9[1]
	Hyperion II 2[15] 2'24 Arleen Auger

← *L'incanto degli occhi* D990e   *Totengräberlied* D44 →

MIT DEM GRÜNEN LAUTENBANDE *see DIE SCHÖNE MÜLLERIN*
D795/13

Der MONDABEND   The moonlit evening
(Ermin) **D141** [H58]
A major   1815

(16 bars)

Rein und freundlich lacht der Himmel	The heavens smile, pure and kindly,
Nieder auf die dunkle Erde;	Upon the dark earth below;
Tausend goldne Augen blinken	A thousand golden eyes shine
Lieblich in die Brust der Menschen,	Fondly into men's hearts,
Und des Mondes lichte Scheibe	And the moon's bright disc
Segelt heiter durch die Bläue.	Sails serenely through the blue.
Auf den goldnen Strahlen zittern	On the golden beams tremble
Süsser Wehmut Silbertropfen,	The silver drops of sweet melancholy;

Dringen sanft mit leisem Hauche	Gently, with soft breath,
In das stille Herz voll Liebe,	They penetrate the silent, loving heart
Und befeuchten mir das Auge	And moisten my eyes
Mit der Sehnsucht zartem Taue.	With the tender dew of longing.
Funkelnd prangt der Stern des Abends	The evening star sparkles resplendently
In den lichtbesäten Räumen,	In the light-strewn expanses of space,
Spielt mit seinem Demantblitzen	And with diamond flashes plays
Durch der Lichte Duftgewebe,	Through the hazy web of light;
Und viel holde Engelsknaben	And many a sweet cherub
Streuen Lilien um die Sterne.	Strews lilies around the stars.
Schön und hehr ist wohl der Himmel	Fair and exalted are the heavens
In des Abends Wunderglanze;	In the wondrous light of evening;
Aber meines Lebens Sterne	But the stars of my life
Wohnen in dem kleinsten Kreise:	Dwell within the smallest circle:
In das Auge meiner Silli	They have all been charmed
Sind sie alle hingezaubert.	Into the eyes of my Silli.

JOHANN GOTTFRIED ERMIN (PSEUDONYM OF JOHANN GOTTFRIED KUMPF) (1781–1862)

This is the first of Schubert's two Ermin settings (1815). See the poet's biography (under Johann Gottfried Kumpf) for a chronological list of all the Ermin settings.

There is nothing particularly noteworthy about this strophic song – apart from the glorious certainty that only Schubert could have written it. It is possible that the composer came across the work of Kumpf thanks to the poet's fellow-Styrian, Anselm Hüttenbrenner. *Der Mondabend* is a silver sliver of a song, a moonlit page in a ternary form so simple that in other hands it would be banal. The running semiquavers of the accompaniment seem at first to suggest water music, but it is moonshine that is on tap with the odd chromatic passing note to paint the glint of a thousand stars. The inspiration for this was undoubtedly the line 'Tausend goldne Augen blinken'. There is so much refraction of moonlight here that the light seems to bounce along the stave together with the accompaniment. We learn in the last strophe that in comparison with the sparkling energy in the eyes of Silli, the poet's beloved, moonbeams come off second best. This night song is thus less about nocturnal splendours than the longing and exaltation of the poet in love. We are aware throughout of an undertow of passionate impatience.

For this reason the song makes rather more of a robust impression than is usual for moon music (compare it to the languid Hölty *An den Mond* D193). The energy of the left hand ostinato (a dotted crotchet and three pulsating quavers) was later to be employed to drive forward such masterpieces as *Der Zwerg* D771 and the first *Suleika* song D720.

Autograph:	Wienbibliothek im Rathaus, Vienna (fragment, bb. 1–18)
First edition:	Published as Op. post. 131 no. 1 by Josef Czerny, Vienna in 1830 (P255)
Subsequent editions:	Peters: Vol. 4/158; AGA XX 43: Vol. 2/20; NSA IV: Vol. 7/86; Bärenreiter: Vol. 6/44
Arrangements:	Arr. Tilman Hoppstock (b. 1961) for guitar accompaniment, in *Franz Schubert: 110 Lieder* (2009)

Discography and timing:　Fischer-Dieskau I 2²¹　1'13　(first two strophes only)

Hyperion I 15²

Hyperion II 4¹⁴　2'09　Margaret Price

← *Ballade* D134　　　　　　　　　　*Geistes-Gruss* D142 (third version) →

MONDENSCHEIN　　　　Moonlight　　　Quintet, TTBBB
(SCHOBER) **D875** [H583]
A♭ major　January 1826

(93 bars)

Des Mondes Zauberblume lacht[1]	The moon's magic flower smiles,
Und ruft mit seelenvollem Blick	And with its blissful gaze restores
In unsre düstre Erdennacht	The paradise of love
Der Liebe Paradies zurück.	To our gloomy earthly night.
Vom mächt'gen Arm des Schlafs besiegt,	Vanquished by the mighty arm of sleep,
Erstarben Sorge, Schuld und Pein,[2]	Care, guilt and pain have perished;
Das Zarte nur und Schöne fliegt	Only tenderness and beauty soar
Entfesselt in den Geisterreih'n.[3]	Unfettered in the ranks of the spirits.
Doch seht! die Fluren sind vertauscht,	See, the meadows are transformed;
Das ist die alte Erde nicht,	This is not the old earth.
O seht ein Silbergarten duftumrauscht,[4]	Behold a scented silver garden,
Voll Nebelschmelz und Zauberlicht.	Filled with shimmering mist and magic light.
Den Geist, vom ird'schen Drucke frei,[5]	Free from earthly burdens, the spirit
Umwallt der Sehnsucht Ätherkleid,	Is enveloped by an ethereal cloak of longing,
Er trinkt in stiller Schwärmerei	And in silent ecstasy
Des Himmels volle Seligkeit.	Drinks in all heaven's rapture.
Doch mahnt das Lied der Nachtigall	But the nightingale's song reminds
An seine Welt das weiche Herz,—	The tender heart of its own world;
In aller Wonne weckt ihr Schall	Blissfully her song awakens
den tiefsten Schmerz,—der Liebe Schmerz!	The deepest sorrow, the sorrow of love.

[1] Schober (*Gedichte*, 1842) has 'Des Mondes *Silberblume* lacht'.
[2] Schober (*Gedichte*, 1842) has '*Entschlummert* Sorge, *Noth* und Pein'.
[3] Schober (*Gedichte*, 1842) has 'Entfesselt in den *Freudenreihn*'.
[4] Schober (*Gedichte*, 1842) has '*Ein Feengarten* duftumrauscht', without 'O seht'.
[5] In *Gedichte* (1842) these two lines are 'Der Busen athmet leicht und frei / Von roher Lebenslast befreit'.

FRANZ VON SCHOBER (1796–1882)

This quintet for two tenors and three basses (the first tenor being a solo part with a challengingly high tessitura) has a chequered history. After its composition in January 1826 the composer put it aside until it was performed (advertised as a 'new' quintet) at a Philharmonic Society concert on 3 January 1828. Ludwig Tietze, renowned for the ease of his top register, sang lead tenor on this occasion. In May 1828 Schubert sent the work to the firm of Schott in Mainz as part of a package of music which he hoped to have published (it included the *Impromptus* for piano D935 that later appeared as Op. post. 142). Schott found the piano pieces 'too difficult for the French market' and eventually sent them back; he was prepared to publish the quintet, but only at half the fee that Schubert had asked for it.

This was not acceptable to the composer (he had written to Schott that 'both compositions have been very well received here') and he asked for it back. It seems that Schott returned the autograph of the vocal score without the supplementary piano part that went with it. We know that the work initially had an accompaniment because it is on record that one Frau Schmiedel played the piano for it at the Philharmonic concert. But the piece also works well unaccompanied, and when it was eventually published posthumously by Diabelli in 1831 the accompaniment was a simple shadowing of the vocal parts in short score. The question is whether this piano part (marked 'ad libitum') was provided by Schubert himself, or whether it was put together by Diabelli in the absence of the composer's own (which had perhaps been more adventurous). That autograph was still probably in the possession of Schott who brought out an unauthorized edition of the quintet in 1831 or 1832 both with and without piano. Sadly, not a single copy of this edition seems to have survived, so we cannot tell whether the accompaniment was different from that of the Diabelli edition recorded for the Hyperion Edition. The AGA chose to publish the work as an unaccompanied quintet.

Schober's text is entitled *Vollmondnacht* in his collected poems (1842). It is clear that Schubert worked from an earlier version, and that the poet changed more than the title when he came to prepare his works for publication many years after they were written. The words put Schubert in mind of water music, as if the stars swim in a heavenly constellation of seas and lakes. The music is cast as a gentle dance, and is in the same key as that most famous of Schubert's barcarolles, *Das Fischermädchen* D957/10 from *Schwanengesang*. Another barcarolle comes to mind, the solo setting of Mayrhofer's poem *Gondelfahrer* D808, also in hypnotic § time.

Four of the five voice parts are written within the normal range of the male part-song, and provide the pulsating heart of the music. The first of the two tenors echoes and elaborates what his colleagues have sung and is a star in every sense. His role is that of both soloist and commentator – one is reminded of the decoration of the second cello part in the slow movement of the String Quintet. There is no doubt that the composer needed this heady tessitura to paint the ethereal nocturnal textures of the words (cf. the Seidl setting *Nachthelle* D892). The runs at bb. 32–4 on 'Entfesselt in den Geisterreih'n' (Schober's printed poem entitled *Vollmondnacht* has the more prosaic 'Freundenreihn') are typical of the somewhat Italianate use of melisma that we find in many songs of the period, although the writing is seldom as florid as this. The piece is full of characteristically Schubertian modulations: the change into A major at 'ein Silbergarten duftumrauscht' (b. 41) is magical, as is the long return to the tonic key of A flat via C flat major in the section beginning 'Er trinkt in stiller Schwärmerei' (bb. 56–8). It is little wonder that Schubert thought this piece worth the sixty florins he asked for it, as opposed to the thirty florins condescendingly offered by Schott.

Autograph: Staatsbibliothek Preussischer Kulturbesitz, Berlin
First edition: Published as Op. post. 102 by Diabelli, Vienna in April 1831
                             (P274)

First known performance: 3 January 1828, Musikverein, Vienna. Performers: Ludwig Tietze,
                            Karl Maria Gross, Karl Greisinger, Anton Obermüller & Alois
                            Fuchs (see Waidelich/Hilmar Dokumente II No. 553)
Subsequent editions: AGA XVI 27: p. 153; NSA III: Vol. 3
Discography and timing: Hyperion I 26[5]   The London Schubert
                            Hyperion II 31[6]   5'10   Chorale (dir. Stephen Layton)

⟵ *Im Jänner 1817 (Tiefes Leid)* D876   *Die Allmacht* D875a ⟶

Die MONDNACHT   The moonlit night
(Kosegarten) **D238** [H130]
F♯ major   25 July 1815

(24 bars)

Siehe, wie die Mondesstrahlen   See, how the moonbeams
Busch und Flur in Silber malen!   Paint bush and meadow silver,
Wie das Bächlein rollt und flimmt!   And how the brook ripples and sparkles.
Strahlen regnen, Funken schmettern   Rays of light pour down, sparks rain
Von den sanftgeregten Blättern,   From the gently stirring leaves,
Und die Tauflur glänzt und glimmt.   And the dewy countryside glistens and
                                           shimmers.

Glänzend erdämmern der Berge Gipfel,   The darkening mountain peaks glimmer,
Glänzend der Pappeln wogende Wipfel.   The swaying tops of the poplars gleam.

Durch die glanzumrauschten Räume   Throughout the luminous spaces,
Flüstern Stimmen, gaukeln Träume,   Voices whisper, dreams hover,
Sprechen mir vertraulich zu.   Speaking confidingly to me.
Seligkeit, die mich gemahnet,   Remembered bliss,
Höchste Lust, die süss mich schwanet, Great joy that fills me with sweet intimations,
Sprich, wo blühst, wo zeitigst du?   Tell me, where do you flourish, where will
                                           your time come?

Sprenge die Brust nicht, mächtiges Sehen![1]   Mighty longing, do not shatter my heart!
Löschet die Wehmut, labende Tränen!   Soothing tears, ease my melancholy!

Wie, ach, wie der Qual genesen?   How, how shall I recover from my torment?
Wo, ach, wo ein liebend Wesen,   Where, oh where is there a loving soul
Das die süssen Qualen stillt?   To calm my sweet anguish?
Eins ins andre gar versunken,   One absorbed in the other,
Gar verloren, gar ertrunken,   Quite lost, quite drowned
Bis sich jede Öde füllt—   Until every wasteland is filled . . .

[1] Kosegarten writes here of 'mächtiges *Dehnen*' (literally, 'mighty stretching').

Solches, ach, wähn' ich, kühlte das Sehnen;
Löschte die Wehmut mit köstlichen Tränen.

I sense that such a soul would cool my longing,
And ease my sorrow with exquisite tears.

Eine weiss ich, ach, nur Eine,
Dich nur weiss ich, dich o Reine,
Die des Herzens Wehmut meint.
Dich umringend, von dir umrungen,
Dich umschlingend, von dir umschlungen,
Gar in Eins mit dir geeint— —
Schon', ach schone den Wonneversunknen!
Himmel und Erde verschwinden dem
    Trunknen.

I know one, ah, only one;
I know only you, purest one,
Who understands the heart's sorrow.
Enfolding you, enfolded by you,
Embracing you, embraced by you,
Joined in unity with you . . .
Spare, oh spare me, sunk in bliss!
For me, in my rapture, heaven and earth vanish.

Ludwig Kosegarten (1758–1818)

This is the eleventh of Schubert's twenty-one Kosegarten solo settings (1815–17). See the poet's biography for a chronological list of all the Kosegarten settings, as well as a discussion of Morten Solvik's Kosegarten Liederkreis and this song's place within it.

As John Reed has written, this enchanting song defies all lieder chronology: so sophisticated its rapturous vocal line and so flexible its constantly modulating underlay, one could not be blamed for thinking of Schumann or even Strauss in his neoclassical vein. The introduction begins in the subdominant, although it does not sound as such to the innocent ear. The music is a haunting succession of sequences, and this pattern is echoed in the work's first page. The second half of the song, with its throbbing accompaniment, has something in common with the second setting of *Stimme der Liebe* D418, or even with the much earlier Körner setting, *Sehnsucht der Liebe* D180.

One sometimes gets the impression that the younger, inexperienced Schubert only read the first verse of a song before setting out on its strophic composition, but here it seems obvious that he has been drawn to the last verse which holds the key to the mood of his setting. The words 'Dich umschlingend, von dir umschlungen' (bb. 11–12, NSA bb. 33–4) are strongly reminiscent of the ecstatic reciprocity of 'Umfangend umfangen' of *Ganymed* D544 from 1817, especially when it continues even more explicitly, 'Gar in Eins mit dir geeint' (bb. 13–14, NSA bb. 35–6). It is little wonder that the eye of an eighteen-year old should be drawn to these earthy lines rather than the ordinary conventions of moonlight poetry, and there is no mention of the midnight hour in *Die Mondnacht* (*cf. Der Geistertanz* D15A and in *Gondelfahrer* D808). However, Brigitte Massin avers that in bb. 11–16 (and in all subsequent verses) the crotchets on the second and fourth beat of each bar in the pianist's right hand represent a chiming clock – twelve precisely timed strokes of the hammer on varied notes spread over seven bars.

This heated atmosphere of early *Liebestod* is perhaps not appropriate for the song's first verse (performers have to underplay the gush here) but the almost orgasmic conclusion of the last verse, the repetition of the final line bringing the whole to a sated conclusion via a chromatically rising bass line (bb. 19–22), is an ideal and bold ending to a most unusual song. The yearning tone suggests that the phrase 'dich, o Reine' (you, o pure one) is a euphemistic figure of speech but the passion of the music is beautifully counterpointed by the texture of the first half of the song, silvery and transparent, that derives from the title. Only the inexplicable exclusion of this work from the Peters Edition, and the fact that the music lies rather mercilessly in a high tessitura, have made it less popular than it deserves to be. As a piece of poetry this is Kosegarten at his most adventurous, displaying an extraordinarily unbuttoned use of imagery, going from 'schwanen' to 'blühen' and from there to 'zeitigen' in the twinkling of an eye. The poem begins each verse in staid trochees all the more effectively to lead into physically pulsating dactyls in the last two lines of each strophe.

Autographs:	Fitzwilliam Museum, Cambridge (first draft);
	Österreichische Nationalbibliothek, Vienna (fair copy)
First edition:	Published as part of the AGA in 1895 (P569)
Subsequent editions:	Not in Peters; AGA XX 102: Vol. 2/208; NSA IV: Vol. 8/142
Bibliography:	Einstein 1951, pp. 47–8
	Massin 1977, p. 602
Discography and timing:	Fischer-Dieskau I 4[18] 1'24 (first strophe only)
	Hyperion I 8[6]
	Hyperion II 8[13] 5'03 Sarah Walker

←— *Abends unter der Linde* D237   *Huldigung* D240 —→

MORGENGRUSS *see DIE SCHÖNE MÜLLERIN* D795/8

Der MORGENKUSS   The morning kiss
(Baumberg) **D264** [H151]

The song exists in two versions, both of which are discussed below:
(1) 22 August 1815; (2) Date unknown, published *c.* 1850

(1)   E♭ major

(9 bars)

(2)   'Langsam'   C major   ¢   [16 bars]

Durch eine ganze Nacht sich nah zu sein,[1]	To be close the whole night long,
So Hand in Hand, so Arm im Arme weilen,	To linger hand in hand, arm in arm,
So viel empfinden, ohne mitzuteilen—	To feel so much, without revealing it in words,
Ist eine wonnevolle Pein!	Is blissful torment.
So immer Seelenblick im Seelenblick	To gaze constantly into each other's soul,
Auch den geheimsten Wunsch des Herzens sehen,	To see into the heart's most secret desire,
So wenig sprechen, und sich doch verstehen—	To speak so little, and yet to understand each other,
Ist hohes martervolles Glück!	Is sublime, anguished happiness.

[1] Baumberg writes 'sich nahe sein'.

Zum Lohn für die im Zwang verschwundne Zeit	Then, in the morning light, to make up for the time
Dann bei dem Morgenstrahl, warm, mit Entzücken	That perforce had passed them by, warmly, rapturously
Sich Mund an Mund, und Herz an Herz sich drücken	To press mouth to mouth and heart to heart –
O dies ist—Engelseligkeit!	Oh, that is angelic bliss!
[. . . 6 . . .]	[. . . 6 . . .]

Gabriele von Baumberg (1775–1839)

This is the fifth of Schubert's seven Baumberg solo settings (1809–10 and 1815). See the poet's biography for a chronological list of all the Baumberg settings.

The first few bars of the introduction set the scene in a ceremonial manner reminiscent of an earlier age. The song is in the 'sunset' key of E flat, but in this piano writing there is a drop of a fourth – E flat to B flat (later incorporated into the vocal line) – which is part of a Schubertian vocabulary found elsewhere in the lieder as a means of hailing the dawn. This opening figure, somewhat *pomposo*, is followed by a series of upward inflections, demisemiquaver runs and rising-and-falling pirouettes gradually edging higher up the stave to reflect the inevitable sunrise that follows the events of a life-changing night. In these three bars of introduction it is as if the whole canvas of the song were becoming gradually flooded with light. The dawn, a wonder of nature, is simultaneously illustrative of the human heart opening itself to new experience – the birth of rapture in a soul that had feared itself isolated. The piano music takes an extravagant decorative turn and the scale passages culminate in an ecstatic trill, symbol for racing heartbeats, that spurs the vocal line into action. With this music so evocative of the eighteenth century, and so right for Baumberg's poetry, one is reminded of the piano writing of Haydn, a composer whom Einstein credits with having influenced all the Baumberg settings.

The floridity of the opening and the high tessitura might well have discouraged nineteenth-century amateur accompanists and singers, or, clearly, so Diabelli thought. When he published the song in the *Nachlass*, not only was it transposed down a third but the introduction was suppressed in favour of a simplified version, re-barred in double note values so as to appear less complex for the performers. This robs the music of its splendidly baroque appearance on the printed page, Schubert's way of paying tribute to Baumberg's position as a leading Viennese figure of the late eighteenth century. This corrupt and flaccid version was printed in the Peters Edition. Singers had to wait another twenty-two years before discovering Schubert's original intentions in the Gotthard volume (1872) and it is this that Mandyczewski reprinted in the AGA, ignoring the so-called second version that had appeared in Peters. Walther Dürr warns us in NSA Vol. 9 that there is no proof that this version goes back to Diabelli alone, but to me the evidence seems overwhelming. The doctored first edition also cut the interludes between the strophes to the detriment of the music and to the discomfort of any interpreter already taxed by a vocal line where there is no respite in the melodic flow, breath having to be snatched in passing. As it is printed in the AGA the pianist must repeat the florid introduction between each of the verses, giving the singer valuable time to regather her poise. The tessitura of these breathlessly ardent lines lies perilously high in what I take to be the authentic E flat major version; Dame Margaret Price sang this song in D flat for Hyperion, avoiding the squeakiness that can render the majesty of the setting toy-like in the hands of thin-voiced nightingales.

The poetess, as if she needs to reprove any base assumptions on the part of her readership, has carefully placed the words 'after a ball' as an afterthought to the title. It would be too scandalous if we were to think that this kiss at dawn was a postlude to a night of unbridled and unchaperoned intimacy! The manuscript source omits any mention of the ball, although the classicism of the setting suggests a formal occasion and feelings suppressed by the exigencies of convention. How familiar Schubert must have been with the frustration at parties of his friends (when he was often relegated to the piano to supply the dance music) where society offered young men little enough opportunity to be alone with the objects of their desires.

Autograph:	Missing or lost
Publication:	First published as No. 33 of *Neueste Folge nachgelassener Lieder und Gesänge* by J. P. Gotthard, Vienna in 1872 (P459; first version)
	First published as Book 45 no. 4 of the *Nachlass* by Diabelli, Vienna in 1850 (P373; second version)
Subsequent editions:	Peters: Vol. 6/45; AGA XX 124: Vol. 3/51; NSA IV: Vol. 9/7 (first version) & 8 (*Nachlass* version)
Bibliography:	Einstein 1951, p. 107
	Youens 1996, pp. 35–40
Discography and timing:	Fischer-Dieskau I 5[9]　1'55　(first two strophes only)
	Hyperion I 15[7]
	Hyperion II 9[12]　　3'20　Margaret Price

← *Cora an die Sonne* D263　　　　　　　　　　　*Abendständchen an Lina* D265 →

MORGENLIED　　　　　　Morning song
(STOLBERG) **D266** [H153]
F major　24 August 1815

(24 bars)

Willkommen, rotes Morgenlicht!
Es grüsset dich mein Geist,
Der durch des Schlafes Hülle bricht,
Und seinen Schöpfer preis't.

Willkommen, goldner Morgenstrahl,
Der schon den Berg begrüsst,
Und bald im stillen Quellental
Die kleine Blume küsst!

O Sonne, sei mir Gottes Bild,
Der täglich dich erneut,

Welcome, rosy light of morning!
My spirit greets you,
Breaking through the veil of sleep
To praise its Creator.

Welcome, golden ray of morning,
Which already greets the mountains,
And in the silent valley, by the stream,
Will soon kiss the little flowers.

O sun, be for me the image of God,
Who renews you each day,

Der immer hehr, und immer mild,	Who, ever noble and gentle,
Die ganze Welt erfreut!	Brings joy to the whole world.
Der, wie die Blum' im Quellental,	Who created you, o sun,
O Sonne, dich erschuf,	As He did the flowers by the valley's streams,
Als deine Schwestern allzumal	When all your sisters
Entflammen seinem Ruf.	Were kindled at his command.
Ihr wandelt auf bestimmter Bahn	You each move on your appointed course,
Einher und strauchelt nicht;	And do not falter;
Denn Gottes Odem haucht euch an,	For God's breath touches you,
Sein Aug' ist euer Licht.	His eye is your light.
[...6...]	[...6...]

Friedrich Leopold, Graf zu Stolberg-Stolberg (1750–1819); poem written in 1793

This is the first of Schubert's nine Stolberg solo settings (1815–23). See the poet's biography for a chronological list of all the Stolberg settings.

This is one of a number of Schubert songs that greet the coming of dawn, and it was obviously conceived for the freshness and purity of the soprano voice. The imagery of first light is linked with newborn innocence, the clean slate of infancy. Something as elemental as sunrise prompts music of flowing naturalness, an ideal depiction of the joy that accompanies the infinite possibilities of a new day. F major is the quintessential pastoral tonality, and Mozartian echoes (not of the grander piano concertos or operas perhaps, but of the lesser-known lieder or wind music) add to the impression of a song in a graceful eighteenth-century frame. In the first bar of the introduction a pleasing little piano figuration in two-fold descent is followed by a graceful triplet in b. 2; in b. 3 the tune is harmonized in euphonious tenths between the hands; while in b. 4 the piano writing in thirds suggests a pair of flutes. The length of the introduction – two extra bars beyond the usual four – avoids any suggestion of the predictable or four-square.

For the first two lines of the poem the piano doubles the voice very much in the old style of earlier lieder composers, but at 'Der durch des Schlafes Hülle bricht' (bb. 11–12) the part-writing diverges and fills out the texture as if stronger light and greater warmth were gradually seeping into the song. The last two lines of the verse are repeated and in bb. 15–16 the voice touches a high A in a marvellous setting of 'Der <u>durch</u> des Schlafes Hülle bricht'. There is something exultant about the voice stepping outside the confines of the stave in this manner, breaking through the veil of sleep while always retaining a measure of classical control (a piano dynamic reigns throughout the setting).

We expect the postlude to finish a bar sooner than it does. With this asymmetrical five-bar ending, Schubert preserves a touch of unconventionality in a song that might otherwise have been written by his forbears. As a whole, *Morgenlied* is conceived in what John Reed terms 'the traditional vernacular style', and yet eight years later this same poet inspired the Romantic masterpieces *Auf dem Wasser zu singen* D774 and *Die Mutter Erde* D788.

Stolberg's poem has eleven strophes of which 1, 2, 3, 4 and 5 are printed here. Only the first of these was written out by the composer, but repeat marks indicate more verses. All eleven of these are printed by the NSA as underlay to the music. For the Hyperion Edition only the first two strophes were recorded.

Autograph:	British Library, London (first draft)
First edition:	Published as part of the AGA in 1895 (P574)
Subsequent editions:	Not in Peters; AGA XX 126: Vol. 3/54; NSA IV: Vol. 9/10
Discography and timing:	Fischer-Dieskau I 5[11] 2'16
	Hyperion I 22[2]
	Hyperion II 9[14] 1'53 Lorna Anderson

← *Abendständchen an Lina D265*   *Trinklied D267* →

MORGENLIED   Morning song
(ANONYMOUS) **D381** [H226]
C major   24 February 1816

Die_ fro - he neu - be - leb - te_ Flur

(17 bars)

Die frohe neubelebte Flur	The newly awakened fields
Singt ihrem Schöpfer Dank.	Sing joyful thanks to their Creator.
O Herr und Vater der Natur.	O Lord and Father of nature,
Dir tön' auch mein Gesang.	Let my song also resound for You!
Der Lebensfreuden schenkst du viel	You bestow many of life's pleasures
Dem, der sich weislich freut.	On him who can enjoy them wisely.
Dies sei, o Vater, stets das Ziel	Let this, O Father, always be my aim
Bei meiner Fröhlichkeit.	In my happiness.
Ich kann mich noch des Lebens freun	I can still enjoy life
In dieser schönen Welt;	In this beautiful world;
Mein Herz soll dem geheiligt sein	My heart shall be consecrated to Him
Der weislich sie erhält.	Who in His wisdom sustains the world.
[. . .]	[. . .]

ANONYMOUS/UNKNOWN

*This is the eighth of Schubert's nineteen solo settings of an anonymous poet. See Anonymous/
Unknown for a chronological list of all the songs for which the poets are unknown.*

This was written on the same day as a companion *Abendlied* (D382) in F major and with a
similar hymn-like quality. Both songs have an unknown (possibly the same) author. The opening
notes of *Morgenlied* suggest a Papageno aria in slow motion, but the piece is not comical and
progresses with well-crafted decorum. A great deal of it consists in the piano dutifully doubling,

or at leasy shadowing, the vocal line, making the ingenious harmonization of bb. 13–15 seem even more inventive. In February 1816 Schubert remained with his nose to the teacher's grindstone, a hard fate considering that the young genius's great song-composing year of 1815 was behind him; but Schubert *père* still failed to see the point of his son's spending a life in music. The symmetry of beginning and ending a schoolday with songs like this *Morgenlied* (or the Claudius setting *Täglich zu singen* D533, composed a year later) seems plausible – although most Schubert songs for the schoolroom (if those provided on occasion for his brother Ferdinand are anything to go by) were not as fresh and graceful as this. 'I can still enjoy life / In this beautiful world' says the anonymous poet, and Schubert seems to have been determined to extricate himself from misery. In April 1816 he made an unsuccessful application for a job as a school music teacher in Laibach, or Ljubljana as it is in present-day Slovenia. Had he won the post, his compositional life might have taken a different course.

Autograph:	Beinecke Rare Book and Manuscript Collection, New Haven
First edition:	Published as part of the AGA in 1895 (P621)
Subsequent editions:	Not in Peters; AGA XX 189: Vol. 4/29; NSA IV: Vol. 10/42
Discography and timing:	Fischer-Dieskau I 6[14] 1'47
	Hyperion I 5[13]
	Hyperion II 12[21] 2'04 Elizabeth Connell

← *Das Grab* D377   *Abendlied* D382 →

MORGENLIED   Morning song
(WERNER) OP. 4 NO. 2, **D685** [H441]
A minor   1820

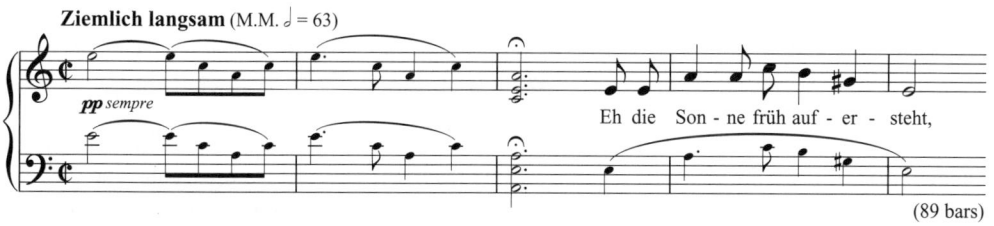

(89 bars)

Eh' die Sonne früh aufersteht,	Before the sun rises early,
Wenn aus dem dampfenden Meer	When from the misty sea
Herauf und herunter das Morgenrot weht,	Dawn wafts in from above and below,
Voranfährt mit dem leuchtenden Speer:—	Surging ahead with shining spear;
Flattern Vöglein dahin und daher,	Little birds flit to and fro,
Singen fröhlich die Kreuz und die Quer	Singing merrily here and there
Ein Lied, ein jubelndes Lied.	A song, a jubilant song.
Was freut ihr Vöglein euch allzumal	Why are you all so delightfully happy, little birds,
So herzig im wärmenden Sonnenstrahl?	In the sun's warming rays?
'Wir freu'n uns, dass wir leben und sind,	'We are happy to be alive,
'Und dass wir luft'ge Gesellen sind,	'And to be companions of the air;
'Nach löblichem Brauch	'In the time-honoured tradition

'Durchflattern wir fröhlich den Strauch;	'We flutter merrily through the bushes,
'Unweht vom lieblichen Morgenwind,	'Fanned by the sweet morning breeze;
'Ergetzet die Sonne sich auch.'	'And the sun, too, rejoices.'
Was sitzt ihr Vöglein so stumm und geduckt	Why do you little birds sit so dumb and hunched up
Am Dach im moosigen Nest?	In your mossy nests on the roof?
'Wir sitzen, weil uns die Sonn' nicht beguckt;	'We sit here because the sun is not looking at us;
'Schon hat sie die Nacht in die Wellen geduckt:	'Night has already dipped it in the waves;
'Der Mond allein,	'The moon alone,
'Der liebliche Schein,	'That sweet light,
'Der Sonne lieblicher Widerschein,	'The sun's sweet reflection,
'Uns in der Dunkelheit nie verlässt,	'Never forsakes us in the dark:
'Darob wir im Stillen uns freu'n.'	'Therefore we quietly rejoice.'
O Jugend, kühlige Morgenzeit,	O youth, cool morning hour,
Wo wir, die Herzen geöffnet und weit,	When, with hearts wide open,
Mit raschem und erwachendem Sinn,	With quickened, awakening senses,
Des Lebens-Frische uns erfreut,	We delighted in life's freshness,
Wohl flohst du dahin—dahin!—	You have fled, alas.
Wir Alten sitzen geduckt im Nest!—	We old ones sit huddled in our nests;
Allein der liebliche Widerschein	But the sweet reflection
Der Jugendzeit,	Of our youth,
Wo wir im Frührot uns erfreut,	When we rejoiced in the dawn,
Uns auch im Alter nie verlässt—	Never forsakes us, even in old age:
Die stille, sinnige Fröhlichkeit!	That calm, pensive happiness.

ZACHARIAS WERNER (1768–1823)

This is the second of Schubert's two Werner solo settings (1817 and 1820). See the poet's biography for a chronological list of all the Werner settings.

The poem comes from Act I Scene 2 of Werner's play, *Die Söhne des Tals* ('The sons of the valley'). It is sung by the gardener Philipp who is really the exiled duke of Anjou. The scene is Cyprus, the year 1306, the plot a quasi-medieval farrago of Knights Templar and secret brotherhoods. It is a very long play and maybe Schubert read it all, or perhaps he had tired of it by the time he reached this lyric. Philipp the noble gardener sings while he works.

The A minor tonality of this song with contrasting episodes in A major is similar to the almost contemporary *Strophe aus 'Die Götter Griechenlands'* D677. A number of works in this most magical of Schubert's tonalities switch between major and minor as between past and present, dream and reality, between 'then' and 'now', or 'here' and 'there'. In *Strophe aus 'Die Götter Griechenlands'* we are left in no doubt that the ethos of classical Greece is heartbreakingly irreconcilable with Schubert's present.

Morgenlied is not quite in that class. But it too is a quasi-philosophical reflection on opposites – man and nature, youth and old age. Its mood might be termed populist, or 'homespun metaphysical' – like the charismatic preaching of Zacharias Werner himself, a famous German playwright who converted to Catholicism and became an honorary canon of St Stephan's cathedral in Vienna. The song must once have been much more popular than it is today to have merited inclusion in Volume 2 of Edition Peters, and Schubert himself must have valued it too:

he chose to publish the work as part of his Op. 4 in 1821 and to dedicate it to the celebrated cleric Ladislaus Pyrker, Patriarch of Venice. Such was Werner's religious celebrity at the time. To this poet, and to Schmidt von Lübeck (who wrote the words for *Der Wanderer* D489), belong the honour of being the first contemporary writers, apart from Goethe of course, whose work was published in conjunction with Schubert's music. (Mayrhofer's *Erlafsee* D586 was in fact the first-ever published Schubert song, but that was only as part of an almanac.) Although *Morgenlied* is today rarely included in recitals, Schubert had high hopes for its popularity. On the autograph the following words are scrawled in the composer's handwriting: 'NB I recommend this song very specially to the singer P and the pianist!! 1820.' In this way, Pepi [Josefine] Koller and her accompanist Albert Stadler in Steyr were sent, probably via Vogl, the manuscript of a new song. There is a naivety in this music (an impression strengthened by the fact that the song is more or less strophic) which is very much a part of the composer's natural response to the words. This may sound twee to some, but audiences of yesteryear, as well as many listeners today, would feel at home with the domestic Schubert and the felicities of this *Morgenlied*.

The solemn opening melody in A minor, doubled by the piano, is expressive of the grey misty hour that precedes the radiance of dawn. The first few bars of this introductory section are heard only once; at 'Herauf und herunter das Morgenrot weht' (bb. 6–8) we hear the dactylic snatch of melody that is incorporated into later strophes and which represents (as always with Schubert when employing this rhythm) the workings of nature – in this case the arrival of dawn and the warming of the sun's rays. Then follows a delightful contrast of speed and colour: the twitterings of birdsong at morningtide. A double bar line changes the key signature and lets in the light; as minor changes to major, the birds, winged messengers of unwitting philosophical bent, take part in a delightfully merry dance (a cancan of worms perhaps) that is so upbeat and pretty that it borders on the kitsch. But no song composer ever lost sales by writing popular tunes, and there may have been an element of consciously wooing the public here. The piano interlude at the end of the first verse (from b. 19) adds chirpy mordents to hopping quavers.

The next section of contrasted panels of minor and major takes the form of a dialogue in question-and-answer form. Jaded mankind can only regard this merriment among the birds as a thing of mystery. 'What makes you so happy?' they ask – in the minor key of course. We may have expected another bird-dance in reply – and this indeed will come – but not before we enjoy a more tranquil moment of vintage, not to say essential, Schubert. 'We rejoice that we live and exist' shows the wisdom of the animal kingdom. It is a simple reply worthy of the composer's own sane attitude to life and his ability to rejoice in the here and now. With another set of double bar lines – and another change to the major key, Schubert makes of 'Wir freu'n uns, dass wir leben und sind' something strangely touching, with soft doublings in the accompaniment relegated exclusively to the treble stave as if the birds, were they pianists, would be too childlike and innocent to play with both hands. This aura of trusting artlessness is underlined by horn music in thirds and sixths. The horn is the quintessential instrument of the great outdoors, its sounds representing the depths of forests and, by extension, the depths of nature itself. Schubert's musical language for the birds owes much to his Schlegel settings where we find similar affectionate simplifications in such songs as *Der Schmetterling* D633, *Die Vögel* D691 and *Der Knabe* D692. This last song also features horn music to describe the free and easy life of our feathered friends.

The music for the poem's third verse follows the same pattern of slow introduction with a minor-key melody, doubled in the piano, and a spirited contribution from the birds. From b. 51 at 'Der Mond allein, / Der liebliche Schein' Schubert loosens the strophic structure and allows a luminous reference to the moon in D major; the plagal relationship to the home key makes this utterly magical moment seem other-worldly, moonstruck. The gentleness of this softly illumined music is emphasized, by way of contrast, with the sudden reappearance of the sun, bright and jolly, in the major key. It is still nightfall of course, but even *thinking* about the sun can make these birds regain their high spirits.

As in a number of songs (*Auf dem Wasser zu singen* D774 comes to mind) it is the last strophe that makes the allegory clear and points out exactly what we human beings have to learn from the natural world. After a rueful repetition of the word 'dahin!' (bb. 71 and 72) which emphasizes that the joys of youth have flown, the middle section ('Wir Alten sitzen geduckt im Nest!' bb. 73–5) is subtly different from the other appearances of this music: instead of a passage in the unambiguous tonic major, Schubert mixes major and minor as if to balance the sad effects of old age with the continuing optimism of youth. The energy of the young may now be only an echo of former glory, but the memory is a sustaining one and it helps Philipp the gardener as he looks back to happier times. The moral is that a life spent happily and on good terms with Nature ensures an old age of equanimity. The three-bar postlude (bb. 87–9) ends on a spread arpeggio in the major key with the fifth of the chord uppermost like a question mark – 'What next?' it asks. 'Whatever it is, we had a happy time while it lasted,' is the implicit reply.

There are two versions of this song, the autograph and the first edition. The differences between them are so slight, however, that the NSA (admittedly in a very early volume of the series) has chosen not to publish the first (autograph) version separately.

Autograph:	Gesellschaft der Musikfreunde, Vienna
First edition:	Published as Op. 4 no. 2 by Cappi & Diabelli, Vienna in May 1821 (P8)
Dedicatee:	Johann Ladislaus Pyrker von Felsö-Eör
Publication reviews:	F. von Hentl 'Blick auf Schubert's Lieder', *Wiener Zeitschrift für Kunst, Literatur, Theater und Mode* No. 36 (23 March 1822), p. 289f. [Waidelich/Hilmar Dokumente I No. 146; Deutsch Doc. Biog. No. 278]
Subsequent editions:	Peters: Vol. 2/4; AGA XX 379: Vol. 6/104; NSA IV: Vol. 1a/30; Bärenreiter: Vol. 1/23
Bibliography:	Capell 1928, p. 168 Einstein 1951, p. 190
Discography and timing:	Fischer-Dieskau II 3[21] 3'58 Hyperion I 29[18] Hyperion II 22[16] 4'13 Marjana Lipovšek

← *Die Sterne* D684   *Nachthymne* D687 →

Der MORGENSTERN   The morning star
(Körner) **D172** [H80]
(Fragment) G♭ major   12 March 1815

(7 bars)

Stern der Liebe, Glanzgebilde,	Star of love, radiant image,
Glühend wie die Himmelsbraut	Glowing like the bride of heaven,
Wanderst durch die Lichtgefilde,	You move through the field of light
Kündend, dass der Morgen graut.	To herald the grey dawn.
Freundlich kommst du angezogen,	You approach in such a kindly manner,
Freundlich schwebst du himmelwärts,	And soar benignly heavenwards;
Glitzernd durch des Äthers Wogen,	Sparkling throught the ether's waves
Strahlst du Hoffnung in das Herz.	You light men's hearts with hope.

THEODOR KÖRNER (1791–1813)

This is the seventh of Schubert's sixteen Körner solo settings (1815–18). See the poet's biography for a chronological list of all the Körner settings.

As with the first version of *Liebesrausch* D164 (also to a Körner text) this hymn to Venus, the star of love, could only be included in the Hyperion Edition thanks to the completion by Reinhard Van Hoorickx of a rather small Schubertian fragment. Only the prelude to the song, and three bars of the vocal line (including the words 'Stern der Liebe, Glanzgebilde'), have survived. The autograph also contains three other complete Körner settings (D168, D169, D170). As is sometimes the case with fragments, it is a possibility that the surviving bars form a preliminary sketch for a song that has been completed elsewhere and subsequently lost. It is more likely, however, that in the heat of inspiration the composer simply moved on to something else that appealed more to him at the time. In the case of *Der Morgenstern* this is a pity because the few bars we have are extremely expressive. The *bel canto* line of the melody in G flat (a key Schubert associates with peace, harmony and rapture) is well suited to the words, and holds out promise of one of those impassioned tenor arias with triplet accompaniment that were a Schubertian speciality of the time.

Reinhard Van Hoorickx solved the problem of completing this fragment by going to the composer's second setting of the words (D203) from May 1815. This was one of five songs, not included in this book (with two texts by Hölty and three by Körner), written for two unaccompanied voices or two horns.[1] These were probably *pièces d'occasion* that Schubert composed for outdoor performance during country excursions beyond Vienna in the warm month of May. The opening of the piano-accompanied version recorded for Hyperion suggests horns anyway with its alternating thirds and sixths and both songs bear the marking 'Lieblich' ('charming'). As the two settings seem related in various ways, Van Hoorickx has taken the vocal line from D203 (from 'Glühend wie die Himmelsbraut' to the end of the song) and transposed it from E flat to G flat. It so happens that the two tunes join up happily and that this transposition provides the tenor voice with a tessitura matching Schubert's original intention. The justification for this completion (if one were needed) is that it would have been a pity to lose the wonderful opening phrase entirely. Although the entire vocal line is genuine Schubert, the text printed above uses italics for the passages completed by Van Hoorickx.

Autograph:	Houghton Library, Harvard University, Cambridge, MA
First edition:	Completed and published privately by Reinhard Van Hoorickx; subsequently as part of the NSA in 2009 (P858)

[1] The songs are *Mailied* D199, *Mailied* D202, *Der Morgenstern* D203, *Jägerlied* D204 and *Lutzows wilde Jagd* D205.

| Subsequent editions: | Not in Peters; Not in AGA; NSA IV: Vol. 8/206 |
| Discography and timing: | Fischer-Dieskau — |

Hyperion I 20[17]

Hyperion II 5[20]   1'39   John Mark Ainsley

← *Gebet während der Schlacht* D171   *Das war ich* D174 →

KARL LUDWIG METHUSALEM MÜLLER (1771–1837)

THE POETIC SOURCES

S1 *Ivanhoe.*, Nach dem Englischen von Walter Scott, Neue verbesserte Auflage, Erster Theil, Wien, Gedruckt bey Anton Strauss, 1825

S2 *Ivanhoe.*, Nach dem Englischen des Walter Scott, von K. L. Meth. Müller, Zweyter Theil, Leipzig, 1820, J. C. Hinrichs'sche Buchhandlung

THE SONG

March 1826   *Romanze des Richard Löwenherz* D907 [S1: Siebzehntes Kapitel, 'Des Kreuzfahrers Ruckkehr' pp. 242–4] [S2: Siebzehntes Kapitel, 'Des Kreuzfahrers Rückkehr', pp. 41–2]

Karl Müller (almost always known by his third name 'Methusalem' to distinguish him from the many other Müllers working in the world of German letters) was born in Steudiz near Leipzig on 16 June 1771. After university he became a private tutor and worked for the duke of Sachsen-Hildburghausen from whom he received the title of *Hofrat*. Between 1795 and 1802 he published eight volumes of poetry and at least three novels, now completely forgotten. Müller's *Historische Gemälde* (1797–1808) is a twenty-volume biographical encyclopaedia of notables, from celebrated courtesans of ancient Greece to Attila, Oliver Cromwell and Warren Hastings. In 1810 he began working for the *Zeitung für die elegante Welt*, an influential Leipzig paper, and in 1816 he took over the editorial reins from August Mahlmann (a poet who combined his own literary work with journalism, as did Müller),

remaining there until 1832. He translated many novels from both English and French. Oskar Wolff notes that although he did not occupy a place of the first rank in the literary world, Müller was an utterly worthy writer. The fact that his name is not even mentioned on the Viennese reprint of the Leipzig-published *Ivanhoe* translation is an indication that he lacked much of a reputation outside his native Leipzig. As the Viennese volume was almost certainly Schubert's source the composer may never have known the name of the man who rendered into German the song of Richard the Lionheart disguised as the Black Knight. On the other hand, as the song was published in 1828 (as Op. 86) there were plenty of chances for Müller to hear his translation set to Schubert's music. Müller died in Leipzig on 15 October 1837.

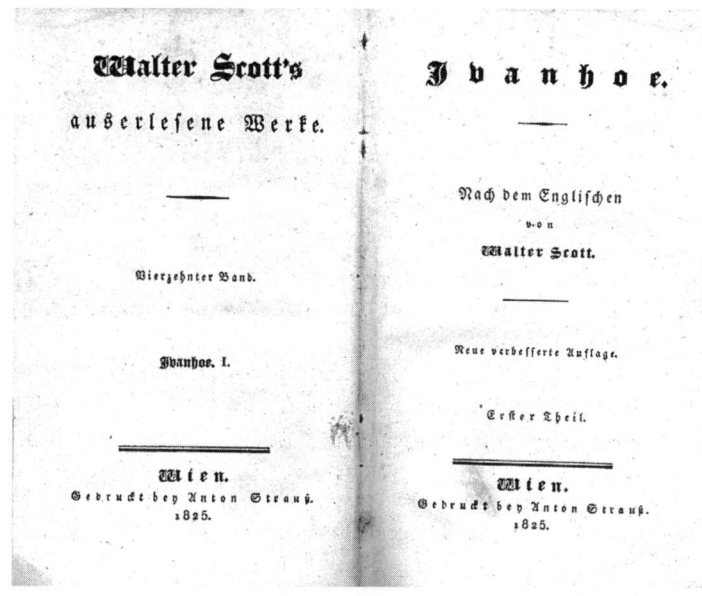

Ivanhoe, Viennese edition (1820) with no mention of the translator, K. M. Müller.

(JOHANN LUDWIG) WILHELM MÜLLER (Griechen-Müller) (1794–1827)

THE POETIC SOURCES

S1 *Sieben und siebzig Gedichte aus den hinterlassenen Papieren eines reisenden Waldhornisten.* Herausgegeben von Wilhelm Müller. Dessau 1821, Bei Christian Georg Ackermann. Druck und Papier von Friedrich Vieweg in Braunschweig

Die schöne Müllerin pp. 1–50 [separate poems had earlier been published in the almanac *Gaben der Milde*, 1818 – Nos 1, 2; in Fouqué's *Frauentaschenbuch für das Jahr 1818* – Nos 5, 10; in Fouqué's *Frauentaschenbuch für das Jahr 1821* No. 7; in the periodical *Der Gesellschafter* May– June 1818, Nos 6, 11, 14, 15, 16, 17, 18, 19, 20]

S2 *Urania. Taschenbuch auf das Jahr 1823.* Neue Folge, fünfter Jahrgang. Mit sieben Kupfern: Böttigers Bildnis gestochen von Schwerdgeburth in Weimar und sechs Darstellungen aus Shakespeare's König Lear, Othello, Macbeth, gestochen, nach Zeichnungen von Opiz, von Adam, Leclerc, Coupé und Delvaux in Paris. Leipzig: F. A. Brockhaus, 1823.

Wanderlieder von Wilhelm Müller. Die Winterreise. In 12 Liedern pp. 209–22
A selection of thirty-three poems from Rückert's *Liebesfrühling* (including poems set by Schumann such as 'Du meine Seele, du mein Herz' and 'Der Himmel hat eine Träne geweint' is printed in the same almanac between pp. 297 and 328

S3 *Gedichte aus den hinterlassenen Papieren eines reisenden Waldhornisten.* Herausgegeben von Wilhelm Müller. Zweites Bändchen, Dessau 1824, Bei Christian Georg Ackermann. Druck und Papier von Joh. Chr. Fritsche in Dessau.

Die Winterreise pp. 75–108, *Ländliche Lieder* pp. 109–36.
Very unusually this book has a second title page: *Lieder des Lebens und der Liebe* herausgegeben
von Wilhelm Müller Dessau 1824. This perhaps indicates that it was a last-minute decision on
the poet's part to make this collection officially a continuation of S1. Because of the binding it
was impossible to remove the *Lieder des Lebens und der Liebe* title, and a new one was simply
added at the front. Just to make the point clear, yet another page was added in front of the new
title: *Gedichte eines reisenden Waldhornisten* II. The dedication page after the title is 'Dem
Meister des deutschen Gesanges Carl Maria von Weber als ein Pfand seiner Freundschaft und
Verehrung gewidmet von dem Herausgeber'. (Dedicated to the master of German Song, Carl
Maria von Weber, as a token of the friendship and esteem of the author [editor]).

S4 *Urania. Taschenbuch auf das Jahr 1822.* Neue Folge, vierter Jahrgang. Mit sieben Kupfern:
Tiecks Bildnis und sechs Darstellungen zu Shakespeare's König Lear, Kaufmann von Venedig,
Othello und Macbeth, gestochen von Coupé, Delvaux, Adam, Bein und Leclerc in Paris. Leipzig:
F. A. Brockhaus, 1822

Sechs ländliche Lieder von Wilhelm Müller (only 5 printed!) pp. 416–25. [This volume of *Urania*
was banned by the Austrian censor in September 1821, as a letter to the publisher Brockhaus
from Müller in October 1821 makes clear. Although it is possible that Schubert had a smuggled
copy of this almanac at his disposal, the use of S3 is much more likely, or even the use of handwritten text provided by Anna Milder-Hauptmann.]

THE SONGS

May–September 1823   *Die Schöne Müllerin* D795/1–20
Das Wandern no. 1 [[the original title in *Gaben der Milde* Vol. IV, 1818,
was *Wanderlust*]; S1: as *Wanderschaft* pp. 7–8]
Wohin? no. 2 [[the original title in *Gaben der Milde* vol. IV, 1818, was
Der Bach]; S1: pp. 9–10]
Halt! no. 3 [S1: p. 11]
Danksagung an den Bach no. 4 [S1: pp. 12–13]
Am Feierabend no. 5 [S1: p. 14] [the original title in *Frauentaschenbuch
für das Jahr 1818* was *Feierabend* pp. 347–8]
Der Neugierige no. 6 [S1: pp. 15–16]
Ungeduld no. 7 [S1: pp. 20–21] this poem appeared in *Frauentaschenbuch
für das Jahr 1821* (p. 401) a few months before the printing of S1.
Morgengruss no. 8 [S1: pp. 22–3]
Des Müllers Blumen no. 9 [S1: pp. 24–5] [the original title in
Frauentaschenbuch für das Jahr 1818 was *Meine Blumen*, pp. 346–7]
Tränenregen no. 10 [S1: pp. 26–7] [*Frauentaschenbuch, 1818* – as above
– pp. 348–9]
Mein! no. 11 [S1: p. 28] [the original title in *Der Gesellschafter*, no. 86,
May 1818, was *Das schönste Lied*]
Pause no. 12 [S1: p. 29]
Mit dem grünen Lautenbande no. 13 [S1: p. 30]
Der Jäger no. 14 [S1: pp. 31–2] [the original title in *Der Gesellschafter*,
no. 87, June 1818, was *Als er den Jäger sah*]
Eifersucht und Stolz no. 15 [S1: p. 33] [the original title in *Der
Gesellschafter*, no. 87, June 1818, was *Trotzige Eifersucht*]
Die liebe Farbe no. 16 [S1: pp. 37–8]

Die böse Farbe no. 17 [S1: pp. 39–40] [the original title in *Der Gesellschafter*, no. 90, June 1818, was *Das böse Grün*]

Trockne Blumen no. 18 [S1: pp. 43–4] [the original title in *Der Gesellschafter*, no. 90, June 1818, was *Müllers trockne Blumen*]

Der Müller und der Bach no. 19 [S1: pp. 45–6]

Des Baches Wiegenlied no. 20 [S1: pp. 47–8] [the original title in *Der Gesellschafter*, no. 91, June 1818, was *Wiegenlied des Baches*]

The poems that Schubert did not set from Müller's *Die schöne Müllerin* are as follows:

Der Dichter als Prolog [S1: pp. 3–6]

Das Mühlenleben [S1: pp. 17–19]

Erster Schmerz, letzter Scherz [S1: pp. 34–6]

Blümlein Vergissmein [S1: pp. 41–2]

Der Dichter, als Epilog [S1: pp. 49–50]

February–October 1827   *WINTERREISE* D911/1–24

Gute Nacht no. 1 [S2: as *Gute Nacht!* pp. 209–10) [S3: pp. 77–8, also no. 1 in Müller's revised order of 1824]

Die Wetterfahne no. 2 [S2: p. 211] [S3: pp. 79–80, also no. 2 in Müller's revised order of 1824]

Gefrorne Tränen no. 3 [S2: p. 212] [S3: p. 80, also no. 3 in Müller's revised order of 1824]

Erstarrung no. 4 [S2: p. 213] [S3: pp. 81–2, also no. 4 in Müller's revised order of 1824]

Der Lindenbaum no. 5 [S2: pp. 214–15] [S3: pp. 83–4, also no. 5 in Müller's revised order of 1824]

Wasserflut no. 6 [S2: p. 216] [S3: p. 86, no. 7 in Müller's revised order of 1824]

Auf dem Flusse no. 7 [S2: p. 217] [S3: p. 87–8, no. 8 in Müller's revised order of 1824]

Rückblick no. 8 [S2: p. 218] [S3: pp. 89–90, no. 9 in Müller's revised order of 1824]

Irrlicht no. 9 [S2: p. 219] [S3: p. 99, no. 18 in Müller's revised order of 1824]

Rast no. 10 [S2: p. 220] [S3: pp. 100–101, no. 19 in Müller's revised order of 1824]

Frühlingstraum no. 11 [S2: pp. 220–21] [S3: pp. 103–4, no. 21 in Müller's revised order of 1824]

Einsamkeit no. 12 [S2: pp. 221–2] [S3: p. 105, no. 22 in Müller's revised order of 1824]

[As all the above twelve songs were found in S2 (and only twelve poems were printed there), the source of the remainder of the songs is exclusively S3 where all twenty-four poems are printed – in a different order however from S2, and thus in a different order from the published song cycle. Schubert decided to preserve the order of the twelve earlier songs as he had found them in S2.]

Die Post no. 13 [S3: p. 85] [no. 6 in Müller's revised order of 1824]

Der greise Kopf no. 14 [S3: p. 91, no. 10 in Müller's revised order of 1824]

Die Krähe no. 15 [S3: p. 92, no. 11 in Müller's revised order of 1824]

Letzte Hoffnung no. 16 [S3: p. 93, no. 12 in Müller's revised order of 1824]

Im Dorfe no. 17 [S3: p. 94, no. 13 in Müller's revised order of 1824]

Der stürmische Morgen no. 18 [S3: p. 95, no. 14 in Müller's revised order of 1824]

Täuschung no. 19 [S3: p. 96, no. 15 in Müller's revised order of 1824]

Der Wegweiser no. 20 [S3: p. 97, no. 16 in Müller's revised order of 1824]

Das Wirtshaus no. 21 [S3: p. 98, no. 17 in Müller's revised order of 1824]

Mut no. 22 [S3: p. 106, no. 23 in Müller's revised order of 1824]

Die Nebensonnen no. 23 [S3: p. 102, no. 20 in Müller's revised order of 1824]

Der Leiermann no. 24 [S3: p. 107, also 24 in Müller's revised order of 1824]

October 1828   *Der Hirt auf dem Felsen* D965. The text set by Schubert for this song is made up of three separate poems, the first and third by Müller. First Section beginning 'Wenn auf dem höchsten Fels ich steh'': [S3: *Der Berghirt* pp. 111–12, only the first four strophes set by Schubert. Third section beginning 'Der Frühling will kommen': *Liebesgedanken* pp. 122–4, only the second strophe set by Schubert] [S4: *Der Berghirt* pp. 419–20 and *Liebesgedanken* pp. 422–3] The author of the two strophes of the song's middle section (beginning 'In tiefem Gram vezehr ich mich') is Karl Varnhagen von Ense (qv).

Wilhelm Müller, nicknamed 'Griechen-Müller' ('Greek Müller') because of his interest in the Greek political cause (see below), was born on 7 October 1794 in Dessau. He was the son of a shoemaker, the only child of six to survive. His parents loved him and were ambitious for him, doing everything to ensure that he had a good start in life. When his mother died (he was eleven) his father remarried and he was fortunate to have an equally affectionate stepmother. At the age of fourteen he prepared a volume of *Elegien, Oden und kleine Lieder* with as much care as if it were about to be printed, and he also wrote a play.

In 1812, at the age of eighteen, he went to Berlin to study philology and history. His studies were interrupted by the outbreak of the patriotic war to rid German-speaking lands of Napoleonic rule. In February 1813 he volunteered for the Prussian army (in the Gardejäger Regiment) and fought in the battles at Lützen, Bautzen, Hanau and Kulm. His regimental duties took him as far afield as Prague and Brussels after which he returned to Dessau. During the time he was stationed in Brussels he had an unhappy relationship with a woman which may have had some bearing on the mood of his later *Winterreise* poems. He resumed his university place in Berlin in 1815 where he made a special study of German literature of the Middle Ages. That year he published an anthology of writings, *Blumenlese aus den Minne Sängern* with a foreword that established his pioneering position in a work of this kind. On 18 October he wrote a famous diary entry that lovers of Schubert's music have always found both touching and uncanny: 'I can neither play nor sing, yet when I write verses I sing and play after all. If I could produce the tunes, my songs would please better than they do now. But courage! A kindred spirit may be found who will hear the tunes behind the words and give them back to me.' As Alec Robertson wrote in a programme note for a Pears–Britten recording, 'They were, indeed, given back to him in undreamt-of measure.'

In actual fact Müller was probably referring to someone he had met already, the composer Ludwig Berger (1777–1829) [*see* COMPOSERS] who was a (slightly older) member of the poet's circle of Berlin friends and later Felix Mendelssohn's piano teacher. This group of lively young minds which gathered at the home of Friedrich von Stägemann included such important personalities as Achim von Arnim and the painter Wilhelm Hensel. The Lieder-spiel games, half poetry and half music, with which these creative young people entertained themselves formed the basis of the work that eventually became *Die schöne Müllerin*. The commentary on that cycle discusses its genesis as well as giving a more detailed account of Müller's life during the Berlin years (1815–17), including his infatuation with Luise Hensel. This lieder circle was dissolved when Napoleon returned from Elba and the Europeans had to take up arms once more. On this occasion Müller stayed in Berlin to finish his studies.

Wilhelm Müller by Julius Schnorr von Carolsfeld, 1818.

Müller's exceptionally personable nature was always at its best in merry company. Contacts with literary luminaries such as Tiedge, Brentano and Fouqué led to the inclusion of his work in the anthology *Bundes-blüthen* in 1816. Müller seems to have had a great gift for languages and at the invitation of Arnim he translated Christopher Marlowe's *Doctor Faustus* from the English with considerable skill. (It would not have escaped Müller's notice that Marlowe, too, was the son of a shoemaker.) The advertisement (probably written by Müller himself) for the book praised 'the godlike freedom from all restrictions that Shakespeare and the British Constitution has made possible'. For his background research on Marlowe he began to read English newspapers and through them a keen interest in politics was awakened.

In August 1817 he set off with Baron Sack on a visit to Egypt, Greece and the Middle East on behalf of the Berlin Academy of Sciences. This included a two-month stop in Vienna where he acquainted himself with the theatrical scene and learned to speak modern Greek (in Vienna there was a large community of deracinated Greeks, refugees from the Turkish rule of their country). Recent research by Rita Steblin has raised the possibility that Müller was in contact with one of Schubert's friends and poets, Franz Xaver von Schlechta, during this Viennese visit. As a result of the plague reported in Constantinople, Müller and Sack changed course for Italy, passing through Venice and Florence and reaching Rome on 4 January 1818. The pair stayed there until Easter but when the poet wanted to revel in Roman life longer still, Sack went on to Egypt with somebody else. This change of plan was to deny Müller the chance to visit Greece, but compensations for the extended Italian sojourn included visits to Naples and Albano, as well as shorter stays in Orvieto and Perugia and the writing of the book *Rom, Römer und Römer-innen* (published in 1820). This was a thoroughly engaging description of everyday life and literature in the Italy of that time that met with disapproval in some German quarters because of its obvious admiration for the free and easy (and openly sensual) Italian lifestyle. Müller was never a man to study things by halves – the grand tour, taking in a great many places in a relatively short space of time, was not for him. He began to study Italian folk poetry and folksong methodically, until all the materials were in place for a book on this subject (*Egeria – Raccolta di Poesie Italiane popolari da Gugliemo Mueller*), published posthumously in 1829. One of his written exercises, listing an Italian verb in all its tenses and moods (with dialect variants) is in my collection. The poet reluctantly left Rome at the end of August 1818, returning via dalliance in Florence to study the paintings there, then Verona, the Tyrol and Munich.

He found himself back in Berlin at the beginning of 1819 and was almost immediately summoned to Dessau by his duke who offered him a post as teacher of classical languages in the newly rebuilt Gymnasium. He was soon appointed librarian to the Hofbibliothek and founded a monthly revue, *Askania*, publishing his poetry regularly in various smaller almanacs and reviews. From this time he began to achieve a great reputation for his ability to adopt in his poetry whatever persona he chose – miller, shepherd, hunter, postillon and so on – always finding an appropriate tone to describe the happiness and sadnesses of such simple folk. In 1821 he married Adelheid Basedow who was a granddaughter of Johann Basedow, the celebrated educational reformer and pioneer of modern teaching methods. This marriage produced a son worthy of both his father and maternal great-grandfather – Max Müller (1823–1900), an orientalist, philologist and linguist who was eventually to live in England where he became one of Oxford's most famous knighted academics.

Wilhelm Müller is chiefly remembered today (outside his musical connections, that is) as the poet of Greece's struggle for emancipation from the Turks. The links with Byron are obvious (although Müller never visited Greece as soldier or even tourist), and both poets number a *Maid of Athens* among their lyrics. Müller's close reading of *Childe Harold's Pilgrimage* greatly influenced his poems published under the title *Die Winterreise*, which the poet was working on at the same time as writing a substantial biographical sketch of Byron for the Brockhaus *Conversations-Lexikon*. It is hardly surprising that with their shared enthusiasm for the Greek cause,

Wilhelm Müller, drawing by Wilhelm Hensel.

Müller regarded the English poet as nothing less than an inspired – and inspiring – hero. *Lieder der Griechen* dates from 1821, and this was followed by *Neue Lieder der Griechen* (1823) and *Neueste Lieder der Griechen* (1824). This progression of 'new' and 'newest' songs ended with *Missolonghi* (1826). These poems demonstrate Müller's own folksy and down-to-earth enthusiasm for Greek life (as he imagined it at least). They also reflect an ongoing German sympathy for the plight of the modern-day Greeks coupled with a sense of shame that the rest of Europe had allowed the country's fortunes to sink to such a low ebb when the Greece of ancient times had been the cradle of Western civilization. The poems devoted to such Greek heroes as Constantine Kanaris and the fallen freedom-fighter Marcos Bozzaris show Müller's strong awareness of modern politics.

Müller's enthusiasm for the Greeks was very different from the loftier Philhellenism that was widespread in this period. The poetry of Anacreon with its earthy hymning of wine, women and song was more to his tastes than the tragedies of Euripides, his frank and open nature in stark contrast to that of aesthetes like Platen who saw in ancient Greek life a mirror of, and justification for, their own forbidden sexual leanings. Müller was no respecter of great reputations and he seems to have been blind to the beauties of neoclassical Goethe; neither would he have enjoyed the classically inspired poems of Mayrhofer. However, among Schubert's poets these two shared liberal sympathies common to the generation that had fought against the yoke of Napoleon. Like Mayrhofer, Müller did not always please the reactionary politicians terrified of any sign of revolution nurtured by students and intellectuals. He was subject to his share of censorship, albeit much less stringent than if he had been, like Schubert's friend Johann Senn, a citizen of Vienna. Fortunately his duke in Dessau remained supportive, even expressing an interest in the suffering of the Greek people thanks to his poet's writings. Müller's overwhelming interest in folk poetry via the Greeks played an important part in developing his taste for a German folk style that influenced many of his followers, Heinrich Heine chief among them. Writing to Müller from Hamburg on 7 June 1826, Heine confessed how much of his newly appeared *Intermezzo* (later the *Lyrisches Intermezzo*, source of *Dichterliebe*) owed to Müller's example:

> I am magnanimous enough to confess to you openly that my small intermezzo metre possesses not merely an accidental similarity with your own accustomed metre, but probably owes its most secret rhythm to your songs – those dear Müller songs which I came to know at the very time I wrote the Intermezzo. *At a very early time I let German folksong exercise its influence upon me. Later on, when I studied at Bonn, August Schlegel opened many metrical secrets to me; but I believe it was in your songs that I found what I looked for – pure tone and true simplicity. How pure and clear your songs are, and they are all true folksongs . . . With the exception of Goethe*

there is no lyric poet whom I love as much as you.

Today, and particularly to the lieder enthusiast, Müller's poetry seems complementary to that of Joseph von Eichendorff (1788–1857). Both fought in the Wars of Liberation against France, and both shared an interest in popular songs and the cult of the wandering lad – the *Wanderbursch*. In this way the minstrel of the Middle Ages was revived in popular fiction (cf. Müller's *Blumenlese* from 1816). Both poets were fond of travel, sharing in particular an affection for Italy. They also both delighted in placing their narrators in the guise of soldier, student, sailor, huntsman, shepherd or fisherman. In the end it is the background and culture of the two men that differentiate them: Eichendorff the Roman Catholic from Silesia, Müller the Protestant from Dessau. The former revealed an overt religiosity in a number of his poems; the latter seldom talked about his faith – indeed Müller presents his winter traveller as a non-believer. Not all musicians found in his work the dark overtones unveiled by Schubert: Müller's poetry was set a great many times by lesser composers, and the singability of his verse encouraged music written for hearty sing-songs rather than the more refined world of art-song in the salon. On 15 December 1822 he wrote a letter congratulating the composer Bernhard Klein (1793–1832), who had set a number of the poems from *Die schöne Müllerin*, on 'the musical animation of my verses'. Müller continued, 'My songs lead but half a life, a paper life of black and white . . . until music breathes life into them, or at least calls it forth and awakens it if it is already dormant in them'. This concern with collaboration with a musician is amply illustrated by the final lines of *Die Winterreise*: the traveller–poet encounters a hurdy-gurdy player and wonders whether it is his destiny to work as part of a song-writing team. It is probably true to say that Müller, who knew nothing of Schubert's music, would have been entranced by much of the composer's *Die schöne Müllerin* – though, like Schubert's friends, he might have been at first bewildered by most of *Winterreise*.

Although Müller was a liberal and thus slightly suspect as far as the German upper classes were concerned, his sheer likeability and good-heartedness won over the Dessau establishment. In 1822 he began the publication of an important anthology of seventeenth-century German poets issued in ten volumes and completed in the year of his death; the third of these, devoted to Paul Flemming (1609–1640), was to be Brahms's source for his two Flemming settings, *O liebliche Wangen* Op. 47/4 and *An die Stolze* Op. 107/1. This profound study of early German lyrics also contributed to the concise and direct style of *Die Winterreise*, a simplicity that is combined, in admittedly unusual manner, with the high-flown Byronic pathos also admired by the poet. Müller was also a tireless contributor to a number of almanacs and yearbooks, both as poet and critic. His poetry had appeared in Förster's famous almanac, *Die Sängerfahrt*, as early as 1818, and numerous other publications and journals.

Müller was regularly employed by the publishing firm of Brockhaus in Leipzig, both as a critic in their journals and as a contributor to their famous encyclopaedia in multiple volumes – the *Conversations-Lexikon*. He was invited to contribute poems to the Brockhaus almanac, *Urania*, their flagship publication. It was in the 1823 edition of *Urania* that Franz Schubert discovered the texts of the first twelve songs of *Winterreise*. All these poems for occasional publications were often reprinted, and often expanded, in more durable book form. In 1821 and 1824 the two volumes of verse appeared for which music lovers will always remember Wilhelm Müller with gratitude: *Sieben und siebzig Gedichte aus den hinterlassenen Papieren eines reisenden Waldhornisten*. This anthology of seventy-seven poems occasioned the admiring letter from Heine quoted above. The two-volume work fancifully purports to be the posthumous papers of a travelling horn-player, and includes the texts of both Schubert cycles: *Die schöne Müllerin* appears in the first volume, and the second contains *Die Winterreise* (note that Schubert dropped the definite article from the title) in

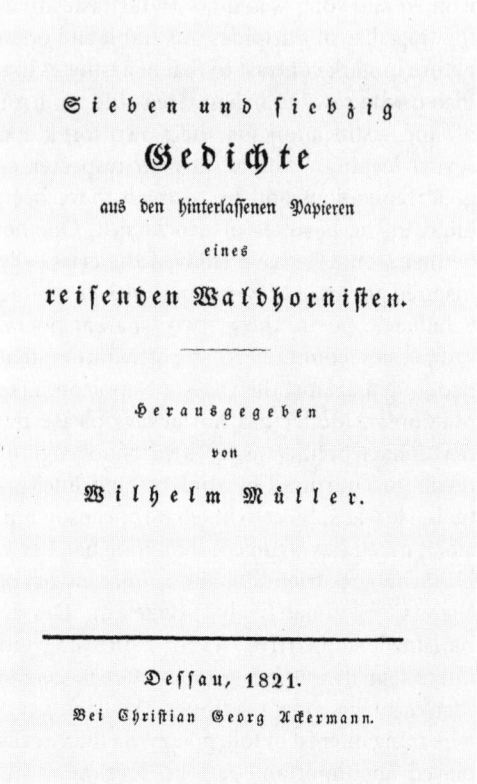

Sieben und siebzig Gedichte by Wilhelm Müller (1821).

its full twenty-four-poem version – thus with twelve more poems than Schubert had first found in *Urania*.

In 1824, shortly after his son's birth, Müller was named a *Hofrat* at the early age of twenty-seven. He established a way of life that kept him busy during the academic year in Dessau and allowed him one protracted *Sommerreise* per year. In 1824 he travelled to Dresden and then Quedlinburg to celebrate Klopstock's centenary. In 1825 his friendship with Tieck deepened, and he spent time on the island of Rügen as the guest of the poet Furchau in Stralsund. In the winter of that year his health took an alarming turn: he developed a cough that was indicative of a lung infection. The duke created a comfortable new apartment for him and his family in the Luisum in Dessau, rooms that the poet Matthisson, another favourite son of Dessau, had occupied for

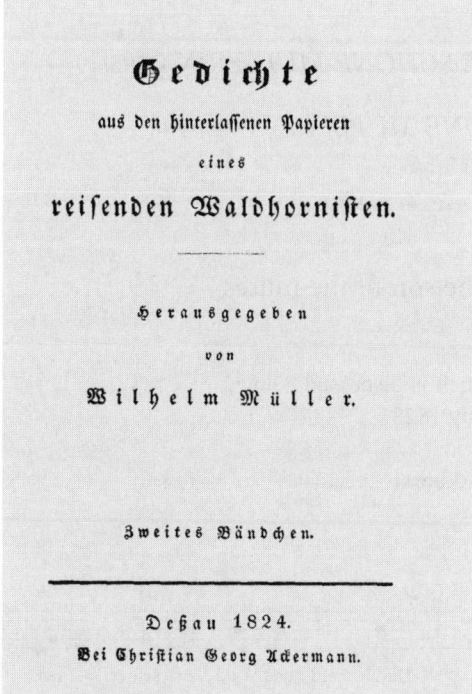

V.

Wanderlieder

von

Wilhelm Müller.

Die Winterreise. In 12 Liedern.

1. Gute Nacht!

Fremd bin ich eingezogen,
Fremd zieh' ich wieder aus.
Der Mai war mir gewogen
Mit manchem Blumenstrauß:
Das Mädchen sprach von Liebe,
Die Mutter gar von Eh' —
Nun ist die Welt so trübe,
Der Weg gehüllt in Schnee.

Ich kann zu meiner Reisen
Nicht wählen mit der Zeit,
Muß selbst den Weg mir weisen
In dieser Dunkelheit.
Es zieht ein Mondenschatten
Als mein Gefährte mit,
Und auf den weißen Matten
Such' ich des Wildes Tritt.

14

Title page for *Die Winterreise* in *Urania* (1823).   *Gute Nacht* from *Urania* (1823).

Gedichte

aus den hinterlassenen Papieren

eines

reisenden Waldhornisten.

Herausgegeben

von

Wilhelm Müller.

Zweites Bändchen.

Dessau 1824.
Bei Christian Georg Ackermann.

Gedichte aus den hinterlassenen Papieren eines reisenden Waldhornisten by Wilhelm Müller (1824).

many years. Aware of this connection with literary history, Müller prepared an entry for Matthisson's *Stammbuch* or autograph album, a dedicatory verse to the older poet ('the dear singer of Nature'), written 'in the room, and at the table, that your muse has consecrated'.

In the summer of 1826 he took a cure at Franzensbad bei Eger, which seemed to be successful. He journeyed back via Bayreuth, Nuremberg, Bamberg and Weimar where he was present at Goethe's seventy-seventh birthday celebrations and met the poet on 24 and 26 September. With his health seemingly restored, Müller enjoyed a sociable winter season in Dessau with a great deal of merriment. He always worked hard as well (in 1826 the poet broadened his scholastic activities and became involved in writing for the monumental *Encyclopädie* of Ersch and Gruber) but the summer of 1827 found him tired and stressed. The doctor prescribed another 'Erholungsreise' and the poet went with his wife on a Rhine journey from Karlsruhe to Stuttgart where they were received by his Swabian friend Gustav Schwab, and also met

Hauff and Uhland. Müller visited Weinsberg's famous doctor, Justinus Kerner (known to lovers of lieder through the songs of Schumann), although he seems to have been disturbed by that poet's spiritualist leanings which were so different from his own rational approach. In Müller's honour Kerner had hung out a Greek flag (a black cross painted on a bright blue and white background) from an old tower outside his house. During the night a rainstorm and autumn mists washed away the blue, leaving on the flag only an ominous black cross – the so-called *Leichenfahn*, or symbol of death in the house. This was a sinister portent, later the subject of a poem by Kerner – *Aus Wilhelm Müllers Besuch* – worthy of the protagonist of *Winterreise*.

The return journey to Dessau was again via Weimar. On 21 September Goethe received the poet, albeit coldly. Two days later, in a letter to a friend, he summed up Müller as 'an awkward personage, arrogant ['süffisant'], and on top of all this, a spectacle wearer'. (Goethe distrusted anyone who wore glasses, possibly because he believed lenses introduced a distortion of the truth in nature.) Müller, whose rough edges were part of his frank and open charm, was probably too ebullient and insufficiently deferential in the older poet's presence. The Müllers, husband and wife, arrived home on 25 September, Wilhelm full of all his travel impressions, perfectly relaxed. On the evening of 30 September he appeared to be in perfect health but shortly before midnight died of a stroke in his sleep. He was only thirty-three. His widow lived until 1883. On 30 September 1891 a memorial statue in Pentelican marble, partly paid for by the Greek government, was erected to him in Dessau. His celebrated son Max travelled from Oxford to deliver the address.

Bibliography: Müller 1898
                Youens 1991, pp. 50–72
                Youens 1992, pp. 1–11
                Youens 1997, pp. 1–41

Der MÜLLER UND DER BACH *see DIE SCHÖNE MÜLLERIN* D795/19

Des MÜLLERS BLUMEN *see DIE SCHÖNE MÜLLERIN* D795/9

Der MUSENSOHN   The son of the muses
(GOETHE) OP. 92 NO. 1, **D764** [H501]

The song exists in two versions, the second of which is discussed below:
(1) Beginning of December 1822; (2) appeared July 1828

(1) 'Ziemlich lebhaft'   A♭ major   §   [73 bars]

(2) G major

Durch Feld und Wald zu schweifen,	Roaming through field and wood,
Mein Liedchen wegzupfeifen,	Whistling my song,
So geht's von Ort zu Ort!	Thus I go from place to place!
Und nach dem Takte reget,	And all keep time with me,
Und nach dem Mass beweget	And all move
Sich alles an mir fort.	In measure with me.
Ich kann sie kaum erwarten,	I can scarcely wait for them,
Die erste Blum' im Garten,	The first flower in the garden,
Die erste Blüt' am Baum.	The first blossom on the tree.
Sie grüssen meine Lieder,	They greet my songs,
Und kommt der Winter wieder,	And when winter returns
Sing ich noch jenen Traum.	I am still singing my dream of them.
Ich sing' ihn in der Weite,	I sing it far and wide,
Auf Eises Läng' und Breite,	The length and breadth of the ice.
Da blüht der Winter schön!	Then winter blooms in beauty!
Auch diese Blüte schwindet,	This blossom, too, vanishes,
Und neue Freude findet	And new joys are found
Sich auf bebauten Höhn.	On the cultivated hillsides.
Denn wie ich bei der Linde	For when, by the linden tree,
Das junge Völkchen finde,	I come upon young folk,
Sogleich erreg' ich sie.	I at once stir them.
Der stumpfe Bursche bläht sich,	The dull lad puffs himself up,
Das steife Mädchen dreht sich	The prim girl whirls
Nach meiner Melodie.	In time to my tune.
Ihr gebt den Sohlen Flügel	You who give my feet wings,
Und treibt, durch Tal und Hügel,	And drive your favourite over hill and dale,
Den Liebling weit von Haus.	Far from home.
Ihr lieben, holden Musen,	Dear, gracious Muses,
Wann ruh' ich ihr am Busen	When shall I at last find rest again
Auch endlich wieder aus?	On her bosom?

JOHANN WOLFGANG VON GOETHE (1749–1832); poem written in 1774

This is the sixty-seventh of Schubert's seventy-five Goethe solo settings (1814–26). See the poet's biography for a chronological list of all the Goethe settings.

December 1822 marked Schubert's rekindled enthusiasm for the texts of Goethe, and *Der Musensohn* is the first of five of his poems that he set within a month. This little group of works marks a farewell to the poet who had been such an inspiring influence in Schubert's life, and they are a worthy conclusion to a momentous partnership. (The final versions of the Mignon songs composed in 1826 are chronologically later, but these may be classified as unfinished business from an earlier time, brought to a successful conclusion after eleven years.) In many ways *Der Musensohn* is the quintessential Schubert song, and it is a constant standby as an encore. It was surely written to woo an audience (rather in the same way that the son of the Muses himself is a charmer, capable of animating even the most unmusical), and it always succeeds in doing so. But audiences tend to enjoy this song more than the performers: the words fly by rather too quickly for the comfort of any singer who has not completely mastered the text, and the pianist has to concentrate hard as the right hand makes audacious little sorties to awkward corners of the keyboard, off the beat, while the left marks the downbeats. These excursions are somewhat perilous, with dives back to home base in the twinkling of an eye. The first version of the song (published in Volume 3b of the NSA) is hardly different from the second save in tonality, A flat major. After constantly playing the song in its original key of G major (or E major for lower voices), any accompanist is grateful not to have to play it in A flat with the resulting awkward keyboard geography. Indeed, perhaps this is why Schubert re-conceived the song in G major for publication.

The principal difficulty facing interpreters of this song is the choice of tempo. At the head of the music Schubert writes 'Ziemlich lebhaft' ('rather lively') which, for a performer without a great deal of experience of this composer's markings, may be taken to mean more or less anything. The American mezzo soprano Jan de Gaetani, for example, chose to record the song incredibly fast, an astonishing feat from both her and her accompanist, but one where the music lost the earthiness and relaxed geniality that is an essential part of Schubert's style. On the other hand the great baritone Gerhard Hüsch favoured a tempo which was so measured that it bordered on the lugubrious. Geoffrey Parsons, Hüsch's last accompanist, also believed in a stately progress for the winged messenger, rightly pointing out that the verb 'schweifen' in the first line of the poem (literally to wander) suggests sauntering rather than running. The lordly insouciance of the young godlike figure (the legend of the lute-playing Orpheus comes to mind) precludes undue haste and unseemly breathlessness; on the other hand the music must have a mercurial quality, an élan suggesting the flight of winged heels ('Ihr gebt den Sohlen Flügel'). As in all fairy-tale figures there is a touch of the demonic here: this music could be sung by a Peter Pan or Pied Piper, and it has something of Puck too, who boasts that he can 'put a girdle round the earth in forty minutes'. The son of the Muses is surely the composer himself, too portly to fly perhaps, but still capable of a beaming smile, a chuckle and, as we shall see, a hidden tear.

As always in matters relating to Schubertian tempi, a compromise is called for to avoid extremes. Thus the song should not be dazzlingly fast in virtuoso manner, and neither should it be self-consciously meaningful – after all it is meant to set the toes tapping and to excite the listener with its irrepressible gaiety. The secret, as always with Schubert, is to be guided by the time signature: here it is §, thus two in a bar in the manner of a folksong. A fast tempo, where we are conscious of only one beat per bar, misses the poise of text and music; a slow one, where six beats, or a leaden two, are heard, denies us the piquancy. One learns that when the composer writes something like 'ziemlich lebhaft' ('ziemlich' being the moderating force) he means us to tread the middle way, curbing our excitement without suppressing it.

The construction of the song is relatively simple. Goethe's five verses are set alternately in G major and B major with actual changes of key signature back and forth. The switch into B major is without the preparatory niceties of modulation. At the beginning of the second verse this abrupt change gives the heart-stopping impression of a sudden momentary dalliance as we are taken into the poet's confidence: at 'Ich kann sie kaum erwarten' (b. 29) the change of key helps depict suspense and impatience as he reflects on the beauties of spring; at the loving repetitions of 'Sing ich noch jenen Traum' (bb. 41–8) he might be closing his eyes (the roving quavers in the accompaniment have temporarily quietened to a gentle throb, as if treading water). He dreams of imaginary sights and fragrances, the very things that inspire him to new melody and keep him ever youthful. Then suddenly we are off again – the second appearance of the G major strain – and the words of the third verse have a breadth and majesty that give the bewitching creator of rhymes and melody a bird's-eye view of the whole world. Here we have a timeless perception of the changing seasons and the cyclical nature of life itself. Another change into B major and we zoom in on the village green like an aerial camera in a documentary about small-town life. Here even the most provincial of yokels, and the most inhibited of girls, are animated by the singer's powers. The pianist can have a moment of discreet fun characterizing the clod-hopping antics of the 'stumpfe Bursche', the left hand slightly accented as the boy earnestly responds to music's call and the girl's stiff limbs loosen a little.

For the last strophe we hear the music in G major for the third and final time. This makes a naturally satisfying and fitting conclusion, a merry recapitulation where the only difference from the first verse initially seems to be the slight rubato at 'am Busen', a ritardando that anticipates the vocal line's concluding phrase. There is an often overlooked 'piano' marking for the vocal line (pianissimo in the accompaniment) at 'Ihr lieben, holden Musen' (b. 100), an important change of dynamic that should be audible to the audience. Close acquaintance with what Goethe is saying in this last verse marks out *Der Musensohn* as no less important a plea for public understanding of the artist than the same poet's *Der Sänger* D149, or Schober's *Trost im Liede* D546. An artist driven by the creative spirit strives unendingly to entertain and move others, but when does he receive his own reward? When will the hard-writing composer–performer too be able to rest on the bosom of someone who loves him? Genius does not ensure happiness and it is all too easy to give out more than one receives.

The conclusion of this song reminds us how seldom Schubert asked for his own needs to be met. How many young people at the Schubertiads danced in happy enjoyment while the composer laboured at the piano to provide them with endless beautiful improvisations? And what loneliness must he have felt as he obliged them! He, more than Goethe ever did, found himself excluded from the joys and satisfactions that are daily enjoyed by those without such an exalted calling. Admired though he was as a composer, there was no one to whom he was overwhelmingly special, for whom he was 'the preferred one'. The repeat of the last two lines of this verse dwells lovingly on the notion of this imaginary moment of tenderness (the ritardando at 'am Busen'), but the song goes back into tempo for its concluding phrase as if these hopes of shared intimacy must be dismissed as a pipe dream.

Performers who really understand the poem will not make of this final page a rollicking peroration; the whole strophe has to have a new colour (aided perhaps by the addition of pedal in the accompaniment that is not necessary elsewhere), a gentle moment of longing tinged with regret, all within the context of the melody that has sauntered happily through the earlier pages. The challenge to performers is to convey, if only for a fleeting moment, the solitary state of being a great artist, someone who merits our compassion as much as our awed admiration. While the cheery postlude restores to view the poet-composer's primary role in life, that of entertainer born to delight us, the final strophe has gently reminded us that the son of the Muses, driven and possessed as he may be by his godlike talents and inner demons, is as vulnerably human as Schubert himself. As if to emphasize this fact, Brian Newbould places this song within the context of the composer's illness, for it was almost certainly towards the end of 1822 that Schubert discovered that he was suffering from syphilis:

> *If the crisis did indeed fall that early, then the Goethe songs of December, including* Der Musen-sohn . . . *could be seen as the first in a line of works, spanning the remaining six years, which seem to gain some of their intensity (be it inherent or imagined on our part) from the composer's stark realization that his existence was under threat.*

Autograph: Staatsbibliothek Preussischer Kulturbesitz, Berlin
Publication: First published as part of the AGA in 1895 (P691; first version)
                        First published as Op. 87 no. 1 (later corrected to Op. 92 no. 1) by
                        M. J. Leidesdorf, Vienna in July 1828 (P162; second version)

Dedicatee:	Josephine von Franck
Publication reviews:	*Münchener Musikzeitung*, No. 14 (3 January 1829), col. 209ff.
	[Waidelich/Hilmar Dokumente I No. 680]
Subsequent editions:	Peters: Vol. 1/253; AGA XX 416a & b: Vol. 7/48; NSA IV: Vol. 5a/3
	& Vol. 5b/182; Bärenreiter: Vol. 3/146
Bibliography:	Bell 1964, pp. 55–6
	Black 2003, p. 70 (discussion of A flat tonality of first version)
	Capell 1928, pp. 180–81
	Einstein 1951, pp. 254–5
	Fischer-Dieskau 1977, p. 161
	Newbould 1997, p. 184
Arrangements:	Arr. Tilman Hoppstock (b. 1961) for guitar accompaniment, in
	Franz Schubert: 110 Lieder (2009)
Discography and timing:	Fischer-Dieskau II 5[14] 2'09
	Hypcrion I 28[18]
	2'20 Christine Schäfer
	Hyperion II 26[6]

← *An die Entfernte* D765   *Am Flusse* D502 →

MUSIKALISCHER SCHWANK: EPISTEL 'AN HERRN JOSEF VON SPAUN' *see* HERRN JOSEF SPAUN, ASSESSOR IN LINZ D749

MUT! *see* *WINTERREISE* D911/22

Die MUTTER ERDE *see* LIED (DES LEBENS TAG IST SCHWER) D788

MUTTER GEHT DURCH IHRE KAMMERN *see* LIED D373

Schubert. A lithograph after W. H. Rieder by Auguste Lemoine.

NACH EINEM GEWITTER

After a storm

(Mayrhofer) **D561** [H370]

F major   May 1817

(29 bars)

Auf den Blumen flimmern Perlen,
P h i l o m e l e n s Klagen fliessen;
Mutiger nun dunkle Erlen
In die reinen Lüfte spriessen.[1]

Pearls glisten on the flowers;
Philomel's lament pours forth.
More boldly now, dark alders
Arise into the pure air.

Und dem Tale, so erblichen,
Kehret holde Röte wieder,
In der Blüten Wohlgerüchen[2]
Baden Vögel ihr Gefieder.

And to the valley, grown so pale,
A fair flush returns.
In the fragrance of the flowers
Birds bathe their plumage.

Hat die Brust sich ausgewittert,
Seitwärts lehnt der Gott den Bogen,—
Und sein golden Antlitz zittert
Reiner auf versöhnten Wogen.

The heart, purged by the storm
The god sets his bow aside,
And his golden countenance glitters
More clearly on the now stilled waves.

JOHANN MAYRHOFER (1787–1836)

This is the twenty-seventh of Schubert's forty-seven Mayrhofer solo settings (1814–24). See the poet's biography for a chronological list of all the Mayrhofer settings.

Schubert took this title to heart; the thunderstorm's musical equivalent is *Sturm und Drang* and *after* the storm there is only a rainbow in the blue sky – the accretions of a passionate outburst have been washed away, leaving a musical language of pristine purity. In Schubert's mind, here and *passim*, this means Mozart. The song describes the felicities of harmony and natural order, and it is perhaps no coincidence that the key of F major and the mood are reminiscent of Papageno's 'Ein Mädchen oder Weibchen' from *Die Zauberflöte*. In describing the Garden of Eden as if before the Fall, Schubert has faced a mini-storm of criticism. Capell goes so far as to doubt the

[1] Mayrhofer (1824) has 'In die *blauen* Lüfte spriessen'. For an explanation of the background to these alternative Mayrhofer readings see Editorial Note at the beginning of Johann MAYRHOFER.
[2] Mayrhofer (1824) has '*Und in duftigen* Gerüchen'.

song's authenticity, but who else but Schubert would have provided an introduction of such enchantment? Underneath a tune of the most artful naivety, the pianist's left hand paints drops of water glistening on the flowers in a chain of repeated Cs – a veritable 'raindrop prelude'. The prosody of the vocal line might be criticized; we may question why such unimportant words as the opening 'Auf den' should be set to a minim and a falling row of quavers. But then we realize that Schubert is creating, before our eyes and ears, the very string of pearls the poet has asked for in the first line of his poem. Other touches of inspiration are gently limned: the expressive lean towards G minor for the plaint of the nightingale (bb. 13–15) and an unpolluted F major arpeggio (b. 19) for the purity of 'reinen Lüfte'. It is true that the words of the subsequent verses suit the tune rather less, but one must recognize and salute Schubert's open-hearted response to one of Mayrhofer's few unreservedly happy texts. In a group of the more intense settings of that poet in recital, *Nach einem Gewitter* would provide a welcome oasis of emotional repose.

Autograph:	Bibliothèque musicale François-Lang, Abbaye de Royaumont, France
First edition:	Published as No. 5 of *Neueste Folge nachgelassener Lieder und Gesänge* by J. P. Gotthard, Vienna in 1872 (P431)
Subsequent editions:	Not in Peters; AGA XX 320: Vol. 5/116; NSA IV: Vol. 11/143
Bibliography:	Capell 1928, p. 139
Discography and timing:	Fischer-Dieskau II 1[6] 2'24
	Hyperion I 19[12]
	Hyperion II 19[4] 1'54 Felicity Lott

⟵ *Der Goldschmiedsgesell* D560   *Die Blumensprache* D519 ⟶

NACHLASS – THE DIABELLI PUBLISHING PROJECT, 1830–50

The Nachlass, the body of unpublished music left behind by a composer, is a general term that one may imagine should be applied to all the songs that Schubert did not see through the press. Many of these songs either acquired late or posthumous opus numbers, or were issued without numbering (*see* POSTHUMOUS SONGS).

However, the 'Nachlass', divided into 'Lieferungen' ('parts'), is a term almost always reserved for the issuing of about 135 of Schubert's posthumous songs and part-songs by Anton Diabelli & Co. in Vienna. The official title of this series was *Franz Schuberts nachgelassene musikalische Dichtungen für Gesang und Pianoforte: mit einer sehr schönen Titel-Vignette*. Advertisements were to be found in periodicals in the summer of 1830 that read as follows: 'Since the above-mentioned publisher [Diabelli] has acquired the complete posthumous songs of Franz Schubert as his exclusive property, there will appear from now on, at fortnightly intervals, "Consignments" containing his most splendid and superb songs, in a uniform and immaculate "Edition de Luxe".'

Diabelli very quickly dropped the idea of issuing these 'parts' at two-weekly intervals. The Nachlass turned into a twenty-year project (1830–50), masterminded by Diabelli himself, a project where musical considerations played a far less important role than did commercial opportunism. During these twenty years fifty 'Nachlass-Hefte', consecutively numbered books of songs, printed in oblong format and of varying length, were issued for sale to the public and were issued simultaneously in Paris by the firm of Richault. There were no Schubert Nachlass issues at all in the years 1834, 1836, 1839, 1841, 1843, 1844 or 1846. Soon after Schubert's death

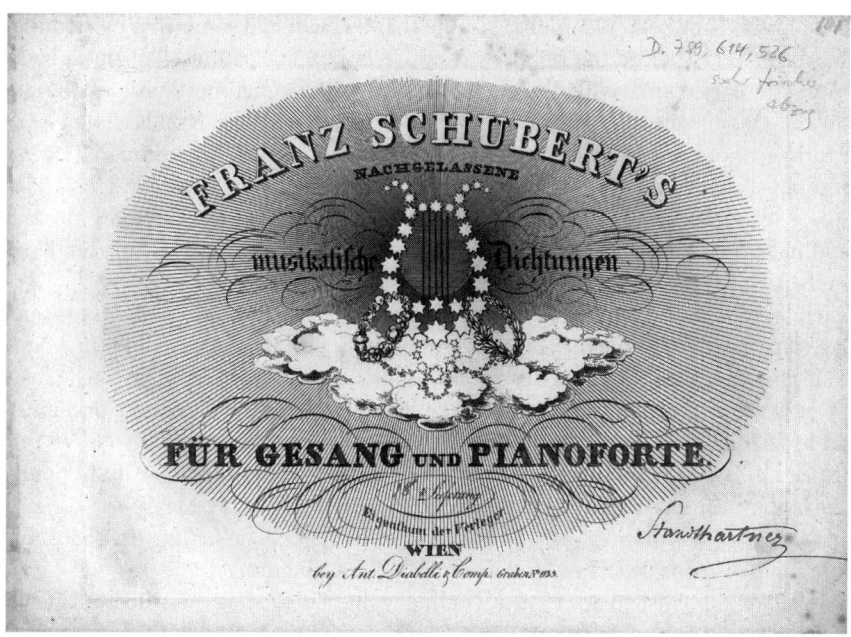

The cover for earlier issues of the Schubert *Nachlass* published by Diabelli.

Diabelli had bought a significant part of Schubert's estate, thus acquiring the rights to several published works and also a large number of important song manuscripts from Ferdinand Schubert. The composer's brother probably received a tidy sum that was useful for his immediate financial needs, but he must have later regretted selling off so much music in a job lot. Schubert manuscripts from different sources also came into Diabelli's possession, and in the course of this period he took over other firms and their stock. He thus acquired something of a Schubert monopoly. He clearly believed that it would not be opportune to issue the songs all at once – 'Make them wait – and pay for it' seems to have been his motto. Thus, many who loved the composer's songs (and impatiently longed to get to know more of them) grew old and died while Diabelli pondered the best way to maximize his investment – a way of operating that took him all the way to the end of 1850, and his own retirement, by which time he still had not published all the Schubert in his possession.

At times Diabelli seems to have felt a sense of responsibility to the composer's legacy; at others he seems to have exacted a posthumous revenge on Schubert for being a composer superior to himself. The result was that it became almost a standing joke when new songs, seemingly written by an obliging phantom in an attic, were dribbled out by the firm twenty-two years after Schubert's death. The British press (the critic of *The Musical World* in London) thought that a 'deep shade of suspicion' hung over the whole enterprise. If Diabelli had indeed had the courage to publish all the available Schubert songs in one fell swoop, the composer's true stature as a master of the lied would have been evident many years earlier.

Diabelli initially enlisted the services of Leopold von Sonnleithner, a genuine Schubert friend and enthusiast, and apparently often asked Sonnleithner's advice about how to go about issuing the songs. For this reason the project got off to a handsome and auspicious start with the issue of five volumes of Ossian settings (these had long been favourites of the older members of the Schubert circle) plus a large Schiller setting, *Elysium*. Such collaboration, however, came at a price, and Sonnleithner was persuaded to effect changes to the composer's manuscripts that he greatly regretted as time went on, making an 'ashamed confession' to the publisher Selmar Bagge in 1867 about his revising role. We might imagine that Diabelli had somewhat twisted his arm. It would be many years before the public was aware how many 'editorial' changes had been made: introductions and finales had been added and texts sometimes substantially altered, above all in the Ossian settings. (The Peters Edition included all the Nachlass songs in their published form without any attempt to remove or untangle Diabelli's revisions.) Two further fascicles of songs (7 and 8) appeared in the autumn of 1830 and included a second major Schiller ballad. If the rate of the first issues of 1830 (seven books) had been maintained the musical world would have been in possession of all these songs after six or seven years, but even this fairly leisurely pace for the unfolding of the Nachlass was not to be.

A complete numbered list of the Nachlass volumes is given below. The songs issued in 1831 included a group of eight put together on a religious theme (10), and a group of four Mayrhofer settings (11). This, and the set of four Mayrhofer songs (22) published in 1833, must have been a source of pleasure and pride to the poet before his death in 1836 – and here one must give some credit to Diabelli. He seems, however, to have made no particular effort to trawl through the treasures at his disposal and find the five further Mayrofer songs therein. Another publisher with greater literary acumen might have produced all seventeen of the Mayrhofer songs in his possession in a series of volumes (as was the case with the Ossian settings in 1830), but the poet's reputation in Vienna seems not to have merited it at the time.

Eight books were published in 1832 including volumes of songs devoted exclusively to settings of Schulze and Schlechta (13 and 15). There were fewer issues in 1833 and none at all in 1834. As if to make up for this, Diabelli issued three books in 1835 including the important Leitner settings (26 and 27). Then there was a gap of eighteen months before the single issue of 1837, five settings of Klopstock (28).

After this the songs often seem to have been issued rather carelessly and without much planning. The selection for Books 29 and 30 (1838) has a rather chaotic and improvised feel. There is a temporary return to a semblance of literary coherence in 1840 with 31 and 32 – a Matthisson volume of songs and Mayrhofer's extended song *Einsamkeit* – but in the nine volumes issued

Cover page of a later issue: No. 33 of the *Nachlass*.

in 1842 there is not the slightest sense of discernment or careful thought. There is some evidence, though, that Diabelli had become aware that Schubert's star was rising all the time, ironically thanks to his other Schubertian publishing ventures. In 1839 he had issued three great Piano Sonatas (D958, D959, D960); eleven years after the composer's death, this was another example of a catastrophically late publication, and one that denied Hummel, who had died, the chance to be the dedicatee of the works as Schubert had intended. The appearance of these great works brought Schubert's name before the public once again, with important critics like Schumann (the new dedicatee chosen by Diabelli) adding to a growing chorus of praise, and an ever-evolving evaluation of the composer's importance.

It is clear that by this time Diabelli believed that the best Schubert songs in his possession had already been issued, and it was now a question of marketing the remainder as cleverly as possible. Of the songs released between 1845 and 1850 (Books 38–50), at least ten were important works, but these were eked out in the most parsimonious manner. While this attitude would appear to indicate a careful husbanding of resources, so sloppy was the firm's control of the material that they issued the unimportant *Lied eines Kriegers* twice, once in Book 35 and again in Book 41. The star of the last year of the Nachlass is Book 47, devoted to five Goethe settings where *Prometheus* and the first version of *An den Mond* D259 appear for the first time.

Besides the Nachlass, Diabelli also began a new series of Schubert publications entitled *Immortellen*, each issue consisting of a single Schubert song mostly transposed for the lower voices encountered in domestic performance; the music for these was taken from the opus numbers published in Schubert's lifetime, as well as the Nachlass. Diabelli was clearly targeting the lucrative market of the younger generation who had not had the chance to collect the Schubert songs the first time round. This series of *Immortellen* continued into the 1860s (several years after Diabelli's death in 1858) and made the firm a lot of money. The remainder of the unpublished songs were handed over to Diabelli's successor Spina who reverted to opus numbers (*see* POSTHUMOUS SONGS) for a further sixteen songs. There were doubtless more songs in the archives of this firm that had to wait further decades for their publication in the Gesamtausgabe of 1894 and 1895.

The following is a list of the fifty 'Nachlass Lieferungen' and their contents. The song titles are given here as they appeared, not always the same as the accepted title today. These earlier titles are cross-referenced in this book.

1830

1. *Die Nacht* (Ossian)
2. *Cronnan, Kolmas Klage*
3. *Lodas Gespenst*
4. *Shilric und Vinvela, Ossians Lied nach dem Falle Nathos', Das Mädchen von Inistore*
5. *Der Tod Oscars*
6. *Elysium*
   [Volumes 1–6 advertised 10 July 1830, and issued between July and September of that year]
7. *Des Sängers Habe, Hippolits Lied, Abendröte, Ständchen* (Shakespeare)
8. *Die Bürgschaft*
   [Volumes 7–8 advertised 26 October 1830]

1831

9. *Der zürnende Barde, Am See* (Bruchmann), *Abendbilder*
10. Acht geistliche Lieder: *Dem Unendlichen, Die Gestirne, Das Marienbild, Vom Mitleiden Mariä, Litanei auf des Fest aller Seelen, Pax vobiscum, Gebet während der Schlacht,*

Himmelsfunken (Volume 10 was accompanied by a specially written preface by Anton Schindler)

11. Vier Lieder von Joh. Mayrhofer: *Orest auf Tauris, Der entsühnte Orest, Philoktet, Freiwilliges Versinken*
    [Volumes 9–11 advertised 21 April 1831]

12. *Der Taucher*
    [Volume 12 advertised 16 June 1831]

1832

13. Zwei Lieder von Ernst Schulze: *An mein Herz, Der liebliche Stern*

14. *Grenzen der Menschheit, Fragment aus dem Aeschylus*

15. Drei Lieder von Franz von Schlechta: *Widerschein, Des Fräuleins Liebeslauschen, Totengräber-Weise*
    [Volumes 13–15 advertised 4 January 1832]

16. *Waldesnacht*
    [Volume 16 advertised 12 March 1832]

17. *Lebensmut* (Schulze), *Der Vater mit dem Kind, An den Tod, Verklärung*
    [Volume 17 advertised 5 May 1832. *An den Tod* was not a first edition, having already been published by Franz von Schober's Lithographishes Institut]

18. *Pilgerweise, An den Mond in einer Herbstnacht, Fahrt zum Hades*
    [Volume 18 advertised 12 July 1832]

19. *Orpheus* (Lied des Orpheus), *Ritter Toggenburg*
    [Volume 19 advertised 9 October 1832]

20. *Im Abendrot, Szene aus Faust, Mignons Gesang* (Kennst du das Land?)
    [Volume 20 advertised 22 December 1832]

1833

21. *Der Blumenbrief, Vergissmeinnicht*
    [Volume 21 advertised 14 February 1833]

22. Vier Lieder von Joh. Mayrhofer: *Der Sieg, Atys, Beim Winde, Abendstern*
    [Volume 22 advertised 4 June 1833. *Beim Winde* was not a first edition as it had already appeared as a supplement to the *Wiener Zeitschrift für Kunst, Literatur, Theater und Mode*]

23. *Schwestergruss, Liedesend*
    [Volume 23 advertised 27 July 1833]

24. *Schiffers Scheidelied, Totengräbers Heimweh*
    [Volume 24 advertised 25 September 1833]

1835

25. *Fülle der Liebe, Im Frühling, Trost in Tränen*

26. *Der Winterabend*

27. Drei Lieder von Carl Gottfr. von Leitner: *Der Wallensteiner Lanzknecht beim Trunk, Der Kreuzzug, Des Fischers Liebesglück*
    [Volumes 25–7 advertised 9 October 1835. *Fülle der Liebe* and *Im Frühling* were not first editions as they had already appeared as supplements to the *Wiener Zeitschrift für Kunst, Literatur, Theater und Mode*. The first two of the Leitner songs above had already appeared elsewhere in smaller publications]

1837

28. Fünf Oden von Klopstock: *Hermann und Thusnelda, Selma und Selmar, Das Rosenband, Edone, Die frühen Gräber*
    [Volume 28 advertised 28 April 1837]

1838

29. *Stimme der Liebe* (Stolberg), *Die Mutter Erde, Gretchens Bitte, Abschied* (Lebe wohl! Du lieber Freund!)
   [Volume 29 published in June 1838]
30. *Tiefes Leid, Clärchens Lied, Grablied für die Mutter*
   [Volume 30 published in 1838]

1840

31. Drei Lieder von Matthisson: *Die Betende, Der Geistertanz* (III), *An Laura, als sie Klopstocks Auferstehungslied sang*
32. *Einsamkeit* (Mayrhofer)
   [Volumes 31–2 advertised 13 June 1840]

1842

33. *Der Schiffer* (Schlegel), *Die gefangenen Sänger*
34. *Auflösung, Blondel zu Marien*
35. *Die erste Liebe, Lied eines Kriegers*
36. *Der Jüngling an der Quelle, Lambertine, Ihr Grab*
37. *Heliopolis* (Fels auf Felsen hingewälzet), *Sehnsucht* (Goethe 'Was zieht mir das Herz so?')
   [Volumes 33–7 advertised 23 June 1842]
40. *Das Mädchen* (Schlegel), *Berthas Lied in der Nacht, An die Freunde*
   [Volume 40 published (out of sequence) *c.* 1842]

1845

38. *Die Einsiedelei, Lebenslied, Versunken*
39. *Als ich sie erröten sah, Das war ich, Ins stille Land*
   [Volumes 38–9 published in the spring of 1845]

1847

41. *Licht und Liebe, Das grosse Halleluja*
   [Volume 41 published *c.* 1847. The first edition of this volume of the Nachlass contained *Lied eines Kriegers* already issued in Volume 35. *Licht und Liebe*, not in itself a first edition, was a substitute for this]

1848

42. *Fragment aus 'Die Götter Griechenlands',*[1] *Das Finden, Cora an die Sonne, Grablied, Adelaide*
   [Volume 42 published *c.* middle of 1848]

1849

43. *Im Gegenwärtigen Vergangenes*
   [Volume 43 published as a single volume in Spring 1849]
44. *Trost* (Mayrhofer), *Die Nacht* (Uz), *Zum Punsche, Das Leben*
   [Volume 44 published as a single volume *c.* middle of 1849]

1850

45. *Frohsinn, Trinklied* (Schäffer), *Klage um Ali Bey, Der Morgenkuss*
46. *Epistel an den Assessor Josef von Spaun in Linz* (Musikalischer Schwank)[2]
   [Volumes 45–6 advertised 8 January 1850]

[1] See under *Strophe aus 'Die Götter Griechenlands'*.
[2] See under *Herrn Joseph Spaun, Assessor in Linz*.

47.   Fünf Lieder von Goethe: *Prometheus, Wer kauft Liebesgötter?, Der Rattenfänger, Nachtge-
      sang, An den Mond* (first version)
48.   *Die Sterne* (Schlegel), *Erntelied, Klage an den Mond, Trinklied* (Shakespeare), *Mignon* (So
      lasst mich scheinen, first version), *Der Goldschmiedsgesell, Tischlerlied*
      [Volumes 47–8 published in Spring 1850]
49.   *Auf der Riesenkoppe, Auf einen Kirchhof*
      [Volume 49 published *c.* 1850]
50.   *An die Apfelbäume wo ich Julien erblickte, Der Leidende, Augenlied*
      [Volume 50 published as a single volume at the end of 1850]

The publishing history of Schubert's lieder is continued, more or less chronologically, in the article on POSTHUMOUS SONGS.

Bibliography: Raab 2002, pp. 217–26

NACH OSTEN! *see* DUBIOUS, MISATTRIBUTED AND LOST SONGS

Die NACHT (Der Unglückliche I)   Night (the forlorn one)
(Pichler)
[Not in Deutsch Catalogue] [H463]
G major   Before 1821

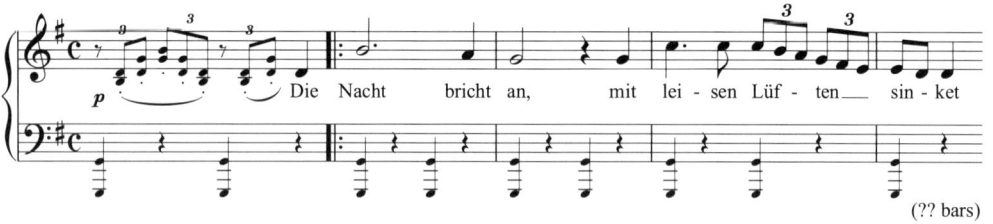

(?? bars)

Die Nacht bricht an; mit leisen Lüften sinket	Night falls, descending with light breezes
Sie auf die müden Sterblichen herab.[1]	Upon weary mortals;
Der sanfte Schlaf, des Todes Bruder, winket,	Gentle sleep, Death's brother, beckons,
Und legt die Menschen in ihr täglich Grab.[2]	And lays them in their daily graves.
Jetzt wachet auf der lichtberaubten Erde	Now only malice and pain
Vielleicht nur noch die Arglist und	Perchance watch over the earth, robbed of light;
der Schmerz;	
Und jetzt, da ich durch nichts gestöret werde,	And now, since nothing may disturb me,
Lass deine Wunden bluten, armes Herz!	Let your wounds bleed, poor heart.
Versenke dich in deines Kummers Tiefen,	Plunge to the depths of your grief,
Und wenn vielleicht in der zerrissnen Brust[3]	And if perchance half-forgotten sorrows
Verjährte, halb vergessne Leiden schliefen,	Have slept in your anguished heart,

[1] Schubert repeats 'müden' in this line.
[2] Pichler writes 'Und legt *sie freundlich* in ihr täglich Grab'.
[3] Schubert repeats 'vielleicht' in this line.

So wecke sie mit grausam süsser Lust!	Awaken them with cruelly sweet delight.
Berechne die verlornen Seligkeiten,	Consider your lost happiness,
Zähl' alle Blumen in dem Paradies,	Count all the flowers in paradise,
Woraus in deiner Jugend goldnen Zeiten	From which, in the golden days of your youth,
Die kalte Hand des Schicksals dich verstiess!	The harsh hand of fate banished you.

Du hast geliebt, du hast das Glück empfunden,	You have loved, you have experienced a happiness
Dem jede Seligkeit der Erde weicht,	Which eclipses all earthly bliss.
Du hast ein Herz, das dich verstand, gefunden,	You have found a heart that understands you,
Des schönsten Glückes höchstes Ziel erreicht.[4]	Your wildest hopes have attained their fair goal.
Da stürzte dich ein trostlos Machtwort nieder,[5]	Then the implacable decree of authority dashed you down
Aus deinen Himmeln, und dein stilles Glück,	From your heaven, and your tranquil happiness,
Das allzu schönes Traumbild, kehrte wieder	Your all-too-lovely dream vision, returned
Zur bessern Welt, aus der es kam, zurück.	To the better world from which it came.

Zerrissen sind nun alle süssen Bande;	Now all the sweet bonds are torn asunder;
Mich hällt kein Herz mehr auf der weiten Welt![6]	No heart now beats for me in the whole world.
Was ist's, das mich in diesem wüsten Lande,[7]	What is it that keeps me still in this wasteland,
In dieser öden Einsamkeit noch hält.[8]	In this barren solitude?
Nur einen Strahl seh' ich von ferne blinken;[9]	Just one ray of light I see shining from afar,
Im Götterglanz erscheint die heil'ge Pflicht:	My sacred duty appears in divine radiance.
Und wenn des müden Geistes Kräfte sinken,	And if the strength of my weary spirit fails,
So sinkt der Mut, den sie mir einflösst, nicht.	Then the courage which that duty inspires in me shall not fail.

KAROLINE PICHLER (1769–1843)

This song of an unknown date is probably the third of Schubert's four Pichler solo settings (otherwise composed between 1816 and 1821). See the poet's biography for a chronological list of all the Pichler settings.

In 2013 this strophic song, rediscovered in the late 1980s, could still claim to be the most recently discovered Schubert lied; it has not yet been assigned a Deutsch number and its authenticity has not been verified. *Die Nacht* was rediscovered as part of a forgotten collection of music that had been gathered together in two volumes by the composer's schoolfriend Franz von Schlechta mainly between 1840 and 1842, with a single item from 1846. This comprised some thirty-nine Schubert songs, alphabetically ordered, in versions for voice and guitar, not in the composer's hand. It also included items by famous composers such as Beethoven, Haydn and Mozart alongside forgotten names like Hermann Proch and Anton Hackl. *Die Nacht* is numbered 72 in the collection. It seems likely that some of the guitar versions were fair copies for the versions of

---

[4] Pichler writes '*Der kühnsten Hoffnung schönes* Ziel erreicht'.
[5] Pichler writes '*grausam* Machtwort'.
[6] Pichler writes '*Mir schlägt* kein Herz'.
[7] Pichler writes 'In diesem *Schattenlande*'.
[8] Pichler writes 'In dieser *toten* Einsamkeit'.
[9] Pichler writes 'Nur Einen *Licht*strahl seh' ich *fernher* blinken'.

the song with this instrument that were published by Diabelli; they are efficiently scored for the instrument to avoid difficulty for the player – the arranger was perhaps Johann Nepomuk Huber. In the absence of an original autograph, dating this song is made more difficult by the bland simplicity of the piano – or rather, guitar – writing (it is possible that this setting of Karoline Pichler's poem once existed in piano-accompanied form, now lost). The lack of a fully developed accompaniment throws more attention on the vocal line which has many Schubertian finger-prints in terms of the rise and fall, as well as the persuasive flexibility, of the melody. The date of the copy is 26 September 1841.

The Italianate melody is typical of the music Schubert was writing around the time of his training with Salieri. But it might be argued that the chain of modulations within the melody sounds too sophisticated for this period. The fact that the famous version of the song, *Der Unglückliche* D713 was composed only in 1821 is another factor in postulating a date later than 1813–16. But the two settings of Pichler's poem are very different. *Der Unglückliche* is an elabo-rate song-cantata made up of various sections in different tempi, and it could not be further from a strophic song in terms of its conception.

Die Nacht, matching the shape of the poem, is cast in four broad and identical musical strophes of thirty bars each. The first, second, third and fourth strophes begin with the opening melody in G major, and for the second half of each of these (the 'B' section) the music changes to stormier mood in E minor. For the performance on Hyperion three of the four strophes were recorded. (It is worth noting that *Der Unglückliche* D713 uses only three strophes and two further lines of the poem, finishing in superbly dramatic fashion.) In this first setting of Pichler's words the composer sets the complete poem, but musically it is infinitely less adven-turous. Pichler's novel *Olivier* (the source of this poem) describes the heroine Adelinde singing this song to her own harp accompaniment – much closer to the guitar as an instrument than the piano.

Aiming at hypnotizing repetition rather than individual detail, Schubert allows the general flow of the cantilena to govern the song's shape. Apart from appropriate moments of vocal melisma (airy triplets for 'mit leisen Lüften sinket', legato syncopation for 'die <u>müden</u> Sterbli-chen'), he does not allow himself to be diverted into the illustrative, word-inspired, commentary that is usually the magical factor in his response to poetry. Indeed, the song is so plain and simple in its marriage of musical and verbal means that one might be tempted to doubt its authenticity; that is, if one did not know how hard it is to write a Schubertian pastiche even half as good as this. The sung text of the poem contains deviations from Pichler's printed text which are different from the composer's changes to the poem for the second setting, *Der Unglückliche*, D713 (qv).

Autograph:	In private possession
First edition:	Published by Universal Edition in 1990 in a version which arranges the guitar accompaniment for piano (P806)
Subsequent editions:	Not in Peters; Not in AGA; Not in NSA
Bibliography:	Partsch/Scheit 1989, p. 15
Arrangements:	Arr. Tilman Hoppstock (b. 1961) for guitar accompaniment, in *Franz Schubert: 110 Lieder* (2009)
Discography and timing:	Fischer-Dieskau —
	Hyperion I 33²²
	Hyperion II 24⁵ 4'48 Catherine Wyn-Rogers

⟵ *Die gefangenen Sänger* D712   *Der Unglückliche* D713 ⟶

Die NACHT
(Uz) **D358** [H210]

The night

The song exists in two versions, the second of which is discussed below:
(1) 1816; (2) Date unknown

(1) 'Langsam'   A♭ major   ¢   [14 bars]

(2)   A♭ major

Du verstörst uns nicht, o Nacht!	You do not disturb us, O night.
Sieh! wir trinken im Gebüsche;	See, we are drinking in the grove,
Und ein kühler Wind erwacht,	And a refreshing breeze arises
Dass er unsern Wein erfrische.	To cool our wine.
Mutter holder Dunkelheit,	Mother of gentle darkness,
Nacht! Vertraute süsser Sorgen,	Night, confidant of our sweet cares,
Die betrogner Wachsamkeit	You have already concealed many a kiss
Viele Küsse schon verborgen!	From cheated vigilance.
Dir allein sei mitbewusst,	You alone shall know
Welch Vergnügen mich berausche,	What rapture overcomes me
Wenn ich an geliebter Brust	When, on my beloved's breast,
Unter Tau und Blumen lausche!	I listen amid the dew and flowers.
Murmelt ihr, wenn alles ruht,	Murmur to her, gently swaying trees,
Murmelt, sanftbewegte Bäume,	Murmur when all is at rest;
Bei dem Sprudeln heisrer Flut,[1]	As the hot flood foams
Mich in wollustvolle Träume!	Murmur me into dreams of ecstasy.

JOHANN PETER UZ (1720–1796); poem written between 1750 and 1754

This is the first of Schubert's five Uz solo settings (1816). See the poet's biography for a chronological list of all the Uz settings.

The manuscript of the first version of *Die Nacht* (as printed in NSA Volume 10, p. 12) was mutilated at some point: much of the vocal line of the opening is cut away as is part of the

---

[1] Uz writes '*heischrer* Flut'.

right-hand piano music. The date was also missing and it is only a matter of conjecture that the song was composed in June 1816, but a relatively safe one given the provenance of the other Uz settings.

As John Reed notes, this song bears a resemblance to another work from 1816, *Abschied, Nach einer Wallfahrtsarie* (D475). The shape of the melodic line is similar, and the accompaniment for both works suggests hunting horns heard in the distance at twilight. Reed finds the music out of keeping with the 'conspiratorial mood' of Uz's lyric. In the hands of the right performers, however, the simplicity of the music can take on a measure of intensity and longing that is perhaps more to do with recitation than singing. It was ever thus with a certain type of Schubertian strophic song – seemingly dull and lifeless on the printed page, the music can spring into life with a singer who understands how to put words across.

The 'horn call' accompanying motif is heard in A flat in the right hand during the first full bar and reappears in the relative minor, in the left hand, immediately afterwards. This canonic effect continues throughout the song, the bass clef answering and echoing the statements of the treble. The song has been cast for two characters: the night does not disturb *us*, the poet says. Just as in *Das Finden* D219 Schubert places music in the treble clef to suggest femininity, the different tessituras of the piano writing here suggest the echoes of personal sympathy and a dialogue of the sexes. Reed opines that the words of this Uz poem have nothing in common with those of *Abschied*, but surely it is reciprocity, the sharing of intimacy and exchange of feelings, that drew the subject matter of the two poems together (and thus their musical depiction) in the composer's mind. There is also something solemn and dignified about a ceremony of farewell, and the advent of night has a similarly majestic portent. The repetition of the line 'Dass er unsern Wein erfrische' is a marvellous touch: the first setting of the words (bb. 7–9) emphasizes 'unsern' and the 'erfrische' falls on the strong first beat; in the repeat (bb. 10–12) the emphases fall in different places (the line has effectively been re-barred) and the result is a colloquy where one person repeats another's statement in a slightly different voice. The haunting elongation of the second syllable of 'erfrische' ('verborgen' in the second verse) takes its cue from the feminine cadence implicit in the rhythm of the poem itself. In the second strophe the emphasis on 'Küsse' at the beginning of b. 8 (for the second time) is countered by an emphasis on 'schon' when the phrase is sung for the second time, adding to the subtly concealed raciness of his confession – there have been many kisses already, but by implication the best are still to come. By 1816 Schubert was becoming increasingly masterful in handling such subtleties of prosody.

All four of Uz's strophes are printed and translated above. For the Hyperion recording Peter Schreier only sang the first two.

Autograph:	University Library of Lund, Sweden (fragment)
Publication:	First published as part of the NSA in 2002 (P825; first version)
	First published as Book 44 no. 2 of the *Nachlass* by Diabelli,
	Vienna in 1849 (P367; second version)
Subsequent editions:	Peters: Vol. 6/40; AGA XX 235: Vol. 4/127; NSA IV: Vol. 10/12
	& 14
Discography and timing:	Fischer-Dieskau I 7²³ 2'29
	Hyperion I 18²
	Hyperion II 12⁵ 2'07 Peter Schreier

← *An Chloen* D363   *Sehnsucht (Mignon)* D359 →

Die NACHT   The night

(Ossian–Macpherson/HAROLD) **D534** [H349]

G minor – A minor   February 1817

(207 bars)

The English version printed below is Macpherson's original text rather than an exact translation of Harold's German

Erster Barde:

Die Nacht ist dumpfig und finster. An den Hügeln ruhn die Wolken. Kein Stern mit grünzitterndem Strahl; kein Mond schaut durch die Luft. Im Walde hör' ich den Hauch; aber ich hör' ihn weit in der Ferne. Der Strom des Tals erbraust; aber sein Brausen ist stürmisch und trüb.[1] Vom Baum beim Grabe der Toten, hört man lang die krächzende Eul.[2] An der Ebne erblick ich eine dämmernde Bildung! es ist ein Geist! er schwindet, er flieht. Durch diesen Weg wird eine Leiche getragen: ihren Pfad bezeichnet das Luftbild. Der fernere Dogge[3] heult von der Hütte des Hügels. Der Hirsch liegt im Moose des Bergs: neben ihm ruht die Hindin.[4] In seinem astigten Geweihe hört sie den Wind; fährt auf, und legt sich zur Ruhe wieder nieder.[5]

[(. . . 3 lines . . .)]

Düster und keuchend, zitternd und traurig, verlor der Wanderer den Weg. Er irrt durch Gebüsche, durch Dornen längs der sprudelnden Quelle. Er fürchtet die Klippe und den Sumpf. Er fürchtet den Geist der Nacht. Der alte Baum ächzt zu dem Windstoss; der fallende Ast erschallt. Die verwelkte, zusammen verworrene Klette, treibt der Wind über das Gras. Es ist der leichte Tritt eines Geists! er bebt in der Mitte der Nacht.

First bard:

Night is dull and dark. The clouds rest on the hills. No star with green trembling beam; no moon looks from the sky. I hear the blast in the wood; but I hear it distant far. The stream of the valley murmurs; but its murmur is sullen and sad.

From the tree at the grave of the dead the long-howling owl is heard. I see a dim form on the plain! It is a ghost! it fades, it flies. Some funeral shall pass this way: the meteor marks the path.

The distant dog is howling from the hut on the hill. The stag lies on the mountain moss: the hind is at his side. She hears the wind in his branchy horns. She starts, but lies again.

[(. . . 3 lines . . .)]

Dark, panting, trembling, sad, the traveller has lost his way. Through shrubs, through thorns, he goes, along the gurgling rill. He fears the rock and the fen. He fears the ghost of night. The old tree groans to the blast; the falling branch resounds. The wind drives the withered burs, clung together, along the grass. It is the light tread of a ghost! He trembles amidst the night.

[1] Harold writes 'störrisch und trüb'.
[2] Harold writes 'hört man *die lang krachzende* Eul'.
[3] Schubert mistakenly writes '*Die* fernere Dogge'.
[4] Schubert changes 'Hindin' to 'Hündinn'.
[5] Harold writes 'legt sich *wieder* zur Ruhe'.

Die Nacht ist düster, dunkel, und heulend;
wolkigt, stürmisch und schwanger mit
Geistern! Die Toten streifen umher! Empfangt
mich von der Nacht, meine Freunde.

Dark, dusty, howling is night, cloudy, windy,
and full of ghosts! The dead are abroad! My
friends, receive me from the night.

[(*Zweyter Barde* . . . 28 lines)]
[(*Dritter Barde* . . . 24 lines)]
[(*Vierter Barde* . . . 25 lines)]
[(*Fünfter Barde* . . . 23 lines)]

[(*Second bard* . . . 24 lines)]
[(*Third bard* . . . 24 lines)]
[(*Fourth bard* . . . 26 lines)]
[(*Fifth bard* . . . 22 lines)]

Der Gebieter:

The chief:

Lass Wolken an Hügeln ruhn; Geister fliegen
und Wandrer beben. Lass die Winde der
Wälder sich heben, brausende Stürme
herabsteigen. Ströme brüllen, Fenster klirren,[6]
grünbeflügelte Dämpfe fliegen; den bleichen
Mond sich hinter seinen Hügeln erheben, oder
sein Haupt in Wolken einhüllen; die Nacht gilt
mir gleich; die Luft sei blau, stürmisch, oder
dunkel. Die Nacht fliegt vorm Strahl, wenn er
am Hügel sich giest. Der junge Tag kehrt von
seinen Wolken, aber wir kehren nimmer
zurück.[7]

Let clouds rest on the hills: spirits fly, and
travellers fear. Let the winds of the woods arise,
the sounding storms blow. Roar streams and
windows flap, and green-winged meteors fly!
Rise the pale moon from behind her hills, or
enclose her head in clouds! night is alike to me,
blue, stormy, or gloomy the sky. Night flies
before the beam, when it is poured on the hill.
The young day returns from his clouds, but we
return no more.

Wo sind unsre Führer der Vorwelt; wo sind
unsre weit beruhmten Gebieter? Schweigend
sind die Felder ihrer Schlachten. Kaum sind
ihre moosigten Gräber noch übrig. Man wird
auch unser vergessen. Dies erhabene Gebäu
wird zerfallen. Unsere Söhne werden die
Trümmer im Grase nicht erblicken. Sie werden
die Greisen befragen, 'Wo standen die Mauern
unsrer Väter?'

Where are our chiefs of old? Where our kings
of mighty name? The fields of their battles are
silent. Scarce their mossy tombs remain. We
shall also be forgot. This lofty house shall fall.
Our sons shall not behold the ruins in grass.
They shall ask of the aged, 'where stood the
walls of our fathers?'

Ertönet das Lied und schlaget die Harfen;
sendet die fröhlichen Muscheln herum. Stellt
hundert Kerzen in die Höhe. Jünglinge,
Mädchen beginnet den Tanz. Nah sei ein
graulockiger Barde, mir die Taten der Vorwelt
zu singen; von Königen berühmt in unserm
Land, von Gebietern, die wir nicht mehr sehn.
Lass die Nacht also vergehen, bis der Morgen in
unsern Hallen erscheine. Dann seien nicht
ferne, der Bogen, die Doggen, die Jünglinge der
Jagd. Wir werden die Hügel mit dem Morgen
besteigen, und die Hirsche erwecken.[8]

Raise the song, and strike the harp; send round
the shells of joy. Suspend a hundred tapers on
high. Youth and maids begin the dance. Let
some grey bard be near me to tell the deeds of
other times; of kings renowned in our land, of
chiefs we behold no more. Thus let the night
pass until morning shall appear in our halls.

Then let the bow be at hand, the dogs, the
youths of the chase. We shall descend the hill
with day, and awake the deer.

---

[6] Harold's original of 'Fenster *schmettern*' is struck through on the autograph and corrected to 'klirren'.
[7] Harold writes '*nicht mehr* zurück'.
[8] Harold writes 'Wir werden *den* Hügel'.

JAMES MACHPHERSON ('OSSIAN') (1736–1796), translated by EDMUND,
BARON VON HAROLD (1737–1800)

This song encompasses a number of different characters who never sing simultaneously (it is thus possible for a single singer to take all the roles in performance). It is accordingly listed here as the last of Schubert's ten Ossian solo settings (1815–17) rather than as an ensemble. See the poet's biography (under Macpherson) for a chronological list of all the Ossian settings.

These rambling epics, short on action and often containing uncertain historical detail, are notable for their poetic descriptions of heath, lake and mountain peopled by a race of noble bearing and magnanimous chivalry. At the time much of the world (with notable exceptions such as Dr Johnson) was prepared to accept the idea of noble savages in Scotland in the third century AD; this was because the poetry of 'Ossian', whether genuinely ancient or not, was full of wild Celtic glamour, strange and 'natural' newness. Although the text of this song is traditionally said to be by 'Ossian', its 'translator', James Macpherson, in a substantial footnote to the epic *Croma* (which includes both the text and the introduction to the song) claimed that the poem dated from a thousand years after Ossian's time. Herder, Goethe and Schiller were delighted with it, and Coleridge and Byron imitated it. Modern scholars admit a genuine background to Ossian and the bardic tradition of Celtic poetry, if not quite the one proposed by Macpherson.

    Die Nacht is the last of Schubert's Ossian settings. The composer abandoned the poet, abruptly, in February 1817. It is also significant that Schubert never offered an Ossian setting for publication in his lifetime. This sudden and complete falling out of love with Ossian might have been influenced by Mayrhofer who would have had strong feelings about the execrable nature of Harold's German translations, and perhaps exhorted the composer to turn his attention to the Greek classics instead. It may be significant that March 1817 opens a new chapter in Schubert's engagement with Mayrhofer's poetry on classical themes. Nevertheless, *Die Nacht* contains so much magnificent music that at its first publication in 1830 Diabelli arranged a performing version that he believed would save the piece for the public. Because of this, the provenance of the musical work is almost as complicated as that of the poetry of Ossian. Both the Peters Edition and the AGA follow Diabelli's reworking of the original. They had no choice because the manuscript itself only re-emerged in Hungary in the late 1960s. This autograph (published in Moscow in 1980) shows that Diabelli changed both Macpherson's text and Schubert's notes at will. The publisher has been particularly execrated by scholars for grafting a hunting song (admittedly a genuine Schubert choral composition), *Jagdlied* D521, onto the body of *Die Nacht* 'in a misguided attempt' (in John Reed's words) 'to give it a rousing finale'.

    When the song was recorded for Hyperion there was much discussion about how best to present the work on disc. John Reed makes the suggestion that the finest music of *Die Nacht* is that of the First Bard, and that the piece could end satisfactorily before the words of the Chieftain. Accordingly Track 1 of the Hyperion disc (Disc 17, Track 27 in Hyperion II) presented this part of the piece (up to b. 100) – the first six and a half pages in the *Gesamtausgabe*. Track 2 (or Track 28) continued the piece. Track 3 offered the *Jagdlied*. The addition of Track 3 showed, more or less, how *Die Nacht* was first published but, because *Jagdlied* is a chorus in its own right, this could also be listened to independently of the context imposed on it by the Diabelli publication.

    Macpherson's own pseudo-scholarly introduction to the poem makes clear the almost impossible task of setting the complete text and why Schubert only attempted two of its six sections: 'The story of it is this: Five bards, passing the night in the house of a chieftain, who was a poet himself, went severally to make their observations on, and returned with a description of, night.' The nocturnal impressions of all five of these bards would have made a song of unmanageable length.

The First Bard: The music of the first part of *Die Nacht* is a high point of Schubert's use of arioso and recitative. The various devices of declamation, and the uses of differing keys and tempi, are so artfully dovetailed that we are scarcely aware of how the whole fits together. But it does – and seamlessly. In the Schiller ballad *Die Erwartung* D159, Schubert displayed a talent for the depiction of the various sounds and feelings of twilight and night, but in that song all was exquisite rococo expectancy – nightfall in the bower of a civilized German garden. In this Ossian piece the composer transplants himself to the Scottish moors of a twilight age where night is a veiled threat; it can almost be embodied and personified as someone sinister. Thirds and sixths glide ominously in the piano part in the beginning, becoming the binding thread of the music for the First Bard. Pianistic illustrations abound: a distant stream murmurs in G flat major (bb. 14–15) and an E flat minor interlude (marked 'Sehr langsam' from b. 18 with a change of key signature into five flats) ends in a dying fall that mimics the hooting owl. Then there is the sudden appearance (and disappearance into pianistic thin air) of a ghost (bb. 27–9), music of dematerialization wonderfully fitted to its purpose. At b. 30 the key signature changes into two sharps and a B minor funeral march passes by with muffled drums, followed by a brave attempt (marked 'Etwas geschwind' from b. 39) to suggest the dog's whining and howling (a sound already depicted in different ways in *Der Geistertanz* D116 and *Minona* D152). All these images give rise to a wealth of pregnant motifs that would have gone a long way if Schubert had chosen to exploit them in instrumental compositions. As it is, he seems to blow all considerations of musical form to the winds and concerns himself only with atmosphere and verbal illustration.

At b. 46 the tempo marking changes to 'Ruhig'. The G major complacency of the stag (b. 47) is contrasted with the nervy (and feminine) movements of the hind – a marvellous passage, marked 'Geschwinder', that shivers with agitation (cf. a similar passage about deer in *Cronnan* D282). Mankind's introduction to the scene (from b. 57, marked 'Etwas geschwinder') is in panicky, short-breathed G-minor phrases that describe someone lost and confused; there is much movement and little direction. The wind music is the quickest in the piece, and some of the most inventive (from b. 75, marked 'Geschwind'). The trepidation before the ghosts ('Langsam' from the middle of b. 81) is rather more conventional, but this leads to a splendid recapitulation of the thirds and sixths of the opening ('Wie oben' from b. 86) with an ominous passage ('Sehr langsam' from b. 94) where we hear the tread of the dead in a low register of voice and piano . The setting of the final two bars of recitative (bb. 97–8, 'My friends, receive me from the night!') has an appropriate Handelian majesty. Schubert now skips a hundred lines of Harold's translation.

The Chief: This section starts well enough, but John Reed is probably right to detect the first signs of flagging invention. After such an extended spell of slow music we long for something faster, and we get it from b. 101 where the marking is 'Mässig' and the tonality is a newly established E flat major. Purling sextuplet semiquavers accompany a rather perfunctory recapitulation of the tales of the First Bard. Moonrise is beautifully depicted in bb. 110–13, the weaving semiquavers in the accompaniment perfect cloud cover for the voice just as the poem describes the obscuring of the moon. The melody at 'sein Haupt in Wolken einhüllen' (b. 113) has been heard in slow motion in death's reassuring words in *Der Tod und das Mädchen* D531 – 'komme nicht zu strafen'. As only three Deutsch numbers separate the two songs we might surmise, putting the two personifications of death side by side, that Schubert regards 'Freund Hain' as a pallid, moonlit figure wreathed in mist rather than something resembling Mozart's Commendatore. This music connects with a recitative for the chieftain ending at bb. 121–2 ('Langsam') in a woebegone and elegiac cadence that leads the music into B flat minor. At

b. 124 ('Geschwind') a conventional scale passage and a pompous succession of chords usher in the idea of the chieftains of old – hackneyed heroics perhaps, although from b. 132 ('Nicht zu langsam') the slow three-part invention for voice and two hands in the passage 'Schweigend sind die Felder' (a kind of 'Tombeau de Bach' to represent the graves of ancient leaders) is a genuine and typical Schubertian inspiration. From b. 148 (marked 'Mässig') the composer attempts to find the right tone for ancient jollification: dance music which is no doubt his idea of an archaic highland fling (the sprightly prancing between bb. 163 and 172). But by now it is easy to see that his heart is no longer in the Highlands, all the fanfares and clatter notwithstanding. What had attracted him to the poem in the first place were the atmospheric possibilities of the poem's opening lines. The closing postlude (bb. 200–7) for all its pomp somehow fails to end the piece conclusively and this accounts for Diabelli's subsequent meddling.

   See also Jagdlied D521.

Autograph:	Hungarian National Library, Budapest
First edition:	Published as Book 1 of the *Nachlass* by Diabelli, Vienna in July 1830; Diabelli appended the music of *Jagdlied* D521 (with new words) to the end of the fragment (P240)
Publication review:	Rellstab 'Ueberblick der Erzeugnisse', *Iris im Gebiete der Tonkunst* (Berlin) No. 39 (12 November 1830) [Waidelich/Hilmar Dokumente II No. 784b]
Subsequent editions:	Peters: Vol. 4/162; AGA XX 305: Vol. 5/39; NSA IV: Vol. 11/90
Bibliography:	Kecskeméti 1968, p. 70
Discography and timing:	Fischer-Dieskau —

Hyperion I 6$^{1-2}$
Hyperion II 17$^{27-28}$ 13'26   Anthony Rolfe Johnson

← *Täglich zu singen* D533   *Philoktet* D540 →

NACHT UND TRÄUME   Night and dreams
(M. von Collin) Op. 43 no. 2, **D827** [H508]

The song exists in two versions, the second of which is discussed below:
(1) 1822/3?; (2) 1822/3?

(1) 'Langsam'   B major   **C**   [28 bars]

(2) B major

(29 bars)

Heil'ge Nacht, du sinkest nieder;	Holy night, you sink down;
Nieder wallen auch die Träume,	Dreams, too, float down,
Wie dein Mondlicht durch die Räume,	Like your moonlight through space,
Durch der Menschen stille Brust.	Through the silent hearts of men.
Die belauschen sie mit Lust;	They listen with delight,
Rufen, wenn der Tag erwacht:	Crying out when day awakes:
Kehre wieder, heil'ge Nacht!	Come back, holy night!
Holde Träume, kehret wieder!	Fair dreams, return!

MATTHÄUS VON COLLIN (1779–1824)

This is the last of Schubert's five Matthäus von Collin solo settings (1816 and 1822–3). See the poet's biography for a chronological list of all the Matthäus von Collin settings.

The date of the song is uncertain; Otto Erich Deutsch placed it in 1825 which accounts for the high D number, but he had overlooked a letter to Schober in June 1823 from Anton von Spaun who reports that he has heard a sequence of 'göttliche Lieder' sung by the baritone Vogl in St Florian. Among these 'god-like' songs were *Der Zwerg* (Collin, D771) and *Nacht und Träume* by the same poet; it is thus likely that the song dates from the winter of 1822–3 alongside the other Collin settings. The autograph has disappeared so we rely on the first edition prepared in Schubert's lifetime; due to a publisher's error the text is there attributed to Schiller. Another slightly different copy belonging to the Spaun family (marked 'Langsam') is published by the NSA as the first version.

The poem for this masterpiece is influenced somewhat by Novalis's *Hymnen an die Nacht*. It is more or less identical to the 'Gesang des Grafen' in Collin's dramatic fragment *Fortunats Abfahrt von Cypern*. This was published in Volume 1 of the *Nachgelassene Gedichte* (1827, p. 65), too late to have been the composer's source, so Schubert must have received the poem from Collin in manuscript form. Nevertheless, this two-volume posthumous collection shows us the genesis of the lyric. Collin evidently went to some trouble to reach the final version, a conflation of two sketches and poems that appeared separately in the different volumes some years after the publication of Schubert's song. In Volume 1 of that set (p. 134) the poem is entitled *Nacht und Träume*. In Volume 2 (p. 149) the title is *Nachtfeyer* (where 'Heil'ge' is a new idea). The word 'Mondlicht' appears in neither of these versions – simple light, rather than moonlight, flits through the trees in *Nachtfeyer*. It seems that the distinguished editor of Collin's posthumous poems (the famous orientalist Hammer-Purgstall) failed to notice that these two works are closely related, although it is not certain which of them came first – the first being a grander ode, the second a more intimate lyric. As an overall title for his song Schubert preferred *Nacht und Träume* to *Nachtfeyer*.

John Reed is right to invoke the 'moon-haunted landscapes' of Samuel Palmer and Caspar David Friedrich when describing this song. He might also have mentioned the word-painting of another contemporary, Percy Bysshe Shelley, from *Queen Mab*:

> How wonderful is Death,
> Death and his brother Sleep!
> One pale as yonder waning moon . . .
> The other rosy as the morn . . .
> Yet both so passing wonderful!

This song about the 'little sleep', whereby men die and are reborn as they dream on their pillows each day of their lives, is indeed 'passing strange and wonderful', although Schubert (setting Wilhelm Müller's verse) was later to mock the escapism of bourgeois dreamers and their cosy pillows in *Im Dorfe* from *Winterreise* D911/17.

Nacht und Träume, drawing by Sorrieu for edition of Richault, Paris (*c.* 1840).

The key of B major glows in a special way in *Nacht und Träume*. The starry heights of the vocal line are poised a long away from the accompaniment – gently rocking semiquavers in both hands cradled in the mellow reaches of the bass clef. Of the four bars of introduction the first is entirely anchored in B major, while the second supports a sighing sequence of right-hand crotchets – the first stirrings of the glorious melody that will soon appear in the vocal line. In bb. 3 and 4 gentle pianistic pulsations continue on their inexorable way into the very heart of the music, as if these subtle harmonic changes were burrowing deep into the unconscious, while the little finger of the pianist's right hand sings like a cello. All of this is preparation for that heart-stopping 'ping' of the first word, 'Heil'ge', that explodes in the vocal firmament with the soft radiance of a shooting star. Because a female voice sounds an octave higher than a male one, it makes a spatial difference if a man rather than a woman sings this song. When a soprano enters on a D sharp, so distant is the voice from the tessitura of the gently rumbling accompaniment that it seems completely unsupported, as if walking a tightrope. That this phrase also requires sovereign breath control, not to mention faultless intonation, is typical of the challenges that Schubert delights to throw at his performers. That initial 'Heil'ge' has to be beautiful, certainly, and it has to be connected to an equally well-sung 'Nacht' that in turn links to 'du sinkest nieder' (with a wonderfully apposite setting of the downwardly gazing 'nieder' in b. 7). Within less than thirty seconds on the recital platform a master singer has announced herself . . . or not. The vocal line both inclines earthwards and stretches upwards into the void, luring moonlight, memories and spirits to visit the realm of dreams.

In the piano, unruffled semiquavers slowly oscillate, as if breathing steadily, and the one significant modulation into G major from the home key of B major (from b. 15) takes the dreamer into even deeper realms of sleep where he or she nestles with the purest delight ('Die belauschen sie mit Lust'). It is notable that the verb 'belauschen' (usually to look out for or be on the watch for) here means to listen intently; Night will make a special sound when it arrives. In Schubert's song the magic of night has been rendered into sound, and the magical shift into G major can only be perceived through the ear. There is a touch of lonely, resounding desolation at b. 20 on the diminished chord of 'Rufen, wenn der Tag erwacht', a sound that resonates mournfully, yet urgently, across the cosmos. We plead for night's return in order to live again in a better world, to recapture the joys that we once possessed – the theme of a number of Schubert's greatest songs. One of the most magical single notes in all Schubert is the melismatic 'Holde', placed almost perversely across the barline between bb. 22 and 23, and requiring a heart-stopping piano dynamic. It is at this other-worldly moment that many a great recitalist, if vocally poised with a favourable wind (or breath) behind her, can win the listener's awestruck admiration. Samuel Beckett chooses this moment to introduce music into his otherwise word-less television play *Nacht und Träume* (1982) where a male voice first hums and sings the last seven bars of this, one of the Irish playwright's most cherished songs by a composer whom he regarded as 'his friend in suffering'.

After this pivotal moment, it remains only for the singer to summon every last ounce of control and to climb up the dangerous ladder of b. 25, part scale, part arpeggio, and then down the other side to bring the song to a rapt close, preferably without breathing before the word 'kehret'.

Many years before Freud's theories, poet and composer understood that sleep is the key to our past joys and troubles. The song is notoriously difficult; all singers and pianists feel that the ideal performance of this music exists only in the imagination. Facing this challenge, and failing, is among an artist's worst nightmares. On the other hand, to give a performance of this song that brings an audible hush to the hall is one of the most thrilling accomplishments for a singer, and the pianist's role in the wielding of the magic is not to be underestimated. The song's post-lude (bb. 27–9) bears an uncanny resemblance to the closing bars of Haydn's English canzonet, *She never told her love* (1795). It is likely that Schubert knew this music; the imagery (Shake-speare's) of 'sitting like Patience on a monument / Smiling at grief' is another state of fathomless contemplation, dreamlike and suspended in musical space.

Autograph:	Missing or lost
Publication:	First published as part of the NSA in 1975 (P764; first version)
	First published as Op. 43 no. 2 by A. Pennauer, Vienna in July 1825 (P84; second version)
Subsequent editions:	Peters: Vol. 1/240 & Vol. 2/971; AGA XX 470: Vol. 8/68; NSA IV: Vol. 2a/184 & Vol. 2b/267; Bärenreiter: Vol. 2/68
Bibliography:	Capell 1928, pp. 208–9
	Fischer-Dieskau 1977, pp. 219–20
	Grindea 1998, p. 183
	Newbould 1997, p. 291
	Youens 2002, pp. 83–92
Arrangements:	Arr. Max Reger (1873–1916) for voice and orchestra (1913–14) [see ORCHESTRATIONS]
	Arr. Colin Matthews (b. 1946) for voice and orchestra (2008)
	Arr. Tilman Hoppstock (b. 1961) for guitar accompaniment, in *Franz Schubert: 110 Lieder* (2009)
Discography and timing:	Fischer-Dieskau II 7[3] 3'27
	Pears-Britten 2[7] 4'00
	Hyperion I 3[13]
	Hyperion II 26[14] 4'40 Ann Murray

← *Der Zwerg* D771   *Wehmut* D772 →

NACHTGESANG
(Goethe) **D119** [H50]
A♭ major   30 November 1814

Song of night

O gib, vom weichen Pfühle, | O lend, from your soft pillow,
Träumend, ein halb Gehör! | Dreaming, but half an ear!

O gib, vom weichen Pfühle,
Träumend, ein halb Gehör!
Bei meinem Saitenspiele
Schlafe! was willst du mehr?

Bei meinem Saitenspiele
Segnet der Sterne Heer
Die ewigen Gefühle;
Schlafe! was willst du mehr?

Die ewigen Gefühle
Heben mich, hoch und hehr,
Aus irdischem Gewühle;
Schlafe! was willst du mehr?

Vom irdischen Gewühle
Trennst du mich nur zu sehr,
Bannst mich in diese Kühle;
Schlafe! was willst du mehr?

Bannst mich in diese Kühle,
Gibst nur im Traum Gehör.
Ach, auf dem weichen Pfühle
Schlafe! was willst du mehr?

O lend, from your soft pillow,
Dreaming, but half an ear!
To the music of my strings
Sleep! What more do you desire?

To the music of my strings
The host of stars
Blesses eternal feelings;
Sleep! What more do you desire?

These eternal feelings
Raise me high and glorious
Above the earthly throng;
Sleep! What more do you desire?

From this earthly throng
You separate me only too well,
You hold me spellbound in this cool remoteness,
Sleep! What more do you desire?

You spellbind me to this coolness,
Giving ear only in your dream,
Ah, on your soft pillow
Sleep! What more do you desire?

JOHANN WOLFGANG VON GOETHE (1749–1832); poem written shortly before 1804

This is the second of Schubert's seventy-five Goethe solo settings (1814–26). See the poet's biography for a chronological list of all the Goethe settings.

It would have been difficult for any composer to follow a work like *Gretchen am Spinnrade* with a second setting of the same poet without it being a let-down. This song is certainly less dramatic, and after the whirrings of the spinning wheel the writing for piano is extremely simple, but Schubert's continuing link with Goethe is still rather miraculous. These fourteen bars in praise of sleep are repeated five times in the hypnotic fashion of an incantation or a mantra; only an insomniac could fully appreciate the sweet reward that is proposed in such beguiling musical fashion. The song would be far better known had it not been banished to the sixth volume of the Peters Edition. The addition of a trite and thoroughly inauthentic prelude and postlude (provided by Diabelli for the first edition), the excision of two of the five marvellous verses and the transposition of the song from its rapt A flat major original, down to the more ordinary key of G (easier to sing perhaps, and thus to sell, but far less effective) have compounded the ill fortunes of the *Nachtgesang*.

In this song by a seventeen-year old, one turns to Zelter's pretty setting for a sign of his influence on Schubert, but in vain; a comparison with the setting by Reichardt (who originally set the Italian folksong, *Tu sei quel dolce fuoco* with the refrain 'Dormi, che vuoi di più', on which Goethe modelled this lyric) is similarly unenlightening. Schubert's music has the winged feet that belong to neither of the older composers. The ending of each verse uses the third of the scale as a question mark for the phrase 'was willst du mehr?', a masterful touch in which the simplest harmonic and melodic means are employed to new effect. It is the forerunner of another sublime Goethe nocturne, *Wandrers Nachtlied* II D768 from ten years later, a work that has the advantage of epigrammatic brevity. All five of Goethe's verses need to be sung in *Nachtgesang*; they make a huge arc, starting at the pillow of the dreamer and returning there after wandering through the nocturnal universe, the third line of each verse becoming the first line of the next. This is a test of technical endurance for the singer, for the song lies in a demanding tessitura, 'high and glorious above the earthly throng', and the marking is pianissimo throughout. This difficulty is another reason for the song's neglect. In the second half of each verse Schubert allows the voice to float free in the starry treble, while the piano slumbers, confined to the five-line grid of the bass stave. In that greatest of nocturnes, *Nacht und Träume* D827, he was once again to place a huge and empty dome of night sky between the song's two protagonists.

Autograph:	Wienbibliothek im Rathaus, Vienna (fair copy)
First edition:	Published as Book 47 no. 4 of the *Nachlass* by Diabelli, Vienna in 1850 (P378)
Subsequent editions:	Peters: Vol. 6/56; AGA XX 32: Vol. 1/197; NSA IV: Vol. 7/55; Bärenreiter: Vol. 6/1
Bibliography:	Capell 1928, p. 86
	Einstein 1951, p. 105
Further settings and arrangements:	Johann Friedrich Reichardt (1752–1814) *Nachtgesang* (1809)
	Carl Friedrich Zelter (1758–1832) *Nachtgesang* (1809)
	Carl Loewe (1796–1869) *Nachtgesang* for SATB chorus Op. 79 no. 2 (1836)
	Wilhelm Petersen (1890–1957) *Nachtgesang* Op. 40 no. 4 (1941)
	Arr. Tilman Hoppstock (b. 1961) for guitar accompaniment, in *Franz Schubert: 110 Lieder* (2009)
Discography and timing:	Fischer-Dieskau I 2[13] 3'32
	Hyperion I 12[20]
	Hyperion II 4[6] 4'10 Adrian Thompson

←— *Gretchen am Spinnrade* D118   *Schäfers Klagelied* D121 —→

NACHTGESANG   Song of night
(Kosegarten) **D314** [H193]

The song exists in two versions, the second of which is discussed below:
(1) 19 October 1815; (2) 1816 (?)

(1) 'Sehr langsam'   E♭ major   ¢   [21 bars]

(2) E♭ major

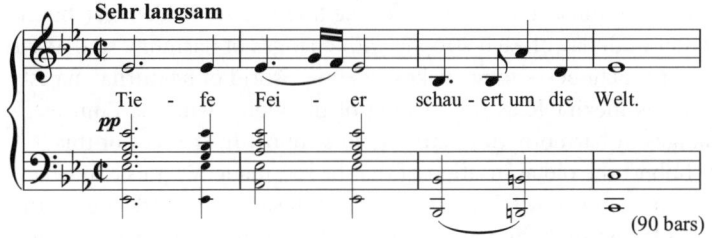

Tiefe Feier	Deep solemnity
Schauert um die Welt.	Hovers over the world.
Braune Schleier	A brown veil
Hüllen Wald und Feld.	Shrouds wood and field.
Trüb' und matt und müde	Unhappy, listless and weary
Nickt jedes Leben ein,	All living creatures drowse off to sleep,
Und namenloser Friede	And ineffable peace
Umsäuselt alles Sein!	Envelops every being.
Wacher Kummer,	Wakeful sorrow,
Verlass ein Weilchen mich!	Leave me a while.
Goldner Schlummer,	Golden slumber,
Komm und umflügle mich!	Come, enfold me in your wings.
Trockne meine Tränen	Dry my tears
Mit deines Schleiers Saum,	With the hem of your veil,
Und täusche, Freund, mein Sehnen	And delude my longing, friend,
Mit deinem schönsten Traum!	With your loveliest dream.
Blaue Ferne	Blue distance
Hoch über mich erhöht!	Raised high above me!
Heilge Sterne	Sacred stars
In hehrer Majestät!	In sublime majesty!
Sagt mir, ist es stiller,	Tell me, twinkling ones,
Ihr Funkelnden, bei euch,	Is it more tranquil with you
Als in der Eitelkeiten	Than in this tumultuous kingdom
Aufruhrvollem Reich?	Of vanities?

Ludwig Kosegarten (1758–1818); poem written in 1787

This is the fifteenth of Schubert's twenty-one Kosegarten solo settings (1815–17). See the poet's biography for a chronological list of all the Kosegarten settings, as well as a discussion of Morten Solvik's Kosegarten Liederkreis and this song's place within it.

There could be no better illustration than this single page of music of how deeply Zumsteeg influenced Schubert, and how completely Schubert surpassed him. Zumsteeg's *Nachtgesang* (a rather beautiful song) appears in the first volume of the *Kleine Balladen und Lieder*, a volume that the younger composer almost certainly owned (or borrowed). The symptoms of Schubert's homage-revisionism are all there: his song is in the same key as Zumsteeg's (E flat), and the rhythmic notation of the first bar is the same (dotted minim plus crotchet). Thus on the printed page the songs do not appear dissimilar, except that Zumsteeg's seems longer and is written for an all-purpose voice in the middle of the range, whereas the tessitura of Schubert's is clearly conceived for the bass or contralto voice. Schubert's setting is completely strophic whereas Zumsteeg has made a curious compromise: the vocal line of the three verses is identical, but he has varied the accompanimental underlay of each strophe with changes of harmony so that the tune is the same, yet not the same. Schubert's song evokes an entire world of nocturnal majesty that makes the musical repeats as inevitable as the turning of the globe, whereas Zumsteeg's setting benefits from the changes in harmony from strophe to strophe. In the face of this it is impossible to level against Schubert the old accusation of that he has made his music unnecessarily complicated in comparison to the 'purity' of his musical forbears. Schubert's superiority lies not only in the simplicity of the accompaniment, but also in his gift for melody and memorable turn of phrase with which the older man could not compete.

The first half of the song has that marvellous combination of stillness and enormity of scale which is a Schubertian speciality; one is reminded that the composer had written *Meeres Stille* D216 four months earlier, and the opening of *Wehmut* D772, a much later song, also comes to mind. At 'Braune Schleier / Hüllen Wald und Feld' (bb. 5–6) the melody lifts momentarily into A flat major only to turn around on itself and slip, as secretively as the words suggest, into the pervasive mist of G minor. The middle section (from b. 10 and the words 'Trüb' und matt und müde') drags its feet in appropriately tortuous chromaticism for two bars before the 'namenloser Friede' of night (bb. 14–15) smooths the harmony back into nocturnal diatonicism. All in all this is a remarkable achievement; as Capell writes, 'The Schubert of *Wandrers Nachtlied* is announced.'

The NSA prints an earlier version of the song that differs only in the tiniest details (without the rolled chords in the second version) but with the same tempo marking and time signature. It is this that is dated 19 October 1815. The second version probably dates from some time in 1816. Of Kosegarten's three strophes printed above, the first two were recorded for the Hyperion Edition.

Autograph:	Library of Congress, Washington (first version)
	Houghton Library of Harvard College, Linbury, Cambridge, MA (second version)
First edition:	Published as Vol. 7 no. 38 in Friedlaender's edition by Peters, Leipzig in 1887 (P499)
Subsequent editions:	Peters: Vol. 7/88; AGA XX 161: Vol. 3/144; NSA IV: Vol. 9/150 (first version) & 151 (second version)
Bibliography:	Capell 1928, p. 95
	Fischer-Dieskau 1977, p. 57
Arrangements:	Arr. Tilman Hoppstock (b. 1961) for guitar accompaniment, in *Franz Schubert: 110 Lieder* (2009)
Discography and timing:	Fischer-Dieskau I 5³⁵ 3'35
	Hyperion I 20¹⁶
	Hyperion II 11⁵ 2'47 Michael George

← *Die Sterne* D313   *An Rosa I* D315 →

NACHTHELLE
(SEIDL) **D892** [H607]
B♭ major   September 1826

Night brightness

Solo and
Chorus (TTBB)

(158 bars)

Die Nacht ist heiter und ist rein,	The night is serene and pure
Im allerhellsten Glanz:	In brightest radiance.
Die Häuser schau'n verwundert drein,	The houses gaze, spellbound,
Steh'n übersilbert ganz.	All bathed in silver.

In mir ist's hell so wunderbar,
  So voll und übervoll,
Und waltet drinnen frei und klar,
  Ganz ohne Leid und Groll.

Ich fass' in meinem Herzenshaus
  Nicht all' das reiche Licht:
Es will hinaus, es muss hinaus,
  Die letzte Schranke bricht.[1]

I am filled to overflowing
  With a wondrous brightness;
Inside I feel free and clear,
  Quite without sorrow or anger.

In my heart's house I cannot contain
  All this abundant light;
It wants to escape, it must escape,
  The last fetters break.

JOHANN GABRIEL VON SEIDL (1804–1875)

In Seidl's *Lieder der Nacht* (1826) this poem occupies a modest place; it consists of three verses that give little clue to the grand setting that Schubert had in store for it. The last line for the poem (as printed) is 'Ich hält' es länger nicht' ('I cannot bear it any longer') which the composer has changed (almost certainly with the poet's permission and collaboration) to the grander and more poetic 'Die letzte Schranke bricht'. In Seidl's poem the narrator is indoors gazing through a window – until he cannot resist the temptation to drink in the beauties of the night sky. With 'Ich hält' es länger nicht' we feel him abruptly throw down his papers, take up his hat and coat, and leave the room, outward bound. And there the poem ends.

  From the very beginning of Schubert's setting, however, we find ourselves outdoors and under the vast cupola of the heavens; a vista of this grandeur cannot be contained or framed by any window; later in the song these windows are the 'eyes' looking out astonished at the stars. Semiquavers pulsate gently in the treble register and they continue to do so throughout *Nachthelle*, signifying the same electrical energy of starlight that Schubert was soon to convey in his Leitner setting *Die Sterne* D939. A continual figuration of this kind underlines the night sky as an all-embracing presence, and one that we are powerless to disturb or influence. These luminous chords, mezzo staccato but bathed in pedal, flood the song in muted, silvery light; open fifths in the left hand prick out the emergence of individual stars which blink at us as we survey the vast sweep of the heavens.

[1] Seidl writes '*Ich halt' es länger nicht!*'.

The solo vocal line ('damnably high' was the somewhat rueful verdict of the composer's friend Ferdinand Walcher) is a creation of great beauty and considerable technical difficulty for the tenor. Ludwig Tietze, who gave the first performance in January 1827, must have had the sort of facility at the top of his range that encouraged the composer to write like this. The chorus echoes the opening solo line at a respectful distance, somewhat lower in the stave. This process, whereby the tightrope-walking of the lead tenor is repeated (in modified form) by the other singers, continues throughout the song. The very houses are moved to expressions of amazement by the night sky (from b. 22), the door of each a mouth, the upstairs windows blinking eyes. This is particularly well illustrated by the choral echo of 'Die Häuser schau'n verwundert drein' (from b. 25): the chromaticism of a C^7 chord slips into a second inversion of E minor with a touch of humour as the composer smiles at the image. (Astonished houses pose little challenge if you are composing songs about speaking graves at the same time – cf. the contemporary *Grab und Mond* D893.) The phrase 'Steh'n übersilbert ganz' is echoed twice to bring the verse to an end.

The second verse (from b. 40) is perhaps the most heroic of the piece   this is real outdoor music with a touch of competitive masculinity with the choral echoes, for once, striving to match the tessitura of the solo phrases. The chorus begins to dovetail with the solo line; the tenor must now undertake valiant stratospheric excursions, supported by his colleagues underneath him (at passages like the first 'Ganz ohne Leid und Groll' from b. 51, for example). The climax of the work is at 'es muss hinaus, / Die letzte Schranke bricht', the last section of Seidl's poem but only the middle of the song. Here soloist and chorus, impatient to break out of everything that constricts them, find themselves almost in unison within an unashamed fortissimo, although the choral singers are spared the soloist's high B flats (bb. 71 and 76).

A magical pianissimo shift to C major at b. 81 sends us back to the beginning of the poem for a modified recapitulation. From now on we hear only the words of the first strophe, but with many elaborations and repetitions. The words 'Steh'n übersilbert ganz' are here set a notch higher, the intrepid soloist touching B flat (bb. 114–15) while turning the corner of the phrase with the utmost delicacy. In the final section Schubert amuses himself with ravishing variations and elaborations of his original ideas. It is like watching a young god at play, rearranging the constellations for pure pleasure, and shifting them back again just as easily. This leisurely sport is a feature of a number of the Seidl settings. The piece ends simply, with a layered effect: the basses sing 'Die Nacht ist heiter und ist rein' in open fifths at b. 147 as do the choral tenors at b. 150. In the middle of this luxuriant Milky Way of sound, the soloist has the same words on the third of the B flat major chord. Once again, and for the last time, he has to brave the heights for a final B flat, five stratospheric beats in all. The composer allows him to sing this for two beats fewer than the chorus's final note. This is to clear the air for the piano's tiny postlude where open fifths in the left hand lead to the depths of the stave, the huge span of the heavens once again illustrated by the distance between the pianist's hands.

The work is one of Schubert's greatest choral pieces. It paints Seidl's words in a manner both magisterial and tender, and far beyond the expectations of the poet. This mastery is typical of the songs of 1826, confirming that Schubert had moved into a new command of his medium and could now fill a canvas of this size with ease, grace and musical power. When music lovers hear *Nachthelle* for the first time (because it is a choral work it is quite easy for even the most devoted song enthusiast to miss) they are invariably smitten with something of the childlike wonder that is so unerringly depicted in this music.

Autograph: Wienbibliothek im Rathaus, Vienna (first draft)
First edition: Published as Op. post. 134 by Diabelli, Vienna in 1839 (P328)

First known performance:	25 January 1827, Musikverein, Vienna. Performers: Ludwig Tietze with unnamed 'Chor' (see Waidelich/Hilmar Dokumente I No. 445 for full concert programme)
Contemporary reviews:	*Berliner allgemeine musikalische Zeitung*, No. 9 (28 February 1827), p. 70ff. [Waidelich/Hilmar Dokumente I No. 455]
Subsequent editions:	AGA XVI 13: p. 98; NSA III: Vol. 3
Bibliography:	Black 2003, p. 146
Arrangements:	Arr. Hans Zender (b. 1936) for tenor, chorus and orchestra [*see* ORCHESTRATIONS]
Discography and timing:	Hyperion I 26[19] 5'52 John Mark Ainsley & The London Hyperion II 32[13] Schubert Chorale (dir. Stephen Layton)

← *Hippolits Lied* D890   *Grab und Mond* D893 →

NACHTHYMNE
(NOVALIS) **D687** [H442]
D major   January 1820

Hymn to the night

(108 bars)

Hinüber wall' ich,	I shall pass over,
Und jede Pein	And all pain
Wird einst ein Stachel	Will be a stab
Der Wollust sein.	Of pleasure.
Noch wenig Zeiten,	In a short while
So bin ich los	I shall be freed
Und liege trunken	And lie enraptured
Der Lieb' im Schoss.	In the bosom of love.
Unendliches Leben	Eternal life
Wogt mächtig in mir,	Will surge powerfully within me;
Ich schaue von oben	I shall gaze down on you
Herunter nach dir.	From above.
An jenem Hügel	Your radiance will fade
Verlischt dein Glanz—	On yonder hill,
Ein Schatten bringet	Shadow will bring
Den kühlenden Kranz.	A cooling wreath.
O! sauge, Geliebter,	Beloved, draw me
Gewaltig mich an,	Powerfully in,
Dass ich entschlummern	That I may fall asleep
Und lieben kann.	And love.

Ich fühle des Todes	I feel the rejuvenating
Verjüngende Flut,	Tide of death,
Zu Balsam und Äther	My blood is changed
Verwandelt mein Blut—	To balm and ether.
Ich lebe bei Tage	By day I live
Voll Glauben und Mut,	Full of faith and courage;
Und sterbe die Nächte	At night I die
In heiliger Glut.	In the sacred fire.

Novalis (pseudonym of Friedrich von Hardenberg) (1772–1801); poem written in 1797

This is the last of Schubert's six Novalis solo settings (1819–20). See the poet's biography for a chronological list of all the Novalis settings.

Whatever reservations exist about the austerity and awkwardness of the four hymns of Novalis (listed in the NSA and this work under the title *Geistliches Lied*) set by Schubert in May 1819, the *Nachthymne* of 1820 is one of his masterpieces. Its inexplicable absence from the Peters Edition makes it almost certainly the least-known of all the composer's great settings of a great poet. It would certainly number among the desert-island choices of many an ardent Schubertian, not only because of the beauty of the music but because the poem is timelessly modern, as relevant to the Symbolists and Expressionists as to Schlegel and Goethe, Freud and Jung. This poem may not have the humanity, good sense and classical control of Goethe, the technical perfection of Rückert or the narrative intensity of Müller, but it is suffused with an incandescence that is both more potent and yet more ethereal than many a work by those masters. Apart from its obvious historical link with Friedrich Schlegel, friend of Novalis, it is nearer, if anything, to Mayrhofer – and this is no coincidence when we count the literary influences at work on that complicated poet. In Novalis the composer has found another dreamer-magician who can match him as he disports himself in the Elysian fields. Not for the first time Schubert combines the deeply spiritual with the erotic, maintaining these two powerful elements in as effortless a musical balance as is achieved by the poet in his verbal imagery. There is something of this delicious combination of opposites in Goethe's *Ganymed* D544, but *Nachthymne* is a more daring work; when the poet lies 'enraptured in the bosom of love' the breadth of the canvas is as broad as the horizon, unrestricted by an eighteenth-century pastoral frame.

Schubert chooses the key of D major – his tonality of pilgrimage and quest – and the music begins with a chorale both simple and inimitable. (Walther Dürr likens the construction of this whole work to an Italian *cavatina* with a concluding *cabaletta*, but such is the intimate import of the words that operatic display is the last thing we think of when hearing this song.) When this composer glimpses heavenly things his Muse begins to dance in dactylic rhythm, and so it is here. A crotchet followed by two quavers (long–short–short) seems a simple enough rhythmic device, but in Schubert's hands it betokens 'letting go'– something outside the control of the singer: the turning of the world, the twinkling of the stars, the gliding footfall of death. Here it is a combination of all these things, and in terms of tonality and pace *Nachthymne* could follow on from a performance of *Der Tod und das Mädchen* D531, as if it were a sequel to the trials of the dying maiden. Where else, except perhaps in the spiritual songs from the *Spanisches Liederbuch* of Hugo Wolf, can we find such an expression of the sweetness of religious (and sexual) masochism as in the first four lines? And who else but Schubert is able to space a chord between the hands with such daring (under 'Hinüber <u>wall</u>' ich' in b. 5) that an accented passing note in the vocal line falls a semitone towards its resolution as in a wide, starry firmament of piano resonance? The music is not fast, yet we float unanchored in a void as we wait impatiently for release; exquisite dominant sevenths in b. 9, before the repeat of 'Hinüber wall' ich', usher us into a vast anteroom of the heavens. At 'Noch wenig Zeiten' (b. 14) the singer says he will only have to wait a little longer; but the astonishing harmonic dislocation in b. 15 of 'So bin ich los' – the upward stretch in the vocal line to encompass an unlikely G sharp – is emblematic of stretching outwards towards release. The repetition of 'Der Lieb' im Schoss' in a rising sequence (bb. 17–18), as if drunk on heavenly ambrosia, is both touching and erotic. This section closes with a repeat of the poem's first four lines. This chorale, where the voice seems to be accompanied by wind and brass, is reminiscent of Brahms's 'St. Antoni' theme, in its andante both stately and other-worldly. The graveside *equali*, music which is the inspiration for *Das Wirtshaus* from *Winterreise*, another dactylic hymn, also comes to mind.

The words 'Unendliches Leben / Wogt mächtig in mir' (from b. 25) usher in a middle section that serves as a wonderful extended transitional passage. It has the visceral power of 'Es schwindelt mir, es brennt / Mein Eingeweide' in the 1826 setting of Mignon's *Nur wer die Sehnsucht kennt* D877/4. Novalis's words are not dissimilar to Goethe's, except that the shocking wave of feeling Mignon experiences is the result of human pain; here the injection of energy is nothing less than the transfiguration that follows death, where the dead are also the quick. Imagine a sci-fi film where someone encountering a race of beings from another planet is unexpectedly filled with their energy and light; we see the metamorphosis in two stages accompanied by marvels of cinematic magic, the second absorption of supernatural light more intensely glowing and other-worldly than the first. So it is with Schubert the film-music composer before his time: special effects include a left-hand tremolo falling in chromatic stages as if the very foundations of our world had melted away, and a repeat of the 'Unendliches Leben' phrase in a powerful and louder sequence. And once we have crossed the barrier into a new state of being we are free to float upwards (from b. 32) into the starry realms of B flat major. (The music for the choral *Nachthelle* D892 is eerily prophesied by the phrase 'Ich schaue von oben / Herunter nach dir'.) There can be few more magisterial sweeps up and down the stave than this remarkable arc of divine observation, as if the singer suddenly has the means to fly. The bar of interlude at b. 34, B flat semiquavers in the right hand and disturbing F sharps deep in the bass, ushers in a repeat of those words, this time in B major. The right-hand chords rise a semitone (b. 36), bringing glimpses of ever-vaster celestial horizons. A remarkable cello-like solo in the piano's left hand (bb. 37–8) sustains this sense of cosmic exploration. As this phrase falls and rises, the music mirrors the poet's yearning to be reunited with his beloved. There is now a masterful ritardando ('langsamer werdend' – becoming slower – is the marking, most unusual for Schubert). To depict the gradual fading of radiance, there is a diminution not only of tempo but of intensity and, once again, sequence and repetition are used. One thinks back to a similar passage in *Cronnan* D282 as the wraith Vinvela vanishes before the eyes of Shilric. The repeat of 'An jenem Hügel / Verlischt dein Glanz' (bb. 41–2) distances itself with the drop of a semitone; the image of the beloved (Novalis's Sophie of course) seems to fade before our ears, as if she were Eurydice. Images of lengthening shadows and the cooling wreath of evening are perfectly caught by a long succession of falling bass minims which sink into the balm of E major on 'kühlenden Kranz' (b. 45). A three-bar interlude of gently pulsating semiquavers continues the idea of healing and acceptance.

The next passage, marked 'Geschwinder' ('quicker' from b. 48), is a short and impassioned plea – Novalis's longing for death as he wishes to rejoin his beloved Sophie. A note of urgency is struck by the syncopated semiquaver figure in the piano on each appearance of 'Gewaltig mich an'. The languishing setting of 'Dass ich entschlummern / Und lieben kann', half sensuous and half impatient, is particularly affecting (bb. 51–3, and repeated in bb. 55–7). A short interlude of exploratory quavers (bb. 58–60) roams around the keyboard as if testing tonality and harmony for the right means of expression. This is music that searches in the dark for the key to the final gateway leading to the heavenly state.

The last section of the song is a marvel. At b. 61 the accompaniment changes to triplets in flowing sixths (a masterstroke, implying release from the bodily state). Mozart had used a similar succession of oscillating sixths (in quavers) in his brooding on life after death in his song *Abendempfindung* K523, and Schubert had already used the same figuration in *Abendbilder* D650. (He was to do so again in *Der Lindenbaum* from *Winterreise* D911/5, a song about life before, and after, the death of love, where the sextuplets signify so much more than the rustling of leaves.) The triplets in *Nachthymne*, glistening up and down the keyboard, gently accompany the voice as it sings a melody based on the euphony of common chords. Leo Black has pointed out that the oscillating thirds in the vocal line here would reappear in 'Wenn ich nur ein Vöglein wäre' (*Der Knabe* D692) and 'Wie soll ich nicht tanzen?' (*Der Schmetterling* D633). In the first of these two Friedrich Schlegel settings the boy longs to take wing as a bird, in other words to free himself from his present mortal incarnation. (This latter point explains a certain similarity between the exaltation of this passage and that of the closing page of *Auflösung* D807.) This music where the soul flies free is some of the most ethereal and rarefied that Schubert ever wrote; the images are of flowing blood, of balsam and ether, and of implied sexual communion, and this music for an altered state has a consistency liquid enough to encompass all of these. When the poet speaks of 'rejuvenating death', of living by day and dying by night in the sacred fire, we are either in the world of nonsense or partaking in mysteries as old as Eleusis where Novalis seeks his Sophie with as much determination as Ceres begs Jupiter for the return of Proserpine. The final vocal line ('Ich fühle des Todes / Verjüngende Flut' bb. 100–4) vanishes into the stratosphere (or more accurately into the top of the stave) and dematerializes before our ears. The postlude follows suit as it climbs higher and higher up the keyboard. The soul is on its way.

At least three of the four earlier *Geistliche Lieder* seem to have been composed within a definite ascetic framework of simple church performance, either imagined or actual. With *Nachthymne*, the composer has allowed himself to respond to Novalis without any preconceived notions about what musical form is appropriate. Novalis and Schubert here reveal themselves to be a perfect match, and the many who revere the poet can only regret that Schubert in this revelatory mood did not lavish his attentions on the other five *Hymnen an die Nacht*.

Autograph:	Gesellschaft der Musikfreunde, Vienna
First edition:	Published as No. 4 of *Neueste Folge nachgelassener Lieder und Gesänge* by J. P. Gotthard, Vienna in 1872 (P430)
Subsequent editions:	Not in Peters; AGA XX 372: Vol. 6/80; NSA IV: Vol. 12/134
Bibliography:	Black 2003, pp. 67–9
	Capell 1928, pp. 159–60
	Fischer-Dieskau 1977, p. 132
	Kohlhäufl 1999, p. 270
Discography and timing:	Fischer-Dieskau II 3[14] 5'24
	Hyperion I 29[8]
	Hyperion II 22[17] 5'39 Marjana Lipovšek

←— *Morgenlied* D685   *Vier Canzonen (Non t'accostar all'urna)* D688/1 —→

Die NACHTIGALL

(Unger) Op. 11 NO. 2, **D724** [H474]

D major   April 1821

The nightingale   Quartet, TTBB

Be - schei - den ver - bor - gen im bu - schich-ten Gang

(139 bars)

Bescheiden verborgen im buschichten Gang	Shyly hidden in the bushy walk,
Erhob Philomele den Zaubergesang;	Philomela raised her voice in enchanted song,
Er schildert der Treue beglückenden[1] Lohn	Hymning the joys of constancy
In hallenden Schlägen, im wirbelnden Ton!	In echoing calls, in warbling tones.

Sanft gleitet die Stimme aus schwellender Brust[2]
Als Hauch der Gefühle, als Zeuge der Lust;

Ach horcht, wie der Seufzer der Sehnsucht
verhallt,
Wenn lieblicher Einklang der Seelen erschallt.

Her voice glides softly from her swelling breast,
An intimation of deep feelings, a witness of
pleasure;
Hark how longing sighs fade

When souls sound in sweet harmony.

So Freunde, verhallte manch himmlisches Lied,[3]
Wenn Cynthias Feuer die Finsternis schied,[4]
Es wehte mit Frieden uns wonnigen Schmerz
Auf Schwingen der Töne ins fühlende Herz.[5]

Thus, friends, did many a heavenly song fade
When Cynthia's fire departed the darkness;
Sweet pains on wings of sound
Wafted peacefully into our sentient hearts.

JOHANN KARL UNGER (1771–1836)

This quartet reworks the story from Ovid's *Metamorphoses* where Philomela turns into a nightingale as she flees her seducer. The work enjoyed an amazing success in Schubert's lifetime; indeed, with the exception of *Erlkönig*, if the number of public performances is anything to go by, it was the most popular of all his works. And why not? It has a very pretty tune, requiring the first tenor to indulge in elegant leaps, jumps, roulades and excursions above the stave which are not only impressive in themselves but which approximate to a non-ornithologist's idea of the song of the nightingale. Above all, the piece has enormous charm and, if performed correctly, delicacy. It is no surprise, however, that the public that clamoured for more performances of this work was also addicted to the Italian intendant Barbaia's diet of *bel canto* opera at the Kärntnertortheater.

The key is D major, undoubtedly the composer's favourite tonality for choral music of this kind; the choice is somewhat practical, being in the comfortable singing range of the tenors and

[1] In the manuscript copy of Unger's compositions (see the biography of the poet) the following differences are noted: *entzückenden* instead of 'beglückenden'.
[2] This line is '*Bald* gleitet die Stimme aus *sanfterer* Brust'.
[3] This line is 'So *Freundinn! ertönte dein* himmlisches Lied'.
[4] This line is '*Als* Cynthia *traulich* die Finsterniss schied'.
[5] This line is 'Auf Schwingen der *Laute* ins fühlende Herz'.

basses. The first verse is gently powered by Schubert's favoured dactylic rhythm in the three lower voices – the metre of the poetry makes this an obvious solution – while the lead tenor fills up the bar with mellifluous quavers that hop from branch to branch within, and later beyond, the fenced-in aviary of the stave. Despite this, there is a folksong-like steadiness and poise to this music that goes well with the background idea of 'Treue' (constancy). After a happy first strophe, the second (with an effective switch to F sharp minor from b. 37) concentrates on the more soulful aspects of nightingale song. At 'Sanft gleitet die Stimme', a figure of a dotted quaver is followed by two demisemiquavers, a figuration descriptive of a tiny shudder or frisson. We find this, also in conjunction with dactylic rhythm, in the middle section of the celebrated *Der Wanderer* D489 (at 'Die Sonne dünkt mich hier so kalt'). Schubertian dactyls always imply ineluctable movement, in nature, of some sort or another, whether of stars in the firmament (*Die Sterne* D939) or the gliding progress of death (*Der Tod und das Mädchen* D531). In *Die Nachtigall* they depict another natural phenomenon that has been with us since time immemorial – birdsong.

This *minore* middle section modulates into A major at b. 53, the better to return to the home key of D major for the third verse. This is a deliciously ornamented recapitulation of the song's opening; indeed it might be called a variation on the first verse, so capriciously inventive are the changes between the two versions. The phrase 'im wirbelnden Ton' is here set as a type of measured trill, hocketing high in the stave on F sharp and G (bb. 86–8). Underneath this warbling the piano reaches an F sharp major chord – the dominant of B minor. And then it is straight into a rollicking final verse (in D major once again, now marked 'Allegro') which has the character of many a Schubertian drinking song. The measured ⅔ of the nightingale's music is replaced by an earthy ⅝. Tenor I begins and, after twelve bars, Tenor II joins at b. 100 as if in a round, using the words of this strophe all over again from the beginning. He sings the same twelve bars while the first voice provides a high descant based on an inversion of the theme. Then comes the turn of the lower voices: Bass II joins in at b. 112, the tune now in G major, and after two bars Bass I takes up an inverted version of the theme, in closer canon this time. This is yet another repetition of the same words, but above them the tenors are singing 'So verhallte manch himmlisches Lied' in augmentation. Tenor I, the erstwhile nightingale, has been relatively unadventurous for this section, but in the final few pages he is liberated from his cage and returns to his high-flying decorative antics. There is an expressive chromatic descent for the words 'ins fühlende Herz' (these words are repeated) with which the piece closes.

The piano part is almost always a straightforward reduction of the vocal parts; so much so that Deutsch was moved to doubt whether the accompaniment, as with those of other pieces like it, was genuine Schubert. It might indeed be that the piano part was insisted on by the publisher, and provided by another hand. (The guitar part printed in the AGA is almost certainly spurious.) The piano writing does not show great imagination or independent invention, suggesting it might have been conceived for rehearsal purposes, but on the other hand it contains a number of tiny but important details – spacing of chords, interludes between the vocal passages and so on – that make it hard to imagine the song entirely without accompaniment. This is particularly true of the music for the beginning of the third verse where the first tenor would sound stranded without the piano's hearty support.

The biographical article on Unger describes the volume of autographs which contains a solo-song setting of *Die Nachtigall* composed by the poet himself. This may well have been Schubert's literary source for Unger's unpublished poem.

Autograph:	Missing or lost
First edition:	Published as Op. 11 no. 2 by Cappi & Diabelli, Vienna in June 1822 (P26)

Dedicatee:	Josef Barth
First known performance:	22 April 1821, Kärntnertortheater, Vienna, as unaccompanied quartet. Performers: Josef Barth, Josef Götz, Johann Umlauf & Wenzel Nejebse (see Waidelich/Hilmar Dokumente I No. 85 for full concert programme)
	The piece was performed with guitar accompaniment on 27 August 1822 at the Theater an der Wien, and with piano on 15 September 1822 in the Redoutensaal, Linz (see Waidelich/Hilmar Dokumente I Nos 168 and 174 for programmes of these performances)
Contemporary reviews:	*Der Sammler* (Vienna) No. 51 (28 April 1821), p. 204 [Waidelich/Hilmar Dokumente I No. 89]
	Conversationsblatt (Vienna) No. 34 (28 April 1821), p. 406 [Waidelich/Hilmar Dokumente I No. 90]
	Wiener allgemeine Theaterzeitung, No. 52 (1 May 1821), p. 207 [Waidelich/Hilmar Dokumente I No. 94]
	Wiener Zeitschrift für Kunst, Literatur, Theater und Mode No. 52 (1 May 1821), p. 452 [Waidelich/Hilmar Dokumente I No. 95]
	Allgemeine musikalische Zeitung (Vienna) No. 39 (16 May 1821), col. 306f. [Waidelich/Hilmar Dokumente I No. 99]
	Allgemeine musikalische Zeitung (Leipzig) No. 22 (30 May 1821), col. 379 [Waidelich/Hilmar Dokumente I No. 103]
	Abend-Zeitung (Dresden) No. 155 (29 June 1821) [Waidelich/Hilmar Dokumente I No. 108; Deutsch Doc. Biog. No. 228]
Subsequent editions:	AGA XVI 5: p. 50; NSA III: Vol. 3
Discography and timing:	Hyperion I 28[7] 3'53 Paul Agnew, Jamie MacDougall, Simon
	Hyperion II 24[16] Keenlyside & Michael George

← *Mignon II (So lasst mich scheinen, bis ich werde) D727*   *Johanna Sebus D728* →

NACHTSTÜCK   Nocturne
(MAYRHOFER) OP. 36 NO. 2, **D672** [H437]

The song exists in two versions, both of which are discussed below:
(1) October 1819; (2) appeared February 1825

(1)   'Langsam   C♯ minor   **C**   [68 bars]

(2)   C minor

(68 bars)

Wenn über Berge sich der Nebel breitet,[1]	When the mists spread over the mountains,
Und Luna mit Gewölken kämpft,	And the moon battles with the clouds,
So nimmt der Alte seine Harfe, und schreitet,[2]	The old man takes his harp, and walks
Und singt waldeinwärts und gedämpft:	Towards the wood, singing in muffled tones:

'Du heilge Nacht!	'Holy night,
'Bald ist's vollbracht.	'Soon it will be done.
'Bald schlaf' ich ihn	'Soon I shall sleep
'Den langen Schlummer,	'The long sleep
'Der mich erlöst	'Which will free me
'Von allem Kummer.'[3]	'From all grief.'

'Die grünen Bäume rauschen dann,	'Then the green trees rustle:
'Schlaf süss, du guter, alter Mann;	'Sleep sweetly, good old man;
'Die Gräser lispeln wankend fort,	'And the swaying grasses whisper:
'Wir decken seinen Ruheort;	'We shall cover his resting place.
'Und mancher liebe Vogel ruft:[4]	'And many a sweet bird calls:
'O lasst ihn ruhn in Rasengruft!'—	'Let him rest in his grassy grave!'

Der Alte horcht, der Alte schweigt—	The old man listens, the old man is silent.
Der Tod hat sich zu ihm geneigt.	Death has inclined towards him.

JOHANN MAYRHOFER (1787–1836)

This is the thirty-sixth of Schubert's forty-seven Mayrhofer solo settings (1814–24). See the poet's biography for a chronological list of all the Mayrhofer settings.

This great song and *Lied eines Schiffers an die Dioskuren* D360 are the most frequently performed of all the Mayrhofer settings. The grandeur of the concept, an ageing minstrel's farewell to life in an imposing aria, and an accompaniment that begins with wonderful scene-setting opportunities, has always attracted singers and pianists. Schubert brought to this song all that he had learned from the Bardic literature of Ossian. Together with Mayrhofer he evokes a somewhat indeterminate age of ancient minstrelsy where life and death were ordained in a pre-Christian manner by the natural cycles of nature, where singing and playing have a 'primal rightness' (as Thomas Hardy might have put it) and where there was no need to hope for a heavenly reward or afterlife. It is enough for the dying musician that his body will become part of the earth again, and that he will merge back into the forest greenery and the beauties of nature from which he and his song have drawn inspiration.

In a letter to his father and stepmother (25 July 1825) written while on holiday in Upper Austria with Vogl, Schubert shows how far this kind of thinking, no doubt inspired by Mayrhofer, had entered into his own philosophy. The composer refers to the hypochondriacal tendencies of his brother Ferdinand:

> . . . *he has undoubtedly been ill 77 times again, and thought 9 times that he was going to die, as though dying were the worst that can happen to a man! If only he could once see these heavenly mountains and lakes, the sight of which threatens to crush or engulf us, he would not be attached to puny human life, nor regard it as otherwise than good fortune to be confided to earth's indescribable power of creating new life.*

[1] Mayrhofer writes '*Wann* über Berge sich der Nebel breitet'. For an explanation of the background to these alternative Mayrhofer readings see Editorial Note at the beginning of Johann MAYRHOFER.
[2] Mayrhofer writes 'So nimmt der Alte seine *Harf*', und schreitet'.
[3] Mayrhofer writes 'Von *jedem* Kummer'.
[4] Mayrhofer writes 'Und mancher *traute* Vogel ruft'.

This aged minstrel, expiring as he sings, will clearly have an unmarked grave. He has a 'good' death, a death without violence, and the moral is that he deserves such an ending because he has fulfilled his role in the community as an artist and seer. As Susan Youens points out, Mayrhofer's noble vision of his going in *Nachtstück* was horrifyingly distant from the reality of his actual suicide.

There is no opportunity with these verses for the wonderfully discursive and descriptive recitative passages of the Ossian settings. Instead, the music has a condensed structure. What could be tighter than the dotted rhythm (verging on double-dotted rhythm) of the opening? The overture to the song (for it is nothing less in terms of its grandeur) is scored as if for string quartet, although the dramatic emphases of a more percussive piano sound are essential to its effect. The topic is the death of an old master, and the regal polyphony of the old masters is accordingly apparent – in particular the oratorios of Handel that were likewise the models for Haydn's *Die Schöpfung*. Schubert's 'Creation' is a bleak and dark mountain landscape shrouded in mists. The clouds gather above, obscuring the moon; we hear their majestic accumulation in the crescendo beginning in b. 2, and the gradually thickening textures of clouds leading to the forte chord halfway through b. 3. The sudden piano dynamic in the middle of b. 4 is like a weak beam of moonlight that filters through the mists, a solitary spotlight on the noble protagonist contemplating his end. When the narrator enters at b. 6 with Mayrhofer's first two lines of poetry, the words have already been interpreted in pianistic terms; for this reason their accompaniment is simply the overture repeated an octave lower (bb. 6–10). The breakthrough of the weaker moon struggling with the mighty clouds now coincides with 'Und Luna mit Gewölken kämpft'.

The *alla breve* sign at b. 11 is crucial to the interpretation here. In effect it gives the performers the permission they need to double the tempo (so that 'Sehr langsam' applies to the minim rather than to the crotchet) and is a chance to inject human purposefulness into the static scene. The old man is determined, but hardly an athlete (in some performances the passage from b. 11 positively whizzes by) – one must sense his creaking old bones as he walks towards the wood. The bare texture here recalls the opening of another Mayrhofer setting from earlier in 1819, *An die Freunde* D654. 'Do not be sorry for me' is the burden of that song, and the austerity of the old man's walk to his death has a similar disdain for musical fuss or sentimentality. With the words 'waldeinwärts und gedämpft' he sings himself into the woods with no one to hear him; at bb. 14–17 (and the empty echo linking these phrases in the accompaniment) it seems as if he is throwing his voice, muted by age, into a dark void. The depth of the forest here is to be equated with something potentially frightening, like the distant howling of wolves. (Mayrhofer's poetry is not without its eccentricities to the modern German ear. 'Gedämpft' is translatable as 'damped down' but in modern German it means 'steamed' as in 'steamed vegetables'; this gave Brigitte Fassbaender an excuse to add to the word a whispered '—es Gemüse' under her breath just before she embarked on the old man's aria, the sudden mention of vegetables wickedly challenging the self-control of her accompanists.)

The invocation to sacred night, deliverer of sleep and eternal repose, is Schubert at his most bardic. Having already composed the *Harfnerlieder* from Goethe's *Wilhelm Meister*, he was well acquainted with the harp as an instrument of tragic confession. In *Nachtstück* the strummed strings inspire a cantilena which goes back to Klopstock's grand hymn, *Dem Unendlichen* D291 of 1815. The fervent religiosity of that address to the author of the universe is not to be found here, but there is something of the same grandeur in the broad curves of the melodic shape that are underpinned by the rolling arpeggios of the accompaniment. These are marked 'mit gehobener Dämpfung', the raised dampers of the piano adding an atmospheric mist to this plea for merciful release. In bb. 26–9 the singer longs for the sleep that will free him ('Der mich erlöst') from all sorrow ('Von allem Kummer'): the tightening of harmonic tension through the rising bass line of bb. 26–7 ('Der mich erlöst') is followed by a miraculous resolution, an unlocking of tension on the grandiose cadence to the relative major (itself like a sob of relief) of 'Von allem Kummer' at b. 28. The vocal stamina required for this extended address is considerable and it is rare to hear a great performance of this song. Those who are strong of voice and lung tend to resort to bellowing (despite there being only a few moments of forte in the whole piece) and those who are less hardy can become winded and short of breath.

After the old man has finished his swansong (at b. 38) the responsibility for the narrative is handed over to the forest's inhabitants who whisper consolatory words and sing his requiem. In piano figurations of the utmost delicacy (almost to the point of winsomeness) semiquaver triplets attached to accented quavers waft between E flat major and A flat minor (at least at first) to represent trees rustling their farewell, whispering grasses, chirping birdsong – all the voices of nature paying tribute to a faithful colleague. At this stage the singer must have reserves of *mezza voce* left to sing the phrases in direct speech (beginning at b. 42 with 'Schlaf süss, du guter, alter Mann'). This writing would not have been possible without the example of Schlegel's *Abendröte* poems where birds, mountains, rivers and streams are anthropomorphized and allowed to address mankind in their own words. It would be wrong to suggest that dainty voices need to be found for these articulate trees and birds, and equally wrong to say that these unworldly participants should be denied a special colour by the interpreter. A great performer will find a way to suggest intimate communing without resorting to vocal tricks.

The final page of the song (from b. 59) is one of the greatest Schubert codas. The poem itself suggests that the bard dies standing up. The music on the other hand seems to allow the old man to sink gradually to his knees, or to slowly melt back into the forest landscape which lovingly reclaims him. The poet tells us that it is 'Der Tod' who bends down towards the old man to gather him into his embrace. Three stages of death are reflected in an extraordinary chain of sequences and modulations grouped in one-bar phrases with a pivotal key change halfway through each. There can be nothing automatic about playing these bars; that tiny hesitation that is Schubertian rubato almost always occurs on the bar line, and there are moments in this passage when the first appearance of a new chord (italicized below) has to be placed by the pianist with great sensibility:

'Der Alte horcht': E flat major to B flat major (b. 59), and then *E flat minor* to B flat major (b. 60). The change to the minor key here suggests the deepest awareness as the old man listens to the call of the infinite.

'Der Alte schweigt': D flat major to A flat major (b. 61) and then *D flat minor* to A flat major (b. 62). The old man falls at last into deathly silence.

'Der Tod hat sich [zu ihm geneigt]': C minor to G major (b. 63) and then *C major* to G major. The comforting balm of death is perfectly depicted in that change to C major that comes like a richly deserved blessing. The music dissolves and dematerializes, leaving an aura of primordial peace.

Schubert first composed this song in C sharp minor. By the time he came to publish it in 1825 his illness had changed his life for ever, and this song from the Mayrhofer years must have reminded him, with some emotion, of the productive times when he and the poet had worked together in the Wipplingerstrasse. Perhaps Schubert decided to recast the piece in C minor for its first edition because he wanted to darken the colour of the music into something more tragic. We have to take it that this was his final decision, but there is a chance that it was a publisher-influenced transposition. The AGA prints only the C sharp minor version, coming as this does from an impeccable manuscript source; the NSA prints both versions, the Peters Edition only the C minor. For a tenor of the right timbre and flexibility the C sharp minor version should still be a carefully considered option.

On 29 March 1869, at a recital in Vienna, Johannes Brahms accompanied Julius Stockhausen in *Nachtstück*; there are surviving fragments in Brahms's papers of an instrumentation of the song.

Autograph:	Gesellschaft der Musikfreunde, Vienna (first draft)
Publication:	First published as part of the NSA in 1975 (P761; first version)
	First published as Op. 36 no. 2 by Cappi & Co., Vienna in February 1825 (P76; second version)
Dedicatee:	Katharina Lászny von Folkusfálva
Subsequent editions:	Peters: Vol. 2/82; AGA XX 368: Vol. 6/62; NSA IV: Vol. 2a/125 & Vol. 2b/222; Bärenreiter: Vol. 2/24
Bibliography:	Capell 1928, p. 161
	Einstein 1951, p. 191
	Fischer-Dieskau 1977, p. 205
	Youens 1996, pp. 209–14
Further settings and arrangements:	Franz Köringer (1921–2000) *Hommage an Franz Schubert* (this song included in mixture of lieder) (1996)
	Arr. Tilman Hoppstock (b. 1961) for guitar accompaniment, in *Franz Schubert: 110 Lieder* (2009)
Discography and timing:	Fischer-Dieskau II 3[11] 5'53
	Pears-Britten 1[3] 6'14
	Hyperion I 4[13] & 11[3] 5'46 Philip Langridge
	5'08 Brigitte Fassbaender
	Hyperion II 22[12] 5'46 Philip Langridge

← *Prometheus* D674   *Strophe aus 'Die Götter Griechenlands'* D677 →

NACHTVIOLEN
(Mayrhofer) **D752** [H484]
C major   April 1822

Dame's violets

(46 bars)

Nachtviolen, Nachtviolen!	Dame's violets,
Dunkle Augen, Seelenvolle,—	Dark, soulful eyes,
Selig ist es, sich versenken[1]	It is blissful to immerse myself
In dem sammtnen Blau.[2]	In your velvety blue.

[1] Mayrhofer writes 'Selig ist es, sich *vertiefen*'. For an explanation of the background to these alternative Mayrhofer readings see Editorial Note at the beginning of Johann Mayrhofer.
[2] Mayrhofer writes 'In *das sammtne* Blau'.

Grüne Blätter streben freudig,	Green leaves strive joyously
Euch zu hellen, euch zu schmücken;	To brighten you, to adorn you;
Doch ihr blicket ernst und schweigend[3]	But you gaze, solemn and silent,
In die laue Frühlingsluft.[4]	Into the mild spring air.
[(. . . 1 line . . .)]	[(. . . 1 line . . .)]
Mit erhabnen Wehmutsstrahlen	With sublime shafts of melancholy
Trafet ihr mein treues Herz,[5]	You have pierced my faithful heart,
Und nun blüht in stummen Nächten,	And now, in silent nights,
Fort die heilige Verbindung.	Our sacred union blossoms.
[(. . . 2 lines . . .)]	[(. . . 2 lines . . .)]

JOHANN MAYRHOFER (1787–1836); poem written in 1821

This is the forty-first of Schubert's forty-seven Mayrhofer solo settings (1814–24). See the poet's biography for a chronological list of all the Mayrhofer settings.

There is some confusion about the identity of the flowers hymned by Mayrhofer. The most obvious candidate is the Dame's violet, the tall wild flower *Hesperis matronalis*, also known sometimes as sweet rocket. In German this is the 'Gemeine Nachtviole'. There are several species of this plant that comes in various colours from white to violet to purple and grows 30–80 centimetres high, the flowers surmounting supporting green foliage on long stems. These flowers give off a wonderful fragrance on summer evenings and can appear to glow in the half-light. In Leopold Trattinnick's anthology of floral verses, *Osterreichischer Blumenkranz* (Vienna, 1819), another Nachtviole, the Afrikanische Nachtviole *(Hesperis africana)* – the so-called African violet – appears on p. 238. We learn from that great Austrian botanist that although this flower comes from 'Barbarian lands' it has been found growing for some years in Hungary where it has been welcomed as a guest resident. Perhaps Schubert encountered an arrangement of these flowers in the drawing room in Zseliz in 1818 – they would almost certainly have been sold in the better flower shops in Vienna. It would help if either variety were unequivocally 'velvety-blue' as Mayrhofer describes the flower.

The sweet-scented violet (whatever its species) has long been a symbol of faithfulness and modesty and the music for this lyric evokes both these things. The small compass of the tune, slender-stemmed, is poised at the top of the stave (Schubert's evocation of the flower's delicately balanced height is an illustrative point that favours *Hesperis matronalis* over the more stumpy *Hesperis africana*). The repetitive nature of the motifs and sequences suggests a type of perennial tenacity, clinging through thick and thin. The simple musical means employed throughout are modest to the point of humility which in Schubert's hands means a deepening rather than an impoverishment of compositional eloquence. All in all, these 'two pages of soft radiance' (Gerald Moore) are acknowledged to be the quintessential Schubert flower song – 'a masterpiece of mysterious intimacy' (Einstein).

Whether the poem should be read as an allegory for something deeper than a flower enthusiast's observations is a moot point. We know that in the spring of 1821 Schubert selected a

---

[3] Mayrhofer writes 'Doch ihr *schauet*, ernst und *ahnend*'.
[4] Mayrhofer writes 'In die laue *Sommer*luft'.
[5] Mayrhofer writes 'Trafet ihr *sein* treues Herz', referring back to himself, 'Der Dichter' mentioned in the cut line.

number of poems from Mayrhofer's handwritten cycle entitled *Heliopolis*; Mayrhofer had put this together by combining new poems with several lyrics he had written earlier. The tenor of the work is summed up by the Blake-like mottos at the head of the manuscript: 'Die Kinder der Welt sind klüger, als die Kinder des Lichts, letztere aber sind seliger'(The children of the world are cleverer than the children of light, but the latter are more blessed); 'Wie die Perser der Sonne, werden die Völker der Kunst huldigen' (Just as the Persians worshipped the sun, so will the peoples worship Art). The cycle concerned the state of the artist in society, imagining a city-state of the sun named Heliopolis where art and artists governed and regulated all things. *Nachtviolen* shared a manuscript with *Heliopolis* I D753 and *Heliopolis* II D754, two songs that specifically describe Mayrhofer's dream. Caught between two such idealistic texts *Nachtviolen* strikes a very personal note. Fischer-Dieskau states unequivocally that *Nachtviolen* 'sorrowfully recalls' the friendship between composer and poet. Another school of thought would regard this song as Schubert's hymn to his putatively romantic friendship with Franz von Schober after they had worked together on *Alfonso und Estella* D732, the shy and modest composer perhaps casting himself as the violet, gazing solemnly and with foreboding ('ahnend' which Schubert changes to 'schweigend' – silently) into the unfriendly outside world?

A glance at Mayrhofer's original shows how at home Schubert was amending his friend's verses to his purposes. He creates three regular four-line strophes by suppressing three of the poem's original lines. One of these had referred rather grandly to the poet in the third person: by changing 'sein treues Herz' to 'mein treues Herz' in the last verse Schubert makes the lyric infinitely easier for a singer to present to an audience. Mayrhofer's original has the violet gazing into the mild *summer* air which is seemingly correct for *Hesperis matronalis*; possibly because wild violets bloom early in the spring Schubert changes 'Sommerluft' to 'Frühlingsluft'. Mayrhofer retained his version of the words as we can see from the 1843 posthumous edition of his poems, but the song was composed in the spring.

Mayrhofer the classicist would have known that the Greeks had chosen the violet as Aphrodite's flower; perhaps he would also have known that the ancients used it as a cure for headaches, melancholia and insomnia, complaints to which the highly strung poet was surely no stranger. He must have been enraptured with this setting (Schubert's alterations to his texts notwithstanding) which is a herbal balm in music, a rescue remedy to soothe and heal wounds of the heart.

The tune, doubling back on itself after each bar, has the simplicity of an immortal nursery rhyme. The accompaniment is remarkable for its airy tessitura: there is almost no music for the bass clef, the pianist's left hand only straying into this region at the end of the song. Purity, innocence and vulnerability are allowed to flourish in a blameless region of childlike rapture. The diminished sevenths that occur twice in the ritornello are harmonic surprises that seem to evoke the surprise of a ravishing fragrance. (We hear this even more eloquently in another more or less contemporary song, *Dass sie hier gewesen* D775, where the east wind bears the scent of his lover to the enraptured poet.) *Nachtviolen* is near enough in ABA form but one of its greatest glories is in the third verse and the modification of the recapitulation. The vocal line changes to make an eloquent coda, but the interplay of voice and piano is most telling here – a variation of surpassing loveliness that seems a tonal analogue for the blossoming of a friendship, with obbligato tendrils of counter-melody signifying togetherness and cooperation.

The bell-like chiming of similar thoughts in the heights of both voice and piano is not unlike the last verse of Brahms's *Wir wandelten* Op. 96 no. 2 where the same idea of unspoken unanimity of thought is expressed. But the music also depicts a gradual but inexorable drifting apart as the pianist is pulled briefly into the bass clef while the flowering vocal line remains in a higher region of the stave. It is possible that these deeper accompanying resonances represent a strengthening of the 'heilige Verbindung' (the flattened ninth at that point is memorably poignant), but the diverging paths of voice and piano could also signify, as Gerald Moore wrote, 'a leave-taking made with affectionate reluctance'.

Autographs:	Udbye Collection, Oslo (first 25 bars);
	Österreichische Nationalbibliothek, Vienna (remaining bars)
First edition:	Published as No. 20 of *Neueste Folge nachgelassener Lieder und*
	Gesänge by J. P. Gotthard, Vienna in 1872 (P446)
Subsequent editions:	Peters: Vol. 7/60; AGA XX 403: Vol. 7/6; NSA IV: Vol. 13/44
Bibliography:	Capell 1928, p. 177
	Einstein 1951, pp. 252–3
	Fischer-Dieskau 1977, pp. 149–50
	Kohlhäufl 1999, p. 303
	Porter 1961, pp. 123–24
Arrangements:	Arr. Tilman Hoppstock (b. 1961) for guitar accompaniment, in
	Franz Schubert: 110 Lieder (2009)
Discography and timing:	Fischer-Dieskau II 5³ 2'49
	Hyperion I 19¹
	Hyperion II 25¹⁰ 3'21 Felicity Lott

← *Frühlingsgesang* D740   *Heliopolis I* D753 →

NÄCHTENS KLANG DIE SÜSSE LAUTE *see DON GAYSEROS* D93/2

NÄHE DES GELIEBTEN   Nearness of the beloved
(GOETHE) OP. 5 NO. 2, **D162** [H70]

The song exists in two versions, the second of which is discussed below:
(1) 27 February 1815; (2) 27 February 1815

(1)   'Langsam, feierlich mit Anmut'   G♭ major   𝄴   [19 bars]

(2)   G♭ major

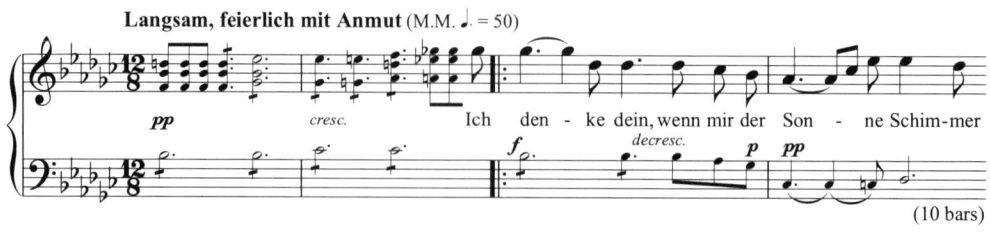

(10 bars)

Ich denke dein, wenn mir der Sonne Schimmer   I think of you when the sunlight
  Vom Meere strahlt;   Glints from the sea.
Ich denke dein, wenn sich des Mondes Flimmer   I think of you when the moon's glimmer
  In Quellen malt.   Is reflected in streams.

Ich sehe dich, wenn auf dem fernen Wege	I see you when, on distant roads,
Der Staub sich hebt;	Dust rises;
In tiefer Nacht, wenn auf dem schmalen Stege	In the depths of the night, when on the
	narrow path
Der Wandrer bebt.	The traveller trembles.
Ich höre dich, wenn dort mit dumpfem Rauschen	I hear you when, with a dull roar,
Die Welle steigt.	The waves surge up.
Im stillen Hain' da geh' ich oft zu lauschen,[1]	I often go to listen in the tranquil grove
Wenn alles schweigt.	When all is silent.
Ich bin bei dir, du seist auch noch so ferne.	I am with you, however far away you are,
Du bist mir nah!	You are close to me!
Die Sonne sinkt, bald leuchten mir die Sterne.	The sun sets, soon the stars will shine for me.
O wärst du da!	Would that you were here!

Johann Wolfgang von Goethe (1749–1832); poem written in April 1795

This is the tenth of Schubert's seventy-five Goethe solo settings (1814–26). See the poet's biography for a chronological list of all the Goethe settings.

The poem, which appeared in Schiller's *Musenalmanach* for 1796, was itself inspired by a song. The three opening words and the mood of the work clearly go back to *Andenken* by Matthisson. Goethe heard a setting of a poem by Matthisson's friend Friederike Brun who had written an 'Ich denke dein' of her own, published in Voss's *Musenalmanach* for 1795. These words had, in turn, been set to music by Zelter, and it was Zelter's song that inspired Goethe. If this had been a setting of Matthisson it is unlikely that Goethe would have adapted the poem in the way he did; perhaps he felt freer to do so in the case of a more or less unknown woman poet, and his title makes clear that the person speaking is a woman (a man would refer to 'Nähe *der* Geliebten', as wrongly printed in an 1864 edition of the poem overleaf). Beethoven sketched a setting of Goethe's poem in 1799 but never completed it; there is another Beethoven setting entitled *Ich denke dein* WoO74 that was composed in two stages, in 1799 and in 1803. This curious work is for voice accompanied by piano duet (only the first verse of the poem) and a set of six variations on the song for the duettists. It is interesting that Beethoven's well-known Matthisson setting *Andenken* WoO136 dates from much later – *c.* 1808.

Schubert had already set Matthisson's *Andenken* (D99) in 1814. Four months after the triumph of *Gretchen am Spinnrade* D118 in October 1814, a perfect example of a through-composed (or 'durchkomponiert') song, Schubert here writes one of the most famous of all strophic songs. In some ways, creating a perfect work of this type was as much of a challenge as following the dictates of a text, line by line, to create Gretchen's immortal setting. Schubert clearly felt something of a sense of responsibility to the strophic song, and *Nähe des Geliebten* is a fine example of how he brought this form, beloved of the North German school of composers, and of Goethe himself, to unprecedented heights.

There had never been a song that combined eighteenth-century musical shape with such modernity. The two bars of pianistic introduction, heard only once because the repeating strophes exclude its reoccurrence, are quite simply a marvel. Within these eight beats there are no fewer than six changes of harmony – two in b. 1 and four (one per crotchet beat) in b. 2.

---

[1] The addition of the word 'da' to Goethe's line is Schubert's. Goethe's original is: 'Im stillen *Haine* geh' ich oft zu lauschen'.

Nähe der [sic] *Geliebten*: Schubert's autograph from the album made for Goethe (1816).

The key signature is that of G flat major, but Schubert approaches the home key from the unexpected vantage point of B flat major. After two beats in that key (six throbbing quaver triplets) there is a switch into a second inversion of E flat minor (retaining the same B flat bass); at b. 2 the left hand rises a semitone (onto C flat) allowing the right hand to form a C flat major chord by leaving out a B flat (in the middle of what had been an E flat minor chord), and without altering the position of the hand on the keyboard. The left hand remains on C flat (= B natural) for the rest of the bar while the right hand climbs in sixths in harmonized semitones. As the chords progress upwards we have E flat at the top, then E natural, F natural and G flat – always with that bass of C flat. The excitement generated by this crescendo, both harmonic and dynamic, is something quite new in lieder (it is to be heard again in the Stolberg setting from 1816, *Stimme der Liebe* D412). At the beginning of b. 3 the pianist's left hand slips down a semitone to B flat and as if by a miracle we have arrived at a first inversion of G flat major. This is the chord that supports 'Ich <u>denke</u> dein'. At this moment just as G flat major is finally attained at the end of the prelude's journey, the vocal line, poised on a high G flat with the arrival of the home key in the accompaniment, seems to explode in the heavens like a shooting star.

When the singer enters on the crest of this harmonic wave, it is as if a promise has been kept, and the power of imagination has surmounted the agony of separation. Something as viscerally exciting yet superbly contained had never happened before in a quiet and intimate strophic song of this kind. The introduction is about the opening of a loving heart, the unfolding realization of deep devotion. 'Ich denke dein' is a confession of love squeezed out of someone who has been rendered virtually inarticulate by emotional intensity, someone with a heart almost too full to be coherent. The composer matches this mixture of frustration and overflowing enthusiasm in a way that scarcely seems possible. It is unusual enough to begin a song with an unprepared high note, but the lead-in that makes that first 'Ich' a crowning glory, the inevitable culmination of two bars of highly unconventional piano writing, is something new and glorious.

Nähe des Geliebten from *Deutsche Lieder in Volkes Herz und Mund* (1864).

The remainder of the song does not disappoint. The vocal line continues on a pathway that is sensuously flexible (the drop of a fifth at the end of each strophe is unusually beautiful) and always rhapsodic. At b. 6 the mirror image between the bass line of the piano and the vocal line provides an element of counterpoint in a structure that is more cleverly planned than it first appears to be.

The poem is a litany, and if the music were to vary too much from verse to verse, Goethe's depiction of a lover's constancy would be undermined. Of course interpreters can choose to vary dynamics (most do) in the spirit of strophic song – 'Ich höre dich' (with its 'Im stillen Hain'') is usually the softest strophe, and 'Ich bin bei dir' the most passionate. Through thought, sight and hearing the narrator persuades herself that her lover is still living, and with her (at least in spirit). The last strophe proves this is self-delusion or a lie – he is dead, or absent or disloyal. And yet, even in these circumstances, there is a triumph of constancy, a belief in love against all the evidence of the senses, that pervades the music. This is a universal emotion of course, and both male and female singers have laid claim to this song with equal success. *Nähe des Geliebten* contains just enough of the Italian manner to render it deliciously singable while remaining German enough to launch a great Goethe text with complete integrity. Here is the much vaunted marriage of the sensibilities of North and South, and a better advertisement for that collaboration could not be found.

Performers know only the second version of the song that Schubert wrote out on 27 February 1815 and published in 1821. He had already expended a great deal of ink writing out essentially the same music in 𝄴 with semiquaver pulsations rather than quaver triplets, making the song look as though it went twice as fast. He crossed this version out with the words 'Gilt nicht' ('not valid') in the margin (published in the NSA in Volume 1b p. 276). The composer was obviously dissatisfied with the appearence of busyness on the printed page. With the change to triplets in quavers the music looks less driven; something about the triplets drags behind the beat and suggests the hopelessness and lassitude that subsumes those who are separated from their beloved. This makes the emotional kick-start of that gathering prelude all the more remarkable, the ardent nature of the singer more believable, in contrast to the calm beginning.

There are a number of possibilities for rubato in music of this kind and within this style – slight hesitations and the careful turning of harmonic corners. In the music of someone like Reichardt this is much less possible, although, after this song of burnished Italianate inspiration, the definition of what was permissible in German song had changed for ever.

Autographs:	Staatsbibliothek Preussischer Kulturbesitz, Berlin (first version)
	In private possession (second version)
	Wienbibliothek im Rathaus (fair copy)
Publication:	First published as part of the AGA in 1895 (P554; first version)
	First published as Op. 5 no. 2 by Cappi & Diabelli, Vienna in July 1821 (P11; second version)
Dedicatee:	Antonio Salieri
Publication reviews:	Rellstab 'Ueberblick der Erzeugnisse', *Iris im Gebiete der Tonkunst* (Berlin), No. 39 (12 November 1830) [Waidelich/Hilmar Dokumente II No. 784b]
Subsequent editions:	Peters: Vol. 1/243; AGA XX 49: Vol. 2/62; NSA IV: Vol. 1a/40 & Vol. 1b/276; Bärenreiter: Vol. 1/32
Bibliography:	Byrne 2003, pp. 172–8
	Capell 1928, pp. 100–101
	Einstein 1951, p. 109
	Fischer-Dieskau 1977, pp. 41–2
	Gülke 1991, p. 73
	Newbould 1997, pp. 397–8
	Reid 2007, pp. 219–20
Further settings and arrangements:	Johann Friedrich Reichardt (1752–1814) *Ich denke dein* (1795)
	Carl Friedrich Zelter (1758–1832) *Ich denke dein* (1808)
	Friedrich Heinrich Himmel (1765–1814) *Nähe des Geliebten* (1807)
	Carl Loewe (1796–1869) *Ich denke dein* Op. 9 Bk 3 no. 1 (1817)
	Robert Schumann (1810–1856) *Ich denke dein*, duet for soprano and tenor Op. 78 no. 3 (1849)
	Stephen Heller (1813–1888) *Nähe des Geliebten* (1836/7)
	Josephine Lang (1815–1880) *Nähe des Geliebten* Op. 5 no. 1 (1830)
	Nikolai Medtner (1880–1951) *Nähe des Geliebten* Op. 15 no. 9 (1907)
	Paul Hindemith (1895–1963) *Nähe des Geliebten* (1914)
	Arr. Tilman Hoppstock (b. 1961) for guitar accompaniment, in *Franz Schubert: 110 Lieder* (2009)
Discography and timing:	Fischer-Dieskau I 3[5] 3'26
	Hyperion I 1[4]
	Hyperion II 5[9] 2'15 Janet Baker

← *An Mignon* D161   *Sängers Morgenlied* D163 →

NAMENSTAGSLIED
(STADLER) **D695** [H451]
A major   March 1820

Name-day song

(68 bars)

Vater, schenk' mir diese Stunde,	Father, grant me this hour,
Hör' ein Lied aus meinem Munde!	Hear a song from my lips!
Dir verdank' ich das Gelingen,	I thank you that my wish
Meine Wünsche heut' zu singen,	To sing today is fulfilled,
Denn du hast mit güt'ger Hand	For with a kindly hand
Mir den Weg dazu gebahnt.	You have prepared the way for me.
O, lass diese Hand mich küssen!	Oh, let me kiss this hand!
Sieh' des Dankes Tränen fliessen!	See how my tears of thanks flow!
Denn sie hat mir mehr gegeben	For your hand has given me more
Als Gesang: ein schönes Leben;	Than song: a fine life;
Und mit kindlich frohem Blick	And with a look of childlike joy
Dank' ich ihr des Lebens Glück.	I thank you for life's happiness.
Himmel, sende deinen Segen	Heaven, bestow your blessing
Dem verehrten Mann entgegen!	On this revered man!
Strahle ihm, des Glückes Sonne!	Shine upon him, sun of happiness!
Schäum' ihm über, Kelch der Wonne!	Overflow for him, cup of joy!
Und von Blumen voll der Pracht	And let a garland of flowers in their full glory
Sei ein Kranz ihm dargebracht.	Be offered him.
Diesen Kranz in deinen Haaren	May God always preserve for us
Möge Gott uns stets bewahren,	This garland in your hair:
Und ich fleh's mit nassen Blicken:	Thus I pray with moist eyes.
Noch ein zweiter soll dich schmücken,	A second garland, blue and gold,
Blau und golden, denn dir spricht	Shall adorn you; for all lips
Jeder Mund: Vergiss mein nicht!	Say to you: Forget me not!

ALBERT STADLER (1794–1888)

This is the second of Schubert's two Stadler solo settings (1815–20). See the poet's biography for a chronological list of all the Stadler settings.

This song reflects the atmosphere of the Schubertiads more than most, a real *pièce d'occasion* (although it is unlikely to have been performed at a Schubertiad in Vienna). The composer's ability and willingness to provide music for his friends when appropriate was, of course, one of the things that endeared him to them. In the absence of court patrons and commissions from the nobility, Schubert wrote the occasional ceremonial piece for middle-class home rather than palace, and out of the goodness of his heart rather than for money. This piece was written for the name-day of the merchant Josef von Koller (1780–1864) of Steyr in Upper Austria. Schubert was not a close friend of the celebrant, but he had been a guest at meals under Koller's roof during a happy visit to Steyr with Vogl in the summer of 1819. Vogl loved to perform in the Kollers' music room and both he and the composer were fond of Koller's eighteen-year-old daughter Josefine (1801–1874, nicknamed Pepi), a reasonably talented soprano who developed a passion for Schubert's music. Albert Stadler was an old schoolmate of the composer, and he accompanied this song at its first performance, having also provided the words. In the summer of 1819 he had also written the words for a vocal trio (Schubert was one of his singers, leaving the piano part to Stadler) honouring Vogl's fifty-first birthday on 10 August (*Cantate zum Geburtstag des Sängers Johann Michael Vogl* D666).

On 17 January 1858 Albert Stadler wrote to Ferdinand Luib (who was gathering personal memories of Schubert from the composer's old friends), stating that he sent a letter to Schubert from Steyr in 1820 asking him to set an enclosed poem to music so that Pepi Koller could sing it on her father's name-day (the saint's day, for those with the name Josef, is 19 March). Schubert complied, but in rather a hurry, adding to his autograph the words 'Stadler is to copy out the voice part and add this for the repeat'.

The introduction has an element of celebratory pomp, albeit framed by the domestic and provincial aspects of the mini-commission. Three bars of ascending arpeggios, matched by a chromatically descending bass, culminate in a gleeful downward chromatic scale (b. 4) such as is not to be found elsewhere in the lieder. This is followed by another bar of swirling semiquavers landing on a protracted cadence initiated by a semibreve. The implication is nothing so much as an obeisance, a daughterly curtsey to the celebrant (indeed Schubert seems to have imagined a balletic entrance for Josefine as if she were coming on stage to deliver her aria). The whole of this rather theatrical seven-bar passage is repeated between verses 2 and 3, and at the end as a postlude. The main body of the song is in Mozartian style, and somewhat in the manner of the Vogl birthday cantata. After the over-the-top introduction, slightly tongue in cheek, the relaxed but heartfelt tone of the sung verses is just right for a loving daughter. The staccato left hand from b. 44 is no doubt meant to illustrate the promised kisses of 'O, lass diese Hand mich küssen'. The revered father praised by his eighteen-year-old daughter is only forty, but for the twenty-six-year-old Stadler this clearly represents venerable old age.

Autograph:	British Library, London
First edition:	Published as part of the AGA in 1895 (P710)
Subsequent editions:	Not in Peters; AGA XX 587: Vol. 10/81; NSA IV: Vol. 12/170
Discography and timing:	Fischer-Dieskau —
	Hyperion I 3[7] 4'36 Ann Murray
	Hyperion II 23[9]

← *Der Schiffer* D694   *Des Fräuleins Liebeslauschen* D698 →

NATURGENUSS
(MATTHISSON) **D188** [H90]
B♭ major   May 1815

Enjoyment of nature

(19 bars)

Im Abendschimmer wallt der Quell	In the soft light of evening the brook flows
Durch Wiesenblumen purpurhell,	Through meadows of bright, purple flowers;
Der Pappelweide wechselnd Grün	The poplar, with its changing shades of green,
Weht ruhelispelnd drüber hin.	Whispers gently above them.
Im Lenzhauch webt der Geist des Herrn!	God's spirit stirs in the spring breeze;
Sieh! Auferstehung nah' und fern,	Behold life's resurrection, near and far,
Sieh! Jugendfülle, Schönheitsmeer,	See, youth's abundance, a sea of beauty
Und Wonnetaumel rings umher!	And teeming joys lie all around.
Ich blicke her, ich blicke hin,	I look about me, close and far away,
Und immer höher schwebt mein Sinn.	And my soul soars ever higher.
Nur Tand sind Pracht und Gold und Ruhm,	Pomp, gold and fame are but dross
Natur, in deinem Heiligtum!	In your sanctuary, Nature!
Des Himmels Ahnung den umweht,	Intimations of heaven envelop him
Der deinen Liebeston versteht;	Who understands your music of love;
Doch, an dein Mutterherz gedrückt,	For he, pressed to your maternal breast,
Wird er zum Himmel selbst entzückt!	Will know the delight of heaven itself!

Friedrich von Matthisson (1761–1831); poem written between 1778 and 1782

This is the nineteenth of Schubert's twenty-nine Matthisson solo settings (1812–17). See the poet's biography for a chronological list of all the Matthisson settings.

This enchanting and contemplative song does not rate a mention with either Capell or Einstein, although Friedlaender thought highly enough of it to include it in Volume 7 of the Peters Edition as a work that deserved to be better known. Simple as it is, it has an inevitability of shape that no one but Schubert could achieve. The vocal line is built around a falling, then rising, B flat arpeggio (bb. 1–3), followed by a scale modulating into F (bb. 5–6). The idea no doubt derives from the word 'Quelle', for this is water music of a gently flowing kind. The slightly wayward five-bar postlude (bb. 15–19) where the left hand delicately joins the right only on the last note of each bar, and is then phrased over to the next beat, adds to a sense of pellucid delight. Schubert later set the poem again (D422), very differently, for male quartet and piano (*see* below). He there attempts to find a new illustrative mood for the intimations of heaven of the last verse, but the earlier strophic barcarolle is more satisfactory as a setting of Matthisson's words, despite the attractive immediacy of the quartet version.

Autograph:	Wienbibliothek im Rathaus, Vienna (fragment, bb. 1–18)
First edition:	Published as Vol. 7 no. 36 in Friedlaender's edition by Peters, Leipzig in 1887 (P497)
Subsequent editions:	Peters: Vol. 7/86; AGA XX 64: Vol. 2/99; NSA IV: Vol. 8/42
Arrangement:	Arr. Tilman Hoppstock (b. 1961) for guitar accompaniment, in *Franz Schubert: 110 Lieder* (2009)
Discography and timing:	Fischer-Dieskau I 3^{16} 2'28
	Hyperion I 7^4
	Hyperion II 6^9 2'46 Lucia Popp

← *Stimme der Liebe* D187   *An die Freude* D189 →

NATURGENUSS   Enjoyment of nature   Quartet, TTBB
(MATTHISSON) OP. 16 NO. 2, **D422** [H480]
D major   1822?

(83 bars)

See previous entry for poem and translation

Friedrich von Matthisson (1761–1831); poem written between 1778 and 1782

This quartet has few rivals in Schubert's works for its depiction of a shared joy in natural surroundings. In the first section words tumble out almost more quickly than the thoughts behind them, suggesting a state of being drunk on nature. The vocal line rises, and with it the sap of springtime excitement, inspiring a mood of wonder and rapture in the outdoors that is infinitely less possible for town dwellers of our time than of Matthisson's. Schubert and his generation were literally able to walk beyond Vienna's city walls and within minutes find themselves surrounded by the beauties of the countryside ('Natur, in deinem Heiligtum').

The key is D major, a tonality which for reasons of vocal range usually signals high As and Bs for the first tenor. The song offers a feast of light and heady singing in running semiquavers that must have been possible only for those few young male singers of the Schubert circle sufficiently in charge of their head voices and falsetto. Nearly two centuries later this exclusivity has not changed. The top line of this quartet is only ever possible for a handful of young tenors before their naturally high-lying voices become fuller and stronger, as well as less flexible. This is definitely music of youth; as the poet exultantly says: 'Sieh! Jugendfülle, Schönheitsmeer / Und Wonnetaumel rings umher!' Age, a kind of hardening of the vocal arteries, undermines many a tenor's ability to undertake this type of filigree work in the giddy heights of *voix mixte*. Schubert did not envisage a tenor singing these high notes from the chest with the force of an operatic aria.

The music, the majority of it written in a piano dynamic, suggests not only shimmering water and the whispering of leafy groves, but the effect of all this beauty on the rapturous poet. This is embodied in four voices intertwined and glancing off each other in tiny details of playful echo (especially between the top and bottom lines at moments like 'Ich blicke her' (b. 24) and 'Nur Tand sind Pracht' (b. 28). In the first and second verses the composer repeats the poet's last line. The third verse is repeated entirely, the key phrase in the last line ('Natur, in deinem Heiligtum') rising to a forte dynamic on both occasions. At the repeat (from b. 37) we hear this phrase in augmentation where those weaving semiquavers, notable for their dazzling profusion, cease at last and give way to a triumphant march in dotted rhythm. The section ends as 'in deinem Heiligtum' is heard (from b. 40) for the last time in crotchet chords that veer between Schubert's magical worlds of A major and minor. This cadence announces a return to D major over the page.

The poem's first three strophes have undoubtedly inspired the best music. Matthisson's fourth verse (beginning 'Des Himmels Ahnung den umweht', from b. 45) is repeated and reworked as the entire inspiration for the second section of some forty bars, marked 'Etwas geschwind'. Rather hearty music, with a touch of the drinking song about it and a rum-ti-tum accompaniment, it is something of a disappointment at first. This regularly happens in Schubert's four-part choruses: wonderful, atmospheric beginnings that satisfy the poetic side of the male singer are followed by a peroration in triple time to appeal to the hearty and the laddish. But even while catering for the popular side of the quartet market, Schubert relieves our disappointment by artfully passing the melody between the tenors and basses antiphonally, by finding a way of setting 'Des Himmels Ahnung' (from b. 62, for the third time) in inspired dramatic augmentation, and by reintroducing those wonderful vocal flights of fancy for the lead tenor on the song's final page. The only high B occurs four bars from the end, reaching heavenwards on the last 'Wird er zum Himmel selbst entzückt' (b. 80). A beautiful and thoroughly Schubertian touch is the further repeat of 'zum Himmel, zum Himmel' where 'entzückt', the past participle at the end of the poet's line, is dropped (a stroke of genius this) in favour of an elongated setting of 'Himmel' which makes its gentle descent of a fifth through the D major ether.

The piano part, however, is little more than an efficient, if discreet (and just occasionally inventive) doubling of the vocal lines and it comes as no surprise to see that the first sketch shows a quartet without accompaniment. This is not a work, like the much later *Gondelfahrer* (D809), where the accompaniment has a life of its own. In fact, Schubert was asked by the publisher Diabelli to supply a piano part in February 1823, and he seems to have complied only because pressed to do so.

Autograph:	Wienbibliothek im Rathaus, Vienna (first draft, without piano)
First edition:	Published as Op. 16 no. 2 by Cappi & Diabelli, Vienna in October 1823 (P49)
Subsequent editions:	AGA XVI 8: p. 76; NSA III: Vol. 3
Bibliography:	Hoorickx 1976, p. 156
Discography and timing:	Hyperion I 32[11] 3'23 Paul Agnew, Jamie MacDougall, Simon
	Hyperion II 25[6] Keenlyside & Michael George

← *Der Wachtelschlag* D742   *Geist der Liebe* D747 →

Die NEBENSONNEN *see* WINTERREISE D911/23

Der NEUGIERIGE *see DIE SCHÖNE MÜLLERIN* D795/6

NIMMER LÄNGER TRAG' ICH *see DUBIOUS, MISATTRIBUTED OR LOST SONGS*

NON T'ACCOSTARE ALL'URNA *see VIER CANZONEN* D688/1

Die NONNE   The nun
(HÖLTY) **D208**

The song exists in two versions, both of which are discussed below:
(1) (Fragment) 29 May 1815; (2) 16 June 1815

(1) 'Mässig, erzählend'   A♭ major   ¢   [153 bars]

(2) A♭ major – F minor

(154 bars)

(1) Es liebt' in Welschland irgendwo	Once upon a time, somewhere in Italy,
Ein schöner junger Ritter	A fair young knight loved
Ein Mädchen, das der Welt entfloh,	A maiden who shunned the world,
Trotz Klostertor und Gitter;	Loved her despite convent gate and iron bars;
Sprach viel von seiner Liebespein,	He spoke much of his anguish in love
Und schwur, auf seinen Knieen,	And vowed, upon his knees,
Sie aus dem Kerker zu befreien,	To free her from her prison,
Und stets für sie zu glühen.	And to love her ardently for ever.
(2) 'Bei diesem Muttergottesbild,	'By the image of the Virgin,
Bei diesem Jesuskinde,	By this child Jesus
Das ihre Mutterarme füllt,	That fills her maternal arms,
Schwör' ich's dir, o Belinde!	I swear to you, Belinda:
Dir ist mein ganzes Herz geweiht,	My whole heart is consecrated to you
So lang ich Odem habe,	As long as I draw breath;
Bei meiner Seelen Seligkeit!	By my soul's salvation
Dich lieb' ich bis zum Grabe.'	I will love you unto the grave.'
(3) Was glaubt ein armes Mädchen nicht,	What will a poor maiden not believe,
Zumal in einer Zelle?	Especially in a convent cell?
Ach! sie vergass der Nonnenpflicht,	Alas, she forgot her duty as a nun,
Des Himmels und der Hölle,	Forgot heaven and hell.

Die, von den Engeln angeschaut,
   Sich ihrem Jesu weihte,
Die reine schöne Gottesbraut,
   Ward eines Frevlers Beute.

(4) Drauf wurde, wie die Männer sind,
   Sein Herz von Stund' an lauer,
Er überliess das arme Kind
   Auf ewig ihrer Trauer.
Vergass der alten Zärtlichkeit,
   Und aller seiner Eide,
Und floh, im bunten Galakleid,
   Nach neuer Augenweide.

(5) Begann mit andern Weibern Reihn,
   Im kerzenhellen Saale,
Gab andern Weibern Schmeichelein,
   Beim lautern Traubenmahle,
Und rühmte sich des Minneglücks
   Bei seiner schönen Nonne,
Und jedes Kusses, jedes Blicks,
   Und jeder andern Wonne.

(6) Die Nonne, voll von welscher Wut,
   Entglüht' in ihrem Mute,
Und sann auf nichts als Dolch und Blut.
   Und träumte nur von Blute.
Sie dingte plötzlich eine Schar
   Von wilden Meuchelmördern,
Den Mann, der treulos worden war,
   Ins Totenreich zu fördern.

(7) Die bohren manches Mörderschwert
   In seine schwarze Seele.
Sein schwarzer, falscher Geist entfährt,
   Wie Schweifeldampf der Höhle.
Er wimmert durch die Luft, wo sein
   Ein Krallenteufel harret.
Drauf ward sein blutendes Gebein
   In eine Gruft verscharret.

(8) Die Nonne flog, wie Nacht begann,
   Zur kleinen Dorfkapelle,
Und riss den wunden Rittersmann
   Aus seiner Ruhestelle.
Riss ihm das Bubenherz heraus,
   Und warf's, den Zorn zu büssen,
Dass dumpf erscholl das Gotteshaus,

   Und trat es mit den Füssen.

She who, watched by the angels,
   Had dedicated herself to Jesus,
The fair, spotless bride of God,
   Fell prey to a sinner.

From this moment, as is the way of men
   His heart grew more tepid;
He abandoned the poor child
   Forever to her sorrow.
Forgetting his former tenderness
   And all his vows,
He went off, in resplendent ceremonial dress,
   To feast his eyes on new delights.

He danced with other women
   In the candlelit ballroom,
Complimented other women
   At the noisy, drunken banquet.
And boasted to his fair nun
   Of his luck in love,
Boasted of every kiss, every glance,
   And every other delight.

The nun, filled with Latin fury,
   Blazed within her heart,
And thought of nothing but dagger and blood,
   And dreamed only of blood.
Then, with sudden resolve, she hired a band
   Of wild assassins,
To dispatch to the realm of the dead
   The man who had turned faithless.

They plunged many a murderous sword
   Into his black soul.
His black, treacherous spirit escaped,
   Like a sulphurous mist from a cavern.
It moaned through the air
   To a devil's awaiting claws.
Then his bleeding corpse
   Was buried in a vault.

As night fell the nun fled
   To the little village chapel,
And seized the dead knight
   From his resting place.
She tore out his wicked heart
   And, to vent her fury, hurled it,
So that the house of God resounded with a
   muffled thud,
   And trampled it underfoot.

(9)   Ihr Geist soll, wie die Sagen gehn,   As legend has it, her spirit
          In dieser Kirche weilen,   Lingers in the church,
       Und, bis im Dorf die Hähne krähn,   Now whimpering, now wailing
          Bald wimmern, und bald heulen.   Until the cocks crow in the village.
       Sobald der Hammer zwölfe schlägt,[1]   As soon as the hammer strikes twelve
          Rauscht sie, an Grabsteinwänden,   She rises up from a vault,
       Aus einer Gruft empor, und trägt   Past tombstones, bearing
          Ein blutend Herz in Händen.   In her hands a bleeding heart.

(10)   Die tiefen, hohlen Augen sprühn   Her sunken, hollow eyes flash
          Ein düsterrotes Feuer,   With sombre red fire,
       Und glühn, wie Schwefelflammen glühn,   Glowing like sulphurous flames
          Durch ihren weissen Schleier.   Through her white veil.
       Sie gafft auf das zerrissne Herz,   She stares at the mutilated heart
          Mit wilder Rachgebärde,   With a gesture of wild revenge,
       Und hebt es dreimal himmelwärts,   Raises it three times towards heaven,
          Und wirft es auf die Erde;   And hurls it to the ground.

(11)   Und rollt die Augen voller Wut,   Filled with rage, she rolls her eyes
          Die eine Hölle blicken,   In which hell blazes,
       Und schüttelt aus dem Schleier Blut,   Shakes blood from her veil
          Und stampft das Herz in Stücken.   And tramples the heart into pieces.
       Ein bleicher Totenflimmer macht[2]   Meanwhile, a pallid deathly gleam
          Indess die Fenster helle.   Lights the windows.
       Der Wächter, der das Dorf bewacht,   The watchman who guards the village
          Sah's oft in der Kapelle.[3]   Has often seen her in the chapel.

LUDWIG HÖLTY (1748–1776); poem written in 1770

This is the ninth of Schubert's twenty-three Hölty solo settings (1813–16). See the poet's biography for a chronological list of all the Hölty settings.

This song of blood and thunder, a tale of energetic and resourceful revenge to gladden the hearts of spurned women everywhere, provides us with all the drama that Schubert had so carefully kept on a leash in composing the Matthisson ballad D114 *Romanze*. Hölty had written one of the very first German horror poems or 'Schauerballaden'. He had received an English-influenced education at Göttingen (Hanover was still an English possession), and the metre of these quatrains – four and three accents per alternate line – is known as the Chevy-Chase strophe (on account of an English sixteenth-century ballad about hunting in Northumberland's Cheviot Hills). Schubert worked hard on his setting, making a first version in late May 1815 and returning to it a fortnight later. It is interesting that in these ballads his revising instincts were almost always to simplify rather than amplify his original illustrative intentions. He knew that the point of a ballad is to get the story across, and anything that gets in the way or slows the pace is detrimental to this aim.

Verses 1–2: The opening of the piece is a good example of the composer's having second thoughts. The earlier version written in May has eight bars of introduction (a genial statement

[1] Hölty has 'Sobald der *Zeiger* zwölfe schlägt'.
[2] Hölty has 'Ein *dunkler* Totenflimmer macht'.
[3] Hölty has 'Sah's in der *Landkapelle*'.

of the main tune) which were ruthlessly cut in June. The vamping two bars of the second version (as recorded in the Hyperion Edition) are the ideal announcement for a more tightly controlled setting up of the proceedings; the marking is 'Erzählend, mässig'. The vocal melody is pleasant enough, but nothing that would distract our attention from the narrative. Dotted rhythms from b. 16 signify the knight's military pretensions, and his exaggerated (and patently insincere) protestations of love are funny – as surely they are meant to be. With passionate outpourings, underscored in triplets, he plights his eternal troth – 'Thy hand, Belinda' (and no doubt other parts of her body) is what he is asking for. The man who loiters in the cloister is a villain and, what's more, an Italian (from 'Welschland'), and we hear it in his slightly over-testosteronic tessitura (high A flats in bb. 32–3).

Verse 3: 'Etwas geschwind', with a change of time-signature to §. The nun believes the words of her seducer, and her fall from grace is unceremoniously described in as much detail as the conventions of the time allow. There is a deliberately heightened declamation here that suggests that the composer is not as shocked by the prospect of an errant nun as an eighteen-year old brought up in the Catholic faith might be.

Verse 4: 'Tändelnd', ⅔. The first version has here a rather fussy and complicated accompaniment in semiquaver triplets. One can see that it was meant to depict the meanderings, the dancing perhaps, of the hard-hearted man, weaving a pack of lies and then boasting of his other conquests. Schubert obviously thought better of all these cascading notes that would have tied the singer to a less flexible style of delivery. The dance, marked 'tändelnd' (playful), is the cat-and-mouse sadism of a game of sexual cruelty, masked in the second version by the courtly rhythm, the civilized veneer, of gentlemanly behaviour. It is nevertheless plain to see (as the section repeats for more details in Verse 5) that the man is an out-and-out cad.

Verses 6–7: Things now move fast! A plunge into recitative scratches the religious veneer and reveals not a nun but a she-devil with a hot Italian temperament. She finds the means (easier said than done, one would have thought, for a woman of the church) to hire a bunch of assassins. Schubert's musical commentary on this is the interval of the augmented fourth, the so-called *diabolus in musica* (two sforzato chords, F and B natural, in bb. 83 and 86). A passage marked 'Wild, schnell' (now in ¾ time) dispatches the blackguard with many a thrust of the dagger. The first version asked for the piano chords to be arpeggiated, but this requirement is abandoned for the second in the interest of sheer speed and power. On the offbeat the piano tears into the body of the victim, whose spirit escapes and is claimed by the devil; the body itself is buried in a vault. The music at b. 109 (marked 'Wie oben') denotes something of a religious ceremony; in terms of rhythm and mood it prophesies the Silbert setting *Himmelsfunken* D651 from 1819.

Verse 8: The nun's thirst for revenge, not to mention her surgical skills, here bring the serious-ness of the piece into question. This is scarcely the gently pastoral Hölty beloved for his portraits of idyllic country life. In the twinkling of a tremolandi passage (bb. 123–5) the enraged nun has recovered the body from the vault and in the space of one chord (in a sforzato C major) she tears out the heart. Giving what might be termed ventricle to her hatred, she executes a Maenad's dance on that unfortunate organ. Schubert, in a series of crazed chords (bb. 129–34) rises manfully (dare one say gleefully?) to the challenge of gush and squelch.

Verses 9–11: It is only here that the family resemblance to the Matthisson *Romanze* D114 becomes apparent: this is after all a ghost story too. In three verses of narrative (from b. 36, in F minor, 'Mässig mit Grauen', §) the performer must maintain the tension already generated in the piece. This is something of a losing battle. The use of repeat marks here clearly indicates that the haunting is a nightly occurrence and that the whole drama is re-enacted with the regu-larity and repetitiveness of a strophic song. The notation of the autograph with the words written out separately at the bottom of the page (NSA Vol. 8 p. XXIV) leaves no doubt that this is indeed how Schubert saw it – a strophic song appended to a ballad. This rather cleverly adopts Zumsteeg's solution for the ending of Schiller's *Ritter Toggenburg*. There is a decided similarity between this last haunting aria (or more accurately an aria of haunting) and the Walter Scott setting *Gesang der Norna* D831, also in F minor, also in § and equally about a witch-like old lady determined to recount her historic tale of woe. In March 1816 when Schubert came to compose his own version of that Schiller ballad, D397, the same strophic device was employed. The nun Belinda's sulphurous presence is less sympathetic perhaps than that of the beautiful Rosalia in *Romanze*, but the erstwhile bride of Christ, still decked in her veil, has a more strenuous role in the Gothic theatre of the absurd. Each night her work, not to mention *his* heart, is cut out. Schubert's own age, less spoiled by a quotidian ration of *grand guignol* on film and television, may have taken this song slightly more seriously than we can, but surely not by a large margin.

Extensive extracts of the first version of D208 are printed in the *Revisionsbericht* of the AGA (it is different enough from the second to have been assigned a separate Deutsch number – 212 – in the first edition of the catalogue) but this earlier version appears in full in Volume 8 p. 207 of the NSA, also numbered D208.

Autographs:	Wienbibliothek im Rathaus, Vienna (first draft and fragment of first version; first draft of second version)
Publication:	First published as part of the AGA Revisionsbericht in 1897 (P724); subsequently published as part of the NSA in 2009 (P859; first version)
	First published as part of the AGA in 1895 (P565; second version)
Subsequent editions:	Not in Peters; AGA XX 77: Vol. 2/124; NSA IV: Vol. 8/60 (second version) & 207 (first version)
Discography and timing:	Fischer-Dieskau —
	Hyperion I 8⁸
	Hyperion II 7⁵ 8'08 Sarah Walker

NORMANS GESANG *see SIEBEN GESÄNGE AUS WALTER SCOTT'S FRÄULEIN VOM SEE* OP. 52 D846

NOVALIS (FRIEDRICH LEOPOLD, FREIHERR VON HARDENBERG) (1772–1801)

THE POETIC SOURCES
S1 *Musen-Almanach für des Jahr 1802*. Herausgegeben von A.W. Schlegel und L. Tieck. Tübingen in der Cotta'sche Buchhandlung, 1802

S2 *Novalis Schriften, Herausgegeben von Ludwig Tieck und Fr. Schlegel*. Dritte Auflage, Erster und Zweiter Theil, Berlin 1815, in der Realschulbuchhandlung

S3 *Novalis Schriften*, Erster und Zweiter Theil, Wien, bei Carl Armbruster, 1820, Gedruckt bei Anton Strauss

THE SONGS

May 1819?   *Geistliches Lied* [formerly known as *Marie*] 'Ich sehe dich in tausend Bildern' D658
             [S2: Zweiter Theil, *Geistliche Lieder* no. XV p. 42] [S3: Zweiter Theil p. 51]

May 1819   *Hymne* [formerly known as *Hymne I*] 'Wenige wissen/Das Geheimnis der Liebe'
             D659 [S1: Section VII *Hymne*: pp. 202–3] [S2: Zweiter Theil, *Geistliche Lieder* No.
             VII pp. 29–30] [S3: Zweiter Theil pp. 36–8]
             Geistliches Lied [formerly known as *Hymne II*] 'Wenn ich ihn nur habe' D660 [S2:
             Zweiter Theil *Geistliche Lieder* no. V pp. 27–8] [S3: Zweiter Theil pp. 33–4]
             Geistliches Lied [formerly known as *Hymne III*] 'Wenn alle untreu werden' D661
             [S2: Zweiter Theil, *Geistliche Lieder* no. VI pp. 28–9] [S3: Zweiter Theil, pp. 35–6]
             Geistliches Lied [formerly known as *Hymne IV*] 'Ich sag es jedem, dass er lebt' D662
             [S2: Zweiter Theil, *Geistliche Lieder* no. IX pp. 33–4] [S3: Zweiter Theil pp. 40–42]

January 1820   *Nachthymne* D687 [S2: Zweiter Theil, pp. 7–8] [S3: Zweiter Theil, pp. 12–13]

Friedrich Leopold, Freiherr von Hardenberg, 'Fritz' to his friends, was born on 2 May 1772 in Oberwiederstedt in Prussian Saxony. For one of his first appearances in print he took the pseudonym Novalis, now pronounced with an emphasis on the second syllable, although he originally stressed the first. 'De Novali' was one of his ancestral names, a four-teenth-century tag that might be translated as 'clearer of the land' or 'ground-breaker'. His family was of the Protestant Saxon nobility and Novalis was brought up to eschew luxury as befitted his evangelical upbringing. Ludwig Tieck described him thus:

Novalis was tall, slender and of noble proportions. He wore his light-brown hair in long clustering locks [. . .] his hazel eyes were clear and glancing; and the colour of his face, especially of the fine brow, almost transparent [. . .] he presented a figure which might be called beautiful. In outline and expression his face strikingly resembled that of the Evangelist John, as we see him in the large noble painting of Albrecht Dürer, preserved at Nuremberg and Munich.

In 1790 young Fritz went to Jena to study law at the celebrated university where he met Johann Gottlieb Fichte as well as Hölderlin and became a close friend and admirer of Schiller. In Leipzig (where he toyed with the idea of becoming a soldier) he met Friedrich Schlegel who was to become his closest friend and supporter, and he was introduced to the philosophical ideas of Kant. This first encounter with the denial of materialism was of crucial importance to the development of a philosophy of 'Magischer Idealismus', a romantic and magical idealism. A large number of Novalis's works from this early period were unearthed in a Cracow library in 1983 and published in 2000. This cache is

Novalis (Friedrich von Hardenberg) by Edward Eichens.

considered by Germanists to have been one of the great literary finds of the last century.

At the end of 1794 Novalis met the twelve-year-old Sophie von Kühn and fell in love with her. She was a precocious child, both stubborn and docile, gifted with a musical ear and taste in matters of dress. 'I gave myself over completely to lust,' he confessed in his journal, but his lust was solitary and the relationship chaste. What would be judged a highly unsuitable pairing in our own time was sanctioned by Sophie's parents. The poet and Sophie were betrothed in May 1795, but later in the year she developed the first symptoms of tuberculosis and died in agony in March 1797. During her illness Novalis wrote poetry while working as auditor to the Saxon government salt works at Weissenfels. From this period date the *Hymnen an die Nacht* ('Hymns to the Night'), published in the Schlegel brothers' periodical *Das Athenäum* in 1800. In these six pieces where prose is interspersed with verse (preparing the way for the modern prose-poem) Novalis celebrates night, or death, as an entry into a higher life. He looks forward to a mystical reunion with Sophie (whom he compares to the Virgin Mary) and with the universe as a whole.

Novalis accomplished the bulk of his work as a result of his obsessive devotion to Sophie's memory. Science, poetry and philosophy were invoked to explain the world by means of a series of allegories and analogies. Some of his most influential writings were two collections of aphorisms and fragments published in his lifetime – *Blütenstaub* ('Pollen', 1798) and *Glauben und Liebe* ('Faith and Love', 1798). He wrote one novel – *Heinrich von Ofterdingen* – which he never completed. This is set in the Middle Ages and is the story of a journey from Eisenach to Augsburg, and a chronicle of the hero's spiritual and artistic development as he discovers that poetry has the power to redeem the world. In the second section of this work Heinrich finds himself in a supernatural world where plants and stones are able to communicate with mankind. For those familiar with Schubert's Schlegel songs from the Novalis-influenced *Abendröte* (qv)

this scenario is already familiar. Novalis wrote *Heinrich von Ofterdingen* partly to refute the worldly urbanity of Goethe's *Wilhelm Meisters Lehrjahre* (where he believed that Nature and Mysticism had been unjustly neglected). It is in the earlier pages of this book that we encounter 'die blaue Blume' – the blue flower (qv *Am Bach im Frühlinge* D361) of which Heinrich dreams in erotic fashion ('the flower bent towards him and the blossom revealed an outstretched blue crown in which floated a tender face'). This flower was soon to be adopted as a symbol of longing among Novalis's fellow-Romantics.

There was further poetry written towards the end of Novalis's short life, and many other things too – fairy-story fragments and learned dissertations. In the essay from 1799, *Die Christenheit oder Europa* ('Christendom or Europe'), he calls for a new Europe free of the strictures of the Reformation and the hard-nosed cynicism of the Enlightenment; in fact he advocates a return to the unified society, cultural, social and intellectual, which had been a characteristic of medieval life. In 1798 Novalis became engaged to Julie von Charpentier, and in 1799 he was promoted to the rank of mine inspector at the Weissenfels saltworks (his poetic life always ran on strange parallel lines with the scientific practicalities of his working career). Before he could marry he died of tuberculosis, after seven months of illness, on 25 March 1801, aged twenty–eight. Many members of his family had been similarly stricken, and of course he shared the fate of his beloved Sophie. He had never left central Germany and, like Schubert, he had never seen the sea.

Schubert's first biographer Kreissle von Hellborn dismissed the Novalis settings as 'not much to speak of . . . more peculiar than beautiful'. With the five song-settings of Novalis the English-speaking Schubertian enters an unfamiliar world. In the first place, none of these songs was published in the Peters Edition; perhaps they were excluded because they were not considered interesting enough on musical grounds, although in the case of the *Nacht-hymne* D687 this is difficult to believe. It is also likely that these texts were judged incomprehensible to singers – it is true that they inhabit an uncomfortable no-man's-land between the sacred and secular. Novalis was a Protestant who freely included the Virgin Mary among his icons, but his liberal use of mythological allusion, and the unbridled invention of his own imagery, irrespective of its doctrinal implications, shocked conventional Roman Catholics. When Friedrich Schlegel was a young man he had welcomed, and helped publish, the *Hymnen an die Nacht*. But as an older man living in Vienna and deeply devoted to Rome, he would have dismissed many of these passages as youthful error (as indeed he dismissed much of his own earlier work).

It is this youthful freedom, however, that now seems truly visionary. Later in the nineteenth century the writings of Novalis played their part in the birth of Wagner's *Tristan und Isolde* and *Parsifal* (the poet Klingsohr is a major character in *Heinrich von Ofterdingen*). In our day Novalis's poetry is valued deeply by Jungians, archetypal psychologists, surrealists and simply lovers of poetry. German-speakers are drawn in by the power and beauty of the language, much of it difficult to understand and astoundingly modern in its effect. Schubert had already been attracted by the pantheism of Goethe (*Ganymed* D544, 1817) and he came across Novalis more or less at the same time as discovering the *Abendröte* settings of Friedrich von Schlegel. For Novalis, nature was 'the veil and mysterious Garment of the Unseen . . . the Voice with which the Deity proclaims himself to man' (Thomas Carlyle, 'Novalis' [1829]).

Novalis was thus an ideal poet to satisfy the metaphysical leanings of the Schubert circle in 1819 – even though the poet had been dead some eighteen years. The popularity of the 1815 edition of Novalis's works, published in Berlin, is attested by a diary entry from Wilhelm Müller's *Tagebuch* from 26 January 1816: 'I have lately been reading a lot of Novalis who has frequently affected me most wondrously. It seemed as if the voice resonating within me were not from the outside, rather as if it came from me. It seemed as if I'd long been wanting to say all that, but had been dumb.' Much of Novalis's imagery is based on doctrines with which the young Roman Catholic men of the Schubert circle had been familiar since childhood – the worship of Mary, Communion, Transubstantiation. Novalis personalized, re-invented and romanticized these and replaced the priest with the artist as chief interpreter and functionary. It is possible that Schubert first read Novalis in German publications from the beginning of the century, but nothing stimulates renewed local interest in a poet more than a reissue of his works, and, in 1820, the two-volume *Schriften* were published in Austria. Schober no doubt organized readings from the works for his *Bildung* circle. The Viennese title page had another Schubertian resonance. It shows

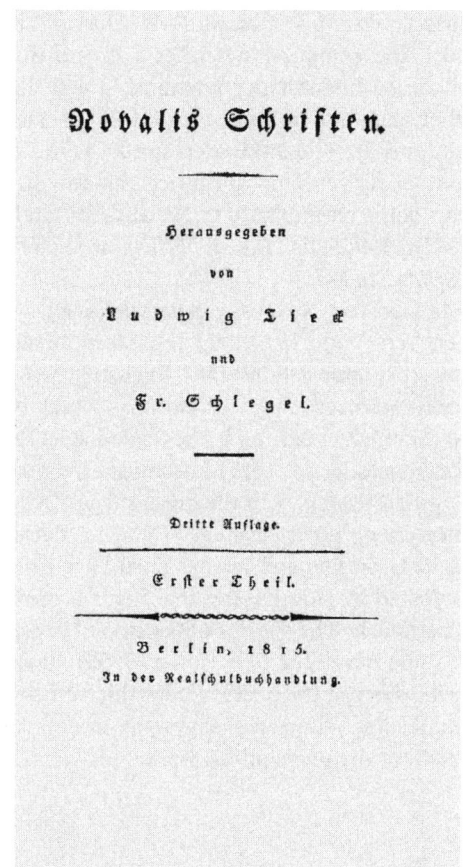

Title page of first edition of the Novalis *Schriften* (1815).

a scene from *Heinrich von Ofterdingen* where the novel's hero converses in a dream with the celebrated blue flower, symbol of German romanticism. But here it is depicted as a sunflower; it is in Schubert's later setting *Heliopolis I* (D753, 1822) that Mayrhofer communes with 'the flower chosen by Helios' and the link between the two flowers, blue and yellow, is evident in this illustration. There is much in the strangeness of that poet (as well as Bruchmann, in *Schwestergruss* D762, and Schober) that has taken its cue from Novalis.

It would not have been lost on Schubert and his friends, raised in a culture of sexual guilt, that Novalis allowed erotic desire into his work as something sublime. In *Hymne* D659 (formerly known as *Hymne* I), the Last Supper is described as the connection between divine

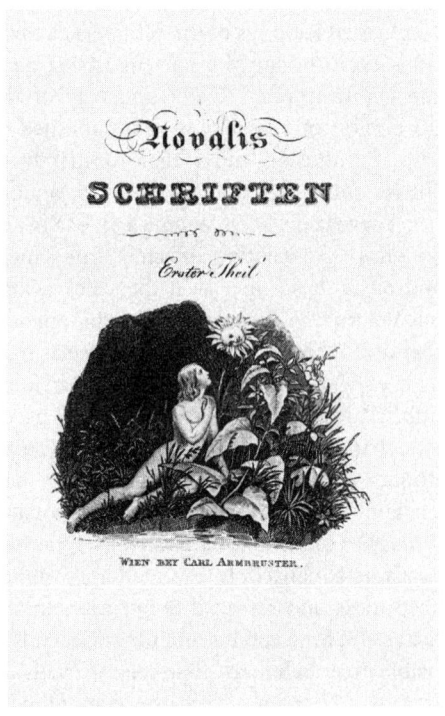

Title page of the Viennese edition of the Novalis *Schriften* (1820).

love and the insatiable thirst for sexual communion. The white-hot conviction with which it is accomplished achieves a verbal (if not musical) rapture akin to someone speaking in tongues, a practice that was common among the Pietists, the evangelical branch of Protestantism in which Novalis was raised. From later periods bereavement-inspired works by Edgar Allan Poe and Vladimir Nabokov come to mind. The nearest we have in the literature of English song are the sonnets of John Donne ('Death be not proud' and so on) which were penned after the poet's wife died.

Novalis defined the words spoken by a poet as 'no mere everyday tokens, magic words that call forth a beautiful circle of kindred spirits' ('Seine Worte sind nicht allgemeine Zeichen – Töne sind es – Zauberworte, die schöne Gruppen um sich her bewegen'). A significant Schubertian after-resonance is the prose-poem *Mein Traum* ('My Dream') in which the composer describes a dream that concerned his unhappy relationship with his father, and where the concluding passage mentions a 'circle of kindred spirits' as in the passage above. This allegorical dream also bears some resemblance to Novalis's fairy tale of *Hyazinth und Rosenblütchen* from *Die Lehrlinge zu Sais*.

In Germany Novalis's reputation has always been very high. In Britain the exceptionally perceptive translations into English (*Twelve of the Spiritual Songs of Novalis*, 1851) by the Scottish poet and theologian George MacDonald (1824–1905) introduced the poet to British readers with the greatest sensitivity. Since then, poets such as Kathleen Raine, David Gascoyne and Jeremy Reed have been fascinated by Novalis, and the 'Night Hymns' in particular. The success of Penelope Fitzgerald's fine novel *The Blue Flower* (1995), based on the story of the poet's relationship with his Sophie, has stimulated a new awareness in Britain of the poet and his work.

NUN LASST UNS DEN LEIB BEGRABEN (Begräbnislied)
(KLOPSTOCK) **D168** [H75]
C minor   9 March 1815

Burial song (Let us now bury the body)

Quartet, SATB

(31 bars)

Begrabt den Leib in seine Gruft,	Bury the body in its grave
Bis ihn des Richters Stimme ruft!	Until the voice of the Supreme Judge summons it;
Wir säen ihn, einst blüht er auf,	We sow it; one day it will blossom forth,
Und steigt verklärt zu Gott hinauf!	And rise up, transfigured, to God.
Grabt mein verwesliches Gebein,	Bury my decaying bones,
O ihr noch Sterblichen nur ein!	You who have yet to die;
Es bleibt, es bleibt im Grabe nicht,	They will not remain in the grave,
Denn Jesus kommt und hält Gericht!	For Jesus will come, and pronounce judgement.
[(. . . 10 . . .)]	[(. . . 10 . . .)]
Ach, Gott, Geopferter! Dein Tod	O Lord, whose life was sacrificed! May your death
Stärk uns in uns'rer letzten Noth,	Strengthen us in our last agony;
Lass' uns're ganze Seele dein,	May our soul be wholly Yours,
Und freudig unser Ende sein.	And our end be joyful!

FRIEDRICH GOTTLOB KLOPSTOCK (1724–1803)

The music of death was never far from the composer's mind in 1815. Schubert chose words by a poet from an earlier epoch who was known as much for his patriotic (and sometimes warlike and jingoistic) poems as for enchanting lyrics like *Das Rosenband* and his religious odes. At first glance the composer's response to these words seems fairly conventional, but there is a brooding drama about the music that shows that Schubert could not help but respond to words. The slow dactyls (a minim plus two crotchets) represent the figure of Death. (The use of this motif was to reach its apotheosis in *Der Tod und das Mädchen* D531.) Note the gradual rise in pitch with Klopstock's imagery: 'sowing' stays on one note in the soprano stave of b. 6 (like so many seeds in the ground); with 'blossoming' the pitch climbs a minor third (on 'blüht er auf', b. 7); finally 'transfiguration' changes B flat to B natural and opens up the music to a grand cadence on 'Gott hinauf' (b. 9).

The opening of the second verse ('Grabt mein verwesliches Gebein', from b. 10) is an eerie dialogue between men's and women's voices. (In fact this is the second half of the first musical verse; *see* paragraph at the end of this commentary.) As one looks at the music on the page, the line of notes on the top two staves (the women mourners, perhaps) seem to be looking down at the buried tenor and basses whose parts are written in coffin outline. The music becomes more lively on 'es bleibt im Grabe nicht', a literal and musical differentiation between the quick and the dead. The pronouncing of judgement ('Jesus kommt und hält Gericht', bb. 15–17) has the solemn grandeur of an old-fashioned Handelian overture. The workings of the Almighty were to be similarly depicted in dotted rhythms in *Dem Unendlichen* D177, a solo setting of the same poet, written a few months later, which has the grandeur of a state occasion; it is quite possible that Schubert was thinking about the poet Körner (who had died a hero's death in battle) when he wrote it.

This quartet was performed in the Hyperion Edition as it was printed in the AGA, as a one-off ABA structure with strophes 1 and 2 set to different music with a variation of the first verse (with a closing *Tierce de Picardie*) to bring the piece to an end. The AGA prints strophes 1, 2 and 13 for this purpose, thus providing a kind of overview of the whole poem. The problem is that even though this shortening of the piece is convenient for performance purposes, it misrepresents Schubert's intentions.

In 1996 the editor of Series III of the NSA, Dietrich Berke, published this work for the first time 'in its authentic shape according to Schubert's autograph'. The inauthentic title of *Begräbnislied* was the first thing to fall away. More importantly this new edition revealed that Schubert intended all thirteen verses of the poem to be sung. This meant six musical verses consisting of Klopstock's paired strophes and antistrophes plus a musical coda for the thirteenth verse. Performers are referred to the new edition where all of Klopstock's verses are printed and underlaid in the correct manner. And the *Tierce de Picardie* printed in the AGA is revealed as bogus.

Autograph:	Houghton Library, Harvard University, Cambridge, MA
First edition:	Published as No. 8 of *Neueste Folge nachgelassener, mehrstimmiger Gesänge mit und ohne Begleitung* by J.P. Gotthard, Vienna in 1872 and subsequently as part of the AGA in 1892 (P519)
Subsequent editions:	AGA XVII 16: p. 241; NSA III: Vol. 2a/11
Discography and timing:	Fischer-Dieskau —

Deutsche Grammophon		Elly Ameling, Janet Baker, Peter
Schubert Quartette	3'16	Schreier & Dietrich Fischer-Dieskau
Hyperion I 20[21]	2'58	Patricia Rozario, Catherine Denley, Ian Bostridge &
Hyperion II 5[15]		Michael George

← *Amphiaraos* D166   *Jesus Christus unser Heiland* D168a →

NUR WER DIE LIEBE KENNT   Only he who knows love
(Impromptu) (WERNER) D₂513A [H330]
(Fragment) A♭ major   1817?

(22 bars)

Nur wer die Liebe kennt, versteht das Sehen	Only those who know love understand the longing
An dem Geliebten ewig fest zu hangen,	Forever to hold fast to the lover,
Und Lebensmut aus seinem Aug' zu trinken;	And to drink life's courage from his eyes.
Er kennt das schmerzlich selige Verlangen,	They know the blissful pain of longing
Dahin zu schmelzen in ein Meer von Tränen,	To dissolve into a sea of tears
Und aufgelöst in Liebe zu versinken! –	And sink, dissolved in love!

[(. . . 7 lines . . .)]   [(. . . 7 lines . . .)]

ZACHARIAS WERNER (1768–1823); poem written 9 August 1806

This is the first of Schubert's two Werner solo settings (1817 and 1820). See the poet's biography for a chronological list of all the Werner settings.

This fragment consists of a partial setting of a thirteen-line poem entitled *Impromptu: in Tharants Ruinen geschrieben*. The title 'In Tharand's Ruinen geschrieben' ('written in Tharant's ruins') might suggest classical allusion, but the poet was almost certainly referring to the ruins of the old castle, a favourite site for painters and illustrators, in the small town of Tharandt, a south-western suburb of Dresden.

It is obvious that Werner modelled his poem on Goethe's celebrated lyric, Mignon's 'Nur wer die Sehnsucht kennt'. Such imitations and parodies were seldom meant to mock the original; rather were they written in homage as the sincerest form of flattery. That the imitation is a sentimental effusion and a pale copy of the original is perhaps why this song remained a fragment: the composer crossed it out before completing it. There are eleven extant bars with full piano accompaniment, and a further eleven bars where only the vocal line is notated. If Schubert had completed the song it is possible that he would have used the complete text. The concluding seven lines make clear that this is a poem of bereavement: what is the use of plucking the golden flowers when these can never adorn the departed beloved?

The key of this fragment is A flat, the tonality of Schubert's first setting of Mignon's lyric (*Sehnsucht* D310), which also has a similar rhythm and comparable vocal line. A feature of the song is a continuing shift between A flat major and minor (the by-play between these two moods was to reach its apotheosis much later in *Auf dem Wasser zu singen* D774 and in the piano Impromptu Op. 90 no. 4 with its cascading arpeggios). There are touches of Schubertian inspiration: at 'Lebensmut' romantic triplets cease in favour of stronger quavers and the idea of melting (at 'Dahin zu schmelzen in ein Meer') is illustrated with a descending chromatic phrase. The melismatic vocal flourish on 'Liebe zu versinken' suggests the Italianate influence quite commonly

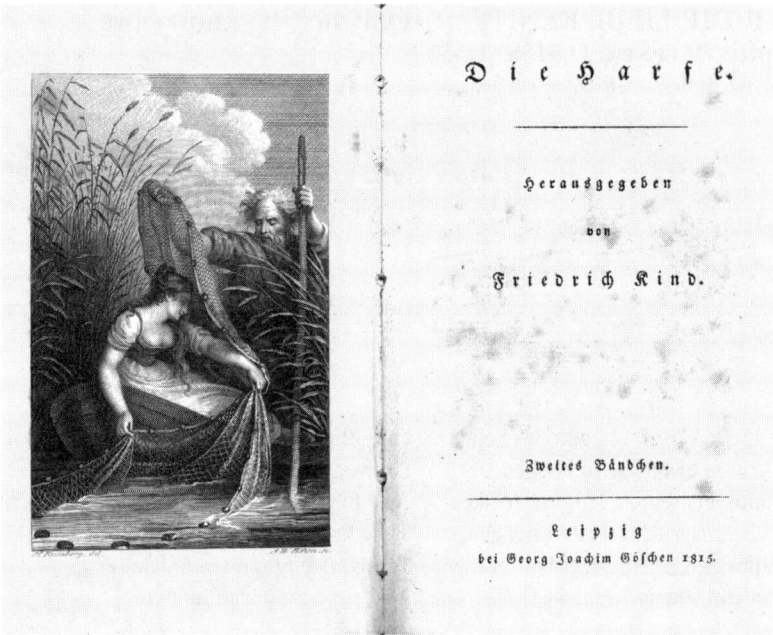

Die Harfe, 1815, source of Werner's *Nur wie die Liebe kennt*.

found in Schubert's music of 1817 (a good example of this is *La pastorella al prato* D528), but in John Reed's opinion the dating of the song is 'highly conjectural'.

The entire vocal line of this fragment as recorded for the Hyperion Edition is genuine Schubert, but only the first twelve bars of the accompaniment (up to and including the words 'Er kennt das') are authentic. From 'schmerzlich selige Verlangen' onwards the piano part (including postlude) has been added by Reinhard Van Hoorickx.

Autograph:	Wienbibliothek im Rathaus, Vienna (fair copy)
First edition:	Published in a performing edition by Reinhard Van Hoorickx in 1974; subsequently issued as part of the NSA in 1999 (P822)
Subsequent editions:	Not in Peters; Not in AGA; NSA IV: Vol. 11/226
Discography and timing:	Fischer-Dieskau —
	Hyperion I 21^5
	Hyperion II 17^8 1'25 Edith Mathis

← *An den Tod* D518   *Die abgeblühte Linde* D514 →

NUR WER DIE SEHNSUCHT KENNT *see*:

SEHNSUCHT (I) D310; SEHNSUCHT (II) D359; SEHNSUCHT (III) D481; SEHNSUCHT (IV) D656 (MALE-VOICE QUINTET); GESÄNGE AUS WILHELM MEISTER: MIGNON UND DER HARFNER D877/1 (DUET); GESÄNGE AUS WILHELM MEISTER: LIED DER MIGNON D877/4; *see* also: MIGNON LIEDER FROM *WILHELM MEISTER*: AN OVERVIEW; *WILHELM MEISTERS LEHRJAHRE*

O

O COMBATS, Ô DÉSORDRE EXTRÊME! *see ECHO ET NARCISSE*
D ANH. II, 3 NO. 2

O QUELL, WAS STRÖMST DU   The flower and the stream
RASCH UND WILD (Die Blume
und der Quell)
(SCHULZE) **D874** [H581]
(Fragment) G major   January? or March 1826?

(18 bars)

Die Blume:
O Quell, was strömst du rasch und wild
Und wühlst in deinem Silbersande
Und drängst, von weichem Schaum verhüllt,
Dich schwellend auf am grünen Rande?
O riesle, Quell,
Doch glatt und hell,
Dass ich, verklärt von zartem Taue,
Mein zitternd Bild in dir erschaue!

Der Quell:
O Blume, kann ich ruhig sein,
Wenn sich dein Bild in mir bespiegelt,
Und wunderbare Liebespein
Mich bald zurückhält, bald beflügelt?
Drum streb' ich auf
Mit irrem Lauf
Und will mit schmachtendem Verlangen,
Du Zarte, deinen Kelch umfangen.

[. . . 2 . . .]

The Flower:
O stream, why do you surge so fast and wild,
Burrowing in your silver sand
And welling up against the green banks,
Masked in soft foam?
Trickle, stream,
Smooth and bright,
That I, transfigured with gentle dew,
Might behold in you my quivering image.

The Stream
O flower, how can I be calm
When your image is reflected in me,
And wondrous pangs of love
Now hold me back, now give me wings?
So I strive upwards
In an uncertain course,
And with languishing yearning
Seek to embrace your calyx, o tender beloved.

[. . . 2 . . .]

ERNST SCHULZE (1789–1817); poem written 8 January 1814

This is the sixth of Schubert's ten Schulze solo settings (1825–6). See the poet's biography for a chronological list of all the Schulze settings. An outline of a suggested performing version for a Schulze cycle is listed under 'Auf den wilden Wegen'.

This fragment consists of four bars of piano introduction and fourteen bars of virtually unaccompanied melody. It is the only one of Schubert's Schulze setting in which the poet does not speak in his own persona. Instead, a flower is in conversation with a stream, not a very promising match for the direct and sometimes searing statements of the other Schulze songs, although it is fairly clear that 'Die Blume' represents the poet's muse, Adelheid Tychsen, and 'Der Quell' the poet himself. This poem is unique among the ninety of Schulze's poetic diary in imagining such a colloquy. *Lebensmelodien* D395 (1816) to a poem by August Schlegel had featured the different thoughts of swan, eagle and doves, but it does not number among the composer's great successes; when anthropomorphizing rivers, mountains, butterflies and birds (as in the Schlegel *Abendröthe* settings) Schubert is happier dealing with one character at a time. The greatest dialogue that is required of a single singer is *Der Müller und der Bach* D795/19, the penultimate song of *Die schöne Müllerin* – and that brings to mind another song from the same cycle, *Eifersucht und Stolz*, in which the turbulent stream mirrors the miller's jealousy. The opening words of that song ('Wohin so schnell, so kraus, und wild, mein lieber Bach?') suggest that Schubert was attracted by the same water imagery that opens the Schulze poem. The piano accompaniment for *O Quell, was strömst du rasch und wild* bubbles excitedly, recalling the Müller setting of 1823.

The fragment has become known by the first line of the poem because there is no indication of another title on the autograph. The title in the *Poetisches Tagebuch* is *Am 8ten Januar 1814*, the earliest poem in the sequence to be set by Schubert. The autograph also contains the first page of *Im Jänner 1817* D876, the only one of the Schulze settings which adopts a date from the *Poetisches Tagebuch* as a song heading. The last two bars of the vocal line (music for the word 'erschaue') and all but the opening five bars of piano writing are provided by Reinhard Van Hoorickx in his completion of the song. In the performance recorded for the Hyperion Edition the first two bars of the introduction are recapitulated as a coda. This modest 'completion' only allows us to hear the flower's words, not the stream's reply. In Schulze's poem there are four strophes in all, the first two of which are printed here. The final verse of the poem brings some kind of quietus to the erotic imagery of the whole: if a kiss is not possible, the stream says, let the flower allow a single petal to fall on my wild depths – I will then silently boil over ('will ich still vorüberwallen').

Autograph:	Bodleian Library, Oxford
First edition:	Published privately by Reinhard Van Hoorickx and subsequently as part of the NSA in 1988 (P802)
Subsequent editions:	Not in Peters; Not in AGA; NSA IV: Vol. 14/267
Bibliography:	Hoorickx 1977, p. 287
Discography and timing:	Fischer-Dieskau —
	Hyperion I 18^{15}
	Hyperion II 31^{4} 0'41 Peter Schreier

←— *Um Mitternacht* D862   *Im Jänner 1817 (Tiefes Leid)* D876 —→

O SO LASST EUCH FROH BEGRÜSSEN *see* DUBIOUS, MISATTRIBUTED AND LOST SONGS

OMBRE AMENE, AMICHE PIANTE (La serenata)

Kind shades, friendly bushes

(Metastasio) **D990f** [H16]
(Composition exercise without accompaniment) A major   1813?

Om - bre a - me - ne   a - mi - che pian - te

(36 bars)

Ombre amene,	Kind shades,
Amiche piante,[1]	Friendly bushes,
Il mio bene,	My darling,
Il caro amante.	My beloved!
Chi mi dice, ove n' andò?	Who can tell me where I should go?
Zeffiretto lusinghiero,	Coaxing zephyr,
A lui vola messaggiero;[2]	Fly to him as a messenger
Dì che torni, e che mi renda	And restore to me
Quella pace, che non ò.[3]	The peace I lack.

PIETRO METASTASIO (1698–1782)

This is the eighth of Schubert's fourteen Metastasio solo settings (1812–27). See the poet's biography for a chronological list of all the Metastasio settings.

This song fragment shares the distinction with the Pichler setting *Die Nacht* (qv) of being the most recent of Schubert song finds. Neither song is mentioned in the second Deutsch catalogue (1978). There, D990F, a companion piece to D990E, is wrongly listed as an early version of the 1827 song for bass, *Il traditor deluso*. Fragments such as this are notoriously difficult to identify, but the confusion here was caused by the disappearance of the autograph that had been sold in Berlin in 1933, and then again in Bern in 1950. Only the first page of the oblong double leaf had been photographed for a sales catalogue. Eventually, in 1988, this manuscript came into the possession of the Viennese collector H. P. Wertitsch. The first song on the double leaf was the first version of *L'incanto degli occhi* D990E. There was a second aria without title (vocal part only) beginning with words that were identified as belonging to Metastasio's cantata *Angelica* with the subtitle *La serenata*. This was actually a lyric that Salieri himself had set as part of the twenty-eighth of his *Divertimenti*. The shepherdess Licori awaits her beloved Tirsi in the midday sun and entreats the gradually lengthening shadows and the gentle winds to find her paramour and tell him to return.

The aria in § shows a developed feel for Italianate melodic line and a sensitivity for the atmosphere of the words (as far as it is possible to tell from the vocal line alone). The autograph is extremely difficult to date, although it must be within the period that Schubert received tuition from Salieri. The second Deutsch catalogue (1978) and Hoorickx place D990E and D990F at the very end of this period in 1816/17, but it is possible that they are earlier works and belong with the other exercises of 1813. Nothing in *L'incanto degli occhi* or *Ombre amene* shows much

[1] Schubert incorrectly changes this to '*Amichi* piante'.
[2] Schubert incorrectly changes this to 'A lui vola *mestaggiero*'.
[3] Schubert changes this to 'Quella pace che non *ho*'.

advance in style and skill on the highly accomplished aria for soprano, *Son fra l'onde* D78 (1813). More significantly, apart from some florid coloratura in D990E, there is little on the level of sophistication that marks out Dido's aria, *Vedi quanto [t']adoro* of 1816 (D510).

Autograph:	Wienbibliothek im Rathaus, Vienna
First edition:	Realized and published privately by Reinhard Van Hoorickx and subsequently as part of the NSA in 1999 (P818)
Subsequent editions:	Not in Peters; Not in AGA; NSA IV: Vol. 11/216 (vocal line only)
Discography and timing:	Fischer-Dieskau —
	Hyperion I 33[14]
	Hyperion II 2[12] 1'38 Ann Murray

← *Die Advokaten* D37   *Misero pargoletto* D42 →

OPUS NUMBERS

The chronological list below is of all the songs and part-songs that were printed in Schubert's lifetime with the publishers and the dates on which they were first advertised for sale. The reader can follow the entire chronology and history of Schubert's song publications (1821–2010) by reading this article first, then the article on the NACHLASS, and then moving on to POSTHUMOUS SONGS. Throughout, each song publication has been given a 'P' number, from P1 to P859 (also to be found in the 'First edition' information following each song commentary). These give the reader an instant, if approximate, idea of how long each song took to reach print. In the list overleaf, poets' names are given only where a song's title (*Sehnsucht* for example) applies to multiple settings by different authors. For the purposes of this list, and for P numbers, the appearance of songs in periodicals, or in Van Hoorickx's privately circulated editions, are not counted as part of the chronology. Part-songs with piano are part of the same sequence.

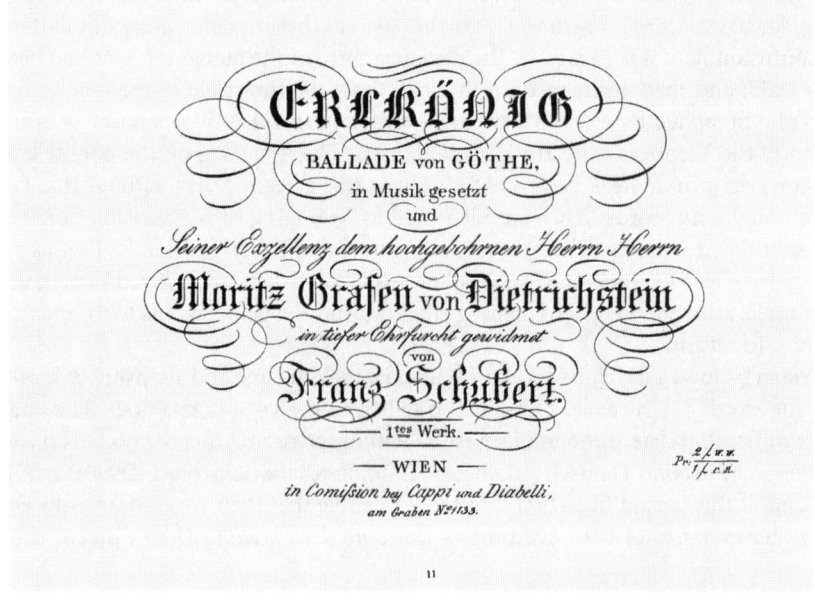

Schubert's Opus 1 – *Erlkönig*, published on commission by Diabelli in 1821.

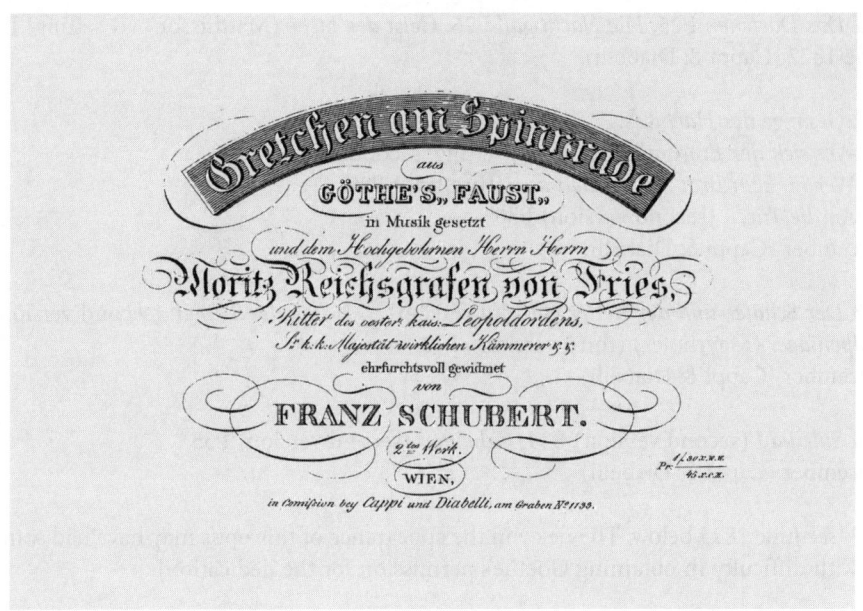

Schubert's Opus 2 – *Gretchen am Spinnrade*, published on commission by Diabelli in 1821.

1821

Op. 1 *Erlkönig* (fourth version) P1
2 April (Cappi & Diabelli)

Op. 2 *Gretchen am Spinnrade* P2
30 April (Cappi & Diabelli)

Op. 3 *Schäfers Klagelied* (first version in C minor) P3, *Meeres Stille* (II setting) P4, *Heidenröslein* P5, *Jägers Abendlied* (II setting) P6
29 May (Cappi & Diabelli)

Op. 4 *Der Wanderer* (third version) P7, *Morgenlied* (Werner) P8, *Wandrers Nachtlied* (D224) P9
29 May (Cappi & Diabelli)

Op. 5 *Rastlose Liebe* (first version in E major) P10, *Nähe des Geliebten* (second version) P11, *Der Fischer* (second version) P12, *Erster Verlust* P13, *Der König in Thule* P14
9 July (Cappi & Diabelli)

Op. 6 *Memnon* P15, *Antigone und Oedip* P16, *Am Grabe Anselmos* (first version) P17
23 August (Cappi & Diabelli)

Op. 7 *Die abgeblühte Linde* P18, *Der Flug der Zeit* P19, *Der Tod und das Mädchen* P20
27 November (Cappi & Diabelli)

1822

Op. 8 *Der Jüngling auf dem Hügel* P21, *Sehnsucht* (Mayrhofer) P22, *Erlafsee*[1] P23, *Am Strome* P24
9 May (Cappi & Diabelli)

---

[1] This song had already been published as a supplement to *Mahlerisches Taschenbuch für Freunde interessanter Gegenden Natur- und Kunst-Merkwürdigkeiten der Österreichischen Monarchie*, Wien, 1818. Verlag von Anton Doll.

Op. 11 *Das Dörfchen* P25, *Die Nachtigall* P26, *Geist der Liebe* (Matthisson) (II setting) P27
12 June 1822 (Cappi & Diabelli)

Op. 12 *Gesänge des Harfners*:
 (i)   *Wer sich der Einsamkeit ergibt* (II setting, second version) P28
 (ii) *Wer nie sein Brot mit Tränen ass* (III setting) P29
 (iii) *An die Türen* (second version) P30
13 December (Cappi & Diabelli)

Op. 13 *Der Schäfer und der Reiter* (second version) P31, *Lob der Tränen* (second version) P32, *Der Alpenjäger* (Mayrhofer) (third version), P33
13 December (Cappi & Diabelli)

Op. 14 *Suleika I* (second version) P34, *Geheimes* (second version) P35
13 December (Cappi & Diabelli)

Op. 19 [*see* June 1825 below. The delay in the appearance of this opus may have had something to do with difficulty in obtaining Goethe's permission for the dedication]

1823

Op. 20 *Sei mir gegrüsst* P36, *Frühlingsglaube* (third version) P37, *Hänflings Liebeswerbung* (third version) P38
10 April (Sauer & Leidesdorf)

Op. 22 *Der Zwerg* P39, *Wehmut* P40
27 May (Sauer & Leidesdorf)

Op. 21 *Auf der Donau* P41, *Der Schiffer* (Mayrhofer) (second version) P42, *Wie Ulfru fischt* (second version) P43
19 June (Sauer & Leidesdorf)

Op. 23 *Die Liebe hat gelogen* P44, *Selige Welt* P45, *Schwanengesang* (Senn) P46, *Schatzgräbers Begehr* (second version) P47
4 August (Sauer & Leidesdorf)

Op. 16 *Frühlingsgesang* P48, *Naturgenuss* P49 (quartet)
9 October (Cappi & Diabelli)

Op. 24 *Gruppe aus dem Tartarus* (II setting) P50, *Schlummerlied* (*Schlaflied*) (second version) P51
27 October (Sauer & Leidesdorf)

1824

Op. 25 *Die schöne Müllerin*
    (i)   *Das Wandern* P52
    (ii) *Wohin?* P53
    (iii) *Halt!* P54
    (iv) *Danksagung an den Bach* P55
    (v)   *Am Feierabend* P56
    (vi) *Der Neugierige* P57

  (vii)   *Ungeduld* P58
 (viii)   *Morgengruss* P59
  (ix)   *Des Müllers Blumen* P60
   (x)   *Tränenregen* P61
  (xi)   *Mein!* P62
 (xii)   *Pause* P63
(xiii)   *Mit dem grünen Lautenbande* P64
 (xiv)   *Der Jäger* P65
  (xv)   *Eifersucht und Stolz* P66
 (xvi)   *Die liebe Farbe* P67
(xvii)   *Die böse Farbe* P68
(xviii) *Trockne Blumen* P69
 (xix)   *Der Müller und der Bach* P70
  (xx)   *Des Baches Wiegenlied* P71
24 March (Sauer & Leidesdorf)

Op. 26 *Romanze (Der Vollmond strahlt)* aus dem Drama *Rosamunde* P72
24 March (Sauer & Leidesdorf). [The *Jägerchor*, *Hirtenchor* and *Geisterchor* from *Rosamunde* appeared in July 1828.]

Op. 28 *Der Gondelfahrer* P73 (quartet)
12 August (Sauer & Leidesdorf)

1825
Op. 32 *Die Forelle* (fourth version) P74[2]
13 January (Anton Diabelli & Co.)

Op. 36 *Die zürnende Diana* (recte: *Den Zurnenden Diana*) (second version) P75, *Nachtstück* (second version) P76
11 February (Cappi & Co.)

Op. 37 *Der Pilgrim* (second version) P77, *Der Alpenjäger* (Schiller) (second version) P78
28 February (Cappi & Co.)

Op. 38 *Der Liedler* P79
9 May (Cappi & Co.)

Op. 19 *An Schwager Kronos* P80, *An Mignon* (second version) P81, *Ganymed* P82
6 June (Cappi & Diabelli)

Op. 43 *Die junge Nonne* P83, *Nacht und Träume* (second version) P84
25 July (Anton Pennauer)

Op. 31 *Suleikas zweiter Gesang* (P85)
12 August (Anton Pennauer)

1826
Op. 39 *Sehnsucht* (Schiller) (II setting, third version) P86
8 February (Anton Pennauer)

---

[2] *Die Forelle* had first appeared as a supplement to the *Wiener Zeitschrift für Kunst, Literatur, Theater und Mode* (issue of 9 December 1820).

Op. 52 *Sieben Gesänge aus Walters Scotts Fräulein vom See*
  (i)   *Ellens Gesang I* P87
  (ii) *Ellens Gesang II* P88
 (iii) *Bootgesang* P89
 (iv) *Coronach* P90
  (v) *Normans Gesang* P91
 (vi) *Ellens Gesang III* P92
(vii) *Lied des gefangenen Jägers* P93
5 April (Matthias Artaria)

Op. 57 *Der Schmetterling* P94, *Die Berge* P95, *An den Mond* (Hölty) (second version) P96
6 April (Thaddäus Weigl)

Op. 58 *Hektors Abschied* (second version) P97, *An Emma* (third version) P98,[3] *Des Mädchens Klage* (II setting, second version) P99
6 April (Thaddäus Weigl)

Op. 60 *Greisengesang* (third version) P100, *Dithyrambe* (II setting) P101
10 June (Cappi & Czerny)

Op. 56 *Willkommen und Abschied* (second version) P102, *An die Leier* P103, *Im Haine* P104
14 July 1826) (Anton Pennauer)

Op. 59 *Du liebst mich nicht* (second version) P105, *Dass sie hier gewesen* P106, *Du bist die Ruh* P107, *Lachen und Weinen* P108
21 September (Sauer & Leidesdorf)

Op. 65 *Lied eines Schiffers an die Dioskuren* P109, *Der Wanderer* (Schlegel) (second version) P110, *Aus Heliopolis* [*Heliopolis* I] P111
24 November (Cappi & Czerny)

1827
Op. 41 *Der Einsame* P112[4]
5 January (Anton Diabelli & Co.)

Op. 44 *An die untergehende Sonne* P113
5 January (Anton Diabelli & Co.)

Op. 62 *Vier Gesänge aus Wilhelm Meister*
  (i)   *Mignon und der Harfner* ('Nur wer die Sehnsucht kennt') (V setting) P114
  (ii) *Heisst mich nicht reden* (II setting) P115
 (iii) *So lasst mich scheinen* (III setting) P116
 (iv) *Nur wer die Sehnsucht kennt* (VI setting) P117
2 March (Anton Diabelli & Co.)

---

[3] *An Emma* had first appeared as a supplement to the *Wiener Zeitschrift für Kunst, Literatur, Theater und Mode* (issue of 30 June 1821).
[4] *Der Einsame* had first appeared as a supplement to the *Wiener Zeitschrift für Kunst, Literatur, Theater und Mode* (issue of 12 March 1825).

Op. 71 *Drang in die Ferne* P118[5]
2 March (Anton Diabelli & Co.)

Op. 72 *Auf dem Wasser zu singen* P119[6]
2 March (Anton Diabelli & Co.)

Op. 68 *Der Wachtelschlag* P120[7]
16 May (Anton Diabelli & Co.)

Op. 73 *Die Rose* (first version in G major) P121[8]
16 May (Anton Diabelli & Co.)

Op. 74 *Die Advokaten* P122
16 May (Anton Diabelli & Co.)

Op. 79 *Das Heimweh* (Pyrker) (second version) P123, *Die Allmacht* (I setting) P124
16 May (Tobias Haslinger)

Op. 80 *Der Wanderer an den Mond* P125, *Das Zügenglöcklein* (second version) P126, *Im Freien* P127
25 May (Tobias Haslinger)

Op. 81 *Alinde* P128, *An die Laute* P129, *Zur guten Nacht* P130
28 May (Tobias Haslinger)

Op. 87 *Der Unglückliche* (second version) P131, *Hoffnung* (Schiller) (II setting) P132, *Der Jüngling am Bache* (III setting, second version) P133
6 August (Anton Pennauer)

Op. 83 *Drei Gesänge für Bassstimme mit Klavier: L'incanto degli occhi* (second version) P134, *Il traditor deluso* (second version) P135, *Il modo di prender moglie* P136
12 September (Tobias Haslinger)

Op. 88 *Abendlied für die Entfernte* P137, *Thekla* (II setting, second version) P138, *Um Mitternacht* (second version) P139, *An die Musik* (second version) P140
12 December (Thaddäus Weigl)

1828
Op. 89 *Winterreise* Part I (Nos 1–12)
  (i)   *Gute Nacht* P141
  (ii) *Die Wetterfahne* P142
  (iii) *Gefrorne Tränen* P143

[5] *Drang in die Ferne* had first appeared as a supplement to the *Wiener Zeitschrift für Kunst, Literatur, Theater und Mode* (issue of 25 March 1823).
[6] *Auf dem Wasser zu singen* had first appeared as a supplement to the *Wiener Zeitschrift für Kunst, Literatur, Theater und Mode* (issue of 30 December 1823).
[7] *Der Wachtelschlag* had first appeared as a supplement to the *Wiener Zeitschrift für Kunst, Literatur, Theater und Mode* (issue of 30 July 1822).
[8] *Die Rose* had first appeared as a supplement to the *Wiener Zeitschrift für Kunst, Literatur, Theater und Mode* (issue of 7 May 1822).

 (iv)   *Erstarrung* P144
  (v)   *Der Lindenbaum* P145
 (vi)   *Wasserflut* P146
(vii)   *Auf dem Flusse* (second version) P147
(viii) *Rückblick* P148
 (ix)   *Irrlicht* P149
  (x)   *Rast* (second version) P150
 (xi)   *Frühlingstraum* (second version) P151
(xii)   *Einsamkeit* (second version) P152
14 January (Tobias Haslinger)

Op. 85 *Lied der Anne Lyle* P153, *Gesang der Norna* P154
14 March (Anton Diabelli & Co.)

Op. 86 *Romanze des Richard Löwenherz* (second version) P155
14 March (Anton Diabelli & Co.)

Op. 90 *Im Walde* (second version in B flat minor) P156, *Auf der Brücke* [*sic*] (second version in A flat major) P157
30 May (J. A. Kienreich, Graz; later corrected to Op. 93 and issued as such by A Diabelli & Co. in Spring 1835)

Op. 106 *Heimliches Lieben* (second version) P158, *Das Weinen* P159, *Vor meiner Wiege* P160, *Gesang (An Silvia)* P161
Spring 1828 (Lithographisches Institut)

Op. 92 *Der Musensohn* (second version in G major) P162, *Auf dem See* (second version) P163, *Geistes-Gruss* (sixth version in E major), P164
11 July (M. J. Leidesdorf)

Op. 96 *Die Sterne* (Leitner) P165, *Jägers Liebeslied* P166, *Wandrers Nachtlied (Über allen Gipfeln)* P167, *Fischerweise* (second version) P168
Summer 1828 (Lithographisches Institut; reissued in March 1829 by Anton Diabelli & Co. as Op. 96)

Op. 95 *Vier Refrain-Lieder*
  (i)   *Die Unterscheidung* P169
 (ii)   *Bei dir allein!* P170
(iii)   *Die Männer sind mechant* P171
 (iv)   *Irdisches Glück* P172
13 August (Thaddäus Weigl)

Op. 97 *Glaube, Hoffnung und Liebe* (Kuffner) P173
6 October (Anton Diabelli & Co.)

Schubert died on 19 November 1828. Strictly speaking any works published after this date are posthumous publications. There were a number of works, however, that were in the process of going through the press at that time, and it is likely that Schubert prepared them and even read the proofs. This applies above all to the second volume of *Winterreise* songs, Op. 89

(in Volume 4 of the NSA both parts of the cycle are treated as having been published within the composer's lifetime). In Volume 5 of the NSA the opus numbers 98, 105 and 108 are also considered to belong to the group of works that were issued while Schubert was still alive. The comic trio of Op. 104 and the choral quintet Op. 102 probably also belong in this category.

Op. 105 *Widerspruch* P174, *Wiegenlied* (Seidl) P175, *Am Fenster* P176, *Sehnsucht* (Seidl) P177
21 November (Josef Czerny – two days after Schubert's death)

Op. 101 *Im Frühling* (2 version) P178,[9] *Trost im Liede* (second version) P179,[10] *Der blinde Knabe* (second version) P180,[11] *Wandrers Nachtlied II* P167[12] (*see* Op. 96)
12 December (H. A. Probst in Leipzig. These four songs had been earlier issued as supplements to the *Wiener Zeitschrift* (*see* footnotes) without opus numbers.)

Op. 89 *Winterreise* Part II (Nos 13–24)
   (i)   *Die Post* P181
   (ii) *Der greise Kopf* P182
   (iii) *Die Krähe* P183
   (iv) *Letzte Hoffnung* P184
   (v)   *Im Dorfe* P185
   (vi) *Der stürmische Morgen* P186
   (vii) *Täuschung* P187
   (vii) *Der Wegweiser* P188
   (ix) *Das Wirtshaus* P189
   (x)   *Mut!* (2nd version) P190
   (xi) *Die Nebensonnen* (2nd version) P191
   (xii) *Der Leiermann* (2nd version) P192
30 December (Tobias Haslinger)

1829

Op. 108 *Über Wildemann* P193, *Todesmusik* (second version) P194, *Erinnerung* [sic] (*Die Erscheinung*) P195[13]
28 January (M. J. Leidesdorf. Schubert had originally intended these songs to be issued as Op. 93, a number that had already been used.)

Op. 98 *An die Nachtigall* (Claudius) P228, *Wiegenlied* (unknown poet) P229, *Iphigenia* (third version) P230
10 July (Anton Diabelli & Co.)

Op. 104 *Der Hochzeitsbraten* (Terzett with piano) P231
10 July (Anton Diabelli & Co.)

---

[9] *Im Frühling* had first appeared as a supplement to the *Wiener Zeitschrift für Kunst, Literatur, Theater und Mode* (issue of 16 September 1828).
[10] *Trost im Liede* had first appeared as a supplement to the *Wiener Zeitschrift für Kunst, Literatur, Theater und Mode* (issue of 23 June 1827).
[11] *Der blinde Knabe* had first appeared as a supplement to the *Wiener Zeitschrift für Kunst, Literatur, Theater und Mode* (issue of 25 September 1827).
[12] *Wandrers Nachtlied II* had first appeared as a supplement to the *Wiener Zeitschrift für Kunst, Literatur, Theater und Mode* (issue of 23 June 1827) and subsequently as Op. 96 no. 3 in the summer of 1828.
[13] This song had first appeared as *Die Erscheinung*, its correct title, as part of an *Album musicale* advertised by Sauer & Leidesdorf on 11 December 1824.

1831

Op. 102 *Mondenschein* (Quintet with piano) P274
21 April (Anton Diabelli & Co.)

Schubert's publishers chose to issue many songs, including some of the most significant ones, as separate items. The songs that had been published as supplements to the *Wiener Zeitschrift* were mostly assigned opus numbers of their own (Opp. 32, 41, 68, 71), although four of these *WZ* songs were grouped together as Op. 101 for Schubert's first song publication in Germany. The other single issues after Opp. 1 and 2 (*Erlkönig* and *Gretchen am Spinnrade* respectively) are Opp. 28, 31, 38, 39, 44, 86, 97, 102 and 104.

There were 209 songs and part-songs published by the end of 1828, thus more or less in Schubert's lifetime. These include the works issued in the weeks after his death, on which he had collaborated during the editorial process. By any standards, this was a remarkable number of songs for a thirty-one-year-old composer to have had in circulation. This figure comprises 192 properly published songs (reflected in the 'P' numbers explained at the beginning of this article), and sixteen songs that first appeared in periodicals, all but four of which (*An den Tod, Der Blumen Schmerz, Die Erscheinung* and *Widerschein*) were published again in permanent form during Schubert's lifetime. There were thus twelve songs (*Erlafsee* and eleven songs published originally as supplements in the *Wiener Zeitschrift*) that were published twice in his lifetime, and one (*Wandrers Nachtlied II*) that appeared three times: once in the *Wiener Zeitschrift* (1827), once in Op. 96 (1828) and again as part of Op. 101 in the same year.

It is interesting to make a tally of the total number of songs that appeared year by year. After the success between 1821 and 1825 (few composers of this or any other time would have been dissatisfied with such a respectable number of songs brought into the public domain) there was a marked yearly increase in publications from 1826 which reached a peak in the last year of the composer's life. This, surely, is an indication of Schubert's steadily growing fame and popularity, and of the fact that he was on the edge of a major career breakthrough at the time of his death.

1818   1 song (*Erlafsee*, published in *Mahlerisches Taschenbuch*)
1820   2 songs (*Die Forelle*, published in the *Wiener Zeitschrift*, and *Widerschein*, published in *Beckers Taschenbuch*)
1821   22 songs (Opp. 1, 2, 3[4 songs], 4[3], 5[5], 6[3], 7[3], 2 songs in *WZ*)
1822   17 songs (Opp. 8[4], 11[3], 12[3], 13[3], 14[2], 2 songs in *WZ*)
1823   18 songs (Opp. 20[3], 22[2], 21[3], 23[4], 16[2], 24[2], 2 songs in *WZ*)
1824   24 songs (Opp. 25[20], 26, 28, 1 song published as a supplement to the *Wiener Allgemeine musikalischen Zeitung*, 1 song published in an *Album Musicale* by Sauer & Leidesdorf)
1825   13 songs (Opp. 32, 36[2], 37[2], 38, 19[3], 43[2], 31, 1 song in *WZ*)
1826   26 songs (Opp. 39, 52[7], 57[3], 58[3], 60[2], 56[3], 59[4], 65[4])
1827   32 songs (Opp. 41, 44, 62[4], 71, 72, 68, 73, 74, 79[2], 80[3], 81[3], 87[3], 83[3], 88[4], 3 songs in *WZ*)
1828   53 songs (Opp. 89 Part One [12], 85[2], 86, 90[2], 106[4], 92[3], 96[4], 95[4], 97, 105[4], 101[3], 89 Part Two [12], 1 song in *WZ*)

The relevance of the old-fashioned opus numbers of Schubert's songs has been overtaken by Deutsch numbers and a far more sophisticated ability to date the music than was available to nineteenth-century musicians. And yet Schubertians must take the opus numbers seriously for a number of reasons. When a song went to press the composer almost invariably revised it to some extent as he prepared the fair copy for publication. This included the reading and correction of proofs where a number of last-minute changes could be made. Thus the actual date of a published song in terms of its creation might encompass a period beginning with its appearance in autograph form and ending only with the date of its publication. In some cases (Op. 38 for instance, the Kenner ballad *Der Liedler*) this represented a gap of over ten years. This process of revision is not allowed for in the chronological H numbers assigned to songs in this book, nor is it by Mandyczewski in the AGA, a strictly chronological survey (as far as it was possible to determine an accurate chronology) relating to each work's first appearance. The significance of opus numbers is taken into account by Dürr's NSA where the works that were issued in Schubert's lifetime were published at the beginning of the survey (volumes 1–5). After these, volumes 6 to 14 were planned to cover, in chronological order, the songs that were *not* published in Schubert's lifetime – songs that may have been revised by the composer as a matter of artistic conscience, but which were never subject to a further stage of pre-publication creative scrutiny.

Another important aspect of the publication of opus numbers is rather more controversial. To what extent was Schubert deliberately putting together thematic garlands of songs that were destined for performance as such? Did he actually envisage performances where the publication groupings should be retained on the concert platform? In an attempt to test these questions the songs, grouped in their original opus numbers, were programmed at the Hohenems Schubertiade some decades ago with mixed results: certain opus numbers worked better in performance than others and some of the groupings were downright dull. In the same way it may be surmised that because Schubert published his Opp. 1 and 2 (and some others) separately, he did not necessarily intend that they should always stand alone in performance. The opus numbers, where the songs are arranged together, do little to spare the hard-working programme planner when it comes to preparing recitals. Nevertheless there are some instances where the groupings do make a kind of sense and one has the impression that careful thought went into the selection of some of the juxtapositions, and very little into others. There is a mixture of altruistic musical and literary thought, and plain commercial expediency.

In any case, the art of the song recital as it is understood today was in its infancy and there was no automatic parallel between printed groupings and what was performed. Even at the end of the nineteenth century, when the lied was an established art form, there was less of a tendency than there is now to think in terms of cycles and quasi-dramatic anthologies. Hugo Wolf published his *Mörike-Lieder* (1888) most carefully in one volume, for example, but there is no evidence that he envisaged a complete concert performance of the work, nor even of his later Spanish and Italian Songbooks. If a set of songs were presented as a single book it was up to the performer to pick and choose, and this also applied to works like *Die schöne Müllerin* and *Winterreise*, too, which were cherry-picked without scruple for many decades. Nevertheless there is no doubt that it was mostly Schubert himself (probably with advice from friends) who selected the songs that went forward to the publishers, and in the more interesting groupings there may be grounds for present-day performers to reflect these choices on the concert platform.

The wishes and the requirements of the composer's publisher are also mostly unknown to us, but they must have played a part in the selection of the songs; if Diabelli was wilful and opinionated during the publication of the Nachlass, there is no reason to suppose that he was any different during Schubert's lifetime. Once we begin to search for justifications for regarding each of these opus numbers as a 'hidden cycle', the possible connections between the printed songs are endless and often ingeniously far-fetched (as is the case in Michael Hall's study of Schubert's song sets). In fact many of these theoretical links seem to be the wishful thinking of modern musicologists determined to marshal disparate songs into cyclic structures.

In a letter to Goethe in 1816 Josef von Spaun outlined a fanciful publication scheme for Schubert's songs (never to be realized), including an initial set of eight books ordered according to poet. The first two of these would be Goethe settings, the third Schiller poems, the fourth and fifth Klopstock works, the sixth containing poets like Matthisson, Hölty and Salis-Seewis, and the seventh and eighth Ossian.

Among the songs published between Op. 1 and Op. 98 (1821–8) there were collections given over to single poets:

Johann Wolfgang von Goethe. Opp. 1, 2, 3, 5, 12, 14, 19, 62, 92 all have exclusively Goethe texts. There are also Goethe songs in Opp. 4, 56 and 96. For performing purposes the best balanced groups are Opp. 5, 12, 62 (the last for soprano with the addition of a tenor for the opening duet).

Johann Mayrhofer. Opp. 21, 36. The three songs of Op. 21 seem to have been chosen to make up a group. They are all to the same poet, and are written for the bass voice. There is, moreover, a water theme uniting the songs. The publisher advertised them as '3 Fischerlieder von Meyerhofer [sic] für den Bass' although there is no mention of a fisherman in the first two songs of the opus. As for Op. 36, according to the advertisement for it in the *Wiener Zeitung* (11 February 1825), the publishers themselves (a different firm from those of Op. 21) selected the two songs from numerous possibilities. Both songs were known to have been performed by Vogl, and this seems to have been at least as important to Cappi & Diabelli as the Mayrhofer connection. To imagine that Schubert was always able to plan his opus number selections meticulously is to reckon without the publishers who probably called the tune on occasion.

Matthäus von Collin. Op. 22. This conjunction of songs, although asymmetrical in terms of length, is perfectly possible in present-day performance.

Friedrich von Schiller. Opp. 37, 58. Op. 37 consists of two substantial songs by a single poet that would go well together on the concert platform. A performance of Op. 58 would be feasible with two singers, one male and one female. The duet *Hektors Abschied* might perhaps be performed last.

Sir Walter Scott. Opp. 52 and 85. Complete performances of Op. 52 are very rare. This group of songs requires a male chorus, a female chorus, a soprano soloist (Ellen), a baritone (Malcolm Graeme) and a tenor (Norman). The two songs of Op. 85 are made for completely different voice types, but might be performed together at a shared concert as an example of two diverse Scott-inspired characters.

Ladislaus Pyrker. Op. 79. It is difficult to imagine the same singer tackling these two songs consecutively in performance. The grouping together of the two works was clearly meant to please the songs' poet and dedicatee.

Johann Gabriel Seidl. Opp. 80, 95, 105. The group of songs that make up Op. 80 could well be performed together although it would take singing of a very concentrated order to avoid dullness in the juxtaposition of the moderato tempi and dreamy mood of the individually marvellous second and third songs. It is possible to imagine the same female singer presenting the first and third songs of Op. 95, and the same male singer the second and fourth – although *Bei dir allein!* is more of a tenor song and *Irdisches Glück* is conceived for lower voice. Op. 105 is a rather wonderful group of Seidl songs that begins with *Widerspruch*, rarely heard as a solo song. In terms of contrasts of tonalities, tempi and mood, it is perfectly possible to imagine this group working in performance. It is said that this was the last of the opus numbers planned by Schubert before his death. It was advertised for sale only two days after the composer's demise.

Friedrich Rochlitz. Op. 81. The third song in the group requires a chorus which rules out ordinary recital performance.

Ernst Schulze. Op. 93. These are two fine Schulze songs, but most singers would wish to include other settings by the same poet in any recital group, and there seems no real reason to confine one's choice to these two which happen to have been published in Graz.

Thematic links

A full performance of Op. 4 presents the possibility of a kind of philosophical trajectory with the subtitle 'Der Wanderer' or 'Das Wandern'.

Op. 6 is a group of songs dedicated to the baritone Vogl – and it may be that its *raison d'être* was simply to gather together a collection of that singer's favourite lieder. The first two of the grouping are *Memnon* and *Antigone und Oedip*, both works on classical subjects. The third song, *Am Grabe Anselmos*, is a lament for the German poet Claudius's son who died when still a child. The possibility arises that whoever assembled the opus number for printing (perhaps someone in the composer's circle like Josef Hüttenbrenner) was attempting to put together a garland of classically inspired songs. It would be easy to imagine that 'Anselmo' – the nickname for Claudius's son Matthias – was a classical character with the poet visiting his grave along the lines of, say, Goethe's poem about the renowned Greek poet Anacreon (*Anakreons Grab*).

The songs of Op. 7 might be interpreted as having a programme encompassing ageing and loyalty, the passage of time and eventual death. There is no denying that the music for *Der Tod und das Mädchen* dwarfs the rest of the opus.

In Op. 13 there is a pastoral aspect to the two outer songs, but *Lob der Tränen* is not the ideal middle panel.

Op. 20, dedicated to a recently bereaved mother, seems designed to convey communication with a soul 'on the other side' (*Sei mir gegrüsst*), while at the same time offering the hope of consolation (*Frühlingsglaube*) with *Hänflings Liebeswerbung* as a slightly inappropriately cheerful epilogue.

Op. 21 has a water theme with boatmen of various kinds – not, as the publisher advertised, an array of fishermen.

Op. 22 might be seen as a diptych of love and loss, with death seen in different ways.

Op. 23 is one of the more interesting 'programmes'. It also works as a suite of keys in performance: the slow dactylic rhythm of *Die Liebe hat gelogen* (C minor), the vigorous bracing idealism of *Selige Welt* (A flat major), a similarly dactylic rhythm in *Schwanengesang* (F minor), and *Schatzgräbers Begehr* an epilogue in a brisk D minor. The whole opus number heard in sequence is like a miniature song sonata with the scherzo placed before the slow movement.

Op. 25, *Die schöne Müllerin*, is clearly meant as a complete piece, and in modern times has always been taken to be a cycle for performance as a whole. The same is true of course of *Winterreise* Op. 89.

Op. 36 might be seen as two views of death among the ancients: the death of Actaeon in mythological times and the death of an Ossianic minstrel. In both cases, and for different reasons, the protagonists are content to die. Elmar Budde believes that the song was printed in C minor (rather than the original C sharp minor) the better to relate it more closely to the A flat major tonality of the first song, *Der zürnenden Diana*. It is unlikely, however, that Cappi & Diabelli, when selecting these songs from Schubert's portfolio (*see* above), would have been thinking along these lines.

Op. 43. The composer might have deliberately placed these two night pieces side by side – a stormy night followed by an epilogue of peace and a different kind of yearning.

Op. 59 would perhaps have been happier as an all-Rückert opus. But the addition of the Platen setting is perhaps an indication of the debt of all the poems to the verse form of the Persian ghazal. In these four poems both Platen and Rückert show their debt to Hammer-Purgstall and the Goethe of the *West-östlicher Divan*.

Op. 60 is clearly written as an opus number for the bass voice. The protagonist is an older man who enjoys the good things of life, including a drink.

Op. 65. The theme is here clearly that of classical journeys and travel of both body and mind. The idea of these slow songs appearing together is better than the actuality of hearing them one after another on the concert platform.

Op. 83. This set of songs was written for a special artist, Luigi Lablache, and hangs together as an opus number for that reason.

Some possible mismatches

There is no real reason why the great classical songs to Mayrhofer poems that open Op. 6 should end with a slim lament for the baby son of Matthias Claudius unless the background theme is somehow about love and loss. Elmar Budde, more convinced of the effectiveness of the opus as a whole, characterizes the three songs as representing speechlessness (*Memnon*), lament (*Antigone und Oedip*) and pain (*Am Grabe Anselmos*).

Similarly Op. 8 would have been happier as a Mayrhofer set without the addition of the setting of Heinrich Hüttenbrenner. The hand of Josef Hüttenbrenner, ever desirous of furthering the artistic cause of his family, is to be discerned in this decision.

In Op. 24 the pairing of *Gruppe aus dem Tartarus* with the Mayrhofer *Schlaflied* is almost grotesque in terms of mood and scale. Perhaps the intention was a deliberate and even ironic contrast, something that works better on paper than in the concert hall. Michael Hall avers that Schubert placed these songs together on account of the alternation between C major and F minor at the end of the Schiller, and the alternating F major and C major in *Schlaflied*. According to Hall the link 'becomes apparent as soon as the voice enters' in the second song, although it seems unlikely that this was the decisive reason for these two songs being published together.

In Op. 56 the juxtaposition of Goethe and Bruchmann is less than happy and *Im Haine*, a fine song in its own right, is an inadequate conclusion to works of such weight. It is unusual for this opus number to have been divided into two books (Heft I and Heft II) with *Willkommen und Abschied* separated from the two Bruchmann songs. All the Goethe settings had hitherto been published in opus numbers devoted entirely to that poet (it was only in Op. 96 that a Goethe song appears in the same grouping as setting by Leitner, Schlechta and Schober (*see below*).

Op. 57 contains three fine songs, but the Hölty *An den Mond* is uncomfortably out on a limb after the Schlegel settings. An all-Schlegel opus might have been better. Michael Hall proposes that the selection of these songs was governed by Schubert's desire to show the contrast between the imaginative aspects of the Schlegel poems and the reality of the Hölty where the moon dispels the fancies and dream-like images which flit before the narrator's eyes.

Op. 87 An alarmingly random assemblage of songs. The opening Pichler setting with its large canvas unbalances the slighter works that follow it.

Op. 88 is similarly a mishmash of four unrelated poets. If there is an intended underlying theme of spiritual alienation healed (with the last song) by music it is not obvious to listeners. The linking tonalities (F major, C minor, B flat major and D major) persuade Elmar Budde that the whole group of songs might represent a small cycle with the subtitle 'Träume'.

Op. 96. This is another almost random gathering together of four poets with different moods and styles. Perhaps Schober, whose lithographical firm published this opus, was pleased to see one of his own poems next to one of Schubert's greatest Goethe settings which, inexplicably, was not published earlier.

Op. 98 (*see* POSTHUMOUS SONGS) was said to have been planned by Schubert but it gives the impression of random shavings from the factory floor. Each song is fine on its own.

Op. 101 (*see* POSTHUMOUS SONGS). The only reason for the publication of these songs together is that they had all appeared separately over the years as supplements to various issues of the *Wiener Zeitschrift für Kunst, Literatur, Theater und Mode*, the so-called *Modezeitung*.

Op. 106 (*see* POSTHUMOUS SONGS). It is a pity perhaps that Schubert did not devote this opus number entirely to the work of Leitner. *Das Weinen* is the weakest of the Leitner songs, *Vor meiner Wiege* is not the happiest conjunction with Klenke's *Heimliches Lieben*, and *Gesang (An Silvia)*, great song though it is, seems an odd epilogue to this particular collection despite being a reflection of the composer's gratitude and affection for the song's dedicatee, Schubert's hostess in Graz, Marie Pachler.

Bibliography: Budde, 1997
                 Hall, 2003

ORCHESTRATIONS: A SELECTIVE SURVEY

Even in a book about the piano-accompanied vocal music of Schubert there should be a moment set aside to consider the orchestration of his songs. The composer himself, constantly working on orchestral scores (symphonies, masses, operas), never felt the need to orchestrate his own lieder (the whole idea of doing so was in any case something that only became fashionable somewhat later). As the first great concert accompanist, Schubert probably enjoyed the flexible possibilities of intimate give and take in the relationship between voice and piano too much to entertain the idea of his songs being placed within the infinitely more cumbersome framework of the orchestra. There is something more bracing about the attack of the piano propelling a song forward compared to the plush and cushioned world of orchestral colour. This can be heard if one considers the song orchestrations of, say, Hugo Wolf and Henri Duparc and their original piano-accompanied versions. In neither case can it be said that the orchestra renders the piano redundant – in fact the opposite is true: the listener longs for the crisper and ultimately more dramatic interchange that is uniquely possible between voice and piano.

Most orchestral conductors, in charge of something much more unwieldy than a single keyboard, are unwilling or unable to fulfil the role of song accompanist effectively (the 'maestro' is by nature a leader rather than a follower). Those who are sufficiently in command of an orchestra truly to control the balance and to exert lightning reflexes on behalf of the singer's interpretative choices – skills taken for granted in an experienced *Liedbegleiter* – are few and far between. The detailed minutiae necessary in the presentation of a song involve a completely different challenge from those of an aria and Schubert understood that difference very well – his many opera arias are never as sharply delineated in terms of musical detail as are his songs. Only Richard Strauss manages to write effulgently beautiful, piano-accompanied songs that transfer effortlessly to the orchestra (and this tells us as much about their occasional lack of psychological depth as about Strauss's orchestrating genius) while, perhaps uniquely, Gustav Mahler (in a work like *Kindertotenlieder* originally conceived for keyboard) makes the listener yearn for the missing orchestral textures.

So why orchestrate a Schubert song? Richard Capell, writing in 1928, regarded it as an 'impropriety', 'and for a reason beyond the difficulty of orchestrating them congruously . . . although the music was frequently conceived by the aid of more or less unconscious thoughts and memories of the tones of real instruments, the expression is very much the affair of one contemplative and concentrated mind, or a pair of chambered collaborating friends, whose closing of their outer door is the opening of the inner world of this music'. Since the demise of the world of the composer-virtuoso pianist like Liszt and Godowsky (*see* TRANSCRIPTIONS), orchestration seems to have been the most usual means by which composers pay tribute to

Schubert. And to orchestrate a Schubert song is not only to invest it with a new array of instrumental colours, but is to introduce it to another arena: when a song moves from the recital room to the concert hall it encounters a wider audience and acquires new glamour. Or so the theory goes. In practical terms the song is often simply taken from a smaller milieu, where it is known and loved, and made to fight for its chances in an environment where a lack of penetrating volume or high notes (not to mention pianistic backup) is a critical handicap. The transition is not always successful: what makes lieder artists special in the ambience, say, of London's Wigmore Hall may seem lost in the wide open spaces of the Royal Albert or Festival halls. Nevertheless, song specialists like Brahms's friend Julius Stockhausen or Schoenberg's friend Julia Culp often welcomed the chance to export their lieder-singing credentials into the concert hall for appreciation by a larger public. Today the most successful singers are those with the ability to sing opera with orchestra and, as a separate discipline, give recitals with piano – versatility, long recognized in Germany and Austria, which has become the touchstone of success in the world of singers.

Until the 1950s it was possible to encounter performances and recordings of Schubert songs with orchestral accompaniment (especially the popular potboilers), but these gradually found less favour with a better-informed public. In modern times one will occasionally find groups of Duparc and Wolf songs with orchestra (the composers made these versions themselves, even if somewhat ill-advisedly) but newly orchestrated Schubert songs now appear only with good reason. Such arrangements often make a strong and novel compositional point, as in the work of Friedrich Goldman, Reimann or Hans Zender (*see* below).

Ferdinand Schubert (1794–1859) was the first to orchestrate his younger brother's songs. Among these were *Der Taucher* D111, *Erlkönig* D328 and *Die junge Nonne* D828. These versions, put together mainly for domestic purposes or small concerts in Vienna, were makeshift affairs and often not in the best of taste. Ferdinand's version of *Ave Maria* D839 features dramatic drum rolls, an inappropriateness that places the hyperbole of Liszt's solo piano version in the shade.

Schubert's close friend, the gifted and prolific Bavarian composer **Franz Lachner** (1803–1890) orchestrated the cantata *Mirjams Siegesgesang* D942, a late Schubert work from 1828. Of all his choral works this is the one which Schubert may arguably have wished to orchestrate himself, and it is possible that Lachner was fulfilling a wish that Schubert had communicated to him before he died.

Hector Berlioz (1803–1869) made an orchestrally accompanied version of *Erlkönig* in 1837. Liszt was such a pioneer in this field that it is unusual to find composers capable of influencing him, but Berlioz did. It is notable that Liszt's first Schubert transcriptions for piano date from more or less the time of this arrangement.

Apart from his many Schubert song arrangements (*see* TRANSCRIPTIONS), **Franz Liszt** (1811–1886) orchestrated six Schubert songs in 1860, four of which were published in 1863. These *Sechs Lieder von Schubert* were (i) *Die junge Nonne* D828 (S375/1), (ii) *Gretchen am Spinnrade* D118 (S375/2), (iii) *Mignon* (*Kennst du das Land?*) D321 (S375/3), (iv) *Erlkönig* D328 (S375/4). Two further songs were in manuscript, but these remained unpublished: (v) *Der Doppelgänger* D957/13 (S375/5) (an extraordinary conception with horns playing a prominent colouristic part, and the soft interpolation of timpani playing a small but dramatic role in the building of tension on the song's second page). This orchestration was first published in the Liszt Society Journal of 2002. The manuscript of the sixth item is lost, but it is almost certainly an arrangement of a *Schwanengesang* song: *Abschied* (Rellstab) D957/7.

Although only related to a song at one remove, mention should be made of Liszt's *Franz Schuberts grosse Fantasie*, Op. 15 (1851) – an arrangement for piano and orchestra of Schubert's solo piano work, *Fantasie in C* (*Wandererfantasie*) D760, which was itself based on themes from the Schmidt von Lübeck setting *Der Wanderer* D489.

In 1872 Liszt arranged *Die Allmacht* [D852] *von Franz Schubert* for tenor, male chorus, orchestra and organ. A certain A. Mayrberg had already published an arrangement of *Die Allmacht* for mixed choir and orchestra on the Latin psalm text 'Domine Dominus noster'. The same work was arranged for choir and orchestra by the German-born American composer **Max Spicker** (1858–1912).

Jacques Offenbach (1819–1880), German-born resident of Paris, made arrangements for voice and orchestra of *Auf dem Wasser zu singen* D774, *Erlkönig* D328, *Gretchen am Spinnrade* D118, *Des Mädchens Klage* D191 and *Ständchen* ('*La Sérénade de Schubert*') D957/4.

In 1862 **Johannes Brahms** (1833–1897) transcribed four Schubert songs for voice (his friend and colleague, baritone Julius Stockhausen) and orchestra. These were *An Schwager Kronos* D369, *Geheimes* I D719, *Greisengesang* D778 and *Memnon* D541. In the same year Brahms orchestrated *Ellens zweiter Gesang* D838 for the soprano Marie Fillunger, later the lifelong companion of Robert Schumann's youngest daughter, Eugenie.

Eduard Kremser (1838–1914) was the conductor of the Wiener Männergesang Verein. He made orchestrally accompanied versions of works that Schubert had originally conceived as part-songs with piano: *Die Nachtigall* D724 (1867), *Gott in der Natur* D757 (1876), *Das Dörfchen* D598 (1880), *Naturgenuss* D422 (1880) and *Geist der Liebe* D747 (1885). He also made choral arrangements of the songs *Pax Vobiscum* D551 and *Am Tage aller Seelen* (*Litanei*) D343.

Felix Weingartner (1863–1942) was a celebrated Austrian conductor, composer and author. For his third wife, the soprano Lucille Marcel, he made arrangements for voice and orchestra of *Ellens dritter Gesang (Ave Maria)* D839, *Die junge Nonne* D828 and *Ständchen* (Rellstab) D957/7. He also arranged *Ständchen* D920 for male chorus and orchestra (1923).

Between 1913 and 1915 **Max Reger** (1873–1916) produced a substantial group of orchestrally accompanied Schubert songs: *An den Mond* D296 (Goethe, second setting), *An die Musik* D547, *Am Tage aller Seelen* (*Litanei*) D343, *Du bist die Ruh* D776, the three *Gesänge des Harfners* D478 [(i) *Wer sich der Einsamkeit ergibt*, (ii) *Wer nie sein Brot mit Tränen ass*, (iii) *An die Türen will ich schleichen*], *Greisengesang* D778, *Gretchen am Spinnrade* D118, *Gruppe aus dem Tartarus* D583, *Im Abendrot* D799, *Memnon* D541, *Nacht und Träume* D827 and *Prometheus* D674.

In September 1912 **Arnold Schoenberg** (1874–1951) orchestrated three songs for the Dutch mezzo-soprano Julia Culp, including *Ständchen* (Shakespeare) D889 and *Der Lindenbaum* D911/5. He had arranged Schubert songs (and the *Rosamunde* music) as hack work in his student years, and in 1921 used the *Ständchen* of Rellstab D957/4 as an exercise for his own pupils (orchestration for clarinet, bassoon, mandolin, guitar and string quartet).

In 1903 a young **Anton von Webern** (1883–1945) orchestrated *Du bist die Ruh* D776, *Erlkönig* D328, *Romanze* from *Rosamunde* D797/3b, *Tränenregen* from *Die schöne Müllerin* D795/10 (a song from this cycle that has been otherwise ignored for transcription), *Ihr Bild* D957/9 (from *Schwanengesang*) and *Der Wegweiser* from *Winterreise* D911/20 (likewise a song from this cycle that has otherwise not found favour for transcription by other composers).

The English composer **Julius Harrison** (1885–1963) wrote *Winter and Spring*, a combination of *Winterreise* D911 and *Schwanengesang* D957 arranged for mixed choir and orchestra.

Hermann Scherchen (1891–1966) was a celebrated German conductor. He arranged *Auf dem Strom* D943 for voice, horn and small orchestra.

Benjamin Britten (1913–1976) made a version of *Die Forelle* D550 – *The Trout* – for voice and string orchestra (with two clarinets) in 1942. Although this was his only foray into Schubert orchestration, he made two versions (1938 and 1942) of his completion of the Schubert song fragment *Gretchen am Zwinger* D564. He later became one of the greatest Schubert song accompanists of all time (*see* PIANISTS).

Paul Angerer (b. 1927), Austrian composer, conductor and violist, arranged the three Metastasio settings that Schubert wrote for Luigi Lablache (*Drei Gesänge von Metastasio* D902) for baritone and strings (1981). Angerer's soprano and string quartet arrangement of the equally Italian *Vier Canzonen* D688 dates from 1997.

Edison Denisov (1929–1996) was a Russian–French composer who transcribed a great deal of Schubert (particularly the dance music). Denisov's arrangement of *Ave Maria* D839 for voice and orchestra dates from 1981. He made a completion of the cantata fragment *Lazarus* D689 in 1995.

Aribert Reimann (b. 1936), the German opera composer best known perhaps for his *Lear*, is also a notable accompanist. He has transcribed Schumann and Brahms lieder for high voice (the German soprano Christine Schäfer) and string quartet accompaniment. His *Mignon* (1995) makes use of various Schubert fragments (D359) and lesser-known Mignon settings (D310) to create a cycle, also with string quartet accompaniment.

The German composer **Hans Zender** (b. 1936) has made a number of arrangements for chorus and orchestra of pieces originally written with piano accompaniment: *Coronach* D836, *Der 23. Psalm* D706, *Gondelfahrer* D809, *Nachthelle* D892. His best-known piece with Schubertian connections is a quirky and inventive reworking of *Winterreise* D911 (far from a mere orchestration) entitled *Schuberts 'Winterreise' – Eine komponierte Interpretation* (for tenor and small orchestra, 1993).

Friedrich Goldmann (1941–2009), born in Dresden, was an eminent composer, resident in Berlin. His *Sechs Heine-Lieder instrumentiert für bariton und Orchester* (the six Heine settings from *Schwanengesang* D957/8–13) date from 1997.

Colin Matthews (b. 1946), the English composer, arranged *Ellens drei Gesänge* (Walter Scott, D837–9) for voice and chamber ensemble in 1984 and *Nacht und Träume* D827 for voice and orchestra in 2008.

The Japanese composer **Yukikazu Suzuki** (1954–2010), also known for his film music, made an arrangement for voice and orchestra of *Winterreise* D911.

Einsamkeit D620 orchestrated by Detlev Glanert, Boosey and Hawkes (2010).

The German composer **Detlev Glanert** (b. 1960), a pupil of Hans Werner Henze, made an orchestration of the great Mayrhofer setting *Einsamkeit* D620 in 2009 which seems calculated simply to broaden the appreciation of a masterpiece that is neglected on the concert platform without aiming, as he puts it, at an 'interpretation der heutigen Zeit' and without adding layers of modernistic interpretation. In writing what is essentially a compact song cycle in six inter-linked sections, Schubert wrote a piece of music that happens to be of ideal length for an orchestral song cycle, and Glanert skilfully adapted the work for that purpose. Glanert also orchestrated *Das Lied im Grünen* D917 and in May 2013 Ian Bostridge premiered the same composer's orchestrations of *Viola* D786 and *Im Walde* (*Waldesnacht*) D708.

OREST (Orest auf Tauris)[1]   Orestes [on Tauris]
(MAYRHOFER) **D548** [H355]
C minor – D major   March 1817

(54 bars)

Ist dies Tauris, wo der Eumeniden[2]	Is this Tauris, where Pythia promised
Wut zu stillen Pythia versprach?—[3]	To appease the anger of the Eumenides?
Weh, die Schwestern mit den Schlangenhaaren	Alas, the snake-haired sisters
Folgen mir vom Land der Griechen nach!	Pursue me from the land of the Greeks.
Rauhes Eiland, kündest keinen Segen:	Bleak island, you announce no blessing:
Nirgends sprosst der Ceres milde Frucht,[4]	Nowhere does Ceres' tender fruit grow;
Keine Reben blüh'n, der Lüfte Sänger,	No vines bloom; the singers of the air,
Wie die Schiffe, meiden diese Bucht.	Like the ships, shun this bay.
Steine fügt die Kunst nicht zu Gebäuden,	Art does not fashion these stones into buildings;
Zelte spannt des Scythen Armut sich;	In their poverty the Scythians erect only tents.
Unter starren Felsen, rauhen Wäldern	Amid harsh rocks and wild forests
Ist das Leben einsam, schauerlich!	Life is lonely and frightening.
'Und hier soll,' so ist ja doch ergangen[5]	'And here,' according to the sacred decree
An den Flehenden der heilige Spruch,	Revealed to the suppliant,
'Eine hohe Priesterin Dianens[6]	'A high priestess of Diana
Lösen meinen und der Väter Fluch.'[7]	Is to lift the curse on me and my fathers.'

[1] Mayrhofer's title is *Der landende Orest*. For an explanation of the background to these alternative Mayrhofer readings see Editorial Note at the beginning of Johann MAYRHOFER.
[2] Mayrhofer writes '*Dieses* Tauris? wo der Eumeniden'.
[3] Mayrhofer writes '*Pythius*' rather than Pythia.
[4] Mayrhofer writes 'Nirgends sprosst der Ceres *goldne* Frucht'.
[5] Mayrhofer writes '*Allhier* soll'.
[6] Mayrhofer writes '*Soll die Bogenspannerin Diana*'.
[7] Mayrhofer writes 'Lösen *deinen* und der Väter Fluch'.

Johann Mayrhofer (1787–1836)

This is the twenty-fourth of Schubert's forty-seven Mayrhofer solo settings (1814–24). See poet's biography for a chronological list of all the Mayrhofer settings.

The third play of the Oresteia trilogy, *The Eumenides*, recounts the trial of Orestes for the slaying of his mother, Clytemnestra, and her lover Aegisthus. Orestes has committed these crimes in order to avenge the murder of his father, Agamemnon. With the casting vote of Athena, he is acquitted, much to the anger of the Furies who pursue him and cause him to suffer bouts of madness. To expiate his guilt Orestes is bidden by the Delphic oracle to go across the Black Sea to Tauris (more recently known as the Crimea) and bring back to Attica the statue of the goddess Diana which had been stolen by the Scythians (in Mayrhofer's poem 'Pythia' refers to the ancient name of Delphi, a surname for Apollo whose oracle is at Delphi). It was the custom of the Taurians to sacrifice all strangers to the goddess Diana. Little does Orestes know that his long-lost sister Iphigenia is the high priestess at Tauris, as she was spirited there when she herself was about to be sacrificed in Aulis with the connivance of her father Agamemnon. Her saviour was the heavenly Diana who also came to the rescue of Orestes and who has watched over these terrible vicissitudes. In the meantime Iphigenia does not know what has happened to the rest of her family, but she will eventually recognize her brother and save him from being another sacrificial victim. (Could there ever have been, apart from the modern-day Wagners, such a tribe of doom-laden siblings as Chrysothemis, Iphigenia, Orestes and Electra?)

Mayrhofer chooses to begin the action of the poem with the moment of Orestes' arrival in Tauris. Orestes is without his beloved companion Pylades who adds a rich musical dimension to Gluck's operatic version of this story, but the legend was so well known to the educated public that the reworking of any fragment of it, as in this case, would have been easily comprehensible. Mayrhofer also wrote a poem about Orestes' sibling which was set by Schubert as *Iphigenia* D573, and is indeed a sister piece to *Orest*. In *Iphigenia*, the unhappy princess sings of her longing to return from exile to her homeland. A similar speech opens the play *Iphigenie auf Tauris* by Goethe (1787), the opening monologue of which was set by Reichardt for soprano and chorus, and was copied out by Schubert himself. Goethe was doubtless one source of Mayrhofer's knowledge of the legend, while the other was the play by Euripides. Schubert knew the story from the Gluck opera, which he first saw in his early teens (the libretto translated into German after the French original by François Guillard). On that memorable occasion in 1813 Schubert and the poet Körner much admired Anna Milder as Iphigenia with Michael Vogl playing opposite her in the role of Orestes. And suddenly in 1817 here Schubert was writing music of his own for the great singer which recalled the exciting circumstances of his first introduction to the Gluck masterpiece.

Orestes with Iphigenia in Tauris, drawing by Ramberg from *Minerva*, 1827, illustrating the scene from Act II of Goethe's play.

It was Schubert's great ambition to write an opera for Vogl of course – he eventually did so in 1819 with *Die Zwillingsbrüder* D647, which had a limited success. It is difficult not to see a number of these classical songs as audition pieces, intended to convince Vogl that here was a fine young opera composer waiting to be discovered – and commissioned! This produces strong-boned music of noble line and import, which lacks however the special relationship of insight and commentary between voice and piano of which Schubert is capable elsewhere. However, despite the feeling that one is playing from an operatic vocal score rather than a lieder album, the music is always inventive and strong.

Mayrhofer's title for the poem in his 1824 *Gedichte* is *Der landende Orest*, a poetic snapshot of the king at the moment of his disembarking at Tauris. The opening chords give Orestes/Vogl a splendidly rhetorical entrance line over a four-bar orchestral phrase (bb. 1–4) that repeats in sequence a fourth higher. This is music worthy of a monarch, albeit a perplexed and weary one;

Vogl would ask for no less in terms of what he would consent to sing at this early stage of the partnership between singer and composer-pianist. The third and fourth lines of this verse are a measured recitative (with a change of key signature to E flat minor, from b. 10) which would have given Vogl ample opportunity for grisly word-painting, the depiction of a touch of madness almost certainly his thespian speciality. The next eight lines describe the surroundings – one vista in G flat major (bb. 15–24), the next in B major (with a change of key signature at b. 27). The vocal line is always regal, the accompaniment as spare as the bleak, inhospitable topography. The beautiful descending vocal line in B major of 'Steine fügt die Kunst' (from b. 27) reveals itself as something of a leitmotif; this is repeated by the piano in D major (another change of key signature at b. 37) as an introduction to the closing four lines of text. Two bars later (b. 41) it is incorporated into the voice part ('An den Flehenden') as we are led to the heart of Orestes' dreams, hopes and prayers to the goddess. The tiny, almost diffident post-lude seems to say 'Who knows? – To be continued!'

Orestes from Düntzer's edition of Goethe's *Werke* (1882).

Until 1999 and the appearance of Volume 11 of the NSA, this song was known as *Orest auf Tauris*, the title given to the song by the Nachlass in 1831. The NSA renamed the song simply *Orest*, arguing that the rest of the title was spuriously added by the posthumous publishers in order to distinguish it from *Der entsühnte Orest* D699, also published in Volume 11 of the Nachlass in 1831.

Autograph:	Österreichische Nationalbibliothek, Vienna
First edition:	Published as Book 11 no. 1 of the *Nachlass* by Diabelli, Vienna in 1831 (P270)
Subsequent editions:	Peters: Vol. 5/40; AGA XX 382: Vol. 6/118; NSA IV: Vol. 11/113

Bibliography: Capell 1928, p. 162
                                 Fischer-Dieskau 1977, p. 199
Discography and timing: Fischer-Dieskau II 4² 2'38
                                 Hyperion I 14¹³
                                                            2'59   Thomas Hampson
                                 Hyperion II 18⁶

← *Antigone und Oedip* D542   *Auf dem See* D543 →

ORNAMENTATION

There are many ornamented vocal lines in the Schubert songs, but they sound so organic and natural – containing nothing extraneous – that they seem scarcely to have been ornamented at all. Another way of putting it is that instead of leaving it to the singers to decorate their vocal lines, the composer did it himself. For example, in *Gesang (An Silvia)* (b. 21) the phrase of four semiquavers that trips down the vocal line on the word 'untertan' ('süsser Ruh' and 'Saitenklang' in subsequent strophes) is Schubert's own ornamentation of the two descending quavers in the song's first draft. This tiny scale has become a beloved part of the song, not an optional adornment. In fact we cannot imagine this passage in its earlier version. Another example: the vocal line of *Der Herbstabend* D405 is plain and simple in bb. 4–6 of the first draft; in the second version Schubert adds a delicate decoration in b. 6 appropriate to the tremulous 'zittern' in the first strophe (which is equally descriptive of the storm-tossed linden branches ('Lindenzweigen') in the third) and the song comes alive. The same principle applies to some of the composer's accompaniments: the first version of *Am Tage Aller Seelen* D343 (*Litanei*) has no turn in the postlude in b. 11; this was only added a few months later. It now seems a necessary part of the song rather than a decorative option. It is possible that Schubert incorporated into his manuscripts some of the ideas of retired opera singer Johann Michael Vogl (1768–1840) (or other singers) regarding ornamentation. All singers of Vogl's generation believed that it was their right, even perhaps their duty, to superimpose their ideas on a composer's music by making their own additions. We have a possible glimpse of a 'before and after' Vogl situation in the three different versions of *Greisengesang* D778: the first (1825) is extremely simple – the noble bare bones of the piece; the second decorated to the nines – and perhaps with Vogl's input; the third (Op. 60 No. 1) a compromise, deleting many of the second version's turns and roulades from the earlier part of the song, but retaining the marvellous melismas (bb. 38–49) which seem to warm the character of the ageing man back into life. Here it is clear that Schubert had the final say as to which of the ornamentations should become part of the printed composition. A list is given at the end of this article of the surviving autographs of Schubert songs ornamented by Vogl. It is certain that Schubert did not agree with all his colleague's adaptations, and equally certain that he did not wish to jeopardize his relationship with Vogl by forbidding the older man to put his own stamp on the music. It is clear the composer understood the difference between live performances and the ongoing legacy of a song in print that was destined for singers of a more modern generation.

VOCAL ORNAMENTS

The Appoggiatura

The vocal lines of Schubert's songs are full of appoggiature, smaller notes nestling next to bigger ones on the stave, as if leaning on them – which is in fact what they are doing. These passing notes – in other words, nominally less important notes – resolve onto the bigger, more significant, ones. In reality, however, it is the passing notes that are often the source of the most beautiful and daring of the composer's effects. Schubert was brought up as a Salieri pupil to notate his vocal lines in a musically grammatical way which was already old-fashioned and eventually abandoned by later composers: he differentiated between notes that were an official part of a chord and harmonically permitted, and extraneous notes, – ones outside the main chord, that had been introduced to decorate the harmony. The correct performance of these appoggiature is simple once this principle is understood, but it remains the most frequent source of error on the concert platform, particularly with student singers.

Here is a phrase from Schubert's *An die Musik* D547 (bb. 13–14):

The reason why the G in this example is notated as an appoggiatura, and not a full note, is because G is not part of the underlying D major harmony. This is the correct way of interpreting this appoggiatura:

On countless occasions I have heard this passage, and hundreds of other similar passages, incorrectly sung like this:

The appoggiatura, usually printed as a small quaver in front of a crotchet or dotted crotchet, replaces the note on which it leans. This is the rule throughout the Schubert songs. Fortunately the NSA, and its offshoot the Bärenreiter Edition, interpret each of these ornaments (and others) in supplementary staves above the music. The appoggiatura is sometimes printed as a small crotchet in front of a minim or dotted minim. Here is another example from the same song, followed by its correct performance:

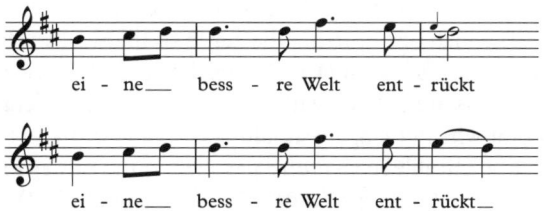

An die Musik, in its opening lines, has another appoggiatura that is often misinterpreted as a long acciaccatura. Here it is (bb. 4–5) followed by its interpretation as printed in the NSA:

In this case the appoggiatura takes on the value of a full crotchet because of the dotted crotchet that follows it. In another famous passage, this time from the final song in *Die schöne Müllerin, Des Baches Wiegenlied* D795/20 (bb. 16–17), the appoggiatura, a B that adventurously decorates a C sharp minor chord, is often sung as an acciaccatura, and even by the most famous singers. As this occurs five times in this long strophic song the quasi-yodelling effect, though perhaps reasonably effective when it comes to the word 'droben' in the final strophe, is not something that Schubert envisaged:

ihr macht mei-nem Schlä - fer die Träu - me

The correct interpretation is as follows:

ihr macht mei-nem Schlä - fer die Träu - me

Two bars later (b. 19) this figuration is sung to the same word ('Schläfer') without an appoggiatura. This is simply because on this occasion both quavers in the vocal line (G sharp and E) are correctly harmonized within the accompanying chord of C sharp minor. This chord is in itself an appoggiatura, functionally a first inversion tonic with an appoggiatura C sharp, resulting in simultaneous, adventurous appoggiature in the voice and piano.

The Acciaccatura

If the appoggiatura is a note that sometimes lingers meaningfully before resolution the acciaccatura is always short. Unfortunately Schubert usually wrote them in the same way (as small quavers and without the stroke through the tail that normally differentiates the acciaccatura). The performer can almost always decide whether such a note is an appoggiatura or acciaccatura purely from its context and its character within the song. The vocal acciaccatura is far less common than the appoggiatura. The most unusual use of it in a vocal line is in *Du liebst mich nicht* D756 (bb. 44 and 48) where the acciaccatura come from the fourth below – the result sounds almost like a gulp, betokening desperation and rage. The acciaccatura in the opening of the first of the *Gesänge des Harfners* D478 allows for the bitter and overwrought mood of the protagonist. In *Erlafsee* D586, by contrast, the piano echoes the vocal acciaccatura in playful mirror-image (bb. 18–22) which also mirrors the sense of the words. This also occurs in the interplay between vocal line and piano in *Der Einsame* D800. In *Erlafsee*, unlike the much later *Der Einsame*, these ornaments are notated with three tails, like small demisemiquavers.

It remains a moot point whether singers should add appoggiature to Schubert's vocal lines. This practice seems safely applicable in *recitativo* passages in the earlier songs, especially where headed with the word *Recit* – in *Szene aus 'Faust'* D126, for example. In *Die Sommernacht* D289, in bb. 3, 8, 11 and 13, the NSA suggests the insertion of appoggiature and the composer himself has written appoggiature in bb. 17 and 18 where the vocal line begins to blossom into arioso. The suggestions of the NSA (and the subsequent Bärenreiter song volumes), which are printed above the vocal line, are especially helpful in cases like these. Such ornamentation being left to the discretion of performers is not usually a feature of Schubert songs composed after 1816.

Cadenzas and grace notes

We have mentioned above that most of the grace notes in Schubert's vocal lines have become so incorporated into the music that they simply appear part of the music rather than as something extra. Exceptions to this are some of the obvious display pieces of Italian or operatic inspiration: in *Vedi quanto adoro* D510 there is an extravagant cadenza on 'tanti affani!' (bb. 52–4); in *La pastorella al prato* D528 there is an ornamented line adorned with demisemiquaver roulades; in *Herrn Josef von Spaun, Assessor in Linz* D749, a parody of an Italian aria, the word 'Barbar' (bb. 42–3) is set to a stirring cadence with a high C followed by a descending chromatic scale. The extraordinary cadence on the word 'Mächte' in *Gesänge des Harfners* II D478 (bb. 29–30), high in the voice and ornamented with a devilishly difficult turn, reminds us that the Harper was an Italian. Flourishes of this kind are sometimes employed in songs like *Der Einsame* D800 with its ornamented ending (bb. 69–70 and 75–6) and where the composer has taken care to write out exactly what he wants. *Blondels Lied zu Marien* D626 is the most florid of all Schubert's lieder for the voice; it is as if the composer were deliberately trying to evoke an earlier age of chivalry with a virtuoso piece for that famed minstrel, Blondel. The words 'Wie in der Liebe Strahlenkranze / Ein holder Stern' receive an extravagant setting where the unimportant word 'ein' is the one which receives the most florid of melismas, not the word 'Stern'; the more important key words are deliberately left untouched (and thus more audible) and ornamentation provided only in their immediate vicinity. This is perhaps deliberate Schubertian policy. In Vogl's ornamented version of the *Ständchen* from *Schwanengesang* (D957/4), the phrase 'in des Mondes Licht' (b. 19) has a pair of grace notes decorating the word 'in' which have survived in Schubert's final version, as have similar grace notes on 'Fürchte, Holde, nicht' (b. 25). Schubert has not, however, adopted Vogl's extravagant turn on 'Mondes Licht' and on the word 'Holde'. The tiny frisson on 'in' is quite enough – a glimmering beam of light that marvellously sets up an unadorned 'Mondes Licht' (the vocal melisma and the beauty of the 'o' vowel are sufficient expressive responsibility for the singer). Similarly, the tiny shudder of fear on 'Fürchte' suffices for the whole bar. These are a composer's decisions; Schubert does not turn his back on the concept of ornamentation but he limits it to its most effective use.

The Mordent
Schubert's use of the vocal mordent was always discerning and powerful. It occurs in *Der König in Thule* D367 (b. 7, first on the words 'an das Grab') where a medieval stylization is suggested as well as Gretchen's unease and foreboding as she sings the ballad in her bedroom. In *Winterreise* it is employed as a shudder in *Der greise Kopf* D911/14 on the words 'Haar' and 'gestreuet' bb. 9–10. A similar sense of something uncannily strange is suggested by its use in *Ihr Bild* D957/9 where perhaps the most expressive of all Schubert's mordents is on the word 'Augenpaar' (b. 21). The nonchalant serenader of *Das Fischermädchen* D957/10 displays at last a certain ironic heartlessness in the single mordent on 'In seiner Tiefe ruht', and only at the end of the song and on the repeat of those words (b. 64).

The Trill
Schubert regards the trill as essentially a pianistic device (*see* below), at least in the lieder; the operas are another matter. An exception to this is in *Bei dem Grabe meines Vaters* D496; on the words 'friede Gottes' (b. 3) there is a trill on the second syllable of 'Gottes' betokening old-fashioned religious reverence. The gamekeeper Kaspar trills ominously in the comic trio *Der Hochzeitsbraten* D930 (bb. 351–3) but this *jeu d'ésprit* is practically a stage work. In *Der Hirt auf dem Felsen* D965 (bb. 217–18) the clarinet trill stands in for the lack of such a challenge for the singer (Anna Milder Hauptmann was no expert triller as Schubert himself noted).

The Turn
The vocal turn was something that Schubert used in various ways, mostly to serious effect. Exceptions to this are the knowing turn on 'meine Nachbarin' (the object of the boy's affection)

in *Der Goldschmiedsgesell* D560 (b. 2), and on the lighthearted words 'leises Angebot' in *Wiedersehen* D855 (b. 11), a vocal effusion that is immediately followed by a turn in the piano in b. 12. There is some disagreement as to whether Schubert intended turns in *Wandrers Nacht-lied* D768 on the word 'balde' (bb. 10 and 12), possibly a Vogl-like idea that the composer thought superfluous – the musical effect without decoration is exalted enough. In *Dass sie hier gewesen* D773 tnere is (on 'Tränen kund') a turn that turns a long held note (b. 48) into some-thing that erupts with emotion. In *Ellens Gesang I* D837, a turn is first heard on 'Schrecken' (b. 17) in Ellen's refrain, somehow giving the character enormous poise and authority. Turns are used to searing effect in *Lied der Mignon* D877/3, one in the major key, the other in the minor (bb. 18 and 38); these moments reveal, in the context of a song of the greatest intro-spection, the full and desperate extent of Mignon's grief. The turn on the word 'Liebe' in the penultimate bar of the vocal line of *Im Freien* D880 (b. 128) seems to set the seal on a long descriptive song, reminding us that its every word and harmony has been motivated by love. In *Der Winterabend* D938 the turn on the word 'Schleiertuch' (b. 53) suggests the moon encom-passing the whole room in the folds of her diaphanous veil. Another turn (on 'verschwund'ne Zeit', b. 76) seems to scan the memory, with infinite tenderness, for precious, remembered images. In *Herbst* D945 we find the longest note-value to which a turn is attached – a dotted semibreve on the words 'Lebens dahin'. The length of time before the singer is required to start the turn seems to indicate the depressive length of life itself. The turn in *Kriegers Ahnung* D957/2 (on the words 'so heiss', b. 20) captures the longing and the nervousness of the warrior who foresees his own death. In *Der Doppelgänger* D957/13 the turn on 'auf dem<u>selben</u> Platz' conjures a whole unspoken and unknown background to the relationship between the lovers. In a similar way the decorated passage on 'so <u>ein</u>sam bin' in *Der Hirt auf dem Felsen* D965 (bb. 151–2) seems to provide a deeper dimension to our understanding of the shepherd's loneliness.

ORNAMENTATION IN THE PIANO WRITING

Grace notes that are meant to sound like ornamentation are reasonably numerous in the songs' accompaniments but a few examples must here suffice. In *Der Liedler* D209 the opening bar has the same turn as Mozart's Rondo in A minor KV511, on the same notes and in the same key – a reminder that Schubert looks to the eighteenth century for much of his inspiration. In *Erlafsee* D586 the piano echoes the voice (bb. 18–22) like water ruffled on the lake. In *Wehmut* D772 the vocal grace notes amplifying 'Frühlingslust' are echoed in the piano (bb. 13–14). *Pause* D795/12 the grace notes of the introduction become a feature of this whole song, a turning point in *Die schöne Müllerin*. *Alinde* D904 begins with a little onrush of grace notes in b. 3 that betoken the lover's impatience and avid desire to find his Alinde. Some of the use of this kind of pianistic ornamentation is unique. In *Der greise Kopf* D911/14 the two little notes in the piano (both hands) as an up-beat to 'Wie weit noch bis zur Bahre!' are extraordinarily eloquent: if performed before the beat (i.e. before the word 'weit') they seem ordinary; if on the beat *with* the singer's word, a feeling of dragging an immense load and great weariness is somehow conveyed. Schubert had had a trial run with this device in bb. 42–4 of *Totengräbers Heimwehe* D842.

The Acciaccatura

Acciaccature almost always convey high spirits in the Schubert accompaniments: the ardent would-be lover in *Ungeduld* D795 (bb. 3 and 6 in the piano introduction); the musical depiction of cosy, flickering flame and convivial insect-music in *Der Einsame* D800 (from b. 2); the cheeki-ness of the rampant butterfly in *Der Schmetterling* D633; the flirtatiouness of the narrator in *Liebhaber in allen Gestalten* D558 (bb. 1–2 of the introduction).

The Mordent

As in the singer's line, the use of the mordent is somewhat more powerful and, as for the voice, carefully rationed for most effective use. The mournful plaint of *An Mignon* D161 is brought to a conclusion by haunting mordents of the postlude (bb. 16–17 and 33–4). In the introduction to *Bootgesang* D835 (b. 2) we feel the gruff determination of the gathering Scottish clans (b. 2) underlined by the mordent. In the opening (and repeating) refrain of *Gute Nacht* D911/1 the single mordent in b. 5 seems somehow to stiffen the winter traveller's determination to set out on his journey. Perhaps the most delicate and dream-like mordents of all occur in the same cycle: with these, in b. 3 of *Frühlingstraum* D911/11, Schubert conveys an other-worldy quasi-Mozartian fragility. The apotheosis of the Schubertian mordent is in *Hippolits Lied* D890 where the decoration is sounded seventy-four times, mostly on E, sometimes on G and D, as an indication of a desperate lover's single-minded obsession. In *Des Fischers Liebesglück* D933 in the piano's introduction the mordent signifies the flickering half-light while also conveying the fisherman's fanciful indolence.

The Trill

Schubert favours the trill as a pianistic device to a certain extent, but he has nothing of Beethoven's death-defying enthusiasm for trills as an expressive medium (as in the closing movement of the Piano Sonata Op. 111 for example). He prefers much shorter trills (maybe as a pianist he was not very good at longer-lasting ones). These are to be found in the introduction to *Der Sänger* D149 (bb. 3–4). The trills in *Der Liedler* D209 are rather more extended (bb. 11–12, and 48–52), but much more typical are the shorter trills, like bursts of defiance, at the beginning of *Lied des Orpheus* D474 where the valorous Orpheus, Tamino-like, faces the fires of hell. The regal nature of Dido's grief is conveyed in the Italianate trills of *Vedi quanto adoro* D510. In a similar way Schubert paints the regal progress of the queen of heaven, the moon, in *An den Mond in einer Herbstnacht* D614 (the quasi-ceremonial trill in bb. 11–12 of the piano's ritornello). In Mayrhofer's *Sehnsucht* D516 the flight-paths of larks are traced in trills in bb. 6–10 – an ornithological parallel to the trilling song of the nightingale in *Ganymed* D544 (bb. 56–9). In *Der Schäfer und der Reiter* D517 we hear the pervasive right-hand trills as a symbol of a former musical age, old-fashioned and courtly. Ominous and disturbing trills for the left hand, a genre famous because of its haunting presence in the first movement of the Sonata in B flat major D960, make their first appearance in *Auf der Donau* D553 (bb. 22–37). The tormented musings of Mayrhofer's poem about the transience of power are mirrored in these rumblings. There are more of these bass trills, thirty-three to be exact, in *Abendröte* D690 and twenty trills in the right hand. Just as *Hippolits Lied* is a study in mordents, *Abendröte* is a study in trills, none of them at all extended and all briefly attached to quavers on the move. The effect is unique – the music seems to shimmer in the light of all these decorations. *Freiwilliges Versinken* D700 is also about light: left- and right-hand trills in the first eleven bars of the song depict the majesty of sunset from the vantage point of Apollo's chariot. There are more deep left-hand trills in *An die Leier* D737; these ironically, even comically, comment on the word 'drohen' (boom or resound) in bb. 64 and 74. In *Heimliches Lieben* D922 the ardent declarations of love are presaged by an introduction, including an effusive trill, which teeters on the edge of parody. There is nothing comical about the angry trills in *Die Wetterfahne* D911/2 (in bb. 4–5) which are like a gust of wind that whirls the weather-vane round and round as if caught in a gale; more than this they perfectly reflect the emotional torment of the traveller faced with such a reminder of his fickle beloved.

The Turn

As in his vocal writing, Schubert uses the turn with greater regularity in accompaniments to his mature lieder, although an earlier appearance of the turn to depict the sheer joy of the harvest is to be found in the postlude to *Erntelied* D434 (b. 14). Also light-hearted is *Lachen und Weinen* D777, where the decorated ritornello implies the weaving of a web of allusion and emotion, all betokening delightful introspection. More typical is the elevated mood of *Im Abendrot* D799 where the piano's turn contributes to the awe of the opening ritornello and which Schubert writes out in full in the later version, perhaps not satisfied that the sign of the turn in the first version sufficiently conveys the seriousness of the music. The most eloquent (and difficult) of all turns for the pianist are to be found in the closing songs of *Winterreise*. In *Das Wirtshaus* D911/21 (b. 5) when it comes to the fingers of the pianist executing that seemingly easy turn they can seem all too easily like the aching and frozen legs of the traveller attempting a pirouette. The turn in the introduction to *Die Nebensonnen* D911/23 (b. 3) is even more difficult to nego-tiate, incorporating, as it does, a change from *piano* to *pianissimo*.

SONGS ORNAMENTED BY JOHANN MICHAEL VOGL – an alphabetical list
Die Allmacht D852 (in A major, a third lower than the C major original). This is scarcely an ornamented version of the song as there arc only a few additional decorations; instead, seven bars of piano writing are added to give the singer time to recover his breath after taxing phrases. This version by Vogl (Schubert himself would not have written the piano interlude in bb. 18–19) reduces the vocal challenges of the original version in every way. This is a version that is viable for modern performance by a less than heroic voice.

An Emma D113 (in F major, the song's original key). This is a complete re-composition (of the accompaniment at least) that shows little understanding of Schubert's remarkable mixture of tender recitative and arioso. Instead the song is hammered into cod-dramatic shape by the addition of cast-iron triplets for the piano. The bizarre semiquaver accompaniment under 'Ach! du liebst im Licht' (bb. 46–9) would no doubt have supported an amazing vocal outburst as if the ghost of Emma were being seen in heaven at last [NSA IV Volume 3b, pp. 250–2].

Antigone und Oedip D542. In the original key of C major, this is probably the most complex of the Vogl ornamentations. The Attic simplicity and grandeur for which Schubert seems to have aimed in this song seems vitiated by the almost constant decorations, particularly in Antigone's aria. If the singer were performing both roles (as seems likely), perhaps he ornamented Anti-gone's music to make it appear more feminine [NSA IV Volume 1b, pp. 284–9].

The first version of *Auf der Bruck* D853 (in G major, possibly the original tonality but a semitone lower than the printed key) is printed with staves showing Vogl's ornamentations, and is particu-larly interesting for the final nine bars of the vocal line with the option of an ornate flourish at the final cadence [NSA IV Volume 5b, pp. 214–22].

Der blinde Knabe D853 (in the original key of B flat major). It is interesting to have this version because we know that the composer Hummel (and his young student, Ferdinand Hiller) were intensely moved by a performance of this song by Vogl and Schubert early in 1827. It departs little from the original apart from a few extra ornaments (heartfelt accaciature, turns and demisemiquaver roulades) and two rallentandi marked at the end of each verse, the second extending over two bars [NSA IV Volume 5b, pp. 252–5].

Der Fischer D225 (G major, transposed a third down from the original). The song is richly ornamented in unexpected and often unlikely ways, and with a number of added fermate [NSA IV Volume 1b, pp. 279–83].

Gesänge des Harfners [note that Vogl re-orders Schubert's cycle with the last song in the sequence here transferred to the opening]

I *An die Türen* (F minor, transposed down a minor third from the original). There is a certain amount of ornamentation and an unexpected fermata in b. 23.

II *Wer sich der Einsamkeit ergibt* (G minor, transposed down a tone from the original). There is some ornamentation, some of it familiar from the definitive edition.

III *Wer nie sein Brot mit Tränen ass* (E minor, transposed a fourth lower than the original).

It seems likely that the definitive edition of Schubert's *Gesänge des Harfners* Op. 12 was to a certain extent influenced by Vogl's ornaments [NSA IV Volume 1b, pp. 292–303].

Gesänge aus Wilhelm Meister: Lied der Mignon D877/2 'Heiss mich nicht reden'. This is a copy of the vocal line alone transposed into D minor from the original E minor. It does not differ greatly from the original apart from the addition of several acciaccature and several turns at the ends of phrases that would necessitate the taking of breath in an awkward part of the phrase. It is unlikely that this song was sung by Vogl himself and it is impossible to say who prepared this version [NSA IV Volume 3b, p. 253].

Jägers Abendlied D368 (A flat major, transposed a fourth down from the original). The three strophes are written out individually the better to encompass Vogl's numerous ornaments [NSA IV Volume 1b, pp. 273–5].

Klage der Ceres D232. In the NSA two ornamented versions of the long Schiller ballad are printed in parallel format so that the differences between them can be seen at a glance. The first is from Franziska Tremier's *Liederalbum* and dates from about 1828/9. The second dates from perhaps four or five years later and is in Otto Biba's collection. Walther Dürr believes it likely that Vogl had a hand in both these versions of the ballad [NSA IV Volume 9, pp. 228–36].

Die schöne Müllerin D795. The editors of the NSA have selected the five songs from Diabelli's 1830 edition of the cycle (published separately by Bärenreiter in facsimile) which differ most from Schubert's original. At some point there was probably at Diabelli's disposal a version of the entire cycle with Vogl's ornamentations but, just like Schubert himself, the publisher decided to use only some of these, clearly believing that the younger singers of the 1830s were no longer interested in ornamentation that was already old-fashioned when the cycle was written. This edition of the cycle was taken to be authentic by two generations of Schubert singers until the reissue of the cycle's first edition, published by Peters and edited by Max Friedlaender, appeared in the 1870s and was gradually adopted by singers.

XI *Mein!* (in the original key of D major). The appoggiature in the first verse seem to create a new melody for the song opening and there are numerous other changes and decorations, some of which have clearly been made primarily for Vogl's vocal convenience.

XIII *Mit dem grünen Lautenbande* (in the original key of B flat major). The added acciaccature of the vocal line make the miller girl seem even more of a minx; when adopted in the later strophes the miller boy sounds even more manic. The fermate in bb. 13 and 17 were clearly inserted to enable Vogl room to breathe, or time to add some extra dramatic characterization.

XVIII *Trockne Blumen* (C minor, a third down from the original). The addition of triplets in the vocal line softens the magnificent austerity of the composer's original conception.

XIX *Der Müller und der Bach* (F minor, a tone down from the original). The various ornaments add nothing expressive to the song and the fermate on the last page, while no doubt contributing to the pathetic tenor of Vogl's interpretation, detract from the flowing river's ineluctable progress and the inevitability of the song's outcome [NSA IV Volume 2b, pp. 275–91].

Ständchen D957/4 (in C minor, transposed a tone down from the original). This is a richly ornamented version of this famous song. Some of the decorations have survived into the definitive printed version (although Schubert did not supervise its publication) so it is likely that here Vogl took Schubert's own decorations and elaborated on them [NSA IV Volume 14b, pp. 290–94].

THE MODERN PERFORMER

On the basis of these artistically uneven results, it remains an open question as to whether the singers and pianists of today should ornament Schubert's songs. The judicious addition of appoggiature in some of the 'recit' passages in the earlier songs is, of course, acceptable (*see Die Sommernacht* D289), but operatic-style additions are another matter. The composer lived in an age of musical transition, but he exerted a modern and fastidious control on his work that looked to Beethoven as preceptor. Vogl was older than Schubert and he took liberties – sometimes outlandish ones – with the music in an eighteenth-century manner when other singing colleagues of the composer did not. This confers no automatic entitlement on today's singers and pianists to attempt the same. If one refrains from ornamenting Mozart's lieder or Beethoven's, or Schumann's (written only twelve years after Schubert's death) there is no real reason to single out Schubert's songs as a special case. Singers or pianists who believe that their ornamentation will improve a Schubert song, rather than undermine it, must be very sure of their ground: it is easy to emulate Vogl's self-importance and narcissism, impossible to replicate his personal link with the composer and the context in which these eccentric ornamented versions came into being and then disappeared from view.

ORPHEUS, ALS ER IN DIE HÖLLE GING *see* LIED DES ORPHEUS D474

'OSSIAN' *see* JAMES MACPHERSON

OSSIANS LIED NACH DEM   Ossian's song after the death of Nathos
FALLE NATHOS'
(MACPHERSON after 'OSSIAN') **D278** [H165]

The song exists in three versions, the second of which is discussed below:
(1) Fragment, date unknown; (2) September(?) 1815; (3) 1816

(1) 'Ruhig'   E major   **C**   [29 bars]

(2) E major

(3) 'Ruhig'   E major   **¢**   [38 bars]

'Beugt euch aus euren Wolken nieder, ihr Geister meiner Väter! beuget euch! legt ab das rote Schrecken eures Laufs! Empfangt den fallenden Führer! Er komme aus einem entfernten Land, oder er steig aus dem tobenden Meer! Sein Kleid von Nebel sei nah', sein Speer aus einer Wolke gestaltet. Sein Schwert ein erloschnes Luftbild.[1] Und ach, sein Gesicht sei lieblich, dass seine Freunde frohlocken in seiner Gegenwart! O beugt euch aus euren Wolken nieder! ihr Geister meiner Väter, beuget euch!'

'Bend forward from your clouds, ghosts of my fathers! Lay the red terror of your course. Receive the falling chief; whether he comes from a distant land or rises from the rolling sea. Let his robe of mist be near; his spear that is formed of a cloud. [Macpherson: Place an half-extinguished meteor by his side in the form of the hero's sword] [Schubert: His sword an extinguished meteor] And oh! let his countenance be lovely, that his friends may delight in his presence. Bend from your clouds,' I said, 'Ghosts of my fathers! Bend!'

JAMES MACPHERSON ('OSSIAN') (1736–1796), translated by EDMUND, BARON VON HAROLD (1737–1800) in 1782

This is the second of Schubert's ten Ossian–Macpherson solo settings (1815–17). See the poet's biography (under Macpherson, James) for a chronological list of all the Ossian settings.

The background to this story is rather convoluted, but nevertheless appropriate to the enthusiasms of a young and patriotic composer mindful of the heroes of his own country's recent war with Napoleon, notably that gifted young bard Theodor Körner who fell in battle. The poem (in reality a piece of prose) is taken from *Darthula*, one of the twenty-two books or subsections that make up *Fingal* (1762), the collection of so-called translations from the Gaelic by James Macpherson which initiated a European craze for Scotland and its past. In one of his 'learned' footnotes Macpherson tells us that Nathos (the Gaelic name 'Nahos' signifies youthfulness) was one of the three sons of Usnoth, Lord of Etha, who were sent to study the arts of warfare with the king of Ulster, their uncle Cuchullin. On arriving in the foreign kingdom the boys discovered that Cuchullin had recently died. Nathos successfully led the armies against the usurper, the villainous Cairbar, and earned the love of Darthula with whom Cairbar was also infatuated. Nathos and Darthula eloped but a storm at sea stranded them within reach of the enemy forces. Despite the great bravery of the three sons of Usnoth, Nathos was slain and Darthula slew herself on her lover's body. 'Ossian' takes up the story the night before the final battle, and tells the whole tale with a number of episodic flashbacks.

This song was written before the composer had established his typical Ossian manner. It is his second setting of the Gaelic bard (*Kolmas Klage* D217 was the first) and one of the simplest. However attractive the complexities of the later settings – extended dramatic scenes of recitative, aria and arioso of which *Cronnan* D282 and *Die Nacht* D534 are perhaps the greatest examples – there is something about the grand and uncomplicated utterance of *Ossians Lied nach dem Falle Nathos* that goes to the heart of the nineteenth century's nostalgia for a distant, mist-enshrouded past, peopled by savages of a fiery yet noble disposition. Hugo Wolf strikes a similar note in his Mörike setting *Gesang Weylas* where the music of the goddess of the mythical realm of Orplid is of an elaborate simplicity, a bardic diatonicism which reflects the eternal verities before man's fall into the chromatic abyss. A similar gravity and clarity of utterance is heard at the end of the Schubert song and of course at the outset; the phrase 'Beugt

---

[1] Harold, faithful to Macpherson, writes '*Stell ein halb* erloschnes Luftbild'. The line continues (not set by Schubert): 'an eine Seite, in Gestalt des Helden-Schwerts'. As Macpherson's original English is printed above, it is necessary also to give in brackets the translation of the truncated line, as Schubert set it.

euch aus euren Wolken' falls and bows in appropriately impressive hymn-like incantation and homage.

By contrast, the music of the section beginning 'Sein Kleid von Nebel sei nah'' (from b. 17) departs from the harmonic simplicity of graveside dirge; there is a restlessness brought about by a chain of relentlessly climbing chromatic sequences. The affectionate fervour of 'Und ach, sein Gesicht sei lieblich' (bb. 23–5) changes the mood once again. Although this passage is safely ensconced in the dominant key (which thus prepares us for the recapitulation in the tonic) it is written for the upper reaches of the bass voice. This tessitura lends the music a heightened emotion as if a normally taciturn and deep-voiced warrior has been stirred to the point of weeping. As Richard Capell pointed out, this is one of the very few Ossian settings that can truly be called a song as opposed to a ballad. Although it may lack the scale and scope of some of the later masterpieces of the genre it demonstrates the composer's ability to create another world from long ago.

There is an incomplete first version of this song entitled *Ossians Lied nach dem Tode Nathos* (with the piece's last nine bars missing). Written in common time rather than *alla breve* it differs in a few details from the second version (e.g. the vocal line bb. 4–5) but it is substantially the same. The NSA (Vol. 9) posits a third version. This is not an autograph but a copy of the song made by Stadler which, in Walther Dürr's opinion, goes back to a long-vanished autograph. This is also substantially the same as the second version.

Autographs:	Österreichische Nationalbibliothek, Vienna (first draft, 29 bars, and fair copy of second version)
Publication:	First published as part of the AGA *Revisionsbericht* in 1897 (P725; first version)
	First published as part of the AGA in 1895 (P589a; second version)
	First published as Book 4 no. 2 of the *Nachlass* by Diabelli, Vienna in 1830 (P245; third version)
Publication reviews:	Rellstab 'Ueberblick der Erzeugnisse', *Iris im Gebiete der Tonkunst* (Berlin), No. 39 (12 November 1830) [Waidelich/Hilmar Dokumente II No. 784b]
Subsequent editions:	Peters: Vol. 4/200; AGA XX 147: Vol. 3/108; NSA IV: Vol. 9/218 (first version), 26 (second version) & 28 (third version)
Bibliography:	Clerk 1870, Vol. 2, p. 534
Discography and timing:	Fischer-Dieskau I 5²⁵ 2'09
	Hyperion I 20² 2'01 Michael George
	Hyperion II 9²⁶

← *Punschlied (Vier Elemente, innig gesellt) D277*   *Das Rosenband D280* →

OSTERLIED *see* JESUS CHRIST UNSER HEILAND D168A

Anton OTTENWALT (1789–1845)

THE POETIC SOURCE
Abend Unterhaltungen für den Winter, Vienna 1816–17, Zum Vortheile der Hausarmen Wiens, für bei Carl Gerold, Wien 1817

THE SONG
September/Autumn 1817   *Der Knabe in der Wiege* D579 [pp. 248–9] [It is unlikely that Schubert received this poem from Ottenwalt himself as the two did not meet until 1819. The composer may have found it as printed in the almanac from 1817 (source listed above), or even more likely, had the small volume handed to him for his perusal by Josef von Spaun.]

Anton Ottenwalt was, according to Deutsch, 'sensitive, serious, somewhat awkward and good-hearted'. In October 1817 he wrote a letter from his home town of Linz to his future brother-in-law Josef von Spaun, which includes the lines 'Schubert . . . has given me great pleasure by having a go at one of my poems. I greatly look forward to hearing the song soon.' The qualifying 'one of my poems' makes it unlikely that Ottenwalt, as is sometimes claimed, was the author of the song *Der Strom* D565 written at about the same time as *Der Knabe in der Wiege*. Puzzlingly, Ottenwalt wrote the poem about the child in its cradle several years before he was a father. (His only child, Karl, was born in 1829, after Schubert's death, and died in 1837 aged only eight.) Spaun was Schubert's trustiest friend, and Ottenwalt, by marrying into the Spaun family in 1819 (his wife Marie, 1795–1847, was sister to the four Spaun brothers), was bound to get to know the composer well. He was a civil servant of some distinction, and was promoted to a post in Vienna in 1830, after Schubert's death.

Outside Vienna, and in the composer's lifetime, Linz was the most important centre of burgeoning Schubert enthusiasm (Graz was to follow suit later). Ottenwalt was already a practised – if unpublished – poet, and Schubert seems to have set his text at Spaun's suggestion. For many years Ottenwalt was at the centre of the composer's unofficial fan club, deeply honoured when Schubert came to stay at his house as a guest, and delighted to see Schubert in Vienna where the poet seems never to have

been readily accepted by the Viennese who no doubt regarded him as provincial. Ottenwalt's letters give the strongest impression of someone who realized that he was entertaining an artist of immortal stature; this was not often the case with many of the circle who while acknowledging the composer's musical genius took him rather for granted on a personal level.

Ottenwalt's most revealing letter about Schubert, an invaluable document giving an insight into how successfully the shy Schubert hid his light under a bushel, was written in the summer of 1825. This was a full eight years after Schubert had set Ottenwalt's poem; the author seems not to have minded that the honour accorded to his talents as a poet was a 'one-off' and not to be repeated:

Linz, 27 July 1825. Schubert was so friendly and communicative . . . We sat together until nearly midnight and never have I seen him like this before, nor heard him; serious, profound and as if inspired. The way he talked about art and poetry, about his youth, his friends and other significant people, about the relationship between the ideal and life, and more in a similar vein. I reacted with ever growing astonishment at this mind, this soul about whom people had said that his artistic achievement had been totally unconscious, a process frequently barely realized or comprehensible even to himself. Yet, how straightforward it all was – I am in no position to talk about the range or any sense of unity in his convictions – but there were glimpses of a world-view that was not second-hand, and any contribution to it which might have been afforded by trusted friends in no way detracts from the characteristic individuality which it reveals.

'Trusted friends' here refers almost certainly to Mayrhofer above all. Like Mayrhofer, Ottenwalt was one of the few people in Schubert's circle who would have been completely unsurprised by the composer's status in later centuries – he seems to have been genuinely in awe of Schubert for all the best artistic reasons and as such comes across as a thoroughly modern and likeable figure. Recent research into his literary work (most of it unpublished) has revealed Ottenwalt to have been a much more gifted and interesting poet than has hitherto been acknowledged. He was also one of Mayrhofer's more important collaborators in the *Beiträge zur Bildung für Jünglinge*, the annual publication issued in 1817 and 1818 for the edification of young men.

Bibliography: Kohlhäufl 1999, pp. 143–8 & 192

Schubert, lithograph by Josef Teltscher (1826).

P

PART-SONGS

Part-songs (vocal trios, quartets or quintets, sometimes piano-accompanied, for male voices in the majority of cases) were an important part of the musical life of the Schubertians. At the beginning of the nineteenth century there was a new demand for *Gesellschaftsmusik* that came with a middle class better educated in the liberal arts. There was a tendency for this kind of *Bildung* to be confined to the young men of the household – for even if women were well educated at home it was only the men who were unchaperoned and fancy-free. These musical gatherings among the young male Schubertians took place first at school, and then at coffee houses and hostelries, or in each other's apartments. By the 1850s, after the seismic political shifts of 1848, young bachelors were far more likely to be invited to domestic gatherings with music where there was the lure of female company (the bigger Schubertiads, such as the famous one given by Spaun in 1826, were early manifestations of this trend). By the middle of the nineteenth century, and certainly when Johannes Brahms composed his *Liebeslieder-Walzer* for SATB and piano duet Op. 52 in 1869 (one might term this Vienna's Victorian era), the vocal quartet for this combination of voices (as opposed to the TTBB so favoured by Schubert) reflected a greater domesticity in the making of music, and a far greater freedom for the participating female members of the family.

Schubert's career, unconcerned with the ultra-formal aristocratic gatherings of Haydn's generation, straddled the two Biedermeier epochs, the second of which (*c.* 1825–48) seems to have been associated with a greater number of marriage ceremonies and a cosier idealization of connubial bliss. Most of the composer's earlier part-songs were written for unattached males, many of whom were too poor to marry according to the Austrian laws of the time. These young men loved to combine singing with a measure of carousing, and frequently sang without the support of a piano. Gatherings of young men in large numbers (as would be necessary for a substantial choral piece) were forbidden by the authorities who were terrified by the prospect of student insurrection; and so works requiring these bigger forces were conceived for public performance; and the number of concerts in Vienna was increasing all the time. The composer was also often called upon to

Schubert singing at the piano, drawing by Ferdinand Georg Waldmüller (1793–1865). Behind the composer stands Johann Michael Vogl, at his right sits the soprano Josefine Fröhlich.

provide music for home consumption, which required the addition of a piano. For example, the intricate quartet *Gebet* D815 was written in 1824 for different members of the Esterházy family – father (bass) and mother (contralto), two daughters (Marie the soprano, Karoline the accompanist) and their house guest, the tenor Baron von Schönstein.

The line-up of SATB was time-honoured of course – it was to be found in every oratorio and mass, and was brought to the pitch of perfection in the work of Joseph Haydn who also composed a set of vocal trios and quartets for voices which was worthy of his greatest writing for strings. But it was the work of Haydn's brother Michael that influenced Schubert. As well as leaving behind an exceptionally large body of sacred choral music, this composer was an avid creator of part-songs for TTBB (more than sixty of them, to texts by such poets as Claudius, Hölty, Matthisson and Schubart). Indeed, we know of Schubert's continuing reverence for the work of Michael Haydn, who seldom garners a mention today, from the fact that Schubert visited that composer's grave in Salzburg in 1825 and wrote home admiringly about his continuing affection. The younger Haydn's unaccompanied part-songs for male voices were written for more or less the same circumstances as many of Schubert's: all-male gatherings that mixed music with poetry readings, philosophical discussions, an element of party pranks and games, and quite a lot of drinking. To Schubert's parties one might add a measure of clandestine political discussion. In Charles Sealsfield's devastating critique of repression, *Austria as it is* (1828), he describes how 'during a dancing, a dining or a whist party' (and he might have included Schubertiads) 'a letter, received from Paris or London – of course not through the post – will glide from hand to hand, in that imperceptible way that Metternich has taught . . .'.

The commentaries in this book include a handful of the composer's unaccompanied vocal pieces. These were recorded for the original Hyperion series because they had some bearing on the solo song settings – for example *Nur wer die Sehnsucht kennt* D656 for unaccompanied male quintet. The list below, however, includes *all* the part-songs, both unaccompanied and accompanied, presented in Deutsch's chronological order. The few unaccompanied part-songs that were recorded for the Hyperion Edition are accorded an H number with a plus sign (H+) so as not to disturb the overall numbering of the solo vocal works with piano. The titles of the piano-accompanied part-songs and ensembles (as well as D80 and D81 with instrumental accompaniment and several unaccompanied items) are printed in bold type; this indicates works that have been allocated a separate commentary in this book.

1812

> *Quell' innocente figlio (Aria dell' angelo)* (Metastasio) D17/3, composition exercise, unaccompanied trio, SAT, *c.* 1812
>
> *Quell' innocente figlio (Aria dell' angelo)* (Metastasio) D17/4, composition exercise, unaccompanied quartet, SATB, *c.* 1812
>
> *Quell' innocente figlio (Aria dell' angelo)* (Metastasio) D17/5, composition exercise, unaccompanied trio, SAT, *c.* 1812
>
> *Quell' innocente figlio (Aria dell' angelo)* (Metastasio) D17/6, composition exercise, unaccompanied trio, SAT, *c.* 1812
>
> *Quell' innocente figlio (Aria dell' angelo)* (Metastasio) D17/7, composition exercise, unaccompanied quartet, SATB, *c.* 1812
>
> *Quell' innocente figlio (Aria dell' angelo)* (Metastasio) D17/8, composition exercise, unaccompanied quartet, SATB, *c.* 1812
>
> *Quell' innocente figlio (Aria dell' angelo)* (Metastasio) D17/9, composition exercise, unaccompanied quartet, SATB, *c.* 1812
>
> [*see also* **solo and duet version of this text, Quell' innocente figlio D17/1 H9 and D17/2 H9a**]

H10   *Viel tausend Sterne prangen* (Eberhard) D642, quartet, SATB, *c.* 1812

    Entra l'uomo allor che nasce ('Aria di Abramo') (Metastasio) D33/3, composition exercise, unaccompanied trio, SAT, September–October 1812

    Entra l'uomo allor che nasce ('Aria di Abramo') (Metastasio) D33/4, composition exercise, unaccompanied quartet, SATB, September–October 1812

    Entra l'uomo allor che nasce (Aria di Abramo) (Metastasio) D33/5, composition exercise, unaccompanied quartet, SATB, September–October 1812 [*see also* **solo and duet versions of this text D33/1 H13 and D33/2 H13a**]

    Te solo adoro ('Aria di Achior' from 'Betulia liberata') (Metastasio) D34, composition exercise, unaccompanied quartet, SATB, 5 November 1812

    Serbate, o Dei custodi (from 'La clemenza di Tito') (Metastasio) D35/1, composition exercise, unaccompanied quartet, SATB, October–December 1812

    Serbate, o Dei custodi (from 'La clemenza di Tito') (Metastasio) D35/2, composition exercise, unaccompanied chorus, SATB, October–December 1812 [*see also* **solo version of this text D35/3 H14**]

H15   *Die Advokaten* (Rustenfeld, Baron Engelhart) D37, comic trio, TTB, after Fischer, 25–7 December 1812

1813

    Totengräberlied (Hölty) first setting D38, unaccompanied trio, TTB, 1813(?) [*see* **second setting for solo voice of this text D44 H20**]

H21   *Dithyrambe* (Schiller) first setting D47, fragment, TB, chorus and piano, 29 March 1813 [*see* **second setting for solo voice D801 H602**]

    Unendliche Freude durchwallet das Herz (Schiller, excerpt from *Elysium*) first setting D51, composition exercise, unaccompanied trio, TTB, 15 April 1813 [*see also* **complete setting of this text for solo voice, *Elysium* D584 H386**]

    Vorüber die stöhnende Klage (Schiller, excerpt from *Elysium*) D53, composition exercise, unaccompanied trio, TTB, 18 April 1813 [*see also* **complete setting of this text for solo voice, *Elysium* D584 H386**]

    Unendliche Freude durchwallet das Herz (Schiller, excerpt from *Elysium*) second setting D54, composition exercise, unaccompanied canon for three male voices, 19 April 1813 [*see also* **complete setting of this text for solo voice, *Elysium* D584 H386**]

    Selig durch die Liebe (Schiller, excerpt from *Die Triumph der Liebe*) D55, composition exercise, unaccompanied trio, TTB, 21 April 1813

    Sanctus (Latin text) D56, composition exercise, unaccompanied canon for three voices, 21 April 1813

    Hier streckt der wallende Pilger (Schiller, excerpt from *Elysium*) D57, composition exercise, unaccompanied trio, TTB, 29 April 1813 [*see also* **complete setting of this text for solo voice, *Elysium* D584 H386**]

    Dessen Fahne Donnerstürme wallet (Schiller, excerpt from *Elysium*) D58, composition exercise, unaccompanied trio, TTB, May 1813 [*see also* **complete setting of this text for solo voice, *Elysium* D584 H386**]

H24+   *Ein jügendlicher Maienschwung* (Schiller, excerpt from *Der Triumph der Liebe*) D61, composition exercise, unaccompanied canon for three voices, 8 May 1813

    Thronend auf erhabnem Sitz (Schiller, excerpt from *Der Triumph der Liebe*) D62, composition exercise, unaccompanied trio, TTB, 9 May 1813

    Wie die stiele Sternenbahn (Schiller, excerpt from *Der Triumph der Liebe*) D63, composition exercise, unaccompanied trio, TTB, 10 May 1813

Majestätsche Sonnenrose (Schiller, excerpt from *Der Triumph der Liebe*) D64, composition exercise, unaccompanied trio, TTB, 10 May 1813

Schmerz verzerret ihr Gesicht (Schiller, excerpt from *Gruppe aus dem Tartarus*) D65, composition exercise, sketch for a canon for three male voices, TTB, 11 May 1813 [*see also* **complete setting of this text for solo voice, *Gruppe aus dem Tartarus* D583** H384]

Frisch atmet des Morgens lebendiger Hauch (Schiller, excerpt from *Der Flüchtling*) D67, composition exercise, unaccompanied trio, TTB, 15 May 1813 [*see also* **complete setting of this text for solo voice, *Der Flüchtling* D402** H234]

Dreifach ist der Schritt der Zeit, Spruch des Konfuzius (Schiller) first setting D43, composition exercise, unaccompanied trio, TTB, 8 July 1813

Dreifach ist der Schritt der Zeit, Spruch des Konfuzius (Schiller) second setting D69, composition exercise, unaccompanied canon for three voices, 8 July 1813

Die zwei Tugendwege (Schiller) D71, composition exercise, unaccompanied trio, TTB, 15 July 1813

Alleluja in F D71A, composition exercise, canon for three voices, July 1813?

H26   ***Trinklied*** (Schäffer) D75, song for bass and chorus, TTB, 29 August 1813

Zur Namensfeier meines Vaters (Schubert) D80, trio, TTB, accompanied by guitar, 27 September 1813

Auf dem Sieg der Deutschen (Anonymous) D81, song accompanied by two violins and cello, October 1813

[*Zur Namensfeier des Herrn Andreas Siller* (Anonymous) D83, song with violin and harp accompaniment, before 4 November 1813]

H28+   ***Verschwunden sind die Schmerzen*** (Anonymous) D88, unaccompanied trio, TTB, 5 November 1813

1815

Mailied (Hölty) first setting D129, unaccompanied trio, TTB, 1815? [*see also* **complete setting of this text for solo voice, *Mailied* D503** H322]

Der Schnee zerrint (Hölty, excerpt from a different *Mailied* from that for D129, D199 and D503) D130, unaccompanied canon for three voices, 1815?

H63   ***Trinklied*** (Castelli) D148, tenor with chorus TTB, February 1815

H75   ***Nun lasst uns den Leib begraben (Begräbnislied)*** (Klopstock) D168, quartet, SATB, 9 March 1815

H76   ***Jesus Christus unser Heiland (Osterlied)*** (Klopstock) D168a, quartet, SATB, 9 March 1815

H77   ***Trinklied vor der Schlacht*** (Körner) D169, chorus, unison, 12 March 1815

H78   ***Schwertlied*** (Körner) D170, chorus, unison, 12 March 1815

H87   ***Trinklied*** (Zettler) D183, solo voice and unison chorus, 12 April 1815

Mailied (Hölty) second setting D199, duet for voices and horn, 24 May 1815 [*see also* **complete setting of this text for solo voice, *Mailied* D503** H322]

Mailied (Der Schnee zerrinnt) (Hölty, excerpt from a different *Mailied* from that for D129, D199 and D503) D202, duet for voices and horn, 26 May 1815

Der Morgenstern (Körner) D203, duet for voices and horn, 26 May 1815 [*see also* **setting of this text (fragment) for solo voice, *Der Morgenstern* D172** H80]

Jägerlied (Körner) D204, duet for voices and horn, 26 May 1815

Lützows wilde Jagd (Körner) D205, duet for voices and horn, 26 May 1815

H123   ***Hymne an den Unendlichen*** (Schiller) D232, quartet, SATB, 11 July 1815

H127   *Das **Abendrot*** (Kosegarten) D236, trio, SSB, 20 July 1815

Lacrimoso son io (unknown text) D131, unaccompanied canon for three voices, August 1815?

Trinklied im Winter (Hölty) D242, unaccompanied trio, TTB, August 1815?

Frühlingslied (Hölty) D243, unaccompanied trio, TTB, August 1815?

Willkommen, lieber schöner Mai (Hölty) D244, unaccompanied trio, TTB, August 1815?

H154   ***Trinklied*** (Anonymous) D267, quartet, TTBB, 25 August 1815

H155   ***Bergknappenlied*** (Anonymous) D268, quartet, TTBB, 25 August 1815

H159   ***Das Leben ist ein Traum*** (Wannovius) D269, trio, SSA, 25 August 1815

H164   ***Punschlied*** (Schiller) D277, trio, TTB, 29 August 1815

Das Grab (Salis-Seewis) D329A, sketch for the first setting as canon for four-part choir, SATB, 28 December 1815?

H206   *Das **Grab*** (Salis-Seewis) second setting D330, chorus, 28 December 1815 [third setting H225, fourth setting H377]

H208   ***Klage um Ali Bey*** (Claudius) D140, trio version, 1815 [*see* quartet version H313a]

1816

H225   *Das **Grab*** (Salis-Seewis) third setting D377, choral song (TTBB), 11 February 1816

H234+ *Der Entfernten* (Salis-Seewis) first setting D331, unaccompanied quartet, TTBB, *c.* 1816 [*see* **second setting for solo voice of this text, *Der Entfernten* D350 H235**]

Die Einsiedelei (Salis-Seewis) first setting D337, unaccompanied quartet, TTBB, *c.* 1816 [*see* **second and third settings for solo voice of this text, *Die Einsiedelei* D393** H238 **and D563** H373]

An den Frühling (Schiller) second setting D338, unaccompanied quartet, TTBB *c.* 1816 [*see* **first and third settings for solo voice of this text, *An den Frühling* D283 H169 and D587 H388**]

Fischerlied (Salis-Seewis) second setting D364, unaccompanied quartet, TTBB, 1816 or 1817? [*see* **first and third settings for solo voice of this text, *Fischerlied* D351 H236 and D562 H372**]

Bardengesang (Ossian/Macpherson) D147, unaccompanied trio, TTB, 20 January 1816?

Trinklied (Anonymous text) fragment D356, solo voice with chorus, TTBB, lost piano accompaniment 1816

Die Schlacht (Schiller) D387, sketch for a second setting as a cantata for solo voices, chorus and piano, March 1816

Goldner Schein (Matthisson) D357, unaccompanied canon for three voices, 1 May 1816

Andenken (Matthisson) second setting D423, unaccompanied quartet, TTBB, May 1816 [*see* **first setting as a solo song, *Andenken* D99 H35**]

Erinnerungen (Matthisson) second setting D424, unaccompanied quartet, TTBB, May 1816 [*see* **first setting as a solo song, *Erinnerungen* D98 H44**]

Trinklied im Mai (Hölty) D427, unaccompanied quartet, TTBB, May 1816

Widerhall (Matthisson) D428, unaccompanied quartet, TTBB, May 1816

H268   ***Beitrag zur fünfzigjährigsten Jubelfeier des Herrn von Salieri, Erstem k.k. Hofkapellmeister in Wien*** (Schubert?) D407, 'Gütigster, Bester!' piano-accompanied trio, TBB, by 16 June 1816 [*see* also **solo tenor aria, D407 H268b**]

H268a ***Beitrag zur fünfzigjährigsten Jubelfeier des Herrn von Salieri, Erstem k.k. Hofkapellmeister in Wien*** (Schubert?) D407, 'Gütigster, Bester!' unaccompanied quartet, TTBB, by 16 June 1816

H268c   *Beitrag zur fünfzigjährigsten Jubelfeier des Herrn von Salieri, Erstem k.k. Hofkapellmeister in Wien* (Schubert?) D407, 'Unser aller Grosspapa', unaccompanied canon for three voices, by 16 June 1816

H269   *An die Sonne* (Uz) D439, quartet, SATB, June 1816

        Chor der Engel (Goethe from *Faust*) D440, unaccompanied chorus, SATB, June 1816

H270   *Das grosse Halleluja* (Klopstock) D442, choral unison, June 1816

H271   *Schlachtlied* (Klopstock) D443, tenor solo or chorus, June 1816

H278   *Gott im Ungewitter* (Uz) D985, quartet, SATB, 1816(?)

H279   *Gott der Weltschöpfer* (Uz) D986, quartet, SATB, 1816(?)

H311+   *Der Geistertanz* (Matthisson) fourth setting D494, quintet, TTBBB, November 1816 [*see* **first setting D15 H7, second setting D15a H8, third setting D116 H47**]

H326   *Licht und Liebe* (Matthäus von Collin) D352, duet, ST, 1816(?)

1817

H334   *Jagdlied* (Werner) D521, solo song or unison choral, January 1817

H344   *La pastorella al prato* (Goldoni) first setting D513, quartet, TTBB, 1817(?) [*see* **second setting as a solo song, *La pastorella al prato* D528 H343**]

        Gesang der Geister über den Wassern (Goethe) second setting D538, unaccompanied quartet, TTBB, March 1817 [**see choral version with piano, *Gesang der Geister über den Wassern* D705 H459**]

H377   *Das Grab* (Salis-Seewis) fourth setting D569, male chorus, unison, June 1817 [*see* **first setting D329A, second setting D330 H206, third setting D377 H225**]

        Lied im Freien (Salis-Seewis) D572, unaccompanied quartet, TTBB, July 1817

H394   *Das Dörfchen* (Bürger) D598 (D641 in D₁), quartet, TTBB, December 1817

1818

H395   *Die Gesellighkeit (Lebenslust)* (Unger) D609, quartet, SATB, January 1818

H400   *Sing-Übungen* (wordless) D619, duet for two equal voices, July 1818

1819

        Leise, leise lasst uns singen (Anonymous) D635, unaccompanied quartet, TTBB, c. 1819

        Das Grab (Salis-Seewis) fifth setting D643A, unaccompanied quartet, TTBB, 1819 [*see* **first setting, *Das Grab* D329A, second setting D330 H206, third setting D377 H225, fourth setting D569 H377**]

H424+   *Sehnsucht (Mignon)* (Goethe) fourth setting D656, quintet for men's voices, TTBBB, April 1819 [*see* **first setting, *Sehnsucht* D310 H190 and 190a, second setting D359 H211, third setting D481 H297, fifth setting (*'Mignon und der Harfner'*) D877/1 H585 and sixth setting D877/4 H588**]

        Ruhe, schönstes Glück der Erde (Anonymous) D657, unaccompanied quartet, TTBB, April 1819

H431   *Cantate zum Geburtstag des Sängers Johann Michael Vogl* (Stadler) D666, trio, STB, before 10 August 1819

1820

        Sechs Antiphonen zum Psalmsonntag (Latin text) D696, unaccompanied chorus, SATB, 26 March 1820

H459   *Gesang der Geister über den Wassern* (Goethe) third setting D705, choral, fragment, December 1820 [*see* **first setting, solo song D484 H307**]

H460   *Der 23. Psalm* (Bible/Mendelssohn) D706, quartet, SSAA, December 1820
         Gesang der Geister über den Wassern (Goethe) fourth setting D714, vocal octet,
         TTTTBBBB with strings, December 1820 [**see first setting, solo song D484 H307**]

1821

H470   *Im gegenwärtigen Vergangenes* (Goethe) D710, tenor and male chorus, TTBB, March 1821?
H474   *Die Nachtigall* (Unger) D724, quartet, TTBB, by April 1821
         Linde Lüfte wehen (Anonymous) D725, fragment, duet, AT, April 1821

1822

H480   *Naturgenuss* (Matthisson) second setting D422, quartet, TTBB, 1822(?) [**see first setting
         as solo song, Naturgenuss D188 H90**]
         Frühlingsgesang (Schober) first setting D709, unaccompanied quartet, TTBB, before April
         1822
H481   *Geist der Liebe* (Matthisson) second setting D747, quartet, TTBB, January 1822 [**see first
         setting, Geist der Liebe D414 H252**]
H483   *Frühlingsgesang* (Schober) second setting D740, quartet, TTBB, January–April 1822
H489   *Gott in der Natur* (Kleist) D757, quartet, SSAA, August 1822
H499   *Schicksalslenker, blicke nieder* (Anonymous) D763, quartet, SATB, 22 November 1822

1823

         Hirtenchor (Hier auf den Fluren) from *Rosamunde* (Chézy) D797/7, choral, SATB,
         orchestral accompaniment arranged for piano, autumn 1823
         Geisterchor (In der Tiefe wohnt das Licht) from *Rosamunde* (Chézy) D794/4, choral,
         TTBB, orchestral accompaniment arranged for piano, autumn 1823
         Jägerchor (Wie lebt sichs so fröhlich) from *Rosamunde* (Chézy) D797/8, choral, SATB,
         orchestral accompaniment arranged for piano, autumn 1823

1824

H550   *Gondelfahrer* (Mayrhofer) second setting D809, quartet, TTBB, March 1824 [**see first
         setting as a solo song, Gondelfahrer D808 H549**]
         Salve Regina in C (Latin text) D811, unaccompanied quartet, TTBB, April 1824
H552   *Gebet* (de la Motte Fouqué) D815, quartet, SATB, September 1824
H553   *Lied eines Kriegers* (Anonymous) D822, solo bass with men's chorus, 31 December 1824

1825

         Wehmut (Heinrich Hüttenbrenner) D825, unaccompanied quartet, SATB, before summer
         1826
         Ewige Liebe (Schulze) D825A, unaccompanied quartet, SATB, before summer 1826
         Flucht (Lappe) D825B, unaccompanied quartet, SATB, summer 1825 at the latest
H566   *Bootgesang* (Scott/Storck) D835, chorus, TTBB, 1825
H567   *Coronach (Totengesang der Frauen und Mädchen)* (Scott/Storck) D836, trio, SSA, 1825
         Trinklied aus dem 16. Jahrhundert (Latin text, Gräffer) D847, unaccompanied quartet,
         TTBB, July 1825

1826

H583   *Mondenschein* (Schober) D875, choral quintet, TTBBB, January 1826
H584   *Die Allmacht* (Pyrker) D875a, second setting, chorus, January 1826 [**see first setting,
         solo song D852 H572**]

H585   *Mignon und der Harfner (Nur wer die Sehnsucht kennt)* (Goethe) fifth setting D877/1,
        duet, January 1826 [*see* **first setting, two versions, D310** H190 and H190a, **second
        setting D359** H211, **third setting D481** H298, **fourth setting D656** H424+, **sixth setting
        D877/4** H588]
H590   *Widerspruch* (Seidl) D865, choral, TTBB, 1826(?)
H607   *Nachthelle* (Seidl) D892, tenor solo and chorus, TTBB, September 1826
H607+   *Grab und Mond* (Seidl) D893, unaccompanied chorus, TTBB, September 1826

1827

        Wein und Liebe (Haug) D901, unaccompanied quartet, TTBB, before June 1827
H608   *Zur guten Nacht* (Rochlitz) D903, tenor solo and chorus, TTBB, January 1827
        Schlachtlied (Klopstock) second setting D912, unaccompanied double chorus, TTBB,
        TTBB, 28 February 1827 [*see* **first setting, *Schlachtlied* D443** H271]
H629   *Ständchen* (Grillparzer) D920, mezzo soprano and male (TTBB) or female (SSAA)
        chorus, July 1827
H647   *Der Hochzeitsbraten* (Schober) D930, trio, STB, November 1827
H656   *Al par del ruscelletto (Cantate für Irene Kiesewetter)* (Anonymous) D936, quartet SATB
        and choral SATB with piano-duet accompaniment, 26 December 1827

1828

H659   *Der Tanz* (Meerau?) D826, quartet, SATB, early 1828
H661   *Mirjams Siegesgesang* (Grillparzer) D942, soprano solo and chorus, SATB,
        March 1828
        Hymne an den heiligen Geist (Schmidl) D948, unaccompanied quartet, TTBB, May 1828?
        (second version of the quartet has wind instrument accompaniment)
        Glaube, Hoffnung und Liebe (Reil) D954, choral SATB, before 2 September 1828 (2
        versions, one with piano accompaniment, the other with wind instruments)
H668+   *Der 92. Psalm* (Bible, in Hebrew) D953, baritone and chorus, SATB, July 1828

PASTORELLA *see* LA PASTORELLA AL PRATO (I) D513 & (II) D528

PAUSE *see* Die SCHÖNE MÜLLERIN D795/12

PAX VOBISCUM   Peace be with you
(SCHOBER) **D551** [H362]
F major   April 1817

(34 bars)

'Der Friede sei mit euch!' das war dein
   Abschiedssegen.
Und so vom Kreis der Gläubigen umkniet,
Vom Siegesstrahl der Gottheit angeglüht,
Flogst du dem ew'gen Heimatland entgegen.—
   Und Friede kam in ihre treuen Herzen,
   Und lohnte sie in ihren grössten Schmerzen,[1]
   Und stärkte sie in ihrem Martertod.

   Ich glaube dich, du grosser Gott!

'Der Friede sei mit euch!' rufst du im
   Rosenglühen
Des Himmels uns an jedem Abend zu,
Wenn alle Wesen zur erwünschten Ruh'
Vom harten Gang des schwülen Tages ziehen;
   Und Berg und Tal und Strom und
      Seeswogen,[2]
   Vom weichen Hauch des Nebels überflogen,
   Noch schöner werden unterm milden Rot;
   Ich liebe dich, du guter Gott!

'Der Friede sei mit euch!' so lacht die erste
   Blume
Des jungen Frühlings uns vertraulich an,
Wenn sie, mit allen Reizen angetan,
Sich bildet in der Schöpfung Heiligthume.
   Wen sollte auch nicht Friede da
      umschweben,
   Wo Erd' und Himmel ringsum sich beleben,
   Und alles aufsteht aus des Winters Tod?

   Ich hoff' auf dich, du starker Gott!

'Peace be with you!' That was your parting
   blessing.
And so, surrounded by the kneeling faithful,
Lit by the rays of the triumphant godhead,
You soared to the eternal homeland.
   Peace entered their devoted hearts,
   Rewarded them in their greatest sorrow,
   And strengthened them in their martyr's
      death.

   I believe in You, Almighty God!

'Peace be with you!' you cry to us each evening

In the roseate glow of sunset,
When all creatures take their longed-for rest
After hard toil in the sultry day,
   When mountain and valley, river and lake
      wave
   Covered by a soft veil of mist,
   Grow still lovelier in the gentle crimson.
   I love you, merciful God!

'Peace be with you!' So tenderly the first flower

Of young spring smiles upon us
When, decked with all its charms,
It unfolds in the sanctuary of creation.
   Who could not feel the aura of peace

   When earth and sky are everywhere reborn,
   And all things rise again from the death of
      winter?
   I hope in You, all-powerful God!

FRANZ VON SCHOBER (1798–1882)

This is the fifth of Schubert's fourteen Schober solo settings (1815–27). See the poet's biography for a chronological list of all the Schober settings.

Only a few weeks (perhaps even less) after the composition of *Der Jüngling und der Tod* D545, an exploration of pantheistic longings, Schubert composed a song fit for use in a church, or at least on a religious occasion. We have no evidence that Franz von Schober was religious (in fact his hedonism seems to have shown a total disregard for the concept of sin) and, indeed, the only real evidence of Schubert's own religious feelings is the quality of his church music. Schubert could nevertheless write *Pax Vobiscum* without any hypocrisy and with the simplicity tradition-ally required for choral music of this kind (see Michael Kube, *Schubert Liedlexikon* pp. 453–4,

[1] In his Gedichte (1842) Schober changes this to 'in ihren *höchsten* Schmerzen'.
[2] The musical underlay of this in the NSA is 'See – es – wogen'. Schober later changed the word to 'Meereswogen'.

who also compares some of the passages of this song with No. 6 – *Nach der Wandlung* – of the *Deutsche Messe* D872). Church music and its full range of colour and emotion was an everyday fact of his life.

Pianists wishing to understand how to play the graveside music for wind and brass instruments depicted in *Das Wirtshaus* D911/21 from *Winterreise* should study *Pax Vobiscum*. It is in the same key of F major and the disposition of the chords at the keyboard, albeit without the chromatic inflections of the later work with its affecting flattened seventh, is remarkably similar; crotchets and quavers in the 'Sehr langsam' of the *Winterreise* song will make for approximately the same tempo as minims and crotchets notated in *alla breve* time. The fact that burials were accompanied by music outdoors (and still are in parts of Austria) is the secret behind both these noble chorales. *Das Wirtshaus* is of course one of the greatest Schubert songs, but *Pax Vobiscum* is also unexpectedly moving, despite its simplicity on the page and the doubling of the voice throughout by the accompaniment.

It is entirely possible that Schubert had only envisaged the performance of the first of Schober's three verses. There are no repeat marks on the autograph; accordingly the second and third verses appear in italics in the NSA. The version of the poem printed in the NSA is taken from a handwritten copy of Schober's poem in the Wienbibliothek im Rathaus that predates the publication of his poems in 1842.

Pax vobiscum was the only Schubert song to be heard at the composer's funeral on 21 November 1828, indicating that it was highly valued by the Schubert circle, including his family. At their request new words were provided by Schober (below) and the song was sung at the graveside with choir and wind instruments under the direction of Johann Baptist Gänsbacher:

AN FRANZ SCHUBERTS SARGE

'Der Friede sei mit dir', du engelreine Seele!
Im frischen Blüh'n der vollen Jugendkraft

Hat dich der Strahl des Todes hingerafft,
Dass er dem reinen Lichte dich vermähle,
Dem Licht, von dem hienieden schon
   durchdrungen,
Dein Geist in heil'gen Tönen uns gesungen,
Das dich geweckt, geleitet und entflammt,

Dem Lichte, das von Gott nur stammt.

O sieh, verklärter Freund, herab auf unsre
   Zähren,
Vergib den Schmerz der schwachen
   Menschenbrust
Wir sind beraubt, *wir* litten den Verlust;
Du schwebst befreit in heimatlichen Sphären.
Für viele Rosen hat dies Erdenleben
Die scharfe Dornen nur zum Lohn gegeben,
Ein langes Leiden und ein frühes Grab, –
Dort fallen alle Ketten ab!

AT FRANZ SCHUBERT'S COFFIN

'Peace be with you', pure, angelic soul.
In the fresh bloom of your full youthful
   powers
The ray of death carried you off
To unite you with the pure light,
The light which your spirit, already suffused
   with it here on earth,
Sang of in sacred tones,
The light that awakened, guided and inspired
   you,
The light that comes from God alone.

Look down, transfigured friend, on our tears,

Forgive the sorrow of feeble human hearts.

We are robbed, *we* have suffered the loss;
Freed, you float in your native spheres.
In reward for so many roses this earthly life
Has given only sharp thorns,
Prolonged suffering and an early grave –
Where all chains fall away!

Und was als Erbteil du uns hast zurückgelassen:	The inheritance you have left us –
Das Wirken heisser Liebe, reiner Kraft,	The work of ardent love, of pure strength,
Die heilge Wahrheit, gross und unerschlafft,	Sacred truth, great and unflagging –
Wir wollen's tief in unsre Seelen fassen.	Let us draw it deep into our souls.
Was du der Kunst, den Deinen du geworden,	What you have become to art, and to your friends,
Ist offenbart in himmlischen Akkorden.	Is revealed in heavenly chords.
Und wenn wir nach den süssen Klängen gehen,	And if we follow those sweet strains
Dann werden wir dich wiedersehen!	We shall see you again!

Deutsch suggests that Schober's mention of 'prolonged suffering' in Verse 2 of the rewritten poem could hardly have been about Schubert's short final illness, and that the poet was referring to the composer's whole life of suffering. But it is also possible that Schober, who knew more about the composer's private life than anyone else, was referring in a deliberately ambiguous manner to the venereal illness that had impaired his friend's health for the previous six years. Whether or not Schubert had intended more than one verse of Schober's original poem to be sung, the poet (never a blushing violet at an important occasion) ensured that all three verses of his specially penned tribute were performed at the burial ceremony.

Autograph:	Wienbibliothek im Rathaus, Vienna (first draft)
First edition:	Published as Book 10 no. 6 of the *Nachlass* by Diabelli, Vienna in April 1831 (P267)
First known performance:	(with Schober's revised poem) 21 November 1828, Kirche St Josef (at Schubert's funeral). Performers unknown [Waidelich/Hilmar Dokumente II No. 642]
Subsequent editions:	Peters: Vol. 2/213; AGA XX 315: Vol. 5/88; NSA IV: Vol. 11/116
Discography and timing:	Fischer-Dieskau II 1[2] 1'44 (first strophe only)
	Hyperion I 3[9]
	Hyperion II 18[13] 5'12 Ann Murray

⟵ *An die Musik* D547   *Hänflings Liebeswerbung* D552 ⟶

PEDALLING

In his masterful *The Romantic Generation* (pp. 21–4) Charles Rosen makes a number of points about use of the pedal in Schubert – although he does not specifically address the issue of the songs:

> *Pedal markings are excessively rare in Schubert . . . The Sonata in G major D894 has only one, in the tenth bar of the first movement, also marked ppp. This suggests that Schubert adheres to the Classical system, in which the dry sound is the norm and the pedalled sound is a special effect [. . .] In the piano writing of the Romantic generation of the 1830s, in fact, a fully pedalled sonority becomes the norm.*

Pedal markings are also relatively rare in the songs. Rosen points out that from about 1830 'the change of pedal is crucial to the conception of rhythmic movement and the sustaining of the melodic line over the bass'. If this is the case the whole of Schubert's output is excused from the tendency among modern pianists to use the pedal as a more or less constant default setting for all music – and for all accompaniments. Schubert songs are conversations between a bass line and the melodic line of the voice. Singers with a fine legato provide their own sustaining pedal as it were; indeed the pedal came into its own in the piano writing of Field and Chopin when it was employed to imitate *bel canto* phrasing. In general terms, therefore, the song accompanist needs to use far less pedal than a solo pianist (and this applies to many composers besides Schubert), the 'pedal effect' in any song being sustained by the intrinsic legato of the voice. In contrast to this legato, the piano should be capable of deploying complementary, sometimes more detached, textures – possible only if freed of unremitting use of the pedal. In this way the piano can achieve an expressive independence precisely because it is capable of providing a textural contrast to vocal legato. A good example of this is the markings in the opening of Schubert's *Ganymed* D544 where only an absence of the sustaining pedal will enable the left-hand staccato to be heard as an independent texture. The song's opening melody demands a singing legato under the fingers of the right hand that is more eloquent for being purely the result of a connection between finger and key, the sound of a spring morning in classical times unclouded (at least for this portion of the song) by a Romantic glow of pedal.

Naturally, there are many passages where use of the pedal is required – to achieve legato in a wide-ranging Schubert song accompaniment, or to avoid undue dryness – and there can be no argument against that. There is scarcely a Schubert song where no pedal is to be used at all. But it is suprising how many pianists use the pedal when the geography of the writing, all the notes safely under the hands, does not require it; when a singer's consonants are smudged and rendered less clear by a competitive blur of piano sound, the pedal is usually the culprit. The cultivation of an unpedalled singing tone in legato piano passages is an essential asset in creating a Schubertian sound world that is clearer and more articulated than might be expected, for example, in Schumann and Brahms. The great accompanist Gerald Moore told me some three decades ago that the older he became the less pedal he used, or felt he needed to use, in Schubert's music, and I have had exactly the same experience.

From the 1770s a number of pianos had pedals operated by knee-levers. Mozart played approvingly on such an instrument by Johann Andreas Stein. How much easier it is to use the pedal on the modern piano when the foot can settle on it for the duration of a piece and provide an automatic means of enriching tone, covering technical lapses and enhancing musical flavour by artificial means – a kind of musical monosodium glutamate! The reflexes required for employing the knee pedal are entirely different, and a great deal less automatic (at least for modern players). In song accompaniment the modern pedal has a far more substantial role than simply providing a connective ligament between chords – it provides atmosphere, magic, a change of colour. Its use as something special, often hugely affecting, is debased by its automatic employment when not actually required for the creation of legato, and when the warmth of singing tone should be created by the pianist's touch alone.

The use of the 'soft pedal' is a separate issue: pianists who use modern instruments would do well to listen to the sometimes spellbinding colours that were produced on the fortepianos of Schubert's time. On some of these Viennese models there was a modification of Bartolomeo Cristifori's una corda mechanism. The pianist could choose whether to strike the normal three strings (tre corde), two strings (due corde) or one string (una corda) depending on the depth to which the pedal was pressed. In a cadenza passage of the slow movement of Beethoven's Piano Concerto No. 4 Op. 58 the composer specifies the use of two of the three strings in bb. 54–9, and in bb. 60–1 two strings with a diminuendo back to one. In Schubert's lieder there are no parallels to Beethoven's futuristically adventurous instructions to his accompanist: in *An die ferue Geliebte*, bb. 202–7 for example, the sustaining pedal is required to be held – as it seldom is in performance – for five bars, resulting in a blur of changing harmonies in the right hand, supported by unchanging Cs and Gs in the left. There was greater flexibility for changes of tonal colour on these early instruments with the added possibilities of further stops to imitate the sound of a lute, bassoon or cembalo. The 'moderator' or celeste stop (popular in Viennese pianos of the time) employed a layer of soft cloth or leather between the hammers and strings to create a muted and ethereal tonal quality. In the late eighteenth century European enthusiasm for the Turkish musical style provided piano-makers with an excuse to build a 'Janissary' stop which added drums, bells or cymbals at the touch of a pedal. A highly selective use of such an exotic device might perhaps be mooted here and there in the *Suleika* settings, D720 and D717 (songs for a Middle Eastern princess) – and then ruled out. The soft pedal of the modern instrument takes the edge off the sound, sometimes disappointingly so, but it comes nowhere near to producing this other-worldly colour. To achieve this on a modern piano the present-day accompanist must apply great subtlety of touch and the use of both pedals.

There are a number of terms to be found in the Schubert songs relating to use of the pedals:

For the sustaining pedal: 'Ped.', 'con pedale', 'Pedale', 'mit Pedale', 'mit gehobener Dämpfung' and
   also 'mit erhobener Dämpfung' (with raised dampers).
For the soft pedal (una corda): 'con sordini' (literally with mutes) and 'mit Verschiebung' (with
   displacement) – descriptive of the the mechanism where the whole keyboard is shifted sideways at the touch of the pedal so that the hammers strike only one string at a time, hence
   the term 'una corda'.

PENSA, CHE QUESTO ISTANTE   Consider that this moment
(METASTASIO) **D76** [H27]

The song exists in two versions, the second of which is discussed below:
(1) 7 September 1813; (2) 13 September 1813

(1)   'Aria: Andante maestoso'   D major   ¾   [46 bars]

(2)   D major

(45 bars)

Pensa che questo istante	Consider that this moment
Del tuo destin decide,	In your destiny will decide
Ch'oggi rinasce Alcide	Whether Alcides is today reborn
Per la futura età.	For future ages.
Pensa che adulto sei,	Consider that you are an adult,
Che sei di Giove un figlio,	That you are a son of Jove,
Che merto e non consiglio	And that your reward
La scelta tua sarà.	Will depend on your merit, not on advice.

PIETRO METASTASIO (1698–1782); poem written in 1760

This is the fifth of Schubert's fourteen Mestastasio solo settings (1812–27). See the poet's biography for a chronological list of all the Metastasio settings.

By the time Schubert composed this little work Salieri probably felt that his young pupil had studied part-writing long enough, and that he was ready to embark on the composition of solo songs. (This despite the fact that Schubert had been setting German texts at home, on his own initiative, for quite some time.) The text is taken from the poet's *Alcide al bivio* ('Hercules at the Crossroads') and is sung by the character of Fronimo, tutor of the young Hercules, to whom the aria is addressed. It is tempting to imagine the unlikely possibility that Salieri selected this text with some understanding of its significance to his own situation vis-à-vis his pupil.

The piece is mentioned in the memoirs of Schubert's schoolfriend Anton Stadler who at one time owned the autograph and who remembered that it was a 'Hausaufgabe' – a homework exercise – for the Italian master. It is, as far as it goes, a very effective piece of music. It has the remarkable virtue of built-in continuity: each phrase organically grows out of what has gone before, and rolls on to the next; nowhere does the music seem to have run its course until it reaches the final bars. And there is something about the dotted rhythm of the accompaniment that encapsulates the heroic posturing of Italian opera. In 1813 this strutting rhythm, taut and dramatic beneath a sinuous *bel canto* cantilena, was probably not yet quite as commonplace as it was later to become, but the mood and manner of this music was to pervade the world of Italian opera for a century. This little piece, so idiomatically conceived for the bass voice, might pass for Rossini, even early Verdi. Schubert's use of the bass clef for the vocal part of *Der Taucher* D77 may have had its beginnings in this exercise. It is a sign of Salieri's profitable teaching that the vocal line is supported by a bass line of such strength and independence. There are a number of corrections in the Italian prosody, clearly the maestro's observations, written into the autograph of the second version in Schubert's hand.

In this song we hear the groundwork that would enable Schubert to write so magnificently, and in a seemingly effortless Italian style, for the great bass Luigi Lablache in 1827. Perhaps less obvious is the fact that without the experience of being required to write music of this kind, Schubert would never have produced *Gretchen am Spinnrade* D118 early in his career or, to take almost a random example, *Ständchen* from *Schwanengesang* D957/4 in his final year. German lieder of this calibre have no choice but to acknowledge their Italian origin sheerly in vocal terms. Such marrying of styles is so much a Schubertian speciality that we scarcely notice when it happens. Just as the Mozartian style encompasses Italy, there is a good deal that has always been thought of as purely Schubertian (and thus Viennese) that also owes its existence to the warmer south.

Autographs:	Wienbibliothek im Rathaus, Vienna (both versions)
Publication:	Published as part of the NSA in 1969 (P743; first version)
	Published as No. 5 of *5 Canti per una sola voce* by J. P. Gotthard, Vienna in 1871 (P424; second version)
Subsequent editions:	Peters: Vol. 10/180; AGA XX 571: Vol. 10/34; NSA IV: Vol. 6/76 & 184; Bärenreiter: Vol. 5/62 (medium/low voice edition only)
Further settings:	Mikhail Glinka (1804–1857) *Pensa che questo istante* (1828)
Discography and timing:	Fischer-Dieskau I 1[8] 2'17
	Hyperion I 33[15]
	Hyperion II 2[24] 1'33 Stephen Varcoe

← *Trinklied* D75   *Son fra l'onde* D78 →

THOMAS PERCY (1729–1811)

THE POETIC SOURCE
S1 *Reliques of Ancient English Poetry* consisting of Old Heroic Ballads, Songs and other Pieces of our early Poets, (chiefly of the lyric kind.) Together with some few of later Date. The Second Edition Volume The First Printed for J. Dodsley in Pall-Mall. MDCCLXVII (1767)

The translation into German of this poem from Percy's *Reliques* was made by Johann Gottfried Herder (qv) and appeared in his *Von deutscher Art und Kunst*. Einige fliegende Blätter, Hamburg, Bode, 1773. The first section of this book is entitled 'Auszug aus einem Briefwechsel über Ossian und die Lieder alter Völker' (Excerpt from a correspondence concerning Ossian and the songs of the ancients) and the translation appears in Herder's work on pp. 25–7. The Scottish poem as it appears in Percy (beginning 'Quhy dois zour brand sae drop wi' bluid, / Edward, Edward?') is reprinted in full by Schochow (1974), Volume 1 pp. 167–9.

THE SONG
September 1827   *Eine altschottische Ballade* D923 [S1: pp. 57–9 – *Edward, Edward* – A Scottish Ballad – from a MS copy transmitted from Scotland]

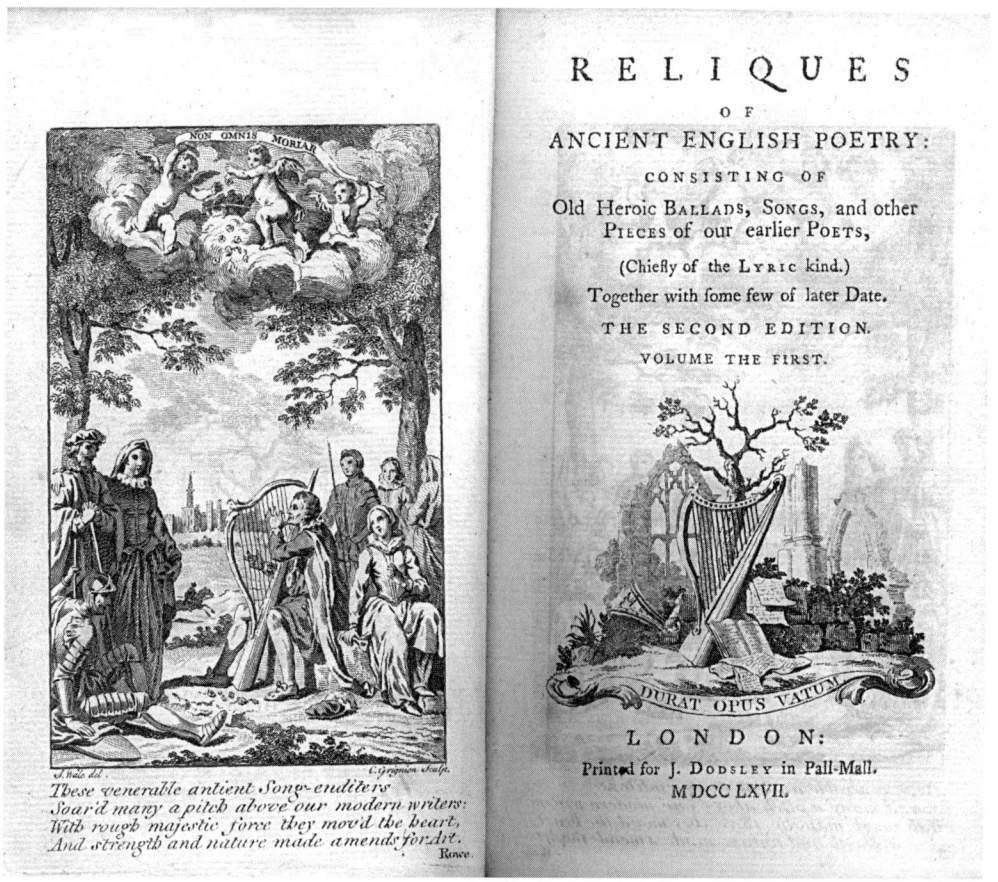

Percy's *Reliques of Ancient English Poetry* (1767).

Thomas Percy, a grocer's son, was born in Bridgnorth, Shropshire, educated at Oxford and became Bishop of Dromore in 1782. As well as publishing his own poetry he had a marked interest in world literature, translating works from the Portuguese and Icelandic languages, and poetry from Hebrew and Spanish originals. Percy's most enduring claim to fame was his good fortune in gaining access to a manuscript in mid-seventeenth-century handwriting that belonged to one Humphrey Pitt of Shifnal. This remarkable source of early ballad literature, one of the most important of its kind to have come down to modern times, is preserved in the British Museum and is known as The Percy Portfolio. Many of the poems in this manuscript first appeared in Percy's *Reliques of Ancient English Poetry* first published in 1765 – only three years after James Macpherson (qv) had published his *Fingal*, purporting to be the work of the ancient Celtic bard Ossian. Like Macpherson, Percy was attacked for being unscholarly and inauthentic but, although they appeared in a period rich in hoax and literary counterfeit, the *Reliques* have stood the test of time as a useful source of time-honoured British texts handed down by oral tradition. The *Edward* poem proved extremely popular with composers: in addition to Schubert it was set by Loewe, Brahms and Tchaikovsky. Bishop Percy died in 1811.

Die PERLE   The pearl
(JACOBI) **D466** [H292]
D minor   August 1816

(18 bars)

Es ging ein Mann zur Frühlingszeit
Durch Busch und Felder weit und breit
Um Birke, Buch' und Erle;
Der Bäume, Grün im Maienlicht,
Die Blumen drunter sah' er nicht;
Er suchte seine Perle.

A man wandered in the springtime
Through bush and field, far and wide,
Past birch, beech and alder;
He did not see the green trees in the May sunlight.
Nor the flowers below;
He was looking for his pearl.

Die Perle war sein höchstes Gut,
Er hatt' um sie des Meeres Flut
Durchschifft, und viel gelitten;
Von ihr des Lebens Trost gehofft,
Im Busen sie bewahrt, und oft
Dem Räuber abgestritten.

The pearl was his most treasured possession;
For it he had sailed the ocean's waters
And suffered much:
He hoped it would be his life's consolation;
He kept it in his heart, and often
Saved it from thieves.

[. . . 2 . . .]

[. . . 2 . . .]

Der arme Pilger! So wie er,
Geh' ich zur Frühlingszeit umher

Poor pilgrim! Like him
I wander at springtime

Um Birke, Buch' und Erle;	Past birch, beech and alder;
Des Maies Wunder seh' ich nicht;[1]	I do not see May's splendour;
Was aber, ach! was mir gebricht,	But alas, what I lack
Ist mehr als eine Perle.	Is more than a pearl.
Was mir gebricht, was ich verlor,	What I lack, what I have lost,
Was ich zum höchsten Gut erkor,	What I counted as my most treasured possession,
Ist Lieb' in treuem Herzen.	Is love from a faithful heart.
Vergebens wall' ich auf und ab;	In vain I roam hither and thither;
Doch find' ich einst ein kühles Grab,	But one day I shall find a cool grave
Das endet alle Schmerzen.	To end all my suffering.

JOHANN GEORG JACOBI (1740–1814); poem written between 1775 and 1782

This is the sixth of Schubert's seven Jacobi solo settings (1816). See the poet's biography for a chronological list of all the Jacobi settings.

Leo Black compares this song to the Friedrich Schlegel setting *Vom Mitleiden Mariä* D632; both are 'self-consciously archaic', and *Die Perle* has a 'three-part texture that could almost be an exercise in species counterpoint'. It is the penultimate of the 1816 Jacobi settings and is rather unlike the others, but it is a reminder that the musical style of the eighteenth century had a rigour that accommodated the introspective self-pity of the Romantics only with difficulty. The composer's influence here is neither Reichardt nor Zumsteeg, but the earlier C. P. E. Bach. The key of D minor has a toughness and bitterness that prophesies the Schober setting *Schatzgräbers Begehr* D761 with its walking basses, and *Gute Nacht* in *Winterreise* D911/1 – both D minor songs with the same determined stride in words and music. The Mayrhofer setting, *Wie Ulfru fischt* D525, in the same key, is similar also in terms of its binary rhythm and the gait of the piano part. The theme of both the Jacobi and Mayrhofer songs is patient, unrewarded effort.

The 'Sehnsucht' inherent in this 'Frühlingsreise' song inevitably exceeds the boundaries of an eighteenth-century pastoral frame, but it is the older garb of the setting that leaves the listener with the impression of a story sternly told. The stride accompaniment, left-hand octaves, all carefully detached as separate quavers, is best described by the unusual marking 'Schreitend', more about manner than actual speed. This is Schubert exploring the thrusting and more masculine side of his personality. The traveller described here is the antecedent of Wilhelm Müller's winter traveller and equally doomed to loneliness and disappointment. The difference is that Müller allows the protagonist of *Winterreise* to speak for himself whereas Jacobi begins by describing someone, with greater Classical distance, in the third person, before adopting a confessional tone.

Jacobi's poem has six strophes. These are all printed with the music in NSA. Translated here (and recorded for Hyperion) are 1, 2, 5 and 6.

Autograph:	Conservatoire collection, Bibliothèque Nationale, Paris
First edition:	Published as No. 31 of *Neueste Folge nachgelassener Lieder und Gesänge* by J. P. Gotthard, Vienna in 1872 (P457)
Subsequent editions:	Not in Peters; AGA XX 248: Vol. 4/153; NSA IV: Vol. 10/210
Bibliography:	Black 2003, p. 65
	Capell 1928, p. 118
	Fischer-Dieskau 1977, p. 76
	Porter 1961, pp. 117–18

[1] Jacobi has 'Des *Maien* Wunder seh' ich nicht'.

Discography and timing: Fischer-Dieskau I 7[34]   1'14   (strophes 1 and 3 only)
                              Hyperion I 8[13]
                              Hyperion II 15[19]   2'25   Sarah Walker

⟵ *Trauer der Liebe* D465   *Am Tage Aller Seelen (Litanei)* D343 ⟶

FRANCESCO PETRARCA ('PETRARCH') (1304–1374)

THE POETIC SOURCE
S1 *Blumensträusse, Italienischer, Spanischer und Portugiesischer Poesie von August Wilhelm Schlegel*, Berlin in der Realschulbuchhandlung, 1804

This book contains a majority of translations from the Italian, Spanish and Portuguese by August Wilhelm Schlegel (qv); D628 and D629 are translations by that poet. In the Petrarch section, *Or che 'l ciel e la terra e 'l vento tace* is translated as 'Nunmehr, da Himmel, Erde schweigt' and signed Gries (qv). This was set as D630. Three further Petrarch translations (on pp. 52, 56 & 67) are similarly attributed but they were not set by Schubert.

THE SONGS
November 1818   *Sonett I* 'Apollo, lebet noch dein hold Verlangen' D628 [translated A. W. von Schlegel qv] This is a translation of Sonetto XXXIV beginning 'Apollo, s'ancor vive il bel desio' [S1: p. 51, listed as Sonett XVIII]
                       Sonett II 'Allein, nachdenklich' D629 [translated by A. W. von Schlegel qv] This is a translation of Sonetto XXXV beginning 'Solo e pensoso i più deserti campi'. [S1: p. 22, Sonett XL: 'Allein nachdenklich, wie gelähmt vom Krampfe'] [There is another translation of this sonnet by Johann Mayrhofer in *Fortuna. Ein Taschenbuch für das Jahr 1828* Herausgegeben von Franz Xav. Told, Wien bey Tenderl und Manstein. This begins 'Ich wandle in entlegensten Gefilden / Gemessnen Schrittes, einsam, immer denkend']

December 1818   *Sonett III* 'Nunmehr, da Himmel Erde schweigt' D630 [translated by J. D. Gries qv] This is a translation of the Sonetto CLXIV beginning 'Or che 'l ciel e la terra e 'l vento tace.' [S1: p. 94, listed as Sonett VI]

Francesco Petrarca was among the most important of the world's poets and men of letters. He was born in Arezzo, Tuscany. When he was a boy his family moved to Avignon and he went to school in Montpellier, returning to Italy to further his studies in Bologna in 1320. After his father's death he was free to abandon the legal career that had been planned for him and took minor ecclesiastical orders in Avignon where he lived a life of elegance and dissipation. It was reputedly there on 6 April 1327 that he first saw Laura in the church of Ste Claire. Petrarch's chaste and distant love for Laura became a lifelong obsession. She has traditionally been identified as Laura de Noves but this is uncertain, and some scholars have even doubted her existence. Petrarch travelled throughout Europe, became increasingly famous in his own lifetime as a writer and thinker, and was undoubtedly one of the founders of European humanism. He mixed with the powerful and mighty, but found refuge in the beauties of the Vaucluse – as is demonstrated by his description of his climb to the summit of Mount Ventoux with his brother in 1336. As well as the poems in the vernacular

PETRARCA.

Unattributed drawing of Petrarch from August von Schlegel's *Blumensträusse Italienischer, Spanischer und Portugiesicher Poesie* (1804).

she reputedly died during the Black Death on 6 April 1348, exactly twenty-one years after the poet had first seen her.

Petrarch's *Canzoniere* are divided between the 263 poems of *Rime in vita Laura* and the 103 poems of *Rime in morte Laura*, more than 300 of which are sonnets. These were imitated everywhere, particularly among the Elizabethans. One of Petrarch's achievements was to evolve a sequence of poems where each single unit was part of a larger cycle – something that was also eventually to have significance for music (Schubert also sought a solution to this question of cyclic unity). His poems traced a biographical story, evolving from his falling in love with Laura to his final invocation of the Virgin and his trust in God as he realizes that 'worldly pleasure is a dream'. Writers from all over Europe accepted the strict discipline of Petrarchan forms and the evolution of the modern lyric owes much to him, as do the sonnet cycles of English writers like Sydney, Spenser, Drayton and Shakespeare. This poet, second only to Dante in the Italian pantheon (Boccaccio also has an honoured place there), was one of the most important founding fathers of the European literary renaissance.

for which he is most famous, he also wrote a great deal in Latin, and his writing covered many aspects of history, philosophy and religion. He continued to write of Laura even after

GOTTLIEB CONRAD PFEFFEL (1736–1809)

THE POETIC SOURCES

S1 *Sammlung Deutscher Beyspiele zur Bildung des Styls. Erster Band* Wien Im Verlagsgewölbe des k.k. Schulbücher-Verschliesses bey St. Anna in der Johannis-Gasse, 1811

This school textbook, the first of a set of two which Schubert almost certainly used (the second for three settings in 1813) contains many poems and fables by Pfeffel.

S2 *Poetische Versuche von Gottlied Conrad Pfeffel*, der Königlich Preussischen Academie der Künste und der freyen literarischen Gesellschaften des Ober-und Nieder-Rheins Mitgliede. Sechster Theil. Tübingen in der J. F. Cotta'schen Buchhandlung. 1802

S3 *Poetische Versuche von Gottlied Conrad Pfeffel*, der Königlich Preussischen Academie der Künste und der freyen literarischen Gesellschaften des Ober-und Nieder-Rheins Mitgliede. Sechster Theil. Wien, 1809. Im Verlag bey Johann Baptist Wallishasser.

This edition in six volumes (usually bound as three) was issued in Vienna in 1809 as a reprint of the German edition of Cotta. The text Schubert set is to be found towards the end of the third double volume. This unique setting of Pfeffel's work suggests that the composer was not particularly attracted to his poetry as such, but was drawn to *Der Vatermörder* on account of its subject matter.

THE SONG

26 December 1811   *Der Vatermörder* D10 [S1: pp. 40–41] [S2: pp. 65–6] [S3: pp. 48–9] In both S2 and S3 the final strophe of the ballad is different from the one Schubert set. Only in S1 is the final strophe of the poem the same, and there are also certain phrases and words that differ from other Pfeffel editions, but which Schubert clearly took from S1.

Gottlieb Conrad Pfeffel was born in Colmar in Alsace on 28 June 1736 (he was thus born, and remained, a French citizen) and studied law at the University of Halle. Afflicted with a disease of the eyes, he became blind at twenty-two but pursued a diligent career in his home town as an administrator of a Protestant institute and later an 'Académie militaire' for boys wishing to pursue careers as soldiers. He is best remembered for his *Fabeln* in which he shows sympathy for the revolutionary ideals of France. Indeed, his knowledge of French literature was immense, as might be expected of someone from Alsace. A great many of his poems have animal themes (taking their cue from Aesop and La Fontaine), the better to

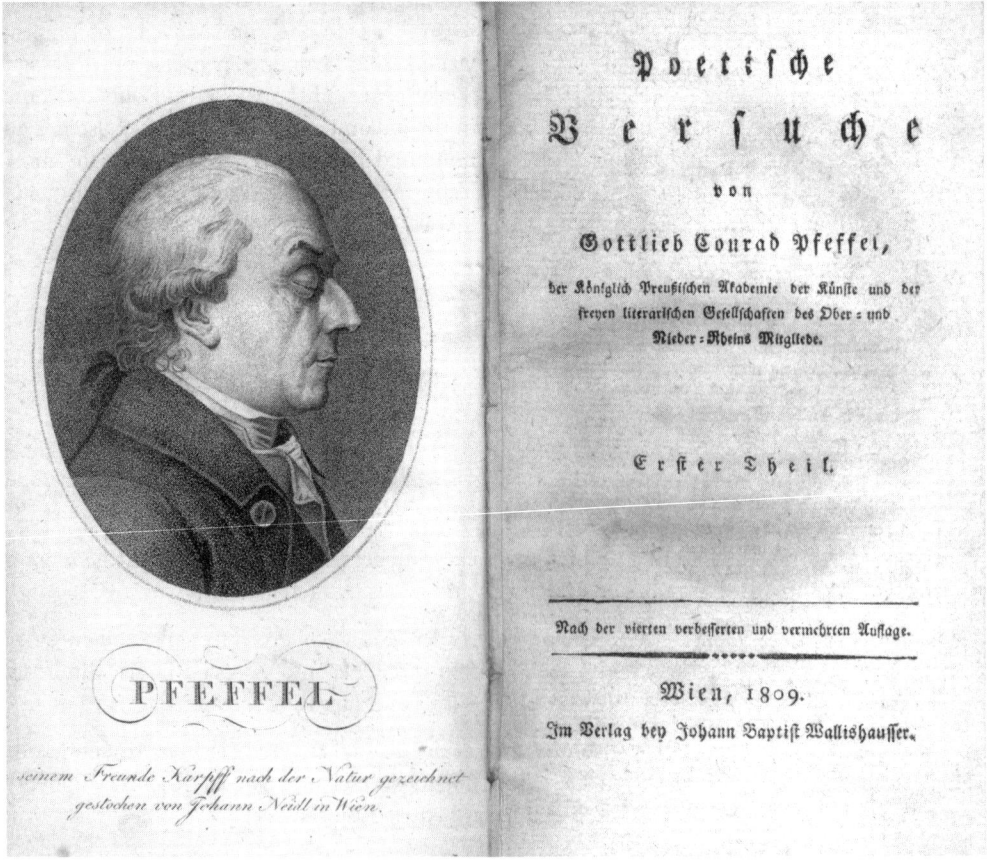

Pfeffel's *Poetische Vesuche*, Vienna (1809).

illustrate moral homilies. He was a prolific author, publishing the first instalment of his *Poetische Versuche* in Frankfurt in 1761. The second instalment contained a poem dedicated to the Viennese singer, pianist and composer Maria Theresa Paradies (1759–1824) who lost her sight in adolescence. Pfeffel imagines this famous pupil of Salieri being visited by Saint Cecilia in a poem whose sentimentality seems acceptable only because it was written for a blind person by someone with the same affliction. Pfeffel's *Prosaische Versuche* appeared posthumously in Tübingen in 1810. Some of his work has been thought interesting enough to be republished in Germany in the last twenty years. He died on 1 May 1809.

PFLICHT UND LIEBE

(GOTTER) **D467** [H287]
(Fragment) C minor   August 1816

Duty and love

(27 bars)

Du, der ewig um mich trauert,
Nicht allein, nicht unbedauert,
Jüngling, seufzest du;
Wann vor Schmerz die Seele schauert,
Lüget meine Stirne Ruh.

Deines nassen Blickes Flehen
Will ich, darf ich nicht verstehn;[1]
Aber zürne nicht!
Was ich fühle, zu gestehen,
Untersagt mir meine Pflicht.

[...2...]

Freund, schweif' aus mit deinen Blicken!
Lass dich die Natur entzücken,
Die dir sonst gelacht!
Ach, sie wird auch mich beglücken,
Wenn sie dich erst glücklich macht.

Trauter Jüngling, lächle wieder!
Sieh, beim Grusse frohen Sangs[2]
Steigt die Sonn' empor!
Trübe sank sie gestern nieder;
Herrlich geht sie heut' hervor.

O youth, who endlessly grieves for me,
You do not sigh
Alone and unpitied;
When your soul is racked with pain
My brow's calm is feigned.

I will not, should not understand
The entreaty of your moist eyes;
But do not be angry!
What I feel, my duty
Forbids me to confess.

[...2...]

Friend, avert your eyes!
Take pleasure in nature,
Which always used to smile on you.
Ah, it will make me happy too
Once it has made you happy.

Dearest youth, smile once more!
See, the sun is rising,
Greeted by joyous songs!
Yesterday it set bedimmed;
Today it emerges in splendour.

[1] Gotter writes 'verste*hen*'.
[2] Schubert unaccountably changes Gotter's 'Sieh, beim Grusse *froher Lieder*' (with its rhyme with the line above) to 'Sangs' preferring, perhaps, the strong alliteration of 'Sangs', 'steigt' and 'Sonn'' which links the power of song with the rising of the sun.

FRIEDRICH WILHELM GOTTER (1746–1797); poem written in 1774

This is Schubert's only setting of a Gotter text. See the poet's biography.

This fragment of twenty-seven bars, probably once a complete song, was written on the other side of a sketch for *An die untergehende Sonne* D457. It is perhaps too fanciful to suppose that Schubert was attracted to the text because it had some relevance to his own relationship to Therese Grob with whom he was said to have been in love. Nevertheless, the composer might have imagined the words spoken to him by a young girl who felt it her duty to discourage his suit; she offers him comfort by directing his gaze away from her and towards the beauties of nature.

Gotter was famous as a librettist, and the anguished feel of this music suggests a *bel canto* opera aria, the piano part in flowing triplets reinforcing this impression. It is as if the young composer is heeding earlier advice (from Salieri perhaps) to concentrate on creating beautiful vocal lines rather than attempting to fill the accompaniment with too much distracting detail. (It is not hard to imagine Salieri taking Schubert to task for writing over-complicated accompaniments.) The piano writing is supportive of the harmonic twists and turns of the vocal line and makes no commentary of its own to deepen the significance of the setting. It is left to the voice part to paint emotion with such devices as the expressive downward sigh (A flat to D natural) on the word 'seufzest' (at b. 8) in the first verse.

The composer uses two of Gotter's verses to make a single musical strophe. The work is technically a fragment only because the final bar of the vocal line is lacking, as well as any postlude. Max Friedlaender provided these when the song was first printed in Volume 7 of the Peters Edition. Gotter's original poem is in six strophes. Verses three and four tell us that the lovers had 'played like lambs' together, and that the young man is himself to blame for the break-up of the relationship because of his new love for Philaide. It is possible that Schubert brought his setting to a close before lines that were scarcely apposite to his own emotional situation at the time. The 'fragment' as it stands is simply a song about a girl who has decided to end a relationship. But Friedlaender clearly believed that Schubert had intended to write a strophic song (which is not at all certain) and while ignoring the third and fourth strophes he uses the last two (the fifth and sixth) of Gotter's poem to create a second musical verse. This version was recorded in the Hyperion Schubert Edition with text as printed above. In the NSA the song remains the fragment without an ending: strophes 3–6 are printed at the end of the song, and only the first two strophes appear as underlay to music.

Autograph:	Wienbibliothek im Rathaus, Vienna (bb. 1–27)
First edition:	Published as Vol. 7 no. 17 in Friedlaender's edition by Peters, Leipzig in 1885 with a newly composed piano postlude by Friedlaender (also serving as an interlude between verses) (P488) Subsequently published in its original form as part of the AGA in 1895
Subsequent editions:	Peters: Vol. 7/37; AGA XX 593: Vol. 10/104; NSA IV: Vol. 10/284
Discography and timing:	Fischer-Dieskau —
	Hyperion I 17¹³
	Hyperion II 15¹⁴ 2'52 Lucia Popp

← *Aus 'Diego Manazares': 'Ilmerine'* D458   *An Chloen* D462 →

PFLÜGERLIED
(Salis-Seewis) **D392** [H237]
C major   March 1816

Ploughman's song

(16 bars)

Arbeitsam und wacker,
Pflügen wir den Acker,
Singend, auf und ab.
Sorgsam trennen wollen
Wir die lockern Schollen,
Unsrer Saaten Grab.

Auf und abwärts ziehend
Furchen wir, stets fliehend
Das erreichte Ziel.
Wühl', o Pflugschaar, wühle!
Aussen drückt die Schwüle;
Tief im Grund ists kühl.

[...]

Säet, froh im Hoffen;
Gräber harren offen,
Fluren sind bebaut;
Deckt mit Egg' und Spaten
Die versenkten Saaten,
Und dankt Gott vertraut!

Gottes Sonne leuchtet,
Lauer Regen feuchtet
Das entkeimte Grün.
Flock', o Schnee und strecke
Deine Silberdecke
Schirmend drüber hin!

[... 3 ...]

Hardworking and stouthearted
We plough the fields,
Singing as we go.
Carefully we separate
The loose clods,
The grave for our seeds.

Moving up and down
We make the furrows, always turning back
From our achieved goal.
Dig, o ploughshare, dig!
Outside the sultriness is oppressive;
Deep in the earth it is cool.

[...]

Sow in joyful hope;
Open graves lie waiting,
Fields are tilled.
Cover the scattered seeds
With harrow and spade,
And give heartfelt thanks to God.

God's sun shines;
Warm rain moistens
The burgeoning green shoots.
Come, flaky snow, and drape
Over them
Your protecting silver blanket.

[... 3 ...]

Johann Gaudenz von Salis-Seewis (1762–1834); poem written in 1794/8

This is the fourth of Schubert's thirteen Salis-Seewis solo settings (1816–?21). See the poet's biography for a chronological list of all the Salis-Seewis settings.

This is one of Schubert's work-songs, a relative of *Fischerweise* D881, *Tischlerlied* D274 and the two settings of *Fischerlied* D351 and D562 (also to a Salis-Seewis text), and so on. Those who make an honest day's living by working with their hands are usually given to a touch of amateur philosophizing. A common theme is that of Death the Leveller: all men are equal because they all end up in the same place – the grave. The inevitability of death features high on the list of German ruminations (even when drink is not on the agenda) and this song is no exception; the coolness of the earth mentioned at the end of the poem is a refuge from a life of hard labour and a staging post for the good in heart who await resurrection. Schubert has a way of musically suggesting the slower thought process – in this case big feet and a heavy tread are signs of the amiable rustic who is the salt of the earth. Shakespeare handles some of his working-class characters in a similar manner, a lesson that was not lost on the German-speaking poets. Salis-Seewis was Swiss of course, and an aristocrat to boot, but his observations on the life of the 'little' people are what Schubert takes to his heart.

The strong bass line of crotchets cuts a furrow through the song's simple texture. A task like ploughing is essentially repetitive and we hear this in the song's four-square structure and its solid, no-nonsense sequences. The man here is a far less mercurial, and certainly less ambitious, German cousin of Britten's 'flaxen-headed' ploughboy who has his eye on a more important destiny. Schubert's ploughman is supremely contented with his lot; we hear his whistle in the little piano interlude in bb. 7 and 8. This figure descends into the piano's left hand at bb. 10 and 12 as if such cheeriness were being ploughed into the soil. Towards the end of each verse (bb. 13–16) there is an indication of hearty musical pleasure in the accomplishment of his task, a descent from G to middle C, first in the voice then echoed by the piano, as if the earth were being fertilized and enriched with music. The pianistic layout is untypical but entirely appropriate to the subject.

This is one of the seventeen songs that formed part of the lieder album for Therese Grob, probably intended as a birthday gift, put together by the composer in November 1816. A number of contemporary copies of the song exist (a sign that it was popular in Schubert's circle) but the NSA regards the Grob album source as the most reliable.

There are eight strophes in Salis-Seewis's poem. All of these appear as underlay to music in the NSA. Translated here (and recorded for the Hyperion Edition) are 1, 2, 4 and 5. Strophes 7 and 8, when the ploughman turns his thoughts to death and burial, may seem less suited to the mood of a song of this kind, but Schubert's robust and effortlessly masterful music can encompass even these darker thoughts.

Autograph:	In private possession (part of the Therese Grob album)
First edition:	Published as part of the AGA in 1895 (P626)
Subsequent editions:	Not in Peters; AGA XX 197: Vol. 4/58; NSA IV: Vol. 10/64
Discography and timing:	Fischer-Dieskau I 6[20] 1'15 (3 strophes)
	Hyperion I 23[4]
	Hyperion II 13[11] 1'48 Christoph Prégardien

← *Fischerlied* D351   *Die Einsiedelei* D393 →

PHIDILE

(CLAUDIUS) **D500** [H318]
G♭ major   November 1816

Phidile

(15 bars)

Ich war erst sechzehn Sommer alt,	I was only sixteen summers old,
Unschuldig und nichts weiter,	Nothing more than an innocent,
Und kannte nichts als unsern Wald,	And knew nothing but our woods,
Als Blumen, Gras und Kräuter.	Flowers, grass and herbs.
Da kam ein fremder Jüngling her;	Then a youthful stranger came along;
Ich hatt' ihn nicht verschrieben,	I had not bid him come
Und wusste nicht wohin noch her;	And knew not where to turn.
Der kam und sprach von Lieben.	He came and spoke of love.
[. . . 3 . . .]	[. . . 3 . . .]
Er ging mir allenthalben nach,	He followed me everywhere,
Und drückte mir die Hände,	And pressed my hands,
Und sagte immer O und Ach,	And kept saying 'Oh' and 'Alas',
Und küsste sie behende.	And kissed them quickly.
Ich sah ihn einmal freundlich an,	One day I looked at him kindly
Und fragte, was er meinte;	And asked what he meant;
Da fiel der junge schöne Mann	Then the fair young man
Mir um den Hals und weinte.	Fell upon my neck and wept.
Das hatte niemand noch getan;	No one had ever done that;
Doch war's mir nicht zuwider	But I did not find it unpleasant,
Und meine beiden Augen sahn	And my two eyes
In meinen Busen nieder.	Looked down at my bosom.
Ich sagt' ihm nicht ein einzig Wort,	I did not say a single word to him
Als ob ich's übel nähme,	To indicate that I took it amiss,
Kein einzig's, und – er flohe fort;	Not a single word – and he fled;
Wenn er doch wieder käme!	If only he would come back again!

MATTHIAS CLAUDIUS (1740–1815); poem issued in 1770

This is the eighth of Schubert's thirteen Claudius solo settings (1816–17). See the poet's biography for a chronological list of all the Claudius settings.

Claudius takes his readership on a journey that combines discreet sexual excitement with the narrative modesty of an ingénue. The poet was a good-hearted and solid citizen, no pornographer, but he cannot resist toying with a comedy of double standards where sophistication masquerades as innocence. How innocent is this Phidile exactly? Her name promises no more reassurance in this sphere than if it had been Bilitis (as hymned by Pierre Louÿs and Debussy). The schoolgirl of precocious development (who teases her public as to how great her experience of life may, or may not, be) is disguised as a Greek nymph. There is a tradition, recounted by Deutsch in the first (1951) edition of his catalogue, that Schubert's mother used to sing an early setting of these words by the Bohemian composer Josef Anton Steffan (Štěpán), published in 1778. If this was so, we can only wonder what she made of it, and whether the poem in any way reflected her own experience. She was certainly a lot older than sixteen, and already 'on the shelf', when she accepted a proposal of marriage from the composer's father – someone rather beneath her within the social ranks of their shared Silesian background.

Haydn, with all the insouciance of the Enlightenment, wrote a number of lieder and part-songs about nymphs and shepherds that would have made Schubert's Biedermeier middle classes blush. In an attempt to court popular success with a more ordinary public, Schubert was to compose two substantial, and somewhat suggestive, songs (the words by Johann Gabriel Seidl) in the last year of his life: *Die Unterscheidung* D866/1 and *Die Männer sind mechant* D866/3. While the Claudius poem has a gentle sweetness that is a long way from Seidl's manner, it is an early example of a comedy song that depends greatly on the daring of singer and accompanist for interpretation.

The marking is a rather provocative (at least for Schubert) 'Unschuldig' ('Innocent'), but this obviously applies more to the green girl who sings the first verse than to the young lady, learning fast, who sings the last. Schubert's setting of that very word 'unschuldig' in the song's second line (bb. 2–3) incorporates an arch high note which is the musical equivalent of the sort of look from a wide-eyed ingénue that would suggest she is more delighted than shocked. The melody in G flat and the gently undulating accompaniment are all that might be desired of a pastoral song along the lines of Haydn's *My mother bids me bind my hair*. The postlude with its prancing and whimsical inflection at b. 14 is one of the more extended and inventive in the strophic songs of 1816.

Walther Dürr mentions the popularity of this text with eighteenth-century composers such as Hiller, Reichardt (his setting also marked 'Unschuldig'), Schulz and Zumsteeg. Even Beethoven (in a letter to the publisher Schott in March 1825) quotes the poem's second line in humorous reference to the innocence of his youth. In Othmar Schoeck's more modern setting the unusual alternation of $\frac{3}{4}$ and $\frac{6}{4}$ time illustrates the narrator's loss of equilibrium as she breathlessly discovers the heady facts of life. *Phidylé*, the sumptuous setting by Henri Duparc of Leconte de Lisle's poem about an equally generous nymph (1882), might be said to represent the culmination of a long musical tradition inspired by the pastoral cavorting of ancient Greece. Reichardt made a setting of a different Claudius poem (also entitled *Phidile*); the poem comes later (Volume 3, p. 54) in the poet's *Asmus omnia*. The full title is 'Phidile. Als sie nach der Kopulation allein in ihr Kämmerlein gegangen war' (. . . as she went alone into her bedroom following her marriage) and seems to have been written as a sequel to the first, an amalgamation of the worlds of the nymph and shepherdess and Christian religion. The poet appears to have breathed a huge sigh of relief as he thus married off his potentially ruined maid. Gottfried August Bürger wrote a poem called *Robert* which re-tells Claudius's story from the would-be seducer's point of view; in the opening line Robert confesses to being a 'Springinsfeld' (a young rogue), a word that also appears in the opening of *Die Männer sind mechant* mentioned above. In that case the 'Springinsfeld' is spied on by a semi-horrified ingénue as he meets a girl (perhaps a professional) who is prepared to accede to his desires.

There are nine strophes in the poem by Claudius, all printed as musical underlay by the NSA. Translated here (and performed in the Hyperion Edition) are 1, 2, 6, 7, 8 and 9. Strophes 3, 4 and 5 describe the long hair, eyes and face of Phidile's handsome seducer and are thus more or less expendable to the narrative.

Autograph:	Missing or lost
First edition:	Published as part of the AGA in 1895 (P661)
Subsequent editions:	Not in Peters; AGA XX 279: Vol. 4/242; NSA IV: Vol. 11/34
Further settings:	Johann Freidrich Reichardt (1752–1814) *Phidile* (1789)
	Johann Rudolph Zumsteeg (1760–1802) *Phidile* (1805)
	Othmar Schoeck (1886–1957) *Phidile* Op. 52 no. 2 (1937)
Discography and timing:	Fischer-Dieskau —
	Hyperion I 17²⁰
	Hyperion II 16²² 4'20 Lucia Popp

← *Am Grabe Anselmos* D504   *Zufriedenheit* D501 →

PHILOKTET   Philoctetes
(MAYRHOFER) **D540** [H350]
B minor   March 1817

(81 bars)

Da sitz' ich ohne Bogen,	I sit here without my bow,
Und starre in den Sand.	Staring at the sand.
Was tat ich dir, Ulysses?	What did I do to you, Ulysses,
Dass du sie mir entwandt	That you took from me
Die Waffe, die den Trojern[1]	The weapon that was the harbinger
Des Todes Bote war;	Of death to the Trojans,
Die auf der wüsten Insel	That gave me sustenance
Mir Unterhalt gebar.	On this desolate island?
Es rauschen Vögelschwärme	Flocks of birds sweep
Mir überm greisen Haupt;[2]	Over my grey head;
Ich greife nach dem Bogen—	I reach for my bow:
Umsonst – er ist geraubt.	In vain, it has been stolen.

[1] Mayrhofer writes 'Die Waffe, die *dem Feinde*'. For an explanation of the background to these alternative Mayrhofer readings see Editorial Note at the beginning of Johann MAYRHOFER.
[2] Mayrhofer writes 'Mir *übers greise* Haupt'.

Aus dichtem Busche raschelt	The brown stag rushes
Der braune Hirsch hervor:	From the dense thicket;
Ich strecke leere Arme	I stretch bare arms
Zur Nemesis empor.	Up to Nemesis.
Du schlauer König scheue	Cunning king, beware
Der Göttin Rächerblick!	The vengeful goddess's gaze!
Erbarme dich – und stelle	Take pity
Den Bogen mir zurück.	And restore to me my bow.

JOHANN MAYRHOFER (1787–1836)

This is the twenty-first of Schubert's forty-seven Mayrhofer solo settings (1814–24). See the poet's biography for a chronological list of all the Mayrhofer settings.

Philoctetes was a tragedy by Sophocles, produced in Athens in 409 BC. Perhaps Mayrhofer studied this play in the original Greek but it is more likely, as with his translation from Aeschylus where he had Stolberg's efforts to hand, that he read it in German. Lessing had published a life of Sophocles as early as 1790, and the first printed editions of the ancient master's plays in German translation date from 1815. Mayrhofer was almost certainly abreast of these recent developments – after all, no book was published in Austria, or even allowed in, without permission from the censor's office, where the poet worked for many years.

Philoctetes, in possession of the bow of Heracles, set out for the Trojan war in command of seven ships from Methone, Thaumacia, Meliboea and Olizon. Later versions of the story describe him as having been one of Helen's suitors and consequently obliged to take part in the Trojan expedition; all we know from Homer is that he failed to reach Troy because he was wounded by a snakebite during his journey. According to some writers Philoctetes had inherited the bow of Heracles from his father Poeas; others say he obtained it, and its never-erring poisoned arrows, from Heracles himself in gratitude for help in setting fire to his funeral pyre on Mount Oeta. The story in the later versions ascribes the catastrophe of the snakebite to the serpent guarding the temple of the goddess Athena on the island of Chyrse, and to the goddess Hera who was furious at Philoctetes for having helped Heracles. Following his terrible injury, Philoctetes was left by his men on the island of Lemnos. The archer's incessant and pitiful moaning had alarmed the sailors and hardened their hearts to his fate; in some accounts the putrid smell of the ulcerated wound also played a part in their decision to desert their commander. This harsh abandonment was sanctioned by command of the Artreidae and by Odysseus (Ulysses) himself who proves to be the villain of the Philoctetes story.

Finding himself thus alone on his inhospitable island, the archer was at least in possession of his bow and arrows, and could still hunt – despite his limited mobility. In some versions of the story Philoctetes perished in these harsh conditions, but another legend has it that he remained on Lemnos for nine years of the Trojan war. In yet another version he was cured by the local priests of Hephaestus, and recovered well enough to undertake military expeditions that would eventually leave him ruler of the entire region, including Lemnos itself. In the tenth year on the battle front in Troy a seer revealed that the city would fall only with the help of Heracles' bow and arrows. Odysseus and the honourable Neoptolemus, second husband of Andromache after Hector's demise, were dispatched to Lemnos to bring the bow back. Of the two, Odysseus was more ruthlessly determined to achieve this end, even if it meant leaving Philoctetes helpless (for in Sophocles' play he had remained a cripple). Philoctetes protested that he was in too much pain to undertake the journey back to Troy, and a huge argument ensued between the crafty Odysseus and Neoptolemus who had the scruples of an old soldier and demurred from betraying a comrade. Odysseus made off with the bow and it is at this point in the story that Mayrhofer's poem takes up the thread from Sophocles and presents us with Philoctetes incandescent with helpless rage.

As befits a song with a very long off-stage prologue, we are plunged into the middle of the story with chords that manage to sound angry and impotent at the same time. They are far from their home key of B minor, and despite their rage they, like Philoctetes, seem stuck in one place. John Reed observes that in the opening vocal line (bb. 5–9) the composer uses his 'favourite tonal image of fate/death, plunging down from B minor to the dominant F sharp major'. Philoctetes is not depicted as a complicated character – he has the ancient virtue of unornamented directness, and the barren island where he has lived for so long has thinned down his vocal line to the bone: 'Die auf der wüsten Insel' (bb. 20–22) is supported by an accompaniment of under-nourished, white-faced minims. The most exceptional harmonic change of gear in the song is at the second verse where D major suddenly veers to a B flat pedal in the key of E flat minor (a new key signature at b. 31). The juxtaposition of tonalities is eerily modern, but the music for the flight of birds (from b. 33) now safe from Philoctetes' bow, with its majestic, whirring accompaniment rooted on solid blocks of chords, seems to be a homage to that rare old bird Gluck. The movement of the stag in the bushes, two bars before the words that describe it (bb. 47–8), is delicate and fleet. The invoking of Nemesis from b. 51 lacks total conviction, and it is no surprise to discover at the beginning of Mayrhofer's third verse that Schubert has composed this piece to something of a classical formula: a *da capo* aria. The music of grounded anger returns, as does the fate/death motif. The demand for the return of the bow is imperious, mirrored by the peremptory four-bar postlude.

To continue the story beyond the song, Neoptolemus, ashamed to have been associated with the treachery of his colleague, returns the bow to Philoctetes, hotly pursued by Odysseus who is nearly shot by the wounded archer wielding his newly restored weapon. In the end Heracles, by now a god, intervenes and commands Philoctetes to go with the bow to Troy where he is promised a cure. The song's protagonist is eventually healed by the surgeon Machaon (with Apollo standing by as anaesthetist) who cuts out the wound, washes it with wine and applies healing herbs. After his recovery Philoctetes helps win the Trojan war by slaying Paris, after which Troy falls into Greek hands. The famous archer ends his days on the coast of Italy building the cities of Petelia and Crimissa; in the latter he erects a temple to Apollo Alaeus to whom he dedicates his bow.

Mayrhofer delighted in looking at the classics from a new perspective, a means of measuring – and not generally favourably – the political and moral climate of the present times against that of the ancients. The appeal of this particular story to the poet is difficult to assess; he perhaps equated Philoctetes' bow with the writer's art, the only thing that enables the otherwise handicapped artist to survive. The attempt to stifle a poet's writing and condemn him to censored silence is an offence against the gods – like stealing the bow away from the helpless Philoctetes. That the bow is restored to its rightful owner by someone other than the power-crazed authorities might be seen as a metaphor for the idea that there is still room for decency and dignity in the way that artists are treated. Goethe was also fascinated by this Philoctetes story: in 1826 he made a little study ('Philoktetes, dreifach') comparing the Sophocles play with what has come down to us (through the criticisms of Dion) concerning the vanished plays on the subject by Aeschylus (the first to tackle the story as a drama) and Euripides. The three parallel columns that Goethe employed for this study are an example of how he tried to solve even literary problems while employing the precision of his scientific training. The Philoctetes Project presented by 'The Theater of War' based in New York City combines readings of Sophocles' play with

discussions and workshops that explore the relationship between the war-wounded and their
carers in present-day conflicts.

Autograph: Wienbibliothek im Rathaus, Vienna (first draft, first 37 bars)
First edition: Published as Book 11 no. 3 of the *Nachlass* by Diabelli, Vienna in
                              April 1831 (P272)
Subsequent editions: Peters: Vol. 5/45; AGA XX 307: Vol. 5/56; NSA IV: Vol. 11/105
Bibliography: Capell 1928, p. 137
Discography and timing: Fischer-Dieskau I 9[23]   2'12
                              Hyperion I 14[9]
                              Hyperion II 18[1]   3'31   Thomas Hampson

← *Die Nacht* D534   *Memnon* D541 →

PIANISTS

The lied is as much a piano form as a vocal one, and there have always been pianists who feel
happier playing song accompaniments, and working with singers, than playing the solo and
chamber music repertory.

The first important accompanist was Schubert himself. A frequent performer at musical
parties, the so-called Schubertiads, it seems that the composer appeared only seven times in public
concerts: 22 April 1827 in Vienna playing *Normans Gesang* D846; 29 April 1827 in Vienna playing
Der Einsame D800; 8 September in Graz playing *Normans Gesang*; 16 March 1828 playing the
same song again in Vienna; 26 March 1828 playing at his own private concert in Vienna where
he accompanied *Der Kreuzzug* D932, *Die Sterne* (Leitner), *Fischerweise* D881, *Fragment aus dem
Aeschylus*, *Ständchen* (Grillparzer), *Auf dem Strom* D943, *Die Allmacht* D852 and *Schlachtgesang*
D912; and on 20 April 1828, *Auf dem Strom* again in Vienna. The composer appeared on countless
other, less formal, occasions as well as those famous private recitals given in the monasteries and
great houses of Upper Austria when he accompanied the baritone Vogl. He wrote to his father
and stepmother from Steyr on 25 July 1825 where his manner of piano playing occasioned some
uniquely self-analytical commentary: 'Several people assured me that the keys become singing
voices under my hands which, if true, pleases me greatly, since I cannot endure the accursed
chopping in which even distinguished pianoforte players indulge and which delights neither the
ear nor the mind.' If this referred to his piano playing in general there is a further revelatory remark
regarding his duo with Vogl: 'The manner in which Vogl sings and I accompany, as though we
were one at such a moment, is something new and unheard-of for these people.' Albert Stadler,
writing thirty years after Schubert's death, described his friend's playing thus:

> *A beautiful touch, a quiet hand, clear, neat playing, full of insight and feeling. He still belonged
> to the old school of good pianoforte players, whose fingers had not yet begun to attack the poor
> keys like birds of prey.*

Schubert was also clearly able to inspire the singers with whom he worked: on one occasion
in 1822 the composer, initially unwilling, was persuaded to accompany Franz Stohl in the song
Der Zwerg. 'Schubert's accompanying enflamed me,' wrote Stohl many years later, 'and I
performed with true enthusiasm.' In July 1825 Anton Ottenwalt, writing to Josef von Spaun,
remarked of the composer's performances of his German dances during Schubert's holiday
sojourn in Linz that 'they take on incredible life under his hands'. On the other hand the young

Ferdinand Hiller, pupil of Hummel, averred that 'Schubert's piano playing, in spite of a not inconsiderable fluency, was very far from being that of a master'. By the standards of the solo pianist Schubert was no virtuoso, but he had other things to offer – imaginative understanding, empathy and experience in making the piano stand in for the thousand other things it must represent and illustrate in the song repertoire.

In this way it may be said that Schubert was the first lied accompanist, and since his time almost every great song composer (Brahms, Britten, Debussy, Fauré, Mendelssohn, Poulenc, Strauss, Wolf) has written accompaniments for himself to play. (Most would have felt less happy as advocates of their solo piano music.) Nevertheless, even in Schubert's time there were others who gladly took on the task of playing his songs. At the musical gatherings of the Kiesewetters and of Ignaz Sonnleithner, and at the evening gatherings of the Musikverein, the Czech composer **Ian Václav Voříšek** (1791–1825), whom Schubert knew as Johann Hugo Worzischek, had a considerable reputation as an accompanist. After his untimely death his place at these regular concerts was taken by Schubert's close friend **Johann Baptist Jenger** (1793–1856) who was a fine musician and faithful friend to the composer from as early as 1817 (it was thanks to Jenger that Schubert visited Graz in 1827, making the rewarding acquaintance there of the pianist Marie Pachler). Apart from playing at various concerts during Schubert's lifetime, Jenger was the regular accompanist of Baron von Schönstein after the composer's death (*see* SINGERS). Faust Pachler, son of Marie, made a fitting tribute to Jenger in 1866: 'The name of this man became inextricably interwoven with the history of music-making in Vienna. Although an amateur pianist of no more than average accomplishments, Jenger was drawn into all circles of society, including eventually the very highest, because he knew better than anyone else how to provide sensitive

Johann Baptist Jenger, lithograph by Josef Teltscher (1801–1837).

accompaniment for the singer's voice and how to transpose music, while playing, to another key.' Leopold von Sonnenleithner observed that Jenger continued to accompany Schubert songs most beautifully after the composer's death, as did the young lady whose health had once given everyone in the Schubert circle so much cause for concern, and for whom Schubert had written a little cantata in praise of her recovery, **Irene Kiesewetter** (1811–1872) who became Baroness Prokesch (qv *Al par del ruscelletto* D936).

Another composer with a Graz connection was **Anselm Hüttenbrenner** (1794–1868) (qv composers) – gifted, good-looking and charming, but ultimately jealous of Schubert's success. Hüttenbrenner must have had considerable keyboard facility as he accompanied *Erlkönig*, clearly when Schubert himself declined to do so in public. He played for performances of this song by Johann Michael Vogl (baritone) – notably on 7 March 1821 at the Kärntnertortheater – and Ludwig Tietze (tenor) in Vienna, as well as in Graz where he also accompanied Jakob Wilhelm Rauscher in *Der Wanderer* D489.

After Schubert's death, at the Schubertiads organized by Josef Wilhelm Witteczek in the Wallfischgasse, Vogl was accompanied by a distinguished lawyer and botanist, **Emmanuel Mikschik**.

Karl Maria von Bocklet, photograph, 1873.   Josef von Gahy with a portable piano, a comic sketch by
                                                   Moritz von Schwind, 1830.

It is clear that even in Schubert's day some pianists were delighted to play the composer's solo piano pieces or chamber music, but less happy to accompany singers. Such a virtuoso was **Karl Maria von Bocklet** (1801–1881), born in Prague and of enormous importance to Schubert as a performer of the solo piano sonatas and pieces, and difficult chamber music such as the two piano trios and the *Fantasie* for violin and piano D959. It is perhaps significant that Bocklet had started off as a violinist and had first attracted Beethoven's attention as such.

Schubert was closer, however, to another, somewhat older, Viennese pianist, **Josef von Gahy** (1793–1864), known as an exceedingly modest man and with whom Schubert delighted in playing piano duets. Gahy was an indefatigable pianist for the social gatherings of the Schubertians, as was the composer himself, and would energize the whole room with his playing for dancing. His nickname was 'Gahidi', a variation on the sound of the linnet that opens the song *Hänflings Liebeswerbung* D552 ('Ahidi! ich liebe'), but there is no record of Gahy's having accompanied singers. According to Kreissle von Hellborn (*The Life of Franz Schubert*, trans. Coleridge, p. 132), not only did Gahy 'learn a great deal that he had never known before, but the pure rapid playing, the bold free conception, the alternately tender and fiery energetic playing of his short, fat friend raised his spirits to the highest pitch'. Here was a perspicacious solo pianist indeed – not too proud to learn from someone whose performing métier was song accompaniment.

On 19 March 1821 the young virtuoso pianist **Karl Schunke** (b. 1801 in Magdeburg) accompanied the tenor Franz Ruess in a performance of *Erlkönig* as part of a concert. The review in the *Wiener Zeitschrift* indicates that he had a few difficulties ('Anstrengungen') in playing the part. On 8 September of the same year Schunke accompanied Vogl in the same song at the Kärntnertortheater. Karl Schunke was the first cousin of the composer Ludwig Schunke who was to become one of Robert Schumann's dearest friends.

Carl Loewe made a sensation in Vienna in 1844 (he was called 'the Schubert of the North') when he accompanied his own singing voice at the piano. Robert Schumann had his wife Clara to play his songs (as well as his solo piano music); Brahms was a dab hand at accompanying singers, as was Wolf. In Schubert's time, and for decades afterwards, accompanying songs in social situations (often sight-reading) was simply regarded as musical good manners (and the result of an appropriate musical education) when there was a gathering of like-minded music lovers. The actual quality of the playing varied from minimal competence to what must have been the dazzling spectacle of the young Mendelssohn accompanying *Erlkönig*. As the lied gradually became independent of social circumstances and was more regularly heard in the concert hall, the task of accompanying songs, the job of the so-called *Liedbegleiter* or song accompanist, assumed an increasing importance. Eventually it would turn into more or less a profession in its own right – but to this day it remains the lucky artist who can make a living from full-time recital work. Most accompanists must have a portfolio of jobs in order to make a living – these may include teaching (almost de rigueur), church work, choral training and, of course, operatic coaching and even writing.

Neither Jenger nor Hüttenbrenner was a full-time concert accompanist. The task of accompanying songs usually fell to those who were familiar with the singer and their ways – thus operatic coaches and conductors. There was a strong tradition in Germany and Austria (as in Italy) whereby singers would appear in recitals with a piano-playing colleague, the maestro who had helped them prepare their operatic roles. This was also the period when opera conductors, indeed all aspiring conductors, worked in the opera house in order to learn about singers and singing at first hand. Playing the piano for recitals and social occasions was simply part of the job. Accompanists, such as **Hanns Udo Müller** (d. 1943) (Gerhard Hüsch's long-standing duo partner with whom the singer recorded Schubert's song-cycles for EMI between the two world wars), **Sebastian Peschko** (1909–1987, the pianist of Heinrich Schlusnus), the composer **Manfred Gurlitt** (1890–1973, Heinrich Rehkemper's pianist, and later Hüsch's) and the conductor **Ferdinand Leitner** (1912–1996), were inheritors of a tradition of training and versatility that produced efficient, if not always inspired, results. This multi-faceted 'Kapellmeister' role was brought to its most distinguished level in modern times by the conductor and lied pianist **Wolfgang Sawallisch** (1923–2013), who inherited the mantle of Richard Strauss, if not as a composer, then as Bavaria's favourite son in terms of opera conducting and song accompaniment. Sawallisch as a pianist worked with artists such as Dietrich Fischer-Dieskau, Margaret Price and Thomas Hampson. The recordings of Ian Bostridge with the conductor **Antonio Pappano** are a recent British collaboration in the same tradition.

By the second decade of the twentieth century, and with the beginning of the recording industry, accompanists began to come into their own. It was still a struggle to be taken seriously, with a sometimes insurmountable prejudice in the music world against artists who volunteered for a role that seemed demeaning in the eyes of those who valued only solo pianists. As a result a number of rather good pianists were employed by the early record labels as hacks, filling the roles of conductors, arrangers, pianists. An example is the unsung **Friedrich Kark** who worked for Odeon and Parlophone *c.* 1918: much of his work was anonymous and not even acknowledged on the record label. Another such artist was **Bruno Seidler-Winkler** (1880–1960). Although he was the named partner of the great tenor Karl Erb, Seidler-Winkler was the anonymous conductor and pianist on numerous recordings for the G&T, HMV, Polydor and Tri-Ergon labels.

No one fought more tirelessly, or successfully, for the proper recognition of the accompanist than the Englishman **Gerald Moore** (1899–1987) who had a lifelong relationship with Schubert's lieder, and a happy propinquity to the EMI recording studios at Hayes, Middlesex at the beginning of the serious recording era. The German accompanist **Michael Raucheisen** (1889–1984) was

Michael Raucheisen.

Elisabeth Schwarzkopf with Gerald Moore in the 1960s.

also a giant of the field; a one-time string player, he was hugely knowledgeable about the repertoire and, as head of Song and Chamber music of the Berlin Radio during the war, pursued a vast lieder recording project of his own devising in the 1940s. This was supported by Goebbels and, as bombs rained down on Berlin, the best singers were given leave to return from the front to record Schubert songs and those of many other composers (not including Mendelssohn or Mahler of course). Raucheisen's regrettably high standing with the Nazis more or less put an end to his inter-national performing career after the war. His musical achievement nevertheless remains, documented on an impressive number of reis-sued discs.

Raucheisen's colleague, **Hans Udo Müller,** was killed in an air raid. The war and its cas-ualties inevitably changed the musical balance of Europe, and this included the balance of accompanists. In the wake of the Holocaust, the Allies, and artists who were on the anti-Nazi side, occupied the moral high ground. Justly, or unjustly, this was to the benefit of English artists in a field formerly dominated by Germans. Supported from the early years by another Englishman, the wily recording magnate Walter Legge, it was Raucheisen's rival, Gerald Moore, who was now better placed, both geographically and tempera-mentally, to become the leading song pianist of his time, and perhaps of all time – certainly on record. Famous well before the war, he now found himself in a position almost to corner the market. His list of stellar partners was immense, ranging from Elena Gerhardt to Elisabeth Schumann, from Hans Hotter to Elisabeth Schwarzkopf and, of course, Dietrich Fischer-Dieskau. The culmination of Moore's lifelong association with Schubert and his partnership with Fischer-Dieskau was the recording of about 500 Schubert songs for Deutsche Grammophon in the early 1970s. There had been distinguished English song accompanists before Moore, although none of them (with the possible exception of George Reeves, *see* below) had particularly specialized in the Schubert repertoire. The depth of his sound, his wonderful legato playing with minimal pedal, his sensitivity to the finest shades of tempo in terms of setting a mood, his ease and

Gerald Moore with Dietrich Fischer-Dieskau.

affability with a wide range of colleagues from all countries – these things marked Moore out as the leading accompanist of his time. After Moore, British accompanists, including his immediate successor, the Australian-born **Geoffrey Parsons** (1929–1995), have taken it for granted that German lieder, and Schubert in particular, are part of their working lives. The Wigmore Hall, nerve centre and barometer of the lieder singer's art in Britain, consecrates 31 January to a Schubert birthday concert, and the composer makes countless other appearances throughout the year. On these occasions singers from all over the world are now accompanied by younger pianists, many of them resident in London, who have increasingly become specialists in this field.

The growth of an English school of song accompanists in the last sixty years may stem from a quiet pleasure in what is perceived as background work, and a certain aspect of the English character that is suited to wielding

Geoffrey Parsons, 1980.

influence discreetly behind the scenes. There have been some important German imports into England of course: **Sir George Henschel** (1850–1934), composer, conductor and singer, accompanied himself for his famous recording of *Der Leiermann*; one of the many important Viennese exiles to come to London in 1938 was the pianist and coach **Paul Hamburger** (1920–2004), like his BBC colleague, **Ernest Lush** (1908–1988), a prolific radio accompanist and a less frequent participant in commercial recordings. But there is something about the English temperament that admires, and feels comfortable with, understatement. This is not to be confused with reticence – after all, a great accompanist has the hidden power and influence of a redoubtable civil-service mandarin. Important British names include **Harold Craxton** (1885–1971), later a famous piano teacher, **Ivor Newton** (1892–1981) and **George Reeves** (who recorded Schubert *in extenso* with Elisabeth Schumann).

There has been another, more immediately glamorous, example for the British accompanist to follow, although attempts at emulation are bound to fail. This was a once-in-a-century conjunction of compositional genius combined with a Schubertian empathy for the art of accompaniment. **Benjamin Britten** (1913–1976) was incomparable in insight and keyboard command (a master of colour and nuance) when it came to the accompaniment of Schubert. Britten was neither a full-time nor a professional accompanist – he was able to pick and choose the singers with whom he collaborated, but his greatest work was with a single singer – his partner in life and in music, the tenor Peter Pears. If any two people of the twentieth century were able to stand in for Schubert and Vogl in terms of the magic of their music-making, it was Pears and Britten at the height of their powers (their thirty-year recording career went from the early forties to the early seventies). To hear this duo perform *Die schöne Müllerin* D795 or *Winterreise* D911 was an utterly unforgettable experience. Britten's reverence for Schubert was total. At a very formal dinner party in Germany,

Benjamin Britten and Peters Pears, 1969.

following a concert (with invited personages of great importance), the bejewelled lady seated next to Britten, thinking to pay the composer an enormous compliment, compared Schubert's songs unfavourably with his own. The composer banged the table in fury and shouted 'Du Depp' ('You nitwit'), nearly provoking a major diplomatic incident. Such an outburst from a normally mild-mannered man when confronted with philistine pretentiousness was worthy of Schubert himself who seldom lost his temper, but when he did so his anger was volcanic.

It goes without saying that British-based accompaniment is only one corner of a vast field of this aspect of Schubertian activity. There have always been parallel (and rival) schools of accompaniment in Germany and Austria – the historical, cultural and linguistic home, after all, of the lied repertoire. Accompanists, properly supported by state teaching positions (with decent pensions) have established their bases in the capital cities of various German *Länder*. In modern times there are many motivated younger European accompanists schooled by conservatory classes in Berlin, Munich, Cologne, Karlsruhe, Vienna, Zurich (to name only a few of the cities where tuition in this field is available), each desiring one day to head a lied class of their own. The civic respectability of the teaching positions in these countries is indicative of the status serious song enjoys in the modern musical life of German-speaking countries.

This development is only new in terms of its scale. Fischer-Dieskau had collaborated with Moore in Schubert, but also, from the beginning of his career, with a number of important German-speaking pianists including **Karl Engel** (1923–2006), the Austrian solo pianist **Jörg Demus** (b. 1928), and the composer **Aribert Reimann** (b. 1936) whose *Winterreise* with Brigitte Fassbaender was a famous, if controversial, recording. The pianist **Erik Werba** (1918–1992) was central fixture in lieder accompaniment in Austria during the middle years of the century, as well as an important teacher. The Viennese-born pianist **Martin Isepp** (1930–2011), exiled from his home country as a child, made his career in England where his mother became an influential singing teacher. In this way English-speaking artists during and after the war were given first-hand access to the lieder traditions that were formerly only available to those who went abroad to study.

France has struggled to find an autonomous approach to the German lied, but Holland has a long song-performing tradition that goes back to **Julius Röntgen** (1855–1932) who was accompanist to the great lieder-singing baritone Johannes Masschaert. This national sympathy with the art of accompaniment continued with the pianists **Felix de Nobel** (1907–1981) and **Coenraad Valentijn Bos** (1875–1955) and culminated in modern times with **Rudolf Jansen** (b. 1940) whose career was a pianistic parallel to that of the great Schubert singer Elly Ameling.

America and Canada have always had large numbers of gifted accompanists: **Frank La Forge** (1879–1953); the composer–accompanist **Celius Dougherty** (1902–1986); **David Garvie** (1923–1995); and **John Wustman** (b. 1930) – this last completing, in 1997, a nine-year project of accompanying the complete Schubert songs. A few have decided to make their lives and careers in Europe: **Dalton Baldwin** (b. 1931) based in France for many years, initially as a partner to Gérard Souzay, for many distinguished Schubert recitals and recordings, and later to many other singers; **Norman Shetler** (b. 1931) in Vienna; and **Irwin Gage** (b. 1939) in Zurich. Gage was a student of Otto Erich Deutsch and has an enormous knowledge of Schubert lieder and a large Schubert discography to his credit.

Irwin Gage.

Leonard Hokanson (1931–2003), a regular partner of the baritone Hermann Prey in Schubert, combined his life as a teacher at Bloomington, Illinois, with a career as a touring pianist. The same is true of **Samuel Sanders** (1937–1999) and **Martin Katz** (b. 1945): the first was professor at the Juilliard School in New York, the second is professor of collaborative piano at Ann Arbor, Michigan. Katz was taught by **Gwendoline Koldofsky** (1906–1998), a Scottish Canadian, and a fine accompanist, who had married an emigré pupil of Schoenberg and moved to Los Angeles. The song pianists of America have continually been nurtured by the rivers of emigration from other lands. At least two distinguished accompanist–immigrants took refuge in the United States from Nazi persecution: **Franz Rupp** (1901–1992) played for Heinrich Schlusnus on countless visits to the USA from his native Germany throughout the 1930s, before moving to America permanently in 1938 where his artists included Marian Anderson; and **Paul**

Ulanowsky (1908–1968) established a duo with Lotte Lehmann (also an exile from Germany, though not Jewish), as well as many other artists.

The status of *primus inter pares* enjoyed by Moore who was able to work with almost every important singer in the world is something that probably no one else will ever achieve; this role was inherited to a greatly reduced extent by Parsons and Gage, but times were already changing by the 1980s with a resurgence of younger German talent. In the present day there are many gifted pianists attracted by this genre of music-making, and singers are generally less tied to the idea of a lifetime accompanist or even a regular concert partner, preferring to ring the changes. Added to this, solo pianists no longer find participation in vocal recitals the career-threatening humiliation it was once felt to be. Although in the 1950s renowned solo pianist **Edwin Fischer** (1886–1960) recorded Schubert with Schwarzkopf (who also made song discs with Gieseking and Fürtwängler), and **Artur Schnabel** (1882–1951) accompanied his wife in recitals, as Richard Strauss had accompanied his, these were special cases at the time. However, the barriers between solo pianists and career accompanists have increasingly broken down over the decades since, providing mixed artistic results.

Incidentally, earlier husband and wife teams included the French baritone Pierre-François Wartel and his wife **Atala Thérèse Wartel** (1814–1865) as well as the soprano Jenny Lind and her husband **Otto Goldschmidt** (1829–1907). The famous German soprano Elisabeth Schumann was married to her accompanist, also a conductor, **Karl Alwin** (1891–1945). The French baritone Charles Panzéra was accompanied by his wife **Magdeleine Panzéra** (b. 1893), as was the Austrian tenor Anton Dermota by his, **Hilde Dermota** (b. 1912, née Berger-Weyerwald).

Such partnerships are not merely based on commercial considerations. The pairing of singers and pianists for reasons of record sales is a relatively recent phenomenon whereby famous solo pianists make recordings with singers while disdaining to share the educative process that is the rough and tumble of their everyday concert lives. There are of course versatile soloists who take this work extremely seriously (**Daniel Barenboim**, **Imogen Cooper**, **Christoph Eschenbach**, **András Schiff** and a few other famous names), but in recent years a great deal of matchmaking in this field has had little justification beyond commercial expediency.

The demarcation lines between what was done superbly in the 1820s by Bocklet and Gahy (playing Schubert's solo piano pieces), and by Schubert himself, or his friends Jenger or Hütten-brenner (playing the song accompaniments), have remained more or less the same in artistic, if not entrepreneurial, terms. In certain obvious pianistic ways the solo pianist has a much harder job, but to imagine that the art of accompanying can be encompassed within a few minutes of sight-reading, or even a few hours of rehearsal, is to dishonour the infinite subtleties of the repertoire that Schubert made his own, both as composer and performer.

In the meantime there are plenty of artists of the present generation, dedicated professional accompanists, who daily do their best to promote this repertoire and perform Schubert songs whenever they can. One of the issues we must increasingly face is the impending collapse of the conventional record industry as we have known it over the last fifty years. Life has moved on from the Gerald Moore days when a series of EMI 78 r.p.m. discs could be the source of a worldwide reputation for an accompanist, and when an organization like the BBC was a major instigator of recitals. But so many artists – too many to list here with any hope of completeness – have proved their devotion to the Schubertian cause, in some cases over very many years, and their names should be included on any roll of honour in an article devoted to Schubert's song pianists. In some cases their best work is yet to come:

In Britain: **Eugene Asti** (an American who is permanently resident in London), **Iain Burnside**, **Julius Drake**, **Christopher Glynn**, **Malcolm Martineau**, **Jennifer Partridge**, **Roger Vignoles**; in America: **Margo Garrett**, **Warren Jones**, **Cameron Stowe**, **Brian Zeger**; in Germany: **Helmut Deutsch**, **Ulrich Eisenlohr** (who has initiated a complete Schubert song series on Naxos Records), **Hartmut Höll** (the youngest accompanist to have worked with Fischer-Dieskau), **Gerhard Huber**, **Phillip Moll** (an American long resident in Berlin and Leipzig), **Wolfram Rieger**, **Eric Schneider**, **Andreas Staier**, **Justus Zeyen**; in Austria: **David Lutz** (another American in charge of training lied pianists in Vienna), **Charles Spencer** (English-born); in France **Jeff Cohen** (another American), **Christian Ivaldi** and **Françoise Tillard**; in Sweden, **Bengt Forsberg**. The list is far from complete and there is no shortage of avid and enthusiastic younger Schubertians; the problem is not finding accompanists able to take on the Schubert songs, but finding the audiences willing to listen to them.

See also ACCOMPANIMENT AND ACCOMPANYING and SINGERS.

PIANOS

The vast majority of song recitals today are accompanied by pianos of modern design, whether or not Schubert lieder appear on the programme. Some thirty or forty years ago, when the passion for original string instruments – sometimes badly played and out of tune – was at its peak, it briefly seemed inevitable that the modern concert grand piano in the accompaniment of lieder of the earlier nineteenth century would be superseded by pianos from Schubert's time, or at least of period design. This was the era when the well-informed music lover was persuaded that the playing of Bach on a modern piano was an inexcusable anachronism – as was the unashamed use of tonality by a twentieth-century composer like Benjamin Britten whose music was nearer to being dismissed by the young when he was at the end of his life (1976) than at any time since. These were uncompromising times when it seemed possible to relegate all musical matters into stylistic boxes, an affordable luxury of that era: the arts were more heavily subsidized than seems possible now to imagine, and the result was an altruism that, while admirable in its idealism, was often as inflexible in its application as the so-called purest Marxist theory. Times have much changed. It was inevitable that market considerations and the dwindling commercial power of the classical music industry would play their part in the loosening of the stays; the rigidity of those who insisted on writing in the style of Webern or Pierre Boulez in the 1970s has been replaced by the prolixity of unashamedly neo-Romantic composers – a more tuneful succession perhaps, but one not always suggestive of great depth, self-questioning or discipline. A by-product of a shift in zeitgeist, and laissez-faire regarding the use of old tonal patterns in modern music, is a far less censorious attitude towards the use of the modern piano in old music – indeed, in the broader scheme of things, this no longer seems to be a controversial issue. Fortepiano-accompanied live recitals and recordings are now very much more the exception than the rule. Some of the old guard, the early-music pioneers, must regard this as a catastrophic retreat, but a pianist like András Schiff, having played a significant role in insisting on performing Bach on a modern instrument in solo appearances, is unlikely to have insisted on a fortepiano for the many Schubert lieder recitals he has accompanied over the years. Of course it is possible that the pendulum will swing again in the direction of 'authenticity', but practical considerations in the organization of song recitals in the real world make this unlikely. When the songs of Schubert (or earlier composers) form an entire concert programme it might make sense to import a fortepiano and someone capable of playing it. But the majority of Schubert songs appear as part of a programme with other, later composers whose music could not be accompanied by period instruments.

The question of whether Schubert would have enjoyed hearing his music played on the modern piano remains open: there are those who claim he would have been delighted by the expressive possibilities and the range of tonal colour offered by the present-day instrument, and those who argue that because his music was conceived with the sound of the earlier piano in mind, it is the duty of present-day performers to re-create that sound. Of the unique beauties of the fortepiano sonority there is no doubt: it has a plangent astringency that makes up for what it might lack in power compared with modern instruments. The colour of the soft pedal 'stop' is particularly beautiful, underlining the use of that pedal for special, magical effect at appropriate times in the music rather than as a vade mecum for everyday legato playing. The easier balance between voice and less powerful piano is another factor, although it is perfectly possible, with any instrument, for a singer to be drowned by a pianist whose ears are not working assiduously. On the other hand the instrument is more fragile, with strings that break relatively easily, and the expressive possibilities are very different, and by no means easy for the player of modern instruments to assimilate without a great deal of experience. A player who is used to the modern Steinway grand with its double-escapement mechanism will find the fortepiano appreciably more 'stringy' and less yielding of nuance and colour – and so it also seems to the average modern listener, no matter how masterfully the player deploys touch, finger legato and rubato.

In Schubert's time the piano, far from being the established classic of the drawing room, was at the cutting edge of brand-new technology that was only beginning to make its way into the homes of the newly affluent middle classes. Like the ever-improving mobile phone of today, or the emergent automobile at the beginning of the twentieth century, the piano was an increasingly popular accessory that was constantly improving (and thus in a continual state of technical flux) with a great many builders and technicians employed in a highly competitive search for an ever-more refined sound and technology. This was a far cry from today where the professional market for pianos is dominated by a handful of brands led by the American–German firm of Steinway & Sons. Schubert was aware that piano manufacture was in a continuing state of evolution, as can be seen from a letter of 23 February 1824 from Anna Hartmann to her fiancé where she recounts a conversation between her brother Fritz and Schubert on her desire to acquire a suitable piano: 'He [Schubert] says that the new innovations are not at all bad, but believes that as long as these are still in their cradle it would be better to buy one of the older variety.' Schubert advised that there was a greater choice of piano in Vienna than Linz and that for 500 florins it would be possible to acquire an instrument from one of the local 'Masters': those mentioned were Conrad Graf (1782–1851), Wilhelm Leschen (from whom a bill for piano repair for 20 florins was one of the composer's outstanding debts at his death) and Graf's later partner, Kaspar Pfaff (1787–1827).

Schubert does not mention other famous Viennese piano builders (among these were Johann Schantz, Matthäus Stein and Johann Baptist Streicher) because he seems to have had a particularly close relationship with the firm of Graf whose workshop was in Währing, an area fairly local to the Schubert family. In 1994 Rita Steblin uncovered evidence of a new Schubert relative, the piano builder Johann Gottfried Schubert (b. 1792), who came as a carpenter from Breslau to live in Vienna *c.* 1805, and who worked assiduously at the Graf factory in Währing before leaving Vienna to establish his own successful firm of piano builders in Germany. This ties in with the memories of Schubert's sister Therese (1801–1878) who recounted that as a little boy Franz wanted to be a carpenter's apprentice, and that he was often taken by a relative, also named Schubert, to a piano factory in the neighbourhood, a ten-minute walk from the Schubert home in the Säulengasse. After the successful performance of the Mass in F, D105 in 1814, Schubert *père* decided to buy a piano for his son, and it made perfect sense, bearing in mind the family connection, that this five-octave instrument came from the Graf factory. This piano later came into the possession of Ferdinand Schubert, ostensibly a gift from the composer who already had a good instrument at his disposal at the Schober family residence. Schubert might have regretted this generosity: he was often without a piano at the fourteen various addresses at which he lived between 1816 and 1828. We know that when he was a lodger at the Fruhwirthhaus in 1825/6 he used the table piano built by the firm of Anton Walter, which was housed in the home of the painter Wilhelm August Rieder. All of this is an indication that whereas a piano was indispensable for Schubertiads and other social occasions, the composer's prolific compositional prowess was unaffected by the lack of one. Nevertheless Schubert took a keen interest in what instruments were available on the market and seems always to have been willing to try the newest models. An entry in Josef Karl Rosenbaum's diary for 28 October 1823 mentions a visit to the furniture maker Reimann to try out a piano made by Reimann's partner Johann Jakob Goll. This instrument had a soundboard over the strings and was the subject of a special imperial patent. Schubert was not the only composer present – this was the occasion on which he offended Carl Maria

The piano by Johann Alois Graf of Vienna which was owned by Schubert.

Schubert's room (and piano), pen drawing by Moritz von Schwind, 1821.

Schubert at the piano at Atzenbrugg. Detail from Leopold Kupelwieser's much larger watercolour 'Gesellschaftsspiel der Schubertianer', 1821.

von Weber with his low opinion of *Euryanthe*; Conradin Kreutzer, already famous for his song settings, also played the instrument. Rosenbaum noted the piano's pleasing tone and secure mechanics and ordered one forthwith.

While he was employed as music master at Zseliz, the summer residence of the Esterházy family, Schubert used an 1810 piano by Karl Schmidt of Pressburg. This was probably the only piano he played that was not of Viennese construction. Perhaps Anton Schindler would have permitted him to try Beethoven's Broadwood after that composer's death but, by all accounts, the instrument had been hammered so hard it was unplayable. Other evidence of the pianos played by Schubert has come down to us through iconography. The played-out instrument that is described by Mayrhofer as having been part of his apartment's furniture when Schubert was lodging with him is the same old-fashioned, pedalless instrument, with a box of books underneath it, to be seen in Moritz von Schwind's drawing of Schubert's poorly furnished room ('Schuberts Zimmer'). Another pedalless instrument was painted by Kupelwieser when he depicted the composer seated at the piano at Atzenbrugg while the Schubertians played charades ('Gesell-schaftspiel der Schubertianer'). In this depiction there is a dog seated where the piano's pedals might otherwise have been. (This instrument survives today in a private Viennese collection.)

Schubert (despite one's inclinations to link his feelings to those of the Schubart setting *An mein Klavier*) seems to have been remarkably unsentimental about pianos, and there is no evidence that he was particularly attached to any one sound or mechanism, no doubt believing – correctly – that there were ongoing improvements in the technical aspects of these matters. His preference for Graf pianos seems to have stemmed from a childhood association rather than an overwhelming devotion to their sound.

While most accompanists of today are unlikely to become specialists on the fortepiano, a feeling for the sound of these pioneering instruments should inform and strengthen the aural imagination of players of modern instruments. It is no longer possible to play Schubert in a way that resembles Brahms at his most effulgent, but because the Steinway is a versatile instrument whose sound can vary in the hands of different players, it can be played in a way that takes into account various aspects of the fortepiano, above all in the judicious use of pedal (which goes hand in hand with respect for the composer's articulation), and the magical sound of the una corda (reserved for passages of magical tenderness, *see* PEDALLING). An accompanist with a sensitive and imaginative ear and touch should be able to incorporate into modern performance an aspect of the fortepiano by preventing the larger modern instrument from wallowing in the more grandiose and exaggerated areas of its potential power and resonance. In this way the pianos of the composer's time become part of the composer's style, a style that it is possible to re-create on pianos other than period instruments.

Bibliography: Litschauer 1993, pp. 133–6
                Steblin 1994, pp. 49–53

KAROLINE (sometimes Caroline or Carolina) PICHLER (1769–1843)

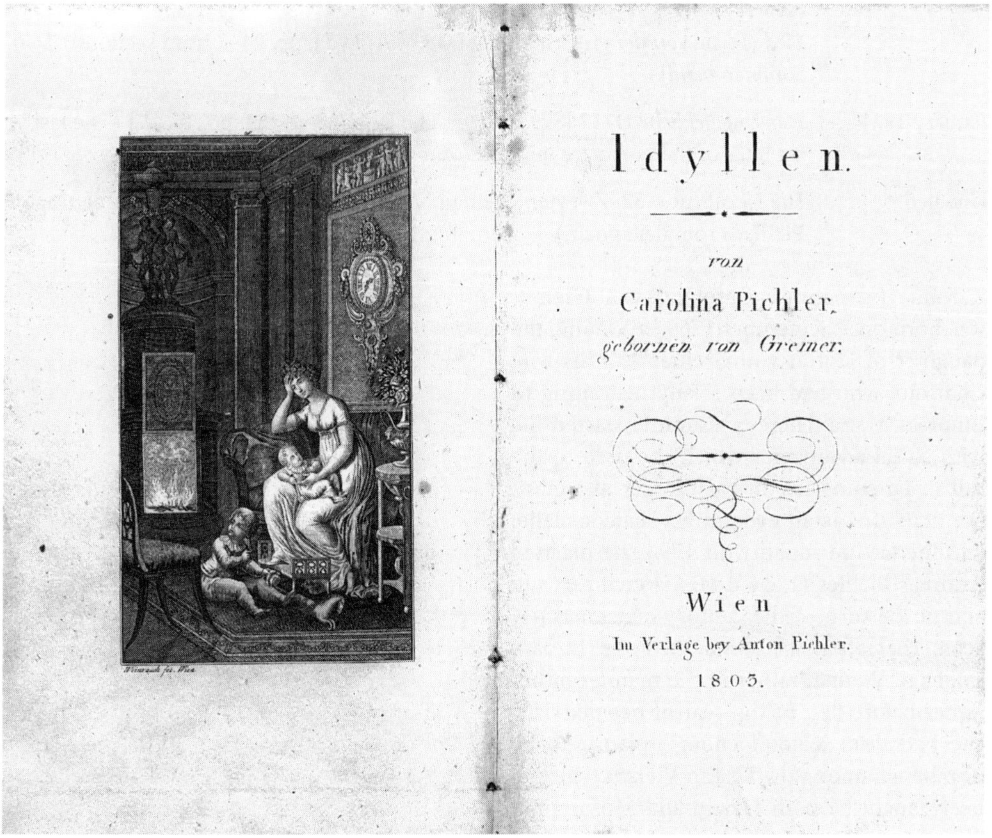

Idyllen, Vienna (1803), Pichler's first publication.

THE POETIC SOURCES

S1 *Idyllen* von Carolina Pichler, gebornen von Greiner. Wien Im Verlage bey Anton Pichler. 1803.

There is also an undated Leipzig reprint of this edition. There are nine *Idylle* in this collection. Schubert sets texts from the second and third of these (*see* below). The second is dedicated 'An meine Freundinn, das Fräulein Josepha von Ravenet'. The eighth idyll is modelled on Virgil's first Eclogue, and the tenth (*Der Tanz*) is dedicated to the first poet ever set by Schubert, Gabriele von Baumberg.

S2 *Olivier oder Die Rache der Elfe* von Carolina Pichler gebornen von Greiner. Erster und Zweyter Theil. Wien Im Verlage bey Anton Pichler. 1803

S3 *Olivier* (Sämmtliche Werke von Caroline Pichler, gebornen von Greiner. Achter Band. Neue verbesserte Auflage. Wien, 1821, Gedruckt und im Verlage von Anton Pichler)

S4 *Idyllen* (Sämmtliche Werke von Caroline Pichler gebornen von Greiner. Fünfzehnter Band. Wien bei Anton Pichler 1822)

THE SONGS

September 1816	*Der Sänger am Felsen* D482 [S1: Alexis, pp. 28–9 from section III *Der Sänger am Felsen*] *Lied (Ferne von der grossen Stadt)* D483 [S1: Lyda, pp. 24–7 from section II *Der Sommerabend*]
January 1821	*Der Unglückliche* D713 [S2: Zweyter Theil, pp. 83–4] [S3: pp. 166–7] (The last six lines of the poem are omitted from this setting)
Undated	*Die Nacht* (qv) [S2: Zweyter Theil, pp. 83–4] [S3: pp. 166–7] (This is a setting of Pichler's complete poem)

Karoline (sometimes Caroline) von Greiner was born on 7 September 1769 in Vienna, the daughter of Hofrat von Greiner and his wife Charlotte who had been a lady-in-waiting to Empress Maria Theresa. Karoline started life with social advantages which she used to the full in pursuing her literary career as well as her activities as an ever-enthusiastic socialite and literary personality. In 1796 she married Andreas Pichler (1764–1837), a civil servant, and at the turn of the century and for thirty years thereafter she dominated the literary salons of Vienna, rather in the manner of her father before her. In the year of her marriage she had been a good enough pianist to be numbered among the best in Vienna (she had been taught by both Haydn and Mozart) but from her middle twenties she concentrated on writing and her salon.

Karoline Pichler, watercolour by Julius Schoppe, 1818.

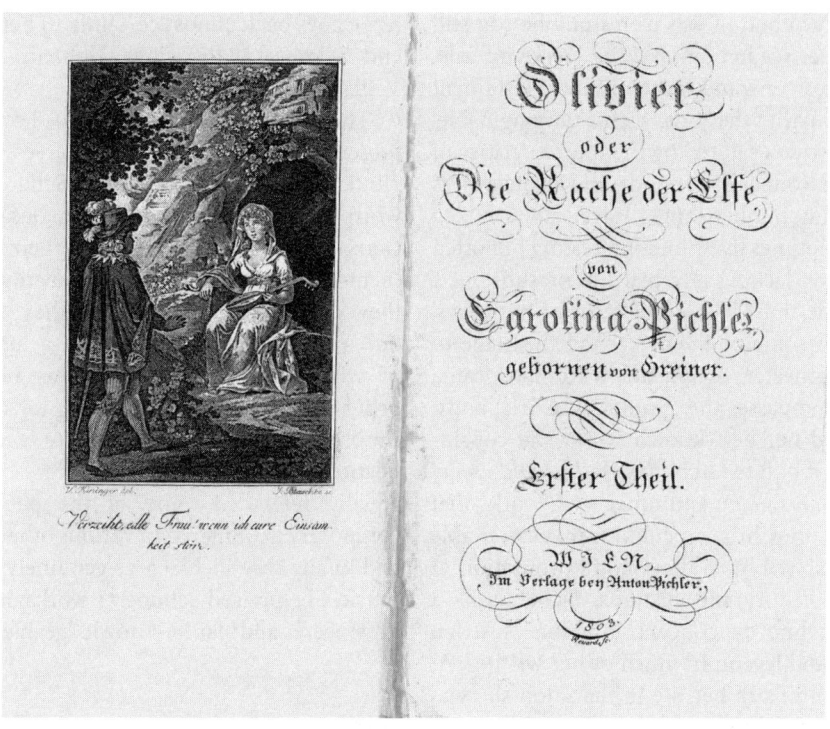

First edition of *Olivier oder Die Rache der Elfe* (1803).

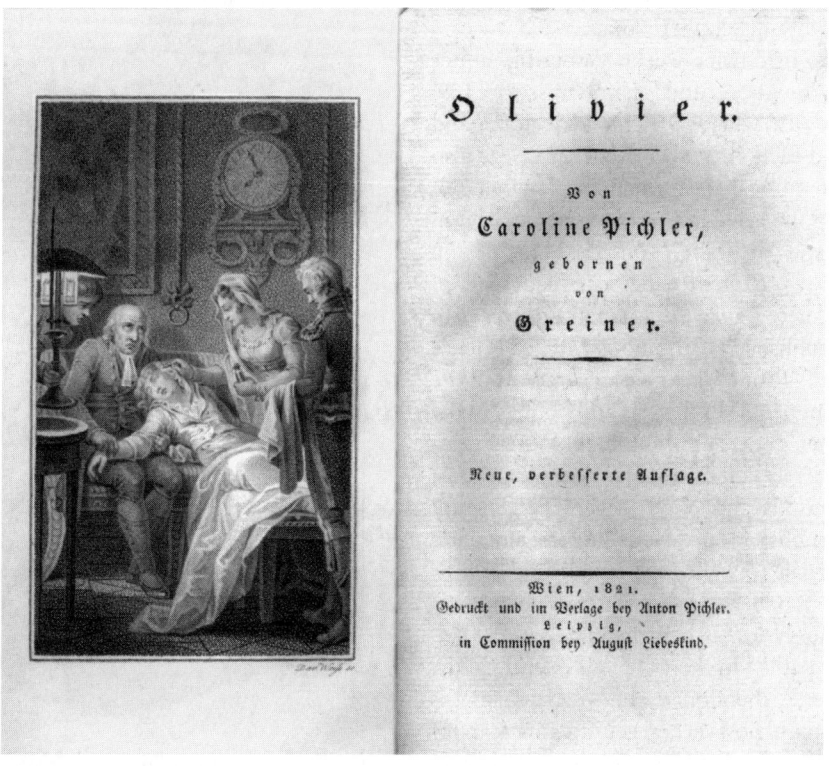

A later edition of *Olivier* (1821), the eighth volume in the poet's twenty-four volume *Sämmtliche Werke*.

Her own output was plentiful: one can still sometimes see her *Sämmtliche Werke* for sale, a long row of some sixty volumes, testament to a popularity that now seems unimaginable. Her work was saluted by the literary critics of the time (often her friends and protégés) as significant, but her longer novels are a mixed bag, sometimes lively and interesting but often derivative, lacking any real life or substance. The same must be said of most of her plays, although some of them reached the stage of the Burgtheater. *Agathokles*, a Roman drama that encompasses the triumph of Christianity, remained her best-known work; she considered it a rebuff to Gibbons's *Decline and Fall of the Roman Empire* and other such works that vaunted pre-Christian cultures in a favourable light. Inspired by Walter Scott's promotion of Scottish history and customs, Pichler took a patriotic line by concentrating on Austrian history and legend in much of her writing. At the beginning of her life in the salon she was a friend of Gabriele von Baumberg, and many years later of Helmina von Chézy (qqv). Pichler's daughter (also Karoline) played the piano and sang Schubert songs.

Pichler held twice-weekly gatherings at her home in the Alsergrund (Hauptstrasse no. 109, formerly 90) where writers read aloud and discussed each other's works. There were also frequent musical performances. Though not equalling the brilliance of Madame de Staël in Switzerland or Rahel von Ense in Berlin, Pichler was a force to be reckoned with in Vienna; her *Denkwürdigkeiten aus meinem Leben* (published posthumously in 1844) leave a detailed, if somewhat gossipy, account of the important people in the arts and politics in the Biedermeier era. These autobiographical writings are lively and more interesting than most of her novels and plays (as are her shorter stories published in various literary almanacs and journals) but they tell us nothing of how she and Schubert got on. He had already set two of her lyrics (1816) when in 1820 the two crossed paths. In her copious writings the composer is mentioned almost in passing as an example of how certain geniuses are scarcely aware of what they have created. This *idée*

reçue goes back almost certainly to her friend, and Schubert's, the singer Johann Michael Vogl.

The composer is certain to have been present at a number of Pichler's soirées. Anselm Hüttenbrenner recorded what Schubert had whispered to him on one such occasion: 'I cannot stand these women with their compliments. They know nothing about music and they don't really mean what they say. Go on, Anselm, slip in and get me a little glass of wine.' Fischer-Dieskau in his book on Schubert takes 'these women' to refer to Karoline Pichler herself, but there is no justification for this. Hüttenbrenner's account equally refers to some of the people the composer encountered in various other salons, and in any case Pichler was genuinely fond of music. She praised Schubert's works, it seems, in sincere and fairly knowledgeable terms:

Karoline Pichler, watercolour by L. Krones, 1829.

according to Hüttenbrenner she was 'complimentary and encouraging' and 'captivated by Schubert's muse'. On this occasion in 1820 she had heard the Schmidt von Lübeck setting *Der Wanderer* D489 sung at the home of Matthäus von Collin. It was soon to be published and dedicated to another close friend of Pichler's, Ladislav Pyrker, two of whose poems Schubert later set to music. According to the diaries of Peter Ivanovich Keppen, when Pichler spoke of Schubert she 'highly praised his talent. On one occasion Schubert turned pages for the Pichlers, *mère et fille*, for a performance of one of his duets, and Karoline flattered him by saying that it was as if "Mozart had once more come to turn the pages while I played one of his sonatas".'

Schubert's only substantial Pichler setting, *Der Unglückliche* D713, has a number of things in common with the famous Schmidt von Lübeck setting: it shares the theme of the outcast and loner in society, it is a mini-cantata in a number of contrasted sections, and the very opening triplets, dragging their feet through the unfriendly world, have a similar portentous power. Moreover, Schubert had originally found the poem for *Der Wanderer* in a Viennese almanac, *Dichtungen für Kunstredner*, where it had been misattributed to the playwright Zacharias Werner (qv, another good friend of Pichler) and entitled *Der Unglückliche*. The confusion was cleared up by 1821 when *Der Wanderer* was published under its correct title and with the correct name of its poet. There was now a vacancy for a song entitled *Der Unglückliche* and it seems possible that Schubert might have written something in Pichler's honour, in the manner (and with the original title) of the song she had admired. Perhaps Schubert took Pichler's enthusiasm to be well informed and genuine, but she was very much a socialite and inhabited a level of society too different from his to have become a true friend.

Bibliography: Clive 1997, pp. 151–2

PILGERWEISE
(SCHOBER) **D789** [H515]
F♯ minor   April 1823

Pilgrim's song

(159 bars)

(1) Ich bin ein Waller auf der Erde
Und gehe still von Haus zu Haus,
O reicht mit freundlicher Gebärde
Der Liebe Gaben mir heraus!

I am a pilgrim on this earth
And go silently from house to house.
O bestow on me with a friendly gesture
Tokens of your love.

(2) Mit offnen teilnahmsvollen Blicken,
Mit einem warmen Händedruck
Könnt ihr dies arme Herz erquicken,
Und es befrei'n von langem Druck.

With open, sympathetic glances,
With a warm grasp of the hand
You can refresh this poor heart
And free it from long oppression.

(3) Doch rechnet nicht, dass ich euch's lohnen,   But do not count on me rewarding you,
     Mit Gegendienst vergelten soll;   Or repaying you with service in return;
     Ich streue nur mit Blumenkronen,   I shall only strew your thresholds
     Mit blauen, eure Schwelle voll;   With wreaths of blue flowers.

(4) Und geb' ein Lied euch noch zur Zither,[1]   And I shall give you a song, to my zither,
     Mit Fleiss gesungen und gespielt,   Sung and played with vigour,
     Das euch vielleicht nur leichter Flitter,   Which will seem to you, perhaps, like flimsy
                                                               tinsel,
     Ein leicht entbehrlich Gut euch gilt—   Something easily done without.

(5) Mir gilt es viel, ich kann's nicht missen,[2]   To me it means much, I cannot do without it,
     Und allen Pilgern ist es wert;[3]   And it is valued by every pilgrim;
     Doch freilich ihr—ihr könnt nicht wissen,   But you, of course, cannot know
     Was d e n beseligt, der entbehrt.   What makes *him* happy who does without.

(6) Vom Überfluss seid ihr erfreuet,   You rejoice in abundance,
     Und findet tausendfach Ersatz;   Which can be replenished a thousandfold;
     Ein Tag dem andern angereihet   Each successive day
     Vergrössert euren Liebesschatz.   Increases the treasury of your love.

(7) Doch mir—so wie ich weiter strebe   But for me, as I strive onwards
     An meinem harten Wanderstabe,[4]   With my hardy pilgrim's staff,
     Reisst in des Glückes Lustgewebe[5]   One thread after another is torn off
     Ein Faden nach dem andern ab.   From the tissue of my happiness.

(8) Drum kann ich nur von Gaben leben,   So I can only live on gifts,
     Von Augenblick zu Augenblick,   From moment to moment.
     O wollet vorwurfslos sie geben!   O, give them without reproach!
     Zu eurer Lust—zu meinem Glück.   For your pleasure, for my happiness.

(9) Ich bin ein Waller auf der Erde   I am a pilgrim on this earth
     Und gehe still von Haus zu Haus,   And go silently from house to house.
     O reicht mit freundlicher Gebärde   O bestow on me with a friendly gesture
     Der Liebe Gaben mir heraus!   Tokens of your love!

FRANZ VON SCHOBER (1796–1882)

*This is the eleventh of Schubert's fourteen Schober solo settings (1815–27). See the poet's
biography for a chronological list of all the Schober settings.*

This shy and resigned song, like the slightly earlier *Schwestergruss* D762 in F sharp minor, is an
example of the 'heavenly length' (Schumann's phrase) of Schubert's music. When he is in this

[1] The fourth strophe contains so many adjustments to Schober's published version (1842) that this needs to be quoted
in full: 'Und *sing ein stilles* Lied zur Zither, / *Das Stammelnd mit dem Seufzer ringt,* / Das euch *wohl gar wie* leichter
Flitter, / *Wie überflüss'ges Spielwerk klingt*—'. A rewrite on this level suggests the original hand of Schober himself.
[2] Schober writes '*Mir klingt es süss,* ich kann's nicht missen'.
[3] Schober writes 'Und *jedem Pilger* ist es wert'.
[4] Schober writes 'An meinem harten *Wanderstab*'.
[5] Schober writes 'Reisst in des Glückes *Luftgewebe*'.

expansive mood it matters little to him whether the public has the patience, or the attention span, to follow his fancy. Fortunately, present-day Schubertians confront such challenges more readily than nineteenth-century audiences. The song was almost certainly never considered for publication in Schubert's lifetime: it is one of the works that he wrote for himself and his inner circle. His greatest friend, Franz von Schober, came up with a poem that chimed with the composer's own sense of suffering and isolation in the wake of his illness, and the resulting music is withdrawn yet heartfelt, almost too obsessive for public consumption. Whether Schober wrote the poem expressly to encourage Schubert to make an autobiographical statement in music is not known; but it seems possible. His friends knew that as long as the composer was working he had a measure of happiness. The pilgrim's plaints do not reflect the poet's circum-stances, but they fit Schubert's story exactly: going from 'house to house' he was continually reliant on the hospitality of friends, and his shortage of money obliged him to 'live on gifts'; his friends' sympathy (and their love) were what he needed most at this time. He was always only able to reward them with music. At this point in 1823, with so much going wrong in his life, it did indeed seem that he could say that 'one thread after another' is 'torn off from the tissue of my happiness'. It was as if the composer had become one of his own song characters, the harper of 'An die Türen will ich schleichen' (*Gesänge des Harfners* III D478/3).

In September 1828, when Schubert came to compose the slow movement of his great A major Sonata (D959), he chose to remember this song – in the same key and (if allowance is made for the two-in-the-bar § of the song, and the slower ⅜ of the piano piece) a similar *Bewegung*, the deliberate and slightly dragging gait of the pilgrim supported by his 'Wanderstab', his trusty stick. That movement's middle section is an untypical outburst of pain and violent anger, a passage bristling with demisemiquavers and chromatic scales that seem wildly out of control. There is nothing like this expressionistic nightmare-in-sound in all Schubert; certainly *Pilger-weise* seems repressed in comparison. The song, and its text, probably brought bad memories of the events of the awful winter of 1822/3 when the disease first made itself apparent. Five years later in the piano sonata of 1828, Schubert has allowed himself to re-experience the panic and desperation, and to commit them to manuscript paper – the pilgrim, no longer silent and long suffering, is able to express his rage at last. In drawing attention to the similarities between song and sonata, Alfred Einstein writes, 'I hope no one will accuse me of suggesting that Schubert had the text of the song in mind when he was writing this movement.' And yet, why not? Such a suggestion seems entirely plausible.

Perhaps Einstein would have thought differently if the text had been by Goethe. But Schober's limited literary gifts are a separate issue from the love felt for him by Schubert which overruled all other considerations. It is likely that these words mattered to the composer precisely because they *were* by Schober, even if they were not the greatest poetry. It is said that Schober had played a part in the background to Schubert's infection (traditionally encouraging the compos-er's ill-fated visit to a prostitute), but who knows how true this is? And who knows how many conversations and barings of the soul had preceded the writing of this poem? It is possible that it was memories of these, and other never-to-be-known twists to the story, that prompted the volcanic outburst in the sonata. In any case, this relationship, with all its ups and downs, was much more complex than we could ever know. In later life Schober, a normally loquacious individual, keen to consort with the famous and to claim his place in history, was remarkably reticent about it. We shall never find out whether this was simple laziness in responding to scholars' questionnaires or a fear of re-opening doors long shut behind which lurked ghosts and skeletons.

The song's original key is F sharp minor. There is another autograph copy in D minor, and when Diabelli published it he chose E minor, an infinitely more comfortable key for singers; consequently this is the one printed in the Peters Edition. There are nine strophes to the song (the last verse a repeat of the first) and the musical form is somewhat palindromic, with each verse representing a letter thus: A, B, C (adopting two lines of A, transposed), D, E (incorporating the last line of C, derived from A), D (with modified vocal line and extension), F (the heart of the pilgrim's plaint), then B, and A plus coda. In this way the music for the first two verses acts as bookends (in reverse order at the end) for a rather more rambling structure at the heart of the song. It is as if the pilgrim returns to his starting point, having gone nowhere in particular and coming full circle. How different this is from the striding determination of the Schiller settings *Der Pilgrim* D794 or *Sehnsucht* D636 written in cantata form, where one new musical vista succeeds another. In the eight-bar introduction of *Pilgerweise* the bass pivots between F sharp and E sharp, the first inversion of the dominant chord. The melody for 'Ich bin ein Waller auf der Erde' is beautiful and memorable; at first it is built on the same harmonic plan as the *Vorspiel*, but it moves into A major at bb. 15–16. The infinitely sad use of the relative major is a feature of this song, bringing an air of philosophic resignation. A short interlude leads to the conclusion of the verse in F sharp major (the 'tokens of love' at b. 22 have a special radiance). The last phrase of this verse's vocal line is repeated in the piano as a *Zwischenspiel*.

So far there has been a tranquillity in the music, but the second strophe is more imploring and needy and Schubert is not ashamed to provide music to match the words. The repeated C sharps of the voice's opening bars ('Mit offnen' bb. 27–8) promise a strophic repeat of what has come before, but instead there are restless, if tiny, harmonic excursions initiated by a roving bass line, and a reckless outpouring of new melody in the vocal line, like a wringing of hands in music. Eric Sams remarked that the toing and froing in the flowing quavers for the setting of the words 'Könnt ihr dies arme Herz erquicken' recalls Mozart's *Dove sono* (at 'mi portasse una speranza') from *Le Nozze di Figaro*. Certainly the Countess is as emotionally vulnerable at this point in the opera as Schober's pilgrim. At times the music seems like a distant variation of the first verse, but there is something more improvised than planned about this organic renewal as each rise and fall of verbal nuance is accommodated afresh. Melody is one thing that Schubert is rich in, which, as it happens, is the message of the song.

By the beginning of the third strophe (b. 42) we have settled into D major, but not for long. At the third and fourth line (beginning from b. 47 'Ich streue nur mit Blumenkronen'), mention of the Novalis-inspired blue flower (also to be found in the 1816 Schober setting *Am Bach im Frühlinge* D361) occasions a recycling of the music from the corresponding passage in the first verse, this time a semitone higher. The same *Zwischenspiel*, also a semitone higher, leads the music into G major (from b. 57).

The central section of the song is given over to the pilgrim's description of his own music-making and the ear has a rest from those undulating accompanying triplets. Instead, a rippling arpeggio figure with a zither-like drone of fifths in the bass (from b. 57) accompanies the phrase beginning 'Und geb' ein Lied euch noch zur Zither'. The words 'Mit Fleiss gesungen und gespielt' (bb. 60–62) come across as Schober's compliment to Schubert's unceasing musical industry; he was perhaps one of the few people in Vienna who knew how hard the composer worked, and how many pieces he composed – many more than ever saw the light of performance. The suddenly rising tessitura of 'Ein leicht entbehrlich Gut euch gilt' (bb. 64–7), with a crescendo, registers a protest, as if the singer were preparing himself to defend music as something essential, vital for his well-being. The fifth strophe, joined closely to the fourth in continuous musical construction, retreats from this assertive position, as if the pilgrim has remembered his place and feels entitled only to state his case gently. The harmonic legerdemain on the change to 'Mir' in b. 68, a curious transition that progresses from D sharp^7 to G sharp minor, is the perfect analogue for an apologetic change of subject. Once again the final line of this section ('was d e n beseligt, der entbehrt' bb. 77–80) with its softly drooping cadence repeats the music for the closing of the first and third strophes, the song's most identifiable musical tag.

The sixth strophe begins in much the same way as the fourth. The accompaniment is a variant of the G major music of that passage and only the vocal line is changed to accommodate different inflections. It is the least convincing verse of a rather unconvincing poem when judged purely as literature and here, perhaps, even the most ardent Schubertian may begin to complain of longueurs. The end of this strophe is differently composed from the fourth; the elongation of 'Vergrössert euren Liebesschatz' (bb. 89–92) is a *bel canto* treasure chest of melisma and decoration, an analogue for the personal blessings enjoyed by others. After this the focus again shifts to the protagonist with the haltingly sung words 'Doch mir' (bb. 96–7) at the beginning of the seventh verse. The music here is entirely new as befits the most personal section of the poem, words which seem most tailored to Schubert's plight. A strong bass line turns the harmonic screw ever tighter; the words 'Reisst in des Glückes Lustgewebe / Ein Faden nach dem andern ab' are repeated and then, as if enumerating the breaking threads one by one, there is a final 'Ein Faden nach dem andern ab' (bb. 111–13). This insistence betokens real desperation; the tessitura is high enough in any case, but here the music seems to climb higher with each breath, phrase by phrase, eventually insisting on a succession of phrases dominated by high Fs. Here is the reason why most singers choose to perform this song, if at all, in a lower key: music for the tearing of threads can sound uncomfortably like the shredding of vocal chords. It is significant that the mood of this word-setting seems more angry than regretful.

At the end of Verse 7 we find ourselves in the distant key of F minor. This changes back to F sharp minor with Schubertian virtuosity as the third note of the scale (A flat) changes enharmonically to G sharp, fifth note of C sharp minor. This in turn is the dominant of the home key. A three-beat setting of the word 'Drum' (bb. 114–15) sustained over a held C sharp presides over this change. The music for this eighth strophe goes back to that of the song's second verse. The words propose a nice exchange of benefits between musician and sponsor, the giver of money deriving pleasure, the artist happiness. The ninth strophe exactly repeats the first, in both words and music. The last two lines of the poem are repeated to make a coda of entirely new musical material anchored in F sharp major. The piano postlude (from b. 155) comprises a segment of the accompaniment, music of deep sighs and a pilgrim's humility, transposed down a minor third from the immediately preceding bars. The whole song, still something of an enigma, is a curious mixture of prolific one-off invention and carefully recycled material. Moreover, there is something of a parallel between the pre-ordained progress of this pilgrim and the daemonic drive that motivates *Der Musensohn* D764 written some months earlier.

Autograph:	Wienbibliothek im Rathaus, Vienna (first draft)
First edition:	Published as Book 18 no. 1 of the *Nachlass* by Diabelli, Vienna in July 1832 (P289)
Subsequent editions:	Peters: Vol. 3/175; AGA XX 429: Vol. 7/108; NSA IV: Vol. 13/95
Bibliography:	Capell 1928, pp. 185–6
	Einstein 1951, pp. 326–7
	Fischer-Dieskau 1977, p. 173
	Kohlhäufl 1999, p. 177
Discography and timing:	Fischer-Dieskau II 6^5 6'00
	Hyperion I 35^4
	Hyperion II 27^3 6'49 Lynne Dawson

← *Lied (Des Lebens Tag ist schwer)* D788   *Vergissmeinnicht* D793 →

Der PILGRIM   The pilgrim
(SCHILLER) OP. 37 NO. 1, **D794** [H518]

The song exists in two versions, the second of which is discussed below:
(1) May 1823; (2) appeared February 1825

(1) 'Mässig'   E major – C♯ minor   𝄵   [106 bars]

(2) D major – B minor

(106 bars)

(1)	Noch in meines Lebens Lenze	I was still in the springtime of my life
	War ich, und ich wandert' aus,	When I journeyed forth,
	Und der Jugend frohe Tänze	And left the merry dances of youth
	Liess ich in des Vaters Haus.	In my father's house.
(2)	All mein Erbteil, all mein Habe	All my inheritance, all my possessions
	Warf ich fröhlich glaubend hin,	I cast away in cheerful faith,
	Und am leichten Pilgerstabe	And with childlike heart
	Zog ich fort mit Kindersinn.	Set off with my pilgrim's staff.
(3)	Denn mich trieb ein mächtig Hoffen	For a mighty hope drove me on,
	Und ein dunkles Glaubenswort:	And a dark word of faith,
	'Wandle,' rief's 'der Weg ist offen,	'Journey onwards', came the cry, 'the way is open,
	Immer nach dem Aufgang fort.'	ever onwards towards the East.'
(4)	'Bis zu einer goldnen Pforten	'Until you reach a golden gate;
	Du gelangst, da gehst du ein,	There you will enter,
	Denn das Irdische wird dorten	For there earthly things
	Himmlisch, unvergänglich sein.'	Become celestial, immortal.'
(5)	Abend ward's und wurde Morgen,	Evening came, and morning,
	Nimmer, nimmer stand ich still,	Never, never did I stop;
	Aber immer blieb's verborgen,	Yet what I seek, what I long for,
	Was ich suche, was ich will.	Always remained hidden.
(6)	Berge lagen mir im Wege,	Mountains loomed in my path,
	Ströme hemmten meinen Fuss,	Rivers checked my step;
	Über Schlünde baut ich Stege,	I built bridges over the abyss
	Brücken durch den wilden Fluss.	And across the turbulent river.
(7)	Und zu eines Stroms Gestaden	And I came to the bank of the river
	Kam ich, der nach Morgen floss;	That flowed eastwards:

| Froh vertrauend seinem Faden, | Joyfully trusting to its current |
| Warf ich mich in seinen Schoss.[1] | I threw myself upon its bosom. |

(8) Hin zu einem grossen Meere   The play of its waves
    Trieb mich seiner Wellen Spiel;   Bore me to a great ocean;
    Vor mir liegt's in weiter Leere,   It lies before me in its vast emptiness.
    Näher bin ich nicht dem Ziel.   I am no nearer my goal.

(9) Ach, kein Steg will dahin führen,   Ah, no bridge will take me there,
    Ach, der Himmel über mir   Ah, the sky above me
    Will die Erde nicht berühren,[2]   Will not touch the earth,
    Und das Dort ist niemals hier!   And the There is never Here!

Friedrich von Schiller (1759–1805); poem written in May 1803

This is the forty-third of Schubert's forty-four Schiller solo settings (1811–24). See the poet's biography for a chronological list of all the Schiller settings.

This is the penultimate Schiller setting. (The last, *Dithyrambe* D801 is considerably less serious.) It stands next to the great song cycle *Die schöne Müllerin* D795 in the Deutsch catalogue and was composed about six months after the devastating diagnosis of Schubert's illness. At first glance the two works may appear incongruent bedfellows, but they share a number of characteristics apart from being the products of a genius at the height of its powers. Common themes are: journeying forth in the springtime of life (both miller boy and pilgrim are walking towards a new destiny); water music (admittedly of different kinds) and, despite the happiest of beginnings, the ultimate defeat of idealism and hope. How the composer's view of the world had changed since his early Schiller songs!

Verses 1–4: The song is made up of an ingenious chain of related melodies somewhat reminiscent (for eight bars or so) of Haydn's 'St Anthony Chorale', immortalized by Brahms. It is cleverly constructed to incorporate elements of the strophic song and to suggest thereby homespun simplicity and goodness. But the hand of the composer is ever present to modify and redirect; what appears at first to be merely simple is shown to be infinitely subtle. The first section, four verses long, establishes the traveller's good-hearted optimism and his background. The pilgrims' chorale is taken at a measured pace but it should not be too slow. It is all too easy to make this music elegiac; without a bracing impetus behind it (two, not four in a bar – and here the first version marked *alla breve* is surely correct) the music seems interminable and heavy. Verses 1 and 3 are musically identical, and so are Verses 2 and 4. There are strong pre-echoes of Leitner's *Der Kreuzzug* D932, in mood and tonality (D major) rather than in tempo. Leitner's monk is contemplative, watching from his cell as the crusade sets out, but there is little doubt that Schiller's pilgrim, like Bunyan's in *Pilgrim's Progress*, is a man of action. His is a song of the open road. He is not necessarily a Christian, however: mention of a 'dunkles Glaubenswort' in Verse 3 suggests that this supplicant had been in the thrall of an exotic religion which has required him to rid himself of his earthly possessions and travel towards the East. The poem as a whole is a warning against believing in a golden gate and celestial Nirvana as earthly destinations.

[1] Schiller writes '*Werf* ich mich in seinen Schoss'.
[2] Schiller writes 'Will die Erde *nie* berühren'.

Verses 5–6: The second part of the song's three-part structure throws obstacles in the path of the pilgrim's progress, as well as the performer's peace of mind. Their journey is relentlessly driven ('Nimmer, nimmer stand ich still' bb. 51–2) by a hopeless quest for the Golden Gate linking earth and heaven. Verse 5 is relatively simple tonally, but at Verse 6 a complex harmonic terrain makes the going tough. The section beginning 'Berge lagen mir im Wege' (b. 57) brings a dazzling sequence of modulations in quick succession, making the keyboard as dangerous a place as the mountaineer's slippery rock face. We emerge from the chromatic crevasse with an imposing modulation (at b. 65) into a more settled F major – more settled at least from the point of view of harmony, if not movement.

Verses 7–8: From b. 66 oscillating quavers replace crotchets in the accompaniment and announce water music: first a gentle stream which, being a natural medium, repeats the tune (transposed into F major) of Verses 1 and 3. As the river falls to the great sea (Verse 8), left-hand broken octaves plunge to the bottom of the keyboard (first at bb. 70–72, and then ever more dramatically at bb. 79–81). The beginning of Verse 8 recycles the vocal line heard at the beginning of Verse 5, transposed a minor third higher. Schubert's structure is a cat's cradle of ingenuity, weaving contrasting melodic strands together in the manner of a rondo. This roundabout excursion has led nowhere. The awful realization that the journey has all been in vain ('Näher bin ich nicht dem Ziel' from b. 85) stops the traveller in his tracks. He sings the words twice as if he can scarcely believe that all his hopes have been utterly betrayed. There is no ritardando, only a suspension on the semibreve of b. 91.

Verse 9: The music, now marked 'Sehr Langsam', changes to ¾ time and, in a spacious and elegaic B minor, is searing in its intensity. Mention of the unattainable 'Himmel über mir' in the major key (bb. 94–6) seems savagely masochistic, and the words 'There is never Here' are pronounced as if from on high, a heavy sentence against which there is no appeal. The final 'ist niemals hier', where the third of the scale is sharpened to suggest the major key (b. 103), is almost triumphant. There is a fierce joy, perhaps even a madness, in facing reality head on. The final whiplash piano chord (now unequivocally in the minor) closes all exploration with cruel finality. The dotted rhythms of this eloquent page are extremely reminiscent of the final verse of *Der Unglückliche* D713 (also in D major–B minor) from 1821.

The poetry of Schiller is part of a German tradition where control and industry, the ethical unimpeachability of the great and good, were valued. This certainly applied to the rigorous moral values of Schubert's father. If we never feel that our hero was as close to Schiller as to Goethe or indeed to Mayrhofer, it is perhaps because Schiller, part of Schubert's song-composing life from almost the very beginning, represented the guiding ideals of a type of literary paternal authority. The invitation to escape into new expressive pastures of sensuality and innovation came from other poets, and the composer had to leave home to achieve his full potential. But Schubert loved his father whatever their difficulties. On the evidence of the quality of much of the music, and because he kept returning to the poet, it is clear that he loved Schiller too. It cannot be denied, however, that other relationships in his life, both personal and literary, were easier.

Autograph:	Staatsbibliothek Preussischer Kulturbesitz, Berlin (first draft)
Publication:	First published in *Der Merker*, Wien 1909. In the AGA (1895), this E major version was corrected to include aspects of the second version in D major. First published thereafter as part of the NSA in 1975 (P762; first version)
	Published as Op. 37 no. 1 by Cappi & Co., Vienna in February 1825 (P77; second version)

Dedicatee:	Ludwig Ferdinand Schnorr von Carolsfeld
Subsequent editions:	Peters: Vol. 4/24; AGA XX 432: Vol. 7/130; NSA IV: Vol. 2a/132 & Vol. 2b/229; Bärenreiter: Vol. 2/29
Bibliography:	Black 2003, p. 108
	Capell 1928, pp. 186–7
	Einstein 1951, p. 255
	Fischer-Dieskau 1977, p. 189
Further settings:	Johann Friedrich Reichardt (1752–1814) *Der Pilgrim* (1809)
Discography and timing:	Fischer-Dieskau II 6[7] 4'26
	Hyperion I 1[18] & 16[15] 4'34 Janet Baker
	4'21 Thomas Allen
	Hyperion II 27[6] 4'21 Thomas Allen

←— *Das Geheimnis* D793   *Auf dem Wasser zu Singen* D774 —→

AUGUST GRAF VON PLATEN HALLERMÜNDE (1796–1835)

THE POETIC SOURCES

S1 *Ghaselen* von August Graf von Platen Hallermünde. Erlangen, Carl Heyder, 1821

This book of 38 pages contains thirty ghazals with a concluding poem addressed to Goethe.

S2 *Vermischte Schriften* von August Graf von Platen Hallermünde, Erlangen, bey Carl Heyder. 1822

This book of 174 pages contains: the play *Marats Tod*, 1820; *Oden und Cantaten* 1816–20; *Lieder* 1813–18; the parody *Die neuen Propheten* 1817; *Colombos Geist* 1818; *Elegische Gedichte* 1813–20; 24 *Ghaselen*; *Abschied von der Zeit* als Epilogus.

THE SONGS

Before 17 April 1822   *Die Liebe hat gelogen* D751 [S2: p. 90, no. XXXIV of *Lieder 1813–1818*]

July 1822   *Du liebst mich nicht* D756 [S1: p. 15, no. 9 of the *Ghaselen*]

Karl August Georg Maximilian, Graf von Platen Hallermünde was born on 24 October 1796 in Ansbach, also the home town of the poet Johann Peter Uz (qv), the only child of Protestant aristocrats. However, the family fortunes were at a low ebb, and Platen never enjoyed the financial means that should have accompanied his birth and status, being brought up to be more or less unaware of his family's position. His mother doted on him, holding herself responsible for much of his early education. As a little boy he wrote plays and poems and was fascinated by legends and fairy tales. He became fiercely patriotic, railing against against Napoleon's invasion of Germany; his parents accordingly thought it a good idea to place him in a highly disciplined academy in Munich (the *Kadettenkorps*) where he was brought up in a military manner, sleeping on straw and punished a good deal for his wilful temperament. The only compensation in this hard life was special friendships with other boys – Max von Gruber and Gustav Jacobs, both anti-authority and both protective towards the younger August, as well as the Fugger brothers. All these students were passionate about literature and were admirers of Goethe and Schiller. From the age of thirteen until the end of his life Platen kept a *Tagebuch*, a diary in thirty-three books and eighteen volumes (published only in 1896) that is one of the most important and self-revealing documents ever undertaken by a German writer. From this we can read of his many private passions, both literary and personal, beginning with his affection for fellow student Joseph Xylander whom he met in 1810, and to whom he dedicated many poems. Much of the poetry he wrote in these years was destroyed.

Instead of immediately going into military service on leaving the *Kadettenkorps*, Platen entered royal service as one of the king of Bavaria's pages – a life of comfort and luxury for good-looking boys of noble birth – where he played a willing part in what was in effect a piece of royal theatre. He learned Italian from one of the other pages, Graf Lodeon Laterano (this was to stand him in good stead later in life) and his duties were more like those of an extra in a sumptuously produced opera. In 1814 the political circumstances of the time, and the poet's continuing passion for a free Germany, resulted in his enlisting in the army. He saw no military service, however, and his increasingly evident homosexual disposition alienated him from the authoritarianism of a military environment. (His life-long dislike of tyranny and forcefully imposed authority is demonstrated by the remarkable lyrics he wrote in favour of Polish freedom – the so-called *Polenlieder* – in 1830–31.) In 1818 he obtained indefinite leave of absence from his regiment – with some rules still attached, as he was to discover later (*see* below). He studied law, botany and zoology at the university of Würzburg, a period that came to a head in a crisis over his embarrassingly passionate attachment to a fellow student, Eduard Schmidtlein, whom he named 'Adrast' (interestingly enough also the title of a *Singspiel* by Schubert, D137, written to Mayrhofer's libretto between 1817 and 1819).

In October 1819 Platen moved to Erlangen to study with, among others, the philosopher Friedrich Wilhelm Joseph von Schelling (1775–1854). In 1820 he made a short visit to Vienna where he possibly encountered another young poet from the Schubert circle, Franz von Bruchmann. Or it may have been that the two met at the home of Schelling in Erlangen, Bruchmann having defied Austrian law in moving from Vienna to study in the Franconian city. For a time Bruchmann and Platen got on famously, Bruchmann delivering poems for Schubert to set to music and, once composed, sending these on to Platen much to the poet's delight. Platen's decision to begin piano lessons in November 1821 could have been influenced by Bruchmann's love of music; the young Viennese had been enthusiastic about the pleasures of being one of Schubert's friends and the beauties of Schubert's Goethe settings.

During Platen's sojourn in Erlangen (where he remained until 1826 with various side-trips into other parts of Germany) he learned Persian and Arabic, and encountered such luminaries

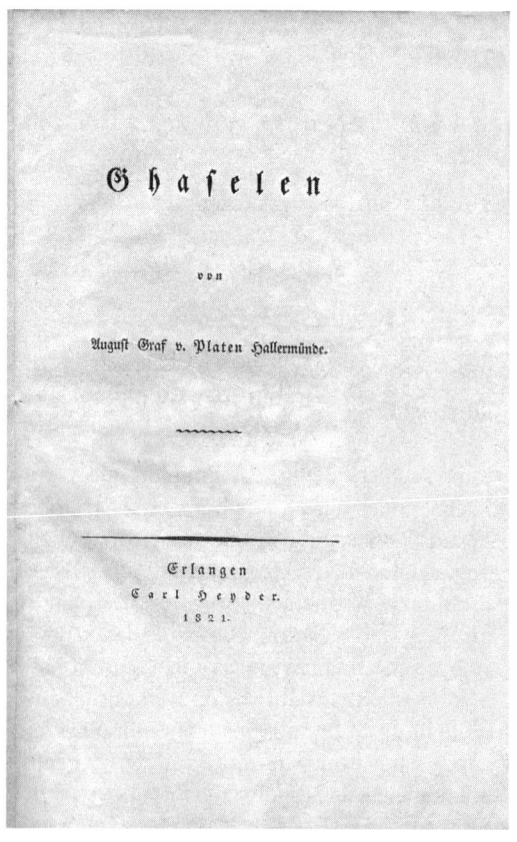

Ghaselen, Erlangen (1821). The Arabic quotation is printed on the obverse side of the title page.

as Goethe, the novelist Jean Paul, the philologist Jacob Grimm and the poet Friedrich Rückert. Platen published his *Ghaselen* in 1821 with a frontispiece printed in Arabic. On leaving Erlangen, Bruchmann was given a copy inscribed with a sonnet – he had, after all, enlisted the help of Joseph von Hammer-Purgstall (qv *West-östlicher Divan*) in obtaining for Platen copies of manuscripts of Persian poetry in the Vienna court library. *Lyrische Blätter* followed in the same year. *Vermischte Schriften* appeared in 1822 and *Neue Ghaselen* in 1823. At sometime during this period there seems to have been a falling-out between Platen and Bruchmann where the affectionate 'Du' form of address to be found in the sonnet (later printed as 'An F. von B. Mit den Gaselen') reverted to a cold 'Sie' on Bruchmann's side. If this estrangement had not occurred perhaps there would have been further Platen settings; given the quality of this poetry it is regrettable that there were only two.

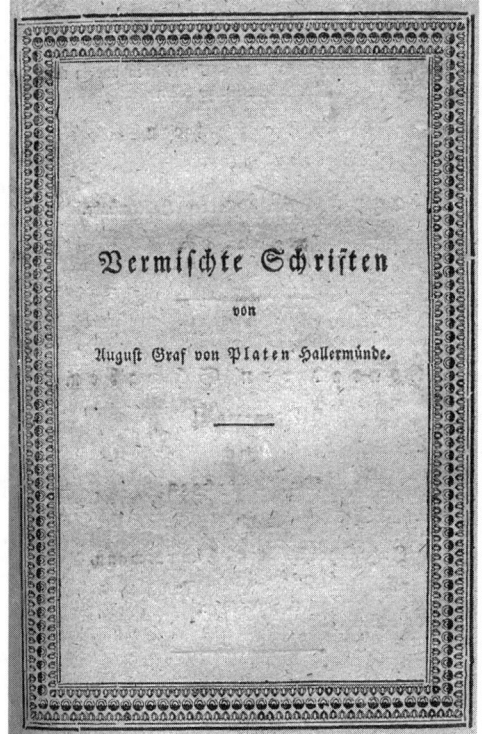

Cover of Platen's *Vermischte Schriften* (Miscellaneous Writings) (1822).

All this time Platen was effectively on leave from his Bavarian regiment in order to pursue his studies. In autumn 1824 he spent two sybaritic months in Venice. As a result of overstaying his military leave (by this time he seemed to have forgotten that he had any military obligations whatever) he was arrested in Nuremberg the following January and jailed until March. Fortunately the new king of Bavaria, Ludwig I, himself a poet and an admirer of Platen's gifts, offered to set the poet free and provide him with enough money to live in Italy and further his talents. Accordingly Platen left Erlangen on 3 September 1826 and began a new life. He believed that in Italy he would find a more tolerant ambience in which to live, but in practical terms he found nothing less than exile. His *Gedichte* were printed in 1828, and he spent a great deal of time polishing and re-polishing his earlier works. Although partly supported by royal grants, Platen was never able to live in comfort, and his stay in Italy was never as fruitful as he (and his royal patron) might have wished. He wrote a number of stage pieces that eventually found some favour at the end of the nineteenth century, but interest in them was relatively short lived.

Platen lived in Naples as well as Florence (returning in between to Munich), but he eventually fled to Sicily, tormented by a hypochondriacal fear of catching cholera. He believed erroneously that he had contracted the disease and took massive amounts of a strong remedy, exacerbating a gastric condition from which he died in Syracuse on 5 December 1835. His schoolfriend Franz Fugger was the first to gather all his writings into a posthumous edition.

Schubert only set two of Platen's poems, although it seems that he had intended to set further lyrics, interestingly enough, on the theme of winter. (The Platen songs, with their tone of disappointed and bitter emotional turmoil, could be seen as forerunners to *Winterreise*.) The other major composer to interest himself in Platen's poetry was Johannes Brahms in four songs of Opus 32; there are also a handful of Schumann settings (all choral except the strangely beautiful *Ihre Stimme*

Graf August von Platen. Engraving by C. Barth.

Op. 96 no. 3), and some Cornelius and Hindemith. He was a poet admired more for fluency and technical command of form (an aspect of his talent that was praised by Goethe) than for depth of feeling. In this verdict was contained a certain amount of animus regarding his notorious lifestyle at a time when homosexuality was hidden and driven underground. The vicious ad hominem attack on Platen by Heinrich Heine in that writer's *Die Baden von Lucca* contained a large element of what would now be termed homophobia, itself aggravated by what Heine took to be Platen's anti-Semitism in a review. In reality this represented the unedifiying spectacle of Germany's outsiders attacking one another to the delight of those who detested them both. In recent years Platen's works, and in particular his confessional diaries, have taken on a new resonance in the light of his lifelong emotional struggles. The poetry itself, normally a model of objectivity, is seldom as self-revealing as the two lyrics that Schubert received through Bruchmann. Platen is admired above all for his command of language and metre. It is for this reason that John G. Robertson (*A History of German Literature*, 1902) calls him 'the most perfect artist among German poets'.

Bibliography: Dürhammer 1999, p. 203
                Robertson 1902, p. 500

EDUARD PLATNER (1786–1860) or **ANTON PLATTNER** (1787–1855)

THE POETIC SOURCE
Taschenbuch zum geselligen Vergnügen. Fünfzehnter Jahrgang 1805. Herausgegeben von W. G. Becker, Leipzig bei Christian Adolph Hempel

THE SONG
No later than October 1817   *Die Blumensprache* D519 [pp. 165–6]

In Becker's almanac of 1805 the poem for *Die Blumensprache* is signed with the letters 'Pl'. Since Mandyczewski this was thought to have referred to a poet named Anton Platner (although the spelling of his name was actually Plattner), who was born in Innsbruck on 3

Becker's *Taschenbuch zum geselligen Vergnügen* (Pocketbook for sociable Pleasures) (1805). The poem *Die Blumensprache* is printed on pp. 165–6, and signed simply with 'Pl.'

November 1787 and died in Brixen on 27 January 1855. His career, which finds a short entry in Goedeke (Vol. 6 p. 676), was summed up by Fischer-Dieskau thus: 'He had been a shepherd near Innsbruck. He had taken Holy Orders after University, but then turned eccentric, writing poems and diaries in his isolation.' This does not sound very hopeful bearing in mind that Plattner was not known to have published anything before 1858, much less a valentine verse written at the age of eighteen! Another possible author (a theory backed by the NSA) is Eduard Platner (1786–1860) who came from Marburg and was professor for Jurisprudence at the early age of twenty-five. He did contribute to alamanacs, and if the author was indeed named Platner, a preco-cious contribution to Becker from Eduard (he would have been nineteen) seems more believable. But the 1805 almanac contains another contribution from 'Pl.' entitled *Die Heimath* (p. 315) which hymns the mountains and valleys of 'Schweizerland', an area that is nearer Plattner in Tyrol than Platner in Marburg! Even more confusing is a contribution from 'Pl' entitled *Phantasien auf Rügen* (stamping ground of Kosegarten and Lappe) printed in the almanac for 1804 when the two putative Plat(t)ners would have been even younger. There is a further 'Pl.' contribution in the almanac for 1809 entitled *Harmonia*. All this suggests a pseudonym and a mystery not yet satisfactorily unravelled.

AARON POLLAK (1764–1829)

THE POETIC SOURCE
Allgemeine Theaterzeitung, 8 April 1828 (No. 43)

THE SONG
April–June 1827   *Frühlingslied* D919 [p. 169]

Pollak was born in 1764 in Prague and made his career in Vienna as an occasional poet and a proofreader of Hebraic script, first in the firm of Georg Holzinger (see *Wiens Buchdrucker-Geschichte* 1882–1882, by Anton Mayer, 1887, p. 190), and then in the firm of Anton Schmid (pp. 143–4). This publisher became Anton, Edler von Schmid in 1825 and his business was famed throughout German-speaking lands for its printing of books in oriental languages (including a complete bible in Hebrew with a German translation by Moses Mendelssohn). Schmid's offices were in the Strudelhof in the Währingergasse. According to the directory of poets printed in Böckh's *Wiens lebende Schriftsteller, Künstler und Dilettanten* (1822), Pollak himself lived in the Wipplingerstrasse, not far from where Schubert and Mayrhofer had shared an apartment. It is tempting to imagine some personal contact between the composer and the considerably older, unmarried poet, and it is not impossible that they met through Salomon Sulzer as a result of the composer's engagement with the Jewish community towards the end of his life that culminated in the composition of *Der 92. Psalm* D953 (qv). The biblical subject matter of Pollak's writing (the titles of his poems are listed in Goedeke, Vol. 17), as well as mention of King Solomon in the original version of *Frühlingslied*, suggest an Orthodox Jewish background and sensibility.

Pollak was a sometime contributor to the *Allgemeine Theaterzeitung*, a Viennese publication founded in 1806 by Adolf Bäuerle. The *Wiener Zeitschrift* of Johann Schickh, founded in 1816, was a rival publication that also included supplementary Viennese fashion plates in colour, and in which Schubert published a number of his songs for the first time. The poem of *Frühlingslied* (with the rubric 'Komp v. Franz Schubert') appeared in the *Allgemeine Theaterzeitung* of 8 April 1828; according to the manuscript, Schubert had composed the unaccompanied choral version of the poem (D914) almost exactly a year earlier, and possibly the solo song version at more or less the same time. Pollak died of tuberculosis, deeply in debt, in the Judenspital, Vienna's Jewish hospital, on 6 February 1829. He was buried in the Währinger Friedhof, where Schubert had been laid to rest three months earlier, although probably in a different part of the cemetery reserved for those of Pollak's faith.

ALEXANDER POPE (1688–1744)

THE POETIC SOURCE
The Works of Alexander Pope, Henry Lintott, London, 1736 (in three volumes) Volume 1 p. 100: *The Dying Christian to his Soul* – Ode

THE SONG
4 May 1813   *Verklärung* D59 based on Pope's *The Dying Christian to his Soul* translated by Johann Gottfried von Herder [*see also* HERDER]

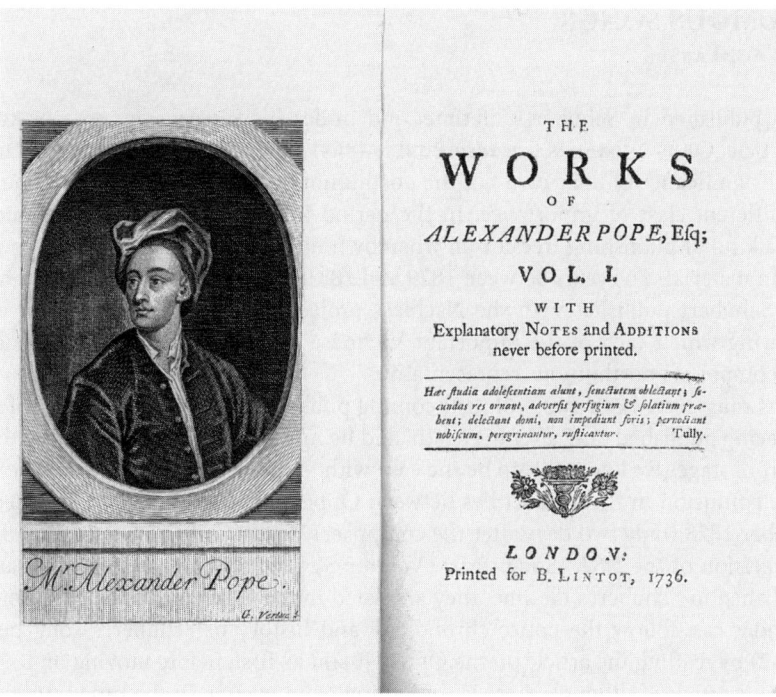

THE

WORKS

O F

ALEXANDER POPE, Efq;

VOL. I.

WITH

Explanatory Notes and Additions
never before printed.

*Hæc ftudia adolefcentiam alunt, fenectutem oblectant; fe-
cundas res ornant, adverfis perfugium & folatium præ-
bent; delectant domi, non impediunt foris; pernoctant
nobifcum, peregrinantur, rufticantur.*   Tully.

LONDON:
Printed for B. Lintot, 1736.

The Works of Alexander Pope, Vol. I (1736). The Ode, *The Dying Christian to his soul* is printed on pp. 100–1 of this volume.

The poem by Pope that Schubert set in Herder's German translation was written in 1712 and published in 1730 (revised 1736). Pope had initially composed a poem entitled 'Adriani morientis ad animam' – or *The Heathen to his dying Soul* (in this case referring to the Roman Emperor Hadrian). This began 'Ah, fleeing spirit! wandering fire / That long has warmed my tender breast'. Richard Steele, editor of the *Spectator*, encouraged Pope to write a Christian equivalent, 'an ode, as of a cheerful dying spirit' and he complied with a lyric that has remained one of his most famous.

Alexander Pope, born on 21 May in 1688 in London, is one of the select band of British writers who featured in Schubert's song-writing catalogue (the others are William Shakespeare, Walter Scott, Colley Cibber and Abraham Cowley, qqv and *see* Great Britain and British Literature). Pope's *Essay on Man* was translated into German in 1822 after which he joined the ranks of Milton, Ossian, Goldsmith, Byron and Marlowe as a European classic. Herder's translation of *The Dying Christian to his Soul* dates from as early as 1786 and was part of an essay entitled *How the Ancients looked at Death*. Pope's greatness as poet, satirist, epigrammist and polemicist needs no explication here. In May 1813, when Schubert added the words 'nach Pope von Herder' to the song autograph, he could not have known anything of Pope's character which was somewhat at odds with these elevated lines. The poet's body was twisted by ill-health and his mind was equivalently maimed by resentments, real and imaginary. It was said of 'the wasp of Twickenham' that he was always taking offence, scheming, reviling, and that he could not so much as take tea without a stratagem. As a trendsetter for the savagery of London's literary scene in the mid-eighteenth century, Pope would have surmounted the comparatively provincial back-biting perils of Viennese artistic life with virtuosic ease. He died on 30 May 1744.

Die POST *see WINTERREISE* D911/13

POSTHUMOUS SONGS
[*see also* NACHLASS]

The songs published in Schubert's lifetime, and under his supervision, are considered in a separate article: OPUS NUMBERS (*see also* PUBLISHERS). The numbers listed in that article have a historical significance of their own but the posthumous opus numbers are more questionable and in a different class of importance. In the period immediately following Schubert's death there was a kind of publishing free-for-all whereby no firm could claim to have a monopoly of Schubertian material. The years between 1829 and 1831 (before Diabelli established his ascendancy as a Schubert publisher with the Nachlass project, qv) were remarkable for a flurry of activity during which each of the important Viennese publishers seems to have laid claim to being the composer's posthumous representative.

Schubert must have been aware of forthcoming publishing plans for a number of songs that ended up being published only after his death, and he might well have seen some of these works through proof stage (we know this to be the case with the second part of *Winterreise*). The area of possible confusion in this respect lies between Opp. 98 and 108 – songs published between 21 November 1828 (only two days after the composer's death) and as late as April 1831. In line with the decision of the NSA (Song series, Volume 5) to treat these songs in the same way as those published in Schubert's lifetime, they are listed in the article on OPUS NUMBERS.

The reader can follow the entire chronology and history of Schubert's song publications (1821–2012) by reading the article on the OPUS NUMBERS first, before moving on to NACHLASS and lastly this article – although there is something of an overlap in the time frame covered in NACHLASS and POSTHUMOUS SONGS. Each song publication has been given a 'P' number from P1 (*Erlkönig*) to P866 (these numbers are also to be found in the song commentaries) which gives the reader an idea, if only approximate, of how long it took for each song to reach print.

1829
Op. 110 *Der Kampf* (for the bass voice) P196
31 January (Josef Czerny)

Op. 111 *An die Freude* P197, *Lebensmelodien* P198, *Die vier Weltalter* P199
5 February (Josef Czerny)

Op. 112 *Gott im Ungewitter* P200, *Gott der Weltschöpfer* P201, *Hymne an den Unendlichen* P202
11 March (Josef Czerny)

Op. 116 *Die Erwartung* P203
13 April (M. J. Leidesdorf)

Schwanengesang (without opus number)
(i)   *Liebesbotschaft* P204
(ii)   *Kriegers Ahnung* P205
(iii)   *Frühlingssehnsucht* P206
(iv)   *Ständchen* P207
(v)   *Aufenthalt* P208
(vi)   *In der Ferne* P209
(vii)   *Abschied* P210

(viii)   *Der Atlas* P211
(ix)   *Ihr Bild* P212
(x)   *Das Fischermädchen* P213
(xi)   *Die Stadt* P214
(xii)   *Am Meer* P215
(xiii)   *Der Doppelgänger* P216
(xiv)   *Die Taubenpost* P217
4 May (Tobias Haslinger). The copyright to this work was later acquired by Diabelli.

Op. 115 *Das Lied im Grünen* P218, *Wonne der Wehmut* P219, *Sprache der Liebe* P220
18 June (M. J. Leidesdorf)

Op. 117 *Der Sänger* (second version) P221
19 June (Josef Czerny)

Op. 118 *Geist der Liebe* P222, *Der Abend* (Kosegarten) P223, *Tischlied* P224, *Lob des Tokayers* P225, *An die Sonne* (Baumberg) P226, *Die Spinnerin* P227
19 June (Josef Czerny)

Op. 109 *Am Bach im Frühling* (sic) (first version) P232, *Genügsamkeit* P233, *An eine Quelle* P234
10 July (A. Diabelli & Co.). This publisher was to become the major player in the publication of the posthumous songs but had not yet come up with his idea of a Schubert *Nachlass*, to be advertised and issued under this title. Op. 109 was thus advertised alongside Op. 98 (*see* OPUS NUMBERS).

Op. 119 *Auf dem Strom* P235
27 October (M. J. Leidesdorf)

Op. 124 *Zwey Scenen* aus dem *Schauspiele: Lacrimas von A. W. Schlegel* [sic]: *Delphine* P236, *Florio* P237
30 October (A. Pennauer). These were the last songs to be offered in 1829.

1830

Op. 126 *Ballade* 'Ein Fräulein schaut vom hohen Thurm' (Kenner) P238
5 January (Josef Czerny)

Op. 129 *Der Hirt auf dem Felsen* P239
1 June (Tobias Haslinger). This publisher, having failed to assign an opus number to *Schwanengesang*, must now have deemed it necessary to give one to this important work in order to keep up with his competitors.

Op. 130 *Das Echo* P249
12 July (Thaddäus Weigl). This publisher had been associated with publishing Schubert's lighter songs.

Even after Diabelli had begun his overwhelmingly important Nachlass series in the summer and autumn of 1830 there remained other publishers still holding a handful of Schubert manuscripts who were determined not to allow him to dominate the field entirely. Their possessions however were small beer in comparison with the piles of important music that Diabelli had up his sleeve (*see* NACHLASS).

Op. 131 *Der Mondabend* P255, *Trinklied* P256, *Klaglied* P257
9 November (Josef Czerny)

Op. 123 *Viola* P258
26 November (A. Pennauer). There is little surprise that with so many publishers using posthumous opus numbers, this work was assigned an earlier number than either the Schütz songs issued in 1829, or the Kenner *Ballade* issued in early 1830.

1832
Even Diabelli himself chose not to include several important Schubert works in his ongoing Nachlass (qv) project. These were usually bigger choral items and were issued side by side with the *Nachlass* song volumes, appearing with opus numbers at a similarly leisurely pace:

Op. 132 *Psalm XXIII* P284
12 March (A. Diabelli & Co.)

1839
Op. 133 *Gott in der Natur* P327
11 November (A. Diabelli and Co.)

Op. 134 *Nachthelle* P328
Middle of 1839(?) (A. Diabelli & Co.)

Op. 136 *Mirjams Siegesgesang* P329
c. 1839 (A. Diabelli & Co.)

1840
Op. 135 *Ständchen* (Grillparzer) (second version) (mezzo soprano and choir) P330
Op. 139 *Gebet* (quartet for SATB and piano) P331
Beginning of 1840 (A. Diabelli & Co.)

1842
Op. 146 *Des Tages Weihe (Schicksalslenker, blicke nieder)* P336
5 January (A. Diabelli and Co.)

1845
Op. 151 *Schlachtlied*
c. 1845 (A. Diabelli & Co.). Diabelli reverted to an opus number for this unaccompanied double chorus (with an optional accompaniment by Ferdinand Schubert) because this type of work was not included in the Nachlass. Unaccompanied choral works of this kind mostly fall outside the scope of this book.

1849
Op. 158 *Der Frühlingsmorgen* (new words attached to *Cantata zum Geburtstag des Sängers Johann Michael Vogl*) P364
(A. Diabelli & Co.)

With Diabelli's retirement in 1850, his firm was taken over by C. A. Spina (1827–1906), the son of a colleague from his earliest days in publishing. Diabelli & Co. were clearly still in possession of a number of song manuscripts. A set of Schubert songs had been engraved in 1852 but were only issued in 1862. Diabelli had probably decided that the fifty volumes of his *Nachlass* should be regarded as something complete in themselves.

1860

Die Wehmut [*Die Herbstnacht*] (first version) P394, *Abschied von der Harfe* (second version) P395 (C. A. Spina)

1862

Op. 165 *Liederkranz* Sammlung von Liedern aus dem Nachlass für eine Singstimme mit Begleitung des Pianoforte: *Die Liebende schreibt* (second version) P396,[1] *Die Sternennächte* (second version) P397, *Das Bild* P398, *Die Täuschung* P399,[2] *Altschottische Ballade* [Eine altschottische Ballade] (first version) P400
6 June (C. A. Spina). The word 'Liederkranz' is clearly merely a marketing ploy; the inference that the four songs published in Op. 165 were somehow connected in terms of theme, poet or date is self-evidently false.

1865

Op. 172 *Sechs Lieder: Der Traum* P401, *Die Laube* P402, *An die Nachtigall* (Hölty) P403, *Das Sehnen* P404, *An den Frühling* (Schiller) (I setting) P405, *Die Vögel* P406
2 December (C. A. Spina)

1867

Op. 173 *Sechs Lieder: Amalia* P407, *Das Geheimniss* (II setting) P408, *Vergebliche Liebe* P409, *Der Blumen Schmerz* P410,[3] *Die Blumensprache* P411, *Das Abendroth* (Schreiber) P412
Published in 1867 (C. A. Spina). With the issuing of Op. 173, thirty-nine years after Schubert's death, the firm of Diabelli finally published its last song by the composer via its successor, Spina. This is also the last of the posthumous opus numbers. In the meantime the firm of Diabelli–Spina had introduced a 'complete' Schubert songs in six volumes encompassing Opp. 1 to 110, and including the two Müller cycles and *Schwanengesang*. A gift of this edition was made by the singer Julius Stockhausen to Johannes Brahms in 1861.

THE RIETZ EDITION

At this point Schubert's reputation was growing to such an extent that for the first time a German – as opposed to Austrian – publisher became involved on a big scale. In 1867 the Leipzig firm of Bartholf Senff issued a handsome 'complete' edition of Schubert's songs edited by Julius Rietz of Dresden (1812–1877), pupil of Zelter, composer and conductor. Rietz had recently involved himself with the complete edition of Bach's works and would go on to edit Mendelssohn's. The preface to this edition berates other publishers for the confusion that was beginning to emerge concerning conflicting versions of Schubert's songs; those in possession of manuscript copies and even autographs found that these sources often failed to line up with the published versions. It was clearly impossible for Rietz to solve these problems even if he was aware of them. His edition is in twenty slim hardback volumes, printed on fine paper, and bound in silk endpapers. These were in 'portrait' format, the 'landscape' printing of earlier Schubert editions having for

---

[1] *Die Liebende schreibt* had first appeared as a supplement to the *Wiener Zeitschrift für Kunst, Literatur, Theater und Mode* (issue of 26 June 1832).
[2] *Die Täuschung* was first issued as a supplement to *Zellners Blätter für Musik, Theater und Kunst* (C. A. Spina) in 1855.
[3] *Der Blumen Schmerz* had first appeared as a supplement to the *Wiener Zeitschrift für Kunst, Literatur, Theater und Mode* (issue of December 1821).

Franz Schubert, *Complete Songs*, Volume 1 of twenty in
the Julius Rietz Edition (1867).

The Sattler Edition of Schubert's works, in German and
French.

some time been considered impossibly old-
fashioned, associated as they were with the
smaller, oblong music stands to be found on
fortepianos. In Volumes 1–10, Rietz organized the songs chronologically in the order of
their opus numbers (1–131, with the later
opus numbers issued by Diabelli and Spina
ignored). After *Schwanengesang* (Volume 11)
his Volumes 12–20 print the Nachlass in
Diabelli's order (Books 1–50) without any
reference, however, to the numbering of these
Viennese fascicles. Although an edition such
as this that tried to impose order on the chaos
of Schubert song publication was inevitable
(given that pirated editions appeared with
impunity), Rietz's desire to give the public the
chance to own Schubert's songs as a single
body of work, and at one fell swoop, was a
challenge to the Viennese publishers who
perhaps had not envisaged a rival edition as
sumptuous as this.

THE HOLLE EDITION

Mention should be made of another, commercial, attempt to publish a 'complete Schubert'
in Germany, this time by the firm of Louis
Holle in Braunschweig (Wolfenbüttel to be
exact), edited by Sattler. Five rather crudely
printed folio volumes of *Lieder, Gesänge und
Balladen* contain the same material as Rietz's
edition (opp. 1 to 131, followed by the *Nachlass*) although this much more populist publication was destined for the whole European
market. Holle had links with Augener in
London and Hagen in New York, and the
songs included French singing translations.
There were also separate editions for special
voice types – the Holle volume for bass
contains transpositions that are still not available elsewhere.

1868

*Sechs bisher ungedruckte Lieder für eine Sing-
stimme mit Begleitung des Pianoforte* without
opus number: *Sehnsucht* (Schiller) (I setting)
P413, *Thekla* (I setting) P414, *An den Mond*
(Goethe) (II setting) P415, *An die Entfernte*
P416, *Romanze* (Matthisson) (2 version) P417,
Abendlied der Fürstin P418

Published in 1868 (Wilhelm Müller, Berlin). The archivist of the Prussian State Library in Berlin, Franz Espagne, had edited six songs in the library's possession.

1870

Mignon-Lieder ('Heiss mich nicht reden' I, P419, 'So lasst mich scheinen' II)
April (J. P. Gotthard). Of these two songs, only the early version of *Heiss mich nicht reden* D726 was a first edition – *So lasst mich scheinen* D727 had been published in the *Nachlass* in 1850.

1870–74: THE PETERS EDITION, VOLUMES 1 TO 6

The Peters Edition has been part of the life of so many generations of lovers of Schubert's songs that a brief history of the Leipzig firm should be given here. It was founded in 1800 by Hoffmeister & Kühnel as the Bureau de la Musique and bought by Carl Friedrich Peters in 1813 (he corresponded with Josef Hüttenbrenner concerning Schubert's music in a long letter written in Leipzig on 12 November 1822, but the negotiations came to nothing). The firm was run as Bureau de Musique C. F. Peters until the owner's death in 1827. His daughter sold it to C. G. Böhme who kept the name Peters and who then sold it on to the Berlin publisher Julius Fried-laender (no relation to Max). Friedlaender was joined in 1863 by Max Abraham who had modern plans for the firm, and Edition Peters was founded in 1867 as a musical equivalent of the popular publishing firm of Reklam – music for the people and mass propagation of culture.

Beginning in 1870 the Leipzig publishers C. F. Peters produced a set of six Schubert lieder volumes, 383 songs in all, clearly designed to compete with the other complete editions; each volume was more substantial than Rietz's slim instalments but avoided the unwieldy clumsiness of Holle's crudely printed folios. The volumes were portable and opened easily on the piano's music stand (in portrait, rather than landscape, format); the easy to read print and the compact format were so popular with the public that almost the whole lieder repertoire itself was to become synonymous with Peters' typesetting and style for generations to come. Abandoning the chronological sequence of opus numbers (of little interest to singers who simply wanted to get their hands on the most famous songs) Peters eventually included all the lieder published in Schubert's lifetime, and much of the material from Diabelli's *Nachlass*. An important editor of this edition was the Leipzig musicologist Alfred Dörffel (1821–1905) whose extensive music library was eventually taken over by Peters. Nevertheless, the Peters Schubert edition was later to become entirely identified with Max Friedlaender (1852–1934) who did not initiate the project but expanded and somewhat rearranged it. Volume 1 had initially opened with *Die schöne Müllerin*, *Winterreise* and *Schwanengesang* followed by a selection of twenty-two 'famous' songs (as opposed to the thirty-four in the later Friedlaender edition); these began with *Erlkönig* and *Gretchen am Spinnrade* (Opp. 1 and 2), but were mostly chosen irrespective of their opus numbers or chronology. These 'Ausgewählte Lieder' had originally appeared in 1870 as a volume on their own. It was a selection that was to stand the test of time – the same songs (in more or less the same sequence) are included in Peters Volume 1 to this day. The second volume contained many great songs, but these were generally rather less well known than those printed in the first; Volume 3 represented a further step away from familiar popularity, and so on. This edition was the most successful of all time as far as the Schubert songs were concerned because it prioritized the amateur singer's performing needs, and enabled people to collect the complete editions gradually if they so preferred, buying each volume as their Schubertian enthusiasm grew.

1871

5 Canti per una sola voce con accompagnamento di Pianoforte composti da Fr. Schubert without opus number: *Non t'accostar all'urna* P420, *Guarda, che bianca luna* P421, *Da quel sembiante appresi* P422, *Mio ben ricordati* P423, *Pensa che questo istante* (2 version) P424

Published in 1871 (J. P. Gotthard, Vienna). The four songs of D688 were thus put together with the early D76.

1872

Neueste Folge nachgelassener mehrstimmiger Gesänge mit und ohne Begleitung von Franz Schubert: An die Sonne (Uz) P425, *Das Grab* (III setting) P426
Published in 1872 (J. P. Gotthard, Vienna). In this collection of nine choral items there were two first editions of ensemble songs with piano.

Neueste Folge nachgelassener Lieder und Gesänge von Franz Schubert: (1) *Wiedersehn* P427,[4] (2) *Gondelfahrer* (I setting, solo song) P428, (3) *Am Flusse* (II setting) P429, (4) *Nachthymne* P430, (5) *Nach einem Gewitter* P431, (6) *Grablied auf einen Soldaten* P432 [the Schubart text is wrongly ascribed to 'Jakobi' (*sic*)], (7) *Der gute Hirt* P433, (8) *Das gestörte Glück* P434, (9) *An die Sonne* (Tiedge) P435, (10) *Abends unter der Linde* (II setting) P436, (11) *Liebeständelei* P437, (12) *Ammenlied* P438, (13) *Sehnsucht (Mignon)* (II setting) P439, (14) *Hoffnung* (Goethe) (1 version) P440, (15) *Rückweg* P441, (16) *Der Knabe in der Wiege* (1 version) P442, (17) *Lebensmut* (Rellstab) P443, (18) *Der Jüngling und der Tod* (2 version) P444, (19) *La Pastorella* (II setting, solo song) P445, (20) *Nachtviolen* P446, (21) *Klage* D436 (2 version) P447 [the anonymous text wrongly ascribed to Hölty], (22) *Der Knabe* P448, (23) *Hoffnung* (Schiller) (I setting) P449, (24) *Herbstlied* P450, (25) *Aus 'Diego Manzanares'*[5] P451, (26) *Die verfehlte Stunde* (1 version) P452, (27) *Der Fluss* P453, (28) *Das Geheimnis* (Schiller) (I setting) P454, (29) *Liebesrausch* (II setting) P455, (30) *Die Sterne* (Fellinger) P456, (31) *Die Perle* P457, (32) *Leiden der Trennung* P458, (33) *Der Morgenkuss nach einem Ball* (1 version) P459, (34) *Clärchens Lied* (already published in Book 30 of the Nachlass), (35) *Sängers Morgenlied* (II setting) P460, (36) *Der Flüchtling* P461 (37–40) *Hymne* I, II, III & IV (Novalis) P462, P463, P464, P465
Published in 1872 (J. P. Gotthard, Vienna).

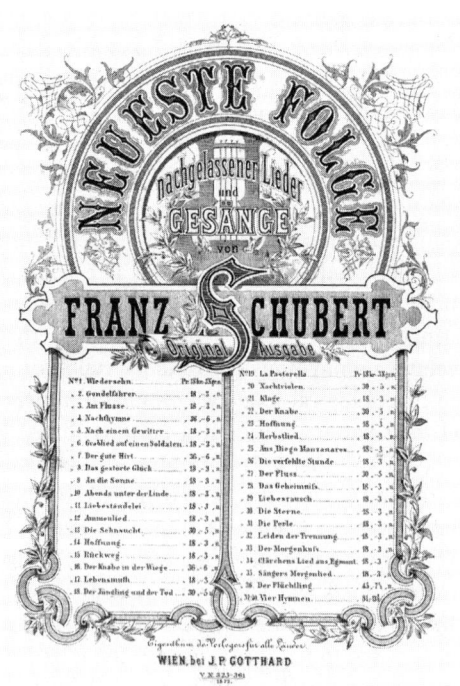

Forty Songs (*Neueste Folge nachgelassener Lieder und Gesänge*) published by J. P. Gotthard, Vienna (1872).

This substantial addition to the Schubert catalogue – thirty-seven of these completely new to the public – was published to coincide with the composer's seventy-fifth birthday celebrations.

---

[4] This was first issued as part of a musical supplement to *Lebensbilder aus Oesterreich – Ein Denkbuch vaterländischer Erinnerungen*, edited by Andreas Schumacher, Wien Tauer und Sohn, 1843.
[5] Someone at the firm of Gotthard must have decided to ignore Schubert's spelling of *Diego Manazares* on the autograph, favouring instead the correct spelling of Madrid's river. This is perfectly accurate as it happens, as the recent discovery of the song's literary source makes clear.

Gotthard took the opportunity to dedicate each of these songs to a well-known Viennese musical personality: thus songs 2, 3, 4 and 28 were dedicated to the baritone Julius Stockhausen, famous for his link with Brahms; 9, 10, 11, 14, 16, 17 to the tenor Gustav Walter; 22, 23, 29, 31, 36 to the great Schubertian collector Nikolaus von Dumba (the owner of the manuscripts of these particular songs). Other Kammersänger and Kammersängerinnen of the time such as Helene Magnus and Luise Dustmann (well-known Brahms singers) were similarly honoured.

1873

Franz Schubert: Sein Leben und seine Werke by August Reissmann
(J. Guttentag, Berlin). This biography contained first printings of *Schwertlied* P466, *Szene aus 'Faust'*, (1 version) P467, *Des Mädchens Klage* (III setting) P468, *Abschied von der Erde* P469. It also included a facsimile of the first page only of the second version of *Die Entzückung an Laura*.

1876

The Viennese firm of Kratochwill published two sets of Schubert songs (eighteen in all) arranged by Gotthard for piano solo, or pianoforte duet; the texts of the songs were printed above the piano staves. This venture must have been influenced by the mania for transcriptions at the time – something initiated by Liszt, as far as the Schubert songs were concerned, nearly thirty years earlier. Of these eighteen songs, six had never been published before: *Der Entfernten* P470, *Blanka [Das Mädchen]* P471, *Täglich zu singen* P472, *Abschied, nach einer Wallfahrtsarie* P473, *An mein Klavier* P474 and *Trauer der Liebe* P475. All, with the exception of *Täglich zu singen*, were published in their original vocal versions in the seventh volume of Friedlaender's edition for Peters in 1885 (*see* below).

In 1884 or a little earlier Max Abraham had invited Max Freidlaender to make a newly revised edition of Schubert's songs. The revised Volume 1 of the Peters set was soon published, this time with a foreword by Max Müller, the world-famous philologist who lived in England, and who was the son of the poet Wilhelm Müller. Bringing such a personal link to the edition was typical of Friedlaender's flair (*see* SCHOLARS). Friedlaender was also soon able to offer Peters a selection of Schubert songs that had never before been published (*see* below).

1885

Nachgelassene, bisher ungedrückte Lieder von F. Schubert: (1) *Die Gebüsche* P476, (2) *Trost (Nimmer lange weil ich hier)* P477, (3) *Minnelied* P478, (4) *Die Wehmuth (Die Herbstnacht)* P394 (published by Spina in 1860), (5) *Liebe schwärmt auf allen Wegen* P479, (6) *Hin und wieder fliegen Pfeile* P480, (7) *Abschied, nach einer Wallfahrtsarie* (published by Kratochwill in 1876), (8) *Idens Nachtgesang* P481, (9) *An mein Klavier* (Kratochwill, 1876), (10) *Furcht der Geliebten* (2 version) P482, (11) *Trauer der Liebe* (Kratochwill, 1876), (12) *Bei dem Grabe meines Vaters* P483, (13) *Abendlied* (Claudius) P484, (14) *Lieb Minna* P485, (15) *An den Frühling* (II setting, 1 version) P486, (16) *Schweizerlied* P487, (17) *Pflicht und Liebe* P488, (18) *Der Entfernten* (Kratochwill, 1876), (19) *Am See* (Mayrhofer, shortened version; thus this cannot be considered a first edition of the song), (20) *Blanka* (Kratochwill, 1876)
1 October 1885 (C. F. Peters, Leipzig). This collection, originally published in two slim volumes, was edited by Max Friedlaender, drawing on various sources, including songs that had appeared as piano arrangements in the Kratochwill edition of 1876.

1887

Without opus numbers. *Der Gott und die Bajadere* P489, *Bundeslied* P490
(Weinberger & Hofbauer, Vienna). Three Schubert songs were part of an anthology published by this Viennese firm in 1887. Two of these were the first editions of the above songs.

THE PETERS EDITION ENLARGED

In 1887 Max Friedlaender produced a second edition of his 1885 volume of unpublished songs (*see* above) by adding a further thirty numbers to make fifty in all. This expanded volume was issued as Volume 7 of the old and established Peters song edition in six volumes. Of the thirty songs, eight, although new to the Peters Edition, had already been published elsewhere, two by Müller of Berlin in 1868, one by Diabelli and one issued as a supplement (*Abschied von der Erde*) to A. Reissman's biography of Schubert that had appeared in 1873. The new songs, apart from two arias (32 and 33) arranged from operas were (21) *Geheimnis* (Mayrhofer) P491, (28) *Das Heimweh* (Hell) P492, (29) *Der Strom* P493,[6] (30) *Trinklied* (Zettler) P494, (31) *Die Einsiedelei* (II setting) P495, (35) *Freude der Kinderjahre* P496, (36) *Naturgenuss* P497, (37) *Daphne am Bach* P498, (38) *Nachtgesang* (Kosegarten) P499, (39) *Frühlingslied* (Hölty) P500, (40) *Der Jüngling am Bache* (II setting) P501, (41) *Das Mädchen aus der Fremde* (II setting) P502, (42) *Punschlied (Im Norden zu singen)* (Schiller) P503, (43) *Gott im Frühlinge* (1 version) P504, (44) *Liebhaber in allen Gestalten* P505, (45) *Die Liebesgötter* P506, (46) *Blumenlied* P507, (47) *Der Schatzgräber* P508, (49) *An die Geliebte* P509. The song *Seligkeit* (51 in later versions of this edition) was added only once it had appeared in Mandyczewski's *Gesamtausgabe*.

This seemingly definitive edition of Schubert's songs in seven volumes was commercially viable, but scholastically unfortunate in that it appeared some years before the definitive (for its time) *Gesamtausgabe*. There were no fewer than 200 songs that were to be published for the first time in that mighty work, so the seven-volume Peters Edition was far from complete, a fact that can still surprise the novice Schubert performer or collector who has invested in what he or she has erroneously believed to be a complete edition. Nevertheless, it was (and remains) handy to use, and enjoyed a sustained commercial success that must have made Diabelli and his successor Spina green with envy. It became an article of faith, especially for British Schubertians, proudly to possess 'all seven volumes'. This means of grading the depth of enthusiasm for Schubert lieder pertained until the end of the twentieth century. (America had rival Schubert anthologies in the International and Schirmer Editions.)

It was known throughout the music publishing industry that a new complete edition of Schubert's work was being prepared by Breitkopf & Härtel. As a result there were no new Schubert songs published between 1887 and 1894.

THE BREITKOPF & HÄRTEL GESAMMTAUSGABE (AGA)

The stage was now set for the historical moment when Eusebius Mandyczewski, editor of the lieder volumes of Breitkopf & Härtel's *Gesamtausgabe* (AGA), would impose some order on the chaos that existed around the songs and

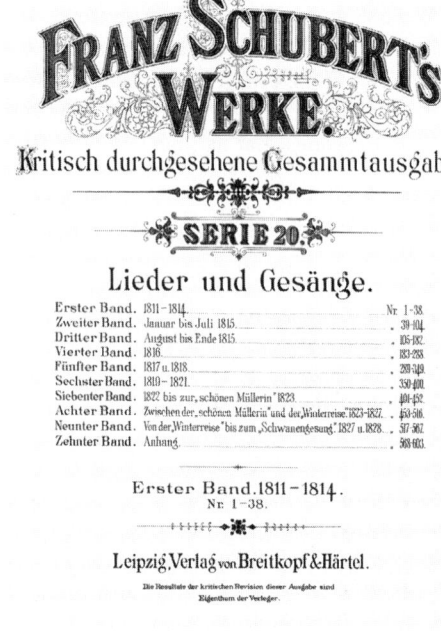

Complete Edition (AGA), edited by Eusebius Mandyczewski.

---

[6] *Der Strom* was edited by Johannes Brahms in the autumn of 1876 as a supplement to *Blätter für Hausmusik* (E. W. Fritzsch, Leipzig).

part-songs in terms of their variants and their chronology. He was supported by the long-viewed and generous provisions of his publishers who were in turn underwritten by Nikolaus von Dumba. Mandyczewski decided to untangle the songs from their respective opus and *Nachlass* numbers and opted for a strictly chronological approach (according to the information available at the time) in the ten mighty volumes of Series XX. This vast task was accomplished with almost superhuman skill and discernment (even if with hindsight, and more recent scholarship, one can detect various errors in Mandyczewski's work). Some 200 Schubert songs appeared in print for the first time and the flood of songs that suddenly overtook the musical world in 1894–5 made this period an especially exciting one for all Schubertians. Completely unknown songs appeared side by side with earlier versions of the famous ones.

1891
FIRST PUBLICATIONS IN SERIES XVI (MUSIC FOR MALE CHORUS):
Ständchen (Grillparzer) (1 version) P510, *Trinklied* (Anon.) P511, *Bergknappenlied* P512, *La Pastorella* (I setting for vocal ensemble) P513, *Beitrag zur 50 Jubelfeier Salieris* (this piece published partly in Series XVI and partly in Series XIX) P514

1892
FIRST PUBLICATIONS IN SERIES XVII (MUSIC FOR MIXED ENSEMBLES):
Glaube, Hoffnung und Liebe (Reil) P515, *Die Geselligkeit* P516, *Der Tanz* P517, *Kantate für Irene Kiesewetter* P518, *Begräbnislied* (*Nun lasst uns den Leib begraben*) P519, *Osterlied* (*Jesus Christ unsrer Heiland*) P520, *Psalm 92* P521

FIRST PUBLICATIONS IN SERIES XIX (SMALLER VOCAL WORKS):
Cantate zum Geburtstag des Sängers Johann Michael Vogl (with original text) P522,[7] *Zur Namensfeier des Vaters* P523, *Das Abendrot* (Kosegarten) (quartet) P524, *Punschlied* (*Vier Elemente*) P525, *Sing-Übungen* P526

1894
FIRST PUBLICATIONS IN SERIES XX
VOLUME I (SONGS OF 1811–14):
Hagars Klage P527, *Des Mädchens Klage* (I setting) P528, *Leichenfantasie* P529, *Der Vatermörder* P530, *Der Jüngling am Bache* (I setting) P531, *Totengräberlied* P532, *Die Schatten* P533, *Der Taucher* (2 version) P534, *Don Gayseros* (three songs, P535, P536, P537), *Andenken* P538, *Geisternähe* P539, *Erinnerung (Todtenopfer)* P540, *Trost. An Elisa* P541, *Lied aus der Ferne* (1 version) P542, *Der Abend* (Matthisson) P543, *Lied der Liebe* P544, *Erinnerungen* (2 version) P545, *An Emma* (1 version) P546, *Das Mädchen aus der Fremde* (I setting) P547, *Schäfers Klagelied* (2 version) P548, *Am See* (Mayrhofer) P549

1895
VOLUME II (SONGS OF 1815):
Der Sänger (2 version) P550, *Minona* P551, *Am Flusse* (1 version) P552, *An Mignon* (1 version) P553, *Nähe des Geliebten* (1 version) P554, *Sängers Morgenlied* (I setting) P555, *Amphiaraos* P556, *Trinklied vor der Schlacht* P557, *Sehnsucht der Liebe* P558, *Die Sterbende* P559, *Stimme der Liebe* (Matthisson) (I setting) P560, *Des Mädchens Klage* (II setting, 1 version) P561, *Die Mainacht* P562, *Seufzer* P563, *Der Liebende* P564, *Die Nonne* (2 version) P565, *Adelwold und Emma* P566, *Von Ida* P567, *Abends unter der Linde* (I setting) P568, *Die Mondnacht* P569, *Huldigung* P570, *Alles um Liebe* P571

---

[7] This trio had already been published as *Der Frühlingsmorgen* Op. 158 (1849). The work thus has two P numbers – the first on account of its music, the second on account of its text.

VOLUME III (SONGS OF 1815):

An den Frühling (II setting, 2 version) P572, *Abendständchen an Lina* P573, *Morgenlied* (Stolberg) P574, *Der Weiberfreund* P575, *Lilla an die Morgenröte* P576, *Totenkranz für ein Kind* P577, *Abendlied* (Stolberg) P578, *Die Fröhlichkeit* P579, *Lied* (Es ist so angenehm) P580, *Furcht der Geliebten* (1 version) P581, *Selma und Selmar* (1 version) P582, *Vaterlandslied* (1 version) P583, (2 version) P584, *An Sie* P585, *Die Sommernacht* (1 version) P586, (2 version) P587, *Dem Unendlichen* (1 version) P588, (3 version) P589, *Ossians Lied nach dem Falle Nathos* (2 version) P589A, *Labetrank der Liebe* P590, *Wiegenlied* ('Schlumm're sanft') P591, *Mein Gruss an den Mai* P592, *Skolie* (Deinhard-Deinhardstein) P593, *Die Sternenwelten* P594, *Die Macht der Liebe* P595, *Sehnsucht (Mignon)* (I setting, 1 version) P596, (2 version) P597, *Hektors Abschied* (1 version) P598, *Die Sterne* ('Wie wohl ist mir') (Kosegarten) P599, *An Rosa I* (I setting) P600, *An Rosa II* (II setting, 1 version) P601 and (2 version) P602, *Idens Schwanenlied* (2 version) P603, *Schwangesang* P604, *Luisens Antwort* P605, *Der Zufriedene* P606, *Liane* P607, *Augenlied* (1 version) P608, *Klage der Ceres* P609, *Harfenspieler* (*Wer sich der Einsamkeit ergibt*) (I setting) P610, *Geistes-Gruss* (1 version) P611, (4 version) P612, *Hoffnung* (Goethe) (2 version) P613, *Erlkönig* (1 version) P614, (2 version) P615, *Das Grab* (II setting) D330, P617[8]

VOLUME IV (SONGS OF 1816):

An die Natur (1 version) P618, *Lied* (Mutter geht durch ihre Kammern) P619, *Klage* (Trauer umfliesst) (1 version) P620, *Morgenlied* (Die frohe neubelebte Flur) P621, *Abendlied* (Sanft glänzt die Abendsonne) P622, *Laura am Klavier* (1 version) P623, (2 version) P624, *Die Entzückung an Laura* (I setting) P625, *Pflügerlied* P626, *An die Harmonie* (*Gesang an die Harmonie*) P627, *Ins stille Land* (Lied: Ins stille Land) (2 version) P628, *Der Herbstabend* (1 version) P629, *Fischerlied* (I setting) P630, *Entzückung* P631, *Geist der Liebe* (Matthisson) (I setting) P632, *Klage* (Die Sonne steigt) (Matthisson) P633, *Stimme der Liebe* (Matthisson) (II setting) P634, *Julius an Theone* P635, *Auf den Tod einer Nachtigall* (II setting) P636, *Die Knabenzeit* P637, *Winterlied* P638, *Die frühe Liebe* (1 version) P639, *Der Leidende* (2 version) P640, *Seligkeit* P641, *Schlachtlied* P642, *An den Schlaf* P643, *Fragment aus dem Aeschylus* (1 version) P644, *An den Mond* (Was schauest du so hell und klar) P645, *An Chloen* (Jacobi) P646, *Hochzeit-Lied* P647, *In der Mitternacht* P648, *Liedesend* (1 version) P649, *Lied des Orpheus* (1 version) P650, *Alte Liebe rostet nie* P651, *Harfenspieler I* (Wer sich der Einsamkeit ergibt) (II setting, 1 version) P652, *Harfenspieler II* (*An die Türen*) (1 version) P653, *Harfenspieler III* (Wer nie sein Brot mit Tränen ass) (I setting) P654, (II setting) P655, *Sehnsucht (Mignon)* (III setting) P656, *Der Sänger am Felsen* P657, *Lied* (Ferne von der grossen Stadt) P658, *Der Wanderer* (1 version) P659, *Der Hirt* P660, *Phidile* P661, *Lied* (Ich bin vergnügt) [*Zufriedenheit*] (I setting) P662, (II setting) (1 version) P663, *Skolie* (Matthisson) P664

VOLUME V (SONGS OF 1817 AND 1818):

Frohsinn (1 version) P665, *Jagdlied* P666, *Die Liebe* (Leon) P667, *Der Alpenjäger* (Mayrhofer) (1 version) P668, *Das Lied vom Reifen* P669, *Auf dem See* (Goethe) (1 version) P670, *Der Jüngling und der Tod* (1 version) P671, *An die Musik* (1 version) P672, *Uraniens Flucht* P673, *Fischerlied* (II setting) P674, *Das Grab* (IV setting) P675, *Die Forelle* (1 version) P676, (2 version) P677, (3 version) P678, *Thekla* (II setting) (1 version) P679, *Sonett I* P680, *Sonett II* P681, *Sonett III* P682

---

[8] The first setting of *Das Grab*, D329a, is for unaccompanied chorus.

VOLUME VI (songs of 1819–21):
Sehnsucht (Schiller) (2 version) P683, *Der Jüngling am Bache* (III setting, 1 version) P684, *Marie* P685, *Strophe aus 'Die Götter Griechenlands'* (1 version) P686, *Der zürnenden Diana* (1 version) P687, *Der Unglückliche* (1 version) P688

VOLUME VII (songs of 1822 to Die schöne Müllerin 1823):
Du liebst mich nicht (1 version) P689, *Die Rose* (2 version, F major) P690,[9] *Der Musensohn* (1 version, A flat major) P691, *Willkommen und Abschied* (1 version, D major) P692, *Schatz-gräbers Begehr* (1 version) P693

VOLUME VIII (songs between Die schöne Müllerin and Winterreise 1827):
Dithyrambe (II setting, 1 version) P693A, *Der blinde Knabe* (1 version) P694, *Das Heimweh* (Pyrker) (1 version) P695, *Fischerweise* (1 version) P696

VOLUME IX (SONGS FROM WINTERREISE TO SCHWANENGESANG, 1827 AND 1828):
Winterreise: (II) *Wasserflut* (version printed in F sharp minor) P697, (IX) *Rast* (1 version) P698, (XII) *Einsamkeit* (1 version printed in B minor) P699, (XXIV) *Der Leiermann* (1 version) P700; *Heimliches Lieben* (1 version) P701, *Eine altschottische Ballade* (2 version) P702

VOLUME X (APPENDIX OF ITALIAN SONGS, FRAGMENTS ETC.):
Misero Pargoletto (2 version) P703, *Son fra l'onde* P704, *Vedi quanto t'adoro* (*Didone abbando-nata*) (4 version) P705, *Auf den Sieg der Deutschen* P706, *Zur Namensfeier des Herrn Andreas Siller*, P707, *Die Befreier Europas in Paris* (3 version) P708, *Lied* (*Brüder, schrecklich brennt die Träne*) P709, *Namenstagslied* P710, *Herbst* P711
Fragments:
Der Geistertanz (I setting) P712, (II setting) P713, *Die drei Sänger* P714, *Lorma* (II setting) P715, *Gesang der Geister über den Wassern* (I setting) P716, *Mahomets Gesang* (I setting) P717, (II setting) P718, *Die Entzückung an Laura* (II setting) P719, *Lied eines Kindes* P720, *Über allen Zauber Liebe* P721, *Johanna Sebus* P722

1897
FIRST PUBLICATIONS IN REVISIONBERICHT:
Romanze (In der Väter Hallen ruhte) P723, *Die Nonne* (1 version) P724, *Ossians Lied nach dem Falle Nathos* (1 version) P725, *Mignon* (So lasst mich scheinen) (I setting, fragments) P726, *Der Knabe in der Wiege* (2 version) P727, *Der Alpenjäger* (Schiller) (1 version) P728

FIRST PUBLICATION IN SUPPLEMENTARY VOLUME OF SERIES XX:
Frühlingslied (Pollak) P729, *Gesang der Geister* (II setting, fragment) P730

1899
Breitkopf & Härtel had already issued several volumes of Schubert songs for popular use. There had been a three-volume edition with the first volume comprising fifty Goethe lieder and the second and third each devoted to a Müller cycle. In 1899 Mandyczewski's great work was used by Breitkopf & Härtel as the basis for a new *Volkstümliche Ausgabe* of the songs. The earlier and less definitive versions of the lieder were left out of what was, in effect, a slimmed-down and rearranged edition of the *Gesamtausgabe* volumes. These volumes were printed in a smaller format (approximating the size of those of the Peters Edition) and the songs were sorted into

---

[9] *Die Rose* had first appeared as a supplement to the *Wiener Zeitschrift für Kunst, Literatur, Theater und Mode* (issue of 7 May 1822, and then as Op. 73).

voice categories (cycles, soprano, tenor, mezzo, baritone, bass and duets). This was a noble attempt to ensure that the Schubert songs were kept in their original tonalities, and that baritones, for example, sang only those songs that had been written for their voice range. Songs were also allocated between the sexes according to the suitability of their texts. The idealistic Mandyczewski seems not to have understood that most singers do not choose their repertoires on the basis of original keys. The lack of transpositions in this edition of Breitkopf's *Volkstümliche Ausgabe* did little to displace the ascendancy of Edition Peters in the market for the ordinary lieder-buying public.

Peters declined to enlarge their seven-volume edition to include the songs found only in the Breitkopf edition, presumably considering it popular enough to be left to sell as it was. Nevertheless, Friedlaender was recruited to re-edit the series (without significantly changing its layout) and in 1922 he provided something of a critical apparatus for the edition by publishing a study of *Die schöne Müllerin* and generally becoming identified with the firm of Peters as a kind of alternative to Mandyczewski's magisterial position with Breitkopf & Härtel. Although Peters could not rival the Breitkopf edition, its link with the celebrated Friedlaender placed it, in the eyes of the public, in a superior position to its many other competitors.

By this time Max Abraham's nephew, Heinrich Hinrichsen, was the proprietor of Edition Peters and he became a great figure in Leipzig's musical life; the instrumental collection to be seen to this day in the Grassistrasse, next to the music Hochschule, was Hinrichsen's gift to the grateful city in 1926. Heinrich perished in Auschwitz (fourteen family members died in the Holocaust) but two of his sons emigrated in 1936–7 – Max Hinrichsen, who founded the Hinrichsen Edition in London, and Walter Hinrichsen, who founded C. F. Peters in New York in 1948. After the war the Leipzig firm continued to trade under its original name in East Germany.

For almost a hundred years most artists in the performing world worked from the Peters Schubert, aware perhaps of the existence of Mandyczewski's *Gesamtausgabe* but unable to get their hands on it for everyday use (unless they were subscribers to the complete edition). In the late 1960s, despite the *Neue Schubert-Ausgabe* being in the pipeline, the American firm of Dover decided to reprint the old *Gesamtausgabe* in order to alleviate this situation, but the hardback volumes were expensive and not directed at the popular or domestic market. As a result, Mandyczewski's wonderful edition stubbornly remained the province of specialists (or those lucky enough to acquire a copy of the lieder series). Peters' arbitrarily arranged hierarchy of importance, a descending order of worth in Volumes 1 to 6 established over 120 years ago, held sway throughout most of the twentieth century.

It is only with the relatively recent appearance of the *Neue Schubert-Ausgabe* (Bärenreiter), with its parallel volumes designed for practical use (since 2005), that younger performers have encountered the songs arranged not for reasons of commercial viability but according first to opus number and then chronolgy. It is a welcome development that these singers' volumes have recently become available in three different keys – the secret, after all, of Peters' success. Indeed for the first time ever, the higher voice volumes of the Bärenreiter series make available many songs in keys higher than Schubert's originals, a development that permits sopranos to sing the bass repertoire, sometimes unwisely. Free (and sometimes unreliable) downloads on the Internet have proved a mixed blessing albeit an improvement on the days when many songs were simply unavailable.

Nothing can obscure Mandyczewski's massive achievement in bringing the Schubert songs to the world's attention in a way that had never before been attempted. His thoroughness is proven by the relatively small number of new songs that have emerged since his work at the end of the nineteenth century. Some of these were published in various journals and periodicals between 1902 and the late 1960s (noted in footnotes in this article). With the publication by Bärenreiter of the *Neue Schubert-Ausgabe*, beginning in 1968, the stage was set for the second

1797–1828

Therese Grob Collection

The Therese Grob Album, privately published by Reinhard Van Hoorickx (1967).

great wave of Schubert song studies, and the appearance of the remaining pieces of the jigsaw. This has taken more than forty years, the life's work of Walther Dürr (*see* SCHOLARS). During this period many have been impatient for a quicker release of the remaining material, and the indefatigable Schubert scholar Reinhard Van Hoorickx issued a large number of the fragments with his own completions, some more successful than others. These were home-made private publications, generously shared with friends and fellow-Schubertians. They never achieved widespread circulation and the average singing student would have had no access to this material without possessing Hoorickx's contact details. These days the Internet would be a boon to this type of amateur activity, but Hoorickx's work pre-dated the technology that would have assured it greater dissemination. On 31 January 1967 Hoorickx achieved quite a coup: the Wilhelm family in Bottmingen – the owners of the autograph – permitted him to issue a privately printed version of the album for Therese Grob (Hoorickx called it *Therese Grob Collection*) which included versions of a number of songs that took a further thirty-five years to reach publication in the NSA. This too had very limited circulation, but it was largely thanks to Van Hoorickx that the Hyperion Schubert Edition (the first of its thirty-seven discs was issued in 1987) managed to offer a more or less complete recording of the fragments before they appeared in the relevant volumes of the NSA. Now that these are all available in the NSA, the way is open to a new generation of scholars and performers to attempt to out-do Hoorickx in terms of creating performing editions of this material, some of it too precious to be lost to the concert hall on account of its present fragmentary status.

1968

Die Erde P731

Vollendung P732

These two songs were published separately by Bärenreiter before they appeared in the pages of the NSA.

THE NEUE SCHUBERT-AUSGABE (NSA) SERIES IV: THE SOLO SONGS

FIRST PUBLICATIONS IN VOLUME 7 (Songs unpublished in Schubert's lifetime, D95–D159, 1814–15):

Lied aus der Ferne (2 version) P733, *Romanze* (Matthisson) (1 version) P734,[10] *Klage um Ali Bey* (solo song version) P735, *Die Erwartung* (1 version) P736, *Erinnerungen* (1 version) P737, *Die Befreier Europas in Paris* (1 version) P738, (2 version) P739

1969

FIRST PUBLICATIONS IN VOLUME 6 OF THE NSA (Songs unpublished in Schubert's lifetime, D5–D78, 1810–13):

Ich sass an einer Tempelhalle [*Lebenstraum*] (II setting) P740, *Gesang in c* [*Lebenstraum*] (I setting without word underlay) P741, *Misero pargoletto* (1 version) P742, *Pensa che questo istante* (1 version) P743

1970

FIRST PUBLICATIONS IN VOLUMES 1A AND 1B OF THE NSA (Songs published in Schubert's lifetime, Opp. 1–21, with alternative and parallel versions to those songs):

Meeres Stille (I setting) P744,[11] *Suleika I* (1 version) P745, *Jägers Abendlied* (I setting) P746,[12] *Der Wanderer* (2 version, B minor) P747, *Rastlose Liebe* (2 version, D major) P748, *Der Fischer* (1 version) P749, *Am Grabe Anselmos* (2 version) P750, *Lob der Tränen* (1 version) P751, *Der Alpenjäger* (Mayrhofer) (2 version) P752, *Frühlingsglaube* (1 version) P753,[13] (2 version) P754,[14] *Hänflings Liebeswerbung* (1 version) P755, *Der Schiffer* (Mayrhofer) (1 version) P756, *Wie Ulfru fischt* (1 version) P757, *Der Schäfer und der Reiter* (1 version) P758

1975

FIRST PUBLICATIONS IN VOLUMES 2A AND 2B OF THE NSA (Songs published in Schubert's lifetime, Opp. 23–43, with alternative and parallel versions to those songs):

Schlaflied (1 version) P759, *Die Forelle* (5 version) P760, *Nachtstück* (1 version) P761, *Der Pilgrim* (1 version, E major) P762,[15] *Sehnsucht* (Schiller) (II setting, 1 version) P763, *Nacht und Träume* (1 version) P764, *Gruppe aus dem Tartarus* (I setting, fragment) P765, *Die schöne Müllerin*: (XI) *Mein!* (ornamented version) P766, (XIII) *Mit dem grünen Lautenbande* (ornamented version) P767, (XVIII) *Trockne Blumen* (ornamented version) P768, (XIX) *Der Müller und der Bach* (ornamented version) P769

---

[10] *Das Fräulein im Thurme (Romanze)* (first version) published as a supplement to *Die Musik*, Berlin, May 1902.

[11] *Meeres Stille* (1 version) published in November 1952 in *Schweizerische Musikzeitung*, edited by Otto Erich Deutsch.

[12] *Jägers Abendlied* (1 version) published 15 January 1907, as supplement to *Die Musik*, Berlin, edited by Eusebius Mandyczewski.

[13] *Frühlingsglaube* (1 version), facsimile in 'Zu Schuberts Frühlingsglaube' by Andreas Holschneider in *Festschrift für Otto Erich Deutsch* (1963).

[14] *Frühlingsglaube* (2 version), facsimile in E. Schreiber, Stuttgart, edited by Hans Halm, May 1958.

[15] *Der Pilgrim* (1 version) first published in *Der Merker*, Wien, November 1909, edited Richard Heuberger.

1979

FIRST PUBLICATIONS IN VOLUMES 4A AND 4B OF THE NSA (SONGS PUBLISHED IN SCHUBERT'S LIFETIME, OPP. 80–89, WITH ALTERNATIVE AND PARALLEL VERSIONS TO THOSE SONGS):

Das Zügenglöcklein (1 version) P770, *Romanze des Richard Löwenherz* (1 version) P771, *Um Mitternacht* (1 version) P772, *Winterreise*: (XXII) *Mut* (1 version) P773, (XXIII) *Die Nebensonnen* (1 version) P774; *L'incanto degli occhi* (I setting, partial) P775, *Il traditor deluso* (1 version) P776, *Winterreise*: (VII) *Auf dem Flusse* (1 version) P777, (XI) *Frühlingstraum* (1 version) P778

1982

FIRST PUBLICATIONS IN VOLUMES 3A AND 3B OF THE NSA (SONGS PUBLISHED IN SCHUBERT'S LIFETIME, OPP. 44–79, WITH ALTERNATIVE AND PARALLEL VERSIONS TO THOSE SONGS):

An den Mond (Hölty) (1 version) P779, *An Emma* (2 version) P780,[16] *Greisengesang* (1 version) P781,[17] (2 version) P782, *Der Wanderer* (Schlegel) (1 version) P784

1985

FIRST PUBLICATIONS IN VOLUMES 5A AND 5B OF THE NSA (SONGS PUBLISHED IN SCHUBERT'S LIFETIME, OPP. 92–108, WITH ALTERNATIVE AND PARALLEL VERSIONS TO THOSE SONGS – VOLUME 5B):

Widerschein (1 version, D major) P785,[18] *Trost im Liede* (1 version) P786, *Im Frühling* (1 version) P787, *Geistes-Gruss* (2 version) P788,[19] (3 version) P789, (5 version) P790, *Iphigenia* (1 version) P791, (2 version) P792, *Todesmusik* (1 version) P793

1986

FIRST PUBLICATION IN SERIES III (ENSEMBLE WORKS FOR VOICES) VOLUME 2A OF THE NSA:

Viel tausend Sterne prangen P794[20]

FIRST PUBLICATIONS IN SERIES VIII (SUPPLEMENT) VOLUME 2 (SCHUBERTS STUDIEN) OF THE NSA:

Quell' innocente figlio P795, *Entra l'uomo* P796, *Serbate, o dei custodi* P797[21]

1988

FIRST PUBLICATIONS IN SERIES IV VOLUMES 14A AND 14B OF THE NSA (SONGS UNPUBLISHED IN SCHUBERT'S LIFETIME, D869–D990, 1826–8. SONGS WITH INSTRUMENTAL ACCOMPANIMENT, AND SONGS FROM OPERAS ARRANGED BY THE COMPOSER FOR VOICE AND PIANO):

[16] *An Emma* (2 version) first published as a supplement to *Wiener Zeitschrift für Kunst, Literatur, Theater und Mode*, June 1821.
[17] *Greisengesang* (1 version) first issued as a facsimile in 'Schubertiade' by Walter Gerstenberg in *Festschrift für Otto Erich Deutsch* (1936).
[18] *Widerschein* (1 version) first published as a supplement to W. G. Becker's *Taschenbuch zum geselligen Vergnügen*, edited Friedrich Kind, Leipzig 1821 (advertised in September 1820).
[19] *Geistes-Gruss* (2 version). This appeared in the 1885 edition of Peters Volume 7 edited by Max Friedlaender, but was removed for the 1887 edition of the same volume.
[20] *Viel tausend Sterne prangen*, first published by Universal Edition in 1937, edited by Alfred Orel.
[21] *Serbate, o dei custodi*, first published by Alfred Orel in *Der junge Schubert* (1940).

Eine altschottische Ballade (3 version) P798,[22] *Der vierährige Posten*: 'Gott, höre meine Stimme' P799, *Alfonso und Estrella*: 'Doch im Getümmel' P800, 'Wenn ich dich, Holde' P801, *O Quell, was strömst du rasch und wild* (fragment) P802, *Fröhliches Scheiden* (fragment) P803,[23] *Sie in jedem Liede* (fragment) P804, *Wolke und Quelle* (fragment) P805

1990

Die Nacht (Der Unglückliche) (I setting) P806
Edited by Erich Wolfgang Partsch, published by Universal Edition (this song not in the Deutsch catalogue)

1992

FIRST PUBLICATIONS IN VOLUME 13 OF THE NSA (SONGS UNPUBLISHED IN
SCHUBERT'S LIFETIME, D712–D861, 1821–5):
Versunken (2 version, D major) P807, *Die Wallfahrt* P808[24]

1996

FIRST PUBLICATIONS IN VOLUME 12 OF THE NSA (SONGS UNPUBLISHED IN
SCHUBERT'S LIFETIME, D611–D708, 1818–20):
Die Sternennächte (1 version) P809, *Die Liebende schreibt* (1 version) P810, *Abend* (Tieck) (fragment) P811, *Das Mädchen* (Schlegel) (2 version) P812, *Der 13. Psalm*[25] P813

1999

FIRST PUBLICATIONS IN VOLUME 11 OF THE NSA (SONGS UNPUBLISHED IN
SCHUBERT'S LIFETIME, D475–D594, SEPTEMBER 1816–NOVEMBER 1817):
Zufriedenheit (Claudius, D501) (2 version, G major) P814, *Mailied* P815, *Leiden der Trennung* (1 version) P816, *L'incanto degli occhi* (I setting, longer fragment than appeared in Volume 4) P817, *Ombre amene* P818, *Vedi quanto t'adoro (Didone abbandonata)* (1 version) P819, (2 version) P820, (3 version) P821, *Nur wer die Liebe kennt* P822

2002

FIRST PUBLICATIONS IN VOLUME 10 OF THE NSA (SONGS UNPUBLISHED IN
SCHUBERT'S LIFETIME, D342–D474, JANUARY–SEPTEMBER 1816):
Am Tage Aller Seelen (Litanei) (2 version) P823, *Am ersten Maimorgen* P824, *Die Nacht* (Uz) (1 version) P825, *Am Bach im Frühlinge* (2 version) P826, *An die Natur* (2 version) P827, *Ritter Toggenburg* (2 version) P828, *Lied (Ins stille Land)* (3 version) P829, (4 version) P830, *Die Herbstnacht* (2 version) P831, *Der Herbstabend* (2 version) P832, *Abschied von der Harfe* (1 version) P833, *Die verfehlte Stunde* (2 version) P834, *Stimme der Liebe* (Stolberg) (1 version) P835, *Die frühe Liebe* (2 version) P836, *Der Leidende* (3 version, A minor) P837, *Klage (An den Mond)* (2 version) P838, *Gott im Frühlinge* (2 version) P839, *Trauer der Liebe* (2 version) P840, *An Chloen* (fragment) P841, *Lorma* (I setting) P842, *Auf den Tod einer Nachtigall* (I setting, fragment) P843, *Lied in der Abwesenheit* P844[26]

---

[22] *Eine altschottische Ballade* (3 version) first published in Budapest in 1971 edited, with facsimile, by Istvan Kecskeméti.
[23] First published as a facsimile in *Franz Schubert* by Richard Heuberger (1902).
[24] First published in a Bärenreiter collection in 1969, edited by Reinhard Van Hoorickx.
[25] Psalm 13, published as a facsimile in *Festblätter für das 10. Deutsche Sängerbundfest*, Wien, 1928, edited Otto Erich Deutsch.
[26] *Lied in der Abwesenheit*, first published in *Moderne Welt* (Wien) December 1925, edited by Otto Erich Deutsch.

2006

FIRST PUBLICATION IN SERIES III (ENSEMBLE WORKS FOR VOICES) VOLUME 2B OF THE NSA:

Die Allmacht (2 setting, choral) P845, *Die Schlacht* (2 setting, choral) P846, *Linde Lüfte wehen* (fragment, duet) P847, *Rosamunde: Jägerchor* P848, *Hirtenchor* P849; *Die Schlacht* (1 version) P850

2009

FIRST PUBLICATIONS IN VOLUME 8 OF THE NSA (SONGS UNPUBLISHED IN SCHUBERT'S LIFETIME, D163–D261, 22 FEBRUARY–21 AUGUST 1815):

Gebet während der Schlacht (1 version) P851, *Abends unter der Linde* (II setting) (2 version) P852, *Winterlied* D deest P853, *Punschlied. Im Norden zu singen* (1 version for solo voice) P854, *Wer kauft Liebesgötter* D261 (2 version) P855, *Liebesrausch* D164 (I setting) P856,[27] *Das war ich* (II setting) D deest P857, *Der Morgenstern* P858, *Die Nonne* (1 version) P859

2012

FIRST PUBLICATIONS IN VOLUME 9 OF THE NSA (SONGS UNPUBLISHED IN SCHUBERT'S LIFETIME, D262–D323 22 AUGUST–DECEMBER 1815):

Das Mädchen von Inistore (2 version) P860, *Nachtgesang* (Kosegarten) (1 version) P861, *An Rosa I* (1 version) P862, *Idens Schwanenlied* (1 version) P863, *Luisens Antwort* (1 version) P864, *Mignon (Kennst du das Land?)* (1 version) P865, *Hermann und Thusnelda* (1 version) P866. This volume also contains two major Ossian settings where Walther Dürr treats the Diabelli *Nachlass* versions of the songs as valid second versions, believing that these were possibly based on autographs that have since vanished – *Cronnan* D282, *Shilric und Vinvela* D293.

With the publication of Voume 9 in Series IV of the NSA a great publishing venture, initiated in 1968 – the solo songs of Franz Schubert in fourteen volumes – was completed. In Series III, Volumes 1 and 3, encompassing the work for male and female ensembles, are yet to appear (Volumes 2A and 2B are dedicated to works for mixed voices). There are also volumes awaited in Series VIII (Supplement) which will publish *Evangelium Johannis* D607 (which first appeared in facsimile, edited by Heuberger, in 1902), Schubert's Gluck arrangements with piano (for the first time), and his arrangement of Maximilian Stadler's *Der 8. Psalm*.

MARTIN JOSEF PRANDSTETTER (1760–1798)

THE POETIC SOURCE

S1 *Wiener Musenalmanach auf das Jahr 1787*. Herausgegeben von J. F. Ratschky und A. Blumauer. Wien, bey Rudolph Gräffer, und Compagnie

THE SONG

22 August 1815 *Die Fröhlichkeit* D262 [S1: pp. 100–104]

Martin Josef Prandstetter, born on 5 October 1760 in Vienna, was of Hungarian origin but achieved high status in the Austrian civil service. Like Mayrhofer from a later generation, Prandstetter was against the absolutist government of the time and belonged to a

---

[27] *Liebesrausch*, first published in *Musik aus aller Welt für Haus und Heim*, Heft 1 (Wien), 1928, edited by Otto Erich Deutsch.

Jacobin group in Vienna that professed open sympathy with the French Revolution. His poetry appeared in the *Wiener Musenalmanach* and also in Masonic publications. His lighter works (such as *Die Fröhlichkeit*) were influenced by Anacreon's Odes, but he also wrote poems in the style of Klopstock and ballads inspired by Bürger and Schiller. Publication of his work ceased in 1794 when he was arrested for treasonable activities and sentenced to three days in the stocks, deportation and thirty years in prison. He died in prison in Munkács in his native Hungary in 1798. His fate bears a certain similarity to that of the poet Schubart who was imprisoned for many years by the duke of Württemburg. A plaque in the Wiener Rathaus was erected to Prandstetter's memory in 1923 when he was celebrated as a 'Freiheitsdichter' and his death ascribed to judicial murder. It is interesting to speculate as to whether Schubert knew anything about the poet's fate when he came across these verses.

ADOLF PRATOBEVERA VON WIESBORN (1806–1875)

THE POETIC SOURCE
Der Falke (1825)

This dramatic poem or play was never printed. It ends with the speech of Mechthild as her father-in-law Hugo, Ritter von Eicheck is dying. The play was performed on 17 February 1826 in the family flat in Vienna, not far from the Kärntnertor, in honour of the birthday of Karl Josef Pratobevera von Wiesborn (1769–1853), the father of the nineteen-year-old author.

THE MELODRAMA
For 17 February 1826   *Abschied ('Leb' wohl, du schöne Erde')* D829

Pratobevera was born to a distinguished Viennese family on 12 June 1806 and trained as a lawyer. By the end of a long and successful life he had reached the highest positions available to a civil servant (governor of Lower Austria and a member of the Upper Chamber of the Reichsrat). His satirical poems on political matters were valued by those who understood the vicissitudes of Austrian politics. In late 1825, he requested that Schubert write some music to accompany the closing speech of his play *Der Falke* (*see* above). The poet himself characterized this drama in one act as 'ein romantisches Spiel, lyrisch, plastisch, in einem langen Aufzug'. Deutsch believed that Schubert was paid for the commission, but Walther Dürr takes the view that the composer was a friend of the family through their daughter, Franziska von Pratobevera (later Tremier), an enthusiastic Schubert singer. The poet's other sister, Berthe, married Kreissle von Hellborn, author of the first Schubert biography. The

Adolf Pratobevera, Freiherr von Wiesborn, unsigned oil painting of 1829.

composer had already used melodrama in his operas *Des Teufels Lustschloss* D184, *Die Zauberharfe* D644 and *Fierabras* D796 but this was the only occasion on which he wrote for the spoken voice and piano.

In regard to musical matters Pratobevera was typical of the well-educated Viennese of the time; he had studied music up to a point, revered Mozart and regarded Beethoven (as was normal for his generation) as a god. A diary entry (quoted in Clive) passes judgement on Schubert's songs after he had died: 'Few of his numerous songs filled me with enthusiasm: many were beautiful, but quite a few did not appeal to me at all, in fact revolted me with their frightful sentimentality' (*Gefrorne Tränen* in *Winterreise*, for example). The poet's wife Katherine (1818–1897) published in 1858 *Die süddeutsche Küche* which became the standard cookbook of its time for southern Germany and Austria. Pratobevera died in Vienna on 16 February 1875.

Bibliography: Clive 1997, pp. 155–6 where the Schubertian credentials and reactions of Pratobevera's extended family are recounted
Dürr, Introduction to NSA IV Volume 13 p. XXI

PROMETHEUS   Prometheus
(Goethe) **D674** [H436]
B♭ major – C major   October 1819

(109 bars)

(1) Bedecke deinen Himmel, Zeus,	Conceal your heaven, Zeus,
Mit Wolkendunst,	Behind a gauze of cloud.
Und übe, dem Knaben gleich,	And, like a boy beheading thistles,
Der Disteln köpft,	Practise on oak trees
An Eichen dich und Bergeshöhn;	And mountain peaks;
Musst mir meine Erde	But you will have to leave
Doch lassen stehn,	My world standing,
Und meine Hütte, die du nicht gebaut,	And my hut, which you did not build,
Und meinen Herd,	And my fireside,
Um dessen Glut	Whose glow
Du mich beneidest.	You envy me.
(2) Ich kenne nichts Ärmeres	I know nothing more wretched
Unter der Sonn' als euch, Götter!	Beneath the sun than you gods!
Ihr nährt kümmerlich	Meagrely you nourish
Vom Opfersteuern[1]	Your majesty
Und Gebetshauch	With offerings
Eure Majestät,	And the breath of prayer,

[1] Goethe writes 'Ihr *nähret* kümmerlich / *Von* Opfersteuern'.

Und darbtet, wären	And would starve
Nicht Kinder und Bettler	If children and beggars
Hoffnungsvolle Toren.	Were not ever-hopeful fools.

(3) Da ich ein Kind war,   When I was a child
     Nicht wusste wo aus noch ein,   And did not know a thing,
     Kehrt' ich mein verirrtes Auge   I turned my perplexed gaze
     Zur Sonne, als wenn drüber wär'   To the sun, as if beyond it
     Ein Ohr, zu hören meine Klage,   There were an ear to listen to my lament,
     Ein Herz wie meins,   And a heart like mine
     Sich des Bedrängten zu erbarmen.   To pity the distressed.

(4) Wer half mir   Who helped me
     Wider der Titanen Übermut?   Against the overweening pride of the Titans?
     Wer rettete vom Tode mich,   Who saved me from death
     Von Sklaverei?   And from slavery?
     Hast du nicht Alles selbst vollendet,   Did you not accomplish it all yourself,
     Heilig glühend Herz?   Sacred, ardent heart?
     Und glühtest jung und gut,   And, deceived in your youthful goodness,
     Betrogen, Rettungsdank   Were you not fired with gratitude for your
                                           deliverance
     Dem Schlafenden da droben?   To the sleeper up above?

(5) Ich dich ehren? Wofür?   I honour you? What for?
     Hast du die Schmerzen gelindert   Have you ever eased the suffering
     Je des Beladenen?   Of him who is oppressed?
     Hast du die Tränen gestillet   Have you ever dried the tears
     Je des Geängsteten?   Of him who is troubled?
     Hat nicht mich zum Manne geschmiedet Did not almighty Time
     Die allmächtige Zeit   And eternal Fate,
     Und das ewige Schicksal,   My masters and yours,
     Meine Herrn und deine?   Forge me into a man?

(6) Wähntest du etwa,   Did you perhaps imagine
     Ich sollte das Leben hassen,   That I would hate life,
     In Wüsten fliehen,   Flee into the wilderness,
     Weil nicht alle   Because not all
     Blütenträume reiften?   My blossoming dreams bore fruit?

(7) Hier sitz' ich, forme Menschen   Here I sit, forming men
     Nach meinem Bilde,   In my own image,
     Ein Geschlecht, das mir gleich sei, A race that shall be like me,
     Zu leiden, zu weinen,   That shall suffer, weep,
     Zu geniessen und zu freuen sich   Enjoy and rejoice,
     Und dein nicht zu achten,   And ignore you,
     Wie ich!   As I do!

JOHANN WOLFGANG VON GOETHE (1749–1832); poem written in late autumn 1773, revised 1774

This is the fifty-sixth of Schubert's seventy-five Goethe solo settings (1814–26). See the poet's biography for a chronological list of all the Goethe settings.

The myth of Prometheus (the main classical sources are Hesiod, Aeschylus, Apollodorus and Pausanias) has attracted western artists since the fourteenth century: the unfortunate Titan appears in John Gower's *Confessio amantis* (*c.* 1390); he was painted by Botticelli and drawn by Parmigianino; Francis Bacon, Ben Jonson, Edmund Spenser, Pierre de Ronsard and Jonathan Swift wrote about him. Gottfried August Bürger and Christoph Martin Wieland took up the subject in 1770, shortly followed by Goethe who wrote his dramatic fragment *Prometheus* in 1773. August von Schlegel wrote an epic poem on Prometheus in 1797, and Johann Gottfried Herder treated the subject in 1803. Beethoven wrote the ballet music for *Die Geschöpfe des Prometheus* in 1801, and Johann Friedrich Reichardt composed a setting of Goethe's poem in 1809 which much influenced Schubert's setting (*see* below). Prometheus features in Byron's *Childe Harold's Pilgrimage*

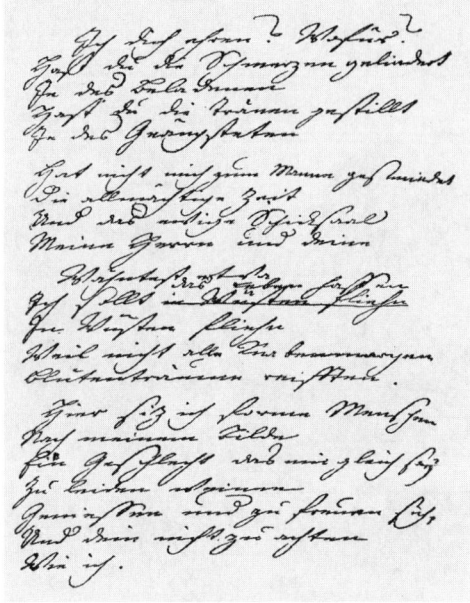

Autograph of Goethe's *Prometheus*, Verses 5–7.

and elsewhere (from 1812), and Wordsworth broaches the subject in 1814. We should also remember that the full title of Mary Wollstonecraft Shelley's famous novel was *Frankenstein, or the Modern Prometheus* (1817).

Schubert's first confrontation with Prometheus was a cantata he composed by that name in 1816 with text by Philipp Dräxler von Carin (D451). The manuscript of this substantial work for two soloists, chorus and orchestra was mislaid even in the composer's lifetime, and we must now consider it lost to posterity. The solo setting of Goethe's poem dates from 1819. During the early Romantic period, Prometheus continued to fascinate artists: in poetry Percy Bysshe Shelley – with his epic and idealistic *Prometheus Unbound* (1820) – as well as Giacomo Leopardi (1824) and Elizabeth Barrett Browning (1833). It was only later in the century that music caught up. The main rival of Schubert's setting – Hugo Wolf's – appeared in the *Goethe-Lieder* of 1889. The *tragédie lyrique* with music, *Prométhée*, written by Gabriel Fauré for forces uncharacteristically vast for his tastes, was conceived for open-air performance in 1900. Alexander Scriabin's *Prométhée: Le poème du feu* dates from 1908–10. Other engagements with the legend from the more recent past are found in the poetry of Pablo Neruda and Robert Lowell; in the writings of Carl Jung who was much taken with Spitteler's *Prometheus und Epimetheus*; in the art of Henry Moore (lithographs for André Gide's translation of Goethe's poem) and Oskar Kokoschka (a triptych of paintings of the 'Prometheus Saga' in 1950); and in the music of Carl Orff (an opera, *Prometheus*, written in 1968) and Luigi Nono (*Prometeo*, 1984).

There are many versions and variants of the story. For our purposes it is enough to know that the Titan (his name means 'forethinker') was a champion of men against the gods. It was said (by Apollodorus) that he was the creator of the human race, fashioning men out of clay, and he taught men the arts and crafts necessary to improve their primitive existence. Legend has it that after Zeus decided to deprive mankind of fire, Prometheus stole a spark from the gods and carried it on a slow-burning fennel stalk in order to give it to mankind. In return for this and other acts of defiance, Zeus punished him in two ways: he created the first woman, Pandora, who brought with her all the world's evils, and he chained the Titan to a rock in the Caucasus where an eagle daily plucked out his liver which grew again each night, ensuring his perpetual agony. Prometheus'

Prometheus, engraving by Stöber after painting by Schedy, published in Vienna (1815). The Titan brandishes fire, his own discovery, and by his side sits a man whom he has created.

release from captivity was eventually secured when Heracles, on the way to his eleventh labour (fetching the golden apples of the Hesperides), shot the eagle that tormented Prometheus; in return, Prometheus advised Heracles to offer to hold up the sky for Atlas, and was sent to fetch the apples on his behalf. Zeus, proud of his son Heracles' achievements, allowed this to happen and forgot his old enmity. There are thus two definite phases to the Prometheus story – Bound and Unbound – which have been variously treated by artists, only a selection of whom are mentioned above.

From the point of view of Goethe's poem, the Titan, still in his workshop, might be named *Prometheus Defiant*. The poet sketched three scenes of an incomplete Promethean drama in 1773. The first of these is an extended conversation in blank verse between Prometheus and Mercury; then the goddess Minerva enters who, although loyal to her father Zeus, loves Prometheus and is his protector. The second scene begins on Olympus: Zeus speaks with Mercury, and then we see Prometheus in his role as creator of mankind. There is also a long exchange between Prometheus and the newly created Pandora. The third scene is set in the workshop of Prometheus and consists of nothing more than the poem that we know, which Goethe rescued from this context and placed in his *Gedichte*.

As is usually the case in Goethe's use of mythology, the ancient tale is an allegory for concerns very much in the present. As Nicholas Boyle puts it, the poem 'showed an awareness and affirmation of the anti-Christian logic at the heart of the contemporary philosophical and theological reflection in Germany'. The poet's *Sturm und Drang* denial of a personal creator-God caused considerable controversy for some time in Germany's literary circles. Added to this was a hint of arrogant celebration of the self-sufficiency of genius, a great artist's independence of the patronage and support of others, and his right to 'go it alone'. Goethe later softened the effect of the poem by publishing it before *Ganymed* in the *Gedichte*. This accented its mythological aspect, and the behaviour of the recklessly defiant Prometheus was counterbalanced by the submissive shepherd-boy, the poet as worshipper of nature. The middle course, the sensible realization of mankind's limitations – not aspiring to be too close to the gods, but not confronting them either – was demonstrated by the third of the triptych, *Grenzen der Menschheit*. Hugo Wolf was to publish them together, in this order, as the three final songs of his *Goethe-Lieder* (1889).

The poem was set by Schubert when he was very much under the intellectual influence of Mayrhofer (he had just taken up residence in the poet's small apartment in the Wipplinger-strasse). Perhaps more surprising is the composer's debt, as late as 1819, to the setting of the text by Johann Friedrich Reichardt (1752–1814): the tonality and voice type, the marking at the head of the music (Reichardt has 'Kräftig deklamiert'), the shape of the whole and the dotted-rhythm defiance of the final section all take their cue from a work written ten years earlier. (So much for Schubert 'growing out' of Reichardt in his teens.) The challenge to conventional reli-

gion, Goethe's pantheism, leaning towards
Spinoza and Leibniz, would have resonated with a composer who had recently
set to music the texts of Novalis and Friedrich von Schlegel. Schubert's difficult relationship with his father was also full of
Promethean overtones. Another factor
was the paternalistic authoritarianism of
Clemens von Metternich's regime, a
permanent source of irritation and intimi-
dation for Austrians of student age, as well
as for Mayrhofer whose work as a censor
was completely at odds with his liberal
private beliefs. The poem could be thought
of as an artist's gesture of defiance against
the overweening power of the state that
meddled in the lives of individuals. This
meant a revolt against authority, not only
in terms of political belief, but also social
mores. In Biedermeier Austria, the Church
and the State were so intertwined, and
matters of private morality so often the
subject of police interference, that it is

Prometheus, engraving by C. Teichendorff from *Goethes Werke*, edited by H. Düntzer (1882).

possible that Schubert and Mayrhofer read into Goethe's defiant words more than a challenge
to conventional religion. In post-Revolutionary Europe the poem resounds like a battle-cry for
individuality, mocking as it does the notion that our official protectors and guardians (whether
God, parents, priests or police) are all-powerful, claiming to care for our good. But every person
is responsible for their own feelings, and what they love is sacred to them. The sole pleasure
known to these false and selfish gods is destroying what is good and beautiful so that they can
maintain control over their helots. They have to be confronted, no matter the cost, and
Prometheus was the first hero to do so.

Schubert was encouraged by Goethe's free verse (the strophes are of uneven length) to find
a musical form that is equally free, reflecting the Titan's defiance of convention and hierarchical
order. This music is the paradigm of feelings vented spontaneously. Accordingly, there is nothing
that looks back to the past – the song thrusts relentlessly forward, each section having its own
atmosphere and logic, the disparate movements melded together less by subtle planning than
by an ongoing intensity in the white heat of the moment.

Verse 1: The song begins with music of self-assertion, a grimly triumphant fanfare-like phrase
of octaves between the hands (bb. 1 and 4). This is a one-bar cell of strutting dotted rhythms
that occurs seven times in all in the opening section. But we are never allowed to feel harmonically safe and settled. The opening bar seems to announce the key of B flat major, but the second
is a series of hammered chords in A flat which lead to E flat major. Another stormy fanfare in
this key (the same dotted rhythm) leads to a bar of similarly insistent D major chords (b. 5)
which, in turn, lead to the G minor tremolo that underpins the opening recitative. Zeus' rage
is depicted in all this at the same time as being the subject of the singer's mockery. These shifting
tonal centres suggest the search for a firm foothold from which to launch an attack, the turn of
the harmonic screw a metaphor for the screwing-up of courage. The singer has not uttered a
note and yet we are already in the presence of a dangerously restless individual with an attitude
problem. When the singer begins with 'Bedecke deinen Himmel, Zeus' (marked 'Recit' from

b. 6) there is a snarl built in, anger and contempt seldom found in Schubert. The setting of the word 'Zeus' on the fourth beat, and tied across the bar line, produces a syncopated casualness, the swaggering insolence of blasphemy.

After 'Wolkendunst' the thundering dotted-rhythm motif of the introduction returns as an interlude, as if played by trombones (bb. 10–11). Mention of beheading thistles has Schubert responding to a visual image: the right-hand tremolo (B flat–D from b. 10) is also beheaded as if a destructive hand were skimming the music's surface. This results in the flattening effect of shrinking and diminishing intervals, a minor, rather than a major, third (B flat–D flat oscillations halfway through b. 11) followed by B flat–C in b. 12. (Goethe took the image from Tarquinius Superbus, last king of Rome, who beheaded thistles as a spoiled and petulant boy.) Further majestic interludes after 'köpft' (bb. 13–14) and 'Bergeshöhn' (bb. 17–18) punctuate the accusation that Zeus' behaviour is childishly petulant; indeed, they may be taken as a parody of the god throwing his weight around to no good purpose. After this, Prometheus really gets into his stride; the sentiments recall 'They shall not build, and another inhabit; they shall not plant, and another eat' of *Isaiah* Chapter 65, words that may be pronounced with the venom of a biblical seer or a trade-union prophet. With the phrases 'Und meine Hütte, die du nicht gebaut' and 'Und meinen Herd / Um dessen Glut / Du mich beneidest' the confrontation between Prometheus and Zeus takes on the revolutionary aspect of worker against boss, of organized labour challenging Olympian capitalism. Each sentence in this section is pitched slightly higher than its predecessor, and adds to the feeling of almost hysterical accusation. After 'beneidest' (bb. 24–5) the storm motif has its last appearance and it is as if Prometheus has become so heated that arioso is abandoned in favour of recitative ('Ich kenne nichts Ärmeres / Unter der Sonn'als euch, Götter!'), almost spluttered in its frustrated anger. In Goethe's versification, this is the beginning of the second strophe, but Schubert reserves his change of mood and tempo ('Etwas langsamer') for 'Ihr nährt kümmerlich' at b. 29.

Verse 2: This strange passage is full of irony and sarcasm, something very rare in Schubert. The 'offerings' and the 'breath of prayer' mentioned here obviously encourage the composer to think of church ceremonial as he knew it. Thus the Titan's continuing accusations and put-downs are accompanied by music in four parts that could have been written for organ; the creeping chromaticisms suggest extreme servility as they genuflect in an elaborate parody of the learned 'old style' of church music. The vocal line is the descant above this four-part writing, but the exaggeratedly woebegone setting of 'kümmerlich' (bb. 29–30), and the sarcasm built into 'Eure Majestät' (bb. 34–5) make it clear that, far from identifying with the solemnity of his accompaniment, the singer scorns it. The picture of superstitious church ceremonial is conjured up in order to be debunked. This passage resembles the time-travelling religious orthodoxy of *Vom Mitleiden Mariä* D632, also in G minor, written ten months earlier and, with the image of the 'Bettler' (b. 38), also with echoes of the supplicant's song 'An die Türen will ich schleichen' sung by the Harper from Goethe's *Wilhelm Meister* (D478/3). Old-fashioned subservience is the theme uniting all these works.

Verse 3: At b. 40 a shift to D minor (and *alla breve* time signature) signals a moment of respite. Schubert knew that a break in the invective was necessary, and that he would have to *reculer pour mieux sauter*. The flashback to childhood – 'Da ich ein Kind war' – allows a moment of tenderness, and we identify more closely with Prometheus as he shows this vulnerable streak. The accompaniment here is very simple, as if it might be played by a child. The emotive accented passing notes on 'Ein *Herz* wie *meins*' (bb. 49–51) and on the final 'erbarmen' emphasize the human compassion of which the Titan, unlike the uncaring Zeus, is capable.

Verse 4: At 'Wer half mir' ('Recit' b. 54) we return without warning to the tirade, although Zeus here is silent – like some dismayed father who has been bossy for years and is unexpectedly confronted with the wrathful onslaught of his once-timid offspring. Here the past is brought up and thrown in his face, the recitative requiring the singer almost to spit out the words. The harmonic basis for this, massive in its effect, as if carved out of marble, is made up of three blocks of diminished-seventh chords with their basses on G, A and then B. The questions of 'Who helped, who saved me?' are answered not in the god's favour; it is to his own heart, and not as he had once believed to the 'sleeper up above', that Prometheus owes his deliverance. In 'Wider der Titanen Übermut' (b. 55) Goethe has invented a background without basis in mythology; Prometheus is himself a Titan, and only in Aeschylus do we hear of him fighting, not his siblings, but Kronos on the side of Zeus. Once again the word 'Herz' is set on a passing note, denoting compassion; this time (at 'Heilig glühend Herz', b. 60) it is an F, the highest note in the song and usually the most difficult to sing. This adds to the heart-rending effect of this passage where Prometheus realizes that he can only look to his own resources for his salvation. After 'Schlafenden da droben?' (bb. 63–4) the piano chords are the most grandiose in the piece. The music is left suspended on the dominant of E flat minor.

Verse 5: This is never to be resolved. In perhaps the most exciting passage of the piece (marked 'Geschwinder', b. 66) the harangue continues on a succession of diminished sevenths pivoting at first on that hanging bass B flat. The rhythmic effect suggests the taunts of a physical challenge – 'Ich dich ehren? Wofür?' – with raised fists and jabs into the air. The diminished-seventh harmony (here associated with the selfish and disruptive god) is contrasted with the major-key wholeness and health of humanity. 'Hast du die Schmerzen gelindert' (bb. 69–70) is written out in C flat major, but 'Je des Beladenen?' effects an enharmonic change to B major symptomatic of transformation and eased suffering (bb. 70–71). The next four bars are a sequence of what we have already heard, notched excrutiatingly a semitone higher. For the repeat of 'Ich dich ehren? Wofür?' the diminished sevenths, rocking back and forth with a boxer's alert footwork, are built on a bank of B naturals in the bass (bb. 72–3). In this context, hearing the consolatory C major of 'Hast du die Tränen gestillet / Je des Geängsteten?' (set in the trickiest part of the voice, requiring much control in *mezza voce*) is like emerging from a forest bristling with accidentals to find comfort and help in a sunlit clearing. Schubert underlines Goethe's point that Prometheus is capable of human compassion, something beyond the understanding of the jealous gods. The hammer-blow chords at the passage beginning 'Hat nicht mich zum Manne geschmiedet' are built on four descending sequences of chromatic harmony: left-hand octaves, starting on a B flat, stride downwards in tones and semitones. This pattern is repeated in the next bars beginning on B, and then C and then C sharp. These basses are harmonized with a blistering array of harmonies, logical but daring, in a sequence where flats change to sharps and sharps to naturals. In this relentless succession of chords we hear the very process of mankind being forged in the smithy of Creation. The sparks fly also thanks to the singer's invective: 'Die allmächtige Zeit' and 'Das ewige Schicksal' refer to the Greek figures Chronos and Moira, who are greater than all the gods. The meaningful appoggiatura of the cadential 'und deine?' (a G sharp major chord) reminds Zeus, with sarcastic obeisances, that he too is subject to the laws of nature.

Verse 6: 'Etwas langsamer' (from b. 83). There are now five bars of respite, although still heavily laden with irony, before the final onslaught. We are in G sharp minor at the beginning of the section (b. 83), and somehow find ourselves in G major after only five bars (b. 87). It is as if the words are whispered to Zeus with a smile of triumph, informing the god that one of his ploys has not worked. He had hoped that Prometheus would hate life on earth, unable to cope with the setbacks regularly endured by human beings, as a disapproving parent might decide to let the hard knocks of life bang some sense into an errant child. The tone of this music is full of taunting politeness with isolated left-hand quavers punctuating the bass line like the muffled drum of a dead march. The honeyed sweetness of 'Weil nicht alle / Blütenträume reiften?' (bb. 85–7) is the most richly sarcastic phrase that Schubert ever wrote, and we might imagine him saying to his own father, 'Do you imagine that because I am not an instant success, because I have been disappointed with some failures, that I am going to give up my life in music?'

Verse 7: The crowning glory of this piece is, at last, grounded in a solid tonality; and what could be more elemental than C major? The marking is 'Kräftig' and something about these hammered chords, massive in their effect and a contrast to all preceding chromaticism, suggests Beethoven, surely the most Promethean of all artists, and one who might have been forgiven for turning on his Creator for the cruel trick played on his hearing. When Schubert wrote this song, the most recent Beethoven work published in Vienna (mid-September 1819) had been the *Hammerklavier* Sonata Op. 106. That work opens with an upward leap from bass to treble, and massive chords like an imperious call to arms, hammered and then snatched away in an implacable Allegro tempo. This is followed by silence for a dotted crotchet, making the succeeding sequence, crashing upon the ear and leaping yet higher up the keyboard, even more dramatic. In this song we have a similar effect: Schubert uses the silence between snatched and leaping chords to depict the magnificent recklessness of the Titan's utterance. And we are reminded that for the composer this is the heart of the song, showing Prometheus at work, sitting in his workshop fashioning a new race of men, just as Schubert daily fashioned a new type of music. One can best be defiant not by shouting about it, but by *doing* something different. How differently Hugo Wolf later organized the accentuation of these words, showing a different reading of the poet's meaning: Schubert's 'Hier <u>sitz</u>' ich' is replaced with Wolf's '<u>hier</u> sitz' ich' and Schubert's 'Ein Ge<u>schlecht</u>, das mir gleich sei' with 'Ein Geschlecht, das <u>mir</u> gleich sei'.

In the absence of Wagnerian-inspired hindsight, Schubert serves the poem in other ways. The energy field set up by this alternation of loud, leaping chords and eerie intermittent silence is immense, as if the very stuff of which men are made is being *thrown* against the potter's wheel. (It was Britten's playing of this passage as he accompanied Fischer-Dieskau at a recital in Aldeburgh in 1972 that brought this image to mind, the higher of the two chords in the recurring pattern not carefully placed but hurled recklessly up the octave.) Time and trouble are taken to paint 'Zu leiden, zu weinen', with mournfully descending intervals on both verbs as if Prometheus were attempting to teach Zeus a new emotional vocabulary. There is a hint of shudder beneath the first 'Wie ich!' (suddenly piano in dynamic) as if Prometheus, aware of his hubris, has a premonition of his punishment. But of course there is to be no punishment, and this is the message of Goethe's poem. Divine retribution is a fairy tale, and we are all responsible for our own destinies. The second 'Wie ich!' makes this clear – the jump of a fifth from G to C is as unambiguous and assured a cadence as one could wish for. All the chromatic doubt of previous pages has been clarified and focused into enlightened rationalism. The piano's two thundering C major chords set the seal on one of Schubert's most remarkable works. We may all be made of Promethean clay, but only genius can be fired to produce a work as extraordinarily rich and highly coloured as this (*see Lob der Tränen* D711, Verse 3).

Autograph:	Gesellschaft der Musikfreunde, Vienna
First edition:	Published as Book 47 no. 1 of the *Nachlass* by Diabelli, Vienna in 1850 (P375)
Subsequent editions:	Peters: Vol. 3/212; AGA XX 370: Vol. 6/71; NSA IV: Vol. 12/120
Bibliography:	Capell 1928, pp. 149–52
	Einstein 1951, p. 192
	Fischer-Dieskau 1977, pp. 130–31
	Mackworth-Young 1952, p. 53
	Robertson 1946, p. 165

Further settings and Arrangements:	Johann Freidrich Reichardt (1752–1814) *Prometheus* (1809)
	Hugo Wolf (1860–1903) *Prometheus* (1889)
	Arr. Max Reger (1873–1916) for voice and orchestra (1915) [*see* ORCHESTRATIONS]
Discography and timing:	Fischer-Dieskau II 3[12] 5'28
	Hyperion I 34[15]
	Hyperion II 22[11] 5'31 Simon Keenlyside

← *Die Liebende schreibt* D673   *Nachtstück* D672 →

Der 8. PSALM   The eighth Psalm

(TRANS. MENDELSSOHN) **D ANHANG II, 4**   [NOT IN HYPERION]

B♭ major   29 August 1823; final arrangement of composition fragment by Maximilian Stadler (1748–1833)

Dem Sangmeister auf Gittith ein Psalm Davids[1]	To the chief musician upon Gittith [or playing the gittith], A Psalm of David [translation from the Authorized Version]

1   Unendlicher! Gott, unser Herr!
      Wie mächtig ist dein Nam' auf Erden:
      Da deine Majestät am Himmel glänzt!

2   Der Säuglinge und Kinder Lallen[2]
      Befestiget dein Reich, beschämt
         den Sünder,
      Und stürzt den Feind, der Nacht
         schnaubt.

3   Betracht' ich deiner Finger Werk,
         den Himmel,
      Den Mond, die Sterne, die du
         eingesetzt:—

4   Was ist der Mensch, dass du noch sein
         gedenkest;
      Der Erdensohn, dass du dich seiner
         annimmst?

O lord! Our Lord,
   How excellent is thy name in all the earth!
   Who has set thy glory above the heavens.

Out of the mouths of babes and sucklings
   Hast thou ordained strength because of thine
      enemies
   That thou mightest still the enemy and the
      avenger.

When I consider the heavens, the work of
   thy fingers,
   The moon and stars which thou hast ordained:

What is man, that thou are mindful of him?

And the son of man that thou visitest him?

---

[1] Gittith refers to the city of Gath. The Gittith is also a lute-like instrument, probably manufactured in Gath.

[2] The English of the Authorized Version is at particular variance with the German here. The literal translation is: The babble of the babes and sucklings / Strengthens thy kingdoms, casts shame upon the sinner / And brings low the enemy who breathes the air of darkness.

5	Hast ihn den Engeln wenig nachgesetzt;	For thou hast made him a little lower than the angels,
	Hast ihn mit Ehr' und Schmuck gekrönt:	And has crowned him with glory and honour;
6	Ernennst ihn zum Beherrscher deiner Werke,	Thou madest him to have domination over the works of thy hands
	Und legst zu seinen Füssen alles:	Thou hast put all things under his feet
7	Das Lamm, den Stier, und auch Gewild:	All sheep and oxon, yea, and the beasts of the field:
8	Was in der Luft, was sich im Wasser regt,	The fowl of the air and the fish of the sea
	Er bahnt sich Wege durch die Meere!	And whatever passeth through the paths of the sea
9	Unendlicher! Gott unser Herr!	O Lord our Lord
	Wie ruhmvoll ist dein Nam' auf Erden!	How excellent is thy name in all the earth!

OLD TESTAMENT, TRANSLATED BY MOSES MENDELSSOHN (1729–1786)

This work falls into the same category as the comic trio *Die Advokaten* D37 in that it is Schubert's arrangement of another composer's work. In this case the composer is Maximilian Stadler (*see* COMPOSERS) who favoured religious music of this kind. Stadler's Latin title is *Domine Dominus Noster*, but he uses the Moses Mendelssohn translation of the biblical Psalms. This work is thus separate from Stadler's *Zwölf Psalmen Davids nach Mendelsohn's* [sic] *Üibsertzung* [sic] *für eine und mehr Singstimmen m. Begleitung d. Pianoforte* that was published in four books in Vienna by P. Mecchetti between 1815 and 1819. It is hard not to believe that it was Stadler's example that led Schubert to this same collection for Psalms 13 and 23. Albert Stadler (no relation to Maximilian) remembers Schubert arranging this music in 1819 for a performance in Steyr, but the manuscript is firmly dated 1823, the summer of which Schubert also spent in Steyr. It may be of course that the work was performed in Steyr in both those years, and that it was the final arrangement that was made in 1823. The work is clearly conceived for Vogl's voice, catering to that singer's taste for grandiose declamation. It is a thundering good sing for a high baritone – hardly musically sophisticated by Schubertian standards but effective in its alternation of *pomposo* rhetoric and recitative. A comparison with Stadler's original shows how Schubert has 'opened out' the composition, retaining most of Stadler's original ideas but creating a more spacious time frame in which to hear or perform them. Schubert clearly enjoys Stadler's work for what it is, a simple and heartfelt paean of praise, but he understands Vogl's desire for a grand vehicle and so tweaks the over-compressed original to give it a broader musical perspective. Schubert's piano part was perhaps meant as a short score for an orchestrated version of the Psalm with strings, woodwind, timpani and organ.

Autograph:	Pierpont Morgan Library, New York (copy of Stadler's work with Schubert's handwritten changes and corrections)
First edition:	Published privately by Reinhard Van Hoorickx
Subsequent editions:	Not in Peters; Not in AGA; NSA VIII: Vol. 1
Discography and timing:	Fischer-Dieskau —
	Hyperion I —
	Hyperion II

Der 13. PSALM[1]   The thirteenth Psalm

(Trans. Mendelssohn) **D663** [H430]
(Fragment) B♭ minor – B♭ major   June 1819

Ach Herr, wie lan-ge willst du mein so ganz ver - ges- sen?

(40 bars)

1 Der Sangmeister ein Psalm Davids	[A Psalm of David] [translation from the Authorized Version]
2 Ach, Herr! wie lange willst du mein so ganz vergessen? Wie lange noch dein Antlitz mir verbergen?	How long wilt thou forget me, O Lord? For ever? How long wilt thou hide thy face from me?
3 Wie lange muss ich meinen Geist mit Sinnen, Mein Herz mit Sorgen täglich quälen? Wie lange noch mein Feind obsiegen?	How long shall I take counsel in my soul, Having sorrow in my heart daily? How long shall mine enemy be exalted over me?

***   ***

4 Schau herab! erhöre mich! Ach Ewiger! mein Gott! Erleuchte meine Augen wieder, Dass ich des Todes nicht entschlafe.	Consider and hear me, O Lord my God: Lighten mine eyes, Lest I sleep the sleep of death;
5 Sonst spricht mein Feind: 'den überwand ich!' Frohlocken Widersacher meines Falles.	Lest mine enemy say I have prevailed against him; And those that trouble me rejoice when I am moved.

***   ***

6 Doch ich vertraue deiner Güte, Mein Herz frohlockt ob deiner Hülfe, Dem Ewigen singe ich; denn er tat mir wohl.	But I have trusted in thy mercy; My heart shall rejoice in thy salvation. I will sing unto the Lord, because he hath dealt bountifully with me.

---

[1] On Schubert's autograph the title (as in the Moses Mendelssohn source) has been overwritten with the words *12. Psalm*. This is the numbering in the Roman Catholic and Greek Orthodox Vulgate as opposed to the Hebraic and Lutheran traditions.

OLD TESTAMENT, TRANSLATED BY MOSES MENDELSSOHN (1729–1786)

This is the second of Schubert's two solo biblical settings. See entry under 'Bible' for a list of all songs setting texts either directly drawn from, or inspired by, the Bible.

This song belongs to a period when Schubert seems to have been exploring new forms of religious music, as well as new styles for writing it. From 1818, apart from the *Deutsches Requiem* D621, there is the unusual fragment titled *Evangelium Johannis* D607, a selection from the Gospel according to St John and Schubert's only work for voice and piano that is a setting of prose (apart from the Ossian settings, of course, but Schubert took those to be poetry). Numerous songs about the Virgin Mary, as well as settings of the religious poet Silbert, date from the same period and in May 1819, a month before writing *Der 13. Psalm*, he set the four *Geistliche Lieder* (D659–662) of Novalis (formerly published under the title of *Hymnen*). Soon afterwards Schubert began work on the big Mass in A flat (not finished until 1822); then there is the unfinished cantata *Lazarus* begun in February 1820.

The Esterházy count and countess with whom he spent the summers of 1818 and 1824 were deeply devout, as were their two daughters, and the composer was susceptible to the enthusiasms of people he liked and admired. But there may be another explanation, and this lies in the rather unusual character of Anton von Pettenkoffer (1788–1834) who, on Thursday evenings in 1819 and 1820, hosted musical gatherings at his third-floor apartment in a house in the Bauernmarkt. These gatherings, which were precursors of the genuine Schubertiads that date from 1821 or so, were an opportunity to hear much unfamiliar music. Handel's *Messiah*, Haydn's *Die Schöpfung* and *Die sieben letzten Worte unseres Erlösers am Kreuze* were all performed, and Schubert himself took part, playing the viola. The host had a penchant for sacred music and it seems likely that at least some of Schubert's religious compositions of the time, including *Der 13. Psalm* and *Lazarus*, were conceived for performance at Pettenkoffer's.

Another important factor was the holiday that Vogl and Schubert took in Steyr in the summer of 1819. It may be that the arrangement Schubert made of Maximilian Stadler's *Psalm 8* in Moses Mendelssohn's translation was completed for the 1819 Steyr holiday alongside this Psalm for solo voice. It seems likely that the song is only a fragment because part of it has been lost. Although it has never been questioned that the work was written for voice and piano, the andante triplet arpeggios drifting down the stave, and the subsequent gently undulating semiquavers, seem infinitely more like harp writing. If the song is genuinely for piano, it is certainly Schubert's most anonymous writing for the instrument. The lack of pianistic detail and elaboration is astonishing considering how often the words might have suggested something more interesting. The harp would have been a highly appropriate instrument to accompany the Psalms of King David (who was a harpist after all) and it seems possible that there would have been a harp among the orchestral instruments available at von Pettenkoffer's (and perhaps also in Steyr). The piece as it stands is entirely performable on the harp, and the key of B flat minor with its five flats, rare in Schubert songs, is an ideal tonality for performance on that instrument. (Around this time people were beginning to play Erard's splendid new double-action harps tuned to the key of C flat.)

There are tiny touches of word-painting – for example the held G flat suspended in mid-air at 'Wie *lange* noch mein Feind obsiegen?' (bb. 3–6) and the softening modulation into the tonic major at 'Schau herab!' (b. 15). The recitative at 'Sonst spricht mein Feind' (b. 25) is disappointingly stiff. The final section of the song (from b. 29) is a gentle dance in $\frac{6}{8}$. Here the atmosphere is that of a charmingly unpretentious *Singspiel* aria in Schubert's *Claudine von Villa Bella* style, although the metre of Mendelssohn's translation is an awkward fit for this sort of pastoral simplicity, with too many words and too few opportunities for the singer to breathe. The last six bars in the performance recorded for the Hyperion Edition are by the eminent Schubert scholar Eusebius Mandyczewski (printed at the end of the NSA version) and are no more than an adequate continuation of the ideas already unfolded. It is likely that Schubert would have composed a postlude, but Mandyczewski was wise enough not to try to provide one.

Autograph:	Missing or lost
First edition:	Fragment completed by Eusebius Mandyczewski; subsequently published privately by Reinhard Van Hoorickx and as part of the NSA in 1996 (P813)
Subsequent editions:	Not in Peters; Not in AGA; NSA IV: Vol. 12/212
Discography and timing:	Fischer-Dieskau —
	Hyperion I 31[8]
	Hyperion II 22[5] 3'04 Christine Brewer

⟵ *Geistliches Lied* ('Ich sag es jedem, dass er lebt') D662

Cantate zum Geburtstag des Sängers Johann Michael Vogl D666 ⟶

Der 23. PSALM (Gott ist mein Hirt)
(Trans. Mendelssohn) **D706** [H460]
A♭ major   December 1820

The twenty-third   Chorus, ssaa
Psalm: The Lord is
my shepherd

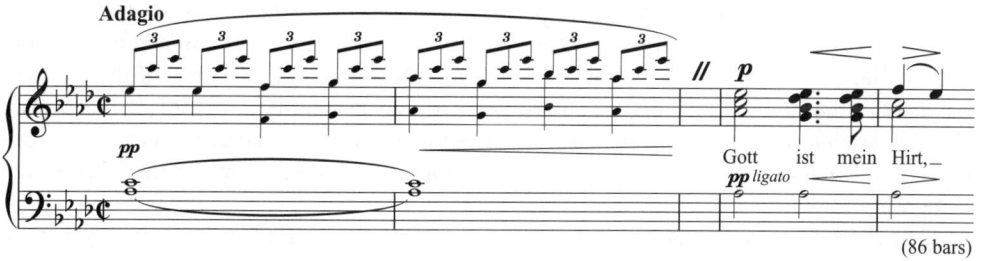

(86 bars)

1   Psalm Davids

[A Psalm of David] [translation from the] Authorized Version]

2   Gott ist mein Hirt, mir wird nichts mangeln.

3   Er lagert mich auf grüne Weide;
Er leitet mich an stillen Bächen:

4   Er labt mein schmachtendes Gemüt,
Er führt mich auf gerechtem Steige,
Zu seines Namens Ruhm.—

5   Und wall' ich auch im Todesschattentale,

So wall' ich ohne Furcht
Denn du beschützest mich;[1]
Dein Stab und deine Stütze
Sind mir immerdar mein Trost.[2]

The Lord is my shepherd, I shall not want.

He maketh me to rest in green pastures;
He leadeth me beside still waters;

He giveth peace unto my soul.
He leadeth me in paths of goodness
For his name's sake.

Yea, though I walk through the valley of
the shadow of death
I will fear no evil,
For thou art with me.
Thy rod and staff,
They comfort me.

[1] Mendelssohn writes 'Denn du *begleitest* mich'.
[2] 'Mir' is not in the Mendelssohn translation.

6   Du richtest mir ein Freudenmahl   Thou preparest a table for me
        Im Angesicht der Feinde zu,   In the presence of mine enemies;
        Du salbst mein Haupt mit Öle   My head with oil thou anointest;
        Und schenkst mir volle, volle Becher ein,   My cup runneth over.
7   Mir folget Heil und Seligkeit   Yea, surely peace and mercy all my life
        In diesem Leben nach.   Shall follow me,
        Einst ruh' ich ew'ge Zeit,   And I will dwell for evermore
        Dort in des Ew'gen Haus.   In the house of the Lord.

OLD TESTAMENT, TRANSLATED BY MOSES MENDELSSOHN (1729–1786)

This well-loved piece, heard in many a church over the last 150 years and at many an *eisteddfod, feis* or village festival, owes its existence to a commission – or at least a request (we are not sure whether money changed hands or whether Schubert merely provided the score out of personal kindness). It was written for the pupils of Anna Fröhlich (1793–1880), a singing teacher at the Wiener Konservatorium. It was also she who cajoled Schubert into composing the Grillparzer *Ständchen* D920 for mezzo and women's chorus in July 1827 when Josefine, her sister, was the soloist. The four Fröhlich sisters were either very insistent (although Schubert never seems to have composed against his will) or very charming and persuasive (Grillparzer was hopelessly in love with one of them, Katharina). The composer delivered the score of *Der 23. Psalm* on completion in December 1820, and the work was first heard the following August at a pupils' concert in the Gundelhof. It achieved immediate popularity, taken up by older artists and performed on several further occasions in Schubert's lifetime, most notably on 7 February 1828 when it was part of the programme at the Musikverein under the direction of Franz or Josef Chiami. This music is in the style of the Austrian *Landmesse*, the homespun liturgical music heard in small country churches of the period. That it was conceived for a concert illustrates how the barriers between performance of sacred music and secular, once rigidly upheld by the authorities, were disintegrating during the composer's lifetime.

Male choruses were a long-established Viennese tradition, and it is hardly surprising that the majority of Schubert's choral music is for men's voices. About a third of the ninety or so works that fall into this category are piano-accompanied, and are thus included in this book, as are the seventeen works for mixed voices and piano. The list of songs for women's voices is much shorter. Only seven works specifically require an all-female cast, five of these with piano. When Schubert came to compose this Psalm he had written only one such work, five years previously in 1815 (*Das Leben* D269) but others were to follow, including the haunting *Coronach* from Scott's *Lady of the Lake* settings. The *Ständchen* mentioned above is probably the most substantial work in this genre. Probably from force of habit the composer originally conceived it for men's chorus and female soloist, but he immediately rectified this by providing another version for women's voices.

Schubert chooses the key of A flat major to express calm and glowing faith. The opening piano triplets waft and weave with the utmost delicacy as a tonic pedal underpins subtle harmonic changes. (Some years later he was to use this device even more effectively in the introduction to *Im Abendrot* D799.) The entry of the four voices at b. 5 is a magical moment: the composer exploits the lack of a vocal bass line to conjure a tessitura that seems unconnected to the earth and its worldly concerns. The spacing of the voices gives an ethereal quality to the music and it is difficult for the ear to disentangle this insinuating blend of close feminine harmony, an effect that has also been much exploited in popular music.

In the beginning, so smooth is the vocal line and so soothing the accompaniment that we see only unending vistas of gently rolling Elysian fields. From b. 12, at 'Er lagert mich auf grüne Weide' ('He maketh me to rest in green pastures'), the pianist's fingers become more active and dancing little dotted-rhythm sequences, where the sopranos and altos are briefly separated in imitation, are buoyed up by gentle Schubertian water music. At this heavenly banquet the waters are sparkling rather than still. There is a sudden outbreak of forte singing at 'seines Namens Ruhm' (literally, 'for the fame of his name', bb. 26–9), accompanied by grandiose triplets that anticipate *Die Allmacht* D852. At 'Und wall' ich auch im Todesschattentale' ('Yea, though I walk through the valley of the shadow of death') the music becomes mysterious and tense, the triplets now pulsating in the bass, a tessitura of the piano which the piece so far has pointedly failed to exploit; in this we hear a ghostly premonition of the song *Schwestergruss* D762 where Franz von Bruchmann's sister supposedly returned with a message from the grave. These central sections provide the only passing moments of doubt and drama, and the music soon returns to the higher regions, in terms of both tessitura and spirit. The piece as a whole seems to be the music of angels, materializing out of thin air and returning to the ether – but not before an apt setting of the final words 'in des Ew'gen Haus' (literally, 'the home of the Eternal One') where the idea of immortality occasions a broadening of the word-setting and a lengthening of note values. Six bars from the end the first soprano holds a high E flat for six beats as the second climbs a chromatic scale as if aspiring to eternal heavenly light. The piano's arpeggios become more ecstatic for a moment, but it is not long before the gently plucked harps of Seraphim re-establish themselves. It is as if they have been resounding for all eternity, and we have been permitted to tune in to them for only the allotted time of five minutes and twenty-three seconds.

Autograph:	Wienbibliothek im Rathaus, Vienna (fragment)
First edition:	Published as Op. post. 132 by Diabelli, Vienna in March 1832 (P284)
First known performance:	30 August 1821 in a Conservatorium public exam at the Gesellschaft der Musikfreunde, Vienna. Singers: Louise Fabiani, Emerenzia Heinrich, Amalia Tevils and Josefine Fleischmann (see Waidelich/Hilmar Dokumente I No. 121 for full programme)
Contemporary reviews:	*Allgemeine Musikalische Zeitung* (Leipzig), 26 September 1821, where the piece is incorrectly identified as '14. Psalm' [Waidelich/Hilmar Dokumente I No. 124; Deutsch Doc. Biog. No. 250] *Allgemeine Musikalische Zeitung* (Vienna), 29 September 1821 [Waidelich/Hilmar Dokumente I No. 125; Deutsch Doc. Biog. No. 251]
Subsequent editions:	AGA XVIII 2: p. 3; NSA III: Vol. 3
Arrangements:	Arr. Hans Zender (b. 1936) *Coronach, 23. Psalm und Der Gondelfahrer* for choir and orchestra [*see* ORCHESTRATIONS]
Discography and timing:	Hyperion I 31^9 / Hyperion II 24^1 — 5'23 — Patricia Rozario, Lorna Anderson, Catherine Denley & Catherine Wyn-Rogers

← *Gesang der Geister über den Wassern* D705   *Im Walde* D708 →

Der 92. PSALM[1]

D953 [H668+]
C major   July 1828

The ninety-second
Psalm: A song for
the Sabbath

Baritone, solo
SATB and
unaccompanied
chorus SATB

tôw   l'hô - dôs la - dô - noj   u - l'sam - mer   le - schi - me - cho el - jôn

(89 bars)

1	Tov lehôdôs ladonoi	It is a good thing to give thanks unto the Lord,
	Ulzameir leshimcho elyôn.	and to sing praises unto thy name, O Most High;
2	lehagid babôker chasdecho	to declare thy loving kindness in the morning,
	Ve-emunoscho baleilôs.	and thy faithfulness in the night seasons,
3	alei osôr va-alei	with an instrument of ten strings, and with the psaltery;
	Novel alei higoyôn bechinôr.	with a solemn sound upon the harp.
4	ki simachtani adônoi befo-olecho	For thou, Lord, hast made me glad through thy work;
	Bema-asei yodecho aranein.	I will exult in the works of thy hands.
5	ma godlu ma-asecho adônoi	How great are thy works, O Lord!
	Meôd omku machshvôsecho.	Thy thoughts are very deep.
6	isch ba-ar lô yeido	A brutish man knoweth not,
	Uchsil lô yovin es zôs.	neither doth a fool understand this.
7	bifrôach rshoim kmô eisev	When the wicked spring up as the grass,
	Vayotzitzu kol pôalei oven	and when all the workers of iniquity do flourish;
	lhishomdom adei ad.	it is that they may be destroyed for ever.
8	veato morôm leôlom [adônoi].	But thou, O Lord, art on high for evermore.

OLD TESTAMENT, IN HEBREW

This is one of the most unusual pieces in the Schubert repertoire. How many people even know that Schubert wrote a Psalm setting in Hebrew? This came about because of the composer's acquaintance with Salomon Sulzer (1804–1890), a young Jewish baritone whose extraordinary talents brought him to Vienna in 1826. Sulzer was born in Hohenems in Vorarlberg where he was appointed cantor at the age of thirteen. (This is the only historical link with Schubert that can be traced back to this tiny Austrian town, renowned today as the cradle of a yearly Schubert festival that has since expanded to nearby Schwarzenberg.) As a young man Sulzer was a music student in Karlsruhe and travelled widely to perfect his calling as a cantor; he also worked on conducting and composition. At only twenty-two he was invited to take up the post of *chazzan*, or cantor, in the newly built Viennese synagogue in the Seitenstettengasse. After his arrival in the capital he studied further with Ignaz von Seyfried, Kapellmeister at the Theater an der Wien

---

[1] The transliteration of the Hebrew in the incipit is given as it is found in the Deutsch catalogue. The transliteration of the full text was prepared for the performance recorded for the Hyperion Edition.

and a distinguished composer of religious music. It was probably through Seyfried that Sulzer was introduced to Schubert.

The 1820s, although a very repressive period politically for most Austrians, marked increasing religious tolerance for the Jewish community, at least in legal terms. The *Heskalah*, the process of Jewish Enlightenment in Vienna, gathered momentum as the walls of the ghetto crumbled away. In 1821 the emperor had ennobled nine Jews, and he agreed to the erection of a new synagogue, the first officially recognized building of its kind since 1671. A new rabbi for this large house of worship was selected by a process of trial sermons; the choice fell on a remarkable man from Copenhagen, Rabbi Isaak Noah Mannheimer, a radical reformer who preferred to preach in German rather than Hebrew. It was Mannheimer's wish to modernize the life of the religious community, including the important musical side of the services. He invited Beethoven, no less, to compose something for the consecration of the house, but the ailing composer could not be persuaded. In the end it was Josef Drechsler, Kapellmeister at St Stephen's, who provided a cantata for the opening of the temple on 9 April 1826. As Elaine Brody points out in *Schubert Studies*, Mannheimer and Sulzer, the precocious young cantor who was the new rabbi's adventurous but canny choice, proved a fine team. Sulzer was less in favour of sweeping changes than Mannheimer; he preferred to modify only certain aspects of the service, while keeping to tradition in other respects. Thus a compromise was reached which balanced the wishes of the reformers with those of the conservatives: Sulzer insisted that the Eastern style of cantillation should be conserved, and that the music should continue to be unaccompanied (it was only much later that an organ was installed). For High Holidays the traditional melodies of the synagogue continued to be used, but Sulzer felt that music by non-Jewish composers might be heard at the Friday night and Saturday services (hence Schubert's setting of this Psalm for the Sabbath).

As Sulzer had been charged with the reorganization of the musical side of the service in the new synagogue, he set about commissioning pieces of music from well-known composers to be used for liturgical purposes. The first volume of his anthology *Schir Zion* ('The Harp of Zion', 1839) consists of 159 musical items of religious music; 122 of these are by Sulzer himself, but the collection also includes works by Josef Drechsler, Josef Fischer and Michael Umlauf, as well

as this Schubert Psalm. It is self-evident that Vienna's leading Jewish composers should have taken an interest in such a project, but it remains unclear what led Schubert to compose this Psalm in July 1828. He was always short of money and it is possible that the arrangement was purely financial. But the composer is also said to have admired the beauty of Sulzer's voice and his artistry. There is an apocryphal story that Schubert insisted on hearing the young singer perform the famous *Der Wanderer* D489 three times in succession, and was astounded by Sulzer's rendition of *Die Allmacht*. Liszt certainly admired Sulzer at a later date and, perhaps as a result, arranged *Die Allmacht* for tenor solo and large male chorus. Someone at the end of the nineteenth century saw fit to provide evidence that Schubert had been the cantor's fervent admirer in the form of a letter to Sulzer, purportedly from the composer, which lauds the cantor

Salomon Sulzer, lithograph by August Prinzhofer, 1846.

extravagantly – and rather uncharacteristically (Schubert tended to be sparing in his praise of younger artists). Otto Erich Deutsch pronounced the letter a forgery, and it was thus not included in the *Documentary Biography*.

But one thing is clear: Schubert could have delivered this Psalm to Sulzer in German, but chose instead to set it in Hebrew. As an unaccompanied work, it strictly speaking falls outside the scope of this book (and of the Hyperion series) but it is a companion piece to the settings of Psalms 13 and 23 and shows the composer at the end of his life to have been open-minded regarding religious viewpoints other than those of his own cultural background. Schubert seems to have gone to some trouble to honour Jewish traditions and language with serious attention to detail, providing Sulzer with a piece that was as authentic as he could make it.

The technical difficulties of setting Hebrew to Western music are not to be underestimated. Hebrew poetry is in fact poetical prose, and traditional Jewish melodies with their freely flowing characteristics resist being confined in the straitjackets of exact Western notation. The composer omitted the first verse of the Psalm and set the next eight (2 to 9) for a group of soloists and chorus in alternation. A baritone solo for Sulzer was included at the heart of the piece. There is nothing like this in Schubert's other choral music, and it is obviously based on the tradition of the *meshorim*, where the cantor sang his melodies, accompanied by a boy soprano and a bass on either side of him. It is clear that the composer consulted Sulzer on matters of Hebrew accentuation and meaning. Although Schubert made no attempt to use any traditional melodic material for the setting (this was Sulzer's compositional speciality), the music is tinged with a trace of what might be termed 'Middle-Eastern exoticism'. It is the consensus that Schubert did rather well in his handling of Hebrew: for example, correct accentuations of the syllables 'noi' and 'yôn'; the florid word-painting at 'babôker' ('in the morning') and the downward cadence on 'baleilôs' ('at night'). As Elaine Brody points out, 'at "lhishomdom" Schubert brings the music to a climax; the setting's highest pitch and *forte* dynamics combine to stress the meaning of the words here: "It is that they shall be destroyed for ever." '

The ninth verse contains only a single line – a four-word Hebrew sentence that is repeated six times. The piece concludes with a simple (and appropriate) repetition of the word 'leôlom' ('for evermore'). It is likely that Schubert deliberately stopped at this verse to enable Sulzer to chant the remainder of the Psalm in recitative. According to Brody, the ending here rather than on the written 'adônoi' ('Lord') has counted against later performances in synagogues.

The manuscript, extant in the 1870s, has since been lost, but the Psalm, and the setting of an unfamiliar language, provides a fascinating glimpse of the composer's intellectual curiosity as he looks beyond the borders of his own background and experience. If it is tempting to think of 'Schwammerl' (the little mushroom of his nickname) as a sedentary soul, this work proposes another Schubert – one who would have made an enthusiastic and fascinated traveller had he been given a chance to explore the wide world beyond Austria's borders. More than this, even in his own lifetime there were signs of something that we now take for granted: Schubert's musical genius enabled him to be a mediator and link between different cultures and faiths.

Autograph:	Missing or lost
First edition:	Published as No. 6 of *Schir Zion, gottesdienstliche Gesänge der Israeliten von S. Sulzer* in 1841; subsequently published by J. P. Gotthard (with German text by Moses Mendelssohn) as 'Der 92. Psalm (Lied für den Sabbath)' in 1870 and as part of the AGA in 1892 (P521)
First known performance:	Summer (July/August) 1828 at the Synagogue an Kienmarkt, Vienna. Soloist: Salomon Sulzer [Waidelich/Hilmar Dokumente II No. 627a]

| Subsequent editions: | AGA XVIII 19: p. 247; NSA III: Vol. 2b/252 (Hebrew) & 375 (German) |
| Bibliography: | Brody 1982, pp. 47–60 |

Discography and timing: Hyperion I 31[10]   5'27   Paul Robinson, Julie Cooper, Joanna
Hyperion II 36[9]   Gamble, Ashley Catling, Charles Gibbs
& Holst Singers (dir. Stephen Layton)

← *Das Echo* D990C   *Glaube, Hoffnung und Liebe* D955 →

PUBLISHERS

If only honest dealing were possible with these *** music publishers, but the wise and benevolent regulations of our Government have taken care that the artist shall remain the eternal slave of these miserable shopkeepers.

Franz Schubert, in a letter to his parents from Steyr, 25 July 1825

The story of Schubert's dealings with the music publishers of Vienna provides a cross section of activity in the Biedermeier age that perfectly illustrates the business conditions of the time. These often represented an uphill struggle for the composer, and some unwholesome aspects of music publishing in Vienna emerge when one looks beyond the simple facts of these transactions: lack of musical idealism and taste, prospensity to double-dealing, the slavish attention to following, rather than creating, market trends and, in the worst cases, greed combined with inefficiency and downright laziness. There were honourable exceptions, but many Viennese publishers, also subject to the debilitating presence of censorship, were guilty of some of these things. Towards the end of his life Schubert attempted to break free from them and establish connections in Germany, where men like Schott of Mainz and Probst of Leipzig, though hard businessmen, had a go-ahead attitude lacking in the self-satisfaction found in the Austrian firms. The composer died before he could bring off an acceptable deal with a German publisher, but by the end of 1828 such an arrangement was perhaps only months away.

Schubert saw his first song in print in February 1818. The Mayrhofer setting *Erlafsee* (composed in September 1817) was issued as a supplement to an almanac that appeared once a year under the title *Mahleriches Taschenbuch für Freunde interessanter Gegenden Natur- und Kunst-Merkwürdigkeiten der Österreichischen Monarchie*. The Viennese publisher was **Anton Doll**, the same firm that had in 1810 issued the complete edition of Schiller's works that was almost certainly used by Schubert for his settings of that poet. This was the sixth year of the periodical's appearance and it contained a frontispiece illustration of 'Der Erlafsee' together with a printing of Mayrhofer's poem (pp. 185–6). At the beginning of the volume, 'Auf der Donau' can be found, a text that Schubert had also set in 1817.

The second song in print, also as a supplement to an almanac, was the Schlechta setting *Widerschein*, the first and only Schubert song to appear outside Austria for many years, and very rarely to be found in extant copies of the almanac. It was issued as a supplement to *W. G. Becker's Taschenbuch zum geselligen Vergnügen* published in Leipzig by **Georg Joachim Göschen**. This was issued on 28 September 1820. The editor, the poet Kind qv (Schubert was later to set one of his poems), also engaged another Franz Schubert to set a poem entitled *Die Lebensgefährten*. It amused Kind to have two musical supplements for his almanac, one with a song by Franz Schubert of Vienna, another with a song by Franz Schubert of Dresden (qv COMPOSERS).

At the end of 1820 an important friend and publisher emerged in Schubert's story. This was the flamboyant figure of **Johann Schickh** (1770–1835). Since 1816 Schickh had edited a remarkable publishing venture that combined all his interests – Art, Literature, Theatre and Fashion – with music very much included in that list of enthusiasms. This *Wiener Zeitschrift für Kunst, Literatur, Theater und Mode* appeared on Tuesdays, Thursdays and Saturdays and was printed by the famous Viennese publisher **Anton Strauss**. Each issue comprised eight pages of closely printed short stories, articles, reviews of theatrical and musical performances from all over the German-speaking world, and poems – usually, but not always, by local Viennese literati. The Thursday issue would always include a spectacularly coloured plate of 'Wiener Moden' – mostly

Johann Schickh, proprietor and editor of the *Wiener Zeitschrift für Kunst, Literatur, Theater und Mode.*

women's fashions. The quality of these plates makes these books (the *Zeitschrift* was reprinted and bound in quarterly volumes) expensive collectors' items today. Once a quarter there would be a musical supplement published, almost always a song. This was on good-quality card-like paper that folded into the main publication but which could also be detached and used for performance.

On occasion it pleased Schickh to offer poems that had come his way, probably for review, to composers for setting. It was Schickh who supplied Beethoven with Goeble's hitherto unknown poem *Abendlied unterm gestirnten Himmel* as a song text, and the work was published as a supplement to the *Zeitschrift* in March 1820. In the same way it was Schickh who first made Schubert aware of Leitner's poetry in 1823, and of Lappe's at the end of 1824. The composer had been a schoolfriend of Killian, Schickh's nephew, and the perspicacious editor was quick to recognize Schubert's genius. No fewer than twelve songs were first published as supplements in the *Wiener Zeitschrift* in Schubert's lifetime. Those songs which were later published during the composer's lifetime are also detailed below:

Die Forelle (*WZ*, 9 December 1820, later reissued as Op. 32)
An Emma (*WZ*, 30 June 1821, later reissued as Op. 58 no. 2)
Der Blumen Schmerz (*WZ*, 8 December 1821)
Die Rose (*WZ*, 7 May 1822, later reissued as Op. 73)
Der Wachtelschlag (*WZ*, 30 July 1822, later reissued as Op. 68)
Drang in die Ferne (*WZ*, 25 March 1823, later reissued as Op. 71)
Auf dem Wasser zu singen (*WZ*, 30 December 1823, later reissued as Op. 72)
Der Einsame (*WZ*, 12 March 1825, later reissued as Op. 41)
Trost im Liede (*WZ*, 23 June 1827, later reissued as Op. 101 no. 3)
Wandrers Nachtlied II (*WZ*, 23 June 1827, later reissued as Op. 96 and Op. 101 no. 4)
Der blinde Knabe (*WZ*, 25 September 1827, later reissued as Op. 101 no. 3)
Im Frühling (*WZ*, 16 September 1828, later reissued as Op. 101 no. 1)

There are two further songs that appeared as supplements in Viennese almanacs, both in 1824. The first of these was the Schubart setting *An den Tod,* published on 26 June 1824 as a supplement to *Wiener Allgemeine musikalische Zeitung.* Interestingly enough the song was printed for this purpose by the Lithographisches Institut, the firm that Franz von Schober would buy and take over in 1826 (*see* below).

The second song appeared on 11 December 1824 in an *Album musicale* Volume 2 published by Sauer and Leidesdorf (*see* below). This was *Die Erscheinung* (later republished posthumously by M. J. Leidesdorf (*see* below) as Op. 108 no. 3. A later title of the song is *Erinnerung.*

Occasional appearances in almanacs were all very well, but they were no substitute for proper publication. It was the first public performance of *Erlkönig* in December 1820 that persuaded some of Schubert's more influential friends, including Leopold von Sonnleithner (*see* FRIENDS AND FAMILY) that it was a matter of the highest priority to have the composer's songs properly published and circulated in the musical world. Approaching such firms as Steiner & Co. and Haslinger (*see* below), they attempted without success to find a publisher who would take a risk on *Erlkönig* (the piano part was considered too difficult); as a result Sonnleithner, together with Josef Hüttenbrenner, Johann Schönauer and Johann Schönpichler, decided to take the gamble themselves. The publishing firm of **Cappi & Diabelli** agreed to act as 'agents on commission' for *Erlkönig,* the copyright remaining with the composer. The consortium would pay for all the printing costs and would also be free to sell copies of the music privately to their friends. The music would also be available for the general public at the firm's establishment and would be advertised in the *Wiener Zeitung* as their publication. In return for this the publishers would take a commission for each copy sold.

Cappi & Diabelli was the partnership of **Pietro Cappi** (whose father had been a partner in the famous music publishing firm of Artaria) and **Anton Diabelli** (1781–1858), a minor composer and music teacher with a highly developed business streak. Their firm operated between 1818 and 1823. The first run of *Erlkönig* was 225 copies, all of which sold quickly (even at the high price of 2 florins). This enabled the consortium of friends to underwrite further publications and Schubert found himself comfortably in pocket. It would not be long before Diabelli realized that there was much more potential in the Schubert song market than he had first thought.

Anton Diabelli, lithograph by Josef Kriehuber, 1841.

SONGS PUBLISHED BY CAPPI & DIABELLI (Kunst- und Musikhändler, Graben Nr. 1133):

Op. 1 *Erlkönig* on commission. Price 2 florins (2 April 1821)

Op. 2 *Gretchen am Spinnrade* on commission. Price 1 florin 30 kreuzer (30 April 1821)

Op. 3 *Schäfers Klagelied, Meeres Stille, Heidenröslein, Jägers Abendlied* on commission. Price 1 florin 30 kreuzer (29 May 1821)

Op. 4 *Der Wanderer* (Schmidt), *Morgenlied* (Werner), *Wandrers Nachtlied* on commission. Price 1 florin 30 kreuzer (29 May 1821)

Op. 5 *Rastlose Liebe, Nähe des Geliebten, Der Fischer, Erster Verlust, Der König in Thule* on commission. Price 1 florin 30 kreuzer (9 July 1821)

Op. 6 *Memnon, Antigone und Oedip, Am Grabe Anselmos* on commission. Price 1 florin 30 kreuzer (23 August 1821)

Op. 7 *Die abgeblühte Linde, Der Flug der Zeit, Der Tod und das Mädchen* on commission. Price 1 florin 30 kreuzer (27 November 1821)

Op. 8 *Der Jüngling auf dem Hügel, Sehnsucht* (Mayrhofer), *Erlafsee, Am Strome*. Price 2 florins (9 May 1822)

Op. 11 *Das Dörfchen, Die Nachtigall, Geist der Liebe* (Matthisson). Price 2 florins (12 June 1822)

Op. 12 *Gesänge des Harfners* on commission. Price 1 florin 30 kreuzer (13 December 1822)

Op. 13 *Der Schäfer und der Reiter, Lob der Tränen, Der Alpenjäger* (Mayrhofer) on commission. Price 1 florin 30 kreuzer (13 December 1822)

Op. 14 *Suleika* I, *Geheimes* on commission. Price 2 florins (13 December 1822)

Op. 16 *Frühlingslied, Naturgenuss* (quartets). The inside title of the first song is, correctly, *Frühlingsgesang*. Price 4 florins 30 kreuzer (9 October 1823)

During this period, up to the end of 1822, Cappi & Diabelli had decided to take the risk of publishing Opp. 8 and 11 on their own account, and clearly found it worth their while (charging 2 florins for each volume). Sonnleithner and his consortium were convinced that their unusual business model with the private publication of the songs was a good one, and to Schubert's permanent advantage. Diabelli knew better than to approach these skilled men of business, so he went behind their backs directly to Schubert and some time at the end of 1822 or beginning of 1823 offered him cash in hand for the copyright of the songs that were already published by Cappi & Diabelli, and the promise of ready payments for later works. This was a singularly bad time in the composer's life (he had recently discovered the disastrous nature of his illness) and Diabelli's clearly disingenuous offer came at a moment when he was at his most insecure and vulnerable. Schubert might have imagined that he would need the money urgently, or perhaps he argued to himself that Diabelli's offer would mean a more 'grown-up' way of publishing his music – after all, Beethoven's works were not sold on commission. He gave in to Diabelli's probably pressurizing negotiation (much to the bitter disappointment of Sonnleithner who regarded it as something of a betrayal on Schubert's part) and sold the copyright of Opp. 1–7 for 800 florins.

Once in the firm's clutches, the composer was beaten down to a proportionately smaller sum for the songs of Opp. 12–14. He would have made much more money from his songs if he had retained their copyright and it was not long before Schubert realized (probably thanks to his friends doing the sums with him) that he had been duped. He was in any case highly dissatisfied with aspects of the publication of Op. 18 ('Walzer, Ländler and Ecossaisen') and left the firm of Cappi & Diabelli in high dudgeon as his letters to Diabelli personally (21 February 1823) and to the firm in general (10 April 1823) testify.

One reason that Schubert could afford to show his real feelings to powerful publishers like Cappi & Diabelli was that he had been in touch with another publishing firm, **Sauer and Leidesdorf**, since October 1822, only a few months after the founding of that firm in July. The partnership between Sauer and Leidesdorf lasted three and a half years, being dissolved in February 1826. Schubert had known **Ignaz Sauer** (1759–1833) since 1818, through his brother Ferdinand, and he was also a friend of the firm's leading light, Marcus (officially **Maximilian Josef) Leidesdorf** (1787–1840), a composer of Jewish extraction and a Salieri pupil. It seems that Schubert was fond of Leidesdorf and may even have confided in him regarding his illness, but Leidesdorf was a depressive (as Schubert explained to Kupelwieser in a letter of 31 March 1824) and thus not the best person to cheer him up. Like the composer, Leidesdorf was always short of money, but he was a much nicer person than Diabelli, and in a few respects a better publisher. The firm seemed to offer everything that Diabelli did not – a sensitivity to the composer's wishes and an aesthetic interest in the appearance and quality of their productions. But there was also a fatal lack of business acumen and attention to detail that soon wrecked the enterprise. It was said that the arrangement between composer and publisher was that Leidesdorf would pay Schubert a yearly sum, like a salary, for the provision of music.

Maximillian Ignaz ('Marcus') Leidesdorf, publisher. Pencil drawing by F. Leidesdorf, 1845, after a painting by Josef Kriehuber, 1829.

Despite liking Leidesdorf personally, Schubert became disenchanted with him during 1824 when the publication of the last three (of five) books of *Die schöne Müllerin* was delayed to August of that year, the first two having appeared in different weeks in February. In a letter to Schober from Zseliz (21 September 1824) Schubert complains that 'with Leidesdorf things have gone badly so far; he cannot pay, nor does a single soul buy anything'. The publisher's lack of ability to capitalize on this new and important work, and his failure to market it efficiently as an entity, was one of the major disappointments of the composer's career. The four songs of Op. 59 were consigned to the failing publisher, presumably for old times' sake, by 1826 and their late appearance (they were only issued after the firm's break-up) is a further indication of Leidesdorf's prevaricating inefficiency. The opus number was inserted by hand, a sign that there was uncertainty on the publisher's part as to what it should be. This particular firm has earned the opprobrium of Schubert scholars, Ernst Hilmar chief among them, for its dilatory attitude towards the composer's manuscripts. It was the normal custom for publishers to return autographs to the composer; it seems that all the fair copies of the works published by Sauer and Leidesdorf, including *Die schöne Müllerin* and the A minor String Quartet D804, were discarded as waste paper.

SONGS PUBLISHED BY SAUER & LEIDESDORF (Kunst-, Alabaster- und Musikalienhandlung, Kärntnerstrasse Nr. 941):

Op. 20 *Sei mir gegrüsst, Frühlingsglaube, Hänflings Liebeswerbung.* Price 1 florin 15 kreuzer (10 April 1823)

Op. 21 *Auf der Donau, Der Schiffer* (Mayrhofer), *Wie Ulfru fischt.* Price 1 florin 30 kreuzer (19 June 1823)

Op. 22 *Der Zwerg, Wehmut.* Price 1 florin 30 kreuzer (27 May 1823)

Op. 23 *Die Liebe hat gelogen, Selige Welt, Schwanengesang* (Senn), *Schatzgräbers Begehr* (4 August 1823)

Op. 24 *Gruppe aus dem Tartarus, Schlummerlied (Schlaflied)* (27 October 1823). The name of the poet Mayrhofer is misspelled as 'Mayerhofer' on the title page

Op. 25 *Die schöne Müllerin* (Book 1 advertised 17 February 1824, price 2 florins; Book 2 on 24 March 1824, price 2 florins; Books 3–5 on 12 August, 1824, 2 florins each)

Op. 28 *Der Gondelfahrer* (quartet). Price 3 florins (12 August 1824)

Op. 59 *Du liebst mich nicht, Dass sie hier gewesen, Du bist die Ruh, Lachen und Weinen.* Price 2 florins (21 September 1826)

The partnership between Sauer and Leidesdorf was dissolved on February 1826 although the songs of Op. 59, published in September of that year, still bear the firm's imprint. A new firm, **M. J. Leidesdorf**, was registered on 7 May 1827. This published up until 1833 when it was taken over by Anton Berka & Co. which was acquired in turn by Anton Diabelli & Co. in 1835. Schubert's fondness for Leidesdorf, despite his inefficiency, meant he let the publisher issue a significant opus of Goethe settings, the last such published in his lifetime (Op. 92). The firm survived long enough also to issue the songs as Op. 108 (*see* OPUS NUMBERS). Leidesdorf left Vienna and settled with his family in Florence. It is unknown whether he took any unpublished Schubert manuscripts with him, but it seems quite possible.

SONGS PUBLISHED BY M. J. LEIDESDORF (Kunst- und Musikalienhandlung, Kärntnerstrasse Nr. 941):

Op. 92 *Der Musensohn, Auf dem See, Geistes-Gruss.* Price 1 florin (converted currency = *c.* 4 florins of old currency) (11 July 1828)

Although Otto Erich Deutsch maintains that Schubert's quarrel with Cappi & Diabelli was with the hard businessman Pietro Cappi and not Diabelli, it is surely significant that the composer was now prepared to do business with Cappi in a new firm (Cappi & Diabelli had been dissolved in 1823) rather than with Diabelli. **Cappi & Co.** was directed by Pietro and his cousin Carlo Cappi between September 1824 and the spring of 1826. The firm was responsible for the major song publications of 1825 before Schubert went away on his summer holiday, one of the issues containing two title-page misprints.

SONGS PUBLISHED BY CAPPI & CO. (privil. Kunst- und Musikalienhändlern, am Graben Nr. 1122):

Op. 36 *Die* [*sic*] *zürnenden Diana, Nachtstück. Gedichtet von Joh: Mayerhofer* [*sic*]. Price 2 florins 30 kreuzer (11 February 1825)

Op. 37 *Der Pilgrim, Der Alpenjäger* (Schiller). Price 2 florins 30 kreuzer (28 February 1825)

Op. 38 *Der Liedler.* Price 2 florins 30 kreuzer (9 May 1825)

Anton Pennauer (1784–1837) seems to have been in touch with Schubert shortly before the newly established music publisher was granted leave to establish his business in the centre of Vienna in July 1825. Pennauer clearly headhunted composers, including Schubert, as he prepared to set up his firm, and he must have found the composer disillusioned by the idea of belonging to one publisher, beginning to realize that the best way forward was to play one off against the other. Pennauer published works by such established composers as Kreutzer and Randhartinger as well as up-and-coming newcomers like Franz Lachner. His publications were admired more for the quality of their title pages and their clear graphic design than for their reliability in matters of musical and verbal detail. Schubert seems to have had much less contact with Pennauer himself than with the manager of the firm, Franz Hüther, who is the author of a sympathetically worded letter to Schubert sent to Steyr on 27 July 1825. There is some valuable information in this letter, including the fact that the composer was able to see three sets of proofs before publication, that the firm was capable of withdrawing issues of songs if there were mistakes in them, and that Pennauer was very interested in the Scott songs to texts from *The Lady of the Lake* (eventually published by Matthias Artaria). The title page shown opposite of a Pennauer publication contains a mistake – the addition of an inauthentic 'Die' to *Sehnsucht*.

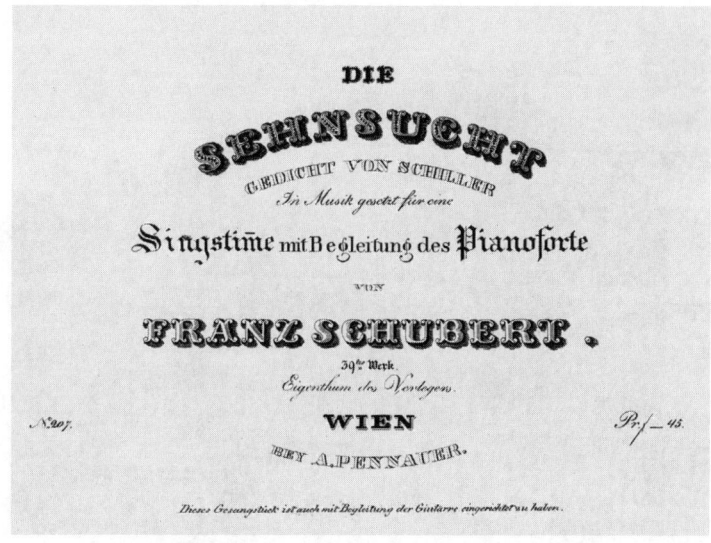

First edition of Schubert's Op. 39 (published by A. Pennauer).

Schubert seems to have been content to allow Pennauer to purchase music from time to time, although he appears never to have considered giving him exclusivity. After Schubert's death Pennauer was in possession of three substantial works (the flower ballad *Viola* D786, the two songs from Schütz's *Lacrimas* D857 and the Piano Sonata in E flat D568) and these were issued posthumously in 1829 and 1830. The firm folded in 1834 and Diabelli bought up its remaining stock, which might have included further Schubert items.

SONGS PUBLISHED BY ANTON PENNAUER (Kunst- und Musikalienhändler, untere Bräunerstrasse, im Fischerischen Hause):

Op. 43 *Die junge Nonne, Nacht und Träume*. Price 1 florin 30 kreuzer (25 July 1825)

Op. 31 *Suleikas zweiter Gesang*. Price 1 florin 30 kreuzer (12 August 1825)

Op. 39 *Die* [sic] *Sehnsucht* [II] (Schiller). Price 1 florin 30 kreuzer (8 February 1826)

Op. 56 *Willkommen und Abschied, An die Leier, Im Haine*. Published in two books, each 1 florin 30 kreuzer (14 July 1826)

Op. 87 *Der Unglückliche, Hoffnung* (Schiller), *Der Jüngling am Bache*. Price 1 florin AC (= 4 florins VC) (6 August 1827)

Matthias Artaria (1793–1835) was the son of the famous Domenico Artaria with whose firm, Artaria & Co., Schubert published several instrumental works in 1827 and 1828. Matthias had gone to London to gather experience in publishing and had returned to Vienna where he became associated with the art dealer Julius Sprenger. He married Sprenger's widow and established a publishing firm under his own name. This operated between 1822 and 1833 when it was taken over by Diabelli. Matthias Artaria published two important piano works by Schubert, but only one vocal work, albeit a big one. The brevity of Schubert's dalliance with the firm may be explained in a letter to him of 26 August 1826, by Artaria's agent in Germany, H. A. Probst: 'I must frankly confess to you that our public does not yet sufficiently and generally understand the peculiar, often ingenious, but perhaps now and then somewhat curious procedures of your mind's creations.'

The music shop of Artaria in Vienna, on the corner of the Paternostergassel and the Kohlmarkt.

SONGS PUBLISHED BY MATTHIAS ARTARIA (Kunst- und Musikalienhändler, am Kohlmarkt Nr. 258):

Op. 52 *Sieben Gesänge aus Walter Scotts Fräulein vom See*. Published in two books for 3 florins 30 kreuzer and 2 florins 30 kreuzer (5 April 1826)

When Cappi & Co., the joint venture between the Cappi cousins, Carlo and Pietro, folded in 1826 Carlo Cappi went into business with **Josef Czerny** (1785–1831) (no relation to the famous pianist and composer Karl Czerny). The firm of **Cappi & Czerny** operated between the spring of 1826 and November 1827. Schubert had clearly been persuaded that this new firm had a future.

SONGS PUBLISHED BY CAPPI UND CZERNY (Privil. Kunsthändler, am Graben Nr. 1134):

Op. 60 *Greisengesang, Dithyrambe*. Price 2 florins (10 June 1826)

Op. 65 *Lied eines Schiffers an die Dioskuren, Der Wanderer* (Schlegel), *Aus Heliopolis* (I). Price 1 florin 30 kreuzer (24 November 1826)

When this venture dissolved, Josef Czerny operated as a publisher under his own name from March 1828 to February 1831. The firm of **Josef Czerny** issued a number of posthumously published songs (the first of these only *just* posthumous – it was issued two days after the composer's death) but the publication of the songs had been planned by Schubert himself.

SONGS PUBLISHED BY JOSEF CZERNY (Privil. Kunst- und Musikalienhändler, am Graben Nr. 1134):

Op. 105 *Widerspruch, Wiegenlied* (Seidl), *Am Fenster, Sehnsucht* (Seidl). Price 4 florins AC (= 8 florins VC) (21 November 1828)

Thaddäus Weigl (1776–1844) was the brother of the famous Viennese composer Josef Weigl, and himself a composer and skilled musician. He founded his publishing firm in 1803 (specializing in Viennese composers) and had an eye for the more popular – and not too demanding – end of the market. Accordingly, the advertisement on 6 April 1827 in the *Wiener Zeitung* claims that Schubert 'has directed his attention to the elimination of any difficulty in the pianoforte accompaniment'. (In *An die Musik* he might not have realized that he was publishing the most popular Schubert song of all.) His business survived until 1831 when it went bankrupt and was bought up, inevitably, by Diabelli, but not before he had issued another posthumous (and 'easy') Schubert song, *Das Echo*, in 1830.

SONGS PUBLISHED BY THADDÄUS WEIGL (Kunst- und Musikverlag, am Graben Nr. 1144, neben dem 'König von England'):

Op. 57 *Der Schmetterling, Die Berge, An den Mond* (Hölty). Price 1 florin 30 kreuzer (6 April 1826)

Op. 58 *Hektors Abschied, An Emma, Des Mädchens Klage*. Price 2 florins – originally advertised as Op. 56, a number that had already been allocated to Pennauer (6 April 1826)

Op. 88 *Abendlied für die Entfernte, Thekla, Um Mitternacht, An die Musik*. Price 45 kreuzer AC (= 3 florins VC) (12 December 1827)

Op. 95 *Vier Refrain-Lieder: Die Unterscheidung, Bei dir allein!, Die Männer sind mechant, Irdisches Glück*. Price for the set of four songs 54 kreuzer AC (= c. 4 florins 40 kreuzer VC). Songs available separately at 20 kreuzer each, with the exception of *Bei dir allein!*, on sale at 30 kreuzer (13 August 1828)

It must have been clear to Schubert that a reconciliation with Diabelli was necessary, as this wily fox was the most successful and astute of all Viennese publishers – and he seemed able to issue Schubert works with or without the composer's cooperation. Although the official date of the reconciliation is said to have coincided with the publication of the *Wilhelm Meister* songs (Op. 62) in March 1827, Diabelli's new firm, **A. Diabelli & Co.** (he had entered into a partnership with Anton Spina in 1824 that would survive until 1851) had been issuing Schubert songs, to which Diabelli owned the copyrights, since 1825. This means that Diabelli, working under one company name or another, published solo songs by Schubert in 1821, 1822, 1825, 1827 and 1828.

A. Diabelli & Co. had opened with a fanfare by publishing the second of two books of Variations for Piano that Diabelli had commissioned from many composers to a theme of his own. The first book was of course the immortal 33 'Diabelli' Variations Op. 120 of Beethoven (brought out by Cappi & Diabelli in 1823). The second instalment, issued on 9 June 1824, contained the variations of Karl Czerny, Anselm Hüttenbrenner, Franz Liszt, Moscheles, Pixis, Tomášek (Tomaschek), Voříšek (Worzischek) and many others including Schubert (D718). Diabelli had published *Die Forelle* in a separate edition as Op. 32 (it had first appeared as a supplement to the *Wiener Zeitschrift*, and then in a Diabelli song anthology named *Philomele*). After this, three Goethe songs, the long delayed Op. 19, had at last appeared, with a dedication to the poet. A. Diabelli & Co. prepared two special copies with gold titles printed on satined paper and sent them to Goethe with a covering letter from Schubert which he had written before departing for his long holiday in Upper Austria in the summer of 1825. Schubert received no reply from Goethe, but it is probable that the publisher did as it would have been illegal under Austrian law to dedicate such a work without the permission of its dedicatee.

Such was Diabelli's place in the music-publishing business as the king of takeovers that it was impossible to avoid him. Apart from the Op. 62 songs, Diabelli's main concern with Schubert's songs in the remainder of the composer's lifetime was the republication of works that had appeared in the *Wiener Zeitschrift*. For Diabelli's role in the publication of Schubert's songs after the composer's death, *see* Nachlass and Posthumous Songs.

SONGS PUBLISHED BY A. DIABELLI & CO. (Kunst- und Musikalienhändler, Graben Nr. 1133):

Op. 32 *Die Forelle*. Price 1 florin. Diabelli adds the words 'Property of the publisher' to the advertisement in both January and June 1825, as if to emphasize that his arrangement with Schubert was no longer on a commission basis (13 January 1825)

Op. 19 *An Schwager Kronos, An Mignon, Ganymed*. Price 2 florins 30 kreuzer (6 June 1825)

Op. 41 *Der Einsame*. Price 1 florin 30 kreuzer (5 January 1827)

Op. 44 *An die untergehende Sonne*. Price 1 florin (5 January 1827)

Op. 62 *Vier Gesänge aus Wilhelm Meister*. Price 1 florin AC (= 4 florins VC) (2 March 1827)

Op. 68 *Der Wachtelschlag*. Price 30 kreuzer AC (= 2 florins VC) (16 May 1827)

Op. 71 *Drang in die Ferne*. Price 30 kreuzer AC (= 2 kreuzer VC) (2 March 1827)

Op. 72 *Auf dem Wasser zu singen*. Price 30 kreuzer AC (= 2 kreuzer VC) (2 March 1827)

Op. 73 *Die Rose*. Price 30 kreuzer AC (= 2 florins VC). A list of all Schubert's works (Opp. 1–74), including those published by other firms, was included with this song (16 May 1827)

Op. 74 *Die Advokaten*. Price 1 florin AC (= 4 florins VC) (16 May 1827)

Op. 85 *Lied der Anne Lyle, Gesang der Norna*. Price 45 kreuzer AC (= 3 florins VC) (14 March 1828)

Op. 86 *Romanze des Richard Löwenherz*. Price 45 kreuzer AC (= 3 florins VC) (14 March 1828)

Op. 97 *Glaube, Hoffnung und Liebe* (Kuffner). Price 30 kreuzer AC (= 3 florins VC) (6 October 1828)

Op. 98 *An die Nachtigall* (Claudius), *Wiegenlied, Iphigenia*. Price 30 kreuzer AC (= 2 Florins VC) (10 July 1829)

Op. 104 *Der Hochzeitsbraten* (terzett with piano). Price 1 florin 45 kreuzer AC (= 7 florins VC) (10 July 1829)

Op. 102 *Mondenschein* (quintet with piano) (21 April 1831)

[The last opus numbers are included on this list, although published posthumously, because it is thought that Schubert himself assigned them to these works.]

There is one further publisher of real substance in the story of Schubert's songs, and that is **Tobias Haslinger** (1787–1842). Brought up in Linz like so many of Schubert's close friends, he was engaged by the firm of Senefelder & Steiner as manager of their art and music business, and became a partner. When the annoyed Schubert informed Diabelli in a letter of 10 April 1823 that 'Herr von Steiner has repeatedly conveyed to me an offer to publish my works' it was no doubt Haslinger to whom the composer had been speaking. Having come to regret his rejection of the Schubert songs in 1821 when they were unsuccessfully touted by Leopold von Sonnleithner and Josef Hüttenbrenner, it is likely that Haslinger now saw in Schubert a genius that the senior Steiner had

Tobias Haslinger, lithograph by Josef Kreihuber, 1842.

failed to perceive. In order to offer Schubert support, Haslinger first had to allow Steiner to retire. By 1826 he was in full command of the firm which now traded under his name. When still working for Steiner, Haslinger had enjoyed an exceptionally cordial relationship with Beethoven (who made merciless fun of his provincial dialect), and he was renowned as a man of considerable charm and geniality, skilled in calming Beethoven's rages and disarming his threats. Unfortunately Beethoven fell out with Steiner on business matters, but Haslinger now seems to have brought his charm to bear on Schubert. The composer was no doubt only too happy to find a publisher of reliability and substance other than Diabelli. It must have been rather delicious for Schubert to read the *Wiener Zeitung* of 16 May 1827 when Diabelli advertised 'new' Schubert publications (actually rather old songs that had already been issued by Schickh's *Wiener Zeitschrift*) while in the very same issue Haslinger advertised the much more recent settings of Ladislaus Pyrker, a famous personage in Austria. Diabelli must have been furious.

Apart from the songs listed below, Haslinger published the G major Piano Sonata D894 and the Impromptus D899. After the composer's death Ferdinand Schubert sold Haslinger the fourteen songs that were published under the title *Schwanengesang* (without opus number), *Der Hirt auf dem Felsen* (published posthumously as Op. 129) and the three final Piano Sonatas D958–60. Haslinger seems to have had an uncharacteristic failure of nerve regarding these piano works and he sold them on to Diabelli who issued them only in 1839. Nevertheless, Haslinger was not one of the many publishing minnows whose destiny was to be swallowed by the ever-voracious Diabelli. His business employed over fifty people and he had ongoing and highly profitable relationships with such composers as Johann Strauss the Elder and Josef Lanner. He also published works by Liszt, Weber and Spohr. He died leaving his family a large fortune, and his firm survived until the death of his son in 1868.

SONGS PUBLISHED BY TOBIAS HASLINGER (Musikverleger, am Graben im Hause der ersten Österr. Sparkasse Nr. 572):

Op. 79 *Das Heimweh* (Pyrker), *Die Allmacht*. Price 1 florin AC (= 4 florins VC) (16 May 1827)

Op. 80 *Der Wanderer an den Mond, Das Zügenglöcklein, Im Freien*. Price 1 florin AC (= 4 florins VC) (25 May 1827)

Op. 81 *Alinde, An die Laute, Zur guten Nacht*. Price 45 kreuzer AC (= 3 florins VC) (28 May 1827)

Op. 83 *Drei Gesänge für Bass-stimme mit Klavier: L'incanto degli occhi, Il traditor deluso, Il modo di prender moglie*. Priced separately as 24, 36, 36 kreuzer. The complete set at 1 florin 36 kreuzer AC (= 6 florins 24 kreuzer VC) (12 September 1827)

Op. 89 *Winterreise*. Price for Part One 3 florins AC (= 12 florins VC), Part Two 2 florins 30 AC = (10 florins VC) (Part One 14 January 1828, Part Two 30 December 1828)

The only Austrian publisher outside Vienna to issue Schubert songs in the composer's lifetime was **Johann Kienreich** (1759–1845) of Graz. Schubert met Kienreich on his visit to the Styrian capital in 1827 when he was a guest of Marie Pachler. The Op. 93 songs (initially wrongly printed as Op. 90 – the number assigned to Haslinger for the *Four Impromptus* D899) were issued a few months before the composer's death. They were republished by Diabelli under the same opus number in 1835.

SONGS PUBLISHED BY J. A. KIENREICH:

Op. 93 *Im Walde [Auf der Brücke]*. Price 1 florin 20 kreuzer AC (= 6 florins VC) (30 May 1828)

The most unusual episode relating to publishing in Schubert's life was when his close friend Franz von Schober, qv, jack of all trades, decided to become a publisher. In 1826 Schober, home from a fruitless attempt to become an actor in Breslau, bought with family money the **Lithographisches Institut**. This printing firm had been established in 1817 by Count Adolf von Pötting. It was clear that Schubert, a long-standing guest in Schober's home, felt he should do all he could to help the new venture. Accordingly the composer handed over some very fine songs for publication, including a setting of Schober's own verse by way of a compliment.

SONGS PUBLISHED BY LITHOGRAPHISCHES INSTITUT:
Op. 96 *Die Sterne* (Leitner), *Jägers Liebeslied, Wanderers [sic] Nachtlied* II, *Fischerweise* (Summer 1828)
Op. 106 *Heimliches Lieben, Das Weinen, Vor meiner Wiege* (Spring 1828)
[These publications seem not to have been advertised in the Viennese press, perhaps to save money.]

The only publisher outside Austria who issued a volume of songs *almost* in the composer's lifetime was **H. A. Probst** (1791–1846) of Leipzig, who was also the German agent for the Viennese firm Artaria. He had been in correspondence with Schubert since 1826 regarding the publication of the composer's works, and even met Schubert on a visit to Vienna. There was a great deal of toing and froing, and when Probst did bring out a posthumous opus number of songs (published a month or so after the composer's death) they were all reissues of works that had originally appeared in the *Wiener Zeitschrift*.

SONGS PUBLISHED BY H. A. PROBST (Leipzig):
Op. 101 *Im Frühling, Trost im Liede, Der blinde Knabe, Wanderers Nachtlied II* (12 December 1828)

The songs mentioned in this article were all published within a time span of seven years. Any notion that Schubert lived a life free from bureaucratic care is scotched by looking at the huge amount of work that was involved in corresponding and negotiating with this array of publishers and proofreading the songs (and the composer had to take care of his entire published output in this way – not just his songs). The majority of correspondence concerning the minutiae of corrections and business dealings has been lost to us, but even a cursory glance through Schubert's publications silences any romantic notion of a composer unknown and undervalued. It is quite clear that a variety of firms were vying for his custom in the final five years of his life, and that his hands were already full with the consequences of his popularity and ever-growing fame. It is notable that tickets for his concert on 26 March 1828 were on sale in the the salesrooms of Haslinger, Diabelli and Leidesdorf, and that all three had an interest in the success of the event. A composer with greater self-esteem would have vaunted his own triumph at the growing number of works in print. In choosing to remain modestly circumspect about his standing in the musical world, Schubert has led many generations of admirers to regard him as a prophet in the wilderness, a man writing screeds of music that would never be heard, struggling valiantly in a vacuum of indifference. The lively nature of his business obligations as outlined here, and the amount of work he would have had to do simply to keep ahead of all his publishers' requirements, paint an entirely different picture of his everyday life.

For songs published after Schubert's death – and thus, with a few exceptions, without his own editorial participation – see POSTHUMOUS SONGS.

As an appendix to this article, mention must be made of the Parisian publisher **Charles-Simon Richault** (1780–1866) who published a work for violin and piano by Schubert in 1827 – thus

Auf dem Wasser zu singen published in French, the translation by Richault, Paris (*c.* 1840).

within the composer's lifetime – and who began to publish song arrangements by Karl Czerny in 1829. Despite the fact that these were, in effect, pirated editions (in those days no payment was due to the Schubert estate), Richault became enamoured of the composer's music and did as much to further his reputation in France as did the singers Wartel and Nourrit. In the 1840s Richault's publications of Schubert songs (with French texts by Bélanger) were praised by

German critics for their elegance and beauty. Each title page boasted a specially commissioned engraving – a mode of song publication that went back to the sumptuous productions of *romance* composers like Louise Puget. By the middle of the nineteenth century there were 336 Schubert songs in Richault's catalogue. He seems to have relied on the Diabelli Nachlass for most of his material. The vogue for Schubert faded somewhat in France after 1850 and with it Richault's plan from the early 1840s to compile a complete edition of the songs. He was an early example of a Schubertian enthusiast from a non-German-speaking country, and he clearly loved the music as much as the money it earned him as publisher.

Bibliography: Raab 2002, p. 217

PUNSCHLIED. IM NORDEN ZU SINGEN (Schiller) D253 [H138]
B♭ major   18 August 1815

On drinking punch (to be sung in the North)

(16 bars)

Auf der Berge freien Höhen,
  In der Mittagssonne Schein,
An des warmen Strahles Kräften
  Zeugt Natur den goldnen Wein

Und noch Niemand hat's erkundet,
  Wie die grosse Mutter schafft,
Unergründlich ist das Wirken,
  Unerforschlich ist die Kraft.

Funkelnd wie ein Sohn der Sonne,
  Wie des Lichtes Feuerquell,
Springt er perlend aus der Tonne,
  Purpurn und kristallenhell.

[...9...]

On the free heights of the mountains,
  In the light of the midday sun,
And by the power of its warm beams,
  Nature produces the golden vine.

And no one has ever divined
  How the Great Mother creates;
Her work is unfathomable,
  Her power inscrutable.

Sparkling like a child of the sun,
  Like the fiery source of light,
It spurts, bubbling, from the barrel,
  Crimson and crystal-bright.

[...9...]

FRIEDRICH VON SCHILLER (1759–1805); poem written in 1803

This is the seventeenth of Schubert's forty-four Schiller solo settings (1811–24). See the poet's biography for a chronological list of all the Schiller settings.

This is one of those hearty drinking songs that the composer seemed delighted to provide for musical gatherings in 1815. It appears in two versions, the first for solo voice and piano and the second as a duet: the solo version appeared for the first time in 2009 in Volume 8 of the NSA; the unaccompanied duet appears in NSA Series III Volume 4. A duet version with piano (as recorded for Hyperion) is printed in the song series of the AGA, but it appears that this is simply a conflation of the two authentic versions, and that the composer actually meant the piece to be performed *either* as a solo with piano, *or* as an unaccompanied duet.

Drinking is a relaxed communal activity and Einstein is probably right to think that a number of the other songs of 'convivial character' in the solo volumes might also be sung as choruses without unduly disturbing Schubert's celestial repose. The addition or absence of piano in such circumstances also seems to be merely a matter of pragmatic availability, something that present-day musicologists would do well to take into account when declaring some versions of music of this domestic genre to be more 'correct' than others. Unlike some of the male chorus songs where the piano accompaniment does no more than shadow the voice part (as if written for rehearsal purposes, which in some cases it almost certainly was), this *Punschlied* has an invigoratingly pianistic underlay that goes well with the marking 'Feurig' (fiery). The proudly repeated chords in B flat major at the beginning (the repetitive assertion of the key has a defiant Beethovenian ring to it) are in the manner of a polonaise, which may be the composer's way of depicting 'the North'. (After all, he used a similar rhythm for *Lied des gefangenen Jägers* D843 set in the cold north of Scotland.) The two-bar postlude, tricky to play, reinforces the polonaise rhythm and adds to the piece's high spirits which sparkle and foam in the jug if the pianist's bartending talents are nimble enough.

Schiller's poem has twelve strophes, the first three of which are printed here, as recorded in the Hyperion Edition. All twelve appear in the AGA, although only the first two are printed under music in that source. In the NSA, in both versions, all twelve verses appear printed under music.

Autograph:	Missing or lost
Publication:	Published as Vol. 7 no. 42 in Friedlaender's edition by Peters, Leipzig in 1887 (P503). Version for solo voice published as part of the NSA in 2009 (P854)
Subsequent editions:	Peters: Vol. 7/93; AGA XX 110: Vol. 3/30; NSA IV: Vol. 8/182 (first version); NSA III: Vol. 4/54 (choral version)
Further settings:	Karl Friedrich Zelter (1758–1832) *Punschlied im Norden zu singen* (1803)
	Johann Friedrich Reichardt (1752–1814) *Punschlied: Im Norden zu singen* (1809)
Discography and timing:	Fischer-Dieskau —
	Hyperion I 20²⁵
	Hyperion II 8²² 1'25 John Mark Ainsley & Jamie MacDougall

← *Das Mädchen aus der Fremde* D252   *Claudine von Villa Bella 'Hin und wieder fliegen Pfeile'* D239/3 →

PUNSCHLIED (Vier Elemente, innig gesellt)   Drinking song   Trio
(SCHILLER) **D277** [H164]
C major   29 August 1815

Feurig

ff

Vier E-le-men-te, in-nig ge-sellt, bil-den das Le-ben, bau-en die Welt.

(16 bars)

Vier Elemente	Four elements,
Innig gesellt,	Inwardly linked,
Bilden das Leben,	Make up life
Bauen die Welt.	And fashion the world.
Presst der Zitrone	Squeeze the lemon's
Saftigen Stern,	Juicy star!
Herb ist des Lebens	Bitter is life's
Innerster Kern.	Innermost core.
Jetzt mit des Zuckers	Now with sugar's
Linderndem Saft	Sweetening juice
Zähmet die herbe	Tame its bitter,
Brennende Kraft.	Stinging power.
Giesset des Wassers	Pour the water's
Sprudelnden Schwall,	Bubbling torrent!
Wasser umfänget	Water calmly
Ruhig das All.	Enfolds the universe.
Tropfen des Geistes	Pour in the drops
Giesset hinein,	Of the spirit,
Leben dem Leben	For the spirit alone
Gibt er allein.	Animates life!
Eh es verdüftet	Take it in quickly,
Schöpfet es schnell,	Before its savour fades!
Nur wenn er glühet,	Only when it glows
Labet der Quell.	Does the stream refresh!

FRIEDRICH VON SCHILLER (1759–1805)

This delightful little chorus is somewhat different from other drinking songs in the Schubert canon, most of which are set on celebrating the grim link between booze and mortality. The German drinker in his cups seems inclined to turn lugubriously philosophical if given half a chance. This song, however, tells us how to make punch; it is concocted step by step as the verses progress. As such, it is the only recipe song in Schubert, and one of the few in the entire song

Illustration for Schiller's *Punschlied* (1859).

repertoire (Bernstein's *La Bonne Cuisine* is another such work) that takes us into the kitchen – a focal point (if his waistline were any indication) of much of the composer's pleasure.

The word 'punch' is of Indian origin and comes from *panca*, meaning five. Punch is traditionally made from a combination of tea, rum, wine, sugar and lemon. Schiller contents himself with four elements – lemon, sugar, water and alcohol – although each of these has a deeper meaning in his recipe of life. As in Schiller's poem *An die Freude* (also set to music by Schubert but not in its entirety), wine is taken to be the drink of the spirit, and spirit (in its alcoholic sense) is an analogy for life – soon to evaporate and so to be taken and enjoyed before it does – 'Eh es verdüftet'. In this *carpe diem* recipe for punch, the poet undertakes to reflect life itself and the things on which the world is built. Only the great German poets (and perhaps only Schiller and his confrère Goethe) can get away with the loftiness of this, but it makes a change from the graveside banalities of bibulous poems from lesser writers.

Schubert rises to the occasion with a heartily memorable tune that broadens into harmony after two bars of portentous unison by voices and piano. Drink is, after all, a serious business. The key is C major, but we meet G sharps as soon as the third beat, the accidental like a sharp ingredient (a twist of lemon peel perhaps) to be thrown into the punchbowl. Each short couplet is repeated to elongate the strophes into usable musical length. The postlude is one of his best in songs of this type, with chords in sixths underpinned by a churning left-hand tonic pedal. The feeling of much earnest mixing, stirring and whisking is vividly conveyed; after one ingredient is mastered (thoroughly squeezed, mashed, dolloped and poured) it is on to the next. There is a deliberate clumsiness here too (Beethovenian, as in so many of Schubert's Schiller settings) as if a group of men, unaccustomed to the niceties of the kitchen, are being a little less careful about the prescribed quantity of ingredients than they should be. One also has the impression that the alcoholic ingredient ('Tropfen des Geistes') is imbibed neat – and rather more than a drop of it – as the punch is prepared.

Autograph:	University Library of Lund, Sweden
First edition:	Published as part of the AGA in 1892 (P525)
Subsequent editions:	AGA XIX 7: p. 58; NSA III: Vol. 3

Discography and timing:	Fischer-Dieskau	—	
	Deutsche Grammophon *Schubert Terzette*	2'54	Peter Schreier, Horst Laubenthal & Dietrich Fischer-Dieskau
	Hyperion I 22[6] Hyperion II 9[25]	3'20	John Mark Ainsley, Jamie MacDougall, Simon Keenlyside & Michael George

← *Abendlied* D276   *Ossians Lied nach dem Fall Nathos'* D278 →

JOHANN LADISLAUS PYRKER (VON FELSÖ-EÖR) (1772–1847)

THE POETIC SOURCES

S1 *Tunisias oder Kaiser Carl V. Heeresfahrt nach Afrika*. Ein Heldengedicht in zwölf Gesängen von Johann Ladislav Pyrker. Verbesserte Ausgabe mit einer Vorrede des Herausgebers. Wien, 1820. Bey Carl Ferdinand Beck. Gedruckt von Anton Strauss.

The passage set by Schubert for *Das Heimweh* is from Canto VI which is at the heart of the story concerning Charles V's battle for Tunis. It is in this canto that the ghost of Hermann (*see Hermann und Thusnelda* D322) appears to the emperor. In the battle against the Turks some of

Title page of *Tunisias* (1820).

Title page of *Perlen der heiligen Vorzeit* (1821).

the bravest men are led by Salis whose regiment receives praise from the emperor. The exotic deployment in Carthage of these 'sons of the mountains' is contrasted with their longing for their Tyrolean homeland, the subject of Schubert's song – although there is no trace in his music of an awareness of, or interest in, the wider context of the words.

S2 *Perlen der heiligen Vorzeit*. Gesammelt durch Johann Ladislav Pyrker. Helias der Thesbit. Eilisa. Die Makkabäer. Ofen, 1821. Gedruckt, aus Kosten des Ofner wohlthätigen Frauen-Vereines, in der kön. Ung. Universitäts-Buchdruckerey, nach Watts'scher Art.

Die Allmacht is an excerpt from *Elisa in zwei Gesängen* (Elisha in Two Cantos) pp. 55–84, here subtitled 'Tod. Unsterblichkeit' (Death, Immortality). In *Elisa* Pyrker elaborates the story of Jehoram's attempt to subjugate the tribes of Moab with the help of Judah and Edom as recounted in the Old Testament (II Kings 3). Elisha has succeeded Elijah as prophet of the Israelites, and Pyrker takes his cue from Verse 15: 'But now bring me a minstrel. And it came to pass, when the minstrel played, that the hand of the Lord came upon him.'

> Erst aufhorchte dem: Elisa mit stillern,
> Ruhigen Blick: doch jetzt entflammt' er sich; glühende Röthe
> Färbte sein blasses Gesicht; er hob in schwebender Haltung
> Von dem Boden sich auf, und begann in hoher Begeisterung:
> 'Gross ist Jehovah, der Herr: denn Himmel und Erde verkünden Seine Macht!'. . .

> *At first Elisha had listened to the sound of the harp with a still,*
> *Serene expression, but now he flared up, a crimson glow*
> *Suffused his pale countenance; swaying unsteadily he rose*
> *from the ground and began in exalted inspiration:*
> *'Great is Jehovah, the Lord: for heaven and earth proclaim his might'. . .*

In the Bible the seer goes on to tactical advice: 'Make this valley full of ditches' (II Kings 16). Pyrker follows suit with a section beginning 'Grabt den Gruben im Thal' but Schubert's music stops before this point; he chooses to repeat words from the beginning of Elisha's hymn of praise instead. This was surely sanctioned, if not suggested, by the poet himself. Leo Black points out that Elisha or Eliezer disappears from the Book of Kings with no account given of his end.

S3 *Perlen der heiligen Vorzeit* von Johann Ladislav Pyrker. Stuttgart und Tübingen
J. F. Cotta 'scher Verlag 1841

Later editions of this work, such as this, contained three additional 'pearls': *Abraham, Moses* and *Samuel*. Schubert's setting of *Die Allmacht* contains certain small changes to the poem that are the same as the later editions. This confirms that Pyrker must have given Schubert handwritten copies of the texts already containing amendments to the first edition that would be incorporated into later printings.

THE SONGS
August 1825   *Das Heimweh* D851 [S1: pp. 141–2]
　　　　　　　Die Allmacht D852 [S2: pp. 60–61] [S3: pp. 127–8]

Ladislaus Pyrker was one of the highest-ranking establishment figures whom Schubert encountered during a career that brought him into contact with a fair number of dignitaries and celebrities. If the memoirs of Beethoven's friend Schindler are to be trusted – and this is a moot point – Schubert's second meeting with Pyrker in Bad Gastein in 1825 (the first had been in 1820 at the home of Matthäus von Collin) was 'one of the most inspiring of his life'.

Pyrker was a cleric of Hungarian birth (he was born on 2 November 1772 in Stuhlweissenburg – today Lángh) and Tyrolean ancestry. He spoke German and Hungarian from an early age, but his schooling was entirely in Latin as was the custom in Hungary at the time. During a visit to Sicily, directly after he had left school, he had a Damascene experience regarding his faith. At twenty he entered the novitiate in the Zisterzienserstift in Lilienfeld, learned how to write in his mother tongue of German, and studied theology in St Pölten. He was ordained as a priest in 1796. Pyrker had a large and charismatic personality and it was clear from the beginning that this egocentric man was destined for those echelons of the church that intersected with the highest offices of state. In 1812, at the age of thirty, he was appointed Abbot of Lilienfeld. In 1819 Emperor Franz I created him Bishop of Zips (the present-day Szepeshely). In 1821, at the astonishingly young age of forty-seven, he was appointed Patriarch of Aquileia (Venice, in less high-flown terms). Here he played the role of

Ladislaus Pyrker, lithograph by Josef Kriehuber, 1834.

all-powerful viceroy in a difficult-to-govern city that had been under Austrian control since Napoleon's demise, and remained so until 1866 (with a short period of insurrection and freedom under Daniel Manin between 1848 and 1849). Pyrker took up his appointment in Venice shortly after Byron brought his sojourn in that city to an end, but the Englishman's hatred of the Austrian occupation was already well known through his verse (this, for example, from *Childe Harold*: 'Venice, lost and won / Her thirteen hundred years of freedom done / Sinks like a seaweed . . .'). Pyrker (automatically loathed by everyone who resented Austria) found himself required to arbitrate in the marital dispute between the English poet's mistress, Teresa Guiccioli, and her husband. By some accounts Pyrker's regency in Venice was remarkable for the pushing-through of such reforms as the draining of marshes and reorganization of the hospitals. The downside of bureaucratic good order was the ruthless suppression of the *carbonari* and all political dissent, and the almost Goering-like gathering of a collection of Italian art (now in the Hungarian National Gallery and Hungarian Museum of Fine Arts) containing treasures that could never have left Venice unless it were, in effect, an occupied territory. After his stint in Venice, Pyrker was elevated to archbishop of Erlau (Eger) in Hungary and received every conceivable honour available to him as a prince of the church.

Like his close friends Matthäus von Collin and Karoline Pichler, Pyrker adopted stirring events in Austrian history for his literary themes. His writing, described by a later critic as belonging to a 'höfisches Biedermeier' style, was partly responsible for his being perceived as a great patriot. For example, the epic poem *Tunisias*, published in 1820, recycled an aspect of Austrian history in a way that burnished the reputation of the Habsburgs. The Emperor Charles V mounted an expedition to North Africa in 1535 as part of his struggle against the Ottoman Empire and Suleiman I; his capture of Tunis was not an unmitigated success in historical terms but, as narrated in Pyrker's rolling hexameters, the campaign against 'Barbrossa' (the Turkish general) and corsair Khayr ad-Din is hymned as a holy crusade to free 20,000 Christian slaves in Tunis, and to rid the Italian towns of the threat of Turkish pirates. Pyrker claimed that as a young man, when returning from a short sojourn in Italy, he had been caught up in a pirate incident off the coast of Genoa; Oskar Wolff's *Literatur Encyclopädie* (1846) solemnly informs us that Pyrker was taken to Algiers to be sold as a slave (a 'fairy tale' according to Goedeke, and an example of how dramatized the poet had allowed the legend of his earlier life to become).

Another deeply patriotic poem, *Rudolph von Habsburg* (Wien, 1825), was published in the year of Schubert and Vogl's Gastein holiday. Pyrker's literary style goes straight back to his beloved Virgilian models. He showed scant awareness of the work of his more modern literary contemporaries, yet he attempted, without success, to attract the praise of Goethe whose equal he believed himself to be. When Goethe failed to be impressed by *Tunisias*, Pyrker's spleen knew no bounds. In a letter to a friend (16 July 1824) he claimed to have found at least a hundred metrical errors in the hexameters of *Hermann und Dorothea*; on a visit to Weimar he wrote that he was more impressed by Schiller's 'little attic room than Hofrat Goethe's entire house'. If Pyrker was pretending to honour Schiller's humility over Goethe's worldly vanity, it was very much the pot blackening the kettle's reputation. The truth is that Pyrker was overweeningly vain, massively ambitious for himself as a writer, and intolerant of criticism. By the time Schubert met him for the second time in Upper Austria in 1825 Pyrker was an enormously influential 'national treasure' who could not be gainsaid. He was also exactly the kind of person to whom Vogl, extremely conscious of hierarchy and prestige, would have bowed the knee. As founder of the 'Kurort' at Bad Gastein he was to all intents and purposes the host of the singer and composer during their holiday sojourn; it is not clear whether they paid for their lodgings or were guests. It is significant that in Pyrker's

autobiography *Mein Leben*, published after his death, neither Schubert nor Vogl rate a mention in his account of that summer in Bad Gastein; the book is full of seemingly more important political and clerical figures. Perhaps Schubert did not hold Pyrker and his ilk in particularly high regard either. In Gmunden, in July of that year, he had set the vocal quartet *Trinklied aus dem 16. Jahrhundert* D847 for his host Ferdinand Traweger. This humorous verse in Latin ('Edit nonna, edit clerus / Ad edendum nemo serus') reveals such a scurrilous view of the Catholic clergy and papacy that the censor only considered it fit for publication in Vienna in 1849, after the insurrection of 1848 had swept away censorship controls. It would certainly have enraged Pyrker had he heard it.

In 1821 Schubert had dutifully dedicated his Op. 4 songs to Pyrker (*Der Wanderer* D493, *Morgenlied* D685 and *Wandrers Nachtlied* D224), for which he received twelve ducats. In a letter to Schubert (18 May 1821) Pyrker, who had been deeply moved by *Der Wanderer* in particular, professed himself proud to belong to the same homeland as the composer. When Vogl and Schubert met up again with Pyrker in Gastein in 1825 it is probable that the poet–cleric was mightily in the mood to have his poetry set to music. The pressure on Schubert, from both Pyrker and Vogl, must have been considerable and he set two texts (making wonderful songs of each) that he almost certainly would not have touched if left to his own devices. When the songs were published together in May 1827 as Op. 79, and dedicated to Pyrker 'with deep reverence', the composer did not receive a penny for his trouble, as Bauernfeld wryly noted in his reminiscences. As Pyrker got older Schubert's posthumous fame grew and his own reputation as a poet waned; he now clung on to the celebrities with whom he had had any connection. By the time Schumann met him in Vienna in 1838 the retired cleric was better known as a supporter of Grillparzer. In the same year the Schubert song transcriptions of Liszt took Vienna by storm. Pyrker's 1842 *Hymn to Austria*, written for the Mozart Festival in

Salzburg (and set to music by Sigismund von Neukomm), contains the line 'Let us also praise Schubert for his magical melodies'. We may be sure that by this time Pyrker had claimed the composer as his close friend and protégé. Afflicted with tic douloureux for the last eleven years of his life, Pyrker died in Vienna on 2 December 1847.

Bibliography: Goedeke 1913, Vol. 10, p. 557
                 Pyrker 1966
                 Wolff 1846, Vol. 6, p. 103
                 Youens 2002, pp. 93–201

Franz Schubert, oil painting, 1827, formerly attributed to J. W. Mähler.

QUELL' INNOCENTE FIGLIO
(Aria dell'angelo)
(METASTASIO) **D17/1&2** [H9 & H9A]
(Composition exercises) *c.* 1812

This innocent son

Solo:	'Andante'	F major	𝄴	[26 bars]
Duet:	No tempo indication	F major	𝄴	[18 bars]

Quell' in - no-cen - te fi - gli-o
(26 bars)

Quell' in - no-cen - te fi - gli-o
(18 bars)

Quell'innocente figlio,	This innocent son,
Dono del Ciel si raro,	Such a rare gift from heaven,
Quel figlio a te sì caro	This son, so dear to you,
Quello vuol Dio da te.	God demands from you.
Vuol che rimanga esangue	He demands that he bleeds
Sotto al paterno ciglio,	Before his father's eyes;
Vuol che ne sparga il sangue	He demands that he who once gave him life
Chi vita già gli diè.	Should shed his blood.

PIETRO METASTASIO (1698–1782); poem written in 1740

These two items constitute the first of Schubert's fourteen Metastasio settings, solo and duet (1812–27). See the poet's biography for a chronological list of all the Metastasio settings.

Schubert's study of composers such as Gluck and Zumsteeg was undertaken through his own enthusiasm. But one cannot overestimate the importance to the young composer's development of Antonio Salieri (1750–1825). Indeed, it is easier to *under*estimate the fruits of Salieri's guidance and, later, his increasingly formal approach to teaching the teenage Schubert. In his memoirs written in 1858, Schubert's schoolfriend Anton Holzapfel was rather snide about the Italian composer's methods:

It was arranged for Schubert to devote himself entirely to the study of music and for him to be allowed to have composition lessons twice a week with the Imperial Court Kapellmeister Salieri, even when he was still in the Seminary. This was a special concession on the part of the directors as it was contrary to the school rules for a pupil to go out by himself. The instruction that now began, instruction which according to ancient usage the Imperial Court Kapellmeister could not refuse and which, so far as I know, was given free, took place at first only twice a week, but after leaving the Seminary Schubert took advantage of it assiduously. I recall clearly that the instruction was but very scanty, a fact easy to understand in view of Salieri's character, with which older musicians were thoroughly conversant and that, on the whole, it consisted only in the superficial correction of small exercises in part writing, though most of it, and this may have been the most successful aspect, consisted in the reading and playing of scores. At the beginning Schubert was obliged, first and foremost, to work through a large number of extremely dull old Italian scores.

The anti-Salieri bias in this memoir (by 1858 Salieri was already being unfairly cast as a villain in Mozart's demise) cannot disguise two things: that Schubert was Salieri's willing and 'assiduous' pupil, and that the young composer was expected to steep himself in Italian music. Schubert's technical education with Salieri is among the best documented of teaching regimes undertaken by a great composer, but the marked exercises alone can give little idea of the verbal instruction between teacher and pupil, or of the coaching in certain professional aspects of composition. For example, in the middle of these exercises we come across a stave, in Schubert's youthful writing, which is not devoted to exercises in Italian word-setting. The following advice seems to have come directly from the old master himself – note Salieri's old-fashioned use of the soprano and tenor clefs:

At a stroke Schubert is categorically informed that certain voices are capable of certain ranges. After this, the unreasonable vocal demands of earlier pieces (such as *Hagars Klage* D5 and *Leichenfantasie* D7) cease to be a troubling feature of the young composer's work. If only for example, Robert Schumann had been given similar instruction at a young age, his earlier lieder would have been written better for different voice types, and easier to sing.

The two settings of *Quell'innocente figlio* that were recorded for the Hyperion Edition (from Metastasio's oratorio *Isacco* where these words have the subtitle *Aria dell'angelo*) were submitted to Salieri as part of a much larger set of composition exercises. Schubert set these words some ten times: for soprano alone; for two sopranos; for soprano, alto and tenor; for soprano, alto, tenor and bass; then another three versions for soprano, alto and tenor followed by three further versions for vocal quartet. The tune of each setting (all are in F or G major) is subtly different: four are in common time, five are in ¾. The manuscript shows many corrections from Salieri. Since this project was conceived as an exercise in prosody and part-writing, there is no piano accompaniment. From the point of view of occasional concert performance this is a pity, and Van Hoorickx rectified the situation with privately printed realizations of the songs.

In this music we hear the beginnings of Schubert's genius for melody. For example, in the first of these two versions (for solo soprano) the vocal line is prophetic of the first setting of Schiller's *Der Jüngling am Bache* D30. In the second, a duet for two sopranos (where Ann Murray recorded both voices) it is impossible not to hear an echo of Mozart's Fiordiligi and Dorabella. Schubert has been taught much (and encouraged to experiment for himself) in the realm of Italian word-setting, and has grafted the fluidity and sensuality fostered by the Italian language on to the impressionable and young German lied. This, then, is the beginning of the miracle that was to reach its first immortal manifestation in *Gretchen am Spinnrade* D118.

The story of Abraham and Isaac is an extremely dramatic one (cf. Britten's second Canticle, *Abraham and Isaac* Op. 51). Schubert had composed a long song based on another biblical story – the concubine Hagar's expulsion into the desert with her child (*Hagars Klage* D5) – and the young composer had reacted to these words with ardour, and perhaps a bit too much dramatic flair for the singer's comfort. Here, though, the emotion behind the imminent death of Isaac at

Abraham's hand is not allowed to get out of control. Everything is subordinated to the comfort of the singer and the pure vowels of the Italian language. Salieri wants polish and poise, not raw Germanic truth. Schubert attempts to inject a bit of passion into this suave music (the high note at the end of the solo version, for example, at 'Quello <u>vuol</u> Dio da te') but he is beginning to learn how to create emotional tension through *melody*. This is a lesson that composers like Zumsteeg and Reichardt never absorbed. Schubert, in his own way, was to be the equal of Mozart (another Metastasio collaborator) in bringing together Italian sensibility and German learning, in marrying Italian polish in the *galant* style with the passion of Germany's burgeoning Romanticism.

Autograph:	Wienbibliothek im Rathaus, Vienna
First edition:	Published in Alfred Orel's *Der junge Schubert* (1940); additional piano accompaniments by Reinhard Van Hoorickx. Subsequently issued as part of the NSA in 1986 (P795)
Subsequent editions:	Not in Peters; Not in AGA; NSA VIII: Vol. 2/185 & 186
Discography and timing:	Fischer-Dieskau —
	Hyperion I 33⁵ & 33⁶ 1'18 Ann Murray (solo version)
	Hyperion II 2³ & 2⁴ 0'59 Ann Murray (duet version, both voices)

← *Der Geistertanz* D15a   *Viel tausend Sterne prangen* D642 →

Schubert. Oil painting of 1827 by Gábor Melegh.

R

RAST *see WINTERREISE* D911/10

RASTE KRIEGER, KRIEG IST AUS *see SIEBEN GESÄNGE AUS WALTER SCOTT'S FRÄULEIN VOM SEE* Op. 52 no. 1

RASTLOSE LIEBE   Restless love
(GOETHE) Op. 5 no. 1, **D138** [H96]

The song exists in two versions, both of which are discussed below:
(1) 19 May 1815; (2) May 1821

(1)   E major

(2)   'Schnell'   D major   2/4   [93 bars]

Dem Schnee, dem Regen,	Into the snow, the rain,
Dem Wind entgegen,	And the wind,
Im Dampf der Klüfte,	Through steamy ravines,
Durch Nebeldüfte,	Through mists,
Immer zu! Immer zu!	Onwards, ever onwards!
Ohne Rast und Ruh!	Without respite!
Lieber durch Leiden	I would sooner fight my way
Wollt' ich mich schlagen,[1]	Through suffering,
Als so viel Freuden	Than endure so much
Des Lebens ertragen.	Of life's joy.
Alle das Neigen	This affection
Von Herzen zu Herzen,	Of one heart for another,
Ach, wie so eigen	Ah, how strangely
Schaffet es Schmerzen![2]	It creates pain!

[1] Goethe writes 'Möcht' ich mich schlagen'.
[2] Goethe writes 'Schaffet *das* Schmerzen'.

Wie soll ich flieh'n?[3]	How shall I flee?
Wälderwärts zieh'n?	Into the forest?
Alles vergebens!	It is all in vain!
Krone des Lebens,	Crown of life,
Glück ohne Ruh,	Happiness without peace –
Liebe, bist du!	This, O love, is you!

JOHANN WOLFGANG VON GOETHE (1749–1832); poem written 6 May 1776

This is the eleventh of Schubert's seventy-five Goethe solo settings (1814–26). See the poet's biography for a chronological list of all the Goethe settings.

The poem has unlikely English origins – *Love will find out a way* from Volume 3 of *Reliques of Ancient English Poetry* (1765) by Bishop Percy (qv):

Over the mountains,
    And over the waves;
Under the fountains,
    And under the graves;
Over floods that are deepest,
    Which Neptune obey;
Over rocks that are steepest,
    Love will find out the way.

This was translated into German by Herder (who conflates Percy's third and fourth verses) under the title *Weg der Liebe*, later set by Brahms as a duet for two female voices, Op. 20 no. 1:

Über die Berge,
    Über die Wellen,
Unter den Gräbern,
    Unter den Quellen etc.

Goethe's *Rastlose Liebe* is a rhythmical parody (similar in terms of title, mood and metre) of a poem he knew in both the original English and its German translation. To match the poet's impetuous response, Schubert summons up a storm of raw energy ('a whirl of feeling, not a logical statement', as Capell writes) within a time frame of less than a minute and a half. The song was an immediate hit with his circle (the composer reportedly wrote it in a transport of ecstasy) and it has been at the centre of the Schubert repertoire ever since. The poem itself was written during a freak May snowstorm in 1776 and charts Goethe's reactions to his burgeoning relationship with Charlotte von Stein – a mixture of fear and excitement, pain and elation, just as snow in May is in itself unexpected. Charlotte was a married woman whose influence Goethe profoundly needed in his life. He was not afraid to declare his feelings in a way that was new in the context of inhibited, and predominantly Christian, German love poetry of the time. In the poet's previous affairs there had been a good deal of self-dramatizing and posturing, but suddenly he felt newly sensitized – open to a relationship of equals rather than one where he took the

---

[3] In the first two lines of this strophe, Goethe writes '*fliehen*' and '*ziehen*'.

The autograph of *Rastlose Liebe* from the album made for Goethe, 1816.

leading role. He felt himself out of control – exhilarated by that strange and unfamiliar feeling, but also anxious. Schubert in 1815 was inexperienced in love, yet he was clearly aware of its excitements and torments. He was already a great composer, a great Goethe composer moreover, and he remained proud enough of this song to dedicate it to his former teacher, Antonio Salieri, as the first of the Op. 5 songs published in 1821.

The text suggests a moto perpetuo with a flurry of semiquavers. Reichardt set it thus in 1794, as did Zelter in 1812. Schubert of course followed suit; he might have known these settings but it seems more likely that it was Goethe's text alone that suggested the restless *Bewegung*. Nevertheless the whole song has the characteristics of the North German school. It is seldom that one finds real *speed* of this kind in a Schubert lied, but it is heard often enough in those by Mendelssohn (Zelter's pupil), such as *Hexenlied* Op. 8 no. 8, *Neue Liebe* Op. 19 no. 4, *Reiselied* Op. 31 no. 6, and so on. There is little room for a pause for thought in this music, and where it is necessary to take one it requires real effort to control the mercurial flow. The construction of the whole is very tight, the piano ceaselessly occupied in its role as rhythmic power-generator. The effect of this brief scherzo would, in instrumental terms, be like the whirrings of a faultlessly oiled piece of machinery were it not for the anguish and elation that the human voice alone can express.

The introduction is a miracle of harmonic legerdemain and very hard to play, as generations of accompanists have discovered. The whirling semiquavers in the right hand are marked sempre legato; the ascending scale in the left, in crotchets and quavers, partially chromatic and marked sempre staccato, sturdily underpins the flurry and pushes the music forward. It is infinitely preferable to play this passage without pedal so the left-hand articulation is audible. These six bars (over in a trice) present a bewildering succession of harmonies starting in E major and returning there with the entry of the voice. During this prelude we feel that the protagonist has attempted to find an exit from the emotional maze in which he is trapped, but having failed to do so must stand his ground, his back against the wall, and explain his case. This is far from easy because a vocal heroism is required that is comparatively rare in Schubert. The high-lying 'Ohne Rast und Ruh' (bb. 19–23) can only be attempted by singers with something of an operatic top. The gifted tenor Ludwig Tietze sang it at a concert in Vienna in 1824; it would have been less suited to the baritone Vogl, even in transposition.

The second verse is marked piano, a dynamic that is essential for the introspective phrase 'Lieber durch Leiden / Wollt' ich mich schlagen' and for the contrast with the wildness of nature described in the first verse. For the second verse ('Alle das Neigen / Von Herzen zu Herzen') the key signature changes to G major and the semiquavers of the accompaniment are replaced by triplets (b. 33). This tiny adjustment gives an impression of relative repose – we are transported with the poet back to an intimate moment with Charlotte, the musical sequence – the second phrase a tone higher than the first – an analogue for leaning and yearning. After a sudden reversion to passionate vehemence, the words 'Wie soll ich flieh'n? / Wälderwärts zieh'n?' are brilliantly set as wildly rhetorical phrases. Taking to the woods is no serious option and 'Alles, alles vergebens!' is a howl of pain that is almost animal-like in its intensity. Note the stretched-out cadence (Alles, b. 51) and the strength of the modulation into C sharp minor at b. 53 ('vergebens'), returning to a key signature of four sharps. The effect of this moment, dominant to tonic, is powerfully suggestive of physical movement, like punching the air in frustration. There are challenges around every corner here: the two bars of 'Krone des Lebens' (bb. 57–8, marked mezzo forte) are juxtaposed with two bars of 'Glück ohne Ruh' (marked piano), a mercurial change for both singer and pianist where any real difference in dynamic is seldom audible in performance. The elongated setting of 'Liebe' (bb. 77–81), an E held high over the stave for four bars, is a masterstroke, suggesting both rapture and pain. This is achieved by the tiniest changes in the supporting harmonies (Lachen und Weinen-like), all contained within one plangent note held in the vocal line as if to emphasize that love is an umbrella word for myriad feelings. The eleven-bar postlude (from b. 83) descends into the lower regions of the keyboard and scurries to its offbeat and puckish conclusion, a frisson under the pianist's hands. Despite all the talk of pain, the final impression is that it is all worth it, that love is an adventure both painful and delicious.

The NSA prints a second version of the song in D major in Vol. 1b p. 208. This dates from May 1821 and was clearly a copy made by the composer because he did not fancy transposing the song (probably for the high baritone Vogl) at sight. Baritones with a secure top should try this version instead of the rather too comfortable C major transposition in the middle voice version of the Peters Edition.

It is a curious footnote to the history of the song that in 1823 Beethoven more or less promised a setting of this poem to Goethe in a letter written on 8 March of that year. He made extensive sketches for a song in E flat major but, as with so many of Beethoven's attempts to set fine poetry, he seems to have been as much initimidated by such texts as inspired by them. Paul Reid in The Beethoven Song Companion raises the possibility that the composer may have come across, and been put off by, Schubert's setting of the lyric published in 1821. It is also possible that he was all too aware of the not inconsiderable achievements of Reichardt and Zelter with the same lyric.

Autograph:	Stadtarchiv, Linz
Publication:	First published as Op. 5 no. 1 by Cappi & Diabelli, Vienna in July 1821 (P10; first version)
	First published as part of NSA in 1970 (P748; second version)
Dedicatee:	Antonio Salieri

First known performance:	Schubert performed the song privately on 13 June 1816, recording the event in his diary and comparing his own performance of *Rastlose Liebe* with the Schiller setting *Amalia*. [Deutsch Doc. Biog. No. 86]
	First public performance: 29 January 1824, Gesellschaft der Musikfreunde, Vienna. Soloist: Ludwig Tietze [Waidelich/Hilmar Dokumente II No. 245; Deutsch Doc. Biog. No. 432]
Publication reviews:	F. von Hentl 'Blick auf Schubert's Lieder', *Wiener Zeitschrift für Kunst, Literatur, Theater und Mode* No. 36 (23 March 1822), p. 289f. [Waidelich/Hilmar Dokumente I No. 146; Deutsch Doc. Biog. No. 278]
Subsequent editions:	Peters: Vol. 1/222; AGA XX 177: Vol. 3/198; NSA IV: Vol. 1a/35 & Vol. 1b/208; Bärenreiter: Vol. 1/28
Bibliography:	Bell 1964, p. 24
	Byrne 2003, pp. 108–12
	Capell 1928, p. 106
	Dürr 1971, pp. 215–30
	Einstein 1951, p. 116
	Fischer-Dieskau 1977, pp. 68–70
	Reid 2007, pp. 237–8
Further settings and arrangements:	Johann Friedrich Reichardt (1752–1814) *Rastlose Liebe* (1794 and 1808)
	Carl Friedrich Zelter (1758–1832) *Rastlose Liebe* (1812)
	Robert Schumann (1810–1856) *Rastlose Liebe* Op. 35 no. 5 for unaccompanied male chorus (1840)
	Arr. Franz Liszt (1811–1886) for solo piano, no. 10 of *Zwölf Lieder von Schubert* (1837–8) [*see* Transcriptions]
	Robert Franz (1815–1892) *Rastlose Liebe* Op. 33 no. 6 (1864)
	Joachim Raff (1822–1882) *Rastlose Liebe* Op. 98 no. 23 (1855–63)
	Othmar Schoeck (1886–1957) *Rastlose Liebe* Op. 19a no. 5 (1912)
Discography and timing:	Fischer-Dieskau I 6[7] 1'23
	Hyperion I 24[5]
	Hyperion II 6[16] 1'29 John Mark Ainsley

← *Die Mainacht* D194   *Amalia* D195 →

JOSEPH FRANZ VON RATSCHKY (1757–1810)

THE POETIC SOURCES

S1 *Taschenbuch zum geselligen Vergnügen* herausgegeben von W.G. Becker für 1795. Mit Churfürstl. Sächsischem Privilegio. Leipzig bei Voss und Compagnie.

The same almanac is also the source of the Tiedge setting *An die Sonne* D272, composed on the same day as *Der Weiberfreund*.

S2 *Neuere Gedichte von Joseph Franz Ratschky*, Wien Bey J.V. Degen Buchdrucker und Buchhändler 1805

The first verse of the translation of *Der Weiberfreund* in this later version reads:

Nie müde, spiel' ich mit den Schaaren
Der Töchter Evens Amors Spiel;
Von fünfzehn bis zu fünfzig
Ist jede meiner Wünsche Ziel.

With Eve's daughters at all stages of playing love's
game. I never tire
Be it fifteen or fifty that their age is
Each is the object of my desire.

Ratschky thus tactfully removes his previous assertion that no female existed who did not please him – setting the lower age at fifteen years old is bad enough by today's standards. Verse 5 of the almanac translation is also here revised; verses 2, 4 and 6 are retained, with the earlier Verse 3 becoming Verse 5.

THE SONG
25 August 1815   *Der Weiberfreund* D271 [S1: 'Nach dem Englischen des Cowley', pp. 201–2] [S2: pp. 21–2]

Ratschky was born in Vienna on 21 August 1757. He worked as a civil servant, also in Linz, and was in charge of the Viennese lottery. In 1796 he became Hofsekretär and was elevated to the nobility in 1806 when he became Hofrat. Like many of the important officials of the time, he was a freemason. He had been acquainted with Mozart who had set his Masonic-inspired *Lied zur Gesellenreise* K468 in 1785, as it happens the same year in which Ratschky's *Gedichte* were published; a second volume of poems followed in 1791 where the poem set by Mozart is to be found. Ratschky was an industrious translator, particularly enjoying works from the English theatre (he translated works by David Garrick for example). He was perhaps most famous for his mock-heroic epic poem *Melchior Striegel* (1793–5) which was modelled on another, even earlier, English work, Samuel Butler's *Hudibras* (1663). He died on 31 May 1810. (*See also* ABRAHAM COWLEY)

J. F. Ratschky, 1791.

Der RATTENFÄNGER   The rat-catcher
(GOETHE) **D255** [H141]
G major   19 August 1815

Etwas geschwind

Ich bin der wohl-be-kann-te Sän-ger, der viel-ge-reis-te Rat-ten-fäng-er,

(21 bars)

Ich bin der wohlbekannte Sänger,	I am the well-known singer,
Der vielgereiste Rattenfänger,	The much-travelled rat-catcher,
Den diese altberühmte Stadt	Of whom this famous old city
Gewiss besonders nötig hat.	Certainly has special need.
Und wären's Ratten noch so viele,	However many rats there are,
Und wären Wiesel mit im Spiele;	And even if there are weasels too,
Von allen säubr' ich diesen Ort,	I'll clear the place of them all;
Sie müssen miteinander fort.	They must go, every single one.
Dann ist der gutgelaunte Sänger	Now, this good-humoured singer
Mitunter auch ein Kinderfänger,	Is also occasionally a child-catcher,
Der selbst die wildesten bezwingt,	Who can tame even the most unruly
Wenn er die goldnen Märchen singt.	When he sings his golden tales.
Und wären Knaben noch so trutzig,	However defiant the boys,
Und wären Mädchen noch so stutzig,	However suspicious the girls,
In meine Saiten greif' ich ein,	When I pluck my strings
Sie müssen alle hinter drein.	They must all follow me.
Dann ist der vielgewandte Sänger	Now, this versatile singer
Gelegentlich ein Mädchenfänger;	Is occasionally a catcher of girls.
In keinem Städtchen langt er an,	He never enters a town
Wo er's nicht mancher angetan.	Without captivating many.
Und wären Mädchen noch so blöde,	However shy the girls,
Und wären Weiber noch so spröde;	And however aloof the ladies,
Doch allen wird so liebebang	They all become lovesick
Bei Zaubersaiten und Gesang.	At the sound of his magic lute and his singing.

JOHANN WOLFGANG VON GOETHE (1749–1832); poem written in 1784/1803

This is the twenty-second of Schubert's seventy-five Goethe solo settings (1814–26). See the poet's biography for a chronological list of all the Goethe settings.

Goethe read about the legend of the Pied Piper of Hamelin in Gottfried's *Chronika* of 1642. The story seems to have its roots in the Children's Crusade of 1212 when forty thousand German children set off over the Alps for Italy. Although the pope ordered them home, many were never seen again by their parents and some were sold into slavery. The legend goes that Hamelin in Westphalia was infested with rats in 1284. A piper in multi-coloured clothes offered to rid the town of them for a sum agreed by the townspeople. He kept his side of the bargain but

Der Rattenfänger.

Ich bin der wohlbekannte Sänger,
Der vielgereiste Rattenfänger,
Den diese weltberühmte Stadt
Gewiß besonders nöthig hat;

Vignette for *Der Rattenfänger* (1864).

when no payment was forthcoming he led all the children into a mountain cave – never to be seen again according to one version, and into Transylvania to found a German colony according to another. The story first appeared in England in James Howell's *Familiar Letters* (1645–55), which was probably the source of Browning's famous poem on the subject. Goethe's debt to the legend is oblique. *Der Rattenfänger* is a reworking of the story in the way that the same poet's *Ganymed* and *Prometheus* are a new take on Greek myth. Goethe's rat-catcher, for example, is not a piper at all but a player of a stringed instrument – probably a lute. The story is not told in full (as in Browning), and the poet introduces the character as if ignorant of the sequel. This is only possible because, as the rat-catcher boasts, he is well known to us – 'wohlbekannt' – and notorious. While the minstrel's ability with rats and children is familiar, Goethe is unable to resist a third strophe that turns him into a ladykiller also.

The music is in Schubert's best *Singspiel* manner; it is a merry and boastful little song with undertones of later developments in the story written in: even in the first full bar, under 'wohlbekannte', an F natural in the left hand slyly undermines the G major tonality – we cannot trust this man. The slithering of rats is marvellously caught in the setting of 'Und wären's Ratten noch so viele', with double thirds in the right hand to show that these creatures move in swarms (bb. 9–10). The phrase 'Und wären Wiesel mit im Spiele' (bb. 12–13) scurries to a cadence that might suggest a vocal cadenza, and is of sinister charm. The accompaniment to the phrase 'säubr' ich', high in the voice, is deliciously ornamented in b. 14, the crushed grace notes of the right hand betokening the imperious sweep of a new broom in the first verse, and the twanging of lute strings in the second.

Perhaps this song would be better known if Hugo Wolf had not composed his masterpiece of 1889 in which the malice is positively diabolical and where we hear rats at every turn in the accompaniment, as King Rat in human form sings his honeyed serenade. Schubert's song cannot compete with that, but on its own terms it is a success. The composer thought highly enough of it to include it in the second of his two lieder albums for Goethe.

Autograph:	University Library of Lund, Sweden (first draft)
	Conservatoire collection, Bibliothèque Nationale, Paris (fair copy made for Goethe)
First edition:	Published as Book 47 no. 3 of the *Nachlass* by Diabelli, Vienna in 1850 (P377)
Subsequent editions:	Peters: Vol. 6/54; AGA XX 112: Vol. 3/34; NSA IV: Vol. 8/192
Further settings and arrangements:	Václav Jan Tomášek (1774–1850) *Der Rattenfänger* Op. 54 no. 5 (1815)
	Hugo Wolf (1860–1903) *Der Rattenfänger* (1888; orchestrated 1890)
	Arr. Tilman Hoppstock (b. 1961) for guitar accompaniment, in *Franz Schubert: 110 Lieder* (2009)
Discography and timing:	Fischer-Dieskau I 5[1] 1'58
	Hyperion I 24[9]
	Hyperion II 9[2] 2'26 Simon Keenlyside

← *Der Gott und die Bajadere* D254   *Der Schatzgräber* D256 →

JOHANN ADAM (or Anton) FRIEDRICH REIL (1773–1843)

THE POETIC SOURCES

S1 *Allgemeine Theaterzeitung und Unterhaltungsblatt für Freunde der Kunst, Literatur und des geselligen Lebens.* Zwanzigster Jahrgang, Nr. 123. Wien, Sonnabend, den 13 October 1827

Schubert composed *Das Lied im Grünen* about four months earlier than the appearance of the poem in this periodical and had clearly been given a handwritten copy of the poem by Reil himself. The various differences there are between the text in the musical setting and the one printed in the *Theaterzeitung* may go back to Reil himself changing the text after Schubert had received it from him.

S2 *Allgemeine Theaterzeitung und Unterhaltungsblatt für Freunde der Kunst, Literatur und des geselligen Lebens.* Ein und zwanzigster Jahrgang, Nr.127. Wien, Sonnabend, den 27 September 1828

The poem for *Glaube, Hoffnung und Liebe* was printed in this newspaper as part of a general report of the consecration of the new bell in the Dreifaltigkeitkirche.

S3 *Glaube, Hoffnung, Liebe Zur Weihe der neuen Glocke an der Kirche zur allerheiligsten Drey-faltigkeit in der Alsergrund Von F.A. Friedrich Reil (Mit Musik von Franz Schubert) Wien 1828.* Gedruckt bey Georg Überreuther.

Pamphlet distributed to the public on 2 September 1828.

THE SONGS

June 1827 — *Das Lied im Grünen* D917. Poem received from the poet in handwritten form [S1: p. 501]

1828, before 2 September — *Glaube, Hoffnung und Liebe* D954. Poem received from the poet in handwritten form [S2: p. 468f.]

Friedrich Reil was born in Tal Ehrenbreitstein near Koblenz on 2 February 1773. An energetic Rhinelander, he was a jack of all trades – jobbing actor (he had worked as far afield as Brno and Ljubljana), author, librettist and entrepreneur – and he clearly had the gift of the gab. He moved to Vienna in his late twenties in 1801. He had a talent for writing occasional poems (for example, in honour of the sixtieth birthday of the Emperor Franz in 1828, and an oration for the same emperor's death in 1835) which were then published in pamphlet form. He was probably in contact with Schubert in May and June 1827 when both men found themselves relaxing in Dornbach, a village to the west of Vienna near the Wiener Wald. It is certain that the composer set *Das*

Lied im Grünen from the manuscript. When the poem was published in October 1827 (well before the song's publication) Reil added the words, 'Was often sung here and there in the meadows during the summer by a merry company to a lively and agreeable tune by Schubert'.

There is some confusion as to how many of the verses of *Das Lied im Grünen* should be performed: the posthumous first edition inserted a verse, not to be found in the autograph, mentioning the poet's studious boyhood acquaintance with the works of Horace, Plato, Wieland and Kant. This can be fun, but it could be argued that it turns an already extensive country ramble into an overnight stopover, and that it adversely affects the song's rondo-

Johann Anton Friendrich Reil, portrait by Friedrich von Hamerling of 1838.

form structure. In any case it is likely that Reil added these words after Schubert's death. After all it was he who added spurious verses to the Shakespeare settings *Ständchen* D889 ('Hark, hark, the lark') and *Trinklied* D888. Like Schlechta, Reil seems to have been aware that the more he had to do with the departed master's music, the more his rather meagre words would be assured of immortality. By the time the song reached publication Schubert had already died and Reil could not resist appending three further strophes to the first edition – rather more to be read by Schubert's admirers, one suspects, than to be sung:

Dem Schläfer im Grünen

O Schubert! Im Grünen
Hat öfter dies Liedchen dich Heitern erquicket;

Uns aber, wo je du gesungen, entzücket.
Ha! nimmer vergisst sich der Geist, das
   Gemüth,
Das deinen Akkorden und Liedern entglüht,
Die nimmer vergrünen.

[. . . 2 . . .]

To the sleeper in nature's green

O Schubert, in nature's green
This song has often refreshed your cheerful
   heart;
But wherever you sang, it delighted us.
Ah! The spirit, the feeling, that glows from your
   imperishable tones and songs
Will never be forgotten.

[. . . 2 . . .]

Reil was better known in Vienna as a librettist of fairly succesful operas for the composers Joseph Weigl and Conradin Kreutzer (qv COMPOSERS). He was also involved with Schubert in providing a sung musical piece,

Glaube, Hoffnung und Liebe, for the consecration of the new bell at the Dreifältigkeit church in the Alsergrund in September 1828. He died in Penzing near Vienna on 2 July 1843.

Bibliography: Clive 1997, p. 162
              Youens 2002, pp. 301–24

CHRISTIAN LUDWIG REISSIG (1784–1847)

THE POETIC SOURCES
S1 Ludwig van Beethoven *Sechs Gesänge* Op. 75 [no. 6 *Der Zufriedene*]

On the same day as composing *Der Zufriedene* Schubert also composed Goethe's *Mignon* (*Kennst du das Land?*) (Beethoven's Op. 75 no. 1 – *Mignon*). This suggests that he took both texts directly from a printed copy of Op. 75. There are also various musical similarities between the two composers' settings.

S2 *Blümchen der Einsamkeit*. Von Christian Ludwig Reissig. Wien, auf Kosten und im Verlag bey Johann Baptist Wallishausser. 1809

THE SONG
23 October 1815　*Der Zufriedene* D320 [S2: p. 62]

Christian Reissig was born in Kassel in Germany on 24 July 1784. In 1809, while on his way to Italy, he stopped in the Imperial City, enlisting as a volunteer in the Austrian army during the Napoleonic wars. Three months later he was wounded in action in the Spanish campaign and returned to live in Hietzing, just outside Vienna, where his war-veteran status clearly helped his career. Nothing is known about his literary activity in Germany before his arrival in Austria apart from his appearance in Becker's Taschenbuch for 1809, published in Leipzig. His collection *Blümchen der Einsamkeit* was published in Vienna, also in 1809. His works include several translations of English poets. Over a period of fifteen years (roughly 1810–25) Reissig made his living as a provider of song texts to such composers as Beethoven, Conradin Kreutzer, Wenzel Müller, Nikolaus von Krufft and Salieri. He arranged for a number of song collections to be printed, inviting various composers to contribute to musical antholo-gies exclusively of his own verse. His poems even seem to have interested Zelter in Berlin. Beethoven is the most famous and most prolific of the Reissig composers, producing between 1809 and 1816 no fewer than eight settings from *Blümchen der Einsamkeit*. It is likely that Schubert was inspired to compose his single Reissig setting, *Der Zufriedene*, after

finding himself in possession of a copy of Beethoven's Op. 75 songs, where this was no. 6. This collection also included the great man's setting of Goethe's *Mignons Lied (Kennst du das Land?)*, a text that Schubert set on the same day in 1815.

Reissig took a highly unconventional approach to business dealings: he sent com-posers his work and canvassed settings from them without paying a fee. He quickly pub-lished the results and took money from gullible dedicatees who were no doubt surprised to find the same songs published elsewhere (by the composer) with another dedication altogether. This behaviour enraged Beethoven, who referred to the wounded 'Captain' Reissig in a letter to Breitkopf & Härtel of 11 October 1810, regarding ownership of songs to the poet's texts. He called Reissig's claim to have paid him for these settings an 'abominable lie'. 'I com-posed these works for him as an act of friend-ship, because he was then a cripple, and aroused my sympathy.' Despite his anger with 'this scoundrel of a captain' (letter of 16 January 1811), Beethoven was drawn back to the poetry in 1815–16 for his *Sehnsucht* WoO 146. Reis-sig's brand of piracy was only possible before the advent of copyright. He left the city in 1822 because of financial difficulties, and moved with his family to Hungary. He died in Stein-amanger (Szombatheley) on 5 December 1847.

REITERLIED *see* LIED EINES KRIEGERS D822

RELIGION AND RELIGIOUS MUSIC

Man comes into the world armed with faith, which is far superior to knowledge and understanding: for in order to understand a thing one must first of all believe in it. Faith is that higher foundation on which the weaker intellect erects the pillars of conviction. Intelligence is nothing else than analysed faith.

Franz Schubert, from his *Tagebuch* for 28 March 1824

Was Franz Schubert religious? Even if we must define 'religion' in order to answer that question, there is no such thing in this case as a straightforward, unequivocal 'Yes' (as with Haydn and Bruckner, for example, or Duparc and Chausson). Indeed, the bits and pieces of documentation at our disposal are so various and contradictory that the conundrum seems almost insoluble. Rationality and the Enlightenment had somewhat loosened the grip of the Church on Austrian life in the last decades of the eighteenth century, but during Metternich's mercilessly reactionary regime the Church was associated with the backlash and was an essential part of the power structure. Schubert and his contemporaries were caught between these opposing historical forces. There is some evidence that the composer was sceptical about the dogma of the Roman Catholic Church but, on the other hand, the list of his liturgical music, together with songs and choral music on religious themes, printed below, also speaks for itself. Setting texts in praise of God was an ever-present part of the composer's musical existence.

Schubert's religious upbringing was all that we might expect of someone born into a lower middle-class but scrupulously upright Viennese family at the end of the eighteenth century. His home was certainly more strictly observant than many (his father was Moravian-born, his mother originally from Silesia – parts of the world that were not so laissez-faire in these matters as metropolitan Vienna). His parents, the father in particular, must have struggled hard to rear God-fearing children, but almost certainly veered towards a strictness which produced a counter-reaction. We know that in one case they failed utterly in their objective: Schubert's elder brother Ignaz (born 1785) was, almost notoriously, a freethinker, but he was careful not to parade this fact before Franz Schubert senior. When Ignaz wrote to his composer brother in 1818 (Schubert was in Hungary) much of his letter was a somewhat scornful description of a ceremony at the family school, involving the erection of a makeshift altar to a saint and the kissing of relics. Some of the guests crept away, unwilling to take part in the ceremony supervised by Schubert's father. Ignaz added a postlude to his letter: 'If you wish to write to Papa and me at the same time, do not touch upon any religious matters.'

The composer's first music lessons were with Michael Holzer, the organist and *Regens chori* of the Lichtental parish church. Schubert's first sacred music was written for Holzer's choir, and his less ambitious church music was always assured a sympathetic hearing in this environment. The ban on women's voices in church had been lifted as recently as 1806, and it was thanks to this new dispensation that Therese Grob, said to have been the composer's first love, was allowed into the choir. Thus it was through church music that Schubert had his first experiences both of love and of being a professional musician. Throughout his life it was to be the one branch of his output that was more or less assured public performance soon after each work was written. Schubert lived at a transitional time when it was still forbidden to perform Masses in the concert hall but when it was becoming acceptable to lavish greater musical resources on the form in the church. Every composer likes – nay, needs – to hear his music performed. Perhaps it is for this reason that Schubert wrote so regularly for the ecclesiastical establishments of a town still hungry for a constant turnover of new religious works, although only four liturgical works were published in his lifetime, all in 1825: a *Tantum ergo*, two *offertoria*, the second of these really a *Salve Regina*, and a Mass (*see* work list below).

It was when he won a scholarship to the Stadtkonvikt as a member of the Hofkapelle choir that the composer encountered new influences. The quiet faith of his local church was replaced by high and mighty manifestations of state religion. At this school daily confession was obligatory, and any signs of political or moral liberalism were quickly suppressed. Schubert no doubt encountered among the priests some good teachers but there were also brutal bigots who vented their frustrations on their pupils with cruelty and violence. The composer's dislike of the priestly tribe comes vividly to the fore in a letter from Hungary to his brother Ferdinand in 1818: 'You have no idea what a gang the priesthood is here: bigoted as mucky old cattle, stupid as arch-donkeys and boorish as bisons. You may hear sermons to which our most venerated *Pater Nepomucene* [Father Maria Johann Nepomuk Priegl in the Rossau] can't hold a candle.'

Most of Schubert's school contemporaries came from wealthier and sometimes less observant families. He was subject to a wide range of influences which no doubt changed his religious views as much as his musical tastes and reading habits. It is here that he must have begun to question some of the more dogmatic aspects of the Roman Catholic faith. In 1813 he had written a poem (since lost) in the style of Klopstock's Odes to God's omnipotence, yet in 1814 his practical knowledge of religion was singled out as being 'bad' in a report at the teacher's training college. He was obviously not an enthusiastic Bible student, but these poor marks are at odds with his extraordinary track record as a precocious composer of religious music.

For almost every sign of Schubert's leanings towards a conventional religious viewpoint, there is a corresponding fact or quotation that seems to oppose it. For example, although he wrote six Masses, he never chose to set the text complete, omitting in every case the phrase 'et unam sanctam catholicam et apostolicam ecclesiam' from the Credo. There are many further variants in his Mass texts. In the second and fourth Masses (G major, D167, and C major, D452) the phrase 'qui sedes ad dexteram Patri' is left out; in the third Mass (B flat major, D324) the phrase 'consubstantialem Patris'. In the two great Masses of Schubert's maturity, his fifth and sixth (A flat, D678, and E flat, D950) we search in vain for 'Patrem omnipotentem' as well as 'genitum non factum'. In the A flat Mass the phrase 'ex Maria virgine' is absent. Perhaps the most unusual phrase in the last five Masses is 'confiteor unum baptisma in remissionem mortuorum'. Schubert constructed this by shortening the much longer 'confiteor unum baptisma in remissionem *peccatorum. Et expecto resurrectionem* mortuorum', thus wiping out mention of sin and resurrection at a stroke. The Masses of 1815 and 1816 shy away from words that bow to the authority of the Father; mention of the Father's omnipotence is finally erased from the text of the late Masses. Some of these changes to the Latin text may have been momentary failures of memory, but the consistent alterations are significant. It is also interesting that the customary words 'Laus Deo' ('Praise be to God') at the end of a Mass are never found on a Schubert manuscript. Despite all this, it is extremely hard to make out a case for a consistently anti-religious attitude. Indeed, apart from the stream of church music and religious songs, there are a number of references to God and Christ in the composer's letters that suggest the opposite viewpoint. During his holiday period in Upper Austria in 1825 with the singer Vogl Schubert wrote to his family about the composition of the Walter Scott setting *Ave Maria*, more properly known as *Ellens Gesang III D839*: 'I never force devotion upon myself and, except when involuntarily overwhelmed by it, never compose hymns or prayers of this kind, but then it is usually the right and true devotion.' Although the letter was specifically intended for parental consumption, there is no reason to doubt the sincerity of the composer's statement. It is still a little known fact, however, that this song was never meant to be squeezed into Latin garb for church performance.

We should not underestimate the extent to which Schubert's beliefs were moved this way or that by the personalities of friends and mentors throughout his life. Was he easily led? Not exactly. He was wary of outside interference and new acquaintances, and he needed to know that new members of the circle were talented and had something to say for themselves. But once he had admitted them to his heart, his mind became receptive to their ideas, and he sometimes found it difficult to see their faults and limitations. The people in whom he put his trust did not always deserve it. Franz von Schober comes to mind, a man who exerted a pull on the composer's affections (both as friend and librettist) that seems out of proportion to his sincerity and talent. As it happens, *Alfonso und Estrella* D732, the opera that the pair wrote together, develops a theme which Schober touches on in the poem *Trost im Liede* D546, also set by Schubert: two of the main characters sing the lines 'through the power of love, joy and sorrow are wedded'. This is a sentiment found elsewhere in Schubert's songs, and the Catholic scholar Robert R. Reilly has pointed out that this is 'the message of the Cross'. The Christian tone of the opera is unmistakable; at the end there is a miraculous chain reaction of forgiveness and repentance set off like bush fire among the main characters. 'Mercy redeems our guilt', sings King Froila, and the opera concludes with redemption for all. It would be hard to imagine such a denouement by artists not raised as Roman Catholics.

It is impossible to know exactly when and how pantheism came up for discussion among the Schubertians, but it is likely to have been in the company of the serious and learned Mayrhofer. This issue had been examined not only by Goethe, but also by such philosophers as Hegel, Fichte and Schelling, names not unknown to Schubert and his friends who attempted, as far as Austrian censorship allowed, to keep abreast of the latest trends in German thought. There seems to have been a pantheistic phase in the composer's development corresponding to his settings of Friedrich von Schlegel, and a related enthusiasm for the mysticism of Novalis. Schubert was not a man attracted to dogmatic extremes of any sort. From time to time he was drawn to writing works for church performance with German texts (*Deutsches Salve Regina*, D379; *Stabat Mater*, D383; the great oratorio fragment *Lazarus*, D689; *Deutsche Messe*, D872), veering towards a more Protestant tradition of church music. Towards the end of his life he was also willing to write music for the synagogue. And the one thing we shall never know – considering the composer's upbringing within a very strict and unyielding Catholicism – is the extent of the guilt he may have felt throughout his life regarding his actions, his sexual behaviour for example, and for his lapses of faith and searches for alternative answers. There is an 'awe and terror' (the words of Leo Black) in Schubert's religious music that suggests that for someone of his background leaving Catholicism was not simply a matter of deciding to do so.

One of the most oft-cited pieces of evidence concerning Schubert's lack of faith comes from a note written to him in 1826 by his friend Ferdinand Walcher (1799–1873). The letter, something of a jest, begins with a stave of Gregorian chant and the phrase 'Credo in unum Deum' ('I believe in one God') penned in old notation. This is followed by Walcher's own words meant for Schubert's eyes: 'Not you, I know well enough.' It is quite possible that a stinging renunciation of faith may have come the night before from the lips of a composer subject to depression and the lingering effects of his illness. He might have felt that he had little to be thankful for in terms of the Almighty's intervention in his affairs. But it seems to me that the words 'one God' are significant. Had Schubert perhaps been talking to Walcher about the fact that God can go by other names? As the words of Mozart's Masonic cantata have it: 'Whether his name is Jehovah ... whether he is named Fu or Brahma.' Or had Schubert proposed a pagan Parnassus that would have appealed to Jung? One of his most haunting songs, *Strophe aus 'Die Götter Griechenlands'* D677, had bemoaned the end of the beautiful civilization which acknowledged the gods of Greece.

What is clear is that at any one time Schubert felt different things about the question of religion. At one moment he seems overcome by a musical feeling which we (and he) could only call devout; at others – as in the late cycles – he sees the world as a dark and unfriendly place where man can expect no redemption by divine intervention. Sometimes he seems happy to set to music conventional depictions of God's power and grace; at other times he is drawn to alternatives. It is clearly nonsense to put forward a case for a cheery composer comforted by church ritual, secure in his place in the divine order of things. He was far too metropolitan, his life too complicated, to embrace the unquestioning faith of his forebears. He had moments of real anger and bitterness associated with religion and its hypocrisies and false promises. The mortal blow of his illness, contracted in late 1822 or early 1823, must have affected his philosophical outlook on life. On the other hand, Schubert seems to have been too much of a mystic, and at heart too much of a life-embracing optimist, to enter the grimly nihilistic world of, say, Brahms's *Vier ernste Gesänge*, music that purports to be religious but which in fact uses biblical words to show the bleakness of the abyss into which that composer saw himself descending.

In Schubert's music we hear, time and time again, that there is nearly always a way out, an alternative enharmonic modulation to provide consolation. (It might be argued that *Winterreise* D911 is shocking because the accustomed Schubertian avenues of escape and redemption are denied us.) Robert R. Reilly avers that Mozart's music has a preternatural purity and perfection that somehow escapes the mark of original sin, a sign of life before the Fall and a promise of Paradise. He continues: 'Schubert's music communicates from the near side of that catastrophic divide. It is the songful lament of the wanderer who has been banished, yet who must find the difficult way back through suffering and death.' Thus a religious scholar perceives the music and the composer's struggle. And there is a side to the composer himself that believed this too, particularly when in desperate straits at the time of his illness. 'It sometimes seems to me', he said, 'as if I did not belong to this world at all.' On the other hand we must not mistake *Der Wanderer* D489 and *Winterreise* as being typical of the entire oeuvre; there is so much joy and promise in Schubert's music, such celebration of the here and now, so little self-pity and self-consciousness, such ineffable grace from we know not where. Or do we?

To say that Schubert 'sat on the fence' seems too inelegant a phrase for a metaphysical question. Throughout his music we hear the vocabulary of charming, and comforting, circumlocution, as if he is saying: 'On the other hand . . . think of it in *this* way.' And we are equally delighted with the alternative. The hedging of bets, in any case, is something typically, even deliciously, Viennese. Religious thought and speech came easily to Schubert; it was part of the language of his upbringing, and at times he reverted to this vocabulary of easy faith with the pleasure of someone coming home to something familiar. At other times he seemed angry and on fire, doubting and questioning like Goethe's Prometheus, making a stand as an angry young man, determined to find a new path for a new era. On occasion he was no doubt ready to denounce God and deny His very existence. (One has only to listen to the unaccompanied Seidl choral setting *Grab und Mond* D893 to hear this.) But whatever he said, and whatever he believed from time to time, he was always able to journey into musical realms that must have touched him, as they touch us, with the wing-tip of Paradise. We are also reminded of the Platonic ideal, the ascent towards divine perfection which Mayrhofer would have expounded to his young friend. If the determined accomplishment of this journey upwards and onwards is the mark of a religious man, then we can indeed answer the question which opened this essay with a resounding 'Yes'. There are few who have aspired to higher things than Franz Peter Seraphicus Schubert; and there are few who have been such unselfish guides, or who have helped so many others to take the first faltering steps on the same journey – wheresoever it may lead.

THE RELIGIOUS SONGS OF SCHUBERT IN THE CONTEXT OF HIS LITURGICAL WORKS[1]

1811–13

30 March 1811	**D5**	***Hagars Klage*** (Schücking). A poem derived from the biblical story of the bondwoman Hagar and Abraham's illegitimate son Ishmael (Genesis 16)
1811/12	**D6**	***Des Mädchens Klage*** (Schiller). A colloquy between the anguished maiden and the 'heavenly maiden' or Virgin Mary. The later setting of the same poem, D191 (15 May 1815), is better known, and there is a third setting D389 (March 1816)
1812?	D24E	Mass in F. Fragment; end of the Gloria and beginning of the Credo
28 June 1812	D27	*Salve Regina* in F
25 September 1812	D31	*Kyrie* for a Mass in D minor
September–October 1812	**D33**	***Entra l'uomo allor che nasce*** – the *Aria d'Abramo*. Composition exercises from Metastasio's *Isacco* (the biblical story of Abraham and Isaac)
1 March 1813	D45	*Kyrie* in B flat for chorus
15 April 1813	D49	*Kyrie* for a Mass in D minor
21 April 1813	D56	*Sanctus* canon for three voices
4 May 1813	**D59**	***Verklärung*** (Pope). Herder's translation of Pope's *The Dying Christian to his Soul*
12 May 1813	D66	*Kyrie* in F for chorus
July 1813(?)	D71A	*Alleluja* in F. Canon for three voices
22–3 August 1813	**D73**	***Thekla: eine Geisterstimme*** (Schiller). Wallenstein's daughter describes the beauty and security of the afterlife where she is reunited with her father. The second setting of *Thekla* **D595** dates from November 1817

1814

1814	D739	*Tantum ergo* in C for chorus, brass, timpani, strings, organ. Published as Op. 45 in 1825
17 May–22 July 1814	D105	Mass (No. 1) in F for soloists, chorus and orchestra
28 June–1 July 1814	D106	*Salve Regina* in B flat for tenor, strings, wind and organ
24/5 July 1814	D110	*Wer ist gross?* for bass, chorus, wind and strings
September(?) 1814	**D102**	***Die Betende*** (Matthisson). A depiction of Laura praying where her sighs are likened to Abel's sacrifice. 'To behold this saintly maid at prayer / Is to look into the world beyond'
2–7 October 1814	**D115**	***An Laura, als sie Klopstocks Auferstehungslied sang*** (Matthisson). The poet listens to Laura singing – the souls of angels must grow more beautiful; 'Heartless sinners beat their breasts / And pray like the seraph Abbadona'

[1] A title in bold type indicates a work that has a commentary in this book.

c. 1814	**D93**	***Don Gayseros*** (de la Motte Fouqué). 3 songs. A tiny song cycle concerning the conflict of the Christians and Muslims in medieval Spain. The devout Donna Clara is in love with a handsome soldier who eventually admits to being a Moorish prince. The text shows the dangers of rigid and dogmatic Christianity, and Donna Clara, who subjects Don Gayseros to an inquisition-like interrogation, is hardly depicted as a sympathetic character

1815

1815?	D136	*Offertorium* in C (*Totus in corde langueo*) for soprano, tenor, clarinet, wind, strings and organ. Published as 'Erstes Offertorium' Op. 46 in 1825
2 February 1815	**D151**	***Auf einen Kirchhof*** (Schlechta). The poet's mawkish graveside contemplations lead to the final rapturous 'What exalts and delights me / Is the pure spirit of the Godhead / Is his breath, which lives within me'
9 March 1815	D167	Mass (No. 2) in G major for soprano, tenor, bass, chorus, strings and organ. Schubert models the 'Benedictus' on the 'Mir ist so wunderbar' quartet from *Fidelio*, a sign that perhaps, in Leo Black's words, 'Schubert's religious thinking centred around music and its greatest exponents.' Or perhaps the quartet's words have been the inspiration: the awakening of love for another human being is a blessing, no matter what its painful circumstances
9 March 1815	**D168**	***Nun lasst uns den Leib begraben (Begräbnislied)*** (Klopstock) for SATB and piano. 'O Lord whose life was sacrificed! May your death / Strengthen us in our last agony; / May our soul be wholly yours, / And our end be joyful!'
9 March 1815	**D168A**	***Jesus Christus unser Heiland (Osterlied)*** (Klopstock), for SATB and piano: 'The son of God and man is arisen!'
12 March 1815	**D171**	***Gebet während der Schlacht*** (Körner) 'Father I praise You! . . . God I surrender myself to You! . . . Father I cry unto You!'
4/6 April 1815	D175	*Stabat Mater* in G minor for chorus, wind, brass, strings and organ
10/11 April 1815	D181	*Offertorium* in A minor (*Tres sunt, qui testimonium dant in coelo*) for chorus, wind, brass, strings and organ
15/17 April 1815	D184	*Graduale* in C (*Benedictus es, Domine*) for chorus, strings, brass, timpani and organ
May 1815	**D186**	***Die Sterbende*** (Matthisson). 'Already seraphim are weaving flowers of paradise / Into a wreath'
29 May–16 June 1815	**D208**	***Die Nonne*** (Hölty). A bloodthirsty tale about Belinda, a nun with a 'Latin temperament' who wreaks a horrible revenge on

the man who seduced her, then abandoned her. He had sworn his faithfulness to her 'by the image of the Virgin, / By this child Jesus' and thus a 'fair spotless bride of God / Fell prey to a sinner'

5 July 1815	D223	*Salve Regina (Offertorium)* in F for soprano, woodwind, strings and organ. In two versions: second version without woodwind. Published as 'Zweites Offertorium' Op. 47 in 1825
11 July 1815	**D232**	**Hymne an den Unendlichen** (Schiller) for SATB with piano. 'My gaze darts around giddily, / And I think of You, Eternal God . . . May the decent common worm know its God'
15 September 1815	**D291**	**Dem Unendlichen** (Klopstock). 'Lord God, no paeans of thanks are worthy of you'
15 September 1815(?)	D486	*Magnificat* in C for soloists, chorus, wind, brass, timpani, strings and organ
15 October 1815	**D307**	**Die Sternenwelten** (translated by Fellinger). The numberless stars 'proclaim widely the glory of God . . . this great universe proclaims / The hand of the sublime Architect'
Begun 11 November 1815	D324	Mass (No. 3) in B flat for soprano, alto, tenor, bass, chorus, wind, brass, strings, timpani and organ

1816

21 February 1816	D379	*Deutsches Salve Regina* in F for chorus and organ. Unknown poet of German words
Begun 28 February 1816	D383	*Stabat Mater (Jesus Christus schwebt am Kreuze).* Oratorio for soloists, chorus and orchestra, text by Klopstock
Beginning of 1816	D386	*Salve Regina* in B flat for chorus
June 1816	D440	*Chor der Engel* (Goethe, from *Faust*) for chorus (SATB). 'Christ ist erstanden!' ('Christ is risen!')
June 1816	**D442**	**Das grosse Halleluja** (Klopstock) for single voice or chorus with piano. 'Glory to the Exalted One, the First, the Father of Creation'
June 1816	**D444**	**Die Gestirne** (Klopstock). 'Field and forest, valley and mountain sound his praise . . . the Infinite Being, the Glorious One'
June 1816	**D448**	**Gott im Frühlinge** (Uz). 'Birds, with the sweet notes of your songs, / Let my songs also / Soar up to the Father of nature . . . I will sing praises to the Lord / Who made me what I am'
June 1816	**D449**	**Der gute Hirt** (Uz). 'Why are you troubled? Be calm my soul! / For God is a good shepherd'
June/July 1816	D452	Mass (No. 4) in C for soloists, chorus, strings and organ (wind, brass ad libitum). Published as Op. 48 in 1825

July 1816	D453	*Requiem* in C minor. Fragment from *Introitus and Kyrie*. For chorus and orchestra
August 1816	**D343**	***Am Tage aller Seelen (Litanei)*** (Jacobi). 'May all souls rest in peace . . . So that they might one day see God face to face / In the pure light of heaven'
August 1816	D460	*Tantum ergo* in C for soprano solo, chorus, wind, brass, strings and organ
August 1816	D461	*Tantum ergo* in C for soprano, alto, tenor, bass and chorus. Instrumental forces as for D460
October 1816	D488	*Auguste jam coelestium.* Duet for soprano and tenor with orchestra
1816(?) (date unknown)	**D985**	***Gott im Ungewitter*** (qv). Quartet (SATB) with piano. 'Almighty and terrible One, who can stand before You / And Thy thunder?'
1816(?) (date unknown)	**D986**	***Gott der Weltschöpfer*** (Uz). Quartet (SATB) with piano. 'To him source of all beings / Let all beings give praise.'

1817

| April 1817 | **D551** | ***Pax vobiscum*** (Schober). 'Lit by the rays of the triumphant Godhead / You soared to the eternal homeland . . . I believe in You, Almighty God!' |
| May 1817 | **D564** | ***Gretchen im Zwinger (Gretchens Bitte)*** *'Ach neige, du Schmerzensreiche'* (Goethe, from *Faust*). Gretchen's anguished prayer to the Madonna: 'You who are laden with sorrow, / Incline your face graciously / To my distress' |

1818

Spring 1818	**D607**	***Evangelium Johannis*** (New Testament, John 6:53–8). Song with figured bass. 'He that eateth of this bread will live forever'
August 1818	D621	*Deutsches Requiem* in G minor
August 1818	**D623**	***Das Marienbild*** (Schreiber). A devout address to a wayside shrine of the Virgin Mary: 'Hail to thee, Lady of Grace'
September 1818	**D626**	***Blondel zu Marien*** (Anon.). The background to this is not clear. Blondel (almost certainly Richard Coeur de Lion's minstrel) sings a song of devotion to Maria. This is almost certainly the Virgin who has protected him during his quest to find his master
December 1818	**D632**	***Vom Mitleiden Mariä*** (Friedrich von Schlegel). 'As Mary stood by the Cross . . . all Christ's suffering / Was impressed upon her heart'

1819

February 1819	**D650**	*Abendbilder* (Silbert). 'Rest beloved ones from your cares, / Until, at the Great Resurrection, / God in his might / Calls us from the night / to eternal bliss On high'
February 1819	**D651**	*Himmelsfunken* (Silbert). 'The orphan heart . . . longs to return home / To the Father, its Creator'
May(?) 1819	**D658**	*Geistliches Lied (Marie)* (Novalis). 'I see you in a thousand pictures, / Mary, sweetly portrayed; / Yet none of them can depict you / As my soul has seen you'
May 1819	**D659–D662**	*Geistliche Lieder (Hymne I, Hymne II, Hymne III, Hymne IV)* (Novalis)
June 1819	**D663**	*Der 13. Psalm* (The Old Testament, translated by Moses Mendelssohn). 'How long wilt thou forget me, O Lord? . . . I will sing unto the Lord, because he hath dealt bountifully with me'
October 1819	**D674**	*Prometheus* (Goethe). This is hardly a religious song as such, but it contains Goethe's veiled challenge to the concept of an Almighty creating power: 'I honour you? What for? / Have you ever eased the suffering / Of him who is oppressed?'
November 1819	D676	*Salve Regina (Offertorium)* in A for soprano and strings

1820

January 1820	**D687**	*Nachthymne* (Novalis). The charged poetry of Novalis provides a highly personal interpretation of Catholic mysticism from a non-Catholic.
November 1819–September 1822	D678	Mass (No. 5) in A flat for soloists, chorus, wind, brass, strings, timpani and organ
February 1820	D689	*Lazarus, oder Die Feier der Auferstehung* (August Hermann Niemayer) – *Szenisches Oratorium* for three soprano soloists, two tenors and a bass, chorus, woodwind, brass and strings (fragment; first act complete and only part of second)
Written for 26 March 1820	D696	*Sechs Antiphonen zum Palmsonntag* for chorus (SATB)
November 1820	**D702**	*Der Jüngling auf dem Hügel* (Heinrich Hüttenbrenner). 'The youth ceased lamenting, / And his eyes were fixed in prayer . . . He read in those stars high above / A message of hope'
December 1820	**D706**	*Der 23. Psalm* (The Old Testament, translated by Moses Mendelssohn) for quartet of female voices (SSAA). 'The Lord is my shepherd, I shall not want'

1821

March 1821	**D716**	*Grenzen der Menschheit* (Goethe). Goethe's imposing poem about what distinguishes gods (and thus by implication God) from men . . . 'For no mortal / Shall measure himself / Against the gods'

16 August 1821	D730	*Tantum ergo* in B flat for soloists, chorus, woodwind, brass, timpani, strings and organ

1822

20 March 1822	D750	*Tantum ergo* in D for chorus, woodwind, brass, timpani, strings and organ
May 1822	D755	*Kyrie* for a Mass in A minor – sketch, for soloists, chorus, strings and organ
August 1822	**D757**	***Gott in der Natur*** (Kleist) for quartet (SSAA) and piano. 'Great is the Lord! / The dawn is but a reflection / Of the hem of his garment'
November 1822	**D762**	***Schwestergruss*** (Bruchmann). The poet communes with the ghost of his sister. She tells him to relinquish the gods of this earth and floats up to the choir of angels. The narrator concludes: 'Night veils / The holy place; / Filled with God, / I sing the Word'
22 November 1822	**D763**	***Schicksalslenker, blicke nieder*** (unknown author) for quartet (SATB) and piano. ('Des Tages Weihe') 'Through the mists shines the immeasurable radiance / Of your greatness'

1824

April 1824	D811	*Salve Regina* in C for quartet (TTBB)
September 1824	**D815**	***Gebet*** (de la Motte Fouqué). Quartet (SATB) with piano. 'Primal source of all goodness, / Primal source of all might!'

1825

Early 1825	**D799**	***Im Abendrot*** (Lappe). 'How lovely is your world, / Father, in its golden radiance'
Early 1825	**D828**	***Die junge Nonne*** (Craigher). 'I wait, my Saviour, with longing gaze! / Come, heavenly bridegroom, take your bride'
April 1825	**D839**	***Ellens Gesang III (Ave Maria)*** (Walter Scott translated by Adam Storck) (qv *Sieben Gesänge aus Walter Scott's Fräulein vom See*). 'Ave Maria! Maiden Mild! / Listen to a maiden's entreaty'
August 1825	**D852**	***Die Allmacht*** (Pyrker). 'Great is Jehovah the Lord! For heaven and earth proclaim / His might' **D875A** is an incomplete choral setting of the same poem for SATB and piano

1826

1826?	**D871**	***Das Zügenglöcklein*** (Seidl). The passing bell tolls for those who have just died. 'Though he gladly rang the bell / He trembles on the threshold / When a voice cries "Enter".'

1827

| Summer or early autumn 1827 | D872 | *Deutsche Messe* (Johann Philipp Neumann) for chorus (SATB) in versions with organ accompaniment, and also with orchestra. |
| November 1827 | **D932** | *Der Kreuzzug* (Leitner). 'A monk stands in his cell . . . Life's journey through the treacherous waves / And burning desert sands / Is also a crusade / Into the promised land' |

1828

March 1828	**D942**	*Mirjams Siegesgesang* (Grillparzer). Cantata for solo soprano, chorus (SATB) and piano. Grillparzer's poem is based on the episode of the Israelites' flight from Egypt. 'And Miriam the prophetess, the sister of Aaron, took a timbrel in her hand; and all the women went after her with timbrels and with dances. And Miriam answered them, Sing ye to the Lord, for He hath triumphed gloriously; the horse and his rider hath He thrown into the sea' (Exodus 15:20–21)
May 1828	D948	*Hymnus an den Heiligen Geist* (Schmidl) for men's solo quartet (TTBB) in two versions, one unaccompanied and one with woodwind and brass instruments
Begun June 1828	D950	Mass (No. 6) in E flat for soloists, chorus, woodwind, brass, timpani and strings
July 1828	**D953**	*Der 92. Psalm* (Old Testament, Psalm 92:2–9). In Hebrew, for baritone solo, quartet (SATB) and chorus
August 1828	**D955**	*Glaube, Hoffnung und Liebe* (Kuffner). 'Have faith, hope and love! . . . Have steadfast faith in God and in your heart!'
Before 2 September 1828	**D954**	*Glaube, Hoffnung und Liebe* (Reil) for quartet (TTBB) and chorus (SATB) with winds. Written for the consecration of the bells in the Dreifaltigkeitskirche in Vienna
October 1828	D961	*Benedictus*, a replacement movement for the Benedictus of the Mass in C major D452
October 1828	D962	*Tantum ergo* in E flat for soloists and chorus with woodwind, brass, timpani and strings
October 1828	D963	*Tenor-Arie mit Chor* (*Intende voci*) for tenor, chorus, woodwind, brass and strings. The text of this is from Psalm 5: 'Hearken unto the voice of my cry, my King and my God'

~~~~~~~~~~~~~~~~

(HEINRICH FRIEDRICH) LUDWIG RELLSTAB (1799–1860)

THE POETIC SOURCE
S1 *Gedichte*, Erstes Bändchen, Laue, Berlin, 1827

S2 *Gedichte von Ludwig Rellstab*, Leipzig, F.A. Brockhaus, 1844. (*Gesammelte Schriften*, Band XII)

Schubert's source for his setting of the Rellstab poems was doubtless handwritten copies; according to Anton Schindler these had been in the possession of Beethoven until his death. A subsection of Rellstab's *Gedichte* is entitled *Lieder* (from p. 77 of the 1844 edition). All but one of the poems that Schubert set are to be found in this part of the collection. But it is interesting that the poet divides the *Lieder* into a 'Liederkranz' (his own suggestion for a song cycle sequence) and single songs ('Einzelne' from p. 84) which he did not consider to be thematically connected in any way. How little Schubert regarded this ordering and these divisions (if he had any idea of them; it is almost certain he encountered these poems in manuscript before Rellstab had arranged them for publication) is evident from the following list of the published sequence. This is also an interesting insight into a number of songs that may have been part of Schindler's consignment to Schubert, and which were set aside by him as unsuitable for music (perhaps because they did not conform to the 'An die ferne Geliebte' theme that was arguably at the back of Schubert's mind when he composed them).

Liederkranz:
Sehnsucht, Verlangen, Bewusstsein, Ständchen (D957/4), *Liebesbotschaft* (D957/1), *Kriegers Ahnung* (D957/2), *Herbst* (D945), *Trost*.
Einzelne:
Frühlingswonne, Mailied, Frühlingsheimweh, Frühlingssehnsucht (D957/3), *Sehnsüchtiges Beneiden, In der Ferne* (D957/6), *Auf dem Strom* (D943), *Veilchen und Astern, Aufenthalt* (D957/5), *Die Verbundenen, Abbitte, An den Mond, Alpenvergissmeinnicht, Abschied* (D957/7)

The song *Lebensmut* (D937) is the only text that is not part of the 'Lieder' section of the book. It appears as part of the group entitled *Gesellige* that appears at the beginning of the collection.

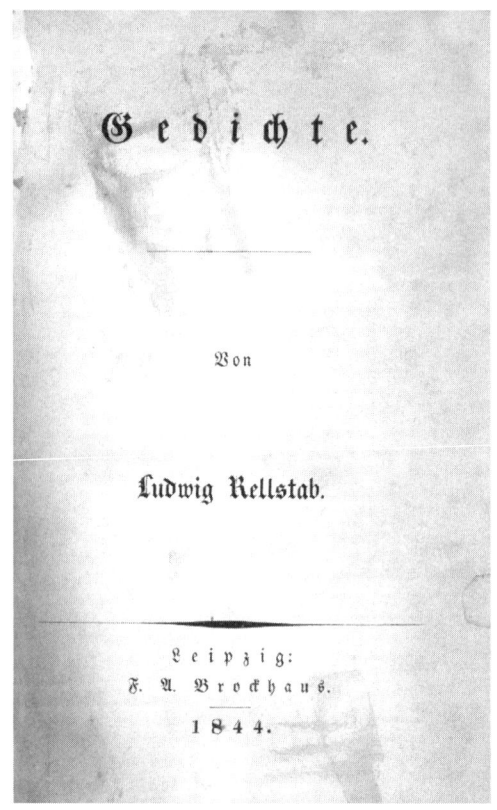

Ludwig Rellstab's *Gedichte* (1844).

THE SONGS
1827 or 1828   *Lebensmut* D937 [S2: 'Gesellige' p. 12]

March 1828   *Auf dem Strom* D943 [S1: p. 120] [S2: Lieder: 'Einzelne' pp. 91–2]

April 1828   *Herbst* D945 [S1: p. 106] [S2: Lieder: 'Liederkranz' p. 82]

August 1828   *SCHWANENGESANG* D957/1–7

    Liebesbotschaft D957/1 [S1: p. 103] [S2: Lieder: 'Liederkranz' p. 80]

    Kriegers Ahnung D957/2 [S1: p. 105] [S2: Lieder: 'Liederkranz' p. 81]

    *Frühlingssehnsuch*t D957/3 [S1: p. 114] [S2: Lieder: 'Einzelne' p. 87–8]

    Ständchen D957/4 [S1: p. 101] [S2: Lieder: 'Liederkranz' p. 79]

    Aufenthalt D957/5 [S1: p. 124] [S2: Lieder: 'Einzelne' p. 94]

    In der Ferne D957/6 [S1: p. 118] [S2: Lieder: 'Einzelne' p. 90]

    Abschied D957/7 [S1: p. 134] [S2: Lieder: 'Einzelnes' pp. 101–2]

Ludwig Rellstab was born in Berlin on 13 April 1799 to a family that was originally from Switzerland. It is interesting to note that he was only twenty-nine when Schubert set his poems, and the astonishingly rapid advance of his career and spread of his influence as a critic was to do with having been born with a musical silver spoon in his mouth. His father, Johann Carl Friedrich Rellstab (1759–1813) was an accomplished composer, pianist and prominent music publisher, intimately connected with every aspect of Prussian musical life. Ludwig's sister Caroline (1786–1814) died young after a distinguished singing career and his cousin was a well-known poet, Wilhelm Häring, 1798–1871, who wrote under the pseudonym of Willibald Alexis. As a boy Rellstab, following in his father's footsteps, performed piano concertos by Mozart and Bach. He was taught by two distinguished composers, both pioneers of the Berlin school of Lieder composition – Ludwig Berger (1777–1839) (who also taught Mendelssohn and was the first to set Müller's *Die schöne Müllerin* texts) and Bernhard Klein (1793–1832). During the upheavals of his youth Rellstab volunteered for the army but was rejected on grounds of weak eyesight. He nevertheless entered military service with a desk job, remaining there until 1821 as a teacher of mathematics and history.

A combined interest in the arts and sciences stood him in good stead as a journalist for the celebrated *Vossische Zeitung* where his knowledge of music, and his readiness to express a strong opinion on almost anything, formed the basis of his enormous reputation as a critic. He became a real celebrity in Berlin as a result of his outspoken writing, giving rise to the saying among his acquaintances that 'a true Berliner only believes in the correctness of his own hard-won opinions once they have been confirmed for him by Rellstab'. In journalistic terms he captured the brusque and controversial aspect of Berlin and its inhabitants, that genial rudeness, blunt and outspoken, that remains an abiding characteristic of the city. *Henriette, oder die schöne Sängerin*, a roman-à-clef (published under the evocative pseudonym of Freimund Zuschauer) featured the soprano Henriette Sontag so thinly disguised that Rellstab's scurrility earned him six months in prison for libel. Some years later (1837) he was imprisoned for six weeks as a result of his campaign against the overweening influence of Berlin's *Generalmusikdirektor*, Gaspare Spontini. Many people on the musical scene today would recognize the eternal phenomenon of the meddling journalist, not exactly fearless but with a nose for scandal, who likes nothing better for their own amusement than to stir up the various factions that live within the rather small pond within which they assume the role of big fish and arbiter. On the more positive side, it might be said that Rellstab was one of the founders of that great European journalistic tradition, the feuilleton.

Rellstab travelled throughout Germany, meeting Weber and Tieck, Jean Paul, Hebel and Goethe. Like a great many men who enjoy success early in life, he remained stuck in his glory days. In 1825 he visited Vienna and made contact with Beethoven. (It was Rellstab's critique of Beethoven's Piano Sonata Op. 27 no. 2 that led to the work being nicknamed 'The Moonlight'.) The poet's posthumously published autobiography *Aus meinem Leben* (1861) ends with a poignant chapter (whether true or accurate is open to question) where Beethoven comes across as a great human being as well as artist, genuinely interested in the poet's work, gravely encouraging, and noble in every aspect (cf. the similarly unsubstantiated pen-portrait of Beethoven by Rellstab's rival critic from Leipzig, Friedrich Rochlitz). Rellstab had hoped to interest the composer in an operatic libretto and although this mission failed, a letter Beethoven wrote to him on 3 May of that year, ending 'Think of me when writing your poems' (quoted in the poet's *Garten und Wald*, 1854), had far-reaching consequences. He seems to have exactly followed Beethoven's advice hence the consignment of poems sent for setting to Beethoven in 1827 or earlier. It was these poems which, according to Schindler, were handed on to Schubert.

Despite his appearance of being a fighter for modern causes, Rellstab was, on the whole, a conservative who resisted the success of the later Romantics. Weber was his idea of a modern composer. Mendelssohn, whom he heard playing for Goethe in Weimar (the great old poet was unencouraging about Rellstab's work), represented the chronological limit of Rellstab's sympathies. Composers such as Chopin and Schumann were weighed in the balance and found wanting. Schumann as a critic had welcomed Chopin's variations on a theme from Mozart's *Don Giovanni* with the words 'Hats off, gentlemen, a genius!', whereas Rellstab, in his review of the same piece, ill-naturedly contended that such violence to Mozart's genius was typical of Slavic barbarity. Liszt (who set some of Rellstab's poems) was excused his venom, and his later relationship with Meyerbeer was less a result of musical sympathy than of business acumen; the poet was a busy translator of that composer's libretti when they found an enormous vogue in

Ludwig Rellstab, engraving by A. Weger after a photograph.

German houses. Rellstab divided composers into two classes: his premier league included Bach, Handel, Gluck, Haydn, Mozart and Beethoven; the best of the also-rans were Cherubini, Spohr, Weber, Mendelssohn and his two teachers Berger and Klein, the former the subject of an appreciative monograph, *Ludwig Berger. Ein Denkmal*, 1846. In the midst of his musical work and writings Rellstab wrote a great deal else, including the highly successful historical novel *1812. Ein historischer Roman* (1834), a minor forerunner of *War and Peace* (and from which Berger set a poem, *Lied aus '1812'*), a guide to the topographical beauties of Berlin, and a collection of stories entitled *Sommerfrüchte*.

Rellstab reviewed Schubert's Ossian settings and *Der Hirt auf dem Felsen* D965 in November 1830 with a condescending tin ear but he never directly commented on Schubert's settings of his own poems. In his lengthy survey of the state of music in Germany (*Über den Zustand der Musik in Deutschland*), published in the *Deutsches Taschenbuch auf das Jahr 1838* – nine years after the publication of *Schwanengesang* – Rellstab devotes only a short paragraph to the composer who would assure his continuing relevance to music lovers: 'Franz Schubert (auch als Balladen-Componist ausgezeichnet) ist höchst eigentümlich in Quartetstil, wenngleich mitunter krankhaft. Seine Arbeiten kommen erst jetzt, nach seinem Tode, in Schwung.' [Franz Schubert (also known as an acclaimed composer of ballads) has a highly individualistic, albeit an occasionally rather morbid style of quartet writing. It is only now, after his death, that his works are beginning to be appreciated.] This damning with faint praise seems to be a classic case of a critic hedging his bets. A few years later, in 1841, he visited Schubert's grave in the Währing cemetery, writing a few complimentary – if patronizing – words, an accolade of the kind reserved at the time for women composers, or mere writers of songs. Rellstab little realized that his creative writing (as opposed to his more significant work as a critic) would take on a degree of immortality thanks only to his connection to Schubert's *Schwanengesang*. He died on 28 November 1860, some thirty-two years after the composer who had been only two years his senior. Rellstab's memoirs, *Aus meinem Leben*, appeared posthumously in 1861.

RIEN DE LA NATURE *see ECHO ET NARCISSE* D ANHANG IIA

RITTER TOGGENBURG
(SCHILLER) **D397** [H232]

The knight of Toggenburg

The song exists in two versions, the first of which is discussed below:
(1) 13 March 1816; (2) Authenticity of this version not fully determined

(1)   F major – B♭ minor

(119 bars)

(2)   'Ruhig'   E♭ major – A♭ major   ¢   [137 bars]

(1)   'Ritter, treue Schwesterliebe
     Widmet euch dies Herz,
   Fordert keine andre Liebe,
     Denn es macht mir Schmerz.
   Ruhig mag ich euch erscheinen,
     Ruhig gehen sehn;
   Eurer Augen stilles Weinen
     Kann ich nicht verstehn.'

'Knight, this heart dedicates to you
   True sisterly love;
Demand no other love,
   For that grieves me.
I would wish to appear calm to you
   And calmly to see you leave.
I cannot understand
   The silent tears in your eyes.'

(2)   Und er hört's mit stummem Harme,
     Reisst sich blutend los,
   Presst sie heftig in die Arme,
     Schwingt sich auf sein Ross,
   Schickt zu seinen Mannen allen
     In dem Lande Schweiz;
   Nach dem heil'gen Grab sie wallen,

     Auf der Brust das Kreuz.

And he listened with silent sorrow
   Tore himself away in anguish,
Pressed her violently in his arms,
   Jumped on his horse
And sent word to all his men
   In the country of Switzerland.
They were to make a pilgrimage to the holy
   sepulchre,
   The cross on their breasts.

(3)   Grosse Taten dort geschehen
     Durch der Helden Arm,
   Ihres Helmes Büsche wehen
     In der Feinde Schwarm,
   Und des Toggenburgers Name
     Schreckt den Muselmann,
   Doch das Herz von seinem Grame
     Nicht genesen kann.

Great deeds were accomplished there
   By the heroes' might;
The plumes on their helmets
   Fluttered amid the teeming foe,
And the name of Toggenburg
   Terrified the Mussulman,
But his heart could not be cured
   Of its grief.

(4)   Und ein Jahr hat er's ertragen,
     Trägt's nicht länger mehr,
   Ruhe kann er nicht erjagen
     Und verlässt das Heer,
   Sieht ein Schiff an Joppes Strande,
     Das die Segel bläht,
   Schiffet heim zum teuren Lande,
     Wo ihr Atem weht.

When he had endured it for one year
   He could endure it no longer;
He could gain no peace,
   And left his army.
He saw a ship on the shore at Joppa,
   Its sails billowing,
And sailed home to the beloved land
   Where she breathed.

(5)   Und an ihres Schlosses Pforte
     Klopft der Pilger an,
   Ach! und mit dem Donnerworte
     Wird sie aufgetan:
   'Die ihr suchet, trägt den Schleier,
     Ist des Himmels Braut,
   Gestern war des Tages Feier,
     Der sie Gott getraut.'

And the pilgrim knocked
   At the gate of her castle.
Alas, it was opened
   With these shattering words:
'She whom you seek wears the veil;
   She is a bride of heaven.
Yesterday was the day of the ceremony
   That wedded her to God.'

(6)   Da verlässet er auf immer
     Seiner Väter Schloss,
   Seine Waffen sieht er nimmer,
     Noch sein treues Ross,

Thereupon he left
   The castle of his fathers for ever.
He never again saw his weapons
   Or his trusty steed.

Von der Toggenburg hernieder
  Steigt er unbekannt,
Denn es deckt die edeln Glieder
  Härenes Gewand.

He descended from Toggenburg
  Unrecognized,
For a hair shirt
  Covered his noble limbs.

(7) Und erbaut sich eine Hütte
  Jener Gegend nah,
Wo das Kloster aus der Mitte
  Düstrer Linden sah;
Harrend von des Morgens Lichte
  Bis zu Abends Schein,
Stille Hoffnung im Gesichte,
  Sass er da allein.

And he built himself a hut
  Near to the place
Where the convent looked out
  From amid sombre linden trees;
Waiting from the light of dawn
  To the glow of evening
With silent hope on his face,
  He sat there alone.

(8) Blickte nach dem Kloster drüben,
  Blickte stundenlang
Nach dem Fenster seiner Lieben,
  Bis das Fenster klang,
Bis die Liebliche sich zeigte,
  Bis das teure Bild
Sich ins Tal herunter neigte,
  Ruhig, engelmild.

He gazed across at the convent –
  Gazed for hours on end
At his beloved's window,
  Until a sound came from the window,
Until his sweetheart appeared;
  Until her dear form
Leant down towards the valley,
  Tranquil and as gentle as an angel.

(9) Und dann legt' er froh sich nieder,
  Schlief getröstet ein,
Still sich freuend, wenn es wieder
  Morgen würde sein.
Und so sass er viele Tage,
  Sass viel Jahre lang,
Harrend ohne Schmerz und Klage
  Bis das Fenster klang.

And then he lay down happily
  And fell asleep, comforted,
Silently looking forward to when
  It would be morning again.
Thus he sat for many days,
  For many long years,
Waiting without sorrow or complaint
  Until the window rattled.

(10) Bis die Liebliche sich zeigte,
  Bis das teure Bild
Sich ins Tal herunter neigte,
  Ruhig, engelmild,
Und so sass er, eine Leiche,
  Eines Morgens da,
Nach dem Fenster noch das bleiche
  Stille Antlitz sah.

Until his sweetheart appeared,
  Until the dear form
Bent down towards the valley,
  Tranquil and gentle as an angel.
And thus he sat there one morning,
  A corpse,
His pale, silent face
  Still gazing at the window.

FRIEDRICH VON SCHILLER (1759–1805); poem completed 31 July 1797

This is the twenty-seventh of Schubert's forty-four Schiller solo settings (1811–24). See the poet's biography for a chronological list of all the Schiller settings.

1816 was very much a transitional time for Schubert. He had already written *Gretchen am Spinnrade* D118 and *Erlkönig* D328, in 1814 and 1815 respectively; but despite these masterpieces, and a number of others, he was not yet ready to abandon his teachers altogether. He lacked the inner confidence of a young Mozart or Beethoven and it is doubtful whether he yet considered himself to be in their league. Salieri had been his teacher until recently, and the celebratory music the younger composer wrote for the fiftieth anniversary of the Italian's arrival in Vienna (*Beitrag zur fünfzigjährigen Jubelfeier des Herrn von Salieri* D407) seems a step or two down from the exalted level of creation of which he had already shown himself capable. For that occasion, and in a spirit of deference, affection and respect, Schubert tailored his style to the occasion, providing music in which the composer of the two immortal Goethe settings named above is simply undetectable.

Zumsteeg was another of his teachers – neither officially nor in person, of course – and in 1816 the nineteen-year old was not yet ready to cut himself free from the Swabian composer's influence. *Ritter Toggenburg* is evidence of a continuing interest in the tradition of the ballad as pioneered by Zumsteeg, and of a certain judicious modesty on Schubert's part that the casual listener may find uninspiring. On the other hand it is the product of an important aspect of the composer's creative nature, the side that listened to others as carefully as he did his own inner voices. 1816 was a period of consolidation. In 1815 his dalliance with song and balladry had the hallmarks of a passionate affair. By 1816 he had settled down into what he knew would be a lifetime's working relationship; his love was no less intense, but it was more responsible and methodical, drawing more on what had gone before. Like the great craftsman that he was, Schubert used 1816 to review the foundations on which he would build his fame, the musical bricks and mortar of the strophic song as constructed by his musical forebears. The strength that lies at the heart of the seemingly simple songs of, for example, *Die schöne Müllerin*, here has its beginnings.

The Schubert ballad – spacious, reckless, sometimes unwieldy, but never less than fascinating – is essentially a phenomenon of the years 1811–15. From the beginning, Schiller was a favourite collaborator. To the dramatic poems of this great playwright we owe some of the most febrile achievements of the composer's youth: *Leichenfantasie* D7, *Der Taucher* D77, *Die Bürgschaft* D246 and so on. Very different from these works is *Die Erwartung* D159 (from the same poet) of May 1816, also influenced by Zumsteeg. *Ritter Toggenburg*, in its economy and lack of extravagance, is a work even more typical of 1816. In its extended static concluding section, a strophic song is welded to the preceding narrative to make a hybrid form unusual in Schubert's output.

The story of a gallant, yet hopeless, passion culminating in faithfulness unto death may have appealed to the composer in 1816 for personal reasons. He was in love with a sweet-voiced soprano in the Liechtental church choir, Therese Grob. Although the date of Schubert's parting from Therese is thought to have been towards the end of 1816, it is likely that the relationship, such as it was, had already run its course earlier in the year. Perhaps the composer saw his devotion as open-ended – that he could win Therese simply by waiting patiently for her like Ritter Toggenburg, despite all the financial difficulties that made their continuing relationship unlikely.

Verse 1: The poet gets straight to the heart of the matter with the words of the young girl (in inverted commas in the poem) whom Toggenburg passionately loves. She can offer him only a sister's affection in return. The key is F major and the music in flowing crotchets is gently tuneful and demure. This is a young lady who has already set her heart on a spiritual life. The music is an example of Schubert's medieval style: while there are no obvious musical archaisms (he reserved touches of learned contrapuntal style for his evocations of the seventeenth and eighteenth centuries), his use of restrained chorale, the equivalent perhaps of a musical fast or renunciation, suggests the epoch of the Crusades. The austerity of hymnody was as near as a nineteenth-century composer dared go to evoke the fourths and fifths of organum. (Informed time travel into the Middle Ages was to be an early twentieth-century speciality, as in the music of Debussy and Satie as well as passages in Pfitzner's *Palestrina*.) Schiller's text tells the story

Ritter Toggenberg, drawing and engraving by A. Müller, 1846.

with the minimum of fuss, and Schubert responds by making the pace of the action move faster than in many of his other ballads; only at the end of the piece does the logic of this become clear where the elongation of time provides the contrast to its former telescoping.

Verse 2: After only a crotchet rest, the music changes into D minor (from b. 18) and a gradual accelerando is indicated ('Mit steigender Bewegung') as the mood changes from serene inaction to the very opposite. Within the space of a few bars Toggenburg has torn himself away and is on his horse, set on deeds of derring-do. What the music lacks in depth it makes up for in breathless pace. Off-the-beat quavers (from b. 21) suggest a pulsating heart; a vocal line in crotchets doubled in both hands by the piano (at 'seinen Mannen', b. 26) paints the rallying of manly determination; and crotchets in alternate hands at 'Nach dem heil'gen Grab sie wallen' (from b. 29) a mixture of impatient energy and religious awe.

Verse 3: This verse is introduced by a short *Zwischenspiel* in the manner of a pilgrims' chorus (bb. 33–7), the basis for the musical setting of the following strophe. Here the music remains in austere crotchets and minims with a few enlivening details: a touch of chromatic colour at 'Ihres Helmes Büsche' (bb. 41–2) and a belligerent left-hand dotted flourish after 'In der Feinde Schwarm' (bb. 43–5), a motif found in other military songs like *Schlachtgesang* D443 or *Lied eines Kriegers* D822. The awe-inspiring effect of the Toggenburg name on the Muslims is emphasized by a vocal line doubled at the octave in both the pianist's hands (bb.45–9). Even if this pilgrims' chorus had derived from Zumsteeg's setting of the ballad, Schubert has made it his own. It is here that we realize that this work is prophetic of *Der Kreuzzug* D932, a Leitner setting that dates from 1827, or *Glaube, Hoffnung und Liebe* D955 from 1828. Even at the end of his life Schubert did not lose his taste for writing music that evoked German history or tradition in an idealized and romanticized fashion. This was perhaps one of Zumsteeg's lasting legacies. Schubert's final opera, the unfinished *Der Graf von Gleichen* D918, is further evidence of an abiding fascination with the medieval past.

Verse 4: The previous section ended in G minor. There is now a sudden change of mood and key. The rigorous crotchets that had cut the music vertically into sections are replaced by forward-moving quavers with a horizontal impetus. It is here that we realize that the whole of this piece is about the relative nature of time – how under some circumstances it drags and, at others, seems to slip away as one year melts into the next. The drooping elongated setting of 'ein Jahr' across two bars (bb. 55–6), and the similarly graphic stretching-out of 'ertragen' and 'länger' are subtle indications of Toggenburg's impatience. Once the knight has decided to leave his troops the music loses its grounded nobility and wanders chromatically – almost aimlessly – through various keys until it encounters a ship bound for home. At b. 67 there is a shift into B flat minor which soon changes into a more optimistic D flat major (from b. 70). If Toggenburg is not exactly piped aboard, the sailing of the homeward-bound vessel is ceremoniously launched by a repeated sequence of rising and falling thirds and sixths (bb. 70–4 and 76–8), reminiscent of Beethoven's motif of horn music in his 'Les Adieux' Sonata Op. 81a. This is not only a farewell to the East, it heralds the dawn of Toggenburg's hopes for a new life.

Verse 5: From b. 83 (marked 'Recit') the music moves swiftly between B flat minor and C major as a journey of many months is accomplished, door to door, in a matter of seconds, a cinematic transformation *avant la lettre*. After these few bars of recitative the poor man's hopes are crushed for ever. The stage is set for the return to the F major of the opening, and once more we hear the opening music of rebuff (marked 'Mässig' at 'Die ihr suchet, trägt den Schleier') that had sent Toggenburg away to the Crusades in the first place. This time the words are not even spoken by the girl herself: this is a message unemotionally delivered and apparently placidly received.

Ritter Toggenberg from Album für Deutschlands Töchter (1853).

In fact, the shock of this news has left him beyond tears, and the stage is now set for one of the strangest conclusions in all of Schubert's lieder.

Verses 6–10: At b. 96 the music, now marked 'Langsam', moves into triple time. A six-bar inter-lude of solemn music in mournful mezzo staccato crotchets effects a modulation from F major back to the elegiac B flat minor tonality that we had briefly visited earlier. The ballad now concludes with a strophic narrative describing the gradual demise of the patiently waiting knight. The fast pace of the earlier pages, where whole battles and long journeys are elided into the space of half a bar, is now replaced by a timeless loop retracing the non-events of Toggen-burg's vigil over a period of years. The music has a *bel canto* shapeliness about it, dignified and infinitely mournful, as befits self-effacing courtly love. There is a brief shift into D flat major (from b. 109) where we hear musical echoes in thirds and sixths of the knight's former voyages and exploits; these do not arise because of the text, but almost despite it. But we soon return to the dying fall of B flat minor, and once again we embark on music of strophic repetition.

Those who have criticized the seeming musical poverty of five unchanging verses have failed to appreciate the static and stoic nature of what is happening to Toggenburg. The music gains a hypnotic power with repetition; if the listener longs for something new, it only serves as reminder of the old warrior's endurance, and his self-appointed fate. It was of course Zumsteeg's discovery, not Schubert's, that strophic technique was ideal for this purpose but this hardly negates its value. The younger composer was rightly taken with the simplicity, as well as the novelty, of the idea. We have the evidence of Josef von Spaun, no less, that as early as 1811 Schubert was absorbed in the study of Zumsteeg's version of this very song:

> 'Listen', he said once, 'to the song I have here', and with a voice already half-breaking he sang Kolma; *then he showed me* Die Erwartung, Maria Stuart *and* Ritter Toggenburg; *he said that he could revel in these songs for days on end.*

It seems that during this period Zumsteeg was able to make time stand still for the young Schubert, as well as for Ritter Toggenburg himself.

In 2002 the NSA published another version of this ballad, a downward transposition into E flat major, although there are doubts concerning its authenticity. In the first version, the music for Verses 9 and 10 is identical, a strophic repeat in B flat minor. In the second there is a change for the final verse where the music is diverted into the major key (A flat in this case). This alters the mood considerably – the terms of Toggenburg's grim and faithful vigil until his death are softened and somehow made sentimental. But the tenderness of this metamorphosis is bought at a price regarding the seriousness of the whole. On these grounds alone one might question whether Schubert himself would ever have authorized this facile and rather banal adjustment.

Autograph:	Deutsche Grammophon Gesellschaft, Hamburg; on loan to Gesellschaft der Musikfreunde, Vienna
Publication:	First published as Book 19 no. 2 of the *Nachlass* by Diabelli, Vienna in October 1832 (P293; first version)
	First published as part of the NSA in 2002 (P828; second version)
Subsequent editions:	Peters: Vol. 5/103; AGA XX 191: Vol. 4/31; NSA IV: Vol. 10/75
Discography and timing:	Fischer-Dieskau —

Hyperion I 32[9]

Hyperion II 13[5]   8'09   Christoph Prégardien

← *Die vier Weltalter* D391   *Gruppe aus dem Tartarus* D396 →

〜〜〜〜〜〜〜

JOHANN FRIEDRICH ROCHLITZ (1769–1842)

THE POETIC SOURCES
S1 *Glycine* von Friedrich Rochlitz. Erster Theil. Mit Kupfern von Schnorr und Böhm, Züllichau und Freystadt bey Darmann, 1805

It is highly unlikely that Schubert set poems from this source. For *Klaglied* (entitled *Sehnsucht* in *Glycine*) it was more likely that he found a contemporary setting, such as that by Sigismund Neukomm, and modelled his own new song on the older work.

S2 *Auswahl des Besten aus Friedrich Rochlitz' sämmtlichen Schriften*. Vom Verfasser veranstaltet, verbessert und herausgegeben. In sechs Bänden. *Vierter Band*. Züllichau, in der Darmannschen Buchhandlung, 1822

The short section of this book entitled *Lyrische Gedichte* is from pp. 145–72. The much longer poem *Der erste Ton* that Rochlitz proposed to Schubert for setting (*see* below) appears in Volume 5 of this collection, pp. 199–202. In 1829 there was a Viennese reprint of these six volumes giving some indication of the author's fame.

THE SONGS
1812   *Klaglied* D23 [S1: pp. 213–14 where the title is *Sehnsucht*]

January 1827 *Zur guten Nacht* D903 [S2: pp. 171–2]
              Alinde D904 [S1: pp. 223–4; S2: pp. 153–4]
              An die Laute D905 [S1: p. 235; S2: p. 163]

The position of revered critic that Ludwig Rellstab occupied in Berlin belonged in Leipzig to the older and more conservative Friedrich Rochlitz. He was born in that city on 12 February 1769 and was educated at the Thomasschule where he was a choirboy. His musical education, in the tradition of Bach, made him one of the first journalists to ponder the lives of creators and composers with any sense of wonder (as well as envy). He was not only a well-known novelist, poet, librettist and playwright but the founder and editor of the *Allgemeine Musikalische Zeitung* of Leipzig from 1798 to 1818; in this period-ical Schubert's music received more favour-able reviews than anywhere else. Rochlitz had an exceptionally good relationship and long correspondence with Goethe who arranged for the poet-critic to be named *Hofrat* at Weimar in 1800 at the age of thirty-one. In 1816 Goethe expressed his admiration for Rochlitz's *Tage der Gefahr* (Days of danger) – an autobiographical account of the Battle of Leipzig three years earlier.

Rochlitz's relationship with Beethoven was more contentious. Beethoven had long been wary of a critic who was in charge of a publica-tion that had given him somewhat mixed reviews. According to Rochlitz they met in 1822 when Rochlitz spent May to August in Vienna. Two weeks after his first brief and unsuccessful encounter with Beethoven, Rochlitz apparently bumped into 'a young composer' on a street corner on 9 July and enlisted his help in finding out when and where the great man dined. The story, initially in a letter to his wife, is recounted again in Volume 4 of the second edition of *Für Freunde der Tonkunst* (1832) where Schubert's name is mentioned for the first time. It does not ring true (as the egocentric Rochlitz claimed) that Schubert (if it were he) had already heard about the poet's visit to Vienna from Beethoven's own lips. Indeed, this piece of embroidery casts into doubt the veracity of much else that follows. At first Rochlitz (there is no further mention of Schubert) sat apart from Beethoven's table (where the composer was sitting with friends) and overheard his pro-English and anti-French monologue. A tête-à-tête followed (with the help of a slate) and then a further meeting in Baden outside Vienna. Rochlitz produced an elegant pen-portrait of the composer as an eccentric but amiable and good-hearted bear. Much later Beethoven mentioned Rochlitz as a possible biographer.

In 1826 Ignaz von Mosel sent some Schubert songs to Rochlitz in Leipzig who replied in positive terms ('highly interesting and estimable'). And yet he could not resist striking that omniscient attitude vis-à-vis an artist, belittling him in the process that seems sometimes to be the preserve of the senior critic. He wrote to Mosel that Schubert needed guidance in order to make something of himself – the implication being that if Rochlitz were in Vienna it would be a simple matter for him to steer the poor young composer in the right direction. Schubert, as was his wont, had little interest in currying favour with powerful individuals, and it is probable that Tobias Haslinger had to push him into writing the three Rochlitz songs (*Alinde* D904, *An die Laute* D905 and *Zur guten Nacht* D903). These were composed

at the beginning of 1827 and rushed into print by May of the same year as Op. 81, with a dedication to the poet from the publisher. This is some indication of the esteem in which Rochlitz was held by those in the musical world who were mindful of their sales.

Rochlitz received the consignment with approval but now, wishing to link his own literary production even closer to that of the composer, went on to propose one of his own texts – *Der erste Ton* – to Schubert, not for musical setting as such but for an orchestrally accompanied melodrama (so as not to resemble Haydn's *Die Schöpfung*, the snag Beethoven had identified when turning down the idea) to be declaimed by the famous actor Anschütz. After insisting that he did not wish to influence Schubert unduly, Rochlitz proceeded to provide a map for the composition in a flurry of musical back-seat driving in one of the most foolish letters in the Schubert documents: 'Overture: a single short, plucked chord, *ff*, and then a note sustained for as long as possible, [here he writes a 'hairpin' symbol for cresc. and symbol for decresc.] for clarinet or horn with a pause. Now a soft opening, darkly inter-

The first of the six volumes of *Auswahl des Besten aus Friedrich Rochlitz' sämmtlichen Schriften* (Selection from the best of Rochlitz's collected writings) (1821). The frontispiece portrait of Rochlitz is an engraving by Böhm of a painting by Schnorr von Carolsfeld.

twined, harmonically rather than melodically...' This directorial advice went on for a further twenty-two lines. Curiously enough, when replying to this letter of 7 November 1827, Schubert made no reference to a former meeting. He declined firmly, saying that melodramas were old-fashioned and that he was only interested in setting words to music to be sung (not strictly true as his interest in operatic melodrama shows). He offered to set part of the poem to music if Rochlitz were agreeable, but only by cutting its first thirty-four lines. The poet, and he thought of himself seriously as such, would have been horrified by such lese-majesty. At the age of fifty-one, he had published no less than six volumes of prose, poetry and critcism as merely a 'selection from the best' of his writings. That Carl Maria von Weber had already set *Der erste Ton* as a melodrama in 1808 might not have been lost on Schubert; having fallen out with Weber, perhaps this made him even less likely to collaborate on such a project. The incident also reinforces the impression of Rochlitz as something of a gatherer of celebrities when it came to composers setting his words.

Schubert's frank response to Rochlitz shows how little he cared towards the end of his life for the useful (and traditionally Viennese) arts of flattery and political opportunism. Rellstab and Rochlitz were the two wordsmiths who owed their inclusion in the composer's mature canon to the fact that they were musical journalists rather than poets *pur sang*. It is unlikely that either would have attracted Schubert's attention on their poetic merit alone. On the other hand, it was foolish for any composer hoping to make a reputation in Germany to offend Rochlitz; the critic must have been extremely miffed with Schubert who was clearly insufficiently grateful for the support he had hitherto received from the *Allgemeine musikalische Zeitung*. Rochlitz died on 16 December 1842, having seen Schubert's music posthumously praised to the skies by his replacement as Leipzig's foremost critic, Robert Schumann, and this in a new journal, the *Neue Zeitschrift für Musik*.

Bibliography: Clive 1997, pp. 166–7
                Stephanie Steiner, *Liedlexikon*, p. 857

ROMANZE   Romance
(MATTHISSON) **D114** [H43]

The song exists in two versions, the second of which is discussed below:
(1) (Fragment) September 1814; (2) 29 September 1814

(1)   'Ziemlich langsam'   G minor   §   [107 bars]

(2)   G minor

(113 bars)

(1)   Ein Fräulein klagt' im finstern Turm,   A maiden wept in a dark tower
      Am Seegestad erbaut.   built on the sea shore.
      Es rauscht' und heulte Wog und Sturm   Waves and storm rushed and howled
      In ihres Jammers Laut.   Through her cries of grief.

(2)   Rosalia von Montanvert   Rosalie of Montanvert
      Hiess manchem Troubadour,   Was, for many a troubadour
      Und einem ganzen Ritterheer   And a whole host of knights
      Die Krone der Natur.   The crown of nature.

(3)   Doch ehe noch ihr Herz die Macht   But before her heart
      Der süssen Minn' empfand,   Had felt the power of sweet love,
      Erlag der Vater in der Schlacht   Her father died in battle
      Am Sarazenenstrand.   On the Saracen shore.

(4)   Der Ohm, ein Ritter Manfry, ward   Her uncle, a knight named Manfry,
      Zum Schirmvogt ihr bestellt;   Was appointed her guardian;
      Dem lacht' ins Herz, wie Felsen hart,   In his rock-hard heart, he rejoiced
      Des Fräuleins Gut und Geld.   At the maiden's gold and wealth.

(5)   Bald überall im Lande ging   Soon the sorrowful news
      Die Trauerkund' umher: Spread throughout the land:
      'Des Todes kalte Nacht empfing[1]   'The cold night of death has enveloped
      Die Rose Montanvert.'[2]   Rose Montanvert.'

(6)   Ein schwarzes Totenfähnlein wallt   A black flag of death flew
      Hoch auf des Fräuleins Burg;   High over the maiden's castle:
      Die dumpfe Leichenglocke schallt   The muffled death-knell sounded
      Drei Tag' und Nächt' hindurch.   For three days and three nights.

(7)   Auf ewig hin, auf ewig tot,   Gone for ever, dead for ever,
      O Rose Montanvert!   O Rose Montanvert!
      Nun milderst du der Witwe Not,   No longer will you soothe the widow's distress,
      Der Waise Schmerz nicht mehr!   The orphan's sorrow.

(8)   So klagt einmütig Alt und Jung,   Thus, from dawn till dusk
      Den Blick von Tränen schwer,   Their eyes heavy with tears,
      Vom Frührot bis zur Dämmerung,   Young and old with one voice
      Die Rose Montanvert.   Mourned Rose Montanvert.

(9)   Der Ohm in einem Turm sie barg,   Her uncle hid her in a tower,
      Erfüllt mit Moderduft;   Filled with the stench of decay!
      Drauf senkte man den leeren Sarg   Then the empty coffin was lowered
      Wohl in der Väter Gruft.   Into her ancestors' vault.

(10) Das Fräulein horchte still und bang   In fear and silence the maiden heard
      Der Priester Litanei'n;   The priests' litanies;
      Trüb' in des Kerkers Gitter drang   The red gleam of the torches
      Der Fackeln roter Schein.   Penetrated dimly through the prison bars

---

[1] Matthisson writes 'umfing'.

[2] In the 1811 edition of his poems, the source of the majority of Schubert's other Matthisson settings, the heroine's name is changed to Rose Mortimer. This suggests the composer used an earlier edition.

(11)   Sie ahnte schaudernd ihr Geschick;   With foreboding she guessed her fate;
Ihr ward so dumpf, ihr ward so schwer,[3] Her senses grew dull and heavy;
In Todesgram erstarb ihr Blick;[4]   Her eyes faded in the darkness of death;
Sie sank und war nicht mehr.   She sank down and was no more.

(12)   Des Turms Ruinen an der See   The ruins of the tower by the sea
Sind heute noch zu schaun.   are still to be seen today;
Den Wandrer fasst in ihrer Näh'   As he draws near,
Ein wundersames Graun.   The traveller is gripped by a strange dread.

(13)   Auch mancher Hirt verkündet euch, And many a shepherd will tell you
Dass er bei Nacht allda   How, at night,
Oft, einer Silberwolke gleich,   He has often seen the maiden
Das Fräulein schweben sah.   Hovering there like a silver cloud.

FRIEDRICH VON MATTHISSON (1761–1831); poem written in 1791

This is the fourteenth of Schubert's twenty-nine Matthisson solo settings (1812–17). See the poet's biography for a chronological list of all the Matthisson settings.

Verses 1–3: There is something about the insinuating gait of this § rhythm that is entirely appropriate to a story that unfolds in a mood of hushed 'once upon a time'. Although the introduction is very brief it is clear that Schubert thought a lot about it; the first version (NSA p. 36) uses different inversions of the chord and allows the leading note to rise, opening out the canvas; the second thoughts lead us harmonically downwards and inwards, to the breathless confidences of the storyteller and the feeling that dark doings are afoot. The exoticism of the word 'Sarazenenstrand' (bb. 23–4) immediately sets Schubert thinking about Mozart's *Entführung aus dem Serail* and Pedrillo's Serenade, also in § and about a young and beautiful girl imprisoned unjustly. Of course Rosalie von Montanvert is not a prisoner in the land of the Moors (her soldier father has been killed in battle there during a crusade), but the very sight of Saracens on the printed page is enough to make the stream of inspiration flow in an easterly direction.

Verses 4–6: Proceedings in § are brought to a halt by the marking 'Recit' and the arrival of Captain Hook on the pantomime stage. The merest mention of Manfry, the dastardly guardian, precursor perhaps of Walter Scott's Templar in *Ivanhoe*, or of Golo in Schumann's opera *Genoveva*, prompts a short and brutal passage, four in a bar, but in the character of a recitative. The passage is introduced by a G^7 chord in third inversion, the F natural in the bass suggestive of villainy like the sudden appearance of a leering face around a door. The creeping piano semiquavers at b. 33 (marked 'Wie oben', slower than they look on the page in this 'Ziemlich langsam' tempo) depict the spreading of news that seeps through the land like blood through a murder victim's clothes. The narrative § rhythm returns (b. 35) with an intoned litany, a succession of Ds bemoaning Rosalie's (supposed) death (bb. 36–8) rising to an E flat in the vocal line that leads us in due course to the distant key of A flat. The depiction in the piano of muffled bells tolling through diminished seventh mists (from b. 45) is an impressionistic masterstroke of Schubertian campanology.

Verses 7–9: As a reminder of how beloved Rosalie was by the populace, we move through the return to F minor (from b. 52) through A flat major (the cadence at bb. 57–8) and back to F minor. The barcarolle rhythm and key are a distant pre-echo of another beautiful girl, *Das Fischermädchen* from *Schwanengesang* D957/10. The reappearance of the ominous 'Ohm'

---

[3] Matthisson's original line is 'Ihr ward so dumpf *und* schwer'.

[4] Mattthisson's original was '*Todesgraun*' and then '*Todesnacht*' (1811 edition).

('Langsam' from b. 69, with a change to common time) disrupts the flow which, of course, is Schubert's intention. The lowering of an empty coffin (for she is condemned to a slow and terrible death walled up in a tower) is most pictorially done, the piano doubling voice, the vocal line swinging pendulously from side to side until it settles on the word 'Gruft' at b. 76.

Verses 10–11: This music (marked 'Wie oben' from b. 77) is the most original of the piece. It combines the § movement with the chromatically creeping semiquavers we heard briefly at the beginning of Verse 5. The horror of the mounting realization of her fate, the claustrophobia, the utter helplessness, are most economically depicted – indeed it is a feature of this ballad that it eschews the grandiose and in so doing paints a more powerful yet feminine picture of the victim. The shudders of fear, like tiny timpani rumbles in the piano's left hand (from b. 84), heighten the grotesque atmosphere as the music journeys inexorably back to its home key of G minor (which it reaches at b. 94). In dying from her initial terror Rosalie is spared the long and protracted death planned for her by her sadistic guardian.

Verses 12–13: The story concludes in an unsentimental, almost matter-of-fact way; the return of the § rhythm that has been a binding force in the piece conveys the timeless quality of a story re-enacted by ghosts across the centuries. Rosalia's presence hovers around shepherds and travellers and it is interesting to see how the composer uses this rhythm as effectively for the floating spirit's dance at the end as for the historical narrative of the beginning (the last four bars of the piece are another prophecy of *Das Fischermädchen*). The metamorphosis of such material is one of the fruits of Schubert's long apprenticeship in strophic song. This piece, with its disciplined restraint and economical organization of material, impresses more than many of his other early ballads.

   The first version of this piece printed in the NSA (we must assume that the second version represents the composer's final thoughts) has different ideas mainly for Verses 10 and 11. The throbbing sextuplet accompaniment here (from b. 76) suggests a mad-scene from a *bel canto* Italian opera. The NSA prints another fragmentary variant of the first version (Volume 7 pp. 186–7) that offers yet another view of Verses 10 and 11 – much stiller and sparing in terms of notes, but dramatic in its own way. All these options are a great deal more imaginative than the musical storytelling of earlier composers in settings of poems of this kind. It is clear that Schubert is composing from an imagination brimming with endless possibilities, and it is somehow heartening that he has the same difficulties as his future performers when it comes to deciding which of his many ideas may be rated as definitive.

Autographs:	Österreichische Nationalbibliothek, Vienna (fair copy);
	Pierpont Morgan Library, New York (fragmentary variant)
Publication:	First published in *Die Musik* (1901–2) and subsequently as part of the NSA in 1968 (P734; first version)
	First published as No. 5 of *Sechs bisher ungedrückte Lieder* by Wilhelm Müller, Berlin in 1868 (P417; second version)
Subsequent editions:	Not in Peters; AGA XX 27: Vol. 1/178; NSA IV: Vol. 7/36, 42 & 186; Bärenreiter: Vol. 5/136 & 142 (high voice); 130 & 136 (medium/low voice)
Bibliography:	Newbould 1997, p. 151
Discography and timing:	Fischer-Dieskau I 2[9] 5'38
	Hyperion I 8[2]
	Hyperion II 3[15] 5'44 Sarah Walker

← *An Emma* D113   *Erinnerungen* D98 →

ROMANZE
(STOLBERG) **D144** [H249]
(Fragment) E major   April 1816

Romance

In der Vä - ter Hal - len ruh - te   Rit - ter Ru - dolf's Hel - den- arm,

(7 bars)

N.B. *In the text printed below, the lines in italics are those for which we do not have Schubert's original music*

In der Väter Hallen ruhte
   Ritter Rudolf's Heldenarm,
Rudolf's, den die Schlacht erfreute,
Rudolf's, welchen Frankreich scheute
   Und der Sarazenen Schwarm.

Er, der Letzte seines Stammes,
   Weinte seiner Söhne Fall:
Zwischen Moosbewachsnen Mauern
Tönte seiner Klage Trauern
   In der Zellen Wiederhall.

In the halls of his fathers
   Rested the heroic arm of Sir Rudolph;
Rudolph, who delighted in battle;
Rudolph, feared by France
   And the Saracen mob.

He, the last of his line,
   Wept for the fall of his sons.
Between mossy walls
His lament rang out
   In the echoing cells.

FRIEDRICH LEOPOLD, GRAF ZU STOLBERG-STOLBERG (1750–1819); poem written in 1774

This is the sixth of Schubert's nine Stolberg solo settings (1815–23). See the poet's biography for a chronological list of all the Stolberg settings.

This fragment consists of five bars of voice and piano and a further two bars of vocal line up to and including the word 'erfreute'. It was written on the obverse side of the manuscript of another Stolberg setting, *Daphne am Bach* D411. These bars were crossed out by the composer who, after painting the grim majesty of Sir Rudolph's baronial hall, lost the inclination to continue the story. It is clear that by April 1816 Schubert's taste for ballads was beginning to wane. The poem has thirteen strophes in all and tells of the love of the fair Agnes, Rudolph's daughter, for Albrecht. The jealous Horst challenges him to a joust and kills him. In the end the father and all three involved in the love triangle are dead in something of a rerun of *Der Tod Oscars* D375. A year or two earlier Schubert would probably have completed the work in the manner of the Matthisson *Romanze* D114 or the Kenner *Ballade* D134.

But all we have is the rather impressive opening bars. Mention of the Saracens in the first verse prompts the composer to the same musical atmosphere that he used in *Der Kreuzzug* D932 over a decade later – a similar solemn march in 4/4 where the Crusades are depicted as a serious and holy business. The completion by Reinhard Van Hoorickx is one of his best; it wisely attempts only to finish the first strophe, and the poem's second verse also fits well enough to this strangely imposing music. One can imagine that Schubert would also have used it for the last strophe of the poem where the stoic Sir Rudolph, without tears and without complaint, holds

gez. u. radirt v. A. Müller.   Verlag v. A. Hofmann & Comp. in Berlin.

Illustration of *Romanze*, drawing and engraving by A. Müller (1846).

the body of his daughter for two days before himself dying. The medieval theme and the atmosphere of almost phlegmatic stoicism bring to mind the Schiller setting *Ritter Toggenburg* D397 from March 1816.

Autograph:	In private possession
First edition:	Published as part of the AGA in 1897; subsequently completed and published privately by Reinhard Van Hoorickx (P723)
Subsequent editions:	Not in Peters; AGA XX 46: Vol. 1/178; NSA IV: Vol. 7/201
Discography and timing:	Fischer-Dieskau —
	Hyperion I 23[9]
	Hyperion II 13[25] 2'05 Christoph Prégardien

← *Stimme der Liebe* D412   *Lied in der Abwesenheit* D416 →

ROMANZE (DER VOLLMOND STRAHLT) *see ROSAMUNDE, FÜRSTIN VON ZYPERN* D797/1

ROMANZE (ICH SCHLEICHE BANG UND STILL HERUM) *see Die VERSCHWORENEN* D787

ROMANZE DES RICHARD LÖWENHERZ
Romance of Richard the Lionheart
(Scott trans. Müller) Op. 86, **D907** [H627]

The song exists in two versions, the second of which is discussed below:
(1) March 1826? (2) appeared March 1828

(1)   No tempo indication   B♭ minor   **C**   [130 bars]

(2)   B minor

Gro-sser Ta-ten tat der Rit - ter fern im heil-gen Lan-de viel.

(125 bars)

A literal rendering of Müller's translation is given here. Scott's original poem,
titled 'The Crusader's Return', from the 1821 edition of Ivanhoe, is printed below in italics

Grosser Taten tat der Ritter	The knight achieved great deeds
Fern im heil'gen Lande viel	Far away in the Holy Land;
Und das Kreuz auf seiner Schulter	The cross on his shoulder
Bleicht' im rauhen Schlachtgewühl.	Had dimmed in the fierce tumult of battle.
Manche Narb' auf seinem Schilde	Many a dent on his shield
Trug er aus dem Kampfgefilde,	He bore from the battlefield;
An der Dame Fenster dicht,	Thus, close by his lady's window,
Sang er so im Mondlicht:	He sang in the moonlight:

Heil der Schönen! aus der Ferne	'Joy to the fair! Your knight
Ist der Ritter heimgekehrt,	Has returned from distant lands,
Doch nichts durft' er mit sich nehmen,	But he could bring nothing with him
Als sein treues Ross und Schwert.	Save his trusty steed and sword;
Seine Lanze, seine Sporen,	His lance, his spurs
Sind allein ihm unverloren,	Are all he has.
Dies ist all sein irdisch Glück,	This is all his earthly wealth –
Dies und Theklas Liebesblick!—	This, and Tekla's loving gaze.
Heil der Schönen! was der Ritter	'Joy to the fair! What your knight has achieved
Tat, verdankt' er ihrer Gunst,	He owes to your favour;
Darum soll ihr Lob verkünden	Therefore the minstrel's sweet art
Stets des Sängers süsse Kunst.[1]	Shall always be to sing her praises.
'Seht, da ist sie', wird es heissen,	"See, it is she," they will proclaim
Wenn sie ihre Schöne preisen,	When they extol the fair beauty,
'Deren Augen Himmelsglanz	"Whose celestial eyes
Gab bei Ascalon den Kranz!'	Won the garland at Askalon."
'Schaut ihr Lächeln, eh'rne Männer[2]	'Behold her smile – it laid men of iron
Streckt es leblos in den Staub!	Lifeless in the dust,
Und Iconium, ob sein Sultan	And Iconium, though his Sultan
Mutig stritt, ward ihm zum Raub!	Fought bravely, became its victim.
Diese Locken, wie sie golden	These golden locks,
Schwimmen um die Brust der Holden,	Flowing around the fair maid's breast,
Legten manchem Muselmann	Cast many a Moslem
Fesseln unzerreissbar an!—	In unbreakable chains.
'Heil der Schönen! dir gehöret,	'Hail, fair lady! To you, my beloved,
Holde, was dein Ritter tat –	Belongs all that your knight has achieved;
Darum öffne ihm die Pforte,[3]	Then open the gate to him,
Nachtwind streift, die Stunde naht.[4]	The night wind blows, the hour approaches.
Dort in Syriens heissen Zonen,	There, in Syria's torrid clime,
Musst' er leicht des Nords entwohnen!	He became a stranger to the cold north.
Lieb' ersticke nun die Scham,[5]	Let love stifle modesty,
Weil von ihm der Ruhm dir kam!'[6]	Since your glory came from him.'

The Crusader's Return
1
High deeds achieved of knightly fame,
From Palestine the champion came;
The Cross upon his shoulders borne,
Battle and blast had dimm'd and torn.
Each dent upon his batter'd shield
Was token of a foughten field;

---

[1] Müller's translation of Scott reads 'Stets des *Minstrels* süsse Kunst'.
[2] The translation has '*Fünfzig* Männer'.
[3] The translation has '*Öffne darum* ihm die Pforte'.
[4] The translation has 'Nacht*luft* streift, die *Stund'* ist spat'.
[5] Here 'nun' replaces the original '*jetzt*'.
[6] The translation has 'Weil von *ihr* der Ruhm dir kam'.

And thus, beneath his lady's bower,
He sung, as fell the twilight-hour:—

2

Joy to the fair! – thy knight behold,
Return'd from yonder land of gold;
No wealth he brings, nor wealth can need,
Save his good arms and battle-steed;
His spurs, to dash against a foe,
His lance and sword to lay him low;
Such all the trophies of his toil,
Such – and the hope of Tekla's smile!

3

Joy to the fair! whose constant knight
Her favour fired to feats of might;
Unnoted shall she not remain
Where meet the bright and noble train;
Minstrel shall sing and herald tell –
'Mark yonder maid of beauty well,
'Tis she for whose bright eyes was won
The listed field at Askalon!'

4

'Note well her smile! – it edged the blade
Which fifty wives to widows made.
When, vain his strength and Mahound's spell,
Iconium's turban'd soldan fell.
Seest thou her locks, whose sunny glow
Half shews, half shades, her neck of snow?
Twines not of them one golden thread,
But for its sake a Paynim bleed.'

5

'Joy to the fair! – my name unknown,
Each deed, and all its praise, thine own;
Then, oh! unbar this churlish gate,
The night dew falls, the hour is late.
Inured to Syria's glowing breath,
I feel the north breeze chill as death;
Let grateful love quell maiden shame,
And grant him bliss who brings thee fame.'

SIR WALTER SCOTT (1771–1832), translated by KARL LUDWIG METHUSALEM MÜLLER (1771–1837); poem written before 1820

This is the last of Schubert's eight Scott solo settings (1825–6) and the only setting of a Müller translation. See Scott's biography for a chronological list of all the Scott settings, and Müller's biography for further information about the poet.

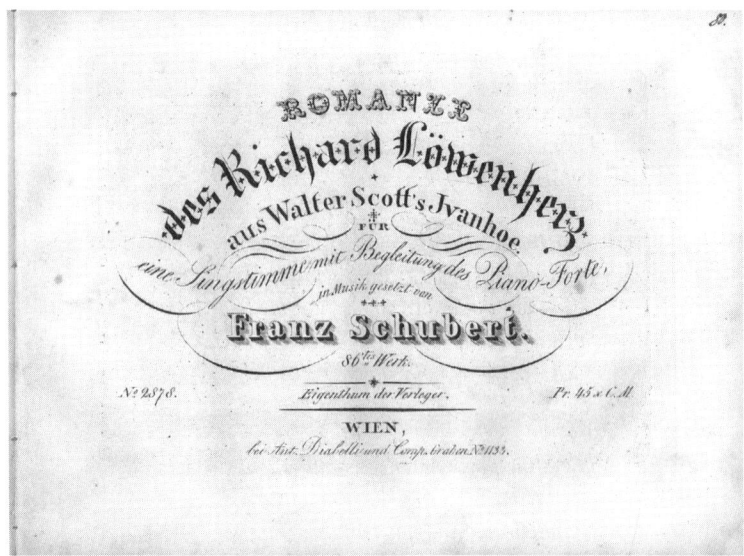

Romanze des Richard Löwenherz, Op. 86.

Not for the first time Schubert reveals his attraction to the epoch of the Crusades and medieval minstrelsy. His opera *Fierabras* (D796, 1823) is set in this period, as is the incomplete *Der Graf von Gleichen* (D918 begun in June 1827), as well as various songs in his output, including *Der Kreuzzug* D932. *Romanze des Richard Löwenherz* is a ballad sung by Richard the Lionheart to Friar Tuck in Book II Chapter 2 of the historical novel *Ivanhoe* (Chapter XVII in the modern one-volume edition). The king, in disguise as a travelling knight, sings in exchange for the hospitality of the 'genial hermit', and is handed the friar's harp to accompany himself. This instrument, somewhat the worse for wear, is missing one of its strings. (Shortly before this it had been too enthusiastically played by Allan-a-Dale, 'the northern minstrel', when in his cups.) In this passage, as elsewhere, Scott cunningly reworks, for his own somewhat anachronistic purposes, the rivalry between Saxon and Norman languages and art-forms in twelfth-century Britain.

> The knight . . . had brought the strings into some order and, after a short prelude, asked his host whether he would choose a sirvente *in the language of* oc, *or a* lai *in the language of* oui, *or a* virelai, *or a ballad in the vulgar English.*
>
> 'A ballad – a ballad,' said the hermit, 'against all the ocs and ouis of France. Downright English am I, Sir Knight, and downright English was my patron St Dunstan, and scorned oc and oui, as he would have scorned the parings of the devil's hoof; downright English alone shall be sung in this cell.'
>
> 'I will assay, then,' said the knight, 'a ballad composed by a Saxon gleeman, whom I knew in the Holy Land.'
>
> It speedily appeared that, if the knight was not a complete master of the minstrel art, his taste for it had at least been cultivated under the best instructors. Art had taught him to soften the faults of a voice which had little compass, and was naturally rough rather than mellow, and, in short, had done all that culture can do in supplying natural deficiencies. His performance, there-fore, might have been termed very respectable by abler judges than the hermit, especially as the knight threw into the notes now a degree of spirit, and now of plaintive enthusiasm, which gave force and energy to the verses which he sung.

> *. . . During this performance, the hermit demeaned himself much like a first-rate critic of the present day at a new opera. He reclined back upon his seat with his eyes half shut: now folding his hands and twisting his thumbs, he seemed absorbed in attention, and anon, balancing his expanded palms, he gently flourished them in time to the music.*

The mention of a 'new opera' prophesies Scott's own bemused attendance at a performance of Rossini's *Ivanhoe* in Paris in October 1826. Scott is such a wonderful author when on form like this, and it is unthinkable that Schubert himself had not read the rest of the story when he set the text. When performing this music the combination of spirit (the marking is 'Mässig, doch feurig') and 'plaintive enthusiasm' (Scott could not have more pithily described an essential aspect of Schubert's art) should be present throughout – also a touch of humour considering the situation, and the cheeky deception of the king in playing at being less than his regal self.

The length of the song, however, invites performances that fail to bring out these subtleties. The moto perpetuo rhythm can easily sound like a joust at full tilt rather than the strumming of a lute. This song has long been the province of the enthusiastic amateur singer determined to 'have a go' in relatively unknown repertoire. As a result it has been cheerily bawled and thumped in makeshift performances that can seem endless to the listener. This is why Capell refers to the song's 'hammered quavers' when a glance at the music shows that these notes in the accompaniment are marked piano in most part, mezzo-forte from time to time, and only very rarely forte. In this amateur mode the song is usually begun too fast but winds down to a sluggish canter as the performers tire. The notion of a king singing about his exploits during the Crusades (even at one remove, as here) implies heroism, but Reed is not correct to say that 'Schubert is clearly content . . . to sustain an image of pageantry and war'. There is also a great deal of charm, even eroticism, in the music, as there is in the poem. Schubert is not belligerent by nature; he clearly sees this piece as a serenade first and foremost, and when it comes to wooing he is masterfully capable of using every trick in the book. Stretches of military-style music (these exploits are recounted to impress the fair Tekla – nothing to do with the Schiller ghost-heroine featured in two Schubert songs) are relieved by gallant little excursions into harmonic highways and byways that recall the more or less contemporary *Das Lied im Grünen* D917.

The translator has chosen to change Scott's iambic tetrameters into trochees; this gives the poem something of a galloping bounce that is not in the original. (If the song, when heard at its worst, seems to be rhythmically repetitive to the point of dullness, this fault goes back to the rum-ti-tum of the translation.) The poem is in five strophes which Schubert varies between minor and major. The key signature of B major appears at b. 21. The six-bar piano introduction (with upbeat) reappears as an interlude between verses 2 and 3 (this time adapted to the major key, bb. 39–45); it returns inflected in the minor for its appearance between Verses 3 and 4 (bb. 64–70), and switches back to the major between verses 4 and 5 (bb. 89–95). It is this music of quasi-fanfare that constantly reminds us of the narrator's military bearing.

The setting of the words allows for greater variety. Verse 1, in B minor, takes us from the battleground to the initiation of the moonlit serenade. This entreaty to the fair one at the heart of the piece is to be heard in Verse 2 ('Heil der Schönen!' – Joy to the fair!) as well as Verse 3. Both strophes use identical music cast in a persuasive B major, suitable for courting a fair damsel. Askalon, mentioned in Verse 3, is a coastal town, Ashkelon, in present-day Israel. Verse 4, with its reminiscences of crusading exploits, returns to B minor – it is related to the harmonic ground plan of Verse 1, although the vocal line is differently pitched; it even takes some of its melodic ideas from verses 2 and 3 in the major key. The composer here allows himself all the freedom he appropriates for modified strophic songs of this kind; a lesser composer would have been satisfied recycling the same melody as before. Schubert cannot resist re-fashioning the rise and fall of the lines better to fit the new words. In this strophe, there is a reference to Iconium, the present-day Konya in Anatolia, Turkey; this city was briefly occupied by Kaiser Friedrich Barbarossa at the end of the twelfth century and was not among King Richard's victories.

Verse 5 returns to B major. This begins with the familiar refrain of 'Heil der Schönen!' (from b. 95) but the music changes with the words 'Darum öffne ihm die Pforte, / Nachtwind streift, die Stunde naht' (bb. 98–100), bringing the knight closer than he has ever been to the fulfilment of his amorous ambitions. The pedal F sharp that underpins 'Dort in Syriens heissen Zonen, / Musst' er leicht des Nords entwohnen' (bb. 101–5) suggests exactly the right amount of pent-up sexual tension and impatience. This champing at the bit is repeated, even more meaningfully, at the repeat of 'Darum öffne ihm die Pforte, / Nachtwind streift' from b. 110 where the words are tellingly changed to 'Öffne darum ihm die Pforte' – the high note on 'Öffne' registering a special pleading. The brave knight, despite apparently upright gallantry, is more interested in horizontal possibilities: using his fame as an excuse, he asks the damsel of his choice to sacrifice her virginal modesty in his honour. This brazen yet charming effrontery must have mightily appealed to the men in the Schubert circle, particularly Schober. The postlude, a mere two bars long and as suggestive as a sly wink, implies that his wish is granted; the song ends as naughtily as Schumann's duet *Unterm Fenster* where the successful serenader slips stealthily through the locked gate in order to storm the fortress, as it were. After all the hustle and bustle of the knight's approach and the petition, the clinching movement that lets him into the boudoir is quick and surreptitious. The embellishment of the final cadence in B major (an arpeggio figure in the left hand at b. 124, cheekily echoed an octave lower in the bass) marks the moment of ingress.

Schubert is fascinated by the challenge of creating unity in diversity – a single structure made up of various strophes (ABBA²C), hanging together as an entity. He may have succeeded too well in that the musical differences between the verses are not very clear on first hearing. Nevertheless this is potentially first-rate Schubert that needs affectionate help, rather than unremitting vigour, from its performers. We are familiar with the through-composed symphonic form in this type of vocal music because of such works as the two *Suleika* lieder (the first of these, D720, is also a B minor work), *Der Zwerg* D771, *Die junge Nonne* D828 and other big songs from about 1823 onwards. These pieces, usually held together by a pervasive accompanying motif, suggest the momentum and unity of orchestral music, and it is for this reason (as well as the matching tonality) that Capell thought that this song might have been adapted to make a good conclusion to the 'Unfinished' Symphony. While this seems optimistic, it is true enough that the *Romanze des Richard Löwenherz* adopts the bustle and elaborate length of a Schubert finale (cf. the final movements of such important works from more or less the same period as the E flat Trio, and the violin *Fantasie*).

The work now seems so bound to its B minor tonality that it is strange to discover that its first version – a less developed variant of the same musical ideas – was originally conceived in B flat minor. This is printed in Volume 4b of the NSA and gives baritones taxed by the original key a good excuse to ask their pianists to play the music down a semitone. The pervasive dotted rhythm of the song was adopted by Brahms in 1862 for his *Sulima* (the thirteenth song of the cycle *Die schöne Magelone* Op. 33). Although that music is windborne rather than horse-powered, the shared theme of these songs is that of journeying lovers (Richard the Lionheart, Peter of Provence) returning from being captives of the Moors.

Autograph:	Wienbibliothek im Rathaus, Vienna (copy of first version in unknown hand with Schubert's handwritten additions)
Publication:	First published as part of the NSA in 1979 (P771; first version)
	First published as Op. 86 by Diabelli, Vienna in March 1828 (P155; second version)

First known performance:	Performed at a Schubertiad at the house of Josef von Spaun on 12 January 1827 (performers unknown, but presumably accompanied by Schubert) [Deutsch Doc. Biog. No. 772] First public performance: 2 February 1828, Landhaussaal, Vienna. Soloist: Ludwig Tietze, accompanied by Franz Schubert [Waidelich/Hilmar Dokumente I No. 584 & Dokumente II No. 583a]
Contemporary reviews:	*Wiener Allgemeine Theaterzeitung* No. 18 (9 February 1828), p. 70f. [Waidelich/Hilmar Dokumente I No. 589; Deutsch Doc. Biog. No. 1027] *Wiener Zeitschrift für Kunst, Literatur, Theater und Mode* No. 20 (14 February 1828), p. 160 [Waidelich/Hilmar Dokumente I No. 591; Deutsch Doc. Biog. No. 1028]
Subsequent editions:	Peters: Vol. 3/45; AGA XX 501: Vol. 8/220; NSA IV: Vol. 4a/70 & Vol. 4b/200; Bärenreiter: Vol. 3/45
Discography and timing:	Fischer-Dieskau II 8[10] 5'21 Hyperion I 36[1] Hyperion II 33[15] 4'36 Gerald Finley

⟵ *Schiffers Scheidelied* D910   *Das Lied im Grünen* D917 ⟶

RICHARD ROOS *see* KARL AUGUST ENGELHARDT

ROSAMUNDE, FÜRSTIN VON ZYPERN
Helmina von Chézy (1783–1856), **D797**
Autumn 1823

The incidental music of *Rosamunde* has achieved an immortality denied to Schubert's other stage music of 1823, but it was far from successful at the time. The story goes that it was the notorious womanizer Josef Kupelwieser, librettist of *Fierabras* and brother of Schubert's painter friend Leopold, who had the idea of teaming up the composer with poetess Wilhelmine (known as Helmina) von Chézy – all in order to give a benefit concert in the Theater an der Wien for a mediocre actress with whom he was in love. The bad luck that dogged almost all of Schubert's theatrical enterprises was once again in evidence: it was a box office and critical disaster at the Theater an der Wien in December 1823, only running for two performances. All the blame for this must fall on the play itself, the original version of which has been lost – the music accounted for a fraction of the work's length. The composer first brought in the overture to his grand opera *Alfonso und Estrella* D732 to serve as opening music, but later the overture of his *Singspiel*, *Die Zauberharfe* D644 was substituted. Apart from this, there are nine numbers including the delicious Entr'acte in B flat (No. 5), the opening melody of which was to serve in 1824 as the opening theme for the Andante of the String Quartet in A minor (where the melody is transposed to C major) and in December 1827 for the third of the four Impromptus D935 which is cast as theme and variations. Four items from this incidental music (nos 3b, 4, 7 and 8) arranged for voice and piano were issued as Op. 26 – the first in 1824 and the remaining three only in July 1828. It is not certain whether the composer himself made the piano reductions. From a stylistic point of view this seems more likely for the *Romanze* than for the three choral items. In a letter to Helmina von Chézy, written at Zseliz on 5 August 1824, Schubert acknowledged receipt of a revised copy of the libretto and made sympathetic noises about the way her play had been 'conspicuously censured' by the critics on acount of 'a few insignificant faults'. It seems that Chézy was interested in purchasing the rights for the music so that she could offer her piece, with Schubert's contributions, to theatres elsewhere. Schubert optimistically asked her for 100 florins for the music, the same amount that Chézy had been paid by the Theater an der Wien for writing the play. We do not know the outcome of these negotiations.

I ROMANZE (ARIETTE)[1]   Romance (Arietta)
Op. 26 no. 1,
D797/3B [H525]
F minor   Autumn 1823

(23 bars)

Der Vollmond strahlt auf Bergeshöhn' –	The full moon beams on the mountain tops;
Wie hab ich Dich vermisst!	How I have missed you!
Du süsses Herz! es ist so schön,	Dearest one, it is so beautiful
Wenn treu die Treue küsst.[2]	When faithfulness truly kisses.
Was frommt des Maien holde Zier?	What are May's fair adornments to me?
D u warst mein Frühlingsstrahl,	*You* were my ray of spring.
Licht meiner Nacht, O lächle mir	Light of my night, o smile upon me
Im Tode noch einmal!	Once more in death.
Sie trat hinein beim Vollmondschein[3]	She entered in the light of the full moon,
Sie blickte himmelwärts:	And gazed heavenwards.
'Im Leben fern, im Tode Dein.'	'In life far away, yet in death yours!'
Und sanft brach Herz an Herz.[4]	And gently heart broke upon heart.

The *Romanze* for Axa was the first of four pieces from *Rosamunde* to be published with a piano accompaniment. Various judicious differences between dynamics in the piano part and the full score, (clarinets, horns and lower strings predominate, with little for the violins) and the skill and economy of the reduction, suggest the composer's own hand. For this reason the haunting little aria must be considered part of his lieder output. It is the simplest of strophic songs and explores the haunting ambivalence between F minor and major. There is a touch of naivety in the gently rocking § rhythm that suggests a bergerette.

[1] The cover title of this song in the First Edition of Op. 26 was originally *Romance* [sic] *aus Rosamunde* while *Ariette* was printed above the music (NSA has reverted to this title). This 'Ariette' was then crossed through with pencil on a rare surviving copy of the first edition (in the Hoboken collection) and changed to *Romanze*. In the absence of a surviving autograph it is possible that these changes of spelling and title were made on the whim of the publisher rather than authorized by Schubert himself.
[2] In the text reassembled and edited in 1996 by Till Gerrit Waidelich the line is 'Wenn *Treu* die Treue küsst'.
[3] Similarly, Chézy's text reads 'beim *hellen Schein*'.
[4] Chézy writes 'Und *süss* brach Herz an Herz'.

That this *Romanze* is a conscious pastoral evocation is borne out by the plot. Kreissle von Hellborn, Schubert's first biographer, extracted the gist of the play (unpublished and entirely lost to us until the recent researches of Till Gerrit Waidelich) from the author's son. It seems that Princess Rosamunde has been brought up ('from some fancy of her father's') as a shepherdess, and in the middle of the stressful and protracted business of regaining her throne, she escapes back to the hut of Axa, 'her old protectress', who sings this song. The soft glinting colours of moonlight on the heath are perfectly caught, and a touch of old-fashioned modality suggests a timeless refuge from the dangers of court life. As one would expect from a composer who numbered *Die schöne Müllerin* D795 among his recent achievements, the strength of the piece is in its flawless melody, seemingly simple but utterly inimitable. The appearance of such a piece is superfluous to the plot; Till Gerrit Waidelich (*Schubert Liedlexikon*) suggests that its inclusion may have been Schubert's idea, or that of the first Axa, Katherina Vogel (according to Schwind a terrible singer).

Autograph:	Missing or lost
First edition:	Published as Op. 26 (Heft 1) by Sauer & Leidesdorf in March 1824 (P72)
Subsequent editions:	Peters: Vol. 1/230; Not in AGA; NSA IV: Vol. 2a/94; Bärenreiter: Vol. 2/2
Bibliography:	Waidelich 1996
Further settings and arrangements:	Charles Ives (1874–1954) *Ballade from Rosamunde* (*c*. 1895 in original German; *De la drama; Rosamunde* (1898, French paraphrase by Bélanger)
	Arr. Anton Webern (1883–1945) for voice and orchestra (1903) [*see* ORCHESTRATIONS]
Discography and timing:	Fischer-Dieskau —
	Hyperion I 9[7] 3'50 Arleen Auger
	Hyperion II 27[13]

← *Die Wallfahrt* D778a   Der Dichter, als Prolog (*Die schöne Müllerin*) →

II GEISTERCHOR   Chorus of spirits   Chorus, TTBB
OP. 26 NO. 3, **D797/4** [NOT IN HYPERION]
D major   Autumn 1823

In der Tiefe wohnt das Licht,
(41 bars)

In der Tiefe wohnt das Licht,
Licht das leuchtet und entzündet;
Wer das Licht des Lichtes findet,
Braucht des eitlen Wissens nicht.

In the depths dwells the light,
Light which shines and kindles.
He who finds the light of light
Has no need of idle knowledge.

Wer vom Licht sich abgewendet,
Der bewillkommt froh die Nacht,
Dass sie selt'ne Gabe spendet,
Ihn belohnt mit dunkler Macht.

He who has turned away from the light
Gladly welcomes the night
That bestows on him precious gifts
And rewards him with dark powers.

Mische, sinne, wirke, strebe,	Mingle, reflect, work, strive,
Mühe dich, du Erdensohn,	Exert yourself, son of the earth,
Dass zu fein nicht dein Gewebe,	That your web is not too finely spun,
Und der Tat nicht gleich der Lohn.	And that you are not rewarded only according to your deeds.

This music for men's voices and brass instruments (TTBB with accompaniment for three horns and three trombones) is almost entirely forgotten. Schubert's piano version (only published in 1828 alongside the other two *Rosamunde* choruses discussed below, a delay typical of Leidesdorf's inefficiency) did not appear in the AGA and has not yet appeared in the NSA. As a result it failed to be included in the Hyperion Edition. Liszt was fascinated by this music, mistakenly imagining that these other-worldly voices (the chorus is sung 'aus der Tiefe' – from the depths, rather than the heavenly heights) were spirits of a heavenly kind, and that the song had some connection with religion. Accordingly he gave his transcription the subtitle *Hymne* and clearly relished its elevated nature that seems to prophesy *Parsifal* in its noble simplicity. The song with its clever part-writing is in Schubert's pilgrimage (or crusade) key of D major and is extremely memorable (the whole of *Rosamunde* is vintage Schubert after all). Chézy cut it entirely from the later, revised edition of her play (as republished in 1996 by Waidelich) on the grounds that she wanted to distance herself from the supernatural element that this chorus had rather gratuitously introduced in the original Viennese production.

Autograph:	Missing or lost
Subsequent editions:	Not in AGA; NSA III: Vol. 3; Neue Ausgabe, Diabelli & Comp. (1832)
Bibliography:	Waidelich 1996
Discography and timing:	Fischer-Dieskau —
	Hyperion —

III HIRTENCHOR   Chorus of shepherds   Chorus, SATB
OP. 26 NO. 4, **D797/7** [NOT IN HYPERION][1]
B♭ major   Autumn 1823

(206 bars)

Hier auf den Fluren mit rosigen Wangen	Here on the meadows, rosy-cheeked
Hirtinnen eilet zum Tanze herbei,[2]	Shepherdesses hasten to dance,
Lasst euch die Wonnen	Let the delights of spring
Des Frühlings umfangen	Embrace you,

---
[1] In Till Gerrit Waidelich's edition of Chézy's revised text this chorus occurs in Act III Scene 5, thus before the *Romanze* which is the last of the three vocal pieces in this version of the libretto (although the first of the vocal items in Schubert's D797).
[2] In Chézy's revised version, '*Jünglinge, Mädchen* zum Tanze herbei'.

Liebe und Freude	Love and joy
Sind ewiger Mai.	Are a never-ending May.
Hierzu den Fussen,	Here at your feet
Holde dir grüssen,[3]	We greet you,
Herrscherin von Arkadien wir dich.	Fair ruler of Arcadia!
Flöten, Schallmeien,	Pipes, shawms
Tönen, es freuen	Sing out; the meadows,
Deiner die Fluren, die blühenden sich.	The flowers delight in you.
Von Jubel erschallen	In jubilation
Die grünenden Hallen	The green expanses resound;
Der Höhen, die luftig,	The airy heights,
Der Fluren die duftig	The fragrant meadows
Erglänzen und strahlen	Shine radiantly
In Liebe und Lust.[4]	In love and pleasure.
In schattigen Talen	In the shaded valleys
Da schweigen die Qualen	The pangs of the loving heart
Der liebenden Brust.	Are stilled.

It is rare for the incidental music for *Rosamunde* to be performed complete, including all the vocal music. This *Hirtenchor* (and its companion pieces *Geisterchor* and *Jägerchor*) make only rare appearances on the concert platform as far as the orchestral music for *Rosamunde* is concerned, and for 180 years they have been lost to recitals for solo singers and small ensembles. The *Romanze* or *Ariette* of Axa 'Der Vollmond strahlt' has survived thanks to its placement in the first volume of the Peters Edition in a time-honoured arrangement for voice and piano. The piano-accompanied versions of *Geisterchor*, *Hirtenchor* and *Jägerchor* were nominally part of Op. 26 of 1824 (the solo song is Op. 26 no. 1) but actually appeared only in 1828. They then disappeared from view, and were not included in the AGA. Two of them reappeared only in 2006 in Volume 2b of Series II of the *Neue Schubert-Ausgabe*, too late to be included in the Hyperion Edition. It is notable that not even the editors of the NSA were able to consult an 1824 Sauer & Leidesdorf printing of these pieces since no copies have survived.

The original scoring of this chorus for shepherds and shepherdesses is for strings, woodwinds and horns – the apotheosis of pastoral music with its rural key of B flat major and its gently insistent dactylic rhythms. The music has a gentle repetitiveness that would be banal from another composer, but in Schubert's hands this celebration of the static becomes hypnotic. In recital conditions the work could very easily be performed by eight or twelve singers to delightful effect: there are passages for solo voices from b. 83 that make a pleasing contrast to the effect of the voices singing tutti. Nevertheless, a performance for a quartet of solo voices – particularly if the soprano were secure in singing a passing high B flat – would also be possible. When looking at the simple piano writing for the solo *Romanze* there is nothing to rule out Schubert himself as the arranger. However, in the *Hirtenchor* the awkwardness of the writing for left hand from b. 115 (while the right hand merely doubles the soprano line) seems uncharacteristic and clumsy. This is even more evident in the graceless and muddy piano writing from b. 145 which is in the worst traditions of piano reductions of orchestral scores. It seems possible that at this time of Schubert's illness someone else was hired by the publishers to make its reduction from the full score.

[3] In Chézy's revised version, '*Hier, Dir zu* Füssen, / Holde *begrüssen*'.
[4] In Chézy's revised version, 'Erglänzen und *prangen* / In Liebe und Lust'.

Autograph:	Missing or lost
First edition:	First published as Op. 26 (Heft 4) by M. J. Leidesdorf in July 1828, but no scores survive. Subsequently published with piano accompaniment as part of the NSA in 2006 (P849)
Subsequent editions:	Not in AGA; NSA III: Vol. 2b/326
Bibliography:	Waidelich 1996
Discography and timing:	Fischer-Dieskau — Hyperion —

IV JÄGERCHOR   Chorus of huntsmen   Chorus, SATB
Op. 26 NO. 2, **D797/8** [NOT IN HYPERION][1]
D major   Autumn 1823

Wie lebt sichs so fröhlich im Grü - nen,

(58 bars)

Wie lebt sichs so fröhlich im Grünen,	How cheerful life is in nature's green,
Im Grünen bei fröhlicher Jagd,	In the green when merrily we hunt,
Von sonnigen Strahlen durchschienen,[2]	Shot through with beams of sunlight,
Wo reizend die Beute uns lacht.	Where the quarry attracts us, mockingly.
Wir lauschen und nicht ist's vergebens,[3]	We listen, not in vain,
Wir lauschen im duftenden Klee,[4]	We listen in the perfumed clover.
O sehet das Ziel unsres Strebens,[5]	Oh, see the goal of our efforts,
Ein schlankes ein flüchtiges Reh![6]	A slender, fugitive roe.
Getroffen bald sinkt es vom Pfeile,	Struck by an arrow, it quickly sinks down,
Doch L i e b e verletzt, dass sie heile,	But *love* wounds only to heal.
Nicht bebe, Du schüchternes Reh,[7]	Do not tremble, timid roe,
Die Liebe gibt Wonne für Weh![8]	Love changes pain into joy.

The reader is referred to the entry for *Hirtenchor* D797/7 above for the background to the work's publication, and its non-availability as a piano-accompanied work until the appearance of the relevant NSA volume in 2006. The music has an attractive energy and a measure of virtuosic skill is required to bring off the sometimes tricky piano writing in swirling semiquavers at the

[1] In Waidelich's edition of Chézy's revised text this chorus opens Act II Scene 1 and is thus the first of the three vocal items in this version of the libretto. In Schubert's D797 it is the last of the three.
[2] In Chézy's revised version: 'Von *goldenen* Strahlen *beschienen*'.
[3] In Chézy's revised edition this sentence is rendered in the past tense: 'Wir *lauschten* und nicht *war's* vergebens'.
[4] Chézy's revision once again has '*lauschten*'.
[5] In Chézy's revised version: '*Bald zeigt sich* das Ziel unsres Strebens'.
[6] In Chézy's revised version: 'Ein schlankes, ein *schüchternes* Reh!'
[7] In Chézy's revised version: '*Horch Mägdlein*, Du schüchternes Reh'.
[8] In Chézy's revised version: '*Süss'* Liebe gibt *Wonnen* für Weh!'

beginning and ending of the piece. The accompaniment otherwise consists of prancing quavers (the inspiration behind it is clearly the galloping of horses) and is relatively simple, often doubling the vocal line in a way that suggests a hand other than Schubert's. Unlike the *Hirtenchor*, performable by a quartet of solo singers, this music needs a choir of at least sixteen voices to make its effect; each one of the SATB lines is divided into two parts. The male voices sing between bb. 9 and 21 and are answered by the women from bb. 21–33. From there on, the two parts of the choir sing together with the first tenor part requiring a certain stamina and ease in the higher tessitura.

Autograph:	Missing or lost
First edition:	Published as Op. 26 (Heft 2) by M. J. Leidesdorf in July 1828; published with piano accompaniment as part of the NSA in 2006 (P848)
Subsequent editions:	Not in AGA; NSA III: Vol. 2b/341; Neue Ausgabe, Diabelli & Co. (1832)
Bibliography:	Waidelich 1996
Discography and timing:	Fischer-Dieskau —
	Hyperion —

Die ROSE   The rose
(F. VON SCHLEGEL) OP. 73, **D745** [H477]

The song exists in two versions, the first of which is discussed below:
(1) Early 1822; (2) Early 1822

(1)   G major

(68 bars)

(2)   No tempo indication   F major $\frac{2}{4}$ [68 bars]

Es lockte schöne Wärme,	Lovely warmth tempted me
Mich an das Licht zu wagen,	To venture into the light.
Da brannten wilde Gluten;	There flames glowed fiercely;
Das muss ich ewig klagen.	I must for ever bemoan that.
Ich konnte lange blühen	I could have bloomed for long
In milden, heitern Tagen;	In mild, bright days.
Nun muss ich frühe welken,	Now I must wither early,
Dem Leben schon entsagen.	Renounce life prematurely.
Es kam die Morgenröte,	The red dawn came;
Da liess ich alles Zagen	I abandoned all timidity
Und öffnete die Knospe,	And opened the bud

Wo alle Reize lagen.	In which lay all my charms.
Ich konnte freundlich duften	I could have spread sweet fragrance
Und meine Krone tragen,	And worn my crown,
Da ward zu heiss die Sonne,	Then the sun grew too hot.
Die muss ich drum verklagen.	Of this I must accuse it.
Was soll der milde Abend?	Of what avail is the mild evening?
Muss ich nun traurig fragen.	I must now ask sadly.
Er kann mich nicht mehr retten,	It can no longer save me,
Die Schmerzen nicht verjagen.	Or banish my sorrows.
Die Röte ist verblichen,	My red colouring is faded;
Bald wird mich Kälte nagen.	Soon cold will gnaw me.
Mein kurzes junges Leben	Though dying, I still wished to tell
Wollt' ich noch sterbend sagen.	Of my brief young life.

FRIEDRICH VON SCHLEGEL (1772–1829); poem written in 1800/1801

This is the the fourteenth of Schubert's sixteen Friedrich von Schlegel solo settings (1818–25). See the poet's biography for a chronological list of all the Friedrich von Schlegel settings. See also the article about the cycle of which this song is part – Abendröte.

For the Romans the rose was the flower of beauty, love and poetry, dedicated to Venus who was said to have coloured the white rose red with her blood when she scratched herself as she ran to comfort her lover Adonis, gored by a wild boar. In western literature it has been both a symbol of gentleness and purity and the sensuous 'bed of crimson joy' described by Blake. Schlegel's poem here refers to more than female virtue besmirched by the heat of male passion. The rose here seems to speak for young people of talent and goodness, or simple childlike beauty, who were gathered before their time, stricken by consumption and other diseases unconquered in the nineteenth century. The poem has the air of Herrick's *To Daffodils* ('. . . we weep to see you haste away so soon') and with hindsight could refer to Schubert himself whose life was blighted by the heat of passion and who died in full flower.

Although it might seem likely that Schubert set the poem in 1819–20, at the same time as other songs from the first part of Schlegel's *Abendröte* sequence, Walther Dürr believes that it was written in early 1822 at the express wish of Johann Schickh, the editor of the *Wiener Zeitschrift* (the journal that appeared on Tuesdays, Thursdays and Saturdays – eight pages of text with a weekly fashion plate, and with lieder supplements four times a year). The Leitner setting *Drang in der Ferne* D770 was to be commissioned in like manner in 1823. As in the other *Abendröte* poems, Schlegel allows the rose to tell us of her plight in her own words. The dangers besetting young ladies who are careless of their virtue may seem rather obvious, but it must have seemed a point worth making at the beginning of the nineteenth century in a world seething with change and greater freedom between the sexes.

The rose itself is given voice in music of demure delicacy, largely accompanied with piano writing where both hands are positioned in the treble clef. Only at the mention of the dangerous heat of the sun does the texture become deeper-hued (as if burnt to a richer colour) with harmonic sequences (as at bb. 8–12) and excursions depicting withering change. From b. 26 the anouncement of dawn ('Es kam die Morgenröte') inspires a delightful little dance-like figure of delicately prancing semiquavers. This is immediately recognizable as music that will reappear four years later with the dawn imagery of *Ständchen* D889, Schubert's setting of Shakespeare's 'Hark, hark the lark'. The sensual left-hand line in singing crotchets at bb. 34–40 seems indicative of a perfume gently and lazily wafting through the air, competing with the energy of the spark-

Liszt's transcription of *Die Rose* for solo piano.

ling sun that stands above it in the treble clef. The change into the minor key at b. 46 is predictable but affecting. After the rose dies on a sighing ritardando ('ich noch sterbend sagen' bb. 64–5) Schubert adds a tiny two-bar postlude as an afterthought, a change to the major key placing the 'tragedy' in a lighter perspective (the fate of the trout comes to mind): we have to accept death as part of nature. As such it seems to be a Schubertian reworking of another flower, the violet that perishes while recounting its own fate in Mozart's *Das Veilchen* K476. The closing bars of *Die Rose* are surely Schubert's equivalent, and perhaps consciously so, of the little interjection-postlude to *Das Veilchen*: 'Das arme Veilchen' Mozart interpolates, not too seriously, 'the poor violet', his own miniature commentary on Goethe's poem. Schubert, as he reverts to the major key, seems to be saying 'Die arme Rose' without using these actual words.

When *Die Rose* appeared in the *Wiener Zeitschrift*, the tonality was a fresh and fragile G major (the key of *Das Veilchen* of course). In 1827 it was published by Diabelli, as Op. 73, in the same key. The second version in F major (published in Volume 3b of the NSA) acknowledges the vocal difficulties of the original key, particularly in the tessitura of the middle section. There are some differences in the second version (the chords of the final two bars, for example) but it is likely to have been made for sheerly practical reasons. When it came to publication Schubert seems to have preferred the original G major tonality. It is notable that this song mightily impressed Franz Liszt whose three versions of it – not perhaps the most obvious candidate for Lisztian metamorphosis – are among that composer's most adventurous and inspired transcriptions.

Autographs:	Missing or lost (first version, G major)
	Wienbibliothek im Rathaus, Vienna (second version, F major)
Publication:	First published as a supplement to the *Wiener Zeitschrift für Kunst, Literatur, Theater und Mode* on 7 May 1822; subsequently issued as Op. 73 by Diabelli, Vienna in May 1827 (P121; first version)
	First published as part of the AGA in 1895 (P690; second version)
Subsequent editions:	Peters: Vol. 2/140; AGA XX 408a & b: Vol. 7/18; NSA IV: Vol. 3a/146 & Vol. 3b/246; Bärenreiter: Vol. 2/166
Bibliography:	Capell 1928, pp. 177–8
	Einstein 1951, p. 253
	Kohlhäufl 1999, p. 302
Arrangements:	Arr. Franz Liszt (1811–1886) for solo piano (three versions, 1838) [*see* TRANSCRIPTIONS]

Discography and timing: Fischer-Dieskau   —
                          Hyperion I 19[6] & 27[13]   3'07   Felicity Lott
                                                2'41   Christine Schäfer
                          Hyperion II 25[3]   3'07   Felicity Lott

← *Der Blumen Schmerz* D731   *Ihr Grab* D736 →

Vignette for the second edition of *Die Rose* Op. 73 (1827).

Das ROSENBAND   The rosy ribbon
(KLOPSTOCK) **D280** [H166]
A♭ major   September 1815(?)

(35 bars)

Im Frühlingsgarten fand ich sie;[1]   I found her in the spring garden,
Da band ich sie mit Rosenbändern: And bound her with rosy ribbons;
Sie fühlt' es nicht und schlummerte.   Oblivious, she slept on.

Ich sah sie an; mein Leben hing   I looked at her; with that gaze
Mit diesem Blick an ihrem Leben: My life was bound to hers:
Ich fühlt' es wohl und wusst' es nicht.   This I felt, yet did not know.

Doch lispelt' ich Ihr leise zu[2]   But I whispered softly to her
Und rauschte mit den Rosenbändern.   And rustled the rosy ribbons.
Da wachte sie vom Schlummer auf.   Then she woke from her slumber.

Sie sah mich an; ihr Leben hing   She looked at me; with that gaze
Mit diesem Blick an meinem Leben,   Her life was bound to mine,
Und um uns ward Elysium.[3]   And all around us was paradise.

---

[1] In Klopstock's original it is 'Im Frühlings*schatten* fand ich sie'.
[2] In Klopstock: 'Doch lispelt' ich Ihr *sprachlos* zu'. The unusual upper case for 'Ihr' is in the original.
[3] In Klopstock: 'Und um uns *ward's* Elysium'.

FRIEDRICH GOTTLOB KLOPSTOCK (1724–1803); poem written in late 1753

This is the first of Schubert's thirteen Klopstock solo settings (1815–16). See the poet's biography for a chronological list of all the Klopstock settings.

This poem, addressed to Klopstock's beloved Meta Moller (whom he referred to as Cidli) was set to music by both Goethe's mistress, the actress Corona Schröter, and his close friend Carl Friedrich Zelter in 1810. Challier's Lieder Catalogue of 1885 lists seven other settings – apart from that of the American Edward MacDowell, all utterly obscure. Still to be written at that time was the Richard Strauss setting (by far the most famous) of 1897. Strauss's effulgent version is a vocal splendour, but its desire to charm in a self-consciously anachronistic manner approaches kitsch without crossing that threshold (the Marschallin in *Der Rosenkavalier* might have possessed a volume of Klopstock's *Oden*). The fact is that nothing can approach Schubert's song for fragrance and shy delight.

Schubert had already set two Klopstock texts (religious choruses for SATB and piano) in March 1815. In September the composer seems to have come across the poet's Odes for the first time – probably in the great Leipzig edition of 1798 but possibly in a collection by the Viennese Trattner. Schubert's arioso, apparently poised between speech and song, and certainly experimental in this respect, veers in the direction of prophetic modernity: out of context one might guess the composer of the chromatically underpinned line 'mein Leben hing / Mit diesem Blick an ihrem Leben' (bb. 9–12) to be Schumann rather than Schubert. Underneath this modernity however there is an old-fashioned discipline: the song is strictly strophic, an ABAB structure for the four verses from the point of view of the vocal line. The accompaniment changes texture halfway through and even incorporates some different basses in bb. 16–18. (A typical example of Schubert's reluctance to take the time-saving path for any musical journey.) It is the rustling of the ribbons at the beginning of the third strophe that clearly occasions the piano's wonderfully flexible quavers which cling and adapt to the contours of the vocal line at every turn. This creates an illusion of improvisation (as if we were to believe that anything could happen as a result of the narrator's game-playing), and the sensuality of the girl's sleeping shape is captured in the music's soft, feminine undulations. These, and the chromatically ascending bass line (bb. 4–6 and 21–2) where the lover approaches his prey as if on tiptoe, reflect the teasing eroticism of the text. The rapturous elongation of the vocal line into minims is superbly effective for the sleeping girl at 'schlummerte' (b. 6) and for the heart-stopping gaze at 'Ich sah sie an' (bb. 7–9) and so on. This works less well at b. 29 for 'um uns ward' but this is the price of uniformity that composers almost always pay in strophic form where the poet's verses are not equally well-suited to the fixed pattern of music. Those performers who understand this style will achieve a feeling of ebb and flow, and it is perfectly possible to smoothe over any moments of awkwardness. This is quite simply a miniature masterpiece which lies slumbering in many an edition of Schubert songs, longing to be awoken and embraced by ardent singers and listeners.

Autograph:	Missing or lost
First edition:	Published as Book 28 no. 3 of the *Nachlass* by Diabelli, Vienna in April 1837 (P317)
Subsequent editions:	Peters: Vol. 5/160; AGA XX 139: Vol. 3/72; NSA IV: Vol. 9/30
Bibliography:	Capel 1928, p. 95
	Einstein 1951, p. 111
	Fischer-Dieskau 1977, p. 48
	Reid 2007, pp. 93–4

Further settings and arrangements:	Josef Antonín Štěpán (1726–1797) *An Cidly* (1778)
	Carl Friedrich Zelter (1758–1832) *Das Rosenband* (1810)
	Ludwig van Beethoven (1770–1827) *Das Rosenband* (incomplete sketch, 1803)
	Edward MacDowell (1860–1902) *Das Rosenband* Op. 12 no. 2 (1880–81)
	Richard Strauss (1864–1949) *Das Rosenband* Op. 36 no. 1 (1897; also orchestrated in 1897)
	Arr. Tilman Hoppstock (b. 1961) for guitar accompaniment, in *Franz Schubert: 110 Lieder* (2009)
Discography and timing:	Fischer-Dieskau I 5[20] 1'38
	Hyperion I 7[17]
	Hyperion II 10[1] 1'47 Elly Ameling

← *Ossians Lied nach dem Falle Nathos' D278*   *Das Mädchen von Inistore D281* →

RUBATO

The *Oxford Companion to Music* (1955) states that 'there can be no term of which the definition is more troublesome to a conscientious musical lexicographer'. In Italian the word literally means 'robbed' but, as Percy Scholes points out, 'nobody is richer or poorer' for this 'crime'. Whatever the etymology, rubato in practice is the slight retardation and acceleration of an established musical pulse to add point to phrasing, or accentuate emotional expression. In truth, this is something that happens almost imperceptibly in eloquent, unselfconscious music-making, and only a trained ear would realize that it had happened at all. As far as most audiences are concerned they have simply heard a vital, engaged performance.

In the fifth edition of *Grove's Dictionary of Music and Musicians* (1954), rubato is defined as 'a matter of fine judgement', and then, as if in warning, 'a golden opportunity for the exercise of economy, without which it is apt to defeat its own end'. The practice of rubato is, therefore, a question of degree. The songs of Schubert are delicately susceptible to it, enhanced by its judicious use and ruined by its exaggeration. Who can imagine *Am See* D746, *Auf dem Wasser zu singen* D774 or *Des Fischers Liebesglück* D933 – the latter almost an etude in the deployment of rubato for both singer and pianist – performed absolutely strictly in time? Rubato is a *sine qua non* in these songs because the waterborne vessels (from which their protagonists supposedly deliver their texts) are subject to the gentle vagaries of lakeside winds and currents ('gentle' is the operative word). In composing songs Schubert was always a practical man, and there is a reason, usually text-related, for everything that happens. He did not look to his performers (as was the case with many later composers) for a displacement of tempi triggered by their own random emotional responses to his music. Each song mentioned above is a sensuous barcarolle, and Schubert would have expected his performers instinctively to feel the infinitesimally subtle ebb and flow in such pieces – above all on account of the poetry that had inspired them in the first place.

At what point, then, does the subtle art of rubato turn into 'messing about with the music'? So personal is this judgement, so much a matter of taste, that aberrations as defined by one listener might appear perfectly acceptable licence to another. In his rubato article for the second edition of *The New Grove* (2001), Richard Hudson writes, 'During the later Romantic period there was a gradual increase in the use of tempo fluctuation for subjective expressive purposes. Rhythm became the principal element in expressive performances.' This is borne out in masterful detail by Edward F. Kravitt in his *The Lied: Mirror of Late Romanticism* (1996). Taking some of his evidence from *fin de siècle* gramophone recordings, Kravitt writes of 'a mannered art . . . Singers tended to emphasize emotive words through sobs, audible breathing, slur, portamenti and tremolos.' The singers in question also clearly regarded a large dose of rubato as an automatic part of the performer's legitimate expressive apparatus.

By 1900, as a result of enormous changes in the language and presentation of music, the way of performing lieder in the 1820s had disappeared from memory (although Schubert's music has a habit of revealing its true nature to its interpreters, irrespective of the zeitgeist). The fading of the authentic tradition (as detailed by Leopold von Sonnleithner below) was gradual but ineluctable, and hugely accelerated by the mid-century advent of Wagner. A composer like Schubert's protégé Franz Lachner (*see* COMPOSERS), later based in Munich, was firmly sidelined once Wagner arrived in that city. The early Romantic tradition, of which Lachner's songs were fine exemplars, was unceremoniously swept away. Schubert's songs survived, of course, but by 1880 most of the composer's circle were dead, some of whom, like Sonnleithner, had been vigorous defenders of a simple, direct performing style. Singers who sang Wagner's operas regarded the lied in an entirely different light. Wagner scornfully dubbed those people who favoured uniformity of tempo 'the temperance league', or 'eunuchs of classical chastity'.

As Kravitt summarizes it, 'Late romantics had applied aspects of theatrical declamation to the lied'. With this declamation came a freedom that encompassed a breadth of rubato in song performance that we have scarcely encountered even in our own time. In the Wagnerian era singers with precarious vocal techniques were able to rely on declamation backed up by acting. At this point it must be admitted that our understanding of song performance in Schubert's own time is slightly confused by the fact that the most famous of the composer's singers, Johann Michael Vogl (1768–1840) was also described (and sometimes decried) as something of a declaimer and over-actor. The singing of the larger-than-life retired opera singer had become less dependable with age, and contemporary accounts describe how he relied on exaggeration and his charisma to put the songs across. He also attempted to ornament Schubert's songs, 'improvements' which the composer tactfully overlooked for the most part when it came to the songs' publication. Vogl first deigned to work with Schubert in 1817, became a convert to his songs and then their most ardent advocate. In any era there are various types of singer, with different temperaments and different interpretative strengths. Vogl was more flamboyant and daring than many of his contemporaries, but it would be a mistake to compare his exaggerations and mannerisms with the style of performance prevalent circa 1900; after all, this singer, essentially a man of the eighteenth century, never heard a note of Wagner in his life.

Fin de siècle singers belonged to another musical world. They clearly believed that Schubert songs sounded more meaningful when rendered in contemporary fashion – contemporary to them, that is – and thus nearer to the realism of opera, or rather Wagnerian music drama. They 'liberated' Schubert from Biedermeier corsetry, and were supposedly more creative than their forebears, 'more in touch with their feelings' to use a modern catchphrase, and less in awe of the purportedly schoolmasterish rendition of written rhythms. At the beginning of the twentieth century, singers' emotional reactions to the music (on the recital platform, at least, and in the absence of the controlling baton of a conductor) were considered paramount – licence and leeway were the order of the day. Indeed, it may be said that rubato had become the singer's right, the new alternative to ornamentation. The burgeoning tradition of the *Liederabend* (at its height in Germany and Austria between 1900 and 1914) was largely a cult of competitive personalities. In a sense every recitalist had become his own conductor, and some singers are very bad conductors indeed. This seems to have applied more to the music of German-speaking countries – tempo is hardly 'an expressive element' in the songs of Fauré and Debussy, for example, although away from this cutting edge in French contemporary music of that era there was no doubt many a Gallic singer determined to wallow in rubato-fuelled sentimentality.

In the absence of radio and the widespread dissemination of recordings there was no performing consensus, no authoritative means of imprinting stylistic desiderata on the public, either nationally or internationally. A feel for a composer's music was something taken away from one-off live performances that were exasperatingly evanescent. But lest it seem as though performers of the time had gone 'rogue' and against the wishes of their composers, it should be pointed out that Wagner himself had been the driving force behind the new fashion of declaimed and acted singing, and Mahler and Strauss accepted it – even required it. Julius Stockhausen (1826–1906), who had sung songs from *Die schöne Müllerin* to the accompaniment of Johannes Brahms in 1856 was considered to be of the old school (more reserved and 'a bit cool' according to the great Viennese critic Eduard Hanslick). Later on even Brahms came to admire singing of a very different kind – that of the controversial Ludwig Wüllner (1858–1938), a barnstorming singing actor who, it seems, had little voice per se but was master of a 'deep inner agitation' (as Felix Weingartner put it) that affected his audience in like manner. 'Deep inner agitation' suggests to me the use of quite a bit of wayward rubato.

One of the difficulties of defining a performing style for Schubert's songs is the fact that they stand in the no-man's-land of the late classical/early Romantic era, between the expiration of the performer's sovereign right to employ ornamentation (already old-fashioned in Schubert's lifetime, *see* ORNAMENTATION) and the inauguration of what Richard Hudson calls 'the later rubato' (associated with Schumann and Chopin) to differentiate it from what he terms 'the earlier rubato' of the eighteenth century. During Schubert's creative lifespan (and despite Vogl's often egregious attempts to ornament his songs in eighteenth-century style) it seems likely that the composer felt more or less in control of how he wanted his music to sound: performers, on the whole, took what was printed on the page and gave voice to the music in a simple and literal way, however heartfelt. This had not been the case in the age of a star like Farinelli, and was no longer the case in the age of a star like Liszt. The interpretation of music approached in a straightforward, rational manner (a knock-on effect perhaps of the Josephinian Enlightenment) is perhaps something that Schubert took for granted as Beethoven's contemporary. He also benefited from the older composer's success in bringing to heel the entire Viennese musical establishment who waited to put into effect the master's latest musical demands, however unrealistic and incomprehensible they appeared at times. It was difficult enough for contemporary performers to get anywhere near to what Beethoven required, without their adding another layer of complexity. 'Der Komponist hat immer recht' ('The composer is always right') was something to be believed and put into practice.

Music changed a great deal in Vienna after the deaths of Beethoven and, eighteen months later, Schubert. Johann Strauss senior and then his son became the guiding spirits of a new age of musical consumption by the masses and a laissez-faire that reflected increasing middle-class prosperity. So there was the rise of popular music on one hand and, later on, the precipitous ascent of the deeply serious Richard Wagner who had no abiding interest in piano-accompanied song, but whose music and aesthetic had a huge influence on both lied composition and performance. The change was gradual and the gap between popular songs and seriously complex lieder inexorably widened. As early as the 1830s the songs published as supplements to the *Wiener Zeitschrift für Kunst, Literatur und Mode* (where eleven of Schubert's finest songs appeared in his own lifetime) showed a sharp downward trend in quality. This music was now aimed at a growing mass market and increasingly inclined to late Biedermeier sentimentality – quasi-Victorian kitsch. Songs of this kind are often well served by rubato – indeed a personalized interpretation by a skilful performer can often improve such music no end.

Some decades after Schubert's death, to the dismay of several of his friends, increasingly wayward performances of his music had become the rule. Rubato came to be accepted, and lauded, as an intrinsically Viennese characteristic, almost a 'magic ingredient' – as native to the city as *The Blue Danube*, for example, a waltz famously shaped by artful displacements of rhythm. Of course, the use of rubato was not confined to Vienna – the new freedom granted to singers enthralled by their own mystique and credited with prophetic powers was largely fuelled by German composers. But Vienna, that most conservative of cities, gilded the rubato myth as if it were its personal escutcheon while jealously cherishing the aura of rubato-charm long after it was outmoded or distrusted elsewhere. There was a belief that only someone Viennese, or at least schooled in Vienna, sounded authentic as a performer of Schubert's songs. It was the German, Dietrich Fischer-Dieskau who, almost unilaterally, established a post-war style of lieder singing in the 1950s, driving a coach and horses (as far as the international lieder public was concerned) through the idea of the primacy of a specifically Viennese performing tradition. Compare, for instance, his restrained use of rubato in *Die schöne Müllerin* with that of the Viennese-born tenor Julius Patzak, a member of a generation that had been brought up to take Vienna's musical superiority for granted (this is not to cast aspersions on the extraordinary magnetism of Patzak as a performer). The playing of this cycle by Michael Raucheisen, a German, for Patzak is no less wayward. Many displaced Viennese musicians who, after 1938, became powerful personalities in the teaching and performing of song in Britain and the United States, took with them into exile some of the city's coquettish characteristics that were emblematic of their own nostalgia for a tragically vanished way of life. In the meantime, Schubert – like Shakespeare – had long been the property of the wider world. The musical eloquence of the English accompanist Gerald Moore (*see* PIANISTS) stemmed less from his use of rubato than from perfectly judged tempi and a deeply nuanced control of touch and tonal colour. He once confided to me that on his first visits to the Salzburg Festival after the war, playing for such artists as Fischer-Dieskau and Schwarzkopf, he was taken to task by the Austrian press for being a cold fish, without charm and catastrophically un-Schubertian. (It was unhelpful that one of his rival accompanists was also a local part-time critic.) Moore was treated as a rank outsider who had failed to understand the *real* Schubert.

The rubato mannerisms current for the latter two-thirds of the nineteenth century in the singing and playing of Schubert songs, and the effulgent pedalling typical of the late Romantics (*see* PEDALLING), were taken to be authentic throughout the world. In Vienna this arch-romanticization of Schubert was passed on by performer to performer as a word-of-mouth tradition. After the First World War and the beginnings of a modern age there were shifts in performing practice. And yet it had been the tendency, especially (but not exclusively) in Vienna, to preserve lieder performance in a bubble that was impervious to the changes in performance practice happening elsewhere on the concert platform – research into the classical style and early music, for example. Symphonic music, piano music, all moved on; lieder tended to be a ring-fenced zone, except for those who advocated recitals with period instruments. It was almost impossible for new ideas, even regarding tempi, to encroach into the sleekly complacent world of Bösendorfer-accompanied star singers. Hearing Schubert's lieder performed in the old style somehow recreated the spirit of the imperial days when Vienna was at its height – a period long after Schubert's death.

Until relatively recently there were teachers in Vienna, or of Viennese origin, who could speak authoritatively and almost at first hand about the musical styles of Mahler, Wolf, Alban Berg and Schoenberg. However admirable this was, Schubert was wrongly considered to be part of the same historical continuum – as if Vienna had always been the post-1848 Ruritanian paradise of increasingly decadent *Gemütlichkeit* it became under Franz Joseph. While it is true that the city's reputation for charm goes back to before Schubert's time, the musical life of Schubert's Vienna was ruled by the shades – living or dead – of Haydn, Mozart, Gluck and Beethoven, not Johann Strauss and later Gustar Mahler. There are many fascinating things to be learned in Vienna about Schubert's songs, but the employment of heart-on-sleeve rubato, bending the composer's rhythms in winsome manner, is not one of them. For very many years the resuscitated shade of the 'Viennese' Schubert, that button-mushroom of a man, Schwammerl, justified performances of soft-edged fuzziness, emollient, amiably overweight, music-making far less stark, powerful and confrontational than it might have been.

Of course, one must mention here that the employment of 'Viennese' rubato in Schubert's instrumental works (especially in the dance-inspired movements, and where there are no words to get in the way) can often seem supremely appropriate. The Scherzo of the D major Piano Sonata D850 is a case in point: the delicate time displacements (utterly Viennese) in the passage beginning b. 51 in the hands of Clifford Curzon, via his Austrian teacher, Artur Schnabel, are magical – and very different from the more straightforward approach of, say, a German pianist like Wilhelm Kempff. This goes to show that Viennese rubato can be employed by an Englishman, and that the success or failure of rubato is always linked to the distinction, or otherwise, of the musical intelligence that either engineers or advises it – when it feels right it seems unanswerable but, once again, this is a matter of personal taste.

Each composer inhabits a subtly different world when it comes to rubato. The arrival of Brahms in Vienna in 1862 gave a new focus to the serious musical life of the city. He was an avid Schubert admirer and in some ways his music was related to Schubert's – but not in terms of the kind of rubato required for its performance. Brahms's songs are rather sparing of markings (and he himself counselled discretion regarding flexibility of tempo), leaving performers remarkably free to add their own interpretative gloss. They require a depth of feeling and empathy for the composer that encompasses time displacements never officially asked for on the page. In Brahms, well-employed rubato adds, rather than subtracts, meaning. This is also true of Mahler who, as Kravitt points out, called for no fewer than ten pauses in his short piano-accompanied setting, *Urlicht* (*c.* 1892). Rubato is an integral part of Mahler's songs, and without it the music sounds inauthentic. Hugo Wolf, a contemporary of both Brahms and Mahler, was entirely unlike Brahms, and more obsessively controlling than Mahler, in the manner in which he put his musical thoughts on paper. Time displacements, the result of an exquisite feeling for prosody, are all painstakingly noted down in the way the words are set to music, and his songs are full of explicit instructions to his performers regarding nuances of tempo – *his* rubato, not theirs – keeping his interpreters on a very tight leash. Wolf required the effects of flexible tempo in his music (and how!) but insisted on his right to control singers' use of it down to the smallest detail. In fact, adherence to these copious markings (as well as to the designated metronome speeds in the *Italienisches Liederbuch*) lead to far better performances of the Wolf songs than would otherwise be possible. I learned this invaluably from many hours spent in the rigorous company of Walter Legge and Elisabeth Schwarzkopf. Their Schubert outlook, however, was rather too literal – as if this composer had been of the same mindset as Wolf, their great hero, and had lived in the same musical epoch (this was partly their stern reaction against the sentimental exaggerations of their own contemporaries). As far as they were concerned, if there was no rubato marked on the page in Schubert there was none to be done in performance, but this (*pace* Sonnleithner below) is surely as ill-advised as a pervasively elastic Schubert.

Rubato *does* exist in the performance of Schubert songs, but the question is how much? Schubert never wrote at the beginning of a song, as some other later composers did, 'with rubato'. A comical mistake was that of the non-German-speaking musicologist who interpreted the words 'Mit Verschiebung' at the beginning of *Suleika I* D720 as 'with rubato'. It is true that 'Verschiebung' is the act of displacement, and that rubato is a kind of a shifting or displacement of rhythm, but in fact the 'Verschiebung' is the left-hand pedal on old pianos that physically shifts the whole keyboard an inch or so to the left so that only one of the strings (una corda) might be struck. Only in very rare cases does Schubert specifically request rubato from his performers. In *Als ich sie erröten sah* D153 (February 1815) the eighteenth-century-style marking, 'Mit Liebes-Affekt', would seem to give performers a free hand in the ardent delivery of a poem where the singer is bewitched by love (in reality the exigency of the long-breathed lines leaves little room for manoeuvre). One also thinks of the unsettled tempo required for *An die Nachtigall* (Hölty) D196 where the marking is 'Unruhig, klagend. Im Zetimasse wachsend bis zur Haltung'. Schubert asks for a gradual 'winding up' of the tempo until the fermata in the middle of the song; the effect is of a kind of rhapsodic desperation with which the composer seems to have associated the key of F sharp minor (cf. the slow, then suddenly frenetic, second movement of the A major Piano Sonata D959). The gradual increase of tempo and tension in this song reminds us that rubato is not only about retarding the tempo but also about pushing ahead, a kind of 'forward rubato'. This is famously required during the ascent to the heavens in *Ganymed* D544, and there is another instance from b. 75 of *Lied des Orpheus, als er in die Hölle ging* D474, where motor rhythms in the manner of a Gluck opera are made gradually to speed up. The marking is 'Geschwinder werdend' – something Schubert seldom asks for. A case where rubato is required (and where the inflection is not covered by *ritenuto* or *rallentando*) is the recurring strophic phrase marked 'nachgebend' ('giving way') in *Heidenröslein* D257 on the little ascending phrase 'Röslein, Röslein, Röslein rot'. Left to their own devices, performers can make of this refrain something mysterious and magical, or cutely winsome. Therein lies the danger: because this is time taken *during* the bar, the effect of stretching the rhythm sometimes seems, in the wrong hands or mouth, like musical chewing gum. Kravitt (p. 285) mentions a recorded performance of this from 1902 where 'sudden retards and excessively long holds reduce fin de siècle performance to caricature'.

Hudson tells us that both Hummel and Czerny – members of the old school – complained of an excessive use of rubato (Hudson's 'later rubato') as early as 1829 and 1839 respectively. The most valuable contemporary writing on this point comes from an essay published in Vienna in November 1860 entitled 'Über den Vortrag des Liedes mit besonderer Beziehung auf Franz Schubert' ('On the performance of songs in particular relationship to those of Franz Schubert'). The author is Schubert's exact contemporary and friend, Leopold von Sonnleithner (1797–1873) (*see* FRIENDS AND FAMILY), who came from an intensely musical background and was the first person, in 1821, to come up with an ingenious solution to the publication of Schubert's lieder, considered commercially unviable by the Viennese firms (see PUBLISHERS). Sonnleithner claimed to have heard Schubert accompany and rehearse his songs more than a hundred times, and he insisted that the composer never allowed violent expression in performance. He believed that the lieder singer's job was to relate the experience and feelings of others without impersonating the characters whose feelings he describes:

> Schubert, from the start, called for his songs to be voiced not so much in a rhetorical style, but rather to be sung flowingly, each note, stripped completely of all unmusical conventions of speech, now given its due by the singing voice, and that in this way the musical idea would be given currency in all its purity. Essentially linked to that is the strictest adherence to tempo. Schubert has everywhere indicated precisely where he wanted or would permit a slowing down or a speeding up or a generally freer rendition. Where he has not indicated this, he was not prepared to countenance even the smallest extravagant gesture, not even the slightest deviation from the tempo. Even if this were not verifiable from the unanimous evidence evinced by his contemporaries, anyone with specialist knowledge would have to recognize this indubitable fact from the nature of the style of his accompaniments. A trotting or galloping horse cannot be made to miss a beat [Erlkönig D328]; a whirring spinning-wheel can suddenly stop if the spinster, moved by passion, momentarily forgets to maintain its momentum, but it cannot from one second to the next change from running fast to slow, viz. alternating from one bar to the next [Gretchen am Spinnrade D118]; a vigorously beating heart cannot (save when suffering apoplexy) stand still so that the

singer, at the words 'Dein ist mein Herz, und wird es ewig bleiben' ('My heart is yours and ever shall remain so'), may let his high A sound out long and loud and moan to its conclusion his excess of emotion [Ungeduld D795/7]; when the march of the pilgrims is heard in the distance and the monk relates his observations to these sounds, so he will have to sing away in strict tempo – the march will not adapt itself to his sentimental accesses of hesitancy [Der Kreuzzug D932]. These wretched instances, which we have the misfortune to listen to all too often, shall serve as mere samples, as this meaningless approach has unfortunately already become the norm. The perpetrators of such artistic sacrilege pride themselves to no small extent on their profound under- standing of the immortal master who, were he still alive, would stop his ears or run a mile, his sweet nature not allowing him to mete out on the offenders the appropriate punishment with his conductor's baton. This is in no way to say that Schubert would have wanted his songs churned out mechanically as on a barrel organ. A faithful, purely musical performance does not in any way preclude feeling and emotion. It is just that the singer must not presume, must not attempt to be more poetic or more insightful than the composer who, by the use of clear signs and symbols has specified precisely what he wants sung and how, and whose work, through any arbitrary high-handedness, will be harmed, spoilt to its very core.

Sonnleithner is clear that songs with characterful accompaniments in moto perpetuo style were not to be messed around with, certainly not in the gross manner he suggests was frequently the case. But even he states that Schubert's music is not to be performed mechanically. The modern performer is left confused, perhaps, about what latitude, if any, they may be allowed in this matter.

In the first place one must recognize, as Sonnleithner points out, that the composer has already furnished his score with a great many requirements regarding dynamics, articulation and tempo. And there remain choices within these many interpretative freedoms that require fine judgement from those in the performers' hot seat. In connection with *Winterreise* D911 (and not referring to large-scale rubato) Benjamin Britten writes of 'the innumerable small vari- ants of rhythm and phrasing which makes up the performer's contribution . . . the length of rests or pauses . . . the colour of the singer's voice or the clarity or smoothness of consonants . . . the responsibility of each individual performer'.[1] If singers and pianists concern themselves with the realization of all the demands that are on the page – in front of their noses, yet often ignored – they will usually find themselves too busy to add their own gratuitous gloss to the proceedings. Instead they may be surprised to discover a kind of glow from within, music-making both natural and sincere. In many cases scrupulous respect for the composer's wishes will automati- cally obviate temptation to add further time displacements in the manner of an amateur cook sprinkling spice at the last minute in a desperate attempt to make a dish palatable. Schubert, like all great composers, is superbly adept at putting his thoughts on paper and making his wishes clear – if only one takes the trouble to learn how to decipher those wishes.

As Britten implies, however, there are times when the performer has to think, and feel, beyond the markings. This applies above all to that subtle hesitation in the music, an agogic adjustment or displacement of time (a 'suspirium' in early music) that occurs – only in very special cases – on, or just before, the bar line. This minuscule hiatus signposts moments of awe, wonder, reverence. Its eighteenth-century equivalent is described in C. P. E. Bach's *Essay on the True Manner of Playing Keyboard Instruments* (1753), where he writes of 'the finest lapses from metre [that] can often be industriously produced'. In Schubert's songs it is also the person at the keyboard who must juggle with fragments of silence while making decisions about the place- ment of chords (*see* commentary for the last strophe of *Nachtstück* D672). Bach *fils*, some of

[1] Benjamin Britten, *On Receiving the Aspen Award* (London, 1964), p. 19.

whose music was known to Schubert, goes on to write of 'an alteration in one's own part alone, running against the organization of the metre, while the main movement of the metre must be preserved precisely'. Bach's Enlightenment rationality is married, in the performance of Schubert's music, with the ardour of nascent romanticism. An often-magical hesitancy is usually at a turning point in the harmony, as if a new vista had opened up to the singer (and thus the listener's ears) in an unexpected direction. In *Der Neugierige* D795/6 from *Die schöne Müllerin*, for example, there is an implied caesura, like an intake of breath (a 'suspirium') on the bar line between bb. 41 and 42, just before the pianissimo 6-4 B major chord (before the repeat of 'O Bächlein meiner Liebe'). The *placing* and *balancing* of this chord, together with its *colour*, is something so crucial as to give the pianist the impression of walking on eggshells. This is not preceded by a large ritardando of the previous semiquavers (b. 41), although an imperceptible easing is necessary, but the listener must be made to feel (in the microsecond before that chord sounds, and the microsecond after) that in this bar, leading up to the recapitulation of 'O Bächlein meiner Liebe', a deeper level of trust and intimacy has been attained between the brook and the enraptured miller boy.

Not all moments in the cycle are as heart-stopping as this. In *Des Müllers Blumen* D795/9, for example, it may be tempting to add expressive rubato to the undulations of the little piano interludes in bb. 15 and 35. These, though, are to be avoided: they would impede the overall flow of the brook (and the piece) as well as the song's musical unity. In the postlude to the following song, *Tränenregen* D795/10, however, there should be a tiny expressive caesura before the last quaver of b. 34, the moment when there is a change to the minor key.

Perhaps the most famous agogic hesitation of all occurs in *Gute Nacht* D911/1 from *Winterreise*, with the famous change to the major key (on the bar line between bb. 90 and 91). This is one of the most challenging moments for accompanists. It requires considerable musical courage *not* to slow down the four quavers of b. 90 to any great extent, and instead to *dare* to take time to place the D major chord (beginning of b. 91) in a newly conjured, radiant pool of musical moonlight. At a moment like this all the pianist's faculties are working together – the timing mechanisms of a conductor as well as fingertips and feet – conspiring to provide the appropriately pedalled touch and colour for this ravishing change of key – 'an epiphany that should happen at the moment and not before' (Susan Youens).[2] This represents a lieder version of 'tread softly, for you tread on my dreams' – as well as the gentle and generous (and masochistic) impulse whereby the protagonist blesses the girl who has rejected him but whom he still loves. One would scarcely believe there was so much behind replacing a D minor chord with a D major one. One thing is certain: the shift from minor to major will never be effected eloquently enough in that miraculous split second if the composer's generosity of spirit is not re-experienced firsthand by the pianist. It is at the keyboard that the coalescence of the accompanist's hot seat and the traveller's cold shoes bring about one of music's most melting moments.

Sonnleithner's 1858 essay describes an exaggerated taking of liberties in moto perpetuo songs that is no longer to be heard today. Many other bad habits have faded away: Kravitt quotes Frederick Niecks (1913) describing how pianists played 'even-rhythmed reiterations' deliberately unevenly in order to avoid monotony – 'not two bars of the same length, nor within the bars, two beats alike'. (This strikes me as an ill-advised attempt on the part of a particularly downtrodden generation of accompanists to stake their claim for expressivity.) Hearing aimless shilly-shallying of this kind it is little wonder that Sonnleithner was at the end of his tether. Nevertheless, even in the moto perpetuo songs of Schubert, music is a living, not a mechanical thing, and there is no question of unsmiling metronomic inflexibility.

[2] Letter to the author, March 2013.

Die Sterne D939 is a moto perpetuo where the whole song is powered by the dactylic hum of a universe pulsating with heavenly light. When playing the accompaniment I might be tempted to take time over the turns at the end of the ritornello (occurring in bb. 23, 60, 105, 150), but I refrain from doing so. To expand their significance (other than ensuring these ornaments do not sound mechanical, facile or squib-like) serves little expressive purpose beyond showing my own winsome pleasure in the music. The song proceeds at its 'Etwas geschwind' pace – fast but not *too* fast. The key changes at bb. 31–2 and 76–7 are shifts that cannot be forced; the music must be allowed to breathe, and the tiny agogical adjustments owe far more to C. P. E. Bach than to Johann Strauss. In the third musical verse (beginning 'Sie blicken / Dem Dulder / Recht mild in's Gesicht') are moments of real magic, and mainly because of the text. At bb. 121–2, for 'Und weisen / Von Gräbern / Gar tröstlich und hold', more time has to be taken on the bar line, between the last quaver of the bar and the crotchet at the beginning of the next, because of the key-shift and the confrontation with mortality represented by the words. Something similar occurs in the last musical verse between bb. 167 and 168 – the tempo is eased, as if the music were turning an astral corner. This creation of extra space in the starry weave may not feel like 'rubato' to performers, but that is exactly what it is in Schubertian terms. It has not come about thanks to a generalized reaction of singer or pianist to the beauty of the music and their pleasure in singing or playing it. It represents, rather, an informed and affectionate acknowledgement of Schubert's musical legerdemain as he leads us on a journey via the text (studied in every detail by the performers) through the harmonic pathways of outer space: a kind of homage. In cases like this a measure of concomitant delight at the keyboard is a natural consequence of being in the presence of music of this calibre.

I have indicated above, by way of example, where I might feel the need to take time *at* the time, and not as something solemnly pre-planned. It goes against the grain to talk of these inflections in terms of numbered bars, for this kind of planned robbery leads to a prison sentence. In my experience it is also impossible to map out Schubertian rubato to a cast-iron degree in a rehearsal situation as if it were an actual written requirement. The most I can ever bring myself to write on my music is a pencilled wavy line, and that only sometimes. A distinguished American singer once visited me with her copy of the songs full of ferocious arrows going in different directions, the result of assiduous coachings. She expected these to guide us both in the taking of time at crucial points, as if she had received gospel truths about what to do. Indeed, I was not certain what made her teacher so sure of his fulsomely detailed advice. Nothing could be more fatal to the essential simplicity of Schubert's music than to pull it hither and thither by intensively discussed prior arrangement. Schubertian rubato is something of the moment, an instinctive response to the rise and fall of a particular phrase that seems necessary at the time – a spontaneous, even opportunistic, theft, if you like, rather than a meticulously planned heist. It is where pianist follows singer, and singer follows pianist, in an exchange of mutual delight – non-choreographed dancing rather than a drilled Broadway production. The execution of this swift, and scarcely noticeable, pickpocketing of tempo requires experience, confidence, daring, above all the kind of musicality that trusts in itself and a charm that stems from gratitude for the music's beauties rather than any need for self-promotion.

Rubato in Schubert seems always wrong when applied from the outside, like the icing of a cake, a piece of plaster decoration added on to the edifice of the music. The challenge to the performer is to employ rubato only when *inwardly* necessary, either musically or because of the words (or, ideally, both). Even the tiniest and most subtle of tempo displacements should be an organic part that does not impede the progress of an exquisitely engineered musical construction. This is often a moto perpetuo in some guise or other, carefully put in train by Schubert. Performers should first learn to enjoy the inevitability of his multifarious rhythmical constructions before plotting how to disrupt or derail them. They may very well so enjoy the ride, and be so enchanted by the inherent vitality and truthful simplicity of the music as it unfolds, that they will leave well enough alone.

If a singer needs a little more time to ensure the clarity of the words, of course this is permissible – indeed such considerations also mitigate against some of the ridiculously fast tempi to be heard from members of the broadband generation (*see* TEMPO). On many an occasion an accompanist, working on behalf of his or her singer, must open up a space in the music, cosmetic surgery of a kind, to facilitate the clearer, and more meaningful, phonation of a passage of text. (To be more accurate it is the singer who first takes the time and the pianist who accommodates it.) In cases like these the priority is putting over the poem in a comprehensible and audible manner, although this is no carte blanche to the singer to render a text more dramatic, or more 'moving', by playing fast and loose with the tempo.

In his 1933 essay that enraged the Nazis, *Leiden und Grösse Richard Wagners*, Thomas Mann employs Nietzsche's 'Pathos der Distanz' to describe the difference between music of the classical and Romantic ages. As the nineteenth century progressed music became longer, louder and more sensational, with less and less concern for that 'pathos of distance'. Performers were made to feel that their role was to crash through barriers in order to abolish the distance between music and audience that had characterized the smaller Romantic forms – lieder among them – and where distance is also to do with scale. Modern-day performers of Schubert in exploring the mindset of a pre-Wagnerian age might do well to keep their respectful distance; in essence this is what Leopold von Sonnleithner, on Schubert's behalf, seems to be exhorting them to do – as if paying closer attention to the markings and keeping stricter time were essential to that distance, and part of that pathos.

There will always be highly talented singers to whom this distance seems a step too far back. And it is undeniable that spontaneity, lack of self-consciousness and a kind of selfless immersion in the music can render certain stylistic faults and taking-of-freedoms, however misguided, exciting and compelling. I suspect that Johann Michael Vogl and Ludwig Wüllner were, in their different ways, this kind of singer – magicians who broke the rules but carried the day as a result of their convictions (in the opinion of many in their audience, that is, and to the utter disapproval of others). There are, at most, one or two singers of this kind in every generation, and they seem never to be entirely happy with their voices (thus at least spared the vocal self-satisfaction fatal to lieder singers). I find myself imagining the glorious results if singers of this kind truly attempted to focus their formidable energies on doing exactly what the composer wanted, rather than yielding so unashamedly to their inner demons. The Schubertian singer never satisfied with his own performances who, with the help of an equally great pianist, came nearest, in my view, to balancing the conflicting demands of duty to the composer and obeying his own demons' musical demands is one of the dedicatees of this book.

Bibliography: Sonnleithner 1860
                Hudson 2001, 'Rubato' in *The New Grove* 21/832–5
                Kravitt 1996, p. 71 and Chapter 10, 'Expressive Aesthetics in Performance',
                pp. 177–98
                Scholes 1955 (ninth edition), Rubato p. 889

RÜCKBLICK *see* WINTERREISE D911/8

FRIEDRICH RÜCKERT
(1788–1866)

THE POETIC SOURCES
S1 *Oestliche Rosen von Friedrich Rückert. Drei Lesen.* Leipzig: F.A Brockhaus 1822

After a dedicatory poem addressed 'To Goethe's West-östlicher Divan', Rückert divides his book into three 'Lesen' – selections or readings. There are no titles to any of the poems in this collection so the song titles are Schubert's own.

S2 *Gesammelte Gedichte von Friedrich Rückert.* Vierter Band. Mit Königl. Würtembergischem Privilegium gegen den Nachdruck. Erlangen. Verlag von Carl Heyder 1837

Heyder of Erlangen was the same publisher who, sixteen years earlier, had produced the two volumes of Platen's poetry that were the source of Schubert settings. This collection was printed too late to be Schubert's source (in any case Rückert did not reproduce the text for D775 in this edition) but it is possible that the poet's choice of title for his own 'Sei mir gegrüsst!' (untitled in S1) may have gone back to the Schubert song published as Op. 20 no. 1 in 1823.

Daß der Ostwind Düfte
Hauchet in die Lüfte,
Dadurch thut er kund,
Daß du hier gewesen.

Weil hier Thränen rinnen,
Dadurch wirst du innen,
Wär's dir sonst nicht kund,
Daß ich hier gewesen.

Schönheit oder Liebe,
Ob versteckt sie bliebe?
Düfte thun es und
Thränen kund,
Daß sie hier gewesen.

The text for *Dass sie hier gewesen* from *Östliche Rosen*, Leipzig (1822).

THE SONGS
1822   *Sei mir gerüsst!* D741 [S1: Zweite Lese: pp. 320–21] [S2 as 'Sei mir gerüsst!' in 'Gasele' section p. 187]

1823   *Dass sie hier gewesen* D775 [S1 Dritte Lese: p. 368]
        Du bist die Ruh D776 [S1: Erste Lese: pp. 125–6] [S2: as 'Kehr' ein bei mir!' pp. 107–8]
        Lachen und Weinen D777 [S1: Erste Lese: p. 132] [S2: as 'Lachens und Weinens Grund' p. 111]
        Greisengesang D778 [S1: Zweite Lese: pp. 272–4] [S2: as 'Vom künftigen Alter' in 'Gasele' section, p. 177]

1823(?)   *Die Wallfahrt* D₂778a [S1: Dritte Lese: p. 369]

Rückert was one of the most significant men of letters of his time and, together with the work of Heinrich Heine, his poetry forms a link between the songs of Schubert and those of Schumann. He was born in Schweinfurt on 16 May 1788. His parents were well educated and his father was a lawyer, but his antecedents were farmers which may account for his phys-ical strength and build of a gentle giant. He grew up in Oberlaunigen on the banks of the Main, and enjoyed an idyllic childhood in country surroundings that he described in his forty-poem cycle *Erinnerungen aus den Kinderjahren eines Dorfamtmannsohns* (1829). He studied at the universities of Würzburg and Heidelberg. It was in Heidelberg that he came into contact with Voss to whose influence he owed his formidable mastery of metrics. His extraordinarily high intellect and somewhat people-shy nature marked him out for an academic career, but he found the groves of academe stifling and insufficiently challenging. He was an astonishing auto-didact, seemingly able to learn more by himself than any institution could teach him. He came into contact with Fouqué, Jean Paul, Ludwig Uhland and Friedrich von Schlegel (whose work he admired while disregarding its Roman Catholic slant) and began to publish his poems in almanacs. From the beginning of his career he was amazingly prolific in his output. He worked for a while as an editor of the *Morgenblatt* for the famous publisher Cotta in Stuttgart before spending a year in Rome (1817–18), having been granted a stipend by the Bavarian king. According to Dorothea Schlegel, his old-fashioned German dress, long uncombed hair and moustache, as well as his exceptionally tall and imposing build, caused some consternation among the inhabitants of the Italian capital – it was as if the northern Barbarians had returned to sack the city.

On his way back from Italy, in the autumn of 1818, he spent a few months in Vienna and met the great orientalist Hammer-Purgstall who encouraged him to study eastern languages. (It was the publications of Hammer-Purgstall that had persuaded Goethe to work on his *West-östlicher Divan*, a Hafiz-inspired collection that had only been published in tantalizing excerpts at the time of Rückert's encounter in Vienna.) The meeting with this great scholar was a turning point for Rückert and he went back to work for Cotta with a vast project in mind: the mastery of Persian, and the writing of a book of poetry that took the writings of Hafiz as its model. In this respect he was only a few steps behind Goethe who had conceived the same idea (without even trying to learn Persian) some five years earlier. When Goethe's work appeared in 1819 Rückert's first reaction was anger – the famous 'alter Herr' had taken so many lines almost word for word from his teacher's pioneering translation (letter to Hammer-Purgstall, 12 December

Friedrich Rückert in Rome, 1818, drawn in ink over pencil by Julius Schnorr von Carolsfeld (1794–1872).

1819). Goethe had always been a skilful magpie; his knowledge of eastern poetry was superficial in comparison to Hammer-Purgstall's, but this venerable scholar was no great poet in his own right. Rückert, though not quite a Goethe, was a fabulously gifted writer; he combined aspects of the abilities of the two older men, and his industry and appetite for work enabled him to become a master in a field that was small in terms of public interest but vast in terms of scholarship. Rückert not only came to an intimate understanding of every branch of oriental poetry (he had a genius for learning new languages) but he wrote poetry, with ever-increasing fluency, in the same metrical forms that had been used by the old Persian poets. The form of the ghazal had already been taken up by August von Platen (qv) whose *Ghaselen* (Erlangen, 1821) preceded Rückert's oriental publications. Platen was in turn influenced by Rückert in his *Neue Ghaselen* (Erlangen, 1823), which contained the heading: 'The Orient is over and done with, may the form now be regarded as ours'. That 'ours' included Rückert of course who was one of Platen's most regular correspondents.

The *Östliche Rosen* owed a great deal to Rückert's contacts in Vienna; the collection received a fine review from Matthäus von Collin (*Jahrbuch von Literatur*, 1822) and Schubert was well placed (also perhaps through Bruchmann) to have cottoned on to their significance immediately, setting the poems when they were hot off the press. The continuation of an oriental phase in his lieder composition must have seemed fortuitous after having so recently worked on poems from Goethe's great *West-östlicher Divan*. For a while Rückert worked as an editor of the *Frauentaschenbuch*, but he later took up posts at the universities of Erlangen (from 1826) and Berlin (from 1841), lecturing on oriental philology. Among his many distinguished pupils was Max Müller (son of his friend, the poet Wilhelm Müller) who was to become one of the greatest of philologists at Oxford and an English knight.

At the end of 1821 Rückert had married Luise Wiethaus-Fischer. The many hundreds of *Liebesfrühling* poems that were the result of his love for Luise, and his almost obsessive celebration of the state of matrimony, made this part of his output truly famous in later years. These poems had a particularly strong effect on Robert Schumann (the *Liebesfrühling* cycle Op. 37, and the *Minnespiel* Op. 101) who found in them a reflection of his own love for Clara Wieck. (Schumann was in touch with Rückert by letter although they never met personally.) In his earlier life Rückert's love affairs had always resulted in similarly copious literary reactions: for example, the seventy-six Sonnets of *Amaryllis* (penned in 1812, published in 1825) described the poet's hopeless love for an innkeeper's daughter, and are considered by some modern writers to be among the greatest of German love lyrics.

Wilhelm Müller (poet of Schubert's *Die schöne Müllerin* and *Winterreise*) was a great admirer of Rückert but he voiced concern at the poet's inability to live in the real world and to inject his output with an understanding of prevailing commercial conditions. Some of the translations Rückert made from Persian and other languages are almost superhumanly

Title page of *Östliche Rosen*, Leipzig (1822).

clever; his ability to match complicated oriental metres, not to mention wordplay and puns, with their German equivalents takes the breath away. The ingenuity of the man knew no bounds in the tasks he set himself in his writing, but the effect of all this dazzling command of knowledge and resource was to exhaust and alienate his potential readership – it was all 'too much'. (Rückert penned some ten thousand poems in all.) Müller saw the danger of his friend's diffuseness early on and Oskar Wolff in his *Encyclopädie der deutschen Nationalliteratur* (1846) is almost at a loss to describe Rückert's output and his technical mastery of rhyme, assonance, alliteration and so on. Wolff compares the poetry to a vast field of flowers blooming in disorganized but magnificent profusion, or a fecund Brazilian rainforest where plants of every hue and variety are entwined around trees as old as time itself. To this day no one has entered that forest in order to classify its vegetation and bring its species to order – a new edition of the *Nachlass* is planned, but there is still no complete collection of Rückert's work.

In the winter of 1833–4 there was a domestic tragedy: two of his ten children with Luise died. A substantial collection of poems entitled *Kindertotenlieder* was published only in 1872, posthumously, and five of these achieved musical immortality through the settings of Gustav Mahler who was a devoted admirer of Rückert's work. This was an unlikely collaboration between hugely different men from different backgrounds and epochs, united only, perhaps, by their burning intelligence and scorn for the rewards and prizes of the world. A text from *Liebesfrühling* like 'Ich bin der Welt abhanden gekommen' (set by Mahler as the last of the *Fünf Rückert-Lieder*) was something to which this composer could truly respond. Other fans of Rückert's verse were Carl Loewe and Richard Strauss who set no fewer than sixteen of his texts to music. But it was Schubert who first saw the poet's musical potential, and the *Östliche Rosen* songs *Dass sie hier gewesen* D775, *Du bist die Ruh* D776, *Lachen und Weinen* D777 and *Greisengesang* D778 are all masterpieces. Few of Schubert's poets, outside Goethe, Mayrhofer, Heine and Müller, could claim to have inspired such a sequence of great songs.

In 1848 Rückert took early retirement from his university posts and settled near Coburg (in Neuses bei Coburg) to follow his own scholastic interests. He remained a prolific poet, publishing many successful collections, although his more ambitious epic poems, comedies and historical dramas were never popular. The death of Luise in 1857 left him solitary and he was almost a recluse in his later years. He died of stomach cancer on 31 January 1866 (the day that would have been Schubert's sixty-ninth birthday). At the turn of the century

Rückert, the only photograph, *c*. 1840.

Rückert's reputation stood high, with many a gold-embossed volume of the *Liebesfrühling* poems available in the bookshops as a wedding or engagement present. The six volumes of *Gedichte* on which his fame as a poet rests were published between 1834 and 1837, although a twelve-volume edition appeared in 1868. His absorption in the celebration of domestic life (he could, and would, write poems on such banal subjects as toothache) made Rückert in retrospect appear to have been the cosy Biedermeier poet par excellence, but this is unjust in light of his liberal credentials, the depth of his philosophical understanding and his early concern (like Uhland and Kerner) with 'green' issues. He is less read today than ever although he sometimes receives praise from contemporary authors who are struck by his integrity of utterance and a technical brilliance (above all as a translator) that has scarcely ever been equalled in German letters.

Bibliography: Aderhold 2002, pp. 59–81
                  Wolff 1846, pp. 318–19

RÜCKWEG

(MAYRHOFER) **D476** [H301]
D minor   September 1816

The return

(30 bars)

Zum Donaustrom, zur Kaiserstadt
Geh' ich in Bangigkeit:
Denn was das Leben Schönes hat,
Entweichet weit und weit.[1]

To the river Danube, to the imperial city
I go with apprehension;
For the beauty of life
Recedes further and further behind me.

Die Berge schwinden allgemach,[2]
Mit ihnen Wald und Fluss;[3]
Der Kühe Glocken läuten nach,
Und Hütten nicken Gruss.

The mountains gradually disappear,
And with them forests and rivers;
The tinkling of cowbells lingers in the air,
And the huts nod their greeting.

Was starrt dein Auge tränenfeucht
Hinaus in blaue Fern'?
Ach, dorten weilt ich, unerreicht,
Frei unter Freien gern!

Why do your eyes, moist with tears,
Stare out into the blue distance?
Ah, there I dwelt happily, in seclusion,
A free man among free men.

Wo Liebe noch und Treue gilt,
Da öffnet sich das Herz;
Die Frucht an ihren Strahlen schwillt,
Und strebet himmelwärts.

Where love and faith are still cherished
The heart will open;
The fruit will ripen in their light,
And aspire towards heaven.

JOHANN MAYRHOFER (1787–1836)

*This is the sixth of Schubert's forty-seven Mayrhofer solo settings (1814–24). See the poet's
biography for a chronological list of all the Mayrhofer settings.*

During the recording sessions for the Hyperion Edition, Ann Murray playfully rehearsed this
song in a rasping cabaret voice, à la Marlene Dietrich. It was astonishingly convincing not only
as vocal imitation: despite the obvious anachronism, the song seemed perfectly suited to the
world-weary style of the *chansonnière* or *diseuse*. The poet drags his feet on his return to Vienna
from the country, and D minor (with which the *Winterreise* cycle opens) is Schubert's key of
melancholy journeys. For Mayrhofer, native of Linz and the mountains of Upper Austria, the
capital city meant politics and intrigue and a harrowing job as a book censor. It was a place

[1] In the 1824 *Gedichte*, Mayrhofer writes '*Entschwindet* weit und weit'. For an explanation of the background to these
alternative Mayrhofer readings see Editorial Note at the beginning of Johann MAYRHOFER.
[2] Mayrhofer (1824 *Gedichte*) writes 'Die Berge *weichen* allgemach'.
[3] Mayrhofer (1824 *Gedichte*) writes 'Mit ihnen *Tal* und Fluss'.

where political repression made it increasingly difficult to be a free man able to express an honest opinion among free men. The popular touch is deliberate, a *Singspiel* style owing something to the street ballad, and a gentle forerunner of the bitter-sweet German cabaret songs that were to voice their political resentments in cynical world-weary terms – music for a Weill, perhaps. The retreating harmonic sequences from b. 12 are perfectly tailored to suggest country scenery dwindling into the distance. Indeed the whole musical shape of the piece lives up to its title – moving away from something, and towards a place that makes for a heavy heart. Even the cowbells seem to be a few more steps in the distance at bb. 21 and 22 than when they are first heard in bb. 19 and 20. The NSA proposes a postlude (a repeat of the prelude) that does not appear in AGA.

Autograph:	Wienbibliothek im Rathaus, Vienna (first draft)
First edition:	Published as No. 15 of *Neueste Folge nachgelassener Lieder und Gesänge* by J. P. Gotthard, Vienna in 1872 (P441)
Subsequent editions:	Not in Peters; AGA XX 252: Vol. 4/178; NSA IV: Vol. 11/4
Discography and timing:	Fischer-Dieskau I 8[4] 1'56
	Hyperion I 3[4]
	Hyperion II 16[2] 2'01 Ann Murray

← *Abschied, nach einer Wallfahrtsarie* D475   *Alte Liebe rostet nie* D477 →

Schubert portrait on plaster (1870) by Moritz von Schwind.

S

Der SÄNGER
(GOETHE) **D149** [H61]

The minstrel

The song exists in two versions, the second of which is discussed below:
(1) February 1815; (2) Date unknown

(1) 'Mässig, heiter'   D major – B♭ major   𝄵   [129 bars]

(2) 'Heiter, mässig geschwind'   D major – B♭ major   𝄵   [151 bars]

(151 bars)

(1)	Was hör' ich draussen vor dem Tor,	'What do I hear outside the gate,
	Was auf der Brücke schallen?	What sounds are those on the bridge?
	Lass den Gesang vor unserm Ohr	Let that song echo in our ears
	Im Saale widerhallen!	Throughout the hall!'
	Der König sprach's, der Page lief;	Thus spake the king, the page ran out;
	Der Page kam	
	der Konig rief:[1]	The page returned, the king cried:
	Lasst mir herein den Alten!	'Let the old man enter!'
(2)	Gegrüsset seid mir, edle Herrn,	'Greetings, noble lords,
	Gegrüsst ihr, schönen Damen![2]	Greetings, fair ladies!
	Welch' reicher Himmel! Stern bei Stern!	How rich is this galaxy! Star upon star!
	Wer kennet ihre Namen?	Who can know their names?
	Im Saal voll Pracht und Herrlichkeit	In this hall of pomp and splendour
	Schliesst, Augen, euch, hier ist nicht Zeit,	Eyes, close, now is not the time
	Sich staunend zu ergötzen	To feast yourselves in wonder.'
(3)	Der Sänger druckt' die Augen ein,	The minstrel closed his eyes
	Und schlug in vollen Tönen;	And struck up in resonant tones;
	Die Ritter schauten mutig drein,	Resolutely the knights looked on,
	Und in den Schoss die Schönen.	While the fair ladies looked down into their laps.
	Der König, dem es wohgefiel;[3]	The king, well pleased with the song,
	Liess, ihn zu ehren	
	für sein Spiel,	Sent for a gold chain
	Eine goldne Kette holen.	To reward him for his singing.

[1] In other editions, Goethe writes 'Der *Knabe* kam, der König rief' – but Schubert sets this line as above, exactly as he found it in the *Gedichte*, Anton Strauss, Wien, 1810.
[2] Goethe has '*schöne* Damen'.
[3] Goethe later changed this to 'Der König dem *das Lied* gefiel'.

(4) Die goldne Kette gib mir nicht; Die Kette gib den Rittern, Vor deren kühnem Angesicht[4] Der Feinde Lanzen splittern! Gib sie dem Kanzler, den du hast, Und lass ihn noch die goldne Last, Zu andern Lasten tragen.	'Do not give the golden chain to me But to your knights, Before whose bold countenance Enemy lances shatter. Give it to your chancellor And let him bear its golden burden With his other burdens.
(5) Ich singe, wie der Vogel singt, Der in den Zweigen wohnet; Das Lied, das aus der Kehle dringt, Ist Lohn, der reichlich lohnet. Doch darf ich bitten, bitt' ich eins: Lass mir den besten Becher Weins, In purem Golde reichen.	I sing as the bird sings Who lives among the branches; The song that pours from my throat Is its own rich reward. But if I may, I will ask one thing: Bring me your best wine In a chalice of pure gold.
(6) Er setzt ihn an, er trank ihn aus: 'O, Trank voll süsser Labe! O, wohl dem höchbeglückten Haus, Wo das ist kleine Gabe! Ergeht's euch wohl, so denkt an mich, Und danket Gott so warm, als ich Fur diesen Trünk euch danke.'	He raised it to his lips and drained it: 'O draught of sweet refreshment Happy the blessed house Where that is but a trifling gift! If you fare well, think of me, And thank God as warmly as I Thank you for this drink.'

JOHANN WOLFGANG VON GOETHE (1749–1832); poem written *c.* 1783

This is the seventh of Schubert's seventy-five Goethe solo settings (1814–26). See the poet's biography for a chronological list of all the Goethe settings.

The Challier lieder catalogue of songs written before 1885 lists fourteen settings of this poem; by 1953 this had expanded to twenty-three. One would not perhaps rush to unearth the versions by Grimmer, Grönland and Schlottmann because even the great lieder composers (Loewe, Schumann, Wolf and of course Schubert) had a hard time with this text, which comes from Chapter 11 of the second book of Goethe's *Wilhelm Meisters Lehrjahre* (1795). It is doubtful whether Schubert had read the novel by 1815 – he almost certainly found the poem in the 1810 Viennese edition of Goethe's *Gedichte* where it is printed separately as the first item in the *Balladen und Romanzen* section. Some time later, as Schubert embarked on exploring the character of Mignon, he would have realized that this lyric signals the first appearance of the Harper, the morbid and crazed man of aged appearance who is the father, by an unwitting incestuous relationship, of that waif-like girl. The poem falls outside the usual group of texts that form the accepted trilogy of Goethe's Harper songs. This is hardly surprising because, unlike the Harper's other highly subjective Ich-Lieder, *Der Sänger* is not at all gloom-laden or pessimistic. At this point in the novel the mysterious musician is anxious to please and sings 'in the most sprightly style' (as Thomas Carlyle puts it in the first translation of the novel into English). Wilhelm Meister declares that the old man's voice 'blesses and revives'. After delivering the ballad to the

---

[4] Goethe writes 'Vor deren *kühnen* Angesicht'.

assembled company (some of whom had been making 'sundry very shallow observations, debating whether the Harper is a Papist or a Jew'), the minstrel calls for a glass of wine and quaffs it before continuing to entertain the assembled company.

The theme of the poem is the glory of art for its own sake, and the reward that an artist finds in his work without needing to contaminate his ideals with material greed. Enlightened patronage is acceptable up to a point but state subsidy for the arts is only a distant spectre. Nevertheless, Goethe must have been aware that artistic humility had been, and would continue to be, exploited at every turn by holders of official purse strings. He was all too conscious of his multifarious obligations to the Weimar court in the 1770s and 1780s, and of how he had become a civil servant to the duke – however well rewarded – at the expense of his artistic freedom. On his return from Italy he had insisted on a complete revision of these working conditions. This ballad, written in 1783, was published soon after the aftershocks of the French Revolution as experienced in Germany had begun to change the relationship between noble employers and their lackeys.

It is immediately apparent that the poet here takes seriously the theme of altruism; he casts his ballad in an idealized and imaginary medieval epoch, full of chivalry and fine feeling. (In reality the Harper is here a modern figure, expressing views of artistic independence that a composer of Schubert's generation would have understood.) Before he sings this song in *Wilhelm Meister*, the Harper deplores man's 'repulsive selfishness'. Novalis had foreseen the return of a golden age of harmonious society, a union of spirit and power, where the artist's role was that of mediator, tempering and enlightening those with political might. Goethe was writing in a world as yet incapable of imagining the financial dealings and fights for artistic independence of a Beethoven, let alone a Wagner. Richard Capell wonders how it was that the impoverished Schubert should have taken up this poem without irony. It was all very well, Capell says (not quite accurately), that the poem should have been written by Goethe who 'never in all his life had to think of ways and means'. The answer is that Schubert was at the time hardly thinking of patronage and financial reward, but rather gearing himself up to face up to his father and insist on his right to give up schoolmastering to become a full-time composer.

For any composer, the main problem with this text is that there are no words for the powerful minstrel's sung performance. Although he is described as a singer ('Der Sänger' indeed), his ability to play his harp (as in the introduction bb. 1–12 and the interlude from b. 53) is all that we, as his audience at one remove, are permitted to hear. The song that receives the approbation of king and court is inaudible to us because Goethe provides no words for it. This is a paradox: the whole of *Der Sänger* is sung of course, but it describes the circumstances leading up to the minstrel's performance, and its aftermath, without allowing us to hear the performance itself. In his extended setting Hugo Wolf gets around this problem by creating a wordless vocal melody in the tenor register of the piano part: the minstrel on the bridge sings 'outside' the vocal texture and the king inside it notices him and comments (in song – how else?). In Schumann's *Ballade des Harfners* Op. 98a no. 1 we hear only a series of rhetorical harp-like spread chords in the piano, as though the singer's skills lie in instrumental virtuosity alone. Loewe's setting is short and to the point, but that is the best thing that might be said of it. Only in Anton Rubinstein's setting (the first of his Op. 91 cycle composed in 1872 which includes every single item of verse in *Wilhelm Meister*) are four pages of piano solo provided to represent the minstrel's performance in real time to the assembled courtiers. But this is not an ideal solution either as it only reminds us that the poem's protagonist is supposed to be renowned for his singing voice rather than simply his instrumental prowess. It is clear that Schubert also had difficulties with the poem, but what is surprising is that a boy of eighteen should have grappled so manfully with its challenges, even if he failed to conquer them entirely. He provides a piano interlude for the performance where the accompanist has to sing his heart out on behalf of the soloist.

Verse 1: John Reed describes the opening bars as 'court music', but the minstrel is not yet inside the palace: in the first *Fassung* the piano writing is marked pianissimo and 'In der Ferne' – 'in the distance'. The sound of the minstrel's voice filters through the palace gate into the king's chamber. Unlike in the Wolf setting, and perhaps nearer to Goethe's intent, the king and court are made to listen to the music in silence, rather than talking through it. This song in the form of an extended piano interlude is recapitulated in the third verse, when the minstrel gives a repeat performance, this time within the audience chamber. Schubert's response to a medieval background is often to conjure an eighteenth-century style – old-fashioned music that a masterful old man from an earlier generation (like Haydn himself, surely Schubert's idea of a musical father figure) might have played. The king's observations cut into the song at a convenient cadence at b. 2 (a fragment of the minstrel's melody returns between his sentences at bb. 15–16). This mixture of outdoor and indoor shots, as if in a film, is one of the great advantages of a song unencumbered by operatic scenery. The young page runs dutifully enough for Schubert: in cartoon fashion the music ascends when he is summoned at bb. 19–20 – the marking is 'Rasch' and then 'staccato'; when his job is accomplished off he goes in the opposite direction, bb. 21–4. (Here Wolf's version is more vivid: there is the same ascending and descending pattern, but the minion's scurrying is depicted by the pianist's left hand crossing over into the treble clef to suggest the squeaky obedience of a lad with an unbroken voice.)

Verses 2–4: From b. 27 the marking is 'Freundlich, mässig'; there is a change of key signature to F major and the music is now in ¾. It is apparent that the old minstrel has been musically trained in the formality of another age. His aria of greeting manages many a vocal flourish and gentlemanly turn. He addresses the beautiful ladies (bb. 32–3) as one not entirely unacquainted with the pleasures of the fairer sex, but it has clearly all been a long time ago. One cannot help wondering whether Wagner had this poem in mind when he wrote Wolfram's opening stanza to the singing contest in the second act of *Tannhäuser*: 'Es wird der Blick wohl trunken mir vom Schauen . . . Da blick' ich auf zu *einem* nur der Sterne'. Wagner seems to have been more impressed by stars as a metaphor for ladies, while Goethe was youthfully impressed with mighty lords and knights. The fanfares of formality die away; the emptiness of C major ceremonial octaves (bb. 41–6) melts into recitative. At b. 47 the change to 'Recit.' and the re-emergence of B flat within a C major chord are a quick means of changing focus from outer pomp to inner contemplation. The old man closes his eyes. It is as if he has fallen into a trance in preparation for his performance. There is a change of key signature back into D major (from b. 51) for the close of his recitative that prepares for the return of 'a tempo' and, at b. 53, the music of the ballad's opening. This is like a compressed sonata movement (bb. 53–83), including an artful little recapitulation at b. 74. But during the minstrel's solo there are also asides from the narrator; the thunderstruck audience is described in a whisper (bb. 64–8) just as the figuration becomes intricate for the pianist standing in for the singer. It is notable that Schubert's operatic instincts, such as they were, led him to amplify the length of the song at this point in order to incorporate a vocal-cum-instrumental solo of credible length from the minstrel (the first version is ten bars shorter here). A cadence in D major at bb. 82–3 brings this set piece to an end, but the two quiet chords that follow, leading into recitative in B flat (a change of key signature), beautifully capture that moment of astonished silence – the audience has been deeply moved. In fast-moving recitative the minstrel refuses the king's offer of a golden chain as a reward (bb. 89–98). By now Schubert had learned that, in this type of ballad, if he lingered in one section he must make up for the dalliance in the next. With a passing reference to the dangers of medieval joust and battle, the music moves on to its next moment of repose.

Verse 5: It is this verse that Wolf seized upon to make a fully sung version of the minstrel's tune which has up until now only occurred in the accompaniment. Yet these words betoken no

Illustration for Goethe's *Der Sänger* (1853).

performance: they are an explanation of the minstrel's motives, once the formal performance is over. Schubert makes of it a charming and unpretentious arietta ('Angenehm, etwas geschwind' from b. 99), very much 'off-duty' music for a serious artist, in his pastoral key of F and a time signature of §. This 'faux-naïf' music is almost too self-consciously simple, but it is apt for the words, and in no danger of swamping the grandeur of the minstrel's central utterance. Both Schubert and Wolf make their accompaniments blossom into flowing semiquavers at this point. As soon as the idea of asking for refreshment occurs to the minstrel he breaks off from his song (as if he has remembered, just in time, that he must not outstay his welcome or bore his hosts). The time has come to claim his modest reward and he returns to recitative (at b. 110) to ask that some of the best wine be served to him in a golden chalice. This is a point of contention in various Goethe editions where pure glass ('reinem Glas') can often be found. Goethe seems to have preferred gold for the poem in ballad form, reverting to glass within the context of the novel in its various forms.

Verse 6: At b. 114 ('Nicht zu langsam, lieblich') there is a change to B flat major and *alla breve* time. The narrator takes over for the line that introduces the old man's final say – the most civilized and measured of drinking songs beginning at b. 118 ('O, Trank voll süsser Labe'). This is probably one song too many as far as the king is concerned who, like Mr Bennet in Jane Austen's *Pride and Prejudice*, may have felt that the singing had 'delighted us long enough'. And yet there is nothing rumbustious here; this is the music of the enraptured wine connoisseur who can seldom afford to taste the best vintages. We distinctly feel that the jaded king and court have been quaffing the same wine without fully appreciating its quality. During this salute to the drink (the repeat of the words 'O, Trank voll süsser Labe' is only to be found in Schubert) the melismas on 'süsser' and 'Labe' (bb. 121–2) suggest liquid ambrosia tasted and rolled around the mouth in sheer wine-tasting delight. Here is a young composer who already knows how to sit in a corner and relish his drink in friendly and thoughtful company. We do not need to be told that the singer has sat down – the music suggests it; indeed we may wonder how the king will get rid of the musician once he has struck this philosophizing form. The garrulous word repetitions on the last page leave us with the impression of an old man enjoying his libation, allowing it to render him fond and sentimental. The affectionate strains with triplet accompaniment of this section are reminiscent of another bardic song – the rejection of violence in favour of love in *An die Leier* D737. The manner of the minstrel's exit in the last five bars suggests he is being gently guided out of the audience chamber. As he withdraws, the final feminine cadence suggests a gracious parting bow. The last 'so denkt an mich' seems significantly pointed, perhaps because there is no hint of a postlude (there is a rolled chord, however, to close the first version). Could Schubert be saying that he too aspires to the role of bard, that he too wishes to be allowed to sing as freely as a bird in the branches, if only his father would permit him? The power of song can educate and civilize those of our rulers susceptible to music; it seems that the composer was hoping for a change of heart much nearer to home.

Autograph:	Conservatoire collection, Bibliothèque Nationale, Paris
Publication:	First published as part of the AGA in 1895 (P550; first version)
	First published as Op. post. 117 by Josef Czerny, Vienna in June 1829 (P221; second version)
Publication reviews:	*Berliner allgemeine musikalische Zeitung*, No. 44 (31 October 1829) p. 347 [Waidelich/Hilmar Dokumente I No. 750]
Subsequent editions:	Peters: Vol. 3/94; AGA XX 45a & b: Vol. 2/33; NSA IV: Vol. 7/90 & 97; Bärenreiter: Vol. 6/137 (first version) & 48 (second version)
Bibliography:	Byrne 2003, pp. 297–304
	Capell 1928, p. 98
	Fischer-Dieskau 1977, p. 42
Further settings:	Johann Friedrich Reichardt (1752–1814) *Aus Wilhelm Meisters Lehrjahre* (1795–6)
	Carl Friedrich Zelter (1758–1832) *Der Sänger* (1803)
	Carl Loewe (1796–1869) *Der Sänger* Op. 59 no. 2 (1836)
	Robert Schumann (1810–1856) *Ballade des Harfners* Op. 98a no. 2 (1849)
	Anton Rubinstein (1829–1894) *Der Sänger* Op. 91 no. 1 (1872)
	Hugo Wolf (1860–1903) *Der Sänger* (1888)
Discography and timing:	Fischer-Dieskau I 3^1 7'06
	Hyperion I 10^1 8'04 Martyn Hill
	Hyperion II 4^{18}

← *Genügsamkeit* D143   *Der Liedler* D209 →

Der SÄNGER AM FELSEN
(PICHLER) **D482** [H305]
E minor   September 1816

The singer on the rock

(21 bars)

[A L E X I S]
Klage, meine Flöte, klage[1]
Die entschwundnen schönen Tage,
Und des Frühlings schnelle Flucht,

Hier auf den verwelkten Fluren,
Wo mein Geist umsonst die Spuren
Süss gewohnter Freuden sucht.

Klage, meine Flöte, klage!
Einsam rufest du dem Tage,
Der dem Schmerz zu spät erwacht.
Einsam schallen meine Lieder,
Nur das Echo hallt sie wieder
Durch die Schatten stiller Nacht.

[. . . 2 . . .]

Klage, meine Flöte, klage!
Kürzt den Faden meiner Tage
Bald der strengen Parze Stahl;
Klage dann auf Lethes Matten[2]
Irgend einem guten Schatten
Meine Lieb' und meine Qual!

[*ALEXIS*]
Mourn, my flute, mourn
The beautiful, vanished days,
And the swift flight of spring

Here on the faded meadows,
Where in vain my spirit seeks the traces
Of sweet, familiar pleasures.

Mourn, my flute, mourn!
All alone you cry out to the day
Which too late awakes to pain.
My lonely songs ring out;
Only the echo carries them back
Through the shades of the silent night.

[. . . 2 . . .]

Mourn my flute, mourn!
Should the blade of the harsh fates
Soon shorten the thread of my days
Then, on Lethe's meadows,
Sing to a kindly shade
Of my love and my torment.

KAROLINE PICHLER (1769–1843)

*This is the first of Schubert's four Pichler solo settings (1816, a song of an unknown date, and
1821). See the poet's biography for a chronological list of all the Pichler settings.*

Benjamin Britten used to 'orchestrate' the accompaniments he played – mostly in his head, but
sometimes with pencilled instrumental cues on the printed music. Here we have the sole
instance of Schubert doing the same on a manuscript – the opening pianoforte ritornello
prompted by the opening words of the poem is marked with the word 'Flöte' (flute) in brackets.
The introduction is nevertheless wonderful piano music with a touch of Mozartian drama and

[1] Pichler writes (*Idyllen*, 1803) '*Klag*, *o meine Flöte, klage*' at the beginning of each strophe.
[2] AGA has '*O dann sing* auf Lethe's Matten', but NSA prints Pichler's original as above.

rhetoric. (This six-bar passage is also designated as the postlude.) The song is marked 'restless and plaintive' and the key of E minor is often associated by Schubert with dejection and unhappiness. One is tempted to regard the passionate melismatic semiquavers and triplets of the vocal line as Italian in inspiration.

The inspiration of the poem is certainly from classical times: Karoline Pichler's 135-line 'Idylle', a dialogue between the shepherds Alexis and Mycon, is set in pastoral Greece. The dialogue begins with this plaint sung by Alexis in five verses (actually the only part of the 'Idylle' that would suit musical setting) and the story unfolds only after this. Drawn by the sound of the music, Mycon approaches the rock, remarking that the murmuring of the stream and the song of the nightingale are nothing like as sad as the music of Alexis, and that his own happy disposition has been moved to sadness by it. Alexis pours out his woes to his friend: he has been betrayed by the beautiful shepherdess Delia and death now seems the only option. Mycon is horrified that a mere girl should have caused such a reaction and he talks to Alexis, man to man, reminding him that there are plenty of pretty girls who could take his mind off Delia. Alexis counters with every possible reason to wallow in his sadness, but Mycon's viewpoint triumphs in the end – with the passing of winter and the coming of the new spring, life will renew itself and Alexis will be released from grief. The song dates from the same time as another Pichler setting – *Lied* ('Ferne von der grossen Stadt') D483.

The NSA prints all five of Pichler's strophes, laid under music. Of these strophes 1, 2 and 5 are translated here as recorded in the Hyperion Edition.

Autograph:	Pierpont Morgan Library, New York (first draft)
First edition:	Published as part of the AGA in 1895 (P657)
Subsequent editions:	Not in Peters; AGA XX 264: Vol. 4/210; NSA IV: Vol. 11/8
Discography and timing:	Fischer-Dieskau I 8[12] 2'46 (first two strophes only)
	Hyperion I 9[18]
	Hyperion II 16[7] 3'21 Arleen Auger

←— *Wer nie sein Brot mit Tränen ass*   *Lied (Ferne von der grossen*
   (Harfenspieler III) D478/2b   *Stadt) D483* —→

Des SÄNGERS HABE[1]   The minstrel's gift
(SCHLECHTA) **D832** [H559]
B♭ major   February 1825

[1] The seven-strophe version of this poem as printed in a later Schlechta publication (*Ephemeren*, 1876) differs in strophes 2–5. The first strophe is identical, and apart from Schlechta's use of 'er' rather than 'ich' at the end of the poem, the final verse is very similar. Even with the changes in the middle verses the gist of the poem has not been significantly altered. Schlechta tended to fuss endlessly over changing details that neither improved his poetry nor seriously altered its meaning.

Schlagt mein ganzes Glück in Splitter,	Break my happiness in pieces,
Nehmt mir alle Habe gleich,	Take from me all I possess;
Lasset mir nur meine Zither,	Leave me only my zither,
Und ich bleibe froh und reich.	And I shall remain glad and rich.
Wenn des Grames Wolken ziehen,	When clouds of sorrow approach
Haucht sie Trost in meine Brust,	It breathes comfort into my heart,
Und aus ihrem Golde blühen	And from its golden strings
Alle Blumen meiner Lust.	Bloom all the flowers of my joy.
Will die Liebe nicht gewähren,	If love is not forthcoming,
Freundschaft brechen ihre Pflicht,	And friendship fails in its duty,
Kann ich beide stolz entbehren,	Then I can proudly forego them both,
Aber meine Zither nicht.	But not my zither.
Reisset meines Lebens Sehne,	When the sinews of my life are torn
Wird sie mir ein Kissen sein,	It will be a pillow for me;
Lullen mich die süssen Töne	Its sweet tones will lull me
In den letzten Schlummer ein.	To my last sleep.
In den Grund des Tannenhaines	Then in the grove of fir trees
Senkt mich leise dann hinab;	Lower me gently into the earth;
Und statt eines Leichensteines	And instead of a tombstone
Stellt die Zither auf mein Grab,	Place my zither upon my grave,
Dass ich, wenn zum stillen Reigen,	So that when at midnight
Aus des Todes dunklem Bann,	The spirits rise from death's dark spell
Mitternachts die Geister Steigen,	For their silent dance,
Ihre Saiten rühren kann.	I may stir its strings.

FRANZ XAVER VON SCHLECHTA (1796–1875)

This is the fourth of Schubert's six Schlechta solo settings (1815–26). See the poet's biography for a chronological list of all the Schlechta settings.

We are always told that it is dangerous to link the mood of a piece of music with biographical circumstances. This may well be true of symphonies, string quartets, sonatas and so on – works that have a relatively long genesis. It is also true that composers do not necessarily write happy music when happy, or tragic music when they have suffered a personal blow. The shape of the work, and its musical needs, take precedence over the vicissitudes of life. The shape of a song, however, is dictated by a poem, and any composer will occasionally be attracted to a lyric or ballad because it chimes with his feelings at the time. When Johannes Brahms, for instance, was moved by a poem, whether or not he later set it, he scratched the margin with his thumbnail, indenting the printed page with the pressure of his emotion. Why should a composer be any different from the rest of us? The vast majority of Schubert's songs were set without a sense of personal involvement, beyond that which he employed constantly in the vast theatre of his imagination. On the whole his creative need was to reflect life simply as it was, his different musical styles the natural result of setting different poets with different temperaments. From time to time, however, particularly at moments of personal crisis, Schubert was moved to write poetry himself. Similarly, he would sometimes look to the poetry of others to mirror his distress and to give him comfort. And when he found something that seemed to speak for him, he set it to music as part of a cathartic process. The choice of Müller's *Die schöne Müllerin* was no accident at a time when the composer was gravely ill, and the composition of *Des Sängers Habe* seems to be in the same category. Indeed a comparison between *Pause* D795/12 in that cycle and *Des Sängers Habe* is fascinating. Both songs are in B flat major; the first refers to a lute, no longer in use and hanging on the wall, the second to a minstrel's zither that is placed on the dead musician's grave. There is a striking similarity between the melismatic vocal lines of 'Soll es das Vorspiel neuer Lieder sein?' (*Pause*, bb. 66–9 and 74–7) and 'Stellt die Zither auf mein Grab' and 'Ihre Seiten rühren kann' (*Des Sängers Habe*, bb. 46–7 and 55–6).

It is possible that in early 1825 Schubert had to return to hospital after a relapse in his condition. Life seemed to be going ill for him on personal and material levels. His one consolation was that his songs were being talked about throughout Vienna and he was becoming increasingly well known, even if he had little to show for it financially. It was at this time that he wrote *Des Sängers Habe*, a work that John Reed calls 'despairing, defiant and triumphant by turns' – a fairly accurate assessment of the composer's mood. Schlechta had been a schoolfriend of Schubert's, and the composer had access to his poems in manuscript; indeed it is vaguely possible that Schlechta wrote the poem with his friend's plight in mind. The text does not appear in the poet's published *Dichtungen* (1824), so if *Des Sängers Habe* was a new poem in 1825 this is quite likely to have been the case. The printed version of the poem (*Ephemeren*, 1876) differs greatly from the one that Schubert set, almost certainly from a handwritten copy. It is possible that the composer himself made the important change from third person to first in the last verse ('Dass ich' rather than 'Dass er'), underlining the status of this song as artistic credo.

The introduction is a mixture of a falling figure in octaves, loud decisive chords and strutting repeated notes as an upbeat to jaunty triplets with a touch of staccato, suggesting an instrument with a brighter, steelier twang than a harp's. This might be the zither mentioned in the poem, or it might be Schubert's piano. That this was above all meant to sound as piano music is emphasized by the re-employment of these right-hand triplets in the first movement of the Piano Trio in B flat, Op. 99 (D898). The song of course is in the same key. This introduction paints a picture of man sweeping aside his misfortune with a touch of anger and defiance, but also with grace and gallant bravado. Here is the spirit of Mozart standing up to the Archbishop of Salzburg; here is the brandished fist of Beethoven who menaces his aristocratic patrons and warns them that he is their superior. But here is also Schubert, who cannot keep up an angry stance for long, and who takes us, as we go deeper into the song, into his secret world of consolation and happiness through music. We are reminded of *An die Leier* D737 which begins in thunderous mood but, despite itself, softens into love music. Dotted rhythms and jumps of an octave in the vocal line (b. 5) reinforce the feeling of pride and grandeur, and there is also a great deal of doubling between voice and piano part – often Schubert's way of emphasizing that he has something of great import to say. The ominous nature of this doubling in the penultimate verse (from b. 38) recalls the central section of another burial song from this period, *Totengräbers Heimwehe* D842. The battling spirit of the Scott songs is also evident, notably in the polonaise-like sprung rhythms found in *Lied des gefangenen Jägers* D843 composed in the same year. In a sense this minstrel is a warrior against life, but he is first and foremost a poet. The most striking modulation in the song is at the repeat of the words 'Aber meine Zither nicht' at the end of the third verse (bb. 26–7). This shift into the submediant – the key of G flat major – is a means of illustrating the difference between temporal and spiritual (and thus sheerly musical) realms. This same relationship of keys is also to be found in the contemporary song *Der Einsame* D800 where it underlines the difference between fireside reality and pipe dreams.

From now on the song pivots between these two tonal centres and the rhythms begin to smooth out: jagged phrases and leaps are replaced by fanciful melismas (as at 'In den letzten Schlummer ein', bb. 34–5). On the phrase 'In den Grund des Tannenhaines / Senkt mich leise dann hinab' mention of a burial prompts a slow descent down the stave for four bars, from D flat to the B flat a tenth below in b. 41 (this is the *Totengräbers Heimwehe* phrase mentioned above). The voice is required not only to sink into the depths but also to float in a higher register over the grave at 'Und statt eines Leichensteines / Stellt die Zither auf mein Grab' (bb. 43–4). The triplet motif returns in the piano, no longer in strident octaves, an ethereal echo of its former self. Within the space of a few minutes we have progressed from anger and determination to an other-worldly picture of the dance of spirits in the afterlife. Schubert has the musical means to take us there: from b. 55 a rapt ostinato of dotted crotchets and quavers underpins a masterly vocal line that seems to recede into a murmur as the song reaches its end. In the piano's left hand there are open fifth chords in the song's final two lines (bb. 58–9 and 61–2). Goethe tells us that Mignon sings her *So lasst mich scheinen* to zither accompaniment, and we know that a left-hand drone is part of the character of that instrument. Wolf gives us these open fifths throughout his setting of that lyric, and here Schubert suggests that instrumental sound also. For no fewer than eight bars the song settles into the tonic key, somehow suggesting the Elysian fields of eternity.

The postlude (bb. 63–4) consists of the triplet figure in the higher reaches of the piano followed by wide-spaced chords prophetic of the hushed endings of certain Wolf songs – *Ganymed* comes to mind as well as his *Mignon III* already mentioned. We are either in fairyland or heaven. Benjamin Britten achieves a similar effect in the last section of his Hardy setting, *The Choirmaster's Burial* Op. 52 no. 5 (by chance in the same key) which also describes spirits paying homage at the graveside of a former musician.

The whole work, despite its relative brevity, gives the strongest impression of having moved through various states of life and spiritual development. Here surely can be discerned Schubert's own voice telling us that life is supportable for him as long as he can make music. His greatest fear was surely not of dying itself, but the process of dying where a degenerative disease such as syphilis might take from him the ability to play his lyre. Anything but that. Instead of being a minstrel with his trusty zither he would be no better than an organ-grinder repeating his tuneless ditties in a desolate winter landscape. But that image, as the composer looked once more into the abyss, belongs to another year and an even greater phase in his development as man and artist.

Autograph:	Conservatoire collection, Bibliothèque Nationale, Paris
First edition:	Published as part of Book 7 no. 1 of the *Nachlass* by Diabelli, Vienna in 1830 (P250)
Subsequent editions:	Peters: Vol. 5/2; AGA XX 466: Vol. 8/46; NSA IV: Vol. 13/152
Bibliography:	Capell 1928, p. 214
	Einstein 1951, p. 317
	Kohlhäufl 1999, p. 178
Discography and timing:	Fischer-Dieskau II 6[20] 3'06
	Hyperion I 26[2]
	Hyperion II 29[14] 2'59 Richard Jackson

← *Gesang der Norna* D831   *Auf der Bruck (Auf der Brücke)* D853 →

SÄNGERS MORGENLIED (I)
(KÖRNER) **D163** [H71]
G major   27 February 1815

The minstrel's morning song

Lieblich, etwas geschwind

Sü - sses Licht! Aus gol - de-nen Pfor - ten

(17 bars)

Süsses Licht! Aus goldnen Pforten[1]
  Brichst du siegend durch die Nacht.
  Schöner Tag! Du bist erwacht.
Mit geheimnisvollen Worten,
In melodischen Akkorden
  Grüss'ich deine Rosenpracht!

Ach! der Liebe sanftes Wehen
  Schwellt mir das bewegte Herz,
  Sanft, wie ein geliebter Schmerz.
Dürft'ich nur auf goldnen Höhen
Mich im Morgenduft ergehen!
  Sehnsucht zieht mich himmelwärts.

Und der Seele kühnes Streben
  Trägt im stolzen Riesenlauf
  Durch die Wolken mich hinauf.
Doch mit sanftem Geisterbeben
Dringt das Lied ins inn're Leben,
  Löst den Sturm melodisch auf.

Vor den Augen wird es helle;
  Freundlich auf der zarten Spur
  Weht der Einklang der Natur,
Und begeistert rauscht die Quelle,
Munter tanzt die flücht'ge Welle
  Durch des Morgens stille Flur.

Und von süsser Lust durchdrungen
  Webt sich zarte Harmonie
  Durch des Lebens Poesie.
Was die Seele tief durchklungen,
Was berauscht der Mund gesungen,
  Glüht in hoher Melodie.

Sweet light! Through golden portals
  You break victoriously through the night.
  Fairest day! You are awakened.
With mysterious words
And melodious strains
  I greet your roseate splendour!

Ah, the soft breath of love
  Swells my full heart,
  As softly as a beloved pain.
If only I could wander on those golden heights
In the fragrant morning!
  A yearning draws me heavenwards.

And the soul's bold striving
  Draws me upwards through the clouds
  In its proud giant's course.
But with a soft, magical quivering
The song penetrates the inner life,
  And with its melodies dispels the storm.

It grows bright before my eyes;
  In harmony nature wafts tenderly
  Upon its gentle course,
And the stream murmurs excitedly;
The fleeting waves dance merrily
  Through the silent morning meadows.

Filled with sweet joy,
  Tender harmonies weave
  Through the poetry of life.
The tones that deeply pierced the soul,
That were sung by enraptured lips,
  Glow in sublime melody.

[1] Schubert sets Körner's 'goldnen' as 'goldenen' only in the first setting of the song.

Des Gesanges muntern Söhnen	Every sorrow in this life fades
Weicht im Leben jeder Schmerz,	Before the cheerful sons of song;
Und nur Liebe schwellt ihr Herz.	Love alone swells their hearts.
In des Liedes heil'gen Tönen	The soul soars heavenwards
Und im Morgenglanz des Schönen	Amid the song's holy strains
Fliegt die Seele himmelwärts.	And beauty's morning radiance.

THEODOR KÖRNER (1791–1813)

This is the first of Schubert's sixteen Körner solo settings (1815–18). See the poet's biography for a chronological list of all the Körner settings.

Many of Schubert's Körner songs have poems taken from the collection *Knospen* (1810) – a title meaning 'buds' that is appropriate for a collection of freshly youthful, if not fully mature or original, poetry. The same charge could not be made against Schubert during this extraordinary year of 1815; the song on the other side of this autograph is none other than the famous, and famously original, *Nähe des Geliebten* D162. The trilling of birdsong in the introduction to *Sängers Morgenlied* allows a hint of pianistic virtuosity high in the treble clef, and the melismas of the vocal line are equally appropriate to the prima donnas of the dawn. This pianistic exuberance, also the interlude at b. 16, is rather reminiscent of Weber, although how much of that master's piano music Schubert knew at this stage (when Weber was yet to write his most famous works for the instrument) is debatable. In any case, this is music of high spirits which takes its cue from the exclamation mark after the first two words – 'Süsses Licht!'; it sparkles like bright light breaking through darkness. The build-up to a modulation to D major is masterfully managed so that the wakening of the day (on the word 'erwacht' b. 8) arrives with a forte dynamic just as the music shifts into the dominant. (In this strophic song the music does not suit the meaning and atmosphere of the second verse nearly so well.) The secretive nature of the following 'geheimnisvollen Worten' is underlined by the accompaniment doubling the voice as if in conspiracy. The singer's greetings are thrown off in insouciant roulades of semiquavers at bb. 12–13 and again at bb. 14–15 with reckless energy. If sung by a good tenor a portrait emerges of the young Körner, as Schubert might have seen him, with his unquenchable lust for life.

Körner's poem has six strophes as printed above. For the Hyperion Edition the first four were recorded for this setting. For the second setting (*see* below) Strophes 1, 5 and 6 were chosen. In Schubert's autograph of both the first and second settings, only the first verse of the poem appears – although the composer has clearly intended the songs to be strophic.

Autograph:	Wienbibliothek im Rathaus, Vienna (fair copy)
First edition:	Published as part of the AGA in 1895 (P555)
Subsequent editions:	Not in Peters; AGA XX 50: Vol. 2/64; NSA IV: Vol. 8/2; Bärenreiter: Vol. 6/102
Bibliography:	Youens 1996, pp. 120–21
Discography and timing:	Fischer-Dieskau —
	Hyperion I 4^2
	Hyperion II 5^{10} 2'23 Philip Langridge

← *Nähe des Geliebten* D162   *An Mignon* D161 →

SÄNGERS MORGENLIED (II)
(KÖRNER) **D165** [H73]
C major   1 March 1815

The minstel's morning song

(22 bars)

See previous entry for poem and translation

THEODOR KÖRNER (1791–1813)

This is the third of Schubert's sixteen Körner solo settings (1815–18). See the poet's biography for a chronological list of all the Körner settings.

Only two days after composing the first setting of this poem, Schubert returned to the text with new ideas, as if he suddenly wondered whether the poem he had initially taken to be a paean of joy was in fact intended as a prayer. (The earlier poems of Körner tend to polarize into one or the other of the two extremes.) As in the two *Fischerlied* settings of Salis-Seewis (D351 and D562), the second is not a reworking of similar material, it is a totally different song. The singer of this spacious aubade is no cheery youth but rather a priest of Apollo, or even one of Norma's druid colleagues spinning a vocal line of Bellini-like suppleness. Writing of this kind goes back to Salieri's teaching of course: Schubert developed an understanding of Italian *bel canto* that other great lieder composers might have envied. A good performance of this deceptively simple-looking setting requires a very good singer. The arrival of dawn at 'Du bist erwacht' in b. 8 is marked by left-hand chords in dotted rhythm – here they have the serious ceremonial duty of trombones in a sacred aria. C major is Schubert's key of clear morning skies: *Morgengruss* D795/8 from *Die schöne Müllerin* had its beginnings here and the postludes to both songs stem from the same creative impulse. The opening of the C major Ottenwalt song *Der Knabe in der Wiege* D579 (1817) also looks back to the opening of this Körner setting whether or not as a conscious act of self-quotation.

For the Hyperion Edition Strophes 1, 5 and 6 were recorded. The spiritual import of the last strophe (and it is surely this that gave Schubert pause for thought when he decided to compose a second setting) must have seemed more appropriate to the music for D165 than for D163. Strophes 1–4 were assigned to the Hyperion recording of the swifter first setting of this lyric, thus the whole of Körner's poem may be heard shared between the two very different songs.

Autograph: Staatsbibliothek Preussischer Kulturbesitz, Berlin
First edition: Published as No. 35 of *Neueste Folge nachgelassener Lieder und Gesänge* by J. P. Gotthard, Vienna in 1872 (P460)
Subsequent editions: Not in Peters; AGA XX 51: Vol. 2/66; NSA IV: Vol. 8/4; Bärenreiter: Vol. 6/104
Bibliography: Youens 1996, pp. 120–21

Discography and timing: Fischer-Dieskau I 3⁶   2'36   (first two strophes only)
                          Hyperion I 4³
                          Hyperion II 5¹³   3'38   Philip Langridge

← *Liebesrausch* D164   *Amphiaraos* D166 →

JOHANN GAUDENZ VON SALIS-SEEWIS (1762–1834)

THE POETIC SOURCES
S1 *Gedichte von J. G. von Salis*. Neueste Auflage, Wien 1815, bey B. Ph. Bauer

This book of poems is divided into four sections ('Zeiträume') according to the date of the poems plus an appendix entitled 'Blumen am Wege' – Flowers at the wayside.

S2 *Gedichte von J. G. Salis*. Neue Auflage. Zürich, bey Orell, Füssli und Compagnie. 1808

The absence of *Der Jüngling an der Quelle* D300 from this edition makes it less likely to have been Schubert's source – it is possible that Schubert used different volumes for the 1815 and 1816 songs.

Gedichte by Salis-Seewis (1808).

THE SONGS

12 October 1815? 1816 or 1821?	*Der Jüngling an der Quelle* D300 [S1: 'Vierter Zeitraum 1800–1806' with the title 'Blumen am Wege' p. 149]
28 December 1815	*Das Grab* D330 (second setting) [S1: 'Erster Zeitraum 1780–1786' pp. 36–7] [S2: pp. 41–2]
1816?	*Fischerlied* D351 (second setting) [S1: 'Zweyter Zeitraum 1787–1792' pp. 54–6] [S2: pp. 82–5]
	Der Entfernten D350 (first setting) [S1: 'Zweyter Zeitraum 1787–1792' pp. 85–6] [S2: pp. 115–17]
11 February 1816	*Das Grab* D377 (third setting) Choir TTBB with piano [S1: 'Erster Zeitraum 1780–1786' pp. 36–7] [S2: pp. 41–2]
March 1816	*Pflügerlied* D392 [S1: 'Dritter Zeitraum 1794–1798' pp. 105–7] [S2: pp. 86–8]
	Die Einsiedelei D393 (second setting) [S1: 'Zweyter Zeitraum 1787–1792' pp. 57–9] [S2: pp. 70–2]
	An die Harmonie D394 [S1: 'Vierter Zeitraum 1800–1806' pp. 129–33] [S2: pp. 138–43]
27 March 1816	*Lied (Ins stille Land)* D403 (four versions) [S1: 'Vierter Zeitraum 1800–1806' p. 138] [S2: pp. 146–7]
End of March/April 1816	*Die Herbstnacht* D404 [S1: 'Dritter Zeitraum 1794–1798' pp. 12–122] [S2: pp. 17–20]. [Salis's title, altered by Schubert, is *Die Wehmut.* In the seventh strophe of the poem Hölty and Matthisson are mentioned by name in literary homage.]
	Abschied von der Harfe D406 [S1: 'Vierter Zeitraum 1800–1806' pp. 139–40] [S2: pp. 148–9]
	Der Herbstabend D405 [S1: 'Zweyter Zeitraum 1787–1791' pp. 87–8] [S2: pp. 39–40]
November 1816	*Herbstlied* D502 [S1: 'Erster Zeitraum 1780–1786' pp. 3–4] [S2: pp. 62–3]
May 1817	*Fischerlied* D562 (third setting) [S1: 'Zweyter Zeitraum 1787–1792' pp. 54–6] [S2: pp. 82–5]
	Die Einsiedelei D563 (third setting) [S1: 'Zweyter Zeitraum 1787–1792' pp. 57–9] [S2: pp. 70–72]
June 1817	*Das Grab* D569 (fourth setting) Unison chorus TTBB with piano [S1: 'Erster Zeitraum 1780–1786' pp. 36–7] [S2: pp. 41–2]

Mention should also be made of other Salis-Seewis settings for unaccompanied voices that are outside the scope of this book: *Das Grab* D329 sketch for the first version of a canon for four-part choir 28 December 1815; *Der Entfernten* D331 (first setting) quartet TTBB *c.* 1816; *Die Einsiedelei* D337 (first setting) quartet *c.* 1816 – the similarity of this melody to the introduction to the Mayrhofer setting *Atys* D585 has been pointed out; *Fischerlied* D364 (second setting) quartet TTBB 1816 or 1817; *Das Grab* D643A (fifth setting) SATB 1819; *Zum Rundetanz* D983B Op. 17 no. 3 TTBB undated

Salis-Seewis, born on 26 December 1762, was the son of Swiss landed gentry. He received his education from private teachers in his father's castle. His mother was an ardent Pietist, and the son was influenced by this religion but without hindrance of the breadth and depth of his education. In 1779, after a short period studying in Lausanne, he went to Paris and began an officer's career in the Swiss Guard Regiment at Versailles. From there he wrote poems of homesickness for Switzerland: he found the bustle of the city and the decadence of life at the Parisian court like being on stage in a play (according to Matthisson). During this time he was already publishing poetry in the German almanacs. On a visit to Germany in 1789/90 he met Goethe, Schiller, Wieland and Herder – these were the great years of Weimar when all these luminaries could be visited, one after another, in the space of a few days.

Salis-Seewis was a first-hand observer of the fall of Louis XVI and the French aristocracy. He wanted to remain in the newly established French Republican army, initially inspired and excited by the idea of Freedom and the Rights of Man, but with the deepening of the Reign of Terror he had no choice but to leave France (he himself was an 'aristo') and he returned to Switzerland in 1793, where he married Ursina von Pestalozzi. He had no intention of changing his career as a professional soldier, albeit a soldier who wrote and published poetry. He was known as 'der dichtende General' and took enormous pains to shape and reshape his work into a form that he found satisfying. He was a man of action who wanted to fight for peace so that poetry could influence and change men's lives. He joined the Swiss army officially in 1798 and over the years he advanced through the ranks. By 1801 he was a member of the Swiss government and here too he rose to distinction while maintaining a cultured and happy household. Salis's poems were published in Zurich in 1793 under the aegis of the German poet Friedrich Matthisson (qv, not yet 'von') who had much more facility than Salis-Seewis and who had made Switzerland his temporary home. Matthisson wrote an introduction to the edition; there were more poems by Salis than

Gedichte by Salis-Seewis, Viennese paperback edition (1815).

he thought worth publishing (the earlier relationship between Hölty and his well-meaning, but over-controlling, 'editor' Johann Heinrich Voss comes to mind). Salis-Seewis shared Matthisson's preoccupation with classical metre and antique poetic forms, but the poems by the Swiss general show a feeling for the countryside and the life of ordinary people that is earthier and more honest – if less elegant – than those of his German mentor. Goedeke speaks of Salis as being 'manlier' than Matthisson, and mentions his modesty in relation to his work. The poet died on 29 January 1834 in his birthplace, his family estate at Bothmar Castle, near Malans, Grisons.

Because Salis-Seewis spent most of his life in his native Switzerland he stands outside the mainstream of German literature despite his gift for friendship and regular correspondence with contemporaries like Matthisson. It is perhaps *because* he was not German that he seems to have been favoured by the Austrian authorities of Schubert's time, and his verse

plays an important part in the school textbook published in Vienna, *Sammlung Deutscher Beyspiele zur Bildung des Styls* which was an early source of texts (Hölty, Schiller, Pfeffel) for the young composer. The volume contains Matthisson's verse tribute to Salis (*An Salis*) as well as a laudatory biographical paragraph about the poet and his military background. Schubert encountered the *Gedichte* of Salis-Seewis at the end of 1815 and went on to set ten of his lyrics, some of them in two or three versions. The last of the Salis-Seewis songs possibly dates from as late as 1821, but the majority were composed in the spring of 1816. Schubert was particularly attracted to Salis in his light-hearted folksong mood, but he also responded well to the streak of philosophical melancholy that subtly insinuates itself into the work. Verse of this kind must have made a relaxing change from the blood-and-thunder writing of Schiller with which the composer also busied himself in March 1816.

SAMUEL FRIEDRICH SAUTER (1766–1846)

THE POETIC SOURCES
S1 *Almanach und Taschenbuch für haeusliche u. gesellschaftl. Freuden*, 1799 von Carl Lang, mit Kupfern von D. Chodowieki H. Güttenberg &. Heilbronn am Nekar im Industrie Comtoir

Facing the printed version of the poem is a musical supplement, a fold-out setting of *Der Wachtelschlag* without any accreditation of composer. It is possible that the dotted rhythms found here on repeated notes were adopted and then a thousandfold improved by Beethoven. Notably Schubert also takes up this rhythm from Beethoven.

S2 *Der Wachtelschlag*, Mit Begleitung des Pianoforte von Ludwig van Beethoven . . . Im Verlage des Kunst- und Industrie Comptoirs zu Wien (1804)

This song, composed in 1803, was assigned the catalogue number WoO 129. It was certainly Schubert's source of text as Schubert follows Beethoven's deviations from Sauter's text in S1, and even leaves out the same line from the poet's last verse 'Tröstet mich wieder der Wachtelgesang'.

THE SONG
1822? *Der Wachtelschlag* D742 Op. 68 [In the first edition of this piece published by Diabelli there is an overlay of a separate system (as printed in the NSA) with an Italian translation of this lyric ('Il Canto della Quaglia' – see Schochow 1974, vol. 2, p. 503). At one time it was thought that Sauter's text was a translation from Metastasio, but this is not so. The

Lang's almanac of 1799, the source of Beethoven's *Der Wachtelschlag* which was, in turn, Schubert's inspiration.

translator of Sauter's text into Italian for the bilingual edition of Op. 68 was probably Craigher de Jachelutta who was attempting to broaden the marketing appeal of Schubert's music in different countries.]

The poet of *Der Wachtelschlag* is not to be confused with Ferdinand Sauter (1804–1854), a friend of Moritz von Schwind who rubbed Schober up the wrong way on occasion, and who was a sometimes rowdy and drunken member of the Schubert circle from 1826. The poet Samuel Sauter would have been horrified that someone like this shared his surname. He was a German of the older generation, born in Flehingen, Baden on 10 November 1766. For most of his life he was a schoolmaster in his home town, as well as in Zaisenhausen. He died in Flehingen on 14 July 1846. His work is mainly in a naive folk-like style, some of it unintentionally funny to those who mock the earnest literary solemnity of the provinces, and of that part of southern Germany in particular. The collection *Volkslieder und andere Reime* was published in 1811 and his collected poems were issued in 1845. In 1855

Samuel Sauter, unsigned lithograph.

some of Sauter's poems were issued by the publishers Eichrodt and Kussmaul as the work of one Gottlieb Biedermaier [*sic*], a fictional Swabian schoolmaster, and his friend Horatius Treuherz (True-Heart). Their reception, which gave rise to an enthusiasm, sometimes ironic, for the banal simplicities of a vanished age, prompted the coining of the term 'Biedermeier' to denote that uneventful period of German and Austrian history between the fall of Napoleon and the political upheavals of 1848 (the term is also applied to literature, painting, furniture and so on). As Schubert's whole life and career fall within these parameters, he is, on a superficial level at least, the Biedermeier composer par excellence. This false image of the safety and small-town cosiness of the Biedermeier epoch, actually a politically repressive period for Austrians, has tended to obscure many important details in Schubert's life. It is interesting that the kitsch simplifications of the musical *Das Dreimäderlhaus* ('Lilac Time') were an indirect result of Sauter's poetry and style and of the Viennese falling in love with the spuriously nostalgic idea of Biedermeier *Gemütlichkeit*.

Der SCHÄFER UND DER REITER[1]
(FOUQUÉ) OP. 13 NO. 1, **D517** [H364]

The shepherd and the horseman

The song exists in two versions, the second of which is discussed below:
(1) April 1817? (2) April 1817?

(1) 'Langsam'   E major – E minor   **C**   [68 bars]

(2) E major – E minor

(74 bars)

Ein Schäfer sass im Grünen,	A shepherd sat amid the greenery,
Sein Liebchen süss im Arm;	His sweetheart in his arms;
Durch Buchenwipfel schienen[2]	Through the tops of the beech trees
Der Sonne Strahlen warm.	Shone the sun's warm rays.
Sie kosten froh und heiter[3]	Joyfully, blithely,
Von Liebeständelei.	They dallied and caressed.
Da ritt bewehrt ein Reiter	Then a horseman, armed,
Den Glücklichen vorbei.[4]	Rode by the happy pair.

[1] De la Motte Fouqué's title is *Schäfer und Reiter*.
[2] Schubert changed this by mistake to 'Buchenwipfel*n*'. Neither this change nor the one given in note 4 below should be performed.
[3] De la Motte Fouqué writes '*Er kos'te* froh und heiter' (*Gedichte*, Wien, Bauer, 1816).
[4] Schubert wrote by mistake '*Die* Glücklichen'.

'Sitz ab und suche Kühle,'
  Rief ihm der Schäfer zu.
'Des Mittags nahe Schwüle
  Gebietet stille Ruh.'

'Noch lacht im Morgenglanze
  So Strauch als Blume hier,
  Und Liebchen pflückt zum Kranze
  Die schönsten Blüten dir.'

Da sprach der finst're Reiter:
  'Nie hält mich Wald und Flur.
  Mich treibt mein Schicksal weiter,
  Und ach, mein ernster Schwur!

'Ich gab mein junges Leben
  Dahin um schnöden Sold;
  Glück kann ich nicht erstreben,
  Nur höchstens Ruhm und Gold.

'Drum schnell, mein Ross, und trabe
  Vorbei wo Blumen blüh'n,
  Einst lohnt wohl Ruh' im Grabe
  Des Kämpfenden Bemüh'n.'

'Dismount and come to the cool shade,'
  The shepherd called to him.
  'Midday's oppressive sultriness
  Bids us rest quietly.

'Here bush and flower
  Still smile in the radiant morning,
  And my sweetheart will pick the loveliest flowers
  To make you a garland.'

Then the gloom-laden rider spoke:
  'Woods and meadows can never keep me:
  My fate drives me onwards,
  And, ah, my solemn vow.

'I gave up my young life
  For vile money.
  I can never aspire to happiness;
  At best only to gold and glory.

'Make haste then, my steed, and trot
  Past the flowers in bloom.
  One day the peace of the grave
  May reward the warrior's toil.'

FRIEDRICH DE LA MOTTE FOUQUÉ (1777–1843)

This is the last of Schubert's five Fouqué solo settings (c. 1814–17). See the poet's biography for a chronological list of all the Fouqué settings.

The contrast between town and country, low and high birth, pastoral and military, is a favourite folksong theme. The pace of life is different for those who tread outdoor paths and those who walk the corridors of power in search of money and honours. In Benjamin Britten's French folksong arrangement *Le roi s'en va-t'en chasse* the beautiful shepherdess Nanon, despite the hectoring of hunting triplets and horn-calls, refuses to become the king's darling. With music from another world, slower in tempo and infinitely more gentle, she graciously declines his rumbustious offer of a life at court. Schubert similarly employs one mood and speed for the shepherd's unworldly music and a contrasting one for the bitter plaint of the passing knight. Fouqué's scenario suggests that the armed traveller may not be attached to any court or country; he is not driven by patriotism or a specific cause. The solemn vow he has made seems to be to himself and his own best interests – financial if not spiritual. If we place the poem in the seventeenth century (and the music suggests that Schubert has envisaged an archaic background to the words) this might be one of the many mercenaries who sold their services to various warring factions during the Thirty Years War. The earning power of these professional soldiers was dependent on their military reputations.

    The pianist opens the song and we find ourselves in the Arcadia of sensuous embrace (a languid left hand) and cooing doves (a trilling right). There is an ornate fussiness about the accompaniment that suggests rococo prettiness and ornamentation. The composer has taken some trouble to make this scene almost a textbook illustration of pastoral life; indeed it is so much set within a gilt frame that it seems a musical equivalent of a painting by Boucher or Fragonard. The subject matter is frivolous perhaps, but its tone as a work of art is serious. The scoring of the song, if it were to be transferred to wind instruments, would call out for Damon's flute to trill and swoon. The key is E major, the tonality of a number of songs in the canon that depict the pastoral idyll; these include *Blumenlied* D431, *Erntelied* D434 and *Elysium* D584. It is perhaps no accident that Hugo Wolf was also to cast his shepherdess in four sharps for *Die Spröde* (Goethe), and that the accompaniment of that song should employ similar light, airy semiquavers to provide a filigree of feminine delicacy.

The picture-book approach continues from b. 14 for the entry of the knight who canters up in what might be termed § triplets for children (compare these to the truly menacing 'adult' triplets of *Erlkönig* D328 and *An Schwager Kronos* D369 for example). There is here a new marking of 'Geschwind' and a change of key to E minor. This is the type of rocking-horse music that Schumann uses in his *Aus alten Märchen winkt es*, the penultimate song from *Dichterliebe* Op. 48 no. 15, which refers to fairy tales of the type conjured by Fouqué. The music for the cavalier's entry has something in common with that for the contemporary *Der Flug der Zeit* D515, as if the rider, pressed for time, is propelled through life by forces outside his control. This mood continues for the poem's third strophe: Schubert cleverly makes the shepherd sing from b. 22, if not exactly in the rider's musical style, then at least within the faster section that introduced him. This allows for the contrast of a return to the pastoral music ('Wie oben' from b. 33, Verse 4 of the poem) with a change of key signature to G major, as the shepherd continues to expound the virtues of country life. As this hedonistic mood reasserts itself we can only wonder that the rider, driven as he is, has the patience to hear words extended into languid melismas and supported by a web of delicate trills.

After this there is no formal option but for the rest of the song (three more verses) to be given over to the rider and his earnest music. The style is impeccable for this type of ballad, yet after we have grasped the point that the rider is obsessed by the search for glory and riches we long to hear a reprise of the music of the shepherd who has presumably been silenced by what he has heard of the unsatisfactory cut and thrust of a roving military life. The poem does not allow for such a recapitulation, however, and the work ends in a serious and gloomy manner. The postlude (bb. 68–74) sounds a gruff and querulous note. Alas, we are unable to take the cavalier's plight entirely seriously: his capitulation to Mammon has been rendered less tragic and less believable by the proximity of the shepherd. This is another of those musical experiments, characteristic of 1817, where Schubert allows the shape of a poem to lead him where it may with variable success.

The first version of the song (marked 'Langsam') is to be found in the *Quellen und Lesarten* booklet to Volume 1 of the NSA on p. 43 (Anhang). The date of April 1817 comes from the index to the Witteczek-Spaun collection. The autograph has vanished and the extant copies of the songs are undated.

Autograph:	Missing or lost
Publication:	First published as part of the NSA in 1970 (P758; first version)
	First published as Op. 13 no. 1 by Cappi & Diabelli, Vienna in December 1822 (P31; second version)
Dedicatee:	Josef von Spaun
Subsequent editions:	Peters: Vol. 3/7; AGA XX 293: Vol. 5/6; NSA IV: Vol. 1a/95 (second version); Vol. 1a and b *Quellen und Lesarten* booklet p. 43 (first version); Bärenreiter: Vol. 1/76
Discography and timing:	Fischer-Dieskau I 9[10] 2'54
	Hyperion I 21[12]
	Hyperion II 18[15] 3'15 Edith Mathis

← *Hänflings Liebeswerbung* D552   *Auf der Donau* D553 →

SCHÄFERS KLAGELIED   Shepherd's lament
(GOETHE) OP. 3 NO. 1, **D121** [H51 & H418A]

The song exists in two versions, the first of which is discussed below:
(1) 30 November 1814; (2) February 1819?

(1) C minor

(61 bars)

(2) 'Mässig'   E minor   𝄴   [65 bars]

Da droben auf jenem Berge	On yonder hill
Da steh ich tausendmal,	I have stood a thousand times,
An meinem Stabe hingebogen[1]	Leaning on my staff
Und schaue hinab in das Tal.	And looking down into the valley.
Dann folg' ich der weidenden Herde,	I have followed the grazing flocks;
Mein Hündchen bewahret mir sie.	My dog looks after them for me.
Ich bin herunter gekommen	I have come down here
Und weiss doch selber nicht wie.	And do not know how.
Da stehet von schönen Blumen	The whole meadow is so full
Da steht die ganze Wiese so voll,[2]	Of lovely flowers;
Ich breche sie, ohne zu wissen,	I pluck them without knowing
Wem ich sie geben soll.	To whom I should give them.
Und Regen, Sturm und Gewitter	During rain, storm and tempest
Verpass' ich unter dem Baum.	I just sit under the tree.
Die Türe dort bleibet verschlossen;	The door there remains locked;
Doch alles ist leider! ein Traum.	For, alas, it is all a dream.
Es stehet ein Regenbogen	There is a rainbow
Wohl über jenem Haus!	Above that house!
Sie aber ist fortgezogen,[3]	But she has moved away,
Und weit in das Land hinaus.[4]	To distant regions.
Hinaus in das Land und weiter,	To distant regions and beyond,
Vielleicht gar über die See.	Perhaps even over the sea.
Vorüber, ihr Schafe, nur vorüber![5]	Move on, sheep, move on!
Dem Schäfer ist gar so weh.	Your shepherd is so wretched.

[1] Goethe (*Gedichte*, Wien, Strauss, 1810) writes 'An meinem Stabe *gebogen*'.
[2] Goethe (*Gedichte*, Wien, Strauss, 1810) writes 'Die ganze Wiese so voll'. The modified repeat of 'Da stehet' (da steht)
is Schubert's.
[3] Goethe writes 'Sie aber ist *weggezogen*'.
[4] In the second version of the song Schubert changes the line's first word 'Und' to 'Gar'.
[5] The insertion of the word 'nur' in this line is Schubert's.

JOHANN WOLFGANG VON GOETHE (1749–1832); poem written in spring 1801

This is the fourth of Schubert's seventy-five Goethe solo settings (1814–26). See the poet's biography for a chronological list of all the Goethe settings.

Schäfers Klagelied was the first Schubert song to be performed at a public concert, astonishingly as late as 1819. It must have gone down well – it is one of Schubert's least challenging songs from the point of view of modernity, yet it is full of delicious and subtle musical detail. The song received a surprising amount of critical attention, even in German publications. It is a textbook *siciliana* with a lilting rhythm that describes a scene both pastoral and melancholy, something familiar to early nineteenth-century audiences. The quality of the new wine poured into old bottles should not go unnoticed, however. The same is true of Goethe's poem which is a simple folksong concealing modern psychological insight. In fact Goethe had written the poem (to be sung to an extant Rhenish folksong) as a deliberate attempt to enrich and modernize the concept of folksong. In 1803 the singer and actor Wilhelm Ehlers (1774–1845) published a version of *Schäfers Klagelied* in his *Gesänge mit Begleitung der Chitarre*, a publication supervised by Goethe himself. The music for this setting must have been similar to the ditty that had been Goethe's original inspiration. Lorraine Byrne argues persuasively that this lyric expresses the poet's grief and deep sense of loss of his sister Cornelia (1750–1777), albeit some twenty-seven years after her death. The text does not immediately suggest bereavement but, reading between the lines, the intervention of death seems as likely a reason for the shepherd's abandonment as the girl moving away to another village, or wherever 'weit in das Land' may signify. Perhaps Goethe looked back on the childhood years spent with his sister with the kind of nostalgia that suggested a pastoral idyll from long ago. In any case the poem turns on its head the conventional story of a restless man deserting the stay-at-home girl.

Schubert's musical form is a palindromic ABCBA: the outer sections in C minor constitute the plaint, the B sections in the relative major are slightly more vivacious and the big central section (the middle two verses) begins with a flower-picking idyll in A flat major so that the shepherd can present his beloved with a bouquet. The left-hand staccati (from b. 21) here denote the sound made by the breaking of their stems. (This staccato sound is heard again, also in the pianist's left hand, when the narrator picks flowers in the first, semiquaver-accompanied, variation of *Im Frühling* D882.) The middle section of the song continues with a sudden storm (from b. 28) that begins in A flat minor and returns, after its brief outburst, to the E flat major of the repeated B section (b. 39). This return is effected only after a delicious detour into C flat major, a key that is always in Schubert's mind when broaching A flat minor. The appearance of a consolatory rainbow leads us back to the rueful mood of the opening, and the whole effect is of a rise and fall of the emotions, a great arc of feeling spanning the horizon. Capell called this song 'a priceless little object of virtù' which is perhaps to underestimate its power and cast it as a dainty *bergerette*. Schubert's shepherd is no Dresden figurine and the intensity of feeling is comparable with that of Gretchen who had sprung to life only six weeks earlier. Till Gerrit Waidelich observes that the dotted rhythm of the song's opening, as well as its whole mood, is inspired by 'Vom weit entfernten Schweizerland / Komm ich voll Gram hieher', the aria of the shepherd Jacob Friburg in Act II Scene 6 of Joseph Weigl's *Die Schweizerfamilie*, a *Singspiel* known to Schubert from boyhood with his admired Johann Michael Vogl in the role of Jacob.

As we have noted, this was the first of Schubert's songs to receive a public performance. The fact that the singer was a tenor on that occasion accounts for the existence of a second version in E minor, a major third higher than the original, and prepared some four years after it. When presented with the chance of an important public performance by a high tenor who liked this song, the composer had no compunction in adapting its tonality. He probably did so, as an accompanist of his own work, more times than we shall ever know. Singers and their pianists

Schäfers Klagelied by Eugen Neureuther (1829–30).

Four Schubert Lieder, Op. 3 (1821).

have always had to live in the real world in this respect, musicologists less so. The latter would duly (and correctly) argue that the transposition upwards alters the character of the song: the change of tessitura turns something brooding and introspective into a more openly dramatic utterance. Apart from the key there is little substantial difference between the two versions, apart from the addition of a four-bar introduction fashioned from the tune of the opening of the vocal line. This arguably indicates that an accompanist was expected to improvise an opening if none was provided.

The composer had the final say, however: when he published this already popular song in May 1821 as the first of his Op. 3, it was the original C minor version, without introduction, that was printed and scrupulously furnished with dynamic and phrasing markings. Schubert had also included the song in C minor in the lieder album sent to Goethe in 1816. It is thus that we are able to detect his distinct preference for the first version.

Autographs:	Österreichische Nationalbibliothek, Vienna (first version, fair copy)
	Wienbibliothek im Rathaus, Vienna (second version, fair copy)
Publication:	First published as Op. 3 no. 1 by Cappi & Diabelli, Vienna in May 1821 (P3; first version)
	First published as part of the AGA in 1894, where it is erroneously catalogued as the first version (P548; second version)

Dedicatee:	Ignaz von Mosel
First known performance:	28 February 1819 at the inn 'Zum römischen Kaiser', Vienna in a programme of musical works and recitations presented by Edward Jaell. Soloist: Franz Jäger (see Waidelich/Hilmar Dokumente II No. 18a)
Contemporary reviews:	*Wiener allgemeine Theaterzeitung*, No. 27 (4 March 1819), p. 107 [Waidelich/Hilmar Dokumente I No. 19; Deutsch Doc. Biog. No. 143]
	Allgemeine musikalische Zeitung (Vienna) No. 19 (6 March 1819), col. 147f. [Waidelich/Hilmar Dokumente I No. 20; Deutsch Doc. Biog. No. 144]
	Der Gesellschafter (Berlin) No. 47 (22 March 1819), p. 188 [Waidelich/Hilmar Dokumente I No. 21; Deutsch Doc. Biog. No. 145]
	Allgemeine musikalische Zeitung (Leipzig) No. 12 (24 March 1819), col. 199f. [Waidelich/Hilmar Dokumente I No. 22]
Publication reviews:	*Wiener allgemeine Theaterzeitung*, No. 61 (22 May 1821), p. 244 [Waidelich/Hilmar Dokumente I No. 101; Deutsch Doc. Biog. No. 238]
	F. von Hentl 'Blick auf Schubert's Lieder', *Wiener Zeitschrift für Kunst, Literatur, Theater und Mode* No. 36 (23 March 1822), p. 289f. [Waidelich/Hilmar Dokumente I No. 146; Deutsch Doc. Biog. No. 278]
Subsequent editions:	Peters: Vol. 1/225; AGA XX 34a & b: Vol. 1/200 & 203; NSA IV: Vol. 1a/20 & Vol. 1b/194; Bärenreiter: Vol. 1/14
Bibliography:	Byrne 2003, pp. 178–88
	Capell 1928, pp. 86–7
	Fischer-Dieskau 1977, pp. 115–16
	Hirsch 1993, pp. 98–115
	Newbould 1997, pp. 145–6
	Sternfeld 1979, pp. 9–13
Further settings and arrangements:	Carl Friedrich Zelter (1758–1832) *Schäfers Klagelied* (1802)
	Václav Tomášek (1774–1850) *Schäfers Klagelied* Op. 56 no. 1 (1815)
	Arr. Tilman Hoppstock (b. 1961) for guitar accompaniment, in *Franz Schubert: 110 Lieder* (2009)
Discography and timing:	Fischer-Dieskau I 2[15] 3'07
	Hyperion I 1[3] & 24[1] 2'47 Janet Baker (first version)
	3'39 John Mark Ainsley (second version)
	Hyperion II 4[7] & 21[13] 2'47 Janet Baker
	3'39 John Mark Ainsley

← *Nachtgesang* D119   *Trost in Tränen* D120 →
← *Der Schmetterling* D633   *Abendbilder* D650 →

FRIEDRICH SCHÄFFER (1772–1800)

THE POETIC SOURCE
S1 *Taschenbuch für häusliche und gesellschaftliche Freuden von Carl Lang.* Heilbronn am Neckar beim Verfasser, 1797

THE SONG
29 August 1815   *Trinklied* D75 (Bass and chorus TTB with piano) [S1: p. 273 with title 'Lied im Kreise der Freundschaft zu singen']

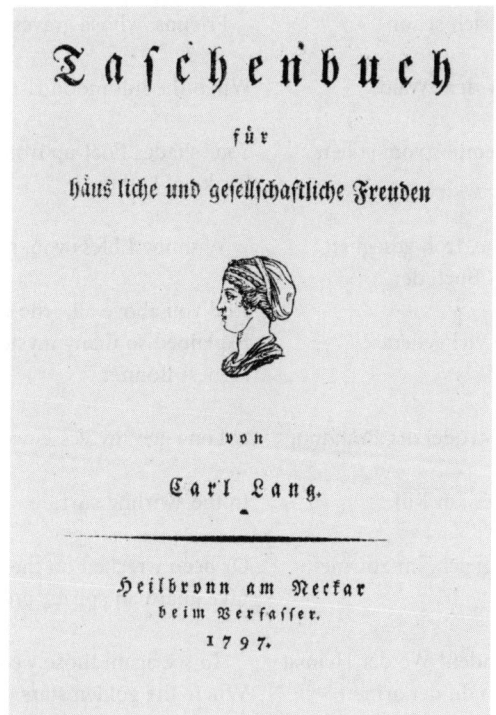

Lang's almanac of 1797. For *Trinklied* see Vol. 3/408–10 below.

Very little is known about Friedrich Schäffer other than that he was a doctor of medicine and was born in Stuttgart and died in Ulm. He was an occasional contributor to almanacs such as the one listed above, and he lived for a time in Vienna.

Die SCHATTEN

The shades

(MATTHISSON) **D50** [H22]
A major – C major   12 April 1813

Freunde, deren Grüfte sich schon
    bemoosten!
Wann der Vollmond über dem Walde
    dämmert,
Schweben eure Schatten empor vom stillen
Ufer der Lethe.

Seid mir, Unvergessliche, froh gesegnet!
Du vor Allen, welcher im Buch der
    Menschheit
Mir der Hieroglyphen so viel gedeutet,
Redlicher Bonnet!

Längst verschlürft im Strudel der Brandung
    wäre
Wohl mein Fahrzeug, oder am Riff
    zerchmettert
Hättet ihr nicht, Genien gleich, im Sturme
Schirmend gewaltet!

Wiedersehn der Liebenden! Wo der Heimat
Goldne Sterne leuchten, o du der armen
Psyche, die gebunden im Grabtal schmachtet,
Himmlische Sehnsucht!¹

Friends, whose graves are already mossy!

When the full moon rises over the forest,

Your shades float up from the silent
Banks of Lethe.

With joy I bless you, my unforgettable ones!

And you above all, who in the book of life

Explained so many mysteries to me,
Honest Bonnet.

Long ago my vessel would have sunk

In the swirling surf,

Or been wrecked on the reef, had you not,
Like guardian spirits, protected me in the storm.

To see again those we love,
Where the golden stars of the homeland shine!
O celestial longing of the poor soul
Which languishes, captive, in the grave.

FRIEDRICH VON MATTHISSON (1761–1831); poem written *c.* 1797

*This is the third of Schubert's twenty-nine Matthisson solo settings (1812–17). See the poet's
biography for a chronological list of all the Matthisson settings.*

This song has the distinction of being the first complete Matthisson setting. After the failures
of the two attempts at *Der Geistertanz* D15 and D15A, Schubert evidently decided to eschew
Zumsteeg's manner and invent something new. In *Die Schatten* he attempts to build a bridge
between what he had learned in his composition exercises with Salieri (for whom he set a large

¹ Matthisson writes '*Heiligste* Sehnsucht'. The young composer's disinclination to describe longing as 'most holy' may be
revealing.

number of Italian texts in various vocal permutations), and the world of contemporary German poetry. The perfection of *Gretchen am Spinnrade* D118 (still nearly eighteen months in the future at this stage) was not achieved without practice; *Die Schatten* is one of the first steps towards the cultivation of the hybrid that we have come to accept as typically Schubertian – the kind of song where German declamation from the intellectually lively North is infused with the warm blood of the South. Here is a tune with curves and shapes and fioriture; a flexible vocal line is supported by strong basses and a sensuous flow. Like *Der Vatermörder* D10 the vocal line lies perilously high – the composer had not yet enough experience of voices to write considerately for them. (It is little wonder that there is another copy of the song in the Witteczek–Spaun collection in the more accessible key of F major that spares the singer two high Bs, and many more As.) Schubert seems to have found the poem in the second volume of a school textbook printed in Vienna entitled *Sammlung Deutscher Beyspiele zur Bildung des Styls*, alongside the poems for *Dithyrambe* D47 (Schiller) and *Totengräberlied* D44 (Hölty). The fifteen-year-old composer made life difficult for himself by choosing this text which is an occasional poem honouring the memory of the poet's friend. Charles Bonnet (1720–1793) was a distinguished botanist and dear to Matthisson, but a French surname set to music seems the wrong sort of surprise in the context of a lied (see bb. 50–51; the copy of the song in the Witteczek collection substitutes the word 'Mentor' for Bonnet at this point). Schubert was later to discover Goethe and choose poems that had universal human significance, however occasional their origin.

The unusual vocabulary (the 'Hieroglyphen' of bb. 45–6 were presumably topical because the Rosetta Stone had been discovered by Napoleon's troops as recently as 1799) and the Sapphic metre, tricky to render into musical phrases of equal length, gave the composer further problems. All in all *Die Schatten* is a strange song but nevertheless has something lyrical and ethereal about it with its unearthly tessitura, beautiful modulations that are already becoming Schubert's trademark and phrases that unfold asymmetrically. The latter characteristic, the result of turning poetry into prose, makes the song sound improvised. The flowing quavers in the right-hand accompaniment, as they support and propel the vocal line, are also on the point of sounding genuinely Schubertian. There is a faster and louder middle section for the avoided shipwreck of Verse 3 (from b. 53, marked 'più allegro'), and then a return to the opening tempo at b. 73. At this point the three sharps of the key signature melt away as if only stainless and accidental-free C major is suitable to bid farewell to a man who has been honoured with such a poem, and is thus absolved of all sin. This is a wistful ending (with a marking of 'dolce' that is devilishly difficult to achieve in this tessitura) in which the words 'Himmlische Sehnsucht' have a passion and dying fall worthy of Italian *bel canto*.

Autograph:	University Library of Lund, Sweden
First edition:	Published as part of the AGA in 1894 (P533)
Subsequent editions:	Not in Peters; AGA XX 8: Vol. 1/58; NSA IV: Vol. 6/68; Bärenreiter: Vol. 5/60 (high voice), 56 (medium/low voice) & 156 (additional lower transposition in high voice edition)
Discography and timing:	Fischer-Dieskau I 1[5] 2'43
	Hyperion I 12[5]
	Hyperion II 2[18] 3'17 Adrian Thompson

← *Dithyrambe* D47   *Sehnsucht* D52 →

Der SCHATZGRÄBER

(GOETHE) **D256** [H142]

D minor   19 August 1815

The treasure-seeker

(46 bars)

Arm am Beutel, krank am Herzen,	Empty of purse, sick of heart,
Schlepp' ich meine langen Tage.	I dragged out my long days.
Armut ist die grösste Plage,	Poverty is the greatest ill,
Reichtum ist das höchste Gut!	Wealth the highest good.
Und zu enden meine Schmerzen,	And to end my suffering
Ging ich, einen Schatz zu graben.	I went to dig for treasure.
Meine Seele sollst du haben!	'You shall have my soul!'
Schrieb ich hin mit eignem Blut.	I wrote in my own blood.
Und so zog ich Kreis' um Kreise,	I drew circle upon circle,
Stellte wunderbare Flammen,	And mixed herbs and bones
Kraut und Knochenwerk zusammen:	In magic flames:
Die Beschwörung war vollbracht.	The spell was cast.
Und auf die gelernte Weise	In the decreed manner
Grub ich nach dem alten Schatze,	And in the appointed place
Auf dem angezeigten Platze.	I dug for the old treasure;
Schwarz und stürmisch war die Nacht.	The night was black and stormy.
Und ich sah ein Licht von weiten;	I saw a far-off light;
Und es kam, gleich einem Sterne,	It came like a star
Hinten aus der fernsten Ferne,	From the remote distance
Eben als es Zwölfe schlug.	On the stroke of twelve.
Und da galt kein Vorbereiten.	Then, without warning,
Heller ward's mit einemmale	It suddenly grew brighter
Von dem Glanz der vollen Schale,	From the radiance of the filled cup
Die ein schöner Knabe trug.	Borne by a fair youth.
Holde Augen sah ich blinken	I saw his kindly eyes sparkling
Unter dichtem Blumenkranze;	Beneath a close-woven garland of flowers;
In des Trankes Himmelsglanze	In the potion's celestial glow
Trat er in den Kreis herein.	He stepped into the circle.
Und er hiess mich freundlich trinken;	Graciously he bade me drink;
Und ich dacht': es kann der Knabe	And I thought: that boy
Mit der schönen lichten Gabe,	With his fair, shining gift
Wahrlich! nicht der Böse sein.	Can surely not be the Devil.

Trinke Mut des reinen Lebens!	Drink the courage of pure life!
Dann verstehst du die Belehrung,	Then you will understand my words,
Kommst, mit ängstlicher Beschwörung,	And never, with anxious incantation,
Nicht zurück an diesen Ort.	Return to this place.
Grabe hier nicht mehr vergebens:	Dig here no more in vain;
Tages Arbeit! Abends Gäste!	Work by day, conviviality in the evening,
Saure Wochen! Frohe Feste!	Weeks of toil and joyous holidays!
Sei dein künftig Zauberwort.	Let this from now on be your magic spell.

JOHANN WOLFGANG VON GOETHE (1749–1832); poem written in May 1797

This is the twenty-third of Schubert's seventy-five Goethe solo settings (1814–26). See the poet's biography for a chronological list of all the Goethe settings.

Goethe wrote this poem in May 1797, apparently as an ironic reaction to the fact that he had been persuaded to take part in a Hamburg lottery where there was a chance to win a house with land. It initiated a whole series of ballads which were to be published in the 1798 *Musenalmanach*. Schiller was immediately enthusiastic about it and made an urgent request to his friend Zumsteeg in Stuttgart to set it to music. It is no surprise that the text had to be learned by heart

Der Schatzgräber by Moritz von Schwind, 1849.

by countless schoolchildren in the German Democratic Republic during the 1950s: one need only glance at the last three lines and the poem's sarcastic attitude to material riches. Goethe got the idea from a sixteenth-century woodcut in Spalatin's German translation of Petrarch's dialogue *De remidiis utriusque fortunae*. It shows three groups of treasure-seekers and satanists, including four men in a magic circle terrified by a visitation from the Devil. Another group consults a magic book and is approached by a boy with a Holy Grail-like chalice surrounded by glorious rays of light.

The rhyme scheme (ABBCADDC) is ingenious: in the first verse for example the ear expects a rhyme at the end of the fourth line to match 'Herzen' at the end of the first, but this comes only at the end of the *fifth* line; similarly 'Gut' seems abandoned at the end of the fourth line and only finds its echo right at the end of the strophe. This technical device exactly mirrors the falsely aroused hopes of the treasure-seeker and the deceptions of his calling. Schubert's chorus-like repetition of the last line to make effectively a nine-line strophe is not the happiest of inspirations, for it seems to turn the ballad into a drinking song.

It is easy to see why this poem appealed to the young composer. The second verse in particular casts a spell that is reminiscent of some of his early ballads with their ghostly encounters, black-hearted villains and maidens in distress. But because the poem was by Goethe it seems that Schubert felt inhibited and lacked the confidence to treat it in a more openly narrative manner. The restraint he displayed in setting *Der Gott und die Bajadere* D254 had some point, but here we require a touch more musical magic, particularly at the moment when a money-grabbing life is changed into one of spiritual enlightenment. (In Loewe's setting of twenty years later the treasure-seeker's A minor world is suddenly dislocated and transformed by a succession of exquisitely daring G sharps.) Of course Schubert's version is fine as far as it goes: he finds an effective bass voice tessitura for the character, and the minor-key melody is a good one. There are nice decorative touches like the trills in the postlude to each verse. It is just that the rippling quaver accompaniment is rather sedate and, at the appearance of the Grail-like light and the angelic boy, the simple change to the major key seems predictable and tame. This is one of the few Goethe settings that did not find its way into either of the two volumes that Schubert prepared for the poet in 1816. It seems fair to deduce therefore that the composer himself did not consider it a complete success.

Autograph:	University Library of Lund, Sweden
First edition:	Published as Vol. 7 no. 47 in Friedlaender's edition by Peters, Leipzig in 1887 (P508)
Subsequent editions:	Peters: Vol. 7/102; AGA XX 113: Vol. 3/35; NSA IV: Vol. 8/194; Bärenreiter: Vol. 6
Bibliography:	Capell 1928, p. 105
Further settings:	Johann Friedrich Reichardt (1752–1814) *Der Schatzgräber* (1811) Carl Loewe (1796–1869) *Der Schatzgräber* Op. 59 no. 3 (1836) Hanns Eisler (1898–1962) *Der Schatzgräber* (1942)
Discography and timing:	Fischer-Dieskau I 5² 3'43
	Hyperion I 24⁸
	Hyperion II 9³ 4'50 Michael George

← *Der Rattenfänger* D255   *Heidenröslein* D257 →

SCHATZGRÄBERS BEGEHR

(SCHOBER) OP. 23 NO. 4, **D761** [H497]

The treasure-hunter's desire

The song exists in two versions, the second of which is discussed below:
(1) November 1822; (2) appeared July–August 1823

(1) 'In mässiger Bewegung'   D minor – D major   **C**   [50 bars]

(2) D minor – D major

In tiefster Erde ruht ein alt Gesetz,	Deep in the earth sleeps an old law.
Dem treibt mich's rastlos immer nachzuspüren;	I feel a restless, ceaseless urge to seek it out,
Und grabend kann ich Andres nicht vollführen.	And as I dig I can accomplish nothing else.
Wohl spannt auch mir die Welt ihr goldnes Netz,	Let the world spread its golden net to lure me, too;
Wohl tönt auch mir der Klugheit seicht Geschwätz:	Let wisdom's shallow prattle ring in my ears:
'Du wirst die Müh' und Zeit umsonst verlieren;'	'You are wasting your time and efforts to no avail!'
Das soll mich nicht in meiner Arbeit irren,[1]	That shall not turn me aside from my labour;
Ich grabe glühend fort, so nun, wie stets.	I go on digging ardently, now as ever.
Und soll mich nie des Findens Wonne laben,	And even if the joy of discovery never rewards me,
Sollt' ich mein Grab mit dieser Hoffnung graben:	If I am digging my own grave with this hope,
Ich steige gern hinab, gestillt ist dann mein Sehnen.[2]	Yet will I gladly climb down, for then my longing will be stilled.
Drum lasset Ruhe mir in meinem Streben!	So leave me in peace with my endeavour.
Ein Grab mag man wohl jedem gerne geben,[3]	Surely a grave is gladly given to every man;
Wollt ihr es denn nicht mir, ihr Lieben, gönnen?[4]	Will you then not grant me one, friends?

[1] This line is correct as it is to be found in Schober's *Gedichte*, 1842. For the 1865 edition of the *Gedichte* Schober changes the line to 'Das hemme nicht mein emsiges Hantiren' ('That will not distract me from my assiduous Labours').
[2] Schober (1842) writes 'Es löscht die Flammen doch, die martend brennen' (It will surely put out the flames whose burns torment me').
[3] Schober writes 'doch' instead of 'wohl' in this line.
[4] Schober writes 'Wollt ihr es *mir* denn nicht, ihr Lieben, gönnen?'.

FRANZ VON SCHOBER (1796–1882)

This is the ninth of Schubert's fourteen Schober solo settings (1815–27). See the poet's biography for a chronological list of all the Schober settings.

Most of the commentators are agreed that this is an unusual song, and that this is because of the poet. Capell is frank in apportioning the blame: 'All that invalidates it is something puerile in Schober's intention – something would-be blood-curdling and grotesque . . '. But there seems to be some hidden agenda in these stanzas which, though fairly typical of their time (Eichendorff was to write his own *Der Schatzgräber*, set to music wonderfully by Schumann, where a treasure-seeker digs his own grave) appear to be aimed at a specific audience. The likelihood is that the poem was conceived in anger and self-pity as a type of rebuttal, and that it was written, if not versified, in sonnet form, in order to reinforce Schober's intellectual credentials. We have no way of knowing how far in advance of the music the words were written, but if they date from earlier in 1822 they would be contemporary with the composition of *Alfonso und Estrella* D732 (qv), the most substantial collaboration between Schubert and Schober.

In later years Schober more or less admitted that the libretto was a botched job, and that he was responsible for the work's failure. The person who was convinced from the start that the whole project was wrong-headed and ill-conceived was the singer Johann Michael Vogl, the most experienced of all Schubert's friends in the world of opera. 'You are wasting your time', he had more or less said, no doubt loftily, and Schober no doubt replied with something along the lines of 'Nothing ventured, nothing gained'. The pair of young creators were fired by an ambitious enthusiasm to get on with something mighty. This poem defends the position of the aspiring artist as something glorious, averring that the metaphorical search for treasure, even unto death, is as fulfilling as its discovery. There is a slightly makeshift and defensive air as if the poem were aimed at unsympathetic ears. The use of the words 'ihr Lieben' in the last strophe suggests that the entire *Freundeskreis* had grumbled about the new project, and that the poem was meant as a general explanation and apologia on behalf of poet and composer. In fact it was probably Vogl who scotched whatever chance the opera had of being heard, and one cannot help wondering whether vanity, pride and the singer's jealousy of the composer's intimate friendship with Schober played as much of a part in this as musical perspicacity.

The song itself may not be Schubert's most distinguished but, appropriate to its name, it is a veritable treasure-trove of ideas for future use and recycling. (In the same way, *Alfonso und Estrella* is full of musical marvels, whatever its failings as drama.) Schubert's *Der Pilgrim* D794 (1823), the restless striding left-hand bass octaves in the old baroque manner, and the texture of a chorale with richly woven inner voices, stems from the same workbench where *Schatzgräbers Begehr* was hammered into shape. And of course, the key of D minor/major (interchangeable with D major/minor) had been a sign of the travelling quest for some time in Schubert's song-writing syntax – as early as the composition of Goethe's *Der Schatzgräber* D256 in 1815. The solemn *Der Kreuzzug* D932 from 1827 is another such song, as is of course the opening song of *Winterreise*, *Gute Nacht* D911/1.

Indeed, *Gute Nacht* joins hands with *Schatzgräbers Begehr*, both in tonality and tempo marking: Schubert marks the Schober setting 'Gehend', and the initial marking for the opening of *Winterreise* was 'Mässig, in gehender Bewegung'. The winter traveller sets out in the dead of night on an impossible mission of self-discovery under adverse circumstances – he is as doomed as the equally determined Schober the librettist. There is a magical – and crucial – change from D minor to D major towards the end of both songs. Other works that derive indirectly from the restless harmonic burrowings of *Schatzgräbers Begehr* are *Totengräbers Heimwehe* D842 and *Totengräber-Weise* D869.

The solemn walking mood is established right at the beginning, the melody a manly chorale with most of the struggle implied in the piano writing. Both hands delve into the bass clef as if in the act of digging, with the occasional semiquavers running through the fingers like earth sifted and scrutinized to no purpose. (The reading of a G sharp at the top of the first right-hand chord in b. 2 of the NSA should be observed.) At bb. 10–11 we move into the major key for the lure of the golden net of earthly temptation, and the judgemental tone of 'Du wirst die Müh' und Zeit umsonst verlieren' (bb. 14–17) suggests the finger-wagging of unimaginative pedantry as it sticks largely to one note. But the poet gives as good as he gets, and his riposte ('Das soll mich nicht in meiner Arbeit irren', bb. 17–19) is equally obstinate, centred around a single note a fourth higher as if parodying the tone of his accuser. The rising sequence for the two 'Ich grabe glühend fort' phrases (bb. 19–21) turns the screw of tension and suggests the tenacity of the fanatic. For this second version of the song, Schubert expands the transitional interlude by adding an extra bar to the draft of 1822 – no doubt all part of reviewing the song as it was made ready for publication in 1823. This helps to set up the third strophe as a moment of unexpected calm. Acceptance of fate is suggested by the gentle undulations of B flat[7] (from b. 27) under the vocal line, an indeterminate sea of cloudy harmony. This passage progresses through a sequence of dreaming flat keys until G flat major turns into F sharp minor at b. 32, and the wistful fantasy of repose returns to a more active mood as the voice plunges an octave to illustrate 'Ich steige gern hinab'.

The final strophe, with its change of key signature to D major at b. 38, can be most affecting in performance, despite the gloomy message. Here the music is at its most demanding for the singer with a *mezza voce* line at the top of the stave as earthbound cares give way to a longing for the peace of the grave. There is an air of self-indulgent bathos to these lines suggesting that the unsuccessful artist is somehow a martyr to be admired as much as the successful one (Schober covers himself on all fronts). Even Schubert's genius, and his loyal enthusiasm for his friend's portentous utterances, cannot quite turn the base metal of this rhetoric into unalloyed gold. The open fifth of the last bar of the postlude suggests a bleak and empty end to a career of fruitless striving. The whole of Schober's life – as unsuccessful businessman, bad actor, dud librettist, social sponge and eventually redundant assistant to Liszt in Weimar (he thus attached himself to the coat-tails of another great musician) – seemed to be a defence of the concept of 'mediocrity with as much honour as possible'. But Schubert loved Schober and, in trying to understand why, we should try to see the best of him – good-looking, charming, diverting, energetic, of an enviable personal magnetism and, above all, deeply musical.

Autograph:	Missing or lost
Publication:	First published as part of the AGA in 1895 (P693; first version)
	Published as Op. 23 no. 4 by Sauer & Leidesdorf, Vienna in
	August 1823 (P47; second version)
Publication reviews:	*Allgemeine musikalische Zeitung* (Leipzig) No. 26 (24 June 1824),
	col. 425–8 [Waidelich/Hilmar Dokumente I No. 282; Deutsch Doc.
	Biog. No. 479]
Subsequent editions:	Peters: Vol. 4/22; AGA XX 412: Vol. 7/35; NSA IV: Vol. 2a/10 &
	Vol. 2b/189; Barenreiter: Vol. 1/40 (medium voice) 1/139 (low voice)
Bibliography:	Capell 1928, p. 174
	Einstein 1951, p. 253
	Fischer-Dieskau 1977, p. 164
	Porter 1961, p. 118
Discography and timing:	Fischer-Dieskau II 5[11] 3'02
	Hyperion I 28[17]
	Hyperion II 26[2] 3'51 Maarten Koningsberger

← *Todesmusik D758*   *Schwestergruss D762* →

SCHICKSALSLENKER, BLICKE NIEDER (Des Tages Weihe)
(ANONYMOUS) **D763** [H499]
A♭ major   22 November 1822

Guides of fate,   Quartet, SATB
look down

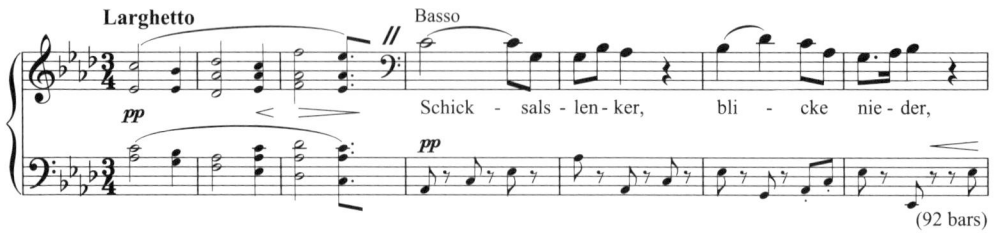

(92 bars)

Schicksalslenker, blicke nieder,	Guider of fate, look down
Auf dein dankerfülltes Herz;	On this grateful heart of yours.
Uns belebt die Freude wieder,	We are stirred anew by joy;
Fern entfloh'n ist jeder Schmerz.	All suffering has fled far away.
Und das Leid, es ist vergessen.	And sorrow is forgotten.
Durch die Nebel strahlt der Glanz	Through the mists shines the immeasurable radiance
Deiner Grösse unermessen,	Of your greatness,
Wie aus hellem Sternenkranz.	As if from a brilliant wreath of stars.
Liebevoll nahmst du der Leiden	Lovingly you took the bitter cup
Herben Kelch von Vaters Mund;	Of sorrows from your Father's lips,
Darum ward in Fern und Weiten	And your supreme merciful kindness
Deine höchste Milde kund.	Was made known far and wide.

ANONYMOUS/UNKNOWN

This quartet was one of the few pieces of occasional music for which Schubert was specially commissioned and paid, and its background is interesting, if rather obscure. We only know something about it through Gerhard von Breuning (the son of Beethoven's friend Stefan von Breuning) who was told the story by Anna Fröhlich, one of Schubert's friends and responsible for encouraging the composer to write a number of part songs for female voices from about 1821. Anna Fröhlich was a piano teacher at the Conservatorium, but she also taught privately at the home of one Baroness Geymüller. The baroness was particularly keen to have a poem set to music in honour of a friend named Ritter who had recently recovered from a serious illness. (Fröhlich had never met Herr Ritter and had no idea who he was, and neither do we to this day.) Fröhlich promised to ask Schubert on Barbara von Geymüller's behalf if he would under-take the task. He did so, apparently composing the piece in a single day, and received fifty Gulden for his trouble. Fröhlich told Breuning the composer was delighted with the money. The first performance must have pleased Herr Ritter (again, we do not know when). The work did not surface again until 1842, as *Des Tages Weihe* and with new words suitable for a name-day or birthday celebration. It was probably the ever-interfering Anton Diabelli who had adapted the text to make it more suitable for commercial consumption (people had birthdays more often than recoveries from serious illnesses, even in unhealthy Vienna). According to the Nottebohm catalogue, Diabelli also took the liberty of adding violin and cello parts to the quartet's accompaniment.

This is a beautiful, if not over-characteristic, piece of occasional music. At least we know that the composer was not responsible for the choice of text with its slightly mawkish religious overtones. The key is A flat which Schubert also chose for his much greater four-part song *Gebet* D815 (1824). In Schubert's output the worship of God (*Im Abendrot* D799) and Zeus (*Ganymed* D544) are linked by this tonality. There may be some argument that Schubert regarded the sensual rituals of *Versunken* D715 and *Geheimes* D719 (both songs also in A flat major) as another kind of worship.

The piece begins with a six-bar introduction. At b. 7 a gentle and mellifluous solo for the bass is initiated, the piano suggestive of string accompaniment with pizzicato lower notes. After fifteen measures (from b. 22) we hear all four voices (SATB) together for the first time, and the accompaniment breaks into semiquavers. The part-writing for the voices is particularly effective, gentle wafting harmony that is exactly right for a song about recovering from illness. For the great moment of God revealing himself ('Durch die Nebel strahlt der Glanz' bb. 40–42) the music shifts into C flat major, an almost obligatory progression in those A flat songs by Schubert where there is a moment of sensual magic or epiphany (in *Ganymed* the narrator imagines himself to be languishing on the breast of Zeus in C flat major). At 'Liebevoll nahmst du der Leiden' there is a short tenor solo (bb. 48–53) before the four-part texture re-establishes itself. A recapitulation of the main tune at b. 68 is marked 'Mit halber Stimme' and, in the *mezza voce* form, strikes the ear as the most restorative of balms. The final setting of 'Schicksalslenker ... blicke nieder ... Auf dein dankerfülltes Herz' (the first strophe of the anonymous text is repeated) dies away in solemn augmentation. Schubert has taken the trouble to write a beautifully turned miniature cantata, somewhat conservative in style (no doubt to fit the musical tastes of his clients) but nevertheless containing many a turn of phrase that could only have come from his hand. The tragic irony is that as the composer sat down to write this piece about the happy cure of Herr Ritter, his own appalling health problem, the syphilis that was to change his life for ever, was about to emerge; indeed it was probably only a matter of weeks before he would notice the first symptoms. The anonymous lines about a 'bitter cup of sorrows' must have have struck him as the most terrible of prophecies. If Elizabeth McKay's theory that the illness was already well advanced by December 1822 is correct, the irony is stronger still.

Autograph:	Missing or lost		
First edition:	Published as Op. post. 146 by Diabelli, Vienna in 1842 (P336)		
Subsequent editions:	Not in Peters; AGA XVII 11: p. 212; NSA III: Vol. 2a/97		
Discography and timing:	Deutsche Grammophon *Schubert Quartette*	4'55	Elly Ameling, Janet Baker, Peter Schreier & Dietrich Fischer-Dieskau
	Hyperion I 28²²		Patricia Rozario, Catherine
	Hyperion II 26⁴	5'16	Denley, Ian Bostridge & Michael George

← *Schwestergruss* D762   *An die Entfernte* D765 →

Die SCHIFFENDE *see* DUBIOUS, MISATTRIBUTED AND LOST SONGS

Der SCHIFFER   The boatman
(MAYRHOFER)[1] OP. 21 NO. 2, **D536** [H352]

The song exists in two versions, the second of which is discussed below:
(1) 1817?; (2) appeared June 1823

(1) 'Feurig'   E♭ major $\frac{2}{4}$ [113 bars]

(2) E♭ major

(115 bars)

Im Winde, im Sturme befahr ich den Fluss,	In wind and storm I row on the river,
Die Kleider durchweichet der Regen im Guss;	My clothes are soaked by the pouring rain;
Ich peitsche die Wellen mit mächtigem Schlag,[2]	I lash the waves with powerful strokes,
Erhoffend, erhoffend mir heiteren Tag.[3]	Hoping for a cheerful day.

Die Wellen, sie jagen das ächzende Schiff,[4]	The waves drive the creaking boat,
Es drohet der Strudel, es drohet das Riff.[5]	Whirlpool and reef threaten;
Gesteine entkollern den felsigen Höh'n,	Rocks roll down from the craggy heights,
Und Tannen erseufzen wie Geistergestöh'n.[6]	And fir trees sigh like moaning ghosts.

So musste es kommen – ich hab es gewollt,	It had to come to this, I wished it so;
Ich hasse ein Leben behaglich entrollt;	I hate a life that unfolds comfortably.
Und schlängen die Wellen den ächzenden Kahn,[7]	And if the waves devoured this creaking boat,
Ich priese doch immer die eigene Bahn.	I would still extol my chosen course.

Drum tose des Wassers ohnmächtiger Zorn,[8]	So let the water roar with impotent rage;
Dem Herzen entquillet ein seliger Born,	A fountain of bliss gushes from my heart,
Die Nerven erfrischend – o himmlische Lust!	Refreshing my nerves – o celestial joy,
Dem Sturme zu trotzen mit männlicher Brust![9]	To defy the storm with manly heart!

[1] The textual differences noted below are all to be found in the printing of the poem in *Beiträge zur Bildung für Jünglinge* (1818) and in the Mayrhofer *Gedichte* (1824). For an explanation of the background to these alternative Mayrhofer readings see Editorial Note at the beginning of Johann MAYRHOFER.
[2] Mayrhofer writes '*Ich lenke – ich peitsche* mit mächtigem Schlag'.
[3] Mayrhofer writes '*Die Wellen*, erhoffend mir heiteren Tag'.
[4] Mayrhofer writes '*Die Fluten*, sie jagen das *schwankende* Schiff'.
[5] Mayrhofer writes 'es drohet *der* Riff'.
[6] Mayrhofer writes 'Und *Fichten, sie sausen* wie Geistergestöh'n'.
[7] Mayrhofer writes 'Und schlängen die *Fluten der drohenden* Kahn'.
[8] Mayrhofer writes '*Es* tose . . .'.
[9] Mayrhofer writes 'Dem Sturme *gebieten* mit männlicher Brust'.

JOHANN MAYRHOFER (1787–1836)

This is the thirteenth of Schubert's forty-seven Mayrhofer solo settings (1814–24). See the poet's biography for a chronological list of all the Mayrhofer settings.

Schubert almost certainly set this poem as early as 1817 and from a handwritten copy. It (the poem, not the song) went into print the following year in the second and final issue of a literary annual – *Beiträge zur Bildung für Jünglinge*, a short-lived publication that was doomed to be banished by the censor and cleared from the shelves. In Susan Youens's words this was 'a "missionary outreach" program expressly for youths', with contributions from Anton von Spaun, Anton Ottenwalt (qv), Josef Kenner (qv) and others in the Linz circle. It is clear that the authorities were petrified by anything with political over- or undertones that was aimed at a student readership, even if it was nearer to a *Boy's Own Paper* in the British tradition (self-reliance, freedom of thought). At first glance this boatman is a role model for the brave, manly behaviour in which Biedermeier morals comfortably meet the Victorian values of British life fifty years later. Wyndham Lewis described what might have been a complementary English scenario: 'Tough conquering Nordics ... crammed with experience and philosophy ... blundering through trackless forests and lethal swamps foiling villains of Latin origin.' Illustrations from British boys' papers usually depicted these gallants in heroic profile: resolute, good-looking, in control of life's tempests – in short all the things that this poet and composer were not but perhaps would have liked to be. Mayrhofer's passionate espousal of the ideals of Greek antiquity provides another clue to his desired self-image. His boatman hero is worthy of the employment of Odysseus at the very least; this man would never have been diverted by the sirens. The wish-fulfillment fantasy of this picture perhaps robs us of the complete engagement we feel when a poem allows Schubert to create more vulnerable characters. But there is no doubt that this is a splendid piece of bravura, a good 'sing' composed, as Einstein says, 'in a *single* stroke'. In *Der Strom* D565, from the same year, the poet's life is compared to the water's erratic meandering; in *Der Schiffer* the water, however terribly it rages, is powerless to alter the boatman's course. Man is well on the way to taming nature.

Der Schiffer, illustration of Schubert's song by Leopold Kupelwieser, 1820.

The piano writing here is extremely invigorating. A single bar of E flat major followed by one shared between G^7 and C minor, a bar of A flat major and then B flat^7 back to E flat major in two beats, followed by the entry of the voice on the upbeat to the next bar, invokes an astonishing degree of excitement. The secret is in the workout given to the fingers, and the unique melodic shape with which Schubert fashions his whiplash right-hand figurations. Here sequences of ingenious arpeggio patterns are heard as a kind of melody. The only accompaniment that is anywhere like this is in *Die schöne Müllerin* – the song *Eifersucht und Stolz* D795/15, also water music in a stormy hurry and similarly marked 'Geschwind' (accompanists tempted to play that song too fast – and most are – should refer to the speed of *Der Schiffer* as a benchmark). The entry of the voice at b. 4 (written in the bass clef as if to emphasize the formidable masculinity of the singer) announces a memorable tune, but nothing too fancy; bb. 5–7 are built around an E flat major chord, the tune leapfrogging in stages up the stave, and bb. 8–11 repeat the process on a B flat^7 background. This plain sailing can only last for a little while. At the harmonic clashes on 'Ich peitsche die Wellen' (bb. 13–14, and equivalent places), the voice is doubled by determined piano octaves; rogue C flats that have forced their way into the harmony, like waves breaking cheekily over the side of the boat, are eventually flattened through sheer determination. The triumphant paean sounded by the stretch in the vocal line when the boatman reaches for his highest note (the E flat on 'er<u>hoff</u>end' in b. 21) is tremendously satisfying for the singer, and the phrase that rolls down from the crest of this sound wave (bb. 21–3) a perfect means of rounding off the strophe.

Der Schiffer is a modified strophic song whose many subtle variations in word-setting do not detract from the forward impetus and no-nonsense simplicity of the whole. The first seventeen bars of music are the same for the first three verses; in fact the music for the whole of Verse 3 is identical to that for Verse 1, giving the climactic word 'priese' (b. 75) a similarly ecstatic quality on the high E flat as we heard on 'erhoffend' in the first strophe. In Verse 2 the new direction taken from b. 46 for 'Und Tannen erseufzen wie Geistergestöh'n' provides a chance for the singer to use a conspiratorial piano dynamic to tell us about the whispering fir-trees high above the river banks. In Verse 4 the music changes course after only nine bars with an interpolation between bb. 93 and 96 that surprises and delights: 'Die Nerven erfrischend' flows upwards to reach a high E flat on '<u>himm</u>lische Lust'. It is as if the poet's imagery of refreshed nerves had led Schubert to imagine blood circulating through the singer's body, thus a smoothly ascending scale, the only such moment in the piece. The song's postlude is simply a repetition of the bracing introduction.

The second version of the song is the one that went into print in 1823. There is a first version published in Volume 1b of the NSA. This includes an *ossia* with variants of the melody – taken from an autograph in the Staatsbibliothek Preussischer Kulturbesitz, Berlin in which the composer has written out only the vocal line (see photograph of score on p. XXXV of Volume 1a).

If *Der Schiffer* has an ever so slightly hollow ring to it, one must blame Mayrhofer's battle against the elements (or more particularly, the elements in society that he despised). His was a Walter Mitty fantasy: however much he tried donning the costume, he was no intrepid boatman. He never quite dared to stand openly against the prejudice of his times, and was already working for that most authoritarian of employers, the Imperial Censor's Office. Mayrhofer's resentment and political frustration lay festering in his troubled mind, hidden from most of his contemporaries. Writing poetry like this, and imagining himself a man of action, was a not entirely convincing means of escape and release.

Autograph:	Staatsbibliothek Preussischer Kulturbesitz (antograph of vocal line)
	Männergesang-Verein, Vienna (first version)
Publication:	First published as part of the NSA in 1970 (P756; first version)
	First published as Op. 21 no. 2 by Sauer & Leidesdorf in June 1823
	(P42; second version)

Dedicatee:	Johann Mayrhofer
Publication reviews:	*Allgemeine musikalische Zeitung* (Leipzig) No. 26 (24 June 1824), col. 425–8 [Waidelich/Hilmar Dokumente I No. 282; Deutsch Doc. Biog. No. 479]
	Of version with guitar accompaniment: *Allgemeiner musikalischer Anzeiger* (Frankfurt) No. 14 (30 September 1826), p. 107 [Waidelich/Hilmar Dokumente I No. 410]
Subsequent editions:	Peters: Vol. 2/52; AGA XX 318: Vol. 5/95; NSA IV: Vol. 1a/152 & Vol. 1b/263; Bärenreiter: Vol. 1/121
Bibliography:	Capell 1928, pp. 139–40
	Einstein 1951, p. 164
	Fischer-Dieskau 1977, p. 98
	Kohlhäufl 1999, p. 307
Discography and timing:	Fischer-Dieskau II 1[5] 1'54
	Hyperion I 2[11]
	Hyperion II 18[3] 1'59 Stephen Varcoe

← *Memnon* D541   *Am Strome* D539 →

Der SCHIFFER

The boatman

(F. von Schlegel) **D694** [H450]
D major   March 1820

(56 bars)

Friedlich lieg' ich hingegossen,	Peacefully I lie stretched out,
Lenke hin und her das Ruder,	Turning the rudder this way and that,
Atme kühl im Licht des Mondes,	Breathing the cool air in the moonlight,
Träume süss im stillen Mute;	Tranquil in spirit, dreaming sweetly.
Gleiten lass' ich auch den Kahn,	And I let the boat drift,
Schaue in die blanken Fluten,	Gazing into the shining waters
Wo die Sterne lieblich schimmern,	Where the stars shimmer enchantingly;
Spiele wieder mit dem Ruder.	And again I play with the rudder.
Sässe doch das blonde Mägdlein	If only that fair-haired girl
Vor mir auf dem Bänkchen ruhend,	Were reclining on the seat before me,
Sänge schmachtend zarte Lieder.	Singing tenderly soulful songs,
Himmlisch wär' mir dann zu Mute.	Then I should feel blissfully happy.
Liess mich necken von dem Kinde,	I should let the child tease me
Wieder tändelnd mit der Guten. –	And flirt again with the girl.
Friedlich lieg' ich hingegossen,	Peacefully I lie stretched out,
Träume süss im stillen Mute,	Tranquil in spirit, dreaming sweetly,
Atme kühl im Licht des Mondes,	Breathing the cool air in the moonlight,
Führe hin und her das Ruder.	Moving the rudder this way and that.

FRIEDRICH VON SCHLEGEL (1772–1829); poem written in 1800/1801

This is the the twelfth of Schubert's sixteen Friedrich von Schlegel solo settings (1818–25). See the poet's biography for a chronological list of all the Friedrich von Schlegel songs.

It seems that in the middle of his work on the *Abendröte* sequence Schubert was drawn by this poem (printed further on in the Schlegel *Gedichte* 1809, and twenty pages after *Die Gebüsche* in the 1816 Viennese edition) which is not part of that set: the poem's water imagery linked with starlight lured him away, for a short while, from the earlier poems in the book. We are grateful that he put aside thoughts of a cycle, one morning in March 1820, to lavish his attentions on the indolent boatman dreaming of his girl. This song could not be more different from that of 1817 with the same title, *Der Schiffer* D536 of Mayrhofer, which is full of almost manic energy and determination. Here we find another boatman, relaxing after hours, whose mood Schubert has caught and immortalized.

Most of the composer's water songs move forwards, like a stream gushing from its source en route to the sea; but here we have a waterborne stillness, and Schubert relishes the challenge. Poulenc's *La Grenouillère* has a similar feel, a song to Apollinaire's poem about a former water-side haunt of Renoir and the Impressionists, where the laziest of minims and crotchets (in the same key of D major as it happens) conjure the sound of lapping water and tethered boats as they gently bump against each other. Much of the special beauty of Schubert's barcarolle lies in the accompaniment, which is one of those one-off inspirations of which he was capable when confronted with a poem with strong imagery. The idea of stretching and drifting here inspires a layout in the piano writing that the composer was never to repeat in quite the same manner. The tessitura of the accompaniment is low and dark as befits the depths of the waters by night, the voice poised above it like moonlight. In the bass can be heard the boat's subtle undulations, slowly rocking between tonic and dominant with an occasional slip into the subdominant. The texture of this bottom line is occasionally enlivened by a tiny tremor of semiquavers deep in the left hand (as in bb. 7 and 10) as the current swells and subsides. Drifting semiquavers are also to be found in the alto and tenor voices of the accompaniment, moving hither and thither in the inner fingers of the pianist's right hand – by implication the same fingers the boatman uses as he plays aimlessly with the rudder. The slight splashing sound this makes is intimated by the piquant accidentals of G sharp and D sharp in the key of D major that break the surface of the tonal waters (bb. 4 and 5 and *passim*). This does not have the ebullience of *Die Forelle* D550, where G natural in the key of D flat adds the necessary glint and splash, but is more of a splosh – sensual and deliciously lazy.

This relaxed feel is to be found in the pacing of the vocal line where the singer can only bring himself to utter a two-bar phrase before the piano takes over for an interlude. The idea of breathing the cool evening air ('Atme kühl im Licht des Mondes') is emphasized by a pause to do just that after singing about it; miraculously the following bar of piano music, originally designed for a gently moving rudder, here seems perfectly descriptive of a deep breath, in and out. The setting of 'Träume süss im stillen Mute' (bb. 14–15, exquisitely prophetic of the floating filigree of a later barcarolle, *Des Fischers Liebesglück* D933) is rather high in tessitura, particularly in comparison with bb. 17–18 where the voice plunges almost two octaves lower. As this happens, the accompaniment slides down in a chromatic scale in sixths between the hands. The boatman thus abandons the rudder and allows his vessel to float free for a moment or two as he looks at the stars. They shine back at him as if in a mirror, and the descent into the vocal and pianistic depths places the heavenly light as far under the waters as the stars themselves are high in the sky. The combination of water and starlight was always a heady cocktail for this composer: the playful semiquavers in the vocal line that ornament 'Wo die Sterne lieblich schimmern, / Spiele wieder mit dem Ruder' remind us of the intoxicated (with nature) melismata of 'Tausend schwebende Sterne' that bring the Goethe setting *Auf dem See* D543 to a dancing conclusion. The final delightful touch in this first section, a detail that is unique to *Der Schiffer*, is a bar of vocal music without words, marked 'ppp' (b. 25). While it is possible that the composer had meant the final words of the strophe to be repeated here, an attempt to do this makes for an awkward underlay; Schubert surely meant the singer to hum, a once-in-a-career device that perfectly fits the mood of this musing boatman, too deep in his reverie to articulate his feelings verbally.

There is one thing missing, however – the boatman's girl. In *Des Fischers Liebesglück* thoughts of love are followed by the real thing, but in *Der Schiffer* the singer can only dream, and he does so in the middle section. Syncopated semiquavers in the relative minor (from b. 28) depict the first stirrings of sexual longing. 'Das blonde Mägdlein' is conjured before our eyes, the gracious upward inflection of 'Mägdlein' (b. 30) perfectly descriptive of the alluring will-o'-the-wisp who is out of his reach. There is suddenly a more urgent, even Italianate, cast to the vocal line: 'Sänge schmachtend zarte Lieder' (b. 33), with just a hint of male bravado and impatience (bordering on exaggeration), is worthy of a professional serenader. For an instant the boatman sees himself in this role and smiles with us at the idea, for he is probably far too lazy to sing anything at all. The change from B minor to B major at 'Himmlisch wär' mir dann zu Mute' (b. 35) implies that the wooer has received his reward, in his fantasy at least. The flirtatious sense of the verb 'tändelnd' (b. 39) is perfectly caught by the rocking rhythm between the hands, the semiquaver syncopations expressive of racing heartbeat, the exchange of cheeky smiles and the choppier waters engendered by two in a boat rather than one. Between bb. 41 and 43 this restless movement subsides, and two dotted crotchets in b. 43 (a long sigh as the boatman accepts that he is alone after all) lead us back to a recapitulation of the opening music. This is a conventional cadence from B minor back to the relative major via a dominant seventh, but it is magical nevertheless. The first section is abbreviated here, but happily so, for we hear just enough music to imagine the singer settled back in his reverie, playing once again with the rudder and whiling away the night in his dreams. Schubert wrote many water songs and many nocturnes, but in this one, as in *Gondelfahrer* D808, he memorably unites the two genres. The sparkling colours that paint his various streams by day in other songs now give way to the glow of moonlight, and deep pools of longing, intermittently and languorously ruffled by the stirrings of desire.

Autograph:	In private possession
First edition:	Published as Book 33 no. 1 of the *Nachlass* by Diabelli, Vienna in June 1842 (P337)
Subsequent editions:	Peters: Vol. 5/190; AGA XX 377: Vol. 6/98; NSA IV: Vol. 12/165
Bibliography:	Capell 1928, p. 166
	Fischer-Dieskau 1977, p. 123
Discography and timing:	Fischer-Dieskau II 3[19] 3'07
	Hyperion I 27[20] 4'04 Matthias Goerne
	Hyperion II 23[8]

← *Der Knabe* D692   *Namenstagslied* D695 →

SCHIFFERS NACHTLIED *see* LIED EINES SCHIFFERS AN DIE DIOSKUREN D360

SCHIFFERS SCHEIDELIED[1]   The sailor's farewell
(SCHOBER) **D910** [H626]
E minor   February 1827

(149 bars)

(1) Die Wogen am Gestade schwellen,
       Es klatscht der Wind das Segeltuch,
     Und murmelt in den weissen Wellen,
       Ich höre seinen wilden Spruch.
     Es ruft mich fort, es winkt der Kahn,[2]

     Vor Ungeduld schaukelnd, auf weite
       Bahn.

(2) Dort streckt sie sich in öder Ferne,

       Du kannst nicht mit, siehst du, mein
         Kind;
     Wie leicht versinken meine Sterne,
       Wie leicht erwächst zum Sturm
         der Wind,
     Dann droht in tausend Gestalten
         der Tod,
       Wie trotzt' ich ihm, wüsst' ich dich
         in Not?

(3) O löse deiner Arme Schlinge
       Und löse auch von mir dein Herz!
     Weiss ich es denn, ob ich's vollbringe
       Und siegreich kehre heimatwärts?
     Die Welle, die jetzt so lockend singt,
     Vielleicht ist's dieselbe, die mich
         verschlingt.

(4) Noch ist's in deine Hand gegeben,
       Noch gingst du nichts unlösbar ein,
     O trenne schnell dein junges Leben
       Von meinem ungewissen Sein,
     O wolle, o wolle, bevor du musst,[3]
     Entsagung ist leichter als Verlust!

The waves surge on the shore,
  The wind beats against the canvas
And murmurs amid the white waves;
  I hear its wild voice.
It calls me away, and the boat, rocking
    impatiently,
Bids me embark on a distant course.

That course stretches far across the empty
    wastes;
  You cannot come with me, my child; do you
    not see
How easily my stars may sink,
  How easily the wind may grow to a tempest?

Then death will threaten in a thousand forms.

How could I defy it if I knew you were in peril?

O loose your arms' embrace
  And free your heart of me.
How do I know if I shall triumph
  And return home victorious?
The very wave that now sings so enticingly
May be the one that engulfs me.

It still lies in your hands;
  You have still not embarked irrevocably.
O sever your young life quickly
  From my uncertain existence.
Do it of your own free will, before you have to;
Renunciation is easier than loss.

[1] The alternative readings listed here are all taken from Schober's *Gedichte*, Cotta, Stuttgart, 1842.
[2] Schober writes 'Es ruft mich *fest*, es winkt *mir* der Kahn'.
[3] The repeat of 'O' (the second 'o wolle') is Schubert's.

(5) O lass mich im Bewusstsein steuern,[4]
     Dass ich allein auf Erden bin,
  Dann beugt sich vor dem Ungeheuern,
     Vorm Unerhörten nicht mein Sinn.
  Ich treibe mit dem Entsetzen Spiel
  Und stehe plötzlich vielleicht am Ziel.

Let me navigate in the knowledge
    That I am alone on this earth,
Then my mind will not flinch
    Before terrors, before the unknown.
I shall sport with horrors,
And shall perhaps stand suddenly at my goal.

(6) Denn hoch auf meiner Maste Spitzen
     Wird stets dein Bild begeisternd stehn,
  Und, angeflammet von den Blitzen,
     Mit seinem Glanz den Mut erhöhn.
  Der Winde Heulen auch noch so bang,[5]
  Übertäubet nicht deiner Stimme Klang.[6]

For your image will always be
    High on my mast, inspiring me,
And, illuminated by lightning,
    Will raise my spirits with its radiance.
However fearfully the winds howl,
They will never drown the sound of your voice.

(7) Und kann ich dich nur sehn und hören,
     Dann hat's mit mir noch keine Not,[7]
  Das Leben will ich nicht entbehren,
     Und kämpfen werd ich mit dem Tod.
  Wie würde mir eine Welt zur Last,[8]
  Die Engel so schön, wie dich umfasst?

And if I can but see and hear you,
    I have no other needs;
I do not wish to forego my life,
    And shall fight with death.
How could a world ever become a burden to me
Which contains angels as fair as you?

(8) Auch du sollst nicht mein Bild
     zerschlagen,
     Mit Freundschaftstränen weih es ein,
  Es soll in Schmerz- und Freudetagen[9]
     Dein Trost und dein Vertrauter sein.
  Ja bleibe, wenn mich auch alles verliess,
  Mein Freund im heimischen Paradies.

You, too, must not destroy my image;

    Consecrate it with tears of friendship.
May it be your comfort and close companion
    In times of sorrow and joy.
If all else has deserted me,
You shall remain my friend in this paradise
    of home.

(9) Und spült dann auch die falsche Welle
     Mich tot zurück zum Blumenstrand,
  So weiss ich doch an lieber Stelle
     Noch eine, eine treue Hand,
  Der weder Verachtung noch Schmerz
     es wehrt,
  Dass sie meinen Resten ein Grab
     beschert.

And if a treacherous wave should wash
    My dead body back upon the flowery shore,
Then I shall know that at the beloved spot
    There will still be one hand
Which neither disdain nor sorrow will prevent

From granting my remains a grave.

FRANZ VON SCHOBER (1796–1882)

*This is the last of Schubert's fourteen Schober solo settings (1815–27). See the poet's biography
for a chronological list of all the Schober settings.*

In his *Schubert: A Biographical Study of his Songs*, Fischer-Dieskau states that this was one of
the works performed by Schubert and Vogl at the gathering for Hummel at the home of Frau

[4] Schubert substitutes 'O' at the beginning of the line for Schober's 'Und'.
[5] Schober writes '*Und heulen die Winde* auch noch so bang'.
[6] Schober writes '*Sie übertäuben* nicht deiner Stimme Klang'.
[7] Schober writes '*So hat's* mit mir noch keine Not'.
[8] Schober writes 'Wie würde mir *je* eine Welt zur Last'.
[9] Schober writes 'Es soll in Schmerz- und *Freuden*tagen'.

von László in March 1827. The young Ferdinand Hiller's report of the occasion avers that 'Schubert had little technique, Vogl had not much of a voice'. Some 150 years later Fischer-Dieskau writes, 'It is not surprising to read that the performers had technical difficulties, for they were interpreting *Schiffers Scheidelied*.' Whether this song was actually performed on that occasion (it had been written the month before) is not to be found in the sources at my disposal. But what is revealing is that Fischer-Dieskau acknowledges that even a great artist of our own time found the work challenging. It is hard enough to sing, but the stamina demanded of the accompanist far outweighs anything required in the pianistically notorious *Erlkönig* D328. That horse-ride etude in triplets is over in a flash in comparison to *Schiffers Scheidelied* with its long stretches of relentlessly rattling semiquavers, even more tiring for the pianist's overworked right arm. With some justification Leo Black hears in this piano ritornello 'the wind howling through the rigging of a ship at sea'. Rather like a seasick voyager caught in the middle of an ocean storm, the pianist longs for these battering waves to let up. Perhaps this is one of the reasons why even Fischer-Dieskau and Gerald Moore elected to leave out three strophes from their recording. For the Hyperion Edition the song was recorded in its complete form.

The song deserves a complete performance for the sake of the poem which, like the contemporary *Jägers Liebeslied* D909, tells us a great deal about Schober. The two songs are twinned in every way, and even their contrasting moods and tempi seem designed by the admiring Schubert to show off the 'Florestan' and 'Eusebius' sides of the poet's nature. The egocentric Schober was partial to poems in the first person that cast him as the intrepid narrator in various dashing disguises, and this seaman calls forth more invigorating music than the musing hunter. (The poem was written a decade before the better known of German seaman's farewells, Eichendorff's *Seemanns Abschied*.)

A reading of Schober's entire poem is sufficient to contest Capell's interpretation of the scenario: he sees the sailor as being 'full of apprehension about his coming voyage, and he urges his young woman to renounce a tie with one so almost certainly doomed'. Young woman? One searches in vain in the long text for such a character. There is no pronoun or adjectival ending that shows that the person to whom this poem is addressed is female, and one can only think that this ambiguity seems too studied not to be deliberate. In the strophe missing in the Fischer-Dieskau recording, the gender of 'Mein Freund [not 'Meine Freundin'] im heimischen Paradies' (Verse 8) seems crucial. The poem's vigorous language of comradeship suggests that it is addressed to a younger man ('Mein Kind' is again ambiguous) of whom he is the mentor. This person is less experienced, no match for the courage of Schober the narrator, perhaps, though he is physically capable, as is implied in the last verse, of burying the remains of the sailor washed up at last upon the shore (hardly a task for a woman).

On the subject of heroic friendship one might think of lines by A. E. Housman with their overtones of ancient Greek-inspired eroticism ('Oh were he and I together / Shipmates on the fleeted main . . . Oh were he and I together / Locking hands and taking leave'). But Schober is far too self-absorbed to long for a shipmate with whom he might be required to share his emotions or his journey and its solitary, reckless glory. Not for him the adhesive love on the open road, or open seas, of Walt Whitman ('Camerado, I give you my hand!'). The concern for the well-being of his disciple, someone clearly in his thrall, is a device merely meant to throw the poet-narrator into more heroic relief.

Schober recoils from commitment, even on paper. He wants to have his cake and eat it: the devotion of an admiring friend at home doting on his picture is combined with a need for freedom. Of course this is rationalized as concern for the safety of his younger companion, although the concern and stagey renunciation expressed in such lines as 'O sever your young life quickly / From my uncertain existence' is hardly to be taken seriously. The tenor of the poem is typical of the quasi-romantic tone of the correspondence between Schober and the younger

Moritz von Schwind. This youthful painter was also referred to as 'My beloved' by Schubert, and Schwind's letter to Schober on Schubert's death (25 November 1828) is revealing of the highly emotional vocabulary employed by some of the members of this circle of friends when writing to each other:

> *You know how much I loved him, so you will understand that I can hardly bear the thought that I have lost him ... You are still here, and you still love me with the same love which in those unforgettable times bound us to our beloved Schubert. To you I offer all the love which has not been buried with him ...*

Male friendship, and the romantic expression of it, was governed by a very different, less guarded, set of rules in Schubert's time than in our own, with its hyper-awareness of psychological and sexual nuance. The poet Kenner disapprovingly referred to Schober's 'disciples' ('Anhänger' with its connotation of a sect) and this poem seems to be addressed to such an adoring disciple. While the language is highly idealistic, it is awash with self-dramatizing egoism, the beloved friend only useful as a mirror in which the would-be seaman can discern his own portrait. Capell finds the character 'unsailorly', someone who was 'simply never cut out for seafaring'. The poem is about an ego trip rather than a trip by sea. The more the poet develops his argument, the more isolated and self-involved he becomes, and it all happens in his head, far from the rigours of the deep. In this context, Schwind's later disenchantment with Schober and everything to do with him seems inevitable.

No matter: Schubert must have believed up to a point in the nobility of what is being said. Schober's credo of living life within (and sometimes apart from) a circle of loving friendship obviously strikes many a chord with the composer. *Schiffers Scheidelied* is another of his 'symphonic' songs, albeit one of the simpler ones. What it lacks in subtlety and illustration of individual images (it goes by too quickly for such typically Schubertian dallying) it makes up for in terms of energy and sheer audacity of scale. The binary construction is familiar from such works as *Romanze des Richard Löwenherz* D907. There B minor alternates with B major; here the change of axis is a shift between E minor and B major. In both songs the use of B major is reserved for music that is fashioned as a refuge from the storm of battle or the battering seas. (In *Schiffers Scheidelied* the fatigue-inducing semiquavers are replaced by quavers at this point, a moment of respite for the pianist.)

The form of the song is the following: Verse 1, bb. 4–22 (storm music in E minor with touches of the major key); Verse 2, bb. 25–43 (the same music as for Verse 1 but without any major key modifications); Verse 3, bb. 47–65 (a new section, with a change of key signature to B major, which is exactly repeated for Verse 4, bb. 69–87); Verse 5, bb. 90–108 (a reversion to a key signature of E minor, only slightly varied from Verse 1 with just a touch of major-key harmony – this is exactly repeated for Verse 6, bb. 111–29); Verses 7, bb. 133–51, and 8, bb. 155–73 (back to the B major music of Verses 3 and 4); Verse 9 begins at b. 176 with the same E minor music as for Verses 1, 2, 5 and 6, but after thirteen bars (from b. 189) the direction changes where the final words of the poem are repeated to make a more extended coda section. The form is thus AABBAABB with a final A modified as a coda.

The effect of this gigantic structure is vitiated in performance if some of the strophes are cut out. In his recording with Gerald Moore, Fischer-Dieskau leaves out 4, 6 and 8 to make AABABA which promotes the storm-lashed E minor music at the expense of the moments of respite in B major. The storm interludes in the piano are sometimes coloured by major-key harmony, sometimes not, according to the mood of the words. In employing a piano figuration of broken octaves (which more often than not double the shape of the vocal line), Schubert brings something new to his songs. It would have been a brave man who played this work to an audience that included Hummel, but the song pays some tribute to the pianistic style of such a master, a self-conscious virtuosity that Schubert usually avoided in his own works, unless he had a certain pianist in mind. As it happened there was one such on the scene at exactly this time – Karl Maria von Bocklet (1801–1881). With Josef Slavík, Bocklet had given a performance of Schubert's *Rondo* in B minor (D895) for violin and piano at the beginning of 1827. He was also to perform numerous piano duets with the composer, and to give the first performance of the *Fantasie* D934 for violin and piano early in 1828. Is it possible that Schubert imagined *Schiffers Scheidelied*, so different from any of the contemporary *Winterreise* songs, in Bocklet's capable hands rather than his own.

Autograph:	Missing or lost
First edition:	Published as Book 24 no. 1 of the *Nachlass* by Diabelli, Vienna in September 1833 (P305)
Subsequent editions:	Peters: Vol. 3/181; AGA XX 516: Vol. 8/267; NSA IV: Vol. 14/26; Bärenreiter: Vol. 4/69
Bibliography:	Black 2001, p. 89
	Capell 1928, p. 226
	Fischer-Dieskau 1977, p. 245
Discography and timing:	Fischer-Dieskau II 9² 4'40 (Strophes 1–3, 5, 7 and 9)
	Hyperion I 36³
	Hyperion II 33¹⁴ 6'35 Gerald Finley

⟵ *Jägers Liebeslied* D909   *Romanze des Richard Löwenherz* D907 ⟶

JOHANN CHRISTOPH FRIEDRICH VON SCHILLER (1759–1805)

THE POETIC SOURCES
S1 *Gedichte von Schiller Erster Theil* (also published within the context of the Viennese edition of Schiller's complete works: *Friedrich Schillers sämmtliche Werke* Neunter Band), Wien, Anton Doll, 1810

S2 *Gedichte von Schiller Zweiter Theil* (also published within the context of the Viennese edition of Schiller's complete work: *Friedrich Schillers sämmtliche Werke* Zehnter Band), Wien, Anton Doll, 1810

S3 *Die Räuber, Ein Schauspiel*, Frankfurt und Leipzig, 1781

S4 *Sammlung Deutscher Beyspiele zur Bildung des Styls*, Zweyter Band, Wien, im Verlagsgewölbe des k.k. Schulbücher-Verchleisses bey St. Anna in der Johannis Gasse. 1812

This school text book may also have been Schubert's source for settings by Pfeffel, Hölty and Matthisson.

THE SONGS
c. 1811	*Leichenfantasie* D7 [S2: pp. 223–6, printed in 'Anhang' (Supplement) to poems
1811? or 1812	*Des Mädchens Klage* D6 [S1: pp. 56–7]

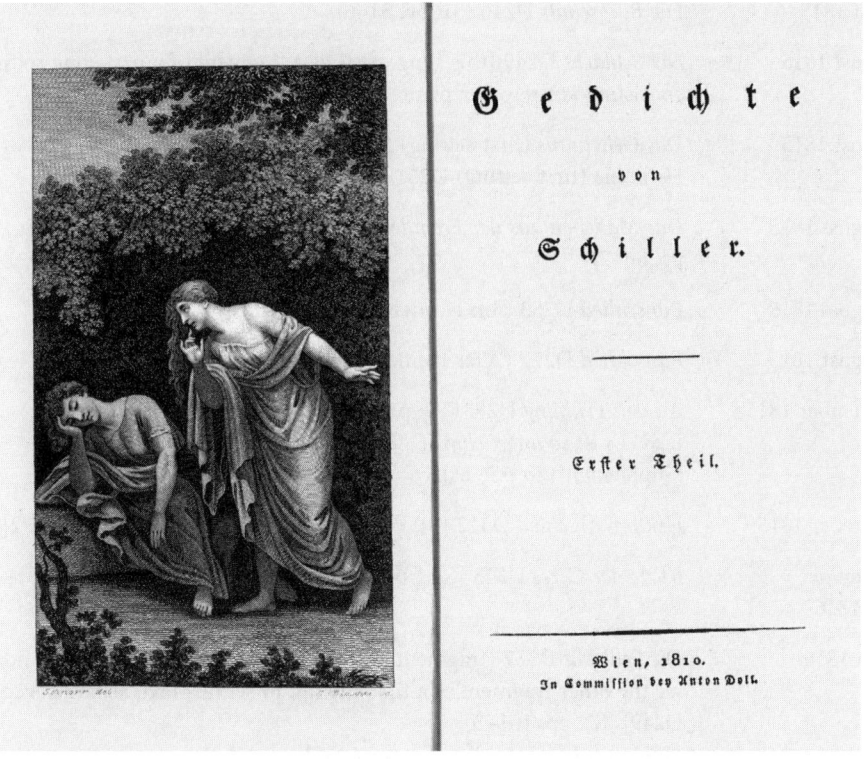

Schiller's *Gedichte*, Viennese edition by Anton Doll (1810). The frontispiece, an engraving after Schnorr von Carolsfeld, depicts the final strophe of the poem *Die Erwartung*, set by Schubert in 1816 (D159).

24 September 1812	*Der Jüngling am Bache* (First setting) D30 [S2: pp. 210–11]
29 March 1813	*Dithyrambe* (first setting) D47 (for tenor, bass, chorus and piano) [S1: pp. 119–20] [S4: pp. 56–7]
15–17 April 1813	*Sehnsucht* (first setting) D52 [S2: pp. 21–2]
22–3 August 1813	*Thekla* (first setting) D73 [S2: pp. 27–8]
17 September 1813–5 April 1814	*Der Taucher* D77 the second version earlier designated D111 [S1: pp. 103–9]
17 September 1814	*An Emma* D113 [as 'Elegie an Emma'] [S1: p. 236]
16 October 1814	*Das Mädchen aus der Fremde* (first version) D117 [S1: pp. 7–8]
May 1815	*An die Freude* D189 [S1: pp. 280–84]
15 May 1815	*Des Mädchens Klage* (second setting, *see* D6) D191 [S1: pp. 56–7] *Der Jüngling am Bache* (second setting, *see* D30) D192 [S2: pp. 210–11]
19 May 1815	*Amalia* D195 [S2: p. 59] [S3: p. 112, Act III Scene 1]
11 July 1815	*Hymne an den Unendlichen* D232 [S2: p. 231, printed in 'Anhang' (Supplement) to poems]

August 1815	*Die Bürgschaft* D246 [S1: pp. 31–6]
1 August 1815	*Die Schlacht* D249 [this song exists as a fragment of a part song setting consisting entirely of a piano introduction of 35 bars] [S2: pp. 101–3]
7 August 1815	*Das Geheimnis* (first setting) D250 [S1: pp. 16–17]
	Hoffnung (first setting) D251 [S1: p. 163]
12 August 1815	*Das Mädchen aus der Fremde* (second setting, *see* D117) D252 [S1: pp. 56–7]
18 August 1815	*Punschlied* D253 ('Im Norden zu singen') [S2: pp. 205–7]
29 August 1815	*Punschlied* D277 ('Vier Elemente, innig gesellt') [S2: pp. 141–2]
6 September 1815	*An den Frühling* D283 [S2: p. 100]
	Lied (Es ist so angenehm) D284 [S2: p. 263, printed in 'Anhang' (Supplement) to poems]
19 October 1815	*Hektors Abschied* D312 [S1: pp. 237–8] [S3: pp. 64–5, Act II Scene 2]
9 November 1815–1816	*Klage der Ceres* D323 [S1: pp. 9–13]
March 1816	*Die Schlacht* D387 [fragment for a Cantata for solo voices, choir and piano, *see* the other fragment of a first attempt to set this text, also unsuccessfully, D249] [S2: pp. 101–3]
	Laura am Klavier D388 [S2: pp. 64–5]
	Des Mädchens Klage (third setting, *see* D6 and D191) D389 [S1: pp. 56–7]
	Die Entzückung an Laura (first setting) D390 [S2: pp. 6–7]
	Die vier Weltalter D391 [S2: pp. 29–31]
	Gruppe aus dem Tartarus (first setting) D396 fragment [S2: p. 106]
13 March 1816	*Ritter Toggenburg* D397 [S1: pp. 62–5]
18 March 1816	*Der Flüchtling* D402 [S2: pp. 104–5]
May 1816	*Die Erwartung* D159 [S1: pp. 130–32]
August 1817	*Die Entzückung an Laura* (second setting, *see* D390) D577 [S2: pp. 66–7]
September 1817	*Gruppe aus dem Tartarus* (second setting, *see* D396) D583 [S2: p. 106]
	Elysium D584 [S2: pp. 107–8]
October 1817	*An den Frühling* (second setting, *see* D283) D587
November 1817	*Der Alpenjäger* D588 [S2: pp. 208–9]
	Der Kampf D594 [S1: pp. 219–20]
	Thekla (second setting, *see* D73) D595 [S2: pp. 27–8]
Undated (1818?)	*Der Graf von Habsburg* D990 fragment [S2: pp. 194–8]
1819?	*Hoffnung* (second setting, *see* D251) D637 [S1: p. 165]
April 1819	*Der Jüngling am Bache* (third setting, *see* D30 and D192) D638 [S2: pp. 210–11]

November 1819	*Strophe aus 'Die Götter Griechenlands'* D677 [the whole poem S1: pp. 221–5, the strophe set S1: p. 224] [S2: the whole poem again, pp. 292–300, but this was not the version Schubert set: in this second version, 'fabelhafte Spur' (as set by Schubert) is replaced by 'gold'ne Spur'; 'Blieb *der Schatten* [shadow] nur zurück' becomes 'Blieb nur *das Gerippe* [skeleton] mir zurück'.
Early 1821?	*Sehnsucht* (second setting, *see* D52) D636 [S2: pp. 21–2]
May 1823	*Das Geheimnis* (second setting, *see* D250) D793 [S1: pp. 16–17] *Der Pilgrim* D794 [S2: pp. 190–91]
1824	*Dithyrambe* (second setting, *see* D52) D801 [S1: pp. 119–20]

Mention should also be made of other Schiller settings for unaccompanied voices, mostly from Schubert's period as a student of Salieri, that are outside the scope of this book:
Dreifach ist der Schritt der Zeit, Spruch des Konfuzius D43 Terzett (TTB) 8 July 1813; *Unendliche Freude durchwallet das Herz* D51 Terzett (TTB) 15 April 1813; *Vorüber die stöhende Klage* D53 Terzett (TTB) 18 April 1813; *Unendliche Freude durchwallet das Herz* D54 (second setting) Terzett (TTB) 19 April 1813; *Selig durch die Liebe* D55 Terzett (TTB) 21 April 1813; *Hier strecket der wallende Pilger* D57 Terzett (TTB) 29 April 1813; *Dessen Fahne Donnerstürme wallte* D58 Terzett (TTB) May 1813; *Hier umarmen sich getreue Gatten* D60 Terzett (TTB) 3 October 1813; *Ein jugendlicher Maienschwung* D61 Canon for 3 voices 8 May 1813; *Thronend auf erhabnem Sitz* D62 Terzett (TTB) 9 May 1813; *Wer die steile Sternenbahn* D63 Terzett (TTB) 10 May 1813; *Majestätsche Sonnenrosse* D64 Terzett (TTB) 10 May 1813; *Schmerz verzerret ihr Gesicht* D65 Sketch for a canon (TTB) 11 May 1813; *Frisch atmet des Morgens lebendiger Hauch* D67 Terzett (TTB) 15 May 1813; *Dreifach ist der Schritt der Zeit, Spruch des Konfuzius* (second version) D69 Canon for three voices, 8 July 1813; *Dreifach ist der Schritt der Zeit, Spruch des Konfuzius* (Third version) D70 Terzett (TTB) 8 July 1813; *Die zwei Tugendwege* D71 Terzett (TTB) 15 July 1813; *An den Frühling* D338 (second setting) Quartet (TTBB) *c.* 1816; *Liebe* D983B Op. 17 no. 2 Quartet (TTBB) undated

Friedrich Schiller's influence on the young Schubert pre-dates the Goethe epiphany, *Gretchen am Spinnrade*, by at least four years; the first Schiller songs were composed in 1811, but the young composer had already copied out a song with a Schiller text, *Die Teilung der Erde*, in 1810, believing the music to be by Haydn. (It was, in fact by the Austrian Franz de Paula Roser (1779–1830), though very much in Haydn's manner.) This wonderful Schiller poem tells how artists, overlooked by Zeus when allocating the wealth of the world, were granted a powerful compensation: they were permitted to visit heaven, as often as they wished, in order to live with Zeus himself. Denied material bounty all his life, but able to inhabit at will a world of heavenly communion with his Muse, the thirteen-year-old Schubert seems to have taken these words very much to heart.

Just as Zelter was the composer friend of Goethe's old age, Schiller enjoyed the friend-ship of the Swabian composer Johann Rudolf Zumsteeg from his school years. Zumsteeg's ballads were fanatically admired by the young Schubert for their adventurous use of form and harmony (by the standards of those days at least) and it was through these that Schubert gained a closer acquaintance with Schiller's verse. On more than one occasion he used the Zumsteeg-Schiller settings as models (as in *Die Erwartung* D159), carefully copying the older composer's choice of tempo and key, but inevitably amplifying and surpassing Zumsteeg's worthy ideas. Forty-four Schiller songs were written between D6 and D801.

Johann Christoph Friedrich Schiller was born just over ten years after Goethe on 10 November 1759. Robert Burns was born earlier in the same year. It was also in 1759 that Voltaire wrote *Candide*. Artists born in this era and who lived beyond middle age straddled two centuries with entirely different priorities and characteristics; those of Schiller's generation were children of the old order and adults of the new. His father had been in the army of the despotic Karl Eugen, duke of Württemberg, and after his soldiering days were over he continued in the duke's employ as a horticulturalist in the gardens at Ludwigsburg. The duke took it upon himself to control the smallest details of the lives of his subjects and their children, and so Schiller was born into intellectual serfdom. His mother was of artistic bent and fond of the poetry of Uz and Gellert. The boy, already fascinated by the theatre, was destined for the priesthood as far as his parents were concerned but the duke decided otherwise. In 1773, at the age of fourteen, Schiller was summarily enrolled into the military academy, the Karlschule, and it was decided that he was to be a lawyer. The regime of discipline, silence and punishment endured by the students would have made a Victorian prison seem an eminently humanitarian institution. The staff were too terrified to exercise any leniency because the duke had spyholes installed in the building through which, from the comfort of his palace, he could observe everything that went on. For six years the young Schiller was subject to the 'perverted discipline' of 'Greek, seclusion and law'. There should be no reason to apologize for quoting here and elsewhere from Thomas Carlyle's grandly resonant biography of Schiller (1825), a work that Goethe himself admired (he wrote a preface for the German translation) and in which Schiller is seen through the eyes of one of Schubert's contemporaries.

After two years Schiller managed to change his course of study to that of medicine. Not that he had any enthusiasm for that subject, but it seemed to him better at least than servitude of the law. He eventually graduated with a medical degree that enabled him to diagnose

his later maladies, only to ignore them. The only possibly useful fruit of these years was a self-preserving and rigid self-control which was to enable him to work through thick and thin. A strong head of concealed resentment boiled over with the composition of his first significant work, *Die Räuber* ('The Robbers'), an explosive play about (not surprisingly) the use and abuse of power. 'For eight years,' he wrote, 'my enthusiasm struggled with military discipline; but the passion for poetry is vehement and fiery as a first love. What discipline was meant to extinguish, it blew into a flame . . . my heart sought refuge in the world of ideas, when I was as yet unacquainted with the world of realities, from which iron measures excluded me.' Schubert's letter home to his brother in 1812, describing the trials of his schooling, is light-hearted by comparison. *Die Räuber* emerged in 1781, just at the right time to make a tremendous impression on a public (especially the young) who could sense political change in the air and who had had enough of the petty tyrannies of the German princes. Schiller became quite famous overnight, but as Carlyle says, 'the characters of the

Schiller, oil painting by Christian Jakob Höflinger, 1781.

piece, though traced in glowing colours, are outlines rather than pictures'. In this sense another comparison with Schubert is evident: the composer's early ballads sometimes have the same over-the-top 'strange mixture of extravagance and true energy' that is noted by Carlyle of Schiller's youthful work.

The poem *Amalia* which comes from *Die Räuber* was reshaped only in 1803 for publication in the poet's *Gedichte*. Schubert set poems from every phase of Schiller's career but Schiller often improved and adapted earlier works for publication, which accounts for various changes in the versions. In 1780 were written *Leichenfantasie, An den Frühling, Gruppe aus dem Tartarus* and *Elysium* while *Die Entzückung an Laura* and *Laura am Klavier* date from 1781. These six poems were included in the astonishingly accomplished *Anthologie auf das Jahr 1782*, the poet's first verse publication. Another poem written in 1781 was *Hektors Abschied*, revised and published in 1800. Other poems from this period were *Die Schlacht* and *Der Flüchtling* (both first published in 1803) and the famous *An die Freude* (1785).

Schiller was skating on thin ice with the duke, endangering the livelihoods of his parents, by the sentiments of *Die Räuber*. The fate of Christian Schubart (the author of *Die Forelle*), who was imprisoned for ten years in the fortress of Hohenasperg for similar literary insubordination, must have been much in his mind. Schiller was reprimanded by the duke, who offered his own 'literary advice', but the headstrong poet went incognito to Mannheim to see the first stage production of his play and was briefly imprisoned for his trouble. It was obvious that he had to get away, whatever the cost, and in October 1782 he fled Stuttgart for Mannheim in the company of the musician Andreas Streicher, his new play *Fiesco*, a Genoese tragedy, under his arm. Neither the playwright nor his new work were altogether welcome in Mannheim, at least not at that moment. He found refuge in Thuringia in the home of Henriette von Wolzogen and worked on his next play *Kabale und Liebe*, a tragedy of everyday life about the love of Ferdinand for

the music master's daughter, Luise. This, with its original title of *Luisa Miller*, was much later to find its composer in Giuseppe Verdi (1849), who was also to base his *I masnadieri* (1847) on *Die Räuber*.

In 1783 Schiller was welcomed back to Mannheim where he became a naturalized subject of the Elector Palatine and was appointed poet to the theatre. He was at last what he had always wanted to be, a man of letters. 'The public is now all to me,' he wrote '. . . my study, my sovereign, my confidant. To the public alone I henceforth belong.' At last Schiller had the leisure time (if any moment of his day – or night – might so be termed) to read Corneille, Racine and Voltaire. The first three acts of *Don Carlos* appeared in *Dahlia*, an almanac for which he wrote between 1785 and 1794, and which was devoted to the history and philosophy of the theatre. A number of Schiller's poems also made their first appearance in this periodical. He left Mannheim after eighteen months (in March 1785) and moved to Saxony where he stayed with his closest friend Christian Gottfried Körner, the father of the poet Theodor Körner whom Schubert met in 1813. At that time it was Körner's advice that gave the young composer the confidence to embrace music as a profession. Perhaps they talked about Schiller, a number of whose poems Schubert had already set to music. It is possible that young Körner, born after Schiller had left Dresden, had visited the poet in Weimar with his parents. The two families certainly kept in touch.

Don Carlos was immediately counted Schiller's greatest success. It initiates what were to be two characteristics of his plays for the rest of his life – increasingly detailed historical research and the creative energy of blank verse (previous works had been in prose). The fourth and fifth acts of the completed play (which was to be the basis of Verdi's greatest Schiller creation in 1867) show a very different artist from the writer of the first three. Although *Don Carlos* is in many ways a masterpiece of Schiller's maturity, Carlyle puts his finger on certain negative factors: 'We have not those careless felicities, those varyings from high to low, that air of living freedom which Shakespeare has accustomed us, like spoiled children, to look for in every perfect work of the species. Schiller is too elevated, too regular and sustained in his elevation, to be altogether natural.' (This might also be considered a fair critique of some of the Schiller settings of Schubert whose music often takes on the characteristics, even the weaker ones, of his chosen poets.) Nevertheless there was a sign in Schiller's work that 'the love of contemplating things as they should be began to yield to the love of knowing things as they are'. The poet was now ready for the last and greatest phase of his career.

In 1787 he first visited Weimar, the undisputed literary epicentre of Germany, where he was received courteously by Johann Gottfried Herder and even more warmly by Christoph Martin Wieland. Poems from this period include the first version of *Die Götter Griechenlands* (1788, revised 1793) but the real outpouring of poetry and ballads was to occur some time later, and as a result of a coming-together of two great minds. At this time Goethe was away on his famed Italian journey and Schiller had made up his mind that he would have little to say to his celebrated elder colleague. Carlyle contrasted Shakespeare with Milton and, by analogy, Goethe with Schiller: 'The first is endowed with an all-comprehending spirit; . . . tolerant of all; peaceful, collected; . . . allowing men of every shape and hue to have their own free scope in his conception . . . The other is earnest, devoted; struggling with a thousand mighty projects of improvement . . . rejecting vehemently, choosing vehemently, at war with the one half of things, in love with the other half.'

'He who would write heroic poems should make his whole life a heroic poem.' So wrote Milton, and Schiller is one of the small band of creative men who lived up to these words. Thanks to his plays and ballads Schiller enjoyed popular success throughout German-speaking lands. By the beginning of the nineteenth century (and despite the fact that some of his greatest work was yet to come) the writer's name was almost a byword for exciting theatre and narrative poetry that was stirring and memorable. Schiller had a low estimation of his own talents in relation to Goethe's, and was excessively modest in this regard. There is little doubt that he was the playwright with the greater sense of theatre, and that his works have held the stage more than Goethe's – in their own right and as inspirations for opera composers including Donizetti (*Maria Stuarda*), Verdi (*Don Carlos*) and Tchaikovsky (*Orleanskaya deva – The Maid of Orleans*).

Encouraged by Wieland and Herder, Schiller moved to Jena, very near Weimar, in 1789, five years before he became friends with Goethe. On the strength of a treatise on the subject of the revolt of the Dutch against the Spanish in the Netherlands (the background to *Don Carlos*) he was appointed professor of history at the University of Jena. He further enhanced his reputation as a serious historian in 1791 by embarking on a history of the Thirty Years War. This was to furnish him with the background for his greatest drama, *Wallenstein*. In 1790 he had married Charlotte von

Schiller, lithograph after the painting by Anton Graff, 1791.

Lengefeld who came from a more elevated social milieu and was an accomplished amateur pianist. Peter Branscombe has suggested that music could not have been a high priority in Schiller's life: only five years after the marriage Charlotte's piano playing skills were decidedly on the wane, probably because she had no instrument on which to practise. Nevertheless, theirs was a devoted and happy relationship and two sons and two daughters were born of the union.

No doubt Charlotte, a tough character who disapproved of the unmarried Goethe's ongoing liaison with Christiane Vulpius, had to undergo many trials in dealing with the deteriorating health of her husband and his heroic (though no doubt seemingly foolhardy) determination to work on regardless. His health problems, a debilitating chest condition and a serious digestive disorder, were exacerbated by his habit of rationing his sleep and writing through the night in a garden house specially built for his solitary nocturnal toil. Carlyle's words on the poet's heroism under these circumstances might also apply to Schubert after the onset of his illness, and in this regard too the fates of composer and poet seem connected: 'His spirit was too vigorous and ardent to yield . . . he declined to dwindle into a pining valetudinarian; in the midst of his infirmities he persevered with unabated zeal in the great business of life. As he partially recovered he returned as strenuously as ever to his intellectual occupations; and often, in the glow of poetical conception, he almost forgot his maladies . . . he did not lose his relish for the beautiful, the grand or the good, in any of their shapes; he loved his friends as formerly and wrote his finest and sublimest works when his health was gone.'

The Schubertian need only apply these words to the miraculous musical productivity of the composer's last years to understand their relevance to a man who had discovered Schiller's poetry at the age of fourteen and felt somehow drawn to a kindred spirit. This affinity between poet and composer, though no match for that between Schubert and Goethe, may have been linked to Schiller's awareness of the musical potential of his poems, which he fashioned accordingly. He was scarcely the best-informed poet about music in general (he was not at all driven by a desire for musical knowledge as was Goethe). Indeed, his tastes in this field were extremely conservative; he valued Gluck's music and thought that Haydn's *Die Schöpfung* was a 'Mischmasch'. But he had written that poems must be 'capable of being *sung*, as the *Iliad* was sung by the peasants of Greece, as the stanzas of *Jerusalem Delivered* are still sung by the Venetian gondoliers'.

The dark cloud of Schiller's ill health brought one silver lining – a large pension from aristocratic Danish admirers that released him from immediate financial worries and enabled him to embark on yet another phase in a life of relentless intellectual exploration and self-improvement. This was a study of the philosophy of Immanuel Kant which resulted, over the next eight years (1793–1801) in a series of papers on weighty philosophical and aesthetic matters. Kant suited Schiller down to the ground: philosopher and poet saw nature and man as opposites – on the one hand, as Isaiah Berlin encapsulates it, nature as a 'capricious, perhaps casual, perhaps chance-directed entity', and on the other, man who 'distinguishes between desire and will, duty and interest, the right and the wrong, and acts accordingly, if need be against nature'. This writing met with much opposition, but even Carlyle, implacably opposed to Kant, owned that Schiller's essays were redeemed by moments that shone like 'bright verdant islands in the misty sea of metaphysics' and proved that Schiller was without doubt Goethe's intellectual equal.

In 1794 these opposites were at long last profoundly attracted to each other, rather than repelled, although there is no doubt that their instinctive antipathy was great at first. Goethe, long before, had written disdainfully that *Die Räuber* had 'been poured in a boundless rushing flood all over the country'. The elder man was frosty and distant, the younger disinclined to play the courtier or sycophant, but chance (or clever friends) brought them together and they began to talk. The subject of their first conversation was Goethe's theory on the metamorphosis of plants and Goethe was stunned to be quietly but firmly challenged on a number of scientific and philosophical premises. The citizens of Weimar were often later to see the two deep in conversation under the shade of a spreading tree at Triesnitz.

Goethe had recently returned from Italy. He knew that one phase of his life was over and another had to begin but was at a loss as to how to proceed. Schiller was the midwife to one of his many artistic rebirths; indeed, in January 1829 Goethe wrote to C. L. F. Schultz, 'I really do not know what would have become of me without Schiller's stimulus.' In 1798 he had written to Schiller himself, 'You have given me a second poetic youth.' The younger poet's determination and vitality, his ability to carry projects through with burning idealistic conviction, his encouragement over the matter of resuming work on *Faust*, rejuvenated the older man. In turn Schiller benefited from the breadth of Goethe's perspective, his urbanity, perspicacity and encouragement. Rousseau thought that the best material for friendship was the 'same sentiments and different opinions', and the friendship between these two men is the best illustration of this premise. In the last years of the eighteenth century there was an exchange between Schiller and Goethe of remarkable letters, almost certainly unequalled as a colloquy between two great artists – 'probably the greatest treasures I possess' Goethe wrote years later of these documents. Spurred on by each other, and in a spirit of friendly rivalry, they wrote a series of ballads, many of which have been set by the great song composers. Schiller was not as musically knowledgeable as Goethe but he knew that certain poetry needed music to enable it to reach the people. He had known the composer Zumsteeg since he was a young man and valued Reichardt as a friend and correspondent, without particularly liking his music. He actually approved of Zelter's setting of *Der Taucher*. The poems of this period gave rise to many of the Schiller–Schubert settings,

and a good number of the Goethe–Schubert works too. They were first published in various of the *Musen-Almanach* or the *Horen* that had replaced *Thalia* as the means of airing Schiller's – and now Goethe's – thoughts. Even listing only the poems that Schubert set to music shows how productive for Schiller were the last years of the century. In 1796 he wrote *Klage der Ceres, Dithyrambe, Die Erwartung, An Emma, Das Mädchen aus der Fremde*, all published in the *Musen-Almanach* for 1797; in 1797, *Hoffnung, Der Taucher, Das Geheimnis, Ritter Toggenburg* (these were published in the 1798 edition of the same publication). The *Musen-Almanach* for 1799 included *Die Bürgschaft*, written in 1798. In reply to criticisms of their work, the two men composed the *Xenien*, the most famous of their public collaborations. These satirical epigrams, a type of German version of Pope's *Dunciad*, attacked mean-minded critics and the general mediocrities of the age, and caused a furore.

In Schiller's last years there was an astonishing outburst of activity as he returned to his homeland, the theatre. If he did not exactly rage against the dying of the light, he used all the hours of darkness to write a major play in almost each of the years of the new century that were left to him. Neither was he idle in writing poetry. The lyrics that Schubert set from the last three years of the poet's life include *Thekla, Die vier Weltalter* (1802), *Der Jüngling am Bache, Sehnsucht, Der Pilgrim*, the two *Punschlieder* (1803) and *Der Alpenjäger* (1804). These, and most of the earlier poems, found their way into the *Gedichte* (1805) which turned out to be a summation of Schiller's work as a poet. Schubert's source, the Viennese edition of 1810, was a reprint of this important collection. The success of the triptych of 'Wallenstein' plays (based on Schiller's painstaking historical researches) was immense and worldwide. Samuel Taylor Coleridge made a remarkable translation of it, a highly suitable example of implacable intellectual English energy to parallel Schiller's industry in translating Shakespeare's *Macbeth*, Gozzi's *Turandot* and Racine's *Phèdre*. Then followed in quick succession two great plays:

Schiller.

Bust of Friedrich Schiller, lithograph after the statue of the poet by Johann Heinrich von Danneker (1758–1841). This engraving is the frontispiece to the first volume of the Viennese complete edition of Schiller's works (1810).

Maria Stuart (on which Donizetti based his opera) and *Die Jungfrau von Orleans* (Tchaikovsky's opera from 1879) which was greeted with cries of 'long live Schiller', and the success of which led to his ennoblement. The last of the historical dramas to be completed was *Wilhelm Tell* in 1804 (also interestingly, Rossini's last opera, 1829). At the time of the poet's death (9 May 1805, at the age of forty-five) he was working on a play about Dmitri of Russia and another about Perkin Warbeck, pretender to the throne of Henry VII.

The poet's work, elevated and stilted though it can sometimes seem to our jaded ears, was a major influence on the young men of Schubert's age. The composer's friend, the

poet Johann Senn, worked bravely (and in vain) for Tyrolean independence, almost certainly with the words of Schiller's William Tell ringing in his ears. The plays of Franz Grillparzer (qv) were immeasurably influenced by the classical age of Weimar, and Schiller in particular. *Schillers Manen, Bilder aus dem Dichterleben* ('Schiller's Shade, Pictures from the Poet's Life') was a set of five poems about Schiller at various stages of his life by the young Johann Gabriel Seidl (qv), published in 1826. In 1828 the German literary historian Wolfgang Menzel portrayed Schiller, with all the zeal of his youthful strength and a virginal purity of heart, entering into a corrupt and tired epoch, a decaying period fit for revolutionary change: 'He has cleansed German poetry, and rejuvenated it.' Schiller had written, 'We would be ashamed if people were to say that things shaped us and not we them'. For Schiller, in Carlyle's words, 'genuine Literature includes the essence of philosophy, religion, art; whatever speaks to the immortal part of man'. For Schubert, music too was about everything in life, an *omnium gatherum* – a phrase Coleridge coined that may be used to describe Goethe's eclectic search for knowledge and Schiller's efforts to make sense of the great issues of life by making them part of a structured plan.

The courageous anti-authoritarianism of Schiller's youth, and the unremitting industry of a maturity blighted by ill-health, but utterly without self-pity, might well have rendered him a role model for more than one young composer. In a rather more glamorous (or just plain dangerous) way than Schubert, he escaped from the terrible drudgery of his school years, only to impose on himself a punishing regime of work and creativity that led to his early death. Both men had to break free from certain shackles in order to have the freedom to function as artists; both had a highly developed sense of duty to their art; both were prodigiously prolific. In these respects the stories of the short, round composer and the tall, aquiline poet have a great deal more in common than those of, say, Schubert and Goethe. And because Schiller

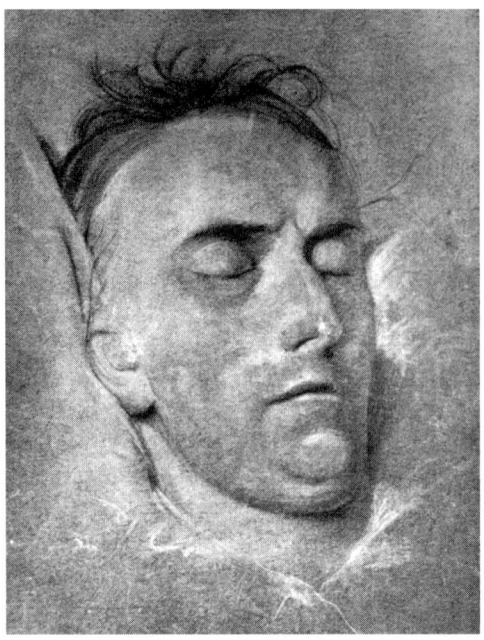

Schiller on his deathbed, 1805, pastel drawing by
F. Jagemann.

Richard Capell in reference to Schiller's 'mode of conceiving things' was convinced that the poet's intellectuality often blocked Schubert's creative flair, but it is obvious that the composer thought it worth trying repeatedly to match these literary challenges. As John Reed observed, 'The proportion of once-and-for-all settings is lower in the case of Schiller than for any other poet. On the other hand Schubert's persistence is sometimes gloriously rewarded.' We can hear Schubert's heroic (and sometimes fruitless) search for a musical translation of this in some of his settings of Schiller. Schiller's was the spirit who showed Schubert that his musical energy could be marshalled as a force for good; indeed, that in its own way music had the power to change the world. We may admit that other writers inspired Schubert to greater heights, but in doing so we must remain grateful for those Schiller masterpieces (such as *Gruppe aus dem Tartarus*, *Strophe aus 'Die Götter Griechenlands'* and *Dithyrambe*) that stand at the apex of Schubert's creative achievement.

had died when Schubert was eight years old there was never any question of the disappointment (and perhaps resentment) that hung over Schubert's relationship, or rather non-relationship, with Goethe.

Bibliography: Berlin 1999, p. 81
               Carlyle 1893
               Menzel 1828, vol. 4, p. 107

Die SCHLACHT
(SCHILLER) **D249** & **D387** [NOT IN HYPERION]

The battle

Bass, tenor & chorus, TTBB

The song exists in two versions, both fragments, the second of which is discussed below:
(D249) 1 August 1815; (D387) March 1816

D249   B minor

D387 B minor

Schwer und dum-pfig ei-ne Wet - ter - wol - ke

(522 bars)

1 Schwer und dumpfig,	Heavy, louring,

1 Schwer und dumpfig,
  Eine Wetterwolke,
Durch die grüne Eb'ne schwankt
  der Marsch.
  Zum wilden eisernen Würfelspiel
Streckt sich unabsehlich das Gefilde.
  Blicke kriechen niederwärts,
An die Rippen pocht das Männerherz,
  Vorüber an hohlen Totengesichtern
Niederjagt der Front der Major:
  Halt!
Und Regimenter fesselt das starre
  Kommando.
  Lautlos steht die Front.

Heavy, louring,
  A thunder cloud,
The line of march comes roiling across the green
  plain.
  The open land stretches further than sight
To the savage, iron-cast game of dice.
  Men's gaze slinks to earth,
Men's hearts beat against their ribs.
  Passing hollowed out, dead faces
The Major gallops down to the front:
  Halt!
And regiments are curbed by the stark
  command;
  The front line stands in silence.

2 Prächtig im glühendem Morgenrot
Was blitzt dorther vom Gebirge?
Seht ihr des Feindes Fahnen wehn?
Wir sehn des Feindes Fahnen wehn,
Gott mit euch, Weib und Kinder!
Lustig! hört ihr den Gesang?
Trommelwirbel, Pfeifenklang
Schmettert durch die Glieder,
Wie braust es fort im schönen wilden Takt!
Und braust durch Mark und Bein.

Magnificent in the glow of dawn,
What is that flashing from the hills?
D'you see the fluttering enemy flags?
We see the fluttering enemy flags!
God be with you, wives and children!
Rejoice! Do you hear the song?
The drum rolls, the sound of pipes
Enters into our limbs;
How it surges with a glorious savage beat!
Surges through bone to the marrow.

  Gott beholfen, Brüder!
  In einer andern Welt wieder.

  God be with you, Brothers!
  We'll meet again in a different world.

3 Schon fleugt es fort wie Wetterleucht,
Dumpf brüllt der Donner schon dort,
Die Wimper zuckt, hier kracht er laut,
Die Losung braust von Heer zu Heer,
Lass brausen in Gottes Namen fort,
Freier schon atmet die Brust.

Now it takes flight – like sheet-lightning,
There, and already the rumbling roar of thunder,
Here, the blink of an eye and a loud crack,
The battle-cry roaring from corps to corps –
Roar away – in God's name,
Already, in our breast, we can breathe more
  freely.

  Der Tod ist los – schon wogt sich
    der Kampf;
  Eisern im wolkigten Pulverdampf.
  Eisern fallen die Würfel.

  Death sets to – already the fight is in spate,

  Iron resolve in the cloud of powder-smoke,
  The fall of the dice cast in iron.

4   Nah umarmen die Heere sich,
    Fertig! heults von P'loton zu P'loton;
    Auf die Knie geworfen.
    Feur'n die Vordern, viele stehen nicht
        mehr auf,
    Lücken reisst die streifende Kartetsche,
    Auf Vormanns Rumpfe springt der
        Hintermann,
    Verwüstung rechts und links und um
        und um
    Bataillone niederwältzt der Tod.

    Close now, the men embrace,
    Ready! the yell goes from platoon to platoon;
    On their knees,
    Those up ahead fire, many do not rise again,

    Gaps are rent by the strafe of bullets,
    The men behind scramble onto the backs of
        those in front,
    Devastation right and left and again and again

    Battallions are crushed by death.

        Die Sonne löscht aus – heiss brennt
            die Schlacht,
        Schwarz brütet auf dem Heer die Nacht.
        Gott befohlen, Brüder!
        In einer andern Welt wieder.

        The sun goes out – the slaughter burns red
            hot,
        Black, the night lies over the army.
        May God help you, Brothers!
        We'll meet again in a different world.

5   Hoch spritzt an den Nacken das Blut,
    Lebende wechseln mit Toten, der Fuss
    Strauchelt über den Leichnamen –
    'Und auch du, Franz?' – 'Grüsse mein
        Lottchen, Freund!'
    Wilder immer wütet der Streit,
    'Grüssen will ich' – Gott! Kamaraden! seht,
    Hinter uns wie die Kartetsche springt!
    'Grüssen will ich dein Lottchen, Freund!
    Schlummre sanft! wo die Kugelsaat
    Regnet, stürz ich Verlassner hinein.'

    We're up to our necks in spurting blood,
    The living replace the dead, feet
    Stumble over corpses –
    'So, you too, Franz?' – 'My friend, give my love
        to my dear Lotte!'
    The conflict rages ever more intensely,
    'I'll give . . .' – in heaven's name, comrades, see
    There behind us, that shell exploding!
    'I'll give your love to your Lotte, dear friend!
    Sleep in peace. I, alone now, will plunge
    Into the field where the rain of bullets is being
        sown.'

        Hieher, dorthin schwankt die Schlacht,
        Finst'rer brütet auf den Heer die Nacht,

        Gott befohlen, Brüder!
        In einer andern Welt wieder.

        The battle pitches this way and that,
        Even more darkly the night is lying over the
            army.
        Go with God, Brothers!
        We'll meet again in a different world!

6   Horch! was strampft im Galopp vorbei?
        Die Adjutanten fliegen,
    Dragoner rasseln in den Feind,
        Und seine Donner ruhen.
    Victoria, Brüder !
    Schrecken reisst die feigen Glieder.
        Und seine Fahne sinkt –

    But listen, what is that galloping past?
        The Adjutants are flying,
    The Dragoons are rattling into the enemy.
        And its thunder has stopped.
    Victory, Brothers!
    Fear is tugging at their cowardly limbs.
        And their flag droops –

7   Entschieden ist die scharfe Schlacht,
    Der Tag blickt siegend durch die Nacht!

    The bitter battle has been concluded,
    Daylight peers victoriously through the night!

Horch! Trommelwirbel, Pfeifenklang!	Listen! Drum rolls, the sound of pipes!
Stimmen schon Triumphgesang!	Already voicing the song of triumph!
Lebt wohl ihr gebliebenen Brüder!	Farewell, you Brothers who stayed!
In einer andern Welt wieder.	We'll meet again in a different world.

FRIEDRICH VON SCHILLER (1759–1805)

This extraordinarily vivid poem might have been Schubert's greatest Schiller setting, and certainly his most ambitious. He set about composing it first in August 1815 but got no further than an extended piano introduction of some thirty-five bars. It is thought that the composer had a solo setting in mind but this can hardly be proved – the music breaks off with the words 'Singstimme' in b. 36. The second version begins in like manner and it is only after some time that the chorus is introduced. The composer was clearly planning an extended work – this much can be seen from the length and scope of the introductory 'Marcia' with its striding bass octaves, ornamental trills and horn-like chords. This music, incomplete though it is, depicts large and imposing forces gathering for battle and Schubert clearly thought it too good to waste. Not only did he retain it as the introduction for his unfinished second setting, he also recycled it as the first of his *Marches héroiques* D602 for piano duet.

The second attempt, D387, is one of the great might-have-beens among the Schubert songs. A real *scena*, and a battle scene at that, for solo voice and male chorus, the composer cared enough about it to sketch it to the very end of the long and involved poem (it extends to some fourteen pages in the NSA). The whole thing is planned in short score on two staves, showing us how Schubert typically mapped out a work in general terms before providing the detail. What is written down here as piano music may indeed be just that, but with a work of this size and for these forces it is possible that the composer envisaged an orchestral accompaniment in the manner of his lost cantata *Prometheus* D451, composed three months later.

Verse 1: A real bass voice is chosen as narrator. (More than one soloist is implied because the solo line later includes music in the tenor tessitura.) The original title of Schiller's poem of 1781 was *In einer Bataille - von einem Offizier* and the composer clearly imagines such a doughty officer singing heroically in the F clef. The first three lines of the strophe are in the prevailing march rhythm already established in the *Vorspiel*. With 'Zum wilden eisernen Würfelspiel' there are four bars marked *Rec.* (recitative) before 'Blicke kriechen niederwärts' continues in tempo ('Im Tempo'). The trepidation of the manly heart ('An die Rippen pocht das Männerherz', a phrase repeated by Schubert) prompts a wild outburst from the piano that is notated in the treble clef – a 'Presto' scale in C major that traverses the keyboard and introduces more recitative. The whole of this passage moves in and out of martial rhythm; the appearance of the Major and his command 'Halt' occasions yet more recitative. As the whole platoon stands silently to attention the marking is 'Sehr langsam' and for a few seconds the music is frozen in a mood of dramatic tension.

Verse 2: With a double bar line the key signature changes to B flat major. For six bars the composer notes down his ideas for the piano interlude – music in prancing dotted rhythms for fife and drum ('Trommelwirbel, Pfeifenklang'), the right hand whistling high in the treble clef. At b. 93, on the words 'Was blitzt dort her von Gebirge?', the men's chorus enters in four parts, written partially in the tenor clef. This choral passage wafts with the movement of the enemy's flag, moving into closer harmony at the mention of wives and children. All in all it develops into what would have been a remarkable duet between soloist and ensemble. The editors of both the NSA and AGA provide a word underlay where Schubert himself had neglected to do so. At

Die Schlacht, illustration from 1859.

b. 145 there is a change of marking to 'Moderato'. Two bars of drum roll are indicated in the accompaniment, leading to a rich four-part setting for chorus of 'Gott beholfen, Brüder! / In einer andern Welt wieder' (the phrase is repeated in bb. 157–64).

Verses 3–7: After this point the sketch becomes decidedly sketchier. It has not so far been possible to complete this work for performance; someone of great ability and imagination might do so one day, but it was clearly beyond the powers of the otherwise indefatigable Reinhard Van Hoorickx. What marvellous interesting musical details are hinted at here: the sunset of Strophe 4 at bb. 273–5; the nervous and slippery quavers underpinning a change to G minor and $\frac{3}{4}$ at b. 304; the pathetic undertone of the exchanges between the dying soldiers and the living involving messages to 'mein Lottchen' – with perhaps a change to recitative; a galloping motif in ascending quavers (and a return to common time) for 'Horch! was strampft im Galopp vorbei?' and the appearance of the Adjutants. At b. 419 Schubert engineers what seems like an offstage choral cry of 'Victoria'; he obviously has an unusual mingling of solo and chorus in mind to reflect the nature of the disorganized mêlée of battle. From b. 452 there are some splendid *Fidelio*-like fanfares to introduce the last verse. Although the vocal line is sketched to the end of this long poem, the personality of the music becomes harder to discern as the piece progresses. The words are more interesting and nuanced than mere jingoism, and it is highly likely that the *Leier und Schwert* poems later penned by Theodor Körner were influenced by this epic description of a battle in all its excitement, as well as its pathos. Why Schubert abandoned the fight is not certain – he left so much of the piece, but sadly not quite enough to enable us to stage a rescue mission. One has the feeling that the poem was just too long for him to feel that he could maintain the listener's interest.

Autographs:	Ibach-Hausarchiv, Schwelm (D249)
	Wienbibliothek im Rathaus, Vienna (D387)
Publication:	First published as part of the NSA in 2006 (P850; D249)
	First published as part of the AGA and subsequently as part of the NSA in 2006 (P846; D387)
Subsequent editions:	AGA XXI Supplement, p. 341; NSA III: Vol. 2b/309 & 311
Discography and timing:	Hyperion I
	Hyperion II

SCHLACHTGESANG

Battle song

(Klopstock) **D443** [H271]
E major   June 1816

(40 bars)

Mit unserm Arm ist nichts getan;	Our arm is powerless
Steht uns der Mächtige nicht bei,	If the Almighty does not stand by us.
Der Alles ausführt!	For He accomplishes all things.
Umsonst entflammt uns kühner Mut,	In vain are we fired by bold courage
Wenn uns der Sieg von Dem nicht wird,	If victory does not come from Him.
Der Alles ausführt!	For He accomplishes all things.
Vergebens fliesset unser Blut	In vain does our blood flow
Fürs Vaterland, wenn Der nicht hilft,	For the Fatherland if He does not help us.
Der Alles ausführt!	For He accomplishes all things.
[...2...]	[...2...]

Auf, in den Flammendampf hinein!	Up now, into the smoking flames!
Wir lächelten dem Tode zu	We have smiled at death,
Und lächeln, Feind', euch zu!	And we smile at you, our foe!
Der Tanz, den unsre Trommel schlägt,	The dance of our drum-beat,
Der laute schöne Kriegestanz,	The glorious resounding war dance,
Er tanzet hin nach euch!	Is dancing towards you.
[. . . 5 . . .]	[. . . 5 . . .]
Durch ihn und uns ist nichts getan,	But we and our dance are powerless
Steht uns der Mächtige nicht bei,	If the Almighty does not stand by us.
Der Alles ausführt!	For He accomplishes all things.
Dort dampft es noch. Hinein, hinein!	The smoke is still rising there. Into the fray!
Wir lächelten dem Tode zu	We smiled at death,
Und lächeln, Feind' euch zu!	And we smile at you, our foe!

FRIEDRICH GOTTLOB KLOPSTOCK (1724–1803); poem written in 1767

This song is almost always performed as a choral piece, but the work's designation is 'for single voice or chorus'. Accordingly it is listed here as the eleventh of Schubert's thirteen Klopstock solo settings (1815–16). See the poet's biography for a chronological list of all the Klopstock settings.

In 1816 Europe was at peace for the first time in many years, but memories of the battles against Napoleon lingered. Vienna was still full of old soldiers and those who had been wounded during the campaigns. Schubert was too young to have gone to war himself – and he would have been disqualified from military service on grounds of height and eyesight alone – but like any other young man in Vienna he had rejoiced in Austrian military successes. When the allied forces had reached Paris in 1814 he wrote a joyful paean (*Die Befreier Europas in Paris* D104) where patriotism proves stronger than musical inspiration.

The poem of *Schlachtgesang* has fourteen verses in all although only seven (as printed above) were recorded for the Hyperion Schubert Edition. The mixture of religious feeling and jingoism is an uncomfortable combination by today's standards, but it was a stock-in-trade, for English poets too, well into the twentieth century. Although Klopstock is better known for his purely religious works, a gruesome historical *scena* like *Hermann und Thusnelda* D322 shows his nationalistic side: the legendary tale of a bloody battle against the Romans was intended as an augury of German victories in contemporary times. That Schubert should have set this poem, and others in the same vein, shows he was not immune (as a teenager at least) to the mood of triumphalism that swept through Vienna after Napoleon's defeat.

Like that other Klopstock setting *Das grosse Halleluja* D442, the musical notation of *Schlachtgesang* goes back to that of the composers of the poet's own time. In the earliest lieder, before the development of independent and significant accompaniments, the words were printed between the two piano staves. In like manner, this song looks like a piano piece with added text. It is fragmented into three separate parts – effectively an ABA (varied to include elements of B, with coda). The A section of fifteen bars is repeated. Five strophes are printed beneath this section, and are to be sung to stirring E major music. Each of Klopstock's three-line strophes is sung twice to make one musical verse. Section B is shorter – nine bars that briefly pass through the relative minor. This music is allocated to seven further strophes printed beneath the music, but each is sung only once, accelerating the song's progress. This is typical of Schubert's interest in tinkering with conventional strophic form. The final section sets the remaining two strophes – a combination of melodies we have heard in A and B. The tiny postlude for piano is made up of martial horn-calls, the double-dotted rhythm suggesting battle music.

As in *Das grosse Halleluja*, nothing in the autograph specifically states that the composer had a choral song in mind (Schubert writes the words 'Gesang und Pianoforte'). It is accordingly published in the solo series of the *Gesamtausgabe*. But men do not fight such battles as solo engagements, and it seems obvious that at least part of this song is choral, the notes on the two staves suggesting that Schubert had in mind a male chorus in five parts. (It is thus allocated to Series III of the NSA.) Unlike *Das grosse Halleluja*, where it is clear that the composer envisaged the whole top stave sung in parts, the repeat of the words within each musical verse might suggest a song for soloist and chorus.

In the penultimate year of his life (1827), Schubert returned to this poem and set it as a work for eight-part unaccompanied double chorus (D912), this time in D major. Of the many poems from 1816 that he might have chosen to set again, this would not seem the most obvious, but it does remind us, historical reasons apart, that this is a colourful and stirring subject for men's voices. It is this choral work, no less, which the composer chose as the conclusion for the one and only public concert in Vienna during his lifetime that was devoted to his works (26 March 1828). Incorporating some of the rhythmic and melodic features of the earlier version, Schubert named that setting (after the poet's own title) *Schlachtlied* (D912). For that reason the Deutsch catalogue of 1978 uses this as the title for both versions. As the manuscript of the earlier work is clearly marked *Schlachtgesang*, that title is retained here.

Klopstock's poem is in fourteen three-line strophes, all printed in the AGA, but not all placed beneath the vocal line. Of these strophes, 1, 2, 3, 6, 7, 13 and 14 are printed here, as recorded in the Hyperion Edition.

Autograph:	Staatsbibliothek Preussischer Kulturbesitz, Berlin
First edition:	First published as part of the AGA in 1895 (P642)
Subsequent editions:	Not in Peters; AGA XX 228: Vol. 4/112; NSA III: Vol. 3
Further settings:	Robert Schumann (1810–1856) *Schlachtgesang* Op. 62/3 (1847) for male chorus ('Patriotische Lieder')
Discography and timing:	Fischer-Dieskau —

Hyperion I 32^{16} 2'00   John Mark Ainsley & The London
Hyperion II 14^{26} Schubert Chorale (dir. Stephen Layton)

← *Das grosse Halleluja* D442   *Die Gestirne* D444 →

SCHLAFLIED (Schlummerlied)   Slumbersong
(MAYRHOFER)[1] OP. 24 NO. 2, **D527** [H342]

The song exists in two versions, the second of which is discussed below:
(1) January 1817; (2) appeared October 1823

(1)   'Langsam'   F major   ℂ   [15 bars] with the title *Abendlied*

(2)   F major

(15 bars)

Es mahnt der Wald, es ruft der Strom:	The woods exhort, the river cries out:
'Du liebes Bübchen, zu uns komm!'[2]	'Sweet boy, come to us!'
Der Knabe kommt, und staunend weilt,[3]	The boy approaches, marvels and tarries,
Und ist von jedem Schmerz geheilt.[4]	And is healed of all pain.
Aus Büschen flötet Wachtelschlag,[5]	The quail's song echoes from the bushes,
Mit irren Farben spielt der Tag;[6]	The day makes play with shimmering colours;
Auf Blümchen rot, auf Blümchen blau[7]	On flowers red and blue
Erglänzt des Himmels feuchter Tau.	The moist dew of heaven glistens.
Ins frische Gras legt er sich hin:[8]	He lies down in the cool grass
Lässt über sich die Wolken ziehn —	And lets the clouds drift above him;
An seine Mutter angeschmiegt,[9]	Nestling close to his mother
Hat ihn der Traumgott eingewiegt.	He is lulled to sleep by the god of dreams.

JOHANN MAYRHOFER (1787–1836)

This is the nineteenth of Schubert's forty-seven Mayrhofer solo settings (1814–24). See the poet's biography for a chronological list of all the Mayrhofer settings.

Schlaflied, known to generations as *Schlummerlied* which is its name in the Peters Edition, is justly celebrated as one of the few genuinely enchanting Mayrhofer songs. However great and

---

[1] The textual differences noted below are all to be found in the printing of the poem in Mayrhofer's *Gedichte* (1824). For an explanation of the background to these alternative Mayrhofer readings see Editorial Note at the beginning of Johann MAYRHOFER.
[2] Mayrhofer writes 'Du *holdes* Bübchen, zu uns Komm!'
[3] Mayrhofer writes 'Der Knabe *naht, und staunt, und weilt*'.
[4] Mayrhofer writes 'Und ist von *allem* Schmerz geheilt'.
[5] Mayrhofer writes 'Aus *Saaten* flötet Wachtelschlag'.
[6] Mayrhofer writes 'Mit irren *Lichtern* spielt der Tag'. The Peters Edition, unlike the NSA, prints 'ihren' (their) instead of 'irren'.
[7] Mayrhofer writes the whole line differently: '*Und auf den Blümlein in der Au*'.
[8] Mayrhofer writes 'Ins *hohe* Gras'.
[9] Mayrhofer writes '*An Mutter Erde* angeschmiegt'.

beautiful the other settings of that poet, they are seldom as ingratiating as this. The dark side of the poet's muse, given to introspection, pessimism and self-doubt, seems banished for a few magical moments as he turns to nature to be healed of his ennui. For the minstrel in *Nachtstück* D672 (Mayrhofer in another guise) death is the solution to his sorrows: the old man strides into the woods and is surrounded by birdsong and the whispering of the grasses as he prepares himself for his end. *Schlaflied* has a different scenario: unless we are meant to believe that this 'Bübchen' has also fallen asleep for ever in the arms of Mother Earth, the boy here finds a more temporary solution to his pain. Most commentators hear it as a lullaby pure and simple, but from the very beginning there is more to this song than meets the ear. The opening of the vocal line with its octave leaps on 'Es mahnt' and 'es ruft' exhorts and lures: in Schubert's depiction Nature is a Lorelei, a seductive force as well as a soothing and restful one. The locale of the forest occasions the music of distant horns, thus the mezzo staccato articulation. A number of the Mayrhofer songs are contemporary with Schubert's flirtation with the Italian operatic muse and the sinuous vocal line with traces of melismatic decoration suggests homage to *bel canto*. Beneath the singer's creamy legato we might imagine a string accompaniment where gently detached chords are given added colour by the tonguing of flutes (at bb. 9 and 10) as well as oboes and bassoons.

Everything in the shape of the opening phrases suggests smiling invitation; a cradling alternation of chords, largely between tonic and dominant, supports octave leaps in the vocal line in which the singer stands on vocal tiptoe. The song can be sung by both sexes of course, but it is a gift for a charming female singer. For the third and fourth lines of the strophe the harmonies become more complex as the boy is welcomed into Flora's embrace; his discoveries are mapped out by a daisy chain of supporting harmonies (at bb. 9–10) on dominant sevenths (on A, B flat, C). He approaches the marvels of Nature on tiptoe (mezzo staccato triplets played by the left hand crossing over the right). The horn music here is in a tessitura that suggests dreams and magic; forest bugles of this kind would later be described by Tennyson as 'the horns of Elfland faintly blowing'. But because Schubert is such a clever manipulator of strophic songs and their multi-purpose accompaniments, those three repeated quavers, high in the treble clef, might also be taken to represent the fluting sound of the quail's call in the second verse – albeit without the dotted rhythms to be heard in *Der Wachtelschlag* D742.

The boy tarries in growing fascination; he ascends to the pivot of 'von jedem Schmerz', and then gives in to promised blandishments (the plummeting vocal line in the second half of b. 11). At the end of the strophe, bb. 12–14 ('Und ist von jedem Schmerz geheilt') are grounded on an F pedal. Beneath the languid vocal line we can hear Nature going about its work in the healing process; those mezzo staccato triplets now seem infinitely soothing, as if sweat were being lovingly wiped from the boy's brow. The idea of being healed of pain by Nature anticipates the poetry of Justinus Kerner as set by Schumann in his Op. 35 (*Erstes Grün* and *Wer machte dich so krank?*).

As we have seen it is unlikely that the poem could represent an elegy, however disguised by Mayrhofer's layers of ambiguous meaning, and Schubert has not taken it as such. But it is possible that the song is a type of miniature *Liebestod* inspired by Goethe's *Ganymed*. Mayrhofer's 'liebes Bübchen' (a diminutive that in this context seems suggestive of a shepherd boy or classical cherub) is enchanted by God-in-Nature in the same way as Ganymede is enveloped by morning radiance. *Schlaflied* (composed only a few months before *Ganymed* D544) also seems to be an early-morning piece decorated with shimmering colours and dew. In both songs the gentle movement of Nature is depicted as a grave dance in which every movement and invitation suggests the workings of a subtle seduction. Flowers and grass play their part in both songs, and Mayrhofer's quail warbles in the place of Goethe's nightingale. 'Die Mutter' (Mother Earth as Mayrhofer later makes clear) stands in for Goethe's 'Alliebender Vater'.

There is a pre-echo of another, much later, song in the lieder repertoire. The opening of the third strophe ('Ins frische Gras legt er sich hin') is reminiscent of 'Ich ruhe still im hohen grünen Gras' in Brahms's *Feldeinsamkeit* p. 86 no. 2. In both cases the boy's gaze drifts heavenwards to the clouds, as if they were transported to another realm, and in both songs the words 'Wolken ziehn' occur. Brahms too casts his song in a spacious and hypnotic F major, a pavane of grave beauty, with chords in the accompaniment also marked mezzo staccato. This may be coincidence of course, but Brahms knew his Schubert very well, so it is possible that his setting is the conscious acknowledgement of a debt to his most revered forebear.

The first version of the song (published in Volume 2b of the NSA) is written out in common time *alla breve* with the tempo marking of 'Langsam'. It is interesting how even on the page the triplets in this version look jauntier and less restful than quavers unfurling smoothly in the spacious realms of ⅛. In *alla breve* songs there is sometimes a temptation to emphasize the second beat. Schubert's decision to recast the whole song in compound time is, from the performer's point of view, completely justified.

Autographs:	Sibley Music Library, University of Rochester, New York (first version)
	Missing or lost (second version)
Publication:	First published as part of the NSA in 1975 (P759; first version)
	First published as Op. 24 no. 2 by Sauer & Leidesdorf, Vienna in October 1823; reprinted by Diabelli (and later Peters) as *Schlummerlied* (P51; second version)
Publication reviews:	*Allgemeine musikalische Zeitung* (Leipzig) No. 26 (24 June 1824), col. 425–8 [Waidelich/Hilmar Dokumente I No. 282; Deutsch Doc. Biog. No. 479]
Subsequent editions:	Peters: Vol. 2/66 as *Schlummerlied*; AGA XX 298: Vol. 5/24; NSA IV: Vol. 2a/20 & Vol. 2b/193; Bärenreiter 1/146
Arrangements:	Arr. Tilman Hoppstock (b. 1961) for guitar accompaniment, in *Franz Schubert: 110 Lieder* (2009)

Detail of the cover for *Schlummerlied*, Karl Czerny's solo piano arrangement of *Schlaflied*, published by Diabelli in the 1840s.

Discography and timing: Fischer-Dieskau I 9[15]   2'42
                           Hyperion I 21[1]
                           Hyperion II 17[20]   2'49   Edith Mathis

← *Sehnsucht* D516   *La pastorella al prato* D528 →

FRANZ XAVER, BARON SCHLECHTA VON WSSEHRD [WSCHERD]
(1796–1875)

THE POETIC SOURCES
Many of the Schlechta poems that were set by Schubert came to the composer in handwritten copies.

S1 *Wiener Zeitschrift für Kunst, Literatur, Theater und Mode*, 18 August 1818

S2 *W.G. Beckers Taschenbuch zum geselligen Vergnügen*. Herausgegeben von Friedrich Kind. Auf das Jahr 1821. Leipzig bei Georg Joachim Gösschen. Wien in der Carl Geroldschen Buchhandlung

There was a musical supplement added to this publication with Schubert's Schlechta setting *Widerschein*. On this fragile insert the composer is named as 'Franz Schubert in Vienna'. It clearly

Becker's *Taschenbuch zum geselligen Vergnügen* (Pocketbook for sociable pleasures) (1821). One of the two musical supplements loosely inserted into this book was *Widerschein* (Schlechta) by 'Franz Schubert in Vienna'.

amused the editor (Friedrich Kind) to engage another Franz Schubert (this time from Dresden) to compose another musical supplement to a poem by Nordstern entitled *Die Lebensgefährten*, with the heading 'Musik von Franz Schubert in Dresden'. This was the same composer, Franz Anton Schubert (1768–1827) who achieved immortality by professing himself to be insulted when a copy of *Erlkönig* was erroneously returned to him from Breitkopf & Härtel. He wrote that he wished to seek out the imposter who had been 'abusing his name in composing such rubbish'.

S3 *Conversationsblatt*. Zeitschrift für wissenschaftliche Unterhaltung III., 1821

S4 *Dichtungen vom Freyherrn Franz von Schlechta*, Erster Band, Wien, 1824. Im v. Hirschfeld'schen Verlage

S5 *Ephemeren. Dichtungen von weiland* [the late] *Franz Freiherrn von Schlechta-Wssehrd*. Mit einem Vorwort von Heinrich Laube. Wien, Pest, Leipzig. A Hartleben's Verlag, 1876

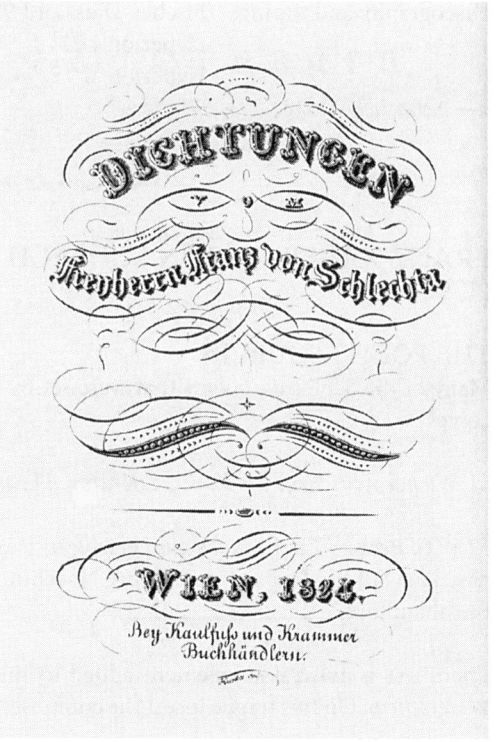

Schlechta's *Dichtungen* (1824).

THE SONGS

2 February 1815   *Auf einen Kirchhof* D151 [S4: pp. 7–8 in a considerably different version]

September 1820   *Widerschein* D639 (second version under D949 in D₁) [S1: p. 804 with the opening 'Fischer harrt am Brückenbogen'] [S2: p. 399] [S4: p. 90 with a new text beginning 'Harrt ein Fischer auf der Brücke'] [S5: p. 9 with yet another new text beginning 'Tom lehnt harrend auf der Brücke']
   Des Fräuleins Liebeslauschen D698 [S3: Heft I pp. 7–8] [S4: pp. 10–11 as No. II ('Das Fräulein') of *Zwey Romanzen*] [S5: pp. 129–30 headed *Fräulein*, part of a two-part poem (pp. 128–30) with the general heading *Liebeslauschen*]

February 1825   *Des Sängers Habe* D832 [The thorough revision of the text Schubert set, probably from a handwritten copy, appears in S5: pp. 30–31 and is printed in full in NSA Volume 13 p. 247. The first verse remains the same, the second begins 'Wenn des Grames Wolken ziehen']

1826   *Totengräber-Weise* D869 [S4: pp. 14–15] [This was certainly Schubert's source with which it agrees in the smallest detail. Certain changes from the original text were incorporated into the *Nachlass* printing and the AGA. These changes were almost certainly initiated by the poet after Schubert's death. The poem is not included in S5]

March 1826   *Fischerweise* D881 [S4: pp. 115–16] [S5: p. 113 with the title *Fischerlied* and with a further number of changes]

Franz Xaver von Schlechta-Wssehrd (sometimes also written Wscherd) was born in Pisek (now in the Czech republic) on 20 October 1796. His father was an army officer who was created a baron in 1819, his son acceding to the title in 1831. He was educated at the school in Kremsmünster and in 1813 became a boarder at Schubert's school in Vienna, the Imperial Konvikt, before going to university to read philosophy and law. There is a certain thoughtless misogyny in some of his work where women appear as dangerous and seductive temptresses (as in the song *Fischerweise* D881), but this was, after all, also a theme in some of the educative poetry of Mayrhofer (*Der Schiffer* D536) whom the young Franz Xaver undoubtedly knew. Schlechta entered the ranks of the civil service in 1818, a year after he began contributing poems to almanacs. Despite his title his family was poor – they were only new nobility after all – and the poet had to earn his own living. He was also a playwright, and – something that was important for Schubert at the time – a theatre reviewer who included music and opera in his remit. It was thanks to Schlechta that Schubert's name appeared in print for the first time – in a poem published in the *Wiener allgemeine Theaterzeitung* on 27 September 1817. This panegyric in four quatrains in the composer's honour (*An Herrn Franz Schubert*) recalled the poet's emotions on hearing a performance of the lost cantata *Prometheus* D451 commissioned by Heinrich Josef Watteroth in July 1816.

In 1818 Schlechta wrote another review, this time of one of the Overtures in Italian style (D590 or D591) arranged for eight hands and two pianos. The poet, only a year older than the composer, described Schubert's 'rich gifts . . . profound feeling, disciplined yet spontaneous force and appealing charm'. He also penned positive reviews in the summer of 1820 for Schubert's two ill-fated operas *Die Zauberharfe* D644 and *Die Zwillingsbrüder* D647. This kind of benign literary activity continued to the 1830s at the latest. As he grew more senior in the civil service and the finance ministry (he eventually reached the ranks of

Hofsekretä in 1834 and Hofrat in 1843) Schlechta seems to have become far less active as a writer. He had already tried extremely hard to succeed as a playwright with the unpublished (and now lost) *Die Freunde*, then with a melodrama entitled *Josue, der Sieger am Jordan, oder Der Brand und die Zerstörung von Jericho* ('Joshua, the Warrior at the Jordan or The Burning and Destruction of Jericho') which was performed in Lemberg (Lvov in the Ukraine) in 1819, but not in Vienna. In May 1820 two of his works, *Die Rückkehr* and *Der Grünmantel von Venedig* reached the stage of the Theater an der Wien, but were not successful with the public. His largest effort, a so-called *Minnespiel* in four acts entitled *Cimburga von Masovien*, was performed at the Burgtheater on 3 November 1825 and published in 1826. Although the celebrated actress Sophie Müller (qv SINGERS), friend of Vogl and Schubert, was in the title role of Cimburga, the work survived for only three performances. The critic Julius Seidlitz, writing in 1836 (the year Schlechta was appointed a court steward), was generally dismissive of the poet, but he believed that Schlechta would achieve something more meaningful if only he could for once look beyond his 'sentimental forget-me-not period' and his 'clear' (meaning over-simplified) view of nature.

He was fortunate in an affectionate wife, the appropriately named Katharina Gutherz, with whom he had two sons and two daughters (Emilie died in childbirth and Sidonie devoted her life to looking after her parents). The elder son Kamil, or Camillo (1822–1880), was undoubtedly known to Schubert as a child, and the younger Ottokar (1825–1894) was named after the thirteenth-century king in the Grillparzer play *König Ottokars Glück und Ende*, clearly Schlechta doffing his hat to a much greater playwright. Camillo began under his father's wing as a civil servant but became involved in radical politics; he was condemned to death for his part in the revolution of 1848, but his sentence was commuted to life imprisonment (no doubt thanks to his father's rank and influence) and he was released in 1854. After returning to Vienna from Hamburg he

Franz von Schlechta, frontispiece to the posthumous
edition of his *Ephemeren* (1876).

he went on to have a career as a writer and
publisher under the pseudonym Camillo Hell.
Although Camillo eventually inherited the
baronetcy, his father refused to receive him in
the family home; the apple of his eye was
Ottokar, the younger son, who became a
distinguished and widely published orientalist
in the mould of Hammer-Purgstall. Schlechta
senior retired in 1864 and enjoyed his old age,
just occasionally returning to verse. He
remained by all accounts (and according to
Heinrich Laube who contributed a preface
to *Ephemeren*) a cheery old soul, delighted to
hunt, shoot or fish, interested in all things, well
informed but, as Laube informs us, also somewhat naïve in his opinions. He died in Vienna
on 23 August 1875, a little more than a month
after the death of another Schubert poet with
moderate longevity, Johann Gabriel Seidl (qv).

Schlechta was one of a handful of Schubert's schoolfriends who remained in Vienna
as members of the Schubert circle until the

composer's death (so many others came and
went according to the dictates of their lives).
He was also one of the few men of the circle to
have married and had a family by the 1820s.
This would account for the fact that he seems
to have attended fewer social gatherings,
although he was gifted enough as a tenor to
have taken part in the Schubertiads. He was
also a member of the *Ludlamshöhle*, that
madcap gathering of pranksters and parodists,
where his nickname was 'Gutauch' – a pun on
the fact that 'schlecht' means 'bad', so the poet
was 'good also', the kind of tag to be affixed to
someone who was essentially genial. He is not
depicted in Schwind's large sepia drawing
from 1868, *Schubert-Abend bei Josef von Spaun*
(it is possible that Schwind did not remember
him, or simply did not rate him) but he did
take part in the unveiling of the 1872 monument to Schubert in the Stadtpark. He contributed a quatrain to the *Wiener Zeitschrift für
Kunst, Literatur, Theater und Mode* for the
issue of 9 December 1828 in honour of Schubert, a few weeks after his death:

> Die Muse weint; ein Liebling folgt
> 　dem andern;
> 　　Warum so jung, so hoffnungsreich
> 　　　auch du?
> Der Winter herrscht; die Nachtigallen
> 　wandern
> 　　Dem Frühling eines schön'ren Landes zu!

> The muse is weeping: one dearest friend
> 　after another;
> 　　Why you, when still so young and full of
> 　　　promise?
> Winter reigns; the nightingales are
> 　moving on
> 　　To spring-time in a lovelier land.

This poem serves as well as any other to illustrate Schlechta's habit of changing tiny details
in his writings. He allowed it to be included
in his last (posthumously published) printing
of the poetry in 1876 (S5: p. 82), but altered
the affectionate word 'Liebling' to the more
neutral 'Sänger'. The language of easy affection
between men was no longer fashionable later
in the century. The last line is changed to 'Den

Wonnen eines steten Frühling's zu' and thus 'the wonders of an eternal spring' replace the 'spring-time in a lovelier land'. Such indecisive tinkering (neither line is distinguished) has the whiff of the amateur and the second rate, and it is a problem in more than one of the Schlechta songs where it has sometimes proved perplexing to decide which is the correct text to be sung in the light of the poet's second, or even third, thoughts, above all in the song *Widerschein* D639. Schlechta's tendency to indulge in ongoing self-revision to no great purpose is discussed at greater length in some of the other individual song commentaries.

Bibliography: Ottner 1999, pp. 183–202
Seidlitz [Jeitteles] 1837,
Vol. 1, pp. 162–4
Waidelich, *Liedlexikon* 2012,
p. 858
Youens 2002, pp. 324–63

AUGUST WILHELM [VON] SCHLEGEL (1767–1845)

THE POETIC SOURCES
S1 *A. W. Schlegel's poetische Werke* Erster und Zweyter Theil. Neueste Auflage, Wien B. Ph Bauer, 1816

S2 *Blumensträusse Italienischer, Spanischer und Portugiesischer Poesie* von August Wilhelm Schlegel. Berlin in der Realschulbuchhandlung, 1804

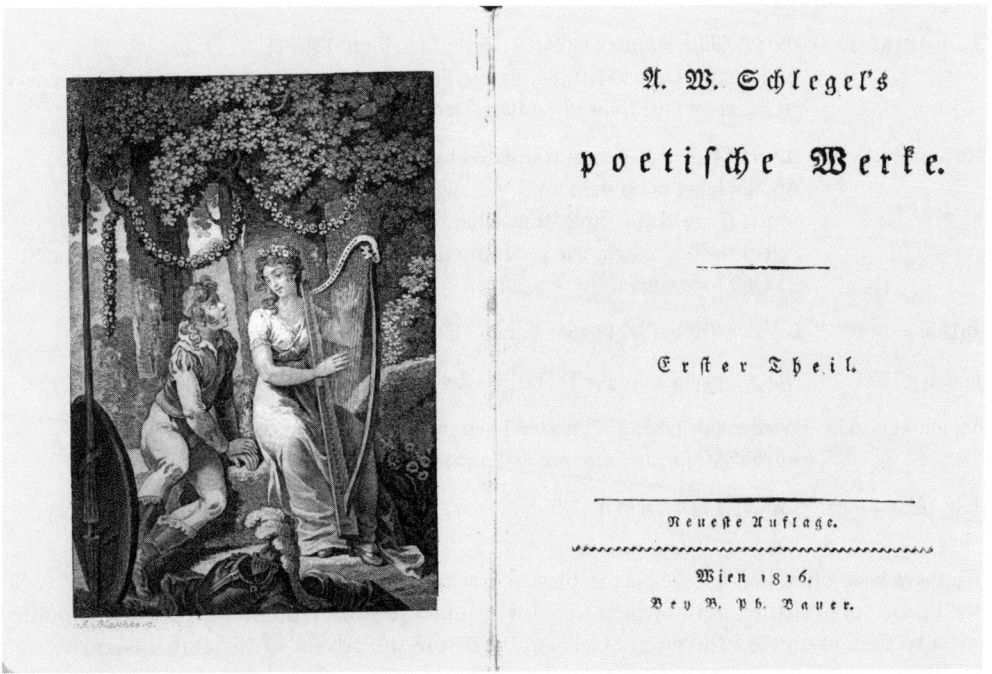

Poetische Werke by A. W. von Schlegel, Vienna paperback edition of 1816.

S3 *William Shakspeare's sæmmtliche drama-tische Werke*, übersetzt im Metrum des Origi-nals. XXVI Bändchen. Wien. Druck und Verlag von J. P. Sollinger, 1825. *Cymbelin* von A. W. Schlegel. Titel und Vignetten lith-ographirt bei Joseph Trentsensky in Wien

S4 *William Shakspeare's sämmtliche dram-tische Werke* Übersetzt im Metrum des Origi-nals in einem Bande nebst Supplement, ent-haltend Shakspeare's Leben, nebst Anmerkun-gen und Kritischen Erläuterungen zu seinen Werken Wien, 1826

This is a handsome one-volume edition of the Viennese Shakespeare edition in Gr 8vo format, very much bigger than the small paperbacks of the individual plays (as S3), issued by the same publisher, Sollinger, without vignettes. It is not impossible that the Schober family acquired this single large volume in 1826 and that it was Schubert's source.

Frontispiece of Schlegel's *Blumensträusse Italienischer, Spanischer und Portugiesischer Poesie* (Flower bouquets of Italian, Spanish and Portugese Poetry) (1804).

THE SONGS

March 1816	*Lebensmelodien* D395 [S1: Erster Theil pp. 51–5]
April 1816	*Die verfehlte Stunde* D409 [S1: Erster Theil pp. 135–7]
	Sprache der Liebe D410 [S1: Erster Theil pp. 123–7 'Zweyte Weise' – the poem is prefaced by four lines of Ludwig Tieck]
November 1818	*Sonett I* D628 (Petrarca, translated by A. W. von Schlegel) [S2: Sonett X – 'Apollo, lebet noch dein hold Verlangen' p. 21]
	Sonett II D629 (Petrarca, translated by A. W. von Schlegel) [S2: Sonett XL – 'Allein nachdenklich, wie gelähmt vom Krampfe' p. 22] For translator of Sonett III D630 *see* GRIES.
1818?	*Lob der Tränen* D711 [S1: Erster Theil pp. 14–16]
January 1821	*Die gefangenen Sänger* D712 [S1: Zweyter Theil pp. 31–2]
September 1825	*Wiedersehn* D855 [S1: Erster Theil pp. 18–19]
	Abendlied für die Entfernte D856 [S1: Erster Theil pp. 10–12]
July 1826	*Ständchen* ('Horch! horch! die Lerch') D889 [S3: Act II Scene 3 p. 33] [S4: p. 606]

Brothers have often had a large part to play in the history of literature, but nowhere was this more so than in nineteenth-century Germany. The Goncourts were a great French phenom-enon, of course, but they were no more remarkable than the brothers Grimm (who adorned the banknotes of their country before the advent of the euro). Germany can boast many other pairs of siblings: the Stol-bergs, the Humboldts, the Manns and, of course, the Schlegels, August and Friedrich. For a great deal of their respective careers they were mutually dependent on each other, and known as the 'Dioscuri of critics', 'die beiden Götter-Buben' ('the two heavenly lads'). Although neither was a poet *pur sang*, their lyrics inspired Schubert to music frequently enough to make them both significant players in his development as a composer of lieder.

The Schlegel family, Protestant and traditional, simple yet intellectually ambitious, came from Meissen in Saxony. The father Johann Adolf Schlegel merits an entry in the reference books in his own right as theologian, translator, fabulist and aesthetician. There was also an uncle, Johann Elias, one of the most distinguished playwrights and literary critics before Lessing. The family of seven children included two gifted girls who from time to time played a lively part in their brothers' lives, pouring cold water on some of their more pompous ideas and helping them out of financial difficulties. An older brother, Carl August Schlegel (1761–89), displayed typical family fortitude: he was an engineer in a Hanoverian regiment in the service of George III, made a map of the Indian interior and died in Madras. The first edition of August Schlegel's poetry (Tübingen, 1800) includes a memoir of Carl August and a note about the sad circumstances of his death.

For the earlier period of their careers, the lives of August und Friedrich ran in biographical tandem. They both had a highly developed sense of family destiny, which is hardly surprising considering the intellectual distinction of their lineage. Friedrich found in his elder brother a 'father, friend and teacher', and they wrote verses to each other bolstering an unashamedly elitist Schlegelian pride. They saw themselves (as Friedrich wrote) 'So wie zwei Kämpfer, die heimlich steigen / Zur Nacht die Felsenkluft empor, / Den Waffenbrüdern den Weg zu zeigen, / Und zu erspäh'n das stille Thor' ('Like two warriors stealthily climbing the ravine by night to show their comrades-in-arms the way, and to espy the silent gate'). August wrote to Friedrich in the autumn of

1802: 'Du folgest deinen Zielen, / Und jedes Unternehmen / Des Forschersinns ist dein' ('You follow your goals, and every venture of the inquiring mind is yours'). This poem continues:

Und was wir beide ernten
Dem andern aufzuspeichern
Ist uns wilkomm'ne Pflicht.
So mögen wir Entfernten
Einander doch bereichern.

And what we both reap
To store up for the other
Is our welcome duty,
Thus we may enrich each other
Though we are far apart.

August Wilhelm was born in Hanover on 8 September 1767. Friedrich's elder by five years, he seemed at first to be the more gifted of the two, and in some ways he was – if not actually as a poet. He studied theology and philology at the university in Göttingen where his teacher Bürger (qv) named him his 'Son in Apollo'. Together, professor and pupil worked on translating Dante and Shakespeare's *A Midsummer Night's Dream*. This was to set the pattern for August's greatest achievements in his later career. After four years as a private teacher in Amsterdam (where Friedrich wrote to him: 'We stick to our habits in that you write a great deal and I read a great deal'), he moved to Jena in 1795 and, with his brother, established the journal *Das Athenäum*, one of the most important organs of the new Romantic school. He married the forthright widow Caroline Böhmer (née Michaelis) who was his fiercest critic and who tactlessly revealed the brothers' low estimation of Schiller (in contrast to their strong admiration for Goethe). August contributed to Schiller's *Horen und Musenalmanach*, but the great poet memorably named Caroline 'Dame Lucifer'. In 1803 she was to leave Schlegel for the philosopher Schelling. In 1798 August was professor of philology in Jena. In 1801 he had a series of readings in Berlin ('Über schöne Litteratur und Kunst') which established him as a literary historian of some importance throughout Europe (these

August von Schlegel, engraving by G. Zumpe.

essays influenced Coleridge and Hazlitt, among others). In 1803 his classical drama *Ion* (inspired by Euripides) was produced in Weimar without much success. The importance of this period for the brothers, and for the fledgling school of Romanticism, is taken up in the commentary on Friedrich Schlegel below.

It was after the Jena years that their paths diverged. August spent fourteen years in the company of Madame de Staël, as a companion on her many travels or at Coppet, her estate near Geneva. It seems that they were not lovers (she had a liaison with Benjamin Constant at this time) but that Schlegel was Staël's counsellor and mentor in all matters pertaining to Germany; he was responsible for the education of her children and the source of many of the ideas that emerged in her masterful *De l'Allemagne* (1813). It was a life that suited him: evening conversation at the highest level with the greatest minds of the age (visitors came to visit Madame de Staël in a never-ending stream), days largely free for reading and study ('I can immerse myself for days at a time in Latin

etymology' he wrote in 1805) and a feeling, in mixing with the great and the good, that he was occupying the centre stage of European thought. In 1808 he gave an important series of lectures in Vienna, anticipating his brother's success in that city, and in 1812 he undertook a dramatic journey to St Petersburg and Moscow in the retinue of the Swedish King Bernadotte.

Between 1797 and 1810 August Schlegel produced his greatest work, the translation of seventeen Shakespeare plays. In sending his brother's version of *Romeo und Julia* to a friend, Friedrich proudly wrote, 'Were I [the literary critic] Körner I would say "This Goethe cannot do". But as I am Friedrich Schlegel I say to you "Friend, this is more than poetry".' These translations represent one of the greatest literary achievements of nineteenth-century Germany. Some of the most complicated passages, including English wordplay, seem effortlessly rendered with a grace and ease (and accuracy) that beggars belief. Novalis remarked of his earlier efforts, 'I am convinced that the German Shakespeare is now better than the English one.' August was not unaware of his own importance in this field, as may be deduced from these lines which rather underestimate the importance of Lessing, Wieland and Bürger in providing a solid foundation for his work in Shakespearean translation (*see* SHAKESPEARE):

Der Erste, der's gewagt auf deutscher Erde
Mit Shakespeares Geist zu ringen und mit
    Dante,
Zugleich der Schöpfer und das Bild der Regel:
Wie ihn der Mund der Zukunft nennen werde,
Ist unbekannt, doch dies Geschlecht erkannte
Ihn bei dem Namen August Wilhelm Schlegel.

The first who ventured on German soil,
To vie with Shakespeare's spirit and with Dante,
At once the creator of the rules and the
    exemplifier of them,
How Posterity will judge him
Only time will tell, but this generation knows
Him by the name of August Wilhelm Schlegel.

Sadly there is no August von Schlegel version of some of the greatest tragedies like *Macbeth*

A. W. von Schlegel's translation of *Cymbeline*, re-issued as part of the Viennese edition of Shakespeare's works with a lithograph by Joseph Trentsensky, Vienna (1825).

or *King Lear* (although there is a remarkable *Hamlet*). His work was completed by Dorothea, Ludwig Tieck's daughter, and her husband Graf Wolf Baudissin.

After the death of Madame de Staël, August took up an appointment as professor of Oriental literature at the newly established University of Bonn where he was renowned for his lectures given in the most elegant riding attire, attended by liveried servants. When he was granted patent of nobility in 1815 (and thus able to add the 'von' to his name) he refused even to open letters which omitted this courtesy. Such vanity in matters of personal appearance and station made him the butt of Heine's mockery. This slightly

ridiculous self-absorption, a family trait it seems, should not obscure Schlegel's important contributions to the study of language and literature from all ages and countries. His translations of Spanish and Italian were almost as popular as his work on Shakespeare, and his devotion to Sanskrit and other Oriental studies in the later part of his life broke new ground. He was one of the first to see writers in the broader terms of historical and national contexts. While this may have caused him to underestimate Milton, for example, who came from a Puritan and thus 'unromantic' background, Schlegel's work in contrasting such writers as Euripides and Racine established a new concept of comparative literature. His role as one of the founding fathers of romanticism ensures for him an enduring place in German literary history. Schlegel died in Bonn on 12 May 1845.

As a poet in his own right August von Schlegel was never particularly highly estimated. His profound understanding of the ways and means of literature was not matched by a natural gift for original poetry. However, his work as a theorist and apologist contributed in no small way to the intellectual climate in which Schubert's talents were to flourish, and it is inevitable that Schlegel's poems reflect the new mood of literary and personal freedom that warmed the composer into musical action. This poet's work appears rather haphazardly in the composer's oeuvre over a nine-year period. There are ten August von Schlegel settings and translations. Schubert returned to Friedrich von Schlegel's work in August 1825, and then set two further poems by August a little while later (D855 and 856). This might imply that the composer continued to associate the brothers in his own mind, long after they had ceased to be truly sympathetic to each other's work.

KARL WILHELM FRIEDRICH VON SCHLEGEL (1772–1829)

THE POETIC SOURCES
S1 *Poetisches Taschenbuch für das Jahr 1806* von Friedrich Schlegel, Berlin, Johann Friedrich Unger, 1806

S2 *Musen-Almanach für das Jahr 1802*. Herausgegeben von A. W. Schlegel und L. Tieck. Tübingen, in der Cotta'schen Buchhandlung, 1802

S3 *Fridrich [sic] Schlegels Gedichte*, Erster und Zweyter Theil, Neueste Auflage, Wien 1816, Bey B. Ph. Bauer

S4 *Friedrich Schlegels Gedichte*, Berlin, bei Julius Eduard Hitzig, 1809 (*Friedrich Schlegels sämmtliche Werke*: Erster Band, Gedichte)

S5 *Gedichte von Friedrich Schlegel*. Zweyte vermehrte Ausgabe. Zweyter Theil. Wien Jakob Meyer und Compagnie 1823 (Friedrich Schlegel's sämmtliche Werke). Neunter Band

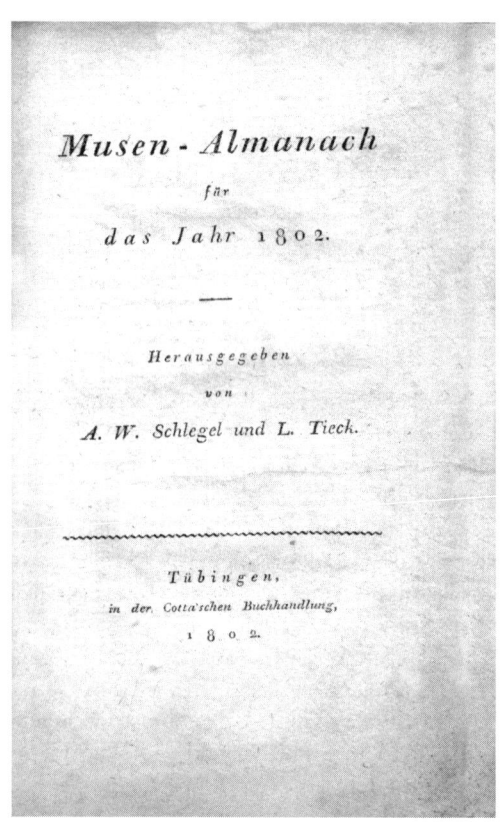

The celebrated *Musen-Almanach für das Jahr 1802* to which Schlegel contributed the *Abendröte* poems.

Schlegel's *Gedichte* (1809).

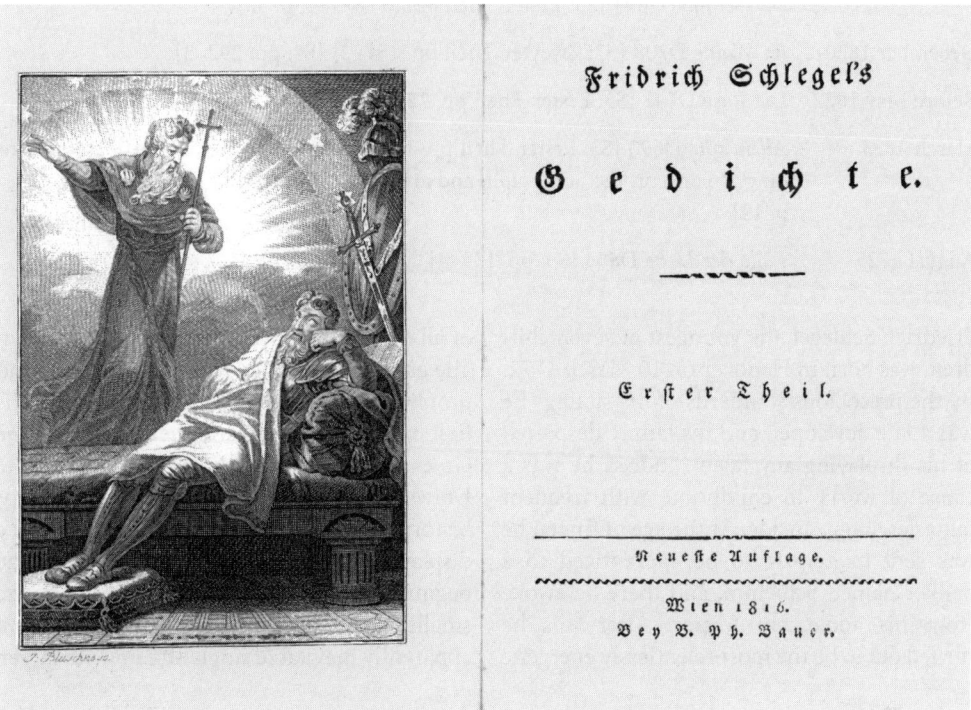

Schlegel's *Gedichte*, paperback edition (Vienna, 1816).

THE SONGS

December 1818	*Blanka* D631 [S1: p. 398 – as the third poem in the fourth and final section of the *Poetisches Taschenbuch* (1806) entitled *Vermischte Gedichte* – this is the only source that uses the poem title *Blanka*. In other sources the title of the poem is *Das Mädchen*.]
	Vom Mitleiden Mariä D632 [S1: pp. 200–201 as No. 13 of the second section of the *Poetisches Taschenbuch* (1806) entitled *Trutznachtigall. Eine Auswahl geistlicher Volkslieder nach Friedrich Spee und einigen andern*. This is a somewhat misleading heading: of the twenty-three poems in this section, seven (including *Vom Mitleiden Mariä*) do not appear in Spee's celebrated *Trutznachtigall*, Cöllen [*sic*] 1649. In his foreword Schlegel admits that texts 9, 10, 12–15 and 19 in his selection of twenty-three are not by Spee; by this he means that these poems do not appear in *Trutznachtigall*. Nevertheless it seems probable that Spee is indeed the author of the text in its original form – *see* SPEE.]
January 1819	*Die Gebüsche* D646 [S2: p. 156] [S3 Erster Theil p. 37] [S4: p. 33]
February 1819	*Der Wanderer* D649 [S2: pp. 146–7] [S3: Erster Theil p. 28] [S4: p. 24]
	Das Mädchen D652 [S2: p. 151] [S3: Erster Theil p. 32] [S4: p. 28]
1820	*Die Sterne* D684 [S2: pp. 155–6] [S3: Erster Theil p. 36] [S4: p. 32]
March 1820?	*Der Schmetterling* D633 [S2: pp. 140–1] [S3: Erster Theil pp. 23–4] [S4: p. 19]
	Die Berge D634 [S2: p. 134] [S3: Erster Theil pp. 17–18] [S4: p. 13]
March 1820	*Die Vögel* D691 [S3: Erster Theil p. 18] [S2: p. 135] [S4: p. 14]
	Der Knabe D692 [S3: Erster Theil p. 19] [S2: p. 156] [S4: p. 15]
	Der Fluss D693 [S3: Erster Theil p. 20] [S2: pp. 137–8] [S4: p. 16]
	Der Schiffer D694 [S3: Erster Theil pp. 57–8] [S4: p. 52]
December 1820	*Im Walde* D708 [S3: Zweyter Theil pp. 151–2] [S4: pp. 292–3]
Before May 1822	*Die Rose* D745 [S3: Erster Theil pp. 22–3] [S4: p. 18]
March 1823	*Abendröte* D690 [S3: Erster Theil pp. 16–17; the words 'Erster Theil' are present on p. 16 and on the autograph, and are not to be found in S2] [S2: p. 133] [S4: p. 12]
August 1825	*Fülle der Liebe* D854 [S5: pp. 132–4]

Friedrich Schlegel, the youngest of seven children, was born in Hanover on 10 March 1772. By the precocious standards of his siblings he was a late developer, and his family despaired of his displaying any talent. Indeed he was a cause of worry in childhood, with frequent fantasies about suicide. At the age of fifteen he was sent to Leipzig to be apprenticed to a banker named Schlemm, and there he awoke from his adolescent torpor. After this he turned out to be the most relentlessly energetic of all the Schlegels, according to Isaiah Berlin 'the greatest harbinger, the greatest herald and prophet of romanticism that ever lived'. His first passion was Plato and the literature of the Greeks, and he joined his brother at the University of Göttingen to study philology, history and philosophy. As a student he displayed stunning mastery of detail and the beginnings of a lifelong ability to synthesize smaller currents of history or thought into an apparently inevitable single stream with larger, even universal, significance. Schlegel aimed to be the Winckelmann of Greek literature, expounding the classical writers in the same way that the great art historian had brought alive the achievements of the ancients in the representational arts. He went on to study in Leipzig where he met Novalis (Friedrich von Hardenberg) who made a deep impression on him. The respect was mutual, for Novalis wrote to him, 'I have never known a man like you. For me you have been the High Priest of Eleusis. Through you I have learned of heaven and hell.' Four years later Novalis was more critical of Schlegel's writings: 'Sie reizen ohne zu befriedigen – sie brechen da ab, wo wir nun gerade aufs Beste gefasst sind – Andeutungen – Vesprechungen ohne Zahl' ('They charm without satisfying: they break off at the exact moment when we were attuned to expect the highest – just an infinity of allusions and promises'). Even at this early stage Schlegel's admirers regretted that greater achievements did not flower as a result of the strivings of his ever-active brain.

Friedrich Schlegel, drawing by his stepson Philipp Veit, cousin of Felix Mendelssohn.

In Berlin Friedrich Schlegel attended the salons of Henriette Herz and Rahel Levin. It was there that he met Dorothea Veit (1763–1839), the married daughter of Moses Mendelssohn and aunt of the as yet unborn composer Felix Mendelssohn. Eight years older than Friedrich, Dorothea left her husband for him (the relationship occasioned an anti-Semitic rant from Schlegel *père*). She became his lifelong companion (they were married only in 1804) and his most ardent and long-suffering propagandist. Friedrich's dream of collaborating with his brother on a large project came to fruition with the publication of *Das Athenäum*. In six issues of this periodical (1798–1800) were united the talents of the early Romantic school. Friedrich Schlegel was the theorist and philosopher, August Schlegel the philologist and critic; Friedrich Schleiermacher was the moralist and theologian of the Romantic academy, Ludwig Tieck its storyteller and Novalis the esoteric mystic. At the core of *Das Athenäum* were Novalis's *Hymnen an die Nacht* (one of which was set by Schubert in 1820), Friedrich Schlegel's aphorisms under the title of *Ideen*, and his *Gespräch über Poesie*. His stream of thoughts written down in a large number of notebooks become the famous *Kritische Fragmente* which enlarged on the irony of Lichtenberg and brought the aphoristic style of Chamfort to German literature. In the tantalizing and elusive art of the fragment, Schlegel's mastery of small forms found its best expression; the fragment would later turn out to be (as Charles Rosen points out in *The Romantic Generation*) central to romanticism itself, in music as much as literature.

Schlegel wrote: 'Our poetry lacks a focus in the way that mythology was a focus for the ancients'; his aim was to seek a new mythology for new times. A new language was to be invented where poetry became a hieroglyphical expression of nature transfigured by 'Phantasie und Liebe'. In his mysticism and redefinition of the meaning of symbolic forms, Schlegel opened a path that was to lead to the early work of Nietzsche and the French symbolists. This *Schlegelianismus der Physik* paired electrical sparks with flowers, and blossoms with the female form; precious stones were 'mineral flowers', and so on. Novalis and Schlegel planned a 'Symphilosophie' in which would occur wondrous 'Mischungen und Entmischungen in physikalischem Chaos' ('blendings and unblendings in physical chaos'). This reflected Dr Johnson's definition, as Friedrich himself noted, of 'Witz', or humour – 'a combination of dissimilar images or discovery of occult resemblances in things apparently unlike' where 'the most heterogeneous ideas are yoked by violence together'.

The Romantic circle soon centred on August's house in Jena. In September 1799 Friedrich moved in, followed by Dorothea, then by Ludwig Tieck who had been more or less discovered by the brothers (his masterful translation of Cervantes's *Don Quixote* stems from August Schlegel's interest in Spanish literature). They were joined by the philosopher Schelling (this was to break up August's marriage) who, like Friedrich Schlegel, suddenly found himself writing lyrics for the first time. Both were considered rather clumsy poets, but here poetry was not considered an end in itself, rather it was a vehicle for ideas. Schleiermacher wrote of Friedrich, 'Transcendence pervaded him, the eternal was his beginning and end, the universal his only and everlasting love.' This description has a strong whiff of Schlegel as a cult guru which was to be amply confirmed by later developments. The majority of the Schlegel texts that Schubert was later to set were written during this heady period. In Schlegel's *Sehnsucht nach dem Unendlichen* there is for the first time a religious and pantheistic note to his writings, and it is this, and the binding thread of the anthropomorphic *Abendröte* poems, which inspired Schubert to give an enduring musical voice to the part-time poet.

Members of the Schubert circle might also have been able to lay their hands on a copy of Schlegel's notorious novel *Lucinde*, famous throughout the German-speaking world since its appearance in 1799. Capable of raising even modern eyebrows, the work was considered scabrous at the time, particularly since its author had recently taken up with a married woman. (Dorothea had to endure its publication at this least tactful of times, but as always she put Friedrich's career before her own dignity.) *Lucinde* advocates a type of sexual freedom that must have appealed to Schubert's generation, for it scornfully denigrated the pretence of innocence where none existed, and placed women in a new light as responsible and responsive sexual beings. It is a plea for an exchange of roles between the sexes, and an androgynous understanding of love. Unashamed eroticism seems part of Schlegel's depiction of a universal pantheism, and this too surely played its part in the composer's enthusiasm (and that of some his friends – Schober for example) for Schlegel's work. Richard Littlejohns encapsulates the message of this powerful book which Isaiah Berlin refers to as the '*Lady Chatterley* of its time . . . a pornographic novel of the fourth order':

> The image of the plant is prominent in Lucinde *and embodies the central theme of the text, namely, the belief that human behaviour should be organic and spontaneous rather than planned and directed at some objective [. . .] In education the emphasis is on the free growth of the individual. Sexual conduct, too, should be based on spontaneity and naturalness: sexual partners should discard inhibition and convention in glorious self-expression and fulfil the divine destiny of all life forms to mate and reproduce.*

At this point the Schlegels were uneasy guests in Goethe's domain. Their opposition to Schiller embarrassed the great man, but Friedrich had written that 'Goethe's poetry is the dawn of true art and pure beauty' and the lion of Weimar was not impervious to the brothers' admiration and its value for his standing among the younger generation. Indeed the Schlegels proclaimed Goethe as more than just the author of *Götz* and *Werther* – they placed the work published since his return from Italy (above all *Wilhelm Meisters Lehrjahre*) at the forefront of literature. Goethe, in endeavouring to return the compliment, encouraged Friedrich's efforts as a playwright. The play *Alarcos* (influenced by Calderón) was given in Weimar in 1802, but its experiments in assonant rhyme resulted in its being laughed off the stage, despite Goethe's thundering efforts to bring the house to order. Apart from this, Goethe (whom Friedrich Schlegel nicknamed 'Der alte Herr') regarded him as a 'stirrer' and a 'stinging nettle', and there was never much personal sympathy between them. He no doubt felt supremely uncomfortable with Friedrich's inventive propensity for 'Ironie' – the mocking of respectable institutions, the debunking of pomposity, according to Isaiah Berlin 'his weapon against ossification and against any form of the stabilisation and freezing of the life stream'.

Shortly after the *Alarcos* debacle Friedrich Schlegel moved with Dorothea to Paris which was his base for a series of lectures and a serious study of Sanskrit with the young Scottish scholar Alexander Hamilton. This coming to terms with the Orient was to bear fruit with his celebrated study *Über Sprache und Weisheit der Inder*. With unrelenting industry he also mastered the history of art and architecture in this period. At this point he had astonishing and serious visions of European unity. These seem surprisingly modern today, and remind us that the close French–German axis in present-day European politics is not new; indeed, writers like Stefan Zweig and Romain Rolland nurtured similar ideals later in the nineteenth century. Schlegel moved to Cologne where he gave a series of readings (the brothers seem to have made as much of a stir with their lectures as Liszt was later to make with his piano recitals) which formed the basis of his equally famous history of German literature. It was here that he married Dorothea, and this concern with religious formality, and an attempt to establish a new age of medieval faith and aesthetics, signalled the next decisive change in his life.

In April 1808 Friedrich and Dorothea converted to Catholicism. This occasioned a scandal similar to that of the publication of *Lucinde*. Soon afterwards the couple made their way to Vienna where brother August had given a series of lectures. Friedrich, not to be outdone, planned a set of talks on recent history (1810), establishing himself as a Viennese social lion as well as a publisher of various papers that were increasingly conservative and royalist. He met Eichendorff (suggesting the title for that poet's novel *Ahnung und Gegenwart*) and became increasingly interested in the trappings of public life. Firmly renouncing Napoleon and adopting the stance of a patriotic Austrian, he also took part in field campaigns in Hungary in 1809, not neglecting to study that nation's language and literature while there. He came to the notice of Metternich himself, and dabbled as a civil servant (no doubt attempting to emulate Goethe's mid-life role in the administration of Weimar), taking an active part in background diplomacy during the Congress of Vienna. It is notable that the secret police were detailed to follow Schlegel (Metternich trusted no one), writing long reports concerning his visits to various hostelries (sometimes as many as fourteen in one day). He ate a great deal (this was reflected in his ever-more portly figure) and was a heavy drinker. His sense of self-importance knew no bounds, although he failed ever to achieve any position of real significance in the Austrian government.

As early as 1808 Schlegel had vigorously recanted his former beliefs: 'Diese aesthetische Träumerei, unmännliche pantheistiche Schwindel, diese Formenspielerei müssen aufhören; sie sind der grossen Zeit unwürdig und nicht mehr angemessen' ('This aesthetic daydreaming, this unmanly pantheistic fraudulence, this playing around with formulae, all these must cease: they are unworthy of these great times and no longer appropriate'). Thus long before Schubert discovered Schlegelian pantheism, the poet himself had firmly renounced it, and in the composer's home town no less. Similarly, Schubert had discovered *Faust* at the moment (1814) when a much older Goethe in Weimar was already engaged in the *West-östlicher Divan*; the reader (or composer) sometimes takes a long time to catch up with the author's latest ideas. By 1809, drawn to the great Redemptorist priest (and later saint) Clemens Hofbauer (1751–1820), who was now resident in Vienna, Schlegel was a crony of Metternich, a knight of the Papal Order of Christ and a member of the Wiener Akademie der bildenden Künste (Academy of Fine Arts). He had achieved far more in terms of rank than any of his relatives, and the noble 'von' was to follow in 1815.

Not everyone was impressed, least of all August who, for all his vanity, remained a liberal, falling into a rage on reading Friedrich's religious articles in the journal *Concordia*. Goethe wrinkled his forehead sceptically on hearing of the conversion from Friedrich's own lips, later writing that 'such a kind of man' simply became 'more and more coarse'. Heine was scornful of Friedrich's 'religiöse Privatmarotten' ('private religious quirks') and Friedrich von Gentz observed that 'For some years now his religious or rather sectarian mania has thoroughly made a fool of him, to which his wife has greatly contributed. The present difference between the two brothers is vast, and in my view wholly in favour of A. W. He's certainly very vain, but full of life, activity and talent.' Gentz continues, playing on the meaning of 'Schlegel', 'F. ist jetzt . . . der wahre Blei-Schlegel, der andre mehr als je, ein Stahl-Schlegel' (F. is now the leaden drumstick, the other more than ever a steel drumstick').

The very things in Schlegel's work that had appealed to the Schubert circle (and which were later to appeal to Schumann) – *Lucinde* and the *Athenäums-Fragmente* – were excluded from the new Schlegel *Gesamtausgabe* in a spirit of unashamed revisionism. Because Schubert was not *au fait* with the most recent literary developments, we cannot be certain whether he knew of Schlegel's change of heart, or that a man of such liberal and universal sympathies had turned into an insufferably grand member of the establishment. We can only imagine how eagerly Schubert might have grasped the opportunity to meet Schlegel in person, having read the poet's earlier works. Many of Schubert's friends were in contact with Schlegel: Helmina von Chézy (authoress of *Rosamunde*) had been one of his students in

his pre-conversion Paris days, and Matthäus von Collin, Karoline Pichler and Craigher de Jachelutta had all been connected to him in one way or another. As late as 1876 Franz von Schober claimed that Schlegel had praised his libretto for *Alfonso und Estrella* (Schubert's opera, D732). We know that Schubert encountered the poet personally during 1825 at one of Schlegel's evenings of telepathy and musical therapy where he liked to demonstrate the healing powers of animal magnetism (a phenomenon that prefigured Freud's therapeutic work) and where music (perhaps Schubert's) was used to place a subject in a trance.

It was in the summer of 1825 that Schubert set his last Schlegel text, *Fülle der Liebe* D854. Perhaps this was at the instigation of the patriarch Pyrker in Gastein, a Schlegel admirer, but it is impossible to rule out a connection between this stray Schlegel setting and a

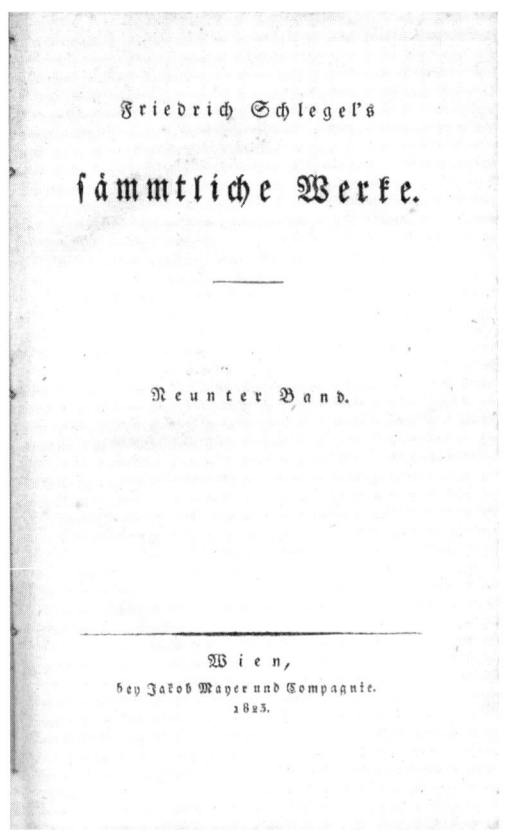

Volume 9 of Schlegel's *Sämmtliche Werke* (1823), source of *Fülle der Liebe*.

personal exchange between composer and poet.

The poet Franz von Bruchmann had reflected Schlegel's pattern of conversion, renouncing the lifestyle of his former friends with vehemence. There is no doubt that he was under the influence of Schlegel, whose latest writings were an antidote to 'the new pagan era . . . a great pantheism' (itself Schlegel-inspired) which, according to the self-flagellating Bruchmann, had been disastrously embraced by the Schubert circle. In the light of the new Catholicism Franz von Schober, who had been a close friend, became the Devil incarnate in Bruchmann's eyes, and the affair between his sister Justina and Schober was ruthlessly suppressed. In the background stands Friedrich von Schlegel, a type of newly sanctimonious *éminence grise* representing the power of the religious backlash that characterized the period.

By 1827 the poet Johann Senn (qv) in a heated correspondence with Bruchmann denounced the 'reformed' Schlegel in no uncertain terms as a fraud and a humbug. At this late stage of the composer's career Schlegel no longer played any part in Schubert's musical life, although he was a witness at Bruchmann's ill-fated wedding to Juliana von Weyrother in June 1827. If Schubert encountered Schlegel in the flesh (as we now believe is likely), there would have been little trace of the poet of the *Abendröte* poems. Now he was a man aspiring to spiritual ecstasy via a completely different route, relishing the panoply of worldly power and wishing to slam shut the doors that he had previously been anxious to open. There is also evidence that Schlegel was a sexual hypocrite, 'helping' young ladies spiritually in the manner of the bogus monk who takes the dying girl's confession in Wolf's *Italienisches Liederbuch*. In short, Schlegel, the adopted Viennese, ended up by personifying the Austrian establishment and many of the things that Schubert and his friends disliked about their country's government.

This move from Left to Right has happened time without number to writers but seldom as precipitously as to Schlegel, whose change over the years from an open-hearted and rebellious

Friedrich Schlegel, engraving after the drawing by Auguste von Buttlar.

young man into a rigid pillar of the establishment was a spectacular volte-face. Nevertheless the literary theories formulated in his prime bore fruit in all sorts of unexpected directions. The neo-Marxism of Walter Benjamin, György Lukács and Theodor Adorno looks back to Schlegel, as does the literary theory of Péter Szondi, the philosophy of Wilhelm Dilthey and Hans-Georg Gadamer, as well as more recent trends in feminism and the theory of literary deconstruction. Schlegel's story is one of restless questing and searching, and a fruitless attempt to fill a personal void which no amount of work and success could achieve. As Ludwig Tieck wrote to August von Schlegel after Friedrich's death: 'As you well know, he found fulfilment neither in scholarship and art, nor faith and religion.' This one-time 'Dictator of Philosophy' had become 'The Dictator of Catholicism' and in

changing the world of thought, and continually reinventing his role in it, he had somehow
failed to change himself. He died less than two
months after Schubert, in Dresden on 12
January 1829.

Bibliography: Berlin 1999, pp. 15, 113–14 &
                117
                Dürhammer 1996, pp. 59–93
                Dürhammer 1999, p. 337
                Littlejohns 2000, p. 873

SCHLUMMERLIED *see* SCHLAFLIED D527

Der SCHMETTERLING   The butterfly
(F. VON SCHLEGEL) OP. 57 NO. 1, **D633** [H418]
F major   March 1820(?) or 1819?

Wie soll ich nicht tanzen?
Es macht keine Mühe,
Und reizende Farben
Schimmern hier im Grünen.
Immer schöner glänzen
Meine bunten Flügel,
Immer süsser hauchen
Alle kleinen Blüten.
Ich nasche die Blüten,
Ihr könnt sie nicht hüten.

   Wie gross ist die Freude.
Sei's spät oder frühe,
Leichtsinnig zu schweben
Über Tal und Hügel.
Wenn der Abend säuselt,
Seht ihr Wolken glühen;
Wenn die Lüfte golden,
Scheint die Wiese grüner.
Ich nasche die Blüten,
Ihr könnt sie nicht hüten.

Why should I not dance?
It costs me no effort,
And enchanting colours
Shimmer here amid the verdure.
Ever lovelier
My brightly coloured wings glisten;
Ever sweeter is the scent
From each tiny blossom.
I sip from the blossoms;
You cannot protect them.

   How great my joy,
Be it early or late,
To flit so blithely
Over hill and dale.
When the evening murmurs
You see the clouds glow;
When the air is golden
The meadows are more radiantly green.
I sip from the blossoms;
You cannot protect them.

FRIEDRICH VON SCHLEGEL (1772–1829); poem written in 1800/1801

*This is the seventh of Schubert's sixteen Friedrich von Schlegel settings (1818–25). See the poet's
biography for a chronological list of all the Friedrich von Schlegel settings. See also the article
about the cycle of which this song is part - Abendröte.*

This enchanting song, the most elegant of trifles, is often sung by women, but this butterfly,
despite his lightness and grace, is a predatory male rogue, make no mistake – never mind the

androgyny of the illustration below. The mood of the music is what the Germans would call 'schelmisch'. Just as the rose is a metaphor for the fallen woman, the butterfly is the inconstant man, going from bloom to bloom without care or regret. The introduction depicts dalliance perfectly: an upbeat of two semiquavers leads to a dotted crotchet, then an answering phrase a fifth lower with a tiny hunting-horn motif in the piano's left hand (the butterfly is a hunter after all, a 'Schürzenjäger' or skirt-chaser); then the same process all over again (he is still hovering, still sipping nectar) with a tiny change of harmony for the horns as they switch to the dominant. Will he stay? Certainly not! The closing bars of the introduction (bb. 5–6) see him fly away in glee, chuckling (if only a butterfly could) and ready to sing us his ditty.

The greater part of the song is underpinned by Schubert's favourite dactylic rhythm in the left hand of the accompaniment, as if to underline that the creature is driven by instinct: his behaviour cannot be other than it is, and it would be as futile to blame the stars for shining as to expect anything other than flitting from a butterfly. What makes the piano writing special is the delicious weaving of the semiquavers in the inner fingers of the right hand; the effect is of a fluttering of wings. At 'Immer schöner glänzen / Meine bunten Flügel' (bb. 15–18) the right thumb provides the suggestion of a chromatic scale that perfectly paints the image of glistening

Illustration for *Der Schmetterling*, 1921, by Erich Schütz.

wings, reminding us that one of the meanings of the word 'chromatic' is many-coloured. Capell (who, taking Mandyczewski as his guide, erroneously places this among the 1815 songs) thinks that the butterfly's ramblings take rather a square form, but this is not always so. In the poem's first four lines (bb. 6–12) the two-bar phrases begin with an upbeat, and end with the stress on an important verb or noun: 'Wie soll ich nicht tanzen? / Es macht keine Mühe, / Und reizende Farben'. This may be square, but it is deliberately so, like a square dance. For the next two lines (bb. 13–18) there is no upbeat, but the same rules of accentuation apply. When we come to the seventh line the ear expects to hear 'Immer süsser hauchen / Alle kleinen Blüten'. Instead Schubert dislocates the rhythm by elongating the 'im' of 'immer' to a dotted crotchet, taking up a whole bar with the word 'süsser' (b. 20). This means that the remaining words in the two-line phrase come together in eight tripping quavers (bb. 21–2), the speed of the syllables on the tip of the tongue making the flowers sound ever smaller, even more sweetly vulnerable to the butterfly's advances. In accenting the first word of each bar and changing Schlegel's prosody we get 'Immer süsser / hauchen alle / kleinen Blüten'. The word 'Blüten' seems carelessly thrown away, and the adjective 'kleinen' (small) is emphasized. The tiny piano interlude strikes a note of triumph in a fanfare that betokens the butterfly's work successfully accomplished before the strophe continues to its end with a varied recapitulation of the opening material. (There is something much more abrasive here than we find in Goethe's *Gleich und gleich* – set by Hugo Wolf – which describes the meeting of flower and bee as an affectionate encounter between two creatures made for each other.)

The song is a purely strophic one, and so the second verse provides no surprises. The tune continues to delight of course, and the chromatic accompaniment at 'Wenn der Abend säuselt' (b. 15 onwards) is highly effective for the rustling sounds of evening. At 'Wenn die Lüfte golden, / Scheint die Wiese grüner' (from b. 19) we hear the same capricious dislocation of the rhythm of the words. All in all there is a Cherubino-like charm to this music with an appropriately Mozartian response from Schubert. The butterfly loves the flowers but he also exploits them. As he is only fulfilling his destiny according to nature he is not to be blamed. If he were human his adventures would perhaps be excusable, like Cherubino's, on account of his youth, where an older philanderer, judged in human terms, would deserve to be run through with a lepidopterist's pin.

Autograph:	Missing or lost
First edition:	Published as Op. 57 no. 1 by Thaddäus Weigl, Vienna in April 1826 (P94)
Publication reviews:	*Allgemeiner musikalischer Anzeiger* (Frankfurt) No. 33 (10 February 1827), p. 317f. [Waidelich/Hilmar Dokumente I No. 452; Deutsch Doc. Biog. No. 798]
Subsequent editions:	Peters: Vol. 4/49; AGA XX 179: Vol. 3/225; NSA IV: Vol. 3a/76; Bärenreiter: Vol. 2/110
Discography and timing:	Fischer-Dieskau I 6^9 1'27
	Hyperion I 27^{14}
	Hyperion II 21^{12} 1'29 Mattthias Goerne

← *Der Wanderer* D649   *Schäfers Klagelied* D121 →

GEORG PHILLIP SCHMIDT ('SCHMIDT VON LÜBECK') (1766–1849)

THE POETIC SOURCES
S1 *Taschenbuch zum geselligen Vergnügen*. Achtzehnter Jahrgang 1808. Herausgegeben von W. G. Becker. Leipzig in der Niemannschen Buchhandlung

S2 *Dichtungen für Kunstredner*. Herausgegeben von Deinhardstein. Wien und Triest, 1815. Im Verlage der Geistingerschen Buchhandlung

In the autograph of the first version of *Der Wanderer* Schubert attributes the poem to Werner, replicating what is printed in S2.

S3 *Lieder von Schmidt von Lübeck*. Herausgegeben von H. C. Schumacher. Altona, bei J. F. Hammerich, 1821 (Zweite vermehrte Auflage, 1826)

THE SONG
October 1816   *Der Wanderer* D489 [S1: p. 143 as *Des Fremdlings Abendlied* ('Mit Musik von Herrn Zelter')] [S2: pp. 149–50, printed with the title *Der Unglückliche*, and with the incorrect name of the poet Werner] [S3: *Des Fremdlings Abendlied* pp. 76–7]

Georg Philipp Schmidt was born in Lübeck on 1 January 1766, thus earning himself the informal title ('von Lübeck') that distinguishes him from other Schmidts. The son of a merchant, he studied law (1786–90) at the universities of Göttingen (taking his poetical style from that of the Göttingen Hainbund – in particular the lyrics of Hölty) and Jena (where he met Goethe and Schiller). He came into contact with Christian Stolberg during a sojourn in Copenhagen. He journeyed in Sweden and then became interested in medicine, qualifying as a doctor at Kiel University in 1797 and later practising in Warsaw. He returned to Hamburg-Altona in the later years of his life, interesting himself in the history of Schleswig-Holstein (*Historische Studien*, 1827), as well as becoming a prosperous businessman and bank director. His poetical output is not considered of great importance – he was an amateur who rejoiced in being in contact with the poets of the time. Although Zelter also set his poetry, it was Schubert who ensured Schmidt's immortality. There is no record of the poet's reaction to the music that launched his most famous poem into the world. He died in Altona near Hamburg on 28 October 1849.

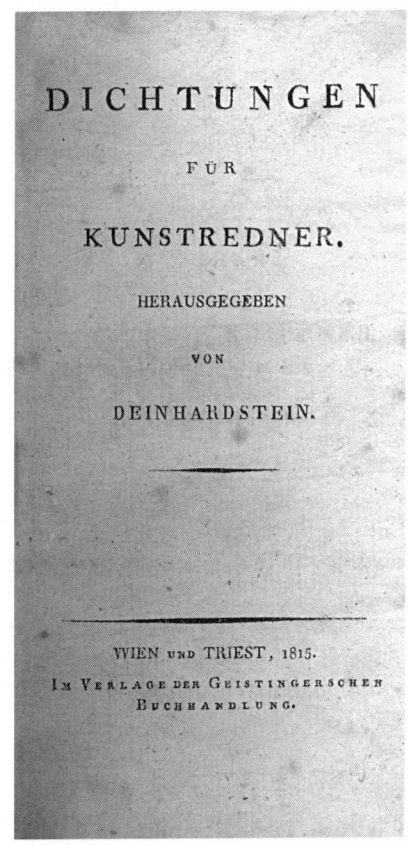

Dichtung für Kunstredner (Poetry for Declamation) (1815).

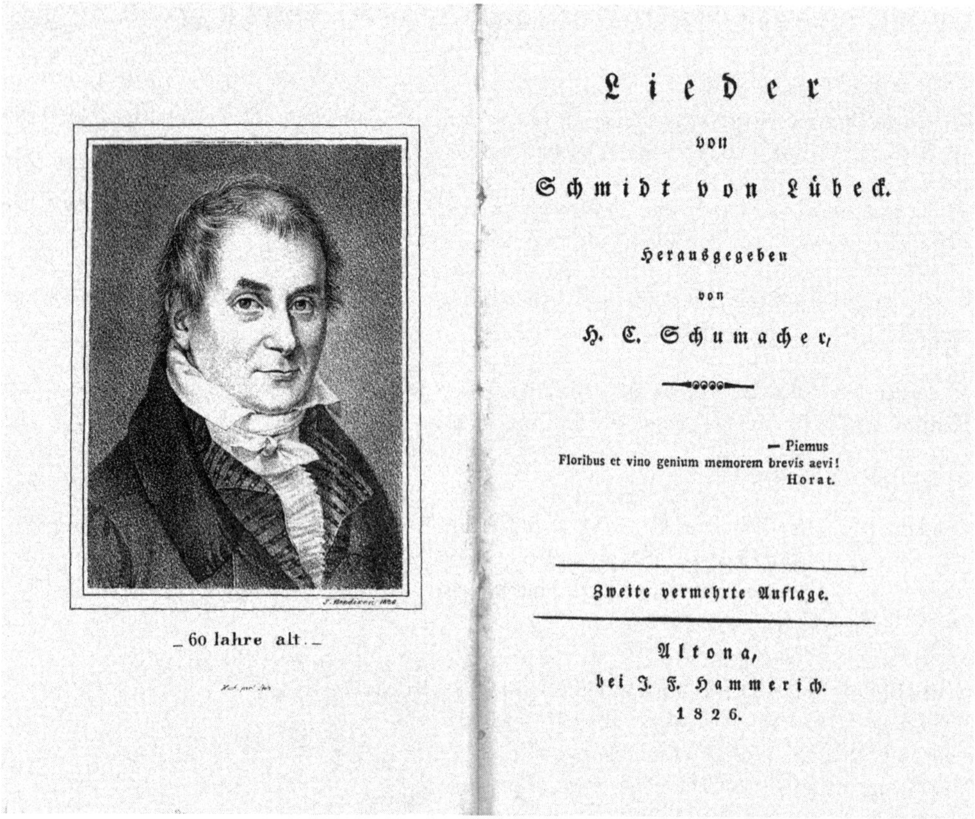

Lieder by Schmidt von Lübeck (1826). The frontispiece by S. Bindixeri shows the poet at sixty years old.

FRANZ ADOLPH FRIEDRICH VON SCHOBER (1796–1882)

THE POETIC SOURCE
All Schober's poems that Schubert set came to the composer in handwritten copies

LATER POETIC SOURCE
S1 *Gedichte* von Franz von Schober, Stuttgart und Tübingen, J.G. Cotta'scher Verlag, 1842

This volume of 267 pages remains the only printed source of the Schober poems set to music by Schubert. All the poems are to be found here with the exception of *An die Musik* and *Der Hochzeitsbraten*. The poem *An Franz Schubert*, not set to music by the composer, appears on pp. 110–12.

THE SONGS
1815	*Genügsamkeit* D143 [S1: p. 8]
1816	*Am Bach im Frühlinge* D361 [S1: p. 9, as no. 1 of Six *Frühlingslieder* pp. 9–18, and with the title *Am Bache*]

| March 1817 | *Trost im Liede* D546 [S1: p. 6] |
| | *An die Musik* D547 |

| April 1817 | *Pax Vobiscum* D551 [S1: p. 79] |

| 1822, before April | *Frühlingsgesang* D740 Quartet for TTBB with piano (between January and the beginning of April 1822) [S1: p. 10, as no. 3 of Six *Frühlingslieder* pp. 9–18] |

| September 1822 | *Todesmusik* D758 [S1: pp. 70–71] |

| November 1822 | *Schatzgräbers Begehr* D761 [S1: p. 161, no. 5 of 'Sonette'] |

| March 1823 | *Viola* D786 [S1: pp. 12–15, as no. 5 of Six *Frühlingslieder* pp. 9–18, and with the subtitle *Blumenballade*] |

| April 1823 | *Pilgerweise* D789 [S1: pp. 4–5] |

| May 1823 | *Vergissmeinnicht* D792 [S1: pp. 15–18, as no. 6 of Six *Frühlingslieder* pp. 9–18] |

| January 1826 | *Mondenschein* D875 Quartet for TTBB and piano [S1: p. 42 as *Vollmondnacht*] |

| February 1827 | *Jägers Liebeslied* D909 [S1: pp. 30–31] |
| | *Schiffers Scheidelied* D910 [S1: pp. 36–8] |

| November 1827 | *Der Hochzeitsbraten* D930 Comic trio for STB |

Mention should also be made of another Schober setting for unaccompanied voices that is outside the scope of this book, as well as the opera that he wrote together with Schubert: *Frühlingsgesang* D709 Quartet (TTBB) before April 1822; *Alfonso und Estrella* – Opera in 3 acts D732, 20 September 1821 to 27 February 1822

The *Gedichte* contains a poem *Die Wolkenbraut* (S1: p. 57). This is in fact an excerpt from *Alfonso und Estrella* D732 (no. 11, Troila's baritone aria at the beginning of Act II). In the second edition of the poems (1865) there is mention of a Schubert setting, but apart from the music for the opera there is no record of this, nor any reason to suppose it ever existed as a separate lied. *Die Wolkenbraut* was nevertheless assigned the catalogue number D683 by Deutsch in 1951; the number is retained as a phantom song [*see* DUBIOUS, MISATTRIBUTED AND LOST SONGS].

Franz von Schober was born to an Austrian family in Torup Castle, near Malmö, Sweden, on 17 May 1796. His father, also Franz, had been manager of Baron Alexius Stierblad's estate since 1780, and was ennobled in 1801; he died in 1802 when the future poet was only six. After a spell in Hamburg, Altona, where she met Klopstock and Claudius (qqv), his mother, Katharina Schober (née Dörfel or Derfl) moved back to her native Austria with her four children (Franz's siblings were his older brother Axel, his older sister Ludovica (Ludwiga) and his younger sister Sophie, all of whom were fated to die before reaching thirty). In 1803 Schober had followed his elder brother's footsteps into one of the most progressive educational establishments in Germany – Schnepfental, near Gotha, not far from Weimar, the town that was to be his home some forty years later. The school was run by Christian Gotthilf Salzmann, a teacher famed for his liberal ideas concerning the upbringing of children. We detect in this choice, and throughout Schober's life, the hand of an indulgent mother who doted on this son in particular. The family returned to Vienna in 1807 (his parents had been married there) and Schober spent a year at school in the city before becoming a boarder at Kremsmünster in Upper Austria. In 1810 Schober's sister Ludovica, living in Baden outside Vienna at the time, was the subject of covert police observation on account of her relationships with various men that officially identified her as a 'Kokotte'. (Frau Schober also had affairs; attitudes to sex in Sweden were clearly different from those in Catholic Austria.) Documents unearthed by Rita Steblin throw light on the bumbling and infinitely costly antics of the Austrian secret service with their intercepting of letters and written reports to Metternich. The Schober family, while committing no illegal offence, was thus known by the state as loose living, an opinion mirrored by Josef Kenner in 1858 concerning his memories of the clan: 'There reigned in this whole family a deep moral depravity ['eine tiefe sittliche Verdorbenheit'], so that it was not to be wondered that Franz von Schober went the same way.'

The twelve-year-old Franz must have found the discipline at Kremsmünster stiflingly different from the liberal regime at Schnepfental, but the arrival of a free spirit from a totally different background would have represented a breath of fresh air for the boy's contemporaries. His fellow pupils and their older acquaintances were all destined to become his friends and later also members of the Schubert circle: Johann Mayrhofer, Josef Kenner and Anton Ottenwalt (qqv) and the Spaun brothers, Anton and Josef (qv), in whose home in Linz Schober first heard some of Schubert's songs. This was as early as 1813. It is not clear when poet and composer first met, but they certainly knew each other by 1815 and, if the drawing of the young Schubert in profile from 1814 (*see* Vol. I 338) attributed to Schober is truly by him, it must have been earlier. In the memoirs of Thekla von Gumpert, who was married to Schober for a short time (many years after Schubert's death), she claims that her former husband had been first impressed by the brilliance of the young Schubert's singing voice, a sound that overwhelmed the other boys' voices in the Hofburg choir. If this is true, Schober was aware of Schubert's existence, without perhaps knowing him personally, some time before July 1812 when the composer's voice broke.

Schober returned to Vienna to study law at the university from 1816, but he failed to complete the course, impulsively undertaking

Franz von Schober, oil painting by Kupelwieser. In the background is Schober's birthplace, the castle of Torup in Sweden.

a nostalgic journey to Sweden, a typical escape route for someone easily bored by scholastic discipline. From 1818 he dabbled in the art of landscape painting. The poet's portrait as eventually painted by Leopold Kupelwieser featured Schloss Torup in the background, an image based on Schober's own drawings of his former Swedish home.

Money for Schober seems never to have been particularly short; on the other hand he did not have the means to lead the life of untrammelled luxury that he clearly believed was his due. A reverse in the family fortunes had left Frau von Schober less wealthy than she had once been, but there always seemed to be enough money for her adored younger son to live comfortably, and to extend hospitality to friends. Schober was good-looking and a superb talker, he was well read and lively, and he had personal charisma that effectively masked the laziness of a dilettante and the complexities of a narcissistic personality. He was interested in contemporary poetry and he loved to organize evenings where he read to his friends and educated them into his way of thinking – this was a pose in itself because Schober, for all his verbal fluency and intermittent *joie de vivre*, was far from a deep thinker in his own right.

From the outset the aspiring poet and the young composer seem to have enjoyed a special relationship. Schubert resided in the Schobers' apartment in the Landskrongasse off the Tuchlauben from the autumn of 1816 to August 1817. Frau von Schober was sympathetic to the composer, who was condemned to earn his crust as a schoolteacher when all he wanted to do was write music, and agreed that he should come and live in the inner city as part of her family. For Schubert the possibility of an address within close walking distance of the building where the Gesellschaft der Musikfreunde held their concerts must have seemed like heaven. Having encountered opposition to the idea from the composer's father, Schober, ever the ladies' man, claimed half a century later to have personally persuaded the mother (actually Schubert's step-mother), after much discussion, to allow the young man to make the move (Waidelich 2008, pp. 41–2). Ready-made patronage of this kind seldom comes a composer's way (one can compare it to the Sitwell family's open-ended hospitality to the young William Walton in the 1920s). This was the first time since his boarding-school days that Schubert had lived away from home and been free from his father's schoolhouse. During this period Schober engineered a meeting between the composer and Johann Michael Vogl, the baritone who was to become Schubert's chief interpreter. It is said that the initial contact with Vogl was brought about through Schober's former brother-in-law, the Italian tenor Giuseppe Siboni who had married Schober's sister Ludovica in 1811. (That she had accidentally killed herself in 1812 while cleaning her husband's gun is one of several bizarre twists in the Schober family history.) The drawing of Vogl by Schober, made more or less at this time, is another indication of his reasonable skill as a draughtsman.

Schubert's sojourn at the Schober household came to an end in August 1817 when he had to vacate his room due to the impending

Schober's drawing of the baritone J. M. Vogl.

return to Vienna of Axel von Schober, Franz's older brother. The poet had to leave Vienna to look after him (Axel was ill and in the event never made it back, dying later that year) and the song *Abschied (Lebe wohl! Du lieber Freund!)* D578, dated 24 August 1817, was clearly written as a parting gift for Schober; it is the only solo song-setting made by the composer of his own words – a heartfelt lyric of farewell clouded by sad family circumstances. By this time Schubert might truly have considered himself part of the Schober family.

Between late 1818 and the beginning of 1821 Schubert shared a room with Johann Mayrhofer in the Wipplingerstrassse. He quit this arrangement in order to live for a while on his own, also in the Wipplingerstrasse, and perhaps for as long as a year, but in 1822 we find him again sharing rooms with Schober, in the Göttweiger Hof (Spiegelgasse 9, very near to where Salieri lived), an arrangement that lasted, on and off, for eighteen months. As well as providing this fairly long-term hospitality in the city centre, Schober called on his family connections to provide accommodation outside Vienna for him and his friends: the three summers of 1820, 1821 and 1822 were periods of great conviviality for the Schubertians, spent at Atzenbrugg Castle (just outside Vienna) which was owned by the poet's uncle, Josef Derfell. In September and October 1821, when Schubert and Schober were working on *Alfonso und Estrella* D732, they spent a month together at St Pölten where another of Schober's friends (actually a former lover of his mother's), Johann Nepomuk von Dankesreither, was bishop. This was the most intense period of collaboration between Schubert and Schober; they happily shared a room and wrote the opera at astonishing speed. The composer seems to have had absolute faith in his friend's ability as a librettist, a confidence not shared by Vogl who was

convinced that for a project of this size and importance Schober was far from an ideal choice. In this Vogl was sadly correct. Schober's verse may have been more accomplished than Kenner's, Schlechta's or Bruchmann's, but he should not have presumed (or accepted the invitation) to collaborate with Schubert on a project as big as an opera.

Writing in the *Schubertliedlexicon* (2012) Siegfried Schmalzriedt goes so far as to posit a full homosexual affair between the poet and composer whom he names a 'Dioscurenpaar' (twinned like Castor and Pollux) during the period of the composition of *Alfonso und Estrella* D732 in St Pölten – and even later, when the flower ballads *Viola* D786 and *Vergissmeinnicht* D792 contained references to a romantic attachment that was doomed, by the mores of the time, to impermanence. Perhaps this is completely untrue, but Schubert's blindness to Schober's limitations, or his resolve to ignore them, might be seen as the result of an enduring schoolboy crush at the very least. One thinks here of how Dickens's David Copperfield hero-worships the fascinating but fatally flawed Steerforth. Schober had all the attributes of height and looks that Schubert lacked. He was free of many of the mind-shackles (otherwise termed 'morality' or 'decency') that bound his contemporaries, he was affluent enough to follow his own caprice and he attracted everyone's attention when he entered the room. This was perhaps the man whom Schubert would have liked to be: Schubert's genius and Schober's appearance, united in one person, would have been the Byronic ideal – including that touch of lameness shared by Byron and Schober. Ilja Dürhammer has unearthed evidence that Schober had fostered adoration in his male friends for years. The love letters (for they are scarcely less) written to Schober by Adam Mittermayr, contemporary at the Kremsmünster school (see Dürhammer, 2006, pp. 184ff.) reveal the poet to have been the ultimate manipulative charmer, cool and in control, almost toying with the devotion he aroused in others. In later years he seems to have inspired a similarly romanticized hero-worship in the

Franz von Schober, pencil drawing by Leopold Kupelwieser, 12 July 1821, shortly before Schubert and Schober went off together to St Pölten to work intensively on *Alfonso und Estrella*.

young Moritz von Schwind. One senses that for Schober sex was more to do with mind-games and the wielding of power than with action. Even his reputation as a womanizer was largely built on hot air: he was far too narcissistic to commit himself to anyone else and all his relationships seem to have been doomed to failure. Nevertheless, music was the powerful adhesive between Schubert and Schober, and whatever the poet's failings, he was intensely musical and perspicacious enough to realize that Schubert was very special.

1822 was the year when the composer had a certain amount of money at his disposal from recently published compositions as well as copyrights recklessly sold off, and with Schober's help he lived life in greater style than ever before. With hindsight some contemporary observers referred to this period in the composer's life as 'dissolute'. After the rigours of sharing a small room with the prickly Mayrhofer, and then living on his own for the first time, life with Schober seems to have offered a heady combination of material comfort and the relaxation that is only possible in the company of very close friends. If the composer found a prostitute with the encouragement of Schober (who is usually blamed for having made the suggestion, as if such an idea could never have occurred to Schubert himself), he was unucky enough to have chosen badly. It was typical of Schober, however, that the judicious long view was usually sacrificed to the quick fix of short-term enjoyment. Throwing parties was a speciality. At this time a number of Schubertiads were organized at Schober's behest, as well as the reading gatherings ('Lesegesellschaften'), inspired by the Bildung circle of Mayrhofer and Ottenwalt, which took place three times a week at Schober's house. Among the works read aloud were Shakespeare's *Henry V*, Goethe's *Torquato Tasso* and Fouqué's *Der Zauberring* (which Schubert had actually read long before, *see Don Gayseros* D93). These gatherings are first mentioned by the composer in December 1822. It was at this time that Schubert's Goethe songs, Op. 14, dedicated to Schober, including the great love

songs *Suleika I* D720 and *Geheimes* D719, first appeared in print. It was perhaps the dedicatee who had introduced Schubert to the glories of Goethe's *West-östlicher Divan*. In the same month Schubert encountered the terrible symptoms of syphilis, the illness that was to change his life for ever.

Schober's reaction to this catastrophe is not directly recorded. We know from the way he avoided visiting Schubert on his deathbed that he was not at his best when dealing with sickness. But it is also true that Schubert was living with the Schobers at this time and they must have had no choice but to be deeply involved in the crisis and its fallout. Three of the most important Schober settings were composed in Spring 1823 – the lengthy flower ballads *Viola* D786 and *Vergissmeinnicht* D792, as well as *Pilgerweise* D789. The texts of all these songs reflect an atmosphere of fear and crisis – the allegory of *Viola* in particular is a powerful elegy for blighted hopes whatever significance it may have had regarding the relationship of poet and composer.

By August 1823 Schober had perhaps experienced enough stress regarding Schubert and his health crisis and he decided to make a new life in Breslau in Silesia (Wroclaw in present-day Poland) in an apparently do-or-die attempt to forge a career as an actor (he assumed the name 'Torupson' during this phase of his life). While he was away, and probably before, he seems to have pursued a plan that was the cause of a major scandal among the Schubertians: he had become secretly engaged to Justina von Bruchmann, sister of Franz von Bruchmann, another of Schubert's poet friends. On discovering this subterfuge during Schober's absence from Vienna, Bruchmann was horrified and scotched the lovers' plans without further ado. The result was the break-up of the original Schubert circle with Schubert taking Schober's side against Bruchmann. '[Schober] had the outrageous temerity', Bruchmann later wrote, 'to seek to sully one of the most precious jewels of my family.' It is notable that some years earlier the Spaun family had similarly put an end to Schober's relationship with Marie, the daughter of the house, albeit in a less dramatic manner.

Until recently Schober's life in Breslau has been something of a mystery. Research by Till Gerrit Waidelich (2008) reveals that, while in that city, Schober appeared on stage every three days or so, some 120 times in all, and in thirty-four different roles. None of these appearances was accorded more than a luke-warm reception by the press, and on one occa-sion his acting was described as that of a 'complete beginner'. While in Breslau Schober published a book of poetry entitled *Paligen-esien aus den heiligen Büchern des alten Bundes* (1826). This collection of forty-seven religious sonnets in the style of Pyrker's *Perlen der heiligen Vorzeit* without the hexameters, its title an imitation of Jean Paul, was clearly written to give its author further performing opportunities in Breslau within a fairly conven-tional religious community. In these portraits of the prophets, taken mainly from the book of Genesis, Schober puts words into the mouths of Abraham, David, Moses, Samuel and so on. As for the 'Lesegesellschaften' in Vienna, they were organized by others during Schober's absence, but they seem to have deteriorated according to the comments of both Moritz von Schwind and Schubert himself. The occasions were now dominated by a group of rabble-rousing 'hearties' who were there for the social fun and drinking rather than literary edification. In Schober's absence Schubert eventually disassociated himself from these gatherings.

The Breslau episode did not turn out as planned – nothing in Schober's life ever did. After an absence of two years he returned to Vienna in 1825, taking up where he had left off with his friends – apart from the enraged Bruchmann of course. No one welcomed the poet back more warmly than Schubert, who had written to him during his absence: 'you dear Schober I shall never forget, for what you meant to me no one else can mean, alas!' (Vienna, 30 November 1823) as well as the heartfelt lament for 'the good old days' begin-ning 'I hear you are not happy . . . this makes me extraordinarily sad' (Zseliz, 21 September

1824). Schober's sojourn in Breslau had one great advantage: new literature was available there untrammelled by Austrian censorship. He returned full of new literary ideas and enthusiasms, and perhaps even a suitcase of books smuggled across the border. The 'Lesegesellschaften' were re-established and Schober, firmly in charge from 1827 or early 1828, no doubt declaimed his *Paligenesien* poems to the circle. During this period, at weekly Saturday meetings, four works by Heinrich von Kleist were presented, as well as works by Ludwig Tieck (whom Schober had met in Dresden). Apart from the regular Goethe contributions, it was doubtless Heine's *Reisebilder* that made the strongest impression on Schubert. It was here that the six Heine songs, posthumously published in *Schwanen-gesang* D957/8–13, had their beginnings.

In the summer of 1826, and possibly that of 1828, Schubert stayed in Währing, just outside Vienna, once again at the invitation of the Schobers. In the autumn of 1826 Schober and Schubert shared a home like the old days, this time an apartment in the Bäckerstrasse (appro-priately enough the Schobers' money had originally come from a successful bakery). Subsequently, after a period on his own, Schubert moved back to the inner city to lodge once again ('beim blauen Igel') at the Schobers' family apartment in the Tuchlauben (from March 1827 until August 1828). Here he lived more comfortably than anywhere he had ever known, and had at his disposal a music room with piano and two further rooms. At this time Schubert, Schober and Schwind considered themselves something of an artistic triumvirate. The composition and publication, adorned with a Schwind vignette, of the comic trio *Der Hochzeitsbraten* D930, a setting of a Schober poem that may have been designed for an actual wedding in Austria or perhaps Breslau, represents unique evidence of this three-way collaboration.

Another aspect of Schober's life was his interest in the burgeoning art of lithography – the printing of images (often his own designs, drawings and portraits) via engrav-ings on limestone. He seems to have devel-

'Lieber Schober, ich höre, Du bist nicht glücklich?' ('Dear Schober, I hear you are not happy?'). Martha Griebler depicts Schubert writing to Schober from Zseliz on 21 September 1824.

oped a passion for this more practical side of art while living in Breslau. After a typically directionless period back in Vienna, during which time his friends despaired of his inactivity, he became absorbed in the making of lithographs, taking some trouble to master the time-consuming technical side of the printing process. In 1828 he purchased the Lithographisches Institut from Ferdinand Count Pálffy who had lost all his money in speculation and had to leave Vienna in a hurry. This firm had printed the Schubart setting *An den Tod* D518 in 1824 as a supplement to the *Allgemeine musikalische Zeitung* (26 June 1824), also offering the song for separate sale. It was almost certainly the Lithographisches Institut, under Schober's personal direction, that printed the invitations to Schubert's one and only private concert in March 1828 and the firm also issued the four songs of Op. 106 soon after. In the summer of the same year four further songs (Op. 96) were issued in rather amateur fashion, an indication of

Schober's fledgling status in the field of music publishing, and also of Schubert's willingness to support his friend's new venture, come what may. The firm eventually went into bankruptcy, due mainly to Schober's slow and cautious attitude to business decisions – a sad failure considering this was the one time in the poet's life when he seems to have lavished concentrated effort on an enterprise.

In the last weeks of his life the ailing Schubert left his comfortable inner-city abode with the Schobers to stay (he thought temporarily) with his brother Ferdinand in Neu-Wieden, where the air was supposedly better. He had every intention of returning to the bosom of the Schober family after he had recovered, but he never did so. Schober's apparent reluctance to visit the stricken composer at this time, perhaps through fear of infection, has contributed to the poet's bad reputation with posterity.

Schubert's music was not immune to Schober's criticism: the poet's displeasure with

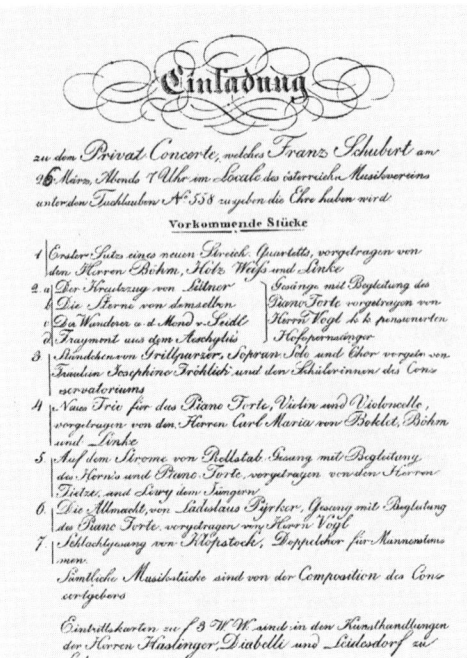

Invitation to the Schubert concert, March 1828, printed
by Schober's Lithographical Institute.

the piano sonatas in A minor and D major
(D845 and D850) was reported in Franz von
Hartmann's diary for 6 January 1827 (Schubert
was not present so these criticisms were made
entirely behind his back). Schober railed at
this music in such a manner that he almost
began an argument with Spaun. It is not hard
to detect jealousy here, or perhaps resentment
at these wordless works that had nothing
whatever to do with him or his literary
influence.

Schubert housed his scores at the Schober
home, and it was there that most of his manuscripts were to be found at his death. In a
letter written twenty years later to Ferdinand
Schubert, Schober points out that he had
returned the manuscripts to the family without
being asked to do so, and that – this with a
touch of retrospective regret – he had kept
only one, the autograph of *Jägers Liebeslied*
D909, a song to his own poem. At Schubert's
death Schober was one of the foremost
mourners, and the supportive role he had
played in the composer's life was gratefully

acknowledged by the Schubert family. They
asked the poet to provide a new version of his
poem *Pax Vobiscum* D551 so that it could be
performed at the funeral service in an arrangement for chorus with wind band accompaniment. Schober also designed the funeral
monument at the Währing cemetery with the
help of the architect Ludwig Förster.

Schober's later life seems to have rolled
along on an improvised wing and a charming,
if insincere, prayer. His mother died in 1833
and he became immersed in a court battle
regarding her will. He visited Hungary and
Bavaria (where his younger friend Moritz von
Schwind was making a great name for himself
as a painter), as well as Italy, France and
Belgium. He was never short of new friends:
in 1835 he became close to Ottilie, Goethe's
daughter-in-law, who was interested in his
Schubertian connections, and it was thanks to
Schober's later encouragement that Goethe's
grandchildren, Alma and Walther, became
interested in the new photographic techniques
of the Daguerrotype (Waidelich 2008, p. 173).
He probably became friendly with Liszt in
1838 when the latter played Schubert song
transcriptions in the Austrian capital. Schober
clearly saw the chance of a new career at the
side of the great pianist, and in the 1840s
attached himself increasingly to Liszt's circle.
At the beginning of 1845 he left Vienna for
good to make a new life in Weimar where Liszt
had been appointed a kind of Kapellmeister at
the ducal court. Here Schober became cham-
berlain and legation councillor.

Despite his ability to write poems, sometimes for music that saluted his new employer's genius, Schober was never to prove as
indispensable to Liszt as he had once been to
Schubert. People have often accused Liszt of
being a charlatan, but his new secretary,
the life and soul of the party, the charming
dilettante with a lazy streak and an ability to
'get away with murder', was his match in
this regard while having little of his talent.
Schober's derivative writing was fluent enough
and had a flair that might have been developed
with greater self-criticism and harder work,
but these are attributes that Schober never

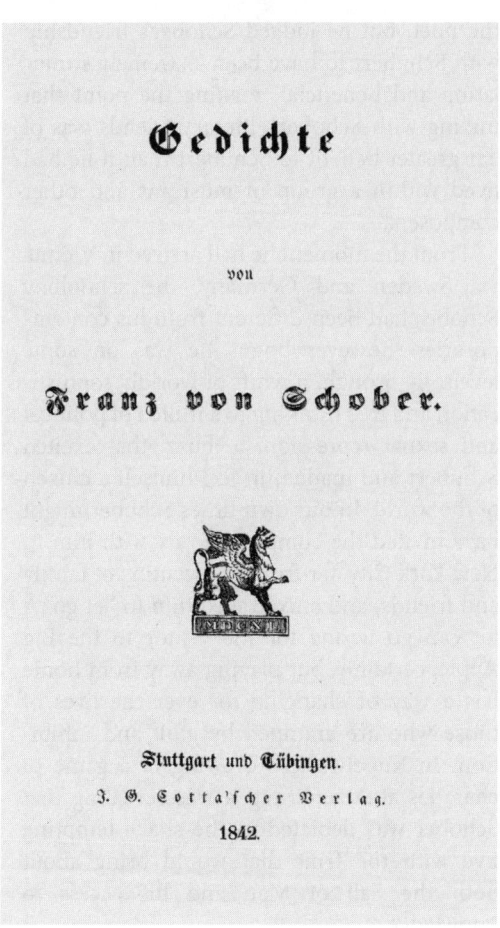

Gedichte

von

Franz von Schober.

Stuttgart und Tübingen.
J. G. Cotta'scher Verlag.
1842.

Schober's *Gedichte* (1842).

learnt from Schubert. Neverthless, in 1842 his *Gedichte* were issued by the firm of Cotta, Goethe's old publisher, a hugely flattering conjunction that was a typically Schoberian public-relations coup. The great poet, dead for only a decade, might have turned in his grave. A section of the volume entitled *Schattenrisse* is devoted to eleven word-portraits of the poets (again in Schober's favourite sonnet form) whom Schober most admired: Walter Scott, Byron, Goethe, Schiller, Jean Paul, Börne, Heine, E. T. A Hoffmann, J. H. Voss, Rückert and Mayerhofer [*sic*]. Both Schober and his mother had been subscribers to Mayrhofer's privately printed *Gedichte* in 1824, but the spelling mistake reveals

an indifference to detail especially when it concerned someone who had once been a close friend.

In 1848 Schober persuaded Liszt to mount a production of his and Schubert's opera, *Alfonso und Estrella* D732, but Liszt soon realized that the music was 'crushed by the weight of the text' (as he wrote on 24 February 1850 to Breitkopf & Härtel). Liszt was all for making a new text in French and superimposing it on the music but this would have removed Schober's main reason for promoting the opera – his own libretto. The incident led to a break between composer and poet. In the end, a one-off performance was given in Weimar on 24 June 1854 with Schober's text in truncated form. By then the poet had become something of a laughing stock as far as Liszt was concerned (Liszt's mistress, Marie d'Agoult, had earlier warned the great pianist that Schober's literary efforts were 'pedantic and mediocre').

Schober moved to Dresden in 1856 where he was married for a short time to Thekla von Gumpert, a reasonably gifted, middle-aged writer who longed for the type of love and respect that Schober was clearly unable to offer. He was terrified of loneliness in old age but his dealings with Thekla (as revealed by Waidelich) were self-centred and cruel. In May 1872 he received a 'golden' invitation from the Wiener Männergesang-Verein to the unveiling of the new Schubert statue by Carl Kundmann that had been erected in the Stadtpark, but he did not feel up to making the journey to Vienna. By this time Schubert's fame must have felt increasingly like a reproach to his own slender achievements.

Schober died in Dresden on 13 December 1882. It is said that he had written down his memories of Schubert soon after the composer's death but that these had been lost. This document might have been of the greatest importance to all students of the composer's life, for later on Schober could never be persuaded to reply to questions on the subject. He doubtless took with him to the grave many secrets concerning a man who was to be the sole reason for his own immortality. Whether

Schober aged seventy-three, photograph, J. Rumner & Co., Vienna 1869.

the poet, but he judged Schober's friendship with Schubert to have been 'extremely stimulating and beneficial', making the point that mixing with Schober's literary friends was of 'far greater benefit to Schubert than if he had lived within a group of musicans and other composers'.

From the moment he had arrived in Vienna via Sweden and Germany, the schoolboy Schober had been different from his contemporaries: however bogus he was on some levels, he brought a whiff of worldly sophistication and free thinking to a milieu of political and sexual repression, a 'buzz' that excited Schubert and made him feel himself a citizen of the world. In our own times Schober might have invited the composer to fly with him to New York City, far from the scrutiny of family and friends, and encouraged him to 'let go'. A lot can go wrong for the visitor to the Big Apple, certainly, but playing away from home has a way of changing for ever the lives of those who are cramped by guilt and inhibition. In Kupelwieser's drawing of a game of charades at Atzenbrugg it was revealing that Schober was depicted as the snake tempting Eve with the fruit that would bring about both the Fall of Man and his access to knowledge.

Perpetual Eden with its sin-free life is not the best milieu for artists. In a world without Schober we would perhaps have lost more than we gained: a less daring and enraptured Schubert might have been a less inspired creator – although he might have found a better opera librettist in 1821 and just possibly been spared syphilis in 1822. On the other hand, without that crisis and turning point the very existence of the two great Müller cycles (and much more besides) is doubtful, and without Schober we would have to face the bleak thought of a life without *An die Musik* D547.

his silence was due to loyalty, or simply because he could not be bothered, is impossible to fathom.

There were plenty who fell for Schober's charm (the young Moritz von Schwind, for example) and plenty who did not (the more sceptical Eduard von Bauernfeld). Many others, including Mayrhofer, Bruchmann and Josef Kenner (*see* the commentary on the song *Jägers Liebeslied* D909), seem to have been dazzled by Schober's friendship at one time or other. Several later turned against him, sometimes vehemently, like Bruchmann and Schwind. Whether Schubert, had he lived longer, would have revised his opinion of Schober is a moot point, but as it is there seems to have been scarcely a cloud in their friendship. The poet was clearly someone who made the composer feel more alive, more informed, more in the swim of culture, more daring and perhaps more *modern*. That most sane of men, Josef von Spaun, had his disagreements with

Bibliography: Eckhardt 1997
                Gunkel 1999
                Steblin 2002
                Waidelich 2008
                Schmalzriedt 2012

Detail from *Gesellschaftsspiel der Schubertianer in Atzenbrugg* (The Schubertans party games at Atzenbrugg). Watercolour by Leopold Kupelwieser, 1821. The charade is the Fall of Man with Schober as the snake, Kupelwieser the Tree of Knowledge and Jenger as Adam.

Die SCHÖNE MÜLLERIN
(Müller) Op. 25, **D795**
Completed by October/November 1823

The fair maid of the mill

Das Wandern D795/1, the first two lines of the first edition, 1824.

The origin of the story about the beautiful maid of the mill is difficult to trace. It was the subject of Paisiello's opera *L'amor contrastato* or *La bella Molinara* (1788) which made its triumphant progress through Germany under the title *Die schöne Müllerin*. In 1795 the young Beethoven wrote two sets of piano variations (WoO69 and 70) based on arias (the second of these based on the celebrated aria 'Nel cor più non mi sento') from this work. Paisiello's opera was performed in Vienna in 1822 when Schubert may well have seen it. Goethe had also written a sequence of poems entitled *Der Edelknabe und die Müllerin* ('The young lord and the miller maid') on this theme but he was not the only poet to write of romance at the mill; Brentano had used the same subject, as had Justinus Kerner. The famous anthology of folk poetry *Des Knaben Wunderhorn* has an entire sequence devoted to millers and miller maids. In his *Jugendlieder* (1810–13) Friedrich Rückert has a poem that contains these four lines which should be compared to the opening of *Am Feierabend*:

O wenn ich doch das Rädlein wär,	Oh if only I were that mill wheel
So wollt ich Lieb' ihr sausen;	How I'd whizz my love to her;
Und wär ich der Mühlbach unterher,	And if I were the millstream below
So wollt ich Lieb' ihr brausen.	I would roar my love to her.

Rückert's poem ends with the following lines that encapsulate the miller's fate in Schubert's cycle:

Und wenn ich nicht ruh' in der Müllerin Arm,	And if I can't rest in the miller maid's arms
So ruh' ich in ihren Wassern.	I shall rest in her stream.

Paisiello's opera was a great success in Berlin. It is to the lively cultural life in that city of salons immediately after the Napoleonic wars that we owe the birth of the narrative song cycle – if not as we know it then in its first incarnation as an amateur *Liederspiel* – a type of party game with music. A number of young artists gathered under the roof of Friedrich August von Stägemann, an important civil servant and supporter of the arts. Among his protégés were Achim von Arnim (co-editor of *Des Knaben Wunderhorn*) and Wilhelm Hensel who was later to be a notable painter and the husband of Fanny Mendelssohn, Felix's sister. At that time Hensel, still unmarried, was a close friend of the young poet Wilhelm Müller who had been a fellow private volunteer in the war to free the Germans from French domination. Also present at Stägemann's gatherings was the young Ludwig Rellstab (qv) who was to become a famous critic and one of the last poets to be set by Schubert. The circle was enlivened by Luise, Hensel's eighteen-year-old sister, and the sixteen-year-old daughter of the house, Hedwig von Stägemann. Luise Hensel is a crucial part of the genesis of this cycle because Müller was deeply and hopelessly in love with her at the time that some of the poems were written. Some of the moods in the cycle of poems seem to have been suggested by incidents during Müller's shy and diffident courtship of Luise. We know this because of a diary Müller kept for the last three months of 1815 and part of 1816 (quoted in some of the commentaries below). This *Tagebuch*, which resurfaced in 1900, happens to have survived the fire in Dessau that destroyed the majority of the poet's books and papers.

Someone in the circle of young friends hit on the idea of making a collaborative play in the form of a poetry contest where each character had to write his or her own words. The story was to be about Rose, the miller's daughter, and her rival suitors – the miller, the hunter, the gardener and the country squire. At the end Rose was to be so shocked by the miller's suicide that she too would throw herself into the brook, after which the hunter would sing a lament at the lovers' graves. In this concept, uncomfortably reminiscent of Pyramus and Thisbe, Hedwig played the

Müllerin, Hensel the hunter, his sister the gardener, Förster a publisher and another member of the circle the squire. Wilhelm Müller was somewhat predictably assigned the role of the miller.

Ludwig Berger (1777–1839) (*see* COMPOSERS) was persuaded to write the music for this *Lied-erspiel*. Much older than the rest of the circle, he probably had little patience with the amateur nature of the enterprise and the inevitably uneven accomplishment of the literary contributions. We do not know much of the performance of the work as first envisaged, but Berger must quickly have seen that young Müller's poems, which were written in the first person and from the miller's point of view, were better than the others. Thanks to Berger, who, according to Rellstab, took Müller in hand and mercilessly nagged him until he felt the poems were right, a metamorphosis took place and a poetic cycle gradually emerged – one, moreover, which was specially crafted for music. The Berger cycle consists of ten songs. Five of these use Müller's texts, beginning with *Wanderlied* (which we now know as *Wohin?*) and ending with *Des Baches Lied* (Schubert's *Des Baches Wiegenlied*). Although not comparable to Schubert's cycle, Berger's work deserves a hearing; it is considerably more interesting than later songs to these texts by Spohr, Klein, Reissiger and Curschmann.

After his dealings with Berger the poet gradually expanded the concept, filling in narrative gaps, and the text for *Die schöne Müllerin* came into being more or less as we know it. There are moments in Müller's work where some of his cohorts' ideas have been taken on board, particularly those of Luise Hensel whose poems were published alongside Müller's in an almanac soon after their composition. In 1817 Müller left Berlin for Egypt (although he got no further than Rome) and the party days among the young people were over. The poems were published in small groups in various newspapers before the final version of the complete cycle (with the words 'to be read in winter' printed under the title) was assembled. Müller read it aloud to

Hedwig von Stägemann, the original schöne Müllerin, a sepia drawing by her mother, 1807.

Hedwig von Stägemann, pencil drawing by Wilhelm Hensel, 1821.

Ludwig Tieck in a meeting outside Dresden in 1820. Tieck, the greatest literary authority of the day, was generally encouraging (Müller later expressed his gratitude for the part Tieck had played in the poems reaching publication) although he disapproved of the tragic ending of *Die schöne Müllerin*. Nevertheless, Müller retained the miller boy's suicide, probably because this had been an essential part of the *Liederspiel* from its inception. The cycle of poems appeared in print in 1821 as part of a much bigger collection of Müller poems entitled *Sieben und siebzig Gedichte aus den hinterlassenen Papieren eines reisenden Waldhornisten* ('Seventy-seven poems from the posthumous papers of a travelling horn-player').

Schubert's first biographer, Kreissle von Hellborn, recounts a story which, because of several inconsistencies, is probably apocryphal: Schubert is said to have come across the Müller book in the library of Benedict Randhartinger and been so taken with the poetry that he simply pocketed it and went home. Randhartinger called on him the next day to retrieve his property and was astonished to receive from the composer not only apologies for his strange behaviour but the first songs in the cycle.[1] There are other theories about the work's genesis. Susan Youens

Luise Hensel, drawing by her brother Wilhelm Hensel, 1828.

suggests the possibility that Schubert was introduced to Müller's poetry by no less a celebrity than Carl Maria von Weber (the dedicatee of Müller's second *Waldhornisten* anthology) who visited Vienna in 1822. When attempting to date the composition of the cycle exactly, we are stymied on account of its having been composed during the most stressful year of the composer's life. The one surviving autograph of a single song from the set is dated October 1823. Walther Dürr argues that this was more or less the time when Schubert found himself in hospital as a result of his venereal infection, and there is some contemporary evidence (the memoirs of Spaun corroborated by Schober) that the composer worked on *Die schöne Müllerin* when he was in such an institution. On the other hand, June and July 1823 are shrouded with mystery – this time slot seems to have disappeared from the Schubertian calendar in terms of surviving documents. A veil drawn over this period perhaps conceals another sojourn in hospital. In late July, Schubert went on holiday, returning to Vienna only in mid-September. John Reed thinks that the holiday in Upper Austria is likely to have been recuperative – following, rather than preceding, hospital treatments – but the question remains open. The diary of Franz von Hartmann (quite possibly reliable in this instance) mentions the *Müller-lieder* performed by Vogl and Schubert at the end of July in Linz. Even if the cycle had not been completed by this point, we can be certain that the work was safely finished well before

---

[1] It was Randhartinger who accompanied Julius Stockhausen in the first complete performance of the cycle in Vienna in 1856.

the end of November when Schubert wrote to Schober in Breslau informing him that the 'mill songs' were due to be printed 'in four books, with vignettes by Schwind'.

Müller's cycle contains five more items than Schubert chose to set (there is also a sixth poem, *Ein ungereimtes Lied*, which Müller originally planned as part of the work and which was restored to the sequence in the Hyperion recording): in *Der Dichter, als Prolog* and *Der Dichter, als Epilog* the poet offers an apologia before and after the main body of the work in the form of speeches in front of the curtain. As well as these gently ironic pieces there are three sizeable poems that Schubert left out of his setting. The first adds a great deal to our understanding of the miller girl's daily life (*Das Mühlenleben*), while the other two illuminate the despair of the boy towards the end of the work (*Erster Schmerz, letzter Scherz* and *Blümlein Vergissmein*). In this commentary the poems are interpolated in Müller's order. Schubert's music does not need prologue or epilogue to achieve its full effect, but the poems' domestic origins as explained above are very much clearer when the cycle is heard framed by these readings. The composer missed out *Das Mühlenleben* so that the girl's character was not as fully drawn and is therefore more mysterious, and the two other poems, fascinating commentaries on the boy's disturbed mental condition, were sacrificed to aid the dramatic tension of the whole and to conserve a tight structure as the cycle moves inexorably to its conclusion.

In this book the poems of *Die schöne Müllerin* are versified and punctuated as they are to be found in Schubert's source, the 1821 edition of *Sieben und siebzig Gedichte aus den hinterlassenen Papieren eines reisenden Waldhornisten*. This includes the use of bold script for the beginning of each poem. For the 1826 edition Müller made a number of changes and many subsequent printings of these poems have adopted those changes, thus unwittingly increasing the number of the deviations Schubert appeared to have made from the poet's original text.

The composition of the cycle was overshadowed by the composer's illness and his recuperation in the Allgemeines Krankenhaus in the ninth district. This is more fully discussed at the end of the commentary on this cycle. The publication of the work in the following year, 1824, was also beset with difficulties. The publishers Sauer & Leidesdorf experienced several production problems and dragged their feet with continuing inefficiency. The planned vignettes by Moritz von Schwind either failed to materialize or were never used. The first book (of five) appeared in mid-February 1824, the second more than a month later and the three remaining books were not advertised until mid-August whereas it would have made much more sense for a narrative cycle of this kind to have been issued without large gaps between instalments. By the summer of 1824 Schubert was resident in Zseliz, the country castle of Count Esterházy, where he was employed as music tutor, and so the proofreading of the last three books was left in the hands of Ferdinand Schubert who was not up to the task. The composer found the actions of Leidesdorf incomprehensible and asked Mortiz von Schwind to scold the publisher 'scandaleusement' on his behalf – only partly in jest. The haphazard publication schedule adversely affected the work's reception, much to Schubert's disappointment. Even Schober in faraway Breslau bemoaned the fact that the Müllerin songs had failed to make an impression.

Shortly after Schubert's death the copyright for the work passed from Leidesdorf to the publisher Anton Diabelli who was not content to use the existing plates and ordered a new engraving for a second edition that appeared in 1830. This gave him the chance to alter the content of the music by publishing a version of the cycle that included ornamented variants of certain songs, stemming partly from those used in performance by the baritone Johann Michael Vogl and partly from Diabelli himself. We know this from the singer Josef Gänsbächer (*see* SINGERS) who, in 1864, was unimpressed that Diabelli (whom he calls 'the hero of the potpourri') should have seen fit to hatch 'the cuckoo's eggs that Vogl had laid in the Müller songs'. This edition was later condemned as a forgery by Max Friedlaender and from the 1880s

The title page of the first edition of *Die schöne Müllerin* (1824).

singers slowly reverted to the text of the first edition as reprinted by Peters. Nevertheless, for fifty years Diabelli's version was taken to be an accurate reflection of Schubert's intentions. Corrupt as it is, its value today is that it gives us a glimpse (incomplete and rather arbitrary) into the performing practice of singers of the generation before Schubert's. The old art of ornamenting a vocal line *ad libitum* was fast going out of fashion, and the composer presumably only put up with it out of respect for Vogl, a senior artist recently retired from the opera stage. On occasion, however, Schubert would adopt Vogl's suggested changes and incorporate them into the music when it was published. Eduard von Bauernfeld remembered 'amicable disputes' on matters such as these between singer and composer. The NSA separately prints (Volume 2b) the four songs in the cycle most affected by these changes. A complete facsimile of the 1830 edition edited by Walther Dürr was published by Bärenreiter in 1996.

The covers of Diabelli's 1830 edition boast a rather bizarre vignette (not by Moritz von Schwind) where the maid of the mill is the wrong size and out of proportion with the mill buildings, trees and animals in the background, clearly a scissors and paste job (see below, p. 881). It is a collage that bears an anachronistic resemblance to Peter Blake's design for the cover of the *Sgt. Pepper* LP. This is a perhaps a stronger connection between the Beatles and Schubert than the one famously proposed in the 1960s by the *Times* critic, William Mann.

Poet:	Wilhelm Müller (1794–1827); poems written in 1817
Autograph:	Missing or lost apart from XV *Eifersucht und Stolz* (first draft) dated October 1823, Gesellschaft der Musikfreunde, Vienna
First edition:	Published as Op. 25 by Sauer & Leidesdorf, Vienna in 1824 (issued in five books between February and August)
Second edition:	Published as Op. 25 by Ant. Diabelli & Co., Vienna, 1830. The allocation of songs to five separate books is the same as for the first edition, although the volumes were issued together rather than at intervals
Dedicatee:	Karl Baron von Schönstein [both editions]
First known performance:	Items from the cycle were performed at a semi-private event at the Stift St Florian, Vienna by Antonie Adamberger and Anton Kattinger

in early October 1826 (see Waidelich/Hilmar Dokumente II No. 410b; Deutsch Doc. Biog. No. 708)

First known complete performance given by Julius Stockhausen & Benedict Randhartinger on 6 May 1856 at the Musikverein, Vienna.

Publication reviews: *Wiener-Zeitung*, No. 38 (17 February 1824), p. 168 [Waidelich/Hilmar Dokumente I No. 248]

Subsequent editions: Peters: Vol. 1/4–53; AGA XX 433–52: Vol. 7/134; NSA IV: Vol. 2a/21–93; Bärenreiter: Vol. 1/147–201

Bibliography: Goertz 2002, pp. 73–81

Gülke 1991, pp. 216–61

Hilmar 1993², p. 35 (newly discovered manuscripts in Karoline Esterházy's collection)

Hilmar-Voit 1991², p. 19

Mayer 1991, pp. 29–36

Newbould 1997, pp. 293–7

Youens 1992

Youens 1997, pp. 1–42 & 159–203

Further settings: Rainer Bredemeyer (1929–1995) *Die schöne Müllerin. Monodramatische Szene für Bariton, Streich- und Hornquartett* (1986)

DER DICHTER, ALS PROLOG [H525+]

The poet, by way of prologue

This poem was not set to music by Schubert.

Ich lad' euch, schöne Damen, kluge Herrn,	Fair ladies, wise gentlemen,
Und die ihr hört und schaut was Gutes gern,	And all who enjoy a good spectacle,
Zu einem funkelnagelneuen Spiel	I invite you to a brand-new entertainment
Im allerfunkelnagelneusten Stil;	In an absolutely brand-new style.
Schlicht ausgedrechselt, kunstlos zugestutzt,	Simply fashioned, artlessly arranged,
Mit edler deutscher Hoheit aufgeputzt,	Adorned with noble German simplicity,
Keck wie ein Bursch im Stadtsoldatenstrauss,	As jaunty as a lad in a town soldier's uniform;
Dazu wohl auch ein wenig fromm für's Haus:	And there's also a little pious humility for the Audience.
Das mag genug mir zur Empfehlung sein,	For me that's enough of a recommendation;
Wem die behagt, der trete nur herein.	If you too like the sound of it, then come in.
Erhoffe, weil es grad' ist Winterzeit,	As it's wintertime I expect
Tut euch ein Stündlein hier im Grün nicht leid;	You won't regret a brief hour here in the countryside;
Denn wisst es nur, dass heut' in meinem Lied	For just let me say that in my song today
Der Lenz mit allen seinen Blumen blüht.	Spring blooms with all its flowers.
Im Freien geht die freie Handlung vor,	The impromptu action takes place outside,
In reiner Luft, weit von der Städte Tor,	In the fresh air, far from city gates,
Durch Wald und Feld, in Gründen, auf den Höhn;	Through the woods and fields, in the hills and valleys,
Und was nur in vier Wänden darf geschehn,	And whatever can only happen between four walls
Das schaut ihr halb durch's offne Fenster an,	You'll half see through the open window;

So ist der Kunst und euch genug gethan.	Thus Art is satisfied, and you too.
Doch wenn ihr nach des Spiels Personen fragt,	Yet if you ask about the characters in the play
So kann ich euch, den Musen sei's geklagt,	The Muses are to blame: I can
Nur e i n e präsentiren recht und ächt,	Really and truly present to you but *one*,
Das ists ein junger blonder Müllersknecht.	A young, blond miller's lad.
Denn, ob der Bach zuletzt ein Wort auch spricht,	For, though the brook also speaks at the end,
So wird ein Bach deshalb Person noch nicht.	This doesn't make a brook into a character.
Drum nehmt nur heut' das Monodram vorlieb:	So today you must make do with a one-man drama.
Wer mehr giebt, als er hat, der heisst ein Dieb.	He who gives more than he has is a thief.
Auch ist dafür die Szene reich geziert,	The set, too, is richly decorated,
Mit grünem Sammet unten tapeziert,	Carpeted with green velvet,
Der ist mit tausend Blumen bunt gestickt,	Colourfully embroidered with a thousand flowers,
Und Weg und Steg darüber ausgedrückt.	With road and path marked out over them.
Die Sonne strahlt von oben hell herein	The sun shines down brightly
Und bricht in Tau und Tränen ihren Schein,	And refracts its light in dew and in tears;
Und auch der Mond blickt aus der Wolken Flor	And the moon, too, looks out from the veil of cloud,
Schwermütig, wie's die Mode will, hervor.	Melancholy, as fashion demands.
Den Hintergrund umkränzt ein hoher Wald,	The background is wreathed in tall woods;
Der Hund schlägt an, das muntre Jagdhorn schallt;	A dog barks, a hunting-horn rings out cheerfully;
Hier stürzt vom schroffen Fels der junge Quell	Here the infant spring gushes from the steep rock
Und fliesst im Tal als Bächlein silberhell;	And, now a silvery brook, flows in the valley.
Das Mühlrad braust, die Werke klappern drein,	The mill-wheel roars, the machinery rattles,
Man hört die Vöglein kaum im nahen Hain.	And you can hardly hear the birds in the nearby grove
Drum denkt, wenn euch zu rauh manch Liedchen klingt,	So if you find many of these ditties too rough-and-ready,
Dass das Lokal es also mit sich bringt.	Bear in mind that this goes with the setting.
Doch, was das Schönste bei den Rädern ist,	But the fairest thing about these wheels
Das wird euch sagen mein Monodramist;	My solo actor will reveal.
Verrieth' ich's euch, verdürb' ich ihm das Spiel:	If I were to give it away, it would spoil his play.
Gehabt euch wohl und amüsiert euch viel!	Farewell, and enjoy yourselves!

Bibliography:	Youens 1997, pp. 164–9		
Discography and timing:	Fischer-Dieskau	—	
	Hyperion I 25[1]		
	Hyperion II 28[1]	2'50	Dietrich Fischer-Dieskau

← *Romanze (Der Vollmond strahlt)* D797/3b   *Das Wandern* D795/1 →

I Das WANDERN

OP. 25 NO. 1, **D795/1** [H526]
B♭ major

Wandering

Das Wan-dern ist des Mül-lers Lust, das Wan-dern,

(24 bars)

Das Wandern ist des Müllers Lust,	To wander is the miller's delight;
Das Wandern!	To wander!
Das muss ein schlechter Müller sein,	A poor miller he must be
Dem niemals fiel das Wandern ein,	Who never thought of wandering,
Das Wandern.	Of wandering.
Vom Wasser haben wir's gelernt,	We have learnt it from the water,
Vom Wasser!	From the water!
Das hat nicht Rast bei Tag und Nacht,	It never rests, by day or night,
Ist stets auf Wanderschaft bedacht,	But is always intent on wandering,
Das Wasser.	The water.
Das sehn wir auch den Rädern ab,	We can see it in the wheels too,
Den Rädern!	The wheels!
Die gar nicht gerne stille stehn,	They never care to stand still
Die sich mein Tag nicht müde gehn,	But turn tirelessly the whole day long,
Die Räder.	The wheels.
Die Steine selbst, so schwer sie sind,	The stones themselves, heavy as they are,
Die Steine!	The stones!
Sie tanzen mit den muntern Reihn	They join in the merry dance
Und wollen gar noch schneller sein,	And seek to move still faster,
Die Steine.	The stones.
O Wandern, Wandern, meine Lust,	O wandering, my delight,
O Wandern!	O wandering!
Herr Meister und Frau Meisterin,	Master and mistress,
Lasst mich in Frieden weiter ziehn	Let me go my way in peace,
Und wandern.	And wander.

This is the first of Schubert's forty-six Müller solo settings (1823, 1827 and 1828). See the poet's biography for a chronological list of all the Müller settings.

At the start of the journey the pianist's hands shift to the lower half of the keyboard; the feeling is of rolling up the sleeves to begin the miller's journey with earthy, homespun music, simple

Das Wandern: The miller boy addresses the miller and his wife ('Frau Meister und Frau Meisterin') to whom he has
been apprenticed. Woodcut from the 'Prachtausgabe' of the cycle (1872).

and good-hearted. There is no other opening like it in all song literature. The pianist's right hand grips the rippling notes of a B flat major chord, briefly adds the third above, then twists back at the beginning of b. 2 to an awkwardly placed E flat (the second finger crosses over the thumb in an unusual figuration and then back again); this launches a tricky leap to an F major chord before a return to the tonic. This figure, all over in a matter of seconds, is repeated many times. In these rotations of the hand it is as if the accompanist is kneading musical dough before patting and cajoling blocks of simple wholemeal chords into shape. The lower reaches of the keyboard here suggest a masculine heartiness, even roughness. With a vocal line of immortal, yet seemingly obvious, tunefulness the protagonist introduces himself. The young miller is feeling the need to get away from his home town; cap in hand he asks permission of his present master and mistress – the 'Herr Meister und Frau Meisterin' (bb. 32–4) of the last strophe. He explains that millers have always delighted in roving; it was customary for young workers to gain their work experience by moving from mill to mill while at the same time seeing a bit of the world, and he points out that he would indeed be a bad miller if he did not feel this wanderlust. The use of the word 'Müller' signifies an in-joke: the poet is also referring to his own taste for travel to far-flung places. Not surprisingly Müller took the role of the miller in the party games associated with the presentation of the story in Berlin, and Schubert's cycle is known in Germany and Austria as *Müllerlieder*.

Müller has his protagonist enthusiastically outlining for his master and mistress the joys of travel. Schubert, on the other hand, knowing that it would be ill-advised to delay the journey from a dramatic point of view, has imagined the young man immediately on the open road. This can be felt in the sheer energy of the music with its infectious bounce and swinging nonchalance. The insistent tonic harmony is so simple that in other hands it might make a static impression, but the beats that change to the dominant are all the more powerful where they are cunningly placed to propel the music forward. The playful joy of physical activity is reflected in the leapfrogging phrase of 'Das Wandern ist des' (b. 5) to which is appended a little arpeggio on 'Müllers Lust' (b. 6) that expresses an overflowing happiness in the first and last verse. The same figure is also an ideal analogue in the second verse for the tumbling movement of cascading water harnessed to the mill-wheel, and for the circular movement of the wheels themselves in the third.

This all-purpose expressiveness, where a tune is made to serve more than one illustrative purpose, is a sign of Schubert's hard-won mastery of the strophic song – the fruit of many years' work in the medium, particularly between 1814 and 1816. The piano of course is a helpful accomplice in all this: its rippling semiquavers are ideal for water music, something in which Schubert was expert; left-hand striding quavers can be gently supportive, playful for the cascading water or brought out in honour of the heavy millstones. As Gerald Moore suggested, hairpin dynamics in the third verse can suitably illustrate the turn of the mill-wheel over each two-bar phrase.

It is interesting that we hardly glimpse here the real character of the young miller as we will come to know him. He is putting on his most rational face to the 'Herr Meister' and his wife. He feels he *ought* to be devoted to the idea of going forth and becoming a better miller, but because romance is not yet on the agenda he has not found his real purpose. As we discover in the fifth song, *Am Feierabend*, his body is not best suited to the hard physical work of the mill but, as a working-class boy, he knows little else of life and he will gladly do what is expected of him. We are told nothing of his earlier background or home life; it remains a mystery whether it is neglect on the part of his family or overprotectiveness that has inspired his desire to travel. This cheery music is sung by the character that others expect him to be – determined, industrious, a man's man and a good member of the Guild. At the beginning of the cycle at least the young miller feels himself part of a community and an ongoing tradition.

Das Wandern, woodcut in *Lieder, Balladen und Romanzen* (1871).

As any visitor to Germany or Austria will know, walking is a communal activity with knapsack and a jolly ditty (rather like this one) sung in harmony. As Charles Rosen writes in *The Romantic Generation*, 'The country walk and its ideology as a direct contact with nature through physical activity often pushed to the point of exhaustion, dominated German and, less powerfully, English culture from the mid-eighteenth century until the Second World War.' Throughout the song there is a distinct feel of folk music to be sung in the open air. At bb. 12–16, 'Das muss ein schlechter Müller sein, / Dem niemals fiel das Wandern ein' (a phrase that sounds like received wisdom rather than original thought), we hear complicitous thirds and tenths between the vocal and bass lines; the harmony, as if sung by chums harmonizing at a party, betokens an uncomplicated view of the world as seen from the middle of the tracks.

Only perhaps in the seventh song, *Ungeduld*, do we hear again such hearty masculine confidence. In the context of the rest of the cycle this back-slapping bonhomie is thoroughly unconvincing; indeed this, despite later titles to the contrary, is probably the greenest song in the set. The miller boy is not yet an outsider, but there is a sign that he is already a dreamer. The challenges faced by the singer in terms of control of dynamics and colour in this song led Julius Stockhausen (the first singer to perform the complete cycle in public some thirty years after its composition) to consider it a revealing test of vocal technique. The tricky echoes of the final words at the end of each strophe ('Das Wandern, das Wandern' bb. 19–20 and so on), profoundly Schubertian, are a sign that here is a protagonist whose waters run deeper than one might expect.

These are metaphors for new freedoms that the young apprentice can scarcely imagine but for which his soul longs. Countless great artists and creative dreamers, whose names we shall never know, have been locked into a way of life because of an accident of birth and upbringing that has utterly obliterated their gifts. This young man's ability is to see, and indeed feel, significances in his mind's eye where his peers see only what is in front of their noses: his poetic streak enables him to experience the deepest emotion, but the subtlety of his responses, so at odds with his station in life, will also be instrumental in his downfall.

First edition:	Published as Op. 25 by Sauer & Leidesdorf, Vienna in 1824 (advertised in February), Book 1, no. 1 (P52)
Second edition:	Published as Op. 25 by Ant. Diabelli & Co., Vienna in 1830. The allocation of songs to five separate books is the same as for the first edition, although the volumes were issued together rather than at intervals.
Subsequent editions:	Peters: Vol. 1/4; AGA XX 433: Vol. 7/134; NSA IV: Vol. 2a/21; Bärenreiter: Vol. 1/147
Bibliography:	Black 2003, pp. 13–14 Youens 1992, pp. 4–35 & 74
Arrangements:	Arr. Franz Liszt (1811–1886) for solo piano, no. 1 of *Müllerlieder* (1846) [*see* TRANSCRIPTIONS] Arr. Leopold Godowsky (1870–1938) for solo piano, *Wandering* (1927, 2nd revised edition 1937) [*see* TRANSCRIPTIONS] Arr. Tilman Hoppstock (b. 1961) for guitar accompaniment, in *Franz Schubert: 110 Lieder* (2009), 2 versions
Discography and timing:	Fischer-Dieskau III 1[1] 2'31 Pears–Britten 2'28 Hyperion I 25[2] Hyperion II 28[2] 2'35 Ian Bostridge

← *Der Dichter, als Prolog*   *Wohin?* D795/2 →

II WOHIN?   Where to?
OP. 25 NO. 2, **D795/2** [H527]
G major

Ich hört' ein Bächlein rauschen   I heard a little brook babbling
Wohl aus dem Felsenquell,   From its rocky source,
Hinab zum Tale rauschen   Babbling down to the valley,
So frisch und wunderhell.   So bright, so wondrously clear.

Ich weiss nicht, wie mir wurde,
Nicht, wer den Rat mir gab,
Ich musste auch hinunter[1]
Mit meinem Wanderstab.

Hinunter und immer weiter
Und immer dem Bache nach,
Und immer heller rauschte,[2]
Und immer heller der Bach.

Ist das denn meine Strasse?
O Bächlein, sprich, wohin?
Du hast mit deinem Rauschen
Mir ganz berauscht den Sinn.

Was sag' ich denn vom Rauschen?[3]
Das kann kein Rauschen sein:
Es singen wohl die Nixen
Tief unten ihren Reihn.[4]

Lass singen, Gesell, lass rauschen,
Und wandre fröhlich nach!
Es gehn ja Mühlenräder
In jedem klaren Bach.

I know not what came over me,
Nor who prompted me,
But I too had to go down
With my wanderer's staff.

Down and ever onwards,
Always following the brook
As it babbled ever brighter
And ever clearer.

Is this, then, my path?
O brook, say where it leads.
With your babbling
You have quite befuddled my mind.

Why do I speak of babbling?
That is no babbling.
It is the water nymphs singing
As they dance their round far below.

Let them sing, my friend; let the brook babble
And follow it cheerfully.
For mill-wheels turn
In every clear brook.

This is the second of Schubert's forty-six Müller solo settings (1823, 1827 and 1828). See the poet's biography for a chronological list of all the Müller settings.

From the beginning we are aware that this is only a little brook, of no great consequence perhaps but nevertheless 'a *dear* little stream' as our nineteenth-century forbears would not have blushed to call it. Moreover the brook is, as yet, free of the mill-wheel, not yet put to work for man's purposes. Schubert conveys this leisurely characteristic in the gently bubbling sextuplets, all contained within the span of a relaxed right hand; the left in quavers is also contained in the drone of a fifth, the pull of a current that gently yet firmly underpins the water's flow. Everything here is of moderate dimensions (this is no Wagnerian salute to Father Rhine) but this very simplicity is eloquently indicative of the German modesty and folksiness of the period, conceived 'Mit edler deutscher Hoheit' as Müller's prologue to Die schöne Müllerin puts it. Accompanists who are not born to this tradition have to enter into its German spirit. It is far too easy to make this stream glint and dart in invigorating manner, as bracingly energetic as a mountain stream in the Scottish Highlands, but Müller's stream does not flow in the wild land of Fingal, with a sweeping and heroic landscape peopled by warriors. Instead this is a fairy-tale forest in which every corner is animated with anthropomorphic life.

[1] This line is correct as Schubert found it in Müller's *Gedichte* (1821). In the second edition of these *Gedichte* (1826) Müller changes the line to 'Ich musste *gleich* hinunter'.
[2] The last two lines of this strophe are correct as Schubert found them in *Gedichte* (1821). Müller changes this (*Gedichte*, 1826) to 'Und immer *frischer* rauschte' to avoid the repetition of 'heller'. The performer has to make a choice whether to incorporate the poet's later changes into Schubert's work.
[3] Müller writes 'Was sag' ich denn *von* Rauschen'. The change to 'vom' is Schubert's.
[4] In the second edition of *Gedichte* Müller changes this line to 'Dort unten ihren Reihn'.

Earnest students of nature of this period in Germany, the first 'Greens', felt then as now that small is beautiful: concentrate on a tiny area, they reasoned, and careful scrutiny will reveal many layers of life. These poets and philosophers refused to be rushed in unseemly manner; they needed time and space in which to express themselves meaningfully. In this moderation we understand the nineteenth-century German reputation for *thoroughness*. Mercurial thought was not a characteristic of the Biedermeier mentality and the composer, perfectly capable of donning the winged shoes of Mercury should he so wish, has thought himself into a deliberately moderate folk style for these songs. His indication of *Mässig* (moderato – two in a bar) serves as a warning against the breakneck tempo favoured by almost every pianist who comes new to this piece. Each note of the accompaniment should be distinct, in gently purling fashion. This stream, companion of homespun sages, should flow in what might be termed a state of Schubertian equilibrium – neither too slow nor too fast.

'Ich hört' ein Bächlein rauschen', the miller says, immediately showing us that with his highly sensitized nature he has ears to hear what others might miss or take for granted, proving himself a true Romantic in the line of Novalis and Schlegel. How different this is from *Das Wandern*, a straightforward strophic song in five verses. There is no such mechanical formula here: the traveller is able to leave the machinery of mill-wheels behind and follow his fancy wherever it may lead him. His choice of words is eloquent: the 'Bächlein' of the opening is the diminutive of 'Bach' and the miller can later claim that this brooklet is *his*, probably because it is humble and unnoticed by many rather than being a glittering prima donna of the waterways. Significantly, as it gathers force in the third strophe 'Bächlein' gives way to 'Bach', but even then we are still talking about a small stream. The singer's melody is a world-famous miracle, so well known that it has the status of folksong. Only Schubert can make up a simple tune to such effect; in other hands it would be simply banal. Blessed by the master's touch this insouciant alternation between tonic and dominant achieves immortality, for this is the sort of melody that Nature herself sings: it seems always to have been there.

As the miller explains how it is that he came to follow the stream, having heard its babbling from the main path, one of Schubert's great achievements in this song is made plain: far from being a set piece, the music has the flexibility to mirror the boy's thoughts as they occur to him. The first two lines of the second strophe, 'Ich weiss nicht, wie mir wurde, / Nicht, wer den Rat mir gab' (bb. 10–14), are in fact recitative cleverly disguised as aria. The singer takes us into his confidence in conversational manner, yet we are not aware of a break in the melody – only that the harmony has strayed from the main path of G major in such a way as to suggest an aside (the diminished seventh on 'wurde' in b. 12, for example). Indeed the continuity of the accompaniment and the plastic nature of the vocal line hide a refined and rather complex formal structure that combines elements of the strophic song with the *durchkomponiert*. The first section consists of the first two strophes. The second section comprises the third strophe, which introduces new material – a sinuous vocal line at 'Hinunter und immer weiter' (bb. 22–4), doubled by the bass of the accompaniment, which is suited to the downward movement described by the words. The next two lines are a highly playful setting of 'Und immer heller rauschte, / Und immer heller der Bach' (bb. 26–30) which is repeated with even more ornamental coloratura for the voice, a high point in the song for semiquaver vocal writing of this kind. At the third section from b. 35 we revert to a recitative feeling with a dislocation of harmony to suggest a new thought ('Ist das denn meine Strasse? / O Bächlein, sprich, wohin?'), a question addressed to the brook but also obliquely to the audience. There is a yearning repeat of the word 'Wohin?' (bb. 39–40) that gives the song its title. The third and fourth lines of this strophe are set to the music of the sinuous vocal line referred to above. By importing this material more than once into later sections the composer builds up the song using a subtle web of musical cross references. We are now ready for a good old-fashioned recapitulation of the opening material (fourth section, fifth strophe, 'Es singen wohl die Nixen' from b. 57), although the singer (and the pianist, aided perhaps by pedal) have to find a new colour to suggest the singing of underwater sprites. It is the only time in the cycle that we hear of these nixies. Although Müller makes the stream itself the young miller's confidant and interlocutor, it is possible that throughout the cycle the stream, sometimes silent, sometimes turbulent, is doing the bidding of the spirits that live beneath the waters. Perhaps Müller had been influenced by his friend de la Motte Fouqué's *Undine* (1811), a tale of a water sprite who aquires a soul by wedding a mortal:

> *In den Seen, und Strömen und Bächen lebt der Wassergeister ausgebreitetes Geschlecht. In klingenden Krystallgewölben, durch die der Himmel mit Himmel mit Sonn' und Sternen hereinsieht, wohnt sich's schön[. . .] Die aber dorten wohnen sind gar hold und lieblich auszuschauen, weit schöner als die Menschen sind.*

> *(A vast family of water-spirits live in the lakes and streams and brooks. In domes of crystal, echoing with many sounds, through which heaven looks in with its sun and its stars, they find their beautiful home. . . Those who dwell there are very fair and lovely to behold – most of them more beautiful than human beings.)*

The final strophe *starts* with the 'sinuous vocal line' (as in the third strophe) and *ends* with a modified version of the opening music. Of course the innocent ear perceives none of this cross-weaving, only an endless stream of melody, divinely inevitable and immediately memorable. It is revealing that Leo Black (also acknowledging Brian Newbould) hears this song as the most miniature of sonata forms – with exposition, development and recapitulation. This explains the music's sense of completeness, and the listener certainly feels a satisfaction with the overall shape of the song. The tune at the opening is to be found note for note at the beginning of J. F. Christmann's *Ich ging im Mondenschimmer* (1784) and (for the upbeat and opening bar at least) in Mozart's 1787 masterpiece *An Chloe* K524. Schubert almost certainly knew the Mozart song but the similarity is not a sign of plagiarism so much as an indication that the repeated notes at 'Ich hört' ein Bächlein' belong to a fairly common folksong formula. The miracle is that Schubert, Mozart-like, was able to create so much magic from such a conventional opening.

The heartiness of *Das Wandern* is now forgotten although the composer has deliberately linked the two songs with the same time signature, a similar quaver *Bewegung* in the left hand and such features as dominant harmony over a tonic bass. If the songs belong together it is as a type of yin and yang, representing the boy's outer and inner worlds. In *Wohin?* his poetic nature is revealed: he hears voices and spirits; in true Romantic style he perceives life and mystery in all things; he is not afraid to give rein to his fantasies. The stream, his new friend, is cast as seducer and adviser, companion and accomplice. Some might detect the first hints that the young miller's is a delicate psyche, that there is a gap between how he really thinks and feels and how an uncomplicated working lad is expected to think and feel. In this song we hear the first references to the depths of the stream (in such phrases as the third strophe's 'Hinunter und immer weiter' bb. 23–5) where he will tragically come to rest at the end of the cycle. (The doubling of the vocal line with the piano bass in this passage is also to be found in other water music both ominous and mysterious – *Der Zwerg* D771 and *Aufenthalt* D957/5 from *Schwanengesang* come to mind.) Reference to the singing of the water nymphs also implants the prophetic idea of lovely sirens who lure men to their destruction. In the cycle's scenario the brook itself performs the seductive tasks normally given to the supernatural beings who swim beneath the surface. In the song's very last phrase, a succession of Ds on the final 'fröhlich nach' (the last note at b. 79 felicitously held for three beats over the rippling accompaniment) beautifully conveys the idea of a traveller wandering down the river path for ever. This is a deliberate ploy to reinforce the impact of the opening of *Halt!* where the protagonist is stopped in his tracks on coming upon the mill that lies further downstream.

First edition:	Published as Op. 25 by Sauer & Leidesdorf, Vienna in 1824 (advertised in February), Book 1, no. 2 (P53)
Second edition:	Published as Op. 25 by Ant. Diabelli & Co., Vienna in 1830
Subsequent editions:	Peters: Vol. 1/6; AGA XX 434: Vol. 7/136; NSA IV: Vol. 2a/23; Bärenreiter: Vol. 1/149
Bibliography:	Youens 1992, pp. 35–7 & 75–6
Further settings and arrangements:	Ludwig Berger (1777–1839) *Des Müllers Wanderlied* (1816)
	Arr. Franz Liszt (1811–1886) for solo piano, no. 5 of *Müllerlieder* (1846) [*see* TRANSCRIPTIONS]
	Edward James Loder (1813–1865) *I heard a brooklet rushing* (1850) [Müller poem translated by Longfellow]
	Arr. Leopold Godowsky (1870–1938) for solo piano, *The Brooklet* (1927, 2nd revised edition 1937) [*see* TRANSCRIPTIONS]
	Arr. Sergei Rachmaninoff (1873–1943) for solo piano, *Wohin?* (1925) [*see* TRANSCRIPTIONS]
	Arr. Tilman Hoppstock (b. 1961) for guitar accompaniment, in *Franz Schubert: 110 Lieder* (2009)
Discography and timing:	Fischer-Dieskau III 1² 2'24
	Pears-Britten 2'03
	Hyperion I 25³
	Hyperion II 28³ 2'30 Ian Bostridge

← *Das Wandern* D795/1   *Halt!* D795/3 →

III HALT!

Op. 25 no. 3, **D795/3** [H528]
C major

Halt!

(60 bars)

Eine Mühle seh' ich blinken[1]	I see a mill gleaming
Aus den Erlen heraus,	Amid the alders;
Durch Rauschen und Singen	The roar of mill-wheels
Bricht Rädergebraus.	Cuts through the babbling and singing.

[1] Müller writes (in both the 1821 and 1826 editions of the *Gedichte*) 'Eine Mühle seh' ich *blicken*'.

Ei willkommen, ei willkommen,   Welcome, welcome,
Süsser Mühlengesang!   Sweet song of the mill!
Und das Haus, wie so traulich!   How inviting the house looks,
Und die Fenster, wie blank!   How sparkling its windows!

Und die Sonne, wie helle   And how brightly the sun
Vom Himmel sie scheint!   Shines from the sky.
Ei, Bächlein, liebes Bächlein,   Now, dear little brook,
War es also gemeint?   Is this what you meant?

*This is the third of Schubert's forty-six Müller solo settings (1823, 1827 and 1828). See the poet's
biography for a chronological list of all the Müller settings.*

After the aqueous meanderings of the brook we suddenly perceive something substantial on
dry land (and in down-to-earth C major) which appears through the alders at a bend of the
river. The song title with its exclamation mark is apt: Schubert makes us hear that the miller
is suddenly confronted with his destiny. The exciting first sighting of the mill is conveyed to
us by the whirring sound of the wheel as the brook abandons the innocent insouciance of its
upstream incarnation in favour of taking its turn at a job of work. This is as much a surprise
to our ears as it is a shock to the eyes of the miller – a thrilling frisson of inner recognition.
The little seven-note motif, a roulade of semiquavers within the compass of a sixth, suggests
the turning of a wheel and is doubled in both hands to give the image a certain grandeur and
solidity. In antithesis to this forte phrase that illustrates the workings of early nineteenth-
century technology, there is a piano passage which shows the workings of the miller's
emotions: at the same time as providing an image of the mill, Schubert gives musical voice to
the invisible landscape of the soul. At b. 2 the right hand gently oscillates on its own, unsupported by the left. It is as if time stands still with the river gently flowing in the background,
having passed through its ride on the mill-wheel. On the last quaver of that bar an accented
low F sharp in the left hand forms the upbeat to a dotted minim G which then falls in an
arpeggio of staccato quavers into the depths of the bass clef (b. 4). This little phrase depicts
fear, uncertainty, excitement and, in the light of what we know about the part that this mill
will play in our hero's life and death, an ominous frisson. It is as if the miller is aware that he
is in the hands of fate and is powerless to resist it. This alternation of the mill-wheel's action
and the boy's inner reaction is repeated in the dominant minor, heightening the suspense.
Two further bars of right-hand semiquavers and pizzicato-like bass notes are needed to clear
the miller's thoughts that briefly move into the submediant (an A minor oscillation in b. 9).
He quickly pulls himself together via the dominant (G major) in b. 10 and steers himself back
to the tonic – the C major of reality – and what stands before him. From now on the mill-
wheel motif that opened the song pervades the left hand while the stream remains represented in the right.

The vocal line is enchanting and full of felicities. What could be more indicative of open-
hearted singing than the Italianate phrase 'Durch Rauschen und Singen' (bb. 15–17) for example?
'Bricht Rädergebraus' (bb. 17–19) describes the movement of the wheel in quavers that rise and
fall. We have by now moved into the dominant (G major). At b. 23, with the phrase 'Ei
willkommen', accompanied by the mill-wheel motif, we return to that mystical realm into which
the miller slips when he imagines portents and voices. With a harmonic focus softened by the
bass note of C (the third inversion of D^7) Schubert perfectly captures the other-worldly whimsy
of a mill's imaginary song. Everything about the place seems just right to the boy's enchanted

Halt! Woodcut from the 'Prachtausgabe' of the cycle (1872).

gaze. Phrases on the cosiness of the house ('Und das Haus, wie so traulich!' bb. 31–3) and the sparkling windows ('Und die Fenster, wie blank!' bb. 34–6) form an extended upbeat to a paean of grateful praise, in the warmest C major, to the sun which shines from heaven as if to bless this fortuitous discovery. This passage has an almost desperate happiness about it. There is no doubt that the miller hankers after security and that his desire to 'wander' has been short-lived. Throughout there is an element of exaggeration that perhaps betrays an unstable personality that might be termed manic-depressive in the light of later developments. Even after this apparent whole-hearted acceptance of the mill's attractive qualities, he does not quite have the courage of his convictions and has to ask the stream whether this was meant to be. The move from C major to F major–D minor at 'Ei, Bächlein, liebes Bächlein, / War es also gemeint?' (bb. 49–51) is similar in effect to 'Ist das denn meine Strasse? / O Bächlein, sprich, wohin?' in *Wohin?*. It is as if the miller is addressing an inner demon, externalized by the brook of course, but nevertheless buried deep within himself. Certainly the shift of key in both songs suggests an internal monologue rather than an ordinary conversation. The alternating major and minor repetitions of 'also gemeint' show a twinge of doubt in an otherwise radiant picture. At the end of the song the question 'Is this what you meant?' hangs in the air; the last things to be heard are the gentle rumble of the mill-wheel in the left hand and the neutral and equivocal C major oscillations of the brook in the right. This is the last opportunity for the miller to extricate himself from his tragedy, but he goes like a lamb to the slaughter. As he says in the next song, 'Ich gebe mich drein' – 'I yield to my fate.'

First edition:	Published as Op. 25 by Sauer & Leidesdorf, Vienna in 1824 (advertised in February), Book 1, no. 3 (P54)
Second edition:	Published as Op. 25 by Ant. Diabelli & Co., Vienna in 1830
Subsequent editions:	Peters Vol. 1/10; AGA XX 435: Vol. 7/140; NSA IV: Vol. 2a/29; Bärenreiter: Vol. 1/153
Bibliography:	Youens 1992, pp. 37–8 & 76–7
Discography and timing:	Fischer-Dieskau III 1[3] 1'34
	Pears–Britten 1'31
	Hyperion I 25[4]
	Hyperion II 28[4] 2'30 Ian Bostridge

← *Wohin?* D795/2   *Danksagung an den Bach* D795/4 →

IV DANKSAGUNG AN DEN BACH Op. 25 no. 4, D795/4 [H529]   Thanksgiving to the brook
G major

Etwas langsam

War es al - so ge - meint, mein rau-schen-der Freund,

(41 bars)

War es also gemeint,	Is this what you meant,
Mein rauschender Freund,	My babbling friend?
Dein Singen, dein Klingen,	Your singing, your murmuring –
War es also gemeint?	Is this what you meant?
'Zur Müllerin hin!'	'To the maid of the mill!'
So lautet der Sinn.	This is your meaning;
Gelt, hab' ich's verstanden?	Have I understood you?
'Zur Müllerin hin!'	'To the maid of the mill!'
Hat s i e dich geschickt?	Did *she* send you,
Oder hast mich berückt?	Or have you entranced me?
Das möcht' ich noch wissen,	I should like to know this, too:
Ob s i e dich geschickt.	Did *she* send you?

Nun wie's auch mag sein,	However it may be,
Ich gebe mich drein:	I yield to my fate:
Was ich such', hab' ich funden,[1]	What I sought I have found,
Wie's immer mag sein.	However it may be.
Nach Arbeit ich frug,	I asked for work;
Nun hab' ich genug,	Now I have enough
Für die Hände, für's Herze	For hands and heart;
Vollauf genug!	Enough, and more besides.

This is the fourth of Schubert's forty-six Müller solo settings (1823, 1827 and 1828). See the poet's biography for a chronological list of all the Müller settings.

Something has happened between the end of the previous song and the beginning of this: the young apprentice has met the miller's daughter and is immediately drawn to her, infatuated, in love. She will remain a fixation, for better or worse, for the rest of his short life. This encounter is understood to be a sacred, predestined moment, an event worthy of a hymn of thanksgiving. The instrumental line of the opening yields to and mingles with the vocal descant in a stately flowing manner. The piano writing has melodic interest in its own right which becomes supportive figuration when the singer takes over the shape of the introductory tune at b. 4 and modifies it a third higher. The whole is like a contrapuntal duet for two male voices, the entire right-hand accompaniment written in the bass clef to emphasize the colloquy. The word 'Danksagung' (thanksgiving) with its religious overtones has prompted the composer to write a hymn of gratitude in an old-fashioned, quasi-sacred manner. In the third bar of this introduction there is the first of two mordents in the cycle, highlighting the intentional antique style. Such an ornament also appears in *Am Feierabend* in the section depicting the time-honoured custom of sitting in a circle at an evening meal. At times (at the end of the first strophe on 'War es also gemeint?', for example) *Danksagung an den Bach* has the texture of a three-part invention of the greatest economy and lucidity.

We have returned to the G major tonality of *Wohin?* and this seems appropriate as attention has shifted from the discovery of the mill back to the brook. The opening of the vocal line is of course a recapitulation of the closing words of the previous poem ('War es also gemeint') but the meaning has changed as if italics had now been added – 'Is *this* what you meant?' The miller had simply been hoping for a safe place to stay and work; instead he has encountered love. Thus these words now credit the omniscient brook with even greater prophetic powers than before. The opening of the second strophe ('Zur Müllerin hin!' bb. 10–11) mentions the girl for the first time, and for the first time a C sharp is introduced into the prevailing G major harmony as if to emphasize that this really is a new direction, and a new character in the drama has been introduced. This brings about a brief dalliance in the direction of D major, but there is an almost immediate and shy retreat from this tonality on 'So lautet der Sinn', b. 12, as if the miller suddenly wonders if he has been pushing his luck to believe that this is what the stream has really meant. On the word 'Gelt' (b. 13), a German colloquial equivalent of 'n'est-ce pas?', or in this case 'Isn't that it?', the stream's melody in the piano's right hand anticipates the accompaniment for 'hab' ich's verstanden?' as if to answer the question before it has even been spoken. The ecstasy of love, and its pain, are beautifully caught in the two utterances of 'Zur Müllerin hin!', the first

---

[1] Müller changes this line in *Gedichte*, 1826: 'Was ich such', *ist gefunden*'.

soaring to the top of the stave (bb. 16–17), the second in a cadence an octave lower, suggesting the humility of religious gratitude (bb. 17–18). At bb. 18–20 the piano's opening music is recapitulated like a ritornello.

But now doubt sets in. In this middle section (the song is basically written in an ABA form) we move into G minor (from b. 22), and we see with ever-increasing clarity the lack of confidence and the susceptibility of the young man's emotions. A shadow crosses the music as he wonders if a plot is afoot ('Hat s i e dich geschickt? / Oder hast mich berückt?') where 'she' is printed in the German manner of emphasis, as if the very idea of the girl occupies a larger and holier place. Is there some sort of collusion between the brook and the girl? Could they be in cahoots to fool or humiliate him? This is only a passing thought. When he repeats 'Ob s i e dich geschickt' (bb. 25–6) he can only think that the girl just might have cared enough to send the brook as her messenger. This is music of infinite longing underlined by 'sie' falling on the beginning of b. 26 which places a halo of emphasis around the all-important word.

All his speculative self-torture must now cease, for he has a job of work to do. All he knows, in the absence of a coherent answer from the stream, is that he must yield to his fate. Note how Schubert yields in the harmony as he softens F sharp to F natural on 'Ich gebe mich drein' (bb. 28–9). So we hear a touch of masochism no more suitable for a man of action than are these words of surrender. In any case, how can the miller claim so easily to have found what he has been seeking? He is obviously not the ever-searching poet driven on by an image of beauty; instead he has put all his hopes on the first girl he has met on his travels, a sign of his inexperience and immaturity. His nature is not without its poetic side, but it is also one that craves instant solutions and the comforts of an easy life. Is it possible that the composer saw something of himself in this mixture? The apposition and contrast of 'Für die Hände, für's Herze' (bb. 34 and 35) are beautifully done, the first out in the open high in the stave, the other buried deep in the body of the music. The closing words 'Vollauf genug!' reinforce the impression of the thanksgiving of a Lutheran chorale, and the piano's postlude is a repeat of the ritornello. We are filled with wonder that Schubert can make such a subtle commentary on the young man's nature within the context of a seemingly artless and simple song. It is perhaps worth noting that the other famous 'Danksagung' in music, the 'Heiliger Danksagung' from Beethoven's String Quartet in A minor, Op. 132, was composed in 1825. It is not impossible that Beethoven leafed through the score of Schubert's work in 1824 (on display at Sauer & Leidesdorf perhaps) and was taken by the song's title.

First edition:	Published as Op. 25 by Sauer & Leidesdorf, Vienna in 1824 (advertised in February), Book 1, no. 4 (P55)
Second edition:	Published as Op. 25 by Ant. Diabelli & Co., Vienna in 1830
Subsequent editions:	Peters: Vol. 1/12; AGA XX 436: Vol. 7/143; NSA IV: Vol. 2a/34; Bärenreiter: Vol. 1/156
Bibliography:	Youens 1992, pp. 38–9 & 77–9
Further settings and arrangements:	Karl Friedrich Curschmann (1805–1841) *Danksagung an den Bach* Op. 5 no. 1 (1833) Arr. Tilman Hoppstock (b. 1961) for guitar accompaniment, in *Franz Schubert: 110 Lieder* (2009)
Discography and timing:	Fischer-Dieskau III 1[4] 2'19
	Pears–Britten 2'27
	Hyperion I 25[5]
	Hyperion II 28[5] 2'16 Ian Bostridge

← *Halt!* D795/3   *Am Feierabend* D795/5 →

V AM FEIERABEND

OP. 25 NO. 5, **D795/5** [H530]

A minor

After work

Hätt' ich tausend	If only I had a thousand
Arme zu rühren!	Arms to wield!
Könnt' ich brausend	If only I could drive
Die Räder führen!	The rushing wheels!
Könnt' ich wehen	If only I could blow like the wind
Durch alle Haine,	Through every wood,
Könnt' ich drehen	And turn
Alle Steine!	Every millstone,
Dass die schöne Müllerin	So that the fair maid of the mill
Merkte meinen treuen Sinn!	Would see my true love.
Ach, wie ist mein Arm so schwach!	Ah, how weak my arm is!
Was ich hebe, was ich trage,	What I lift and carry,
Was ich schneide, was ich schlage,	What I cut and hammer –
Jeder Knappe tut mir's nach.[1]	Any apprentice could do the same.
Und da sitz' ich in der grossen Runde,	And there I sit with them, in a circle,
In der stillen kühlen Feierstunde,	In the quiet, cool hour after work,
Und der Meister sagt zu Allen:[2]	And the master says to us all:
'Euer Werk hat mir gefallen;'	'I am pleased with your work.'
Und das liebe Mädchen sagt	And the sweet maid
Allen eine gute Nacht.	Bids us all goodnight.

[Schubert repeats the first strophe of the poem in order to complete his setting]

This is the fifth of Schubert's forty-six Müller solo settings (1823, 1827 and 1828). See the poet's biography for a chronological list of all the Müller settings.

This is the only song in the cycle with a large cast of characters and extras. Amateur singers have always been attracted to it, not only because of its stirring tune but because it gives them the chance to play the mill's pompous owner for a few bars, and to indicate the girl's tones in falsetto as she says goodnight to all the apprentices. The young miller is here shown to have a working life with a group of other people. On another level, however, his nascent obsession with

---

[1] Müller writes 'Jeder Knappe tut *es* nach'.
[2] Müller has '*spricht* zu Allen' in both editions of his poems, but the NSA adopts Schubert's autograph change to '*sagt*'. Peters and AGA prefer 'spricht' probably because 'sagt' occurs again only two lines later in the poem.

the maid of the mill has already sealed him off in his own world of fantasy and longing. Even at this stage, before the appearance of the hunter, he sees other men as rivals. Later in the cycle he will sit with the girl on one unhappy occasion by the brook (*X. Tränenregen*) and he will recount her brief visit to him in his room (*XIII. Mit dem grünen Lautenbande*), but otherwise, apart from communing with the brook, he is a loner.

As evening approaches, the new apprentice looks back on his day's work with some dissatisfaction. The song has a time signature of § and the pianist starts with heavy chords in groups of two, plus a panting quaver rest; these denote not only the hard physical activity mentioned in the second verse, but also frustration and self-directed anger. Perhaps he is still too young, too much of what the Germans call a 'Kaulquappe' (tadpole) to compete with the other boys. The poem is full of conditional verbs rendered by the subjunctive ('Hätt' ich'. . . 'Könnt' ich' – 'If only I had'. . . 'If only I could'). The accompaniment whirrs energetically because, in our hero's mind, the stream at his behest is driving the mill-wheels twice as fast as usual (compare the more leisurely turn of the wheel in *Halt!*). If he *could* do the stream's work single-handed, if he *were* a force of nature to be reckoned with, *if* his own efforts were to drive the mill with such force that it was twice as productive and twice as prosperous, *then* the girl would be sure to notice him. And thus we are given to suppose that she has not noticed him yet, and that he is perhaps not one of the strongest or most beautiful specimens of manhood.

This song has energy and determination certainly, but it is not to be presented in a towering Beethovenian rage. In some performances we can scarcely believe that this is the same boy who has sung *Danksagung an den Bach*, and who will go on to sing *Der Neugierige*. Many singers perform this music so heroically and manfully that the whole point of the boy's limited strength is lost. The pianist too must be careful not to attack the music with the bravura and *Schwung* that suggests an all-conquering hero. This melody is almost identical to that of an 1815 Goethe setting *An Mignon* D161 in which the poet refers to the 'secret, silent power' of sorrows: 'In my heart of hearts I am racked by savage pain', he says, 'I must weep in secret, yet I can appear happy, even glowing and healthy.' The adoption of this old tune for *Am Feierabend*, eight years later, is a sure sign that the composer saw the texts as having something in common – a worm in the bud, healthy physical activity combined with unhealthily suppressed feeling. The key is Schubert's favourite tonality of A minor and, true to form, he reserves a special effect for 'Dass die *schöne Müllerin* / Merkte meinen treuen Sinn!' (bb. 16–19) where mention of his beloved (the only time in the work where she is referred to by the title that gives the cycle its name) prompts a brief yet magical change into A major. We feel him sigh inwardly with pleasure at the very thought of her.

We return to reality in the second verse via a change back into A minor (b. 25) for the rippling semiquavers that are soon replaced by a recurrence of the two-quaver figure of the introduction. It is astonishing how effectively this simple motif conveys both hard physical work and, when combined with an intervening gasping rest, the resulting exhaustion. At this point in the poem there is a comma after every three words ('Was ich hebe, was ich trage, / Was ich schneide, was ich schlage') giving the vocal line an impression of breathlessness as the miller strains to complete his tasks. We surmise that the young man, who was only too happy to stop walking at first sight of a mill, is not going to surpass any of his colleagues in terms of physical prowess.

The change into the next section is extraordinary, for in the matter of half a bar we are transported to the relative major and to a calmer time of day (from b. 36). The fraught A minor semiquavers are replaced by quavers in the more neutral key of C major, and in this change we can almost see the twilight and feel the cool of evening. It is notable however that there is no suggestion that this section should be performed any slower than the main tempo (which is marked 'Ziemlich geschwind' – *rather* fast). The German word 'Feierabend' has no easy translation into English because it is a tradition that has no real equivalent in English-speaking lands. It denotes the almost sacred significance of sharing time with family, loved ones or colleagues after a good day's work – a celebration of friendship and comradeship. In the mill the workers who have shared arduous toil relax and eat together, sitting in a big circle like knights of the round table, or in this case the round wheel. There is a solemnity to this breaking of bread, for *Die schöne Müllerin* is set in a time when the old-fashioned German virtues were observed, and grace was certain to have been said at table. At 'Und der Meister sagt zu Allen' (from b. 45) Schubert provides one of his most convincing character sketches, vividly limned in the space of a few bars. The girl's father is paterfamilias to his young charges (the use of the familiar plural 'euer' for 'your' shows this), overweight and florid (the accompaniment is reduced to large and ponderous dotted minims) and somewhat self-important as befits his station as proprietor of the mill. He is pleased with his apprentices' work and, all in all, is a good-hearted Hans Sachs on a small scale. The miller's rotundity suggests a gruffer bass, and so the tenor descends to the lower half of the stave. At b. 51 the sudden shift an octave higher for 'Und das liebe Mädchen sagt' takes magical flight into the feminine world. The singer goes on to a high G (marked pianissimo, b. 54) for 'Allen eine gute Nacht' and we cannot help but hear her own voice in this tessitura. This phrase is repeated from b. 57 and the second time we feel the boy's resentment that the girl is not directing the greeting to him exclusively.

Müller ends the poem here as the girl slips away from the gathering (given the description of a 'kühle Feierstunde' it seems likely that the evening meal has been taken out of doors in the mill courtyard). Schubert uses the boy's frustration to launch into a recapitulation of the opening music and sets the first verse of the poem again. This gives new life to the apprentice's determination to do everything possible to win the miller girl's attention. At b. 59 those mill-wheels begin turning again (as if summoned back to life by a phantom slave-driver on a night shift) and the marking is 'Etwas geschwinder'. In most performances this direction is simply treated as an 'a tempo' – a corrective to the slower tempo (unmarked) that tradition has wrongly come to accept for the middle section from b. 36; in other words there is usually no difference between the speed of the swirling semiquavers at the beginning of the song and for those of the closing section. And yet there surely should be, and the composer could not have been clearer in his stated requirements. If the opening is performed only '*Ziemlich* geschwind' as marked (as opposed to the less equivocal 'Geschwind') the miller boy's disillusionment at his lack of energy can be more truthfully depicted, particularly in the litany of futile activity in bb. 26–36. A less than precipitous tempo at the beginning, sadly seldom heard, also enables the middle section (when the apprentices sit in a circle for the evening meal) to be performed without a massive meno mosso – although this section taken at the same speed as the opening is still rather faster than the somnolent tempo often employed for this far-from-happy episode for the new boy at the mill. If everyone else is relaxed at the end of the day, the newcomer is still on tenterhooks.

The recapitulation, on the other hand, represents the purely imaginary redoubled efforts of the boy, now refreshed by a break, to vie with his working rivals. At the beginning of the song, the left-hand quavers had limped with a rest between every group of three; at the recapitulation the music is driven forwards by a different left-hand rhythm: two quavers placed together (without the limp) make for something rather more vigorous than at the opening. There is no melting change into A major this time at mention of the miller girl; indeed we can almost detect the boy's anger with his 'beloved' for not singling him out with a goodnight glance. 'Dass die schöne Müllerin / Merkte meinen treuen Sinn!' is heard no fewer than three times, and for the first two of these the word 'meinen' is repeated as if to emphasize 'If only she would notice my, *my* genuine feelings'. At b. 79 time stands still as, lost in dreaming, the boy repeats these words for the third and last time. These flights of moonstruck fancy are interrupted and contrasted with music of frustration – the muscular semiquavers of the mill-wheels. The piece ends on an extended sigh as the pianist plays a descending scale, twelve notes that reach into the depths of the keyboard (bb. 86–7) before two angry cadential chords. Thus is completed a picture of emotional ambivalence: the young man revels in the fantasy world he has constructed around himself while longing to be someone different – a man of resolution and action. In the next song he will ask if this love is to be or not to be. Müller was such an expert on English literature that it is possible that these parallels with *Hamlet* were created deliberately.

Paul Reid in *The Beethoven Song Companion* has pointed out the similarity beween certain features of *Am Feierabend* (above all the cascade of semiquavers at the beginning of the song) and Beethoven's Goethe setting *Sehnsucht* ('Was zieht mir das Herz so?') Op. 83 no. 2 (1810).

First edition:	Published as Op. 25 by Sauer & Leidesdorf, Vienna in 1824 (advertised in March), Book 2, no. 1 (P56)
Second edition:	Published as Op. 25 by Ant. Diabelli & Co., Vienna in 1830
Subsequent editions:	Peters: Vol. 1/14; AGA XX 437: Vol. 7/145; NSA IV: Vol. 2a/36; Bärenreiter: Vol. 1/158
Bibliography:	Reid 2007, pp. 252–4
	Youens 1992, pp. 40–41 & 79–81
Arrangements:	Arr. Tilman Hoppstock (b. 1961) for guitar accompaniment, in *Franz Schubert: 110 Lieder* (2009)
Discography and timing:	Fischer-Dieskau III 1[5] 2'36
	Pears–Britten 2'30
	Hyperion I 25[6]
	Hyperion II 28[6] 2'29 Ian Bostridge

← *Danksagung an den Bach* D795/4   *Der Neugierige* D795/6 →

VI Der NEUGIERIGE   The inquisitive one
Op. 25 NO. 6, **D795/6** [H531]
B major

(55 bars)

Ich frage keine Blume,	I ask no flower,
Ich frage keinen Stern,	I ask no star;
Sie können mir alle nicht sagen,[1]	None of them can tell me
Was ich erführ' so gern.	What I would so dearly like to know.
Ich bin ja auch kein Gärtner,	For I am no gardener,
Die Sterne stehn zu hoch;	And the stars are too high;
Mein Bächlein will ich fragen,	I will ask my little brook
Ob mich mein Herz belog.	If my heart has lied to me.

[1] In his *Gedichte* (1826) Müller removed the word 'alle' from this line. Schubert set it as he found it in the 1821 edition.

O Bächlein meiner Liebe,	O brook of my love,
Wie bist du heut' so stumm!	How silent you are today!
Will ja nur Eines wissen,	I wish to know just one thing,
Ein Wörtchen um und um.	One small word, over and over again.
Ja, heisst das eine Wörtchen,	One word is 'yes',
Das andre heisset Nein,	The other is 'no';
Die beiden Wörtchen schliessen	These two words contain for me
Die ganze Welt mir ein.	The whole world.
O Bächlein meiner Liebe,	O brook of my love,
Was bist du wunderlich!	How mysterious you are.
Will's ja nicht weiter sagen,	I will tell no one else:
Sag', Bächlein, liebt sie mich?	Say, brook, does she love me?

This is the sixth of Schubert's forty-six Müller solo settings (1823, 1827 and 1828). See the poet's biography for a chronological list of all the Müller settings.

The Teutonic 'neugierig' is stronger than the Latin-derived 'inquisitive' or 'curious', although it is convenient to translate the word thus rather than as the cumbersome (but more accurate) 'greedy for something new'. 'Curiosity' is too lukewarm a word to describe the emotional precipice on which the boy finds himself stranded; the girl's feelings for him have become a matter of life and death. Significantly the miller does not ask *her* whether she loves him; no doubt fearful of rejection, he considers talking to the trees and stars and places his faith in portents. The pianist's introduction comprises two juxtaposed propositions of two bars each: the first ends hopefully in the air in b. 2; the next, separated from the first by a crotchet rest, sinks to a resigned cadence in b. 4. There is diffidence and hesitation in both these exquisite phrases; each seems to describe a physical action like the tearing of petals off a flower in a self-teasing game of 'she loves me, she loves me not'. In fact there is a passage from Wilhelm Müller's *Tagebuch* (23 October 1815) which shows the kind of games the poet played with himself in regard to his love for Luise Hensel: 'I had first toyed with her name, intertwined it with mine, I'd written down questions, then closed my eyes, turned the paper over several times, then had blindly written down the answers – and oh, how delighted I was when it worked out. I had written: "Luise, do you love me?" And directly below was the word, "Ja". But then wicked misfortune had altered the "'Mein' Wilhelm" into "Nein . . ." And so, it said: yes, no Wilhelm and I was back to square one.'[2]

The first two verses of this poem are set as both song and recitative, but this is a recitative in a million and only Schubert could set words with such skill. Only when the real aria comes (at 'O Bächlein meiner Liebe') do we realize that this lilting little tune has been but an extended upbeat to a glorious effusion of melody. Years of experience have enabled the composer to blend two genres, song and recitative, into one, and in this case the words and melody appear to be invented on the spur of the moment, as though the singer is thinking as he goes along. It is this which gives the piece its astonishing freshness. The lightest and least obtrusive of accompani-

---

[2] The original German for this passage is as follows: 'Ich hatte erst mit ihrem Namen gespielt, ihn mit dem meinigen verschlungen, Fragen aufgeschrieben, dann die Augen zugemacht, das Papier mehrmals herumgedreht, dann die Antwort blindings geschrieben und – ach, wie freute ich mich, als es zutraf. Ich hatte aufgeschrieben: Luise, liebst du mich? Und gerade darunter stand das Ja. Aber wieder ein böser Zufall hatte das "mein Wilhelm" in nein verwandelt. Und so hiess es: ja, nein, Wilhelm und ich war so weit wie vorher.'

ments, quavers alternating in each hand, makes for an airy uncluttered texture in which the singer is free to shape the phrases with a gently ruminative rubato. We can almost see him looking at the flowers (in the middle of the stave, bb. 5–6), shifting his gaze to the stars (bb. 6–8 at the top of the stave) and then adopting an expression of dejection as the passage reaches mid point (the end of the first strophe) at 'Was ich erführ' so gern', bb. 10–12. Here the vocal line falls wistfully to the dominant, and the conditional mood of the verb ('erführ') is highlighted by the harmonic stretch of the setting. The next verse ('Ich bin ja auch kein Gärtner') is a simple repeat of the first two lines musically speaking; the words state the obvious, that the miller is neither gardener nor astronomer (mention of a gardener harks back to the original form of the Berlin *Liederspiel* that included such a character), and then inspiration strikes in the third line of the verse. Yes of course, he should ask the *brooklet* rather than the flowers and stars. The unexpected turn of harmony at 'Mein Bächlein' indicates the surprise of someone who has overlooked the obvious; the phrase plunges down the stave as the miller boy's eyes shift from sky and field to look at something that lies glistening and shimmering at his feet. At b. 17, after uncertainty and diffidence, vocal melismas flower, delightedly mirroring the movement of water in an outpouring of confidence. But a warning note is struck at 'Ob mich mein Herz belog' (bb. 18–20): treason and betrayal are around every corner – the stream has already been accused of befuddling the miller (in the second song) and of entrancing him (in the fourth song), but the boy's self-deception will prove worse. The two bars of piano writing in semiquavers that echo the voice part (bb. 20–21) are among Schubert's most beautiful transitions. The chord of F sharp^7 is reached before the watery semiquavers suddenly stop midstream and we have three quaver rests of pregnant silence (b. 22). The brook is 'stumm' and has not responded to the boy's indirect question. In order to give up its secrets it seems that it will have to be coaxed and wooed by the miller almost on bended knee, and with very special music.

At this magical turning point Schubert changes tempo (the marking is 'Sehr langsam') as well as metre (with a time signature change from $\frac{2}{4}$ to $\frac{3}{4}$). Performers must be careful to keep the stream flowing with three 'very slow' crotchets, not twelve very slow semiquavers! To write such an aria within a song the composer draws on all his knowledge of the great Italian vocal tradition that he acquired from Salieri and which marks him out as different from the earlier North German lieder composers. To Schubert it seemed appropriate that a man deeply in love with love should be moved to music of this kind. The beauty and accessibility of this cantilena have deceived many an Italian singer into believing, on first hearing *Der Neugierige*, that he too can master lieder challenges without much difficulty. Bellini might have been proud of this melody, its long lines simple yet eloquent, the underlying harmony unfussy and changing at just the right moment to underline the poignancy of the text. The accompaniment is the simplest of water music with a beautiful little obbligato note sounded in the right hand (in the manner of an oboe perhaps) after the word 'stumm' (b. 26, second beat) and later after 'wunderlich' (b. 46) to betoken the pangs of longing felt by the boy and his heartfelt pleading with the stream to give him an answer.

Next comes a return (at b. 33) to recitative at 'Ja, heisst das eine Wörtchen' which corresponds to the equivocation of the opening bars of the accompaniment. With the word 'Ja' the stream falls ominously silent. For a moment the miller turns away from the brook and nurses his best and worst scenarios in music of almost masochistic sweetness. The movement of the harmony upwards on 'Das andre heisset Nein' (bb. 34–5) is a lift into the unthinkable: the shift from the first inversion of F sharp major for 'Yes' to a first inversion of G major for 'No' is like the bottom dropping out of the singer's world – the uplift and hope of many sharps cancelled at a stroke by the bleak reality of naturals as the pianist's hands sag despondently on to the white keys. After static and empty chords for the 'Yes' section, the accompaniment rises and swells in quavers at 'No', as if threatening to overflow the river banks. As is customary in the spirit of recitative, this section moves forward impatiently without strict tempo; when contemplating the 'Ja' with enthusiasm the singer moves considerably faster than the 'Sehr langsam' of the main cantilena, slowing down in agonized hesitation as 'Nein' is approached. 'Die beiden Wörtchen schliessen / Die ganze Welt mir ein', uncertain of tempo because the ebb and flow of water knows no controlled measure, wavers first in one direction and then in another, getting nowhere in terms of harmonic progression. There is no choice but to ask the brook for advice once again, and the return of the beautiful tune 'O Bächlein meiner Liebe' is prepared in a manner worthy of it. Here, after the second 'schliessen / Die ganze Welt mir ein' at bb. 39–41, is another miraculous transitional interlude – from G major back to F sharp major (on its way back to B major) in two bars (bb. 41–2) where the water music and its exquisite modulations are the gentlest balm for the troubled soul.

The brook's aria is heard once again, but it is modified after six bars (at b. 49) when it changes musical direction and moves into new harmonic territory to include the miller's final heart-rending phrases, 'Sag', Bächlein, liebt sie mich?' Up till now he has talked of wanting to know only one word, lacking the courage to ask his question directly. But at the end, helped by the brook's sympathetic yet non-committal murmurings, he finally comes out with it – 'Does she love me?' This is sung twice, the first time (b. 49) touching an F sharp high in the stave that soars in hope; the repeat at bb. 50–52 is more modest but no less poignant. Both exclamations are so vulnerably voiced that we can no longer feel impatience with the boy's timidity. He wins our heart with his poetry and depth of feeling.

The postlude transfers the brook's gently undulating semiquavers to the left hand, leaving the right free to sing a touching progression of crotchet chords that continue the questioner's concern wordlessly: we can almost see his expression. Even here the pianist's right-hand tune is divided into three parts of three crotchets each, a section that seems to say 'yes' (bb. 52–3), a more muted counterbalance that could be 'no' (bb. 53–54) and a final neutral summing up on three B major chords. These conflicting possibilities have pervaded every aspect of the song's form. The enigmatic brook has failed to answer the question but its musical speech remains full of charm and mystery, empathy and watery danger. Semiquavers in the final bar gently sidle downwards under the pianist's left hand, prophetic of the very end of *Der Müller und der Bach* D795/19 where the young miller's body will slip to the depths accompanied by a similar figuration.

First edition:	Published as Op. 25 by Sauer & Leidesdorf, Vienna in 1824 (advertised in March), Book 2, no. 2 (P57)
Second edition:	Published as Op. 25 by Ant. Diabelli & Co., Vienna in 1830
Subsequent editions:	Peters: Vol. 1/18; AGA XX 438: Vol. 7/149; NSA IV: Vol. 2a/42; Bärenreiter: Vol. 1/161
Bibliography:	Youens 1992, pp. 41–2 & 81–3
Further settings:	Fanny Mendelssohn (1805–1847) *Der Neugierige* (1823)
Discography and timing:	Fischer-Dieskau III 1[6] 4'20
	Pears–Britten 4'21
	Hyperion I 25[7]
	Hyperion II 28[7] 3'56 Ian Bostridge

← *Am Feierabend* D795/6   *Das Mühlenleben* →

DAS MÜHLENLEBEN
[H531+]

Life in the mill

[*This poem was not set to music by Schubert.*]

Seh' ich sie am Bache sitzen,
Wenn sie Fliegennetze strickt,
Oder Sonntags für die Fenster
Frische Wiesenblumen pflückt;

Seh' ich sie zum Garten wandeln,
Mit dem Körbchen in der Hand,
Nach den ersten Beeren spähen
An der grünen Dornenwand:

Dann wird's eng' in meiner Mühle,
Alle Mauern ziehn sich ein,
Und ich möchte flugs ein Fischer,
Jäger oder Gärtner sein.

Und der Steine lustig Pfeifen,
Und des Wasserrads Gebraus,
Und der Werke emsig Klappern,
'S jagt mich fast zum Tor hinaus.

Aber wenn in guter Stunde
Plaudernd sie zum Burschen tritt,
Und als kluges Kind des Hauses
Seitwärts nach dem Rechten sieht;

Und verständig lobt den Einen,
Dass der Andre merken mag,
Wie er's besser treiben solle,
Geht er ihrem Danke nach –

Keiner fühlt sich recht getroffen,
Und doch schiesst sie nimmer fehl,
Jeder muss von Schonung sagen,
Und doch hat sie keinen Hehl.

Keiner wünscht, sie möchte gehen,
Steht sie auch als Herrin da,
Und fast wie das Auge Gottes
Ist ihr Bild uns immer nah. –

Ei, da mag das Mühlenleben
Wohl des Liedes würdig sein,
Und die Räder, Stein' und Stampfen
Stimmen als Begleitung ein.

When I see her by the brook
Sewing fly-nets,
Or, on Sundays, picking fresh meadow flowers
For her windows;

Or going into the garden
With her basket in her hand
Looking for early berries
Amongst the green brambles,

Then the mill seems too cramped,
Its walls close in on me,
And at once I want to be
A fisherman, a huntsman or a gardener:

And the merry grinding of the stones,
The roar of the waterwheel
And the busy clatter of the machinery
Almost drive me out of the gate.

But when the pleasant time comes
When she chats with one of the boys,
And, being the good girl of the house,
Glances sideways as is only right and proper,

And she judiciously praises one of them
So that another can see
How he must do better
If he is to earn her thanks,

Then nobody feels victimized,
Though she always makes her point;
They all talk of her consideration,
Though there's nothing guarded about her.

Nobody wants her to go,
Although she's the mistress
And almost like the eye of God
Her image is always close to us.

Well, I think life in the mill
Could be made into a song,
With the wheels, stones and all the pounding
Joining in as the accompaniment!

Alles geht in schönem Tanze	Everything goes up and down,
Auf und ab, und ein und aus:	To and fro, as if in a lovely dance;
Gott gesegne mir das Handwerk	May God bless my work,
Und des guten Meisters Haus!	And the good master's house.

Bibliography: Youens 1992, pp. 42–3
                            Youens 1997, pp. 169–91
Discography and timing: Fischer-Dieskau —
                            Hyperion I 25[8]
                            Hyperion II 28[8]   1'42   Dietrich Fischer-Dieskau

← *Der Neugierige* D795/6   *Ungeduld* D795/7 →

VII UNGEDULD   Impatience
Op. 25 no. 7, **D795/7** [H532]
A major

Ich schnitt' es gern in alle Rinden ein,	I should like to carve it in the bark of every tree,
Ich grüb' es gern in jeden Kieselstein,	I should like to inscribe it on every pebble,
Ich möcht' es sä'n auf jedes frische Beet	Sow it in every fresh plot
Mit Kressensamen, der es schnell verrät,	With cress seed that would quickly reveal it;
Auf jeden weissen Zettel möcht' ich's	I should like to write it on every scrap of white
schreiben:	paper:
Dein ist mein Herz, und soll es ewig bleiben.	My heart is yours, and shall ever remain so.
Ich möcht' mir ziehen einen jungen Star,	I should like to train a young starling
Bis dass er spräch' die Worte rein und klar,	Until it spoke the words, pure and clear;
Bis er sie spräch' mit meines Mundes Klang,	Until it spoke with the sound of my voice,
Mit meines Herzens vollem, heissem Drang;	With my heart's full, ardent yearning.
Dann säng' er hell durch ihre Fensterscheiben:	Then it would sing brightly at her window:
Dein ist mein Herz, und soll es ewig bleiben.	My heart is yours, and shall ever remain so.
Den Morgenwinden möcht' ich's hauchen	I should like to breathe it to the morning
ein,	winds,
Ich möcht' es säuseln durch den regen Hain;	And whisper it through the rustling grove.
O, leuchtet' es aus jedem Blumenstern!	If only it shone from every flower;
Trüg' es der Duft zu ihr von nah und fern!	If only fragrant scents could bear it to her from
	near and far.
Ihr Wogen, könnt ihr nichts als Räder treiben?	Waves, can you drive only mill-wheels?
Dein ist mein Herz, und soll es ewig bleiben.	My heart is yours, and shall ever remain so.

Ich meint', es müsst' in meinen Augen stehn,	I should have thought it would show in my eyes,
Auf meinen Wangen müsst' man's brennen sehn,	Could be seen burning on my cheeks,
Zu lesen wär's auf meinem stummen Mund,	Could be read on my silent lips;
Ein jeder Atemzug gäb's laut ihr kund;	I should have thought my every breath would proclaim it to her;
Und sie merkt nichts von all' dem bangen Treiben:	But she notices none of these anxious signs:
Dein ist mein Herz, und soll es ewig bleiben!	My heart is yours, and shall ever remain so.

This is the seventh of Schubert's forty-six Müller solo settings (1823, 1827 and 1828). See the poet's biography for a chronological list of all the Müller settings.

The preceding six songs in the cycle have all been concerned, in one way or another, with the brook. An unbroken thread runs through them of water imagery reflected musically in a stream of semiquavers in different time signatures and of different speeds. *Ungeduld* takes place on dry land, for we now suddenly hear talk of trees and pebbles, flowers and groves. Having previously revealed that he is no gardener, the miller here proposes the tricky task of planting cress seeds in the shape of the words 'Dein ist mein Herz'. This is all hypothetical of course, but the young man's new-found independence from his watery mentor suggests he has acquired greater confidence. A change has taken place since *Der Neugierige* where he could scarcely allow himself to ask whether or not the girl loved him. But he is still the same miller boy: there have already been signs in his nature of mood swings between manic enthusiasm and depression, and in this song he is on an 'up'. *Ungeduld* has suffered from being treated as a display piece of Italianate passion, beloved by tenors because of the two high As at the end of each strophe. It has often been sung out of context, and with operatic enthusiasm, as a single item in a recital. Were the miller as masterful and insistent as we sometimes hear in louder performances of this song, there would be no tragic story – he would simply have swept the maid of the mill off her feet and kept her! The reality is that he is only this virile in his fantasy, that here he is imagining himself as the ardent suitor, singing the song to himself because he lacks the courage to sing it to her face. The song's title probably refers to the miller's impatience for fantasy to turn into reality, particularly in the fourth verse ('I should have thought my every breath would proclaim it to her') where he sounds frustrated by the girl's inability to read the signs. As Susan Youens writes, the song shows the miller's 'frantic striving to force reciprocated love into being where it can only be given as a gift'. Whatever the enthusiasm and passionate overreaction of the miller, there are three major warning signs to performers against taking the title too literally and bashing through the piece on a wing and a prayer: the prevailing dynamic marking is piano; Schubert's moderating tempo marking is 'Etwas geschwind' (*quite* fast); and the vocal line is so densely packed with words that incomprehensibility is a real danger at too precipitous a tempo. The English-speaking listener will be proud to learn that Müller (a scholar of English literature whose first publication was a German translation of Marlowe's *Dr Faustus*) took his inspiration for *Ungeduld* from Edmund Spenser's *Colin Clout's come home again* (1591):

Her name in every tree I will endosse,
That as the trees do grow, her name may grow:
And in the ground each where will it engrosse,

And fill with stones, that all men may it know.
The speaking woods and murmuring waters fall,
Her name Ile teach in knowen termes to frame:
And eke my lambs, when for their dams they call,
Ile teach to call for *Cynthia* by name.

The idea for the poem's second verse derives from lines voiced, with less than loving intent, by Hotspur in Shakespeare's *Henry IV Part One* Act I Scene 3: 'I'll have a starling shall be taught to speak / Nothing but "Mortimer," and give it him / To keep his anger still in motion.' The miller's intent is more affectionate, but his equally obsessive starling will be trained to repeat his message with similar insistence.

The accompaniment is one of the composer's most famous creations. In the *Vorspiel* lightly throbbing triplet chords in the right hand seem at first to be mere vamp or harmonic filler, but after five beats they blossom unexpectedly into melody with a charming change to the dominant. At the end of the first bar we hear a marvellous left-hand counter-melody in the bassoon register that has something of that instrument's roguish charm. The idea of impatience is beautifully caught when, after the left hand has nudged the right into melodic life and precipitated the modulation (A major to E major), it unexpectedly re-emerges in the middle of the third bar to have another say – this time legato, but still mischievous, like an irrepressible petitioner popping up under the pianist's arm. The change to E minor in the fourth bar modifies the feeling of rapture with a moment of pain as if facing the fact, however briefly, that in all this adoration there is no certainty of reciprocation. The vocal line is written in a pattern of successive repetitions of dotted quaver + semiquaver. At this tempo it is almost inevitable that these should more or less synchronize with the piano's triplets, cunningly displaced between left and right hands to allow the accompanist the best chance of remaining exactly with the voice.

Apart from the ritornello at the beginning of each verse the piano writing is extremely simple, a mere harmonic support, as befits a tune so weighed down with words. The voice part on the other hand is complex and demanding. Each line of the strophe climbs slightly higher (highest notes of C sharp, D and E successively in the first three lines), effectively depicting mounting enthusiasm. In the fourth line and b. 15 the tenor touches a high G (at 'Mit Kres<u>sen</u>samen, der es schnell verrät'), a pitch at which clear diction is far from easy. The fifth line falls back down the stave but it is a case of *reculer pour mieux sauter* as the verse is brought back to the tonic in preparation for the refrain. This consists of the last line of the strophe that provides the vocal paean of praise that the public has been waiting for; it must be said that this is something of a test piece for the singer. The first 'Dein ist mein Herz' (in the middle of the stave, bb. 19–20) is a superb warm up for the second phrase which touches high A twice (on 'Dein' at b. 21 and again on the first 'ewig' at b. 23). The piano writing in the left hand here is taken from the bassoon-like phrases of the opening bars, but now seems filled out with imaginary cellos and horns.

It is indicative of how well Schubert understands the voice, and a singer's needs, that at this vocally challenging point the accompaniment is designed to provide much-needed support before each of the high As. In the upbeat to b. 23 a triplet in *both* hands of the piano encourages the singer to gather all his resources and launch himself up to this high note. If the ascent has been exciting the descent is no less so. The 'ewig' on a high A in b. 23 falls in an arpeggio to the A an octave below; with a tug in b. 24 the second 'ewig' plunges down a seventh (D to E) and the word 'bleiben' bounces from this E up the octave for a moment before descending at last to the tonic. The effect is like an exhilarating bungee jump where the first big leap into a chasm (the equivalent of the singer launching himself to the top of the stave) gives rise to a succession of bouncing aftershocks before the elasticized rope straightens and comes to rest.

Ungeduld, woodcut from the 'Prachtausgabe' of the cycle (1872). The engraving illustrates the first line of the poem.

Schubert would have expected performers to vary the dynamics of each of these strophes according to the meaning of the words (the third verse in particular calls for softer colours). It is neither possible nor desirable to sing the song 'piano' throughout any more than it is effective to shout it from the rooftops. The challenge to the interpreter is to give the song something of the display qualities expected by the public, without losing an overall vision of the young miller's character in the process.

In May 1992 the Viennese collector H. P. Wertisch (*see* AUTOGRAPHS, ALBUMS AND COLLEC-TIONS) acquired from a sale at Sotheby's a newly discovered Schubert autograph of the songs *Ungeduld*, *Morgengruss* and *Des Müllers Blumen* (songs VII, VIII and IX in the sequence) bound together as if they constituted a small cycle within a cycle, and all transposed into medium-voice keys. These songs had been written out in 1824. It is possible that they were meant for the baritone voice of Karl von Schönstein, the dedicatee of the cycle, but Ernst Hilmar (in *Schubert durch die Brille*) believes they were written out for the mezzo-soprano voice of Countess Karoline Esterházy while Schubert was in Zseliz as music master to her and her sister, and that they constitute a discreet declaration of love by the composer for the younger daughter of his employer, Count Esterházy. This also reminds us of how common it was in the nineteenth century to find women singers including excerpts from this cycle in their programmes.

First edition:	Published as Op. 25 by Sauer & Leidesdorf, Vienna in 1824 (advertised in March), Book 2, no. 3 (P58)
Second edition:	Published as Op. 25 by Ant. Diabelli & Co., Vienna in 1830. This song is printed here in F major – certainly Vogl's key, but no doubt also to encourage sales among amateur singers
First known performance:	The first recorded public performance of *Ungeduld* was at an Abend-Unterhaltung of the Gesellschaft der Musikfreunde, Vienna on 29 January 1829, sung by Columban von Schnitzer (see Waidelich/Hilmar Dokumente II No. 686)
Subsequent editions:	Peters: Vol. 1/20; AGA XX 439: Vol. 7/152; NSA IV: Vol. 2a/46; Bärenreiter: Vol. 1/164
Bibliography:	Hilmar 1993[2] Youens 1992, pp. 43–5 & 83–5
Further settings and arrangements:	Louis Spohr (1784–1859) *Ungeduld* Op. 94 no. 4 (1835–6) Karl Friedrich Curschmann (1805–1841) *Ungeduld* Op. 3 no. 6 (1830) Arr. Franz Liszt (1811–1886) for solo piano, no. 5 of *Sechs Melodien von Schubert* (1844) [*see* TRANSCRIPTIONS] Arr. Franz Liszt (1811–1886) for solo piano, no. 6 of *Müllerlieder* (1846) (2 versions) [*see* TRANSCRIPTIONS] Arr. Leopold Godowsky (1870–1938) for solo piano, *Impatience* (1927, 2nd revised edition 1937) [*see* TRANSCRIPTIONS] Arr. Tilman Hoppstock (b. 1961) for guitar accompaniment, in *Franz Schubert: 110 Lieder* (2009)
Discography and timing:	Fischer-Dieskau III 1[7] 2'47 Pears–Britten 2'41 Hyperion I 25[9] Hyperion II 28[9] 2'38 Ian Bostridge

← *Das Mühlenleben*   *Morgengruss* D795/8 →

VIII MORGENGRUSS

Morning greeting

OP. 25 NO. 8, **D795/8** [H533]
C major

(23 bars)

Guten Morgen, schöne Müllerin!	Good morning, fair maid of the mill!
Wo steckst du gleich das Köpfchen hin,	Why do you quickly turn your head away
Als wär' dir was geschehen?	As if something was wrong?

Verdriesst dich denn mein Gruss so schwer?	Does my greeting annoy you so deeply?
Verstört dich denn mein Blick so sehr?	Does my glance upset you so much?
So muss ich wieder gehen.	If so, I must go away again.
O lass mich nur von ferne stehn,	O just let me stand far off
Nach deinem lieben Fenster sehn,	And gaze at your beloved window
Von ferne, ganz von ferne!	From the far distance!
Du blondes Köpfchen, komm hervor!	Little blonde head, come out!
Hervor aus eurem runden Tor,	Come out from your arched doorways,
Ihr blauen Morgensterne!	Blue morning stars.
Ihr schlummertrunknen Äugelein,	Little eyes, drunk with slumber,
Ihr taubetrübten Blümelein,	Little flowers, saddened by the dew,
Was scheuet ihr die Sonne?	Why do you fear the sun?
Hat es die Nacht so gut gemeint,	Has night been so good to you
Dass ihr euch schliesst und bückt und weint	That you close and droop, and weep
Nach ihrer stillen Wonne?	For its silent bliss?
Nun schüttelt ab der Träume Flor,	Shake off now the veil of dreams
Und hebt euch frisch und frei empor	And rise up, refreshed and free,
In Gottes hellen Morgen!	To God's bright morning!
Die Lerche wirbelt in der Luft,	The lark is trilling in the sky,
Und aus dem tiefen Herzen ruft	And from the depths of the heart
Die Liebe Leid und Sorgen.	Love draws grief and care.

This is the eighth of Schubert's forty-six Müller solo settings (1823, 1827 and 1828). See the poet's biography for a chronological list of all the Müller settings.

This song at first hearing seems to be addressed directly to the 'schöne Müllerin'. Subsequent hearings reveal, as in all the songs of the Müller cycles, different layers of meaning. There is some suggestion that the opening incident where the miller stands adoringly underneath the girl's bedroom window has actually happened; reality and fantasy are so blurred in this cycle that it is difficult to be sure. If he does say these words as she gazes sleepily out of the window, we must assume that he has kept an all-night vigil to catch sight of her drawing back the curtains. What would the girl think of finding the miller looking up at her window so early in the morning? There is a hint in this song that she finds the young man odd and disturbing; this is hardly surprising as the second verse begins with the words of a voyeur, the first of a number of occasions in the cycle when the boy watches helplessly from afar, too shy to approach her and with a potentially unhealthy fixation. Perhaps she turns away because she is aware of this. Interestingly though, this implied rejection ('Verdriesst dich denn mein Gruss so schwer?') occasions no real change in the miller's spirits, only a slightly crestfallen and teasing musical response that remains well within the boundaries of courtship. To pretend to be shocked by a young man's attentions could well be the correct reaction for a demure maiden; and for the young man to pretend to be wounded is also part of the chase, the technique of a worldly suitor wooing a shy and inexperienced virgin. This makes it likely that *Morgengruss*, like *Ungeduld*, is a rehearsal of a declaration performed in front of a mirror, rather than a recounting of fact.

The use of the 'du' form of the verb throughout implies a rather unlikely intimacy with the daughter of the protagonist's employer. In the controlled circumstances of a Walter Mitty-like fantasy, the rejection regarded as inevitable deep in the psyche can be assimilated and dismissed. In any case, as Susan Youens has pointed out, the ultra-poetic language of this poem is at odds with true feeling and spontaneous emotion. This is poetry to be recited aloud, with a strummed lute perhaps, but it is not the language of real intimacy. The maid of the mill as described and created by the miller is unreal: as Youens writes, 'she is a blank slate on which he writes his own desires and ideas'.

Schubert here uses the strictest strophic form and the simplest harmony to weave a golden early morning spell in a sunlit C major (the sun has already shone in this key in *Halt!*). The music is all perfect innocence, a countryside idyll that only needs corn 'as high as an elephant's eye' to make it a Biedermeier equivalent of 'Oh what a beautiful mornin'' from *Oklahoma!* Both songs are easy to patronize and absolutely inimitable, for both Schubert and Richard Rogers had the so-called popular touch. The radiance and freshness of the music are as breathtaking as the economy of means. As it happens, Donizetti, another great populist, chanced on the opening of Schubert's melody for Edgardo's aria 'Fra poco a me ricovero' from *Lucia di Lammermoor* (1835).

Morgengruss is divided into three sections. The first three lines of the strophe (bb. 4–10) are the greeting (the piano's introduction is extrapolated from the opening melody); the second section (bb. 11–14, from 'Verdriesst dich denn mein Gruss so schwer?') has a *lamentoso* bass that falls in semitones from B flat (first inversion of a G minor chord) to G, the song's dominant. The last section, bb. 15–21, uses the last line of the strophe. 'So muss ich wieder gehen' ('If so, I must go away again') sings the miller, but instead of being a man of his word he sings the words again, with a third 'wieder gehen' to boot; he is rooted to the spot and has no intention of going anywhere. A lovely touch is the canonical writing between voice and piano at the distance of a bar; perhaps this implies the unbridgeable distance between the two 'lovers' but also perhaps between dream and reality. On first hearing, the song seems to have an ABC structure; in fact the form is a carefully planned ABA in which the repeated A section ('So muss ich wieder gehen') is modified in shape and harmony while retaining the essential characteristics (the jump of a major sixth, the feminine cadences) of the opening. This gives a subtle sense of unity and folk-song simplicity.

Like *Der Neugierige*, this is one of those Schubert pieces that sits on the fence between two genres of vocal writing: it has all the tunefulness of song and all the flexibility of recitative. The accompaniment is extremely sparse throughout, giving a great interpretative freedom to a creative singer. If this simplicity belies the complexities of the textual interpretation, it must be remembered that idealized relationships and conversations are much less complex than real ones. There is something pristine about the song, and also something very staged with its flowery language and striking of attitudes. Its undeniable perfection and simplicity are the perfection and simplicity of delusion and fantasy.

First edition:	Published as Op. 25 by Sauer & Leidesdorf, Vienna in 1824 (advertised in March), Book 2, no. 4 (P59)
Second edition:	Published as Op. 25 by Ant. Diabelli & Co., Vienna in 1830
Subsequent editions:	Peters: Vol. 1/22; AGA XX 440: Vol. 7/154; NSA IV: Vol. 2a/50; Bärenreiter: Vol. 1/168
Bibliography:	Youens 1992, pp. 46–7 & 85–7
Arrangements:	Arr. Leopold Godowsky (1870–1938) for solo piano, *Morning Greeting* (1927, 2nd revised edition 1937) [*see* TRANSCRIPTIONS]
	Arr. Tilman Hoppstock (b. 1961) for guitar accompaniment, in *Franz Schubert: 110 Lieder* (2009)

Discography and timing: Fischer-Dieskau III 1[8]   4'25
                          Pears–Britten   3'57
                          Hyperion I 25[10]
                          Hyperion II 28[10]   4'00   Ian Bostridge

← *Ungeduld D795/7*   *Des Müllers Blumen D795/9* →

IX Des MÜLLERS BLUMEN   The miller's flowers
OP. 25 NO. 9, **D795/9** [H534]
A major

Am Bach viel kleine Blumen stehn,	Many small flowers grow by the brook,
Aus hellen blauen Augen sehn;	Gazing from bright blue eyes.
Der Bach der ist des Müllers Freund,	The brook is the miller's friend,
Und hellblau Liebchens Auge scheint;	And my sweetheart's eyes are bright blue,
Drum sind es meine Blumen.	Therefore they are my flowers.
Dicht unter ihrem Fensterlein	Right under her window
Da will ich pflanzen die Blumen ein,[1]	I will plant the flowers.
Da ruft ihr zu, wenn alles schweigt,	There you shall call to her when all is silent,
Wenn sich ihr Haupt zum Schlummer neigt,	When she lays down her head to sleep,
Ihr wisst ja, was ich meine.	For you know what I wish to say.
Und wenn sie tät die Äuglein zu,[2]	And when she closes her eyes
Und schläft in süsser, süsser Ruh',	And sleeps in sweet repose,
Dann lispelt als ein Traumgesicht	Then whisper to her as a dream:
Ihr zu: 'Vergiss, vergiss mein nicht!'	'Forget me not!'
Das ist es, was ich meine.	That is what I wish to say.
Und schliesst sie früh die Laden auf,	And when, early in the morning, she opens the shutters,
Dann schaut mit Liebesblick hinauf:	Then gaze up lovingly;
Der Tau in euren Äugelein,	The dew in your eyes
Das sollen meine Tränen sein,	Shall be the tears
Die will ich auf euch weinen.	That I will weep upon you.

[1] Müller changes this line in the *Gedichte*, 1826: 'Da *pflanz' ich meine* Blumen ein'. Schubert set the line as printed above, exactly as he found it in the 1821 edition.
[2] 'Tät' is here an archaic form of 'tut'.

This is the ninth of Schubert's forty-six Müller solo settings (1823, 1827 and 1828). See the poet's biography for a chronological list of all the Müller settings.

The boy continues to be obsessed with the daughter of the house, just as Schubert seems to have been in Zseliz in 1824. The opening of the second verse shows that he is still hanging around under her window, planting flower seed, *faute de mieux*, and in the wrong type of bed. *Des Müllers Blumen* is something of a mirror image of the other song in the cycle in A major, *Ungeduld*, which proclaims 'Dein ist mein Herz'. Here, in music of a very different kind, the miller lays claim to the girl. He does this in the most fanciful way, his line of reasoning something like this: it is my brook; the small blue flowers that grow by the brook are like her eyes; therefore they are my flowers. The repeated phrase 'Drum sind es meine Blumen' seems to imply emphasis – 'Therefore they are *my* flowers' – and the word 'flowers' has become a metaphor for the girl herself. 'Drum' ('therefore') is placed on an important downbeat and its dotted crotchet constitutes half a bar of melody. The length of the setting adds to the feeling that the miller has taken pains to sort this out in his mind; the repetition of the phrase sets the seal on it like a magic incantation or spell, not dissimilar to a successfully resolved game of 'She loves me, she loves me not'. It is significant that in a harmonic scheme of great simplicity Schubert reserves the most telling moment (a brief but pointed modulation into the relative minor at 'meine Bl<u>ume</u>n', bb. 17–18) for these deluded words.

   This is yet another instance of the miller not allowing the girl herself (or not *daring* to allow her) to have any say in the matter of a relationship; it is sufficient that *he* loves, and a side of him expects the strength of his own longing to solve all difficulties. There is in this self-sufficient obsession something deeply narcissistic, and this song provides everything that a Narcissus might require: a stream to mirror his emotions and music that is reflective in every sense. Schubert seems to have taken the cue for his musical setting from the crucial line 'Der Bach der ist des Müllers Freund', for here we have music of friendship where the closely entwined vocal line and piano glide together in a succession of thirds, sixths and other harmonies of smooth complicity. If the brook shows its ability to bewitch the boy at any point in the cycle before *Der Müller und der Bach* (the nineteenth song) it is surely here and in the third verse of the next song.

   In some ways this is the simplest song in the cycle. The form is strophic like its predecessor *Morgengruss*, and the music for each verse is in a straightforward AAB form. One feels that this simplicity is absolutely deliberate and that Schubert has carefully made certain subdivisions within the cycle. Songs I to VI belong together because they establish the miller in his milieu, united as they are by the brook and the semiquaver figuration that appears in different guises. Songs VII to X on the other hand are concerned with his courtship, or rather non-courtship, of the girl, his powerfully self-deluding construction of castles in the air. It is because these have such a poor foundation in reality that the whole edifice crumbles in the second half of the cycle. These four songs are united by the simplicity of their structure. The miller boy would so like his love for the girl to be pure and simple, and so it is, except for the tiny matter of her reciprocation. By excluding her from the scene the way is open for an uncomplicated idyll. Schubert builds within his cycle a temporary dreamland where the strophic form, beloved of yore, reflects the innocence of the emotional landscape. This is more effectively to emphasize the disintegration of the miller's world later in the cycle.

   For the moment we have calm and seductive peace, and the song in its own right is very beautiful. The introduction starts with an A major arpeggio that reflects the brook's watery depths but also seems to come deep from the realms of dreams. As Susan Youens has pointed out, a very similar passage for piano (in the same key) introduces the fourth strophe ('Ich träumte von Lieb' um Liebe') of *Frühlingstraum* from *Winterreise* D911/11. In that song the winter traveller *in extremis* has dreamed of mutual love and a lovely maiden, and on waking

Am Bache viel kleine Blumen stehn,
Aus hellen blauen Augen sehn;
Der Bach, der ist des Müllers Freund,
Und hellblau Liebchens Auge scheint,
Drum sind es meine Blumen.

Dicht unter ihrem Fensterlein
Da pflanz' ich meine Blumen ein;
Da ruft ihr zu, wenn Alles schweigt,
Wenn sich ihr Haupt zum Schlummer neigt,
Ihr wißt ja, was ich meine.

Und wenn sie thut die Aeuglein zu
Und schläft in süßer, süßer Ruh',
Dann lispelt als ein Traumgesicht
Ihr zu: Vergiß, vergiß mein nicht!
Das ist es, was ich meine.

Des Müllers Blumen, woodcut from the 'Prachtausgabe' of the cycle (1872). The engraving illustrates the second verse of the poem.

finds his life empty as before. This motivic link is a further indication, if any were needed, that the composer saw *Des Müllers Blumen* as happening within a daydream from which the miller would awaken with tragic consequences. But in the meantime the reverie is beguiling. The words of the third verse, with images of dreams and sleep especially suited to soft dynamics, are a gift to the imaginative interpreter. On one of the song's autographs Schubert added a footnote to the effect that the accompaniment can be played an octave higher if desired ['NB Die Begleitung dieses Liedes kann füglich um eine Oktave höher gespielt werden – Franz Schubert']. In the Hyperion recording we adopted this suggestion for the third strophe, the change of colour well suited to the words.

The fourth verse introduces the idea of tears, a sign perhaps that the miller boy's delusion of happiness is not so complete that he is incapable of weeping. The whole of this song is conceived in such flowery metaphors, however, that the mutable images of tears and dew are probably simply part of the miller's fantasy language of courtship. Flowering forget-me-nots occur in Schober's ballad *Vergissmeinnicht* D792, also from 1823.

First edition:	Published as Op. 25 by Sauer & Leidesdorf, Vienna in 1824 (advertised in March), Book 2, no. 5 (P60)
Second edition:	Published as Op. 25 by Ant. Diabelli & Co., Vienna in 1830
Subsequent editions:	Peters: Vol. 1/24; AGA XX 441: Vol. 7/155; NSA IV: Vol. 2a/52; Bärenreiter: Vol. 1/170
Bibliography:	Youens 1992, pp. 47–9 & 87–8
Further settings and arrangements:	Ludwig Berger (1777–1839) *Müllers Blumen* (1816) Fanny Mendelssohn (1805–1847) *Des Müllers Blumen* (1823) Arr. Tilman Hoppstock (b. 1961) for guitar accompaniment, in *Franz Schubert: 110 Lieder* (2009)
Discography and timing:	Fischer-Dieskau III 1[9] 3'18
	Pears–Britten 3'32
	Hyperion I 25[11]
	Hyperion II 28[11] 3'13 Ian Bostridge

← *Morgengruss* D795/8   *Tränenregen* D795/10 →

X TRÄNENREGEN   Shower of tears
Op. 25 no. 10, **D795/10** [H535]
A major

(36 bars)

Wir sassen so traulich beisammen	We sat together in such harmony
Im kühlen Erlendach,	Beneath the cool canopy of alders,
Wir schauten so traulich zusammen	And in harmony gazed down
Hinab in den rieselnden Bach.	Into the rippling brook.

Der Mond war auch gekommen,	The moon had appeared too,
Die Sternlein hinterdrein,	And then the stars.
Und schauten so traulich zusammen	They gazed down in harmony
In den silbernen Spiegel hinein.	Into the silvery mirror.
Ich sah nach keinem Monde,	I did not look at the moon;
Nach keinem Sternenschein,	I did not look at the stars.
Ich schaute nach ihrem Bilde,	I gazed only at her reflection,
Nach ihren Augen allein.	And her eyes.
Und sahe sie nicken und blicken	I saw them nod and gaze up
Herauf aus dem seligen Bach,	From the happy brook;
Die Blümlein am Ufer, die blauen,	The little blue flowers on the bank
Sie nickten und blickten ihr nach.	Nodded and glanced at her.
Und in den Bach versunken	The whole sky seemed
Der ganze Himmel schien,	Immersed in the brook
Und wollte mich mit hinunter	And sought to drag me down
In seine Tiefe ziehn.	Into its depths.
Und über den Wolken und Sternen	Above the clouds and stars
Da rieselte munter der Bach,	The brook rippled merrily,
Und rief mit Singen und Klingen:	And called me with its singing and ringing:
Geselle, Geselle, mir nach!	'Friend, follow me!'
Da gingen die Augen mir über,	Then my eyes filled with tears
Da ward es im Spiegel so kraus;	And the mirror became blurred.
Sie sprach: Es kommt ein Regen,	She said: 'It's about to rain.
Ade, ich geh' nach Haus.	Goodbye. I'm going home.'

This is the tenth of Schubert's forty-six Müller solo settings (1823, 1827 and 1828). See the poet's biography for a chronological list of all the Müller settings.

It is notable that *Des Müllers Blumen* ends on the word 'weinen' without a *Nachspiel* of any kind. It is the only song in the cycle to do so. *Tränenregen* begins on an upbeat in the same key and with the same time signature; it is clear that the composer wished to link these two songs, although *Tränenregen* is marked 'Ziemlich langsam' – a touch slower than the 'Mässig' of *Des Müllers Blumen*. The second book of the first edition, issued in February 1824, ended with *Des Müllers Blumen*. *Tränenregen* opened the third book, creating an unfortunate caesura from the musical point of view and one that could have been avoided. No wonder Schubert was frustrated that Sauer & Leidesdorf made the public wait until the following August for the third book. These two songs belong together and should have followed seamlessly one after the other.

Within its more leisurely tempo, *Tränenregen* has a more adventurous and disturbed harmonic palette than its predecessor. The prevalence of E sharp, which we hear as part of the very first upbeat chord, confers a melancholy ambivalence as if the music, officially in A major, threatens to modulate into the relative minor at certain moments. It does not do so, and this perhaps lends greater surprise to the change to the tonic minor in the last verse. This slightly disturbed musical landscape is in great contrast to the two strophic songs that have come before it. At last we have something different from castles in the air: the small but significant incident by the brook described here seems actually to have happened.

Both *Morgengruss* and *Des Müllers Blumen* have seen the miller take up vigil beneath the girl's window (whether in imagination or reality is a moot point) as he waits to greet her awakening or to plant flowers. Now at last there is a real development: the two young people are sitting together in the early evening on the riverbank. The musical stage is set for a lovers' meeting. An entry in Müller's *Tagebuch* (23 November 1815), when he was unsuccessfully wooing Luise Hensel, may describe the occasion which inspired this song: 'She was so lovely tonight; I don't know whether it was because of that that I was not really happy because she didn't actually say anything dismissive to me. But I was miserable, wasn't able to talk much and that also put me on edge. This can't go on for much longer, I must declare my love to her.'[1] The accompaniment is a tender three-part invention that occasionally blossoms into four parts. For the most part the right hand doubles the voice, emphasizing the quality of intimacy and *Traulichkeit*. The bass line has a real independent life, often running in contrary motion to the vocal line as is appropriate for reflection in water (the same idea had been used by Beethoven in the fourth song of *An die ferne Geliebte* Op. 98). At the end of each of the poet's first six strophes Schubert has invented a truly exquisite *Zwischenspiel* (in the dominant after Verses 1, 3 and 5, bb. 11–13; in the tonic in a slightly higher tessitura after Verses 2, 4 and 6, bb. 22–4) which denotes the gentle murmurings of flowing water. The enchanting transparency of this figuration is reminiscent of *Der Jüngling an der Quelle* D300, another water song in A major and also in 𝄴.

As in a number of the songs in this cycle that initially seem to promise to take the action forward to some happy resolution of the miller's emotional crisis, there is something crucial missing in this scenario. Like two people embarrassed at having nothing much to say, the main characters, united at last in a song, look away from each other and gaze into the brook. Is the boy, ardently in love with the maid of the mill, simply shy? Perhaps this is the whole problem, but one is tempted to look beneath the surface. Although he is sitting by her side it seems that he can only see her by courtesy of the brook's reflection. If there was ever an example of being in love with the idea of love more than the object of love itself, this is it. The miller lad has his heart's desire at his side, and all he can do is look at her reflection! Even then he seems not to see the whole person: the girl's eyes, and their similarity to the brook's flowers, have become almost a fetish. We wait for a comment on her beautiful mouth, her snow-white breast or her maidenly figure, but even these clichés are denied us. Amazingly, in the fifth and sixth strophes of the poem (the third musical verse – Schubert uses two strophes of Müller to make one of his own) the miller's attention wanders away from his beloved and becomes more and more taken up with the brook itself.

Although it is not mentioned in the poem, he can of course see his own reflection, as well as the sky's, in the water and the self-absorption of a latter-day Narcissus takes over. The brook in a moment of jealousy seems to be wooing him away from the girl's side, saying, 'Come here, follow me rather than stay with her' (Verse 6, bb. 20–22). Here we have the strongest indication of the sinister role that the brook will play in the story of the miller boy's life and death. Does the inevitability of his end, a presentiment of doom, now strike our protagonist? In the seventh of Müller's strophes (which Schubert fashions into a half verse of music that stands on its own), the miller begins to cry so he can no longer see the reflection. The key changes from A major

---

[1] The original German for this passage is as follows: 'Sie war so schön heute Abend; ich weiss nicht ob dass gerade Schuld war, das ich nicht recht fröhlich war, da sie mir doch eigentlich nichts Niedergeschlagendes sagte. Aber ich war unglücklich, konnte auch wenig reden und das machte mich wieder ängstlich. Es kann nicht lange mehr so dauern, ich muss ihr meine Liebe gestehen.'

to A minor (bb. 25–6) and tears drip into the water like the first drops of a summer shower. Suddenly the girl gets up as if responding to a change in the weather and with the utmost banality (insensitive to the ambient mood, *her* uncaring words remain in A major) she leaves him and goes back to the house.

But one can feel a degree of sympathy for the girl. She has been sitting wordlessly on the bank as her companion stares into the water, absorbed in his own thoughts. Why doesn't he *look* at her? Then suddenly and silently he begins to cry. By now she has had enough of an evening's ordeal and she makes her excuses (perhaps it is a little unkind to refer to the tears as an imminent rainstorm, but coming from solid working stock she can't be doing with men who cry for no reason) and returns to the house with a sigh of relief.

The everyday explanation of her peremptory exit is that she is simply 'playing hard to get', but such coquettish behaviour belongs at the end of a song a great deal less subtle than this one. In this confrontation the prosaic, down-to-earth girl encounters a poetic, highly strung sensibility and finds it inexplicable and thus not much to her liking. It is not the fact that the girl leaves him alone on the bank of the stream that prompts the lad's tears, for he is already grappling with a melancholy and a sense of impending doom in which she plays no real part. It is significant that her only words, 'Ade, ich geh' nach Haus' (Schubert sets these in a manner that suggests both curt annoyance and limited emotional horizons), neither occasion a musical reaction of despair, nor stop the song in its tracks. The haunting little ritornello (in A major as at the opening) is heard again at the same reflective speed. We might assume that whether the girl herself comes or goes is all the same to the young miller, so strongly is she fixed as an icon in his mind. There is a haunting addition to this postlude which slips into the minor for two eloquent bars (bb. 35–6). While this could be interpreted as a sad musical commentary on her withdrawal, the intense and unruffled concentration of the music suggests that the miller is so absorbed with what the brook is saying to him that he scarcely notices. Or perhaps he has expected to be abandoned in a preordained story that must take its course with its inevitable conclusion in the depths of the stream.

The second edition of this song (Diabelli, 1830) is printed as a *durchkomponiert*, rather than a strophic, song. This makes clear that the opening piano ritornello is not heard between each strophe, even though the repeat mark at the end of the song would seem to indicate that it is to be played. In fact this seems to have been one of the casualties of Ferdinand Schubert's inexperienced proofreading for the first edition, an oversight that was perpetuated in the Peters Edition and the AGA. There should of course be another double bar and repeat mark before the last quaver of b. 4 so that in each strophe the voice re-enters after the rippling brook interlude (bb. 22–4) is over. This mistake is at last rectified in the NSA.

First edition:	Published as Op. 25 by Sauer & Leidesdorf, Vienna in 1824 (advertised in August), Book 3, no. 1 (P61)
Second edition:	Published as Op. 25 by Ant. Diabelli & Co., Vienna in 1830
Subsequent editions:	Peters: Vol. 1/26; AGA XX 442: Vol. 7/156; NSA IV: Vol. 2a/54; Bärenreiter: Vol. 1/172
Bibliography:	Youens 1992, pp. 49–51 & 88–90
Arrangement:	Arr. Anton Webern (1883–1945) for voice and orchestra, *Tränenregen* (1903) [*see* ORCHESTRATIONS]
Discography and timing:	Fischer-Dieskau III 1[10] 4'10
	Pears–Britten 5'09
	Hyperion I 25[12]
	Hyperion II 28[12] 4'11 Ian Bostridge

← *Des Müllers Blumen* D795/9   *Ein ungereimtes Lied* →

EIN UNGEREIMTES LIED   An unrhymed song
[H535+]

This poem was not set to music by Schubert. First published in the periodical
Der Gesellschafter *in May 1818, it is not included in any of Müller's published collections,*
although at some point it clearly belonged to Die schöne Müllerin. *Perhaps the poet removed*
it because it depicted the relationship between the miller and the girl (perhaps entirely imaginary)
as being something too conventionally romantic.

Kein Liedchen mehr!	Enough of ditties!
Aber Küsse, Küsse!	But kisses! kisses!
Und Herz an Herz,	And heart against heart,
Und schwimmende Blicke,	And swooning glances
Und Tränen drin!	Filled with tears,
Und Tränen so selig,	Blissful tears,
Und Seufzer dazu,	And sighs,
Und Seufzer so süss!	Sighs so sweet!
Und wer sie sucht –	And he who seeks those ditties
Und will nicht plaudern –	(And can hold his tongue)
Am Erlenbach,	By the alder brook
Wo die Blümlein stehn,	Where the flowers grow,
Die kleinen, die blauen,	The little blue flowers,
Und unter der Linde	Beneath the linden tree
Im Mühlengarten:	In the miller's garden –
Da wird er sie finden,	He will find them
Da wehen sie hin	Wafting
Und wehen sie her,	To and fro
Im Abendwind,	In the evening breeze,
Im Sternenschimmer!	Under the shimmering stars!
Ach, wer sie hörte,	Ah, who might hear them,
Und recht verstände,	And understand them?
Und wieder sänge	Who might sing them again
In Vers und Reim:	In rhyming verse,
Die Lieder dort!	Those songs?

Discography and timing: Fischer-Dieskau   —
                           Hyperion I 25¹³
                           Hyperion II 28¹³   0'45   Dietrich Fischer-Dieskau

← *Tränenregen* D795/10   *Mein!* D795/11 →

XI MEIN! Mine!

Op. 25 no. 11, **D795/11** [H536]
D major

(103 bars)

Bächlein, lass dein Rauschen sein!	Brook, cease your babbling!
Räder, stellt eu'r Brausen ein!	Wheels, stop your roaring!
All' ihr muntern Waldvögelein,	All you merry wood-birds
Gross und klein,	Great and small,
Endet eure Melodein!	End your warbling!
Durch den Hain	Throughout the wood,
Aus und ein	Within it and beyond,
Schalle heut' e i n Reim allein:	Let *one* rhyme alone ring out today:
Die geliebte Müllerin ist m e i n!	My beloved, the maid of the mill, is *mine!*
M e i n!	*Mine!*
Frühling, sind das alle deine Blümelein?	Spring, are these all of your flowers?
Sonne, hast du keinen hellern Schein?	Sun, do you have no brighter light?
Ach, so muss ich ganz allein,	Ah, then I must remain all alone
Mit dem seligen Worte m e i n,	With that blissful word '*mine*',
Unverstanden in der weiten Schöpfung sein!	Understood nowhere in the whole of creation!

This is the eleventh of Schubert's forty-six Müller solo settings (1823, 1827 and 1828). See the poet's biography for a chronological list of all the Müller settings.

Müller was almost certainly inspired to this merciless reiteration of the 'ei' (or 'ai') vowel by a poem entitled *Der Mondschein* by Friedrich Wilhelm Gotter (qv). The result is a lyric that suggests obsession. The fragment *Ein ungereimtes Lied*, read by Dietrich Fischer-Dieskau for the Hyperion Edition (*see* above) was reinstated at this point in the story by Max Friedlaender in his study of the cycle, but it is not part of Müller's published work. We have to wonder whether it, like *Mein!* itself, is merely an extension of the boy's fantasies. By what right, we might ask, can the miller suddenly proclaim the girl to be his? Has there been some crucial development that has been left out of Schubert's (as opposed to Müller's) cycle? After all, as in *Winterreise* D911, this work is a succession of moments that taken together make up something of a story, but it is not necessarily a blow-by-blow account of the actions of the characters. Between *Tränenregen* and *Mein!* something might have happened – but what? A reasonable guess is that the miller girl, being kind at heart and somewhat ashamed of her peremptory behaviour at the brook's edge, has made an effort to be nice to the apprentice who has been mooning around the mill, prone to tears. She has taken the trouble to say a few kind words, and has perhaps even made an effort to smile at him. In a generous mood she might even have given him a kiss. For the highly strung young man these crumbs from the table might have been enough to turn depression into elation, her friendly behaviour interpreted as something much more significant.

Because he avoids asking her directly whether she loves him, he is gloriously free to assume that she does, shouting it from the rooftops and dancing for joy.

If the girl were really his, the miller would want to have her by his side. Instead his proclamation is solitary, and he even admits to the strong possibility, at the end of the poem, that he will be left all alone with the *word*, misunderstood by the rest of creation. It seems that the concept of laying claim to someone as 'his' and celebrating the idea is more important to him than the communing and sharing that flow from a reciprocated relationship. The boy has been in a slough of despond but here the other side of his manic-depressive condition shows itself. In case this statement sounds unduly influenced by twentieth-century psychiatry, it is worth noting that the great singer Julius Stockhausen (as Susan Youens points out) referred to this song in his diary (1862) as 'true insanity' ['Das ist ein wahres Rasen']. Thus one of the earliest interpreters of the cycle was able to see in it the disturbing depths that remain hidden from the majority of performers, not to mention the public, to this day.

The music of the opening is somewhat reminiscent of the clacking mill-wheels of the first song of the cycle. It recaptures the energy of *Das Wandern* as if this were a new beginning to a new cycle. Müller's poem, with lines of unequal length and its obsessive insistence on the sound 'ein' at the end of each line (so that everything in the world seems to rhyme with 'Mein'), gives a much stronger indication of what Youens calls the boy's 'disordered mind' than a first hearing of Schubert's music. Müller's use of metre suggests speed: with its breathless short lines *Mein!* is a fast poem, and Schubert follows this hint with relish. Indeed from a sheerly musical point of view this song overflows with the bloom of healthy, physical exuberance. An unusual feature that appears throughout the song is that most of the groups of four quavers making up the bouncing accompaniment have a minim doubling as their first note – a note, in other words, that is held over its three quaver neighbours, making a descant of sorts played by the right thumb and the left little finger. This internal, hidden melody exactly translates into musical terms the poet's image of *one* persisting rhyme that lies at the heart of everything. This is particularly true from b. 22 at 'Durch den Hain / Aus und ein / Schalle heut' ein Reim allein' where we hear no fewer than fifteen Es tolling bell-like at every half-bar. The phrase 'Die geliebte Müllerin' gives rise to a flurry of coloratura where the voice at last matches the flowing quaver movement of the accompaniment. When 'ist mein, ist mein' is sung, however, the vocal line soars to F sharp for the first time (b. 32) and the note values are longer; this reminds us how the complementary word 'Dein' in *Ungeduld* occasioned both change of tessitura and broadening of tempo.

Of course musically elongating this word, as if truly to drive it home, reflects the sense of the proprietary insistence of 'Mein' as it is used in the poem. Schubert both repeats Müller's phrase and adds another 'ist mein' at the end of each repeat. This is justified by the poet's use of the German equivalent of italics for emphasis, the widely spaced 'M e i n'. Müller places another 'Mein!' (printed in the same way) on a line of its own, and Schubert highlights this by setting the world twice: the first appearance is an arching phrase over six beats that changes the harmonic direction of the song (another sign of the power of the miller's determination that 'Mine!' should mean that *he* is in control); the second triumphantly marks a successful landing into the next section of the song (in B flat major).

This section, from b. 40, has a playfully pugnacious air. The miller accuses nature of not doing enough to celebrate his victory. Why is it that spring has failed to produce more flowers or to make the sun shine more brightly? Schubert sets these lines superbly as rhetorical questions, the upward inflection of the voice just right for this hectoring. Müller ends his poem with the miller masochistically embracing the idea of being alone with his special word, so all-encompassing that it is simply misunderstood by everyone else. Schubert knows that he will have to return to the elated mood of the opening, therefore these questions should not be too desperate. Although he darkens the music into G minor at 'Ach, so muss ich ganz allein' (bb. 47–8), the change of mood passes. Despite a slightly woeful colour in B flat minor for 'Unverstanden' (bb. 51–2) the composer seems less concerned with emphasizing this word than in depicting, with the broadest of brushes, the young man's exhilaration at being part of Nature's grand plan. 'Schöpfung', a very big concept, is elongated (bb. 53–4) with suitable grandeur. 'Unverstanden in der weiten Schöpfung sein' is repeated, the second time with a marvellously apt decorative turn on 'Schöpfung' (b. 59). (This decoration may have been one of those ornaments initially proposed by Vogl which the composer decided to incorporate into his autograph – *see* below.) Here is the devil-may-care gallantry of a young man willing to embrace the whole of creation at the same time as defying it to take away his happiness. This impression is confirmed by the *Zwischenspiel* of four bars (bb. 60–63) that brings us back to the home key with a sense of mounting enthusiasm. The song has a straightforward ABA structure and we hear essentially the same music again, varied only at the end to ensure that the piece finishes resoundingly in D major, the final vocal phrase ('ist m e i n, / [ist] M e i n!') containing a quixotic triplet as a final flourish.

This recapitulation betokens a disparity between the intentions of poet and composer, but musical imperatives win the day over literary considerations. At this point the cycle requires physical energy to win the battle, however briefly, over tortured introspection. Before this there have been three songs in moderate tempo (VIII, IX and X) and Richard Capell's advice was that they are 'best not dawdled over by the singer'. There speaks a critic who had seen many an audience slide towards boredom because of too much slow music. Although these strophic songs lie at the heart of the cycle and are infinitely precious to the Schubertian, there is the danger that a wider public, less atuned to their beauties, might find them a little tedious. By 1823 Schubert was far too practical a man not to realize this; whatever the underlying madness of the poem, the invigorating *Bewegung* of *Mein!*, and the re-emergence of the mill-wheels in good working order, were planned as a temporary relief to both ear and heart.

The version of *Mein!* appearing in the cycle's second edition (1830) is sufficiently different to be printed separately in Volume 2b of the NSA. In places the vocal line is entirely rewritten. The familiar melody is recast in the same way that a jazz singer, Billie Holiday for example, would remodel the melodic details of a well-known standard while retaining its familiar overall shape. But this version contains a curious anomaly: in bb. 22–4 (and in the later equivalent passage) Schubert's rollicking quavers have been *simplified* by Diabelli, as if he were unaware that the decoration of the vocal line stemmed from the composer himself. In any case, he decided that what he must have imagined was Vogl's version was too difficult to print. This is an illustration of how arbitrary this edition is. Had it been simply a faithful record of Vogl's version throughout it would have been a far more valuable document than this opportunistic mishmash of Schubert, Vogl and the egregious Diabelli acting as umpire between the two extremes, and often opting for the advantages of neither.

First edition:	Published as Op. 25 by Sauer & Leidesdorf, Vienna in 1824 (advertised in August), Book 3, no. 2 (P62)
Second edition:	Published as Op. 25 by Ant. Diabelli & Co., Vienna in 1830. The ornamented version of *Mein!* is reprinted in NSA Vol. 2b/275 (1975), the first printing in modern times (P766)
Subsequent editions:	Peters: Vol. 1/28; AGA XX 443: Vol. 7/158; NSA IV: Vol. 2a/57; Bärenreiter: Vol. 1/174
Bibliography:	Youens 1992, pp. 51–2 & 91–2
	Youens 1997, pp. 191–8
Further settings:	Karl Friedrich Curschmann (1805–1841) *Mein!* Op. 3 no. 4 (1830)

Discography and timing: Fischer-Dieskau III 1[11]   2'18
                          Pears–Britten   2'10
                          Hyperion I 25[14]   2'23   Ian Bostridge
                          Hyperion II 28[14]

← *Ein ungereimtes Lied*   *Pause* D795/12 →

XII PAUSE   Pause
OP. 25 NO. 12, **D795/12** [H537]
B♭ major

Mei - ne Lau - te hab ich ge - hängt an die Wand,

(81 bars)

Meine Laute hab' ich gehängt an die Wand,
Hab' sie umschlungen mit einem grünen Band –
Ich kann nicht mehr singen, mein Herz ist zu voll,
Weiss nicht, wie ich's in Reime zwingen soll.
Meiner Sehnsucht allerheissesten Schmerz
Durft' ich aushauchen in Liederscherz,
Und wie ich klagte so süss und fein,
Glaubt' ich doch, mein Leiden wär' nicht klein.[1]
Ei, wie gross ist wohl meines Glückes Last,
Dass kein Klang auf Erden es in sich fasst?

   Nun, liebe Laute, ruh' an dem Nagel hier!
Und weht ein Lüftchen über die Saiten dir,
Und streift eine Biene mit ihren Flügeln dich,
Da wird mir so bange und es durchschauert mich.[2]
Warum liess ich das Band auch hängen so lang'?
Oft fliegt's um die Saiten mit seufzendem Klang.

Ist es der Nachklang meiner Liebespein?
Soll es das Vorspiel neuer Lieder sein?

I have hung my lute on the wall,
And tied a green ribbon around it.
I can sing no more, my heart is too full;
I do not know how to force it into rhyme.
The most ardent pangs of my longing
I could express in playful song,
And as I lamented, so sweetly and tenderly,
I believed my sorrows were not trifling.
Ah, how great can my burden of joy be
That no song on earth will contain it?

   Rest now, dear lute, here on this nail,
And if a breath of air wafts over your strings,
Or a bee touches you with its wings,
I shall feel afraid, and shudder.
Why have I let this ribbon hang down so far?
Often it flutters across the strings with a
   sighing sound.
Is this the echo of my love's sorrow,
Or could it be the prelude to new songs?

*This is the twelfth of Schubert's forty-six Müller solo settings (1823, 1827 and 1828). See the
poet's biography for a chronological list of all the Müller settings.*

I once accompanied a performance of *Die schöne Müllerin* in England which had only nineteen
songs on the printed programme. The titles of songs I to XI were correctly listed, as were those
for XIII to XX. Indented in the middle of this list was 'Pause' (which, as it happens, is also the

---

[1] Müller writes '*Meint'* ich doch, mein Leiden wär' nicht klein'.
[2] The word 'so' in this line is Schubert's addition to Müller's text.

German for concert interval). On this occasion the English-speaking public assumed the performers would leave the stage and tea would be served. As the word occured more or less halfway down the page this optimism (soon dashed by an announcement) seemed entirely logical – apart from the fact that the cycle is seldom, if ever, performed with a break.

Bruno Hake informs us that Müller only introduced the lute motive into his poetic sequence when he was in Italy in 1817/18 – thus some time after the original Berlin version. This led Franz Valentin Damian to propose that the entire poem was written from the poet's standpoint rather than that of the miller boy – that the words of the poem are addressed to the reader by Müller himself, rather than by the cycle's miller protagonist. An argument against this theory is that these serious verses are in an entirely different tone from the playful and ironic prologue and epilogue to the work provided by the poet as bookends to the cycle (and not set by Schubert). Damian is undeterred by this and points out that the lute is an instrument that appears only in this one song, that it is never heard of again. In *Eifersucht und Stolz* (XV) the miller boy refers to himself as piping, not strumming. The sophisticated yet introspective perceptions of *Pause*, Damian continues, are inappropriate to the miller boy himself (although we may reply that generations of listeners have thrilled to the revelation of the boy's hidden depths). He avers that the green ribbon that is common to *Pause* and the following song (where the lute seems no longer to be hanging on the wall) is the connective thread that allows Müller to switch roles, once again donning the mask of the miller boy, having allowed the public to see him as a creative artist at the crossroads of his own work. One may point out that the lute is no longer on the wall because it is once again in use, but Damian's theory is persuasive enough on a number of literary levels. Whether Schubert understood it this way, as Damain also believes, is a moot point, and the theory is not at all helpful for the singer. On film, and with a change of costume and lighting, it may be possible to counterpoint poet and protagonist, perhaps sung by the same singer, but on the concert platform the narrative thread of the piece, and the audience's engagement with the fate of the miller boy, are so strong that to engineer (and explain) a sudden change of character midstream would be a ruinous disruption. The commentary that follows is based on the almost universally held assumption that *Pause* was intended by the composer to be performed and heard as part of the miller boy's own story. If the protagonist is able here to assume and adopt the self-awareness of Müller's own musings the result is a more rounded character with whom the listener can identify. When the boy dies in the stream our emotional reactions to his demise are intensified because of what he has shared with us in *Pause*.

The song does indeed stand apart from its fellows in terms of both poetic content and musical style. John Reed considers it 'the most subtle and inspired song in the cycle' and it is easy to see why. For the first time in what has been essentially an outdoor work we are allowed into the miller's room, and in this inner sanctum we are at the heart of his longing as well as at the heart of the cycle. We are given a new view of the protagonist off duty as it were: although he is a singer in Schubert's work, it is a paradox that we have had no idea until now that Müller's miller is musical and that he expresses himself with the help of a lute or guitar. He must have carried it in his knapsack as he made his way downstream to his new employers. Although this streak of creativity is not surprising in one we already know to be sensitive, it is further indication of a secret inner life of which his workmates know nothing.

The musical depiction of silence is a challenge for any composer. In *Pause* voice and piano, usually closely entwined in the cycle, are given separate identities as if to underline the miller's separation from his muse. The lute hangs on the wall so it is obvious that the miller is *not* strumming it as he sings to us – that is the point of the poem. The piano opening starts with a tiny cell of nascent melody that consists of a motif of four beats (crotchet, dotted quaver + semiquaver crotchet, quaver, quaver rest). This occurs no fewer than eighteen times in the key of B flat major, and eight times in slightly varied or tranposed form. The motif, which signifies the swelling and dying away of sound, always promises to launch into real melody, but the promise is never fulfilled, an apt illustration of something which Schubert was seldom to know personally – a writer's block of the musical imagination. The performing range of the mute lute is hemmed in within the compass of the pianist's hand and unable to proceed from these confines into a full-flowering tune of its own. Even the little triplet figure in the third and fourth bars of the introduction is harmonically unadventurous and still rooted in the home key of B flat major. The tiny accents on the third beat of the bar underline a sense of yearning, as if the instrument itself is straining at the leash, or rather pulling at its ribbon, waiting to serve its master. The repetitions of this little figuration pervade the song and are the binding threads that unify the piece. The charm and delicacy of this music uncannily suggest the soft and haunting sounds of a small, intimate instrument brought to life by a gust of wind or something brushing against the strings. This ostinato accompaniment, playing in the miller's mind without a vocal melody to match it, is thus a prototype of the magical piano parts of Brahms, Wolf and Cornelius describing the Aeolian harp (*Lerchengesang* Op. 70 no. 2, *An eine Äeolsharfe, Mörike-Lieder* no. 11, *Auftrag* Op. 5 no. 6) untouched by human hand and yet prompted by nature into soft ethereal sounds.

The singer provides a melody in apposition to the lute's strumming as a type of song-in-waiting. Voice and lute thus move on different planes. It is of course paradoxical that as he complains that he can no longer sing, he does so most beautifully. But even here Schubert has not invented a real melody: the vocal line is limited, recitative-like in character and strangely repetitive as if also stuck in one groove. The second line of the strophe is a musical repeat of the first, and the music of the third line ('Ich kann nicht mehr singen, mein Herz ist zu voll') is reworked with the same melodic contours in the fourth ('Weiss nicht, wie ich's in Reime zwingen soll'). The slight differences of harmony in these two similar passages illustrate Müller's lines about not being able to rhyme his feelings, though he does rhyme the words that describe the predicament. Both pianist and singer disclaim their ability to make music and yet their music-making, when combined, is of surpassing beauty – twin depictions of a creative impasse adding up to something greater than their parts. In this way Schubert is true both to Müller's poem, and to his *amour propre* as a composer.

There was a time of course when all was well; the miller remembers when he was able to write songs. This passage ('Meiner Sehnsucht allerheissesten Schmerz' from b. 21) prompts a change into G minor where voice and piano are lovingly married in thirds, a stark contrast to the previous bars where they have gone their separate ways. There is a distinct exoticism about this music: the exaggerated adjective 'allerheissest', the drone of fifths in the left hand, the sobbing melismas on 'Meiner Sehnsucht', the dotted rhythms in the left hand at cadences and the pointed change between major and minor chords at 'Liederscherz' all suggest the charged intensity of Eastern European folk music, the voice a violin obbligato to the piano's cimbalom or zither. After 'mein Leiden wär' nicht klein' the piano has a small but meaningful cadenza (with fermata) that echoes the vocal line. Even more extraordinary is the passage at 'Ei, wie gross ist wohl meines Glückes Last' from b. 35 where the singer bursts into impassioned recitative and then, violin-like, takes off in a virtuoso cadenza of wayward tripping quavers. Such extended hocketing with two notes per syllable is rare in Schubert and one wonders if Vogl's style of ornamentation has played a part in the conception. It seems this passage of rhapsodic intensity may well have been inspired by Hungarian music, a brooding *lassu* succeeded by a more extrovert *friss* (Max Friedlaender claimed to detect a Hungarian influence in the introduction to *Mein!*). Schubert had associated Karoline Esterházy with Hungary since 1818 and a self-confessional passage about pangs of longing may well have prompted a Hungarian stylization. Another possibility moves the musical influence much further south, towards the Aegean – more believably so because this weaving vocal line is somewhat reminiscent of the middle section of *Strophe aus 'Die Götter Griechenlands'* D677 (bb. 24–34) where the modern reality of Greece is contrasted with its former glories. In 1823 the Greek War of Independence was raging; Vienna was full of expatriates and their music. Schubert was almost certainly aware that his poet (known as Griechen-Müller) was a passionate advocate of Greek freedom. Such a reference to Müller's own sympathies, if true, would add weight to Damian's theory outlined at the beginning of this commentary.

Meine Laute hab' ich gehängt an die Band,
Haß' sie umschlungen mit einem grünen Band —
Ich kann nicht mehr singen, mein Herz ist zu voll,
Weiß nicht, wie ich's in Reime zwingen soll.
Meiner Sehnsucht allerheißesten Schmerz
Durft' ich aushauchen in Liederscherz,
Und wie ich klagte so süß und fein,
Meint' ich doch, mein Leiden wär' nicht klein.
Ei, wie groß ist wohl meines Glückes Last,
Daß kein Klang auf Erden es in sich faßt?

Pause, woodcut from the 'Prachtausgabe' of the cycle (1872).

From b. 46, at 'Nun, liebe Laute, ruh' an dem Nagel hier!' the music of the opening is recapitulated, but it takes a tiny imagined intervention of nature to change the song's course. Nothing can make the miller create new music, but a breath of wind or the chance brush of a bee's wing shocks him into a new tonality of thought. There is an impassioned cadence in C minor on 'es dur<u>ch</u>schauert mich' (b. 55) which shows his susceptibility to portents and omens. At b. 56 the lute figuration of the opening is heard in A flat major, a change of key that seems to plunge the boy deep into introspective thought. (It is impossible not to believe that Brahms first heard in these bars the seed of the opening of the slow movement – in A flat – of his Piano Quintet Op. 34.) The green ribbon around the miller's lute that will later play a part in his betrayal suddenly seems significant here, for it has a life of its own, a ghostly presence that brushes the strings of its own accord. A flat major cedes to A flat minor (b. 63) and the first inversion of F flat major (E major), heralding another passage of recitative, a miracle of vulnerability and openness. The 'Hungarian' (or 'Greek') passage had the boy playing the part of an itinerant musician, but here the professional mask drops and we are more aware than we have been in the whole cycle of his insecurity, his fear and his need to be loved. How different this is from the carolled certainties of *Mein!*, but how much more real it all is. The heart-rending chord on the word 'Liebespein' (bb. 65–6) is one of those musical moments in Schubert when we can feel the spirit of Wagner hovering nearby.

Not least of Schubert's many achievements in this song is the superb musical solution he finds to the shaping of the final question. On 'Soll es das <u>Vor</u>spiel neuer Lieder sein?' (from b. 66) the voice rises to a soft high F as the bass falls a semitone from G flat to F (the second inversion of the home key of B flat major). This is one of the cycle's most magical moments; time seems to stand still, which is exactly what the words themselves imply, for here we have a void of uncertainty, a question that only time will answer. A similarly shaped melismatic vocal line, also in B flat major, this time referring to the uncertain musical future of a dead performer's zither, can be heard in bb. 46–7 and 55–6 of *Des Sängers Habe* D832, a song from early 1825 that was possibly composed during a relapse in Schubert's illness. In the postlude to *Pause* the strumming motif in B flat major (b. 78) is followed by a repeat of it in B flat minor (b. 79, a typically Schubertian juxtaposition that reminds us of 'Liederscherz' earlier) and then in sighing triplets the song gently winds down to a conclusion.

Only in *Der Leiermann* D911/24, the concluding song in *Winterreise*, do we have such daring in the depiction of frozen inspiration where the closing verse ('Wunderlicher Alter, / Soll ich mit dir gehn? / Willst zu meinen Liedern / Deine Leier drehn?') is equally heart-rending. The final lines of both songs concern the future fates of their wounded protagonists and in each case this question concerns the ability *somehow* to continue making music. This thought must also have been in Schubert's mind in 1823 as he lay in hospital with a life-threatening illness, a disease notorious for its abilities to blight the creative faculties of those unlucky enough to be caught in its thrall. Keeping going as a musician, at all costs, is the priority of the miller boy, the winter traveller and Schubert himself.

First edition: Published as Op. 25 by Sauer & Leidesdorf, Vienna in 1824
                          (advertised in August), Book 3, no. 3 (P63)
Second edition: Published as Op. 25 by Ant. Diabelli & Co., Vienna in 1830
Subsequent editions: Peters: Vol. 1/32; AGA XX 444: Vol. 7/162; NSA IV: Vol. 2a/63;
                          Bärenreiter: Vol. 1/178
Bibliography: Damian 1928, pp. 35–43
                          Hake 1908, p. 41
                          Hirsch 1993, pp. 127–35
                          Youens 1992, pp. 53–4 & 92–5
Arrangement: Arr. Tilman Hoppstock (b. 1961) for guitar accompaniment, in
                          Franz Schubert: 110 Lieder (2009)
Discography and timing: Fischer-Dieskau III 1[12]   4'26
                          Pears–Britten   4'31
                          Hyperion I 25[15]
                          Hyperion II 28[15]   4'30   Ian Bostridge

← *Mein!* D795/11   *Mit dem grünen Lautenbande* D795/13 →

XIII MIT DEM GRÜNEN LAUTENBANDE Op. 25 no. 13, D795/13 [H538]
Bb major

To accompany the green ribbon

Mässig

"Schad um das schö-ne   grü-ne Band,

(19 bars)

'Schad' um das schöne grüne Band,
Dass es verbleicht hier an der Wand,
Ich hab' das Grün so gern!'
So sprachst du, Liebchen, heut' zu mir;
Gleich knüpf' ich's ab und send' es dir:
Nun hab' das Grüne gern!

  Ist auch dein ganzer Liebster weiss,
Soll Grün doch haben seinen Preis,
Und ich auch hab' es gern.
Weil unsre Lieb' ist immer grün,
Weil grün der Hoffnung Fernen blühn,
Drum haben wir es gern.

'What a pity that the lovely green ribbon
Should fade on the wall here;
I am so fond of green!'
That is what you said to me today, my love.
I'll take it down and send it to you straight away:
Now you can delight in green!

  Though your sweetheart is all in white,
Green shall have its reward,
And I, too, am fond of it.
For our love is evergreen,
For distant hope blossoms green.
That is why we are fond of it.

Nun schlinge in die Locken dein[1]
Das grüne Band gefällig ein,
Du hast ja's Grün so gern.
Dann weiss ich, wo die Hoffnung grünt,
Dann weiss ich, wo die Liebe tront,
Dann hab' ich's Grün erst gern.

Now plait the green ribbon
Prettily into your hair,
For you are so fond of green.
Then I shall know where hope dwells,
Then I shall know where love reigns,
Then I shall truly delight in green.

This is the thirteenth of Schubert's forty-six Müller solo settings (1823, 1827 and 1828). See the poet's biography for a chronological list of all the Müller settings.

This song is linked to its predecessor in a way that suggests a certain symmetry with the connected pair of songs (*Des Müllers Blumen* and *Tränenregen*) before *Mein!*. The miller's question at the end of *Pause* is 'Could it [the fluttering of the ribbon across the lute strings] be the prelude to new songs?' And now there comes his answer in the shape of an introductory chord in the same key (B flat major) announcing what is in effect the second half of the cycle, rather like a minstrel striking up after the interval. Alfred Einstein avers that there is no need to play this opening chord if *Pause* has just been performed. For some time I adopted this advice but I have come to see this reiteration of B flat major as an answer to the question – yes, the story will continue and there will be new songs. It also reflects the sheer surprise occasioned by the sudden appearance of the miller girl at the door, like an apparition summoned by the boy's hopes and dreams. There *are* to be new songs, but not to his liking and not always of his own making. It is significant that after a period of creative silence the impetus for these new sounds is neither a breath of air nor a bee striking the strings (as described in *Pause*) but a fleeting visit by the miller girl. So, directly after the chord, the first thing we hear is *her* music and *her* voice: the playful introduction suggests the insouciance of capricious charm, the dotted rhythms indicative of a tripping feminine gait. The miller's new era of songs is thus kick-started by an outside influence; he takes up her melodic line and experiences a last moment of innocence and hope in circumstances over which he has no control.

What occasions her visit we do not know. Is this mere coquetry on her part? This would fit the theory of those who see in the girl a heartless trifler with the boy's affections, but there are other explanations. There is no mention anywhere in the cycle of the miller's wife, and it is apparent from the poem *Das Mühlenleben* that the girl has taken over the duties of mistress of the house. In this capacity she no doubt has the right to inspect the apprentices' rooms from time to time. The carefree, indeed casual, nature of the music is a cruel reminder of how little the girl cares for him, but she is not to be blamed, for as far as we know she has made no promises and told no lies. Unlike the winter traveller the miller cannot claim that the girl spoke of love; in *Winterreise* there is an element of betrayal, but here there seems only to be self-deception and a reading of significance into events where none is meant. It is likely that the girl has already met the hunter and, in falling in love with him, has fallen for the colour of his livery. The first three lines of the strophe in inverted commas are the girl's words. Her phrase in B flat is answered by the miller in F, a subtle suggestion of a time shift to remind us that he is recounting her words some time after they have been said to him. She must know by now that the miller is infatuated with her, and is trying to tell him obliquely that her affections are elsewhere; he is nevertheless deaf to anything that will spoil this unexpected moment of intimacy. Green has become the

[1] Müller (*Gedichte*, 1826) changes the line to 'Nun *schlingst du* in die Locken dein'. Schubert sets the line as he found it in the *Gedichte*, 1821.

emblem of her new relationship and we wince for him as he enthusiastically takes it up as the entirely inappropriate symbol of a romance that has never been. His eagerness to send her the fading green ribbon (bleached by the sun because the lute has not been used recently, and that too because of her) is tragically self-wounding, and the setting of 'Gleich knüpf' ich's ab und send' es dir' is full of impetuous haste (bb. 12–13). In this succession of quick consonants, particularly the onomatopoeic 'knüpf', we can almost hear the ribbon being torn off the wall. Each time the refrain comes at 'Ich hab' das Grün so gern' the piano doubles the voice; what is at first a display of solidarity quickly seems to be mockery, particularly at the end of the second verse when he says that '*We* are fond of it'. The title implies that the manuscript of the song is sent to the girl with the gift of the ribbon – yet more evidence of a courtship at one remove, where face to face confrontation is avoided at all costs.

Earlier in the verse the miller's confused thinking is apparent. He refers to their love as 'immer grün' – 'evergreen', and yet in the next breath talks of 'distant hope', almost as if he does not wish for the moment of consummation to come too soon. Not for the first time do we suspect that he finds sexual reality frightening and much less palatable than romantic gesture. The suggestion of a sexual thrill in the third verse is purely vicarious. The lad may not himself dare touch the miller girl, whom he has placed on a pedestal, but he wishes to see his ribbon tied to her person, intimately embracing her hair. We may guess how much he would like to run his fingers through it, but he is prepared to wait. Is this because he is frightened perhaps? In the meantime it is enough that she will wear it in the manner of a medieval lady who sports the colours of her champion. The girl is only too willing to do this but the poor miller does not yet realize that another much more powerful green knight has entered the lists with a stronger lance, and a willingness to use it.

First edition:	Published as Op. 25 by Sauer & Leidesdorf, Vienna in 1824 (advertised in August), Book 4, no. 1 (P64)
Second edition:	Published as Op. 25 by Ant. Diabelli & Co., Vienna in 1830. The ornamented version of *Mit dem grünen Lautenbande* is reprinted in NSA Vol. 2b/280 (1975), the first printing in modern times (P767)
Subsequent editions:	Peters: Vol. 1/35; AGA XX 445: Vol. 7/165; NSA IV: Vol. 2a/68; Bärenreiter: Vol. 1/181
Bibliography:	Einstein 1951, p. 258 Norton-Welsh 1996, pp. 117–22 Youens 1992, pp. 55–6 & 95–7
Arrangement:	Arr. Tilman Hoppstock (b. 1961) for guitar accompaniment, in *Franz Schubert: 110 Lieder* (2009)
Discography and timing:	Fischer-Dieskau III 1[13] 1'59 Pears–Britten 2'09 Hyperion I 25[16] Hyperion II 28[16] 2'05 Ian Bostridge

← *Pause* D795/12   *Der Jäger* D795/14 →

XIV Der JÄGER   The huntsman
OP. 25 NO. 14, **D795/14** [H539]
C minor

(32 bars)

Was sucht denn der Jäger am Mühlbach hier?

Bleib', trotziger Jäger, in deinem Revier!
Hier gibt es kein Wild zu jagen für dich,
Hier wohnt nur ein Rehlein, ein zahmes,
   für mich.
Und willst du das zärtliche Rehlein sehn,
So lass deine Büchsen im Walde stehn,
Und lass deine klaffenden Hunde zu Haus,
Und lass auf dem Horne den Saus und Braus,
Und scheere vom Kinne das struppige Haar,
Sonst scheut sich im Garten das Rehlein
   fürwahr.

   Doch besser, du bleibest im Walde dazu,

Und liessest die Mühlen und Müller in Ruh'.
Was taugen die Fischlein im grünen Gezweig?
Was will denn das Eichhorn im bläulichen
   Teich?
Drum bleibe, du trotziger Jäger, im Hain,
Und lass mich mit meinen drei Rädern allein;
Und willst meinem Schätzchen dich machen
   beliebt
So wisse, mein Freund, was ihr Herzchen
   betrübt:
Die Eber, die kommen zur Nacht aus dem Hain
Und brechen in ihren Kohlgarten ein,
Und treten und wühlen herum in dem Feld:
Die Eber, die schiesse, du Jägerheld!

What does the huntsman seek here by the
   millstream?
Stay in your own territory, insolent hunter!
Here is no game for you to hunt;
Here dwells only a tame fawn for me.

And should you wish to see that gentle fawn,
Leave your guns in the forest,
Leave your baying hounds at home,
Stop that raucous din on your horn
And shave that unkempt beard from your chin,
Or the fawn in the garden will take fright.

   But it would be better if you stayed in the
      forest
And left mills and millers in peace.
How can fish thrive among green branches?
What can the squirrel want in the blue pond?

Stay in the wood, then, defiant hunter,
And leave me alone with my three mill-wheels,
And if you wish to make yourself popular with
   my sweetheart,
Then, my friend, you should know what
   distresses her heart:
Wild boars come out of the wood at night,
And break into her cabbage patch,
Rooting about and trampling over the field.
Shoot the wild boars, you heroic hunter!

*This is the fourteenth of Schubert's forty-six Müller solo settings (1823, 1827 and 1828). See the
      poet's biography for a chronological list of all the Müller settings.*

This piece strikes the cycle like lightning; even the sudden change from the B flat major of the
preceding song to C minor is a surprise. We have heard nothing like this from the miller before.
At last our hero has found out about the hunter and his role in the girl's life. He has probably
been the last at the mill to know, so absorbed has he been in his own daydreams and wishful
thinking. The song's tessitura is low and suitable for a baritone, as if the miller, in abandoning

the tenor's higher reaches, is demonstrating his masculinity in this man-to-man confrontation. And yet surely this too is happening only in the young miller's mind: a stream of invective that has all the signs of being rehearsed and performed at home – a corollary to *Morgengruss*. As in that song, the imagery is metaphorical, too high-flown for a straightforward fight of the 'You have stolen my girl' variety. The deluded miller regards the miller girl as his property in his description of her as *his* tame fawn ('ein zahmes, für mich'), yet he fights shy of a direct locking of horns, expounding instead for the hunter what Susan Youens calls a 'miniature manual on etiquette'. In this catalogue of 'dos and don'ts' the miller accuses his rival of being the enemy of the natural world, a despoiler of the beauties of nature like the insensitive hunters in *Bambi* who bring death and destruction to the forest. It really distresses the girl that the wild boar destroys her cabbages – why doesn't the hunter do something useful and kill the boar?

We learn a lot about the boy in this poem, above all that he has been given a decent – if conservative – upbringing (we will hear even more of this in the next song). He believes that everything has its place and that different layers of society were not made to mix, much less interbreed. He hates noise and feels threatened by unshaven and unkempt displays of machismo. In short his world is ruled by Apollo, and Dionysus is repressed, and this inability to come to terms with his own masculinity both enrages him (particularly when he sees the magnetic pull of someone who is aggressively male) and probably renders him less attractive to the girl. To illustrate how out of place the hunter is in the mill environment the miller uses the image of a fish in a tree, reminding one of the feminist adage 'A woman needs a man like a fish needs a bicycle'. The beautiful miller girl herself, as is perhaps appropriate for the unenlightened heroine of a nineteenth-century romance, does not seem to agree.

The introduction is a splendid evocation of the hunt, both in its biting $\frac{6}{8}$ rhythm and its use of canon as the right hand chases the left at the distance of a bar. This device, fleetingly suggestive of the fugal *caccia* of Bach's time, is abandoned after its first appearance – far too many words and images are now spat out (a syllable on each fleet quaver) to countenance such contrapuntal complexities. It is interesting that Schubert had already used exactly the same rhythm of these opening four bars (plus upbeat) in his 1816 masterpiece *An Schwager Kronos* D369. Leo Black has pointed out that the Duet (for Eginhard and Brutamonte) from the opera *Fierabras* D796 (Act 2 No. 8, bb. 208–15 'Wir folgen der Spur im hastigen Lauf') anticipates this song by a few months and has the same rhythm and very similar atmosphere – the Frankish knights are 'hunting' Eginhard after all.

The first line of the strophe is perhaps the most direct in the song – a straightforward question ('Was sucht denn der Jäger am Mühlbach hier?') – and is countered in the second by a direct invitation to 'get lost' ('Bleib', trotziger Jäger, in deinem Revier!'). The 'du' form of the verb is calculatedly contemptuous. The third and fourth lines, which contain the miller's claim to possess the girl, are a repeat of this music. From this point one musical phrase (and one line of the poem) at a time is repeated instead of two, and these shorter-breathed statements wonderfully convey not only a sense of mounting anger but also the miller's impotence to influence events. The 'miniature manual on etiquette' is launched by the conditional clause of the strophe's fifth line ('Und willst du das zärtliche Rehlein sehn', bb. 12–14), the music for which is repeated in the sixth.

The right-hand accompaniment has doubled the voice for much of the time, but now the pianist has a burgeoning alto line that tumbles chromatically down the stave as an inner voice, a musical analogy for a slew of words that tumble out of control in pique and petulance. The setting of the seventh line ('Und lass deine klaffenden Hunde zu Haus', bb. 16–18) ventures higher into the stave and is musically repeated in the eighth. The ninth and tenth, similarly paired, are the most dramatic of all and the singer touches a high G at b. 23. In a masterstroke of formal planning Schubert then almost exactly repeats the words and music of these last two lines (as if the miller is in such a rage that he can only splutter what he has already said) so that the vocal line is made up of a symmetrical twenty-four bars. This also has the advantage of accommodating the extra two lines of the second verse (for some reason Müller wrote ten lines in the first and twelve in the second). It is thus Schubert's unusual achievement that he has written a strophic song to a non-strophic text. The hunting phrase that has served as introduction makes a reappearance as a postlude. All here is of the utmost simplicity and economy but this terse, even brutal, music (note the Freudian menace of 'brechen in ihren Kohlgarten ein', bb. 23–24, where users of the Peters Edition would do well to adopt the better word underlay of the NSA) packs a powerful punch all the same. Never again will the miller view the world with a Pollyanna-like innocence. Mention of the defective underlay in the first edition (and thus carried over to the Peters Edition) reminds us that Schubert was away in Zseliz in 1824 when these songs emerged in proof form and he was unable to correct them. The task went to his brother Ferdinand who was not nearly as efficient as he should have been.

First edition:	Published as Op. 25 by Sauer & Leidesdorf, Vienna in 1824 (advertised in August), Book 4, no. 2 (P65)
Second edition:	Published as Op. 25 by Ant. Diabelli & Co., Vienna in 1830
Subsequent editions:	Peters: Vol. 1/36; AGA XX 446: Vol. 7/166; NSA IV: Vol. 2a/70; Bärenreiter: Vol. 1/182
Bibliography:	Black 1998, pp. 27–8
	Youens 1992, pp. 56–9 & 97–9
Arrangements:	Arr. Franz Liszt (1811–1886) for solo piano, no. 3 of *Müllerlieder* (1846) [*see* TRANSCRIPTIONS]
	Arr. Tilman Hoppstock (b. 1961) for guitar accompaniment, in *Franz Schubert: 110 Lieder* (2009)
Discography and timing:	Fischer-Dieskau III 1[14] 1'12
	Pears–Britten 1'18
	Hyperion I 25[17]
	Hyperion II 28[17] 1'15 Ian Bostridge

⟵ *Mit dem grünen Lautenbande* D795/13   *Eifersucht und Stolz* D795/15 ⟶

XV EIFERSUCHT UND STOLZ   Jealousy and pride
Op. 25 no. 15, **D795/15** [H540]
G minor – G major

Wohin so schnell, so kraus und wild, mein
    lieber Bach?[1]
Eilst du voll Zorn dem frechen Bruder
    Jäger nach?

Whither so fast, so ruffled and
    fierce, my beloved brook?
Do you hurry full of anger after our insolent
    huntsman friend?

[1] Müller writes 'Wohin so schnell, so kraus, *so* wild, mein lieber Bach?'

Kehr' um, kehr' um, und schilt erst deine Müllerin	Turn back, and first reproach your maid of the mill
Für ihren leichten, losen, kleinen Flattersinn.	For her frivolous, wanton inconstancy.
Sahst du sie gestern Abend nicht am Tore stehn,	Did you not see her standing by the gate last night,
Mit langem Halse nach der grossen Strasse sehn?	Craning her neck as she looked towards the high road?
Wenn von dem Fang der Jäger lustig zieht nach Haus,	When the huntsman returns home merrily after the kill
Da steckt kein sittsam Kind den Kopf zum Fenster 'naus.	A nice girl does not put her head out of the window.
Geh', Bächlein, hin und sag' ihr das, doch sag' ihr nicht,	Go, brook, and tell her this; but breathe not a word –
Hörst du, kein Wort, von meinem traurigen Gesicht;	Do you hear? – about my unhappy face;
Sag' ihr: Er schnitzt bei mir sich eine Pfeif' aus Rohr,	Tell her: he has cut himself a reed pipe on my banks,
Und bläst den Kindern schöne Tänz' und Lieder vor.	And is piping pretty songs and dances for the children.

This is the fifteenth of Schubert's forty-six Müller solo settings (1823, 1827 and 1828). See the poet's biography for a chronological list of all the Müller settings.

The brook dominates four of the six remaining songs in the cycle and it returns here with a vengeance; during its leave of absence from the cycle the miller has reached crisis point on dry land. Once more he goes to the stream and asks 'Wohin?', but this time he cries all the way to the bank, as it were. Instead of the G major of *Wohin?* in which we encounter the murmuring and beguiling waters, we have G minor to represent another mood altogether; in sympathy with the miller's predicament the brook seems roused to turbulent fury. The piano's right-hand arpeggio figurations are reminiscent of the bustling meanderings of *Das Wandern* although here they are no longer supported by genial striding octaves in the left hand. Instead we hear stringent chords beneath (beginning with open fifths) where an insistent quaver upbeat to a strong first beat of the bar propels the song forward. The courtship of the girl has been a patent failure, and here we see the initiation of the second phase of the boy's relationship with the brook. He will identify himself more and more with his 'friend' until he can scarcely tell the difference between his own words and those whispered to him by the stream.

The tempo is 'Geschwind' and $\frac{2}{4}$. Many performances remove a bar line from every two bars of Schubert's music and find a tempo that is virtually an *alla breve* $\frac{2}{2}$ and far too fast. Not only does this reduce the words to gabble, but it destroys the tempo relationship with *Der Jäger* which is also marked 'Geschwind' and where a dotted crotchet in that song should approximately equal a crotchet of *Eifersucht und Stolz*. After all, the two songs are linked. (In the commentary to the Mayrhofer setting *Der Schiffer* D536 I suggest a similarity of moods and tempi between that song and this one.) This is the brook's commentary on the hunter's (and the girl's) unacceptable behaviour, a mirror of the boy's fury in *Der Jäger*. It makes no sense, however, for the pianist suddenly to give the brook the power of the Hoover Dam – it is still only a stream after all. The semiquavers of *Eifersucht und Stolz* should thus be faster than those of *Das Wandern* but not *twice* as fast as is often the case – for reasons of audibility of the text as much as anything. It is obvious that the tempo of *Der Jäger* is also governed by these practical considerations.

Schubert keeps the swirling accompaniment on the move with the most remarkable combination of standard devices (arpeggio figures and scale passages) given many a new twist of direction by his ingenuity. There is nothing predictable or automatically repetitive about these patterns. The idea of turning around in midstream ('Kehr' um' as the miller commands the brook, bb. 12–14) is admirably caught in the third and fourth bars that first plunge toward the bass clef and then change direction upwards. As in his settings of Goethe's *Gesang der Geister über den Wassern* D484 and D705 Schubert has imagined a course of water as it goes through different terrains, sometimes on the flats and sometimes hilly; a lesser composer would have been content to invent an all-purpose water figuration. The word-setting is particularly subtle: the syncopation of contempt on 'Jäger' (b. 11); the flightiness of the quavers at 'leichten, losen, kleinen Flattersinn' (where he is critical of the miller girl for the first time), illustrative of inconstancy and unreliability; the almost hysterical tessitura of the first two 'Kehr' um' interjections (bb. 22–4). There is more than a suggestion of subterfuge at 'Sahst du sie gestern Abend nicht am Tore stehn' (bb. 26–30). The accompaniment's sneaky left-hand chromatics help to imply that the miller has been spying on the girl (that voyeur again!) and we hear a disconcerting mixture of jealousy and scorn that introduces a note of derangement into the cycle. The octave stretch of 'Mit langem Halse' at bb. 30–32 superbly paints both the miller girl's craned neck as she waits for the hoped-for return of the hunter, and the boy's contempt for her behaviour. Note that the water music ceases as soon as the hunter is announced at b. 36 ('Wenn von dem Fang der Jäger lustig zieht nach Haus') and that this character is strong and independent enough to need only the barest accompaniment. The vocal line is punctuated by miniature horn-fanfare motifs that are imperious and decisive as the miller mocks the hunter's exaggerated machismo (there is enough aggressive masculine exaggeration in this passage to suggest parody). Yet we are only too aware that he is envious. His choice of vocabulary is revealing: when he tells the brook that the miller girl is 'kein sittsam Kind' ('no nice girl') we can see that an insistence on the niceties of behaviour protect him from facing up to reality. He seems unable to cope with the realities of sexual attraction, an electricity that, at a distance, and to his great distress, he can see sparking between his beloved and the hunter. In *Morgengruss* the girl had turned her head away at the window after an imagined ardent greeting; perhaps there is a side to the miller that liked the shyness of that response. He would prefer the girl to remain as inhibited as he is about the physical expression of attraction until he himself is ready to take the plunge. When that will be we do not know – and neither, we suspect, does he.

Throughout the song the miller talks to the brook as his servant and messenger. Rather than chase after the hunter his watery friend is bidden to turn back and reproach the girl who is now 'deine Müllerin' ('*your* miller girl'). He considers that the brook owes him this favour: who else led him to the girl's door, and who else is responsible for the whole debacle? As soon as the lesson in ladylike manners has been formulated, and with literally no pause for breath, the brook is sent on its way ('Geh', Bächlein, hin und sag' ihr das') with a change into the major at b. 67, showing how pleased the boy is to have delivered his reproving lecture. At this point Schubert's abilities as a setter of words are once again proven to be beyond compare. The miller, concerned for his *amour propre* and fearing that the brook might tell the girl more than is necessary, has a last-minute inspiration. At 'doch sag' ihr nicht, / Hörst du, kein Wort, von meinem traurigen Gesicht' the stream is put 'on hold' at the miller's behest. The accompaniment flows on and yet it seems obediently to wait and listen, treading water as the boy takes time to formulate his exact message. The urgent parenthesis of 'Hörst du, kein Wort' is superbly effective, with just the right suggestion of finger-wagging in the dotted rhythm of 'kein Wort'. The music moves back briefly into G minor here and 'traurigen Gesicht' (bb. 61–3) has just a tiny suggestion of self-pity consistent with the boy's tendency throughout to

Eifersucht und Stolz, woodcut from the 'Prachtausgabe' of the cycle (1872).

theatricalize his plight. The elongation of the final 'sag' ihr' takes the time needed to hatch a plot, or at any rate to string together a tall story before our very ears. It is in exactly this way that Brahms, in his *Botschaft* Op. 47 no. 1 (bb. 39–40), no doubt inspired by Schubert's example, prolongs the word 'Sprich' ('Say') before coming up with a sufficiently convincing formulation of words for the breezes to convey to his beloved. This improvised message is preceded (in both songs) by a musically engineered hesitation that might be verbally expressed as follows: 'Tell her . . . wait a minute . . . yes, I've *got* it!' (clinched by a strong modulation to a major key).

And then he plumps for his tall story: the change back into G major (b. 67 at 'Er schnitzt') is like a trap springing shut, superbly evocative of this flash of inspiration. The word-setting and prosody of this whole section is as masterly as anything the composer ever achieved. The last passage, the poem's final two lines, evokes a little pastoral idyll with the insouciance of forced jollity. The water motif is pressed into service as warbling pipe music to which entirely imaginary children dance, but tears are never far away. The vehement return of 'Sag' ihr' (bb. 87–9) shatters the pretence – the first two of these revert to the minor key, and the final outbursts, high in the voice and in G major, seem intoxicated with this face-saving message. Nevertheless these are *cris de cœur* which pierce the heart. The postlude tumbles in arpeggios to the bottom of the piano before a perfect cadence, two loud and defiant chords, reminds us that pride, after all, is the second part of the song's title. In his *Tagebuch* entry for 30 November 1815 Müller reveals what might have been the beginnings of this poem in regard to his protracted (and unsuccessful) wooing of Luise Hensel: 'But to no one else so-ever on this earth shall you belong! Is that jealousy, envy? What if you were to be happy with another? Ah, so just show me that other who deserves you, who can make you happy!'[1]

---

[1] The original German of this passage is as follows: 'Aber, nur keinem Andern musst du auf Erden angehören! Ist das Eifersucht, Neid! Wenn du nun glücklich wärest mit einem Andern? Ach, so zeige mir jenen Andern, der dich verdient, der dich glücklich machen kann?'

First edition:	Published as Op. 25 by Sauer & Leidesdorf, Vienna in 1824
	(advertised in August), Book 4, no. 3 (P66)
Second edition:	Published as Op. 25 by Ant. Diabelli & Co., Vienna in 1830
Subsequent editions:	Peters: Vol. 1/38; AGA XX 447: Vol. 7/168; NSA IV: Vol. 2a/72;
	Bärenreiter: Vol. 1/184
Bibliography:	Youens 1992, pp. 59–60 & 99–102
Discography and timing:	Fischer-Dieskau III 1[15] 1'32
	Pears–Britten 1'35
	Hyperion I 25[18]
	Hyperion II 28[18] 1'36 Ian Bostridge

← *Der Jäger D795/14*   *Erster Schmerz, letzter Scherz* →

ERSTER SCHMERZ, LETZTER SCHERZ   First pain, last happiness
[H540+]

This poem was not set to music by Schubert

Nun sitz' am Bache nieder	So sit by the stream
Mit deinem hellen Rohr,	With your cheerful reed
Und blas' den lieben Kindern	And play pretty songs
Die schönen Lieder vor.	For the dear children!
Die Lust ist ja verrauschet,	Pleasure has flowed away
Das Leid hat immer Zeit:	Sorrow always has its turn;
Nun singe neue Lieder	So sing new songs
Von alter Seligkeit.	Of my old happiness.
Noch blühn die alten Blumen,	The same flowers are in bloom,
Noch rauscht der alte Bach,	The same stream rushes by,
Es scheint die liebe Sonne	The dear sun shines now
Noch wie am ersten Tag.	As it did on that first day.
Die Fensterscheiben glänzen	The window panes sparkle
Im klaren Morgenschein,	In the bright morning light,
Und hinter den Fensterscheiben	And behind the panes
Da sitzt die Liebste mein.	Sits my sweetheart.
Ein Jäger, ein grüner Jäger,	A huntsman, dressed in green,
Der liegt in ihrem Arm –	Lies in her arms –
Ei, Bach, wie lustig du rauschest,	Ah, my stream, how merrily you murmur,
Ei, Sonne, wie scheinst du so warm!	Ah, sun, how warmly you shine!
Ich will einen Strauss dir pflücken,	My love, I will pick you
Herzliebste, von buntem Klee,	A posy of bright clover:[1]
Den sollst du mir stellen an's Fenster,	Put it in your window
Damit ich den Jäger nicht seh'.	So I cannot see the huntsman.

[1] Among much else, a symbol of first love.

Ich will mit Rosenblättern	I will scatter rose-petals
Den Mühlensteg bestreun:	On the mill-bridge,
Der Steg hat mich getragen	For that bridge brought me
Zu dir, Herzliebste mein!	To you, my dear love:
Und wenn der stolze Jäger	And if that arrogant huntsman
Ein Blättchen mir zertritt,	Steps on one of my petals,
Dann stürz', o Steg, zusammen	I want the bridge to collapse
Und nimm den Grünen mit!	And take the green huntsman with it,
Und trag ihn auf dem Rücken	And carry him on his back
In's Meer, mit gutem Wind,	Out to sea; and with a strong wind
Nach einer fernen Insel,	Take him to a far-off island
Wo keine Mädchen sind.	Where there are no girls.
Herzliebste, das Vergessen,	My love, forgetfulness
Es kommt dir ja nicht schwer –	Is not so hard for you –
Willst du den Müller wieder?	Will you take your miller back again?
Vergisst dich nimmermehr.	He will never forget you.

Bibliography: Youens 1992, p. 60
                          Youens 1997, pp. 169–91
Discography and timing: Fischer-Dieskau   –
                          Hyperion I 25[19]
                          Hyperion II 28[19]   1'39   Dietrich Fischer-Dieskau

⟵ *Eifersucht und Stolz* D795/15   *Die liebe Farbe* D795/16 ⟶

XVI Die LIEBE FARBE   The beloved colour
Op. 25 no. 16, **D795/16** [H541]
B minor

In Grün will ich mich klei - den,

(26 bars)

In Grün will ich mich kleiden,	I shall dress in green,
In grune Tränenweiden,	In green weeping willows:
Mein Schatz hat's Grün so gern.	My love is so fond of green.
Will suchen einen Zypressenhain,	I shall seek out a cypress grove,
Eine Heide von grünem Rosmarein,[1]	A heath full of green rosemary:
Mein Schatz hat's Grün so gern.[2]	My love is so fond of green.

[1] In both editions of the poem (1821 and 1826) Müller uses the older spelling of 'Haide'. In the 1826 edition of the *Gedichte* he changes the line slightly: 'Eine *Haide voll* grünem Rosmarein'.
[2] Müller adapts this line from *Rose die Müllerin* by Hedwig von Stägemann (from the original Berlin *Liederspiel*) where it is 'Ich hab' das Grün so gern'. This later appeared in Hedwig's *Gedichte* published under her married name of Hedwig von Olfers.

Wohlauf zum fröhlichen Jagen![3]	Up, away to the merry hunt!
Wohlauf durch Heid' und Hagen!	Away over heath and hedge!
Mein Schatz hat's Jagen so gern.	My love is so fond of hunting.
Das Wild, das ich jage, das ist der Tod,	The game I hunt is death.
Die Heide, die heiss ich die Liebesnot,	The heath I call Love's Torment:
Mein Schatz hat's Jagen so gern.	My love is so fond of green.
Grabt mir ein Grab im Wasen,	Dig me a grave in the grass.
Deckt mich mit grünem Rasen,	Cover me with green turf.
Mein Schatz hat's Grün so gern.	My love is so fond of green.
Kein Kreuzlein schwarz, kein Blümlein bunt,	No black cross, no colourful flowers,
Grün, Alles grün so rings und rund!	Green, everything green, all around.
Mein Schatz hat's Grün so gern.	My love is so fond of green.

This is the sixteenth of Schubert's forty-six Müller solo settings (1823, 1827 and 1828). See the poet's biography for a chronological list of all the Müller settings.

It is at this point in the cycle that the music achieves tragic stature: from now on there is no detail that does not seem to point to the miller's inevitable doom, and Schubert rises to every challenge brought about by this crescendo of pathos and heartbreak. The time signature is $\frac{2}{4}$ – the same as for *Eifersucht und Stolz*. There are also eight relentless semiquavers in every bar of the accompaniment as in that song, but here there is a complete transformation of *Bewegung* and deepening of mood. The key is B minor. John Reed writes that Schubert uses this tonality for music of 'alienation and derangement' (*Der Doppelgänger* D957/13 is another example) and both these words seem appropriate here. We might also mention the B minor of the 'Unfinished' Symphony D759 in relation to the architecture of a song which, over its three strophes, achieves the inevitability and sweep of a symphonic movement.

There is no more dissembling in this song, no more half-hearted attempts at pretending to play the pipes to happy children. Here we have a young man overwhelmed by grief and obsessed by its cause. The previous poem in the cycle, unset by Schubert, has described how the miller has to watch his beloved in the hunter's arms, and that he must simply learn to live with it. At least Schubert spares his hero this masochism. All he can think of is the word 'green' and its implications: 'Mein Schatz hat's Grün so gern' at the end of the first and last strophes is a bitter echo of the words that tripped off her tongue in *Mit dem grünen Lautenbande*. Thinking back he realizes that she was teasing him with an announcement of her attraction to the hunter even then. Every time we hear this phrase in this song it is first in B major rising to a high F sharp on the vocal line, and then in crestfallen echo in B minor and lower in the voice. This may seem like hackneyed musical practice, but in Schubert's hands the juxtaposition of masochistic sweetness and dark brooding is magical. It also suggests the contrast between the girl's happy reaction to the colour, reported ironically by the miller in the major, and his own minor-key emotions in counterpoint. The colour that once represented freshness and innocence now stands for jealousy and everything that the hunter has and the miller lacks. He might just as well say 'My love is so fond of strong, tall men', 'men with an exciting career', 'men with decisive personalities' and so on.

---

[3] Müller adapts this line from a military poem by de la Motte Fouqué for a regiment of hunters: *Kriegslied für die freiwilligen Jäger* (1813).

Another possibility is more literal: 'My love is so fond of green' could imply that he believes that it is the green garb that has beguiled and seduced rather than the intrinsically worthless person who wears it. An arid world is implied, where human attributes are less important than rank or dress. Would the miller like to believe that the girl is beguiled by nothing more serious than the hunter's costume, that she is in the grip of a fetish for green rather than truly in love? This would make her just as unbalanced as he is, her fixation a counterpart of his. From our viewpoint this is unlikely; from his, highly desirable, for such crushes and passions for uniforms are more likely to fade than real love.

The most famous feature of this strictly strophic song is the 532 repeated F sharps (miscounted as 536 by Richard Capell) which softly yet insistently sound in the right hand throughout the accompaniment. These F sharps are buried within chords during the remarkably beautiful four-bar ritornello that is a miracle of emotional depth and harmonic simplicity – essentially a simple tune built on an oscillation between tonic and dominant, conveying heartbreak and yearning with quiet grandeur. In the main body of the song the F sharps emerge to be played singly by the right hand, the obsession exposed. The left hand supports this threnody with bare quavers and a contrapuntal effect is produced between the hands of hunting-horn motifs in thirds and sixths (under the first 'Mein Schatz hat's Grün so gern' and at 'Will suchen einen Zypressenhain' – the cypress being the tree of death). This gives the first verse a pervasive elegiac quality, like the melancholy echoes of a hunt at dusk in a dark green forest. The performers have the licence to vary the dynamics and intensity of the horn-writing to make this passage truly ominous. (It is interesting that the composer had already written unaccompanied songs for voices or horns – presumably for outdoor performance – in 1815.) These quasi-horn effects come into their own in the second strophe where it is even clearer that the young man has death on his mind – not the hunter's but his own. Charles Rosen in *The Romantic Generation* has drawn attention to the fact that repetitions on one note in both vocal line and accompaniment also occur in *Der Wegweiser* D911/20 from *Winterreise* and that these too denote the inexorable path to death. A more modern piece of music with the same bleakly repetitive imagery is *Le Gibet*, one of Ravel's *Gaspard de la nuit* (1908) for piano.

The voice part is also miraculous. Schubert's highly charged but essentially tranquil vocal line takes away from Müller's words their inherent sarcasm, spite and petulance, even their rage, and replaces them with something monumental and universal. The song is often performed too slowly (it is the crotchet that is 'rather slow' which does not mean dragging semiquavers) but at the right tempo the long soaring phrases confer on the singer a tragic dignity, disturbed and unhinged rather than comatose. As happens often in this cycle, the composer writes music for the words which is as real as the miller's belief in them. This is surely the key to depicting madness on stage with true pathos. It is for us, the audience, to see the larger scenario, to spot the self-deception and identify the pathological condition. As far as the hero of this cycle is concerned it is all *real*: the moments where he sees love to be his for the taking are set to music (*Ungeduld* and *Mein!*) that reflects his certainties rather than our doubts. It is *our* perception of the gap between his shining confidence and what we know to be the truth which is the stuff of tragedy. Shakespeare understood this by creating for his mad men and women an inner world that makes perfect sense for them, however disturbed we know them to be. We have already spoken of a link between the young miller and Hamlet and, as Susan Youens has pointed out, in this song he seeks a place to die with weeping willow and rosemary, a locale that mirrors the watery grave of Ophelia. A reading of Müller's poem might make of these words a manipulative threat designed to shock the girl into regret. With Schubert's music and the other-worldly spell that it weaves with its hypnotic and haunting repetitions (not only of the F sharps, but of the strophes themselves) we hear all too clearly that this boy is not only threatening suicide, he is capable of it at any time.

First edition:	Published as Op. 25 by Sauer & Leidesdorf, Vienna in 1824 (advertised in August), Book 4, no. 4 (P67)
Second edition:	Published as Op. 25 by Ant. Diabelli & Co., Vienna in 1830
Subsequent editions:	Peters: Vol. 1/41; AGA XX 448: Vol. 7/172; NSA IV: Vol. 2a/76; Bärenreiter: Vol. 1/188
Bibliography:	Youens 1992, pp. 61–2 & 102–4
	Youens 1997, pp. 198–203
Further settings and arrangements:	Fanny Mendelssohn (1805–1847) *Die liebe Farbe* (1823)
	Arr. Tilman Hoppstock (b. 1961) for guitar accompaniment, in *Franz Schubert: 110 Lieder* (2009)
Discography and timing:	Fischer-Dieskau III 1[16] 3'50
	Pears–Britten 4'02
	Hyperion I 25[20]
	Hyperion II 28[20] 4'05 Ian Bostridge

← *Erster Schmerz, letzter Scherz*   *Die böse Farbe* D795/17 →

XVII Die BÖSE FARBE   The loathsome colour
Op. 25 no. 17, **D795/17** [H542]
B major

Ich möchte ziehn in die Welt hinaus,
Hinaus in die weite Welt,
Wenn's nur so grün, so grün nicht wär'
Da draussen in Wald und Feld!

  Ich möchte die grünen Blätter all'
Pflücken von jedem Zweig,
Ich möchte die grünen Gräser all'
Weinen ganz totenbleich.

  Ach Grün, du böse Farbe du,
Was siehst mich immer an,
So stolz, so keck, so schadenfroh,
Mich armen, weissen Mann?[1]

  Ich möchte liegen vor ihrer Tür,
Im Sturm und Regen und Schnee,[2]

I should like to go out into the world,
Into the wide world.
If only it were not so green
Out there in field and forest!

  I should like to pluck the green leaves
From every branch;
I should like to make the green grass
Deathly pale with my weeping.

  O green, you loathsome colour,
Why do you look at me,
So proud, so insolent, so gloating –
At me, a poor white miller?

  I should like to lie at her door
In storm and rain and snow,

[1] In this line Schubert sets the word 'armen' twice.
[2] Müller writes '*In* Sturm und Regen und Schnee'.

Und singen ganz leise bei Tag und Nacht	And sing softly, day and night,
Das eine Wörtchen Ade!	One single word, 'Farewell!'
Horch, wenn im Wald ein Jagdhorn schallt,[3]	Hark! When a hunting horn sounds in the wood,
Da klingt ihr Fensterlein,	I can hear her window.
Und schaut sie auch nach mir nicht aus,	And though she is not looking out for me,
Darf ich doch schauen hinein.	Yet I can look in.
O binde von der Stirn dir ab	O untie the green ribbon
Das grüne, grüne Band,	From your brow.
Ade, Ade! und reiche mir	Farewell! And in parting
Zum Abschied deine Hand!	Give me your hand.

This is the seventeenth of Schubert's forty-six Müller solo settings (1823, 1827 and 1828). See the poet's biography for a chronological list of all the Müller settings.

This song is a mirror image of *Die liebe Farbe*, and not only in terms of its title. Where *Die liebe Farbe* is slow, *Die böse Farbe* is rather fast ('Ziemlich geschwind'); where the first seems drained of energy, the second is vehement; the first in B minor, the second in B major, for Schubert has paradoxically used the minor key for a song about the beloved colour, and the major for this tirade against the same loathsome colour. Everything in the miller's world is topsy-turvy and this view of life 'through the looking glass' reveals itself as increasingly unhinged. Throughout the cycle the miller has been the opposite of a man of action: he has shied away from direct confrontation, whether with the girl with whom he has fallen in love, or with the hunter. This timidity has been balanced by a fevered imagination and a great deal of rage – or impotent anger – which finds no outlet in reality. No one at the mill has any idea of his hidden depths, or the ecstatic highs and terrible lows of which he is capable. This song is the apotheosis of that manic-depressive pattern where ironic enthusiasm and desperate panic stand side by side. It is pervaded by the phrase 'Ich möchte' – 'I would like'; indeed it is a catalogue of what he *would* do if he had the will and energy. The boy has always had a tendency to fantasize and daydream, but now he is locked into a world of words where the idea of green, a poetic conceit that was first used with delight (XIII) and then with irony, sarcasm and heartbreak (XVI) has taken the form of a nightmare obsession. The colour becomes anthropomorphized into a living, dangerous thing.

    The composer takes the opportunity to juxtapose two important motifs in this song. In contrast to *Eifersucht und Stolz* where the description of the hunter's courting is kept quite separate from the main colloquy with the stream, the brook's water music and the music of the hunt here run into each other like colours merging on a painter's palette. The deadly rival has stormed the fortress of the boy's secret world and nowhere is safe from his influence. Accordingly the first two bars of the *Vorspiel* introduce watery sextuplets (marked 'piano') in B major, followed immediately by a bar of strident B minor sextuplets (marked 'forte') in hunting-horn style and then three snatched and angry quaver Bs, the second supported by an arpeggiated minor chord. This underlines the hunter's ubiquitous presence in the miller's thoughts. The opening vocal phrase ('Ich möchte ziehn in die Welt hinaus') is also forte, a bold outdoor tune built from a B major arpeggio and accompanied by quaver chords alternating in each hand. At 'Hinaus in die weite Welt' the effortful vocal line at the top of the stave on 'weite' (b. 7) conveys

---

[3] Müller writes 'Horch, wenn im Wald ein Jagdhorn *ruft*'.

the miller trying in vain to encompass the entire world; here the voice's Herculean task is supported by the piano doubling the vocal line. At 'Wenn's nur so grün' (bb. 9–10) the quaver accompaniment is reminiscent of that for 'Ich frage keine Blume' in *Der Neugierige*, as if harking back to the world of flowers and gardeners, now a part of the hated terrain of green. This section modulates to the dominant and the hunting-horn figure in the piano, a shudder of revulsion in this context (b. 12), leads us back to the tonic and introduces the second strophe ('Ich möchte die grünen Blätter all''). From the musical point of view this is a modified repeat of the first; note the staccato chords under 'Pflücken' (b. 15) that onomatopoeically suggest leaves plucked from branches, and the astonishing shift of harmony – a tonal analogue for a sea change or an altered state of matter – on 'toten<u>bleich</u>' (b. 20). Here the colour is bleached from B minor by a sudden sideways shift into the whiteness of C major, the flattened supertonic.

The third strophe ('Ach Grün, du böse Farbe du') contains new music in the manner of an accusatory recitative. This denunciation of the loathsome colour shifts focus from the operatic flow of the 'Ich möchte' phrases, which have to be sung in long lines. Despite a certain freedom of expression as the singer moves away from cantilena to much shorter phrases in speech rhythms spat out between clenched teeth, the rhythm remains strictly governed by the throbbing ostinato of horn-like sextuplets in the piano's tenor register (from b. 21). This passage makes an almost orchestral effect as the outer fingers of the right hand play legato quavers from b. 23, the left staccato, while the right thumb hammers away, driving the point home about the miller's obsession with his *bête verte*. The hunter lies under the skin of the music here, his motif like Blake's rose-devouring invisible worm that flies in the night. This passage, working on three levels at once, is truly fractured into self-defeating warring factions, almost a clinical description in music of the miller's paranoic imaginings. His physical description of himself is revealing: 'Mich armen, armen weissen Mann'. Not only is he covered with flour (an occupational hazard, and as much a sign of his calling as is the hunter's green), he is pale with shock and white with fury.

For the fourth strophe (from b. 32) we have a repeat of the opening tune, this time marked pianissimo; indeed for the rest of the song there is no further dynamic marking, but it would be a brave singer who obeyed the composer in this respect. In most performances the phrase is seldom less than mezzo forte, the song's ending never less than forte. For 'Ich möchte liegen vor ihrer Tür' the brook makes an appearance as accompanist, gently murmuring the sextuplets that we heard in the prelude. Instead of violent action this whispering proposes passive resistance. It is highly significant that the brook is the boy's sponsor when he first uses the word 'Ade!' – 'farewell' – a tiny word with large implications. It is the same word, one of the few which the miller girl has exchanged with her apprentice employee, spoken to him in *Tränenregen*. He has not answered her until now, but his 'Ade' is irrevocable. The idea of lying in front of the girl's door is one which Susan Youens avers that 'nineteenth-century readers would have construed as feminine in nature'. Such passivity in abject male suitors is found in other songs in the lieder repertory (for instance, Schumann's *Der Page* Op. 30 no. 2 and *O wüsstest Du* from Wolf's *Italienisches Liederbuch*). As it is sung here in the major key and with a certain bitter sweetness, the miller, gripped by a masochistic delight, wishes for his own *Liebestod* with Isolde-like euphoria.

The fifth strophe is one of the most extraordinary passages in the cycle. A new hunting-horn figure appears in the form of ninety-five feverish repetitions of the same F sharp (from b. 41) that lie at the centre of *Die liebe Farbe*. Here supporting chords evoke music of the chase with alternating major and minor harmonies. This covert reference to the previous song that was all about the girl's preference for green is a sign that the miller girl herself will now enter the picture, on the hunter's arm as it were. The boy all but foams at the mouth at the thought that the raucous, priapic sound of the horn will bring her expectantly to her window, with eyes only for the man in green. Not for the first time the miller shows his propensity for voyeurism, although he will of course only be peering in at the window in his thoughts. He can fancy that in her hair she is wearing the green ribbon from his lute like an obscene trophy. He tells her to take it off with such desperation ('O binde von der Stirn dir ab / Das grüne, grüne Band') that it is as though he believes that in wearing it she has some talismanic power over him: when she removes it he will die perhaps, but he will also be released. The melody of the last strophe is more or less a musical repeat of the second. The brook music still forms the basis of the accompaniment but with greater assurance, as if it has seized control of the situation and has the power to wash the sound of the hunter away. The goodbye is now almost noble, and hysteria yields to eloquence and real pathos. The melody has gained stature in repetition and here sounds heroic and manly. Schubert speaks up for the boy, making us respect him when Müller would sometimes have us laugh at him. This farewell in the major key conveys the same recklessness and touching gallantry found in the poem by A. E. Housman (England's Müller and Heine combined) about an enemy soldier 'That took the sabre straight and took it striking / And laughed and kissed his hand to me and died'. It is interesting that the words of this verse are the last, and the most decisive, addressed to the girl. With steely determination the miller asks her to give him her hand – if not in marriage, then in final farewell. At last he imagines actually telling – nay commanding – *her* to do something for *him*, and it is only in accepting the inevitability of death that he can summon the courage to do so. He would die as he touched her for the first and last time. The postlude, an exact repetition of the introduction, leaves us in the same place in which we started – the song has solved nothing and has only exacerbated the crisis.

First edition:	Published as Op. 25 by Sauer & Leidesdorf, Vienna in 1824 (advertised in August), Book 4, no. 5 (P68)
Second edition:	Published as Op. 25 by Ant. Diabelli & Co., Vienna in 1830
Subsequent editions:	Peters: Vol. 1/43; AGA XX 449: Vol. 7/174; NSA IV: Vol. 2a/78; Bärenreiter: Vol. 1/190
Bibliography:	Youens 1992, pp. 62–4 & 104–6
Further settings and arrangements:	Ludwig Berger (1777–1839) *Der Müller* (1816) Arr. Franz Liszt (1811–1886) for solo piano, no. 4 of *Müllerlieder* (1846) [*see* TRANSCRIPTIONS]
Discography and timing:	Fischer-Dieskau III 1[17] 1'59
	Pears–Britten 1'55
	Hyperion I 25[21]
	Hyperion II 28[21] 2'01 Ian Bostridge

← *Die liebe Farbe* D795/16   *Blümlein Vergissmein* →

BLÜMLEIN VERGISSMEIN   The forget-me flower
[H542+]

This poem was not set to music by Schubert.

Was treibt mich jeden Morgen	What drives me every morning
So tief in's Holz hinein?	So deep into the woods?
Was frommt mir, mich zu bergen	What is the use of hiding myself
Im unbelauschten Hain?	In secluded groves?

Es blüht auf allen Fluren	In all the meadows
Blümlein V e r g i s s m e i n n i c h t,	*Forget-me-nots* flower;
Es schaut vom heitern Himmel	From the cloudless sky
Herab in blauem Licht.	Their blue radiance glows,
Und soll ich's niedertreten,	And if I nearly step on one,
Bebt mir der Fuss zurück,	My trembling foot hesitates,
Es fleht aus jedem Kelche	For beseeching from every chalice
Ein wohlbekannter Blick.	It is that well-known look
Weisst du, in welchem Garten	Do you know a garden
Blümlein V e r g i s s m e i n steht?	Where a *forget-me* flower grows?
Das Blümlein muss ich suchen,	I must search for that flower,
Wie auch die Strasse geht.	Wherever it might be.
'S ist nicht für Mädchenbusen,	It is not for a girl's breast,
So schön sieht es nicht aus:	It is not pretty enough for that –
Schwarz, schwarz ist seine Farbe,	Black, black is its colour;
Es passt in keinen Strauss.	It wouldn't be right in any posy.
Hat keine grüne Blätter,	It has no green leaves,
Hat keinen Blütenduft,	No flower scent,
Es windet sich am Boden	It writhes on the ground
In nächtig dumpfer Luft.	In the musty night air.
Wächst auch an einem Ufer,	It grows on a bank
Doch unten fliesst kein Bach,	But no stream flows below –
Und willst das Blümlein pflücken,	If you try to pick the flower
Dich zieht der Abgrund nach.	An abyss drags you down.
Das ist der rechte Garten,	That's the proper place for it,
Ein schwarzer, schwarzer Flor:	A bright black plant;
Darauf magst du dich betten –	You could make your bed on it –
Schleuss zu das Gartentor!	Lock the garden gate.

Bibliography: Youens 1992, p. 64
                         Youens 1997, pp. 169–91
Discography and timing: Fischer-Dieskau   –
                         Hyperion I 25[22]
                         Hyperion II 28[22]   1'27   Dietrich Fischer-Dieskau

← *Die böse Farbe* D795/17   *Trockne Blumen* D795/18 →

XVIII TROCKNE BLUMEN

Op. 25 no. 18, **D795/18** [H543]

E minor – E major

Withered flowers

(57 bars)

Ihr Blümlein alle,	All you flowers
Die sie mir gab,	That she gave to me,
Euch soll man legen	You shall be laid
Mit mir ins Grab.	With me in the grave.
Wie seht ihr alle	How sorrowfully
Mich an so weh,	You all look at me,
Als ob ihr wüsstet,	As though you knew
Wie mir gescheh'?	How I was feeling!
Ihr Blümlein alle,	All you flowers,
Wie welk, wie blass?	How faded and pale you are!
Ihr Blümlein alle	All you flowers,
Wovon so nass?	Why are you so moist?
Ach, Tränen machen	Alas, tears will not create
Nicht maiengrün,	The green of May,
Machen tote Liebe	Nor make dead love
Nicht wieder blühn.	Bloom anew.
Und Lenz wird kommen	Spring will come,
Und Winter wird gehn,	And winter will pass,
Und Blümlein werden	And flowers
Im Grase stehn,	Will grow in the grass.
Und Blümlein liegen	And flowers will lie
In meinem Grab,	In my grave –
Die Blümlein alle,	All the flowers
Die sie mir gab.	That she gave me.
Und wenn sie wandelt	And when she walks
Am Hügel vorbei,	Past that mound
Und denkt im Herzen:	And reflects in her heart,
'D e r meint' es treu!'	'*His* love was true.'
Dann Blümlein alle,	Then, all you flowers,
Heraus, heraus!	Come forth, come forth!
Der Mai ist kommen,	May is here,
Der Winter ist aus.	Winter is over!

This is the eighteenth of Schubert's forty-six Müller solo settings (1823, 1827 and 1828). See the poet's biography for a chronological list of all the Müller settings.

The previous song has had a watery flow; the brook comes to the miller's side at the moment that he decides to say goodbye, as if pulling at his sleeve like a suitor who has a solution to all his problems. There is also a certain sexual quality to the music of *Die böse Farbe*, a lubricity that imagines (as subtext at least) what the hunter and girl are getting up to, and the frustration felt by the boy who cannot reconcile lust with love. Here by contrast is the triumph of asceticism: everything (in the first part of the song at least) is dry and desiccated. It is significant that at this point the miller still imagines that his grave will be on terra firma. The preceding poem in Müller's cycle, *Blümlein Vergissmein* (not set by Schubert), has referred to copses, groves and gardens but not to the stream. Before going to the waterside and yielding to the persuasive murmurings of the brook, the miller allows himself one more fantasy scenario that builds into one of the cycle's high points in terms of both emotion and decibels. We are not aware that the girl has ever given our lad flowers (surely that is the role of the man in a courtship?) but he refers here to 'all the flowers that she gave to me'. Of course these may be real forget-me-nots, but the very premise that gives rise to this song may well be imaginary and metaphoric, the withered flowers a symbol of glances and smiles that he has wrongly interpreted as signs of love.

The movement of *Die böse Farbe* was flowingly horizontal but here everything is vertical; the recurring ictus of the beat, emphasized by the accompaniment's lifeless quavers, constructs a musical straitjacket. In no other song in the cycle is strictness of tempo more important for the performers. The mood is one of a funeral cortège and the melody has a measured tread, progressing disconcertingly from quiet dignity (which masks hysteria) to rapturous euphoria. This song must have appealed to Mahler who was also taken by funeral music as a mixture of the grotesque and religious, folksong in the context of age-old, primitive ceremonial. That Schubert was proud of this melody, as simple as it is memorable, is suggested by the fact that he soon re-used it as the basis of his 'Trockne Blumen' Variations in E minor for flute and piano (D802, January 1824), notably keeping the key of the song as an essential part of the tune's character. His use of the melody for variation is a further indication that he thought of it as dried seed which, when watered by the miller's tears, or the composer's imagination, could quickly blossom into more luxuriant foliage. The sparseness of the original inspiration, with its strong tonal skeleton, allows much amplification, and the instrumental writing of these Variations is among the composer's most ornate and virtuosic. In the same way the final page of this song is certainly the most heroic in the cycle, the underlying tempo and shape indivisible from the opening, and yet astonishingly different in scale and emotional range.

Schubert uses three strophes of the poem to make a musical verse that unwinds as if on automatic pilot, expressing numbness of emotion and the irrevocable march of fate. Simple yet heart-rending modulations at the end of each of Müller's strophes punctuate this tune without giving much pause for thought or breath. Thus at 'Mit mir ins Grab' (b. 6) and 'Wie mir gescheh'?' (b. 10) the music slips into the relative major with wonderful pathos. At the end of the third strophe the cadence at 'Wovon so nass?' is positively agonized, the voice high on the stave and the accompaniment in sad echo a bar later. With confidence in his melodic gift, Schubert uses almost exactly the same music for the next three strophes. There is a slight ornamentation of the vocal line at 'Lenz wird kommen / Und Winter wird gehn': two demisemiquavers on 'wird' are set in such a way as superficially to suggest a brief wintry shudder, but it is more likely that this new eruption in the vocal line represents a thaw, the rhythm of the vocal line enlivened by the spring sunshine.

At the seventh strophe the key signature changes to E major (from b. 30) and we are plunged into the future, a happier time even though – or perhaps because – the miller is depicted as dead and buried. Here *Der Lindenbaum* D911/5 from *Winterreise* comes to mind, a song that also veers between two time zones (past and present in that case) as expressed by E major and E minor with repetitive figures in the accompaniment. At 'Und wenn sie wandelt / Am Hügel vorbei' the right-hand accompaniment retains the same holding pattern of quaver + semiquaver rest + semiquaver that has dryly shadowed the vocal line in the rest of the song. In the left hand a marvellous little E major tune in dotted rhythm begins to extend its tendrils across the bass-clef trellis, a tonal analogue for the stirring power of seed about to sprout. It is given its final encouragement to emerge by the girl's imagined words 'D e r meint' es treu!' and at 'Dann Blümlein alle, / Heraus!' (bb. 34–6) the dotted semiquaver figure makes its way above ground into the treble clef. The music now begins to take on a bracing quality bordering on the menacing: the rolled 'r' of 'heraus' makes the word a frightening command and what has started as a small cortège turns into a triumphalist rally. This galvanizing outburst reaches its apotheosis on 'Der Mai ist kommen, / Der Winter ist aus' (bb. 36–8), the piano supporting the voice in strong dactylic rhythm. This is not only a deranged fantasy of power after death but a metaphor for the miller's sexual power which has frightened and tormented him and which, repressed throughout the cycle, is here liberated by words he imagines from *her* ('D e r meint' es treu!'), justifying his love at last. The emphasis in this printing underlines the miller's fantasy about being the chosen one after all, his fidelity standing in triumphant contrast to that of the hunter who in the long run will certainly be revealed as untrustworthy. The priapic forces that rise into action are more than a match for the masculinity of the miller's rival. The singer's loudest moments in the cycle occur here; after this terrifying climax there is nothing left to say in the forte dynamic, and piano and pianissimo govern the last six bars of *Trockne Blumen*, continuing for the remainder of the cycle. The detumescence brought about by reality at the end of the song deflates the moment of glory that has come too late. The dotted semi-quaver motif which has initiated the change to E major makes a final forlorn appearance in E minor (from b. 54) and we first hear the tonic chord in this key on a weak beat in the penultimate bar. The left-hand figuration descends to the bottom of the stave in a direction that signifies the grave.

A. E. Housman must have known this song, or at least the poem, when he wrote the following lines (published after his death as XXXI of *More Poems*). 'Forget me!' the lover has said, and the poet obeys this command to a masochistic extent that outdoes the German poet: the flowers are not even permitted to spring up in rebuke (an obvious sexual metaphor, as in Müller) as the unreciprocating beloved passes the suicide's grave:

> If here, where clover whitens
>   The dead man's knoll, you pass,
> And no tall flower to meet you
>   Starts in the trefoiled grass,
>
> Halt by the headstone naming
>   The heart no longer stirred,
> And say the lad that loved you
>   Was one that kept his word.

First edition:	Published as Op. 25 by Sauer & Leidesdorf, Vienna in 1824 (advertised in August), Book 5, no. 1 (P69)
Second edition:	Published as Op. 25 by Ant. Diabelli & Co., Vienna in 1830. The ornamented version of *Trockne Blumen* is reprinted in NSA Vol. 2b/284 (1975), the first printing in modern times (P768)

Subsequent editions:	Peters: Vol. 1/46; AGA XX 450: Vol. 7/178; NSA IV: Vol. 2a/83; Bärenreiter: Vol. 1/193
Bibliography:	Youens 1992, pp. 64–5 & 107–8
Further settings and arrangements:	Ludwig Berger (1777–1839) *Müllers Trockne Blumen* (1816) Arr. Franz Liszt (1811–1886) for solo piano, no. 4 of *Sechs Melodien von Schubert* (1844) [*see* TRANSCRIPTIONS] Arr. Tilman Hoppstock (b. 1961) for guitar accompaniment, in *Franz Schubert: 110 Lieder* (2009)
Discography and timing:	Fischer-Dieskau III 1[18] 3'37
	Pears–Britten 3'34
	Hyperion I 25[23]
	Hyperion II 28[23] 3'51 Ian Bostridge

← *Blümlein Vergissmein*   *Der Müller und der Bach* D795/19 →

XIX Der MÜLLER UND DER BACH   The miller and the brook
OP. 25 NO. 19, **D795/19** [H544]
G minor – G major

(89 bars)

Der Müller.
Wo ein treues Herze
In Liebe vergeht,
Da welken die Lilien
Auf jedem Beet.

Da muss in die Wolken
Der Vollmond gehn,
Damit seine Tränen
Die Menschen nicht sehn.

Da halten die Englein
Die Augen sich zu,
Und schluchzen und singen
Die Seele zu Ruh'.

Der Bach.
Und wenn sich die Liebe
Dem Schmerz entringt,
Ein Sternlein, ein neues,
Am Himmel erblinkt.

The Miller:
Where a true heart
Dies of love,
The lilies wilt
In their beds.

There the full moon
Must disappear behind clouds
So that mankind
Does not see its tears.

There angels
Cover their eyes
And, sobbing, sing
The soul to rest.

The Brook:
And when love
Struggles free of sorrow,
A new star
Shines in the sky.

Da springen drei Rosen,
Halb rot und halb weiss,[1]
Die welken nicht wieder,
Aus Dornenreis.

Und die Engelein schneiden
Die Flügel sich ab,
Und gehn alle Morgen
Zur Erde herab.

Der Müller.
  Ach, Bächlein, liebes Bächlein,
Du meinst es so gut:
Ach, Bächlein, aber weisst du,
Wie Liebe tut?

  Ach, unten, da unten,
Die kühle Ruh'!
Ach, Bächlein, liebes Bächlein,
So singe nur zu.

Three roses,
Half-red, half-white,
Spring from thorny stems
And will never wither.

And the angels
Cut off their wings,
And every morning
Descend to earth.

The Miller:
  Ah, brook, beloved brook,
You mean so well:
Ah, brook, but do you know,
How love feels?

  Ah, below, down below,
Is cool rest!
Brook, beloved brook,
Sing on.

This is the nineteenth of Schubert's forty-six Müller solo settings (1823, 1827 and 1828). See the poet's biography for a chronological list of all the Müller settings.

Throughout *Die schöne Müllerin* the boy has attempted to establish his independence from his watery mentor: in moments of optimism and cheerful fantasy – *Ungeduld* (VII), *Morgengruss* (VIII), *Pause* (XII) and *Mit dem grünen Lautenbande* (XIII) – the stream plays no part in the story or the musical imagery. Even when the horizon darkens with the appearance of a rival – *Der Jäger* (XIV) – and when the idea of death as a solution to his problems comes into his mind – *Die liebe Farbe* (XVI) and *Trockne Blumen* (XVIII) – the miller dispenses with the stream's counsel. More importantly, in *Tränenregen* (XI) the idea of a watery grave seems not yet to have occurred to him despite the brook's hints and blandishments ('Geselle, Geselle, mir nach!'). It is never made clear whether the boy is taken from the stream and given a burial after his suicide, but in *Trockne Blumen* he imagines a grave mound that might be visited by a hopefully guilt-ridden miller girl. In these 'dry' songs the young man envisages the joys of courtship, the pain of rivalry and the acceptance of death, unprompted by the silvery whisperings of the brook. These seven waterproof songs, however, are a minority; one feels that despite the boy's attempts to live a normal earthbound life the brook has long claimed him as belonging to the watery depths. In *Die liebe Farbe* the miller confesses to hunting death ('Das Wild, das ich jage, das ist der Tod') as a means of putting a stop to his pain, but this search places no weapon of self-mutilation in his hands. Indeed, despite the suppressed violence of *Die böse Farbe* and the terse rhythmic grandeur of *Trockne Blumen*, we find it hard to imagine the boy doing anything decisive at all, let alone with knife, rope or the hated hunter's gun. Of course the solution, suicide by drowning, a death requiring none of these instruments, has been waiting there all the time; as early as *Wohin?* the miller has heard the voices of the beguiling Lorelei-like river sprites.

[1] The word 'und' in this line is Schubert's. Müller writes 'Halb rot, halb weiss'.

Schubert links and contrasts Songs XVIII and XIX – death on land and death in the water – in cunning fashion: *Trockne Blumen* is in E minor, *Der Müller und der Bach* G minor changing to G major (the relative major of E minor) for the middle section, the brook's aria 'Und wenn sich die Liebe'; *Trockne Blumen* is in an unyielding, landlocked duple metre (²⁄₄) while *Der Müller und der Bach* flows in watery triple time (³⁄₈); both songs are built on protracted pedal points to underline the miller's narrow options on his one-way street to death; in *Trockne Blumen* the pianist's opening chord (E minor with B and G in the right hand) is *on* the beat, both of the pianist's hands frozen together to co-ordinate the funeral cortège, whereas in *Der Müller und der Bach* the opening chord is subtly altered (G minor with B *flat* and G in the right hand) and is *off* the beat, right hand trailing left. The vocal entry at b. 3 is marked 'Der Müller' to distinguish him from the singing stream later in the song. In the displacement of the rhythm we sense the tragic instability of the singer; the limp inherent in the music depicts the wounded psyche which now seeks the comfort and safety of oblivion. This wonderful music had been prophesied, four years earlier, in the opening pages of the Mayrhofer setting *Beim Winde* D669 – a nocturne similarly poised between G minor and, after twelve bars, G major, and where the imagery of clouds, moon, stars and water are to be found in that song's opening phrase: 'Es träumen die Wolken, / Die Sterne, der Mond'.

Despite – or because of – the muted colours of *Der Müller und der Bach* there is no doubt that here we have the most disturbed music in the cycle. As all great composers of mad scenes have known, there is nothing frightening about deranged characters who foam at the mouth. Instead we have music to be sung at the waterside by a male Ophelia (Goethe's Mignon also comes to mind in the combination of tragedy and acceptance) tinged with an other-worldly melancholy beyond joy or rage, and all the more haunting for its lucidity and understatement. The tune is one of ravishing beauty, the extraordinary melody underlined by the sparseness of the accompaniment which is prophetic of the repetitious drone of *Der Leiermann* D911/24, the closing song of *Winterreise*. A succession of 'wild' or 'blue' notes in the vocal line provides plaintive twists of the most gentle derangement. For example the word 'Liebe' in the poem's second line (b. 5) rises to an F sharp utterly at odds with the G in the bass and seems to voice all the pain and terrible sweetness of that emotion. The flattened supertonic, an A flat on 'Lilien' (b. 8) provides another strange and exotic colour. The modulation into the relative major from b. 10, as veiled moonlight infiltrates the song at 'Da muss in die Wolken / Der Vollmond gehn', is heartbreakingly beautiful. The musical form of this strophe is a simple ABA. At the return of the A section the mention of the weeping angels ('Da halten die Englein / Die Augen sich zu', from b. 19) seems entirely appropriate for this music of the spheres that manages to suggest depression and radiance at the same time.

In the middle section the brook (over b. 28 the words 'Der Bach' are noted in the score) has an aria of its own. Müller's poem was later set as a duet by K. N. Kunz and O. Tiesen among others, but Schubert insists that his miller should also take up this role. It is of course the voice of the brook singing *through* the boy, as if the water demon has possessed him. To insist on the literal existence of a second character is to take away from the boy's hearing of inner voices, and the depiction of the gentle (and at times not so gentle) madness that precedes his suicide. This page is for the singer perhaps the most technically challenging in the whole cycle. Its high-lying tessitura comes towards the end of a demanding evening, and there is very little time to breathe between the phrases. Melismas on the first 'Himmel erblinkt' and an extraordinary decorative turn of phrase on the second add to the difficulties where wonderful breath control is imperative. The brook makes these superhuman demands precisely because it *is* superhuman. It is the general custom to sing the brook's music at a slightly faster speed, not only to mitigate these difficulties, but to emphasize the change of character.

From b. 29 the key is G major, the tonality that has been associated with the brook since the cycle's second song. Watery semiquavers make up the accompaniment for a song within a song without the slightest trace of sentimentality. Coaxed into speech for the first time (in contrast to its equivocal silence in *Der Neugierige*) the brook seems to be saying 'Your suffering is not in vain' and yet this is said almost happily, and certainly without commiseration. It whispers of the emergence of a new star in the heavens (the piano's left hand reflects the vocal line in mirror image from b. 32 at 'Ein Sternlein, ein neues') and imperishable roses in a text that might have yielded a corny and heartfelt musical response from almost any other composer. But Schubert's music, although of great beauty, is almost matter of fact, as if to remind us that dying is part of a natural sequence of events. The continual flowing of the water does not allow us to dwell on this tragedy, nor the many others before it. The brook, which has seen everything pass and everything healed, is not to be compared to a dangerous or deceitful human being; it is simply one of Death's many inscrutable agents, serving the greatest and most inevitable of deliverers. Gustav Mahler was also continually to be fascinated by the folk-like and terrible simplicity of the forces of Nature.

With a simple but unforgettable change from major back to minor between bb. 60 and 61 the miller boy now sings his last verse. This is an almost exact musical recapitulation of the opening strophe for the first four lines, with the telling difference that the boy's tune is now accompanied by the millstream's semiquavers. Never has the boy been so affectionate with his 'liebes Bächlein'. 'War es also gemeint?' he had asked in songs III and IV and, bearing no resentment for the advice that has led him to these crossroads, he here says, 'Du meinst es so gut' (bb. 63–5). We can almost see the two dramatis personae melt into one as the boy is gradually submerged. At 'Ach, unten, da unten' the F natural at the top of the stave at b. 71 is a natural mirror image of the stream's depth as the miller looks into its watery abyss. In order to be absorbed into the brook completely there is only one citadel left to fall – the boy's insistence on his lamenting minor key. The lure of 'Die kühle Ruh'!' is rendered irresistible by a brief but persuasive modulation into B flat major (bb. 72–4). After this, the B naturals at 'Ach, Bächlein, liebes Bächlein, / So singe nur zu' and the E natural on the second 'Bächlein' (with a bend in the melody at b. 76 that takes the breath away in a touching performance) allow him to slide gently into G major. As flats yield to naturals, the miller acquiesces to the brook at last, the accidentals, signs of total capitulation. Perhaps Müller unconsciously secreted into his work a sliver of the scenario of de la Motte Fouqué's *Undine* whereby a male hero is loved both by an earthbound mortal (in this case the miller girl) and the water sprite who eventually claims him. At the end of the tale the grave of Knight Huldbrand is magically surrounded by water, allowing Undine perpetual access to her beloved; in Schubert's cycle the stream first sings a lullaby that entices the young miller to commit suicide, then cradles him lovingly in its depths. Both could be seen as variations on the Lorelei story, seemingly an age-old myth but actually invented by Clemens Brentano in 1801.

Here it is perhaps curious that the choice is not between a female nixie and her equally female earthly rival, but rather between feminine and masculine nouns, 'die Müllerin' and 'der Bach'. In the next song the brook will shoo away the 'böses Mägdelein' while claiming the boy as its (his) own. This is held to be a significant detail by some modern scholars, but it is doubtful that Müller meant anything by it (both Mägdelein and Bächlein are neuter nouns after all) beyond the fact that the miller boy is now at one with a trusted friend as opposed to a treacherous lover. This calm and close identification, all passion spent, is mirrored by the melismas on bb. 80–2 at 'singe nur zu', notes which until now have only been sung by the brook. The music's vulnerability, sweetness and lack of bathos at this point have made enough eyes water over the years to fill a second stream. The miller is transfigured: if he has been self-indulgent, melodramatically calling out for love and attention, he is no longer so, and this is no manipulative suicide. Suddenly this is a man like Schubert himself in 1823 – youthful, gifted and sensitive, and confronted with a terminal condition. In the process of singing, someone about to die has surrendered to the inevitable with an acceptance rendered radiant by music. From madness to an epiphany in so few pages is a journey only to be undertaken by the greatest of composers. To eavesdrop on this coming to terms with death seems almost improper, and it breaks the listener's heart.

The postlude juxtaposes two figurations: the depths of the stream are heard in the piano's middle register in a G major arpeggio (bb. 82, 84, 86); alternating with this, and higher on the keyboard, is the tune (bb. 83 and 85) we have already heard on the first 'Himmel erblinkt' in b. 35. This alternating pattern is heard twice. That new star, it seems, is already shining in the heavens as the boy slips into the stream. In the penultimate bar the piano arpeggios discreetly depict this downward movement as they shift from treble to bass, where the figure in the left hand is graced with two demisemiquavers in b. 88. This tiny shudder adds the final impetus to the descent. The right-hand chord is tied, allowing the final left-hand chord to resound mournfully, all alone deep in the bass clef.

The survival of the manuscript of Vogl's own 'Veränderung' (literally change or transformation) of this song offers a rare insight into the singer's performing practice. Presumably Diabelli, when preparing the second edition of 1830, had access to an entire set of Vogl's working copies which he modified according to his own tastes and what he believed would be acceptable to the public. The importance of this manuscript is such that the NSA declines to print the song as it appears in the Diabelli edition and opts instead to publish the Vogl version as it stands. In terms of taking liberties with the original text the Diabelli version (in the original G minor, rather than Vogl's transposition to F minor) is considerably toned down. Diabelli's delight in ornamentation seems to stand somewhere between Vogl's and Schubert's as reflected by their relative ages – the singer was born in 1768, the publisher in 1781 and the composer in 1797. It is clear that this kind of singer's decoration was a slowly dying art, becoming less practised, and less acceptable, with each succeeding generation.

First edition:	Published as Op. 25 by Sauer & Leidesdorf, Vienna in 1824 (advertised in August), Book 5, no. 2 (P70)
Second edition:	Published as Op. 25 by Ant. Diabelli & Co., Vienna in 1830. The ornamented version of *Der Müller und der Bach* reprinted in NSA Vol. 2b/288 (1975) is not from this edition but derives from a manuscript of J. M. Vogl, the first printing in modern times (P769)
Subsequent editions:	Peters: Vol. 1/49; AGA XX 451: Vol. 7/181; NSA IV: Vol. 2a/87; Bärenreiter: Vol. 1/196
Bibliography:	Youens 1992, pp. 66–7 & 108–9
Arrangements:	Arr. Franz Liszt (1811–1886) for solo piano, no. 2 of *Müllerlieder* (1846) (2 versions) [*see* TRANSCRIPTIONS]
	Arr. Tilman Hoppstock (b. 1961) for guitar accompaniment, in *Franz Schubert: 110 Lieder* (2009)
Discography and timing:	Fischer-Dieskau III 1[19] 3'42
	Pears–Britten 4'12
	Hyperion I 25[24]
	Hyperion II 28[24] 3'56 Ian Bostridge

← *Trockne Blumen* D795/18   *Des Baches Wiegenlied* D795/20 →

XX Des BACHES WIEGENLIED — The brook's lullaby
OP. 25 NO. 20, **D795/20** [H545]
E major

Gu-te Ruh, gu-te Ruh, tu die Au - gen zu,

(24 bars)

Gute Ruh', gute Ruh'!
Tu' die Augen zu!
Wandrer, du müder, du bist zu Haus.
Die Treu' ist hier,
Sollst liegen bei mir,
Bis das Meer will trinken die Bächlein aus.

Will betten dich kühl,
Auf weichen Pfühl,[1]
In dem blauen krystallenen Kämmerlein.
Heran, heran,
Was wiegen kann,
Woget und wieget den Knaben mir ein!

Wenn ein Jagdhorn schallt
Aus dem grünen Wald,
Will ich sausen und brausen wohl um dich her.
Blickt nicht herein,
Blaue Blümelein!
Ihr macht meinem Schläfer die Träume so
  schwer.

Hinweg, hinweg
Von dem Mühlensteg,
Böses Mägdelein, dass ihn dein Schatten
  nicht weckt![2]
Wirf mir herein
Dein Tüchlein fein,
Dass ich die Augen ihm halte bedeckt!

Gute Nacht, gute Nacht!
Bis alles wacht,
Schlaf' aus deine Freude, schlaf' aus dein Leid!
Der Vollmond steigt,
Der Nebel weicht,
Und der Himmel da droben, wie ist er so weit!

Rest well, rest well!
Close your eyes!
Weary wanderer, this is your home.
Here is constancy;
You shall lie with me,
Until the sea drinks up all brooks.

I shall make you a cool bed
On a soft pillow
In this blue crystal chamber.
Come, come,
All you who can lull,
Rock and lull this boy for me!

When a hunting-horn echoes
From the green forest,
I shall surge and roar about you.
Do not peep in,
Little blue flowers!
You will give my slumberer such bad dreams.

Away, away
From the mill-path,
Wicked girl, lest your shadow should wake him!

Throw me
Your fine shawl,
That I may keep his eyes covered!

Good night, good night,
Until all awaken;
Sleep away your joy, sleep away your sorrow!
The full moon rises,
The mist vanishes,
And the sky above, how vast it is.

[1] Müller writes 'Auf *weichem* Pfühl'.
[2] Müller writes 'Mägdlein' and Schubert adds an extra syllable to the word, thus 'Mägdelein'.

This is the twentieth of Schubert's forty-six Müller solo settings (1823, 1827 and 1828). See the poet's biography for a chronological list of all the Müller settings.

The last song in the cycle, one of Schubert's most telling and mesmeric utterances, is given over to the brook which – who – continues to sing in unison with the miller. It is purely strophic in form, and a true epilogue in that it seems utterly separate from the rest of the cycle. The boy is released from all human concerns and sufferings, and the composer himself seems free of obligation to divert and entertain us. With the greatest courage and an assurance seen only in fools and geniuses, Schubert allows a simple melody to be repeated five times with the tiniest adjustments between strophes (made necessary by the prosody and word-setting) which in any case are not perceptible to the listener. We thus have a seamless lament that in the wrong hands can be very boring; in the right perform-ance it quietly builds in stature, strophe by strophe, unbearably moving in its simplicity.

Des Baches Wiegenlied, woodcut from the 'Prachtausgabe' of the cycle (1872).

The tempo indication is 'Mässig' (Moderato) and *alla breve* ($\frac{2}{2}$) – a warning to those performers who allow themselves to be moved by the cycle to such an extent that this last hymn is made maudlin and lachrymose by an excessively slow tempo. This is absolutely the wrong moment for an accomplished singer to use this music as a means of displaying his stun-ning breath control. The point of this music is that the brook is incapable of such self-indul-gence: it is human beings who have let the miller boy down and human emotions that have led to his downfall, so here we encounter nature singing, free at last of human interference. The music has a sweep of inevitability where there is no place for subjective emotion and gratuitous rubato.

It is true that Müller's strophes are varied; at one point the hunter enters and in the next verse the blue-eyed maid of the mill is duly sent away lest she disturb the young man's sleep. But the music goes way beyond the pathetic fallacy and the anthropomorphizing of the mill-stream's 'thoughts'; Schubert makes no attempt to illustrate these ideas, and any efforts by the performers to do so should be extremely subtle. The hunting-horn motif is built into the accompaniment's thirds and sixths and the temptation for the accompanist is to bring them out, hunter-like, in strident fashion. And yet, as Charles Rosen has pointed out in *The Romantic Generation*, these harmonies, *softly* played as if from far away (and heard as such by visitors to the forest) were already a metaphor for distance, and thus absence, when Beethoven composed his 'Les Adieux' Sonata Op. 81a; at the end of *Suleika I* D720 and in the prelude and interludes of *Der Lindenbaum* D911/5 Schubert used horn music of this type to denote the separation of lovers. The music of the hunt, by a supreme irony, is thus summoned to denote the unbridge-able gap between the living and the dead. Schubert gets to the heart of the matter with music in which we are free to imagine we hear a thousand things in the water – including Müller's text – while all that is *really* happening is the eternal flow that whispers nature's wisdom beyond our comprehension. Similarly, Benjamin Britten understood that Peter Grimes's suicide by drowning, far out at sea, should not be followed by tragic music; far more eloquently, the opera's opening chorus is recapitulated in matter-of-fact fashion to demonstrate that life in the village simply goes on.

The key is E major (what a different outcome the boy had envisaged – in the same key – at the end of *Trockne Blumen*) which confers a brightness on the music after the G minor of the preceding piece. There is an audaciously long pedal-point on a succession of left-hand Es (bb. 1–9) with inner voices in the alto and tenor register (gently rocking eddies and currents) sheltering beneath accented minims (Bs in the right hand). These sounds are bell-like and pierce the accompaniment's texture. Whatever Schubert's estimation of the Roman Catholic

Woodcut for *Des Baches Wiegenlied* from 'Prachtausgabe' of *Die schöne Müllerin*.

Church in Austria he was influenced by its customs (the suicide that he here treats so sympathetically would of course have been a sin in the eyes of the priests). Can it be that these repeated notes represent the old-fashioned custom of the passing bell (cf. *Das Zügenglöcklein* D871) which traditionally sounded in any village at the news of a death? This thought allows us momentarily to imagine the consternation and horror at the mill when the boy's colleagues learn of his suicide, and it would explain why the miller girl should come to the edge of the brook clutching a shawl or possibly a delicate neckerchief (is there a parallel symbolism between the green ribbon, fading and sterile in its disuse, and the delicate, attractive, flattering neckerchief?). At 'Wandrer, du <u>müder</u>, du <u>bist</u> zu <u>Haus</u>' there is a marvellous yet simple sequence – B major to C sharp minor, then the dominant of that key – a G sharp major chord. As this bass G sharp moves up a semitone into A major we find we have modulated to the security of the subdominant at 'Die Treu' ist hier, / Sollst liegen bei mir'. This change of key draws the boy even more intimately to the brook's deeper currents, and lures us into the very heart of the song.

The third section now follows (the song's structure is ABC, a simple but rare form in Schubert) and is amazingly original. Based entirely on dactylic rhythms (a crotchet plus two quavers), it takes on the characteristic of a dance of the utmost gravity and portent and illustrates the 'Woget und wieget' of the second strophe to perfection (bb. 16–19). *Des Baches Wiegenlied* is written largely in anapaestic rhythm, but the emergence of these dactyls places the song among those by Schubert that are connected to the great whirring dynamo of nature. In depicting certain big ideas, these songs (for example *Der Tod und das Mädchen* D531 – death, *Die Sterne* D939 – the stars and *An mein Klavier* D342 – the phenomenon of music itself) are oblivious to trifling human concerns. The accompaniment is made up of chords thick with notes, yet airily, and slightly eerily, mezzo staccato; the third inversion of the dominant seventh chord, thus a seventh on the seventh of D sharp, is embellished with a yearning passing note of C sharp at the top which resolves on to a B major chord (b. 16). This initiates a solemn dactylic dance that seems as old as the hypnotic Allegretto of Beethoven's Symphony no. 7, and is really as old as time itself. This music pivots around that C sharp–B alternation with changing harmonies underneath. This passage is strongly reminiscent of the 'Andante' movement of the A major piano Sonata D664; as the piano combines with the plangent eloquence of the voice the music seems unconnected with the earth, so serenely does it float in harmonic limbo, unanchored by root-position chords. The vocal line rises to an extraordinary high G sharp on the word '<u>trinken</u>' (in the first verse, b. 17), but the composer must surely have been thinking of the last strophe where it exactly mirrors 'da dr<u>oben</u>' to heart-stopping effect (b. 35 in the NSA). There is a brief moment of sadness with a C natural on the repeat of 'Bis das <u>Meer</u> will trinken' but this is only a passing colour and the strophe ends in an uncomplicated cadence, perfect in every way. The postlude is simply a repetition of the introduction which in itself is the unchanging pattern on which the vocal line is grafted.

Benjamin Britten, a superb interpreter of this cycle, wrote one of his most important songs, *Before Life and After*, to a text of Thomas Hardy:

> A time there was – as one may guess
> And as, indeed, earth's testimonies tell –
>   Before the birth of consciousness,
>   When all went well.
>
>   None suffered sickness, love, or loss,
> None knew regret, starved hope, or heart-burnings;
>   None cared whatever crash or cross
>   Brought wrack to things.

If something ceased, no tongue bewailed,
If something winced and waned, no heart was wrung;
If brightness dimmed, and dark prevailed,
No sense was stung.

But the disease of feeling germed,
And primal rightness took the tint of wrong;
Ere nescience shall be reaffirmed
How long, how long?

In *Des Baches Wiegenlied* the 'disease of feeling' is vanquished in favour of what was, according to Hardy, a primordial state of grace – a return perhaps to the conditions pertaining in the Garden of Eden, before the birth of consciousness that brings with it pain and human suffering. Schubert here creates his own musical evocation of nescience – for death is too negative a term for this state of release. The miller boy is at last free from pain and danger, and the listener too is released by this music from his own woes and allowed into a new realm of calm and acceptance. At the end we find we have been transported to a loftier place, 'da droben', but without a hint of a heavenly afterlife. Such a journey could never have been envisaged by the poor miller boy when he first set off, and such a work could never have been written by the Schubert of 1815. It seems clear at last that the cycle marks a turning point in the composer's life and output. It is as if, in order to face life once again in the wake of his illness, he had to allow the miller boy to die in his stead. It is a formidable challenge for performers to play their part in the re-creation of these feelings. As the great accompanist Gerald Moore wrote: 'Only a humble approach and a reverence for Schubert will reveal the music's secrets. Thus and thus only will singer and pianist find inspiration, exalt the listener and, incidentally, ennoble themselves.'

Title page of the second edition of *Die schöne Müllerin*, published by Diabelli (1830).

First edition: Published as Op. 25 by Sauer & Leidesdorf, Vienna in 1824
(advertised in August), Book 5, no. 3 (P71)

Second edition:	Published as Op. 25 by Ant. Diabelli & Co., Vienna in 1830. This song is printed here in C major – certainly Vogl's key, but no doubt also to encourage sales among amateur singers
Subsequent editions:	Peters: Vol. 1/52; AGA XX 452: Vol. 7/184; NSA IV: Vol. 2a/90; Bärenreiter: Vol. 1/199
Bibliography:	Youens 1992, pp. 67–70 & 109–11
Further settings and arrangements:	Ludwig Berger (1777–1839) *Des Baches Lied* (1816) Arr. Tilman Hoppstock (b. 1961) for guitar accompaniment, in *Franz Schubert: 110 Lieder* (2009)
Discography and timing:	Fischer-Dieskau III 1[20] 6'21
	Pears–Britten 7'15
	Hyperion I 25[25]
	Hyperion II 28[25] 6'17 Ian Bostridge

← *Der Müller und der Bach* D795/19   *Der Dichter, als Epilog* →

DER DICHTER, ALS EPILOG   The poet, by way of epilogue
[H545+]

Woodcut from the 'Prachtausgabe' of the cycle (1872).

This poem was not set to music by Schubert.

Weil gern man schliesst mit einer runden Zahl,	Since we like to end with a round number
Tret' ich noch einmal in den vollen Saal,	I again enter this full room
Als letztes, fünf und zwanzigstes Gedicht,[1]	As the twenty-fifth, and final, poem,
Als Epilog, der gern das Klügste spricht.	As Epilogue, which likes to come up with the wisest observation.
Doch pfuschte mir der Bach in's Handwerk schon	But the brook has already queered my pitch
Mit seiner Leichenred' im nassen Ton.	With the sodden tones of its funeral oration.
Aus solchem hohlen Wasserorgelschall	From the hollow sounds of this watery organ
Zieht jeder selbst sich besser die Moral;	Each man had better draw the moral for himself;
Ich geb' es auf und lasse diesen Zwist,	I give in, and bury the hatchet,
Weil Widerspruch nicht meines Amtes ist.	For conflict is not my province.
So hab' ich denn nichts lieber hier zu thun,	So all that remains for me to do
Als euch zum Schluss zu wünschen, wohl zu ruhn.	Is to end by wishing you goodnight.
Wir blasen unsre Sonn' und Sternlein aus –	We blow out our sun and stars.
Nun findet euch im Dunkel gut nach Haus,	Find your way home safely in the dark;
Und wollt ihr träumen einen leichten Traum,	And if you wish to dream a light dream
So denkt an Mühlenrad und Wasserschaum,	When you shut your eyes for a long night's sleep,
Wenn ihr die Augen schliesst zu langer Nacht,	Think of the mill-wheel and the foaming water
Bis es den Kopf zum Drehen euch gebracht.	Until your head whirls.
Und wer ein Mädchen führt an seiner Hand,	And if you lead a maiden by the hand,
Der bitte scheidend um ein Liebespfand,	Ask for a pledge of love in parting,
Und gibt sie heute, was sie oft versagt,	And if today she gives you what she has often denied,
So sei des treuen Müllers treu gedacht	Think faithfully of the faithful miller.
Bei jedem Händedruck, bei jedem Kuss,	At every squeeze of the hand, at every kiss,
Bei jedem heissen Herzensüberfluss:	At every passionate surge of the heart,
Geb' ihm die Liebe für sein kurzes Leid	Grant him love for his brief sorrow;
In eurem Busen lange Seligkeit!	Grant him lasting bliss in your hearts.

Bibliography: Youens 1992, pp. 70–71
                     Youens 1997, pp. 164–9
Discography and timing: Fischer-Dieskau   –
                     Hyperion I 25²⁶
                     Hyperion II 28²⁶   1'40   Dietrich Fischer-Dieskau

← *Des Baches Wiegenlied* D795/20   *Abendstern* D806 →

AFTERWORD

It is perhaps after hearing *Die schöne Müllerin* that the listener is best able to take into account the sad circumstances of its composition. Early in 1823 (or towards the end of 1822) Schubert contracted syphilis. Legend has it that one of his closest friends, Franz von Schober, had encouraged him to visit a prostitute, but who can say whether this was an isolated incident? Several of

---

[1] In the 1872 edition, reproduced on the previous page, 'funf und zwanzigstes' is all one word.

Schubert's contemporaries refer to his 'burning sensuality' and his schoolfriend Josef Kenner wrote that the composer's 'craving for pleasure dragged his soul down to the slough of moral degradation'. These remarks seem excessively censorious at a time when it was quite common for young men, frustrated by the purity of their chaperoned wives to be, to make alternative arrangements. Perhaps Kenner was referring to something more forbidden. Many years ago, long before there was any scholastic controversy regarding the composer's sexuality, the late Walter Legge (who admittedly delighted in shocking people) informed me that in the Vienna of the 1930s, where he was researching Hugo Wolf and meeting some of that composer's surviving friends, he had been told 'on the best authority' that Schubert's illness was a result of a homosexual encounter. This is of course hearsay at more than one remove, but it is an indication that discussion of these matters is no modern phenomenon. What we do know is that Schubert had a spell in hospital, and that he lost his hair due to the mercury treatment that was then the only palliative for the disease although dangerously poisonous. He thus had to suffer not only the symptoms of syphilis (particularly unpleasant, though not yet fatal, in the secondary stage) but all the significant changes it brought into his life: the fear of infection and the moral condemnation of those he had thought to be friends; the belief that he no longer had the right to have a relationship for fear of passing on the infection; above all the knowledge that the time remaining to him as a composer might be limited, and that his life was to end prematurely and in the most harrowing circumstances. Parallels with HIV and Aids have given Schubert's tragic plight many modern resonances. 'I have brought it on myself', he probably thought, and many people, then as now, would agree with him. It was probably during his hospital stay in 1823 that he composed parts of *Die schöne Müllerin*.

Schubert went through terrible patches of despair – and for quite some time after the initial diagnosis. We know this from a letter he wrote to his friend Leopold Kupelwieser in Rome as late as March 1824 where he quoted part of the Goethe poem *Gretchen am Spinnrade* in relation to his own emotional predicament:

> *I feel myself to be the most unhappy and wretched creature in the world. Imagine a man whose health will never be right again, and who in sheer despair over this ever makes things worse and worse, instead of better; imagine a man, I say, whose most brilliant hopes have perished, to whom the happiness of love and friendship have nothing to offer but pain [. . .] 'My peace is gone, my heart is sore, I shall find it never and nevermore' I may well sing now, for each night, on retiring to bed, I hope I may not wake again . . .*

In May 1823 Schubert also wrote an astonishing poem entitled *Mein Gebet* ('My Prayer'); he seems to have needed to express himself in words only at moments of the greatest stress when the music had dried up (*see* SCHUBERT THE COMPOSER AS POET). His familiarity with Greek mythology is used to express what seems to be a suicidal depression. The last strophe runs thus:

Tödt' es und mich selber tödte,	Kill it and me, myself kill,
Stürz' nun Alles in die Lethe,	Cast everything into the Lethe
Und ein reines kräft'ges Sein	And then, great god allow
Lass', o Grosser, dann gedeih'n.	A pure and powerful being to flourish.

It is at this moment, when the composer talks of plunging into the Lethean waters, that his connection with the boy in *Die schöne Müllerin* seems most intense. As a result of the 1823 crisis Schubert felt himself at a dead end in both his life and his career. His operatic hopes had recently been dashed and he was massively depressed. His well-documented lack of self-esteem in non-musical matters fits with the conventional psychological portrait of those who pay for sex. He was almost certainly prey to secret crushes and passionate fantasies. Even before his illness he seems to have been a terrible disappointment to his father on personal, if not musical, grounds. In July 1822 he had written down a dream (*Mein Traum* [My Dream] – Deutsch 1946, pp. 226–8) in which he refuses to eat a banquet provided for him by his father and is duly banished into the wilderness; on his return he is shown his father's favourite garden and he also rejects this, saying that it is repulsive. This must surely represent the composer's inability to live life in the manner expected of him by Schubert senior.

Despite a loyal circle of friends Schubert was in many ways a loner and a misfit, and this is doubtless why, in the depths of his crisis, he felt so much in common with the miller boy whom he makes a much more complex creation than Müller intended. (The poet's *Prologue* and *Epilogue* barely conceal a chuckle; the composer's music ignores these parts of the cycle and allows many a tear.) The difficulty in reconciling love with sex, an inability to differentiate between fantasy and reality, and a lack of decisive masculine confidence seem to be common ground for the composer and the protagonist of his cycle. In some of the songs (*Ungeduld, Mein!*) the exaggerated rhapsodic intensity of *La Bonne chanson* comes to mind, love poems written by Paul Verlaine to his fiancée in an effort to convince himself (unsuccessfully in the long run) that their life together would be idyllic. Does the miller really long for the girl or, as with Verlaine and Mathilde Mauté, is it the *idea* of her, the concept of fitting into an everyday normality, that appeals? Is she his 'rêve familier', his redemptive archetype?

Schubert's music adds to *Die schöne Müllerin* many dimensions undreamed of by its poet and creator. The eponymous heroine, who represents the normality so elusive to the miller, hardly plays a leading role. The composer chose not to set the poem *Das Mühlenleben* that rounds her character; he wanted her to be more enigmatic, less real. In this way the miller's passion becomes mysterious and self-deluding, less reasonable, more obsessive. For all the boy's passionate projections, the girl herself is but a shadowy presence and it is the brook, a friend and confidant, who wins the boy in the end. It is as if the hero were being pulled in two directions: an ambivalence and sexual diffidence run beneath the surface throughout the cycle and the boy is attracted by rival forces – the female *Müllerin* and the asexual brook which (or who) eventually claims him.

If we were to believe that this young man has committed suicide simply because the girl he loves has gone off with someone else, we should be diminishing the importance of this work. The composer's agenda here is infinitely deeper. He has created a lament both for what he has lost and what he will never attain; it is a salute to those who fail to live up to what is expected of them, particularly in terms of the stereotypes of manliness, success and heroism. In this respect the young miller is an anti-hero: Schubert's work is a compassionate portrait of a 'loser' and a reminder that those who make nothing of their lives are often people who are are simultaneously enriched and damned by a poetic nature, and who cannot face the everyday world. It is also a farewell to the composer's youthful belief that he could trust to chance to look after him, that something good was bound to be around the corner. Alone and terminally ill, Schubert had to face the stark realities of the future as he worked on this cycle. From the tone of *Mein Gebet* there must have been a great danger that feelings of bitterness would poison the sweet wellspring of his creative inspiration. He had no psychiatrist to whom he could pour out his problems, but he had the self-preserving instincts given to the greatest of artists: Schubert did not drown himself and he kept his talents not only intact but more finely honed than ever before. From 1823 he wrote less music, perhaps, but there is scarcely a note that is not *meant* and of significance. In writing *Die schöne Müllerin* the composer was in effect his own psychiatrist: he worked through his problems by transferring his disappointments and grief on to the shoulders of the young miller. As a part of this process of self-forgiveness and reconciliation it is the miller who dies in Schubert's stead, leaving the composer free to continue with his life's work. That the composer was somehow transfigured by this death-at-one-remove can be heard in the depth and quality of music, never a note wasted, that flowed from his pen in the last five years of his life.

If listening to music can change a life, how much truer must that be for the person writing that music and hearing it for the first time in the act of creation? *Die schöne Müllerin* is a watershed work that appears to divide the composer's life into 'before' and 'after'. The 'after' years were extraordinarily rich in terms of compositions, suggesting that Schubert experienced some kind of spiritual healing. Many music lovers and performers would claim to have benefited from the regenerative powers of Schubert's music, and so – thank heavens – did the composer himself when most in need.

SCHÖNE WELT, WO BIST DU? *see* STROPHE AUS 'DIE GÖTTER GRIECHENLANDS' D677

SCHOLARS

Writing new songs was Schubert's metier, but it was copies of the old ones that his friends, always one step behind him, required for their enlightenment or entertainment. Fortunately there were also those in the Schubert circle who understood that their generation had a responsibility to safeguard his legacy. This aspect of Schubertian history is discussed in the article AUTOGRAPHS, ALBUMS AND COLLECTIONS where one name in particular stands out from the earliest days – that of **Josef Wilhelm Witteczek** (1787–1859) whose meticulously assembled collection of copies rendered the composer's cause the greatest imaginable long-term service – a labour of love that evolved into a great act of scholarship.

There have always been those whose love for Schubert has been expressed in eminently practical terms. In Witteczek's case it was in the collecting and cataloguing of manuscripts; others have demonstrated their affection by singing, playing or conducting. The performing scholar, or the scholar–performer, has work to do apart from singing and playing – thinking and, on occasion, writing – that involves more scholarship than is generally realized. Books on Schubert songs by such celebrated performers as **Dietrich Fischer-Dieskau** (1925–2012) and **Gerald Moore** (1899–1986) have brought their 'hands-on' perspective to the round table of Schubertian discussion. In fact many of the names listed in this article have been active in making music. One thinks above all of an early Schubertian hero, a distinguished conductor who saw his role as a kind of missionary; his name appears here not because of his work with the symphonies but on account of his important connection with the composer's part-songs. **Johann, Ritter von Herbeck** (1831–1877) both collected and discovered manuscripts. At the age

Johann von Herbeck.

of twenty-six he unearthed the score of *Gesang der Geister über den Wassern* D714 for voices and strings and performed it soon after. He found the oratorio *Lazarus* D689, made a piano reduction for the work from the full score and performed it in 1863. He also rediscovered the sketches for the composer's last opera *Der Graf von Gleichen* D918. His editions of the choral music, both accompanied and unaccompanied, took into account the reminiscences and tempo indications of some of the singers who had performed them in Schubert's lifetime. Like a knight rescuing a princess from a tower, Herbeck confronted the Hüttenbrenner brothers, Anselm and Josef, prised the 'Unfinished' Symphony D759 from their grasp and carried it aloft into the concert hall (1865). Herbeck also conducted performances of the opera *Die Verschworenen* D787 (qv), as well as excerpts from many of Schubert's other forgotten dramatic works. He was a tireless man whose exceptional service to the music of Wagner and Bruckner lies outside the scope of this article.

Another type of practical scholar was the one who wanted to tell the story of Schubert's life in order to win for his music greater understanding and more frequent performances. The first biographical article was by the composer's sometime friend, **Anton Schindler** (1795–1864) in 1857. **Ludwig Gottfried Neumann** (1813–1865) gathered together material for a biography that was never published. **Aloys Fuchs** (1799–1853), an avid collector of manuscripts, was the first to attempt a catalogue of Schubert's works, making in 1842 a valiant effort to list the lost manuscripts with a view to their recovery. **Ferdinand Luib** (1811–1877) gathered together much valuable information in 1857–8 by sending out questionnaires and letters to those who survived within the Schubert circle. Much of Luib's material was used (with scant acknowledgement) by **Heinrich Kreissle von Hellborn** (1822–1869), the composer's first real biographer. Kreissle was a civil servant who married into the Pratobevera (qv) family which once had connec-

Kreissle von Hellborn.

tions with Schubert himself. He later became the director of the Gesellschaft der Musikfreunde in Vienna. In 1860 Kreissle published *Eine biografische Skizze* of Schubert with a quotation from Robert Schumann on the title page. It was only a beginning, but it gave the world an appetite to discover more about the man behind the music, and also occasioned a feud with Franz von Schober (qv) over some inaccurate information regarding *Alfonso und Estrella*. Undaunted, Kreissle followed the *Skizze* with a full-scale biography, *Franz Schubert* (1865), published by the Viennese firm of Carl Gerold; French and English translations soon followed. Kreissle's work is essential reading for any Schubert lover, but it has its flaws: in its desire to defend the composer from the charge that he was merely a song-writer, it gives too much attention perhaps to the operas and too little to the great song cycles. Nevertheless, for its time, it represents an indispensable achievement.

It was not long before writers from other countries staked their claim to Schubertian expertise. The first of these was the composer **August Friedrich Wilhelm Reissmann** (1825–1903)

Title page of Franz Schubert by Kreissle von Hellborn, the first full-scale biography of the composer.

Title page of August Reissmann's study of Schubert's life and works (1873).

who was a professor of music at the Stern Conservatoire in Berlin. He had issued a pioneering biography of Schumann in 1865, and followed suit with *Franz Schubert. Sein Leben und seine Werke* (Berlin, 1873). The Viennese Kreissle had enjoyed unrivalled access to personal information, but Reissmann was better qualified, in technical terms at least, to write a work in which the music was placed to the fore. In his study of German song, *Das deutsche Lied in seiner historischen Entwicklung* (in its English translation 'German Song in its Historical Development', 1861), Reissmann had discussed Schubert's songs at length in Chapter 5 under the heading *Das deutsche Lied in höchster Blüte* ('German song in full flower'). He claimed, with some justification, that Kreissle had depended on that work when writing his

August Reissmann.

own comments on Schubert's songs. In Reissmann's book the lieder are a central point of discussion, and a handful of rare vocal works, including first editions, are offered as supplements. On the other hand Reissmann underestimated Schubert's achievements as an instrumental composer – more, it seems, as a matter of taste than oversight. With regard to the symphonies the pioneering efforts of Herbeck, and those of a conductor–composer like Mendelssohn, were already well-enough known. From now on almost all commentary would tend to take sides between the instrumental and vocal canons according to the author's own musical preferences.

In nineteenth-century musical life Felix Mendelssohn's name was synonymous with England. That composer had attempted to introduce Schubert's 'Great' C major Symphony D944 to London audiences, but the recalcitrant orchestra stymied the project in rehearsal. Nevertheless, it was logical that many non-German speakers should have been first drawn to that side of Schubert's music – symphonies, piano and chamber music – without the challenge of words in an unfamiliar language to deal with. One of these enthusiasts was **Sir George Grove** (1820–1900), that great Victorian powerhouse of good works, among which was the propagation of music. He was the first director of the Royal College of Music, and was the force behind the writing and editing of a musical dictionary named after him that remains a pre-eminent reference work. In October 1867 Grove made a pilgrimage to Vienna in the company of Arthur Sullivan, and the pair, a vanguard party of British Schubertians, were royally received by Eduard Schneider, Schubert's nephew and the owner of many manuscripts, and by the publisher Spina. This visit, a magical experience for the two

Sir George Grove.

Englishmen, had many fruitful consequences for the reception of Schubert's music in the English-speaking world. On a later visit to Vienna in 1892 Grove was fortunate to have Eusebius Mandyczewski (*see* below) as his guide and advisor. Many Schubert works were performed in England thanks to Grove's influence, and he contributed a Schubert work list as an appendix to Arthur Coleridge's English translation of Kreissle von Hellborn's biography (1869). In recent years it has been revealed that some of Grove's vaunted achievements in terms of original discovery (above all his so-called unearthing of the score of *Rosamunde* D797 in a cupboard) were much exaggerated; he was a popularizer and gentleman-scholar rather than a full-time musicologist. Nevertheless, his extensive article about Schubert in the first edition of his celebrated dictionary remains wonderfully readable on account of its enthusiasm, and his affection for Schubert was soon to be echoed by countless grateful compatriots. Grove's correspondence with the song scholar Max Friedlaender (*see* below) was gathered together by Franz Krautwurst and published by the International Franz Schubert Institute in 2002.

Every generation brings its own scholars, each with an ambition to sort out a tangled web of conflicting information. One of the greatest of these was **Martin Gustav Nottebohm** (1817–1882) who gave a life of invaluable service to a field that would now be termed musicology. His teachers were Mendelssohn and Schumann in Leipzig, and later Simon Sechter, the composer and counterpoint expert with whom Schubert had studied in the last weeks of his life. Nottebohm became the greatest Beethoven scholar of his generation, but his thematic catalogue of Schubert's work (1874), arranged in order of the published opus numbers, is a model of its kind and still of interest today.

The study of Schubert was soon to become a worldwide phenomenon; it was inevitable that specialists should arise within the overall discipline, and in various fields. Max Friedlaender and Eusebius Mandy-

M. G. Nottebohm.

czewksi, a pupil of Nottebohm, were the first truly to specialize in Schubert's songs. These men were of quite different temperaments: Friedlaender was the greater popularizer and energetic enthusiast, Mandyczewski the more thorough scholar, and ultimately the greater Schubertian. The two editions of the lieder connected with their life-work remain similarly differentiated.

From the very beginning **Max Friedlaender** (sometimes spelled Friedländer) (1852–1934) was eminently practical in the manner of a performing musician: he had begun his career as a singing student of Manuel Garcia in London and later of Julius Stockhausen in Frankfurt, although the majority of his professional life was spent in Berlin. He had an astonishing knowledge of the repertoire, and published works on Beethoven and Goethe, as well as a still-famous study of the lied in the eighteenth century, *Das deutsche Lied im 18. Jahrhundert* (1902). He made contributions to knowledge of Schubertian performing practice and ornamentation, but he had a light hand – some would say too light – when it came to detailed textual research. His name was linked inextricably with the volumes of Schubert songs issued by the Leipzig firm of

C. F. Peters, although Friedlaender was too young to have been responsible for the original planning of this edition which first appeared between 1871 and 1874. In the early 1880s, Peters (or rather its proprietor Max Abraham; *see* POSTHUMOUS SONGS), mindful of the commercial competition, engaged Friedlaender to revise the entire edition, a process that went on in various stages until the 1920s. In 1885 Friedlaender prepared two slim volumes of songs for Peters that contained a number of first editions. Two years later this volume was the basis of an expanded collection of songs that became the supplementary Volume 7, a kind of musical 'afterword' to the original six-volume set, and containing hitherto unpublished material. Friedlaender's introductions and supplementary volume to his 'newly' revised edition made much of his research into manuscripts and primary sources, but the main body of the Peters Edition never received a truly radical overhaul. Instead its scope was broadened (if not deepened): the publisher, no doubt encour-

Nottebohm's Schubert catalogue (1874).

Max Friedlaender, 1885.

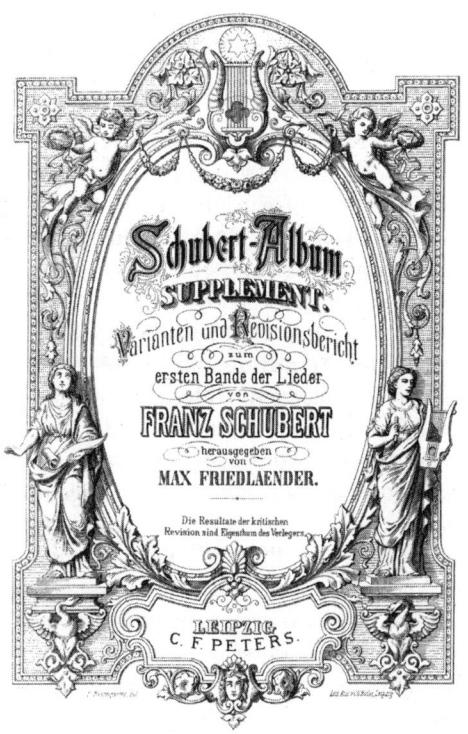

Friedlaender's 'Schubert-Album Supplement' (1884).

aged by Friedlaender, now offered four different key-variants available for Volume 1 (the three cycles and selected famous songs), and three each for Volumes 2 and 3. By the turn of the century a single volume of selected transpositions (issued as *52 Ausgewählte Lieder . . . aus dem Schubert Album IV–VII*, edited by Friedlaender in collaboration with Eduard Behm) offered lower tonalities for forty-six further songs from the last four volumes of the Peters Edition, plus six further songs (also transposed) that had so far only appeared in Mandyczewski's *Gesamtausgabe*. These six songs were never available in the Peters Edition in their original keys, such was the seemingly improvised nature of the enterprise. Nevertheless, Friedlaender's work for Peters prospered: the transpositions were chosen with a secure knowledge of the different voice categories, and of the capabilities and performing needs of singers within each different *Fach*. These different tonalities kept domestic Schubert singers happy for generations, and still do, although fewer amateurs sing lieder nowadays, sadly, and there is less call for the almost comically low-lying comforts of the 'Tiefer Alt oder Bass' volume. For the same firm Friedlaender edited the complete songs of Schumann in three volumes, and a selection of songs by Mendelssohn and Loewe. His name became a byword for lieder, and was displayed on every music lover's shelf.

Friedlaender was also a notable collector. His knowledge of the whereabouts of Schubert manuscripts was akin to being au fait with the latest gossip and, even as a very young man, his acquaintance with the facts had been useful to Nottebohm in the compilation of his catalogue. Brahms, initially alarmed at the new fashion for musicological completeness in Schubert studies, referred to Friedlaender (in a letter to Simrock of 2 June 1886) as 'the most dangerous "Schubert scholar" . . . who almost daily makes a huge fuss about unprinted and unknown things . . . this kind of enthusiasm should be confined to the bedroom . . . it is irreverent to distribute such bumph in public'. This type of excavation, the excitement of the chase, was something in which Friedlaender excelled. He possessed a huge amount of Schubertian material and information, but he seems to have lacked the concentration to put it together in a biography – a project that was long rumoured to be in the pipeline. Nevertheless, he was renowned as someone who was generous with advice and who was humble and courteous with his colleagues. Valuable items in his collection were later sold into private hands, some of them disappearing for ever; this has earned the resentment of some modern scholars, but there was a reason for Friedlaender's hasty attempts to provide for himself. As my accompanist colleague Phillip Moll wrote to me, 'Friedlaender lived just long enough, after a lifetime of patriotic service to his country, to German culture and in particular to German song, to be stripped of his well-deserved titles and offices a year before his death in 1934 at the age of 82'.

Eusebius Mandyczewski (1857–1929) was of a completely different temperament: where Friedlaender had flair, Mandyczewski had patience. He was both a composer and a conductor; a protégé of Brahms, he had worked as that composer's amanuensis. On Brahms's recommendation Mandyczewski was employed as a member of staff for the preparation of the Schubert *Gesamtausgabe* published by Breitkopf & Härtel, being given special responsibility for the lieder series, as well

Eusebius Mandyczewski in middle life.

Mandyczewski in 1928.

as the masses, smaller church works and string quartets. It was fortunate that the *Gesamtausgabe* was financially supported by the generous and altruistic Nikolaus von Dumba (*see* AUTOGRAPHS, ALBUMS AND COLLECTIONS); this enabled the reserved young scholar to do what he did best – to work with a combination of fervour and painstaking thoroughness.

The religiously devout Mandyczewski cut rather a saintly figure – certainly a contrast to the worldly Friedlaender. He was born in the Ukraine in a far-flung corner of the Austrian empire, and his Eastern Orthodox religious background might account for the fact that he seems to have been singularly without vanity or any kind of overweening personal ambition. He contented himself with editorial work and short articles – he was the Viennese correspondent of the *Musical Times* – and had no interest in writing a book to add to the shelf of immortality. Maurice Brown observed that those areas of the Breitkopf & Härtel complete edition with which Mandyczewski was involved were successful, and those that were published without his participation were much less so. His special relationship to the Schubert lied was emphasized by his later marriage to Albine von Vest, a lieder singer. His eminence in the field was hard won and his editorial decisions for the song volumes contentious. Brahms, for one, was initially horrified by the notion (outlandishly modern for the time) that all Schubert's juvenilia should be treated as seriously as his later work, that every available version of every song should be included in the work and that fragments should be made available to the public just as they were. The great composer, very hard on his own failed efforts, favoured a selective process that weeded out weaker material, whereas Mandyczewski argued that it was not for scholars to make such selective judgements. As a result, Schubert's entire achievement in song unfolds within the 'park-like pages' (Capell's description) of ten chronologically arranged volumes that contain every variant version available at the time. Mandyczewski silenced his critics with the scale of his achievement and the logic and elegance with which it was presented. Indeed, it is said that on seeing Mandyczewski's work on the lieder, Brahms was ashamed that he had not spent a great deal more time editing Schubert's symphonies. The listener, turning the pages of the volumes, can almost feel the development and growth of Schubert as an artist – and even Brahms admitted as much. The *Revisionsbericht*, published as a separate volume, is also a remarkable achievement for its time.

It goes without saying that Mandyczewski made a number of errors, but these can be discerned only with hindsight, and in the light of modern scholarship. It is utterly commendable that after more than a hundred years Mandyczewski's edition remains splendidly beautiful to look at, and is still very useful. It was especially indispensable in the last decades of the twentieth century and the start of the twenty-first, when the appetite for Schubert songs was growing all the time, and the publication of the Lieder series of the *Neue Schubert-Ausgabe* (its first volume having appeared in 1968, its last in 2012) seemed remarkably slow. The present-day editors would remind us of the hard tasks they face with the exigencies of modern musicology (and the song aspect of the new edition certainly suffered a severe setback with the death in a tragic accident of the distinguished scholar and discoverer of unknown Schubert autographs, **Christa Landon**, 1921–1978). But the fact remains that Mandyczewski's work, without the help of modern technology, was completed within a single decade. This stands as a huge tribute to his industry and gives credence to reports that he worked himself to the bone. He was heavily involved with both the exhibition and the musicological congress that were planned in 1928 in honour of the centenary of Schubert's death. Sadly he seems to have exhausted himself in the pursuit of excellence and died only months after this important event. The musicological report on the 1928 Schubert conference is dedicated to Mandyczewski's memory.

Any number of writers on music who were contemporary with Mandyczewski benefited from his work. The biography of Schubert (in the series 'Die berühmten Musiker', 1902) by **Richard Heuberger** (1850–1914) was the first to make use of the findings of Breitkopf & Härtel's *Gesamtausgabe*. That the composer of the charming *Im chambre séparée* from *Der Opernball* should have counted himself a Schubert scholar seems unlikely, but Heuberger was distantly related to the Schubert family (Schubert's half-brother Andreas had married a Heuberger) and throughout his career busied himself with Schubert studies and making Schubert arrangements and completions.

After the appearance of Mandyczewski's magnificent Lieder Series XX, a gift to the world of singers and their pianists, it was inevitable that the songs should be singled out for special attention by musicologists. *Die Lieder Franz Schuberts* (1915), the first volume of an incomplete study by **Moritz Bauer** (1875–1932), was available just after the First World War. One of the most influential books on the subject to be written outside Germany and Austria was *Schubert's Songs* by **Richard Capell** (1856–1954). Published in London in 1928 (Schubert's centenary year), it is an indirect tribute to Mandyczewski's achievement (for it follows that great scholar's chronology) and it remains a model of Schubertian devotion. Capell was the music critic of the *Daily Telegraph* in London and a fine amateur musician; he punctiliously played through all the music in the *Gesamtausgabe* volumes, although his musical perceptions are sometimes skewed by the fact that he had never heard good performances, or any performances come to that, of many of the works of which he wrote. When he loved and understood a song, Capell's descriptions can be supremely memorable; this was writing that shaped the Schubertian responses of generations of British music lovers – indeed, his study has been called 'one of the best books on music in the English language'. There have been later studies of the Schubert songs by English writers (for example *The Songs of Schubert* by **Arnold Craig Bell**, 1964, and the slim but learned study by Maurice Brown, *see* below) but none approaches Capell as an introduction to the subject. It was Capell who was clearly an inspiration to Dietrich Fischer-Dieskau in preparing his own similarly chronological study of Schubert's songs.

A Vienna that could boast so many music lovers was certain to be ever more fertile ground for Schubert scholarship of different kinds. Mandyczewski's energies had, to all intents, been focused primarily on the textual questions raised by the manuscripts, and by the sound and effect of the music itself when he conducted it. In the dissemination of biographical information he was far less interested. Many years later, one of his grateful students, the musicologist **Hans Gál** (1890–1987), himself the author of a moving study (*Franz Schubert und die Melodie*, 1970, translated as *Franz Schubert and the Essence of Melody*, 1974) had the following to say about his former teacher: 'If you had asked him [Mandyczewski] about Schubert, he would have smiled and said: Schubert? Play his music, sing his songs, and you will know more about him than I can tell you . . . His lack of ambition is the reason why he left no literary monument: his encyclopaedic knowledge went to the benefit of anyone who wanted information, suggestion, guidance. He never took the trouble of writing down what he knew.' (This remark is reproduced in Brown's *Essays on Schubert*, 1966, p. 193.)

In fact, much of what Mandyczewski knew was almost certainly taken down, very punctiliously, by a young man who had the patience and ears of a folksong-gatherer when it came to Schubertian information. **Otto Erich Deutsch** (1883–1967) was born in Vienna and died in the same city. He was one of the members of the Jewish intelligentsia who survived the Holocaust and returned to the city of his birth – or, perhaps more importantly for him, Schubert's birth. He had a passion for lively and personal historical detail combined with the rigours of dispassionate scholarship. Gustav Nottebohm had already provided a list of Schubert's works, but he was not the composer's Köchel: Nottebohm's catalogue relied on opus numbers that took no account of the chronology of the music, an option that Mandyczewski had rendered obsolete. It was Deutsch whose name would eventually be connected with Schubert's in terms of the numbering of his every work (the so-called 'D' numbers) in as near to a chronological order as was possible.

Deutsch had found his way to Schubert studies via an early interest in the artist and painter Moritz von Schwind; as a teenager he attended the famous Schubert exhibition mounted in Vienna in 1897 on the occasion of the centenary of the composer's birth. He took as a challenge Max Friedlaender's remark that 'material for a biography was, and still is, wanting', and began to assemble facts in a quietly methodical way. In Vienna he was more favourably placed to do so than Friedlaender, who lived and worked in Berlin. Very soon the material for a biography, rather than a biography itself, became its own means to an end. Deutsch's passionate researches were supported by a number of older scholars who valued his work, among them the Brahms biographer **Max Kalbeck** (1850–1921). The young Deutsch was asking questions of older people when it was still possible to garner vital information about Schubert and his circle from living memory if not at first hand (as had been available to Ferdinand Luib; *see* above). The full extent of Deutsch's patient and punctilious research during this period is only evident in work that appeared many decades later.

In 1905, at the age of twenty-two, Deutsch published a *Schubert-Brevier*. This small Schubert Reader, part of a 'Breviary' series published by Schuster & Loeffler on famous writers and musicians, was issued in an attractive yellow-striped cover that resembled Biedermeier wallpaper. This is the first-ever assemblage of Schubert documents as such, sometimes with commentary, and containing very useful appendices on pictures, personalities and works. It is Deutsch's most lighthearted book (although one must not forget his marvellously funny German translation of Gilbert and Sullivan's *The Mikado* made towards the end of his life). If the *Schubert-Brevier* was not always accurate in the light of his later scholarship, it must have been seized on by lovers of Schubert as a small treasure trove of first-hand information. Deutsch's

Otto Deutsch's *Brevier* (1905).

early work no doubt encouraged other writers to provide the interconnecting biographical thread that he himself refrained from writing. The Berlin musicologist **Walter Dahms** (1887–1973) wrote a Schubert biography in 1912 that was very successful with the public. That Dahms had prepared his work from the research notes of yet another Schubert scholar, **Alois Fellner**, is an indication of the richness and variety of Schubertian scholarship at the time.

For Deutsch, the pathway to knowledge was more circuitous and altruistic; by his middle twenties he was the art critic for the newspaper *Die Zeit* and worked in the Kunsthistorisches Institut of the University of Vienna. This connection with pictures, and a knowledge of, and access to, pictorial archives, enabled him to publish his first masterpiece shortly before the First World War – Schubert's life in pictures, entitled *Franz Schubert. Sein Leben in Bildern* (1913). There had been nothing like this sumptuous iconographical volume before, and there has scarcely been anything like it since for any other composer (although nearly half a century later Deutsch issued a pictorial volume on the life of Mozart, with the addition of colour). A first encounter with this collection of beautifully presented Schubertian images, the triumphant intersection of musicology and art history, covering every conceivable aspect of the composer's life and work, invariably takes the breath away. Pictured within this tome is almost every person who played a role, however small, in Schubert's life and work (Walter Dahms, having recently published his biography, is the last person to appear on the volume's pages). To be found therein is an image of almost every Schubertian site, every artefact, every known portrait, including pictures of Schubert's exhumed skull photographed from different angles. The songs are served by portraits of their poets, where available, and illustrations of vignettes, title pages and so on.

This volume was the first instalment of a huge project entitled *Franz Schubert. Die Dokumente seines Lebens und Schaffens*. The second volume, which appeared in 1914, was a documentary biography – in this case simply the documents themselves published without explication or commentary. More than in the case of the *Brevier* we encounter here a style of presentation that lies at the heart of all Deutsch's work, the motto of which could be 'let the facts speak for themselves'. Readers, presented with documents arranged in chronological order, are left to build up their own picture of the composer's life without the critic acting as interpretative middleman. The advertised catalogue, or *Verzeichnis*, of Schubert's works that had been initially advertised as being part of this project failed to appear at this time – **Ludwig Scheibler** (1848–1921), the Schubert scholar with whom Deutsch had been collaborating on this vast task, died unexpectedly in 1921.

With the documentary volume, backed up by the book of pictures, Deutsch had assembled a Luther's bible of Schubertiana whereby the interpretative role of priest-musicologist was no longer exclusively the preserve of professionals. This had far-reaching consequences for both the liveliness and the unruliness of Schubert studies where there are more amateur commentators than for almost any other composer. Deutsch had unleashed the means for everyone, worldwide, to become his or her own Schubertian expert. He had also succeeded in providing a true picture of the composer that might counter the fictitional misconceptions fostered by the hugely successful novel *Schwammerl* by Rudolf Bartsch (1873–1952), published in 1912, and eventually the basis of the operetta *Das Dreimäderlhaus* with music by Heinrich Berté. By 1922 there was an English version of this, the musical *Lilac Time*, running on the London stage. Deutsch was bitterly disappointed that his own hard work on the composer enjoyed nothing like the financial success of Bartsch's saccharine fantasy, and did little to stem the flow of ill-informed kitsch that flooded the market in a crescendo leading to the centenary of Schubert's death in 1928. Between the wars Deutsch retreated into a scholarly world; his work took the form of multitudinous articles in musical journals and newspapers (some 150 in all) and the publication of facsimiles of Schubert's works. As well as managing his own publishing business

in Vienna, he became the librarian of Antony Hoboken (who later compiled the Haydn catalogue) and an esteemed 'Herr Professor' in Viennese life – a title conferred on him by the grateful
Viennese musical establishment in the 'Schubert Year' of 1928.

Deutsch was no musicologist in the normal definition of the word; his unwillingness to tackle a full-scale biography with commentary on the music itself stemmed, no doubt, from the fact that his training had been first and foremost as an art and literature historian. (By the time his eightieth-birthday *Festschrift* appeared Deutsch was, of course, accepted as an equal by great musicologists throughout the world.) However, in Vienna, Berlin and elsewhere in the German-speaking countries there were between the wars countless scholars willing to discuss the music itself in any amount of detail. **Alfred Orel** (1889–1967), pupil of Guido Adler, published many articles on Schubert from 1926 and made a special study of the exercises undertaken by the composer for Salieri in his student years (*Der junge Schubert*, 1940). **Willi Kahl** (1893–1962) published *Verzeichnis des Schrifttums über Franz Schubert* in 1938, a copious bibliography of writings on Schubert. Another Adler pupil was **Bernhard Paumgartner** (1887–1971), a close colleague of Deutsch and the author of *Franz Schubert: Eine Biographie* (1943). Paumgartner was a descendant of Silvester Paumgartner of Steyr to whom Schu-

The young Otto Erich Deutsch at the time of his first Schubert publications.

bert had dedicated the 'Trout' Quintet. The biography of Schubert by **Walther Vetter** (1891–1967) appeared in 1934, and nearly twenty years later his study of *Der Klassiker Schubert* (1953). The lifelong devotion to Schubertian studies of the Swiss musicologist **Harry Goldschmidt** (1910–1986) should also be mentioned: *Schubert: Ein Lebensbild* (1954) appeared the year after Vetter's two-volume work.

Deutsch had been happy to allow decades to go by while painstakingly building up his Schubertian knowledge without publishing the large books more characteristic of his ambitious colleagues. This leisurely, and somewhat Olympian, view was disrupted by anti-Semitism and war. In 1939, when in his active mid fifties, Deutsch was forced to emigrate to England. Cambridge became the temporary headquarters of Schubert studies, a displacement that provided the impetus for the second wave of his publications on a larger scale. The first fruit of his work in exile was the English edition of the *Documentary Biography* (London, 1946; the American edition – *The Schubert Reader*, 1947; updated German edition, 1964). This was a hugely expanded version of the 1914 edition with a host of new publications, including eleven Schubert letters. Deutsch's detailed notebooks, happily shipped from Vienna and returned to their possessor in England after a spell in New York harbour, were mined to provide the invaluable commentaries on the documents. It is these paragraphs, printed in modestly smaller type, a style that goes back to the *Schubert-Brevier* of 1905, that reveal the unfathomable depth of Deutsch's knowledge of Viennese life in the Biedermeier period. It must have been an intensely

SCHUBERT

A DOCUMENTARY BIOGRAPHY

by
OTTO ERICH DEUTSCH

Translated by
ERIC BLOM

Being an English version of
FRANZ SCHUBERT: DIE DOKUMENTE SEINES LEBENS
Revised and augmented with a commentary
by the author

Illustrated with
4 COLOURED PLATES
36 BLACK AND WHITE PLATES
&
42 LINE DRAWINGS

LONDON
J. M. DENT & SONS LTD.

Franz Schubert

Thematisches
Verzeichnis
seiner Werke
in chronologischer
Folge

von Otto Erich Deutsch

Neuausgabe in deutscher Sprache
bearbeitet und herausgegeben
von der Editionsleitung
der Neuen Schubert-Ausgabe
und Werner Aderhold

 Bärenreiter

The English edition of Deutsch's *Documentary Biography* (1946).

Title page of Deutsch's catalogue of Schubert's works (second version, 1978).

nostalgic experience for him to prepare this work while exiled from the city whose civilizing influence in happier times can be felt on every page. The *Documentary Biography* appeared of course in English: all the documents and their commentaries had been translated from the German by Swiss-born English critic **Eric Blom** (1888–1959). Blom enjoyed a close collaboration with Deutsch, and was partly responsible for the new and expanded shape of the work (he was soon to go on to be the editor of the fifth edition of *Grove's Dictionary*). With the publication of the *Documentary Biography* the English-speaking music lover's understanding of Schubert was transformed and deepened almost overnight. It was followed in 1951 with the work that the public had been expecting Deutsch to publish for the past thirty years: *Schubert. Thematic Catalogue of all his Works* in chronological order. At last, every Schubert work was attached to a Deutsch number that indicated its chronology, as far as was known at the time, within the composer's output.

The emigration of distinguished Jewish musicologists from Germany and Austria had other Schubertian side effects. The next important Schubert biographer, **Alfred Einstein** (1880–1952), who was a cousin of the great physicist, moved to Italy in 1933 and to the United States in 1939. In America he turned his attentions to both Mozart and Schubert, and his biography of the latter, intended as a guide for the man in the street rather than his fellow musicologists, was published in 1951 in America (*Schubert – A musical portrait*) and in 1952 in Germany. Shortly before this, Einstein's study, *The Italian Madrigal* (1949), was published and quickly welcomed as the standard work on the subject. Although the Schubert biography was published just too early to take account of Deutsch's catalogue, Einstein had a wonderful way of walking the reader through Schubert's life and works, stopping on the way to remark on the unfolding beauties. His coverage of the songs is selective but methodical, and what he has to say about them is often revelatory.

Although Deutsch had taken British nationality in 1949, the lure of his native city was irresistible. He returned to Vienna in 1952 where he continued to work (Mozart and Handel were his chosen subjects outside Schubert) and teach. He enjoyed coaching lieder in particular, though singers and pianists, the American accompanist Irwin Gage among them, tended to be awed by his presence. His last important book was *Schubert. Die Erinnerungen seiner Freunde* (1957, revised 1966, translated as *Memories of his Friends*, London, 1958). In 1978, some eleven years after his death, a second edition of the catalogue was produced (this time in German) in time for the 150th anniversary of Schubert's death. This edition in turn has become outdated and stands in urgent need of revision.

Deutsch never wrote a biography of Schubert as such, but in a sense he did much more than that: he opened the door to Schubert's life

Otto Erich Deutsch in Vienna, in old age in the 1950s, after his return from England.

and work so that the most humble admirer of the composer's music felt able to create an emotional link with the composer as a person. In confessing in the preface to the *Documentary Biography* that he lacked 'the gift of analysis' and disliked 'the aesthetic approach to matters of art', Deutsch laid down a challenge to others to provide that very analysis. The love and veneration felt the world over for Schubert (as a man, as much as for his music) is partly the result of this audacious and liberating 'freedom of information' act.

With the passing of the years Schubert studies have become increasingly competitive and the ways of looking at Schubert's music have proliferated. There are many musicians – in several countries – who would claim to have got not a whit nearer the composer's music as a result of Deutsch's life's work; these same scholars would claim that biographical considerations are irrelevant to the study of a composer's music. There is an entire school of writing about music that has developed more or less independently of the tradition fostered by Deutsch, as well as his predecessors and successors. In looking at Schubert's work in musical terms alone, this school of 'pure' musicology offers revelations of a different kind – although one man's revelation is often another's confusion. Since the earliest times there have been those whose service to music, and to Schubert in particular, has been expressed in terms of analytical discussion where musicology is both science and art – in some cases, rather more of the former than the latter.

Perhaps the first theoretician in Schubert studies was **Hans Georg Nägeli** (1773–1836), a Swiss composer, choral trainer and educationalist who founded the 'Singinstitut' in Zurich. Nägeli's writing on song (*Die Lieder Kunst*, 1817) makes imaginative new demands and predictions for the medium that were fulfilled by Schubert, and his support for Michael Haydn's work chimed with Schubert's own enthusiasm for that composer. By 1826 Nägeli was aware of Schubert and admired his piano works. His acute ear and interest in the younger generation marks him out as a pioneer Schubertian.

Heinrich Schenker (1868–1935) is one of the most important of all musical theoreticians. As a young man he came to Vienna from Galicia to study with Bruckner, and was a teacher of such figures as Hoboken and Furtwängler. In his thirties he accompanied the great Dutch baritone Messachaert in *Die schöne Müllerin* D795. Most of his work as a musical analyst favoured the examination of instrumental music rather than vocal, but in the journal he founded in 1921 entitled *Der Tonwille* he turned his attention to two Schubert songs – *Ihr Bild* D957/9 and *Gretchen am Spinnrade* D118. In various issues of the same publication Schenker analysed important pieces of Schubert's chamber music, and at least four of the piano sonatas.

Very different from Schenker was **Paul Mies** (1875–1976), a powerful analyst of the lied form (*Schubert: der Meister des Liedes: Die Entwicklung von Form und Inhalt im Schubertschen Lied*, 1928). His work also encompassed biographical considerations. Between 1928 and 1969 a handful of important articles embracing theoretical and philosophical matters of great interest to the Schubertian were written by **Theodor Adorno** (1903–1969). The Greek scholar **Thrasybulos Georgiades** (1907–1977), who spent his working life in Germany, was specifically a lied scholar whose analyses in *Schubert, Musik und Lyrik* (1967) were highly influential in their observations on the relationship between words and music. Georgiades formulated a notable theory concerning the similarity of Schubert's creative and working practices with those of his poets – and thereby his specific mastery of the art of song composition. A scholar who developed Georgiades's theories was his pupil **Arnold Feil** (b. 1925) whose researches into rhythm in Schubert's music are central to his work. Feil's study of the Müller song cycles (*Franz Schubert. 'Die schöne Müllerin' 'Winterreise'*, 1975) is a standard work that has been translated into English and French. He was also responsible for facsimile editions of the two great Müller cycles, and was on the editorial board of the *Neue Schubert-Ausgabe*. Of the relatively recent Schubert studies in Germany, *Franz Schubert und seine Zeit* (1991) by **Peter Gülke** (b. 1934) has perhaps been the most successful; this work discusses Schubert analytically, philosophically and historically, without attempting a conventional biography. Gülke also contributed twenty-three articles to the *Schubert Liedlexikon* (2012).

With strong claims from both sides of the debate regarding the practice of musicology it is all but impossible to award the 'greatest-living-Schubert-scholar' accolades that seemed applicable in the times of Mandyczewski, Deutsch and Maurice Brown (*see* below). **Walther Dürr** (b. 1932) is the 'grand old man' of present-day Schubert studies. Like Alfred Einstein he has contributed a great deal to the study of the Italian madrigal, and throughout his career has continued to publish articles on early Italian music. Since the late 1960s he has given his attention to Schubert, and in particular the lieder, and he has also written papers on such composers as Schumann, Loewe and Josephine Lang. His kindness and generosity in helping other Schubertians (not to mention performers) marks him out as both scholar and

Walther Dürr.

gentleman. His lifelong work in Tübingen on the song volumes of the *Neue Schubert-Ausgabe* (now complete, apart from the preparation of one further volume of *Kritischer Bericht*) included the introductions and notes on each song. This has been combined with the exploration of other areas of the composer's oeuvre, such as the opera *Alfonso und Estrella* and some of the piano music. With so much responsibility he has sometimes stood in the musical firing line – musicology has never been a particularly friendly or trouble-free realm, even in the time of Mandyczewski. Dürr's numerous publications in journals are in the Otto Erich Deutsch tradition in terms of their profuse variety – nearly eighty articles on Schubert alone are listed in the *Festschrift* issued for his seventieth birthday, *Schubert und das Biedermeier* (Bärenreiter, 2002). He is also the moving spirit and editor of the *Schubert Liedlexikon* (2012) and a massive contributor to the work. As a scholar Dürr stands very much in the dignified and judicious tradition of Mandyczewski and Maurice Brown. Dürr's work in Tübingen is ably assisted by **Christine Martin** who is also an expert on the Schubert operas (she also contributes thirty-two articles to the *Schubert Liedlexikon*, 2012). Mention should be made here of **Michael Kube**, **Uwe Schweikert** and **Stefanie Steiner** who are contributing editors to the same Lexikon. **Dietrich Berke** has also played an important part in the NSA particularly with the part song and choral repertoire and as contributor to the *Schubert Liedlexikon*.

The Schubertian scholar, **Ernst Hilmar** (b. 1938), was a contributor to Dürr's *Festschrift* but is distinguished in rather a different way. Born in Graz and trained in Germany he was perhaps the most energetic Schubertian of his generation – a powerhouse of activity, some of it controversial, none of it dull. There is scarcely any field of Schubert study with which Hilmar has not been involved. He considered himself a musicologist in the mould of Fritz Racek (1911–1975) of whom he was a protégé in Vienna, and who fought in vain for a new complete edition of Schubert's works in the 1950s. During Hilmar's period in charge at the Stadt- und Landesbibliothek in Vienna (now the Wienbibliothek im Rathaus) between 1975 and 1994, the library, already in possession of the majority of the song manuscripts, acquired many further treasures. He established an impressive network of international Schubert societies under the general umbrella of the *International Franz Schubert Institute* (IFSI) and was editor, between 1987 and 2003, of the often invaluable twice-yearly journal, *Schubert durch die Brille*. Like Deutsch he has shied away from writing a Schubert biography, but the volume *Franz Schubert in seiner Zeit* (1985) serves as an introduction to the composer with many new viewpoints, and there is a handsome iconographical volume (*Schubert*, 1989) with a certain biographical thread to it. Hilmar's largest publication was a copious volume of commentary (2003) on a substantial new volume of documents (a modern-day supplement to Deutsch's far from complete catalogue) that had been compiled by **Till Gerrit Waidelich** (b. 1969) in 1993. Both were published as a matching set by Schneider. (Waidelich, also a major contributor to the *Schubert Liedlexikon* 2012, is among the very finest of the younger Schubert scholars.) An earlier *Schubert-Lexikon* (1996, not specializing only in the songs) can also be numbered among Ernst Hilmar's achievements. This was later expanded into a profusely illustrated *Schubert-Encyclopädie* in two volumes (Schneider, 2004), an indispensable reference book that was assembled in collaboration with **Margaret Jestremski** (also a great Wolf scholar). Hilmar was clearly in the vanguard of those who see musicology as a kind of practical activism. In his successful efforts to preserve Atzenbrugg castle outside Vienna, the site of Schubertian excursions to the countryside in the 1820s, as well as a less fruitful campaign to preserve and repair the ruin of the Esterházy family residence at Zseliz, Hilmar was at his practical best. In his case the excitement of discovering new material – the archaeological side of musicology – trumped the Deutsch-like observations of the art historian. Impatient with the ivory tower, Hilmar has never shied away from a fight. An example of this is his argument about the so-called 'Paraphe' (*see* INITIALS AND SIGNATURES). Hilmar succeeded more than once in shaking up received opinion – sometimes to the irritation of his fellow scholars.

All this contrasts with the quiet and smooth scholarship of **Otto Biba** (b. 1946), distinguished director of the Archive of the Gesellschaft der Musikfreunde. He is younger than Hilmar, but essentially a scholar in the ongoing Viennese tradition in which Hilmar never felt comfortable. The distinguished Austrian musicologist and Schubert expert **Walburga Litschauer** (b. 1954), responsible for the publication of new documents in 1986 and 1993 (*Neue Dokumente zum Schubert-Kreis*), is the doyenne of highly regarded Schubert scholars. She has a lively spirit in Schubert studies while remaining part of the ongoing Viennese tradition, as well as of the German school led by Dürr. She contributed to the *Schwanengesang* publication edited for Yale University Press (2000) by Martin Chusid (*see* below) and is a contributor to the *Schubert Liedlexikon* (2012). Somewhat to the bemusement of English-speaking Schubertians the list of German and Austrian scholars engaged with this composer grows daily. Thirty years ago it was possible to read everything written about Schubert but now it is impossible to keep up with the books published on the subject, let alone the articles in musical journals. In this overview I have done little enough justice to the scholars already mentioned, and less to those names that I can only list here: **Marie Agnes Dittrich** for detailed studies of individual songs (in the lieder section of the *Schubert Handbuch*); **Ira Schulze-Ardey** (Matthisson settings); **Astrid Tschense-Oesterle** (Goethe settings); **Michael Kohlhäufl** for an in-depth study of the poets in Schubert's circle; **Friedrich Dreckmann** and **Michael Stegemann** for general studies of the composer. Contributors to the *Schubert Liedlexicon* (2012), other than the ten authors mentioned elsewhere in this article, include an extraordinary mixture of musicologists and Germanists: **Werner Aderhold, Michael Bauer, Christiane Braun, Moritz Chelius, Gerhard Dietel, Christian Geltinger, Andreas Holzer, Annegret Huber, Christoph Huber, Manuela Jahrmärker, Hans Joachim Kreutzer, Stefan Lindinger, Helga Lühning, Dieter Martin, Almut Ochsmann, Michael Raab, Reinhard Saller, Siegfried Schmalzriedt, Thomas Seedorf, Thomas Seybolt, Morten Solvik** (*see* Kosegarten Liederkreis), **Mirjam Springer, Wolfgang Stähr, Christian Strehk**. The future of Schubert studies in German-speaking countries is assured.

It is perhaps natural that the musicologists of Austria and Germany should feel superior to those based far from the countries where new discoveries of Schubert letters, manuscripts and so on might be expected to be made. There are scholars who regard this first-hand exhumation as the only kind of interesting musicology. It is true that Schubert lovers of Britain, France and America are often unable to speak Schubert's language fluently, much less read the composer's handwriting. On the other hand, wherever a score of Schubert's work is to be found the stirrings of the heart are also to be felt. Someone in whom these are combined with musical and literary perspicacity will have opinions on Schubert and the ability – and surely the right – to express them. The English had to swallow the proprietary nature of the Germans in Shakespeare studies ('Unser Shakespeare'); in return, the Germans and Austrians have had to concede that Schubert in terms of his music and life is nationally uncontainable: he belongs to the world at large.

The presence of Otto Erich Deutsch in England as the result of the *Anschluss*, and the appearance of the *Documentary Biography* and *Thematic Catalogue*, provided a huge fillip to Schubert studies in England. This period set the seal on Britain's 'special relationship' with Schubert that had been initiated by Sir George Grove. Deutsch's arrival in England just overlapped with the life of **Sir Donald Tovey** (1875–1940), one of the most enthusiastic of the Schubertian English musicologists. His six volumes of *Essays in Musical Analysis* appeared between 1935 and 1939; in a supplementary volume to that series there is an essay on the song *Viola* D786. **Arthur Hutchings** (1906–1989) contributed a *Schubert* to the *Master Musicians* series in 1945 and **Gerald Abraham** (1904–1988) edited his *Schubert Symposium* (1946); Deutsch contributed an essay on *Schubert the Man* to the latter book and **Alec Robertson** (1892–1982) wrote the gentle chapter on the songs in post-Capell mode. These studies just missed the publication of the

Documentary Biography, after which Schubert scholarship became more complicated and technically more demanding.

One Englishman in particular, **Maurice J. E. Brown** (1906–1975), emerged as the Schubert specialist of his generation. Many other British musicologists of the time numbered Schubert among their different interests but Brown more or less gave his life to this composer's music. He became a close colleague of Deutsch and helped to prepare the English edition of the *Erinnerungen*, published in Britain as *Memoirs*. A science master at Marlborough Grammar School, Brown – rather like Grove – was a part-time scholar whose work often outshone the achievements of full-time musicologists in other countries. He published his *Schubert, A Critical Biography* in 1958 (translated into German in 1969) as well as copious articles in the journals and *Essays on Schubert* in 1966. During the 1960s and '70s, after Deutsch's death, Brown was generally considered the greatest living authority on Schubert. He wrote a monograph on the songs for the BBC in 1967 (reprinted many times), and there is much in his occasional writings that examines musicological issues regarding the composer's lieder output.

Maurice J. E. Brown.

Brown's example was an inspiration to his contemporaries. **John Reed** (1909–1999), another teacher-turned-musicologist, published an important study about the end of Schubert's life, *The Final Years* (1972). Reed had the ability to write about musicological matters in a clear and simple way: his *Schubert* for the 'Great Composers' series (Faber and Faber, 1978) is a model of how to connect with the younger reader. The English-speaking lieder enthusiast is indebted to Reed chiefly for his pioneering *The Schubert Song Companion* (1985) where a great deal of important information is assembled in a

John Reed.

concise form. It was an invaluable guide during the making of the Hyperion Song Edition (begun in 1987). Reed also wrote a 'grown-up' study of Schubert's life and work for the Dent 'Master Musicians' series (1987).

A contemporary and friend of Maurice Brown was the scholar **Eric Sams** (1926–2004) (pictured overleaf) whose published work on the songs of Schumann, Wolf and Brahms made him a unique figure in lieder scholarship. Sams was also hugely knowledgeable about Schubert and wrote a number of articles on the composer; sadly a projected book on the songs was never

completed, but he is one of the revered dedicatees of this book. A world authority on the
Viennese theatre in the time of Nestroy, and
a renowned Germanist, **Peter Branscombe**
(1929–2009) has made many a telling contribution to the examination of Schubert's life
and times; that he was co-editor, with **Eva
Badura-Skoda**, of *Schubert Studies* (1982) is
an indication of the increasingly international nature of Schubertian co-operation.
Leo Black (b. 1937) is a scholar and radio
producer who for many years oversaw broad-
casts by countless singers of the composer's
music at the BBC. With his wide hands-on
knowledge of the song repertoire it is little
wonder that his *Franz Schubert: Music and*

Eric Sams.

Belief (2003) contains many illuminating references to the songs. These are made mainly in the
context of a discussion of Schubert's religious music, breaking new ground, although **Elizabeth
Norman McKay** (b. 1931) also entered this field of exploration when she made a case for linking
Winterreise with *Die deutsche Messe* D872 (*Schubert durch die Brille*, 1999). McKay's *Franz
Schubert – A Biography* (1996) is a useful and level-headed gathering together of various strands
of modern scholarship and opinion. She has written a book on Schubert's operas, as well as one
on the darker tonalities used by the composer, and published several articles on the songs.
Together with the musicologist and conductor **Brian Newbould** (b. 1936), whose main Schubertian explorations have been into the larger-scale works including the symphonies, McKay
has proved herself over the years, and after the death of John Reed, to be Britain's leading Schubert scholar.

    That title in France would almost certainly go to **Brigitte Massin** (b. 1927) whose copious
biography *Franz Schubert* (1977, republished 1993) was a best-seller. *Franz Schubert: Le naïf et
la mort* (1997) by **Rémy Stricker** is notable for its personal and touching empathy with its
subject, qualities also to be found in *Le Rapt de Ganymède* by **Dominique Fernandez** (1989),
a book that addresses the controversial issues of sexuality and sexual shame in Schubert's life in
a way that has not been attempted elsewhere. In France there has been a long line of Schubertian
commentary that goes back to the nineteenth century, most of it imitated from German or
Austrian publications. A typical work of Fauré's time, for example, heavily reliant on Kreissle,
was *Franz Schubert: sa vie et ses œuvres* by **Mme Agathe Audley** (1871), written at a time when
the icons of German musical culture were establishing themselves strongly in France, despite
recent political catastrophes.

    In Belgium, the work of the Ghent-born **Reinhard Van Hoorickx** (1918–1997) took a for
more practical turn. He was consecrated as a priest in 1943 and spent many years following his
vocation in the Middle East. Apart from his frequent contributions to musicological journals
– in the region of forty essays including much work on Ferdinand Schubert – Van Hoorickx
published his first completion of a Schubert song fragment in 1959. Eventually he made
performing versions of almost all the fragmentary songs. These are of no great intrinsic musical
merit but, in not attempting to match the sophistication of the composer's own work, Van
Hoorickx's material fades into the background, allowing these fragments to be heard in arrangements where everything the composer had written is retained. Apart from his role as a modest
composer at one remove, Van Hoorickx was a tenacious scholar determined to unearth details
overlooked by everyone else. At times his single-minded devotion to his Schubert studies put

him at odds with his church superiors – he was 'exiled' to Corsica for some years but carried on his researches regardless.

Schubertian musicology in Russia, including work on *Winterreise*, was led by **Juri Chochlow** (b. 1922), a name not to be confused with that of **Maximillian and Lilly Schochow** whose two-volume work *Franz Schubert: Die Texte seiner einstimmig komponierten Lieder und ihre Dichter* (1974) gathered together all the Schubert song texts while attempting with varying success to identify their sources and Schubert's departures from the originals. The sequel to that book (*Band III: Die Texte der mehrstimmigen Lieder*) was edited by **Werner Bodendorff** and published in 2006.

A new country enters the stakes in terms of sustained Schubert scholarship with the work of the Irish musicologist and Germanist **Lorraine Byrne** (b. 1968), author of *Schubert's Goethe Settings* (2003) and editor of *Goethe Musical Poet, Musical Catalyst* (2004). She has also issued a performing version for voices and piano of what remains to us of Schubert's *Claudine von Villa Bella* (2002). Lorraine Byrne's colleague in the shared editorship of *The Unknown Schubert* (2008) was the Canadian scholar **Barbara M. Reul** (b. 1967).

American Schubert studies need a chapter on their own: a short article can only scratch the surface. It is strange perhaps that in a country where the performance of Schubert's lieder seems to be a diminishing priority for singers and their audiences, the amount of published writing on the subject is almost overwhelming. This academic enthusiasm has not been without its dramatic moments. The greatest controversy of recent years, that of Schubert's sexuality, was sparked off in 1988 by a lecture for the American Musicological Society (followed in 1989 by an article in *19th-Century Music*) by **Maynard Solomon** (b. 1930). Solomon offered a passage in a letter of Eduard von Bauernfeld in August 1826 (referring to the 'peacocks of Benvenuto Cellini') as evidence of the composer's homosexuality. This triggered all-out scholastic war with much of the German-speaking musicological establishment, above all with the blistering retort to Solomon in 1993 of **Rita Steblin** (b. 1951), a Canadian Schubert scholar working in Vienna at the time, who was determined to defend Schubert's name against what she clearly regarded as a serious calumny. The researches of **Ilija Dürhammer** (b. 1969) in *Schuberts literarische Heimat* (1999) have gone much deeper into the pros and cons of this topic (and many others) in regard to the Schubert circle as a whole, with many new documents, but have not produced an incontrovertible answer concerning the composer himself. Steblin, who has made a speciality of biographical research, unearthed evidence of Schubert's membership (1817–18) of the *Unsinnsgesellschaft*; this required complicated unravelling and has added a dimension to our knowledge of the composer's Viennese existence unremarked by Deutsch. It also has relevance to some of the songs that were perhaps composed for the society's

Reinhard Van Hoorickx.

proceedings. In addition, Steblin has contributed significant scholarship on Schubert's relationship with Therese Grob and her family.

The debate on the composer's sexuality has continued, with scholars on either side of the Atlantic often, but not always, taking opposite viewpoints. (A German scholar who unusually supports the thesis of Schubert's homosexuality is **Christoph Schwandt** (b. 1956).) There used to be some consensus between American and European musicology as far as Schubert was concerned; in modern times some aspects of transatlantic scholarship appear to have the characteristics of a breakaway Anglican diocese – and for some of the same reasons. It is now more or less accepted that even if Solomon were correct, or even partly correct (Schubert's bisexuality is sometimes posited as a kind of middle position), the arguments he used to make his case were flawed. This quarrel, however, helped open the floodgates of cultural theory as applied to Schubert and his songs on a much broader level, a postmodernist approach to writing about the composer of which **Lawrence Kramer** (b. 1946) is the leading American exponent (*Franz Schubert: Sexuality, Subjectivity, Song*, 1998). A more recent example of this genre is *Schubert and the European Imagination* (2006) by **Scott Messing**. Lawrence Kramer's work is not to be confused with that of **Richard Kramer** whose *Distant Cycles: Schubert and the Conceiving of Song* (1994) is also controversial, although firmly connected with a detailed discussion of the music itself. The Schubertian writings of **Kristina Muxfeldt**, a pupil of Richard Kramer, include a dissertation for SUNY Stony Brook entitled 'Schubert Song Studies' and *Vanishing Sensibilities* (2012).

This is not to say that such analyses as those of the New York academic and Verdi scholar **Martin Chusid** (1925–2013) in his facsimile edition of *Schwanengesang* (with an accompanying book of analytical essays) are not in the mainstream European tradition – it depends, after all, on *which* European tradition. The same could be said of the challenging analyses of **Edward Cone** (1917–2004) as in '"Am Meer" reconsidered: Strophic, Binary or Ternary?', published in *Schubert Studies* (1998). Cone also contributed a chapter of commentary to Chusid's *Schwanengesang*. The sympathies of most American Schubert scholars tend to fall in either biographical or analytical (often Schenkerian) directions.

Something new in Schubertian musicology, and emanating not unnaturally from a country where the employment of technology is second nature, was the work contributed by **Robert Winter** (b. 1945), professor of music at UCLA, on paper studies whereby the dating of works is determined by the paper that the composer used. The process is quite fallible in that music paper can be used a long time after the date of its watermark. However Winter is celebrated in many areas of Schubert detective work. A musicologist using more conventional means is **Rufus Hallmark** (b. 1943) of Queen's College, City University of New York, who has written numerous articles about Schubert (including a study of *Auf dem Strom*); he was editor of *German Lieder in the Nineteenth Century* (1996, rev. 2009). In the same year appeared *The Lied, Mirror of Late Romanticism* by **Edward F. Kravitt** (1926–2002). Though not exclusively about Schubert, it is full of original perceptions about the composer's music. **Christopher Gibbs** (b. 1958) has edited the *Cambridge Companion to Schubert* (1997). An expert on the reception of Schubert lieder, he is also the author of *The Life of Schubert* (2000) which emphasizes the importance of Schubert's relationship to Beethoven. Other important Schubertians from North America are **David Gramit** (b. 1959), who teaches in Canada and who wrote a dissertation for Duke University on Schubert's *Bildungskreis*, and **David Montgomery** who authored *Franz Schubert's Music in Performance* (2003). His views regarding appoggiaturas in Schubert's music, as well as his disagreement concerning rhythmic assimilation (whereby the semiquaver after a dotted quaver is brought into line with the third of a set of triplets, as in *Wasserflut* D911/6 from *Winterreise*) conflict with the editorial policy of the NSA (see also *Schubert durch die Brille*, 27, 2001).

The American to have written the most consistently and fully about Schubert's songs (for publishers both in the USA and Great Britain) is **Susan Youens** (b. 1947), professor of musicology at Notre Dame, Indiana. Apart from many contributions to learned journals and books, she has written studies on both Müller song cycles: one for the Cornell University Press about *Winterreise* (1991) and two for Cambridge University Press on *Die schöne Müllerin* (1992 and 1997). Also by her are *Schubert's Poets and the Making of Lieder* (1996), *Schubert's Late Lieder: Beyond the Song Cycles* (2002) and, most recently, *Heinrich Heine and the Lied* (2007), a study of settings of that great poet that includes Schubert's. She has of course written about other lieder composers, notably Hugo Wolf, but her working life has been primarily devoted to Schubert's songs. Her writing is poised between the intersecting worlds of music and literature, exactly the interdisciplinary area

Susan Youens.

inhabited by the lied, and testily ignored by those who insist on treating song as a 'pure' or abstract musical form. Musicologists of the latter kidney may complain about Youens's literary excursions, but interpreters of the lied find her detailed and imaginative explications enlightening; her journeys in the company of Schubert's poets always lead somewhere interesting for the performer. It is no surprise to learn that Youens has been a singer herself, and that listening to song is as important to her as writing about it. This practical side of her devotion to the composer and his works, while not precluding poetic description and insight, is palpable in everything she writes. The useful writings on Schubert by **Marjorie Wing Hirsch** (b. 1960) (*Schubert's Dramatic Lieder*, 1993 and *Romantic Lieder and the Search for Lost Paradise*, 2007) are in the Youens tradition of combined musicological and literary perception, as are the writings of **Lorraine Byrne Bodley** (*see* above).

Bibliography: Everett 1988

JOHANNA HENRIETTE SCHOPENHAUER (1766–1838)

THE POETIC SOURCE

S1 *Gabriele*, Ein Roman von Johanna Schopenhauer. In drei Theilen. Dritter Theil. Leipzig F. A. Brockhaus, 1821

In the foreword to Volume 1 of this two-volume edition Schopenhauer admits that heaven had not blessed her with the 'gift of song' and that the poetry to be found in her novel was not by her. She gladly names her friend Friedrich von Gerstenbergk (qv) as the author of the lyrics. These are to be found on pp. 177–9 and p. 322 of Volume 1, and p. 146 (*Hippolits Lied*) and pp. 257–8 (*Gabrielens Abendlied*) of Volume 3 of the novel. It is possible that Schubert's source was a later reprint of the novel published in Vienna in 1825 by Chr. Fr. Schade in the Classische Cabinets-Bibliothek series.

THE SONG
July 1826   *Hippolits Lied* D890 [S1: p. 146]

Johanna Trosiener was born on 3 July 1766 in Danzig. When she was scarcely nineteen she married the rich merchant Heinrich Floris Schopenhauer. She travelled throughout Europe with him and the couple moved to Hamburg where Arthur Schopenhauer, the future philosopher, was born on 22 February 1788. Johanna's husband died in 1805 and she decided to move to Weimar – unfortunately at the time of the French invasion. She arrived there when most people were fleeing the town and was a pillar of strength to those in need. Her salons held on Thursdays and Saturdays became a focal point of intellectual life in Weimar. She lived with Friedrich von Gerstenbergk for a number of years; the relationship was the cause of a rupture between Johanna and her son Arthur. She moved to Bonn in 1828 to be with her daughter, but returned to Weimar at the specific invitation of the Grand Duke (she was missed as a hostess and genial literary spirit). She died in Weimar on 17 April 1838. Schopenhauer was a prolific authoress of novels and short stories. No less than nine closely printed pages in Goedeke are required to list her work.

See also FRIEDRICH VON GERSTENBERGK.

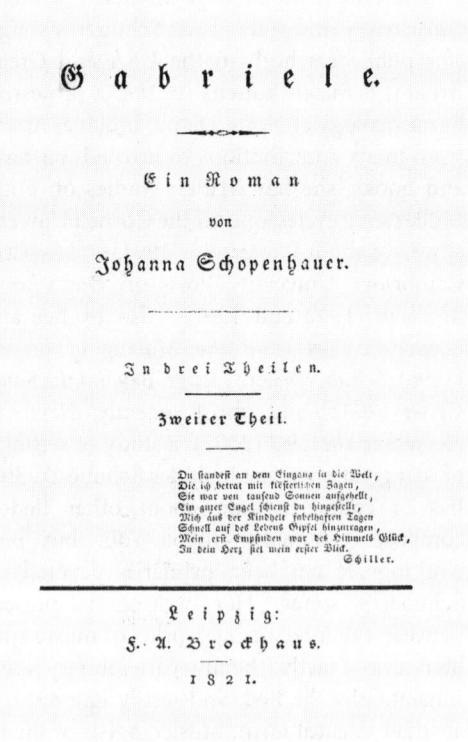

Gabriele (1821).

Johanna Schopenhauer, drawing by Gustav Guibert, 1794.

ALOYS [ALOIS] WILHELM SCHREIBER (1761–1841)

THE POETIC SOURCES

S1 *Gedichte von Aloys Schreiber*, Erster und Zweyter Teil, Neueste Auflage, Wien, 1817, Bey B. Ph. Bauer

This is one of the series of the works of German poets printed in small, pink paper-covered volumes, and which Schubert clearly found extremely handy. Other poets published in this Viennese series used by Schubert included Salis-Seewis, Kosegarten, A. W. Schlegel and Jacobi. The title of this ninety-volume series as a whole was *Deutscher Parnass. Die vollständigste, correcteste und wohlfeilste Ausgabe Deutscher Dichter des goldenen Zeitalters, in 90 Theilen* ('The most complete, most correct and least expensive edition of German poets from the golden age in ninety parts'). Schubert probably obtained it from the book dealer Ignaz Klang – Dorotheergasse, 1105 'im linken Eckhause von Graben hinein' ('in the corner house in from the Graben, on the left-hand side'). This would place Klang's bookshop almost opposite where the music firm of Doblinger has its premises today.

S2 *Poetische Werke von Aloys Schreiber*. Erster Band (Mit Kupfer). Tübingen, bei Heinrich Laupp, 1817

THE SONGS

April 1818   *An den Mond in einer Herbstnacht* D614 [S1: Zweyter Teil, pp. 68–9] [S2: pp. 366–7] In the last strophe (as printed only in Schreiber's *Gedichte und Erzählungen*, 1812) the line 'Du wirst sehn noch manches Lächeln' (bb. 110–11) is followed by 'Und seh'n noch manche Träne'. The absence of the latter line in the Schubert setting indicates that the composer did not use the earlier source.

August 1818   *Der Blumenbrief* D622 [S1: Erster Teil, pp. 86–7] [S2: p. 90]
Das Marienbild D623 [S1: pp. 14–15 printed there with the title *Das Marien-Bild in einem Baume*] [S2: pp. 6–7 printed there with the title *Das Marienbild in einem Baume*]

November 1818   *Das Abendrot* D627 [S1: pp. 68–9] [S2: p. 67]

Alois Schreiber was born in Bühl near Baden-Baden on 12 October 1761. He was destined for a life in the Church but, influenced by the works of the Enlightenment (Salomon Gessner, Uz, Claudius, Bürger, Klopstock), he became very critical of conservative Catholicism. Schreiber became a teacher of aesthetics at the Gymnasium in his home town of Baden-Baden, and then moved on to Mainz. From 1797 he lived in Rastatt. He at first supported the ideals of the French Revolution but from 1793 turned against left-wing politics. His revered models were Rousseau and Goethe, and in the last decade of the eighteenth century he published novellas, tales and poetic works including a volume of *Gedichte*. In 1805 he was appointed Professor of Aesthetics in Heidelberg where he came under the influence of Johann Heinrich Voss (qv) whose son became his best friend. In this lively university town he engaged in polemical battles with the Romantics supporting the Rationalists. His poetry stands nearer the eighteenth century than the nineteenth in style and sympathy. The *Werke* were published in 1817/18 and consisted of three books containing one volume of poems and two of Erzählungen, or Tales (a few of which also contain lyrics). The Viennese edition (issued at the same time) was an inexpensive Austrian reprint of this edition.

Schreiber made his greatest reputation as a writer specializing in topography (he was an authority on the Rhineland and Baden); some of his guide books to the Rhine with their accompanying fold-out maps are particularly sumptuous and appeared in various English editions for foreign tourists. He was also the editor of the Heidelberg-based almanac *Cornelia* (from 1816 until his death), a 'Taschenbuch für Frauen' which untypically survived until 1873. For this famous publication he called on the collaboration of such writers as the brothers Stolberg, Rückert and Uhland. Schreiber eventually went on to work in Karlsruhe, achieving the title of Hofrat, and returned to a position in Baden-Baden at the end of his life, giving readings and lectures to foreign visitors. His life exemplified the typical cycle of a poet returning to his birthplace and converting to conservative ideals in older age after a lifetime of distinguished promotions and youthful liberalism. Schreiber died on 21 October 1841 at the ripe old age of eighty.

Aloys Schreiber, engraving by Lange after portrait of Eduard Schuler.

Schreiber was one of those poets whose work influenced Schubert for a very definite and limited period (another example is Rückert where six settings all date from 1822–3). All the Schreiber settings date from 1818, a period when the composer was comparatively unprolific but when his song texts reflected a search for a philosophical centre, ranging from the pantheism of Friedrich von Schlegel and Mayrhofer's classically influenced poetry to the Christian piety of Schreiber's poems. An important consideration here is the influence of the Esterházy family (*Das Abendrot* D627 was written for Count Esterházy, who was a bass). The religious tone of some of the other Schreiber settings might be explained by the Esterházy family's preference for music with a link to the church. Emilie Zumsteeg also set a text by Schreiber in 1819, and Carl Loewe's famous *Odins Meeresritt* (Op. 118, 1851) has a text by him. Other Schreiber settings by Loewe are *Maria und das Milchmädchen*, Op. 36 no. 4, and *Der ewige Jude* Op. 36 no. 3.

Bibliography: Porhansl 1989, pp. 12–14

CHRISTIAN FRIEDRICH DANIEL SCHUBART (1739–1791)

THE POETIC SOURCE

S1 *Christian Friedrich Daniel Schubart's Gedichte*, herausgegeben von seinem Sohne Ludwig Schubart. Erster und Zweiter Theil. Frankfurt am Main 1802, bey F. C. Hermann

It is also possible that Schubert used a contemporary Viennese edition of the Schubart poems (a reprint of the above German edition), two small pocket volumes issued in the Deutscher Parnass series – Nos 67 and 68 – and published by Bauer und Dirnböck.

THE SONGS

c. 1816   *An mein Klavier* D342 [S1: Zweiter Theil pp. 84–6 with the title *Serafina an ihr Klavier*]

July 1816   *Grablied auf einen Soldaten* D454 [S1: Zweiter Theil in section 'Impromptus, Zeitstücke, Epigramme' pp. 325–7 with the title *Todtenmarsch*]

1816 or 1817   *An den Tod* D518 [S1: Erster Theil pp. 262–5]

1817   *Die Forelle* D550 [S1: Zweiter Theil in section 'Impromptus, Zeitstücke, Epigramme' pp. 302–3]

Schubart was born in Obersontheim, Limburg, on 24 March 1739, the son of a schoolteacher. He showed musical talent when very young as a composer and performer, but his reverence for the *Messias* of Klopstock was an early indication of gifts that were evenly divided between music and poetry. It was later said of him that he was a 'born poet', but only that: he was not a poet who knew how to cultivate and refine his talent, cursed as he was by a wild personality and an unlucky fate. Too clever and outspoken for his own good, his radical stance and sharp tongue were his downfall. Schubart, for all his attractive qualities, is generally considered to have squandered his rich abilities in both music and literature. It was the latter side of his life that got him into trouble and if Schubart had kept to music he would have had a much happier life. He rates a substantial entry in *The New Grove Dictionary of Music* (2001) in his own right. Charles Burney praised his virtuosity as a player of the organ and harpsichord, and nineteenth-century composers (including Beethoven and Schumann) were interested in his writings on musical aesthetics. He believed that folksong was the real music of the people and he was also one of the only writers of his period fully to estimate the greatness of both

J. S. and C. P. E. Bach. Among his numerous compositions, Schubart made a musical setting of his own poem, *Die Forelle*, as well as of his charming *Weihnachtslied der Hirtin*, a poem later set to music by the six-year-old Richard Strauss.

His student days in Erlangen were spent drinking, dancing, playing and womanizing. Schubart was a *bon viveur* to say the least, and although he tried being a part-time preacher and schoolteacher, he tended towards a dissipated lifestyle. He married Helene Bühler, daughter of a customs official, who hardly realized what she had taken on, but who managed to stay the course with her errant, and ultimately martyred, husband. Schubart landed the job of organist and director of music in Ludwigsburg and had the time of his life. It was while he was there that his reputation attracted Goethe's attention – not yet as a writer, but as a piano virtuoso (the great poet was then journeying in Italy). But making music was not nearly diverting enough for Schubart who, as he later ruefully admitted, cavorted in Ludwigsburg between the Scylla and Charibdis of wine and women, and ended up being caught in the whirlpool. He angered the clergy by attacking aspects of the church and, as a result, lost his job in May 1773 and was exiled from the town.

He ended up in Augsburg, and then in Ulm, as editor of *Die deutsche Chronik*. By this time he had already published some volumes of his own poetry – relatively innocuous verse – but in taking on the 'editorship' of such an enterprise (where, like Matthias Claudius in Wandsbek, he effectively had to write all the copy himself – eight pages twice a week) he developed a taste for social and political commentary of an acerbic kind. He rejoiced in expounding a worldwide view of events. In 1775, for example, he wrote that North America was the land of the future, and that much more could be expected from it than of Europe. Schubart courted controversy in his writing, and his sharp tongue and literary wit made him famous throughout Germany, with some 20,000 regular readers. Unfortunately for him these included people whose power he had drastically underestimated; no doubt he felt himself untouchable in the free imperial city of Ulm.

Die deutsche Chronik was something of a combination of *Private Eye* and *Der Spiegel*; among its targets were the famously tyrannical Karl Eugen, Duke of Württemberg, and his mistress, Franziska von Hohenheim. The so-called defamation of such famous people in the region had terrible consequences. In a story worthy of Alexander Dumas, Schubart was lured by a seemingly innocent invitation on 27 January 1777 to the town of Blaubeuren (as this lay within the borders of Duke Karl Eugen's domain, the reckless poet should have known better). Once Schubart was within the reach of a ruler with absolute powers, his fate was sealed. Without a hearing or trial he was summarily thrown into the grim Hohenasperg prison near Ludwigsburg (open to this day as a museum in memory of its many inmates until the 1940s). The deception that led to his incarceration was a real muddying of the waters and puts the fate of the unfairly captured trout (the poem *Die Forelle* was written in prison in 1783) into a different perspective. In fact, all Schubart's poems that Schubert set to music were written when in captivity.

Schubart spent the first year in solitary confinement. For four years he was not allowed to write but he dictated part of his autobiography to a fellow inmate through a hole in his cell wall. After eight years' imprisonment he was allowed to see his family – they were being supported meanwhile by the duke whose reputation for quixotic and dangerously contradictory behaviour was well earned. (Schubart's fate was meant to be a warning to other writers; the punishment was a constant and fearful reminder to Friedrich Schiller, twenty years younger, whose destiny as a schoolboy and teenager lay in the hands of the same petty despot.) As time went on Schubart was allowed writing materials in his cell and some of his best work was written under appalling conditions, including a masterwork on musical theory and history, *Ideen zu einer Ästhetik der Tonkunst*, published posthumously in 1806, which is still regarded as an important work (*see* TONALITY AND TRANSPOSITION). It is said that Schubart also dictated this latter work through an opening in the wall.

On 11 May 1787, after more than ten years' imprisonment, Schubart was released. The perversity of the duke knew no bounds: he immediately appointed Schubart director of the theatre and court poet as if nothing had happened. Of course Schubart was now one of Europe's most famous prisoners of conscience, a hugely popular man throughout Germany, especially with the young. The duke was probably nervously aware of a changing zeitgeist where such absolutist cruelty by the aristocracy was becoming impossible to sustain. Within two years the Bastille in Paris would be torn apart by the mob. Although Schubart immediately took up *Die Deutsche Chronik* again, his spirit and health had been broken by his ordeal and the years that were left to him were not productive. He had become religious during his imprisonment. He lived long enough to see the publication of his first volume of autobiography (his son Ludwig subsequently took up his cause) but died on 10 October 1791, a few months before Mozart.

Mention of that composer in connection with Schubart is a timely reminder of the

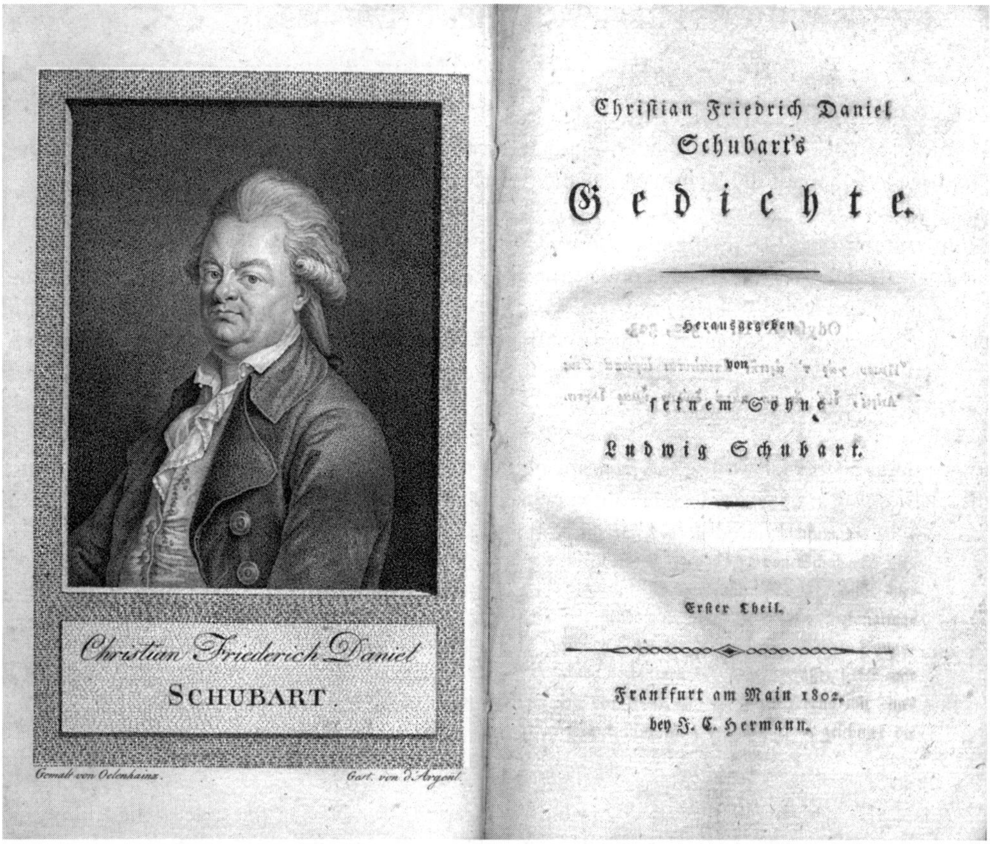

Christian Friedrich Daniel
Schubart's

Gedichte.

Herausgegeben
von
seinem Sohne
Ludwig Schubart.

Erster Theil.

Frankfurt am Main 1802,
bey J. C. Hermann.

Schubart's *Gedichte* (1802). Frontispiece of the poet after painting by Oelenhainz.

dangers regularly faced by artists in the employ of rulers whose local powers were unconstrained. While Mozart was quarrelling with Archbishop Colloredo of Salzburg in 1781, Schubart was four years into what might be termed his 'Guantanamo' experience. Mozart was playing with fire in defying the archbishop, and might well have suffered a great deal more than a metaphorical kick down the stairs. It is tempting to imagine that Schubart's work was made known to Schubert by Johann Mayrhofer, the imperial censor who detested his job, and who probably owned a copy of the posthumous *Gedichte* of 1802, pictured above. Those of liberal disposition admired the many facets of the poet's lyrics (among his charming poems there were also some grimly political plaints written in prison). The almost legendary story of Schubart's fate became a fable about 'the bad old days' and something of a rallying cry to those in Biedermeier Vienna who felt their freedoms were once again threatened.

FRANZ SERAPHICUS PETER SCHUBERT (1797–1828)
as Poet

THE POETIC SOURCES
S1 Autograph of D80 marked 'Terzetto' and at the end 'Fine, den 27 September, 1813 [line above the three letters]. Auf die Nahmenfeyer meines Vaters!!!'

S2 Autograph of D407 in three sections: I: first draft of the tenor solo with piano ('Güt as Weisheit strömen mild'); II: fair copy of three sections of the work incorporating the opening unaccompanied vocal quartet (Gütigster, Bester! Weisester, Grösster!'), the tenor solo with piano, and the unaccompanied canon for three voices ('Unser aller Grosspapa / Bleibe noch recht lange da'); III: an earlier draft of the first item ('Gütigster, Bester!' etc.) in a version for vocal trio (TTB) and piano

S3 Autograph of D578 where the first strophe of the song is written out under the music and the further three verses are written out very neatly on the second page. The autograph is signed 'Franz Schubert' and dated 'Wien, am 8 August 1817'

THE SONGS
27 September 1813   *Zur Namensfeier meines Vaters* D80 [S1]

16 June 1816   *Beitrag zur fünfzigjährigsten Jubelfeier des Herrn von Salieri* D407 [S2]

8 August 1817   *Abschied ('Lebe wohl! Du lieber Freund')* D578 [S3]

Abschied, the text by Schubert to mark his friend Franz von Schober's departure from Vienna in 1817, is the only piece of his own poetry that he set as a solo song. The two other works with Schubert's texts are for ensembles of different kinds and are less well known. The first of these, *Zur Namensfeier meines Vaters* D80, is a small piece for three male voices with guitar accompaniment written in September 1813 in celebration of the name-day of the composer's father. There are four strophes in this poem: the first, an invocation to Apollo with his lyre, is written with an AABB rhyme scheme, and the following three strophes are ABBA. The writing is reasonably sophisticated but is not faultless ('Freude' is made to rhyme with 'Leide' in the third strophe).

The majority of Schubert's poetic writings had nothing to do with music. We do not know the reason he turned to poetry in May 1813; Anton Holzapfel, a friend from Schubert's youth, remembers the composer having written two poems at that time. The lost second poem was in the style of the Klopstock Odes. The surviving one reads:

Die Zeit
Unaufhaltsam rollt sie hin,
Nicht mehr kehrt die Holde wieder,
Stät im Lebenslauf Begleiterin
Senkt sie sich mit uns ins Grab hernieder.

Nur ein Hauch! – und er ist Zeit
Hauch! schwind' würdig ihr dort nieder
Hin zum Stuhle der Gerechtigkeit
Bringe deines Mundes Tugendlieder!

Nu rein Schall! und er ist Zeit
Schall! Schwind' würdig ihr dort nieder
Hin zum Sitze der Barmherzigkeit
Schütte reuig Flehen vor ihm nieder!

Unaufhaltsam rollt sie hin
Nicht mehr kehrt die Holde wieder
Stät im Lebenslauf Begleiterin
Senkt sie sich mit uns ins Grab hernieder.

Time
Inexorably rolling on,
Precious Time will return no more,
Our constant companion in life,
It descends with us into the grave.

Just one breath! – and it is time.
A breath! then down, vanish with dignity,
And bring to the Seat of Justice
The songs of virtue from your mouth!

Now a ringing sound! – and it is time.
A sound! Then down, vanish with dignity,
And pour out before the Seat of Mercy
Your contrite supplication.

Inexorably rolling on,
Precious Time will return no more,
Our constant companion in life,
It descends with us into the grave.

It is sometimes suggested that the composer was also responsible for the text of *Auf den Sieg der Deutschen* D81 beginning 'Verschwunden sind die Schmerzen', a cantata celebrating the allied victory in the autumn of 1813. This is difficult to believe, not only because of the skill with which the verse is written, but because it shows an all-embracing view of history with which it is hard to credit a sixteen-year-old boy. On the other hand the poem that was displayed on the door of the Schubert family home in the Säulengasse on the night of 16 June 1814 could very easily have been written by the young composer. The rhyme between 'Kaiser' and 'Lorbeerreiser', and the idea of a heart sprouting like a laurel tree, display a less than professional literary elegance, although there has been some skill employed in the arranging of the Latin epithet so that the total of the enlarged Roman numbers added together comes to 1814:

O könnt' ich, wie ich wollte,
Ich ehrte, wie man sollte,
F r a n z den besten Kaiser!
Es brennen hier nur Kerzen
Allein aus meinem Herzen
Spriessen Lorbeerreiser.

FRANCISCO MAGNO, VICTORI
    REDEVNTI!

Oh, if I but could, as I would,
I'd honour as one should
Franz the best Kaiser!
Here, they merely burn candles.
Alone from my heart
Do sprigs of laurel grow.

Hundreds of such tributes to the emperor, great and small, were displayed by loyal members of the public on that night of festive illuminations throughout the capital. These were gathered together in Joseph Rossi's *Denkbuch für Fürst und Vaterland* published in Vienna later in the same year, 1814. Three years before any of Schubert's songs appeared in print, this poem, possibly by the young composer, appeared on p. 161 of the first volume of Rossi's two-volume compendium, although only the composer's father's name is mentioned (see overleaf).

That Schubert's Latin was of a high standard is proven by his extended dedicatory inscription in that language to the composer Assmayer in March 1818 (Documentary Biography No. 123, p. 89).

Curiously, the second piece of music involving Schubert's words, *Beitrag zur fünfzigjährigsten Jubelfeier des Herrn von Salieri* D407, was written for an event on 16 June 1816, exactly two years to the day after the illuminations and festivities for the emperor described above. This was the fiftieth anniversary celebration of Antonio Salieri's arrival in Vienna in 1766, as a sixteen-year-old boy, under the tutelage and guidance of his mentor Florian Leopold Gassmann (1729–1774). Schubert had been Salieri's composition pupil since 1812, although the Italian maestro had known of his musical talents since the auditions for a place at the choir school in 1808. Many composers of different ages took part in these celebrations, and Schubert's homage was almost certainly performed. No doubt he gave the fair copy of the work to Salieri (S2 Part II) with the handwritten dedication.

The next piece of verse we encounter from Schubert is in his diary for 8 September 1816. It concludes a long list of earnest reflections and epithets that are the sign of a young man awakened to philosophical thought and

161 〜〜〜

Nr. 10. In der Säulengasse. Bey Herrn
Schubert, Schullehrer:

O könnt' ich, wie ich wollte,
Ich ehrte, wie man sollte,
Franz den besten Kaiser!
Es brennen hier nur Kerzen,
Allein aus meinem Herzen
Sprießen Lorberreiser.

FRANCIsCo MAGNO, VICtorI
REDEVNTI!

A poem possibly by Schubert aged sixteen, from Rossi's *Denkbuch für Fürst und Vaterland*, Vienna (1814).

self-examination (there are references that clearly derive from Marcus Aurelius). Some of the observations have the air of *idées reçues* recycled into Schubert's prose after discussions with some of his friends, above all his learned mentor, Johann Mayrhofer (Documentary Biography No. 98, p. 70). These thoughts are terminated with nothing much more than rhyming doggerel – some might say a refreshing return from elevated thought to a cosier Schubertian normality:

Sonderbare Fragen,
Hör ich alle sagen?
Es lässt sich hier nicht wagen,
Wir müssens duldend tragen.
    Nun gute Nacht,
    Bis ihr erwacht.

Strange questions,
Is that what I hear everyone say?
No chance of being provocative here,
We must bear with it patiently.
    And now Good Night,
    Sleep till first light.

Schubert was often asked to write out his most popular music for friends. Here is a dedicatory verse (*c.* 1817) on an album leaf containing an Ecossaise and a German dance D365/3. On one side of the manuscript,

together with the Ecossaise, he wrote the following:

Springen Sie mit diesem Eccossaise [*sic*]
Durch jedes Wohl und Weh!

Dance along to this Eccossaise
Through every joy and sore dismay!

This rhyme shows that Schubert probably mis-pronounced the name of the dance as 'Eccosais'. On the other side, underneath his autograph of the German dance, he wrote:

Tanzen Sie stets bei diesen Walzer;
Werden sie Russe oder gar Pfalzer.

If you keep dancing to these waltzes
You'll become a Russian or even a man of the
    Pfalz (Palatinate).

Ernst Hilmar considers it a possibility that the text of the song *Der Strom* D565, officially cast in the 'Anonymous' category, could be by Schubert himself. If this were so it would be among his most self-revealing documents, describing as it does a life as turbulent and twisted as the course of a river, a life of inner torment and lack of fulfilment. A logistical argument in favour of this theory is that the only solo setting that is certainly by Schubert (*Abschied* D578, *see* below) was composed only a short time later and it is possible that at that point the composer was intending to provide his own song texts.

When Franz von Schober had to leave Vienna in August 1817 on account of the health of his brother Axel, Schubert wrote a poem and song by way of a farewell gift (*Abschied* D578). It is possible that Schober had been planning to go on to Sweden after visiting Axel (in the event he returned to Vienna on account of his brother's death) which would explain the composition of a song that seems to envisage a long absence between friends. The circumstances also meant that Schubert's idyllic stay as a guest in the Schober household for more than a year was coming to an end (it was intended that he would give up his room to Axel). For a number of reasons this was an emotional departure and we notice that the more mature composer was inclined to turn to poetry as an expressive medium only when driven to do so by a situation in which he felt himself *in extremis*. His abilities as a poet were nowhere near his sovereign gifts as a composer, but one feels that when confronted with certain crises his creative faculties in terms of music dried up, if only very temporarily, in favour of the written word.

We have no idea why and under what circumstances Schubert wrote a poem entitled *Der Geist der Welt*, probably in September 1820. Was it the result of the fate of his friend Johann Senn, or was it a gift to another friend, Johann Huber? The title seems prophetic of Thomas Hardy, and the content suggests an attempt to write in Mayrhofer's style:

Der Geist der Welt
Lasst sie mir in ihrem Wahn,
Spricht der Geist der Welt,
Er ists, der im schwanken Kahn
So sie mir erhält.

Lasst sie rennen, jagen nur
Hin nach einem fernen Ziel,
Glauben viel, beweisen viel
Auf der dunkeln Spur.

Nichts ist wahr von allen dem,
Doch ists kein Verlust;

Menschlich ist ihr Weltsystem,
Göttlich, bin ich's mir bewusst.

The Spirit of the World
Let them carry on in all their folly,
Says the Spirit of the World,
It is that which, in their frail boat,
Keeps them safe for me.

Just let them run, chasing off
Towards a distant goal,
Believing much, proving much
In pursuit of the dark trail.

None of it is true,
But that's of no account;
Their world-view is human,
God-like, of that I am aware.

A copy of the poem in Schubert's hand was given by Ferdinand Schubert to Robert Schumann when that composer visited Vienna in 1838.

An extraordinary document should be mentioned next that is something of a poem in prose. This is *Mein Traum* (My Dream), dated 3 July 1822 (Documentary Biography No. 298, p. 226) in which Schubert recounts a dream in the form of an allegorical tale. This is chiefly concerned with the composer's relationship with his father and the latter's disappointed expectations. It seems extremely modern for its time and for psychiatrists and psychoanalysts it is by far the most interesting of all the documents relating to the composer's life. This is a dream fit for analysis by Freud or Jung at least three-quarters of a century before they were in a position to find such a confessional deserving of study.

The next surviving poetry in Schubert's hand (though not by him) is an album leaf inscription for Albert Schellmann dated 18 November 1822, one of the last months of Schubert's period of riotous living after his move away from Mayrhofer's apartment, and very shortly before he was to discover his venereal infection:

Wer nicht liebt Wein, Mädchen und Gesang,
Bleibt ein Narr sein Lebenlang.

He who loves not wine, girls and song
Will be a fool his whole life long.
                                   (Martin Luther)

Lest these words should be taken as an unequivocal statement of the composer's own preferences (as well they may be) he complicates the
situation for scholars by quoting a Goethe
quatrain from the poem *Beherzigung* (set to
music by Hugo Wolf in 1888) on the other side
of the page – perhaps (and perhaps not) meant
as an amplification, or even a contradiction, of
Luther's words in terms of choice of lifestyle:

Eines schickt sich nicht für Alle.
Sehe jeder wie er's treibe,
Siehe jeder, wo er bleibe
Und wer steht, dass er nicht falle.

One way is not right for all.
Each must take heed how he acts,
Each take heed how he impacts
And he who stops, mind lest he fall.

The fall from grace predicted in Goethe's biblically inspired words (1 Corinthians 10) was to
come all too soon. Some time towards the end
of 1822 or the beginning of 1823, Schubert
discovered he was suffering from syphilis. In
the ensuing shock and depression he turned
once more to poetry, penning on 5 May 1823
the most desperate words he was ever to write:

Mein Gebet

Tiefer Sehnsucht heil'ges Bangen
Will in schön're Welten langen;
    Möchte füllen dunklen Raum
    Mit allmächt'gem Liebestraum.

Grosser Vater! reich' dem Sohne,
Tiefer Schmerzen nun zum Lohne,
    Endlich als Erlösungsmahl
    Deiner Liebe ew'gen Strahl.

Sieh, vernichtet liegt im Staube,
Unerhörtem Gram zum Raube,
    Meines Lebens Martergang
    Nahend ew'gem Untergang.

Tödt' es und mich, selber tödte,
Stürz' nun Alles in die Lethe,
    Und ein reines kräft'ges Sein
    Lass', o Grosser, dann gedeih'n.

My Prayer

From deepest longing, with holy fear
To reach more beautiful worlds is my desire;
    My wish to fill the dark void
    With pure love's dream now unalloyed.

Offer, O mighty father, to your son,
Whose sole reward has been deep pain,
    The sustenance at last that means
        redemption,
    The light eternal of your love.

See, lying in the dust, reduced to nought,
A victim of inexpressible grief,
    The martyr's road that was my life
    Approach its never-ending doom.

Kill it and me, myself kill,
Cast everything into the Lethe
    And then, great god, allow
    A pure and powerful being to flourish.

   In complete contrast to this outpouring of
starkly subjective, some would say suicidal,
feeling is the poem that Schubert included as
part of a letter sent to Schober from Zseliz on
21 September 1824 (this was during the period
that Schober was more or less out of touch
with his Viennese friends and living in
Breslau). This attempts to comment on the
times as well as on the composer's individual
circumstances. Although he tells Schober that
he has been healthy for the last five months
(since shortly after he wrote a desperate letter
concerning his health to Kupelwieser in Rome
at the end of March 1824, Documentary Biography No. 456, p. 338) he misses his friends
and is still depressed: 'I often live through days
of great misery', he writes ('verlebe manchmal
durch sehr elende Tage'). The invocation to
'heil'ge Kunst' in the last verse is clearly a broad
reference to art in general, but it echoes the
address to music in Schober's poem *An die*

Musik ('Du holde Kunst'). For the first time Schubert seems aware that his poem might be judged as a work of art, and knows all too well that in comparison to Schober he is an amateur writer. However, he knows that Schober's reprimands about his weaknesses as a poet will be tempered by affection and indulgence ('weil ich weiss, dass Du selbst meine Schwächen mit Liebe u. Schonung rügst'). The poem seems to be a heartfelt lament on the political situation in Metternich's Austria where a sclerotic and repressive government regarded youth as a potential troublemaking enemy and where young people, not for the last time in Austrian history, felt disabled by the ultra-conservative zeitgeist. Apart from the support of his friends and a handful of powerful patrons, Schubert clearly felt that his compositions had been written in a kind of vacuum as far as the appreciation of the older generation was concerned. Schober seems not to have commented on the poem (certainly not in any extant letter), although it may have been the subject of discussion between poet and composer-poet when Schober returned to Vienna. Somewhat overburdened with a grandeur of diction that did not come naturally to Schubert, this poem was probably the last he was to write:

Klage an das Volk!
O Jugend unsrer Zeit, Du bist dahin!
Die Kraft zahllosen Volks, sie ist vergeudet,
Nicht e i n e r von der Meng' sich unterscheidet,
Und nichtsbedeutend all' vorüberzieh'n.

Zu grosser Schmerz, der mächtig mich verzehrt,
Und nur als Letztes jener Kraft mir bleibet;
Denn tatlos mich auch diese Zeit zerstäubet,
Die jedem Grosses zu vollbringen wehrt.

Im siechen Alter schleicht das Volk einher,
Die Taten seiner Jugend wähnt es Träume,
Ja spottet töricht jener gold'nen Reime,
Nichtsachtend ihren kräft'gen Inhalt mehr.

Nur Dir, o heil'ge Kunst, ist's noch gegönnt
Im Bild' die Zeit der Kraft u. Tat zu schildern,
Um weniges den grossen Schmerz zu mildern,
Der nimmer mit dem Schicksal sie versöhnt.

An Elegy for the People
Youth of today, you are broken!
The strength of countless peoples; it has been
    squandered,
Not *one* from in among the crowd stands out,
And insignificant, they all pass by.

Pain that is too great consumes me mightily,
And is the last vestige left to me of that
strength;
For without achievement I too am made as dust
By these times that stop us all from
    accomplishing great things.

In sickly old age the people creep around;
Youthful achievement perceived as dreams,
Foolishly they even mock its golden rhymes,
Without regard now for its powerful content.

Only to you, o holy art, is it still granted
To depict the age of power and achievement,
To ameliorate a little the great pain
Which no longer reconciles it with Fate.

CLEMENS AUGUST JOSEPH MARIA SCHÜCKING (1759–1790)

THE POETIC SOURCES
S1 *Hagars Klage in der Wüste Bersaba*. Johann Rudolf Zumsteeg, Leipzig, bey Breitkopf und Härtel [January 1797]

This ballad by Zumsteeg was undoubtedly Schubert's source (Zumsteeg's source was S2 below). The entire work is reprinted in NSA Volume 6 pp. 186–94.

S2 *Poetische Blumenlese. Auf das Jahr 1781*. Göttingen bey Johann Christian Dietrich (Göttinger Musenalmanach)

Göttingen *Musenalmanach* (1781). The poem of *Hagars Klage* is on p. 123 (Zumsteeg's source).

There are four contributions to this almanac by Schücking; the other titles, apart from *Hagars Klage*, are *Der Abschied, Lied zur Einsaat, Josts mit der Schelle (Bettellied)*.

THE SONG
30 March 1811   *Hagars Klage* D5 [S2: pp. 123–6, under the title *Hagars Klage in der Wüste Bersaba*]

Until it was discovered that Schubert had set the poetry of Gabriele von Baumberg for his first ballad, the honour of having been Schubert's first-ever poet had gone to the very little-known Clemens Schücking, poet of *Hagars Klage* D5. He was born on 5 January 1759 in Münster, younger brother to the better-known writer Christoph Bernhard Joseph Schücking (1753–1778). Clemens went to Vienna to study law, as well as Heidelberg and Göttingen (where he met the poets of the Göttingen Hainbund and considered himself among their number). Schücking went on to become a lawyer in his home city and became a well-known Freemason as well as the leader in Münster of the *Illuminatenorden*, the secret society (banned in Bavaria) that furthered the ideals of the Enlightenment. He became advisor and counsellor to Graf von Merveldt. He died on 22 January 1790 in Bonn. Schücking published poems in the Göttingen almanac of 1781 (where only the abbreviated signature 'Schg' appears) and in the Voss almanac of 1788.

CHRISTIAN WILHELM VON SCHÜTZ (1776–1847)

THE POETIC SOURCE

S1 *Lacrimas, Ein Schauspiel.* Herausgegeben von August Wilhelm Schlegel. Berlin, Im Verlage der Realschulbuchhandlung, 1803

The first edition of *Lacrimas* has no author's name on the title page. The fact that the series of plays was edited (herausgegeben) by A. W. Schlegel led Schubert to believe that the author was Schlegel: the title page of the songs' first edition in 1829 is *Zwey Scenen aus dem Schauspiele 'Lacrimas' von A. W. Schlegel.* It is possible that Schubert found the play in Johann Michael Vogl's library in Steyr.

THE SONGS

September 1825   *Delphine* D857/1 [S1: Act IV Scene 2, pp. 118–19]
                          Florio D857/2 [S1: Act III Scene 6, pp. 92–3]

The commentaries for both of these songs in Volume 3 of this work are to be found under *Zwei Szenen aus Lacrimas.*

Wilhelm von Schütz was born in Berlin on 13 April 1776 into a Prussian noble family. He studied law, later entering into government service. In 1807 he was appointed Landrat at Ziebingen, near Frankfurt an der Oder. He was a political conservative and opposed the state reforms of King Friedrich Wilhlem III. Although he was suspended from his position in Ziebingen in 1811, he lived there for most of the rest of his life. It was mainly in his earlier years, and thanks to his friendship with August von Schlegel and Ludwig Tieck, that Schütz dabbled in the theatre, writing a few pieces that were popular in their time. *Lacrimas* was the first of his tragedies. The play, which was brought out under the imprimatur and aegis of Schlegel, achieved such success for its author that he was referred to as 'Schütz-Lacrimas' after that. His fascination with the interaction between the Christian and the Muslim worlds was shared by Schubert who wrote a large opera, *Fierabras* D796, on the subject. In 1820 Schütz wrote that in his play he had intended to reflect the fate of mankind where the connection between God, and human nature's closeness to God, something shared by early Christians and Muslims, had been torn asunder in modern times. Later plays included *Karl der Kühne, Der Graf und die Gräfin von*

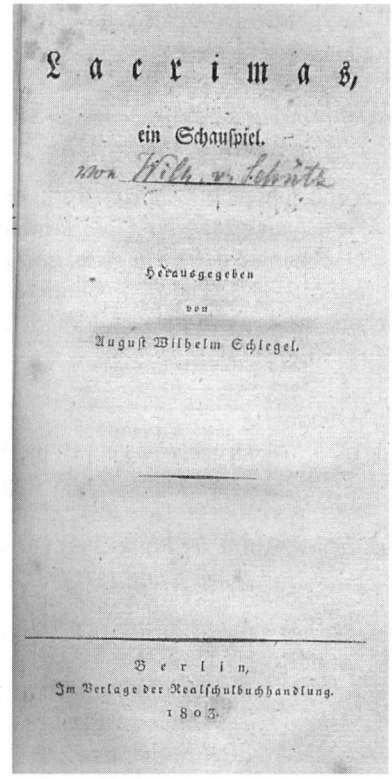

Schütz's *Lacrimas* (1803). The first edition was published without the author's name (added here in pencil).

Gleichen (D918, the subject of Schubert's last opera), *Graf von Schwarzenberg* and *Niobe*.

Schütz visited Vienna in 1825 and was in contact with Friedrich von Schlegel, a meeting that perhaps led to his conversion to Catholicism in 1830. He moved to Dresden in 1833, and penned articles and tracts on such diverse subjects as industry and religion. He was responsible for publishing the first German translation in twelve volumes of Casanova's works. He died in Leipzig on 9 August 1847. A somewhat grotesque footnote to the life of Schütz (for which he himself is not to blame) is that in 1922 Joseph Goebbels wrote his doctoral thesis on the works of this poet: *Wilhelm von Schütz als Dramatiker. Ein Beitrag zur Geschichte des Dramas der Romantischen Schule.* Perhaps Goebbels had become fascinated with Schütz's philosophical work which included books on laws governing the press (1821) and on mixed marriages in Prussia (1839).

ERNST KONRAD FRIEDRICH SCHULZE (1789–1817)

THE POETIC SOURCES
S1 *Ernst Schulze's sämmtiche Poetische Schriften*, Dritter Band. I Poetisches Tagebuch. II Reise durch das Weserthal. III Psyche, ein griechisches Märchen. Leipzig F. A. Brockhaus 1819

This first edition of Schulze's works is in four volumes. The work was issued with an unusual binding: a combination of dappled pale blue covers (the effect is that of a lightly cloudy sky) while the volumes have pale yellow spines. Unlike the second edition, there are no vignettes or illustrations.

S2 *Sämmtliche poetische Werke von Ernst Schulze*. Neue Ausgabe mit sechzehn Kupfern. Dritter Theil. Leipzig F. A. Brockhaus 1822

This second volume of Schulze's works (Part Three) is shared between the *Poetisches Tagebuch vom 29sten Junius 1814 bis 17ten Februar, 1817* (pp. 1–208), *Reise durch das Weserthal* 1814 (pp. 209–24) and *Psyche, ein griechisches Märchen in sieben Büchern. Angefangen im Sommer 1807* (pp. 225–334). The first volume of Schulze's works (Parts One and Two) is given over entirely to the massive poem *Cäcilie*. It is not clear whether Schubert had the first or second edition at his disposal.

THE SONGS
March 1825   *Im Walde* D834 [S1: pp. 66–70 with the title *Im Walde hinter Falkenhagen. Den 22sten Julius, 1814*] [S2: pp. 70–71]

August 1825   *Auf der Bruck* D853 Op. 93 no. 2 [S1: pp. 74–5 with the title *Auf der Bruck. Den 25sten Julius, 1814*] [S2: pp. 75–6]

December 1825   *An mein Herz* D860 [S1: pp. 121–2 with the title *Am 23sten Januar 1816*] [S2: pp. 123–4]
                   Der liebliche Stern D861 [S1: p. 63 with the title *Am 28sten April, 1814*] [S2: p. 64]
                   Um Mitternacht D862 Op. 88 no. 3 [S1: pp. 89–90 with the title *Am 5ten März 1815, Nachts um 12 Uhr*] [S2: pp. 90–91]

January? 1826   *O Quell, was strömst du rasch und wild* D874 [S1: pp. 45–6 with the title *Am 8ten Januar, 1814*] [S2: pp. 46–7]

January 1826   *Im Jänner 1817* D876 [S1: p. 196 with the title *Am 17ten Januar 1817*] [S2: p. 200] [Schubert's title uses the Austrian form of the month for his title – Jänner – rather than Schulze's German Januar. This is perhaps the reason that there has long been an alternative title for the song: *Tiefes Leid*]

March 1826   *Im Frühling* D882 [S1: pp. 98–9 with the title *Am 31sten März 1815*] [S2: pp. 99–100]
                  Lebensmut D883 [S1: pp. 100–101 with the title *Am 1sten April 1815*] [S2: pp. 101–2]
                  Über Wildemann D884 Op. 108 no. 1[S1 pp. 172–3 with the title *Über Wildemann, einem Bergstädchen am Harz. Den 28sten April, 1816*] [S2 pp. 176–7]

Mention should also be made of another Schulze setting for unaccompanied voices that is outside the scope of this book: *Ewige Liebe* D825A Op. 64 no. 2 Quartet (TTBB) composed before the summer of 1826.

Ernst Schulze was born in Celle, Lower Saxony, on 22 March 1789. He lost his mother when two years old, and a loveless home environment (his father remarried) may have accounted for many of his subsequent emotional problems. As a child he was withdrawn and bookish with adults, and a reckless daredevil with his peers. During his university years (he studied theology, philology and aesthetics at Göttingen) he wrote that he could have had 'twelve mistresses without loving any less than the others'; at the same time properly brought-up young ladies found him and his ever-fluent verse sensitively soulful. His writing took its cue from Hölty, Matthisson and Schiller. Self-confidence and worldly cynicism is common enough in young men of undergraduate age (some of the Schubert circle, Schober for example, might be accused of manipulative insincerity with the opposite sex). Schulze's debaucheries (by which he confessed that he was frequently exhausted) went hand in hand with a capacity to inhabit a fantasy world where the borders between truth and reality were blurred. The poet's half-sister Sophie died of consumption in 1811 and this tragedy seems to have precipitated a need for a relationship with someone who resembled her physically.

Schulze had met the Tychsen sisters, Adelheid and Cäcilie, in early 1811. They were the daughters of Thomas Tychsen, a well-known orientalist and archaeologist. At the time Schulze described Adelheid (the later inspiration of the *Poetisches Tagebuch*) as 'rather like a bagpipe that does not sound equally pleasant to all listeners' and as having 'a monkey's face'. On the other hand he found Cäcilie attractive and mounted a campaign to seduce her (he referred to her as 'booty'), playing on her gift for foreign languages and her love of music, particularly that of Bach. (Schulze too was rather musical.) At about the time of his sister's death Schulze seems to have fallen genuinely in love with Cäcilie, seeing himself as Petrarch to her Laura. If he saw her as a saviour and an antidote to his dissolute life, the self-conscious declarations in his diaries and letters suggest an ongoing literary game rather than any depth of real feeling.

Cäcilie gave him no especial encouragement (indeed it was obvious they had little in common); she was not Schulze's fiancée, as has often been stated in biographical articles about the poet, but her early death in December 1812 cast her as his lost Muse ('I will weep for her eternally'). He took four years to write *Cäcilie, Ein romantisches Gedicht*, an epic poem in which the story of the minstrel Reinald and his beloved Cäcilie is played out against the background of the Danes' conversion to Christianity by the Germans in the tenth century. This vast work (twenty cantos of unequal lengths, made up of 1,985 eight-line stanzas) reflected the medieval preoccupations of many poets of the time. The courtly theme of star-crossed lovers was almost fundamental to the German romanticism of Jean Paul, Kleist and Tieck, while Hölderlin and Novalis had brought a mystical and religious significance to the twinned themes of love and death. Schulze's poetry, as good as some of it is, seems openly imitative of his great literary predecessors.

The Tychsen family tolerated Schulze's devotion to Cäcilie's memory through poetry, but when he began transferring his intense emotional attentions to the formerly despised Adelheid, alarm bells rang. From the start she told him frankly that his suit was hopeless (she was in love with someone else), and when we read Schulze's letter to a friend that states 'we love each other – she has told me so herself and treats me as her fiancé as does the entire city' we know that the poet has moved into an area of fantasy and self-delusion. The poems of the *Poetisches Tagebuch* (there are exactly 100 of them) were written in the form of diary entries between 29 June 1813 and 17 February 1817. Both sisters, the living and the dead, inhabit its pages. At times Schulze admits that he is 'the faithful minstrel who, though never loved, sang only of love' but the reader is subtly led to believe what the deluded poet himself imagined: that the poems chart an ongoing relationship – the good times and the bad, separations, hope of returning to the beloved's arms (*Auf der Bruck*), the memories of a happy past (*Im Frühling*) that had never in fact truly existed, and so on. Schulze was weaving his poetic magic out of the slenderest slivers of reality. His meetings with Adelheid became less and less frequent; contact with her by letter (his to her were long and emotionally manipulative – we know because he kept copies of them all) was mostly one-sided. And all the while the poems flow forth, remarkable works in different metres and forms. Like the Petrarch of the *Rime* (and Schulze cultivated the similarity) the one-track poet could say, 'I wept and sang; I cannot change my style, but day and night I vent through my tongue and my eyes the sorrow accumulated in my soul.' A Novalis epigram also comes to mind: 'Whoever loves must everlastingly remain

Ernst Schulze, portrait drawn by Opitz, engraved by Coupé.

aware of the surrounding void, and keep the wound open. May God grant that I shall preserve this pain which is exquisitely dear to me.' Schulze clearly worked hard to preserve the pain that was his constant companion and exquisite Muse.

Things, however, had gone too far for the Tychsens. Gifts of flowers were returned and in July 1815 Schulze was banned from the house by Adelheid herself. Although she was probably not entirely blameless in her dealings with the poet (many people disliked her), one feels sympathy for her decision. Schulze believed that he had immortalized the Tychsen family in verse (as indeed he had in a way) and that it was their own emotional limitations that prevented them from feeling things at his exalted level. This is a textbook case for the twentieth-century psychiatrist, but death was the nineteenth's way of solving the problem. Poor Schulze died on 29 June 1817, still only in his twenties, having succumbed to tuberculosis, the disease that had killed his mother, sister and Cäcilie Tychsen. On his deathbed he was offered a professorship in Lüneberg. He also received news that he had won the prize offered by the editors of the Leipzig almanac *Urania* for his romantic poem *Die bezauberte Rose* (the story of how Princess Klothilde turns into a rose and back again), and the publicity surrounding this award made him famous throughout Germany. Schubert considered this work for operatic treatment in 1824. It is not certain where the composer first encountered Schulze's name but he was almost certainly aware of the poet's reputation before he discovered the poetry itself. For example, in the *Taschenbuch zum geselligen Vergnügen* of 1822 where Schubert found *Ihr Grab* D736 (p. 91), there is on p. 101 a poem in honour of Ernst Schulze's grave.

The poet's older contemporary Friedrich Bouterwek expunged much of the truth from the first biographical essay published at the

Ernst Schulze's

sämmtliche

poetische Schriften.

Dritter Band.

I. Poetisches Tagebuch.
II. Reise durch das Weserthal.
III. Psyche, ein griechisches Märchen.

Leipzig:
F. A. Brockhaus.

1 8 1 9.

Schulze's *Sämmtliche poetische Schriften* (1819). The *Poetisches Tagebuch* is in the third volume of this collection.

beginning of both editions of the collected works [S1 and S2] of 1819 and 1822. It was a later nineteenth-century scholar Karl Emil Franzos (who also re-discovered the *Woyzeck* manuscript of Büchner) who published a great deal of suppressed material. Mental illness is no longer considered shameful, and it is especially moving to know about it when (as in Schulze's case and that of Hugo Wolf) it is part of a pattern that generates a high level of artistic accomplishment. Schulze as a poet has always been admired by those who know his work, such as Schumann, who referred to 'dear Schulze' and even wrote a poem about him.

The grim reality of the Napoleonic wars in which Schulze fought seems seldom to have touched the world of the *Tagebuch* that purported to be a diary of events. One of the rare poems in which war is mentioned was actually set by Schubert – the male quartet (TTBB) *Ewige Liebe* D825A. This work uses a poem entitled '27 Oktober 1814', where Schulze employs the image of 'Leier und Schwert' – lyre and sword – signifying that he knew the collection of war poems by Theodor Körner published under that title. Körner was one of the admired role models of Schubert's youth, and it is not impossible that the composer wrote this unaccompanied work before the Schulze songs with piano, and that this homage to Körner's memory led Schubert to explore further the poet's work.

A cursory glance through the *Poetisches Tagebuch*, however, shows why it was impossible for the composer to set a great many more poems from the sequence: they display a variety of metrical forms, some of which (the hexameter for example) Schubert tended to avoid as unsuitable for music. There is no discernible storyline, only a succession of diary entries in verse, varied by season, locale and metaphor rather than any plot development. While Schulze returns again and again to the misery of love locked out, love fulfilled, however self-deluded, is also a favourite theme. Schubert cannot have been aware of the precise biographical background when he came to set these songs, beyond the fact that, as is clear from the words themselves, the poet is obsessed

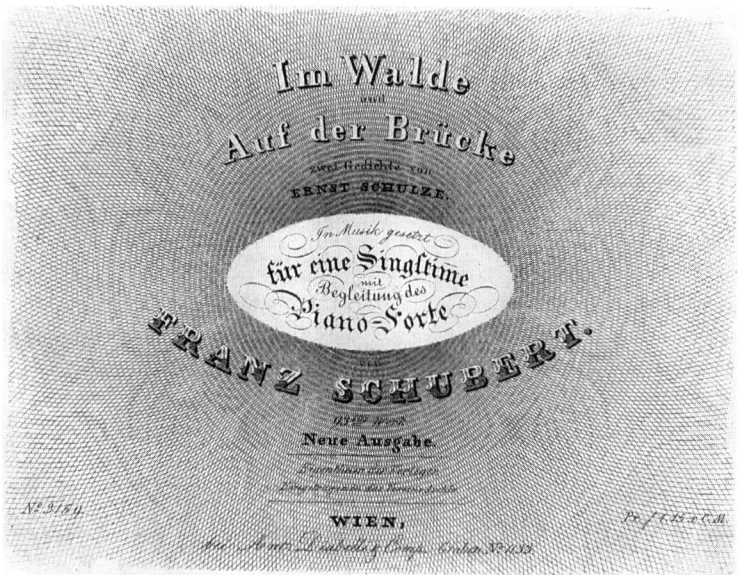

Im Walde and *Auf der Brücke*, two Schulze songs Op. 93.

with love and refers to 'zwei Namen' in his introduction – two names that he claims for Muses. Nevertheless, as Susan Youens notes, the composer seems to have caught 'the whiff of insanity in Schulze's poetic diary'.

The nine songs were written within a year (March 1825–March 1826) and as works of the composer's maturity they stand together not only in terms of their formal procedures (all strophic in one modified way or another) but also in terms of a homogeneity of tone – despite the wild mood swings – that stems from the unifying voice of Ernst Schulze himself. When the songs are performed together it is arguable that the group needs a working title. In a less audacious spirit than that of the publisher Tobias Haslinger, who took it upon himself to invent a new cycle by publishing the last Schubert songs under the

title *Schwanengesang* D957 and D965A (thus juxtaposing three poets who are not the most obvious of bedfellows), I tentatively proposed the title 'Auf den wilden Wegen' (qv) for the recording of the songs in the Hyperion Schubert Edition. These words were taken from the first verse of the opening song of the suggested sequence, *Auf der Bruck* D853. The 'wild paths' of this phrase suggest a journey through tough terrain, but they also imply the poet's unbalanced state of mind. Many of the poems were written on journeys, and away from home, but the title also reinforces the close relationship of the Schulze songs to the greatest of all journeying lieder, *Winterreise*.

See also AUF DEN WILDEN WEGEN.

Bibliography: Youens 1996, pp. 228–330